lonely planet

Europe

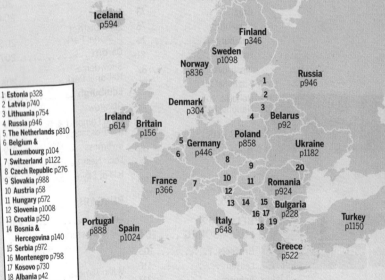

Iceland
p594

Finland
p346

Sweden
p1098

Norway
p836

Russia
p946

Denmark
p304

1

2

Belarus
p92

3

4

Ireland
p614

Britain
p156

Germany
p446

Poland
p858

Ukraine
p1182

5

6

8

9

20

France
p366

7

10

11

Romania
p924

12

13   14   15

Bulgaria
p228

16 17

18   19

Turkey
p1150

Portugal
p888

Spain
p1024

Italy
p648

Greece
p522

Alexis Averbuck, James Bainbridge, Mark Baker, Oliver Berry, Greg Bloom,
Gregor Clark, Marc Di Duca, Peter Dragicevich, Duncan Garwood, Anita
Isalska, Catherine Le Nevez, Tom Masters, Hugh McNaughtan, Korina
Miller, John Noble, Becky Ohlsen, Lorna Parkes, Leonid Ragozin, Tim Rich-
ards, S   heward, Andy
                                                           erman

ICELAND P594

A P946

NATTHAWAT/ GETTY IMAGES ©

Contents

Contents

ON THE ROAD

Contents

Welcome to Europe

There simply is no way to tour Europe and not be awestruck by its scenic beauty, epic history and dazzling artistic and culinary diversity.

Cultural Heritage

Europe's almost unmanageable wealth of attractions is its biggest single draw: the birthplace of democracy in Athens, the Renaissance art of Florence, the graceful canals of Venice, the Napoleonic splendour of Paris, and the multilayered historical and cultural canvas of London. Less obvious but no less impressive attractions include Moorish palaces in Andalucía, the fascinating East-meets-West brew of İstanbul in Turkey, the majesty of meticulously restored imperial palaces in Russia's former capital St Petersburg and the ongoing project of Gaudí's La Sagrada Família in Barcelona.

Glorious Scenery

There's a huge diversity of natural scenery: rugged Scottish Highlands with glens and lochs; Norway's fabulous fjords, seemingly chipped to jagged perfection by giants; the vine-raked valleys of the Loire; and the steppe-like plains of central Spain. If you're looking for beaches, a circuit of the Mediterranean's northern coast reveals one gem after another. Or strike out to lesser known, yet beautiful coastal regions such as the Baltic and Black Seas. Mountain lovers should head to the Alps: they march across central Europe taking in France, Switzerland, Austria, northern Italy and tiny Liechtenstein.

Raise a Glass

Europe has some of the best nightlife in the world. Globally famous DJs keep the party going in London, Berlin and Paris, all of which also offer top-class entertainment, especially theatre and live music. Other key locations for high-energy nightlife include Moscow, Belgrade, Budapest and Madrid, while those hankering for something cosier can add Dublin's pubs or Vienna's cafes to their itinerary. Continue to party on the continent's streets at a multiplicity of festivals and celebrations, from city parades attended by hundreds of thousands to intimate concerts in an ancient amphitheatre.

Magnificent Menus

Once you've ticked off the great museums, panoramic vistas and energetic nightlife, what's left? A chance to indulge in a culinary adventure to beat all others, that's what! Who wouldn't want to snack on pizza in Naples, souvlaki in Santorini or even haggis in Scotland? But did you also know that Britain has some of the best Indian restaurants in the world; that Turkey's doner kebab is a key part of contemporary German food culture; and that in the Netherlands you can gorge on an Indonesian *rijsttafel* (rice table)? Once again Europe's diversity and global reach is its trump card.

Why I Love Europe

By Brendan Sainsbury, Writer

As with many young travellers, Europe is where my life on the road began in the late 1980s with a £140 Inter-rail ticket. Not having travelled outside Britain as a child, I'll never forget the excitement of arriving at Paris' Gare du Nord after dark to explore the 'City of Light'. Since then, I've travelled around Europe multiple times returning regularly to my favourite places (Andalucía, the Loire, the Dolomites, London and the English Lake District) and revelling in the diversity, intensity and complexity of this multilayered continent that I'll need at least 10 lifetimes to explore properly.

For more about our writers, see p1245

Above: Catedral de Mallorca (p1073), Mallorca, Spain

Europe

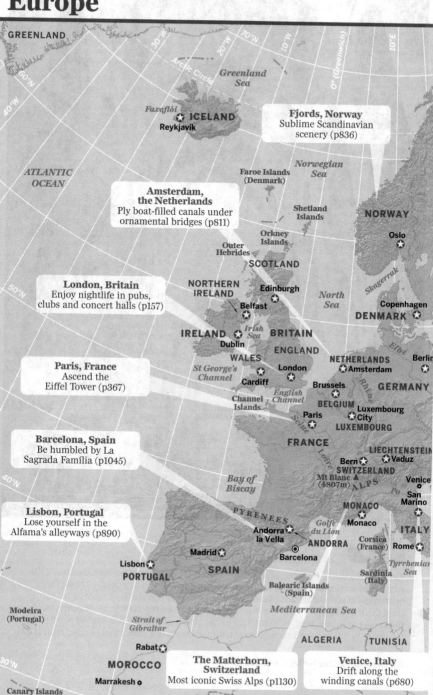

GREENLAND

Greenland
Sea

Fjords, Norway
Sublime Scandinavian
scenery (p836)

Faxaflói ✪ ICELAND
Reykjavík

ATLANTIC
OCEAN

Norwegian
Sea

Faroe Islands
(Denmark)

**Amsterdam,
the Netherlands**
Ply boat-filled canals under
ornamental bridges (p811)

Shetland
Islands

NORWAY

Oslo
✪

Orkney
Islands

Outer
Hebrides

SCOTLAND

London, Britain
Enjoy nightlife in pubs,
clubs and concert halls (p157)

NORTHERN
IRELAND

Edinburgh
✪

Belfast
✪

North
Sea

Skagerrak

Copenhagen
✪

DENMARK ✪

IRELAND ✪ Irish
Sea

BRITAIN

Dublin

ENGLAND

Elbe

Berlin
✪

Paris, France
Ascend the
Eiffel Tower (p367)

WALES

St George's
Channel

Cardiff
✪

London
✪

NETHERLANDS
✪ Amsterdam

Brussels
✪

GERMANY

Rhine

Channel
Islands

English
Channel

BELGIUM

Luxembourg
✪ City

Seine

Paris
✪

LUXEMBOURG

Barcelona, Spain
Be humbled by La
Sagrada Família (p1045)

FRANCE

Loire

LIECHTENSTEIN

Bern ✪ ✪ Vaduz
SWITZERLAND

Bay of
Biscay

Mt Blanc ▲
(4807m) ALPS

Venice
○

San
Marino ✪

Lisbon, Portugal
Lose yourself in the
Alfama's alleyways (p890)

PYRENEES

Golfe
du Lion

MONACO
✪
Monaco

Po

ITALY

Lisbon ✪

Andorra ✪
la Vella

ANDORRA

Corsica
(France)

Rome ✪

Madrid ✪

Barcelona

PORTUGAL

SPAIN

Balearic Islands
(Spain)

Sardinia
(Italy)

Tyrrhenian
Sea

Modeira
(Portugal)

Strait of
Gibraltar

Mediterranean Sea

ALGERIA

TUNISIA

Rabat ✪

MOROCCO

Marrakesh ○

Canary Islands
(Spain)

**The Matterhorn,
Switzerland**
Most iconic Swiss Alps (p1130)

Venice, Italy
Drift along the
winding canals (p680)

Berlin, Germany
Historic encounters at the
Berlin Wall (p447)

St Petersburg, Russia
Imperial palaces
packed with art (p959)

Tallinn, Estonia
Soak up the city's
vibrant vibe (p330)

Prague, Czech Republic
Iconic castle, diverse
neighbourhoods, and art (p278)

Budapest, Hungary
Museums, thermal baths
and nightlife (p573)

Transylvania, Romania
Explore the mountains and
spooky castles (p931)

İstanbul, Turkey
Marvel at the
stunning mosques (p1151)

Ohrid, Macedonia
Wander the sublime
Old Town (p777)

Dubrovnik, Croatia
Walk the old city walls
at dusk (p268)

0 — 1000 km
0 — 500 miles

SWEDEN

FINLAND

White Sea

Gulf of Bothnia

Helsinki
St Petersburg
Tallinn
ESTONIA
RUSSIA
Volga
Stockholm
Baltic Sea
LATVIA
Rīga
Moscow
KAZAKHSTAN
LITHUANIA
Vilnius
Minsk
Don
Kaliningrad
RUSSIA
BELARUS
POLAND
Warsaw
Kiev
Dnieper
Caspian Sea
CZECH
REPUBLIC
Kraków
UKRAINE
Prague
CARPATHIAN MOUNTAINS
Vienna
SLOVAKIA
MOLDOVA
Bratislava
Chișinău
Crimea
AUSTRIA
HUNGARY
SLOVENIA
Budapest
TRANSYLVANIA
GEORGIA
AZERBAIJAN
Ljubljana
ROMANIA
Black Sea
Zagreb
Bucharest
ARMENIA
CROATIA
Sarajevo
Belgrade
SERBIA
BOSNIA &
BULGARIA
IRAN
HERCEGOVINA
KOSOVO
Sofiya
Dubrovnik
Pristina
İstanbul
Podgorica
MACEDONIA
Ankara
MONTENEGRO
Skopje
Adriatic Sea
Tirana
TURKEY
SYRIA
ALBANIA
IRAQ
Aegean Sea
GREECE
Sicily
Ionian Sea
Athens
Cyclades Islands
Nicosia
LEBANON
Ionian Islands
Dodecanese Islands
CYPRUS
Valletta
Crete
JORDAN
MALTA
Mediterranean Sea
SAUDI
ARABIA
EGYPT

Europe's
Top 24

London's Nightlife, Britain

1 Can you hear that, music lovers? That's London calling – from the numerous theatres, concert halls, nightclubs, pubs and even tube stations, where on any given night hundreds, if not thousands, of performers are taking to the stage. Search for your own iconic London experience, whether it's the Proms at the Royal Albert Hall (pictured; p183), an East End singa-long around a clunky pub piano, a theatre performance in the West End, a superstar DJ set at Fabric or a floppy-fringed guitar band at a Hoxton boozer.

Eiffel Tower, France

2 Seven million people visit the Eiffel Tower (pictured; p367) annually and most agree that each visit is unique. From an evening ascent amid twinkling lights to lunch in the company of a staggering city panorama, there are 101 ways to 'do' it. Pedal beneath it, skip the lift and hike up, buy a crêpe from a stand or a key ring from the street, snap yourself in front of it, visit at night or – our favourite – experience the odd special occasion when all 324m of it glows a different colour.

ROB BALL / GETTY IMAGES ©

Venice, Italy

3 There's something magical about Venice (p680) on a sunny winter's day. With far fewer tourists around and the light sharp and clear, it's the perfect time to lap up the city's unique and magical atmosphere. Ditch your map and wander the shadowy backlines of Dorsoduro while imagining secret assignations and whispered conspiracies at every turn. Then visit two of Venice's top galleries, the Gallerie dell'Accademia and the Peggy Guggenheim Collection, which houses works by many of the giants of 20th-century art.

Remembering the Berlin Wall, Germany

4 Even after 25 years, the sheer magnitude and disbelief that the Berlin Wall (p453) really cut through this city doesn't sink in. But the best way to examine its role in Berlin is to make your way – on foot or by bike – along the Berlin Wall Trail. Passing the Brandenburg Gate, analysing graffiti at the East Side Gallery (pictured) or learning about its history at the Documentation Centre: the path brings it all into context. It's heartbreaking, hopeful and sombre, but integral in trying to understand Germany's capital.

LITTLEAOM / SHUTTERSTOCK ©

MIHAI-BOGDAN LAZAR / SHUTTERSTOCK ©

Santorini, Greece

5 On first view, startling Santorini grabs your attention and doesn't let it go. The submerged caldera, surrounded by lava-layered cliffs topped by villages that look like a sprinkling of icing sugar, is one of nature's great wonders, best experienced by a walk along the clifftops from the main town of Fira (p547) to the northern village of Oia (pictured). The precariousness and impermanence of the place is breathtaking. Recover from your efforts with Santorini's ice-cold Yellow Donkey beer in Oia as you wait for its famed picture-perfect sunset.

St Petersburg, Russia

6 Marvelling at how many masterpieces there are in the Hermitage; window-shopping and people-watching along Nevsky Prospekt (p964); gliding down canals past the grand facades of palaces and golden-domed churches; enjoying a ballet at the beautiful Mariinsky Theatre (pictured); having a banquet fit for a tsar then dancing till dawn at a dive bar in a crumbling ruin – Russia's imperial capital is a visual stunner and hedonist's delight, best visited at the height of summer when the White Nights see the city party around the clock.

7

8

JAKL LUBOS /SHUTTERSTOCK ©

LUCIANO MORTULA - LGM / SHUTTERSTOCK ©

The Matterhorn, Switzerland

7 It graces Toblerone packages and evokes stereotypical *Heidi* scenes, but nothing prepares you for the allure of the Matterhorn (pictured; p1130). As soon as you arrive at the timber-chalet-filled village of Zermatt, this mighty mountain looms above you, mesmerising you with its chiselled, majestic peak. Gaze at it from a tranquil sidewalk cafe, hike in its shadow along the tangle of alpine paths above town with cowbells clinking in the distance, or pause to admire its sheer size from a ski slope..

Prague, Czech Republic

8 Prague's big attractions – Prague Castle (p278) and Old Town Square – are highlights of the Czech capital, but for a more insightful look at life two decades after the Velvet Revolution, head to local neighbourhoods around the centre. Working-class Žižkov and energetic Smíchov are crammed with pubs, while elegant tree-lined Vinohrady features a diverse menu of cosmopolitan restaurants. Prague showcases many forms of art, from iconic works from the last century to more recent but equally challenging pieces.

Fjords, Norway

9 The drama of Norway's fjords is difficult to overstate. They cut deep gashes into the Norwegian interior, adding texture and depth to the map of northwestern Scandinavia. Sheer rock walls plunge from high, green meadows into water-filled canyons shadowed by pretty fjord-side villages. Sognefjorden (p849), more than 200km long, and Hardangerfjord are Norway's most extensive fjord networks, but the quiet, precipitous beauty of Nærøyfjord, Lysefjord and – the king of fjords – Geirangerfjord (pictured), are prime candidates for Scandinavia's most beautiful corner.

Granada's Alhambra, Spain

10 The palace complex of the Alhambra (pictured; p1083) is close to architectural perfection. It is perhaps the most refined example of Islamic art anywhere in the world, not to mention the most enduring symbol of 800 years of Moorish rule in what was then known as Al-Andalus. From afar, the Alhambra's red fortress towers dominate the Granada skyline, set against a backdrop of the Sierra Nevada's snowcapped peaks. Up close, the Alhambra's perfectly proportioned Generalife gardens complement the exquisite detail of the Palacio Nazaríes. Put simply, this is Spain's most beautiful monument.

Imperial Vienna, Austria

11 Imagine what you could do with un-limited riches and Austria's top archi-tects at your hands for 640 years: you have the Vienna of the Habsburgs. The graceful Hofburg (pictured; p59) whisks you back to the age of empires as you marvel at the treasury's imperial crowns, the equine ballet of the Spanische Hofreitschule (Spanish Riding School) and Empress Elisabeth's chandelier-lit apartments. The palace is rivalled in grandeur only by Schloss Schönbrunn and also the baroque Schloss Belvedere, both set in exquisite landscaped gardens.

Dubrovnik's Old City Walls, Croatia

12 Get up close and personal with the city by walking the spectacular city walls (p268), as history is unfurled from the battlements. No visit is complete without a leisurely walk along these ramparts, the finest in the world and Dubrovnik's main claim to fame. Built between the 13th and 16th centuries, they are still remarkably intact today, and the vistas over the terracotta rooftops and the Adriatic Sea are sublime, especially at dusk when the sundown makes the hues dramatic and the panoramas unforgettable.

EMI CRISTEA / SHUTTERSTOCK ©

EMI CRISTEA / SHUTTERSTOCK ©

Moscow's Red Square, Russia

13 With the gravitational pull of a black hole, Red Square (p949) sucks in every visitor to Russia's capital, leaving them slack-jawed with wonder. Standing on the rectangular cobble-stoned expanse – surrounded by the candy-coloured swirls of the cupolas atop St Basil's Cathedral (pictured), the red-star-tipped towers of the Kremlin, Lenin's squat granite mausoleum, the handsome red-brick facade of the State History Museum, and GUM, a grand emporium of consumption – you are literally at the centre of Russia's modern history.

Amsterdam's Canals, The Netherlands

14 To say Amster-dammers love the water is an understate-ment. Sure, the city (p811) made its first fortune in maritime trade, but that's ancient history. You can stroll next to the canals and check out some of the thousands of houseboats. Or, better still, go for a ride. From boat level you'll see a whole new set of archi-tectural details such as the ornamentation bedecking the bridges. And when you pass the canalside cafe terraces, you can just look up and wave.

Ancient Rome, Italy

15 Rome's famous seven hills (actu-ally, there are nine) offer some superb vantage points. A favourite is the Palatino (pictured; p650), a gorgeous green expanse of evocative ruins, tower-ing umbrella pines and unforgettable views over the Roman Forum. This is where it all began, where Romulus supposedly founded the city and where the ancient Roman emper-ors lived in unimaginable luxury. Nowadays, it's a truly haunting spot; as you walk the gravel paths you can almost sense the ghosts in the air.

Budapest, Hungary

16 Straddling both sides of the Danube River, with the Buda Hills to the west and the start of the Great Plain to the east, Budapest (p573) is perhaps the most beautiful city in Eastern Europe. Parks brim with attractions, the architecture is second to none and museums are filled with treasures. And with Turkish-era thermal baths belching steam and a nightlife throbbing till dawn most nights, it's easy to see why the Hungarian capital is one of the continent's most delightful and fun cities to visit.

Top: Széchenyi Baths (p577)

Barcelona's La Sagrada Família, Spain

17 One of Spain's top sights, La Sagrada Família (pictured; p1049), modernist brainchild of Antoni Gaudí, remains a work in progress more than 90 years after its creator's death. Fanciful and profound, inspired by nature and barely restrained by a Gothic style, Barcelona's quirky temple soars skyward with an almost playful majesty. The improbable angles and departures from architectural convention will have you shaking your head in disbelief.

Bay of Kotor, Montenegro

18 There's a sense of secrecy and mystery to the Bay of Kotor (p800). Grey mountain walls rise steeply from steely blue waters, getting higher and higher as you progress through their folds to the hidden reaches of the inner bay. Here, ancient stone settlements hug the shoreline, with Kotor's ancient alleyways concealed in its innermost reaches behind hefty stone walls. Talk about drama! But you wouldn't expect anything else of the Balkans, where life is exuberantly Mediterranean and lived full of passion on these ancient streets.

Athens, Greece

19 Magnificent ruins of its ancient civilisation are scattered across the mainland and islands of Greece, but it's in its capital Athens that the greatest and most iconic of those monuments still stands. High on a rocky outcrop overlooking the city, the Acropolis (p524) epitomises the glory of ancient Greece. Other impressive ruins littering this resilient, vibrant city include the mammoth Temple of Olympian Zeus and two agoras (marketplaces – one Greek, one Roman) mingling with first-rate museums.

Tallinn, Estonia

20 The Estonian capital (p330) is rightly famous for its two-tiered chocolate-box Old Town with landscapes of intertwining alleys, picturesque courtyards and red-rooftop views from medieval turrets. But be sure to step outside the Old Town walls and experience Tallinn's other treasures: its stylish restaurants plating up fashionable New Nordic cuisine, its buzzing Scandinavian-influenced design community, its ever-growing number of museums or its progressive contemporary architecture.

İstanbul, Turkey

21 Straddling Europe and Asia, and serving stints as the capital of the Byzantine and Ottoman Empires, İstanbul is one of the world's great cities. The historical highlights cluster in Sultanahmet – the Aya Sofya (p1151), Blue Mosque, Topkapı Palace and Grand Bazaar. After marvelling at their ancient domes and glittering interiors, it's time to experience the vibrant contemporary life of this huge metropolis. Cross the Galata Bridge, passing ferries and fish-kebab stands, to Beyoğlu, where the nightlife thrives from chic rooftop bars to rowdy taverns.

SCANRAIL / SHUTTERSTOCK ©

ARTUR BOGACKI / SHUTTERSTOCK ©

Lisbon's Alfama, Portugal

22 The Alfama (p890), with its labyrinthine alleyways, hidden courtyards and curving, shadow-filled lanes, is a magical place to lose all sense of direction and delve into the soul of the city. On the journey, you'll pass breadbox-sized grocers, brilliantly tiled buildings and cosy taverns filled with easygoing chatter, with the scent of chargrilled sardines and the mournful rhythms of fado drifting in the breeze. Then you round a bend and catch sight of steeply pitched rooftops leading down to the glittering Tejo and you know you're hooked.

Ohrid, Macedonia

23 Whether you come to sublime, hilly Ohrid (p777) for its sturdy medieval castle, to wander the stone laneways of its Old Town or to gaze at its restored Plaošnik, every visitor pauses for a few moments at the Church of Sveti Jovan at Kaneo, set high on a bluff overlooking Lake Ohrid and its popular beaches. It's the prime spot for absorbing the town's beautiful architecture, idling sunbathers and distant fishing skiffs – all framed by the rippling green of Mt Galičica to the southeast and the endless expanse of lake stretching out elsewhere.

Castles & Mountains of Transylvania, Romania

24 The Romanian region (p931) that so ghoulishly inspired Irish writer Bram Stoker to create his *Dracula* has some seriously spooky castles. Monumental Bran Castle (pictured), south of Braşov, is suitably vampiric, but our favourite haunt has to be the 13th-century Râşnov fortress just down the road. The castles are nestled high amid the Carpathians, a relatively underexplored mountain range that's ideal for all manner of outdoor activity, including hiking, trekking, mountain biking and skiing.

Need to Know

For more information, see Survival Guide (p1195)

Currency
Euro (€), Pound (£), Swiss franc (Sfr), Rouble (R)

Language
English, French, German, Italian, Spanish, Russian, Hungarian, Greek, Turkish

Visas
EU citizens don't need visas for other EU countries. Australians, Canadians, New Zealanders and Americans don't need visas for visits of less than 90 days.

Money
ATMs are common; credit and debit cards are widely accepted.

Mobile Phones
Europe uses the GSM 900 network. If you're coming from outside Europe it's worth buying a prepaid local SIM.

Time
Britain, Ireland and Portugal (GMT), Central Europe (GMT plus one hour), Greece, Turkey and Eastern Europe (GMT plus two hours), Russia (GMT plus three hours)

When to Go

desert, dry climate
warm to hot summers, mild winters
warm to hot summers, cold winters
mild summers, cold winters
cold climate

Sweden GO May-Sep

Russia GO May-Sep & Dec-Jan

Britain GO Apr-Oct

Germany GO May-Sep

Czech Republic GO Apr-Oct

France GO Apr-Jun & Sep-Oct

Italy GO Apr-Jun & Sep-Oct

High Season (Jun–Aug)

➡ Everybody comes to Europe and all of Europe hits the road.

➡ Hotel prices and temperatures are their highest.

➡ Expect all the major attractions to be nightmarishly busy.

Shoulder (Apr–May & Sep–Oct)

➡ Crowds and prices drop, except in Italy where it's still busy.

➡ Temperatures are comfortable but it can be hot in southern Europe.

➡ Overall these are the best months to travel in Europe.

Low Season (Nov–Mar)

➡ Outside ski resorts, hotels drop their prices or close down.

➡ The weather can be cold and days short, especially in northern Europe.

➡ Some places, such as resort towns, are like ghost towns.

Useful Websites

Lonely Planet (www.lonely planet.com/europe) Destination information, hotel bookings, traveller forum and more.

The Man in Seat Sixty-One (www.seat61.com) Encyclopedic site dedicated to train travel plus plenty of other tips.

Hidden Europe (www.hidden europe.co.uk) Fascinating magazine and online dispatches from all the continent's corners.

Couchsurfing (www.couch surfing.org) Find a free bed and make friends in any European country.

VisitEurope (www.visiteurope. com) With information about travel in 33 member countries.

Spotted by Locals (www.spot tedbylocals.com) Insider tips for cities across Europe.

What to Take

Flip-flops (thongs) for overnight trains, hostel bathrooms and the beach.

Hiking boots for Europe's walks.

Ear plugs – especially helpful in hostels.

Antimosquito plugs – useful in summer, particularly in the Baltic and Scandinavia.

European plug adapters.

Unlocked mobile phone for use with a local SIM card.

Casual-smart clothes – look the part when breaking the budget.

Exchange Rates

AU	A$1	€0.69	£0.58
CA	C$1	€0.70	£0.60
JAP	¥100	€0.81	£0.69
NZ	NZ$1	€0.66	£0.56
US	US$1	€0.96	£0.81

For current exchange rates see www.xe.com.

Daily Costs
Budget: Less than €60
➡ Dorm beds: €10–20
➡ Admission to museums: €5–15
➡ Pizza or pasta: €8–12

Midrange: €60–200
➡ Double room in a small hotel: €50–100
➡ Short taxi trip: €10–20
➡ Meals in good restaurants: around €20 per person

Top end: More than €200
➡ Stay at iconic hotels: from €150
➡ Car hire: from around €30 per day
➡ Theatre tickets: €15–150

Accommodation
Europe offers the fullest possible range of accommodation for all budgets. Book up to two months in advance for a July visit, or for ski resorts over Christmas and New Year.

Hotels Range from the local pub to restored castles.

B&Bs Small, family-run houses generally provide good value.

Hostels Enormous variety from backpacker palaces to real dumps.

Homestays and farmstays A great way to really find out how locals live.

Arriving in Europe
Schiphol Airport, Amsterdam (p834) Trains to the centre (20 minutes).

Heathrow Airport, London (p186) Trains (15 minutes) and tube (one hour) to the centre.

Aéroport de Charles de Gaulle, Paris (p388) Many buses (one hour) and trains (30 minutes) to the centre.

Frankfurt Airport, Frankfurt (p495) Trains (15 minutes) to the centre.

Leonardo da Vinci Airport, Rome (p667) Buses (one hour) and trains (30 minutes) to the centre.

Barajas Airport, Madrid (p1038) Buses (40 minutes) and metro (15 minutes) to the centre.

Getting Around
In most European countries, the train is the best option for internal transport.

Train Europe's train network is fast and efficient but rarely a bargain unless you book well in advance or use a rail pass wisely.

Bus Usually taken for short trips in remoter areas, though long-distance intercity buses can be cheap.

Car You can hire a car or drive your own through Europe. Roads are excellent but petrol is expensive.

Ferry Boats connect Britain and Ireland with mainland Europe; Scandinavia to the Baltic countries and Germany; and Italy to the Balkans and Greece.

Air Speed things up by flying from one end of the continent to the other.

Bicycle Slow things down on a two-wheeler; a great way to get around just about anywhere.

For much more on **getting around**, see 1208

If You Like...

Castles & Palaces

Versailles, France The vast formal palace against which all others are measured includes the Hall of Mirrors and sumptuous gardens. (p390)

Neuschwanstein, Germany In the heart of the Bavarian Alps, this is everybody's (including Disney's) castle fantasy. (p481)

Winter Palace, Russia Forever associated with the Russian Revolution, this golden-green baroque building in St Petersburg is unmatched for tsarist splendour. (p963)

Bran Castle, Romania Better known as Dracula's Castle, this Transylvanian beauty is straight out of a horror movie. (p934)

Alhambra, Spain This exquisite Islamic palace complex in Granada is a World Heritage–listed wonder. (p1083)

Gravensteen, Belgium The turreted stone castle of the Counts of Flanders looms over the beautiful Belgian city of Ghent. (p121)

Windsor Castle, Britain The world's largest and oldest occupied fortress is one of the British monarch's principal residences. (p187)

Topkapı Palace, Turkey Tour the opulent pavilions and jewel-filled Treasury of the former court of the Ottoman empire in İstanbul. (p1151)

Beaches & Islands

Cyclades, Greece The names Mykonos, Santorini and Naxos all conjure up images of perfect golden beaches and the reality will not disappoint. (p541)

Riviera, Albania The white-sand beaches on Albania's fast-disappearing undeveloped coastline is sublime. (p54)

Menorca, Spain Beaches so beautiful you think they might be dreams are tucked away in little coves in the prettiest of the Balearic Islands. (p1073)

Black Sea Coast, Bulgaria Bulgaria guards the best beaches on the Black Sea, especially if you avoid the big resorts and head to smaller Sozopol. (p244)

Hvar Island, Croatia Famed for its verdancy and lilac fields, this luxurious and sunny island is the jumping-off point for the wooded Pakleni Islands. (p266)

Isle of Skye, Scotland A 50-mile-long smorgasbord of velvet moors, jagged mountains, sparkling lochs and towering sea cliffs. (p221)

Spectacular Scenery

The Alps, Switzerland There's no competition for the most stunning landscape in Europe – beautiful Switzerland. (p1122)

Fjords, Norway Like steep gashes cutting into a precipitous coastline, Norway's fjords are simply unmissable. (p836)

West Coast of Ireland Wind-whipped headlands, hidden bays and mossy green clifftops battle against the wild Atlantic. (p633)

High Tatras, Slovakia Pristine snowfields, ultramarine mountain lakes, thundering waterfalls, undulating pine forests and shimmering alpine meadows. (p998)

Vatnajökull National Park, Iceland Skaftafell is the jewel in the crown of this breathtaking collection of peaks and glaciers. (p608)

Nightlife

Berlin, Germany There's nothing quite like arriving at superclub **Berghain** to dance from sunrise to sundown. (p462)

London, Britain A multifarious scene from a quiet session down the local pub to a full-blown night on the tiles of East London. (p157)

Moscow, Russia Once famed for its strict door policies, Moscow has spawned a slew of new democratically run bars and clubs. (p948)

Madrid, Spain Has more bars per capita than anywhere else on earth and no one goes to

bed here before killing the night. (p1025)

Mykonos, Greece There are party pockets dotted throughout the Greek islands; summer revellers flock to the bars and clubs of Mykonos. (p541)

Reykjavík, Iceland Join in the *djammið*, a raucous weekend pub crawl around the Icelandic capital's vibrant cafe-bar scene. (p595)

Belgrade, Serbia The Serbian capital is one of the liveliest places to party the night away, especially in its summer *splavovi* (floating clubs) on the Danube. (p974)

Great Food

Copenhagen, Denmark Yes, Denmark's capital is the place to sample Europe's most sought-after menus and cool New Nordic cuisine.

Naples, Italy Pizza, the peasant dish that ate the world, is still the best in the city of its birth: accept no imitations. (p707)

San Sebastián, Spain The Basque powerhouse hosts an impressive array of Michelin-starred restaurants. (p1062)

Lyon, France Forget Paris, the gastronomic capital of La Belle France is undoubtedly Lyon, a city that will have gourmands swooning. (p407)

Seafood, Greece Swig on ouzo while snacking on grilled octopus; not a bad way to pack away some calories. (p522)

İstanbul, Turkey Grilled meats, kebaps and a marvellous array of meze (small dishes) can be sampled in this paradise for food lovers. (p1151)

Top: A typically Greek menu: fresh seafood, Greek salad, olive oil and bread
Bottom: Cala Macarella, Menorca (p1073), Spain

Outdoor Fun

Bovec and Bled, Slovenia
The capital of active sports in Eastern Europe is Slovenia, with everything from canyoning to hydrospeeding. (p1015)

Cycling the Loire Valley, France There's a gorgeous château around every bend in the river in this beautiful valley. (p401)

Skiing year-round, Austria Experience Olympic-sized skiing in Innsbruck, the Alpine city ringed by famous year-round pistes. (p58)

Bridge diving, Bosnia and Hercegovina Screw up your courage and learn from professional divers how to safely jump off Mostar's **Stari Most** (old bridge). (p149)

Snowmobiling and dog-sledding, Sweden Explore the icy wastelands of northern Sweden in the most thrilling way possible. (p1098)

Caving, Slovakia The **Slovenský Raj National Park** includes one of only three aragonite caves in the world, as well as the Dobšinská Ice Cave. (p1002)

Art Collections

Louvre, France It's not just Paris' museum, it's the world's; treasures collected from Europe and all over the planet in exhaustive quantity. (p371)

Florence, Italy From the Duomo, to the Uffizi, to the Ponte Vecchio – the entire Renaissance in one city. (p692)

Hermitage, Russia Housed in the Winter Palace lies one of the world's greatest art collections, stuffed full of treasures from

Egyptian mummies to Picasso. (p963)

Van Gogh Museum, Netherlands Despite his troubled life and struggles with madness, Van Gogh's superb creations are gloriously easy to enjoy in Amsterdam. (p813)

Madrid, Spain With the Prado, Thyssen and Reina Sofia within a single golden mile of art, Madrid is a premier destinations for art lovers. (p1025)

Music

Vienna's Staatsoper, Austria The premier venue in a city synonymous with opera and classical music. (p69)

Berlin, Germany Everything from the world's most acclaimed techno venue to the **Berlin Philharmonic** can be seen in Germany's music-obsessed capital. (p462)

Irish music, Ireland The Irish love their music and it takes little to get them singing; the west coast hums with music pubs, especially in Galway. (p633)

Fado, Portugal Portuguese love the melancholic and nostalgic songs of fado; hear it in Lisbon's Alfama district. (p890)

Trubači, Serbia While this wild brass music is celebrated en masse at Guča each August, ragtag *trubači* bands wander the streets of many Serbian towns year-round. (p972)

Seville, Spain Few musical forms capture the spirit of a nation quite like passionate flamenco, and Seville is its cradle. (p1076)

Mariinsky Theatre, Russia There's nowhere like St Petersburg's Mariinsky for world-class opera and ballet. (p966)

Cafes & Bars

Vienna's coffee houses, Austria Unchanged in decades and heavy with the air of refinement; pause for a cup served just so. (p59)

Irish pubs, Ireland Come and join the warm and gregarious crowds of locals in any pub in Ireland for a true cultural experience. (p614)

Paris' cafe society, France What's more clichéd: the practised curtness of the Parisian waiter or the studied boredom of the customer? (p367)

Amsterdam's tiny havens, Netherlands The Dutch call them 'brown cafes' for the former tobacco stains on the walls, but they're still cosy, warm and invariably friendly. (p811)

Bourse cafes, Belgium Many of Brussels' most iconic cafes are within stumbling distance of the city's Bourse and are great places to sample Belgian beer. (p104)

Budapest's ruin pubs, Hungary So-called 'ruin pubs' – essentially pop-up bars in abandoned buildings – are popular seasonal outdoor venues in summer. (p573)

Architecture

Notre Dame, France Paris' gargoyle-covered cathedral is a Gothic wonder. (p371)

Meteora, Greece Late 14th-century monasteries perch dramatically atop enormous rocky pinnacles. (p537)

La Sagrada Família, Spain Gaudí's singular work in progress, Barcelona's mighty cathedral defies imagination. (p1049)

Pantheon, Rome Commissioned during Augustus' reign,

Pantheon (p651), Rome, Italy

the portico of this ancient wonder is graced by Corinthian columns. (p651)

Grand Place, Belgium Brussels' suitably grand central square is ringed by gilded houses. (p105)

St Basil's Cathedral, Moscow The Red Square's iconic mixture of colours, patterns and shapes is the culmination of a style unique to Russian architecture. (p949)

Art nouveau, Budapest Budapest hits its stride with art nouveau masterpieces. (p573)

Blue Mosque, İstanbul Islamic style finds perfect form in the Blue Mosque, one of İstanbul's most recognisable buildings. (p1154)

Historical Sites

Stonehenge, Britain The UK's most iconic – and mysterious – archaeological site, dating back some 5000 years. (p190)

Pompeii, Italy Wander the streets and alleys of this great ancient city, buried by a volcanic eruption. (p713)

Athens, Greece Ancient wonders include the Acropolis, Ancient Agora, Temple of Olympian Zeus and more. (p523)

Amsterdam's Canal Ring, Netherlands Stroll the Dutch capital's Golden Age canals lined with gabled buildings. (p811)

Moscow's Kremlin, Russia The seat of power to medieval tsars and modern tyrants alike, Moscow's vast Kremlin offers incredible history lessons. (p948)

Dachau, Germany The first Nazi concentration camp is a harrowing introduction to WWII's horrors. (p478)

Sarajevo, Bosnia Hercegovina Enjoy the bustling old Turkish quarter of arguably the Balkans' most charming town – and a proud survivor. (p142) (p142)

Month by Month

January

It's cold but most towns are relatively tourist-free and hotel prices are rock bottom. Head to Eastern Europe's ski slopes for wallet-friendly prices, with Bosnia and Bulgaria your best bets.

✯✯ Orthodox Christmas, Eastern Europe

Christmas is celebrated in different ways in Eastern Europe: many countries celebrate on Christmas Eve (24 December), with an evening meal and midnight Mass. In Russia, Ukraine, Belarus, Moldova, Serbia, Montenegro and Macedonia, Christmas falls in January, as per the Julian calendar.

✯✯ Kiruna Snöfestivalen, Sweden

In the last weekend of January this Lapland snow festival (www.snofestivalen.com), based around a snow-sculpting competition, draws artists from all over Europe. There's also a husky-dog competition and a handicrafts fair.

✯✯ Küstendorf Film & Music Festival, Serbia

Created and curated by Serbian director Emir Kusturica, this international indie-fest (http://kustendorf-filmandmusicfestival.org) in the town of Drvengrad, near Zlatibor in Serbia, eschews traditional red-carpet glitz for oddball inclusions vying for the 'Golden Egg' prize.

February

Carnival in all its manic glory sweeps the Catholic regions. Cold temperatures are forgotten amid masquerades, street festivals and general bacchanalia. Expect to be kissed by a stranger.

✯✯ Carnavale, Italy

In the period before Ash Wednesday, Venice goes mad for masks (www.venice-carnival-italy.com). Costume balls, many with traditions centuries old, enliven the social calendar in this storied old city. Even those without a coveted invite are swept up in the pageantry.

✯✯ Carnival, Croatia

For colourful costumes and nonstop revelry head to Rijeka, where Carnival is the pinnacle of the year's calendar (www.rijecki-karneval.hr). Zadar and Samobor host Carnival celebrations too, with street dancing, concerts and masked balls.

✯✯ Karneval/ Fasching, Germany

Germany doesn't leave the pre-Lent season solely to its neighbours. Karneval is celebrated with abandon in the traditional Catholic regions including Bavaria, along the Rhine and particularly vibrantly in Cologne (www.koelnerkarneval.de).

March

Spring arrives in southern Europe. Further north the rest of the continent continues to freeze, though days are often bright.

✈ St Patrick's Day, Ireland

Parades and celebrations are held on 17 March in Irish towns big and small to honour the beloved patron saint of Ireland. While elsewhere the day is a commercialised romp of green beer, in his home country it's time for a parade and celebrations with friends and family.

✈ Budapest Spring Festival, Hungary

This two-week festival in March/April is one of Europe's top classical-music events (www.springfestival. hu). Concerts are held in a number of beautiful venues, including stunning churches, the opera house and the national theatre.

🏃 Ski-Jumping World Cup, Slovenia

This exciting international competition (www.plan ica.si) takes place on the world's largest ski-jumping hill, in the Planica Valley at Rateče near Kranjska Gora. Held the third weekend in March, it's a must for adrenaline junkies.

April

Spring arrives with a burst of colour, from the glorious bulb fields of Holland to the blooming orchards of Spain. On the most southern beaches it's time to shake the sand out of the umbrellas.

✈ Semana Santa, Spain

There are parades of penitents and holy icons in Spain, notably in Seville, during Easter week (www. semana-santa.org). Thousands of members of religious brotherhoods parade in trad garb before thousands of spectators. Look for the pointed *capirotes* (hoods).

✈ Settimana Santa, Italy

Italy celebrates Holy Week with processions and passion plays. By Holy Thursday Rome is thronged with the faithful and even nonbelievers are swept up in the emotion and piety of hundreds of thousands thronging the Vatican and St Peter's Basilica.

✈ Orthodox Easter, Greece

The most important festival in the Greek Orthodox calendar has an emphasis on the Resurrection, so it's a celebratory event. The most significant part is midnight on Easter Saturday, when candles are lit and fireworks and a procession hit the streets.

✈ Feria de Abril, Spain

Hoods off! A week-long party in Seville in late April counterbalances the religious peak of Easter (http://feriadesevilla.anda-lunet.com). The beautiful old squares of this gorgeous city come alive during the long, warm nights for which the nation is known.

✈ Koningsdag (King's Day), Netherlands

The nationwide celebration on 27 April is especially fervent in Amsterdam, awash with orange costumes and fake Afros, beer, dope, leather boys, temporary roller coasters, clogs and general craziness.

May

May is usually sunny and warm and full of things to do – an excellent time to visit. It's not too hot or too crowded, though you can still expect the big destinations to feel busy.

🍺 Beer Festival, Czech Republic

An event dear to many travellers' hearts, this Prague beer festival (www. ceskypivnifestival.cz) offers lots of food, music and – most importantly – around 70 beers from around the country from mid- to late May.

☆ Brussels Jazz Marathon, Belgium

Around-the-clock jazz performances hit Brussels during the second-last weekend in May (www.facebook.com/ brusselsjazzmarathon). The saxophone is the instrument of choice for this international-flavoured city's most joyous celebration.

✈ Queima das Fitas, Portugal

Coimbra's annual highlight is this boozy week of fado music and revelry that begins on the first Thursday in May (www.queimadas-fitascoimbra.pt), when students celebrate the end of the academic year.

June

The huge summer travel season hasn't started yet, but the sun has broken through the clouds and the weather is generally gorgeous across the continent.

★ Karneval der Kulturen, Germany

This joyous street carnival (www.karneval-berlin.de) celebrates Berlin's multicultural tapestry with parties, global nosh and a fun parade of flamboyantly costumed dancers, DJs, artists and musicians.

★ Festa de São João, Portugal

Elaborate processions, live music on Porto's plazas and merrymaking all across Portugal's second city. Squeaky plastic hammers (for sale everywhere) come out for the unusual custom of whacking one another. Everyone is fair game – expect no mercy.

☆ White Nights, Russia

By mid-June the Baltic sun just sinks behind the horizon at night, leaving the sky a grey-white colour and encouraging locals to forget routines and party hard. The best place to join the fun is St Petersburg, where balls, classical-music concerts and other summer events keep spirits high.

★ Glastonbury Festival, Britain

The town's youthful summer vibe peaks for this long weekend of music, theatre and New Age shenanigans (www.glastonburyfestivals.co.uk). It's one of England's favourite outdoor events and more than 100,000 turn up to writhe around in the grassy fields (or deep mud) at Pilton's (Worthy) Farm.

★ Roskilde Festival, Denmark

Northern Europe's largest music festival (www.roskilde-festival.dk) rocks Roskilde each summer. It takes place in late June but advance ticket sales are on offer in December and the festival usually sells out.

★ Festa de Santo António, Portugal

Feasting, drinking and dancing in Lisbon's Alfama in honour of St Anthony (12–13 June) top the even grander three-week Festas de Lisboa (www.festasdelisboa.com), which features processions and dozens of street parties.

☆ Hellenic Festival, Greece

The ancient theatre at Epidavros and the Odeon of Herodes Atticus are the headline venues of Athens' annual cultural shindig (www.greekfestival.gr). The festival, which runs from mid-June to August, features music, dance, theatre and much more.

July

One of the busiest months for travel across the continent with outdoor cafes, beer gardens and beach clubs all hopping. Expect beautiful – even steamy – weather anywhere you go.

★ Il Palio, Italy

Siena's great annual event is the Palio (2 July and 16 August; www.thepalio.com), a pageant culminating in a bareback horse race round Il Campo. The city is divided into 17 *contrade* (districts), of which 10 compete for the *palio* (silk banner), with emotions exploding.

★ Sanfermines (Running of the Bulls), Spain

Fiesta de San Fermín (Sanfermines) is the week-long nonstop Pamplona festival (www.bullrunpamplona.com) with the daily *encierro* (running of the bulls) as its centrepiece. Anything can happen, but it rarely ends well for the bull. The anti-bullfighting event, the Running of the Nudes (www.runningofthenudes.com), takes place two days earlier.

★ Bastille Day, France

Fireworks, balls, processions, and – of course – good food and wine, for France's national day on 14 July, celebrated in every French town and city. Go to the heart of town and get caught up in this patriotic festival.

☆ EXIT Festival, Serbia

Eastern Europe's most talked-about music festival (www.exitfest.org) takes place within the walls of the Petrovaradin Citadel in Serbia's second city, Novi Sad. Book early as it attracts music lovers from all over the continent with big international acts headlining.

☆ Gentse Feesten, Belgium

Ghent is transformed into a 10-day party of music and theatre, a highlight of which is a vast techno celebration called 10 Days Off (www.gentsefeesten.be).

⚔ Medieval Festival of the Arts, Romania

The beautiful Romanian city of Sighişoara hosts open-air concerts, parades and ceremonies, all glorifying medieval Transylvania and taking the town back to its fascinating 12th-century origins.

☆ Bažant Pohoda, Slovakia

Slovakia's largest music festival (www.pohodafestival. sk) represents all genres of music from folk and rock to orchestral over eight different stages. It's firmly established as one of Europe's biggest and best summer music festivals.

☆ Ultra Europe, Croatia

Held over three days in Split's Poljud Stadium this electronic music fest (www. ultraeurope.com) includes a huge beach party.

☆ Východná, Slovakia

Slovakia's standout folk festival, Východná (www. festivalvychodna.sk) is held in a village nestled just below the High Tatras.

☆ Paléo Festival Nyon, Switzerland

More than 250 shows and concerts are staged for this premier music festival (http://yeah.paleo.ch) held above the town of Nyon.

August

It's cooling off in every sense, from the northern countries to the romance started on a dance floor in Ibiza. Maybe the best time to visit: the weather's still good and crowds have thinned.

Everybody's going someplace as half of Europe shuts down to enjoy the traditional month of holiday with the other half. If it's near the beach, from Germany's Baltic to Spain's Balearics, it's mobbed and the temperatures are hot, hot, hot!

⚔ Amsterdam Gay Pride, Netherlands

Held at the beginning of August, this is one of Europe's best GLBT events (www.amsterdamgaypride. nl). It's more about freedom and diversity than protest.

☆ Salzburg Festival, Austria

Austria's most renowned classical-music festival (www.salzburgfestival.at) attracts international stars from late July to the end of August. That urbane person sitting by you having a glass of wine who looks like a famous cellist, probably is.

⚔ Zürich Street Parade, Switzerland

Zürich lets its hair down with an enormous techno parade (www.streetparade.com). All thoughts of numbered accounts are forgotten as bankers, and everybody else in this otherwise staid burg, party to orgasmic, deep-base thump, thump, thump.

⚔ Notting Hill Carnival, Britain

This is Europe's largest – and London's most vibrant – outdoor carnival, where London's Caribbean community shows the city how to party (www.thelondonnottinghillcarnival.com). Food, frolic and fun are just a part of this vast multicultural two-day celebration.

☆ Edinburgh International Festival, Britain

Three weeks of innovative drama, comedy, dance, music and more (www.eif.co.uk). Two weeks overlap with the celebrated Fringe Festival (www.edfringe.com), which draws acts from around the globe. Expect cutting-edge productions that often defy description.

☆ Guča Trumpet Festival, Serbia

Guča's Dragačevo Trumpet Assembly (www.guca.rs) is one of the most exciting and bizarre events in all of Eastern Europe. Hundreds of thousands of revellers descend on the small Serbian town to damage their eardrums, livers and sanity in four cacophonous days of revelry.

☆ Sziget Music Festival, Hungary

A week-long, great-value world-music festival (www.sziget.hu) held all over Budapest. Sziget features bands from around the world playing at more than 60 venues.

September

It's cooling off in every sense, from the northern countries to the romance started on a dance floor in Ibiza. Maybe the best time to visit: the weather's still good and crowds have thinned.

☆ Venice International Film Festival, Italy

The Mostra del Cinema di Venezia (www.labiennale.

org) is Italy's top film fest and one of the world's top indie-film fests. The judging here is seen as an early indication of what to look for at the next year's Oscars.

🍺 Oktoberfest, Germany

Despite its name, Germany's legendary beer-swilling party (www.oktoberfest. de) starts mid-September in Munich and finishes a week into October. Millions descend for litres of beer and carousing that has no equal. If you didn't plan ahead, you'll have to sleep in Austria.

☆ Dvořák Autumn, Czech Republic

This festival of classical music (www.kso.cz) honours the work of the Czech Republic's favourite composer, Anton Dvořák. The event is held over three weeks in the spa town of Karlovy Vary.

☆ Festes de la Mercè, Spain

Barcelona knows how to party until dawn and it outdoes itself for the Festes de la Mercè (around 24 September). The city's biggest celebration has four days of concerts, dancing, *castellers* (human-castle builders), fireworks and *correfocs* – a parade of fireworks-spitting dragons and devils.

October

Another good month to visit – almost everything is still open, while prices and visitor numbers are way down. Weather can be unpredictable, though, and even cold in northern Europe.

☆ Belfast International Arts Festival, Northern Ireland

After 50 years of being hosted at Queen's University, this huge arts festival (www.belfastinternationalartsfestival.com) reinvented itself in 2015 and is now held at a wider cache of Belfast venues. The city sheds its gritty legacy, and celebrates the intellectual and the creative without excessive hype.

🍷 Wine Festival, Moldova

Wine-enriched folkloric performances in Moldova draw oenophiles and anyone wanting to profit from the 10-day visa-free regime Moldova introduces during the festival.

November

Leaves have fallen and snow is about to in much of Europe. Even in the temperate zones around the Med it can get chilly, rainy and blustery. Most seasonal attractions have closed for the year.

🎆 Guy Fawkes Night, Britain

Bonfires and fireworks erupt across Britain on 5 November, recalling the foiling of a plot to blow up the Houses of Parliament in the 1600s. Go to high ground in London to see glowing explosions erupt everywhere.

☆ Iceland Airwaves, Iceland

Roll on up to Reykjavík for Iceland Airwaves (www.icelandairwaves.is), a great music festival featuring both Icelandic and international acts.

December

Despite freezing temperatures this is a magical time to visit Europe, with Christmas decorations brightening the dark streets. Prices remain surprisingly low provided you avoid Christmas and New Year's Eve.

🎆 Natale, Italy

Italian churches set up an intricate crib or a *presepe* (nativity scene) in the lead-up to Christmas. Some are quite famous, most are works of art, and many date back hundreds of years and are venerated for their spiritual ties.

Itineraries

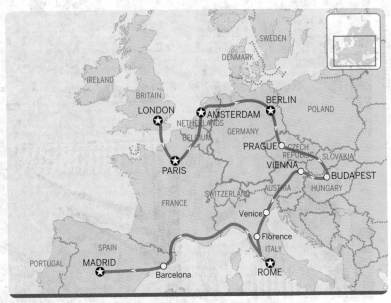

5 WEEKS : First-Time Europe

If you only visit Europe once in your life, you'll want to experience its famous cultural cities.

London is calling. The former capital of a huge empire is a city of massive museums, regal parks and electrifying nightlife.

Take the Eurostar to **Paris** and prepare to be seduced by the Eiffel Tower, Versailles and the Louvre. The art theme continues in **Amsterdam** where you can admire works by Van Gogh and Rembrandt and cycle alongside shimmering canals. Next travel to cosmopolitan, hedonistic **Berlin** in Germany where it's possible to see the remains of the wall.

Prague in the Czech Republic is a city of intangible medieval magic. **Budapest** could be Prague's twin offering refined music, riverside architecture and a youthful nocturnal scene. **Vienna** is known for its Habsburg history and gilded coffee bars.

Time to hit southern Europe. Start in glorious **Venice** with its canals and gondoliers, jump on a train to the Renaissance time capsule of **Florence**, and then proceed to **Rome**, home to the Vatican and Colosseum.

Leapfrog southern France to Spain stopping in **Barcelona** where Gaudí meets Gothic, before having a grand finale in **Madrid**, HQ of heavyweight art and all-night partying.

Above: Dubrovnik (p268), Croatia

Left: Santorini (p546), Greece

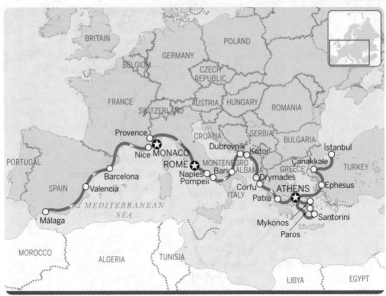

Mediterranean Europe

5 WEEKS

Think Europe doesn't do beaches? Think again – it does, but with lashings of culture on the side, as you'll find during this romp along its southern shores.

Fly to Spain and claim your sun-lounger at one of Europe's warmest year-round beaches in **Málaga**, an emerging art city with a museum to native son, Picasso. Follow the coast up to **Valencia** next, a complex mix of antique and modern, and the culinary home of paella. Pay homage to Catalonia in **Barcelona** where you can soak up the seaside ambience of Gaudí's city, while investigating the pedestrianised La Rambla and another Picasso museum. Cross the border into France, then beach-hop along the Côte d'Azur to **Nice** with its palm-lined seafront. Take the twisty coastal corniches to beguiling **Monaco** and, afterwards, spend a day or two inland in the beautiful villages of **Provence**.

Return to Nice and take the train southeast to historic **Rome**. Continue south to energetic **Naples**, peer into ill-fated **Pompeii** and explore the narrow footpaths and ancient staircases of the precipitous Amalfi Coast. Cross Italy to understated **Bari**, from where you head across the Adriatic by ferry to the Croatian pearl of **Dubrovnik** with its marble streets, baroque buildings and spectacular city walls.

Bus it south through Montenegro and Albania – two of Europe's lesser known but underrated destinations. Pause at the walled town of **Kotor** in the former and the white crescent-shaped beaches of **Drymades** in the latter.

Greece's Ionian Islands are next and the best is **Corfu** where Greek mythology and ancient castles are complemented by some fine scimitars of sand. Take a ferry to Patra and a bus on to venerable **Athens**, capital of the ancient world, guarded by the Acropolis. Move on to the port of Piraeus for an island-hopping expedition of the Cyclades, dreamy islands that include sophisticated **Mykonos**, laid-back **Paros** and volcanic **Santorini**. When you've had enough of Greek salads, set sail for Turkish port Kuşadası from lush, mountainous Samos.

Visit ancient **Ephesus**, one of the greatest surviving Graeco-Roman cities. Travel by bus north along the Aegean coast to the ruins of Troy and **Çanakkale**, the harbour town that's the base for visiting Gallipoli Peninsula. Finish in beautiful, chaotic **İstanbul**: when you've had your fill of sightseeing you can relax in a *hammam* (Turkish bath).

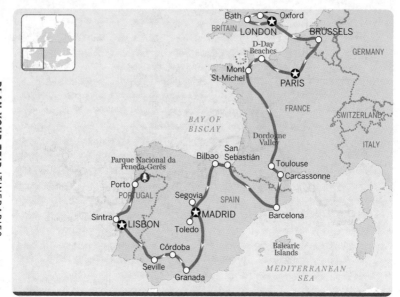

3 WEEKS From London to the Sun

Combining the best of both worlds, this itinerary begins with the urban powerhouse of London and ends with soaking up the sun in Spain and Portugal.

Enjoy several days in **London** for museums, galleries, street markets and clubbing, then take a train to **Bath** to appreciate Roman and Georgian architecture and thermal baths. Save time on the way back for **Oxford**, the fabled university town.

Back in London, take the Eurostar from grand St Pancras station to **Brussels**, the ethnically diverse headquarters of the EU known for its chocolate, art nouveau architecture and French-Flemish culture.

The Eurostar will whisk you southwest to romantic **Paris**. Having dipped into the City of Light's cultural sights and gourmet delights, make side trips to **D-Day beaches** north of Bayeux and the iconic abbey of **Mont St-Michel**, which reaches for the sky from its rocky island perch.

Head by rail south, stopping at lively **Toulouse**. Detour to the fairy-tale fortified city of **Carcassonne**. Cross into Spain, pausing at supercool **Barcelona**, where you can indulge in traditional Catalan cooking as well as more avant-garde Spanish cuisine.

Zip north to Basque seaside resort **San Sebastián**, with its envelope-pushing food scene, and then to the curvaceous Museo Guggenheim in happening **Bilbao**. Turn south, making a beeline for energetic **Madrid**, for some of Europe's best galleries and bars. From here plan day trips to **Toledo**, the so-called 'city of three cultures', and enchanting **Segovia**.

Continue south to **Granada** to explore the exquisite Alhambra. Continue your Andalucian adventures with the one-of-a-kind Mezquita of **Córdoba**, before dancing flamenco in **Seville**. Get the bus to Portugal's captivating hillside capital **Lisbon** where you can eat custard tarts by the sea, or listen to fado in the lamplit lanes of the Alfama. Sidestep to the wooded hills of **Sintra**, home to fairy-tale-like palaces and gardens.

Further north lies Unesco World Heritage–listed **Porto**, a lovely city to explore on foot. Finish off your Iberian ramblings in the **Parque Nacional da Peneda-Gerês**, where you can hike amid scenery little changed since the 12th-century founding of Portugal.

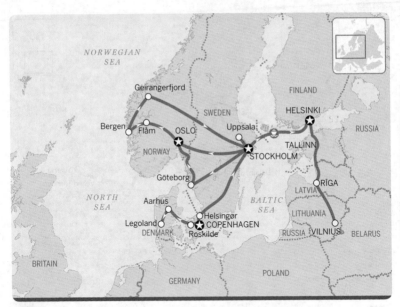

Scandinavian & Baltic Highlights

Three weeks is sufficient for the classic sights of northern Europe, though you can easily spend longer. Extra time allows detailed exploration and side trips to quieter places.

Start in Danish capital **Copenhagen**, the hipster of the Nordic block, admiring the waterfront and museums, and enjoying world-class eating options. Make day trips to the cathedral and Viking-boat museum at **Roskilde**, 'Hamlet's' castle Kronborg Slot at **Helsingør**; Denmark's second but no-less-trendy city **Aarhus** with its incredible art at ARoS Aarhus Kunstmuseum; and the country's top tourist attraction, **Legoland**.

Take the train to charming **Stockholm**. Sweden's capital spills across 14 islands with Gamla Stan the oldest and most beautiful. Side-trip to university town **Uppsala**, Sweden's spiritual heart, and spend the night. Creative and happening **Göteborg**, the country's second city, has interesting galleries and museums.

It's a 3½-hour bus ride to **Oslo**, where you can check out Munch's work in a stunning setting. Norway's capital has plenty of museums and galleries, plus the iconic Oslo Opera House, the centre of its massive waterfront redevelopment project.

From Oslo, take the long but scenic 'Norway in a Nutshell' rail day trip to **Flåm** and ride the world's steepest railway that runs without cable or rack wheels. Continue by boat and bus along the stunning Sognefjord – Norway's deepest fjord with rock walls rising up to 1000m over the water, to **Bergen**. Admire this pretty town from a cable car and explore the quayside Bryggen district of historic buildings. From Bergen take a side trip to the mighty 20km-long emerald-green **Geirangerfjord**, a spectacular Unesco World Heritage Site.

Return to Stockholm for a cruise circuit of the Baltic. First stop in quirky, design-diva **Helsinki**, a great base for exploring the natural wonders of Finland. Don't miss Unesco World Heritage–listed Suomenlinna, a fortress set on a tight cluster of islands connected by bridges.

Wind up proceedings in the Baltic States starting in **Tallinn**, the charming Estonian capital. Next is Latvia's gorgeous art nouveau **Rīga** followed by Lithuania's capital **Vilnius**, the baroque bombshell of the Baltics, a fitting finale.

4 WEEKS   The Alps to the Balkans

If you fancy visiting gorgeous towns on the shores of brilliant-blue lakes surrounded by turreted Alpine peaks, followed by a sojourn through the capitals of Eastern Europe, then head to Switzerland and jump on this itinerary.

Start with a few days in the spectacular **Swiss Alps**, ideal for hiking in summer and skiing in winter. Visit the oft-overlooked Swiss capital of **Bern**, and sophisticated, lakeside **Zürich**. Take the train to the top of Jungfrau (it's Europe's highest station) before heading down to visit lovely **Lucerne** where candy-coloured houses are reflected in a cobalt lake.

Turn east into Austria next where, on the banks of the Danube, you'll find elegant **Vienna** where you can tour the Habsburg palace Hofburg, world-class museums and the city's legendary coffee houses. Track south into Slovenia, pausing by emerald-green **Lake Bled** and nearby, but much less-developed **Lake Bohinj** with the picturesque Julian Alps as the backdrop. Both locations are great for outdoor activities, offering kayaking, mountain biking and trekking.

Time to decamp to Croatia's **Dalmatian Coast**, a holiday paradise of sun-dappled islands, limestone cliffs, ancient towns and Mediterranean cuisine. Aptly named **Split** on the Adriatic displays an interesting split between tradition and modernity, and guards Diocletian's Palace, one of Europe's most incredible Roman ruins. Further south, the walled marble town of **Dubrovnik** is heavy with history and tourists. Inland and across the border in Bosnia and Hercegovina lies **Sarajevo**. Forget its grisly recent past, this is a city on the rebound and a good place for winter activities, especially skiing in the nearby mountains.

Travel east through Serbia stopping off in gritty but lively **Belgrade** to experience its famous nightlife and explore historic Kalemegdan Citadel. Then take a train to the relaxed Bulgarian capital of **Sofia** with its cityscape of onion-domed churches and Cold War–era monuments.

A train zips you through the mountains to Bulgaria's loveliest town, **Veliko Târnovo**, laced with cobbled lanes and surrounded by forested hills. Finish off in seaside **Varna**, your base for Black Sea beaches, archaeology museums and enormous parks.

Above: Jungfrau (p1136), Switzerland

Right: Sofia (p230), Bulgaria

ROSSHELEN / SHUTTERSTOCK ©

Eastern Europe Today

Forget the stereotypes of the grim and grey 'Eastern Bloc' of the early 1990s – this half of Europe is one of the most dynamic and fast-changing places in the world.

The natural starting point is **Berlin**, once a city divided but now a veritable music, art and nightlife mecca. Despite wartime bombing, there is plenty of history here from the Reichstag to the Holocaust Memorial and Checkpoint Charlie.

Cross the now nonexistent iron curtain to Poland's capital **Warsaw**, a vibrant city that's survived all that history could throw at it and was meticulously restored after WWII. Further south is beautiful **Kraków**, the amazingly preserved royal capital which miraculously was spared destruction in WWII.

Cut across Slovakia into the Czech Republic and another remarkably intact medieval city **Prague** which has one of Eastern Europe's most romantic and architecturally impressive historical centres.

Moving back east, you'll encounter the Hungarian capital, **Budapest**, where you can freshen up at the thermal baths and party at numerous pubs and bars.

Romania had to wait a long time for its place in the sun, but it has come, especially in dynamic capital **Bucharest** with its emerging museums, trendy cafes and the world's largest parliament building.

For another side of Romania, make a beeline for **Transylvania** where you can sharpen your fangs at 'Dracula's' castle in **Bran** and enjoy the gorgeous old towns nearby.

Head north into Western Ukraine where epiphanies are rife in charming Unesco World Heritage–listed **Lviv**. Continue on to bustling Ukrainian capital **Kyiv**, one of the former Soviet Union's more pleasant metropolises, before journeying into the past on a train to **Minsk** in Belarus to see how things were under communism.

Take another train to modern-day supercity **Moscow**, where the imposing Kremlin and adjacent Red Square are guaranteed to strike you with awe. Finally, head north to the old imperial capital of **St Petersburg**, where you can spend several days touring the Hermitage and other gorgeously restored palaces.

On the Road

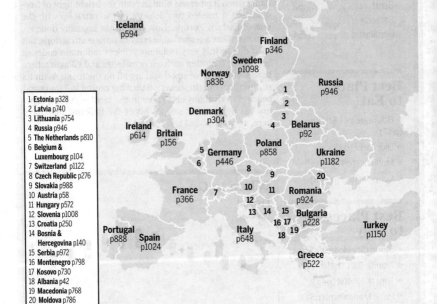

Albania

Best Places to Eat

➜ Boutique de l'Artiste (p47)

➜ Uka Farm (p48)

➜ Mullixhiu (p47)

➜ Mare Nostrum (p53)

Best Places to Stay

➜ Stone City Hostel (p55)

➜ Tradita G&T (p49)

➜ Trip 'N' Hostel (p45)

➜ Hotel Mangalemi (p52)

Why Go?

Albania has natural beauty in such abundance that you might wonder why it took 20 years for the country to take off as a tourist destination since the end of a particularly brutal strain of communism in 1991. So backward was Albania when it emerged blinking into the bright light of freedom that it needed two decades just to catch up with the rest of Eastern Europe. Now that it has arguably done so, Albania offers a remarkable array of unique attractions, not least due to this very isolation: ancient mountain codes of behaviour, forgotten archaeological sites and villages where time seems to have stood still are all on the menu. With its stunning mountain scenery, a thriving capital in Tirana and beaches to rival any elsewhere in the Mediterranean, Albania has become the sleeper hit of the Balkans. But hurry here, as word is well and truly out.

When to Go
Tirana

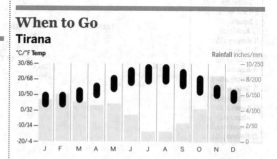

Jun Enjoy the perfect Mediterranean climate and deserted beaches.

Jul–Aug Albania's beaches may be packed, but this is a great time to explore the mountains.

Dec See features and shorts at the Tirana Film Festival, while the intrepid can snowshoe to Theth.

Albania Highlights

1 Lake Koman Ferry (p50) Join the hardy locals on this magical boat ride through stunning mountain scenery across an immense man-made lake.

2 Accursed Mountains (p50) Do the wonderful day trek between the isolated mountain villages of Valbona and Theth and experience some of Albania's best scenery.

3 Berat (p52) Explore this Unesco World Heritage–listed museum town, known as the 'city of a thousand windows'.

4 Albania Riviera (p54) Catch some sun at one of the many gorgeous beaches and coves on Albania's Ionian coast.

5 Tirana (p44) Feast your eyes on the wild colour schemes and experience Blloku cafe culture in the plucky Albanian capital.

6 Gjirokastra (p54) Take a trip to this traditional Albanian mountain town, with its spectacular Ottoman-era mansions and impressive hilltop fortress.

TIRANA

04 / POP 835,000

Lively, colourful Tirana is the beating heart of Albania, where this tiny nation's hopes and dreams coalesce into a vibrant whirl of traffic, brash consumerism and unfettered fun. Having undergone a transformation of extraordinary proportions since awaking from its communist slumber in the early 1990s, Tirana's centre is now unrecognisable, with buildings painted in primary colours, and public squares and pedestrianised streets that are a pleasure to wander.

Trendy Blloku buzzes with the well-heeled and flush hanging out in bars and cafes, while the city's grand boulevards are lined with fascinating relics of its Ottoman, Italian and communist past – from delicate minarets to loud socialist murals. Add to this some excellent museums and you have a compelling list of reasons to visit. With the traffic doing daily battle with both itself and pedestrians, the city is loud, crazy, colourful and dusty, but Tirana is never dull.

◉ Sights & Activities

★ Bunk'Art   MUSEUM
(067 2072 905, 068 4834 444; www.bunkart.al; Rr Fadil Deliu; with/without audio guide 700/500 lekë; ⊘9am-5pm) This fantastic conversion – from a massive Cold War bunker on the outskirts of Tirana into a history and contemporary art museum – is Albania's most exciting new sight and easily a Tirana highlight. With almost 3000 sq metres of space underground spread over several floors, the bunker was built for Albania's political elite in the 1970s and remained a secret for much of its existence. Now it hosts exhibits that combine the modern history of Albania with pieces of contemporary art.

★ National History Museum   MUSEUM
(Muzeu Historik Kombëtar; www.mhk.gov.al; Sheshi Skënderbej; adult/student 200/80 lekë; ⊘9am-2pm & 4-7pm) The largest museum in Albania holds many of the country's archaeological treasures and a replica of Skanderbeg's massive sword (how he held it, rode his horse and fought at the same time is a mystery). The excellent collection is almost entirely signed in English and takes you chronologically from ancient Illyria to the postcommunist era. One highlight of the museum is a terrific exhibition of icons by Onufri, a renowned 16th-century Albanian master of colour.

★ National Gallery of Arts   GALLERY
(Galeria Kombëtare e Arteve; www.galeriakombetare.gov.al/en/home/index.shtml; Blvd Dëshmorët e Kombit; adult/student 200/100 lekë; ⊘9am-2pm & 5-8pm May-Sep, 10am-8pm Oct-Apr) Tracing the relatively brief history of Albanian painting from the early 19th century to the present day, this beautiful space also has temporary exhibitions. Downstairs there's a small but interesting collection of 19th-century paintings depicting scenes from daily Albanian life, while upstairs the art takes on a political dimension with some truly fabulous examples of Albanian socialist realism. Don't miss the small collection of communist statues in storage behind the building, including two rarely seen statues of Uncle Joe Stalin himself.

Sheshi Skënderbej   SQUARE
(Skanderbeg Sq) Sheshi Skënderbej is the best place to start witnessing Tirana's dai-

---

ITINERARIES

One Week
Spend a day in busy Tirana, checking out the various excellent museums as well as the Blloku bars and cafes. On day two, make the three-hour trip to the Ottoman-era town of Berat. Overnight there before continuing down the coast to spend a couple of days on the beach in Himara or Drymades. Loop around for one last night in charming Gjirokastra before returning to Tirana.

Two Weeks
Follow the first week itinerary and then head north into Albania's incredible 'Accursed Mountains'. Start in Shkodra, from where you can get transport to Koman for the stunning morning ferry ride to Fierzë. Continue the same day to the charming mountain village of Valbona for the night, before trekking to Theth and spending your last couple of nights in the beautiful Theth National Park before heading back to Tirana.

BUNKER LOVE

On the hillsides, beaches and generally most surfaces in Albania, you will notice small concrete domes (often in groups of three) with rectangular slits. Meet the bunkers: Enver Hoxha's concrete legacy, built from 1950 to 1985. Weighing in at 5 tonnes of concrete and iron, these little mushrooms are almost impossible to destroy. They were built to repel an invasion and can resist full tank assault – a fact proved by their chief engineer, who vouched for his creation's strength by standing inside one while it was bombarded by a tank. The shell-shocked engineer emerged unscathed and tens of thousands were built. Today, some are creatively painted, one houses a tattoo artist and some even house makeshift hostels.

Two enormous bunkers, the scale of which do not compare to these tiny sniper installations, can be found in Tirana and Gjirokastra. In Tirana, Bunk'Art (p44) is the city's most fascinating site, a history museum housed inside a vast government bunker. In Gjirokastra, the Cold War Tunnel (p55), in fact a similarly massive government bunker, can also be visited, though minus the history museum and art display.

ly goings-on. Until it was pulled down by an angry mob in 1991, a 10m-high bronze statue of Enver Hoxha stood here, watching over a mainly car-free square. Now only the **equestrian statue of Skanderbeg** remains, and the 'square' – once Tirana's most popular meeting point in the decades where 99% of people were forced to get around on foot – is now a huge traffic roundabout.

Et'hem Bey Mosque   MOSQUE
(Sheshi Skënderbej; ⊙8am-11am) To one side of Sheshi Skënderbej, the 1789–1823 Et'hem Bey Mosque was spared destruction during the atheism campaign of the late 1960s because of its status as a cultural monument. Small and elegant, it's one of the oldest buildings left in the city. Take your shoes off to look inside at the beautifully painted dome.

Mt Dajti National Park   NATIONAL PARK
Just 25km east of Tirana is Mt Dajti National Park (1611m). It is the most accessible mountain in the country and many Tiranans go there to escape the city rush and have a spit-roast lamb lunch. A sky-high, Austrian-made cable car, **Dajti Express** (⏲04 2379 111; www.dajtiekspres.com; return 800 lekë; ⊙9am-10pm Wed-Mon, to 7pm Oct-Apr), takes 15 minutes to make the scenic trip to (almost) the top. Once there, you can avoid all the touts and their minibuses and take the opportunity to stroll through lovely, shady beech and pine forests.

☞ Tours

Tirana Free Tour   TOURS
(⏲069 6315 858; www.tiranafreetour.com) This enterprising tour agency has made its name by offering a free daily tour of Tirana that leaves at 10am year-round. In July, August and September a second tour is offered at 6pm. Tours meet outside the National History Museum on Sheshi Skënderbej. Tips are appreciated if you enjoy the two-hour tour, and further (paid) tours are available.

🛏 Sleeping

⭐**Trip'n'Hostel**   HOSTEL €
(⏲068 2055 540, 068 3048 905; www.tripnhostel. com; Rr Musa Maci 1; dm/d from €10/30; ☞) Tirana's coolest hostel is on a small side street, housed in a design-conscious, self-contained house with a leafy garden out the back, a bar, a kitchen and a cellar-like chill-out lounge downstairs. Dorms have handmade fixtures, curtains between beds for privacy and private lockable drawers, while there's also a roof terrace strewn with hammocks.

⭐**Tirana Backpacker Hostel**   HOSTEL €
(⏲068 4682 353, 068 3133 451; www.tiranahostel. com; Rr e Bogdaneve 3; dm €10-13, d €35, cabin per person €14; ❋@☞) Albania's first-ever hostel goes from strength to strength and remains one of the best-value and most enthusiastically run places in the country. Housed in a charmingly decorated house, with a garden, in which there are several cute cabins for those wanting more than a dorm room, the place is stylishly designed, excellently located and superfriendly.

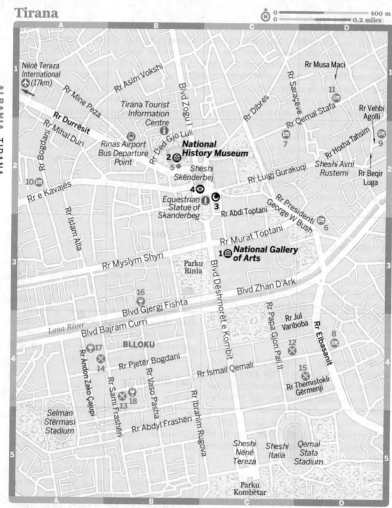

ALBANIA TIRANA

Destil Hostel

HOSTEL €

(☑069 8852 388; www.destil.al; Rr Qamil Guranja-ku; dm €8-12; ✳🛜) If you seek a rather cool place to lay your head and aren't concerned about a cultivated hostel vibe, then Destil may just be the antihostel for you. The four minimal yet stylish rooms are all dorms, but each has its own bathroom. There's no kitchen, but instead there's a fantastic restaurant/cafe/bar/chill-out area downstairs where guests can mingle with the city's creative classes.

Milingona Hostel

HOSTEL €

(☑067 6748 779; www.milingonahostel.com; Rr Vehbi Agolli 5; dm €8-10, d €28; @🛜) This superchilled villa in a side street in the middle of Tirana's old town is a friendly place with small four- and six-person dorms, though the basement's 10-bed dorm is the coolest spot in summer. There's a communal kitchen, plus an outside bar with hammocks slung between trees and lots of space for socialising. Extras include free yoga in summer, individual lockable boxes under each bed and free use of computers.

Tirana

◎ **Top Sights**
1 National Gallery of Arts.........................C3
2 National History Museum.....................B2

◎ **Sights**
3 Et'hem Bey Mosque C2
4 Sheshi Skënderbej.................................B2

◎ **Activities, Courses & Tours**
5 Tirana Free Tour B2

◎ **Sleeping**
6 Brilant Antik Hotel D3
7 Capital Tirana Hotel...............................C2
8 Destil Hostel D4

9 Milingona Hostel.....................................D2
10 Tirana Backpacker Hostel.....................A2
11 Trip'n'Hostel..D1

◎ **Eating**
12 Boutique de l'Artiste C4
13 Era B4
14 Juvenilja...A4
15 New York Tirana Bagels D4

◎ **Drinking & Nightlife**
16 BUFE..B3
17 Bunker 1944...A4
18 Radio..B4

Capital Tirana Hotel　　　HOTEL €€
(☑ 069 2080 931, 04 2258 575; www.capitaltirana-hotel.com; Rr Qemal Stafa; s/d incl breakfast from €35/55; ☐ ✳ ☎) This thoroughly modern 29-room hotel just a stone's throw from Sheshi Skënderbej is very good value given its centrality. It may be a little sterile and business-like, but the rooms are of good quality with flat-screen TVs and minibars, staff are very helpful and the busy shopping street outside is great for local atmosphere.

★**Brilant Antik Hotel**　　BOUTIQUE HOTEL €€€
(☑ 04 2251 166; www.hotelbrilant.com; Rr Jeronim de Rada 79; s/d incl breakfast €60/90; ✳ ☎) Easily one of Tirana's best midrange offerings, this charming house-cum-hotel has plenty of character, a central location and welcoming English-speaking staff to ease you into Tirana life. Rooms are spacious, decently furnished with the odd antique, and breakfast downstairs is a veritable feast each morning.

✖ Eating

New York Tirana Bagels　　CAFE €
(☑ 069 540 7583; http://newyorktiranabagels.com/; Rr Themistokli Gërmenji; bagels & sandwiches 80-300 lekë; ☺ 7.30am - 9.30pm; ☎ ✐) Believe it or not, Tirana is home to the Balkans' best bagels. Pick up one for breakfast from the aptly named New York Tirana Bagels, a cafe and social enterprise whose profits go towards supporting people in need.

Era　　ALBANIAN, ITALIAN €€
(☑ 04 225 7805; www.era.al; Rr Ismail Qemali; mains 400-900 lekë; ☺ 11am-midnight; ✐) This local institution serves traditional Albanian and Italian fare in the heart of Blloku. The

inventive menu includes oven-baked veal and eggs, stuffed eggplant, pizza and pilau with chicken and pine nuts. Be warned: it's sometimes quite hard to get a seat as it's fearsomely popular. There's a second branch near the Stadium.

Juvenilja　　ALBANIAN €€
(Rr Sami Frashëri; mains 200-950 lekë; ☺ 10am-11.30pm; ☎) This fairly unassuming Blloku establishment actually has a range of excellent traditional Albanian dishes on the menu, including veal escalope with wine and lemon, and piglet ribs with broad beans. There's an English menu and superhelpful, liveried staff.

★**Mullixhiu**　　ALBANIAN €€€
(☑ 069 666 0444; Shëtitore Parku i Madh; mains 1000-2000 lekë; ☺ noon-4pm & 6-11pm; ☎ ✐) Around the corner from the chic cafes of Blloku neighbourhood, Chef Bledar Kola's Albanian food metamorphosis is hidden behind a row of grain mills and a wall of corn husks. Opened in February 2016, the restaurant is one of the pioneers of Albania's slow-food movement.

★**Boutique de l'Artiste**　　MEDITERRANEAN €€€
(Rr Ismail Qemali 12; mains 750-1500 lekë; ☺ noon-midnight Mon-Fri, from 9am Sat & Sun; ☎) Despite its rather pretentious name, this place is all understatement, with a restrained decor and passionate staff who effortlessly translate the daily specials from a giant blackboard into English for guests. There's also a full à la carte menu taking in various aspects of Mediterranean cooking with a strong Italian flavour. Brunch is popular here, as is the in-house patisserie.

Uka Farm ALBANIAN €€€

(☑ 067 203 9909; Rr Adem Jashari, Laknas; mains 900-2500 lekë; ⊘ by reservation only) Uka Farm was founded in 1996 by former Minister of Agriculture Rexhep Uka, who started organic cultivation of agricultural products on a small plot of land. His son Flori, a trained winemaker and standout amateur chef, is now the driving force behind the restaurant, which opened in 2014. Guests can enjoy fresh, flavourful vegetables and locally sourced cheese and meat as well as quality homemade wine.

🍷 Drinking

★**Radio** BAR

(Rr Ismail Qemali 29/1; ⊘ 9am-1am; 🛜) Named for the owner's collection of antique Albanian radios, Radio is an eclectic dream with decor that includes vintage Albanian film posters and even a collection of communist-era propaganda books to read at the bar over a cocktail. It attracts a young, intellectual and alternative crowd. It's set back from the street, but it is well worth finding in otherwise rather mainstream Blloku.

Bunker 1944 BAR

(Rr Andon Zako Çajupi; ⊘ 4pm-midnight Mon-Fri, to 3am Fri & Sat) This former bunker is now a bohemian bolthole amid a sea of fairly predictable Blloku bars. Inside it's stuffed full of communist-era furniture and antiques/junk including homemade paintings, old vinyl, clocks and radios. There's a great selection of beers available, including IPA, London Porter and London Pride, and a friendly international crowd.

BUFE WINE BAR

(☑ 069 459 1203; Rr Reshit Çollaku; ⊘ 10am-midnight; 🛜) Get a full *aperitivo* spread at this famed Tirana wine bar.

ℹ️ Information

Tirana Tourist Information Centre (☑ 04 2223 313; www.tirana.gov.al; Rr Ded Gjo Luli; ⊘ 9am-6pm Mon-Fri, to 2pm Sat) A friendly English-speaking staff makes getting information easy at this government-run initiative just off Sheshi Skënderbej.

ℹ️ Getting There & Away

AIR

The modern **Nënë Tereza International Airport** (Mother Teresa Airport; ☑ 04 2381 800; www.tirana-airport.com; Rinas) is at Rinas, 17km northwest of Tirana. The Rinas Express airport bus operates an on-the-hour (7am to 6pm) service, with departures from the corner of Rr Mine Peza and Rr e Durrësit (a few blocks from the National History Museum) for 250 lekë one way. The going taxi rate is 2000 lekë to 2500 lekë.

BUS

There is no official bus station in Tirana. Instead, there are a large number of bus stops around the city centre from which buses to specific destinations leave. Do check at your hostel or hotel for the latest departure points, as they have been known to change.

Most international services depart from various points of Blvd Zogu I, with multiple services to Skopje, Macedonia (€20, eight hours), and Pristina (via Prizren), Kosovo (€10, four hours), leaving from near the Tirana International Hotel, and services to Budva, Kotor and Podgorica in Montenegro (€15 to €25, four hours) leaving from in front of the **Tirana Tourist Information Centre** (p48).

Furgons (shared minibuses) to Durrës and Bajram Curri leave the Zogu i Zi roundabout at the intersection of Rr Durrësit and Rr Muhamet Gjollesha. Services to Shkodra leave from what's known as the Northern Bus Station on Rr Dritan Hoxha, a short distance from the Zogu i Zi roundabout.

Departures to the south leave from Rr Myhedin Llegami near the corner with Blvd Gjergj Fishta. These include services to Berat, Himara, Saranda and Gjirokastra. Services to Himara and Saranda will drop you off at any of the coastal villages along the way.

DESTINATION	PRICE (LEKË)	DURATION	DISTANCE (KM)
Berat	400	2½hr	122
Durrës	130	1hr	38
Elbasan	150	1½hr	54
Fier	600	2hr	113
Gjirokastra	1000	7hr	232
Korça	500	4hr	181
Kruja	150	30min	32
Pogradec	500	3½hr	150
Saranda	1500	7hr	284
Shkodra	300	2hr	116
Vlora	500-700	4hr	147

ℹ️ Getting Around

There's now a good network of city buses running around Tirana costing 30 lekë per journey (payable to the conductor), although most of the sights can be covered easily on foot.

NORTHERN ALBANIA

Shkodra

📞 022 / POP 111,000

Shkodra, the traditional centre of the Gheg cultural region, is one of the oldest cities in Europe. The ancient Rozafa Fortress has stunning views over Lake Shkodra, while a concerted effort to renovate the buildings in the Old Town has made wandering through Shkodra a treat for the eyes. Many travellers pass through here between Tirana and Montenegro, or en route to the Lake Koman Ferry and the villages of Theth and Valbona, but it's worth spending a night or two to soak up this welcoming place before hurrying on to the mountains, the coast or the capital.

⊙ Sights

★ **Rozafa Fortress**   CASTLE
(200 lekë; ⊙ 8am-8pm summer, until 4pm winter) With spectacular views over the city and Lake Shkodra, the Rozafa Fortress is the most impressive sight in town. Founded by the Illyrians in antiquity and rebuilt much later by the Venetians and then the Turks, the fortress takes its name from a woman who was allegedly walled into the ramparts as an offering to the gods so that the construction would stand.

★ **Marubi National
Photography Museum**   GALLERY
(Muzeu Kombëtari i Fotografise Marubi; Rr Kolë Idromeno 32; adult/student 700/200 lekë; ⊙ 9am-2pm & 4-7pm) Since moving to brand new premises on the *pedonalja* (pedestrianised Rr Kolë Idromeno) in 2016, the Marubi Museum has sealed its reputation as Albania's best photography collection. Here you can find the impressive work of the Marubi 'dynasty', Albania's first and foremost family of photographers, as well as high-quality temporary exhibits. The collection includes the first-ever photograph taken in Albania, by Pjetër Marubi in 1858, as well as fascinating portraits, street scenes and early photojournalism, all giving a fascinating glimpse into old Albania.

🛏 Sleeping

Wanderers Hostel   HOSTEL €
(📞 069 2121 062; www.thewanderershostel.com; Rr Gjuhadol; dm/d incl breakfast €8/25; ❄ 🐾 🛜) Stealing a march on much of the longer-established hostel competition in town, Wanderers is currently Shkodra's most pop-

ular budget accommodation and attracts a young and fun crowd year-round. The place is a natural hangout, with a chilled-out garden, a bar area and a shared kitchen. Dorms are comfortable and clean, bike hire is €2 per day and the location is superb.

Mi Casa Es Tu Casa   HOSTEL €
(📞 069 3812 054; www.micasaestucasa.it; Blvd Skenderbeu 22; dm €9-13, d/apt €30/40, campsite per person with/without own tent €5/7; @ 🛜) English-speaking Alba is the matriarch of this impressive place, which has a central location, traditional atmosphere, a large kitchen, bright colour schemes and a garden where you can also pitch or hire a tent. Dorms can be a little crowded, but the cosy private rooms upstairs are excellent and are stuffed full of communist-era Albanian furniture. Bike hire is available for €5.

Lake Shkodra Resort   CAMPGROUND €
(📞 069 2750 337; www.lakeshkodraresort.com; campsite per tent €12, per person €5-6, cabins €65-85, glamping d €30; 🛜) Frequently appearing in lists of Europe's best campsites, this gorgeously located and superbly run place is not in Shkodra itself, but on the lakeside 7km from the city. There are spotless facilities, a huge range of activities including watersports on offer and, best of all, access to a great sandy beach perfect for swimming. There are also new cabins sleeping up to four people and even a glamping lodge to choose from.

★ **Tradita G&T**   BOUTIQUE HOTEL €€
(📞 068 2086 056, 022 809 683; www.hoteltradita.com; Rr Edith Durham 4; s/d/tr incl breakfast €43/64/81; 🅿 ❄ 🐾 🛜) By far the best choice in town, this innovative, well-managed guesthouse is a delight. Housed in a painstakingly restored 17th-century mansion that once belonged to a famous Shkodran writer, the Tradita heaves with Albanian arts and crafts and has traditional yet very comfortable rooms with terracotta-roofed bathrooms and locally woven bed linen.

🍴 Eating

Sofra   ALBANIAN €
(Rr Kolë Idromeno; mains 200-500 lekë; ⊙ noon-midnight; 🛜) Right in the middle of the busy *petonalja* (pedestrianised Rr Kolë Idromeno), with tables on the street as well as a cosy upstairs dining room, this traditional place is an excellent opportunity to try a range of Albanian dishes, with the set meals being particularly good value.

San Francisco ALBANIAN €€

(Rr Kolë Idromeno; mains 300-800 lekë; ⊙6am-11pm; 🕾) This grand old place has a touch of the old world about it, particularly in its more formal upstairs dining room and spacious terrace where the best tables have superb views over the Great Mosque. This makes a great spot for breakfast, but full meals of traditional Albanian cooking are served all day long.

Çoçja ITALIAN €€

(Vila Bekteshi; Rr Hazan Riza; mains 250-1000 lekë; ⊙7am-11pm; 🕾) This classy converted mansion on a pleasant piazza in the centre of town is all gleaming white tablecloths, timber floors and smart design choices. The menu encompasses great pizza as well as more exciting fare such as veal ribs, grilled frogs, grilled trout, and chicken fillet with mushrooms and cream. There's also a courtyard garden that's perfect for summer drinks.

❶ Getting There & Away

BUS

There is no bus station in Shkodra, but most services leave from around Sheshi Demokracia in the centre of town. There are hourly *furgons* (minibuses; 400 lekë) and buses (300 lekë) to Tirana (two hours, 6am to 5pm), which depart from outside Radio Shkodra near Hotel Rozafa. There are also several daily buses to Kotor, Ulcinj and Podgorica in Montenegro (€5 to €8, two to three hours) from outside the Ebu Bekr Mosque.

To get up into the mountains, catch the 6.30am bus to Lake Koman (600 lekë, two hours) in time for the wonderful Lake Koman Ferry to Fierzë. Several *furgons* also depart daily for Theth between 6am and 7am (1200 lekë, four hours). In both cases hotels can call ahead to get the *furgon* to pick you up on its way out of town.

TAXI

It costs between €40 and €50 for the trip from Shkodra to Ulcinj in Montenegro, depending on your haggling skills.

The Accursed Mountains

The 'Accursed Mountains' (Bjeshkët e Namuna) offer some of Albania's most impressive scenery, and the area has exploded in recent years as a popular backpacker destination. It's a totally different side of the country here: that of blood feuds, deep tradition, extraordinary landscapes and fierce local pride. It's absolutely a highlight of any trip to Albania and, indeed, it's quite extraordinary to get this far removed from modern life in 21st-century Europe.

Valbona

Valbona has a gorgeous setting on a wide plain surrounded by towering mountain peaks, and its summer tourism industry is

---

CROSSING LAKE KOMAN

One of Albania's undisputed highlights is this superb three-hour ferry ride (www.komanilakeferry.com/en/ferry-lines-in-the-komani-lake) across vast Lake Koman, connecting the towns of Koman and Fierza. Lake Koman was created in 1978 when the Drin River was dammed, with the result being that you can cruise through spectacular mountain scenery where many incredibly hardy people still live as they have for centuries, tucked away in tiny mountain villages.

The best way to experience the journey is to make a three-day, two-night loop beginning and ending in Shkodra, and taking in Koman, Fierza, Valbona and Theth. To do this, arrange to have the morning 6.30am *furgon* (shared minibus) from Shkodra to Koman (600 lekë, two hours) pick you up at your hotel, which will get you to the ferry departure point by 8.30am. There are normally two ferries daily (700 lekë, 2½ hours) and both leave from Koman at 9am. One of the two, the *Berisha*, carries up to 10 cars, which cost 700 lekë per square metre of space they occupy. There's also a big car ferry that leaves at 1pm, but it only runs when demand is high enough – call ahead to make a reservation.

On arrival in Fierza, the boats are met by *furgons* that will take you to either Bajram Curri (200 lekë, 15 minutes) or to Valbona (400 lekë, 15 minutes). There's no real reason to stop in Bajram Curri unless you plan to head to Kosovo. Hikers will want to head straight for Valbona, where you can stay for a night or two before doing the stunning day hike to Theth. After the hike you can stay for another night or two in glorious Theth before taking a *furgon* back to Shkodra.

increasingly well organised. The village itself consists virtually only of guesthouses and camping grounds, nearly all of which have their own restaurants attached. Most travellers just spend a night here before trekking to Theth, which is a shame as there are a wealth of other excellent hikes to do in the area – ask for guides or information at the superhelpful Hotel Rilindja (p51), or check out the excellent www.journeytovalbona. com website, a DIY-kit for the entire area.

🛏 Sleeping & Eating

★ **Hotel Rilindja**   GUESTHOUSE €
(☑ 067 3014 637; www.journeytovalbona. com; Quku i Valbonës; tent/dm/d incl breakfast €4/12/35; 🛜) Pioneering tourism in Valbona since 2005, the Albanian–American–run Rilindja is hugely popular with travellers, who love the comfortable accommodation and excellent food. The five simple rooms in the atmospheric farmhouse share a bathroom, except for one with private facilities. The new Rezidenca up the road offers a far more upscale experience with en suite singles, double and triples.

Hotel & Camping Tradita   CHALET €
(☑ 067 3380 014, 067 3014 567; Valbona; dm/chalet €10/25) This collection of five chalets in the middle of the village has extraordinary views in all directions. The pine cabins each sleep three and come with hot water and private facilities. The owner, Isa, also offers six further rooms in his adjacent stone house. The good on-site restaurant is the social centre of the village.

ℹ Getting There & Away

Valbona can be reached from Shkodra via the Lake Koman Ferry and a connecting *furgon* (minibus) from Fierzë (400 lekë, one hour). Alternatively it can be reached by *furgon* from Bajram Curri (200 lekë, 45 minutes).

Theth

This unique mountain village easily has the most dramatic setting in Albania. Just the journey here is quite incredible, whether you approach over the mountains on foot from Valbona or by vehicle from Shkodra. Both a sprawling village along the valley floor amid an amphitheatre of distant mountains and a national park containing stunning landscapes and excellent hiking routes, Theth is now well on its way to being Albania's next big thing. An improved – though still incomplete – asphalt road from Shkodra has made access to this once virtually unknown village far easier in recent years, bringing with it the familiar problem of overdevelopment. Come quickly while Theth retains its incomparable romance and unique charm.

🛏 Sleeping & Eating

There are no normal restaurants in town, but nearly all guesthouses and homestays offer three meals a day.

★ **Guesthouse Rupa**   GUESTHOUSE €
(☑ 068 2003 393, 022 244 077; rorupaog@yahoo. com; r per person incl full board €25; ⊘ Apr-Oct) This traditional stone guesthouse with a large garden is run by the formidable Roza, who speaks good English and is a great source of information about the area. There are only five rooms, but – rarely for Theth – all have private facilities, even if some of them are not in great shape. The excellent meals are taken communally around a big table.

Vila Zorgji   GUESTHOUSE €
(☑ 068 3617 309; pellumbkola@gmail.com; r incl breakfast/full board per person €15/25; ⊘ Apr-Oct) One of the best new guesthouses in town, Zorgji is on the main track towards the church as you enter the village, next to the pink-painted school. The building on the road is the restaurant (which also has two rooms upstairs), while Zorgji's best accommodation is a couple of minutes up the hillside, where great wood-panelled rooms enjoy outstanding views.

ℹ Getting There & Away

A new asphalt road from Shkodra ends 15km before reaching Theth. Do not attempt the last part unless you have a 4WD.

A daily *furgon* (1000 lekë, two hours) leaves from Shkodra at 7am and will pick you up from your hotel if your hotel owner calls ahead for you. The return trip leaves Theth between 1pm and 2pm, arriving late afternoon in Shkodra. During the summer months it's also easy to arrange a shared *furgon* transfer to Shkodra with other hikers from Valbona.

CENTRAL ALBANIA

Berat

📍 032 / POP 35,000

Berat weaves its own very special magic and is easily a highlight of visiting Albania. Its most striking feature is the collection of white Ottoman houses climbing up the hill to its castle, earning it the title of 'town of a thousand windows' and helping it join Gjirokastra on the list of Unesco World Heritage sites in 2008. Its rugged mountain setting is particularly evocative when the clouds swirl around the tops of the minarets or break up to show the icy peak of Mt Tomorri. Despite now being a big centre for tourism in Albania, Berat has managed to retain its easygoing charm and friendly atmosphere.

◎ Sights

★ **Kalaja**   CASTLE

(100 lekë; ⊙24hr) The Kala neighbourhood inside the castle's walls still lives and breathes; if you walk around this busy, ancient neighbourhood for long enough you'll invariably stumble into someone's courtyard thinking it's a church or ruin (no one seems to mind, though). In spring and summer the fragrance of camomile is in the air (and underfoot) and wildflowers burst from every gap between the stones, giving the entire site a magical feel.

★ **Onufri Museum**   GALLERY

(200 lekë; ⊙9am-2pm & 4-7pm Mon-Sat, 9am-7pm Sun May-Sep, to 4pm Oct-Apr) The Onufri Museum is situated in the Kala quarter's biggest church, **Church of the Dormition of St Mary** (Kisha Fjetja e Shën Mërisë). The church itself dates from 1797 and was built on the foundations of an earlier 10th-century chapel. Today Onufri's spectacular 16th-century religious paintings are displayed along with the church's beautifully gilded 19th-century iconostasis. Don't miss the chapel behind the iconostasis, or its painted cupola, whose frescoes are now faded almost to invisibility.

Ethnographic Museum   MUSEUM

(200 lekë; ⊙9am-2pm & 4-7pm Mon-Sat, 9am-7pm Sun May-Sep, to 4pm Oct-Apr) On the steep hillside that leads up to the castle is this excellent museum, which is housed in an 18th-century Ottoman house that's as interesting as the exhibits. The ground floor has displays of traditional clothes and the tools used by silversmiths and weavers, while the upper storey has kitchens, bedrooms and guest rooms decked out in traditional style.

🛏 Sleeping

★ **Berat Backpackers**   HOSTEL €

(📞069 7854 219; www.beratbackpackers.com; 295 Gorica; tent/dm/r €6/10/30; ⊙mid-Mar–Oct; @🛜) This transformed traditional house in the Gorica quarter houses one of Albania's friendliest hostels. The vine-clad establishment contains a basement bar and restaurant, an alfresco drinking area and a relaxed atmosphere that money can't buy. There are two airy dorms with original ceilings, and four gorgeous, excellent-value double rooms with antique furnishings. Shaded camping area and cheap laundry also available.

Hotel Restaurant Klea   GUESTHOUSE €

(📞032 234 970; Rr Shën Triadha, Kala; s/d/ incl breakfast €20/30) From the castle gates go straight ahead and you'll find this gorgeous hilltop hideaway, run by a friendly English-speaking family. There are just five compact wood-panelled rooms, each with its own clean and modern bathroom. The downstairs restaurant adjoins a wonderful garden and has a daily changing specials menu featuring tasty Albanian fare (200 lekë to450 lekë).

★ **Hotel Mangalemi**   HOTEL €€

(📞068 2323 238; www.mangalemihotel.com; Rr Mihail Komneno; s/d/tr from €30/40/55; 🅿✴@🛜) A true highlight of Berat is this gorgeous place inside two sprawling Ottoman houses where all the rooms are beautifully furnished in traditional Berati style and balconies give superb views. Its terrace restaurant (mains 400 lekë to 600 lekë; reserve on summer evenings) is the best place to eat in town and has great Albanian food with bonus views of Mt Tomorri.

🍴 Eating

★ **Lili Homemade Food**   ALBANIAN €

(📞069 234 9362; mains 500-700 lekë; ⊙11am-10pm) This charming family home deep into the Mangalem Quarter underneath the castle is the setting for one of Berat's best restaurants. Lili speaks English and will invite you to take a table in his backyard where you can order a meal of traditional Berati cooking. We heartily recommend the *gjize ferges,* a delicious mash of tomato, garlic and cheese.

Mangalemi Restaurant ALBANIAN €€
(Rr Mihail Komneno; mains 300-800 lekë; ⊙ noon-11pm; ☎) The restaurant of the excellent Hotel Mangalemi is the best place in town for traditional Albanian cooking, and summer nights on its breezy verandah are not to be missed. The large menu serves simple, home-cooked traditional Berati fare, including an excellent veal kebab, mouth-watering grilled halloumi cheese and *tavë kosi* (lamb and rice baked in yoghurt and eggs).

ⓘ Information

Information Centre (Rr Antipatrea; ⊙ 9am-noon & 2-6pm Mon-Fri) This brand new and rather sleek tourist information centre can be found on Berat's main square, and has lots of local information and English-speaking staff.

ⓘ Getting There & Away

Berat now has a bus terminal, around 3km from the town centre on the main road to Tirana. Bus services run to Tirana (400 lekë, three hours, half-hourly until 3pm). There are also buses to Saranda (1600 lekë, six hours, two daily at 8am and 2pm), one of which goes via Gjirokastra (1000 lekë, four hours, 8am). To get to the bus station from the centre, ask locals to put you on a bus to 'Terminali Autobusave'.

SOUTHERN COAST

Saranda

✍ 0852 / POP 38,000

Saranda is the unofficial capital of the Albanian Riviera, and come the summer months it seems like half of Tirana relocates here to enjoy the busy beach and busier nightlife along its crowd-filled seaside promenade. What was once a sleepy fishing village is now a thriving city, and while Saranda has lost much of its charm in the past two decades, it has retained much of its charisma.

⊙ Sights

★ **Butrint** RUINS
(http://butrint.al/eng/; 700 lekë; ⊙ 8am-7.30am) The ancient ruins of Butrint, 18km south of Saranda, are famed for their size, beauty and tranquillity. They're in a fantastic natural setting and are part of a 29-sq-km

national park. The remains – Albania's finest – are from a variety of periods, spanning 2500 years. Set aside at least two hours to explore. Buses from Saranda (100 lekë, 20 minutes, hourly from 8.30am to 5.30pm) leave from outside the ZIT Information Centre (p54), returning from Butrint hourly on the hour.

⌕ Sleeping

Hairy Lemon HOSTEL €
(✍ 069 889 9196; www.hairylemonhostel.com; cnr Mitat Hoxha & E Arberit, 8th floor; dm incl breakfast from €10; ☎) With a prime 8th-floor location, a clean beach at its base and a friendly, helpful atmosphere, this Irish-run backpacker hostel is a good place to chill. There's an open-plan kitchen and lounge, and two dorm rooms with fans and sea breezes, not to mention unlimited pancakes for breakfast.

Hotel Titania HOTEL €€
(✍ 069 689 7826, 085 222 869; hoteltitania@yahoo.com; Rr Jonianët 13; r incl breakfast from €50; ❄☎) This place is a great bargain given that most of its rooms have sea views and the seafront promenade begins just meters from its front door. The rooms are spacious and modern, all with balconies and good bathrooms. An excellent breakfast is served on the delightful roof terrace that looks over the bay.

✕ Eating

Gërthëla SEAFOOD €€
(Rr Jonianët; mains 300-1000 lekë; ⊙ 11am-midnight; ☎) One of Saranda's original restaurants, 'The Crab' is a long-standing taverna that only has fish and seafood on the menu, and locals will tell you with certainty that it offers the best-prepared versions of either available in town. The cosy glass-fronted dining room is full of traditional knick-knacks and there's a big wine selection to boot.

★ **Mare Nostrum** INTERNATIONAL €€€
(Rr Jonianët; mains 700-1200 lekë; ⊙ 7am-midnight Mar-Dec) This sleek restaurant immediately feels different to the others along the seafront. Here there's elegant decor that wouldn't look out of place in a major European capital; the buzz of a smart, in-the-know crowd; and an imaginative menu that combines the seafood and fish you'll find everywhere else with dishes such as Indonesian chicken curry and burgers.

THE ALBANIAN RIVIERA

The Albanian Riviera was a revelation a decade or so ago, when backpackers discovered the last virgin stretch of the Mediterranean coast in Europe, flocking here in droves, setting up ad hoc campsites and exploring scores of little-known beaches. Since then, things have become significantly less pristine, with overdevelopment blighting many of the once-charming coastal villages. But worry not, while Dhërmi and Himara may be well and truly swarming, with a little persistence there are still spots to kick back and enjoy the empty beaches the region was once so famous for.

One such place is **Vuno**, a tiny hillside village above picturesque Jal Beach. Each summer Vuno's primary school is filled with blow-up beds and it becomes **Shkolla Hostel** (☑ 069 2119 596; www.tiranahostel.com/south-hostel; Vuno; tent/dm €4/8; ☺ May-Sep). What it lacks in infrastructure and privacy it makes up for with its goat-bell soundtrack and evening campfire. Jal has two beaches; one has free camping while the other has a camping ground set back from the sea (including tent 2000 lekë). Fresh seafood is bountiful in Jal and there are plenty of beachside restaurants in summer.

ℹ Information

ZIT Information Centre (☑ 069 324 3304; Rr Skënderbeu; ☺ 8am-8pm Jul-Aug, to 4pm Mon-Fri Sep-Jun) Saranda's tiny but excellent ZIT information centre provides information about transport and local sights and is staffed by friendly and helpful English-speaking staff.

ℹ Getting There & Away

BUS

Most buses leave just uphill from the ruins on Rr Vangjel Pando, right in the centre of town. Buses to Tirana (1300 lekë, eight hours) go inland via Gjirokastra (300 lekë, two hours) and leave regularly between 5am and 10.30am There are later buses at 2pm and 10pm. The 7am Tirana bus takes the coastal route (1300 lekë, eight hours). There is also one bus a day to Himara at 11.30am (400 lekë, two hours), which can stop at any point along the way to let you off at riviera villages.

Municipal buses go to Butrint via Ksamil hourly on the half hour from 8.30am (100 lekë, 30 minutes), leaving opposite ZIT and returning from Butrint on the hour each hour.

FERRY

Finikas Lines (☑ 085 226 057, 067 2022 004; www.finikas-lines.com; Rr Mithat Hoxha) at the port sells hydrofoil and ferry tickets for Corfu (adult/child €24/13, 45 minutes) with a daily departure 9am, 10.30am and 4pm in the summer months. From Corfu there are three ferries per day in summer: 9am, 1pm and 6.30pm. Note that Greek time is one hour ahead of Albanian time.

EASTERN ALBANIA

Gjirokastra

☑ 084 / POP 43,000

Defined by its castle, roads paved with chunky limestone and shale, imposing slate-roofed houses and views out to the Drina Valley, Gjirokastra is a magical hillside town described beautifully by Albania's most famous author, Ismail Kadare (b 1936), in *Chronicle in Stone*. There has been a settlement here for 2500 years, though these days it's the 600 'monumental' Ottoman-era houses in town that attract visitors. The town is also synonymous for Albanians with former dictator Enver Hoxha, who was born here and ensured the town was relatively well preserved under his rule; though he is not memorialised in any way here today. Far less touristy than Berat, the town is equally as charming and has several fascinating sights, as well as some excellent accommodation options.

◉ Sights

★ **Gjirokastra Castle**   CASTLE

(200 lekë; ☺ 9am-8pm summer, 9am-4pm winter) Gjirokastra's eerie hilltop castle is one of the biggest in the Balkans and is definitely worth the steep walk up from the Old Town. The castle remains somewhat infamous due to its use as a prison under the communists. Inside there's an eerie collection of armoury, two good museums, a recovered US Air Force jet shot down during the communist era, and a hilariously hard-to-use audio tour

that's included in your entry fee. The views across the valley are simply superb.

★ Cold War Tunnel
TUNNEL

(200 lekë; ⊗8am-4pm Mon-Fri, 10am-2pm Sat, 9am-3pm Sun) Gjirokastra's most interesting sight in no way relates to its traditional architecture, but instead to its far more modern kind: this is a giant bunker built deep under the castle for use by the local authorities during the full-scale invasion Hoxha was so paranoid about. Built in secret during the 1960s, it has 80 rooms and its existence remained unknown to locals until the 1990s. Personal guided tours run from the tourist information booth on the main square all day.

★ Zekate House
HISTORIC BUILDING

(200 lekë; ⊗9am-6pm) This incredible three-storey house dates from 1811 and has twin towers and a double-arched facade. It's fascinating to nose around the almost totally unchanged interiors of an Ottoman-era home, especially the upstairs galleries, which are the most impressive. The owners live next door and collect the payments; to get here, follow the signs past the Hotel Kalemi and keep zigzagging up the hill.

🛏 Sleeping

★ Stone City Hostel
HOSTEL €

(☑069 348 4271; www.stonecityhostel.com; Pazar; incl breakfast dm €10-11, d €25; ⊗closed Nov-Mar; ❄🕏) This brand new hostel is a fantastic conversion of an Old Town house created and run by Dutchman Walter. The attention to detail and respect for traditional craftsmanship is extremely heartening, with beautiful carved wooden panels in all the rooms. Choose between the dorm rooms with custom-made bunks or the one double room, all of which share spotless communal facilities.

★ Gjirokastra Hotel
HOTEL €

(☑068 4099 669, 084 265 982; hhotelgjirokastra@yahoo.com; Rr. Sheazi Çomo; s/d €25/35, ste €40; ❄🕏) A great option that combines modern facilities with traditional touches, this lovely family-run hotel inside a 300-year-old house has rooms that boast huge balconies and gorgeously carved wooden ceilings. The suite is gorgeous, with a long Ottoman-style sofa, original wooden doors and ceiling, and magnificent stone walls: it's an absolute bargain at €40.

Hotel Kalemi 2
HOTEL €€

(www.kalemihotels.com; Rr Alqi Kondi; incl breakfast d €40-45, tr €55, ste €65-100; @🕏) The second of the two Kalemi hotels, this brand new place is a total renovation of a large stone mansion that has some beautiful fittings in its 16 individually decorated rooms. Modern bathrooms contrast with the elaborate traditional ceilings. The huge suite is easily worth its price and must rank among the most atmospheric sleeping options in Albania.

🍴 Eating

★ Kujtimi
ALBANIAN €€

(mains 350-650 lekë; ⊗11am-11pm) This wonderfully laid-back outdoor restaurant, run by the Dumi family, is an excellent choice. Try the delicious *trofte* (fried trout; 400 lekë), the *midhje* (fried mussels; 350 lekë) and *qifqi* (rice balls fried in herbs and egg, a local speciality). The terrace is the perfect place to absorb the charms of the Old Town with a glass of local wine.

Taverna Kuka
ALBANIAN €€

(Rr Astrit Karagjozi; mains 300-750 lekë; ⊗11am-midnight; 🕏) Just beyond Gjirokastra's old mosque, this largely outdoor terrace restaurant has a wonderful location and a menu full of delicious Albanian cooking, including *qofte* (meatballs), Saranda mussels, pork pancetta and grilled lamb. There's a surprisingly cool decor given the rural Albanian setting and its terrace is a firm local favourite on summer evenings.

ESSENTIAL FOOD & DRINK

Byrek Pastry with cheese or meat.

Fergesë Baked peppers, egg and cheese, and occasionally meat.

Konjak Local brandy.

Midhje Wild or farmed mussels, often served fried.

Paçë koke Sheep's head soup, usually served for breakfast.

Qofta Flat or cylindrical minced-meat rissoles.

Raki Popular spirit made from grapes.

Raki mani Spirit made from mulberries.

Sufllaqë Doner kebab.

Tavë Meat baked with cheese and egg.

ⓘ Information

Information Centre (⊙ 8am-4pm Mon-Fri, to 2pm Sat, to 3pm Sun) In a kiosk on the main square at the entrance to the Old Town, the staff here don't speak a word of English, which isn't very helpful, but there are town maps for sale and well as information about tours in the local area. Tickets for the Cold War Tunnel are also on sale here.

ⓘ Getting There & Away

Buses stop at the ad hoc bus station just after the Eida petrol station on the new town's main road. Services include Tirana (1200 lekë, seven hours, every one to two hours until 5pm), Saranda (300 lekë, one hour, hourly) and Berat (1000 lekë, four hours, 9.15am and 3.45pm). A taxi between the Old Town and the bus station is 300 lekë.

ⓘ Getting Around

The new town (no slate roofs here) is on the main Saranda–Tirana road, and a taxi up to or back from the Old Town is 300 lekë.

SURVIVAL GUIDE

ⓘ Directory A–Z

ACCOMMODATION

Hotels and guesthouses are easily found throughout Albania, as tourism continues to grow and grow. You will almost never have trouble finding a room for the night, though seaside towns are often booked out in late July and August.

COUNTRY FACTS

Area 28,748 sq km

Capital Tirana

Country Code ☏ 355

Currency Lek (plural lekë); the euro (€) is widely accepted.

Emergencies ☏ 127 (Ambulance); ☏ 128 (Fire); ☏ 129 (Police)

Language Albanian

Money ATMs in most towns.

Population 2.77 million

Visas Nearly all visitors can travel visa-free to Albania.

EATING PRICE RANGES

The following price categories are based on the cost of a main course.

€ less than 300 lekë

€€ 300 lekë to 600 lekë

€€€ more than 600 lekë

MONEY

The lek (plural lekë) is the official currency of Albania, though the euro is widely accepted; you'll get a better deal for things in general if you use lek. Accommodation is generally quoted in euros but can be paid in either currency. ATMs can be found in all but the most rural of Albania's towns, and many dispense cash in both currencies. Credit cards are accepted only in the larger hotels, shops and travel agencies, and few of these are outside Tirana.

OPENING HOURS

Banks 9am to 3.30pm Monday to Friday

Cafes & Bars 8am to midnight

Offices 8am to 5pm Monday to Friday

Restaurants 8am to midnight

Shops 8am to 7pm; siesta time can be any time between noon and 4pm

PUBLIC HOLIDAYS

New Year's Day 1 January

Summer Day 16 March

Nevruz 23 March

Catholic Easter March or April

Orthodox Easter March or April

May Day 1 May

Mother Teresa Day 19 October

Independence Day 28 November

Liberation Day 29 November

Christmas Day 25 December

TELEPHONE

Albania's country phone code is ☏ 355.

Mobile Phones

Albania has a good level of mobile coverage, though there are still some areas where getting a signal can be hard. It's very straightforward to buy a SIM card with mobile data from any internet provider. Prepaid SIM cards cost around 500 lekë and include credit. Mobile numbers begin with 06. To call an Albanian mobile number from abroad, dial +☏ 355 then either 67, 68 or 69 (ie drop the 0).

🅘 Getting There & Away

AIR

Nënë Tereza International Airport is a modern, well-run terminal 17km northwest of Tirana. There are no domestic flights within Albania. Airlines flying to and from Tirana include Adria Airways (www.adria.si), Alitalia (www.alitalia.com), Austrian Airlines (www.austrian.com), Lufthansa (www.lufthansa.com), Olympic Air (www.olympicair.com), Pegasus Airlines (www.flypgs.com) and Turkish Airlines (www.turkishairlines.com).

LAND

There are no passenger trains into Albania, so your border-crossing options are buses, *furgons* (minibuses), taxis or walking to a border and picking up transport on the other side.

Border Crossings

Montenegro The main crossings link Shkodra to Ulcinj (via Muriqan, Albania and Sukobin, Montenegro) and to Podgorica (Hani i Hotit).

Kosovo The closest border crossing to the Lake Koman Ferry terminal is Morina, and further south is Qafë Prush. Near Kukës use Morinë for the highway to Tirana.

Macedonia Use Blato to get to Debar, and Qafë e Thanës or Tushemisht, each to one side of Pogradec, for accessing Ohrid.

Greece The main border crossing to and from Greece is Kakavija on the road from Athens to Tirana.

SLEEPING PRICE RANGES

The following price categories are based on the cost of a double room in high season.

€ less than €40

€€ €40–€80

€€€ more than €80

Bus

From Tirana, regular buses head to Pristina, Kosovo; to Skopje in Macedonia; to Ulcinj in Montenegro; and to Athens and Thessaloniki in Greece. *Furgons* and buses leave Shkodra for Montenegro, and buses head to Kosovo from Durrës. Buses travel to Greece from Albanian towns on the southern coast as well as from Tirana.

SEA

Two or three boats per day ply the route between Saranda and Corfu, in Greece, and there are plenty of ferry companies making the journey to Italy from Vlora and Durrës. There are additional ferries from Vlora and Himara to Corfu in the summer.

Austria

Best Places to Eat

➜ Lingenhel (p68)
➜ Griechenbeisl (p68)
➜ Punks (p68)
➜ Magazin (p80)
➜ Die Wilderin (p84)

Best Places to Stay

➜ Grand Ferdinand Hotel (p67)
➜ Magdas (p67)
➜ Hotel am Brillantengrund (p67)
➜ Haus Ballwein (p79)
➜ Hotel Weisses Kreuz (p84)

Why Go?

For such a small country, Austria is ridiculously large on in-spiration. This is the land where Mozart was born, Strauss taught the world to waltz and Julie Andrews grabbed the spotlight with her twirling entrance in *The Sound of Mu-sic*. It's where the Habsburgs ruled over their spectacular, sprawling 600-year empire.

These past glories still shine in the resplendent baroque palaces and chandelier-lit coffee houses of Vienna, Inns-bruck and Salzburg, but beyond its storybook cities, Aus-tria's allure is one of natural beauty and outdoors adven-ture. Whether you're schussing down the legendary slopes of Kitzbühel, climbing high in the Alps of Tyrol or cycling the banks of the mighty Danube, you'll find the kind of land-scapes that no well-orchestrated symphony or singing nun could ever quite do justice.

When to Go
Vienna

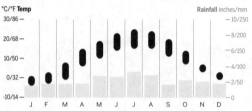

Jul–Aug Alpine hiking in Tyrol, lake swimming in Salzkammergut and lots of sum-mer festivals.

Sep–Oct New wine in vineyards near Vienna, golden forest strolls and few crowds.

Dec–Jan Christ-mas markets, skiing in the Alps and Vienna waltzing into the New Year.

VIENNA

♩ 01 / POP 1,766,750

Few cities in the world waltz so effortlessly between the present and the past like Vienna. Its splendid historical face is easily recognised: grand imperial palaces and bombastic baroque interiors, revered opera houses and magnificent squares. But Vienna is also one of Europe's most dynamic urban spaces. A stone's throw from Hofburg (the Imperial Palace), the MuseumsQuartier houses provocative and high-profile contemporary art behind a striking basalt facade. In the Innere Stadt (Inner City), up-to-the-minute design stores sidle up to old-world confectioners, and Austro-Asian fusion restaurants stand alongside traditional *Beisl* (small taverns).

◉ Sights

Vienna's magnificent series of boulevards, the Ringstrasse, encircles the Innere Stadt, with many of the city's most famous sights situated on or within it, including the monumental Hofburg palace complex. Just outside the Ringstrasse are exceptional museums including the Kunsthistorisches Museum and the ensemble making up the MuseumsQuartier, while attractions further afield include the sumptuous palaces Schloss Schönbrunn and Schloss Belvedere.

★ **Hofburg**   PALACE

(Imperial Palace; www.hofburg-wien.at; 01, Michaelerkuppel; 🚋 1A, 2A Michaelerplatz, 🚊 D, 1, 2, 46, 49, 71 Burgring, Ⓤ Herrengasse) **FREE** Nothing symbolises Austria's resplendent cultural heritage more than its Hofburg, home base of the Habsburgs from 1273 to 1918. The oldest section is the 13th-century Schweizerhof (Swiss Courtyard), named after the Swiss guards who used to protect its precincts. The Renaissance Swiss gate dates from 1553. The courtyard adjoins a larger courtyard, In der Burg, with a monument to Emperor Franz II adorning its centre. The palace now houses the Austrian president's offices and a raft of museums.

★ **Kaiserappartements**   PALACE

(Imperial Apartments; www.hofburg-wien.at; 01, Michaelerplatz; adult/child €12.90/7.70, incl guided tour €15.90/9.20; ⊘ 9am-6pm Jul & Aug, to 5.30pm Sep-Jun; Ⓤ Herrengasse) The Kaiserappartements (Imperial Apartments), once the official living quarters of Franz Josef I and Empress Elisabeth, are dazzling in their chandelier-lit opulence. The highlight is the Sisi Museum (♩ 01-533 75 70; 01, Michaelerkuppel; adult/child €12.90/7.70, incl guided tour €15.90/9.20; ⊘ 9am-6pm Jul & Aug, to 5.30pm Sep-Jun), devoted to Austria's most beloved empress, which has a strong focus on the clothing and jewellery of Austria's monarch. Multilingual audio guides are included in the admission price. Guided tours take in the Kaiserappartements, the Sisi Museum and the Silberkammer (Silver Depot; 01, Michaelerkuppel; adult/child €12.90/7.70, incl guided tour €15.90/9.20; ⊘ 9am-6pm Jul & Aug, to 5.30pm Sep-Jun), whose largest silver service caters to 140 dinner guests.

★ **Kaiserliche Schatzkammer**   MUSEUM

(Imperial Treasury; www.kaiserliche-schatzkammer.at; 01, Schweizerhof; adult/child €12/free; ⊘ 9am-5.30pm Wed-Mon; Ⓤ Herrengasse) The Kaiserliche Schatzkammer contains secular and ecclesiastical treasures, including devotional images and altars, particularly from the baroque era, of priceless value and splendour – the sheer wealth of this collection of crown jewels is staggering. As you walk through the rooms you see magnificent treasures such as a golden rose, diamond-studded Turkish sabres, a 2680-carat Colombian emerald and, the highlight of the treasury, the imperial crown.

> **ITINERARIES**
> ....
>
> **Two Days**
> Make the most of Vienna, spending your first day visiting the Habsburg palaces and Stephansdom before cosying up in a *Kaffeehäus* (coffee house). At night, check out the pumping bar scene.
>
> **One Week**
> Plan for two long and lovely days in Vienna, plus another day exploring the Wachau (Danube Valley) wine region, a day each in Salzburg and Innsbruck, a day in St Anton am Arlberg or Kitzbühel hiking or skiing and then a final day exploring the Salzkammergut lakes.

AUSTRIA VIENNA

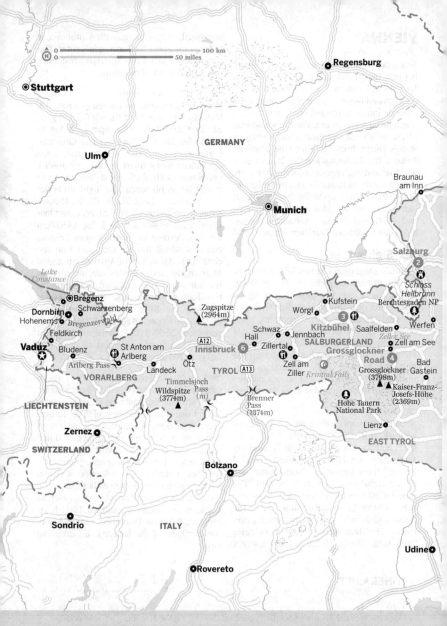

Austria Highlights

1 Vienna (p59) Discover opulent Habsburg palaces, coffee houses and cutting-edge galleries.

2 Salzburg (p76) Survey the baroque cityscape from the giddy height of 900-year-old Festung Hohensalzburg.

3 Kitzbühel (p86) Send your spirits soaring from peak to peak hiking and skiing.

4 Grossglockner Road (p87) Buckle up for a rollercoaster ride of Alps and glaciers on one of Austria's greatest drives.

★ **Stephansdom** CATHEDRAL
(St Stephen's Cathedral; ☑ tours 01-515 323 054; www.stephanskirche.at; 01, Stephansplatz; main nave adult & one child €6, additional child €1.50; ☺ public visits 9-11.30am & 1-4.30pm Mon-Sat, 1-4.30pm Sun; Ⓤ Stephansplatz) Vienna's Gothic masterpiece Stephansdom – or Steffl (Little Stephan), as it's ironically nicknamed – is Vienna's pride and joy. A church has stood here since the 12th century, and reminders of this are the Romanesque **Riesentor** (Giant Gate) and **Heidentürme**. From the exterior, the first thing that will strike you is the glorious tiled **roof**, with its dazzling row of chevrons and Austrian eagle. Inside, the magnificent Gothic stone **pulpit** presides over the main nave, fashioned in 1515 by Anton Pilgrim.

★ **Kunsthistorisches Museum** MUSEUM
(KHM, Museum of Art History; www.khm.at; 01, Maria-Theresien-Platz; adult/child incl Neue Burg museums €15/free; ☺ 10am-6pm Fri-Wed, to 9pm Thu Jun-Aug, closed Mon Sep-May; Ⓤ Museumsquartier, Volkstheater) One of the unforgettable experiences of any trip to Vienna is a visit to the Kunsthistorisches Museum, brimming with works by Europe's finest painters, sculptors and artisans. Occupying a neoclassical building as sumptuous as the art it contains, the museum takes you on a time-travel treasure hunt from Classical Rome to Egypt and the Renaissance. If your time's limited,

---

SPIN OF THE RING

One of the best deals in Vienna is a self-guided tour on tram 1 or 2 of the monumental **Ringstrasse** boulevard encircling much of the Innere Stadt, which turned 150 in 2015. For the price of a single ticket you'll take in the neo-Gothic **Rathaus** (City Hall; www. wien.gv.at; 01, Rathausplatz 1; ☺ tours 1pm Mon, Wed & Fri Sep-Jun, 1pm Mon-Fri Jul & Aug; ☒ D, 1, 2 Rathaus, Ⓤ Rathaus) **FREE**, the Greek Revival–style parliament, the 19th-century **Burgtheater** (National Theatre; ☑ 01-514 44 4440; www. burgtheater.at; 01, Universitätsring 2; seats €7.50-61, standing room €3.50, students €9; ☺ box office 9am-5pm Mon-Fri; ☒ D, 1, 2 Rathaus, Ⓤ Rathaus) and the baroque **Karlskirche** (St Charles Church; www. karlskirche.at; 04, Karlsplatz; adult/child €8/free; ☺ 9am-6pm Mon-Sat, noon-7pm Sun; Ⓤ Karlsplatz), among other sights.

---

skip straight to the **Picture Gallery**, where you'll want to dedicate at least an hour or two to Old Masters.

★ **MuseumsQuartier** MUSEUM
(Museum Quarter; MQ; www.mqw.at; 07, Museumsplatz; ☺ information & ticket centre 10am-7pm; Ⓤ Museumsquartier, Volkstheater) The MuseumsQuartier is a remarkable ensemble of museums, cafes, restaurants and bars inside former imperial stables designed by Fischer von Erlach. This breeding ground of Viennese cultural life is the perfect place to hang out and watch or meet people on warm evenings. With over 60,000 sq metres of exhibition space – including the Leopold Museum, MUMOK, Kunsthalle (p71), **Architekturzentrum** (Vienna Architecture Centre; ☑ 01-522 31 15; www.azw. at; exhibition prices vary, library admission free; ☺ architecture centre 10am-7pm, library 10am-5.30pm Mon, Wed & Fri, to 7pm Sat & Sun, closed Thu) and **Zoom** (☑ 01-524 79 08; www.kinder museum.at; exhibition adult/child €4/free, activities child €4-6, accompanying adult free; ☺ 12.45-5pm Tue-Sun Jul & Aug, 8.30am-4pm Tue-Fri, 9.45am-4pm Sat & Sun Sep-Jun, activity times vary) – the complex is one of the world's most ambitious cultural hubs.

★ **MUMOK** GALLERY
(Museum Moderner Kunst; Museum of Modern Art; www.mumok.at; 07, Museumsplatz 1; adult/child €11/free; ☺ 2-7pm Mon, 10am-7pm Tue, Wed & Fri-Sun, 10am-9pm Thu; ☒ 49 Volkstheater, Ⓤ Volkstheater, Museumsquartier) The dark basalt edifice and sharp corners of the Museum Moderner Kunst are a complete contrast to the MuseumsQuartier's historical sleeve. Inside, MUMOK contains Vienna's finest collection of 20th-century art, centred on fluxus, nouveau realism, pop art and photo-realism. The best of expressionism, cubism, minimal art and Viennese Actionism is represented in a collection of 9000 works that are rotated and exhibited by theme – but note that sometimes all this Actionism is packed away to make room for temporary exhibitions.

Leopold Museum MUSEUM
(www.leopoldmuseum.org; 07, Museumsplatz 1; adult/child €13/8; ☺ 10am-6pm Fri-Wed, to 9pm Thu Jun-Aug, 10am-6pm Wed & Fri-Mon, to 9pm Thu Sep-May; Ⓤ Volkstheater, Museumsquartier) Part of the MuseumsQuartier (p62), the Leopold Museum is named after ophthalmologist Rudolf Leopold, who, after buying his first Egon Schiele for a song as a young student

in 1950, amassed a huge private collection of mainly 19th-century and modernist Austrian artworks. In 1994 he sold the lot – 5266 paintings – to the Austrian government for €160 million (individually, the paintings would have made him €574 million), and the Leopold Museum was born. **Café Leopold** (www.cafe-leopold.at; ⊙10am-midnight Sun-Wed, to 4am Thu, to 6am Fri & Sat; 🛜) is located on the top floor.

Haus der Musik MUSEUM
(www.hausdermusik.com; 01, Seilerstätte 30; adult/child €13/6, with Mozarthaus Vienna €18/8; ⊙10am-10pm; 🚊D, 1, 2, 71, Ⓤ Karlsplatz) The Haus der Musik explains the world of sound and music to adults and children alike in an amusing and interactive way (in English and German). Exhibits are spread over four floors and cover everything from how sound is created, from Vienna's Philharmonic Orchestra to street noises. The staircase between floors acts as a piano; its glassed-in ground-floor courtyard hosts musical events. Admission is discounted after 8pm. The nearest tram stop is Kärntner Ring/Oper.

Secession MUSEUM
(www.secession.at; 01, Friedrichstrasse 12; adult/child €9/5.50; ⊙10am-6pm Tue-Sun; Ⓤ Karlsplatz) In 1897, 19 progressive artists swam away from the mainstream Künstlerhaus artistic establishment to form the *Wiener Secession* (Vienna Secession). Among their number were Klimt, Josef Hoffman, Kolo Moser and Joseph M Olbrich. Olbrich designed the new exhibition centre of the Secessionists, which combined sparse functionality with stylistic motifs. Its biggest draw is Klimt's exquisitely gilded *Beethoven Frieze*. Guided tours in English (€3) lasting one hour take place at 11am Saturday. An audio guide costs €3.

⭐**Schloss Belvedere** PALACE
(www.belvedere.at; adult/child Oberes Belvedere €14/free, Unteres Belvedere €12/free, combined ticket €20/free; ⊙10am-6pm; 🚊D, 71 Schwarzenbergplatz; Ⓤ Taubstummengasse, Südtiroler Platz) A masterpiece of total art, Schloss Belvedere is one of the world's finest baroque palaces. Designed by Johann Lukas von Hildebrandt (1668–1745), it was built for the brilliant military strategist Prince Eugene of Savoy, conqueror of the Turks in 1718. What giddy romance is evoked in its sumptuously frescoed halls, replete with artworks by Klimt,

Schiele and Kokoschka; what stories are conjured in its landscaped gardens, which drop like the fall of a theatre curtain to reveal Vienna's skyline.

⭐**Sigmund Freud Museum** MUSEUM, HOUSE
(www.freud-museum.at; 09, Berggasse 19; adult/child €10/4; ⊙10am-6pm; 🚊D, Ⓤ Schottentor, Schottenring) Sigmund Freud is a bit like the telephone – once he happened, there was no going back. This is where Freud spent his most prolific years and developed the most significant of his groundbreaking theories; he moved here with his family in 1891 and stayed until forced into exile by the Nazis in 1938.

⭐**Schloss Schönbrunn** PALACE
(www.schoenbrunn.at; 13, Schönbrunner Schlossstrasse 47; adult/child Imperial Tour €13.30/9.80, Grand Tour €16.40/10.80, Grand Tour with guide €19.40/12.30; ⊙8.30am-6.30pm Jul & Aug, to 5.30pm Sep, Oct & Apr-Jun, to 5pm Nov-Mar; Ⓤ Hietzing) The Habsburgs' overwhelmingly opulent summer palace is now a Unesco World Heritage site. Of the palace's 1441 rooms, 40 are open to the public; the Imperial Tour takes you into 26 of these, including the private apartments of Franz Josef and Sisi, while the Grand Tour covers all 40 and includes the precious 18th-century interiors from the time of Maria-Theresia. These mandatory tours are done with an audio guide or, for an additional charge, a tour guide.

🏃 **Activities**

The **Donauinsel** (Danube Island) features swimming areas and paths for walking and cycling. The **Alte Donau** is a landlocked arm of the Danube, a favourite of sailing and boating enthusiasts, swimmers, walkers, fisherfolk and, in winter (when it's cold enough), ice skaters.

Central Vienna

Bauernmarkt
Yppenplatz
(1.3km)

Ostarichi
Park

Alser Str

26

Schlösselgasse

Wickenburggasse

Landesgerichtsstr

Rooseveltplatz

Universitätsstr

Liebiggasse

Reichsratstr

Ebendorferstr

Votivpark

Währinger Str

Sigmund Freud
Museum (500m);
Flein (750m)

Schottentor

Schottentor

Börsegasse/
Wipplingerstrasse

Börseplatz

Börsegasse

Punks
(500m)

Buchfeldgasse

Schlüsselgasse

Friedrich-
Schmidt-Platz

Tulpengasse

Rathaus

Felderstr

Friedrich-Schmidt-
Platz

Reichsratstr

13

Rathauspark

Rathausplatz/
Burgtheater

41

34

INNERE
STADT 1

Mölker Bastei

Helferstorferstr

39

Freyungasse

Herrengasse

Renngasse

Tiefer Graben

Am Hof

Hohenstaufengasse

27

Bankgasse

Färbergasse

Strauchgasse

Naglergasse

Bognergasse

Weinstube
Josefstadt
(150m)

Lenaugasse

Josefstädter Str

Stadiongasse

Stadiongasse/
Parlament

Minoritenplatz

Herrengasse

Löwelstr

Fähnengasse

Kohlmarkt

Lange Gasse

Josefsgasse

Auerspergstr

Doblhoffgasse

Schmerlingplatz

Volksgarten

Ballhausplatz

Schauflergasse

Kaiserappartements

In der Burg

2

Michaelerplatz

Hofburg

1

Trautsongasse

Dirndlherz
(250m)

Lerchenfelder Str

18

Museumstr

Museumstr

Volksgartenstr

Hansenstr

Dr Karl-
Renner-
Ring

Bellariastr

Burgring (Ringstrasse)

Heldenplatz

33

Neue
Burg

15

Josefsplatz

3

Kaiserliche
Schatzkammer

Reitschulestr

Augustinerstr

Neustiftgasse

Volkstheater

Maria-
Theresien-
Platz

10

MUMOK

6

7

MuseumsQuartier

Kunsthalle Wien

12

Breite Gasse

Stiftgasse

Burggasse

my MOjO
vie (800m)

Kunsthistorisches
Museum

5

Babenbergerstr

Burgring

Burggarten

Goethegasse

32

22

Helmut-
Zilk-Platz
(Albertinaplatz)

Opernring

Siebensterngasse

Karl-Schweighofer-Gasse

17

NEUBAU 7

Museumsquartier

Elisabethstr

Schillerplatz

Opernring
(Ringstrasse)

Hotel am
Brillantengrund (550m)

Kirchengasse

Schloss
Schönbrunn
(3.2km)

Mariahilfer Str

Barnabitengasse

Mariahilfer Str

Windmühlgasse

Fillgradergasse

Theobaldgasse

Gumpendorfer Str

Rahlgasse

Mariahilfer Str

Getreidemarkt

Lehargasse

29

MARIAHILF
6

14

Friedrichstr

Karlsplatz

Treitlstr

38

Gumpendorfer Str

Laimgrubengasse

Girardigasse

Rechte Wienzeile

25

Schleifmühlgasse

Opernring

Opernring

Wiedner Hauptstr

Schadekgasse

Esterházy
Park

Fritz-
Grünbaum-
Platz

Pension Kraml (250m);
Mini (550m)

Linke Wienzeile

Kettenbrückengasse

21

Schikanedergasse

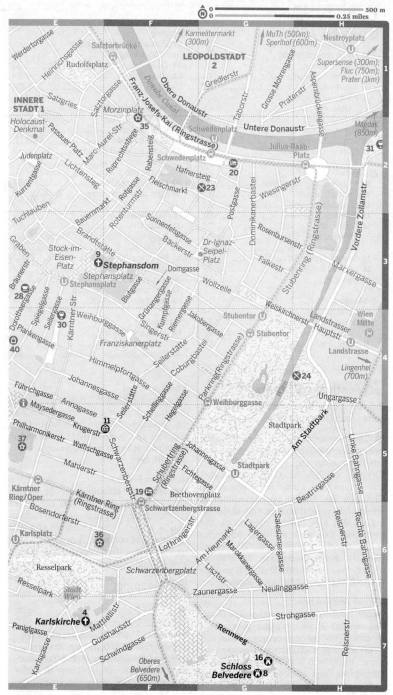

Karmelitermarkt (300m)

MuTh (500m); Sperlhof (600m)

Nestroyplatz

Supersense (300m); Fluc (750m); Prater (1km)

LEOPOLDSTADT 2

Salztorbrücke

Werdertorgasse

Heinrichsgasse

Rudolfsplatz

Salztorgasse

Franz-Josefs-Kai (Ringstrasse)

Donaukanal

Obere Donaustr

Gredlerstr

Taborstr

Grosse Mohrengasse

Praterstr

Aspernbrückengasse

INNERE STADT 1

Salzgries

Morzinplatz 35

Marc-Aurel-Str

Ruprechtsstiege

Rabensteig

Schwedenplatz

Untere Donaustr

Magdas (850m)

Holocaust-Denkmal

Passauer Platz

Lichtensteg

Rotgasse

Rotenturmstr

Hafnersteig

Fleischmarkt

Julius-Raab-Platz

31

Judenplatz

Kurrentgasse

Tuchlauben

Bauernmarkt

Brandstätte

Sonnenfelsgasse

Bäckerstr

Dr-Ignaz-Seipel-Platz

Postgasse

Dominikanerbastei

Wiesingerstr

Rosenbursenstr

Schwedenplatz 20

23

Graben

Bräunerstr

Stock-im-Eisen-Platz

9 Stephansdom

Domgasse

Falkestr

Stubenring (Ringstrasse)

Marxergasse

Vordere Zollamtstr

28

Stephansplatz

Stephansplatz

Blutgasse

Wollzeile

Landstrasser Hauptstr

Wien Mitte

Dorotheergasse

Spiegelgasse

Sellergasse

30

Weihburggasse

Kärntner Str

Grünangergasse

Kumpfgasse

Singerstr

Riemergasse

Jakobergasse

Weiskirchnerstr

Stubentor

Stubentor

Landstrasse

Plankengasse

40

Franziskanerplatz

Seilerstätte

Parkring (Ringstrasse)

Lingenhel (700m)

Führichgasse

Himmelpfortgasse

Coburgbastei

24

Ungargasse

Maysedergasse

Johannesgasse

Annagasse

Seilerstätte

Schellinggasse

Hegelgasse

Weihburggasse

Philharmonikerstr

Krugerstr

11

Stadtpark

Am Stadtpark

37

Walfischgasse

Schwarzenbergstr

Johannesgasse

Fichtegasse

Mahlerstr

Schubertring (Ringstrasse)

Stadtpark

Linke Bahngasse

Kärntner Ring/Oper

Kärntner Ring (Ringstrasse)

19

Beethovenplatz

Beatrixgasse

Bösendorferstr

Schwartzenbergstrasse

Karlsplatz

36

Lothringerstr

Am Heumarkt

Marokkanergasse

Salesianergasse

Rechte Bahngasse

Resselpark

Schwarzenbergplatz

Lisztstr

Reisnerstr

Resselpark

Stadt Wien

Zaunergasse

Neulinggasse

Paniglgasse

4 Karlskirche

Mattiellistr

Gusshausstr

Schwindgasse

Rennweg

Strohgasse

Reisnerstr

Karlsgasse

Oberes Belvedere (650m)

16

Schloss Belvedere 8

Central Vienna

✨ Festivals & Events

Pick up a copy of the monthly booklet of events from the tourist office.

★ Christkindlmärkte   CHRISTMAS MARKET
(www.wien.info/en/shopping-wining-dining/markets/christmas-markets; ⊘ mid-Nov–25 Dec) Vienna's much-loved Christmas market season runs from around mid-November to Christmas Eve. Magical *Christkindlmärkte* set up in streets and squares, with stalls selling wooden toys, holiday decorations and traditional food such as *Wurst* (sausages) and *Glühwein* (mulled wine). The centrepiece is the **Rathausplatz Christkindlmarkt** (www.christkindlmarkt.at; ⊘ 10am-10pm 13 Nov–26 Dec; 🚋 D, 1, 2 Rathaus, Ⓤ Rathaus).

Wiener Festwochen   ART
(Vienna Festival; www.festwochen.at; ⊘ mid-May–mid-Jun) A wide-ranging program of theatrical productions, concerts, dance performances and visual arts from around the world, the month-long Wiener Festwochen takes place from mid-May to mid-June at various venues city-wide.

Donauinselfest   MUSIC
(https://donauinselfest.at; ⊘ late Jun) FREE Held over three days on a weekend in late June, the Donauinselfest features a feast of rock, pop, folk and country performers, and attracts almost three million onlookers. Best of all, it's free!

Musikfilm Festival   FILM
(http://filmfestival-rathausplatz.at; 01, Rathausplatz; ⊘ mid-Jul–early Sep; 🚋 D, 1, 2 Rathaus, Ⓤ Rathaus) Once the sun sets, the Rathausplatz is home to free screenings of operas, operettas and concerts. Turn up early for a good seat. Food stands and bars create a carnival-like atmosphere.

🛏 Sleeping

★ my MOjO vie   HOSTEL €
(☑ 0676-551 11 55; www.mymojovie.at; 07, Kaiserstrasse 77; dm €24-28, d/tr/q with private bathroom €80/120/160, s/d/tr/q with shared bathroom €40/60/90/116; @ 🛜; Ⓤ Burggasse-Stadthalle) An old-fashioned cage lift rattles up to these design-focused backpacker digs.

Everything you could wish for is here – well-equipped dorms with two power points per bed, a self-catering kitchen, netbooks for surfing, guidebooks for browsing and musical instruments for your own jam session. There's no air-con but fans are available in summer.

Hotel am Brillantengrund HOTEL €

(☑ 01-523 36 62; www.brillantengrund.com; 07, Bandgasse 4; s/d/tr/q from €69/79/99/119; @ 🛜; 🚋 49 Westbahnstrasse/Zieglergasse, Ⓤ Zieglergasse) In a lemon-yellow building set around a sociable courtyard strewn with potted palms, this community linchpin works with local artists and hosts regular exhibitions, along with DJs, live music and other events such as pop-up markets and shops. Parquet-floored rooms are simple but decorated with vintage furniture, which variously incorporate local artworks, funky wallpapers and retro light fittings. Breakfast included.

Hotel Drei Kronen PENSION €

(☑ 01-587 32 89; www.hotel3kronen.at; 04, Schleifmühlegasse 25; s/d from €69/92; @ 🛜; Ⓤ Kettenbrückengasse) Within stumbling distance of the Naschmarkt (some rooms overlook it), this family-owned abode is one of Vienna's best-kept secrets. Palatial touches (shiny marble, polished brass, white-and-gold wallpaper) are distinctly Viennese, but nonetheless a casual feel prevails. Rooms are fitted with *Jugendstil* (Art Nouveau) furniture and art (including many prints by Gustav Klimt).

★Grand Ferdinand Hotel DESIGN HOTEL €€€

(☑ 01-918 804 00; www.grandferdinand.com; 01, Schubertring 10-12; dm/d/ste from €30/180/500; ❄️🛜♨️; 🚋 2, 71) An enormous taxidermied horse stands in the reception area of this ultrahip newcomer, which is shaking up Vienna's accommodation scene by offering parquet-floored dorms with mahogany bunks alongside richly coloured designer rooms with chaises longues and chandeliered suites with private champagne bars. Breakfast (€29) is served on the panoramic rooftop terrace, adjacent to the heated, open-air infinity pool.

★Hotel Capricorno HOTEL €€

(☑ 01-533 31 04-0; www.schick-hotels.com/hotel-capricorno; 01, Schwedenplatz 3-4; s/d incl breakfast from €118/146; 🅿🛜; 🚋 1, 2, Ⓤ Schwedenplatz) Set behind an unpromising mid-20th-century facade, Hotel Capricorno was stunningly made over in 2015 in lustrous velveteens in zesty lime, orange, lemon and aubergine shades. Most of its 42 rooms have balconies (front rooms overlook the Danube Canal; rear rooms are quieter). On-site parking – rare for Vienna – is available for just €24 per day. It's a 10-minute walk from Stephansdom.

★Magdas BOUTIQUE HOTEL €€

(☑ 01-720 02 88; www.magdas-hotel.at; 02, Laufbergergasse 2; d €70-150) How clever: the Magdas is a hotel making a social difference as here the staff who welcome guests are refugees. The former retirement home turned boutique hotel opened its doors in 2016 and hit the ground running. The rooms are retro cool, with one-of-a-kind murals, knitted cushions and upcycling. The pick of them have balconies overlooking the Prater, just around the corner.

✗ Eating

Würstelstande (sausage stands) are great for a cheap bite on the run, and the city has a booming international restaurant scene and many multiethnic markets. Self-caterers can also stock up at central Hofer, Billa and Spar supermarkets. Some have delis that make sandwiches to order.

DON'T MISS

FOOD MARKET FINDS

The sprawling **Naschmarkt** (06, Linke & Rechte Wienzeile; ⊙ 6am-7.30pm Mon-Fri, to 6pm Sat; Ⓤ Karlsplatz, Kettenbrückengasse) is the place to *nasch* (snack) in Vienna. Stalls are piled high with meats, fruits, vegetables, cheeses, olives, spices and wine. There are also plenty of cafes dishing up good-value lunches, along with delis and takeaway stands.

Bio-Markt Freyung (01, Freyungasse; ⊙ 9am-6pm Fri & Sat; Ⓤ Herrengasse, Schottentor) 🍃 sells farm-fresh produce, as does the bustling **Karmelitermarkt** (02, Karmelitermarkt; ⊙ 6am-7.30pm Mon-Fri, to 5pm Sat; 🚋 2 Karmeliterplatz, Ⓤ Taborstrasse). Head to the Saturday farmers market at the latter for brunch at one of the excellent deli-cafes or, if you like you're markets with a little more edge, head to **Bauernmarkt Yppenplatz.** (16, Yppenplatz; ⊙ 9am-1pm Sat; 🚋 2, Ⓤ Josefstädter Strasse).

★**Bitzinger Würstelstand
am Albertinaplatz** STREET FOOD €
(www.bitzinger-wien.at; 01, Albertinaplatz; sausages €3.40-4.40; ⊙8am-4am; ⬚Kärntner Ring/Oper, ⓊKarlsplatz, Stephansplatz) Behind the Staatsoper, Vienna's best sausage stand has cult status. Bitzinger offers the contrasting spectacle of ladies and gents dressed to the nines, sipping beer, wine (from €2.30) or Joseph Perrier Champagne (€19.90 for 0.2L) while tucking into sausages at outdoor tables or the heated counter after performances. Mustard (€0.40) comes in *süss* (sweet, ie mild) or *scharf* (fiercely hot).

★**Griechenbeisl** BISTRO €€
(☎01-533 19 77; www.griechenbeisl.at; 01, Fleischmarkt 11; mains €15-28; ⊙11.30am-11.30pm; ⬚; ⬚1, 2, ⓊSchwedenplatz) Dating from 1447 and frequented by Beethoven, Brahms, Schubert and Strauss among other luminaries, Vienna's oldest restaurant has vaulted rooms, wood panelling and a figure of Augustin trapped at the bottom of a well inside the front door. Every classic Viennese dish is on the menu, along with three daily vegetarian options. In summer, head to the plant-fringed front garden.

★**Lingenhel** MODERN EUROPEAN €€
(☎01-710 15 66; www.lingenhel.com; 03, Landstrasser Hauptstrasse 74; mains €19-24; ⊙shop 8am-8pm, restaurant 8am-10pm Mon-Sat; ⓊRochusgasse) One of Vienna's most exciting gastro newcomers, Lingenhel is an ultra-slick deli-shop-bar-restaurant, lodged in a 200-year-old house. Salamis, wines and own-dairy cheeses tempt in the shop, while much-lauded chef Daniel Hoffmeister helms the kitchen in the pared-back, whitewashed restaurant. The season-inflected food – simple as char with kohlrabi and pork belly with aubergines – tastes profoundly of what it ought to.

★**Punks** MODERN EUROPEAN €€
(☎0664 275 70 72; www.punks.wien; 08, Florianigasse 50; small plates €4.50) The name might be a giveaway, but this guerilla-style restaurant *is* indeed shaking up an otherwise genteel neighbourhood. Patrick Müller, Anna Schwab and René Steindachner have 'occupied' a former wine bar and eschewed the usual refit or any form of interior decoration; the focus is, quite literally, on the kitchen, with a menu of inventive small dishes prepared behind the bar.

Meierei im Stadtpark AUSTRIAN €€
(☎01-713 31 68; http://steirereck.at; 03, Am Heumarkt 2a; set breakfasts €20-24, mains €11.50-22; ⊙8am-11pm Mon-Fri, 9am-7pm Sat & Sun; ⬚; ⓊStadtpark) In the green surrounds of Stadtpark, the Meierei is most famous for its goulash served with lemon, capers and creamy dumplings (€18) and its selection of 120 types of cheese. Served until noon, the bountiful breakfast features gastronomic show-stoppers such as poached duck egg with sweet potato, cress and wild mushrooms, and warm curd-cheese strudel with elderberry compote.

DON'T MISS

COFFEE HOUSE CULTURE

Vienna's legendary *Kaffeehäuser* (coffee houses) rank on the Unesco list of Intangible Cultural Heritage, which defines them as 'places where time and space are consumed, but only the coffee is found on the bill'. Grand or humble, poster-plastered or chandelier-lit, this is where you can join the locals for coffee, cake and a slice of living history.

Café Sperl (www.cafesperl.at; 06, Gumpendorfer Strasse 11; ⊙7am-11pm Mon-Sat, 11am-8pm Sun; ⬚; ⓊMuseumsquartier, Kettenbrückengasse)

Café Central (www.palaisevents.at; 01, Herrengasse 14; ⊙7.30am-10pm Mon-Sat, 10am-10pm Sun; ⬚; ⓊHerrengasse)

Café Leopold Hawelka (www.hawelka.at; 01, Dorotheergasse 6; ⊙8am-midnight Mon-Wed, to 1am Thu-Sat, 10am-midnight Sun; ⓊStephansplatz)

Sperlhof (02, Grosse Sperlgasse 41; ⊙4pm-1.30am; ⓊTaborstrasse)

Supersense (02, Praterstrasse 70; lunch special €5.50-6.50, breakfast €3.80-8; ⊙9am-7pm Mon-Fri, 10am-5pm Sat)

Drinking & Nightlife

Bars pump north and south of the Naschmarkt, around Spittelberg and along the Gürtel (mainly around the U6 stops of Josefstädter Strasse and Nussdorfer Strasse). Vienna's great-value *Heurigen*, or wine taverns, cluster in the wine-growing suburbs to the north, southwest, west and northwest of the city.

★**Loos American Bar**   COCKTAIL BAR
(www.loosbar.at; 01, Kärntner Durchgang 10; ☻noon-5am Thu-Sat, to 4am Sun-Wed; U Stephansplatz) Loos is *the* spot in the Innere Stadt for a classic cocktail such as its signature dry martini, expertly whipped up by talented mixologists. Designed by Adolf Loos in 1908, this tiny 27-sq-metre box (seating just 20-or-so patrons) is bedecked from head to toe in onyx and polished brass, with mirrored walls that make it appear far larger.

Dachboden   BAR
(www.25hours-hotels.com; 07, Lerchenfelder Strasse 1-3; ☻3pm-1am; ☎; U Volkstheater) Housed in the **25hours Hotel** (☏01-521 51; www.25hours-hotels.com; 07, Lerchenfelder Strasse 1-3; d €160-190, ste €195-330; P ☎; U Volkstheater), Dachboden has stunning views of Vienna's skyline from its beach bar–style decked terrace. DJs spins jazz, soul and funk on Wednesday and Friday nights. Inside, wooden crates and mismatched vintage furniture are scattered across the raw-concrete floor beneath chandeliers. Besides Fritz cola and an array of wines, beers and speciality teas, there are tapas-style snacks.

★**Achtundzwanzig**   WINE BAR
(www.achtundzwanzig.at; 08, Schlösslegasse 28; ☻4pm-1am Mon-Thu, to 2am Fri, 7pm-2am Sat; ᾬ5, 43, 44, U Schottentor) Austrian wine fans with a rock-and-roll sensibility will feel like they've found heaven at this black-daubed *vinothek* (wine bar) that vibes casual but takes its wines super seriously. Wines by the glass are all sourced from small producers – many of them are organic or minimal-intervention and friends of the owners – and are well priced at under €4 a glass.

★**Strandbar Herrmann**   BAR
(www.strandbarherrmann.at; 03, Herrmannpark; ☻10am-2am Apr-early Oct; ☎; ᾬ O Hintere Zollamtsstrasse, U Schwedenplatz) You'd swear you're by the sea at this hopping canalside beach bar, with beach chairs, sand, DJ beats and hordes of Viennese livin' it up on sum-

mer evenings. Cool trivia: it's located on Herrmannpark, named after picture-postcard inventor Emanuel Herrmann (1839–1902).

Weinstube Josefstadt   WINE BAR
(08, Piaristengasse 27; ☻4pm-midnight Apr-Dec, closed Jan-Mar; U Rathaus) Weinstube Josefstadt is one of the loveliest *Stadtheurigen* (city wine taverns) in Vienna. A leafy green oasis spliced between towering residential blocks, its tables of friendly, well-liquored locals are squeezed in between the trees and shrubs looking onto a pretty, painted *Salettl*, or wooden summerhouse. Wine is local and cheap, food is typical, with a buffet-style meat and fritter selection.

Fluc   CLUB
(www.fluc.at; 02, Praterstern 5; ☻6pm-4am; U Praterstern) Located on the wrong side of the tracks (Praterstern can be rough around the edges at times) and housed in a converted pedestrian passage, Fluc is the closest that Vienna's nightlife scene comes to anarchy – without the fear of physical violence.

☆ **Entertainment**

Vienna is, was and will always be the European capital of opera and classical music. The line-up of music events is never-ending and even the city's buskers are often classically trained musicians.

Box offices generally open from Monday to Saturday and sell cheap (€3 to €6) standing-room tickets around an hour before performances.

For weekly listings, visit Flater (www.falter.at), while Tourist Info Wien (http://events.wien.info/en) lists concerts up to 18 months in advance.

★**Staatsoper**   OPERA
(☏01-514 44 7880; www.wiener-staatsoper.at; 01, Opernring 2; tickets €10-208, standing room €3-4; ᾬ D 1, 2, 71 Kärntner Ring/Oper, U Karlsplatz) The glorious Staatsoper is Vienna's premiere opera and classical-music venue. Productions are lavish, formal affairs, where people dress up accordingly. In the interval, wander the foyer and refreshment rooms to fully appreciate the gold-and-crystal interior. Opera is not performed here in July and August (tours still take place). Tickets can be purchased (☏01-514 44 7810; www.bundestheater.at; 01, Operngasse 2; ☻8am-6pm Mon-Fri, 9am-noon Sat & Sun; U Stephansplatz) up to two months in advance.

IMPERIAL ENTERTAINMENT

The world-famous Vienna Boys' Choir performs on Sunday at 9.15am (late September to June) in the **Burgkapelle** (Royal Chapel) in the Hofburg. **Tickets** (☑ 01-533 99 27; www. hofmusikkapelle.gv.at; 01, Schweizerhof; tickets €10-36; Ⓤ Herrengasse) should be booked around six weeks in advance. The group also performs on Friday afternoons at the **MuTh** (☑ 01-347 80 80; www.muth.at; 02, Obere Augartenstrasse 1e; Vienna Boys' Choir Fri performance €39-89; ⊙ 4-6pm Mon-Fri & 1 hour before performances; Ⓤ Taborstrasse).

Another Habsburg legacy is the **Spanish Riding School** (Spanische Hofreitschule; ☑ 01-533 90 31-0; www.srs.at; 01, Michaelerplatz 1; performances €25-217; ⊙ hours vary; 🚌 1A, 2A Michaelerplatz, Ⓤ Herrengasse), where Lipizzaner stallions gracefully perform equine ballet to classical music. For morning training sessions, same-day tickets are available at the nearby visitor centre.

★ **Musikverein** CONCERT VENUE
(☑ 01-505 81 90; www.musikverein.at; 01, Musikvereinsplatz 1; tickets €24-95, standing room €4-6; ⊙ box office 9am-8pm Mon-Fri, to 1pm Sat Sep-Jun, 9am-noon Mon-Fri Jul & Aug; Ⓤ Karlsplatz) The opulent Musikverein holds the proud title of the best acoustics of any concert hall in Austria, which the Vienna Philharmonic Orchestra embraces. The lavish interior can be visited by 45-minute guided tour (in English and German; adult/child €6.50/4) at 10am, 11am and noon Monday to Saturday. Smaller-scale performances are held in the Brahms Saal. There are no student tickets.

Theater an der Wien THEATRE
(☑ 01-588 85; www.theater-wien.at; 06, Linke Wienzeile 6; tickets €10-160, standing room €7, student tickets €10-15; ⊙ box office 10am-6pm Mon-Sat, 2-6pm Sun; Ⓤ Karlsplatz) The Theater an der Wien has hosted some monumental premiere performances, including Beethoven's *Fidelio*, Mozart's *Die Zauberflöte* and Strauss Jnr's *Die Fledermaus*. These days, besides staging musicals, dance and concerts, it's re-established its reputation for high-quality opera, with one premiere each month.

Student tickets go on sale 30 minutes before shows; standing-room tickets are available one hour prior to performances.

Jazzland LIVE MUSIC
(☑ 01-533 25 75; www.jazzland.at; 01, Franz-Josefs-Kai 29; cover €11-20; ⊙ 7pm-2am Mon-Sat mid-Aug–mid-Jul, live music from 9pm; 🚌 1, 2, Ⓤ Schwedenplatz) Buried in a former wine cellar beneath Ruprechtskirche, Jazzland is Vienna's oldest jazz club, dating back nearly 50 years. The music covers the whole jazz spectrum, and features both local and international acts. Past performers have included Ray Brown, Teddy Wilson, Big Joe Williams and Max Kaminsky.

🛍 Shopping

In the alley-woven Innere Stadt, go to Kohlmarkt for designer chic, Herrengasse for antiques and Kärntnerstrasse for high-street brands. Tune into Vienna's creative pulse in the idiosyncratic boutiques and concept stores in Neubau, especially along Kirchengasse and Lindengasse along with the edgier still around Yppenplatz.

Dorotheum ANTIQUES
(www.dorotheum.com; 01, Dorotheergasse 17; ⊙ 10am-6pm Mon-Fri, 9am-5pm Sat; Ⓤ Stephansplatz) The Dorotheum is among the largest auction houses in Europe and for the casual visitor it's more like a museum, housing everything from antique toys and tableware to autographs, antique guns and, above all, lots of quality paintings. You can bid at the regular auctions held here, otherwise just drop by (it's free) and enjoy browsing.

★ **Dirndlherz** CLOTHING
(http://dirndlherz.at; 07, Lerchenfelder Strasse 50; ⊙ 11am-6pm Thu & Fri, to 4pm Sat; Ⓤ Volkstheater) Putting her own spin on Alpine fashion, Austrian designer Gabriela Urabl creates one-of-a-kind, high-fashion *Dirndls* (women's traditional dress), from sassy purple-velvet bosom-lifters to 1950s-style gingham numbers and *Dirndls* emblazoned with quirky motifs like pop-art and punk-like conical metal studs. T-shirts with tag-lines like *'Mei Dirndl is in da Wäsch'* ('My *Dirndl* is in the wash') are also available.

ℹ Information

Most hostels and hotels in Vienna offer free wi-fi, called WLAN (pronounced vee-lan) in German. As well as 400 city hotspots which can be found at www.wien.gv.at/stadtplan, cafes, coffee houses and bars also offer free wi-fi; check locations at www.freewave.at/en/hotspots.

Tourist Info Wien (☑ 01-245 55; www.wien.
info; 01, Albertinaplatz; ☺ 9am-7pm; ☎; ☒ D,
1, 2, 71 Kärntner Ring/Oper, ⓤ Stephansplatz)
Vienna's main tourist office has free maps and
racks of brochures.

ℹ Getting There & Away

AIR

Located 19km southwest of the city centre,
Vienna International Airport (VIE; ☑ 01-700
722 233; www.viennaairport.com; ☎) is a
well-serviced international hub. The fastest
transport into the centre is **City Airport Train**
(CAT; www.cityairporttrain.com; single/return
€11/19), which runs every 30 minutes and takes
16 minutes between the airport and Wien Mitte;
book online for a discount. The S-Bahn (S7)
does the same journey (single €4.40) but in 25
minutes.

BOAT

Fast hydrofoils travel eastwards to Bratislava
(one way €20 to €35, 1¼ hours) daily from April
to October. From May to September, they also
travel twice weekly to Budapest (one way/return
€109/125, 5½ hours). Bookings can be made
through **DDSG Blue Danube** (☑ 01-58 880;
www.ddsg-blue-danube.at; Handelskai 265,
Vienna; Ⓜ Vorgartenstrasse).

BUS

National Bundesbuses arrive and depart from
several different locations, depending on the
destination. Bus lines serving Vienna include
Eurolines (☑ 0900 128 712; www.eurolines.
at; 03, Erdbergstrasse 200; ☺ office 8am-6pm;
ⓤ Erdberg).

CAR & MOTORCYCLE

The Gürtel is an outer ring road that joins up with
the A22 on the north bank of the Danube and the
A23 southeast of town. All the main road routes
intersect with this system, including the A1 from
Linz and Salzburg, and the A2 from Graz.

TRAIN

Vienna is one of central Europe's main rail hubs.
Österreichische Bundesbahn has connections to
many European cities, including Budapest (€29
to €37, 2½ to 3¼ hours), Munich (€93, 4½ to
five hours), Paris (€51 to €142, 11½ to 13 hours),
Prague (€49, 4¼ hours) and Venice (€49 to
€108, seven to 11 hours).

Vienna's main train station, the Wien Hauptbahnhof, 3km south of Stephansdom, handles
all international trains as well as trains Austria's
provincial capitals, apart from Salzburg.

ℹ Getting Around

BICYCLE

Citybike Wien (Vienna City Bike; www.city
bikewien.at; 1st/2nd/3rd hr free/€1/2, per
hr thereafter €4) has more than 120 bicycle
stands across the city. A credit card is required
and after a €1 registration fee bikes are free for
the first hour.

PUBLIC TRANSPORT

Vienna's unified public transport network
encompasses trains, trams, buses, and underground (U-Bahn) and suburban (S-Bahn) trains.
Free maps and information pamphlets are available from **Wiener Linien** (☑ 01-7909-100; www.
wienerlinien.at).

All tickets must be validated at the entrance to
U-Bahn stations and on buses and trams (except
for weekly and monthly tickets).

Singles cost €2.20. A 24-hour ticket costs
€7.60, a 48-hour ticket €13.30 and a 72-hour
ticket €16.50. Weekly tickets (valid Monday to
Sunday) cost €16.20.

THE DANUBE VALLEY

The stretch of Danube between Krems and
Melk, known locally as the Wachau, is arguably the loveliest along the entire length of
the long, long river. Both banks are dotted
with ruined castles and medieval towns,
and lined with terraced vineyards. Further
upstream is the industrial city of Linz, Austria's avant-garde art and new technology
trailblazer.

Krems an der Donau

☑ 02732 / POP 23,900

Sitting on the northern bank of the Danube
against a backdrop of terraced vineyards,
Krems marks the beginning of the Wachau.
It has an attractive cobbled centre, some
good restaurants and the gallery-dotted
Kunstmeile.

◉ Sights & Activities

Kunsthalle Krems   GALLERY
(www.kunsthalle.at; Franz-Zeller-Platz 3; €10;
☺ 10am-5pm Tue-Sun) The flagship of Krems'
Kunstmeile, an eclectic collection of galleries and museums, the Kunsthalle has a program of changing exhibitions. These might
be mid-19th-century landscapes or hardcore
conceptual works, but are always well curated. Guided tours (€3) run on Sundays at 2pm.

ⓘ ON YOUR BIKE

Register online for Danube Valley's bike-hire network **Nextbike** (☑ 02742-229 901; www.nextbike.at; per hr €1, 24hr €8).

Domäne Wachau
WINE

(☑ 02711-371 15; www.domaene-wachau.at; ⊙ 10am-5pm Mon-Sat Apr-Oct, closed Sat Nov-Mar) If you're intent on tasting the best of what the Wachau has to offer, it's a good idea to do a broad range of vineyards, from the innovative family-run operations to the big boys like Domäne Wachau, one of the region's most well known producers internationally. A large modern tasting room is set back just from the river and staffed by an army of keen young assistants. It also stocks some nice local food products if wine's not your thing.

🛏 Sleeping

Hotel-Garni Schauhuber
HOTEL €

(☑ 0660 4003 412; Steiner Landstrasse 16; s/d €40/72; ☯ 🎧) The Schauhuber is charmingly old-fashioned, with sparkling tiled surfaces, whitewashed walls and large rooms. Breakfast is hearty.

Kolpinghaus
ACCOMMODATION SERVICES €

(☑ 02732-835 41; www.kolpingkrems.at; Alauntalstrasse 95 & 97; s/d €40/75; ⊙ reception 8am-5pm Mon-Fri, to noon Sat & Sun; 🅿 🎧) These super student quarters are available to travellers any time of year: a great deal if you don't mind the trek up to the university. Some of the basic but comfortable rooms are huge, with bathrooms the size of some hotel singles, as well as their own kitchens. Only con is the institutional checkout time of 10am.

ⓘ Information

Krems Tourismus
(☑ 02732-82 676; www.krems.info; Utzstrasse 1; ⊙ 9am-6pm Mon-Fri, 11am-6pm Sat, 11am-4pm Sun, shorter hours in winter) Helpful office well stocked with info and maps.

ⓘ Getting There & Away

Frequent daily trains connect Krems with Vienna (€17.60, one hour). **Wachau Linien** (☑ 0810 222 324; www.vor.at) runs buses along the Danube Valley and the Wachau Ticket (€10, purchase from the driver) gives you a day's unlimited travel on all buses and the Danube ferries.

Melk

☑ 02752 / POP 5260

With its blockbuster abbey-fortress set high above the valley, Melk is a high point of any visit to the Danube Valley. Separated from the river by a stretch of woodland, this pretty town makes for an easy and rewarding day trip from Krems or even Vienna. Post abbey visit, you'll find plenty of restaurants and cafes with alfresco seating line the Rathausplatz.

◎ Sights

Stift Melk
ABBEY

(Benedictine Abbey of Melk; www.stiftmelk.at; Abt Berthold Dietmayr Strasse 1; adult/child €11/6, with guided tour €13/8; ⊙ 9am-5.30pm, tours 10.55am & 2.55pm May-Sep, tours only 11am & 2pm Nov-Mar) Of the many abbeys in Austria, Stift Melk is the most famous. Possibly Lower Austria's finest, the monastery church dominates the complex with its twin spires and high octagonal dome. The interior is baroque gone barmy, with regiments of smirking cherubs, gilt twirls and polished faux marble. The theatrical high-altar scene, depicting St Peter and St Paul (the church's two patron saints), is by Peter Widerin. Johann Michael Rottmayr created most of the ceiling paintings, including those in the dome.

ⓘ Information

Melk Tourist Office
(☑ 02752-511 60; www.stadt-melk.at; Kremser Strasse 5; ⊙ 9.30am-6pm Mon-Sat, to 4pm Sun Apr-Oct, 9am-5pm Mon-Thu, to 2.30pm Fri Nov-Mar)

ⓘ Getting There & Away

Boats leave from the canal by Pionierstrasse, 400m north of the abbey. There are hourly trains to Vienna (€16.50, 1¼ hours).

Linz

☑ 0732 / POP 197,500

'It begins in Linz' goes the Austrian saying, and it's true. The technology trailblazer and European Capital of Culture 2009 is blessed with a leading-edge cyber centre and world-class contemporary-art gallery.

◉ Sights & Activities

★ Ars Electronica Center
MUSEUM

(www.aec.at; Ars-Electronica-Strasse 1; adult/child €9.50/7.50; ☺9am-5pm Tue, Wed & Fri, 9am-9pm Thu, 10am-6pm Sat & Sun) The technology, science and digital media of the future are in the spotlight at Linz' biggest crowd-puller. In the labs you can interact with robots, animate digital objects, print 3D structures, turn your body into musical instruments, and (virtually) travel to outer space. Kids love it. Designed by Vienna-based architectural firm Treusch, the centre resembles a futuristic ship by the Danube after dark, when its LED glass skin kaleidoscopically changes colour.

★ Lentos
GALLERY

(www.lentos.at; Ernst-Koref-Promenade 1; adult/child €8/4.50, guided tours €3; ☺10am-6pm Tue, Wed & Fri-Sun, 10am-9pm Thu) Overlooking the Danube, the rectangular glass-and-steel Lentos is strikingly illuminated by night. The gallery guards one of Austria's finest modern-art collections, including works by Warhol, Schiele, Klimt, Kokoschka and Lovis Corinth, which sometimes feature in the large-scale exhibitions. There are regular guided tours in German and 30-minute tours in English at 4pm on the first Saturday of the month. Alternatively, download Lentos' app from the website.

🛏 Sleeping & Eating

★ Hotel am Domplatz
DESIGN HOTEL €€

(☑0732-77 30 00; www.hotelamdomplatz.at; Stifterstrasse 4; d €111-175, ste €280-340; ❄🌐) ⚑ Adjacent to the neo-Gothic Mariendom (ask for a room overlooking the cathedral), this glass-and-concrete cube filled with striking metal sculptures has streamlined, Nordic-style pristine-white and blonde-wood rooms with semi-open bathrooms. Wind down with a view at the rooftop spa. In fine weather, the cathedral-facing terrace is a prime spot for breakfast (€18), which includes a glass of bubbly.

★ Cafe Jindrak
CAFE €

(www.jindrak.at; Herrenstrasse 22; dishes €3-8.80; ☺8am-6pm Mon-Sat, 8.30am-6pm Sun; 🚸) Join the cake-loving locals at this celebrated cafe – the original shop (1929) of a now nine-strong chain that produces over 100,000 of its famous *Linzer Torte* each year made to its family recipe. You'd need a huge fork (and appetite) to tackle the torte that set a

---

Guinness World Record in 1999, measuring 4m high and weighing 650kg.

ⓘ Information

Tourist Information Linz (☑0732-7070 2009; www.linztourismus.at; Hauptplatz 1; ☺9am-7pm Mon-Sat, 10am-7pm Sun May-Sep, 9am-5pm Mon-Sat, 10am-5pm Sun Oct-Apr) Upper Austria information as well as brochures and accommodation listings.

ⓘ Getting There & Around

AIR

Ryanair flies to the **Blue Danube Airport** (LNZ; ☑07221-60 00; www.linz-airport.at; Flughafenstrasse 1, Hörsching), 13km southwest of Linz. An hourly shuttle bus (€3.10, 20 minutes) links the airport to the main train station.

PUBLIC TRANSPORT

Single bus and tram tickets cost €1.10, and day passes €4.40 and must be pre-purchased.

TRAIN

Linz is halfway between Salzburg and Vienna on the main road and rail routes. Trains to Salzburg (€12.80, 1¼ hours) and Vienna (€18.90, 1½ hours) leave at least twice hourly.

THE SOUTH

Austria's southern states often feel worlds apart from the rest of the country, both in climate and attitude. Styria (Steiermark) is a blissful amalgamation of genteel architecture, rolling green hills, vine-covered slopes and soaring mountains. Its capital, Graz, is one of Austria's most attractive cities. A glamorous crowd heads to sun-drenched Carinthia (Kärnten) in summer. Sidling up to Italy, its sparkling lakes and pretty lidos are as close to Mediterranean as this landlocked country gets.

Graz

☑0316 / POP 265,780

Austria's second-largest city is relaxed and good-looking, with ample green spaces, red rooftops and a narrow, fast-flowing river gushing through its centre. Architecturally, Graz hints at nearby Italy with its Renaissance courtyards and baroque palaces. But there's a youthful, almost Eastern European energy too, with a handful of edgily modern buildings, a vibrant arts scene and great nightlife (thanks in part to its large student population).

◎ Sights

Graz is a city easily enjoyed by simply wandering aimlessly. Admission to all of the Joanneum museums with a 24-hour ticket costs €11/4 for adults/children.

★ **Kunsthaus Graz**   GALLERY
(www.kunsthausgraz.at; Lendkai 1; adult/child €9/3; ◎ 10am-5pm Tue-Sun; 🚊 1, 3, 6, 7 Südtiroler Platz) Designed by British architects Peter Cook and Colin Fournier, this world-class contemporary-art space is known as the 'friendly alien' by locals. The building is signature Cook, a photovoltaic-skinned sexy biomorphic blob that is at once completely at odds with its pristine historic surroundings but sits rather lyrically within in it as well. Exhibitions change every three to four months.

Neue Galerie Graz   GALLERY
(www.museum-joanneum.at; Joanneumsviertel; adult/child €9/3; ◎ 10am-5pm Tue-Sun; 🕾; 🚊 1, 3, 4, 5, 6, 7 Hauptplatz) The Neue Galerie is the crowning glory of the three museums inside the Joanneumsviertel complex. The stunning collection on level 0 is the highlight. Though not enormous, it showcases vibrant works by painters such as Ernst Christian Moser, Ferdinand Georg Waldmüller and Johann Nepomuk Passini. Egon Schiele is also represented here.

★ **Schlossberg**   VIEWPOINT
(1hr ticket for lift or funicular €2.10, lift adult/child €1.40/0.90; 🚊 4, 5 Schlossbergplatz) **FREE** Rising to 473m, Schlossberg is the site of the original fortress where Graz was founded and is marked by the city's most visible icon – the **Uhrturm** (Clock Tower; 🚊 4, 5 Schlossplatz/Murinse, for lift) **FREE**. Its wooded slopes can be reached by a number of bucolic and strenuous paths, but also by lift or Schlossbergbahn funicular. It's a brief walk or take tram 4 or 5 to Schlossplatz/Murinsel for the lift.

Schloss Eggenberg   PALACE
(www.museum-joanneum.at; Eggenberger Allee 90; adult/child €11.50/5.50; ◎ tours hourly 10am-

4pm, apart from 1pm Tue-Sun late Mar-Oct, exhibitions 10am-5pm Wed-Sun; 🚊 1 Schloss Eggenberg) Graz' elegant palace was created for the Eggenberg dynasty in 1625 by Giovanni Pietro de Pomis (1565–1633) at the request of Johann Ulrich (1568–1634). Admission is on a highly worthwhile guided tour during which you learn about the idiosyncrasies of each room, the stories told by the frescoes and about the Eggenberg family itself.

🛏 Sleeping

★ **Hotel Wiesler**   HOTEL €€
(🕿 0316-70 66-0; www.hotelwiesler.com; Grieskai 4; d €155-210; 🅿 @; 🚊 1, 3, 6, 7 Südtiroler Platz) The riverside Wiesler, a *Jugenstil* (art nouveau) gem from 1901, has been recently transformed into Graz' most glamorous hotel. Hotelier Florian Weltzer has shaken up everything, including the notion of room categories, and ensured that this is a luxury experience that is far from stuffy.

Hotel Daniel   HOTEL €
(🕿 0316-71 10 80; www.hoteldaniel.com; Europaplatz 1; d €65-350; 🅿 ✳ @ 🕿; 🚊 1, 3, 6, 7 Hauptbahnhof) The Daniel's rooms are well designed and super simple, and while its small 'smart' rooms scrape into budget territory, it also now offers the super exclusive loft cube on the roof if you're looking for something out of the ordinary. The lobby area is a lot of fun, a great space to work or just hang out.

✕ Eating

Graz does fine dining with aplomb, but you'll also find plenty of cheap eats near Universität Graz, particularly on Halbärthgasse, Zinzendorfgasse and Harrachgasse.

Stock up for a picnic at the farmers markets on Kaiser-Josef-Platz and Lendplatz. For fast-food stands, head for Hauptplatz and Jakominiplatz.

★ **Aiola Upstairs**   INTERNATIONAL €€
(www.aiola.at; Schlossberg 2; pasta €14.50-16.50, mains €19.50-27.50; ◎ 9am-midnight Mon-Sat; 🕿; 🚊 4, 5 Schlossbergplatz/Murinsel (for lift)) Ask locals for the best outdoor dining experience in Graz, and they'll direct you to Aiola. This wonderful restaurant on Schlossberg has great views from both its glass box interior and its beautiful summer terrace. Even better, the cooking up here is some of the city's best, with interesting international flavours and seasonal ingredients.

★ **Der Steirer** AUSTRIAN, TAPAS €€
(☑0316-70 36 54; www.dersteirer.at; Belgiergasse 1; weekday lunch menu €8.90, mains €10.90-22; ☺11am-midnight; ☑; ☒1, 3, 6, 7 Südtiroler Platz) This neo-*Beisl* (bistro pub) and wine bar has a beautiful selection of Styrian dishes, including a great goulash, lamb cutlets and stuffed peppers, all done in a simple, contemporary style. Its Styrian tapas concept works, and is a nice way to sample local flavours if you just feel like nibbling.

Kunsthauscafé INTERNATIONAL €
(☑0316-71 49 57; www.kunsthauscafe.co.at; Südtirolerplatz 2; mains €6-16.50; ☺9am-11pm Sun-Thu, to 1am Fri & Sat) A happy, young crowd fills the long tables here for a menu that incorporates burgers (from big beef to goat cheese), vaguely Mexican dishes, main-sized salads and the house special 'Styrian Sandwich', a combination of crispy pork belly, creamy sauerkraut and horseradish. It's very, very loud, but fun if you're in the mood.

🍷 Drinking & Nightlife

The bar scene in Graz is split between three main areas: around the university; east of the Kunsthaus in hipster Lend; and on Mehlplatz and Prokopigasse (dubbed the 'Bermuda Triangle').

Blendend COFFEE
(www.blendend.at; Mariahilferstrasse 24; ☺4pm-2am Mon-Fri, from 9am Sat & Sun) A rambling, warm and endearingly boho addition to Lend's usual lineup of grungy bars, Blendend is a great drinking and snacking spot during the week and then turns all day cafe on weekends with beautiful homemade cakes and desserts competing with the spritzs and excellent local beers. In warmer weather all the action happens at the courtyard tables.

Freiblick Tagescafe ROOFTOP BAR
(☑0316-83 53 02; freiblick.co.at; Sackstrasse 7-11, Kastner & Öhler; ☺9.30am-7pm Mon-Fri, to 6pm Sat) This huge terrace cafe-bar tops the Kastner & Öhler department store and has the best view in the city. Enjoy the clouds and rooftops over breakfast platter and coffee or a lunchtime soup or salad. Or stop by in the afternoon for something from the Prosecco spritz menu or a Hugo Royal – Moët Chandon splashed with elderflower (€15).

STYRIAN TUSCANY

Head south of Graz to what's known as *Steirische Toskana* (Styrian Tuscany), for lush wine country that's reminiscent of Chianti: gentle rolling hills cultivated with vineyards or patchwork farmland, dotted with small forests where deer roam. Apart from its stellar whites, it's also famous for Kürbiskernöl, the rich pumpkin-seed oil generously used in Styrian cooking. The picturesque 'capital' of **Ehrenhausen**, on the road to the Slovenian border, makes a fine base for wine tasting and exploring.

ℹ Information

Graz Tourismus (☑0316-807 50; www.graztourismus.at; Herrengasse 16; ☺10am-7pm Apr-Oct & Dec, to 6pm Nov & Jan-Mar; phone line 10am-5pm; ☎; ☒1, 3, 4, 5, 6, 7 Hauptplatz) Graz' main tourist office, with loads of free information on the city and helpful and knowledgeable staff.

ℹ Getting There & Away

AIR

Graz airport (GRZ; ☑0316-290 20; www.flughafen-graz.at) is located 10km south of the centre and is served by European carriers including Air Berlin, which connects the city with Berlin.

TRAIN

Trains to Vienna depart hourly (€37.30, 2½ hours), and six daily go to Salzburg (€48, four hours). International train connections from Graz include Ljubljana (€41, 3½ hours) and Budapest (€70, 5½ hours).

ℹ Getting Around

BICYCLE

Bicycle rental is available from **Bicycle** (☑0316-82 13 57; www.bicycle.at; Körösistrasse 5; per 24hr €10, Fri-Mon €16, per week €49; ☺7am-1pm & 2-6pm Mon-Fri).

PUBLIC TRANSPORT

Single tickets (€2.10) for buses, trams and the Schlossbergbahn are valid for one hour, but you're usually better off buying a 24-hour pass (€4.70).

Klagenfurt

☑ 0463 / POP 95,450

With its captivating location on Wörthersee and more Renaissance than baroque beauty, Klagenfurt has a distinct Mediterranean feel and is suprisingly lively. Carinthia's capital makes a handy base for exploring Wörthersee's lakeside villages and elegant medieval towns to the north.

◎ Sights & Activities

Boating and swimming are usually possible from May to September.

Europapark   PARK

The green expanse and its *Strandbad* (beach) on the shores of the Wörthersee are centres for aquatic fun and especially great for kids. The park's biggest draw is **Minimundus** (www.minimundus.at; Villacher Strasse 241; adult/child €18/10; ◎ 9am-7pm Mar & Apr, to 8pm May-Sep; 👪), a 'miniature world' with 140 replicas of the world's architectural icons, downsized to a scale of 1:25. To get here, take bus 10, 11, 12 or 22 from Heiligengeistplatz.

🛏 Sleeping & Eating

When you check into accommodation in Klagenfurt, ask for a *Gästekarte* (guest card), entitling you to discounts.

★ Stand No. 17   ITALIAN, AUSTRIAN €

(☑ 0677 617 129 65; Benediktiner Platz; €8-14; ◎ 8am-4pm Tue-Sat) Nini Loudon's kitchen springs in to service from 11.30am to 2pm. Her small, market-fresh menu has beloved regional specialities but more often crosses the border to include seasonal Italian classics (white truffle risotto if you're lucky) as well as occasionally ranging further to include couscous and tagines.

ⓘ REACHING EUROPAPARK

Take bus 10 from Heiligengeistplatz via Minimundus to Strandbad. To get to Wörthersee by bicycle, avoid Villacher Strasse and take the bicycle path running along the northern side of Lendl Canal. Access from the small streets running west from Villacher Ring and Villacher Strasse.

★ Das Domizil   APARTMENT €€

(☑ 0664 843 30 50; www.das-domizil.at; Bahnhofstrasse 51; apt €98; 🅿🛜) This large, light and sweetly decorated apartment is in a grand 19th-century building just beyond the ring of the historic centre. It's extremely well equipped with a full kitchen, laundry facilities and lots of space. Owner Ingo Dietrich is a friendly and fashionable young local who is generous with his insider tips and time. Courtyard parking is €12 per day extra.

ⓘ Information

Tourist Office (☑ 0463-537 22 23; www.visit klagenfurt.at; Neuer Platz 1, Rathaus; ◎ 8am-6pm Mon-Fri, 10am-5pm Sat, to 3pm Sun) Sells Kärnten Cards and books accommodation.

ⓘ Getting There & Around

AIR

Klagenfurt's **airport** (www.klagenfurt-airport. com; Flughafenstrasse 60-66) is 3km north of town. Germanwings flies to Vienna and Berlin, Hamburg and Cologne in Germany.

BUS

Bus drivers sell single, hourly or 24-hour tickets (€1.40/2.10/4.80).

TRAIN

Two hourly direct trains run from Klagenfurt to Vienna (€52.60, four hours) and Salzburg (€41.25, 3¼ hours). Trains to Graz depart every two to three hours (€41.25, 2¾ hours). Trains to western Austria, Italy, Slovenia and Germany go via Villach (€7.10, 24 to 37 minutes, two to four per hour).

SALZBURG

☑ 0662 / POP

The joke 'If it's baroque, don't fix it' is a perfect maxim for Salzburg; the tranquil Old Town burrowed below steep hills looks much as it did when Mozart lived here 250 years ago.

A Unesco World Heritage site, Salzburg's overwhelmingly 17th-century Altstadt – old town – is entrancing both at ground level and from Hohensalzburg fortress high above. Across the fast-flowing Salzach River rests Schloss Mirabell, surrounded by gorgeous manicured gardens.

You can of course, bypass the baroque grandeur and head straight for kitsch-country via a tour of *The Sound of Music* film locations.

⊙ Sights

Dom
CATHEDRAL

(Cathedral; www.salzburger-dom.at; Domplatz; ⊙8am-7pm Mon-Sat, 1-7pm Sun May-Sep, shorter hours rest of year) FREE Gracefully crowned by a bulbous copper dome and twin spires, the Dom stands out as a masterpiece of baroque art. Bronze portals symbolising faith, hope and charity lead into the cathedral. In the nave, both the intricate stucco and Arsenio Mascagni's ceiling frescoes recounting the Passion of Christ guide the eye to the polychrome dome.

★Residenz
PALACE

(www.domquartier.at; Residenzplatz 1; DomQuartier ticket adult/child €12/5; ⊙10am-5pm Wed-Mon) The crowning glory of Salzburg's new DomQuartier, the Residenz is where the prince-archbishops held court until Salzburg became part of the Habsburg Empire in the 19th century. An audio-guide tour takes in the exuberant **state rooms**, lavishly adorned with tapestries, stucco and frescoes by Johann Michael Rottmayr. The 3rd floor is given over to the **Residenzgalerie**, where the focus is on Flemish and Dutch masters. Must-sees include Rubens' *Allegory on Emperor Charles V* and Rembrandt's chiaroscuro *Old Woman Praying*.

★Salzburg Museum
MUSEUM

(www.salzburgmuseum.at; Mozartplatz 1; adult/child €8.50/3; ⊙9am-5pm Tue-Sun, to 8pm Thu; 🖼) Housed in the baroque Neue Residenz palace, this flagship museum takes you on a fascinating romp through Salzburg past and present. Ornate rooms showcase everything from Roman excavations to royal portraits. There are free **guided tours** at 6pm every Thursday.

★Festung Hohensalzburg
FORT

(www.salzburg-burgen.at; Mönchsberg 34; adult/child/family €12/6.80/26.20, incl funicular €15.20/8.70/33.70; ⊙9am-7pm) Salzburg's most visible icon is this mighty, 900-year-old cliff-top fortress, one of the biggest and best preserved in Europe. It's easy to spend half a day up here, roaming the ramparts for far-reaching views over the city's spires, the Salzach River and the mountains. The fortress is a steep 15-minute jaunt from the centre or a speedy ride up in the glass Festungsbahn funicular.

Stift Nonnberg
CONVENT

(Nonnberg Convent; Nonnberggasse 2; ⊙7am-dusk) FREE A short climb up the Nonnbergstiege staircase from Kaigasse or along Festungsgasse brings you to this Benedictine convent, founded 1300 years ago and made famous as the nunnery in *The Sound of Music*. You can visit the beautiful rib-vaulted **church**, but the rest of the convent is off-limits. Take €0.50 to switch on the light that illuminates the beautiful **Romanesque frescoes**.

Mozarts Geburtshaus
MUSEUM

(Mozart's Birthplace; www.mozarteum.at; Getreidegasse 9; adult/child €10/3.50; ⊙8.30am-7pm Jul & Aug, 9am-5.30pm Sep-Jun) Wolfgang Amadeus Mozart, Salzburg's most famous son, was born in this bright yellow townhouse in 1756 and spent the first 17 years of his life here. Today's museum harbours a collection of instruments, documents and portraits. Highlights include the mini-violin he played as a toddler, plus a lock of his hair and buttons from his jacket. In one room, Mozart is shown as a holy babe beneath a neon-blue halo – we'll leave you to draw your own analogies.

Mozart-Wohnhaus
MUSEUM

(Mozart's Residence; www.mozarteum.at; Makartplatz 8; adult/child €10/3.50; ⊙8.30am-7pm Jul & Aug, 9am-5.30pm Sep-Jun) Tired of the cramped living conditions on Getreidegasse, the Mozart family moved to this more spacious abode in 1773, where a prolific Wolfgang composed works such as the *Shepherd King* (K208) and *Idomeneo* (K366). Emanuel Schikaneder, a close friend of Mozart and the librettist of *The Magic Flute*, was

> ### ⓘ DOMQUARTIER
>
> Salzburg shines more brightly than ever since the opening of the DomQuartier (www.domquartier.at) in 2014, showcasing the most fabulous baroque monuments and museums in the historic centre. A single ticket (adult/child €12/5) gives you access to the **Residenz** state rooms and gallery, the upper galleries of the **Dom**, the **Dommuseum** and **Erzabtei St Peter**. The multilingual audio guide whisks you through the quarter in 90 minutes, though you could easily spend half a day absorbing all of its sights.

AUSTRIA SALZBURG

Salzburg

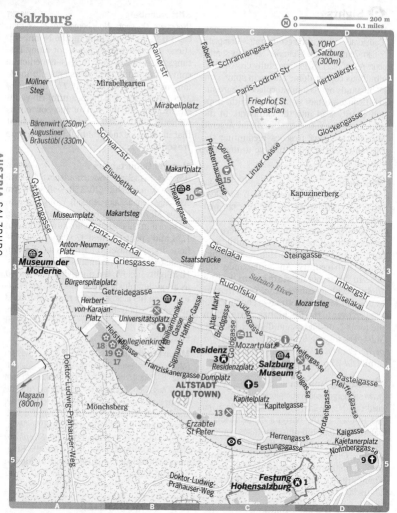

a regular guest here. An audio guide accompanies your visit, serenading you with opera excerpts. Alongside family portraits and documents, you'll find Mozart's original fortepiano.

★ **Museum der Moderne**   GALLERY
(www.museumdermoderne.at; Mönchsberg 32; adult/child €8/6; ⊙10am-6pm Tue-Sun, to 8pm Wed) Straddling Mönchsberg's cliffs, this contemporary glass-and-marble oblong of a gallery stands in stark contrast to the fortress, and shows first-rate temporary exhibitions of 20th- and 21st-century art. The

works of Alberto Giacometti, Dieter Roth, Emil Nolde and John Cage have previously been featured. There's a free **guided tour** of the gallery at 6.30pm every Wednesday. The **Mönchsberg Lift** (Gstättengasse 13; one-way/ return €2.30/3.60, incl gallery entry €9.10/6.50; ⊙8am-7pm Mon, to 9pm Tue-Sun) whizzes up to the gallery year-round.

☞ Tours

One-hour guided tours (in German and English; €10) of the historic centre depart daily at 12.15pm and 2pm from Mozartplatz.

Salzburg

⭐ Festivals & Events

Salzburg Festival   ART

(Salzburger Festspiele; www.salzburgerfestspiele.at; ⊙ Jul & Aug) The absolute highlight of the city's events calendar is the Salzburg Festival. It's a grand affair, with some 200 productions – including theatre, classical music and opera – staged in the impressive surrounds of the **Grosses Festpielhaus** (☑ 0662-804 50; Hofstallgasse 1), **Haus für Mozart** (House for Mozart; ☑ 0662-804 55 00; www.salzburgerfestspiele.at; Hofstallgasse 1) and the baroque **Felsenreitschule** (Summer Riding School; Hofstallgasse 1). Tickets vary in price between €11 and €430; book well ahead.

🛏 Sleeping

⭐ **Haus Ballwein**   GUESTHOUSE €

(☑ 0662-82 40 29; www.haus-ballwein.at; Moosstrasse 69a; s €55-59, d €69-83, tr €85-90, q €90-98; P �🛜) With its bright, pine-filled rooms, mountain views, free bike hire and garden, this place is big on charm. The largest, quietest rooms face the back and have balconies and kitchenettes. It's a 10-minute trundle from the *Altstadt;* take bus 21 to Gsengerweg. Breakfast is a wholesome spread of fresh rolls, eggs, fruit, muesli and cold cuts.

YOHO Salzburg   HOSTEL €

(☑ 0662-87 96 49; www.yoho.at; Paracelsusstrasse 9; dm €19-23, d €72-93; @🛜) Free wi-fi, secure lockers, comfy bunks, plenty of cheap beer and good-value schnitzels – what more could a backpacker ask for? Except, perhaps, a merry sing-along with *The Sound of Music* screened daily (yes, *every* day) at 7pm. The friendly crew can arrange tours, adventure

sports such as rafting and canyoning, and bike hire.

Hotel Am Dom   BOUTIQUE HOTEL €€

(☑ 0662-84 27 65; www.hotelamdom.at; Goldgasse 17; s €109-219, d €119-349; ❄🛜) Antique meets boutique at this *Altstadt* hotel, where the original vaults and beams of the 800-year-old building contrast with razor-sharp design features. Artworks inspired by the musical legends of the Salzburg Festival grace the rooms, which sport caramel-champagne colour schemes, funky lighting, velvet throws and ultra-glam bathrooms.

Arte Vida   GUESTHOUSE €€

(☑ 0662-87 31 85; www.artevida.at; Dreifaltigkeitsgasse 9; s €69-129, d €89-145, apt €160-220; 🛜) Arte Vida has the boho-chic feel of a Marrakech *riad*, with its lantern-lit salon, communal kitchen and serene garden. Asia and Africa have provided the inspiration for the rich colours and fabrics that dress the individually designed rooms. Your affable hosts Herbert and Karoline happily give tips on Salzburg and its surrounds, and can arrange massages and private yoga sessions.

⭐ **Villa Trapp**   HOTEL €€€

(☑ 0662-63 08 60; www.villa-trapp.com; Traunstrasse 34; s €65-130, d €114-280, ste €290-580; P 🛜) Marianne and Christopher have transformed the original von Trapp family home into a beautiful guesthouse (for guests only, we might add). The 19th-century villa is elegant, if not *quite* as palatial as in the movie, with tasteful wood-floored rooms and a balustrade for sweeping down à la Baroness Schräder.

Eating

Self-caterers can find picnic fixings at the **Grünmarkt** (Green Market; Universitätsplatz; ⊙7am-7pm Mon-Fri, to 3pm Sat).

★Magazin
MODERN EUROPEAN €€€

(✆0662-841 584 20; www.magazin.co.at; Augustinergasse 13a; 2-course lunch €16, mains €27-41, tasting menus €71-85; ⊙11.30am-2pm & 6-10pm Tue-Sat) In a courtyard below Mönchsberg's sheer rock wall, Magazin shelters a deli, wine store, cookery school and restaurant. Chef Richard Brunnauer's menus fizz with seasonal flavours: dishes like marinated alpine char with avocado and herb salad and saddle of venison with boletus mushrooms are matched with wines from the 850-bottle cellar, and served alfresco or in the industrial-chic, cave-like interior.

★Bärenwirt
AUSTRIAN €€

(✆0662-42 24 04; www.baerenwirt-salzburg.at; Müllner Hauptstrasse 8; mains €9-19; ⊙11am-11pm) Sizzling and stirring since 1663, Bärenwirt is Austrian through and through. Go for hearty *Bierbraten* (beer roast) with dumplings, locally caught trout or organic wild boar *Bratwurst*. A tiled oven warms the woody, hunting-lodge-style interior in winter, while the river-facing terrace is a summer crowd-puller. The restaurant is 500m north of Museumplatz.

Zwettler's
AUSTRIAN €€

(✆0662-84 41 99; www.zwettlers.com; Kaigasse 3; mains €9.50-21; ⊙11.30am-1am Tue-Sat, to midnight Sun) This gastro-pub has a lively buzz on its pavement terrace. Local grub such as schnitzel with parsley potatoes and venison ragout goes well with a cold, foamy Kaiser Karl wheat beer. The two-course lunch is a snip at €7.90.

M32
FUSION €€

(✆0662-84 10 00; www.m32.at; Mönchsberg 32; 2-course lunch €16, mains €23-40; ⊙9am-1am Tue-Sun; ⚲⛟) Bold colours and a veritable forest of stag antlers reveal architect Matteo Thun's imprint at the Museum der Moderne's ultra-sleek restaurant. The food goes with the seasons with specialities like organic local beef with sautéed porcini and lime-chilli risotto with roasted octopus. The glass-walled restaurant and terrace take in the full sweep of Salzburg's mountain-backed skyline.

Stiftsbäckerei St Peter
BAKERY €

(Kapitelplatz 8; ⊙7am-5pm Mon-Tue & Thu-Fri, to 1pm Sat) Next to the monastery, where the watermill turns, this 700-year-old bakery turns out Salzburg's best sourdough loaves from a wood-fired oven.

🍷 Drinking & Nightlife

You'll find the biggest concentration of bars along both banks of the Salzach, the most lively are around Gstättengasse.

★Augustiner Bräustübl
BREWERY

(www.augustinerbier.at; Augustinergasse 4-6; ⊙3-11pm Mon-Fri, from 2.30pm Sat & Sun) Who says monks can't enjoy themselves? Since 1621, this cheery, monastery-run brewery has been serving potent homebrews in beer steins in the vaulted hall and beneath the chestnut trees in the 1000-seat beer garden. Get your tankard filled at the foyer pump and visit the snack stands for hearty, beer-swigging grub like *Stelzen* (ham hock), pork belly and giant pretzels.

★Enoteca Settemila
WINE BAR

(Bergstrasse 9; ⊙5-11pm Tue-Sat) This bijou wine shop and bar brims with the enthusiasm and passion of Rafael Peil and Nina Corti. Go to sample their well-curated selection of wines, including Austrian, organic and biodynamic ones, with *taglieri* – sharing plates of cheese and *salumi* – salami, ham, prosciutto and the like – from small Italian producers.

★Kaffee Alchemie
CAFE

(www.kaffee-alchemie.at; Rudolfskai 38; ⊙7.30am-6pm Mon-Fri, 10am-6pm Sat & Sun) Making coffee really is rocket science at this vintage-cool cafe by the river, which plays up high-quality, fair-trade, single-origin beans. Talented baristas knock up spot-on espressos (on a Marzocco GB5, in case you wondered), cappuccinos and speciality coffees, which go nicely with the selection of cakes and brownies. Not a coffee fan? Try the super-smooth coffee-leaf tea.

ⓘ SALZBURG CARD

If you're planning on doing lots of sightseeing, grab a Salzburg Card (1-/2-/3-day card €27/36/42) and get free entry to all of the major sights and attractions, unlimited use of public transport (including cable cars) and numerous discounts on tours and events. The card is half-price for children and €3 cheaper in the low season.

ⓘ Information

Most hotels and bars offer free wi-fi, and there are several cheap internet cafes near the train station. *Bankomaten* (ATMs) are all over the place.

Tourist Office (☏ 0662-88 98 70; www.salzburg.info; Mozartplatz 5; ⊙ 9am-7pm Mon-Sat, 10am-6pm Sun) Helpful tourist office with a ticket-booking service (www.salzburgticket.com) in the same building.

ⓘ Getting There & Away

AIR

Flights from the UK and the rest of Europe, including low-cost airlines **Ryanair** (www.ryanair.com) and **easyJet** (www.easyjet.com) service **Salzburg airport** (☏ 0662-858 00; www.salzburg-airport.com; Innsbrucker Bundesstrasse 95; 🖀), 5.5km west of the city centre.

BUS

Salzburger Verkehrsverbund (☏ 24hr hotline 0662-63 29 00; www.svv-info.at) Coaches depart from just outside the Hauptbahnhof on Südtiroler Platz.

TRAIN

Fast trains leave frequently for Vienna (€51, 2½ hours) via Linz (€25, 1¼ hours). There is a two-hourly express service to Klagenfurt (€39, three hours). There are hourly trains to Innsbruck (€45, two hours).

ⓘ Getting Around

BICYCLE

A Velo (Mozartplatz; bicycle rental half-day/full day/week €12/18/55, e-bike €18/25/120; ⊙ 9am-6pm mid-Apr–Oct) Just across the way from the tourist office.

BUS

Buses 1 and 4 start from the Hauptbahnhof and skirt the pedestrian-only Altstadt, Bus 2 runs to the airport. Bus drivers sell single (€2.40) and 24-hour (€5.30) tickets; these are cheaper when purchased in advance from machines and cheaper still in packs of five from *Tabak* (€1.60 each).

SALZKAMMERGUT

A wonderland of deep blue lakes and tall craggy peaks, the Lake District has long been a favourite holiday destination for Austrians, luring a throng of summertime visitors to boat, fish, swim, hike or just laze on the shore.

WORTH A TRIP

SCHLOSS HELLBRUNN
••••••••••••••••••••••••••••••

A prince-archbishop with a wicked sense of humour, Markus Sittikus built Italianate **Schloss Hellbrunn** (www.hellbrunn.at; Fürstenweg 37; adult/child/family €12.50/5.50/26.50, gardens free; ⊙ 9am-5.30pm Apr-Oct, to 9pm Jul & Aug; 🖪) as a 17th-century summer palace and an escape from his Residenz functions.

While the whimsical palace interior is worth a peek, the eccentric Wasserspiele (trick fountains) are the big draw in summer. Be prepared to get soaked with no statue quite as it seems, including the emblematic tongue-poking-out Germaul mask.

Look out for *The Sound of Music* pavilion of 'Sixteen Going on Seventeen' fame.

Bus 25 ((€2, every 20 minutes) runs to Hellbrunn, 4.5km south of Salzburg, from Mozartsteg/Rudolfskai in the Altstadt.

Bad Ischl is the region's hub, but Hallstatt is its true jewel. For info visit **Salzkammergut Touristik** (☏ 06132-24 00 00; www.salzkammergut.co.at; Götzstrasse 12; ⊙ 9am-7pm summer, 9am-6pm Mon-Fri, to 5am Sat rest of year). The Salzkammergut Card (€4.90, available May to October) provides up to 30% discounts on sights, ferries, cable cars and some buses.

Hallstatt
☏ 06134 / POP 790

With pastel-coloured houses that cast shimmering reflections onto the glassy waters of the lake and with towering mountains on all sides, Hallstatt is a beauty with a great back story. Now a Unesco World Heritage site, Hallstatt was settled 4500 years ago and over 2000 Iron Age graves have been discovered in the area, most of them dating from 1000 to 500 BC.

◉ Sights & Activities

Salzwelten — MINE
(☏ 06134-200 24 00; www.salzwelten.at; Salzbergstrasse 21; return funicular plus tour adult/child/family €30/10/75; ⊙ 9.30am-4.30pm Apr-Sep, to 3pm Oct, to 2.30pm Nov) The fascinating *Salzbergwerk* (salt mine) is situated high above

WORTH A TRIP

OBERTRAUN

Across the lake from the Hallstatt throngs, down-to-earth Obertraun is the gateway for some geological fun. The many 1000 year old caves of the **Dachstein Rieseneishöhle** (www.dachstein-salzkammergut.com; tour packages adult €12.30-37.40, child €10.80-20.60; ☺9am-4pm May-Sep) extend into the mountain for almost 80km in places.

From Obertraun it's also possible to catch a cable car to **Krippenstein** (www.dachstein-salzkammergut.com; cable car return adult/child €29.30/16.10; ☺mid-Jun–Oct), where you'll find the freaky but fabulous **5 Fingers viewing platform**, which protrudes over a sheer cliff face – not for sufferers of vertigo.

Hallstatt on **Salzberg** (Salt Mountain) and is the lake's major cultural attraction. The bilingual German-English tour details how salt is formed and the history of mining, and takes visitors down into the depths on miners' slides – the largest is 60m (on which you can get your photo taken).

Beinhaus CHURCH
(Bone House; Kirchenweg 40; €1.50; ☺10am-6pm May-Oct) This small ossuary contains rows of neatly stacked skulls, painted with decorative designs and the names of their former owners. Bones have been exhumed from the overcrowded graveyard since 1600, and although the practice waned in the 20th century, the last joined the collection in 1995. It stands in the grounds of the 15th-century Catholic **Pfarrkirche** (parish church), which has some attractive Gothic frescoes and three winged altars inside.

🛏 Sleeping & Eating

Pension Sarstein GUESTHOUSE €€
(✆06134-82 17; Gosaumühlstrasse 83; d €81-101, apt for 2/3/4 people excl breakfast €100/130/150; 🛜) The affable Fischer family take pride in their little guesthouse, a few minutes' walk along the lakefront from central Hallstatt. The old-fashioned rooms are not flash, but they are neat, cosy and have balconies with dreamy lake and mountain views. Family-sized apartments come with kitchenettes.

Balthazar im Rudolfsturm AUSTRIAN €€
(Rudolfsturm; mains €10.50-20; ☺9am-5pm May-Oct) Balthazar is situated 855m above Hallstatt and has the most spectacular terrace in the region. The menu is Austrian comfort food and the service is charming, but you're here for the gobsmacking views. It's best accessed by the funicular.

Heritage Hotel Hallstatt HOTEL €€€
(✆06134-20 03 60; www.heritagehotel.at; Landungsplatz 102; s €145, d €200-335; 🛜) Rooms in this luxury hotel are spread across three buildings. The main building may claim the town's prime position at the landing stage on the lake, but 500-year-old Stocker House, a greystone beauty up the hill, is by far the most atmospheric. Rooms across all three buildings offer stunning views and have modern, rather reserved, decor.

❶ Getting There & Away

BOAT

Ferry excursions do the circuit of Hallstatt Lahn via Hallstatt Markt, Obersee, Untersee and Steeg return (€10, 90 minutes) three times daily from July to early September.

TRAIN

About a dozen trains daily connect Hallstatt and Bad Ischl (€4.30, 27 minutes). Hallstatt Bahnhof (train station) is across the lake from the village, and boat services coincide with train arrivals (€2.40, 10 minutes, last ferry to Hallstatt Markt 6.50pm).

TYROL

Tyrol (or *Tirol*) is as pure Alpine as Austria gets, with mountains that make you want to yodel out loud and patchwork pastures chiming with cowbells. Nowhere else in the country is the downhill skiing as exhilarating, the après-ski as pumping, the wooden chalets as chocolate box, the food as hearty.

Innsbruck

✆0512 / POP 124,580

Tyrol's capital is a sight to behold. Jagged rock spires are so close that within 25 minutes it's possible to travel from the heart of the city to over 2000m above sea level. Summer and winter outdoor activities abound, and it's understandable why some visitors only take a peek at Innsbruck proper before heading for the hills. But to do so is a shame, for Innsbruck is in many ways Austria in microcosm, with an authentic late-medieval Altstadt (Old Town), inventive architecture and vibrant student-driven nightlife.

◎ Sights

★ Hofkirche
CHURCH

(www.tiroler-landesmuseum.at; Universitätstrasse 2; adult/child €7/free; ⊙ 9am-5pm Mon-Sat, 12.30-5pm Sun) Innsbruck's pride and joy is the Gothic Hofkirche, one of Europe's finest royal court churches. It was commissioned in 1553 by Ferdinand I, who enlisted top artists of the age such as Albrecht Dürer, Alexander Colin and Peter Vischer the Elder. Top billing goes to the empty **sarcophagus of Emperor Maximilian I** (1459–1519), a masterpiece of German Renaissance sculpture, elaborately carved from black marble.

★ Goldenes Dachl Museum
MUSEUM

(Golden Roof Museum; Herzog-Friedrich-Strasse 15; adult/child €4.80/2.40; ⊙ 10am-5pm May-Sep, closed Mon Oct-Apr) Innsbruck's golden wonder and most distinctive landmark is this Gothic oriel, built for Holy Roman Emperor Maximilian I (1459–1519), lavishly festooned with murals and glittering with 2657 fire-gilt copper tiles. It is most impressive from the exterior, but the museum is worth a look – especially if you have the Innsbruck Card – with an audio guide whisking you through the history. Keep an eye out for the grotesque tournament helmets designed to resemble the Turks of the rival Ottoman Empire.

★ Hofburg
PALACE

(Imperial Palace; www.hofburg-innsbruck.at; Rennweg 1; adult/child €9/free; ⊙ 9am-5pm) Grabbing attention with its pearly white facade and cupolas, the Hofburg was built as a castle for Archduke Sigmund the Rich in the 15th century, expanded by Emperor Maximilian I in the 16th century and given a baroque makeover by Empress Maria Theresia in the 18th century. The centrepiece of the lavish rococo state apartments is the 31m-long **Riesensaal** (Giant's Hall).

Bergisel
VIEWPOINT

(www.bergisel.info; adult/child €9.50/4.50; ⊙ 9am-6pm Jun-Oct, 10am-5pm Nov-May) Rising above Innsbruck like a celestial staircase, this glass-and-steel ski jump was designed by much-lauded Iraqi architect Zaha Hadid. It's 455 steps or a two-minute funicular ride to the 50m-high **viewing platform**, with a

DON'T MISS

FREE GUIDED HIKES

From late May to October, Innsbruck Information (p85) arranges daily guided hikes, from sunrise walks to half-day mountain jaunts. The hikes are free with a Club Innsbruck Card, which you receive automatically when you stay overnight in Innsbruck. Pop into the tourist office to register and browse the program.

breathtaking panorama of the Nordkette range, Inntal and Innsbruck. Tram 1 trundles here from central Innsbruck.

★ Schloss Ambras
PALACE

(www.schlossambras-innsbruck.at; Schlosstrasse 20; palace adult/child €10/free, gardens free; ⊙ palace 10am-5pm, gardens 6am-8pm; ♿) Picturesquely perched on a hill and set among beautiful gardens, this Renaissance pile was acquired in 1564 by Archduke Ferdinand II, then ruler of Tyrol, who transformed it from a fortress into a palace. Don't miss the centrepiece **Spanische Saal** (Spanish Hall), the dazzling **Armour Collection** and the gallery's Velázquez and Van Dyck originals.

𝌂 Activities

Anyone who loves playing in the great outdoors will be itching to head up into the Alps in Innsbruck.

Nordkettenbahnen
FUNICULAR

(www.nordkette.com; 1 way/return to Hungerburg €4.80/8, to Seegrube €17.30/28.80, to Hafelekar €19.20/32; ⊙ Hungerburg 7am-7.15pm Mon-Fri, 8am-7.15pm Sat & Sun, Seegrube 8.30am-5.30pm daily, Hafelekar 9am-5pm daily) Zaha Hadid's space-age funicular runs every 15 minutes, whizzing you from the Congress Centre to the slopes in no time. Walking trails head off in all directions from **Hungerburg** and **Seegrube**. For more of a challenge, there is a downhill track for mountain bikers and two fixed-rope routes *(Klettersteige)* for climbers.

Inntour
ADVENTURE SPORTS

(www.inntour.com; Leopoldstrasse 4; ⊙ 9am-6pm Mon-Sat) Based at Die Börse, Inntour arranges all manner of thrillseeking pursuits, including canyoning (€80), tandem paragliding (€105), whitewater rafting (€45) and bungee jumping from the 192m Europabrücke (€140).

🛏 Sleeping

The tourist office has lists of private rooms costing between €20 and €40 per person.

Nepomuk's   HOSTEL €
(☑ 0512-584 118; www.nepomuks.at; Kiebachgasse 16; dm/d from €24/58; 🛜) Could this be backpacker heaven? Nepomuk's sure comes close, with its Altstadt location, well-stocked kitchen and high-ceilinged dorms with homely touches like CD players. The delicious breakfast in attached Cafe Munding, with homemade pastries, jam and fresh-roasted coffee, gets your day off to a grand start.

Pension Paula   GUESTHOUSE €
(☑ 0512-292 262; www.pensionpaula.at; Weiherburggasse 15; s €36-48, d €62-72; Ⓟ) This pension occupies an alpine chalet and has super-clean, homely rooms (most with balcony). It's up the hill towards the zoo and has great vistas across the city.

★ Hotel Weisses Kreuz   HISTORIC HOTEL €€
(☑ 0512-594 79; www.weisseskreuz.at; Herzog-Friedrich-Strasse 31; s/d from €77/119, with shared bathroom from €41/75; Ⓟ @ 🛜) Beneath the arcades, this atmospheric Altstadt hotel has played host to guests for 500 years, including a 13-year-old Mozart. With its wood-panelled parlours, antiques and twisting staircase, the hotel oozes history with every creaking beam. Rooms are supremely comfortable, staff charming and breakfast is a lavish spread.

🍴 Eating

★ Breakfast Club   BREAKFAST €
(www.breakfast-club.at; Maria-Theresien-Strasse 49; breakfast €5-13; ⊗ 7.30am-4pm; 🛜 ☑) Hip, wholesome and nicely chilled, the Breakfast Club does what it says on the tin: all-day breakfast and brunch. And boy are you in for a treat: free-range eggs, Tyrolean mountain cheese, organic breads, homemade spreads, cinnamon-dusted waffles with cranberries and cream, French toast, Greek omelette – take your pick. It also does fresh-pressed juices and proper Italian coffee.

★ Die Wilderin   AUSTRIAN €€
(☑ 0512-562 728; www.diewilderin.at; Seilergasse 5; mains €9.50-20; ⊗ 5pm-2am Tue-Sat, to midnight Sun) 🌱 Take a gastronomic walk on the wild side at this modern-day hunter-gatherer of a restaurant, where chefs take pride in local sourcing and using top-notch farm-fresh and foraged ingredients. The menu sings of the seasons, be it asparagus, game, strawberries or winter veg. The vibe is urbane and relaxed.

Chez Nico   VEGETARIAN €€
(☑ 0650 4510624; www.chez-nico.at; Maria-Theresien-Strasse 49; 2-course lunch €14.50, 7-course menu €60; ⊗ 6.30-10pm Mon & Sat, noon-2pm & 6.30-10pm Tue-Fri; ☑) Take a petit bistro and a Parisian chef with a passion for herbs, *et voilà*, you get Chez Nico. Nicolas Curtil (Nico) cooks seasonal, all-vegetarian

OTHER TOWNS WORTH A VISIT

Fancy exploring further? Here are some towns, resorts and valleys in Austria that you may want to consider for day trips or longer visits.

Zillertal Storybook Tyrol, with a steam train, snow-capped Alps and outdoor activities aplenty.

Zell am See An alpine beauty on the shores of its namesake lake. Gateway to the epic Grossglockner Road.

Eisenstadt The petite capital of Burgenland is known for its wonderful palace and famous former resident, composer Haydn.

Schladming Laid-back Styrian gem in the glacial Dachstein mountains. Great for skiing, hiking, biking and white-water rafting on the Enns River.

WORTH A TRIP

KRIMML FALLS

The thunderous, three-tier **Krimmler Wasserfälle** (Krimml Falls; ☑06564-72 12; www.wasserfaelle-krimml.at; adult/child €9.20/4.60 incl WasserWelten Krimml; ⊙9am-5pm May-Oct) is Europe's highest waterfall at 380m, and one of Austria's most unforgettable sights. The **Wasserfallweg** (Waterfall Trail), which starts at the ticket office and weaves gently uphill through mixed forest, has numerous viewpoints with photogenic close-ups of the falls. It's about a two-hour round-trip walk.

The pretty Alpine village of Krimml has a handful of places to sleep and eat – contact the **tourist office** (☑06564-72 39; www.krimml.at; Oberkrimml 37; ⊙8am-6pm Mon-Fri, 8.30-11.30am Sat) for more information.

Buses run year-round from Krimml to Zell am See (€10.20, 1¼ hours, every two hours), with frequent onward train connections to Salzburg (€19.60, 1½ hours). The village is about 500m north of the waterfall, on a side turning from the B165. There are parking spaces near the falls.

---

delights along the lines of tomato and argan oil consommé and watermelon and chanterelle carpaccio with pine nuts and parmesan. You won't miss the meat, we swear.

Il Convento　　　　　ITALIAN €€
(☑0512-581 354; www.ilconvento.at; Burggraben 29; mains €13.50-25, 2-course lunch €17.50-18.50; ⊙11am-3pm & 5pm-midnight Mon-Sat) Neatly tucked into the old city walls, this Italian newcomer is run with passion by Peppino and Angelika. It's a winner, with its refined look (white tablecloths, wood beams, Franciscan monastery views from the terrace) and menu. Dishes such as clam linguine, braised veal and salt-crusted cod are cooked to a T and served with wines drawn from the well-stocked cellar.

🍷 Drinking & Nightlife

Tribaun　　　　　CRAFT BEER
(www.tribaun.com; Museumstrasse 5; ⊙6pm-2am Mon-Sat) This cracking new bar taps into craft-beer culture, with a wide variety of brews – from stouts and porters to IPA, sour, amber, honey and red ales. The easygoing vibe and fun-loving crew add to its appeal. For more insight, hook onto a 90-minute, seven-beer tasting (€19).

Moustache　　　　　BAR
(www.cafe-moustache.at; Herzog-Otto-Strasse 8; ⊙11am-2am Tue-Sun; 🕾) Playing Spot-the-Moustache (Einstein, Charlie Chaplin and co) is the preferred pastime at this retro bolthole, with table football and a terrace overlooking pretty Domplatz. They knock up a mean pisco sour.

360°　　　　　BAR
(Rathaus Galerien; ⊙10am-1am Mon-Sat) Grab a cushion and drink in 360-degree views of the city and Alps from the balcony that skirts this spherical, glass-walled bar. It's a nicely chilled spot for a coffee or sundowner.

ℹ Information

Innsbruck Information (☑0512-53 56-0, 0512-59 850; www.innsbruck.info; Burggraben 3; ⊙9am-6pm) Main tourist office with truckloads of info on the city and surrounds, including skiing and walking.

ℹ Getting There & Away

AIR
EasyJet flies to **Innsbruck Airport** (INN; ☑22 52 50; www.innsbruck-airport.com; Fürstenweg 180), 4km west of the city centre.

CAR & MOTORCYCLE
The A12 and the parallel Hwy 171 are the main roads heading west and east. The B177, to the west of Innsbruck, continues north to Germany and Munich whilte the A13 toll road (€8.50) runs south through the Brenner Pass to Italy.

TRAIN
Fast trains depart daily every two hours for Bregenz (€37.50, 2¾ hours) and Salzburg (€45.50, two hours); from Innsbruck to the Arlberg, the best views are on the right-hand side of the train. Express trains serve Munich (€41.20, 1¾ hours) and Verona (€40.20, 3½ hours). Direct services to Kitzbühel also run every two hours (€15.80, 1¼ hours) and hourly to Lienz (€23.50, three to five hours).

WORTH A TRIP

BREGENZERWALD

Only a few kilometres southeast of Bregenz, the forest-cloaked slopes, velvet-green pastures and limestone peaks of the Bregenzerwald unfold. In summer it's a glorious place to spend a few days hiking the hills and filling up on homemade cheeses in alpine dairies. Winter brings plenty of snow, and the area is noted for its downhill and cross-country skiing. The **Bregenzerwald tourist office** (☑ 05512-23 65; www.bregenzerwald.at; Impulszentrum 1135, Egg; ⊙ 9am-5pm Mon-Fri, 8am-1pm Sat) has information on the region.

ⓘ Getting Around

Single tickets on buses and trams cost €2, day passes are €4.

Kitzbühel

☑ 05356 / POP 8135

Ever since Franz Reisch slipped on skis and whizzed down the slopes of Kitzbüheler Horn way back in 1893, so christening the first alpine ski run in Austria, Kitzbühel has carved out its reputation as one of Europe's foremost ski resorts. It's renowned for the white-knuckled Hahnenkamm downhill ski race in January and the reliable excellence of its slopes.

🏃 Activities

In winter there's first-rate intermediate skiing and freeriding on **Kitzbüheler Horn** to the north and **Hahnenkamm** to the south of town. One-/three-/six-day passes cost €53/147/256 in the high winter season and €47.50/132.50/230.50 at all other times.

Dozens of summer **hiking trails** thread through the Kitzbühel Alps; the tourist office gives walking maps and runs free guided hikes for guests staying in town. Cable cars cost €18.80/23.50 one way/return in summer.

🛏 Sleeping & Eating

Rates leap by up to 50% in the winter season.

Snowbunny's Hostel   HOSTEL €
(☑ 067 67940233; www.snowbunnys.co.uk; Bichlstrasse 30; dm €22-25, d €66; @ 🕽) This friendly, laid-back hostel is a bunny-hop from the slopes. Dorms are fine, if a tad dark; breakfast is DIY-style in the kitchen. There's a TV lounge, a ski storage room and cats to stroke.

★**Villa Licht**   HOTEL €€
(☑ 05356-622 93; www.villa-licht.at; Franz-Reisch-Strasse 8; apt €120-210; 🅿 @ 🕽 🗴) Pretty gardens, spruce modern apartments with pine trappings, living rooms with kitchenettes, balconies with mountain views, peace – this charming Tyrolean chalet has the lot, and owner Renate goes out of her way to please. Kids love the outdoor pool in summer.

★**Restaurant Zur Tenne**   AUSTRIAN €€
(☑ 05356-644 44-0; www.hotelzurtenne.com; Vorderstadt 8-10; mains €18-43; ⊙ 11.30am-1.30pm & 6.30-9.30pm) Choose between the rustic, beamed interior where an open fire crackles and the more summery conservatory at Hotel Tenne's highly regarded restaurant. Service is polished and the menu puts a sophisticated twist on seasonal Tyrolean dishes such as catfish with wild garlic pasta and artichokes.

ⓘ Getting There & Away

Trains run frequently from Kitzbühel to Innsbruck (€15.80, 1¼ hours) and Salzburg (€30.30, 2½ hours). For Kufstein (€10.20, one hour), change at Wörgl.

Lienz

☑ 04852 / POP 11,900

The Dolomites rise like an amphitheatre around Lienz, which straddles the Isel and Drau Rivers just 40km north of Italy. The capital of East Tyrol is a scenic staging point for travels through the Hohe Tauern National Park.

◎ Sights & Activities

A €45 day pass covers skiing on the nearby **Zettersfeld** and **Hochstein** peaks. However, the area is more renowned for its many kilometres of cross-country trails; the town fills up for the annual Dolomitenlauf cross-country skiing race in mid-January.

🛏 Sleeping & Eating

The tourist office can point you in the direction of good-value guesthouses and camping grounds.

Gasthof Schlossberghof
HOTEL €€

(☑04852-632 33; schlossberghof.at; Iseltaler-
strasse 21; s/d €65/100) The location of this
simple, freshly renovated hotel might seem
unprepossessing at first, but it's great if
you're in a car (free parking and undercover parks for bikes), plus the ten-minute
stroll into the centre takes you past Tyrolean 19th-century villas watched over by the
Dolomites.

Weinphilo
WINE BAR

(☑04852-612 53; www.weinphilo.com; Messing-
gasse 11; ☉10am-10pm Mon-Fri, to 3pm Sat) A
proper Italian wine shop and bar, where
you can join locals for a glass of a beautiful
small-producer wine from the Veneto, Friu-
li, Südtirol or even further south. There are
meat and cheese platters and you can also
pop in here in the morning for an expertly made coffee from Tuscany's Cafe Baratto
beans.

ℹ Information

Tourist Office (Lienzer Dolimiten; ☑050
212 400; www.osttirol.com; Europaplatz 1;
☉8am-6pm Mon-Fri, 9am-noon & 4-6pm Sat,
9.30-midnight Sun mid-June–end Sep, closed
Sat afternoon & Sun Oct-May) Staff will help you
find accommodation (even private rooms) free
of charge. They also have hiking maps and brochures on all the adventure sports operators.

ℹ Getting There & Away

There are several daily services to Innsbruck
(€15.40 to €20.40, 3¼ to 4½ hours). Trains run
every two hours to Salzburg (€38.90, 3½ hours).
To head south by car, you must first divert west
or east along Hwy 100.

Hohe Tauern National Park

Straddling Tyrol, Salzburg and Carinthia,
this national park is the largest in the Alps;
a 1786-sq-km wilderness of 3000m peaks,
alpine meadows and waterfalls. At its heart
lies **Grossglockner** (3798m), Austria's
highest mountain, which towers over the
8km-long Pasterze Glacier, best seen from
the outlook at **Kaiser-Franz-Josefs-Höhe**
(2369m).

The 48km **Grossglockner Road** (www.
grossglockner.at; day ticket car/motorbike €35/25;
☉5am-9.30pm) from Bruck in Salzburger-
land to Heiligenblut in Carinthia is one of
Europe's greatest Alpine drives. A feat of
1930s engineering, the road swings gid-
dily around 36 switchbacks, passing jew-
el-coloured lakes, forested slopes and wondrous glaciers.

The major village on the Grossglockner Road is **Heiligenblut**, famous for its
15th-century pilgrimage church. Here the
tourist office (☑04824-27 00; www.heiligen
blut.at; Hof 4; ☉9am-6pm Mon-Fri, 2-6pm Sat
& Sun) can advise on guided ranger hikes,
mountain hiking and skiing. The village
also has a spick-and-span **Jugendherberge**
(☑04824-22 59; www.oejhv.or.at; Hof 36; dm/s/d
€22.50/30.50/52; ℗ 🖥).

Bus 5002 runs frequently between Lienz
and Heiligenblut on weekdays (€16.40, one
hour), less frequently at weekends.

NATIONAL PARKS IN THE AUSTRIAN ALPS

For an area of such mind-blowing natural beauty, it may come as a surprise to learn that
there are just three national parks (Hohe Tauern, Kalkalpen and Gesäuse) as well as one
major nature reserve (Nockberge) in the Austrian Alps. But statistics aren't everything,
particularly when one of these national parks is the magnificent Hohe Tauern, the Alps'
largest and Europe's second-largest national park, which is a tour de force of 3000m
peaks, immense glaciers and waterfalls.

The national-park authorities have managed to strike a good balance between preserving the wildlife and keeping local economic endeavours such as farming, hunting
and tourism alive. The website www.nationalparksaustria.at has links to all national
parks and a brochure in English to download.

Aside from national parks, protected areas and nature reserves are dotted all over
the Austrian Alps, from the mesmerising mountainscapes of Naturpark Zillertaler Alpen
in Tyrol to the lakes of the Salzkammergut. See www.naturparke.at for the lowdown on
Austria's nature parks.

VORARLBERG

Cut off from the rest of Austria by the snow-capped Arlberg massif, the westerly region of Vorarlberg has more than the touch of nearby Switzerland about it.

The capital, **Bregenz**, sits prettily on the shores of Lake Constance and holds the **Bregenzer Festspiele** (Bregenz Festival; ☑ 05574-40 76; www.bregenzerfestspiele.com; ⊘ mid-Jul–late Aug) in July/August, when opera is performed on a floating stage on the lake.

The real action here, though, is in the Arlberg region, shared by Vorarlberg and neighbouring Tyrol. Some of the country's best downhill and off-piste skiing – not to mention après-ski partying – is in **St Anton am Arlberg**, where the first ski club in the Alps was founded in 1901. The centrally located **tourist office** (☑ 05446-226 90; www.stantonamarlberg.com; Dorfstrasse 8; ⊘ 8am-6pm Mon-Fri, 9am-6pm Sat, 9am-noon & 2-5pm Sun) has maps, and information on accommodation and activities.

A single ski pass (one-/three-/six-day pass €52/148/262) covers the whole Arlberg region and is valid for all 87 ski lifts.

Accommodation is mainly in small B&Bs. Most budget places book out months in advance.

St Anton is on the main railway route between Bregenz (€12.80, 1¼ hours) and Innsbruck (€16.80, 1¼ hours). It's close to the eastern entrance of the Arlberg Tunnel, the toll road connecting Vorarlberg and Tyrol (€8.50). This region is also a convenient gateway to Germany and Liechtenstein.

SURVIVAL GUIDE

ⓘ Directory A–Z

ACCOMMODATION

From simple mountain huts to five-star hotels fit for kings – you'll find the lot in Austria. Tourist offices invariably keep lists and details, as do the sites listed here.

SLEEPING PRICE RANGES

The following price ranges refer to a double room with a bathroom for two people, including breakfast.

€ less than €80

€€ €80–€200

€€€ more than €200

Austrian Hotelreservation (www.austrian-hotelreservation.at)

Austrian National Tourist Office (www.austria.info)

Bergfex (www.bergfex.com)

Camping in Österreich (https://www.camping.info/österreich)

Accommodation Types

Hostels In Austria around 100 hostels (*Jugendherberge*) are affiliated with Hostelling International (HI). Facilities are often excellent. Four- to six-bed dorms with shower/toilet are the norm, though some places also have doubles and family rooms. See www.oejhv.or.at or www.oejhw.at for details.

Private rooms *Privatzimmer* (private rooms) are cheap (often about €50 per double). On top of this, you will find *Bauernhof* (farmhouses) in rural areas, and some *Öko-Bauernhöfe* (organic farms).

Alpine huts There are over 400 huts maintained by the Österreichischer Alpenverein. Bed prices for nonmembers are from €20. Open roughly late June to mid-September with advance bookings essential; meals or cooking facilities are often available.

Rental accommodation *Ferienwohnungen* (self-catering apartments) are ubiquitous in Austrian mountain resorts. Contact a local tourist office for lists and prices.

Camping Austria has some 500 camping grounds, many well equipped and scenically located. Prices can be as low as €5 per person or small tent and as high as €20. Many close in winter, so phone ahead to check.

DISCOUNT CARDS

Student & Youth Cards International Student Identity Cards (ISIC) and European Youth Card (formerly Euro<26; check www.euro26.org for discounts) will get you discounts at most museums, galleries and theatres. Admission is generally a little higher than the price for children.

Discount Rail Cards See the Getting Around section.

MONEY

Austria's currency is the euro. An approximate 10% tip is expected in restaurants. Pay it directly to the server; don't leave it on the table.

OPENING HOURS

Banks 8am or 9am to 3pm Monday to Friday, to 5.30pm Thursday

Cafes 7am to 8pm; hours vary widely

Clubs 10pm to late

Post offices 8am to noon and 2pm to 6pm Monday to Friday, 8am to noon Saturday

Pubs 6pm to 1am or later

Restaurants 11am to 2.30pm and 6pm to 11pm
Shops 9am to 6.30pm Monday to Friday, 9am to 5pm Saturday
Supermarkets 9am to 8pm Monday to Saturday

PUBLIC HOLIDAYS

New Year's Day (Neujahr) 1 January
Epiphany (Heilige Drei Könige) 6 January
Easter Monday (Ostermontag) March/April
Labour Day (Tag der Arbeit) 1 May
Whit Monday (Pfingstmontag) Sixth Monday after Easter
Ascension Day (Christi Himmelfahrt) Sixth Thursday after Easter
Corpus Christi (Fronleichnam) Second Thursday after Whitsunday
Assumption (Maria Himmelfahrt) 15 August
National Day (Nationalfeiertag) 26 October
All Saints' Day (Allerheiligen) 1 November
Immaculate Conception (Mariä Empfängnis) 8 December
Christmas Day (Christfest) 25 December
St Stephen's Day (Stephanitag) 26 December

TELEPHONE

➡ Austrian telephone numbers consist of an area code followed by the local number.

➡ The country code is 📞 43 and the international access code is 📞 00.

➡ Phone shops sell prepaid SIM cards from around €15.

➡ Phone cards in different denominations are sold at post offices and *Tabak* (tobacconist) shops. Call centres are widespread in cities, and many internet cafes are geared for Skype calls.

TOURIST INFORMATION

Tourist offices, which are dispersed far and wide in Austria, tend to adjust their hours from one year to the next, so business hours may have changed slightly by the time you arrive. Most offices have at least one English speaker on staff.

VISAS

Schengen visa rules apply. The Austrian Foreign Ministry website www.bmeia.gv.at lists embassies.

❶ Getting There & Away

AIR

Among the low-cost airlines, Air Berlin and Nikki flys to Graz, Innsbruck, Linz, Salzburg and Vienna, easyJet to Innsbruck, Salzburg and Vienna, and Ryanair to Linz, Salzburg and Bratislava (for Vienna).

LAND

Bus

Buses depart from Austria for as far afield as England, the Baltic countries, the Netherlands, Germany and Switzerland. Most significantly, they provide access to Eastern European cities small and large – from the likes of Sofia and Warsaw, to Banja Luka, Mostar and Sarajevo.

Services operated by **Eurolines** (www.euro lines.at) leave from Vienna and from several regional cities.

Car & Motorcycle

There are numerous entry points into Austria by road from Germany, the Czech Republic, Slovakia, Hungary, Slovenia, Italy and Switzerland. All border-crossing points are open 24 hours.

Standard European insurance and paperwork rules apply.

EATING PRICE RANGES

The following price ranges refer to the cost of a two-course meal, excluding drinks.

€ less than €15

€€ €15–€30

€€€ more than €30

Train

Austria has excellent rail connections. The main services in and out of the country from the west normally pass through Bregenz, Innsbruck or Salzburg en route to Vienna. Trains to Eastern Europe leave from Vienna. Express services to Italy go via Innsbruck or Villach; trains to Slovenia are routed through Graz.

For online timetables and tickets, visit the **ÖBB** (Österreichische Bundesbahnen; Austrian Federal Railways; [phone] 24hr hotline 05 1717; www.oebb.at) website. SparSchiene (discounted tickets) are often available when you book online in advance. Deutsche Bahn (www.bahn.com) is also useful.

RIVER & LAKE

Hydrofoils run to Bratislava and Budapest from Vienna; slower boats cruise the Danube between the capital and Passau. The **Danube Tourist Commission** (www.danube-river.org) has a country-by-country list of operators and agents who can book tours.

🛈 Getting Around

AIR

Austrian Airlines (www.austrian.com) offers several flights daily between Vienna and Innsbruck, Graz, Klagenfurt, Linz and Salzburg.

BICYCLE

➡ All cities have at least one bike shop that doubles as a rental centre; expect to pay around €15 to €25 per day.

➡ You can take bicycles on any train with a bicycle symbol at the top of its timetable. Bikes cost an extra 10% on your ticket price on regional and S-Bahn trains, or reserve ahead (€3.50) for a space on long-distance trains.

BOAT

Services along the Danube are generally slow, scenic excursions rather than functional means of transport.

BUS

Rail routes are often complemented by **Postbus** ([phone] 24hr hotline 0810 222 333; www.postbus.at) services, which really come into their own in the more inaccessible mountainous regions.

CAR & MOTORCYCLE

A *Vignette* (toll sticker) is imposed on all motorways; charges for cars/motorbikes are €8.80/5.10 for 10 days and €25.70/12.90 for two months. *Vignette* can be purchased at border crossings, petrol stations and *Tabak* shops. There are additional tolls (usually €2.50 to €10) for some mountain tunnels.

Speed limits are 50km/h in built-up areas, 130km/h on autobahn and 100km/h on other roads.

ESSENTIAL FOOD & DRINK

Make it meaty Go for a classic Wiener schnitzel, *Tafelspitz* (boiled beef with horseradish sauce) or *Schweinebraten* (pork roast). The humble *Wurst* (sausage) comes in various guises.

On the side Lashings of potatoes, either fried (*Pommes*), roasted (*Bratkartoffeln*), in a salad (*Erdapfelsalat*) or boiled in their skins (*Quellmänner*); or try *Knödel* (dumplings) and *Nudeln* (flat egg noodles).

Kaffee und Kuchen Coffee and cake is Austria's sweetest tradition. Must-tries: flaky apple strudel, rich, chocolatey *Sacher Torte* and *Kaiserschmarrn* (sweet 'scrambled' pancakes with raisins).

Wine at the source Jovial locals gather in rustic *Heurigen* (wine taverns) in the wine-producing east, identified by an evergreen branch above the door. Sip crisp Grüner Veltliner whites and spicy Blaufränkisch wines.

Cheese fest Dig into gooey *Käsnudeln* (cheese noodles) in Carinthia, *Kaspressknodel* (fried cheese dumplings) in Tyrol and *Käsekrainer* (cheesy sausages) in Vienna. The hilly Bregenzerwald is studded with dairies.

The minimum age for hiring small cars is 19 years, or 25 years for larger, 'prestige' cars. Customers must have held a driving licence for at least a year. Many contracts forbid customers to take cars outside Austria, particularly into Eastern Europe.

Crash helmets are compulsory for motorcyclists.

TRAIN

Austria has a clean, efficient rail system, and if you use a discount card it's very inexpensive.

➡ **ÖBB** (p90) is the main operator, supplemented with a handful of private lines. Tickets and timetables are available online.

➡ Disabled passengers can use the 24-hour 05-17 17 customer number for special travel assistance; do this at least 24 hours ahead of travel (48 hours ahead for international services). Staff at stations will help with boarding and alighting.

RESOURCES

ÖAV (www.alpenverein.at) Austrian Alpine Club

ÖBB (www.oebb.at) Austrian Federal Railways

Österreich Werbung (www.austria.info) National tourism authority

➡ It's worth seeking out RailJet train services connecting Vienna, Graz, Villach, Salzburg, Innsbruck, Linz and Klagenfurt, as they travel up to 200km/h.

➡ Reservations in 2nd class within Austria cost €3.50 for most express services; recommended for travel on weekends.

➡ Fares quoted are for 2nd-class tickets.

AUSTRIA GETTING AROUND

Belarus

Best Places to Eat

➡ Bistro de Luxe (p97)

➡ Jules Verne (p101)

➡ Kamyanyitsa (p96)

➡ Time's Cafe (p101)

➡ Lido (p96)

Best Places to Stay

➡ Hotel Manastyrski (p95)

➡ Hermitage Hotel (p101)

➡ Revolución Hostel (p95)

➡ Kamyanyuki Hotel Complex (p102)

➡ Neman Hotel (p100)

Why Go?

Eastern Europe's outcast, Belarus (Беларусь) lies at the edge of the region and seems determined to avoid integration with the rest of the continent at all costs. Taking its lead from the Soviet Union rather than the European Union, this little-visited dictatorship may seem like a strange choice for travellers, but its isolation lies at the heart of its appeal.

While the rest of Eastern Europe has charged headlong into capitalism, Belarus allows the chance to visit a Europe with minimal advertising and no litter or graffiti. Outside the monumental Stalinist capital of Minsk, Belarus offers a simple yet pleasing landscape of cornflower fields, thick forests and picturesque villages. The country also has two excellent national parks and is home to Europe's largest mammal, the *zubr* (European bison). While travellers will always be the subject of curiosity, they'll also be on the receiving end of warm hospitality and a genuine welcome.

When to Go
Minsk

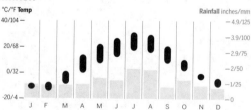

Jun–Aug Come to Belarus to escape the crowds elsewhere in Eastern Europe.

Early Jul On 6 July stay up all night for Kupalle, a fortune-telling festival with pagan roots.

Oct Pleasantly cool climate and fall foliage in Belavezhskaya Pushcha National Park near Brest.

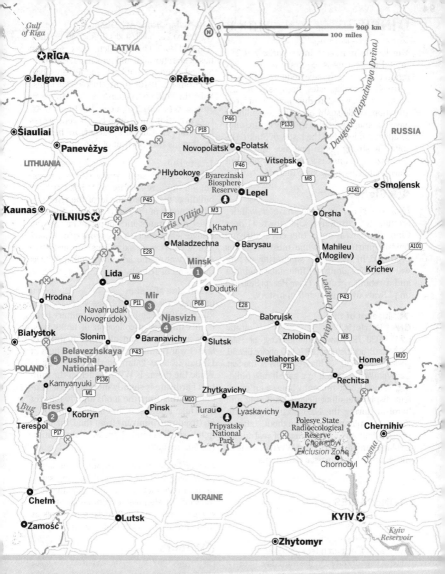

Belarus Highlights

1 **Minsk** (p94) Getting under the skin of Belarus' friendly and accessible capital, a showcase of Stalinist architecture.

2 **Brest** (p100) Strolling through the mellow pedestrian streets of this cosmopolitan city and gaping at its epic WWII memorials.

3 **Mir Castle** (p100) Training your lens on this fairy-tale 16th-century castle – and its equally famous reflection.

4 **Njasvizh** (p99) Exploring this tranquil provincial town's parks and impeccably restored castle.

5 **Belavezhskaya Pushcha National Park** (p102) Touring Europe's oldest wildlife refuge in search of rare European bison.

MINSK   МIНCК

📱17 / POP 1.915 MILLION

Minsk will almost certainly surprise you. The capital of Belarus is, contrary to its dreary reputation, a progressive, modern and clean place. Fashionable cafes, impressive restaurants and crowded nightclubs vie for your attention, while sushi bars and art galleries have taken up residence in a city centre once totally remodelled to the tastes of Stalin. Despite the strong police presence and obedient citizenry, Minsk is a thoroughly pleasant place that's easy to become fond of.

Sights

If you're short on time, have a wander around the attractive Old Town (Upper City). This was once the city's thriving Jewish quarter, and while most of it was destroyed in the war, a smattering of pre-war buildings along vul Internatsyanalnaya and a rebuilt ratusha (Town Hall; pl Svobody) on pl Svobody emit a whiff of history.

★ Museum of the Great Patriotic War   MUSEUM

(📱17 2030 792; www.warmuseum.by; pr Peremozhtsau 8; adult/student BR7/3.50, photos BR1.50, guided tours BR30; ⊙10am-6pm Tue & Thu-Sun, 11am-7pm Wed) Located in a garish new building, Minsk's best museum houses an excellent display detailing Belarus' suffering and heroism during the Nazi occupation. With English explanations throughout, atmospheric dioramas and a range of real tanks, airplanes and artillery from WWII, it's one of the capital's few must-see attractions.

ITINERARIES

···

Three Days

Spend two days getting to know Minsk, whose Stalinist architecture belies a lively, friendly city. On the third day, take a day trip to Njasvizh and Mir with their historic castles and charming Belarusian countryside feel.

One Week

Take a train to Brest and spend a couple of days there, including a day trip to Belavezhskaya Pushcha National Park. If you still have time, head north to pleasant Hrodna before exiting via Poland.

Belarusian State Art Museum   MUSEUM

(vul Lenina 20; adult/student BR5/2.50; ⊙11am-7pm Wed-Mon) This excellent state museum has been renovated and now includes a light-bathed extension out back that features local art from the 1940s to the 1970s. Don't miss Valentin Volkov's socialist realist *Minsk on July 3, 1944* (1944–5), depicting the Red Army's arrival in the ruined city. Several works by Yudel Pen, Chagall's teacher, are here, including his 1914 portrait of Chagall.

Trinity Hill   HISTORIC SITE

(Traetskae Pradmestse) Trinity Hill is a pleasant – if tiny – re-creation of Minsk's pre-war buildings on a pretty bend of the river just a little north of the centre. It has a few little cafes, restaurants and shops, and a walking bridge leads over to the Island of Courage & Sorrow (Island of Tears), an evocative Afghan war memorial known colloquially as the Island of Tears by locals.

Stalin Line Museum   MUSEUM

(http://stalin-line.by; Rt 28, Lashany; adult/student R10/5; ⊙10am-6pm) A must for military buffs is this impressive collection of tanks, missiles, helicopters and all other manner of Soviet war paraphernalia in an open field in Lashany, about 25km northwest of Minsk. While the theme is WWII, much of the military hardware is slightly more modern, generally dating from the 1960s and '70s. To get here take a Maladzechna-bound *marshrutka* (fixed-rate minivan) from the Druzhnaya (p98) stop behind Minsk's train station (R3.50, frequent).

Zaslavsky Jewish Monument   MONUMENT

(vul Melnikayte) This extremely moving sight, rather hidden away in a sunken gully amid trees off vul Melnikayte, commemorates the savage murder of 5000 Jews from Minsk at the hands of the Nazis on 2 March 1942.

Tours

City Tour   BUS

(📱17 392 5999; http://citytour.by; adult/child BR30/15; ⊙tours 11am, 1.30pm, 4pm & 6.30pm) Much of Minsk's most jaw-dropping architecture from the Soviet and Lukashenko eras is outside the centre, so these two-hour double-decker bus tours are a great way to see several of them at once. Tours kick off at the classic Stalinist 'City Gates' opposite the train station.

MINSK'S MAIN DRAG

A walk along Minsk's inconspicuous **pr Nezalezhnastsi** (Independence Avenue) is a good way to take Minsk's pulse while also taking in a few sights. Formerly pr Francyska Skaryny, it runs the length of the modern city, from stubbornly austere pl Nezalezhnastsi to the pinnacle of Lukashenko-approved hubris, the rhombicuboctahedron-shaped **National Library of Belarus**.

Heading out from pl Nezalezhnastsi, you'll pass the iconic Minsk Hotel, the ominous **KGB headquarters** (pr Nezalezhnastsi 17) and daunting **Oktyabrskaya pl** (pl Kastrychnitskaya) before crossing the Svislach River, straddled by the city's two main parks. Just across the bridge, on the west bank, is the **former residence of Lee Harvey Oswald** (vul Kamyunistychnaya 4) – it's the bottom left apartment). The alleged assassin of former US president John F Kennedy lived here for a couple of years in his early 20s. He arrived in Minsk in January 1960 after leaving the US Marines and defecting to the USSR. Once here, he truly went native: he got a job in a radio factory, married a Minsk woman, had a child – and even changed his name to Alek. But soon he returned to the United States and...you know the rest.

Just 100m northeast of here, **pl Peramohi** (Victory Sq), ploshchad Pobedy in Russian), is marked by a giant **Victory Obelisk** and its eternal flame, which is directly beneath the obelisk underground. From here you can continue walking to **pl Jakuba Kolasa**, a leafy square occupied by an elephantine monument to the Belarusian writer, or hop on the Metro to go out to the National Library 5km away.

🛏 Sleeping

If you're here for more than a couple of nights, consider renting an apartment. You can go through online booking sites, but dealing with agents directly is better, especially if you require visa support. Two of the best are **Belarus Rent** (www.belarusrent.com; apts from US$45) and **Minsk4rent** (☑ 29 1114 817; www.minsk4rent.com; apts from US$35).

⭐ Revolución Hostel   HOSTEL €

(☑ 29 6146 465; www.revolucion.by; vul Revalyutsiynaya 16; dm US$8-10, d US$24-31; ⊛🛜) Right in the heart of the Old Town, this friendly and pleasingly quirky hostel is festooned with photographs of various revolutionaries and even has a pet tortoise called Marseillaise. The excellent four- to 12-bed dorms feature solid wooden bunk beds with individual plugs, and there are a couple of equally pleasing double rooms as well.

Trinity Hostel   HOSTEL €

(☑ 29 3112 783; www.hostel-traveler.by; vul Staravilenskaya 12; dm from US$11, r without bathroom US$28-33; ⊛🛜) This well-run hostel in a quiet courtyard is a great option. It's centrally located on Trinity Hill (p94), and has 40 beds in four- to eight-bed dorms and several excellent-value private rooms distributed between the main building and an adjoining riverside annex. There's a no-alcohol rule and a strict ban on making noise after 11pm.

⭐ Hotel Manastyrski   HISTORIC HOTEL €€

(☑ 17 3290 300; http://monastyrski.by/en; vul Kirilla i Mefodya 6; s/d incl breakfast from US$75/$96; ⊛❋🛜) Housed in the converted remains of a Benedictine Monastery in the heart of Minsk's bustling Old Town, this 48-room gem cannot be beat for location or atmosphere. Rooms are smart and comfortably furnished with dark-wood fittings, while the impressive corridors are decorated with frescoes (found during the renovation) and wrought-iron chandeliers. Booking directly on its website nets a 10% discount.

Hampton by Hilton   BUSINESS HOTEL €€

(☑ 17 2154 000; http://hamptoninn3.hilton.com; vul Talstoha 8; r incl breakfast from US$70; 🅿⊛ ❋@🛜) While not quite in the centre, the advantages of this shiny business-class hotel are many: slick service, comfortable beds, contemporary design, nice desks and functioning everything. Rooms are slightly on the cosy (as in small) side, but for this price and level of amenities, you're not complaining.

🍴 Eating

Minsk has a decent eating scene and plenty of choice – don't believe the hype about food in Belarus; in the capital, at least, you'll eat well. Consider reserving tables at weekends.

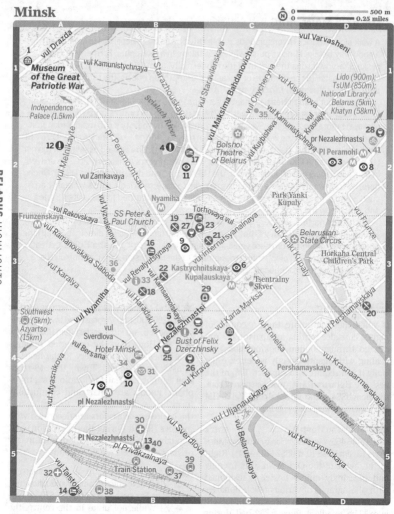

★**Lido**   CAFETERIA €
(pr Nezalezhnastsi 49/1; mains BR2.50-5; ⊙8am-
11pm Mon-Fri, from 11am Sat & Sun; ⊜☑) This
large, upscale *stolovaya* (cafeteria) with Latvian roots has a huge array of food on display, so it's easy for non-Russian speakers:
just point at what you want. Classic Russian
soups and salads, grilled trout and chicken
meatballs are highlights.

Stolle   PIES €
(www.stolle.by; vul Rakovskaya 23; pies from BR2.50;
⊙10am-11pm; ☎) Stolle is a great option, with
delicious, freshly baked sweet and savoury

pies to eat in or take away. Unlike the many
other branches in town, this well-located one
features a full non-pie menu of traditional
Russian and Belarusian cuisine.

Other central branches include those at **vul
Internatsyonalnaya** (vul Internatsyonalnaya 23;
⊙10am-11pm; ☎), **vul Sverdlova** (vul Sverdlova
22; ⊙10am-10pm; ☎) and **pr Nezalezhnastsi**
(pr Nezalezhnastsi 38; ⊙8am-9pm).

Kamyanitsa   BELARUSIAN €€
(☑17 2945 124; vul Pershamaskaya 18; mains
BR10-20; ⊙noon-11pm; ⊜) Wander a couple
blocks southeast of the centre for some

Minsk

of the best traditional Belarusian cuisine in town. The *draniki* (potato pancakes) here are top-notch, or go for the *koldumy* (stuffed *draniki*) or quirky house specials like Granny Dunya's Meat Pot.

Tapas Bar SPANISH €€
(☑ 29 3991 111; vul Internatsyanalnaya 9/17; mains BR10-20; ☺ 11am-midnight; ❂ ☎ 🖊) This stylish joint with olive-coloured walls, friendly service and bright dining areas serves up good tapas from a large menu. All the classics are present, as well as a range of meaty mains and excellent *paella* (good for two).

Gambrinus BELARUSIAN €€
(pl Svabody 2; mains BR15-25; ☺ noon-midnight) This dungeon pub serves a mix of delicious Belarusian and European food and has a 'beer book' with over 100 beers (and about as many cocktails, to boot). In the summer months you'll want to roost on the terrace and watch the action around the *ratusha* (town hall) directly opposite on central pl Svobody.

★**Bistro de Luxe** BISTRO €€€
(44 7891 111; vul Haradski Val 10; mains BR20-45; ☺ 8am-midnight Mon-Fri, from 11am Sat & Sun; ☎) Housed in a gorgeous space with chandeliers, sleek brasserie-style furnishings, a chessboard floor and luxury toilets, Bistro de Luxe has charm and atmosphere that's hard to find elsewhere in Minsk. The food is excellent – it leans towards Italian – and service is impeccable. Breakfast served daily until midday.

🍷 Drinking

Minsk's party scene is conveniently centred in the heart of the Old Town around pl Svobody. On summer weekend nights, vul Zybitskaya turns into a giant street party and the surrounding bars heave with life.

★**Sweet & Sour** COCKTAIL BAR
(vul Karla Marksa 14; ☺ 4pm-2am Mon-Sat; ☎) This dimly lit hideaway is for serious cocktail aficionados. Kick back in scuffed leather couches or belly up to the bar and order

US prohibition-era classics from smartly dressed bartenders. Some of the best cocktails are off-menu, and there's a good selection of single malts too.

U Ratushi
PUB

(pl Svabody; cover BR10 Fri & Sat; ⊙10am-2am; 🐾) This multilevel pub-style restaurant is packed with a raucous, fun-loving crowd who come to drink cheap drinks and dance to live rock music. It's one of the few places in the Old Town that caters to a not-so-young clientele and is a great place to meet fellow travelers and locals alike.

Bessonitsa
COCKTAIL BAR

(Insomnia; vul Hiersena 1; ⊙noon-late) *The* place in the Old Town for professional cocktails (try the bourbon sour or a gimlet) and late-night eats. It has Minsk's longest bar, a lively interior and a bustling patio tailor-made for people-watching.

Stary Mensk
CAFE

(pr Nezalezhnastsi 14; ⊙10am-midnight Sun-Thu, to 2am Fri & Sat) Itsy-bitsy Stary Mensk and its teeny-weeny cousin, London (pr Nezalezhnastsi 18; ⊙10am-midnight Sun-Thu, to 2am Fri & Sat; 🐾), are two of the hippest cafes in town, serving up coffees, fresh teas, imported beer, wine and hot grogs that are just the tonic when the temperatures drop.

🛍 Shopping

★ ў Gallery & Shop
GIFTS & SOUVENIRS

(pr Nezalezhnastsi 37a; gallery BR5; ⊙10am-10pm) This cool space, named after a letter unique to the Belarusian language (called '*u niesklado-vaye*', and pronounced as a 'v') is about as counter-cultural as Minsk gets. The design, souvenir and clothes shop is the ideal place for that quirky gift or T-shirt to bring home. The gallery is attached to ў Bar (www.ybar.by; pr Nezalezhnastsi 37A; ⊙10am-midnight) and showcases local contemporary art.

Minskikh Maestroy Souvenir Market
GIFTS & SOUVENIRS

(pl Svabody; ⊙11am-9pm) This outdoor souvenir market on pl Svabody is where you can haggle for local art, folk crafts, Soviet posters and coins, matryoshka dolls, etc.

ℹ Information

MEDICAL SERVICES

Apteka #4 (vul Kirava 3; ⊙24hr) All-day and all-night pharmacy.

Ecomedservice (📋17 2077 474; www.ems.by; vul Talstoha 4; ⊙8am-9pm) Reliable, Western-style clinic. Bring a translator.

MONEY

ATMs can be found throughout the city. Exchange bureaux dot the centre, while most banks and hotels can change euros and US dollars.

POST

Central Post Office (pr Nezalezhnastsi 10; ⊙8am-8pm Mon-Fri, 10am-5pm Sat & Sun) In the centre of town.

TOURIST INFORMATION

BelarusTourService (📋29 6770 011; www.visa.by) Daria is an excellent source for visa support, hotel bookings and transfers.

Minsk Tourist Information Centre (📋17 2033 995; www.minsktourism.by; vul Revalyutsiynaya 13-119; ⊙8.45am-1pm & 2-6pm Mon-Fri) The friendly staff speak English, give out free maps and can help find guides in English and other languages.

ℹ Getting There & Away

AIR

Minsk-2 International Airport (📋17 2791 300; www.airport.by) Minsk is well connected to the rest of Europe and the Middle East from this airport about 40km east of the centre. There are no domestic flights in Belarus.

BUS

Ecolines (📋29 3533 060; www.ecolines.net; vul Babruyskaya 21) has useful international buses to Kyiv (BR35, 11 hours, one daily), Riga (BR30, nine hours, one daily), Vilnius (BR15, four hours, one daily) and Warsaw (BR55, 11 hours, three daily).

The vast majority of intercity domestic and international services leave from the **Central bus station** (Tsentralny Awtavakzal; 📋114; vul Babruyskaya 6), while the smaller **Southwest bus station** (Yugo-Zapadnaya Awtavakzal; Chyhunachnaya vul) and the **Druzhnaya bus stop** serve some of Minsk's suburbs.

TRAIN

The busy and modern **Minsk train station** (📋17 2257 000, 105; pl Privakzalnaya; ⊙24hr) is pretty easy to deal with. You can buy tickets here, or opposite the station at the less crowded **International Train Ticket Office** (vul Kirava 2; ⊙7am-8pm).

Most services are standard Soviet *pasazhyrsky* (passenger) trains with *platskart* (3rd-class, hard sleeper) and pricier *kupe* (2nd-class, soft sleeper) options. Business-class express trains, with airplane-style seating, are an option on some intercity routes.

ESSENTIAL FOOD & DRINK

Belarusian cuisine rarely differs from Russian cuisine, although there are a few dishes unique to the country.

Belavezhskaya A bitter herbal alcoholic drink.

Draniki Potato pancakes, usually served with sour cream (*smetana*).

Khaladnik A local variation on cold *borshch*, a soup made from beetroot and garnished with sour cream, chopped-up hard-boiled eggs and potatoes.

Kindziuk A pig-stomach sausage filled with minced pork, herbs and spices.

Kletsky Dumplings stuffed with mushrooms, cheese or potato.

Kolduni Potato dumplings stuffed with meat.

Kvas A mildly alcoholic drink made from black or rye bread and commonly sold on the streets.

Manchanka Pancakes served with a meaty gravy.

❶ Getting Around

TO/FROM THE AIRPORT

From Minsk-2 International Airport, handy bus 300Э goes to the train station in the centre of town via pr Nezalezhnastsi (BR3.80, 55 minutes, every 30 to 60 minutes until 10pm). A taxi from the airport costs BR40 to BR60.

BICYCLE

Cycling is an ideal way to explore Minsk and its vast boulevards. **Speedy Go** (☑ 29 1445 030; http://speedygo.by; pr Nezalezhnastsi 37A; bicycles per day BR15; ⊙ 10am-10pm) hires out bicycles, or you can find more expensive bike rentals in most major parks.

CAR

Rental cars are widely available and work great for day trips out of town. As well as outlets at the airport, both **Avis** (☑ 17 2099 489; www.avis.by) and **Europcar** (☑ 29 1336 553; www.europcar. by ⊙ 9am-6pm) can be found at Hotel Minsk at Nezalezhnastsi 11; for a cheaper local option try **AvtoGurman** (☑ 29 6887 070; http://auto-rent. by; vul Chycheryna 4; from €25 per day).

PUBLIC TRANSPORT

Minsk's metro system isn't hugely useful to travellers unless you're exploring the vast suburbs. It's open daily from dawn until just after midnight. One ride costs BR0.55.

Buses, trams and trolleybuses also cost 55 kopeks per ride, while swifter *marshrutky* (fixed-route minivans) cost BR0.80 to BR1.

TAXI

Ordering a taxi by phone will cost just BR8 to BR10 for trips within the centre. Dial ☑ 035 or ☑ 007. Drivers that hang out at taxi stands usually charge considerably more.

AROUND MINSK

Mir and Njasvizh are near each other but are not connected by public transport so hiring a car makes sense to see them both in one day. Other worthwhile trips from the capital include **Khatyn** (www.khatyn.by; photo exhibit BR1; ⊙ complex 24hr, photo exhibit 11am-4pm Tue-Sun) FREE, a sobering memorial to a village wiped out by the Nazis 60km north of Minsk (accessible only by private transport); and **Dudutki** (☑ 29 602 5250; www.dudutki.by; adult/child BR10/6; audioguide BR3; ⊙ 10am-5pm Tue-Wed, to 6pm Thu-Sun), an open-air folk museum 40km south of Minsk (take bus 323 from Minsk's Southwest bus station).

Njasvizh   Нясвіж

This green and attractive town 120km southwest of Minsk is home to the splendid **Njasvizh Castle** (☑ 1770 20 602; www.nias-vizh.by; adult/student BR13/6.50, excursion R36; ⊙ 10am-7pm). It was erected by the Radziwill family in 1583 but was rebuilt and restored often over the centuries and encompasses many styles. With more than 30 fully refurbished state rooms, a very impressive inner courtyard and clearly labelled displays, you can easily spend a couple of hours looking around. Access to the castle is via a causeway leading away from the parking lot, with lovely lakes on either side.

From Minsk's Central bus station, there are four daily buses to and from Njasvizh (BR8, two hours).

WORTH A TRIP

HRODNA ГРОДНА

If you're entering Belarus from northern Poland, or if you have extra time in the country, think about visiting Hrodna (or Grodno in Russian). It was one of the few Belarusian cities that *wasn't* bombed during WWII, so it's rife with old wooden homes and, although it's a major city, it definitely has a 'big village' sort of feel to it. The best hotel in terms of location and value is the **Neman Hotel** (☑ 152 791 700; www.hotel-neman.by; vul Stefana Batoryya 8; s/d from US$44/65; P ➔ ඔ), which has functional rooms, including some cavernous suites, and two restaurants – one being a huge basement beer pub.

Five daily trains serve Minsk (from BR8, five to eight hours). For Brest, you're best off with a *marshrutka* (BR17, four hours, six daily) from the **Central bus station** (vul Chyrvonaarmeyskaya 7). To cross the Hrodna–Kuźnica border to Bialystok in Poland (about three hours), there are several minibuses (BR25) and a daily Ecolines bus (BR37). About four buses per day serve Vilnius (BR30, four hours).

Mir   Mip

The charming small town of Mir, 85km southwest of Minsk, is dominated by the impossibly romantic 16th-century **Mir Castle** (☑ 1596 28 270; www.mirzamak.by; adult/student BR7/3.50; ☉ castle 10am-6pm, closed last Wed of month; courtyard 24hr), which overlooks a small lake at one end of the town. It was once owned by the powerful Radziwill princes and has been under Unesco protection since 1994. A recent renovation has the place looking simply lovely, with gorgeous grounds, impressively restored interiors and a huge display on the life and times of the Radziwills.

The town of Mir itself is a delightful backwater and a great place to break your journey and experience a slice of rural Belarusian life. From Minsk's Central bus station, buses to Navahrudak (Novogrudok in Russian) stop in Mir (BR7, 1½ hours, at least hourly).

BREST   БРЕСТ

☑ 0162 / POP 309,800

This prosperous and cosmopolitan border town looks far more to the neighbouring EU than to Minsk. It has plenty of charm and has performed a massive DIY job on itself over the past few years in preparation for its millennial celebrations in 2019.

⊙ Sights

Most sights are in and around Brest Fortress, which flanks the Bug and Mukhavets rivers just a whisper from the Polish border. The fortress is about a 4km walk from central vul Savetskaya, a pleasant walking street lined with bars and restaurants.

★ **Museum of Railway Technology**   MUSEUM
(pr Masherava 2; adult/student BR2.50/2; ☉ 9am-9pm Tue-Sun May-Sep, 8.30am-5.30pm Tue-Sun Oct-Apr) One of Brest's most popular sights is the outdoor Museum of Railway Technology, where there's a superb collection of locomotives and carriages dating from 1903 (eg the Moscow–Brest Express, with shower rooms and a very comfy main bedroom) to 1988 (far more proletarian Soviet passenger carriages).

St Nikolaiv Church   CHURCH
(cnr vul Savetskaya & vul Mitskevicha) With its gold cupolas and yellow-and-blue facades shining gaily in the sunshine, the finely detailed 200-year-old Orthodox church is one of several lovely churches in Brest.

Museum of Confiscated Art   MUSEUM
(vul Lenina 39; adult/student BR22/15; ☉ 10am-6pm Tue-Sun) This museum has an extraordinary display of mostly 17th- to 18th-century icons, jewellery, antique furniture and Chinese porcelain seized from smugglers trying to get them across the border to Poland during the 1990s.

⊨ Sleeping

★ **Dream Hostel**   HOSTEL €
(☑ 162 531 499, 33 3610 315; www.dreamhostel.by; Apt 5, vul Mayakowskaha 17/1; dm US$10; ➔ ඔ) Brest's finest hostel is housed in an apartment building right in the middle of town. It's modern and bright, with clean bunks, a large TV room, kitchen and laundry. The entrance is 50m east of Bike N' Roll on vul Mayakowskaha; go through the first of two adjacent archways and follow the footpath around to the right.

Hotel Molodyozhnaya
HOTEL €

(☑162 216 376; www.molodezhnaya.by; vul Kamsamolskaya 6; s/d US$27/37; ⊜🕾) This small renovated Soviet-era hotel is ideally located opposite the train station, although it is susceptible to street noise. The rooms are comfortable and clean, all have private facilities, and the welcome is warm.

Hermitage Hotel
HOTEL €€€

(☑162 276 000; www.hermitagehotel.by; vul Chkalava 7; s/d incl breakfast from US$115/143; P⊜❀🕾) This 55-room hotel is heads above the local competition and is priced accordingly. Housed in a sensitively designed modern building, it has more than a little old-world style, with spacious, grand and well-appointed rooms, as well as impressive public areas.

✕ Eating & Drinking

It's hard to beat dining outside on pedestrianized vul Savetskaya, but on summer evenings it can be hard to find a seat.

★ Jules Verne
INTERNATIONAL €€

(vul Hoholya 29; mains BR10-25; ⊙noon-1am Sun-Thu, 5pm-1am Fri & Sat; 🕾🍴) It's almost a miracle that such a great restaurant exists in Brest. Decked out like a traditional gentlemen's club and with a travel theme, this dark, atmospheric joint manages to be refined without being stuffy. It serves up cracking dishes, from mouthwatering Indian curries and French specialities to sumptuous desserts and the best coffee in town. Don't miss it.

Time's Cafe
EUROPEAN €€

(vul Savetskaya 30; mains BR10-20; ⊙8.30am-11pm Mon-Fri, 11am-11pm Sat & Sun; 🕾) This friendly and self-consciously cool place has a jazz and blues soundtrack and a summer terrace with views of pedestrianized vul Savetskaya. Dishes range from steak in a balsamic reduction to salmon carpaccio with scallops – quite different from the offerings of most places nearby.

Korova
COCKTAIL BAR

(vul Savetskaya 73; ⊙noon-2am Sun-Thu, to 4am Fri & Sat) Just an average grill and bar along vul Savetskaya by day, Korova morphs at night into a superb lounge-club, with slick bartenders serving expertly made cocktails and craft beer, while an all-types crowd gets their groove on to talented DJ acts and/or live bands.

Coyote Bar
BAR

(vul Dzyarzhynskaha 14; BR10 after 11pm Fri & Sat; ⊙noon-midnight Sun-Thu, to 3am Fri & Sat) Bartenders dancing on the bar and loud live music are the calling cards of this raucous bar. Terrific fun any night of the week, it really gets going on weekends, when the best bands play and shots fly.

ℹ Information

24-hour Pharmacy (vul Hoholya 32; ⊙24 hrs)
Brest Intourist (☑162 205 571, 162 200 510; Hotel Intourist, pr Masherava 15; ⊙9am-6pm Mon-Fri) The super-friendly English-speaking staff can arrange city tours, including 'Jewish Brest', and trips to the Belavezhskaya Pushcha National Park.

BELARUS MIR

BREST FORTRESS

The city's main sight is the **Brest Fortress** (Brestskaya krepost; www.brest-fortress.by; pr Masherava) FREE, a moving WWII memorial where Soviet troops held out far longer than expected against the Nazi onslaught in the early days of Operation Barbarossa.

The fortress was built between 1833 and 1842, but by WWII it was being used mainly as a barracks. The two regiments bunking here when German troops launched a surprise attack in 1941 defended the fort for an astounding month and became venerated as national legends thanks to Stalin's propaganda machine.

Enter the Brest Fortress complex through a tunnel in the shape of a huge socialist star, then walk straight ahead several hundred metres to the fortresses' most iconic site – **Courage**, a chiselled soldier's head projecting from a massive rock, flanked by a skyscraping memorial obelisk.

There are several museums in and around the sprawling grounds, the most interesting of which are a pair museums that commemorate the siege and related events in WWII: the comprehensive **Defence of Brest Fortress Museum** (adult/student BR4/2, English-language audioguide BR3; ⊙9am-6pm Tue-Sun) inside the fortresses' northern bastion; and the newer, more visual **Museum of War, Territory of Peace** (adult/student BR4/2, English-language audioguide BR3; ⊙10am-7pm Wed-Mon) in the southern bastion.

Post Office (pl Lenina; ⊘8am-8pm Mon-Sat, to 5pm Sat, to 3pm Sun)

❶ Getting There & Away

BUS

The **bus station** (☑114; vul Mitskevicha) is in the centre of town. There are *marshrutky* (fixed-route minivans) to Hrodna (BR17, four hours, six daily), plus a slower bus or two. Buses serve Minsk (BR5 to BR8, five hours, three daily) but trains are preferable.

Ecolines (www.ecolines.net) buses to Warsaw (BR30, five hours, two daily) originate in Minsk. To Vilnius there are three midnight buses per week (BR35, 9½ hours).

TRAIN

The **train station** (☑105) is a short walk from the centre. There's a morning express train (BR9.50, 3¼ hours, one daily), and slower passenger (*pasazhirsky*) trains to Minsk (from BR8, 4½ hours to nine hours, frequent).

The number 9 train trundles to Warsaw (BR25, six hours, one daily).

❶ Getting Around

For a taxi, call ☑5656 or have your hotel call for you.

Bike N' Roll (☑29 5051 286; http://bikenroll.net; vul Mayakowskaha 17/1; bicycles per day BR19.50; ⊘10am-7pm Mon-Fri, to 5pm Sat & Sun) Nice selection of mountain and city bikes available for hourly or daily rental.

Easyday (☑29 8882 007; www.easyday.by) Car rental for as low as €20 per day. No English.

COUNTRY FACTS

Currency Belarusian rouble (BR)

Language Belarusian and Russian

Money ATMs taking international cards are widely available.

Visas Five-day visa-free travel for citizens of 80 countries arriving by air.

Population 9.57 million

Area 207,600 sq km

Capital Minsk

Country Code ☑375

Emergency Ambulance ☑03, Fire ☑01, Police ☑02

AROUND BREST

Belavezhskaya Pushcha National Park Белавежская Пушча

Unesco World Heritage Site Belavezhskaya Pushcha National Park (☑16 3156 200, 16 3156 398; www.npbp.by; varies per activity; ⊘ticket office 9am-5pm) is the oldest wildlife refuge in Europe and the pride of Belarus. At the National Park headquarters in Kamyanyuki, 55km north of Brest, you can arrange to tour the park by bus, bicycle or private car, and you can spend the night at one of several comfortable hotels in the Kamyanyuki Hotel Complex (☑1631 56 200; beltour07@mail.ru; d US$35-44; ⊛ ☎ ☒) near the park entrance.

Some 1300 sq km of primeval forest survives in Belavezhskaya Pushcha National Park, half of which lies in Poland. At least 55 mammal species call this park home, but the area is most celebrated for its 300 or so European bison, the continent's largest land mammal. They were driven to near extinction then bred back from the 52 animals surviving in zoos. Now a total of about 3000 *zubr* exist, of which more than 300 are wild in the Belavezhskaya Pushcha.

You have a chance to spot these beasts in the wild on a tour of the park, although you have to be a bit lucky. The October-to-April period offers the best odds.

To get to the park from Brest take a bus or *marshrutka* from the bus station to the village of Kamyanyuki (BR3.80, 1¼ hours, about seven daily). An altogether easier option for visiting the park is to book a day trip from Brest with an English-speaking guide through Brest Intourist (p101).

SURVIVAL GUIDE

❶ Directory A–Z

BUSINESS HOURS

Banks 9am–5pm Monday to Friday
Office hours 9am–6pm Monday to Friday
Shops 9am/10am – 9pm Monday to Saturday, to 6pm Sunday (if at all)

INSURANCE

You'll need a policy from an authorised state health-insurance provider as a requirement for obtaining a visa. This is best done through a travel agent. If you're eligible for the five-day visa-free scheme, then this health-insurance requirement is waived. However, we do recommend obtaining a legitimate international health-insurance policy that covers Belarus.

MONEY

The Belarusian rouble is pinned to the US dollar at BR2-to-US$1 and is relatively stable. ATMs are widespread and most banks, supermarkets and higher-end hotels have currency-exchange facilities. Credit cards are widely used for payment in Minsk and other cities but are unlikely to be accepted in rural areas.

TELEPHONE

There are four mobile-phone companies that can sell you a SIM-card package with oodles of data for next to nothing. Bring your passport, a Belarusian address and your unlocked phone.

To place a call or send a text from a local mobile phone, dial either +☑375 or ☑80, plus the nine-digit number.

VISAS

From 2017, citizens of 80 countries can travel in Belarus visa-free for five days if arriving by air. For longer stays and if not arriving by air, most travellers need visas.

If you require a visa, you'll need to enlist the services of a Belarusian travel agency or pre-booked hotel for letters of invitation and other visa-support documentation. For visa support, we recommend BelarusTourService (p98) or Belarus Rent (p95).

Belarusian visa regulations change frequently, so check the website of your nearest Belarusian embassy for the latest bureaucratic requirements.

Registration

Keep the white slip you receive upon arrival in Belarus: you must have it registered and present it again upon departure if you are staying for more than five working days. Hotels do this automatically and the service is included in the room price.

ⓘ Getting There & Away

Flights into Minsk are the most popular means of entering Belarus. Common overland routes include bus or train to Brest or Hrodno from Poland; bus or train to Minsk from Vilnius, Lithuania, and train to Homel or Minsk from Ukraine. Arriving overland from Russia is problematic as there are no border checkpoints between Russia and Belarus, so you won't be able to obtain a proper entry stamp.

AIR

Minsk-2 International Airport (p98) is well connected by direct flights to Europe, the Middle East and the former Soviet Union.

Belarus' national airline, **Belavia** (☑17 2202 555; www.belavia.by; vul Nyamiha 14, Minsk), has lots of flights to Moscow and the Commonwealth of Independent States (CIS), and it also serves a few Western European cities including Amsterdam, Berlin, Frankfurt, London, Paris and Vienna. Belavia has a good safety record and modern planes. Other airlines that fly to Minsk include Aeroflot, Air Baltic, Austrian Airlines, El Al, LOT Polish Airlines and Lufthansa.

LAND

Belarus has good overland bus and train links to all neighbouring countries and borders are generally hassle-free provided your papers are in order. Queues can plague any overland border crossing, of course, but they are usually not too bad. The one exception is the Hrodna–Kuźnica (Bialystok, Poland) crossing, where we've heard reports of long waits when crossing by train. We recommend taking the bus instead.

ⓘ Getting Around

Trains are extremely cheap and plenty comfortable, buses cheap but less comfortable. For train schedules and prices, www.rw.by and www.rzd.ru are great sites if you read Russian, or try www.bahn.de if you don't.

Train Super-cheap, efficient and usually on time. Try the business-class express trains for quick hops between cities.

Car Hiring a car is recommended for exploring around Minsk, with car hire widely available.

Bus A bit cheaper than trains, but can be slower. Zippy *marshrutky* (public minivans), on the other hand, are less comfortable but generally faster than buses or trains.

Belgium & Luxembourg

Best Places to Eat

➡ L'Ogenblik (p113)

➡ La Cristallerie (p134)

➡ Den Gouden Harynck (p127)

➡ De Stove (p127)

➡ De Ruyffelaer (p130)

Best Places to Stay

➡ Chambres d'Hôtes du Vaudeville (p109)

➡ Main Street Hotel (p129)

➡ Guesthouse Nuit Blanche (p125)

➡ Auberge Aal Veinen (p135)

➡ Bed, Bad & Brood (p119)

Why Go?

Stereotypes of comic books, chips and sublime chocolates are just the start in eccentric little Belgium, its self-deprecating people have quietly spent centuries producing some of Europe's finest art and architecture. Bilingual Brussels is the dynamic yet personable EU capital, but also sports what's arguably the world's most beautiful city square. Flat, Flemish Flanders has many other alluring medieval cities, all easily linked by regular train hops. In hilly, French-speaking Wallonia, the attractions are contrastingly rural – castle villages, outdoor activities and extensive cave systems. Independent Luxembourg, the EU's richest country, is compact and hilly with its own wealth of castle villages. The grand duchy's capital city is famed for banking but also sports a fairy-tale Unesco-listed historic Old Town. And from the brilliant beers of Belgium to the sparkling wines of Luxembourg's Moselle Valley, there's plenty to lubricate some of Europe's best dining.

When to Go
Brussels

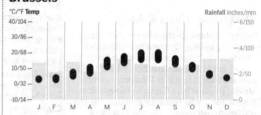

Pre-Easter weekends Belgium hosts many of Europe's weirdest carnivals, not just at Mardi Gras.

Feb–Mar Both countries symbolically burn the spirit of winter on the first weekend after Carnival.

Jul–Aug Countless festivals, hotels packed at the coast but cheaper in Brussels and Luxembourg City.

BRUSSELS

POP 1.2 MILLION

Belgium's fascinating capital, and the administrative capital of the EU, Brussels is historic yet hip, bureaucratic yet bizarre, self-confident yet unshowy, and multicultural to its roots. All this plays out in a cityscape that swings from majestic to quirky to rundown and back again. Organic art nouveau facades face off against 1960s concrete developments, and regal 19th-century mansions contrast with the brutal glass of the EU's Gotham City. This whole maelstrom swirls out from Brussels' medieval core, where the Grand Place is surely one of the world's most beautiful squares.

One constant is the enviable quality of everyday life, with a *café*–bar scene that never gets old.

◉ Sights

◉ Central Brussels

Grand Place SQUARE

(Ⓜ Gare Centrale) Brussels' magnificent Grand Place is one of the world's most unforgettable urban ensembles. Oddly hidden, the enclosed cobblestone square is only revealed as you enter on foot from one of six narrow side alleys: Rue des Harengs is the best first approach. The focal point is the spired 15th-century city hall, but each of the antique guildhalls (mostly 1697–1705) has a charm of its own. Most are unashamed exhibitionists, with fine baroque gables, gilded statues and elaborate guild symbols.

Manneken Pis MONUMENT

(cnr Rue de l'Étuve & Rue du Chêne; Ⓜ Gare Centrale) Rue Charles Buls – Brussels' most unashamedly touristy shopping street, lined with chocolate and trinket shops – leads the hordes three blocks from the Grand Place to the Manneken Pis. This fountain-statue of a little boy taking a leak is comically tiny and a perversely perfect national symbol for surreal Belgium. Most of the time the statue's nakedness is hidden beneath a costume relevant to an anniversary, national day or local event: his ever-growing wardrobe is partly displayed at the **Maison du Roi** (Musée de la Ville de Bruxelles; Grand Place; Ⓜ Gare Centrale).

Musées Royaux des Beaux-Arts GALLERY

(Royal Museums of Fine Arts; ☑ 02-508 32 11; www.fine-arts-museum.be; Rue de la Régence 3; adult/6-25yr/BrusselsCard €8/2/free, with Magritte Museum €13; ⊙ 10am-5pm Tue-Fri, 11am-6pm Sat & Sun; Ⓜ Gare Centrale, Parc) This prestigious museum incorporates the Musée d'Art Ancien (ancient art); the Musée d'Art Moderne (modern art), with works by surrealist Paul Delvaux and Fauvist Rik Wouters; and the purpose-built Musée Magritte (p105). The 15th-century Flemish Primitives are wonderfully represented in the Musée d'Art Ancien: there's Rogier Van der Weyden's *Pietà* with its hallucinatory sky, Hans Memling's refined portraits, and the richly textured *Madonna With Saints* by the Master of the Legend of St Lucy.

Musée Magritte MUSEUM

(☑ 02-508 32 11; www.musee-magritte-museum.be; Rue de la Régence 3; adult/under 26yr/BrusselsCard €8/2/free; ⊙ 10am-5pm Tue-Fri, 11am-6pm Sat & Sun; Ⓜ Gare Centrale, Parc) The beautifully presented Magritte Museum holds the world's largest collection of the surrealist pioneer's paintings and drawings. Watch his style develop from colourful Braque-style cubism in 1920 through a Dali-esque phase and a late-1940s period of Kandinsky-like brushwork to his trademark bowler hats of the 1960s. Regular screenings of a 50-minute documentary provide insights into the artist's unconventionally conventional life.

MIM MUSEUM

(Musée des Instruments de Musique; ☑ 02-545 01 30; www.mim.be; Rue Montagne de la Cour 2; adult/concession €8/6; ⊙ 9.30am-5pm Tue-Fri, 10am-5pm Sat & Sun; Ⓜ Gare Centrale, Parc) Strap on a pair of headphones, then step on the automated floor panels in front of the precious instruments (including world instruments and Adolphe Sax's inventions) to hear them being played. As much of a highlight as the museum itself are the premises – the art-nouveau Old England Building. This former department store was built in 1899 by Paul Saintenoy and has a panoramic rooftop *café* and outdoor terrace.

★ Musée du Costume et de la Dentelle MUSEUM

(Costume & Lace Museum; ☑ 02-213 44 50; www.costumeandlacemuseum.brussels; Rue de la Violette 12; adult/child/BrusselsCard €8/free/free; ⊙ 10am-5pm Tue-Sun; Ⓜ Gare Centrale) Lacemaking has been one of Flanders' finest crafts since the 16th century. While *kloskant* (bobbin lace) originated in Bruges, *naaldkant* (needlepoint lace) was developed in Italy but was predominantly made

Belgium & Luxembourg Highlights

1 Bruges (p124)
Coming on weekdays off-season to appreciate the picture-perfect canal scenes of this medieval city, without the tourist overload.

2 Ghent (p121)
Being wooed by one of Europe's greatest underappreciated all-round discoveries.

3 Brussels (p105) Savouring the 'world's most beautiful square', then seeking out remarkable *cafés*, chocolate shops and art nouveau survivors.

4 Antwerp (p117) Following fashion to this hip yet historic city.

5 Luxembourg City (p131) Spending the weekend in the UNESCO-listed Old Town then heading out to the grand duchy's evocative castle villages.

6 Ypres (p128) Pondering the heartbreaking futility of WWI in Flanders' fields around its meticulously rebuilt medieval core.

7 Wallonia (p130) Exploring the caves and castles of Belgium's rural southern half.

in Brussels. This excellent museum reveals lace's applications for under- and outerwear over the centuries, as well as displaying other luxury textiles in beautifully presented changing exhibitions. Ask for an English-language booklet.

Beyond the Centre

Musée Horta MUSEUM

(02-543 04 90; www.hortamuseum.be; Rue Américaine 25; adult/child €10/3; 2-5.30pm Tue-Sun; Horta, 91, 92) The typically austere exterior doesn't give much away, but Victor Horta's former home (designed and built 1898–1901) is an art nouveau jewel. The stairwell is the structural triumph of the house: follow the playful knots and curlicues of the banister, which become more exuberant as you ascend, ending at a tangle of swirls and glass lamps at the skylight, glazed with citrus-coloured and plain glass.

Cantillon Brewery BREWERY

(Musée Bruxellois de la Gueuze; 02-520 28 91; www.cantillon.be; Rue Gheude 56; admission €7; 10am-5pm Mon, Tue & Thu-Sat; Clemenceau) Beer lovers shouldn't miss this unique living brewery-museum. Atmospheric and family run, it's Brussels' last operating lambic brewery and still uses much of the original 19th-century equipment. After hearing a brief explanation, visitors take a self-guided tour, including the barrel rooms where the beers mature for up to three years in chestnut wine casks. The entry fee includes two taster glasses of Cantillon's startlingly acidic brews.

★Musée du Cinquantenaire MUSEUM

(02-741 73 01; www.kmkg-mrah.be; Parc du Cinquantenaire 10; adult/child/BrusselsCard €8/2/free; 9.30am-5pm Tue-Fri, from 10am Sat & Sun; Mérode) This astonishingly rich collection ranges from ancient Egyptian sarcophagi to Meso-American masks to icons to wooden bicycles. Decide what you want to see before coming or the sheer scope can prove overwhelming. Visually attractive spaces include the medieval stone carvings set around a neo-Gothic cloister and the soaring Corinthian columns (convincing fibreglass props) that bring atmosphere to an original AD 420 mosaic from Roman Syria. Labelling is in French and Dutch, so the English-language audio guide (€3) is worth considering.

★Musée des Sciences Naturelles MUSEUM

(02-627 42 11; www.naturalsciences.be; Rue Vautier 29; adult/concession/child/BrusselsCard €7/6/4.50/free; 9.30am-5pm Tue-Fri, 10am-6pm Sat & Sun; 38 (direction Homborch, departs from next to Gare Centrale) to De Meeus on Rue du Luxembourg) Thought-provoking and highly interactive, this museum has far more than the usual selection of stuffed animals. But the undoubted highlight is a unique 'family' of iguanodons – 10m-high dinosaurs found in a Hainaut coal mine in 1878. A computer simulation shows the mudslide that might have covered them, sand boxes allow you to play dino hunter and multilingual videos give a wonderfully nuanced debate on recent palaeontology.

ITINERARIES

Four Days

Just long enough to get a first taste of Belgium's four finest 'art cities': Bruges, Ghent, Brussels and Antwerp, all easy jump-offs or short excursions while you're train-hopping between Paris and Amsterdam. **Bruges** is the fairy-tale 'Venice of the north', **Ghent** has similar canalside charms without the tourist hordes, and **Brussels'** incomparable Grand Place is worth jumping off any train for, even if you have only a few hours to spare. Cosmopolitan **Antwerp** goes one further, adding in fashion and diamonds. If you're overnighting make sure to hit Brussels on a weekend and Bruges on a weekday to get the best deals on accommodation.

Ten Days

Add in a side trip to **Leuven**, then swing into Wallonia, visiting **Waterloo**, the excellent museums of **Mons**, the picturesque castles and views of the Ardennes, especially **Bouillon**, then pretty **Luxembourg**. All while trying the excellent local beers along the way, of course.

Atomium
MONUMENT

(☑02-475 47 75; www.atomium.be; Av de l'Atomium; adult/teen/child €12/8/6; ☺10am-6pm; Ⓜ Heysel, 🚌51) The space-age Atomium looms 102m over north Brussels' suburbia, resembling a steel alien from a '60s Hollywood movie. It consists of nine house-sized metallic balls linked by steel tube-columns containing escalators and lifts. The balls are arranged like a school chemistry set to represent iron atoms in their crystal lattice... except these are 165 billion times bigger. It was built as a symbol of postwar progress for the 1958 World's Fair and became an architectural icon, receiving a makeover in 2006.

🧭 Tours

Groovy Brussels Bike Tours
CYCLING

(☑0484 89 89 36; www.groovybrussels.com/bike; tour incl bicycle rental €25; ☺10am daily Apr-Oct, plus 2pm weekends) Many first-time visitors love this tour for the ride and for the beer and *frites* stops along the way (food and drink cost extra). Tours start from the Grand Place and take 3½ hours; the maximum group size is 12. The outfit also offers chocolate and beer walking tours.

🛏 Sleeping

Many business hotels drop their rates dramatically at weekends and in summer. Double rooms with September midweek rates of €240 might cost as little as €69 in August. Brussels has a reasonable network of B&Bs, many listed and bookable through Bed & Brussels (www.bnb-brussels.be), or try sites like Airbnb (www.airbnb.com) and Wimdu (www.wimdu.co.uk).

★ Captaincy Guesthouse
HOSTEL €

(☑0496 59 93 79; www.thecaptaincybrussels. be; Quai à la Chaux 8; dm €31-37, d €90; Ⓜ Ste-Catherine) An idiosyncratic, warm and friendly venture, housed in a 17th-century mansion with a hip Ste-Catherine location and a mix of dorms (some mixed sex) and rooms. A generous €7.50 breakfast is served in the spacious living area. The wooden attic housing an en-suite four-bed female dorm has a fabulous boutique-hotel feel, and the attic double is a winner too.

Centre Vincent van Gogh
HOSTEL €

(☑02-217 01 58; www.chab.be; Rue Traversière 8; dm €22-26, s/tw/tr €35/60/90; @ 🛜; Ⓜ Botanique) The lobby bar and pool-table veranda are unusually hip for a hostel, but rooms are less glamorous and, from some, reaching the toilets means crossing the garden courtyard. No membership is required, but you have to be under 35 years unless in a group.

★ Chambres d'Hôtes du Vaudeville
B&B €€

(☑0484 59 46 69; www.theatreduvaudeville.be; Galerie de la Reine 11; d from €120; 🛜; 🚇 Bruxelles Central) 🅿 This classy B&B has an incredible location right within the gorgeous (if reverberant) Galeries St-Hubert. Delectable decor styles include African, modernist and 'Madame Loulou' (with 1920s nude sketches). Larger front rooms have claw-foot bathtubs and *galerie* views but can be noisy, with clatter that continues all night. Get keys via the art deco–influenced Café du Vaudeville, where breakfast is included.

Vaudeville's unique house beer is provided free in the minibar.

La Vieille Lanterne
B&B €€

(☑02-512 74 94; www.lavieillelanterne.be; Rue des Grands Carmes 29; s €118-168, d €130-180; 🛜; 🚇 Anneessens) Look out at the Manneken Pis from the window of room 5 in this neat, unsophisticated six-room B&B-style 'hotel', accessed by steep spiral stairs from an archetypal gift shop. Check in before 10pm.

Downtown-BXL
B&B €€

(☑0475 29 07 21; www.downtownbxl.com; Rue du Marché au Charbon 118-120; r €109-119; 🛜; 🚇 Anneessens) Near the capital's gay district, this B&B is superbly located if you're dancing the night away. From the communal breakfast table and help-yourself coffee bar, a classic staircase winds up to good-value rooms featuring zebra-striped cushions and Warhol Marilyn prints. One room features a round bed. Adjacent Casa-BXL (r €109-119) offers three rooms in a more Moroccan-Asian style.

★ Hôtel Métropole
HOTEL €€€

(☑02-217 23 00, reservations 02-214 2424; www.metropolehotel.com; Place de Brouckère 31; r €170-350, weekend rates from €130; ☺ ❄ 🛜; Ⓜ De Brouckère) This 1895 showpiece has a jaw-droppingly sumptuous French Renaissance–style foyer with marble walls, coffered ceiling and beautifully etched stained-glass back windows. The *café* is indulgent and the bar (with frequent live music) features recently 'rediscovered' murals by a student of Horta. One of the lifts is an 1895 original.

Central Brussels

200 m
0.1 miles

Pl Ste Gudule
Blvd Pachéco
Pl de Louvain
Centre Vincent van Gogh (1km)
R de la Loi
R Royale
Parc
2
Blvd de Berlaimont
R des Sables
R du Meiboom
R du Marais
R des Comédiens
R des Boiteux
R du Persil
R des Herbes Potagères
R du Bois Sauvage
Pl Ste Gudule
R de Ligne
R des Colonies
Gare Centrale
R Ravenstein
R de Loxum
R Cardinal Mercier
Bruxelles-Central
Pl des Martyrs
R d'Argent
R Léopold
R du Fossé aux Loups
R Neuve
R des Princes
R de la Reine
R de l'Écuyer
R d'Arenberg
Galerie du Roi
Galerie des Princes
R des Dominicains
R de la Montagne
Blvd de l'Impératrice
Pl d'Espagne
R de l'Infante Isabelle
R de la Madeleine
23
16
35
3
10
21
26
12
Pl de Brouckère
De Brouckère
R des Augustins
Pl de la Monnaie
R de l'Écuyer
R de la Fourche
Petite R des Bouchers
R des Bouchers
R des Harengs
ÎLOT SACRÉ
R de la Colline
R du Marché aux Fromages
R de la Violette
13
25
24
5
4
27
Eurolines (1km)
Bruxelles-Nord (1.1km)
STE-CATHERINE
R de l'Évêque
Blvd Anspach
R Grétry
R des Fripiers
R du Marché aux Herbes
R au Beurre
R de la Tête d'Or
R des Brasseurs
R Chair et Pain
Visit Brussels
Musée du Costume et de la Dentelle
30
1
R des Halles
Pl du Samedi
R de la Vierge Noire
R de la Bourse
Pl de la Bourse
Bourse
R Henri Maus
R J-van Praet
R des Pierres
R du Midi
R de la Tête d'Or
R du Marché au Charbon
R de l'Amigo
22
29
19
34
31
37
20
Pl Ste-Catherine
R Ste-Catherine
R des Poissonniers
R Paul Devaux
ST-GÉRY
Borgval
Pl St-Géry
R St-Géry
R Plattesteen
R des Teinturiers
R des Grands Carmes
R du Marché au Charbon
Blvd Anspach
Henri (200m); Captaincy (450m)
Marché aux Poissons
R Melsens
R Antoine Dansaert
R Van Artevelde
R des Chartreux
R du Vieux Marché aux Grains
R St-Christophe
R de la Grande Île
R des Riches Claires
ST-GÉRY
R des 6 Jetons
Pl Fontainas
BarBeton (80m)
R de la Braie
R Pletinckx
Cantillon Brewery (1km)
36
18
17
33
38

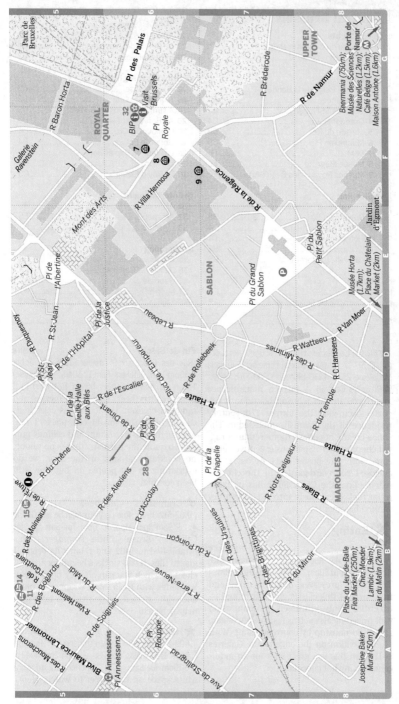

Central Brussels

★ **Hôtel Le Dixseptième** BOUTIQUE HOTEL €€€
(☑02-517 17 17; www.ledixseptieme.be; Rue de la Madeleine 25; r €130-190, ste €200-370; ❋ 🐾; 🚇 Bruxelles Central) A hushed magnificence greets you in this alluring boutique hotel, partly occupying the former 17th-century residence of the Spanish ambassador. The coffee-cream breakfast room retains original cherub reliefs. Spacious executive suites come with four-poster beds. Across a tiny enclosed courtyard-garden in the cheaper rear section, the Creuz Suite has its bathroom tucked curiously into a 14th-century vaulted basement.

✖ **Eating**

★ **Arcadi** BRASSERIE €
(☑02-511 33 43; Rue d'Arenberg 1b; mains €10-15; ⊙9.30am-10.30pm Tue-Sun; 🚇Gare Centrale) The jars of preserves, beautiful cakes and fruit tarts of this classic and charming bistro entice plenty of Brussels residents, as do well-priced meals such as lasagne and steak, all served nonstop by courteous staff. With a nice location on the edge of the Galeries St-Hubert, this is a great spot for an indulgent, creamy hot chocolate.

Fin de Siècle BELGIAN €
(Rue des Chartreux 9; mains €11.25-20; ⊙bar 4.30pm-1am, kitchen 6pm-12.30am; 🚇Bourse) From *carbonade* (beer-based hot pot) and *kriek* (cherry beer) chicken to mezzes and tandoori chicken, the food is as eclectic as the decor in this low-lit cult place. Tables are rough, music constant and ceilings purple. To quote the barman, 'there's no phone, no bookings, no sign on the door...we do everything to put people off but they still keep coming'.

★ **Cremerie De Linkebeek** DELI €
(☑02-512 35 10; Rue du Vieux Marché aux Grains 4; ⊙9am-3pm Mon, to 6pm Tue-Sat; 🚇Ste-Catherine) Brussels' best *fromagerie* was established in 1902 and retains its original glazed tiles. It still stocks a beguiling array of cheeses, which you can also try on crunchy baguettes with fresh salad, wrapped in blue-and-white-striped paper ready to take to a nearby bench.

★ **Henri** FUSION €€
(☑02-218 00 08; www.restohenri.be; Rue de Flandre 113; mains €16-23; ⊙noon-2pm Tue-Fri & 6-10pm Tue-Sat; 🚇Ste-Catherine) In an airy white space on this street to watch, Henri

BOURSE CAFES

Many of Brussels' most iconic *cafés* are within stumbling distance of the Bourse. Don't miss **Le Cirio** (☑02-512 13 95; Rue de la Bourse 18; ⊙10am-midnight; 🚊Bourse), a sumptuous yet affordable 1866 marvel full of polished brasswork serving great-value pub meals. Three more classics are hidden up shoulder-wide alleys: the medieval yet unpretentious **A l'Image de Nostre-Dame** (Rue du Marais 3; ⊙noon-midnight Mon-Fri, 3pm-1am Sat, 4-10.30pm Sun; 🚊Bourse); the 1695 Rubenseque **Au Bon Vieux Temps** (☑02-217 26 26; Impasse St-Nicolas; ⊙11am-midnight; 🚊Bourse), which sometimes stocks ultra-rare Westvleteren beers (€10!); and lambic specialist **À la Bécasse** (☑02-511 00 06; www. alabecasse.com; Rue de Tabora 11; ⊙11am-midnight, to 1am Fri & Sat; Ⓜ Gare Centrale), with its vaguely Puritanical rows of wooden tables.

concocts tangy fusion dishes such as tuna with ginger, soy and lime, artichokes with scampi, lime and olive tapenade, or Argentine fillet steak. There's an astute wine list, and staff who know their stuff.

Le Cercle des Voyageurs   BRASSERIE **€€**
(☑02-514 39 49; www.lecercledesvoyageurs. com; Rue des Grands Carmes 18; mains €15-21; ⊙11am-midnight; 🛜; 🚊Bourse, Anneessens) Delightful bistro featuring globes, an antique-map ceiling and a travel library. If your date's late, flick through an old *National Geographic* in your colonial leather chair. The global brasserie food is pretty good, and there are documentary screenings and free live music: piano jazz on Tuesday and experimental on Thursday. Other gigs in the cave have a small entrance fee.

★L'Ogenblik   FRENCH **€€€**
(☑02-511 61 51; www.ogenblik.be; Galerie des Princes 1; mains €25-33; ⊙noon-2.30pm & 6.30pm-midnight Mon-Sat; 🚊Bourse) It may be only a stone's throw from Rue des Bouchers, but this timeless bistro with its lace curtains, resident cat, marble-topped tables and magnificent wrought-iron lamp feels a world away. They've been producing French classics here for more than 30 years, and the expertise shows. Worth the price for a special meal in the heart of town.

Drinking & Nightlife

Café culture is one of Brussels' greatest attractions. On the Grand Place itself, 300-year-old gems, like **Le Roy d'Espagne** (☑02-513 08 07; www.roydespagne.be; Grand Place 1; ⊙9.30am-1am; Ⓜ Gare Centrale) and **Chaloupe d'Or** (☑02-511 41 61; Grand Place 24; ⊙11am-1am; Ⓜ Gare Centrale) are magnificent but predictably pricey. Go out of the centre a little to explore the city's new brand

of laid-back hipster bars, most decorated in minimal upcycled style, and hosting DJ nights and live music events: try **Café Belga** (☑02-640 35 08; Place Eugène Flagey 18; ⊙8am-2am Sun-Thu, to 3am Fri & Sat; 🚊81, 82), **BarBeton** (☑02-513 83 63; www.barbeton. be; Rue Antoine Dansaert 114; ⊙10am-midnight; 🛜; Ⓜ Ste-Catherine) or **Bar du Matin** (☑02-537 71 59; bardumatin.blogspot.com; Chaussée d'Alsemberg 172; ⊙8am-1am Sun-Thu, 8am-2am Fri & Sat; Ⓜ Albert).

★Chez Moeder Lambic   PUB
(☑02-544 16 99; www.moederlambic.com; Rue de Savoie 68; ⊙4pm-3am; Ⓜ Horta) An institution. Behind windows plastered with beer stickers, this tattered, quirky old brown *café* is the ultimate beer spot in Brussels. Sample some of its hundreds of brews while flipping through its collection of dog-eared comics.

CHIP CHAMPS

Frying since 1948, **Maison Antoine** (☑02-230 54 56; www.maisonantoine.be; Place Jourdan; chips €2.60-3; ⊙11.30am-1am Sun-Thu, to 2am Fri & Sat; Ⓜ Schuman) is a classic little *fritkot* (take-away chip kiosk) whose reputation as 'Brussels' best' is self-perpetuating. 'Best' or not, its chips are certainly top notch and such is their popularity that *cafés* on the surrounding square (including beautifully wrought-iron-fronted L'Autobus) allow *frites* eaters to sit and snack so long as they buy a drink. Handily central **Fritland** (☑02-514 06 27; www.fritland brussels.be; Rue Henri Maus 49; ⊙11am-1am Sun-Thu, 10am-dawn Fri & Sat; 🚊Bourse) keeps frying till the wee hours.

★ **Goupil le Fol** BAR

(☑ 02-511 13 96; www.goupillefol.com; Rue de la Violette 22; ☺ 4pm-2am Sun & Mon, 4pm-3am Tue-Sat; Ⓜ Gare Centrale) Overwhelming weirdness hits you as you acid-trip your way through this sensory overload of rambling passageways, ragged old sofas and inexplicable beverages mostly based on madly fruit-flavoured wines (no beer is served). Unmissable.

La Fleur en Papier Doré CAFE

(☑ 02-511 16 59; www.goudblommekeinpapier. be; Rue des Alexiens 53; ☺ 11am-midnight Tue-Sat, to 7pm Sun; 🚇 Bruxelles Central) The nicotine-stained walls of this tiny *café*, adored by artists and locals, are covered with writings, art and scribbles by Magritte and his surrealist pals, some of which were reputedly traded for free drinks. *'Ceci n'est pas un musée'*, quips a sign on the door reminding visitors to buy a drink and not just look around.

À la Mort Subite CAFE

(☑ 02-513 13 18; www.alamortsubite.com; Rue Montagne aux Herbes Potagères 7; ☺ 11am-1am Mon-Sat, noon-midnight Sun; Ⓜ Gare Centrale) An absolute classic unchanged since 1928, with lined-up wooden tables, arched mirror panels and entertainingly brusque service.

☆ Entertainment

L'Archiduc JAZZ

(☑ 02-512 06 52; www.archiduc.net; Rue Antoine Dansaert 6; ☺ 4pm-5am; 🚇 Bourse) This intimate, split-level art deco bar has been playing jazz since 1937. It's an unusual two-tiered circular space that can get incredibly packed but remains convivial. You might need to ring the doorbell. Saturday concerts (5pm) are free; Sunday brings in international talent and admission charges vary.

AB LIVE MUSIC

(Ancienne Belgique; ☑ 02-548 24 84; www.ab concerts.be; Blvd Anspach 110; 🚇 Bourse) The AB's two auditoriums are favourite venues for mid-level international rock bands and acts such as Jools Holland and Madeleine Peyroux, plus plenty of home-grown talent. The ticket office is located on Rue des Pierres. There's a good on-site bar-restaurant that opens at 6pm (bookings essential).

🔒 Shopping

Tourist-oriented shops selling chocolate, beer, lace and Atomium baubles stretch between the Grand Place and Manneken Pis. For better chocolate shops in calmer, grander settings, peruse the resplendent **Galeries St-Hubert** (☑ 02-545 09 90; www.grsh.be; Rue du Marché aux Herbes; Ⓜ Gare Centrale) or the upmarket Sablon area, or visit the daily flea market (p115). Antwerp more than Brussels is Belgium's fashion capital, but Rue Antoine Dansaert has several cutting-edge boutiques including **Stijl** (☑ 02-512 03 13; www.stijl.be; Rue Antoine Dansaert 74; ☺ 10.30am-6.30pm Mon-Sat; Ⓜ Ste-Catherine).

Supermarkets sell a range of Belgian beers relatively cheaply but for wider selections and the relevant glasses, try **Beermania** (☑ 02-512 17 88; www.beermania.be; Chaussée de Wavre 174; ☺ 11am-9pm Mon-Sat; Ⓜ Porte de Namur) or the very personal little **Délices et Caprices** (☑ 02-512 14 51; www.the -belgian-beer-tasting-shop.be; Rue des Bouchers 68; ☺ 2-8pm Thu-Sat & Mon; Ⓜ Gare Centrale).

COMIC-STRIP CULTURE

In Belgium, comic strips *(bandes dessinées)* are revered as the 'ninth art'. Serious comic fans might enjoy Brussels' comprehensive **Centre Belge de la Bande Dessinée** (Belgian Comic Strip Centre; ☑ 02-219 19 80; www.comicscenter.net; Rue des Sables 20; adult/ concession €10/7; ☺ 10am-6pm Tue-Sun; Ⓜ Rogier) in a distinctive Horta-designed art-nouveau building.

Dozens of cartoon murals enliven Brussels buildings. Comic shops include **Brüsel** (www.brusel.com; Blvd Anspach 100; ☺ 10.30am-6.30pm Mon-Sat, from noon Sun; 🚇 Bourse) and **Multi-BD** (☑ 02-513 72 35; www.multibd.com; Blvd Anspach 122-124; ☺ 10.30am-7pm Mon-Sat, 12.30-6.30pm Sun; 🚇 Bourse).

For an immersive Tintin experience, a trip to Louvain-la-Neuve's **Musée Hergé** (☑ 010-48 84 21; www.museeherge.com; Rue du Labrador 26; adult/child €9.50/5; ☺ 10.30am-5.30pm Tue-Fri, 10am-6pm Sat & Sun) is highly recommended. Trains from Brussels (€5.30, 50 minutes) generally require a change at Ottignies.

★ **Place du Jeu-de-Balle**
Flea Market   MARKET
(www.marcheauxpuces.be; Place du Jeu-de-Balle;
⊙ 6am-2pm Mon-Fri, 6am-3pm Sat & Sun; Ⓜ Porte
de Hal, 🚋 Lemonnier) The quintessential Ma-
rolles experience is haggling at this chaotic
flea market, established in 1919. Weekends
see it at its liveliest, but for the best bargains,
head here early morning midweek.

★ **Place du Châtelain Market**   MARKET
(Place du Châtelain; ⊙ afternoon Wed; Ⓜ Louise)
Fabulous food stalls cluster around an elongated, leafy square at this market. Cheese,
charcuterie, fresh fruit and veg, seasonal
fodder – truffles, mushrooms, berries and
so on – a Middle Eastern food van, Turkish
bread, vats of Congolese stew, a wine bar
and cake stalls: it's a true foodie heaven, well
worth a special trip.

★ **Gabriele**   VINTAGE
(📞 02-512 67 43; www.gabrielevintage.com; Rue
des Chartreux 27; ⊙ 1-7pm Mon & Tue, 11am-7pm
Wed-Sat; 🚋 Bourse) For amazing vintage finds,
try eccentric, elegant Gabriele. There's a gorgeous jumble of cocktail dresses, hats, Chinese shawls and accessories; only original
clothes from the '20s to the '80s are stocked.

ℹ Information

Exchange agency rates are usually best around
the Bourse. As well as the following there are
info counters at Brussels Airport and Bruxelles-
Midi station.

BIP (📞 02-563 63 99; bip.brussels; Rue Royale
2-4; ⊙ 9.30am-5.30pm Mon-Fri, 10am-6pm Sat
& Sun; Ⓜ Parc) Official Brussels-region tourist
office. Hotel bookings and lots of information.

Visit Brussels (📞 02-513 89 40; www.visit.
brussels; Hôtel de Ville, Grand Place; ⊙ 9am-
6pm; 🚋 Bourse) Visit Brussels has stacks
of city-specific information as well as handy
fold-out guides (independently researched) to
the best shops, restaurants and pubs in town.
The Rue Royale (📞 02-513 89 40; www.visit.
brussels; Rue Royale 2; ⊙ 9am-6pm; Ⓜ Parc)
office is much less crowded than the Grand
Place one. Here you'll also find the Arsène50
(www.arsene50.be; Rue Royale 2; ⊙ 12.30-5pm
Tue-Sat; Ⓜ Parc) desk, which provides great
discounts for cultural events.

ℹ Getting There & Away

BUS

Eurolines (📞 02-274 13 50; www.eurolines.be;
Rue du Progrès 80; 🚋 Gare du Nord) International bus service Eurolines has buses departing from Bruxelles-Nord train station.

WORTH A TRIP

BRUSSELS TO ANTWERP

Direct Brussels–Antwerp trains take
just over half an hour. But if you're not
in a hurry consider stopping en route
at a couple of other historic cities, not
more than a minor diversion by train:
Leuven (30 minutes) then Mechelen (22
minutes). In both towns the station is
around 15 minutes' walk from the centre. And both have imaginative accommodation, including hostels, if you're
too charmed to move on.

TRAIN

Bruxelles-Midi (Gare du Midi; luggage office
per day €2.50, luggage lockers
per article per day €2.50, luggage lockers
per 24hr small/large €3/4; ⊙ luggage office
6am-9pm; Ⓜ Gare du Midi, 🚆 Bruxelles-Midi)
is the main station for international connections; high-speed trains only stop here. Most
other mainline trains stop in quick succession
at Bruxelles-Midi, **Bruxelles-Central** (Gare
Centrale) and, except for Amsterdam trains,
also at **Bruxelles-Nord** (Gare du Nord). For all
enquiries, consult www.b-rail.be.

The following fares (one way, 2nd class) are for
standard trains from Bruxelles-Central:

DESTINA-TION	FARE (€)	DURATION (MIN)	FRE-QUENCY (HR)
Antwerp	7.30	35-49	5
Bruges	14.10	62	2
Ghent	8.90	36	2
Leuven	5.30	24-36	4
Luxembourg City	37.80	180	1
Mechelen	4.50	15-28	2
Mons	9.40	55	2
Ypres	17.50	105	1

ℹ Getting Around

TO/FROM BRUSSELS AIRPORT
Taxi

Fares start around €40. Very bad idea in rush-
hour traffic.

Train

Airport City Express (tickets €8.70;
⊙ 5.30am-12.20am) trains run four times
hourly to the city's three main stations,
Bruxelles-Nord (15 minutes), Bruxelles-Central
(€8.50, 20 minutes) and Bruxelles-Midi (25
minutes).

TO/FROM CHARLEROI AIRPORT

Around 6km north of Charleroi, **Charleroi Airport** (www.charleroi-airport.com; 🕾), also known as Brussels-South, is Belgium's main hub for budget airlines, notably Ryanair. Two or three **coaches** (www.brussels-city-shuttle.com; around €14; ☺7.50am-midnight) per hour take 55 minutes to Brussels.

BICYCLE

FietsPunt/PointVelo (🖉 02-513 04 09; www. recyclo.org; Carrefour de l'Europe 2; per 1/3 days €7.50/15; ☺7am-7pm Mon-Fri; 🚊 Brux-elles-Central) Rents long term: it's on the left as you leave Bruxelles-Central station by the (daytime-only) Madeleine exit.

Villo! (🖉 078-05 11 10; en.villo.be; subscription day/week €1.60/7.90) Has 180 automated pickup/drop-off short-term-rental stands. Credit card required; read the online instructions carefully.

PUBLIC TRANSPORT

STIB/MIVB (www.stib-mivb.be) tickets are sold at metro stations, newsagents and on buses and trams. Single-/five-/10-journey tickets valid for one hour from validation cost €2.10/8/14 including transfers. Unlimited one-/two-/three-day passes cost €7.50/14/18. Airport buses are excluded.

FLANDERS

Leuven

POP 97,600

Lively, self-confident Leuven (Louvain in French; www.leuven.be) is Flanders' oldest university town and home to the vast **Stella Artois brewery** (www.breweryvisits.com; Vuurkruisenlaan; adult/concession €8.50/7.50; ☺9am-7.30pm Tue-Sat). Its greatest attraction is a flamboyant 15th-century **Stadhuis** (Grote Markt 9; tours €4; ☺tours 3pm) lavished with exterior statuary. Other architectural attractions are patchy due to heavy damage sustained in 20th-century wars, but the iconic **university library** (University Library; http://bib.kuleuven.be; Monseigneur Ladeuzeplein 21; tower entrance €7; ☺tower 10am-5pm) FREE has been rebuilt. Twice. **Muntstraat** is a loveable medieval alley popular with locals and visitors alike and **Oude Markt** is a very lively square of wall-to-wall bars that hum till the wee hours.

The most interesting option for accommodation is the grand mansion housing **Oude Brouwerei Keyser Carel** (🖉 016-22 14 81; www.keysercarel.be; Lei 15; s/d €115/130), while homely **Leuven City Hostel** (🖉 016-84 30 33; www.leuvencityhostel.com; Ravenstraat 37; dm/d from €25/55; ☺reception 4-8pm; @🕾) and peaceful **Martin's Klooster Hotel** (🖉 016-21 31 41; www.martins-hotels.com; Onze-Lieve-Vrouwstraat 18; d €169-209; @🕾) are good, relatively central accommodation choices.

Terrace cafes surround the stadhuis, and perpetually packed, casually stylish restaurants and bars spill tables onto cosy flag-decked Munstraat.

Mechelen

POP 82,300

Belgium's religious capital, Mechelen (Malines in French) has the **St-Romboutskathedraal cathedral** (http://sintrombout storen.mechelen.be; Grote Markt; tower adult/youth €8/3; ☺1-6pm Mon-Fri, 10am-6pm Sat) FREE featuring a 97m, 15th-century tower that soars above a particularly memorable central market square. There are other splendid churches on Keizerstraat where the courthouse and theatre were both once royal palaces in the days when the Low Countries were effectively run from Mechelen. Other top sights include the brilliant **Speelgoedmuseum Toy Museum** (🖉 015-55 70 75; www.speelgoedmuseum. be; Nekkerstraat 21; adult/child €9.80/7.30; ☺10am-5pm Tue-Sun) and the **Schepenhuis gallery tower** (🖉 015-29 40 30; Steenweg 1) on IJzerenleen, a street of fine baroque facades leading towards the main station passing close to **Vismarkt**, the compact bar-cafe zone. There's a modern HI Hostel, the **Hostel De Zandpoort** (🖉 015-27 85 39; www.mechelen-hostel.com; Zandpoortvest 70; dm €23-26, tw €55-58; ☺check-in 5-10pm; 🅿🕾), or try stylish **Martins Patershof** (🖉 015-46 46 46; www.martinshotels.com; Karmelietenstraat 4; d €149-249; ❋🕾), set in a 1867 Franciscan monastery.

Mechelen's agricultural specialities include *witloof* (endives) and especially *asperges* (asparagus), prominent on restaurant menus mid-April to late June.

WORTH A TRIP

WATERLOO

Tourists have been swarming to Waterloo ever since Napoleon's 1815 defeat, a seminal event in European history. Inaugurated for the 2015 bicentenary, **Memorial 1815** (☑ 02-385 19 12; www.waterloo1815.be; Rte du Lion, Hameau du Lion; adult/child €16/13, with Wellington & Napoleon headquarters museums €19/15; ⊘ 9.30am-6.30pm Apr-Sep, 9.30am-5.30pm Oct-Mar) is a showpiece underground museum and visitor centre at the main battlefield area (known as Hameau du Lion). There's a detailed audio guide and some enjoyable technological effects. The climax is an impressive 3D film that sticks you right into the middle of the cavalry charges. It includes admission to various other battlefield attractions, including the Butte du Lion, a memorial hill from which you can survey the terrain, and the recently restored Hougoumont farmhouse that played a key part in the battle.

TEC bus W runs every 30 minutes from Ave Fonsny at Bruxelles-Midi to Braine-l'Alleud train station, passing through Waterloo town and stopping near Hameau du Lion (€3.20, one hour). If coming by train, get off at Braine-l'Alleud rather than awkwardly located Waterloo station, then switch to bus W to reach the battlefield.

Antwerp

POP 503,200

Belgium's second city and biggest port is Antwerp (Antwerpen/Anvers in Dutch/French) and without a doubt, this charming city is the country's capital of cool. It's long been a powerful magnet for everyone from fashion moguls and club queens to art lovers and diamond dealers. In the mid-16th century it was one of Europe's most important cities and home to baroque superstar painter Pieter Paul Rubens – there are numerous places to admire his works across the city.

⊙ Sights

◉ City Centre

⭐**Grote Markt**   SQUARE

As with every great Flemish city, Antwerp's medieval heart is a classic Grote Markt (Market Sq). Here the triangular, pedestrianised space features the voluptuous, baroque **Brabo Fountain** depicting Antwerp's giant-killing, hand-throwing legend. Flanked on two sides by very photogenic guildhalls, the square is dominated by an impressive Italo-Flemish Renaissance-style **stadhuis** (Town Hall; Grote Markt), completed in 1565.

Het Steen   CASTLE

(Steenplein) On a riverside knoll, Het Steen is a dinky but photogenic castle dating from 1200 and occupying the site of Antwerp's original Gallo-Roman settlement. Outside is a humorous **statue of Lange Wapper**, a tall folkloric 'peeping Tom' figure showing off his codpiece to two diminutive onlookers. Directly north, the misnamed **Maritime Park** is a long, open-sided wrought-iron shed displaying a historic barge collection. There is nothing to see inside the castle.

⭐**Onze-Lieve-Vrouwekathedraal**   CATHEDRAL

(☑ 03-213 99 51; www.dekathedraal.be; Handschoenmarkt; adult/reduced €6/4; ⊘ 10am-5pm Mon-Fri, to 3pm Sat, 1-4pm Sun) Belgium's finest Gothic cathedral was 169 years in the making (1352–1521). Wherever you wander in Antwerp, its gracious, 123m-high spire has a habit of popping unexpectedly into view and it rarely fails to prompt a gasp of awe. The sight is particularly well framed when looking up Pelgrimstraat in the afternoon light.

⭐**Museum Plantin-Moretus**   HISTORIC BUILDING

(☑ 03-221 14 50; www.museumplantinmoretus.be; Vrijdag Markt 22; adult/reduced/child €8/6/free; ⊘ 10am-5pm Tue-Sun) Giving a museum Unesco World Heritage status might seem odd – until you've seen this astonishing, recently renovated place. Once home to the world's first industrial printing works, it's been a museum since 1876. The medieval building and 1622 courtyard garden alone would be worth a visit, but the world's oldest printing press, priceless manuscripts and original type sets make for a giddy experience indeed. Other highlights include the 1640 library, a bookshop dating to 1700 and rooms lined with gilt leather.

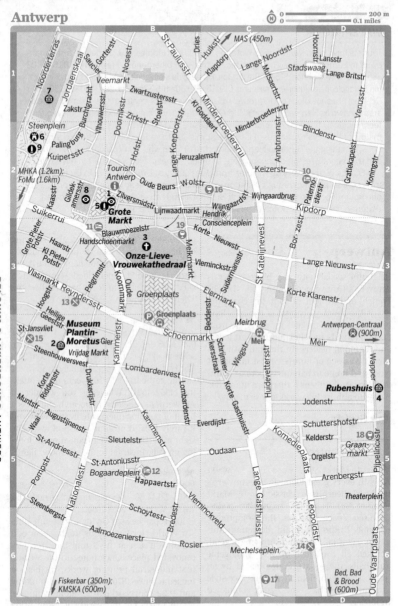

★ **Rubenshuis**   MUSEUM
(☎03-201 15 55; www.rubenshuis.be; Wapper 9-11; adult/concession €8/6, audioguide €2; ⊙10am-5pm Tue-Sun) The 1611 building was built as home and studio by celebrated painter Pieter Paul Rubens. Rescued from ruins in 1937, and extensively and sensitively restored, the building is a delightfully indulgent one, with baroque portico, rear facade and exquisite formal garden. The furniture all dates from Rubens' era, although it's not part of the original decor. Fourteen Rubens canvases

Antwerp

are displayed, along with some wonderful period ephemera, such as the metal frame of a ruff collar and a linen press.

⭐ **Antwerpen-Centraal**   LANDMARK
(Koningin Astridplein 27) With its neo-Gothic facade, vast main hall and splendidly proportioned dome, the 1905 Antwerpen-Centraal train station is one of the city's premier landmarks. It was rated by *Newsweek* as one of the world's five most beautiful stations. It's also very practical, the multilevel platforms having had a full 21st-century makeover.

◉ 't Zuid

South of the centre, this is a conspicuously prosperous area dotted with century-old architecture, hip bars, fine restaurants and museums. The classic centrepiece art gallery, **KMSKA** (www.kmska.be; Leopold de Waelplaats), is closed for renovation until late 2017, but meanwhile there's still **MHKA** (☑03-238 59 60; www.muhka.be; Leuvenstraat 32; adult/child €10/1; ⊙11am-6pm Tue-Sun, to 9pm Thu) for contemporary conceptual art and outstanding **FoMu** (FotoMuseum; ☑03-242 93 00; www.fotomuseum.be; Waalsekaai 47; adult/child €8/3; ⊙10am-6pm Tue-Sun) for photography.

◉ 't Eilandje

⭐ **MAS**   MUSEUM
(Museum aan de Stroom; ☑03-338 44 00; www.mas.be; Hanzestedenplaats; adult/reduced €10/8; ⊙10am-5pm Tue-Sun, to 6pm Sat & Sun Apr-Oct) Opened in 2011, MAS is a 10-storey complex that redefines the idea of a museum-gallery. Floors are designed around big-idea themes using a barrage of media, from old master paintings through to tribal artefacts to video installations.

🛏 Sleeping

Antwerp offers a staggering range of stylish, well-priced B&Bs. Many are listed on www.bedandbreakfast.eu.

Pulcinella   HOSTEL €
(☑03-234 03 14; www.jeugdherbergen.be; Bogaardeplein 1; dm €25-28, tw €60-63; @ 🐱) This giant, tailor-made HI hostel is hard to beat for its Fashion District location and cool modernist decor. It's a little cheaper for HI members and under-30s; breakfast is included.

⭐ **Bed, Bad & Brood**   B&B €€
(☑03-248 15 39; www.bbantwerp.com; Justitiestraat 43; s/d/q €70/80/120, budget s/d €57/68; ⊖@) In a 1910, belle époque–era townhouse near the vast Gerechtshof (former courthouse), this B&B impresses with authentic wooden floors, high ceilings and beautifully eclectic furniture. Rooms are remarkably spacious and comfortable for the price – all but the budget rooms have a bath, and the family room is a separate two-bedder tucked away up a mysterious little staircase.

Hotel O   HOTEL €€
(☑03-500 89 50; www.hotelokathedral.com; Handschoenmarkt 3; s €99, d €119-159) The immediate selling point here is an unbeatable location, staring across a square at the cathedral frontage. A little foyer bar lined with 1950s radios and audio equipment leads to midsize rooms with black and moody decor, giant Rubens reproductions spilling onto the ceilings, and baths in black-framed glass boxes.

⭐ **De Witte Lelie**   DESIGN HOTEL €€€
(☑03-226 19 66; www.dewittelelie.be; Keizerstraat 16-18; d €245-525; ⊖❄🐱) A trio of renovated 16th-century mansions houses 10 luxurious rooms at this elegant family-run hotel. Design choices are bold, mixing 20th-century

THE FASHION DISTRICT

Antwerp may seem far more sartorially laid-back than fashion heavyweights Paris or Milan, but it punches above its weight. In the space of just a few streets you'll find dozens of designer boutiques, along with a variety of streetwear, end-of-line discounters, upmarket vintage and designer consignment shops and more mainstream labels. Few places in the world have such a convenient and covetable concentration.

The tourist office has a fashion-walk directory pamphlet. Or simply stroll Nationalestraat, Lombardenvest, Huidevettersstraat and Schuttershofstraat, not missing Kammenstraat for streetwear and up-and-coming designers.

pieces with grand original features and each of the rooms has a distinct look and layout. The public areas – two salons, a reading room, a pretty courtyard and a super-sexy private bar – are incredibly lavish considering the hotel's handful of guests.

Eating

Locals head to 't Zuid to dine, with restaurants lining Leopold de Waelplaats, Vlaamsekaai and Marnixplaats and fanning out through surrounding streets.

LOA INTERNATIONAL, FAST FOOD €

(☑03-291 64 85; www.loa.be; Hoogstraat 77; dishes €5-10; ☺noon-10pm Mon & Wed-Thu, to 11pm Fri & Sat, to 8pm Sun) International 'street food' – pad thai, Moroccan pancakes, tortillas, croquettes – are made with love and care in this bright cafe. There's complimentary mint tea to sip with your meal and front-row seats onto the square.

De Groote Witte Arend BELGIAN €€

(☑03-233 50 33; www.degrootewittearend.be; Reyndersstraat 18; mains €15-24; ☺11.30am-midnight, kitchen 11.30am-3pm & 5-10pm; ☜) Retaining the Tuscan stone arcade of a 15th- and 17th-century convent building, as well as a little family chapel, this place combines the joys of a good beer bar with the satisfaction of well-cooked, sensibly priced Flemish home cuisine, notably *stoemp* (potato hash), *stoofvlees/carbonade* (beef, beer and onion

stew) and huge portions of rabbit in rich Westmalle sauce.

Fiskebar SEAFOOD €€

(☑03-257 13 57; http://fiskebar.be; Marnixplaats 12; mains €24-36; ☺restaurant 6-8.30pm Mon-Thu, 6-9.30pm Fri, noon-3pm & 6-9.30pm Sat, noon-3pm & 6-8pm Sun) Locals swear that Fiskebar serves Antwerp's best seafood, meaning there's always an almighty crush for tables in this bustling, fashionably dishevelled former fishmongers' shop. If you can't get a booking, try its oyster bar next door, which serves a more limited selection and works without reservations.

★Het Gebaar BELGIAN €€€

(☑03-232 37 10; www.hetgebaar.be; Leopoldstraat 24; mains €34-48; ☺noon-5.30pm) Chef Roger van Damme only does fancy and only does lunch. At the entrance to Antwerp's petite botanical gardens, the former gardener's house is a deeply romantic setting to write off an afternoon. The Flemish stew and tartars retain the essence of the original but use the best produce and are prettily presented. Highly theatrical desserts are a house speciality.

🍷 Drinking & Nightlife

To sound like a local, stride into a pub and ask for a *bolleke*. Don't worry, that means a 'little bowl' (ie glass) of De Koninck, the city's favourite ale. Cheap places to try it include classic *cafés* **Oud Arsenaal** (Pijpelincxstraat 4; ☺10am-10pm Wed-Fri, 7.30am-7.30pm Sat & Sun), **De Kat** (☑03-233 08 92; www.facebook.com/cafeDeKat; Wolstraat 22; ☺noon-2am Mon-Sat, 5pm-2am Sun) and the livelier **Pelikaan** (Melkmarkt 14; ☺8.30am-3am). Mechleseplein bars including **Korsåkov** (☑0485 46 45 06; facebook.com/vokasrov; Mechelseplein 21; ☺11am-3am Mon-Wed, to 4am Thu, to 5am Fri & Sat, noon-midnight Sun) open till very late as do countless other great options around KMSKA in the 't Zuid area.

ⓘ Information

Tourism Antwerp (☑03-232 01 03; www.visitantwerpen.be; Grote Markt 13; ☺9am-5.45pm Mon-Sat, to 4.45pm Sun) Tourism Antwerp has a large, central office with helpful staff – pick up maps, buy tram/bus passes and book tickets here. There is also a booth on the ground floor of Antwerpen-Centraal station.

❶ Getting There & Away

BUS
Buses for Lier and many other destinations start from Antwerpen-Berchem bus station, although trains are generally much faster.

TRAIN
Regular services to Bruges (€14.80, 75 minutes), Brussels (€7.30, 35 to 49 minutes) and Ghent (€9.40, 46 minutes). High speed service to Amsterdam.

❶ Getting Around
Franklin Rooseveltplaats and Koningin Astridplein are hubs for the integrated network of De Lijn (www.delijn.be) buses and trams (some running underground metro-style).

Ghent

POP 247,500

Ghent (www.visitgent.be) is one of Europe's greatest discoveries – small enough to feel cosy but big enough to stay vibrant. It has enough medieval frivolity to create a spectacle but retains a gritty industrial edge that keeps things 'real'. Tourists remain surprisingly thin on the ground, yet with its fabulous canalside architecture, wealth of quirky bars and some of Belgium's most fascinating museums, this is a city you really won't want to miss.

◉ Sights

Most major sights are strolling distance from Korenmarkt, the westernmost of three interlinked squares that form the heart of Ghent's historic core.

St-Baafskathedraal   CATHEDRAL
(www.sintbaafskathedraal.be;   St-Baafsplein;
⊙8.30am-6pm Mon-Sat, 10am-6pm Sun Apr-Oct, to 5pm Nov-Mar) St-Baafs cathedral's towering interior has some fine stained glass and an unusual combination of brick vaulting with stone tracery. A €0.20 leaflet guides you round the cathedral's numerous art treasures, including a big original Rubens opposite the stairway that leads down into the partly muralled crypts. However, most visitors come to see just one magnificent work – the Van Eycks' 1432 'Flemish Primitive' masterpiece, *The Adoration of the Mystic Lamb* (adult/child/audio guide €4/1.50/1).

Belfort   HISTORIC BUILDING
(☑09-375 31 61; www.belfortgent.be; Botermarkt; adult/concession/child €8/2.70/free; ⊙10am-6pm) Ghent's soaring, Unesco-listed, 14th-century belfry is topped by a large dragon. That's a weathervane not a fire breather and it's become something of a city mascot. You'll meet two previous dragon incarnations on the climb to the top (mostly by lift) but other than some bell-making exhibits, the real attraction is the view. Enter through the Lakenhalle, Ghent's cloth hall that was left half-built in 1445 and only completed in 1903.

Gravensteen   CASTLE
(http://gravensteen.stad.gent;   St-Veerleplein;
adult/concession/child €10/6/free; ⊙10am-6pm Apr-Oct, 9am-5pm Nov-Mar) The counts of Flanders' quintessential 12th-century stone castle comes complete with moat, turrets and arrow slits. It's all the more remarkable considering that during the 19th century the site was converted into a cotton mill. Meticulously restored since, the interior sports the odd suit of armour, a guillotine and torture devices. The relative lack of furnishings is compensated with a hand-held 45-minute movie guide, which sets a tongue-in-cheek historical costumed drama in the rooms, prison pit and battlements.

★MSK   GALLERY
(Museum voor Schone Kunsten; ☑09-323 67 00; www.mskgent.be; Citadelpark; adult/youth/child €8/2/free; ⊙9.30am-5.30pm Tue-Fri, 10am-6pm Sat & Sun) Styled like a Greek temple, this superb 1903 fine-art gallery introduces a veritable A-Z of great Belgian and Low Countries' painters from the 14th to mid-20th centuries. Highlights include a happy family of coffins by Magritte, Luminist canvases by Emile Claus, and Pieter Breughel the Younger's 1621 *Dorpsadvocaat* – a brilliant portrait of a village lawyer oozing with arrogance. English-language explanation cards are available in each room.

---

❶ PARTY TIME IN GHENT

During mid-July's raucous Gentse Feesten (http://gentsefeesten.stad. gent; ⊙Jul) festival, the city's many squares become venues for a variety of street-theatre performances and there are big associated techno and jazz festivals. Those wanting a merrily boozy party atmosphere will love it. But consider avoiding Ghent at this time if you don't.

Ghent Centre

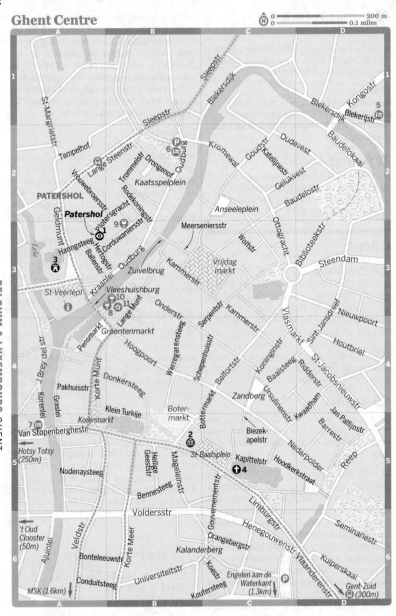

★ **The Adoration of the Mystic Lamb**   ARTWORK

(Het Lam Gods; www.sintbaafskathedraal.be; St- Baafskathedraal; adult/child/audio guide €4/ 1.50/1; ⊗ 9.30am-5pm Mon-Sat, 1-5pm Sun Apr- Oct, 10.30am-4pm Mon-Sat, 1-4pm Sun Nov-Mar) Formidable queues form to see *The Adoration of the Mystic Lamb (De Aanbidding van het Lams God)*, a lavish representation of medieval religious thinking that is one of

Ghent Centre

the earliest-known oil paintings. Completed in 1432, it was painted as an altarpiece by the Flemish Primitive artists, the Van Eyck brothers, and has 20 panels (originally the interior panels were displayed only on important religious occasions, but these days they're always open to view).

🛏 Sleeping

Ghent offers innovative accommodation in all budget ranges. Websites www.gent-accommodations.be and www.bedandbreakfast-gent.be help you gauge availability in the city's numerous appealing B&Bs.

★ Uppelink HOSTEL €
(☑09-279 44 77; www.hosteluppelink.com; Sint-Michielsplein 21; dm €21-37) Within a classic step-gabled canalside house, the show-stopping attraction at this super-central new hostel is the unbeatable view of Ghent's main towers as seen from the breakfast room and from the biggest, cheapest dorms. Smaller rooms have little view, if any.

Hostel 47 HOSTEL €
(☑0478 71 28 27; www.hostel47.com; Blekerijstraat 47-51; dm €26.50-29.50, d/tr €66/€90; ⊕) Unusually calm yet pretty central, this inviting hostel has revamped a high-ceilinged historic house with virginal white walls, spacious bunk rooms and designer fittings. Free lockers and cursory breakfast with Nespresso coffee; no bar.

★ Engelen aan de Waterkant B&B €€
(☑0476 40 25 23; www.engelenaandewaterkant.be; Ter Platen 30; r €110) Two 'angel' rooms are an opportunity for the interior-designer owner to experiment and for guests to soak up the special atmosphere in a 1900 townhouse overlooking the tree-lined canal.

★ Simon Says GUESTHOUSE €€
(☑09-233 03 43; www.simon-says.be; Sluizeken 8; d from €130; ☎) Two fashionably styled guest rooms above an excellent coffee shop in a brightly coloured corner house with art nouveau facade.

🍴 Eating

Enchanting Patershol is a web of twisting cobbled lanes with old-world houses that are now interspersed with small restaurants. Others jostle for summer terrace space on Graslei's gorgeous canalside terrace. There's fast food around Korenmarkt and great-value Turkish options along Sleepstraat. Numerous vegetarian and organic choices feature on the tourist office's free *Veggieplan Gent* guide map.

't Oud Clooster CAFE €
(☑09-233 78 02; www.toudclooster.be; Zwarte-zusterstraat 5; mains €12-21; ⊕11.45am-2.30pm & 6-10.30pm Mon-Fri, 11.45am-2.30pm & 5.30-10.30pm Sat, 5.30-9.30pm Sun) Mostly candle-lit at night, this atmospheric double-level 'pratcafe' is built into sections of what was long ago a nunnery, hence the sprinkling of religious statues and cherub lampholders. Well-priced *café* food is presented with unexpected style.

🍸 Drinking & Entertainment

Try the snug Hot Club de Gand (☑09-256 71 99; www.hotclub.gent; Schuddevisstraatje - Groentenmarkt 15b; ⊕3pm-late) for live jazz, gyspy or blues music; Hotsy Totsy (☑09-224 20 12; www.facebook.com/Hotsy.Totsy.Gent; Hoogstraat 1; ⊕6pm-1am Mon-Fri, 8pm-2am Sat & Sun, opens 8pm Jul & Aug) for free Thursday jazz; and beautifully panelled Rococo (☑09-224 30 35; Corduwaniersstraat 5; ⊕9pm-late Tue-Sun) for candle-lit conversation. Het Waterhuis aan de Bierkant (☑09-225 06 80; www.waterhuisaandebierkant.be; Groentenmarkt 12; ⊕11am-1am) has the best beer choice including their own brews, while 't Dreupelkot (☑09-224 21 20; www.dreupelkot.be; Groentenmarkt 12; ⊕4pm-late Mon-Sat) is a traditional *jenever* bar with a hundred concoctions.

ℹ Information

Ghent Tourist Office (☑ 09-266 56 60; www.
visit.gent.be; Oude Vismijn, St-Veerleplein
5; ⊙ 9.30am-6.30pm mid-Mar–mid-Oct, to
4.30pm mid-Oct–mid-Mar) Very helpful for free
maps and accommodation bookings.

ℹ Getting There & Away

BUS

Some longer distance buses depart from **Gent-
Zuid bus station** (Woodrow Wilsonplein), others
from various points around Gent-St-Pieters train
station.

TRAIN

Gent-Dampoort, 1km west of the old city, is the
handiest station with useful trains to the following destinations:

Antwerp (€9.40, fast/slow 42/64 minutes,
three per hour)

Bruges (€6.50, 36 minutes, hourly)

Gent-St-Pieters, 2.5km south of the centre and
Ghent's main station, has more choices:

Bruges (€6.50, fast/slow 24/42 minutes, five
per hour)

Brussels (€8.90, 36 minutes, twice hourly)

ℹ Getting Around

BICYCLE

Biker (☑ 09-224 29 03; www.bikerfietsen.be;
Steendam 16; per day €9; ⊙ 9am-12.30pm &
1.30-6pm Tue-Sat)

Max Mobiel (☑ 09-242 80 40; www.max
-mobiel.be; Vokselslaan 27; per half-day/day/
week €7/10/30) Two minutes' walk south of
Gent-St-Pieters station. Branch kiosk at Gent-
Dampoort station.

BUS & TRAM

Tickets are cheaper bought from machines, De
Lijn (www.delijn.be) or the **ticket kiosk** (www.
delijn.be; ⊙ 7am-1.30pm & 2-7pm Mon-Fri)
outside Gent-St-Pieters. **Tram 1** runs from
Gent-St-Pieters to and through the centre, passing walkably close to most major sites.

Bruges

POP 117,000

Cobblestone lanes, dreamy canals, soaring
spires and whitewashed almshouses combine to make central Bruges (Brugge in
Dutch) one of Europe's most picture-perfect
historic cities. The only problem is that
everyone knows of these charms, and the
place gets mobbed.

◉ Sights

The real joy of Bruges is simply wandering
alongside the canals, soaking up the atmosphere. To avoid the worst crowds, explore
east of pretty Jan van Eyckplein.

Markt   SQUARE

The heart of ancient Bruges, the old market
square is lined with pavement cafes beneath
step-gabled facades. The buildings aren't
always quite as medieval as they look, but
together they create a fabulous scene and
even the neo-Gothic **post office** is architecturally magnificent. The scene is dominated
by the **Belfort**, Belgium's most famous belfry, whose iconic octagonal tower is arguably
better appreciated from afar than by climbing 366 claustrophobic steps to the top.

Historium   MUSEUM

(☑ 050-27 03 11; www.historium.be; Markt; adult/
child €13/7.50; ⊙ 10am-6pm) The Historium occupies a neo-Gothic building on the northern
side of the Markt. Taking visitors back to 1435,
it is a multimedia experience, claiming to be
more medieval movie than museum. The
'immersive' one-hour audio and video tour
aims to take you back to medieval Bruges: a
fictional love story gives narrative structure,
and you can nose around Van Eyck's studio,
among other pseudo historic experiences.

Brugse Vrije   HISTORIC BUILDING

(Burg 11a; included in Stadhuis entry; ⊙ 9.30am-
noon & 1.30-5pm) Most eye-catching with its
early baroque gabling, gilt highlights and
golden statuettes, this was once the palace
of the 'Liberty of Bruges', the large autonomous territory and administrative body that
ruled from Bruges (1121–1794). Much of the
building is still used for city offices, but you
can visit the former aldermen's room, the
Renaissancezaal, to admire its remarkable
1531 carved chimney piece.

Stadhuis   HISTORIC BUILDING

(City Hall; Burg 12; adult/child €4/3; ⊙ 9.30am-
5pm) The beautiful 1420 stadhuis features
a fanciful facade that's second only to Leuven's for exquisitely turreted Gothic excess.
Inside, an audio guide explains numerous
portraits in somewhat excessive detail before leading you upstairs to the astonishing
Gotische Zaal (Gothic Hall). Few rooms
anywhere achieve such a jaw-dropping first
impression as this dazzling hall with its
polychrome ceiling, hanging vaults, romantically historic murals and upper frieze of
gilt figures.

★ **Groeningemuseum** GALLERY
(☎ 050-44 87 43; www.museabrugge.be; Dijver 12; adult/concession €8/6; ◷ 9.30am-5pm Tue-Sun) Bruges' most celebrated art gallery boasts an astonishingly rich collection whose strengths are in superb Flemish Primitive and Renaissance works, depicting the conspicuous wealth of the city with glitteringly realistic artistry. In room 2 are meditative works including Jan Van Eyck's 1436 radiant masterpiece *Madonna with Canon George Van der Paele* (1436) and the *Madonna* by the Master of the Embroidered Foliage, where the rich fabric of the Madonna's robe meets the 'real' foliage at her feet with exquisite detail.

Begijnhof HISTORIC BUILDING
(Wijngaardstraat; ◷ 6.30am-6.30pm) `FREE`
Bruges' delightful *begijnhof* originally dates from the 13th century. Although the last *begijn* has long since passed away, today residents of the pretty, whitewashed garden complex include a convent of Benedictine nuns. Despite the hordes of summer tourists, the *begijnhof* remains a remarkably tranquil haven. In spring, a carpet of daffodils adds to the quaintness of the scene. Outside the 1776 gateway bridge lies a tempting, if predictably tourist-priced, array of terraced restaurants, lace shops and waffle peddlers.

🖝 Tours

Canal Tour BOATING
(☎ 050-33 32 93; www.boottochten-brugge.be; adult/child €8/4; ◷ 10am-6pm Mar–mid-Nov) Taking a Canal Tour is a must. Yep, it's touristy, but what isn't in Bruges? Viewing the city from the water gives it a totally different feel than by foot. Cruise down Spiegelrei towards Jan Van Eyckplein and it's possible to imagine Venetian merchants entering the city centuries ago and meeting under the slender turret of the Poortersloge building up ahead.

🛏 Sleeping

Almost all options can get seriously overbooked from Easter to October and over Christmas. Things get especially tough at weekends when two-night minimum stays are often required. Many cheaper B&Bs charge around €10 per room less if you stay more than one night.

't Keizershof HOTEL €
(☎ 050-33 87 28; www.hotelkeizershof.be; Oostermeers 126; s €40-50, d €54-65; P ☎) Remarkably tasteful and well kept for this price, the seven simple rooms with shared bathrooms are above a former brasserie-cafe decorated with old radios (now used as the breakfast room). Free parking.

Bauhaus HOSTEL €
(St Christopher's Hostel; ☎ 050-34 10 93; www.bauhaus.be; Langestraat 145; dm €21-31, d €87-97; @ ☎) One of Belgium's most popular hangouts for young travellers, this backpacker 'village' incorporates a hostel, apartments, a nightclub, internet cafe and a little chill-out room that's well hidden behind the reception and laundrette section at Langestraat 145. Simple and slightly cramped dorms are operated with key cards; hotel-section double rooms have private shower cubicles; bike hire is also available.

★ **B&B SintNik** B&B €€
(☎ 050-61 03 08; www.sintnik.be; St-Niklaasstraat 18; s €125-155, d €135-165; ☎) Room 1 has a claw-foot bath and antique glass panel, but it's the other two rooms' remarkable Pisa-like belfry views that make this welcoming B&B so special and popular.

★ **B&B Dieltiens** B&B €€
(☎ 050-33 42 94; www.bedandbreakfastbruges.be; Waalsestraat 40; s €60-80, d €70-90, tr €90-115) Old and new art fills this lovingly restored classical mansion, which remains an appealingly real home run by charming musician hosts. Superbly central yet quiet. It also operates a holiday flat (from €75 per night) nearby in a 17th-century house.

★ **Guesthouse Nuit Blanche** B&B €€€
(☎ 0494 40 04 47; www.bb-nuitblanche.com; Groeninge 2; d €175-195) Pay what you like, nowhere else in Bruges can get you a more romantic location than this fabulous B&B, which started life as a 15th-century tannery. It oozes history, retaining original Gothic fireplaces, stained-glass roundels and some historic furniture, while bathrooms and beds are luxury-hotel standard.

★ **B&B Huyze Hertsberge** B&B €€€
(☎ 050-33 35 42; www.bruges-bedandbreakfast.be; Hertsbergestraat 8; d €165-175) Very spacious and oozing good taste, this late-17th-century house has a gorgeous period salon decked with antiques and sepia photos of the charming owner's great-great-grandparents (who first moved in here in 1901). The four guest rooms are comfortably grand, each with at least partial views of the tranquil little canalside garden.

Bruges

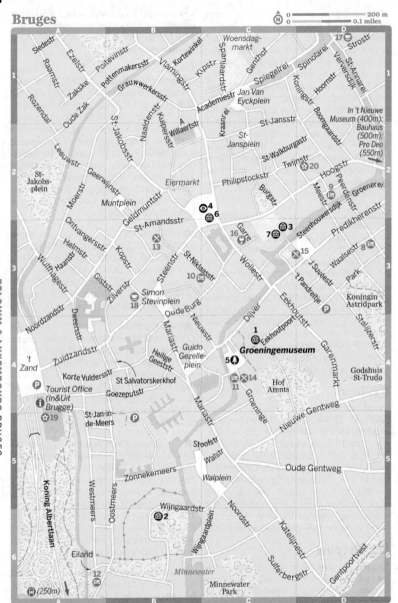

✕ Eating

Den Gouden Karpel SEAFOOD €

(📞050-33 33 89; www.dengoudenkarpel.be; Vismarkt 9-11; dishes from €4; ⊙11am-6pm Tue-Sat) Takeaway or eat in, this sleek little *café*–bar is a great location for a jumpingly fresh seafood lunch, right by the fish market. Crab sandwiches, smoked salmon salads, shrimp croquettes and oysters are on the menu.

Bruges

★ **De Stove** INTERNATIONAL €€
(☑050-33 78 35; www.restaurantdestove.be; Kleine St-Amandsstraat 4; mains €19-36, menu without/with wine €51/69; ⊙7-9pm Fri-Tue, plus noon-1.30pm Sun) Just 20 seats keep this gem intimate. Fish caught daily is the house speciality, but the monthly changing menu also includes the likes of wild boar fillet on oyster mushrooms. Everything, from the bread to the ice cream, is homemade. Despite perennially rave reviews, this calm, one-room, family restaurant remains friendly, reliable and inventive, without a hint of tourist-tweeness.

★ **In 't Nieuwe Museum** CAFE €€
(☑050-33 12 80; www.nieuw-museum.com; Hooistraat 42; mains €17-25; ⊙6-11pm Fri-Tue, plus 12.30-2.30pm Sun) So called because of the museum-like collection of brewery plaques, money boxes and other mementos of *café* life adorning the walls, this family-owned local favourite serves succulent meat cooked on a 17th-century open fire. Specials include veggie burgers, eel dishes, ribs, steaks and creamy *vispannetje* (fish casserole).

★ **Pro Deo** BELGIAN €€
(☑050-33 73 55; www.bistroprodeo.be; Langestraat 161; mains €17-27; ⊙11.45am-1.45pm & 6-9.30pm Tue-Fri, 6-10pm Sat) A snug and romantic restaurant in a 16th-century whitewashed gabled building. The owner couple brings a personal touch, and serve up superb Belgian dishes such as *stoofvlees* (traditional stew).

★ **Den Gouden Harynck** INTERNATIONAL €€€
(☑050-33 76 37; www.goudenharynck.be; Groeninge 25; set lunch menu €45, midweek dinner €65, surprise menu €95; ⊙noon-1.30pm & 7-8.30pm Tue-Fri, 7-8.30pm Sat) Behind an ivy-clad facade, this uncluttered Michelin-starred restaurant garners consistent praise and won't hurt the purse quite as severely as certain better-known competitors. A lovely location: both central and secluded; exquisite dishes might include noisettes of venison topped with lardo and quince purée or seed-crusted fillet of bream.

🍷 **Drinking & Nightlife**

Beer-specialist *cafés* include **'t Brugs Beertje** (☑050-33 96 16; www.brugsbeertje.be; Kemelstraat 5; ⊙4pm-midnight Mon, Thu & Sun, to 1am Fri & Sat) and alley-hidden **De Garre** (☑050-34 10 29; www.degarre.be; Garre 1; ⊙noon-midnight Sun-Thu, noon-12.30am Fri, 11am-12.30am Sat) serving its own fabulous 11% Garre house brew. Old-world classic **Herberg Vlissinghe** (☑050-34 37 37; www.cafevlissinghe.be; Blekerstraat 2; ⊙11am-10pm Wed-Sat, to 7pm Sun) dates from 1515. Eiermarkt, just north of Markt, has many plain but lively bars, with DJs and seemingly endless happy hours.

☆ **Entertainment**

★ **Retsin's Lucifernum** LIVE MUSIC
(☑0476 35 06 51; www.lucifernum.be; Twijnstraat 6-8; admission incl drink €10; ⊙8-11pm Sun) A former Masonic lodge owned by a self-proclaimed vampire: ring the bell on a Sunday night, pass the voodoo temple and hope you're invited inside where an otherworldly candle-lit bar may be serving potent rum cocktails and serenading you with live Latin music. Or maybe not. It's always a surprise. Don't miss the graves in the tropical garden.

Concertgebouw CONCERT VENUE
(☑070-22 33 02; www.concertgebouw.be; 't Zand 34; tickets from €10) Bruges' stunning 21st-century concert hall is the work of architects Paul Robbrecht and Hilde Daem and takes

its design cues from the city's three famous towers and red bricks. Theatre, classical music and dance are regularly staged. The tourist office is situated at street level.

ℹ Information

There are two offices; both sell extensive €2 guide booklets and €0.50 city maps.

Tourist Information Counter (☑ 050-44 46 46; www.visitbruges.be; Train Station; ⊙10am-5pm)

Tourist Office (In&Uit Brugge) (☑ 050-44 46 46; www.visitbruges.be; 't Zand 34; ⊙10am-5pm Mon-Sat, 10am-2pm Sun)

ℹ Getting There & Away

Bruges' train station is about 1.5km south of the Markt, a lovely walk via the Begijnhof.

Antwerp (€14.80, 75 minutes) Twice hourly.

Brussels (€14.10, one hour) Twice hourly.

Ghent (€6.50, fast/slow 24/42 minutes) Five hourly, two continue to more central Gent-Dampoort.

Ypres (Ieper in Dutch) Take a train to Roeselare (€5, fast/slow 22/33 minutes), then bus 94 or 95: both buses pass key WWI sites en route.

ℹ Getting Around

BICYCLE

B-Bike (☑ 0479 971 28; www.b-bike.be; Zand Parking 26; per hr/day €5/15; ⊙10am-7pm Apr-Oct)

Rijwielhandel Erik Popelier (☑ 050-34 32 62; www.fietsenpopelier.be; Mariastraat 26; per hr/half-/full day €5/10/15, tandem €10/20/30; ⊙10am-6pm) Good bicycles for adults and kids; helmets for hire, free map, no deposit.

WHAT'S A BEGIJNHOF?

Usually enclosed around a central garden, a *begijnhof* (*béguinage* in French) is a pretty cluster of historic houses originally built to house lay sisters. The idea originated in the 12th century when many such women were left widowed by their crusader-knight husbands. Today 14 of Flanders' historic *begijnhoven* have been declared Unesco World Heritage Sites with great examples at Diest, Lier, Turnhout, Kortrijk and Bruges, which also has dozens of smaller *godshuizen* (almshouses).

BUS

To get from the train station to Markt, take any bus marked 'Centrum'. For the way back, buses stop at Biekorf, just northwest of Markt on Kuiperstraat.

Ypres

POP 35,100

Only the hardest of hearts are unmoved by historic Ypres (Ieper in Dutch). In the Middle Ages it was an important cloth town ranking alongside Bruges and Ghent. In WWI some 300,000 Allied soldiers died in the 'Salient', a bow-shaped bulge that formed the front line around town. Ypres remained unoccupied by German forces, but was utterly flattened by bombardment. After the war, the beautiful medieval core was convincingly rebuilt and the restored Ypres Lakenhalle is today one of the most spectacular buildings in Belgium. Most tourism still revolves around WWI; the Salient is dotted with cemeteries, memorials, bunkers and war museums.

◉ Sights

◉ Central Ypres

★ **In Flanders Fields**   MUSEUM

(☑ 057-23 92 20; www.inflandersfields.be; Lakenhalle, Grote Markt 34; adult/under 26yr/child €9/5/4; ⊙10am-6pm Apr-mid-Nov, to 5pm Tue-Sun mid-Nov-Mar) No museum gives a more balanced yet moving and user-friendly introduction to WWI history. It's a multi-sensory experience combining soundscapes, videos, well-chosen exhibits and interactive learning stations at which you 'become' a character and follow his/her progress through the wartime period. An electronic 'identity' bracelet activates certain displays.

Lakenhalle   HISTORIC BUILDING

(Cloth Hall; Grote Markt 34) Dominating the Grote Markt, the enormous reconstructed Lakenhalle is one of Belgium's most impressive buildings. Its 70m-high belfry has the vague appearance of a medieval Big Ben. The original version was completed in 1304 beside the Ieperslee, a river that, now covered over, once allowed ships to sail right up to the Lakenhalle to unload their cargoes of wool. These were stored beneath the high gables of the 1st floor, where you'll find the unmissable In Flanders Fields museum.

Menin Gate MEMORIAL
(Menenpoort) A block east of Grote Markt, the famous Menin Gate is a huge stone gateway straddling the main road at the city moat. It's inscribed with the names of 54,896 'lost' British and Commonwealth WWI troops whose bodies were never found.

Ypres Salient

Many WWI sites are in rural locations that are awkward to reach without a car or tour bus. But the following are all within 600m of Ypres–Roeselare bus routes 94 and 95 (once or twice hourly weekdays, five daily weekends), so could be visited en route between Ypres and Bruges.

Memorial Museum Passchendaele 1917 MUSEUM
(www.passchendaele.be; Ieperstraat 5; admission €8.50; ⊙9am-6pm Feb–mid-Dec; ☐94) In central Zonnebeke village, Kasteel Zonnebeke (www.zonnebeke.be) is a lake-fronted Normandy chalet-style mansion built in 1922 to replace a castle bombarded into rubble during WWI. It hosts a tourist office, cafe and particularly polished WWI museum charting local battle progressions with plenty of multilingual commentaries. The big attraction here is descending into its multiroom 'trench experience' with low-lit, wooden-clad subterranean bunk rooms and a soundtrack. Explanations are much more helpful here than in 'real' trenches elsewhere.

Tyne Cot CEMETERY
(⊙24hr, visitor centre 9am-6pm Feb-Nov; ☐94) **FREE** Probably the most visited Salient site, this is the world's biggest British Commonwealth war cemetery, with 11,956 graves. A huge semicircular wall commemorates another 34,857 lost-in-action soldiers whose names wouldn't fit on Ypres' Menin Gate. The name Tyne Cot was coined by Northumberland Fusiliers who fancied that German bunkers on the hillside here looked like Tyneside cottages. Two such dumpy concrete bunkers sit amid the graves, with a third visible through the metal wreath beneath the white Cross of Sacrifice.

Deutscher Soldatenfriedhof CEMETERY
FREE The area's main German WWI cemetery is smaller than Tyne Cot but arguably more memorable, amid oak trees and trios of squat, mossy crosses. Some 44,000 corpses were grouped together here, up to 10 per granite grave slab, and four eerie silhouette

LAST POST
At 8pm daily, traffic through the Menin Gate is halted while buglers sound the Last Post (www.lastpost.be) in remembrance of the WWI dead, a moving tradition started in 1928. Every evening the scene is different, possibly accompanied by pipers, troops of cadets or maybe a military band.

statues survey the site. Entering takes you through a black concrete 'tunnel' that clanks and hisses with distant war sounds, while four short video montages commemorate the tragedy of war.

Tours
Over the Top BUS
(☑057-42 43 20; www.overthetoptours.be; Meensestraat 41; tours €40; ⊙tours 9am-1.30pm & 2.30-5.30pm) A WWI specialist bookshop towards the Menin Gate, offering twice-daily, half-day guided minibus tours of the Ypres Salient, the north salient tour is in the morning, the south in the afternoon.

British Grenadier BUS
(☑057 21 46 57; www.salienttours.be; Meensestraat 5; standard tour €38; ⊙10am-1.30pm & 2.15-5.45pm) Offers three different Ypres tours, with morning and afternoon departures for various sites on the Salient. It also offers full-day tours (€110) around the Somme region and/or Vimy Ridge.

Sleeping & Eating
Ariane Hotel HOTEL €€
(☑057-21 82 18; www.ariane.be; Slachthuisstraat 58; r €125-167; 🅿🛜) This peaceful, professionally managed, large hotel has a designer feel to the rooms and popular restaurant, while wartime memorabilia dots the spacious common areas.

B&B Ter Thuyne B&B €€
(☑057-36 00 42; www.terthuyne.be; Gustave de Stuersstraat 19; s/d from €80/95; @) Three comfortable rooms that are luminously bright and scrupulously clean, but not overly fashion-conscious.

★ Main Street Hotel GUESTHOUSE €€€
(☑057-46 96 33; www.mainstreet-hotel.be; Rijselstraat 136; d €180-260; 🛜) Jumbling funky eccentricity with historical twists and luxurious

comfort, this is a one-off that simply oozes character. The smallest room is designed like a mad professor's experiment, the breakfast room has a Tiffany glass ceiling...and so it goes on!

★ **De Ruyffelaer** FLEMISH €€
(☑ 057-36 60 06; www.deruyffelaer.be; Gustave de Stuersstraat 9; mains €15-21; ⊙ 11.30am-3.30pm Sun, 5.30-9.30pm Fri-Sun) Traditional local dishes served in an adorable, wood-panelled interior with old chequerboard floors and a brocante decor, including dried flowers, old radios and antique biscuit tins.

❶ Information

Tourist Office (☑ 057-23 92 20; www.toerism eieper.be; Lakenhalle; ⊙ 9am-6pm Mon-Fri, 10am-6pm Sat & Sun Apr–mid-Nov, to 5pm mid-Nov–Mar) Tourist office for Ypres and surrounds with an extensive bookshop.

❶ Getting There & Around

BICYCLE

Hire bikes from **Hotel Ambrosia** (☑ 057-36 63 66; www.ambrosiahotel.be; D'Hondtstraat 54; bike per day €15; ⊙ 7.30am-7.30pm).

BUS

Services pick up passengers in Grote Markt's northeast corner (check the direction carefully!). For Bruges take Roeselare-bound routes 94 or 95 then change to train.

TRAIN

Services run hourly to Ghent (€11.50, one hour) and Brussels (€17.50, 1¾ hours) via Kortrijk (€5.30, 30 minutes), where you could change for Bruges or Antwerp.

WALLONIA

Make some time for hilly Wallonia, Belgium's French-speaking southern half. Wallonia's cities have plenty of charm, but the region's standout attractions are mostly rural – outdoor activities, fabulous caves and venerable castles.

Mons

POP 93,400

With a characterful medieval centre climbing up a hill and a fine Grand Place, Mons (Bergen in Dutch) had a substantial facelift in 2015, when it was a European Capital of Culture. The legacy is a handful of entertaining modern museums that make Mons an excellent visit, with plenty to keep you busy for two or three days. One museum covers war in excellent fashion, while another celebrates the riotous Doudou festival, which stars St George, a dragon, St Waudru, devils and thousands of beery revellers.

◉ Sights

★ **Mons Memorial Museum** MUSEUM
(☑ 065-40 53 20; www.monsmemorialmuseum. mons.be; Blvd Dolez 51; adult/child €9/2; ⊙ 10am-6pm Tue-Sun; ☜) A superb new museum, this extensive display mostly covers Mons' experience of the two world wars, though the constant sieges of this town's turbulent history are also mentioned. It gets the balance just right between military history, personal testimony of civilians and soldiers, and thought-provoking items on display. Some seriously good visuals make the to-and-fro (and stuck for years in the mud) of WWI instantly comprehensible, and there's an animated 3D film on the legend of the Angels of Mons.

Musée du Doudou MUSEUM
(☑ 065-40 53 18; www.museedudoudou.mons.be; Jardin du Mayeur; adult/child €9/2; ⊙ 10am-6pm Tue-Sun) Head through the Hôtel de Ville on the Grand Place to reach this museum, dedicated to Mons' riotous **Ducasse festival** (www.doudou.mons.be). All aspects of this curious event, as well as background on St George, St Waudru and dragons, are covered in entertaining interactive fashion, and there are interesting cultural musings on the festival's changing nature over time. During the audiovisual, showing the climactic Lumeçon battle, you can almost smell the beer and sweat. There's audio content in French, Dutch and English.

🛏 Sleeping & Eating

Auberge de Jeunesse HOSTEL €
(☑ 065-87 55 70; www.lesaubergesdejeunesse. be; Rampe du Château 2; dm/s/d €28/46/68; ℗ @ ☜) Just before the base of the belfry, this modern, well-equipped HI hostel has an attractive tiered design making good use of the sloping terrain. Worth booking ahead. Prices drop significantly in quieter months. Rates are €2 less per person for those aged 26 and under; 10% HI discount.

BOULLON

Wallonia has some magnificent castles dotted right across it. If you're only going to visit one, though, make it this. Dreamily arrayed around a tight loop of the Semois River, Bouillon is protected by its gloriously medieval stronghold, gnarled and grim up on the hill. On a summer evening, limpid light and reflections in the water can make this one of Belgium's prettiest towns. The **Château de Bouillon** (☑ 061 46 62 57; www.bouillon-initia-tive.be; Rue du Château; adult/child €7/5; ⊙ 10am-6.30pm Jul & Aug, 10am-5pm or 6pm Mar-Jun & Sep-Nov, see website for winter opening; P⌂), Belgium's finest feudal castle, accessed by two stone bridges between crags, harks back to 988, but is especially associated with Crusader knight Godefroid (Godefroy) de Bouillon. The super-atmospheric castle still has everything you might wish for – dank dripping passageways tunnelling into the hill-side, musty half-lit cell rooms, rough-hewn stairwells and many an eerie nook and cranny to discover. To reach Bouillon, train to Libramont, then take bus 8 (€3.20, 45 minutes, roughly hourly weekdays, two-hourly weekends).

★ **Dream Hôtel** HOTEL €€
(☑ 065-32 97 20; www.dream-mons.be; Rue de la Grand Triperie 17; s/d €94/113; P❄@⛾) Centrally located in a revamped 19th-century chapel, Dream Hôtel combines a good level of comfort with more than a dash of Belgian eccentricity, including multilingual murals, bowler-hat lamps and side tables made from drums. Bathrooms, with separate toilet, are excellent, and noise insulation is relatively good. There's a lovely little spa to wallow in, and free (valet) parking.

★ **Vilaine Fille,
Mauvais Garçon** MODERN FRENCH €€€
(Naughty Girl, Bad Boy; ☑ 065-66 67 62; www.vilainefillemauvaisgarcon.be; Rue de Nimy 55; mains €25-28, set meals €27-55; ⊙ noon-3pm & 7-10.30pm Tue-Fri, 7-10.30pm Sat, noon-3pm Sun) Artful gastronomic takes on traditional plates, with familiar ingredients appearing in surprising ways, are the hallmarks of this enjoyable restaurant. The smart contemporary interior in a historic building makes for relaxed, quality dining. The menu is short, and there are various set meals depending on which day it is.

❶ Information

Maison du Tourisme (☑ 065-33 55 80; www.visitmons.be; Grand Place 27; ⊙ 9am-5.30pm daily; ⛾) On the main square, with lots of booklets and information, and bike rental.

❶ Getting There & Away

Mons' **train station** (Place Léopold; provisional until the new Calatrava design is finally finished) and neighbouring **TEC bus station** (☑ 065-38 88 15) are 700m west of the Grand Place. There are very regular services to Brussels (€9.40, 50 minutes), among other destinations.

LUXEMBOURG

Ruled by its own monarchy, the Grand Duchy of Luxembourg is famed for its banks but visually it's mostly an undulating series of pretty wooded hills dotted with castle villages. These are made accessible from the attractive capital city by excellent roads and a very well-organised single-price public transport system. Luxembourg has its own language, Lëtzebuergesch, but most Luxembourgers also speak French and German.

Luxembourg City

POP 111,300

If you thought that the Grand Duchy's capital was nothing more than banks and EU offices, you'll be delighted at discovering the attractive reality. The Unesco-listed Old Town is one of Europe's most scenic capitals, thanks largely to its unusual setting, draped across the deep gorges of the Alzette and Pétrusse rivers. It's full of weird spaces, tunnels and surprising nooks to explore. Good museums and a great dining scene makes this a top city to visit. It's worth visiting on a weekend, when hotel prices drop and on-street parking is free.

❂ Sights

The Old Town counterpoints some fine old buildings with modern museums and an offering of high-end restaurants. The

Luxembourg City

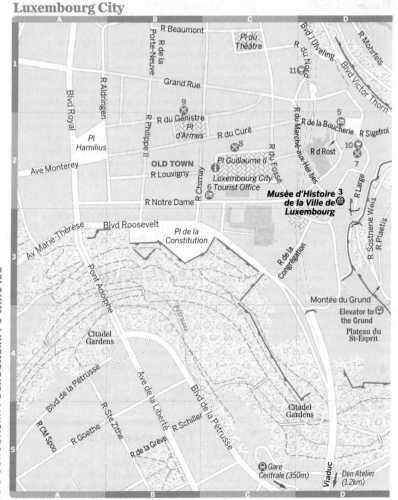

picturesque Grund area lies riverside, way below at the base of a dramatic fortified escarpment.

★ Chemin de la Corniche   AREA

This pedestrian promenade has been hailed as 'Europe's most beautiful balcony'. It winds along the course of the 17th-century city ramparts with views across the river canyon towards the hefty fortifications of the Wenzelsmauer (Wenceslas Wall). The rampart-top walk continues along Blvd Victor Thorn to the Dräi Tier (Triple Gate) tower.

★ Bock Casemates   FORTRESS

(www.lcto.lu; Montée de Clausen; adult/child €6/3; ⊗10am-5.30pm mid-Feb–Mar & Oct-early Nov, 10am-8.30pm Apr-Sep) Beneath the Montée de Clausen, the cliff-top site of Count Sigefroi's once-mighty fort, the Bock Casemates are a picturesque, atmospheric honeycomb of rock galleries and passages – yes, kids will love it – initially carved by the Spaniards between 1737 and 1746. Over the years the casemates have housed everything from garrisons to bakeries to slaughterhouses; during WWI and WWII they sheltered 35,000 locals.

free; ⊙10am-8pm Wed, 10am-6pm Thu-Mon; 🛜) Groundbreaking exhibitions of modern, installation and experiential art are hosted in this airy architectural icon designed by IM Pei. The collection includes everything from photography to fashion, design and multimedia. The glass-roofed cafe makes a decent lunch/snack spot. To reach Mudam, take bus 1, 8 or 16.

★ US Military Cemetery CEMETERY
(www.abmc.gov; 50 Val du Scheid; ⊙9am-5pm) In a beautifully maintained graveyard near Hamm lie over 5000 US WWII war dead, including George Patton, the audacious general of the US Third Army who played a large part in Luxembourg's 1944 liberation. It's a humbling sight, with its long rows of white crosses (and the odd Star of David). It's just near the airport off the N2; bus 15 gets you close. Take it to the second-last stop, Käschtewee.

🛏 Sleeping

Luxembourg City's accommodation scene is heavy with business options but online rates are slashed at weekends and in summer.

Auberge de Jeunesse HOSTEL €
(☎26 27 66 650; www.youthhostels.lu; 5 Rue du Fort Olisy; dm/s/d €25/40/60, €3 per person off for HI members; ℗❄@🛜) This state-of-the-art hostel has very comfortable, sex-segregated dorms with electronic entry. There are good-sized lockers (bring padlock), laundry facilities and masses of space including a great terrace from which

★ Musée d'Histoire
de la Ville de Luxembourg MUSEUM
(Luxembourg City History Museum; ☎47 96 45 00; www.mhvl.lu; 14 Rue du St-Esprit; adult/under 21 yr €5/free; ⊙10am-6pm Tue-Sun, to 8pm Thu) This remarkably engrossing and interactive museum hides within a series of 17th-century houses, including a former 'holiday home' of the Bishop of Orval. A lovely garden and open terrace offers great views.

★ Mudam GALLERY
(Musée d'Art Moderne; ☎45 37 85 1; www.mudam.lu; 3 Parc Dräi Eechelen; adult/under-21 €7/

to admire views to the Old Town. En-suite dorms cost €1 more.

★**Hôtel Simoncini** HOTEL €€€
(🖉22 28 44; www.hotelsimoncini.lu; 6 Rue Notre-Dame; s/d incl breakfast Mon-Thu from €160/180, Fri-Sun €130/150; @ 🔊) A delightful contemporary option in the city centre, the Simoncini's foyer is a modern art gallery and the smart, bright rooms have slight touches of retro-cool. As it's not very big, and prices are pretty low for central Luxembourg, it gets booked up midweek well ahead.

★**Hôtel Parc Beaux-Arts** BOUTIQUE HOTEL €€€
(🖉44 23 23 23 23; www.parcbeauxarts.lu; 1 Rue Sigefroi; ste Mon-Thu advance/rack rates €229/430, Fri-Sun from €159; @ 🔊) Exuding understated luxury, this charming little hotel comprises a trio of 18th-century houses containing 10 gorgeous suites. Each features original artworks by contemporary artists, oak floors, Murano crystal lamps and a fresh rose daily. Seek out the 'secret' lounge hidden away in the original timber eaves. In the heart of the bar and restaurant zone, so expect some street noise at weekends.

✕ Eating

Eating is expensive in Luxembourg, but there's a lively dining scene. For characterful options, hunt around in the alleys and passages collectively nicknamed 'Îlot Gourmand' directly behind the Royal Palace. There are interesting alternatives in Grund and the Clausen area. Daily in summer, tables spill merrily onto leafy Place d'Armes, with everything from burger chains to classy seafood on offer. Inexpensive but mostly characterless places for Asian food are in the train station area.

Am Tiirmschen FRENCH €€
(🖉26 27 07 33; www.amtiirmschen.lu; 32 Rue de l'Eau, Îlot Gourmand; mains €18-25; ⊘noon-2pm Tue-Fri, 7-10.30pm Mon-Sat) This is a great place to sample typical Luxembourg dishes, but it also serves good fish and French options in case your companions don't fancy *kniddelen* (dumplings) or smoked pork. It has a semi-successful mix of old and pseudo-old decor, with heavy, bowed beams.

Brasserie Guillaume SEAFOOD €€€
(🖉26 20 20 20; www.brasserieguillaume.lu; 12 Place Guillaume II; mains €18-40; ⊘11.30am-midnight; 🔊🍴) With tables on this emblematic square, this could be another tourist trap eatery. But far from it: so seriously do

they take their seafood here, they drive over to Paris' famed Rungis wholesale market. Cakestand-like seafood platters are popular and delicious, but the beef carpaccios and fish dishes are also sublime. Service is busy and competent, and the kitchen's open later than most.

★**La Cristallerie** MODERN FRENCH €€€
(🖉27 47 37 42 1; www.hotel-leplacedarmes.com; 18 Place d'Armes; menus €78-178; ⊘noon-2pm & 7-9.30pm Tue-Fri, 7-9.30pm Sat; 🔊🍴) This indulgent gastronomic restaurant is hidden on the 1st floor of the Place d'Armes Hotel, lit with original stained glass and decor picked out in relatively subtle gilt. One of the degustation menus is vegetarian, and wine flights are available for all.

🍷 Drinking & Entertainment

★**Dipso** WINE BAR
(🖉26 20 14 14; www.dipso.lu; 4 Rue de la Loge; ⊘5pm-1am Tue-Sat; 🔊) This has genuine atmosphere under its vaulted ceiling and on its tiny, fight-for-a-seat terrace. With 20-something wines by the glass, you might need the platters of cold cuts, sushi etc (€18 to €25) to soak it all up. Beware expensive bottles: it's the sort of place that, after quaffing a few looseners, the three-figure burgundy might seem like a sound plan.

Konrad Cafe BAR
(🖉26 20 18 94; www.facebook.com/Konradcafe; 7 Rue du Nord; ⊘11am-midnight Sun-Thu, 11am-1am Fri, 10am-1am Sat; 🔊) Relaxed and happily bohemian, this sweet cafe is a cordial spot to drop in at any time of day for juices, light meals (€4 to €10) or a coffee and something sweet. At night it becomes more of a bar, with a downstairs space hosting regular comedy and live music.

ℹ Information

Luxembourg City Tourist Office (LCTO; 🖉22 28 09; www.lcto.lu; Place Guillaume II; ⊘9am-6pm Mon-Sat, 10am-6pm Sun Oct-Mar, 9am-7pm Mon-Sat, 10am-6pm Sun Apr-Nov) Sells city guides (€2), and has maps, walking-tour pamphlets and event guides.

ℹ Getting There & Away

BUS
Useful international connections from beside the train station include Bitburg (bus 401, 1¼ hours) and Trier (bus 118, one hour).

TRAIN

Trains are run by CFL (www.cfl.lu), with good connections all through northern Europe. Sample fares from Gare Centrale, 1km south of the Old Town:

Brussels (€39, three hours, hourly) Via Arlon and Namur.

Paris (2¼ hours, €82-€104) Direct five to six times daily via Metz.

Trier (€18, one hour, hourly) Continuing to Koblenz (€46.20, 2½ hours).

ℹ️ Getting Around

TO/FROM LUXEMBOURG AIRPORT

Luxembourg Airport (www.lux-airport.lu) is 6km east of Place d'Armes, 20 minutes by bus 16.

BICYCLE

Velóh (☑ 800 611 00; www.en.veloh.lu; subscription per week/year €1/15, plus €1 per hour.; ☺ 24hr) Short-hop bike-rental scheme.

Vélo en Ville (☑ 47 96 23 83; 8 Bisserwée; per half-/full day/weekend/week €12.50/20/37.50/100; ☺ 8am-noon & 1-8pm Mon-Fri, 10am-noon & 1-8pm Sat & Sun Apr-Sep, 7am-3pm Mon-Fri Oct-Mar) Hires mountain bikes and city bikes.

BUS

Frequent buses shuttle to Gare Centrale (the train station) and Kirchberg (for Mudam) from Place Hamilius, the main bus stand for the Old Town. Fewer on Sundays.

Northern Luxembourg

Understandably popular as a weekend getaway, magical little **Vianden** (www.vianden-info.lu) is dominated by a vast slate-roofed **castle** (☑ 83 41 08; www.castle-vianden.lu; adult/child €7/2; ☺ 10am-4pm Nov-Feb, to 5pm Mar & Oct, to 6pm Apr-Sep) and its impregnable stone walls glow golden in the evening's floodlights. Cobbled Grand Rue descends 700m from there to the riverside tourist office passing the HI Hostel, **Auberge de Jeunesse** (☑ 26 27 66 80 0; www.youthhostels.lu; 3 Montée du Château; HI members dm/s/d €19.20/34.20/49.40, nonmembers €22.20/37.20/55.40; ☺ 🍴 🛜), and several appealling family hotels, notably unique **Auberge Aal Veinen** (☑ 83 43 68; http://vianden.beimhunn.lu; 114 Grand Rue; s/d €60/80; ☺ closed mid-Dec–mid-Jan; 🛜) and **Hôtel Heintz** (☑ 83 41 55; www.hotel-heintz.lu; 55 Grand Rue; s €65-95, d €75-105; ☺ Easter-Sep; 🅿 🛜).

Bus 570 (18 minutes) connects at least hourly to **Diekirch**, which is home to **Musée National d'Histoire Militaire** (☑ 80 89 08; www.mnhm.net; 10 Rue Bamertal; adult/child €5/3; ☺ 10am-6pm Tue-Sun), the most comprehensive and visual of many museums commemorating 1944's devastating midwinter Battle of the Ardennes. Diekirch has twice-hourly trains to Luxembourg City (40 minutes) via **Ettelbrück** (10 minutes). From there you can catch buses to **Bastogne** (Belgium) for other major WWII sites and the excellent new **Bastogne War Museum** (☑ 061 21 02 20; www.bastognewarmuseum.be; Colline du Mardasson, 5; adult/child €14/8; ☺ 9.30am-6pm, to 7pm Jul & Aug, closed Jan & Mon mid-Nov–mid-Mar).

Bus 545 from Ettelbrück gets you within 2km of isolated **Château de Bourscheid** (www.chateau.bourscheid.lu; adult/youth/child €5/4/3; ☺ 9.30am-5.30pm Apr–mid-Oct, 11am-3.30pm mid-Oct–Mar), Luxembourg's most evocative medieval ruined castle, and trains run north towards Liège via pretty **Clervaux**, home to a convincingly rebuilt castle that hosts the world-famous **Family of Man photography exhibition** (☑ 92 96 57; www.steichencollections.lu; Château de Clervaux; over /under 21 €6/free; ☺ noon-6pm Wed-Sun Mar-Dec), established in 1955 and intended as a manifesto for peace. Bus 663 (32 minutes) departs for Vianden at 8.30am, 10am, 2pm and 5pm.

Moselle Valley

Smothering the Moselle River's steeply rising banks are the neatly clipped vineyards that produce Luxembourg's balanced Rieslings, fruity rivaners and excellent *crémants* (sparkling *méthode traditionelle* wines). Taste a selection at the grand **Caves Bernard-Massard** (☑ 75 05 45 1; www.bernard-massard.lu; 8 Rue du Pont; tours €6-9; ☺ tours 9.30am-6pm Tue-Sun Apr-Oct) in central **Grevenmacher** where frequent 20-minute winery tours are multilingual and spiced with humour. The Enner der Bréck bus stop outside is on bus routes 130 from Rue Heine in Luxembourg City (55 minutes, once or twice hourly).

A good way of visiting the wine route is renting a bicycle with **Rentabike Miselerland** (entente-moselle.lu/rentabike-miselerland; per day €10), free if you have a Luxembourg Card. Pick-up at one of numerous points and drop off at another: just make sure that you check closing times and take ID.

SURVIVAL GUIDE

ℹ️ Directory A–Z

ACCOMMODATION

Tourist offices often provide free accommodation-booking assistance.

Hotels Availability and prices vary markedly by area. Bruges, for example, is terribly busy in summer and weekends, while Brussels and Luxembourg City are quieter at those times.

B&Bs Rooms rented in local homes (*gastenkamers/chambres d'hôtes*) can be cheap and cheerful but some offer standards and prices equivalent to a boutique hotel.

Holiday houses (*gîtes*) Are easily rented in **Wallonia** (www.gitesdewallonie.be) and **Luxembourg** (www.gites.lu), but minimum stays apply and there's a hefty 'cleaning fee' on top of quoted rates.

Hostels Typically charge around €18 to €28 for dormitory beds. Luxembourg has an excellent network of HI hostels (http://youth hostels.lu).

Camping Opportunities are plentiful, especially in the Ardennes. For extensive listings see www.campingbelgique.be (Wallonia), www.camping.be (Flanders) and www.camping.lu (Luxembourg).

ACTIVITIES

In mostly-flat **Flanders** (www.fietsroute.org), bicycles are a popular means of everyday travel and many roads have dedicated cycle lanes. In **Wallonia** (www.wallonie.be), the hilly terrain favours mountain bikes (VTT).

Canoeing and kayaking are best in the Ardennes, but don't expect rapids of any magnitude.

Local tourist offices have copious information about footpaths and sell regional hiking maps.

MONEY

➡ Credit cards are widely accepted. ATMs are plentiful, and are the best way of accessing cash.

➡ Tipping is not expected in restaurants or cabs: service and VAT are always included.

SLEEPING PRICE RANGES

Ranges are based on the cost of a double room in high season.

€ less than €60

€€ €60–€140

€€€ more than €140

EATING PRICE RANGES

The following price ranges are based on the cost of a typical main course.

€ less than €15

€€ €15 to €25

€€€ more than €25

OPENING HOURS

Many sights close on Monday. Restaurants normally close one full day per week. Opening hours for shops, bars and cafes vary widely.

Banks 8.30am–3.30pm or later Monday to Friday, some also Saturday morning

Bars 10am–1am, but hours very flexible

Restaurants noon–2.30pm and 7pm–9.30pm

Shops 10am–6.30pm Monday to Saturday, sometimes closed for an hour at lunchtime

PUBLIC HOLIDAYS

New Year's Day 1 January

Easter Monday March/April

Labour Day 1 May

Iris Day 8 May (Brussels region only)

Ascension Day 39 days after Easter Sunday (always a Thursday)

Pentecost Monday 50 days after Easter Sunday

Luxembourg National Day 23 June (Luxembourg only)

Flemish Community Day 11 July (Flanders only)

Belgium National Day 21 July (Belgium only)

Assumption Day 15 August

Francophone Community Day 27 September (Wallonia only)

All Saints' Day 1 November

Armistice Day 11 November (Belgium only)

Christmas Day 25 December

TELEPHONE

➡ Country code 32 (Belgium), 352 (Luxembourg). International access code 00.

➡ If you've got an unlocked smartphone, you can pick up a local SIM card for a few euros and charge it with a month's worth of data at a decent speed for under €20.

TOURIST INFORMATION

Almost every town and village has its own tourist office – *dienst voor toerisme*, *toeristische dienst* or simply *toerisme* (in Flanders), *maison du tourisme*, *office du tourisme* or *syndicat d'initiative* (in Wallonia and Luxembourg).

Useful contacts:

Visit Wallonia (www.belgiumtheplaceto.be)
Wallonia and Brussels
Visit Flanders (www.visitflanders.com)
Flanders
Visit Luxembourg (www.vlsitluxembourg.com)
Luxembourg

VISAS

Schengen visa rules apply. Embassies are listed at www.diplomatie.belgium.be/en and www.mae.lu.

Getting There & Away

AIR

Brussels airport (BRU; www.brusselsairport.be) is Belgium's main long-haul gateway.

Budget airlines use Charleroi Airport (p116), 55km south of Brussels.

Luxembourg airport (www.lux-airport.lu) has various European connections.

You may sometimes find it cheaper or more convenient to fly into one of the major airports in neighbouring countries – in Frankfurt, Amsterdam or Paris, for example – and continue into Belgium/Luxembourg by train.

LAND
Bus

Eurolines (www.eurolines.eu) Large international bus network; usually cheaper than equivalent train tickets. Useful routes served at least daily include London–Brussels (seven to eight hours), London–Bruges/Ghent (six to seven hours), Brussels–Paris (four hours), Brussels–Amsterdam (three to four hours) and Brussels–Berlin (10 hours). Liège and Antwerp also served.

Ecolines (www.ecolines.net) Consortium of mostly Baltic or Eastern European coach lines.

Car & Motorcycle

➡ Northern Europe is one vast web of motorways, so Belgium and Luxembourg are easily accessed from anywhere.

➡ There's no problem bringing foreign vehicles into Belgium or Luxembourg, provided you have registration papers and valid insurance ('Green Card').

➡ Most car-hire companies in the Netherlands, France, Germany or other EU nations won't have a problem with your taking their car into Belgium or Luxembourg, but check rental conditions before you do so.

Train

There are excellent train links with neighbouring countries.

➡ Internet bookings save you a few euros over Belgian pay-and-go tickets for most international tickets. Check out www.b-europe.com and www.cfl.lu or operator websites of the country of origin.

➡ Railcards are valid on standard services but there are surcharges for high-speed lines including **Eurostar** (www.eurostar.com) to London (two hours) and Lille, **Thalys** (www.thalys.com) to Cologne, Amsterdam and Paris.

➡ **Deutsche Bahn** (www.bahn.com) runs high-speed ICE trains Brussels Midi–Liège–Aachen–Cologne–Frankfurt (3 hours) while **SNCF** (www.sncf.com) has TGV links to numerous French destinations, albeit bypassing central Paris.

➡ To avoid high-speed surcharges, useful 'ordinary' cross-border services include Liège–Aachen, Liège–Maastricht, Tournai–Lille, Brussels Central–Amsterdam and Luxembourg–Trier.

SEA

P&O (www.poferries.com) operates a Zeebrugge–Hull route. Fourteen hours overnight. The quickest way across the Channel is to travel via the French port of Calais, around an hour's drive west of Ostend.

> ### 🅘 LUXEMBOURG'S SIMPLIFIED TRANSPORT SYSTEM
>
> Luxembourg has a one-price domestic ticket system. Wherever you go by public transport within Luxembourg the price is the same, €2 for up to two hours, €4 for the day. See www.cfl.lu for timetables.

ESSENTIAL FOOD & DRINK

Belgium's famous lagers (eg Stella Artois) and white beers (Hoegaarden) are now global brands. But what has connoisseurs really drooling are the robust, rich 'abbey' beers (originally brewed in monasteries), and the 'Trappist beers' (that still are). Chimay, Rochefort, Westmalle and Orval are the best known. But for beer maniacs the one that really counts is ultra-rare Westvleteren XII.

Dining is a treat in Belgium and Luxembourg, where meals are often described as being French in quality, German in quantity. Classic, home-style dishes include the following:

Chicons au gratin Endive rolled in ham and cooked in cheese/béchamel sauce.

Filet Américain A blob of raw minced beef, typically topped with equally raw egg yolk.

Judd mat gaardebounen Luxembourg's national dish; smoked pork neck in a cream-based sauce with chunks of potato and broad beans.

Kniddelen Dumplings.

Mosselen/moules Steaming cauldrons of in-the-shell mussels, typically cooked in white wine and served with a mountain of *frites* (chips).

Paling in 't groen Eel in a sorrel or spinach sauce.

Stoemp Mashed veg-and-potato dish.

Vlaamse stoverij/carbonade flamande Semi-sweet beer-based meat casserole.

Waterzooi A cream-based chicken or fish stew.

ⓘ Getting Around

BICYCLE

Cycling is a great way to get around in flat Flanders, less so in chaotic Brussels or undulating Wallonia. The Belgian countryside is riddled with cycling routes and most tourist offices sell helpful regional cycling maps.

» Bike hire is available in or near most major train stations. Short-hop hire schemes are available in cities.

» Bikes on the train are free in Luxembourg. In Belgium it costs €5 one-way (or €8 all day) on top of the rail fare. A few busy city-centre train stations don't allow bicycle transportation.

ⓘ CONNECTIONS

Amsterdam, Paris, Cologne and London are all under 2½ hours from Brussels by high-speed train. Liège, Luxembourg City and Antwerp are also on high-speed international routes. Go via Tournai to reach France, or via Luxembourg City to reach Germany by train if you want to avoid such lines and their compulsory reservations. Budget airlines offer cheap deals to numerous European destinations, particularly from Charleroi.

BUS & TRAM

Regional buses are well coordinated with Belgium's rail network, but in rural regions you can still find that relatively short distances can involve long waits. In Brussels and Antwerp, trams that run underground are called *premetro*.

The route planner at www.belgianrail.be gives useful bus suggestions where that's the logical choice for your route. In Luxembourg, use www.mobiliteit.lu.

CAR & MOTORCYCLE

» Motorways are toll free.

» Speed limits are 50km/h in most towns (30km/h near schools), 70km/h to 90km/h on inter-town roads, and 120km/h on motorways in Belgium (130km/h in Luxembourg).

» The maximum legal blood alcohol limit is 0.05%.

» Car hire is available at airports and major train stations, but is usually cheaper from city-centre offices.

» Fill up in Luxembourg for big savings.

TAXI

Taxis must usually be pre-booked but there are ranks near main stations. Tips and taxes are always included in metered fares.

TRAIN

Belgium's trains are run by **SNCB** (Belgian Railways; ☎ 02-528 28 28; www.belgianrail.be (domestic trains)). Luxembourg's joint railway-bus network is coordinated by **CFL** (☎ 24 89 24 89; www.cfl.lu).

Return tickets are normally twice the price of singles except on weekends from 7pm Friday, when a return ticket getting back by Sunday night costs little more than a single.

Under-26s can buy a Go-Pass 1, which costs €6 and is valid for any one-way trip within Belgium.

---

❶ LUXEMBOURG CARD

The worthwhile **Luxembourg Card** (www.visitluxembourg.com; 1-/2-/3-day adult €13/20/28, family €28/48/68) gives free admission to over 50 of the country's top attractions, discounts on some others, plus unlimited use of public transport. You'll save money if visiting more than two museums or castles a day. Purchase online, from tourist offices, train stations or major hotels. The website details what's included.

Bosnia & Hercegovina

Best Places to Eat

➡ Mala Kuhinja (p147)
➡ Hindin Han (p152)
➡ Manolo (p147)
➡ Babilon (p153)
➡ Park Prinčeva (p147)

Best Places to Stay

➡ Muslibegović House (p152)
➡ Isabegov Hamam Hotel (p146)
➡ Ovo Malo Duše (p146)
➡ Hostel Balkanarama (p152)

Why Go?

This craggily beautiful land retains some lingering scars from the heartbreaking civil war in the 1990s. But today visitors will more likely remember Bosnia and Hercegovina (BiH) for its deep, unassuming human warmth and for the intriguing East-meets-West atmosphere born of fascinatingly blended Ottoman and Austro-Hungarian histories.

Major drawcards are the reincarnated antique centres of Sarajevo and Mostar, where rebuilt historical buildings counterpoint fashionable bars and wi-fi–equipped cafes. Captivating Sarajevo is an architectural gem, with countless minarets amid the tile-roofed houses that rise steeply up its river flanks. Mostar is world famous for its extraordinary arc of 16th-century stone bridge, photogenically flanked by cute mill-house restaurants. The town is set at the heart of Hercegovina's sun-baked wine country, with waterfalls, a riverside sufi-house and an Ottoman fortress all nearby.

When to Go
Sarajevo

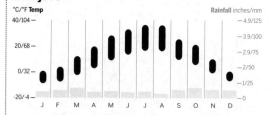

Apr–Jun Beat the heat in Hercegovina; blooming flowers in Bosnia.

Jul–Aug Gets sweaty and accommodation fills, but festivals keep things lively.

Mid-Jan–mid-Mar Skiing gets cheaper after the New Year holidays.

Bosnia & Hercegovina Highlights

1 Stari Most (p149)
Gawping as young men throw themselves off Mostar's magnificently rebuilt stone arc.

2 Baščaršija (p142)
Padding around Old Sarajevo's fascinating Turkic era alleyways on soft flagstones that feel like chilled butter underfoot.

3 Tunnel Museum (p146)
Discovering more about the hopes and horrors of the 1990s civil war at this intensely moving museum.

4 Mostar's Hinterland (p153) Making a satisfyingly varied day trip from Mostar to Kravice Waterfalls and other gems of Hercegovina.

5 Mountain Escapes (p148) Heading for resorts like Jahorina and Bjelašnica in the hills around Sarajevo to ski in winter or hike in the summer sunshine.

SARAJEVO

📞 033 / POP 395,000

In the 1990s Sarajevo was besieged and on the edge of annihilation. Today, its restored historic centre is full of welcoming cafes and good-value lodgings, the bullet holes largely plastered over on the city's curious architectural mixture of Ottoman, Yugoslav and Austro-Hungarian buildings.

The antique stone-flagged alleys of Baščaršija give the delightful Old Town core a certain Turkish feel. Directly north and south, steep valley sides are fuzzed with red-roofed Bosnian houses and prickled with uncountable minarets, climbing towards green-topped mountain ridges. In winter, Sarajevo's mountain resorts Bjelašnica and Jahorina offer some of Europe's best-value skiing, barely 30km away.

⊙ Sights & Activities

⊙ Old Sarajevo

★ Baščaršija AREA

Centred on what foreigners nickname Pigeon Sq, Baščaršija is the heart of old Sarajevo with pedestrians padding pale stone alleys and squares between lively (if tourist-centric) coppersmith alleys, grand Ottoman mosques, *caravanserai*-restaurants and lots of inviting little cafes and *ćevapi* serveries.

★ Sarajevo City Hall ARCHITECTURE

(Vijećnica; www.nub.ba; adult/child 5/3KM; ⊙10am-8pm Jun-Sep, to 5pm Oct-May) Storybook neo-Moorish facades make the 1898 Vijećnica Sarajevo's most beautiful Austro-Hungarian–era building. Seriously damaged during the 1990s siege, it finally reopened in 2014 after laborious reconstruction. Its colourfully restored multi-arched interior and stained-glass ceiling are superb. And the ticket also allows you to peruse the excellent *Sarajevo 1914-1981* exhibition in the octagonal basement. This gives well-explained potted histories of the city's various 20th-century periods, insights into fashion and music subcultures, and revelations about Franz Ferdinand's love life.

Gazi-Husrevbey Mosque MOSQUE

(www.vakuf-gazi.ba; Saraći 18; 3KM; ⊙9am-noon, 2.30-3.30pm & 5-6.15pm May-Sep, 9am-11am only Oct-Apr, closed Ramadan) Bosnia's second Ottoman governor, Gazi-Husrevbey, funded a series of splendid 16th-century buildings of which this 1531 mosque, with its 45m minaret, forms the greatest centrepiece. The interior is beautifully proportioned and even if you can't look inside, it's worth walking through the courtyard with its lovely fountain and the tomb tower of Gazi-Husrevbey off to one side.

Franz Ferdinand's Assassination Spot HISTORIC SITE

(cnr Obala Kulina Bana & Zelenih Beretki) On 28 June 1914, Archduke Franz Ferdinand, heir to the Habsburg throne of Austro-Hungary, was shot dead by 18-year-old Gavrilo Princip. This assassination, which would ultimately be the fuse that detonated WWI, happened by an odd series of coincidences on a street corner outside what is now the small **Sarajevo 1878–1918 museum** (Zelenih Beretki 2; 4KM; ⊙10am-6pm Mon-Fri, to 3pm Sat mid-Apr–mid-Nov, to 4pm Mon-Fri, to 3pm Sat mid-Nov–mid-Apr).

BOSNIA & HERCEGOVINA SARAJEVO

ITINERARIES

Two Days

If you only have two days you're best concentrating your time on the two main cities. In **Sarajevo**, take time to wander the streets of the Old Town and visit the beautifully restored City Hall, but make sure you also venture out to the **Tunnel Museum**, perhaps as part of a guided tour. In **Mostar** you'll want plenty of time to take in views of the famous bridge, perhaps drinking or dining by the riverside. Both cities have plenty of quirky bars and cafes where you can get to know the locals.

Four Days

With more time on your hands, extend your itinerary by joining a day tour ex-Mostar to visit historic **Počitelj**, quaint **Blagaj** and the impressive **Kravice** waterfalls. In Sarajevo, cafe-hop around Baščaršija's *caravanserais* and consider venturing up into the surrounding hills and mountains at Jahorina or Bjelašnica.

Despića Kuća MUSEUM
(☑ 033-215531; http://muzejsarajeva.ba; Despićeva 2; adult/child 3/1KM, guide 5KM; ☻10am-6pm Mon-Fri (to 4pm winter), to 3pm Sat) The Despića Kuća is one of the oldest surviving residential buildings in central Sarajevo, though you'd never guess so from the ho-hum facade. Inside, it's a house within a house, the original 1780 section retaining even the prison-style bars on stone window frames.

Galerija 11-07-95 MUSEUM
(☑ 033-953170; http://galerija110795.ba; Trg fra Grge Martića 2, 3rd fl; admission/audioguide/tour 12/3/2KM; ☻9am-10pm, guided tours 11.15am & 7.15pm) This new gallery uses stirring visual imagery and video footage to create a powerful memorial to more than 8000 victims of the Srebrenica massacre, one of the most infamous events of the Bosnian civil war. You'll need well over an hour to make the most of a visit, and it's worth paying the extra for the guide to get more insight.

☻ Bjelave & Vratnik

Bristling with little minarets amid tile-roofed houses and *doksat* box-windows, the appealingly untouristed areas of Bjelave and former citadel Vratnik (p143) rise steeply above the Old Town to the north and northeast. Random exploration highlights the fine viewpoints at Žuta Tabija and the eerie but even higher Bijela Tabija (p143).

★ Svrzo House MUSEUM
(Svrzina Kuća; ☑ 033-535264; http://muzejsarajeva.ba; Glođina 8; 3KM; ☻10am-6pm Mon-Fri, to 3pm Sat, closes early off-season) An oasis of white-washed walls, cobbled courtyards and partly vine-draped dark timbers, this 18th-century house-museum is brilliantly restored and appropriately furnished, helping visitors imagine Sarajevo life in eras past.

War Childhood Museum MUSEUM
(http://museum.warchildhood.com; Logavina 32; adult/child 10/5KM; ☻11am-7pm Tue-Sun) A fascinating new museum focusing on the experiences of children who grew up during the 1990s conflict. Poignantly personal items donated by former war children, such as diaries, drawings and ballet slippers, are displayed alongside written and video testimonies.

Vratnik AREA
Built in the 1720s and reinforced in 1816, Vratnik Citadel once enclosed a whole area of the upper city. Patchy remnants of wall fragments, military ruins and gatehouses remain. The urban area is appealingly untouristed with many mosques and tile-roofed houses, and several superb viewpoints. Start with a 3KM taxi hop up to the graffiti-daubed **Bijela Tabija** (Poddžebhana bb) fortress-ruin viewpoint (or take buses 52 or 55 to **Višegradski Kapija** (Carina 57a) gatehouse), then walk back.

Žuta Tabija VIEWPOINT
(Yellow Bastion; Jekovac bb) To gaze out across Sarajevo's red-roofed cityscape, one of the most appealing yet accessible viewpoints is from this chunk of old rampart-bastion, now sprouting mature trees and a popular place for picnickers and canoodling lovers.

☻ Novo Sarajevo

During the 1992–95 siege, the city's wide east–west artery road (Zmaja od Bosne) was dubbed 'sniper alley' because Serb gunmen in surrounding hills could pick off civilians as they tried to cross it. Most of the embattled journalists who covered that conflict sought refuge in what's now the Hotel Holiday, built in 1984 as the Holiday Inn and looking like a cubist still life of pudding and custard. Completely rebuilt, this business-oriented area now sports the nation's **tallest skyscraper** (www.avaztwisttower.ba; Tešanjska 24a; coffee/beer from 2/3KM; ☻7am-11pm) and newest **shopping mall** (Sarajevo City Center; www.scc.ba; Vrbanja 1; ☻10am-10pm, cafes 8am-11pm, parking 24hr; ⛟1, 3 Marijin Dvor) but is most interesting for two excellent museums.

National Museum MUSEUM
(Zemaljski Muzej Bosne-i-Hercegovine; www.zemaljskimuzej.ba; Zmaja od Bosne 3; adult/child 6/3KM; ☻10am-7pm Tue-Fri, to 2pm Sat & Sun) Bosnia's biggest and best-endowed museum of ancient and natural history is housed in an impressive, purpose-built quadrangle of neoclassical 1913 buildings. It's best known for housing the priceless Sarajevo Haggadah but there's much more to see. Highlights include Illyrian and Roman carvings, Frankish-style medieval swords, beautifully preserved 19th-century room interiors and meteorites among the extensive cabinets full of geological samples. Many explanatory panels have English translations.

Central Sarajevo

200 m
0.1 miles

BJELAVE

BAŠČARŠIJA

Baščaršija
Tram Stop Kračule

Svrzo House

Sarajevo City Hall

Žuta Tabija (200m);
Caffe Kamarija (300m);
Jajce Barracks (500m);
Bijela Tabija (1.1km)

Megara

Šahinaginca

Dugi Sokak
Talirovića

Isevića

Obala Isa-bega Išakovića

Konak

Park Prinčeva
(800m)

Bistrik

Austrijski
Trg

Latin
Bridge

Atmejdan
Park

Miljacka River

Orthodox Cathedral of
the Holy Mother

Catholic
Cathedral

Trg
Oslobođenja

Gimnazijska

Čemaluša

Obala Kulina Bana

Hamidije Kreševljakovića

Skenderija

Čobanija

Branilaca Sarajeva

Kulovića

National
Bank Building

Alije Isaković

Šenoina

Maršala Tita

Pruscakova

Mehmeda Spahe

Radićeva

SCC (800m);
National Museum (1.2km);
History Museum
of BiH (1.4km);
Tito Cafe (1.5km)

Avaz Twist
Tower (1.4km);
Main (1.7km);
(1.8km)

Dunja Balkan
House (275m)

Academy
of Arts

Mula Mustafe Bašeskije

Central Sarajevo

History Museum of BiH MUSEUM
(☎033-226098; www.muzej.ba; Zmaja od Bosne 5; 5KM, person with disability 1KM; ☉9am-7pm) Somewhat misleadingly named, this small but engrossing museum has three exhibition rooms. Two feature changing themes, but while these are often fascinating (recently on German 1980s subcultures), the main attraction is the third hall's permanent *Surrounded Sarajevo* exhibition. This charts the Sarajevo people's life-and-death battle for survival between 1992 and 1995. Personal effects include self-made lamps, examples of food aid, stacks of Monopoly-style 1990s dinars and a makeshift siege-time 'home'.

☞ Tours

Various companies run a range of tours in and beyond Sarajevo, many including the otherwise awkward-to-reach Tunnel Museum. Reliable operators include Sarajevo Funky Tours (☎062-910546; www.sarajevo-funkytours.com; Besarina Čikma 5) and Insider

(☎061-190591; www.sarajevoinsider.com; Zelenih Beretki 30; ☉9am-6pm Mon-Fri, 9.30am-2pm Sat & Sun).

✸ Festivals & Events

Sarajevo Film Festival FILM
(www.sff.ba; ☉mid-Aug) During this globally acclaimed film fest, the whole city turns into a giant party with countless concerts and many impromptu bars opening on street counters.

▭ Sleeping

★ **Seven Heavens** GUESTHOUSE €
(☎062-191508; 3rd fl, Štrossmayerova 3; dm/d €12/30) Three floors up in the grand mansion above the Monument Jazz Club, this boutique hostel-guesthouse has bathrooms that would put a five-star hotel to shame, shared by just three smart rooms and one spacious dorm.

DON'T MISS

TUNNEL MUSEUM

The most visceral of Sarajevo's many 1990s war-experience 'attractions' is the unmissable **Tunnel Museum** (Tunel Spasa; http://tunelspasa.ba; Tuneli bb 1; adult/student 10/5KM; ⊙9am-5pm, last entry 4.30pm Apr-Oct, 3.30pm Nov-Mar). The museum's centrepiece and raison d'être is a 25m section of the 1m wide, 1.6m high hand-dug tunnel under the airport runway. That acted as the city's lifeline to the outside world during the 1992–95 siege, when Sarajevo was virtually surrounded by hostile Serb forces.

Getting here by public transport is a bit of a fiddle. Take tram 3 to Ilidža, the far terminus (35 minutes), then take a taxi, the infrequent Kotorac-bound bus 12 (10 minutes) or walk (around 30 minutes). If you're alone, a group tour can prove cheaper than a taxi.

★ War Hostel
THEME HOSTEL €

(☑060-3171908; https://warhostel.com; Hrvatin 21; dm/d €10/40) 'You're not here just to sleep', says agent Zero-One who answers the door in a bulletproof vest. 'I want to change your experience'. A constant crackle of walkie-talkie messages form the soundscape to the seatless common room where you can discuss the immersion experience. Unforgettable.

Hostel For Me
HOSTEL €

(☑062 328658, 033-840135; www.hostelforme. com; 4th fl, Prote Bakovica 2; dm €10; ❋ 🔊) Right within the Old Town, hidden away up four flights of stairs, this is one of Sarajevo's best-appointed modern hostels. It's worth the climb for good-headroom bunks, huge lockers, a decent lounge and a kitchen with fine views across the Old Town roofs to the Gazi-Husrevbegov Mosque.

★ Isabegov Hamam Hotel
HERITAGE HOTEL €€

(☑033-570050; www.isabegovhotel.com; Bistrik 1; s/d/q €80/100/120; ❋) After many years of restoration the classic 1462 Isabegov Hamam (bathhouse) reopened in 2015 with 15 hotel rooms designed to evoke the spirit of the age with lashings of handcrafted darkwood furniture, ornately carved bedsteads and tube-glass chandeliers.

★ Ovo Malo Duše
BOUTIQUE GUESTHOUSE €€

(☑061-365100, 033-972800; http://ovo-malo-duse.com; Ćurčiluk Veliki 3; s/d 103/146KM; ⊙7am-10.30pm; ❋ 🔊) The six-room former Villa Wien has been rebranded and given a minor makeover but it retains an appealing mixture of comfort and old-world charm. Each room has its own idiosyncrasies. There's no reception so you will need to check in at the Wiener Café downstairs before 10.30pm when that closes.

Hotel Latinski Most
HOTEL €€

(☑033-572660; www.hotel-latinskimost.com; Obala Isabega Isakovića 1; s/d/tr 117/158/178KM, off season 99/138/158KM) This cosy hotel is ideal for WWI aficionados who want to survey the Franz Ferdinand assassination spot from directly across the river. Three of the smaller rooms have petite balconies offering just that, and their double-glazing works remarkably well against street noise.

★ Hotel Central
HOTEL €€€

(☑033-561800; www.hotelcentral.ba; Ćumurija 8; d/ste 220/260KM; ❋ 🔊 ▨) Behind a grand Austro-Hungarian facade, most of this snazzy 'hotel' is in fact an amazing three-floor gym complex with professional-standard weight rooms, saunas and a big indoor pool manned by qualified sports training staff. The huge guest rooms are fashionably appointed but there are only 15. Book well in advance.

★ Hotel Michele
BOUTIQUE HOTEL €€€

(☑033-560310; www.hotelmichele.ba; Ivana Cankara 27; s/d €75/85, apt €120-175; ❋ 🔊) Behind the exterior of an oversized contemporary townhouse, this offbeat guesthouse-hotel welcomes you into a lobby-lounge full of framed portraits, pinned butterflies and elegant fittings. Antique-effect elements are in the 12 standard rooms but what has drawn celebrity guests such as Morgan Freeman and Kevin Spacey are the vast, indulgently furnished apartments with antique (if sometimes mismatching) furniture.

✖ Eating

Bravadžiluk
STREET FOOD €

(mains from 3KM) For inexpensive snack meals look along Bravadžiluk or nearby Kundurdžiluk: **Buregdžinica Bosna** (Bravadžulik; potato/cheese/meat pies per 8/10/12kg, meal portions

2-3.50KM; ☺7am-11pm) is excellent for cheap, fresh *burek* sold by weight. Locals argue whether **Hodžić** (Sebilj Sq; small/large čevapi 3.50/7KM; ☺8am-10pm), **Željo** (Kundurdžiluk 17 & 20; small/medium/large ćevapi 3.5/7/10KM; ☺8am-10pm) or **Mrkva** (www.mrkva.ba; Bravadžulik 15; small/large čevapi 3.5/7KM; ☺8am-10pm) serves the best *ćevapi*, and there is plenty of attractively styled competition.

Barhana
PIZZA, BOSNIAN €
(Đugalina 8; pizza 5-12KM; ☺10am-midnight, kitchen to 11.30pm) Tourist-centric Barhana's remarkably reasonable prices pair unbeatably with its charming part-wooden cottage interior. The centrepiece is the large brick pizza oven and open kitchen, partly masked by collections of bottles and candles.

★Mala Kuhinja
FUSION €€
(☎061-144741; www.malakuhinja.ba; Tina Ujevića 13; mains 12-25KM; ☺10am-11pm Mon-Sat; 🛜🍴) Run by former TV celebrity chefs, the novel concept here is to forget menus and simply ask you what you do/don't like. Spicy? Vegan? No problem. And armed with this knowledge the team makes culinary magic in the show-kitchen. Superb.

Manolo
INTERNATIONAL €€
(Maršala Tita 21; mains 12-20KM, steaks 17-33KM; ☺8am-11pm) An exciting star in Sarajevo's culinary firmament, Manolo's panache for '60s and '70s retro design is backed by magicians in the kitchen. Beyond steaks and Italian mainstays, the menu's more imaginative dishes include wok-fried prawn and ginger, mustard chicken and spicy veal with sun-dried tomatoes. On colder days, closable glass panels convert the garden yard into a bright, wraparound veranda. No alcohol.

Inat Kuća
BOSNIAN €€
(Spite House; ☎033-447867; www.inatkuca.ba; Velika Alifakovac 1; mains 10-20KM; ☺11am-10pm; 🛜📱) This Sarajevo institution occupies a classic Ottoman-era house that's a veritable museum piece with central stone water trough, a case of antique guns and fine metal-filigree lanterns. A range of Bosnian specialities is served using pewter crockery at glass-topped display tables containing traditional local jewellery.

Dunja Balkan House
INTERNATIONAL €€
(☎033-214318; www.facebook.com/dunjasarajevo; Sumbala Avde 3; salads 6.20-13KM, mains 9-25KM; ☺8am-midnight Mon-Sat, 11am-6pm Sun) The house and garden seem to meld into one another in this smart yet relaxed restaurant-cafe with a tree growing through the roof, birdcages, decanters on tables, and riding caps hanging on a hatstand. The menu includes excellent salads, some Bosnian fare, fish, grills and much to please the staff of the nearby Italian embassy.

Pivnica HS
INTERNATIONAL €€
(☎033-239740; Franjevačka 15; mains 14-23KM; ☺10am-1am, kitchen 10.30am-midnight; 🛜📱) Wild West saloon, Munich bierkeller, Las Vegas fantasy or Willy Wonka masterpiece? However you describe its decor, Pivnica HS is a vibrant place for dining on well-presented (mainly meat-based) dishes or sampling the full range of Sarajevskaya tap beers brewed next door.

Park Prinčeva
BALKAN, EUROPEAN €€€
(☎033-222708; www.parkprinceva.ba; Iza Hidra 7; meals 16-32KM; ☺9am-11pm; 📱; 🚌56) Gaze out over a superb city panorama from this hillside perch, like Bono and Bill Clinton before you. From the open-sided terrace the City Hall is beautifully framed between rooftops, mosques and twinkling lights. Waiters in bow ties and red waistcoats deliver dishes that go beyond Bosnian usuals, such as chicken in cherry sauce or *pizzaiolo* roll with capers and olives.

🍷 Drinking & Entertainment

★Zlatna Ribica
BAR
(☎033-836348; Kaptol 5; ☺8am-late) Sedate and outwardly grand, this tiny and eccentric bar adds understated humour to a cosy treasure trove of antiques and kitsch, reflected in big art nouveau mirrors.

★Dekanter
WINE BAR
(☎033-263815; www.facebook.com/vinoteka. dekanter; Radićeva 4; ☺8am-midnight Mon-Sat, 6pm-midnight Sun; 🛜) It's easy to sit for hours sampling from more than 100 local and world vintages in this glorious, low-lit wine bar decorated with bottles, chateau-boxes and swirling ceiling sculptures of intertwined wires.

Čajdžinica Džirlo
TEAHOUSE
(www.facebook.com/cajdzinicadzirlo; Kovači 16; ☺8am-10pm) Minuscule but brimming with character, Džirlo brews some 50 types of tea, many of them made from distinctive Bosnian herbs. They are served in lovely little pots, each distinctive according to the blend.

AROUND SARAJEVO

Mountains rise directly behind Sarajevo, offering convenient access to winter skiing and charming summer rambles. **Jahorina** is the larger resort, with multiple pistes and seven main ski lifts, whilst the more modest **Bjelašnica** offers night skiing and a web of magical mountain villages to explore.

To the east, **Visoko** attracts new-age mystics and curious tourists with its mysterious 'pyramid' and crystal vendors. To the south, **Konjic** is the nearest rafting centre to Sarajevo, with a gigantic atomic bunker that cost Yugoslavia billions to build.

Cafe Barometar   BAR
(www.facebook.com/cafebarometar; Branilaca Sarajeva 23; ☺ 7am-midnight Sun-Thu, to 2am Fri & Sat) Like an image of HG Wells' *Time Machine*, this little cafe-bar weaves together dials, pipes and wacky furniture crafted from axels, compressors and submarine parts.

★ **Pink Houdini**   JAZZ
(www.facebook.com/jazzbluesclubpinkhoudini; Branilaca Sarajeva 31; ☺ 24hr) One of Sarajevo's rare 24-hour drinking spots, this quirky basement jazz bar has a tree of guitars, a wacky-fiesta themed abstract ceiling sculpture and UV lighting that makes your gin-and-tonic luminescent. Romping live blues gigs start at 10.30pm on Wednesdays, Fridays and Sundays.

★ **National Theatre**   PERFORMING ARTS
(Narodno Pozorište; ☑ 033-226431; www.nps.ba; Obala Kulina Bana 9; ☺ box office 9am-noon & 4-7.30pm) Classically adorned with fiddly gilt mouldings, this proscenium-arched theatre hosts a ballet, opera, play or philharmonic concert virtually every night from mid-September to mid-June.

🛍 Shopping

★ **Isfahan Gallery**   CARPETS
(☑ 033-237429; www.isfahans.com; Sarači 77, Morića Han; ☺ 9am-11pm) Specialising in high-quality Persian carpets (with certificate), along with richly glazed ceramic work, this entrancing shop brings a barrage of beautiful colours to the already enticing Morića Han *caravanserai*.

★ **Di Vina**   WINE
(☑ 033-267400; www.divina.ba; Josipa Stadlera 10; 4-wine tasting 15KM; ☺ 10am-8pm Mon-Fri, to 6pm Sat) There's nowhere better to start a wine-shopping spree than this well-stocked, super-friendly store run by a Bosnian family who returned to Sarajevo having lived in Canada. Drop-in wine tastings lasting around 20 minutes are available till an hour before closing.

Bezistan   MARKET
(http://vakuf-gazi.ba/english/index.php; Gazi Husrevbegova; ☺ 8am-9pm Mon-Sat, 10am-3pm Sun) The 16th-century stone-vaulted covered bazaar is little more than 100m long but squint and you could be in İstanbul. Many of the 70-plus shops sell inexpensive souvenirs, scarves, cheap handbags and knock-off sunglasses.

ⓘ Information

Official Tourist Info Centre (Turistički Informativni Centar; ☑ 033-580999; www.sarajevo-tourism.com; Sarači 58; ☺ 9am-8pm Mon-Fri, 10am-6pm Sat & Sun, varies seasonally) Helpful tourist information centre. Beware of commercial imitations.

ⓘ Getting There & Away

AIR

Sarajevo International Airport (Aerodrom; www.sia.ba; Kurta Schorka 36; ☺ closed 11pm-5am) Sarajevo's modern but compact international airport is about 12km southwest of Baščaršija. An hour is usually ample for check-in.

BUS

From Sarajevo's **main bus station** (☑ 033-213100; www.centrotrans.com; Put Zivota 8; ☺ 6am-10pm), beside the train station, there are frequent buses to Mostar (20KM, 2½ hours), several daily services to Zagreb, Split an Dubrovnik in Croatia, plus daily buses to Belgrade (Serbia). There are five more Belgrade services from the inconveniently distant **East Sarajevo (Lukovica) bus station** (Autobuska Stanica Istočno Sarajevo; ☑ 057-317377; www.balkanexpress-is.com; Srpskih Vladara bb; ☺ 6am-11.15pm), 400m beyond the western terminus stop of trolleybus 103 or bus 31E. That bus station also has buses to Podgorica and Herceg Novi in Montenegro.

TRAIN

There is a daily service to Zagreb (56KM, 9½ hours). Trains to Mostar were suspended at the time of research pending track reconstruction.

BOSNIA & HERCEGOVINA SARAJEVO

ⓘ Getting Around

TO/FROM THE AIRPORT

Taxis should charge around 20KM for the 12km drive to Baščaršija. Beware taxi drivers refusing to use the meter and asking for vastly inflated fares.

An infrequent **Centrotrans** (www.centrotrans.com; Ferhadija 16) bus service marked Aerodrom-Baščaršija (5KM, pay on-board) departs from outside the terminal taking around 30 minutes to the Old Town area. A more frequent and cheaper alternative from the airport area is to take bus 31E or trolleybus 103 (1.80KM), which run every few minutes till around 11.30pm. The nearest stop to the airport is Konzum Dobrijna, around a 700m walk from the terminal.

PUBLIC TRANSPORT

Single-ride tickets for bus, tram or trolleybus cost 1.60KM from kiosks, 1.80KM from drivers. They must be stamped once aboard.

Tram 3 (every four to seven minutes) is the most useful for sightseeing. It loops anticlockwise around Baščaršija before heading out west past the National Museum to Ilidža, where you can catch bus 12 onward to the Tunnel Museum.

TAXI

Paja Taxis (☑ 1522, 033-412555) This reliable taxi company charges on-the-metre fares of 2KM plus about 1KM per kilometre.

MOSTAR

☑ 036 / POP 105,800

Mostar's world-famous 16th-century stone bridge is the centrepiece of its alluring, extensively restored Old Town where, at dusk, the lights of numerous mill-house restaurants twinkle across gushing streamlets. Further from the centre a scattering of shattered building shells remain as a moving testament to the terrible 1990s conflict that divided the city. The surrounding sundrenched Herzegovinian countryside produces excellent wines and offers a series of tempting day-trip attractions.

⊙ Sights & Activities

★ Stari Most   BRIDGE

World-famous Stari Most (Old Bridge) is Mostar's indisputable visual focus. Its pale stone magnificently throws back the golden glow of sunset or the tasteful night-time floodlighting. The bridge's swooping arch was originally built between 1557 and 1566 on the orders of Suleyman the Magnificent. The current structure is a very convincing 21st-century rebuild following the bridge's 1990s bombardment during the civil war. Numerous well-positioned cafes and restaurants tempt you to sit and savour the splendidly restored scene.

BOSNIA & HERCEGOVINA MOSTAR

BIH & THE 1990S CONFLICT

Today's BiH remains deeply scarred by a 1990s civil war that began when post-Tito-era Yugoslavia imploded. Seen very simply, the core conflict was a territorial battle between the Bosnians, Serbs and Croats. The war that ensued is often portrayed as 'ethnic', but in fact all sides were Slavs, differing only in their (generally secularised) religious backgrounds. Indeed, many Bosniaks (Muslims), Serbs (Orthodox Christians) and Croats (Catholics) had intermarried or were friends. Yet for nearly four years a brutal and extraordinarily complex civil war raged, with atrocities committed by all sides.

Best known is the campaign of 'ethnic' cleansing in northern and eastern BiH, which aimed at creating a Serb republic. Meanwhile in Mostar, Bosnian Croats and Bosniaks traded fire across a 'front line' with Croat bombardment eventually destroying the city's world-famous old bridge. Sarajevo endured a long siege and, in July 1995, Dutch peacekeepers monitoring the supposedly 'safe' area of Srebrenica proved unable to prevent a Bosnian Serb force from killing an estimated 8000 Muslim men in Europe's worst mass killings since WWII. By this stage, Croats had renewed their own offensive, expelling Serbs from western BiH and the Krajina region of Croatia.

Finally two weeks of NATO air strikes in September 1995 added force to an ultimatum to end the Serbs' siege of Sarajevo and a peace conference was held in Dayton, Ohio. The resultant accords maintained BiH's pre-war external boundaries but divided the country into a complex jigsaw of semi-autonomous 'entities' and cantons to balance 'ethnic' sensibilities. This succeeded in maintaining the fragile peace but the complex political structure resulting from the war has led to bureaucratic tangles and economic stagnation.

Mostar

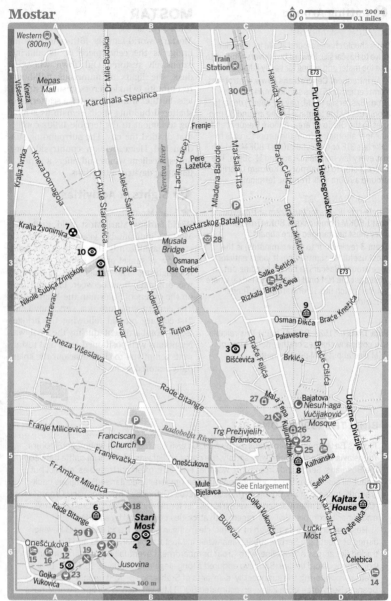

Bridge Diver's Club SPECTACLE
(☎061-388552; Stari Most; ☉10am–dusk) In summer, young men leap from the parapet of Stari Most, falling more than 20m into the freezing cold Neretva. That's not a suicide attempt but a professional sport – donations are expected from spectators and the divers won't leap until 50KM has been collected.

Mostar

Crooked Bridge BRIDGE
(Kriva Ćuprija) Built as a miniature test run for Stari Most, the pint-sized Crooked Bridge crosses the tiny Rabobolja creek amid a series of picturesque mill-house restaurants.

Hammam Museum MUSEUM
(Džejvanbeg Bathhouse; Rad Bitange bb; adult/student 5/3KM; ⊙10am-6pm Tue-Sun) This late-16th-century bathhouse has been attractively restored with whitewashed interior, bilingual panels explaining *hammam* (Turkish bath) culture and glass cabinets displaying associated traditional accoutrements.

★**Kajtaz House** MUSEUM
(Gaše Ilića 21; adult/child 4KM/free; ⊙9am-6pm Apr-Oct) Hidden behind tall walls, Mostar's most historic old house was once the harem section of a larger homestead built for a 16th-century Turkish judge. Full of original artefacts, it still belongs to descendants of the original family albeit now under Unesco protection. A visit includes a very extensive, personal tour.

Bišćevića Ćošak HOUSE
(Turkish House; Bišćevića 13; adult/student 4/3KM; ⊙8.30am-7pm Apr-Oct, winter by tour only) Built in 1635, Bišćevića Ćošak is one of very few traditional Turkic-styled houses to retain its original appearance, albeit now with trin-

kets for sale and a fountain made of metal *ibrik* jugs. Three rooms are colourfully furnished with rugs, metalwork and carved wooden furniture. Spot the two tortoises.

Spanski Trg HISTORIC SITE
In the early 1990s, Croat and Bosniak forces bombarded each other into the rubble across a 'front line' which ran along the Bulevar and Alese Šantića St. Even now, several shell-pocked skeletal buildings remain in ruins around Spanski Trg, notably the triangular tower that was once **Ljubljanska Banka** (Snipers' Nest; Kralja Zvonimira bb) but is now a concrete skeleton plastered with graffiti.

⌗ Tours

Virtually all hostels offer walking tours around town and/or great-value full-day Hercegovina trips visiting Blagaj, Počitelj and the Kravice Waterfalls (for around €30).

Requiring only a two-person minimum, **i-House** (☑036-580048, 063-481842; ihouse-mostar.com; Oneščukova 25; ⊙9am-9pm Jun-Sep, reduced hours Mar-May & Oct-Nov) has a similar around-Mostar option, does a fascinating 'Death of Yugoslavia' tour and offers numerous alternative possibilities, including wine tasting, paragliding, rafting and a Wednesday trip to **Tito's Nuclear Bunker**.

BOSNIA & HERCEGOVINA MOSTAR

🛏 Sleeping

There are numerous small hostels, though some are dormant between November and April.

★Hostel Balkanarama · HOSTEL €
(☑063-897832; www.facebook.com/balkanarama-hostel; Braće Seva 1A; dorm 20-30KM; ☺bar 6pm-11pm, hostel closed Oct-Mar; 🛜) Run by a very creative Anglo-Bosnian, this excellent new hostel has quickly become one of Mostar's most popular. Quirky features include a central kitchen table fashioned from beer crates and seats made from container pallets augmenting floor cushions in the candle-lamp rooftop bar.

Hostel Nina · HOSTEL €
(☑036-550520, 061-382743; www.hostelnina.ba; Čelebica 18; dm/s/d without bathroom €10/16/21; ❄@🛜) This popular homestay-hostel is run by an obliging English-speaking lady whose husband is a war survivor and former bridge-jumper who pioneered and still runs regional Hercegovina day tours (€30) that just might end up with drinks at his Tabhana bar.

Pansion Oskar · GUESTHOUSE €
(☑061-823649; www.pansionoskar.com; Onešćukova 33; per person €20; ❄🛜) Pansion Oskar is essentially a pair of family homes above a delightful open-air garden bar-restaurant slap bang in the historic centre. The nine

---

ENTITIES & AREAS

Geographically BiH comprises Bosnia in the north and Hercegovina (pronounced her-tse-go-vina) in the south. However, the term 'Bosnian' refers to anyone from BiH, not just from Bosnia proper.

Politically, BiH is divided into two entirely different entities. Southwest and central BiH falls mostly within the Federation of Bosnia and Hercegovina, usually shortened to 'the Federation'. Meanwhile most areas bordering Serbia, Montenegro and the northern arm of Croatia are within the Serb-dominated Republika Srpska (abbreviated RS). A few minor practicalities (stamps, phonecards) appear in different versions and the Cyrillic alphabet is more prominent in the RS, but these days casual visitors are unlikely to notice immediately visible differences between the entities.

---

rooms are fairly simple – three have shared bathroom. Touches of oriental decor echo the feel of the impressive summer garden below. You might have to look for staff in reception if the bell remains unanswered.

★Muslibegović House · HISTORIC HOTEL €€
(☑036-551379; www.muslibegovichouse.com; Osman Đikća 41; s/d/ste €60/90/105; ☺museum 10am-6pm mid-Apr–mid-Oct; ❄🛜) In summer, tourists pay 4KM to visit this beautiful, late-17th-century Ottoman courtyard house (extended in 1871). But it's also an extremely charming boutique hotel. Room sizes and styles vary significantly, mixing excellent modern bathrooms with elements of traditional Bosnian, Turkish or even Moroccan design.

★Pansion City Star · HOTEL €€
(☑060-3328821, 036-580080; www.citystar.ba; Onešćukova 35; s/d/tr/q from 102/124/156/248KM, breakfast 10KM; ❄🛜) Brand new in 2016, the building is designed to exacting traditional standards as befits the Unesco-protected Old Town zone, but room interiors are immaculately contemporary with a variety of mood lighting. The Swiss-made beds are super-comfortable and sepia wall photos of Mostar add visual focus.

★Shangri-La · GUESTHOUSE €€
(☑061-169362; www.shangrila.com.ba; Kalhanska 10; r €49-65; 🅿❄🛜) Behind an imposing 19th-century style facade, eight individually themed rooms are appointed to hotel standards, and there's a fine roof terrace with comfy parasol-shaded seating, dwarf citrus trees and panoramic city views. The English-speaking hosts are faultlessly welcoming without being intrusive. Breakfast costs €6 extra.

🍴 Eating

Cafes and restaurants with divine views of Stari Most cluster along the riverbank. Along Mala Tepa and the main central commercial street Braće Fejića you'll find supermarkets, a **vegetable market** (Mala Tepa; ☺6.30am-5pm) and several inexpensive places for *ćevapi* and other Bosnian snacks.

Hindin Han · BALKAN €€
(☑061-153054, 036-581054; Jusovina bb; mains 10-18KM, seafood 14-24KM, ćevapi 7KM, wine per litre 15KM; ☺9am-11pm; 🛜📱) Hindin Han is a rebuilt historic mill-cottage building with several layers of summer terrace perched

AROUND MOSTAR

Many Mostar agencies and hostels combine the following for a satisfying day trip:

Blagaj This village's signature sight is a half-timbered sufi-house (*tekija*) standing beside the surreally blue-green Buna River, where it gushes out of a cliff-cave.

Počitelj A steeply layered Ottoman-era fortress village that's one of BiH's most picture-perfect architectural ensembles.

Međugorje Curious for its mixture of pilgrim piety and Catholic kitsch ever since the Virgin Mary was reputedly spotted in a series of 1981 visions.

Kravice Waterfalls BiH's splendid 25m mini Niagara. Some tours give you several hours here to swim in natural pools.

---

pleasantly above a side stream. Locals rate its food as better than most equivalent tourist restaurants. The stuffed squid we tried was perfectly cooked and generously garnished.

Šadrvan
BALKAN €€

(☑036-579057; www.restoransadravan.ba; Jusovina 11; mains10-25KM; ⊙8am-11pm Feb-Dec; 🛜🅿) On a vine- and tree-shaded corner where the pedestrian lane from Stari Most divides, this delightful tourist favourite has tables set around a trickling fountain made of old Turkish-style metalwork. Obliging costumed waiters can help explain a menu that covers many bases and takes a stab at some vegetarian options. Meat-free *đuveč* (KM8) tastes like ratatouille on rice.

Babilon
BALKAN €€

(☑061-164912; Tabhana; mains 8-20KM; ⊙9am-11pm summer, 11am-4pm Dec-Feb; 🅿) The Babilon has stupendous views across the river to the Old Town and Stari Most from an extensive series of terraces on five different layers.

Urban Grill
BOSNIAN €€

(Mala Tepa 26; mains 8-18KM; ⊙8am-11pm Mon-Sat, 9am-11pm Sun; 🅿) From street level Urban Grill seems to be a slightly upmarket Bosnian fast-food place. But the menu spans a great range and the big attraction is the lower terrace with unexpectedly perfectly framed views of the Old Bridge.

🍷 Drinking & Nightlife

Black Dog Pub
PUB

(Crooked Bridge; beer/wine from 2/4KM; ⊙10am-late) Old Mostar's best hostelry is a historic mill-house decked with flags and car number plates. It's about the only place you'll find draft ales from the local Oldbridz mi-cro-brewery (www.facebook.com/oldbridz.ale). Live bands play regularly midsummer, more rarely off season.

Caffe Marshall
BAR

(www.apartmanimarshall.com; Oneščukova bb; coffee/beer from 2/3KM; ⊙8am-1am) With a ceiling draped in musical instruments, this music-pumping box bar is named for an ancient Marshall speaker in the owner's collection, rather than for Tito, though a copper Tito head does now grace the cute stone building's facade.

Terasa
CAFE

(Maršala Tita bb; coffee from 2KM; ⊙weather-dependent) Half a dozen tables on an open-air perch-terrace survey Stari Most and the Old Town towers from photogenic yet unexpected angles. Enter beside MUM (Museum of Mostar & Herzegovina; ☑036-551432; www.muzejhercegovine.ba; Maršala Tita 156; adult/student 5/3KM; ⊙10am-4pm Tue-Sun).

Ali Baba
BAR

(Kujundžiluk; beer/shots from 3/2KM; ⊙7am-3am Jun-Sep) Take a gaping cavern in the raw rock, add fat beats and colourful flashing globe lamps and hey presto, you have this one-off party bar. A dripping tunnel leads out to a second entrance on Maršala Tita.

🛍 Shopping

Edo Kurt's Workshop
ART

(☑061-772173; https://mostar-art.com; Kujundžiluk 5; ⊙7.30am-4pm) For decades, coppersmith Ismet Kurt beat metal – notably shell casings – into beautiful works of art. His son Edo has now taken on the trade with similar skill in an intriguing little workshop on Kujundžiluk that's a veritable craft museum.

ⓘ Information

Bosniak Post Office (Braće Fejića bb; ⊙8am-8pm Mon-Fri, to 3pm Sat) The main BH Pošta office is right in the heart of town.

Tourist Info Centre (☑036-580275; www.her cegovina.ba; Trg Preživjelih Branioco; ⊙8am-8pm May–early Oct) This office is usefully central but not gushingly helpful.

ⓘ Getting There & Around

BUS

The **main bus station** (☑036-552025; Trg Ivana Krndelja) beside the train station handles half a dozen daily services to Sarajevo, Split and Zagreb plus early morning departures to Belgrade, Herceg Novi, Kotor and Vienna. For Dubrovnik there are three or four direct buses (40KM, 4½ hours) each day.

TRAIN

Trains to Sarajevo should leave morning and evening but services are currently suspended pending track renewal.

SURVIVAL GUIDE

ⓘ Directory A–Z

INTERNET ACCESS

Almost all hotels and most cafes offer free wi-fi.

MONEY

Bosnia's convertible mark (KM or BAM), pronounced *kai-em* or *maraka*, is tied to the euro at

COUNTRY FACTS

Area 51,129 sq km

Capital Sarajevo

Country code ☑387

Currency Convertible mark (KM, BAM)

Emergency Ambulance ☑124, Fire ☑123, Police ☑122

Languages Bosnian, Serbian and Croatian (all variants of the same language)

Money ATMs accepting Visa and MasterCard are ubiquitous

Population 3.53 million

Useful phrases *zdravo* (hello); *hvala* (thanks); *molim* (please), *koliko to košta?* (how much does it cost?)

Visas not required for most visitors (see www.mfa.ba)

ESSENTIAL FOOD & DRINK

Burek Bosnian *burek* are cylindrical or spiral lengths of filo pastry filled with minced meat. *Sirnica* is filled instead with cheese, *krompiruša* with potato and *zeljanica* with spinach. Collectively these pies are called *pita*.

Ćevapi (Ćevapčići) Minced meat formed into cylindrical pellets and served in fresh bread with melting *kajmak*.

Hurmastica Syrup-soaked sponge fingers.

Kajmak Thick semi-soured cream.

Pljeskavica Patty-shaped *ćevapi*.

Rakija Grappa or fruit brandy.

Sarma Steamed dolma-parcels of rice and minced meat wrapped in cabbage or other green leaves.

Tufahija Whole stewed apple with walnut filling.

approximately €1=1.96KM. Though no longer officially sanctioned, many businesses still unblinkingly accept euros for minor purchases.

OPENING HOURS

Banks 8am–6pm Monday to Friday, 8.30am–1.30pm Saturday

Office hours 8am–4pm Monday to Friday

Shops 8am–6pm daily; many stay open later

Restaurants 7am–10.30pm or last customer

POST

BiH has three parallel postal organisations, each issuing their own stamps: BH Pošta (Federation; www.posta.ba), Pošte Srpske (RS; www.postes-rpske.com) and HP Post (Croat areas, western Mostar; www.post.ba).

PUBLIC HOLIDAYS

Nationwide holidays:

New Year's Day 1 January

Independence Day 1 March

May Day 1 May

National Statehood Day 25 November

Additional holidays in the Federation:

Kurban Bajram (Islamic Feast of Sacrifice) 1 September 2017, 22 August 2018, 12 August 2019

Ramazanski Bajram (end of Ramadan) 26 June 2017, 15 June 2018, 5 June 2019

Gregorian Easter 14 and 17 April 2017, 31 March and 2 April 2018, 19 and 22 April 2019

Gregorian Christmas 25 December

Additional holidays in the Republika Srpska (RS):
Orthodox Easter 14 and 17 Apr 2017, 6 and 9 April 2018, 22 and 29 April 2019
Orthodox Christmas 6 January

SAFE TRAVEL

Landmines and unexploded ordnance still affect 2.3% of Bosnia and Hercegovina's area (see www.bhmac.org). Stick to asphalt/concrete surfaces or well-worn paths and avoid exploring war-wrecked buildings.

VISAS

Currently stays of less than 90 days require no visa for citizens of 77 counties including most European nations, plus Australia, Canada, Israel, New Zealand and the US. Other nationals should check www.mfa.ba for details.

Transit through Neum (coastal BiH between Split and Dubrovnik) is possible without a Bosnian visa assuming you have a double- or multiple-entry Croat visa.

ⓘ Getting There & Away

The main gateway by air is busy little **Sarajevo International Airport** (p148). WizzAir budget flights from several north-European destinations arrive at **Tuzla International Airport** (TZL; ☏ 035-814605; http://tuzla-airport.ba; Dubrave Gornje; ⊘ closed midnight-3.30am or longer), there are regular summer links to several Italian cities from **Mostar Airport** (OMO; ☏ 036-350992; www.mostar-airport.ba), and

---

EATING PRICE RANGES

The following price ranges refer to a main course.

€ less than 10KM

€€ 10KM–25KM

€€€ more than 25KM

SLEEPING PRICE RANGES

Except for in hostels, the following price ranges refer to a double room with bathroom during high season (June to September). Unless otherwise stated, breakfast is included in the price.

€ less than 80KM

€€ 80KM–190KM

€€€ more than 190KM

Banja Luka Airport (☏ 051-535210; www.banjaluka-airport.com) has an Air Serbia service to Belgrade with possible onward connections.

BiH cities have plenty of international bus services (notably to Belgrade, Dubrovnik, Munich, Split, Vienna and Zagreb), but the only international train is the daily Zagreb–Sarajevo service.

Britain

Best Traditional British Pubs

➡ Star Inn (p193)

➡ Bear Inn (p196)

➡ Old Thatch Tavern (p198)

➡ Blue Bell (p203)

➡ Café Royal Circle Bar (p212)

Best Museums

➡ Victoria & Albert Museum (p165)

➡ Ashmolean Museum (p194)

➡ National Railway Museum (p201)

➡ Kelvingrove Art Gallery & Museum (p214)

➡ Science Museum (p165)

Why Go?

Few places cram so much history, heritage and scenery into such a compact space as Britain. Twelve hours is all you'll need to travel from one end to the other, but you could spend a lifetime exploring – from the ancient relics of Stonehenge and Avebury, to the great medieval cathedrals of Westminster and Canterbury, and the magnificent mountain landscapes of Snowdonia and Skye.

In fact, Britain isn't really one country at all, but three. While they haven't always been one easy bedfellows, the contrasts between England, Wales and Scotland make this a rewarding place to visit. With a wealth of rolling countryside, stately cities, world-class museums and national parks to explore, Britain really is one of Europe's most unmissable destinations. And despite what you may have heard, it doesn't rain *all* the time – but even so, a brolly and a raincoat will certainly come in handy.

When to Go

London

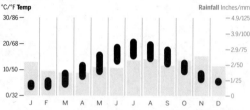

Easter–May Fewer crowds, especially in popular spots like Bath, York and Edinburgh.

Jun–Aug The weather is at its best but the coast and national parks are busy.

Mid-Sep–Oct Prices drop and the weather is often surprisingly good.

ENGLAND

By far the biggest of the three nations that comprise Great Britain, England offers a tempting spread of classic travel experiences, from London's vibrant theatre scene and the historic colleges of Oxford, to the grand cathedrals of Canterbury and York and the mountain landscapes of the Lake District.

London

POP 8.7 MILLION

Everyone comes to London with preconceptions shaped by a multitude of books, movies, TV shows and pop songs. Whatever yours are, prepare to have them exploded by this endlessly intriguing city. Its streets are steeped in fascinating history, magnificent art, imposing architecture and popular culture. When you add a bottomless reserve of cool to this mix, it's hard not to conclude that London is one of the world's great cities, if not the greatest.

The only downside is increasing cost: London is now Europe's most expensive city for visitors, whatever their budget. But with some careful planning and a bit of common sense, you can find excellent bargains and freebies among the popular attractions. And many of London's finest assets – its wonderful parks, bridges, squares and boulevards, not to mention many of its landmark museums – come completely free.

History

London first came into being as a Celtic village near a ford across the River Thames, but the city really only took off after the Roman invasion in AD 43. The Romans enclosed Londinium in walls that still find an echo in the shape of the City of London (the city's central financial district) today. Next came the Saxons, and the town they called Lundenwic prospered.

London grew in global importance throughout the medieval period, surviving devastating challenges such as the 1665 plague and the 1666 Great Fire. Many of its important landmarks such as St Paul's Cathedral were built at this time by visionary architect Christopher Wren.

By the early 1700s, Georgian London had become one of Europe's largest and richest cities. It was during the Victorian era that London really hit its stride, fuelled by vast mercantile wealth and a huge global empire.

The ravages of WWI were followed by the economic troubles of the 1920s and 1930s, but it was WWII that wrought the greatest damage: huge swathes of the city were reduced to rubble during a series of devastating bombings known as the Blitz.

During the 1960s, Swinging London became the world's undisputed cultural capital, with an explosion of provocative art, music, writing, theatre and fashion. The 1970s proved more turbulent than innovative, with widespread unrest and economic discontent, while the 1980s were marked by an economic boom in London's financial district (known as the City), which brought a forest of skyscrapers to the city's skyline.

In 2000 London got its first elected Mayor, left-wing Ken Livingstone, who served for two terms before being ousted in 2008 by his Eton-educated Conservative rival, Boris Johnson, who oversaw the city's hugely successful stint as Olympics host. The pendulum swung back leftwards in 2016 when former Labour MP Sadiq Khan took office, the first Muslim to be mayor of a major Western capital city.

ITINERARIES

One Week

With just seven days, you're pretty much limited to sights in England. Spend three days seeing the sights in London, then head to Oxford for a day, followed by a day each at Stonehenge and historic Bath, before returning for a final day in London.

Two Weeks

Follow the one-week itinerary, but instead of returning to London on day seven, head north to Stratford-upon-Avon for everything Shakespeare. Continue north with a day in the Lake District, followed by two days in Scotland's capital, Edinburgh. After a day trip to Loch Ness, recross the border for two days to see York and Castle Howard. Next, stop off in Cambridge on the way back to London.

Britain Highlights

1 London (p157)
Exploring the streets of one of the world's greatest capital cities.

2 Bath (p190)
Visiting Roman baths and admiring grand Georgian architecture.

3 Stratford-upon-Avon
(p196) Enjoying a Shakespeare play in the town of his birth.

4 Snowdonia National Park
(p208) Marvelling at the mountainous landscape of Wales' first national park.

5 York (p201)
Delving into the city's history – Roman, Viking and medieval .

6 Oxford (p193)
Getting lost among the city's dreaming spires.

ATLANTIC OCEAN

NORTH SEA

The Minch

Sea of the Hebrides

North Channel

SHETLAND ISLANDS

Mainland

ORKNEY ISLANDS

Mainland

John O'Groats
Thurso
Wick
Durness
Ullapool
Sutherland
Elgin
Inverness
Moray Firth
Spey
Aberdeen
Don
Cairngorms National Park
Aviemore
Strathfarrar
Kyle of Lochalsh
Isle of Skye
Rhum
Ben Nevis
Fort William
Oban
Tobermory
Mull
Coll
Tiree
Loch Ness
Loch Linnhe
Loch Awe
SCOTLAND
Perth
Dundee
St Andrews
Loch Lomond & Trossachs National Park
Stirling
Loch Lomond
Edinburgh
Glasgow
Melrose
Arran
Alloway
Galloway Forest
Stranraer
Lewis
Harris
North Uist
South Uist
St Kilda
OUTER HEBRIDES
INNER HEBRIDES
Jura
Islay
Newcastle-upon-Tyne
Northumberland National Park
Hadrian's Wall
Carlisle

7 Stonehenge
(p190) Stepping back in time wandering around the great trilithons of this ancient site.

8 Edinburgh
(p209) Joining the party in Scotland's festival city.

9 Isle of Skye
(p221) Heading north through the Scottish Highlands to experience the epic scenery of this rugged island.

10 Lake District National Park
(p205) Following in the footsteps of Romantic poet William Wordsworth.

London

Sights

Westminster & St James's

★ Westminster Abbey CHURCH

(Map p166; ☑ 020-7222 5152; www.westminster
-abbey.org; 20 Dean's Yard, SW1; adult/child £20/9,
verger tours £5, cloister & gardens free; ⊙ 9.30am-
4.30pm Mon, Tue, Thu & Fri, to 7pm Wed, to 2.30pm
Sat; ⊜ Westminster) A splendid mixture of
architectural styles, Westminster Abbey
is considered the finest example of Early
English Gothic (1190–1300). It's not merely
a beautiful place of worship – the Abbey
also serves up the country's history cold on
slabs of stone. For centuries the country's
greatest have been interred here, including
17 monarchs from Henry III (died 1272) to
George II (1760). Never a cathedral (the seat
of a bishop), Westminster Abbey is what is
called a 'royal peculiar', administered by the
Crown.

★ Houses of Parliament HISTORIC BUILDING

(Palace of Westminster; Map p166; www.parlia
ment.uk; Parliament Sq, SW1; ⊜ Westminster)
FREE A visit here is a journey to the heart of
UK democracy. Officially called the Palace
of Westminster, the Houses of Parliament's
oldest part is 11th-century **Westminster
Hall**, one of only a few sections that survived a catastrophic fire in 1834. Its roof,
added between 1394–1401, is the earliest-known example of a hammerbeam roof.
The rest is mostly a neo-Gothic confection
built by Charles Barry and Augustus Pugin
(1840–58).

The palace's most famous feature is its
clock tower, Elizabeth Tower, aka **Big Ben**
(Map p166; ⊜ Westminster).

★ Tate Britain GALLERY

(www.tate.org.uk; Millbank, SW1; ⊙ 10am-6pm, to
10pm 1st Fri of month; ⊜ Pimlico) **FREE** Splendidly reopened a few years back with a
stunning new art deco–inspired staircase
and a rehung collection, the older and more
venerable of the two Tate siblings celebrates
paintings from 1500 to the present, with
works from Blake, Hogarth, Gainsborough,
Barbara Hepworth, Whistler, Constable
and Turner, as well as vibrant modern and
contemporary pieces from Lucian Freud,
Francis Bacon and Henry Moore. Join a free
45-minute **thematic tour** (11am daily) and
15-minute **Art in Focus talks** (1.15pm Tuesday, Thursday and Saturday).

West End

★ Trafalgar Square   SQUARE
(Map p166; ⊜ Charing Cross) In many ways Trafalgar Sq is is the centre of London, where rallies and marches take place, tens of thousands of revellers usher in the New Year and locals congregate for anything from communal open-air cinema and Christmas celebrations to various political protests. It is dominated by the 52m-high **Nelson's Column** and ringed by many splendid buildings, including the National Gallery and St Martin-in-the-Fields. The Nazis once planned to shift Nelson's Column to Berlin in the wake of a successful invasion.

★ National Gallery   GALLERY
(Map p166; www.nationalgallery.org.uk; Trafalgar Sq, WC2; ⊙ 10am-6pm Sat-Thu, to 9pm Fri; ⊜ Charing Cross) **FREE** With some 2300 European paintings on display, this is one of the world's great art collections, with seminal works from every important epoch in the history of art – from the mid-13th to the early 20th century, including masterpieces by Leonardo da Vinci, Michelangelo, Titian, Van Gogh and Renoir.

Many visitors flock to the East Wing (1700–1900), where works by 18th-century British artists such as Gainsborough, Constable and Turner, and seminal Impressionist and post-Impressionist masterpieces by Van Gogh, Renoir and Monet await.

★ National Portrait Gallery   GALLERY
(Map p166; ☑ 020-7321 0055; www.npg.org.uk; St Martin's Pl, WC2; ⊙ 10am-6pm Sat-Wed, to 9pm Thu & Fri; ⊜ Charing Cross, Leicester Sq) **FREE** What makes the National Portrait Gallery so compelling is its familiarity; in many cases you'll have heard of the subject (royals, scientists, politicians, celebrities) or the artist (Andy Warhol, Annie Leibovitz, Lucian Freud). Highlights include the famous 'Chandos portrait' of William Shakespeare, the first artwork the gallery acquired (in 1856) and believed to be the only likeness made during the playwright's lifetime, and a touching sketch of novelist Jane Austen by her sister.

★ Madame Tussauds   MUSEUM
(☑ 0870 400 3000; www.madame-tussauds.com/london; Marylebone Rd, NW1; adult/child 4-15yr £35/30; ⊙ 8.30/10am-4/6pm (seasonal); ⊜ Baker St) It may be kitschy and pricey (book online for much cheaper rates), but Madame Tussauds makes for a fun-filled day. There

---

BIG BEN

The Houses of Parliament's most famous feature is the clock tower known as Big Ben. Strictly speaking, however, Big Ben is the tower's 13-ton bell, named after Benjamin Hall, commissioner of works when the tower was completed in 1858.

---

are photo ops with your dream celebrity (Daniel Craig, Miley Cyrus, Audrey Hepburn, the Beckhams), the Bollywood gathering (studs Hrithik Roshan and Salman Khan) and the Royal Appointment (the Queen, Harry, William and Kate).

Piccadilly Circus   SQUARE
(Map p166; ⊜ Piccadilly Circus) John Nash had originally designed Regent St and Piccadilly in the 1820s to be the two most elegant streets in town but, curbed by city planners, couldn't realise his dream to the full. He may be disappointed, but suitably astonished, with Piccadilly Circus today: a traffic maelstrom, deluged with visitors and flanked by flashing advertisements. 'It's like Piccadilly Circus', as the expression goes, but it's certainly fun.

The City

★ Tower of London   CASTLE
(Map p162; ☑ 0844 482 7777; www.hrp.org.uk/toweroflondon; Petty Wales, EC3; adult/child £25/12, audio guide £4/3; ⊙ 9.30am-5pm; ⊜ Tower Hill) The unmissable Tower of London (actually a castle of 22 towers) offers a window into a gruesome and compelling history. This was where two kings and three queens met their death and countless others were imprisoned. Come here to see the colourful Yeoman Warders (or Beefeaters), the spectacular Crown Jewels, the soothsaying ravens and armour fit for a *very* large king.

★ Tower Bridge   BRIDGE
(Map p162; ⊜ Tower Hill) London was a thriving city in 1894 when elegant Tower Bridge was built. Designed to be raised to allow ships to pass, electricity has now taken over from the original steam and hydraulic engines. A lift leads up from the northern tower to the **Tower Bridge Exhibition**, where the story of its building is recounted within the upper walkway. You then walk down to the fascinating Victorian Engine Rooms, which powered the bridge lifts.

BRITAIN LONDON

Central London

500 m
0.25 miles

ST PANCRAS

FINSBURY

Rosebery Ave

Lloyd Baker St
Margery St
Wharton St

33
11

CLERKENWELL

Gray's Inn Rd
Phoenix Pl
Gray's Inn Gardens

HOLBORN

Spa Fields
Skinner St
St John St
Aylesbury St
Sekforde St
St James's
Clerkenwell Rd
Clerkenwell Green
Farringdon Rd

Leather Lane Market
Leather Lane
Cross St
Hatton Garden
26
Brooke St
Fetter La
High Holborn
Lincoln's Inn Fields
Portugal St
Carey St

Moreland St
Spencer St
St John St
Central St
Goswell Rd
Gt Sutton St
Compton St
Pear Tree St
Percival St
Dingley Rd
Lever St
Bath St
Peerless St
Nile St
Britannia Wk
City Rd
East Rd
Old St
25
13
HOXTON
Pitfield St
SHOREDITCH
Great Eastern St
Curtain Rd
Leonard St
Tabernacle St
St Paul St
Worship St
24
City Rd
Old St
Banner St
Bunhill Fields
Bunhill Row
Whitecross St
Golden La
Beech St
Chiswell St
Wilson St
Sun St
Finsbury Sq
Finsbury Circus
South Pl
Moorgate
London Wall
Wood St
Gresham St
St Martin's Le-Grand
Cheapside
Poultry
Princes St
Threadneedle St
Cornhill
Lothbury

28
Barbican
Aldersgate St
Lion La
Little Britain
King Edward St
Newgate St
St Paul's Cathedral
3

Goswell Rd
Aldersgate St
St John St
Clerkenwell Rd
18
20
27
Farringdon
Charterhouse St
Snow Hill
Holborn Viaduct
Farringdon St
Bride St
Fleet St
Ludgate Hill
Gough Sq
Bell La

Columbia Rd
1
Columbia Road Flower Market
Hackney Rd
Bethnal Green Rd
Austin St
Swanfield St
Calvert Ave
Boundary St
Shoreditch High St
Kingsland Rd
Curtain Rd
Great Eastern St
Shoreditch High St
Exchange Sq
Appold St
Bishopsgate
Liverpool St
Liverpool St
Eldon St
Old Broad St
Wormwood St

SPITALFIELDS
Spital St
Quaker St
Brick La
Lamb St
Commercial St
Folgate St
Brushfield St
Commercial St
Hanbury St
Fournier St
Brick La
Commercial St
37
38
17
36
Middlesex St
New St
Houndsditch
Bevis Marks
Leadenhall St
Wentworth St
Goulston St
Aldgate
Whitechapel
Docklands (2.1mi);
Greenwich (4.6mi);
London City (5.8mi)

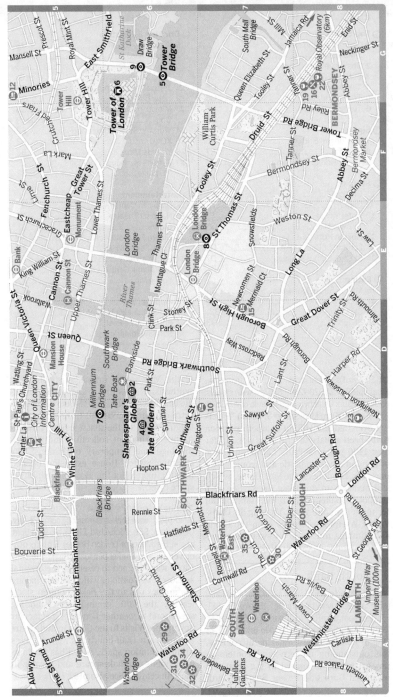

Central London

★ **St Paul's Cathedral** CATHEDRAL
(Map p162; ☑020-7246 8357; www.stpauls.
co.uk; St Paul's Churchyard, EC4; adult/child £18/8;
⊙8.30am-4.30pm Mon-Sat; ⊜St Paul's) Towering over Ludgate Hill, in a superb position that's been a place of Christian worship for over 1400 years, St Paul's Cathedral is one of London's most majestic and iconic buildings. For Londoners, the vast dome, which still manages to dominate the skyline, is a symbol of resilience and pride, standing tall for more than 300 years. Viewing Sir Christopher Wren's masterpiece from the inside and climbing to the top for sweeping views of the capital is an exhilarating experience.

⊙ South Bank

★ **Tate Modern** MUSEUM
(Map p162; www.tate.org.uk; Bankside, SE1;
⊙10am-6pm Sun-Thu, to 10pm Fri & Sat; 🛜🚼;
⊜Blackfriars, Southwark or London Bridge) FREE
One of London's most amazing attractions, this outstanding modern- and contemporary-art gallery is housed in the creatively revamped **Bankside Power Station** south of the Millennium Bridge. A spellbinding synthesis of modern art and capacious industrial brick design, Tate Modern has been extraordinarily successful in bringing challenging work to the masses, both through its free permanent collection and fee-paying big-name temporary exhibitions. The stunning Switch House extension opened in 2016, increasing the available exhibition space by 60%.

★ **Shakespeare's Globe** HISTORIC BUILDING
(Map p162; www.shakespearesglobe.com; 21 New Globe Walk, SE1; adult/child £16/9; ⊙9am-5pm;
🚼; ⊜Blackfriars or London Bridge) Unlike other venues for Shakespearean plays, the new Globe was designed to resemble the original as closely as possible, which means having the arena open to the fickle London skies, leaving the 700 'groundlings' (standing spectators) to weather London's spectacular downpours. Visits to the Globe include tours of the theatre (half-hourly) as well as access to the exhibition space, which has fascinating exhibits on Shakespeare and theatre in the 17th century. See also p182.

★**London Eye** VIEWPOINT
(Map p166; ☑0871-222 4002; www.londoneye.
com; adult/child £23.45/18.95; ⊙11am-6pm Sep-
May, 10am-8.30pm Jun-Aug; ⊜Waterloo or Westminster) Standing 135m high in a fairly flat
city, the London Eye affords views 25 miles
in every direction, weather permitting.
Interactive tablets provide great information
(in six languages) about landmarks as they
appear in the skyline. Each rotation – or
'flight' – takes a gracefully slow 30 minutes.
At peak times (July, August and school holidays) it can feel like you'll spend more time
in the queue than in the capsule; book premium fast-track tickets to jump the queue.

★**Imperial War Museum** MUSEUM
(www.iwm.org.uk; Lambeth Rd, SE1; ⊙10am-6pm;
⊜Lambeth North) FREE Fronted by a pair of
intimidating 15in naval guns, this riveting
museum is housed in what was the Bethlehem Royal Hospital, a psychiatric hospital
also known as Bedlam. Although the museum's focus is on military action involving
British or Commonwealth troops largely
during the 20th century, it rolls out the carpet to war in the wider sense. Highlights
include the state-of-the-art First World War
Galleries and Witnesses to War in the
forecourt and atrium above.

Shard NOTABLE BUILDING
(Map p162; www.theviewfromtheshard.com; 32
London Bridge St, SE1; adult/child £30.95/24.95;
⊙10am-10pm; ⊜London Bridge) Punctur-
ing the skies above London, the dramatic
splinter-like form of the Shard has rapidly
become an icon of London. The viewing
platforms on floors 69 and 72 are open to
the public and the views are, as you'd expect
from a 244m vantage point, sweeping, but
they come at a hefty price – book online at
least a day in advance to save £5.

◎ Kensington & Hyde Park

This area is called the Royal Borough of
Kensington and Chelsea, and residents are
certainly paid royally, earning the highest
incomes in the UK (shops and restaurants
will presume you do too).

★**Natural History Museum** MUSEUM
(Map p170; www.nhm.ac.uk; Cromwell Rd, SW7;
⊙10am-5.50pm; ☎; ⊜South Kensington) FREE
This colossal and magnificent-looking building is infused with the irrepressible Victorian spirit of collecting, cataloguing and inter-
preting the natural world. The Dinosaurs

Gallery (Blue Zone) is a must for children,
who gawp at the animatronic T-Rex, fossils
and excellent displays. Adults for their part
will love the intriguing Treasures exhibition in the Cadogan Gallery (Green Zone),
which houses a host of unrelated objects
each telling its own unique story, from a
chunk of moon rock to a dodo skeleton.

★**Science Museum** MUSEUM
(Map p170; www.sciencemuseum.org.uk; Exhibition Rd, SW7; ⊙10am-6pm; ☎; ⊜South Kensington) FREE With seven floors of interactive
and educational exhibits, this scientifically
spellbinding museum will mesmerise adults
and children alike, covering everything from
early technology to space travel. A perennial favourite is Exploring Space, a gallery
featuring genuine rockets and satellites and
a full-size replica of 'Eagle', the lander that
took Neil Armstrong and Buzz Aldrin to the
Moon in 1969. The Making the Modern
World Gallery next door is a visual feast of
locomotives, planes, cars and other revolutionary inventions.

★**Victoria & Albert Museum** MUSEUM
(V&A; Map p170; ☑020-7942 2000; www.vam.
ac.uk; Cromwell Rd, SW7; ⊙10am-5.40pm Sat-
Thu, to 10pm Fri; ⊜South Kensington) FREE The
Museum of Manufactures, as the V&A was
known when it opened in 1852, was part of
Prince Albert's legacy to the nation in the
aftermath of the successful Great Exhibition
of 1851. It houses the world's largest collection of decorative arts, from Asian ceramics
to Middle Eastern rugs, Chinese paintings,
Western furniture, fashion from all ages and
modern-day domestic appliances. The temporary exhibitions are another highlight,
covering anything from David Bowie retro-
spectives to designer Alexander McQueen,
special materials and trends.

★**Hyde Park** PARK
(Map p170; www.royalparks.org.uk/parks/hyde-
park; ⊙5am-midnight; ⊜Marble Arch, Hyde Park
Corner or Queensway) At 145 hectares, Hyde
Park is central London's largest open space,
expropriated from the Church in 1536
by Henry VIII and turned into a hunting
ground and later a venue for duels, executions and horse racing. The 1851 Great Exhibition was held here, and during WWII
the park became an enormous potato field.
These days, there's boating on the Serpentine, summer concerts (Bruce Springsteen,
Florence + The Machine, Patti Smith), film
nights and other warm-weather events.

West End & Westminster

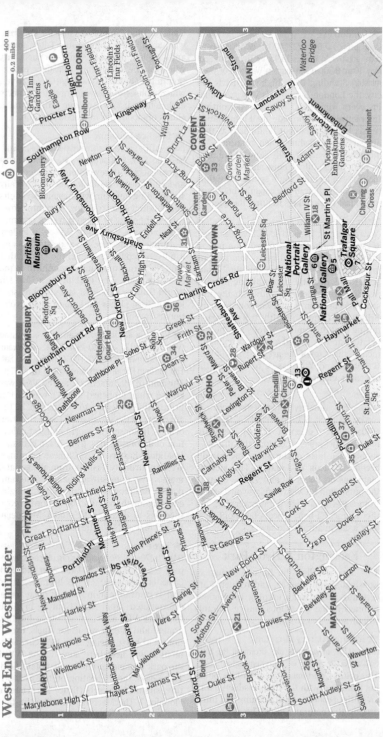

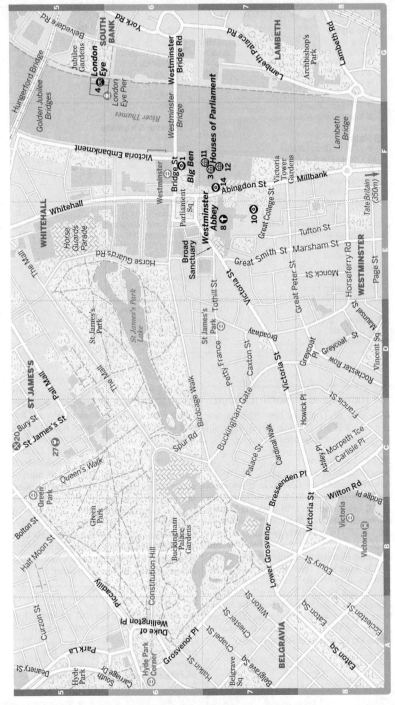

West End & Westminster

⊙ Hampstead & North London

With one of London's best high streets and plenty of green space, increasingly hip Marylebone is a great area to wander.

★ ZSL London Zoo   ZOO
(www.zsl.org/zsl-london-zoo; Outer Circle, Regent's Park, NW1; adult/child £29.75/22; ⊙10am-6pm Apr-Sep, to 5.30pm Mar & Oct, to 4pm Nov-Feb; ⊞; ⊒274) Established in 1828, these 15-hectare zoological gardens are among the oldest in the world. The emphasis nowadays is firmly placed on conservation, education and breeding. Highlights include Penguin Beach, Gorilla Kingdom, Tiger Territory, the walkthrough In with the Lemurs, In with the Spiders and Meet the Monkeys. Land of the Lions is a new enclosure to house its Asiatic lions. Feeding sessions and talks take place throughout the day – join in with a spot of afternoon tea (adult/child £19.75/10).

Regent's Park   PARK
(www.royalparks.org.uk; ⊙5am-dusk; ⊜Regent's Park or Baker St) The most elaborate and formal of London's many parks, Regent's Park is one of the capital's loveliest green spaces. Among its many attractions are London Zoo (p168), Regent's Canal, an ornamental lake and sports pitches where locals meet to play football, rugby and volleyball. **Queen Mary's Gardens**, towards the south of the park, are particularly pretty, especially in June when the roses are in bloom. Performances take place here in an **open-air theatre** (☑0844 826 4242; www.openairtheatre.org; Queen Mary's Gardens, Regent's Park, NW1; ⊙May-Sep; ⊞; ⊜Baker St) during summer.

⊙ Greenwich

An extraordinary cluster of buildings has earned 'Maritime Greenwich' its place on Unesco's World Heritage list. It's also famous for straddling the hemispheres; this is the degree zero of longitude, home of the Greenwich Meridian and Greenwich Mean Time.

Greenwich is easily reached on the DLR train (to Cutty Sark station), or by boat – Thames Clippers (www.thamesclippers.com; all zones adult/child £9/4.50) depart from the London Eye every 20 minutes.

★**Royal Observatory** HISTORIC BUILDING
(www.rmg.co.uk; Greenwich Park, Blackheath Ave, SE10; adult/child £9.50/5, with Cutty Sark £18.50/8.50; ⊙10am-5pm Sep-Jun, to 6pm Jul & Aug; 🚇DLR Cutty Sark, DLR Greenwich or Greenwich) Rising south of Queen's House, idyllic **Greenwich Park** (www.royalparks.org.uk; King George St, SE10; ⊙6am-6pm winter, to 8pm spring & autumn, to 9pm summer; 🚇DLR Cutty Sark, 🚇Greenwich or Maze Hill) climbs up the hill, affording stunning views of London from the Royal Observatory, which Charles II had built in 1675 to help solve the riddle of longitude. To the north is lovely **Flamsteed House** and the **Meridian Courtyard**, where you can stand with your feet straddling the western and eastern hemispheres; admission is by ticket. The southern half contains the highly informative and free **Weller Astronomy Galleries** and the **Peter Harrison Planetarium** (📞020-8312 6608; www.rmg.co.uk/whats-on/planetarium-shows; Greenwich Park, SE10; adult/child £7.50/5.50; 🚇Greenwich or DLR Cutty Sark).

★**Old Royal Naval College** HISTORIC BUILDING
(www.ornc.org; 2 Cutty Sark Gardens, SE10; ⊙grounds 8am-6pm, to 11pm in summer; 🚇DLR Cutty Sark) FREE Designed by Christopher Wren, the Old Royal Naval College is a magnificent example of monumental classical architecture. Parts are now used by the University of Greenwich and Trinity College of Music, but you can still visit the **chapel** and the extraordinary **Painted Hall**, which took artist Sir James Thornhill 19 years to complete. Hour-long, yeomen-led tours (£6) leave at noon daily, taking in areas not otherwise open to the public. Free 45-minute tours take place at least four times daily.

★**National Maritime Museum** MUSEUM
(www.rmg.co.uk/national-maritime-museum; Romney Rd, SE10; ⊙10am-5pm; 🚇DLR Cutty Sark) FREE Narrating the long, briny and eventful history of seafaring Britain, this excellent museum's exhibits are arranged thematically, with highlights including *Miss Britain III* (the first boat to top 100mph on open water) from 1933, the 19m-long golden state barge built in 1732 for Frederick, Prince of Wales, the huge ship's propeller and the colourful

BRITISH MUSEUM

The vast British Museum (Map p166; 📞020-7323 8299; www.britishmuseum.org; Great Russell St, WC1; ⊙10am-5.30pm Sat-Thu, to 8.30pm Fri; 🚇Russell Sq or Tottenham Court Rd) FREE isn't just the nation's largest museum, it's one of the oldest and finest anywhere in the world. Among the must-see antiquities are the Rosetta Stone, the key to deciphering Egyptian hieroglyphics, discovered in 1799; the controversial Parthenon Sculptures, stripped from the walls of the Parthenon in Athens by Lord Elgin (the British ambassador to the Ottoman Empire); and the Anglo-Saxon Sutton Hoo relics. The Great Court was restored and augmented by Norman Foster in 2000 and now has a spectacular glass-and-steel roof.

You'll need multiple visits to savour even the highlights here; take advantage of the 15 free 30- to 40-minute eye-opener tours of individual galleries per day. Audio guides (£5) can be found at the audio-guide desk in the Great Court.

figureheads installed on the ground floor. Families will love these, as well as the ship simulator and the 'All Hands' children's gallery on the 2nd floor.

★**Cutty Sark** MUSEUM
(📞020-8312 6608; www.rmg.co.uk/cuttysark; King William Walk, SE10; adult/child £13.50/7; ⊙10am-5pm Sep-Jun, to 6pm Jul & Aug; 🚇DLR Cutty Sark) This Greenwich landmark, the last of the great clipper ships to sail between China and England in the 19th century, saw £25 million of extensive renovations largely precipitated by a disastrous fire in 2007. The exhibition in the ship's hold tells her story as a tea clipper at the end of the 19th century (and then wool and mixed cargo).

⊙ Outside Central London

★**Kew Gardens** GARDENS
(www.kew.org; Kew Rd; adult/child £15/3.50; ⊙10am-6.30pm Apr-Aug, closes earlier Sep-Mar; 🚤Kew Pier, 🚇Kew Bridge, 🚇Kew Gardens) In 1759 botanists began rummaging around the world for specimens to plant in the 3-hectare Royal Botanic Gardens at Kew. They never

Hyde Park to Chelsea

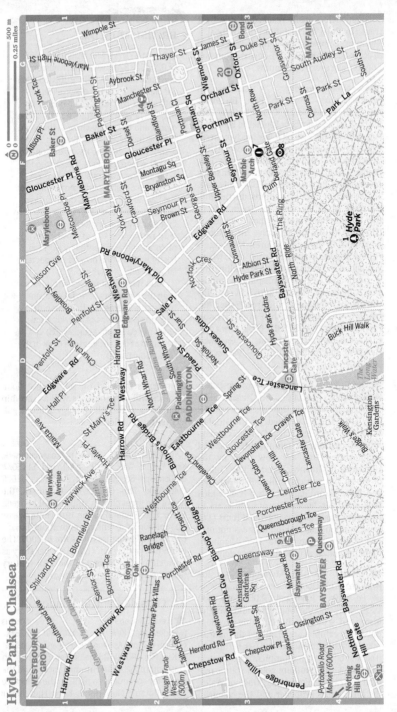

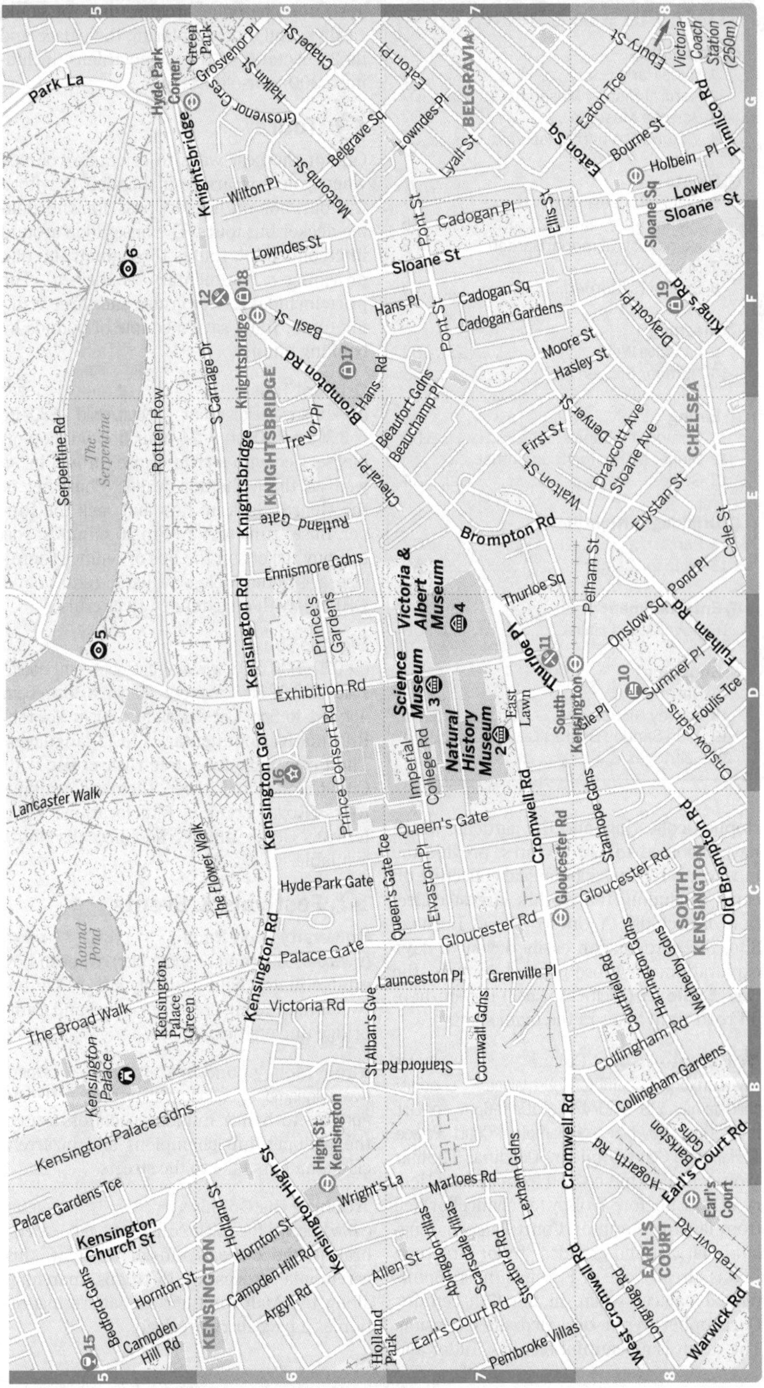
Park La
Hyde Park Corner
Green Park
Grosvenor Pl
Chapel St
Halkin St
Grosvenor Cres
Eaton Pl
BELGRAVIA
Ebury St
Victoria Coach Station (250m)
Eaton Tce
Eaton Sq
Lowndes Pl
Belgrave Sq
Lyall St
Motcomb St
Wilton Pl
Knightsbridge
Bourne St
Holbein Pl
Pimlico Rd
Lower Sloane St
Sloane Sq
Cadogan Pl
Pont St
Ellis St
Lowndes St
Sloane St
6
12
18
19
King's Rd
Hans Pl
Cadogan Sq
Cadogan Gardens
Basil St
Draycott Pl
S Carriage Dr
Brompton Rd
17
Hans Rd
Moore St
Hasley St
Rotten Row
Serpentine Rd
The Serpentine
KNIGHTSBRIDGE
Trevor Pl
Beaufort Gdns
Beauchamp Pl
Denyer St
First St
Draycott Ave
Sloane Ave
CHELSEA
Cheval Pl
Walton St
Rutland Gate
Elystan St
Brompton Rd
Ennismore Gdns
Victoria & Albert Museum
4
Thurloe Sq
Pelham St
Cale St
Pond Pl
Kensington Rd
Prince's Gardens
Onslow Sq
Fulham Rd
5
Thurloe Pl
11
Exhibition Rd
Science Museum
3
10
Sumner Pl
Foulis Tce
South Kensington
Natural History Museum
2
East Lawn
Onslow Gdns
Kensington Gore
Prince Consort Rd
Imperial College Rd
16
Lancaster Walk
Queen's Gate
Cromwell Rd
Gloucester Rd
Stanhope Gdns
Old Brompton Rd
The Flower Walk
Hyde Park Gate
Queen's Gate Tce
Elvaston Pl
Gloucester Rd
SOUTH KENSINGTON
Round Pond
Palace Gate
Gloucester Rd
Kensington Rd
Kensington Palace Green
Launceston Pl
Grenville Pl
Courtfield Rd
Harrington Gdns
Wetherby Gdns
The Broad Walk
Victoria Rd
St Alban's Gve
Cornwall Gdns
Collingham Rd
Kensington Palace
Stanford Rd
Collingham Gardens
Kensington Palace Gdns
High St Kensington
Cromwell Rd
Barkston Gdns
Hogarth Rd
Earl's Court Rd
Palace Gardens Tce
Kensington High St
Wright's La
Marloes Rd
Lexham Gdns
Earl's Court
Kensington Church St
Holland St
Hornton St
Abingdon Villas
Scarsdale Villas
Stratford Rd
EARL'S COURT
Trebovir Rd
KENSINGTON
Campden Hill Rd
Allen St
West Cromwell Rd
Longridge Rd
Warwick Rd
Bedford Gdns
Hornton St
Argyll Rd
Holland Park
Earl's Court Rd
Pembroke Villas
15
Campden Hill Rd
A
B
C
D
E
F
G
5
6
7
8

Hyde Park to Chelsea

stopped collecting, and the gardens, which have bloomed to 120 hectares, provide the most comprehensive botanical collection on earth (including the world's largest collection of orchids). A Unesco World Heritage Site, the gardens can easily devour a day's exploration; for those pressed for time, the Kew Explorer (adult/child £5/2) hop-on/hop-off road train takes in the main sights.

★ Hampton Court Palace   PALACE
(www.hrp.org.uk/hamptoncourtpalace; adult/child/family £19/9.50/47; ⊙10am-6pm Apr-Oct, to 4.30pm Nov-Mar; ▣Hampton Court Palace, ▣Hampton Court) Built by Cardinal Thomas Wolsey in 1514 but coaxed from him by Henry VIII just before Wolsey (as chancellor) fell from favour, Hampton Court Palace is England's largest and grandest Tudor structure. It was already one of Europe's most sophisticated palaces when, in the 17th century, Christopher Wren designed an extension. The result is a beautiful blend of Tudor and 'restrained baroque' architecture. You could easily spend a day exploring the palace and its 24 hectares of riverside gardens, including a 300-year-old maze.

☞ Tours

One of the best ways to orientate yourself when you first arrive in London is with a 24-hour hop-on/hop-off pass for the double-decker bus tours. The buses loop around interconnecting routes throughout the day, providing a commentary as they go. The price includes a river cruise and three walking tours. You'll save a couple of pounds by booking online.

Original Tour   BUS
(www.theoriginaltour.com; adult/child £30/15; ⊙8.30am-8.30pm) A 24-hour hop-on, hop-off bus service with a river cruise thrown in, as well as three themed walks: Changing of the Guard, Rock 'n' Roll and Jack the Ripper. Buses run every five to 20 minutes; you can buy tickets on the bus or online. There's also a 48-hour ticket available (adult/child £40/19), with an extended river cruise.

Big Bus Tours   BUS
(✆020-7808 6753; www.bigbustours.com; adult/child £30/12.50; ⊙every 20min 8.30am-6pm Apr-Sep, to 5pm Oct & Mar, to 4.30pm Nov-Feb) Informative commentaries in 12 languages. The ticket includes a free river cruise with City Cruises and three thematic walking tours (Royal London, film locations, mysteries). Good online booking discounts available.

✺ Festivals & Events

University Boat Race   ROWING
(www.theboatrace.org; ⊙late Mar) A posh-boy grudge match held annually since 1829 between the rowing crews of Oxford and Cambridge universities.

Virgin Money London Marathon   SPORTS
(www.virginmoneylondonmarathon.com; ⊙late Apr) Up to half a million spectators watch the whippet-thin champions and bizarrely clad amateurs take to the streets.

Trooping the Colour   PARADE
(www.trooping-the-colour.co.uk; ⊙Jun) Celebrating the Queen's official birthday, this ceremonial procession of troops, marching along the Mall for their monarch's inspection, is a pageantry overload.

Meltdown Festival   MUSIC
(www.southbankcentre.co.uk; ☺late Jun) The Southbank Centre hands over the curatorial reigns to a legend of contemporary music (such as Morrissey, Patti Smith or David Byrne) to pull together a full program of concerts, talks and films.

Wimbledon Championships   SPECTATOR SPORT
(☑020-8944 1066; www.wimbledon.com; Church Rd, SW19; grounds admission £8-25, tickets £41-190) The world's most splendid tennis event.

Pride   GAY & LESBIAN
(www.prideinlondon.org; ☺late Jun or early Jul) The big event on the gay and lesbian calendar, a technicolour street parade heads through the West End, culminating in a concert in Trafalgar Sq.

Notting Hill Carnival   CARNIVAL
(www.thelondonnottinghillcarnival.com; ☺Aug) Every year, for three days during the last weekend of August, Notting Hill echoes to the calypso, ska, reggae and soca sounds of the Notting Hill Carnival. Launched in 1964 by the local Afro-Caribbean community, keen to celebrate its culture and traditions, it has grown to become Europe's largest street festival (up to one million people) and a highlight of London's calendar.

🛏 Sleeping

When it comes to accommodation, London is one of the most expensive places in the world. Budget is pretty much anything below £100 per night for a double; double rooms ranging between £100 and £200 per night are considered midrange; more expensive options fall into the top-end category. Public transport is good, so you don't need to sleep at Buckingham Palace to be at the heart of things.

🛏 West End

★Clink78   HOSTEL £
(Map p162; ☑020-7183 9400; www.clinkhostels.com/london/clink78; 78 King's Cross Rd, WC1; dm/r incl breakfast from £16/65; @ ⓦ; ☺King's Cross St Pancras) This fantastic 630-bed hostel is housed in a 19th-century magistrates courthouse where Dickens once worked as a scribe and members of the Clash stood trial in 1978. Rooms feature pod beds (including overhead storage space) in four- to 16-bed dormitories. There's a top kitchen with a huge dining area and the busy Clash bar in the basement.

YHA London Oxford Street   HOSTEL £
(Map p166; ☑020-7734 1618; www.yha.org.uk/hostel/london-oxford-street; 14 Noel St, W1; dm/tw from £18-36, tw £50-85; @ ⓦ; ☺Oxford Circus) The most central of London's eight YHA hostels is also one of the most intimate with just 104 beds, and excellent shared facilities, including the fuchsia kitchen and the bright, funky lounge. Dormitories have three and four beds and there are doubles and twins. The in-house shop sells coffee and beer. Wifi (common areas) is free. Free daily walking tours too.

London St Pancras YHA   HOSTEL £
(☑0345 371 9344; www.yha.org.uk; 79-81 Euston Rd, NW1; dm/r from £16/60; ⓦ; ☺King's Cross St Pancras) This hostel with 186 beds spread over eight floors has modern, clean dorms sleeping four to six (nearly all with private facilities) and some private rooms. There's a good bar and cafe, although there are no self-catering facilities. Check out time is 10am.

Arosfa Hotel   B&B ££
(☑020-7636 2115; www.arosfalondon.com; 83 Gower St, WC1; s/tw/tr/f from £90/135/155/210, d £140-175, incl breakfast; @ⓦ; ☺Goodge St) The Philippe Starck furniture and modern look in the lounge is more lavish than the decor in the hotel's 16 rooms, with cabin-like bathrooms in many of them. About half have been refurbished; they are small but remain good value. There are a couple of family rooms; room 4 looks on to a small but charming garden. Prices rise on Saturdays.

Jesmond Hotel   B&B ££
(☑020-7636 3199; www.jesmondhotel.org.uk; 63 Gower St, WC1; s £75-95, d £95-125, tr £140-165, q £150-185, all incl breakfast; @ⓦ; ☺Goodge St) The rooms – cheapest with shared bathroom – at this popular, 15-room family-run Georgian hotel in Bloomsbury are basic but clean and cheerful, there's a small, pretty garden and the price tag is very attractive indeed. There's also laundry service, free wi-fi and good breakfasts for kicking off your London day. Location is highly central.

★Haymarket Hotel   HOTEL £££
(Map p166; ☑020-7470 4000; www.firmdalehotels.com/hotels/london/haymarket-hotel; 1 Suffolk Pl, off Haymarket, SW1; r/ste from £335/505; ✲ⓦ✲; ☺Piccadilly Circus) With the trademark colours and lines of hoteliers and designers Tim and Kit Kemp, the Haymarket is beautiful, with hand-painted Gournay wallpaper, signature fuchsia and green

Bloomsbury, St Pancras & Camden

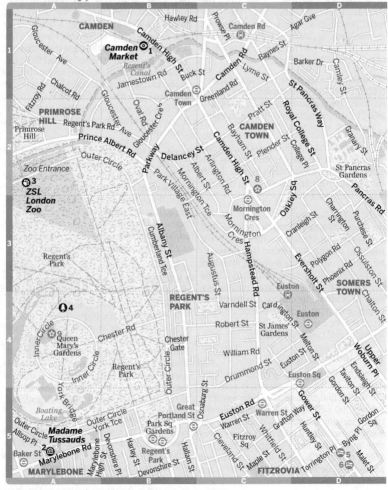

Bloomsbury, St Pancras & Camden

◎ Top Sights
1 Camden Market	B1
2 Madame Tussauds	A5
3 ZSL London Zoo	A2

◎ Sights
4 Regent's Park	A4

◉ Sleeping
5 Arosfa Hotel	D5
6 Jesmond Hotel	D5
7 London St Pancras YHA	E4

✪ Entertainment
8 KOKO	C2
9 Regent's Park Open Air Theatre	A4

designs in the 50 guest rooms, a sensational 18m pool with mood lighting, an exquisite library lounge with honesty bar, and original artwork throughout. Just love the dog silhouettes on the chairs and bar stools.

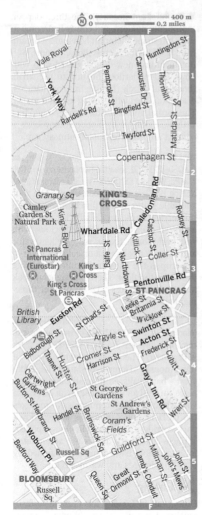

Hotel Indigo London – Tower Hill HOTEL **££**
(Map p162; ☑ 020-7265 1014; www.hotelindigo. com; 142 Minories, EC3; r from £166; ❋ 🐾; ⊖ Aldgate) This branch of the US InterContinental group's boutique-hotel chain offers 46 differently styled rooms, all with four-poster beds and iPod docking stations. Larger-than-life drawings and photos of the neighbourhood won't let you forget where you are.

🛏 South Bank

Immediately south of the river is good if you want to immerse yourself in workaday London and still be central.

St Christopher's Village HOSTEL **£**
(Map p162; ☑ 020-7939 9710; www.st-christo phers.co.uk; 163 Borough High St, SE1; dm/r incl breakfast from £11.40/50; 🐾; ⊖ London Bridge) This 230-bed party-zone hostel has new bathrooms, fresh paint, pod beds with privacy curtains, reading lights, power sockets (British and European) and USB ports, and refurbished common areas. Its two bars, Belushi's and Dugout, are perennially popular. Dorms have four to 33 beds (following the introduction of triple bunks); breakfast and linen are included.

★ Citizen M BOUTIQUE HOTEL **££**
(Map p162; ☑ 020-3519 1680; www.citizenm. com/london-bankside; 20 Lavington St, SE1; r £109-249; ❋ @ 🐾; ⊖ Southwark) If Citizen M had a motto, it would be 'Less fuss, more comfort'. The hotel has done away with things it considers superfluous (room service, reception, heaps of space) and instead has gone all out on mattresses and bedding (heavenly super-king-sized beds), state-of-the-art technology (everything from mood lighting to TV is controlled through a tablet computer) and superb decor.

🛏 The City

London St Paul's YHA HOSTEL **£**
(Map p162; ☑ 020-7236 4965; www.yha.org.uk/ hostel/london-st-pauls; 36 Carter Lane, EC4; dm/ tw/d from £18/65/89; @ 🐾; ⊖ St Paul's) This 213-bed hostel is housed in the former boarding school for choirboys from St Paul's Cathedral, almost next door. Dorms have between three and 11 beds, and twins and doubles are available. There's a great lounge, licensed cafeteria (breakfast £5.25, dinner from £7 to £10) but no kitchen – and lots and lots of stairs (and no lift). Seven-night maximum stay.

🛏 Kensington & Hyde Park

This classy area offers easy access to the museums and big-name fashion stores, but at a price that reflects the upmarket surroundings.

Lime Tree Hotel BOUTIQUE HOTEL **££**
(☑ 020-7730 8191; www.limetreehotel.co.uk; 135-137 Ebury St, SW1; s incl breakfast £120-160, d & tw £180-210, tr £230; @ 🐾; ⊖ Victoria) Family run for 30 years, this beautiful 25-bedroom Georgian town-house hotel is all comfort, British designs and understated elegance. Rooms are individually decorated, many with open fireplaces and sash windows, but

some are smaller than others, so enquire. There is a lovely back garden for late-afternoon rays (picnics encouraged on summer evenings). Rates include a hearty full-English breakfast. No lift.

★ **Number Sixteen** HOTEL £££
(Map p170; 020-7589 5232; www.firmdale hotels.com/hotels/london/number-sixteen; 16 Sumner Pl, SW7; s from £192, d £240-396; ❄ @ ⦿; ⦿ South Kensington) With uplifting splashes of colour, choice art and a sophisticated-but-fun design ethos, Number Sixteen is simply ravishing. There are 41 individually designed rooms, a cosy drawing room and a fully stocked library. And wait till you see the idyllic, long back garden set around a fountain, or sit down for breakfast in the light-filled conservatory. Great amenities for families.

🛏 Clerkenwell, Shoreditch & Spitalfields

★ **Hoxton Hotel** HOTEL ££
(Map p162; 020-7550 1000; www.hoxtonho tels.com; 81 Great Eastern St, EC2; r £69-259; ❄ ⦿; ⦿ Old St) In the heart of hip Shoreditch, this sleek hotel takes the easyJet approach to selling its rooms – book long enough ahead and you might pay just £49. The 210 renovated rooms are small but stylish, with flatscreen TVs, a desk, fridge with complimentary bottled water and milk, and breakfast (orange juice, granola, yoghurt, banana) in a bag delivered to your door.

🛏 Notting Hill & West London

West London's Earl's Court district is lively, cosmopolitan and so popular with travelling Antipodeans that it's been nicknamed Kangaroo Valley.

Safestay Holland Park HOSTEL £
(020-3326 8471; www.safestay.co.uk; Holland Walk, W8; dm £20, r from £60; ⦿; ⦿ High St Kensington or Holland Park) This new place replaced the long-serving YHA hostel running here since 1958. With a bright and bold colour design, the hostel has four- to eight-bunk dorm rooms, twin-bunk and single-bunk rooms, free wi-fi in the lobby and a fabulous location in the Jacobean east wing of Holland House in **Holland Park** (Ilchester Pl).

★ **Barclay House** B&B ££
(077 6742 0943; www.barclayhouselondon. com; 21 Barclay Rd, SW6; s from £110, d £135-168;

@ ⦿; ⦿ Fulham Broadway) The three dapper, thoroughly modern and comfy bedrooms in this ship-shape Victorian house are a dream, from the Phillipe Starck shower rooms, walnut furniture, new double-glazed sash windows and underfloor heating to the small, thoughtful details (fumble-free coat hangers, drawers packed with sewing kits and maps). The cordial, music-loving owners – bursting with tips and handy London knowledge – concoct an inclusive, homely atmosphere.

★ **Main House** HOTEL ££
(020-7221 9691; www.themainhouse.co.uk; 6 Colville Rd, W11; ste £120-150; ⦿; ⦿ Ladbroke Grove, Notting Hill Gate or Westbourne Park) The four adorable suites at this peach of a Victorian midterrace house on Colville Rd make this a superb choice. Bright and spacious, with vast bathrooms, rooms are excellent value and include endless tea or coffee. Cream of the crop is the uppermost suite, occupying the entire top floor. There's no sign, but look for the huge letters 'SIX'. Minimum three-night stay.

La Suite West BOUTIQUE HOTEL £££
(Map p170; 020-7313 8484; www.lasuitewest. com; 41-51 Inverness Tce, W2; r £129-279; ❄ @ ⦿; ⦿ Bayswater) The black-and-white foyer of the Anouska Hempel–designed La Suite West – bare walls, a minimalist slit of a fireplace, an iPad for guests' use on an otherwise void white-marble reception desk – presages the OCD neatness of rooms hidden down dark corridors. The straight lines, spotless surfaces and sharp angles are accentuated by impeccable bathrooms and softened by comfortable beds and warm service.

✖ Eating

Dining out in London has become so fashionable that you can hardly open a menu without banging into a celebrity chef. The range and quality of eating options has increased enormously over the last few decades.

✖ West End

★ **Shoryu** NOODLES £
(Map p166; none; www.shoryuramen.com; 9 Regent St, SW1; mains £9.50-14.90; ⊙ 11.15am-midnight Mon-Sat, to 10.30pm Sun; ⦿ Piccadilly Circus) Compact, well-mannered noodle-parlour Shoryu draws in reams of noodle diners to feast at its wooden counters and small tables. It's busy, friendly and efficient, with helpful

and informative staff. Fantastic *tonkotsu* pork-broth ramen is the name of the game here, sprinkled with *nori* (dried, pressed seaweed), spring onion, *nitamago* (soft-boiled eggs) and sesame seeds. No bookings.

★Mildreds   VEGETARIAN £
(Map p166; ✆020-7484 1634; www.mildreds. co.uk; 45 Lexington St, W1; mains £7-12; ☺noon-11pm Mon-Sat; 🛜🖉; ⊖Oxford Circus, Piccadilly Circus) Central London's most inventive vegetarian restaurant, Mildred's heaves at lunchtime so don't be shy about sharing a table in the skylit dining room. Expect the likes of Sri Lankan sweet-potato and cashew-nut curry, pumpkin and ricotta ravioli, Middle Eastern meze, wonderfully exotic (and filling) salads and delicious stir-fries. There are also vegan and gluten-free options.

★Brasserie Zédel   FRENCH ££
(Map p166; ✆020-7734 4888; www.brasserie zedel.com; 20 Sherwood St, W1; mains £13.50-25.75; ☺11.30am-midnight Mon-Sat, to 11pm Sun; 🛜; ⊖Piccadilly Circus) This brasserie in the renovated art deco ballroom of a former hotel is the Frenchest eatery west of Calais. Favourites include *choucroute Alsacienne* (sauerkraut with sausages and charcuterie £14) or a straight-up *steak haché, sauce au poivre et frites* (chopped steak with pepper sauce; £9.75). Set menus (£9.75/12.75 for two/three courses) and *plats du jour* (£14.25) offer excellent value, in a terrific setting.

★Palomar   ISRAELI ££
(Map p166; ✆020-7439 8777; http://thepalomar. co.uk; 34 Rupert St, W1; mains £7-16.50; ☺noon-2.30pm & 5.30-11pm Mon-Sat, 12.30-3.30pm & 6-9pm Sun; 🛜; ⊖Piccadilly Circus) The buzzing vibe at this good-looking celebration of modern-day Jerusalem cuisine (in all its inflections) is infectious, but we could enjoy the dishes cooked up here in a deserted warehouse and still come back for more. The Jerusalem-style polenta and Josperised aubergine are fantastic, but portions are smallish, so sharing is the way to go. Reservations essential.

★Cafe Murano   ITALIAN ££
(Map p166; ✆020-3371 5559; www.cafemu rano.co.uk; 33 St James's St, SW1; mains £18-25, 2/3-course set meal £19/23; ☺noon-3pm & 5.30-11pm Mon-Sat, 11.30am-4pm Sun; ⊖Green Park) The setting may seem somewhat demure at this superb and busy restaurant, but with such a sublime North Italian menu on offer, it sees no need to be flash and of-the-mo-

ment. You get what you come for, and the beef carpaccio, crab linguine and lamb ragu are as close to culinary perfection as you can get. Reserve.

★Barrafina   SPANISH ££
(Map p166; ✆020-7440 1456; www.barrafina. co.uk; 10 Adelaide St, WC2; tapas £6.50-15.80; ☺noon-3pm & 5-11pm Mon-Sat, 1-3.30pm & 5.30-10pm Sun; ⊖Embankment or Leicester Sq) With no reservations, you may need to get in line for an hour or so at this restaurant that does a brisk service in some of the best tapas in town. Divine mouthfuls are served on each plate, from the stuffed courgette flower to the suckling pig and crab on toast, so diners dig their heels in, prepared to wait.

★Claridge's Foyer & Reading Room   BRITISH £££
(Map p166; ✆020-7107 8886; www.claridges. co.uk; 49-53 Brook St, W1; afternoon tea £68, with champagne £79; ☺afternoon tea 2.45-5.30pm; 🛜; ⊖Bond St) Extend that pinkie finger to partake in afternoon tea within the classic art deco–style foyer of this landmark hotel where the gentle clink of fine porcelain and champagne glasses could be a defining memory of your trip to London. The setting is gorgeous and dress is elegant, smart casual (ripped jeans and baseball caps won't get served).

🍴 South Bank

For a feed with a local feel, head to Borough Market or Bermondsey St.

M Manze   BRITISH £
(www.manze.co.uk; 87 Tower Bridge Rd, SE1; mains from £2.95; ☺11am-2pm Mon, 10.30am-2pm Tue-Thu, 10am-2.30pm Fri & Sat; ⊖Borough) Dating to 1902, M Manze started off as an ice-cream seller before moving on to selling its legendary staples: minced-beef pies. It's a classic operation, from the ageing tilework to the traditional workers' menu: pie and mash, pie and liquor (a parsley-based sauce), and you can take your eels jellied or stewed. Vegetarian pies available. Eat in or take away.

★Skylon   MODERN EUROPEAN ££
(Map p162; ✆020-7654 7800; www.skylon-rest aurant.co.uk; 3rd fl, Royal Festival Hall, South-bank Centre, Belvedere Rd, SE1; 3-course menu grill/restaurant £25/30; ☺grill noon-11pm Mon-Sat, to 10.30pm Sun, restaurant noon-2.30pm & 5.30-10.30pm Mon-Sat & noon-4pm Sun; 🛜; ⊖Waterloo) This excellent restaurant inside

the Royal Festival Hall is divided into grill and fine-dining sections by a large **bar** (⊘ noon-1am Mon-Sat, to 10.30pm Sun). The decor is cutting-edge 1950s: muted colours and period chairs (trendy then, trendier now) while floor-to-ceiling windows bathe you in magnificent views of the Thames and the city. The six-course restaurant tasting menu costs £59. Booking is advised.

Kensington & Hyde Park

★ Pimlico Fresh   CAFE £
(☑ 020-7932 0030; 86 Wilton Rd, SW1; mains from £4.50; ⊘ 7.30am-7.30pm Mon-Fri, 9am-6pm Sat & Sun; ⊖ Victoria) This friendly two-room cafe will see you right whether you need breakfast (French toast, bowls of porridge laced with honey or maple syrup), lunch (homemade quiches and soups, 'things' on toast) or just a good old latte and cake.

Comptoir Libanais   LEBANESE £
(Map p170; ☑ 020-7225 5006; www.comptoirliba nais.com; 1-5 Exhibition Rd, SW7; mains from £8.50; ⊘ 8.30am-midnight Mon-Sat, to 10.30pm Sun; 🛜; ⊖ South Kensington) If your battery's flat hoovering up South Kensington's museums, this colourful, good-looking and brisk restaurant just round the corner from the tube station is excellent for Lebanese meze, wraps, tagine (slow-cooked casseroles), *mana'esh* (flatbreads), salads and fine breakfasts. When the sun's shining, the outside tables quickly fill with munchers and people-watchers. There are no reservations, so just pitch up (elbows sharpened).

★ Rabbit   MODERN BRITISH ££
(☑ 020-3750 0172; www.rabbit-restaurant.com; 172 King's Rd, SW3; mains £6-24, set lunch £13.50; ⊘ noon-midnight Tue-Sat, 6-11pm Mon, noon-6pm Sun; 🖋; ⊖ Sloane Sq) Three brothers grew up on a farm. One became a farmer, another a butcher, while the third worked in hospitality. So they pooled their skills and came up with Rabbit, a breath of fresh air in upmarket Chelsea. The restaurant rocks the agrichic (yes) look and the creative, seasonal modern British cuisine is fabulous.

★ Dinner by Heston
Blumenthal   MODERN BRITISH £££
(Map p170; ☑ 020-7201 3833; www.dinnerby heston.com; Mandarin Oriental Hyde Park, 66 Knightsbridge, SW1; 3-course set lunch £45, mains £28-44; ⊘ noon-2pm & 6-10.15pm Mon-Fri, noon-2.30pm & 6-10.30pm Sat & Sun; 🛜; ⊖ Knights-

bridge) Sumptuously presented Dinner is a gastronomic tour de force, taking diners on a journey through British culinary history (with inventive modern inflections). Dishes carry historical dates to convey context, while the restaurant interior is a design triumph, from the glass-walled kitchen and its overhead clock mechanism to the large windows looking onto the park. Book ahead.

Clerkenwell, Shoreditch & Spitalfields

From the hit-and-miss Bangladeshi restaurants of Brick Lane to the Vietnamese strip on Kingsland Rd, the East End's cuisine is as multicultural as its residents. Clerkenwell's hidden gems are well worth digging for; Exmouth Market is a good place to start.

★ St John   BRITISH ££
(Map p162; ☑ 020-7251 0848; www.stjohngroup. uk.com/spitalfields; 26 St John St, EC1M; mains £14.80-24.90; ⊘ noon-3pm & 6-11pm Mon-Fri, 6-11pm Sat, 12.30-4pm Sun; ⊖ Farringdon) Whitewashed brick walls, high ceilings and simple wooden furniture keep diners free to concentrate on St John's famous nose-to-tail dishes. Serves are big, hearty and a celebration of England's culinary past. Don't miss the signature roast bone marrow and parsley salad (£8.90).

Poppie's   FISH & CHIPS ££
(Map p162; www.poppiesfishandchips.co.uk; 6-8 Hanbury St, E1; mains £12.20-15.90; ⊘ 11am-11pm; ⊖ Liverpool St) This glorious re-creation of a 1950s East End chippy comes complete with waitresses in pinnies and hairnets, and Blitz memorabilia. As well as the usual fishy suspects, it does those old-time London staples – jellied eels and mushy peas – plus kid-pleasing, sweet-tooth desserts (sticky toffee pudding or apple pie with ice cream) and a wine list.

Notting Hill & West London

★ Potli   INDIAN £
(☑ 020-8741 4328; www.potli.co.uk; 319-321 King St, W6; weekday 1-/2-course set lunch £7.95/10.95, mains £7.50-15; ⊘ noon-2.30pm Mon-Sat, 6-10.15pm Mon-Thu, 5.30-10.30pm Fri & Sat, noon-10pm Sun; 🛜; ⊖ Stamford Brook or Ravenscourt Park) With its scattered pieces from Mumbai's Thieves Market, Indian-market-kitchen/bazaar cuisine, home-made pickles and spice mixes, plus an accent on genuine fla-

ROLL OUT THE BARROW

London has more than 350 markets selling everything from antiques and curios to flowers and fish. Some, such as Camden and Portobello Road, are full of tourists, while others exist just for the locals.

Portobello Road Market (www.portobellomarket.org; Portobello Rd, W10; ⊙8am-6.30pm Mon-Wed, Fri & Sat, to 1pm Thu; ⊜Notting Hill Gate or Ladbroke Grove) Lovely on a warm summer's day, Portobello Road Market is an iconic London attraction with an eclectic mix of street food, fruit and veg, antiques, curios, collectables, vibrant fashion and trinkets. Although the shops along Portobello Rd open daily and the fruit and veg stalls (from Elgin Cres to Talbot Rd) only close on Sunday, the busiest day by far is Saturday, when antique dealers set up shop (from Chepstow Villas to Elgin Cres).

Columbia Road Flower Market (Map p162; www.columbiaroad.info; Columbia Rd, E2; ⊙8am-3pm Sun; ⊜Hoxton) A wonderful explosion of colour and life, this weekly market sells a beautiful array of flowers, pot plants, bulbs, seeds and everything you might need for the garden. It's a lot of fun and the best place to hear proper Cockney barrow-boy banter ('We got flowers cheap enough for ya muvver-in-law's grave' etc). It gets really packed, so go as early as you can, or later on, when the vendors sell off the cut flowers cheaply.

Camden Market (www.camdenmarket.com; Camden High St, NW1; ⊙10am-6pm; ⊜Camden Town or Chalk Farm) Although – or perhaps because – it stopped being cutting-edge several thousand cheap leather jackets ago, Camden Market attracts millions of visitors each year and is one of London's most popular attractions. What started out as a collection of attractive craft stalls by Camden Lock on the Regent's Canal now extends most of the way from Camden Town tube station to Chalk Farm tube station.

Old Spitalfields Market (Map p162; www.oldspitalfieldsmarket.com; Commercial St, E1; ⊙10am-5pm Mon-Fri & Sun, 11am-5pm Sat; ⊜Liverpool St) Traders have been hawking their wares here since 1638 and it's still one of London's best markets. Today's covered market was built in the late 19th century, with the more modern development added in 2006. Sundays are the biggest and best days, but Thursdays are good for antiques and Fridays for independent fashion. There are plenty of food stalls, too.

Sunday UpMarket (Map p162; www.sundayupmarket.co.uk; Old Truman Brewery, 91 Brick Lane, E1; ⊙11am-6pm Sat, 10am-5pm Sun; ⊜Shoreditch High St) The best of all the Sunday markets, this workaday covered car park fills up with young designers selling their wares, quirky crafts and a drool-inducing array of food stalls.

Broadway Market (www.broadwaymarket.co.uk; Broadway Market, E8; ⊙9am-5pm Sat; ⊒394) There's been a market down this pretty street since the late 19th century. The focus these days is artisan food, arty knick-knacks, books, records and vintage clothing. Stock up on edible treats then head to **London Fields** (Richmond Rd, E8; ⊜Hackney Central) for a picnic.

vour, tantalising Potli deftly captures the aromas of its culinary home. Downstairs there's an open kitchen and service is friendly, but it's the alluring menu – where flavours are teased into a rich and authentic India culinary experience – that's the real crowd-pleaser.

★**Geales**　　　　　　　　SEAFOOD **££**
(Map p170; ☏020-7727 7528; www.geales.com; 2 Farmer St, W8; 2-course express lunch £9.95, mains £9-37.50; ⊙noon-3pm & 6-10.30pm Tue-Fri, noon-10.30pm Sat, noon-4pm Sun; ☜; ⊜Notting Hill Gate) Frying since 1939 – a bad year for the restaurant trade – Geales has endured with

its quiet location on the corner of Farmer St in Hillgate Village. The succulent fish in crispy batter is a fine catch from a menu which also runs to other British faves such as pork belly with apple sauce and crackling, and beef and bacon pie.

🍷 Drinking & Nightlife

As long as there's been a city, Londoners have loved to drink, and – as history shows – often immoderately. Clubland is no longer confined to the West End, with megaclubs scattered throughout the city wherever there's a venue big enough, cheap enough or quirky enough to hold them. The big nights are Friday and Saturday. Admission prices vary widely; it's often cheaper to arrive early or pre-book tickets.

🍸 West End

★ Dukes London   COCKTAIL BAR

(Map p166; ☑️ 020-7491 4840; www.dukeshotel. com/dukes-bar; Dukes Hotel, 35 St James's Pl, SW1; ⏰ 2-11pm Mon-Sat, 4-10.30pm Sun; 📶; 🚇 Green Park) Sip to-die-for martinis like royalty in a gentleman's-club-like ambience at this tidily tucked-away classic bar where white-jacketed masters mix up some awesomely good preparations. Ian Fleming used to drink here, perhaps perfecting his 'shaken, not stirred' Bond maxim. Smokers can ease into the secluded Cognac and Cigar Garden to light up (but cigars must be purchased here).

★ American Bar   BAR

(Map p166; www.thebeaumont.com/dining/american-bar; The Beaumont, Brown Hart Gardens, W1; ⏰ 11.30am-midnight Mon-Sat, to 11pm Sun; 📶; 🚇 Bond St) Sip a bourbon or a classic cocktail in the classic 1930s art-deco striped-walnut ambience of this stylish bar at the hallmark Beaumont hotel (☑️ 020-7499 1001; d/studio/ste incl breakfast from £395/625/900; ❋📶). It's central, period and like a gentleman's club, but far from stuffy. Only a few years old, the American Bar feels like its been pouring drinks since the days of the Eton Crop and the Jazz Age.

Purl   COCKTAIL BAR

(Map p170; ☑️ 020-7935 0835; www.purl-london .com; 50-54 Blandford St, W1; ⏰ 5-11.30pm Mon-Thu, to midnight Fri & Sat; 🚇 Baker St, Bond St) Purl is a fabulous underground drinking den. Decked out in vintage furniture, it serves original and intriguingly named cocktails (What's Your Poison? or Mr Hyde's No 2) and a punch of the day. It's all subdued lighting and hushed-tone conversations, which only adds to the mysterious air. Booking recommended.

Connaught Bar   COCKTAIL BAR

(Map p166; ☑️ 020-7314 3419; www.the-connaught.co.uk/mayfair-bars/connaught-bar; Connaught Hotel, Carlos Pl, W1; ⏰ 11am-1am Mon-Sat, to midnight Sun; 🚇 Bond St) Drinkers who know their stuff single out the Martini trolley for particular praise, but almost everything at this sumptuous bar at the exclusive and very British Connaught Hotel gets the nod: lavish deco-inspired lines, excruciating attention to detail, faultless service, and some of the best drinks in town. Cocktails, classic and those given a thoroughly contemporary twist, start at £17.

Village   GAY

(Map p166; ☑️ 020-7478 0530; www.village-soho. co.uk; 81 Wardour St, W1; ⏰ 5pm-1am Mon & Tue, to 2am Wed-Sat, to 11.30pm Sun; 🚇 Piccadilly Circus) The Village is always up for a party, whatever the night of the week. There are karaoke nights, 'discolicious' nights, go-go-dancer nights – take your pick. And if you can't wait to strut your stuff until the clubs open, there is a dance floor downstairs, complete with pole, of course. Open till 3am on the last weekend of the month.

🍸 South Bank

★ Little Bird Gin   COCKTAIL BAR

(Map p162; www.littlebirdgin.com; Maltby St, SE1; ⏰ 10am-4pm Sat, from 11am Sun; 🚇 London Bridge) This South London–based distillery opens a pop-up bar in a workshop at Maltby Street Market (www.maltby.st; dishes £5-10; ⏰ 9am-4pm Sat, 11am-4pm Sun) to ply merry punters with devilishly good cocktails (£5 to £7), served in jam jars or apothecary's glass bottles.

★ Oblix   BAR

(Map p162; www.oblixrestaurant.com; 32nd fl, Shard, 31 St Thomas St, SE1; ⏰ noon-11pm; 🚇 London Bridge) On the 32nd floor of the Shard (p165), Oblix offers mesmerising vistas of London. You can come for anything from a coffee (£3.50) to a cocktail (from £10) and enjoy virtually the same views as the official viewing galleries of the Shard (but at a reduced cost and with the added bonus of a drink). Live music every night from 7pm.

★ 40 Maltby Street   WINE BAR

(Map p162; www.40maltbystreet.com; 40 Maltby St, SE1; ⏰ 5.30-10pm Wed & Thu, 12.30-2.30pm & 5.30-10pm Fri, 11am-10pm Sat; 🚇 London Bridge) 🍷 This tunnel-like wine-bar-cum-kitchen sits under the railway arches that take trains in and out of London Bridge. It is first and foremost a wine importer focusing on organic vintages but its hospitality venture has become incredibly popular. The wine recommendations are obviously top-notch (most of them by the glass) and the food – simple, gourmet bistro fare – is spot on.

GAY & LESBIAN LONDON

Generally, London's a safe place for lesbians and gays. It's rare to encounter any problem with sharing rooms or holding hands in the inner city, although it would pay to keep your wits about you at night and be conscious of your surroundings.

The West End, particularly Soho, is the visible centre of gay and lesbian London, with numerous venues clustered around Old Compton St – but many other areas have their own miniscenes.

The easiest way to find out what's going on is to pick up the free press from a venue (*Boyz*, *QX*); the gay section of *Time Out* (www.timeout.com/london/lgbt) is also useful.

⚘ Clerkenwell, Shoreditch & Spitalfields

★ XOYO
CLUB
(Map p162; www.xoyo.co.uk; 32-37 Cowper St, EC2A; ⊘9pm-4am Fri & Sat, hours vary Sun-Thu; ⊖Old St) This fantastic Shoreditch warehouse club throws together a pulsingly popular mix of gigs, club nights and art events. Always buzzing, the varied line-up – expect indie bands, hip-hop, electro, dubstep and much in between – attracts a mix of clubbers, from skinny-jeaned hipsters to more mature hedonists (but no suits).

★ Zetter Townhouse
Cocktail Lounge
COCKTAIL BAR
(Map p162; ☑020-7324 4545; www.thezetter townhouse.com; 49-50 St John's Sq, EC1V; ⊘7.30am-12.45am; ☎; ⊖Farringdon) Tucked away behind an unassuming door on St John's Sq, this ground-floor bar is quirkily decorated with plush armchairs, stuffed animal heads and a legion of lamps. The cocktail list takes its theme from the area's distilling history – recipes of yesteryear and homemade tinctures and cordials are used to create interesting and unusual tipples. House cocktails are all £10.50.

Fabric
CLUB
(www.fabriclondon.com; 77a Charterhouse Street, EC1M; £5-25; ⊘11pm-7am Fri-Sun; ⊖Farringdon or Barbican) London's leading club, Fabric's three separate dance floors in a huge converted cold store opposite Smithfield meat market draws impressive queues (buy tickets online). FabricLive (on selected Fridays) rumbles with drum and bass and dubstep, while Fabric (usually on Saturdays but also on selected Fridays) is the club's signature live DJ night. Sunday's WetYourSelf! delivers house, techno and electronica.

★ Jerusalem Tavern
PUB
(Map p162; www.stpetersbrewery.co.uk; 55 Britton St, EC1M; ⊘11am-11pm Mon-Fri; ☎; ⊖Farringdon) Pick a wood-panelled cubicle to park yourself in at this tiny and highly atmospheric pub housed in a building dating to 1720, and select from the fantastic beverages brewed by St Peter's Brewery in North Suffolk. Be warned, it's hugely popular and often very crowded.

★ Ye Olde Mitre
PUB
(Map p162; www.yeoldemitreholborn.co.uk; 1 Ely Ct, EC1N; ⊘11am-11pm Mon-Fri; ☎; ⊖Farringdon) A delightfully cosy historic pub with an extensive beer selection, tucked away in a backstreet off Hatton Garden, Ye Olde Mitre was built in 1546 for the servants of Ely Palace. There's no music, so the rooms only echo with amiable chit-chat. Queen Elizabeth I danced around the cherry tree by the bar, they say. Closed Saturday and Sunday.

★ Worship St Whistling Shop
COCKTAIL BAR
(Map p162; ☑020-7247 0015; www.whistling shop.com; 63 Worship St, EC2A; ⊘5pm-midnight Mon & Tue, to 1am Wed & Thu, to 2am Fri & Sat; ⊖Old St) While the name is Victorian slang for a place selling illicit booze, this subterranean drinking den's master mixologists explore the experimental outer limits of cocktail chemistry and aromatic science, as well as concocting the classics. Many ingredients are made with the rotary evaporators in the on-site lab. Cocktail masterclasses also run.

⚘ Notting Hill, Bayswater & Paddington

★ Troubadour
BAR
(☑020-7341 6333; www.troubadour.co.uk; 263-267 Old Brompton Rd, SW5; ⊘cafe 8.30am-12.30am, club 8pm-12.30am or 2am; ☎; ⊖Earl's Court) On a compatible spiritual plane to Paris' Shakespeare and Company Bookshop, this

eccentric, time-warped and convivial boho bar-cafe has been serenading drinkers since the 1950s. (Deep breath) Adele, Paolo Nutini, Joni Mitchell and (deeper breath) Jimi Hendrix and Bob Dylan have performed here, and there's still live music (folk, blues) and a large, pleasant garden open in summer.

Windsor Castle
PUB

(Map p170; www.thewindsorcastlekensington. co.uk; 114 Campden Hill Rd, W11; ⊙ noon-11pm Mon-Sat, to 10.30pm Sun; 🐾; ⊖ Notting Hill Gate) A classic tavern on the brow of Campden Hill Rd, this place has history, nooks and charm on tap. It's worth the search for its historic compartmentalised interior, roaring fire (in winter), delightful beer garden (in summer) and affable regulars (most always). According to legend, the bones of Thomas Paine (author of *Rights of Man*) are in the cellar.

Earl of Lonsdale
PUB

(277-281 Portobello Rd, W11; ⊙ noon-11pm Mon-Fri, 10am-11pm Sat, noon-10.30pm Sun; ⊖ Notting Hill Gate or Ladbroke Grove) Named after the *bon vivant* founder of the AA (Automobile Association, *not* Alcoholics Anonymous), the Earl is peaceful during the day, with both old biddies and young hipsters inhabiting the reintroduced snugs. There are Samuel Smith's ales, a fantastic backroom with sofas, banquettes, open fires and a magnificent beer garden: all in all, a perfect bolthole for those traipsing Portobello Rd.

Greenwich & South London

★ Cutty Sark Tavern
PUB

(📞 020-8858 3146; www.cuttysarkse10.co.uk; 4-6 Ballast Quay, SE10; ⊙ 11.30am-11pm Mon-Sat, noon-10.30pm Sun; 🐾; 🚆 DLR Cutty Sark) Housed in a delightful bow-windowed, wood-beamed Georgian building directly on the Thames, the Cutty Sark is one of the few independent pubs left in Greenwich. Half a dozen cask-conditioned ales on tap line the bar, there's an inviting riverside seating area opposite and an upstairs dining room looking out on to glorious views. It's a 10-minute walk from the DLR station.

Ministry of Sound
CLUB

(Map p162; 📞 020-7740 8600; www.ministryof sound.com; 103 Gaunt St, SE1; £10-22; ⊙ 10pm-6.30am Fri, 11am-7am Sat; 🐾; ⊖ Elephant & Castle) This legendary club-cum-enormous-global-brand (four bars, three dance floors) lost some 'edge' in the early noughties but, after pumping in top DJs, firmly rejoined the top club ranks. Fridays is the Gallery trance night, while Saturday sessions offer the crème de la crème of house, electro and techno DJs.

☆ Entertainment

Theatre

London is a world capital for theatre and there's a lot more than mammoth musicals to tempt you into the West End. On performance days, you can buy half-price tickets for West End productions (cash only) from the official agency **Tkts Leicester Sq** (www.tkts. co.uk/leicester-square; The Lodge, Leicester Square, WC2; ⊙ 10am-7pm Mon-Sat, 11am-4.30pm Sun; ⊖ Leicester Sq). The booth is the one with the clock tower; beware of touts selling dodgy tickets. For more, see www.officiallondon theatre.co.uk or www.theatremonkey.com.

★ Shakespeare's Globe
THEATRE

(Map p162; 📞 020-7401 9919; www.shakes pearesglobe.com; 21 New Globe Walk, SE1; seats £20-45, standing £5; ⊖ Blackfriars or London Bridge) If you love Shakespeare and the theatre, the Globe (p164) will knock your theatrical socks off. This authentic Shakespearean theatre is a wooden 'O' without a roof over the central stage area, and although there are covered wooden bench seats in tiers around the stage, many people (there's room for 700) do as 17th-century 'groundlings' did, and stand in front of the stage.

National Theatre
THEATRE

(Royal National Theatre; Map p162; 📞 020-7452 3000; www.nationaltheatre.org.uk; South Bank, SE1; ⊖ Waterloo) England's flagship theatre showcases a mix of classic and contemporary plays performed by excellent casts in three theatres (Olivier, Lyttelton and Dorfman). Artistic director Rufus Norris, who started in April 2015, made headlines in 2016 for announcing plans to stage a Brexit-based drama.

Old Vic
THEATRE

(Map p162; 📞 0844 871 7628; www.oldvictheatre. com; The Cut, SE1; ⊖ Waterloo) American actor Kevin Spacey took the theatrical helm of this London theatre in 2003, giving it a new lease of life. He was succeeded in April 2015 by Matthew Warchus (who directed *Matilda the Musical* and the film *Pride*), whose aim is to bring an eclectic program to the theatre: expect new writing, as well as dynamic revivals of old works and musicals.

Young Vic
THEATRE

(Map p162; ☑ 020-7922 2922; www.youngvic.org; 66 The Cut, SE1; ⊜ Southwark or Waterloo) This ground breaking theatre is as much about showcasing and discovering new talent as it is about people discovering theatre. The Young Vic features actors, directors and plays from across the world, many tackling contemporary political and cultural issues, such as the death penalty, racism or corruption, and often blending dance and music with acting.

Donmar Warehouse
THEATRE

(Map p166; ☑ 0844 871 7624; www.donmarware house.com; 41 Earlham St, WC2; ⊜ Covent Garden) The cosy Donmar Warehouse is London's 'thinking person's theatre'. Current artistic director Josie Rourke has staged some intriguing and successful productions, including the well-received comedy *My Night with Reg*.

Live Music

★606 Club
BLUES, JAZZ

(☑ 020-7352 5953; www.606club.co.uk; 90 Lots Rd, SW10; ⊘ 7-11.15pm Sun-Thu, 8pm-12.30am Fri & Sat; ⧉ Imperial Wharf) Named after its old address on King's Rd, which cast a spell over jazz lovers London-wide back in the '80s, this fantastic, tucked-away basement jazz club and restaurant gives centre stage to contemporary British-based jazz musicians nightly. The club can only serve alcohol to people who are dining and it is highly advisable to book to get a table.

★KOKO
LIVE MUSIC

(www.koko.uk.com; 1a Camden High St, NW1; ⊜ Mornington Cres) Once the legendary Camden Palace, where Charlie Chaplin, the Goons and the Sex Pistols performed, KOKO is maintaining its reputation as one of London's better gig venues. The theatre has a dance floor and decadent balconies and attracts an indie crowd with Club NME on Friday. There are live bands most nights and it has a great roof terrace.

Ronnie Scott's
JAZZ

(Map p166; ☑ 020-7439 0747; www.ronniescotts. co.uk; 47 Frith St, W1; ⊘ 7pm-3am Mon-Sat, 1-4pm & 8pm-midnight Sun; ⊜ Leicester Sq or Tottenham Court Rd) Ronnie Scott originally opened his jazz club on Gerrard St in 1959 under a Chinese gambling den. It moved here six years later and became widely known as Britain's best jazz club. Gigs are at 8.15pm (8pm Sunday) with a second sitting at 11.15pm Friday and Saturday (check though), followed by the more informal Late, Late Show until 3am.

100 Club
LIVE MUSIC

(Map p166; ☑ 020-7636 0933; www.the100club. co.uk; 100 Oxford St, W1; admission £8-20; ⊘ check website for gig times; ⊜ Oxford Circus or Tottenham Court Rd) This legendary London venue has always concentrated on jazz, but also features swing and rock. It's showcased Chris Barber, BB King and the Stones, and was at the centre of the punk revolution and the '90s indie scene. It hosts dancing swing gigs and local jazz musicians, the occasional bigname, where-are-they-now bands and topleague tributes.

Comedy

Comedy Store
COMEDY

(Map p166; ☑ 0844 871 7699; www.thecomedy store.co.uk; 1a Oxendon St, SW1; admission £8-22.50; ⊜ Piccadilly Circus) One of the first (and still one of the best) comedy clubs in London. Wednesday and Sunday night's Comedy Store Players is the most famous improvisation outfit in town, with the wonderful Josie Lawrence; on Thursdays, Fridays and Saturdays Best in Stand Up features the best on London's comedy circuit.

Soho Theatre
COMEDY

(Map p166; ☑ 020-7478 0100; www.sohotheatre. com; 21 Dean St, W1; admission £8-25; ⊜ Tottenham Court Rd) The Soho Theatre has developed a superb reputation for showcasing new comedy-writing talent and comedians. It's also hosted some top-notch stand-up or sketch-based comedians including Alexei Sayle and Doctor Brown, plus cabaret.

Classical Music, Opera & Dance

Royal Albert Hall
CONCERT VENUE

(Map p170; ☑ 0845 401 5034; www.royalalbert hall.com; Kensington Gore, SW7; ⊜ South Kensington) This splendid Victorian concert hall hosts classical-music, rock and other performances, but is famously the venue for the BBC-sponsored Proms. Booking is possible, but from mid-July to mid-September Proms punters queue for £5 standing (or 'promenading') tickets that go on sale one hour before curtain-up. Otherwise, the box office and prepaid-ticket collection counter are through door 12 (south side of the hall).

Royal Festival Hall
CONCERT VENUE

(Map p162; ☑ 020-7960 4200; www.south bankcentre.co.uk; Southbank Centre, Belvedere Rd, SE1; ☎; ⊜ Waterloo) Royal Festival Hall's amphitheatre seats 2500 and is one of the best places for catching world- and classical-music artists. The sound is fantastic, the programming impeccable and there are frequent free gigs in the wonderfully expansive foyer.

Barbican Centre PERFORMING ARTS
(Map p162; ☑ 020-7638 8891; www.barbican.org. uk; Silk St, EC2; ⊗ box office 10am-8pm; ⊜ Barbican) Home to the wonderful London Symphony Orchestra and its associate orchestra, the lesser-known BBC Symphony Orchestra, the arts centre also hosts scores of other leading musicians, focusing in particular on jazz, folk, world and soul artists. Dance is another strong point here, while film covers recent releases as well as film festivals and seasons.

Royal Opera House OPERA
(Map p166; ☑ 020-7304 4000; www.roh.org.uk; Bow St, WC2; tickets £4-270; ⊜ Covent Garden) The £210 million redevelopment for the millennium gave classic opera a fantastic setting in London, and coming here for a night is a sumptuous – if pricey – affair. Although the program has been fluffed up by modern influences, the main attractions are still the opera and classical ballet – all are wonderful productions and feature world-class performers.

Sadler's Wells DANCE
(Map p162; ☑ 020-7863 8000; www.sadlerswells. com; Rosebery Ave, EC1R; ⊜ Angel) A glittering modern venue that was, in fact, first established in 1683, Sadler's Wells is the most eclectic modern-dance and ballet venue in town, with experimental dance shows of all genres and from all corners of the globe. The Lilian Baylis Studio stages smaller productions.

Southbank Centre CONCERT VENUE
(Map p162; ☑ 0844 875 0073; www.southbank centre.co.uk; Belvedere Rd, SE1; ⊜ Waterloo) The Southbank Centre comprises several venues – Royal Festival Hall (p183), **Queen Elizabeth Hall** (QEH) and Purcell Room – hosting a wide range of performing arts. As well as regular programming, it organises fantastic festivals, including **London Wonderground** (circus and cabaret), **Udderbelly** (a festival of comedy in all its guises) and **Meltdown** (a music event curated by the best and most eclectic names in music).

🔒 Shopping

Department Stores

London's famous department stores are an attraction in themselves, even if you're not interested in buying.

⭐ **Fortnum & Mason** DEPARTMENT STORE
(Map p166; ☑ 020-7734 8040; www.fortnum andmason.com; 181 Piccadilly, W1; ⊗ 10am-8pm Mon-Sat, 11.30am-6pm Sun; ⊜ Piccadilly Circus) With its classic eau de nil colour scheme, London's oldest grocery store (established 1707), refuses to yield to modern times. Its staff still clad in old-fashioned tailcoats, its glamorous food hall supplied with hampers, cut marmalade, speciality teas and so forth, Fortnum and Mason is *the* quintessential London shopping experience.

Harrods DEPARTMENT STORE
(Map p170; ☑ 020-7730 1234; www.harrods. com; 87-135 Brompton Rd, SW1; ⊗ 10am-9pm Mon-Sat, 11.30am-6pm Sun; ⊜ Knightsbridge) Garish and stylish in equal measures, perennially crowded Harrods is an obligatory stop for visitors, from the cash-strapped to the big spenders. The stock is astonishing, as are many of the price tags. High on kitsch, the 'Egyptian Elevator' resembles something out of an *Indiana Jones* epic, while the memorial fountain to Dodi and Di (lower ground floor) merely adds surrealism.

Selfridges DEPARTMENT STORE
(Map p170; www.selfridges.com; 400 Oxford St, W1; ⊗ 9.30am-10pm Mon-Sat, 11.30am-6pm Sun; ⊜ Bond St) Selfridges loves innovation – it's famed for its inventive window displays by international artists, gala shows and, above all, its amazing range of products. It's the trendiest of London's one-stop shops, with labels such as Boudicca, Luella Bartley, Emma Cook, Chloé and Missoni; an unparalleled food hall; and Europe's largest cosmetics department.

Liberty DEPARTMENT STORE
(Map p166; www.liberty.co.uk; Great Marlborough St, W1; ⊗ 10am-8pm Mon-Sat, noon-6pm Sun; ⊜ Oxford Circus) An irresistible blend of contemporary styles in an old-fashioned mock-Tudor atmosphere, Liberty has a huge cosmetics department and an accessories floor, along with a breathtaking lingerie section, all at very inflated prices. A classic London souvenir is a Liberty fabric print, especially in the form of a scarf.

Harvey Nichols DEPARTMENT STORE
(Map p170; www.harveynichols.com; 109-125 Knightsbridge, SW1; ⊙10am-8pm Mon-Sat, 11.30am-6pm Sun; ⊜Knightsbridge) At London's temple of high fashion, you'll find Chloé and Balenciaga bags, the city's best denim range, a massive make-up hall with exclusive lines and great jewellery. The food hall and in-house restaurant, **Fifth Floor**, are, you guessed it, on the 5th floor. From 11.30am to midday, it's browsing time only.

Music

As befitting a global music capital, London has a wide range of music stores.

★**Rough Trade East** MUSIC
(Map p162; www.roughtrade.com; Old Truman Brewery, 91 Brick Lane, E1; ⊙9am-9pm Mon-Thu, to 8pm Fri, 10am-8pm Sat, 11am-7pm Sun; ⊜Shoreditch High St) No longer directly associated with the legendary record label (home to The Smiths, The Libertines and The Strokes, among many others), but this huge record store is still the best place to come for music of an indie, soul, electronica and alternative bent. Apart from the impressive selection of CDs and vinyl, it also dispenses coffee and stages promotional gigs.

Ray's Jazz MUSIC
(Map p166; www.foyles.co.uk; 2nd fl, 107 Charing Cross Rd, WC2; ⊙9.30am-9pm Mon-Sat, 11.30am-6pm Sun; ⊜Tottenham Court Rd) Quiet and serene with friendly and helpful staff, this shop on the 2nd floor of Foyles (p185) bookshop has one of the best jazz selections in London.

Bookshops

★**John Sandoe Books** BOOKS
(Map p170; ☑020-7589 9473; www.johnsandoe. com; 10 Blacklands Tce, SW3; ⊙9.30am-6.30pm Mon-Sat, 11am-5pm Sun; ⊜Sloane Sq) The perfect antidote to impersonal book superstores, this atmospheric three-storey bookshop in 18th-century premises is a treasure trove of literary gems and hidden surprises. It's been in business for almost 60 years and loyal customers swear by it, while knowledgeable booksellers spill forth with well-read pointers and helpful advice.

Hatchards BOOKS
(Map p166; ☑020-7439 9921; www.hatchards. co.uk; 187 Piccadilly, W1; ⊙9.30am-8pm Mon-Sat, noon-6.30pm Sun; ⊜Green Park or Piccadilly Circus) London's oldest bookshop dates to 1797. Holding three royal warrants (hence

the portrait of the Queen), it's a stupendous independent bookstore, with a solid supply of signed editions and bursting at its smart seams with very browsable stock. There's a strong selection of first editions on the ground floor as well as regular literary events.

Foyles BOOKS
(Map p166; ☑020-7434 1574; www.foyles.co.uk; 107 Charing Cross Rd, WC2; ⊙9.30am-9pm Mon-Sat, 11.30am-6pm Sun; ⊜Tottenham Court Rd) With four miles of shelving, you can bet on finding even the most obscure of titles in London's most legendary bookshop. Once synonymous with chaos, Foyles long ago got its act together and in 2014 moved just down the road into the spacious former home of Central St Martins. Thoroughly redesigned, its stunning new home is a joy to explore.

ⓘ Information

City of London Information Centre (Map p162; www.visitthecity.co.uk; St Paul's Churchyard, EC4; ⊙9.30am-5.30pm Mon-Sat, 10am-4pm Sun; 🛜; ⊜St Paul's) Multilingual tourist information, fast-track tickets to City attractions and guided walks (adult/child £7/6).

ⓘ Getting There & Away

BUS & COACH

The London terminus for long-distance buses (called 'coaches' in Britain) is **Victoria Coach Station** (164 Buckingham Palace Rd, SW1; ⊜Victoria).

TRAIN

Most of London's main-line rail terminals are linked by the Circle line on the tube. The terminals listed here serve the following destinations:

Charing Cross Canterbury

Euston Manchester, Liverpool, Carlisle, Glasgow

King's Cross Cambridge, Hull, York, Newcastle, Edinburgh, Aberdeen

Liverpool Street Stansted airport (Express), Cambridge

London Bridge Gatwick airport, Brighton

Marylebone Birmingham

Paddington Heathrow airport (Express), Oxford, Bath, Bristol, Exeter, Plymouth, Cardiff

St Pancras Gatwick and Luton airports, Brighton, Nottingham, Sheffield, Leicester, Leeds, Paris Eurostar

Victoria Gatwick airport (Express), Brighton, Canterbury

Waterloo Windsor, Winchester, Exeter, Plymouth

ℹ Getting Around

TO/FROM THE AIRPORTS

Gatwick

National Rail (www.nationalrail.co.uk) has regular train services to/from London Bridge (30 minutes, every 15 to 30 minutes), London King's Cross (55 minutes, every 15 to 30 minutes) and London Victoria (30 minutes, every 10 to 15 minutes). Fares vary depending on the time of travel and the train company, but allow £10 to £20 for a single.

EasyBus (www.easybus.co.uk) runs 19-seater minibuses to Gatwick every 15 to 20 minutes on two routes: one from Earl's Court/West Brompton and from Waterloo (one-way from £5.95). The service runs round the clock. Journey time averages 75 minutes.

Heathrow

The cheapest option from Heathrow is the Underground (tube). The Piccadilly line is accessible from every terminal (£6, one hour to central London, departing from Heathrow every five minutes from around 5am to 11.30pm).

Faster, and much more expensive, is the **Heathrow Express** (www.heathrowexpress. com; 1-way/return £22/36) train to Paddington station (15 minutes, every 15 minutes, 5.12am to 11.48pm). You can purchase tickets on board (£5 extra), from self-service machines (cash and credit cards accepted) at both stations, or online.

London City

The Docklands Light Railway (DLR) connects London City Airport to the tube network, taking 22 minutes to reach Bank station (£4 to £5). A black taxi costs around £35 to/from central London.

Luton

National Rail (www.nationalrail.co.uk) services (one-way from £10, 35 to 50 minutes, every six to 30 minutes, from 7am to 10pm) run from London Bridge and London King's Cross to Luton Airport Parkway station, where an airport shuttle bus (one-way £1.60) will take you to the airport in 10 minutes.

ℹ MAPS

There was a time when no Londoner would be without a pocket-sized *London A–Z* map-book. It's a great resource if you don't have a smartphone. You can buy them at newsstands and shops everywhere. For getting around the London Underground system (the tube), maps are free at underground stations.

EasyBus (www.easybus.co.uk) minibuses head from Victoria, Earl's Court and Baker St to Luton (from £4.95); allow 1½ hours, every 30 minutes. A taxi costs around £110 to £110.

Stansted

The **Stansted Express** (☑ 0845 8500150; www. stanstedexpress.com; one-way/return £19/32) train connects with Liverpool Street station (one way/return £19.10/31, 45 minutes, every 15 to 30 minutes, 5.30am to 12.30am).

EasyBus (www.easybus.co.uk) has services between Stansted and Baker St (from £4.95, 1¼ hours, every 15 minutes).

National Express (www.nationalexpress. com) runs buses to Stansted – the A9 goes to Liverpool Street station (from £10, 80 minutes, every 30 minutes). The A6 links with Victoria Coach Station (from £12, allow 1¾ hours, every 20 minutes).

BICYCLE

Central London is mostly flat, relatively compact and the traffic moves slowly – all of which makes it surprisingly good for cyclists. It can get terribly congested though, so you'll need to keep your wits about you – and lock your bike (including both wheels) securely.

Bikes can be hired from numerous self-service docking stations through **Santander Cycles** (☑ 0343 222 6666; www.tfl.gov.uk/modes/cycling/santander-cycles). The access fee is £2 for 24 hours. All you need is a credit or debit card. The first 30 minutes are free. It's then £2 for any additional period of 30 minutes.

CAR

Don't. As a visitor, it's very unlikely you'll need to drive in London. If you do, you'll incur an £11.50 per day congestion charge (7am to 6pm weekdays) simply to take a car into central London. If you're hiring a car to continue your trip around Britain, take the tube or train to a major airport and pick it up from there.

PUBLIC TRANSPORT

London's public transport is excellent, with tubes, trains, buses and boats getting you wherever you need to go. **TFL** (www.tfl.gov.uk), the city's public transport provider, is the glue that binds the network together. Its website has a handy journey planner and information on all services, including taxis.

Boat

Thames Clippers (www.thamesclippers.com) run regular services between Embankment, Waterloo, Blackfriars, Bankside, London Bridge, Tower Bridge, Canary Wharf, Greenwich, North Greenwich and Woolwich piers (adult/child £7.50/3.75), from 6.55am to around midnight (from 9.29am weekends).

① OYSTER CARD

The Oyster Card is a smart card on which you can store credit towards 'prepay' fares, as well as Travelcards valid for periods from a day to a year. Oyster Cards are valid across the entire public transport network in London. When entering a station, simply touch your card on a reader (they have a yellow circle with the image of an Oyster Card on them) and then touch again on your way out. The system will deduct the appropriate amount of credit from your card. For bus journeys, you only need to touch once upon boarding.

The benefit is that fares for Oyster Card users are lower than standard ones. If you make many journeys during the day, you will never pay more than the appropriate Travelcard (peak or off peak) once the daily 'price cap' has been reached.

Oyster Cards can be bought (£5 refundable deposit required) and topped up at any Underground station, travel information centre or shop displaying the Oyster logo.

To get your deposit back along with any remaining credit, simply return your Oyster Card at a ticket booth.

Bus

Buses run regularly during the day, while less-frequent night buses (prefixed with the letter 'N') wheel into action when the tube stops. Cash is not accepted; instead you must pay with an Oyster Card, Travelcard or a contactless payment card. Fares are a flat £1.50, no matter the distance travelled. Buses stop on request, so clearly signal the driver with an outstretched arm.

Underground & Docklands Light Railway

The tube extends its subterranean tentacles throughout London and into the surrounding counties, with services running every few minutes from roughly 5.30am to 12.30am (7am to 11.30pm Sunday). Selected lines (the Victoria and Jubilee lines, plus most of the Piccadilly, Central and Northern lines) run all night on Fridays and Saturdays, with trains every 10 minutes or so.

The Docklands Light Railway (DLR) links the City to Docklands, Greenwich and London City Airport.

Lines are colour-coded (red for the Central Line, yellow for the Circle Line, black for the Northern Line and so on). It helps to know the direction you're travelling in (ie northbound or southbound, eastbound or westbound) as well as the terminus of the line you're travelling on. If you get confused, don't worry, as copies of the tube's famous map are posted everywhere, showing how the 14 different routes intersect. Be warned, however – the distances between stations on the tube map aren't remotely to scale.

Single fares cost from £2.40/4.90 with/without an Oyster Card.

TAXI

London's famous black cabs are available for hire when the yellow light above the windscreen is lit. Fares are metered, with flag fall of £2.60 and the additional rate dependent on time of day, distance travelled and taxi speed. A 1-mile trip will cost between £6 and £9.

Minicabs are a cheaper alternative to black cabs and will quote trip fares in advance. Only use drivers from proper agencies; licensed minicabs aren't allowed to tout for business or pick you up off the street without a booking. Apps such as **Uber** (www.uber.com) or **Kabbee** (www.kabbee.com) allow you to book a minicab in double-quick time.

Around London

'When you're tired of London, you're tired of life' said 18th-century Londoner Samuel Johnson. But he wasn't living in an age when too many days on the tube can leave you exhausted and grouchy. Luckily, the capital is surprisingly close to some excellent day trips; Windsor and Eton are two gems that are an easy train ride from the capital.

Windsor & Eton

POP 31,225

Dominated by the massive bulk of Windsor Castle, these twin towns have a rather surreal atmosphere, with the morning pomp and ceremony of the changing of the guards in Windsor and the sight of school boys dressed in formal tailcoats wandering the streets of Eton.

⊙ Sights

★ **Windsor Castle**   CASTLE

(☑ 0303 123 7304; www.royalcollection.org.uk; Castle Hill; adult/child £20.50/12; ⊙ 9.30am-5.30pm Mar-Oct, 9.45am-4.15pm Nov-Feb; ⓘ; ☒ 702 from London Victoria, ☒ London Waterloo to Windsor & Eton Riverside, ☒ London Paddington to Windsor & Eton Central via Slough) The world's largest and oldest continuously occupied fortress, Windsor Castle is a majestic vision of battlements and towers. It's used for state occasions and is one of the Queen's principal residences; if she's home, the Royal Standard flies from the Round Tower. Take a free guided tour (every half-hour) of the wards or a handheld multimedia tour of the lavish State Apartments and beautiful chapels. Sections may be off limits if in use. Book tickets online to avoid queues.

Eton College NOTABLE BUILDING
(☑01753-370100; www.etoncollege.com; High St, Eton; adult/child £10/free; ☺tours Fri 2pm & 4pm May-Aug) The largest and most famous public (meaning private and fee-paying) boys' school in England, and arguably the most enduring symbol of England's class system. High-profile alumni include 19 British prime ministers, countless princes, kings and maharajas, famous explorers, authors, actors and economists – among them Princes William and Harry, George Orwell, Ian Fleming, John Maynard Keynes, Bear Grylls and Eddie Redmayne.

ⓘ Information

Tourist Office (☑01753-743900; www.windsor.gov.uk; Old Booking Hall, Windsor Royal Shopping Arcade, Thames St; ☺10am-5pm Apr-Sep, to 4pm Oct-Mar) Pick up a heritage walk map (£2.20).

ⓘ Getting There & Away

Trains from Windsor & Eton Riverside (Dachet Rd) go directly to London Waterloo (£10, one hour). Trains from Windsor & Eton Central (Thames St), changing at Slough for London Paddington (£10, 28 to 46 minutes), are quicker.

> **WORTH A TRIP**
>
> ### THE MAKING OF HARRY POTTER
>
> Whether you're a fairweather fan or a full-on Pothead, this studio tour (☑0345 084 0900; www.wbstudiotour.co.uk; Studio Tour Dr, Leavesden, WD25; adult/child £39/31; ☺9am-8pm, hours vary; ℗) is well worth the admittedly hefty admission price. You'll need to pre-book your visit for an allocated timeslot and then allow two- to three hours to do the complex justice. It starts with a short film before you're ushered through giant doors into the actual set of Hogwarts' Great Hall – the first of many 'wow' moments. It's near Watford, northwest of London.

Canterbury

POP 55,240

Canterbury tops the charts for English cathedral cities. Many consider the World Heritage–listed cathedral that dominates its centre to be one of Europe's finest, and the town's narrow medieval alleyways, riverside gardens and ancient city walls are a joy to explore.

◉ Sights

★**Canterbury Cathedral** CATHEDRAL
(www.canterbury-cathedral.org; adult/concession £12/10.50, tours £5/4, audio guide £4/3; ☺9am-5.30pm Mon-Sat, 12.30-2.30pm Sun) A rich repository of more than 1400 years of Christian history, the Church of England's mother ship is a truly extraordinary place with an absorbing history. This Gothic cathedral, the highlight of the city's World Heritage Sites, is southeast England's top tourist attraction as well as a place of worship. It's also the site of English history's most famous murder: Archbishop Thomas Becket was done in here in 1170. Allow at least two hours to do the cathedral justice.

⌸ Sleeping

Kipp's Independent Hostel HOSTEL £
(☑01227-786121; www.kipps-hostel.com; 40 Nunnery Fields; dm £16.50-24.50, s £25-35, d £50-70; @☜) Occupying a red-brick town house in a quietish residential area less than a mile from the city centre, these superb backpacker digs enjoy a homely atmosphere, clean (though cramped) dorms and rave reviews.

Arthouse B&B B&B ££
(☑07976-725457; www.arthousebandb.com; 24 London Rd; r from £65; ℗☜) A night at Canterbury's most laid-back digs, housed in a 19th-century fire station, is a bit like sleeping over at a really cool art student's pad. The theme is funky and eclectic, with furniture by local designers and artwork by the instantly likeable artist owners, who have a house-studio out the back.

✕ Eating & Drinking

★**Tiny Tim's Tearoom** CAFE £
(www.tinytimstearoom.com; 34 St Margaret's St; mains £6-10.50; ☺9.30am-5pm Tue-Sat, 10.30am-4pm Sun) It's no mean feat to be declared 'Kent Tearoom of the Year', but this swish 1930s cafe was awarded the accolade in 2015. It offers hungry shoppers big break-

fasts bursting with Kentish ingredients, and tiers of cakes, crumpets, cucumber sandwiches and scones plastered in clotted cream. On busy shopping days you are guaranteed to queue for a table.

★ **Deeson's**   BRITISH ££
(☑ 01227-767854; www.deesonsrestaurant.co.uk; 25-26 Sun St; mains £15-24; ⊗ noon-3pm & 5-10pm) Put the words 'local', 'seasonal' and 'tasty' together and you have this superb British eatery. Local fruit and veg; award-winning wines, beers and ciders; fish from Kent's coastal waters; and the odd ingredient from the proprietor's own allotment are all served in a straightforward, contemporary setting just a Kentish apple's throw from the Canterbury Cathedral gates.

ℹ Information

Tourist Office (☑ 01227-862162; www.canterbury.co.uk; 18 High St; ⊗ 9am-5pm Mon-Wed, Fri & Sat, to 7pm Thu, 10am-5pm Sun) Located in the Beaney House of Art & Knowledge. Staff can help book accommodation, excursions and theatre tickets.

ℹ Getting There & Away

There are two train stations: Canterbury East for London Victoria and Dover; and Canterbury West for London's Charing Cross and St Pancras stations. Connections include Dover Priory (£8, 25 minutes, half-hourly), London St Pancras (£34.80, one hour, hourly) and London Victoria/Charing Cross (£29.30, 1¾ hours, two hourly).

Salisbury

POP 40,300

Centred on a majestic cathedral topped by the tallest spire in England, the gracious city of Salisbury has been an important provincial city for more than 1000 years.

◉ Sights

★ **Salisbury Cathedral**   CATHEDRAL
(☑ 01722-555120; www.salisburycathedral.org.uk; Cathedral Close; requested donation adult/child £7.50/free; ⊗ 9am-5pm Mon-Sat, noon-4pm Sun) England is endowed with countless stunning churches, but few can hold a candle to the grandeur and sheer spectacle of 13th-century Salisbury Cathedral. This early English Gothic–style structure has an elaborate exterior decorated with pointed arches and flying buttresses, and a sombre, austere interior designed to keep its congregation

AVEBURY

While the tour buses usually head straight to Stonehenge, prehistoric purists make for **Avebury Stone Circle**. Though it lacks the dramatic trilithons ('gateways') of its sister site across the plain, Avebury is the largest stone circle in the world and a more rewarding place to visit simply because you can get closer to the giant boulders.

A large section of Avebury village is actually inside the circle, meaning you can sleep, or at least have lunch and a pint, inside the mystic ring.

Buses run from Salisbury via Devizes (£7.50, 1¾ hours, hourly Monday to Saturday, five on Sunday).

suitably pious. Its statuary and tombs are outstanding; don't miss the daily tower tours (p189) and the cathedral's original, 13th-century copy of the **Magna Carta** (⊗ 9.30am-4.30pm Mon-Sat, noon-3.45pm Sun).

★ **Salisbury Museum**   MUSEUM
(☑ 01722-332151; www.salisburymuseum.org.uk; 65 Cathedral Close; adult/child £8/4; ⊗ 10am-5pm Mon-Sat year-round, plus noon-5pm Sun Jun-Sep) The hugely important archaeological finds here include the Stonehenge Archer, the bones of a man found in the ditch surrounding the stone circle – one of the arrows found alongside probably killed him. With gold coins dating from 100 BC and a Bronze Age gold necklace, it's a powerful introduction to Wiltshire's prehistory.

🛏 Sleeping & Eating

★ **Chapter House**   INN ££
(☑ 01722-412028; www.thechapterhouseuk.com; 9 St Johns St; r £100-140) In this 800-year-old boutique beauty, wood panels and wildly wonky stairs sit beside duck-your-head beams. The cheaper bedrooms are swish but the posher ones are stunning, starring slipper baths and the odd heraldic crest. The pick is room 6, where King Charles is reputed to have stayed. Lucky him.

Cathedral View   B&B ££
(☑ 01722-502254; www.cathedral-viewbandb.co.uk; 83 Exeter St; s £75-85, d £80-100; 🅿 🛜) Admirable attention to detail defines this Georgian town house, where miniature flower displays and home-baked biscuits

sit in quietly elegant rooms. Breakfasts include prime Wiltshire sausages and the B&B's own bread and jam, while homemade lemon drizzle cake will be waiting for your afternoon tea.

Cloisters PUB FOOD ££
(www.cloisterspubsalisbury.co.uk; 83 Catherine St; mains £9-19; ⊘noon-9pm) The building dates from 1350, it's been a pub since the 1600s and, today, improbably warped beams reinforce an age-old vibe. It's a convivial spot for beefy burgers and homemade pies, or classier evening fare such as pesto-dusted salmon fillet, and lamb steaks with redcurrant sauce.

ⓘ Information

Tourist Office (☑01722-342860; www.visitsalisbury.co.uk; Fish Row; ⊘9am-5pm Mon-Fri, 10am-4pm Sat, 10am-2pm Sun)

ⓘ Getting There & Away

BUS

National Express services include Bath (£11, 1¼ hours, one day), Bristol (£11, 2¼ hours, one daily) and London (£17, three hours, three daily) via Heathrow. Tour buses leave Salisbury for Stonehenge regularly.

TRAIN

Trains run half-hourly from London Waterloo (£25, 1½ hours), Bath (£10, one hour), Bristol (£15, 1¼ hours) and Exeter (£20, two hours).

Stonehenge

This compelling ring of monolithic stones has been attracting a steady stream of pilgrims, poets and philosophers for the last 5000 years and is easily Britain's most iconic archaeological site.

An ultramodern makeover at ancient Stonehenge (EH; ☑0370 333 1181; www.english-heritage.org.uk; adult/child same-day tickets £18/11, advance booking £15.50/9.30; ⊘9am-8pm Jun-Aug, 9.30am-7pm Apr, May & Sep, 9.30am-5pm Oct-Mar; Ⓟ) has brought an impressive visitor centre and the closure of an intrusive road (now restored to grassland). The result is a far stronger sense of historical context; dignity and mystery returned to an archaeological gem.

Stonehenge is one of Britain's great archaeological mysteries: despite countless theories about the site's purpose, ranging from a sacrificial centre to a celestial timepiece, in truth, no one knows for sure what

> **ⓘ STONE CIRCLE ACCESS VISITS**
>
> Visitors to Stonehenge normally have to stay outside the stone circle. But on **Stone Circle Access Visits** (☑0370 333 0605; www.english-heritage.org.uk; adult/child £32/19) you get to wander round the core of the site, getting up-close views of the bluestones and trilithons. The walks take place in the evening or early morning, so the quieter atmosphere and the slanting sunlight add to the effect. Each visit only takes 26 people; to secure a place book at least two months in advance.

drove prehistoric Britons to expend so much time and effort on its construction.

Stonehenge now operates by timed tickets, meaning if you want guaranteed entry you have to book in advance. If you're planning a high-season visit, it's best to secure your ticket well in advance.

ⓘ Getting There & Around

BUS

There is no public transport to the site. The **Stonehenge Tour** (☑01202-338420; www.thestonehengetour.info; adult/child £27/17) leaves Salisbury's train station half-hourly from June to August, and hourly from September to May.

Bath

POP 88,900

Britain is littered with beautiful cities, but precious few compare to Bath, founded on top of natural hot springs that led the Romans to build a magnificent bathhouse here. Bath's heyday was during the 18th century, when local entrepreneur Ralph Allen and the father-and-son architects John Wood the Elder and Younger turned this sleepy backwater into the toast of Georgian society, and constructed fabulous landmarks such as the Circus and Royal Crescent.

◉ Sights

★**Roman Baths** HISTORIC BUILDING
(☑01225-477785; www.romanbaths.co.uk; Abbey Churchyard; adult/child £15.50/9.80; ⊘9.30am-6pm Sep-Jun, 9am-10pm Jul & Aug) In typically ostentatious style, the Romans constructed a complex of bathhouses above Bath's three natural hot springs, which emerge at a steady

46°C (115°F). Situated alongside a temple dedicated to the healing goddess Sulis-Minerva, the baths now form one of the best-preserved ancient Roman spas in the world, and are encircled by 18th- and 19th-century buildings. Bath's premier attraction can get very busy. To dodge the worst crowds, avoid weekends, July and August.

★ **Royal Crescent** ARCHITECTURE
(Royal Cres) Bath is famous for its glorious Georgian architecture, and it doesn't get any grander than this semicircular terrace of majestic town houses overlooking the green sweep of Royal Victoria Park. Designed by John Wood the Younger (1728–82) and built between 1767 and 1775, the houses appear perfectly symmetrical from the outside, but the owners were allowed to tweak the interiors, so no two houses are quite the same. **No 1 Royal Crescent** (☑01225-428126; www.no1royalcrescent.org.uk; 1 Royal Cres; adult/child/family £10/4/22; ☺noon-5.30pm Mon & 10.30am-5.30pm Tue-Sun Feb–early Dec) offers you an intriguing insight into life inside.

Jane Austen Centre MUSEUM
(☑01225-443000; www.janeausten.co.uk; 40 Gay St; adult/child £11/5.50; ☺9.45am-5.30pm Apr-Oct, 10am-4pm Nov-Mar) Bath is known to many as a location in Jane Austen's novels, including *Persuasion* and *Northanger Abbey*. Although Austen lived in Bath for only five years, from 1801 to 1806, she remained a regular visitor and a keen student of the city's social scene. Here, guides in Regency costumes regale you with Austen-esque tales as you tour memorabilia relating to the writer's life in Bath.

🛏 Sleeping

Bath YHA HOSTEL £
(☑0845 371 9303; www.yha.org.uk; Bathwick Hill; dm £13-22, d from £39; ☺reception 7am-11pm; 🅿@🛜) Split across an Italianate mansion and a modern annex, this impressive hostel is a steep climb (or a short hop on bus U1 or U18) from the city. The listed building means the rooms are huge, and some have period features such as cornicing and bay windows.

★ **Three Abbey Green** B&B ££
(☑01225-428558; www.threeabbeygreen.com; 3 Abbey Green; d £90-200, apt £160; 🛜) Rarely in Bath do you get somewhere as central as this Georgian town house with such spacious rooms. Elegant, 18th-century-style furnishings are teamed with swish wet-room

---

DON'T MISS

THE THERMAE BATH SPA
....
Taking a dip in the Roman Baths might be off-limits, but you can still sample the city's curative waters at this fantastic modern **spa complex** (☑01225-331234; www.thermaebathspa.com; Hot Bath St; Mon-Fri £35, Sat & Sun £38; ☺9am-9.30pm, last entry 7pm), housed in a shell of local stone and plate glass. Ticket includes steam rooms, waterfall showers and a choice of two swimming pools. The showpiece attraction is the open-air rooftop pool, where you can bathe with a backdrop of Bath's cityscape – a don't-miss experience, best enjoyed at dusk.

---

bathrooms, and the opulent Lord Nelson suite features a vast four-poster bed. There's also a two-person, self-catering apartment nearby (two-night minimum stay).

★ **Queensberry Hotel** HOTEL £££
(☑01225-447928; www.thequeensberry.co.uk; 4 Russell St; r £125-185, ste £225-275; 🛜) Award-winning, quirky Queensberry is Bath's best boutique spoil. Four Georgian town houses have been combined into one seamlessly stylish whole, where heritage roots meet snazzy designs; expect everything from gingham checks and country creams to bright upholstery, original fireplaces and free-standing tubs. Rates exclude breakfast; parking is £7.

🍴 Eating & Drinking

Adventure Cafe Bar CAFE £
(www.adventurecafebar.co.uk; 5 Princes Bldgs, George St; mains £5-10; ☺8am-3am Mon-Fri, 9am-3am Sat & Sun; 🍴) This cool cafe-bar, just a slipper's throw from the Assembly Rooms, offers something to everyone at most times of the day: morning cappuccino, lunchtime ciabatta and late-night beer and cocktails. There's great outdoor seating in the back.

Café Retro CAFE £
(☑01225-339347; www.caferetro.co.uk; 18 York St; mains £5-11; ☺9am-5pm Mon-Sun) A poke in the eye for the corporate coffee chains. The paint job's scruffy, the crockery's ancient and none of the furniture matches, but that's all part of the charm: this is a cafe from the old school, and there are few places better for burgers, butties or cake. Takeaways (in biodegradable containers) are available from Retro-to-Go next door.

Bath

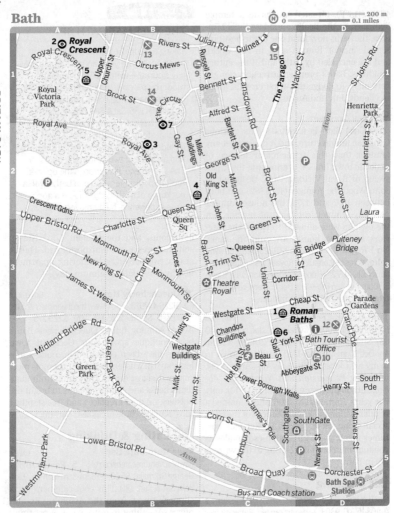

★ **Circus** MODERN BRITISH **££**
(📞01225-466020; www.thecircusrestaurant.
co.uk; 34 Brock St; mains lunch £10-15, dinner
£17-21; ⊙10am-midnight Mon-Sat) Chef Ali
Golden has turned this bistro into one of
Bath's destination addresses. Her taste is
for British dishes with a continental twist,
à la Elizabeth David: rabbit, Wiltshire lamb
and West Country fish are all infused with
herby flavours and rich sauces. It occupies
an elegant town house near the Circus. Reservations recommended.

Chequers GASTROPUB **££**
(📞01225-360017; www.thechequersbar.com; 50
Rivers St; mains £10-25; ⊙bar noon-11pm daily, food
6-9pm daily, noon-2.30pm Sat & Sun) A discerning crowd inhabits Chequers, a pub that's
been in business since 1776, but which has a
menu that's bang up to date thanks to head
chef Tony Casey. Forget bar-food staples,
here it's hake with octopus and wild rice.

★ **Menu Gordon Jones** MODERN BRITISH **£££**
(📞01225-480871; www.menugordonjones.co.uk;
2 Wellsway; 5-course lunch £40, 6-course dinner

Bath

⦿ Top Sights

⦿ Sights

✪ Activities, Courses & Tours

⬚ Sleeping

⊗ Eating

⊖ Drinking & Nightlife

£55; ⊙12.30-2pm & 7-9pm Tue-Sat) If you enjoy dining with an element of surprise, then Gordon Jones' restaurant will be right up your culinary boulevard. Menus are dreamt up daily and showcase the chef's taste for experimental ingredients (eel, haggis and smoked milk foam) and madcap presentation (test tubes, edible cups, slate plates). It's superb value given the skill on show. Reservations essential.

★Star Inn   PUB
(www.abbeyales.co.uk; 23 The Vineyards, off the Paragon; ⊙noon-2.30pm & 5.30-11pm Mon-Fri, noon-midnight Sat, to 10.30pm Sun) Not many pubs are registered relics, but the Star is – it still has many of its 19th-century bar fittings. It's the brewery tap for Bath-based Abbey Ales; some ales are served in traditional jugs, and you can even ask for a pinch of snuff in the 'smaller bar'.

ⓘ Information

Bath Tourist Office (☑ 0844 847 5256; www.visitbath.co.uk; Abbey Chambers, Abbey Churchyard; ⊙9.30am-5.30pm Mon-Sat, 10am-4pm Sun) Calls are charged at the premium rate of 50p per minute.

ⓘ Getting There & Away

BUS

Bath's **bus and coach station** (Dorchester St) is near the train station. National Express coaches run directly to London (£33, 3½ hours, eight to 10 daily) via Heathrow.

TRAIN

Bath Spa station is at the end of Manvers St. Many services connect through Bristol (£7.30, 15 minutes, three per hour), especially to the north of England. Direct services include London Paddington/London Waterloo (£38, 1½ hours, half-hourly) and Salisbury (£18, one hour, hourly).

Oxford

POP 159,994

One of the world's most famous university cities, Oxford is both beautiful and privileged. It's a wonderful place to wander: the elegant honey-toned buildings of the university's 38 colleges wrap around tranquil courtyards and narrow cobbled lanes where a studious calm reigns. But along with the rich history, tradition and energetic academic life, there is a busy, lively town beyond the college walls.

⦿ Sights

Not all of Oxford's colleges are open to the public. Check www.ox.ac.uk/colleges for full details.

★Bodleian Library   LIBRARY
(☑01865-277162; www.bodleian.ox.ac.uk/bodley; Catte St; tours £6-14; ⊙9am-5pm Mon-Sat, 11am-5pm Sun) Oxford's Bodleian Library is one of the oldest public libraries in the world and quite possibly the most impressive one you'll ever see. Visitors are welcome to wander around the central quad and the foyer exhibition space. For £1 you can visit the Divinity School, but the rest of the complex is only accessible on guided tours. Check timings online or at the information desk. Advance tickets are only available for extended tours; others must be purchased on the day.

★Christ Church   COLLEGE
(☑01865-276492; www.chch.ox.ac.uk; St Aldate's; adult/child £9/8; ⊙10am-5pm Mon-Sat, 2-5pm Sun) The largest of all of Oxford's colleges, with 650 students, and the one with the grandest quad, Christ Church is also its most popular. Its magnificent buildings, illustrious history and latter-day fame as a location for the *Harry Potter* films have

tourists visiting in droves. The college was founded in 1524 by Cardinal Thomas Wolsey, who suppressed the 9th-century monastery existing on the site to acquire the funds for his lavish building project.

★ **Pitt Rivers Museum** MUSEUM
(☑ 01865-270927; www.prm.ox.ac.uk; South Parks Rd; ⊙noon-4.30pm Mon, 10am-4.30pm Tue-Sun) **FREE** Hidden away through a door at the back of the **Oxford University Museum of Natural History** (☑ 01865-272950; www.oum. ox.ac.uk; Parks Rd; ⊙10am-5pm; 🛜📶) **FREE**, this wonderfully creepy anthropological museum houses a treasure trove of half a million objects from around the world – more than enough to satisfy any armchair adventurer. One of the reasons it's so brilliant is the fact there are no computers, interactive displays or shiny modern gimmicks. Dim lighting lends an air of mystery to glass cases stuffed with the prized booty of Victorian explorers.

★ **Ashmolean Museum** MUSEUM
(☑ 01865-278000; www.ashmolean.org; Beaumont St; ⊙10am-5pm Tue-Sun) **FREE** Britain's oldest public museum, second in repute only to London's British Museum, was established in 1683 when Elias Ashmole presented the university with the collection of curiosities amassed by the well-travelled John Tradescant, gardener to Charles I. Today its four floors feature interactive displays, a giant

MESSING ABOUT ON THE RIVER

An unmissable Oxford experience, punting is all about sitting back and quaffing Pimms (the quintessential English summer drink) as you watch the city's glorious architecture float by. Which, of course, requires someone else to do the hard work – punting is far more difficult than it appears. If you decide to go it alone, a deposit is usually charged. Most punts hold five people including the punter. Hire them from **Magdalen Bridge Boathouse** (☑ 01865-202643; www.oxfordpunting.co.uk; High St; chauffeured 4-person punts per 30min £32, punt rental per hr £22; ⊙9.30am-dusk Feb-Nov) or **Cherwell Boat House** (☑ 01865-515978; www.cherwellboathouse.co.uk; 50 Bardwell Rd; punt rental per hour £16-18; ⊙10am-dusk mid-Mar–mid-Oct).

atrium, glass walls revealing galleries on different levels and a beautifully sited rooftop restaurant. Collections, displayed in bright, spacious, attractive galleries within one of Britain's best examples of neoclassical architecture, span the world.

Magdalen College COLLEGE
(☑ 01865-276000; www.magd.ox.ac.uk; High St; adult/child £6/5; ⊙1pm-dusk Oct-Jun, 10am-7pm Jul & Aug, noon-7pm Sep) Set amid 40 hectares of private lawns, woodlands, river walks and deer park, Magdalen (*mawd*-lin), founded in 1458, is one of the wealthiest and most beautiful of Oxford's colleges. It has a reputation as an artistic college. Some of its notable students have included writers Julian Barnes, Alan Hollinghurst, CS Lewis, John Betjeman, Seamus Heaney and Oscar Wilde, not to mention Edward VIII, TE Lawrence 'of Arabia', Dudley Moore and Cardinal Thomas Wolsey.

🛏 Sleeping

Central Backpackers HOSTEL **£**
(☑ 01865-242288; www.centralbackpackers.co.uk; 13 Park End St; dm £20-25; 🛜) A welcoming budget option between the train station and town centre, above a bar. This small hostel has basic, bright and cheerful dorms, with lockers, for four to 12 people, a rooftop terrace and a small TV lounge. There's a six-bed girls-only dorm.

★ **Oxford Coach & Horses** B&B **££**
(☑ 01865-200017; www.oxfordcoachandhorses. co.uk; 62 St Clement's St; s/d/tr £125/135/165; 🅿🛜) Once an 18th-century coaching inn, this fabulous English-Mexican-owned boutique B&B hides behind a fresh powder-blue exterior, just a few metres from the Cowley Rd action. The eight light-filled rooms are cosy, spacious and individually styled in soothing pastels with the odd splash of purple, turquoise or exposed wood. The converted ground floor houses an airy, attractive breakfast room.

Galaxie Hotel B&B **££**
(☑ 01865-515688; www.galaxie.co.uk; 180 Banbury Rd, Summertown; s/d from £82/88; 🛜) A breezy reception hall leads past black-and-white photos to homey, boutique-y rooms at this smartly updated B&B, spread across two interconnecting Victorian town houses. Rooms, in various sizes, are styled in creams and greys offset by lime-green cushions; some come equipped with desks, fridges and

GLASTONBURY

To many people, Glastonbury is synonymous with the **Glastonbury Festival of Contemporary Performing Arts** (www.glastonburyfestivals.co.uk; tickets from £228; ⊘ Jun or Jul), a majestic (and frequently mud-soaked) extravaganza of music, theatre, dance, cabaret, carnival, spirituality and general all-round weirdness that's been held on and off farmland in Pilton, just outside Glastonbury, for the last 40-something years (bar the occasional off year to let the farm recover).

The town owes much of its spiritual fame to nearby **Glastonbury Tor** (NT; www.nationaltrust.org.uk) FREE, a grassy hump about a mile from town, topped by the ruins of St Michael's Church. According to local legend, the tor is said to be the mythical Isle of Avalon, King Arthur's last resting place. It's also allegedly one of the world's great spiritual nodes, marking the meeting point of many mystical lines of power known as ley lines.

There is no train station in Glastonbury, but bus 37/375/376 runs to Wells (£3.50, 15 minutes, several times per hour) and Bristol (£5.50, 1½ hours, every half hour).

kitchenettes. Sculptures, fire burners and tiki-bar-style benches dot the garden. It's 1.5 miles north of the centre.

Burlington House B&B ££
(☎ 01865-513513; www.burlington-hotel-oxford.co.uk; 374 Banbury Rd, Summertown; s/d from £70/96; 🅿🛜) Twelve elegantly contemporary rooms with patterned wallpaper, immaculate bathrooms, dashes of colour and luxury touches are available at this beautifully refreshed Victorian merchant's house. Personal service is as sensational as the delicious breakfast, complete with organic eggs, fresh orange juice and homemade bread, yoghurt and granola. It's 2 miles north of central Oxford, with good public transport links.

✖ Eating

★**Edamamé** JAPANESE £
(☎ 01865-246916; www.edamame.co.uk; 15 Holywell St; mains £6-9.50; ⊘ 11.30am-2.30pm Wed, 11.30am-2.30pm & 5-8.30pm Thu-Sat, noon-3.30pm Sun; 🖉) The queue out the door speaks volumes about the food quality at this tiny, deliciously authentic place. All light wood, dainty trays and friendly bustle, this is Oxford's top spot for gracefully simple, flavour-packed Japanese cuisine. Dishes include fragrant chicken-miso ramen, tofu stir-fry and, on Thursday night, sushi. No bookings; arrive early and be prepared to wait. Cash only at lunch.

★**Vaults & Garden** CAFE £
(☎ 01865-279112; www.thevaultsandgarden.com; University Church of St Mary the Virgin, Radcliffe Sq; mains £7-10; ⊘ 8.30am-6pm; 🛜🖉) Hidden away in the vaulted 14th-century Old Congregation House of the University Church, this buzzy local favourite serves a wholesome seasonal selection of soups, salads, pastas, curries, sandwiches and cakes, including plenty of vegetarian and gluten-free options. It's one of Oxford's most beautiful lunch venues, with additional tables in a pretty garden overlooking Radcliffe Sq. Arrive early to grab a seat.

Turl St Kitchen MODERN BRITISH ££
(☎ 01865-264171; www.turlstreetkitchen.co.uk; 16-17 Turl St; mains £11-19; ⊘ 8-10am, noon-2.30pm & 6.30-10pm; 🖉) 🖊 A twice-daily-changing menu transforms meals into exquisite surprises at this lively, super-central multilevel cafe-restaurant. Fresh, organic, sustainable and locally sourced produce is thrown into creative contemporary combinations, perhaps starring veggie tajines, roast beef, hake-and-chorizo skewers or fennel-infused salads. Proceeds support a local charity. The interior is a rustic-chic mix of blue-tiled floors, faded-wood tables and fairy lights. Good cakes and coffee.

Café Coco MEDITERRANEAN ££
(☎ 01865-200232; www.cafecoco.co.uk; 23 Cowley Rd; breakfast £4.50-9, mains £7-12; ⊘ 10am-10pm Mon-Thu, to midnight Fri, 9am-midnight Sat, 9am-10pm Sun; 🖉) This Cowley Rd institution is a hugely popular brunching destination, decorated with classic posters, warm yellow walls, chunky mirrors and a plaster-cast clown in an ice bath. The globetrotting menu ranges from cooked and 'healthy' breakfasts to pizzas, salads, burgers, pastas, meze platters, Mediterranean mains and zingy fresh juices. Or just swing by for cocktails (happy hour 5pm to 7.30pm).

DON'T MISS

BLENHEIM PALACE

One of the country's greatest stately homes, Blenheim Palace (☑01993-810530; www.blenheimpalace.com; Woodstock; adult/child £24.90/13.90, park & gardens only £14.90/6.90; ⊙ palace 10.30am-5.30pm, park & gardens 9am-6pm; P) is a monumental baroque fantasy designed by Sir John Vanbrugh and Nicholas Hawksmoor between 1705 and 1722. Now a Unesco World Heritage Site, it's home to the 12th Duke of Marlborough. Highlights include the Great Hall, a vast space topped by 20m-high ceilings adorned with images of the first duke in battle; the most important public room, the various grand state rooms with their plush decor and priceless china cabinets; and the magnificent 55m Long Library. You can also visit the Churchill Exhibition, dedicated to the life, work and writings of Sir Winston, who was born at Blenheim in 1874.

Blenheim Palace is near the town of Woodstock, a few miles northwest of Oxford. To get there, Stagecoach bus S3 (£3.70, 30 minutes, every half hour, hourly on Sunday) runs from George St in Oxford.

Drinking & Nightlife

Eagle & Child
PUB

(☑01865-302925; www.nicholsonspubs.co.uk/theeagleandchildoxford; 49 St Giles; ⊙noon-11pm) Affectionately known as the 'Bird & Baby', this quirky pub dates from 1650 and was once a favourite haunt of authors JRR Tolkien and CS Lewis and a few other Inklings. Its narrow wood-panelled rooms and selection of real ales, craft beers and gins still attracts a mellow crowd.

Bear Inn
PUB

(☑01865-728164; www.bearoxford.co.uk; 6 Alfred St; ⊙11am-11pm Sun-Thu, to midnight Fri & Sat) Arguably Oxford's oldest pub (there's been a pub on this site since 1242), the atmospherically creaky Bear requires all but the most vertically challenged to duck their heads when passing through doorways. A curious tie collection covers the walls and ceilings, and there are usually a couple of worthy guest ales and artisan beers.

Turf Tavern
PUB

(☑01865-243235; www.turftavern-oxford.co.uk; 4-5 Bath Pl; ⊙11am-11pm; 🐾) Squeezed down a narrow alleyway, this tiny medieval pub (from at least 1381) is one of Oxford's best loved. It's where US president Bill Clinton famously 'did not inhale'; other patrons have included Oscar Wilde, Stephen Hawking and Margaret Thatcher. Home to 11 real ales, it's always crammed with students, professionals and the odd tourist. Plenty of outdoor seating.

ⓘ Information

Tourist Office
(☑01865-686430; www.experienceoxfordshire.com; 15-16 Broad St; ⊙9.30am-5pm Mon-Sat, 10am-4pm Sun) Covers the whole of Oxfordshire, stocks printed Oxford walking guides and books official walking tours.

ⓘ Getting There & Away

BUS
Oxford's main bus/coach station is at Gloucester Green, with frequent services to London (£15, 1¾ hours, every 15 minutes). There are also regular buses to/from Heathrow and Gatwick airports.

TRAIN
Oxford's train station has half-hourly services to London Paddington (£25, 1¼ hours) and roughly hourly trains to Birmingham (£18, 1¼ hours). Hourly services also run to Bath (£28, 1½ hours) and Bristol (£30, one to two hours), but require a change at Didcot Parkway.

Stratford-upon-Avon

POP 27,455

The author of some of the most quoted lines ever written in the English language, William Shakespeare was born in Stratford in 1564 and died here in 1616. Experiences linked to his life in this unmistakably Tudor town range from the touristy (medieval re-creations and Bard-themed tearooms) to the humbling (Shakespeare's modest grave in Holy Trinity Church) and the sublime (taking in a play by the world-famous Royal Shakespeare Company).

◉ Sights

★Shakespeare's
Birthplace
HISTORIC BUILDING

(✆01789-204016; www.shakespeare.org.uk; Henley St; incl Shakespeare's New Place & Halls Croft adult/child £17.50/11.50; ⊙9am-5.30pm Jul & Aug, to 5pm Sep-Jun) Start your Shakespeare quest at the house where the world's most popular playwright supposedly spent his childhood days. In fact, the jury is still out on whether this really was Shakespeare's birthplace, but devotees of the Bard have been dropping in since at least the 19th century, leaving their signatures scratched on to the windows. Set behind a modern facade, the house has restored Tudor rooms, live presentations from famous Shakespearean characters and an engaging exhibition on Stratford's favourite son.

★Shakespeare's New Place
HISTORIC SITE

(✆01789-204016; www.shakespeare.org.uk; cnr Chapel St & Chapel Lane; incl Shakespeare's Birthplace & Hall's Croft adult/child £17.50/11.50; ⊙9am-5.30pm Jul & Aug, 9am-5pm mid-Mar–Jun, Sep & Oct, 10am-4pm Nov–mid-Mar) When Shakespeare retired, he swapped the bright lights of London for a comfortable town house at New Place, where he died of unknown causes in April 1616. The house was demolished in 1759, but an attractive Elizabethan knot garden occupies part of the grounds. A major restoration project has uncovered Shakespeare's kitchen and incorporated new exhibits in a reimagining of the house as it would have been. You can also explore the adjacent Nash's House, where Shakespeare's granddaughter Elizabeth lived.

Shakespeare's School Room
HISTORIC SITE

(www.shakespearesschoolroom.org; King Edward VI School, Church St; adult/child £8.90/5.50; ⊙11am-5pm Mon-Fri during school term, 10am-5pm Sat, Sun & school holidays) Shakespeare's alma mater, King Edward VI School (still a prestigious grammar school today), incorporates a vast black-and-white timbered building, dating from 1420, that was once the town's guildhall. Upstairs, in the Bard's former classroom, you can sit in on mock-Tudor lessons, watch a short film and test yourself on Tudor-style homework.

It's adjacent to the 1269-built **Guild Chapel** (cnr Chapel Lane & Church St; ⊙services 10am Wed, noon 1st Sat of month Apr-Sep).

THE COTSWOLDS

Rolling gracefully across six counties, the Cotswolds are a delightful tangle of gloriously golden villages, thatch-roofed cottages, evocative churches, rickety almshouses and ancient mansions of honey-coloured stone. If you've ever lusted after exposed beams, cream teas or cuisine crammed full of local produce, look no further.

Travel by public transport requires careful planning and patience; for the most flexibility and the option of getting off the beaten track, your own car is unbeatable. Alternatively, the **Cotswolds Discoverer card** (www.escapetothecotswolds.org.uk/discoverer; one-/three-day pass £10/25) gives you unlimited travel on participating bus or train routes.

Anne Hathaway's Cottage
HISTORIC BUILDING

(✆01789-204016; www.shakespeare.org.uk; Cottage Lane, Shottery; adult/child £10.25/6.50; ⊙9am-5pm mid-Mar–Oct, closed Nov–mid-Mar) Before tying the knot with Shakespeare, Anne Hathaway lived in Shottery, 1 mile west of the centre of Stratford, in this delightful thatched farmhouse. As well as period furniture, it has gorgeous gardens and an orchard and arboretum, with examples of all the trees mentioned in Shakespeare's plays. A footpath (no bikes allowed) leads to Shottery from Evesham Pl. The **City Sightseeing** (✆01789-299123; www.city-sightseeing.com; adult/child £13.90/6.95; ⊙every 30min Apr-Sep, less frequently Oct-Mar) bus stops here.

Holy Trinity Church
CHURCH

(✆01789-266316; www.stratford-upon-avon.org; Old Town; Shakespeare's grave adult/child £2/1; ⊙8.30am-6pm Mon-Sat, 12.30-5pm Sun Apr-Sep, shorter hours Oct-Mar) The final resting place of the Bard is said to be the most visited parish church in all of England. Inside are handsome 16th- and 17th-century tombs (particularly in the Clopton Chapel), some fabulous carvings on the choir stalls and, of course, the grave of William Shakespeare, with its ominous epitaph: 'cvrst be he yt moves my bones'.

🛌 Sleeping

Stratford-upon-Avon YHA HOSTEL £
(📞0845 371 9661; www.yha.org.uk; Hemmingford House, Wellesbourne, Alveston; dm/d/camping pod from £19/90/89; 🅿@🛜) Set in a large 200-year-old mansion 1.5 miles east of the town centre, this superior hostel attracts travellers of all ages. Of its 32 rooms and dorms, 16 are en suite, as are four-person camping pods with kitchenettes. There's a canteen, bar and kitchen. Buses X15, X18 and 18A run here from Bridge St. Wi-fi is available in common areas.

Falcon Hotel HOTEL ££
(📞01789-279953; www.sjhotels.co.uk; Chapel St; d/f from £85/145; 🅿🛜) Definitely request a room in the original 15th-century building, not the soulless modern annex or dingy 17th-century garden house of this epicentral hotel. This way you'll get the full Tudor experience – creaky floorboards, wonky timbered walls and all. Open fires blaze in the public areas but the best asset is the bargain-priced-for-Stratford car park (£5). Family rooms sleep three people.

Church Street Townhouse BOUTIQUE HOTEL £££
(📞01789-262222; www.churchstreet-th.co.uk; 16 Church St; d from £110; 🛜) Some of the dozen rooms at this exquisite hotel have free-standing claw-foot bathtubs, and all have iPod docks, flatscreen TVs and luxurious furnishings. Light sleepers should avoid room 1, nearest the bar. The building itself is a centrally located 400-year-old gem with a first-rate restaurant and bar. There's a minimum two-night stay on weekends.

ⓘ SHAKESPEARE HISTORIC HOMES

Five of the most important buildings associated with Shakespeare contain museums that form the core of the visitor experience at Stratford. All are run by the **Shakespeare Birthplace Trust** (www.shakespeare.org.uk).

Tickets for the three houses in town – **Shakespeare's Birthplace**, **Shakespeare's New Place** and **Halls Croft** – cost adult/child £17.50/11.50. If you also visit **Anne Hathaway's Cottage** and **Mary Arden's Farm**, buy a combination ticket covering all five properties (adult/child £26.25/17).

🍴 Eating & Drinking

Sheep St is clustered with eating options, mostly aimed at theatregoers (look out for good-value pretheatre menus).

Fourteas CAFE £
(📞01789-293908; www.thefourteas.co.uk; 24 Sheep St; dishes £4-7, afternoon tea with/without Prosecco £18.50/14; ⏱9.30am-5pm Mon-Sat, 11am-4pm Sun) 🍴 Breaking with Stratford's Shakespearean theme, this tearoom takes the 1940s as its inspiration with beautiful old teapots, framed posters and staff in period costume. As well as premium loose-leaf teas and homemade cakes, there are hearty breakfasts, delicious sandwiches (fresh poached salmon, brie and grape), a hot dish of the day and indulgent afternoon teas (gluten-free options available).

Church Street Townhouse BISTRO ££
(📞01789-262222; www.churchstreettownhouse. com; 16 Church St; mains £11-24; ⏱kitchen noon-3pm & 5-9.45pm, bar 8am-midnight Mon-Sat, to 10.30pm Sun; 🛜) This lovely restaurant is a fantastic place for immersing yourself in Stratford's historic charms. The food is delightful and the ambience impeccably congenial and well presented. Music students from Shakespeare's old grammar school across the way tinkle the piano ivories daily at 5.30pm, though it can be hard to hear over the bar noise.

★Old Thatch Tavern PUB
(www.oldthatchtavernstratford.co.uk; Greenhill St; ⏱11.30am-11pm Mon-Sat, noon-6pm Sun; 🛜) To truly appreciate Stratford's olde-worlde atmosphere, join the locals for a pint at the town's oldest pub. Built in 1470, this thatched-roofed, low-ceilinged treasure has great real ales and a gorgeous summertime courtyard.

Dirty Duck PUB
(Black Swan; Waterside; ⏱11am-11pm Mon-Sat, to 10.30pm Sun) Also called the 'Black Swan', this enchanting riverside alehouse is the only pub in England to be licensed under two names. It's a favourite thespian watering hole, with a roll-call of former regulars (Olivier, Attenborough et al) that reads like a who's who of actors.

☆ Entertainment

★Royal Shakespeare Company THEATRE
(RSC; 📞box office 01789-403493; www.rsc.org. uk; Waterside; tours adult £6.50-8.50, child £3-4.50, tower adult/child £2.50/1.25; ⏱tour times

vary, tower 10am-6.15pm Sun-Fri, 10am-12.15pm & 2-6.15pm Sat Apr-Sep, 10am-4.30pm Sun-Fri, 10am-12.15pm & 2-4.30pm Sat Oct-Mar) Stratford has two grand stages run by the world-renowned Royal Shakespeare Company – the Royal Shakespeare Theatre and the Swan Theatre (☑ 01789-403493) on Waterside – as well as the smaller Other Place (☑ box office 01789-403493; www.rsc.org.uk; 22 Southern Lane). The theatres have witnessed performances by such legends as Lawrence Olivier, Richard Burton, Judi Dench, Helen Mirren, Ian McKellan and Patrick Stewart. Various one-hour guided tours take you behind the scenes.

ⓘ Information

Tourist Office (☑ 01789-264293; www.discover-stratford.com; Bridge Foot; ⊙ 9am-5.30pm Mon-Sat, 10am-4pm Sun) Just west of Clopton Bridge.

ⓘ Getting There & Away

BUS

National Express coaches and other bus companies run from Stratford's Riverside bus station (behind the Stratford Leisure Centre on Bridgeway). Destinations include Birmingham (£8.50, one hour, twice daily), London Victoria (£7, three hours, three daily) and Oxford (£10.80, one hour, twice daily).

TRAIN

From Stratford train station, trains run to Birmingham (£7.70, 50 minutes, half-hourly), and London Marylebone (£28.90, two hours, up to two per hour) and Warwick (£6.60, 30 minutes, hourly).

Cambridge

POP 123,900

Abounding with exquisite architecture, oozing history and tradition, and renowned for its quirky rituals, Cambridge is a university town extraordinaire. The tightly packed core of ancient colleges, the picturesque 'Backs' (college gardens) leading on to the river and the leafy green meadows that surround the city give it a far more tranquil appeal than its historic rival Oxford.

◉ Sights

Cambridge University comprises 31 colleges, though not all are open to the public. Opening hours are only a rough guide, so contact the colleges or the tourist office for more information.

WORTH A TRIP

WARWICK

Regularly namechecked by Shakespeare, the town of Warwick is a treasure-house of medieval architecture. It is dominated by the soaring turrets of **Warwick Castle** (☑ 0871 265 2000; www.warwick-castle.com; Castle Lane; castle adult/child £25.20/22.20, castle & dungeon £30.20/27.20; ⊙ 10am-6pm Apr-Sep, to 5pm Oct-Mar; P �ⓦ), founded in 1068 by William the Conqueror, and later the ancestral home of the Earls of Warwick. It's now been transformed into a major tourist attraction by the owners of Madame Tussauds, with family-friendly activities and waxworks populating the private apartments.

Stagecoach bus 18A goes to Stratford-upon-Avon (£4.30, 45 minutes, half-hourly). Trains run to Birmingham (£6.80, 40 minutes, half-hourly), Stratford-upon-Avon (£6.60, 30 minutes, hourly) and London Marylebone (£31.80, 1½ hours, every 20 minutes).

★ **King's College Chapel**   CHURCH
(☑ 01223-331212; www.kings.cam.ac.uk; King's Pde; adult/child £9/free; ⊙ 9.30am-3.30pm Mon-Sat & 1.15-2.30pm Sun term time, 9.30am-4.30pm daily university holidays) In a city crammed with showstopping buildings, this is the scene-stealer. Grandiose, 16th-century King's College Chapel is one of England's most extraordinary examples of Gothic architecture. Its inspirational, intricate 80m-long, fan-vaulted ceiling is the world's largest and soars upwards before exploding into a series of stone fireworks. This hugely atmospheric space is a fitting stage for the chapel's world-famous choir; hear it during the magnificent, free, evensong (term time only; 5.30pm Monday to Saturday, 10.30am and 3.30pm Sunday).

★ **Trinity College**   COLLEGE
(www.trin.cam.ac.uk; Trinity St; adult/child £3/1; ⊙ 10am-3.30pm Nov-Mar, to 5pm Jul-Oct) The largest of Cambridge's colleges, Trinity offers an extraordinary Tudor gateway, an air of supreme elegance and a sweeping Great Court – the largest of its kind in the world. It also boasts the renowned and suitably musty **Wren Library** (⊙ noon-2pm Mon-Fri year-round, plus 10.30am-12.30pm Sat term time) FREE, containing 55,000 books dated before 1820 and

PUNTING ON THE BACKS

Gliding a self-propelled punt along the Backs is a blissful experience – once you've got the hang of it. It can also be a manic challenge to begin. If you wimp out you can always opt for a relaxing chauffeured punt.

Punt hire costs around £20 to £28 per hour; 45-minute chauffeured trips of the Backs cost about £15 to £19 per person. One-way trips to Grantchester (1½ hours) start at around £18 per person.

more than 2500 manuscripts. Works include those by Shakespeare, St Jerome, Newton and Swift – and AA Milne's original *Winnie the Pooh;* both Milne and his son, Christopher Robin, were graduates.

★ **The Backs**   PARK
Behind the Cambridge colleges' grandiose facades and stately courts, a series of gardens and parks line up beside the river. Collectively known as the Backs, the tranquil green spaces and shimmering waters offer unparalleled views of the colleges and are often the most enduring image of Cambridge for visitors. The picture-postcard snapshots of student life and graceful bridges can be seen from the riverside pathways and pedestrian bridges – or the comfort of a chauffeur-driven punt.

★ **Fitzwilliam Museum**   MUSEUM
(www.fitzmuseum.cam.ac.uk; Trumpington St; by donation; ⊗10am-5pm Tue-Sat, noon-5pm Sun) **FREE** Fondly dubbed 'the Fitz' by locals, this colossal neoclassical pile was one of the first public art museums in Britain, built to house the fabulous treasures that the seventh Viscount Fitzwilliam bequeathed to his old university. Expect Roman and Egyptian grave goods, artworks by many of the great masters and some more-quirky collections: banknotes, literary autographs, watches and armour.

🛏 Sleeping

Cambridge YHA   HOSTEL £
(☑0845-371 9728; www.yha.org.uk; 97 Tenison Rd; dm £18-26, d £39-59; @ 🛜) Smart, friendly, recently renovated, deservedly popular hostel with compact dorms and good facilities. Handily, it's near the train station.

Benson House   B&B ££
(☑01223-311594; www.bensonhouse.co.uk; 24 Huntingdon Rd; s £75-115, d £110-115; 🅿 🛜) Lots of little things lift Benson a cut above – sleep among feather pillows and Egyptian cotton linen, sip tea from Royal Doulton bone china, then tuck into award-winning breakfasts featuring kippers, croissants and fresh fruit.

★ **Varsity**   BOUTIQUE HOTEL £££
(☑01223-306030; www.thevarsityhotel.co.uk; Thompson's Lane; d £190-350; @ 🛜) In the 44 individually styled rooms of riverside Varsity, wondrous furnishings and witty features (Union Jack footstools, mock-flock wallpaper) sit beside floor-to-ceiling glass windows, espresso machines and smartphone docks. The views out over the colleges from the roof terrace are frankly gorgeous.

🍴 Eating & Drinking

★ **Urban Shed**   SANDWICHES £
(www.theurbanshed.com; 62 King St; sandwiches from £4.25; ⊗8.30am-5pm Mon-Thu, 8.30am-4.30pm Fri, 9am-6pm Sat, 10am-4pm Sun) Somewhere between a retro goods shop and a sandwich bar, at unorthodox Urban Shed the personal service ethos is so strong regular customers have a locker for their own mug. Decor teams old aeroplane seats with cable-drum tables, their own-blend coffee is mellow and the sandwiches range is superb.

Chop House   BRITISH ££
(www.cambscuisine.com/cambridge-chop-house; 1 King's Pde; mains £15-22; ⊗noon-10.30pm Mon-Sat, to 9.30pm Sun) The window seats here deliver some of the best views in town – on to King's College's hallowed walls. The food is pure English establishment too: hearty steaks and chops and chips, plus a scattering of fish dishes and suet puddings. It's also open from 10am to noon for coffee and cakes.

Pint Shop   MODERN BRITISH ££
(☑01223-352293; www.pintshop.co.uk; 10 Peas Hill; mains £12.50-25.50; ⊗noon-10pm Mon-Fri, 11am-10.30pm Sat, 11am-10pm Sun) Popular Pint Shop's vision is to embrace eating and drinking equally. So it's created both a busy bar specialising in craft beer (10 on keg and six on draft) and a stylish dining room serving classy versions of traditional grub (dry aged steaks, gin-cured sea trout, charcoal-grilled plaice). All in all, hard to resist.

★ **Midsummer House**   MODERN BRITISH £££
(☑ 01223-369299; www.midsummerhouse.co.uk;
Midsummer Common; 5/8 courses £56.50/120;
⊘ noon-1.30pm Wed-Sat, 7-8.30pm Tue-Thu,
6.30-9.30pm Fri & Sat; ☑) At the region's top
table Chef Daniel Clifford's double Michelin-starred creations are distinguished by
depth of flavour and immense technical
skill. Sample transformations of coal-baked
celeriac, Cornish crab, and roast pigeon
with wild garlic before a pear, blueberry and
white chocolate delight.

★ **Eagle**   PUB
(www.eagle-cambridge.co.uk; Benet St; ⊘ 8am-
11pm Mon-Sat, to 10.30pm Sun; 🛜🖐) Cambridge's most famous pub has loosened the
tongues and pickled the grey cells of many
an illustrious academic; among them Nobel
Prize–winning scientists Crick and Watson,
who discussed their research into DNA
here (note the blue plaque by the door).
Fifteenth-century, wood-panelled and rambling, its cosy rooms include one with WWII
airmen's signatures on the ceiling.

ℹ️ **Information**

Tourist Office (☑ 01223-791500; www.
visitcambridge.org; The Guildhall, Peas Hill;
⊘ 10am-5pm Mon-Sat Nov-Mar, 10am-5pm
Mon-Sat, 11am-3pm Sun Apr-Oct)

ℹ️ **Getting There & Away**

BUS

From Parkside there are regular National Express buses to London Gatwick airport (£37, 3¾
hours, nine daily), Heathrow airport (£25, 2¾
hours, hourly) and Oxford (£12, 3½ hours, every
30 minutes).

TRAIN

The train station is off Station Rd, which is off
Hills Rd. Destinations include London Kings
Cross (£23, one hour, two to four per hour) and
Stansted airport (£10, 35 minutes/hourly).

York

POP 198,000

Nowhere in northern England says 'medieval' quite like York, a city of extraordinary
historical wealth that has lost little of its pre-
industrial lustre. Its spider's web of narrow
streets is enclosed by a magnificent circuit
of 13th-century walls and the city's rich heritage is woven into virtually every brick and
beam.

◉ **Sights**

If the weather's good, don't miss the chance
to walk York's **City Walls** (www.yorkwalls.
org.uk), which follow the line of the original Roman walls and give a whole new perspective on the city. Allow 1½ to two hours
for the full circuit of 4.5 miles or, if you're
pushed for time, the short stretch from
Bootham Bar to Monk Bar is worth doing
for the views of the minster.

★ **York Minster**   CATHEDRAL
(www.yorkminster.org; Deangate; adult/child £10/
free, incl tower £15/5; ⊘ 9am-5.30pm Mon-Sat,
12.45-5pm Sun, last admission 30min before closing) The remarkable York Minster is the
largest medieval cathedral in all of Northern
Europe, and one of the world's most beautiful Gothic buildings. Seat of the archbishop
of York, primate of England, it is second in
importance only to Canterbury, seat of the
primate of *all* England – the separate titles
were created to settle a debate over the true
centre of the English church. If this is the
only cathedral you visit in England, you'll
still walk away satisfied.

★ **Jorvik Viking Centre**   MUSEUM
(www.jorvik-viking-centre.co.uk; Coppergate;
adult/child £10.25/7.25; ⊘ 10am-5pm Apr-Oct,
to 4pm Nov-Mar) Interactive multimedia
exhibits aimed at bringing history to life often achieve exactly the opposite, but the
much-hyped Jorvik manages to pull it off
with aplomb. Thoroughly restored and re-
imagined following flood damage in 2015,
it's a smells-and-all reconstruction of the
Viking settlement unearthed here during
excavations in the late 1970s, experienced
via a 'time-car' monorail that transports
you through 9th-century Jorvik (the Viking
name for York). You can reduce time waiting
in the queue by booking your tickets online.

★ **National Railway Museum**   MUSEUM
(www.nrm.org.uk; Leeman Rd; ⊘ 10am-6pm;
🅿️🖐) **FREE** While many railway museums
are the sole preserve of lone men in anoraks
comparing dog-eared notebooks and getting
high on the smell of machine oil, coal smoke
and nostalgia, this place is different. York's
National Railway Museum – the biggest in
the world, with more than 100 locomotives
– is so well presented and crammed with
fascinating stuff that it's interesting even
to folk whose eyes don't mist over at the
thought of a 4-6-2 A1 Pacific class thundering into a tunnel.

> ### ℹ YORK PASS
>
> If you plan on visiting a number of sights, you can save yourself some money by using a YorkPass (www.yorkpass.com). It gives you free access to more than 30 pay-to-visit sights in and around York, including York Minster, Jorvik and Castle Howard. You can buy it at York tourist office or online; prices for one/two/three days are adult £38/50/60, child £20/26/30.

Yorkshire Museum   MUSEUM
(www.yorkshiremuseum.org.uk; Museum St; adult/child £7.50/free; ⊙10am-5pm) Most of York's Roman archaeology is hidden beneath the medieval city, so the superb displays in the Yorkshire Museum are invaluable if you want to get an idea of what Eboracum was like. There are maps and models of Roman York, funerary monuments, mosaic floors and wall paintings, and a 4th-century bust of Emperor Constantine. Kids will enjoy the dinosaur exhibit, centred around giant ichthyosaur fossils from Yorkshire's Jurassic coast.

The Shambles   STREET
The Shambles takes its name from the Saxon word *shamel,* meaning 'slaughterhouse' – in 1862 there were 26 butcher shops on this street. Today the butchers are long gone, but this narrow cobbled lane, lined with 15th-century Tudor buildings that overhang so much they seem to meet above your head, is the most picturesque in Britain, and one of the most visited in Europe, often crammed with visitors intent on buying a tacky souvenir before rushing back to the tour bus.

🚩 Tours

Ghost Hunt of York   WALKING
(www.ghosthunt.co.uk; adult/child £6/4; ⊙tours 7.30pm) The kids will just love this award-winning and highly entertaining 75-minute tour laced with authentic ghost stories. It begins at the top end of The Shambles, whatever the weather (it's never cancelled) and there's no need to book, just turn up and wait till you hear the handbell ringing...

Yorkwalk   WALKING
(www.yorkwalk.co.uk; adult/child £6/5; ⊙tours 10.30am & 2.15pm Feb-Nov) Offers a series of two-hour walks on a range of themes, from the classics – Roman York, the snickelways

(narrow alleys) and City Walls – to walks focused on chocolates and sweets, women in York, and the inevitable graveyard, coffin and plague tour. Walks depart from Museum Gardens Gate on Museum St; there's no need to book.

🛏 Sleeping

Despite the inflated prices of the high season, it is still tough to find a bed during midsummer.

★Fort   HOSTEL £
(☎01904-620222; www.thefortyork.co.uk; 1 Little Stonegate; dm/d from £18/74; 🛜) This boutique hostel showcases the work of young British designers, creating affordable accommodation with a dash of character and flair. There are six- and eight-bed dorms, along with half a dozen doubles, but don't expect a peaceful retreat – the central location is in the middle of York's nightlife, and there's a lively club downstairs (earplugs are provided!).

Safestay York   HOSTEL £
(☎01904-627720; www.safestayyork.co.uk; 88-90 Micklegate; dm/tw from £18/75; @🛜) Housed in a Grade I Georgian building that was once home to the High Sheriff of Yorkshire, this is a large and well-equipped boutique hostel with cool decor and good facilities. It's popular with school groups and stag and hen parties – don't come here looking for peace and quiet!

★Hedley House Hotel   HOTEL ££
(☎01904-637404; www.hedleyhouse.com; 3 Bootham Tce; d/f from £105/115; 🅿🛜) 🅿 This red-brick terrace-house hotel sports a variety of smartly refurbished, family-friendly accommodation, including rooms that sleep up to five, and some self-catering apartments – plus it has a sauna and spa bath on the outdoor terrace at the back, and is barely five minutes' walk from the city centre through the Museum Gardens.

Bar Convent   B&B ££
(☎01904-643238; www.bar-convent.org.uk; 17 Blossom St; s/d £67/96; 🛜) This elegant Georgian mansion just outside Micklegate Bar, less than 10 minutes' walk from the train station, houses a working convent, a cafe, a conference centre and exhibition, and also offers excellent B&B accommodation. Open to visitors of all faiths and none. Charming bedrooms are modern and well equipped, breakfasts are superb, and there's a garden and hidden chapel to enjoy.

★ Middlethorpe Hall HOTEL £££

(☑ 01904-641241; www.middlethorpe.com; Bishopthorpe Rd; s/d from £118/126; P ⚛ 📶) This breathtaking 17th-century country house is set in 8 hectares of parkland, once the home of diarist Lady Mary Wortley Montagu. The rooms are divided between the main house, restored courtyard buildings and three cottage suites. All are beautifully decorated with original antiques and oil paintings that have been carefully selected to reflect the period.

✗ Eating & Drinking

★ Mannion's CAFE, BISTRO £

(☑ 01904-631030; www.mannionandco.co.uk; 1 Blake St; mains £6-11; ⊙ 9am-5.30pm Mon-Fri, to 6pm Sat, 10am-5pm Sun) Expect to queue for a table at this busy bistro (no reservations), with its maze of rustic, wood-panelled rooms and selection of daily specials. Regulars on the menu include eggs Benedict for breakfast, a chunky Yorkshire rarebit made with home-baked bread, and lunch platters of cheese and charcuterie from the attached deli. Oh, and pavlova for pudding.

★ No 8 Bistro BISTRO ££

(☑ 01904-653074; www.no8york.co.uk/bistro; 8 Gillygate; 3-course lunch/dinner £16/25; ⊙ noon-10pm Mon-Thu, 9am-10pm Fri-Sun; 📶 🍴) 🍸 A cool little place with modern artwork mimicking the Edwardian stained glass at the front, No 8 offers a day-long menu of classic bistro dishes using fresh local produce, including Jerusalem artichoke risotto with fresh herbs, and Yorkshire lamb slow-cooked in hay and lavender. It also does breakfast daily (mains £6 to £9) and Sunday lunch (two courses £18). Booking recommended.

★ Parlour at Grays Court CAFE, BRITISH ££

(www.grayscourtyork.com; Chapter House St; mains £9-20; ⊙ 10am-5pm & 6-9pm; 📶) An unexpected pleasure in the heart of York, this 16th-century mansion (now a hotel) has more of a country house atmosphere. Relax with coffee and cake in the sunny garden, enjoy a light lunch of Yorkshire rarebit, or indulge in a dinner of scallops and sea bass in the oak-panelled Jacobean gallery. The daytime menu includes traditional afternoon tea (£18.50).

★ Cochon Aveugle FRENCH £££

(☑ 01904-640222; www.lecochonaveugle.uk; 37 Walmgate; 6-/9-course tasting menu £40/60; ⊙ 6-9pm Tue-Sat) 🍸 Black pudding maca-

roon? Strawberry and elderflower sandwich? Blowtorched mackerel with melon gazpacho? Fussy eaters beware – this small restaurant with huge ambition serves an ever-changing tasting menu (no á la carte) of infinite imagination and invention. You never know what will come next, except that it will be delicious. Bookings essential.

★ Blue Bell PUB

(☑ 01904-654904; bluebellyork@gmail.com; 53 Fossgate; ⊙ 11am-11pm Mon-Thu, to midnight Fri-Sat, noon-10.30pm Sun) This is what a proper English pub looks like – a tiny, 200-year-old wood-panelled room with a smouldering fireplace, decor untouched since 1903, a pile of ancient board games in the corner, friendly and efficient bar staff, and Timothy Taylor and Black Sheep ales on tap. Bliss, with froth on top – if you can get in (it's often full).

❶ Information

York Tourist Office (☑ 01904-550099; www.visityork.org; 1 Museum St; ⊙ 9am-5pm Mon-Sat, 10am-4pm Sun) Visitor and transport info for all of Yorkshire, plus accommodation bookings, ticket sales and internet access.

❶ Getting There & Away

BUS

York does not have a bus station; intercity buses stop outside the train station, while local and regional buses stop here and also on Rougier St, about 200m northeast of the train station.

There are **National Express** (☑ 08717 818181; www.nationalexpress.com) coaches to London (from £25, 5½ hours, three daily), Birmingham (£29, 3½ hours, one daily) and Newcastle (£15.40, 2¼ hours, two daily).

TRAIN

York is a major railway hub with frequent direct services to Birmingham (£45, 2¼ hours, half-hourly), Newcastle (£25, one hour, half-hourly), Leeds (£13.90, 25 minutes, four per hour), London's King's Cross (£80, two hours, half-hourly), Manchester (£25, 1½ hours, four per hour) and Scarborough (£14, 50 minutes, hourly). There are also trains to Cambridge (£71, three hours, hourly), changing at Peterborough.

Castle Howard

Stately homes may be two a penny in England, but you'll have to try hard to find one as breathtakingly stately as Castle Howard (www.castlehoward.co.uk; adult/child house & grounds £17.50/9, grounds only £9.95/7; ⊙ house

10.30am-4pm (last admission), grounds 10am-5pm; P), a work of theatrical grandeur and audacity, and one of the world's most beautiful buildings. It's instantly recognisable from its starring role in the 1980s TV series *Brideshead Revisited* and in the 2008 film of the same name. It's 15 miles northeast of York; **Stephenson's of Easingwold** (www.stephensonsofeasingwold.co.uk) bus 181 links York with Castle Howard (£10 return, 40 minutes, four times daily Monday to Saturday year-round, three on Sunday May to September).

Chester

POP 79,645

With a red-sandstone, Roman wall wrapped around a tidy collection of Tudor and Victorian buildings, Chester is one of English history's greatest gifts to the contemporary visitor. The walls were built when this was Castra Devana, the largest Roman fortress in Britain.

⊙ Sights

★ **City Walls**   LANDMARK

A good way to get a sense of Chester's unique character is to walk the 2-mile circuit along the walls that surround the historic centre. Originally built by the Romans around AD 70, the walls were altered substantially over the following centuries but have retained their current position since around 1200. The tourist office's *Walk Around Chester Walls* leaflet is an excellent guide and you can also take a 90-minute guided walk.

★ **Rows**   ARCHITECTURE

Besides the City Walls, Chester's other great draw is the Rows, a series of two-level galleried arcades along the four streets that fan out in each direction from the **Central Cross**. The architecture is a handsome mix of Victorian and Tudor (original and mock) buildings that house a fantastic collection of individually owned shops.

Chester Cathedral   CATHEDRAL

(✆ 01244-324756; www.chestercathedral.com; 12 Abbey Sq; ⊙9am-6pm Mon-Sat, 11am-4pm Sun) **FREE** Originally a Benedictine abbey built on the remains of an earlier Saxon church dedicated to St Werburgh (the city's patron saint), it was shut down in 1540 as part of Henry VIII's dissolution frenzy, but reconsecrated as a cathedral the following year.

Despite a substantial Victorian facelift, the cathedral retains much of its original 12th-century structure. You can amble about freely, but the **tours** (adult/child full tour £8/6, short tour £6; ⊙full tour 11am & 3pm daily, half tour 12.30pm & 1.15pm Mon-Tue, also 2pm & 4pm Wed-Sat) are excellent, as they bring you to to the top of the panoramic bell tower.

🛌 Sleeping

Chester Backpackers   HOSTEL £

(✆ 01244-400185; www.chesterbackpackers.co.uk; 67 Boughton; dm/s/d from £16/22/34; ☎) Comfortable dorm rooms with nice pine beds in a typically Tudor white-and-black building. It's just a short walk from the city walls and there's also a pleasant garden.

★ **Stone Villa**   B&B ££

(✆ 01244-345014; www.stonevillachester.co.uk; 3 Stone Pl, Hoole Rd; s/d from £60/85; P☎; ▣9) This award-winning, beautiful 1850 villa has everything you need for a memorable stay. Elegant bedrooms, a fabulous breakfast and welcoming, friendly owners all add up to one of the best lodgings in town. The property is about a mile from the city centre.

🍴 Eating

Joseph Benjamin   MODERN BRITISH ££

(✆ 01244-344295; www.josephbenjamin.co.uk; 140 Northgate St; mains £13-17; ⊙noon-3pm Tue-Sat, also 6-9.30pm Thu-Sat & noon-4pm Sun) A bright star in Chester's culinary firmament is this combo restaurant, bar and deli that delivers carefully prepared local produce to take out or eat in. Excellent sandwiches and gorgeous salads are the mainstay of the takeaway menu, while the more formal dinner menu features fine examples of modern British cuisine.

★ **Simon Radley at the Grosvenor**   MODERN BRITISH £££

(✆ 01244-324024; www.chestergrosvenor.com; 58 Eastgate St, Chester Grosvenor Hotel; tasting menu £99, à la carte menu £75; ⊙6.30-9pm Tue-Sat) Simon Radley's formal restaurant (you're instructed to arrive 30 minutes early for drinks and canapés) has served near-perfect Modern British cuisine since 1990, when it was first awarded the Michelin star that it has kept ever since. The food is divine and the wine list extensive. One of Britain's best, but why no second star? Smart attire, no children under 12.

ℹ Information

Tourist Office (📞01244-402111; www.visitchester.com; Town Hall, Northgate St; ⊙9am-5.30pm Mon-Sat, 10am-5pm Sun Mar-Oct, 9.30am-4.30pm Mon-Fri, 9am-4ppm Sat, 10am-4pm Sun Nov-Feb)

ℹ Getting There & Away

BUS

National Express (📞08717 81 81 81; www.nationalexpress.com) coaches stop on Vicar's Lane, opposite the tourist office. Destinations include Liverpool (£8, one hour, four daily), London (£27.60, 5½ hours, three daily) and Manchester (£7.60, 1¼ hours, three daily).

TRAIN

The train station is about a mile from the city centre. City Rail Link buses are free for people with rail tickets. Destinations include Liverpool (£6.90, 45 minutes, hourly), London Euston (£69, 2½ hours, hourly) and Manchester (£12.60, one hour, hourly).

Lake District National Park

A dramatic landscape of ridges, lakes and peaks, including England's highest mountain, Scafell Pike (978m), the Lake District is one of Britain's most scenic corners. The awe-inspiring geography here shaped the literary personae of some of Britain's best-known poets, including William Wordsworth.

Often called simply the Lakes, the national park and surrounding area attract around 15 million visitors annually. But if you avoid summer weekends it's easy enough to miss the crush, especially if you do a bit of hiking.

There's a host of B&Bs and country-house hotels in the Lakes, plus more than 20 YHA hostels, many of which can be linked by foot if you wish to hike.

ℹ Information

Brockhole National Park Visitor Centre (📞015394-46601; www.lake-district.gov.uk; ⊙10am-5pm Easter-Oct, to 4pm Nov-Easter) In a 19th-century mansion 3 miles north of Windermere on the A591, this is the Lake District's flagship visitor centre. It also has a teashop, an adventure playground and gardens.

ℹ Getting There & Around

BUS

There's one daily National Express coach from London Victoria to Windermere (£31.50, eight hours) via Lancaster and Kendal. Local bus services include the following:

Bus 555/556 Lakeslink Runs hourly between Kendal and Windermere, stopping at all the main towns including Keswick, Grasmere and Ambleside.

Bus 505 Coniston Rambler Runs hourly between Kendal, Windermere, Ambleside and Coniston.

TRAIN

To get to the Lake District by train, you need to change at Oxenholme (on the London Euston to Glasgow line) for Kendal and Windermere, which has connections from London Euston (£103, 3½ hours), Manchester Piccadilly (£36.20, 1½ hours) and Glasgow (£54, 2¾ hours).

Windermere

POP 5423

Stretching for 10.5 miles between Ambleside and Newby Bridge, Windermere isn't just the queen of Lake District lakes – it's also the largest body of water anywhere in England. It's been a centre for tourism since the first trains chugged into town in 1847 and it's still one of the national park's busiest spots.

Windermere Lake Cruises (📞015394-43360; www.windermere-lakecruises.co.uk; tickets from £2.70) offers scheduled boat trips across the lake from the lakeside settlement of Bowness-on-Windermere.

🛏 Sleeping

Lake District Backpackers Lodge HOSTEL £ (📞015394-46374; www.lakedistrictbackpackers.co.uk; High St, Windermere Town; dm/r £16.50/39; @) In a small, old-style house down a little lane near the train station, this basic hostel lacks pizzazz, but it's pretty much the only option in town for budgeteers. There are two small four-bed dorms, plus two private rooms with a double bed and a single bed above. The kitchen is tiny but the lounge is cosy.

★ Boundary B&B ££ (📞015394-48978; www.boundaryonline.com; Lake Rd, Windermere Town; d £99-210; 🅿 🛜) A refined choice, sleek and chic, with neutral-toned rooms all named after great English cricketers: top picks are Hobbs, with bay window and vast bathroom, and Ranji, with cute flamingo wallpaper and a free-standing in-room bathtub. The downstairs lounge has a trendy wood burner and copies of *Wisden's Almanac* to browse.

★ **Rum Doodle**   B&B **££**

(☎ 015394-45967; www.rumdoodlewindermere. com; Sunny Bank Rd, Windermere Town; d £85-119; P ?) Named after a classic travel novel about a fictional mountain in the Himalayas, this B&B zings with imagination. Its rooms are themed after places and characters in the book, with details like book-effect wallpaper, vintage maps and old suitcases. Top of the heap is The Summit, snug under the eaves with a separate sitting room. Two-night minimum in summer.

Grasmere

POP 1458

Grasmere is a gorgeous little Lakeland village, all the more famous because of its links with Britain's leading Romantic poet, William Wordsworth.

Literary pilgrims come to **Dove Cottage** (☎ 015394-35544; www.wordsworth.org.uk; adult/child £7.50/4.50; ⊙ 9.30am-5.30pm), his former home, where highlights include some fine portraits of the man himself, a cabinet containing his spectacles, and a set of scales used by his pal de Quincey to weigh out opium. At **St Oswald's Church** (Church Stile) you'll see a memorial to the poet, and in the churchyard you'll find his grave.

To cure any sombre thoughts, head for **Sarah Nelson's Gingerbread Shop** (☎ 015394-35428; www.grasmeregingerbread. co.uk; Church Cottage; ⊙ 9.15am-5.30pm Mon-Sat, 12.30-5pm Sun) and stock up on Grasmere's famous confectionery.

DON'T MISS

HILL TOP

The cute-as-a-button farmhouse of **Hill Top** (NT; ☎ 015394-36269; www.national trust.org.uk/hill-top; adult/child £10/5, admission to garden & shop free; ⊙ house 10am-5.30pm Mon-Thu, 10am-4.30pm Fri-Sun, garden to 5.45pm Mon-Thu, to 5pm Fri-Sun) is a must for Beatrix Potter fans: it was her first house in the Lake District, and is also where she wrote and illustrated several of her famous tales.

The cottage is in Near Sawrey, 2 miles from Hawkshead and Ferry House. The **Cross Lakes Experience** (www. mountain-goat.co.uk/Cross-Lakes-Experi ence; adult/child return £12.45/7.15; ⊙ Apr-Nov) stops en route from Ferry House to Hawkshead.

Keswick

POP 4821

The main town of the north Lakes, Keswick sits beside lovely Derwent Water, a silvery curve studded with wooded islands and criss-crossed by puttering cruise boats, operated by the **Keswick Launch** (☎ 017687-72263; www.keswick-launch.co.uk; round-the-lake adult/child/family £10.25/5.15/24).

🛏 Sleeping

Keswick YHA   HOSTEL **£**

(☎ 0845-371 9746; www.yha.org.uk; Station Rd; dm £18-30; ⊙ reception 7am-11pm; ?) Right along the River Greta, the town's YHA took a battering during the 2015 storms; much of the ground floor, including the cafe, was swamped and is yet to reopen (although the self-catering kitchen remains). The upper levels of the hostel largely escaped damage: choose from two- to six-bed dorms and relax in the lounge overlooking Fitz Park.

★ **Howe Keld**   B&B **££**

(☎ 017687-72417; www.howekeld.co.uk; 5-7 The Heads; s £60-85, d £112-130; P ?) This gold-standard B&B pulls out all the stops: goose-down duvets, slate-floored bathrooms, chic colours and locally made furniture. The best rooms have views across Crow Park and the golf course, and the breakfast is a pick-and-mix delight. Free parking is available on The Heads if there's space.

★ **Lookout**   B&B **££**

(☎ 017687-80407; www.thelookoutkeswick.co.uk; Chestnut Hill; d £95-120; P ?) The clue's in the name: this fine B&B is all about the views – there's a stunning panorama of fells filling every window. It's in a gabled 1920s house but feels modern with cappuccino-and-cream colour schemes, wooden beds and minimalist glass showers. Take Penrith Rd west and turn right onto Chestnut Hill; the B&B is on the left.

WALES

Lying to the west of England, Wales is a nation with Celtic roots, its own language and a rich historic legacy. While some areas in the south are undeniably scarred by coal mining and heavy industry, Wales boasts a scenic landscape of wild mountains, rolling hills and rich farmland, and the bustling capital city of Cardiff.

OTHER BRITISH PLACES WORTH A VISIT

Some places in Britain we recommend for day trips or longer visits:

Cornwall The southwestern tip of Britain is ringed with rugged granite seacliffs, sparkling bays, picturesque fishing villages and white sandy beaches.

Liverpool The city's waterfront is a World Heritage Site crammed with top museums, including the International Slavery Museum and the Beatles Story.

Hadrian's Wall One of the country's most dramatic Roman ruins, a 2000-year-old procession of abandoned forts and towers marching across the lonely landscape of northern England.

Glen Coe Scotland's most famous glen combines those two essential qualities of Highlands landscape: dramatic scenery and deep history.

Pembrokeshire Wales' western extremity is famous for its beaches and coastal walks, as well as being home to one of Britain's finest Norman castles.

Cardiff

POP 346,000

The capital of Wales since only 1955, Cardiff has embraced its new role with vigour, emerging as one of Britain's leading urban centres in the 21st century.

◉ Sights

★**Cardiff Castle** CASTLE
(☑ 029-2087 8100; www.cardiffcastle.com; Castle St; adult/child £12/9, incl guided tour £15/11; ⊙ 9am-5pm) There's a medieval keep at its heart, but it's the later additions to Cardiff Castle that really capture the imagination. During the Victorian era, extravagant mock-Gothic features were grafted onto this relic, including a clock tower and a lavish banqueting hall. Some but not all of this flamboyant fantasy world can be accessed with a regular castle entry; the rest can be visited as part of a guided tour.

★**National Museum Cardiff** MUSEUM
(☑ 0300 111 2 333; www.museumwales.ac.uk; Gorsedd Gardens Rd; ⊙ 10am-4pm Tue-Sun) FREE Devoted mainly to natural history and art, this grand neoclassical building is the centrepiece of the seven institutions dotted around the country that together form the Welsh National Museum. It's one of Britain's best museums; you'll need at least three hours to do it justice, but it could easily consume the best part of a rainy day.

★**Wales Millennium Centre** ARTS CENTRE
(☑ 029-2063 6464; www.wmc.org.uk; Bute Pl, Cardiff Bay; tours adult/child £6/free; ⊙ 9am-7pm) The centrepiece and symbol of Cardiff Bay's regeneration is the superb Wales Millennium Centre, an architectural masterpiece of stacked Welsh slate in shades of purple, green and grey topped with an overarching bronzed steel shell. Designed by Welsh architect Jonathan Adams, it opened in 2004 as Wales' premier arts complex, housing major cultural organisations such as the Welsh National Opera, National Dance Company, BBC National Orchestra of Wales, Literature Wales, HiJinx Theatre and Tŷ Cerdd (Music Centre Wales).

Doctor Who Experience GALLERY
(☑ 0844 801 2279; www.doctorwhoexperience.com; Porth Teigr; adult/child £15/11; ⊙ 10am-5pm (last admission 3.30pm) daily Jul & Aug, Tue-Sun Mar-Jun, Sep & Oct, Wed-Sun Nov-Feb) The huge success of the reinvented classic TV series *Doctor Who,* produced by BBC Wales, has brought Cardiff to the attention of sci-fi fans worldwide. City locations have featured in many episodes; and the first two series of the spin-off *Torchwood* were also set in Cardiff Bay. Capitalising on Timelord tourism, this interactive exhibition is located right next to the BBC studios where the series is filmed – look out for the Tardis hovering outside.

🛏 Sleeping

★**Safehouse** HOSTEL £
(☑ 029-2037 2833; www.safehousehostel.com; 3 Westgate St; dm/s/d without bathroom from £14/35/37; ☜) There aren't too many hostels with a grand Victorian sitting room to rival Safehouse's. Built in 1889, this lovely red-brick office building has been thoughtfully converted into a boutique hostel with private rooms and four- to 12-bed dorms.

WORTH A TRIP

CONWY CASTLE

On the north coast of Wales, the historic town of Conwy is utterly dominated by the Unesco-designated cultural treasure of Conwy Castle (Cadw; ☑ 01492-592358; www.cadw.wales.gov.uk; Castle Sq; adult/child £7.95/5.60; ☺ 9.30am-5pm Mar-Jun, Sep & Oct, to 6pm Jul & Aug, to 4pm Nov-Feb; ℗), the most stunning of all Edward I's Welsh fortresses. Built between 1277 and 1307 on a rocky outcrop, it has commanding views across the estuary and Snowdonia National Park.

Each bunk bed has its own built-in locker and electrical socket. It's on a busy road, so earplugs are a sensible precaution.

★ **Lincoln House** HOTEL ££
(☑ 029-2039 5558; www.lincolnhotel.co.uk; 118 Cathedral Rd, Pontcanna; r £90-150; ℗ ☎) Walking a middle line between a large B&B and a small hotel, Lincoln House is a generously proportioned Victorian property with heraldic emblems in the stained-glass windows of its sitting room, and a separate bar. For added romance, book a four-poster room.

★ **Number 62** GUESTHOUSE ££
(☑ 07974 571348; www.number62.com; 62 Cathedral Rd, Pontcanna; s/d from £68/77; ☎) The only thing stopping us calling Number 62 a B&B is that breakfast is only offered as an add-on. The cosy, comfortable rooms come with thoughtful extras such as body lotion, make-up wipes and cotton buds. It also has one of the most lovingly tended front gardens of all of the converted town houses on this strip.

✗ Eating

★ **Riverside Market** MARKET £
(www.riversidemarket.org.uk; Fitzhamon Embankment, Riverside; ☺ 10am-2pm Sun; ☑) What it lacks in size, Riverside Market makes up for in sheer yumminess, its stalls heaving with cooked meals, cakes, cheese, organic meat, charcuterie and bread. There are lots of options for vegetarians and an excellent coffee stall.

★ **Mint & Mustard** INDIAN ££
(☑ 029-2062 0333; www.mintandmustard.com; 134 Whitchurch Rd, Cathays; mains £8.25-15; ☺ noon-2pm & 5-11pm; ☑) Specialising in seafood dishes from India's southern state of Kerala, this excellent restaurant combines an upmarket ambience with attentive service and delicious, beautifully presented food. If you're not enticed by the lobster, prawn and fish dishes, there are plenty of vegetarian options and an excellent crusted lamb biryani.

★ **Fish at 85** SEAFOOD £££
(☑ 029-2023 5666; www.fishat85.co.uk; 85 Pontcanna Rd, Pontcanna; mains £19-24; ☺ noon-2.30pm & 6-9pm Tue-Sat) By day a fishmongers (hence the lingering smell), by night an elegant restaurant with Cape Cod-ish decor and candles floating in water-filled jars, Fish at 85 is Cardiff's premier spot for a seafood dinner. The menu cherry-picks the best of the day's catch, offering half-a-dozen varieties, exquisitely cooked and in huge portions.

❶ Information

Tourist Office (☑ 029-2087 3573; www.visitcardiff.com; Wales Millennium Centre, Bute Pl, Cardiff Bay; ☺ 10am-6pm Mon-Sat, to 4pm Sun) Information, advice and souvenirs.

❶ Getting There & Away

BUS
Cardiff's central bus station has closed for a major redevelopment and is due to reopen near the train station in a revitalised Central Sq in 2018.

National Express coaches travel to London (from £5, 3½ hours, four daily) and Bristol (£6.10, one hour, four daily).

TRAIN
Direct services from Cardiff include London Paddington (from £40, two hours, two per hour) and Bristol (£12.50, 50 minutes, half-hourly).

Snowdonia National Park

Snowdonia National Park (Parc Cenedlaethol Eryri; www.eryri-npa.gov.uk) was founded in 1951 (making it Wales' first national park). Around 350,000 people travel to the national park to climb, walk or take the train to the summit of Mt Snowdon, Wales' highest mountain.

Snowdon (Yr Wyddfa)

No Snowdonia experience is complete without coming face-to-face with Snowdon (1085m) – 'Yr Wyddfa' in Welsh (pronounced uhr-*with*-vuh, meaning 'the Tomb'). On a clear day the views stretch to Ireland and the Isle of Man. Even on a gloomy day you could find yourself above the clouds. At the top is the striking Hafod Eryri (☺10am–20min before last train departure; ☎) visitor centre, opened in 2009 by Prince Charles.

Six paths of varying length and difficulty lead to the summit, all taking around six hours return, or you can cheat and catch the Snowdon Mountain Railway (☑01286-870223; www.snowdonrailway.co.uk; Llanberis; adult/child return diesel £29/20, steam £37/27; ☺9am-5pm mid-Mar–Nov), opened in 1896 and still the UK's only public rack-and-pinion railway.

However you get to the summit, take warm, waterproof clothing, wear sturdy footwear and check the weather forecast before setting out.

🛏 Sleeping

YHA Snowdon Ranger HOSTEL £
(☑08453-719659; www.yha.org.uk; Rhyd Ddu; d/tw £29/55; P☎) On the A4085, 5 miles north of Beddgelert at the trailhead for the Snowdon Ranger Path, this former inn has its own adjoining lakeside beach, and is close to Llanberis too. Accommodation is basic but dependable.

Pen-y-Gwryd HOTEL ££
(☑01286-870211; www.pyg.co.uk; Nant Gwynant; s/d from £45/90; P☎) Eccentric but full of atmosphere, this Georgian coaching inn was used as a training base by the 1953 Everest team, and memorabilia from their stay includes signatures on the restaurant ceiling. TV, wi-fi and mobile-phone signals don't penetrate here; instead, there's a comfy games room, sauna and a lake for those hardy enough to swim.

❶ Getting There & Away

The **Welsh Highland Railway** (☑01766-516000; www.festrail.co.uk; adult/child return £38/34.20; ☺Easter-Oct, limited winter service) and Snowdon Sherpa buses link various places in Snowdonia with the town of Caernarfon, which can be reached by train from London Euston (£86, 3¼ hours, hourly).

SCOTLAND

Despite its small size, Scotland has many treasures crammed into its compact territory – big skies, lonely landscapes, spectacular wildlife, superb seafood and hospitable, down-to-earth people. From the cultural at-

tractions of Edinburgh to the heather-clad hills of the Highlands, there's something for everyone.

Edinburgh

POP 498,810

Edinburgh is a city that just begs to be explored. From the imposing castle to the Palace of Holyroodhouse to the Royal Yacht Britannia, every corner turned reveals sudden views and unexpected vistas – green sunlit hills, a glimpse of rust-red crags, a blue flash of distant sea. But there's more to Edinburgh than sightseeing – there are top shops, world-class restaurants and a bacchanalia of bars to enjoy.

◉ Sights

★Edinburgh Castle CASTLE
(www.edinburghcastle.gov.uk; Castle Esplanade; adult/child £16.50/9.90, audioguide additional £3.50; ☺9.30am-6pm Apr-Sep, to 5pm Oct-Mar, last admission 1hr before closing; ⚇23, 27, 41, 42) Edinburgh Castle has played a pivotal role in Scottish history, both as a royal residence – King Malcolm Canmore (r 1058–93) and Queen Margaret first made their home here in the 11th century – and as a military stronghold. The castle last saw military action in 1745; from then until the 1920s it served as the British army's main base in Scotland. Today it is one of Scotland's most atmospheric and popular tourist attractions.

★Real Mary King's Close HISTORIC BUILDING
(☑0845 070 6244; www.realmarykingsclose.com; 2 Warriston's Close, High St; adult/child £14.50/8.75; ☺10am-9pm daily Apr-Oct, 10am-5pm Sun-Thu, 10am-9pm Fri & Sat Nov-Mar; ⚇23, 27, 41, 42) Edinburgh's 18th-century City Chambers were built over the sealed-off remains of Mary King's Close, and the lower levels of this medieval Old Town alley have survived almost unchanged amid the foundations for 250 years. Now open to the public, this spooky, subterranean labyrinth gives a fascinating insight into the everyday life of 17th-century Edinburgh. Costumed characters lead tours through a 16th-century town house and the plague-stricken home of a 17th-century gravedigger. Advance booking recommended.

★National Museum of Scotland MUSEUM
(www.nms.ac.uk; Chambers St; fee for special exhibitions varies; ☺10am-5pm; ♿; ⚇2, 23, 27, 35, 41, 42, 45) FREE Broad, elegant Chambers St is dominated by the long facade of the

National Museum of Scotland. Its extensive collections are spread between two buildings, one modern, one Victorian – the golden stone and striking modern architecture of the new building, opened in 1998, is one of the city's most distinctive landmarks. The five floors of the museum trace the history of Scotland from its geological beginnings to the 1990s, with many imaginative and stimulating exhibits. Audio-guides are available in several languages.

★**Scottish Parliament Building** NOTABLE BUILDING
(☎0131-348 5200; www.scottish.parliament.uk; Horse Wynd; ⊕9am-6.30pm Tue-Thu & 10am-5pm Mon, Fri & Sat in session, 10am-5pm Mon-Sat in recess; 🚉; 🚌6, 35) FREE The Scottish parliament building, on the site of a former brewery, was officially opened by HM the Queen in October 2005. Designed by Catalan architect Enric Miralles (1955–2000), the ground plan of the parliament complex is said to represent a 'flower of democracy rooted in Scottish soil' (best seen looking down from Salisbury Crags). Free, one-hour guided tours (advance booking recommended) include a visit to the Debating Chamber, a committee room, the Garden Lobby and an MSP's (Member of the Scottish Parliament) office.

★**Royal Yacht Britannia** SHIP
(www.royalyachtbritannia.co.uk; Ocean Terminal; adult/child £15/8.50; ⊕9.30am-6pm Jul-Sep, to 5.30pm Apr-Jun & Oct, 10am-5pm Nov-Mar, last admission 90min before closing; 🚉; 🚌11, 22, 34, 35, 36) Built on Clydeside, the former Royal Yacht *Britannia* was the British royal family's floating holiday home during their foreign travels from the time of her launch in 1953 until her decommissioning in 1997, and is now moored permanently in front of Ocean Terminal (☎0131-555 8888; www.oceanterminal.com; Ocean Dr; ⊕10am-8pm Mon-Fri, to 7pm Sat, 11am-6pm Sun; 🚉). The tour, which you take at your own pace with an audioguide (included in the admission fee and available in 20 languages), lifts the curtain on the everyday lives of the royals, and gives an intriguing insight into the Queen's private tastes.

★**Palace of Holyroodhouse** PALACE
(www.royalcollection.org.uk; Horse Wynd; adult/child incl audioguide £12/7.20; ⊕9.30am-6pm Apr-Oct, to 4.30pm Nov-Mar; 🚉; 🚌6, 35) This palace is the royal family's official residence in Scotland, but is more famous as the 16th-century home of the ill-fated Mary, Queen of Scots. The highlight of the tour is **Mary's Bed Chamber**, home to the unfortunate queen from 1561 to 1567. It was here that her jealous second husband, Lord Darnley, restrained the pregnant queen while his henchmen murdered her secretary – and favourite – Rizzio. A plaque in the neighbouring room marks the spot where he bled to death.

🛏 Sleeping

★**Malone's Old Town Hostel** HOSTEL £
(☎0131-226 7648; www.maloneshostel.com; 14 Forrest Rd; dm £12-20; @🚉; 🚌2, 23, 27, 41, 42, 45) No fancy decor or style credentials here, but they've got the basics right: it's clean, comfortable and friendly, and set upstairs from an Irish pub where guests get discounts on food and drink. The cherry on the cake is its superbly central location, an easy walk from the Royal Mile, the castle, the Grassmarket and Princes St.

Code Hostel HOSTEL £
(☎0131-659 9883; www.codehostel.com; 50 Rose St N Lane; dm from £25, d £99; 🚉; 🚌Princes St) This upmarket hostel, bang in the middle of the New Town, combines cute designer decor with innovative sleeping cubicles that offer more privacy than bunks (four to six people per dorm, each with en suite shower room). There's also a luxurious double apartment called the Penthouse, complete with kitchenette and roof terrace.

★**Southside Guest House** B&B ££
(☎0131-668 4422; www.southsideguesthouse.co.uk; 8 Newington Rd; s/d from £80/105; 🚉; 🚌all Newington buses) Though set in a typical Victorian terrace, the Southside transcends the traditional guesthouse category and feels more like a modern boutique hotel. Its eight stylish rooms ooze interior design, standing out from other Newington B&Bs through the clever use of bold colours and modern

THE QUEENSFERRY CROSSING

The famous Forth Bridge (1890) and Forth Road Bridge (1964), which soar across the Firth of Forth to the west of Edinburgh have been joined by the impressive Queensferry Crossing (a new bridge opening May 2017).

furniture. Breakfast is an event, with Bucks Fizz (cava mixed with orange juice) on offer to ease the hangover!

★ Wallace's Arthouse
B&B ££

(📞 07941 343714; www.wallacesarthousescotland.com; 41/4 Constitution St; s/d £99/120; 🗑; 🖵 12, 16) This Georgian apartment, housed in the neoclassical Leith Assembly Rooms (a Grade A listed building), offers two beautifully nostalgic bedrooms styled by former fashion designer Wallace, who comes as part of the package – your charming host and breakfast chef is an unfailing source of colourful anecdotes and local knowledge.

★ Sheridan Guest House
B&B ££

(📞 0131-554 4107; www.sheridanedinburgh.com; 1 Bonnington Tce, Newhaven Rd; r from £95; 🅿 🗑; 🖵 7, 11, 14) Flowerpots filled with colourful blooms line the steps of this little haven hidden away to the north of the New Town. The eight bedrooms (all en suite) blend crisp colours with contemporary furniture, stylish lighting and colourful paintings, which complement the house's clean-cut Georgian lines, while the breakfast menu adds omelettes, pancakes with maple syrup, and scrambled eggs with smoked salmon to the usual offerings.

✕ Eating

★ Mums
CAFE £

(📞 0131-260 9806; www.monstermashcafe.co.uk; 4a Forrest Rd; mains £8-11; ⊙ 9am-10pm Mon-Sat, 10am-10pm Sun; 🗑 👭; 🖵 23, 27, 41, 42) 🍴 This nostalgia-fuelled cafe serves up classic British comfort food that wouldn't look out of place on a 1950s menu – bacon and eggs, bangers and mash, shepherd's pie, fish and chips. But there's a twist – the food is all top-quality nosh freshly prepared from local produce. There's also a good selection of bottled craft beers and Scottish-brewed cider.

★ Aizle
SCOTTISH ££

(📞 0131-662 9349; http://aizle.co.uk; 107-109 St Leonard's St; 5-course dinner £45; ⊙ 6-9.30pm Wed, Thu & Sun, 5-9.30pm Fri & Sat; 🗑; 🖵 14) If you're the sort who has trouble deciding what to eat, Aizle will do it for you (the name is an old Scots word for 'spark' or 'ember'). There's no menu, just a five-course dinner conjured from a monthly 'harvest' of the finest and freshest of local produce (listed on a blackboard), and presented beautifully – art on a plate.

FESTIVAL CITY

Edinburgh boasts a frenzy of festivals throughout the year, including the world-famous **Edinburgh Festival Fringe** (📞 0131-226 0026; www.edfringe.com), held over 3½ weeks in August. The last two weeks overlap with the first two weeks of the **Edinburgh International Festival** (📞 0131-473 2000; www.eif.co.uk). See www.edinburghfestivals.co.uk for more.

★ Cannonball Restaurant
SCOTTISH ££

(📞 0131-225 1550; www.contini.com/contini-cannonball; 356 Castlehill, Royal Mile; mains £15-25; ⊙ noon-5pm & 5.30-10pm Tue-Sat; 🗑 👭; 🖵 23, 27, 41, 42) The historic Cannonball House next to Edinburgh Castle's esplanade has been transformed into a sophisticated restaurant (and whisky bar) where the Contini family work their Italian magic on Scottish classics to produce dishes such as haggis balls with spiced pickled turnip and whisky marmalade, and lobster with wild garlic and lemon butter.

★ Gardener's Cottage
SCOTTISH ££

(📞 0131-558 1221; www.thegardenerscottage.co; 1 Royal Terrace Gardens, London Rd; lunch mains £16-17, dinner set menu £40; ⊙ noon-2pm & 5-10pm Mon & Wed-Fri, 10am-2pm & 5-10pm Sat & Sun; 🖵 all London Rd buses) 🍴 This country cottage in the heart of the city, bedecked with flowers and fairy lights, offers one of Edinburgh's most interesting dining experiences – two tiny rooms with communal tables made of salvaged timber, and a menu based on fresh local produce (most of the vegetables and fruit are grown in a local organic garden). Bookings essential; brunch served at weekends.

★ Ondine
SEAFOOD £££

(📞 0131-226 1888; www.ondinerestaurant.co.uk; 2 George IV Bridge; mains £17-40, 2-/3-course lunch £25/30; ⊙ noon-3pm & 5.30-10pm Mon-Sat; 🗑; 🖵 23, 27, 41, 42) Ondine is one of Edinburgh's finest seafood restaurants, with a menu based on sustainably sourced fish. Take a seat at the curved Oyster Bar and tuck into oysters Kilpatrick, smoked haddock chowder, lobster thermidor, a roast shellfish platter or just good old haddock and chips (with minted pea purée, just to keep things posh).

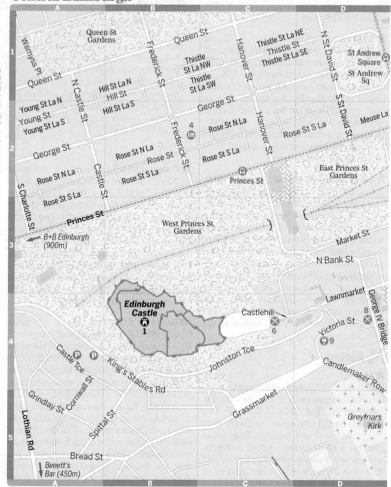

🍷 Drinking & Nightlife

Café Royal Circle Bar PUB

(www.caferoyaledinburgh.co.uk; 17 West Register St;
⊙ 11am-11pm Mon-Wed, to midnight Thu, to 1am Fri
& Sat, 12.30-11pm Sun; 🛜; 🚌 Princes St) Perhaps
the classic Edinburgh pub, the Café Royal's
main claims to fame are its magnificent oval
bar and its Doulton tile portraits of famous
Victorian inventors. Sit at the bar or claim
one of the cosy leather booths beneath the
stained-glass windows, and choose from the
seven real ales on tap.

★ Bow Bar PUB

(www.thebowbar.co.uk; 80 West Bow; ⊙ noon-midnight Mon-Sat, to 11.30pm Sun; 🚌 2, 23, 27, 41, 42)
One of the city's best traditional-style pubs
(it's not as old as it looks), serving a range of
excellent real ales, Scottish craft gins and a
vast selection of malt whiskies, the Bow Bar
often has standing-room only on Friday and
Saturday evenings.

★ Bennet's Bar PUB

(📞 0131-229 5143; www.bennetsbaredinburgh.
co.uk; 8 Leven St; ⊙ 11am-1am; 🚌 all Tollcross buses) Situated beside the King's Theatre, Ben-

china (cocktails are served in teapots), the real ales and bottled beers are complemented by a range of speciality teas, coffees and fruit drinks (including rose lemonade), and well-above-average pub grub (served from 10am to 10pm).

★**Cabaret Voltaire**　　　　　CLUB
(www.thecabaretvoltaire.com;　36-38　Blair　St; ⊙5pm-3am Mon-Thu, noon-3am Fri-Sun; 📶; 🚌all South Bridge buses) An atmospheric warren of stone-lined vaults houses this self-consciously 'alternative' club, which eschews huge dance floors and egotistical DJ worship in favour of a 'creative crucible' hosting an eclectic mix of DJs, live acts, comedy, theatre, visual arts and the spoken word. Well worth a look.

☆ Entertainment

The comprehensive source for what's on is *The List* (www.list.co.uk).

★**Sandy Bell's**　　　　TRADITIONAL MUSIC
(www.sandybellsedinburgh.co.uk;　25　Forrest　Rd; ⊙noon-1am Mon-Sat, 12.30pm-midnight Sun; 🚌2, 23, 27, 41, 42, 45) This unassuming pub is a stalwart of the traditional music scene (the founder's wife sang with the Corries). There's music almost every evening at 9pm, and from 3pm Saturday and Sunday, plus lots of impromptu sessions.

★**Summerhall**　　　　　　THEATRE
(📞0131-560 1580; www.summerhall.co.uk; 1 Summerhall; 🚌41, 42, 67) Formerly Edinburgh

net's has managed to hang on to almost all of its beautiful Victorian fittings, from the leaded stained-glass windows and ornate mirrors to the wooden gantry and the brass water taps on the bar (for your whisky – there are over 100 malts from which to choose).

★**Roseleaf**　　　　　　　　　BAR
(📞0131-476 5268; www.roseleaf.co.uk; 23-24 Sandport Pl; ⊙10am-1am; 📶📶; 🚌16, 22, 35, 36) Cute, quaint and verging on chintzy, the Roseleaf could hardly be further from the average Leith bar. Decked out in flowered wallpaper, old furniture and rose-patterned

University's veterinary school, the Summerhall complex is a major cultural centre and entertainment venue, with old halls and lecture theatres (including an original anatomy lecture theatre) now serving as venues for drama, dance, cinema and comedy performances. It's also one of the main venues for Edinburgh Festival events.

ℹ Information

Edinburgh Information Centre (☏ 0131-473 3868; www.edinburgh.org; Waverley Mall, 3 Princes St; ⊙ 9am-7pm Mon-Sat, 10am-7pm Sun Jul & Aug, to 6pm Jun, to 5pm Sep-May; ☏; ☒ St Andrew Sq) Includes an accommodation booking service, currency exchange, gift and bookshop, internet access and counters selling tickets for Edinburgh city tours and Scottish Citylink bus services.

ℹ Getting There & Away

AIR

Edinburgh Airport (EDI; ☏ 0844 448 8833; www.edinburghairport.com), 8 miles west of the city, has numerous flights to other parts of Scotland and the UK, Ireland and mainland Europe.

BUS

Scottish Citylink (☏ 0871 266 3333; www.citylink.co.uk) buses connect Edinburgh with all of Scotland's cities and major towns, including Glasgow (£7.50, 1¼ hours, every 15 minutes), Stirling (£8.20, one hour, hourly) and Inverness (£31, 3½ to 4½ hours, hourly). National Express operates a direct coach service from London (from £28, 10 hours, two daily).

It's also worth checking with **Megabus** (☏ 0141-352 4444; www.megabus.com) for cheap intercity bus fares from Edinburgh to London, Glasgow and Inverness.

TRAIN

The main terminus in Edinburgh is Waverley train station, in the heart of the city. Trains arriving from, and departing for, the west also stop at Haymarket station, which is more convenient for the West End.

ScotRail (☏ 0344-811 0141; www.scotrail.co.uk) operates a regular shuttle service between Edinburgh and Glasgow (£12.50, 50 minutes, every 15 minutes), and frequent daily services to all Scottish cities, including Stirling (£8.60, one hour, twice hourly Monday to Saturday, hourly Sunday) and Inverness (£38, 3½ hours, eight daily). There are also regular trains to London Kings Cross (from £82, 4½ hours, at least hourly) via York.

Glasgow

POP 596,500

With a population around 1½ times that of Edinburgh, and a radically different history rooted in industry and trade rather than politics and law, Glasgow stands in complete contrast to the capital. The city offers a unique blend of friendliness, energy, dry humour and urban chaos, and also boasts excellent art galleries and museums – including the famous Burrell Collection (currently closed for refurbishment, due to reopen in 2020) – as well as numerous good-value restaurants, countless pubs, bars and clubs, and a lively performing-arts scene.

Just 50 miles to the west of Edinburgh, Glasgow makes an easy day trip by train or bus.

⊙ Sights

Glasgow's main square in the city centre is grand **George Square**, built in the Victorian era to show off the city's wealth, and dignified by statues of notable Scots, including Robert Burns, James Watt, John Moore and Sir Walter Scott.

★ **Kelvingrove Art Gallery & Museum** GALLERY, MUSEUM
(www.glasgowmuseums.com; Argyle St; ⊙ 10am-5pm Mon-Thu & Sat, 11am-5pm Fri & Sun; ☏) **FREE** A magnificent stone building, this grand Victorian cathedral of culture is a fascinating and unusual museum, with a bewildering variety of exhibits. You'll find fine art alongside stuffed animals, and Micronesian shark-tooth swords alongside a Spitfire plane, but it's not mix 'n' match: rooms are carefully and thoughtfully themed, and the collection is a manageable size. It has an excellent room of Scottish art, a room of fine French Impressionist works, and quality Renaissance paintings from Italy and Flanders.

★ **Riverside Museum** MUSEUM
(☏ 0141-287 2720; www.glasgowmuseums.com; 100 Pointhouse Pl; ⊙ 10am-5pm Mon-Thu & Sat, 11am-5pm Fri & Sun; ☏ ♿) **FREE** This visually impressive modern museum at Glasgow Harbour owes its striking curved forms to late British-Iraqi architect Zaha Hadid. A transport museum forms the main part of the collection, featuring a fascinating series of cars made in Scotland, plus assorted railway locos, trams, bikes (including the world's first pedal-powered bicycle from

DON'T MISS

STIRLING CASTLE

Hold Stirling and you control Scotland. This maxim has ensured that a fortress of some kind has existed here since prehistoric times. You cannot help drawing parallels with Edinburgh Castle, but many find **Stirling Castle** (HS; www.stirlingcastle.gov.uk; Castle Wynd; adult/child £14.50/8.70; ⌚9.30am-6pm Apr-Sep, to 5pm Oct-Mar; P) more atmospheric – the location, architecture, historical significance and commanding views combine to make it a grand and memorable sight.

The current castle dates from the late 14th to the 16th century, when it was a residence of the Stuart monarchs. The undisputed highlight of a visit is the fabulous, recently restored **Royal Palace**. The idea was that it should look brand new, just as when it was constructed by French masons under the orders of James V in the mid-16th century with the aim of impressing his new (also French) bride and other crowned heads of Europe.

The suite of six rooms – three for the king, three for the queen – is a sumptuous riot of colour. Particularly notable are the fine fireplaces, the **Stirling Heads** – modern reproductions of painted oak discs in the ceiling of the king's audience chamber – and the fabulous series of **tapestries** that have been painstakingly woven over many years.

Stirling is 35 miles northwest of Edinburgh, and easily reached by train (£8.60, one hour, half-hourly Monday to Saturday, hourly Sunday).

1847) and model Clyde-built ships. An atmospheric recreation of a Glasgow shopping street from the early 20th century puts the vintage vehicles into a social context. There's also a cafe.

★**Glasgow Cathedral** CATHEDRAL
(HES; ☎0141-552 8198; www.historicenvironment.scot; Cathedral Sq; ⌚9.30am-5.30pm Mon-Sat & 1-5pm Sun Apr-Sep, 10am-4pm Mon-Sat & 1-4pm Sun Oct-Mar) FREE Glasgow Cathedral has a rare timelessness. The dark, imposing interior conjures up medieval might and can send a shiver down the spine. It's a shining example of Gothic architecture, and unlike nearly all of Scotland's cathedrals, survived the turmoil of the Reformation mobs almost intact. Most of the current building dates from the 15th century.

★**Glasgow Science Centre** MUSEUM
(☎0141-420 5000; www.glasgowsciencecentre.org; 50 Pacific Quay; adult/child £11/9, IMAX, tower or planetarium extra £2.50-3.50; ⌚10am-5pm Wed-Sun Nov-Mar, 10am-5pm daily Apr-Oct; 📶👪) This ultramodern science museum will keep the kids entertained for hours (that's middle-aged kids, too!). It brings science and technology alive through hundreds of interactive exhibits on four floors: a bounty of discovery for inquisitive minds. There's also an **IMAX theatre** (see www.cineworld.com for current screenings), a rotating 127m-high **observation tower**; a **planetarium**, and a **Science Theatre**, with live science demonstrations. To get here, take bus 89 or 90 from Union St.

✕ Eating & Drinking

★**Ox & Finch** FUSION £
(☎0141-339 8627; www.oxandfinch.com; 920 Sauchiehall St; portions £4-8; ⌚noon-10pm; 📶) This fashionable place could almost sum up the thriving modern Glasgow eating scene, with a faux-pub name, sleek but comfortable contemporary decor, tapas-sized dishes and an open kitchen. Grab a cosy booth and be prepared to have your tastebuds wowed with innovative, delicious creations aimed at sharing, drawing on French and Mediterranean influences but focusing on quality Scottish produce.

★**Saramago Café Bar** CAFE £
(☎0141-352 4920; www.facebook.com/saramagocafebar; 350 Sauchiehall St; light meals £3-9; ⌚food noon-10pm Sun-Wed, noon-11.30pm Thu-Sat; 📶🌿) In the airy atrium of the Centre for Contemporary Arts, this place does a great line in eclectic vegan fusion food, with a range of top flavour combinations from around the globe. The upstairs bar has a great deck on steep Scott St and packs out inside with a friendly hipstery crowd enjoying the DJ sets and quality tap beers.

★**Mother India** INDIAN ££
(☎0141-221 1663; www.motherindia.co.uk; 28 Westminster Tce, Sauchiehall St; mains £8-16; ⌚5.30-10.30pm Mon-Thu, noon-11pm Fri, 1-11pm Sat, 1-10pm Sun; 📶🌿👪) Glasgow curry buffs forever debate the merits of the city's numerous excellent South Asian restaurants, and this features in every discussion. It may lack the

Glasgow

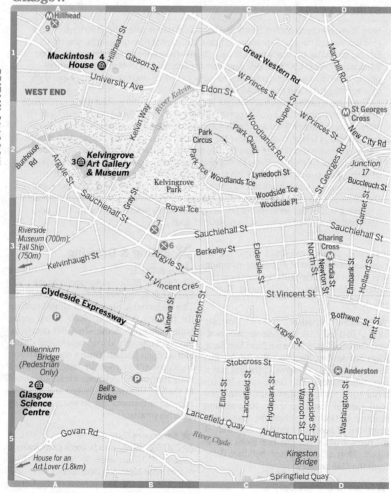

trendiness of some of the up-and-comers, but it's been a stalwart for years, and the quality and innovation on show are superb. The three dining areas are all attractive and it makes an effort for kids, with a separate menu.

★ **Ubiquitous Chip**   SCOTTISH **£££**
(☎0141-334 5007; www.ubiquitouschip.co.uk; 12 Ashton Lane; 2-/3-course lunch £17/21, mains £22-35, brasserie mains £10-15; ⊗noon-2.30pm & 5-11pm Mon-Sat, 12.30-3pm & 5-11pm Sun; 🕾) 🖋 The original champion of Scottish produce, this is legendary for its unparalleled Scot-

tish cuisine and lengthy wine list. Named to poke fun at Scotland's culinary reputation, it offers a French touch but resolutely Scottish ingredients, carefully selected and following sustainable principles. The elegant courtyard space offers some of Glasgow's best dining, while, above, the cheaper brasserie offers exceptional value for money.

Horse Shoe   PUB
(www.horseshoebar.co.uk; 17 Drury St; ⊗10am-midnight Sun-Fri, 9am-midnight Sat) This legendary city pub and popular meeting

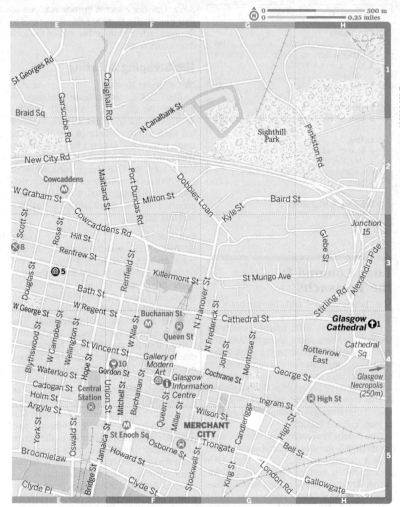

place dates from the late 19th century and is largely unchanged. It's a picturesque spot, with the longest continuous bar in the UK, but its main attraction is what's served over it – real ale and good cheer. Upstairs in the lounge is some of the best-value pub food (three-course lunch £4.50) in town.

❶ Information

Glasgow Information Centre (www.visit scotland.com; Gallery of Modern Art, Royal Exchange Sq; ⊙10am-4.45pm, till 7.45pm Thu,

from 11am Fri & Sun; 🛜) In the **Gallery of Modern Art** (GoMA; ☑0141-287 3050; www. glasgowmuseums.com; Royal Exchange Sq; ⊙10am-5pm Mon-Thu & Sat, until 8pm Thu, 11am-5pm Fri & Sun; 🛜).

❶ Getting There & Away

Glasgow is easily reached from Edinburgh by bus (£7.50, 1¼ hours, every 15 minutes) or train (£13.60, 50 minutes, every 15 minutes).

Glasgow

⊙ Top Sights
1 Glasgow Cathedral H4
2 Glasgow Science Centre.....................A4
3 Kelvingrove Art Gallery &
   Museum A2
4 Mackintosh House...............................A1

⊙ Sights
5 Willow Tearooms E3

✖ Eating
6 Mother India B3
7 Ox & Finch...B3
8 Saramago Café Bar E3
9 Ubiquitous Chip A1

⊙ Drinking & Nightlife
10 Horse Shoe..F4

Loch Lomond & the Trossachs

The 'bonnie banks' and 'bonnie braes' of **Loch Lomond** have long been Glasgow's rural retreat. The main tourist focus is on the loch's western shore, along the A82. The eastern shore, followed by the West Highland Way long-distance footpath, is quieter. The region's importance was recognised when it became the heart of **Loch Lomond & the Trossachs National Park** (www.lochlomond-trossachs.org) – Scotland's first national park, created in 2002.

The nearby **Trossachs** is a region famous for its thickly forested hills and scenic lochs. It first gained popularity in the early 19th century when curious visitors came from across Britain, drawn by the romantic language of Walter Scott's poem *Lady of the Lake,* inspired by Loch Katrine, and his novel *Rob Roy,* about the derring-do of the region's most famous son.

The main centre for Loch Lomond boat trips is Balloch, where **Sweeney's Cruises** (☑01389-752376; www.sweeneyscruiseco.com; Balloch Rd) offers a range of outings, including a one-hour cruise to Inchmurrin and back (adult/child £10.20/7, five times daily April to October, twice daily November to March).

Loch Katrine Cruises (☑01877-376315; www.lochkatrine.com; Trossachs Pier; 1hr cruise adult £11-13, child £5.50-6.50; ⊙Easter-Oct) runs boat trips from Trossachs Pier at the eastern end of Loch Katrine, some aboard the fabulous centenarian steamship *Sir Walter*

Scott. One-hour scenic cruises run one to four times daily; there are also departures to Stronachlachar at the other end of the loch (two hours return).

🛏 Sleeping & Eating

★ Callander Hostel
HOSTEL £

(☑01877-331465; www.callanderhostel.co.uk; 6 Bridgend; dm £18.50-23.50, d £60-70; ☑@🖙) 🖉 This hostel in a mock-Tudor building has been a major labour of love by a local youth project and is now a top-class facility. Well-furnished dorms offer bunks with individual light and USB charge ports, while en suite doubles have super views. Staff are welcoming and friendly, and it has a spacious common area and share kitchen as well as a cafe and garden.

Oak Tree Inn
INN ££

(☑01360-870357; www.theoaktreeinn.co.uk; Balmaha; dm/s/d £30/70/90; ☑🖙) An attractive traditional inn built in slate and timber, this offers bright modern guest bedrooms for pampered hikers, plus super-spacious superior chambers, self-catering cottages and two four-bed bunkrooms for hardier souls. The rustic restaurant brings locals, tourists and walkers together and dishes up hearty meals that cover lots of bases (mains £9 to £12; food noon to 9pm). There's lots of outdoor seating.

★ Callander Meadows
SCOTTISH ££

(☑01877-330181; www.callandermeadows.co.uk; 24 Main St; 2-/3-course lunch £12/17, mains £13-17; ⊙10am-9pm Thu-Mon; 🖙) Informal and cosy, this well-loved restaurant in the centre of Callander occupies the front rooms of a main-street house. It's truly excellent; there's a contemporary flair for presentation and unusual flavour combinations, but a solidly British base underpins the cuisine. There's a great beer/coffee garden out the back, where you can also eat. Opens daily from June to September.

Drover's Inn
PUB FOOD ££

(☑01301-704234; www.thedroversinn.co.uk; Ardlui; bar meals £9-14; ⊙11.30am-10pm Mon-Sat, 11.30am-9.30pm or 10pm Sun; 🖙) Don't miss this low-ceilinged howff (drinking den) just north of Ardlui with its smoke-blackened stone, kilted bartenders, and walls festooned with moth-eaten stags' heads and stuffed birds. The bar, where Rob Roy allegedly dropped by for pints, serves hearty hill-walking fuel and hosts live folk music at weekends. Recommended more as an atmospheric place to eat and drink than somewhere to stay.

ⓘ Getting There & Away

Balloch, at the southern end of Loch Lomond, can be easily reached from Glasgow by bus (£5, 1½ hours, at least two per hour) or train (£5.30, 45 minutes, every 30 minutes).

For exploring the Trossachs, your own transport is recommended.

Inverness

Inverness, the primary city and shopping centre of the Highlands, has a great location astride the River Ness at the northern end of the Great Glen. It's a jumping-off point for exploring Loch Ness and northern Scotland, with the railway line from Edinburgh branching east to Elgin and Aberdeen, north to Thurso and Wick, and west to Kyle of Lochalsh (the nearest train station to the Isle of Skye). The latter route is one of Britain's great scenic rail journeys.

🛏 Sleeping

Bazpackers Backpackers Hotel HOSTEL £
(✆ 01463-717663; www.bazpackershostel.co.uk; 4 Culduthel Rd; dm/tw £18/50; @🕿) This may be Inverness' smallest hostel (34 beds), but it's hugely popular. It's a friendly, quiet place – the main building has a convivial lounge centred on a wood-burning stove, and a small garden and great views (some rooms are in a separate building with no garden). The dorms and kitchen can be a bit cramped, but the showers are great.

★ Trafford Bank B&B ££
(✆ 01463-241414; www.traffordbankguesthouse. co.uk; 96 Fairfield Rd; d £120-140; P🕿) Lots of word-of-mouth rave reviews for this elegant Victorian villa, which was once home to a bishop, just a mitre-toss from the Caledonian Canal and 10 minutes' walk west from the city centre. The luxurious rooms include fresh flowers and fruit, bathrobes and fluffy towels – ask for the Tartan Room, which has a wrought-iron king-size bed and Victorian roll-top bath.

★ Rocpool Reserve BOUTIQUE HOTEL £££
(✆ 01463-240089; www.rocpool.com; Culduthel Rd; s/d from £195/230; P🕿) Boutique chic meets the Highlands in this slick and sophisticated little hotel, where an elegant Georgian exterior conceals an oasis of contemporary cool. A gleaming white entrance hall lined with red carpet and contemporary art leads to designer rooms in shades of chocolate, cream and gold; a restaurant by Albert Roux completes the luxury package.

🍴 Eating

★ Café 1 BISTRO ££
(✆ 01463-226200; www.cafe1.net; 75 Castle St; mains £13-25; ⊘ noon-2.30pm & 5-9.30pm Mon-Fri, noon-2.30pm & 6-9.30pm Sat; 🖫) 🥄 Café 1 is a friendly, appealing bistro with candlelit tables amid elegant blonde-wood and wrought-iron decor. There is an international menu based on quality Scottish produce, from Aberdeen Angus steaks to crisp pan-fried sea bass and meltingly tender pork belly. The set lunch menu (two courses for £12) is served noon to 2.30pm Monday to Saturday.

THE GENIUS OF CHARLES RENNIE MACKINTOSH

Charles Rennie Mackintosh (1868–1928) is to Glasgow what Gaudí is to Barcelona. A designer, architect and master of the art nouveau style, his quirky, linear and geometric designs are seen all over Glasgow.

Many of his buildings are open to the public, though his masterpiece, the **Glasgow School of Art**, was extensively damaged by fire in 2014 and is due to reopen in 2018. If you're a fan, the **Mackintosh Trail ticket** (£10), available at the tourist office or any Mackintosh building, gives you a day's free admission to all his creations, plus unlimited bus and subway travel. Highlights include the following:

Willow Tearooms (217 Sauchiehall St; 🕿) `FREE`

Mackintosh House (www.hunterian.gla.ac.uk; 82 Hillhead St; adult/child £5/3; ⊘10am-5pm Tue-Sat, 11am-4pm Sun)

House for an Art Lover (✆ 0141-353 4770; www.houseforanartlover.co.uk; Bellahouston Park, Dumbreck Rd; adult/child £4.50/3; ⊘10am-4pm Mon-Wed, to 12.30pm Thu-Sun)

THE NORTH COAST 500

This 500-mile circuit of northern Scotland's stunning coastline (www.northcoast500.com) has become hugely popular, with thousands of people completing the route by car, campervan, motorbike or bicycle.

Kitchen Brasserie
MODERN SCOTTISH ££

(☑ 01463-259119; www.kitchenrestaurant.co.uk; 15 Huntly St; mains £9-20; ☺ noon-3pm & 5-10pm; ☎ 🍴) This spectacular glass-fronted restaurant offers a great menu of top Scottish produce with a Mediterranean or Asian touch, and a view over the River Ness – try to get a table upstairs. Great value two-course lunch (£9, noon to 3pm) and early-bird menu (£13, 5pm to 7pm).

ⓘ Information

Inverness Tourist Office (☑ 01463-252401; www.visithighlands.com; Castle Wynd; internet access per 20min £1; ☺ 9am-5pm Mon-Sat, 10am-3pm Sun, longer hours Mar-Oct) Bureau de change and accommodation booking service; also sells tickets for tours and cruises.

ⓘ Getting There & Away

BUS

Buses depart from **Inverness bus station** (Margaret St). Coaches from London (£45, 13 hours, one daily direct) are operated by **National Express** (☑ 08717-818181; www.nationalexpress.com); more frequent services require a change at Glasgow. Other routes include Edinburgh (£31, 3½ to 4½ hours, hourly) and Portree on the Isle of Skye (£25, 3¼ hours, three daily).

TRAIN

Trains depart from Inverness for Kyle of Lochalsh (£18, 2½ hours, four daily Monday to Saturday, two Sunday), one of Britain's most scenic railway lines.

There's one direct train from London each day (£120, eight to nine hours); others require a change at Edinburgh.

Loch Ness

Deep, dark and narrow, Loch Ness stretches for 23 miles between Inverness and Fort Augustus. Its bitterly cold waters have been extensively explored in search of the elusive Loch Ness monster, but most visitors see her only in cardboard cut-out form at the monster exhibitions. The village of **Drumnadrochit** is a hotbed of beastie fever, with two monster exhibitions battling it out for the tourist dollar.

⊙ Sights & Activities

Loch Ness Centre & Exhibition
MUSEUM

(☑ 01456-450573; www.lochness.com; adult/child £7.95/4.95; ☺ 9.30am-6pm Jul & Aug, to 5pm Easter-Jun, Sep & Oct, 10am-3.30pm Nov-Easter; 🅿 🍴) This Nessie-themed attraction adopts a scientific approach that allows you to weigh the evidence for yourself. Exhibits include the original equipment – sonar survey vessels, miniature submarines, cameras and sediment coring tools – used in various monster hunts, as well as original photographs and film footage of sightings. You'll find out about hoaxes and optical illusions, as well as learning a lot about the ecology of Loch Ness – is there enough food in the loch to support even one 'monster', let alone a breeding population?

Urquhart Castle
CASTLE

(HS; ☑ 01456-450551; adult/child £8.50/5.10; ☺ 9.30am-6pm Apr-Sep, to 5pm Oct, to 4.30pm Nov-Mar; 🅿) Commanding a superb location 1.5 miles east of Drumnadrochit, with outstanding views (on a clear day), Urquhart Castle is a popular Nessie-hunting hot spot. A huge visitor centre (most of which is beneath ground level) includes a video theatre (with a dramatic 'reveal' of the castle at the end of the film) and displays of medieval items discovered in the castle. The site includes a huge gift shop and a restaurant, and is often very crowded in summer.

Nessie Hunter
BOATING

(☑ 01456-450395; www.lochness-cruises.com; adult/child £15/10; ☺ Easter-Oct) One-hour monster-hunting cruises, complete with sonar and underwater cameras. Cruises depart from Drumnadrochit hourly (except 1pm) from 9am to 6pm daily.

ⓘ Getting There & Away

Scottish Citylink (☑ 0871-266 3333; www.citylink.co.uk) and Stagecoach buses from Inverness to Fort William run along the shores of Loch Ness (six to eight daily, five on Sunday); those headed for Skye turn off at Invermoriston. There are bus stops at Drumnadrochit (£3.30, 30 minutes) and Urquhart Castle car park (£3.60, 35 minutes).

Isle of Skye

POP 10,000

The Isle of Skye is the biggest of Scotland's islands (now linked to the mainland by a bridge at Kyle of Lochalsh), a 50-mile-long smorgasbord of velvet moors, jagged mountains, sparkling lochs and towering sea cliffs. It takes its name from the old Norse *sky-a*, meaning 'cloud island', a Viking reference to the often mist-enshrouded Cuillin Hills, Britain's most spectacular mountain range. The stunning scenery is the main attraction, including the cliffs and pinnacles of the Old Man of Storr, Kilt Rock and the Quiraing, but there are plenty of cosy pubs to retire to when the rainclouds close in.

Portree is the main town, with Broadford a close second; both have banks, ATMs, supermarkets and petrol stations.

◉ Sights & Activities

Dunvegan Castle   CASTLE
(☑ 01470-521206; www.dunvegancastle.com; adult/child £12/9; ◷ 10am-5.30pm Apr–mid-Oct; P) Skye's most famous historic building, and one of its most popular tourist attractions, Dunvegan Castle is the seat of the chief of Clan MacLeod. In addition to the usual castle stuff – swords, silver and family portraits – there are some interesting artefacts, including the Fairy Flag, a diaphanous silk banner that dates from some time between the 4th and 7th centuries, and Bonnie Prince Charlie's waistcoat and a lock of his hair, donated by Flora MacDonald's granddaughter.

Skye Tours   BUS
(☑ 01471-822716; www.skye-tours.co.uk; adult/child £35/30; ◷ Mon-Sat) Five-hour sightseeing tours of Skye in a minibus, taking in the Old Man of Storr, Kilt Rock and Dunvegan Castle. Depart from Kyle of Lochalsh train station at 11.30am (connects with 8.55am train from Inverness, returns to Kyle by 4.45pm in time to catch the return train at 5.13pm).

🛏 Sleeping

Portree, the island's capital, has the largest selection of accommodation, eating places and other services.

★ Cowshed Boutique Bunkhouse HOSTEL £
(☑ 07917 536820; www.skyecowshed.co.uk; Uig; dm/tw £20/80, pod £70; P 🛜) This new hostel enjoys a glorious setting overlooking Uig Bay, with superb views from its ultra-stylish lounge. The dorms have custom-built wooden bunks that offer comfort and privacy, while the camping pods (sleeping up to four, but more comfortable with two) have heating and en suite shower rooms; there are even mini 'dog pods' for your canine companions.

Portree Youth Hostel   HOSTEL £
(SYHA; ☑ 01478-612231; www.syha.org.uk; Bayfield Rd; dm/tw £24/66; P 🛜) This brand-new SYHA hostel (formerly Bayfield Backpackers) has been completely renovated and offers brightly decorated dorms and private rooms, a stylish lounge with views over the bay, and outdoor seating areas, with an ideal location in the town centre just 100m from the bus stop.

★ Tigh an Dochais   B&B ££
(☑ 01471-820022; www.skyebedbreakfast.co.uk; 13 Harrapool; d £105; P 🛜) 🅿 A cleverly designed modern building, Tigh an Dochais is one of Skye's best B&Bs – a little footbridge leads to the front door, which is on the 1st floor. Here you'll find the dining room (gorgeous breakfasts) and lounge offering a stunning view of sea and hills; the bedrooms (downstairs) open onto an outdoor deck with that same wonderful view.

★ Toravaig House Hotel   HOTEL ££
(☑ 01471-820200; www.toravaig.com; Toravaig; d £110-149; P 🛜) This hotel, 3 miles south of Isleornsay, is one of those places where the owners know a thing or two about hospitality – as soon as you arrive you'll feel right at home, whether relaxing on the sofas by the log fire in the lounge or admiring the view across the Sound of Sleat from the lawn chairs in the garden.

🍴 Eating

★ Scorrybreac   MODERN SCOTTISH ££
(☑ 01478-612069; www.scorrybreac.com; 7 Bosville Tce; 2-/3-course dinner £27.50/32.50; ◷ 5-9.30pm Tue-Sat) 🅿 Set in the front rooms of what was once a private house, and with just eight tables, Scorrybreac is snug and intimate, offering fine dining without the faff. Chef Calum Munro (son of Donnie Munro, of Gaelic rock band Runrig fame) sources as much produce as possible from Skye, including foraged herbs and mushrooms, and creates the most exquisite concoctions.

★ Creelers   SEAFOOD ££
(☑ 01471-822281; www.skye-seafood-restaurant.co.uk; Lower Harrapool; mains £14-19; ◷ noon-8.30pm Tue-Sat Mar-Oct; 🚼) 🅿 Broadford has

several places to eat but one really stands out: Creelers is a small, bustling, no-frills restaurant that serves some of the best seafood on Skye. The house speciality is traditional Marseille *bouillabaisse* (a rich, spicy seafood stew). Best to book ahead.

ℹ Getting There & Away

BOAT

Despite the bridge, there are still a couple of ferry links between Skye and the mainland. Ferries also operate from Uig on Skye to the Outer Hebrides.

The **CalMac** (☑ 0800 066 5000; www.calmac. co.uk; per person/car £2.80/9.40) ferry between Mallaig and Armadale (30 minutes, eight daily Monday to Saturday, five to seven on Sunday) is very popular on weekends and in July and August. Book ahead if you're travelling by car.

Skye Ferry (www.skyeferry.co.uk; car with up to 4 passengers £15; ☺ Easter–mid Oct) runs a tiny vessel (six cars only) on the short Kylerhea to Glenelg crossing (five minutes, every 20 minutes). The ferry operates from 10am to 6pm daily (till 7pm June to August).

BUS

There are buses from Glasgow to Portree (£42, seven hours, three daily), plus a service from Inverness to Portree (£25, 3¼ hours, three daily).

SURVIVAL GUIDE

ℹ Directory A–Z

ACCOMMODATION

Accommodation can be difficult to find during holidays (especially around Easter and New Year) and major events (such as the Edinburgh Festival). In summer, popular spots (York, Canterbury, Bath etc) get very crowded, so booking ahead is essential. Local TICs often provide an accommodation booking service for a small fee.

SLEEPING PRICE RANGES

Reviews of places to stay use the following price ranges, all based on double room with private bathroom in high season. Hotels in London are more expensive than the rest of the country, so have different price ranges.

£ less than £65 (London less than £100)

££ £65–130 (London £100–200)

£££ more than £130 (London more than £200)

Hostels There are two types of hostels in Britain: those run by the **Youth Hostels Association** (www.yha.org.uk) and **Scottish Youth Hostels Association** (www.syha.org.uk), and independent hostels, most of which are listed in the **Independent Hostels Guide** (www. independenthostelguide.co.uk). The simplest hostels cost around £15 per person per night. Larger hostels with more facilities are £18 to £30. London's YHA hostels cost from £32.

B&Bs The B&B (bed and breakfast) is a great British institution. At smaller places it's pretty much a room in somebody's house; larger places may be called a 'guesthouse' (halfway between a B&B and a full hotel). Prices start from around £30 per person for a simple bedroom and shared bathroom; for around £35 to £45 per person you get a private bathroom – either down the hall or an en suite.

Hotels There's a massive choice of hotels in Britain, from small town houses to grand country mansions, from no-frills locations to boutique hideaways. At the bargain end, single/double rooms cost from £45/60. Move up the scale and you'll pay £100/150 or beyond.

Camping Campsites range from farmers' fields with a tap and basic toilet, costing from £5 per person per night, to smarter affairs with hot showers and many other facilities, charging up to £15. You usually need all your own equipment.

ACTIVITIES

Britain is a great destination for outdoor enthusiasts. Walking and cycling are the most popular activities – you can do them on a whim, and they're the perfect way to open up some beautiful corners of the country.

Cycling

Compact Britain is an excellent destination to explore by bike. Popular regions to tour include southwest England, the Yorkshire Dales, Derbyshire's Peak District, Mid-Wales and the Scottish Borders. Bike-hire outlets are widespread; rates are typically around £15 per day or £80 per week.

The 10,000-mile **National Cycle Network** (www.nationalcyclenetwork.org.uk) is a web of quiet roads and traffic-free tracks that pass through busy cities and remote rural areas.

Sustrans (www.sustrans.org.uk) is another useful organisation, and publishes a wide range of maps, guides and planning tools.

Walking & Hiking

Hiking is a hugely popular pastime in Britain, especially in scenic areas such as Snowdonia, the Lake District, the Yorkshire Dales and the Scottish Highlands. Various long-distance routes cross the countryside, including the **Coast to Coast** (www.wainwright.org.uk/coasttocoast. html), the **Cotswold Way** (www.nationaltrail. co.uk/cotswold), the **West Highland Way** (www.

west-highland-way.co.uk) and the **South West Coast Path** (www.southwestcoastpath.com).

The **Ramblers Association** (www.ramblers.org.uk) is the country's leading walkers' organisation.

GAY & LESBIAN TRAVELLERS

Britain is a generally tolerant place for gays and lesbians. London, Manchester and Brighton have flourishing gay scenes, and in other sizeable cities (even some small towns), you'll find communities not entirely in the closet. That said, you'll still find pockets of homophobic hostility in some areas. Resources include the following:

Diva (www.divamag.co.uk)

Gay Times (www.gaytimes.co.uk)

Switchboard LGBT+ Helpline (www.switchboard.lgbt; ☑ 0300 330 0630)

INTERNET RESOURCES

Visit Britain (www.visitbritain.com) Comprehensive national tourism website.

Traveline (www.traveline.org.uk) Timetables and travel advice for public transport across Britain.

Lonely Planet (www.lonelyplanet.com/great-britain) Destination info, hotel bookings, traveller forum and more.

MONEY

➡ The currency of Britain is the pound sterling (£). Paper money (notes) comes in £5, £10, £20 and £50 denominations, although some shops don't accept £50 notes.

➡ ATMs, often called cash machines, are easy to find in towns and cities.

➡ Most banks and some post offices offer currency exchange.

➡ Visa and MasterCard credit and debit cards are widely accepted in Britain. Nearly everywhere uses a 'Chip and PIN' system (instead of signing).

➡ Smaller businesses may charge a fee for credit-card use, and some take cash or cheque only.

➡ Tipping is not obligatory. A 10% to 15% tip is fine for restaurants, cafes, taxi drivers and pub meals; if you order drinks and food at the bar, there's no need to tip.

➡ Travellers cheques are rarely used.

OPENING HOURS

Standard opening hours:

Banks 9.30am–4pm or 5pm Monday to Friday; main branches 9.30am–1pm Saturday

Post offices 9am–5pm (5.30pm or 6pm in cities) Monday to Friday, 9am–12.30pm Saturday (main branches to 5pm)

Pubs Noon–11pm Monday to Saturday (many till midnight or 1am Friday and Saturday, especially in Scotland), 12.30pm–11pm Sunday

Restaurants Lunch is noon–3pm, dinner 6pm–9pm or 10pm (or later in cities)

Shops 9am–5.30pm (or 6pm in cities) Monday to Saturday, and often 11am–5pm Sunday. Big city convenience stores open 24/7

PUBLIC HOLIDAYS

In many areas of Britain, bank holidays are just for the banks – many businesses and visitor attractions stay open.

New Year's Day 1 January (plus 2 January in Scotland)

Easter March/April (Good Friday to Easter Monday inclusive)

May Day First Monday in May

Spring Bank Holiday Last Monday in May

Summer Bank Holiday Last Monday in August

Christmas Day 25 December

Boxing Day 26 December

COUNTRY FACTS

Area 88,500 sq miles

Capitals London (England and the United Kingdom), Cardiff (Wales), Edinburgh (Scotland)

Country Code ☑ 44

Currency Pound sterling (£)

Emergency ☑ 999 or ☑ 112

Languages English, Welsh, Scottish Gaelic

Money ATMs widespread; credit cards widely accepted

Population 61.4 million

Visas Schengen rules do not apply

SCHOOL HOLIDAYS

Roads get busy and hotel prices go up during school holidays.

Easter Holiday Week before and week after Easter.

Summer Holiday Third week of July to first week of September.

Christmas Holiday Mid-December to first week of January.

There are also three week-long 'half-term' school holidays – usually late February (or early March), late May and late October. These vary between Scotland, England and Wales.

SAFE TRAVEL

Britain is a remarkably safe country, but crime is not unknown in London and other cities.

➡ Watch out for pickpockets and hustlers in crowded areas popular with tourists, such as around Westminster Bridge in London.

➡ When travelling by tube, tram or urban train services at night, choose a carriage containing other people.

➡ Many town centres can be rowdy on Friday and Saturday nights when the pubs and clubs are emptying.

➡ Unlicensed minicabs – a bloke with a car earning money on the side – operate in large cities, and are worth avoiding unless you know what you're doing.

TELEPHONE

The UK uses the GSM 900/1800 network, which covers the rest of Europe, Australia and New Zealand, but isn't compatible with the North American GSM 1900. Most modern mobiles can function on both networks – but check before you leave home just in case.

Though roaming charges within Britain and the EU were entirely eliminated in June 2017, other international roaming charges can be prohibitively high.

Area codes in the UK do not have a standard format or length (eg Edinburgh 0131, London 020, Ambleside 015394). In our reviews, area codes and phone numbers have been listed together, separated by a hyphen.

➡ Dial ☎100 for an operator and ☎155 for an international operator as well as reverse-charge (collect) calls.

➡ To call outside the UK, dial ☎00, then the country code (1 for USA, 61 for Australia etc), the area code (you usually drop the initial zero) and the number.

➡ For directory enquiries, a host of agencies offer this service – numbers include ☎118 118, ☎118 500 and ☎118 811 – but fees are extortionate (around £6 for a 45-second call); search online for free at www.thephonebook.bt.com.

TIME

Britain is on GMT/UTC. The clocks go forward for 'summer time' one hour at the end of March and go back at the end of October. The 24-hour clock is used for transport timetables.

VISAS

➡ Generally not needed for stays of up to six months. Not a member of the Schengen Zone.

➡ If you're a citizen of the EEA (European Economic Area) nations or Switzerland, you don't need a visa to enter or work in Britain – you can enter using your national identity card.

➡ Currently, if you're a citizen of Australia, Canada, New Zealand, Japan, Israel, the USA and several other countries, you can stay for up to six months (no visa required), but are not allowed to work.

➡ For more info see www.gov.uk/check-uk-visa.

🛈 Getting There & Away

AIR
London Airports

London is served by five airports; Heathrow and Gatwick are the busiest.

Gatwick (LGW; www.gatwickairport.com) Britain's number-two airport, mainly for international flights, 30 miles south of central London.

London City (LCY; www.londoncityairport.com)

London Heathrow Airport (LHR; www.heathrow airport.com) The UK's major hub welcoming flights from all over the world.

Luton (LTN; www.london-luton.co.uk) Some 35 miles north of central London, well known as a holiday-flight airport.

Stansted (STN; www.stanstedairport.com) About 35 miles northeast of central London, mainly handling charter and budget European flights.

Regional Airports

Bristol Airport (BRS; www.bristolairport.co.uk) Flights from all over Europe.

Cardiff Airport (CWL; www.cardiff-airport. com) 12 miles southwest of Cardiff, past Barry.

Edinburgh Airport (EDI; www. edinburghair port.com) Numerous flights to other parts of the UK, Ireland and mainland Europe. Daily flights to Inverness, Wick, Orkney, Shetland and Stornoway.

Glasgow International Airport (GLA; www. glasgowairport.com) Handles domestic traffic and international flights.

Liverpool John Lennon Airport (LPL; www. liverpoolairport.com) Serves a variety of UK and international destinations.

Manchester Airport (MHT; www.manchester airport.co.uk) The largest airport outside London with flights to the US and Canada.

Newcastle International Airport (NCL; www. newcastleairport.com) Direct services to many UK and European cities.

LAND
Bus & Coach

The international network **Eurolines** (www. eurolines.com) connects a huge number of European destinations via the Channel Tunnel or ferry crossings.

Services to and from Britain are operated by **National Express** (www.nationalexpress.com).

Train

High-speed **Eurostar** (www.eurostar.com) passenger services shuttle at least 10 times daily between London and Paris (2½ hours) or Brussels (two hours) via the Channel Tunnel. The normal one-way fare between London and Paris/Brussels costs around £145; advance booking and off-peak travel gets cheaper fares as low as £29 one-way.

Vehicles use the **Eurotunnel** (www.eurotunnel.com) at Folkestone in England or Calais in France. The trains run four times an hour from 6am to 10pm, then hourly. The journey takes 35 minutes. The one-way cost for a car and passengers is between £75 and £100 depending on time of day; promotional fares often bring it down to £59 or less.

Travelling between Ireland and Britain, the main train–ferry–train route is Dublin to London, via Dun Laoghaire and Holyhead. Ferries also run between Rosslare and Fishguard or Pembroke (Wales), with train connections on either side.

SEA

The main ferry routes between Britain and mainland Europe include Dover to Calais or Boulogne (France), Harwich to Hook of Holland (Netherlands), Hull to Zeebrugge (Belgium) or Rotterdam (Netherlands), and Portsmouth to Santander or Bilbao (Spain). Routes to and from Ireland include Holyhead to Dun Laoghaire.

Competition from the Eurotunnel and budget airlines means ferry operators discount heavily at certain times of year. The short cross-channel routes such as Dover to Calais or Boulogne can be as low as £45 for a car plus two passengers, although around £75 to £105 is more likely. If you're a foot passenger, or cycling, fares cost about £30 to £50 each way.

Broker sites covering all routes and options include www.ferrybooker.com and www.directferries.co.uk. Ferry companies include the following:

Brittany Ferries (www.brittany-ferries.com)
DFDS Seaways (www.dfds.co.uk)
Irish Ferries (www.irishferries.com)
P&O Ferries (www.poferries.com)
Stena Line (www.stenaline.com)

ESSENTIAL FOOD & DRINK

Britain once had a reputation for bad food, but the nation has enjoyed something of a culinary revolution in the last decade or so, and you can often find fine dining based on fresh local produce.

Fish and chips Long-standing favourite, best sampled in coastal towns.

Haggis Scottish icon, mainly offal and oatmeal, traditionally served with 'tatties and neeps' (potatoes and turnips).

Sandwich Global snack today, but an English invention from the 18th century.

Laverbread Laver is a type of seaweed, mixed with oatmeal and fried to create this traditional Welsh speciality.

Ploughman's lunch Bread and cheese – pub menu regular, perfect with a pint.

Roast beef & Yorkshire pudding Traditional lunch on Sunday for the English.

Cornish pasty Savoury pastry, southwest speciality, now available countrywide.

Real ale Traditionally brewed beer, flavoured with malt and hops and served at room temperature.

Scotch whisky Spirit distilled from malted and fermented barley, then aged in oak barrels for at least three years.

CONNECTIONS

The quickest way to Europe from Britain is via the Channel Tunnel, which has direct Eurostar rail services from London to Paris and Brussels. Ferries sail from southern England to French ports in a couple of hours; other routes connect eastern England to the Netherlands, Germany and northern Spain, and Ireland from southwest Scotland and Wales.

ⓘ Getting Around

For getting around Britain, your first choice is car or public transport. Having your own car makes the best use of time and helps reach remote places, but rental, fuel costs and parking can be expensive – so public transport is often the better way to go.

Cheapest but slowest are long-distance buses (called coaches in Britain). Trains are faster but much more expensive.

AIR

Britain's domestic air companies include the following:

British Airways (www.britishairways.com)
EasyJet (www.easyjet.com)
FlyBe (www.flybe.com)
Loganair (www.loganair.co.uk)
Ryanair (www.ryanair.com)

On most shorter routes (eg London to Newcastle, or Manchester to Bristol), it's often faster to take the train once airport downtime is factored in.

BUS

Long-distance buses (coaches) nearly always offer the cheapest way to get around. Many towns have separate stations for local buses and intercity coaches; make sure you're in the right one.

National Express (www.nationalexpress.com) is England's main coach operator. North of the border, **Scottish Citylink** (www.citylink.co.uk) is the leading coach company. Tickets are cheaper if you book in advance and travel at quieter times. As a rough guide, a 200-mile trip (eg London to York) will cost around £15 to £25 if booked a few days in advance.

Also offering cheap fares is **Megabus** (www.megabus.com), which serves about 30 destinations around Britain.

Bus Passes

National Express offers discount passes to full-time students and under-26s, called **Young Persons Coachcards**. They cost £10 and give 30% off standard adult fares. Also available are coachcards for people over 60 years, families and travellers with a disability.

For touring the country, National Express offers **Brit Xplorer** passes, allowing unlimited travel for seven days (£79), 14 days (£139) and 28 days (£219).

CAR & MOTORCYCLE

Most overseas driving licences are valid in Britain for up to 12 months from the date of entry.

Rental

Car rental is expensive in Britain; you'll pay from around £130 per week for the smallest model, or £190 per week and upward for a medium-sized car (including insurance and unlimited mileage). All the major players including Avis, Hertz and Budget operate here.

Using a rental-broker site such as **UK Car Hire** (www.ukcarhire.net) or **Kayak** (www.kayak.com) can help find bargains.

It's illegal to drive a car or motorbike in Britain without (at least) third-party insurance. This is included with all rental cars.

Road Rules

The *Highway Code*, available in bookshops (or at www.gov.uk/highway-code), contains everything you need to know about Britain's road rules. The main ones to remember:

➡ Always drive on the left.

➡ Give way to your right at junctions and roundabouts.

➡ Always use the left-hand lane on motorways and dual carriageways, unless overtaking (passing).

➡ Wear seat belts in cars and crash helmets on motorcycles.

➡ Don't use a mobile phone while driving.

➡ Don't drink and drive; the maximum blood-alcohol level allowed is 80mg/100mL (0.08%) in England and Wales, 50mg/100mL (0.05%) in Scotland.

➡ Yellow lines (single or double) along the edge of the road indicate parking restrictions, red lines mean no stopping whatsoever.

➡ Speed limits are 30mph in built-up areas, 60mph on main roads, and 70mph on motorways and dual carriageways.

TRAIN

About 20 different companies operate train services in Britain, while Network Rail operates track and stations. For some passengers this system can be confusing at first, but information and ticket-buying services are mostly centralised. If you have to change trains, or use two or more train operators, you still buy one ticket – valid for the whole journey. The main railcards and passes are also accepted by all train operators.

National Rail Enquiries (www.nationalrail. co.uk) provides booking and timetable information for Britain's entire rail network.

Classes

Rail travel has two classes: 1st and standard. Travelling 1st class costs around 50% more than standard. At weekends some train operators offer 'upgrades' to 1st class for an extra £5 to £25 on top of your standard class fare, payable on the spot.

Costs & Reservations

The earlier you book, the cheaper it gets. You can also save if you travel 'off-peak' (ie the days and times that aren't busy). If you buy online, you can have the ticket posted (UK addresses only), or collect it from station machines on the day of travel.

There are three main fare types:

Anytime Buy anytime, travel anytime – usually the most expensive option.

Off-peak Buy anytime, travel off-peak (what is off-peak depends on the journey).

Advance Buy in advance, travel only on specific trains (usually the cheapest option).

Train Passes

If you're staying in Britain for a while, passes known as railcards (www.railcard.co.uk) are available:

16–25 Railcard For those aged 16 to 25, or a full-time UK student.

> ### TRAVELINE
>
> **Traveline** (www.traveline.info) is a very useful information service covering bus, coach, taxi and train services nationwide.

Senior Railcard For anyone aged over 60.

Family & Friends Railcard Covers up to four adults and four children travelling together.

Railcards cost £30 (valid for one year, available from major stations or online) and get 33% discount on most train fares, except those already heavily discounted. With the Family card, adults get 33% and children get 60% discounts, so the fee is easily repaid in a couple of journeys.

The following train passes are available:

Regional Passes Various local train passes are available covering specific areas and lines – ask at a local train station to get an idea of what's available.

National Passes For country-wide travel, **BritRail** (www.britrail.net) passes are available for visitors from overseas. They must be bought in your country of origin (not in Britain) from a specialist travel agency. Available in seven different versions (eg England only; Scotland only; all Britain; UK and Ireland) for periods from four to 30 days.

Bulgaria

Best Places to Eat

➔ MoMa Bulgarian Food & Wine (p234)

➔ Shtastliveca (p243)

➔ Rosé (p246)

➔ Made In Home (p234)

➔ Memory (p240)

Best Places to Stay

➔ Hotel-Mehana Gurko (p242)

➔ At Renaissance Square (p239)

➔ Canapé Connection (p231)

➔ Hostel Old Plovdiv (p239)

➔ Yo Ho Hostel (p244)

Why Go?

Soul-stirring mountains, golden beaches and cities that hum with music and art. There's a lot to love about Bulgaria (България): no wonder the Greeks, Romans, Byzantines and Turks all fought to claim it as their own. Billed as the oldest nation on the continent, Bulgaria is rich with ancient treasure. The mysterious Thracians left behind dazzling hauls of gold and silver, and tombs that can be explored to this day. The Romans built cities of breathtaking scale, the bathhouses, walls and amphitheatres of which sit nonchalantly in the midst of modern cities.

Centuries later, Bulgaria still beguiles with its come-hither coastline and fertile valleys laden with vines and roses. Plovdiv is the European Capital of Culture for 2019, Sofia has cool cred to rival any major metropolis, and lively Black Sea resorts teem with modern-day pleasure pilgrims.

When to Go
Sofia

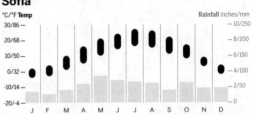

Feb Pop your cork at Melnik's Golden Grape Festival.

Jun Celebrate the sweetest harvest at Kazanlâk's Rose Festival.

Jul–Sep Spend lazy days on the Black Sea beaches and nights at Bulgaria's best clubs.

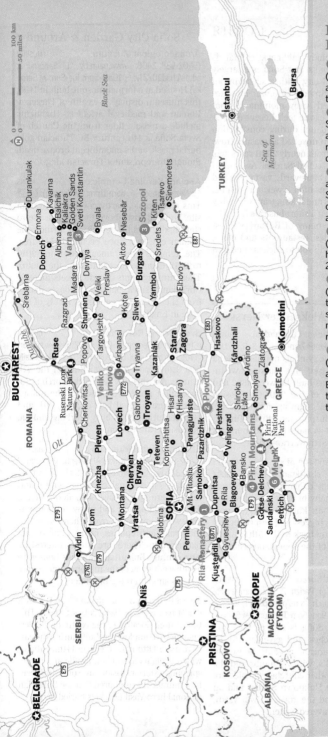

Bulgaria Highlights

1 Rila Monastery (p237) Exploring artistic and religious treasures.

2 Plovdiv (p000) Soaking up the city's ancient ambience and revitalised artistic quarter.

3 Sozopol (p247) and **Varna** (p244) Sun-worshipping or clubbing all night long at Black Sea resorts.

4 Pirin Mountains (p237) Skiing or hiking among the 2000m peaks.

5 Veliko Târnovo (p242) Visiting the Tsars' medieval stronghold in this monumental, riverside town.

6 Melnik (p237) Sipping a glass or three of Bulgarian *vino* in this photogenic wine town.

SOFIA СОФИЯ

02 / POP 1.2 MILLION

Bulgaria's pleasingly laid-back capital is no grand metropolis, but Sofia is a largely modern, youthful city, with a scattering of onion-domed churches, Ottoman mosques and stubborn Red Army monuments that lend an eclectic, exotic feel. Recent excavation work carried out during construction of the city's metro unveiled a treasure trove of Roman ruins from nearly 2000 years ago, when the city was called 'Serdica'. Away from the buildings and boulevards, vast parks and manicured gardens offer a welcome respite, and the ski slopes and hiking trails of mighty Mt Vitosha are just a short bus ride from the centre. Home to many of Bulgaria's finest museums, galleries, restaurants and clubs, Sofia may persuade you to stick around and explore further.

Sights

Ploshtad Aleksander Nevski

★ **Aleksander Nevski Cathedral** CHURCH
(pl Aleksander Nevski; ⊙ 7am-7pm; M Sofiyski Universitet) One of *the* symbols not just of Sofia but of Bulgaria itself, this massive, awe-inspiring church was built between 1882 and 1912 in memory of the 200,000 Russian soldiers who died fighting for Bulgaria's independence during the Russo-Turkish War (1877–78). It is named in honour of a 13th-century Russian warrior-prince.

Aleksander Nevski Crypt GALLERY
(Museum of Icons; pl Aleksander Nevski; adult/child 6/3 lv; ⊙ 10am-5.30pm Tue-Sun; M Sofiyski Universitet) Originally built as a final resting place for Bulgarian kings, this crypt now houses Bulgaria's biggest and best collection of icons, stretching back to the 5th century. Enter to the left of the eponymous church's main entrance.

★ **Sveta Sofia Church** CHURCH
(02-987 0971; ul Parizh 2; museum adult/child 6/2 lv; ⊙ church 7am-7pm Apr-Oct, to 6pm Nov-Mar, museum 9am-5pm Tue-Sun; M Sofiyski Universitet) Sveta Sofia is one of the capital's oldest churches, and gave the city its name. A subterranean museum houses an ancient necropolis, with 56 tombs and the remains of four other churches. Outside are the Tomb of the Unknown Soldier and an eternal flame, and the grave of Ivan Vazov, Bulgaria's most revered writer.

Sofia City Garden & Around

Archaeological Museum MUSEUM
(02-988 2406; www.naim.bg; ul Saborna 2; adult/child 10/2 lv; ⊙ 10am-5pm Tue-Sun; M Serdika) Housed in a former mosque built in 1496, this museum displays a wealth of Thracian, Roman and medieval artefacts. Highlights include a mosaic floor from the Church of Sveta Sofia, a 4th-century BC Thracian gold burial mask, and a magnificent bronze head, thought to represent a Thracian king.

Ancient Serdica Complex RUINS
(pl Nezavisimost; ⊙ 6am-11pm; M Serdika) FREE This remarkable, partly covered excavation site, situated just above the Serdika metro station, displays the remains of Serdica, the Roman city that once occupied this area. The remains were unearthed from 2010 to 2012 during construction of the metro. There are fragments of eight streets, an early Christian basilica, baths and houses dating from the 4th to 6th centuries. Plenty of signage in English.

Sveti Georgi Rotunda CHURCH
(Church of St George; 02-980 9216; www.svgeorgi-rotonda.com; bul Dondukov 2; ⊙ services daily 8am, 9am & 5pm; M Serdika) Built in the 4th century AD, this tiny red-brick church is Sofia's oldest preserved building. The murals inside were painted between the 10th and 14th centuries. It's a busy, working church, but visitors are welcome.

Ethnographical Museum MUSEUM
(02-988 1974; pl Knyaz Al Batenberg 1; adult/child 3/1 lv; ⊙ 10am-6pm Tue-Sun; M Serdika) Displays on regional costumes, crafts and folklore are spread over two floors of the former royal palace, and many of the rooms are worth pausing over themselves for their marble fireplaces, mirrors and ornate plasterwork. There are some interesting 19th-century Bulgarian paintings housed in an adjacent wing of the museum, and there's a crafts shop on the ground floor.

Sveta Petka Samardzhiiska Church CHURCH
(bul Maria Luisa 2; ⊙ 9am-5pm; M Serdika) This tiny church, located in the centre of the Serdika metro complex, was built during the early years of Ottoman rule (late 14th century), which explains its sunken profile and inconspicuous exterior. Inside are some 16th-century murals. It's rumoured that the Bulgarian national hero Vasil Levski is buried here.

Sveta Nedelya Cathedral — CHURCH
(🕿02-987 5748; pl Sveta Nedelya; ⊗8am-6pm; Ⓜ Serdika) Completed in 1863, this magnificent domed church is one of the city's major landmarks, and is noted for its rich, Byzantine-style murals. The church was targeted by communists on 16 April 1925 in a failed bomb attack aimed at assassinating Tsar Boris III.

Museum of Socialist Art — MUSEUM
(🕿02-980 0093; ul Lachezar Stanchev 7, Iztok; 6 lv; ⊗10am-5.30pm Tue-Sun; Ⓜ GM Dimitrov) If you wondered where all those unwanted statues of Lenin ended up, you'll find some here, along with the red star from atop Sofia's Party House (pl Nezavisimost; Ⓜ Serdika). There's a gallery of paintings, where you'll rejoice in catchy titles such as *Youth Meeting at Kilifarevo Village to Send Worker-Peasant Delegation to the USSR,* and stirring old propaganda films are shown.

☞ Tours

Free Sofia Tour — WALKING
(🕿0988920461; www.freesofiatour.com; cnr ul Alabin & bul Vitosha; ⊗11am & 6pm; Ⓜ Serdika) FREE Explore Sofia's sights in the company of friendly and enthusiastic English-speaking young locals on this two-hour guided walk. No reservation is needed; just show up outside the Palace of Justice.

Balkan Bites — FOOD & DRINK
(🕿0877613992; www.balkanbites.bg; by donation; ⊗tours 2pm; Ⓜ Sofiyski Universitet, ⓐ9) This two-hour guided walking tour focuses on food and includes tastings and drinks at restaurants around town. The basic tour is free but a donation is expected. Walks depart at 2pm from the statue of Stefan Stambolov in Crystal Park.

New Sofia Pub Crawl — TOURS
(🕿0877613992; www.thenewsofiapubcrawl.com; tours 20 lv; ⊗9pm-1am; Ⓜ Sofiyski Universitet, ⓐ9) Explore Sofia's secret haunts on this nightly knees-up. Expect lots of good chat and surprising insights into the social side of the city (plus the odd free drink). Meet by the statue of Stefan Stambolov in Crystal Park.

🛏 Sleeping

Accommodation in Sofia tends to be more expensive than elsewhere in Bulgaria, with hotel prices comparable to those in other large European cities. There are several modern hostels that offer dorm-bed accommodation (and often a couple of private rooms), plus free wi-fi, shared kitchens, and other perks.

Art Hostel — HOSTEL €
(🕿02-987 0545; www.art-hostel.com; ul Angel Kânchev 21a; dm/s/d from 20/47/66 lv; @🛜; ⓐ12) This bohemian hostel stands out from the crowd with its summertime art exhibitions, live music, dance performances and more. Dorms are appropriately arty and bright; private rooms are airy and very welcoming. There's a great basement bar and peaceful little garden at the back.

★Canapé Connection — GUESTHOUSE €
(🕿02-441 6373; www.canapeconnection.com; ul William Gladstone 12a; s/d from 50/64 lv; 🛜🛗; ⓐ1, 6, 7) Formerly a hostel, Canapé reinvented itself as a guesthouse in 2016, retaining its same attention to cleanliness and a refreshingly simple, rustic design. The six rooms are divided into singles and doubles, with a larger room upstairs to accommodate families. There's a quiet garden outside to relax in. Note there's no breakfast, but you'll find several coffee places nearby.

★Hotel Niky — HOTEL €€
(🕿02-952 3058; www.hotel-niky.com; ul Neofit Rilski 16; r/ste from 90/130 lv; P🐾❄🛜🛗; Ⓜ NDK, ⓐ1) Offering excellent value and a good city-centre location, Niky has comfortable rooms and gleaming bathrooms; the smart little suites come with kitchenettes. It's a very popular place and frequently full; be sure to book ahead.

ITINERARIES

One Week
Take a full day to hit Sofia's main attractions, then take the bus to Veliko Târnovo for a few days of sightseeing and hiking. For the rest of the week, head to Varna for some sea and sand, or veer south to the ancient beach towns of Nesebâr and Sozopol.

Two Weeks
Spend a few extra days in Sofia, adding in a day trip to Rila Monastery, then catch a bus to Plovdiv to wander the cobbled lanes of the Old Town. From there, take the mountain air in majestic Veliko Târnovo. Make for the coast, with a few nights in Varna and lively Sozopol.

BULGARIA SOFIA

Sofia

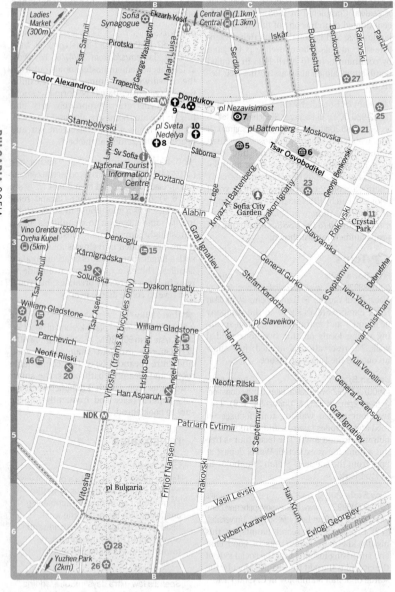

Hotel Les Fleurs BOUTIQUE HOTEL **€€€**
(☎02-810 0800; www.lesfleurshotel.com; bul Vitosha 21; r from 220 lv; P⊖✳☎; MSerdika, ☐10)
You can hardly miss this very central hotel with gigantic blooms on its facade. The flow-ery motif is continued in the large, carefully styled rooms, and there's a very good restaurant on-site. The location, right at the start of the pedestrian-only stretch of bul Vitosha, is ideal.

✕ Eating

Sofia has some of the country's best restaurants, including traditional and international cuisines. In summer, cafes occupy every piece of garden and footpath, the best ones offering a refined setting for cocktails and cakes. Kiosks around town sell tasty local fast food such as *banitsa* (cheese pasties) and *palachinki* (pancakes).

Vila Rosich BAKERY €
(☑02-954 3072; www.vilarosiche.com; ul Neofit Rilski 26; sandwiches & cakes 5-7 lv; ☺8am-9pm; ☎🖉; Ⓜ︎NDK) Step into the back garden of this hidden bakery and enter what feels like a secret world of fresh-made breads and cakes. It's a perfect spot for an afternoon sweet, or a light cheese-stuffed croissant sandwich.

★**MoMa Bulgarian
Food & Wine** BULGARIAN €€

(☑0885622020; www.moma-restaurant.com; ul Solunska 28; mains 8-22 lv; ⊘11am-10pm; 🛜🍴; Ⓜ Serdika) An update on the traditional *mehana* (taverna), serving typical Bulgarian foods, such as grilled meats and meatballs, and wines, but in a more modern and understated interior. The result is one of the best nights out in town. Start off with a shot of *rakia* (Bulgarian brandy) and a salad, and move on to the ample main courses. Book ahead – this restaurant is popular.

★**Made In Home** INTERNATIONAL €€

(☑0876884014; ul Angel Kânchev 30a; mains 12-22 lv; ⊘11am-9pm Mon, to 10pm Tue-Sun; 🛜🍴; Ⓜ NDK) Sofia's very popular entrant into the worldwide, locally sourced, slow-food trend (the name refers to the fact that all items are made in-house). The cooking is eclectic, with dollops of Middle Eastern (eg hummus) and Turkish items, as well as ample vegetarian and vegan offerings. The playfully rustic interior feels straight out of a Winnie-the-Pooh book. Reservations essential.

Manastirska Magernitsa BULGARIAN €€

(☑02-980 3883; www.magernitsa.com; ul Han Asparuh 67; mains 8-18 lv; ⊘11-2am; Ⓜ NDK) This traditional *mehana* (tavern) is among the best places in Sofia to sample authentic Bulgarian cuisine. The enormous menu features recipes collected from monasteries across the country, with dishes such as 'drunken rabbit' stewed in wine, as well as salads, fish, pork and game options. Portions are generous and the service attentive. Dine in the garden in nice weather.

🍷 **Drinking & Nightlife**

Raketa Rakia Bar BAR

(☑02-444 6111; ul Yanko Sakazov 15-17; ⊘11am-midnight; 🛜; 🚃11, Ⓜ Sofiyski Universitet) Unsurprisingly, this rakish communist-era retro bar has a huge selection of *rakia* (Bulgarian brandy) on hand; before you start working your way down the list, line your stomach with meat-and-cream-heavy snacks and meals. Reservations essential.

One More Bar BAR

(☑0882539592; ul Shishman 12; ⊘8.30am-2.30am; 🛜; Ⓜ Sofiyski Universitet) Inside a gorgeous old house, this shabby-chic hot spot wouldn't be out of place in Melbourne or Manhattan: an extensive cocktail list, a delightful summer garden and jazzy background music add to its cosmopolitan appeal.

DaDa Cultural Bar BAR

(☑0877062455; http://blog.dadaculturalbar.eu; ul Georgi Benkovski 10; ⊘24hr; 🛜; Ⓜ Serdika, 🚃20, 22) A local institution, DaDa bar is far more than a place to drink. The mission here is culture, and expect to find live music, art installations, readings or happenings. The website usually has an up-to-date program. Friendly staff and a welcoming vibe.

☆ **Entertainment**

If you read Bulgarian, or can decipher some Cyrillic, *Programata* is the most comprehensive source of entertainment listings; otherwise check out its excellent English-language website, www.programata.bg. You can book tickets online at www.ticketpro.bg.

Live Music

RockIT LIVE MUSIC

(☑0888666991; ul Georgi Benkovski 14; ⊘9pm-4am Mon-Sat; Ⓜ Serdika, 🚃20, 22) If you're into rock and metal, get your horns up here. This huge two-level building shakes beneath the weight of heavy live bands, DJs, and lots and lots of hair.

Sofia Live Club LIVE MUSIC

(☑0886661045; www.sofialiveclub.com; pl Bulgaria 1; ⊘8pm-7am; Ⓜ NDK) This slick venue, located in the National Palace of Culture (NDK), is the city's largest live-music club. All swished up in cabaret style, it hosts local and international jazz, alternative, world-music and rock acts.

Bulgaria Hall CLASSICAL MUSIC

(☑tickets 02-987 7656; www.sofiaphilharmonie. bg; ul Aksakov 1; ⊘box office 9.30am-2.30pm, 3-7.30pm Mon-Fri, 9.30am-2.30pm Sat; Ⓜ Serdika) Home of the excellent Sofia Philharmonic Orchestra.

Performing Arts

Ticket prices for theatre and live music vary enormously. For shows at the Opera House or the Ivan Vazov National Theatre, you might pay anything from 10 lv to 30 lv; shows at the National Palace of Culture (NDK) vary much more, with tickets costing from 30 lv to 80 lv for international acts and around 10 lv to 30 lv for local ones.

National Palace of Culture CONCERT VENUE

(NDK; ☑02-916 6300; www.ndk.bg; pl Bulgaria; ⊘ticket office 10am-8pm; 🛜; Ⓜ NDK) The NDK (as it's usually called) has 15 halls and is the country's largest cultural complex. It maintains a regular program of events throughout the year, including film screenings, trade shows and big-name international music acts.

National Opera House
OPERA

(☑ tickets 02-987 1366; www.operasofia.bg; bul Dondukov 30; ☺ box office 9am-2pm & 2.30-7pm Mon-Fri, 11am-7pm Sat, 11am-4pm Sun; ☒ 20, 22) Opened in 1953, this monumental edifice is the venue for classical opera and ballet performances, as well as special concerts for children. Enter from ul Vrabcha.

Cultural Centre G8
CINEMA

(☑ 02-995 0080; www.g8cinema.com; ul William Gladstone 8; tickets 6-8 lv; ☺ 9am-11pm; ☒ 1, 6, 7) This trendy, art-house cinema does triple duty as a contemporary art gallery and secluded, garden drinking spot.

🔒 Shopping

Bulevard Vitosha is Sofia's main shopping street, mostly featuring international brand-name boutiques interspersed with restaurants.

Vino Orenda
WINE

(☑ 0889623606; www.vinoorenda.com; bul Makedonia 50a; ☺ 10.30am-7.30pm Mon-Fri; ☒ 4, 5) Small, knowledgeable wine shop offering products from a variety of independent producers around the country. The engaging owner is more than happy to guide you through your options.

Centre of Folk Arts & Crafts
GIFTS & SOUVENIRS

(☑ 02-989 6416; www.craftshop-bg.com; ul Parizh 4; ☺ 9.30am-6.30pm Mon-Sat, by appointment Sun; ☒ Serdika, ☒ 20, 22) Typical Bulgarian souvenirs such as hand-woven rugs, pottery, silver jewellery, woodcarvings and CDs of Bulgarian music are available in this crowded shop, though prices are rather high. There's another branch inside the Royal Palace, at the exit from the Ethnographic Museum.

Ladies' Market
MARKET

(Zhenski Pazar; ul Stefan Stambolov; ☺ dawn-dusk; ☒ Lavov most, ☒ 20, 22) Stretching several blocks between ul Ekzarh Yosif and bul Slivnitsa, this is Sofia's biggest market for fresh produce, meats, fish, cheeses and spices, with lots of Turkish items tossed into the mix. It's a great spot for self-caterers. Beware pickpockets.

ℹ️ Information

National Tourist Information Centre (☑ 02-933 5826; www.bulgariatravel.org; pl Sveta Nedelya 1; ☺ 9am-5pm Mon-Fri; ☒ Serdika) The office is hidden near a small side street, a few steps southwest of pl Sveta Nedelya.

Sofia Tourist Information Centre (☑ 02-491 8344; www.info-sofia.bg; Sofiyski Universitet metro underpass; ☺ 8am-8pm Mon-Fri, 10am-6pm Sat & Sun; ☒ Sofiyski Universitet) Lots of free leaflets and maps, and helpful English-speaking staff.

Pirogov Hospital (☑ emergency 02-915 4411; www.pirogov.bg; bul General Totleben 21; ☒ 4, 5) Sofia's main public hospital for emergencies.

ℹ️ Getting There & Away

AIR

Sofia Airport (☑ info 24hr 02-937 2211; www.sofia-airport.bg; off bul Brussels; ☎; ☒ 84, ☒ Sofia Airport) is 10km east of the city centre. The only domestic flights within Bulgaria are between Sofia and the Black Sea coast.

Bulgaria Air (☑ call centre 02-402 0400; www.air.bg; ul Ivan Vazov 2; ☺ 9.30am-noon & 12.30pm-5.30pm Mon-Fri; ☒ Serdika) flies daily to Varna, with two or three daily flights between July and September; the airline also flies to Burgas.

BUS

Sofia's **central bus station** (Tsentralna Avtogara; ☑ info 0900 63 099; www.centralnaavtogara.bg; bul Maria Luisa 100; ☺ 24hr; ☎; ☒ Central Railway Station) is beside the train station and accessed by the same metro stop. There are dozens of counters for individual private companies, an information desk and an **OK-Supertrans taxi desk** (☑ 02-973 2121; www.oktaxi.net; Centrali Bus Station; ☺ 6am-10pm; ☒ Central Railway Station). Departures are less frequent between November and April. Frequent buses depart Sofia for Plovdiv (14 lv, 2½ hours), Veliko Târnovo (22 lv, four hours), Varna (33 lv, seven hours) and more; the easy-to-navigate www.bgrazpisanie.com/en has full local and international timetables and fare listings.

TRAIN

The **central train station** (☑ info 02-931 1111, international services 02-931 0972, tickets 02-932 2270; www.bdz.bg; bul Maria Luisa 102a; ☺ ticket office 7am-8.15pm; ☒ Central Railway Station) has been extensively renovated but lacks many basic services. It's located in an isolated part of town about 1km north of the centre, though it's the terminus of a metro line and easy to reach. It's 100m (a five-minute walk) from the Central Bus Station.

Destinations for all domestic and international services are listed on timetables in Cyrillic, but

MT VITOSHA & BOYANA

The Mt Vitosha range, 23km long and 13km wide, lies just south of Sofia; it's sometimes referred to as the 'lungs of Sofia' for the refreshing breezes it deflects onto the capital. The mountain is part of the 227 sq km Vitosha Nature Park (www.park-vitosha.org), the oldest of its kind in Bulgaria (created in 1934). The main activities are hiking in summer and skiing in winter (mid-December to April). All of the park's areas have good hiking; Aleko, the country's highest ski resort, is best for skiing.

On weekends chairlifts, starting around 4km from the village of **Dragalevtsi**, run all year up to Goli Vrâh (1837m); take bus 66 or 93. Another option is the six-person gondola at Simeonovo, reachable by buses 122 or 123 (also weekends only).

A trip out here could be combined with a visit to **Boyana**, home to the fabulous, Unesco-listed **Boyana Church** (☑ 02-959 0939; www.boyanachurch.org; ul Boyansko Ezero 3, Boyana; adult/child 10/1 lv, combined ticket with National Historical Museum 12 lv, guides 10 lv; ☉ 9.30am-5.30pm Apr-Oct, 9am-5pm Nov-Mar; ☐ 64, 107) (en route between central Sofia and the mountains). This tiny church is adorned with 90 colourful murals dating to the 13th century, considered among the most important examples of medieval Bulgarian art. A combined ticket includes entry to both the church and the **National Museum of History** (☑ 02-955 4280; www.historymuseum.org; ul Vitoshko Lale 16, Boyana; adult/child 10/1 lv, combined ticket with Boyana Church 12 lv, guided tours in English 30 lv; ☉ 9.30am-6pm Apr-Oct, 9am-5.30pm Nov-Mar; ☐ 63, 107, 111, ☑ 2), 2km away. Take bus 64 or 107 to reach Boyana.

departures (for the following two hours) and arrivals (for the previous two hours) are listed in English on a large screen on the ground floor.

Same-day tickets are sold at counters on the ground floor, while advance tickets are sold in the gloomy basement, accessed via an unsigned flight of stairs near some snack bars. Counters are open 24 hours, but normally only a few are staffed and queues are long, so don't turn up at the last moment to purchase your ticket, and allow some extra time to work out the confusing system of platforms (indicated with Roman numerals) and tracks.

Sample fast train routes include Sofia to Plovdiv (8 lv to 10 lv, 2½ to 3 hours) and Varna (31 lv to 39 lv, 7½ to 9 hours): see www.bgrazpisanie.com/en or www.bdz.bg/en for all domestic and international routes.

ⓘ Getting Around

TO/FROM THE AIRPORT

Sofia's metro connects Terminal 2 to the centre (Serdika station) in around 20 minutes. Buy tickets in the station, which is located just outside the terminal exit. Bus 84 also shuttles between the centre and both terminals. Buy tickets (1 lv, plus an extra fare for large luggage) from the driver. A taxi to the centre will cost anywhere from 10 lv to 15 lv. Prebook your taxi at the **OK-Supertrans Taxi** (p235) counter.

CAR & MOTORCYCLE

Sofia's public transport is excellent and traffic can be heavy, so there's no need to drive a private or rented car in Sofia. If you wish to ex-

plore further afield, however, a car might come in handy. The **Union of Bulgarian Motorists** (☑ 02-935 7935, road assistance 02-91 146; www.uab.org) provides emergency roadside service. Numerous car-rental outlets have desks at Sofia Airport.

PUBLIC TRANSPORT

Sofia has a comprehensive public transport system based on trams, buses, trolleybuses and underground metro. Public transport generally runs from 5.30am to around 11pm every day. The **Sofia Urban Mobility Centre** (☑ info 0700 13 233; www.sofiatraffic.bg) maintains a helpful website with fares and an updated transport map.

Tickets for trams, buses and trolleybuses cost 1 lv each (8 lv for 10 trips) and can be purchased at kiosks near stops or from on-board ticket machines. Consider buying a day pass (4 lv) to save the hassle of buying individual tickets.

See www.sofiatraffic.bg for more information on public transport.

TAXI

By law, taxis must use meters, but those that wait around the airport, luxury hotels and within 100m of pl Sveta Nedelya will often try to negotiate an unmetered fare – which, of course, will be considerably more. All official taxis are yellow, have fares per kilometre displayed in the window, and have obvious taxi signs (in English or Bulgarian) on top. **OK-Supertrans** (☑ 02-973 2121; www.oktaxi.net; 0.79/0.90 day/night rate) or **Yellow Taxi** (☑ 02-91 119; www.yellow333.com) are reliable operators.

SOUTHERN BULGARIA

Some of Bulgaria's most precious treasures are scattered in the towns, villages and forests of the stunning south. The must-visit medieval Rila Monastery is nestled in the deep forest but easily reached by bus; tiny Melnik is awash in ancient wine; and the cobbled streets of Plovdiv, Bulgaria's second city, are lined with timeless reminders of civilisations come and gone.

The region is a scenic and craggy one; the Rila Mountains (www.rilanationalpark.bg) are just south of Sofia, the Pirin Mountains (www.pirin-np.com) rise towards the Greek border, and the Rodopi Mountains loom to the east and south of Plovdiv. There's great hiking to be had, and the south is also home to three of Bulgaria's most popular ski resorts: Borovets, Bansko and Pamporovo; see www.bulgariaski.com for information.

Rila Monastery
Рилски Манастир

Many Bulgarians say you haven't really been to Bulgaria until you've paid your respects to the truly heavenly, Unesco-listed **Rila Monastery**, 120km south of Sofia. Founded in AD 927 and inspired by the powerful spiritual influence of hermit monk Ivan Rilski, the monastery complex was heavily restored in 1469 after raids. It became a stronghold of Bulgarian culture and language during Ottoman rule. Set in a magnificent forested valley ideal for hiking, the monastery is rightfully famous for its mural-plastered **Church of Rozhdestvo Bogorodichno** (Church of the Nativity; Rila Monastery) dating from the 1830s. The attached **museum** (Rila Monastery; 8 lv; ⊙8.30am-4.30pm) is home to the astonishing **Rafail's Cross**, an early 19th-century double-sided crucifix, with biblical scenes painstakingly carved in miniature. The monastery compound is open from 6am to 10pm. Visitors should dress modestly.

If you have time, hike up to the **Tomb of St Ivan**, the founder of the monastery. The 15-minute walk begins along the road 3.7km east behind the monastery.

You can stay in simple **rooms** (☑ 0896872010; www.rilamonastery.pmg-blg.com; r 30-60 lv) at the monastery or, for something slightly more upmarket, try **Gorski Kut** (☑ 07054-2170, 0888710348; www.gorski-kut.eu; d/tr/ste 51/61/76 lv; P ✳), 5km west.

Tour buses such as **Rila Monastery Bus** (☑ 02-489 0883; www.rilamonasterybus.com; 50 lv) are a popular option for a day trip from Sofia. By public transport, one daily morning bus (22 lv, 2½ hours) goes from Sofia's Ovcha Kupel bus station, returning in the afternoon.

Melnik   Мелник
☑ 07437 / POP 390

Steep sandstone pyramids form a magnificent backdrop in tiny Melnik, 20km north of the Bulgaria–Greece border. But it's a 600-year-old wine culture that has made Melnik famous, and the village's wonderfully restored National Revival architecture looks all the better through a haze of cabernet sauvignon.

★ Festivals & Events

Golden Grapes Festival   WINE
(⊙2nd weekend Feb) It's hardly Bacchanalian – this is small-town Bulgaria, after all – but this annual knees-up gathers local wine producers to showcase their wares and tempt tourists with wine tastings, all set to a backdrop of singing competitions and other folkish entertainment. It's usually on the second weekend of February; ask at the tourist office for details.

⊙ Sights

The major sights here, unsurprisingly, are wineries. Melnik's wines, celebrated for more than 600 years, include the signature dark red, Shiroka Melnishka Loza; it was a favourite tipple of Winston Churchill. Shops and stands dot Melnik's cobblestone paths, with reds and whites starting from around 3 lv; better yet, learn the history and tools of Melnik's winemaking trade at the **Museum of Wine** (www.muzei-na-vinoto.com; ul Melnik 91; 5 lv; ⊙10am-7pm).

Kordopulov House   MUSEUM
(☑ 0877576120, 0887776917; www.kordopulova-house.com; 3 lv; ⊙9.30am-6.30pm Apr-Sep, to 4pm Oct-Mar) Reportedly Bulgaria's largest Revival-era building, this whitewashed and wooden mansion beams down from a cliff face at the eastern end of Melnik's main road. Dating to 1754, the four-storey mansion was formerly the home of a prestigious wine merchant family. Its naturally cool rooms steep visitors in luxurious period flavour, from floral stained-glass windows to

Oriental-style fireplaces and a sauna. There are touches of intrigue, too, such as the secret cupboard that allowed the whole family to eavesdrop on wine-trading deals.

🛏 Sleeping

Private rooms are a budget, no-frills option (15 lv to 20 lv per person), usually with shared bathrooms; look for English-language 'Rooms' signs.

★ **Hotel Bolyarka**   HOTEL €€
(✆ 07437-2383; www.melnikhotels.com; ul Melnik 34; s/d/apt 40/60/100 lv; P ❋ @ ❂) The right blend of old-world nostalgia and modern comfort has made this one of Melnik's favourite hotels. The Bolyarka has elegant rooms, a snug lobby bar, a Finnish-style sauna and one of Melnik's best restaurants. For a touch of added charm, reserve a deluxe apartment (130 lv) with fireplace.

Hotel Melnik   HOTEL €€
(✆ 07437-2272, 0879131459; www.hotelmelnik.com; ul Vardar 2; s/d/apt 40/60/120 lv; P ❋ ❂) This pleasant hotel is shaded by fig and cherry trees, and peeps down over Melnik's main road. White-walled rooms with simple furnishings don't quite match the old-world reception and the *mehana* (tavern) with a bird's-eye view. But it's great value, smartly run and the location – up a cobbled lane, on the right as you enter the village – is convenient whether you arrive by car or bus.

🍴 Eating

★ **Mehana Chavkova Kâshta**   BULGARIAN €€
(✆ 0893505090; www.themelnikhouse.com; 7-12 lv) Sit beneath 500-year-old trees and watch Melnik meander past at this superb spot. Like many places in town, grilled meats and Bulgarian dishes are specialities (try the *satch*, a sizzling flat pan of meat and vegetables); the atmosphere and friendly service give it an extra nudge above the rest. It's 200m from the bus stop, along the main road.

ℹ Information

Melnik Tourist Information Centre (Obshtina Building; ⊙9am-5pm) Located behind the bus stop, on the *obshtina* (municipality) building's upper floor, this centre advises on accommodation and local activities, though opening times can be spotty (especially outside summer). Bus and train timetables are posted outside.

Informative (but unofficial) tourism website http://melnik-bg.eu details history and local attractions.

ℹ Getting There & Away

One daily direct bus connects Melnik with Sofia (17 lv, 4½ hours), though times vary. Two daily direct buses serve Blagoevgrad (7 lv, two hours) near the border with Macedonia.

Plovdiv   Пловдив

☏ 032 / POP 341,560

With an easy grace, Plovdiv mingles invigorating nightlife with millennia-old ruins. Like Rome, Plovdiv straddles seven hills; but as Europe's oldest continuously inhabited city, it's far more ancient. It is best loved for its romantic old town, packed with colourful and creaky 19th-century mansions that house museums, galleries and guesthouses.

Bulgaria's cosmopolitan second city has always been hot on the heels of Sofia, and a stint as European Capital of Culture 2019 seems sure to give Plovdiv the edge. Music and art festivals draw increasing crowds, while renovations in the Kapana artistic quarter and Tsar Simeon Gardens have given the city new confidence.

⊙ Sights

Most of Plovdiv's main sights are in and around the fantastic Old Town. Its meandering cobblestone streets, overflowing with atmospheric house museums, art galleries, antique stores, are also home to welcoming nooks for eating, drinking and people-watching.

★ **Roman Amphitheatre**   HISTORIC SITE
(ul Hemus; adult/student 5/2 lv; ⊙9am-6pm Apr-Oct, to 5pm Nov-Mar) Plovdiv's magnificent 2nd-century AD amphitheatre, built during the reign of Emperor Trajan, was uncovered during a freak landslide in 1972. It once held about 6000 spectators. Now largely restored, it's one of Bulgaria's most magical venues, once again hosting large-scale special events and concerts. Visitors can admire the amphitheatre for free from several lookouts along ul Hemus, or pay admission for a scarper around.

Balabanov House   MUSEUM
(✆ 032-627 082; ul K Stoilov 57; 3 lv; ⊙9am-6pm Apr-Oct, to 5.30pm Nov-Mar) One of Plovdiv's most beautiful Bulgarian National Revival-era mansions, Balabanov House is an enjoy-

MYSTERIES OF THRACE

Plovdiv makes an excellent base for half-day trips to the windblown ruins and spiritual sights of Bulgarian Thrace.

Magnificent **Bachkovo Monastery** (www.bachkovskimanastir.com; Bachkovo; monastery free, refectory 6 lv, museum 2 lv, ossuary 6 lv; ☺6am-10pm) **FREE**, founded in 1083, is about 30km south of Plovdiv. Its church is decorated with 1850s frescoes by renowned artist Zahari Zograf and houses a much-cherished icon of the Virgin Mary. Take any bus to Smolyan from Plovdiv's Rodopi bus station (4 lv), disembark at the turn-off about 1.2km south of Bachkovo village and walk about 500m uphill.

Asen's Fortress (Assenovgrad; adult/student 3/2 lv; ☺10am-6pm Wed-Sun Apr-Oct, to 5pm Nov-Mar), 19km southeast of Plovdiv, squats precariously on the edge of a cliff. Over the centuries, Roman, Byzantine and Ottoman rulers admired its impenetrable position so much that they continued to build and rebuild, adding chapels and thickening its walls to a battering-ram-proof 3m. Taxis from Plovdiv will charge about 35 lv to 40 lv for a return trip to the fortress; better yet, negotiate for a driver to take you to both fortress and Bachkovo Monastery.

BULGARIA PLOVDIV

able way to experience old town nostalgia as well as contemporary art. The house was faithfully reconstructed in 19th-century style during the 1970s. The lower floor has an impressive collection of paintings by local artists, while upper rooms are decorated with antiques and elaborately carved ceilings.

Ethnographical Museum　　　MUSEUM
(☎032-624 261; www.ethnograph.info; ul Dr Chomakov 2; adult/student 5/2 lv; ☺9am-6pm Tue-Sun May-Oct, to 5pm Nov-Apr) Even if you don't have time to step inside, it would be criminal to leave Plovdiv's old town without glancing into the courtyard of this stunning National Revival–era building. Well-manicured flower gardens surround a navy-blue mansion, ornamented with golden filigree and topped with a distinctive peaked roof. There is more to admire inside, especially the upper floor's sunshine-yellow walls and carved wooden ceiling, hovering above displays of regional costumes. The ground-floor displays of agrarian instruments are a shade less interesting.

☞ Tours

Hristo Petrov
(☎0879694681; hristo.petroff@yahoo.com) Knowledgeable Hristo can take small groups on day trips by car to surrounding attractions. A typical rate for visiting Buzludzha, a UFO-shaped Soviet relic in the central mountains, is around 150 lv.

Patrick Penov
(☎0887364711; www.guide-bg.com) For a tour with a personal touch, licensed guide Svet-

lomir 'Patrick' Penov crafts superb itineraries from Thracian treasures and wineries to horse riding, mountain biking and village life. Average daily rates are 200 lv to 250 lv.

🛏 Sleeping

Hikers Hostel　　　HOSTEL €
(☎0896764854; www.hikers-hostel.org; ul Sǎborna 53; 18-/12-bed dm 18/20 lv; @🛜) In a mellow Old-Town location, Hikers has wood-floored dorms and standard hostel perks such as a laundry and a shared kitchen. Bonuses such as a garden lounge, hammocks and mega-friendly staff make it a worthy option. Staff can help organise excursions to Bachkovo Monastery (southern mountains), Buzludzha Monument (central mountains) and more. Off-site private rooms (from 43 lv) are available in the Kapana area.

★Hostel Old Plovdiv　　　HOSTEL €€
(☎032-260 925; www.hosteloldplovdiv. com; ul Chetvarti Yanuari 3; dm/s/d/tr/q 26/60/90/110/130 lv; P🛜) This marvellous old building (1868) is more akin to a boutique historical hotel than a run-of-the-mill hostel. Remarkably restored by charismatic owner Hristo Giulev and his wife, this genial place smack bang in the middle of the Old Town is all about warm welcomes and old-world charm.

★At Renaissance Square　　　BOUTIQUE HOTEL €€€
(☎032-266 966; www.renaissance-bg.com; pl Vǎzhrazhdane 1; s/d from 115/145 lv; P✳@🛜) Re-creating National Revival–era grandeur is a labour of love at this charming little

TOMBS & BLOOMS: KAZANLÂK

For centuries Kazanlâk has been the sweet-smelling centre of European rose-oil production. This nondescript town is also the gateway to the Valley of the Thracian Kings, meaning you can combine fragrant flowers with awe-inspiring tombs in a single visit.

Roses (the aromatic *Rosa damascena*, to be precise) bloom around mid-May to mid-June. Their delicate oils are used in everything from moisturising balms, liqueurs, jams and candies. Kazanlâk's **Rose Festival** (⊙first weekend Jun) is the highlight of the season. You can explore the history of rose-oil production year-round at the **Museum of Roses** (☑0431-64 057; bul Osvobozhdenie 10; adult/student 3/1 lv; ⊙9am-6.30pm), or on a visit to **Enio Bonchev Rose Distillery** (☑02-986 3995; www.eniobonchev.com; Tarnichene; admission with/without rose picking 9.60/6 lv), 27km west of Kazanlâk (call or email in advance to fix a time).

Long before a single seed was sown, the Thracians – a fierce Indo-European tribe – ruled the roost. Archaeologists believe there are at least 1500 Thracian burial mounds and tombs in the vicinity. Most visitors head to the **Replica Thracian Tomb of Kazanlâk** (Tyulbe Park; adult/child 3/1 lv; ⊙9am-5.30pm); at the time of research, the original was inaccessible to visitors. More tombs can be reached via tour bus or your own vehicle: between Kazanlâk and the village of Shipka you can step inside 4th-century BC **Shushmanets Tomb** (adult/student 3/1 lv; ⊙9am-5pm May-Nov) and the mysterious **Ostrusha Tomb** (adult/student 3/1 lv; ⊙9am-5pm May-Nov), whose sarcophagus was carved from a single slab of stone.

Day trips taking in both regions can be arranged at the Kazanlâk **tourist information centre** (☑0431-99 553; ul Iskra 4; ⊙9am-1pm & 2-6pm Mon-Fri, 10am-4pm Sat & Sun). The **Roza Hotel** (☑0431-50 005; www.hotelrozabg.com; ul Rozova Dolina 2; r 50-110 lv; P❋@🛜) in town makes a comfortable and good-value base.

Buses run from Kazanlâk to Sofia (17 lv, three hours, five daily) and Plovdiv (9 lv, two hours, three daily). See www.bdz.bg/en for train schedules.

hotel, between the old town and Plovdiv's shopping streets. Its five rooms are individually decorated with handsome wood floors, billowy drapes, and floral wall and ceiling paintings. Friendly, English-speaking owner Dimitar Vassilev is a font of local knowledge who extends the warmest of welcomes.

✖ Eating

Klebarnitsa Kapana   BAKERY €
(☑0882330773; ul Ioakim Gruev 20; ⊙9am-7pm; ☑) This bakery has a sociable twist, with places to perch while you tuck into oven-warm bread, fresh pastries and other goodies.

Happy Bar & Grill   INTERNATIONAL €€
(☑0888181073; http://happy.bg; ul Patriarh Evtimii 13; mains 8-12 lv; ⊙11am-11pm Mon-Sat, 11.30am-11.30pm Sun) Despite having the outward appearance of a Bulgarian TGI Friday's, this popular place serves impressive sushi, American-inspired caesar salads and steaks, alongside a gamut of fresh Bulgarian fare. Service is scantily clad but operates with razor-sharp efficiency.

Memory   EUROPEAN €€€
(☑032-626 103; http://memorybg.net; pl Saedinenie 3; mains 15-25 lv; ⊙11am-1am) Candlelit tables in a secluded courtyard make Memory a venue to impress, with soul and jazz tunes completing the sultry mood. Its forte is creative interpretations of Western European flavours, such as lamb with mint risotto, and duck nestled in parsnip purée. Everything is lovingly presented and whisked to tables by polite (if slightly stiff) waiting staff.

🍷 Drinking & Nightlife

There are some great haunts in the Kapana district; the name means 'the trap', referring to its tight streets (north of pl Dzhumaya, between ul Rayko Daskalov to the west and bul Tsar Boris Obedinitel to the east).

★Basquiat Wine & Art   WINE BAR
(☑0895460493; https://basquiat.alle.bg; ul Bratya Pulievi 4; ⊙9am-midnight) A smooth funk soundtrack and great selection of local wines lure an arty crowd to this small Kapana bar. House wines start at 2 lv per glass; for something more memorable, the *malina* (raspberry-scented) wine packs a syrupy punch.

Kotka i Mishka BAR

(☑0878407578; ul Hristo Dyukmedjiev 14; ⊘10am-midnight) The crowd at this hole-in-the-wall craft-beer hang-out spills onto the street – such is the bar's deserved popularity, even against stiff competition in buzzing Kapana, but it's too chilled to warrant its hipster label. Decorations – such as hamster cages hanging from the ceiling – in the industrial-feel brick bar are a nod to the name, meaning 'cat and mouse'.

ⓘ Information

Tourist Information Centre (☑032-656 794; www.visitplovdiv.com; pl Tsentralen 1; ⊘9am-6pm Mon-Fri, 10am-5pm Sat & Sun) Helpful centre near the post office; provides maps and info. There's another **office** (☑032-620 453; ul Sâborna 22; ⊘9am-1pm & 2pm-6pm Mon-Fri, 10am-1pm & 2-5pm Sat & Sun) in the Old Town.

ⓘ Getting There & Away

BUS

Plovdiv's main station is **Yug bus station** (☑032-626 937; bul Hristo Botev 47). Yug is diagonally opposite the train station and a 15-minute walk from the centre. Taxis cost 5 lv to 7 lv; local buses 7, 20 and 26 stop across the street. Routes include Plovdiv to Sofia (8 lv to 14 lv, 2½ hours, half-hourly), Bansko (14 lv, 3½ hours, two daily) and Varna (22 lv to 26 lv, seven hours, two to five daily). Check out www.bgrazpisanie.com/en for full destination and fare info.

The **Sever bus station** (☑032-953 705; www.hebrosbus.com; ul Dimitar Stambolov 2) in the northern suburbs is accessed by bus route 99. It serves destinations to the north of Plovdiv, including Veliko Târnovo (18 lv, 4½hours).

TRAIN

Daily direct services from the **train station** (bul Hristo Botev) include trains to Sofia (9 lv, three hours, 15 daily) and Burgas (14.60 lv, six hours, two daily); see www.bgrazpisanie.com/en or www.bdz.bg/en for all fares and timetables.

CENTRAL BULGARIA

Bulgaria's mountainous centre is arguably the country's historic heart. Dramatic past events played out on both sides of the Stara Planina range: to the west is museum village Koprivshtitsa, while the lowlands town of Kazanlâk accesses Thracian tombs and the famously fragrant Valley of the Roses. The hub is magnificent Veliko Târnovo, former capital of the Bulgarian tsars, crowned with one of Europe's most spectacular citadels.

Koprivshtitsa Копривщица

☑07184 / POP 2300

This museum-village immediately pleases the eye with its numerous restored National Revival–period mansions. It's a peaceful, touristy place, but Koprivshtitsa was once the heart of Bulgaria's revolution against the Ottomans. Historic houses are interspersed with rambling, overgrown lanes, making it a romantic getaway and a safe and fun place for children.

⊙ Sights

Koprivshtitsa boasts six house museums. To buy a combined ticket for all (adult/student 5/3 lv), visit the souvenir shop Kupchinitsa, near the **tourist-information centre** (☑07184-2191; www.koprivshtitza.com; pl 20 April 6; ⊘9.30am-5.30pm Tue, Wed & Fri-Sun Apr-Oct, to 5pm Nov-Mar).

Oslekov House MUSEUM

(ul Gereniloto 4; admission 3 lv; ⊘9.30am-5.30pm Apr-Oct, 9am-5pm Nov-Mar, closed Mon) With its triple-arched entrance and interior restored in shades from scarlet to sapphire blue, Oslekov House is arguably the most beautifully restored example of Bulgarian National Revival–period architecture in Koprivshtitsa. It was built between 1853 and 1856 by a rich merchant executed after his arrest during the 1876 April Uprising. Now a house museum, it features informative, multilingual displays (Bulgarian, English and French) about 19th-century Bulgaria.

Kableshkov House MUSEUM

(ul Todor Kableshkov 8; adult/student 4/2 lv; ⊘9.30am-5.30pm Tue-Sun Apr-Oct, to 5pm Nov-Mar) Todor Kableshkov is revered as having (probably) been the person who fired the first shot in the 1876 uprising against the Turks. After his arrest, he committed suicide rather than allow his captors to decide his fate. This, his glorious former home (built 1845), contains exhibits about the April Uprising.

🛏 Sleeping & Eating

Hotel Astra GUESTHOUSE €

(☑07184-2033; www.hotelastra.org; bul Hadzhi Nencho Palaveev 11; d/apt incl breakfast 45/66 lv; ℗) Set beautifully in a garden at the northern end of Koprivshtitsa, the hospitable Astra has large, well-kept rooms and serves an epic homemade breakfast spread of pancakes, thick yogurt and more.

BULGARIA KOPRIVSHTITSA

Dyado Liben
BULGARIAN €€

(📞 0887532096; bul Hadzhi Nencho Palaveev 47; mains 8-15 lv; ⏰ 11am-midnight; 🐾) Traditional fare is served at this atmospheric 1852 mansion with tables set in a warren of halls, graced with ornate painted walls and heavy, worn wood floors. Find it just across the bridge leading from the main square inside the facing courtyard.

ℹ️ Information

There are ATMs and a post office/telephone centre in the village centre.

ℹ️ Getting There & Away

Without private transport, getting to Koprivshtitsa can be inconvenient. Being 9km north of the village, to get to the train station requires a shuttle bus (2 lv, 15 minutes), which isn't always timed to meet trains. Trains come from Sofia (6 lv to 9 lv, 2½ hours, eight daily) and Karlovo (3 lv to 4 lv, one to 1½ hours, two to four daily). Koprivshtitsa's **bus stop** (📞 07184-3044; bul Palaveev 76) is more central; there are six daily buses to Sofia (13 lv, two hours) and one daily to Plovdiv (12 lv, two hours).

Veliko Târnovo
Велико Търново

📞 062 / POP 68,780

Medieval history emanates from Veliko Târnovo's fortified walls and cobbled lanes. One of Bulgaria's oldest towns, Veliko Târnovo has as its centrepiece the breathtaking restored Tsarevets Fortress, citadel of the Second Bulgarian Empire.

⊙ Sights

★ Tsarevets Fortress
FORTRESS

(adult/student 6/2 lv, scenic elevator 2 lv; ⏰ 8am-7pm Apr-Oct, 9am-5pm Nov-Mar) The inescapable symbol of Veliko Târnovo, this reconstructed fortress dominates the skyline and is one of Bulgaria's most beloved monuments. The former seat of the medieval tsars, it boasts the remains of more than 400 houses, 18 churches, the royal palace, an execution rock and more. Watch your step: there are lots of potholes, broken steps and unfenced drops. The fortress morphs into a psychedelic spectacle with a magnificent night-time **Sound & Light Show** (📞 0885080865; www.soundandlight.bg; ul N Pikolo 6; admission 20-25 lv).

Ulitsa Gurko
HISTORIC SITE

The oldest street in Veliko Târnovo, ul Gurko is a must-stroll with arresting views towards the Yantra River and Asen Monument. Its charmingly crumbling period houses – which appear to be haphazardly piled on one another – provide a million photo ops and conversations that start with 'Imagine living here...' Sturdy shoes a must.

Sarafkina Kâshta
MUSEUM

(ul General Gurko 88; adult/student 6/2 lv; ⏰ 9am-6pm Tue & Thu-Sat, noon-6pm Wed) Built for a wealthy banker in 1861, this National Revival–style house museum spans five storeys (when viewed from the river). Within, 19th-century earrings, bracelets and other delicate silverware are on display, alongside antique ceramics, woodcarvings and traditional costumes and jewellery.

🛏️ Sleeping

Hostel Mostel
HOSTEL €

(📞 0897859359; www.hostelmostel.com; ul Iordan Indjeto 10; campsites/dm/s/d incl breakfast 18/20/46/60 lv; @🐾) The famous Sofia-based Hostel Mostel has a welcoming branch in Târnovo, with clean, modern dorm rooms and doubles with sparkling bathrooms. It's just 150m from Tsarevets Fortress – good for exploring there, but a long walk from the city centre. Service is cheerful and multilingual, and there's barbecue equipment out back.

Hotel Anhea
HOTEL €

(📞 062-577713; www.anheabg.com; ul Nezavisimost 32; s/d/tr from 30/45/55 lv; ❄️🐾) This superb budget hotel in an early 1900s building has a restful air, despite its central location. Crisp beige and cream rooms are arranged across two buildings, between which lies a peaceful courtyard and breakfast area – this secret garden is decorated with pretty iron railings, fountains and overseen by resident rabbit Emma.

★ Hotel-Mehana Gurko
HISTORIC HOTEL €€

(📞 0887858965; www.hotel-gurko.com; ul General Gurko 33; s/d/apt incl breakfast from 70/90/130 lv; 🅿️❄️@🐾) Sitting pretty on Veliko Târnovo's oldest street, with blooms spilling over its wooden balconies and agricultural curios littering the exterior, the Gurko is one of the best places to sleep (and eat) in town. Its 21 rooms are spacious and soothing, each individually decorated and offering great views.

Eating

⭐ Shtastliveca   BULGARIAN €€
(☑ 062-606 656; www.shtastliveca.com; ul Stefan Stambolov 79; mains 10-20 lv; ⏰11am-1am; 🐾) 🌿 Inventive dishes and amiable service have solidified the 'Lucky Man' as a favourite among locals and expats. Sauces pairing chocolate and cheese are drizzled over chicken, while strawberry and balsamic vinegar lend piquancy to meaty dishes, and there is a pleasing range for vegetarians.

⭐ Han Hadji Nikoli   INTERNATIONAL €€€
(☑ 062-651 291; www.hanhadjinikoli.com; ul Rakovski 19; mains 17-30 lv; ⏰10am-11pm; 🐾) Countless Veliko Târnovo inns were ransacked under Ottoman rule, as they were popular meeting places for revolution-minded locals. Fortunately Han Hadji Nikoli survived, and today the town's finest restaurant occupies this beautifully restored 1858 building with an upstairs gallery. Well-executed dishes include Trakia chicken marinated in herbs and yoghurt, mussels sautéed in white wine and exquisitely prepared pork neck.

Drinking & Nightlife

⭐ Tam   BAR
(☑ 0889879693; ul Marno Pole 2A; ⏰4pm-3am Mon-Sat) Open the nondescript door, and up the stairs you'll find the city's friendliest, most-open-minded hang-out. Tam is the place to feel the pulse of VT's arty crowd. You might stumble on art installations, movie screenings or language nights in English, French or Spanish. Punters and staff extend a genuine welcome and drinks flow late.

Sammy's Bar   BAR
(☑ 0885233387; ul Nezavisimost; ⏰11am-3am) The lofty views from this bar and beer garden are as refreshing as the selection of herb-garnished lemonades (2.80 lv). So it's no wonder that Sammy's, just off busy ul Nezavisimost, has become a trusted local haunt.

☆ Entertainment

Melon Live Music Club   LIVE MUSIC
(☑ 062-603 439; bul Nezavisimost 21; ⏰6pm-2am) Popular spot for live music, from rock and R&B to Latin jazz. Admission to live events is around 4 lv or 5 lv.

🛍 Shopping

⭐ Samovodska Charshiya   ARTS & CRAFTS
(ul Rakovski) Veliko Târnovo's historic quarter is a true centre of craftsmanship, with genuine blacksmiths, potters and cutlers, among other artisans, still practising their trades here. Wander the cobblestone streets to discover bookshops and purveyors of antiques, jewellery and art, housed in appealing National Revival houses.

ⓘ Information

Tourist Information Centre (☑ 062-622 148; www.velikoturnovo.info; ul Hristo Botev 5; ⏰9am-6pm Mon-Sat Apr-Oct, Mon-Fri Nov-Mar) Helpful English-speaking staff offering local info and advice.

ⓘ Getting There & Away

BUS

The most central bus terminal is **Hotel Etar Bus Station** (www.etapgroup.com; ul Ivailo 2), served by hourly buses to Sofia (20 lv, three to 3½ hours) and Varna (20 lv, 3½ hours). The station is just south of the tourist information centre.

Two non-central bus stations also serve Veliko Târnovo, with a broader range of destinations and services. **Zapad Bus Station** (☑ 062-640 908, 062-620 014; ul Nikola Gabrovski 74), about 3km southwest of the tourist information centre, is the main intercity one, serving Plovdiv (19 lv, four hours, four daily), Kazanlâk (9 lv, 2½ hours, five daily) and Burgas (18 lv to 25 lv, four hours, four daily). Local buses 10, 12, 14, 70 and 110 go to Zapad. Closer to the centre is **Yug Bus Station** (☑ 062-620 014; ul Hristo Botev 74), 700m south of the tourist information centre, serving Sofia and Varna.

TRAIN

The slightly more walkable of the town's two stations is **Veliko Târnovo Train Station** (☑ 062-620 065), 1.5km west of town, served by one daily direct train to Plovdiv (12 lv, 4½ hours; alternatively, travel via Stara Zagora) and one direct service to Varna (14 lv, four hours).

Gorna Oryakhovitsa train station (☑ 062-826 118), 8.5km northeast of town, is along the main line between Sofia and Varna. There are daily services to/from Sofia (14.60 lv, four to five hours, eight daily), some via Tulovo or Mezdra. Direct trains also reach Varna (13 lv, 3½ to four hours, five daily). From Veliko Târnovo, minibuses wait opposite the market along ul Vasil Levski to get to this train station. Taxis cost about 12 lv to 15 lv.

BLACK SEA COAST

Bulgaria's long Black Sea coastline is the country's summertime playground. The big, purpose-built resorts here have become serious rivals to those of Spain and Greece, while independent travellers will find plenty to explore away from the parasols and jet skis. Sparsely populated sandy beaches to the far south and north, the bird-filled lakes around Burgas, and picturesque ancient towns such as Nesebâr and Sozopol are rewarding destinations. The 'maritime capital' of Varna and its seaside rival, Burgas, are two of Bulgaria's most vibrant cities. Both are famous for summer festivals and nightlife.

Varna   Варна

📞 052 / POP 334,700

Cosmopolitan Varna is by far the most interesting town on the Black Sea coast. A combination of port city, naval base and seaside resort, it's an appealing place to while away a few days, packed with history yet thoroughly modern, with an enormous park to amble around and a lengthy, white-sand beach to lounge on. In the city centre you'll find Bulgaria's largest Roman baths complex and its finest archaeological museum, as well as a dynamic cultural and restaurant scene.

⊙ Sights & Activities

★ Archaeological Museum   MUSEUM

(📞052-681 030; www.archaeo.museumvarna.com; ul Maria Luisa 41; adult/child 10/2 lv; ⊙10am-5pm Tue-Sun Apr-Sep, Tue-Sat Oct-Mar; 🚌8, 9, 109, 409) Exhibits at this vast museum, the best of its kind in Bulgaria, include 6000-year-old bangles, necklaces and earrings said to be the oldest worked gold found in the world.

Beach   BEACH

(⊙9am-6pm) Varna has a long stretch of public beach, starting in the south, near the port, and stretching north some 4km. Generally, the quality of the sand and water improve and the crowds thin as you stroll north. The easiest way to access the beach is to walk south on bul Slivnitsa to Primorski Park and follow the stairs to the beach.

Baracuda Dive Center   DIVING

(📞052-610 841; www.baracudadive.com; half-day beginning instruction from 110 lv) Offers diving instruction for beginners and advanced divers, as well as guided diving excursions along the Black Sea coast. Rates include equipment.

🛏 Sleeping

★ Yo Ho Hostel   HOSTEL €

(📞0884729144; www.yohohostel.com; ul Ruse 23; dm/s/d from 14/30/40 lv; @🛜; 🚌8, 9, 109) Shiver your timbers at this cheerful, pirate-themed place, with four- and 11-bed dorm rooms and private options. Staff offer free pick-ups and can organise camping and rafting trips. The location is an easy walk to the main sights.

Hotel Odessos   HOTEL €€

(📞052-640 300; www.odessos-bg.com; bul Slivnitsa 1; s/d from 75/90 lv; 🅿❄🛜) Enjoying a great location opposite the main entrance to Primorski Park, this is an older establishment with smallish and pretty average rooms, but it's convenient for the beach. Only the pricier 'sea view' rooms have balconies.

✗ Eating

Morsko Konche   PIZZA €

(📞052-600 418; www.morskokonche.bg; pl Nezavisimost, cnr ul Zamenhof; pizzas 5-10 lv; ⊙8.30am-10pm; 🛜🍴; 🚌8, 9, 109) The 'Seahorse' is a cheap and cheerful pizza place with a big menu featuring all the standard varieties, as well as some inventive creations of its own: the 'exotic' pizza comes with bananas and blueberries.

★ Stariya Chinar   BULGARIAN €€

(📞0876520500; www.stariachinar.com; ul Preslav 11; mains 10-20 lv; ⊙8am-midnight) This is upmarket Balkan soul food at its best. Try the baked lamb, made to an old Bulgarian recipe, or the divine barbecue pork ribs; it also boasts some rather ornate salads. Outdoor seating is lovely in summer; park yourself in the traditional interior when the cooler weather strikes.

🍷 Drinking & Nightlife

Some of Varna's best bars exist only during the summer: head down to Kraybrezhna aleya by the beach and take your pick.

Sundogs   PUB

(📞0988936630; www.sundogspub.com; ul Koloni 1; ⊙9am-midnight; 🛜) Big with expats and locals, this very welcoming watering hole is a great place to make new friends, chase down excellent pub grub with a good selection of beers, or show off your smarts at quiz nights.

Palm Beach   CLUB

(📞0889422553; www.facebook.com/PalmBeachVarna; Kraybrezhna aleya; ⊙24hr) By day, a great place to relax by the beach and enjoy coffee and drinks at the bar. By night, a beachside nightclub, with music and dancing that can go all the way till morning.

☆ Entertainment

Varna Opera Theatre OPERA
(☑box office 052-665 022; www.tmpcvarna.com; pl Nezavisimost 1; ⊙ticket office 10am-1pm & 2-7pm; ⌨8, 9, 109, 409) Varna's grand opera house hosts performances by the Varna Opera and Philharmonic Orchestra all year, except July and August, when some performances are staged at the Open-Air Theatre in Primorski Park.

ⓘ Information

Tourist Information Centre (☑052-820 690; www.visit.varna.bg; pl Kiril & Metodii; ⊙9am-7pm; ⌨8, 9, 109, 409) Plenty of free brochures and maps, and helpful multilingual staff. The Tourist Information Centre also operates free three-hour walking tours of the city on select days from June to September.

ⓘ Getting There & Away

AIR

Varna's international **airport** (VAR; ☑052-573 323; www.varna-airport.bg; Aksakovo; ⌨409) has scheduled and charter flights from all over Europe, as well as regular flights to and from Sofia. From the centre, bus 409 goes to the airport.

BUS

Varna's **central bus station** (Avtoexpress; ☑information 052-757 044, tickets 052-748 349; www.bgrazpisanie.com; bul Vladislav Varenchik 158; ⊙24hr; ⌨148, 409) is about 2km northwest of the city centre. There are regular buses to Sofia (33 lv, seven hours), Burgas (14 lv, 2½ hours) and other major destinations in Bulgaria: see www.bgrazpisanie.com/en for fares and schedules.

TRAIN

Trains depart Varna's **train station** (☑052-662 3343; www.bdz.bg; pl Slaveikov; ⌨8, 9, 109) for Sofia (24 lv, seven to eight hours, seven daily) and Plovdiv (24 lv, seven hours, three daily).

Nesebâr   Несебър

☑0554 / POP 11,600

Postcard-pretty Nesebâr (Ne-*se*-bar) – about 40km northeast of Burgas – was settled by Greek colonists in 512BC, though today it's more famous for its (mostly ruined) medieval churches. Though beautiful, Nesebâr is heavily commercialised, and transforms into one huge, open-air souvenir market during the high season. The Sunny Beach megaresort is 5km to the north.

◉ Sights & Activities

All of Nesebâr's main sights are in the Old Town; around 1.5km southwest of the peninsula is **South Beach**, where all the usual water sports are available, including jet-skiing and waterskiing.

Archaeological Museum MUSEUM
(☑0554-46 019; www.ancient-nessebar.com; ul Mesembria 2; adult/child 6/3 lv; ⊙9am-7pm Mon-Fri, 9.30am-2pm & 2.30-7pm Sat & Sun Jun-Sep, reduced hours Oct-May) Explore the rich history of Nesebâr – formerly Mesembria – at this fine museum. Greek and Roman pottery, statues and tombstones, as well as Thracian gold jewellery and ancient anchors, are displayed here. There's also a collection of icons recovered from Nesebâr's numerous churches.

Sveti Stefan Church CHURCH
(☑0554-46 019; www.ancient-nessebar.com; ul Ribarska; adult/child 6/3 lv; ⊙9am-7pm Mon-Fri, 10.30am-2pm & 2.30-7pm Sat & Sun May-Sep, 9am-5pm Mon-Fri, 10am-5pm Sat & Sun Oct-Apr) Built in the 11th century and reconstructed 500 years later, this is the best-preserved church in town. If you only visit one, this is the church to choose. Its beautiful 16th- to 18th-century murals cover virtually the entire interior. Come early, as it's popular with tour groups.

Aqua Paradise WATER PARK
(☑0885208055; www.aquaparadise-bg.com; adult/child 40/20 lv, after 3pm 30/15 lv; ⊙10am-6.30pm; ☒) Organised watery fun is on hand at Aqua Paradise, a huge water park on the southern outskirts of Sunny Beach just as you enter Nesebâr, with a variety of pools, slides and chutes. A free minibus, running every 15 minutes, makes pick-ups at signed stops around Nesebâr and Sunny Beach.

🛏 Sleeping & Eating

★**Boutique Hotel**
St Stefan BOUTIQUE HOTEL €€
(☑0554-43 603; www.hotelsaintstefan.com; ul Ribarska 11; r/ste 80/160 lv; ☒❄☎) One of the nicest hotels in Nesebâr, the St Stefan offers rooms with views out over the harbour and Black Sea. There's a small sauna on the premises as well as a terrace for drinks and light meals. Rooms feature original artwork by Bulgarian artists. Breakfast costs 8 lv. Book well in advance for summer dates.

★ **Gloria Mar** BULGARIAN €€€

(☑ 0893550055; www.gloriamar-bg.com; ul Krajbrezhna 9; mains 12-30 lv; ⊙ 11am-11pm) For our money, the best dining option in touristy Nesebâr. Fresh seafood, wood-fired pizzas and grilled meats, as well as harder-to-find risottos and paellas. There's an extensive wine list and dining on three levels, including a rooftop terrace. It's on the southern side of old Nesebâr, facing the marina and passenger ferry terminal.

ⓘ Getting There & Away

Nesebâr is well connected to coastal destinations by public transport; its bus station is on the small square just outside the city walls. The stop before this on the mainland is for the new town. There are buses every few minutes to Sunny Beach (1 lv, 10 minutes), and to Burgas (6 lv, one hour, hourly), Varna (14 lv, two hours, four daily) and Sofia (37 lv, seven hours, three daily).

Fast Ferry (☑ 0885808001; www.fastferry. bg; Passenger Ferry Port; ⊙ 8.30am-8.30pm Jun-Sep) operates a high-speed hydrofoil service to the uncrowded resort of Pomorie (one way/return from 11/20 lv, 25 minutes, three daily) and Sozopol (one way/return from 27/50 lv, 40 minutes, three daily).

Burgas Бургас

☑ 056 / POP 200,000

For most visitors, the port city of Burgas (sometimes written as 'Bourgas') is no more than a transit point. But if you do decide to stop over, you'll find a well-kept city with a neat, pedestrianised centre, a long, uncrowded beach and some small but interesting museums. Nature lovers also arrive for the four lakes just outside the city, which are havens for bird life.

Burgas is also the jumping-off point for visits to St Anastasia Island (☑ 0882004124; www.anastasia-island.com; return boat trip adult/child 12/7 lv; ⊙ departures 10am, 11.30am, 1pm, 3pm Jun-Aug), a small volcanic island that has served as a religious retreat, a prison and pirate bait (according to legend, a golden treasure is buried in its sands). Today it is dominated by a lighthouse and a monastery, where visitors can sample various healing herb potions.

⌂ Sleeping & Eating

Old House Hostel HOSTEL €

(☑ 056-841 558; www.burgashostel.com; ul Sofroniy 3; dm/d 17/33 lv; ▣ ⊛) This charming hostel makes itself right at home in a lovely 1895 house. Dorms are airy and bright (and bunk-free!), while doubles have access to a sweet little courtyard. The location is central and about 400m from the beach.

Hotel Bulair HOTEL €

(☑ 056-844 389; www.hotelbulair.com; ul Bulair 7; r 60 lv; ▣ ⊛ ⊛) In a converted 19th-century townhouse on a busy road, the 14-room Bulair is very handy for the bus and train stations. Guests have access to the spa and wellness centre at the nearby Primoretz Grand Hotel & Spa.

★ **Rosé** INTERNATIONAL €€

(☑ 0885855099; bul Aleko Bogoridi 19; mains 8-20 lv; ⊙ 8am-11pm; ⊛) Choose from a wide menu of grilled meats and fish, including a superlative lamb-shank offering, or fresh pasta, at this superb restaurant in the city centre. Finish off with a cake or homemade ice cream. Rosé also does a very good breakfast, including a rarity for Bulgaria: gluten-free muesli.

ⓘ Getting There & Away

AIR

Bulgaria Air (www.air.bg) links **Burgas Airport** (BOJ; ☑ information 056-870 248; www. bourgas-airport.com; Sarafovo; ⊛; ▣ 15), 10km northeast of town, with Sofia daily (April to October). In summer, **Wizz Air** (www.wizzair. com) connects Burgas with London Luton, Budapest, Prague and Warsaw. Other carriers fly to destinations in Germany and Russia.

BUS

Yug bus station (☑ 0884981220; www. bgrazpisanie.com; pl Tsaritsa Yoanna), outside the train station at the southern end of ul Aleksandrovska, is where most travellers arrive or leave. There are regular buses to coastal destinations, including Nesebâr (6 lv, 40 minutes, half-hourly), Varna (14 lv, two hours, half-hourly) and Sozopol (5 lv, 40 minutes, every 45 minutes). Several daily buses also go to and from Sofia (30 lv, seven to eight hours) and Plovdiv (20 lv, four hours). Departures are less frequent outside summer.

TRAIN

The **train station** (☑ information 056-845 022; www.bdz.bg; ul Ivan Vazov; ⊙ information office 6am-10pm) has clearly marked ticket windows for buying advance tickets for domestic and international services. Trains run to Plovdiv (16 lv, five to six hours, five daily) and Sofia (21 lv, seven to eight hours, five daily).

Sozopol · Созопол

☑ 0550 / POP 5700

Ancient Sozopol, with its charming old town of meandering cobbled streets and pretty wooden houses huddled together on a narrow peninsula, is one of the coast's real highlights. With two superb beaches, a genial atmosphere, plentiful accommodation and good transport links, it has long been a popular seaside resort and makes an excellent base for exploring the area. Although not quite as crowded as Nesebâr, it is becoming ever more popular with international visitors.

Festivals

Apollonia Arts Festival　　　　　ART, MUSIC
(www.apollonia.bg; ⊙ end Aug–mid-Sep) This is the highlight of Sozopol's cultural calendar, with concerts, theatrical performances, art exhibitions, film screenings and more held across town.

◉ Sights & Activities

Sozopol has two great beaches: **Harmanite Beach** has all the good-time gear (waterslide, paddle boats, beach bar), while to the north, the smaller **Town Beach** packs in the serious sun-worshippers.

Archaeological Museum　　　　　MUSEUM
(☑ 0550-22 226; ul Han Krum 2; adult/child 7/3 lv; ⊙ 8.30am-6pm Jun-Sep, 8.30am-6pm Mon-Fri Oct-May) Housed in a drab concrete box near the port, this museum has a small but fascinating collection of local finds from its Apollonian glory days and beyond. In addition to a wealth of Hellenic treasures, the museum occasionally exhibits the skeleton of a local 'vampire', found with a stake driven through its chest. Enter from the building's northern side.

Sveti Ivan　　　　　ISLAND
The largest Bulgarian island in the Black Sea (0.7 sq km), Sveti Ivan lies 3km north of Sozopol's Old Town. The island's history stretches back to Thracian and Roman times, and includes a monastery from the 4th century AD. Sveti Ivan made international headlines in 2010 with the purported discovery of the remains of St John the Baptist. There are no scheduled excursions to the island, but private trips can be arranged along the **Fishing Harbour**; expect to pay from around 50 lv.

ESSENTIAL FOOD & DRINK

Fresh fruit, vegetables, dairy produce and grilled meat form the basis of Bulgarian cuisine, which has been heavily influenced by Greek and Turkish cookery. Pork and chicken are the most popular meats, while tripe also features heavily on traditional menus. You will also find recipes including duck, rabbit and venison, and fish is plentiful along the Black Sea coast, but less common elsewhere.

Banitsa Flaky cheese pastry, often served fresh and hot.

Beer You're never far from a cold beer in Bulgaria. Zagorka, Kamenitza and Shumensko are the most popular nationwide brands.

Kavarma This 'claypot meal', or meat stew, is normally made with either chicken or pork and is one of the country's most popular dishes.

Kebabche Thin, grilled pork sausage, a staple of every *mehana* (tavern) in the country.

Mish Mash Summer favourite made from tomatoes, capsicum, eggs, feta and spices.

Musaka Bulgarian moussaka bears more than a passing resemblance to its Greek cousin, but it's a delicious staple of cheap cafeteria meals.

Shishcheta Shish kebab consisting of chunks of chicken or pork on wooden skewers with mushrooms and peppers.

Shkembe chorba Traditional stomach soup is one of the more adventurous and offbeat highlights of Bulgarian cuisine.

Tarator On a hot day there's nothing better than this delicious chilled cucumber and yoghurt soup, served with garlic, dill and crushed walnuts.

Wine They've been producing wine here since Thracian times and there are some excellent varieties to try.

🛏 Sleeping & Eating

Hotel prices drop considerably in the off-season, when visitors will have Sozopol all to themselves. Cheap eats abound along the harbourfront ul Kraybrezhna in the Old Town; more upmarket restaurants are found on ul Morski Skali.

★ **Justa Hostel** HOSTEL **€**
(☑ 0550-22 175; ul Apolonia 20; dm 20 lv; ☎) This clean, cosy, centrally located hostel sits in the centre of the Old Town, a few minutes' walk from the beach and offers dorm-bed accommodation with shared bath and shower. The price includes traditional breakfast (pancakes) and coffee.

★ **Art Hotel** HOTEL **€€**
(☑ 0550-24 081, 0878650160; www.arthotel-sbh. com; ul Kiril & Metodii 72; d/studios 80/100 lv; ❄☎) This peaceful old house, belonging to the Union of Bulgarian Artists, is within a walled courtyard toward the tip of the peninsula, away from the crowds. It has a small selection of bright, comfortable rooms with balconies, most with sea views; breakfast is served on the terraces overlooking the sea.

Panorama SEAFOOD **€€**
(ul Morski Skali 21; mains 8-20 lv; ⊙11am-11pm) This lively place has an open terrace with a fantastic view toward Sveti Ivan island. Fresh, locally caught fish is the mainstay of the menu. It's one of the best of many seafood spots on this street.

ⓘ Getting There & Away

The small public **bus station** (☑ 0550-23 460; www.bgrazpisanie.com; ul Han Krum) is just south of the Old Town walls. Buses leave for Burgas (5 lv, 40 minutes) about every 30 minutes between 6am and 9pm in summer, and about once an hour in the low season. Buses run two to three times a day to Sofia (32 lv, seven hours).

Fast Ferry (☑ 0988908629, booking 0885808001; www.fastferry.bg; Sozopol Harbour) runs three ferries per day to/from Nesebâr (single/return from 27/54 lv, 40 minutes) between June and September.

SURVIVAL GUIDE

ⓘ Directory A–Z

ACCOMMODATION

Sofia, Plovdiv, Veliko Târnovo, Varna and Burgas all have hostels; for cheap accommodation

---

elsewhere, look out for signs reading 'стаи под наем' (rooms for rent). Many hotels offer discounts for longer stays or on weekends; prices may rise during summer.

GAY & LESBIAN TRAVELLERS

Homosexuality is legal in Bulgaria but gay culture is very discreet as a result of prevailing macho attitudes and widespread homophobia. Attitudes among younger people are slowly changing, and there are a few gay clubs and bars in Sofia and in other major cities. Useful websites include www.gay.bg and www.gay-bulgaria.info.

INTERNET RESOURCES

Ministry of Tourism (www.tourism.government.bg)

National tourism portal (www.bulgariatravel.org)

TRAVELLERS WITH DISABILITIES

Bulgaria is not an easy destination for travellers with disabilities. Uneven and broken footpaths are common in towns and wheelchair-accessible toilets and ramps are rare outside the more expensive hotels.

VISAS

Citizens of other EU countries, as well as Australia, Canada, New Zealand, the USA and many other countries do not need a visa for stays of up to 90 days. Other nationals should contact the Bulgarian embassy in their home country for current visa requirements.

ⓘ Getting There & Away

AIR

Most international visitors come and/or go via **Sofia Airport** (p235); there are frequent flights between Sofia and other European cities. The national carrier is **Bulgaria Air** (www.air.bg).

LAND

Although Sofia has international bus and train connections, it's not necessary to backtrack to the capital if you're heading to, for example,

Athens or İstanbul: Plovdiv offers regular buses to both. Heading to Belgrade by train means going through Sofia; for Skopje, you'll need to catch a bus from there, too.

Bus

Most international buses arrive in Sofia. You'll have to get off the bus at the border and walk through customs to present your passport. When travelling out of Bulgaria by bus, the cost of entry visas for the countries concerned are not included in the prices of the bus tickets.

Car & Motorcycle

In order to drive on Bulgarian roads, you will need to purchase a vignette (15/30 lv for one week/month), sold at all border crossings into Bulgaria, petrol stations and post offices. Rental cars hired within Bulgaria should already have a vignette.

Train

There are a number of international trains from Bulgaria, including services to Serbia, Romania and Turkey. Sofia is the main hub, although trains stop at other towns.

ℹ Getting Around

AIR

The only scheduled domestic flights within Bulgaria are between Sofia and Varna and Sofia and Burgas. Both routes are operated by **Bulgaria Air** (www.air.bg).

BICYCLE

➡ Many roads are in poor condition; some major roads are always choked with traffic and bikes aren't allowed on highways.

➡ Many trains will carry your bike for an extra 2 lv.

➡ Spare parts are available in cities and major towns, but it's better to bring your own.

BUS

Buses link all cities and major towns and connect villages with the nearest transport hub. Though it isn't exhaustive, many bus and train schedules can be accessed at www.bgrazpisanie.com/en.

CAR & MOTORCYCLE

Bulgaria's roads are among the most dangerous in Europe, and the number of road deaths each year is high. Speeding and aggressive driving habits are common; during summer (July to September), an increase in drink-driving and holiday traffic can contribute further to accidents.

The **Union of Bulgarian Motorists** (p236) offers 24-hour road assistance.

Road Rules

➡ Drive on the right.

EATING PRICE RANGES

The following price ranges refer to a standard main course. Unless otherwise stated, service charge is included in the price.

€ less than 10 lv

€€ 10–20 lv

€€€ more than 20 lv

➡ Drivers and passengers in the front must wear seat belts; motorcyclists must wear helmets.

➡ Blood-alcohol limit is 0.05%.

➡ Children under 12 are not allowed to sit in front.

➡ Headlights must be on low beam at all times, year-round.

➡ Speed limits are 50km/h within towns, 90km/h on main roads and 130km/h on motorways.

TRAIN

The Bulgarian State Railways (БДЖ; www.bdz.bg) boasts more than 4070km of tracks across the country, linking most sizeable towns and cities. Most trains tend to be antiquated and not especially comfortable, with journey times often slower than buses. On the plus side you'll have more room in a train compartment and the scenery is likely to be more rewarding.

Trains are classified as *ekspresen* (express), *bârz* (fast) or *pâtnicheski* (slow passenger). Unless you absolutely thrive on train travel or want to visit a more remote town, use a fast or express train.

COUNTRY FACTS

Area 110,879 sq km

Capital Sofia

Country Code ☑ 359

Currency Lev (lv)

Emergency ☑ 112

Language Bulgarian

Money ATMs are everywhere.

Population 7.19 million

Visas Not required for citizens of the EU, USA, Canada, Australia and New Zealand for stays of less than 90 days.

Croatia

Best Places to Eat

➜ Pantarul (p271)

➜ Male Madlene (p258)

➜ Vinodol (p256)

➜ Restaurant 360° (p272)

➜ Zinfandel's (p256)

Best Places to Stay

➜ Antique Split Luxury Rooms (p264)

➜ Art Hotel Kalelarga (p260)

➜ Karmen Apartments (p270)

➜ Studio Kairos (p255)

➜ Villa Skansi (p266)

Why Go?

If your Mediterranean fantasies feature balmy days by sapphire waters in the shade of ancient walled towns, Croatia is the place to turn them into reality. The extraordinary Adriatic coastline, speckled with 1244 islands and strewn with historic towns, is Croatia's main attraction. The standout is Dubrovnik, its remarkable Old Town ringed by mighty defensive walls. Coastal Split showcases Diocletian's Palace, one of the world's most impressive Roman monuments, where dozens of bars, restaurants and shops thrive amid the old walls. In the heart-shaped peninsula of Istria, Rovinj is a charm-packed fishing port. The Adriatic isles hold much varied appeal, from glitzy Hvar Town on its namesake island to the secluded naturist coves of the Pakleni Islands just offshore. Away from the coast, Zagreb, Croatia's lovely capital has a booming cafe culture and art scene, while Plitvice Lakes National Park offers a verdant maze of turquoise lakes and cascading waterfalls.

When to Go
Zagreb

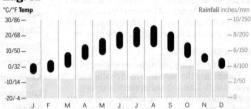

May & Sep Good weather, less tourists, full events calendar, great for hiking.

Jun Best time to visit: beautiful weather, fewer people, lower prices, the festival season kicks off.

Jul & Aug Lots of sunshine, warm sea and summer festivals; many tourists and highest prices.

ZAGREB

POP 790,000

Zagreb has culture, arts, music, architecture, gastronomy and all the other things that make a quality capital city – it's no surprise that the number of visitors has risen sharply in recent years. Croatia's coastal attractions aside, Zagreb has finally been discovered as a popular city-break destination in its own right.

Visually, Zagreb is a mixture of straight-laced Austro-Hungarian architecture and rough-around-the-edges socialist structures, its character a sometimes uneasy combination of the two elements. This small metropolis is made for strolling the streets, drinking coffee in the permanently full cafes, popping into museums and galleries, and enjoying the theatres, concerts and cinema. It's a year-round outdoor city: in spring and summer everyone scurries to Jarun Lake in the southwest to swim or sail, or dance the night away at lakeside discos, while in winter Zagrebians go skiing at Mt Medvednica (only a tram or bus ride away).

◉ Sights

As the oldest part of Zagreb, the Upper Town (Gornji Grad) offers landmark buildings and churches from the earlier centuries of Zagreb's history. The Lower Town (Donji Grad) has the city's most interesting art museums and fine examples of 19th- and 20th-century architecture.

★ **Museum of Broken Relationships**   MUSEUM
(www.brokenships.com; Ćirilometodska 2; adult/concession 30/20KN; ⊙ 9am-10.30pm Jun-Sep, 9am-9pm Oct-May) Explore mementoes that remain after a relationship ends at Zagreb's quirkiest museum. The innovative exhibit toured the world until it settled here in its permanent home (it recently opened a second location in Hollywood). On display are donations from around the globe, in a string of all-white rooms with vaulted ceilings and epoxy-resin floors.

Funicular Railway   FUNICULAR
(ticket 4KN; ⊙ 6.30am-10pm) The funicular railway, which was constructed in 1888, connects the Lower and Upper Towns of Zagreb.

Dolac Market   MARKET
(⊙ open-air market 6.30am-3pm Mon-Sat, to 1pm Sun, covered market 7am-2pm Mon-Fri, 7am-3pm Sat, 7am-1pm Sun) Zagreb's colourful fruit and vegetable market is just north of Trg Bana Jelačića. Traders from all over Croatia come to sell their products at this buzzing centre of activity. Dolac has been heaving since the 1930s, when the city authorities set up a market space on the 'border' between the Upper and Lower Towns.

Zrinjevac   SQUARE
Officially called Trg Nikole Šubića Zrinskog but lovingly known as Zrinjevac, this verdant square at the heart of the city has become a vital part of Zagreb. It's filled with stalls almost year-round, and features festivals and events, be it summer or winter. Most are centred on the music pavilion (dating from 1891).

Art Pavilion   GALLERY
(Umjetnički Paviljon; 🖉 01-48 41 070; www.umjetnicki-paviljon.hr; Trg Kralja Tomislava 22; adult/concession 40/25KN; ⊙ 11am-8pm Tue-Thu, Sat & Sun, to 9pm Fri) The yellow Art Pavilion presents changing exhibitions of contemporary art. Constructed in 1897 in stunning art nouveau style, the pavilion is the only space in Zagreb that was specifically designed to host large exhibitions.

Museum of Contemporary Art   MUSEUM
(Muzej Suvremene Umjetnosti; 🖉 01-60 52 700; www.msu.hr; Avenija Dubrovnik 17; adult/concession 30/15KN; ⊙ 11am-6pm Tue-Fri & Sun, to 8pm Sat) Housed in a stunning city icon designed by local star architect Igor Franić, this swanky museum displays both solo and thematic group shows by Croatian and international artists in its 17,000 sq metres. The permanent display, *Collection in Motion*, showcases 620 edgy works by 240 artists, roughly half of whom are Croatian. There's a packed year-round schedule of film, theatre, concerts and performance art.

Maksimir Park   PARK
(🖉 01-23 20 460; www.park-maksimir.hr; Maksimirski perivoj bb; ⊙ info centre 10am-4pm Tue-Fri, to 6pm Sat & Sun) The park, a peaceful wooded enclave covering 18 hectares, is easily accessible by trams 11 and 12 from Jelačić square. Opened to the public in 1794, it was the first public promenade in southeastern Europe. It's landscaped like an English garden, with alleys, lawns and artificial lakes.

Mirogoj   CEMETERY
(Aleja Hermanna Bollea 27; ⊙ 6am-8pm Apr-Oct, 7.30am-6pm Nov-Mar) A 10-minute ride north of the city centre (or a 30-minute walk

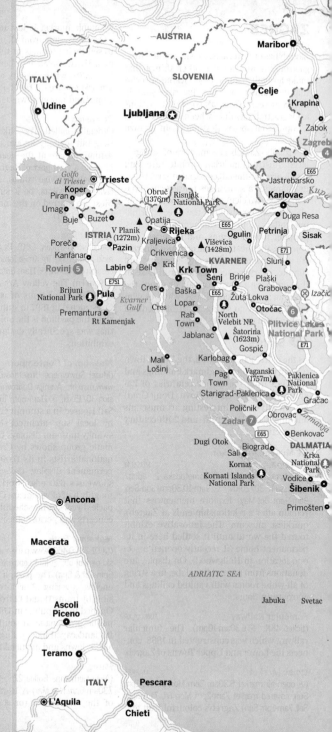

Croatia Highlights

1 Dubrovnik
(p268) Circling the historic city's mighty walls and then catching the cable car up Mt Srđ for breathtaking views from above.

2 Hvar Town
(p266) Capping off endless beach days with sunset cocktails and back-lane boogie sessions.

3 Split (p261)
Discovering the city's ancient heart in Diocletian's Palace, a quarter that buzzes day and night.

4 Zagreb (p251)
Exploring the quirky museums and cafes of Croatia's cute little capital.

5 Rovinj (p258)
Roam the steep cobbled streets and piazzas of Istria's showpiece coastal town.

6 Plitvice Lakes National Park
(p261) Marvelling at the otherworldly turquoise lakes and dramatic waterfalls of arguably Croatia's top natural attraction.

7 Zadar (p259)
Exploring Roman ruins, intriguing museums, local eateries and hip bars within the marbled streets of the old town.

Zagreb

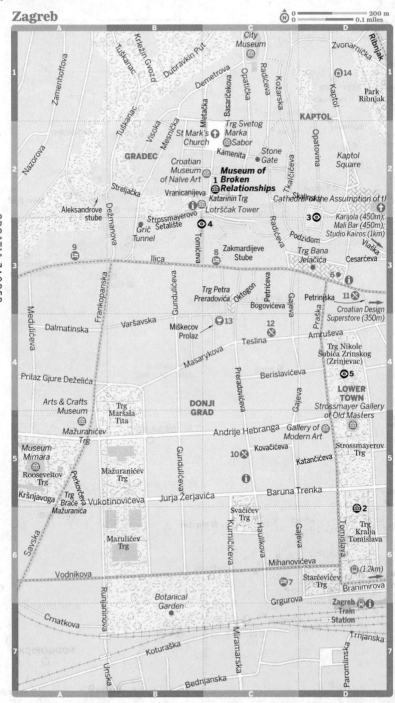

Zagreb

through leafy streets) takes you to one of the most beautiful cemeteries in Europe, sited at the base of Mt Medvednica. It was designed in 1876 by Austrian-born architect Herman Bollé, who created numerous buildings around Zagreb. The majestic arcade, topped by a string of cupolas, looks like a fortress from the outside, but feels calm and graceful on the inside.

☞ Tours

Secret Zagreb TOURS
(www.secret-zagreb.com; per person 75KN) A thorough ethnographer and inspiring storyteller, Iva Silla is the guide who reveals the Zagreb of curious myths and legends and peculiar historical personalities. Take her hit walking tour Zagreb Ghosts and Dragons (which runs year-round) to peek into the city's hidden corners or forgotten graveyards, all set in the city centre.

Blue Bike Tours CYCLING
(☑ 098 18 83 344; www.zagrebbybike.com; Trg Bana Jelačića 15) To experience Zagreb on a bike, book one of the tours that run twice

daily at 10am and 5pm from May through September (2pm only from October to April); choose between Ancient or Novi Zagreb. Tours last around 2½ hours and cost 190KN. The four-hour combo tour of both options costs 290KN. They also rent bikes for 100KN per day between 10am and 8pm.

🛏 Sleeping

★Studio Kairos B&B $$
(☑ 01-46 40 680; www.studio-kairos.com; Vlaška 92; s 340-420KN; d 520-620KN; ❄ 🛜) This adorable B&B in a street-level apartment has four well-appointed rooms decked out by theme – Writers', Crafts, Music and Granny's – and there's a cosy common space where a delicious breakfast is served. The interior design is gorgeous and the friendly owners are a fountain of knowledge. Bikes are also available for rent.

Swanky Mint Hostel HOSTEL $$
(☑ 01-40 04 248; www.swanky-hostel.com/mint; Ilica 50; dm from 150KN, s/d 360/520KN, apt 650-800KN; ❄ @ 🛜 ⛲) Inside a restored textile-dye factory from the 19th century, this cool hostel in the heart of town combines industrial chic with creature comforts in its rooms, dorms and apartments. Freebies include wi-fi, lockers, towels and a welcome shot of *rakija* (grappa). The garden bar serves breakfast and drinks, and there's even a small pool on site.

★Esplanade Zagreb Hotel HOTEL $$$
(☑ 01-45 66 666; www.esplanade.hr; Mihanovićeva 1; s/d 1165/1700KN; Ⓟ ❄ @ 🛜) Drenched in history, this six-storey hotel was built next to the train station in 1925 to welcome the *Orient Express* crowd in grand style. It has hosted kings, artists, journalists and politicians ever since. The art deco masterpiece is replete with walls of swirling marble, immense staircases and wood-panelled lifts.

Hotel Jägerhorn HOTEL $$$
(☑ 01-48 33 877; www.hotel-jagerhorn.hr; Ilica 14; s/d/apt 890/1000/1300KN; Ⓟ ❄ @ 🛜) A charming little hotel that sits right underneath Lotrščak Tower, the 'Hunter's Horn' has friendly service and 18 spacious, classic rooms with good views (you can gaze over leafy Gradec from the top-floor attic rooms). The downstairs terrace cafe is lovely. It's the oldest hotel in Zagreb, around since 1827.

CROATIA ZAGREB

✕ Eating

Bistro 75
BISTRO $

(☑01-48 40 545; Preradovićeva 34; mains 36-42KN; ☺11am-11pm Mon-Thu, to 1am Fri & Sat) Tasty bites like oxtail sandwiches and falafel wraps, a set of daily specials, twisted cocktails and a great range of local craft beers (like Zmajska and Varionica) are all reasons to check out this sleek little bistro. It has a colourful wall mural and a banquette inside, plus tables on a streetside deck.

★ Vinodol
CROATIAN $$

(☑01-48 11 427; www.vinodol-zg.hr; Teslina 10; mains 48-160KN; ☺10am-midnight) The well-prepared, central-European fare here is much-loved by local and overseas patrons. On warm days, eat on the covered patio (entered through an ivy-clad passageway off Teslina); the cold-weather alternative is the dining hall with vaulted stone ceilings. Highlights include the succulent lamb or veal and potatoes cooked under *peka* (a domed baking lid), as well as *bukovače* (local mushrooms).

★ Mundoaka Street Food
INTERNATIONAL $$

(☑01-78 88 777; Petrinjska 2; mains 65-85KN; ☺9am-midnight Mon-Sat) This tiny eatery clad in light wood, with tables outside, serves up American classics – think chicken wings and pork ribs – and a global spectrum of dishes, from Spanish tortillas to *shakshuka* eggs. Great breakfasts, muffins and cakes, all prepared by one of Zagreb's best-known chefs. Reserve ahead.

Mali Bar
TAPAS $$

(☑01-55 31 014; Vlaška 63; dishes 45-120KN; ☺12.30pm-midnight Mon-Sat) This spot by star chef Ana Ugarković shares the terraced space with **Karijola** (☑01-55 31 016; www.pizzeria-karijola.com; Vlaška 63; pizzas 46-70KN; ☺11am-midnight Mon-Sat, to 11pm Sun), hidden away in a *veža* (alleyway). The interior is cosy and earth-tone colourful, and the food is focused on globally inspired tapas-style dishes.

Zinfandel's
INTERNATIONAL $$$

(☑01-45 66 644; www.zinfandels.hr; Mihanovićeva 1; mains 150-295KN; ☺6am-11pm Mon-Sat, 6.30am-11pm Sun) Some of the tastiest, most creative dishes in town are conjured up by chef Ana Grgić and served with flair here in the dining room of the Esplanade Zagreb Hotel (p255).

🍷 Drinking & Nightlife

In the Upper Town, the chic Tkalčićeva is throbbing with bars and cafes. With half a dozen bars and sidewalk cafes between Trg Petra Preradovića (known locally as Cvjetni trg) and Bogovićeva in the Lower Town, the scene on summer nights resembles a vast outdoor party. Things wind down by midnight though, and get quieter from mid-July through late August.

Kino Europa
BAR

(www.kinoeuropa.hr; Varšavska 3; ☺8.30am-midnight Mon-Thu, to 4am Fri & Sat, 11am-11pm Sun; 📶) Zagreb's oldest cinema, from the 1920s, now houses a splendid cafe, wine bar and *grapperia*. At this glass-enclosed space with an outdoor terrace you can enjoy great coffee, over 30 types of grappa and free wi-fi. The cinema hosts film screenings and occasional dance parties.

ITINERARIES

Three Days

Spend a day in dynamic **Zagreb**, delving into its vibrant cafe culture and nightlife and fascinating museums, then head down to **Rovinj** in Istria to spend a couple of days unwinding by the sea, wandering the cobbled streets and sampling the celebrated Istrian cuisine.

One Week

Start with a weekend in Zagreb, then head south to take in one of the region's best sights: the Roman ruins of Diocletian's Palace in **Split** are a living part of this exuberant seafront city. Base yourself here for two days of sightseeing, beach fun and nightlife action. Next, take the winding coastal road to **Dubrovnik**, a magnificent walled city whose beauty is bound to blow you away with the jaw-dropping sights of its Old Town.

🛍 Shopping

Croatian Design Superstore DESIGN
(www.croatiandesignsuperstore.com; Martićeva
4; ⊘9am-9pm Mon-Sat) This one-stop shop
for the best of Croatian design stocks more
than 130 curated items by 150 different creators. Clad in all red, the store showcases the
cream of Croatia's homegrown design, from
accessories and gifts to wine and lighting. It
doubles as a platform for promoting Croatian design and also has a sweet little cafe
serving healthy bites.

Bornstein WINE
(www.bornstein.hr; Kaptol 19; ⊘9am-8pm Mon-Fri,
to 4.30pm Sat) If Croatia's wine and spirits
have gone to your head, get your fix here.
Stocks an astonishing collection of brandy,
wine and gourmet products. There's also a
wine bar on site.

ℹ Information

Main Tourist Information Centre (☑infor-
mation 0800 53 53, office 01-48 14 051; www.
infozagreb.hr; Trg Bana Jelačića 11; ⊘8.30am-
9pm Mon-Fri, 9am-6pm Sat & Sun Jun-Sep,
8.30am-8pm Mon-Fri, 9am-6pm Sat, 10am-
4pm Sun Oct-May) Distributes free city maps
and leaflets. There are also tourist information
centres at **Lotrščak Tower** (☑01-48 51 510;
⊘9am-9pm Mon-Fri, 10am-9pm Sat & Sun
Jun-Sep, 9am-5pm Mon-Fri, 10am-5pm Sat
& Sun Oct-May); the **main railway station**
(⊘9am-9pm Mon-Fri, 10am-5pm Sat & Sun);
the **main bus station** (☑01-61 15 507; ⊘9am-
9pm Mon-Fri, 10am-5pm Sat & Sun); and
Zagreb Airport (☑01-62 65 091; ⊘9am-9pm
Mon-Fri, 10am-5pm Sat & Sun).

Zagreb County Tourist Association (☑01-
48 73 665; www.tzzz.hr; Preradovićeva 42;
⊘8am-4pm Mon-Fri) Has information and
materials about attractions in Zagreb's surroundings, including wine roads and bike trails.

KBC Rebro (☑01-23 88 888; Kišpatićeva 12;
⊘24hr) East of the city; provides emergency aid.

ℹ Getting There & Away

AIR

Zagreb Airport (☑01-45 62 170; www.za-
greb-airport.hr) Located 17km southeast of
Zagreb, this is Croatia's major airport, offering
a range of international and domestic services.

BUS

Zagreb's **bus station** (☑060 313 333; www.
akz.hr; Avenija M Držića 4) is 1km east of the
train station. If you need to store bags, there's
a **garderoba** (☑01-60 08 649; Bus Station; per
hour 5KN; ⊘24hr). Trams 2 and 6 run from the
bus station to the train station. Tram 6 goes to
Trg bana Jelačića.

Domestic destinations include: Dubrovnik
(191KN to 231KN, 9½ to 11 hours, nine to 12
daily), Rovinj (100KN to 195KN, 4 to 6 hours, 20
daily), Zadar (90KN to 135KN, 3½ to five hours,
31 daily) and Split (115KN to 205KN, five to 8½
hours, 32 to 34 daily).

TRAIN

The **train station** (☑060 333 444; www.hzpp.
hr; Trg Kralja Tomislava 12) is in the southern
part of the city; there's a **garderoba** (locker per
24hr 15KN; ⊘24hr). It's advisable to book train
tickets in advance because of limited seating.

Domestic trains head to Split (190KN to
208KN, five to seven hours, four daily). There are
international departures to Belgrade (184KN,
6½ hours, two daily), Ljubljana (68KN, 2½ hours,
five daily), Sarajevo (165KN, eight to 9½ hours,
daily) and Vienna (549KN, six to seven hours,
two daily).

ℹ Getting Around

TO/FROM THE AIRPORT

The Croatia Airlines bus to the airport (30KN)
leaves from the bus station every half-hour or
hour from about 4.30am to 8pm, and returns
from the airport on the same schedule.

Taxis cost between 110KN and 200KN to the
city centre.

PUBLIC TRANSPORT

Zagreb's public transport (www.zet.hr) is based
on an efficient network of trams, although the
city centre is compact enough to make them
almost unnecessary. Tram maps are posted
at most stations, making the system easy to
navigate.

Buy tickets at newspaper kiosks or from the
driver for 10KN (15KN at night). You can use your
ticket for transfers within 90 minutes, but only
in one direction. A *dnevna karta* (day ticket) is
valid on all public transport until 4am the next
morning; it's available for 30KN at most newspaper kiosks.

Make sure you validate your ticket when you
get on the tram by pressing it on the yellow box.

ISTRIA

Continental Croatia meets the Adriatic in
Istria (Istra to Croats), the heart-shaped,
3600-sq-km peninsula just south of Trieste in
Italy. While the bucolic interior of rolling hills
and fertile plains attracts artsy visitors to its
hilltop villages, rural hotels and farmhouse
restaurants, the verdant indented coastline

is enormously popular with the sun'n'sea set. Vast hotel complexes line much of the coast and its rocky beaches are not Croatia's best, but the facilities are wide-ranging, the sea is clean and secluded spots are still plentiful.

The coast gets flooded with tourists in summer, but you can still feel alone and undisturbed in 'Green Istria' (the interior), even in mid-August. Add acclaimed gastronomy (starring fresh seafood, prime white truffles, wild asparagus, top-rated olive oils and award-winning wines), sprinkle it with historical charm and you have a little slice of heaven.

Rovinj

POP 14,300

Rovinj (Rovigno in Italian) is coastal Istria's star attraction. While it can get overrun with tourists in summer, it remains one of the last true Mediterranean fishing ports. Wooded hills and low-rise hotels surround the old town, which is webbed with steep cobbled streets and piazzas. The 14 green islands of the Rovinj archipelago make for a pleasant afternoon away; the most popular islands are Sveta Katarina and Crveni Otok (Red Island), also known as Sveti Andrija.

The old town is contained within an egg-shaped peninsula. About 1.5km south is the Punta Corrente Forest Park and the wooded cape of Zlatni Rt (Golden Cape), with its age-old oak and pine trees and several large hotels. There are two harbours: the northern open harbour and the small, protected harbour to the south.

⊙ Sights

★ **Church of St Euphemia**   CHURCH
(Sveta Eufemija; Petra Stankovića; ⊙10am-6pm Jun-Sep, to 4pm May, to 2pm Apr) **FREE** The town's showcase, this imposing church dominates the old town from its hilltop location in the middle of the peninsula. Built in 1736, it's the largest baroque building in Istria, reflecting the period during the 18th century when Rovinj was its most populous town. Inside, look for the marble **tomb of St Euphemia** behind the right-hand altar.

Punta Corrente Forest Park   PARK
(Zlatni Rt) Follow the waterfront on foot or by bike past Hotel Park to this verdant area, locally known as Zlatni Rt, about 1.5km south. Covered in oak and pine groves and boasting 10 species of cypress, the park was established in 1890 by Baron Hütterott, an

Austrian admiral who kept a villa on Crveni Otok. You can swim off the rocks or just sit and admire the offshore islands.

🛏 Sleeping

Porton Biondi   CAMPGROUND **$**
(☑052-813 557; www.portonbiondirovinj.com; Aleja Porton Biondi 1; campsites per person/tent 57/50KN; ⊙Apr-Oct; ⛺) This beachside camping ground, which sleeps 1200, is about 700m north of the old town. It has a restaurant, snack bar and, oddly enough, a massage service.

Villa Baron Gautsch   GUESTHOUSE **$$**
(☑052-840 538; www.baron-gautsch.com; IM Ronjgova 7; s/d 293/586KN; ❄🖥) This German-owned *pansion* (guesthouse), on the leafy street leading up from Hotel Park, has 17 spick-and-span rooms, some with terraces and views of the sea and the old town. Breakfast is served on the small terrace out the back. It's cash (kuna) only and prices almost halve in low season.

Monte Mulini   HOTEL **$$$**
(☑052-636 000; www.montemulinihotel.com; A Smareglia bb; d from 3500KN; 🅿❄🖥🏊) This swanky and extremely pricey hotel slopes down towards Lone Bay, a 10-minute stroll from the old town along the Lungomare. Balconied rooms all have sea views and upscale trimmings. The spa and Wine Vault restaurant are both tops. There are three outdoor pools, and the design is bold and bright, but you'll need a fat wallet to enjoy it.

✕ Eating

★ **Male Madlene**   TAPAS **$$**
(☑052-815 905; Sv Križa 28; 5 courses fingerfood & wine 150KN; ⊙11am-2pm & 7-11pm May-Sep) This adorable and popular spot is in the owner's tiny jumble sale of a living room hanging over the sea, where she serves creative finger food with market-fresh ingredients, based on old Italian recipes. Think tuna-filled zucchini, goat's-cheese-stuffed peppers and bite-size savoury pies and cakes. It has great Istrian wines by the glass. Reserve ahead, especially for evenings.

★ **Barba Danilo**   MEDITERRANEAN **$$$**
(☑052-830 002; www.barbadanilo.com; Polari 5; mains 90-280KN; ⊙6-11.30pm) The last place you might expect to find one of Rovinj's best restaurants is on a campsite 3km from the centre, but that's where you'll find Barba Danilo. With just 45 seats in summer, book-

WORTH A TRIP

MORE TO EXPLORE

Poreč This ancient Istrian town has at its heart a World Heritage–listed basilica and a medley of Gothic, Romanesque and baroque buildings.

Pula Don't miss Istria's main city, with its wealth of Roman architecture. The star of the show is the remarkably well-preserved amphitheatre dating back to the 1st century. About 10km south along the indented shoreline, the Premantura Peninsula hides a spectacular nature park, the protected cape of Kamenjak with its lovely rolling hills, wild flowers, low Mediterranean shrubs, fruit trees and medicinal herbs, and around 30km of virgin beaches and coves.

Opatija Genteel Opatija was the most chic seaside resort for the elite during the days of the Austro-Hungarian Empire – as evidenced by the many handsome belle-époque villas that the period bequeathed. The town sprawls along the coast between forested hills and the sparkling Adriatic, and the whole waterfront is connected by a promenade.

Korčula The Southern Dalmatian island of Korčula, rich in vineyards and olive trees, is the largest in an archipelago of 48, with plenty of opportunities for scenic drives, many quiet coves and secluded beaches, as well as Korčula Town, a striking walled town of round defensive towers, narrow stone streets and red-roofed houses that resembles a miniature Dubrovnik.

ing several days ahead is essential. Dishes by head chef Goran Glavan are modern takes on traditional Mediterranean fare with net-fresh seafood taking a star turn.

ℹ Information

Medical Centre (☏ 052-840 702; Istarska bb; ⏰ 24hr)

Tourist Office (☏ 052-811 566; www.tzgrovinj.hr; Pina Budicina 12; ⏰ 8am-10pm Jun-Sep, to 8pm Apr-May & Oct-Nov) Just off Trg Maršala Tita.

ℹ Getting There & Away

The bus station (Mattea Benussi) is just to the southeast of the old town. Destinations include Dubrovnik (402KN, 16 hours, one daily), Poreč (36KN to 47KN, 35 minutes to one hour, eight daily), Pula (33KN, 40 minutes, at least hourly), Split (285KN, 11 hours, one daily) and Zagreb (109KN to 150KN, 3¼ to 5½ hours, nine daily).

DALMATIA

Roman ruins, spectacular beaches, old fishing ports, medieval architecture and unspoilt offshore islands make a trip to Dalmatia (Dalmacija) unforgettable. Occupying the central 375km of Croatia's Adriatic coast, Dalmatia offers a matchless combination of hedonism and historical discovery. The jagged coast is speckled with lush offshore islands and dotted with historic cities.

Zadar

POP 75,100

Boasting a historic old town of Roman ruins, medieval churches, cosmopolitan cafes and quality museums set on a small peninsula, Zadar is an intriguing city. It's not too crowded, it's not overrun with tourists and its two unique attractions – the sound-and-light spectacle of the *Sea Organ* and the *Sun Salutation* – need to be seen and heard to be believed.

While it's not a picture-postcard kind of place, the mix of ancient relics, Habsburg elegance, coastal setting and unsightly tower blocks is what gives Zadar so much character. It's no Dubrovnik, but it's not a museum town either – this is a living, vibrant city, enjoyed by residents and visitors alike.

Zadar is also a key transport hub with superb ferry connections to the surrounding islands.

⊙ Sights

★**Sea Organ**   MONUMENT

(Morske orgulje; Istarska Obala) **FREE** Zadar's incredible *Sea Organ*, designed by local architect Nikola Bašić, is unique. Set within the perforated stone stairs that descend into the sea is a system of pipes and whistles that exudes wistful sighs when the movement of the sea pushes air through it. The effect is hypnotic, the mellifluous tones increasing in volume when a boat or ferry passes by. You

DON'T MISS

TROGIR

Gorgeous Trogir (called *Trau* by the Venetians) is set within medieval walls on a tiny island, linked by bridges to both the mainland and to the far larger Čiovo Island. On summer nights everyone gravitates to the wide seaside promenade, lined with bars, cafes and yachts – leaving the knotted, maze-like marble streets gleaming mysteriously under old-fashioned streetlights.

The old town has retained many intact and beautiful buildings from its age of glory between the 13th and 15th centuries. In 1997 its profuse collection of Romanesque and Renaissance buildings earned it World Heritage status.

While it's easily reached on a day trip from Split, Trogir also makes a good alternative base to the big city and a relaxing place to spend a few days.

Buses head here from Zagreb (from 149KN, 6½ hours, 11 daily), Zadar (80KN, 2½ hours, every half-hour), Split (21KN, 30 minutes, frequent) and Dubrovnik (140KN, 5½ hours, five daily).

can swim from the steps off the promenade while listening to the sounds.

★ Sun Salutation   MONUMENT

(Pozdrav Suncu; Istarska Obala) Another wacky and wonderful creation by Nikola Bašić (along with the nearby Sea Organ; p259), this 22m-wide circle set into the pavement is filled with 300 multilayered glass plates that collect the sun's energy during the day. Together with the wave energy that makes the *Sea Organ's* sound, it produces a trippy light show from sunset to sunrise that's meant to simulate the solar system. It also collects enough energy to power the entire harbour-front lighting system.

St Donatus' Church   CHURCH

(Crkva Sv Donata; Šimuna Kožičića Benje bb; 20KN; ⊙9am-9pm May-Sep, to 4pm Oct-Apr) Dating from the beginning of the 9th century, this unusual circular Byzantine-style church was named after the bishop who commissioned it. As one of only a handful of buildings from the early Croatian kingdom to have survived the Mongol invasion of the 13th century, it's a particularly important cultural relic. The simple and unadorned interior includes two complete Roman columns, recycled from the Forum. Also from the Forum are the paving slabs that were revealed after the original floor was removed.

🛏 Sleeping

★ Drunken Monkey   HOSTEL $

(☑023-314 406; www.drunkenmonkeyhostel. com; Jure Kastriotica Skenderbega 21; dm/r from 165/424KN; ☀@☎☎) Snuck away in a suburban neighbourhood, this friendly little

hostel has brightly coloured rooms, a small pool, a guest barbecue and an all-round funky vibe. Staff can arrange trips to the Plitvice Lakes and the Krka National Park. If it's full, try the Drunken Monkey's nearby sister – the Lazy Monkey, with similar standards and rates.

★ Art Hotel Kalelarga   HOTEL $$$

(☑023-233 000; www.arthotel-kalelarga.com; Majke Margarite 3; s/d 1340/1640KN; ☀☎) Built and designed under strict conservation rules due to its old-town location, this 10-room boutique hotel is an understated and luxurious beauty. Exposed stonework and mushroom hues imbue the spacious rooms with plenty of style and character. The gourmet breakfast is served in the hotel's own stylish restaurant (Široka 23; breakfast 25-60KN; mains 60-140KN; ⊙7am-10pm).

🍴 Eating & Drinking

★ Kaštel   MEDITERRANEAN $$

(☑023-494 950; www.hotel-bastion.hr; Bedemi Zadarskih Pobuna 13; mains 80-170KN; ⊙7am-11pm) Hotel Bastion's fine-dining restaurant offers contemporary takes on classic Croatian cuisine (octopus stew, stuffed squid, Pag cheese). France and Italy also make their presence felt, particularly in the delectable dessert list. Opt for the white-linen experience inside or dine on the battlements overlooking the harbour for a memorable evening's dining.

★ Pet Bunara   DALMATIAN $$

(☑023-224 010; www.petbunara.com; Stratico 1; mains 60-165KN; ⊙11am-11pm) With exposed stone walls inside and a pretty terrace lined with olive trees, this is an atmospheric place to tuck into Dalmatian soups and stews, homemade pasta and local faves such as octopus and turkey. Save room for a traditional Zadar fig cake or cherry torte.

Foša
SEAFOOD $$$

(☑ 023-314 421; www.fosa.hr; Kralja Dmitra Zvonimira 2; mains 95-225KN; ⊗noon-1am) With a gorgeous terrace that juts out into the harbour and a sleek interior that combines ancient stone walls with 21st-century style, Foša is a very classy place. The main focus of chef Damir Tomljanović is fresh fish, plucked from the Adriatic and served grilled or salt-baked.

★ La Bodega
WINE BAR

(www.labodega.hr; Široka 3; ⊗7am-1am Sun-Thu, to 1.30am Fri & Sat) With its slick, eccentric, semi-industrial decor, a bar with a line of hams and garlic hanging above, Portuguese-style tiles and welcoming, open-to-the-street approach, this is one of Zadar's hippest bars. There's a good range of Croatian wines by the glass and an extraordinary selection by the bottle – to be enjoyed with a variety of cheese and prosciutto.

ⓘ Information

Tourist Office (☑ 023-316 166; www.zadar. travel; Mihe Klaića 5; ⊗8am-11pm May-Jul & Sep, to midnight Aug, 8am-8pm Mon-Fri, 9am-2pm Sat & Sun Oct-Apr; ☎) Publishes a good colour map and rents audio guides (35KN) for a self-guided tour around the town. Also offers free wi-fi.

Zadar General Hospital (Opća Bolnica Zadar; ☑ 023-505 505; www.bolnica-zadar.hr; Bože Peričića 5)

ⓘ Getting There & Away

The **bus station** (☑ 060 305 305; www.liburnija-zadar.hr; Ante Starčevića 1) is about 1km southeast of the old town. Destinations include **Dubrovnik** (173KN, eight hours, six daily), **Pula** (176KN, seven hours, two daily), **Split** (80KN, three hours, hourly) and **Zagreb** (110KN, 3½ hours, hourly).

Split

POP 178,000

Croatia's second-largest city, Split (*Spalato* in Italian) is a great place to see Dalmatian life as it's really lived. Always buzzing, this exuberant city has just the right balance of tradition and modernity. Step inside Diocletian's Palace (a Unesco World Heritage Site and one of the world's most impressive Roman monuments) and you'll see dozens of bars, restaurants and shops thriving amid the atmospheric old walls where Split life has been humming along for thousands of years.

To top it off, Split has a unique setting. Its dramatic coastal mountains act as the perfect backdrop to the turquoise waters of the Adriatic and help divert attention from the dozens of shabby high-rise apartment blocks that fill its suburbs. It's this thoroughly lived-in aspect of Split that means it will never be a fantasy land like Dubrovnik, but you could argue that it's all the better for that.

WORTH A TRIP

PLITVICE LAKES NATIONAL PARK

The absolute highlight of Croatia's Adriatic hinterland, this glorious expanse of forested hills and turquoise lakes is exquisitely scenic – so much so that in 1979 Unesco proclaimed the **park** (☑ 053-751 015; www.np-plitvicka-jezera.hr; adult/child 180/80KN Jul & Aug, 110/55KN Apr-Jun, Sep & Oct, 55/35KN Nov-Mar; ⊗7am-8pm) a World Heritage Site.

Sixteen crystalline lakes tumble into each other via a series of waterfalls and cascades, whilst clouds of butterflies drift above. It takes upwards of six hours to explore the the 18km of wooden footbridges and pathways which snake around the edges of the rumbling water on foot, but you can slice two hours off by taking advantage of the park's free boats and buses (departing every 30 minutes from April to October).

While the park is beautiful year-round, spring and autumn are the best times to visit. In spring and early summer the falls are flush with water, while in autumn the changing leaves put on a colourful display. Winter is also spectacular, although snow can limit access and the free park transport doesn't operate. If possible, avoid the peak months of July and August, when the falls reduce to a trickle, parking is problematic and the sheer volume of visitors can turn the walking tracks into a conga line.

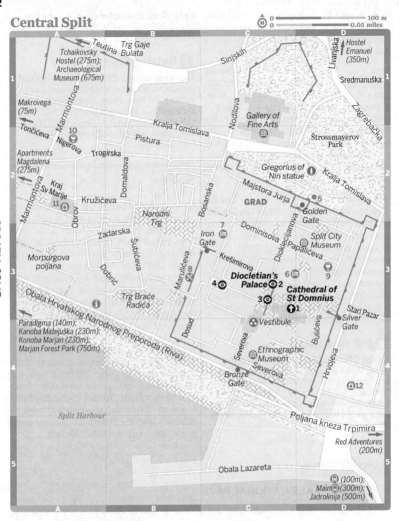

Central Split

⦿ Sights & Activities

◎ Diocletian's Palace

Facing the harbour, **Diocletian's Palace** is one of the most imposing Roman ruins in existence. Don't expect a palace though, nor a museum – this is the living heart of the city, its labyrinthine streets packed with people, bars, shops and restaurants.

It was built as a military fortress, imperial residence and fortified town, with walls reinforced by square corner towers. There are 220 buildings within the palace boundaries, which is home to about 3000 people.

Peristil   SQUARE
This picturesque, colonnaded, ancient Roman courtyard (or peristyle) lies at the very heart of Diocletian's Palace. In summer you can almost be guaranteed a pair of strapping local lads dressed as legionaries adding to the scene. Notice the black-granite sphinx sitting between the columns near the cathedral; dating from the 15th century BC, it was one of several imported from Egypt when the palace was constructed.

Central Split

★ **Cathedral of St Domnius**   CHURCH
(Katedrala Sv Duje; Peristil; cathedral/belfry 35/20KN; ⊙8am-7pm Mon-Sat, 12.30-6.30pm Sun) FREE Split's octagonal cathedral is one of the best-preserved ancient Roman buildings standing today. It was built as a mausoleum for Diocletian, the last famous persecutor of the Christians, who was interred here in 311 AD. The Christians got the last laugh, destroying the emperor's sarcophagus and converting his tomb into a church in the 5th century, dedicated to one of his victims. Note that a ticket for the cathedral includes admission to its crypt, treasury and baptistery (Temple of Jupiter).

Temple of Jupiter   TEMPLE
(Jupiterov Hram; 10KN; ⊙8am-7pm Mon-Sat, 12.30-6.30pm Sun) Although it's now the cathedral's baptistery, this wonderfully intact building was originally an ancient Roman temple, dedicated to the king of the gods. It still has its original barrel-vaulted ceiling and a decorative frieze on the walls, although a striking bronze statue of St John the Baptist by Ivan Meštrović now fills the spot where the god once stood. Of the columns that once supported a porch, only one remains.

⊙ Other Areas

Meštrović Gallery   GALLERY
(Galerija Meštrović; ☎021-340 800; www.mestrovic.hr; Šetalište Ivana Meštrovića 46; adult/child 40/20KN; ⊙9am-7pm Tue-Sun May-Sep, to 4pm Tue-Sun Oct-Apr) At this stellar art museum, you'll see a comprehensive, well-arranged collection of works by Ivan Meštrović, Croatia's premier modern sculptor, who built the gallery as a personal residence in the 1930s. Although Meštrović intended to retire here, he emigrated to the USA soon after WWII. Admission includes entry to the nearby **Kaštelet** (☎021-358 185; www.mestrovic.hr; Šetalište Ivana Meštrovića 39; admission by Meštrović Gallery ticket; ⊙9am-7pm Tue-Sun May-Sep), a fortress housing other Meštrović works.

Archaeological Museum   MUSEUM
(Arheološki Muzej; ☎021-329 340; www.armus.hr; Zrinsko-Frankopanska 25; adult/concession 30/15KN; ⊙9am-2pm & 4-8pm Mon-Sat) A treasure trove of classical sculpture and mosaic is displayed at this excellent museum, a short walk north of the town centre. Most of the vast collection originated from the ancient Roman settlements of Split and neighbouring Salona (Solin), and there's also some Greek pottery from the island of Vis. There are displays of jewellery and coins, and a room filled with artefacts dating from the Paleolithic to the Iron Age.

Salona   ARCHAEOLOGICAL SITE
(☎021-213 358; Don Frane Bulića bb, Solin; adult/child 30/15KN; ⊙9am-7pm Mon-Sat, to 2pm Sun) The ruins of the ancient city of Salona, situated at the foot of the mountains just northeast of Split, are the most archaeologically important in Croatia. Start by paying your admission fee at the **Tusculum Museum**, near the entrance to the reserve, as you'll need the map from its brochure to help you navigate the vast, sprawling site. This small museum has lots of ancient sculpture and interesting displays on the archaeological team that uncovered the site.

Marjan Forest Park   WALKING
(Park šuma Marjan) Considered the lungs of the city, this hilly nature reserve offers trails through fragrant pine forests to scenic lookouts, medieval chapels and cave dwellings once inhabited by Christian hermits. For an afternoon away from the city buzz, consider taking a long walk through the park and descending to Kašjuni beach to cool off before catching the bus back.

CROATIA SPLIT

ACTIVITIES

Croatia is a great destination for outdoor activities. Cycling is tops, especially in Istria, which has over 60 marked trails through stunning scenery. Hiking is also incredible, particularly in the national parks like Plitvice. Croatia also has some great dive sites, including many wrecks. Other activities worth trying in Croatia are kayaking, rafting, rock climbing and caving.

☞ Tours

Red Adventures   ADVENTURE
(☑ 091 79 03 747; www.red-adventures.com; Kralja Zvonimira 8) Specialising in active excursions, this crew offers sea kayaking (from €38), rock climbing (from €50), hiking (from €30) and bike tours (from €45) around Split. It also rents bikes, kayaks and cars, charters yachts, provides transfers and arranges private accommodation.

Split Walking Tours   TOURS
(☑ 099 82 15 383; www.splitwalkingtour.com; Golden Gate; ☉ Apr-Oct) Leads walking tours in English, Italian, German, Spanish and French, departing from the Golden Gate at set times during the day (check its website). Options include the 75-minute Diocletian's Palace Tour (100KN) and the two-hour Split Walking Tour (160KN), which includes the palace and the medieval part of town. It also offers kayaking, diving, cycling tours, boat trips and excursions.

🛌 Sleeping

Hostel Emanuel   HOSTEL $
(☑ 021-786 533; hostelemanuel@gmail.com; Tolstojeva 20; dm €29; ❄ @ 🛜) Run by a friendly couple, this hip little hostel in a suburban apartment block has colourful contemporary interiors and a relaxed vibe. In the two dorms (one sleeping five, the other 10), each bunk has a large locker, curtains, a reading light and a power outlet.

Tchaikovsky Hostel   HOSTEL $
(☑ 021-317 124; www.tchaikovskyhostel.com; Čajkovskoga 4; dm 180-200KN; ❄ @ 🛜) This four-dorm hostel in an apartment block in the neighbourhood of Špinut is run by a German-born Croat. Rooms are neat and tidy, with bunks featuring built-in shelves. Freebies include cereal, espresso and tea.

★ Apartments Magdalena   APARTMENT $$
(☑ 098 423 087; www.magdalena-apartments.com; Milićeva 18; 450-580KN; ❄ 🛜) You may never want to leave Magdalena's top-floor apartment once you see the old-town view from the dormer window. The three apartments are nicely furnished and the hospitality offered by the off-site owners is exceptional: chocolates on arrival, beer in the fridge, a back-up toothbrush in the cupboard and even a mobile phone with credit on it.

★ Villa Split   B&B $$$
(☑ 091 40 34 403; www.villasplitluxury.com; Bajamontijeva 5; r from €207; P ❄ 🛜) Built into the Roman-constructed wall of Diocletian's Palace, this wonderful boutique B&B has only three rooms – the best of which is the slightly larger one in the attic. If you're happy to swap the ancient for the merely medieval, there are six larger rooms in a 10th-century building on the main square.

★ Antique Split Luxury Rooms   HOTEL $$$
(☑ 021-785 208; www.antique-split.com; Poljana Grgura Ninskog 1; r 2690-3845KN; ❄ 🛜) Palace living at its most palatial, this boutique complex has eight chic rooms with stone walls and impressive bathrooms. In some you'll wake up to incredible views over the cathedral.

🍴 Eating

Makrovega   VEGETARIAN $
(☑ 021-394 440; www.makrovega.hr; Leština 2; mains 50-75KN; ☉ 9am-9.30pm Mon-Fri, to 5pm Sat) Hidden away down a lane and behind a courtyard, this meat-free haven serves macrobiotic, vegetarian and some raw food. Think lots of seitan, tofu and tempeh, and excellent cakes.

★ Konoba Matejuška   DALMATIAN $$
(☑ 021-355 152; www.konobamatejuska.hr; Tomića Stine 3; mains 85-160KN; ☉ noon-11pm) This cosy, rustic tavern in an alleyway minutes from the seafront specialises in well-prepared seafood – as epitomised in its perfectly cooked fish platter for two. There are only four small tables outside and a couple of larger ones inside, so book ahead.

★ Zinfandel   EUROPEAN $$
(☑ 021-355 135; www.zinfandelfoodandwinebar.com; Marulićeva 2; mains 90-145KN; ☉ 8am-1am) The vibe might be more like an upmarket wine bar but the food is top-notch here, too. The menu includes delicious risotto, home-

made pasta, veal cheek *pašticada* (traditional Dalmatian stew), burgers, steaks and fish, and there's a huge choice of local wine by the glass to wash it down. The beer selection is good, too.

Konoba Marjan   DALMATIAN $$
(📞 098 93 46 848; www.facebook.com/konobamarjan; Senjska 1; mains 78-139KN; ⊙noon-11pm; 🖃) Offering great-quality Dalmatian fare, this friendly little Veli Varoš tavern features daily specials such as cuttlefish *brujet* (fish stew), goulash and prawn pasta. The wine list is excellent, showcasing some local boutique wineries, and there are a few seats outside on the street leading up to Marjan Hill.

Paradigma   MEDITERRANEAN $$$
(📞 021-645 103; www.restoranparadigma.hr; Bana Josipa Jelačića 3; mains 100-175KN; ⊙11am-midnight Jun-Sep, 11.30am-10.30pm Mon-Sat, to 4.30pm Sun Oct-May) Bringing culinary innovation to Split, this restaurant sports modern interiors with colourful paintings and a rooftop terrace with sea glimpses in an old building resembling a ship's bow. Dishes are presented like mini works of art – and while not everything tastes as exquisite as it looks, most of the dishes are sublime.

🍸 Drinking & Nightlife

Marcvs Marvlvs Spalatensis   WINE BAR
(www.facebook.com/marvlvs; Papalićeva 4; ⊙5pm-midnight; 🖃) Fittingly, the 15th-century Gothic home of the 'Dante of Croatia', Marko Marulić, now houses this wonderful little 'library jazz bar' – two small rooms crammed with books and frequented by ageless bohemians, tortured poets and wistful academics. Cheese, chess, cards and cigars are all on offer, and there's often live music.

To Je To   BAR
(www.tojetosplit.com; Nigerova 2; ⊙8.30am-1am; 🖃) If you're up for loud rock and hip hop, Croatian craft beer and Mexican food, this effortlessly hip little bar is the place to come. The chilled-out Honduran/US owners engender a feel-good Latin American party vibe, there's live music most nights and a crazy karaoke session on Fridays.

🛍 Shopping

Green Market   MARKET
(Hrvojeva bb; ⊙6.30am-2pm) This open-air market is the place to come to stock up on fruit, vegetables and cut flowers. While it's

busiest in the mornings, a few stallholders stay open to sell cherries and strawberries to tourists throughout the afternoon in summer.

Fish Market   MARKET
(Ribarnica; Obrov 5; ⊙6.30am-2pm) As stinky and chaotic a scene as you could possibly imagine, Split's indoor/outdoor fish market is a spectacle to behold. Locals head here on a daily basis to haggle for all their scaly and slimy requirements from their favourite chain-smoking vendors. It's all over by about 11am, bar the dregs.

Information

Tourist Office (📞 021-360 066; www.visitsplit.com; Obala hrvatskog narodnog preporoda 9; ⊙8am-9pm Mon-Sat, to 7pm Sun Jun-Sep, 8am-8pm Mon-Sat, to 5pm Sun Apr, May & Oct, 9am-4pm Mon-Fri, to 1pm Sat Nov-Mar) Has info on Split and sells the Split Card (70KN), which offers free and reduced prices to Split attractions, plus discounts on car rental, restaurants, shops and theatres. You get the card for free if you're staying in Split more than three nights from October to May.

University Hospital Split (Klinički Bolnički Centar (KBC) Split; 📞 021-556 111; www.kbsplit.hr; Spinčićeva 1)

🛈 Getting There & Away

AIR
Split airport (Zračna Luka Split; 📞 021-203 507; www.split-airport.hr; Cesta dr Franje Tuđmana 1270, Kaštel Štafilić, Kaštela) is 20km west of town, just 6km before Trogir. **Croatia Airlines** (📞 072 500 505; www.croatiaairlines.com) operates flights to Zagreb year-round and to Dubrovnik in summer, as well as various international destinations. In summer, dozens of airlines fly here from all over Europe, but the only year-round carriers are Germanwings (www.germanwings.com) and Lufthansa CityLine (www.lufthansacityline.com).

BOAT
Split's ferry harbour is extremely busy and can be hard to negotiate, so you're best to arrive early. Most domestic ferries depart from Gat Sv Petra, the first of the three major piers, which has **ticket booths** for both Jadrolinija and Kapetan Luka. The giant international ferries depart from Gat Sv Duje, the second of the piers, where there's a large **ferry terminal** with ticketing offices for all the major lines.

For most domestic ferries you can't reserve tickets ahead of time; they're only available for purchase on the day of departure. In July and August it's often necessary to appear hours before departure for a car ferry, and put your car in the line for boarding. There is rarely a problem or a long wait obtaining a space off-season.

Jadrolinija (☏ 021-338 333; www.jadrolinija. hr; Gat Sv Duje bb) operates most of the ferries between Split and the islands, including catamarans to Hvar Town (55KN, one hour, two to four daily) and Korčula Town (80KN, three hours, daily).

Kapetan Luka (p268) has a fast catamaran operating daily from June to September, heading to **Hvar Town** (70KN, 65 minutes), **Korčula Town** (120KN, 1¾ hours) and **Dubrovnik** (190KN, 4¼ hours); services drop to four times per week in May and three per week in October.

BUS

Most intercity and international buses arrive at and depart from the **main bus station** (Autobusni Kolodvor Split; ☏ 060 327 777; www.ak-split.hr; Obala kneza Domagoja bb) beside the harbour. In summer, it's best to purchase bus tickets with seat reservations in advance. If you need to store bags, there's a **garderoba** (Obala kneza Domagoja 12; 1st hr 5KN, then 1.50KN per hr; ⊗ 6am-10pm) nearby.

Domestic destinations include Zagreb (130KN, five hours, at least hourly), Pula (300KN, 10 hours, three daily), Zadar (100KN, 3½ hours, at least hourly) and Dubrovnik (130KN, 4½ hours, 21 daily).

TRAIN

Five trains a day head to Split's **train station** (☏ 021-338 525; www.hzpp.hr; Obala kneza Domagoja 9; ⊗ 6am-10pm) from Zagreb (112KN, six hours, six daily). The train station has lockers (per day 15KN) that will fit suitcases but you can't leave bags overnight. There's another **garderoba** (☏ 098 446 780; Obala kneza Domagoja 6; per day 15KN; ⊗ 6am-10pm Jul & Aug, 7.30am-9pm Sep-Jun) nearby, out on the street.

Hvar Island

POP 11,080

Long, lean Hvar is vaguely shaped like the profile of a holidaymaker reclining on a sun lounger, which is altogether appropriate for the sunniest spot in the country (2724 sunny hours each year) and its most luxurious beach destination.

Hvar Town, the island's capital, offers swanky hotels, elegant restaurants and a general sense that, if you care about seeing and being seen, this is the place to be. Rubbing shoulders with the posh yachties are hundreds of young partygoers, dancing on tables at the town's legendary beach bars.

The northern coastal towns of Stari Grad and Jelsa are far more subdued and low-key.

Hvar's interior hides abandoned ancient hamlets, craggy peaks, vineyards and the lavender fields that the island is famous for. It's worth exploring on a day trip, as is the southern end of the island, which has some of Hvar's most beautiful and isolated coves.

◉ Sights & Activities

St Stephen's Cathedral　　　　CATHEDRAL
(Katedrala svetog Stjepana; Trg Sv Stjepana bb; 10KN; ⊗ 9am-1pm & 5-9pm) Providing a grand backdrop to the main square, this baroque cathedral was built in the 16th and 17th centuries at the height of the Dalmatian Renaissance to replace one destroyed by the Turks. Parts of the older building are visible in the nave and in the carved 15th-century choir stalls. Its most distinctive feature is its tall, rectangular bell tower, which sprouts an additional window at each level, giving it an oddly top-heavy appearance.

Fortica　　　　FORTRESS
(Tvrđava Španjola; ☏ 021-742 608; Biskupa Jurja Dubokovica bb; adult/child 30/15KN; ⊗ 8am-9pm) Looming high above the town and lit with a golden glow at night, this medieval castle occupies the site of an ancient Illyrian settlement dating from before 500BC. The views looking down over Hvar and the Pakleni Islands are magnificent, and well worth the trudge up through the old-town streets. Once you clear the town walls it's a gently sloping meander up the tree-shaded hillside to the fortress – or you can drive to the very top.

⊨ Sleeping

Hvar Town has the lion's share of the island's best accommodation, but expect to pay more than you would at most places on the Dalmatian coast. However, a good crop of hostels and private apartments helps to keep things more affordable. Stari Grad and Jelsa are poorly served for both hotels and hostels; consider private accommodation as an alternative.

★**Villa Skansi**　　　　HOSTEL **$**
(☏ 021-741 426; hostelvillaskansi1@gmail.com; Domovinskog rata 18; dm/r from 250/750KN; ❄ @ ⊛) Hvar's biggest and best hostel has brightly coloured dorms, fancy bathrooms, a great terrace with sea views, a barbecue, a bar, a book exchange and a laundry service,

PAKLENI ISLANDS

Most visitors to Hvar Town visit the crystal-clear waters, hidden beaches and deserted lagoons of the Pakleni Islands (Pakleni Otoci), a gorgeous chain of wooded isles that stretch out immediately in front of the town. Although the name is often translated as 'Hell's Islands', its meaning is thought to derive from *paklina*, a pine resin that was once harvested here to waterproof boats.

The largest of the Pakleni Islands by far is **Sveti Klement**, which supports three villages in its 5 sq km. Palmižana village has a marina, accommodation, restaurants and a pebbly beach.

The closest of the islands to Hvar is **Jerolim**, which has a popular naturist beach. Stipanska bay on the nearby island of **Marinkovac** (40KN, 10 to 15 minutes), also has a clothing-optional section, although it's better known for its raucous beach club. Other popular options on Marinkovac include Ždrilca bay and pretty Mlini beach.

and rents scooters and boats. The private rooms are in a separate, newly built block next door, surrounded by citrus trees, pomegranates and bougainvillea. Plus there's a free pub crawl every night.

⭐**Apartments Ana Dujmović**　　APARTMENT $
(☑098 838 434; www.visit-hvar.com/apart-ments-ana-dujmovic; Biskupa Jurja Dubokovića 36; apt from €55; P ✳ 🔊) This brilliant brace of comfortable holiday apartments are set behind an olive grove, only a 10-minute walk from the centre of town and, crucially, five minutes from the beach and Hula-Hula bar. Call ahead and the delightful owner will pick you up from the town centre.

⭐**Earthers Hostel**　　HOSTEL $$
(☑099 26 79 889; www.earthershostel.com; Martina Vučetića 11; dm/r 250/640KN; ⊘Apr-Sep; P ✳ 🔊) The advantages of Earthers' south-end-of-town location are the spacious surrounds and brilliant sunset views. The main hostel occupies a comfortable family home (which in the off-season reverts to being just that), and the well-appointed private rooms have their own swish house next door. A simple breakfast is included, and the friendly young owners host a barbecue every few days.

Apartments Komazin　　APARTMENT $$$
(☑091 60 19 712; www.croatia-hvar-apartments. com; Nikice Kolumbića 2; apt from 1025KN; P ✳ @ 🔊 ✦) With five bright apartments and one private room to rent, bougainvillea-draped Komazin is an attractive option at the upper end of the private-apartment heap.

🍴 Eating

⭐**Fig Cafe Bar**　　CAFE $$
(☑099 42 29 721; www.figcafebar.com; Ivana Frane Biundovića 3; mains 60-100KN; ⊘9am-10pm mid-Apr–Oct; 🔊🍴) Run by an Aussie-Croat and an American, this great little place serves up delicious stuffed flatbreads (fig and farm cheese, pear and blue cheese, brie and prosciutto), vegetarian curries and, our favourite Hvar breakfast, spiced eggs. There are even some vegan options – a rarity in these parts.

⭐**Dalmatino**　　DALMATIAN $$$
(☑091 52 93 121; www.dalmatino-hvar.com; Sv Marak 1; mains 70-250KN; ⊘noon-3pm & 5pm-midnight; 🔊) Calling itself a 'steak and fish house', this place is always popular – due, in part, to the handsome waiters and the free-flowing *rakija* (brandy). Thankfully the food is also excellent; try their *gregada*, a fish fillet served on potatoes with a thick, broth-like sauce.

🍸 Drinking & Nightlife

⭐**Hula-Hula Hvar**　　BAR
(www.hulahulahvar.com; Šetalište Antuna Tomislava Petriča 10; ⊘9am-11pm) *The* spot to catch the sunset to the sound of techno and house music, Hula-Hula is known for its après-beach party (4pm to 9pm), where all of young trendy Hvar seems to descend for sundowner cocktails. Dancing on tables is pretty much compulsory.

⭐**Kiva Bar**　　BAR
(www.kivabarhvar.com; Fabrika 10; ⊘9pm-2am) A happening place in an alleyway just off the Riva, Kiva is packed to the rafters most nights, with crowds spilling out and filling

up the lane. DJs spin a crowd-pleasing mix of old-school dance, pop and hip-hop classics to an up-for-it crowd.

ℹ️ Information

Tourist Office (☏ 021-741 059; www.tzhvar. hr; Trg Sv Stjepana 42; ⊙ 8am-9pm Jul & Aug, 8am-8pm Mon-Sat, 8am-1pm & 4-8pm Sun Jun & Sep, 8am-2pm Mon-Fri, to noon Sat Oct-May) In the Arsenal building, right on St Stephen's Sq.

Tourist Office Information Point (☏ 021-718 109; Trg Marka Miličića; ⊙ 8am-9pm Mon-Sat, 9am-1pm Sun Jun-Sep) A summertime annex of the main tourist office in the bus station.

ℹ️ Getting There & Away

Hvar has two main car-ferry ports: one near Stari Grad and the other at Sućuraj on the eastern tip of the island. **Jadrolinija** (☏ 021-773 433; www. jadrolinija.hr) operates from both, with ferries from Split to Stari Grad (per adult/child/car/ motorcycle/bike 47/24/318/78/45KN, two hours, six daily June to September, three daily at other times) and from Drvenik to Sućuraj (16/8/108/30/16KN, 34 minutes, 10 daily). Note: bus services to/from Sućuraj are extremely limited.

Jadrolinija also has high-speed catamaran services to Hvar Town from Korčula Town (70KN, 1½ hours, two daily) and Split (55KN, 65 minutes, seven daily). From July to mid-September, there's also a daily catamaran to Hvar Town from Dubrovnik (190KN, four hours).

Kapetan Luka (Krilo; ☏ 021-645 476; www. krilo.hr) has a fast catamaran to Hvar Town from Dubrovnik (190KN, three hours), Korčula Town (90KN, 65 minutes) and Split (70KN, 65 minutes). Tickets can be purchased from **Pelegrini Tours** (☏ 021-742 743; www.pelegrini-hvar.hr; Obala Riva 20).

ℹ️ Getting Around

Buses meet most ferries that dock at the ferry port near Stari Grad and go to Hvar Town (27KN, 20 minutes), central Stari Grad (13KN, 10 minutes) and Jelsa (33KN, 40 minutes). Buses also connect Hvar Town with Stari Grad (30KN, 30 minutes, 10 daily) and Jelsa (33KN, 50 minutes, eight daily); and Stari Grad with Jelsa (30KN, 25 minutes, 13 daily). Services are less frequent in the low season.

Dubrovnik

POP 28,500

No matter whether you are visiting Dubrovnik for the first time or if you're returning to this marvellous city, the sense of awe and beauty when you set eyes on the Stradun (the Old Town's main street) never fades. It's hard to imagine anyone becoming jaded by the marble streets and baroque buildings or failing to be inspired by a walk along the ancient city walls that once protected a civilised, sophisticated republic for five centuries and that now look out onto the endless shimmer of the peaceful Adriatic.

⊙ Sights

★ **City Walls & Forts**   FORT
(Gradske zidine; adult/child 120/30KN; ⊙ 8am-7.30pm Apr-Oct, 9am-3pm Nov-Mar) No visit to Dubrovnik would be complete without a walk around the spectacular city walls, the finest in the world and the city's main claim to fame. From the top, the view over the Old Town and the sparkling Adriatic is sublime. You can get a good handle on the extent of the shelling damage in the 1990s by gazing over the rooftops: those sporting bright new terracotta suffered damage and had to be replaced.

The first set of walls to enclose the city was built in the 9th century. In the middle of the 14th century the 1.5m-thick defences were fortified with 15 square forts. The threat of attacks from the Turks in the 15th century prompted the city to strengthen the existing forts and add new ones, so that the entire Old Town was contained within a stone barrier 2km long and up to 25m high. The walls are thicker on the land side – up to 6m – and range from 1.5m to 3m on the sea side.

The round **Minčeta Tower** (Tvrđava Minčeta; City Walls) protects the landward edge of the city from attack, the **Bokar Tower** (Tvrđava Bokar) and **Fort Lawrence** (Tvrđava Lovrjenac; admission 30KN; ⊙ 8am-7.30pm) look west and out to sea, while **Fort Revelin** (Trg Oružja) and **Fort St John** (Tvrđava sv Ivana) guard the eastern approach and the Old Harbour.

There are entrances to the walls from near the Pile Gate, the Ploče Gate and the Maritime Museum. The Pile Gate entrance tends to be the busiest, and entering from the Ploče side has the added advantage of getting the steepest climbs out of the way first (you're required to walk in an anticlockwise direction). Don't underestimate how strenuous the wall walk can be, especially on a hot day. There's very little shelter and the few vendors selling water on the route tend to be overpriced.

CAVTAT

Without Cavtat, there'd be no Dubrovnik, as it was refugees from the original Cavtat who established the city of Dubrovnik in 614. But Cavtat is interesting in itself. A lot more 'local' than Dubrovnik – read, not flooded by tourists on a daily basis – it has its own charm. Wrapped around a very pretty harbour that's bordered by beaches and backed by a curtain of imposing hills, the setting is lovely.

Cavtat's most famous personality is the painter Vlaho Bukovac (1855–1922), one of the foremost exponents of Croatian modernism. His paintings are liberally distributed around the town's main sights.

From June to September there are 11 sailings a day between Dubrovnik's Old Harbour and Cavtat (one way/return 50/80KN, 45 minutes). For the rest of the year this reduces to three to five a day, weather dependent. Bus 10 runs roughly half-hourly to Cavtat (25KN, 25 minutes) from Dubrovnik's bus station; the last buses return at 12.45am.

★ **Rector's Palace**   PALACE
(Knežev dvor; ☎020-321 422; www.dumus.hr; Pred Dvorom 3; adult/child multimuseum pass 100/25KN; ⊙9am-6pm Apr-Oct, to 4pm Nov-Mar) Built in the late 15th century for the elected rector who governed Dubrovnik, this Gothic-Renaissance palace contains the rector's office, his private chambers, public halls, administrative offices and a dungeon. During his one-month term the rector was unable to leave the building without the permission of the senate. Today the palace has been turned into the **Cultural History Museum**, with artfully restored rooms, portraits, coats of arms and coins, evoking the glorious history of Dubrovnik.

★ **War Photo Limited**   GALLERY
(☎020-322 166; www.warphotoltd.com; Antuninska 6; adult/child 40/30KN; ⊙10am-10pm daily Jun-Sep, 10am-4pm Wed-Mon May & Oct) An immensely powerful experience, this gallery features intensely compelling exhibitions curated by New Zealand photojournalist Wade Goddard, who worked in the Balkans in the 1990s. Its declared intention is to 'expose the myth of war...to let people see war as it is, raw, venal, frightening, by focusing on how war inflicts injustices on innocents and combatants alike'. There's a permanent exhibition on the upper floor devoted to the wars in Yugoslavia, but the changing exhibitions cover a multitude of conflicts.

★ **Lokrum**   ISLAND
(www.lokrum.hr; adult/child incl boat 100/20KN; ⊙Apr-Nov) Lush Lokrum is a beautiful, forested island full of holm oaks, black ash, pines and olive trees, and is an ideal escape from urban Dubrovnik. It's a popular swimming spot, although the beaches are rocky.

To reach the nudist beach, head left from the ferry and follow the signs marked FKK; the rocks at the far end are Dubrovnik's de facto gay beach. Also popular is the small saltwater lake known as the **Dead Sea**.

🏃 Activities

★ **Cable Car**   CABLE CAR
(Žičara; ☎020-414 355; www.dubrovnikcablecar. com; Petra Krešimira IV bb; return adult/child 120/50KN; ⊙9am-5pm Nov-Mar, to 9pm Apr, May, Sep & Oct, to midnight Jun-Aug) Dubrovnik's cable car whisks you from just north of the city walls to Mt Srđ in under four minutes. At the end of the line there's a stupendous perspective of the city from a lofty 405m, taking in the terracotta-tiled rooftops of the old town and the island of Lokrum, with the Adriatic and distant Elafiti Islands filling the horizon.

Banje Beach   SWIMMING
(www.banjebeach.eu; Frana Supila 10) Banje Beach is the closest beach to the old town, just beyond the 17th-century Lazareti (a former quarantine station) outside Ploče Gate. Although many people rent lounge chairs and parasols from the beach club, there's no problem with just flinging a towel on the beach if you can find a space.

Outdoor Croatia   KAYAKING
(☎020-418 282; www.outdoorcroatia.com; Sv Križa 3; day trip 400KN) Rents kayaks and offers day trips around the Elafiti Islands, along with multiday excursions and kayaking-cycling combos.

🛏 Sleeping

Dubrovnik is the most expensive city in the country, so expect to pay more for a room

Dubrovnik

here (even hostels fall into our midrange category), and you should book well in advance, especially in summer. There's limited accommodation in the compact old town itself. If you want to combine a beach holiday with your city stay, consider the leafy Lapad peninsula, 4km west of the centre.

Hostel Angelina   HOSTEL $

(☑ 091 89 39 089; www.hostelangelinaoldtown-dubrovnik.com; Plovani skalini 17a; dm 208KN; ✳ 🛜) Hidden away in a quiet nook of the old town, this cute little hostel offers bunk rooms, a small guest kitchen and a bougain-

villea-shaded terrace with memorable views over the rooftops. Plus you'll get a great glute workout every time you walk up the lane.

★ Karmen Apartments   APARTMENT $$

(☑ 098 619 282; www.karmendu.com; Bandure-va 1; apt from €95; ✳ 🛜) These four inviting apartments enjoy a great location a stone's throw from Ploče harbour. All have plenty of character with art, splashes of colour, tasteful furnishings and books to browse. Apartment 2 has a little balcony while apartment 1 enjoys sublime port views. Book well ahead.

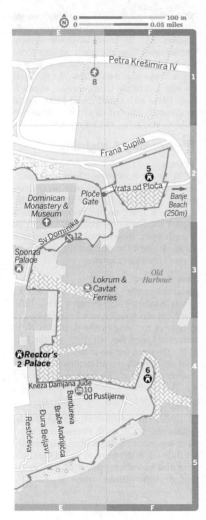

big hotel has more personality that you'd expect for its size, due in large part to its interesting art, slick design and charming staff. The breakfast buffet is excellent and the outdoor pool is pleasantly cool on a scorching day (the indoor one's warmer).

★ **Villa Dubrovnik** HOTEL **$$$**
(☑ 020-500 300; www.villa-dubrovnik.hr; Vlaha Bukovca 6; r from €581; P❄☎☎) Gazing endlessly at the old town and Lokrum from its prime waterfront position, this elegant, low-slung boutique hotel gleams white against a backdrop of honey-coloured stone. The windows retract completely to bring the indoor pool into the outdoors, but sunseekers can laze on a lounger by the sea or commandeer a day bed in the rooftop prosciutto-and-wine bar.

✗ Eating

★ **Pantarul** MODERN EUROPEAN **$$**
(☑ 020-333 486; www.pantarul.com; Kralja Tomislava 1; mains 70-128KN; ☺ noon-4pm & 6pm-midnight) This breezy bistro serves exceptional homemade bread, pasta and risotto, alongside the likes of pork belly, steaks, ox cheeks, burgers and a variety of fish dishes. There's a fresh modern touch to most dishes, but chef Ana-Marija Bujić knows her

★ **Villa Klaić** B&B **$$**
(☑ 091 73 84 673; www.villaklaic-dubrovnik.com; Šumetska 9; s/d from €70/90; P❄☎☎) Just off the main coast road, high above the old town, this outstanding guesthouse offers comfortable modern rooms and wonderful hospitality courtesy of the owner, Milo Klaić. Extras include a small swimming pool, continental breakfast, free pick-ups and free beer!

★ **Hotel Kompas** HOTEL **$$$**
(☑ 020-299 000; www.adriaticluxuryhotels.com; Kardinala Stepinca 21; r/ste from €210/542; P❄☎☎) Right by the beach at Lapad, this

way around traditional Dalmatian cuisine too – she's got her own cookbook to prove it.

★ Nishta
VEGETARIAN $$

(📋 020-322 088; www.nishtarestaurant.com; Prijeko 29; mains 77-85KN; ⊘11.30am-11.30pm; 📶🍴) The popularity of this tiny old-town eatery (expect to queue) is testament not just to the paucity of options for vegetarians and vegans in Croatia but to the excellent, imaginative food produced within. Alongside the expected curries, pastas and vegie burgers, the menu delivers more unusual options such as delicious eggplant tartare, 'tempehritos' and pasta-free zucchini 'spaghetti'.

★ Shizuku
JAPANESE $$

(📋 020-311 493; www.facebook.com/Shizuku-Dubrovnik; Kneza Domagoja 1f; mains 65-99KN; ⊘noon-midnight Tue-Sun; 📶) Tucked away in a residential area between the harbour and Lapad Bay, this charming little restaurant has an appealing front terrace and an interior decorated with silky draperies, paper lampshades and colourful umbrellas. The Japanese owners will be in the kitchen, preparing authentic sushi, sashimi, udon and gyoza. Wash it all down with Japanese beer or sake.

★ Restaurant 360°
MODERN EUROPEAN $$$

(📋 020-322 222; www.360dubrovnik.com; Sv Dominika bb; mains 240-290KN, 5-course degustation 780KN; ⊘6.30-11pm) Dubrovnik's glitziest restaurant offers fine dining at its finest, with flavoursome, beautifully presented, creative cuisine and slick, professional service. The setting is unrivalled, on top of the city walls with tables positioned so you can peer through the battlements over the harbour.

★ Amfora
INTERNATIONAL $$$

(📋 020-419 419; www.amforadubrovnik.com; Obala Stjepana Radića 26; mains 145-185KN; ⊘noon-4pm & 7-11pm) From the street, Amfora looks like just another local cafe-bar, but the real magic happens at the six-table restaurant at the rear. Dalmatian favourites such as *pašticada* (stew with gnocchi) and black risotto sit alongside fusion dishes such as swordfish sashimi, veal kofte, and miso fish soup.

🍷 Drinking & Nightlife

★ Bard
BAR

(off Ilije Sarake; ⊘9am-3am) The more upmarket and slick of two cliff bars pressed up against the seaward side of the city walls, this one is lower on the rocks and has a shaded terrace where you can lose a day quite happily, mesmerised by the Adriatic vistas. At night the surrounding stone is lit in ever-changing colours.

Cave Bar More
BAR

(www.hotel-more.hr; Hotel More, Šetalište Nika i Meda Pucića; ⊘10am-midnight) This little beach bar serves coffee, snacks and cocktails to bathers reclining by the dazzlingly clear waters of Lapad Bay, but that's not the half of it – the main bar is set in an actual cave. Cool off beneath the stalactites in the side chamber, where a glass floor exposes a water-filled cavern.

D'vino
WINE BAR

(📋 020-321 130; www.dvino.net; Palmotićeva 4a; ⊘10am-late; 📶) If you're interested in sampling top-notch Croatian wine, this upmarket little bar is the place to go. As well as a large and varied wine list, it offers themed tasting flights (three wines for 50KN)

ESSENTIAL FOOD & DRINK

Croatia's cuisine reflects the varied cultures that have influenced the country over the course of its history. You'll find a sharp divide between the Italian-style cuisine along the coast and the flavours of Hungary, Austria and Turkey in the continental parts. Istrian cuisine has been attracting international foodies in recent years for its long gastronomic tradition, fresh ingredients and unique specialities.

Here are a few essential food and drink items to be aware of while in Croatia:

Beer Two popular brands of Croatian pivo (beer) are Zagreb's Ožujsko and Karlovačko from Karlovac.

Burek Pastry stuffed with ground meat, spinach or cheese.

Ćevapčići Small spicy sausages of minced beef, lamb or pork.

Rakija Strong Croatian grappa comes in different flavours, from plum to honey.

Ražnjići Small chunks of pork grilled on a skewer.

accompanied by a thorough description by the knowledgable staff.

Buža BAR

(off Od Margarite; ⊘8am-2am) Finding this ramshackle bar on a cliff feels like a real discovery as you duck and dive around the city walls and finally see the entrance tunnel. However, Buža's no secret – it gets insanely busy, especially around sunset. Wait for a space on one of the concrete platforms, grab a cool drink in a plastic cup and enjoy the vibe and views.

ⓘ Information

Dubrovnik's tourist board has offices in **Pile** (⌨ 020-312 011; www.tzdubrovnik.hr; Brsalje 5; ⊘8am-9pm Jun-Sep, 8am-7pm Mon-Sat, 9am-3pm Sun Oct-May), **Gruž** (⌨ 020-417 983; www.tzdubrovnik.hr; Obala Pape Ivana Pavla II 1; ⊘8am-9pm Jun-Sep, to 3pm Mon-Sat Oct-May) and **Lapad** (⌨ 020-437 460; www.tzdubrovnik. hr; Kralja Tomislava 7; ⊘8am-8pm Mon-Fri, 9am-noon & 5-8pm Sat & Sun Jun-Sep) that dispense maps, information and advice.

Dubrovnik General Hospital (Opća bolnica Dubrovnik; ⌨ 020-431 777; www.bolnica-du. hr; Dr Roka Mišetića 2; ⊘emergency department 24hr) On the southern edge of the Lapad peninsula.

Travel Corner (⌨ 020-492 313; Obala Stjepana Radića 40; internet per hr 25KN, left luggage 2hr 10KN then per hr 4KN, per day 40KN; ⊘9am-8pm Mon-Sat, 9am-4.30pm Sun) This handy one-stop shop has a left-luggage service and internet terminals, dispenses tourist information, books excursions and sells Kapetan Luka ferry tickets.

ⓘ Getting There & Away

AIR

Daily flights to/from Zagreb and Split are operated by **Croatia Airlines** (⌨ 01-66 76 555; www. croatiaairlines.hr). Dubrovnik airport is served by over a dozen other airlines from across Europe.

BOAT

The **ferry terminal** (Obala Pape Ivana Pavla II 1) is in Gruž, 3km northwest of the old town. Ferries for **Lokrum and Cavtat** depart from the Old Harbour.

From July to mid-September, there's a daily **Jadrolinija** (⌨ 020-418 000; www.jadrolinija. hr; Obala Stjepana Radića 40) catamaran to Korčula (120KN, 2¼ hours) and Hvar (190KN, four hours).

From June to September **Kapetan Luka** (Krilo; ⌨ 021-872 877; www.krilo.hr) has a daily fast

boat to/from Korčula (120KN, 1¾ hours), Hvar (190KN, three hours) and Split (190KN, 4¼ hours), dropping to four times per week in May and three per week in October.

BUS

Buses out of Dubrovnik **bus station** (⌨ 060 305 070; Obala Pape Ivana Pavla II 44a; 🔊) can be crowded, so book tickets ahead in summer. All bus schedules are detailed at www.libertas-dubrovnik.hr.

ⓘ Getting Around

Dubrovnik Airport (DBV, Zračna luka Dubrovnik; ⌨ 020-773 100; www.airport-dubrovnik.hr) is in Čilipi, 19km southeast of Dubrovnik. Atlas runs the airport bus service (40KN, 30 minutes), timed around flights. Buses to Dubrovnik stop at the Pile Gate and the bus station; buses to the airport pick up from the bus station and from the bus stop near the cable car.

A taxi to the old town costs up to 280KN.

SURVIVAL GUIDE

ⓘ Directory A-Z

ACCOMMODATION

Croatia is traditionally seen as a summer destination and good places book out well in advance in July and August. It's also very busy in June and September.

Hotels These range from massive beach resorts to boutique establishments.

Apartments Privately owned holiday units are a staple of the local accommodation scene, especially for families.

Guesthouses Usually family-run establishments where spare rooms are rented at a bargain price – sometimes with their own bathrooms, sometimes not.

Hostels Mainly in the bigger cities and more popular beach destinations, with dorms and sometimes private rooms, too.

Campgrounds Tent and caravan sites, often fairly basic.

SLEEPING PRICE RANGES

The following price ranges refer to a double room with a bathroom in July and August.

€ less than 450KN

€€ 450–800KN

€€€ more than 800KN

CROATIA DIRECTORY A-Z

Registration & Sojourn Tax

Accommodation providers will handle travellers' registration with the local police, as required by Croatian authorities. To do this, they will ask for your passport when you check in. Normally they will note the details they require and photocopy or scan the relevant page, and then hand your passport straight back.

Part of the reason for this process is so that the correct 'sojourn tax' can be paid. This is a small amount (usually less than 10KN) that is charged for every day you stay in Croatia, no matter what type of accommodation you're staying in. It's quite normal for this to be additional to the room rate you've been quoted.

OPENING HOURS

Opening hours vary throughout the year. We've provided high-season opening hours; hours generally decrease in the shoulder and low seasons.

Banks 8am or 9am to 8pm weekdays and 7am–1pm or 8am–2pm Saturdays.

Cafes and Bars 8am or 9am to midnight.

Offices 8am–4pm or 8.30am–4.30pm weekdays.

Post Offices 7am–8pm weekdays and 7am–1pm Saturdays. Longer hours in coastal towns in summer.

Restaurants Noon to 11pm or midnight. Often closed Sundays outside peak season.

Shops 8am–8pm weekdays, 8am to 2pm or 3pm Saturdays. Some take a 2pm–5pm break. Shopping malls have longer hours.

PUBLIC HOLIDAYS

Croats take their holidays very seriously. Shops and museums are shut and boat services are reduced. On religious holidays, the churches are full; it can be a good time to check out the artwork in a church that is usually closed.

COUNTRY FACTS

Area 56,538 sq km

Capital Zagreb

Country Code 385

Currency Kuna (KN)

Emergency Ambulance ☑94, police ☑92

Language Croatian

Money ATMs available; credit cards accepted in most hotels and many restaurants.

Population 4.3 million

Visas Not required for most nationalities for stays of up to 90 days.

EATING PRICE RANGES

The following price ranges refer to a main course.

€ less than 70KN

€€ 70–120KN

€€€ more than 120KN

New Year's Day 1 January

Epiphany 6 January

Easter Sunday & Monday March/April

Labour Day 1 May

Corpus Christi 60 days after Easter

Day of Antifascist Resistance 22 June

Statehood Day 25 June

Homeland Thanksgiving Day 5 August

Feast of the Assumption 15 August

Independence Day 8 October

All Saints' Day 1 November

Christmas 25 & 26 December

TELEPHONE
Mobile Phones

Users with unlocked phones can buy a local SIM card, which are easy to find. Otherwise, you may be charged roaming rates.

Phone Codes

➡ To call Croatia from abroad, dial your international access code, then ☑385 (the country code for Croatia), then the area code (without the initial 0) and the local number.

➡ To call from region to region within Croatia, start with the area code (with the initial 0); drop it when dialling within the same code.

➡ Phone numbers with the prefix 060 are either free or charged at a premium rate, so watch out for the small print. Phone numbers that begin with 09 are mobile phone numbers.

TOURIST INFORMATION

The Croatian National Tourist Board (www.croatia.hr) is a good source of info.

VISAS

Citizens of many countries, including EU member states, Australia, Brazil, Canada, Israel, Japan, New Zealand, Singapore and the USA do not need a visa for stays of up to 90 days within a 180-day period. (Note that this means that leaving the country just to get a stamp and return isn't a legal option.)

Other nationalities can check whether they need a visa and download application forms on the website of the Croatian Ministry for Foreign & European Affairs (www.mvep.hr).

ⓘ Getting There & Away

There are direct flights to Croatia from a variety of European cities year-round, with dozens of seasonal routes and charters added in summer

LAND

Croatia has border crossings with Slovenia, Hungary, Serbia, Bosnia and Hercegovina, and Montenegro.

Direct bus connections link Croatia to all of its neighbours and to as far afield as Norway. Useful websites include www.eurolines.com, www.buscroatia.com, www.getbybus.com and www.vollo.net.

Zagreb is Croatia's main train hub, with connections to Austria, Bosnia, Germany, Hungary, Serbia, Slovenia and Switzerland. Useful websites include www.raileurope.com and www.eurail.com.

SEA

Regular ferries connect Croatia with Italy. Split is the main hub.

ⓘ Getting Around

Transport in Croatia is reasonably priced, quick and generally efficient.

Air A surprisingly extensive schedule of domestic flights, especially in summer.

Boat Extensive network of car ferries and faster catamarans all along the coast and the islands.

Bus Reasonably priced, with extensive coverage of the country and frequent departures.

Car Useful for travelling at your own pace or for visiting regions with minimal public transport. Cars can be hired in every city or larger town. Drive on the right.

Train Less frequent and much slower than buses, with a limited network.

Czech Republic

Best Places to Eat

➡ U Kroka (p286)

➡ Field (p286)

➡ Buffalo Burger Bar (p291)

➡ Pavillon (p297)

Best Places to Stay

➡ Hotel 16 (p285)

➡ Savic Hotel (p285)

➡ Hotel garni Myší Díra (p294)

➡ Hostel Mitte (p296)

Why Go?

Since the fall of communism in 1989 and the opening up of Central and Eastern Europe, Prague has evolved into one of Europe's most popular travel destinations. The city offers an intact medieval core that transports you back – especially when strolling the hidden streets of the Old Town – some 600 years. The 14th-century Charles Bridge, traversing two historic neighbourhoods across a slow-moving river, is one of the continent's most beautiful sights.

The city is not just about history. It's a vital urban centre with a rich array of cultural offerings. Outside the capital, in the provinces of Bohemia and Moravia, castles and palaces abound – including the audacious hilltop chateau at Český Krumlov – which illuminate the stories of powerful dynasties whose influence was felt throughout Europe. Olomouc, the historic capital of Moravia to the east, boasts much of the beauty of Prague without the crowds.

When to Go
Prague

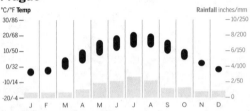

May Prague Spring Festival makes this the capital's most popular month.

Sep Autumn brings lovely strolling weather to West Bohemia's spa towns.

Dec *Svařák* (mulled wine) and music at Christmas markets in towns across the country.

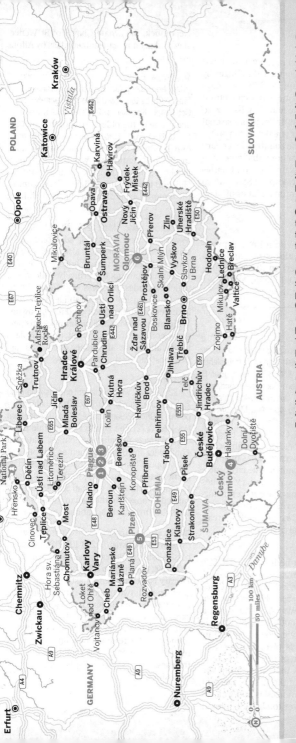

Czech Republic Highlights

1 Charles Bridge (p280) Strolling across in the early morning or late evening when the crowds thin out.

2 U Kroka (p286) Enjoying an evening in an old-school Czech pub.

3 Astronomical Clock (p279) Joining the appreciative throngs at the top of the hour.

4 Český Krumlov (p292) Walking the streets of one of the prettiest towns in Central Europe.

5 Pilsner Urquell Brewery (p291) Touring this brewery in Plzeň to see where it all started.

6 Olomouc (p298) Ambling through this stately town, the most amazing place you've never heard of.

PRAGUE

POP 1.3 MILLION

It's the perfect irony of Prague: you are lured here by the past, but compelled to linger by the present and the future. Fill your days with its illustrious artistic and architectural heritage – from Gothic and Renaissance to art nouveau and cubist. If Prague's seasonal legions of tourists wear you down, that's OK. Just drink a glass of the country's legendary lager, relax and rest reassured that quiet moments still exist: a private dawn on Charles Bridge, the glorious cityscape of Staré Město or getting lost in the intimate lanes of Malá Strana.

⊙ Sights

Prague nestles on the Vltava River, separating **Hradčany** (the Castle district) and **Malá Strana** (Lesser Quarter) on the west bank, from **Staré Město** (Old Town) and **Nové Město** (New Town) on the east.

⊙ Hradčany

★ Prague Castle   CASTLE
(Pražský hrad; Map p279; ☑ 224 372 423; www.hrad.cz; Hradčanské náměstí 1; grounds free, sights adult/concession Tour A & C 350/175Kc, Tour B 250/125Kc; ☺ grounds 6am-11pm year-round, gardens 10am-6pm Apr-Oct, closed Nov-Mar, historic bldg 9am-5pm Apr-Oct, to 4pm Nov-Mar; Ⓜ Malostranská, 🚊22) Prague Castle – Pražský hrad, or just *hrad* to Czechs – is Prague's most popular attraction. Looming above the Vltava's left bank, its serried ranks of spires, towers and palaces dominate the city centre like a fairy-tale fortress. Within its walls lies a varied and fascinating collection of historic buildings, museums and galleries that are home to some of the Czech Republic's greatest artistic and cultural treasures.

★ St Vitus Cathedral   CHURCH
(Katedrála sv Víta; Map p279; ☑ 257 531 622; www.katedralasvatehovita.cz; Third Courtyard, Prague Castle; admission incl with Prague Castle Tour A & B tickets; ☺ 9am-5pm Mon-Sat, noon-5pm Sun Apr-Oct, to 4pm Nov-Mar; 🚊22) Built over a time span of almost 600 years, St Vitus is one of the most richly endowed cathedrals in central Europe. It is pivotal to the religious and cultural life of the Czech Republic, housing treasures that range from the 14th-century mosaic of the Last Judgement and the tombs of St Wenceslas and Charles IV, to the baroque silver tomb of St John of Nepomuck, the ornate Chapel of St Wenceslas, and art nouveau stained glass by Alfons Mucha.

Old Royal Palace   PALACE
(Starý královský palác; Map p279; admission with Prague Castle tour A & B tickets; ☺ 9am-5pm Apr-Oct, to 4pm Nov-Mar; 🚊22) The Old Royal Palace is one of the oldest parts of Prague Castle, dating from 1135. It was originally used only by Czech princesses, but from the 13th to the 16th centuries it was the king's own palace. At its heart is the grand Vladislav Hall and the Bohemian Chancellery, scene of the famous Defenestration of Prague in 1618.

Lobkowicz Palace   MUSEUM
(Lobkovický palác; Map p279; ☑ 233 312 925; www.lobkowicz.com; Jiřská 3; adult/concession/family 275/200/690Kč; ☺ 10am-6pm; 🚊22) This 16th-century palace houses a private museum known as the Princely Collections, which includes priceless paintings, furniture and musical memorabilia. Your tour includes an audio guide dictated by owner William Lobkowicz and his family – this personal connection really brings the displays to life, and makes the palace one of the castle's most interesting attractions.

★ Loreta   CHURCH
(☑ 220 516 740; www.loreta.cz; Loretánské náměstí 7; adult/child/family 150/80/310Kč, photography permit 100Kč; ☺ 9am-5pm Apr-Oct, 9.30am-4pm Nov-Mar; 🚊22) The Loreta is a baroque place of pilgrimage founded by Benigna Kateřina Lobkowicz in 1626, designed as a replica of the supposed Santa Casa (Sacred House; the home of the Virgin Mary) in the Holy Land. Legend says that the original Santa Casa was carried by angels to the Italian town of Loreto as the Turks were advancing on Nazareth.

★ Strahov Library   HISTORIC BUILDING
(Strahovská knihovna; ☑ 233 107 718; www.strahovskyklaster.cz; Strahovské nádvoří 1; adult/child 100/50Kč; ☺ 9am-noon & 1-5pm; 🚊22) Strahov Library is the largest monastic library in the country, with two magnificent baroque halls dating from the 17th and 18th centuries. You can peek through the doors but, sadly, you can't go into the halls themselves – it was found that fluctuations in humidity caused by visitors' breath was endangering the frescoes. There's also a display of historical curiosities.

Prague Castle

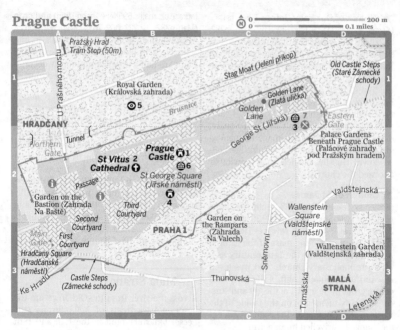

◎ Staré Město

The Old Town (Staré Město) is the city's oldest quarter and home to its main market, Old Town Square (Staroměstské náměstí; Map p282; Ⓜ Staroměstská), often simply called Staromák. The square has functioned as the centre of the Old Town since the 10th century.

★ **Old Town Hall** HISTORIC BUILDING

(Staroměstská radnice; Map p282; ☏ 236 002 629; www.staromestskaradnicepraha.cz; Staroměstské náměstí 1; guided tour adult/child 100/70Kč, incl tower 180Kč; ◷ 11am-6pm Mon, 9am-6pm Tue-Sun; Ⓜ Staroměstská) Prague's Old Town Hall, founded in 1338, is a hotchpotch of medieval buildings acquired piecemeal over the centuries, presided over by a tall Gothic tower with a splendid Astronomical Clock. As well as housing the Old Town's main tourist information office, the town hall has several historic attractions, and hosts art exhibitions on the ground floor and the 2nd floor.

★ **Astronomical Clock** HISTORIC SITE

(Map p282; Staroměstské náměstí; ◷ chimes on the hour 9am-9pm; Ⓜ Staroměstská) Every hour, on the hour, crowds gather beneath the Old

Prague Castle

◉ Top Sights

◎ Sights

⊗ Eating

Town Hall Tower (Věž radnice; Map p282; ☏ 236 002 629; www.staromestskaradnicepraha. cz; Staroměstské náměstí 1; adult/child 130/80Kč, incl Old Town Hall tour 180Kč; ◷ 11am-10pm Mon, 9am-10pm Tue-Sun; Ⓜ Staroměstská) to watch the Astronomical Clock in action. Despite a slightly underwhelming performance that takes only 45 seconds, the clock is one of Europe's best-known tourist attractions, and a 'must-see' for visitors to Prague. After all, it's historic, photogenic and – if you take time to study it – rich in intriguing symbolism. The clock is scheduled to be out of action from spring 2017 to summer 2018 while the clock tower undergoes renovations.

★ Church of Our Lady Before Týn   CHURCH
(Kostel Panny Marie před Týnem; Map p282; ☑222 318 186; www.tyn.cz; Staroměstské náměstí; suggested donation 25Kč; ◎10am-1pm & 3-5pm Tue-Sat, 10am-noon Sun Mar-Dec; Ⓜ Staroměstská) Its distinctive twin Gothic spires make the Týn Church an unmistakable Old Town landmark. Like something out of a 15th-century – and probably slightly cruel – fairy tale, they loom over the Old Town Square, decorated with a golden image of the Virgin Mary made in the 1620s from the melted-down Hussite chalice that previously adorned the church.

★ Church of St James   CHURCH
(Kostel sv Jakuba; Map p282; http://praha.minorite.cz; Malá Štupartská 6; ◎9.30am-noon & 2-4pm Tue-Sat, 2-4pm Sun; Ⓜ Náměstí Republiky) FREE The great Gothic mass of the Church of St James began in the 14th century as a Minorite monastery church, and was given a beautiful baroque facelift in the early 18th century. But in the midst of the gilt and stucco is a grisly memento: on the inside of the western wall (look up to the right as you enter) hangs a shrivelled human arm.

★ Municipal House   HISTORIC BUILDING
(Obecní dům; Map p282; ☑222 002 101; www.obecnidum.cz; náměstí Republiky 5; guided tour adult/concession/child under 10yr 290/240Kč/free; ◎public areas 7.30am-11pm, information centre 10am-8pm; ☎; Ⓜ Náměstí Republiky, 🚋6, 8, 15, 26) Restored in the 1990s after decades of neglect, Prague's most exuberantly art-nouveau building is a labour of love, every detail of its design and decoration carefully considered, every painting and sculpture loaded with symbolism. The **restaurant** (Map p282; ☑222 002 770; www.francouzskares-

taurace.cz; mains 695Kč; ◎noon-11pm) and **cafe** (Map p282; ☑222 002 763; www.kavarnaod.cz; ◎7.30am-11pm; ☎) here are like walk-in museums of art-nouveau design, while upstairs there are half a dozen sumptuously decorated halls that you can visit by guided tour.

★ Apple Museum   MUSEUM
(Map p282; ☑774 414 775; www.applemuseum.com; Husova 21; adult/child 300/140Kč; ◎10am-10pm; Ⓜ Staroměstská) This shrine to all things Apple claims to be the world's biggest collection of Apple products, with at least one of everything made by the company between 1976 and 2012. Sleek white galleries showcase row upon row of beautifully displayed computers, laptops, iPods and iPhones like sacred reliquaries; highlights include the earliest Apple I and Apple II computers, an iPod 'family tree', and Steve Jobs' business cards.

◉ Malá Strana

Across the river from the Old Town are the baroque backstreets of Malá Strana (the Lesser Quarter), built in the 17th and 18th centuries by victorious Catholic clerics and noblemen on the foundations of their predecessors' Renaissance palaces.

★ Charles Bridge   BRIDGE
(Karlův most; Map p282; ◎24hr; 🚋2, 17, 18 to Karlovy lázně, 12, 15, 20, 22 to Malostranské náměstí) Strolling across Charles Bridge is everybody's favourite Prague activity. However, by 9am it's a 500m-long fairground, with an army of tourists squeezing through a gauntlet of hawkers and buskers beneath the impassive gaze of the baroque statues that line the parapets. If you want to experience the

---

ITINERARIES
··

One Week
Experience **Prague's** exciting combination of its tumultuous past and energetic present. Top experiences include the grandeur of Prague Castle, Josefov's Prague Jewish Museum, and getting lost amid the bewildering labyrinth of the Old Town. Take an essential day trip to **Karlštejn**, and then head south to **Český Krumlov** for a few days of riverside R&R.

Two Weeks
Begin in **Prague** before heading west for the spa scene at **Karlovy Vary**. Balance the virtue and vice ledger with a few Bohemian brews in **Plzeň** before heading south for relaxation and rigour around **Český Krumlov**. Head east to the Renaissance grandeur of **Telč** and **Brno's** cosmopolitan galleries and museums. From Moravia's largest city, it's just a skip to stately **Olomouc**.

bridge at its most atmospheric, try to visit it at dawn.

★**St Nicholas Church**   CHURCH
(Kostel sv Mikuláše; ☑ 257 534 215; www.stnicholas. cz; Malostranské náměstí 38; adult/child 70/50Kč; ☺ 9am-5pm Mar-Oct, to 4pm Nov-Feb; ⛆ 12, 15, 20, 22) Malá Strana is dominated by the huge green cupola of St Nicholas Church, one of Central Europe's finest baroque buildings. (Don't confuse it with the other Church of St Nicholas on Old Town Square.) On the ceiling, Johann Kracker's 1770 *Apotheosis of St Nicholas* is Europe's largest fresco (clever trompe l'oeil technique has made the painting merge almost seamlessly with the architecture).

★**Museum of the
Infant Jesus of Prague**   MUSEUM
(Muzeum Pražského Jezulátka; ☑ 257 533 646; www.pragjesu.cz; Karmelitská 9; ☺ church 8.30am-7pm Mon-Sat, to 8pm Sun, museum 9.30am-5.30pm Mon-Sat, 1-6pm Sun, closed 1 Jan, 25 & 26 Dec & Easter Mon; ⛆ 12, 15, 20, 22) **FREE** The Church of Our Lady Victorious (kostel Panny Marie Vítězné), built in 1613, has on its central altar a 47cm-tall waxwork figure of the baby Jesus, brought from Spain in 1628 and known as the Infant Jesus of Prague (Pražské Jezulátko). At the back of the church is a museum, displaying a selection of the frocks used to dress the Infant.

★**John Lennon Wall**   HISTORIC SITE
(Velkopřevorské náměstí; ⛆ 12, 15, 20, 22) After his murder on 8 December 1980, John Lennon became a pacifist hero for many young Czechs. An image of Lennon was painted on a wall in a secluded square opposite the French Embassy (there is a niche on the wall that looks like a tombstone), along with political graffiti and Beatles lyrics.

★**Petřín**   HILL
(⛆ Nebozízek, Petřín) This 318m-high hill is one of Prague's largest green spaces. It's great for quiet, tree-shaded walks and fine views over the 'City of a Hundred Spires'. Most of the attractions atop the hill, including a lookout tower and mirror maze, were built in the late 19th to early 20th century, lending the place an old-fashioned, fun-fair atmosphere.

👁 Nové Město

Nové Město (New Town) surrounds the Old Town on all sides and was originally laid out

in the 14th century. Its main public area is **Wenceslas Square** (Václavské náměstí; Map p282; Ⓜ Můstek, Muzeum), lined with shops, banks and restaurants, and dotted by a **statue of St Wenceslas** (sv Václav; Map p282; Václavské náměstí; Ⓜ Muzeum) on horseback. The **National Museum** (Národní muzeum; Map p282; ☑ 224 497 111; www.nm.cz; Václavské náměstí 68; Ⓜ Muzeum), which dominates the top of the square, is closed for long-term renovation.

★**Mucha Museum**   GALLERY
(Muchovo muzeum; Map p282; ☑ 221 451 333; www.mucha.cz; Panská 7; adult/child 240/160Kč; ☺ 10am-6pm; ⛆ 3, 5, 6, 9, 14, 24) This fascinating (and busy) museum features the sensuous art-nouveau posters, paintings and decorative panels of Alfons Mucha (1860–1939), as well as many sketches, photographs and other memorabilia. The exhibits include countless artworks showing Mucha's trademark Slavic maidens with flowing hair and piercing blue eyes, bearing symbolic garlands and linden boughs.

★**National Memorial to the
Heroes of the Heydrich Terror**   MUSEUM
(Národní památník hrdinů Heydrichiády; ☑ 224 916 100; www.pamatnik-heydrichiady.cz; Resslova 9; ☺ 9am-5pm Tue-Sun Mar-Oct, 9am-5pm Tue-Sat Nov-Feb; Ⓜ Karlovo Náměstí) **FREE** The Church of Sts Cyril & Methodius houses a moving memorial to the seven Czech paratroopers who were involved in the assassination of Reichsprotektor Reinhard Heydrich in 1942, with an exhibit and video about Nazi persecution of the Czechs. The church appeared in the 2016 movie based on the assassination, *Anthropoid*.

★**Prague City Museum**   MUSEUM
(Muzeum hlavního města Prahy; ☑ 224 816 773; www.muzeumprahy.cz; Na Poříčí 52; adult/child 120/50Kč; ☺ 9am-6pm Tue-Sun; Ⓜ Florenc) This excellent museum, opened in 1898, is devoted to the history of Prague from prehistoric times to the 20th century (labels are in English as well as Czech). Among the many intriguing exhibits are an astonishing scale model of Prague, and the Astronomical Clock's original 1866 calendar wheel with Josef Mánes' beautiful painted panels representing the months – that's January at the top, toasting his toes by the fire, and August near the bottom, sickle in hand, harvesting the corn.

Central Prague

JOSEFOV

22

Kozí

U obecního dvora

Eliška Krásnohorské

Dušní

Bílkova

Vlava River

Dvořákovo nábřeží

17.listopadu

Josefov

U starého hřbitova

Červená

13

Prague Jewish Museum

6

Pařížská

Vězeňská

Franz Kafka Monument

V Kolkovně

Masná

Dušní

Týnská

Máchova Bridge
(Máchesův most)

14

Alšovo nábřeží

Jan Palach Square
(Náměstí
Jana Palacha)

Široká

Maiselova

M **Staroměstská**

27

Valentinská

Žatecká

Kaprova

Uradnice

Dlouhá

Týnská ulička

25

T·ýnská

Týn Courtyard
(Týnský dvůr)

15

Veleslavínova

Platnéřská

Linhartská

Jan Hus Statue

12

Church of
Our Lady
Before Týn

3

John Lennon Wall (650m);
St Nicholas Church (700m);
Museum of the Infant
Jesus of Prague (850m);
Loreta (1.7km);
Strahov Library (2km)

Mariánské
náměstí

11

**Astronomical
Clock**

5

Celetná

Křížovnická

2

**Charles
Bridge**

18

Křížovnické
náměstí

Karlova

**Old
Town Hall**

STARÉ MĚSTO

Little Square
(Malé náměstí)

Železná

Former Fruit
Market
(Ovocný trh)

Havířská

7

Anenská

Liliová

Řetězová

Husova

Jílská

Zlatá

Michalská

Melantrichova

Open-Air
Market

Rytířská

Provaznická

Anenské
náměstí

21

29

Bethlehem Square
(Betlémské
náměstí)

Skořepka

Havelská

V Kotící

Uhelný
trh

Perlová

Můstek M

Náprstkova

Betlémská

Konviktská

Na Perštýně

Martinská

28. října

Jungmannovo
náměstí

M **Můstek**

Smetanovo nábřeží

Karolíny Světlé

Bartolomějská

Divadelní

19

31

**Národní
Třída**

30

K (David
Černý
Sculpture)

Franciscan Garden
(Františkánská
zahrada)

Legion
Bridge
(Legií
most)

Jazz Dock (750m);
Petřín Funicular
Railway (850m)

Národní třída

Mikulandská

Vorsilská

Purkyňova

Jungmannova

Palackého

P

34

Masarykovo nábřeží

Ostrovní

V Jirchářích

Spálená

Vladislavova

Vodičkova

Slav Island
(Slovanský
ostrov)

Dancing
House (300m);
U Kroka (1.5km);
Vyšehrad
Citadel (2km)

Nastruze

Pštrossova

Křemencova

National Memorial
to the Heroes of the
Heydrich Terror (300m)

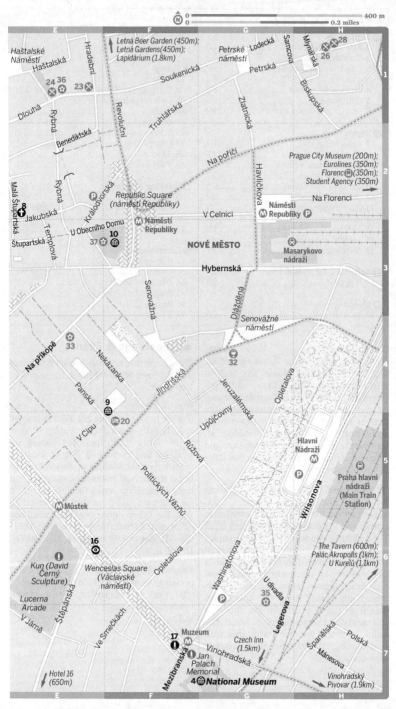

0   400 m
0   0.2 miles

Haštalské Náměstí

Haštalská

Hradební

Letná Beer Garden (450m);
Letná Gardens(450m);
Lapidárium (1.8km);

Petrské náměstí

Lodecká

Samcova

Mlynářská

28
26

24 36   23

Soukenická

Petrská

Dlouhá

Rybná

Benediktská

Revoluční

Truhlářská

Zlatnická

Biskupská

1

Na poříčí

Prague City Museum (200m);
Eurolines (350m);
Florenc (350m);
Student Agency (350m)

2

Malá Štupartská

Rybná

Královdorská

Republic Square
(náměstí Republiky)

V Celnici

Havlíčkova

Na Florenci

Náměstí
Republiky P

8
Jakubská

P

Štupartská

Temylová

U Obecního Domu

37   10

M Náměstí
Republiky

NOVÉ MĚSTO

Hybernská

M Náměstí
Republiky P

Masarykovo
nádraží

3

Senovážná

Dlážděná

Senovážné
náměstí

Na příkopě

33

Nekázanka

Jindřišská

Jeruzalémská

Opletalova

32

4

Panská

9
20

V Cípu

Upujčovny

Růžová

Hlavní
Nádraží

M

Praha hlavní
nádraží
(Main Train
Station)

5

M Můstek

Politických Vězňů

Washingtonova

Wilsonova

16

Kuň (David
Černý
Sculpture)

Wenceslas Square
(Václavské
náměstí)

Opletalova

The Tavern (600m);
Palác Akropolis (1km);
U Kurelů (1.1km)

6

Lucerna
Arcade

V Jámě

Štěpánská

Ve Smečkách

P

U divadla

Legerova

35

Španělská

Polská

Hotel 16
(650m)

Mezibranská

17

Muzeum
M

Jan
Palach
Memorial

Vinohradská

Czech Inn
(1.5km)

Mánesova

4 National Museum

Vinohradský
Pivovar (1.9km)

7

Central Prague

Dancing House ARCHITECTURE
(Tančící dům; http://tadu.cz; Rašínovo nábřeží 80; 🚊5, 17) The Dancing House was built in 1996 by architects Vlado Milunić and Frank Gehry. The curved lines of the narrow-waisted glass tower clutched against its more upright and formal partner led to it being christened the 'Fred & Ginger' building, after legendary dancing duo Fred Astaire and Ginger Rogers. It's surprising how well it fits in with its ageing neighbours.

★**Vyšehrad Citadel** FORTRESS
(🖉261 225 304; www.praha-vysehrad.cz; information centre at V pevnosti 159/5b; admission to grounds free; ⊙grounds 24hr; Ⓜ Vyšehrad) FREE The Vyšehrad Citadel refers to the complex of buildings and structures atop Vyšehrad Hill that have played an important role in Czech history for over 1000 years as a royal residence, religious centre and military fortress. While most of the surviving structures date from the 18th century, the citadel is still viewed as the city's spiritual home. The sights are spread out over a wide area, with commanding views out over the Vltava and surrounding city.

⭐ Festivals & Events

Prague's pretty Christmas market dominates the Old Town Square through the month of December.

Prague Spring MUSIC
(Pražské jaro; 🖉box office 227 059 234, program 257 314 040; www.festival.cz; ⊙May) Prague Spring is the Czech Republic's biggest annual cultural event and one of Europe's most important festivals of classical music. Concerts are held in theatres, churches and historic buildings across the city. Tickets go on sale from mid-December the preceding year. Buy tickets online or at the festival box office at the **Rudolfinum** (Map p282; 🖉227 059 270; www.ceskafilharmonie.cz; Alšovo nábřeží 12; 🚊2, 17, 18).

Prague Fringe Festival ART
(www.praguefringe.com; ⊙late May/early Jun) A wild week of happenings, theatre pieces, concerts and comedy shows. Much of it is in English.

🛏 Sleeping

★ Czech Inn
HOSTEL, HOTEL €

(☑ reception 267 267 612, reservations 267 267 600; www.czech-inn.com; Francouzská 76, Vršovice; dm 280-450Kč, s/d 1200/1600Kč, apt from 3000Kč; ℗ ☻ @ 奈; 🚊 4, 22) The Czech Inn calls itself a hostel, but the boutique label wouldn't be out of place. Everything seems sculpted by an industrial designer, from the iron beds to the brushed-steel flooring and minimalist square sinks. It offers a variety of accommodation, from standard hostel dorm rooms to good-value doubles (with or without private bathroom) and apartments.

Ahoy! Hostel
HOSTEL €

(Map p282; ☑ 773 004 003; www.ahoyhostel. com; Na Perštýně 10; dm/tw 460/1350Kč; @ 奈; Ⓜ Národní Třída, 🚊 2, 9, 18, 22) No big signs or branding here, just an inconspicuous card by the blue door at No 10. But inside is a very pleasant, welcoming and peaceful hostel (definitely not for the party crowd), with eager-to-please staff, some self-consciously 'arty' decoration, clean and comfortable six- or eight-bed dorms, and a couple of private twin rooms. Ideal location, too.

★ Hotel 16
HOTEL €€

(☑ 224 920 636; www.hotel16.cz; Kateřinská 16; s/d from 2400/3500Kč; ☻ ✳ @ 奈 🚹; 🚊 4, 6, 10, 16, 22) Hotel 16 is a friendly, family-run little place with just 14 rooms, tucked away in a very quiet corner of town where you're more likely to hear birdsong than traffic. The rooms vary in size and are simply but smartly furnished; the best, at the back, have views onto the peaceful terraced garden. Staff are superb, and can't do enough to help.

★ Fusion Hotel
BOUTIQUE HOTEL €€

(Map p282; ☑ 226 222 800; www.fusionhotels. com; Panská 9; r from 2650Kč; @ 奈; 🚊 3, 5, 6, 9, 14, 24) Fusion has style in abundance, from the revolving bar and spaceship-like UV corridor lighting, to the individually decorated bedrooms that resemble miniature modern-art galleries. As well as doubles, triples and family rooms, there are 'theme rooms' decorated in vintage or romantic style, with works by young Czech artists; one even offers a communal bed for up to six people!

★ Savic Hotel
HOTEL €€€

(Map p282; ☑ 224 248 555; www.savic.eu; Jilská 7; r from 4800Kč; ✳ @ 奈; Ⓜ Můstek) From the complimentary glass of wine when you arrive to the comfy king-size beds, the Savic certainly knows how to make you feel pampered. Housed in the former monastery of St Giles, the hotel is bursting with character and full of delightful period details including old stone fireplaces, beautiful painted timber ceilings and fragments of frescoes.

PRAGUE'S JEWISH MUSEUM

The **Prague Jewish Museum** (Židovské muzeum Praha; Map p282; ☑ 222 749 211; www. jewishmuseum.cz; Reservation Centre, Maiselova 15; ordinary ticket adult/child 300/200Kč, combined ticket incl entry to Old-New Synagogue 480/320Kč; ☺ 9am-6pm Sun-Fri Apr-Oct, to 4.30pm Nov-Mar; Ⓜ Staroměstská), a collection of four synagogues – the **Maisel**, **Pinkas**, **Spanish** and **Klaus** – the former **Ceremonial Hall** and the **Old Jewish Cemetery**, is one of the city's treasures. The monuments are clustered together in Josefov, a small corner of the Old Town that was home to Prague's Jews for some 800 years before an urban renewal project at the start of the 20th century and the Nazi occupation during WWII brought this all to an end.

The monuments cannot be visited separately but require a combined-entry ticket good for all of the sights and available at ticket windows throughout Josefov. A fifth synagogue, the **Old-New Synagogue** (Staronová synagóga; Map p282; www.jewishmuseum.cz; Červená 2; adult/child 200/140Kč; ☺ 9am-6pm Sun-Fri Apr-Oct, to 4.30pm Nov-Mar; 🚊 17), is still used for religious services, and requires a separate ticket or additional fee.

The museum was first established in 1906 to preserve objects from synagogues that were demolished during the slum clearance at the turn of the 20th century. The collection grew richer as a result of one of the most grotesquely ironic acts of WWII. During the Nazi occupation, the Germans took over management of the museum in order to create a 'museum of an extinct race'. To that end, they brought in objects from destroyed Jewish communities throughout Bohemia and Moravia.

✖ Eating

Lokál
CZECH €

(Map p282; ☑222 316 265; http://lokal-dlouha.
ambi.cz; Dlouhá 33; mains 115-235Kč; ⊙11am-1am
Mon-Sat, noon-midnight Sun; ☎; ☐6, 8, 15, 26)
Who'd have thought it possible? A classic
Czech beer hall (albeit with slick modern
styling); excellent *tankové pivo* (tanked
Pilsner Urquell); a daily-changing menu
of traditional Bohemian dishes; and smiling, efficient, friendly service! Top restaurant chain Ambiente has turned its hand
to Czech cuisine, and the result has been
so successful that the place is always busy,
mostly with locals.

★ Mistral Café
BISTRO €

(Map p282; ☑222 317 737; www.mistralcafe.cz;
Valentinská 11; mains 130-250Kč; ⊙10am-11pm;
☎ 🖐; Ⓜ Staroměstská) Is this the coolest bistro in the Old Town? Pale stone, bleached
birchwood and potted shrubs make for
a clean, crisp, modern look, and the clientele of local students and office workers clearly appreciate the competitively
priced, well-prepared food. Fish and chips
in crumpled brown paper with lemon and
black-pepper mayo – yum!

Maitrea
VEGETARIAN €

(Map p282; ☑221 711 631; www.restau-
race-maitrea.cz; Týnská ulička 6; mains 200-240Kč;
weekday lunch 135Kč; ⊙11.30am-11.30pm Mon-Fri,
noon-11.30pm Sat & Sun; ⊝ 🖉 🖐; Ⓜ Staroměstská) Maitrea (a Buddhist term meaning 'the
future Buddha') is a beautifully designed
space full of flowing curves and organic
shapes, from the sensuous polished-oak furniture and fittings to the blossom-like lampshades. The menu is inventive and wholly
vegetarian, with dishes such as Tex-Mex
quesadillas, spicy goulash with wholemeal
dumplings, and spaghetti with spinach,
crispy shredded tofu and rosemary pesto.

★ Nejen Bistro
BISTRO €€

(☑222 960 515; www.nejenbistro.cz; Křižíkova 24,
Karlín; mains 200-380Kč; ⊙10am-11pm; ☐3, 8,
24) 🖉 Nejen (Not Only) is emblematic of
the new breed of restaurant that is transforming Karlín into one of Prague's hottest
neighbourhoods. Its quirky interior was
nominated for a slew of design awards. But
just as much attention is lavished on the
food, which makes the most of the kitchen's
fancy Josper grill, turning out superb steaks,
beef ribs and Nejen's signature Black Angus
burger.

★ Sansho
ASIAN, FUSION €€

(Map p282; ☑222 317 425; www.sansho.cz;
Petrská 25; lunch mains 190-245Kč, 6-course dinner 900-1200Kč; ⊙11.30am-2pm Tue-Fri, 6-11pm
Tue-Sat, last orders 10pm; ⊝ 🖉; ☐3, 8, 14, 24) 🖉
'Friendly and informal' best describes the
atmosphere at this groundbreaking restaurant where British chef Paul Day champions
Czech farmers by sourcing all his meat and
vegetables locally. There's no menu as such –
the waiter will explain what dishes are available, depending on market produce. Typical
dishes include curried rabbit, pork belly
with watermelon and hoisin, and 12-hour
beef rendang. Reservations recommended.

U Kroka
CZECH €€

(☑775 905 022; www.ukroka.cz; Vratislavova 12,
Vyšehrad; mains 170-295Kč; ⊙11am-11pm; ⊝ ☎;
☐2, 3, 7, 17, 21) Cap a visit to historic Vyšehrad
Citadel with a hearty meal at this traditional
pub that delivers not just excellent beer but
very good food as well. Classic dishes like
goulash, boiled beef, rabbit and duck confit
are served in a festive setting. Daily lunch
specials (around 140Kč) are available from
11am to 3pm. Reservations (advisable) are
only possible after 3pm.

★ La Bottega Bistroteka
ITALIAN €€

(Map p282; ☑222 311 372; www.bistroteka.cz;
Dlouhá 39; mains 265-465Kč; ⊙9am-10.30pm
Mon-Sat, to 9pm Sun; ☐6, 8, 15, 26) You'll find
smart and snappy service at this stylish de-
li-cum-bistro, where the menu makes the
most of all that delicious Italian produce
artfully arranged on the counter; the beef
cheek canneloni with parmesan sauce and
fava beans, for example, is just exquisite. It's
best to book, but you can often get a walk-in
table at lunchtime.

★ Field
CZECH €€€

(Map p282; ☑222 316 999; www.fieldrestau-
rant.cz; U Milosrdných 12; mains 590-620Kč,
6-course tasting menu 2800Kč; ⊙11am-2.30pm
& 6-10.30pm Mon-Fri, noon-3pm & 6-10.30pm Sat,
noon-3pm & 6-10pm Sun; ⊝; ☐17) 🖉 Prague's
third Michelin-starred restaurant is its least
formal and most fun. The decor is an amusing art-meets-agriculture blend of farmyard
implements and minimalist chic, while the
chef creates painterly presentations from
the finest of local produce along with freshly
foraged herbs and edible flowers. You'll have
to book at least a couple of weeks in advance
to have a chance of a table.

V Zátiší
CZECH, INDIAN €€€

(Map p282; 222 221 155; www.vzatisi.cz; Liliová 1; 2-/3-course meal 990/1190Kč; noon-3pm & 5.30-11pm; ; 2, 17, 18) 'Still Life' is one of Prague's top restaurants, famed for the quality of its cuisine. The decor is bold and modern, with quirky glassware, boldly patterned wallpapers and cappuccino-coloured crushed-velvet chairs. The menu ranges from high-end Indian cuisine to gourmet versions of traditional Czech dishes – the South Bohemian duck with white cabbage and herb dumplings is superb.

Drinking & Nightlife

Czech beers are among the world's best. The most famous brands are Plzeňský Prazdroj (Pilsner Urquell), Budvar and Prague's own Staropramen. Independent microbreweries and regional Czech beers are also becoming more popular in Prague.

★Vinograf
WINE BAR

(Map p282; 214 214 681; www.vinograf.cz; Senovážné náměstí 23; 11.30am-midnight Mon-Sat, 5pm-midnight Sun; ; 3, 5, 6, 9, 14, 24) With knowledgeable staff, a relaxed atmosphere and an off-the-beaten-track feel, this appealingly modern wine bar is a great place to discover Moravian wines. There's good finger food to accompany your wine, mostly cheese and charcuterie, with food and wine menus (in Czech and English) on big blackboards behind the bar. Very busy at weekends, when it's worth booking a table.

Vinohradský Pivovar
PUB

(222 760 080; www.vinohradskypivovar.cz; Korunní 106, Vinohrady; 11am-midnight; ; 10, 16) This popular and highly recommended neighbourhood pub and restaurant offers its own home-brewed lagers as well as a well-regarded IPA. There's seating on two levels and a large events room at the back for concerts and happenings. The restaurant features classic Czech pub dishes (like *Wienerschnitzel* and pork medallions) at reasonable prices (180Kč to 230Kč). Book in advance for an evening meal.

★Letná Beer Garden
BEER GARDEN

(233 378 208; www.letenskyzamecek.cz; Letenské sady 341; 11am-11pm May-Sep; 1, 8, 12, 25, 26) No accounting of watering holes in the neighbourhood would be complete without a nod toward the city's best beer garden, with an amazing panorama, situated at the eastern end of the **Letná Gardens** (Letenské sady; 24hr; ; 1, 8, 12, 25, 26 to Letenské náměstí). Buy a takeaway beer from a small kiosk and grab a picnic table, or sit on a small terrace where you can order beer by the glass and decent pizza.

★Cross Club
CLUB

(736 535 010; www.crossclub.cz; Plynární 23; admission free-200Kč; cafe noon-2am, club 6pm-4am; ; Nádraží Holešovice) An industrial club in every sense of the word: the setting in an industrial zone; the thumping music (both DJs and live acts); and the interior, an absolute must-see jumble of gadgets, shafts, cranks and pipes, many of which move and pulsate with light to the music. The program includes occasional live music, theatre performances and art happenings.

U Kurelů
PUB

(www.ukurelu.cz; Chvalova 1, Žižkov; 5-11pm Tue-Sun; ; 5, 9, 15, 26) This reinvention of a classic Žižkov pub, originally opened in 1907, is the brainchild of the good folk at **The Tavern** (www.eng.thetavern.cz; Chopinova 26, Vinohrady; burgers 140-200Kč; 11.30am-10pm Mon-Fri, brunch from 11am Sat & Sun; ; Jiřího z Poděbrad, 11, 13), and the well-priced Pilsner Urquell (46Kč for 0.5L) and range of Czech microbrews is underpinned by the Tavern's famous smokehouse burgers, nachos and quesadillas.

Pivnice U Černého Vola
PUB

(220 513 481; Loretánské náměstí 1; 10am-10pm; 22) Many religious people make a pilgrimage to the Loreta, but just across the road, the 'Black Ox' is a shrine that pulls in pilgrims of a different kind. This surprisingly inexpensive beer hall is visited by real-ale aficionados for its authentic atmosphere and lip-smackingly delicious draught beer, Velkopopovický Kozel (31Kč for 0.5L), brewed in a small town southeast of Prague.

Cafe Louvre
CAFE

(Map p282; 224 930 949; www.cafelouvre.cz; 1st fl, Národní třída 22; 8am-11.30pm Mon-Fri, 9am-11.30pm Sat & Sun; 2, 9, 18, 22) The French-style Cafe Louvre is arguably the most amenable of Prague's grand cafes, as popular today as it was in the early 1900s when it was frequented by the likes of Franz Kafka and Albert Einstein. The atmosphere is wonderfully olde-worlde, and it serves good food as well as coffee. Check out the billiard hall and the ground-floor art gallery.

U Medvídků BEER HALL
(At the Little Bear; Map p282; ☑224 211 916; www.umedvidku.cz; Na Perštýně 7; ☺beer hall 11.30am-11pm, museum noon-10pm; ☎; Ⓜ Národní Třída, ☖2, 9, 18, 22) The most micro of Prague's microbreweries, with a capacity of only 250L, U Medvídků started producing its own beer in 2005, though its trad-style beer hall has been around for many years. What it lacks in size, it makes up for in strength – the dark lager, marketed as X-Beer, is the strongest in the country, with an alcohol content of 11.8%.

☆ Entertainment

From dance to classical music to jazz, Prague offers plenty of entertainment options. Try the following ticket agencies to see what might be on during your visit, and to snag tickets online, check out **Bohemia Ticket** (Map p282; ☑224 215 031; www.bohemiaticket. cz; Na příkopě 16, Nové Město; ☺10am-7pm Mon-Fri, to 5pm Sat, to 3pm Sun; Ⓜ Můstek).

Performing Arts

National Theatre OPERA, BALLET
(Národní divadlo; Map p282; ☑224 901 448; www.narodni-divadlo.cz; Národní třída 2; tickets 100-1290Kč; ☺box offices 10am-6pm; ☖2, 9, 18, 22) The much-loved National Theatre provides a stage for traditional opera, drama and ballet by the likes of Smetana, Shakespeare and Tchaikovsky, sharing the program alongside more modern works by composers and playwrights such as Philip Glass and John Osborne. The box offices are in the Nový síň building next door, in the Kolowrat Palace (opposite the Estates Theatre) and at the State Opera.

Prague State Opera OPERA, BALLET
(Státní opera Praha; Map p282; ☑224 901 448; www.narodni-divadlo.cz; Wilsonova 4; ☺box office 10am-6pm; Ⓜ Muzeum) The impressive neo-rococo home of the Prague State Opera provides a glorious setting for performances of opera and ballet. The building is closed for renovation work until 2018.

Dvořák Hall CONCERT VENUE
(Dvořákova síň; Map p282; ☑227 059 227; www. ceskafilharmonie.cz; náměstí Jana Palacha 1, Rudolfinum; tickets 120-900Kč; ☺box office 10am-12.30pm & 1.30-6pm Mon-Fri; Ⓜ Staroměstská) The Dvořák Hall in the neo-Renaissance Rudolfinum (p284) is home to the world-renowned Czech Philharmonic Orchestra (Česká filharmonie). Sit back and be impressed by some of the best classical musicians in Prague.

Live Music

★ **Palác Akropolis** LIVE MUSIC
(☑296 330 913; www.palacakropolis.cz; Kubelíkova 27, Žižkov; tickets free-250Kč; ☺club 6.30pm-5am; ☎; ☖5, 9, 15, 26) The Akropolis is a Prague institution, a smoky, labyrinthine, sticky-floored shrine to alternative music and drama. Its various performance spaces host a smorgasbord of musical and cultural events, from DJs to string quartets to Macedonian Roma bands to local rock gods to visiting talent – Marianne Faithfull, the Flaming Lips and the Strokes have all played here.

Roxy LIVE MUSIC
(Map p282; ☑224 826 296; www.roxy.cz; Dlouhá 33; tickets 150-700Kč; ☺7pm-5am; ☖6, 8, 15, 26) Set in the ramshackle shell of an art deco cinema, the legendary Roxy has nurtured the more independent and innovative end of Prague's club spectrum since 1987 – this is the place to see the Czech Republic's top DJs. On the 1st floor is NoD, an 'experimental space' that stages drama, dance, performance art, cinema and live music. Best nightspot in Staré Město.

Jazz Dock JAZZ
(☑774 058 838; www.jazzdock.cz; Janáčkovo nábřeží 2, Smíchov; tickets 150-300Kč; ☺4pm-3am; ☎; Ⓜ Anděl, ☖9, 12, 15, 20) Most of Prague's jazz clubs are smoky cellar affairs, but this riverside club is a definite step up, with clean, modern decor and a decidedly romantic view out over the Vltava. It draws some of the best local talent and occasional international acts. Go early or book to get a good table. Shows normally begin at 7pm and 10pm.

❶ Information

The major banks are best for changing cash, but using a debit card in an ATM gives a better exchange rate. Avoid *směnárna* (private exchange booths), which advertise misleading rates and have exorbitant charges.

Na Homolce Hospital (☑257 271 111; www. homolka.cz; 5th fl, Foreign Pavilion, Roentgenova 2, Motol; ☖167, 168 to Nemocnice Na Homolce) Widely considered to be the best hospital in Prague, equipped and staffed to Western standards, with staff who speak English, French, German and Spanish.

Prague City Tourism (Prague Welcome; Map p282; ☑221 714 714; www.prague. eu; Staroměstské náměstí 5, Old Town Hall;

⊘ 9am-7pm; Ⓜ Staroměstská) The busiest of the Prague City Tourism branches occupies the ground floor of the Old Town Hall (enter to the left of the Astronomical Clock).

Relax Café-Bar (☑224 211 521; www.re-laxcafebar.cz; Dlážděná 4; per 10min 10Kč; ⊘ 8am-10pm Mon-Fri, 2-10pm Sat; 🕾; Ⓜ Náměstí Republiky) A conveniently located internet cafe. Wi-fi is free.

ⓘ Getting There & Away

There are very efficient overland and air routes to Prague and the Czech Republic.

ⓘ Getting Around

TO/FROM THE AIRPORT

To get into town from Prague airport, buy a full-price public transport ticket (32Kč) from the **Prague Public Transport Authority** desk in the arrivals hall and take bus 119 (20 minutes, every 10 minutes, 4am to midnight) to the Nádraží Veleslavín metro stop (line A), then continue by metro into the city centre (another 10 to 15 minutes; no new ticket needed).

If you're heading to the southwestern part of the city, take bus 100, which goes to the Zličín metro station (line B).

There's also an Airport Express bus (AE; 60Kč, 35 minutes, every half-hour from 5am to 10pm) that runs to Prague main train station, where you can connect to metro line C (buy ticket from driver, luggage goes free).

Several taxi companies operate from the airport. Count on about 30 minutes' drive time, depending on traffic, and a fare of 600Kč to and from the centre. You'll find taxi stands outside both arrivals terminals. Drivers usually speak some English and accept credit cards.

PUBLIC TRANSPORT

Prague's excellent public-transport system combines tram, metro and bus services. It's operated by the **Prague Public Transport Authority** (DPP; ☑296 191 817; www.dpp.cz; ⊘7am-9pm), which has information desks in both terminals of Prague's Václav Havel Airport and in several metro stations, including the Můstek, Anděl, Hradčanská and Nádraží Veleslavín stations. The metro operates daily from 5am to midnight.

Tickets valid on all metros, trams and buses are sold from machines at metro stations (coins only), as well as at DPP information offices and many newsstands and kiosks. Tickets can be purchased individually or as discounted day passes valid for one or three days.

A full-price individual ticket costs 32/16Kč per adult/senior aged 65 to 70 and is valid for 90 minutes of unlimited travel. For shorter journeys, buy short-term tickets that are valid for 30 minutes of unlimited travel. These cost 24/12Kč

per adult/senior. One-day passes cost 110/55Kč per adult/senior; three-day passes cost 310Kč (no discount for seniors).

TAXI

Taxis are frequent and relatively inexpensive. The official rate for licensed cabs is 40Kč flagfall plus 28Kč per kilometre and 6Kč per minute while waiting. On this basis, any trip within the city centre – say, from Wenceslas Sq to Malá Strana – should cost around 170Kč. A trip to the suburbs, depending on the distance, should run from 200Kč to 400Kč, and to the airport between 500Kč and 700Kč.

The following companies offer 24-hour service and English-speaking operators:

AAA Radio Taxi (☑14014, 222 333 222; www.aaataxi.cz) Operates a 24-hour taxi service from the airport, charging around 500Kč to 650Kč to get to the centre of Prague. You'll find taxi stands outside both arrivals terminals. Drivers usually speak some English and accept credit cards.

City Taxi (☑257 257 257; www.citytaxi.cz)
ProfiTaxi (☑14015; www.profitaxi.cz)

AROUND PRAGUE

Karlštejn

Rising above the village of Karlštejn, 30km southwest of Prague, medieval **Karlštejn Castle** (Hrad Karlštejn; ☑tour bookings 311 681 617; www.hradkarlstejn.cz; adult/child Tour 1 270/180Kč, Tour 2 330/230Kč, Tour 3 150/100Kč; ⊘9am-6.30pm Jul & Aug, 9.30am-5.30pm Tue-Sun May, Jun & Sep, to 5pm Apr, to 4.30pm Oct, to 4pm Mar, shorter hrs Sat & Sun only Dec-Feb) is in such good shape it wouldn't look out of place at Disneyworld. The crowds come in theme-park proportions as well, but the peaceful surrounding countryside offers views of Karlštejn's stunning exterior that rival anything you'll see on the inside.

The castle was born of a grand pedigree, originally conceived by Emperor Charles IV in the 14th century as a bastion for hiding the crown jewels. Run by an appointed burgrave, the castle was surrounded by a network of landowning knight-vassals, who came to the castle's aid whenever enemies moved against it.

Karlštejn again sheltered the Bohemian and the Holy Roman Empire crown jewels during the Hussite Wars of the 15th century, but fell into disrepair as its defences became outmoded. Considerable restoration work in the late-19th century returned the castle to its former glory.

Castle visits are by guided tour only. Some tours must be reserved in advance by phone or via the castle website.

Three tours are available: **Tour 1** (50 minutes) passes through the Knight's Hall, still daubed with the coats-of-arms and names of the knight-vassals, Charles IV's Bedchamber, the Audience Hall and the Jewel House, which includes treasures from the Chapel of the Holy Cross and a replica of the St Wenceslas Crown.

Tour 2 (70 minutes, May to October only) takes in the Marian Tower, with the Church of the Virgin Mary and the Chapel of St Catherine, then moves to the Great Tower for the castle's star attraction, the exquisite Chapel of the Holy Cross, its walls and vaulted ceiling adorned with thousands of polished semiprecious stones set in gilt stucco in the form of crosses, and with religious and heraldic paintings.

Tour 3 (40 minutes, May to October only) visits the upper levels of the Great Tower, the highest point of the castle, which provides stunning views over the surrounding countryside.

From Prague, there are frequent train departures daily from Prague's main station. The journey takes 45 minutes and costs around 55Kč each way.

Kutná Hora

In the 14th century, Kutná Hora, 60km southeast of Prague, rivalled the capital in importance because of the rich deposits of silver ore below the ground. The ore ran out in 1726, leaving the medieval townscape largely unaltered. Now with several fascinating and unusual historical attractions, the Unesco World Heritage–listed town is a popular day trip from Prague.

Interestingly, most visitors come not for the silver splendour but rather to see an eerie monastery, dating from the 19th century, with an interior crafted solely from human bones. Indeed, the remarkable **Sedlec Ossuary** (Kostnice; ☑ information centre 326 551 049; www.ossuary.eu; Zámecká 127; adult/concession 90/60Kč; ☺8am-6pm Mon-Sat, 9am-6pm Sun Apr-Sep, 9am-5pm Mar & Oct, 9am-4pm Nov-Feb), or 'bone church', features the remains of no fewer than 40,000 people who died over the years from wars and pestilence.

Closer to the centre of Kutná Hora is the town's greatest monument: the Gothic **Cathedral of St Barbara** (Chrám sv Barbora; ☑775 363 938; www.khfarnost.cz; Barborská; adult/concession 85/40Kč; ☺9am-6pm Apr-Oct, 10am-5pm Mon-Fri, 10am-6pm Sat & Sun Nov-Dec, 10am-4pm Jan-Mar). Rivalling Prague's St Vitus in size and magnificence, its soaring nave culminates in elegant, six-petalled ribbed vaulting, and the ambulatory chapels preserve original 15th-century frescoes. Other leading attractions include the **Hrádek** (České muzeum stříbra; ☑327 512 159; www.cms-kh.cz; Barborská 28; adult/concession Tour 1 70/40Kč, Tour 2 120/80Kč, combined 140/90Kč; ☺10am-6pm Jul & Aug, 9am-6pm May, Jun & Sep, 9am-5pm Apr & Oct, 9am-4pm Nov, closed Mon year-round) from the 15th century, which now houses the Czech Silver Museum.

Both buses and trains make the trip to Kutná Hora from Prague, though the train is usually a better bet. Direct trains depart from Prague's main train station to Kutná Hora hlavní nádraží every two hours (209Kč return, 55 minutes). It's a 10-minute walk from here to Sedlec Ossuary, and a further 2.5km (30 minutes) to the Old Town. Buses (136Kč return, 1¾ hours) depart from Prague's Háje bus station on the far southern end of the city. On weekdays, buses run hourly, with reduced services on weekdays.

BOHEMIA

The Czech Republic's western province boasts surprising variety. Český Krumlov, with its riverside setting and dramatic Renaissance castle, is in a class by itself. Big cities like Plzeň offer urban attractions like great museums and restaurants. The spa towns of western Bohemia, such as Karlovy Vary, were world famous in the 19th century and retain old-world lustre.

Plzeň

POP 188,190

Plzeň, the regional capital of western Bohemia and the second-biggest city in Bohemia after Prague, is best known as the home of the Pilsner Urquell Brewery, but it has a handful of other interesting sights and enough good restaurants and night-time pursuits to justify an overnight stay. Most of the sights are located near the central square, but the brewery itself is about a 15-minute walk outside the city centre.

⊙ Sights

★ Pilsner Urquell Brewery
BREWERY
(Prazdroj; ☑377 062 888; www.prazdrojvisit.cz;
U Prazdroje 7; guided tour adult/child 200/120Kč;
☺8.30am-6pm Apr-Sep, to 5pm Oct-Mar, English
tours 1pm, 2.45pm & 4.30pm) Plzeň's most popular attraction is the tour of the Pilsner Urquell
Brewery, in operation since 1842 and arguably home to the world's best beer. Entry is by
guided tour only, with three tours in English
available daily. Tour highlights include a trip
to the old cellars (dress warmly) and a glass
of unpasteurised nectar at the end.

Underground Plzeň
TUNNEL
(Plzeňské historické podzemí; ☑377 235 574; www.
plzenskepodzemi.cz; Veleslavínova 6; tour in English adult/child 120/90Kč; ☺10am-6pm Apr-Sep,
to 5pm Oct-Dec & Feb-Mar, closed Jan, English tour
2.20pm daily Apr-Oct) This extraordinary tour
explores the passageways below the old city.
The earliest were probably dug in the 14th
century, perhaps for beer production or defence; the latest date from the 19th century.
Of an estimated 11km that have been excavated, some 500m of the tunnels are open to
the public. Bring extra clothing – it's a chilly
10°C underground.

★ Techmania Science Centre
MUSEUM
(☑737 247 585; www.techmania.cz; cnr Borská &
Břeňkova, Areál Škoda; adult/child incl 3D planetarium 180/110Kč; ☺8.30am-5pm Mon-Fri, 10am-
7pm Sat, 10am-6pm Sun; P☎♿; ☐15, 17) Kids
will have a ball at this high-tech, interactive
science centre where they can play with infrared cameras, magnets and many other
instructive and fun exhibits. There's a 3D
planetarium (included in the full-price admission) and a few full-sized historic trams
and trains manufactured at the Škoda engineering works. Take the trolleybus; it's a
2km hike southwest from the city centre.

Brewery Museum
MUSEUM
(☑377 224 955; www.prazdrojvisit.cz; Veleslavínova 6; guided tour adult/child 120/90Kč, English text
90/60Kč; ☺10am-6pm Apr-Sep, to 5pm Oct-Mar)
The Brewery Museum offers an insight into
how beer was made (and drunk) in the days
before Pilsner Urquell was founded. Highlights include a mock-up of a 19th-century
pub, a huge wooden beer tankard from Siberia and a collection of beer mats. All have
English captions and there's a good printed
English text available for those not taking
the tour.

Great Synagogue
SYNAGOGUE
(Velká Synagoga; ☑377 223 346; www.zoplzen.
cz; sady Pětatřicátníků 11; adult/child 70/40Kč;
☺10am-6pm Sun-Fri Apr-Oct) The Great
Synagogue, west of the Old Town, is the
third-largest in the world – only those in
Jerusalem and Budapest are bigger. It was
built in the Moorish style in 1892 by the
2000 Jews who lived in Plzeň at the time.
The building is now used for concerts and
art exhibitions.

⌂ Sleeping

Hotel Roudna
HOTEL €
(☑377 259 926; www.hotelroudna.cz; Na Roudné
13; s/d 1150/1400Kč; P@☎) Perhaps the city's
best-value lodging, across the river to the
north of the old town, the Roudna's exterior
isn't much to look at, but inside rooms are
well proportioned with high-end amenities
such as flat-screen TV, minibar and desk.
Breakfasts are fresh and ample, and reception is friendly. Note there's no lift.

Hotel Rous
BOUTIQUE HOTEL €€
(☑602 320 294; www.hotelrous.cz; Zbrojnicka
113/7; s/d from 1750/2150Kč; P@☎) This
600-year-old building combines the historic
character of the original stone walls alongside modern furnishings. Bathrooms are art
deco cool in black and white. Breakfast is
taken in a garden cafe concealed amid remnants of Plzeň's defensive walls. Downstairs,
the Caffe Emily serves very good coffee.

✗ Eating & Drinking

Na Parkánu
CZECH €
(☑377 324 485; www.naparkanu.com; Veleslavínova 4; mains 100-330Kč; ☺11am-11pm Mon-Thu, to
1am Fri & Sat, to 10pm Sun; ☎) Don't overlook
this pleasant pub-restaurant, attached to the
Brewery Museum. It may look a bit touristy,
but the traditional Czech food is top rate,
and the beer, naturally, could hardly be better. Try to snag a spot in the summer garden.
Don't leave without trying the *nefiltrované
pivo* (unfiltered beer). Reservations are an
absolute must.

★ Buffalo Burger Bar
AMERICAN €€
(☑733 124 514; buffaloburgerbar@gmail.com;
Dominikánská 3; mains 165-385Kč; ☺11am-11pm;
☺☎) Tuck in to some of the best burgers
in the Czech Republic at this American-style
diner, with cool timber decor the colour
of a well-done steak. Everything is freshly
made, from the hand-cooked tortilla chips,

zingy salsa and guacamole, to the perfect french fries, coleslaw and the juicy burgers themselves.

★ **Aberdeen Angus Steakhouse**   STEAK €€
(✆725 555 631; www.angussteakhouse.cz; Pražská 23; mains 215-715Kč; ⊙11am-11pm Sun-Thu, to midnight Fri & Sat; ☺🛜) For our money, this may be the best steakhouse in all of the Czech Republic. The meats hail from a nearby farm, where the livestock is raised organically. There are several cuts and sizes on offer; lunch options include a tantalising cheeseburger. The downstairs dining room is cosy; there's also a creek-side terrace. Book in advance.

★ **Měšťanská Beseda**   PUB
(✆378 035 415; http://web.mestanska-beseda. cz; Kopeckého sady 13; ⊙9am-10pm Mon-Fri, 11am-10pm Sat & Sun; 🛜) Cool heritage cafe, sunny beer garden, expansive exhibition space and occasional art-house cinema – the elegant Art Nouveau Měšťanská Beseda is hands-down Plzeň's most versatile venue. The beautifully restored 19th-century pub is perfect for a leisurely beer or cafe. Check out who's performing at the attached theatre.

Galerie Azyl   BAR
(✆377 235 507; www.galerieazyl.cz; Veleslavínova 17; ⊙8am-11pm Mon-Thu, to 1am Fri, 6pm-1am Sat; 🛜) Locals kick off the morning with an excellent espresso here. Later in the day, Galerie Azyl morphs into Plzeň's classiest cocktail bar. Quirky artwork surrounds conversation-friendly booths.

ℹ Information

City Information Centre (Informační centrum města Plzně; ✆378 035 330; www.pilsen.eu/ tourist; náměstí Republiky 41; ⊙9am-7pm Apr-Sep, to 6pm Oct-Mar; 🛜) Plzeň's well-stocked tourist information office is a first port of call for visitors. Staff here can advise on sleeping and eating options, and there are free city maps and a stock of brochures on what to see and do.

ℹ Getting There & Away

Several trains leave daily from Prague's main train station (Hlavní nádraží; 160Kč, 1½ hours) to Plzeň's **train station** (Plzeň hlavní nádraží; www. cd.cz; Nádražní 102), which is 1km east of the historic centre.

From Prague, **Student Agency** (✆841 101 101; www.studentagency.cz; náměstí Republiky 9; ⊙9am-6pm Mon-Fri) runs half-hourly buses

during the day to Plzeň (100Kč, one hour). Plzeň **bus station** (Centrální autobusové nádraží, CAN; ✆377 237 237; www.csadplzen.cz; Husova 60), marked on maps and street signs as CAN, is 1km west of the centre.

Český Krumlov

POP 61,100

Český Krumlov, in Bohemia's deep south, is one of the most picturesque towns in Europe. It's a little like Prague in miniature – a Unesco World Heritage Site with a stunning castle above the Vltava River, an old town square, Renaissance and baroque architecture, and hordes of tourists milling through the streets – but all on a smaller scale; you can walk from one side of town to the other in 20 minutes. Český Krumlov is best approached as an overnight destination; it's too far for a comfortable day trip from Prague. Consider staying at least two nights, and spend one of the days hiking or biking in the surrounding woods and fields.

◉ Sights

★ **Český Krumlov State Castle**   CASTLE
(✆380 704 711; www.zamek-ceskykrumlov.eu; Zámek 59; adult/concession Tour 1 250/160Kč, Tour 2 240/140Kč, Theatre Tour 300/200Kč; ⊙9am-6pm Tue-Sun Jun-Aug, to 5pm Apr, May, Sep & Oct) Český Krumlov's striking Renaissance castle, occupying a promontory high above the town, began life in the 13th century. It acquired its present appearance in the 16th to 18th centuries under the stewardship of the noble Rožmberk and Schwarzenberg families. The interiors are accessible by guided tour only, though you can stroll the grounds on your own.

Castle Museum & Tower   MUSEUM, TOWER
(✆380 704 711; www.zamek-ceskykrumlov.eu; Zámek 59; combined entry adult/child 130/60Kč, museum only 100/50Kč, tower only 50/30Kč; ⊙9am-5pm Jun-Aug, to 4pm Apr, May, Sep & Oct, to 3pm Tue-Sun Nov-Mar) Located within the castle complex, this small museum and adjoining tower is an ideal option if you don't have the time or energy for a full castle tour. Through a series of rooms, the museum traces the castle's history from its origins through to the present day. Climb the tower for perfect photo-ops of the town below.

Český Krumlov

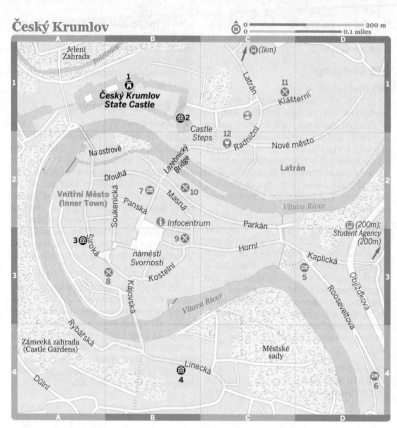

Egon Schiele Art Centrum MUSEUM
(📞380 704 011; www.schieleartcentrum.cz; Široká 71; adult/child under 6yr 160Kč/free; ⊙10am-6pm Tue-Sun) This excellent private gallery houses a small retrospective of the controversial Viennese painter Egon Schiele (1890–1918), who lived in Krumlov in 1911, and raised the ire of the townsfolk by hiring young girls as nude models. For this and other sins he was eventually driven out. The centre also houses interesting temporary exhibitions.

Museum Fotoateliér Seidel MUSEUM
(📞736 503 871; www.seidel.cz; Linecká 272; adult/child 100/40Kč; ⊙9am-noon & 1-6pm May-Sep, to 5pm Apr & Oct-Dec, to 5pm Tue-Sun Jan-Mar) This photography museum presents a moving retrospective of the work of local photographers Josef Seidel and his son František. Especially poignant are the images recording early-20th-century life in nearby villages. In

Český Krumlov

⊚ Top Sights
1 Český Krumlov State Castle B1

⊚ Sights
2 Castle Museum & Tower B1
3 Egon Schiele Art Centrum A3
4 Museum Fotoateliér Seidel B4

🛏 Sleeping
5 Hotel garni Myší Díra D3
6 Krumlov House D4
7 U Malého Vítka B2

🍴 Eating
8 Hospoda Na Louži B3
9 Krčma v Šatlavské B3
10 Laibon B2
11 Nonna Gina C1

🍷 Drinking & Nightlife
12 Zapa Cocktail Bar C2

the high season you should be able to join an English-language tour; if not, let the pictures tell the story.

🛏 Sleeping

★**Krumlov House** HOSTEL €
(☎380 711 935; www.krumlovhostel.com; Rooseveltova 68; dm/d/tr 335/785/935Kč; ◉@🛜) 🍃 Perched above the river, Krumlov House is friendly and comfortable, and has plenty of books, DVDs and local information to feed your inner wanderer. Accommodation is in a six-bed en suite dorm as well as private double and triple rooms or private, self-catered apartments. The owners are English-speaking and traveller-friendly.

★**Hotel garni Myší Díra** HOTEL €€
(☎380 712 853; http://cz.ubytovani.ceskykrumlov-info.cz; Rooseveltova 28; s/d/tr 2150/2450/2950Kč; 🅿🛜) This place has a superb location overlooking the river, and bright, spacious rooms with lots of pale wood and quirky handmade furniture; room No 12, with a huge corner bath and naughty decorations on the bed, is our favourite. Limited parking in front of the hotel costs 190Kč.

U Malého Vítka HOTEL €€
(☎380 711 925; www.vitekhotel.cz; Radniční 27; s/d 1050/1600Kč; 🅿◉🛜) We like this small hotel in the heart of the Old Town. The simple room furnishings are of high-quality, hand-crafted wood, and each room is named after a traditional Czech fairy-tale character. The downstairs restaurant and cafe are very good too.

🍴 Eating & Drinking

★**Nonna Gina** ITALIAN €
(☎380 717 187; www.pizzerianonnagina.wz.cz; Klášterní 52; mains 100-200Kč; ⊙11am-11pm; ◉) Authentic Italian flavours from the Massaro family feature at this long-established pizzeria, where the quality of food and service knock the socks off more expensive restaurants. Superb antipasti, great pizza and Italian wines at surprisingly low prices make for a memorable meal. Grab an outdoor table and pretend you're in Naples, or retreat to the snug and intimate upstairs dining room.

Laibon VEGETARIAN €
(☎775 676 654; www.laibon.cz; Parkán 105; mains 130-200Kč; ⊙11am-11pm; ◉🛜🍴) One of the town's rare meat-free zones, this snug veggie oasis offers great hummus, couscous, curry and pasta dishes, and local specialities such as *bryndzové halušky* (tiny potato dumplings with sheep's-milk cheese). Book in advance in summer and request an outside table with a view of the castle.

WORTH A TRIP

UNESCO HERITAGE ARCHITECTURE IN TELČ

The Unesco-protected town of Telč, perched on the border between Bohemia and Moravia, possesses one of the country's prettiest and best-preserved historic town squares.

The main attraction is the beauty of the square, **Náměstí Zachariáše z Hradce**, itself, which is lined with Renaissance burghers' houses. Most of the structures were built in the 16th century after a fire levelled the town in 1530. Famous houses include No 15, which shows the characteristic Renaissance sgraffito. The house at No 48 was given a baroque facade in the 18th century.

Telč Chateau (Zámek; ☎567 243 943; www.zamek-telc.cz; náměstí Zachariáše z Hradce 1; adult/concession Route A 120/80Kč, Route B 90/70Kč; ⊙10am-3pm Tue-Sun Apr & Oct, to 4pm May, Jun & Sep, to 4.30pm Jul & Aug), another Renaissance masterpiece, guards the northern end of the square. Entry is by guided tour only.

If you decide to spend the night, the **Hotel Celerin** (☎567 243 477; www.hotelcelerin.cz; náměstí Zachariáše z Hradce 43; s/d 980/1700Kč; ◉❄🛜) offers 12 comfortable rooms, with decor ranging from cosy wood to white-wedding chintz (take a look first).

There are a handful of daily buses that run from Prague's Florenc bus station (175Kč, 2½ hours), though many connections require a change in Jihlava. The situation is marginally better for bus travel to/from Brno (125Kč, two hours). Check the online timetable at http://jizdnirady.idnes.cz for times.

Hospoda Na Louži   CZECH €

(☑380 711 280; www.nalouzi.cz; Kájovská 66; mains 120-240Kč; ☻) Nothing's changed in this wood-panelled *pivo* (beer) parlour for almost a century. Locals and tourists pack Na Louži for huge plates of Czech staples such as chicken schnitzels or roast pork and dumplings, as well as dark (and light) beer from the local Eggenberg brewery. Get the fruit dumplings for dessert if you see them on the menu.

★**Krčma v Šatlavské**   CZECH €€

(☑380 713 344; www.satlava.cz; Horní 157; mains 150-325Kč; ☺11am-midnight) This medieval barbecue cellar is hugely popular with visitors and your table mates are much more likely to be from Austria or China than from the town itself. The grilled meats served up with gusto in a funky labyrinth illuminated by candles are excellent and perfectly in character with Český Krumlov. Advance booking is essential.

Zapa Cocktail Bar   COCKTAIL BAR

(☑380 712 559; www.zapabar.cz; Latrán 15; ☺6pm-1am; ☜) Most of Český Krumlov empties out after dinner, but Zapa keeps going until after midnight. Expect a relaxed vibe and the town's best cocktails.

ℹ **Information**

Infocentrum (☑380 704 622; www.ckrumlov. info; náměstí Svornosti 2; ☺9am-7pm Jun-Aug, to 6pm Apr, May, Sep & Oct, to 5pm Nov-Mar, closed lunch Sat & Sun) One of the country's best tourist offices. Good source for transport and accommodation info, maps, internet access (per five minutes 5Kč) and audio guides (per hour 100Kč). A guide for disabled visitors is also available.

ℹ **Getting There & Away**

The train from Prague (275Kč, 3½ hours, four to six daily) requires a change in České Budějovice. There's regular train service between České Budějovice and Český Krumlov (51Kč, 45 minutes). It is quicker and cheaper to take the bus. Český Krumlov **train station** (Vlakové nádraží; ☑840 112 113; www.cd.cz; Třída Míru 1) is located 2km north of the historic centre.

By bus, **Student Agency** (☑841 101 101; www. studentagency.cz; Nemocniční 586) coaches (200Kč, three hours, hourly) leave from Prague's Na Knížecí bus station at Anděl metro station (Line B). Book in advance for weekends or in July and August. Český Krumlov **bus station** (Autobusové nádraží; Nemocniční 586) is about a 10-minute walk east of the historic centre.

MORAVIA

The Czech Republic's eastern province, Moravia is yin to Bohemia's yang. If Bohemians love beer, Moravians love wine. If Bohemia is towns and cities, Moravia is rolling hills and pretty landscapes. The Moravian capital, Brno, has the museums, but the northern city of Olomouc has the captivating architecture.

Brno

POP 370,440

Among Czechs, Moravia's capital has a dull rep: a likeable enough place where not much actually happens. The reality, however, is very different. Tens of thousands of students who attend university here ensure a lively cafe and club scene that easily rival Prague's. The museums are great, too. Brno was one of the leading centres of experimental architecture in the early 20th century, and the Unesco-protected Vila Tugendhat is considered a masterwork of functionalist design.

◉ **Sights**

★**Vila Tugendhat**   ARCHITECTURE

(Villa Tugendhat; ☑515 511 015, tour bookings 731 616 899; www.tugendhat.eu; Černopolní 45; adult/concession basic tour 300/180Kč, extended tour 350/210Kč; ☺10am-6pm Tue-Sun Mar-Dec, 9am-7pm Wed-Sun Jan & Feb; ☐3, 5, 9) Brno had a reputation in the 1920s as a centre for modern architecture in the Bauhaus style. Arguably the finest example is this family villa, designed by modern master Mies van der Rohe for Greta and Fritz Tugendhat in 1930. The house was the inspiration for British author Simon Mawer in his 2009 bestseller *The Glass Room*. Entry is by guided tour booked in advance by phone or email. Two tours are available: basic (one hour) and extended (1½ hours).

Capuchin Monastery   CEMETERY

(Kapucínský klášter; ☑511 145 796; www.kapucini.cz; Kapucínské náměstí; adult/concession 70/35Kč; ☺9am-noon & 1-6pm Mon-Sat, 11am-5pm Sun Apr-Oct, 10am-4pm Mon-Sat, 11am-4.30pm Sun Nov-Mar; ☐4, 8, 9) One of the city's leading attractions is this ghoulish cellar crypt that holds the mummified remains of several city noblemen from the 18th century. Apparently the dry, well-ventilated crypt has the natural ability to turn dead bodies into mummies. Up to 150 cadavers were deposited here prior to 1784, the desiccated corpses including monks, abbots and local notables.

Old Town Hall
HISTORIC BUILDING

(Stará radnice; ☑542 427 150; www.ticbrno.cz; Radnická 8; tower adult/concession 60/30Kč; ☺10am-6pm; ☑4, 8, 9) No visit to Brno would be complete without a peek inside the city's medieval Old Town Hall, parts of which date back to the 13th century. The tourist office (p297) is here, plus oddities including a crocodile hanging from the ceiling (known affectionately as the Brno 'dragon') and a wooden wagon wheel with a unique story. You can also climb the tower.

Labyrinth under the Cabbage Market
TUNNELS

(Brněnské podzemí; ☑542 427 150; www.ticbrno. cz; Zelný trh 21; adult/concession 160/80Kč; ☺9am-6pm Tue-Sun; ☑4, 8, 9) In recent years, the city has opened several sections of extensive underground tunnels to the general public. This tour takes around 40 minutes to explore a number of cellars situated 6m to 8m below the Cabbage Market, which has served as a food market for centuries. The cellars were built for two purposes: to store goods and to hide in during wars.

Špilberk Castle
CASTLE

(Hrad Špilberk; ☑542 123 611; www.spilberk.cz; Špilberk 210/1; combined entry adult/concession 280/170Kč, casements only 90/50Kč, tower only 50/30Kč; ☺9am-5pm May & Jun, 10am-6pm Jul-Sep, 9am-5pm Tue-Sun Oct-Apr) Brno's spooky hilltop castle is considered the city's most important landmark. Its history stretches back to the 13th century, when it was home to Moravian margraves and later a fortress. Under the Habsburgs in the 18th and 19th centuries, it served as a prison. Today it's home to the Brno City Museum, with several temporary and permanent exhibitions.

🛏 Sleeping

In February, April, August, September and October, Brno hosts major international trade fairs, and hotel rates increase by 40% to 100%. Book ahead if possible.

★ Hostel Mitte
HOSTEL €

(☑734 622 340; www.hostelmitte.com; Panská 22; dm 400-500Kč, s/d 1000/1300Kč, all incl breakfast; ☺@🛜; ☑4, 8, 9) Set in the heart of the Old Town, this clean and stylish hostel smells and looks brand new. The rooms are named after famous Moravians (eg Milan Kundera) or famous events (Austerlitz) and decorated accordingly. There are six-bed dorms and private singles and doubles. Cute cafe on the ground floor.

Hostel Fléda
HOSTEL €

(☑731 651 005; www.hostelfleda.com; Štefánikova 24; dm/d from 250/800Kč; ☺🛜; ☑1, 2, 4, 6, 8) One of Brno's best music clubs (p297) offers funky and colourful rooms and a good cafe and good bar reinforce the social vibe. It's a quick tram ride from the centre to the Hrnčířská stop.

Hotel Europa
HOTEL €€

(☑515 143 100; www.hotel-europa-brno.cz; třída kpt Jaroše 27; s/d 1400/1800Kč; ☑P☺🛜; ☑3, 5, 9) Set in a quiet neighbourhood a 10-minute walk from the city centre, this self-proclaimed 'art' hotel (presumably for the futuristic furniture at the entrance) offers clean and tastefully furnished modern rooms in a historic 19th-century building. Rooms come in 'standard' and more expensive 'superior', with the chief difference being size. There is free parking out the front and in the courtyard.

Barceló Brno Palace
LUXURY HOTEL €€€

(☑national hotline 800 222 515, reception 532 156 777; www.barcelo.com; Šilingrovo nám 2; r from 3600Kč; ☑P☺❄@🛜; ☑1, 12) Five-star heritage luxury comes to Brno at the Barceló Brno Palace. The reception area blends glorious 19th-century architecture with thoroughly modern touches, and the spacious rooms are both contemporary and romantic. The location on the edge of Brno's Old Town is excellent.

Eating

Špaliček
CZECH €

(☑542 211 526; www.facebook.com/restaurace. spalicek; Zelný trh 12; mains 80-160Kč; ☺11am-11pm; ☺🛜; ☑4, 8, 9) Brno's oldest (and maybe its 'meatiest') restaurant sits on the edge of the Cabbage Market. Ignore the irony and dig into huge Moravian meals, partnered with a local beer or something from the decent list of Moravian wines. The old-school tavern atmosphere is authentic and the daily lunch specials are a steal.

Spolek CZECH €
(📞774 814 230; www.spolek.net; Orli 22; mains 80-180Kč; ⊙9am-10pm Mon-Fri, 10am-10pm Sat & Sun; 🛜📶👶; ♿4, 8, 9) You'll get friendly, unpretentious service at this coolly 'bohemian' (yes, we're in Moravia) haven with interesting salads and soups, and a concise but diverse wine list. Photojournalism on the walls is complemented by a funky mezzanine bookshop. It has excellent coffee, too.

Bistro Franz CZECH €€
(📞720 113 502; www.bistrofranz.cz; Veveří 14; mains 155-220Kč; ⊙8am-11pm Mon-Fri, 10am-11pm Sat, 10am-9pm Sun; 🍴🛜📶; ♿1, 3, 9, 11, 12) Colourfully retro Bistro Franz is one of a new generation of restaurants that focuses on locally sourced, organic ingredients. The philosophy extends to the relatively simple menu of soups, baked chicken drumsticks, curried lentils and other student-friendly food. The wine is carefully chosen and the coffee is sustainably grown. Excellent choice for morning coffee and breakfast.

★**Pavillon** INTERNATIONAL €€
(📞541 213 497; www.restaurant-pavillon.cz; Jezuitská 6; mains 250-385Kč; ⊙11am-11pm Mon-Sat, noon-10pm Sun; 🍴🛜📶; ♿1, 2, 4, 8) High-end dining in an elegant, airy space that recalls the city's heritage in functionalist architecture. The menu changes with the season, but usually features one vegetarian entree as well as mains with locally sourced ingredients, such as wild boar or lamb raised in the Vysočina highlands. Daily lunch specials (200Kč) including soup, main and dessert are a steal.

🍷 **Drinking**

★**Cafe Podnebi** CAFE
(📞542 211 372; www.podnebi.cz; Údolní 5; ⊙8am-midnight Mon-Fri, from 9am Sat & Sun; 🛜👶; ♿4) This homey, student-oriented cafe is famous citywide for its excellent hot chocolate, but it also serves very good espresso drinks. There are plenty of baked goods and sweets to snack on. In summer the garden terrace is a hidden oasis, and there's a small play area for kids.

Bar, Který Neexistuje COCKTAIL BAR
(📞734 878 602; www.barkteryneexistuje.cz; Dvořákova 1; ⊙5pm-2am; 🛜; ♿4, 8, 9) 'The bar that doesn't exist' boasts a long, beautiful bar backed by every bottle of booze imagina-

ble. It anchors a row of popular, student-oriented bars along trendy Dvořákova. For a bar that 'doesn't exist', it gets quite crowded, so it's best to book ahead.

Super Panda Circus COCKTAIL BAR
(📞734 878 603; www.superpandacircus.cz; Šilingrovo náměstí 3, enter from Husova; ⊙6pm-2am Mon-Sat; 🛜; ♿1, 12) From the moment the doorman ushers you through an unmarked door into this bar, you feel you've entered a secret world like out of the movie *Eyes Wide Shut*. The dark interior, lit only in crazy colours emanating from the bar, and inventive drinks add to the allure. Hope for an empty table since it's not possible to book.

U Richarda PUB
(📞775 027 918; www.uricharda.cz; Údolní 7; ⊙3.30pm-2.30am Mon-Sat; 🛜; ♿4) This microbrewery is highly popular with students, who come for the great house-brewed, unpasteurised yeast beers, including a rare cherry-flavoured lager, and decent bar food like burgers and ribs (mains 110Kč to 149Kč). Book ahead.

☆ **Entertainment**

Fléda LIVE MUSIC
(📞533 433 432; www.fleda.cz; Štefánikova 24; tickets 200-400Kč; ⊙7pm-2am; ♿1, 2, 4, 6, 8) Brno's best up-and-coming bands, occasional touring performers and DJs all rock the stage at Brno's top music club. Buy tickets at the venue. Shows start around 9pm. Take the tram to the Hrnčířská stop.

Brno Philharmonic Orchestra CLASSICAL MUSIC
(Besední dům; 📞tickets 539 092 811; www.filharmonie-brno.cz; Komenského náměstí 8; tickets 290-390Kč; ⊙box office 9am-2pm Mon & Wed, 1-6pm Tue, Thu & Fri, plus 1hr before performances; ♿12, 13) The Brno Philharmonic is the city's leading orchestra for classical music. It conducts some 40 concerts each year, plus tours around the Czech Republic and Europe. It's particularly strong on Moravian-born, early 20th-century composer Leoš Janáček. Most performances are held at Besední dům concert house. Buy tickets at the box office, located around the corner from the main entrance on Besední.

ℹ **Information**

Tourist Information Centre (TIC Brno; 📞542 427 150; www.gotobrno.cz; Radnická 8, Old

Town Hall; ⊗8.30am-6pm Mon-Fri, 9am-6pm Sat & Sun) Brno's main tourist office is located within the Old Town Hall complex. The office has loads of great information on the city in English, including events calendars and walking maps, and staff can help find accommodation. Lots of material on the city's rich architectural heritage is also available, as well as self-guided tours. There's a free computer to check email.

ⓘ Getting There & Away

Express trains to Brno depart Prague's Hlavní nádraží (219Kč, three hours) every couple of hours during the day. Brno is a handy junction for onward train travel to Vienna (220Kč, two hours) and Bratislava (210Kč, 1½ hours).

There's regular coach service throughout the day to Prague (210Kč, 2½ hours), Bratislava (180Kč, two hours), Olomouc (100Kč, one hour) and Vienna (200Kč, two hours). **Student Agency** (☑ Brno office 539 000 860, national hotline 800 100 300; www.studentagency.cz; náměstí Svobody 17; ⊗9am-6pm Mon-Fri) buses serve Prague, as well as other domestic and international destinations.

Olomouc

POP 100,150

Olomouc (ol'-la-moats) is a sleeper. Practically unknown outside the Czech Republic and underappreciated even at home, the city is surprisingly majestic. The main square is among the country's nicest, surrounded by historic buildings and blessed with a Unesco-protected trinity column. The evocative central streets are dotted with beautiful churches, testament to the city's long history as a bastion of the Catholic church.

◎ Sights

Holy Trinity Column   MONUMENT
(Sloup Nejsvětější Trojice; Horní náměstí; ⊗closed to the public) The town's pride and joy is this 35m-high (115ft) baroque sculpture that dominates Horní náměstí and is a popular meeting spot for local residents. The trinity column was built between 1716 and 1754 and is allegedly the biggest single baroque sculpture in Central Europe. In 2000 the column was added to Unesco's World Heritage Site list.

Archdiocesan Museum   MUSEUM
(Arcidiecézni muzeum; ☑585 514 111; www.olmuart. cz; Václavské náměstí 3; adult/concession 70/35Kč,

Sun free, combined admission with Museum of Modern Art 100/50Kč; ⊗10am-6pm Tue-Sun; 🚍2, 3, 4, 6) The impressive holdings of the Archdiocesan Museum trace the history of Olomouc back 1000 years. The thoughtful layout, with helpful English signage, takes you through the original Romanesque foundations of Olomouc Castle, and highlights the cultural and artistic development of the city during the Gothic and baroque periods. Don't miss the magnificent Troyer Coach, definitely the stretch limo of the 18th century.

St Moritz Cathedral   CHURCH
(Chrám sv Mořice; www.moric-olomouc.cz; Opletalova 10; ⊗tower 9am-5pm Mon-Sat, noon-5pm Sun; 🚍2, 3, 4, 6) **FREE** This vast Gothic cathedral is Olomouc's original parish church, built between 1412 and 1540. The western tower is a remnant of its 13th-century predecessor. The cathedral's amazing sense of peace is shattered every September with an International Organ Festival; the cathedral's organ is Moravia's mightiest. The tower (more than 200 steps) provides the best view in town.

Museum of Modern Art   MUSEUM
(Muzeum moderního umění; ☑585 514 111; www. olmuart.cz; Denisova 47; adult/child 70/35Kč, Sun & 1st Wed of month free, combined admission with Archdiocesan Museum 100/50Kč; ⊗10am-6pm Tue-Sun; 🚍2, 3, 4, 6) On two floors, the museum showcases art from the 20th century under the heading 'A Century of Relativity'. The top floor focuses on movements from the first half of the century, including expressionism, cubism and surrealism. A second part, one floor below, features postwar movements such as abstraction and Czech trends from the 1970s and '80s.

Civil Defence Shelter   HISTORIC SITE
(Kryt Civilní Obrany; www.tourism.olomouc.eu; Bezručovy sady; 30Kč; ⊗tours at 10am, 1pm & 4pm Thu & Sat mid-Jun–mid-Sep) Olomouc is all about centuries-old history, but this more-recent relic of the Cold War is also worth exploring on a guided tour. The shelter was built between 1953 and 1956 and was designed to keep a lucky few protected from the ravages of a chemical or nuclear strike. Tours are arranged by Olomouc Information Centre (p300), which is also where they start.

🛏 Sleeping

Cosy Corner Hostel   HOSTEL €
(☑ 777 570 730; www.cosycornerhostel.com; 4th fl,
Sokolská 1; dm/s/d 300/700/900Kč; ⊝ 🛜; 🚌 2, 3,
4, 6) The Australian-Czech couple who mind
this friendly and exceptionally well-run hostel are a wealth of local information. There
are dorms in eight-bed rooms, as well as
private singles and doubles. Bicycles can be
hired for 100Kč per day. In summer there's
sometimes a two-night minimum stay, but
Olomouc is worth it, and there's plenty of
day-trip information on offer.

★ Penzión Na Hradě   PENSION €€
(☑ 585 203 231; www.penzionnahrade.cz; Michalská 4; s/d 1490/1990Kč; ⊝ ❄ 🛜) In terms of
price/quality ratio, this may be Olomouc's
best deal, and worth the minor splurge if
you can swing it. The location, tucked away
in the shadow of St Michael's Church, is ideally central and the sleek, cool rooms have
a professional design touch. There's also
a small garden terrace for relaxing out the
back. Book ahead in summer.

Pension Royal   PENSION €€
(☑ 734 200 602; www.pension-royal.cz; Wurmova
1; r 1600/2000Kč; 🅿 ⊝ 🛜; 🚌 2, 3, 4, 6) With
antique furniture, crisp white duvets and
Oriental rugs on wood floors, the Royal is
a spacious and splurge-worthy romantic
getaway. Each room has a separate name
and unique furnishings, though all go for an
updated old-world feel. To get here catch a
tram from the train station, jumping off at
the U Domú stop.

🍴 Eating & Drinking

★ Svatováclavský Pivovar   CZECH €€
(☑ 585 207 517; www.svatovaclavsky-pivovar.cz;
Mariánská 4; mains 180-290Kč; ⊙ 9am-midnight
Mon-Fri, 11am-midnight Sat, 11am-10pm Sun; ⊝ 🛜;
🚌 2, 3, 4, 6) This warm and inviting pub
makes its own beer and serves plate-loads
of Czech specialities such as duck confit and
beer-infused goulash. Stop by for lunch midweek for an excellent value soup and main
course for around 150Kč. Speciality beers
include unpasteurised wheat and cherry-flavoured varieties. Useful for washing down
some of Olomouc's signature stinky cheese,
tvarůžky.

Plan B   CZECH €€
(☑ 773 046 454; www.bar-planb.cz; Palachovo
náměstí 1; mains 150-250Kč; ⊙ 11am-midnight
Mon-Fri, 4pm-midnight Sat; ⊝ 🛜 🍴; 🚌 1, 3, 4, 6, 7)
This homey, low-key bistro puts the emphasis on organic, locally sourced ingredients
and traditional recipes. The daily lunch specials served during the week (11am to 2pm)
feature a choice of four to five entrées (at
least one vegetarian) plus soup for 120Kč.
The evening menu changes week to week, so
check the door or the website to see what's
cooking during your visit.

Vila Primavesi   INTERNATIONAL €€
(☑ 585 204 852; www.primavesi.cz; Univerzitní 7;
mains 160-280Kč; ⊙ 11am-11pm Mon-Sat, to 4pm
Sun; ⊝; 🚌 2, 3, 4, 6) In an art nouveau villa
that played host to Austrian artist Gustav
Klimt in the early 20th century, the Vila
Primavesi enjoys one of Olomouc's most exclusive settings. On summer evenings dine
on dishes such as tuna steak and risotto on
the terrace overlooking the city gardens.
Lunch specials are better value than evening
meals.

★ Cafe 87   CAFE
(☑ 585 202 593; www.cafe87.cz; Denisova 47; coffee 40Kč; ⊙ 7.30am-9pm Mon-Fri, 8am-9pm Sat &
Sun; 🛜; 🚌 2, 3, 4, 6) Locals come in droves to
this funky cafe beside the Olomouc Museum of Modern Art for coffee and its famous
chocolate pie (50Kč). Some people still apparently prefer the dark chocolate to the
white chocolate. When will they learn? It's a
top spot for breakfast and toasted sandwiches, too. Seating is over two floors and there's
a rooftop terrace.

The Black Stuff   PUB
(☑ 774 697 909; www.blackstuff.cz; 1 máje 19;
⊙ 4pm-2am Mon-Fri, 5pm-3am Sat, 5-11pm Sun;
🛜; 🚌 2, 3, 4, 6) Cosy, old-fashioned Irish bar
with several beers on tap and a large and
growing collection of single malts and other choice tipples. Attracts a mixed crowd of
students, locals and visitors.

⭐ Entertainment

Jazz Tibet Club   LIVE MUSIC
(☑ 585 230 399; www.jazzclub.olomouc.com;
Sokolská 48; tickets 100-300Kč; 🛜) Blues, jazz
and world music, including occasional international acts, feature at this popular spot,
which also incorporates a good restaurant

and wine bar. See the website for the program during your visit. Buy tickets at the venue on the day of the show or in advance at the Olomouc Information Centre (p300).

Moravian Philharmonic Olomouc CLASSICAL MUSIC
(Moravská Filharmonie Olomouc; ☑ 585 206 520, tickets 585 513 392; www.mfo.cz; Horní náměstí 23; tickets 80-220Kč) The local orchestra presents regular concerts and hosts Olomouc's International Organ Festival. Buy tickets one week in advance at the Olomouc Information Centre (p300) or at the venue one hour before the performance starts.

ℹ️ Information

Olomouc Information Centre (Olomoucká Informační Služba; ☑ 585 513 385; www.tourism.olomouc.eu; Horní náměstí; ☺ 9am-7pm) Though Olomouc's information centre is short on language skills, it's very helpful when it comes to securing maps, brochures and tickets for events around town. It also offers regular daily sightseeing tours of the Town Hall (30Kč), and from mid-June to mid-September daily guided one-hour sightseeing tours of the city centre (70Kč).

ℹ️ Getting There & Away

Olomouc is on a main international rail line, with regular services from both Prague (220Kč, two to three hours) and Brno (100Kč, 1½ hours). From Prague, you can take normal trains or faster, high-end private trains run by **Student Agency's RegioJet** (RegioJet; ☑ 841 101 101; www.studentagency.cz; Riegrova 28; ☺ 9am-6pm Mon-Fri; 🚋 2, 3, 4, 6) or **LEO Express** (☑ 220 311 700; www.le.cz; Jeremenkova 23, Main Train Station; ☺ 5.45am-9.45pm; 🚋 1, 2, 3, 4, 5, 6, 7). Olomouc's train station is 2km east of the centre and accessible via several tram lines.

Olomouc is well-connected by bus to and from Brno (90Kč, 1¼ hours). The best way of getting to Prague, however, is by train. The **bus station** (Autobusové nádraží Olomouc; ☑ 585 313 848; www.vlak-bus.cz; Sladkovského 142/37; 🚋 1, 2, 3, 4, 5, 6, 7) is located just behind the train station, about 2km east of the centre.

SURVIVAL GUIDE

ℹ️ Directory A–Z

ACCOMMODATION

The Czech Republic has a wide variety of accommodation options, from luxury hotels to pensions and camping grounds. Prague, Brno and Český Krumlov all have decent backpacker-oriented hostels.

➡ In Prague, hotel rates peak in spring and autumn, as well as around the Christmas and Easter holidays. Midsummer is considered 'shoulder season' and rates are about 20% off peak.

➡ The capital is a popular destination, so book in advance. Hotels are cheaper and less busy outside of Prague, but try to reserve ahead of arrival to get the best rate.

BUSINESS HOURS

Banks 9am to 4pm Monday to Friday.
Bars and clubs 11am to 1am Tuesday to Saturday.
Museums 9am to 6pm Tuesday to Sunday; some attractions closed or have shorter hours October to April.
Post offices 8am to 7pm Monday to Friday, 9am to 1pm Saturday (varies)
Restaurants 11am to 11pm daily.
Shops 9am to 6pm Monday to Friday, 9am to 1pm Saturday (varies).

GAY & LESBIAN TRAVELLERS

The Czech Republic is a relatively tolerant destination for gay and lesbian travellers. Homosexuality is legal, and since 2006, same-sex couples have been able to form registered partnerships.

Prague has a lively gay scene and is home to Europe's biggest gay pride march (www.prague pride.cz). Useful websites include **Travel Gay Europe** (www.travelgayeurope.com) and **Prague Saints** (www.praguesaints.cz).

INTERNET RESOURCES

CzechTourism (www.czechtourism.com)
National Bus & Train Timetable (http://jizdni-rady.idnes.cz)
Prague Events Calendar (www.pragueevents-calendar.com)
Prague City Tourism (www.prague.eu)

SLEEPING PRICE RANGES

The following price ranges refer to the cost of a standard double room per night in high season.

€ less than 2000Kč

€€ 2000Kč to 4000Kč

€€€ more than 4000Kč

MONEY

➡ The currency is the *koruna* (crown), abbreviated as Kč. The euro does not circulate.

➡ The best places to exchange money are banks or use your credit or debit card to withdraw money as needed from ATMs.

➡ Never exchange money on the street and avoid private exchange offices, especially in Prague, as they charge high commissions.

➡ Keep small change handy for use in public toilets and metro-ticket machines.

PUBLIC HOLIDAYS

New Year's Day 1 January
Easter Monday March/April
Labour Day 1 May
Liberation Day 8 May
Sts Cyril & Methodius Day 5 July
Jan Hus Day 6 July
Czech Statehood Day 28 September
Republic Day 28 October
Struggle for Freedom & Democracy Day 17 November
Christmas 24 to 26 December

TELEPHONE

➡ All Czech phone numbers have nine digits. Dial all nine numbers for any call.

➡ The Czech Republic's country code is 420.

➡ Mobile-phone coverage (GSM 900/1800) is compatible with most European, Australian or New Zealand handsets (though generally not with North American or Japanese models).

➡ Purchase a Czech prepaid SIM card from any mobile-phone shop. These allow you to make local calls at cheaper local rates.

COUNTRY FACTS

Area 78,866 sq km

Capital Prague

Country Code 420

Currency Crown (Kč)

Emergency 112

Language Czech

Money ATMs all over; banks open Monday to Friday

Population 10.6 million

Visas Schengen rules apply; visas not required for most nationalities

➡ Local mobile numbers can be identified by prefix. Mobiles start with 601–608 or 720–779.

➡ Public phones operate via prepaid magnetic cards purchased at post offices or newsstands from 300Kč.

VISAS

➡ The Czech Republic is part of the EU's Schengen area, and citizens of most developed countries can spend up to 90 days in the country in a six-month period without a visa.

ℹ Getting There & Away

The Czech Republic lies at the centre of Europe and has good rail and road connections to surrounding countries. Prague's international airport is a major air hub for Central Europe. Flights, cars and tours can be booked online at lonelyplanet.com/bookings.

CZECH REPUBLIC GETTING THERE & AWAY

ESSENTIAL FOOD & DRINK

Becherovka A shot of this sweetish herbal liqueur from Karlovy Vary is a popular way to start (or end) a big meal.

Beer Modern *pils* (light, amber-coloured lager) was invented in the city of Plzeň in the 19th century, giving Czechs bragging rights to having the best beer (*pivo*) in the world.

Braised Beef Look out for svíčková na smetaně on menus. This is a satisfying slice of roast beef, served in a cream sauce, with a side of bread dumplings and a dollop of cranberry sauce.

Carp This lowly fish (kapr in Czech) is given pride of place every Christmas at the centre of the family meal. Kapr na kmíní is fried or baked carp with caraway seed.

Dumplings Every culture has its favourite starchy side dish; for Czechs it's *knedliky* – big bread dumplings that are perfect for mopping up gravy.

Roast Pork Move over beef, pork (*vepřové maso*) is king here. The classic Bohemian dish, seen on menus around the country, is vepřo-knedlo-zelo, local slang for roast pork, bread dumplings and sauerkraut.

EATING PRICE RANGES

The following price ranges refer to the price of a main course at dinner:

€ less than 200Kč

€€ 200Kč to 500Kč

€€€ more than 500Kč

AIR

Prague's **Václav Havel Airport** (Prague Ruzyně International Airport; ☑ 220 111 888; www.prg. aero; K letišti 6, Ruzyně; ☎; ☐ 100, 119) is one of Central Europe's busiest airports, and daily flights connect the Czech capital with major cities throughout Europe, the UK, the Middle East and Asia. From April to October, direct flights link Prague to a handful of cities in North America.

LAND

The Czech Republic has border crossings with Germany, Poland, Slovakia and Austria. These are all EU member states within the Schengen zone, meaning there are no passport or customs checks.

Bus

➡ The main international terminal is Florenc bus station in Prague.

➡ Leading international bus carriers include Student Agency and Eurolines.

Eurolines (☑ 731 222 111; www.elines. cz; Křižíkova 2110/2b, ÚAN Praha Florenc; ⊙ 6.30am-7pm Sat-Thu, to 9pm Fri; ☎; Ⓜ Florenc) International bus carrier links Prague to cities around Europe. Consult the website for a timetable and prices. Buy tickets online or at Florenc bus station.

Florenc Bus Station (ÚAN Praha Florenc; ☑ 900 144 444; www.florenc.cz; Křižíkova 2110/2b, Karlín; ⊙ 5am-midnight; ☎; Ⓜ Florenc) Prague' s main bus station, servicing most domestic and long-haul international routes. There's an information counter, ticket windows, a left-luggage office and a small number of shops and restaurants. You can also usually purchase tickets directly from the driver.

Student Agency (☑ bus information 841 101 101, info 800 100 300; www.studentagency.cz; Křižíkova 2110/2b, ÚAN Praha Florenc; ⊙ 5am-11.30pm) This modern, well-run company operates comfortable, full-service coaches to major Czech cities as well as 60 destinations around Europe. Buses usually depart from Florenc bus station, but may depart from other stations as well. Be sure to ask which station when you purchase your ticket.

Train

➡ The country's main international rail gateway is **Praha hlavní nádraží** (Prague main train station). The station is accessible by public transport on metro line C.

➡ There is regular rail service from Prague to and from Germany, Poland, Slovakia and Austria. Trains to/from the south and east, including from Bratislava, Vienna and Budapest, also stop at Brno's main train station.

➡ In Prague, buy train tickets at ČD Centrum, located on the lower level of the station. Credit cards are accepted.

➡ Both InterRail and Eurail passes are valid on the Czech rail network.

ČD Centrum (☑ 840 112 113; www.cd.cz; Wilsonova 8, Praha hlavní nádraží; ⊙ 3am-midnight; Ⓜ Hlavní nádraží) The main ticket office for purchasing train tickets for both domestic (vnitrostátní jízdenky) and international (mezínárodní jízdenky) destinations is located on the lower (park) level of the Prague's main train station. It also sells seat reservations, as well as booking couchettes and sleeping cars.

LEO Express (☑ 220 311 700; www.le.cz; Wilsonova 8, Praha hlavní nádraží; ⊙ ticket office 7.15am-9.30pm; Ⓜ Hlavní Nádraží) Private company offering low-cost rail and bus transport to Brno, Olomouc and Ostrava, with onward bus connections to Lviv, Ukraine, and Kraków, Poland, among other destinations. Buy tickets online or at the ticket office in Prague's main train station (Praha hlavní nádraží).

Praha hlavní nádraží (Prague Main Train Station; ☑ 840 112 113; www.cd.cz; Wilsonova 8, Nové Město; ⊙ 3.30am-12.30am; Ⓜ Hlavní nádraží) Prague's main train station, handling most international and domestic arrivals and departures.

ⓘ Getting Around

BUS

➡ Buses are often faster, cheaper and more convenient than trains.

➡ Many bus routes have reduced frequency (or none) on weekends.

➡ Check bus timetables and prices at http:// jizdnirady.idnes.cz.

➡ In Prague, many (though not all) buses arrive at and depart from Florenc bus station. Be sure to double-check the correct station.

➡ Try to arrive at the station well ahead of departure to secure a seat. Buy tickets at the station ticket window or directly from the driver.

Student Agency is the most popular, private bus company. It runs clean, comfortable coaches to cities around the country.

CAR & MOTORCYCLE

➡ For breakdown assistance anywhere in the country, dial 1230.

➡ The minimum driving age is 18 and traffic moves on the right. Children aged under 12 are prohibited from sitting in the front seat.

➡ Drivers are required to keep their headlights on at all times. The legal blood-alcohol limit is zero.

TRAIN

➡ Czech Railways provides efficient train services to almost every part of the country.

➡ Private rail operators, such as LEO Express (p302) offer fast, high-speed trains between Prague and Olomouc, among other destinations.

➡ For an online timetable, go to http://jizdni-rady.idnes.cz or www.cd.cz.

Denmark

Includes ➜

Best Places to Eat

➜ Höst (p314)

➜ Schønnemann (p314)

➜ Torvehallerne KBH (p313)

➜ Aarhus Street Food (p322)

➜ St Pauls Apothek (p322)

Best Places to Stay

➜ Hotel Nimb (p313)

➜ Generator Hostel (p312)

➜ Hotel Guldsmeden (p321)

➜ Badepension Marienlund (p324)

Why Go?

Denmark is the bridge between Scandinavia and northern Europe. To the rest of Scandinavia, the Danes are chilled, frivolous party animals, with relatively liberal, progressive attitudes. Their culture, food, architecture and appetite for conspicuous consumption owe as much, if not more, to their German neighbours to the south than to their former colonies (Sweden, Norway and Iceland) to the north.

Packed with intriguing museums, shops, bars, nightlife and award-winning restaurants, Denmark's capital, Copenhagen, is one of the hippest, most accessible cities in Europe. And while Danish cities such as Odense and Aarhus harbour their own urbane drawcards, Denmark's other chief appeal lies in its photogenic countryside, sweeping coastline and historic sights.

When to Go
Copenhagen

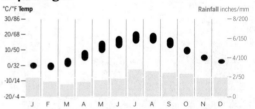

Jun & Jul Long days, buzzing beachside towns, Copenhagen Jazz and A-list rock fest Roskilde.

Sep & Oct Fewer crowds, golden landscapes and snug nights by crackling open fires.

Dec Twinkling Christmas lights, ice-skating rinks and gallons of warming *gløgg* (mulled wine).

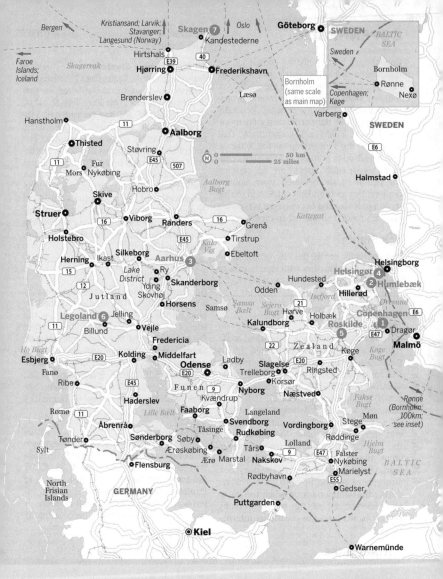

Denmark Highlights

1 Copenhagen (p306)
Lapping up the good looks of the capital of cool.

2 Louisiana (p307)
Being inspired by the art and the views at the gallery in Humlebæk.

3 Aarhus (p319) Visiting the 2017 Capital of Culture

and home of showpiece art museum ARoS.

4 Kronborg Slot (p316)
Snooping around Hamlet's epic home in Helsingør.

5 Roskilde Festival
(p317) Letting loose at summer music festivals around the country, including

Scandinavia's largest music festival.

6 Legoland (p322)
Marveling at the microcosmic miniland before jumping on a few rides.

7 Skagen (p323) Witnessing treasured artworks and clashing seas in the holiday haven.

COPENHAGEN

POP 562,379

Copenhagen is not only the coolest kid on the Nordic block, but also gets constantly ranked as the happiest city in the world. Ask a dozen locals why and they would probably all zone in on the *hygge*, which generally means cosiness, but encompasses far more. But it is this laid-back contentment that helps give the Danish capital the X factor. The backdrop is pretty cool as well: its cobbled, bike-friendly streets are an enticing concoction of sherbet-hued town houses, craft studios and candlelit cafes. Add to this its compact size and Copenhagen is possibly Europe's most seamless urban experience.

◉ Sights

You can walk across the city centre in an hour, and travel further with ease thanks to the cycle paths, metro, trains and buses.

◉ Tivoli & Around

★Tivoli Gardens   AMUSEMENT PARK
(www.tivoli.dk; Vesterbrogade 3, Vesterbro; adult/child under 8yr Mon-Thu Dkr110/free, Fri-Sun Dkr120/free; ⊙11am-11pm Sun-Thu, to midnight Fri & Sat Apr-Sep, reduced hours rest of year; 🛜🚼; 🚌2A, 5A, 9A, 12, 26, 250S, 350S, 🚆S-train København H) Dating from 1843, tasteful Tivoli wins fans with its dreamy whirl of amusement rides, twinkling pavilions, carnival games and open-air stage shows. Visitors can ride the renovated, century-old **rollercoaster**, enjoy the famous Saturday-evening **fireworks display** or just soak up the storybook atmosphere. A good tip is to go on Fridays during the summer season when the open-air Plænen stage hosts free rock concerts by Danish bands (and the occasional international superstar) from 10pm – go early if it's a big-name act.

★Ny Carlsberg Glyptotek   MUSEUM
(www.glyptoteket.dk; Dantes Plads 7, Vesterbro, HC Andersens Blvd; adult/child Dkr95/free, Tue free; ⊙11am-6pm Tue-Sun, until 10pm Thu; 🛜; 🚌1A, 2A, 11A, 33, 40, 66, 🚆S-train København H) Fin-de-siècle architecture dallies with an eclectic mix of art at Ny Carlsberg Glyptotek. The collection is divided into two parts: northern Europe's largest booty of antiquities, and an elegant collection of 19th-century Danish and French art. The latter includes the largest collection of Rodin sculptures outside of France and no fewer than 47 Gauguin paintings. These are displayed along with works by greats like Cézanne, Van Gogh, Pissarro, Monet and Renoir.

◉ Slotsholmen

An island separated from the city centre by a moatlike canal on three sides and the harbour on the other side, Slotsholmen is the site of **Christiansborg Slot** (Christiansborg Palace; 📞33 92 64 92; www.christiansborg.dk; Slotsholmen, Christianshavn; adult/child Dkr90/45, joint ticket incl royal reception rooms, ruins, kitchens & stables Dkr150/75; ⊙10am-5pm Apr-Oct; 🚼; 🚌1A, 2A, 9A, 26, 40, 66, 🚊Det Kongelige Bibliotek, 🅼Christianshavn), home to Denmark's parliament.

★Nationalmuseet   MUSEUM
(National Museum; www.natmus.dk; Ny Vestergade 10, Slotsholmen; adult/child Dkr75/60; ⊙10am-5pm Tue-Sun; 🛜🚼; 🚌1A, 2A, 11A, 33, 40, 66, 🚆S-train København H) For a crash course in Danish history and culture, spend an afternoon at Denmark's National Museum. It has first claims on virtually every antiquity

---

ITINERARIES

One Week

You could comfortably spend four days in Copenhagen exploring the museums, hunting down Danish design and taste-testing its lauded restaurants and bars. A trip north along the coast to the magnificent modern-art museum Louisiana, and then further north still to Kronborg Slot, before returning south via Roskilde, would be a great way to spend the other three days.

Two Weeks

After time in and around Copenhagen, head west, stopping off to see Hans Christian Andersen's birthplace in Odense. Continue further west to the Jutland peninsula for the understated hipster cool of Aarhus and plastic-fantastic Legoland, then head north to luminous Skagen.

LOUISIANA: MODERN-ART MUST

Even if you don't have a consuming passion for modern art, Denmark's outstanding **Louisiana** (www.louisiana.dk; Gammel Strandvej 13, Humlebæk; adult/child Dkr115/free; ☺11am-10pm Tue-Fri, to 6pm Sat & Sun; ☎) should be high on your 'to do' list. It's a striking modernist gallery made up of four huge wings, which stretch across a sculpture-filled park, burrowing down into the hillside and nosing out again to wink at the sea (and Sweden). The collection itself is stellar, covering everything from constructivism, CoBrA movement artists and minimalist art to abstract expressionism, pop art and photography.

Louisiana is in the leafy town of Humlebæk, 30km north of Copenhagen. From Humlebæk train station, the museum is a 1.5km signposted walk along Gammel Strandvej. Trains to Humlebæk run at least twice hourly from Copenhagen (Dkr115, 35 minutes) and Helsingør (Dkr36, 10 minutes). If day-tripping it from Copenhagen, the 24-hour ticket (adult/child Dkr130/65) is much better value.

uncovered on Danish soil, including Stone Age tools, Viking weaponry, rune stones and medieval jewellery. Among the many highlights is a finely crafted 3500-year-old Sun Chariot, as well as bronze *lurs* (horns), some of which date back 3000 years and are still capable of blowing a tune.

⭐ **De Kongelige Repræsentationslokaler** HISTORIC BUILDING
(Royal Reception Rooms at Christiansborg Slot; www.christiansborg.dk; Slotsholmen, Christianshavn; adult/child Dkr90/45; ☺10am-5pm May-Sep, closed Mon Oct-Apr, guided tours in Danish/English 11am/3pm; ☎; ☐1A, 2A, 9A, 11A, 26, 40, 66) The grandest part of Christiansborg Slot is De Kongelige Repræsentationslokaler, an ornate Renaissance hall where the queen holds royal banquets and entertains heads of state. Don't miss the beautifully sewn and colourful wall tapestries depicting Danish history from Viking times to today. Created by tapestry designer Bjørn Nørgaard over a decade, the works were completed in 2000. Look for the Adam and Eve–style representation of the queen and her husband (albeit clothed) in a Danish Garden of Eden.

⭐ **Thorvaldsens Museum** MUSEUM
(www.thorvaldsensmuseum.dk; Bertel Thorvaldsens Plads; adult/child Dkr40/free, Wed free; ☺10am-5pm Tue-Sun; ☐1A, 2A, 11A, 26, 40, 66) What looks like a colourful Greco-Roman mausoleum is in fact a museum dedicated to the works of illustrious Danish sculptor Bertel Thorvaldsen (1770–1844). Heavily influenced by mythology after four decades in Rome, Thorvaldsen returned to Copenhagen and donated his private collection to the Danish public. In return the royal fam-ily provided this site for the construction of what is a remarkable complex housing Thorvaldsen's drawings, plaster moulds and statues. The museum also contains Thorvaldsen's own collection of Mediterranean antiquities.

Ruinerne under Christiansborg RUINS
(Ruins under Christiansborg; www.christiansborg.dk; Slotsholmen, Christianshavn; adult/child Dkr50/25, joint ticket incl royal reception rooms, kitchens & stables Dkr150/75; ☺10am-5pm, closed Mon Oct-Apr, guided tours in English/Danish noon Sat/Sun; ☐1A, 2A, 9A, 11A, 26, 40, 66) A walk through the crypt-like bowels of Slotsholmen, known as Ruinerne under Christiansborg, offers a unique perspective on Copenhagen's well-seasoned history. In the basement of the current palace, beneath the tower, are the remains of two earlier castles. The most notable are the ruins of Absalon's fortress, Slotsholmen's original castle, built by Bishop Absalon in 1167.

ℹ COPENHAGEN CARD

The **Copenhagen Card** (www.copenhagencard.com; adult/child 10-15yr 24hr Dkr379/199, 48hr Dkr529/269, 72hr Dkr629/319, 120hr Dkr839/419), available at the Copenhagen Visitors Centre or online, gives you free access to 72 museums and attractions in the city and surrounding area, as well as free travel for all S-train, metro and bus journeys within the seven travel zones. Note, though, that several of the city's attractions are either free or at least free one day of the week.

Central Copenhagen (København)

NØRREBRO

Assistens Kirkegård

Coffee Collective Nørrebro (400m)

Møllegade
Guldbergsgade
Sankt Hans Torv
Blegdamsvej
Læssøesgade
Ryesgade
Fredensbro
37

Elmegade
Fælledvej
Nørrebrogade
Skt Hans Gade
Ravnsborggade
Sortedam Dossering
Sortedams Sø
Øster Søgade
Solvgade

Rantzausgade
Kapelvej
Griffenfeldsgade
Stengade
Baggesensgade
Korsgade
Blågårds Plads
Dronning Louises Bro
Frederiksborggade
Romersgade
Gothersgade
Øster Farimagsgade

Åblvd

Coffee Collective Frederiksberg (1km)

Peblinge Dossering
Peblinge Sø
Vendersgade
Limegade
Nørreport
Israels Plads
29
33
M
S

Åblvd
Gyldenløvesgade
Nørre Søgade
Nansensgade
Nørre Farimagsgade
Rosengården
Nørre Voldgade
Nørregade
Fiolstræde

H C Ørsteds Vej
Rosenørns Allé
Forum
M
VESTERBRO
23
Sankt Marcus Allé
Turesensgade
Ørsteds Parken
Larslejstræde
Krystalgade
Kannikestræde

22
Danasvej
Vester Søgade
Nyropsgade
Vester Farimagsgade
H C Andersens Blvd
Nørre Voldgade
Studiestræde
Vor Frue Plads
15

Niels Ebbesens Vej
Vodroffsvej
Kampmannsgade
Gammeltorv
Vestergade
Frederiksberggade
Rådhusstræde

Fortåbningsholms Allé
Sankt Jørgens Sø
Vesterport
S
Hammerichsgade
Jernbanegade
Vestergade
STRØGET
Bag Rådhuset

Gammel Kongevej
Jernbanegade
Rådhuspladsen
17
Lavendelstræde
Regnbuepladsen
Stormgade

24
Vesterbrogade
Axeltorv
10
Tivoli Gardens
TIVOLI
Dantes Plads

Bertrams Guldsmeden (250m)

Ved Vesterport
Copenhagen Visitors Centre
27
Banegårdspladsen
5
Ny Carlsberg Glyptotek

19
28
Bernstorffsgade
Tietgensgade

35
Viktoriagade
Istedgade
Central Station (København Hovedbanegården)
Eurolines
Otto Mønstedsgade
21
Hambrogade

Dannebrogsgade
Eskildsgade
Absalonsgade
Gasværksvej
Halmtorvet
Sønder Blvd
Kødbyen (Meatpacking District)
VESTERBRO
Ingerslevsgade
Carsten Niebuhrs Gade
Mitchellsgade
Kalvebod Brygge

Vega Live (350m); Carlsberg Visitors Centre (1.6km)

DENMARK COPENHAGEN

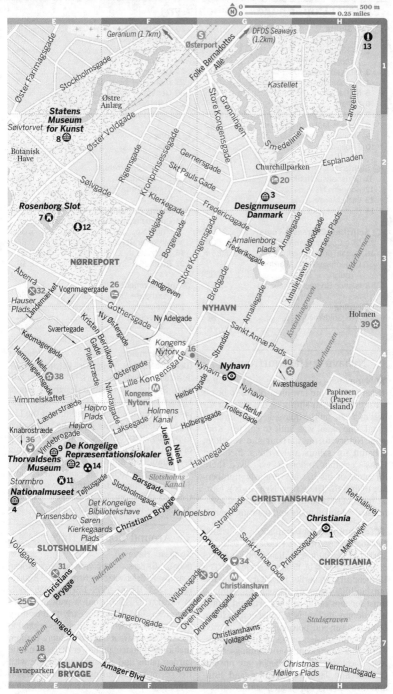

DENMARK COPENHAGEN

Central Copenhagen (København)

◉ Nyhavn & Harbourfront

★**Nyhavn**   CANAL

(Nyhavn) There are few nicer places to be on a sunny day than sitting at the outdoor tables of a cafe on the quayside of the Nyhavn canal. The canal was built to connect Kongens Nytorv to the harbour and was long a haunt for sailors and writers, including Hans Christian Andersen, who lived there for most of his life at, variously, numbers 20, 18 and 67. These days Nyhavn is a tourist magnet of brightly coloured gabled town houses, colourful boats and foaming beers.

★**Designmuseum Danmark**   MUSEUM

(www.designmuseum.dk; Bredgade 68, Østerport; adult/child Dkr100/free; ⊙11am-5pm Tue & Thu-Sun, to 9pm Wed; 🚌1A, 15, Ⓜ Kongens Nytorv) The 18th-century Frederiks Hospital is now the outstanding Denmark Design Museum. A must for fans of the applied arts and industrial design, its extensive collection includes Danish silver and porcelain textiles, as well as the iconic design pieces of modern innovators like Kaare Klint, Poul Henningsen and Arne Jacobsen. Also on display are ancient Chinese and Japanese ceramics, and 18th- and 19th-century European decorative arts.

Little Mermaid   MONUMENT

(Den Lille Havfrue; Langelinie, Østerport; 🚌1A, 🚢Nordre Toldbod) New York has its Lady Liberty, Sydney its (Danish-designed) Opera House. When the world thinks of Copenhagen, chances are they're thinking of the Little Mermaid. Love her or loathe her (watch Copenhageners cringe at the very mention of her), this small, underwhelming statue is arguably the most photographed sight in the country, as well as the cause of countless 'is that it?' shrugs from tourists who have trudged the kilometre or so along an often windswept harbourfront to see her.

◉ Around Kongens Have

Kongens Have   PARK

(King's Gardens; http://parkmuseerne.dk/kongens-have/; Øster Voldgade, Nørreport; ⊙8.30am-6pm; 🚌6A, 11A, 42, 150S, 173E, 184, 185, 350S, Ⓜ Nørreport) FREE The oldest park in Copenhagen was laid out in the early 17th century by Christian IV, who used it as his vegetable patch. These days it has a little more to offer, including immaculate flower beds, romantic garden paths and a marionette theatre with free performances during the summer season (2pm and 3pm Tuesday to Sunday). Located on the northeastern side of the park, the theatre occupies one of the neoclassical pavilions designed by Danish architect Peter Meyn.

★ Statens Museum for Kunst   MUSEUM
(www.smk.dk; Sølvgade 48-50, Østerport; adult/child Dkk110/free; ⏱ 11am-5pm Tue & Thu-Sun, to 8pm Wed; 🚇; 🚌 6A, 26, 42, 173E, 184, 185) **FREE** Denmark's National Gallery straddles two contrasting, interconnected buildings: a late-19th-century 'palazzo' and a sharply minimalist extension. The museum houses medieval and Renaissance works, and impressive collections of Dutch and Flemish artists including Rubens, Breughel and Rembrandt. It claims the world's finest collection of 19th-century Danish Golden Age artists, among them Eckersberg and Hammershøi, foreign greats like Matisse and Picasso, and modern Danish heavyweights including Per Kirkeby.

★ Rosenborg Slot   CASTLE
(www.kongernessamling.dk/en/rosenborg; Øster Voldgade 4A, Nørreport; adult/child Dkr105/free, incl Amalienborg Slot Dkr145/free; ⏱ 10am-5pm Jun-Aug, to 4pm May, Sep & Oct, reduced hours rest of year; 🚇; 🚌 6A, 11A, 42, 150S, 173E, 184, 185, 350S, 🚇 Nørreport) A 'once-upon-a-time' combo of turrets, gables and moat, the early-17th-century Rosenborg Slot was built in Dutch Renaissance style between 1606 and 1633 by King Christian IV to serve as his summer home. Today, the castle's 24 upper rooms are chronologically arranged, housing the furnishings and portraits of each monarch from Christian IV to Frederik VII. The pièce de résistance is the basement Treasury, home to the dazzling crown jewels, among them Christian IV's glorious crown and Christian III's jewel-studded sword.

⊙ Christianshavn

★ Christiania   AREA
(Prinsessegade, Christianshavn; 🚌 9A, 2A, 40, 350S, 🚇 Christianshavn) Escape the capitalist crunch at Freetown Christiania, a dreadlocks-heavy commune straddling the eastern side of Christianshavn. Since its establishment by squatters in 1971, the area has drawn nonconformists from across the globe, attracted by the concept of collective business, workshops and communal living. Explore beyond the settlement's infamous 'Pusher St' – lined with shady hash and marijuana dealers – and you'll stumble upon a semibucolic wonderland of whimsical DIY

homes, cosy gardens and craft shops, eateries, beer gardens and music venues.

⊙ Outer Copenhagen

Den Blå Planet   AQUARIUM
(www.denblaaplanet.dk; Jacob Fortlingsvej 1, Kastrup; adult/child 3-11yr Dkr170/95; ⏱ 10am-9pm Mon, to 5pm Tue-Sun; 🚇; 🚌 5A, 🚇 Kastrup) Designed to look like a whirlpool from above, Copenhagen's aluminium-clad aquarium is the largest in northern Europe. The space is divided into climatic and geographic sections, the most spectacular of which is 'Ocean/Coral Reef'. Home to swarms of technicolor tropical fish, the exhibition is also home to the centre's largest tank, a massive 4-million-litre showcase brimming with sharks, stingrays and other majestic creatures. If possible, visit the aquarium on a Monday evening when it's at its quietest and most evocative.

Carlsberg Visitors Centre   BREWERY
(📞 33 27 12 82; www.visitcarlsberg.dk; Gamle Carlsberg Vej 11, Vesterbro; adult/child Dkr95/70; ⏱ 10am-5pm Tue-Sun; 🚌 18, 26) Adjacent to the architecturally whimsical Carlsberg brewery, the Carlsberg Visitors Centre explores the history of Danish beer from 1370 BC (yes, they carbon-dated a bog girl who was found in a peat bog caressing a jug of well-aged brew). Dioramas give the lowdown on the brewing process and en route to your final destination you'll pass antique copper vats and the stables with a dozen Jutland dray horses.

⫝̸ Tours

Canal Tours Copenhagen   BOATING
(📞 32 66 00 00; www.stromma.dk; Nyhavn; adult/child Dkr80/40; ⏱ 9.30am-9pm late Jun-late Aug, reduced hours rest of year; 🚻; 🚇 Kongens Nytorv) Canal Tours Copenhagen runs one-hour

SUPERKILEN

The fascinating one-kilometre-long Superkilen (Nørrebrogade 210; 🚌 5A, 66, Ⓢ Nørrebro) park showcases objects sourced from around the globe with the aim of celebrating diversity and uniting the community. Items include a tile fountain from Morocco, bollards from Ghana, and swing chairs from Baghdad, as well as neon signs from Russia and China. Even the benches, manhole covers, and rubbish bins hail from foreign lands.

cruises of the city's canals and harbour, taking in numerous major sights, including Christiansborg Slot, Christianshavn, the Royal Library, Opera House, Amalienborg Palace and the Little Mermaid. Embark at Nyhavn or Ved Stranden. Boats depart up to six times per hour from late June to late August, with reduced frequency the rest of the year.

Copenhagen Free Walking Tours WALKING
(www.copenhagenfreewalkingtours.dk; Rådhus (City Hall), Strøget, H C Andersens Blvd; ☉noon) FREE Departing daily at noon from outside rådhus (City Hall), these free three-hour walking tours take in famous landmarks and include interesting anecdotes. Tours are in English and require a minimum of five people. Free 90-minute tours of Christianshavn depart at 4pm Friday to Monday from the base of the Bishop Absalon statue on Højbro Plads. A tip is expected.

Bike Copenhagen with Mike CYCLING
(☑26 39 56 88; www.bikecopenhagenwithmike. dk; Sankt Peders Stræde 47, Strøget; per person Dkr299) If you don't fancy walking, Bike Mike runs three-hour cycling tours of the city, departing Sankt Peders Stræde 47 in the city centre, just east of Ørstedsparken (which is southwest of Nørreport station). The tour cost includes bike and helmet rental. Seasonal options are also offered, including a Saturday-evening 'Ride & Dine' tour from June to September. Cash only.

✯✦ Festivals & Events

Distortion MUSIC
(www.cphdistortion.dk) Taking place over five heady days in early June, Copenhagen Distortion celebrates the city's street life and club culture. Expect raucous block parties and top-name DJs spinning dance tracks in bars and clubs across town.

FANCY A SWIM?

Copenhagen's coolest outdoor pool complex, **Islands Brygge Havnebadet** (Islands Brygge, Sunby; ☉7am-7pm Mon-Fri, 11am-7pm Sat & Sun Jun-Aug; ☑); ☑5A, 12, Ⓜ Islands Brygge) FREE comprises five pools and sits right in the central city's main canal. Water quality is rigorously monitored and the lawns, BBQ facilities and eateries make it a top spot to see and be seen on a warm summer day, whether you get wet or not.

Copenhagen Jazz Festival MUSIC
(www.jazz.dk) Copenhagen's single largest event, and the largest jazz festival in northern Europe, hits the city over 10 days in early July. The programme covers jazz in all its forms, with an impressive line-up of local and international talent.

Copenhagen Cooking FOOD & DRINK
(www.copenhagencooking.dk) Scandinavia's largest food festival serves up a gut-rumbling programme spanning cooking demonstrations from A-list chefs to tastings and foodie tours of the city. Events are held in venues and restaurants across town, usually in August. A month-long winter edition takes place in February.

🛏 Sleeping

Copenhagen's design legacy is not limited to higher-end establishments, with a number of excellent budget hotels and hostels also available, mainly centred on the western side of Central Station. It's a good idea to reserve rooms in advance, especially hostels, during the busy summer season. The Copenhagen Visitors Centre (p313) can book rooms in private homes (Dkr350/500 for singles/doubles); there is a Dkr100 booking fee if you do it via this office when you arrive, otherwise it's free online.

★ Urban House HOSTEL, HOTEL €
(☑89 88 32 69; www.urbanhouse.me; Colbjørnsensgade 5-11, Vesterbro; dm/s/d Dkr174/586/671; @ 🎅; ☑2A, 5A, 9A, 350S, Ⓜ Central Station) This hostel is huge, encompassing three historic buildings in hip Vesterbro. Step into the entrance and you instantly pick up on the vibe; there is a vast sitting room with comfy chairs and sofas, plus full bar with snacks. Accommodation ranges from single rooms to dorms with bunk beds for up to 10 people; all have private bathrooms.

Danhostel Copenhagen City HOSTEL €
(☑33 11 85 85; www.danhostel.dk/copenhagen city; HC Andersens Blvd 50, Vesterbro; dm/d Dkr240/675; @ 🎅; ☑12, 33, 1A, 2A, 11A, 40, 66) Step into the lobby here with its cafe-bar and it resembles more of a hotel than hostel. Set in a tower block overlooking the harbour just south of Tivoli Gardens (did we mention the views?), the dorms and private rooms are bright, light and modern, each with bathroom. Book ahead.

★ Generator Hostel HOSTEL €€
(☑78 77 54 00; www.generatorhostel.com; Adelgade 5-7, Nyhavn; dm Dkr150-350, r Dkr800-1200;

@🛜; 🖥11A, 350S, Ⓜ Kongens Nytorv) A solid choice for 'cheap chic', upbeat, design-literate Generator sits on the very edge of the city's medieval core. It's kitted out with designer furniture, slick communal areas (including a bar and outdoor terrace) and friendly, young staff. While the rooms can be a little small, all are bright and modern, with bathrooms in both private rooms and dorms.

Guldsmeden Hotels
HOTEL €€

(www.guldsmedenhotels.com) The gorgeous eco-chain Guldsmeden hotels (there are four in town) include **Bertrams** (📞70 20 81 07; Vesterbrogade 107, Frederiksberg; s/d from Dkr915/1025; @🛜; 🖥6A, 3A) 🏆, **Axel** (📞33 31 32 66; Helgolandsgade 7-11, Kødbyen; s/d Dkr865/995; @🛜; 🖥6A, 26, 🚆S-train København H.) 🏆, **Babette** (📞33 14 15 00; Bredgade 78, Østerport; s/d from Dkr795/995; P@🛜; 🖥1A) 🏆 and **Carlton** (📞33 22 15 00; Vesterbrogade 66, Frederiksberg; s/d from Dkr695/795; P@🛜♿; 🖥6A).

Cabinn Hotels
HOTEL €€

(www.cabinn.com) Well managed, functional and cheap, the Cabinn chain has four hotels in Copenhagen. The most central, **Cabinn City** (📞33 46 16 16; Mitchellsgade 14, Vesterbro; s/d/tr Dkr565/700/815; @🛜; 🖥5A, 9A, 11A, 30, 🚆S-train København H), is just south of Tivoli. Both **Cabinn Scandinavia** (📞35 36 11 11; Vodroffsvej 57, Frederiksberg; s/d/tr Dkr565/700/815; @🛜; 🖥2A, 68, 250S, Ⓜ Forum) and **Cabinn Express** (📞33 21 04 00; Danasvej 32, Frederiksberg; s/d/tr Dkr565/700/815; @🛜; 🖥3A, 30, Ⓜ Forum) are less than 2km west of Tivoli. **Cabinn Metro** (📞32 46 57 00; Arne Jakobsens Allé 2, Ørestad; s/d/tr Dkr565/700/815; P@🛜; Ⓜ Ørestad) is a short walk from Ørestad metro station, and close to the airport.

★ Hotel Nimb
BOUTIQUE HOTEL €€€

(📞88 70 00 00; www.nimb.dk; Bernstorffsgade 5, Vesterbro; r from Dkr2750; P@🛜; 🖥2A, 5A, 9A, 12, 26, 250S, 350S, 🚆S-train København H) Located at Tivoli, this boutique belle offers 17 individually styled rooms and suites fusing clean lines, beautiful art and antiques, luxury fabrics and high-tech perks such as Bang & Olufsen TVs and sound systems. All rooms except three also feature a fireplace, while all bar one come with views over the amusement park.

✕ Eating

Copenhagen remains one of the hottest culinary destinations in Europe, with more Michelin stars than any other Scandinavian city. You'll find many of the coolest spots in

---

> ### ℹ️ LAST-MINUTE CHEAP SLEEPS
>
> If you arrive in Copenhagen without a hotel booking, luck may yet be on your side. The **Copenhagen Visitors Centre** (📞70 22 24 42; www.visitcopen hagen.com; Vesterbrogade 4A, Vesterbro; ⏱9am-8pm Jul-Sep, to 5pm Mon-Fri, to 2pm Sat Oct-Feb, to 5pm Mon-Fri, to 4pm Sat & Sun Mar-Jun; 🛜; 🖥2A, 5A, 9A, 12, 26, 250S, 350S, 🚆S-train København H) books unfilled hotel rooms at discounted rates of up to 50%. These discounts, however, are based on supply and demand, and are not always available during busy periods.

the Vesterbro neighbourhood, while bohemian Nørrebro has its fair share of cheaper, student-friendly eateries.

Beyond New Nordic cult restaurants like **Geranium** (📞69 96 00 20; geranium.dk; Per Henrik Lings Allé 4, Østerbro; lunch/dinner tasting menu Dkr1250/1550, lighter lunch tasting menu Dkr950; ⏱lunch noon-1pm Thu-Sat, dinner 6.30-9pm Wed-Sat; ✉) 🏆 and **Kadeau** (📞33 25 22 23; www.kadeau.dk; Wildersgade 10a; 4-/8-course menu Dkr550/850; ⏱noon-3.30pm Wed-Fri & 6pm-late Tue-Sun), contemporary Danish innovation is also driving a growing number of casual, midrange eateries.

Torvehallerne KBH
MARKET €

(www.torvehallernekbh.dk; Israels Plads, Nørreport; snacks from Dkr80; ⏱10am-7pm Mon-Thu, to 8pm Fri, to 6pm Sat, 11am-5pm Sun; Ⓜ Nørreport) Food market Torvehallerne KBH is an essential stop on the Copenhagen foodie trail. A delicious ode to the fresh, the tasty and the artisanal, the market's beautiful stalls peddle everything from seasonal herbs and berries to smoked meats, seafood and cheeses, smørrebrød (open sandwiches), fresh pasta and hand-brewed coffee. You could easily spend an hour or more exploring its twin halls. As well as a market, you can also eat here; several of the vendors prepare inexpensive meals.

★ Lillian's Smørrebrød
DANISH €

(www.facebook.com/lillianssmorrebrod; Vester Voldgade 108, Slotsholmen; smørrebrød Dkr17-50; ⏱6am-1.30pm Mon-Thu, to 1am Fri; 🖥1A, 2A, 9A) One of the best, the oldest (dating from 1978) and least costly smørrebrød places in the city, but word is out so you may have to opt for a takeaway as there are just a handful of tables inside and out. The piled-high, open-face sandwiches are classic and include marinated herring, chicken salad and roast beef with remoulade.

Coffees are also cheap here with a cappuccino costing just Dkr16 – a steal in this town. Note that there's nothing fancy about the decor, in fact the place resembles a seafood market stall with its floor-to-ceiling white tiling and stainless-steel counter. No worries, you're here for the food.

★ **Schønnemann**   DANISH €€
(☑33 12 07 85; www.restaurantschonnemann.dk; Hauser Plads 16, Nørreport; smørrebrød Dkr89-185; ⏱11.30am-5pm Mon-Sat; 🖥; 🚌6A, 11A, Ⓜ Nørreport) A verified institution, Schønnemann has been lining bellies with smørrebrød (open sandwiches) and snaps (small shot of a strong alcoholic beverage) since 1877. Originally a hit with farmers in town peddling their produce, the restaurant's current fan base includes revered chefs like Noma's René Redzepi (try the smørrebrød named after him: smoked halibut with creamed cucumber, radishes and chives on caraway bread).

Bæst   ITALIAN €€
(☑35 35 04 63; www.baest.dk; Guldbergsgade 29; pizzas Dkr85-150; ⏱5-10.30pm; 🚌5A, 3A) Bæst uses organic meats and produce to create tasty Italian fare. The menu features charcuterie using Danish meats and cheeses from their own dairy, as well as pizzas topped with hand-pulled mozzarella and cooked in their wood-fired oven. The sharing menu (small/large Dkr375/450) gives diners the opportunity to sample a variety of dishes. Bæst has an adjoining bakery and cafe called Mirabelle.

★ **Höst**   DANISH €€€
(☑89 93 84 09; www.hostvakst.dk; Nørre Farimagsgade 41, Nørrebro; mains Dkr205-245, 5-course set menu Dkr395; ⏱5.30pm-midnight, last order 9.30pm; 🚌40, Ⓜ Nørrebro) Höst's phenomenal popularity is a no-brainer: warm, award-winning interiors and New Nordic food that's equally as fabulous and filling. The set menu is superb, with three smaller 'surprise dishes' thrown in and evocative creations like beef tenderloin from Grambogaard with onion compote, gherkins, cress and smoked cheese. The 'deluxe' wine menu is significantly better than the standard option. Book ahead, especially later in the week.

🍷 **Drinking & Nightlife**

Copenhagen is packed with a diverse range of drinking options. Vibrant drinking areas include Kødbyen (the 'Meatpacking District') and Istedgade in Vesterbro; Ravnsborggade, Elmegade and Sankt Hans Torv in Nørrebro; and especially gay-friendly Studiestræde. And, of course, on a sunny day there is always touristic Nyhavn, although prices are higher and locals tend to head elsewhere. The line between cafe, bar and restaurant is often blurred, with many places changing role as the day progresses. And while you can hit the dance floor most nights of the week, the club scene really revs into gear from Thursday to Saturday.

★ **Coffee Collective Nørrebro**   CAFE
(www.coffeecollective.dk; Jægersborggade 10, Nørrebro; ⏱7am-7pm Mon-Fri, 8am-7pm Sat & Sun; 🚌18, 12, 66) In a city where lacklustre coffee is as common as perfect cheekbones, this microroastery peddles the good stuff – we're talking rich, complex cups of caffeinated magic. The baristas are passionate about their beans and the cafe itself sits on creative Jægersborggade in Nørrebro. There are two other outlets, at food market Torvehallerne KBH (p313) and in Frederiksberg (Godthåbsvej 34b; ⏱7.30am-9pm Mon-Fri, from 9am Sat, from 10am Sun).

Christianshavns Bådudlejning og Café BAR
(☑32 96 53 53; www.baadudlejningen.dk; Overgaden Neden Vandet 29, Christianshavn; ⏱9am-midnight Jun–mid-Aug, reduced hours Apr, May & mid-Aug–Sep, closed Oct-Mar; 🖥; 🚌2A, 9A, 40, 350S, Ⓜ Christianshavn) Right on Christianshavn's main canal, this festive, wood-decked cafe-bar is a wonderful spot for drinks by the water. It's a cosy, affable hang-out, with jovial crowds, strung lights and little rowing boats (available for hire) docked like bath-time toys. There's grub for the peckish, and gas heaters and tarpaulins to ward off any northern chill.

Mikkeller Bar   BAR
(www.mikkeller.dk; Viktoriagade 8B-C, Frederiksberg; ⏱1pm-1am Sun-Wed, to 2am Thu & Fri, noon-2am Sat; 🖥; 🚌6A, 10, 14, 26, 🚆S-train København H) Low-slung lights, moss-green floors and 20 brews on tap: cult-status Mikkeller flies the flag for craft beer, its rotating cast of suds including Mikkeller's own acclaimed creations and guest drops from microbreweries from around the globe. The bottled offerings are equally inspired, with cheese and snacks to soak up the foamy goodness.

Ruby COCKTAIL BAR

(www.rby.dk; Nybrogade 10, Strøget; ⏱4pm-2am Mon-Sat, from 6pm Sun; 🚇; 🚌1A, 2A, 11A, 26, 40, 66) Cocktail connoisseurs raise their glasses to high-achieving Ruby. Here, hipster-geek mixologists whip up near-flawless libations such as the Green & White (vodka, dill, white chocolate and liquorice root) and a lively crowd spills into a labyrinth of cosy, decadent rooms. For a gentlemen's club vibe, head downstairs into a world of chesterfields, oil paintings and wooden cabinets lined with spirits.

Rust CLUB

(☎35 24 52 00; www.rust.dk; Guldbergsgade 8, Nørrebro; ⏱hours vary, club usually 11pm-5am Fri & Sat; 🚇; 🚌3A, 5A, 350S) A smashing place attracting one of the largest, coolest crowds in Copenhagen. Live acts focus on alternative or upcoming indie rock, hip-hop or electronica, while the club churns out hip-hop, dancehall and electro on Wednesdays, and house, electro and rock on Fridays and Saturdays. From 11pm, entrance is only to over 18s (Wednesday and Thursday) and over 20s (Friday and Saturday).

☆ Entertainment

Copenhagen is home to thriving live-music and club scenes that span intimate jazz and blues clubs to mega rock venues. Blockbuster cultural venues such as Operaen (Copenhagen Opera House; ☎box office 33 69 69 69; www. kglteater.dk; Ekvipagemestervej 10; 🚌9A, 🛥Opera) and Skuespilhuset (Royal Danish Playhouse; ☎33 69 69 69; kglteater.dk; Sankt Anne Plads 36; 🚌11A, M Kongens Nytorv) deliver top-tier opera and theatre. For listings, scan www.aok.dk and www.visitcopenhagen.com. Most events can be booked through Billetnet (☎70 15 65 65; www.billetnet.dk), which has an outlet at Tivoii. You can also try Billetlugen (☎70 26 32 67; www.billetlugen.dk).

★ Jazzhouse JAZZ

(☎33 15 47 00; www.jazzhouse.dk; Niels Hemmingsensgade 10, Strøget; 🚇; 🚌11A) Copenhagen's leading jazz joint serves up top Danish and visiting talent, with music styles running the gamut from bebop to fusion jazz. Doors usually open at 7pm, with concerts starting at 8pm. On Friday and Saturday, late-night concerts (from 11pm) are also offered. Check the website for details and consider booking big-name acts in advance.

Vega Live LIVE MUSIC

(☎33 25 70 11; www.vega.dk; Enghavevej 40, Frederiksberg; 🚇; 🚌3A, 10, 14) The daddy of Copenhagen's live-music venues, Vega hosts everyone from big-name rock, pop, blues and jazz acts to underground indie, hip-hop and electro up-and-comers. Gigs take place on either the main stage (Store Vega), small stage (Lille Vega) or the revamped ground-floor Ideal Bar.

The venue is a 1950s former trade union HQ revamped by leading Danish architect Vilhelm Lauritzen. Performance times vary; check the website.

ℹ Information

Copenhagen Visitors Centre (p313) Copenhagen's excellent and informative information centre has a superb cafe and lounge with free wi-fi; it also sells the Copenhagen Card (p307).

ℹ Getting There & Away

AIR

Copenhagen Airport (www.cph.dk) is Scandinavia's busiest hub, with direct connections to other destinations in Denmark, as well as in Europe, North America and Asia. It is in Kastrup, 9km southeast of the city centre.

BOAT

DFDS Seaways (☎33 42 30 10; www.dfdsseaways.com; Dampfærgevej 30; 🚇S-train Nordhavn) operates daily ferries to Oslo.

BUS

Long-distance buses leave from opposite the DGI-byen sports complex on Ingerslevsgade, a quick walk southwest of Central Station. Advance reservations on most international routes can be made at **Eurolines** (☎33 88 70 00; www. eurolines.dk; Halmtorvet 5).

TRAIN

Long-distance trains arrive and depart from Central Station, known officially as Københavns Hovedbanegård. A billetautomat (coin-operated ticket machine) is the quickest way to purchase a ticket. **DSB Billetsalg** (DSB Ticket Office; ☎70 13 14 15; www.dsb.dk; Copenhagen Central Station, Bernstorffsgade 16-22; ⏱7am-8pm Mon-Fri, 8am-6pm Sat & Sun) is best for reservations and for purchasing international train tickets. Alternatively, make reservations on DSB's website.

ℹ Getting Around

By far the best way to see Copenhagen is on foot. There are few main sights or shopping quarters more than a 20-minute walk from the city centre.

TO/FROM THE AIRPORT

➡ **DSB** (www.dsb.dk) trains link the airport with Copenhagen's Central Station (Dkr36, 14 minutes, every 12 minutes).

➡ The 24-hour **metro** (www.m.dk) runs every four to 20 minutes between the airport arrival terminal (station name is Lufthavnen) and the eastern side of the city centre. It doesn't stop at København H (Central Station) but is handy for Christianshavn and Nyhavn (get off at Kongens Nytorv for Nyhavn). Journey time to Kongens Nytorv is 14 minutes (Dkr36).

BICYCLE

Copenhagen vies with Amsterdam as the world's most bike-friendly city. Most streets have cycle lanes and, more importantly, motorists tend to respect them. The city has a superb citywide rental system: **Bycyklen** (City Bikes; www.bycyklen.dk) has high-tech 'Smart Bikes' featuring touchscreen tablets with GPS, multispeed electric motors, puncture-resistant tyres and locks. The bikes must by paid for by credit card via their website or the bike's touchscreen.

BUS & TRAIN

➡ Buses, metro and trains use a common fare system based on zones. The basic fare of Dkr24 for up to two zones covers most city runs and allows transfers between buses and trains on a single ticket within one hour.

➡ If you plan on exploring sights outside the city, including Helsingør and Roskilde, you're better off buying a 24-hour ticket (all zones Dkr130) or a seven-day FlexCard (all zones Dkr675).

➡ The website www.rejseplanen.dk offers a handy journey planner, with transport routes, times and prices.

ZEALAND

Though Copenhagen is the centre of gravity for most visitors to Denmark's eastern island, there is no shortage of drawcards beyond the city limits, especially Kronborg Slot (famously known as Hamlet's castle, Elsinore) and the remarkable Viking ships of Roskilde.

Helsingør (Elsinore)

POP 46,830

Generally, visitors come to the harbour town of Helsingør, at the northeastern tip of Zealand, for one of two reasons. If they are Swedish, they come to stock up on cheap(er) booze (this is the closest point to Sweden, and ferries shuttle back and forth across the Øresund frequently). Or, more often, they come to soak up the atmosphere of Denmark's most famous and awe-inspiring castle.

⊙ Sights

★Kronborg Slot   CASTLE

(www.kronborg.dk; Kronborgvej; interior incl guided tour adult/child Dkr90/45; ⊙10am-5.30pm Jun-Sep, 11am-4pm Apr-May, 11am-4pm Tue-Sun Oct-Mar) The Unesco World Heritage–listed Kronborg Slot began life as Krogen, a formidable tollhouse built by Danish king Erik of Pomerania in the 1420s. Expanded by Frederik II in 1585, the castle was ravaged by fire in 1629, leaving nothing but the outer walls. The tireless builder-king Christian IV rebuilt Kronborg, preserving the castle's earlier Renaissance style and adding his own baroque touches. The galleried chapel was the only part of Kronborg that escaped the flames in 1629 and gives a good impression of the castle's original appearance.

★M/S Museet for Søfart   MUSEUM

(Maritime Museum of Denmark; www.mfs.dk; Ny Kronborgvej 1; adult/child Dkr110/free; ⊙10am-5pm Jul & Aug, 11am-5pm Tue-Sun rest of year; 🛜) Ingeniously built in and around a dry dock beside Kronborg Slot, Denmark's subterranean Maritime Museum merits a visit as much for its design as for its enlightened, multimedia galleries. The latter explore Denmark's maritime history and culture in dynamic, contemporary ways. Alongside the usual booty of nautical instruments, sea charts and wartime objects, exhibitions explore themes as varied as the representation of sailors in popular culture, trade and exploitation in Denmark's overseas colonies, and globe-crossing journeys of modern shipping containers.

🛏 Sleeping & Eating

Danhostel Helsingør   HOSTEL €

(🗹49 28 49 49; danhostelhelsingor.dk; Nordre Strandvej 24; dm/s/d/tr Dkr225/495/550/595; 🅿🛜; 🚌842) This 180-bed hostel is based in a coastal manor house 2km northwest of town on a little beach looking directly across to Sweden. The run-of-the-mill dorms are in one of the smaller attached buildings. Facilities include a self-catering kitchen, small playground and outdoor ping-pong tables to keep kids amused. From Helsingør, bus 842 (Dkr24) will get you there.

Café Hyacinth   DANISH €

(Bjergegade 4; lunch Dkr99; ⊙noon-5pm Mon-Thu, to 6pm Fri & Sat; 🛜) Perfect for indecisive types, the inexpensive lunch choice here comprises three smørrebrød (open sandwiches), plus a glass of beer from a local microbrewery and a shot of snaps. The toppings are piled high works of art, each based on Danish classics like fried fish, shrimp and roast beef, with all the extras like pickles, remoulade and crispy onions.

Cafe Richs DANISH €
(www.barrichs.dk; Kampergade 1; smørrebrød from Dkr99; 🛜) The decor has a classic old-fashioned feel and the smørrebrød is superb, with huge portions and some simple-sounding but great combinations, like eggs, potatoes and tomatoes, which is about as far removed from egg and chips as you can get, and includes boiled new potatoes, hard-boiled eggs, cherry tomatoes, red onions, chives, rucola, bacon...and more.

Cafe Richs is named after a brand of substitute coffee that was used during food shortages in Denmark during World War II. Nostalgic types can buy it here for Dkr50.

❶ Information

Tourist Office (📞 49 21 13 33; www.visitnordsjaelland.com; Havnepladsen 3; ⊙10am-5pm Mon-Fri, to 2pm Sat & Sun Jul-Aug, reduced hours rest of year) The helpful tourist office is located opposite the train station.

❶ Getting There & Away

Trains between Copenhagen and Helsingør run about three times hourly (Dkr115, 45 minutes). If you're day-tripping from Copenhagen, buy a 24-hour pass (Dkr130).

Roskilde

POP 50,046

Most foreigners who have heard of Roskilde know it either as the home of one of northern Europe's best music festivals, or the site of several remarkable Viking ship finds. To the Danes, however, it is a city of great royal and religious significance, as it was the capital city long before Copenhagen. The **Roskilde Festival** (www.roskilde-festival.dk; tickets from Dkr1965) takes place over a long weekend in early July, in fields just outside the city centre. It attracts the biggest international rock and pop names, along with 75,000 music fans, and is renowned for its relaxed, friendly atmosphere. Most visitors camp on-site.

◉ Sights

★**Viking Ship Museum** MUSEUM
(Vikingskibsmuseet; 📞 46 30 02 00; www.vikingeskibsmuseet.dk; Vindeboder 12; adult/child May–mid-Oct Dkr120/free, mid-Oct–Apr Dkr85/free, boat trip excl museum Dkr100; ⊙10am-5pm late Jun–mid-Aug, to 4pm mid-Aug–late Jun, boat trips daily mid-May–Sep; 🅿🚻) Viking fans will be wowed by the superb Viking Ship Museum, displaying five Viking ships discovered at the bottom of Roskilde Fjord. The museum consists of two main sections – the Viking Ship Hall, where the boats themselves are kept; and Museumsø, where archaeological work takes place. There are free 45-minute guided tours in English at noon and 3pm daily from late June to the end of August and at noon on weekends from May to late June and in September.

★**Ragnarock** MUSEUM
(www.museumragnarock.dk; Rabalderstræde 1; adult/child Dkr90/free; ⊙10am-6pm Tue, Thu-Sun, to 10pm Wed; 🅿🛜; 🚌202A, 212) This museum is dedicated to pop, rock and youth culture and delivers a multisensory journey through the evolution of rock music from the 1950s to the present. Interactive exhibitions have visitors laying and remixing hits, practising various dance steps and rocking to a virtual Roskilde Festival crowd. You can also marvel at the largest mirrorball in the world. From Roskilde train station, buses 202A and 212 stop 350m from the museum.

★**Roskilde Domkirke** CATHEDRAL
(www.roskildedomkirke.dk; Domkirkepladsen; adult/child Dkr60/free; ⊙10am-6pm Mon-Sat, 1-6pm Sun Apr-Sep, to 4pm Oct-Mar) Not merely the crème de la crème of Danish cathedrals, this twin-towered giant is a designated Unesco World Heritage site. Started by Bishop Absalon in 1170, the building has been rebuilt and tweaked so many times that it's now a superb showcase of 800 years' worth of Danish architecture. As the royal mausoleum, it contains the crypts of 37 Danish kings and queens – contemplating the remains of so many powerful historical figures is a moving memento mori.

🛏 Sleeping & Eating

Danhostel Roskilde HOSTEL €
(📞 46 35 21 84; www.danhostel.dk/roskilde; Vindeboder 7; dm/s/d Dkr225/475/525; 🅿🛜) Roskilde's modern hostel has a superb position, on the waterfront right next door to the Viking Ship Museum. Pimped with funky black-and-white murals, each of the 40 large rooms has its own shower and toilet. The staff is friendly and pets are allowed. Unusually, however, wi-fi is an extra Dkr20 per hour (Dkr100 per 24 hours).

DENMARK ROSKILDE

Café Vivaldi INTERNATIONAL €€

(Stændertorvet 8; sandwiches & salads Dkr99-109, mains Dkr169-199; ☺10am-10pm Sun-Thu, to 11pm Fri & Sat; ☏) Slap bang on the main square (cathedral views included), this faux-bistro is a good place to sit back and people-watch over abundant servings of tasty cafe grub. Edibles include soup, sandwiches, wraps, burgers and salads, as well as more substantial pasta and meat dishes. It's particularly handy on Sundays, when most of the town shuts down.

❶ Information

Tourist Office (☑46 31 65 65; www.visi-troskilde.com; Stændertorvet 1; ☺10am-4pm or 5pm Mon-Fri, to 1pm Sat) The tourist office provides information as well as accommodation options.

❶ Getting There & Away

Trains from Copenhagen to Roskilde are frequent (Dkr30, 20 minutes). If you're day-tripping from Copenhagen, buy a 24-hour pass (Dkr130).

FUNEN

Funen is Denmark's proverbial middle child. Lacking Zealand's capital-city pull or Jutland's geographic dominance, it's often overlooked by visitors, who perhaps make a whistle-stop visit to Hans Christian Andersen's birthplace in Odense.

Odense

POP 175,245

Currently undergoing a major revamp, Funen's millennium-old capital is a cheerful, compact city, ideal for feet and bicycles, and with enough diversions to keep you hooked for a day or two. It was here that Hans Christian Andersen entered the world, once upon a time...

◉ Sights

★HC Andersens Hus MUSEUM

(www.museum.odense.dk; Bangs Boder 29; adult/child Dkr95/free; ☺10am-5pm Jul & Aug, to 4pm Tue-Sun Sep-Jun; ⊞) Lying amid the miniaturised streets of the former poor quarter, this museum delivers a thorough, lively telling of Andersen's extraordinary life and times. His achievements are put into an interesting historical context and leavened by some engaging audiovisual material and quirky exhibits (such as the display on his height – HCA was 25cm taller than the national average at the time).

The ticket gets you same-day entry to **HC Andersens Barndomshjem** (www.museum. odense.dk; Munkemøllestræde 3-5; adult/child Dkr30/free; ☺10am-5pm Jul & Aug, to 3pm or 4pm Tue-Sun Sep-Jun).

The attraction incorporates Andersen's rather sparse birthplace. There's also a reconstruction of his Copenhagen study, displays of his pen-and-ink sketches and paper cuttings, and a voluminous selection of his books, which have been translated into some 140 languages (more than any other author).

★Brandts MUSEUM

(www.brandts.dk; Brandts Torv 1; combined ticket with Brandts 13 adult/child Dkr90/free; ☺10am-5pm Tue, Wed & Fri-Sun, noon-9pm Thu) The former textile mill on Brandts Passage has been beautifully converted into a sprawling art centre, with thought-provoking, well-curated changing displays.

Brandts Samling (the permanent collection) traces 250 years of Danish art, from classic to modern, and includes an impressive assemblage of international photography. For more edgy and contemporary art, head to Brandts' second venue: Brandts 13.

Art highlights include portraits by Christoffer Wilhelm Eckersberg (the 'father of Danish painting'), plus HA Brendekilde's powerful *Udslidt* (Worn Out; 1889), depicting a collapsed farm worker, and PS Krøyer's radiant *Italienske markarbejdere* (Italian Field Labourers; 1880). Funen artists also feature – Johannes Larsen's *Svanerne letter, Fiil Sø* is a stunning depiction of swans taking flight.

On the 3rd floor, **Danmarks Mediemuseum** traces the history of the Danish media (primarily in Danish, but with a tablet provided for coverage in other languages).

The area around Brandts is worth a wander for great street art and murals.

Note: there's free entry after 5pm on Thursday.

🛏 Sleeping

Billesgade B&B €

(www.billesgade.dk; Billesgade 9; s/d Dkr437/546; ℗☏) This spotless B&B is run by charming Brian and Anette, who offer good-sized, well-equipped rooms with shared bathroom plus a communal kitchen, free parking, bikes to rent and cable TV. It's a 15-minute walk from the centre and a couple of minutes to a supermarket; breakfast is an agreeable extra (Dkr60) with eggs laid by their own chickens.

Eating & Drinking

Cafe Skt Gertrud
CAFE €€

(www.gertruds.dk; Jernbanegade 8; mains Dkr110-145; ⊙9am-1pm Mon-Wed, to 3pm Thu-Sat, 10am-midnight Sun; 🛜) This grand dame of a cafe is a place to be seen by young and old alike, with an elegant interior and outside terrace. This is a good place for morning coffee (along with one of the buttery croissants) or a light lunch – try steamed mussels in white wine, salmon mousse or a classic salad niçoise.

Restaurant no.61
EUROPEAN €€€

(☑61 69 10 35; www.no61.dk; Kongensgade 61; 2/3 courses Dkr255/295; ⊙from 5pm Tue-Sat; 🛜) Winning plaudits for its embrace of classic European cooking, this family-friendly, farmhouse-chic bistro has a menu that changes monthly and is short, simple and seasonal. Each course presents two options: dishes plucked straight from the Funen fields might include white asparagus with truffle-infused hollandaise sauce or a confection of strawberry, rhubarb, white chocolate and crème anglaise. Reservations recommended.

Nelle's Coffee & Wine
BAR

(www.nellesbar.dk; Pantheonsgade; ⊙9am-10pm Mon-Thu, to midnight Fri & Sat, to 5.30pm Sun; 🛜) Get your morning caffeine fix here (Nelle's brews the city's best coffee), along with a buttery pastry, then return at wine-time to select from some 20 wines by the glass (from Dkr55), accompanied by nuts or boards with cheese and cold cuts to share.

There are art books to browse and lazy jazz on the soundtrack; it's the sort of place you stay a while.

Information

Tourist Office (☑63 75 75 20; www.visitodense.com; Vestergade 2; ⊙9.30am-6pm Mon-Fri, 10am-3pm Sat, 11am-2pm Sun Jul & Aug, 10am-4.30pm Mon-Fri, to 1pm Sat Sep-Jun; 🛜) Helpful, well-stocked office in the town hall, about 700m from the train station.

Getting There & Away

Odense is on the main railway line between Copenhagen (Dkr278, 1½ hours, at least hourly) and Aarhus (Dkr255, 1¾ hours, at least hourly).

JUTLAND

Denmark doesn't have a north–south divide; culturally, spiritually and to a great extent politically, it is divided into Jutland... and all the rest. Home of historic villages, it is a picture-book destination where you can enjoy thatch-roofed houses, blooming gardens and cobblestone streets lined with boutiques, galleries and cafes.

Aarhus

POP 319,680

Always the bridesmaid, never the bride, Aarhus (*oar*-hus) stands in the shadow of its bigger, brasher sibling, Copenhagen. Yet savvy travellers are coming to appreciate the city's charms – as well as its constantly evolving, exuberant foodie scene. Its designation of the Capital of Culture in 2017 (www.aarhus2017.dk) means that the city's stature is destined to continue to grow, along with its reputation, profile – and popularity.

Sights

ARoS Aarhus Kunstmuseum
MUSEUM

(☑87 30 66 00; www.aros.dk; Aros Allé 2; adult/child Dkr130/free; ⊙10am-5pm Tue & Thu-Sun, to 10pm Wed; ♿) Inside the cubist, red-brick walls of Aarhus' showpiece art museum are nine floors of sweeping curves, soaring spaces and white walls showcasing a wonderful selection of Golden Age works, Danish modernism and an abundance of arresting and vivid contemporary art. The museum's cherry-on-top is the spectacular **Your Rainbow Panorama**, a 360-degree rooftop walkway offering technicolour views of the city through its glass panes in all shades of the rainbow.

Intriguingly, ARoS' main theme is Dante's *The Divine Comedy;* the entrance is on level 4 and from there you either descend into Hell or climb towards Heaven. Hell is **De 9 Rum** (The 9 Spaces), on the bottom floor, painted black and home to moody installation pieces; Heaven is the rooftop rainbow halo, the brainchild of Olafur Eliasson, a Danish-Icelandic artist famed for big, conceptual pieces.

Another iconic piece is Ron Mueck's **Boy** on level 1, an astoundingly lifelike, oversized (5m-high) sculpture of a crouching boy.

The museum stages varied special exhibitions – check what's on when you're in town. ARoS also houses a great gift shop and

DENMARK AARHUS

light-filled cafe on level 4 (free entry), and a restaurant on level 8.

★ **Moesgaard Museum** MUSEUM
(📞87 39 40 00; www.moesgaardmuseum.dk; Moesgård Allé; adult/child Dkr140/free; ⏰10am-5pm Tue & Thu-Sun, to 9pm Wed; 📶) Don't miss

the reinvented Moesgård Museum, 10km south of the city. It is located in a spectacularly designed, award-winning modern space, next door to the manor house that once accommodated its excellent prehistory exhibits. The museum's star attraction is the 2000-year-old **Grauballe Man**, whose as-

Aarhus

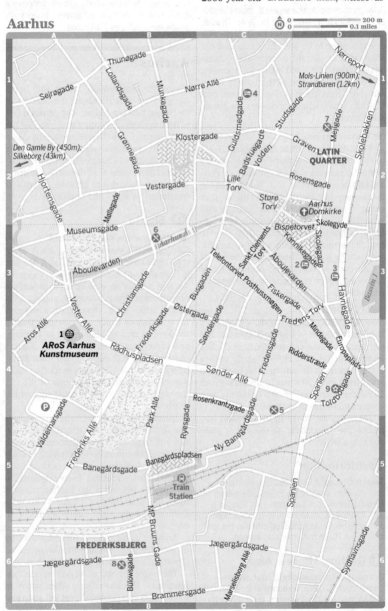

tonishingly well-preserved body was found in 1952 in the village of Grauballe, 35km west of Aarhus.

Den Gamle By
MUSEUM

(The Old Town; ☑86 12 31 88; www.dengamleby.dk; Viborgvej 2; adult/child Dkr135/free; ☺10am-5pm, hours vary by season; 🚋) The Danes' seemingly limitless enthusiasm for dressing up and re-creating history reaches its zenith at Den Gamle By. It's an engaging, picturesque open-air museum of 75 half-timbered houses brought here from all corners of Denmark and reconstructed as a provincial market town from the era of Hans Christian Andersen. Re-created neighbourhoods from 1927 and 1974 are the latest additions.

🛏 Sleeping

City Sleep-In
HOSTEL €

(☑86 19 20 55; www.citysleep-in.dk; Havnegade 20; dm Dkr190, d without/with bathroom Dkr460/520; @🛜) This central hostel used to house seamen and is a real one-off with its rambling layout of sitting rooms, terraces, rooms and dorms. There is a large communal kitchen and a bar-cafe with regular live music. Colourful murals cover the walls, and the furnishings are an eclectic and comfortable mishmash of styles and era.

Rooms are white on white and sparkling clean.

★Hotel Guldsmeden
BOUTIQUE HOTEL €€

(☑86 13 45 50; http://guldsmedenhotels.com/aarhus; Guldsmedgade 40; d with/without bathroom from Dkr1395/995; 🛜) 🍴 A top pick for its excellent location, warm staff, French Colonial–style rooms with Persian rugs, pretty garden oasis and relaxed, stylish ambience. Bumper

breakfasts (mainly organic) are included, as is Guldsmeden's own organic toiletries range. *Guldsmed* means both goldsmith and dragonfly in Danish – look for sweet use of the dragonfly motif in the decor.

Originally a family home, this was the first of a small chain of 27 hotels located throughout Denmark, all named after this street, which used to house goldsmiths and jewellers.

Cabinn Aarhus Hotel
HOTEL €

(☑86 75 70 00; www.cabinn.com; Kannikegade 14; s/d/tr/f from Dkr495/625/805/950; 🅿@🛜) 'Best location, best price' is the Cabinn chain's motto and, given that this branch overlooks the river and is in the centre of town, it is about spot on. The functional rooms are based on ships' cabins (hence the name) – the cheapest is *tiny*, but all come with bathroom, kettle and TV.

The public areas are vast, with comfortable seats and sofas throughout.

🍴 Eating

The Latin Quarter is good for bistro-style cafes; Skolegade (and its extension, Mejlgade) delivers a handful of excellent budget options.

★Oli Nico
INTERNATIONAL €

(www.olinico.dk; Mejlgade 35; dishes Dkr55-125; ☺11.30am-2pm & 5.30-9pm Mon-Fri, noon-2pm & 5.30-9pm Sat, 5.30-9pm Sun; 🛜) You may need to fight for one of the sought-after tables at Oli Nico, a small deli-restaurant with a menu of classic dishes at astoundingly good prices (*moules frites* for Dkr65, rib-eye steak for Dkr130 – both with homemade chips!). The daily-changing, three-course dinner menu (for a bargain Dkr135) may be Aarhus' best-kept food secret. No reservations; takeaway available.

F-Høj
DELI €

(www.fhoj.dk; Gronnegade 2; smørrebrød Dkr65; ☺11am-4pm Tue-Sat; 🛜) This cool little deli overlooks the river and has a reassuringly brief menu of smørrebrød. Expect imaginative combos like shrimp salad, topped with a poached egg and watercress, and shredded cod with tarragon and Jerusalem artichoke. Plus there are wonderful cakes (try the cream puff) and hot and cold drinks; they also serve wine by the glass.

It's a popular takeaway place, but there are a few tables in an intimate dining room clad in typical Scandi-style light wood.

★ **St Pauls Apothek** SCANDINAVIAN €€
(☑ 86 12 08 33; www.stpaulsapothek.
dk; Jægergårdsgade 76; 2-/3-course menu
Dkr265/345; ⊙ 5.30pm-midnight Tue-Thu, to 2am
Fri & Sat; 🕾) What was once a pharmacy is
now one of Aarhus' hottest, best-value dining destinations: a Brooklyn-esque combo
of hipster mixologists, vintage architectural detailing and slinky mood lighting. The
menu is small on choice but big on Nordic
produce and confident food pairings – and
for Dkr645, you can enjoy three courses
matched with inspired, delicious cocktails.
Book ahead.

The Apothek is also in hot demand as a
luxe drinking den – visit in the wee hours to
sample a few of the killer cocktails.

★ **Aarhus Street Food** FOOD HALL €€
(www.aarhusstreetfood.com; Ny Banegårdsgade
46; mains Dkr80-150; ⊙ 11.30am-9pm Mon-Fri, to
midnight Sat & Sun; 🕾🍴) 🍴 Opened in September 2016, this former bus garage at the
back of the station now houses a vibrant
street food venue serving everything from
Mexican to Thai and Indian meals, plus
cafes and bars. The place is fast becoming
one of *the* places to meet, greet and graze in
town. Prices obviously vary but are generally
cheaper than restaurant food.

There are about 50 venues in all, with
plenty of communal dining space and live
music taking place regularly at weekends.

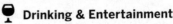

🍷 Drinking & Entertainment

Aarhus is the nation's music capital, with
quality music gigs in venues from dignified
concert halls to beer-fuelled boltholes. For
the lowdown on what's happening, click
onto www.visitaarhus.com or www.stiften.
dk/kultur

★ **Strandbaren** BAR
(www.facebook.com/strandbarenaarhus; Havne-
bassin 7, pier 4; ⊙ May-Sep) Plonk shipping containers and sand on a harbourfront spot and
voila: beach bar. This chilled hang-out at
Aarhus Ø (just beyond the ferry port) offers
food, drink, flirting and weather-dependent
activities and events. Check hours and location on the Facebook page (harbour redevelopment may require an annual location
change; opening hours are 'when the sun is
shining').

Bus 33 runs out this way. While you're
here, check out the new architectural developments of Aarhus Ø, including the
head-turning 'Iceberg'.

Train LIVE MUSIC
(www.train.dk; Toldbodgade 6; ⊙ club from midnight Fri & Sat; 🕾) Aarhus' premier club, Train
is first and foremost a concert venue, with
shows a couple of nights a week and some
big international acts on the program. Train
opens as a late-night club as well on Friday
and Saturday nights, with room for up to

LEGOLAND

Revisit your tender years at Denmark's most visited tourist attraction (beyond Copenhagen), Legoland (www.legoland.dk; Nordmarksvej; adult/child Dkr349/329; ⊙ 10am-8pm
or 9pm Jul–mid-Aug, shorter hours Apr-Jun & mid-Aug–Oct, closed Nov-Mar; 🅿🕾🎗). Located
1km north of the Lego company town of Billund, the sprawling theme park is a gobsmacking ode to those little plastic building blocks, with everything from giant Lego
models of famous cities, landmarks and wild beasts to re-created scenes from the *Star
Wars* film series.

Legoland closing times vary – from 6pm to 9pm. Also worth knowing (and not well
publicised) is that the park opens its gates a half-hour before the rides close, and no
ticket is necessary to enter. Rides normally close one or two hours before the park itself
(check the website), so with a bit of luck you could end up with 2½ hours to browse and
check out Miniland for free.

In late 2017 the 'experience centre' Lego House is set to open in Billund town itself.
Featuring a bold, inspired design that resembles a stack of gigantic Lego bricks, it will
incorporate exhibition areas, rooftop gardens, a cafe, a Lego store and a covered public
square, and is expected to attract 250,000 visitors annually.

Billund lies in central Jutland. By train, the most common route is to disembark at
Vejle and catch a bus from there (take bus 43 or 143). Buses run up to 10 times daily
between Aarhus and Billund airport (Dkr165, one hour), close to the park. To plan your
travel, use www.rejseplanen.dk.

1700 party-people and top-notch DJ talent. The complex also incorporates Kupé, a funky lounge club.

ℹ️ Information

VisitAarhus provides information online (www.visitaarhus.com), by phone (87 31 50 10), at summer booths and via touchscreens around town. Smartphone users can download the free VisitAarhus app.

ℹ️ Getting There & Away

Aarhus is well connected by train. Services to Copenhagen (one way Dkr388, three to 3½ hours) via Odense (Dkr255, 1¾ hours) leave Aarhus roughly half-hourly.

Skagen

POP 8200

With its rich art heritage, fresh seafood and photogenic neighbourhoods, Skagen (pronounced *Skain*) is a delicious slice of Denmark. In the mid-19th century, artists flocked here, charmed by the radiant light's impact on the ruggedly beautiful landscape. Now tourists come in droves, drawn by an intoxicating combination of the busy working harbour, long sandy beaches and buzzing holiday atmosphere.

⊙ Sights

★ Skagens Museum   MUSEUM
(☑98 44 64 44; www.skagensmuseum.dk; Brøndumsvej 4; adult/child Dkr100/free; ⊙10am-5pm, to 9pm Wed May-Aug, reduced hrs Sep-Apr) This wonderful gallery showcases the outstanding art that was produced in Skagen between 1870 and 1930. Artists discovered Skagen's luminous light and its wind-blasted heath-and-dune landscape in the mid-19th century, and fixed eagerly on the romantic imagery of the area's fishing life that had earned the people of Skagen a hard living for centuries. Their work established a vivid figurative style of painting that became known internationally as the 'Skagen School'.

Anchers Hus   GALLERY
(www.skagenkunstmuseer.dk; Markvej 2; adult/child Dkr80/free, incl Skagens Museum & Drachmanns Hus Dkr170/free; ⊙11am-4pm Tue-Sun) Visit the fascinating former home of famous Skagen painters Anna and Michael Ancher, preserved in time exactly the same as when Anna Ancher died in 1935, along with their personal possessions and more than

280 pieces of art. There is also a cafe, small shop and a separate gallery for temporary exhibitions. The nearby **Drachmanns Hus** was the former house of another renowned Skagen painter (and author), Holger Drachmann, and is also open to the public.

Gammel Skagen   VILLAGE, BEACH
There's a touch of Cape Cod in refined Gammel Skagen ('Old Skagen', also known as Højen), renowned for its gorgeous sunsets, upmarket hotels and well-heeled summer residents.

It was a fishing hamlet before sandstorms ravaged this windswept area and forced many of its inhabitants to move to Skagen on the more protected east coast. It's a pleasant bike ride 4km west of Skagen: head towards Frederikshavn and turn right at Højensvej, which takes you to the waterfront.

Grenen   BEACH
Appropriately enough for such a neat and ordered country, Denmark doesn't end untidily at its most northerly point, but on a neat finger of sand just a few metres wide. You can actually paddle at its tip, where the waters of the Kattegat and Skagerrak clash, and you can put one foot in each sea – but not too far. Bathing here is forbidden because of the ferocious tidal currents.

🛏️ Sleeping

Danhostel Skagen   HOSTEL €
(☑98 44 22 00; www.danhostelskagen.dk; Rolighedsvej 2; dm/s/d Dkr180/525/625; ⊙Mar-Nov; 🅿️🛜) Always a hive of activity, this hostel is modern, functional and spick-and-span.

It's decent value, particularly for families or groups. Low-season prices drop sharply. It's 1km towards Frederikshavn from the Skagen train station (if you're coming by train, get off at Frederikshavnsvej).

★**Badepension Marienlund** GUESTHOUSE €€
(☑28 12 13 20; www.marienlund.dk; Fabriciusvej 8; s/d incl breakfast Dkr680/1190; ☺Apr-Oct; P�) A cosy atmosphere, idyllic garden and pretty lounge and breakfast areas make Marienlund a top option. There are only 14 rooms, all light, white and simply furnished (all with bathrooms). You'll find the hotel in a peaceful residential neighbourhood west of the centre; bike hire available.

✗ Eating

Perhaps a dozen seafood shacks line the harbour, selling fresh seafood. Prawns/shrimp *(rejer)* are the favourite order, costing around Dkr100 for a generous helping. Aside from seafood, there are plenty of eating choices in town, as well as a supermarket, **SuperBrugsen** (Sankt Laurentii Vej 28; ☺8am-10pm), with an excellent bakery, plus a couple of good delis where you can pick up picnic fare to take to the beach.

Jorgens Spisehus DANISH €
(www.joergensspisehus.dk; Sardinvej 7; mains Dkr75-99; ☺10am-7.30pm Tue-Fri, from 11am Sat & Sun) A terrific down-to-earth local restaurant where you can depend on no-fuss traditional dishes and cheerful service. The decor and ambience are nothing to get excited about but the Dkr75 dish of the day will surely put a smile on your face; bet on specialities like *Luksus Stjerneskud* (pan-fried breaded plaice and shrimp served on toast with all the trimmings).

ℹ Information

Tourist Office (☑98 44 13 77; www. skagen-tourist.dk; Vestre Strandvej 10; ☺9am-4pm Mon-Sat, 10am-2pm Sun late Jun–mid-Aug, shorter hours rest of year) The tourist office is located in front of the harbour and carries loads of info on regional sights, attractions and activities.

ℹ Getting There & Away

Trains run hourly to Frederikshavn (Dkr60, 35 minutes), where you can change for destinations further south.

The summertime (late June to mid-August) bus 99 connects Skagen with other northern towns and attractions, including Hirtshals.

SURVIVAL GUIDE

ℹ Directory A–Z

ACCOMMODATION
Camping & Cabins
➡ Denmark is well set up for campers, with nearly 600 campgrounds. Some are open only in the summer months. Many campgrounds offer cabins for rent.

➡ The per-night charge typically costs around Dkr75 for an adult, and about half that for each child. In summer some places also tack on a site charge of Dkr50 per tent/caravan; some also have a small eco tax.

ESSENTIAL DANISH FOOD & DRINK

Beer Carlsberg may dominate, but Denmark's expanding battalion of microbreweries include Mikkeller, Amager Bryghus and Bryghuset Møn.

Kanelsnegle A calorific delight, the 'cinnamon snail' is a sweet, buttery pastry, sometimes laced with chocolate.

Koldskål A cold, sweet buttermilk soup made with vanilla and traditionally served with crunchy biscuits such as kammerjunkere.

New Nordic flavours Sample Nordic produce cooked with groundbreaking creativity at hotspot restaurants like Copenhagen's Kadeau (p313) or Geranium (p313).

Sild Smoked, cured, pickled or fried, herring is a local staple, best washed down with generous serves of akvavit (an alcoholic spirit commonly made with potatoes and spiced with caraway).Smoked, cured, pickled or fried, herring is a local staple, best washed down with generous serves of akvavit (an alcoholic spirit commonly made with potatoes and spiced with caraway).

Smørrebrød Rye or white bread topped with anything from beef tartar to egg and shrimp, the open sandwich is Denmark's most famous culinary export.

* You need a camping card (Dkr110) for stays at all campgrounds. You can buy a card at the first campground you arrive at, at local tourist offices, or from the Danish Camping Board.
* Best online resources: www.danishcamp sites.dk, www.dkcamp.dk and www.smaa pladser.dk

Hostels

* Some 88 hostels make up the **Danhostel** (www.danhostel.dk) association, which is affiliated with Hostelling International (HI). Some are dedicated hostels in holiday areas, others are attached to sports centres.
* Advance reservations are advised, particularly in summer. In a few places, reception closes as early as 6pm. In most hostels the reception office is closed, and the phone not answered, between noon and 4pm.
* Typical costs are Dkr200 to Dkr275 for a dorm bed. For private rooms, expect to pay Dkr450 to Dkr720 per double, and up to Dkr100 for each additional person in larger rooms. All hostels offer family rooms. Many rooms come with bathrooms.
* You'll save money with a sleep sheet or your own linen, as most hostels charge for this.
* All hostels provide breakfast costing around Dkr70.
* If you hold a valid national or international hostel card, you receive a 10% discount on rates (these can be purchased from hostels and cost Dkr70 for Danish residents, Dkr160 for foreigners). We list prices for non-cardholders.

Hotels

* Some hotels have set rates published on their websites; others have rates that fluctuate according to season and demand. Most hotel websites offer good deals, as do booking engines such as booking.com.
* Many business hotels offer cheaper rates on Friday and Saturday nights year-round, and during the summer peak (from about midsummer in late June until the start of the school year in early/mid-August).
* There is no hard-and-fast rule about the inclusion of breakfast in rates – many hotels include it, but for others it is optional. At budget hotels like Cabinn you can purchase it for around Dkr70.

Other Accommodation

* Many tourist offices book rooms in private homes for a small fee, or provide a list of local rooms on their website.
* Hundreds of places (summer cottages, inner-city apartments, family-friendly houses) can be rented direct from the owner via **AirBnB** (www.airbnb.com).

SLEEPING PRICE RANGES

The following price ranges refer to a double room in high season. Unless otherwise noted, rooms have private bathrooms.

€ less than Dkr700

€€ Dkr700–1500

€€€ more than Dkr1500

EATING PRICE RANGES

The following price ranges refer to the cost of a standard main course.

€ less than Dkr125

€€ Dkr125–250

€€€ more than Dkr250

ACTIVITIES

* Denmark is well set up for outdoor activities, from island-hopping cycling adventures to Lake District canoeing. The **Visit Denmark** (www.visitdenmark.com) website offers great information and links.
* The best way to tour Denmark by bike is by grabbing a map and planning it yourself – a fantastic resource is the **Cyclistic** (http://cyclistic.dk/en/) website. Each county produces its own detailed 1:100,000 cycle touring maps; many of them come with booklets detailing accommodation, sights and other local information. These maps cost around Dkr129, and are available at tourist offices or online via the Danish cycling federation, Dansk Cyklist Forbund (shop at http://shop.dcf.dk).

INTERNET RESOURCES

Denmark.dk (www.denmark.dk) Hugely informative on diverse subjects.
Rejseplanen (www.rejseplanen.dk) Great journey planner.
Visit Copenhagen (www.visitcopenhagen.com) For the capital's highlights.
Visit Denmark (www.visitdenmark.com) Denmark's official tourism website, lists tourist offices throughout the country.

MONEY

ATMs Major bank ATMs accept Visa, MasterCard and the Cirrus and Plus bank cards.
Credit cards Visa and MasterCard are widely accepted in Denmark (American Express and Diners Club less so). A surcharge of up to 3.75% is imposed on foreign credit-card transactions in some restaurants, shops and hotels.

DENMARK DIRECTORY A-Z

Tipping Restaurant bills and taxi fares include service charges in the quoted prices. Further tipping is unnecessary, although rounding up the bill is not uncommon when service has been especially good.

OPENING HOURS

→ Opening hours vary throughout the year. We've provided high-season opening hours; hours will generally decrease in the shoulder and low seasons.

→ Family-friendly attractions (museums, zoos, fun parks) in holiday hotspots generally open from June to August (possibly May to September), plus for the spring and autumn school holidays.

Banks 10am to 4pm Monday to Friday

Bars 4pm to midnight, to 2am or later Friday and Saturday (clubs on weekends may open until 5am)

Cafes 8am to 5pm or later

Restaurants noon to 10pm (maybe earlier on weekends for brunch)

Shops 10am to 6pm Monday to Friday (possibly until 7pm on Friday), to 4pm Saturday. Some larger stores may open on Sunday.

Supermarkets 8am to 9pm (many with bakeries opening around 7am)

PUBLIC HOLIDAYS

Banks and most businesses close on public holidays and transport schedules are usually reduced.

New Year's Day 1 January

Maundy Thursday Thursday before Easter

Good Friday to Easter Monday March/April

Great Prayer Day Fourth Friday after Easter

Ascension Day Sixth Thursday after Easter

Whitsunday Seventh Sunday after Easter

Whitmonday Seventh Monday after Easter

Constitution Day 5 June

Christmas From noon 24 December until 26 December

New Year's Eve 31 December (from noon)

TELEPHONE

→ There are no regional area codes within Denmark.

→ To call Denmark from abroad: dial your country's international access code, then ☑ 45 (Denmark's country code), then the local number.

→ To call internationally from Denmark: dial ☑ 00, then the country code for the country you're calling, followed by the area code and local number.

→ Public payphones are elusive, but they accept coins, phonecards and credit cards.

Phonecards are available from kiosks and post offices.

TIME

→ Denmark is one hour ahead of GMT/UTC. Clocks are moved forward one hour for daylight-saving time from late March to late October.

→ Denmark uses the 24-hour clock and timetables and business hours are posted accordingly.

→ *Klokken*, which means o'clock, is abbreviated as kl (kl 19.30 is 7.30pm).

VISAS

→ No entry visa is needed by citizens of EU and Nordic countries.

→ Citizens of the USA, Canada, Australia and New Zealand don't need a visa for tourist stays of less than 90 days.

→ Citizens of many African, South American, Asian and former Soviet bloc countries do require a visa. See www.nyidanmark.dk.

ⓘ Getting There & Away

AIR

→ The majority of overseas flights into Denmark land at **Copenhagen International Airport** (www.cph.dk; Lufthavnsboulevarden 6, Kastrup) in Kastrup, about 9km southeast of central Copenhagen.

→ A number of international flights, mostly those coming from other Nordic countries or the UK, land at smaller regional airports, in Aarhus, Aalborg, Billund, Esbjerg and Sønderborg.

LAND

→ Denmark's only land crossing is with Germany, although the bridge over the Øresund from Sweden functions in the same way. If travelling by road, there's a toll per vehicle (Dkr350) to cross the Øresund bridge linking Copenhagen with Malmö. Trains run this route frequently (Dkr95, 35 minutes).

→ **Eurolines Scandinavia** (www.eurolines.dk) offers connections to more than 500 major European cities in 26 countries. Destinations, timetables and prices are all online; advance reservations advised.

→ Reliable, regular train services link Denmark to Sweden, Germany and Norway. Tickets booked online in advance can be cheaper. See www.dsb.dk for details.

SEA

→ Ferry connections are possible between Denmark and Norway, Sweden, Germany, Poland (via Sweden), Iceland and the Faroe Islands.

→ Fares on these ships vary wildly, by season and by day of the week. The highest prices tend to occur on summer weekends and the lowest on winter weekdays. Discounts are often available, including for holders of rail passes or student cards and for seniors. Child fares are usually half the adult fares. Bookings are advised.

Major operators and their routes are listed here.

Faroe Islands & Iceland

Smyril Line (www.smyrilline.com) Route: Hirtshals to Seyðisfjörður (Iceland) via Tórshavn (Faroe Islands).

Germany

BornholmerFærgen (www.bornholmerfaergen. dk) Route: Rønne (on Bornholm) to Sassnitz.

Scandlines (www.scandlines.com) Routes: Rødbyhavn (on Lolland) to Puttgarden; Gedser (on Falster) to Rostock.

SyltExpress (www.syltfaehre.de) Route: Havneby (on Rømø) to the German island of Sylt.

Norway

Color Line (www.colorline.com) Routes: Hirtshals to Kristiansand; to Larvik.

DFDS Seaways (www.dfdsseaways.com) Route: Copenhagen to Oslo.

Fjordline (www.fjordline.com) Routes: Hirtshals to Kristiansand; to Bergen via Stavanger; to Langesund.

Stena Line (www.stenaline.com) Route: Frederikshavn to Oslo.

Sweden

BornholmerFærgen (www.bornholmerfaergen. dk) Route: Rønne (Bornholm) to Ystad.

Scandlines (www.scandlines.com) Route: Helsingør to Helsingborg.

Stena Line (www.stenaline.com) Routes: Frederikshavn to Gothenburg (Göteborg); Grenaa to Varberg.

❶ Getting Around

BICYCLE

➡ Denmark is the most cycle-friendly country in the EU, and cyclists are very well catered for with excellent cycling routes throughout the country.

➡ You'll be able to hire a bike in almost every Danish town and village. Bike-rental prices average around Dkr100/400 per day/week for something basic.

➡ Bicycles can be taken on ferries and trains for a modest fee.

---

❶ THE ESSENTIAL TRANSPORT WEBSITE

For getting around in Denmark, the essential website is **www.rejseplanen. dk**. It allows you to enter your start and end point, date and preferred time of travel, and will then give you the best travel option, which may involve walking or taking a bus or train. Bus routes are linked, travel times are given, and fares listed. Download the app for easy mobile access.

BOAT

➡ Ferries link virtually all of Denmark's populated islands.

BUS

➡ Long-distance buses run a distant second to trains. Still, some cross-country bus routes work out to about 25% cheaper than trains.

➡ Popular routes include Copenhagen to Aarhus or Aalborg. A useful operator is **Abildskou** (www.abildskou.dk).

CAR & MOTORCYCLE

➡ Denmark is perfect for touring by car. Roads are high quality and usually well signposted. Traffic is manageable, even in major cities such as Copenhagen (rush hours excepted).

➡ Denmark's network of ferries carries vehicles for reasonable rates. It's a good idea to make reservations, especially in summer.

TRAIN

➡ **Danske Statsbaner** (DSB; ☎ 70 13 14 15; www.dsb.dk; Taastrup) runs virtually all Danish train services. Overall, train travel isn't expensive, in large part because distances are short.

➡ Most long-distance trains on major routes operate at least hourly throughout the day. During morning and evening peak times, it's advisable to make reservations (Dkr30) if travelling on the speedy InterCityLyn (ICL) and Intercity (IC) trains.

➡ There are various discounts available for students, children, seniors and groups travelling together. Good advance-purchase discounts are sometimes available – look for 'Orange' tickets.

Estonia

Best Places to Eat

➡ Mr Jakob (p340)

➡ Ö (p336)

➡ Rataskaevu 16 (p336)

➡ Retro (p344)

➡ Altja Kõrts (p338)

Best Places to Stay

➡ Pädaste Manor (p342)

➡ Antonius Hotel (p340)

➡ Georg Ots Spa Hotel (p343)

➡ Tabinoya (p334)

➡ Merekalda (p338)

Why Go?

Estonia doesn't have to struggle to find a point of difference; it's completely unique. It shares a similar geography and history with Latvia and Lithuania, but it's culturally very different. Its closest ethnic and linguistic buddy is Finland, yet although they both may love to get naked together in the sauna, 50 years of Soviet rule have separated the two. For the past 300 years Estonia has been linked to Russia, but the two states have as much in common as a barn swallow and a bear (their respective national symbols).

In recent decades, and with a new-found confidence, Estonia has crept from under the Soviet blanket and leapt into the arms of Europe. The love affair is mutual: Europe has fallen for the chocolate-box allure of Tallinn and its Unesco-protected Old Town, while travellers seeking something different are tapping into Estonia's captivating blend of Eastern European and Nordic appeal.

When to Go
Tallinn

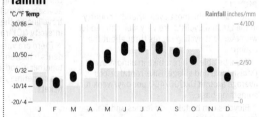

Apr & May See the country shake off winter's gloom.

Jun–Aug White nights, beach parties and loads of summer festivals.

Dec Christmas markets, mulled wine and long, cosy nights.

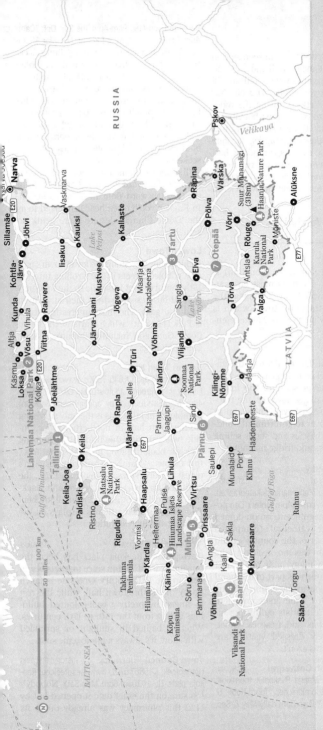

Estonia Highlights

1 Tallinn (p330)
Embarking on a medieval quest for atmospheric restaurants and hidden bars in the history-saturated lanes.

2 Lahemaa National Park (p338) Wandering the forest paths, bog boardwalks, abandoned beaches and manor-house halls.

3 Tartu (p339) Furthering your education among the museums and student bars of Estonia's second city.

4 Saaremaa (p342) Unwinding among the windmills and exploring the island's castles, churches, cliffs, coast and crater.

5 Muhu (p342) Hopping over for frozen-in-island-time Koguva village and the gastronomic delights of Pädaste Manor.

6 Pärnu (p341) Strolling the golden sands and genteel streets of Estonia's 'summer capital'.

7 Otepää (p340) Getting back to nature, even if the snow's a no-show, at the 'winter capital'.

TALLINN

POP 414,000

If you're labouring under the misconception that 'former Soviet' means dull and grey and that all tourist traps are soulless, Tallinn will delight in proving you wrong. This city has charm by the bucketload, fusing the modern and medieval to come up with a vibrant vibe all of its own. It's an intoxicating mix of church spires, glass skyscrapers, baroque palaces, appealing eateries, brooding battlements, shiny shopping malls, run-down wooden houses and cafes set on sunny squares – with a few Soviet throwbacks in the mix.

◉ Sights & Activities

◉ Old Town

Tallinn's medieval Old Town (Vanalinn) is without doubt the country's most fascinating locality. It's divided into Toompea (the upper town) and the lower town, which is still surrounded by much of its 2.5km defensive wall.

Toompea

Lording it over the Lower Town is the ancient hilltop citadel of Toompea. In German times this was the preserve of the feudal nobility, literally looking down on the traders and lesser beings below. It's now almost completely given over to government buildings, churches, embassies and shops selling amber knick-knacks and fridge magnets.

★Alexander Nevsky
Orthodox Cathedral   CATHEDRAL
(☑644 3484; http://tallinnanevskikatedraal.eu; Lossi plats 10; ⊙8am-7pm, to 4pm winter) The positioning of this magnificent, onion-domed Russian Orthodox cathedral (completed in 1900) at the heart of the country's main administrative hub was no accident: the church was one of many built in the last part of the 19th century as part of a general wave of Russification in the empire's Baltic provinces. Orthodox believers come here in droves, alongside tourists ogling the interior's striking icons and frescoes. Quiet, respectful, demurely dressed visitors are welcome but cameras aren't.

St Mary's Lutheran Cathedral   CHURCH
(Tallinna Püha Neitsi Maarja Piiskoplik toomkirik; ☑644 4140; www.toomkirik.ee; Toom-Kooli 6; church/tower €2/5; ⊙9am-5pm daily May & Sep, 9am-6pm Jun-Aug, 9am-4pm Tue-Sun Oct, 10am-4pm Tue-Fri, 9am-4pm Sat & Sun Nov-Mar, 10am-5pm Tue-Fri, 9am-5pm Sat & Sun Apr) Tallinn's cathedral (now Lutheran, originally Catholic) was founded by at least 1233, although the exterior dates mainly from the 15th century, with the tower completed in 1779. This impressive building was a burial ground for the rich and titled, and the whitewashed walls are decorated with the elaborate coats-of-arms of Estonia's noble families. Fit viewseekers can climb the tower.

Toompea is named after the cathedral – the Estonian word 'toom' is borrowed from the German word 'dom' meaning cathedral. In English you'll often hear it referred to as the 'Dome Church', despite there being no actual dome.

Lower Town

Picking your way along the lower town's narrow, cobbled streets is like strolling into the 15th century – not least due to the tendency of local businesses to dress their staff up in medieval garb. The most interesting street is Pikk (Long St), which starts at the Great Coast Gate and includes Tallinn's historic guild buildings.

Tallinn Town Hall   HISTORIC BUILDING
(Tallinna raekoda; ☑645 7900; www.raekoda.tallinn.ee; Raekoja plats; adult/student €5/2; ⊙10am-4pm Mon-Sat Jul-Aug, by appointment Sep-Jun) Completed in 1404, this is the only surviving Gothic town hall in northern Europe. Inside, you can visit the Trade Hall (housing a visitor book dripping in royal signatures), the Council Chamber (featuring Estonia's oldest woodcarvings, dating from 1374), the vaulted Citizens' Hall, a yellow-and-black-tiled councillor's office and a small kitchen. The steeply sloped attic has displays on the building and its restoration.

★Town Hall Square   SQUARE
(Raekoja plats) Raekoja plats has been the pulsing heart of Tallinn since markets began here in the 11th century. One side is taken up by the Gothic town hall, while the rest is ringed by pretty pastel-coloured buildings dating from the 15th to 17th centuries. Whether bathed in sunlight or sprinkled with snow, it's always a photogenic spot.

Town Council Pharmacy   HISTORIC BUILDING
(Raeapteek; ☑5887 5701; www.raeapteek.ee; Raekoja plats 11; ⊙10am-6pm Mon-Sat) Nobody's too sure on the exact date it opened but by 1422 this pharmacy was already on to its

third owner, making it the oldest continually operating pharmacy in Europe. In 1583 Johann Burchardt took the helm, and a descendant with the same name ran the shop right up until 1913 – 10 generations in all! Inside there are painted beams and a small historical display, or you can just drop in to stock up on painkillers and prophylactics.

St Olaf's Church   CHURCH
(Oleviste kirik; ☑ 641 2241; www.oleviste.ee; Lai 50; tower adult/child €2/1; ◔ 10am-6pm Apr-Oct, to 8pm Jul & Aug) From 1549 to 1625, when its 159m steeple was struck by lightning and burnt down, this (now Baptist) church was one of the tallest buildings in the world. The current spire reaches a still respectable 124m and you can take a tight, confined, 258-step staircase up the tower for wonderful views of Toompea over the Lower Town's rooftops.

Lower Town Wall   FORTRESS
(Linnamüür; ☑ 644 9867; Väike-Kloostri 3; adult/child €2/0.75; ◔ 11am-7pm Jun-Aug, 11am-5pm Fri-Wed Apr, May, Sep & Oct, 11am-4pm Fri-Tue Nov-Mar) The most photogenic stretch of Tallinn's remaining walls connects nine towers lining the western edge of the Old Town. Visitors can explore the barren nooks and crannies of three of them, with cameras at the ready for the red-rooftop views.

◉ Kalamaja

Immediately northwest of the Old Town, this enclave of tumbledown wooden houses and crumbling factories has swiftly transitioned into one of Tallinn's most interesting neighbourhoods. The intimidating hulk of Patarei Prison had seemed to cast a malevolent shadow over this part of town, so its transformation over the last few years has been nothing short of extraordinary. Major road

projects and the opening of an impressive museum at Lennusadam are only the most visible elements of a revolution started by local hipsters opening cafes and bars in abandoned warehouses and rickety storefronts.

Lennusadam   MUSEUM
(Seaplane Harbour; ☑ 620 0550; www.meremuuseum.ee; Vesilennuki 6; adult/child €14/7, incl Fat Margaret €16/8; ◔ 10am-7pm daily May-Sep, 10am-6pm Tue-Sun Oct-Apr; ℗) When this triple-domed hangar was completed in 1917, its reinforced-concrete shell frame construction was unique in the world. Resembling a classic Bond-villain lair, the vast space was completely restored and opened to the public in 2012 as a fascinating maritime museum, filled with interactive displays. Highlights include exploring the cramped corridors of a 1930s naval submarine, and the icebreaker and minehunter ships moored outside.

Telliskivi Creative City   AREA
(Telliskivi Loomelinnak; www.telliskivi.eu; Telliskivi 60a; ◔ shops 8.30am-9pm Mon-Sat, 9am-7pm Sun) Once literally on the wrong side of the tracks, this set of 10 abandoned factory buildings is now Tallinn's most alternative shopping and entertainment precinct. All the cliches of hipster culture can be found here: cafes, a bike shop, bars selling craft beer, graffiti walls, artist studios, food trucks etc. But even the beardless flock to Telleskivi to peruse the fashion and design stores, sink espressos and rummage through the stalls at the weekly flea market.

◉ Kadriorg Park

About 2km east of the Old Town (take tram 1 or 3), this beautiful park's ample acreage is Tallinn's favourite patch of green. Together with the baroque Kadriorg Palace, it was commissioned by the Russian tsar Peter the

---

ITINERARIES

Three days
Base yourself in **Tallinn** and spend your first day exploring all the nooks and crannies of the **Old Town**. The following day, do what most tourists don't – step out of Old Town. Explore **Kadriorg Park** for a first-rate greenery and art fix, then hit the wonderful Estonian Open-Air Museum. On your last day, hire a car or take a day tour to **Lahemaa National Park**.

One week
Spend your first three days in **Tallinn**, then allow a full day to explore **Lahemaa** before bedding down within the national park. The following day, continue on to **Tartu** for a night or two and then finish up in **Pärnu**.

Tallinn

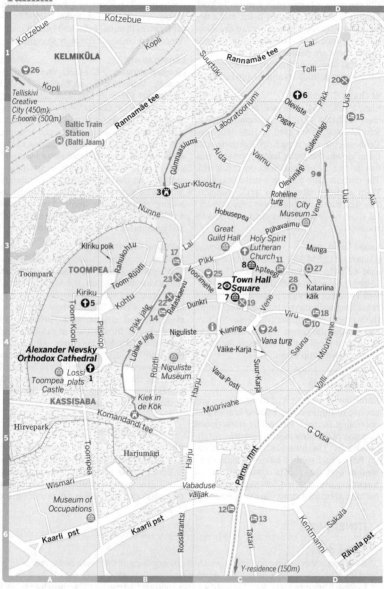

Great for his wife Catherine I soon after his conquest of Estonia (Kadriorg means Catherine's Valley in Estonian). Nowadays the oak, lilac and horse chestnut trees provide shade for strollers and picnickers, the formal pond and gardens provide a genteel backdrop for romantic promenades and wedding photos, and the children's playground is a favourite off-leash area for the city's youngsters.

Oct-Apr) Kadriorg Palace, built by Peter the Great between 1718 and 1736, now houses a branch of the Estonian Art Museum devoted to Dutch, German and Italian paintings from the 16th to the 18th centuries, and Russian works from the 18th to early 20th centuries (check out the decorative porcelain with communist imagery upstairs). The building is exactly as frilly and fabulous as a palace ought to be and there's a handsome French-style formal garden at the rear.

★ **Kadriorg Art Museum** PALACE
(Kadrioru kunstimuuseum; ☑ 606 6400; www. kadriorumuuseum.ekm.ee; A Weizenbergi 37; adult/ child €6.50/4.50; ☺ 10am-6pm Tue & Thu-Sun, to 8pm Wed May-Sep, 10am-8pm Wed, to 5pm Thu-Sun

If tourists won't go to the countryside, let's bring the countryside to them. That's the modus operandi of the **Estonian Open-Air Museum** (Eesti vabaõhumuuseum; ☑ 654 9101; www.evm.ee; Vabaõhumuuseumi tee 12, Rocca Al Mare; adult/child May-Sep €8/5, Oct-Apr €6/4; ☺10am-8pm May-Sep, to 5pm Oct-Apr), an excellent, sprawling complex, where historic buildings have been plucked and transplanted among the tall trees. In summer the time-warping effect is highlighted by staff in period costume performing traditional activities among the wooden farmhouses and windmills.

★**Kumu**   GALLERY

(☑ 602 6000; www.kumu.ekm.ee; A Weizenbergi 34; all galleries adult/student €8/6, 5th floor only €4/3; ☺10am-8pm Thu, 10am-6pm Fri-Sun year-round, plus 10am-6pm Tue Apr-Sep, 10am-6pm Wed Oct-Mar) This futuristic, Finnish-designed, seven-storey building (2006) is a spectacular structure of limestone, glass and copper, nicely integrated into the landscape. Kumu (the name is short for *kunstimuuseum* or art museum) contains the country's largest repository of Estonian art as well as constantly changing contemporary exhibits.

◉ Pirita

Pirita's main claim to fame is that it was the base for the sailing events of the 1980 Moscow Olympics; international regattas are still held here. It's also home to Tallinn's largest and most popular beach.

Buses 1A, 8, 34A and 38 all run between the city centre and Pirita, with the last two continuing on to the TV Tower.

Tallinn TV Tower   VIEWPOINT

(Tallinna teletorn; ☑ 686 3005; www.teletorn.ee; Kloostrimetsa tee 58a; adult/child €10/6; ☺10am-7pm) Opened in time for the 1980 Olympics, this futuristic 314m tower offers brilliant views from its 22nd floor (175m). Press a button and frosted glass disks set in the floor suddenly clear, giving a view straight down. Once you're done gawping, check out the interactive displays in the space-age pods. Daredevils can try the open-air 'edge walk' (€20).

☞ Tours

Tallinn Traveller Tours   TOURS

(☑ 5837 4800; www.traveller.ee) Entertaining, good-value tours – including a two-hour Old Town walking tour that departs at midday from outside the tourist information centre (it's nominally free but tips are encouraged). There are also ghost tours (€15), bike tours (from €19) and day trips to as far afield as Rīga (€55).

City Bike   CYCLING

(☑ 511 1819; www.citybike.ee; Vene 33; ☺10am-7pm, to 6pm Oct-Apr) 'Welcome to Tallinn' tours (€19, two hours) depart at 11am year-round and include Kadriorg and Pirita. 'Other Side' tours take in Kalamaja and Stroomi Beach (from €19, 2½ hours), while 'Countryside Cycling & Old Town Walking' tours head out as far as the Open-Air Museum (€57, four hours). It also co-ordinates self-guided day trips and longer itineraries.

Epic Bar Crawl   TOURS

(☑ 5624 3088; www.freetour.com; tour €12-15; ☺10pm Wed-Sat) The Epic Bar Crawl bills itself as 'the most fun and disorderly pub crawl in Tallinn' and the price includes a welcome beer or cider, a shot in each of three bars and entry to a nightclub. It also offers particularly ignominious packages designed for stags.

🛏 Sleeping

🛏 Old Town

★**Tabinoya**   HOSTEL €

(☑ 632 0062; www.tabinoya.com; Nunne 1; dm €17-19, d €50; @ 🛜) The Baltic's first Japanese-run hostel occupies the two top floors of a charming old building, with dorms and a communal lounge at the top, and spacious private rooms, a kitchen and a sauna below. Bathroom facilities are shared. The vibe's a bit more comfortable and quiet than most of Tallinn's hostels. Book ahead.

Red Emperor   HOSTEL €

(☑ 615 0035; www.redemperorhostel.com; Aia 10; dm/s/d from €13/22/34; @ 🛜) Situated above a wonderfully grungy live-music bar, Red Emperor is Tallinn's premier party hostel for those of a beardy, indie persuasion. Facilities are good, with brightly painted rooms, wooden bunks and plenty of showers, and there are organised activities every day (karaoke, shared dinners etc). Pack heavy-duty earplugs if you're a light sleeper.

Old House Hostel & Guesthouse   HOSTEL €

(☑641 1281; www.oldhouse.ee; Uus 22 & Uus 26; dm/s/d €20/40/56; P@⊚) Although one is called a hostel and one a guesthouse, these twin establishments both combine a cosy guesthouse feel with hostel facilities (bunk-less dorm rooms, shared bathrooms, guest kitchens and lounges). The homey, old-world decor (antiques, wacky wallpaper, plants, lamps) and the relatively quiet Old Town location will appeal to budget travellers who like things to be nice and comfortable.

Old House Apartments   APARTMENT €€

(☑641 1464; www.oldhouseapartments.ee; Rataskaevu 16; apt €99-109; P⊚) Old House is an understatement for this wonderful 14th-century merchant's house. It's been split into eight beautifully furnished apartments (including a spacious two-bedroom one with traces of a medieval painted ceiling). There are a further 21 apartments scattered around the Old Town in similar buildings, although the quality and facilities vary widely.

Viru Backpackers   HOSTEL €€

(☑644 6050; www.virubackpackers.com; 3rd fl, Viru 5; s/d €38/54; ❋⊚) This small, much flasher sibling of Monk's Bunk (p335) offers cosy, brightly painted private rooms, some of which have their own bathrooms. It's a quieter environment than the Monk, albeit in a noisier part of town.

★Hotel Cru   HOTEL €€€

(☑611 7600; www.cruhotel.eu; Viru 8; s/d/ste €105/130/270; ⊚) Behind its pretty powder-blue facade, this boutique 14th-century offering has richly furnished rooms with plenty of original features (timber beams and stone walls) scattered along a rabbit warren of corridors. The cheapest are a little snug.

Hotel Telegraaf   HOTEL €€€

(☑600 0600; www.telegraafhotel.com; Vene 9; r €225-255; P❋⊚≋) This upmarket hotel in a converted 19th-century former telegraph station delivers style in spades. It boasts a spa, a pretty courtyard, an acclaimed restaurant, swanky decor and smart, efficient service. 'Superior' rooms, in the older part of the building, have more historical detail but we prefer the marginally cheaper 'executive' rooms for their bigger proportions and sharp decor.

🛏 City Centre

Monk's Bunk   HOSTEL €

(☑636 3924; www.themonksbunk.com; Tatari 1; dm €13-17, r €44-50; @⊚) Very much a party hostel; the only monk we can imagine fitting in here is, perhaps, Friar Tuck. There are organised activities every night, including legendary pub crawls. The facilities are good, with high ceilings, free lockers and underfloor heating in the bathrooms.

★Y-residence   APARTMENT €€

(☑502 1477; www.yogaresidence.eu; Pärnu mnt 32; apt €65-150; ⊚) The 'Y' stands for 'yoga', which is a strange name for what's basically a block of very modern, fresh and well-equipped apartments, a short stroll from the Old Town. You can expect friendly staff, a kitchenette and a washing machine. There is a second block north of the Old Town.

Hotell Palace   HOTEL €€€

(☑680 6655; www.tallinnhotels.ee; Vabaduse Väljak 3; r €135-180; ❋⊚≋) A recent renovation has swept through this architecturally interesting 1930s hotel, leaving comfortable, tastefully furnished rooms in its wake. It's directly across the road from Freedom Sq and the Old Town. The complex includes an indoor pool, a spa, saunas and a small gym, although they're only free for those staying in superior rooms or suites.

Swissôtel Tallinn   HOTEL €€€

(☑624 0000; www.swissotel.com; Tornimäe 3; r €235-390; ❋⊚≋) Raising the standards at the big end of town while stretching up 30 floors, this 238-room hotel offers elegant, sumptuous rooms with superlative views. The bathroom design is ultra-cool and, if further indulgence is required, there's an in-house spa. Friendly staff, too.

✕ Eating

✕ Old Town

★Vegan Restoran V   VEGAN €

(☑626 9087; www.vonkrahl.ee; Rataskaevu 12; mains €6-10; ⊙noon-11pm Sun-Thu, noon-midnight Fri & Sat; ☑) Visiting vegans are spoilt for choice in this wonderful restaurant. In summer everyone wants one of the four tables on the street but the atmospheric interior is just as great. The food is excellent; expect the likes of sweet potato peanut curry, spicy tofu with quinoa and stuffed zucchini.

III Draakon
CAFE €

(www.kolmasdraakon.ee; Raekoja plats 1; mains €1-3; ⊘9am-midnight) There's bucketloads of atmosphere at this Lilliputian tavern below the Town Hall, and super-cheap elk soup, sausages and oven-hot pies baked fresh on site. The historic setting is amped up – expect costumed wenches with a good line in tourist banter, and beer served in ceramic steins.

★ Rataskaevu 16
ESTONIAN €€

(☑642 4025; www.rataskaevu16.ee; Rataskaevu 16; mains €10-17; ⊘noon-11pm Sun-Thu, noon-midnight Fri & Sat; ☑) If you've ever had a hankering for braised roast elk, this is the place to come. Although it's hardly a traditional eatery, plenty of Estonian faves fill the menu – fried Baltic herrings, grilled pork fillet and Estonian cheeses among them. Finish with a serve of its legendary chocolate cake.

Von Krahli Aed
MODERN EUROPEAN €€

(☑626 9088; www.vonkrahl.ee; Rataskaevu 8; mains €13-17; ⊘noon-midnight Mon-Sat, noon-11pm Sun; ☎☑) You'll find plenty of greenery on your plate at this rustic, plant-filled restaurant (aed means 'garden'). The menu embraces fresh flavours and wins fans by noting vegan, gluten-, lactose- and egg-free options.

★ Tchaikovsky
RUSSIAN, FRENCH €€€

(☑600 0610; www.telegraafhotel.com; Vene 9; mains €24-26; ⊘noon-3pm & 6-11pm Mon-Fri, 1-11pm Sat & Sun) Located in a glassed-in pavilion at the heart of the Hotel Telegraaf, Tchaikovsky offers a dazzling tableau of blinged-up chandeliers, gilt frames and greenery. Service is formal and faultless, as is the classic Franco-Russian menu, all accompanied by live chamber music.

★ Leib
ESTONIAN €€€

(☑611 9026; www.leibresto.ee; Uus 31; mains €13-22; ⊘noon-3pm & 6-11pm Mon-Fri, noon-11pm Sat) An inconspicuous gate opens onto a large lawn guarded by busts of Sean Connery and Robert Burns. Welcome to the former home of Tallinn's Scottish club (really!), where 'simple, soulful food' is served along with homemade leib (bread). The slow-cooked meat and grilled fish dishes are exceptional.

City Centre

★ Ö
NEW NORDIC €€€

(☑661 6150; www.restoran-o.ee; Mere pst 6e; degustations €59-76; ⊘6-11pm Mon-Sat, closed Jul) Award-winning Ö (pronounced 'er') has carved a unique space in Tallinn's culinary world, delivering inventive degustation menus showcasing seasonal Estonian produce. There's a distinct 'New Nordic' influence at play, and the understated dining room nicely counterbalances the theatrical cuisine.

Kalamaja

F-hoone
PUB FOOD €

(☑5322 6855; www.fhoone.ee; Telliskivi 60a; mains €5-10; ⊘kitchen 9am-11pm Mon-Sat, 9am-9pm Sun; ☎☑) The trailblazer of the über-hip Telliskivi complex, this cavernous place embraces industrial chic and offers a quality menu of pasta, burgers, stews, grilled vegies and felafels. Wash it down with a craft beer from the extensive selection.

★ Moon
RUSSIAN €€

(☑631 4575; www.restoranmoon.ee; Võrgu 3; mains €10-20; ⊘noon-11pm Mon-Sat, 1-9pm Sun, closed Jul) The best restaurant in ever-increasingly hip Kalamaja, Moon is informal but excellent, combining Russian and broader European influences to delicious effect. Save room for dessert.

Klaus
CAFE €€

(☑5691 9010; www.klauskohvik.ee; Kalasadama; mains €9.50-14; ⊘9am-11pm; ☎) There's a fresh, designery feel to this informal cafe down by the water. The menu is full of tasty snacks and more substantial meals, including lamb koftas, pasta and steaks. We wholeheartedly endorse the 'Cubanos' pulled pork sandwich, although we don't suggest tackling this messy beast on a date.

Pirita

★ NOA
INTERNATIONAL €€€

(☑508 0589; www.noaresto.ee; Ranna tee 3; mains €12-24; ⊘noon-11pm Mon-Thu, noon-midnight Fri & Sat, noon-10pm Sun; ☑) It's worth the trek out to the far side of Pirita to this elegant eatery which opened in 2014 and was rated the best in Estonia that very year. It's housed in a stylish low-slung pavilion that gazes back over Tallinn Bay to the Old Town. Choose between the more informal à la carte restaurant and the degustation-only Chef's Hall.

🍷 Drinking & Nightlife

Speakeasy by Põhjala
BAR

(www.speakeasy.ee; Kopli 4; ⊘6pm-2am Wed-Sat) It's pretty basic – particleboard walls, junkstore furniture and a courtyard surrounded by derelict buildings – but this hip little bar is a showcase for one of Estonia's best microbreweries. Expect lots of beardy dudes discussing the relative merits of the India Pale Ale over the Imperial Baltic Porter.

DM Baar BAR

(☑ 644 2350; www.depechemode.ee; Voorimehe 4; ⊙ noon-4am) If you just can't get enough of Depeche Mode, this is the bar for you. The walls are covered with all manner of memorabilia, including pictures of the actual band partying here. And the soundtrack? Do you really need to ask? If you're not a fan, leave in silence.

Clazz BAR

(☑ 666 0003; www.clazz.ee; Vana turg 2; ⊙ 6pm-2am Tue-Thu, noon-3am Fri & Sat) Behind the cheesy name (a contraction of 'classy jazz') is a popular lounge bar featuring live music every night of the week, ranging from jazz to soul, funk, blues and Latin.

🛒 Shopping

Viru Keskus SHOPPING CENTRE

(www.virukeskus.com; Viru väljak 4; ⊙ 9am-9pm) Tallinn's showpiece shopping mall is home to fashion boutiques, a great bookstore (Rahva Raamat) and a branch of the Piletilevi event ticketing agency. At the rear it connects to the Kaubamaja department store. The main terminal for local buses is in the basement.

Masters' Courtyard ARTS & CRAFTS

(Meistrite Hoov; www.hoov.ee; Vene 6; ⊙ 10am-6pm) Rich pickings here, with the cobbled courtyard not only home to a cosy cafe but also small stores and artisans' workshops selling quality ceramics, glass, jewellery, knitwear, woodwork and candles.

Katariina käik ARTS & CRAFTS

(St Catherine's Passage; www.katariinagild.eu; off Vene 12) This lovely lane is home to the Katariina Gild comprising several artisans' studios where you can happily browse ceramics, textiles, patchwork quilts, hats, jewellery, stained glass and beautiful leatherbound books.

ℹ️ Information

East-Tallinn Central Hospital (Ida-Tallinna Keskhaigla; ☑ 666 1900; www.itk.ee; Ravi 18) Offers a full range of services, including a 24-hour emergency room.

Tallinn Tourist Information Centre (☑ 645 7777; www.visittallinn.ee; Niguliste 2; ⊙ 9am-5pm Mon-Sat, 10am-3pm Sun Oct-Mar, 9am-6pm Mon-Sat, 9am-4pm Sun Apr, May & Sep, 9am-7pm Mon-Sat, 9am-6pm Sun Jun-Aug) Brochures, maps, event schedules and other info.

ℹ️ Getting There & Away

BUS

The **Central Bus Station** (Tallinna bussijaam; ☑ 12550; www.bussijaam.ee; Lastekodu 46; ⊙ 5am-1am) is about 2km southeast of the Old Town (tram 2 or 4). Destinations include Rakvere (€3.50 to €7, 1½ hours, 19 daily), Tartu (€7 to €12, 2½ hours, at least every half-hour), Otepää (€13, 3½ hours, daily), Pärnu (€6.50 to €11, two hours, at least hourly) and Kuressaare (€15 to €17, four hours, 11 daily). **TPilet** (www.tpilet.ee) has times and prices for all national bus services.

TRAIN

The **Central Train Station** (Balti Jaam; Toompuiestee 35) is on the northwestern edge of the Old Town. Destinations include Rakvere (€5.50, 1½ hours, three daily), Tartu (€11, two to 2½ hours, eight daily) and Pärnu (€7.60, 2¼ hours, three daily).

ℹ️ Getting Around

TO/FROM THE AIRPORT

➡ **Tallinn Airport** (Tallinna Lennujaam; ☑ 605 8888; www.tallinn-airport.ee; Tartu mnt 101) is 4km from the centre.

➡ Bus 2 runs every 20 to 30 minutes (6am to around 11pm) from the A Laikmaa stop, opposite the Tallink Hotel, next to Viru Keskus. From the airport, bus 2 will take you to the centre. Buy tickets from the driver (€1.60); journey time depends on traffic but rarely exceeds 20 minutes.

➡ A taxi between the airport and the city centre should cost less than €10.

PUBLIC TRANSPORT

Tallinn has an excellent network of buses, trams and trolleybuses that run from around 6am to midnight. The major **local bus station** is on the basement level of the Viru Keskus shopping centre, although some buses terminate their routes on the surrounding streets. All local public transport timetables are online at www.tallinn.ee.

Public transport is free for Tallinn residents. Visitors still need to pay, either from the driver with cash (€1.60 for a single journey) or by using the e-ticketing system. Buy a plastic smartcard (€2 deposit) and top up with credit, then validate the card at the start of each journey using the orange card-readers. Fares using the e-ticketing system cost €1.10/3/6 for an hour/day/five days.

The Tallinn Card includes free public transport. Travelling without a valid ticket runs the risk of a €40 fine.

TAXI

Taxis are plentiful, but each company sets its own fare. The base fare ranges from €2 to €5, followed by 50c to €1 per kilometre. To avoid suprises, try **Krooni Takso** (☑1212; www.kroonitakso.ee; base fare €2.50, per km 6am-11pm €0.50, 11pm-6am €0.55) or **Reval Takso** (☑1207; www.reval-takso.ee; base fare €2.29, per km €0.49).

LAHEMAA NATIONAL PARK

The perfect country retreat from the capital, Lahemaa takes in a stretch of coast indented with peninsulas and bays, plus 475 sq km of pine-fresh forested hinterland. Visitors are looked after with cosy guesthouses, remote seaside campgrounds and a network of pine-scented forest trails.

◎ Sights

Palmse Manor HISTORIC BUILDING

(☑5559 9977; www.palmse.ee; adult/child €7/5; ⊙10am-5pm, to 6pm summer) Fully restored Palmse Manor is the showpiece of Lahemaa National Park, housing the visitor centre in its former stables. The pretty manor house (1720, rebuilt in the 1780s) is now a museum containing period furniture and clothing. Other estate buildings have also been restored and put to new use: the distillery is a hotel, the steward's residence is a guesthouse, the lakeside bathhouse is a summertime restaurant and the farm labourers' quarters became a tavern.

Altja VILLAGE

First mentioned in 1465, this fishing village has many restored or reconstructed traditional buildings, including a wonderfully ancient-looking tavern that was actually built in 1976. Altja's Swing Hill (Kiitemägi), complete with a traditional Estonian wooden swing, has long been the focus of Midsummer's Eve festivities in Lahemaa. The 3km circular **Altja Nature & Culture Trail** starts at Swing Hill and takes in net sheds, fishing cottages and the stone field known as the 'open-air museum of stones'.

⊨ Sleeping & Eating

Lepispea Caravan & Camping CAMPGROUND €

(☑5450 1522; www.lepispea.eu; Lepispea 3; tent per person €6, caravan €17, plus per person €2; ⊙May-Sep; 🅿🛜) In Lepispea, 1km west of Võsu, this campground is spread over a large field fringed by trees and terminating in a little reed-lined beach. Facilities are good, including a sauna house for rent. It also hires bikes (per day €10).

★Merekalda APARTMENT €€

(☑323 8451; www.merekalda.ee; Neeme tee 2, Käsmu; r €49, apt €69-99; ⊙May-Sep; 🅿🛜) At the entrance to Käsmu, this peaceful retreat is set around a lovely large garden right on the bay. Ideally you'll plump for an apartment with a sea view and terrace, but you'll need to book ahead. Boat and bike hire are available.

★Toomarahva Turismitalu GUESTHOUSE, CAMPGROUND €€

(☑505 0850; www.toomarahva.ee; Altja; tent/hayloft per person €3/5, caravan €10, cottage €30, d €50, apt €70-120; 🛜) This atmospheric farmstead comprises thatch-roofed wooden buildings and a garden full of flowers and sculptures. Sleeping options include two cute and comfortable rooms that share a bathroom, and an apartment that can be rented with either one or two bedrooms, or you can even doss down in the hayloft in summer. Plus there's a traditional sauna for hire.

★Altja Kõrts ESTONIAN €

(☑324 0070; www.palmse.ee; Altja; mains €6-8; ⊙noon-8pm) Set in a thatched, wooden building with a large terrace, this uber-rustic place serves delicious plates of traditional fare (baked pork with sauerkraut etc) to candlelit wooden tables. It's extremely atmospheric and a lot of fun.

ℹ Information

Lahemaa National Park Visitor Centre (☑329 5555; www.loodusegakoos.ee; ⊙9am-5pm or 6pm daily mid-Apr–mid-Oct, 9am-5pm Mon-Fri mid-Oct–mid-Apr) This excellent centre stocks the essential map of Lahemaa (€1.90), as well as information on hiking trails, accommodation and guiding services. It's worth starting your park visit with the free 17-minute film titled *Lahemaa – Nature and Man*.

ℹ Getting There & Away

Hiring a car will give you the most flexibility, or you could take a tour from Tallinn. Exploring the park using public transport requires patience and time. Buses to destinations within the park leave from the town of Rakvere (connected by bus to Tallinn, Tartu and Pärnu), which is 35km southeast of Palmse. Once you've arrived in the park, bike hire is easy to arrange.

TARTU

POP 98,000

Tartu was the cradle of Estonia's 19th-century national revival and lays claim to being the nation's cultural capital. Locals talk about a special Tartu *vaim* (spirit), created by the time-stands-still feel of its wooden houses and stately buildings, and by the beauty of its parks and riverfront. It's also Estonia's premier university town, with students making up nearly one fifth of the population – guaranteeing a vibrant nightlife for a city of its size.

⊙ Sights

Rising to the west of the town hall, Toomemägi (Cathedral Hill) is the original reason for Tartu's existence, functioning on and off as a stronghold from around the 5th or 6th century. It's now a tranquil park, with walking paths meandering through the trees and a pretty-as-a-picture rotunda which serves as a summertime cafe.

★ University of Tartu Museum MUSEUM
(Tartu Ülikool muuseum; ☑737 5674; www.muuse-um.ut.ee; Lossi 25; adult/child €5/4; ⊙10am-6pm Tue-Sun May-Sep, 11am-5pm Wed-Sun Oct-Apr) Atop Toomemägi are the ruins of a Gothic cathedral, originally built by German knights in the 13th century. It was substantially rebuilt in the 15th century, despoiled during the Reformation in 1525, used as a barn, and partly rebuilt between 1804 and 1809 to house the university library, which is now a museum. Inside there are a range of interesting exhibits chronicling student life.

★ Town Hall Square SQUARE
(Raekoja plats) Tartu's main square is lined with grand buildings and echoes with the chink of glasses and plates in summer. The centrepiece is the Town Hall itself, fronted by a statue of students kissing under a spouting umbrella. On the south side of the square, look out for the communist hammer-and-sickle relief that still remains on the facade of number 5.

Science Centre AHHAA MUSEUM
(Teaduskeskus AHHAA; www.ahhaa.ee; Sadama 1; adult/child €13/10, planetarium €4, flight simulator €1, 4D theatre €2.50; ⊙10am-7pm Sun-Thu, 10am-8pm Fri & Sat) Head under the dome for a whizz-bang series of interactive exhibits that are liable to bring out the mad scientist in kids and adults alike. Allow at least a couple of hours. And you just haven't lived until you've set a tray of magnetised iron filings

'dancing' to Bronski Beat's *Smalltown Boy*. Upstairs there's a nightmarish collection of pickled organs and deformed foetuses courtesy of the university's medical faculty.

★ Estonian National Museum MUSEUM
(Eesti rahva muuseum; ☑736 3051; www.erm.ee; Muuseumi tee 2; adult/child €12/8; ⊙10am-7pm Tue & Thu-Sun, 10am-9pm Wed) This immense, low-slung, architectural showcase is a striking sight and had both Estonian patriots and architecture-lovers purring when it opened in late 2016. The permanent exhibition covers national prehistory and history in some detail. Fittingly, for a museum built over a former Soviet airstrip, the Russian occupation is given in-depth treatment, while the 'Echo of the Urals' exhibition gives an overview of the various peoples speaking tongues in the Estonian language family. There's also a restaurant and cafe.

🛏 Sleeping & Eating

Terviseks HOSTEL €
(☑565 5382; www.terviseksbbb.com; top fl, Raekoja plats 10; dm €15-17, s/d €22/44; @🖥) Occupying a historic building in a perfect main-square location, this excellent 'backpacker's bed and breakfast' offers dorms (maximum four beds, no bunks), private rooms, a full kitchen and lots of switched-on info about the happening places in town. It's like staying in your rich mate's cool European pad. *Terviseks* (cheers) to that.

★ Domus Dorpatensis APARTMENT €€
(☑733 1345; www.dorpatensis.ee; Raekoja plats 1; apt €50-85; 🖥) Run by an academic foundation, this block of 10 apartments offers an unbeatable location and wonderful value for money. The units range in size but all have writing desks (it's run by scholars, after all) and almost all have kitchenettes. The staff are particularly helpful – dispensing parking advice and directing guests to the communal laundry. The entrance is on Ülikooli.

Tampere Maja GUESTHOUSE €€
(☑738 6300; www.tamperemaja.ee; Jaani 4; s/d/tr/q from €45/72/89/132; 🅿🌀@🖥) With strong links to the Finnish city of Tampere (Tartu's sister city), this cosy guesthouse features six warm, light-filled guest rooms. Breakfast is included and each room has access to cooking facilities. And it wouldn't be Finnish if it didn't offer an authentic sauna (one to four people €15; open to nonguests).

Villa Margaretha
BOUTIQUE HOTEL €€

(📞731 1820; www.margaretha.ee; Tähe 11/13; s €55-85, d €65-95, ste €175; 🅿🛜) Like something out of a fairy tale, this wooden art nouveau house has a sweet little turret and romantic rooms decked out with sleigh beds and artfully draped fabrics. The cheaper rooms in the modern extension at the rear are bland in comparison. It's a little away from the action but still within walking distance of the Old Town.

★ Antonius Hotel
HOTEL €€€

(📞737 0377; www.hotelantonius.ee; Ülikooli 15; s/d/ste from €95/120/220; ❇🛜) Sitting plumb opposite the main university building, this first-rate, 18-room boutique hotel is loaded with antiques and period features. Breakfast is served in the 18th-century vaulted cellar, which in the evening morphs into a top-notch restaurant.

Cafe Truffe
MODERN EUROPEAN €€

(📞742 8840; www.truffe.ee; Raekoja plats 16; mains €11-19; ☺11am-11pm Mon-Thu, 11am-1am Fri & Sat, 11am-10pm Sun) Truffe calls itself a cafe, although it feels more like an upmarket bar, and the food is absolutely restaurant quality. One thing's for certain, it's the best eatery on Town Hall Sq and one of Tartu's finest. In summer, grab a seat on the large terrace and tuck into a steak with truffle sauce or a delicately smoked duck breast.

ⓘ Information

Tartu Tourist Information Centre (📞744 2111; www.visittartu.com; Town Hall, Raekoja plats; ☺9am-6pm Mon-Fri, 10am-5pm Sat & Sun May–mid-Sep, 9am-6pm Mon, 9am-5pm Tue-Fri, 10am-2pm Sat mid-Sep–Apr) Stocks local maps and brochures, books accommodation and tour guides, and has free internet access.

ⓘ Getting There & Away

BUS

From the **bus station** (Tartu Autobussijaam; Turu 2 (enter from Soola); ☺6am-9pm), buses run to and from Tallinn (€7 to €12, 2½ hours, at least every half hour), Rakvere (€7 to €9, three hours, eight daily), Otepää (€2 to €3.50, one hour, 10 daily), Pärnu (€9.60 to €12, 2¾ hours, 12 daily) and Kuressaare (€18, 5½ hours, two daily).

TRAIN

Tartu's beautifully restored **train station** (📞673 7400; www.elron.ee; Vaksali 6) is 1.5km southwest of the old town (at the end of Kuperjanovi street). Four express (2½-hour) and four regular (two-hour) services head to Tallinn daily (both €11),

OTEPÄÄ
POP 1900

The small hilltop town of Otepää, 44km south of Tartu, is the centre of a picturesque area of forests, lakes and rivers. The district is beloved by Estonians for its natural beauty and its many possibilities for hiking, biking and swimming in summer, and cross-country skiing in winter. It's often referred to as Estonia's winter capital, and winter weekends here are busy and loads of fun. Some have even dubbed the area (tongue firmly in cheek) the 'Estonian Alps' – a reference not to its peaks but to its excellent ski trails. The 63km Tartu Ski Marathon kicks off here every February but even in summer you'll see professional athletes and enthusiasts hurtling around on roller skis.

The main part of Otepää is centred on the intersection of the Tartu, Võru and Valga highways, where you'll find the main square, shops and some patchy residential streets. A small swathe of forest separates it from a smaller settlement by the lakeshore, 2km southwest.

🛏 Sleeping & Eating

Murakas
HOTEL €€

(📞731 1410; www.murakas.ee; Valga mnt 23a; s/d €50/60; 🅿🛜) With only 10 bedrooms, Murakas is more like a large friendly guesthouse than a hotel. Stripey carpets, blonde wood and balconies give the rooms a fresh feel and there's a similarly breezy breakfast room downstairs.

★ Mr Jakob
MODERN ESTONIAN €€€

(📞5375 3307; www.otepaagolf.ee; Mäha küla; mains €14-18; ☺noon-9pm, closed Mon-Thu Nov-Mar; 🛜) Otepää's best restaurant is hidden away at the golf club, 4km west of Pühajärv. The menu is as contemporary and playful as the decor, taking Estonian classics such as pork ribs and marinated herring fillets and producing something quite extraordinary. Add to that charming service and blissful views over the course and surrounding fields.

ⓘ Information

Otepää Tourist Information Centre (📞766 1200; www.otepaa.eu; Tartu mnt 1; ☺10am-5pm Mon-Fri, to 3pm Sat & Sun mid-May–mid-Sep, 10am-5pm Mon-Fri, to 2pm Sat rest of year) A well-informed staff distribute maps and brochures, and make recommendations for activities, guide services and lodging in the area.

ℹ Getting There & Away

The bus station (Tartu mnt 1) is next to the tourist office. Destinations include Tallinn (€13, 3½ hours, daily) and Tartu (€2 to €3.50, one hour, 10 daily).

PÄRNU

POP 39,800

Local families, young party-goers and German, Swedish and Finnish holidaymakers join together in a collective prayer for sunny weather while strolling the golden-sand beaches, sprawling parks and picturesque historic centre of Pärnu (*pair*-nu), Estonia's premier seaside resort.

The main thoroughfare of the old town is Rüütli, lined with splendid buildings dating back to the 17th century.

◎ Sights

★ Pärnu Beach   BEACH

Pärnu's long, wide, sandy beach – sprinkled with volleyball courts, cafes and changing cubicles – is easily the city's main drawcard. A curving path stretches along the sand, lined with fountains, park benches and an excellent playground. Early-20th-century buildings are strung along Ranna pst, the avenue that runs parallel to the beach. Across the road, the formal gardens of **Rannapark** are ideal for a summertime picnic.

★ Museum of New Art   GALLERY

(Uue kunstimuuseum; ☑443 0772; www.mona.ee; Esplanaadi 10; adult/child €4/2; ◎9am-9pm Jun-Aug, 9am-7pm Sep-May) Pärnu's former Communist Party headquarters now houses one of Estonia's edgiest galleries. As part of its commitment to pushing the cultural envelope, it stages an international nude art exhibition every summer. Founded by film-maker Mark Soosaar, the gallery also hosts the annual Pärnu Film Festival.

⌖ Sleeping

In summer it's worth booking ahead; outside high season you should be able to snare a good deal (rates can be up to 50% lower).

Embrace   B&B €€

(☑5887 3404; www.embrace.ee; Pardi 30; r €110; ◎Mar-early Jan; P☀🤖) Snuggle up in an old wooden house in a suburban street, close to the beach and water park. Rooms strike a nice balance between antique and contemporary,

and there's a set of four modern, self-contained apartments in a neighbouring annex.

Inge Villa   GUESTHOUSE €€

(☑443 8510; www.ingevilla.ee; Kaarli 20; s/d/ste €56/70/82; ☀🤖) Describing itself as a 'Swedish-Estonian villa hotel', low-key and lovely Inge Villa occupies a prime patch of real estate near the beach. Its 11 rooms are simply decorated in muted tones with Nordic minimalism to the fore. The garden, lounge and sauna seal the deal.

Villa Ammende   HOTEL €€€

(☑447 3888; www.ammende.ee; Mere pst 7; s/d/ste €225/275/475; P☀🤖) Luxury abounds in this refurbished 1904 art nouveau mansion, which lords it over handsomely manicured grounds. The gorgeous exterior – looking like one of the cooler Paris metro stops writ large – is matched by an elegant lobby and individually antique-furnished rooms. Rooms in the gardener's house are more affordable but lack a little of the wow factor. It's a lot cheaper outside of July.

✗ Eating

★ Piccadilly   CAFE €

(☑442 0085; www.kohvila.com; Pühavaimu 15; dishes €4-6; ◎9am-7pm Mon-Thu, 11am-midnight Fri-Sat, 11am-7pm Sun; ☑) Piccadilly offers a down-tempo haven for wine-lovers and vegetarians and an extensive range of hot beverages. Savoury options include delicious salads, sandwiches and omelettes, but really it's all about the sweeties, including moreish cheesecake and handmade chocolates.

★ Lime Lounge   INTERNATIONAL €€€

(☑449 2190; www.limelounge.ee; Hommiku 17; mains €8-19; ◎noon-11pm Mon-Thu, noon-midnight Fri & Sat; 🤖🍴) Bright and zesty Lime Lounge feels more like a cocktail bar than a restaurant, although the food really is excellent. The well-travelled menu bounds from Russia (borscht) to France (duck breast), Italy (delicious pasta) and all the way to Thailand (*tom kha gai* soup).

ℹ Information

Pärnu Tourist Information Centre (☑447 3000; www.visitparnu.com; Uus 4; ◎9am-6pm mid-May–mid-Sep, 9am-5pm Mon-Fri, 10am-2pm Sat & Sun mid-Sep–mid-May) A very helpful centre stocking maps and brochures, booking accommodation and rental cars (for a small fee), and providing a left-luggage service (per day €2). There's a small gallery attached as well as a toilet and showers.

Getting There & Away

Pärnu's **bus station** is right in the centre of town, with services to/from Tallinn (€6.50 to €11, two hours, at least hourly), Rakvere (€9 to €11, 2¾ to four hours, three daily), Tartu (€9.60 to €12, 2¾ hours, 12 daily) and Kuressaare (€13, 3½ hours, four daily).

MUHU

POP 1560

Connected to Saaremaa by a 2.5km causeway, the island of Muhu has the undeserved reputation as the 'doormat' for the bigger island – lots of people passing through on their way from the ferry, but few stopping. In fact, Estonia's third-biggest island offers plenty of excuses to hang around, not least one of the country's best restaurants and some excellent accommodation options. There's no tourist office on the island, but there's lots of good information online at www.muhu.info.

Sights

Muhu Museum　　　　　　　　　　MUSEUM
(454 8872; www.muhumuuseum.ee; Koguva; adult/concession €3/2; 9am-6pm mid-May–mid-Sep, 10am-5pm Tue-Sat rest of year) Koguva, 6km off the main road on the western tip of Muhu, is an exceptionally well-preserved, old-fashioned island village, now protected as an open-air museum. One ticket allows you to wander through an old schoolhouse, a house displaying beautiful traditional textiles from the area (including painstakingly detailed folk costumes) and a farm that was the ancestral home of author Juhan Smuul (1922–71). You can poke around various farm buildings, one of which contains a collection of Singer sewing machines.

Sleeping & Eating

★ **Pädaste Manor**　　　　　　　HOTEL €€€
(454 8800; www.padaste.ee; Pädaste; r €254-481, ste €416-875; Mar-Oct; P🐾) If money's no object, here's where to part with it. This manicured bayside estate encompasses the restored manor house (14 rooms and a fine-dining restaurant), a stone carriage house (nine rooms and a spa centre) and a separate stone 'sea house' brasserie. The attention to detail is second-to-none, from the pop-up TVs to the antique furnishings and Muhu embroidery.

Getting There & Away

BOAT

➠ Car ferries run by **Praamid** (1310; www.praamid.ee; adult/child/car €3/1.50/8.40) make the 25-minute crossing between Virtsu on the mainland and Kuivastu on Muhu.

➠ Boats depart Virtsu from roughly 5.35am until midnight, with at least one or two sailings per hour up until 10.15pm.

➠ A 50% surcharge applies to vehicles heading to the island after 1pm on Fridays and departing the island after 1pm on Sundays.

➠ Up to 70% of each boat's capacity is presold online; the website has a real-time indicator showing what percentage has already been sold. The remaining 30% is kept for drive-up customers and offered on a first-in, first-on basis. You should definitely consider prebooking at busy times, particularly around weekends in summer.

➠ Tickets purchased online must either be printed out or loaded as an electronic ticket onto a smartphone.

➠ If you miss your prebooked boat, your ticket will be valid for the regular queue on subsequent boats for up to 48 hours.

BUS

Buses take the ferry from the mainland and continue through to Saaremaa via the causeway, stopping along the main road. Major destinations include Tallinn (€12 to €14, three hours, 11 daily), Tartu (€17, five hours, two daily), Pärnu (€8.80, 2½ hours, four daily) and Kuressaare (€5 to €5.60, one hour, 18 daily).

SAAREMAA

POP 31,600

Saaremaa (literally 'island land') is synonymous to Estonians with space, spruce and fresh air – and bottled water, vodka and killer beer. Estonia's largest island (roughly the size of Luxembourg) is still substantially covered in forests of pine, spruce and juniper, while its windmills, lighthouses and tiny villages seem largely unbothered by the passage of time.

During the Soviet era the entire island was off limits to visitors (due to an early-radar system and rocket base stationed there), even to 'mainland' Estonians, who needed a permit to visit. This resulted in a minimum of industrial build-up and the unwitting protection of the island's rural charm.

This unique old-time setting goes hand-in-hand with inextinguishable Saaremaan pride. Saaremaa has always had an inde-

ESSENTIAL FOOD & DRINK

Estonian gastronomy mixes Nordic, Russian and German influences, and prizes local and seasonal produce.

Desserts On the sweet side, you'll find delicious chocolates, marzipan and cakes.

Favourite drinks Õlu (beer) is the favourite alcoholic drink. Popular brands include Saku and A Le Coq, and aficionados should seek out the product of the local microbreweries such as Tallinn's Põhjala. Other tipples include vodka (Viru Valge and Saremaa are the best-known local brands) and Vana Tallinn, a syrupy sweet liqueur, also available in a cream version.

Other favourites Include black bread, sauerkraut, black pudding, smoked meat and fish, creamy salted butter and sour cream, which is served with almost everything.

Pork and potatoes The traditional stodgy standbys, prepared a hundred different ways.

Seasonal In summer, berries enter the menu in both sweet and savoury dishes, while everyone goes crazy for forest mushrooms in the autumn.

pendent streak and was usually the last part of Estonia to fall to invaders. Its people have their own customs, songs and costumes. They don't revere mainland Estonia's *Kalevipoeg* legend, for Saaremaa has its own hero, Suur Tõll, who fought many battles around the island against devils and fiends.

Kuressaare, the capital of Saaremaa, is on the south coast (75km from the Muhu ferry terminal) and is a natural base for visitors. It's here among the upmarket hotels that you'll understand where the island got its nickname, 'Spa-remaa'. When the long days arrive, so too do the Finns and Swedes, jostling for beach and sauna space with Estonian urban-escapees. More information is online at www.saaremaa.ee.

⊙ Sights

The long stretch of pine-lined sand from **Mändjala** to **Järve**, west of Kuressaare, is Saaremaa's main beach resort. The shallow beach curves languidly towards the south, where the 32km **Sõrve Peninsula** takes over. This beautiful but sparsely populated finger of land comes to a dramatic end at **Sääre**, with a lighthouse and a narrow sand spit extending out to sea.

The peninsula saw heavy fighting during WWII and the battle scars remain. Various abandoned bunkers and battlements, and the remnants of the Lõme-Kaimri anti-tank defence lines, can still be seen.

★**Kuressaare Castle**   CASTLE
(www.saaremaamuuseum.ee) Majestic Kuressaare Castle stands facing the sea at the southern end of the town, on an artificial is-

land ringed by a moat. It's the best-preserved castle in the Baltic and the region's only medieval stone castle that has remained intact. The castle grounds are open to the public at all times but to visit the keep you'll need to buy a ticket to Saaremaa Museum.

Panga Pank   VIEWPOINT
Saaremaa's highest cliffs run along the northern coast near Panga for 3km. The highest point (21.3m) was a sacred place where sacrifices were made to the sea god; gifts of flowers, coins, vodka and beer are still sometimes left here. It's a pretty spot, looking down at the treacherous waters below.

🛏 Sleeping & Eating

The tourist office can organise beds in private apartments and farms across the island. Hotel prices are up to 50% cheaper from September through April. Most hotel spa centres are open to nonguests. All of the following are in Kuressaare, unless otherwise noted.

★**Georg Ots Spa Hotel**   HOTEL **€€**
(Gospa; ☑ 455 0000; www.gospa.ee; Tori 2; r €185-225, ste €295; P ❄ 🛜 ♨ 🐾) Named after a renowned Estonian opera singer, Gospa has modern rooms with wildly striped carpet, enormous king-sized beds and a warm but minimalist design. Most rooms have balconies and there's a fitness centre and excellent spa centre, including a pool and multiple saunas. Separate freestanding 'residences' are also available, and families are very well catered for. Prices vary widely.

★ **Piibutopsu** APARTMENT €€

(✒ 5693 0288; www.piibutopsu.ee; Ülejõe 19a, Nasva; d/tr/q €60/90/120; P ⛾) Set on the ample lawn of a private residence down a side street in Nasva (the first little settlement west of Kuressaare), Piibutopsu offers four well-equipped holiday apartments in a new custom-built block. The units are grouped around a central lounge with a wood fire, and there's even a mini spa centre on site. All in all, an excellent option.

★ **Ekesparre** BOUTIQUE HOTEL €€€

(✒ 453 8778; www.ekesparre.ee; Lossi 27; r €172-215; ⊙ Apr-Oct; P ⛾) Holding pole position on the castle grounds, this elegant 10-room hotel has been returned to its art nouveau glory. Period wallpaper and carpet, Tiffany lamps and a smattering of orchids add to the refined, clubby atmosphere, while the 3rd-floor guests' library is a gem. As you'd expect from the price, it's a polished operator.

★ **Retro** CAFE €

(✒ 5683 8400; www.kohvikretro.ee; Lossi 5; mains €7.50-14; ⊙ noon-10pm Mon-Thu, to midnight Fri & Sat, to 8pm Sun; ⛾⛾) The menu at this hip little cafe-bar is deceptively simple (pasta, burgers, steak, grilled fish), but Retro takes things to the next level, making its own pasta and burger buns and using the best fresh local produce. Desserts are delicious, too. There's also a great selection of Estonian craft beer, perfect for supping on the large rear terrace.

❶ Information

Kuressaare Tourist Office (✒ 453 3120; www.kuressaare.ee; Tallinna 2; ⊙ 9am-6pm Mon-Fri, 10am-4pm Sat & Sun mid-May–mid-Sep, 9am-5pm Mon-Fri rest of year) Inside the old town hall, it sells maps and guides, arranges accommodation and has information on boat trips and island tours.

Leisi Tourist Office (✒ 457 3073; www.leisivald.ee; Kuressaare mnt. 11; ⊙ 1-7pm Jun-Aug; ⛾) If you're arriving from Hiiumaa via the Sõru-Triigi ferry, pick up maps and get general Saaremaa information at the tiny Leisi tourist office, inside the pretty, vine-covered restaurant, Sassimaja.

❶ Getting There & Away

Most travellers reach Saaremaa by taking the ferry from Virtsu to Muhu and then crossing the 2.5km causeway connecting the islands.

❶ Getting Around

Local buses putter around the island, but not very frequently. The main terminus is **Kuressaare bus station** (Kuressaare Bussijaam; ✒ 453 1661; www.bussipilet.ee; Pihtla tee 2) and there's a route planner online at www.bussipilet.ee.

SURVIVAL GUIDE

❶ Directory A–Z

ACCOMMODATION

If you like flying by the seat of your pants when you're travelling, you'll find July and August in Estonia very problematic. The best accommodation books up quickly and in Tallinn, especially on weekends, you might find yourself scraping for anywhere at all to lay your head. In fact, Tallinn gets busy most weekends, so try to book about a month ahead anytime from May through to September (midweek isn't anywhere near as bad).

High season in Estonia means summer. Prices drop off substantially at other times. The exception is Otepää, when there's also a corresponding peak in winter.

GAY & LESBIAN TRAVELLERS

Today's Estonia is a fairly tolerant and safe home to its gay and lesbian citizens, but only Tallinn has any gay venues. Homosexuality was decriminalised in 1992 and since 2001 there has been an equal age of consent for everyone (14 years). In 2014 Estonia became the first former Soviet republic to pass a law recognising same-sex registered partnerships.

TELEPHONE

There are no area codes in Estonia. All landline numbers have seven digits; mobile numbers have seven or eight digits, beginning with 5.

TOURIST INFORMATION

Most major destinations have tourist offices. The national tourist board has an excellent website (www.visitestonia.com).

SLEEPING PRICE RANGES

The following price ranges refer to a double room in high (but not necessary peak) seaon.

€ less than €35

€€ €35–100

€€€ more than €100

VISAS

EU citizens can spend unlimited time in Estonia, while citizens of Australia, Canada, Japan, New Zealand, the USA and many other countries can enter visa-free for a maximum 90-day stay over a six-month period. Travellers holding a Schengen visa do not need an additional Estonian visa. For information, see the website of the Estonian Ministry of Foreign Affairs (www.vm.ee/en).

Getting There & Away

AIR

Eleven European airlines have scheduled services to Tallinn year-round, with additional routes and airlines added in summer. There are also direct flights from Helsinki to Tartu Airport.

LAND

Bus

The following bus companies all have services between Estonia and the other Baltic states:

Ecolines (www.ecolines.net) Major routes: Tallinn–Pärnu–Rīga (seven daily), two of which continue on to Vilnius; Tallinn–St Petersburg (four daily); Tartu–Valga–Rīga (daily); Vilnius–Rīga–Tartu–Narva–St Petersburg (daily).

Lux Express & Simple Express (www.luxexpress.eu) Major routes: Tallinn–Pärnu–Rīga (10 to 12 daily), six of which continue on to Panevėžys and Vilnius; Tallinn–Rakvere–Sillamäe–Narva–St Petersburg (six to nine daily); Tallinn–Tartu–Võru–Moscow (daily); Rīga–Valmiera–Tartu–Sillamäe–Narva–St Petersburg (nine to 10 daily).

UAB Toks (www2.toks.lt) Tallinn–Pärnu–Rīga–Panevėžys–Vilnius buses (two daily), with one continuing on to Kaunas and Warsaw.

Train

GoRail (www.gorail.ee) has direct trains to Tallinn from St Petersburg and Moscow. There are no direct trains to Latvia; you'll need to change at Valga.

SEA

Eckerö Line (www.eckeroline.fi; Passenger Terminal A, Varasadam; adult/child/car from €19/12/19) Twice-daily car ferry from Helsinki to Tallinn (2½ hours).

Linda Line (☑ 699 9331; www.lindaliini.ee; Linnahall Terminal) Small, passenger-only hydrofoils travel between Helsinki and Tallinn at least two times daily from late March to late December (from €25, 1½ hours). Weather dependent.

Tallink (☑ 640 9808; www.tallink.com; Terminal D, Lootsi 13) Four to seven car ferries daily between Helsinki and Tallinn (passenger/vehicle from €31/26). The huge *Baltic Princess* takes 3½ hours; newer high-speed ferries take two hours. They also have an overnight ferry between Stockholm and Tallinn, via the Åland islands (passenger/vehicle from €39/62, 18 hours).

Viking Line (☑ 666 3966; www.vikingline.com; Terminal A, Varasadam; passenger/vehicle from €29/26) Two daily car ferries between Helsinki and Tallinn (2½ hours).

Getting Around

BUS

Buses are a good option domestically, as they're more frequent than trains and cover many destinations not serviced by the limited rail network. **TPilet** (www.tpilet.ee) has schedules and prices for all services.

TRAIN

Trains are handy for getting between Tallinn and Tartu, but services to Pärnu are extremely limited.

COUNTRY FACTS

Area 45,226 sq km

Capital Tallinn

Country Code 372

Currency euro €

Emergency Ambulance & fire ☑ 112, police ☑ 110

Language Estonian

Money ATMs all over.

Visas Not required for citizens of the EU, USA, Canada, New Zealand and Australia.

EATING PRICE RANGES

The following Estonian price ranges refer to a standard main course.

€ less than €10

€€ €10 to €15

€€€ more than €15

Finland

Best Places to Eat

➡ Vanha Kauppahalli (p352)

➡ Olo (p350)

➡ Aanaar (p362)

➡ Hella & Huone (p356)

➡ Musta Lammas (p359)

➡ Smor (p354)

Best Places to Stay

➡ Hotel F6 (p349)

➡ Arctic Light Hotel (p360)

➡ Dream Hostel (p356)

➡ Lapland Hotel (p356)

➡ Lossiranta Lodge (p357)

➡ Hotelli Helka (p349)

Why Go?

Inspired design, technology and epicurean scenes meet epic stretches of wilderness here in Europe's deep north, where summer's endless light balances winter's eerie frozen magic.

Whatever the season, there's something pure in the Finnish air and spirit that's vital and exciting. With towering forests, speckled by picture-perfect lakes, Suomi offers some of Europe's best hiking, kayaking and canoeing. After the snowfall, pursuits include skiing, sledding with dogs or reindeer, snowmobiling or trekking across snowy solitudes, lit by a beautiful, pale winter sun. And of course, there's catching the majestic aurora borealis (Northern Lights).

Vibrant cities stock the south, headlined by the capital, Helsinki, a cutting-edge urban space with world-renowned design and music scenes where 'new Suomi' cuisine is flourishing, bringing locally foraged flavours to the fore. Beyond Helsinki, Tampere and Turku are especially engaging, with spirited university-student populations.

When to Go

Helsinki

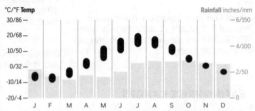

Mar–Apr There's still plenty of snow, but enough daylight to enjoy winter sports.

Jul Everlasting daylight, countless festivals and summer budget accommodation.

Sep The stunning *ruska* (autumn colours) season make this prime hiking time up north.

Finland Highlights

1 Helsinki (p348) Exploring Finland's harbourside capital, a creative melting pot for the latest in Finnish food, drink, design and nightlife.

2 Savonlinna (p357) Marvelling at the shimmering lakescapes of picturesque Savonlinna, and catching top-quality opera in its medieval castle.

3 Kuopio (p359) Cruising Lakeland waterways, dining on tiny lake fish, and sweating in the huge, sociable smoke sauna.

4 Rovaniemi (p360) Crossing the Arctic Circle, hitting the awesome Arktikum museum, and visiting Santa in his grotto.

5 Inari (p361) Learning about Sámi culture, husky-sledding and meeting reindeer in this northern Lapland village.

HELSINKI

⏱ 09 / POP 628,208

It's fitting that harbourside Helsinki, capital of a country with such watery geography, entwines so spectacularly with the Baltic's bays, inlets and islands.

While Helsinki can seem a younger sibling to the Scandinavian capitals, it's the one that went to art school, scorns pop music and works in a cutting-edge studio. The design scene here is one of the most electrifying in the world today, with boutiques, workshops and galleries proliferating in the Design District, Helsinki's thoroughfares and intriguing backstreets. The city's foodie scene is also flourishing, with hip eateries offering locally sourced tasting menus, craft-beer bars, coffee roasteries and microdistilleries popping up at dizzying speed.

◉ Sights

★ Tuomiokirkko
CHURCH

(Lutheran Cathedral; www.helsinginseurakunnat.fi; Unioninkatu 29; ⊙ 9am-midnight Jun-Aug, to 6pm Sep-May) FREE One of CL Engel's finest creations, the chalk-white neoclassical Lutheran cathedral presides over Senaatintori. Created to serve as a reminder of God's supremacy, its high flight of stairs is now a popular meeting place. Zinc statues of the 12 apostles guard the city from the roof of the church. The spartan, almost mausoleum-like interior has little ornamentation under the lofty dome apart from an altar painting and three stern statues of Reformation heroes Luther, Melanchthon and Mikael Agricola.

★ Ateneum
GALLERY

(www.ateneum.fi; Kaivokatu 2; adult/child €13/free; ⊙ 10am-6pm Tue & Fri, to 8pm Wed & Thu, to 5pm Sat & Sun) Occupying an 1887 building, Finland's premier art gallery offers a crash course in the nation's art. The top floor houses Finnish paintings and sculptures from the 'golden age' of the late 19th century through to the 1950s, including works by Albert Edelfelt, Hugo Simberg, Helene Schjerfbeck, the Von Wright brothers and Pekka Halonen. Pride of place goes to the prolific Akseli Gallen-Kallela's triptych from the *Kalevala* depicting Väinämöinen's pursuit of the maiden Aino.

Helsinki Art Museum
MUSEUM

(HAM; www.hamhelsinki.fi; Eteläinen Rautatiekatu 8; adult/child €10/free; ⊙ 11am-7pm Tue-Sun) Recently reopened after extensive renovations,

Helsinki's contemporary art museum oversees 9000 works including 3500 city-wide public artworks. The overwhelming majority of its 20th- and 21st-century works are by Finnish artists; it also presents rotating exhibitions by emerging artists. There's always at least one free exhibition that doesn't require a ticket to the museum's main section.

Kamppi Chapel
CHAPEL

(www.helsinginseurakunnat.fi; Simonkatu 7; ⊙ 8am-8pm Mon-Fri, 10am-6pm Sat & Sun) FREE Built in 2012 by Helsinki architectural firm K2S, this exquisite, ultra-contemporary curvilinear chapel is constructed entirely from wood (wax-treated spruce outside; oiled alder planks inside, with pews crafted from ash), and offers a moment of quiet contemplation in cocoon-like surrounds. Its altar cross is the work of blacksmith Antti Nieminen. Known as the Chapel of Silence, the Lutheran chapel is ecumenical and welcomes people of all (or no) faiths.

🏃 Activities

★ Allas Sea Pool
SWIMMING

(www.allasseapool.fi; Katajanokanlaituri 2; day ticket adult/child €9/6, towel/swimwear rental each €5; ⊙ 6.30am-10pm Mon-Thu, 6.30am-midnight Fri, 8am-midnight Sat, 8am-10pm Sun) Built from Finnish fir, this swimming complex opened in 2016 and sits right on the harbour against a spectacular city backdrop. It incorporates a bracing Baltic sea-water pool, two freshwater pools (one for adults, one for kids; both heated to 27°C) and three saunas (male, female and mixed). Regular events include DJs or full-moon all-night nude swimming. Its restaurant serves Nordic cuisine.

⌖ Tours

Cruise companies depart on various harbour jaunts from the *kauppatori* (market square) in summer.

An excellent budget tour is to do a circuit of town on Tram 2; pick up the free route map from the tourist office as your guide.

🛏 Sleeping

From mid-May to mid-August bookings are strongly advisable, although July is a quieter time for business and high-end hotels.

Hostel Diana Park
HOSTEL €

(⏱ 09-642169; www.dianapark.fi; Uudenmaankatu 9; dm/s/d from €31/55/68; ☎) More like a guesthouse, Helsinki's most characterful and laid-back hostel occupies the top floor of a building in a lively street of bars and restaurants. Its 50 beds are spread across 15 rooms; all share bathrooms but have in-room sinks. Private rooms offer more peace and there's a great lounge for socialising. HI members get 10% off; breakfast costs €7.

★ **Hotelli Helka**   HOTEL €€
(✆ 09-613580; www.hotelhelka.com; Pohjoinen Rautatiekatu 23; s €110-150, d €140-180, ste from €206; P ♠) One of the centre's best mid-range hotels, the Helka has friendly staff and excellent facilities, including parking (€28) if you can bag one of the 28 spots. Best are the rooms, with Alvar Aalto–designed furniture, ice-block bedside lights and a backlit print of a rural Suomi scene over the bed. Saunas are situated on the top floor adjoining the rooftop terrace.

Hotel Indigo   BOUTIQUE HOTEL €€
(✆ 020-048-105; www.ihg.com; Bulevardi 26; d/ste from €149/207; P ✴ @ ♠) Helsinki's first branch of branded boutique chain Hotel Indigo opened in the heart of the Design District in 2016. Local artists designed and painted unique murals that splash colour across all 120 rooms; suites have tubs with spa jets. Free bikes are available for guests; there's also a free on-site gym. Bröd, its restaurant, serves Nordic cuisine. Breakfast costs €15.

★ **Hotel F6**   BOUTIQUE HOTEL €€€
(✆ 09-6899-9666; www.hotelf6.fi; Fabianinkatu 6; s/d incl breakfast from €120/150; ✴ ♠) 🖉 Stunningly designed, this hotel opened in 2016 and ranges around an internal courtyard (some rooms have direct access and patios); superior rooms come with French balconies. All 66 rooms are spacious (even the smallest are 27 sq metres) and stylishly furnished with cushion-strewn sofas. The courtyard also has a herb garden supplying the bar. Breakfast is organic; wind and water powers all electricity.

✗ **Eating**

Good budget options are in short supply but lunch specials are available in most places and there are plenty of self-catering opportunities.

Karl Fazer Café   CAFE €
(www.fazer.fi; Kluuvikatu 3; dishes €4-12; ⏲ 7.30am-10pm Mon-Fri, 9am-10pm Sat, 10am-6pm Sun; ♠🖉) Founded in 1891 and fronted by a striking art deco facade, this cavernous classic cafe is the flagship for Fazer's chocolate empire. The glass cupola reflects sound, so locals say it's a bad place to gossip. It's ideal, however, for buying dazzling confectionery, fresh bread, salmon or shrimp sandwiches, or digging into towering sundaes or spectacular cakes. Gluten-free dishes are available.

★ **Kuu**   FINNISH €€
(✆ 09-2709-0973; www.ravintolakuu.fi; Töölönkatu 27; mains €19-30, 2-/3-course lunch menus €24/28, 4-course dinner menus €48-51; ⏲ 11.30am-midnight Mon-Fri, 2pm-midnight Sat, 2-10pm Sun) Traditional Finnish fare is given a sharp, contemporary twist at Kuu, which creates dishes from local ingredients such as smoked reindeer heart with pickled forest mushrooms, poached pike-perch with Lappish fingerling potatoes, and liquorice ice cream with cloudberry soup. Wines are pricey, but there are some interesting choices. Its casual bistro sibling KuuKuu is located 800m south.

The Cock   PUB FOOD €€
(✆ 050-352-3486; www.thecock.fi; Fabianinkatu 17; mains lunch €12-22, dinner €22-28; ⏲ kitchen 7.30am-11pm Mon-Fri, noon-11pm Sat, bar to 2am Mon-Sat; ♠) Newcomer The Cock combines a free-wheeling bar with ping-pong tables (hosting regular tournaments) and brilliant cocktails (such as a Helsinki G&T with pink

ITINERARIES

One Week

Helsinki demands at least a couple of days and is a good base for a day trip to **Tallinn** (Estonia) or **Porvoo**. In summer head to the **Lakeland** and explore **Savonlinna** and **Kuopio** (catch a lake ferry between them). In winter take an overnight train or budget flight to **Lapland**, visiting Santa, exploring Sámi culture and mushing with huskies. A Helsinki–Savonlinna–Kuopio–Rovaniemi–Helsinki route is a good option.

Two Weeks

Spend a few days in **Helsinki** and **Porvoo**, visit the harbour town of **Turku** and lively **Tampere**. Next stops are **Savonlinna** and **Kuopio** in the beautiful **Lakeland**. Head up to **Rovaniemi**, and perhaps as far north as the Sámi capital **Inari**. You could also fit in a summer festival, some hiking, or a quick cycling trip to **Åland**.

grapefruit, lingonberry and Helsinki dry gin) together with seriously good food, from breakfast (sweet-potato toast with hummus and avocado) through to lunch (seared locally caught salmon with kale) and dinner (herb-crusted Åland lamb with truffle risotto).

⭐Olo   FINNISH €€€
(☏010-320-6250; www.olo-ravintola.fi; Pohjois-esplanadi 5; 4-course lunch menu €52, dinner tasting menus €73-149, with paired wines €153-315; ⊗11.30am-3pm & 6pm-midnight Tue-Fri, 6pm-midnight Sat) Considered Helsinki's best restaurant, Michelin-starred Olo occupies a handsome 19th-century harbourside mansion. It's at the forefront of modern Suomi cuisine, and its memorable degustation menus incorporate both the forage ethos and molecular gastronomy, and feature culinary jewels such as herring with fermented cucumber, Åland lamb with blackcurrant leaves, juniper-marinated reindeer carpac-

cio, and Arctic crab with root celery. Book a few weeks ahead.

🍷 Drinking & Nightlife

The city centre is full of bars and clubs. For the cheapest beer in Helsinki (€3 to €4 a pint), hit working-class Kallio (near Sörnäinen metro station), north of the centre.

⭐Birri   MICROBREWERY
(Il Birrificio; www.ilbirri.fi; Fredrikinkatu 22; ⊗11am-11pm Mon-Thu, to 1am Fri & Sat, to 4pm Sun) Birri brews three of its own beers on-site at any one time, stocks a fantastic range of Finnish-only craft beers, and also handcrafts its own seasonally changing sausages. The space is strikingly done out with Arctic-white metro tiles, brown-and-white chequerboard floor tiles, exposed timber beams and gleaming silver kegs. Weekend brunch, from 11am to 1.30pm, is among Helsinki's best.

Andante
CAFE

(Fredrikinkatu 20; ⊙11am-6pm Mon, Thu & Fri, to 5.30pm Sat & Sun; 🛜) Design District hang-out Andante is both a fragrant florist selling pot plants and bouquets of blooms and a cafe brewing organic, fair-trade coffee etched with intricate coffee art (oat milk available). There's also a wide range of Chinese teas, seasonal smoothies and juices, and snacks such as raw cakes with raspberry and goji berry or green tea and lingonberry.

Bar Loose
BAR, CLUB

(www.barloose.com; Annankatu 21; ⊙6pm-2am Tue, to 4am Wed-Sun; 🛜) The scarlet-coloured interior seems too stylish for a rock bar, but that's what Bar Loose is, with portraits of guitar heroes lining one wall and an eclectic crowd upstairs, served by two bars. Downstairs is a club area, with live music more nights than not and DJs spinning everything from metal to mod/retro classics. Drinks are decently priced.

☆ Entertainment

★ Musiikkitalo
CONCERT VENUE

(Helsinki Music Centre; www.musiikkitalo.fi; Mannerheimintie 13; tickets free to €30) Home to the Helsinki Philharmonic Orchestra, Finnish Radio Symphony Orchestra and Sibelius Academy, the glass- and copper-fronted Helsinki Music Centre, opened in 2011, hosts a diverse program of classical, jazz, folk and pop music. The 1704-capacity main auditorium, visible from the foyer, has stunning acoustics. Five smaller halls seat 140 to 400. Tickets are available at the door and from www.ticketmaster.fi.

Tavastia
LIVE MUSIC

(www.tavastiaklubi.fi; Urho Kekkosenkatu 4; ⊙8pm-1am Sun-Thu, to 3am Fri, to 4am Sat) One of Helsinki's legendary rock venues, Tavastia attracts both up-and-coming local acts and bigger international groups, with a band every night of the week. Also check out what's on at its adjoining venue, Semifinal, where new talent and young local bands take the stage.

🛍 Shopping

Helsinki is a design epicentre, from fashion to furniture and homewares. Its hub is the Design District Helsinki (https://designdistrict.fi), spread out between chic Esplanadi to the east, retro-hipster Punavuori to the south and Kamppi to the west. Hundreds of shops, studios and galleries are mapped on its website; you can also pick up a map at the tourist office.

★ Tre   DESIGN
(www.worldoftre.com; Mikonkatu 6; ⏰ 11am-9pm Mon-Fri, to 6pm Sat) If you only have time to visit one design store in Helsinki, this 2016-opened emporium is a brilliant bet, showcasing the works of Finnish designers in fashion, jewellery and accessories including umbrellas, furniture, ceramics, textiles, stationery and art. A superb range of architectural and design books help provide inspiration. Its vegan cafe serves soups, great coffee and scrumptious cakes.

Sweet Story   FOOD
(www.sweetstory.fi; Katariinankatu 3; ⏰ 10am-6pm Tue-Fri, 11am-4pm Sat) 🍴 Handmade caramels, liquorices (including a traditional Finnish variety with tar) and a rainbow of boiled sweets at this fantasyland are all organic and free from gluten, lactose and artificial colours and preservatives. Most are made at Sweet Story's own Helsinki workshop;

there's also a handful of other specialities from Denmark, Lithuania and Austria.

ℹ Information

Large parts of the city centre have free wi-fi.
Helsinki City Tourist Office (📞 09-3101-3300; www.visithelsinki.fi; Pohjoisesplanadi 19; ⏰ 9am-6pm Mon-Sat, to 4pm Sun mid-May–mid-Sep, 9am-6pm Mon-Fri, 10am-4pm Sat & Sun mid-Sep–mid-May) Busy multilingual office with reams of information on the city. Also has an office at the airport (Terminal 2, Helsinki-Vantaa airport; ⏰ 10am-8pm May-Sep, 10am-6pm Mon-Sat, noon-6pm Sun Oct-Apr).

ℹ Getting There & Away

AIR
Helsinki-Vantaa Airport (p364), 19km north of the capital, is Finland's main air terminus. Direct flights serve many major European cities and several intercontinental destinations.

Finnair (www.finnair.com) covers 18 Finnish cities, usually at least once per day.

BOAT
International ferries sail to Stockholm, Tallinn, St Petersburg and German destinations. There is also regular fast-boat service to Tallinn. There are five main ferry terminals.

BUS
Kamppi bus station (www.matkahuolto.fi; Salomonkatu) has a terminal for local buses to Espoo in one wing, while longer-distance buses also depart from here to destinations throughout Finland. From Kamppi bus station, **OnniBus** (p365) runs budget routes to several Finnish cities.

TRAIN
Helsinki's central **train station** (Rautatieasema; www.vr.fi; Kaivokatu 1) is linked to the metro (Rautatientori stop) and situated 500m east of Kamppi bus station.

HELSINKI'S MARKET HALLS

While food stalls, fresh produce and berries can be found at the kauppatori (market square), the real centre of Finnish market produce is the kauppahalli (market hall). There are three in central Helsinki, including **Vanha Kauppahalli** (www.vanhakauppahalli.fi; Eteläranta 1; ⏰ 8am-6pm Mon-Sat; 🚇) 🍴 alongside the harbour. Built in 1888, it's still a traditional Finnish market, with wooden stalls selling local flavours such as liquorice, Finnish cheeses, smoked salmon and herring, berries, forest mushrooms and herbs. Its centrepiece is its superb new cafe, **Story** (www.restaurantstory.fi; Vanha Kauppahalli, Eteläranta; snacks €2.70-9.50, mains €10.50-16.90; ⏰ kitchen 8am-3pm Mon-Fri, to 5pm Sat, bar to 6pm Mon-Sat; 🚇) 🍴 .

Hakaniemen Kauppahalli (www.hakaniemenkauppahalli.fi; Hämeentie 1; ⏰ 8am-6pm Mon-Fri, to 4pm Sat; 🚇) 🍴 and **Hietalahden Kauppahalli** (www.hietalahdenkauppahalli.fi; Lönnrotinkatu 34; ⏰ 8am-6pm Mon & Tue, to 10pm Wed-Sat, 10am-4pm Sun Jun-Aug, closed Sun Sep-May; 🚇) 🍴 are also perfect for picking up picnic ingredients.

The train is the fastest and cheapest way to get from Helsinki to major Finnish centres; there are also daily trains to Russia.

ⓘ Getting Around

TO/FROM THE AIRPORT

Bus 615 (€5, 50 minutes, every 30 minutes, 24 hours) shuttles between Helsinki-Vantaa Airport (platform 21) and platform 3 at Rautatientori next to Helsinki's train station.

Faster **Finnair buses** (www.finnair.com; Elielinaukio) depart from Elielinaukio platform 30 outside Helsinki's train station (€6.30, 30 minutes, every 20 minutes, 5am to midnight). The last service leaves the airport at 1.10am.

Opened in 2015, Helsinki's airport–city rail link (€5.50, 30 minutes, up to six hourly from 5am to 12.15am) serves the central train station.

BICYCLE

With a flat inner city and well-marked cycling paths, Helsinki is ideal for cycling. Pick up the free *Ulkoilukartta* Helsinki cycling map at the tourist office or view it online at www.ulkoilukartta.fi.

Launched in 2016, Helsinki's shared-bike scheme City Bikes (www.hsl.fi/citybikes) has some 1500 bikes at 150 stations citywide. Bikes per 30/60/90/120 minutes are free/€0.50/€1.50/€2.50. Register online, or pick up a bike at five locations – Hakaniemi metro station, Rautatientori bus station, Kiasma, Kaivopuisto or Unioninkatu – with just a credit card. City Bike station locations are mapped at www.reittiopas.fi.

LOCAL TRANSPORT

HSL (www.hsl.fi) operates buses, metro, local trains, trams and the Suomenlinna ferry. A one-hour flat-fare ticket for any HSL transport costs €3.20 when purchased on board or €2.70 when purchased in advance. Day or multiday tickets (per 24/48/72 hours €8/12/16, tickets up to seven days available) are worthwhile. Buy tickets at the Rautatientori and Hakaniemi metro stations, R-kioskis and the tourist office.

TURKU

🖉 02 / POP 185,908

Turku's historic castle and cathedral point to the city's rich cultural history when it was the Finnish capital. Contemporary Turku is a hotbed of experimental art and vibrant festivals, thanks in part to the country's second-largest university population.

FINLAND'S FORTRESS

Suomenlinna (Sveaborg; www.suomenlinna.fi), the 'fortress of Finland', is set on a cluster of islands connected by bridges. The Unesco World Heritage site was originally built by the Swedes as Sveaborg in the mid-18th century. Several museums, former bunkers and fortress walls, as well as Finland's only remaining WWII submarine, are fascinating to explore; its **tourist office** (🖉0295-338 410; www.suomenlinna.fi; ⏱10am-6pm May-Sep, 10am-4pm Oct-Apr) has info. Cafes and picnic spots are plentiful.

Ferries (www.hsl.fi; single/return €2.80/5, 15 minutes, three times hourly, fewer in winter) depart from the passenger quay at Helsinki's **Kauppatori**.

ⓞ Sights

★**Turun Linna**   CASTLE
(Turku Castle; 🖉02-262-0300; www.turku.fi/turunlinna; Linnankatu 80; adult/child €9/5, guided tours €2; ⏱10am-6pm daily Jun-Aug, Tue-Sun Sep-May) Founded in 1280 at the mouth of the Aurajoki, mammoth Turku Castle is easily Finland's largest. Highlights include two dungeons and sumptuous banqueting halls, as well as a fascinating **historical museum** of medieval Turku in the castle's Old Bailey. Models depict the castle's growth from a simple island fortress to a Renaissance palace. Guided tours in English run several times daily from June to August.

★**Turun Tuomiokirkko**   CATHEDRAL
(Turku Cathedral; 🖉040-341-7100; www.turunseurakunnat.fi; Tuomiokirkonkatu 1; cathedral free, museum adult/child €2/1; ⏱cathedral & museum 9am-6pm) The 'mother church' of Finland's Lutheran faith, Turku Cathedral towers over the town. Consecrated in 1300, the colossal brick Gothic building was rebuilt many times over the centuries after damaging fires.

Upstairs, a small **museum** traces the stages of the cathedral's construction, and contains medieval sculptures and religious paraphernalia.

Free **summer organ concerts** (www.turkuorgan.fi) take place at 8pm Tuesday. English-language services are held at 4pm every Sunday except the last of the month year-round.

★ **Aboa Vetus & Ars Nova**   MUSEUM, GALLERY
(www.aboavetusarsnova.fi; Itäinen Rantakatu 4-6; adult/child €9/5.50; ⊘11am-7pm) Art and archaeology unite here under one roof. Aboa Vetus (Old Turku) draws you underground to Turku's medieval streets, showcasing some of the 37,000 artefacts unearthed from the site (digs still continue). Back in the present, Ars Nova (New Art) presents contemporary art exhibitions. The themed Turku Biennaali (www.turkubiennaali.fi) takes place here in summer of odd-numbered years. English-language tours lasting 45 minutes (included in admission) take place daily from 11.30am in July and August.

✹ Festivals & Events

★ **Ruisrock**   MUSIC
(www.ruisrock.fi; 3-day ticket €145) For three days each summer, Finland's oldest and largest annual rock festival – held since 1969 and attracting 100,000-strong crowds – takes over Ruissalo island.

⊨ Sleeping

Laivahostel Borea   HOSTEL €
(☑040-843-6611; www.msborea.fi; Linnankatu 72; dm/s/d/tr/q from €26/41/64/99/125; P♠) Built in Sweden in 1960, the enormous passenger ship SS *Bore* is docked outside the Forum Marinum museum, just 500m northeast of the ferry terminal. It now contains an award-winning HI-affiliated hostel with 120 vintage ensuite cabins. Most are squishy, but if you want room to spread out, higher-priced doubles have a lounge area. Rates include a morning sauna.

★ **Park Hotel**   BOUTIQUE HOTEL €€
(☑02-273-2555; www.parkhotelturku.fi; Rauhankatu 1; s €89-135, d €129-165, ste €180-205; P♠) Overlooking a hilly park, this art nouveau building is a genuine character, with a resident squawking parrot, Jaakko, and classical music playing in the lift/elevator. Its 20 rooms are decorated in a lovably chintzy style and equipped with minibars. Family owners and facilities, such as a lounge with pool table, make it the antithesis of a chain hotel.

✗ Eating

CaféArt   CAFE €
(www.cafeart.fi; Läntinen Rantakatu 5; dishes €2.20-6.40; ⊘10am-7pm Mon-Fri, to 5pm Sat, 11am-5pm Sun) serves superb coffee and sublime cakes.

Tårget   MODERN EUROPEAN €€
(☑040-0522-707; www.matbar.fi; Linnankatu 3A; pizzas €13-16, mains €20-26; ⊘kitchen 11am-9.30pm Mon-Fri, noon-9.30pm Sat, bar to 10pm Mon-Thu, to 2am Fri, 3am Sat) Tårget has a vaulted-cellar wine bar and mezzanine cocktail bar with live funk, jazz or folk on weekends. But above all it's worth hitting for exceptional pizzas (Parma ham, figs, honey and goats cheese; crayfish, lemon crème fraîche, dill and red onion) and à la carte creations (sugar-salted pike-perch with grilled fennel; beef brisket with forest mushrooms; seabuckthorn sorbet with rum-marinated blueberries).

★ **Smor**   GASTRONOMY €€€
(☑02-536-9444; www.smor.fi; Läntinen Rantakatu 3; mains lunch €10-18, dinner €21-30, 3-course lunch menu €28, 4-course dinner menu €57; ⊘11am-2pm & 4.30-10pm Mon-Fri, 4.30-10pm Sat) A vaulted cellar lit by flickering candles makes a romantic backdrop for stunning, often organic, locally sourced cuisine: roast Åland lamb with corn mousse and forest-mushroom jus, pike-perch with cauliflower-and-raw-apple purée, or ox cheek with beetroot and cranberry sauce. Desserts such as blueberry and white-chocolate ganache with cloudberry crème, or lingonberry panna cotta with summer berry sauce are equally inspired.

🍷 Drinking & Nightlife

Boat bars such as Donna (www.donna.fi; Itäinen Rantakatu; ⊘11am-3am Apr-Sep) open along the river from around April to September.

★ **Tiirikkala**   COCKTAIL BAR
(www.tiirikkala.fi; Linnankatu 3; ⊘11am-10pm Tue-Thu, to 2am Fri & Sat, noon-10pm Sun) Fresh from a cool, contemporary Nordic–style makeover, this gorgeous old wooden house opens to a street-level terrace and fabulous roof terrace. Unique cocktails include When You Walk in the Room (Akvavit, rhubarb liqueur and red carrot juice) and Meet Me in the Alleyway (cognac and grape juice). Soul, jazz and blues head up its weekend live-music program. Great weekend brunch.

ℹ Information

Tourist Office (☑02-262-7444; www.visitturku.fi; Aurakatu 4; ⊘8.30am-6pm Mon-Fri, 9am-4pm Sat & Sun Apr-Sep, 8.30am-6pm Mon-Fri, 10am-3pm Sat & Sun Oct-Mar; ♠) Busy but helpful office with information on the entire region.

ℹ️ Getting There & Away

BOAT

The harbour, southwest of the city centre, has terminals for Tallink/Silja and Viking Line services to Stockholm (10½ hours) via the Åland islands.

BUS

From the main **bus station** (www.matkahuolto. fi; Aninkaistenkatu 20) there are frequent services to Helsinki (€25, 2½ hours, up to four hourly) and Tampere (€22, 2½ hours, hourly).

TRAIN

Turku's train station is 400m northwest of the city centre; trains also stop at the ferry harbour.

Destinations include the following:

Helsinki (€20, two hours, every two hours)

Rovaniemi (€96, 12 hours, four daily) With a change in Oulu or Pasila.

Tampere (€20, 1¾ hours, three daily)

ℹ️ Getting Around

The tourist office hires bikes (per half-/full day €15/20) and publishes an excellent free *pyörätiekartta* (bike-route map) of the city and surrounding towns.

Bus 1 runs between the harbour, kauppatori and airport (day/night €3/4).

TAMPERE

📱 03 / POP 225,485

Set between two vast lakes, scenic Tampere has a down-to-earth vitality that makes it a favourite for many visitors. The Tammerkoski rapids churn through the centre, flanked by grassy banks, which contrast with the red brick of the imposing fabric mills that once drove the city's economy. Regenerated industrial buildings now house quirky museums, enticing shops, pubs, cinemas and cafes.

◎ Sights

★**Tuomiokirkko**   CHURCH
(www.tampereenseurakunnat.fi; Tuomiokirkonkatu 3; ⊙10am-5pm May-Aug, 11am-3pm Sep-Apr) **FREE** An iconic example of National Romantic architecture, Tampere's cathedral dates from 1907. Hugo Simberg created the frescoes and stained glass; you'll appreciate that they were controversial. A procession of ghostly childlike apostles holds the 'garland of life', graves and plants are tended by skeletal figures, and a wounded angel is stretchered off by two children. Magnus Enckell's dreamlike Resurrection altarpiece

WORTH A TRIP

PORVOO

Finland's second-oldest town is an ever-popular day trip or weekender from Helsinki. **Porvoo** (Swedish: Borgå) officially became a town in 1380, but even before that it was an important trading post. The town's fabulous historic centre includes the famous brick-red former warehouses along the river that once stored goods bound for destinations across Europe. During the day, Old Town craft shops are bustling with visitors, but staying on a weeknight will mean you could have the place more or less to yourself. The old painted buildings are spectacular in the setting sun.

Buses depart for Porvoo from Helsinki's Kamppi bus station (€9, one hour, up to six per hour).

is designed in similar style. The symbolist stonework and disturbing colours of the stained glass add to the haunting ambience.

★**Amurin Työläismuseokortteli**   MUSEUM
(Amuri Museum of Workers' Housing; www.museo kortteli.fi; Satakunnankatu 49; adult/child €7/3; ⊙10am-6pm Tue-Sun mid-May–mid-Sep) An entire block of wooden houses, including 32 apartments, a bakery, a shoemaker, two general shops and a cafe, is preserved at the Amuri Museum of Workers' Housing, evoking life from 1882 to 1973. Entertaining backstories (English translation available) give plenty of historical information. Its on-site Café Amurin Helmi serves breakfast, soups, breads, cakes and pastries (baked on the premises).

★**Särkänniemi**   AMUSEMENT PARK
(www.sarkanniemi.fi; Laiturikatu 1; adult/child under 100cm day pass €19.90/free, evening ticket from 9pm €9.90/free; ⊙rides mid-May–Aug, hrs vary) This promontory-set amusement park complex offers dozens of rides, an observation tower, art gallery, aquarium, farm zoo and planetarium. Among the best rides are the Tornado roller coaster, super-fast High Voltage, speedboat rides on the lake and an Angry Birds area for younger kids. Opening times are complex; check the website. Indoor attractions stay open year-round. Take bus 20 from the train station or central square.

THE ÅLAND ARCHIPELAGO

The glorious Åland archipelago is a geo-political anomaly: the islands belong to Finland, speak Swedish, but have their own parliament, flag and stamps. Åland is the sunniest spot in northern Europe and its sweeping white-sand beaches and flat, scenic cycling routes have great appeal. Outside the lively capital, Mariehamn, a sleepy haze hangs over the islands' tiny villages and finding your own remote beach among the 6500 skerries and islets is surprisingly easy. A lattice of bridges and free cable ferries connect the central islands, while larg-er car ferries run to the archipelago's outer reaches. Several car ferries head to Åland, including those that connect Turku and Helsinki with Stockholm. Bikes are the best way to explore and are easily rented.

☞ Tours

Boat trips on Tampere's magnificent lakes are extremely popular in summer; the tour-ist office has seasonal schedules.

🛏 Sleeping

★ Dream Hostel   HOSTEL €

(☏ 045-236-0517; www.dreamhostel.fi; Åkerlund-inkatu 2; dm/s/tw/d/q from €19.80/59/62/65/89; ☜) ✎ With its cool, contemporary Nordic design and fantastic facilities, this spacious hostel is consistently ranked Finland's best. It has switched-on staff; super-comfortable wide-berth dorms (unisex and female) in various sizes; amenities including bike hire; free tea and coffee; a fully kitted-out self-catering kitchen; and a book exchange. It's a 200m walk southeast of the train station in a quiet area.

★ Lapland Hotel   DESIGN HOTEL €€

(☏ 03-383-000; www.laplandhotels.com; Yliopis-tonkatu 44; d/ste incl breakfast from €117/313; ℗ ✻ ☜) Although well south of Lapland, this stunning new property 300m east of the train station evokes the country's northern latitudes in its 141 rooms, where themes include Northern Lights, Ruska (autumn leaves), Summer and Winter. Suites have in-room saunas; low-allergen and accessible rooms are available. Its restaurant, Dabbal,

serves Lappish cuisine, such as reindeer with celery root and juniper sauce.

✗ Eating

Tampere's speciality, *mustamakkara,* is a mild, tasty sausage made with cow's blood, normally eaten with lingonberry jam. Try it at the kauppahalli (covered market) or Lau-kontori Market.

Bull   BURGERS €

(www.gastropub.net/bull; Hatanpään valtatie 4; burgers €14.50-18.50; ⏰ 10.30am-11pm Mon-Thu, 10.30am-1am Fri, 1pm-1am Sat, 1pm-11pm Sun; ✎) Patties made from 100% Black Angus beef are the centrepiece of many of Bull's towering burgers, including Dirty Harry (with blue cheese and red onion) and the Highlander (with a whisky-infused patty). It also has a horse meat version, My Little Pony (with smoked cheese and beetroot), as well as veggie and vegan options cooked on a separate grill.

★ Tuulensuu   EUROPEAN €€

(www.gastropub.net/tuulensuu; Hämeenpuisto 23; mains €14-24.50; ⏰ kitchen 3pm-midnight Sun-Fri, noon-midnight Sat, bar to 2am daily; ☜) Tampere's best gastropub overflows with locals thanks to its superb range of Belgian beers, good wines, lengthy port menu and gourmet bar snacks, such as fresh-roasted almonds. Bis-tro fare inspired by Germany, Belgium and northeastern France includes mussels in white wine, smoked pork neck with sauer-kraut, fried frogs' legs and hops-marinated artichokes, and creamy forest-mushroom soup.

★ Hella & Huone   GASTRONOMY €€€

(☏ 010-322-3898; http://hellajahuone.fi; Salho-jankatu 48; 6-/12-course menu €65/95, with paired wines €123/175; ⏰ 6-10pm Thu-Sat) Acclaimed chef Arto Rastas serves cutting-edge molec-ular Nordic cuisine at this minimalistic spot with black high-backed chairs providing a sharp contrast to the stark white tablecloths. Lamb tartare with smoked egg yolk, pike-perch with lichen sauce, lobster with Arctic herb butter, wild duck with blueberry dust, and gin-marinated boysenberries with gin ice cream are among Rastas' seasonal creations.

🍷 Drinking & Nightlife

Mokkamestarit (http://mokkamestarit.fi; Ver-katehtaankatu 9; ⏰ 10am-6pm Mon-Fri, to 4pm Sat; ☜) ✎ roasts its own heavenly coffee. Café

Europa (www.ravintola.fi/cafe-europa; Aleksanterinkatu 29; ☺ noon-midnight Mon & Tue, to 2am Wed & Thu, to 3am Fri & Sat, 1pm-midnight Sun; ☎) is a glorious 1930s-style meeting spot. For cocktails with a view, head to Finland's highest bar, **Moro Sky Bar** (www.sokoshotels.fi/en/tampere/solo-sokos-hotel-torni-tampere/restaurants; Ratapihankatu 43; ☺ 11am-midnight Sun-Tue, to 2am Wed-Sat).

🛍 Shopping

Taito Pirkanmaa GIFTS & SOUVENIRS
(www.taitopirkanmaa.fi; Hatanpään valtatie 4A; ☺ 10am-6pm Mon-Fri, to 3pm Sat) 🌿 Sells handcrafted Finish products.

ℹ Information

Visit Tampere (☑ 03-5656-6800; www.visittampere.fi; Hämeenkatu 14B; ☺ 9am-6pm Mon-Fri, 10am-3pm Sat & Sun Jun-Aug, 10am-5pm Mon-Fri, to 3pm Sat Sep-May; ☎) On the main street in the centre of town. Can book activities and events.

ℹ Getting There & Away

AIR

Tampere-Pirkkala Airport (TMP; www.finavia.fi; Tornikaari 50) is 17km southwest of the city.
AirBaltic Flies to Riga.
Finnair Flies to Helsinki (though the train is more convenient), with connections to other Finnish cities.
SAS Flies to Stockholm.

BUS

From the **bus station** (Hatanpään valtatie 7), express buses serve Helsinki (€27, 2¾ hours, up to four hourly) and Turku (€22, 2½ hours, hourly). There are services to most other major towns in Finland.

TRAIN

Trains link Tampere's central **train station** (www.vr.fi; Rautatienkatu 25) with Helsinki (€21, 1¾ hours, up to three hourly), Turku (€20, 1¾ hours, three daily) and other cities.

LAKELAND

Most of Finland could be dubbed lakeland, but around here it seems there's more aqua than terra firma. Reflecting the sky and forests as clearly as a mirror, the sparkling, clean water leaves an indelible impression.

Savonlinna

📱 015 / POP 35,504

One of Finland's prettiest towns, Savonlinna shimmers on a sunny day as the water ripples around its centre. Set on islands between Haapavesi and Pihlajavesi lakes, its centrepiece is the dramatic castle Olavinlinna, perched on a rocky islet.

⊙ Sights

★ **Olavinlinna** CASTLE
(www.kansallismuseo.fi; Olavinlinna; adult/child €9/4.50; ☺ 11am-6pm Jun–mid-Aug, 10am-4pm Mon-Fri, 11am-4pm Sat & Sun mid-Aug–mid-Dec & Jan-May) Built directly on a rock in the middle of the lake (reached by bridges), this heavily restored 15th-century fortification is also the stunning venue for July's month-long **Savonlinna Opera Festival**. To visit the upper part of the interior, including the towers and chapel, you must join an hour-long guided tour (English tours hourly June to mid-August; check languages at other times). Guides bring the castle to life with vivid details of daily life here.

🛏 Sleeping

★ **Lossiranta Lodge** BOUTIQUE HOTEL €€
(☑ 044-511-2323; www.lossiranta.net; Aino Acktén Puistotie; incl breakfast d €85-145, f €175-210; P ☎ ♨) 🌿 Olavinlinna Castle looms opposite this rural-like retreat offering five doubles in the main building with their own

---

FINLAND SAVONLINNA

SAUNAS

For centuries the sauna has been a place to meditate, warm up and even give birth, and most Finns still use it at least once a week. Saunas are usually taken in the nude (public saunas are nearly always sex-segregated) and Finns are quite strict about its nonsexual – even sacred – nature.

Shower first. Once inside (with a temperature of 80°C to 100°C), water is thrown onto the stove using a *kauhu* (ladle), producing *löyly* (steam). A *vihta* (whisk of birch twigs and leaves, known as a *vasta* in eastern Finland) is sometimes used to lightly strike the skin, improving circulation. Cool off with a cold shower or preferably by jumping into a lake. Repeat. The sauna beer afterwards is also traditional.

OFF THE BEATEN TRACK

THE SEAL LAKES

Easily reached from Savonlinna, the watery Linnansaari and Kolovesi National Parks are great to explore by canoe and are the habitat of a rare inland seal. See www.outdoors.fi for information on the parks, and www.oravivillage.com for transport, accommodation, activities and equipment-hire services in the area.

entrance and terrace, and an annexe, Tavis Inn, housing another two doubles and five family rooms with small kitchens tucked into cupboards. All are stylishly decorated; personal touches include vases and woollen blankets. There's a lakefront spa and sauna and a private pier.

Perhehotelli Hospitz   HOTEL €€

(☑015-515-661; www.hospitz.com; Linnankatu 20; s €88-130, d €98-200, tr €125-195, q €145-215; ☺Apr-Dec; ⓟ🛜) Dating from the 1930s, this cosy Savonlinna classic retains many of its original fittings. Rooms are elegant, although beds are narrow and bathrooms small; larger family rooms are available. Balconies cost a little extra. The apple-tree-shaded terrace overlooks the harbour, with access to a small beach. Opera atmosphere is great with a midnight buffet: book aeons in advance.

🍴 Eating & Drinking

The lakeside kauppatori (market square) is the place for snacking. A traditional *lörtsy* (turnover) comes savoury with meat *(lihalörtsy)* or sweet with apple *(omenalörtsy)* or cloudberry *(lakkalörtsy)*. Savonlinna is also famous for fried *muikku* (vendace, or whitefish, a small lake fish). Restaurants open later during the opera festival; many have reduced hours from September to May and some close altogether.

Café Alegria   CAFE €

(www.cafealegria.net; Puistokatu 3; dishes €3.30-9.60; ☺9am-7pm Mon-Fri, 10am-5pm Sat, noon-4pm Sun Jun-Aug, 10am-7pm Mon-Fri, to 3pm Sat Sep-May; 🍴) Artworks from monthly changing exhibitions are for sale at this snug cafe. Dishes range from scrambled eggs with reindeer blood sausage to goats cheese tarts and home-baked cakes (cherry-chocolate, blueberry and carrot...). Its soup of the day

(which might be paprika and whitefish, sweet potato and lentil, or chanterelle mushrooms), comes with bread, spreads and refillable tea or coffee.

Kahvila Saima   CAFE

(☑015-515-340; www.kahvilasaima.net; Linnankatu 11; dishes €6.50-16.50; ☺10am-7pm Jun-Aug, 10.30am-4.30pm Wed-Sun Sep-May) Set inside a duck egg blue–painted wooden villa with stained-glass windows, and opening to a wide terrace out the back, this charmingly old-fashioned cafe is adorned with striped wallpaper and serves Finnish favourites such as salmon and fennel soup, a reindeer burger with spicy coleslaw and fries, pike-perch with herb-butter sauce and sweet potato mash, and lingonberry-and-apple cake.

★Huvila   FINNISH €€

(☑015-555-0555; www.panimoravintolahuvila.fi; Puistokatu 4; 3-course menu €34.40-37.40; ☺4-11pm Mon-Fri, 2-11pm Sat Jun & Aug, noon-midnight Mon-Sat, noon-10pm Sun Jul; 🛜) Built in 1912, this noble wooden building sits across the harbour from the town centre. Menus (no à la carte) might feature cauliflower soup with trout mousse, braised pork neck with thyme-and-truffle mash, and apple-and-rosemary panna cotta with lingonberry sauce. Home-brewed beers are exquisite and the terrace is a wonderful place on a sunny afternoon. Live music occasionally takes place.

ℹ️ Getting There & Away

AIR

Savonlinna Airport (SVL; www.finavia.fi; Lentoasemantie 50) is situated 15km north of town, and is served by Finnair, with regular services to Helsinki year-round, as well as charter flights during the opera festival.

BOAT

Boats connect Savonlinna with many lakeside towns; check www.oravivillage.com for seasonal schedules. The **M/S Puijo** (☑015-250-250; www.mspuijo.fi; Satamapuistonkatu; one-way €95, return with overnight cabin €180, return by same-day bus €130; ☺mid-Jun–mid-Aug) cruises between Savonlinna and Kuopio in summer.

BUS

Bus services include Helsinki (€24, 5½ hours, up to nine daily).

TRAIN

Trains from Helsinki (€48, 4¼ hours, up to four daily) require a change in Parikkala.

Kuopio

Kuopio is the quintessential summery lakeside town, with pleasure cruises on the azure water, spruce forests to stroll in, wooden waterside pubs, and local fish specialities to taste. And what better than a traditional smoke sauna to give necessary impetus to jump into the chilly waters?

☑ 017 / POP 112,158

☉ Sights

Kuopion Korttelimuseo　　　　MUSEUM
(Old Kuopio Museum; www.korttelimuseo.kuopio.fi; Kirkkokatu 22; adult/child €6/free; ⊙10am-5pm Tue-Sat Jun-Sep, 10am-3pm Tue-Sat Oct-May) This block of 11 wooden town houses dating from the 18th to 19th centuries forms one of Kuopio's delightful museums. Several period-furnished homes represent family life between 1800 and 1930. Apteekkimuseo in building 11 contains old pharmacy paraphernalia, while in another building it's fascinating to compare photos of Kuopio from different decades. Interpretative information is in English and Finnish. Its cafe serves delicious sweet and savoury dishes including a traditional *rahkapiirakka* (a local cheesecake-style pastry).

**Suomen Ortodoksinen
Kirkkomuseo**　　　　MUSEUM
(Finnish Orthodox Church Museum; www.riisa.fi; Karjalankatu 1; adult/child €10/free; ⊙noon-4pm Tue-Sat) Over 800 religious icons and 4000 textiles, along with documents, maps, drawings and photographs depicting Orthodox history in Karelia and ancient Byzantine traditions are displayed across nine rooms at this excellent museum, freshly reopened after extensive renovations. Many items were brought here from monasteries and churches now in Russian-occupied Karelia.

🏃 Activities

★ **Jätkänkämppä**　　　　SAUNA
(☑ 030-60830; www.rauhalahti.fi; Katiskaniementie 8; adult/child €12/6; ⊙4-10pm Tue & Fri Jun-Aug, 4-10pm Tue Sep-May) This giant *savusauna* (smoke sauna) is a memorable, sociable experience. It seats 60 and is mixed: you're given towels to wear. Bring a swimsuit for lake dipping – devoted locals and brave tourists do so even when it's covered with ice. Repeat the process several times.

Then buy a beer and relax, looking out over the lake in Nordic peace.

🛏 Sleeping & Eating

Kuopio City Center　　　　HOTEL €€
(☑ 020-004-8125; www.city.cumulus.fi/hotellit; Haapaniemenkatu 22; s/d/tr from €141/156/186; ❋ 🛜 🕸) Completely remodelled earlier this decade, this historic hotel has a prime location on the kauppatori. Well-soundproofed rooms become more spacious as you head up the price scale; triples have a sofa bed and several come with kitchenettes. Some rooms have views of the market square, while others, more unusually, overlook the interior of a department store.

★ **Musta Lammas**　　　　FINNISH €€€
(☑ 017-581-0458; http://mustalammas.ravintolamestarit.net; Satamakatu 4; mains €29, 5-course tasting menu €59, with paired wines €100; ⊙5pm-11pm Mon-Sat; 🍴) Set in a romantic brick-vaulted space and opening to a roof terrace, fêted gourmet restaurant the Black Sheep uses top-quality Finnish produce in dishes such as wild boar with celery root and apple, coffee-marinated roast pumpkin, and pike-perch with lingonberry sauce. Wines include a fabulous selection of generously priced special bottles. Vegetarian and vegan tasting menus (€49) require prior notice.

ℹ Information

Kuopio Info (☑ 017-182-584; www.kuopio.fi; Apaja Shopping Centre, Kauppakatu 45; ⊙8am-3pm Mon-Fri) Underneath the kauppatori. Information on regional attractions and accommodation.

ℹ Getting There & Away

Buses serve Helsinki (€30, 6½ hours, hourly) and other cities, as do trains (€45, 4½ hours, up to five daily) and flights from **Kuopio Airport** (KUO; www.finavia.fi; Lentokentäntie 275). In summer boats travel between Kuopio and Savonlinna.

LAPLAND

Extending hundreds of kilometres above the Arctic Circle, Lapland is Finland's true wilderness and casts a powerful spell. The midnight sun, the Sámi peoples, the aurora borealis (Northern Lights) and the wandering reindeer are all components of Lapland's magic, as is good old ho-ho-ho himself, who 'officially' resides up here.

FINLAND KUOPIO

Rovaniemi

♪ 016 / POP 61,784

Situated right by the Arctic Circle, Santa Claus' 'official' terrestrial residence is the capital of Finnish Lapland. It's an ideal base for organising activities. and is Lapland's transport hub.

◉ Sights

★ **Arktikum**   MUSEUM

(www.arktikum.fi; Pohjoisranta 4; adult/child €12/5; ⊙ 9am-6pm Jun-Aug, 10am-6pm Tue-Sun mid-Jan–May & Sep-Nov, 10am-6pm Dec–mid-Jan) With its beautifully designed glass tunnel stretching out to the Ounasjoki, this is one of Finland's finest museums. One half deals with Lapland, with information on Sámi culture and the history of Rovaniemi; the other offers a wide-ranging display on the Arctic, with superb static and interactive displays focusing on flora and fauna, as well as on the peoples of Arctic Europe, Asia and North America. Downstairs, an audiovisual – basically a pretty slide show – plays on a constant loop.

☞ Tours

Rovaniemi is Finnish Lapland's most popular base for winter and summer activities, offering the convenience of frequent departures and professional trips with multilingual guides. Check the tourist-office website for activities including river cruises, reindeer- and husky-sledding, rafting, snowmobiling, skiing and mountain biking.

LAPLAND SEASONS

It's important to time your trip in Lapland carefully. In the far north there's no sun for 50 days of the year, and no night for 70-odd days. In June it's very muddy, and in July insects can be hard to deal with. If you're here to walk, August is great and September brings the spectacle of the *ruska* (autumn leaves). There's usually thick snow cover from mid-October to May; December draws charter flights looking for Santa, real reindeer and a white Christmas, but the best time for skiing and husky/reindeer/snowmobile safaris is March and April, when you get a decent amount of daylight and less-extreme temperatures.

🛏 Sleeping

Hostel Rudolf   HOSTEL €

(♪ 016-321-321; www.santashotels.fi; Koskikatu 41; s/d/tr from €49/58/87; P 🖥) Run by Hotel Santa Claus, 700m southeast, where you inconveniently have to go to check-in, this staffless 'hostel' is Rovaniemi's only one and can fill up fast. Rooms are private (no dorms) and good for the price, with spotless bathrooms, solid desks and bedside lamps. There's also a kitchen available but don't expect a hostel atmosphere. HI discount.

Guesthouse Borealis   GUESTHOUSE €

(♪ 044-313-1771; www.guesthouseborealis.com; Asemieskatu 1; s/d/tr/apt from €58/68/99/175; P 🖥) Cordial hospitality and proximity to trains make this family-run spot a winner. Rooms are simple, bright and clean. Guests can use a kitchen; per three hours in winter/summer the sauna costs €89/69. Breakfast, served in an airy dining room, features Finnish porridge. Its two apartments each have their own entrance and full kitchen; one has a private balcony and sauna.

★ **Arctic Light Hotel**   BOUTIQUE HOTEL €€€

(♪ 020-171-0100; www.arcticlighthotel.fi; Valtakatu 18; d/apt incl breakfast from €150/349; P ❄ 🖥 ♿) In Rovaniemi's former 1950s town hall, with original fixtures including wood panelling, a vintage elevator and wrought-iron balustrades, Lapland's top hotel has handcrafted artworks adorning individually designed rooms (some with private saunas). Loft rooms have skylights for aurora borealis views; the two apartments sleep four, with separate living rooms. Buffet breakfasts are designed by Finnish-American TV chef Sara La Fountain.

✗ Eating

Nili   FINNISH €€

(♪ 0400-369-669; www.nili.fi; Valtakatu 20; mains €18.60-34.60; ⊙ 5-11pm Mon-Sat) A timberlined interior with framed black-and-white photos of Lapland, kerosene lamps, traditional fishing nets, taxidermied bear and reindeer heads, and antler chandeliers give this hunting-lodge-style spot a cosy, rustic charm. Local ingredients are used in dishes such as zandar lake fish with tar-and-mustard foam and reindeer with pickled cucumber and lingonberry jam, accompanied by Finnish beers, ciders and berry liqueurs.

Roka INTERNATIONAL €€

(☑ 050-311-6411; www.ravintolaroka.fi; Ainonkatu 3; street food dishes €9.50-12, mains €14.50-26; ⊙ 10.30am-9pm Mon-Thu, 10.30am-11pm Fri, noon-11pm Sat, noon-9pm Sun) With its exposed brick walls, communal tables and blackboard-chalked menus, this post-industrial-style bistro is Rovaniemi's hippest eatery. Street food – such as sandwiches on homemade bread (beef brisket and horseradish mayo; grilled halloumi with red-onion compote and tzatziki), fish and chips, and braised pork belly – is its signature; mains include reindeer with roast beetroot and game sauce, and pan-fried pike.

ⓘ Information

Tourist Information (☑ 016-346-270; www.visitrovaniemi.fi; Maakuntakatu 29; ⊙ 9am-5pm Mon-Fri; 🛜) On the square in the middle of town.

ⓘ Getting There & Away

AIR

Rovaniemi's **airport** (RVN; ☑ 020-708-6506; www.finavia.fi; Lentokentäntie), 8km northeast of the city, has several Finnair and Norwegian flights daily to/from Helsinki.

Major car-rental companies have desks here.

BUS

From the **bus station** (Matkahuolto Rovaniemi; ☑ 020-710-5435; www.matkahuolto.fi; Lapinkävijantie 2), daily connections serve just about everywhere in Lapland, including Norwegian destinations. Night buses serve Helsinki (€130.20, 11½ hours, up to four daily).

TRAIN

One direct train per day runs from Rovaniemi to Helsinki (€80, 8½ hours, up to three daily), with two more requiring a change in Oulu. Helsinki services include overnighters (per berth from €121).

Inari

☑ 016 / POP 550

The tiny village of Inari (Sámi: Anár) is Finland's most significant Sámi centre and the ideal starting point to learn something of their culture.

The village sits on Lapland's largest lake, Inarijärvi, with more than 3000 islands in its 1153-sq-km area.

OTHER PLACES WORTH VISITING

Kemi Come in winter for trips on an icebreaker and the chance to overnight in a spectacular snow castle.

Ruka This ski resort is a great year-round base for outdoor activity, with some of Finland's finest hikes and canoeing routes on the doorstep.

Rauma The Unesco World Heritage–listed Old Town district, Vanha Rauma, is the largest preserved wooden town in the Nordic countries.

Naantali (Swedish: Nådendal) Just 18km west of Turku, Naantali is home to the adorable Muumimaailma (Moominworld) theme park, a quaint Old Town, and the Finnish president's summer residence.

Jyväskylä Lively lakeside university town strongly connected with Finland's most famous architect and designer Alvar Aalto.

Oulu This cheerful city is beautifully located on a series of linked islands.

⊙ Sights

★ **Siida** MUSEUM

(www.siida.fi; Inarintie 46; adult/child €10/5; ⊙ 9am-7pm Jun–mid-Sep, 10am-5pm Tue-Sun mid-Sep–May) One of Finland's finest museums, Siida offers a comprehensive overview of the Sámi and their environment. The main exhibition hall consists of a fabulous nature exhibition around the edge, detailing northern Lapland's ecology by season, with wonderful photos and information panels. In the centre of the room is detailed information on the Sámi, from their former semi-nomadic existence to modern times.

Sajos CULTURAL CENTRE

(www.samediggi.fi; Siljotie 4; ⊙ 9am-5pm Mon-Fri) FREE The spectacular wood-and-glass Sámi cultural centre stands proud in the middle of town. It holds the Sámi parliament as well as a library and music archive, restaurant, exhibitions and craft shop.

SEEING SANTA

The southernmost line at which the sun doesn't set on at least one day a year, the Arctic Circle (Napapiiri in Finnish) crosses the Sodankylä road 7.5km north of Rovaniemi (although the Arctic Circle can actually shift several metres daily). There's an Arctic Circle marker here; surrounding it is the 'official' Santa Claus Village (www.santaclausvillage.info; Sodankyläntie; ⊘9am-6pm Jun-Aug, 10am-5pm mid-Jan–May, Sep & Nov, 9am-7pm Dec–mid-Jan) FREE, a touristy complex of shops, activities and accommodation.

The Santa Claus Post Office (www.santaclaus.posti.fi; Sodankyläntie; ⊘9am-6pm Jun-Aug, 10am-5pm mid-Jan–May, Sep & Nov, 9am-7pm Dec–mid-Jan) FREE receives over half a million letters yearly from children all over the world. Your postcard sent from here will bear an official Santa stamp, and you can arrange to have it delivered at Christmas. For €7.95, Santa will send you a Christmas card.

At the tourist information desk you can get your Arctic Circle certificate (€4.20) or stamp your passport (€0.50).

But the top attraction for most is, of course, Santa himself, who sees visitors year-round in a rather impressive grotto (www.santaclauslive.com; Sodankyläntie; ⊘9am-6pm Jun-Aug, 10am-5pm mid-Jan–May, Sep & Nov, 9am-7pm Dec–mid-Jan) FREE. A private chat (around two minutes) is absolutely free, but you can't photograph the moment, and official photos of your visit start at €20. You can also get a certificate of 'niceness' or of meeting Santa (each €7.95).

Other attractions include Snowman World, with an ice bar and tyre tobogganing; a husky park; reindeer-pulled sleigh rides (on wheels in summer, traditional runners in snow; per adult/child from €17/13 for 400m); ice sculpting; and varying Christmassy exhibitions.

Accommodation options include panoramic glass-walled cabins, and winter igloos. Santamus is an atmospheric seasonal 'experience' restaurant; a cafe serves salmon smoked over an open fire.

Bus 8 heads here from the train station, via the city (Rovakatu P; Poromiehentie) and airport (€3.90; 20 minutes; hourly 6.30am to 6.30pm).

🛏 Sleeping & Eating

Lomakylä Inari   CAMPGROUND €
(☑016-671-108; www.visitinari.fi; Inarintie 26; tent sites from €20, 2-/4-person cabins €67/79, without bathroom €40/50, cottages €85-170; P🐾) Inari's closest campground is 500m south of the town centre and offers a range of 40 cabins and cottages, 40 caravan pitches and 30 tent sites, as well as good facilities including a cafe. Pricier lakeside cabins are worth it for the memorable sunrises. Camping and nonheated cabins are available from June to September only.

Tradition Hotel Kultahovi   HOTEL €€
(☑016-511-7100;   www.hotelkultahovi.fi; Saarikoskentie 2; s/d from €86/110, annexe s/d from €118/136; P🐾) This cosy Sámi family-run place overlooks the Jäniskoski rapids and has 45 spruce-furnished rooms, some with a great river view. Standard rooms have been recently renovated, while annexe rooms have an appealing Nordic decor, a drying cupboard and riverside balcony/terrace; most also contain a sauna. There's also a fantastic riverside sauna. Its restaurant, Aanaar (mains €13.30-31.50, 3-/5-course menu €43.50/62, with paired wines €62/85; ⊘11am-2.30pm & 5-10.30pm) 🐾, serves delicious Lappish specialities.

🛍 Shopping

Inarin Hopea   JEWELLERY
(☑016-671-333; www.inarinhopea.fi; Inarintie 61; ⊘10am-8pm) You can watch gold- and silversmith Matti Qvick at work in his studio, which is filled with his traditional handmade jewellery (rings, bracelets, pendants, earrings and more, at all price points) based on Sámi designs and local wildlife such as Arctic foxes and Scandinavian lynx, which he's been crafting here since 1982. Pieces can be custom fitted while you wait.

ℹ Information

Tourist Office (☑040-168-9668; www.inari.fi; Inarintie 46; ⊘9am-7pm Jun–mid-Sep, 10am-5pm Tue-Sun mid-Sep–May; 🐾) Located in the **Siida** (p361) museum. There's also a nature information point here.

ℹ Getting There & Away

Two daily buses travel to Inari from Rovaniemi (€60.10, five hours) and continue to Norway.

SURVIVAL GUIDE

ℹ Directory A–Z

ACCOMMODATION

Solid Nordic comfort in standard rooms dominates rather than boutique accommodation.

➡ Most campgrounds open from June to August; sites usually cost around €14 plus €5/2 per adult/child. Most have cabins or cottages, usually excellent value; from €40 for a basic cabin to €120 for a cottage with kitchen, bathroom and sauna.

➡ HI members save 10% per night at affiliated hostels.

➡ From June to August many student residences are made over as summer hostels and hotels.

➡ Hotels in Finland charge robustly. But on weekends and during the July summer holidays prices tend to drop by 40% or so. A breakfast buffet is nearly always included. Double beds are rare.

➡ One of Finland's joys is its plethora of cottages for rent, many in romantic lake-and-forest locations. The biggest booker is **Lomarengas** (☑ 030-650-2502; www.lomarengas.fi).

ACTIVITIES

Water sports Every waterside town has a place (frequently the campground) where you can rent a canoe, kayak or rowboat. Rental cottages often have rowboats that you can use free of charge to investigate the local lake. Rafting options abound.

Fishing Several permits are required of foreigners but they are very easy to arrange. See www.mmm.fi for details.

Hiking Finland has some of Europe's greatest hiking, best done from June to September, although in July mosquitoes and other biting insects can be a big problem in Lapland. Wilderness huts line the northern trails. Numerous national parks (www.nationalparks.fi) provide a well-maintained network of marked trails across the nation.

SLEEPING PRICE RANGES

The following price ranges refer to a double room in high season.

€ less than €70

€€ €70–€160

€€€ more than €160

COUNTRY FACTS

Area 338,145 sq km

Capital Helsinki

Country code ☑ 358

Currency euro (€)

Emergency ☑ 112

Languages Finnish, Swedish, Sámi languages

Population 5.5 million

Visas Schengen visa rules apply

Skiing The ski season runs from late November to early May and slightly longer in the north.

Dog-sledding Expeditions can range from one-hour tasters to multiday trips with overnight stays in remote forest huts.

Snowmobiling If you want to drive one, a driving licence is required.

Saunas Many hotels, hostels and campgrounds have saunas that are free with a night's stay. Large towns have public saunas.

INTERNET ACCESS

Wireless internet access is widespread; several cities have extensive free networks and nearly all hotels, as well as many restaurants, cafes and bars, offer free access to customers and guests.

MONEY

ATMs Using ATMs with a credit or debit card is by far the easiest way of getting cash.

Credit cards Widely accepted.

Moneychangers Travellers cheques and cash can be exchanged at banks; in cities, independent exchange facilities such as Forex (www.forex.fi) usually offer better rates.

Tipping Service is considered to be included in bills, so there's no need to tip unless you want to reward exceptional service.

OPENING HOURS

Many attractions in Finland only open for a short summer season, typically mid-June to late August. Opening hours tend to shorten in winter in general.

Alko (state alcohol store) 9am–8pm Monday to Friday, to 6pm Saturday

Banks 9am–4.15pm Monday to Friday

Businesses & shops 9am–6pm Monday to Friday, to 3pm Saturday

Nightclubs 10pm–4am Wednesday to Saturday

Pubs 11am–1am (often later on Friday and Saturday)

Restaurants 11am–10pm; lunch 11am–3pm. Last orders generally an hour before closing.

TELEPHONE

➠ Public telephones basically no longer exist in Finland.

➠ If you have an unlocked phone, the cheapest and most practical solution is to purchase a Finnish SIM card.

➠ You can buy a prepaid SIM card at any R-kioski shop. Top the credit up at the same outlets, online or at ATMs.

➠ The country code for Finland is ☏ 358. To dial abroad, the exit is ☏ 00.

TIME

Eastern European Time (EET), an hour ahead of Sweden and Norway. In winter it's two hours ahead of UTC/GMT; from late March to late October the clocks go forward an hour to three hours ahead of UTC/GMT.

TOURIST INFORMATION

The main website of the Finnish Tourist Board is www.visitfinland.com.

VISAS

Schengen rules apply. Check the website www. formin.finland.fi for details.

ⓘ Getting There & Away

Finland is easily accessed from Europe and beyond. There are direct flights from numerous destinations, while Baltic ferries are another good option.

AIR

Most flights to Finland land at **Helsinki-Vantaa Airport** (www.helsinki-vantaa.fi), 19km north of the capital.

Finland is easily reached by air, with direct flights to Helsinki from many European, American and Asian destinations. It's also served by budget carriers, especially Ryanair, from several European countries. Most other flights are with Finnair or Scandinavian Airlines (SAS).

LAND

There are several border crossings from northern Sweden and Norway to northern Finland, with no passport or customs formalities. Buses link northern Finland and Norway, while the shared bus station at Tornio (Finland) and Haparanda (Sweden) links the public transport systems of those countries.

Between Finland and Russia, there are nine main border crossings, including several in the southeast and two in Lapland. Buses and trains run from Helsinki and other cities to Russia. You must already have a Russian visa.

SEA

Baltic ferries connect Finland with Estonia, Russia, Germany and Sweden. Book ahead in summer, at weekends and if travelling with a vehicle.

Ferry companies have detailed timetables and fares on their websites. Fares vary according to season. Main operators include the following:

Eckerö Line (☏ 06000-4300; www.eckeroline.fi)

Finnlines (☏ 09-231-43100; www.finnlines. com)

Linda Line (☏ 0600-066-8970; www.lindaline.fi)

Tallink/Silja (☏ 0600-15700; www.tallinksilja. com)

Viking Line (☏ 0600-41577; www.vikingline.fi)

ESSENTIAL FOOD & DRINK

Alcoholic drinks Beer is a staple, and great microbreweries are on the increase. Finns also love dissolving things in vodka; try a shot of salmiakkikossu (salty-liquorice flavoured) or fisu (Fisherman's Friend–flavoured).

Brunssi Weekend brunssi (brunch) is all the rage in Helsinki and other cities. Book ahead for these sumptuous all-you-can-eat spreads.

Coffee To fit in, eight or nine cups a day is about right, best accompanied with a *pulla* (cardamom-flavoured pastry).

Fresh food The kauppahalli (market hall) is where to go for a stunning array of produce. In summer, stalls at the kauppatori (market square) sell delicious fresh vegetables and fruit.

Fish Salmon is ubiquitous; tasty lake fish include Arctic char, lavaret, pike-perch and scrumptious fried muikku (vendace).

Gastronomy Helsinki is the best venue for fabulous new-Suomi cuisine, with sumptuous, inventive degustation menus presenting traditional Finnish ingredients in crest-of-the-wave ways.

Offbeat meats Unusual meats appear on menus: reindeer is a staple up north, elk is commonly eaten, and bear is also available.

ℹ Getting Around

AIR

Finnair runs a fairly comprehensive domestic service out of Helsinki. Multitrip journeys can be significantly cheaper than one-way flights.

BICYCLE

Finland is as bicycle friendly as any country you'll find, with plenty of paths and few hills. Bikes can be taken on most trains, buses and ferries. Åland is particularly good for cycling. Helmets are required by law. You can hire a bike in nearly every Finnish town.

BOAT

The most popular lake boat routes are Tampere–Hämeenlinna, Tampere–Virrat, Savonlinna–Kuopio and Lahti–Jyväskylä. The site www.lautta.net is handy for domestic lake-boat and ferry services.

BUS

Bus is the main form of long-distance transport in Finland, with a far more comprehensive network than the train.

Ticketing is handled by **Matkahuolto** (www.matkahuolto.fi), whose excellent website has all the timetables. Matkahuolto offices work normal business hours, but you can always just buy your ticket from the driver.

Towns have a *linja-autoasema* (bus terminal), with local timetables displayed (*lähtevät* is departures, *saapuvat* arrivals).

Separate from the normal system, **OnniBus** (www.onnibus.com; Salomonkatu) runs a variety of budget inter-city routes in comfortable double-decker buses, best booked in advance.

CAR & MOTORCYCLE

Many petrol stations are unstaffed, but machines take cash and most (but not all) chip-and-pin-enabled credit and debit cards.

Hire

A small car costs from €65/205 per day/week with 300km free per day, not including insurance. Weekend rates can yield savings. As ever, the cheapest deals are online.

Car-rental franchises with offices in many Finnish cities:

→ Avis (www.avis.com)
→ Budget (www.budget.com)
→ Europcar (www.europcar.com)
→ Hertz (www.hertz.com)
→ Sixt (www.sixt.com)

Road Hazards

Wildlife Beware of elk and reindeer, which don't respect vehicles and can dash onto the road unexpectedly. This sounds comical, but elks especially constitute a deadly danger. Notify the police if there is an accident involving these animals. Reindeer are very common

in Lapland; slow right down if you see one, as there will be more nearby.

Conditions Snow and ice on the roads, potentially from September to April, and as late as June in Lapland, make driving a serious undertaking. Snow chains are illegal: people use either snow tyres, which have studs, or special all-weather tyres.

Road Rules

→ Finns drive on the right.
→ The speed limit is 50km/h in built-up areas, from 80km/h to 100km/h on highways, and 120km/h on motorways.
→ Use headlights at all times.
→ Seatbelts are compulsory.
→ Blood alcohol limit: 0.05%.

An important feature of Finland is that there are fewer give-way signs than most countries. Traffic entering an intersection from the right has right of way. While this doesn't apply to highways or main roads, in towns cars will often nip out from the right without looking: you must give way, so be careful at smaller intersections in towns.

TRAIN

State-owned Valtion Rautatiet (www.vr.fi) runs Finnish trains: a fast, efficient service, with prices roughly equivalent to buses on the same route.

Major stations have a VR office and ticket machines; tickets can also be purchased online, where you'll find discounted advance fares. You can also board and pay the conductor, but if the station where you boarded had ticket-purchasing facilities, you'll be charged a small penalty fee (€2 to €5).

Train Passes

Eurail and InterRail offer various passes that include train travel within Finland.

The **Eurail Scandinavia** pass gives a number of days in a two-month period, and is valid for travel in Denmark, Sweden, Norway and Finland. It costs €215/248/278/353 for three/four/five/eight days' 2nd-class travel within a one-month period. The **Finland Eurail** pass costs €159/191/220/296 for three/four/five/eight days' 2nd-class travel in a one-month period within Finland.

For EU residents, the **InterRail** Finland pass offers travel only in Finland for three/four/six/eight days in a one-month period, costing €118/149/199/239 in 2nd class.

France

Best Places to Stay

➡ Joke Hôtel (p380)

➡ L'Hôtel Particulier (p417)

➡ Villa des Consuls (p415)

➡ Cour des Loges (p410)

➡ Nice Garden Hôtel (p432)

Best Places for History

➡ Musée du Louvre (p371)

➡ Château de Versailles (p390)

➡ D-Day Beaches (p395)

➡ Château de Chambord (p403)

➡ Pont du Gard (p423)

Why Go?

France has so much to entice travellers – renowned gastronomy, iconic sights, splendid art heritage, a fabulous outdoors: you could sample it all in a week, but you'll invariably feel as though you've only scratched the surface of this big country.

Visiting France is certainly about seeing the big sights, but it's just as much about savouring life's little pleasures: a stroll through an elegant city square, a coffee on a sunny pavement terrace, a meal that lasts well into the afternoon or night, a scenic drive punctuated with photo stops and impromptu farm or vineyard visits. The French are big on their *art de vivre* (art of living) and you should embrace it too – whether you're wandering the boulevards of Paris, exploring the vineyards of Bordeaux and Burgundy or cruising the cliffs of the Côte d'Azur.

On y va, as they say in France!

When to Go
Paris

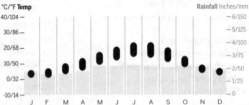

Dec–Mar Christmas markets in Alsace, snow in the Alps and truffles in the south.

Apr–Jun France is at its springtime best, with good weather and far fewer crowds.

Sep Cooling temperatures, abundant local produce and the *vendange* (grape harvest).

PARIS

POP 2.2 MILLION

What can be said about the sexy, sophisticated City of Lights that hasn't already been said myriad times before? Quite simply, this is one of the world's great metropolises – a trendsetter, market leader and cultural capital for over a thousand years and still going strong.

As you might expect, Paris is strewn with historic architecture, glorious galleries and cultural treasures galore. But the modern-day city is much more than just a museum piece: it's a heady hodgepodge of cultures and ideas – a place to stroll the boulevards, shop till you drop, flop riverside or simply do as the Parisians do and watch the world buzz by from a streetside cafe. Savour every moment.

◉ Sights

◔ Left Bank

★ Eiffel Tower   LANDMARK
(Map p372; ☎08 92 70 12 39; www.toureiffel. paris; Champ de Mars, 5 av Anatole France, 7e; adult/ child lift to top €17/8, lift to 2nd fl €11/4, stairs to 2nd fl €7/3; ☉ lifts & stairs 9am-12.45am mid-Jun–Aug, lifts 9.30am-11pm, stairs 9.30am-6.30pm Sep–mid-Jun; Ⓜ Bir Hakeim or RER Champ de Mars–Tour Eiffel) No one could imagine Paris today without it. But Gustave Eiffel only constructed this elegant, 320m-tall signature spire as a temporary exhibit for the 1889 World's Fair. Luckily, the art-nouveau tower's popularity assured its survival. Prebook tickets online to avoid long queues.

Lifts ascend to the tower's three floors; change lifts on the 2nd floor for the final ascent to the top. Energetic visitors can climb as far as the 2nd floor via the south pillar's 704 stairs.

★ Musée d'Orsay   MUSEUM
(Map p372; www.musee-orsay.fr; 1 rue de la Légion d'Honneur, 7e; adult/child €12/free; ☉9.30am-6pm Tue, Wed & Fri-Sun, to 9.45pm Thu; Ⓜ Assemblée Nationale, RER Musée d'Orsay) The home of France's national collection from the impressionist, postimpressionist and art-nouveau movements spanning from 1848 to 1914 is the glorious former Gare d'Orsay railway station – itself an art-nouveau showpiece – where a roll-call of masters and their world-famous works are on display.

Top of every visitor's must-see list is the museum's painting collections, centred on the world's largest collection of impressionist and postimpressionist art.

Musée du Quai Branly   MUSEUM
(Map p372; ☎01 56 61 70 00; www.quaibranly. fr; 37 quai Branly, 7e; adult/child €10/free; ☉11am-7pm Tue, Wed & Sun, 11am-9pm Thu-Sat; Ⓜ Alma Marceau or RER Pont de l'Alma) A tribute to the diversity of human culture, Musée du Quai Branly inspires travellers, armchair anthropologists, and anyone who appreciates the beauty of traditional craftsmanship, through an overview of indigenous and folk art. Spanning four main sections – Oceania, Asia, Africa and the Americas – an impressive array of masks, carvings, weapons, jewellery and more make up the body of the rich collection, displayed in a refreshingly unique interior without rooms or high walls.

FRANCE PARIS

ITINERARIES

One Week

Start with a couple of days exploring **Paris**, taking in the Louvre, the Eiffel Tower, Notre Dame, Montmartre and a boat trip along the Seine. Day trip to magnificent **Versailles** and then spend the rest of the week in **Normandy** to visit WWII's D-Day beaches and glorious Mont St-Michel. Or head east to **Champagne** to sample the famous bubbly and visit Reims' magnificent cathedral.

Two Weeks

With Paris and surrounds having taken up much of the first week, hop on a high-speed TGV to **Avignon** or **Marseille** and take in the delights of Provence's Roman heritage, its beautiful hilltop villages and its famous artistic legacy. Finish your stay with a few days in **Nice**, enjoying its glittering Mediterranean landscapes and sunny cuisine. Alternatively, head southwest to elegant **Bordeaux** and its world-famous vineyards before pushing inland to the **Dordogne** with its hearty gastronomy and unique prehistoric-art heritage.

France Highlights

1 Paris (p367)
Gorging on the iconic sights and sophistication of Europe's most hopelessly romantic city.

2 Loire Valley (p401) Reliving the French Renaissance with extraordinary châteaux built by kings and queens.

3 Chamonix (p412) Doing a Bond and swooshing down slopes in the shadow of Mont Blanc.

4 Mont St-Michel (p395) Dodging tides, strolling moonlit sand and immersing yourself in legend at this island abbey.

5 Provence (p423) Savouring ancient ruins, modern art, markets, lavender and hilltop villages.

6 Épernay (p399) Tasting bubbly in ancient *caves* (cellars) in the heart of Champagne.

7 Lyon (p407) Tucking into France's piggy-driven cuisine in a traditional *bouchon*.

8 Casino de Monte Carlo (p436) Hitting the big time in Monaco's sumptuous gaming house.

ⓘ MUSEUM DISCOUNTS & FREEBIES

Almost all museums and monuments in Paris have discounted tickets (*tarif réduit*) for students and seniors with valid ID; children and students who are EU citizens under 26 usually qualify for free admission. National museums are also free on the first Sunday of each month, except the Arc de Triomphe, Conciergerie, Musée du Louvre, Panthéon and Tours de Notre Dame, which are only free on the first Sunday of the month November to March.

Paris Museum Pass (www.parismuseumpass.com; 2/4/6 days €48/62/74) Gets you into 50-odd venues in and around Paris, and often enables you to bypass (or substantially reduce) long ticket queues.

Paris Passlib' (www.parisinfo.com; 2/3/5 days €109/129/155) Sold at the Paris Convention & Visitors Bureau (p388) and on its website, this handy city pass includes unlimited public transport in zones 1 to 3, a Paris Museum Pass, a one-hour boat cruise, and a one-day bus tour with L'Open Tour (☑ 01 42 66 56 56; www.paris.opentour.com; 1-day pass adult/child €33/17). There's an optional €15 supplement for a skip-the-line ticket to levels one and two of the Eiffel Tower, or €21.50 for all three Eiffel Tower platforms.

Look out for excellent temporary exhibitions and performances.

Musée Rodin   MUSEUM, GARDEN

(Map p372; www.musee-rodin.fr; 79 rue de Varenne, 7e; adult/child museum incl garden €10/free, garden only €4/free; ◷ 10am-5.45pm Tue-Sun; Ⓜ Varenne) Sculptor, painter, sketcher, engraver and collector Auguste Rodin donated his entire collection to the French state in 1908 on the proviso that they dedicate his former workshop and showroom, the beautiful 1730 Hôtel Biron, to displaying his works. They're now installed not only in the magnificently restored mansion itself, but in its rose-filled garden – one of the most peaceful places in central Paris and a wonderful spot to contemplate his famous work *The Thinker*. Prepurchase tickets online to avoid queuing.

Panthéon   MAUSOLEUM

(Map p376; www.paris-pantheon.fr; place du Panthéon, 5e; adult/child €9/free; ◷ 10am-6.30pm Apr-Sep, to 6pm Oct-Mar; Ⓜ Maubert-Mutualité or RER Luxembourg) Overlooking the city from its Left Bank perch, the Panthéon's stately neoclassical dome is an icon of the Parisian skyline. The vast interior is an architectural masterpiece: originally a church and now a mausoleum, it has served since 1791 as the resting place of some of France's greatest thinkers, including Voltaire, Rousseau, Braille and Hugo. A copy of Foucault's pendulum, first hung from the dome in 1851 to demonstrate the rotation of the earth, takes pride of place.

Jardin du Luxembourg   PARK

(Map p376; www.senat.fr/visite/jardin; numerous entrances; ◷ hours vary; Ⓜ Mabillon, St-Sulpice, Rennes, Notre Dame des Champs, RER Luxembourg) This inner-city oasis of formal terraces, chestnut groves and lush lawns has a special place in Parisians' hearts. Napoléon dedicated the 23 gracefully laid-out hectares of the Luxembourg Gardens to the children of Paris, and many residents spent their childhood prodding 1920s wooden sailboats (sailboat rental per 30min €3.50; ◷ Apr-Oct) with long sticks on the octagonal Grand Bassin pond, watching puppets perform *Punch & Judy*-type shows at the Théâtre du Luxembourg (www.marionnettesduluxembourg.fr; tickets €6; ◷ usually 11am & 3.30pm Wed, Sat & Sun, 11am, 3pm & 4.15pm daily during school holidays), and riding the *carrousel* (merry-go-round) or ponies (pony rides €3.50; ◷ 3-6pm Wed, Sat, Sun & school holidays).

Église St-Germain des Prés   CHURCH

(Map p376; www.eglise-stgermaindespres.fr; 3 place St-Germain des Prés, 6e; ◷ 8am-7.45pm; Ⓜ St-Germain des Prés) Paris' oldest standing church, the Romanesque St Germanus of the Fields, was built in the 11th century on the site of a 6th-century abbey and was the main place of worship in Paris until the arrival of Notre Dame. It's since been altered many times, but the Chapelle de St-Symphorien (to the right as you enter) was part of the original abbey and is believed to be the resting place of St Germanus (496–576), the first bishop of Paris.

★ **Les Catacombes** CEMETERY
(Map p372; www.catacombes.paris.fr; 1 av Colonel Henri Roi-Tanguy, 14e; adult/child €12/free, online booking incl audioguide €27/5; ⏱ 10am-8pm Tue-Sun; Ⓜ Denfert Rochereau) Paris' most macabre sight is its underground tunnels lined with skulls and bones. In 1785 it was decided to rectify the hygiene problems of Paris' overflowing cemeteries by exhuming the bones and storing them in disused quarry tunnels and the Catacombes were created in 1810.

After descending 20m (via 130 narrow, dizzying spiral steps) below street level, you follow the dark, subterranean passages to reach the ossuary (2km in all). Exit back up 83 steps onto rue Remy Dumoncel, 14e.

◎ The Islands

Paris' twin set of islands could not be more different. Île de la Cité is bigger, full of sights and very touristy (few people live here).

Smaller Île St-Louis is residential and quieter, with just enough boutiques and restaurants – and legendary ice-cream maker Berthillon – to attract visitors. The area around Pont St-Louis, the bridge across to the Île de la Cité, and Pont Louis-Philippe, the bridge to Le Marais, is one of the most romantic spots in Paris.

★ **Cathédrale Notre Dame de Paris** CATHEDRAL
(Map p376; ☎ 01 42 34 56 10; www.notredamede-paris.fr; 6 place du Parvis Notre Dame, 4e; cathedral free, adult/child towers €10/free, treasury €4/2; ⏱ cathedral 7.45am-6.45pm Mon-Fri, to 7.15pm Sat & Sun, towers 10am-6.30pm Sun-Thu, to 11pm Fri & Sat Jul & Aug, 10am-6.30pm Apr-Jun & Sep, 10am-5.30pm Oct-Mar, treasury 9.30am-6pm Apr-Sep, 10am-5.30pm Oct-Mar; Ⓜ Cité) Paris' most visited unticketed site, with upwards of 14 million visitors per year, is a masterpiece of French Gothic architecture. The focus of Catholic Paris for seven centuries, its vast interior accommodates 6000 worshippers.

Highlights include its three spectacular rose windows, treasury, and bell towers, which can be climbed. From the North Tower, 400-odd steps spiral to the top of the western façade, where you'll find yourself face-to-face with frightening gargoyles and a spectacular view of Paris.

Sainte-Chapelle CHAPEL
(Map p376; ☎ 01 53 40 60 80, concerts 01 42 77 65 65; www.sainte-chapelle.fr; 8 bd du Palais, 1er; adult/child €10/free, joint ticket with Conciergerie €15; ⏱ 9am-7pm Apr-Sep, to 5pm Oct-Mar; Ⓜ Cité)
Try to save Sainte-Chapelle for a sunny day, when Paris' oldest, finest stained glass is at its dazzling best. Enshrined within the Palais de Justice (Law Courts), this gemlike Holy Chapel is Paris' most exquisite Gothic monument. Sainte-Chapelle was built in just six years (compared with nearly 200 years for Notre Dame) and consecrated in 1248.

The chapel was conceived by Louis IX to house his personal collection of holy relics, including the famous Holy Crown (now in Notre Dame).

◎ Right Bank

★ **Musée du Louvre** MUSEUM
(Map p376; ☎ 01 40 20 53 17; www.louvre.fr; rue de Rivoli & quai des Tuileries, 1er; adult/child €15/free; ⏱ 9am-6pm Mon, Thu, Sat & Sun, to 9.45pm Wed & Fri; Ⓜ Palais Royal–Musée du Louvre) Few art galleries are as prized as the Musée du Louvre, Paris' pièce de résistance and the world's most visited museum. The palace rambles over four floors, up and down innumerable staircases, and through three wings. Showcasing 35,000 works of art – from Mesopotamian, Egyptian and Greek antiquities to masterpieces by artists such as Leonardo

> **FRANCE PARIS**

---

❶ THE LOUVRE: TICKETS & TOURS

To best navigate the collection, opt for a self-guided thematic trail (1½ to three hours; download trail brochures in advance from the website) or a self-paced multimedia guide (€5). More formal, English-language guided tours depart from the Hall Napoléon, which also has free English-language maps.

The main entrance and ticket windows are covered by the 21m-high Grande Pyramide, a glass pyramid designed by the Chinese-born American architect IM Pei. If you don't have the Museum Pass (which gives you priority), you can avoid the longest queues (for security) outside the pyramid by entering the Louvre complex via the underground shopping centre Carrousel du Louvre (Map p376; http://carrouseldulouvre.com; 99 rue de Rivoli, 1er; ⏱ 8.30am-11pm, shops 10am-8pm; ☎; Ⓜ Palais Royal–Musée du Louvre). You'll need to queue up again to buy your ticket once inside.

Greater Paris

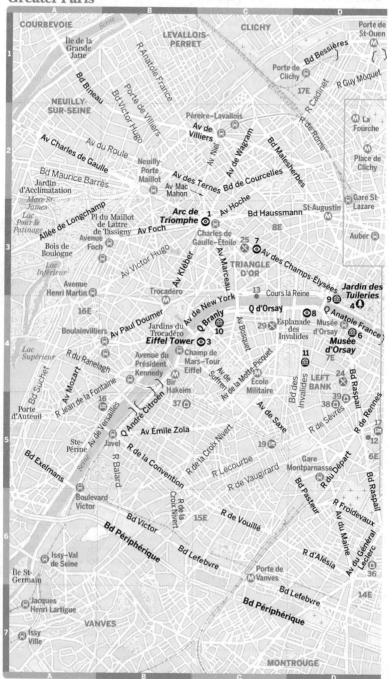

Greater Paris

da Vinci (including his incomparable *Mona Lisa*), Michelangelo and Rembrandt – it would take nine months to glance at every piece, rendering advance planning essential.

★ **Arc de Triomphe**　LANDMARK
(Map p372; www.paris-arc-de-triomphe.fr; place Charles de Gaulle, 8e; viewing platform adult/child €12/free; ⊙10am-11pm Apr-Sep, to 10.30pm Oct-Mar; Ⓜ Charles de Gaulle–Étoile) If anything rivals the Eiffel Tower (p367) as the symbol of Paris, it's this magnificent 1836 monument to Napoléon's victory at Austerlitz (1805), which he commissioned the following year. The intricately sculpted triumphal arch stands sentinel in the centre of the Étoile ('Star') roundabout. From the viewing platform on top of the arch (50m up via 284 steps and well worth the climb) you can see the dozen avenues.

★ **Jardin des Tuileries**　PARK
(Map p372; rue de Rivoli, 1er; ⊙7am-9pm Mar–late Sep, 7.30am-7.30pm Sep–late Mar; ♿; Ⓜ Tuileries, Concorde) Filled with fountains, ponds and sculptures, the formal 28-hectare Tuileries Garden, which begins just west of the Jardin du Carrousel, was laid out in its present form in 1664 by André Le Nôtre, who also created the gardens at Vaux-le-Vicomte and Versailles. The Tuileries soon became the most fashionable spot in Paris for parading about in one's finery. It now forms part of the Banks of the Seine Unesco World Heritage Site.

Centre Pompidou　MUSEUM
(Map p376; ☑01 44 78 12 33; www.centrepompidou.fr; place Georges Pompidou, 4e; museum, exhibitions & panorama adult/child €14/free, panorama ticket only €5; ⊙11am-10pm Wed & Fri-Mon, to 11pm Thu; ☎; Ⓜ Rambuteau) Renowned for its radical architectural statement, the 1977-opened Centre Pompidou brings together galleries and cutting-edge exhibitions, hands-on workshops, dance performances, cinemas and other entertainment venues, with street performers and fanciful fountains outside. The **Musée National d'Art Moderne**, France's national collection of art dating from 1905 onward, is the main draw; a fraction of its 100,000-plus pieces – including fauvist, cubist and surrealist works, pop art and contemporary works – is

on display. Don't miss the spectacular Parisian panorama from the rooftop.

Basilique du Sacré-Cœur BASILICA
(Map p380; ☎01 53 41 89 00; www.sacre-coeur-montmartre.com; Parvis du Sacré-Cœur; basilica free, dome adult/child €6/4, cash only; ⊗basilica 6am-10.30pm, dome 8.30am-8pm May-Sep, to 5pm Oct-Apr; ⓂAnvers, Abbesses) Begun in 1875 in the wake of the Franco-Prussian War and the chaos of the Paris Commune, Sacré-Cœur is a symbol of the former struggle between the conservative Catholic old guard and the secular, republican radicals. It was finally consecrated in 1919, standing in utter contrast to the bohemian lifestyle that surrounded it. The view over Paris from its parvis is breathtaking. If you don't want to walk the hill, you can use a regular metro ticket aboard the funicular (place St-Pierre, 18e; ⊗6am-12.45am; ⓂAnvers, Abbesses).

★ Place des Vosges SQUARE
(Map p376; 4e; ⓂSt-Paul, Bastille) Inaugurated in 1612 as place Royale and thus Paris' oldest square, place des Vosges is a strikingly elegant ensemble of 36 symmetrical houses with ground-floor arcades, steep slate roofs and large dormer windows arranged around a leafy square with four symmetrical fountains and an 1829 copy of a mounted statue of Louis XIII. The square received its present name in 1800 to honour the Vosges *département* (administrative division) for being the first in France to pay its taxes.

★ Musée National Picasso GALLERY
(Map p376; ☎01 85 56 00 36; www.museepicasso paris.fr; 5 rue de Thorigny, 3e; adult/child €12.50/ free; ⊗10.30am-6pm Tue-Fri, 9.30am-6pm Sat & Sun; ⓂSt-Paul, Chemin Vert) One of Paris' most beloved art collections is showcased inside the mid-17th-century Hôtel Salé, an exquisite private mansion owned by the city since 1964. The Musée National Picasso is a staggering art museum devoted to Spanish artist Pablo Picasso (1881–1973), who spent much of his life living and working in Paris. The collection includes more than 5000 drawings, engravings, paintings, ceramic works and sculptures by the *grand maître* (great master), although they're not all displayed at the same time.

★ Cimetière du Père Lachaise CEMETERY
(Map p372; ☎01 55 25 82 10; www.pere-lachaise. com; 16 rue du Repos & 8 bd de Ménilmontant, 20e; ⊗8am-6pm Mon-Fri, 8.30am-6pm Sat, 9am-6pm Sun mid-Mar–Oct, shorter hours Nov–mid-Mar; ⓂPère Lachaise, Gambetta) The world's most visited cemetery, Père Lachaise opened in 1804. Its 70,000 ornate and ostentatious tombs of the rich and famous form a verdant, 44-hectare sculpture garden. The most visited are those of 1960s rock star Jim Morrison (division 6) and Oscar Wilde (division 89). Pick up cemetery maps at the conservation office (Bureaux de la Conservation; Map p372; ☎01 55 25 82 10; 16 rue du Repos, 20e; ⊗8.30am-12.30pm & 2-5pm Mon-Fri; ⓂPhilippe Auguste, Père Lachaise) near the main bd de Ménilmontant entrance. Other notables buried here include composer Chopin; playwright Molière; poet Apollinaire; and writers Balzac, Proust, Gertrude Stein and Colette.

☞ Tours

★ Parisien d'un Jour –
Paris Greeters WALKING
(www.greeters.paris; by donation) See Paris through local eyes with these two- to three-hour city tours. Volunteers – mainly knowledgable Parisians passionate about their city – lead groups (maximum six people) to their favourite spots. Minimum two weeks' notice is needed.

Meeting the French CULTURAL, TOURS
(☎01 42 51 19 80; www.meetingthefrench.com; tours & courses from €25) Cosmetics workshops, backstage cabaret tours, fashion designer showroom visits, French table decoration, art embroidery classes, market tours, baking with a Parisian baker – the repertoire of cultural and gourmet tours and behind-the-scenes experiences offered by Meeting the French is truly outstanding. All courses and tours are in English.

Fat Tire Bike Tours CYCLING
(☎01 82 88 80 96; www.fattiretours.com; tours from €29) Offers day and night bicycle tours of the city, both in central Paris and further afield to Versailles and Monet's Garden (p391) in Giverny.

It also runs a host of other tours and activities, from cookery lessons to flea and food market tours, walking tours, and tours of the Louvre and Château de Versailles.

Bateaux-Mouches BOATING
(Map p372; ☎01 42 25 96 10; www.bateaux-mouches.fr; Port de la Conférence, 8e; adult/child €13.50/6; ⓂAlma Marceau) Bateaux-Mouches, the largest river cruise company in Paris, is a favourite with tour groups. Departing just

Central Paris

0   400 m
0   0.2 miles

RIGHT BANK

LE MARAIS

Musée National Picasso

Place des Vosges

Musée du Louvre

Palais Royal – Musée du Louvre

Q François Mitterrand

Jardin des Tuileries

Jardin du Palais Royal

Av de l'Opéra

Bd St-Martin

Bd du Temple

Bd Jules Ferry

Bd Richard Lenoir

Bd Voltaire

Bd Beaumarchais

Av de la République

Bd de Sébastopol

Q de l'Hôtel de Ville

Q des Gesvres

Q de la Mégisserie

Q de Conti

Q des Grands Augustins

Q Malaquais

République

Oberkampf

St-Sébastien Froissart

Filles du Calvaire

Rambuteau

Châtelet – Les Halles

Châtelet

Hôtel de Ville

Pont au Change

Pont Neuf

Pont des Arts

Île de la Cité

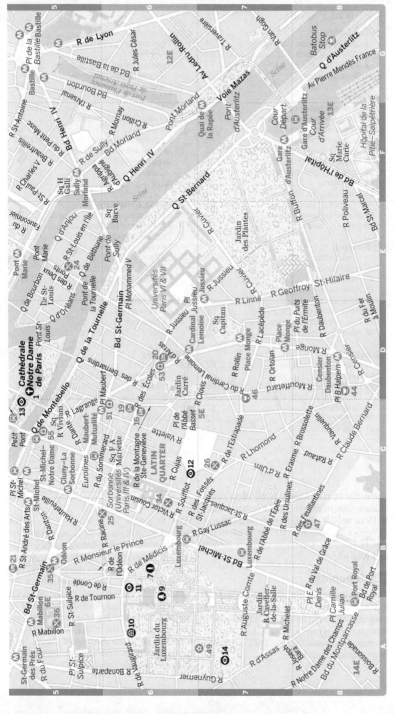

Central Paris

east of the Pont de l'Alma on the Right Bank, cruises (70 minutes) run regularly from 10.15am to 10.30pm April to September and 13 times a day between 11am and 9.20pm the rest of the year. Commentary is in French and English.

🛏 Sleeping

The Paris Convention & Visitors Bureau (p388) can find you a place to stay (no booking fee, but you need a credit card), though queues can be long in high season. To rent an apartment, try **Paris Attitude** (www.parisattitude.com).

🛏 Left Bank

Hôtel St-André des Arts   HOTEL €
(Map p376; ☎01 43 26 96 16; www.hotel-saint andredesarts.fr; 66 rue St-André des Arts, 6e; s/d/tr/q €95/115/156/181; ☎; Ⓜ Odéon) Located on a lively, restaurant-lined thoroughfare, this 31-room hotel is a veritable bargain in the centre of the action opposite the beautiful glass-roofed passage Cour du Commerce St André. The rooms are basic and there's no lift/elevator, but the public areas are very evocative of *vieux Paris* (old Paris), with beamed ceilings and ancient stone walls, and rates include breakfast.

★ **Familia Hôtel**   HOTEL €€

(Map p376; ☑ 01 43 54 55 27; www.familiahotel.com; 11 rue des Écoles, 5e; s €110, d €134-152, tr €191, f €214; ✴ 🛜; Ⓜ Cardinal Lemoine) Sepia murals of Parisian landmarks, flower-bedecked windows and exposed rafters and stone walls make this friendly third-generation family-run hotel one of the most attractive 'almost budget' options on this side of the Seine. Eight rooms (on the 2nd, 5th and 6th floors; there's a lift) have little balconies offering glimpses of Notre Dame. Breakfast costs €7.

Hôtel La Lanterne   BOUTIQUE HOTEL €€

(Map p376; ☑ 01 53 19 88 39; www.hotel-la-lanterne.com; 12 rue de la Montagne Ste-Geneviève, 5e; d/ste from €170/390; ✴ @ 🛜 ⊠; Ⓜ Maubert-Mutualité) A stunning swimming pool and *hammam* (Turkish steambath) in a vaulted stone cellar, a topiary-filled courtyard garden, contemporary guest rooms (some with small balconies) with B&W photos of Parisian architecture, and amenities, including Nespresso machines, and an honesty bar make this a jewel of a boutique hotel. Breakfast (€19) lets you choose from hot and cold buffets and includes Mariage Frères teas.

Hôtel Atmosphères   DESIGN HOTEL €€

(Map p376; ☑ 01 43 26 56 02; www.hotelatmospheres.com; 31 rue des Écoles, 5e; s/d/tr/ste from €126/144/174/229; ✴ @ 🛜; Ⓜ Maubert-Mutualité) Striking images by award-winning French photographer Thierry des Ouches are permanently exhibited at this haven, where cocooning rooms evoke different Parisian 'atmospheres', such as 'nature', 'monuments', the metro-inspired 'urban' and colourful *salon de thé* (tearoom)–style 'macaron'. There's a small gym and a sauna as well as an honesty bar. Breakfast costs €16.

Hôtel Minerve   HOTEL €€

(Map p376; ☑ 01 43 26 26 04; www.parishotelminerve.com; 13 rue des Écoles, 5e; s/d/f from €161/197/394; ✴ @ 🛜; Ⓜ Cardinal Lemoine) Oriental carpets, antique books, frescoes of French monuments and wall tapestries make this family-run hotel a lovely place to stay. Room styles are a mix of traditional and modern (renovated earlier this decade); some have small balconies with views of Notre Dame, while the 1st-floor rooms all have parquet floors.

Hôtel Perreyve   HOTEL €€

(Map p372; ☑ 01 45 48 35 01; www.perreyve-hotel-paris-luxembourg.com; 63 rue Madame, 6e;

s/d €152/197; ✴ 🛜; Ⓜ Rennes) A hop, skip and a jump from the Jardin du Luxembourg, this welcoming 1920s hotel is superb value given its coveted location. Cosy, carpeted rooms have enormous frescoes; on the ground floor, start the day in the pretty breakfast room with herringbone floors and fire-engine-red tables and chairs.

★ **Sublim Eiffel**   DESIGN HOTEL €€

(Map p372; ☑ 01 40 65 95 95; www.sublimeiffel.com; 94 bd Garibaldi, 15e; d from €146; ✴ 🛜; Ⓜ Sèvres-Lecourbe) There's no forgetting what city you're in with the Eiffel Tower motifs in reception and rooms (along with Parisian street-map carpets and metro-tunnel-shaped bedheads) plus glittering tower views from upper-floor windows. Edgy design elements also include cobblestone staircase carpeting (there's also a lift) and, fittingly in *la ville lumière* (the City of Lights), technicoloured in-room fibre-optic lighting. The small wellness centre/ *hammam* offers massages.

🛏 **Right Bank**

★ **Les Piaules**   HOSTEL €

(Map p372; ☑ 01 43 55 09 97; www.lespiaules.com; 59 bd de Belleville, 11e; dm €23-58, d €130-200; @ 🛜; Ⓜ Couronnes) This thoroughly contemporary hostel is the Belleville hot spot to mingle with locals over Parisian craft beer, cosy up in front of the wood-burner with a good book, or lap up sun and stunning views from the 5th-floor rooftop terrace. Dorms are bright and cheery, with custom bunks and ample bedside plugs, but it's the sleek all-white rooftop doubles everyone really gushes over.

Cosmos Hôtel   HOTEL €

(Map p372; ☑ 01 43 57 25 88; www.cosmos-hotel-paris.com; 35 rue Jean-Pierre Timbaud, 11e; s €66, d €72-82, tr €93; 🛜; Ⓜ République) Cheap, brilliant value and just footsteps from the nightlife of rue JPT, Cosmos is a shiny star with retro style on the budget-hotel scene. It has been around for 30-odd years but, unlike most other hotels in the same price bracket, Cosmos has been treated to a thoroughly modern makeover this century. Breakfast costs €8.

Hôtel Tiquetonne   HOTEL €

(Map p376; ☑ 01 42 36 94 58; www.hoteltiquetonne.fr; 6 rue Tiquetonne, 2e; d €80, without shower €65; 🛜; Ⓜ Étienne Marcel) What heart-warmingly good value this 45-room cheapie is. This serious, well-tended address has been in the hotel biz since the 1900s and is much loved by a loyal clientele of all ages. Rooms range across seven floors, are spick and span, and sport an inoffensive mix of vintage decor – roughly 1930s to 1980s, with brand-new bathrooms and parquet flooring in recently renovated rooms.

Mama Shelter DESIGN HOTEL €
(Map p372; ☎01 43 48 48 48; www.mamashelter.com; 109 rue de Bagnolet, 20e; s/d/tr from €89/99/139; ❄@📶; 🚌76, Ⓜ Alexandre Dumas, Gambetta) This former car park was coaxed into its current zany incarnation by uber-designer Philippe Starck. Its 170 cutting-edge rooms feature iMacs, catchy colour schemes, polished-concrete walls and free movies on demand. A rooftop terrace, pizzeria, and huge restaurant with live music and Sunday brunch only add to its street cred. Book as early as possible to get the best deal. Breakfast is €16.

★ Joke Hôtel DESIGN HOTEL €€
(Map p380; ☎01 40 40 71 71; www.astotel.com/hotel; rue Blanche, 9e; s/d €129/150; ❄@📶; Ⓜ Place de Clichy, Pigalle) No joke. This hotel is a serious contender for Paris' best-value, most fun address. Play 'scrabble' or spin the wheel

Montmartre

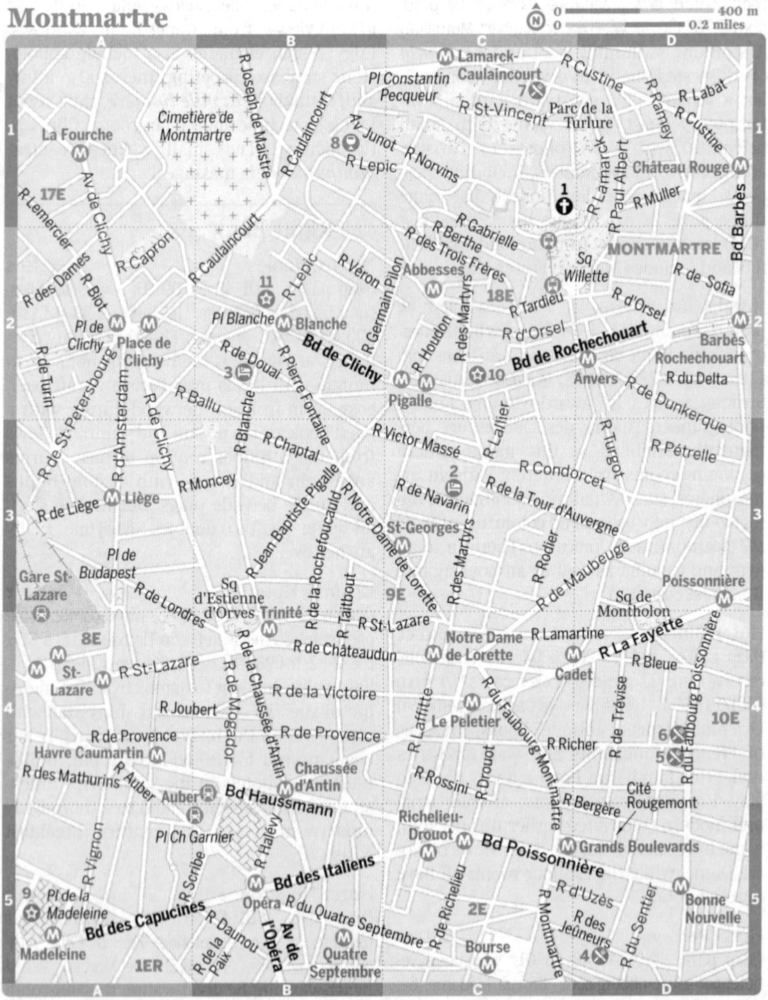

of fortune above your bed each night, hunt for coins stuck in the floor, and generally frolic in the youthful ambience and striking design of this fabulous, childhood-themed hotel. Rates include breakfast and all-day complimentary drinks, cakes and fruit.

★**Hôtel Crayon**   BOUTIQUE HOTEL €€
(Map p376; ☑01 42 36 54 19; www.hotelcrayon. com; 25 rue du Bouloi, 1er; s/d €203/229; ❊ ☎; ⓜLes Halles, Sentier) Line drawings by French artist Julie Gauthron bedeck walls and doors at this creative boutique hotel. *Le crayon* (the pencil) is the theme, with 26 rooms sporting a different shade of each floor's chosen colour – we love the coloured-glass shower doors, and the books on the bedside table guests can swap and take home. On-line deals often slash rates by up to 50%.

★**Hôtel Providence**   BOUTIQUE HOTEL €€
(Map p372; ☑01 46 34 34 04; www.hotelprovidence paris.com; 90 rue René Boulanger, 10e; d from €170; ❊ ☎; ⓜStrasbourg-St-Denis, République) This luxurious hideaway, in a 19th-century townhouse in the increasingly trendy 10e, is exquisite. Its 18 individually decorated rooms come with rich House of Hackney velvet wallpaper and vintage flea-market finds; the smallest rooms are not nearly as 'Mini' (by Paris standards) as the name suggests. Utterly glorious is the bespoke cocktail bar gracing each room, complete with suggested recipes and ingredients.

★**Hôtel Georgette**   DESIGN HOTEL €€
(Map p376; ☑01 44 61 10 10; www.hotelgeorgette. com; 36 rue du Grenier St-Lazare, 3e; d from €190; ❊ ☎; ⓜRambuteau) Clearly seeking inspiration from the Centre Pompidou around the corner, this sweet little neighbourhood hotel is a steal. The lobby is bright and appealing, and rooms are a decorative ode to either Pop Art, Op Art, Dada or New Realism with lots of bold colours and funky touches like Andy Warhol–inspired Campbell's-soup-can lampshades.

Grand Amour Hôtel   DESIGN HOTEL €€
(Map p372; ☑01 44 16 03 10; www.hotelamour paris.fr; 18 rue de la Fidelité, 10e; s/d from €145/230; ☎; ⓜChâteau d'Eau) Younger sister to Pigalle's **Hôtel Amour** (Map p380; ☑01 48 78 31 80; 8 rue Navarin, 9e; d €170-230; ☎; ⓜSt-Georges, Pigalle), this hipster lifestyle hotel mixes vintage furniture from the flea market with phallic-symbol carpets and the striking B&W nude photography of graffiti artist André Saraiva. The result is an edgy hideaway for lovers in one of the city's most up-and-coming neighbourhoods. Breakfast is served in the hotel bistro, a trendy drinking and dining address in itself.

Hôtel Vic Eiffel   BOUTIQUE HOTEL €€
(Map p372; ☑01 53 86 83 83; www.hotelviceiffel. com; 92 bd Garibaldi, 15e; s/d €190/220; ☎; ⓜSèvres-Lecourbe) A short walk from the Eiffel Tower, with the metro on the doorstep, this pristine hotel has chic orange and oyster-grey rooms (two of which are wheelchair accessible). Classic rooms are small but perfectly functional; Superior and Privilege rooms offer increased space. All have Nespresso coffee-making machines. Rates plummet outside high season. Breakfast, served in an atrium-style courtyard, costs €14.

★**Hôtel Félicien**   BOUTIQUE HOTEL €€€
(Map p372; ☑01 55 74 00 00; www.hotelfelicien paris.com; 21 rue Félicien David, 16e; d €280-330, ste from €470; ❊ @ ☎; ⓜMirabeau) The price–quality ratio at this chic boutique hotel, squirrelled away in a 1930s building, is outstanding. Exquisitely designed rooms feel more five-star than four, with 'White' and 'Silver' suites on the hotel's top 'Sky floor' more than satisfying their promise of indulgent cocooning. Romantics, eat your heart out.

FRANCE PARIS

Montmartre

Eating

Left Bank

★ Shakespeare & Company Café
CAFE €

(Map p376; www.shakespeareandcompany. com; 2 rue St-Julien le Pauvre, 5e; dishes €3.50-10.50; ⊘ 9.30am-7pm Mon-Fri, to 8pm Sat & Sun; 🛜 🖉 👪; Ⓜ St-Michel) *Instant history was made when this light-filled, literary-inspired cafe opened in 2015 adjacent to magical bookshop Shakespeare & Company (p387), designed from long-lost sketches to fulfil a dream of late bookshop founder George Whitman from the 1960s. Its primarily vegetarian menu (with vegan and gluten-free dishes available) includes homemade bagels, rye bread, soups, salads and pastries, plus Parisian-roasted Café Lomi (Map p372; 📞 09 80 39 56 24; www.lomi.paris; 3ter rue Marcadet, 18e; ⊘ 10am-7pm; Ⓜ Marcadet–Poissonniers) coffee.

★ L'Avant Comptoir du Marché
TAPAS €

(Map p376; 15 rue Lobineau, 6e; tapas €3.50-19; ⊘ noon-11pm; Ⓜ Mabillon) The latest of Yves Camdeborde's casual 'small plates' eateries is this porcine-specialist tapas bar wedged in one corner of the Marché St-Germain covered market–shopping complex. A flying, fire-engine-red pig is the ceiling's centrepiece, surrounded by suspended menus listing dishes such as Bayonne ham croquettes, Bigorre pâté, and shots of Béarnaise pig's blood; wines are chalked on the blackboard. No reservations.

Camdeborde's neighbouring addresses include bistro Le Comptoir du Relais (Map p376; 📞 01 44 27 07 97; www.hotel-paris-relais-saint-germain.com; 9 Carrefour de l'Odéon, 6e; lunch mains €14-28, dinner menu €60; ⊘ noon-6pm & 8.30-11.30pm Mon-Fri, noon-11pm Sat & Sun; Ⓜ Odéon), tapas bar L'Avant Comptoir (Map p376; www.hotel-paris-relais-saint-germain.com; 3 Carrefour de l'Odéon, 6e; tapas €4-10; ⊘ noon-midnight; Ⓜ Odéon) and seafood tapas bar L'Avant Comptoir de la Mer (Map p376; www.hotel-paris-relais-saint-germain.com; 3 Carrefour de l'Odéon, 6e; tapas €5-25; ⊘ 11am-11pm; Ⓜ Odéon).

★ Café de la Nouvelle Mairie
CAFE €

(Map p376; 📞 01 44 07 04 41; 19 rue des Fossés St-Jacques, 5e; mains €9-19; ⊘ kitchen noon-2.30pm & 8-10.30pm Mon-Thu, 8-10pm Fri; Ⓜ Cardinal Lemoine) Shhhh…just around the corner from the Panthéon (p370) but hidden away on a small, fountained square, this narrow wine bar is a neighbourhood secret, serving blackboard-chalked natural wines by the glass and delicious seasonal bistro fare from oysters and ribs (*à la française*) to grilled lamb sausage over lentils. It takes reservations for dinner but not lunch – arrive early.

★ Bouillon Racine
BRASSERIE €€

(Map p376; 📞 01 44 32 15 60; www.bouillonracine. com; 3 rue Racine, 6e; weekday 2-course lunch menu €17, menus €33-46, mains €18.50-29; ⊘ noon-11pm; 👪; Ⓜ Cluny-La Sorbonne) Inconspicuously situated in a quiet street, this heritage-listed 1906 art-nouveau 'soup kitchen', with mirrored walls, floral motifs and ceramic tiling, was built in 1906 to feed market workers. Despite the magnificent interior, the food – inspired by age-old recipes – is no afterthought but superbly executed (stuffed, spit-roasted suckling pig, pork shank in Rodenbach red beer, scallops and shrimps with lobster coulis).

★ Tomy & Co
GASTRONOMY €€

(Map p372; 📞 01 45 51 46 93; 22 rue Surcouf, 7e; 2-course lunch menu €25, 3-course dinner menu €45, tasting menu €65, with paired wines €100; ⊘ noon-2pm & 7.30-9.30pm Mon-Fri; Ⓜ Invalides) The talk-of-the-town address of the moment is Tomy Gousset's inaugural restaurant (book ahead). Gousset previously cooked in some of Paris' top kitchens and now works his magic here on inspired seasonal dishes like roast duck with candied yellow beets and pickled grapes, and pork neck with spinach, black olives, micro herbs and raw mushrooms, using produce from his organic garden.

La Table de Marie-Jeanne
ROTISSERIE €€

(Map p376; 📞 01 42 49 87 31; www.latable demariejeanne.fr; 4 rue Toullier, 5e; 2-/3-course menus lunch €17/21, dinner €26/31; ⊘ noon-2.15pm & 7-10.30pm Tue-Sat; Ⓜ Cluny–La Sorbonne or RER Luxembourg) Free-range chickens and prime cuts of lamb, beef, pork, duck and veal (plus venison in season) are spit-roasted on these chic Left Bank premises. Adorned with stencilled animals on blond wood-panelled walls, exposed stone and suspended topaz and jade-green glass lights, accompanying sides here include roasted potatoes, salads and fragrant sauces such as rosemary and pepper.

TOP FIVE SWEET TREATS

You couldn't come to Paris and not indulge in something sweet, sticky and delicious. From light-as-air macarons to creamy éclairs, fruity tarts and sinful chocolate confections, the Parisians really know how to indulge a sweet tooth.

Ladurée (Map p372; www.laduree.com; 75 av des Champs-Élysées, 8e; pastries from €1.90,; ⊙7.30am-11.30pm Mon-Thu, 7.30am-12.30am Fri, 8.30am-12.30am Sat, 8.30am-11.30pm Sun; Ⓜ George V) Famous across Paris for its multi-flavoured macarons.

Berthillon (Map p376; www.berthillon.fr; 31 rue St-Louis en l'Île, 4e; 1/2/3 scoops take away €3/4/6.50, eat-in €4.50/7.50/10.50; ⊙10am-8pm Wed-Sun, closed Aug; Ⓜ Pont Marie) Seventy-odd flavours of ice-cream, including seasonal ones.

Jacques Genin (Map p376; ☑01 45 77 29 01; www.jacquesgenin.fr; 133 rue de Turenne, 3e; pastries €9; ⊙11am-7pm Tue-Sun; Ⓜ Oberkampf, Filles du Calvaire) A wildly creative chocolatier with a delightful tea-room.

La Patisserie des Rêves (Map p372; www.lapatisseriedesreves.com; 93 rue du Bac, 7e; ⊙9am-7pm Tue-Thu, to 8pm Fri & Sat, to 2pm Sun; Ⓜ Rue du Bac) The cakes on show here are almost too dreamy to eat.

Le Bonbon au Palais (Map p376; www.bonbonsaupalais.fr; 19 rue Monge, 5e; ⊙10.30am-7.30pm Tue-Sat; Ⓜ Cardinal Lemoine) From stripey *berlingots* to almondy *calissons*, this is Paris' favourite sweet-shop.

🍴 Right Bank

⭐ Chez Alain Miam Miam
SANDWICHES, CRÊPERIE €

(Map p376; www.facebook.com/ChezAlainMiam Miam; Marché des Enfants Rouges, 39 rue de Bretagne & 33bis rue Charlot, 3e; dishes €3-9.50; ⊙9am-3.30pm Wed-Fri, to 5.30pm Sat, to 3pm Sun; ☑; Ⓜ Filles du Calvaire) Weave your way through the makeshift kitchens inside Marché des Enfants Rouges to find Alain, a retired baker sporting T-shirts with attitude, whose passion, humour and food are legendary. Watch him prepare you a monster sandwich or *galette* (savoury pancake) on a sizzling griddle a fresh, organic ingredients – grated fennel, smoked air-dried beef, avocado, sesame salt and prized honeys.

⭐ Café Pinson
CAFE, VEGETARIAN €

(Map p376; ☑09 83 82 53 53; www.cafepinson. fr; 6 rue du Forez, 3e; 2-course lunch menu €17.50, mains €14; ⊙9am-10pm Mon-Fri, 10am-10pm Sat, noon-6pm Sun; 🖥☑; Ⓜ Filles du Calvaire) 🍃 Tucked down a narrow side street in the fashionable Haut Marais, with an interior by celebrity designer Dorothée Meilichzon, this spacious cafe sees a stylish lunchtime crowd flock for its organic vegetarian and vegan dishes such as almond, carrot and ginger soup and dark-chocolate pear crumble. Freshly squeezed juices are excellent, as is Sunday brunch (€27; 12.15pm and 2pm).

⭐ 52 Faubourg St-Denis
MODERN FRENCH €

(Map p372; www.faubourgstdenis.com; 52 rue du Faubourg St-Denis, 10e; mains €16-20; ⊙8am-midnight, kitchen noon-2.30pm & 7-11pm; 🖥; Ⓜ Château d'Eau) This thoroughly contemporary, neighbourhood cafe-restaurant is simply a brilliant space to hang out in at any time of day. Be it for breakfast, coffee, a zingy fresh-sage infusion, dinner or drinks, 52 Faubourg, as locals call it, gets it just right. Cuisine is modern and creative, and the chef is not shy in mixing veg with fruit in every course – including dessert. No reservations.

⭐ Richer
BISTRO €

(Map p380; www.lericher.com; 2 rue Richer, 9e; mains €18-20; ⊙noon-2.30pm and 7.30-10.30pm; Ⓜ Poissonière, Bonne Nouvelle) Richer's pared-back, exposed-brick decor is a smart setting for genius creations like smoked duck breast ravioli in miso broth, and quince and lime cheesecake for dessert. It doesn't take reservations, but it serves up snacks and Chinese tea, and has a full bar (open until midnight). Fantastic value. Run by the same team as across-the-street neighbour **L'Office** (☑01 47 70 67 31; www.office-resto.com; 2-/3-course lunch menus €22/27, mains €19-32; ⊙noon-2pm & 7.30-10.30pm Mon-Fri).

Café Marais
MODERN FRENCH €

(Map p376; ☑01 42 71 61 46; www.cafemarais. fr; 10 rue des Haudriettes, 3e; 2-course lunch/

dinner menu €17.50/19.50; ⊗ noon-3pm Mon-Thu, noon-3pm & 7-11.30pm Fri & Sat; Ⓜ Rambuteau) Exposed stone, a beamed ceiling and silent B&W movies (Charlie Chaplin et al) screened on one wall create an appealing vintage feel in this small and excellent bistro – one of the best-value spots for dining in Le Marais. The round of Camembert roasted with honey, homemade courgette gratin and parmesan crème brûlée are all excellent.

Soul Kitchen

VEGETARIAN €

(Map p380; www.soulkitchenparis.fr; 33 rue Lamarck, 18e; lunch menu €13.90; ⊗ 8.45am-6pm Mon-Fri; 🐾🖉🚻; Ⓜ Lamarck–Caulaincourt) This vegetarian eatery with shabby-chic vintage interior and tiny open kitchen serves market-driven dishes including feisty bowls of creative salads, homemade soups, savoury tarts, burritos and wraps – all gargantuan in size and packed with seasonal veggies. Round off lunch or snack between meals on muffins, cakes and mint-laced *citronnade maison* (homemade lemonade). Families should check out the sage-green 'games' cupboard.

★ Au Passage

BISTRO €€

(Map p376; 🖉 01 73 20 23 23; www.restaurant-au-passage.fr; 1bis passage St-Sébastien, 11e; small plates €7-14, meats to share €18-70; ⊗ 7-11.30pm Mon-Sat; Ⓜ St-Sébastien-Froissart) Spawned by talented Australian chef James Henry, who went on to open Bones then Parisian bistro Belon in Hong Kong, this *petit bar de quartier* (neighbourhood bar) is still raved about. Pick from a good-value, uncomplicated choice selection of *petites assiettes* (small plates designed to be shared) featuring various market produce – cold meats, raw or cooked fish, vegetables and so on. Advance reservations essential.

★ Bambou

SOUTHEAST ASIAN €€

(Map p380; 🖉 01 40 28 98 30; www.bambou-paris.com; 23 rue des Jeûneurs, 2e; mains €19-28; ⊗ noon-2.30pm & 7-11pm, bar to midnight; 🖉; Ⓜ Sentier) One of Paris' most sizzling recent openings, this spectacular Southeast Asian restaurant occupies a 500-sq-metre former fabric warehouse, with vintage birdcages and a giant metal dragon adorning the main dining room, a downstairs billiards room and bar, vast terrace and Zen-like garden. Chef Antonin Bonnet's specialities include squid with black pepper and basil, and aromatic shrimp pad thai.

★ La Bulle

MODERN FRENCH €€

(Map p372; 🖉 01 85 15 21 58; www.restolabulle.fr; 48 rue Louis Blanc, 10e; 2-/3-course lunch menus €18.50/24, 3-/6-course dinner menus €36/55, mains €19-28; ⊗ noon-2.30pm & 7.30-10.30pm Mon-Sat; Ⓜ Louis Blanc) It's worth the short detour to this contemporary corner bistro with lime-green seating on a sunny pavement terrace, and talented young chef Romain Perrollaz in the kitchen. His cuisine is creative and strictly *fait maison* (homemade), with lots of tempting combos like poached salmon and artichoke mousse, squid stuffed with konbu (Japanese seaweed), or pork, pistachio and cuttlefish ink terrine.

★ Le Clown Bar

MODERN FRENCH €€

(Map p376; 🖉 01 43 55 87 35; www.clown-bar-paris.com; 114 rue Amelot, 11e; mains €28-36; ⊗ kitchen noon-2.30pm & 7-10.30pm Wed-Sun, bar 7.30am-1.30am; Ⓜ Filles du Calvaire) The former staff dining room of the city's winter circus, the 1852-built Cirque d'Hiver, is a historic monument with colourful clown-themed ceramics and mosaics, painted glass ceilings and its original zinc bar. Fabulous modern French cuisine spans scallops with smoked rosemary ricotta to Mesquer pigeon, smoked eel with pear and mushrooms and sautéed veal's brains, accompanied by excellent natural wines.

★ Pierre Sang Boyer

MODERN FRENCH €€

(Map p372; 🖉 09 67 31 96 80; www.pierresang-boyer.com; 55 rue Oberkampf, 11e; 2-/3-/5-course lunch €20/25/35, 4-/6-course dinner €35/50; ⊗ noon-3pm & 7-11pm Tue-Sat; Ⓜ Oberkampf) *Top Chef* finalist Pierre Sang Boyer stars at his kitchen restaurant where foodies sit on bar stools and watch the French–South Korean chef perform. Cuisine is modern French with a strong fusion lilt, and the vibe is fun and casual. If the place is full, nip around the corner to Sang's 'atelier' annexe on rue Gambey.

Le Bistrot Paul Bert

BISTRO €€

(Map p372; 🖉 01 43 72 24 01; 18 rue Paul Bert, 11e; 2-/3-course lunch/dinner menu €19/41; ⊗ noon-2pm & 7.30-11pm Tue-Sat; Ⓜ Faidherbe-Chaligny) When food writers list Paris' best bistros, Paul Bert's name consistently pops up. The timeless vintage decor and classic dishes like *steak-frites* and hazelnut-cream Paris-Brest pastry merit booking ahead. Look for its siblings in the same street: **L'Écailler du Bistrot** (🖉 01 43 72 76 77; 22 rue Paul Bert, 11e; weekday lunch menu €19, mains €17-38; ⊗ noon-

2.30pm & 7.30-11pm Tue-Sat) for seafood; **La Cave Paul Bert** (☑01 58 53 30 92; 16 rue Paul Bert, 11e; ⊗noon-midnight, kitchen noon-2pm & 7.30-11.30pm), a wine bar with small plates; and **Le 6 Paul Bert** (☑01 43 79 14 32; 6 rue Paul Bert, 12e; 6-course menu €60; ⊗7-11pm Tue-Sat) for modern cuisine.

Soya
VEGETARIAN, VEGAN €€

(Map p376; ☑01 48 06 33 02; www.facebook.com/soyacantinebio; 20 rue de la Pierre Levée, 11e; weekday lunch menu €15-22, brunch €27; ⊗7-11pm Tue, noon-3.30pm & 7-11pm Wed-Fri, 11.30am-11pm Sat, 11.30am-4pm Sun; ☑; MGoncourt, République) A favourite for its ubercool location in an industrial atelier (with bare cement, metal columns and big windows), Soya is a full-on *cantine bio* (organic eatery) in what was once a staunchly working-class district. Dishes, many tofu-based, are vegetarian and the weekend brunch buffet is deliciously lazy and languid. A glass floor floods the basement area with light.

★Frenchie
BISTRO €€€

(Map p376; ☑01 40 39 96 19; www.frenchie-restaurant.com; 5 rue du Nil, 2e; 4-course lunch menu €45, 5-course dinner menu €74, with wine €175; ⊗6.30-11pm Mon-Wed, noon-2.30pm & 6.30-11pm Fri; MSentier) Tucked down an inconspicuous alley, this tiny bistro with wooden tables and old stone walls is always packed and for good reason: excellent-value dishes are modern, market-driven and prepared with unpretentious flair by French chef Gregory Marchand. Reserve well in advance; arrive at 6.30pm and pray for a cancellation (it does happen); or head to neighbouring **Frenchie Bar à Vins** (6 rue du Nil, 2e; dishes €9-23; ⊗6.30-11pm Mon-Fri).

Drinking & Nightlife

The line between bars, cafes and bistros is blurred at best. It costs more to sit at a table than to stand at the counter, more on a fancy square than a backstreet, more in the 8e than in the 18e. After 10pm many cafes charge a pricier *tarif de nuit* (night rate).

Left Bank

★Little Bastards
COCKTAIL BAR

(Map p376; 5 rue Blainville, 5e; ⊗7pm-2am Mon, 6pm-2am Tue-Thu, 6pm-4am Fri & Sat; MPlace Monge) Only house-creation cocktails are listed on the menu at uberhip Little Bastards – among them Fal' in Love (Beefeater gin, cranberry juice, lime, mint, guava purée and

Falernum clove-, ginger- and almond-syrup), Be a Beet Smooth (Jameson whisky, coriander, sherry, egg white and pepper) and Deep Throat (Absolut vodka, watermelon syrup and Pernod) – but they'll also mix up classics if you ask.

★Les Deux Magots
CAFE

(Map p376; www.lesdeuxmagots.fr; 170 bd St-Germain, 6e; ⊗7.30am-1am; MSt-Germain des Prés) If ever there was a cafe that summed up St-Germain des Prés' early 20th-century literary scene, it's this former hang-out of anyone who was anyone. You will spend *beaucoup* to sip a coffee in a wicker chair on the terrace shaded by dark-green awnings and geraniums spilling from window boxes, but it's an undeniable piece of Parisian history.

Le Verre à Pied
CAFE

(Map p376; 118bis rue Mouffetard, 5e; ⊗9am-9pm Tue-Sat, 9.30am-4pm Sun; MCensier Daubenton) This *café-tabac* is a pearl of a place where little has changed since 1870. Its nicotine-hued mirrored wall, moulded cornices and original bar make it part of a dying breed, but it epitomises the charm, glamour and romance of an old Paris everyone loves, including stallholders from the rue Mouffetard market who yo-yo in and out.

Right Bank

★Le Baron Rouge
WINE BAR

(Map p372; ☑01 43 43 14 32; www.lebaronrouge.net; 1 rue Théophile Roussel, 12e; ⊗5-10pm Mon, 10am-2pm & 5-10pm Tue-Fri, 10am-10pm Sat, 10am-4pm Sun; MLedru-Rollin) Just about the ultimate Parisian wine-bar experience, this wonderfully unpretentious local meeting place where everyone is welcome has barrels

---

BAR-HOPPING STREETS

Prime Parisian streets for a soirée:

Rue Vieille du Temple, 4e Marais cocktail of gay bars and chic cafes.

Rue Oberkampf, 11e Edgy urban hangouts.

Rue de Lappe, 11e Boisterous Bastille bars and clubs.

Rue de la Butte aux Cailles, 13e Village atmosphere and fun local haunts.

Rue Princesse, 6e Student and sports bars.

stacked against the bottle-lined walls and serves cheese, charcuterie and oysters. It's especially busy on Sunday after the Marché d'Aligre (Map p372; rue d'Aligre, 12e; ⊙8am-1pm Tue-Sun) wraps up. For a small deposit, you can fill up 1L bottles straight from the barrel for under €5.

★**Experimental Cocktail Club** COCKTAIL BAR
(ECC; Map p376; www.experimentalevents.com; 37 rue St-Sauveur, 2e; ⊙7pm-2am; MRéaumur–Sébastopol) With a black-curtain façade, this retro-chic speakeasy – with sister bars in London, Ibiza and New York – is a sophisticated flashback to those années folles (crazy years) of Prohibition New York. Cocktails (€13 to €15) are individual and fabulous, and DJs keep the party going until dawn at weekends. It's not a large space, however, and fills to capacity quickly.

★**Candelaria** COCKTAIL BAR
(Map p376; www.quixotic-projects.com; 52 rue de Saintonge, 3e; ⊙bar 6pm-2am Mon-Fri, noon-4pm & 6pm-2am Sat & Sun, taqueria noon-10.30pm Sun-Wed, noon-11.30pm Thu-Sat; MFilles du Calvaire) A lime-green taqueria serving homemade tacos, quesadillas and tostadas (dishes €3.50 to €9) conceals one of Paris' coolest cocktail bars through an unmarked internal door. Evenings kick off with occasional DJ sets, tastings, post-gallery drinks and phenomenal cocktails made from agave spirits including mezcal. Reserve online for cocktail-fuelled weekend brunch (€20; noon to 4pm), featuring a feisty tequila-laced Bloody Maria.

★**Le Très Particulier** COCKTAIL BAR
(Map p380; ☑01 53 41 81 40; www.hotel-particulier-montmartre.com; Pavillon D, 23 av Junot, 18e; ⊙6pm-2am; MLamarck-Caulaincourt) The clandestine cocktail bar of boutique Hôtel Particulier Montmartre is an enchanting spot for a summertime alfresco cocktail. Ring the buzzer at the unmarked black gated entrance and make a beeline for the 1871 mansion's flowery walled garden (or, if it's raining, the adjacent conservatory-style interior). DJs spin tunes from 9.30pm Wednesday to Saturday and from 7pm on Sunday.

★**Le Petit Fer à Cheval** BAR
(Map p376; www.cafeine.com/petit-fer-a-cheval; 30 rue Vieille du Temple, 4e; ⊙9am-2am; MHôtel de Ville, St-Paul) A Marais institution, the Little Horseshoe is a minute cafe-bar with an original horseshoe-shaped zinc bar from

1903. The place overflows with regulars from dawn to dark. Great apéro (predinner drink) spot and great WC – stainless-steel toilet stalls straight out of a Flash Gordon film (actually inspired by the interior of the Nautilus submarine in Jules Verne's 20,000 Leagues under the Sea).

★**Fluctuat Nec Mergitur** CAFE
(Map p376; ☑01 42 06 44 07; www.fluctuat-cafe.paris; place de la République, 10e; ⊙7.30am-2am; 🛜; MRépublique) No address guarantees a fuller immersion into local life than Fluctuat (formerly Café Monde et Média), all shiny, new and rebranded with an edgy name after a kitchen fire in February 2015 wrecked the popular cafe and after-work hot spot. Its enviable location on pedestrian esplanade place de la République means it's always buzzing with Parisians chatting over drinks.

Chez Jeannette BAR
(Map p372; 47 rue du Faubourg St-Denis, 10e; ⊙8am-2am; MChâteau d'Eau) For vintage vibe you don't get better than Jeannette's. Cracked tile floors and original 1950s decor have turned this local neighbourhood cafe-bar into one of the 10e's most popular hot spots. Local hang-out by day, pints by night and reasonably priced meals around the clock.

La Fourmi BAR
(Map p380; 74 rue des Martyrs, 18e; ⊙8.30am-2am Sun-Thu, to 4am Fri & Sat; MPigalle) A Pigalle institution, sociable La Fourmi hits the mark with its high ceilings, long zinc bar, timber-panelled walls and unpretentious vibe. It's a great place to find out about live music and club nights or grab a drink before heading out to a show. Bonus: table football.

☆ Entertainment

To find out what's on, buy Pariscope (€0.50) or L'Officiel des Spectacles (€0.50; www.offi.fr) at Parisian news kiosks. Both are published on Wednesday. The most convenient place to buy concert, performance or event tickets is megastore Fnac (☑08 92 68 36 22; www.fnactickets.com), which has numerous branches in town.

If you go on the day of a performance, you can snag a half-price ticket (plus €3 commission) for ballet, theatre, opera and other performances at the discount-ticket outlet Kiosque Théâtre Madeleine (Map p380; www.kiosqueculture.com; opposite 15 place de la

Madeleine, 8e; ⏰12.30-7.30pm Tue-Sat, to 3.45pm Sun; Ⓜ Madeleine).

⭐**Café Universel**   JAZZ, BLUES
(Map p376; ☎01 43 25 74 20; www.cafeuniversel. com; 267 rue St-Jacques, 5e; ⏰9pm-2am Tue-Sat; 🛜; Ⓜ Censier Daubenton or RER Port Royal) Café Universel hosts a brilliant array of live concerts with everything from bebop and Latin sounds to vocal jazz sessions. Plenty of freedom is given to young producers and artists, and its convivial relaxed atmosphere attracts a mix of students and jazz lovers. Concerts are free, but tip the artists when they pass the hat around.

⭐**Le Batofar**   CLUB
(Map p372; www.batofar.fr; opposite 11 quai François Mauriac, 13e; ⏰club 11.30pm-6am Tue-Sat, bar 6-11pm Tue-Sat May-Sep, 7pm-midnight Tue-Sat Oct-Apr; Ⓜ Quai de la Gare, Bibliothèque) This much-loved, red-metal tugboat has a rooftop bar that's terrific in summer, and a respected restaurant, while the club underneath provides memorable underwater acoustics between its metal walls and portholes. Le Batofar is known for its edgy, experimental music policy and live performances from 7pm, mostly electro-oriented but also incorporating hip hop, new wave, rock, punk and jazz.

Le Bataclan   LIVE MUSIC
(Map p376; www.bataclan.fr; 50 bd Voltaire, 11e; Ⓜ Oberkampf, St-Ambroise) Built in 1864, intimate concert, theatre and dance hall Le Bataclan was Maurice Chevalier's debut venue in 1910. The 1497-capacity venue reopened with a concert by Sting on 12 November 2016, almost a year to the day following the tragic 13 November 2015 terrorist attacks that took place here, and once again hosts French and international rock and pop legends.

La Cigale   LIVE MUSIC
(Map p380; ☎01 49 25 89 99; www.lacigale.fr; 120 bd de Rochechouart, 18e; Ⓜ Pigalle) Now classed as a historical monument, this music hall dates from 1887 but was redecorated 100 years later by Philippe Starck. Artists who have performed here include Ryan Adams, Ibrahim Maalouf and the Dandy Warhols.

Moulin Rouge   CABARET
(Map p380; ☎01 53 09 82 82; www.moulinrouge. fr; 82 bd de Clichy, 18e; show/dinner show from €87/165; ⏰shows 7pm, 9pm & 11pm; Ⓜ Blanche) Immortalised in Toulouse-Lautrec's posters

GAY & LESBIAN PARIS

Le Marais (4e), especially the areas around the intersection of rue Ste-Croix de la Bretonnerie and rue des Archives, and eastwards to rue Vieille du Temple, has been Paris' main centre of gay nightlife for some three decades.

The single best source of info on gay and lesbian Paris is the **Centre Gai et Lesbien de Paris** (Map p376; ☎01 43 57 21 47; www.centrelgbtparis.org; 63 rue Beaubourg, 3e; ⏰centre & bar 3.30-8pm Mon-Fri, 1-7pm Sat, library 2-8pm Mon, Tue & Wed, 5-7pm Fri & Sat; Ⓜ Rambuteau), with a large library and happening bar.

and later in Baz Luhrmann's film, Paris' legendary cabaret twinkles beneath a 1925 replica of its original red windmill. Yes, it's packed with bus-tour crowds. But from the opening bars of music to the last high cancan-girl kick, it's a whirl of fantastical costumes, sets, choreography and Champagne. Book in advance online and dress smartly (no sneakers). No entry for children under six.

Point Éphémère   LIVE MUSIC
(Map p372; ☎01 40 34 02 48; www.point ephemere.org; 200 quai de Valmy, 10e; ⏰12.30pm-2am Mon-Sat, to 10pm Sun; 🛜; Ⓜ Louis Blanc) On the banks of Canal St-Martin in a former fire station and later squat, this arts and music venue attracts an underground crowd for concerts, dance nights and art exhibitions. Its rockin' restaurant, Animal Kitchen, fuses gourmet cuisine with music from Animal Records (Sunday brunch from 1pm is a highlight); the rooftop bar, Le Top, opens in fine weather.

🛍 Shopping

⭐**Shakespeare & Company**   BOOKS
(Map p376; ☎01 43 25 40 93; www.shakespeare andcompany.com; 37 rue de la Bûcherie, 5e; ⏰10am-11pm; Ⓜ St-Michel) Shakespeare's enchanting nooks and crannies overflow with new and secondhand English-language books. The original shop (12 rue l'Odéon, 6e; closed by the Nazis in 1941) was run by Sylvia Beach and became the meeting point for Hemingway's 'Lost Generation'. Readings by emerging and illustrious authors take place at 7pm most Mondays. There's a wonderful cafe (p382) and various workshops and festivals.

★ **Marché aux Puces de St-Ouen**   MARKET

(www.marcheauxpuces-saintouen.com; rue des Rosiers, St-Ouen; ⊙ Sat-Mon; M Porte de Clignancourt) This vast flea market, founded in the late 19th century and said to be Europe's largest, has more than 2500 stalls grouped into 15 *marchés* (markets), each with its own speciality (eg Marché Paul Bert Serpette for 17th-century furniture, Marché Malik for casual clothing, Marché Biron for Asian art). Each market has different opening hours – check the website for details.

★ **Paris Rendez-Vous**   GIFTS & SOUVENIRS

(Map p376; www.rendezvous.paris.fr; 29 rue de Rivoli, 4e; ⊙10am-7pm Mon-Sat; M Hôtel de Ville) This chic city has its own designer line of souvenirs, sold in its own ubercool concept store inside Hôtel de Ville (city hall). Shop here for everything from clothing and homewares to Paris-themed books, wooden toy sailing boats and signature Jardin du Luxembourg Fermob chairs. *Quel style!*

★ **Gab & Jo**   FASHION & ACCESSORIES

(Map p376; www.gabjo.fr; 28 rue Jacob, 6e; ⊙11am-7pm Mon-Sat; M St-Germain des Prés) 🏷 Forget mass-produced, imported souvenirs: for quality local gifts, browse the shelves of the country's first-ever concept store stocking only made-in-France items. Designers include La Note Parisienne (scented candles for each Parisian *arrondissement*, such as the 6e, with notes of lipstick, cognac, orange blossom, tuberose, jasmine, rose and fig), Marius Fabre (Marseille soaps), Germaine-des-Prés (lingerie), MILF (sunglasses) and Monsieur Marcel (T-shirts).

★ **La Grande Épicerie de Paris**   FOOD & DRINKS

(Map p372; www.lagrandeepicerie.com; 36 rue de Sèvres, 7e; ⊙8.30am-9pm Mon-Sat, 10am-8pm Sun; M Sèvres-Babylone) The magnificent food hall of department store **Le Bon Marché** (Map p372; www.bonmarche.com; 24 rue de Sèvres, 7e; ⊙10am-8pm Mon-Wed & Sat, to 8.45pm Thu & Fri, 11am-8pm Sun; M Sèvres-Babylone) sells 30,000 rare and/or luxury gourmet products, including 60 different types of bread baked on site and delicacies such as caviar ravioli. Its fantastical displays of chocolates, pastries, biscuits, cheeses, fresh fruit and vegetables and deli goods are a Parisian sight in themselves. Wine tastings regularly take place in the basement.

Fromagerie Laurent Dubois   CHEESE

(Map p376; www.fromageslaurentdubois.fr; 47ter bd St-Germain, 5e; ⊙8am-7.45pm Tue-Sat, 8.30am-1pm Sun; M Maubert-Mutualité) One of the best *fromageries* in Paris, this cheese-lover's nirvana is filled with to-die-for delicacies, such as St-Félicien with Périgord truffles. Rare, limited-production cheeses include blue Termignon and Tarentaise goat's cheese. All are appropriately cellared in warm, humid or cold environments. There's also a 15e **branch** (Map p372; 2 rue de Lourmel, 15e; ⊙9am-1pm & 4-7.45pm Tue-Fri, 8.30am-7.45pm Sat, 9am-1pm Sun; M Dupleix).

ℹ Information

DANGERS & ANNOYANCES

Metro stations best avoided late at night include Châtelet–Les Halles and its corridors; Château Rouge in Montmartre; Gare du Nord; Strasbourg St-Denis; Réaumur Sébastopol; and Montparnasse Bienvenüe.

Pickpocketing and thefts from handbags and packs is a problem wherever there are crowds (especially of tourists).

MEDICAL SERVICES

Paris has some 50 hospitals including the following:

American Hospital of Paris (📞 01 46 41 25 25; www.american-hospital.org; 63 bd Victor Hugo, Neuilly-sur-Seine; M Pont de Levallois) Private hospital; emergency 24-hour medical and dental care.

Hertford British Hospital (IHFB; 📞 01 46 39 22 00; www.ihfb.org; 4 rue Kléber, Levallois-Perret; M Anatole France) Less expensive, private, English-speaking option.

Hôpital Hôtel Dieu (📞 01 42 34 88 19; www.aphp.fr; 1 place du Parvis Notre Dame, 4e; M Cité) One of the city's main government-run public hospitals; after 8pm use the emergency entrance on rue de la Cité.

TOURIST INFORMATION

Paris Convention & Visitors Bureau (Office du Tourisme et des Congrès de Paris; Map p376; www.parisinfo.com; 25 rue des Pyramides, 1er; ⊙9am-7pm May-Oct, 10am-7pm Nov-Apr; M Pyramides) The main branch is 500m northwest of the Louvre. It sells tickets for tours and several attractions, plus museum and transport passes. Also books accommodation.

ℹ Getting There & Away

AIR

There are three main airports in Paris:

Aéroport de Charles de Gaulle (CDG; 📞 01 70 36 39 50; www.parisaeroport.fr) Most international airlines fly to CDG, 28km north-east of the centre of Paris. In French, the airport is commonly called 'Roissy'.

Aéroport d'Orly (ORY; ☑ 01 70 36 39 50; www. parisaeroport.fr) Located 19km south of Paris but not as frequently used by international airlines.

Aéroport de Beauvais (BVA; ☑ 08 92 68 20 66; www.aeroportbeauvais.com) Not really in Paris at all (it's 75km north of Paris) but used by some low-cost carriers.

BUS

Eurolines (Map p376; www.eurolines.fr; 55 rue St-Jacques, 5e; ☉ ticket office 9.30am-6.30pm Mon-Fri, 10am-1pm & 2-5pm Sat; Ⓜ Cluny–La Sorbonne) connects all major European capitals to Paris' international bus terminal, **Gare Routiére Internationale de Paris-Galliéni** (☑ 08 92 89 90 91; 28 av du Général de Gaulle, Bagnolet; Ⓜ Galliéni). The terminal is in the eastern suburb of Bagnolet; it's about a 15-minute metro ride to the more central République station.

TRAIN

Paris has six major train stations serving both national and international destinations. For mainline train information, check **SNCF** (www. sncf-voyages.com).

Gare du Nord (rue de Dunkerque, 10e; Ⓜ Gare du Nord) Trains to/from the UK, Belgium, Germany and northern France.

Gare de l'Est (bd de Strasbourg, 10e; Ⓜ Gare de l'Est) Trains to/from Germany, Switzerland and eastern areas of France.

Gare de Lyon (bd Diderot, 12e; Ⓜ Gare de Lyon) Trains to/from Provence, the Riviera, the Alps and Italy. Also serves Geneva.

Gare d'Austerlitz (bd de l'Hôpital, 13e; Ⓜ Gare d'Austerlitz) Trains to/from Spain and Portugal, and non-TGV trains to southwestern France.

Gare Montparnasse (av du Maine & bd de Vaugirard, 15e; Ⓜ Montparnasse Bienvenüe) Trains to/from western France (Brittany, Atlantic coast) and southwestern France.

Gare St-Lazare Trains to Normandy.

❶ Getting Around

TO/FROM THE AIRPORTS

Getting into town is straightforward and inexpensive thanks to a fleet of public-transport options. Bus drivers sell tickets. Children aged four to 11 years pay half-price on most services.

Aéroport de Charles de Gaulle

RER B line (€10, 50 minutes, every 10 to 20 minutes) Stops at Gare du Nord, Châtelet–Les Halles and St-Michel–Notre Dame stations. Trains run from 5am to 11pm; there are fewer trains on weekends.

Le Bus Direct line 2 (€17; one hour; every 30 minutes, 5.45am to 11pm) Links the airport with the Arc de Triomphe via the Eiffel Tower and Trocadéro.

Le Bus Direct line 4 (€17; 50 to 80 minutes; every 30 minutes, 6am to 10.30pm from the airport, 5.30am to 10.30pm from Montparnasse) Links the airport with Gare Montparnasse (80 minutes) in southern Paris via Gare de Lyon (50 minutes) in eastern Paris.

RATP bus 350 (€6; 70 minutes; every 30 minutes, 5.30am to 11pm) Links the airport with Gare de l'Est in northern Paris.

Taxi (40 minutes to city centre) €50 to Right Bank and €55 to Left Bank, plus 15% surcharge between 5pm and 10am and on Sundays.

Aéroport d'Orly

RER B and Orlyval (€12.05, 35 minutes, every four to 12 minutes, 6am to 11pm) The nearest RER station to the airport is Antony, where you connect on the dedicated Orlyval.

Le Bus Direct line 1 (€12; one hour, every 20 minutes 5.50am to 11.30pm from Orly, 4.50am to 10.30pm from the Arc de Triomphe) Runs to/from the Arc de Triomphe (one hour) via Gare Montparnasse (40 minutes), La Motte-Picquet and Trocadéro.

Taxi (30 minutes to city centre) €30 to the Left Bank and €35 to the Right Bank, plus 15% between 5pm and 10am and on Sundays.

Aéroport de Beauvais

Beauvais shuttle (€17, 1¼ hours) links the airport with metro station Porte Maillot.

BICYCLE

The **Vélib'** (☑ 01 30 79 79 30; www.velib.paris. fr; day/week subscription €1.70/8, bike hire up to 30/60/90/120min free/€1/2/4) bike-share scheme puts 20,000-odd bikes at the disposal of Parisians and visitors to get around the city. There are about 1800 docking stations; bikes are available around the clock.

BOAT

Batobus (www.batobus.com; adult/child 1-day pass €17/8, 2-day pass €19/10; ☉10am-9.30pm Apr-Aug, to 7pm Sep-Mar) runs glassed-in trimarans that dock every 20 to 25 minutes at nine small piers along the Seine: Beaugrenelle, Eiffel Tower, Musée d'Orsay, St-Germain des Prés, Notre Dame, Jardin des Plantes/Cité de la Mode et du Design, Hôtel de Ville, Musée du Louvre and Champs-Élysées.

Buy tickets online, at ferry stops or at tourist offices. You can also buy a two- or three-day Paris À La Carte Pass that includes L'Open Tour buses for €45 or €49.

PUBLIC TRANSPORT

➡ Paris' public transit system is operated by the **RATP** (www.ratp.fr).

➜ The same RATP tickets are valid on the metro, RER, buses, trams and Montmartre funicular. A ticket – white in colour and called Le Ticket t+ – costs €1.90 (half price for children aged four to nine years) if bought individually and €14.50 for adults for a carnet (book) of 10.

➜ One ticket covers travel between any two metro stations (no return journeys) for 1½ hours; you can transfer between buses and between buses and trams, but not from metro to bus or vice versa.

➜ Keep your ticket until you exit the station or risk a fine.

Bus

➜ Buses run from 5.30am to 8.30pm Monday to Saturday, with certain evening lines continuing until midnight or 12.30am, when the hourly Noctilien (www.noctilien.fr) night buses kick in.

➜ Short bus rides (ie rides in one or two bus zones) cost one ticket; longer rides require two.

➜ Remember to punch single-journey tickets in the composteur (ticket machine) next to the driver.

Metro & RER

Paris' underground network consists of 14 numbered metro lines and the five suburban RER lines (designated by the letters A to E).

Trains usually start around 5.30am and finish sometime between 12.35am and 1.15am (2.15am Friday and Saturday).

Tourist Passes

Mobilis Allows unlimited travel for one day and costs €7.30 (two zones) to €17.30 (five zones). Buy it at any metro, RER or SNCF station in the Paris region.

Paris Visite Allows unlimited travel as well as discounted entry to certain museums and other discounts and bonuses. The 'Paris+Suburbs+Airports' pass includes transport to/from the airports and costs €24.50/37.25/52.20/63.90 for one/two/three/five days. The cheaper 'Paris Centre' pass, valid for zones 1 to 3, costs €11.65/18.95/25.85/37.25 for one/two/three/five days.

Travel Passes

If you're staying in Paris more than three or four days, the cheapest and easiest way to use public transport is to get a rechargeable **Navigo** (www.navigo.fr) pass.

A weekly pass costs €22.15 and is valid Monday to Sunday. You'll also need to pay €5 for the Navigo card and provide a passport photo.

TAXI

➜ The prise en charge (flagfall) is €2.60. Within the city limits, it costs €1.04 per kilometre for travel between 10am and 5pm Monday to Saturday (Tarif A; white light on taxi roof and meter).

➜ At night (5pm to 10am), on Sunday from 7am to midnight, and in the inner suburbs the rate is €1.27 per kilometre (Tarif B; orange light).

➜ The minimum taxi fare for a short trip is €6.86.

➜ There's a €3 surcharge for taking a fourth passenger. The first piece of baggage is free; additional pieces over 5kg cost €1 extra.

➜ To order a taxi, call or reserve online with **Taxis G7** (☑ 3607, 01 41 27 66 99; www.taxisg7.fr), **Taxis Bleus** (☑ 08 91 70 10 10, 3609; www.taxis-bleus.com) or **Alpha Taxis** (☑ 01 45 85 85 85; www.alpha-taxis-paris.fr).

➜ An alternative is the private driver system, Uber taxi (www.uber.com/cities/paris), whereby you order and pay via your smartphone.

AROUND PARIS

Versailles

POP 87,400

Louis XIV – the Roi Soleil (Sun King) – transformed his father's hunting lodge into the monumental Château de Versailles in the mid-17th century, and it remains France's most famous, grandest palace. Situated in the prosperous, leafy and bourgeois suburb of Versailles, 28km southwest of Paris, the baroque château was the kingdom's political capital and the seat of the royal court from 1682 up until the fateful events of 1789, when revolutionaries massacred the palace guard and dragged Louis XVI and Marie Antoinette back to Paris, where they were ingloriously guillotined.

The current €400 million restoration program is the most ambitious yet, and until it's completed in 2020, at least a part of the palace is likely to be clad in scaffolding when you visit.

◉ Sights

★**Château de Versailles**   PALACE

(☑ 01 30 83 78 00; www.chateauversailles.fr; place d'Armes; adult/child passport ticket incl estate-wide access €20/free, with musical events €27/free, palace €15/free; ⊙9am-6.30pm Tue-Sun Apr-Oct, to 5.30pm Tue-Sun Nov-Mar; Ⓜ RER Versailles-Château–Rive Gauche) Amid magnificently landscaped formal gardens, this splendid and enormous palace was built in the mid-17th century during the reign of Louis XIV – the Roi Soleil (Sun King) – to project the absolute power of the French monarchy, which was then at the height of its glory. The château has undergone relatively few alterations since its construction, though almost all the interior furnishings disappeared during the Revolution and many of the rooms were rebuilt by Louis-Philippe (r 1830–48).

❶ Getting There & Away

RER C5 (€4.20, 40 minutes, frequent) goes from Paris' Left Bank RER stations to Versailles-Château–Rive Gauche station. The less convenient RER C8 links Paris with Versailles-Chantiers station, a 1.3km walk from the château.

Chartres

POP 40,216

The magnificent 13th-century **Cathédrale Notre Dame** (www.cathedrale-chartres.org; place de la Cathédrale; ⊙8.30am-7.30pm daily year-round, also to 10pm Tue, Fri & Sun Jun-Aug) of Chartres, crowned by two very different spires – one Gothic, the other Romanesque – rises from rich farmland 88km southwest of Paris and dominates the medieval town.

The cathedral's west, north and south entrances have superbly ornamented triple portals and its 105m-high **Clocher Vieux** (Old Bell Tower), also called the Tour Sud (South Tower), is the tallest Romanesque steeple still standing. Superb views of three-tiered flying buttresses and the 19th-century copper roof, turned green by verdigris, reward the 350-step hike up the 112m-high **Clocher Neuf** (New Bell Tower, also known as North Tower).

Inside, 172 extraordinary stained-glass windows, mainly from the 13th century, form one of the most important ensembles of medieval stained glass in the world. The three most exquisite – renowned for the depth and intensity of their tones, famously known as 'Chartres blue' – are above the west entrance and below the rose window.

❶ Getting There & Away

Frequent SNCF trains link Paris' Gare Montparnasse (€16, 55 to 70 minutes) with Chartres, some of which stop at Versailles-Chantiers (€13.50, 45 to 60 minutes).

---

❶ VERSAILLES TIPS

Versailles is one of the country's most popular destinations, with over five million visitors annually; advance planning will make visiting more enjoyable.

➡ Monday is out for obvious reasons (it's closed).

➡ Arrive early morning and avoid Tuesday, Saturday and Sunday, its busiest days.

➡ Prepurchase tickets on the château's website or at **Fnac** (p386) branches and head straight to **Entrance A** (Château de Versailles).

➡ Versailles is free on the first Sunday of every month from November to March.

➡ Pre-book a **guided tour** (☑01 30 83 77 88; www.chateauversailles.fr; Château de Versailles; tours €7, plus palace entry; ⊙English-language tours 9.30am Tue-Sun) to access areas that are otherwise off limits as well as the most famous parts of the palace.

➡ Free apps can be downloaded from the website.

Giverny

☑518

The tiny village of Giverny, 74km northwest of Paris, was the **home of impressionist Claude Monet** (☑02 32 51 28 21; http://fondation-monet.com; 84 rue Claude Monet; adult/child €9.50/5.50, incl Musée des Impressionnismes Giverny €16.50/8.50; ⊙9.30am-6pm Easter-Oct) for the last 43 years of his life. You can visit the artist's pastel-pink house and famous gardens with lily pond, Japanese bridge draped in purple wisteria, and so on. Early to late spring, daffodils, tulips, rhododendrons, wisteria and irises bloom in the flowery gardens, followed by poppies and lilies. By June, nasturtiums, roses and sweet peas are in flower, while September is the month to see dahlias, sunflowers and hollyhocks.

The closest train station is at Vernon, from where buses, taxis and cycle/walking tracks run to Giverny. Shuttle buses (€8 return, 20 minutes, four daily Easter to October) meet most trains from Paris at Vernon. From Paris' Gare St-Lazare there are up to 15 daily trains to Vernon (€14.70, 45 minutes to one hour).

WORTH A TRIP

MODERN ART MUSEUMS

Two of Paris' foremost art institutions, the Louvre and the Centre Pompidou, have satellite outposts in northern France that art lovers definitely won't want to miss.

Louvre-Lens (☑ 03 21 18 62 62; www.louvrelens.fr; 99 rue Paul Bert; multimedia guide €3; ⊗ 10am-6pm Wed-Mon) **FREE** Showcases hundreds of the Louvre's treasures in a purpose-built, state-of-the-art exhibition space in Lens, 35km southwest of Lille. A second building, the glass-walled **Pavillon de Verre**, displays temporary themed exhibits. Lens is easily reached by train from Paris' Gare du Nord (€40, 1¼ hours) and Lille-Flandres (from €8.30, 45 minutes)

Centre Pompidou-Metz (www.centrepompidou-metz.fr; 1 parvis des Droits de l'Homme; adult/child €7/free; ⊗ 10am-6pm Mon & Wed-Thu, to 7pm Fri-Sun) Concentrates mainly on abstract and experimental art. The building itself is worth the trip, designed by Japanese architect Shigeru Ban, with a curved roof resembling a space-age Chinese hat. Trains run direct from from Paris (€33 to €81, 1½ hours) and Strasbourg (€27.10, 1½ hours).

LILLE & THE SOMME

When it comes to culture, cuisine, beer, shopping and dramatic views of land and sea, the friendly Ch'tis (residents of France's northern tip) and their region compete with the best France has to offer. Highlights include Flemish-style Lille, the cross-Channel shopping centre of Calais, and the moving battlefields and cemeteries of WWI.

Lille

POP 231,500

Lille may be the country's most underrated major city. In recent decades, this once-grimy industrial metropolis has transformed itself – with generous government help – into a glittering and self-confident cultural and commercial hub. Highlights of the city include an attractive old town with a strong Flemish accent, renowned art museums, stylish shopping and a cutting-edge, student-driven nightlife.

◉ Sights

Palais des Beaux Arts GALLERY
(Fine Arts Museum; ☑ 03 20 06 78 00; www.pba-lille.fr; place de la République; adult/child €7/4; ⊗ 2-5.50pm Mon, 10am-5.50pm Wed-Sun; 🛜🚭; Ⓜ République Beaux-Arts) Lille's illustrious Fine Arts Museum displays a truly first-rate collection of 15th- to 20th-century paintings, including works by Rubens, Van Dyck and Manet. Exquisite porcelain and faience (pottery), much of it of local provenance, is on the ground floor, while in the basement you'll find classical archaeology, medieval statuary and 18th-century scale models of the fortified cities of northern France and Belgium.

Vieille Bourse HISTORIC BUILDING
Ornamented with caryatids and cornucopia, this Flemish Renaissance extravaganza was built in 1653. It consists of 24 separate houses set around a richly ornamented interior courtyard that hosts a used-book market and chess games.

Musée d'Art Moderne, d'Art Contemporain et d'Art Brut – LaM GALLERY
(☑ 03 20 19 68 88; www.musee-lam.fr; 1 allée du Musée, Villeneuve-d'Ascq; adult/child €7/5; ⊗ 10am-6pm Tue-Sun) Colourful, playful and just plain weird works of modern and contemporary art by masters such as Braque, Calder, Léger, Miró, Modigliani and Picasso are the big draw at this renowned museum and sculpture park in the Lille suburb of Villeneuve-d'Ascq, 9km east of Gare Lille-Europe. Take metro line 1 to Pont de Bois, then bus L4 six stops to 'LAM'.

⌂ Sleeping

Auberge de Jeunesse HOSTEL €
(☑ 03 20 57 08 94; www.hifrance.org; 235 bd Paul Painlevé; dm incl breakfast & sheets €25; @🛜; Ⓜ Porte de Valenciennes) The good news is that Lille has a youth hostel, opened in 2015, with a façade sporting the colours of Europe. The bad news is that while all 55 rooms have showers, only 12 have attached toilets, and instead of faucets the showers have annoying timer-buttons. Wi-fi is available only in the lobby.

Hôtel de la Treille HOTEL €€
(📞 03 20 55 45 46; www.hoteldelatreille.com; 7-9 place Louise de Bettignies; d €90-140; 📶) In a superb spot smack in the middle of Vieux Lille, a few steps from dining and shopping options galore. The 42 stylish rooms, totally redecorated in 2014, offer views of the lively square out front, the cathedral or a quiet interior courtyard.

✖ Eating

★ Meert PASTRIES €
(📞 03 20 57 93 93; www.meert.fr; 27 rue Esquermoise; waffles from €3; ⊘ shop 9.30am-7.30pm Tue-Sat, 9am-1pm & 3-7pm Sun, tearoom 9.30am-10pm Tue-Sat, 9am-6pm Sun; 📶; Ⓜ Rihour) Famed for its *gaufres* (waffles) made with Madagascar vanilla, Meert has served kings, viceroys and generals since 1761. The sumptuous chocolate shop's coffered ceiling, painted wooden panels, wrought-iron balcony and mosaic floor date from 1839. Inside, the historic *salon de thé* is a delightful spot for a morning Arabica or a mid-afternoon tea. Also has a French gourmet restaurant.

La Petite Table MODERN FRENCH €
(📞 03 20 55 60 47; www.lapetitetable-vieuxlille.com; 59 rue de la Monnaie; mains €1-16; ⊘ noon-2.30pm Tue-Sun, 7.30-10pm or 10.30pm Tue-Sat; 📶) Inspired by the 34 countries he visited during nine years in the French navy, chef Arnaud Duhamel – a Lonely Planet fan – prepares both local (Flemish) favourites and dishes inspired by the tastes he encountered in the Americas, Africa and around the Indian Ocean. A favourite of locals in search of good value.

ⓘ Information

Tourist Office (📞 03 59 57 94 00; www.lille-tourism.com; place Rihour; ⊘ 9am-6pm Mon-Sat, 10am-4.30pm Sun & holidays; Ⓜ Rihour) Has walking itineraries of the city (€3).

ⓘ Getting There & Away

AIR
Aéroport de Lille (www.lille.aeroport.fr) is connected to all major French cities and a number of European destinations too.

TRAIN
Lille's two main train stations, Gare Lille-Flandres and newer Gare Lille-Europe, are 400m apart on the eastern edge of the city centre.

Gare Lille-Europe (📶; Ⓜ Gare Lille-Europe) Topped by what looks like a 20-storey ski boot, this ultramodern station handles Eurostar trains to London, TGV/Thalys/Eurostar trains to Brussels-Midi, half of the TGVs to Paris Gare du Nord and most province-to-province TGVs.

Gare Lille-Flandres (📶; Ⓜ Gare Lille-Flandres) This old-fashioned station, recently spruced up, is used by half of the TGVs to Paris Gare du Nord and all intra-regional TER services.

FRANCE LILLE

WORTH A TRIP

THE SOMME BATTLEFIELDS

The First Battle of the Somme, a WWI Allied offensive waged in the villages and woodlands northeast of Amiens, was designed to relieve pressure on the beleaguered French troops at Verdun. On 1 July 1916, British, Commonwealth and French troops 'went over the top' in a massive assault along a 34km front. But German positions proved virtually unbreachable, and on the first day of the battle an astounding 21,392 British troops were killed and another 35,492 were wounded. By the time the offensive was called off in mid-November, a total of 1.2 million lives had been lost on both sides. The British had advanced 12km, the French 8km.

The battlefields and memorials are numerous and scattered – joining a tour can therefore be a good option, especially if you don't have your own transport. Respected operators include the **Battlefields Experience** (📞 03 22 76 29 60; www.thebattleofthe-somme.co.uk), **Chemins d'Histoire** (📞 06 31 31 85 02; www.cheminsdhistoire.com) and **Terres de Mémoire** (📞 03 22 84 23 05; www.terresdememoire.com).

Between 2014 and 2018, a number of events will commemorate the Centenary of WWI throughout the region.

The tourist offices in **Péronne** (📞 03 22 84 42 38; www.hautesomme-tourisme.com; 16 place André Audinot; ⊘ 10am-noon & 2-5pm or 6pm Mon-Sat Sep-Jun, plus 9am-12.30pm & 1.30-6.30pm Sun Jul & Aug) and **Albert** (📞 03 22 75 16 42; www.tourisme-paysducoquelicot.com; 9 rue Gambetta; ⊘ 9am-12.30pm & 1.30-5pm or 6.30pm Mon-Fri, 9am-noon & 2-5pm or 6.30pm Sat Sep-Apr, plus 9am-1pm Sun May-Aug) can help with booking tours and accommodation.

Services include the following:

Brussels-Midi TGV €30, 35 minutes, at least a dozen daily; regular train €22.50, two hours

London (St Pancras International) Eurostar €110 to €180, 90 minutes, 10 daily

Paris Gare du Nord €50 to €67, one hour, 16 to 24 daily

NORMANDY

Famous for cows, cider and Camembert, this largely rural region (www.normandie-tourisme.fr) is one of France's most traditional, and most visited, thanks to world-renowned sights such as the Bayeux Tapestry, the historic D-Day beaches and spectacular Mont St-Michel.

FRANCE BAYEUX

Bayeux

POP 13,900

Bayeux has become famous throughout the English-speaking world thanks to a 68.3m-long piece of painstakingly embroidered cloth: the 11th-century Bayeux Tapestry, with its 58 scenes that vividly tell the story of the Norman invasion of England in 1066.

The town is also one of the few in Normandy to have survived WWII practically unscathed, with a centre crammed with 13th- to 18th-century buildings, wooden-framed Norman-style houses, and a spectacular Norman Gothic cathedral. It makes a great base for exploring D-Day beaches.

◉ Sights

★ **Bayeux Tapestry** TAPESTRY
(✆02 31 51 25 50; www.bayeuxmuseum.com; rue de Nesmond; adult/child incl audioguide €9/4; ⊙9am-6.30pm Mar-Oct, to 7pm May-Aug, 9.30am-12.30pm & 2-6pm Nov-Feb) The world's most celebrated work of embroidery depicts the conquest of England by William the Conqueror in 1066 from an unashamedly Norman perspective. Commissioned by Bishop Odo of Bayeux, William's half-brother, for the opening of Bayeux' cathedral in 1077, the 68.3m-long cartoon strip tells the dramatic, bloody tale with verve and vividness.

🛌 Sleeping

Hôtel d'Argouges HOTEL €€
(✆02 31 92 88 86; www.hotel-dargouges.com; 21 rue St-Patrice; s/d/tr/f €115/132/175/205; ⊙closed Dec & Jan; P🐾) Occupying a stately

18th-century residence with a lush little garden, this graceful hotel has 28 comfortable rooms with exposed beams, thick walls and Louis XVI–style furniture. The breakfast room, hardly changed since 1734, still has its original wood panels and parquet floors.

Villa Lara BOUTIQUE HOTEL €€€
(✆02 31 92 00 55; www.hotel-villalara.com; 6 place de Québec; d €190-360, ste €390-520; P🐾🌐) Newly constructed in the past decade, this 28-room hotel, Bayeux' most luxurious, sports minimalist colour schemes, top-quality fabrics and decor that juxtaposes 18th- and 21st-century tastes. Amenities include a bar and a gym. Most rooms have cathedral views.

✖ Eating

★ **La Reine Mathilde** PASTRIES €
(47 rue St-Martin; cakes from €2.50; ⊙9am-7.30pm Tue-Sun) This sumptuously decorated patisserie and *salon de thé*, ideal for a sweet breakfast or a relaxing cup of afternoon tea, hasn't changed much since it was built in 1898.

Au Ptit Bistrot MODERN FRENCH €€
(✆02 31 92 30 08; 31 rue Larcher; lunch menu €17-20, dinner menu €27-33, mains €16-19; ⊙noon-2pm & 7-9pm Tue-Sat) Near the cathedral, this friendly, welcoming eatery whips up creative, beautifully prepared dishes that highlight the Norman bounty without a lick of pretension. Recent hits include chestnut soup, duck breast and bulgur with seasonal fruits and roasted pineapple, and black cod with spinach and spicy guacamole. Reservations essential.

Alchimie MODERN FRENCH €€
(lunch menu €12) On a street lined with restaurants, Alchimie has a simple but elegant design that takes nothing from the beautifully presented dishes. Choose from the day's specials listed on a chalkboard menu, which might include hits like *brandade de morue* (baked codfish pie). It's a local favourite, so call ahead.

❶ Information

Tourist Office (✆02 31 51 28 28; www.bayeux-bessin-tourisme.com; pont St-Jean; ⊙9.30am-12.30pm & 2-6pm) Covers both Bayeux and the surrounding region, including D-Day beaches.

ℹ Getting There & Away

Trains link Bayeux with Caen (€7, 20 minutes, hourly), from where there are connections to Paris' Gare St-Lazare and Rouen.

D-Day Beaches

Early on 6 June 1944, Allied troops stormed 80km of beaches north of Bayeux, code-named (from west to east) Utah, Omaha, Gold, Juno and Sword. The landings on D-Day – called *Jour J* in French – ultimately led to the liberation of Europe from Nazi occupation. For context, see www.normandie-memoire.com and www.6juin1944.com.

The most brutal fighting on D-Day took place 15km northwest of Bayeux along the stretch of coastline now known as **Omaha Beach**, today a glorious stretch of fine golden sand partly lined with sand dunes and summer homes. **Circuit de la Plage d'Omaha**, a trail marked with a yellow stripe, is a self-guided tour along the beach, surveyed from a bluff above by the huge **Normandy American Cemetery & Memorial** (☑02 31 51 62 00; www.abmc.gov; Colleville-sur-Mer; ☉9am-6pm mid-Apr–mid-Sep, to 5pm mid-Sep–mid-Apr). Featured in the opening scenes of Steven Spielberg's *Saving Private Ryan,* this is the largest American cemetery in Europe.

Caen's high-tech, hugely impressive **Mémorial – Un Musée pour la Paix** (Memorial – A Museum for Peace; ☑02 31 06 06 44; www.memorial-caen.fr; esplanade Général Eisenhower; adult/child €20/17; ☉9am-7pm early Feb-early Nov, 9.30am-6.30pm Tue-Sun early Nov-early Feb, closed 3 weeks in Jan) uses sound, lighting, film, animation and lots of exhibits to graphically explore and evoke the events of WWII, the D-Day landings and the ensuing Cold War.

🧭 Tours

**Tours by Le Mémorial –
Un Musée pour la Paix**   BUS
(☑02 31 06 06 45; www.memorial-caen.fr; tour morning/afternoon €65/85; ☉9am & 2pm Apr-Sep, 1pm Oct-Mar, closed 3 weeks in Jan) Excellent year-round minibus tours (four to five hours), take in Pointe du Hoc, Omaha Beach, the American cemetery and the artificial port at Arromanches. There are cheaper tours in full-size buses (€45) from June to August. Rates include entry to Le Mémorial – Un Musée pour la Paix. Book online.

Normandy Tours   TOURS
(☑02 31 92 10 70; www.normandy-landing-tours.com; 26 place de la Gare, Bayeux; adult/student €62/55) Offers well-regarded four- to five-hour tours of the main sites starting at 8.15am and 1.15pm on most days, as well as personally tailored trips. Based at Bayeux' Hôtel de la Gare, facing the train station.

Mont St-Michel

It's one of France's most iconic images: the slender spires, stout ramparts and rocky slopes of Mont St-Michel rising dramatically from the sea – or towering over sands laid bare by the receding tide. Despite huge numbers of tourists, both the abbey and the narrow alleys below still manage to transport visitors back to the Middle Ages.

The bay around Mont St-Michel is famed for having Europe's highest tidal variations; the difference between low and high tides – only about six hours apart – can reach an astonishing 15m.

◎ Sights

Abbaye du Mont St-Michel   ABBEY
(☑02 33 89 80 00; www.monuments-nationaux.fr; adult/child incl guided tour €9/free; ☉9am-7pm, last entry 1hr before closing) The Mont's star attraction is the stunning architectural ensemble high up on top: the abbey. Most areas can be visited without a guide, but it's well worth taking the one-hour tour included in the ticket price; English tours (usually) begin at 11am and 3pm from October to March, with three or four daily tours in spring and summer. You can also take a 1½-hour audioguide tour (one/two people €4.50/6), available in six languages.

🛏 Sleeping

La Jacotière   B&B €€
(☑02 33 60 22 94; www.lajacotiere.fr; 46 rue de la Côte, Ardevon; d incl breakfast €75-90, studio €80-95; 🅿🛜) Built as a farmhouse in 1906, this superbly situated, family-run B&B has five comfortable rooms and one studio apartment. Situated just 300m east of the shuttle stop in La Caserne.

Hôtel Du Guesclin   HOTEL €€
(☑02 33 60 14 10; www.hotelduguesclin.com; Grande Rue, Mont St-Michel; d €95-125; ☉closed Wed night & Thu Apr-Jun & Oct–mid-Nov, hotel closed mid-Nov–Mar) One of the most affordable hotels on the Mont itself, the Hôtel Du

Guesclin (geck-*la*) has 10 charming rooms, five with priceless views of the bay.

ℹ️ Getting There & Away

Transdev bus 1 links the Mont St-Michel La Caserne parking lot (2.5km from the Mont itself, which you access by free shuttle) with **Pontorson** (€3.20, 18 minutes), the nearest train station. From Pontorson, there are two to three daily trains to/from Bayeux (€25, 1¾ hours) and Caen (€26.10, 1¾ hours).

BRITTANY

Brittany is for explorers. Its wild, dramatic coastline, medieval towns, thick forests and the eeriest stone circles this side of Stonehenge make a trip here well worth the detour from the beaten track. This is a land of prehistoric mysticism, proud tradition and culinary wealth, where locals remain fiercely independent, where Breton culture (and cider) is celebrated and where Paris feels a very long way away indeed.

Quimper

POP 66,926

Small enough to feel like a village – with its slanted half-timbered houses and narrow cobbled streets – and large enough to buzz as the troubadour of Breton culture, Quimper (pronounced *kam-pair*) is the thriving capital of Finistère (meaning 'land's end').

◉ Sights

⭐ **Cathédrale St-Corentin**   CHURCH
(place St-Corentin; ⊙ 8.30am-noon & 1.30-6.30pm Mon-Sat, 8.30am-noon & 2-6.30pm Sun) At the centre of the city is Quimper's Gothic cathedral with its distinctive dip in the middle where it was built to conform to the land, said to symbolise Christ's inclined head as he was dying on the cross. Construction began in 1239, but the cathedral's dramatic twin spires weren't added until the 19th century. High on the west façade, look out for an equestrian statue of King Gradlon, the city's mythical 5th-century founder.

⭐ **Musée Départemental Breton**   MUSEUM
(☑ 02 98 95 21 60; www.museedepartementalbreton.fr; 1 rue du Roi Gradlon; adult/child €5/free; ⊙ 9am-12.30pm & 1.30-5pm Tue-Sat, 2-5pm Sun Sep-Jun, 9am-6pm daily Jul & Aug) Beside the Cathédrale St-Corentin, recessed behind a magnificent stone courtyard, this superb museum showcases Breton history, furniture, costumes, crafts and archaeology, in a former bishop's palace.

🛏️ Sleeping & Eating

Hôtel Gradlon   HOTEL €€
(☑ 02 98 95 04 39; www.hotel-gradlon.com; 30 rue de Brest; d €130-150; ⊙ mid-Jan-mid-Dec; P 🐾) The rather bland, modern façade belies a charming country manor interior, with excellent service. The smallish but well-furnished rooms differ, but all have plenty of character and individual touches, and bathrooms tend towards the large and modern. Costs drop dramatically in winter; breakfast costs €12. No lift.

⭐ **L'Épée**   CAFE €€
(☑ 02 98 95 28 97; www.quimper-lepee.com; 14 rue du Parc; mains €12-24, lunch menus €24, other menus €29-46; ⊙ brasserie noon-2.30pm & 7-10.30pm, cafe 10.30am-midnight) A Quimper institution – it's one of Brittany's oldest brasseries – L'Épée hits the mark with its buzzy, contemporary dining areas, efficient service and good vibe. Despite the hip interior, the food is by no means an afterthought. Superbly executed dishes include duck breast, lamb shank, shellfish and salads. You can also just stop in for a drink.

ℹ️ Information

Tourist office (☑ 02 98 53 04 05; www.quimper-tourisme.com; place de la Résistance; ⊙ 9am-7pm Mon-Sat, 10am-12.45pm & 3-5.45pm Sun Jul & Aug, 9.30am-12.30pm & 1.30-6.30pm Mon-Sat Sep-Jun, plus 10am-12.45pm Sun Apr-Jun & Sep; 🐾) Has information about the wider area.

ℹ️ Getting There & Away

Frequent trains serve Paris' Gare Montparnasse (€30 to €96, 4¾ hours).

St-Malo

POP 46,589

The mast-filled port of fortified St-Malo is inextricably tied up with the deep briny blue: the town became a key harbour during the 17th and 18th centuries, functioning as a base for merchant ships and government-sanctioned privateers, and these days it's a busy cross-Channel ferry port and summertime getaway.

◉ Sights

Walking on top of the sturdy 17th-century ramparts (1.8km) affords fine views of the old walled city known as **Intra-Muros** (Within the Walls), or Ville Close; access the ramparts from any of the city gates.

★**Château de St-Malo**   CASTLE
Château de St-Malo was built by the dukes of Brittany in the 15th and 16th centuries, and now holds **Musée d'Histoire de St-Malo** (📞02 99 40 71 57; www.ville-saint-malo.fr/culture/les-musees; Château; adult/child €6/3; ⊙10am-12.30pm & 2-6pm daily Apr-Sep, Tue-Sun Oct-Mar), which looks at the life and history of the city. The castle's lookout tower offers eye-popping views of the old city.

**Île du Grand Bé &
Fort du Petit Bé**   ISLAND, CASTLE
(📞06 08 27 51 20; www.petit-be.com; fort guided tours adult/child €5/3; ⊙fort by reservation, depending on tides) At low tide, cross the beach to walk out via Porte des Bés to Île du Grand Bé, the rocky islet where the great St-Malo-born, 18th-century writer Chateaubriand is buried. About 100m beyond the Île du Grand Bé is the privately owned, Vauban-built, 17th-century Fort du Petit Bé. The owner runs 30-minute guided tours in French; leaflets are available in English. Once the tide rushes in, the causeway remains impassable for about six hours; check tide times with the tourist office.

🛏 Sleeping & Eating

★**La Maison des Armateurs**   HOTEL €€
(📞02 99 40 87 70; www.maisondesarmateurs.com; 6 Grand Rue; d €110-210, f/ste from €190/230; ⊙closed Dec; ❄🐾) No language barrier here – La Maison des Armateurs is run by a helpful French-American couple. Despite the austere granite-fronted setting, the inside of this sassy four-star hotel is all sexy, modern minimalism: modern furniture throughout, gleaming bathrooms with power showers and cool chocolate, pale orange and neutral grey tones. Families can plump for the super-sized suites. Check the website for deals.

★**Bistro Autour du Beurre**   BISTRO €€
(📞02 23 18 25 81; www.lebeurrebordier.com; 7 rue de l'Orme; lunch menu €19, mains €18-24; ⊙noon-2pm Tue-Sat, 7-10pm Thu-Sat) This casual bistro showcases the cheeses and butters handmade by the world-famous Jean-Yves Bordier; you'll find his **shop** (www.lebeurrebordier.com; 7 rue de l'Orme; ⊙9am-1pm & 3.30-7.30pm

Tue-Sat, 9am-1pm Mon & Sun) next door. His products are shipped to renowned restaurants around the globe. At the bistro, the butter sampler (€15 in the shop, but included in meals) and bottomless bread basket are just the start to creative, local meals that change with the seasons.

ℹ Information

Tourist Office (📞08 25 13 52 00; www.saint-malo-tourisme.com; esplanade St-Vincent; ⊙9am-7.30pm Mon-Sat, 10am-6pm Sun Jul & Aug, shorter hours Sep-Jun; 🐾) Just outside the walls, near Porte St-Vincent. Has smartphone app, transport info and loads of local advice.

ℹ Getting There & Away

Brittany Ferries (www.brittany-ferries.com) sails between St-Malo and Portsmouth; Condor Ferries (www.condorferries.co.uk) runs to/from Poole via Jersey or Guernsey.

TGV train services go to Paris' Gare Montparnasse (€45 to €79, 3½ hours, three direct TGVs daily).

CHAMPAGNE

Known in Roman times as Campania, meaning 'plain', the agricultural region of Champagne is synonymous these days with its world-famous bubbly. This multimillion-dollar industry is strictly protected under French law, ensuring that only grapes grown in designated Champagne vineyards can truly lay claim to the hallowed title. The town of Épernay, 30km south of the regional capital of Reims, is the best place to head for *dégustation* (tasting); a self-drive **Champagne Routes** (www.tourisme-en-champagne.com) wends its way through the region's most celebrated vineyards.

Reims

POP 186,505

Over the course of a millennium (816 to 1825), some 34 sovereigns – among them two dozen kings – began their reigns in Reims' famed cathedral. Meticulously reconstructed after WWI and again following WWII, the city – whose name is pronounced something like 'rance' and is often anglicised as Rheims – is endowed with handsome pedestrian zones, well-tended parks, lively nightlife and a state-of-the-art tramway.

◉ Sights

★ **Cathédrale Notre Dame** CATHEDRAL
(www.cathedrale-reims.culture.fr; place du Cardinal Luçon; tower adult/child €7.50/free, incl Palais du Tau €11/free; ☉ 7.30am-7.15pm, tower tours hourly 10am-4pm Tue-Sat, 2-4pm Sun May-Sep, 10am-4pm Sat, 2-4pm Sun mid-Mar–Apr) Imagine the egos and extravagance of a French royal coronation. The focal point of such bejewelled pomposity was Reims' resplendent Gothic cathedral, begun in 1211 on a site occupied by churches since the 5th century. The interior is a rainbow of stained-glass windows; the finest are the western façade's 12-petalled **great rose window** – under restoration at the time of research – the north transept's **rose window** and the vivid **Chagall** creations (1974) in the central axial chapel. The tourist office rents audioguides (€6) for self-paced cathedral tours.

★ **Basilique St-Rémi** BASILICA
(place du Chanoine Ladame; ☉ 8am-7pm) **FREE**
This 121m-long former Benedictine abbey church, a Unesco World Heritage Site, mixes Romanesque elements from the mid-11th century (the worn but stunning nave and transept) with early Gothic features from the latter half of the 12th century (the choir, with a large triforium gallery and, way up top, tiny clerestory windows).

Next door, **Musée St-Rémi** (53 rue Simon; adult/child €4/free; ☉ 2-6.30pm Mon-Fri, to 7pm Sat & Sun), in a 17th- and 18th-century abbey, features local Gallo-Roman archaeology, tapestries and 16th- to 19th-century military history.

★ **Palais du Tau** MUSEUM
(www.palais-du-tau.fr; 2 place du Cardinal Luçon; adult/child €7.50/free, incl cathedral tower €11/free; ☉ 9.30am-12.30pm & 2-5.30pm Tue-Sun) A Unesco World Heritage Site, this lavish former archbishop's residence, redesigned in neoclassical style between 1671 and 1710, was where French princes stayed before their coronations – and where they threw sumptuous banquets afterwards. Now a museum, it displays truly exceptional statuary, liturgical objects and tapestries from the cathedral, some in the impressive, Gothic-style Salle de Tau (Great Hall). Treasures worth seeking out include the 9th-century talisman of Charlemagne and Saint Remi's golden, gem-encrusted chalice, which dates to the 12th century.

★ **Taittinger** WINERY
(☐ 03 26 85 45 35; www.taittinger.com; 9 place St-Niçaise; tours €17-45; ☉ 9.30am-5.30pm, shorter hours & closed weekends Oct-Mar) The headquarters of Taittinger are an excellent place to come for a clear, straightforward presentation on how Champagne is actually made – there's no claptrap about 'the Champagne mystique' here. Parts of the cellars occupy 4th-century Roman stone quarries; other bits were excavated by 13th-century Benedictine monks. No need to reserve. Situated 1.5km southeast of Reims centre; take the Citadine 1 or 2 bus to the St-Niçaise or Salines stops.

🛏 Sleeping

★ **Les Telliers** B&B €€
(☐ 09 53 79 80 74; www.telliers.fr; 18 rue des Telliers; s €67-84, d €79-120, tr €116-141, q €132-162; 🅿 🛜) Enticingly positioned down a quiet alley near the cathedral, this bijou B&B extends one of Reims' warmest *bienvenues*. The high-ceilinged rooms are big on art deco character, and handsomely decorated with ornamental fireplaces, polished oak floors and the odd antique. Breakfast costs an extra €9 and is a generous spread of pastries, fruit, fresh-pressed juice and coffee.

La Demeure des Sacres B&B €€
(☐ 06 79 06 80 68; www.la-demeure-des-sacres.com; 29 rue Libergier; d €145, ste €220-245; 🛜) Nuzzled in an art deco townhouse close to the cathedral, this B&B harbours four wood-floored rooms and suites, with pleasing original features like marble fireplaces and free-standing bath-tubs. The Royal Suite has cracking cathedral views. Homemade treats (preserves, crêpes and the like) appear at breakfast, which is included in the room rate. There is a secluded garden for post-sightseeing moments.

🍴 Eating

Anna-S – La Table Amoureuse FRENCH €€
(☐ 03 26 89 12 12; www.annas-latableamoureuse.com; 6 rue Gambetta; 3-course lunch €17.50, dinner menus €29-47; ☉ noon-1.30pm & 7-9pm Tue & Thu-Sat, noon-1.30pm Wed & Sun) So what if the decor is chintzy – there is a reason why this bistro is as busy as a beehive. Friendly service and a menu packed with well-done classics – Arctic char with Champagne jus, fillet of veal in rich, earthy morel sauce – hit the mark every time. The three-course lunch is a steal at €17.50.

Brasserie Le Boulingrin BRASSERIE €€
(☑ 03 26 40 96 22; www.boulingrin.fr; 29-31 rue de Mars; menus €20-29; ☺ noon-2.30pm & 7-10.30pm Mon-Sat) A genuine, old-time brasserie – the decor and zinc bar date back to 1925 – whose ambience and cuisine make it an enduring favourite. From September to June, the culinary focus is on *fruits de mer* (seafood) such as Breton oysters. There's always a €9.50 lunch special.

ℹ Information

Tourist Office (☑ 03 26 77 45 00; www.reims-tourisme.com; 6 rue Rockefeller; ☺ 10am-6pm Mon-Sat, 10am-12.30pm & 1.30-5pm Sun) Find stacks of information on Reims (plus free city maps) and the Champagne region here.

ℹ Getting There & Away

From Reims' train station, 1km northwest of the cathedral, there are services to Paris' Gare de l'Est (€19 to €63, 46 minutes to one hour, 12 to 17 daily) and Épernay (€7, 20 to 42 minutes, 16 daily).

Épernay

POP 23,529

Prosperous Épernay, 25km south of Reims, is the self-proclaimed *capitale du champagne* and home to many of the world's most celebrated Champagne houses. Beneath the town's streets, some 200 million bottles of Champagne are slowly being aged, just waiting to be popped open for some fizz-fuelled celebration.

◉ Sights & Activities

★ **Avenue de Champagne** STREET
Épernay's handsome av de Champagne fizzes with *maisons de champagne* (Champagne houses). The boulevard is lined with mansions and neoclassical villas, rebuilt after WWI. Peek through wrought-iron gates at Moët's private **Hôtel Chandon**, an early 19th-century pavilion-style residence set in landscaped gardens, which counts Wagner among its famous past guests. The haunted-looking **Château Perrier**, a red-brick mansion built in 1854 in neo–Louis XIII style, is aptly placed at No13! The roundabout presents photo ops with its giant cork and bottle-top.

★ **Moët & Chandon** WINERY
(☑ 03 26 51 20 20; www.moet.com; 20 av de Champagne; adult incl 1/2 glasses €23/28, 10-18yr €10; ☺ tours 9.30-11.30am & 2-4.30pm Apr–mid-Nov, 9.30-11.30am & 2-4.30pm Mon-Fri mid-Nov–Mar) Flying the Moët, French, European and Russian flags, this prestigious *maison* offers frequent one-hour tours that are among the region's most impressive, offering a peek at part of its 28km labyrinth of *caves* (cellars). At the shop, you can pick up a 15L bottle of Brut Impérial for just €1500; a standard bottle will set you back €31.

Mercier WINERY
(☑ 03 26 51 22 22; www.champagnemercier.fr; 68-70 av de Champagne; adult incl 1/2/3 glasses €14/19/22 Mon-Fri, €16/21/25 Sat & Sun, 12-17yr €8; ☺ tours 9.30-11.30am & 2-4.30pm, closed mid-Dec–mid-Feb) France's most popular brand was founded in 1847 by Eugène Mercier, a trailblazer in the field of eye-catching publicity stunts and the virtual creator of the cellar tour. Everything here is flashy, including the 160,000L barrel that took two decades to build (for the Universal Exposition of 1889), the lift that transports you 30m underground and the laser-guided touring train.

🛏 Sleeping

Magna Quies B&B €€
(☑ 06 73 25 66 60; www.magnaquies-epernay.jimdo.com; 49 av de Champagne; d/tr/q €140/180/200; 🅿) Nestled in a shuttered manor house on the av de Champagne, this family-run B&B extends the warmest of welcomes. The trio of sunny, wood-floored rooms command fine views of the vineyards. Rates include a generous breakfast spread of pastries, fresh fruit and cold cuts.

Hôtel Jean Moët HISTORIC HOTEL €€
(☑ 03 26 32 19 22; www.hoteljeanmoet.com; 7 rue Jean Moët; d €140-205, ste €230-260; ❄🅰🛁) Housed in a beautifully converted 18th-century mansion, this old-town hotel is big on atmosphere, with its skylit tearoom, antique-meets-boutique-chic rooms and cellar, C. Comme (p400). Spa treatments and a swimming pool await after a hard day's Champagne-tasting.

🍴 Eating & Drinking

★ **La Grillade Gourmande** FRENCH €€
(☑ 03 26 55 44 22; www.lagrilladegourmande.com; 16 rue de Reims; menus €19-59; ☺ noon-2pm & 7.30-10pm Tue-Sat) This chic, red-walled bistro

is an inviting spot to try chargrilled meats and dishes rich in texture and flavour, such as crayfish pan-fried in Champagne and lamb cooked in rosemary and honey until meltingly tender. Diners spill out onto the covered terrace in the warm months.

★ **C. Comme**   WINE BAR
(www.c-comme.fr; 8 rue Gambetta; light meals €7.50-14.50, 6-glass Champagne tasting €33-39; ☺ 10am-8.30pm Sun-Wed, to 11pm Thu, to midnight Fri & Sat) The downstairs cellar has a stash of 300 different varieties of Champagne; sample them (from €6 a glass) in the softly lit bar-bistro upstairs. Accompany with a tasting plate of regional cheese, charcuterie and *rillettes* (pork pâté). We love the funky bottle-top tables and relaxed ambience.

ⓘ Information

Tourist office (☑ 03 26 53 33 00; www. ot-epernay.fr; 7 av de Champagne; ☺ 9am-12.30pm & 1.30-7pm Mon-Sat, 10.30am-1pm & 2-4.30pm Sun, closed Sun mid-Oct–mid-Apr; ☎) Has English brochures and maps.

ⓘ Getting There & Away

The **train station** (place Mendès-France) has direct services to Reims (€7, 24 to 37 minutes, 14 daily) and Paris Gare de l'Est (€24 to €65, 1¼ hours to 2¾ hours, eight daily).

ALSACE & LORRAINE

Teetering on the tempestuous frontier between France and Germany, the neighbouring regions of Alsace and Lorraine are where the worlds of Gallic and Germanic culture collide. Half-timbered houses, lush vineyards and forest-clad mountains hint at Alsace's Teutonic leanings, while Lorraine is indisputably Francophile.

Strasbourg

POP 280,114

Strasbourg is the perfect overture to all that is idiosyncratic about Alsace – walking a fine tightrope between France and Germany and between a medieval past and a progressive future, it pulls off its act in inimitable Alsatian style. Roam the old town's twisting alleys lined with crooked half-timbered houses à la Grimm, feast in cosy *winstubs* (Alsatian taverns), and marvel at how a city that does Christmas markets and gingerbread so

well can also be home to the glittering EU Quarter and France's second-largest student population.

◉ Sights

★ **Cathédrale Notre-Dame**   CATHEDRAL
(www.cathedrale-strasbourg.fr; place de la Cathédrale; adult/child astronomical clock €2/1.50, platform €5/2.50; ☺ 7-11.15am & 12.45-7pm, astronomical clock tickets sold 11.30am-12.25pm Mon-Sat, platform 9am-7.15pm; ᐯ Grand'Rue) Nothing prepares you for your first glimpse of Strasbourg's Cathédrale Notre-Dame, completed in all its Gothic grandeur in 1439. The lace-fine façade lifts the gaze little by little to flying buttresses, leering gargoyles and a 142m spire. The interior is exquisitely lit by 12th- to 14th-century **stained-glass windows**, including the western portal's jewel-like rose window. The Gothic-meets-Renaissance **astronomical clock** strikes solar noon at 12.30pm with a parade of figures portraying the different stages of life and Jesus with his Apostles.

★ **Grande Île**   HISTORIC SITE
(ᐯ Grand'Rue) History seeps through the twisting lanes and cafe-rimmed plazas of Grande Île, Strasbourg's Unesco World Heritage–listed island bordered by the River Ill. These streets – with their photogenic line-up of wonky, timber-framed houses in sherbet colours – are made for aimless ambling. They cower beneath the soaring magnificence of the cathedral (p400) and its sidekick, the gingerbready 15th-century **Maison Kammerzell** (rue des Hallebardes; ᐯ Grand'Rue), with its ornate carvings and leaded windows. The alleys are at their most atmospheric when lantern lit at night.

Petite France   AREA
(ᐯ Grand'Rue) Criss-crossed by narrow lanes, canals and locks, Petite France is where artisans plied their trades in the Middle Ages. The half-timbered houses, sprouting veritable thickets of scarlet geraniums in summer, and the riverside parks attract the masses, but the area still manages to retain its Alsatian charm, especially in the early morning and late evening. Drink in views of the River Ill and the **Barrage Vauban** (Vauban Dam; ☺ viewing terrace 7.15am-9pm, shorter hours winter; ᐯ Faubourg National) FREE from the much-photographed **Ponts Couverts** (Covered Bridges; ᐯ Musée d'Art Moderne) and their trio of 13th-century towers.

★ **Palais Rohan** HISTORIC BUILDING
(2 place du Château; adult/child per museum €6.50/free, all 3 museums €12/free; ⊙10am-6pm Wed-Mon; 🚌 Grand'Rue) Hailed a 'Versailles in miniature', this opulent 18th-century residence is replete with treasures. The basement **Musée Archéologique** takes you from the Palaeolithic period to AD 800. On the ground floor is the **Musée des Arts Décoratifs**, where rooms adorned with Hannong ceramics and gleaming silverware evoke the lavish lifestyle of the nobility in the 18th century. On the 1st floor, the **Musée des Beaux-Arts** collection of 14th- to 19th-century art includes El Greco, Botticelli and Flemish Primitive works.

🛏 Sleeping

Les Artistes GUESTHOUSE €
(☎ 03 88 77 15 53; www.chambre-hotes-les-artistes. fr; 22 rue Vermeer; d €60-80, tr €80-100; 🛜; 🚌 Elsau) Les Artistes offers clean, simple quarters and a good old-fashioned *bienvenue*. Rates include a fab breakfast, with fresh pastries and homemade jam. It's a homely pick, with a garden and barbecue area. Central Strasbourg, 3km away, can be reached on a cycle path or by tram (take B or C from rue du Faubourg National to the Elsau stop).

Hotel D BOUTIQUE HOTEL €€
(☎ 03 88 15 13 67; www.hoteld.fr; 15 rue du Fossé des Treize; d €129-189, ste €219-309; 🅿❄🛜; 🚌 République) Splashes of bold colour and daring design have transformed this townhouse into a nouveau-chic boutique hotel. The slick, spacious rooms are dressed in soothing tones and no comfort stone has been left unturned – you'll find robes, Nespresso machines and iPod docks even in the standard ones. A fitness room and sauna invite relaxation.

🍴 Eating

★ **Vince'Stub** FRENCH €€
(☎ 03 88 52 02 91; www.vincestub.com; 10 Petite rue des Dentelles; mains €14-17; ⊙11.30am-2pm & 7-10.30pm Tue-Sat; 🚌 Grand'Rue) This sweet, petite bistro has a cosy beamed interior, a nicely down-to-earth vibe and a menu packed with Alsatian classics – see the blackboard for daily specials. It does a roaring trade in comfort food, from spot-on *steak-frites* to pork knuckles with Munster cheese.

La Cuiller à Pot FRENCH €€
(☎ 03 88 35 56 30; www.lacuillerapot.com; 18b rue Finkwiller; mains €19.50-26.50; ⊙noon-2.30pm & 7-10.30pm Tue-Fri, 7-10.30pm Sat; 🚌 Musée d'Art Moderne) Run by a talented husband-and-wife team, this little Alsatian dream of a restaurant rustles up fresh regional cuisine. Its well-edited menu goes with the seasons but might include such dishes as fillet of beef with wild mushrooms, and homemade gnocchi and escargots in parsley jus. Quality is second to none.

ℹ Information

Tourist office (☎ 03 88 52 28 28; www. otstrasbourg.fr; 17 place de la Cathédrale; ⊙9am-7pm daily; 🚌 Grand'Rue) Has maps in English (€1).

ℹ Getting There & Away

AIR
Strasbourg's international **airport** (www. strasbourg.aeroport.fr) is 17km southwest of the city centre (towards Molsheim).

TRAIN
Destinations within France:
Lille €98 to €151, four hours, 17 daily
Lyon €38 to €182, 4½ hours, 14 daily
Metz €27.10, 1½ hours, 16 daily
Nancy €26 to €31, 1½ hours, 12 daily
Paris €77 to €144, 2¼ hours, 19 daily

THE LOIRE VALLEY

One step removed from the French capital, the Loire was historically the place where princes, dukes and notable nobles established their country getaways, and the countryside is littered with some of the most extravagant architecture outside Versailles.

Blois

POP 47,500

Blois' historic château was the feudal seat of the powerful counts of Blois, and its grand halls, spiral staircases and sweeping courtyards provide a whistle-stop tour through the key periods of French architecture.

◉ Sights

★ **Château Royal de Blois** CHATEAU
(☎ 02 54 90 33 33; www.chateaudeblois.fr; place du Château; adult/child €10/5, audioguide €4/3; ⊙9am-6pm or 7pm Apr-Oct, 9am-noon & 1.30-5.30pm Nov-Mar) Seven French kings lived in Blois' royal château, whose four grand

FRANCE BLOIS

wings were built during four distinct periods in French architecture: Gothic (13th century), Flamboyant Gothic (1498–1501), early Renaissance (1515–20) and classical (1630s). You can easily spend a half-day immersing yourself in the château's dramatic and bloody history and its extraordinary architecture. In July and August there are free tours in English.

⭐ **Maison de la Magie**   MUSEUM
(📞 02 54 90 33 33; www.maisondelamagie.fr; 1 place du Château; adult/child €9/5; ⊙ 10am-12.30pm & 2-6.30pm Apr-Aug & mid-Oct–2 Nov, 2-6.30pm 1st half Sep; 🚼) Across the square from the château, this museum of magic occupies the one-time home of watchmaker, inventor and conjurer Jean Eugène Robert-Houdin (1805–71), after whom the American magician Harry Houdini named himself. Dragons emerge roaring from the windows every half-hour, while inside the museum has exhibits on Houdin and the history of magic, displays of optical trickery, and several daily magic shows.

🛏 Sleeping

Hôtel Anne de Bretagne   HOTEL €
(📞 02 54 78 05 38; www.hotelannedebretagne. com; 31 av du Dr Jean Laigret; s/d/q €60/69/95; 🅿 🛜) This ivy-covered hotel, in a great location midway between the train station and the château, has friendly staff, a cosy piano-equipped salon and 29 brightly coloured rooms with bold bedspreads. A packed three-course picnic lunch costs €11.50. It also rents out bicycles.

⭐ **La Maison de Thomas**   B&B €€
(📞 09 81 84 44 59; www.lamaisondethomas.fr; 12 rue Beauvoir; s/d/tr incl breakfast €90/100/140;

🛜) A friendly welcome and five spacious rooms with large windows, high ceilings and exposed beams await you at this beautiful B&B, on a pedestrianised street midway between the château and the cathedral. There's bike storage in the interior courtyard and a wine cellar where you can sample local vintages.

🍴 Eating

Les Banquettes Rouges   MODERN FRENCH €€
(📞 02 54 78 74 92; www.lesbanquettesrouges.com; 16 rue des Trois Marchands; lunch/dinner menus from €17.50/27.50; ⊙ noon-1.30pm & 7-9.30pm Tue-Sat) In the St-Nicolas quarter below the château, this restaurant – easy to spot thanks to its bright-red façade – serves French *semi-gastronomique* cuisine. Favourites often available here include pan-fried veal liver with morello cherry and bitter-orange gravy, and *fondant au chocolat*.

L'Orangerie du Château   GASTRONOMY €€€
(📞 02 54 78 05 36; www.orangerie-du-chateau.fr; 1 av Dr Jean Laigret; menus €38-84; ⊙ noon-1.45pm & 7-9.15pm Tue-Sat) This Michelin-starred restaurant serves *cuisine gastronomique inventive* inspired by both French tradition and culinary ideas from faraway lands. The wine list comes on a tablet computer. For dessert try the speciality, soufflé.

ℹ Information

Tourist Office (📞 02 54 90 41 41; www. bloischambord.co.uk; 23 place du Château; ⊙ 9am-7pm Easter-Sep, 10am-5pm Oct-Easter) Has maps of town and sells châteaux combo and concert tickets. Download its smartphone app via the website. Situated across the square from the château.

CHÂTEAUX TOURS

If you don't have your own car, minibus tours are a good way to see the châteaux without being dependent on sometimes infrequent public transport. A variety of private companies offer well-organised itineraries, taking in various combinations of Azay-le-Rideau, Villandry, Cheverny, Chambord, Chenonceau and vineyards offering wine tasting. Many are also happy to create custom-designed tours. Half-day trips cost between €23 and €36 per person; full-day trips range from €50 to €54. These prices don't include admission to the châteaux, though you often get slightly discounted tickets. Reserve online or via the **Tours** (📞 02 47 70 37 37; www.tours-tourisme.fr; 78-82 rue Bernard Palissy; ⊙ 8.30am-7pm Mon-Sat, 10am-12.30pm & 2.30-5pm Sun Apr-Sep, 9am-12.30pm & 1.30-6pm Mon-Sat, 10am-1pm Sun Oct-Mar) or **Amboise** (p404) tourist offices, from where most tours depart.

Getting There & Away

BUS

The tourist office has a brochure detailing public-transport options to nearby châteaux.

A *navette* (shuttle bus; €6) run by **Route 41** (TLC; ☎02 54 58 55 44; www.route41.fr) makes it possible to do a Blois-Chambord-Cheverny-Beauregard-Blois circuit on Wednesday, Saturday and Sunday from early April to 1 November; it also runs daily during school vacation periods and on holidays from early April to August.

TRAIN

The **Blois-Chambord train station** (av Dr Jean Laigret) is 600m west (up the hill) from Blois' château. Destinations include the following:

Amboise €7.20, 15 minutes, 16 to 25 daily

Paris Gare d'Austerlitz €29.40, 1½ hours, five direct daily

Tours €11.20, 40 minutes, 14 to 22 daily

Around Blois

Château de Chambord

For full-blown château splendour, you can't top **Chambord** (☎info 02 54 50 40 00, tour & show reservations 02 54 50 50 40; www.chambord.org; adult/child €11/9, parking near/distant €6/4; ⏲9am-5pm or 6pm; 👪), constructed from 1519 by François I as a lavish base for hunting game in the Sologne forests but eventually used for just 42 days during the king's 32-year reign (1515–47).

The château's most famous feature is its **double-helix staircase**, attributed by some to Leonardo da Vinci, who lived in Amboise (34km southwest) from 1516 until his death three years later. The most interesting rooms are on the 1st floor, including the **king's and queen's chambers** (complete with interconnecting passages to enable late-night hijinks) and a wing devoted to the thwarted attempts of the Comte de Chambord to be crowned Henri V after the fall of the Second Empire.

In summer there may be hour-long guided tours (€5/3 per adult/child) in English – ask at the new Halle d'Acceuil (entrance pavilion).

Chambord is 16km east of Blois.

Château de Cheverny

Thought by many to be the most perfectly proportioned château of all, **Cheverny** (☎02 54 79 96 29; www.chateau-cheverny.fr; av du Château; château & gardens adult/child €10.50/7.50; ⏲9.15am-7pm Apr-Sep, 10am-5.30pm Oct-Mar) has hardly been altered since its construction between 1625 and 1634. Inside is a formal dining room, bridal chamber and children's playroom (complete with Napoléon III–era toys), as well as a guards' room full of pikestaffs, claymores and suits of armour.

Many priceless art works (including the *Mona Lisa*) were stashed in the château's 18th-century **Orangerie** during WWII.

Near the château's gateway, the **kennels** house pedigreed French pointer/English foxhound hunting dogs still used by the owners of Cheverny; feeding time, the **Soupe des Chiens**, takes place daily at 5pm April to September.

Cheverny is 14km southeast of Blois and 18km southwest of Chambord.

Amboise

POP 13,200

The childhood home of Charles VIII and the final resting place of Leonardo da Vinci, elegant Amboise, 23km northeast of Tours, is pleasantly perched along the southern bank of the Loire and overlooked by its fortified château.

Sights

★Château Royal d'Amboise CHATEAU

(☎02 47 57 00 98; www.chateau-amboise.com; place Michel Debré; adult/child €11.20/7.50, incl audioguide €15.20/10.50; ⏲9am-6pm or 7.30pm Mar–mid-Nov, 9am-12.30pm & 2-5.15pm mid-Nov–Feb) Perched on a rocky escarpment above town, Amboise's castle was a favoured retreat for all of France's Valois and Bourbon kings. Only a few of the château's original structures survive, but you can still visit the furnished Logis (Lodge) – Gothic except for the top half of one wing, which is Renaissance – and the Flamboyant Gothic Chapelle St-Hubert (1493), where Leonardo da Vinci's presumed remains have been buried since 1863. The ramparts afford thrilling views of the town and river.

★Le Clos Lucé HISTORIC BUILDING

(☎02 47 57 00 73; www.vinci-closluce.com; 2 rue du Clos Lucé; adult/child €15/10.50; ⏲9am-7pm or 8pm Feb-Oct, 9am or 10am-5pm or 6pm Nov-Jan; 👪) It was on the invitation of François I that Leonardo da Vinci (1452–1519), aged 64, took up residence at this grand manor house (built 1471). An admirer of the Italian Renaissance, the French monarch named Da Vinci 'first painter, engineer and king's architect', and the Italian spent his time here sketching, tinkering and dreaming up ingenious contraptions. Fascinating models of his many inventions are on display inside the home and around its lovely 7-hectare gardens.

🛏 Sleeping

★ Le Vieux Manoir
B&B €€

(☑ 02 47 30 41 27; www.le-vieux-manoir.com; 13 rue Rabelais; d incl breakfast €150-220, f €330, cottages €260-310; ☺ late Mar-Oct; P ❋ ☎) Set in a lovely walled garden, this restored mansion has oodles of old-time charm. The six rooms and two cottages, decorated with antiques, get lots of natural light, and owners Gloria and Bob (expat Americans who once ran an award-winning Boston B&B) are generous with their knowledge of the area.

Le Clos d'Amboise
HISTORIC HOTEL €€€

(☑ 02 47 30 10 20; www.leclosamboise.com; 27 rue Rabelais; r €189-239, 6-person ste €239-289; P ❋ @ ☎ ☒) Overlooking a lovely garden with 200-year-old fir trees and a heated pool, this posh pad – most of it built in the 17th century – offers country living in the heart of town. Stylish features abound, from luxurious fabrics to antique furnishings. Half of the 20 rooms still have their original, now non-functioning, fireplaces.

🍴 Eating

★ Food Market
MARKET €

(quai du Général de Gaulle; ☺ 8am-1pm Sun) Voted France's *marché préféré* (favourite market) in 2015, this riverfront extravaganza, 400m southwest of the château, draws 200 to 300 stalls selling both edibles and durables. Worth timing your visit around.

La Fourchette
FRENCH €€

(☑ 06 11 78 16 98; 9 rue Malebranche; lunch/dinner menus €17/30; ☺ noon-1.30pm Tue-Sat, 7-8.30pm Fri & Sat, plus Tue & Wed evenings summer) Hidden away in a back alley off rue Nationale, this is Amboise's favourite address for family-style French cooking – chef Christine will make you feel as though you've been invited to her house for lunch. The *menu* has just two entrées, two mains and two desserts. The restaurant is small, so reserve ahead.

❶ Information

Tourist office (☑ 02 47 57 09 28; www.amboise-valdeloire.co.uk; cnr quai du Général de Gaulle & allée du Sergent Turpin; internet access per 30min €4; ☺ 9am or 10am-6pm or 7pm Mon-Sat, 10am-12.30pm Sun Apr-Oct, 10am-12.30pm & 2-5pm Mon-Sat Nov-Mar; ☎) Offers walking tours.

❶ Getting There & Around

Amboise's **train station** (bd Gambetta) is 1.5km north of the château, on the opposite side of the Loire.

Destinations include the following:

Blois €7.20, 15 minutes, 16 to 25 daily

Paris Gare d'Austerlitz €33.20, 1¾ hours, four direct daily

Tours €5.70, 17 minutes, 13 to 23 daily

Around Amboise

Château de Chenonceau

Spanning the languid Cher River via a series of supremely graceful arches, the castle of **Chenonceau** (☑ 02 47 23 90 07; www.chenonceau.com; adult/child €13/10, with audioguide €17.50/14; ☺ 9am-7pm or later Apr-Sep, to 5pm or 6pm Oct-Mar; ☎) is one of the most elegant and unusual in the Loire Valley.

The château's interior is crammed with wonderful furniture and tapestries, stunning original tiled floors and a fabulous art collection including works by Tintoretto, Correggio, Rubens, Murillo, Van Dyck and Ribera. The pièce de résistance is the 60m-long window-lined **Grande Gallerie** spanning the Cher.

Make time to visit the **gardens** too: it seems as if there's one of every kind imaginable (maze, English, vegetable, playground, flower...).

The château is 33km east of Tours, 13km southeast of Amboise and 40km southwest of Blois. From the town of Chenonceaux (spelt with an x), just outside the château grounds, trains go to Tours (€7, 25 minutes, nine to 12 daily).

Château d'Azay-le-Rideau

Romantic, moat-ringed **Azay-le-Rideau** (☑ 02 47 45 42 04; www.azay-le-rideau.fr; adult/child €8.50/free, audioguide €4.50; ☺ 9.30am-6pm Apr-Sep, to 7pm Jul & Aug, 10am-5.15pm Oct-Mar) is wonderfully adorned with slender turrets, geometric windows and decorative stonework, wrapped up within a shady landscaped park. Built in the 1500s on a natural island in the middle of a river, the château is one of the Loire's loveliest: Honoré de Balzac called it a 'multifaceted diamond set in the River Indre'.

Its most famous feature is its open **loggia staircase**, in the Italian style, overlooking the central courtyard and decorated with the salamanders and ermines of François I and Queen Claude.

Azay-le-Rideau is 26km southwest of Tours. The château is 2.5km from the train station, where there are eight daily services to Tours (€5.90, 30 minutes).

BURGUNDY & THE RHÔNE VALLEY

If there's one place in France where you're really going to find out what makes the nation tick, it's Burgundy. Two of the country's enduring passions – food and wine – come together in this gorgeously rural region; if you're a sucker for hearty food and the fruits of the vine, you'll be in seventh heaven.

Dijon

POP 157,200

Filled with elegant medieval and Renaissance buildings, dashing Dijon is Burgundy's capital, and the spiritual home of French mustard. Its lively old town is wonderful for strolling and shopping, interspersed with some snappy drinking and dining.

◉ Sights

Palais des Ducs et des États de Bourgogne   PALACE

(Palace of the Dukes & States of Burgundy; place de la Libération) Once home to Burgundy's powerful dukes, this monumental palace with a neoclassical façade overlooks place de la Libération, Old Dijon's magnificent central square dating from 1686. The palace's eastern wing houses the outstanding Musée des Beaux-Arts, whose entrance is next to the **Tour de Bar**, a squat 14th-century tower that once served as a prison. The remainder of the palace houses municipal offices that are off-limits to the public.

★ Musée des Beaux-Arts   MUSEUM

(📞03 80 74 52 09; http://mba.dijon.fr; 1 rue Rameau; audioguide €4, guided tour €6; ⊙9.30am-6pm May-Oct, 10am-5pm Nov-Apr, closed Tue year-round) **FREE** Housed in the monumental Palais des Ducs, these sprawling galleries (works of art in themselves) constitute one of France's most outstanding museums. The star attraction, reopened in September 2013 after extensive renovations, is the wood-panelled **Salle des Gardes**, which houses the ornate, carved late-medieval sepulchres of dukes John the Fearless and Philip the Bold. Other sections focus on Egyptian art, the Middle Ages in Burgundy and Europe, and six centuries of European painting, from the Renaissance to modern times.

🛏 Sleeping

Hôtel du Palais   HOTEL €

(📞03 80 65 51 43; www.hoteldupalais-dijon.fr; 23 rue du Palais; s €59-79, d €65-95, q €109, breakfast €9.90; ✳🕙📶) Newly remodelled and upgraded to three-star status, this inviting hotel in a 17th-century *hôtel particulier* (private mansion) offers excellent value. The 13 rooms range from cosy, inexpensive 3rd-floor doubles tucked under the eaves to spacious, high-ceilinged family suites with abundant natural light. The location is unbeatable, on a quiet side street five minutes' walk from central place de la Libération.

★ La Cour Berbisey   B&B €€€

(📞03 45 83 12 38; www.lacourberbisey.fr; 31 rue Berbisey; r €129-159, junior ste €189-219, ste €249-279; 📶🏊) An arched red doorway in an ivy-draped wall leads to this luxurious B&B, easily Dijon's classiest midcity accommodation. Three enormous suites with parquet floors, beamed ceilings and tall French-shuttered windows are complemented by a lone junior suite and one smaller but equally comfortable double. Other upscale touches include an indoor swimming pool, sauna and an antique-filled salon. Breakfast is included.

✕ Eating

Chez le Bougnat   BURGUNDIAN €

(📞03 80 43 31 17; www.facebook.com/chezlebougnat; 53 rue Berbisey; menus €10.50-18; ⊙noon-2.30pm & 7pm-1am) Chef-owner (and former TV scriptwriter) Cyrille Doudies serves up copious plates of authentic Burgundian food at insanely low prices in this one-room eatery decorated with concert posters and old 45rpm records. It's one of the few eateries in Dijon that opens dependably on Sundays.

DZ'Envies
BURGUNDIAN €€

(📞 03 80 50 09 26; www.dzenvies.com; 12 rue Odebert; mains €16-22, lunch menus €13-20, dinner menus €29-36; ⊘ noon-2pm & 7-10pm Mon-Sat) This zinging restaurant with cheery decorative touches is a good choice if you're tired of heavy Burgundian classics. The menu always involves seasonal, fresh ingredients, and dishes are imaginatively prepared and beautifully presented. At €18, the lunchtime 'I love Dijon' *menu* is a steal.

🛍 Shopping

Moutarde Maille
FOOD

(📞 03 80 30 41 02; www.maille.com; 32 rue de la Liberté; ⊘ 10am-7pm Mon-Sat) When you enter the factory boutique of this mustard company, tangy odours assault your nostrils. Three-dozen varieties of mustard fill the shelves (cassis, truffle, celery etc), along with three rotating flavours on tap for you to sample.

ⓘ Information

Tourist office (📞 08 92 70 05 58; www.visit dijon.com; 11 rue des Forges; ⊘ 9.30am-6.30pm Mon-Sat, 10am-6pm Sun Apr-Sep, 9.30am-1pm & 2-6pm Mon-Sat, 10am-4pm Sun Oct-Mar; 🛜) Offers tours and maps.

ⓘ Getting There & Away

BUS

Transco (📞 03 80 11 29 29; www.cotedor.fr/cms/transco-horaires) Buses stop in front of the train station. Tickets are sold on board (€1.50). Bus 44 goes to Nuits-St-Georges (45 minutes) and Beaune (1¼ hours).

TRAIN

Connections from Dijon's train station include the following:

Lyon-Part Dieu Regional train/TGV from €32/39, two/1½ hours, 25 daily

Marseille TGV from €82, 3½ hours, six direct daily

Paris Gare de Lyon Regional train/TGV from €46/59, three/1½ hours, 25 daily

Beaune

POP 22,540

Beaune (pronounced 'bone'), 44km south of Dijon, is the unofficial capital of the Côte d'Or. This thriving town's *raison d'être* and the source of its *joie de vivre* is wine.

◉ Sights & Activities

Beaune's amoeba-shaped old city is enclosed by **stone ramparts** sheltering wine cellars.

Hôtel-Dieu des Hospices
de Beaune
HISTORIC BUILDING

(📞 03 80 24 45 00; www.hospices-de-beaune.com; rue de l'Hôtel-Dieu; adult/child €7.50/3; ⊘ 9am-6.30pm mid-Mar–mid-Nov, 9-11.30am & 2-5.30pm mid-Nov–mid-Mar) Built in 1443, this magnificent Gothic hospital (until 1971) is famously topped by stunning turrets and pitched rooftops covered in multicoloured tiles. Interior highlights include the barrel-vaulted **Grande Salle** (look for the dragons and peasant heads up on the roof beams); the mural-covered **St-Hughes Room**; an 18th-century **pharmacy** lined with flasks once filled with elixirs and powders; and the multipanelled masterpiece **Polyptych of the Last Judgement** by 15th-century Flemish painter Rogier van der Weyden, depicting Judgment Day in glorious technicolour.

🛏 Sleeping

★ **Les Jardins de Loïs**
B&B €€

(📞 03 80 22 41 97; www.jardinsdelois.com; 8 bd Bretonnière; r €160, ste €185-195, 2-/4-person apt €280/350; 🛜) An unexpected oasis in the middle of the city, this luxurious B&B encompasses several ample rooms, including two suites and a 135-sq-metre top-floor apartment with drop-dead gorgeous views of Beaune's rooftops. The vast garden, complete with rose bushes and fruit trees, makes a dreamy place to sit and enjoy wine grown on the hotel's private domaine. Free parking.

Hôtel des Remparts
HISTORIC HOTEL €€

(📞 03 80 24 94 94; www.hotel-remparts-beaune.com; 48 rue Thiers; d €97-129, ste €134-179; 🅿✳🛜) Set around two delightful courtyards, rooms in this 17th-century townhouse have red-tiled or parquet floors and simple antique furniture. Some rooms come with exposed beams and a fireplace while others have air-con. Most bathrooms have been renovated. Friendly staff can also hire out bikes. Parking costs €10.

🍴 Eating

Food Market
MARKET €

(place de la Halle; ⊘ 7am-1pm Wed & Sat) Beaune's Saturday food market is an elaborate affair, with vendors displaying their wares both indoors and on the cobblestones of place de la Halle. There's a much smaller *marché*

A TRIP BETWEEN VINES

Burgundy's most renowned vintages come from the **Côte d'Or** (Golden Hillside), a range of hills made of limestone, flint and clay that runs south from Dijon for about 60km. The northern section, the **Côte de Nuits**, stretches from Marsannay-la-Côte south to Corgoloin and produces reds known for their robust, full-bodied character. The southern section, the **Côte de Beaune**, lies between Ladoix-Serrigny and Santenay and produces great reds and whites.

Tourist offices provide brochures. The signposted **Route des Grands Crus** (www. road-of-the-fine-burgundy-wines.com) visits some of the most celebrated Côte de Nuits vineyards; mandatory tasting stops for oenophiles seeking nirvana include 16th-century **Château du Clos de Vougeot** (☑03 80 62 86 09; www.closdevougeot. fr; Vougeot; adult/child €7.50/2.50; ⊗9am-6.30pm Sun-Fri & to 5pm Sat Apr-Oct, 10am-5pm Nov-Mar), which offers excellent guided tours, and **L'Imaginarium** (☑03 80 62 61 40; www.imaginarium-bourgogne.com; av du Jura, Nuits-St-Georges; adult incl basic/grand cru tasting €9/17, child €6; ⊗2-7pm Mon, 10am-7pm Tue-Sun), an entertaining wine museum in **Nuits-St-Georges**.

Wine & Voyages (☑03 80 61 15 15; www.wineandvoyages.com; tours €58-114) and **Authentica Tours** (☑06 87 01 43 78; www.authentica-tours.com; tours €65-130) run minibus tours in English; reserve online or at the Dijon tourist office.

gourmand (gourmet market) on Wednesday morning.

Le Bacchus BURGUNDIAN €€
(☑03 80 24 07 78; 6 rue du Faubourg Madeleine; menus lunch €14-16.50, dinner €29-31; ⊗noon-2pm & 7-10pm Tue-Sat) The welcome is warm and the food exceptional at this small restaurant just outside Beaune's centre. Multilingual co-owner Anna works the tables while her partner Olivier whips up market-fresh *menus* that blend classic flavours (steak with Fallot mustard) with tasty surprises (gazpacho with tomato-basil ice cream). Save room for desserts such as Bourbon vanilla crème brûlée, flambéed at your table.

ℹ Information

Tourist office (☑03 80 26 21 30; www. beaune-tourisme.fr; 6 bd Perpreuil; ⊗9am-6.30pm Mon-Sat, to 6pm Sun Apr-Oct, shorter hours Nov-Mar) Has lots of info about nearby vineyards.

ℹ Getting There & Away

BUS

Bus 44, operated by Transco (www.cotedor.fr), links Beaune with Dijon (€1.50, 1¼ hours, two to seven daily), stopping at Côte d'Or villages such as Gevrey-Chambertin, Vougeot, Nuits-St-Georges and Aloxe-Corton.

TRAIN

Trains connect the following places:

Dijon €8, 20 to 30 minutes, 40 daily
Nuits-St-Georges €3.70, 10 minutes, eight daily
Paris €50, 3½ hours, seven direct daily

Lyon
POP 509,000

Gourmets, eat your heart out: Lyon is *the* gastronomic capital of France, with a lavish table of piggy-driven dishes and delicacies to savour. The city has been a commercial, industrial and banking powerhouse for the past 500 years, and is France's third-largest city, with outstanding art museums, a dynamic nightlife, green parks and a Unesco-listed old town.

◉ Sights

⊙ Vieux Lyon

Old Lyon, with its cobblestone streets and medieval and Renaissance houses below Fourvière hill, is divided into three quarters: St-Paul (north), St-Jean (middle) and St-Georges (south). Lovely old buildings languish on **rue du Bœuf, rue St-Jean** and **rue des Trois Maries**.

Deep within Vieux Lyon and Croix Rousse, dark, dingy *traboules* (secret passages) wind their way through apartment blocks, under streets and into courtyards. In all, 315 passages link 230 streets, with a combined length of 50km. The tourist office includes *traboules* on many of its guided walking **tours** (☑ 04 72 77 69 69; www.lyon-france.com; tours adult/child €12/7; ☉ by reservation).

Cathédrale St-Jean CATHEDRAL

(place St-Jean, 5e; ☉ 8.15am-7.45pm Mon-Fri, to 7pm Sat & Sun; Ⓜ Vieux Lyon) Lyon's partly Romanesque cathedral was built between the late 11th and early 16th centuries. The portals of its Flamboyant Gothic façade, completed in 1480 (and recently renovated), are decorated with 280 square stone medallions. Inside, the highlight is the **astronomical clock** in the north transept.

◉ Fourvière

Over two millennia ago, the Romans built the city of Lugdunum on the slopes of Fourvière. Footpaths wind uphill, but the funicular is less taxing.

Basilique Notre Dame de Fourvière CHURCH

(www.fourviere.org; place de Fourvière, 5e; rooftop tour adult/child €7/4; ☉ 8am-6.45pm, guided tours Apr-Nov; Ⓕ Fourvière) Crowning the hill, with stunning city panoramas from its terrace, this superb example of late 19th-century French ecclesiastical architecture is lined

Lyon

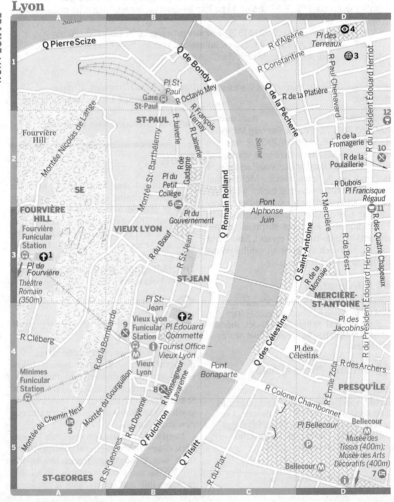

with intricate mosaics. One-hour discovery visits take in the main features of the basilica and crypt; 75-minute rooftop tours ('Visite Insolite') climax on the stone-sculpted roof.

Théâtre Romain ARCHAEOLOGICAL SITE
(rue Cléberg, 5e; [M] Fourvière, Minimes) Lyon's Roman theatre, built around 15 BC and enlarged in AD 120, sat an audience of 10,000. Romans held poetry readings and musical recitals in the smaller, adjacent *odéon*.

☉ Presqu'île, Confluence & Croix-Rousse

Lyon's city centre lies on this 500m- to 800m-wide peninsula bounded by the rivers Rhône and Saône. Past **Gare de Perrache** lies **Lyon Confluence** (www.lyon-confluence.fr) the city's newest neighbourhood. The hilltop quarter of Croix Rousse slinks north up the steep *pentes* (slopes) from place des Terreaux.

Musée des Beaux-Arts MUSEUM
([☎] 04 72 10 17 40; www.mba-lyon.fr; 20 place des Terreaux, 1er; adult/child €8/free; ☉10am-6pm Wed, Thu & Sat-Mon, 10.30am-6pm Fri; [M] Hôtel de Ville) This stunning and eminently manageable museum showcases France's finest collection of sculptures and paintings outside of Paris from antiquity onwards. Highlights include works by Monet, Matisse and Picasso. Pick up a free audioguide and be sure to stop for a drink or meal on the delightful stone terrace off its cafe-restaurant or take time out in its tranquil **cloister garden**.

Place des Terreaux SQUARE
([M] Hôtel de Ville) The centrepiece of the Presqu'île's beautiful central square is a 19th-century **fountain** made of 21 tonnes of lead and sculpted by Frédéric-Auguste Bartholdi (of Statue of Liberty fame). The four horses pulling the chariot symbolise rivers galloping seawards. The **Hôtel de Ville** fronting the square was built in 1655 but was given its present ornate façade in 1702.

FRANCE LYON

Daniel Buren's polka-dot 'forest' of 69 **granite fountains** are embedded in the ground across much of the square.

Musée des Tissus
MUSEUM

(☑04 78 38 42 00; www.mtmad.fr; 34 rue de la Charité, 2e; adult/child €10/7.50; ☺10am-5.30pm Tue-Sun; ⓂAmpère) Extraordinary Lyonnais and international silks are showcased here. Ticket includes admission to the adjoining Musée des Arts Décoratifs (p410), which displays 18th-century furniture, tapestries, wallpaper, ceramics and silver.

Musée des Arts Décoratifs
MUSEUM

(☑04 78 38 42 00; www.mtmad.fr; 34 rue de la Charité, 2e; adult/child €10/7.50; ☺10am-5.30pm Tue-Sun; ⓂAmpère) This well-organised museum displays 18th-century furniture, tapestries, wallpaper, ceramics and silver. Ticket includes admission to the adjoining Musée des Tissus (p410), which showcases extraordinary Lyonnais and international silks.

Musée des Confluences
MUSEUM

(☑04 28 38 11 90; www.museedesconfluences.fr; 86 quai Perrache, 6e; adult/child €9/free; ☺11am-6.15pm Tue, Wed & Fri, 11am-9.15pm Thu, 10am-6.15pm Sat & Sun; ⓐT1) Opened in late 2014, this recent building, designed by the Viennese firm Coop Himmelb(l)au, is the crowning glory of Lyon's newest neighbourhood, the Confluence, at Presqu'île's southern tip. Lying at the confluence of the Rhône and Saône rivers, this ambitious science-and-humanities museum is housed in a futuristic steel-and-glass transparent crystal. Its distorted structure is one of the city's iconic landmarks.

⚐ Tours

★Walking Tours
WALKING

(☑04 72 77 69 69; www.en.lyon-france.com/Guided-Tours-Excursions; adult/child €12/7; ☺by reservation) The tourist office organises a variety of excellent tours through Vieux Lyon and Croix Rousse with local English-speaking guides. Book in advance (online, by phone or in person at the tourist office).

🛏 Sleeping

Auberge de Jeunesse du Vieux Lyon
HOSTEL €

(☑04 78 15 05 50; www.hifrance.org; 41-45 montée du Chemin Neuf, 5e; dm incl breakfast €19.50-25.60; ☺reception 7am-1pm, 2-8pm & 9pm-1am; @🤶; ⓂVieux Lyon, ⓐMinimes) Stunning city views unfold from the terrace of Lyon's HI-affiliated hostel, and from many of the (mostly four- and six-bed) dorms. Bike parking and kitchen facilities are available, and there's an on-site bar. Try for a dorm with city views. To avoid the tiring 10-minute climb from Vieux Lyon metro station, take the funicular to Minimes station and walk downhill.

★Mama Shelter
HOTEL €€

(☑04 78 02 58 00; www.mamashelter.com/en/lyon; 13 rue Domer, 7e; r €69-299; ⓟ❄@🤶; ⓂJean Macé) Lyon's branch of this trendy hotel chain has sleek decor, carpets splashed with calli-graffiti, firm beds, plush pillows, modernist lighting and big-screen Macs offering free in-room movies. A youthful crowd fills the long bar at the low-lit restaurant. The residential location 2km outside the centre may feel remote, but it's only three metro stops from Gare de la Part-Dieu and place Bellecour.

★Jardin d'Hiver
B&B €€

(☑04 78 28 69 34; www.guesthouse-lyon.com; 10 rue des Marronniers, 2e; s/d incl breakfast €110/130, apt per week from €520; ❄🤶; ⓂBellecour) Chic and centrally located, this 3rd-floor B&B (no lift) has two spacious rooms replete with modern conveniences – one in understated purple and pistachio, the other in vivid purple and orange. Friendly owner Annick Bournonville serves 100% organic breakfasts in the foliage-filled breakfast room. In the same building, her son rents out apartments with kitchen and laundry facilities. English and Spanish are spoken.

★Cour des Loges
HOTEL €€€

(☑04 72 77 44 44; www.courdesloges.com; 2-8 rue du Bœuf, 5e; d €200-350, ste €250-600; ❄@🤶❄; ⓂVieux Lyon) Four 14th- to 17th-century houses wrapped around a *traboule* (secret passage) with preserved features such as Italianate loggias make this an exquisite place to stay. Individually decorated rooms woo with designer bathroom fittings and bountiful antiques, while decadent facilities include a spa, a Michelin-starred restaurant (*menus* €95 to €115), a swish cafe and a cross-vaulted bar.

✕ Eating

Lyon's sparkling restaurant line-up embraces all genres: French, fusion, fast and international, as well as traditional Lyonnais *bouchons* (small, friendly bistros serving local city cuisine).

★ **Les Halles de**
Lyon Paul Bocuse   MARKET €
(📞04 78 62 39 33; www.hallespaulbocuse.lyon.fr; 102 cours Lafayette, 3e; ⊗7am-10.30pm Tue-Sat, to 4.30pm Sun; Ⓜ Part-Dieu) Lyon's famed indoor food market has nearly five-dozen stalls selling countless gourmet delights. Pick up a round of runny St Marcellin from legendary cheesemonger Mère Richard, and a knobbly Jésus de Lyon from Charcuterie Sibilia. Or enjoy a sit-down lunch of local produce, especially enjoyable on Sundays when local families congregate for shellfish and white-wine brunches.

★ **L'Instant**   CAFE €
(📞04 78 29 85 08; www.linstant-patisserie.fr; 3 place Marcel Bertone, 4e; breakfast €6.50, lunch mains €6.50-13, weekend brunch €20; ⊗8am-7pm Mon-Sat, to 1pm Sun; 🛜; Ⓜ Croix Rousse) The best spot in Croix Rousse to start the day, this hybrid cafe–pastry shop overlooking lovely place Marcel Bertone packs a punch. The continental breakfast (and brunch on weekends) is the highlight, while the pastries and pies will leave your taste buds reeling. The wonderfully mellow setting and relaxed urban vibe add to the appeal. Ample outdoor seating on warm days.

★ **Le Musée**   BOUCHON €€
(📞04 78 37 71 54; 2 rue des Forces, 2e; lunch mains €14, lunch menus €19-26, dinner menus €23-32; ⊗noon-1.30pm & 7.30-9.30pm Tue-Sat; Ⓜ Cordeliers) Housed in the stables of Lyon's former Hôtel de Ville, this delightful *bouchon* serves a splendid array of meat-heavy Lyonnais classics, including a divine *poulet au vinaigre* (chicken cooked in vinegar). The daily changing *menu* features 10 appetisers and 10 main dishes, plus five scrumptious desserts, all served on cute china plates at long family-style tables.

★ **Daniel et Denise**   BOUCHON €€
(📞04 78 42 24 62; www.danieletdenise-stjean.fr; 36 rue Tramassac, 5e; mains €15-25, lunch menu €21, dinner menus €30-40; ⊗noon-2pm & 7.30-9.30pm Tue-Sat) One of Vieux Lyon's most dependable and traditional eateries, this classic spot is run by award-winning chef Joseph Viola, who was elected president of Lyon's *bouchon* association in 2014. Come here for elaborate variations on traditional Lyonnais themes.

★ **Cinq Mains**   NEOBISTRO €€
(📞04 37 57 30 52; www.facebook.com/cinqmains; 12 rue Monseigneur Lavarenne, 5e; lunch menus €12-19, dinner menus €28-35; ⊗noon-2pm & 8-10pm daily) When young Lyonnais Grégory Cuilleron and his two friends opened this neobistro in early 2016, it was an instant hit. They're working wonders at this cool loft-like space with a mezzanine, serving up tantalising creations based on what they find at the market. A new generation of chefs and a new spin for Lyonnais cuisine.

🍷 Drinking & Entertainment

Grand Café des Négociants   CAFE
(www.lesnegociants.com; 1 place Francisque Régaud, 2e; ⊗7am-4am; Ⓜ Cordeliers) The tree-shaded terrace and Second Empire decor of chandeliers and mirror-lined walls are the big draws at this centrally located cafe-brasserie, a Lyonnais institution since 1864. Food is served from noon to midnight.

Harmonie des Vins   WINE BAR
(www.harmoniedesvins.fr; 9 rue Neuve, 1er; ⊗10am-2.30pm & 6.30pm-1am Tue-Fri, 6.30pm-1am Sat; 🛜; Ⓜ Hôtel de Ville, Cordeliers) Find out all about French wine at this charm-laden wine bar replete with old stone walls, contemporary furnishings and tasty food. A cheese or charcuterie platter will set you back €14.

ℹ️ Information

Tourist Office (📞04 72 77 69 69; www.lyon-france.com; place Bellecour, 2e; ⊗9am-6pm; Ⓜ Bellecour) In the centre of Presqu'île, Lyon's exceptionally helpful, multilingual and well-staffed main tourist office offers a variety of city walking tours and sells the Lyon City Card. It can also book accommodation.

> ### ℹ️ LYON CITY CARD
> ·····································
> The excellent-value Lyon City Card (www.lyon-france.com; 1/2/3 days adult €22/32/42, child €13.50/18.50/23.50) offers free admission to every Lyon museum and a number of attractions. The card also includes unlimited city-wide transport on buses, trams, the funicular and the metro. Full-price cards are available at the tourist office, or save 10% by booking online.

Tourist Office – Vieux Lyon (☑ 04 72 77 69 69; www.lyon-france.com; 4 av du Doyenné, 5e; ⊙10am-5.30pm; Ⓜ Vieux Lyon) A smaller branch of the main tourist office, just outside the Vieux Lyon metro station.

ⓘ Getting There & Away

AIR

Lyon-St-Exupéry Airport (www.lyonaeroports. com), 25km east of the city, serves 120 direct destinations across Europe and beyond, including many budget carriers.

BUS

In the Perrache complex, **Eurolines** (☑ 08 92 89 90 91, 04 72 56 95 30; www.eurolines.fr; Gare de Perrache, 2e; Ⓜ Perrache) and Spain-oriented **Linebús** (☑ 04 72 41 72 27; www.linebus.com; Gare de Perrache) have offices on the bus-station level of the Centre d'Échange (follow the 'Lignes Internationales' signs).

TRAIN

Lyon has two main-line train stations: **Gare de la Part-Dieu** (place Charles Béraudier, 3e; Ⓜ Part-Dieu), 1.5km east of the Rhône, and **Gare de Perrache** (cours de Verdun Rambaud, 2e; Ⓜ Perrache).

Destinations by direct TGV include the following:

Dijon €37, 1½ hours, at least six daily

Marseille €53, 1¾ hours, every 30 to 60 minutes

Paris Charles de Gaulle Airport €97, two hours, at least 11 daily

Paris Gare de Lyon €75, two hours, every 30 to 60 minutes

ⓘ Getting Around

Buses, trams, a four-line metro and two funiculars linking Vieux Lyon to Fourvière and St-Just are operated by TCL (www.tcl.fr). Public transport runs from around 5am to midnight.

Tickets cost €1.80 (€16.20 for a *carnet* of 10) and are available from bus and tram drivers as well as machines at metro entrances. An all-day ticket costs €5.50. Bring coins, as machines don't accept notes (or some international credit cards). Time-stamp tickets on all forms of public transport or risk a fine.

Pick up a red-and-silver bike at one of 200-odd bike stations throughout the city and drop it off at another with Lyon's **Vélo'v** (www.velov. grandlyon.com; 1st 30min free, next 30min €1, each subsequent 30min period €2) bike rental scheme.

THE FRENCH ALPS

Hiking, skiing, majestic panoramas – the French Alps have it all when it comes to the great outdoors. But you'll also find excellent gastronomy, good nightlife and plenty of history.

Chamonix

POP 9050 / ELEV 1037M

With the pearly white peaks of the Mont Blanc massif as a sensational backdrop, being an icon comes naturally to Chamonix. First 'discovered' by Brits William Windham and Richard Pococke in 1741, this is the mecca of mountaineering. Its knife-edge peaks, plunging slopes and massive glaciers have enthralled generations of adventurers and thrill-seekers ever since. Its après-ski scene is equally pumping.

⦿ Sights

★**Aiguille du Midi**   VIEWPOINT

A great broken tooth of rock rearing among the Alpine fastness of the Mont Blanc massif, the Aiguille du Midi (3842m) is one of Chamonix' most distinctive geographical features. If you can handle the altitude, the 360-degree views of the French, Swiss and Italian Alps from the summit are (quite literally) breathtaking. Year-round, you can float in a cable car from Chamonix to the Aiguille du Midi on the vertiginous **Téléphérique de l'Aiguille du Midi** (www.compagniedumont-blanc.co.uk; place de l'Aiguille du Midi; adult/child return to Aiguille du Midi €58.50/49.70, to Plan de l'Aiguille summer €31/26.40, winter €17/14.50; ⊙1st ascent btwn 7.10am & 8.30am, last btwn 3.30pm & 5pm).

Le Brévent   VIEWPOINT

The highest peak on the western side of the Chamonix Valley, Le Brévent (2525m) has tremendous views of the Mont Blanc massif, myriad hiking trails through a nature reserve, ledges to paraglide from and some vertiginous black runs. Reach it by linking the **Télécabine de Planpraz** (☑ 04 50 53 22 75; www.compagniedumontblanc.co.uk; 29 rue Henriette d'Angeville; adult/child return €30.50/25.90; ⊙from 8.50am Dec-Apr, Jun-Sep & late Oct-Nov), 400m west of the tourist office, with the **Téléphérique du Brévent** (www.compagnie-dumontblanc.co.uk; 29 rue Henriette d'Angeville; adult/child one way €23/19.60, return €31/26.40; ⊙mid-Dec–mid-Apr & mid-Jun–mid-Sep). Plenty of family-friendly trails begin at **Planpraz** (2000m), and the Liaison cable car connects to the adjacent ski fields of La Flégère.

Mer de Glace VIEWPOINT
France's largest glacier, the 200m-deep 'Sea of Ice', flows 7km down the northern side of Mont Blanc, moving up to 1cm an hour (about 90m a year). The **Train du Montenvers** (☑04 50 53 22 75; www.compagniedumontblanc.fr; 35 place de la Mer de Glace; adult/child return €31/26.40; ⊘10am-4.30pm), a picturesque, 5km-long cog railway opened in 1909, links Gare du Montenvers with Montenvers (1913m), from where a cable car takes you down to the glacier and the **Grotte de Glace** (⊘closed last half of May & late Sep–mid-Oct). Your ticket also gets you into the Glaciorium, which looks at the birth, life and future of glaciers.

🕴 Activities

The ski season runs from mid-December to mid-April. Summer activities – hiking, canyoning, mountaineering etc – generally start in June and end in September. The **Compagnie des Guides de Chamonix** (☑04 50 53 00 88; www.chamonix-guides.com; 190 place de l'Église, Maison de la Montagne; ⊘8.30am-noon & 2.30-7.30pm, closed Sun & Mon late Apr–mid-Jun & mid-Sep–mid-Dec) is the most famous of all the guide companies and has guides for virtually every activity, whatever the season.

🛏 Sleeping

★**Hôtel Richemond** HOTEL €€
(☑04 50 53 08 85; www.richemond.fr; 228 rue du Docteur Paccard; s/d/tr €66/103/136; ⊘mid-Dec–mid-Apr & mid-Jun–mid-Sep; 🖺) In a grand old building constructed in 1914 (and run by the same family ever since), this hotel – as friendly as it is central – has 52 spacious rooms with views of either Mont Blanc or Le Brévent; some are pleasantly old-fashioned (retaining original furniture and cast-iron bath-tubs), others are recently renovated in white, black and beige. Outstanding value.

★**Hôtel Aiguille du Midi** HOTEL €€
(☑04 50 53 00 65; www.hotel-aiguilledumidi.com; 479 chemin Napoléon, Les Bossons; d €77-158, q €198; ⊘mid-Dec–early Apr & mid-May–Sep; 🖺🏊) Run by the same family since 1908, this welcoming hotel has stunning views of the Aiguille du Midi and Mont Blanc. There are 39 cosy, pine-panelled rooms, an outdoor heated pool and a clay tennis court

for summer fun, and a very good restaurant, accessible on half-board packages. Bus and train stops to Chamonix are right around the corner.

🍴 Eating

Hibou Deli DELI €
(☑04 50 96 65 13; www.hibou-chamonix.com; 416 rue Joseph Vallot; mains €8-10; ⊘11am-9pm mid-Dec–early May & mid-Jun–early Oct; ☑) This tiny shopfront kitchen, owned by a British chef, pumps out fantastic Asian and North African–inflected dishes to takeaway. The lamb *mechoui* is rubbed with spices and cooked over 24 hours to an almost buttery consistency, the Bangkok chicken is fragrant with limes leaves and coconut, and there's always plenty of veggie options and an interesting *plat de jour*.

★**Le Cap Horn** MODERN FRENCH €€
(☑04 50 21 80 80; www.caphorn-chamonix.com; 78 rue des Moulins; menus lunch €20, dinner €32-39; ⊘noon-3pm & 7-10.30pm) Housed in a gorgeous, two-storey chalet decorated with model sailing boats – joint homage to the Alps and Cape Horn – this highly praised restaurant, opened in 2012, serves French and Asian-inflected dishes such as pan-seared duck breast with honey and soy sauce, fisherman's stew and, for dessert, *soufflé au Grand Marnier*. Reserve for dinner Friday and Saturday in winter and summer.

Munchie FUSION €€
(☑04 50 53 45 41; www.munchie.eu; 87 rue des Moulins; mains €22-24; ⊘7pm-2am winter & summer) Franco-Asian-Scandinavian fusion may not be a tried-and-true recipe for success, but this casual, Swedish-skippered restaurant has been making diners happy since 1997. Dishes such as Sichuan-spiced lamb tataki, Japanese coconut rice with egg-yolk confit and Thai 'pesto', and cod with ash and leek are so popular that reservations are recommended during the ski season.

🍷 Drinking & Nightlife

★**MBC** MICROBREWERY
(Micro Brasserie de Chamonix; ☑04 50 53 61 59; www.mbchx.com; 350 rte du Bouchet; ⊘4pm-2am winter & summer, to 1am spring & autumn) Run by the last man standing of four Canadian founders, this buzzing microbrewery is one of Chamonix' most unpretentious and gregarious watering holes. Be it with their phenomenal burgers (€10 to €15), chilli-licked

wings (12 for €5.25 – half-price – on Monday), live music (from 9pm) or great craft beer, MBC delivers. It's busiest from 5pm to 11pm.

Chambre Neuf   BAR
(📱 04 50 53 00 31; www.hotelgustavia.eu; 272 av Michel Croz; ⊙7am-1am; 🛜) Chamonix' most spirited après-ski party (4pm to 8pm), fuelled by a Swedish band and dancing on the tables, spills out the front door of Chambre Neuf. Wildly popular with seasonal workers, it opens its terrace in spring.

Jekyll & Hyde   PUB
(📱 04 50 55 99 70; www.thejekyll.com; 71 rte des Pélerins, Chamonix Sud; ⊙4pm-2am Mon-Fri, opens earlier Sat & Sun; 🛜) This British-owned après-ski mainstay has a split personality: upstairs the 'Jekyll' has really good pub food (try the steak-and-Guinness pie), live music (Wednesday, Thursday and Sunday from 9.30pm) and DJs; downstairs, the 'Hyde' is cosier and more relaxed. Both have good Irish beer and a friendly vibe, and can be found 350m southwest of the Téléphérique de l'Aiguille du Midi.

ℹ️ Information

Tourist Office (📱 04 50 53 00 24; www.chamonix.com; 85 place du Triangle de l'Amitié; ⊙8.30am-7pm winter & summer, 9am-12.30pm & 2-6pm in low season; 🛜) The tourist office has information on accommodation (including various types of B&Bs and *gîtes* in the valley), activities, weather and cultural events.

ℹ️ Getting There & Away

BUS

Chamonix' **bus station** (📱 04 50 53 01 15; 234 av Courmayeur, Chamonix Sud; ⊙8am-noon & 1.15-6.30pm in winter, shorter hours rest of year) has moved to av Courmayeur, Chamonix Sud.

Geneva, Switzerland (airport and bus station) One way/return €25/50, 1½ to two hours, eight daily in winter, six at other times. Operated by **Starshipper** (📱 04 56 12 40 59; www.starshipper.com).

Courmayeur, Italy One way/return €15/21, 45 minutes, four daily. Run by **Savda** (📱 +39 01 65 36 70 11; www.savda.it), with onward connections to Aosta and Milan.

TRAIN

The scenic, narrow-gauge **Mont Blanc Express** glides from St-Gervais-Le-Fayet to the Swiss

town of Martigny, taking in Les Houches, Chamonix, Argentière and Vallorcine en route.

From St-Gervais-Le-Fayet, there are somewhat infrequent trains to cities around France, often with a change in Bellegarde or Annecy.

Annecy €15.70, 1½ hours, 12 daily

Lyon €36.60, 3½ to five hours, 10 daily

Paris €98.50 to €128, 4¾ to seven hours, 11 daily

THE DORDOGNE

Tucked in the country's southwestern corner, the Dordogne fuses history, culture and culinary sophistication in one unforgettably scenic package. The region is best known for its sturdy *bastides* (fortified towns), clifftop châteaux and spectacular prehistoric cave paintings.

Sarlat-La-Canéda

POP 9414

A picturesque tangle of honey-coloured buildings and medieval architecture, Sarlat-La-Canéda is incredibly scenic and perennially popular with visitors.

◉ Sights

Part of the fun of Sarlat is getting lost in its twisting alleyways and backstreets. **Rue Jean-Jacques Rousseau** and **rue Landry** are good starting points, but for the grandest buildings and *hôtels particuliers* explore **rue des Consuls**.

★**Weekly Markets**   MARKET
(place de la Liberté & rue de la République; ⊙8.30am-1pm Wed, 8.30am-6pm Sat) For an introductory French market experience, visit Sarlat's heavily touristed Saturday market, which takes over the streets around Cathédrale St-Sacerdos. Depending on the season, delicacies include local mushrooms and duck- and goose-based products such as foie gras. The Wednesday version is a smaller affair. An atmospheric largely organic **night market** (⊙6-10pm) operates on Thursdays.

★**Église Ste-Marie**   CHURCH, MARKET
(place de la Liberté) Église Ste-Marie was ingeniously converted by acclaimed architect Jean Nouvel, whose parents still live in Sarlat, into the town's touristy **Marché Couvert** (Covered Market; ⊙8.30am-2pm daily mid-Apr–mid-Nov, closed Mon, Thu & Sun rest of year).

PREHISTORIC CAVE ART

The Vézère Valley is littered with some of the most spectacular prehistoric cave art anywhere in Europe, spread over some 175 known sites. The most famous of all is **Grotte de Lascaux**, 2km from Montignac, which features the largest collection of paintings ever discovered. The original cave was closed in 1963 to prevent damage, but in December 2016, an amazing, millimetre-perfect facsimile was opened just a few steps from the site of the original cave. Known as **Lascaux IV** (05 53 50 15 63, reservations 05 53 05 65 60; Montignac; www.lascaux.fr; adult/child €16/10.40; 9am-10pm Jul & Aug, 9.30am-8pm Apr-Jun & Sep,10am-5pm rest of the year), it uses the latest laser technology to re-create the rock paintings in what feels like a real cave – complete with muffled sounds, semi-darkness, damp smells, prehistoric fauna and all.

Several other caves around the valley remain open to the public. Visitor numbers are limited, so you'll need to reserve well ahead.

Grotte de Font de Gaume (☑05 53 06 86 00; www.eyzies.monuments-nationaux.fr; 4 av des Grottes; adult/child €7.50/free; ⊙guided tours 9.30am-5.30pm Sun-Fri mid-May–mid-Sep, 9.30am-12.30pm & 2-5.30pm Sun-Fri mid-Sep–mid-May) About 14,000 years ago, prehistoric artists created the gallery of over 230 figures, including bison, reindeer, horses, mammoths, bears and wolves, of which 25 are on permanent display. Located about 1km northeast of LEs Eyzies.

Abri du Cap Blanc (☑05 53 06 86 00; www.eyzies.monuments-nationaux.fr; adult/child €7.50/free; ⊙guided tours 10am-6pm Sun-Fri mid-May–mid-Sep, 10am-12.30pm & 2-5.30pm Sun-Fri mid-Sep–mid-May) Showcases an unusual sculpture gallery of horses, bison and deer. It's 7km east of Les Eyzies.

Grotte de Rouffignac (☑05 53 05 41 71; www.grottederouffignac.fr; Rouffignac-St-Cernin-de-Reilhac; adult/child €7.50/4.80; ⊙9-11.30am & 2-6pm Jul & Aug, 10-11.30am & 2-5pm Apr-Jun, Sep & Oct, closed Nov-Mar) Sometimes known as the 'Cave of 100 Mammoths' because of its painted mammoths. Access to the caves, hidden in woodland 15km north of Les Eyzies, is aboard a trundling electric train.

Its panoramic lift offers 360-degree views across Sarlat's countryside.

🛏 Sleeping

★La Maison des Peyrat   HOTEL €€
(☑05 53 59 00 32; www.maisondespeyrat.com; Le Lac de la Plane; r €70-112) This beautifully renovated 17th-century house, formerly a nuns' hospital and later an aristocratic hunting lodge, is set on a hill about 1.5km from Sarlat centre. Eleven generously sized rooms are decorated in modern farmhouse style; the best have views over gardens and the countryside beyond. Good restaurant, too.

★Villa des Consuls   B&B €€
(☑05 53 31 90 05; www.villaconsuls.fr; 3 rue Jean-Jacques Rousseau; d €95-110, apt €150-190; @🛜) Despite its Renaissance exterior, the enormous rooms here are modern through and through, with shiny wood floors and sleek furnishings. Several delightful self-contained apartments dot the town, all offering the same mix of period plushness

– some also have terraces overlooking the town's rooftops.

🍴 Eating

Le Petit Manoir   FRENCH €€
(☑05 53 29 82 14; 13 rue de la République; mains €20; ⊙12.40-2pm & 7-9pm Tue-Sun; 🛜🅿) Book ahead for a seat in the ornate 15th-century mansion where the cuisine combines creative Dordogne specialities with a touch of Asian fusion. The Vietnamese chef creates a *menu* that changes with the seasons, and there are always vegetarian options (*menu* €27).

Le Bistrot   FRENCH €€
(☑05 53 28 28 40; www.le-bistrot-sarlat.com; 14 place du Peyrou; menus €18-30; ⊙noon-2pm & 6.30-10pm mid-Mar–Sep) This touristy little bistro is the best of the bunch on cafe-clad place du Peyrou. The menu's heavy on Sarlat classics, especially walnuts, duck breast and finger-lickin' *pommes sarlardaises* (potatoes cooked in duck fat).

ℹ Information

Tourist Office (☑ 05 53 31 45 45; www.
sarlat-tourisme.com; 3 rue Tourny; ◷ 9am-7pm
Mon-Sat, 10am-1pm & 2-6pm Sun May-Sep,
shorter hours Oct-Apr; ☏) Sarlat's tourist
office is packed with info, but often gets overwhelmed by visitors; the website has it all.

ℹ Getting There & Away

The **train station** (av de la Gare) is 1.3km south
of the old city. Many destinations require a
change at Le Buisson or Libourne.

Destinations include the following:

Bordeaux €27.70, 2¾ hours, six daily

Les Eyzies €10.10, 1½ to two hours depending
on connections, four daily

Périgueux €16.30, 1½ to 2½ hours depending
on connections, five daily

THE ATLANTIC COAST

With quiet country roads winding through
vine-striped hills and wild stretches of coastal sands interspersed with misty islands, the
Atlantic coast is where France gets back to
nature. If you're a surf nut or beach bum,
the sandy bays around Biarritz will be right
up your alley, while oenophiles can sample
the fruits of the vine in the high temple of
French winemaking, Bordeaux.

Bordeaux

POP 242,945

The city of Bordeaux is among France's most
exciting, vibrant and dynamic cities. In the
last decade and a half, it's shed its languid,
Belle au Bois Dormant (Sleeping Beauty)
image thanks to the vision of city mayor
Alain Juppé who has pedestrianised boulevards, restored neoclassical architecture,
created a high-tech public transport system
and reclaimed Bordeaux' former industrial
wet docks at Bassin à Flots. Half the city (18
sq km) is Unesco-listed, making it the largest
urban World Heritage Site; while world-class
architects have designed a bevy of striking
new buildings – the Herzog & de Meuron stadium (2015), decanter-shaped La Cité du Vin
(2016) and Jean-Jacques Bosc bridge (2018)
across the Garonne River included.

◉ Sights

Thirsty? The 1000-sq-km wine-growing
area around the city of Bordeaux is, along
with Burgundy, France's most important

producer of top-quality wines. Whet your
palate with one of the tourist office's two-
hour introductory courses (€14), or head
for the nearby wine villages like St-Émilion
and Pauillac, where many châteaux accept
visitors.

★ La Cité du Vin   MUSEUM

(☑ 05 56 81 38 47; www.laciteduvin.com; 1 Esplanade
de Pontac; adult/child €20/free; ◷ 9.30am-7.30pm
Apr-Oct, Tue-Sun Nov-Mar) The complex world of
wine is explored in depth at ground-breaking
La Cité du Vin, a stunning piece of contemporary architecture resembling a wine decant-
er on the banks of the River Garonne. The
curvaceous gold building glitters in the sun
and its 3000 sq metres of exhibits are equally
sensory and sensational. Digital guides lead
visitors around 20 different themed sections
covering everything from vine cultivation,
grape varieties and wine production to ancient wine trade, 21st-century wine trends
and celebrated personalities.

Cathédrale St-André   CATHEDRAL

(www.cathedrale-bordeaux.fr; place Jean Moulin; ◷ 2-6pm Mon, 10am-noon & 2-6pm Tue-Sun)
Lording over the city, and a Unesco World
Heritage Site prior to the city's classification,
the cathedral's oldest section dates from
1096; most of what you see today was built
in the 13th and 14th centuries. Enjoy exceptional masonry carvings in the north portal.

Musée des Beaux-Arts   GALLERY

(☑ 05 56 96 51 60; www.musba-bordeaux.fr; 20
cours d'Albret; adult/child €4/2; ◷ 11am-6pm mid-
Jul–mid-Aug, closed Tue rest of year) The evolution of Occidental art from the Renaissance
to the mid-20th century is on view at Bordeaux' Museum of Fine Arts, which occupies
two wings of the 1770s-built Hôtel de Ville,
either side of elegant city park Jardin de
la Mairie. The museum was established in
1801; highlights include 17th-century Flemish, Dutch and Italian paintings. Temporary
exhibitions are regularly hosted at its nearby annexe, Galerie des Beaux-Arts (place du
Colonel Raynal; adult/child €6.50/3.50; ◷ 11am-
6pm mid-Jul–mid-Aug, closed Tue rest of year).

🛏 Sleeping

Chez Dupont   B&B €€

(☑ 05 56 81 49 59; www.chez-dupont.com; 45 rue
Notre Dame; s/d from €85/100) Five impeccably
decorated rooms, peppered with a wonderful collection of vintage curiosities, inspires
love at first sight at this thoroughly contem-

porary, design-driven B&B in the trendy former wine-merchant quarter of Chartrons. Across the road from, and run by, the bistro of the same name, Chez Dupont is one of the best deals in town.

La Maison du Lierre   BOUTIQUE HOTEL €€
(☑05 56 51 92 71; www.hotel-maisondulierre-bordeaux.com; 57 rue Huguerie; d €95-149; ⊚) The delightfully restored 'House of Ivy' has a welcoming *chambre d'hôte* feel. A beautiful Bordelaise stone staircase (no lift) leads to small, sunlit rooms with polished floorboards, rose-printed fabrics and sparkling bathrooms. The vine-draped garden is a perfect spot to sip fresh orange juice at breakfast (€10).

★**L'Hôtel Particulier**   BOUTIQUE HOTEL €€€
(☑05 57 88 28 80; www.lhotel-particulier.com; 44 rue Vital-Carles; d €189-299; ⊚) Step into this fabulous boutique hotel and be wowed by period furnishings mixed with contemporary design, extravagant decorative touches and an atmospheric courtyard garden. Its five individually designed hotel rooms (breakfast €12) match up to expectations with vintage fireplaces, carved ceilings and bath-tubs with legs. Exceptional value are the suite of equally well-furnished self-catering apartments, sleeping one (€89), two (€109) or four people (€179).

✗ Eating

Place du Parlement, rue du Pas St-Georges, rue des Faussets and place de la Victoire are loaded with dining addresses, as is the old waterfront warehouse district around quai des Marques – great for a sunset meal or drink.

★**Magasin Général**   INTERNATIONAL €
(☑05 56 77 88 35; www.magasingeneral.camp; 87 quai des Queyries; 2-/3-course menu €14/18, mains €9-19; ⊚8.30am-6pm Wed-Fri, 8.30am-midnight Sat, 10am-midnight Sun, kitchen noon-2.15pm & 7-10pm; ⊚) Follow the hip crowd across the river to this huge industrial hangar on the right bank, France's biggest and best organic restaurant with gargantuan terrace complete with vintage sofa seating, ping-pong table and table football. Everything here, from the vegan burgers and super-food salads to smoothies, pizzas, wine and French bistro fare, is *bio* (organic) and sourced locally. Sunday brunch (€24) is a bottomless feast.

★**Le Petit Commerce**   SEAFOOD €€
(05 56 79 76 58; 22 rue Parlement St-Pierre; 2-course lunch menu €14, mains €15-25; ⊚noon-midnight) This iconic bistro, with dining rooms both sides of a narrow pedestrian street and former Michelin-starred chef Stéphane Carrade in the kitchen, is the star turn of the trendy St-Pierre quarter. It's best known for its excellent seafood *menu* that embraces everything from Arcachon sole and oysters to eels, lobsters and *chipirons* (baby squid) fresh from St-Jean de Luz.

★**Potato Head**   MODERN FRENCH €€
(www.potatoheadbordeaux.com; 27 rue Buhan; mains lunch €13, dinner €18-25, 5-course tasting menu €41; ⊚11am-3pm Sun) With its eclectic mix of seating (bar stool, bistro and armchair), moss-clad vegetal wall and industrial-style lighting, this trendy bistro is a fabulous space to dine in. Throw in a creative kitchen known for surprise combos (foie gras, beetroot, ginger and chocolate, anyone?) and the finest summer garden in the city and, well, you need to reserve well in advance.

DON'T MISS

DUNE DU PILAT

This colossal sand dune (sometimes referred to as the Dune de Pyla because of its location in the resort town of Pyla-sur-Mer), 65km west of Bordeaux, stretches from the mouth of the Bassin d'Arcachon southwards for almost 3km. Already the largest in Europe, it's spreading eastwards at 4.5m a year – it has swallowed trees, a road junction and even a hotel. Take care swimming in this area: powerful currents swirl out to sea from the deceptively tranquil *baïnes* (little bays).

Although an easy day trip from Bordeaux, the area around the dune is an enjoyable place to kick back for a while. Most people camp in one of the swag of seasonal campgrounds; see www.bassin-arcachon.com.

ℹ️ Information

Tourist Office (☎ 05 56 00 66 00; www.bordeaux-tourisme.com; 12 cours du 30 Juillet; ⊙ 9am-7.30pm Mon-Sat, 9.30am-6.30pm Sun Jul & Aug, shorter hours Sep-Jun) Runs an excellent range of city and regional tours; reserve online or in situ. It also rents pocket modems to hook you up with wi-fi. There's a small but helpful branch (☎ 05 56 91 64 70; rue Charles Domercq, Parvis Louis Armand; ⊙ 9am-noon & 1-6pm Mon-Sat, 10am-noon & 1-3pm Sun Jul & Aug, shorter hours rest of year) at the train station.

ℹ️ Getting There & Away

AIR

Bordeaux airport (www.bordeaux.aeroport. fr) is in Mérignac, 10km west of the city centre, with domestic and international services.

TRAIN

Bordeaux is one of France's major rail-transit points. The station, **Gare St-Jean** (cours de la Marne), is about 3km from the city centre at the southern terminus of cours de la Marne.

Destinations include the following:

Nantes €52.40, five hours, three daily

Paris Gare Montparnasse €79, 3¼ hours, at least 16 daily

Poitiers €42, 1¾ hours, at least hourly

Toulouse €40 to €50, 2¼ hours, hourly

Biarritz

POP 26,000

Edge your way south along the coast towards Spain and you arrive in stylish Biarritz, just as ritzy as its name suggests. The resort took off in the mid-19th century (Napoléon III had a rather soft spot for the place) and it still shimmers with architectural treasures from the belle époque and art deco eras. Big waves – some of Europe's best – and a beachy lifestyle are a magnet for Europe's hip surfing set.

◉ Sights & Activities

Biarritz' raison d'être is its fashionable beaches, particularly central Grande Plage and Plage Miramar, lined end to end with sunbathing bodies on hot summer days. North of Pointe St-Martin, the adrenaline-pumping surfing beaches of Anglet (the final 't' is pronounced) continue northwards for more than 4km. Take bus 10 or 13 from the bottom of av Verdun (just near av Édouard VII).

Chapelle Impériale CHURCH
(☎ 05 59 22 37 10; 15 rue des 100 Gardes; €3; ⊙ 2.30-6pm) Built in 1864 on the instructions of Empress Eugénie, this glitzy church mixes Byzantine and Moorish styles, and the plaza in front has a great view of the Grande Plage. You can buy tickets online at the tourist office to avoid queues.

Cité de l'Océan MUSEUM
(☎ 05 59 22 75 40; www.citedelocean.com; 1 av de la Plage; adult/child/family €11.50/7.50/39, joint ticket with Musée de la Mer €18.50/13/63; ⊙ 10am-10pm Jul & Aug, 10am-7pm Easter, Apr-Jun, Sep & Oct, shorter hours rest of year) Biarritz' newest sea-themed attraction is part museum, part theme park, part educational centre. It takes a fun approach to learning about the sea in all its forms – attractions range from a chance to explore a marine lab to a simulated dive into the depths in an underwater bathysphere. It's good fun, but probably more of interest to older kids.

🛌 Sleeping

Maison du Lierre HERITAGE HOTEL €€
(☎ 05 59 24 06 00; www.hotel-maisondulierre-biarritz.com; 3 av du Jardin Public; d €129-169; 🛜) What a beauty this mansion is, impressively detached, with a balcony and park view from nearly every room (apart from the very cheapest, which overlook a neighbouring building). It's elegantly simple – wooden floors, cool furnishings, rooms named after flowers – and the central staircase is a listed monument. It's not even expensive for Biarritz. Recommended.

Hôtel St-James HOTEL €€
(☎ 05 59 24 06 36; www.hotel-saintjames.com; 1 rue des Halles; s €55-105, d €65-120, tr €75-140; 🛜) This one won't suit all, but it offers some of the best value in town. It's directly above the Café du Commerce, so inevitably it's got a buzzier (read: noisier) vibe than some of the pricier places – but the simple, smart rooms and central location make it well worthy of consideration.

🍴 Eating

Bar Jean TAPAS €
(☎ 05 59 24 80 38; www.barjean-biarritz.fr; 5 rue des Halles; tapas €2-6; ⊙ noon-3.30pm & 6.30pm-midnight) One of the oldest tapas venues in town (in business since the '30s), traditional and full of atmosphere – from the flamenco soundtrack to the Andalucian murals. Try

the calamari rings wrapped around a stack of lardons and drizzled in olive oil.

⭐ **Restaurant Le Pim'pi**   FRENCH €€
(☑ 05 59 24 12 62; 14 av Verdun; menus €14-28, mains €15-18; ⊘ noon-2pm Tue, noon-2pm & 7-9.30pm Wed-Sat) A small and resolutely old-fashioned place unfazed by all the razzmatazz around it. The daily specials are chalked up on a blackboard – most are of the classic French bistro style but are produced with such unusual skill and passion that many consider this one of the town's better places to eat.

ℹ Information

Tourist Office (☑ 05 59 22 37 10; www.tourisme.biarritz.fr; square d'Ixelles; ⊘ 9am-7pm Jul & Aug, shorter hours rest of year) In July and August there are tourist-office annexes at the airport, train station and at the roundabout just off the Biarritz *sortie* (exit) 4 from the A63.

ℹ Getting There & Away

AIR

Biarritz-Anglet-Bayonne Airport (☑ 05 59 43 83 83; www.biarritz.aeroport.fr), 3km southeast of Biarritz, is served by several low-cost carriers.

BUS

ATCRB (09 70 80 90 74; www.transports-atcrb.com) line 816 buses travel down the coast to St-Jean de Luz, Urrugne and Hendaye. The fare is a flat-rate €2, and buses leave from the **stop** just near the tourist office beside square d'Ixelles.

Buses to Spain, including San Sebastián and Bilbao, also depart from the same stop.

TRAIN

Biarritz-La Négresse train station, 3km south of town, is linked to the centre by bus A1.

TGVs run direct to Paris Gare Montparnasse (€69 to €109, five to six hours, eight daily). Other destinations include Bordeaux and Toulouse. For destinations further south, trains run at least hourly including services to St-Jean de Luz (€4.50, 20 minutes) and Hendaye (€6, 28 minutes), and twice daily to Irún (€6.50, 43 minutes).

LANGUEDOC-ROUSSILLON

Languedoc-Roussillon comes in three distinct flavours: Bas-Languedoc (Lower Languedoc), land of bullfighting, rugby and robust red wines; Haut Languedoc (Upper Languedoc), a mountainous, sparsely populated terrain made for lovers of the great outdoors; and Roussillon, to the south, snug against the rugged Pyrenees and frontier to Spanish Catalonia.

Languedoc's traditional centre, Toulouse, was shaved off when regional boundaries were redrawn almost half a century ago, but we've chosen to include it in this section.

Toulouse

POP 458,298

Elegantly set at the confluence of the Canal du Midi and the Garonne River , this vibrant southern city – nicknamed *la ville rose* (the pink city) after the distinctive hot-pink stone used in many buildings – is one of France's liveliest metropolises. Busy, buzzy and bustling with students, this riverside dame has a history stretching back over 2000 years and has been a hub for the aerospace industry since the 1930s. With a thriving cafe and cultural scene, a wealth of impressive *hôtels particuliers* and an enormously atmospheric old quarter, France's fourth-largest city is one place where you'll love to linger.

◎ Sights & Activities

Place du Capitole   SQUARE
Toulouse's magnificent main square is the city's literal and metaphorical heart, where Toulousiens turn out en masse on sunny evenings to sip a coffee or an early aperitif at a pavement cafe. On the eastern side is the 128m-long façade of the **Capitole** (place du Capitole; ⊘ 8.30am-7pm Mon-Sat, 10am-7pm Sun) 🆓, the city hall, built in the 1750s. Inside is the **Théâtre du Capitole**, one of France's most prestigious opera venues, and the over-the-top, late 19th-century **Salle des Illustres** (Hall of the Illustrious).

To the south of the square is the city's **Vieux Quartier** (Old Quarter), a tangle of lanes and leafy squares brimming with cafes, shops and eateries.

Musée des Augustins   GALLERY
(www.augustins.org; 21 rue de Metz; adult/child €5/free; ⊘ 10am-6pm Thu-Mon, to 9pm Wed) Located within a former Augustinian monastery, this fine-arts museum spans the Roman era through to the early 20th century. Echoing stairwells and high-vaulted chambers are part of the fun, but artistic highlights include the French rooms – with works by Delacroix, Ingres and Courbet – and works

by Toulouse-Lautrec and Monet, among the standouts from the 20th-century collection. Don't skip the 14th-century **cloister gardens**, with gurning gargoyle statues that seem to pose around the courtyard. Temporary exhibitions are €4 extra.

Basilique St-Sernin   CHURCH
(place St-Sernin; ambulatory €2.50; ⊗8.30am-6pm Mon-Sat, to 7.30pm Sun) This well-preserved Romanesque edifice is built from golden and rose-hued stonework up to the tip of the octogonal bell tower. Entry is free, but it's worth the additional charge to explore the **ambulatory**, where marble statues stare out from alcoves in the pink brick walls. The tomb of the basilica's namesake St Sernin (also known as St Saturnin) has pride of place: he was Toulouse's first bishop and met a gruesome end when pagan priests tied him to a bull.

★ Couvent des Jacobins   CHURCH, MONASTERY
(www.jacobins.mairie-toulouse.fr; rue Lakanal; cloister adult/child €4/2; ⊗9am-6pm Tue-Sun) Fresh from celebrating its eighth centenary, this elegant ecclesiastical structure is the mother church of the Dominican order, founded in 1215. First admire the **Église des Jacobins'** ornate stained-glass windows before wandering through the **Cloître des Jacobins**, in which graceful russet-brick columns surround a green courtyard. Pause in chapels and side rooms along the way, like the echoing **Salle Capitulaire**, a 14th-century hall ornamented with a haloed lamb. Don't miss **Chapelle St-Antonin**, with its 14th-century ceiling frescoes showing apocalyptic scenes.

★ Cité de l'Espace   MUSEUM
(www.cite-espace.com; av Jean Gonord; adult €21-25.50, child €15.50-19; ⊗10am-7pm daily Jul & Aug, to 5pm or 6pm Sep-Dec & Feb-Jun, closed Mon in Feb, Mar & Sep-Dec, closed Jan; ⊕) The fantastic space museum on the city's eastern outskirts brings Toulouse's illustrious aeronautical history to life through hands-on exhibits, including a moon-running simulator, a rotating pod to test your tolerance for space travel, a planetarium and an observatory, plus a vast cinema to immerse you in a space mission. The showpieces are the full-scale replicas of iconic spacecraft, including the Mars Rover and a 52m-high Ariane 5 space rocket.

🛏 Sleeping

La Petite Auberge de St-Sernin   HOSTEL €
(⌖09 81 26 63 00; www.lapetiteaubergedesaint-sernin.com; 17 rue d'Embarthe; dm €22, r €45-55; ❋🛜) No-frills but friendly, this backpacker-filled hostel offers boxy dorm rooms of four, six and eight beds, plus a few doubles (winter only). The decor's very plain – tiled floors, bare walls – but there's a garden for barbecues, and you're only a minute's walk from the Basilique St-Sernin. Some rooms have air-conditioning; ask when you book.

★ Hôtel Albert 1er   HOTEL €€
(⌖05 61 21 47 49; www.hotel-albert1.com; 8 rue Rivals; d €65-145; ❋🛜) 🅿 The Albert's central location and eager-to-please staff are a winning combination. A palette of maroon and cream, with marble flourishes here and there, bestows a regal feel on comfortable rooms. Bathrooms are lavished with ecofriendly products. The breakfast buffet is largely organic. Some recently upgraded rooms have mod cons such as USB ports and coffee makers.

Hôtel St-Sernin   BOUTIQUE HOTEL €€
(⌖05 61 21 73 08; www.hotelstsernin.com; 2 rue St-Bernard; d €79-119; 🅿🛜) Red-velvet furnishings and white walls give a classic feel to this hotel's small but sleek rooms. The best rooms have floor-to-ceiling windows overlooking the Basilique St-Sernin. Ask in advance about parking; there's a limited number of on-site spaces.

🍴 Eating

Bd de Strasbourg, place St-Georges and place du Capitole are perfect spots for summer dining alfresco. Rue Pargaminières is the street for kebabs, burgers and other late-night student grub.

Faim des Haricots   VEGETARIAN €
(⌖05 61 22 49 25; www.lafaimdesharicots.fr; 3 rue du Puits Vert; menus €12-14; ⊗noon-3pm & 6-10pm; ⌖) With confit duck and pâté featuring prominently on restaurant menus across Toulouse, this budget vegetarian canteen provides a much-needed palate cleanser. Faim des Haricots serves everything *à volonté* (all you can eat); simply choose whether you'd prefer to tuck into salads, quiches or the dish of the day.

Les Halles Victor Hugo   MARKET
(⌖05 61 22 76 92; www.marchevictorhugo.fr; place Victor Hugo; ⊗7am-1.30pm Tue-Sun) The beating

heart of Toulouse's food scene is this covered market, packed with local producers busily selling cheeses, fresh pasta, meats and take-away nibbles from sushi to spicy curries. For a great-value local dining experience, join streams of hungry market-goers at one of the tiny restaurants on the 1st floor (arrive just before noon or prepare to fight for a table).

La Braisière
BISTRO €€
(☑ 05 61 52 37 13; www.labraisiere.fr; 42 rue Pharaon; mains €14-22; ⊙ noon-2.30pm & 6.30-10pm Mon-Sat, 6.30-11pm Sun) This carnivorous bistro flame-grills beef to perfection, lavishing fine cuts of meat with sauces from green pepper to pungent Roquefort. Right in the middle of one of Toulouse's most historic streets, its interior decorated with watercolours of the city's past, La Braisière exudes comfort and nostalgia. Come hungry.

If you can't muster the appetite for hulking steaks, adjoining **L'Annexe** serves tapas.

★ Le Genty Magre
FRENCH €€€
(☑ 05 61 21 38 60; www.legentymagre.com; 3 rue Genty Magre; mains €18-30, menu €38; ⊙ 12.30-2.30pm & 8-10pm Tue-Sat) Classic French cuisine is the order of the day here, but lauded chef Romain Brard has plenty of modern tricks up his sleeve, too. The dining room feels inviting, with brick walls, burnished wood and sultry lighting. It's arguably the best place in the city to try rich, traditional dishes such as *confit de canard* (duck confit) or *cassoulet* (stew).

Solides
FRENCH €€€
(☑ 05 61 53 34 88; www.solides.fr; 38 rue des Polinaires; lunch menu €18, dinner menus €31-60; ⊙ noon-2pm & 8-10pm Mon-Fri) Ex-contestant on French *MasterChef* Simon Carlier has two excellent restaurants in Toulouse. **Solides Comme Cochons** (☑ 09 67 36 58 16; 49 rue Pargaminières; mains €15-20; ⊙ noon-2pm & 8-10pm Tue-Sat), a diner with a piggy focus, and his flagship, this newly renovated bistro inside the old Rotisserie des Carmes restaurant. Both showcase his imaginative, playful style. Tables here are red-hot, so book ahead.

ℹ Information

Tourist Office (☑ €0.45 per min 08 92 18 01 80; www.toulouse-tourisme.com; square Charles de Gaulle; ⊙ 9am-7pm Mon-Sat, 10.30am-5.15pm Sun Jun-Sep, 9am-6pm Mon-Fri, 9am-12.30pm & 2-6pm Sat, 10am-12.30pm & 2-5pm Sun Oct-Mar) The modern, multilingual tourist office is housed within a spiky, 16th-century belfry on square Charles de Gaulle.

ℹ Getting There & Away

AIR
Toulouse-Blagnac Airport (TLS; www.toulouse.aeroport.fr/en), 8km northwest of the centre, has frequent domestic and European flights. A **Navette Aéroport Flybus** (Airport Shuttle; www.tisseo.fr; single/return €8/15) links it with town.

TRAIN
Gare Matabiau (bd Pierre Sémard), 1km northeast of the centre, is served by frequent TGVs to Bordeaux (€26 to €44 via TGV, two hours, 15 daily) and east to Carcassonne (€16.50 to €22, 45 minutes to 1 hour, 12 to 20 daily).

FRANCE TOULOUSE

DON'T MISS

CARCASSONNE

Perched on a rocky hilltop and bristling with zigzag battlements, stout walls and spiky turrets, the fortified city of Carcassonne looks like something out of a children's storybook from afar. It's most people's perfect idea of a medieval castle, and it's undoubtedly an impressive spectacle – not to mention one of the Languedoc's biggest tourist draws.

The town's main attraction is its rampart-ringed fortress, known as La Cité. Encircled by two sets of battlements and 52 stone towers, it's topped by distinctive 'witch's hat' roofs (added by architect Viollet-le-Duc during 19th-century restorations). Inside the gates, there's a maze of cobbled lanes and courtyards to explore, now mostly lined by shops and restaurants.

Carcassonne also has one of France's oldest bridges: the Pont-Vieux, built during the 14th century.

Carcassonne is on the main train line from Toulouse (€16, 50 minutes, up to three hourly).

Nîmes

POP 154,000

This lively city boasts some of France's best-preserved classical buildings, including a famous Roman amphitheatre, although the city is most famous for its sartorial export, *serge de Nîmes* – better known to cowboys, clubbers and couturiers as denim.

Sights

A **Pass Nîmes Romaine** (adult/child €11.50/9), valid for three days, covers all three sights; buy one at the first place you visit.

★**Les Arènes** ROMAN SITE
(www.arenes-nimes.com; place des Arènes; adult/child incl audioguide €10/8; ⊙ 9am-8pm Jul & Aug, shorter hours Sep-Jun) Nîmes' twin-tiered amphitheatre is the best preserved in France. Built around 100 BC, the arena once seated 24,000 spectators and staged gladiatorial contests and public executions, and it's still an impressive venue for gigs, events and summer bullfights (during which it's closed for visits). An audioguide provides context as you explore the arena, seating areas, stairwells and corridors (known to Romans as *vomitories*), and afterwards you can view replicas of gladiatorial armour and original bullfighters' costumes in the museum.

Sleeping

Hôtel des Tuileries HOTEL €
(☑ 04 66 21 31 15; www.hoteldestuileries.com; 22 rue Roussy; d/tr/f from €72/90/115; P ❋ ❀) Nîmes' best deal is this delightful, bargain-priced 11-room hotel strolling distance from Les Arènes. Individually decorated rooms are spacious and spotless, and some have covered balconies. Breakfast costs €8. Its private parking garage (€10) is located just down the street, but there are only five car spaces, so reserve ahead.

Hôtel de l'Amphithéâtre HOTEL €€
(☑ 04 66 67 28 51; www.hoteldelamphitheatre.com; 4 rue des Arènes; s/d €70/90) Down a narrow backstreet leading away from Les Arènes, this tall town house has rooms in greys, whites and taupes, some with balconies overlooking place du Marché (light sleepers, beware: it can be noisy at night), and great buffet breakfasts (€10) including organic honey and homemade jam. It's run by an expat Cornishman and his trench wife.

Eating

La Petite Fadette CAFE €
(☑ 04 66 67 53 05; 34 rue du Grand Couvent; menus €10-14.50, tapas €3.30-7.50; ⊙ 11am-2.30pm Mon-Wed, 11am-2.30pm & 6-10.30pm Thu-Sat) *Tartines* (open-face toasted sandwiches) such as smoked salmon or cured ham and goat's cheese, as well as huge salads, are specialities of this cosy cafe, which has a cute rococo interior lined with vintage photos, and outside tables on a small courtyard. Contemporary tapas takes over the menu of an evening: crispy duck hearts, mini burgers, courgette *frites* (fries)...

★**Le Cerf à Moustache** BISTRO €€
(☑ 09 81 83 44 33; www.lecerfamoustache.com; 38 bd Victor Hugo; 2-/3-course menus lunch €15.80/19.90, dinner €25.90/30.90; ⊙ 11.45am-2pm & 7.45-10pm Mon-Sat) The Deer with the Moustache has established itself as one of Nîmes' best bistros, with quirky decor (including reclaimed furniture and a wall of sketch-covered old books), matched by chef Julien Salem's creative take on the classics (Aveyronnais steak with St-Marcellin cream, rabbit ballotine with crushed potatoes and garlic, white-chocolate mousse with mandarin meringue) and 60 wines by the glass.

Information

Tourist Office (☑ 04 66 58 38 00; www.ot-nimes.fr; 6 rue Auguste; ⊙ 9am-7.30pm Mon-Fri, 9am-7pm Sat, 10am-6pm Sun Jul & Aug, shorter hours rest of year; ☎) There's also a seasonal annexe (☑ 04 66 58 38 00; www.ot-nimes.fr; esplanade Charles de Gaulle; ⊙ 10am-5pm Jul & Aug) on esplanade Charles de Gaulle.

Getting There & Away

AIR

Aéroport de Nîmes Alès Camargue Cévennes (FNI; ☑ 04 66 70 49 49; www.aeroport-nimes.fr) 10km southeast of the city on the A54, is served only by Ryanair, which flies to/from London Luton, Liverpool, Brussels and Fez.

An airport bus (€6.50, 30 minutes) to/from the train station connects with all flights.

BUS

Edgard runs services to Pont du Gard (Line B21, €1.50, 40 minutes, hourly Monday to Saturday, two on Sunday) from the **bus station** (next to the train station).

TRAIN

TGVs run hourly to/from Paris' Gare de Lyon (€77, three hours) from the **train station** (bd Sergent Triaire).

Local destinations, with at least hourly departures, include the following:

Arles €8.80, 35 minutes
Avignon €10.60, one hour
Montpellier €9.90, 30 minutes

Pont du Gard

Southern France has some fine Roman sites, but for audacious engineering, nothing can top Unesco World Heritage Site Pont du Gard (☑ 04 66 37 50 99; www.pontdugard.fr; car & up to 5 passengers €18, after 8pm €10, by bicycle or on foot €7, after 8pm €3.50; ⊘ site 24hr year-round, visitor centre & museum 9am-8pm Jul & Aug, shorter hours Sep–mid-Jan & mid-Feb–Jun), 21km northeast of Nîmes. This three-tiered aqueduct was once part of a 50km-long system of water channels, built around 19 BC to transport water from Uzès to Nîmes. The scale is huge: 48.8m high, 275m long and graced with 35 precision-built arches, the bridge was sturdy enough to carry up to 20,000 cu metres of water per day. Each block was carved by hand and transported here from nearby quarries – no mean feat, considering the largest blocks weigh over 5 tonnes.

The Musée de la Romanité provides background on the bridge's construction, while kids can try out educational activities in the Ludo play area. Nearby, the 1.4km Mémoires de Garrigue walking trail winds upstream through typically Mediterranean scrubland, and offers some of the best bridge views.

There are large car parks on both banks of the river, about a 400m walk from the bridge.

PROVENCE

Provence conjures up images of rolling lavender fields, blue skies, gorgeous villages, wonderful food and superb wine. It certainly delivers on all those fronts, but it's not just worth visiting for its good looks – dig a little deeper and you'll also discover the multicultural metropolis of Marseille, the artistic haven of Aix-en-Provence and the old Roman city of Arles.

Marseille

POP 858,902

Marseille grows on you with its fusion of cultures, souk-like markets, millennia-old port and *corniches* (coastal roads) along rocky inlets and sun-baked beaches. Once the butt of French jokes, the *cité phocéenne* (in reference to Phocaea, the ancient Greek city located in modern-day Turkey, from where Marseille's settlers, the Massiliots, came) is looking fabulous after its facelift as the European Capital of Culture in 2013.

⊙ Sights

★ Vieux Port   HISTORIC SITE

(Ⓜ Vieux Port) Ships have docked for more than 26 centuries at the city's birthplace, the colourful old port. The main commercial docks were transferred to the Joliette area north of here in the 1840s, but the old port remains a thriving harbour for fishing boats, pleasure yachts and tourists. Guarding either side of the harbour are **Fort St-Nicolas** (⊘8am-7.45pm May-Aug, shorter hours rest of year; Ⓜ Vieux Port) and **Fort St-Jean** (Ⓜ Vieux Port), founded in the 13th century by the Knights Hospitaller of St John of Jerusalem (and now home to the city's flagship MuCEM museum).

★ Musée des Civilisations
de l'Europe et de la Méditerranée   MUSEUM

(MuCEM, Museum of European & Mediterranean Civilisations; ☑ 04 84 35 13 13; www.mucem.org; 7 Promenade Robert Laffont; adult/family/child incl exhibitions €9.50/14/free, 1st Sun of month free; ⊘10am-8pm Wed-Mon Jul & Aug, 11am-7pm Wed-Mon May, Jun, Sep & Oct, 11am-6pm Wed-Mon Nov-Apr; ⛬; Ⓜ Vieux Port, Joliette) The icon of modern Marseille, this stunning museum explores the history, culture and civilisation of the Mediterranean region through anthropological exhibits, rotating art exhibitions and film. The collection sits in a bold, contemporary building, J4, designed by Algerian-born, Marseille-educated architect Rudi Ricciotti. It is linked by a vertigo-inducing footbridge to the 13th-century Fort St-Jean, from which there are stupendous views of the Vieux Port and the Mediterranean. The fort grounds and their gardens are free to explore.

★ Villa Méditerranée   MUSEUM

(www.villa-mediterranee.org; bd du Littoral, esplanade du J4; ⊘noon-6pm Tue-Fri, 10am-6pm Sat & Sun; ⛬; Ⓜ Vieux Port, Joliette) **FREE** This eye-catching white structure next to MuCEM is no ordinary 'villa'. Designed by architect Stefano Boeri in 2013, the sleek white edifice sports a spectacular cantilever overhanging an ornamental pool. Inside, a viewing gallery with glass-panelled floor (look down if you dare!), and two or three temporary multimedia exhibitions evoke aspects of the Mediterranean, be they sea life, history or environmental. But it's the building itself that's the undisputed highlight here.

★ Le Panier
HISTORIC SITE

(Ⓜ Vieux Port) From the Vieux Port, hike north up to this fantastic history-woven quarter, which is fabulous for a wander with its artsy ambience, cool hidden squares and sun-baked cafes. In Greek Massilia it was the site of the agora (marketplace), hence its name, which means 'the basket'. During WWII the quarter was dynamited and afterwards rebuilt. Today it's a mishmash of lanes hiding artisan shops, ateliers (workshops) and terraced houses strung with drying washing.

★ Basilique Notre Dame de la Garde
CHURCH

(Montée de la Bonne Mère; www.notredame lagarde.com; rue Fort du Sanctuaire; ⊙7am-8pm Apr-Sep, to 7pm Oct-Mar; 🚌60) This opulent 19th-century Romano-Byzantine basilica occupies Marseille's highest point, La Garde (162m). Built between 1853 and 1864, it is ornamented with coloured marble, murals depicting the safe passage of sailing vessels and superb mosaics. The hilltop gives 360-degree panoramas of the city. The church's bell tower is crowned by a 9.7m-tall gilded statue of the Virgin Mary on a 12m-high pedestal. It's a 1km walk from the Vieux Port, or take bus 60 or the tourist train.

Château d'If
ISLAND, CASTLE

(www.if.monuments-nationaux.fr; adult/child €5.50/ free; ⊙10am-6pm Apr-Oct, to 5pm rest of year) Located 3.5km west of the Vieux Port, this island fortress-prison was immortalised in Alexandre Dumas' classic 1844 novel *The Count of Monte Cristo*. Many political prisoners were incarcerated here including the Revolutionary hero Mirabeau and the Communards of 1871. Other than the island itself there's not a great deal to see, but it's worth the trip just for the views of the Vieux Port. **Frioul If Express** (www.frioul-if-express.com; 1 quai des Belges) runs boats (€10.50 return, 20 minutes, around nine daily) from the quay.

ⓘ MARSEILLE CITY PASS

The **Marseille City Pass** (www.resa marseille.com; 24/48/72hr €24/31/39) covers admission to city museums, public transport, a guided city tour, a Château d'If boat trip and more, plus other discounts. It's not necessary for children under 12, as many attractions are greatly reduced or free. Buy it online or at the tourist office.

🛏 Sleeping

★ Mama Shelter
DESIGN HOTEL €€

(☑01 43 48 48 48; www.mamashelter.com; 64 rue de la Loubière; d €79-129; ❄🛜; Ⓜ Notre Dame du Mont-Cours Julien) This funky mini-chain of design-forward hotels recently opened its outpost in Marseille, and if you're a cool kid in search of sexy sleeps, this is the address for you. It's all about the details here – Philippe Starck furniture, sleek white-and-chrome colour schemes, in-room iMacs. Smaller rooms are oddly shaped, though, and it's a walk from the old port.

★ Hôtel St-Louis
HOTEL €€

(☑04 91 54 02 74; www.hotel-st-louis.com; 2 rue des Récollettes; r €89-140; ❄🛜; Ⓜ Noailles, 🚊Canebière Garibaldi) With its balconies and curlicues, the handsome 19th-century façade of this old-style hotel sets the vintage tone for the whole place. It's full of imagination: each of the rooms has its own individual style, from flea-market chic to English cottage-cosy, and a few have little balconies.

Hotel Carré Vieux Port
HOTEL €€

(☑04 91 33 02 33; www.hotel-carre-vieux-port. com; 6 rue Beauvau; s €99-112, d €106-119, tr €137-150; ❄🛜) Fresh from a comprehensive refurb, this ultra-central hotel now rates as one of the old port's top choices. It's a block from the buzzy quayside of the Vieux Port, and its rooms are bright, spacious and comfortable, with nice touches like frying-pan-sized shower heads, cube-shaped bath goodies, kettles in every room, and – er – a fibreglass bull in reception.

🍴 Eating

The Vieux Port overflows with restaurants, but choose carefully. Head to cours Julien and its surrounding streets for world cuisine.

★**Les Buffets du Vieux Port** FRENCH €
(☑04 13 20 11 32; www.clubhousevieuxport.
com; 158 quai du Port; adult/child menu €23/13;
☺noon-2.30pm & 7.30-10.30pm; 🚻; Ⓜ Vieux Port)
What a great idea – a high-class, on-trend
self-service canteen, with a vast array of
starters, mains, salads and desserts laid out
like a banquet for diners to help themselves
to. Premium cold cuts, fresh seafood, bouillabaisse, mussels, fish soup – it's all here
and more. Portside tables go fast, but there's
plenty of room inside.

★**Café Populaire** BISTRO €€
(☑04 91 02 53 96; www.cafepopulaire.com; 110
rue Paradis; tapas €6-16, mains €17-22; ☺noon-
2.30pm & 8-11pm Tue-Sat; Ⓜ Estrangin-Préfecture)
Vintage furniture, old books on the shelves
and a fine collection of glass soda bottles
lend a retro air to this trendy, 1950s-styled
jazz comptoir (counter) – a restaurant despite its name. The crowd is chic and smiling
chefs in the open kitchen mesmerise with
daily specials like king prawns *à la plancha*
(grilled) or beetroot and coriander salad.

★**L'Arome** MODERN FRENCH €€
(☑04 91 42 88 80; rue de Trois Rois; mains €16-25;
☺7.30-10pm; Ⓜ Notre Dame du Mont) The current hot tip in the trendy area around cours
Julien is this tiny bistro, on a graffiti-clad
street flanked by ethnic restaurants. The
no-frills decor, relaxed service and focused
menu of French market classics have made
this diner deservedly popular. Chef-owner
Romain has worked in plenty of fancy restaurants, but aims for sophisticated simplicity here. Reservations essential.

★**Le Café des Épices** MODERN FRENCH €€
(☑04 91 91 22 69; www.cafedesepices.com; 4 rue
du Lacydon; lunch/dinner menus from €25/45;
☺noon-3pm & 6-11pm Tue-Fri, noon-3pm Sat;
Ⓜ Vieux Port) One of Marseille's best chefs, Arnaud de Grammont infuses his cooking with
a panoply of flavours: squid-ink spaghetti
with sesame and perfectly cooked scallops,
or coriander- and citrus-spiced potatoes
topped with the catch of the day. Presentation is impeccable, the decor playful, and
the colourful outdoor terrace between giant
potted olive trees nothing short of superb.

🍷 **Drinking & Entertainment**

Options for a coffee or something stronger
abound on both quays at the Vieux Port. Cafes crowd cours Honoré d'Estienne d'Orves,
1er, a large open square two blocks south of
quai de Rive Neuve.

Au Petit Nice BAR
(☑04 91 48 43 04; 28 place Jean Jaurès; ☺6.30pm-
2am Tue-Sat; Ⓜ Notre Dame du Mont-Cours Julien)
This popular pub has loads of beers on tap
and a pleasant courtyard to chill in (note
that this is *not* the hotel of the same name).

Le Montmartre CAFE
(☑04 91 56 03 24; 4 place de Lenche; mains from
€6; ☺9am-11pm; Ⓜ Vieux Port, Joliette) Place de
Lenche is a lovely, small square in Le Panier
with glimpses of the Vieux Port. Among several cafes here, this one captures the neighbourhood vibe and is a fine place to hang
out with a drink on a lazy afternoon.

Dock des Suds LIVE MUSIC
(☑04 91 99 00 00; www.dock-des-suds.org; 12
rue Urbain V; ☺closed Aug; Ⓜ National, 🚇 Arenc

FRANCE MARSEILLE

WORTH A TRIP

LES CALANQUES
••

Marseille abuts the wild and spectacular **Parc National des Calanques** (www.
calanques-parcnational.fr), a 20km stretch of high, rocky promontories, rising from bril-
liant-turquoise Mediterranean waters.

The sheer cliffs are occasionally interrupted by small idyllic beaches, some impossible to reach without a kayak. Amongst the most famous are the calanques of Sormiou,
Port-Miou, Port-Pin and En-Vau.

October to June, the best way to see the Calanques is to hike and the best access is
from the small town of Cassis. The **tourist office** (☑08 92 39 01 03; www.ot-cassis.com;
quai des Moulins; ☺9am-7pm Mon-Sat, 9.30am-12.30pm & 3-6pm Sun Jul & Aug, shorter hours
rest of year; 🚄) has maps. In July and August, trails close because of fire danger: take a
boat tour from Marseille or Cassis; sea kayak with **Raskas Kayak** (☑04 91 73 27 16; www.
raskas-kayak.com; Marseille; half-/full day €35/65); drive; or take a bus.

le Silo) Eclectic live music in a large venue in the Joliette neighbourhood north of the Vieux Port.

ⓘ Tourist Information

Tourist Office (☎ 04 91 13 89 00; www.marseille-tourisme.com; 11 La Canebière; ⏰ 9am-7pm Mon-Sat, 10am-5pm Sun; Ⓜ Vieux Port) Has plenty of information about the city and the Calanques.

ⓘ Getting There & Away

AIR

Aéroport Marseille-Provence (Aéroport Marseille-Marignane; MRS; ☎ 04 42 14 14 14; www.marseille.aeroport.fr) is located 25km northwest of Marseille in Marignane. There are regular year-round flights to nearly all major French cities, plus major conurbations in the UK, Germany, Belgium, Italy and Spain.

Navette Marseille (www.navettemarseille-aeroport.com; ⏰ 4.30am-11.30pm) buses link the airport and Gare St-Charles (adult/child €8.20/4.10) every 15 to 20 minutes.

The airport's train station has direct services to several cities including Arles and Avignon; a free shuttle bus runs to/from the airport terminal.

BOAT

The **passenger ferry terminal** (www.marseille-port.fr; Ⓜ Joliette) is 250m south of place de la Joliette, 1er. **SNCM** (☎ 08 91 70 18 01; www.sncm.fr; 61 bd des Dames; Ⓜ Joliette) boats sail to Corsica, Sardinia and North Africa.

TRAIN

Eurostar (www.eurostar.com) has services one to five times weekly between Marseille and London (from €99, 6½ hours) via Avignon and Lyon. As always, the earlier you book, the cheaper the potential fare.

Regular and TGV trains serve **Gare St-Charles** (⏰ ticket office 5.15am-10pm; Ⓜ Gare St-Charles SNCF), which is a junction for both metro lines. The **left-luggage office** (⏰ 8.15am-9pm) is next to platform A. Sample fares:

Avignon €17 to €20.50, 35 minutes

Nice €28, 2½ hours

Paris Gare de Lyon from €75, three hours on TGV

ⓘ Getting Around

Marseille has two metro lines, two tram lines and an extensive bus network, all run by **RTM** (☎ 04 91 91 92 10; www.rtm.fr; 6 rue des Fabres; ⏰ 8.30am-6pm Mon-Fri, 8.30am-noon & 1-4.30pm Sat; Ⓜ Vieux Port), where you can obtain information and transport tickets (€1.60).

Pick up a bike from 100-plus stations across the city with **Le Vélo** (www.levelo-mpm.fr).

Aix-en-Provence

POP 145,300

Aix-en-Provence is to Provence what the Left Bank is to Paris: a pocket of bohemian chic crawling with students. It's hard to believe that 'Aix' (pronounced ex) is just 25km from chaotic, exotic Marseille. The city has been a cultural centre since the Middle Ages (two of the town's most famous sons are painter Paul Cézanne and novelist Émile Zola), but for all its polish, it's still a laid-back Provençal town at heart.

◎ Sights

A stroller's paradise, Aix highlight is the mostly pedestrian old city, **Vieil Aix**. South of cours Mirabeau, the **Quartier Mazarin** was laid out in the 17th century, and is home to some of Aix finest buildings.

★ Musée Granet   MUSEUM

(☎ 04 42 52 88 32; www.museegranet-aixenprovence.fr; place St-Jean de Malte; adult/child €5/free; ⏰ 11am-7pm Tue-Sun) This fabulous art museum sits right near the top of France's artistic must-sees, housing works by some of the most iconic artists associated with Provence, including Picasso, Léger, Matisse, Monet, Klee, Van Gogh and, perhaps most importantly of all in Aix, nine works by local boy Cézanne. The collection is named after the Provençal painter François Marius Granet (1775–1849), who donated a large number of works, and housed inside a dramatic 17th-century priory.

★ Caumont Centre d'Art   HISTORIC BUILDING

(☎ 04 42 20 70 01; www.caumont-centredart.com; 3 rue Joseph Cabassol; temporary exhibitions €8.50-11; ⏰ 10am-7pm May-Sep, to 6pm Oct-Apr) Aix' newest pride and joy is also one of its oldest: a stellar art space housed inside the Mazarin Quarter's grandest 17th-century *hôtel particulier*. There are three exhibitions every year exploring the region's rich artistic and cultural heritage, but it's the building itself that's the star of the show. Built from honey-coloured stone, its palatial rooms are stuffed with antiques and objets d'art that illustrate the aristocratic lifestyle of the house's most celebrated owner, the Marquise de Caumont.

Atelier Cézanne   MUSEUM
(☑04 42 21 06 53; www.atelier-cezanne.com; 9 av Paul Cézanne; adult/child €6/free; ☺10am-6pm Jul & Aug, shorter hours Sep-Jun) Cézanne's last studio, 1.5km north of the tourist office on a hilltop, was painstakingly preserved (and re-created: not all the tools and still-life models strewn around the room were his) as it was at the time of this death. Though the studio is inspiring, none of his works hang there. Take bus 1 or 20 to the Atelier Cézanne stop or walk from town.

🛏 Sleeping

Hôtel Cardinal   HOTEL €
(☑04 42 38 32 30; www.hotel-cardinal-aix.com; 24 rue Cardinale; s €69, d €79-119; 🛜) Pleasantly removed from the hustle and bustle of central Aix, this quaint Mazarin Quarter hotel is surprisingly elegant considering the price, with heritage rooms featuring original fireplaces, antiques and a surfeit of swag curtains. There are also six large suites in the annexe up the street, each with a kitchenette and dining room – ideal for longer stays.

★L'Épicerie   B&B €€
(☑06 08 85 38 68; www.unechambreenville.eu; 12 rue du Cancel; d €100-140; 🛜) This intimate B&B on a backstreet in Vieil Aix is the creation of born-and-bred Aixois lad Luc. His breakfast room re-creates a 1950s grocery store, and the flowery garden out the back is perfect for excellent evening dining and weekend brunch (book ahead for both). Breakfast is a veritable feast. Two rooms accommodate families of four.

🍴 Eating

★Farinoman Fou   BAKERY €
(www.farinomanfou.fr; 3 rue Mignet; breads €1-3; ☺7am-7pm Tue-Sat) Tucked just off place des Prêcheurs is this truly phenomenal bakery, with a constant queue outside its door. The different crunchy breads baked by artisanal *boulanger* Benoît Fradette are reason enough to sell up and move to Aix. The bakery has no shop as such; customers jostle for space with bread ovens and dough-mixing tubs.

★Le Petit Verdot   FRENCH €€
(☑04 42 27 30 12; www.lepetitverdot.fr; 7 rue d'Entrecasteaux; mains €19-25; ☺7pm-midnight Mon-Sat) Great Provençal food and great Provençal wines – really, what more do you want from a meal in this part of France?

It's all about hearty, honest dining here, with table tops made out of old wine crates, and a lively chef-patron who runs the place with huge enthusiasm. Expect slow-braised meats, seasonal veg, sinful desserts and some super wines to go with.

ℹ️ Information

Tourist Office (☑04 42 16 11 61; www.aixenprovencetourism.com; 300 av Giuseppe Verdi; ☺8.30am-7pm Mon-Sat, 10am-1pm & 2-6pm Sun, to 8pm Mon-Sat Jun-Sep; 🛜) Sells tickets for guided tours and events.

ℹ️ Getting There & Away

BUS
Aix' **bus station** (☑08 91 02 40 25, 04 42 91 26 80; place Marius Bastard) is a 10-minute walk southwest from La Rotonde. Sunday service is limited.
Avignon Line 23, €17.40, 1¼ hours, six daily
Marseille Line 20, €5.60, 25 minutes, every 10 minutes, five daily, three on Sunday
Nice Line 20, €29.40, 3¼ hours, five daily, three on Sunday

TRAIN
The **city centre train station**, at the southern end of av Victor Hugo, serves Marseille (€6.50, 45 minutes).
Aix' **TGV station**, 15km from the centre, is a stop on the high-speed Paris–Marseille line. Bus 40 runs from the TGV station to Aix' bus station (€4.10, 15 minutes, every 15 minutes).

Avignon
POP 91,250

Hooped by 4.3km of superbly preserved stone ramparts, this graceful city is the belle of Provence's ball. Its turn as the papal seat of power has bestowed Avignon with a treasury of magnificent art and architecture, none grander than the massive medieval fortress and papal palace, the Palais des Papes. Famed for its annual performing arts festival, these days Avignon is a lively student city and an ideal spot from which to step out into the surrounding region.

👁 Sights

★Palais des Papes   PALACE
(Papal Palace; www.palais-des-papes.com; place du Palais; adult/child €11/9, with Pont St-Bénezet €13.50/10.50; ☺9am-8pm Jul, to 8.30pm Aug, shorter hours Sep-Jun) The largest Gothic palace ever built, the Palais des Papes was

WORTH A TRIP

VAN GOGH'S ARLES

If the winding streets and colourful houses of Arles seem familiar, it's hardly surprising – Vincent van Gogh lived here for much of his life in a yellow house on place Lamartine, and the town regularly featured in his canvases. His original house was destroyed during WWII, but you can still follow in Vincent's footsteps on the evocative **Van Gogh walking circuit** – the **tourist office** (☑04 90 18 41 20; www.arlestourisme.com; esplanade Charles de Gaulle, Blvd des Lices; ☉9am-6.45pm Apr-Sep, 9am-4.45pm or 5.45pm Mon-Fri, 10am-1pm Sun Oct-Mar; ☎) sells maps (€1). You won't see many of the artist's masterpieces in Arles, however, although the modern art gallery **Fondation Vincent Van Gogh** (☑04 90 49 94 04; www.fondation-vincentvangogh-arles.org; 35ter rue du Docteur Fanton; adult/child €9/4; ☉11am-7pm Tue-Sun Apr–mid-Sep, to 6pm mid-Sep–Mar) always has one on show, as well as contemporary exhibitions inspired by the Impressionist.

Two millennia ago, Arles was a major Roman settlement. The town's 20,000-seat amphitheatre, known as the **Arènes** (Amphithéâtre; ☑08 91 70 03 70; www.arenes-arles.com; Rond-Point des Arènes; adult/child €6/free, incl Théâtre Antique €9/free; ☉9am-8pm Jul & Aug, to 7pm May, Jun & Sep, shorter hours Oct-Apr), is nowadays used for bullfights.

There are buses to/from Aix-en-Provence (€11, 1½ hours) and regular trains to/from Nîmes (€7.50, 30 minutes), Marseille (€13, 55 minutes) and Avignon (€6, 20 minutes).

erected by Pope Clement V, who abandoned Rome in 1309 as a result of violent disorder following his election. It served as the seat of papal power for seven decades, and its immense scale provides ample testament to the medieval might of the Roman Catholic church. Ringed by 3m-thick walls, its cavernous halls, chapels and antechambers are largely bare today, but an audioguide (€2) provides a useful backstory.

★ **Pont St-Bénezet**   BRIDGE
(bd du Rhône; adult/child 24hr ticket €5/4, with Palais des Papes €13.50/10.50; ☉9am-8pm Jul, to 8.30pm Aug, shorter hours Sep-Jun) Legend says Pastor Bénezet had three saintly visions urging him to build a bridge across the Rhône. Completed in 1185, the 900m-long bridge with 20 arches linked Avignon with Villeneuve-lès-Avignon. It was rebuilt several times before all but four of its spans were washed away in the 1600s.

If you don't want to pay to visit the bridge, admire it for free from Rocher des Doms park or Pont Édouard Daladier or on Île de la Barthelasse's chemin des Berges.

⚑ Festivals & Events

Hundreds of artists take to the stage and streets during the world-famous **Festival d'Avignon** (www.festival-avignon.com; ☉Jul) and the fringe **Festival Off** (www.avignonleoff. com; ☉Jul), held early July to early August.

⌑ Sleeping

Les Jardins de Baracane   B&B €€
(☑06 11 14 88 54; www.lesjardinsdebaracane.fr; 12 rue Baracane; r €125-205; P✱⊛⊛) This 18th-century house near place des Corps-Saints is owned by an architect, so it's been sensitively and tastefully renovated. Wood beams, stone walls and period detailing feature in all rooms, but the best are the two suites, which are posh enough for a pope. There's a great pool, and breakfast is served in the garden under a huge wisteria tree.

Hotel Central   HOTEL €€
(☑04 90 86 07 81; www.hotel-central-avignon. com; 31 rue de la République; d €89-119) As its name suggests, this efficient hotel is right in the heart of things, smack bang beside the main thoroughfare of rue de la Republique. It's modern throughout, with smallish but smart rooms, minimal clutter, and tasteful tones of cream and slate predominating, although a few rooms are more floral in style. The interior breakfast courtyard is a boon.

Hôtel de l'Horloge   HOTEL €€
(☑04 90 16 42 00; www.hotels-ocre-azur.com; place de l'Horloge; d €130-220; ✱☎) A refined choice: a spacious and well-run hotel in a lovely building near the town hall just off Avignon's main thoroughfare. The decor is fairly standard – beige walls, tasteful prints – but the terrace rooms are worth the extra for their knockout views (room 505 overlooks the Palais des Papes).

✖ Eating

Maison Violette BAKERY €

(☑ 06 59 44 62 94; place des Corps Saints; ⊙ 7am-7.30pm Mon-Sat) We simply defy you to walk into this bakery and not instantly be tempted by the stacks of baguettes, *ficelles* and *pains de campagnes* loaded up on the counter, not to mention the orderly ranks of éclairs, *millefeuilles*, fruit tarts and cookies lined up irresistibly behind the glass. Go on, a little bit of what you fancy does you good, *non*?

★ Restaurant L'Essentiel FRENCH €€

(☑ 04 90 85 87 12; www.restaurantlessentiel.com; 2 rue Petite Fusterie; menus €32-46; ⊙ noon-2pm & 7-9.45pm Tue-Sat) Snug in an elegant, caramel-stone *hôtel particulier*, the Essential is one of the finest places to eat in town – inside or in the wonderful courtyard garden. Begin with courgette flowers poached in a crayfish and truffle sauce, then continue with rabbit stuffed with candied aubergine, perhaps.

L'Épicerie BISTRO €€

(☑ 04 90 82 74 22; www.restaurantlepicerie.fr; 10 place St-Pierre; lunch/dinner menus from €16/23; ⊙ noon-2.30pm & 8-10pm) Traditional and unashamedly so, this cosy bistro is a fine spot for hearty French dishes, from homemade foie gras to a mixed platter of Provençal produce (€19). All the bistro boxes receive a big tick: checked tablecloths, vintage signs, friendly waiters, great local wines by the glass.

ℹ Information

Tourist Office (☑ 04 32 74 32 74; www.avignon-tourisme.com; 41 cours Jean Jaurès; ⊙ 9am-6pm Mon-Sat, 10am-5pm Sun Apr-Oct, shorter hours Nov-Mar) Offers a range of excellent guided walking tours covering the town's history, architecture and papal buildings. It can also book tickets for boat trips on the Rhône and wine-tasting trips to nearby vineyards.

ℹ Getting There & Away

BUS

The **bus station** (bd St-Roch; ⊙ information window 8am-7pm Mon-Fri, to 1pm Sat) is next to the central train station.

Destinations include the following:

Aix-en-Provence €17.40, LER Line 23, 1¼ hours, six daily Monday to Saturday, two on Sunday

Arles €7.10, LER Line 18, 50 minutes, at least seven daily

TRAIN

Avignon has two train stations: **Gare Avignon Centre** (42 bd St-Roch), on the southern edge of the walled town, and **Gare Avignon TGV** (Courtine), 4km southwest in Courtine. Local shuttle trains link the two every 20 minutes (€1.60, five minutes, 6am to 11pm). Note that there is no luggage storage at the train station.

Destinations served by TGV include Paris Gare du Lyon (€35 to €80, 3½ hours), Marseille (€17.50, 35 minutes) and Nice (€31 to €40, 3¼ hours).

THE FRENCH RIVIERA & MONACO

With its glistening seas, idyllic beaches and fabulous weather, the French Riviera (Côte d'Azur in French) screams exclusivity, extravagance and excess. It has been a favourite getaway for the European jet set since Victorian times and there is nowhere more chichi or glam in France than St-Tropez, Cannes and super-rich, sovereign Monaco.

Nice

POP 343,000

Riviera queen Nice is what good living is all about – shimmering shores, the very best of Mediterranean food, a unique historical heritage, free museums, a charming old town, exceptional art and alpine wilderness within an hour's drive.

⊙ Sights & Activities

★ Promenade des Anglais ARCHITECTURE

The most famous stretch of seafront in Nice – if not France – is this vast paved promenade, which gets its name from the English expat patrons who paid for it in 1822. It runs for the whole 4km sweep of the Baie des Anges with a dedicated lane for cyclists and skaters; if you fancy joining them, you can rent skates, scooters and bikes from **Roller Station** (☑ 04 93 62 99 05; www.roller-station.fr; 49 quai des États-Unis; skates, boards & scooters per hr/day €5/10, bicycles €5/15; ⊙ 9am-8pm Jul & Aug, 10am-7pm Sep-Jun).

★ Vieux Nice HISTORIC SITE

Getting lost among the dark, narrow, winding alleyways of Nice's old town is a highlight. The layout has barely changed since the 1700s, and it's now packed with delis, restaurants, boutiques and bars, but the centrepiece remains **cours Saleya**: a massive market square that's permanently thronging in summer. The **food market** (cours Saleya; ☺6am-1.30pm Tue-Sun) is perfect for fresh produce and foodie souvenirs, while the **flower market** is worth visiting just for the colours and fragrances. A **flea market** (cours Saleya; ☺8am-5pm Mon) is held on Monday.

★ Musée d'Art Moderne et d'Art Contemporain
GALLERY

(MAMAC; ☑04 97 13 42 01; www.mamac-nice.org; place Yves Klein; ☺10am-6pm Tue-Sun) `FREE`

European and American avant-garde works from the 1950s to the present are the focus of this museum. Highlights include many works by Christo and Nice's New Realists: Niki de Saint Phalle, César, Arman and Yves Klein. The building's rooftop also works as an exhibition space (with knockout panoramas of Nice to boot).

Musée Matisse
GALLERY

(☑04 93 81 08 08; www.musee-matisse-nice.org; 164 av des Arènes de Cimiez; ☺10am-6pm Wed-Mon) `FREE` This museum, 2km north in the leafy Cimiez quarter, houses a fascinating assortment of works by Matisse, including

Nice

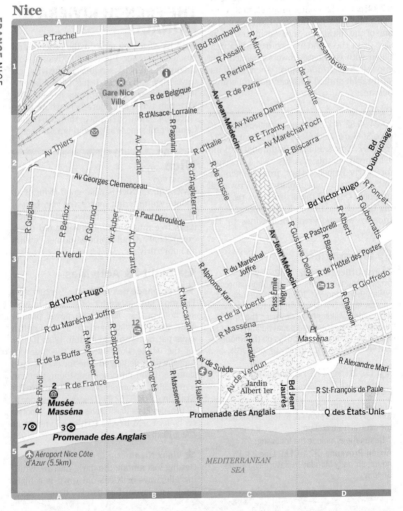

oil paintings, drawings, sculptures, tapestries and Matisse's famous paper cut-outs. The permanent collection is displayed in a red-ochre 17th-century Genoese villa in an olive grove. Temporary exhibitions are in the futuristic basement building. Matisse is buried in the **Monastère Notre Dame de Cimiez** (place du Monastère; ⊘8.30am-12.30pm & 2.30-6.30pm) cemetery, across the park from the museum.

★**Musée Masséna**   MUSEUM
(☑04 93 91 19 10; 65 rue de France; adult/child €6/free; ⊘10am-6pm Wed-Mon) Originally built as a holiday home for Prince Victor d'Essling (the grandson of one of Napoléon's favourite generals, Maréchal Massena), this lavish belle époque building is another of the city's iconic architectural landmarks. Built between 1898 and 1901 in grand neoclassical style with an Italianate twist, it's now a fascinating museum dedicated to the history of the Riviera – taking in everything from holidaying monarchs to expat Americans, the boom of tourism and the enduring importance of Carnival.

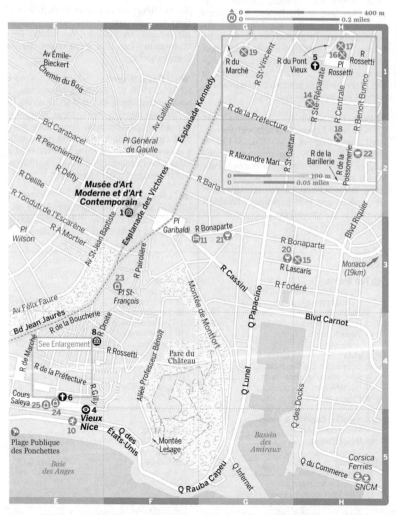

🛏 Sleeping

Villa Saint-Exupéry Beach Hostel   HOSTEL **€**
(☑04 93 16 13 45; www.villahostels.com; 6 rue Sacha Guitry; dm €40-50, d/tr €120/150; 🅿@🛜) It's actually a few blocks from the beach, but this longstanding city hostel has plenty of other pluses: bar, kitchen, free wi-fi, gym, games room etc, plus friendly multilingual staff and a great location. The downside? High prices (at least for a hostel) and occasionally drab decor. All dorms have a private ensuite bathroom, and sleep from three to 14.

⭐Nice Garden Hôtel   BOUTIQUE HOTEL **€€**
(☑04 93 87 35 62; www.nicegardenhotel.com; 11 rue du Congrès; s €75, d €90-123, tr €138; ☺reception 8am-9pm; 🅿🛜) Behind heavy iron gates hides this gem: nine beautifully appointed rooms – the work of the exquisite Marion – are a subtle blend of old and new and overlook a delightful garden with a glorious orange tree. Amazingly, all this charm and peacefulness is just two blocks from the promenade. Breakfast costs €9.

⭐Hôtel Le Genève   HOTEL **€€**
(☑04 93 56 84 79; www.hotel-le-geneve-nice.com; 1 rue Cassini; r €135-169; 🅿🛜) Situated just off place Garibaldi, this renovated corner hotel is bang in the middle of Nice's lively Petit Marais *quartier*. Bedrooms look sleek in cool greys, crimsons and charcoals; bathrooms are modern and well appointed. Breakfast is served in the ground-floor cafe, brimful of vintage bric-a-brac and mismatched furniture. Bars and cafes abound here.

⭐Nice Pebbles   APARTMENT **€€**
(☑04 97 20 27 30; www.nicepebbles.com; 1-/2-/3-bedroom apt from €110/130/200; 🅿🛜) Nice Pebbles offers nearly a hundred apartments and villas to choose from, from one to five bedrooms: all chosen for quirkiness and design, though sizes and location vary. Wi-fi, DVD players and proper kitchens are standard, and some also have luxuries such as a swimming pool, patio or garden. Rates vary widely; low-season deals can be very good.

🍴 Eating

Niçois nibbles include *socca* (a thin layer of chickpea flour and olive oil batter), *salade niçoise* and *farcis* (stuffed vegetables). Restaurants in Vieux Nice are a mixed bag, so choose carefully.

⭐La Rossettisserie   FRENCH **€**
(☑04 93 76 18 80; www.larossettisserie.com; 8 rue Mascoïnat; mains €13.50-14.50; ☺noon-2pm & 7.30-10pm Mon-Sat) Roast meat is the order of the day here: make your choice from beef, chicken, veal or lamb, and pair it with a choice of mashed or sautéed potatoes and ratatouille or salad. Simple and sumptuous, and the vaulted cellar is a delight.

⭐Fenocchio   ICE CREAM **€**
(☑04 93 80 72 52; www.fenocchio.fr; 2 place Rossetti; 1/2 scoops €2.50/4; ☺9am-midnight Feb-Oct) There's no shortage of ice-cream sellers

---

Nice

THE CORNICHES

Some of the Riviera's most spectacular scenery stretches east between Nice and Monaco. A trio of *corniches* (coastal roads) hugs the cliffs between the two seaside cities, each higher up the hill than the last. The middle *corniche* ends in Monaco; the upper and lower continue to Menton near the France/Italy border.

Corniche Inférieure (lower) Skimming the glittering, villa-studded shoreline, this road is all about belle époque glamour, the height of which can be seen at the extravagant **Villa Ephrussi de Rothschild** (☑04 93 01 33 09; www.villa-ephrussi.com/en; St-Jean-Cap Ferrat; adult/child €13/10; ⊙10am-7pm Jul & Aug, 10am-6pm Feb-Jun Sep & Oct, 2-6pm Mon-Fri, 10am-6pm Sat & Sun Nov-Jan) in St-Jean-Cap Ferrat.

Moyenne (middle) Corniche The jewel in the Riviera crown undoubtedly goes to **Èze**, a medieval village spectacularly located on a rocky outcrop with dazzling views of the Med.

Grande (upper) Corniche The epitomy of 'scenic drive', with sublime panoramas unfolding at every bend. Stop in **La Turbie** for dramatic views of Monaco.

FRANCE NICE

in the old town, but this *maître glacier* (master ice-cream maker) has been king of the scoops since 1966. The array of flavours is mind-boggling – olive, tomato, fig, beer, lavender and violet are just a few to try. Dither too long over the 70-plus flavours and you'll never make it to the front of the queue. For a Niçois twist, ask for *tourte de blette* (a sweet chard tart with raisins, pine kernels and parmesan).

Chez Pipo FRENCH €
(☑04 93 55 88 82; 13 rue Bavastro; socca €2.70; ⊙11.30am-2.30pm & 5.30-11pm Tue-Sun) Everyone says the best *socca* (chickpea-flour pancakes) can be found in the old town, but don't believe them – this place near Port Lympia has been in the biz since 1923 and, for our money, knocks *socca*-shaped spots off anywhere else in Nice.

★**Le Bistrot d'Antoine** MODERN FRENCH €€
(☑04 93 85 29 57; 27 rue de la Préfecture; menus €25-43, mains €15-25; ⊙noon-2pm & 7-10pm Tue-Sat) A quintessential French bistro, right down to the checked tablecloths, streetside tables and impeccable service – not to mention the handwritten blackboard, loaded with classic dishes such as rabbit pâté, potcooked pork, blood sausage and duck breast. If you've never eaten classic French food, this is definitely the place to start; and if you have, you're in for a treat.

Bar des Oiseaux FRENCH €€
(☑04 93 80 27 33; 5 rue Saint-Vincent; mains €16-25; ⊙noon-1.45pm & 7.15-9.45pm Tue-Sat) An old town classic, in business since 1961 on

a corner of a shady backstreet (expect to get lost en route). It's been various things down the years, including a bar and nightclub, and still has a few of its original saucy murals left in situ. But today it's a lively bistro serving trad French cuisine spiced up with a modern twist or two. Bookings recommended.

🍷 Drinking & Nightlife

Les Distilleries Idéales CAFE
(☑04 93 62 10 66; www.lesdistilleriesideales.fr; 24 rue de la Préfecture; ⊙9am-12.30am) The most atmospheric spot for a tipple in the old town, whether you're after one of the many beers on tap or a local wine by the glass. Brick-lined and set out over two floors (with a little balcony that's great for peoplewatching), it's packed until late. Happy hour is from 6pm to 8pm.

Comptoir Central Électrique BAR
(☑04 93 14 09 62; www.comptoircentralelectrique.fr; 10 rue Bonaparte; ⊙8.30am-12.30am Mon-Sat) Once a lighting factory (check out the lightbulb collection inside), now a hip-and-happening Port Lympia bar with slouchy sofas, industrial-chic decor and loads of beers and wines by the glass. There's a blackboard menu of snacks to share too.

BaR'Oc WINE BAR
(☑06 43 64 68 05; 10 rue Bavastro; ⊙7pm-12.30am) Fine wine and even finer tapas – from parma ham to oven-baked *figatelli* (a type of salami from Corsica) – plus tasting platters of cheese and cold cuts.

❶ Information

Tourist Office (Gare de Nice; ☑ 08 92 70 74 07; av Thiers; ☺ 9am-7pm daily Jun-Sep, 9am-6pm Mon-Sat & 10-5pm Sun Oct-May) In a booth right beside the train station.

❶ Getting There & Away

AIR

Nice-Côte d'Azur Airport (☑ 08 20 42 33 33; www.nice.aeroport.fr; ☎) is France's second-largest airport and has international flights to Europe, North Africa and the US, with regular and low-cost airlines. The airport has two terminals, linked by a free shuttle bus.

Buses 98 and 99 link the airport's terminal with Promenade des Anglais and Nice train station respectively (€6, 35 minutes, every 20 minutes).

BOAT

Nice is the main port for ferries to Corsica. **SNCM** (www.sncm.fr; quai du Commerce) and **Corsica Ferries** (www.corsicaferries.com; quai du Commerce) are the two main companies.

TRAIN

From Nice's train station, 1.2km north of the beach, there are frequent services to Cannes (€5.90, 40 minutes), Marseille (€35 to €38, 2½ hours), Monaco (€3.30, 25 minutes) and other Riviera destinations.

Cannes

POP 74,626

Most have heard of Cannes and its celebrity film festival. The latter only lasts for two weeks in May, but the buzz and glitz linger all year thanks to regular visits from celebrities who come here to indulge in designer shopping, beaches and the palace hotels of the Riviera's glammest seafront, bd de la Croisette.

◉ Sights & Activities

★ La Croisette   ARCHITECTURE

The multi-starred hotels and couture shops lining the iconic bd de la Croisette (aka La Croisette) may be the preserve of the rich and famous, but anyone can enjoy strolling the palm-shaded promenade – a favourite pastime among Cannois at night, when it twinkles with bright lights. Views of the Baie de Cannes and nearby Estérel mountains are beautiful, and seafront hotel palaces dazzle in all their stunning art deco glory.

Le Suquet   HISTORIC SITE

Follow rue St-Antoine and snake your way up Le Suquet, Cannes' oldest district, for great views of the bay.

Îles de Lérins   ISLAND

Although just 20 minutes away by boat, these tranquil islands feel far from the madding crowd. **Île Ste-Marguerite**, where the mysterious Man in the Iron Mask was incarcerated during the late 17th century, is known for its bone-white beaches, eucalyptus groves and small marine museum. Tiny **Île St-Honorat** has been a monastery since the 5th century: you can visit the church and small chapels and stroll through the monks' vineyards.

Boats leave Cannes from quai des Îles on the western side of the harbour. **Riviera Lines** (☑ 04 92 98 71 31; www.riviera-lines.com; quai Max Laubeuf) runs ferries to Île Ste-Marguerite and **Compagnie Planaria** (www.cannes-ilesdelerins.com; quai Max Laubeuf) covers Île St-Honorat.

🛏 Sleeping

Hôtel Le Mistral   BOUTIQUE HOTEL €€

(☑ 04 93 39 91 46; www.mistral-hotel.com; 13 rue des Belges; s €89-109, d €99-129; ❄ ☎) For super-pricey Cannes, this little 10-roomer is quite amazing value. Rooms are small but decked out in flattering red and plum tones – Privilege rooms have quite a bit more space, plus a fold-out sofa bed. There are sea views from the top floor, and the hotel is just 50m from La Croisette. There's no lift, though.

Hôtel 7e Art   BOUTIQUE HOTEL €€

(☑ 04 93 68 66 66; www.7arthotel.com; 23 rue du Maréchal Joffre; r €82-115; ❄ ☎) Cinema-themed in name and nature: the hotel's styled after the '7th Art' (as French people call film), and the rooms are divided into three filmic categories (Short Film, Long Film and Palme d'Or). Space is tight, but additions like iPod docks and vintage film posters add character. The very noisy road is a major drawback.

🍴 Eating

★ La Boulangerie par Jean-Luc Pelé   BAKERY €

(☑ 04 93 38 06 10; www.jeanlucpele.com; 3 rue du 24 août; lunch menus €6-9.50; ☺ 7.30am-7.30pm Mon-Sat) This swanky bakery by Cannois *chocolatier* and *pâtissier* Jean-Luc Pelé casts a whole new spin on eating cheap in Cannes. Creative salads, sandwiches, wraps and bagels – to eat in or out – burst with local flavours and provide the perfect prelude to the utterly sensational cakes and desserts Pelé is best known for.

★**Bobo Bistro**   MEDITERRANEAN €
(☑04 93 99 97 33; 21 rue du Commandant André; pizza €12-16, mains €15-20; ☺noon-3pm & 7-11pm Mon-Sat, 7-11pm Sun) Predictably, it's a 'bobo' (bourgeois bohemian) crowd that gathers at this achingly cool bistro in Cannes' fashionable Carré d'Or (Golden Sq). Decor is stylishly retro, with attention-grabbing objets d'art including a tableau of dozens of spindles of coloured yarn. Cuisine is local, seasonal and invariably organic: artichoke salad, tuna carpaccio with passion fruit, roasted cod with mash *fait masion* (homemade).

Aux Bons Enfants   FRENCH €€
(☑06 18 81 37 47; www.aux-bons-enfants.com; 80 rue Meynadier; menus €29, mains €16; ☺noon-2pm & 7-10pm Tue-Sat) A people's-choice place since 1935, this informal restaurant cooks up regional dishes, such as *aïoli garni* (garlic and saffron mayonnaise served with fish and vegetables), *daube* (a Provençal beef stew) and *rascasse meunière* (pan-fried rockfish), all in a convivial atmosphere. No credit cards or reservations.

ℹ️ Information

Tourist Office (☑04 92 99 84 22; www. cannes-destination.fr; 1 bd de la Croisette; ☺9am-8pm Jun-Aug, 9am or 10am-7pm Sep-May; 🛜) Runs an informative guided walking tour (€6) of the city at 2.30pm every Monday, and at 9.15am in July and August; there are simultaneous tours in English and French. It also runs a guided tour of the Palais des Festivals, but at the moment it's only run in French.

ℹ️ Getting There & Away

Cannes' gleaming white train station is well connected with other towns along the coast:
Marseille €25, two hours, half-hourly
Monaco €8, one hour, at least twice hourly
Nice €6, 40 minutes, every 15 minutes

St-Tropez

POP 4903

In the soft autumn or winter light, it's hard to believe the pretty terracotta fishing village of St-Tropez is a stop on the Riviera celebrity circuit. It seems far removed from its glitzy siblings further up the coast, but come spring or summer, it's a different world: the population increases tenfold, prices triple and fun-seekers pile in to party till dawn, strut around the luxury-yacht-packed Vieux Port and enjoy the creature comforts of exclusive A-listers' beaches in the Baie de Pampelonne.

◉ Sights & Activities

About 4km southeast of town is the start of **Plage de Tahiti** and its continuation, the famous **Plage de Pampelonne**, studded with St-Tropez' most legendary drinking and dining haunts.

★**Citadelle de St-Tropez**   MUSEUM
(☑04 94 54 84 14; admission €3; ☺10am-6.30pm Apr-Sep, to 5.30pm Oct-Mar) Built in 1602 to defend the coast against Spain, the citadel dominates the hillside overlooking St-Tropez to the east. The views are fantastic. Its dungeons are home to the excellent **Musée de l'Histoire Maritime**, an all-interactive museum inaugurated in July 2013 retracing the history of humans at sea, from fishing, trading, exploration, travel and the navy.

★**La Ponche**   HISTORIC SITE
Shrug off the hustle of the port in St-Tropez' historic fishing quarter, La Ponche, northeast of the Vieux Port. From the southern end of quai Frédéric Mistral, place Garrezio sprawls east from 10th-century **Tour Suffren** to place de l'Hôtel de Ville. From here, rue Guichard leads southeast to sweet-chiming **Église de St-Tropez** (place de l'Ormeau), a St-Trop landmark built in 1785 in Italian baroque style. Inside is a bust of St Torpes, honoured during Les Bravades in May.

🛏️ Sleeping

Hôtel Lou Cagnard   HOTEL €€
(☑04 94 97 04 24; www.hotel-lou-cagnard.com; 18 av Paul Roussel; d €83-176; ☺Mar-Oct; ❄🛜) This old-school hotel stands out in stark contrast against most of the swanky hotels around St-Tropez. Located in an old house shaded by lemon and fig trees, its rooms are unashamedly frilly and floral, but some have garden patios, and the lovely jasmine-scented garden and welcoming family feel make it a home away from home. The cheapest rooms share toilets.

Hôtel Le Colombier   HOTEL €€
(☑04 94 97 05 31; http://lecolombierhotel.free.fr; impasse des Conquettes; d €105-185, tr €235-285;

⊘mid-Apr–mid-Nov; ✳ 🔊) An immaculately clean converted house, a five-minute walk from place des Lices, the Colombier's fresh, summery decor is feminine and uncluttered. Rooms are in shades of white and furnished with vintage furniture.

🍴 Eating

⭐ La Tarte Tropézienne   CAFE €
(📞04 94 97 04 69; www.latartetropezienne.fr; place des Lices; mains €13-15, cakes €3-5; ⊘6.30am-7.30pm & noon-3pm) This newly renovated cafe-bakery is the creator of the eponymous sugar-crusted, orange-perfumed cake. There are smaller branches on **rue Clémenceau** (📞04 94 97 71 42; www.latartetropezienne.fr; 36 rue Clémenceau; mains €13-15, cakes €3-5; ⊘7am-7pm) and near the **new port** (📞04 94 97 19 77; www.latartetropezienne.fr; 9 bd Louis Blanc; mains €13-15, cakes €3-5; ⊘6.30am-7.30pm), plus various other towns around the Côte d'Azur.

La Pesquière   SEAFOOD €
(📞04 94 97 05 92; 1 rue des Remparts; menu €29, mains €14-20; ⊘9am-midnight mid-Mar–Nov) This is the kind of place you wouldn't think could still exist in swanky St-Tropez – a down-to-earth, honest-as-they-come seafood restaurant, which has been been serving up bowls of mussels, stuffed sardines and Provençal vegetables for going on five decades. It's near the old fishing quays of La Ponche, so the fish is guaranteed fresh – but don't expect any frills.

Le Café   CAFE €€
(📞04 94 97 44 69; www.lecafe.fr; place des Lices; lunch/dinner menus €18/32; ⊘8am-11pm) Whetting whistles since 1789, this historic cafe is where artists and painters preferred to hang out back in the days when St-Trop was still a sleepy port. Happily, it's clung on to its no-nonsense roots – you'll find solid dishes such as pot-roasted chicken, mussels and grilled fish on the menu, as well as a lovely interior bar with globe lights and wooden fixtures that still give it a cosy fin-de-siècle vibe. They'll lend you a set of boules if you want to take on some *pétanque* players on the square.

ℹ️ Information

Tourist Office (📞08 92 68 48 28; www.sainttropeztourisme.com; quai Jean Jaurès; ⊘9.30am-1.30pm & 3-7.30pm Jul & Aug, 9.30am-12.30pm & 2-7pm Apr-Jun, Sep & Oct, to 6pm Mon-Sat Nov-Mar) Runs occasional walking tours April to October, and also has a kiosk in Parking du Port in July and August. Rather stingily, you have to pay for a town map (€2).

ℹ️ Getting There & Away

VarLib (📞04 94 24 60 00; www.varlib.fr) tickets cost €3 from the **bus station** (📞04 94 56 25 74; av du Général de Gaulle) for anywhere within the Var département (except Toulon-Hyères airport), including Ramatuelle (35 minutes), St-Raphaël (1¼ hours to three hours, depending on traffic) via Grimaud and Port Grimaud, and Fréjus.

Buses serve Toulon-Hyères airport (€15, 1½ hours), but some require a transfer.

Monaco

POP 37,800

Squeezed into just 200 hectares, this confetti principality might be the world's second-smallest country (the Vatican is smaller), but what it lacks in size it makes up for in attitude. Glitzy, glam and screaming hedonism, Monaco is truly beguiling.

It is a sovereign state but has no border control. It has its own flag (red and white) and national holiday (19 November), and it uses the euro even though it's not part of the EU.

You can easily visit Monaco as a day trip from Nice, a short train ride away.

◉ Sights

⭐ Casino de Monte Carlo   CASINO
(📞98 06 21 21; www.montecarlocasinos.com; place du Casino; 9am-noon €10, from 2pm Salons Ordinaires/Salons Privées €10/20; ⊘visits 9am-noon, gaming 2pm-2am or 4am or when last game ends) Peeping inside Monte Carlo's legendary marble-and-gold casino is a Monaco essential. The building, open to visitors every morning, is Europe's most lavish example of belle époque architecture. Prince Charles III came up with the idea of the casino and in 1866, three years after its inauguration, the name 'Monte Carlo' – Ligurian for 'Mount Charles' in honour of the prince – was coined. To gamble or watch the poker-faced play, visit after 2pm (when a strict over-18s-only admission rule kicks in).

⭐ Le Rocher   HISTORIC SITE
Monaco Ville, also called Le Rocher, is the only part of Monaco to have retained its original old town, complete with small, winding medieval lanes. The old town

thrusts skywards on a pistol-shaped rock, its strategic location overlooking the sea that became the stronghold of the Grimaldi dynasty. There are various staircases up to Le Rocher; the best route up is via Rampe Major, which starts from place aux Armes near the port.

★ Musée Océanographique de Monaco   AQUARIUM

(📌93 15 36 00; www.oceano.mc; av St-Martin; adult €11-16, child €7-12; ⊙9.30am-8pm Jul & Aug, 10am-7pm Apr-Jun & Sep, to 6pm Oct-Mar) Stuck dramatically to the edge of a cliff since 1910, the world-renowned Musée Océanographique de Monaco, founded by Prince Albert I (1848–1922), is a stunner. Its centrepiece is its **aquarium** with a 6m-deep lagoon where sharks and marine predators are separated from colourful tropical fishes by a coral reef. Upstairs, two huge colonnaded rooms retrace the history of oceanography and marine biology (and Prince Albert's contribution to the field) through photographs, old equipment, numerous specimens and interactive displays.

🛌 Sleeping

Monaco is no budget destination when it comes to accommodation. Budget-conscious travellers should stay in nearby Nice and visit as a day trip.

Relais International de la Jeunesse Thalassa   HOSTEL €

(📌04 93 78 18 58; www.clajsud.fr; 2 av Gramaglia, Cap d'Ail; dm €20; ⊙Apr-Oct) This hostel isn't actually in Monaco, it's 2km along the coast at Cap d'Ail, but it's only a quick bus or train ride into the principality. It's got a lot going for it: a fab beachside location, clean four- to 10-bed dorms, home-cooked meals (€12) and takeaway picnics (€9), and a handy location 300m from the station.

Novotel Monte Carlo   HOTEL €€€

(📌99 99 83 00; www.novotel.com/5275; 16 bd Princesse Charlotte; d from €175; ❄@🛜🏊) Put all your chain-hotel preconceptions aside, for the Novotel Monte Carlo is no ordinary chain hotel. Rooms are bright, spacious and colourful, with bath and shower in every bathroom. Even better, up to two children under 16 can stay for free with their parents (and they throw the breakfast in too). The pool is open June to September.

✕ Eating

★ Marché de la Condamine   MARKET €

(www.facebook.com/marche.condamine; 15 place d'Armes; ⊙7am-3pm Mon-Sat, to 2pm Sun) For tasty, excellent-value fare around shared tables, hit Monaco's fabulous market food court, tucked beneath the arches behind the open-air market stalls on place d'Armes. Fresh pasta (€5.50 to €9) from Maison des Pâtes, truffle cuisine from Truffle Gourmet and traditional Niçois *socca* (€2.80 per slice) from Chez Roger steal the show. Check its Facebook page for what's cooking.

★ La Montgolfière   FUSION €€€

(📌97 98 61 59; www.lamontgolfiere.mc; 16 rue Basse; 3-/4-course menu €47/54; ⊙noon-2pm & 7.30-9.30pm Mon, Tue & Thu-Sat) Monegasque chef Henri Geraci has worked in some of the Riviera's top restaurants, but he's now happily settled at his own establishment down a shady alleyway near the palace. Escoffier-trained, he's faithful to the French classics, but his travels have given him a taste for Asian flavours too, so expect some exotic twists. The restaurant's small and sought after, so reserve ahead.

ℹ Information

TELEPHONE

Calls between Monaco and France are international calls. Dial 📌00 followed by Monaco's country code (📌377) when calling Monaco from France or elsewhere abroad. To phone France from Monaco, dial 00 and France's country code (📌33).

TOURIST INFORMATION

Tourist Office (www.visitmonaco.com; 2a bd des Moulins; ⊙9am-7pm Mon-Sat, 11am-1pm Sun) For tourist information by the port, head to the seasonal kiosk run by the tourist office near the cruise-ship terminal on Esplanade des Pêcheurs.

ℹ Getting There & Away

Services run about every 20 minutes east to Menton (€2, 15 minutes) and west to Nice (€3, 25 minutes). Bus 100 (€1.50, every 15 minutes from 6am to 9pm) goes to Nice (45 minutes) and Menton (40 minutes) along the Corniche Inférieure.

CORSICA

The rugged island of Corsica (Corse in French) is officially a part of France but remains fiercely proud of its own culture, history and language. It's one of the Mediterranean's most dramatic islands, with a bevy of beautiful beaches, glitzy ports and a mountainous, maquis-covered interior to explore, as well as a wild, independent spirit all of its own.

Ajaccio

POP 68,265

Ajaccio, Corsica's main metropolis, is all class and seduction. Looming over this elegant port city is the spectre of Corsica's great general: Napoléon Bonaparte was born here in 1769 and the city is dotted with statues and museums relating to him (starting with the main street in Ajaccio, cours Napoléon).

◉ Sights & Activities

Kiosks on the quayside opposite place du Maréchal Foch sell tickets for seasonal **boat trips** around the Golfe d'Ajaccio and Îles Sanguinaires (adult/child €25/15), and excursions to the Réserve Naturelle de Scandola (adult/child €55/35).

Maison Bonaparte   MUSEUM
(☑ 04 95 21 43 89; www.musees-nationaux-napoleoniens.org; rue St-Charles; adult/child €7/free; ☺ 10.30am-12.30pm & 1.15-6pm Tue-Sun Apr-Sep, to 4.30pm Oct-Mar) Napoléon spent his first nine years in this house. Ransacked by Corsican nationalists in 1793, requisitioned by English troops from 1794 to 1796, and eventually rebuilt by Napoléon's mother, the house became a place of pilgrimage for French revolutionaries. It hosts memorabilia of the emperor and his siblings, including a glass medallion containing a lock of his hair. A comprehensive audioguide (included in admission price for adults, €2 for children) is available in several languages.

Palais Fesch –
Musée des Beaux-Arts   GALLERY
(☑ 04 95 26 26 26; www.musee-fesch.com; 50-52 rue du Cardinal Fesch; adult/child €8/5; ☺ 10.30am-6pm Mon, Wed & Sat, noon-6pm Thu, Fri & Sun May-Sep, to 5pm Oct-Apr) One of the island's must-sees, this superb museum established by Napoléon's uncle has France's largest collection of Italian paintings outside the Louvre. Mostly the works of minor or anonymous 14th- to 19th-century artists, there are also canvases by Titian, Fra Bartolomeo, Veronese, Botticelli and Bellini. Look out for *La Vierge à l'Enfant Soutenu par un*

Ange (Mother and Child Supported by an Angel), one of Botticelli's masterpieces. The museum also houses temporary exhibitions.

🛏 Sleeping & Eating

Hôtel Marengo   HOTEL €
(☑ 04 95 21 43 66; www.hotel-marengo.com; 2 rue Marengo; d €78-98; ☺ Apr-Oct; ❄ 🖥) For something near to the sand, try this charmingly eccentric small hotel. Rooms have a balcony, there's a quiet flower-filled courtyard and reception is an agreeable clutter of tasteful prints and personal objects. Find it down a cul-de-sac off bd Madame Mère.

Hôtel Kallisté   HOTEL €
(☑ 04 95 51 34 45; www.hotel-kalliste-ajaccio.com; 51 cours Napoléon; s/d €68/88; ❄ 🖥) Low prices and a central location on Ajaccio's main street, midway between the train station and the port, are the twin draws at this 19th-century Ajaccio town house. The front desk closes after 8pm, but there's an automated reception system for late arrivals.

★ L'Altru Versu   BISTRO €€
(☑ 04 95 50 05 22; rte des Sanguinaires; mains €20-29; ☺ 12.30-2pm Thu-Mon, 7.30-10.30pm daily mid-Jun–mid-Oct, 12.30-2pm Thu-Tue, 7.30-10.30pm Mon, Tue & Thu-Sat rest of year) A phoenix rising from the ashes, this perennial favourite reopened in 2015 on Ajaccio's western waterfront after suffering two devastating winter storms and a fire. Magnificent sea views complement the exquisite gastronomic creations of the Mezzacqui brothers (Jean-Pierre front of house, David powering the kitchen), from crispy minted prawns with pistachio cream to pork with honey and clementine zest.

ℹ Information

Tourist Office (☑ 04 95 51 53 03; www.ajaccio-tourisme.com; 3 bd du Roi Jérôme; ☺ 8am-7pm Mon-Sat, 9am-1pm Sun Apr-Oct, shorter hours Nov-Mar; 🖥)

ℹ Getting There & Away

AIR

Aéroport d'Ajaccio Napoléon Bonaparte
(☑ 04 95 23 56 56; www.2a.cci.fr/Aeroport-Napoleon-Bonaparte-Ajaccio.html), 7km east of town, is linked by bus 8 (€4.50, 15 minutes) with Ajaccio's train station (bus stop marked Marconajo). Count on around €25 for a taxi into town.

BOAT

Boats to/from Toulon, Nice and Marseille depart from Ajaccio's **Terminal Maritime et Routier** (☑ 04 95 51 55 45; quai L'Herminier).

BUS

Local bus companies have ticket kiosks inside the ferry terminal building, the arrival/departure point for buses.

Bonifacio €20, 3hr, two daily Mon-Sat
Porto €12, 2hr, two daily Mon-Sat
Porto-Vecchio €20, 3¼hr, two daily Mon-Sat
Zonza €12, 2hr, two daily Mon-Sat

TRAIN

From the **train station** (place de la Gare), 500m north of town, services include the following:
Bastia €21.60, 3¾ hours, five daily
Calvi €25.10, 4¾ hours, two daily (change at Ponte Leccia)

Bastia

POP 42,948

The bustling old port of Bastia has an irresistible magnetism. Allow yourself at least a day to drink in the narrow old-town alleyways of Terra Vecchia, the seething Vieux Port, the dramatic 16th-century citadel perched up high, and the compelling history museum.

◉ Sights & Activities

★ Terra Vecchia   HISTORIC SITE

A spiderweb of narrow lanes, Terra Vecchia is Bastia's heart and soul. Shady place de l'Hôtel de Ville hosts a lively morning market on Saturday and Sunday. One block west, baroque Chapelle de l'Immaculée Conception (rue des Terrasses), with its elaborately painted barrel-vaulted ceiling, briefly served as the seat of the short-lived Anglo-Corsican parliament in 1795. Further north is Chapelle St-Roch (rue Napoléon), with an 18th-century organ and *trompe l'œil* roof.

★ Terra Nova   HISTORIC SITE

Above Jardin Romieu looms Bastia's amber-hued citadel, built from the 15th to 17th centuries as a stronghold for the city's Genoese masters. Inside, the Palais des Gouverneurs houses the Musée de Bastia (☑ 04 95 31 09 12; www.musee-bastia.com; place du Donjon; adult/child €5/2.50, Oct-Apr free; ◷ 10am-6.30pm Tue-Sun May-Sep, daily Jul & Aug, shorter hours rest of year), which retraces the city's history. A few streets south, don't miss the majestic Cathédrale Ste-Marie (rue de

l'Évêché) and nearby Église Ste-Croix (rue de l'Évêché), featuring gilded ceilings and a mysterious black-oak crucifix found in the sea in 1428.

🛏 Sleeping & Eating

★ Hôtel-Restaurant
La Corniche   HOTEL €€

(☑ 04 95 31 40 98; www.hotel-lacorniche.com; San Martino di Lota; d €78-106; ◷ mid-Feb–Dec; ❄ 🛜 ⛲) Perched high in the hilltop village of San Martino di Lota, Hôtel-Restaurant La Corniche is a brilliant halfway house between city convenience (it's just 8km from Bastia) and Cap Corse wilderness: the sea views will leave you smitten. A family-run hotel since 1934, it woos travellers with its fabulous location and gourmet food (mains €18 to €29, *menus* €24.50 to €31.50).

Hôtel Central   HOTEL €€

(☑ 04 95 31 71 12; www.centralhotel.fr; 3 rue Miot; s €80-90, d €90-110, apt €130; ❄ 🛜) From the vintage, black-and-white tiled floor in the entrance to the sweeping staircase and eclectic jumble of plant pots in the minuscule interior courtyard, this family-run address oozes 1940s grace. The hotel's pedigree dates to 1941 and the vintage furnishings inside the 19th-century building don't disappoint. The three apartments, with fully equipped kitchen, are great for longer stays.

A Scudella   CORSICAN €€

(☑ 04 95 46 25 31, 09 51 70 79 46; 10 rue Pino; menu €25; ◷ 7pm-2am Tue-Sat) Tucked down a back alley between place de l'Hôtel de Ville and the Vieux Port, this is a superb spot to sample traditional mountain fare, from appetisers of fine Corsican charcuterie and *beignets de brocciu* (fritters filled with *fromage frais*) to *veau aux olives* (stewed veal with olives) to *flan à la châtaigne* (chestnut flan).

ℹ Information

Tourist Office (☑ 04 95 54 20 40; www.bastia-tourisme.com; place St-Nicolas; ◷ 8am-6pm Mon-Sat, to noon Sun; 🛜) Organises guided tours of the city and has plenty of information about Cap Corse.

ℹ Getting There & Away

AIR

Aéroport Bastia-Poretta (www.bastia.aeroport.fr) is 24km south of the city. **Société des Autobus Bastiais** (☑ 04 95 31 06 65;

bastiabus.com) operates shuttles (€9, 35 minutes) every hour or two between the airport and Bastia's downtown Préfecture building. **Taxi Aéroport Poretta** (☑ 04 95 36 04 65; www.corsica-taxis.com) charges €48/66 by day/night.

BOAT

Ferry companies have information offices at **Bastia Port** (www.bastia.port.fr); they are usually open for same-day ticket sales a couple of hours before sailings. Ferries sail to/from Marseille, Toulon and Nice (mainland France), and Livorno, Savona, Piombino and Genoa (Italy).

BUS & TRAIN

From the **train station** (av Maréchal Sébastiani), there are daily services to Ajaccio (€21.60, 3¾ hours, four daily) via Corte (€10.10, 1¾ hours), and Calvi (€16.40, 3¼ hours, two daily) via Île Rousse (€13.50, 2¾ hours).

Bonifacio

POP 3016

With its glittering harbour, dramatic perch atop creamy white cliffs, and a stout citadel teetering above the cornflower-blue waters of the Bouches de Bonifacio, this dazzling port is an essential stop. Just a short hop from Sardinia, Bonifacio has a distinctly Italianate feel: sun-bleached townhouses, dangling washing lines and murky chapels cram the web of alleyways of the old citadel, while, down below on the harbourside, brasseries and boat kiosks tout their wares to the droves of day trippers.

◉ Sights

★Citadel   HISTORIC SITE

(Haute Ville) Much of Bonifacio's charm comes from strolling the citadel's shady streets, several spanned by arched aqueducts designed to collect rainwater to fill the communal cistern opposite **Église Ste-Marie Majeure**. From the marina, the paved steps of **montée du Rastello** and **montée St-Roch** bring you up to the citadel's old gateway, **Porte de Gênes**, complete with an original 16th-century drawbridge.

Îles Lavezzi   ISLAND

Paradise! This protected clutch of uninhabited islets were made for those who love nothing better than splashing in tranquil lapis-lazuli waters. The 65-hectare Île Lavez-

zi, which gives its name to the whole archipelago, is the most accessible of the islands.

In summer, various companies organise **boat trips** here; buy tickets at the booths located on Bonifacio's marina and bring your own picnic lunch. Boats also sail to the island from Porto-Vecchio.

🛏 Sleeping & Eating

Hôtel Le Colomba   HOTEL €€

(☑ 04 95 73 73 44; www.hotel-bonifacio-corse. fr; 4-6 rue Simon Varsi; d €112-167; ❋ 🗟) Occupying a tastefully renovated 14th-century building, this hotel enjoys a prime location on a picturesque (steep) street, bang in the heart of the old town. Rooms are simple and smallish, but fresh and individually decorated with amenities including wrought-iron bedsteads, country fabrics, carved bedheads and/or checkerboard tiles. Other pluses include friendly staff and breakfast served in a medieval vaulted cellar.

★Kissing Pigs   CORSICAN €

(☑ 04 95 73 56 09; 15 quai Banda del Ferro; mains €11-23, menus €20-22; ⊗ noon-2.30pm & 7-10.30pm Tue-Sun) Soothingly positioned by the harbour, this widely acclaimed restaurant and wine bar serves savoury fare in a seductively cosy interior, complete with wooden fixtures and swinging sausages. It's famed for its cheese and charcuterie platters; for the indecisive, the combination *moitié-moitié* (half-half) is perfect. The Corsican wine list is another hit.

❶ Information

Tourist Office (☑ 04 95 73 11 88; www. bonifacio.fr; 2 rue Fred Scamaroni; ⊗ 9am-8pm Jul & Aug, shorter hours rest of year; 🗟)

❶ Getting There & Away

AIR

A taxi into town from **Aéroport de Figari-Sud-Corse** (☑ 04 95 71 10 10; www.2a.cci.fr/ Aeroport-Figari-Sud-Corse.html), 20km north, costs about €45.

BOAT

Sardinia's main ferry operator, **Moby** (☑ 04 95 73 00 29; www.mobycorse.com) runs seasonal boats between Bonifacio and Santa Teresa Gallura (Sardinia); sailing time is 50 minutes.

SURVIVAL GUIDE

ℹ Directory A–Z

ACCOMMODATION

Many tourist offices make room reservations, often for a fee of €5; many only do so if you stop by in person. In the French Alps, ski-resort tourist offices operate a central reservation service.

B&Bs

For charm, a heartfelt *bienvenue* (welcome) and home cooking, it's hard to beat a *chambre d'hôte* (B&B). Pick up lists at local tourist offices or online.

Fleurs de Soleil (www.fleursdesoleil.fr) Selective collection of 550 stylish *maisons d'hôte*, mainly in rural France.

Gîtes de France (www.gites-de-france.com) France's primary umbrella organisation for B&Bs and self-catering properties (*gîtes*). Search by region, theme (charm, with kids, by the sea, gourmet, great garden etc), activity (fishing, wine tasting etc) or facilities (pool, dishwasher, fireplace, baby equipment etc).

Samedi Midi Éditions (www.samedimidi.com) Country, mountain, seaside... Choose your *chambre d'hôte* by location or theme (romance, golf, design, cooking courses).

Camping

➡ Most campgrounds open March or April to October.

➡ Euro-economisers should look for good-value but no-frills *campings municipaux* (municipal camping grounds).

➡ Accessing campgrounds without your own transport can be difficult in many areas.

➡ Camping in nondesignated spots (*camping sauvage*) is illegal in France.

SLEEPING PRICE RANGES

The following price ranges refer to a double room in high season, with private bathroom (any combination of toilet, bath-tub, shower and washbasin), excluding breakfast unless otherwise noted.

€ less than €90 (less than €130 in Paris)

€€ €90–190 (€130–250 in Paris)

€€€ more than €190 (more than €250 in Paris)

Hostels

Hostels range from funky to threadbare.

➡ A dorm bed in an *auberge de jeunesse* (youth hostel) costs €20 to €50 in Paris, and anything from €15 to €40 in the provinces, depending on location, amenities and facilities; sheets are always included, breakfast more often than not.

➡ To prevent outbreaks of bed bugs, sleeping bags are no longer permitted.

➡ All hostels are nonsmoking.

Hotels

➡ French hotels almost never include breakfast in their advertised nightly rates.

➡ Hotels in France are rated with one to five stars; ratings are based on objective criteria (eg size of entry hall), not service, decor or cleanliness.

➡ A double room has one double bed (or two singles pushed together); a room with twin beds is more expensive, as is a room with bath-tub instead of shower.

ESSENTIAL FOOD & DRINK

Bordeaux & Burgundy wines You'll find France's signature reds in every restaurant; now find out more by touring the vineyards.

Bouillabaisse Marseille's signature hearty fish stew, eaten with croutons and rouille (garlic-and-chilli mayonnaise).

Champagne Tasting in century-old cellars is an essential part of Champagne's bubbly experience.

Foie gras & truffles The Dordogne features goose and 'black diamonds' from December to March. Provence is also good for indulging in the aphrodisiacal fungi.

Fondue & raclette Warming cheese dishes in the French Alps.

Oysters & white wine Everywhere on the Atlantic coast, but especially in Cancale and Bordeaux.

Piggy-part cuisine Lyon is famous for its juicy *andouillette* (pig-intestine sausage), a perfect marriage with a local Côtes du Rhône red.

COUNTRY FACTS

Area 551,000 sq km

Capital Paris

Country Code ☑33

Currency Euro (€)

Emergency ☑112

Language French

Money ATMs everywhere.

Visas Schengen rules apply.

ACTIVITIES

From glaciers, rivers and canyons in the Alps to porcelain-smooth cycling trails in the Dordogne and Loire Valley – not to mention 3200km of coastline stretching from Italy to Spain and from the Basque country to the Straits of Dover – France's landscapes are ripe for exhilarating outdoor escapes.

➜ The French countryside is crisscrossed by a staggering 120,000km of *sentiers balisés* (marked walking paths), which pass through every imaginable terrain in every region of the country. No permit is needed to hike.

➜ The best-known trails are the *sentiers de grande randonnée* (GR), long-distance paths marked by red-and-white-striped track indicators.

➜ For complete details on regional activities, courses, equipment rental, clubs, companies and organisations, contact local tourist offices.

FOOD

Price indicators refer to the average cost of a two-course meal.

€ less than €20

€€ €20–40

€€€ more than €40

GAY & LESBIAN TRAVELLERS

The rainbow flag flies high in France, one of Europe's most liberal countries when it comes to homosexuality.

➜ Paris has been a thriving gay and lesbian centre since the late 1970s.

➜ Bordeaux, Lille, Lyon, Toulouse and many other towns have active communities.

➜ Attitudes towards homosexuality tend to be more conservative in the countryside and villages.

➜ Same-sex marriage has been legal in France since May 2013.

➜ Gay Pride marches are held in major French cities from mid-May to early July.

Online, try the following websites:

France Queer Resources Directory (www.france.qrd.org) Gay and lesbian directory.

Gaipied (www.gayvox.com/guide3) Online travel guide to France, with listings by region, by Gayvox.

LANGUAGE COURSES

➜ All manner of French-language courses are available in Paris and provincial towns and cities; most also arrange accommodation.

➜ Prices and courses vary greatly; the content can often be tailored to your specific needs (for a fee).

➜ The website www.europa-pages.com/france lists language schools in France.

Alliance Française (Map p372; ☑01 42 84 90 00; www.alliancefr.org; 101 bd Raspail, 6e; intensif/extensif courses per week from €202/91; Ⓜ St-Placide) French courses (minimum one week) for all levels. *Intensif* courses meet for four hours a day five days a week; *extensif* courses involve nine hours' tuition a week.

Eurocentres (www.eurocentres.com) This affiliation of small, well-organised schools has three addresses in France: in Amboise in the charming Loire Valley, in La Rochelle and Paris.

LEGAL MATTERS

➜ French police have wide powers of stop-and-search and can demand proof of identity at any time.

➜ Foreigners must be able to prove their legal status in France (eg passport, visa, residency permit).

➜ French law doesn't distinguish between hard and soft drugs; penalties can be severe (including fines and jail sentences).

MONEY

➜ Credit and debit cards are accepted almost everywhere in France.

➜ Some places (eg 24-hour petrol stations and some *autoroute* toll machines) only take credit cards with chips and PINs.

➜ In Paris and major cities, *bureaux de change* (exchange bureaux) are fast and easy, are open longer hours and offer competitive exchange rates.

OPENING HOURS

➜ French business hours are regulated by a maze of government regulations, including the 35-hour working week.

➜ The midday break is uncommon in Paris but, in general, gets longer the further south you go.

➜ French law requires most businesses to close Sunday; exceptions include grocery stores, *boulangeries*, florists and businesses catering to the tourist trade.

➜ In many places shops close on Monday.

➡ Many service stations open 24 hours a day and stock basic groceries.

➡ Restaurants generally close one or two days of the week.

➡ Museums tend to close on Monday or Tuesday.

PUBLIC HOLIDAYS

The following *jours fériés* (public holidays) are observed in France:

New Year's Day (Jour de l'An) 1 January

Easter Sunday & Monday (Pâques & Lundi de Pâques) Late March/April

May Day (Fête du Travail) 1 May

Victoire 1945 8 May – WWII armistice

Ascension Thursday (Ascension) May – celebrated on the 40th day after Easter

Pentecost/Whit Sunday & Whit Monday (Pentecôte & Lundi de Pentecôte) Mid-May to mid-June – celebrated on the seventh Sunday after Easter

Bastille Day/National Day (Fête Nationale) 14 July – *the* national holiday

Assumption Day (Assomption) 15 August

All Saints' Day (Toussaint) 1 November

Remembrance Day (L'onze Novembre) 11 November – WWI armistice

Christmas (Noël) 25 December

TELEPHONE

➡ French mobile phone numbers begin with ☑ 06 or ☑ 07.

➡ France uses GSM 900/1800, which is compatible with the rest of Europe and Australia but not with the North American GSM 1900 or the totally different system in Japan (though some North Americans have tri-band phones that work here).

➡ It is usually cheaper to buy a local SIM card from a French provider such as Orange, SFR, Bouygues and Free Mobile than to use international roaming. To do this, ensure your phone is 'unlocked'.

➡ Recharge cards are sold at most *tabacs* (tobacconist-newsagents) and supermarkets.

➡ To call France from abroad dial your country's international access code, then ☑ 33 (France's country code), then the 10-digit local number without the initial zero.

➡ To call internationally from France dial ☑ 00, the *indicatif* (country code), the area code (without the initial zero if there is one) and the local number.

VISAS

For up-to-date details on visa requirements, check the **Ministère des Affaires Étrangères** (Ministry of Foreign Affairs; Map p372; www.diplomatie.gouv.fr; 37 quai d'Orsay, 7e; Ⓜ Assemblée Nationale).

➡ EU nationals and citizens of Iceland, Norway and Switzerland need only a passport or national identity card to enter France and stay in the country, even for stays of over 90 days. Citizens of new EU member states may be subject to various limitations on living and working in France.

➡ Citizens of Australia, the USA, Canada, Israel, Hong Kong, Japan, Malaysia, New Zealand, Singapore, South Korea and many Latin American countries do not need visas to visit France as tourists for up to 90 days. For longer stays of over 90 days, contact your nearest French embassy or consulate.

➡ Other people wishing to come to France as tourists have to apply for a **Schengen Visa**.

➡ Citizens of Australia, Canada, Japan and New Zealand aged between 18 and 30 are eligible for a 12-month, multiple-entry **Working Holiday Visa** (Permis Vacances Travail).

ⓘ Getting There & Away

AIR

International airports include the following; there are many smaller ones serving European destinations only.

Aéroport de Charles de Gaulle, Paris (p388)
Aéroport d'Orly, Paris (p389)
Aéroport Lyon-St-Exupéry (p412)
Aéroport Marseille-Provence (p426)
Aéroport Nice Côte d'Azur (p434)

LAND
Bus

Eurolines (☑ 08 92 89 90 91; www.eurolines.eu), a grouping of 32 long-haul coach operators, links France with cities all across Europe and in Morocco and Russia. Discounts are available to people under 26 and over 60. Make advance reservations, especially in July and August.

Car & Motorcycle

A right-hand-drive vehicle brought to France from the UK or Ireland must have deflectors affixed to the headlights to avoid dazzling oncoming traffic.

CONNECTIONS

➡ High-speed trains link Paris' Gare du Nord with London's St Pancras (via the Channel Tunnel/Eurostar rail service) in just over two hours; Gare du Nord is also the point of departure for speedy trains to Brussels, Amsterdam and Cologne.

➡ Rail services link France with virtually every country in Europe.

SNCF TRAIN FARES & DISCOUNTS

The Basics

→ 1st-class travel, where available, costs 20% to 30% extra.

→ Ticket prices for some trains, including most TGVs, are pricier during peak periods.

→ The further in advance you reserve, the lower the fares.

→ Children under four travel for free, or €9 with a *forfait bambin* to any destination if they need a seat.

→ Children aged four to 11 travel for half-price.

Discount Tickets

Prem's The SNCF's most heavily discounted, use-or-lose tickets are sold online, by phone and at ticket windows/machines a maximum of 90 days and a minimum of 14 days before you travel.

Bons Plans A grab-bag of cheap options for different routes/dates, advertised online under the tab 'Dernière Minute' (Last Minute).

iDTGV Cheap tickets on advance-purchase TGV travel between about 30 cities; only sold at www.idtgv.com.

Ouigo (www.ouigo.com) is a low-cost TGV service whereby you can travel on high-speed TGVs for a snip of the usual price.

Discount Cards

Reductions of 25% to 60% are available with several discount cards (valid for one year):

Carte Jeune (€50) Available to travellers aged 12 to 27.

Carte Enfant+ (€75) For one to four adults travelling with a child aged four to 11.

Carte Weekend (€75) For people aged 26 to 59. Discounts on return journeys of at least 200km that either include a Saturday night away or only involve travel on a Saturday or Sunday.

Carte Sénior+ (€60) For travellers over 60.

Departing from the UK, **Eurotunnel Le Shuttle** (☑ in France 08 10 63 03 04, in UK 08443 35 35 35; www.eurotunnel.com) trains whisk bicycles, motorcycles, cars and coaches in 35 minutes from Folkestone through the Channel Tunnel to Coquelles, 5km southwest of Calais. Shuttles run 24 hours a day, with up to three departures an hour during peak periods. The earlier you book, the less you pay. Fares for a car, including up to nine passengers, start at €30.

Train

→ Rail services – including a dwindling number of overnight services to/from Spain, Italy and Germany, and Eurostar services to/from the UK – link France with virtually every country in Europe.

→ Book tickets and get train information from Rail Europe (www.raileurope.com). In France, ticketing is handled by SNCF (www.voyages-sncf.com); internet bookings are possible, but it won't post tickets outside France.

SEA

Regular ferries travel to France from the UK, Ireland and Italy.

Brittany Ferries (www.brittany-ferries.co.uk) Links between England/Ireland and Brittany and Normandy.

P&O Ferries (www.poferries.com) Ferries between England and northern France.

SNCM (www.sncm.fr) Ferries between France and Sardinia.

 Getting Around

AIR

Air France (www.airfrance.com) and its subsidiaries Hop! (www.hop.com) and Transavia (www.transavia.com) control the lion's share of France's domestic airline industry.

Budget carriers offering flights within France include EasyJet (www.easyjet.com), Twin Jet (www.twinjet.net) and Air Corsica (www.air corsica.com).

BUS

Buses are widely used for short-distance travel within *départements*, especially in rural areas with relatively few train lines (eg Brittany and Normandy). Unfortunately, services in some regions are infrequent and slow, in part because they were designed to get children to school rather than transport visitors around the countryside.

BICYCLE

France is a great place to cycle, and French train company SNCF does its best to make travelling with a bicycle easy; see **www.velo.sncf.com** for full details.

Most French cities and towns have at least one bike shop that rents out mountain bikes (VTT; around €15 a day), road bikes (VTCs) and cheaper city bikes. You have to leave ID and/or a deposit (often a credit-card slip) that you forfeit if the bike is damaged or stolen. A growing number of cities have automatic bike-rental systems.

CAR & MOTORCYCLE

A car gives you exceptional freedom and allows you to visit more remote parts of France.

➡ All drivers must carry a national ID card or passport; a valid driving licence (*permis de conduire*; most foreign licences can be used in France for up to a year); car-ownership papers, known as a *carte grise* (grey card); and proof of third-party (liability) insurance.

➡ Many French motorways (*autoroutes*) are fitted with toll (*péage*) stations that charge a fee based on the distance you've travelled; factor in these costs when driving.

➡ To hire a car you'll usually need to be over 21 and in possession of a valid driving licence and a credit card. Automatic transmissions are very rare in France; you'll need to order one well in advance.

TRAIN

➡ France's superb rail network is operated by the state-owned SNCF (www.sncf.com); many rural towns not on the SNCF train network are served by SNCF buses.

➡ The flagship trains on French railways are the superfast TGVs, which reach speeds in excess of 200mph and can whisk you from Paris to the Côte d'Azur in as little as three hours.

➡ Before boarding any train, you must validate (*composter*) your ticket by time-stamping it in a *composteur*, one of those yellow posts located on the way to the platform.

Rail Passes

Residents of Europe (who do not live in France) can purchase an InterRail One Country Pass (www.interrailnet.com; three/four/six/eight days €203/223/283/313, 12–25 years €154/164/208/232), which entitles its bearer to unlimited travel on SNCF trains for three to eight days over the course of a month.

For non-European residents, Rail Europe (www.raileurope-world.com) offers the France Rail Pass (www.francerailpass.com; two/four/five days over one month €102/153/172, 12–25 years €81/123/138).

You need to really rack up the kilometres to make these passes worthwhile.

FRANCE GETTING AROUND

Germany

Best Castles & Palaces

➡ Schloss Neuschwanstein (p481)

➡ Wartburg (p469)

➡ Burg Eltz (p500)

➡ Schloss Sanssouci (p460)

Best Iconic Sights

➡ Brandenburger Tor (p447)

➡ Kölner Dom (p500)

➡ Holstentor (p514)

➡ Hofbräuhaus (p477)

Why Go?

Few countries have had as much impact on the world as Germany. It has given us the printing press, the automobile, aspirin and historic heavyweights from Luther to Bach to Hitler. You'll encounter history in towns where streets were laid out long before Columbus set sail, and in castles that loom above prim, half-timbered villages.

The great cities – Berlin, Munich and Hamburg among them – come in more flavours than a jar of jelly beans but will all wow you with a cultural kaleidoscope that spans the arc from art museums and high-brow opera to naughty cabaret and underground clubs.

Germany's storybook landscapes will also likely leave an even bigger imprint on your memories. There's something undeniably artistic in the way Germany's scenery unfolds from the dune-fringed northern coasts via romantic river valleys to the off-the-charts Alpine splendour. As much fun as it may be to rev up the engines on the autobahn, do slow down to better appreciate this complex and fascinating country.

When to Go
Berlin

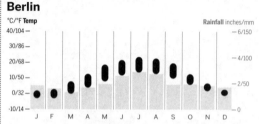

Jun–Aug Warm summers cause Germans to shed their clothes; night never seems to come.

Sep Radiant foliage and often-sunny skies invite outdoor pursuits; festivals galore.

Dec It's icy, it's cold but lines are short and Alpine slopes and twinkly Christmas markets beckon.

BERLIN

♪ 030 / POP 3.61 MILLION

Berlin is a bon vivant, passionately feasting on the smorgasbord of life, never taking things – or itself – too seriously. Its unique blend of glamour and grit is bound to mesmerise anyone keen to connect with its vibrant culture, superb museums, fabulous food, intense nightlife and tangible history.

When it comes to creativity, the sky's the limit in Berlin, Europe's newest start-up capital. In the last 20 years, the city has become a giant lab of cultural experimentation thanks to an abundance of space, cheap rent and a free-wheeling spirit that nurtures and encourages new ideas.

All this trendiness is a triumph for a city that staged a revolution, was headquartered by Nazis, bombed to bits, divided in two and finally reunited – and that was just in the 20th century! Must-sees and aimless explorations – Berlin delivers it all in one exciting and memorable package.

◉ Sights

Key sights such as the Reichstag, Brandenburger Tor and Museumsinsel cluster in the walkable historic city centre – **Mitte** – which also cradles the **Scheunenviertel**, a maze-like hipster quarter around Hackescher Markt. Further north, residential **Prenzlauer Berg** has a lively cafe and restaurant scene, while to the south loom the contemporary high-rises of **Potsdamer Platz**. Further south, gritty but cool **Kreuzberg** and **Neukölln** are party central, as is student-flavoured **Friedrichshain** east across the Spree River. Western Berlin's hub is **Charlottenburg**, with great shopping and a swish royal palace.

◉ Historic Mitte

★**Reichstag**   HISTORIC BUILDING
(www.bundestag.de; Platz der Republik 1, Visitors' Service, Scheidemannstrasse; ⊙lift ride 8am-midnight, last entry 10pm, Visitors' Service 8am-8pm Apr-Oct, to 6pm Nov-Mar; ◻100, Ⓢ Brandenburger Tor, Hauptbahnhof, Ⓤ Brandenburger Tor, Bundestag) FREE It's been burned, bombed, rebuilt, buttressed by the Wall, wrapped in fabric and finally turned into the modern home of the German parliament by Norman Foster: the 1894 Reichstag is indeed one of Berlin's most iconic buildings. Its most distinctive feature, the glittering glass dome, is serviced by a lift and affords fabulous 360-degree city views. For guaranteed access, make free reservations online, otherwise try scoring tickets at the Reichstag Service Centre for the same or next day. Bring ID.

★**Brandenburger Tor**   LANDMARK
(Brandenburger Gate; Pariser Platz; Ⓢ Brandenburger Tor, Ⓤ Brandenburger Tor) A symbol of division during the Cold War, the landmark Brandenburg Gate now epitomises German reunification. Carl Gotthard Langhans found inspiration in Athens' Acropolis for the elegant triumphal arch, completed in 1791 as the royal city gate. It stands sentinel over Pariser Platz, a harmoniously proportioned square once again framed by banks, a hotel and the US, British and French embassies, just as it was during its 19th-century heyday.

★**Holocaust Memorial**   MEMORIAL
(Memorial to the Murdered Jews of Europe; Map p456; ☎030-2639 4336; www.stiftung-denkmal. de; Cora-Berliner-Strasse 1; audioguide adult/

GERMANY BERLIN

ITINERARIES

Three Days
Come on, is that all you got? If the answer is really yes, drive down the **Romantic Road**, stopping in Rothenburg ob der Tauber and Füssen, then spend the rest of your time in **Munich**.

Five Days
Spend a couple of days in **Berlin**, head south to **Dresden** and **Nuremberg** or **Bamberg** for half a day each and wrap up your trip in **Munich** and surrounds.

One Week
This gives you a little bit of time to tailor a tour beyond the highlights mentioned above. Art fans might want to build **Cologne** or **Düsseldorf** into their itinerary; romantics could consider **Heidelberg**, a Rhine cruise or a trip down the **Romantic Road**; while outdoorsy types are likely to be lured by **Garmisch-Partenkirchen**, **Berchtesgaden** or the **Black Forest**.

Germany Highlights

1 Berlin (p447)
Discovering your inner party animal in the capital: save sleep for somewhere else as there's no time here with the clubs, museums and bars.

2 Munich (p471)
Experiencing Oktoberfest, a bacchanale of suds, or just soaking up the vibe in a beer garden.

3 Bamberg
(p486) Going slow in Germany's alluring small towns like this gem, with winding lanes, smoked beer (1) and a lack of cliché.

4 Cologne (p500)
Comparing the soaring peaks of the Dom with the slinky glasses of this city's famous beer.

5 Black Forest
(p490) Going cuckoo in the Black Forest, discovering its chilly

crags, misty peaks and
endless trails.

6 Dresden (p463)
Getting into the swing
of this city, with a
creative culture beyond
the restorations.

7 Hamburg (p507)
Cruising around one
of the world's great
harbours, then following
the trail of the Beatles.

8 Trier (p499)
Discovering the best-
preserved Roman ruins
north of the Alps in this
delightful wine town on
the Moselle.

**9 Schloss
Neuschwanstein**
(p481) Diving into
the mind of a loopy
Bavarian monarch at
this dreamy palace
cradled by the Alps.

10 Nuremberg
(p484) Tapping into
this city's medieval
roots, enjoying the
famous local sausages,
and pondering its
haunting Nazi past.

Berlin

concession €4/2; ⊙ field 24hr, information centre 10am-8pm Tue-Sun Apr-Sep, to 7pm Oct-Mar, last entry 45min before closing; Ⓢ Brandenburger Tor, Ⓤ Brandenburger Tor) FREE Inaugurated in 2005, this football-field-sized memorial by American architect Peter Eisenman consists of 2711 sarcophagi-like concrete columns rising in sombre silence from undulating ground. You're free to access this maze at any point and make your individual journey through it. For context visit the subterranean **Ort der Information** (Information Centre; Map p456; ☎030-7407 2929; www.holocaust-mahnmal.de; Cora-Berliner-Strasse 1) FREE whose exhibits will leave no one untouched. Audioguides and audio translations of exhibit panels are available.

Hitler's Bunker   HISTORIC SITE
(Map p456; cnr In den Ministergärten & Gertrud-Kolmar-Strasse; ⊙24hr; Ⓢ Brandenburger Tor, Ⓤ Brandenburger Tor) Berlin was burning and Soviet tanks advancing relentlessly when Adolf Hitler killed himself on 30 April 1945, alongside Eva Braun, his long-time female companion, hours after their marriage. Today, a parking lot covers the site, revealing its dark history only via an information panel with a diagram of the vast bunker network, construction data and the site's post-WWII history.

Checkpoint Charlie   HISTORIC SITE
(Map p456; cnr Zimmerstrasse & Friedrichstrasse; ⊙24hr; Ⓤ Kochstrasse) FREE Checkpoint Charlie was the principal gateway for foreigners and diplomats between the two Berlins from 1961 to 1990. Unfortunately, this potent symbol of the Cold War has degenerated into a tacky tourist trap, though a free open-air exhibit that illustrates milestones in Cold War history is one redeeming aspect.

◉ Museumsinsel & Scheunenviertel

Museumsinsel (Museum Island) is Berlin's most important treasure trove with five museums showcasing 6000 years worth of art, artefacts, sculpture and architecture from Europe and beyond.

★ Pergamonmuseum   MUSEUM
(☎030-266 424 242; www.smb.museum; Bodestrasse 1-3; adult/concession €12/6; ⊙10am-6pm Fri-Wed, to 8pm Thu; ☒100, 200, TXL, Ⓢ Hackescher Markt, Friedrichstrasse) Opening a fascinating window on to the ancient world, this palatial three-wing complex unites a rich feast of classical sculpture and monumental architecture from Greece, Rome, Babylon and the Middle East, including the radiant-blue **Ishtar Gate** from Babylon, the **Roman Mar-**

ket Gate of Miletus and the Caliph's Palace of Mshatta. Renovations put the namesake Pergamon Altar off limits until 2019. Budget at least two hours for this amazing place and be sure to pick up the free and excellent audioguide.

⭐ **Neues Museum**   MUSEUM
(New Museum; ☎030-266 424 242; www.smb. museum; Bodestrasse 1-3; adult/concession €12/6; ⊙10am-6pm, to 8pm Thu; ☐100, 200, TXL, ⑤Hackescher Markt) David Chipperfield's reconstruction of the bombed-out Neues Museum is now the residence of Queen Nefertiti, the showstopper of the Egyptian Museum, which also features mummies, sculptures and sarcophagi. Pride of place at the Museum of Pre- and Early History (in the same building) goes to Trojan antiquities, a Neanderthal skull and the 3000-year-old 'Berliner Goldhut', a golden conical hat. Skip the queue by buying your timed ticket online. Entry must be made during the designated 30-minute time slot.

Berliner Dom   CHURCH
(Berlin Cathedral; ☎030-2026 9136; www.berliner dom.de; Am Lustgarten; adult/concession/under 18 €7/5/free; ⊙9am-8pm Apr-Oct, to 7pm Nov-Mar; ☐100, 200, TXL, ⑤Hackescher Markt) Pompous yet majestic, the Italian Renaissance–style former royal court church (1905) does triple duty as house of worship, museum and concert hall. Inside it's gilt to the hilt and outfitted with a lavish marble-and-onyx altar, a 7269-pipe Sauer organ and elaborate royal sarcophagi. Climb up the 267 steps to the gallery for glorious city views.

⭐ **DDR Museum**   MUSEUM
(GDR Museum; ☎030-847 123 731; www.ddr -museum.de; Karl-Liebknecht-Strasse 1; adult/ concession €9.50/6; ⊙10am-8pm Sun-Fri, to 10pm Sat; ☐100, 200, TXL, ⑤Hackescher Markt) This interactive museum does an entertaining job of pulling back the iron curtain on an extinct society. You'll learn how, under communism, kids were put through collective potty training, engineers earned little more than farmers, and everyone, it seems, went on nudist holidays. A highlight is a simulated ride in a Trabi (an East German car).

⭐ **Fernsehturm**   LANDMARK
(TV Tower; ☎030-247 575 875; www.tv-turm.de; Panoramastrasse 1a; adult/child €13/8.50, premium ticket €19.50/12; ⊙9am-midnight Mar-Oct, 10am-midnight Nov-Feb, last ascent 11.30pm; 🛜; ☐100, 200, TXL, ⓊAlexanderplatz, ⑤Alexanderplatz) Germany's tallest structure, the TV Tower has been soaring 368m high since 1969 and is as iconic to Berlin as the Eiffel Tower is to Paris. On clear days, views are stunning from the panorama level at 203m or from the upstairs restaurant (☎030-247 5750; www.tv-turm.de/en/bar-restaurant; mains lunch €9.50-18.50, dinner €14.50-28.50; ⊙10am-midnight), which makes one revolution per hour. To shorten the wait, buy a timed ticket online.

⭐ **Hackesche Höfe**   HISTORIC SITE
(☎030-2809 8010; www.hackesche-hoefe.com; enter from Rosenthaler Strasse 40/41 or Sophienstrasse 6; ☐M1, ⑤Hackescher Markt, ⓊWeinmeisterstrasse) FREE The Hackesche Höfe is the largest and most famous of the courtyard ensembles peppered throughout the Scheunenviertel. Built in 1907, the eight

---

BERLIN IN...

One Day
Book ahead for an early lift ride to the Reichstag dome, then snap a picture of the Brandenburger Tor (Gate) before stumbling around the Holocaust Memorial and admiring the contemporary architecture of Potsdamer Platz. Ponder Cold War madness at Checkpoint Charlie, then head to Museumsinsel for an audience with Queen Nefertiti and the Ishtar Gate. Finish up with a night of mirth and gaiety around Hackescher Markt.

Two Days
Kick off day two coming to grips with what life was like in divided Berlin at the Gedenkstätte Berliner Mauer. Intensify the experience at the DDR Museum or on a walk along the East Side Gallery. Spend the afternoon soaking up the urban spirit of Kreuzberg with its sassy shops and street art, grab dinner along the canal, drinks around Kottbusser Tor and finish up with a night of clubbing.

GERMANY BERLIN

Mitte

Invalidenstr

Hannoversche Str

Linienstr 16

Kollwitzplatzmarkt (1km)

Rosa-Luxemburg-Platz

Rosa-Luxemburg-Str

Max-Beer-Str

Alte Schönhauser Str

Mulackstr

Steinstr

Gormannstr

Weinmeisterstr

Weinmeisterstr

La Soupe Populaire (850m)

Gontardstr

Alexanderplatz

Fernsehturm

Berlin Tourist Info TV Tower

3 15 18

Rathausstr

Judenstr

Grunerstr

Molkenmarkt

Poststr

Karl-Liebknecht-Str

Rochstr

Rosenstr

Spandauer Str

DDR Museum 2

Liebknechtbrücke

Spree River

13

Friedrichsbrücke

11

Lustgarten

14

Schlossbrücke

Spreekanal

Oberwallstr

Bebelplatz

Unter den Linden

Rosenthaler Str 17

Gipsstr

Sophienstr

Hackesche Höfe 4

Hackescher Markt

Hackescher Markt

Burgstr

Grosse Hamburger Str

Koppenplatz

Circus Hotel (90m); Weinerei (850m); Konnopke's Imbiss & Prater (1.5km)

Krausnickstr

Augustr 19

SCHEUNENVIERTEL

Neue Synagoge 5

Monbijouplatz

Monbijou Park

9

7 **Pergamonmuseum**

6 **Neues Museum**

10

Am Zeughaus

Am Kupfergraben

20

12

Hegelplatz

Georgenstr

Bodestr

Tucholskystr

Torstr

Linienstr

Oranienburger Str

Oranienburger Str

Johannisstr

Ziegelstr

Kalkscheunenstr

Planckstr

Geschwister-Scholl-Str

Charlottenstr

Dorotheenstr

Mittelstr

Chausseestr

Oranienburger Tor

Friedrichstr

Am Zirkus

Bertolt-Brecht-Platz

Bahnhof Friedrichstr

Friedrichstr

Friedrichstr

Spree River

Gedenkstätte Berliner Mauer (1km)

Hannoversche Str

Schumannstr

Reinhardtstr

Albrechtstr

Marienstr

Schiffbauerdamm

Reichstagufer

Luisenstr

Charité-Platz

Karlplatz

Schumannstr

Brandenburger Tor

Berlin Tourist Info (500m)

Alexanderufer

Spreebogenpark

Otto-von-Bismarck-Allee

Kapelleufer

Paul-Löbe-Allee

Platz der Republik

Bundestag

Reichstag 8

Brandenburger Tor 1

Pariser Platz

Berlin Tourist Info

Platz des 18 März

Scheidemannstr

400 m
0.2 miles

Mitte

interlinked *Höfe* reopened in 1996 with a congenial mix of cafes, galleries, boutiques and entertainment venues. The main entrance on Rosenthaler Strasse leads to **Court I**, prettily festooned with art nouveau tiles, while Court VII segues to the romantic **Rosenhöfe** with a sunken rose garden and tendril-like balustrades.

★**Neue Synagoge** SYNAGOGUE
(☏030-8802 8300; www.centrumjudaicum.de; Oranienburger Strasse 28-30; adult/concession €5/4; ⊙10am-6pm Mon-Fri, to 7pm Sun, closes 3pm Fri & 6pm Sun Oct-Mar; ⒨M1, ⓤOranienburger Tor, ⓈOranienburger Strasse) The gleaming gold dome of the Neue Synagoge is the most visible symbol of Berlin's revitalised Jewish community. The 1866 original was Germany's largest synagogue but its modern incarnation is not so much a house of worship (although prayer services do take place), as a museum and place of remembrance called **Centrum Judaicum**. The dome can be climbed from April to September (adult/concession €3/2.50). An audioguide costs €3.

★**Gedenkstätte Berliner Mauer** MEMORIAL
(Berlin Wall Memorial; ☏030-467 986 666; www.berliner-mauer-gedenkstaette.de; Bernauer Strasse btwn Schwedter Strasse & Gartenstrasse; ⊙visitor & documentation centre 10am-6pm Tue-Sun, open-air exhibit 8am-10pm daily; ⒮Nordbahnhof, Bernauer Strasse, Eberswalder Strasse) FREE For an insightful primer on the Berlin Wall, visit this outdoor memorial, which extends for 1.4km along Bernauer Strasse and integrates an original section of Wall, vestiges of the border installations and escape tunnels, a chapel and a monument. Multimedia stations, panels, excavations and a **Documentation Centre** provide context and explain what the border fortifications looked like and how they shaped the everyday lives of people on both sides of them. There's a great view from the centre's viewing platform.

◉ Potsdamer Platz & Tiergarten

Potsdamer Platz, built from scratch in the 1990s from terrain once bisected by the Berlin Wall, is a showcase of contemporary architecture, with Helmut Jahn's **Sony Center** being the most eye-catching complex. A visit here is easily combined with the **Kulturforum**, a cluster of art museums and the world-famous Berliner Philharmonie. With its rambling paths and hidden beer gardens, the Tiergarten, one of Europe's largest city parks, makes for a perfect sightseeing break.

★**Gemäldegalerie** GALLERY
(Gallery of Old Masters; Map p458; ☏030-266 424 242; www.smb.museum/gg; Matthäikirchplatz; adult/concession €10/5; ⊙10am-6pm Tue, Wed & Fri, 10am-8pm Thu, 11am-6pm Sat & Sun; ⒨; ⒬M29, M48, M85, 200, ⒮Potsdamer Platz, ⓤPotsdamer Platz) This museum ranks among the world's finest and most comprehensive collections of European art with about 1500 paintings spanning the arc of artistic vision from the 13th to the 18th century. Wear comfy shoes when exploring the 72 galleries: a walk past masterpieces by Titian, Dürer, Hals, Vermeer, Gainsborough and many more Old Masters covers almost 2km. Don't miss the Rembrandt Room (Room X).

★**Topographie des Terrors** MUSEUM
(Topography of Terror; Map p456; ☏030-2548 0950; www.topographie.de; Niederkirchner Strasse 8; ⊙10am-8pm, grounds close at dusk or 8pm at the latest; ⒮Potsdamer Platz, ⓤPotsdamer Platz) FREE In the same spot where the most feared institutions of Nazi Germany (including the

Gestapo headquarters and the SS central command) once stood, this compelling exhibit chronicles the stages of terror and persecution, puts a face on the perpetrators and details the impact these brutal institutions had on all of Europe. A second exhibit outside zeroes in on how life changed for Berlin and its people after the Nazis made it their capital.

⊙ Kreuzberg & Friedrichshain

Kreuzberg has a split personality: while its western section (around Bergmannstrasse) has a genteel air, eastern Kreuzberg (around Kottbusser Tor) – as well as northern Neukölln across the canal – is a multicultural mosaic and raucous nightlife hub. You'll find more after-dark action along with some Cold War relics in Friedrichshain across the Spree.

★ East Side Gallery
LANDMARK

(Map p456; www.eastsidegallery-berlin.de; Mühlenstrasse btwn Oberbaumbrücke & Ostbahnhof; ⊙24hr; Ⓤ Warschauer Strasse, Ⓢ Ostbahnhof, Warschauer Strasse) **FREE** The year was 1989. After 28 years, the Berlin Wall, that grim and grey divider of humanity, finally met its maker. Most of it was quickly dismantled, but along Mühlenstrasse, paralleling the Spree, a 1.3km stretch became the East Side Gallery, the world's largest open-air mural collection. In more than 100 paintings, dozens of international artists translated the era's global euphoria and optimism into a mix of political statements, drug-induced musings and truly artistic visions.

★ Jüdisches Museum
MUSEUM

(Jewish Museum; Map p456; ☑030-2599 3300; www.jmberlin.de; Lindenstrasse 9-14; adult/concession €8/3, audioguide €3; ⊙10am-8pm Tue-Sun, to 10pm Mon, last entry 1hr before closing; Ⓤ Hallesches Tor, Kochstrasse) In a landmark building by American-Polish architect Daniel Libeskind, Berlin's Jewish Museum offers a chronicle of the trials and triumphs in 2000 years of Jewish life in Germany. The exhibit smoothly navigates all major periods, from the Middle Ages via the Enlightenment to the community's post-1990 renaissance. Find out about Jewish cultural contributions, holiday traditions, the difficult road to emancipation and outstanding individuals (eg Moses Mendelssohn, Levi Strauss) and the fates of ordinary people.

Stasimuseum
MUSEUM

(☑030-553 6854; www.stasimuseum.de; Haus 1, Ruschestrasse 103; adult/concession €6/4.50; ⊙10am-6pm Mon-Fri, 11am-6pm Sat & Sun; Ⓤ Magdalenenstrasse) This exhibit provides an overview of the structure, methods and impact of the Ministry of State Security (Stasi), former East Germany's secret police, inside the feared institution's fortress-like headquarters. Marvel at cunningly low-tech surveillance devices (hidden in watering cans, rocks, even neckties), a prisoner transport van with tiny, lightless cells, and the stuffy offices of Stasi chief Erich Mielke. Panelling is partly in English. Free English tours at 3pm Saturday and Sunday. The museum is in the eastern district of Lichtenberg, just north of U-Bahn station Magdalenenstrasse.

MORE MUSEUM ISLAND TREASURES

While the Pergamonmuseum and the Neues Museum are the highlights of Museum Island, the other three museums are no slouches in the treasure department either. Fronting the Lustgarten park the Altes Museum (Old Museum; ☑030-266 424 242; www.smb.museum; Am Lustgarten; adult/concession €10/5; ⊙10am-6pm Tue, Wed & Fri-Sun, to 8pm Thu; 100, 200, TXL; Ⓢ Friedrichstrasse, Hackescher Markt) presents Greek, Etruscan and Roman antiquities. At the northern tip of the island, the Bodemuseum (☑030-266 424 242; www.smb.museum; cnr Am Kupfergraben & Monbijoubrücke; adult/concession €12/6; ⊙10am-6pm Tue, Wed & Fri-Sun, to 8pm Thu; Ⓢ Hackescher Markt, Friedrichstrasse) has a prized collection of European sculpture from the Middle Ages to the 18th century. Finally, there's the Alte Nationalgalerie (Old National Gallery; ☑030-266 424 242; www.smb.museum; Bodestrasse 1-3; adult/concession €12/6; ⊙10am-6pm Tue, Wed & Fri-Sun, to 8pm Thu; 100, 200, TXL, Ⓢ Hackescher Markt), whose thematic focus is on 19th-century European painting.

A combined day pass for all five museums costs €18 (concession €9).

BERLIN CITY PALACE: BACK TO THE FUTURE PALACE

Across from Museum Island looms Berlin's biggest construction site: the **Humboldt Forum** (Berlin City Palace; Schlossplatz; 🚇100, 200, TXL, Ⓤ Klosterstrasse), an art and cultural centre built to look like an exact replica of the baroque Berliner Stadtschloss (Berlin City Palace), but with a modern interior. The new space will be a centre of global culture and also harbour famous collections of ethnology and Asian art. If all goes to plan, the entire project should open in 2019.

Although barely damaged in WWII, the palace where Prussian rulers had made their home since 1443 was blown up by East Germany's government in 1950 to drop the final curtain on Prussian and Nazi rule.

Meanwhile, an adjacent information centre called **Humboldt-Box** (☑0180 503 0707; www.humboldt-box.com; Schlossplatz 5; ⊙10am-7pm Apr-Nov, to 6pm Dec-Mar; 🚇100, 200, TXL, Ⓤ Hausvogteiplatz) FREE has changing exhibits on the project and panoramic views from its top-level cafe. An exhibition highlight is a fantastically detailed model that shows how the historic palace fit into the old city centre around 1900.

Stasi Prison MEMORIAL

(Gedenkstätte Berlin-Hohenschönhausen; ☑030-9860 8230; www.stiftung-hsh.de; Genslerstrasse 66; tours adult/concession €6/3, exhibit free; ⊙tours in English 10.30am, 12.30pm & 2.30pm Mar-Oct, 2.30pm daily & 11.30am Sat & Sun Nov-Feb, exhibit 9am-6pm, German tours more frequent; ℗; 🚋M5) Victims of Stasi persecution often ended up in this grim remand prison, now a memorial site officially called Gedenkstätte Berlin-Hohenschönhausen. Tours – often conducted by former inmates – reveal the full extent of the terror and cruelty perpetrated upon thousands of suspected regime opponents, many utterly innocent. A permanent exhibit uses photographs, objects and a free audioguide to document daily life behind bars and also opens up the offices of the prison administration.

⊙ City West & Charlottenburg

★ **Schloss Charlottenburg** PALACE

(☑030-320 910; www.spsg.de; Spandauer Damm 10-22; day passes to all 4 buildings adult/concession €12/9; ⊙hours vary by building; ℗; 🚋M45, 109, 309, Ⓤ Richard-Wagner-Platz, Sophie-Charlotte-Platz) Charlottenburg Palace is one of the few sites in Berlin that still reflects the one-time grandeur of the Hohenzollern clan that ruled the region from 1415 to 1918. Originally a petite summer retreat, it grew into an exquisite baroque pile with opulent private apartments, richly festooned festival halls, collections of precious porcelain and paintings by French 18th-century masters. It's lovely in fine weather when you can fold a stroll in the palace park into a day of peeking at royal treasures.

★ **Kaiser-Wilhelm-Gedächtniskirche** CHURCH

(Kaiser Wilhelm Memorial Church; Map p458; ☑030-218 5023; www.gedaechtniskirche.com; Breitscheidplatz; ⊙church 9am-7pm, memorial hall 10am-6pm Mon-Fri, 10am-5.30pm Sat, noon-5.30pm Sun; 🚇100, 200, Ⓤ Zoologischer Garten, Kurfürstendamm, Ⓢ Zoologischer Garten) FREE Allied bombing in 1943 left only the husk of the west tower of this once magnificent neo-Romanesque church standing. Now an antiwar memorial, it stands quiet and dignified amid the roaring traffic. Historic photographs displayed in the **Gedenkhalle** (Hall of Remembrance), at the bottom of the tower, help you visualise the former grandeur of this 1895 church. The adjacent octagonal hall of worship, added in 1961, has glowing midnight-blue glass walls and a giant 'floating' Jesus.

⋐ Tours

Alternative Berlin Tours WALKING

(☑0162 819 8264; www.alternativeberlin.com; tours €10-20) Not your run-of-the-mill tour company, this outfit runs tip-based subculture tours that get beneath the skin of the city, plus an excellent street-art tour and workshop, an alternative pub crawl, a craft beer tour, the surreal 'Twilight Tour', an ecotour, and a food and drink tour.

Fat Tire Tours Berlin CYCLING

(☑030-2404 7991; www.fattiretours.com/berlin; Panoramastrasse 1a; adult/concession/under 12 incl bicycle from €28/26/14; Ⓢ Alexanderplatz, Ⓤ Alexanderplatz) This top-rated outfit runs English-language tours by bike, e-bike and Segway. Options include a classic city spin;

GERMANY BERLIN

Kreuzberg & Friedrichshain

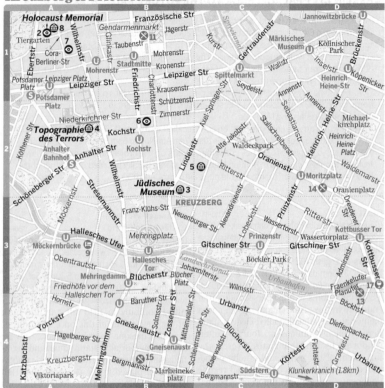

tours with a focus on Nazi Germany, the Cold War or 'Modern Berlin'; a trip to Potsdam; and an evening food tour. Tours leave from the TV Tower main entrance. Reservations advised.

🛏 Sleeping

While hotels in Charlottenburg often have special deals, remember that staying here puts you an U-Bahn ride away from most major sights (which are in Mitte) and happening nightlife in Friedrichshain or Kreuzberg.

🛏 Historic Mitte & Scheunenviertel

Wombat's Berlin　　　　　HOSTEL €
(📞030-8471 0820; www.wombats-hostels.com/berlin; Alte Schönhauser Strasse 2; dm €20-26, d €68-78; ❄@🛜; Ⓤ Rosa-Luxemburg-Platz) Sociable and central, Wombat's gets hostelling

right. From backpack-sized in-room lockers to individual reading lamps and a guest kitchen with dishwasher, the attention to detail here is impressive. Spacious and clean en-suite dorms are as much part of the deal as free linen and a welcome drink, best enjoyed with fellow party pilgrims at sunset on the rooftop.

★Circus Hotel　　　　　HOTEL €€
(📞030-2000 3939; www.circus-berlin.de; Rosenthaler Strasse 1; d €85-120, apt €120-190; ❄@🛜; Ⓤ Rosenthaler Platz) At this super-central budget boutique hotel, none of the compact, mod rooms are alike, but all feature upbeat colours, thoughtful design touches, a small desk, a tea and coffee station and organic bath products. Unexpected perks include a roof terrace, bike rentals and a fabulous breakfast buffet (€9) served until 1pm. Need more space? Go for an apartment.

Kreuzberg & Friedrichshain

◎ Top Sights
1 East Side Gallery......................................F2
2 Holocaust Memorial...............................A1
3 Jüdisches Museum..................................B2
4 Topographie des Terrors.....................A2

◎ Sights
5 Berlinische Galerie.................................C2
6 Checkpoint Charlie.................................B2
7 Hitler's Bunker..A1
8 Ort der Information................................A1

🛏 Sleeping
9 Grand Hostel Berlin...............................A3
10 Michelberger Hotel................................G2

✪ Eating
11 Augustiner am Gendarmenmarkt.........B1
12 Burgermeister..F3
13 Defne...D4
14 Max und Moritz.....................................D2
   Michelberger....................................(see 10)
15 Umami...B4

◎ Drinking & Nightlife
16 ://about blank...H3
17 Ankerklause..D3
18 Berghain/Panorama Bar.......................F1
19 Schwarze Traube...................................E3

✪ Entertainment
20 Kantine am Berghain............................F1

🛏 Kreuzberg & Friedrichshain

★ Grand Hostel Berlin   HOSTEL €
(Map p456; ☎ 030-2009 5450; www.grandhostel
-berlin.de; Tempelhofer Ufer 14; dm €10-32, tw

with/without bathroom from €49/38; ❸@🛜;
Ⓤ Möckernbrücke) Cocktails in the library bar?
Check. Rooms with stucco-ornamented ceilings? Got 'em. Canal views? Yep. Ensconced
in a fully renovated 1870s building, the

Charlottenburg

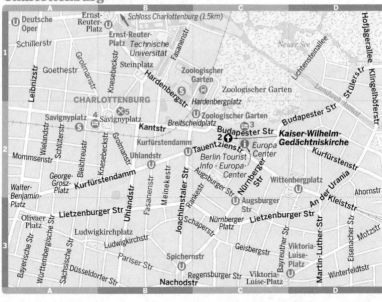

Charlottenburg

◎ Top Sights
- 1 Gemäldegalerie.....................................F1
- 2 Kaiser-Wilhelm-Gedächtniskirche C2

🛏 Sleeping
- 3 25hours Hotel Bikini Berlin.................C2
- 4 Sir Savigny...A2

🍴 Eating
- Butcher ....(see 4)
- 5 Dicke Wirtin B2
- Neni..(see 3)

🍸 Drinking & Nightlife
- Monkey Bar....................................(see 3)

★ Entertainment
- 6 Berliner Philharmonie..........................F1

'five-star' Grand Hostel is one of Berlin's most supremely comfortable, convivial and atmospheric hostels. Private rooms are spacious and nicely furnished and dorms come with freestanding quality beds and large lockers. Breakfast is €6.50.

★ **Michelberger Hotel**   HOTEL **€€**
(Map p456; ☑030-2977 8590; www.michelberger hotel.com; Warschauer Strasse 39; d €90-160; ☎;

Ⓤ Warschauer Strasse, Ⓢ Warschauer Strasse) The ultimate in creative crash pads, Michelberger perfectly encapsulates Berlin's offbeat DIY spirit without being self-consciously cool. Rooms don't hide their factory pedigree, but are comfortable and come in sizes suitable for lovebirds, families or rock bands. Staff are friendly and clued-up, and the **restaurant** (mains lunch €8-10, dinner €12-23; ⊘7-11am, noon-3pm & 7-11pm; ⊖❀🖢) 🖉 is popular with both guests and locals. Breakfast is €16.

🛏 City West & Charlottenburg

Sir Savigny   BOUTIQUE HOTEL **€€**
(Map p458; ☑030-323 015 600; www.hotel-sirsavigny.de; Kantstrasse 144; r €90-160; ⊖❀🖢; Ⓢ Savignyplatz) Not only pictures but also hotels tell a story, and this is the story of Sir FK Savigny, a fictional character who welcomes savvy travellers to his cosmopolitan crash pad with a hip bar and burger joint on the ground floor. Smartly dressed rooms are equipped with such lifestyle essentials as smartphone docks, espresso-pod machines and complimentary minibar. Breakfast is €18.

(Map p458;

★25hours Hotel
Bikini Berlin DESIGN HOTEL €€
(Map p458; ☎030-120 2210; www.25hours-hotels.
com; Budapester Strasse 40; r €130-330; P ❄ @
🛜; ☐100, 200, ⑤ Zoologischer Garten, Ⓤ Zoologischer Garten) The 'urban jungle' theme of
this lifestyle outpost in the iconic 1950s Bikini Haus plays on its location between the
zoo and main shopping district. Rooms are
stylish, if a tad compact, with the nicer ones
facing the animal park. Quirk factors include
an on-site bakery, hammocks in the public
areas and a sauna with zoo view.

✕ Eating

✕ Historic Mitte & Scheunenviertel

★Chèn Chè VIETNAMESE €€
(☎030-2888 4282; www.chenche-berlin.de;
Rosenthaler Strasse 13; dishes €6.50-11; ☺noon-
midnight; ❄🍴; ☐M1, Ⓤ Rosenthaler Platz) In
this exotic Vietnamese tearoom you can
settle down in the charming Zen garden
or beneath the hexagonal chandelier made
from the torn pages of a herbal medicine
book. The compact menu features healthy
and meticulously presented *pho* (soups),
curries and noodle dishes served in traditional clay pots. Exquisite tea selection and
small shop.

★Augustiner am
Gendarmenmarkt GERMAN €€
(Map p456; ☎030-2045 4020; www.augustiner
-braeu-berlin.de; Charlottenstrasse 55; mains €6.50-
26.50; ☺10am-2am; Ⓤ Französische Strasse)
Tourists, concert-goers and hearty-food
lovers rub shoulders at rustic tables in this
authentic Bavarian beer hall. Soak up the
down-to-earth vibe right along with a mug of
full-bodied Augustiner brew. Sausages, roast
pork and pretzels provide rib-sticking sustenance, but there's also plenty of lighter (even
meat-free) fare as well as good-value lunch
specials.

★Katz Orange INTERNATIONAL €€€
(☎030-983 208 430; www.katzorange.com; Bergstrasse 22; mains €18-29; ☺6-11pm; ❄; ☐M8,
Ⓤ Rosenthaler Platz) 🍴 With its gourmet, organic farm-to-table menu, stylish country
flair and top-notch cocktails, the 'Orange
Cat' hits a gastro grand slam. It will have you
purring for such perennial faves as Duroc
pork that's been slow-roasted for 12 hours
(nicknamed 'candy on bone'). The setting
in a castle-like former brewery is stunning,
especially in summer when the patio opens.

✕ Prenzlauer Berg

Konnopke's Imbiss GERMAN €
(☎030-442 7765; www.konnopke-imbiss.de; Schönhauser Allee 44a; sausages €1.30-2; ☺9am-8pm
Mon-Fri, 11.30am-8pm Sat; ☐M1, M10, Ⓤ Eberswalder Strasse) Brave the inevitable queue at
this famous sausage kitchen, ensconced in
the same spot below the elevated U-Bahn
tracks since 1930, but now equipped with
a heated pavilion and an English menu.
The 'secret' sauce topping its classic *Currywurst* comes in a four-tier heat scale from
mild to wild.

Umami VIETNAMESE €€
(☎030-2886 0626; www.umami-restaurant.de;
Knaackstrasse 16-18; mains €7.50-15; ☺noon-
11.30pm; ❄🛜🍴; ☐M2, Ⓤ Senefelderplatz) A
mellow 1950s lounge-vibe and an inspired
menu of Indochine home cooking divided
into 'regular' and 'vegetarian' choices are
the main draws of this restaurant with large
pavement terrace. Leave room for the green-
tea apple pie or a Vietnamese cupcake called
'popcake'. The six-course family meal is a
steal at €20.

SCHLOSS & PARK SANSSOUCI

Easily reached in half an hour from central Berlin, the former royal Prussian seat of Potsdam lures visitors to its splendid Unesco-recognised palaces and parks dreamed up by 18th-century King Friedrich II (Frederick the Great).

Headlining the roll call of royal pads is **Schloss Sanssouci** (☎0331-969 4200; www. spsg.de; Maulbeerallee; adult/concession incl tour or audioguide €12/8; ☺10am-6pm Tue-Sun Apr-Oct, to 5pm Nov-Mar; ☐614, 650, 695), a celebrated rococo palace and the king's favourite summer retreat. Standouts on the audio-guided tour include the whimsically decorated concert hall, the intimate library and the domed Marble Hall. Admission is limited and by timed ticket only; book online (tickets.spsg.de) to avoid wait times and/or disappointment. Tickets must be printed out. Tours run by the Potsdam **tourist office** (☎0331-2755 8899; www.potsdam-tourism.com; Potsdam Hauptbahnhof; ☺9.30am-6pm Mon-Sat; ⑤Potsdam Hauptbahnhof) guarantee entry.

Schloss Sanssouci is surrounded by a sprawling park dotted with numerous other palaces, buildings, fountains, statues and romantic corners. The one building not to be missed is the **Chinesisches Haus** (Chinese House; ☎0331-969 4200; www.spsg.de; Am Grünen Gitter; adult/concession €3/2; ☺10am-6pm Tue-Sun May-Oct; ☐605, 606, ☐91), an adorable clover-leaf-shaped pavilion whose exterior is decorated with exotically dressed gilded figures shown sipping tea, dancing and playing musical instruments.

Another park highlight is the **Neues Palais** (New Palace; ☎0331-969 4200; www.spsg.de; Am Neuen Palais; adult/concession incl tour or audioguide €8/6; ☺10am-6pm Wed-Mon Apr-Oct, to 5pm Nov-Mar; ☐605, 606, 695, ⑤Potsdam Charlottenhof) at the far western end. It has built-to-impress dimensions and is filled with opulent private and representative rooms.

Each building charges separate admission; a day pass to all costs €19 (concession €14).

On a nice day, it's worth exploring Potsdam's watery landscape and numerous other palaces on a **boat cruise** (☎0331-275 9210; www.schiffahrt-in-potsdam.de; Lange Brücke 6; ☺Apr-Oct; ☐605, 610, 631, 694, ☐91, 92, 93, 98). The most popular one is the 90-minute *Schlösserundfahrt* (palace cruise; €14). Boats leave from docks near the Hauptbahnhof.

Regional trains leaving from Berlin-Hauptbahnhof and Zoologischer Garten need only 25 minutes to reach Potsdam Hauptbahnhof. The S-Bahn S7 from central Berlin makes the trip in about 40 minutes. You need an ABC ticket (€3.30) for either service.

✗ Kreuzberg

★**Burgermeister**   BURGERS €
(Map p456; ☎030-2388 3840; www.burger-meister.de; Oberbaumstrasse 8; burgers €3.50-4.80; ☺11am-3am Sun-Thu, to 4am Fri & Sat; ⑪Schlesisches Tor) It's green, ornate, a century old and...it used to be a toilet. Now it's a burger joint beneath the elevated U-Bahn tracks. Get in line for the plump all-beef patties (try the Meisterburger with fried onions, bacon and barbecue sauce) paired with cheese fries and such homemade dips as peanut or mango curry.

Max und Moritz   GERMAN €€
(Map p456; ☎030-6951 5911; www.maxundmoritz berlin.de; Oranienstrasse 162; mains €9.50-17; ☺5pm-midnight; ☺☎; ⑪Moritzplatz) The patina of yesteryear hangs over this ode to old-school brewpub named for the cheeky Wilhelm Busch cartoon characters. Since 1902 it has packed hungry diners and drinkers into its rustic tile-and-stucco ornamented rooms for sudsy home brews and granny-style Berlin fare. A menu favourite is the *Königsberger Klopse* (veal meatballs in caper sauce).

Defne   TURKISH €€
(Map p456; ☎030-8179 7111; www.defne-restaurant.de; Planufer 92c; mains €8.50-20; ☺4pm-1am Apr-Sep, 5pm-1am Oct-Mar; ☺☑; ⑪Kottbusser Tor, Schönleinstrasse) If you thought Turkish cuisine stopped at the doner kebab, canal-side Defne will teach you otherwise. The appetiser platter alone elicits intense cravings (fabulous walnut-chilli paste!), but inventive mains such as *ali nacik* (sliced lamb with puréed eggplant and yoghurt) also warrant repeat visits. Good vegetarian choices too. Lovely summer terrace.

City West & Charlottenburg

Butcher
BURGERS €€

(Map p458; ☑ 030-323 015 600; www.the-butcher.com; Kantstrasse 144; burgers €9-11.50; ☺ 7am-late; ☻ 🕾; ⑤ Savignyplatz) No matter if you fancy the Daddy, the Cow Boy or the Ugly – this place knows how to build one hell of a burger. Prime ingredients like Aberdeen Angus beef, house-baked buns and a secret (what else?) sauce make these patty-and-bun combos shine. With its bar and DJ line-up, the Butcher also injects a dose of hip into the 'hood.

Dicke Wirtin
GERMAN €€

(Map p458; ☑ 030-312 4952; www.dicke-wirtin.de; Carmerstrasse 9; mains €6-16.50; ☺ 11am-late; ☻; ⑤ Savignyplatz) Old Berlin charm oozes from every nook and cranny of this been-here-forever pub, which pours nine draught beers (including the superb Kloster Andechs) and nearly three dozen homemade schnapps varieties. Hearty local and German fare like smoked veal dumplings, boiled eel, beef liver and pork roast keeps brains balanced. Bargain lunches, too.

🍷 Drinking & Nightlife

★ Prater Biergarten
BEER GARDEN

(☑ 030-448 5688; www.pratergarten.de; Kastanienallee 7-9; snacks €2.50-6; ☺ noon-late Apr-Sep, weather permitting; ⑪ Eberswalder Strasse) Berlin's oldest beer garden has seen beer-soaked nights since 1837 and is still a charismatic spot for guzzling a custom-brewed Prater Pilsner beneath the ancient chestnut trees (self-service). Kids can romp around the small play area.

★ Schwarze Traube
COCKTAIL BAR

(Map p456; ☑ 030-2313 5569; www.schwarzetraube.de; Wrangelstrasse 24; ☺ 7pm-2am Sun-Thu, to 5am Fri & Sat; ⑪ Görlitzer Bahnhof) Mixologist Atalay Aktas was Germany's Best Bartender of 2013 and this pint-sized drinking parlour is where he and his staff create their magic potions. Since there's no menu, each drink is calibrated to the taste and mood of each patron using premium spirits, expertise and a dash of psychology.

★ Strandbar Mitte
BAR

(☑ 030-2838 5588; www.strandbar-mitte.de; Monbijoustrasse 3; dancing €4; ☺ 10am-late May-Sep; 🕾 M1, ⑤ Oranienburger Strasse) With a full-on view of the Bodemuseum, palm trees and a relaxed ambience, Germany's first beach bar (since 2002) is great for balancing a surfeit of sightseeing stimulus with a reviving drink and thin-crust pizza. At night, there's dancing under the stars with tango, cha-cha, swing and salsa, often preceded by dance lessons.

★ Clärchens Ballhaus
CLUB

(☑ 030-282 9295; www.ballhaus.de; Auguststrasse 24; ☺ 11am-late; ☻; 🕾 M1, ⑤ Oranienburger Strasse) Yesteryear is right now at this late, great 19th-century dance hall where groovers and grannies hoof it across the parquet without a touch of irony. There are different sounds nightly – salsa to swing, tango to disco – and a live band on Saturday. Dancing kicks off from 9pm or 9.30pm. Easy door but often packed, so book a table.

Ankerklause
PUB

(Map p456; ☑ 030-693 5649; www.ankerklause.de; Kottbusser Damm 104; ☺ from 4pm Mon, from 10am Tue-Sun; ⑪ Schönleinstrasse) Ahoy there! Drop anchor at this nautical kitsch tavern in an old harbour master's shack and enjoy the arse-kicking jukebox, cold beers and surprisingly good German pub fare. The best seats are on the geranium-festooned terrace where you can wave to the boats puttering along the canal. A cult pit stop until the wee hours.

Klunkerkranich
BAR

(www.klunkerkranich.de; Karl-Marx-Strasse 66; ☺ 10am-1.30am Mon-Sat, noon-1.30am Sun, weather permitting; 🕾; ⑪ Rathaus Neukölln) During the warmer months, this club-garden-bar combo is mostly a fab place for day-drinking

GERMANY BERLIN

GAY & LESBIAN BERLIN

Berlin's legendary liberalism has spawned one of the world's biggest and most diverse GLBT playgrounds. The historic 'gay village' is near Nollendorfplatz in Schöneberg (Motzstrasse and Fuggerstrasse especially; get off at U-Bahn station Nollendorfplatz), where the rainbow flag has proudly flown since the 1920s. The crowd skews older and leather. Current hipster central is Kreuzberg, where freewheeling party pens cluster along Oranienstrasse. Check *Siegessäule* (www.siegessaeule.de), the weekly freebie 'bible' to all things gay and lesbian in town, for the latest happenings.

and chilling to local DJs or bands up on the rooftop parking deck of the Neukölln Arcaden shopping mall. It also does breakfast, light lunches and tapas. Check the website – these folks come up with new ideas all the time (gardening workshops anyone?).

To get up here, take the lifts just inside the 'Bibliothek/Post' entrance on Karl-Marx-Strasse to the 5th floor.

★ ://about blank   CLUB
(Map p456; www.aboutparty.net; Markgrafendamm 24c; ⊙ hours vary, always Fri & Sat; S Ostkreuz) At this gritty multifloor party pen with lots of nooks and crannies, a steady line-up of top DJs feeds a diverse bunch of revellers dance-worthy electronic gruel. Intense club nights usually segue into the morning and beyond. Run by a collective, the venue also hosts cultural, political and gender events.

★ Berghain/Panorama Bar   CLUB
(Map p456; www.berghain.de; Am Wriezener Bahnhof; ⊙ midnight Fri-Mon morning; S Ostbahnhof) Only world-class spinmasters heat up this hedonistic bass-junkie hellhole inside a labyrinthine ex-power plant. Hard-edged minimal techno dominates the ex–turbine hall (Berghain) while house dominates at Panorama Bar, one floor up. Strict door, no cameras. Check the website for midweek concerts and record-release parties at the main venue and the adjacent **Kantine am Berghain** (☑ 030-2936 0210; admission varies; ⊙ hours vary).

☆ Entertainment

Berliner Philharmonie   CLASSICAL MUSIC
(Map p458; ☑ tickets 030-254 888 999; www.berliner-philharmoniker.de; Herbert-von-Karajan-Strasse 1; tickets €30-100; ☒ M29, M48, M85, 200, S Potsdamer Platz, U Potsdamer Platz) This world-famous concert hall has supreme acoustics and, thanks to Hans Scharoun's terraced vineyard configuration, not a bad seat in the house. It's the home turf of the Berliner Philharmoniker, which will be led by Sir Simon Rattle until 2018. One year later, Russia-born Kirill Petrenko will pick up the baton as music director.

ⓘ Information

Brandenburger Tor (☑ 030-250 025; www.visitberlin.de; Brandenburger Tor, south wing, Pariser Platz; ⊙ 9.30am-7pm Apr-Oct, to 6pm Nov-Mar; S Brandenburger Tor, U Brandenburger Tor)

ⓘ DISCOUNT CARDS

Berlin Welcome Card (www.berlinwelcomecard.de; travel in AB zones 48/72 hours €19.50/27.50, AB zones 72 hours plus admission to Museumsinsel €42) Valid for unlimited public transport for one adult and up to three children under 14 plus up to 50% discount to 200 sights, attractions and tours. Sold online, at the tourist offices, from U-Bahn and S-Bahn station ticket vending machines and on buses.

Museumspass Berlin (adult/concession €24/12) Buys admission to the permanent exhibits of about 50 museums for three consecutive days, including big draws like the Pergamonmuseum. Sold at tourist offices and participating museums.

Europa-Center (Map p458; ☑ 030-250 025; Tauentzienstrasse 9, Europa-Center, ground fl; ⊙ 10am-8pm Mon-Sat; ☒ 100, 200, U Kurfürstendamm)

Hauptbahnhof (☑ 030-250 025; www.visitberlin.de; Hauptbahnhof, Europaplatz entrance, ground fl; ⊙ 8am-10pm; S Hauptbahnhof, R Hauptbahnhof)

TV Tower (☑ 030-250 025; www.visitberlin.de; Panoramastrasse 1a, TV Tower, ground fl; ⊙ 10am-6pm Apr-Oct, to 4pm Nov-Mar; ☒ 100, 200, TXL, U Alexanderplatz, S Alexanderplatz)

ⓘ Getting There & Away

AIR

Since the opening of the new Berlin Brandenburg Airport has been delayed indefinitely, flights continue to land at the city's **Tegel** (TXL; ☑ 030-6091 1150; www.berlin-airport.de; ☒ Tegel Flughafen) and **Schönefeld** (SXF; ☑ 030-6091 1150; www.berlin-airport.de; R Airport-Express, RE7 & RB14) airports.

BUS

Most long-haul buses arrive at the **Zentraler Omnibusbahnhof** (ZOB; ☑ 030-3010 0175; www.iob-berlin.de; Masurenallee 4-6; S Messe/ICC Nord, U Kaiserdamm) near the trade fair grounds in far western Berlin. The U2 U-Bahn line links to the city centre. Some bus operators also stop at Alexanderplatz and other points around town.

TRAIN

Berlin has several train stations but most trains converge at the Hauptbahnhof (main train station) in the heart of the city.

ⓘ Getting Around

TO/FROM THE AIRPORT
Tegel

Bus TXL bus to Alexanderplatz (Tariff AB, 40 minutes) via Hauptbahnhof (central train station) every 10 minutes. Bus X9 for Charlottenburg (eg Zoo station; Tariff AB, 20 minutes).

U-Bahn Closest U-station is Jakob-Kaiser-Platz, served by bus 109 and X9. From here, the U7 goes straight to Schöneberg and Kreuzberg (Tariff AB).

Schönefeld

The airport train station is about 400m from the terminals. Free shuttle buses run every 10 minutes; walking takes five to 10 minutes.

Airport-Express Regular Deutsche Bahn regional trains, identified as RE7 and RB14 in timetables, go to central Berlin twice hourly (Tariff ABC, 30 minutes).

S-Bahn S9 runs every 20 minutes and is handy for Friedrichshain or Prenzlauer Berg. For the Messe (trade-fair grounds), take the S45 to Südkreuz and change to the S41.Tariff ABC.

PUBLIC TRANSPORT

➡ One ticket is valid on all forms of public transport, including the U-Bahn, buses, trams and ferries. Most rides require a Tariff AB ticket, which is valid for two hours (interruptions and transfers allowed, but not round trips).

➡ Tickets are available from bus drivers, vending machines at U- and S-Bahn stations and on trams and at station offices. Expect to pay cash (change given) and be sure to validate (stamp) your ticket or risk a €60 fine during spot-checks.

➡ Services operate from 4am until just after midnight on weekdays, with half-hourly *Nachtbuses* (night buses) in between. At weekends the U-Bahn and S-Bahn run all night long (except the U4 and U55).

➡ For trip planning, check the website (www.bvg.de) or call the 24-hour hotline.

ⓘ BUS TOUR ON THE CHEAP

Get a crash course in 'Berlinology' by hopping on bus 100 or 200 at Zoologischer Garten or Alexanderplatz and letting the landmarks whoosh by for the price of a standard bus ticket (€2.70, day pass €7). Bus 100 goes via the Tiergarten, 200 via Potsdamer Platz. Without traffic and getting off, trips take about 30 minutes.

CENTRAL GERMANY

Central Germany straddles the states of Thuringia and Saxony, both in the former eastern Germany. It takes in towns like Weimar, Eisenach and Erfurt that have been shaped by some of the biggest names in German history and culture, including Goethe and Martin Luther. Further east, Dresden is a town that defines survival while Leipzig can be justifiably proud of doing its part in bringing about the downfall of East Germany. Expect this region to enlighten, inspire and, above all, surprise you.

Dresden

🎵 0351 / POP 512,000

Proof that there is life after death, Dresden has become one of Germany's most visited cities, and for good reason. Restorations have returned its historic core to its 18th-century heyday when it was famous throughout Europe as 'Florence on the Elbe'. Scores of Italian artists, musicians, actors and master craftsmen flocked to the court of Augustus the Strong, bestowing countless masterpieces upon the city.

The devastating bombing raids in 1945 levelled most of these treasures. But Dresden is a survivor and many of the most important landmarks have since been rebuilt, including the elegant Frauenkirche. Today, there's a constantly evolving arts and cultural scene and zinging pub and nightlife quarters, especially in the Outer Neustadt.

⊙ Sights

Dresden straddles the Elbe River, with the attraction-studded Altstadt (old town) in the south and the Neustadt (new town) pub and student quarter to the north.

★ **Zwinger**   PALACE
(🎵 0351-4914 2000; www.der-dresdner-zwinger.de; Theaterplatz 1; adult/concession €10/7.50; ⊙ 10am-6pm Tue-Sun) FREE A collaboration between the architect Matthäus Pöppelmann and the sculptor Balthasar Permoser, the Zwinger was built between 1710 and 1728 on the orders of Augustus the Strong, who, having returned from seeing Louis XIV's palace at Versailles, wanted something similar for himself. Primarily a party palace for royals, the Zwinger has ornate portals that lead into the vast fountain-studded courtyard, which is framed by buildings lavishly

GERMANY DRESDEN

WORTH A TRIP

SACHSENHAUSEN CONCENTRATION CAMP

A mere 35km north of Berlin, Sachsenhausen was built by prisoners and opened in 1936 as a prototype for other concentration camps. By 1945 some 200,000 people had passed through its sinister gates, most of them political opponents, Jews, Roma people and, after 1939, POWs. Tens of thousands died from hunger, exhaustion, illness, exposure, medical experiments and executions. The camp became a **memorial site** (Memorial & Museum Sachsenhausen; ☑ 03301-200 200; www.stiftung-bg.de; Strasse der Nationen 22, Oranienburg; ⊙ 8.30am-6pm mid-Mar–mid-Oct, to 4.30pm mid-Oct–mid-Mar, museums closed Mon mid-Oct–mid-Mar; **P**; **S** Oranienburg) **FREE** in 1961. A tour of the grounds, remaining buildings and exhibits will leave no one untouched.

Unless you're on a guided tour, pick up a leaflet (€0.50) or, better yet, an audioguide (€3, including leaflet) at the visitor centre to get a better grasp of this huge site. Between mid-October and mid-March avoid visiting on a Monday when all indoor exhibits are closed.

The S-Bahn S1 makes the trip to Oranienburg train station thrice hourly (ABC ticket €3.30, 45 minutes), from where it's a 2km signposted walk or a ride on hourly bus 804 to the site.

festooned with evocative sculpture. Today, it houses three superb museums within its baroque walls.

★ **Historisches Grünes Gewölbe** MUSEUM
(Historic Green Vault; ☑ 0351-4914 2000; www.skd.museum; Residenzschloss; admission incl audioguide €15; ⊙ 10am-6pm Wed-Mon) The Historic Green Vault displays some 3000 precious items in the same fashion as during the time of August der Starke, namely on shelves and tables without glass protection in a series of increasingly lavish rooms. Admission is by timed ticket only, and only a limited number of visitors per hour may pass through the 'dust lock'. Get advance tickets online or by phone since only 40% are sold at the palace box office for same-day admission.

Neues Grünes Gewölbe MUSEUM
(New Green Vault; ☑ 0351-4914 2000; www.skd.museum; Residenzschloss; adult/under 17yr incl audioguide €15/free; ⊙ 10am-6pm Wed-Mon) The New Green Vault presents some 1000 objects in 10 modern rooms. Key sights include a frigate fashioned from ivory with wafer-thin sails, a cherry pit with 185 faces carved into it and an exotic ensemble of 132 gem-studded figurines representing a royal court in India. The artistry of each item is dazzling. To avoid the worst crush of people, visit during lunchtime.

Frauenkirche CHURCH
(☑ 0351-6560 6100; www.frauenkirche-dresden.de; Neumarkt; audioguide €2.50, cupola adult/student €8/5; ⊙ 10am-noon & 1-6pm) **FREE** The domed Frauenkirche – Dresden's most beloved symbol – has literally risen from the city's ashes. The original graced its skyline for two centuries before collapsing after the February 1945 bombing, and was rebuilt from a pile of rubble between 1994 and 2005. A spitting image of the original, it may not bear the gravitas of age but that only slightly detracts from its festive beauty inside and out. The altar, reassembled from nearly 2000 fragments, is especially striking.

★ **Albertinum** MUSEUM
(☑ 0351-4914 2000; www.skd.museum; enter from Brühlsche Terrasse or Georg-Treu-Platz 2; adult/concession/under 17yr €10/7.50/free; ⊙ 10am-6pm Tue-Sun) After massive renovations following severe 2002 flood damage, the Renaissance-era former arsenal became the stunning home of the **Galerie Neue Meister** (New Masters Gallery), which displays an arc of paintings by some of the great names in art from the 18th century onwards. Caspar David Friedrich and Claude Monet's landscapes compete with the abstract visions of Marc Chagall and Gerhard Richter, all in gorgeous rooms orbiting a light-filled courtyard. There's also a superb sculpture collection spread over the lower floors.

Semperoper HISTORIC BUILDING
(☑ 0351-320 7360; www.semperoper-erleben.de; Theaterplatz 2; tour adult/concession €11/7; ⊙ hours vary) One of Germany's most famous opera houses, the Semperoper opened in 1841 and has hosted premieres of famous works by Richard Strauss, Carl Maria von

Weber and Richard Wagner. Guided 45-minute tours operate almost daily (the 3pm tour is in English); exact times depend on the rehearsal and performance schedule. Buy advance tickets online to skip the queue.

🛏 Sleeping

Hostel Mondpalast   HOSTEL €
(☑ 0351-563 4050; www.mondpalast.de; Louisenstrasse 77; dm/d from €14/37, linen €2; @ 🛜) A funky location in the thick of the Äussere Neustadt is the main draw of this out-of-this-world hostel-bar-cafe (with cheap drinks). Each funky and playful room is designed to reflect a sign of the zodiac. Bonus points for the bike rentals and the well-equipped kitchen. Breakfast is €7.

Aparthotel am Zwinger   APARTMENT €
(☑ 0351-8990 0100; www.aparthotel-zwinger. de; Maxstrasse 3; apt from €60; ⊘ reception 7am-10pm Mon-Fri, 9.30am-6pm Sat & Sun, or by arrangement; P 🛜) This excellent option has bright, functional and spacious apartments with kitchens that even come equipped with Nespresso machines. Units are spread over several buildings, but all are super-central and quiet. Access to the buffet breakfast costs €12.90, and it's a good option unless you're self-catering, as the neighbourhood is pretty low on breakfast options.

★Gewandhaus Hotel   BOUTIQUE HOTEL €€
(☑ 0351-494 90; www.gewandhaus-hotel.de; Ringstrasse 1; d from €137; P ❄ @ 🛜 ⛲) Revamped as a boutique hotel a few years ago, the stunning Gewandhaus, an 18th-century trading house of tailors and fabric merchants that burned down in 1945, boasts sleek public areas, beautiful and bright rooms, and a breakfast that sets a high bar for anything else offered in the city. Part of the Marriott group.

🍴 Eating & Drinking

The Neustadt has oodles of cafes and restaurants, especially along Königsstrasse and the streets north of Albertplatz. The latter is also the centre of Dresden's nightlife. Altstadt restaurants are more tourist-geared and pricier.

★Raskolnikoff   INTERNATIONAL €€
(☑ 0351-804 5706; www.raskolnikoff.de; Böhmische Strasse 34; mains €10-15; ⊘ 11am-2am Mon-Fri, 9am-2am Sat & Sun) An artist squat before the Wall came down, Raskolnikoff now brims with grown-up artsy-bohemian flair, especially in the sweet little garden at the back,

complete with bizarre water feature. The seasonally calibrated menu showcases the fruits of the surrounding land in globally inspired dishes, and the beer is brewed locally. Breakfast is served until 2pm, with an excellent brunch (€14.90) on Sundays.

Lila Sosse   GERMAN €€
(☑ 0351-803 6723; www.lilasosse.de; Alaunstrasse 70, Kunsthofpassage; appetisers €3.50-9.50, mains €13-15; ⊘ 4pm-late Mon-Fri, from noon Sat & Sun) This jumping joint puts a new spin on modern German cooking by serving intriguing appetisers in glass preserve jars. You're free to order just a couple (the fennel-orange salad and carp with capers are recommended) or, if your tummy needs silencing, pair them with a meaty main and dessert. Reservations essential. It's part of the charming **Kunsthofpassage courtyard complex** (enter from Alaunstrasse 70 or Görlitzer Strasse 23; ⊘ 24hr) **FREE**.

brennNessel   VEGETARIAN €€
(☑ 0351-494 3319; www.brennnessel-dresden.de; Schützengasse 18; mains €9-15; ⊘ 11am-midnight) This popular, largely vegetarian gastropub in a miraculously surviving 350-year-old building is an oasis in the otherwise empty and anodyne streets of the Altstadt. Indeed, reserve for lunch if you'd like to eat outside in the charming, sun-dappled courtyard as it's something of a favourite hang-out for off-duty Semperoper musicians and nearby office workers.

★Restaurant Genuss-Atelier   GERMAN €€€
(☑ 0351-2502 8337; www.genuss-atelier.net; Bautzner Strasse 149; mains €15-27; ⊘ noon-11pm Wed-Fri, from noon Sat & Sun; 🚋 11 to Waldschlösschen) Lighting up Dresden's culinary scene of late is this fantastic place that's well worth the trip on the 11 tram. The creative menu is streets ahead of most offerings elsewhere, although the best way to experience the 'Pleasure-Atelier' is to book a surprise menu (three/four/five courses €38/48/58) and let the chefs show off their craft. Reservations essential.

ℹ Information

There are tourist office branches inside the **Hauptbahnhof** (☑ 0351-501 501; www.dresden. de; main train station, Wiener Platz; ⊘ 8am-8pm) and near the **Frauenkirche** (☑ 0351-501 501; www.dresden.de; QF Passage, Neumarkt 2; ⊘ 10am-7pm Mon-Fri, to 6pm Sat, to 3pm Sun). Both book rooms and tours and rent out audioguides.

MEISSEN

Straddling the Elbe around 25km upstream from Dresden, Meissen is the cradle of European porcelain, which was first cooked up in 1710 in its imposing castle, the **Albrechtsburg** (☑03521-470 70; www.albrechtsburg-meissen.de; Domplatz 1; adult/concession incl audioguide €8/4, with Dom €10.50/5.50; ⊙10am-6pm Mar-Oct, 10am-5pm Nov-Feb). An exhibit on the 2nd floor chronicles how it all began. Highlights of the adjacent **cathedral** (☑03521-452 490; www.dom-zu-meissen.de; Domplatz 7; adult/concession €4/2.50, with Albrechtsburg €10.50/5.50; ⊙9am-6pm Apr-Oct, 10am-4pm Nov-Mar) include medieval stained-glass windows and an altarpiece by Lucas Cranach the Elder. Both squat atop a ridge overlooking Meissen's handsome Altstadt (old town).

Since 1863, porcelain production has taken place in a custom-built factory, about 1km south of the Altstadt. Next to it is the **Erlebniswelt Haus Meissen** (☑03521-468 208; www.meissen.com; Talstrasse 9; adult/concession €9/5; ⊙9am-6pm May-Oct, 9am-5pm Nov-Apr), a vastly popular porcelain museum where you can witness the astonishing artistry and craftsmanship that makes Meissen porcelain unique. Note that entry is timed and only in groups, so you may have to wait a while during high season.

For details and further information about the town, stop by the **tourist office** (☑03521-419 40; www.touristinfo-meissen.de; Markt 3; ⊙10am-6pm Mon-Fri, 10am-4pm Sat & Sun Apr-Oct, 10am-5pm Mon-Fri, 10am-3pm Sat Nov, Dec, Feb & Mar).

Half-hourly S1 trains run to Meissen from Dresden's Hauptbahnhof and Neustadt train stations (€6, 40 minutes). For the Erlebniswelt, get off at Meissen-Triebischtal. Boats operated by **Sächsische Dampfschiffahrt** (☑03521-866 090; www.saechsische-dampfschiffahrt.de; one way/return €16/21.50; ⊙May-Sep) make the trip to Meissen from the Terrassenufer in Dresden in two hours. Consider going one way by boat and the other by train.

ⓘ Getting There & Away

Dresden Airport (DRS; ☑0351-881 3360; www.dresden-airport.de) is about 9km north of the city centre and linked by the S2 train several times hourly (€2.20, 20 minutes).

Fast trains make the trip to Dresden from Berlin-Hauptbahnhof in two hours (€40) and Leipzig in 1¼ hours (€24.50). The S1 local train runs half-hourly to Meissen (€6.40, 40 minutes) and Bad Schandau in Saxon Switzerland (€6.40, 45 minutes).

Leipzig

☑0341 / POP 532,000

Hypezig! cry the papers. The New Berlin, says just about everybody. Yes, Leipzig is Saxony's coolest city, a playground for nomadic young creatives who have been displaced even by the fast-gentrifying German capital. But Leipzig is also a city of enormous history known as the Stadt der Helden (City of Heroes) for its leading role in the 1989 'Peaceful Revolution' that helped bring the Cold War to an end. A trade-fair mecca since medieval times, the city is solidly in the sights of music lovers due to its intrinsic connection to the lives and work of Bach, Mendelssohn and Wagner.

⊙ Sights

Don't rush from sight to sight – wandering around Leipzig is a pleasure in itself, with many of the blocks around the central Markt criss-crossed by historic shopping arcades, including the classic **Mädlerpassage**.

★**Nikolaikirche**   CHURCH
(Church of St Nicholas; www.nikolaikirche-leipzig. de; Nikolaikirchhof 3; ⊙10am-6pm Mon-Sat, to 4pm Sun) This church has Romanesque and Gothic roots but since 1797 has sported a striking neoclassical interior with palm-like pillars and cream-coloured pews. The design is certainly gorgeous but the church is most famous for playing a key role in the nonviolent movement that led to the downfall of the East German government. As early as 1982 it hosted 'peace prayers' every Monday at 5pm (still held today), which over time inspired and empowered local citizens to confront the injustices plaguing their country.

★**Museum der Bildenden Künste**   MUSEUM
(☑0341-216 990; www.mdbk.de; Katharinenstrasse 10; adult/concession €5/4; ⊙10am-6pm Tue & Thu-Sun, noon-8pm Wed) This imposing modernist glass cube is the home of Leipzig's fine arts

museum and its world-class collection of paintings from the 15th century to today, including works by Caspar David Friedrich, Cranach, Munch and Monet. Highlights include rooms dedicated to native sons Max Beckmann, Max Klinger and Neo Rauch. Exhibits are playfully juxtaposed and range from sculpture and installation to religious art. The collection is enormous, so set aside at least two hours to do it justice.

Zeitgeschichtliches Forum MUSEUM
(Forum of Contemporary History; ☑0341-222 0400; www.hdg.de/leipzig; Grimmaische Strasse 6; ☉9am-6pm Tue-Fri, 10am-6pm Sat & Sun) FREE This fascinating, enormous and very well curated exhibit tells the political history of the GDR, from division and dictatorship to fall-of-the-Wall ecstasy and post-*Wende* blues. It's essential viewing for anyone seeking to understand the late country's political power apparatus, the systematic oppression of regime critics, milestones in inter-German and international relations, and the opposition movement that led to its downfall.

Stasi Museum MUSEUM
(☑0341-961 2443; www.runde-ecke-leipzig.de; Dittrichring 24; ☉10am-6pm) FREE In the GDR the walls had ears, as is chillingly documented in this exhibit in the former Leipzig headquarters of the East German secret police (the Stasi), a building known as the Runde Ecke (Round Corner). English-language audioguides (€4) aid in understanding the all-German displays on propaganda, preposterous disguises, cunning surveillance devices, recruitment (even among children), scent storage and other chilling machinations that reveal the GDR's all-out zeal when it came to controlling, manipulating and repressing its own people.

Thomaskirche CHURCH
(☑0341-222 240; www.thomaskirche.org; Thomaskirchhof 18; tower €2; ☉church 9am-6pm, tower 1pm, 2pm & 4.30pm Sat, 2pm & 3pm Sun Apr-Nov) Johann Sebastian Bach worked as a cantor in the Thomaskirche from 1723 until his death in 1750, and his remains lie buried beneath a bronze plate in front of the altar. The Thomanerchor, once led by Bach, has been going strong since 1212 and now includes 100 boys aged eight to 18. The church tower can be climbed, though the real reason to come here is to absorb the great man's legacy, often played on the church's giant organ.

Bach-Museum Leipzig MUSEUM
(☑0341-913 70; www.bachmuseumleipzig.de; Thomaskirchhof 16; adult/concession/under 16yr €8/6/free; ☉10am-6pm Tue-Sun) This interactive museum does more than tell you about the life and accomplishments of Johann Sebastian Bach. Learn how to date a Bach manuscript, listen to baroque instruments or treat your ears to any composition he ever wrote. The 'treasure room' downstairs displays rare original manuscripts.

🛏 Sleeping

Hostel Blauer Stern HOSTEL €
(☑0341-4927 6166; www.hostelblauerstern.de; Lindenauer Markt 20; dm/s/d/ €18/25/35; 🛜) If you're interested in exploring Leipzig's alternative scene, then this is a great option, in the western district of Plagwitz, a fast up-and-coming, young and arty slice of town. The thoughtfully decorated rooms all have an East German retro style, and big weekly discounts can make them a steal. Take tram 7 or 15 from Hauptbahnhof.

arcona Living Bach14 HOTEL €€
(☑0341-496 140; http://bach14.arcona.de; Thomaskirchhof 13/14; d from €105; 🛜) In this musically themed marvel, you'll sleep sweetly in sleek rooms decorated with sound-sculpture lamps, Bach manuscript wallpaper and colours ranging from subdued olive to perky raspberry. The quietest rooms are in the garden wing, while those in the historic front section have views of the famous Thomaskirche.

🍴 Eating

Pilot INTERNATIONAL €€
(☑0341-9628 9550; Bosestrasse 1; mains €7-20; ☉9am-late; 🛜) This retro-styled and quite charming establishment draws a bohemian crowd with its rustic menu, back-to-basic Saxon dishes and a splash of more contemporary specials and fresh salads. Its extensive drinks selection, including rich espresso from Trieste and a long tea list, is a further draw.

Cafe Puschkin CAFE €€
(☑0341-392 0105; www.cafepuschkin.de; Karl-Liebknecht-Strasse 74; mains €5-12; ☉9am-2am) This charming old pub on the Südvorstadt's super cool Karl-Liebknecht-Strasse (aka 'Karli') is a bit of a local institution. The selection of burgers, nachos and sausages won't blow you away, but it's good comfort food in a friendly and somewhat eccentric

atmosphere. It's also a great breakfast spot following a night out here.

★ Auerbachs Keller
GERMAN €€€

(☑ 0341-216 100; www.auerbachs-keller-leipzig.de; Mädlerpassage, Grimmaische Strasse 2-4; mains Keller €10-26, Weinstuben €33-35; ⊘ Keller noon-11pm daily, Weinstuben 6-11pm Mon-Sat) Founded in 1525, Auerbachs Keller is one of Germany's best-known restaurants. It's cosy and touristy but the food's actually quite good and the setting memorable. There are two sections: the vaulted Grosser Keller for hearty Saxonian dishes and the four historic rooms of the Historische Weinstuben for upscale German fare. Reservations highly advised.

Drinking & Nightlife

Leipzig is Saxony's liveliest city, with several areas noted for their going out options: in the city centre there's the boisterous Barfussgässchen and the more upmarket theatre district around Gottschedstrasse. Younger crowds gravitate towards Karl-Liebknecht-Strasse (aka 'Karli') south of the centre and Karl-Heine-Strasse in the up-and-coming southwestern suburb of Plagwitz.

Moritzbastei
BAR

(☑ 0341-702590; www.moritzbastei.de; Universitätsstrasse 9; ⊘10am-late Mon-Fri, noon-late Sat; ☎) This legendary (sub)cultural centre in a warren of cellars of the old city fortifications keeps an all-ages crowd happy with parties (almost nightly), concerts, art and readings. It harbours stylish cocktail and wine bars as well as a daytime cafe (dishes €2 to €5) that serves delicious coffee, along with healthy and wallet-friendly fare. Summer terrace, too.

★ Distillery
CLUB

(☑ 0341-3559 7400; www.distillery.de; Kurt-Eisner-Strasse 91; ⊘from 11.30pm Fri & Sat; 📮9 to Kurt-Eisner/A-Hoffmann-Strasse) One of the oldest techno clubs in eastern Germany, Distillery has been going for over 20 years and remains among the best. With an unpretentious crowd, cool location, decent drinks prices and occasional star DJs (Ellen Allien, Carl Craig, Richie Hawtin), its popularity is easy to understand. As well as techno, there's house, drum'n'bass and hip hop to be had here.

Noch Besser Leben
PUB

(www.nochbesserleben.com; Merseburger Strasse 25; ⊘4.30pm-late) Despite the address, this locally beloved bar can be found on Plag-witz' main drag, Karl-Heine-Strasse, and is a great, if smokey, spot to join a cool local crowd drinking an impressive selection of beer. It has a communal, friendly atmosphere, for which only the German word *gemütlich* (approximately translated as cosy) will do.

ℹ️ Information

Tourist Office (☑ 0341-710 4260; www.leipzig.travel; Katharinenstrasse 8; ⊘9.30am-6pm Mon-Fri, to 4pm Sat, to 3pm Sun) Room referral, ticket sales, maps and general information. Also sells the **Leipzig Card** (one/three days €11.90/23.50); good for free or discounted admission to attractions, plus free travel on public transport.

ℹ️ Getting There & Away

Leipzig-Halle Airport (LEJ; ☑ 0341-2240; www.leipzig-halle-airport.de) is about 21km west of Leipzig and linked to town by half-hourly S-Bahn trains (€4.30, 35 minutes).

High-speed trains frequently serve Frankfurt (€76, 3½ hours), Dresden (€24.50, 1¼ hours) and Berlin (€47, 1¼ hours), among other cities.

Weimar

☑ 03643 / POP 63,320

Historical epicentre of the German Enlightenment, Weimar is an essential stop for anyone with a passion for German history and culture. A pantheon of intellectual and creative giants lived and worked here: Goethe, Schiller, Bach, Cranach, Liszt, Nietzsche, Gropius, Herder, Feininger, Kandinsky... the list goes on. In summer, Weimar's many parks and gardens lend themselves to quiet contemplation of the town's intellectual and cultural onslaught, or to taking a break from it.

⊙ Sights

★ Goethe-Nationalmuseum
MUSEUM

(☑ 03643-545 400; www.klassik-stiftung.de; Frauenplan 1; adult/concession €12/8.50; ⊘9.30am-6pm Tue-Sun Apr-Oct, to 4pm Nov-Mar) This museum has the most comprehensive and insightful exhibit about Johann Wolfgang von Goethe, Germany's literary icon. It incorporates his home of 50 years, left pretty much as it was upon his death in 1832. This is where Goethe worked, studied, researched and penned *Faust* and other immortal works. In a modern annexe, documents and objects shed light on the man and his achievements,

EISENACH

On the edge of the Thuringian forest, Eisenach is the birthplace of Johann Sebastian Bach, but even the town's **museum** (☑03691-793 40; www.bachhaus.de; Frauenplan 21; adult/concession €9/5; ☉10am-6pm) dedicated to the great composer plays second fiddle to its main attraction: the awe-inspiring 11th-century **Wartburg** (☑03691-2500; www.wartburg-eisenach.de; Auf der Wartburg 1; tour adult/concession €9/5, museum & Luther study only €5/3; ☉tours 8.30am-5pm Apr-Oct, 9am-3.30pm Nov-Mar, English tour 1.30pm) castle.

Perched high above the town (views!), the humungous pile hosted medieval minstrel song contests and was the home of Elisabeth, a Hungarian princess later canonised for her charitable deeds. Its most famous resident, however, was **Martin Luther**, who went into hiding here in 1521 after being excommunicated and placed under papal ban. During this 10-month stay, he translated the New Testament from Greek into German, contributing enormously to the development of the written German language. His modest study is part of the guided tour. Back in town, there's an exhibit about the man and his historical impact in the **Lutherhaus** (☑03691-298 30; www.lutherhaus-eisenach.com; Lutherplatz 8; adult/concession €6/4; ☉10am-5pm, closed Mon Nov-Mar), where he lived as a school boy.

In summer, arrive before 11am to avoid the worst of the crowds. From April to October, bus 10 runs hourly from 9am to 5pm from the Hauptbahnhof to the Eselstation stop, from where it's a steep 10-minute walk up to the castle.

Regional trains run frequently to Erfurt (€12.10, 45 minutes) and Weimar (€15, one hour). The **tourist office** (☑03691-792 30; www.eisenach.info; Markt 24; ☉10am-6pm Mon-Fri, to 5pm Sat & Sun) can help with finding accommodation.

not only in literature, but also in art, science and politics.

★ Herzogin Anna Amalia Bibliothek   LIBRARY

(☑03643-545 400; www.anna-amalia-bibliothek.de; Platz der Demokratie 1; adult/concession incl audioguide €7.50/6; ☉9.30am-2.30pm Tue-Sun) Assembled by literature-loving local duchess Anna Amalia (1739–1807), this Unesco World Heritage library has been beautifully reconstructed after a monumental fire in 2004 destroyed much of the building and its priceless contents. Some of the most precious tomes are housed in the magnificent **Rokokosaal** (Rococo Hall), and were once used by Goethe, Schiller and other Weimar hot shots, who are depicted in busts and paintings.

Bauhaus Museum   MUSEUM

(☑03643-545 400; www.klassik-stiftung.de; Theaterplatz 1; adult/concession €4/3; ☉10am-6pm Apr-Oct, to 4pm Nov-Mar) Considering that Weimar is the 1919 birthplace of the influential Bauhaus school of art, design and architecture, this museum is a rather modest affair. A new, representative museum is expected to open in 2018.

🛏 Sleeping & Eating

★ Design Apartments Weimar   APARTMENT €€

(☑03643-251 8426; www.hier-war-goethe-nie.de; Fuldaer Strasse 85; apt per person from €61; ☞) Get in quick to snap up one of these enormous, self-contained, fully renovated heritage apartments that could have been plucked from the pages of a Taschen design book. Even better is that you'd be hard-pressed to find friendlier, kinder hosts anywhere. This is surely the perfect home base from which to explore the delights of Weimar and Thuringia. Exceptional value.

Residenz-Café   INTERNATIONAL €€

(☑03643-594 08; www.residenz-cafe.de; Grüner Markt 4; breakfast €3.90-8.60, mains €5-18; ☉8am-1am; ☑) Locally adored 'Resi' is a Viennese-style coffeehouse and a jack of all trades – everyone should find something to their taste here, no matter where the hand's on the clock. The 'Lovers' Breakfast' comes with sparkling wine, the cakes are delicious and the salads crisp, but perhaps the most creativity goes into the weekly specials.

Hans und Franz   GERMAN €€

(☑03643-457 3987; www.hanzundfranz.com; Erfurter Strasse 23; mains €8-14; ☉6-11pm Mon-Sat, to 9pm Sun; ☑) There's something of a mid-century vibe at this happy haunt serving up local specialities such as *Thuringian Klösse* (dumplings) with red cabbage, and meaty German favourites, intelligently balanced with a few nice options for vegetarians and vegans. And, yes, the schnitzel here is good.

Zum Weissen Schwan GERMAN €€
(☑ 03643-908 751; Frauentorstrasse 23; mains €9-24; ☺ noon-10pm Tue-Sat) At this venerable inn, you can fill your tummy with Goethe's favourite dish, which actually hails from his home town of Frankfurt (boiled beef with herb sauce, red beet salad and potatoes). The rest of the menu, though, is midrange Thuringian.

ℹ Information

Tourist Office (☑ 03643-7450; www.weimar. de; Markt 10; ☺ 9.30am-7pm Mon-Sat, to 3pm Sun Apr-Oct, 9.30am-6pm Mon-Fri, to 2pm Sat & Sun Nov-Mar) Pick up a great-value Weimar-Card (€27.50 for two days) for free admission to most museums, free iGuides, free travel on city buses and discounted tours.

ℹ Getting There & Away

Frequent regional trains go to Erfurt (€5, 15 minutes), Eisenach (€15, one hour), Gotha (€13, 35 minutes) and Jena (€5, 15 minutes). The town centre is a 20-minute walk or ride on bus 1 away.

Erfurt

☑ 0361 / POP 204,880

A little river courses through this Instagram-pretty medieval pastiche of sweeping squares, time-worn alleyways, a house-lined bridge and lofty church spires. Erfurt also boasts one of Germany's oldest universities, founded by rich merchants in 1392, where Martin Luther studied philosophy before becoming a monk at the local monastery. It's a refreshingly untouristed spot and well worth exploring.

◉ Sights

Erfurt's main sights cluster in the old town, about a 10-minute walk from the train station (or quick ride on tram 3, 4 or 6).

Erfurter Dom CATHEDRAL
(Mariendom; ☑ 0361-646 1265; www.dom-erfurt. de; Domplatz; ☺ 9.30am-6pm Mon-Sat, 1-6pm Sun May-Oct, to 5pm Nov-Apr) Erfurt's cathedral, where Martin Luther was ordained a priest, has origins as a simple 8th-century chapel that grew into the stately Gothic pile you see today. Standouts in its treasure-filled interior include the stained-glass windows; the Wolfram, an 850-year-old bronze candelabrum in the shape of a man; the Gloriosa bell (1497); a Romanesque stucco Madonna; and the intricately carved choir stalls.

★ **Zitadelle Petersberg** FORTRESS
(☑ 0361-664 00; tour adult/concession €8/4; ☺ 7pm Fri & Sat May-Oct) Situated on the Petersberg hill northwest of Domplatz, this citadel ranks among Europe's largest and best-preserved baroque fortresses. It sits above a honeycomb of tunnels, which can be explored on two-hour guided tours run by the tourist office. Otherwise, it's free to roam the external grounds and to enjoy fabulous views over Erfurt.

Krämerbrücke BRIDGE
(Merchants' Bridge) Flanked by cute half-timbered houses on both sides, this charming 1325 stone bridge is the only one north of the Alps that's still inhabited. To this day people live above little shops with attractive displays of chocolate and pottery, jewellery and basic souvenirs. See the bridge from above by climbing the tower of the Ägidienkirche (usually open 11am to 5pm) punctuating its eastern end.

🛏 Sleeping

Opera Hostel HOSTEL €
(☑ 0361-6013 1360; www.opera-hostel.de; Walk-mühlstrasse 13; dm €15-22, s/d/tr €49/60/81, linen €2.50; @ 🛜) This upmarket hostel in a historic building scores big with wallet-watching global nomads. Rooms are bright and spacious, many with an extra sofa for chilling. Make friends in the communal kitchen and on-site lounge-bar.

★ **Hotel Brühlerhöhe** BOUTIQUE HOTEL €€
(☑ 0361-241 4990; www.hotel-bruehlerhoehe -erfurt.de; Rudolfstrasse 48; s/d from €80/95; P 🛜) This Prussian officers' casino turned chic city hotel gets high marks for its opulent breakfast spread (€12.50) and smiling, quick-on-their-feet staff. Rooms are cosy and modern with chocolate-brown furniture, thick carpets and sparkling baths. It's a short tram ride into the town centre.

✕ Eating & Drinking

Faustfood BARBECUE €
(📞0361-6443 6300; www.faustfood.de; Waage-
gasse 1; items from €3.50; ⊙11am-11pm Tue-Sat, to
7pm Sun) It's a clever name and a clever concept: traditional Thuringian grills (*Rostbrä-
tel* and bratwurst) alongside more international meaty treats such as spare ribs, steak
and cheeseburgers. Dine in or take away, but
you might want to head elsewhere if you're
vegetarian.

★ Zum Wenigemarkt 13 GERMAN €€
(📞0361-642 2379; www.wenigemarkt-13.de; Wenigemarkt 13; mains €10-18; ⊙11.30am-11pm) This
upbeat restaurant in a delightful spot serves
traditional and updated takes on Thuringian cuisine, starring regionally hunted and
gathered ingredients where possible. Tender
salt-encrusted pork roast and trout drizzled
with tangy caper-and-white-wine sauce are
both menu stars.

Modern Masters COCKTAIL BAR
(📞0361-550 7255; www.modern-masters.de;
Michaelisstrasse 48; ⊙6pm-2am Tue-Sat) Urbane
and sophisticated, this cocktail bar has been
shaking up Erfurt with flights of fancy in li-
bation, offering an impressive range of more
than 220 concoctions.

ℹ Information

Tourist Office Erfurt (📞0361-664 00; www.
erfurt-tourismus.de; Benediktsplatz 1; ⊙10am-
6pm Mon-Sat, to 3pm Sun) Sells the ErfurtCard
(€14.90 per 48 hours), which includes a city
tour, public transport, and free or discounted
admissions.

ℹ Getting There & Away

Direct IC/ICE trains connect Erfurt with Berlin
(€61, 2½ hours), Dresden (€53, 2½ hours) and
Frankfurt am Main (€55, 2¼ hours). Regional
trains to Weimar (€5, 15 minutes) and Eisenach
(€12.10, 45 minutes) run at least hourly.

BAVARIA

From the cloud-shredding Alps to the fertile
Danube plain, Bavaria (Bayern) is a place
that keeps its clichéd promises. Storybook
castles bequeathed by an oddball king poke
through dark forest, cowbells tinkle in
flower-filled meadows, the thwack of palm
on Lederhosen accompanies the clump of
frothy stein on timber, and medieval walled
towns go about their time-warped business.

But there's so much more than the
chocolate-box idyll. Learn about Bavaria's
state-of-the-art motor industry in Munich,
discover its Nazi past in Nuremberg and
Berchtesgaden, sip world-class wines in
Würzburg or take a mindboggling train
ride up Germany's highest mountains. Destinations are often described as possessing
'something for everyone'. In Bavaria, this is
no exaggeration.

Munich

📞089 / POP 1.38 MILLION

If you're looking for Alpine clichés, they're all
here, but Munich also has plenty of unexpected cards down its Dirndl. Munich's walkable
centre retains a small-town air but holds
some world-class sights, especially art galleries and museums. Throw in royal Bavarian
heritage, an entire suburb of Olympic legacy
and a kitbag of dark tourism, and it's clear
why southern Germany's metropolis is such a
favourite among those who seek out the past
but like to hit the town once they're done.

◉ Sights

Munich's major sights cluster around the
Altstadt, with the main museum district just
north of the Residenz. However, it will take
another day or two to explore bohemian
Schwabing, the sprawling Englischer Garten
and trendy Haidhausen to the east. Northwest of the Altstadt you'll find cosmopolitan
Neuhausen, the Olympiapark and Schloss
Nymphenburg.

◉ Altstadt

★ Munich Residenz PALACE
(📞089-290 671; www.residenz-muenchen.de; Max-
Joseph-Platz 3; Museum & Schatzkammer each
adult/concession/under 18 €7/6/free, combination
ticket €11/9/free; ⊙9am-6pm Apr–mid-Oct, 10am-
5pm mid-Oct–Mar, last entry 1hr before closing)
Generations of Bavarian rulers expanded a
medieval fortress into this vast and palatial
compound that served as their primary residence and seat of government from 1508 to
1918. Today it's an Aladdin's cave of fanciful
rooms and collections through the ages that
can be seen on an audio-guided tour of what
is called the **Residenzmuseum**. Allow at
least two hours to see everything at a gallop.

Highlights include the fresco-smothered
Antiquarium banqueting hall and the exuberantly rococo **Reiche Zimmer** (Ornate

Central Munich

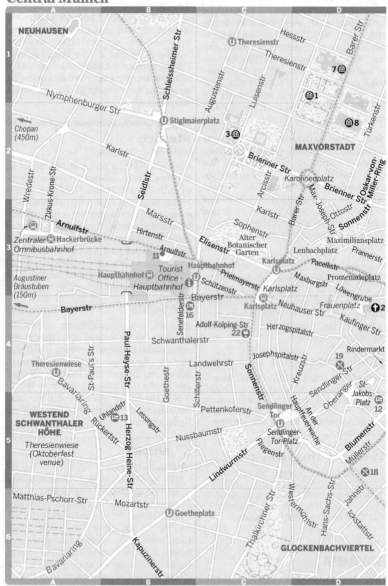

Rooms). **The Schatzkammer** (Treasure Chamber) displays a veritable banker's bonus worth of jewel-encrusted bling of yesteryear, from golden toothpicks to finely crafted swords, miniatures in ivory to gold entombed cosmetics trunks.

Marienplatz SQUARE

(S Marienplatz, U Marienplatz) The epicentral heart and soul of the Altstadt, Marienplatz is a popular gathering spot and packs a lot of personality into a compact frame. It's anchored by the **Mariensäule** (Mary's Col-

Central Munich

GERMANY MUNICH

St Peterskirche CHURCH
(Church of St Peter; Rindermarkt 1; church free, tower adult/concession €3/1; ⊙ tower 9am-6.30pm Mon-Fri, from 10am Sat & Sun; Ⓤ Marienplatz, Ⓢ Marienplatz) Some 306 steps divide you from the best view of central Munich from the 92m tower of St Peterskirche, Munich's oldest church (1150). Inside awaits a virtual textbook of art through the centuries. Worth a closer peek are the Gothic St-Martin-Altar, the baroque ceiling fresco by Johann Baptist Zimmermann and rococo sculptures by Ignaz Günther.

Viktualienmarkt MARKET
(⊙ Mon-Fri & morning Sat; Ⓤ Marienplatz, Ⓢ Marienplatz) Fresh fruit and vegetables, piles of artisan cheeses, tubs of exotic olives, hams and jams, chanterelles and truffles – Viktualienmarkt is a feast of flavours and one of central Europe's finest gourmet markets.

umn), built in 1638 to celebrate victory over Swedish forces during the Thirty Years' War. This is the busiest spot in all Munich, with throngs of tourists swarming across its expanse from early morning till late at night.

Frauenkirche
CHURCH

(Church of Our Lady; www.muenchner-dom.de; Frauenplatz 1; ⊙7am-7pm Sat-Wed, to 8.30pm Thu, to 6pm Fri; ⑤Marienplatz) The landmark Frauenkirche, built between 1468 and 1488, is Munich's spiritual heart and the Mt Everest among its churches. No other building in the central city may stand taller than its onion-domed twin towers, which reach a skyscraping 99m. The south tower can be climbed but was under urgent renovation at the time of writing.

⊙ Maxvorstadt, Schwabing & Englischer Garten

North of the Altstadt, Maxvorstadt is home to Munich's main university and top-drawer art museums. It segues into equally cafe-filled Schwabing, which rubs up against the vast Englischer Garten, one of Europe's biggest city parks and a favourite playground for locals and visitors alike.

Note that many major museums, including all the Pinakothek galleries, charge just €1 admission on Sundays.

Alte Pinakothek
MUSEUM

(☑089-238 0526; www.pinakothek.de; Barer Strasse 27; adult/child €4/2, Sun €1, audioguide €4.50; ⊙10am-8pm Tue, to 6pm Wed-Sun; 回Pinakotheken, 回Pinakotheken) Munich's main repository of Old European Masters is crammed with all the major players that decorated canvases between the 14th and 18th centuries. This neoclassical temple was masterminded by Leo von Klenze and is a delicacy even if you can't tell your Rembrandt from your Rubens. The collection is world famous for its exceptional quality and depth, especially when it comes to German masters.

Neue Pinakothek
MUSEUM

(☑089-2380 5195; www.pinakothek.de; Barer Strasse 29; adult/child €7/5, Sun €1; ⊙10am-6pm Thu-Mon, to 8pm Wed; 回Pinakotheken, 回Pinakotheken) The Neue Pinakothek harbours a well-respected collection of 19th- and early-20th-century paintings and sculpture, from rococo to *Jugendstil* (art nouveau). All the world-famous household names get wall space here, including crowd-pleasing French impressionists such as Monet, Cézanne and Degas as well as Van Gogh, whose boldly pigmented *Sunflowers* (1888) radiates cheer.

Pinakothek der Moderne
MUSEUM

(☑089-2380 5360; www.pinakothek.de; Barer Strasse 40; adult/child €10/7, Sun €1; ⊙10am-6pm Tue, Wed & Fri-Sun, to 8pm Thu; 回Pinakotheken, 回Pinakotheken) Germany's largest modern-art museum unites four significant collections under a single roof: 20th-century art, applied design from the 19th century to today, a graphics collection and an architecture museum. It's housed in a spectacular building by Stephan Braunfels, whose four-storey interior centres on a vast eye-like dome through which soft natural light filters throughout the blanched white galleries.

Lenbachhaus
MUSEUM

(Municipal Gallery; ☑089-2333 2000; www.lenbachhaus.de; Luisenstrasse 33; adult/concession incl audioguide €10/5; ⊙10am-9pm Tue, to 6pm Wed-Sun; 回Königsplatz, 回Königsplatz) Reopened in 2013 to rave reviews after a four-year renovation that saw the addition of a new wing by noted architect Norman Foster, this glorious gallery is once again the go-to place to admire the vibrant canvases of Kandinsky, Franz Marc, Paul Klee and other members of ground-breaking modernist group Der Blaue Reiter (The Blue Rider), founded in Munich in 1911.

⊙ Further Afield

Schloss Nymphenburg
PALACE

(www.schloss-nymphenburg.de; castle adult/concession €6/5, all sites €11.50/9; ⊙9am-6pm Apr–mid-Oct, 10am-4pm mid-Oct–Mar; 回Schloss Nymphenburg) This commanding palace and its lavish gardens sprawl around 5km northwest of the Altstadt. Begun in 1664 as a villa for Electress Adelaide of Savoy, the stately pile was extended over the next century to create the royal family's summer residence. Franz Duke of Bavaria, head of the once royal Wittelsbach family, still occupies an apartment here.

BMW Museum
MUSEUM

(www.bmw-welt.de; Am Olympiapark 2; adult/concession €10/7; ⊙10am-6pm Tue-Sun; 回Olympiazentrum) This silver, bowl-shaped museum comprises seven themed 'houses' that examine the development of BMW's product line and include sections on motorcycles and motor racing. Even if you can't tell a head gasket from a crankshaft, the interior design – with its curvy retro feel, futuristic bridges, squares and huge backlit wall screens – is reason enough to visit.

🐾 Tours

★**Radius Tours & Bike Rental** TOURS
(☑089-543 487 7740; www.radiustours.com; Ar-nulfstrasse 3; Ⓢ Hauptbahnhof, 🚌 Hauptbahnhof, Ⓤ Hauptbahnhof) Entertaining and inform-ative English-language tours include the two-hour Discover Munich walk (€14), the fascinating 2½-hour Third Reich tour (€16), and the three-hour Bavarian Beer tour (€33). The company also runs popular excursions to Neuschwanstein, Salzburg and Dachau and has hundreds of bikes for hire (€14.50 per day).

City Bus 100 BUS
(www.mvv-muenchen.de) Ordinary city bus that runs from the Hauptbahnhof to the Ostbahn-hof via 21 sights, including the Residenz and the Pinakothek museums.

🛏 Sleeping

Room rates in Munich tend to be high, and they skyrocket during the Oktoberfest. Book well ahead.

Wombats City Hostel Munich HOSTEL €
(☑089-5998 9180; www.wombats-hostels.com; Senefelderstrasse 1; dm/d from €19/74; Ⓟ@🛜; 🚌 Hauptbahnhof, Ⓤ Hauptbahnhof) Munich's top hostel is a professionally run affair with a whopping 300 dorm beds plus pri-

vate rooms. Dorms are painted in cheerful pastels and outfitted with wooden floors, en-suite facilities, sturdy lockers and comfy pine bunks, all in a central location near the train station. A free welcome drink awaits in the bar. Buffet breakfast costs €4.50.

Hotel Uhland HOTEL €€
(☑089-543 350; www.hotel-uhland.de; Uhland-strasse 1; s/d incl breakfast from €75/95; Ⓟ🛜; Ⓤ Theresienwiese) The Uhland is an endur-ing favourite with regulars who like their hotel to feel like a home away from home. Free parking, a breakfast buffet with organic products, and minibar drinks that won't dent your budget are just some of the thoughtful features.

Hotel Blauer Bock HOTEL €€
(☑089-231 780; www.hotelblauerbock.de; Sebas-tiansplatz 9; s/d from €47/79; 🛜; Ⓤ Marienplatz, Ⓢ Marienplatz) A pretzel's throw from the Viktualienmarkt, this simple hotel has cun-ningly slipped through the net of Altstadt gentrification to become one of the city centre's best deals. The cheapest, unmodern-ised rooms have shared facilities, the updat-ed en-suite chambers are of a 21st-century vintage, and all are quiet, despite the loca-tion. Superb restaurant.

Flushing Meadows DESIGN HOTEL €€
(☑089-5527 9170; www.flushingmeadowshotel.com; Fraunhoferstrasse 32; studios €115-165; ☺re-ception 6am-11pm; Ⓟ❄🛜; Ⓢ Fraunhoferstrasse) Urban explorers keen on up-to-the-minute design cherish this new contender on the top two floors of a former postal office in the hip Glockenbachviertel. Each of the 11 concrete-ceilinged lofts reflects the vision of a locally known creative type, while three of the five penthouse studios have a private ter-race. Breakfast costs €10.50.

GERMANY MUNICH

Louis Hotel
HOTEL €€€

(☑ 089-411 9080; www.louis-hotel.com; Viktualien-markt 6/Rindermarkt 2; r €159-289; Ⓢ Ma-rienplatz) An air of relaxed sophistication pervades the scene-savvy Louis, where good-sized rooms are furnished in nut and oak, natural stone and elegant tiles and equipped with the gamut of 'electronica', including iPod docks and flat screens with Sky TV. All have small balconies facing either the courtyard or the Viktualienmarkt. Views are also terrific from the rooftop bar and restaurant.

✖ Eating

Schmalznudel
CAFE €

(Cafe Frischhut; Prälat-Zistl-Strasse 8; pastries €2; ⊙ 8am-6pm; Ⓤ Marienplatz, Ⓢ Marienplatz) This incredibly popular institution serves just four traditional pastries, one of which, the Schmalznudel (an oily type of doughnut), gives the place its local nickname. Every baked goodie you munch here is crisp and fragrant, as they're always fresh off the hot-plate. They're best eaten with a steaming pot of coffee on a winter's day.

Tegernseer Tal
BAVARIAN €€

(☑ 089-222 626; www.tegernseer-tal8.com; Tal 8; mains €7-20.50; ⊙ 9.30am-1am Sun-Wed, to 3am Thu-Sat; ☎; Ⓤ Marienplatz, Ⓢ Marienplatz) A blond-wood interior illuminated by a huge skylight makes this a bright alternative to Munich's dark-panelled taverns. And with Alpine Tegernseer beer on tap and an imaginative menu of regional food, this is generally a lighter, calmer beer-hall experience with a less raucous ambience.

★ Fraunhofer
BAVARIAN €€

(☑ 089-266 460; www.fraunhofertheater.de; Fraun-hoferstrasse 9; mains €7-25; ⊙ 4.30pm-1am Mon-Fri, 10am-1am Sat; ☑; Ⓤ Müllerstrasse) With its screechy parquet floors, stuccoed ceilings, wood panelling and virtually no trace that the last century even happened, this wonderfully characterful inn is perfect for exploring the region with a fork. The menu is a seasonally adapted checklist of southern German favourites but also features at least a dozen vegetarian dishes and the odd exotic ingredient.

Prinz Myshkin
VEGETARIAN €€

(☑ 089-265 596; www.prinzmyshkin.com; Hacken-strasse 2; mains €10-20; ⊙ 11am-12.30am; ☑; Ⓤ Marienplatz, Ⓢ Marienplatz) This place is proof, if any were needed, that the vegetarian experience has well and truly left the sandals, beards and lentils era. Ensconced in a former brewery, Munich's premier meat-free dining spot occupies a gleamingly whitewashed, vaulted space where health-conscious eaters come to savour imaginative dishes such as curry-orange-carrot soup, unexpectedly good curries and 'wellness desserts'.

Chopan
AFGHANI €€

(☑ 089-1895 6459; www.chopan.de; Elviras-trasse 18a; mains €7-19.50; ⊙ 6pm-midnight; Ⓤ Maillingerstrasse) Munich has a huge Afghan community, whose most respected eatery is this much-lauded restaurant done out Central Asian caravanserai style with rich fabrics, multihued glass lanterns and geometric patterns. In this culinary Aladdin's cave you'll discover an exotic menu of lamb, lentils, rice, spinach and flatbread in various combinations, but there are no alcoholic beverages to see things on their way.

Alois Dallmayr
FOOD HALL €€

(☑ 089-213 5104; www.dallmayr.de; Dienerstrasse 14; ⊙ 9.30am-7pm Mon-Sat) A pricey gourmet delicatessen right in the thick of the Altstadt action, best known for its coffee but has so much more, including cheeses, ham, truffles, wine, caviar and exotic foods from every corner of the globe.

♇ Drinking & Nightlife

Generally speaking, student-flavoured places abound in Maxvorstadt and Schwabing, while traditional beer halls and taverns cluster in the Altstadt. Haidhausen attracts trendy types, and the Gärtnerplatzviertel and Glockenbachviertel are alive with gay bars and hipster haunts.

Niederlassung
BAR

(☑ 089-3260 0307; www.niederlassung.org; But-termelcherstrasse 6; ⊙ 7pm-1am Tue-Thu, to 3am Fri & Sat, to midnight Sun; Ⓢ Fraunhoferstrasse,

---

GAY & LESBIAN MUNICH

In Munich, the rainbow flag flies especially proudly along Müllerstrasse and the adjoining Glockenbachviertel. Keep an eye out for the freebie mags Our Munich and Sergej, which contain up-to-date listings and news about the community and gay-friendly establishments around town. Another source of info is www.gaytouristoffice.com.

BEER HALLS & BEER GARDENS

Beer drinking is not just an integral part of Munich's entertainment scene, it's a reason to visit. A few enduring faves:

Augustiner Bräustuben (☎089-507 047; www.braeustuben.de; Landsberger Strasse 19; ◷10am-midnight; ☒Holzapfelstrasse) Depending on the wind, an aroma of hops envelops you as you approach this traditional beer hall inside the Augustiner brewery. The Bavarian fare is superb, especially the *Schweinshaxe* (pork knuckle). Due to the location the atmosphere in the evenings is slightly more authentic than that of its city-centre cousins, with fewer tourists at the long tables.

Chinesischer Turm (☎089-383 8730; www.chinaturm.de; Englischer Garten 3; ◷10am-11pm; ☒Chinesischer Turm, ☒Tivolistrasse) This one's hard to ignore because of its English Garden location and pedigree as Munich's oldest beer garden (open since 1791). Camera-toting tourists and laid-back locals, picnicking families and businessmen sneaking a sly brew clomp around the wooden pagoda, showered by the strained sounds of possibly the world's drunkest oompah band.

Hofbräuhaus (☎089-2901 3610; www.hofbraeuhaus.de; Am Platzl 9; 1L beer €8.40, mains €9-19; ◷9am-11.30pm; ☒Kammerspiele, ⑤Marienplatz, ⑪Marienplatz) Every visitor to Munich should make a pilgrimage to this mothership of all beer halls, if only once. Within this major tourist attraction you'll discover a range of spaces in which to do your mass lifting: the horse chestnut–shaded garden, the main hall next to the oompah band, tables opposite the industrial-scale kitchen and quieter corners.

☒Isartor) From Adler Dry to Zephyr, this gin joint stocks an impressive 80 varieties of juniper juice in an unpretentious setting filled with books and sofas and humming with indie sounds. There's even a selection of different tonic waters to choose from. Happy hour from 7pm to 9pm and after midnight.

Zephyr Bar COCKTAIL BAR
(www.zephyr-bar.de; Baaderstrasse 68; ◷8pm-1am Mon-Thu, to 3am Fri & Sat; ⑤Fraunhoferstrasse) At one of Munich's best bars, Alex Schmaltz whips up courageous potions with unusual ingredients such as homemade cucumber-dill juice, sesame oil or banana-parsley purée. Cocktail alchemy at its finest, and a top gin selection to boot. No reservations.

Harry Klein CLUB
(☎089-4028 7400; www.harrykleinclub.de; Sonnenstrasse 8; ◷from 11pm; ☒Karlsplatz, ⑤Karlsplatz, ⑪Karlsplatz) Follow the gold-lined passageway off Sonnenstrasse to what some regard as one of the best *Elektro-clubs* in the world. Nights here are an alchemy of electro sound and visuals, with live video art projected onto the walls Kraftwerk style blending to awe-inspiring effect with the music.

☆ Entertainment

FC Bayern München FOOTBALL
(☎089-6993 1333; www.fcbayern.de; Allianz Arena, Werner-Heisenberg-Allee 25, Fröttmaning; ⑪Fröttmaning) Germany's most successful team both domestically and on a European level plays home games at the impressive Allianz Arena, built for the 2006 World Cup. Tickets can be ordered online.

ℹ Information

Tourist office branches include **Hauptbahnhof** (☎089-2339 6500; www.muenchen.de; Bahnhofplatz 2; ◷9am-8pm Mon-Sat, 10am-6pm Sun; ☒Hauptbahnhof, ⑪Hauptbahnhof, ⑤Hauptbahnhof) and **Marienplatz** (☎089-2339 6500; www.muenchen.de; Marienplatz 2; ◷9am-7.30pm Mon-Fri, 9am-4pm Sat, 10am-2pm Sun; ⑪Marienplatz, ⑤Marienplatz).

ℹ Getting There & Away

AIR
Munich Airport (MUC; ☎089-975 00; www.munich-airport.de) is about 30km northeast of town and linked to the Hauptbahnhof every 10 minutes by S-Bahn (S1 and S8; €10.40, 40 minutes) and every 20 minutes by the Lufthansa Airport Bus (€10.50, 45 minutes, between 5am and 8pm).

WORTH A TRIP

DACHAU CONCENTRATION CAMP

Officially called the **KZ-Gedenkstätte Dachau** (Dachau Concentration Camp Memorial Site; ☑ 08131-669 970; www.kz-gedenkstaette-dachau.de; Peter-Roth-Strasse 2a, Dachau; museum admission free; ☺9am-5pm), the first Nazi concentration camp opened in 1933 in a bucolic village about 16km northwest of central Munich. All in all, it 'processed' more than 200,000 inmates, killing at least 43,000, and is now a haunting memorial. Expect to spend two to three hours exploring the grounds and exhibits. For deeper understanding, pick up an audioguide (€3), join a 2½-hour tour (€3) or watch the 22-minute English-language documentary at the main museum.

From the Hauptbahnhof take the S2 to Dachau station (two-zone ticket; €5.20, 21 minutes), then catch frequent bus 726 (direction: Saubachsiedlung) to the camp.

Ryanair flies into Memmingen's **Allgäu Airport** (FMM; ☑ 08331-984 2000; www.allgaeu -airport.de; Am Flughafen 35, Memmingen), 125km to the west. The Allgäu-Airport-Express bus travels up to seven times daily between here and Munich Hauptbahnhof (€13.50, 1¾ hours).

BUS

Buses, including the Romantic Road Coach, depart from **Zentraler Omnibusbahnhof** (Central Bus Station, ZOB; www.muenchen-zob.de; Arnulfstrasse 21; Ⓢ Hackerbrücke) at S-Bahn station Hackerbrücke near the main train station.

TRAIN

All services leave from the Hauptbahnhof, where **Euraide** (www.euraide.de; Desk 1, Reisezentrum, Hauptbahnhof; ☺10am-7pm Mon-Fri Mar-Apr & Aug-Dec, to 8pm May-Jul; Ⓤ Hauptbahnhof, Ⓢ Hauptbahnhof) is a friendly English-speaking travel agency. Frequent fast and direct services include trains to Nuremberg (€55, 1¼ hours), Frankfurt (€101, 3¼ hours), Berlin (€130, 6½ hours) and Vienna (€93, 4½ hours), as well as thrice-daily trains to Prague (€74, 6¼ hours).

ⓘ Getting Around

For public transport information, consult www. mvv-muenchen.de.

Garmisch-Partenkirchen

☑ 08821 / POP 26,000

A paradise for skiers and hikers, Garmisch-Partenkirchen is blessed with a fabled setting a snowball's throw from Germany's highest peak, the 2962m-high Zugspitze. Garmisch has a more cosmopolitan feel, while Partenkirchen retains an old-world Alpine village vibe. The towns were merged for the 1936 Winter Olympics.

⊙ Sights

Zugspitze   MOUNTAIN
(www.zugspitze.de; return adult/child €53/31; ☺train 8.15am-3.15pm) On good days, views from Germany's rooftop extend into four countries. The round trip starts in Garmisch aboard a cogwheel train (Zahnradbahn) that chugs along the mountain base to the Eibsee, an idyllic forest lake. From here, the Eibsee-Seilbahn, a super-steep cable car, swings to the top at 2962m. When you're done admiring the views, the Gletscherbahn cable car takes you to the Zugspitze glacier at 2600m, from where the cogwheel train heads back to Garmisch.

Partnachklamm   CANYON
(www.partnachklamm.eu; adult/concession €4/ 2.50; ☺8am-6pm May, Jun & Oct, to 7pm Jul-Sep, 9am-6pm Nov-Apr) A top attraction around Garmisch is this narrow and dramatically beautiful 700m-long gorge with walls rising up to 80m. The trail hewn into the rock is especially spectacular in winter when you can walk beneath curtains of icicles and frozen waterfalls.

🛏 Sleeping & Eating

Hotel Garmischer Hof   HOTEL €€
(☑ 08821-9110; www.garmischer-hof.de; Chamonix-strasse 10; s €65-80, d €98-138; 🕾🏊) In the ownership of the Seiwald family since 1928, many a climber, skier and Alpine adventurer has creased the sheets at this welcoming inn. Rooms are elegant and cosy with some traditional Alpine touches, the buffet breakfast is served in the vaulted cafe-restaurant and there's a spa and sauna providing après-ski relief.

★ **Gasthof Fraundorfer** BAVARIAN €€
(www.gasthof-fraundorfer.de; Ludwigstrasse 24;
mains €8-19; ☺ 7am-midnight Thu-Mon, from 5pm
Wed) If you came to the Alps to experience
yodelling, knee slapping and red-faced locals in lederhosen, you just arrived at the
right address. Steins of frothing ale fuel
the increasingly raucous atmosphere as the
evening progresses and monster portions of
plattered pig meat push belt buckles to the
limit. Decor ranges from baroque cherubs
to hunting trophies and the 'Sports Corner'.
Unmissable.

ℹ Information

Tourist Office (☑ 08821-180 700; www.gapa.
de; Richard-Strauss-Platz 2; ☺ 9am-6pm
Mon-Sat, 10am-noon Sun, closed Sun Nov-Mar)
Friendly staff hands out map, brochures and
advice.

ℹ Getting There & Away

Numerous tour operators run day trips to
Garmisch-Partenkirchen from Munich but
there's also at least hourly direct train service
(€20.70, 1¼ hours).

Berchtesgaden

☑ 08652 / POP 7800

Steeped in myth and legend, Berchtesgaden's
and the surrounding countryside (the Berchtesgadener Land) is almost preternatu-
rally beautiful. Framed by six formidable
mountain ranges and home to Germany's
second-highest mountain, the Watzmann
(2713m), its dreamy, fir-lined valleys are filled
with gurgling streams and peaceful Alpine
villages. Alas, Berchtesgaden's history is also
indelibly tainted by the Nazi period. The area
is easily visited on a day trip from Salzburg.

◉ Sights

Berchtesgaden main sights are all a car or
bus ride away from town. Seeing everything
in a day without your own transport is virtually impossible.

Eagle's Nest HISTORIC SITE
(Kehlsteinhaus; ☑ 08652-2969; www.kehlstein
haus.de; Obersalzberg; adult/child €16.10/9.30;
☺ buses 8.30am-4.50pm mid-May–Oct) The Eagle's Nest was built as a mountaintop retreat
for Hitler, and gifted to him on his 50th

birthday. It took some 3000 workers only
two years to carve the precipitous 6km-long
mountain road, cut a 124m-long tunnel and
a brass-panelled lift through the rock, and
build the lodge itself (now a restaurant). It
can only be reached by special shuttle bus
from the Kehlsteinhaus bus station.

Dokumentation Obersalzberg MUSEUM
(☑ 08652-947 960; www.obersalzberg.de; Salzbergstrasse 41, Obersalzberg; adult/concession
€3/free, audioguide €2; ☺ 9am-5pm daily Apr-Oct,
10am-3pm Tue-Sun Nov-Mar, last entry 1hr before
closing) In 1933 the quiet mountain village
of Obersalzberg (3km from Berchtesgaden)
became the second seat of Nazi power after Berlin, a dark period that's given the full
historical treatment at this excellent exhibit. It documents the forced takeover of the
area, the construction of the compound and
the daily life of the Nazi elite. All facets of
Nazi terror are dealt with, including Hitler's
near-mythical appeal, his racial politics, the
resistance movement, foreign policy and the
death camps.

Königssee LAKE
Crossing the serenely picturesque, emerald-
green Königssee makes for some unforgettable memories and once-in-a-lifetime photo
opportunities. Cradled by steep mountain
walls some 5km south of Berchtesgaden,
the emerald-green Königssee is Germany's
highest lake (603m), with drinkably pure
waters shimmering into fjordlike depths. Bus
841/842 makes the trip out here from the Berchtesgaden train station roughly every hour.

☞ Tours

Eagle's Nest Tours TOURS
(☑ 08652-649 71; www.eagles-nest-tours.com;
adult/child €53/35; ☺ 1.15pm mid-May–Oct) This
highly reputable outfit offers a fascinating
overview of Berchtesgaden's Nazi legacy.
Guests are taken not only to the Eagle's Nest
but around the Obersalzberg area and into
the underground bunker system. The four-
hour English-language tour departs from
the tourist office, across the roundabout
opposite the train station. Booking ahead is
advisable in July and August.

GERMANY BERCHTESGADEN

HITLER'S MOUNTAIN RETREAT

Of all the German towns tainted by the Third Reich, the Berchtesgaden area carries a burden heavier than most. Hitler fell in love with the secluded alpine village of Obersalzberg while vacationing here in the 1920s and later bought a small country home that was enlarged into an imposing residence – the Berghof.

After seizing power in 1933, the 'Führer' established a second seat of power here and brought much of the party brass with him. They drove out the local villagers and turned the compound into a *Führersperrgebiet* (an off-limits area). Many important decisions, about war and peace and the Holocaust, were made here.

In the final days of WWII, British and American bombers levelled much of Obersalzberg, although the Eagle's Nest, Hitler's mountaintop eyrie, was left strangely unscathed.

🛏 Sleeping & Eating

Hotel Vier Jahreszeiten   HOTEL €€
(📞 08652-9520; www.hotel-vierjahreszeiten-berchtesgaden.de; Maximilianstrasse 20; s €59-89, d €89-119; ⊙ reception 7am-11pm; 🅿 🎧 ❄) For a taste of Berchtesgaden's storied past, stay at this traditional lodge where Bavarian royalty once crumpled the sheets. Rooms have been updated in the last decade and the south-facing (more-expensive) rooms offer dramatic mountain views. After a day's sightseeing, dinner in the hunting lodge–style Hubertusstube restaurant is a real treat.

Bräustübl   BAVARIAN €€
(📞 08652-976 724; www.braeustueberl-berchtesgaden.de; Bräuhausstrasse 13; mains €7-17; ⊙ 10am-midnight) Past the vaulted entrance painted in Bavaria's white and blue diamonds, this cosy beer hall–beer garden is run by the local brewery. Expect a carnivorous feast with such favourite rib-stickers as pork roast and the house speciality: breaded calf's head (tastes better than it sounds). On Friday and Saturday, an oompah band launches into knee-slapping action.

ℹ Information

Tourist Office (📞 08652-896 70; www.berchtesgaden.com; Königsseer Strasse; ⊙ 8.30am-6pm Mon-Fri, 9am-5pm Sat, 9am-3pm Sun, reduced hours mid-Oct–Mar) Near the train station, this very helpful office has detailed information on the entire Berchtesgaden region.

ℹ Getting There & Away

Travelling from Munich by train involves a change from Meridian to BLB (Berchtesgadener Land Bahn) trains at Freilassing (€33.80, 2½ hours, at least hourly connections). The best option between Berchtesgaden and Salzburg is hourly RVO bus 840 (45 minutes).

Romantic Road

Stretching 400km from the vineyards of Würzburg to the foot of the Alps, the Romantic Road (Romantische Strasse) is by far the most popular of Germany's themed holiday routes. It passes through more than two dozen cities and towns, including Rothenburg ob der Tauber and also takes in Schloss Neuschwanstein, the country's most famous palace.

ℹ Getting There & Around

Frankfurt and Munich are the most popular gateways for exploring the Romantic Road. The ideal way to travel is by car, though many foreign travellers prefer to take Deutsche Touring's **Romantic Road Coach** (📞 09851-551 387; www.romanticroadcoach.de), which can get incredibly crowded in summer. From April to October this special coach runs daily in each direction between Frankfurt and Füssen (for Neuschwanstein); the entire journey takes around 12 hours. There's no charge for breaking the journey and continuing the next day.

Tickets are available for the entire route or for short segments, and reservations are only necessary during peak-season weekends. Buy tickets online or from travel agents, **EurAide** (p478) in Munich or Reisezentrum offices in larger train stations.

Füssen
📞 08362 / POP 14,600

In the foothills of the Alps, Füssen itself is a charming town, although most visitors skip it and head straight to Schloss Neuschwanstein and Hohenschwangau, the two most famous castles associated with King Ludwig II. You can see both on a long day trip from

Munich, although only when spending the night, after all the day-trippers have gone, will you sense a certain Alpine serenity.

⊙ Sights

The castles are served by buses 78 and 73 from Füssen Bahnhof (€4.40 return, eight minutes, at least hourly).

★**Schloss Neuschwanstein**   CASTLE
(🖉 tickets 08362-930 830; www.neuschwanstein. de; Neuschwansteinstrasse 20; adult/concession €12/11, incl Hohenschwangau €23/21; ⊙ 9am-6pm Apr–mid-Oct, 10am-4pm mid-Oct–Mar) Appearing through the mountaintops like a mirage, Schloss Neuschwanstein was the model for Disney's *Sleeping Beauty* castle. King Ludwig II planned this fairy-tale pile himself, with the help of a stage designer rather than an architect. He envisioned it as a giant stage on which to recreate the world of Germanic mythology, inspired by the operatic works of his friend Richard Wagner. The most impressive room is the **Sängersaal** (Minstrels' Hall), whose frescos depict scenes from the opera *Tannhäuser*.

Built as a romantic medieval castle, work started in 1869 and, like so many of Ludwig's grand schemes, was never finished. For all the coffer-depleting sums spent on it, the king spent just over 170 days in residence.

Completed sections include Ludwig's Tristan and Isolde–themed bedroom, dominated by a huge Gothic-style bed crowned with intricately carved cathedral-like spires; a gaudy artificial grotto (another allusion to *Tannhäuser*); and the Byzantine-style **Thronsaal** (Throne Room) with an incredible mosaic floor containing over two million stones. The painting opposite the (throneless) throne platform depicts another castle dreamed up by Ludwig that was never built. Almost every window provides tour-halting views across the plain below.

The tour ends with a 20-minute film on the castle and its creator, and there's a reasonably priced cafe and the inevitable gift shops.

For the postcard view of Neuschwanstein and the plains beyond, walk 10 minutes up to **Marienbrücke** (Mary's Bridge), which spans the spectacular Pöllat Gorge over a waterfall just above the castle. It's said Ludwig enjoyed coming up here after dark to watch the candlelight radiating from the Sängersaal.

ℹ️ CASTLE TICKETS & TOURS

Both Hohenschwangau and Neuschwanstein must be seen on guided 35-minute tours (in German or English). Timed tickets are only available from the **Ticket-Center** (🖉 08362-930 830; www.hohenschwangau.de; Alpenseestrasse 12; ⊙ 8am-5pm Apr–mid-Oct, 9am-3.30pm mid-Oct–Mar) at the foot of the castles and may be reserved online until two days prior to your visit (recommended).

If visiting both castles on the same day, the Hohenschwangau tour is scheduled first with enough time for the steep 30- to 40-minute walk between the castles. The footsore can travel by bus or by horsedrawn carriage.

Schloss Hohenschwangau   CASTLE
(🖉 08362-930 830; www.hohenschwangau.de; Alpenseestrasse 30; adult/concession €12/11, incl Neuschwanstein €23/21; ⊙ 8am-5pm Apr–mid-Oct, 9am-3.30pm mid-Oct–Mar) King Ludwig II grew up at the sun-yellow Schloss Hohenschwangau and later enjoyed summers here until his death in 1886. His father, Maximilian II, built this palace in a neo-Gothic style atop 12th-century ruins left by Schwangau knights. Far less showy than Neuschwanstein, Hohenschwangau has a distinctly lived-in feel where every piece of furniture is a used original. After his father died, Ludwig's main alteration was having stars, illuminated with hidden oil lamps, painted on the ceiling of his bedroom.

🛏️ Sleeping & Eating

★**Hotel Sonne**   DESIGN HOTEL €€
(🖉 08362-9080; www.hotel-fuessen.de; Prinzregentenplatz 1; s/d from €89/109; 🅿 🛜) Although traditional looking from outside, this Altstadt favourite offers an unexpected design-hotel experience within. Themed rooms feature everything from swooping bed canopies to big-print wallpaper, huge pieces of wall art to sumptuous fabrics. The public spaces are littered with pieces of art, period costumes and design features – the overall effect is impressive and unusual for this part of Germany.

Restaurant Ritterstub'n   GERMAN €€
(🖉 08362-7759; www.restaurant-ritterstuben.de; Ritterstrasse 4; mains €6.80-18.50; ⊙ 11.30am-10pm Tue-Sun) This convivial pit stop has

value-priced salads, snacks, lunch specials, fish, schnitzel and gluten-free dishes, and even a cute kids' menu. The medieval knight theme can be a bit grating but kids often love eating their fishsticks with their fingers or seeing mum and dad draped in a big bib.

❶ Information

Tourist Office (☑ 08362-938 50; www.fuessen.de; Kaiser-Maximilian-Platz; ⊙ 9am-5pm Mon-Fri, 9.30am-3.30pm Sat) Can help find rooms.

❶ Getting There & Away

Füssen is the southern terminus of the Romantic Road Coach.

If you want to do the castles in a single day from Munich, you'll need to start early. The first train leaves Munich at 5.53am (€26.20, change in Buchloe), reaching Füssen at 7.52am. Otherwise, direct trains leave Munich once every two hours throughout the day.

Rothenburg ob der Tauber

☑ 09861 / POP 10,900

With its jumble of half-timbered houses enclosed by Germany's best-preserved ramparts, Rothenburg ob der Tauber lays on the medieval cuteness with a trowel. It's an essential stop on the Romantic Road but, alas, overcrowding can detract from its charm. Visit early or late in the day (or, ideally, stay overnight) to experience this historic wonderland sans crowds.

◉ Sights

Jakobskirche CHURCH
(Church of St Jacob; Klingengasse 1; adult/concession €2.50/1.50; ⊙ 9am-5.15pm Mon-Sat, 10.45am-5.15pm Sun Apr-Oct, shorter hours Nov-Mar) One of the few places of worship in Bavaria to charge admission, Rothenburg's Lutheran parish church was begun in the 14th century and finished in the 15th. The building sports some wonderfully aged stained-glass windows but the top attraction is Tilman Riemenschneider's **Heilig Blut Altar** (Altar of the Holy Blood). The gilded cross above the main scene depicting the Last Supper incorporates Rothenburg's most treasured reliquary – a rock crystal capsule said to contain three drops of Christ's blood.

Rathausturm HISTORIC BUILDING
(Town Hall Tower; Marktplatz; adult/concession €2/0.50; ⊙ 9.30am-12.30pm & 1-5pm daily Apr-Oct, 10.30am-2pm & 2.30-6pm daily Dec, noon-3pm Sat & Sun rest of year) The Rathaus on Marktplatz was begun in Gothic style in the 14th century and was completed during the Renaissance. Climb the 220 steps of the medieval town hall to the viewing platform of the Rathausturm to be rewarded with widescreen views of the Tauber.

Stadtmauer HISTORIC SITE
(Town Wall) With time and fresh legs, a 2.5km circular walk around the unbroken ring of town walls gives a sense of the importance medieval people placed on defending their settlement. A great lookout point is the eastern tower, the **Röderturm** (Rödergasse; adult/child €1.50/1; ⊙ 9am-5pm Mar-Nov), but for the most impressive views head to the west side of town, where a sweeping view of the Tauber Valley includes the Doppelbrücke, a double-decker bridge.

Mittelalterliches Kriminalmuseum MUSEUM
(Medieval Crime & Punishment Museum; www.kriminalmuseum.eu; Burggasse 3; adult/concession €7/4; ⊙ 10am-6pm May-Oct, 1-4pm Nov-Apr) Medieval implements of torture and punishment are on show at this gruesomely fascinating museum. Exhibits include chastity belts, masks of disgrace for gossips, a cage for cheating bakers, a neck brace for quarrelsome women and a beer-barrel pen for drunks. You can even snap a selfie in the stocks!

🛏 Sleeping & Eating

⭐ **Burg-Hotel** HOTEL €€
(☑ 09861-948 90; www.burghotel.eu; Klostergasse 1-3; s €100-135, d €125-195; P ⊖ ✳ 🛜) Each of the 17 elegantly furnished guest rooms at this boutique hotel built into the town walls has its own private sitting area. The lower floors shelter a decadent spa with tanning beds, saunas and rainforest showers, and a cellar with a Steinway piano, while phenomenal valley views unfurl from the breakfast room and stone terrace.

Gasthof Butz GERMAN €
(☑ 09861-2201; Kapellenplatz 4; mains €7-15; ⊙ noon-11pm Fri-Wed; 🛜) For a quick, no-nonsense goulash, schnitzel or roast pork, lug your weary legs to this locally adored, family-run inn in a former brewery. In summer two flowery beer gardens beckon. It also

rents a dozen simply furnished rooms (doubles €36 to €75).

Zur Höll FRANCONIAN €€
(☑ 09861-4229; www.hoell.rothenburg.de; Burggasse 8; mains €7-20; ☺ 5-11pm Mon-Sat) This medieval wine tavern is in the town's oldest original building, with sections dating back to the year 900. The menu of regional specialities is limited but refined, though it's the superb selection of Franconian wines that people really come for.

ℹ Information

Tourist Office (☑ 09861-404 800; www.tourismus.rothenburg.de; Marktplatz 2; ☺ 9am-6pm Mon-Fri, 10am-5pm Sat & Sun May-Oct, 9am-5pm Mon-Fri, 10am-1pm Sat Nov-Apr) Helpful office offering free internet access.

ℹ Getting There & Away

The Romantic Road Coach pauses in town for 45 minutes.

You can go anywhere by train from Rothenburg, as long as it's Steinach. Change there for services to Würzburg (€13.30, one hour and 10 minutes). Travel to and from Munich (from €31, three hours) can involve up to three different trains.

Würzburg

☑ 0931 / POP 133,800
Tucked in among river valleys lined with vineyards, Würzburg beguiles long before you reach the city centre and is renowned for its art, architecture and delicate wines. Its crowning architectural glory is the Residenz, one of the finest baroque structures in Germany and a Unesco World Heritage site.

◎ Sights

★ **Würzburg Residenz** PALACE
(www.residenz-wuerzburg.de; Balthasar-Neumann-Promenade; adult/concession/under 18yr €7.50/6.50/free; ☺ 9am-6pm Apr-Oct, 10am-4.30pm Nov-Mar, 45min English tours 11am & 3pm, also 4.30pm Apr-Oct) The vast Unesco-listed Residenz, built by 18th-century architect Balthasar Neumann as the home of the local prince-bishops, is one of Germany's most important and beautiful baroque palaces. Top billing goes to the brilliant zigzagging **Treppenhaus** (Staircase) lidded by what still is the world's largest fresco, a masterpiece by Giovanni Battista Tiepolo depicting allegories of the four then-known continents (Europe, Africa, America and Asia).

The structure was commissioned in 1720 by prince-bishop Johann Philipp Franz von Schönborn, who was unhappy with his old-fashioned digs up in Marienberg Fortress, and took almost 60 years to complete. Today, the 360 rooms are home to government institutions, university faculties and a museum, but the grandest 40 have been restored for visitors to admire.

Besides the Grand Staircase, feast your eyes on the ice-white stucco-adorned **Weisser Saal** (White Hall) before entering the **Kaisersaal** (Imperial Hall), canopied by yet another impressive Tiepolo fresco. Other stunners include the gilded stucco **Spiegelkabinett** (Mirror Hall), covered with a unique mirror-like glass painted with figural, floral and animal motifs (accessible by tour only).

In the residence's south wing, the **Hofkirche** (Court Church) is another Neumann and Tiepolo co-production. Its marble columns, gold leaf and profusion of angels match the Residenz in splendour and proportions.

Entered via frilly wrought-iron gates, the **Hofgarten** (Court Garden; open until dusk, free) is a smooth blend of French- and English-style landscaping teeming with whimsical sculptures of children, mostly by court sculptor Peter Wagner. Concerts, festivals and special events take place here during the warmer months.

The complex also houses collections of antiques, paintings and drawings in the **Martin-von-Wagner Museum** (no relation to Peter) and, handily, a winery in the atmospheric cellar, the **Staatlicher Hofkeller Würzburg**, that is open for tours with tasting.

Dom St Kilian CHURCH
(www.dom-wuerzburg.de; Domstrasse 40; ☺ 8am-7pm Mon-Sat, 8am-8pm Sun) FREE Würzburg's highly unusual cathedral has a Romanesque core that has been altered many times over the centuries. Recently renovated, the elaborate stucco work of the chancel contrasts starkly with the bare whitewash of the austere Romanesque nave, which is capped with a ceiling that wouldn't look out of place in a 1960s bus station.

The whole mishmash creates quite an impression and is possibly Germany's oddest cathedral interior. The **Schönbornkapelle** by Balthasar Neumann returns a little baroque order to things.

GERMANY ROMANTIC ROAD

Festung Marienberg
FORTRESS

(tour adult/concession €3.50/2.50; ⊙ tours 11am, 2pm, 3pm & 4pm Tue-Sun, also 10am & 1pm Sat & Sun mid-Mar–Oct, 11am, 2pm & 3pm Sat & Sun Nov–mid-Mar) Enjoy panoramic city and vineyard views from this hulking fortress whose construction was initiated around 1200 by the local prince-bishops who governed here until 1719. Dramatically illuminated at night, the structure was only penetrated once, by Swedish troops during the Thirty Years' War, in 1631. Inside, the **Fürstenbaumuseum** (closed November to mid-March) sheds light on its former residents' pompous lifestyle, while the **Mainfränkisches Museum** presents city history and works by local late-Gothic master carver Tilmann Riemenschneider and other famous artists.

🍴 Sleeping & Eating

Hotel Rebstock
HOTEL €€€

(☑ 0931-309 30; www.rebstock.com; Neubaustrasse 7; s/d from €131/241; ❉ @ 🛜) Würzburg's top digs, in a squarely renovated rococo townhouse, has 70 unique, stylishly finished rooms with the gamut of amenities, impeccable service and an Altstadt location. A pillow selection and supercomfy 'gel' beds should ease you into slumberland, perhaps after a fine meal in the dramatic bistro or the slick Michelin-star Kuno 1408 restaurant.

Backöfele
FRANCONIAN €€

(☑ 0931-590 59; www.backoefele.de; Ursulinergasse 2; mains €8-20; ⊙ noon-midnight Mon-Thu, to 1am Fri & Sat, to 11pm Sun) This old-timey warren has been serving hearty Franconian food for nearly 50 years. Find a table in the cobbled courtyard or one of four historic rooms, each candlelit and uniquely furnished with local flair. Featuring schnitzel, snails, bratwurst in wine, wine soup with cinnamon croutons, grilled meat and other local faves, the menu makes for mouth-watering reading. Bookings recommended.

Alte Mainmühle
FRANCONIAN €€

(☑ 0931-167 77; www.alte-mainmuehle.de; Mainkai 1; mains €8-25; ⊙ 10am-midnight) Accessed straight from the old bridge, tourists and locals alike cram into this old mill to savour modern twists on Franconian classics (including popular river fish). In summer the double terrace beckons – the upper one delivers pretty views of the bridge and Marienberg Fortress; in winter retreat to the snug timber dining room. Year round, guests spill out onto the bridge itself, Aperol Sprizz in hand.

ℹ️ Information

Tourist Office (☑ 0931-372 398; www.wuerzburg.de; Marktplatz 9; ⊙ 10am-5pm Mon-Fri, 10am-3pm Sat & Sun May-Oct, closed Sun and slightly shorter hours Nov-Apr) Within the attractive Falkenhaus, this efficient office can help you with room reservations and tour booking.

ℹ️ Getting There & Away

Frequent trains run to Bamberg (€20.70, one hour), Frankfurt (€35, one hour), Nuremberg (from €20.90, one hour) and Rothenburg ob der Tauber (via Steinach; €13.30, one hour).

Nuremberg

☑ 0911 / POP 510,600

Nuremberg (Nürnberg) woos visitors with its wonderfully restored medieval Altstadt, its grand castle and, in December, its magical *Christkindlmarkt* (Christmas market).

The town played a key role during the Nazi years. It was here that the fanatical party rallies were held, the boycott of Jewish businesses began and the anti-Semitic Nuremberg Laws were enacted. After WWII the city was chosen as the site of the Nuremberg Trials of Nazi war criminals.

◉ Sights

Nuremberg's city centre is best explored on foot but the Nazi-related sights are a tram ride away.

Hauptmarkt
SQUARE

This bustling square in the heart of the Altstadt is the site of daily markets as well as the famous *Christkindlmarkt* (Christmas market). At the eastern end is the ornate Gothic **Frauenkirche** (church). Daily at noon crowds crane their necks to witness the clock's figures enact a spectacle called the *Männleinlaufen* (Little Men Dancing). Rising from the square like a Gothic spire is the sculpture-festooned **Schöner Brunnen** (Beautiful Fountain). Touch the golden ring in the ornate wrought-iron gate for good luck.

★ Kaiserburg
CASTLE

(Imperial Castle; ☑ 0911-244 6590; www.kaiserburg -nuernberg.de; Auf dem Burg; adult/concession incl Sinwell Tower €7/6, Palas & Museum €5.50/4.50; ⊙ 9am-6pm Apr-Sep, 10am-4pm Oct-Mar) This enormous castle complex above the Altstadt poignantly reflects Nuremberg's medieval might. The main attraction is a tour of the newly renovated residential wing (**Palas**) to see the lavish Knights' and Imperial Hall, a Romanesque double chapel and an exhibit on the inner workings of the Holy Roman Empire. This segues to the **Kaiserburg Museum**, which focuses on the castle's military and building history. Elsewhere, enjoy panoramic views from the **Sinwell Tower** or peer 48m down into the **Deep Well**.

Memorium Nuremberg Trials MEMORIAL
(☑0911-3217 9372; www.memorium-nuremberg. de; Bärenschanzstrasse 72; adult/concession incl audioguide €5/3; ⊙9am-6pm Mon & Wed-Fri, 10am-6pm Sat & Sun Apr-Oct, slightly shorter hours Nov-Mar) Göring, Hess, Speer and 21 other Nazi leaders were tried for crimes against peace and humanity by the Allies in **Schwurgerichtssaal 600** (Court Room 600) of this still-working courthouse. Today the room forms part of an engaging exhibit detailing the background, progression and impact of the trials using film, photographs, audiotape and even the original defendants' dock. To get here, take the U1 towards Bärenschanze and get off at Sielstrasse.

Reichsparteitagsgelände HISTORIC SITE
(Luitpoldhain; ☑0911-231 7538; www.museen. nuernberg.de/dokuzentrum/; Bayernstrasse 110; grounds free, Documentation Centre adult/concession incl audioguide €5/3; ⊙grounds 24hr, Documentation Centre 9am-6pm Mon-Fri, 10am-6pm Sat & Sun) If you've ever wondered where the infamous black-and-white images of ecstatic Nazi supporters hailing their Führer were taken, it was here in Nuremberg. Much of the grounds were destroyed during Allied bombing raids, but enough remains to get a sense of the megalomania behind the regime. The excellent **Dokumentationszentrum** (Documentation Centre) is especially enlightening; it's served by tram 9 from the Hauptbahnhof.

🛏 Sleeping

Hotel Victoria HOTEL €€
(☑0911-240 50; www.hotelvictoria.de; Königstrasse 80; s/d from €82/98; ▣@🛜) A hotel since 1896, the Victoria is a solid option with a central location. With its early-21st-century bathrooms and now ever-so-slightly-dated decor, the price is about right. Popular with business travellers. Parking costs €12.

Beginning in late November every year, central squares across Germany are transformed into Christmas markets or *Christkindlmarkt* (also known as *Weihnachtsmärkte*). Folks stamp about between the wooden stalls, perusing seasonal trinkets (from hand-carved ornaments to plastic angels) while warming themselves with *Glühwein* (mulled, spiced red wine) and grilled sausages. Locals love 'em and, not surprisingly, the markets are popular with tourists, so bundle up and carouse for hours. Markets in Nuremberg, Dresden, Cologne and Munich are especially famous.

Hotel Drei Raben BOUTIQUE HOTEL €€€
(☑0911-274 380; www.hoteldreiraben.de; Königstrasse 63; d incl breakfast from €175; ▣✳🛜) The design of this classy charmer builds upon the legend of the three ravens perched on the building's chimney stack, who tell stories from Nuremberg lore. Art and decor in the 'mythical theme' rooms reflect a particular tale, from the life of Albrecht Dürer to the first railway.

🍴 Eating & Drinking

Don't leave Nuremberg without trying its famous finger-sized *Nürnberger Bratwürste*. You'll find them everywhere around town.

★Albrecht Dürer Stube FRANCONIAN €€
(☑0911-227 209; www.albrecht-duerer-stube.de; cnr Albrecht-Dürer-Strasse & Agnesgasse; mains €6-15; ⊙6pm-midnight Mon-Sat, 11.30am-2.30pm Fri & Sun) This unpretentious and intimate restaurant has a Dürer-inspired dining room, prettily laid tables, a ceramic stove keeping things toasty when they're not outside and a menu of Nuremberg sausages, steaks, sea fish, seasonal specials, Franconian wine and *Landbier* (regional beer). There aren't many tables so booking ahead at weekends is recommended.

Heilig-Geist-Spital BAVARIAN €€
(☑0911-221 761; www.heilig-geist-spital.de; Spitalgasse 16; mains €7-18; ⊙11.30am-11pm) Lots of dark carved wood, a herd of hunting trophies and a romantic candlelit half-light make this former hospital, suspended over the Pegnitz, one of the most atmospheric dining rooms in town. Sample the delicious,

seasonally changing menu inside or out in the pretty courtyard, a real treat if you are looking for somewhere traditional to dine.

Kloster PUB
(Obere Wörthstrasse 19; ⊙5pm-1am) One of Nuremberg's best drinking dens is all dressed up as a monastery replete with ecclesiastic knick-knacks including coffins emerging from the walls. The monks here pray to the god of *Landbier* (regional beer) and won't be up at 5am for matins, that's for sure.

Information

Tourist Office – Hauptmarkt (☎0911-233 60; www.tourismus.nuernberg.de; Hauptmarkt 18; ⊙9am-6pm Mon-Sat year-round, also 10am-4pm Sun Apr-Oct)

Tourist Office – Künstlerhaus (☎0911-233 60; www.tourismus.nuernberg.de; Königstrasse 93; ⊙9am-7pm Mon-Sat, 10am-4pm Sun) Publishes the excellent *See & Enjoy* booklet, a comprehensive guide to the city.

Getting There & Away

Rail connections from Nuremberg include Frankfurt (€55, 2½ hours) and Munich (from €36, one hour).

Bamberg

☎0951 / POP 71,200

Off the major tourist routes, Bamberg is one of Germany's most delightful and authentic towns. It has a bevy of beautifully preserved historic buildings, palaces and churches in its Unesco-recognised Altstadt, a lively student population and its own style of beer.

Sights

Bamberger Dom CATHEDRAL
(www.erzbistum-bamberg.de; Domplatz; ⊙8am-6pm Apr-Oct, to 5pm Nov-Mar) FREE Beneath the quartet of spires, Bamberg's cathedral is packed with artistic treasures, most famously the life-size equestrian statue of the **Bamberger Reiter** (Bamberg Horseman), whose true identity remains a mystery. It overlooks the **tomb of cathedral founders**, Emperor Heinrich II and his wife Kunigunde, splendidly carved by Tilmann Riemenschneider. The **marble tomb of Clemens II** in the west choir is the only papal buried site north of the Alps. Nearby, the **Virgin Mary altar** by Veit Stoss also warrants closer inspection.

Altes Rathaus HISTORIC BUILDING
(Old Town Hall; Obere Brücke; adult/concession €4.50/4; ⊙9.30am-4.30pm Tue-Sun) Like a ship in dry dock, Bamberg's 1462 Old Town Hall was built on an artificial island in the Regnitz River, allegedly because the local bishop had refused to give the town's citizens any land for its construction. Inside is a collection of precious porcelain but even more enchanting are the richly detailed frescos adorning its facades – note the cherub's leg cheekily sticking out from its east facade.

Neue Residenz PALACE
(New Residence; ☎0951-519 390; Domplatz 8; adult/concession €4/3; ⊙9am-6pm Apr-Sep, 10am-4pm Oct-Mar) This splendid episcopal palace gives you an eyeful of the lavish lifestyle of Bamberg's prince-bishops who, between 1703 and 1802, occupied its 40-odd rooms that can only be seen on guided 45-minute tours (in German). Tickets are also good for the **Bavarian State Gallery**, with works by Lucas Cranach the Elder and other old masters. The baroque **Rose Garden** delivers fabulous views over the town.

Sleeping

Hotel Wohnbar BOUTIQUE HOTEL €
(☎0951-5099 8844; www.wohnbar-bamberg.de; Stangsstrasse 3; s/d from €59/79; P ᯤ) 'Carpe Noctem' (Seize the Night) is the motto of this charming 10-room retreat with boldly coloured, contemporary rooms near the university quarter. Those in the 'economy' category are a very tight squeeze. Parking costs €10 per day.

Barockhotel am Dom HOTEL €€
(☎0951-540 31; www.barockhotel.de; Vorderer Bach 4; s/d from €84/99; P ᯤ) The sugary facade, a sceptre's swipe from the Dom, gives a hint of the baroque heritage and original details within. The 19 rooms have sweeping views of the Dom or the roofs of the Altstadt, and breakfast is served in a 14th-century vault.

Eating & Drinking

Obere Sandstrasse near the cathedral and Austrasse near the university are both good eat and drink streets. Try Bamberg's unique style of beer called *Rauchbier* (smoked beer).

Zum Sternla FRANCONIAN €
(☎0951-287 50; www.sternla.de; Lange Strasse 46; mains €5-12; ⊙4-11pm Tue, 11am-11pm Wed-

Sun) Bamberg's oldest *Wirtshaus* (inn; established 1380) bangs down bargain-priced staples including pork dishes, steaks, dumplings and sauerkraut, as well as specials, but it's a great, non-touristy place for a traditional *Brotzeit* (snack), or just a pretzel and a beer. The menu is helpfully translated from Franconian into German.

Schlenkerla   GERMAN €€

(🖉 0951-560 60; www.schlenkerla.de; Dominikanerstrasse 6; mains €6.50-13; ☺ 9.30am-11.30pm) Beneath wooden beams as dark as the superb *Rauchbier* poured straight from oak barrels, locals and visitors dig into scrumptious Franconian fare at this legendary flower-festooned tavern near the cathedral.

ⓘ Information

Tourist Office (🖉 0951-297 6200; www.bamberg.info; Geyersworthstrasse 5; ☺ 9.30am-6pm Mon-Fri, to 4pm Sat, to 2.30pm Sun) Staff sell the Bambergcard (€14.90), valid for three days of free bus rides and free museum entry.

ⓘ Getting There & Away

Getting to and from Bamberg by train usually involves a change in Würzburg.

Regensburg

🖉 0941 / POP 140,300

In a scene-stealing locale on the wide Danube River, Regensburg has relics of historic periods reaching back to the Romans, yet doesn't get the tourist mobs you'll find in other equally attractive German cities. Though big on the historical wow factor, today's Regensburg is a laid-back and unpretentious student town with a distinct Italianate flair.

◉ Sights

Altes Rathaus   HISTORIC BUILDING

(Old Town Hall; Rathausplatz; adult/concession €7.50/4; ☺ tours in English 3pm Easter-Oct, 2pm Nov & Dec, in German every 30min) From 1663 to 1806, the Reichstag (imperial assembly) held its gatherings at Regensburg's old town hall, an important role commemorated by an exhibit in today's **Reichstagsmuseum**. Tours take in the lavish assembly hall and the original **torture chambers** in the cellar.

Buy tickets at the tourist office in the same building. Note that access is by tour only. Audioguides are available for English speakers in January and February.

Dom St Peter   CHURCH

(www.bistum-regensburg.de; Domplatz; ☺ 6.30am-7pm Jun-Sep, to 6pm Apr, May & Oct, to 5pm Nov-Mar) It takes a few seconds for your eyes to adjust to the dim interior of Regensburg's soaring landmark, the Dom St Peter, one of Bavaria's grandest Gothic cathedrals with stunning kaleidoscopic stained-glass windows and an opulent, silver-sheathed main altar.

The cathedral is home of the **Domspatzen**, a 1000-year-old boys' choir that accompanies the 10am Sunday service (only during the school year). The **Domschatzmuseum** (Cathedral Treasury) brims with monstrances, tapestries and other church treasures.

Steinerne Brücke   BRIDGE

(Stone Bridge) An incredible feat of engineering for its day, Regensburg's 900-year-old Stone Bridge was at one time the only fortified crossing of the Danube. Damaged and neglected for centuries, the entire expanse has undergone renovation in recent years.

🛌 Sleeping

Brook Lane Hostel   HOSTEL €

(🖉 0941-696 5521; www.hostel-regensburg.de; Obere Bachgasse 21; dm/s/d from €16/40/50, apt per person €55; 🛜) Regensburg's only backpacker hostel has its very own convenience store, which doubles up as reception, but isn't open 24 hours, so late landers should let staff know in advance. Dorms do the minimum required, but the apartments and doubles here are applaudable deals, especially if you're travelling in a two- or moresome. Access to kitchens and washing machines throughout.

★ **Elements Hotel**   HOTEL €€

(🖉 941-2007 2275; www.hotel-elements.de; Alter Kornmarkt 3; d from €105; 🛜) Four elements, four rooms, and what rooms they are! 'Fire' blazes in plush crimson, while 'Water' is a wellness suite with a Jacuzzi; 'Air' is playful and light and natural wood; and stone and leather reign in colonial-inspired 'Earth'. Breakfast costs an extra €15.

✕ Eating & Drinking

Historische Wurstkuchl   GERMAN €

(🖉 0941-466 210; www.wurstkuchl.de; Thundorferstrasse 3; 6 sausages €9; ☺ 9am-7pm) Completely submerged several times by the Danube's fickle floods, this titchy eatery has been serving the city's traditional finger-size sausages, grilled over beech wood and dished up with the restaurant's own sauerkraut and sweet grainy mustard, since 1135 and lays claim to being the world's oldest sausage kitchen.

Weltenburger am Dom
BAVARIAN €€

(☑0941-586 1460; www.weltenburger-am-dom.de; Domplatz 3; dishes €6.40-20.80; ⊙11am-11pm) Tightly packed gastropub with a mouth-watering menu card of huge gourmet burgers, sausage dishes, beer hall and garden favourites such as *Obazda* (cream cheese on pretzels) and *Sauerbraten* (marinated roast meat), dark beer goulash and a few token desserts. Make sure you are hungry before you come as portions are big.

ⓘ Information

Tourist Office (☑0941-507 4410; www.regensburg.de; Rathausplatz 4; ⊙9am-6pm Mon-Fri, 9am-4pm Sat, 9.30am-4pm Sun Apr-Oct, closes 2.30pm Sun Nov-Mar; ☎) In the historic Altes Rathaus. Sells tickets, tours, rooms and an audioguide for self-guided tours.

ⓘ Getting There & Away

Frequent trains leave for Munich (€27.50, 1½ hours) and Nuremberg (€20.70, one to two hours), among other cities.

STUTTGART & THE BLACK FOREST

The high-tech urbanite pleasures of Stuttgart, one of the engines of the German economy, form an appealing contrast to the historic charms of Heidelberg, home to the country's oldest university and a romantic ruined castle. Beyond lies the myth-shrouded Black Forest (Schwarzwald in German), a pretty land of misty hills, thick forest and cute villages with youthful and vibrant Freiburg as its only major town.

Stuttgart

☑0711 / POP 600,000

Stuttgart residents enjoy an enviable quality of life that's to no small degree rooted in its fabled car companies – Porsche and Mercedes – which show off their pedigree in two excellent museums. Hemmed in by vine-covered hills the city also has plenty in store for fans of European art.

⊙ Sights

Königsstrasse, a long, pedestrianised shopping strip, links the Hauptbahnhof to the city centre with the Schloss and the art museums. The Mercedes-Benz Museum is about 5km northeast and the Porsche Museum 7km north of here.

Kunstmuseum Stuttgart
GALLERY

(☑0711-2161 9600; www.kunstmuseum-stuttgart.de; Kleiner Schlossplatz 1; adult/concession €6/4; ⊙10am-6pm Tue-Thu, Sat & Sun, to 9pm Fri) Occupying a shimmering glass cube, this gallery presents high-calibre special exhibits alongside a permanent gallery filled with a prized collection of works by Otto Dix, Willi Baumeister and Alfred Höltzel. For a great view, head up to the Cube cafe.

Mercedes-Benz Museum
MUSEUM

(☑0711-173 0000; www.mercedes-benz-classic.com; Mercedesstrasse 100; adult/concession/under 15yr €10/5/free; ⊙9am-6pm Tue-Sun, last admission 5pm; ⓡS1 to Neckarpark) A futuristic swirl on the cityscape, the Mercedes-Benz Museum takes a chronological spin through the Mercedes empire. Look out for legends like the 1885 Daimler Riding Car, the world's first gasoline-powered vehicle, and the record-breaking Lightning Benz that hit 228km/h at Daytona Beach in 1909.

Porsche Museum
MUSEUM

(☑0711-9112 0911; www.porsche.com/museum; Porscheplatz 1; adult/concession €8/4; ⊙9am-6pm Tue-Sun; ⓡNeuwirtshaus) Like a pearly white spaceship preparing for lift-off, the barrier-free Porsche Museum is every little boy's dream. Groovy audioguides race you through the history of Porsche from its 1948 beginnings. Stop to glimpse the 911 GT1 that won Le Mans in 1998.

🛏 Sleeping

Hostel Alex 30
HOSTEL €

(☑0711-838 8950; www.alex30-hostel.de; Alexanderstrasse 30; dm €25-29, s/d €43/64; Ⓟ☎) Fun-seekers on a budget should thrive at this popular hostel within walking distance of the city centre. Rooms are kept spick and span, and the bar, sun deck and communal kitchen are ideal for swapping stories with fellow travellers. Light sleepers might want to pack earplugs for thin walls and street noise. Breakfast costs €8.

Kronen Hotel
HOTEL €€€

(☑0711-225 10; www.kronenhotel-stuttgart.de; Kronenstrasse 48; s €115-125, d €160-190; Ⓟ❄☎) Right on the lap of Königsstrasse, this hotel outclasses most in Stuttgart with its terrific location, good-natured staff, well-appointed rooms and funkily lit sauna. Breakfast is above par, with fresh fruit, eggs and bacon, smoked fish and pastries.

✖ Eating & Drinking

Hans-im-Glück-Platz is a hub of bars, while clubs line Theodor-Heuss-Strasse and wine taverns abound in the Bohnenviertel.

Stuttgarter Markthalle　　　　MARKET €
(Market Hall; ☑ 0711-480 410; www.markthalle-stuttgart.de; Dorotheenstrasse 4; ⊙ 7am-6.30pm Mon-Fri, 7am-5pm Sat) Olives, regional cheeses, spices, patisserie, fruit and veg, wine and tapas – you'll find it all under one roof at Stuttgart's large art-nouveau market hall, which also has snack stands.

Ochs'n'Willi　　　　GERMAN €€
(☑ 0711-226 5191; www.ochsn-willi.de; Kleiner Schlossplatz 4; mains €11.50-30; ⊙ 11am-11.30pm) A warm, woody hunter's cottage restaurant just this side of twee, Ochs'n'Willi delivers gutsy portions of Swabian and Bavarian fare. Dig into pork knuckles with lashings of dumplings and kraut, spot-on *Maultaschen* (pasta pockets) or rich, brothy *Gaisburger Marsch* (beef stew). There's a terrace for warm-weather dining.

Weinhaus Stetter　　　　GERMAN €€
(☑ 0711-240 163; www.weinhaus-stetter.de; Rosenstrasse 32; snacks & mains €4-14; ⊙ 3-11pm Mon-Fri, noon-3pm & 5.30-11pm Sat) This traditional wine tavern in the Bohnenviertel quarter serves up no-nonsense Swabian cooking, including flavoursome *Linsen und Saiten* (lentils with sausage) and beef roast with onion, in a convivial ambience. The attached wine shop sells around 500 different vintages.

Cube　　　　INTERNATIONAL €€€
(☑ 0711-280 4441; www.cube-restaurant.de; Kleiner Schlossplatz 1; mains €29-37; ⊙ 10am-midnight Sun-Thu, 10am-2am Fri & Sat) The food is stellar but it actually plays second fiddle to the dazzling decor, refined ambience and stunning views at this glass-fronted cube atop the Kunstmuseum. Lunches are perky, fresh and international, while dinners feature more complex Pacific Rim–inspired cuisine. The lunch special is a steal at around €10.

ℹ Information

Tourist Office (☑ 0711-22 280; www.stuttgart-tourist.de; Königstrasse 1a; ⊙ 9am-8pm Mon-Fri, to 6pm Sat, 11am-6pm Sun)

BOHEMIAN BEANS

To really slip under Stuttgart's skin, mosey through the **Bohnenviertel** (Bean District), one of the city's lesser-known neighbourhoods. Walk south to Hans-im-Glück Platz, centred on a fountain depicting the caged Grimm's fairy-tale character Lucky Hans, and you'll soon reach the boho-flavoured Bohnenviertel, named after beans introduced in the 16th century. Back then they were grown everywhere as the staple food of the poor tanners, dyers and craftsmen who lived here.

ℹ Getting There & Away

Stuttgart Airport (SGT; ☑ 0711-9480; www.stuttgart-airport.com), a major hub for Germanwings, is 13km south of the city and linked to the Hauptbahnhof by S2 and S3 trains (€3.90, 30 minutes).

There are train services to all major German cities, including Frankfurt (€63, 1¼ hours) and Munich (€57, 2¼ hours).

Heidelberg

☑ 06221 / POP 152,435

Germany's oldest and most famous university town is renowned for its lovely Altstadt, its plethora of pubs and its evocative half-ruined castle. Millions of visitors are drawn each year to this photogenic assemblage, thereby following in the footsteps of Mark Twain who kicked off his European travels in 1878 in Heidelberg, later recounting his bemused observations in *A Tramp Abroad*.

◉ Sights

Heidelberg's sites cluster in the Altstadt, which starts to reveal itself only after a charm-free 15-minute walk east from the main train station or a short ride on bus 32 or 38.

★ Schloss Heidelberg　　　　CASTLE
(☑ 072 5174 2770; www.schloss-heidelberg.de; adult/child incl Bergbahn €7/4, tours €4/2, audio-guide €4; ⊙ grounds 24hr, castle 8am-6pm, English tours hourly 11.15am-4.15pm Mon-Fri, 10.15am-4.15pm Sat & Sun Apr-Oct, reduced tours Nov-Mar) Towering over the Altstadt, Heidelberg's ruined Renaissance castle cuts a romantic figure, especially across the Neckar River when illuminated at night. Attractions include the world's largest wine cask

and fabulous views. It's reached either via a steep, cobbled trail in about 10 minutes or by taking the Bergbahn (cogwheel train) from Kornmarkt station. The only way to see the less-than-scintillating interior is by tour, which can be safely skipped. After 6pm you can stroll the grounds for free.

Alte Brücke
BRIDGE

(Karl-Theodor-Brücke) Heidelberg's 200m-long 'old bridge', built in 1786, connects the Altstadt with the river's right bank and the Schlangenweg (Snake Path), whose switchbacks lead to the Philosophenweg (Philosophers' Walk; south bank of the Neckar River).

Next to the tower gate on the Altstadt side of the bridge, look for the brass sculpture of a monkey holding a mirror. It's the 1979 replacement of the 17th-century original sculpture.

Studentenkarzer
HISTORIC SITE

(Student Jail; ☑06221-543 593; www.uni-heidelberg.de; Augustinergasse 2; adult/child incl Universitätsmuseum €3/2.50; ☉10am-6pm Tue-Sun Apr-Sep, 10am-4pm Tue-Sat Oct-Mar) From 1823 to 1914, students convicted of misdeeds such as public inebriation, loud nocturnal singing, freeing the local pigs or duelling were sent to this student jail for at least 24 hours. Judging by the inventive wall graffiti, some found their stay highly amusing. Delinquents were let out to attend lectures or take exams. In certain circles, a stint in the Karzer was considered a rite of passage.

🛏 Sleeping

Steffis Hostel
HOSTEL €

(☑06221-778 2772; www.hostelheidelberg.de; Alte Eppelheimer Strasse 50; dm from €18, s/d/f without bathroom from €45/56/100; ☉reception 8am-10pm; 🅿@🛜) In a 19th-century tobacco factory a block north of the Hauptbahnhof, accessed via an industrial-size lift/elevator, Steffis offers bright, well-lit dorms and rooms (all with shared bathrooms), a colourful lounge that's great for meeting fellow travellers, a spacious kitchen and an old-school hostel vibe. Breakfast costs €3. Perks include tea, coffee and free bike rental.

★ Hotel Villa Marstall
HISTORIC HOTEL €€

(☑06221-655 570; www.villamarstall.de; Lauerstrasse 1; s €95-165, d €115-185; ☉reception 7am-10pm Mon-Sat, 8am-6pm Sun; ✳🛜) A 19th-century neoclassical mansion directly overlooking the Neckar River, Villa Marstall is a jewel with cherrywood floors, solid-

timber furniture and amenities including a lift/elevator. Exquisite rooms are decorated in whites, creams and bronzes, and come with in-room fridges (perfect for chilling a bottle of regional wine). A sumptuous breakfast buffet (€12) is served in the red-sandstone vaulted cellar.

🍴 Eating & Drinking

★'S' Kastanie
GERMAN €€

(☑06221-728 0343; www.restaurant-s-kastanie.de; Elisabethenweg 1; 2-course lunch menu €10, mains €12-30; ☉11.30am-2.30pm & 6-10pm Wed-Fri, 5-10pm Sat, 11.30am-8pm Sun) A panoramic terrace provides sweeping views of the river at this gorgeous 1904-built former hunting lodge, with stained glass and timber panelling, set in the forest near the castle. Chef Sven Schönig's stunning creations include a sweet potato and goat's cheese tower with papaya, and goose-stuffed ravioli.

Schnitzelbank
GERMAN €€

(☑06221-211 89; www.schnitzelbank-heidelberg.de; Baumamtsgasse 7; mains €15-22; ☉5pm-1am Mon-Fri, from 11.30am Sat & Sun) Small and often jam-packed, this cosy wine tavern has you sampling the local tipples (all wines are regional) and cuisine while crouched on wooden workbenches from the time when this was still a cooperage. It's these benches that give the place its name, incidentally, not the veal and pork schnitzel on the menu. Other specialities include Saumagen (stuffed pig's stomach).

ℹ Information

Tourist Office – Hauptbahnhof (☑06221-584 4444; www.heidelberg-marketing.de; Willy-Brandt-Platz 1; ☉9am-7pm Mon-Sat, 10am-6pm Sun Apr-Oct, 9am-6pm Mon-Sat Nov-Mar) Right outside the main train station.

Tourist Office – Marktplatz (www.heidelberg-marketing.de; Marktplatz 10; ☉8am-5pm Mon-Fri year-round, 10am-5pm Sat Apr-Oct) In the old town.

ℹ Getting There & Away

There are at least hourly IC trains to/from Frankfurt (€18 to €29, one hour) and Stuttgart (€19 to €39, 40 minutes).

Black Forest

The Black Forest (Schwarzwald) gets its name from its dark canopy of evergreens. Let winding backroads take you through misty vales, fairy-tale woodlands and villages that radiate earthy authenticity. It's not nature wild and remote, but bucolic and picturesque.

Many of the Black Forest's most impressive sights are in the triangle delimited by the lively university city of Freiburg, 15km east of the Rhine in the southwest; Triberg, cuckoo-clock capital in the north; and the charming river-valley city of St Blasien in the southeast.

Baden-Baden

☎ 07221 / POP 54,500

The northern gateway to the Black Forest, Baden-Baden is one of Europe's most famous spa towns whose mineral-rich waters have cured the ills of celebs from Queen Victoria to Victoria Beckham. An air of old-world luxury hangs over this beautiful town that's also home to a palatial casino.

🏃 Activities

★ Friedrichsbad
SPA

(☎ 07221-275 920; www.carasana.de; Römerplatz 1; 3hr ticket €25, incl soap-&-brush massage €37; ⊙ 9am-10pm, last admission 7pm) If it's the body of Venus and the complexion of Cleopatra you desire, abandon modesty (and clothing) to wallow in thermal waters at this palatial 19th-century marble-and-mosaic-festooned spa. As Mark Twain put it, 'after 10 minutes you forget time; after 20 minutes, the world', as you slip into the regime of steaming, scrubbing, hot-cold bathing and dunking in the Roman-Irish bath.

Caracalla Spa
SPA

(☎ 07221-275 940; www.carasana.de; Römerplatz 11; 2/3hr €16/19, day ticket €23; ⊙ 8am-10pm, last admission 8pm) This modern, glass-fronted spa has a cluster of indoor and outdoor pools, grottos and surge channels, making the most of the mineral-rich spring water. For those who dare to bare, saunas range from the rustic 'forest' to the roasting 95°C 'fire' variety.

🛏 Sleeping & Eating

Schweizer Hof
HOTEL €€

(☎ 07221-304 60; www.schweizerhof.de; Lange Strasse 73; s €69-89, d €99-135) Sitting on one of Baden-Baden's smartest streets, this above-par hotel is a real find, with 34 dapper en-suite rooms, chandelier-lit spaces, and a garden with sun lounges for chilling. The buffet breakfast is a rich affair.

★ Weinstube im Baldreit
GERMAN €€

(☎ 07221-231 36; Küferstrasse 3; mains €12.50-19; ⊙ 5-10pm Tue-Sat) Well hidden down cobbled lanes, this wine-cellar restaurant is tricky to find, but worth looking for. Baden-Alsatian fare such as *Flammkuchen* (Alsatian pizza) topped with Black Forest ham, Roquefort and pears is expertly matched with local wines. Eat in the ivy-swathed courtyard in summer, and the vaulted interior in winter.

ℹ Information

Main Tourist Office (☎ 07221-275 200; www.baden-baden.com; Schwarzwaldstrasse 52; ⊙ 9am-6pm Mon-Sat, 9am-1pm Sun) Situated 2km northwest of the centre. If you're driving from the northwest (from the A5), this place is on the way into town. Sells event tickets.

Triberg

☎ 07722 / POP 5000

Cuckoo-clock capital, Black Forest–cake pilgrimage site and Germany's highest waterfall – Triberg is a torrent of Schwarzwald superlatives and attracts gushes of guests.

👁 Sights

★ Triberger Wasserfälle
WATERFALL

(adult/concession/family €4/3.50/9.50; ⊙ 9am-7pm Mar-early Nov & 25-30 Dec) Niagara they ain't but Germany's highest waterfalls do exude their own wild romanticism. The Gutach River feeds the seven-tiered falls, which drop a total of 163m and are illuminated until 10pm.

🛏 Sleeping & Eating

★ Parkhotel Wehrle
HISTORIC HOTEL €€€

(☎ 07722-860 20; www.parkhotel-wehrle.de; Gartenstrasse 24; s €95-105, d €155-179; P 🕏 ☲) This 400-year-old hotel has a recommended integrated day spa. Often with a baroque or Biedermeier touch, quarters are roomy and beautifully furnished with antiques; the best have Duravit whirlpool tubs. Hemingway once waxed lyrical about the trout he ordered at the hotel's venerable restaurant (mains €15-24; ⊙ 6-9pm daily, noon-2pm Sun).

★ Café Schäfer
CAFE €

(☎ 07722-4465; www.cafe-schaefer-triberg.de; Hauptstrasse 33; cakes €3-4; ⊙ 9am-6pm Mon, Tue, Thu & Fri, 8am-6pm Sat, 11am-6pm Sun) Confectioner Claus Schäfer uses the original 1915 recipe for Black Forest gateau to prepare this sinful treat that layers chocolate cake perfumed with cherry brandy, whipped cream and sour cherries and wraps it all in more cream and shaved chocolate. Trust us, it's worth the calories.

ⓘ Information

Tourist Office (☑ 07722-866 490; www.triberg. de; Wallfahrtstrasse 4; ☉ 9am-5pm Mon-Fri, 10am-5pm Sat & Sun) Inside the Schwarzwald-Museum. Stocks walking, cross-country skiing and mountain-biking maps.

Freiburg im Breisgau

☑ 0761 / POP 224,190

Sitting plump at the foot of the Black Forest's wooded slopes and vineyards, Freiburg is a sunny, cheerful university town whose Altstadt is a storybook tableau of gabled townhouses, cobblestone lanes and cafe-rimmed plazas. Party-loving students spice up the local nightlife and give Freiburg its relaxed air.

◉ Sights

★**Freiburger Münster**   CATHEDRAL

(Freiburg Minster; ☑ 0761-202 790; www.freiburger muenster.info; Münsterplatz; tower adult/concession €2/1.50; ☉ 10am-5pm Mon-Sat, 1-7.30pm Sun, tower 9.30am-4.45pm Mon-Sat, 1-5pm Sun) With its lacy spires, cheeky gargoyles and intricate entrance portal, Freiburg's 11th-century minster cuts an impressive figure above the central market square. It has dazzling kaleidoscopic stained-glass windows that were mostly financed by medieval guilds and a high altar with a masterful triptych by Dürer protégé Hans Baldung Grien. Square at the base, the tower becomes an octagon higher up and is crowned by a filigreed 116m-high spire. On clear days you can spy the Vosges Mountains in France.

Rathausplatz   SQUARE

(Town Hall Square) Join locals relaxing in a cafe by the fountain in chestnut-shaded Rathausplatz, Freiburg's prettiest square. Pull out your camera to snap pictures of the ox-blood-red 16th-century **Altes Rathaus** (Old Town Hall) with the tourist office, the step-gabled 19th-century **Neues Rathaus** (New Town Hall) and the medieval **Martinskirche** with its modern interior.

Augustinermuseum   MUSEUM

(☑ 0761-201 2531; Auginerplatz 1; adult/concession/ under 18yr €7/5/free; ☉ 10am-5pm Tue-Sun) Dip into the past as represented by artists working from the Middle Ages to the 19th century at this superb museum in a sensitively modernised monastery. The **Sculpture Hall** on the ground floor is especially impressive for its fine medieval sculpture and masterpieces by Renaissance artists Hans Baldung Grien and Lucas Cranach the Elder. Head upstairs for eye-level views of mounted gargoyles.

🛏 Sleeping

Black Forest Hostel   HOSTEL €

(☑ 0761-881 7870; www.blackforest-hostel.de; Kartäuserstrasse 33; dm €17-28, s/d €36/60, linen €4; ☉ reception 7am-1am; @) Boho budget digs with chilled common areas, a shared kitchen, bike rental and spacey stainless-steel showers. It's a five-minute walk from the town centre.

Hotel Schwarzwälder Hof   HOTEL €€

(☑ 0761-380 30; www.schwarzwaelder-hof.com; Herrenstrasse 43; s €68-80, d €99-125; 🖥) This bijou hotel has an unrivalled style-for-euro ratio. A wrought-iron staircase sweeps up to snazzy rooms furnished in classic, modern or traditional style. Some have postcard

---

THE BATTLE OF THE BIRDS

Triberg being Germany's undisputed cuckoo-clock capital, it's not surprising that two giant timepieces battle for title of world's largest cuckoo clock.

The older and more charming contender calls itself the **1. Weltgrösste Kuckucksuhr** (First World's Largest Cuckoo Clock; www.1weltgroesstekuckucksuhr.de; Untertalstrasse 28, Schonach; adult/concession €1.20/0.60; ☉ 10am-noon & 1-5pm) and can be found in Schonach. It kicked into gear in 1980 and took a local clockmaker three years to build by hand. A Dold family member is usually around to the explain the mechanism.

It has since been eclipsed in size by its cousin at the **Eble Uhren-Park** (☑ 07722-962 20; www.uhren-park.de; Schonachbach 27; €2; ☉ 9am-6pm Mon-Sat, 10am-6pm Sun), which occupies an entire house on the B33 between Triberg and Hornberg. Although undeniably bigger (and listed in the *Guinness Book of World Records*), it's more of a gimmick to lure shoppers inside a large clock shop.

views of the Altstadt. There's also an on-site restaurant.

✖ Eating & Drinking

Markthalle MARKET **€**
(www.markthalle-freiburg.de; Martinsgasse 235; light meals €4-8; ⊙ 8am-8pm Mon-Thu, to midnight Fri & Sat) Eat your way around the world – from curry to sushi, oysters to antipasti – at the food counters in this historic market hall, nicknamed 'Fressgässle'.

Gasthaus zum Kranz GERMAN **€€**
(⤷ 0761-217 1967; www.gasthauszumkranz.de; Herrenstrasse 40; mains €13-25; ⊙ 11.30am-3pm & 5.30pm-midnight Mon-Sat, noon-3pm & 5.30pm-midnight Sun) There's always a good buzz at this quintessentially rustic Badisch tavern. Pull up a hefty chair at one of the even heftier timber tables for well-prepared regional faves such as roast suckling pig, *Maultaschen* and *Sauerbraten* (beef pot roast with vinegar, onions and peppercorns).

Hausbrauerei Feierling PUB FOOD **€€**
(⤷ 0761-243 480; www.feierling.de; Gerberau 46; mains €5-15; ⊙ 11am-midnight Mon-Thu, to 1am Fri & Sun; ⧸) Thumbs up for the Feierling house brew, which has kept beer lovers lubricated for over a quarter century. In summer grab a table in the lovely beer garden and stave off a hangover with honest-to-goodness German classics or try one of the flavour-packed vegetarian alternatives.

Schlappen PUB
(⤷ 0761-334 94⧸; www.schlappen.com; Löwenstrasse 2; ⊙ 11am-1am Mon-Wed, to 2am Thu, to 3am Fri & Sat, 3pm-1am Sun) In historic digs and crammed with antiques and vintage theatre posters, this rocking, evergreen pub has made the magic happen for generations of students. Check out the skeleton in the men's toilet. Summer terrace.

❶ Information

Tourist Office (⤷ 0761-388 1880; www.freiburg.de; Rathausplatz 2-4; ⊙ 8am-8pm Mon-Fri, 9.30am-5pm Sat, 10.30am-3.30pm Sun) Pick up the three-day WelcomeKarte (€25), covering all public transport and the Schauinslandbahn, at Freiburg's central tourist office.

❶ Getting There & Away

Connections include ICE trains to Basel (from €19, 45 minutes) and Baden-Baden (from €18.10, 45 minutes).

LOCAL KNOWLEDGE

SOARING ABOVE THE FOREST

Freiburg seems tiny as you drift up above the city and a tapestry of meadows and forest on the **Schauinslandbahn** (⤷ 451 1777; www.schauinslandbahn.de; return adult/child €12.50/8, one way €9/6; ⊙ 9am-5pm Oct-Jun, to 6pm Jul-Sep) to the 1284m Schauinsland peak. The lift provides a speedy link between Freiburg and the Black Forest highlands.

FRANKFURT & THE RHINELAND

Defined by the mighty Rhine, fine wines, medieval castles and romantic villages, Germany's heartland speaks to the imagination. Even Frankfurt, which may seem all buttoned-up business, reveals itself as a laid-back metropolis with fabulous museums and pulsating nightlife.

Frankfurt-am-Main

⤷ 069 / POP 709,395

Unashamedly high-rise, Frankfurt-on-the-Main (pronounced 'mine') is a true capital of finance and business and hosts some of Europe's key trade fairs. But despite its business demeanour, Frankfurt consistently ranks high among Germany's most liveable cities thanks to its rich collection of museums, expansive parks and greenery, a lively student scene and excellent public transport.

◉ Sights

★ **Kaiserdom** CATHEDRAL
(Imperial/Frankfurt Cathedral; www.dom-frankfurt.de; Domplatz 1; tower adult/concession €3.50/1.50; ⊙ church 8am-8pm Mon-Thu, noon-8pm Fri, 9am-8pm Sat & Sun, tower 9am-6pm Apr-Oct, 11am-5pm Thu-Mon Nov-Mar; Ⓢ Dom/Römer) Frankfurt's red-sandstone cathedral is dominated by a 95m-high Gothic **tower**, which can be climbed via 324 steps. Construction began in the 13th century; from 1356 to 1792, the Holy Roman Emperors were elected (and, after 1562, consecrated and crowned) in the **Wahlkapelle** at the end of the right aisle (look for the 'skull' altar). The cathedral was rebuilt both after an 1867 fire and after the bombings of 1944, which left it a burnt-out shell.

Frankfurt-am-Main

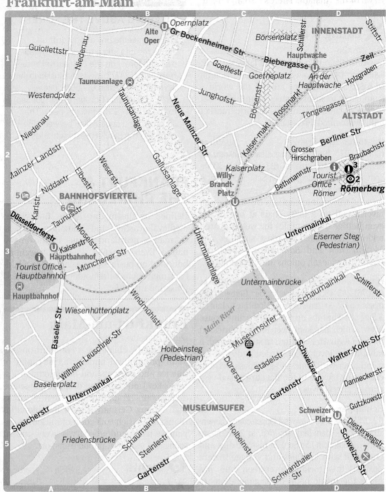

★ **Römberg** SQUARE

(⑤ Dom/Römer) The Römberg is Frankfurt's old central square. Ornately gabled half-timbered buildings, reconstructed after WWII, give an idea of how beautiful the city's medieval core once was.

In the square's centre is the **Gerechtigkeitsbrunnen** (Fountain of Justice; Römberg); in 1612, at the coronation of Matthias, the fountain ran with wine. The Römberg is especially lovely as a backdrop for the **Christmas market** (Weihnachtsmarkt; ⊙ 10am-9pm Mon-Sat, 11am-9pm Sun late Nov-23 Dec).

Museumsufer Frankfurt MUSEUM

(www.museumsufer-frankfurt.de; south bank of the Main River, btwn Eiserner Steg & Friedensbrücke; ⑤ Schweizer Platz) More than a dozen museums line up along the south bank of the Main River, collectively known as the Museumsufer. The most famous is the **Städel Museum** (☑ 069-605 098; www.staedelmuseum. de; Schaumainkai 63; adult/child €14/12; ⊙ 10am-7pm Tue, Wed, Sat & Sun, to 9pm Thu & Fri May-Jun & Sep, 10am-9pm daily Jul & Aug, 10am-6pm Tue, Wed, Sat & Sun, to 9pm Thu & Fri Oct-Apr; ☎; 🚌 16 Otto-Hahn-Platz), a renowned art gallery, but fans of architecture, archaeology, applied arts,

inside the turn-of-the-20th-century gabled building it's a sanctuary of parquet floors, boldly coloured walls and designer furniture. Facilities include a laundry and 24-hour bar with a billiard table; breakfast costs €4.50. A private apartment sleeping up to four people with a private bathroom and kitchen costs €426 per week.

25hours Hotel by Levi's   DESIGN HOTEL €€
(☑069-256 6770; www.25hours-hotels.com; Niddastrasse 58; d weekday/weekend from €149/89; P❄@☎; ®Hauptbahnhof) Inspired by Levi's (yes, the jeans brand), this hipster haven has a rooftop terrace, free bike hire, and a Gibson Music Room for jamming on drums and guitars. Rooms are themed by decade, from the 1930s (calm colours) to the 1980s (tiger-print walls, optical-illusion carpets). Breakfast costs a whopping €18.

★**Villa Orange**   BOUTIQUE HOTEL €€
(☑069-405 840; www.villa-orange.de; Hebelstrasse 1; s/d weekday from €130/160, weekend from €105/129; P❄☎; ⊞12/18 Friedberger Platz) ✿ Offering a winning combination of tranquillity, modern German design and small-hotel comforts (such as a quiet corner library), this century-old, tangerine-coloured villa has 38 spacious rooms, some with free-standing baths and four-poster beds. Everything is organic – the sheets, the soap and the bountiful buffet breakfast.

film and ethnology will also get their fill. Bus 46, which leaves from the Hauptbahnhof several times hourly, links most museums.

🛏 Sleeping

If a big trade show is in town (and it often is) prices can triple. In general, rates drop on weekends.

Five Elements   HOSTEL €
(☑069-2400 5885; www.5elementshostel.de; Moselstrasse 40; dm/s/d from €18/45/56; ☎; ®Hauptbahnhof) The location mightn't be Frankfurt's most salubrious, but once you're

---

LOCAL KNOWLEDGE

APPLE-WINE TAVERNS

Apple-wine taverns are Frankfurt's great local tradition. They serve *Ebbelwei* (Frankfurt dialect for *Apfelwein*), an alcoholic apple cider, along with local specialities like *Handkäse mit Musik* (literally, 'hand-cheese with music'). This is a round cheese soaked in oil and vinegar and topped with onions; your bowel supplies the music. Anything with *Grüne Sosse*, a herb sauce, is also a winner. **Fichtekränzi** (☑069-612 778; www.fichtekraenzi.de; Wallstrasse 5; ⊘5pm-1am Mon-Sat, 4pm-1am Sun; ⓡ14/18 Frankensteiner Platz) and **Adolf Wagner** (☑069-612 565; www.apfelwein -wagner.com; Schweizer Strasse 71; mains €8-18; ⊘11am-midnight; Ⓢ Schweizer Platz) in Alt-Sachsenhausen are recommended traditional taverns.

✗ Eating & Drinking

The pedestrian strip west of Hauptwache square is nicknamed Fressgass (literally 'Grazing Street') thanks to its many (average) eateries. Cosy apple-wine taverns cluster in Alt-Sachsenhausen south of the Main.

★ Kleinmarkthalle
MARKET €

(www.kleinmarkthalle.de; Hasengasse 5-7; ⊘8am-6pm Mon-Fri, to 4pm Sat; Ⓢ Dom/Römer) 🖋 Aromatic stalls inside this bustling traditional market hall sell artisan smoked sausages, cheeses, roasted nuts, breads, pretzels, loose-leaf teas, and pastries, cakes and chocolates, as well as fruit, vegetables, spices, fresh Italian pastas, Greek olives, meat, poultry and, downstairs, fish. It's unmissable for picnickers or self-caterers, or anyone wanting to experience Frankfurt life. The upper-level wine bar opens to a terrace.

Bitter & Zart
CAFE €

(☑069-9494 2846; www.bitterundzart.de; Braubachstrasse 14; dishes €4-8; ⊘10am-7pm Mon-Sat, 11am-6pm Sun; Ⓢ Dom/Römer) Walk past the shelves piled high with chocolate pralines to order espresso, hot chocolate and luscious cakes such as lemon cake, carrot cake and *Frankfurt Kränze* (butter-cream cake), with gluten-free options.

★ Dauth-Schneider
GERMAN €€

(☑069-613 533; www.dauth-schneider.de; Neuer Wall 5; mains €4-14.50; ⊘kitchen 11.30am-midnight; ⓡLokalbahnhof) With a history stretching back to 1849 (the basement housed an apple winery), this convivial tavern is not only a wonderful place to sample the local drop but also classic regional specialities such as *Sulz Fleisch* (cold meat and jelly terrine), pork knuckle with sauerkraut, Frankfurter schnitzel, sausages and various tasting platters. Tables fill the tree-shaded terrace in summer.

ⓘ Information

Tourist Office – Hauptbahnhof (☑069-2123 8800; www.frankfurt-tourismus.de; Main Hall, Hauptbahnhof; ⊘8am-9pm Mon-Fri, 9am-6pm Sat & Sun; ⓡHauptbahnhof) At the main train station.

Tourist Office – Römer (☑069-2123 8800; www.frankfurt-tourismus.de; Römerberg 27; ⊘9.30am-5.30pm Mon-Fri, to 4pm Sat & Sun; Ⓢ Dom/Römer) Smallish office in the central square.

ⓘ Getting There & Away

AIR

Frankfurt Airport (FRA; www.frankfurt-airport.com; 🛜; ⓡFlughafen Regionalbahnhof), 12km southwest of the city centre, is Germany's busiest. S-Bahn lines S8 and S9 shuttle between the airport's regional train station (Regionalbahnhof) and the city centre (€4.55, 15 minutes) several times hourly.

Note that **Frankfurt-Hahn Airport** (HHN; www.hahn-airport.de), served by Ryanair, is actually 125km west of Frankfurt, near the Mosel Valley. Buses to Frankfurt's Hauptbahnhof take 1¾ hours and should be booked ahead.

BUS

The Romantic Road Coach and long-distance buses leave from the south side of the Hauptbahnhof.

TRAIN

There are direct trains to pretty much everywhere, including Berlin (€123, 4¼ hours) and Munich (from €82, 3½ hours).

The Romantic Rhine Valley

Between Bingen and Koblenz, the Rhine cuts deeply through the Rhenish slate mountains. Forested hillsides cradle craggy cliffs and nearly vertical terraced vineyards. Idyllic villages appear around each bend, their neat half-timbered houses and church steeples seemingly plucked from the world of fairy tales. High above the river, busy with barge traffic, are the famous medieval castles, some ruined, some restored, all vestiges from a mysterious past.

Although Koblenz and Mainz are logical starting points, the area can also be explored on a long day trip from Frankfurt.

Bacharach

One of the prettiest of the Rhine villages, Bacharach conceals its considerable charms behind a 14th-century town wall. Beyond the thick arched gateways awaits a beautiful medieval old town graced with half-timbered townhouses lining Oberstrasse, the main thoroughfare. There's no shortage of atmospheric places to eat and sample the local vintages.

For gorgeous views of village, vineyards and river, take a stroll atop the **medieval ramparts**, which are punctuated by guard towers. An especially scenic panorama unfolds from the **Postenturm** at the north end of town, from where you can also espy the filigreed ruins of the **Wernerkapelle**, a medieval chapel, and the turrets of the 12th-century hilltop **Burg Stahleck**, a castle turned **youth hostel** (✆06743-1266; www.jugendherberge.de; dm/s/d €22/27/54; P @).

Another good place to stay is the **Rhein Hotel** (✆06743-1243; www.rhein-hotel-bacharach.de; Langstrasse 50; s €39-68, d €78-136; P ❀ 🛜), which has 14 well-lit rooms with original artwork and a respected restaurant.

St Goar & St Goarshausen

These twin towns face each other across the Rhine. On the left bank, St Goar is lorded over by **Burg Rheinfels** (✆06741-7753; www.st-goar.de; adult/child €5/2.50; ⊗9am-6pm mid-Mar–late Oct, 11am-5pm late Oct–mid-Nov). Once the mightiest fortress on the Rhine, Burg Rheinfels was built in 1245 by Count Dieter V of Katzenelnbogen as a base for his toll-collecting operations. Its size and labyrinthine layout are astonishing.

A ferry links St Goar with St Goarshausen and the most fabled spot along the Romantic Rhine, the **Loreley Rock**. This vertical slab of slate owes its fame to a mythical maiden whose siren songs are said to have lured sailors to their death in the river's treacherous currents. A **Besucherzentrum** (✆06771-599

093; www.loreley-besucherzentrum.de; Loreleyring 7; adult/child €2.50/1.50, parking €2; ⊗10am-6pm Apr-Oct, 10am-5pm Mar, 11am-4pm Sat & Sun Nov-Feb) at the top of the rock reveals more.

A classy spot to spend the night is **Romantik Hotel Schloss Rheinfels** (✆06741-8020; www.schloss-rheinfels.de; Schlossberg 47; s/d weekday from €95/130, weekend €110/140; P @ 🛜 ✉), right by the castle. Its three restaurants enjoy a fine reputation but there are plenty more down in the village.

Braubach

Framed by forested hillsides, vineyards and rose gardens, the 1300-year-old town of Braubach, 8km south of Koblenz, centres on a small, half-timbered market square. High above are the dramatic towers, turrets and crenellations of the 700-year-old **Marksburg** (✆02627-206; www.marksburg.de; adult/child €7/5; ⊗10am-5pm mid-Mar–Oct, 11am-4pm Nov–mid-Mar), which – unique among the Rhine fortresses – was never destroyed. Tours (in English at 1pm and 4pm from late March to October) take in the citadel, the Gothic hall, the kitchen and the torture chamber.

Koblenz

Founded by the Romans, Koblenz sits at the confluence of the Rhine and Moselle Rivers, a point known as **Deutsches Eck** (German Corner) and dominated by a bombastic

GERMANY THE ROMANTIC RHINE VALLEY

ROMANCING THE RHINE

The Romantic Rhine Valley villages have plenty more charmers that deserve at least a quick spin. Just pick one at random and make your own discoveries. Here are some teasers:

Boppard Roman ruins and a cable car to the stunning Vierseenblick viewpoint (left bank).

Oberwesel Famous for its 3km-long medieval town wall punctuated by 16 guard towers (left bank).

Assmannhausen Relatively untouristed village known for its red wines, sweeping views and good hikes (right bank).

Rüdesheim Day-tripper-deluged but handy launchpad for the mighty Niederwalddenkmal monument and Eberbach Monastery (right bank).

> **ℹ EXPLORING THE ROMANTIC RHINE**
>
> Each mode of transport on the Rhine has its own advantages and all are equally enjoyable. Try combining several.
>
> **Boat** From about Easter to October (winter services are very limited), passenger ships run by **Köln-Düsseldorfer** (☑ 0221-208 8318; www.k-d.com) link villages on a set timetable. You're free to get on and off as you like.
>
> **Car** No bridges span the Rhine between Koblenz and Bingen but you can easily change banks by using a car ferry (*Autofähre*). There are five routes: Bingen–Rüdesheim, Niederheimbach–Lorch, Boppard–Filsen, Oberwesel–Kaub and St Goar–Goarshausen.
>
> **Train** Villages on the Rhine's left bank (eg Bacharach and Boppard) are served regularly by local trains on the Koblenz–Mainz run. Right-bank villages such as Rüdesheim, St Goarshausen and Braubach are linked hourly to Koblenz' Hauptbahnhof and Frankfurt by the RheingauLinie train.

19th-century statue of Kaiser Wilhelm I on horseback. On the right Rhine bank high above the Deutsches Eck – and reached by an 850m-long **Seilbahn** (cable car; www.seilbahn-koblenz.de; return adult/child €9/4, incl fortress €11.80/5.60; ⊙ 10am-6pm or 7pm Apr-Oct, to 5pm Nov-Mar) – is the **Festung Ehrenbreitstein** (☑ 0261-6675 4000; www.diefestungehrenbreitstein.de; adult/child €6/3, incl cable car €11.80/5.60; ⊙ 10am-6pm Apr-Oct, to 5pm Nov-Mar), one of Europe's mightiest citadels. Views are great and there's a restaurant and a regional museum inside.

Moselle Valley

Like a vine right before harvest, the Moselle hangs heavy with visitor fruit. Castles and towns with half-timbered buildings are built along the sinuous river below steep, rocky cliffs planted with vineyards. It's one of Germany's most evocative regions, with stunning views revealed at every river bend. Unlike the Romantic Rhine, it's spanned by plenty of bridges. The most scenic section unravels between Bernkastel-Kues and Cochem, 50km apart and linked by the B421.

Cochem

Easily reached by train or boat from Koblenz, Cochem is one of the most popular destinations on the Moselle thanks to its fairytale-like **Reichsburg** (☑ 02671-255; www.burg-cochem.de; Schlossstrasse 36; tours adult/child €6/3; ⊙ tours 9am-5pm mid-Mar-Oct, 10am-3pm Nov & Dec, 11am, noon & 1pm Wed, Sat & Sun Jan-mid-Mar). Like many others, the 11th-century original fell victim to frenzied Frenchmen in 1689, then stood ruined for centuries until a wealthy Berliner snapped it up for a pittance in 1868 and had it restored to its current – if not always architecturally faithful - glory. The 40-minute tours (in German but English leaflet available) take in decorative rooms reflecting 1000 years' worth of tastes and styles.

The **tourist office** (☑ 02671-600 40; www.cochem.de; Endertplatz 1; ⊙ 9am-5pm Mon-Sat, 10am-3pm Sun May-Oct, 9am-5pm Mon-Fri Apr, 9am-1pm & 2-5pm Mon-Fri Nov-Mar) has information about the entire region.

Cochem is 55km from Koblenz via the scenic B327 and B49. Regional trains shuttling between Trier (€15.90, 45 minutes) and Koblenz (€11.90, 50 minutes) stop here as well.

Beilstein

Picture-perfect Beilstein is little more than a cluster of higgledy-piggledy houses surrounded by steep vineyards. Its historic highlights include the **Marktplatz** and the ruined hilltop castle **Burg Metternich** (☑ 02673-936 39; admission €2.50; ⊙ 9am-6pm Apr-Nov) – oh the views! The **Zehnthauskeller** (☑ 02673-900 907; www.zehnthauskeller.de; Marktplatz; ⊙ 11am-10pm Tue-Sat, noon-10pm Sun) houses a romantically dark, vaulted wine tavern owned by the same family that also runs two local hotels. There is no tourist office nor an ATM.

Bus 716 goes from Cochem to Beilstein (€3.65, 20 minutes) almost hourly in season, although the approach by boat is more scenic (€12, one hour).

Bernkastel-Kues

This charming twin town straddles the Moselle about 50km downriver from Trier and is close to some of the river's most famous vineyards. The prettier of the two – Bernkastel on the right bank – is a symphony in half-timber, stone and slate and teems with wine taverns.

Get your heart pumping by hoofing it up to **Burg Landshut**, a ruined 13th-century castle on a bluff above town. Allow 30 minutes to be rewarded with glorious valley views and a cold drink at the beer garden. Alternatively, shuttle buses leave from the riverfront.

The **tourist office** (☑06531-500 190; www. bernkastel.de; Gestade 6, ☺9am-5pm Mon-Fri, 10am-5pm Sat, 10am-1pm Sun May-Oct, 9.30am-4pm Mon-Fri Nov-Apr) is in Bernkastel.

Coming from Trier, drivers should follow the B53. Using public transport involves catching the regional train to Wittlich and switching to bus 300.

Trier

☑0651 / POP 106,544

A Unesco World Heritage site since 1986, Germany's oldest city is home to its finest ensemble of ancient Roman monuments, among them a mighty gate, amphitheater and thermal baths. Architectural treasures from later ages include Germany's oldest Gothic church and Karl Marx' birthplace.

◉ Sights

★ Porta Nigra   GATE
(adult/child €4/3; ☺9am-6pm Apr-Sep, to 5pm Mar & Oct, to 4pm Nov-Feb) This brooding 2nd-century Roman city gate – blackened by time (hence the name, Latin for 'black gate') – is a marvel of engineering since it's held together by nothing but gravity and iron clamps.

In the 11th century, the structure was turned into a church to honour Simeon, a Greek hermit who spent six years walled up in its east tower. After his death in 1134, he was buried inside the gate and later became a saint.

★ Konstantin Basilika   CHURCH
(☑0651-9949 1200; www.ekkt.ekir.de; Konstantinplatz 10; ☺10am-6pm Mon-Sat, 1-6pm Sun Apr-Oct, 10am-noon & 2-4pm Mon-Sat, 1-4pm Sun Nov-Mar) Constructed around AD 310 as Constantine's throne room, the brick-built basilica is now an austere Protestant church. With built-to-impress dimensions (some 67m long, 27m wide and 33m high), it's the largest single-room Roman structure still in existence. A new organ, with 87 registers and 6500 pipes, generates a seven-fold echo.

★ Amphitheatre   ROMAN SITE
(Olewiger Strasse; adult/child €4/3; ☺9am-6pm Apr-Sep, to 5pm Mar & Oct, to 4pm Nov-Feb) Trier's Roman amphitheatre could accommodate 20,000 spectators for gladiator tournaments and animal fights. Beneath the arena are dungeons where prisoners sentenced to death waited next to starving beasts for the final showdown.

★ Kaiserthermen   ROMAN SITE
(Imperial Baths; Weberbachstrasse 41; adult/child €4/3; ☺9am-6pm Apr-Sep, to 5pm Mar & Oct, to 4pm Nov-Feb) Get a sense of the layout of this vast Roman thermal bathing complex with its striped brick-and-stone arches from the corner lookout tower, then descend into an underground labyrinth consisting of cavernous hot and cold water baths, boiler rooms and heating channels.

★ Trierer Dom   CATHEDRAL
(☑0651-979 0790; www.dominformation.de; Liebfrauenstrasse 12, cnr of Domfreihof; ☺6.30am-6pm Apr-Oct, to 5.30pm Nov-Mar) FREE Looming above the Roman palace of Helena (Emperor Constantine's mother), this cathedral is Germany's oldest bishop's church and still retains Roman sections. Today's edifice is a study in nearly 1700 years of church architecture with Romanesque, Gothic and baroque elements. Intriguingly, its floor plan is of a 12-petalled flower, symbolising the Virgin Mary.

To see some dazzling ecclesiastical equipment and peer into early Christian history, head upstairs to the **Domschatz** (Cathedral Treasury; ☑0651-710 5378; adult/child €1.50/0.50; ☺10am-5pm Mon-Sat, 12.30-5pm Sun Mar-Oct & Dec, 11am-4pm Tue-Sat, 12.30-4pm Sun & Mon Nov, Jan&Feb) or around the corner to the **Museum am Dom Trier** (☑0651-710 5255; www.bistum-trier.de/museum; Bischof-Stein-Platz 1; adult/child €3.50/2; ☺9am-5pm Tue-Sat, 1-5pm Sun).

🛏 Sleeping

Evergreen Hostel   HOSTEL €
(☑0651-6998 7026, outside office hours 0157 8856 9594; www.evergreen-hostel.de; Gartenfeldstrasse 7; dm from €17, s/d from €42/52, without bathroom from €38/50; ☺reception 8-11am & 2-7pm May-Oct, 9-11am & 3-6pm Nov-Apr; @ 🛜) This laid-back indie hostel has a piano in the common kitchen and 12 attractive, spacious rooms, most with private bathrooms. Breakfast costs €6. Outside office hours, call ahead to arrange your arrival.

WORTH A TRIP

BURG ELTZ

At the head of the beautiful Eltz Valley, Burg Eltz (☑02672-950 500; www.burg-eltz.de; Burg-Eltz-Strasse 1, Wierschem; tour adult/child €9/6.50; ⊙9.30am-5.30pm Apr-Oct) is one of Germany's most romantic medieval castles. Never destroyed, this vision of turrets, towers, oriels, gables and half-timber has squatted atop a rock framed by thick forest for nearly 900 years and is still owned by the original family. The decorations, furnishings, tapestries, fireplaces, paintings and armour you see during the 45-minute tour are also centuries old.

By car, you can reach Burg Eltz via Munstermaifeld. From the car park it's a shuttle bus ride (€2) or 1.3km walk to the castle. Alternatively, take a boat or train to Moselkern village and approach the castle via a lovely 5km walk (or €24 taxi ride).

Hotel Villa Hügel BOUTIQUE HOTEL €€
(☑0651-937 100; www.hotel-villa-huegel.de; Bernhardstrasse 14; s/d from €108/148; P@🛜🏊) Begin the day with sparkling wine at a lavish breakfast buffet at this stylish hillside villa, and end it luxuriating in the 12m indoor pool and Finnish sauna. The 36 rooms are decorated with honey-toned woods.

✗ Eating & Drinking

de Winkel PUB FOOD €
(☑0651-436 1878; www.de-winkel.de; Johannisstrasse 25; mains €6-9.50; ⊙6pm-1am Tue-Thu, to 2am Fri & Sat) Winny and Morris have presided over this locally adored watering hole for years. Join the locals for Pils and a bite, for instance the crispy chicken wings called 'Flieten' in Trier dialect.

★ Weinwirtschaft Friedrich-Wilhelm GERMAN €€
(☑0651-9947 4800; www.weinwirtschaft-fw.de; Weberbach 75; mains €11-26; ⊙kitchen noon-2pm & 6-10pm Mon-Sat, wine shop 11.30am-3pm & 5.30-8pm Tue-Sat) A historic former wine warehouse with exposed brick and hoists now houses this superb restaurant. Creative dishes incorporate local wines, such as trout poached in sparkling white wine with mustard sauce and white asparagus; and local

sausage with Riesling sauerkraut and fried potatoes. Vines trail over the trellis-covered garden; the attached wine shop is a great place to stock up.

ⓘ Information

Tourist Office (☑0651-978 080; www.trier-info.de; An der Porta Nigra; ⊙9am-6pm Mon-Sat, 10am-5pm Sun May-Oct, shorter hours Nov-Apr)

ⓘ Getting There & Away

Frequent direct train connections include Koblenz (€12 to €24, 1½ to two hours), Cologne (€19 to €45, three hours) and Luxembourg (€14 to €30, 50 minutes).

Cologne

☑0221 / POP 1 MILLION

Cologne (Köln) offers lots of attractions, led by its famous cathedral whose filigree twin spires dominate the skyline. The city's museum landscape is especially strong when it comes to art but also has something in store for fans of chocolate, sports and Roman history. Its people are well known for their joie de vivre and it's easy to have a good time right along with them year-round in the beer halls of the Altstadt.

◉ Sights

★ Kölner Dom CATHEDRAL
(Cologne Cathedral; ☑0221-9258 4720; www.koelner-dom.de; tower adult/concession €4/2; ⊙6am-9pm May-Oct, to 7.30pm Nov-Apr, tower 9am-6pm May-Sep, to 5pm Mar, Apr & Oct, to 4pm Nov-Feb) Cologne's geographical and spiritual heart – and its single-biggest tourist draw – is the magnificent Kölner Dom. With its soaring twin spires, this is the Mt Everest of cathedrals, jam-packed with art and treasures. For an exercise fix, climb the 533 steps up the Dom's south tower to the base of the steeple that dwarfed all buildings in Europe until Gustave Eiffel built a certain tower in Paris. The underground Domforum visitor centre is a good source of info and tickets.

The Dom is Germany's largest cathedral and must be circled to truly appreciate its dimensions. Note how its lacy spires and flying buttresses create a sensation of lightness and fragility despite its mass and height.

This sensation continues inside, where a phalanx of pillars and arches supports the lofty nave. Soft light filters through the medieval stained-glass windows, as well as a much-lauded recent window by contemporary artist Gerhard Richter in the transept. A kaleidoscope of 11,500 squares in 72 colours, Richter's abstract design has been called a 'symphony of light'. In the afternoon especially, when the sun hits it just so, it's easy to understand why.

The pièce de résistance among the cathedral's bevy of treasures is the **Shrine of the Three Kings** behind the main altar, a richly bejewelled and gilded sarcophagus said to hold the remains of the kings who followed the star to the stable in Bethlehem where Jesus was born. The bones were spirited out of Milan in 1164 as spoils of war by Emperor Barbarossa's chancellor and instantly turned Cologne into a major pilgrimage site.

Other highlights include the **Gero Crucifix** (970), notable for its monumental size and an emotional intensity rarely achieved in those early medieval days; the choir stalls from 1310, richly carved from oak; and the altar painting (c 1450) by Cologne artist Stephan Lochner.

During your climb up to the 95m-high viewing platform, take a breather and admire the 24-tonne **Peter Bell** (1923), the largest free-swinging working bell in the world.

★ **Römisch-Germanisches Museum**   MUSEUM
(Roman Germanic Museum; ☑ 0221-2212 4438; www.museenkoeln.de; Roncalliplatz 4; adult/concession €9/5; ⊙ 10am-5pm Tue-Sun) Sculptures and ruins displayed outside the entrance are merely the overture to a full symphony of Roman artefacts found along the Rhine. Highlights include the giant **Poblicius tomb** (AD 30–40), the magnificent 3rd-century **Dionysus mosaic**, and astonishingly well-preserved glass items. Insight into daily Roman life is gained from toys, tweezers, lamps and jewellery, the designs of which have changed surprisingly little since Roman times.

Museum Ludwig   MUSEUM
(☑ 0221-2212 6165; www.museum-ludwig.de; Heinrich-Böll-Platz; adult/concession €11/7.50, more during special exhibits; ⊙ 10am-6pm Tue-Sun) A mecca of contemporary art, Museum Ludwig presents a tantalising mix of works from all major phases. Fans of German expressionism (Beckmann, Dix, Kirchner) will get their fill here as much as those with a penchant for Picasso, American pop art (Warhol, Lichtenstein) and Russian avant-garde painter Alexander Rodchenko. Rothko and Pollock are highlights of the abstract collection, while Gursky and Tillmanns are among the reasons the photography section is a must stop.

Wallraf-Richartz-Museum & Fondation Corboud   MUSEUM
(☑ 0221-2212 1119; www.wallraf.museum; Obenmarspforten; adult/concession €12/8; ⊙ 10am-6pm Tue-Sun) A famous collection of European paintings from the 13th to the 19th centuries, the Wallraf-Richartz-Museum occupies a postmodern cube designed by the late OM Ungers. Works are presented chronologically, with the oldest on the 1st floor where standouts include brilliant examples from the Cologne School, known for its distinctive use of colour. The most famous painting is Stefan Lochner's *Madonna of the Rose Bower*.

Schokoladenmuseum   MUSEUM
(Chocolate Museum; ☑ 0221-931 8880; www.schokoladenmuseum.de; Am Schokoladenmuseum 1a; adult/concession €9/6.50; ⊙ 10am-6pm Tue-Fri, 11am-7pm Sat & Sun, last entry 1hr before closing; ⊕) At this high-tech temple to the art of chocolate-making, exhibits on the origin of the 'elixir of the gods', as the Aztecs called it, and the cocoa-growing process are followed by a live-production factory tour and a stop at a chocolate fountain for a sample.

COLOGNE CARNIVAL

Carnival in Cologne is one of the best parties in Europe and a thumb in the eye of the German work ethic. It all starts with *Weiberfastnacht,* the Thursday before Ash Wednesday, when women rule the day (and do things like chop off the ties of their male colleagues/bosses). The party continues through the weekend, with more than 50 parades of ingenious floats and wildly dressed lunatics dancing in the streets. By the time it all comes to a head with the big parade on *Rosenmontag* (Rose Monday), the entire city has come unglued. Those still capable of swaying and singing will live it up one last time on Shrove Tuesday before the curtain comes down on Ash Wednesday.

Cologne

🛏 Sleeping

Station Hostel for Backpackers HOSTEL €
(☎ 0221-912 5301; www.hostel-cologne.de; Marzellenstrasse 44-56; dm €17-24, s/d from €32/48; @ 🛜) Near the Hauptbahnhof, this is a hostel as hostels should be: central, convivial and economical. A lounge gives way to clean, colourful rooms sleeping one to six people. There's lots of free stuff, including linen, internet access, lockers, city maps and guest kitchen. Some private rooms have their own bathrooms.

★ Hopper Hotel et cetera HOTEL €€
(☎ 0221-924 400; www.hopper.de; Brüsseler Strasse 26; s/d from €75/110; 🅿 @ 🛜) A waxen monk welcomes you to this former monastery whose 49 rooms sport eucalyptus floors, cherry furniture and marble baths along with lots of useful features like fridges. The sauna and bar, both in the vaulted cellars, are great places for reliving the day's exploits. The cheapest singles are dubbed 'monastic cells'.

Cologne

Stern am Rathaus HOTEL €€
(⊉0221-2225 1750; www.stern-am-rathaus.de; Bürgerstrasse 6; s/d from €75/105; ❄ 🛜) This small, contemporary hotel has eight nicely spruced-up, luxuriously panelled rooms spread over three floors. It's in a quiet side street smack dab in the Altstadt yet close to sights and plenty of restaurants. Kudos for the extra-comfortable beds, the personalised service and the high-quality breakfast buffet.

✕ Eating & Drinking

There are plenty of beer halls and restaurants in the tourist-adored Altstadt, but for a more local vibe head to student-flavoured Zülpicher Viertel or the Belgisches Viertel, both in the city centre. Local breweries turn out a variety called *Kölsch*, which is relatively light and served in skinny 200mL glasses.

★**Salon Schmitz** MODERN EUROPEAN €€
(⊉0221-9229 9594; www.salonschmitz.com; Aachener Strasse 28; mains from €10; ⊙9am-late, hours vary by venue) Spread over three historic row houses, the Schmitz empire is your one-stop for excellent food and drink. From the casual bistro to excellent seasonal meals in the restaurant to the takeaway deli, you'll find something you like at Schmitz almost any time of day. Wash it all down with the house-brand *Kölsch*.

★**Bei Oma Kleinmann** GERMAN €€
(⊉0221-232 346; www.beiomakleinmann.de; Zülpicher Strasse 9; mains €13-22; ⊙5pm-midnight Tue-Thu & Sun, to 1am Fri & Sat) Named for its long-time owner, who was still cooking almost to her last day at age 95 in 2009, this perennially booked, graffiti-covered restaurant serves oodles of schnitzel, made either with pork or veal and paired with home-made sauces and sides. Pull up a seat at the small wooden tables for a classic Cologne night out.

★**Päffgen** BEER HALL
(⊉0221-135 461; www.paeffgen-koelsch.de; Friesenstrasse 64-66; mains €6-20; ⊙10am-midnight Sun-Thu, to 12.30am Fri & Sat) Busy, loud and boisterous, Päffgen has been pouring *Kölsch* since 1883 and hasn't lost a step since. In summer you can enjoy the refreshing brew and local specialities (€1.10 to €10.70) beneath starry skies in the beer garden.

❶ Information

Tourist Office (⊉0221-346 430; www.cologne-tourism.com; Kardinal-Höffner-Platz 1; ⊙9am-8pm Mon-Sat, 10am-5pm Sun) Excellent; near the cathedral. The app is well done.

❶ Getting There & Away

AIR

Köln Bonn Airport (CGN; Cologne-Bonn Airport; ⊉02203-404 001; www.koeln-bonn-airport.de; Kennedystrasse) is about 18km southeast of the city centre and connected to the Hauptbahnhof by the S-Bahn S13 train every 20 minutes (€2.80, 15 minutes).

TRAIN

Services to and from Cologne are fast and frequent in all directions. A sampling: Berlin (€117, 4¼ hours), Frankfurt (€71, 1¼ hours) and Munich (€142, 4½ hours). In addition there are fast Thalys and ICE trains to Brussels (where you can connect to the Eurostar for London) and Paris.

Düsseldorf

⊉0211 / POP 594,000

Düsseldorf dazzles with boundary-pushing architecture, zinging nightlife and an art scene to rival many a metropolis. It's a posh and modern city whose economy is dominated by banking, advertising, fashion and telecommunications. However, a couple of hours of partying in the boisterous pubs of the Altstadt, the historical quarter along the Rhine, is all you need to realise that locals have no problem letting their hair down once they slip out of those Boss jackets.

WORTH A TRIP

BONN

South of Cologne on the Rhine River, Bonn served as West Germany's capital from 1949 until 1990. For visitors, the birthplace of Ludwig van Beethoven has plenty in store, not least the great composer's birth house, a string of top-rated museums and the lovely riverside setting.

The **Beethoven-Haus** (☎0228-981 7525; www.beethoven-haus-bonn.de; Bonngasse 24-26; adult/concession €6/4.50; ⏲10am-6pm Apr-Oct, 10am-5pm Mon-Sat, 11am-5pm Sun Nov-Mar), where the composer was born in 1770, is big on memorabilia concerning his life and music. A highlight is his last piano, which was outfitted with an amplified sounding board to accommodate his deafness. Tickets are also good for an adjacent interactive Beethoven-themed 3D multimedia show.

Bonn's most stellar museums line up neatly on Museumsmeile (Museum Mile) in the heart of the former government quarter along Willy-Brandt-Allee just south of the city centre (take U-Bahn lines 16, 63 and 66). A top contender is the **Kunstmuseum Bonn** (Bonn Art Museum; ☎0228-776 260; www.kunstmuseum-bonn.de; Friedrich-Ebert-Allee 2; adult/concession €7/3.50; ⏲11am-6pm Tue & Thu-Sun, to 9pm Wed), which presents 20th-century art, including a standout collection of works by August Macke and other Rhenish expressionists. History buffs gravitate to the **Haus der Geschichte** (Museum of History; ☎0228-916 50; www.hdg.de; Willy-Brandt-Allee 14; ⏲9am-7pm Tue-Fri, 10am-6pm Sat & Sun) FREE for an engaging romp through Germany's post-WWII history.

The **tourist office** (☎0228-775 000; www.bonn-region.de; Windeckstrasse 1; ⏲10am-6pm Mon-Fri, to 4pm Sat, to 2pm Sun) is just off Münsterplatz and a three-minute walk, along Poststrasse, from the Hauptbahnhof.

The U-Bahn lines 16 and 18 (€7.70, one hour) and regional trains (€7.70, 30 minutes) link Cologne and Bonn several times hourly.

Sights

K20 Grabbeplatz MUSEUM
(☎0211-838 1204; Grabbeplatz 5; adult/child €12/2.50; ⏲10am-6pm Tue-Fri, 11am-6pm Sat & Sun) A collection that spans the arc of 20th-century artistic vision gives the K20 an enviable edge in the art world. It encompasses major works by Picasso, Matisse and Mondrian and more than 100 paintings and drawings by Paul Klee. Americans represented include Jackson Pollock, Andy Warhol and Jasper John. Düsseldorf's own Joseph Beuys has a major presence as well.

K21 Ständehaus MUSEUM
(☎0211-838 1204; Ständehausstrasse 1; adult/child €12/2.50; ⏲10am-6pm Tue-Fri, 11am-6pm Sat & Sun) A stately 19th-century parliament building forms a fabulous dichotomy to the cutting-edge art of the K21 – a collection showcasing only works created after the 1980s. Large-scale film and video installations and groups of works share space with site-specific rooms by an international cast of artists including Andreas Gursky, Candida Höfer, Bill Viola and Nam June Paik.

Medienhafen ARCHITECTURE
(Am Handelshafen) This once-dead old harbour area has been reborn as the Medienhafen, an increasingly hip quarter filled with architecture, restaurants, bars, hotels and clubs. Once-crumbling warehouses have turned into high-tech office buildings and now rub shoulders with bold new structures designed by celebrated international architects, including Frank Gehry.

Sleeping

Max Hotel Garni PENSION €€
(☎0211-386 800; www.max-hotelgarni.de; Adersstrasse 65; s/d €75/90; @ 📶) Upbeat, contemporary and run with personal flair, this charmer is a favourite Düsseldorf bargain. The 11 rooms are good-sized and decked out in bright hues and warm woods. Rates include coffee, tea, soft drinks and a regional public transport pass; breakfast costs €7.50. The reception isn't always staffed, so call ahead to arrange an arrival time.

★**Hotel Windsor** HOTEL €€
(☎0211-914 680; www.sir-astor.de; Grafenberger Allee 36; s/d from €89/94; P ⊖ @ 📶) With the same owner as the Sir & Lady Astor, the

Windsor commits itself to the British country tradition. Behind the sandstone facade of this 100-year-old mansion await 18 rooms where you can unwind beneath stucco-ornamented ceilings surrounded by antiques and sedate prints.

✖ Eating & Drinking

The local beverage of choice is *Altbier*, a dark and semisweet beer typical of Düsseldorf.

★ **Brauerei im Füchschen** GERMAN €€
(☑ 0211-137 4716; www.fuechschen.de; Ratinger Strasse 28; mains €6-16; ☺9am-1am Mon-Thu, to 2am Fri & Sat, to midnight Sun) Boisterous, packed and drenched with local colour, the 'Little Fox' in the Altstadt is all you expect a Rhenish beer hall to be. The kitchen makes a mean *Schweinshaxe* (roast pork leg). The high-ceilinged interior echoes with the mirthful roar of people enjoying their meals. This is one of the best *Altbier* breweries in town.

★ **Zum Uerige** BEER HALL
(☑ 0211-866 990; www.uerige.de; Berger Strasse 1; ☺10am-midnight) This cavernous brewpub is the quintessential Düsseldorf haunt to try the city's typical *Altbier*. The suds flow so quickly from giant copper vats that the waiters – called *Köbes* – simply carry huge trays of brew and plonk down a glass whenever they spy an empty. Even on a cold day, the outside tables are alive with merriment.

ℹ Information

Tourist Office – Altstadt (☑ 0211-1720 2840; www.duesseldorf-tourismus.de; cnr Marktstrasse & Rheinstrasse; ☺10am-6pm) Right in the heart of the old centre.

Tourist Office – Hauptbahnhof (☑ 0211-1720 2844; www.duesseldorf-tourismus.de; Immermannstrasse 65b; ☺9.30am-7pm Mon-Fri, to 5pm Sat) The main tourist office, across from the train station; has an exchange window.

ℹ Getting There & Away

Düsseldorf International Airport (DUS; ☑ 0211-4210; www.dus.com) is linked to the city centre by the S-Bahn line 1 (€2.60, 10 minutes).

Regional trains travel to Cologne (€12, 30 minutes), Bonn (€19, one hour) and Aachen (€23, 1½ hours). Fast ICE train links include Berlin (€111, 4¼ hours), Hamburg (€82, 3½ hours) and Frankfurt (€82, 1½ hours).

Aachen

☑ 0241 / POP 240,100

Aachen makes for an excellent day trip from Cologne or Düsseldorf as well as a worthy overnight stop. The Romans nursed their war wounds and stiff joints in the steaming waters of Aachen's mineral springs, but it was Charlemagne who put the city firmly on the European map. His legacy lives on in the stunning Dom, which in 1978 became Germany's first Unesco World Heritage site, as well as the new Centre Charlemagne.

◉ Sights

★ **Aachener Dom** CATHEDRAL
(☑ 0241-447 090; www.aachendom.de; Münsterplatz; ☺7am-7pm Apr-Dec, to 6pm Jan-Mar) It's impossible to overestimate the significance of Aachen's magnificent cathedral. The burial place of Charlemagne, it's where more than 30 German kings were crowned and where pilgrims have flocked since the 12th century. Before entering the church, stop by **Dom Information** (☑ 0241-4770 9145; www.aachendom.de; Johannes-Paul-II-Strasse; ☺10am-5pm Jan-Mar, to 6pm Apr-Dec) for info and tickets for tours and the cathedral treasury.

The oldest and most impressive section is Charlemagne's palace chapel, the **Pfalzkapelle**, an outstanding example of Carolingian architecture. Completed in 800, the year of the emperor's coronation, it's an octagonal dome encircled by a 16-sided

LOCAL KNOWLEDGE

FLINGERN FLING

Once all working-class, Flingern, a neighbourhood east of the Hauptbahnhof, is now the centre of Düsseldorf's stylish hipness. The main strip is a 1km-stretch of leafy Ackerstrasse, where retail therapy gets a unique twist in indie boutiques stocked with vintage frocks, edgy jewellery, whimsical tees, handmade accessories and gourmet foods.

There are cafes by the dozen; try arty, punky **Café Hüftgold** (www.cafehueftgold.de; Ackerstrasse 113; snacks from €3; ☺8am-7pm Mon-Wed, to 10pm Thu & Fri, 9am-10pm Sat, 10am-10pm Sun) or join the mixed and merry mobs on the terrace at **Beethoven** (☑ 0211-2339 8687; Ackerstrasse 106; ☺10am-midnight).

ambulatory supported by antique Italian pillars. The colossal brass chandelier was a gift from Emperor Friedrich Barbarossa, during whose reign Charlemagne was canonised in 1165.

Pilgrims have poured into town ever since that time, drawn as much by the cult surrounding Charlemagne as by his prized relics: Christ's loincloth from when he was crucified, Mary's cloak, the clothes used for John the Baptist when he was beheaded and swaddling clothes from when Jesus was an infant. These are displayed once every seven years (next in 2021) and draw 100,000 or more of the faithful.

To accommodate these regular floods of visitors, a Gothic choir was docked to the chapel in 1414 and filled with such priceless treasures as the pala d'oro, a gold-plated altar-front depicting Christ's Passion, and the jewel-encrusted gilded copper pulpit, both fashioned in the 11th century. At the far end is the gilded shrine of Charlemagne that has held the emperor's remains since 1215. In front, the equally fanciful shrine of St Mary shelters the cathedral's four prized relics.

Unless you join a guided tour (adult/concession €4/3; ☉tours 11am-5.30pm Mon-Fri, 1-5pm Sat & Sun, 2pm tour in English daily), you'll barely get a glimpse of the white marble of Charlemagne's imperial throne in the upstairs gallery. Reached via six steps – just like King Solomon's throne – it served as the coronation throne of those 30 German kings between 936 and 1531.

Rathaus
HISTORIC BUILDING
(Town Hall; ☑0241-432 7310; Markt; adult/concession incl audioguide €5/3; ☉10am-6pm) Fifty life-size statues of German rulers, including 30 kings crowned in town between 936 and 1531 AD, adorn the facade of Aachen's splendid Gothic town hall. It was built in the 14th century atop the foundations of Charlemagne's palace, of which only the eastern tower, the Granusturm, survives. Inside, the undisputed highlight is the Krönungssaal (Coronation Hall) with its epic 19th-century frescos and replicas of the imperial insignia: a crown, orb and sword (the originals are in Vienna). The Rathaus faces the Markt.

Centre Charlemagne
MUSEUM
(☑0241-432 4994; www.route-charlemagne.eu; Katschhof 1; adult/concession €6/3; ☉10am-5pm Tue-Sat) Overlooking the Katschhof square and right in the midst of where the great man walked, this museum looks at not only the life and times of Charlemagne but also Aachen's dramatic history. Multimedia exhibits bring the Roman era to life, and significant moments ever since. Begin your Route Charlemagne walk here; there is a huge amount of info in English.

🛏 Sleeping & Eating

Aachen's students have their own 'Latin Quarter' along Pontstrasse northeast of the Markt.

A&O Aachen
HOSTEL, HOTEL €
(☑0241-463 073 300; www.aohostels.com; Hackländerstrasse 5; dm/s/d from €24/60/70; ☎) Vast and utilitarian, you can't beat this flashpacker haven's location next to the train station and close to the centre. All rooms have private bathrooms and there is a lift. At busy times rates can soar past those of plusher digs in town.

★Hotel Drei Könige
HOTEL €€
(☑0241-483 93; www.h3k-aachen.de; Büchel 5; s €109-139, d €139-169; ☎) The radiant Mediterranean decor is an instant mood-warmer at this family-run favourite with its doesn't-get-more-central location. Some of the nine rooms are a tad twee; the four two-room apartments sleep up to four. Breakfast, on the 4th floor, comes with dreamy views over the rooftops and the cathedral.

Alt-Aachener Café-Stuben
CAFE €
(Van den Daele; ☑0241-357 24; Büchel 18; treats from €3; ☉9am-6.30pm Mon-Fri, 10am-6pm Sat & Sun) Leather-covered walls, tiled stoves and antiques forge the yesteryear flair of this rambling cafe institution that dates from 1890 (the building goes back to 1655). Come for all-day breakfast, a light lunch, divine cakes or just to pick up the housemade *Printen*, Aachen's riff on traditional *Lebkuchen*.

★Am Knipp
GERMAN €€
(☑0241-331 68; www.amknipp.de; Bergdriesch 3; mains €9-23; ☉5-11pm Mon & Wed-Fri, from 6pm Sat & Sun) Hungry grazers have stopped by this traditional inn since 1698, and you too will have a fine time enjoying hearty German cuisine served amid a flea market's worth of knick-knacks or, if weather permits, in the big beer garden.

ℹ Information

Tourist Office (☑ 0241-180 2950; www.
aachen-tourist.de; Friedrich-Wilhelm-Platz;
⊙ 9am-6pm Mon-Fri, to 3pm Sat & Sun Apr-
Dec, shorter hours Jan-Mar) Local tourist
information.

ℹ Getting There & Away

Regional trains to Cologne (€17, one hour) run
twice hourly, with some proceeding beyond.
Aachen is a stop for high-speed trains to/from
Brussels and Paris.

HAMBURG & THE NORTH

Germany's windswept and maritime-
flavoured north is dominated by Hamburg, a
metropolis shaped by water and commerce
since the Middle Ages. Bremen is a fabulous
stop with fairy-tale character, and not only
because of the famous Brothers' Grimm
fairy tale starring a certain donkey, dog, cat
and rooster. Those with a sweet tooth should
not miss a side trip to Lübeck, renowned for
its superb marzipan.

Hamburg

☑ 040 / POP 1.8 MILLION
Hamburg's historic label, 'The gateway to
the world', might be a bold claim, but Germany's second-largest city and biggest port
has never been shy. Hamburg has engaged
in business with the world ever since it
joined the Hanseatic League back in the
Middle Ages. Its maritime spirit infuses the
entire city; from architecture to menus to
the cry of gulls, you always know you're near
the water. The city has given rise to vibrant
neighbourhoods awash with multicultural
eateries, as well as the gloriously seedy Reeperbahn red-light district. Hamburg nurtured
the early promise of the Beatles, and today
its distinctive live- and electronic-music
scene thrives in unique harbourside venues.

⊙ Sights

⭐Speicherstadt   AREA
(Am Sandtorkai; ⊙ 24hr; Ⓢ Rödingsmarkt, Messberg) The seven-storey red-brick warehouses
lining the Speicherstadt archipelago are a
famous Hamburg symbol and the largest
continuous warehouse complex in the world,
recognised by Unesco as a World Heritage
Site. Its distinctive architecture is best appre-

ciated on a leisurely wander or a ride on a flat
tour boat (called *Barkasse*). Many buildings
contain shops, cafes and small museums.

⭐Fischmarkt   MARKET
(Grosse Elbstrasse 9; ⊙ 5-9.30am Sun Apr-Oct,
7-9.30am Sun Nov-Mar; 🚌 112 to Fischmarkt,
Ⓡ Reeperbahn) Here's the perfect excuse to
stay up all Saturday night. Every Sunday in
the wee hours, some 70,000 locals and visitors descend upon the famous Fischmarkt
in St Pauli. The market has been running
since 1703, and its undisputed stars are the
boisterous *Marktschreier* (market criers)
who hawk their wares at full volume. Live
bands also entertainingly crank out cover
versions of ancient German pop songs in the
adjoining Fischauktionshalle (Fish Auction Hall).

⭐Miniatur Wunderland   MUSEUM
(☑ 040-300 6800; www.miniatur-wunderland.de;
Kehrwieder 2; adult/child €13/6.50; ⊙ 9.30am-
6pm Mon, Wed & Thu, to 9pm Tue, to 7pm Fri, 8am-
9pm Sat, 8.30am-8pm Sun; Ⓢ Messberg) Even
the worst cynics are quickly transformed
into fans of this vast miniature world that
goes on and on. The model trains wending
their way through the Alps are impressive –
but slightly predictable. But when you see a
model A380 swoop out of the sky and land
at the fully functional model of Hamburg's
airport, you can't help but gasp and say
OMG! On weekends and in summer holidays, prepurchase your ticket online to skip
the queues.

⭐Hamburger Kunsthalle   MUSEUM
(☑ 040-428 131 257; www.hamburger-kunsthalle.
de; Glockengiesserwall; adult/child weekdays
€12/free, weekends €14/free, Thu 6-9pm €8/
free; ⊙ 10am-6pm Tue, Wed & Fri-Sun, to 9pm Thu;
Ⓢ Hauptbahnhof) A treasure trove of art from
the Renaissance to the present day, the Kunsthalle spans two buildings linked by an
underground passage. The main building
houses works ranging from medieval portraiture to 20th-century classics, such as
Klee and Kokoschka. There's also a memorable room of 19th-century landscapes by
Caspar David Friedrich. Its stark white modern cube, the Galerie der Gegenwart, showcases contemporary German artists.

St Michaelis Kirche   CHURCH
(Church of St Michael; ☑ 040-376 780; www.
st-michaelis.de; Englische Planke 1; tower adult/
child €5/3.50, crypt €4/2.50, combo ticket

GERMANY HAMBURG

Hamburg

€7/4; ⊘9am-7.30pm May-Oct, 10am-5.30pm Nov-Apr, last admission 30min before closing; ⊠ Stadthausbrücke) 'Der Michel', as it is affectionately called, is one of Hamburg's most recognisable landmarks and northern Germany's largest Protestant baroque church. Ascending the tower (by steps or lift) rewards visitors with great panoramas across the city and canals. The crypt has an engaging multimedia exhibit on the city's history.

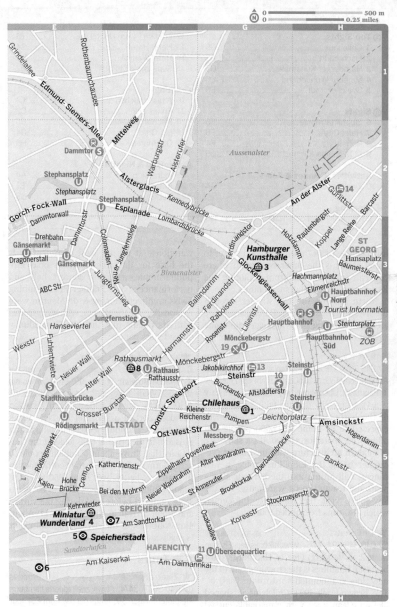

0 — 500 m
0 — 0.25 miles

Grindelallee
Edmund-Siemers-Allee
Rothenbaumchaussee
Mittelweg
Warburgstr
Alsterufer
Aussenalster
Dammtor
Stephansplatz
Stephansplatz
Gorch-Fock-Wall
Alsterglacis
Stephansplatz
Kennedybrücke
An der Alster ⓘ 14
Gurlittstr
Barcastr
Dammtorwall
Esplanade
Lombardsbrücke
Holzdamm
Rautenbergstr
Koppel
Lange Reihe
ST GEORG
Drehbahn
Gänsemarkt
Colonnaden
Ferdinandstor
Hamburger Kunsthalle
Glockengiesserwall
Hansaplatz
Baumeisterstr
Hachmannplatz
Dragonerstall
Gänsemarkt
Neuer Jungfernstieg
Binnenalster
Ballindamm
🏛 3
Ellmenreichstr
Hauptbahnhof-Nord ⓘ
ABC Str
Ferdinandstr
Rabolsen
Lilienstr
Hauptbahnhof
Tourist Information
Hanseviertel
Jungfernstieg Ⓢ
Hermannstr
Rosenstr
Mönckebergstr
Steintorplatz
Hauptbahnhof-Süd
ZOB
Wexstr
Fuhlentwiete
Neuer Wall
Rathausmarkt
Mönckebergstr
19 ⊗
Jakobikirchhof 🖼 13
Steinstr
10
Alter Wall
🏛 8 Ⓤ Rathaus
Rathausstr
Domstr Speersort
Burchardstr
Altstädterstr
Steinstr
Grosser Burstah
Stadthausbrücke
Chilehaus
Kleine Reichenstr
🏛 1
Deichtorplatz
Amsinckstr
Rödingsmarkt
ALTSTADT
Ost-West-Str
Pumpen
Messberg
Högerdamm
Katherinenstr
Zippelhaus Dovenfleet
Alter Wandrahm
Bankstr
Hohe Brücke
Cremon
Bei den Mühren
Neuer Wandrahm
St.Annenufer
Brooktorkai-Oberbaumbrücke
Stockmeyerstr ⊗ 20
Kehrwieder
Miniatur Wunderland 4 🏛
◉ 7 Am Sandtorkai
SPEICHERSTADT
Osakaallee
Koreastr
5 ◉ Speicherstadt
HAFENCITY
11 Ⓤ Überseequartier
Sandtorhafen
◉ 6
Am Kaiserkai
Am Dalmannkai

Rathaus HISTORIC BUILDING
(☎ 040-428 312 064; Rathausmarkt 1; tours adult/under 14yr €4/free; ⊙ tours half-hourly 11am-4pm Mon-Fri, 10am-5pm Sat, to 4pm Sun, English tours depend on demand; Ⓢ Rathausmarkt, Jungfern- stieg) With its spectacular coffered ceiling, Hamburg's baroque Rathaus is one of Europe's most opulent, and is renowned for its **Emperor's Hall** and **Great Hall**. The 40-minute tours take in only a fraction of

Hamburg

this beehive of 647 rooms. A good secret to know about is the inner courtyard, where you can take a break from exploring the Rathaus on comfy chairs with tables.

North of here, you can wander through the **Alsterarkaden**, the Renaissance-style arcades sheltering shops and cafes alongside a canal or 'fleet'.

HafenCity AREA
(⌨ 040-3690 1799; www.hafencity.com; InfoCenter, Am Sandtorkai 30; ⊙ InfoCenter 10am-6pm Tue-Sun; ⓢ Baumwall, Überseequartier) FREE HafenCity is a vast new city quarter taking shape east of the harbour. When fully completed, it's expected to be home to 12,000 people and offer work space for 40,000. It's a showcase of modern architecture with the biggest eye-catcher being the Elbphilharmonie, a vast concert hall jutting into the harbour atop a protected tea-and-cocoa warehouse. For the low-down, visit the HafenCity InfoCenter, which also runs free guided tours.

★**Chilehaus** HISTORIC BUILDING
(⌨ 040-349 194 247; www.chilehaus.de; Fischertwiete 2; ⓢ Messberg) One of Hamburg's most beautiful buildings is the crowning gem of the new Unesco-annointed **Kontorhaus District**. The brown-brick 1924 Chilehaus is shaped like an ocean liner, with remarkable curved walls meeting in the shape of a ship's bow and staggered balconies that look like decks.

Elbphilharmonie ARTS CENTRE
(Elbe Philharmonic Hall; ⌨ 040-3576 6666; www. elbphilharmonie.de; Platz der Deutschen Einheit 4; ⓢ Baumwall) A squat brown-brick former

warehouse at the far west of HafenCity is the base for the architecturally bold Elbphilharmonie, a major concert hall and performance space. Pritzker Prize–winning Swiss architects Herzog & de Meuron were responsible for the design, which captivates with its details like the 1096 individually curved glass panes.

★**Auswanderermuseum BallinStadt** MUSEUM
(Emigration Museum; ⌨ 040-3197 9160; www.ballin stadt.de; Veddeler Bogen 2; adult/child €12.50/7; ⊙ 10am-6pm Apr-Oct, 10am-4.30pm Nov-Mar; ⍰ Veddel) Sort of a bookend for New York's Ellis Island, Hamburg's excellent emigration museum in the original halls looks at the conditions that drove about 5 million people to leave Germany for the US and South America in search of better lives from 1850 until the 1930s. Multilingual displays address the hardships endured before and during the voyage and upon arrival in the New World. About 4km southeast of the city centre, BallinStadt is easily reached by S-Bahn.

🖝 Tours

★**Zweiradperle** CYCLING
(⌨ 040-3037 3474; www.zweiradperle.hamburg; Altstädter Strasse 3-7; rental per day from €14, tour incl rental from €25; ⊙ 10am-6pm daily Apr–mid-Oct, from 11am Tue-Fri, to 3pm Sat mid-Oct–Mar, tour 10.30am daily; ⓤ Steinstrasse) Offers a range of rental bikes (including helmets and locks), as well as tours. The three-hour tour is a great introduction to the city. Has a cool cafe and plenty of cycling info.

🛏 Sleeping

⭐ Superbude St Pauli
HOTEL, HOSTEL €

(📞 040-807 915 820; www.superbude.de; Juliusstrasse 1-7; dm/r from €16/60; @ 🛜; 🚇 Sternschanze, 🚉 Sternschanze, Holstenstrasse) The young and forever-young mix and mingle without a shred of prejudice at this rocking design hotel-hostel combo that's all about living, laughing, partying and, yes, even sleeping well. All rooms have comfy beds and sleek private baths, breakfast is served until noon and there's even a 'rock star suite' with an Astra beer as a pillow treat.

⭐ Henri Hotel
HOTEL €€

(📞 040-554 357 557; www.henri-hotel.com; Bugenhagenstrasse 21; r €110-180; 🛜; 🚇 Mönckebergstrasse) Kidney-shaped tables, plush armchairs, vintage typewriters – the Henri channels the 1950s so successfully that you half expect to run into Don Draper. Its 65 rooms and studios are a good fit for urban lifestyle junkies who like the alchemy of modern comforts and retro design. For more elbow room get an L-sized room with a king-size bed.

⭐ Fritz im Pyjama Hotel
BOUTIQUE HOTEL €€

(📞 040-314 838; www.fritz-im-pyjama.de; Schanzenstrasse 101-103; s/d from €77/120; 🛜; 🚇 Sternschanze) This stylish townhouse hotel sits smack dab in the heart of the Schanzenviertel party zone. Rooms are smallish, with wooden floors, angular furniture and large windows; seven of the 17 have a balcony. Those without are quieter as they face the courtyard.

25hours Hotel HafenCity
HOTEL €€

(📞 040-257 7770; www.25hours-hotel.de; Überseeallee 5; r €100-200; 🅿 🍴 🛜; 🚇 Überseequartier) Offbeat decor, an infectious irreverence and postmodern vintage flair make this pad a top choice among global nomads. Sporting maritime flourishes, the decor channels an old-timey seaman's club in the lobby. There's an excellent restaurant and 170 cabin-style rooms. Enjoy views of the emerging Hafen-City neighbourhood from the rooftop sauna.

⭐ Hotel Wedina
HOTEL €€€

(📞 040-280 8900; www.hotelwedina.de; Gurlittstrasse 23; r €125-245; 🅿 @ 🛜; 🚇 Hauptbahnhof) Margaret Atwood, Jonathan Franzen and Martin Walser are among the literary greats who've stayed at this lovable lair. Rooms are spread over five brightly pigmented buildings

SIGHTSEEING LIKE A REAL HAMBURGER

This maritime city offers a bewildering array of boat trips, but locals will tell you that you don't have to book a cruise to see the port – the city's **harbour ferries** will take you up the river on a regular public transport ticket, and you can avoid hokey narration!

One oft-recommended route is to catch **ferry 62** from Landungsbrücken to Finkenwerder, then change for the 64 to Teufelsbrücke. From Teufelsbrücke, you can wander along the Elbe eastwards to Neumühlen, from where you can catch bus 112 back to the Altona S-Bahn station or ferry 62 back to Landungsbrücken.

On land, the **U3 U-Bahn line** is particularly scenic, especially the elevated track between the St Pauli and Rathaus U-Bahn stations.

that in different ways express the owners' love for literature, architecture and art. It's close to the train station and the Alster lakes. The breakfasts are especially good.

🍴 Eating

The **Schanzenviertel** (U-Bahn to Feldstrasse or Schanzenstern) swarms with cheap eateries; try Schulterblatt for Portuguese outlets or Susannenstrasse for Asian and Turkish. St Georg's **Lange Reihe** (U-Bahn to Hauptbahnhof) offers many characterful eating spots to suit every budget. Fish restaurants around the Landungsbrücken tend to be overrated and touristy.

⭐ Fischbrötchenbude Brücke 10
SEAFOOD €

(📞 040-3339 9339; www.bruecke-10.de; Landungsbrücken, Pier 10; sandwiches €3-9.50; ⏰ 10am-10pm Apr-Oct, to 8pm Nov-Mar; 🚇 Landungsbrücken, 🚉 Landungsbrücken) There are a gazillion fish sandwich vendors in Hamburg, but we're going to stick our neck out and say that this vibrant, clean and contemporary outpost makes the best. Try a classic *Bismarck* (pickled herring) or *Matjes* (brined), or treat yourself to a bulging shrimp sandwich. Lovely tables outside.

ST PAULI & THE REEPERBAHN

No discussion of Hamburg is complete without mentioning St Pauli, home to one of Europe's most (in)famous red-light districts. Sex shops, table-dance bars and strip clubs still line its main drag, the Reeperbahn, and side streets, but the popularity of prostitution has declined dramatically in the internet age. Today St Pauli is Hamburg's main nightlife district, drawing people of all ages and walks of life to live music and dance clubs, chic bars and theatres.

In fact, street walkers are not even allowed to hit the pavement before 8pm and then are confined to certain areas, the most notorious being the gated Herbertstrasse (no women and men under 18 years allowed). Nearby, the cops of the Davidwache police station keep an eye on the lurid surrounds. A short walk west is the side street called Grosse Freiheit, where the Beatles cut their teeth at the Indra Club (No 64) and the Kaiserkeller (No 36). Both are vastly different venues today, but there's a small monument to the Fab Four in a courtyard behind No 35.

★ **Mö-Grill**   GERMAN €
(Mönckebergstrasse 11; mains from €4; ⊙10am-7pm; Ⓢ Mönckebergstrasse) You can smell the curry and see the crowds from two streets away at this very popular venue for that beloved German fast food, the *Currywurst*. Locals agree that the versions here (and at a second stand across the street) are about the best anywhere.

★ **Altes Mädchen**   MODERN EUROPEAN €€
(✑040-800 077 750; www.altes-maedchen.com; Lagerstrasse 28b; mains €6-29; ⊙noon-late Mon-Sat, from 10am Sun; Ⓢ Sternschanze) The lofty red-brick halls of a 19th-century animal market have been upcycled into a hip culinary destination that includes a coffee roastery, a celebrity chef restaurant, and this beguiling brewpub with a central bar, in-house bakery and garden.

Oberhafen Kantine   GERMAN €€
(✑040-3280 9984; www.oberhafenkantine-hamburg.de; Stockmeyerstrasse 39; mains €8.50-19.50; ⊙noon-10pm Mon-Sat, to 5.30pm Sun; Ⓡ Steinstrasse) Since 1925, this slightly tilted brick restaurant has served up the most traditional Hamburg fare. Here you can order a 'Hamburger' and you get the real thing: a patty made with various seasonings and onions. Roast beef and fish round out a trip back to the days when the surrounding piers echoed to the shouts of seafarers.

Erikas Eck   GERMAN €€
(✑040-433 545; www.erikas-eck.de; Sternstrasse 98; mains €6-21; ⊙5pm-2pm Mon-Fri, to 9am Sat & Sun; Ⓡ Sternschanze) This pit-stop institution originally fed hungry workers from the nearby abattoir (today the central meat market)

and now serves wallet-friendly but waist-expanding portions of schnitzel and other German fare to a motley crowd of clubbers, cabbies and cops 21 hours a day (weekdays).

🍷 Drinking & Entertainment

Partying in Hamburg concentrates on the Schanzenviertel and St Pauli, a few streets further south. Most people start the night in the former, then move on to the clubs and bars of the latter around midnight. Online sources: www.szene-hamburg.de and www.neu.clubkombinat.de.

★ **Katze**   BAR
(✑040-5577 5910; Schulterblatt 88; ⊙3pm-midnight Mon-Thu, 6pm-3am Fri, 1pm-3am Sat, 3pm-midnight Sun; Ⓢ Sternschanze) Small and sleek, this 'kitty' (*Katze* = cat) gets the crowd purring for well-priced cocktails (best caipirinhas in town) and great music (there's dancing on weekends). It's one of the most popular among the watering holes on this main Schanzenviertel booze strip.

★ **Indra Club**   CLUB
(www.indramusikclub.com; 64 Grosse Freiheit; ⊙9pm-late Wed-Sun; Ⓡ Reeperbahn) The Beatles' small first venue is open again and has live acts many nights. The interior is vastly different from the 1960s and there is a fine beer garden.

★ **Hafenklang**   MUSIC BAR
(✑040-388 744; www.hafenklang.org; Grosse Elbstrasse 84; Ⓡ Königstrasse) A collective of Hamburg industry insiders present established and emerging DJs and bands, as well as clubbing events and parties. Look for the spray-painted name on the graffiti-covered

dark-brick harbour store above a blank metal door.

★ **Strandperle** BAR
(☑ 040-8809 9508; www.strandperle-hamburg.de; Oevelgönne 60; ⊙ 10am-11pm Mon-Fri, 9am-11pm Sat & Sun May-Sep, shorter hours & Fri-Sun only Oct-Apr; ☑ 112) Hamburg's original beach bar is a must for primo beer, burgers and people-watching. All ages and classes gather, mingle and wriggle their toes in the sand, especially at sunset, right on the Elbe as huge freighters glide past. Get here by taking ferry 62 from Landungsbrücken or bus 112 from Altona station to Neumühlen/Oevelgönne.

Uebel und Gefährlich CLUB
(☑ 040-3179 3610; www.uebelundgefaehrlich.com; Feldstrasse 66; Ⓢ Feldstrasse) DJ sets, live music and parties rock this soundproof WWII bunker. Doors open around 7pm weekdays but as late as midnight on Friday and Saturday.

ℹ️ Information

Tourist Information am Hafen (☑ 040-3005 1701; www.hamburg-travel.com; btwn piers 4 & 5, St Pauli Landungsbrücken; ⊙ 9am-6pm Sun-Wed, to 7pm Thu-Sat; Ⓢ Landungsbrücken) No hotel bookings.

Tourist Information Hauptbahnhof (☑ 040-3005 1701; www.hamburg-travel.com; Hauptbahnhof, near Kirchenallee exit; ⊙ 9am-7pm Mon-Sat, 10am-6pm Sun; Ⓢ Hauptbahnhof, Ⓡ Hauptbahnhof) Busy all the time.

ℹ️ Getting There & Away

AIR

Hamburg's **airport** (HAM; ☑ 040-507 50; www. hamburg-airport.de; Ⓡ Hamburg Airport) is linked to the city centre every 10 minutes by the S-Bahn line S1 (€3.10, 25 minutes). A taxi takes about a half hour and cost around €30.

BUS

The **Zentraler Omnibusbahnhof** (Zentraler Omnibusbahnhof, Central Bus Station; ☑ 040-247 576; www.zob-hamburg.de; Adenauerallee 78; Ⓡ Hauptbahnhof), southeast of the Hauptbahnhof, has many domestic and international departures by Eurolines, Flixbus and many other operators.

TRAIN

Hamburg is a major train hub with four mainline train stations: the Hauptbahnhof, Altona, Dammtor and Harburg. Frequent trains serve Lübeck (€17, 45 minutes), Bremen (from €26, 55 minutes), Berlin-Hauptbahnhof (€78, 1¾ hours), Copenhagen (€110, 4¾ hours) and many other cities.

ℹ️ Getting Around

For public transport information, go to www.hvv. de. The city is divided into zones. Fare zone A covers the city centre, inner suburbs and airport.

Lübeck

☑ 0451 / POP 211,700

Compact and charming Lübeck makes for a great day trip from Hamburg. Looking like a pair of witches' hats, the pointed towers of its landmark Holstentor (Holsten Gate) form the gateway to its historic centre that sits on an island embraced by the arms of the Trave River. The Unesco-recognised web of cobbled lanes flanked by gabled merchants' homes and spired churches is an enduring reminder of Lübeck's role as the one-time capital of the medieval Hanseatic League trading power. Today, it enjoys fame as Germany's marzipan capital.

GERMANY LÜBECK

OFF THE BEATEN TRACK

ANNE FRANK & BERGEN-BELSEN

Nazi-built Bergen-Belsen (Bergen-Belsen Memorial Site; ☑ 05051-475 90; www.bergen-belsen.de; Anne-Frank-Platz, Lohheide; ⊙ Documentation Centre 10am-6pm Apr-Sep, 10am-5pm Oct-Mar, grounds until dusk) began its existence in 1940 as a POW camp, but became a concentration camp after being taken over by the SS in 1943, initially to imprison Jews as hostages in exchange for German POWs held abroad. In all, 70,000 prisoners perished here, most famously Anne Frank. A modern Documentation Centre chronicles the fates of the people who passed through here. A small section deals with Anne Frank, and there's also a memorial grave stone for her and her sister, Margot, near the cemetery's Jewish Monument.

The memorial site is in the countryside about 60km northeast of Hanover and a bit complicated to reach if you don't have your own wheels. See the website for detailed driving and public transport directions.

⦿ Sights

★ Holstentor
LANDMARK

(Holsten Gate) Built in 1464 and looking so settled-in that it appears to sag, Lübeck's charming red-brick city gate is a national icon. Its twin pointed cylindrical towers, leaning together across the stepped gable that joins them, captivated Andy Warhol (his print is in the St Annen Museum), and have graced postcards, paintings, posters and marzipan souvenirs. Discover this and more inside the Museum Holstentor (☑ 0451-122 4129; www. museum-holstentor.de; adult/child €7/2.50; ◐ 10am-6pm Apr-Dec, 11am-5pm Tue-Sun Jan-Mar), which sheds light on the history of the gate and on Lübeck's medieval mercantile glory days.

★ Museumsquartier St Annen
MUSEUM

(Museum Quarter St Annen; ☑ 0451-122 4137; www. museumsquartier-st-annen.de; St-Annen-Strasse; adult/child €12/6; ◐ 10am-5pm Tue-Sun Apr-Dec, 11am-5pm Tue-Sun Jan-Mar) This museum quarter includes an old synagogue, church and medieval buildings along its uneven streets. The namesake St Annen Museum details the diverse history of the neighbourhood as it traces 700 years of art and culture. The adjoining St Annen Kunstalle has ecclesiastical art (including Hans Memling's 1491 *Passion Altar*) and contemporary art including Andy Warhol's print of Lübeck's Holstentor. There's a chic little cafe in the courtyard.

Marienkirche
CHURCH

(St Mary's Church; ☑ 0451-397 700; www.st-marien -luebeck.com; Marienkirchhof 1; adult/child €2/1.50; ◐ 10am-6pm Apr-Sep, to 5pm Oct, to 4pm Tue-Sun Nov-Mar) This fine Gothic church boasts the world's highest brick-vaulted roof and was the model for dozens of churches in northern Germany. Crane your neck to take in the painted cross-vaulted ceilings supported by slender, ribbed pillars. A WWII bombing raid brought down the church's bells, which have been left where they fell in 1942 and have become a famous symbol of the city.

🛏 Sleeping

★ Klassik Altstadt Hotel
BOUTIQUE HOTEL €€

(☑ 0451-702 980; www.klassik-altstadt-hotel.de; Fischergrube 52; s/d from €50/120; 🖨) Each of the 29 rooms at this elegantly furnished boutique hotel is dedicated to a different, mostly German, writer or artist, such as Thomas Mann and Johann Sebastian Bach. Single rooms (some share baths and are great value) feature travelogues by famous authors.

SWEET TEMPTATIONS

Niederegger (☑ 0451-530 1126; www. niederegger.de; Breite Strasse 89; ◐ 9am-8pm Mon-Sat, 10am-6pm Sun) is Lübeck's mecca for marzipan, which has been made locally for centuries. The shop's elaborate displays are a feast for the eyes, and there's even a small museum where you'll learn that marzipan was considered medicine in the Middle Ages. The on-site cafe serves sandwiches and salads alongside sweet treats.

★ Hotel zur Alten Stadtmauer
HOTEL €€

(☑ 0451-737 02; www.hotelstadtmauer.de; An der Mauer 57; s/d from €67/98; P 🖨) With pine furniture and splashes of red and yellow, this simple 24-room hotel is a great place to wake up. Back rooms overlook the lakes and three are in a historic guesthouse. The real star of your stay, however, is the bounteous breakfast buffet, with many homemade preserves and other touches. Be aware that the hotel parking is 200m away.

🍴 Eating & Drinking

★ Grenadine
BISTRO €€

(☑ 0451-307 2950; www.grenadine-hl.de; Wahmstrasse 40; mains €7-15.50; ◐ 9am-4pm Mon, to 10pm Tue-Thu, to midnight Fri & Sat, to 3pm Sun; 🖨) This narrow, elongated bar leads through to a garden out the back. Enjoy bistro fare amid chic, retro-minimalist style. The long drinks menu goes well with tapas choices. Sandwiches, salads and pasta plus a gorgeous breakfast buffet are served.

Brauberger
GERMAN €€

(☑ 0451-714 44; www.brauberger.de; Alfstrasse 36; mains €9-20; ◐ 5pm-midnight Mon-Thu, 5pm-late Fri & Sat) The air is redolent of hops at this traditional German brewery. Get a stein of the one house brew, the superbly sweet, cloudy *Zwickelbier*, and tuck into a sizeable schnitzel or other traditional fare. There are outside tables out the back and student specials for pitchers.

ⓘ Information

Tourist Office (☑ 0451-889 9700; www. luebeck-tourismus.de; Holstentorplatz 1; ◐ 9am-7pm Mon-Fri, 10am-4pm Sat, 10am-3pm Sun May-Aug, reduced hours Sep-Apr) Sells the HappyDay Card (€12/14/17 per

24/48/72 hours) with discounts and free public transport. Also has a cafe and internet terminals.

ⓘ Getting There & Away

Ryanair and Wizzair serve **Lübeck Airport** (LBC; ☑ 0451-583 010; www.flughafen-luebeck.de; Blankenseer Strasse 101).

Regional trains connect to Hamburg hourly (€14, 45 minutes).

Bremen

☑ 0421 / POP 546,450

It's a shame the donkey, dog, cat and rooster in Grimm's *Town Musicians of Bremen* never actually made it here – they would have fallen in love with the place. This little city is big on charm, from the fairy-tale character statue to a jaw-dropping expressionist laneway and impressive town hall. On top of that, the Weser riverside promenade is a relaxing, bistro and beer garden–lined refuge and the lively student district ('Das Viertel') along Ostertorsteinweg is filled with indie boutiques, cafes, art-house cinemas and alt-flavoured cultural venues.

◉ Sights

Bremen's key historic sights cluster around Markt and can easily be explored on foot.

Markt SQUARE

Bremen's Unesco World Heritage–protected Markt is striking, especially for its ornate, gabled and sculpture-festooned **Rathaus** (town hall; 1410). In front stands a 5.5m-high medieval statue of the knight Roland (1404), the symbolic protector of Bremen's civic rights and freedoms.

Dom St Petri CHURCH

(St Petri Cathedral; ☑ 0421-334 7142; www.st petridom.de; Sandstrasse 10-12; tower adult/concession €2/1, museum free; ◷ 10am-5pm Mon-Fri, to 2pm Sat, 2-5pm Sun) Bremen's Protestant main church has origins in the 8th century and got its ribbed vaulting, chapels and two high towers in the 13th century. Aside from the imposing architecture, the intricately carved pulpit and the baptismal font in the western crypt deserve a closer look. For panoramic views, climb the 265 steps to the top of the south tower (April to October). The Dom-museum displays religious artefacts and treasures found here in a 1970s archaeological dig.

Böttcherstrasse STREET

(www.boettcherstrasse.de) The charming medieval coopers' lane was transformed into a prime example of mostly expressionist architecture in the 1920s at the instigation of coffee merchant Ludwig Roselius. Its red-brick houses sport unique facades, whimsical fountains, statues and a carillon; many house artisanal shops and art museums. Its most striking feature is Bernhard Hoetger's golden **Lichtbringer** (Bringer of Light) relief that keeps an eye on the north entrance.

★ Beck's Brewery BREWERY

(☑ 0421-5094 5555; www.becks.de/besucher zentrum; Am Deich 18/19; tours €11.90; ◷ tours 1pm, 3pm & 4.30pm Mon-Wed, 10am, 11.30am, 1pm,

GERMANY BREMEN

WORTH A TRIP

BACK TO THE ROOTS IN BREMERHAVEN

Standing on the spot where more than 7.2 million emigrants set sail for the US, South America and Australia between 1830 and 1942, the spectacular **Deutsches Auswandererhaus** (German Emigration Centre; ☑ 0471-902 200; www.dah-bremerhaven.de; Columbusstrasse 65; adult/concession €13.80/11.80; ◷ 10am-6pm Mar-Oct, 10am-5pm Nov-Feb) museum does a superb job commemorating some of their stories. The visitor relives stages of their journey, which begins at the wharf where passengers huddle together before boarding 'the ship', clutching the biographical details of one particular traveller and heading toward their new life. A second exhibit, opened in 2012, reverses the theme and tells of immigration to Germany since the 17th century. Everything is available in both German and English.

Bremerhaven is some 70km north of Bremen and is served by regional train (€12.10, 40 minutes). From the station, take bus 502, 505, 506, 508 or 509 to 'Havenwelten' to get to the museum and the harbour with its many old vessels (including a WWII sub) and striking contemporary architecture.

WORTH A TRIP

HANOVER'S HERRENHÄUSER GÄRTEN

Proof that Hanover is not all buttoned-down business are the grandiose baroque **Royal Gardens of Herrenhausen** (☑ 0511-1683 4000; www.hannover.de/Herrenhausen; Herrenhäuser Strasse 4; general admission free; ☉ 9am-6pm Apr-Oct, to 4.30pm Nov-Mar, grotto 9am-5.30pm Apr-Oct, to 4pm Nov-Mar; ⓤ Hannover Herrenhäuser Gärten), which rank among the most important historic garden landscapes in Europe. Inspired by the park at Versailles, the sprawling grounds are perfect for slowing down and smelling the roses for a couple of hours, especially on a blue-sky day.

With its fountains, neat flowerbeds, trimmed hedges and shaped lawns, the 300-year-old **Grosser Garten** (Great Garden) is the centrepiece of the experience. Don't miss the **Niki de Saint Phalle Grotto** near the northern end, which provides a magical backdrop for the whimsical statues, fountains and coloured tiles by this late French artist (1930–2002). South of here, the **Grosse Fontäne** (Big Fountain; the tallest in Europe) jets water up to 80m high. In summer, fountains are synchronised during the **Wasserspiele** (water games). During the **Illuminations** the gardens and fountains are atmospherically lit at night.

Across Herrenhäuser Strasse, the **Berggarten** is redolent with a mindboggling assortment of global flora, while east of the Grosser Garten, beyond a small canal, the lake-dotted **Georgengarten** counts the **Wilhelm-Busch-Museum** (☑ 0511-1699 9911; www.karikatur-museum.de; adult/concession €6/4; ☉ 11am-6pm Tue-Sun), with its wealth of caricatures by Busch, Honoré Daumier, William Hogarth and many others' among its treasures.

If you're curious about Hanover's other sights, stop by the **tourist office** (☑ information 0511-1234 5111, room reservations 12 34 55 55; www.hannover.de; Ernst-Aug-Platz 8; ☉ 9am-6pm Mon-Fri, 10am-3pm Sat & Sun).

3pm, 4.30pm & 6pm Thu-Sat) Two-hour tours of one of Germany's most internationally famous breweries must be booked online. The 3pm tour is also in English. Minimum age 16. Meet at the brewery's visitor centre, reached by taking tram 1, 2 or 3 to Am Brill.

Schnoor AREA
This maze of narrow, winding alleys was once the fishermen's quarter and later a red-light district. Now its doll's house–sized cottages contain boutiques, restaurants, cafes and galleries. Though tourist-geared, there are some lovely corners to explore around here on a leisurely amble.

🛏 Sleeping

Prizeotel Bremen City HOTEL €
(☑ 0421-222 2100; www.prizeotel.com/bremen; Theodor-Heuss-Allee 12; s/d from €59/64; ⓟ ✳ 🛜) This funky, fresh and fluoro design hotel won't be everyone's cup of tea, but if you like it, you'll love it. Ultra-modern, compact rooms are quiet despite their proximity to the rail lines (the hotel is a five-minute walk from the station). All rooms feature 32-inch TVs, 'mega beds' and 'maxi showers'.

⭐ **Atlantic Grand** HOTEL €€
(☑ 0421-620 620; www.atlantic-hotels.de; Bredenstrasse 2; r from €114) Pitched around a central courtyard, moments from Bremen's quirky Böttcherstrasse, the simple, effortlessly stylish, dark-wooded rooms with chocolate leather armchairs and top-notch service from attentive staff make this classy hotel an excellent choice.

🍴 Eating & Drinking

Tourist-oriented places cluster around Markt, which is pretty dead after dark. Das Viertel has an alternative, student-flavoured feel, while the waterfront promenade, Schlachte, is pricier and more mainstream.

Engel Weincafe CAFE €
(☑ 0421-6964 2390; www.engelweincafe-bremen. de; Ostertorsteinweg 31; dishes €4.50-12; ☉ 9am-1am Mon-Fri, 10am-1am Sat & Sun; 🛜 🌱) Exuding the nostalgic vibe of a former pharmacy, this popular hang-out gets a good crowd no matter where the hand's on the clock. Come for breakfast, a hot lunch special, crispy *Flammekuche* (French pizza), carpaccio or pasta, or just some cheese and a glass of wine.

★ **Bremer Ratskeller** GERMAN €€

(☑ 0421-321 676; www.ratskeller-bremen.de; Am Markt 11; mains €9-19; ⊙ 11am-midnight) Ratskellers were traditionally built underneath the Rathaus in every German town to keep the citizens and civil servants fed. Bremen's is quite the experience, with high vaulted ceilings, an atmosphere that's the real deal on the historical Richter scale (in business since 1405!) and good, heavy, no-fuss German food and beer. What's not to like?

★ **Kleiner Olymp** GERMAN €€

(☑ 0421-326 667; www.kleiner-olymp.de; Hinter der Holzpforte 20; mains €7-19; ⊙ 11am-11pm) This homely kitchen in Schnoor has a wonderful atmosphere, delicious (and not too heavy) North German cuisine and very reasonable prices. With a selection of mouthwatering soups and starters, seafood (not pork, for a change) features predominantly and appropriately on the menu. Enjoy!

☆ Entertainment

★ **Lila Eule** LIVE MUSIC

(www.lilaeule.de; Bernhardstrasse 10; ⊙ from 8pm) A decade or more is a long time to be a hot tip, but this gem off Sielwall has pulled it off. A student crowd gathers here for parties and events, but it's also a very alternative place to watch the Werder Bremen football team; most Werder matches are shown here. Thursday night is the legendary student bash.

❶ Information

Tourist Office (☑ 0421-308 0010; www.bremen-tourism.de) Branches include **Markt** (Langenstrasse 2-4; ⊙ 9.30am-6.30pm Mon-Fri, to 5pm Sat, 10am-4pm Sun), a full-service tourist office with friendly staff, near Markt, and **Hauptbahnhof** (⊙ 9am-6.30pm Mon-Fri, to 5pm Sat & Sun), handily located at the main train station.

❶ Getting There & Around

Bremen's **airport** (BRE; ☑ 0421-559 50; www.airport-bremen.de) is about 3.5km south of the city and served by tram 6 (€2.60, 15 minutes).

Frequent IC trains go to Hamburg (€28, one hour), Hanover (€33, one hour) and Cologne (€67, three hours). Less frequent IC trains go to Berlin (€79, four hours).

SURVIVAL GUIDE

❶ Directory A–Z

ACCOMMODATION

Reservations are a good idea between June and September, and around major holidays, festivals, cultural events and trade shows.

DISCOUNT CARDS

Tourist offices in many cities sell Welcome Cards, which entitle visitors to discounts on museums, sights and tours, plus unlimited trips on local public transport. They can be good value if you plan on taking advantage of most of the benefits and don't qualify for any of the standard discounts.

GAY & LESBIAN TRAVELLERS

Germany is a magnet for *schwule* (gay) and *lesbische* (lesbian) travellers, with the rainbow flag flying especially proudly in Berlin and Cologne. There are also sizeable communities in Hamburg, Frankfurt and Munich.

INTERNET RESOURCES

Lonely Planet (www.lonelyplanet.com/germany) Hotel bookings, traveller forum and more.

German National Tourist Office (www.germany.travel)

Facts About Germany (www.tatsachen-ueber-deutschland.de/en) Reference tool on all aspects of German society.

Deutschland Online (www.magazine-deutschland.de) Insightful features on culture, business and politics.

Online German course (www.deutsch-lernen.com)

LEGAL MATTERS

➡ The permissible blood-alcohol limit is 0.05%.

➡ Drinking in public is legal, but be discreet.

COUNTRY FACTS

Area 356,866 sq km

Capital Berlin

Country Code 49

Currency euro (€)

Emergency ☑ 112

Language German

Money ATMs common, cash preferred for most purchases

Population 80.7 million

Visas Schengen rules apply

ESSENTIAL FOOD & DRINK

As in Britain, Germany has redeemed itself gastronomically over the past decade. These days culinary offerings are often slimmed down and healthier as many chefs let the trifecta of seasonal-regional-organic ingredients steer their menus. International flavours and cooking techniques further add pizzazz to tried-and-trusted specialities, while vegan and vegetarian selections are becoming commonplace. Of course, if you crave traditional comfort food, you'll still find plenty of pork, potatoes and cabbage on the menus, especially in the countryside. Here are our top-five classic German culinary treats:

Sausage (wurst) Favourite snack food, links come in 1500 varieties, including finger-sized *Nürnbergers*, crunchy *Thüringers* and tomato-sauce-drowned *Currywurst*.

Schweinshaxe The mother of all pork dishes, this one presents itself as entire knuckle roasted to crispy perfection.

Königsberger Klopse A simple but elegant plate of golf-ball-sized veal meatballs in a caper-laced white sauce and served with a side of boiled potatoes and beetroot.

Bread Get Germans talking about bread and often their eyes will water as they describe their favourite type – usually hearty and wholegrained in infinite variations.

Black forest cake (Schwarzwälder Kirschtorte) Multilayered chocolate sponge cake, whipped cream and kirsch confection, topped with cherries and chocolate shavings.

➤ Cannabis *consumption* is not illegal, but the possession, acquisition, sale and cultivation of it is considered a criminal offence. There is usually no prosecution for possessing 'small quantities'.

MONEY

➤ Cash is king in Germany. Always carry some with you and plan to pay cash almost everywhere.

➤ Credit cards are becoming more widely accepted, but it's best not to assume you'll be able to use one – ask first.

➤ Most ATMs (*Geldautomat*) are linked to international networks such as Cirrus, Plus, Star and Maestro.

OPENING HOURS

The following are typical opening hours in Germany, although these may vary seasonally and between cities and villages.

Banks 9am–4pm Monday to Friday, extended hours usually on Tuesday and Thursday, some open Saturday

Bars 6pm–1am

Cafes 8am–8pm

Clubs 11pm to early morning hours

Restaurants 11am–11pm (food service often stops at 9pm in rural areas)

Major stores and supermarkets 9.30am–8pm Monday to Saturday (shorter hours outside city centres)

PUBLIC HOLIDAYS

The following are nationwide *gesetzliche Feiertage* (public holidays):

Neujahrstag (New Year's Day) 1 January

Ostern (Easter) March/April; Good Friday, Easter Sunday and Easter Monday

Christi Himmelfahrt (Ascension Day) Forty days after Easter

Maifeiertag/Tag der Arbeit (Labour Day) 1 May

Pfingsten (Whit/Pentecost Sunday & Monday) Fifty days after Easter

Tag der Deutschen Einheit (Day of German Unity) 3 October

Weihnachtstag (Christmas Day) 25 December

Zweiter Weihnachtstag (Boxing Day) 26 December

TELEPHONE

German phone numbers consist of an area code (three to six digits), starting with 0, and the local number (three to nine digits). If dialling from a

SLEEPING PRICE RANGES

The price indicators in this book refer to the cost of a double room with private bathroom, including taxes.

€ less than €80

€€ €80–€160

€€€ more than €160

landline within the same city, you don't need to dial the area code. You must dial it if using a mobile.

Country code 📞 49
International access code 📞 00

❶ Getting There & Away

AIR

Huge **Frankfurt Airport** (p496) is Germany's busiest, with **Munich** (p477) a close second and **Düsseldorf** (p505) getting a good share of flights as well. Airports in Berlin, Hamburg and Cologne are comparatively small.

LAND
Bus

Long-distance coach travel to Germany from such cities as Milan, Vienna, Amsterdam and Copenhagen has become a viable option thanks to a new crop of companies offering good-value connections aboard comfortable buses with snack bars and free wi-fi. Major operators include **Flixbus** (📞 030-300 137 300; www.flixbus.com), **Megabus** (📞 in the UK 0900 1600 900; www.megabus.com) and Eurolines (www.eurolines.com). For routes, times and prices, check www.busradar.com.

Car & Motorcycle

➡ When bringing your own vehicle to Germany, you need a valid driving licence, car registration and proof of third-party insurance. Foreign cars must display a nationality sticker unless they have official European plates. You also need to carry a warning (hazard) triangle and a first-aid kit.

➡ Most German cities now have environmental zones that may only be entered by vehicles (including foreign ones) displaying an *Umweltplakette* (emissions sticker). Check with your motoring association or buy one at www.umwelt-plakette.de.

Train

➡ Germany has an efficient railway network with excellent links to other European destinations. Ticketing is handled by **Deutsche Bahn** (📞 01806 99 66 33; www.bahn.de).

➡ Seat reservations are a good idea for Friday and Sunday travel on long-distance trains and highly recommended during the peak summer season and around major holidays.

➡ Eurail and Interrail passes are valid on all German national trains.

SEA

➡ Germany's main ferry ports are Kiel, Travemünde (near Lübeck), Rostock and Sassnitz (on Rügen Island). All have services to Scandinavia and the Baltic states. There are no direct ferries between Germany and the UK.

➡ For details and tickets, go to www.ferrysavers.com.

❶ Getting Around

Germans are whizzes at moving people around, and the public transport network is one of the best in Europe. The best ways of getting around the country are by car and by train.

AIR

Unless you're flying from one end of the country to the other, say from Berlin or Hamburg to Munich, planes are only marginally quicker than trains once you factor in the check-in and transit times.

BICYCLE

➡ Cycling is allowed on all roads except autobahns (motorways). Helmets are not compulsory (not even for children).

➡ Bicycles may be taken on most trains but require a separate ticket *(Fahrradkarte)* and a reservation if travelling on an IC/EC train. They are not allowed on ICE trains.

➡ Most towns and cities have a private bicycle-hire station, often at or near the train station. A growing number have automated bike-rental systems.

BOAT

➡ From April to October, boats operate on set timetables along sections of the Rhine, the Elbe and the Danube.

BUS

➡ Domestic buses cover an extensive nationwide network. Fierce competition has kept prices extremely low. Flixbus (www.flixbus.com) is the dominant operator.

➡ In some rural areas buses may be your only option for getting around without your own vehicle. The frequency of services varies from 'rarely' to 'constantly'. Commuter-geared routes offer limited or no service in the evenings and on weekends.

➡ In cities, buses generally converge at the *Busbahnhof* or *Zentraler Omnibus Bahnhof*

EATING PRICE RANGES

The following price ranges refer to a standard main course.

€ less than €8

€€ €8–€18

€€€ more than €18

MILESTONES IN GERMAN HISTORY

800 Charlemagne is crowned emperor by the pope, laying the foundation for the Holy Roman Empire, which will last until 1806.

1241 Hamburg and Lübeck sign a trading agreement, creating the base for the powerful Hanseatic League that dominates politics and trade across much of Europe throughout the Middle Ages.

1455 Johannes Gutenberg invents moveable type, which for the first time allows books to be published in larger quantities.

1517 Martin Luther challenges Catholic church practices by posting his Ninety-Five Theses and ushering in the Reformation.

1618–48 The Thirty Years' War pits Protestants against Catholics in a far-reaching, bloody war that leaves Europe's population depleted and vast regions reduced to wasteland.

1871 A united Germany is created with Prussia at its helm, Berlin as its capital and Wilhelm I as its emperor.

1914–18 WWI: Germany, Austria-Hungary and Turkey go to war against Britain, France, Italy and Russia. Germany is defeated.

1933 Hitler comes to power, ushering in 12 years of Nazi terror that culminates in WWII and the systematic annihilation of Jews, Roma, Sinti and other people deemed 'undesirable'.

1949 Germany is divided into a democratic West Germany under the western Allies (the US, UK and France) and a socialist East Germany under the Soviet Union.

1961 The East German government erects the Berlin Wall, dividing the country into two for the next 28 years.

1989 The Berlin Wall collapses; Germany is reunited the following year.

(ZOB; central bus station), which is often near the Hauptbahnhof (central train station).

➡ From April to October, the tourist-geared **Romantic Road Coach** (☎ 09851-551 387; www.romantic-road.com) runs one coach daily in each direction between Frankfurt and Füssen (for Schloss Neuschwanstein) via Munich; the entire trip takes around 12 hours.

CAR & MOTORCYCLE

➡ Driving is on the right side of the road.

➡ With few exceptions, no tolls are charged on public roads.

➡ Unless posted otherwise, speed limits are 50km/h in cities, 100km/h on country roads and no limit on the autobahn.

➡ Cars are impractical in urban areas. Leaving your car in a central Parkhaus (car park) can cost €20 per day or more.

➡ Visitors from most countries do not need an International Driving Permit to drive in Germany. Automatic transmissions are rare and must be booked well in advance.

LOCAL TRANSPORT

➡ Public transport is excellent within big cities and small towns and may include buses, trams (Strassenbahn), S-Bahn (light rail), U-Bahn (underground/subway trains) and ferries.

➡ Fares are usually determined by zones or time travelled, sometimes both. Multiticket strips (Streifenkarte) and day passes (Tageskarte) usually offer better value than single-ride tickets.

➡ Most tickets must be validated (stamped) upon boarding.

TRAIN

➡ Germany's train network is almost entirely run by **Deutsche Bahn** (p519), although there is a growing number of routes operated by private companies but integrated into the DB network.

➡ Of the several train types, ICE trains are the fastest and most comfortable. IC trains (EC if they cross borders) are almost as fast but older and less snazzy. RE and RB trains are regional.

S-Bahn are suburban trains operating in large cities and conurbations.

➡ At larger stations, you can store your luggage in a locker (*Schliessfach*) or a left-luggage office (*Gepäckaufbewahrung*).

➡ Seat reservations for long-distance travel are highly recommended, especially if you're travelling on a Friday or Sunday afternoon, during holiday periods or in summer. Reservations can be made online and at ticket counters as late as 10 minutes before departure.

➡ Buy tickets online (www.bahn.de) or at stations from vending machines or ticket offices (*Reisezentrum*). Only conductors on ICE and IC/EC trains sell tickets on board at a surcharge.

TIPPING

Hotels €1 per bag is standard. It's also nice to leave a little cash for the room cleaners, say €1 or €2 per day.

Restaurants Restaurant bills always include *Bedienung* (service charge), but most people add 5% or 10% unless the service was truly abhorrent.

Bars About 5%, rounded to the nearest euro. For drinks brought to your table, tip as for restaurants.

Taxis Tip about 10%, rounded to the nearest euro.

Toilet attendants Loose change.

Greece Ελλάδα

Best Places to Eat

➜ Mani Mani (p530)
➜ Koukoumavlos (p548)
➜ Thalassino Ageri (p554)
➜ Klimataria (p566)
➜ Il Vesuvio (p565)

Best Places to Sleep

➜ Nafplion 1841 (p534)
➜ Mill Houses (p548)
➜ Marco Polo Mansion (p557)
➜ Bella Venezia (p565)

Why Go?

It's easy to understand how so many myths of gods and giants originated in this vast and varied landscape, with wide open skies and a sea speckled with islands. Endless kilometres of aquamarine coastline, sun-bleached ancient ruins, strong feta and stronger ouzo – the Greek landscape thrills while the culture captivates with a population passionate about everything from politics to art. Magnificent archaeological sites like the Acropolis, Delphi, Delos and Knossos are easily reached and hiking trails criss-cross Mt Olympus, the Zagorohoria and islands like Crete and Corfu. Meanwhile, the nightlife thrives in Greece's vibrant modern cities and on islands such as Mykonos and Santorini. Add a flourishing arts scene, world-class cuisine and welcoming locals to the mix and it's easy to see why most visitors head home vowing to come back. Travellers to Greece inevitably end up with a favourite site they long to return to – get out there and find yours.

When to Go
Athens

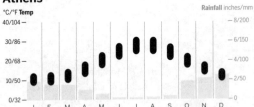

May & Jun Greece opens the shutters in time for Orthodox Easter; the best months to visit.

Jul & Aug Be prepared to battle summer crowds, high prices and soaring temperatures.

Sep & Oct The tourist season winds down; an excellent, relaxing time to head to Greece.

Greece Highlights

1 **Athens** (p523) Tracing the ancient to the modern, from the Acropolis to booming nightclubs.

2 **Cyclades** (p541) Island-hopping under the Aegean sun.

3 **Lesvos (Mytilini)** (p561) Sipping ouzo while munching grilled octopus on this olive-tree-filled island.

4 **Santorini** (p546) Staring dumbfounded at the dramatic volcanic caldera on this incomparable island.

5 **Hania, Crete** (p549) Strolling the lovely Venetian Harbour then supping on some of Greece's best food.

6 **Meteora** (p537) Climbing russet rock pinnacles to exquisite monasteries.

7 **Nafplio** (p534) Basing yourself in this quaint village and exploring the back roads and ruins of the Peloponnese.

8 **Rhodes Town** (p555) Losing yourself within the medieval walls of the Old Town.

9 **Delphi** (p537) Searching for the oracle amid the dazzling ruins.

ATHENS   AΘHNA

POP 3.1 MILLION

Ancient and modern, with equal measures of grunge and grace, bustling Athens is a heady mix of history and edginess. Iconic monuments mingle with first-rate museums, bustling shops and stylish, alfresco dining. Even in the face of current financial issues, Athens is more cosmopolitan than ever before with hip hotels, artsy-industrial neighbourhoods and entertainment quarters showing its modern face.

ITINERARIES

One Week

Explore Athens' museums and ancient sites on day one before spending a couple of days in the Peloponnese visiting Nafplio, Mycenae and Olympia; ferry to the Cyclades and enjoy Mykonos and spectacular Santorini.

One Month

Give yourself some more time in Athens and the Peloponnese, then visit the Ionian Islands for a few days. Explore the villages of Zagorohoria before travelling back to Athens via Meteora and Delphi. Take a ferry from Piraeus south to Mykonos, then island-hop via Santorini to Crete. After exploring Crete, take the ferry east to Rhodes, then north to Kos, Samos and Lesvos. Wrap up in relaxed, cosmopolitan Thessaloniki.

👁 Sights

⭐ Acropolis — HISTORIC SITE

(📞 210 321 4172; http://odysseus.culture.gr; adult/concession/child €20/10/free; ⊙ 8am-8pm Apr-Oct, to 5pm Nov-Mar, last entry 30min before closing; M Akropoli) The Acropolis is the most important ancient site in the Western world. Crowned by the Parthenon, it stands sentinel over Athens, visible from almost everywhere within the city. Its monuments and sanctuaries of Pentelic marble gleam white in the midday sun and gradually take on a honey hue as the sun sinks, while at night they stand brilliantly illuminated above the city. A glimpse of this magnificent sight cannot fail to exalt your spirit.

⭐ Acropolis Museum — MUSEUM

(📞 210 900 0900; www.theacropolismuseum.gr; Dionysiou Areopagitou 15, Makrygianni; adult/child €5/free; ⊙ 8am-4pm Mon, to 8pm Tue-Sun, to 10pm Fri Apr-Oct, 9am-5pm Mon-Thu, to 10pm Fri, to 8pm Sat & Sun Nov-Mar; M Akropoli) This dazzling modernist museum at the foot of the Acropolis' southern slope showcases its surviving treasures still in Greek possession. While the collection covers the Archaic and Roman periods, the emphasis is on the Acropolis of the 5th century BC, considered the apotheosis of Greece's artistic achievement. The museum cleverly reveals layers of history, floating over ruins with the Acropolis visible above, showing the masterpieces in context. The surprisingly good-value restaurant has superb views; there's also a fine museum shop.

⭐ Ancient Agora — HISTORIC SITE

(📞 210 321 0185; http://odysseus.culture.gr; Adrianou 24; adult/student/child €8/4/free, with Acropolis pass free; ⊙ 8am-8pm daily May-Oct, 8am-3pm Nov-Apr; M Monastiraki) The heart of ancient Athens was the Agora, the lively, crowded focal point of administrative, commercial, political and social activity. Socrates expounded his philosophy here, and in AD 49 St Paul came here to win converts to Christianity. The site today is a lush, refreshing respite, with beautiful monuments and temples and a fascinating museum.

⭐ Roman Agora & Tower of the Winds — HISTORIC SITE

(📞 210 324 5220; http://odysseus.culture.gr; cnr Pelopida & Eolou, Monastiraki; adult/student/child €6/3/free, with Acropolis pass free; ⊙ 8am-5pm, reduced hours in low season; M Monastiraki) The entrance to the Roman Agora is through the well-preserved Gate of Athena Archegetis, flanked by four Doric columns. It was financed by Julius Caesar and erected sometime during the 1st century AD. Restored and reopened in 2016, the extraordinary Tower of the Winds was built in the 1st century BC by a Syrian astronomer named Andronicus. The octagonal monument of Pentelic marble is an ingenious construction that functioned as a sundial, weather vane, water clock and compass.

⭐ Temple of Olympian Zeus — TEMPLE

(Olympieio; 📞 210 922 6330; http://odysseus.culture.gr; Leoforos Vasilissis Olgas, Syntagma; adult/student/child €6/3/free, with Acropolis pass free; ⊙ 8am-3pm Oct-Apr, 8am-8pm May-Sep, final admission 30min before closing; M Akropoli, Syntagma) You can't miss this striking marvel smack in the centre of Athens. It is the largest temple in Greece; begun in the 6th century BC by Peisistratos, it was abandoned for lack of funds. Various other leaders had stabs at completing it, but it was left to Hadrian to complete the work in AD 131 – taking more than 700 years in total to build.

★ **Panathenaic Stadium** HISTORIC SITE

(☎210 752 2984; www.panathenaicstadium.gr; Leoforos Vasileos Konstantinou, Pangrati; adult/student/child €5/2.50/free; ☺8am-7pm Mar-Oct, to 5pm Nov-Feb; MᎪkropoli) The grand Panathenaic Stadium lies between two pine-covered hills between the neighbourhoods of Mets and Pangrati. It was originally built in the 4th century BC as a venue for the Panathenaic athletic contests. It's said that at Hadrian's inauguration in AD 120, 1000 wild animals were sacrificed in the arena. Later, the seats were rebuilt in Pentelic marble by Herodes Atticus. There are seats for 70,000 spectators, a running track and a central area for field events.

★ **Parliament &**
Changing of the Guard NOTABLE BUILDING

(Plateia Syntagmatos; MSyntagma) FREE In front of the parliament building on Plateia Syntagmatos (Syntagma Sq), the traditionally costumed *evzones* (guards) of the **Tomb of the Unknown Soldier** change every hour on the hour. On Sunday at 11am, a whole platoon marches down Vasilissis Sofias to the tomb, accompanied by a band.

★ **National Gardens** GARDENS

(cnr Leoforos Vasilissis Sofias & Leoforos Vasilissis Amalias, Syntagma; ☺7am-dusk; MSyntagma) FREE A delightful, shady refuge during summer, the National Gardens were formerly the royal gardens, designed by Queen Amalia. There's a large children's playground, a duck pond and a shady cafe.

★ **Benaki Museum** MUSEUM

(☎210 367 1000; www.benaki.gr; Koumbari 1, cnr Leoforos Vasilissis Sofias, Kolonaki; adult/student/child €9/7/free, Thu free; ☺9am-5pm Wed & Fri, to midnight Thu & Sat, to 3pm Sun; MSyntagma,

---

ⓘ **CHEAPER BY THE HALF-DOZEN**

A €30 unified ticket from the Acropolis (valid for five days) includes entry to the other significant ancient sites: Ancient Agora, Roman Agora, Keramikos, Temple of Olympian Zeus and the Theatre of Dionysos.

Enter the sites free on the first Sunday of the month from November to March, and on certain holidays. Anyone aged under 18 years or with an EU student card gets in free.

Evangelismos) Greece's finest private museum contains the vast collection of Antonis Benakis, accumulated during 35 years of avid collecting in Europe and Asia. The collection includes Bronze Age finds from Mycenae and Thessaly; works by El Greco; ecclesiastical furniture brought from Asia Minor; pottery, copper, silver and woodwork from Egypt, Asia Minor and Mesopotamia; and a stunning collection of Greek regional costumes.

★ **National**
Archaeological Museum MUSEUM

(☎213 214 4800; www.namuseum.gr; 28 Oktovriou-Patision 44, Exarhia; adult/child €10/free; ☺1-8pm Mon, 8am-8pm Tue-Sun Apr-Oct, 1-8pm Mon, 9am-4pm Tue-Sun Nov-Mar; MViktoria, 2, 4, 5, 9 or 11 to Polytechnio) One of the world's most important museums, the National Archaeological Museum houses the world's finest collection of Greek antiquities. Treasures offering a view of Greek art and history – dating from the Neolithic era to classical periods – include exquisite sculptures, pottery, jewellery, frescoes and artefacts found throughout Greece. The beautifully presented exhibits

---

GREECE ATHENS

CONTEMPORARY ART

Athens is not all about ancient art. For a taste of the contemporary, visit:

Taf (The Art Foundation; ☎210 323 8757; www.theartfoundation.gr; Normanou 5, Monastiraki; ☺noon-9pm Mon-Sat, to 7pm Sun; MMonastiraki) Eclectic art and music gallery.

Six DOGS (☎210 321 0510; www.sixdogs.gr; Avramiotou 6-8, Monastiraki; ☺10am-late; MMonastiraki) Theatre meets gallery meets live music venue.

Onassis Cultural Centre (☎info/tickets 210 900 5800; www.sgt.gr; Leoforos Syngrou 107-109, Neos Kosmos; MSyngrou-Fix) Multimillion-euro visual and performing-arts centre.

National Museum of Contemporary Art (☎211 101 9000; www.emst.gr; Kallirrois & Frantzi, Koukaki-Syngrou; adult/student/child €5/3/free, 5-10pm Thu free; ☺11am-7pm Tue, Wed & Fri-Sun, to 10pm Thu; MSyngrou-Fix) In spectacularly renovated quarters, with top-notch rotating exhibits.

Central Athens

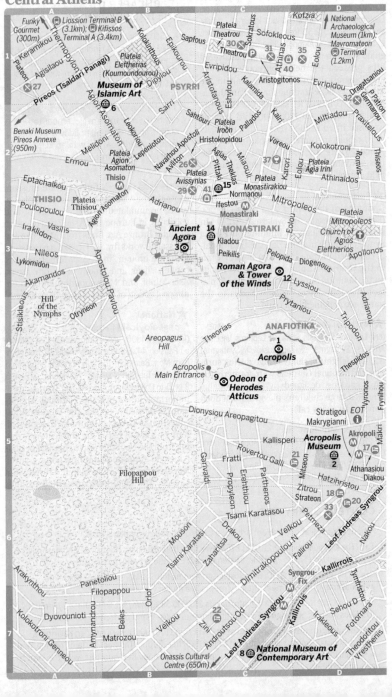

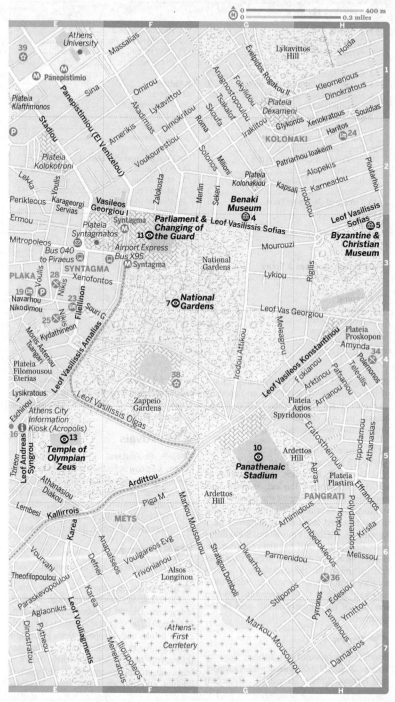

Central Athens

are displayed mainly thematically. Allow plenty of time to view the vast and spectacular collections (more than 11,000 items) housed in this enormous (8000-sq-metre) 19th-century neoclassical building.

★ **Museum of Islamic Art**   MUSEUM
(☎ 210 325 1311; www.benaki.gr; Agion Asomaton 22 & Dipylou 12, Keramikos; adult/student/child €9/7/free; ☉ 8am-6pm Thu-Sun; Ⓜ Thisio) This museum showcases one of the world's most significant collections of Islamic art. Housed in two restored neoclassical mansions near Keramikos, it exhibits more than 8000 items representing the 12th to 19th centuries, including weavings, carvings, prayer rugs, tiles and ceramics. On the 3rd floor is a 17th-century reception room with an inlaid marble floor from a Cairo mansion. You can see part of the Themistoklean wall in the basement.

☞ Tours

Besides open-bus tours try **Athens Segway Tours** (☎ 210 322 2500; www.athenssegwaytours.com; Eschinou 9, Plaka; 2hr tour €59; Ⓜ Akropoli)

or the volunteer **This is My Athens** (http://myathens.thisisathens.org). Hike or kayak with **Trekking Hellas** (☎ 210 331 0323; www.trekking.gr; Gounari 96, Marousi).

🎪 Festivals

★ **Hellenic Festival**   PERFORMING ARTS
(Athens & Epidavros Festival; www.greekfestival.gr; ☉ Jun-Aug) The ancient theatre at Epidavros and Athens' Odeon of Herodes Atticus are the headline venues of Greece's annual cultural festival featuring a top line-up of local and international music, dance and theatre.

🛏 Sleeping

Book well ahead for July and August.

★ **Athens Backpackers**   HOSTEL €
(☎ 210 922 4044; www.backpackers.gr; Makri 12, Makrygianni; dm incl breakfast €27-30; ※@⑤; Ⓜ Akropoli) The popular rooftop bar with cheap drinks and Acropolis views is a major drawcard for this modern and friendly Australian-run backpacker favourite. There's a barbecue in the courtyard, a well-stocked kitchen and a busy social scene. Spotless

dorms with private bathrooms and lockers have bedding, but towel use costs €2. Management also runs well-priced **Athens Studios** (📞210 923 5811; www.athensstudios.gr; Veïkou 3a, Makrygianni; apt incl breakfast €105; @ 🛜; Ⓜ Akropoli), with modern apartments nearby.

Marble House Pension
PENSION €

(📞210 923 4058; www.marblehouse.gr; Zini 35a, Koukaki; s/d/tr €35/45/55, d/tr/q with shared bathroom €40/50/65; ✳@🛜; Ⓜ Syngrou-Fix) Tucked into a quiet cul-de-sac is one of Athens' best-value budget hotels. Rooms have been artfully updated, with wrought-iron beds, and bathrooms are sleek marble. All rooms have a fridge and ceiling fans and some have air-con (€9 extra). It's a fair walk from the tourist drag, but close to the metro. Breakfast available (€5).

★ Hera Hotel
BOUTIQUE HOTEL €€

(📞210 923 6682; www.herahotel.gr; Falirou 9, Makrygianni; d incl breakfast €160-190, ste €250; ✳@🛜; Ⓜ Akropoli) This elegant boutique hotel, a short walk from the Acropolis and Plaka, was totally rebuilt – but the formal interior design is in keeping with the lovely neoclassical facade. There's lots of brass and timber, and stylish classic furnishings. The rooftop garden, restaurant and bar have spectacular views.

Periscope
BOUTIQUE HOTEL €€

(📞210 729 7200; www.periscope.gr; Haritos 22, Kolonaki; d from €120; ✳🛜; Ⓜ Evangelismos) Right in chic Kolonaki overlooking Lykavittos, Periscope is a design hotel with industrial decor. Clever gadgets are sprinkled throughout, including the lobby slide show and aerial shots of the city on the ceilings. Korres organic toiletries and the trendy **Pbox** restaurant add to the vibe. The penthouse's private rooftop spa has sensational views.

★ Herodion
HOTEL €€€

(📞210 923 6832; www.herodion.gr; Rovertou Galli 4, Makrygianni; d incl breakfast from €165; ✳@🛜; Ⓜ Akropoli) This smart four-star hotel is geared towards the well-heeled traveller and business travellers. Rooms are small but decked out with all the trimmings and have super-comfortable beds. The rooftop spa and lounge have unbeatable Acropolis and museum views.

★ Electra Palace
LUXURY HOTEL €€€

(📞210 337 0000; www.electrahotels.gr; Navarhou Nikodimou 18, Plaka; d/ste incl breakfast from €250/350; P✳@🛜🏊; Ⓜ Syntagma) Plaka's smartest hotel is one for the romantics – have breakfast under the Acropolis on your balcony (in higher-end rooms) and dinner in the chic rooftop restaurant. Completely refurbished with classic elegance, the well-appointed rooms are buffered from the sounds of the city streets. There's a gym and an indoor swimming pool, as well as a rooftop pool with Acropolis views.

★ NEW Hotel
BOUTIQUE HOTEL €€€

(📞210 327 3000; www.yeshotels.gr; Filellinon 16, Plaka; d from €150; P✳🛜; Ⓜ Syntagma) Whether you dig the groovy, top-designer Campana Brothers furniture or the sleeping-pillow menu (tell 'em how you like it!), you'll find some sort of decadent treat here to tickle your fancy. Part of a renowned local design-hotel group, NEW Hotel is the latest entry on the high-end Athens scene.

✕ Eating

Eat streets include Mitropoleos, Adrianou and Navarchou Apostoli in Monastiraki, the area around Plateia Psyrri, and Gazi, near Keramikos metro.

The fruit and vegetable **market** (Varvakios Agora; Athinas, btwn Sofokleous & Evripidou; ⏰7am-3pm Mon-Sat; Ⓜ Monastiraki, Panepistimio, Omonia) is opposite the meat market.

★ Akordeon
MEZEDHES €

(📞210 325 3703; Hristokopidou 7, Psyrri; dishes €6-15; ⏰lunch & dinner; Ⓜ Monastiraki, Thisio) Slide into this charming butter-yellow house across from a church in a quiet Psyrri side street for a warm welcome by musician-chefs Pepi and Achilleas (and their spouses), who run this excellent venue on the local music and mezedhes scene. They'll help you order authentic Greek fare, then (at night and on weekends) surround you with their soulful songs.

★ Mavro Provato
MEZEDHES €

(📞210 722 3466; www.tomauroprovato.gr; Arrianou 31-33, Pangrati; dishes €5-12; ⏰lunch & dinner; Ⓜ Evangelismos) Book ahead for this wildly popular modern *mezedhopoleio* (restaurant specialising in mezedhes) in Pangrati, where tables line the footpath and delicious small plates are paired with *raki* (Cretan firewater) or *tsipouro* (distilled spirit similar to ouzo but usually stronger).

★ Kalnterimi
TAVERNA €

(📞210 331 0049; www.kalnterimi.gr; Plateia Agion Theodoron, cnr Skouleniou, Monastiraki; mains €5-8; ⏰noon-11pm Mon-Sat; 🛜; Ⓜ Panepistimio)

WORTH A TRIP

ISLAND IN A DAY: AEGINA & HYDRA

For islands within easy reach of Athens, head to the Saronic Gulf. Aegina (eh-yee-nah; www.aeginagreece.com), just a half hour from Piraeus, is home to the impressive Temple of Aphaia, said to have served as a model for the construction of the Parthenon. The catwalk queen of the Saronics, Hydra (ee-drah; www.hydra.gr, www.hydraislandgreece.com) is a delight, an hour and a half from Piraeus. Its picturesque horseshoe-shaped harbour town with gracious stone mansions stacked up the rocky hillsides is known as a retreat for artists, writers and celebrities. There are no motorised vehicles – apart from sanitation trucks – leading to unspoilt trails along the coast and into the mountains.

From Hydra, you can return to Piraeus, or carry on to Spetses and the Peloponnese (Metohi, Ermione and Porto Heli). Check Hellenic Seaways (www.hsw.gr) and Aegina Flying Dolphins (www.aegeanflyingdolphins.gr).

Find your way behind the Church of Agii Theodori to this hidden, open-air taverna offering Greek food at its most authentic. Everything is freshly cooked and delicious: you can't go wrong. Hand-painted tables spill onto the footpath along a pedestrian street and give a feeling of peace in one of the busiest parts of the city.

⭐ **Diporto Agoras**   TAVERNA €

(210 321 1463; cnr Theatrou & Sokratous; plates €5-7; 7am-7pm Mon-Sat, closed 1-20 Aug; Omonia, Monastiraki) This quirky old taverna is one of the dining gems of Athens. There's no signage, only two doors leading to a rustic cellar where there's no menu, just a few dishes that haven't changed in years. The house speciality is *revythia* (chickpeas), usually followed by grilled fish and washed down with wine from one of the giant barrels lining the wall. The often erratic service is part of the appeal.

⭐ **Avocado**   VEGETARIAN €

(210 323 7878; www.avocadoathens.com; Nikis 30, Plaka; mains €8-13; noon-11pm Mon-Fri, 11am-11pm Sat, noon-7pm Sun; ; Syntagma) This excellent, popular cafe offers a full array of vegan, gluten-free and organic treats – a rarity in Greece. Next to an organic market, and with a tiny front patio, you can enjoy everything from sandwiches to quinoa with eggplant or mixed-veg coconut curry. Fresh juices and mango lassis are all made on the spot.

⭐ **Varvakios Agora**   MARKET €

(Athens Central Market; Athinas, btwn Sofokleous & Evripidou, Omonia; 7am-6pm Mon-Sat; Monastiraki, Panepistimio, Omonia) The streets around the colourful and bustling Varvakios Agora are a sensory delight. The meat and fish market fills the historic building on the eastern side, and the fruit and vegetable market is across the road. The meat market

might sound like a strange place to go for a meal, but its tavernas are an Athenian institution. Clients range from hungry market workers to elegant couples emerging from nightclubs in search of a bowl of hangover-busting *patsas* (tripe soup).

⭐ **2 Mazi**   FUSION €€

(210 322 2839; www.2mazi.gr; Nikis 48, Plaka; mains €17-26; 12.30pm-midnight; Syntagma, Akropoli) Inside a neoclassical mansion, this elegant dining room with white linen and proper crystal is the venue for inventive creations by two young chefs. They incorporate fresh local products such as mountain greens, Greek cheeses and freshly caught seafood to make interesting and beautifully presented dishes spanning the cuisines of Asia, France and the Greek islands.

⭐ **Athiri**   GREEK €€

(210 346 2983; www.athirirestaurant.gr; Plateon 15, Keramikos; mains €12-19; 8pm-1am Tue-Sat, 1-5pm Sun; Thisio) Athiri's lovely garden courtyard is a verdant surprise in this pocket of Keramikos. The small but innovative menu plays on Greek regional classics. Try Santorini fava and the hearty beef stew with *myzithra* (sheep's-milk cheese) and handmade pasta from Karpathos.

⭐ **Mani Mani**   GREEK €€

(210 921 8180; www.manimani.com.gr/english. html; Falirou 10, Makrygianni; mains €15-20; 2-11pm Mon-Sat, 1-6pm Sun; Akropoli) Head upstairs to the relaxing, cheerful dining rooms of this delightful modern restaurant, which specialises in regional cuisine from Mani in the Peloponnese. Standouts include the ravioli with Swiss chard, chervil and cheese, and the tangy Mani sausage with orange. Almost all dishes can be ordered as half portions (at half-price), allowing you to sample widely.

★ **Funky Gourmet** MEDITERRANEAN €€€
(☑ 210 524 2727; www.funkygourmet.com; Paramythias 3, cnr Salaminas, Keramikos; set menu from €150; ⊙7.30pm-1am Tue-Sat, last order 10.30pm; Ⓜ Metaxourgio) Nouveau gastronomy meets fresh Mediterranean ingredients at this two–Michelin star restaurant. Elegant lighting, refinement and sheer joy in food make this a worthwhile stop for any foodie. The degustation menus can be paired with wines. Book ahead.

★ **Spondi** MEDITERRANEAN €€€
(☑ 210 756 4021; www.spondi.gr; Pyrronos 5, Pangrati; mains €44-52, set menus from €73; ⊙8pm-late) Two Michelin–starred Spondi is frequently voted Athens' best restaurant, and the accolades are deserved. It offers Mediterranean haute cuisine, with heavy French influences, in a relaxed, chic setting in a charming old house. Choose from the menu or a range of set dinner and wine *prix fixes*.

🍷 Drinking & Entertainment

One local favoured pastime is going for coffee. Athens' ubiquitous, packed cafes have some of Europe's most expensive coffee (between €3 and €5) – you're essentially hiring the chair and can linger for hours. Many daytime cafes and restaurants turn into bars and clubs at night.

The city's hottest scene masses around Kolokotroni north of Plateia Syntagmatos, and around Plateia Agia Irini in Monastiraki. A cafe-thick area in Monastiraki is Adrianou, along the Ancient Agora, where people fill shady tables. Psyrri has seen a recent resurgence, while Kolonaki steadfastly attracts the trendier set, and Gazi remains tried-and-true. For the best dancing in summer, cab it to beach clubs along the coast near Glyfada – city locations close earlier.

English-language entertainment information appears daily in the 'Kathimerini' supplement in the *International Herald Tribune*; Athens Plus also has listings. For comprehensive events listings, with links to online ticket sales points, try the following:

SUMMER CINEMA

One of the delights of hot summer nights in Athens is the enduring tradition of open-air cinema, where you can watch the latest Hollywood or art-house flick under moonlight. The most historic outdoor cinema is **Aigli** (☑ 210 336 9369; www.aeglizappiou.gr; Zappeio Gardens, Syntagma; €8.50; ⊙films at 9pm & 11pm; Ⓜ Syntagma), in the verdant Zappeio Gardens, where you can watch a movie in style with a glass of wine.

www.breathtakingathens.gr, www.elculture.gr, www.tickethour.com, www.tickethouse.gr, www.ticketservices.gr.

With the current financially strapped climate in Athens, watch your back wherever you go.

🛍 Shopping

Find boutiques around Syntagma, from the Attica department store past Voukourestiou and on Ermou; designer brands and cool shops in Kolonaki; and souvenirs, folk art and leather in Plaka and Monastiraki with its fun **Monastiraki Flea Market** (btwn Adrianou, Ifestou & Ermou, Monastiraki; ⊙daily May-Oct, closed Thu & Sat Nov-Apr; Ⓜ Monastiraki).

ℹ Information

DANGERS & ANNOYANCES

Crime has risen in Athens with the onset of the financial crisis. Though violent crime remains relatively rare, travellers should stay alert on the streets, especially at night.

➡ Streets surrounding Omonia have become markedly seedier, with an increase in prostitutes and junkies; avoid the area, especially at night.

➡ Watch for pickpockets on the metro and at the markets.

➡ When taking taxis, ask the driver to use the meter or negotiate a price in advance. Ignore stories that the hotel you've chosen is closed

REMBETIKA

Athens has some of the best *rembetika* (Greek blues) in intimate, evocative venues. Performances usually include both *rembetika* and *laïka* (urban popular music), start at around 11.30pm and do not have a cover charge, though drinks can be expensive. Most close May to September, so in summer try live-music tavernas around Plaka and Psyrri. There's also live music most weekends at **Café Avyssinia** (☑ 210 321 7047; Kynetou 7, Monastiraki; mains €10-16; ⊙11am-1am Tue-Sat, to 7pm Sun; Ⓜ Monastiraki) and Akordeon (p529).

ⓘ UNCERTAIN TIMES

➡ Due to the financial difficulties in Greece, opening hours, prices and even the existence of some establishments have fluctuated much more than usual.

➡ With businesses associated with tourism, opening hours can always be haphazard; if trade is good, they're open, if not, they shut.

➡ 'High season' is usually July and August. If you turn up in 'shoulder seasons' (May and June; September and October) expect to pay significantly less. Things may be dirt cheap or closed in winter.

or full: they're angling for a commission from another hotel.

➡ Bar scams are commonplace, particularly in Plaka and Syntagma. Beware the over-friendly!

➡ With the recent financial reforms in Greece have come strikes in Athens (check http://livingingreece.gr/strikes). Picketers tend to march in Plateia Syntagmatos.

EMERGENCY

Ambulance/First-Aid Advice (☑166)

Pharmacies (☑in Greek 1434) Check pharmacy windows for details of the nearest duty pharmacy. There's a 24-hour pharmacy at the airport.

SOS Doctors (☑1016, 210 821 1888; ☉24hr) Pay service with English-speaking doctors.

INTERNET RESOURCES

Official visitor site (www.thisisathens.org)

TOURIST INFORMATION

EOT (Greek National Tourist Organisation; ☑210 331 0716, 210 331 0347; www.visit greece.gr; Dionysiou Areopagitou 18-20, Makrygianni; ☉8am-8pm Mon-Fri, 10am-4pm Sat & Sun May-Sep, 9am-7pm Mon-Fri Oct-Apr; Ⓜ Akropoli) Free *Athens* map, transport information and *Athens & Attica* booklet. There's also a desk at **Athens Airport** (☉9am-5pm Mon-Fri & 10am-4pm Sat).

Athens Airport Information Desk (☉24hr) This 24-hour desk has Athens info, booklets and the Athens Spotlighted discount card for goods and services.

Athens City Information Kiosks (www.breath takingathens.com) **Airport** (☑210 353 0390; ☉8am-8pm; Ⓜ Airport); **Acropolis** (☑210 321 7116; Dionysiou Areopagitou & Leoforos Syngrou; ☉9am-9pm May-Sep; Ⓜ Akropoli) Maps, transport information and all Athens info.

ⓘ Getting There & Away

AIR

Modern **Eleftherios Venizelos International Airport** (ATH; ☑210 353 0000; www.aia.gr) is 27km east of Athens.

BOAT

Most ferries, hydrofoils and high-speed catamarans leave from the massive port at Piraeus. Some depart from smaller ports at Rafina and Lavrio.

Purchase tickets at booths on the quay next to each ferry, over the phone or online; travel agencies selling tickets also surround each port.

BUS

Athens has two main intercity **KTEL** (☑210 880 8000; www.ktelattikis.gr) bus stations: **Liossion Terminal B** (☑210 831 7153; Liossion 260, Thymarakia; Ⓜ Agios Nikolaos, Attiki), 5km north of Omonia with buses to central and northern Greece (Delphi, Meteora), and **Kifissos Terminal A** (☑210 515 0025; Leoforos Kifisou 100, Peristeri; Ⓜ Agios Antonios), 7km north of Omonia, with buses to Thessaloniki, the Peloponnese, Ionian Islands and western Greece. The KTEL website and tourist offices have timetables.

Buses for southern Attica (Rafina, Lavrio, Sounio) leave from the **Mavromateon Terminal** (☑210 880 8080, 210 822 5148, 210 880 8000; www.ktelattikis.gr; cnr Leoforos Alexandras & 28 Oktovriou-Patision, Pedion Areos; Ⓜ Viktoria), about 250m north of the National Archaeological Museum.

CAR & MOTORCYCLE

The airport has car rental, and Syngrou, just south of the Temple of Olympian Zeus, is dotted with car-hire firms, though driving in Athens is treacherous.

TRAIN

Intercity trains to central and northern Greece depart from the central **Larisis train station** (Stathmos Larisis; ☑14511; www.trainose.gr; Ⓜ Larisis), about 1km northwest of Plateia Omonias, and served by the metro. For the Peloponnese, take the suburban rail to Kiato and change for other OSE services, or check for available lines at the Larisis station.

GREECE ATHENS

ℹ Getting Around

TO/FROM THE AIRPORT
Bus

Tickets cost €5. Twenty-four-hour services:
Piraeus Port Bus X96, 1½ hours, every 20 minutes
Plateia Syntagmatos Bus X95, 60 to 90 minutes, every 30 minutes (the Syntagma stop is on Othonos)
Terminal A (Kifissos) Bus Station Bus X93, 60 minutes, every 30 to 60 minutes

Metro

Blue line 3 links the airport to the city centre in around 40 minutes; it operates from Monastiraki from 5.50am to midnight, and from the airport from 5.30am to 11.30pm. Tickets (€8) are valid for all public transport for 70 minutes. Fare for two passengers is €14 total.

Taxi

Fixed fares are posted. Expect day/night €35/50 to the city centre, and €47/72 to Piraeus. Both trips often take at least an hour, longer with heavy traffic. Check www.athensairport taxi.com for more info.

PUBLIC TRANSPORT

The metro, tram and bus system makes getting around central Athens and to Piraeus easy. Athens' road traffic can be horrendous. Get maps and timetables at the tourist offices or **Athens Urban Transport Organisation** (OASA; ☑ 11185; www.oasa.gr).

Tickets good for 70 minutes (€1.20), or a 24-hour/five-day travel pass (€4/10) are valid for all forms of public transport except for airport services. The three-day tourist ticket (€20) includes airport transport. Bus/trolleybus–only tickets cannot be used on the metro.

Children under six travel free; people under 18 or over 65 pay half-fare. Buy tickets in metro stations, transport kiosks or most *periptera* (kiosks). Validate the ticket in the machine as you board.

Bus & Trolleybus

Buses and electric trolleybuses operate every 15 minutes from 5am to midnight.

To get to Piraeus: from Syntagma and Filellinon to Akti Xaveriou catch bus 040; from the Omonia end of Athinas to Plateia Themistokleous, catch bus 049.

Metro

Trains operate from 5am to midnight (Friday and Saturday to around 2am), every four to 10 minutes. Get timetables at www.stasy.gr.

TAXI

Taxis are generally reasonable, with small surcharges for port, train and bus station pick-ups, baggage over 10kg or radio taxi. Insist on a metered rate (except for posted flat rates at the airport). Taxi services include **Athina 1** (☑ 210 921 2800, 210 921 0417), **Enotita** (☑ 210 649 5099, 18388; www.athensradio-taxienotita.gr), **Taxibeat** (www.taxibeat.gr) and **Parthenon** (☑ 210 532 3300; www.radio-taxi-parthenon.gr).

TRAIN

Suburban Rail (☑ 14511; www.trainose.gr) A fast suburban rail links Athens with the airport, Piraeus, the outer regions and the northern Peloponnese. It connects to the metro at Larisis, Doukissis Plakentias and Nerantziotissa stations, and goes from the airport to Kiato.

PIRAEUS PORT

Greece's main port and ferry hub fills seemingly endless quays with ships, hydrofoils and catamarans heading all over the country. All ferry companies have online timetables and booths on the quays. EOT (p532) in Athens has a weekly schedule, or check www.openseas.gr. Schedules are reduced in April, May and October, and are radically cut in winter, especially to smaller islands. When buying tickets, confirm the departure point – some Cyclades boats leave from Rafina or Lavrio, and Patras port serves Italy and the Ionian Islands. Igoumenitsa also serves Corfu.

The fastest and most convenient link to Athens is the metro (€1.20, 40 minutes, every 10 minutes, 5am to midnight), near the ferries. Piraeus has a station for Athens' suburban rail. Left luggage at the metro station costs €3 per 24 hours.

The **X96** (Plateia Karaïskaki; tickets €5) Piraeus–Athens Airport Express (€5) leaves from the southwestern corner of Plateia Karaïskaki. Bus 040 goes to Syntagma in downtown Athens.

THE PELOPONNESE
ΠΕΛΟΠΟΝΝΗΣΟΣ

The Peloponnese encompasses a breathtaking array of landscapes, villages and ruins, where much of Greek history has played out.

Nafplio   Ναύπλιο
POP 14,200

Elegant Venetian houses and neoclassical mansions dripping with crimson bougainvillea cascade down Nafplio's hillside to the azure sea. Vibrant cafes, shops and restaurants fill winding pedestrian streets. Crenulated Palamidi Fortress perches above it all. What's not to love?

⊙ Sights

★ **Palamidi Fortress**   FORTRESS
(☑ 27520 28036; adult/concession €4/2; ⊙ 8am-6.45pm May-Oct, 8am-2.45pm Nov-Apr) This vast, spectacular citadel, reachable either by steep ascent on foot or a short drive, stands on a 216m-high outcrop of rock that gives all-encompassing views of Nafplio and the Argolic Gulf. It was built by the Venetians between 1711 and 1714, and is regarded as a masterpiece of military architecture in spite of being successfully stormed in one night by Greek troops in 1822, causing the Turkish garrison within to surrender without a fight.

★ **Archaeological Museum**   MUSEUM
(☑ 27520 27502; Plateia Syntagmatos; adult/child €6/3; ⊙ 8am-3pm Tue-Sun) Inside a splendid Venetian building, this museum traces the social development of Argolis, from the hunter-gatherers of the Fragthi cave to the sophisticated Mycenaean-era civilisations, through beautifully presented archaeological finds from the surrounding area. Exhibits range from Paleolithic fire middens, dating from 32,000 BC, to elaborately painted amphorae (circa 520 BC). You may also spot the only existing bronze armour from near Mycenae (3500 years old and complete with boar-tusk helmet), a wealth of funereal offerings and ceremonial clay masks.

Peloponnesian Folklore Foundation Museum   MUSEUM
(☑ 27520 28379; www.pli.gr; Vasileos Alexandrou 1; adult/child €2/free; ⊙ 9am-2:30pm Mon-Sat, 9:30am-3pm Sun) Established by its philanthropic owner, Nafplio's award-winning museum is a beautifully arranged collection of folk costumes and household items from Nafplio's 19th- and early 20th-century history. Be wowed by the intricate embroidery of traditional costumes and the heavy silver adornments; admire the turn-of-the-century couture and see if you can spot a horse-tricycle. The gift shop sells high-quality local crafts.

🛏 Sleeping

The Old Town is *the* place to stay, but it has few budget options. Cheaper spots dot the road to Argos and Tolo.

★ **Nafplion 1841**   PENSION €
(☑ 27520 24622; www.nafplion1841.gr; Kapodistriou 9; s incl breakfast €50, d incl breakfast €55-85, tr incl breakfast €95; ❊ 🖥) Not only does this delightful pension occupy a 19th-century mansion, but its five bright rooms offer contemporary creature comforts without diminishing the building's character. Expect Cocomat mattresses, superior bed linens, climate control, hydro-massage showers and plasma-screen TVs. The hostess is a delight and so is the breakfast.

Amfitriti Pension   PENSION €€
(☑ 27520 96250; www.amfitriti-pension.gr; Kapodistriou 24; d incl breakfast from €90; ❊ 🖥) Quaint antiques fill these intimate rooms in a house in the Old Town. You can also enjoy stellar views at its nearby sister hotel, **Amfitriti Belvedere**, which is chock-full of brightly coloured tapestries and emits a feeling of cheery serenity.

✖ Eating

Nafplio's Old Town streets are loaded with standard tavernas, with best eats around Vasilissis Olgas.

Ta Fanaria   GREEK €
(☑ 27520 27141; www.fanaria.gr; Staikopoulou 14; mains €7-15; ⊙ noon-midnight; 🖉) This intimate taverna wins points not just for the attentive service but also for its superior selection of vegetarian dishes (think spinach and feta pie, okra stew, oven-baked veggies) alongside the dolmadhes (vine leaves stuffed with rice and sometimes meat) and other Greek classics.

Faro Taverna   SEAFOOD €€
(☑ 27520 27704; Mili; mains €8-15; ⊙ noon-11pm) Locally famous and well worth the 10-minute drive around the bay from Nafplio, this

taverna, run by the grandson of the original owner, sits right on Mili Beach. You can't go wrong with the catch of the day, be it freshly grilled squid, red mullet, fresh sardines or anchovies.

★ 3Sixty°   INTERNATIONAL €€€
(☑ 27525 00501; www.3sixtycafe.gr; Papanikolaou 26 & Koletti; dinner mains €20-64; ☺ 9am-1am; ☏☑) Nafplio punches above its culinary weight at the most imaginative restaurant in town. Sophisticated fare includes the likes of smoky aubergine *imam* with veal, wild mushroom risotto with truffle oil, and lamb stuffed with goat gruyère. Salads are equally creative. The sultry bar serves potent signature cocktails (we're fans of Legendary Star) and numerous Greek wines.

ℹ Information

Staikos Tours (☑ 27520 27950; www.rentacarnafplio.gr; Bouboulinas 50; ☺ 8.30am-2.30pm & 5.30-9pm) A helpful outfit offering Avis rental cars and full travel services.

ℹ Getting There & Away

KTEL Argolis Bus Station (☑ 27520 27323; www.ktelargolida.gr; Syngrou) has the following services:

Argos (for Peloponnese connections) €1.60, 30 minutes, hourly

Athens €13.10, 2½ hours, hourly (via Corinth)

Epidavros €2.90, 45 minutes, four to six Monday to Saturday, one Sunday

Mycenae €2.90, one hour, two to three daily

Epidavros   Επίδαυρος

In its day **Epidavros** (☑ 27530 22009; adult/concession incl museum and Sanctuary of Asclepius €12/6; ☺ 8am-8pm, reduced hours Sep-Mar; ℗) was famed as far away as Rome as a place of miraculous healing. Visitors came great distances to this Sanctuary of Asclepius (god of medicine), set amid pine-clad hills, to seek a cure for their ailments. Don't miss the peaceful Sanctuary of Asclepius, an ancient spa and healing centre.

This World Heritage site's remarkably well-preserved theatre remains a venue during the Hellenic Festival (p528) for Classical Greek theatre, first performed here up to 2000 years ago.

Go as a day trip from Nafplio (€2.90, 45 minutes, four to six buses Monday to Saturday, one Sunday).

Mycenae   Μυκήνες

Although settled as early as the 6th millennium BC, **Ancient Mycenae** (☑ 27510 76585; adult/concession incl Ancient Mycenae museum & Agamemon's Tomb €12/6; ☺ 8am-8pm Apr-Oct, to 3pm Nov-Mar), pronounced mih-*kee*-nes, was at its most powerful from 1600 to 1200 BC. Mycenae's grand entrance, the Lion Gate, is Europe's oldest monumental sculpture.

Two daily buses (excluding Sundays) head to Mycenae from Nafplio (€2.60, one hour) and Argos (€1.60, 30 minutes).

Mystras   Μυστράς

The captivating ruins of churches, libraries, strongholds and palaces in the fortress town of Mystras (miss-*trahss*), a World Heritage-listed site, spill from a spur of the Taÿgetos Mountains 7km west of Sparta. It's among the most important historical sites in the Peloponnese. This is where the Byzantine Empire's richly artistic and intellectual culture made its last stand before an invading Ottoman army, almost 1000 years after its foundation.

Traveller facilities are found in Mystras village, 1km or so below the main gate of ancient Mystras. Staying in the village allows you to beat the crowds and the heat. The stunning **Traditional Guesthouse Mazaraki** (☑ 27310 20414; www.xenonasmazaraki.gr; Pikoulianika; d €85, ste €120-150, apt €190; incl breakfast; ℗☏☒) 🍽 is a destination in itself.

Olympia   Ολυμπία

POP 1000

The compact modern village of Olympia (o-lim-bee-ah), lined with souvenir shops and eateries, caters to the coach-loads of tourists who pass through on their way to the most famous sight in the Peloponnese: Ancient Olympia. This is where myth and fact merge – where Zeus allegedly held the first Olympic Games and where the first Olympics were staged in 776 BC, and every four years thereafter until AD 393, when Emperor Theodosius I banned them.

Just 500m south of the village, across the Kladeos River, the remains of **Ancient Olympia** (☑ 26240 22517; adult/concession site & Olympic museums €12/6; ☺ 8am-8pm Apr-Oct, to 3pm Nov-Mar) rest amid luxurious greenery. The Olympic Flame is lit here every four

GREEK HISTORY IN A NUTSHELL

With its strategic position at the crossroads of Europe and Asia, Greece has endured a vibrant and turbulent history. During the Bronze Age (3000–1200 BC in Greece), the advanced Cycladic, Minoan and Mycenaean civilisations flourished. The Mycenaeans were swept aside in the 12th century BC by the warrior-like Dorians, who introduced Greece to the Iron Age.

By 800 BC, when Homer's *Odyssey* and *Iliad* were first written down, Greece was undergoing a cultural and military revival with the evolution of the city states, the most powerful of which were Athens and Sparta, and the development of democracy. The unified Greeks repelled the Persians twice, which was followed by an era of unparalleled growth and prosperity known as the Classical (or Golden) Age.

The Golden Age

During this period, Pericles commissioned the Parthenon, Sophocles wrote *Oedipus the King* and Socrates taught young Athenians to think. The era ended with the Peloponnesian War (431–404 BC), when the militaristic Spartans defeated the Athenians. They failed to notice the expansion of Macedonia under King Philip II, who conquered the war-weary city states.

Philip's son, Alexander the Great, marched triumphantly into Asia Minor, Egypt, Persia and parts of what are now Afghanistan and India. In 323 BC he met an untimely death at the age of 33, and his generals divided his empire between themselves.

Roman Rule & the Byzantine Empire

Roman incursions into Greece began in 205 BC. By 146 BC Greece and Macedonia had become Roman provinces. In the centuries that followed, Venetians, Franks, Normans, Slavs, Persians, Arabs and, finally, Turks, took turns chipping away at the Byzantine Empire.

The Ottoman Empire & Independence

After the end of the Byzantine Empire in 1453, when Constantinople fell to the Turks, most of Greece became part of the Ottoman Empire. The Greeks fought the War of Independence from 1821 to 1832, and in 1827 Ioannis Kapodistrias was elected the first Greek president.

years. Don't miss the statue of Hermes of Praxiteles, a classical-sculpture masterpiece, at the exceptional **Archaeological Museum** (adult/concession site & Olympic museums €12/6; ◷ 8am-8pm May-Oct, 8am-3pm Nov-Apr).

Sparkling-clean **Pension Posidon** (☑ 26240 22567; www.pensionposidon.gr; Stefanopoulou 9; s/d/tr incl breakfast €35/40/45; ✳) and quiet, spacious **Hotel Pelops** (☑ 26240 22543; www.hotelpelops.gr; Varela 2; s/d/tr incl breakfast €45/60/80; ✳ @ ☎) offer the best value in the centre. Family-run **Best Western Europa** (☑ 26240 22650; www.hoteleuropa.gr; Drouva 1; s/d/tr incl breakfast €75/94/105; P ✳ @ ☎ ☲) above town has sweeping vistas from room balconies and the wonderful swimming pool.

Buses depart from in front of the train station. There are services to Pyrgos (€2.30, 30 minutes, eight to 13 daily), with four or five handy Athens connections, and to Trip-oli (€14.30, three hours) – reserve your seat with KTEL Pyrgos one day in advance. Train services head to/from Pyrgos only – there are five departures daily (€2, 30 minutes).

CENTRAL GREECE (ΚΕΝΤΡΙΚΗ ΕΛΛΑΔΑ)

Central Greece's dramatic landscape of deep gorges, rugged mountains and fertile valleys is home to the magical stone pinnacle-topping monasteries of Meteora and the iconic ruins of ancient Delphi, where Alexander the Great sought advice from the Delphic oracle. Established in 1938, **Parnassos National Park** (☑ 22340 23529; http://en.parnassosnp.gr), to the north of Delphi, attracts naturalists, hikers (it's part of the E4 European long-distance path) and skiers.

Delphi   Δελφοί

POP 854

Modern Delphi and its adjoining ruins hang stunningly on the slopes of Mt Parnassos overlooking the shimmering Gulf of Corinth.

According to mythology, Zeus released two eagles at opposite ends of the world and they met here, thus making Delphi the centre of the world. By the 6th century BC, Ancient Delphi (☑ 22650 82312; site or museum adult/child €6/free, combined €9; ☺ 8am-8pm Apr-Oct, 8am-3pm Nov-Mar) had become the Sanctuary of Apollo. Thousands of pilgrims flocked here to consult the female oracle who sat at the mouth of a fume-emitting chasm. After sacrificing a sheep or goat, pilgrims would ask a question, and a priest would translate the oracle's response into verse. Wars, voyages and business transactions were undertaken on the strength of these prophecies.

In the town centre, Rooms Pitho (☑ 22650 82850; www.pithohotel.gr; Vasileon Pavlou & Friderikis 40a; s/d/tr incl breakfast from €45/55/70; ✹ ⛢) is friendly, and cosy Hotel Sibylla (☑ 22650 82335; www.sibylla-hotel.gr; Vasileon Pavlou & Friderikis 9; s/d/tr €30/35/40; ✹ ⛢) has tidy rooms and views across the gulf. Elegant, modern Hotel Apollonia (☑ 22650 82919; www.hotelapollonia.gr; Syngrou 37-39; s/d incl breakfast €75/90; ✹ @ ⛢) has balcony views all over Delphi.

Apollon Camping (☑ 22650 82762; www.apolloncamping.gr; campsites per person/tent €8.50/5; ℗ @ ⛢ ⛱) is just 2km west of town, with a restaurant, pool and minimarket.

At the excellent, family-run Taverna Vakhos (☑ 22650 83186; www.vakhos.com; Apollonos 31; mains €8-15; ☺ noon-late; ⛢) they serve traditional dishes while locals pack Taverna Gargadouas (Vasileon Pavlou & Friderikis; mains €8-10; ☺ noon-late) for grilled meats and slow-roasted lamb.

Buses depart from the eastern end of Friderikis, opposite the old Hotel Vouza. Tickets must be purchased from The Delphi restaurant between 9am and 8pm. Four to five buses head daily to Athens Liossion Terminal B (€15.10, three hours). For Meteora/Kalambaka, take a bus to Lamia (€9.10, two hours, one daily) to transfer.

Meteora   Μετέωρα

Meteora (meh-teh-o-rah) should be a certified Wonder of the World with its magnificent late-14th-century monasteries perched dramatically atop enormous rocky pinnacles.

◉ Sights

While there were once monasteries on all 24 pinnacles, only six are still occupied: Megalou Meteorou (Grand Meteoron; €3; ☺ 9am-1pm & 3.30-6pm Wed-Mon Apr-Oct, to 5pm Thu-Mon Nov-Mar), Varlaam (€3; ☺ 9am-1pm & 3.30-6pm Sat-Thu Apr-Oct, until 5pm Sat-Wed Nov-Mar), Agiou Stefanou (€3; ☺ 9am-1.30pm & 3.30-6pm Tue-Sun Apr-Oct, 9.30am-1pm & 3-5pm Tue-Sun Nov-Mar), Agias Triados (Holy Trinity; €3; ☺ 9am-5.45pm Fri-Wed Apr-Oct, 9am-12.30pm & 3-5pm Sat-Wed Nov-Mar), Agiou Nikolaou (Monastery of St Nikolaou Anapafsa; €3; ☺ 9am-3.30pm Sat-Thu Nov-Mar, to 2pm Apr-Oct) and Agias Varvaras Rousanou (€3; ☺ 9am-6pm Thu-Tue Apr-Oct, to 2pm Nov-Mar). Strict dress codes apply (no bare shoulders or knees and women must wear skirts; you can borrow a long skirt at the door). Walk the footpaths between monasteries, drive the back asphalt road, or take the bus (€1.20, 20 minutes) that departs from Kalambaka and Kastraki at 9am, and returns at 1pm (12.40pm on weekends).

Meteora's stunning rocks are also a climbing paradise. Visit Meteora (☑ 24320 23820; www.visitmeteora.travel; Patriarchou Dimitriou 2, Kalambaka; ☺ 9am-9pm) offers some excellent opportunities with professional guides Lazaros Botelis and Kostas Liolios.

GREECE DELPHI

MT OLYMPUS

Just as it did for the ancients, Greece's highest mountain, Olympus (☑ 23520 83000; www.olympusfd.gr), the cloud-covered lair of the Greek pantheon, fires the visitor's imagination today. The highest of Olympus' eight peaks is Mytikas (2917m), popular with trekkers, who use Litohoro (305m), 5km inland from the Athens–Thessaloniki highway, as their base. The main route up takes two days, with a stay overnight at one of the refuges (☺ May-Oct). Good protective clothing is essential, even in summer. EOS Litohoro (Greek Alpine Club; ☑ 23520 84544, 23520 82444; http://eoslitohorou.blogspot.com; ☺ 9.30am-12.30pm & 6-8pm Mon-Sat Jun-Sep) has information.

🛏 Sleeping & Eating

The tranquil village of Kastraki, 2km from Kalambaka, is the best base for visiting Meteora.

Pyrgos Adrachti BOUTIQUE HOTEL €€
(☑ 24320 22275; www.hotel-adrachti.gr; d €55-80, tr €85; 🅿 ❄ 🛜) Slick and cool sums up this place – think designer-style touches throughout the rooms, bar and common areas, and an up-close-and-personal rock experience. Plus there's a tidy garden to relax in post-activities. It's at the northern end of the village, nestled under the rocks; follow the signs.

Batalogianni TAVERNA €
(☑ 3202 3253; mains €7-12; ⊗ 8am-late) You know the type of place you wouldn't look twice at 'cos it's slightly off the road and you don't realise it has an oasis of a garden terrace and serves up delicious 100% home-made *mayirefta* (ready-cooked meals)? This charming little spot is all that. Open all year.

ℹ Getting There & Around

Local buses shuttle between Kalambaka and Kastraki (€1.20). Hourly buses go from Kalambaka's **KTEL bus station** (☑ 24320 22432; www.ktel-trikala.gr; Ikonomou) to the transport hub of Trikala (€2.30, 30 minutes), from where buses go to Ioannina (€12.50, 2½ hours, two daily) and Athens (€29, five hours, seven daily).

From Kalambaka **train station** (☑ 24320 22451; www.trainose.gr), trains run to Athens (regular/IC €18 to €29, 4½/five hours, both once daily) and Thessaloniki (€15.20, four hours, three daily). You may need to change in Paleofarsalos.

NORTHERN GREECE
ΒΟΡΕΙΑ ΕΛΛΑΔΑ

Northern Greece is graced with magnificent mountains, thick forests, tranquil lakes and archaeological sites. It's easy to get off the beaten track and experience aspects of Greece noticeably different to other mainland areas and the islands.

Thessaloniki Θεσσαλονίκη

POP 325,200

Dodge cherry sellers in the street, smell spices in the air and enjoy waterfront breezes in Thessaloniki (thess-ah-lo-*nee*-kih), also known as Salonica. The second city of Byzantium and of modern Greece boasts countless Byzantine churches, a smattering of Roman ruins, engaging museums, shopping to rival Athens, fine restaurants and a lively cafe scene and nightlife.

👁 Sights

Check out the seafront **White Tower** (Lefkos Pyrgos; ☑ 2310 267 832; www.lpth.gr; adult/student €3/2; ⊗ 8.30am-3pm Tue-Sun, to 8pm in summer) with its spine-chillling history, and wander *hammams* (Turkish baths), Ottoman and Roman sites like Galerius' **Rotunda** (☑ 2310 218 720; Plateia Agiou Georgiou; ⊗ 9am-5pm Tue-Sun) FREE, and churches such as the enormous, revered 5th-century **Church of Agios Dimitrios** (☑ 2310 270 008; www.inad.gr; Agiou Dimitriou 97; ⊗ 8am-10pm) with its crypt containing the relics of the city's patron saint.

The award-winning **Museum of Byzantine Culture** (☑ 2313 306 400; www.mbp.gr; Leoforos Stratou 2; adult/student €8/4 Apr-Oct, €4 Nov-Mar; ⊗ 8am-8pm Apr-Oct, 9am-4pm Nov-Mar) beautifully displays splendid sculptures, mosaics, icons and other intriguing artefacts. The outstanding **Archaeological Museum** (☑ 2310 830 538; www.amth.gr; Manoli Andronikou 6; adult/concession €8/4; ⊗ 8am-8pm daily) showcases prehistoric, ancient Macedonian and Hellenistic finds.

The compelling **Thessaloniki Centre of Contemporary Art** (☑ 231 059 3270; www.cact.gr; Warehouse B1; adult/child €3/1.50; ⊗ 10am-6pm Tue-Sat, hours vary) and hip **Thessaloniki Museum of Photography** (☑ 2310 566 716; www.thmphoto.gr; Warehouse A, Port; adult/student €2/1; ⊗ 11am-7pm Tue-Sun, to 10pm Fri), beside the port, are worth a look.

🛏 Sleeping

Thess Hostel HOSTEL €
(☑ 6937320162, 2310 554 120; http://thesshostel.gr; Ag Panton 12; dm/apt €18/49; 🛜) This brand-new hostel is a splash of colour tucked into the backstreets behind the train station. The effusive warmth of the staff, the hostel's immaculate cleanliness and its provision of backpacker essentials (good wi-fi, 24-hour reception, a quirkily decorated hang-out area) are all impressive. Thess is well situated if you have an early start at the train or main bus station.

Colors Central Ladadika BOUTIQUE HOTEL €€
(☑ 2316 007 676; www.colorscentral.gr; Oplopiou 1, cnr Katouni; s/d/ste €70/80/100; ❄ 🛜) This stylish boutique hotel, sister to the Colors hotel in Valaoritou, occupies a grand heritage

Thessaloniki

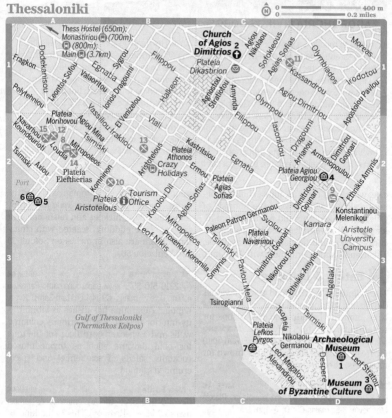

Thessaloniki

◎ Top Sights
1	Archaeological Museum	D4
2	Church of Agios Dimitrios	C1
3	Museum of Byzantine Culture	D4

◎ Sights
4	Rotunda of Galerius	D2
5	Thessaloniki Centre of Contemporary Art	A2
6	Thessaloniki Museum of Photography	A2
7	White Tower	C4

🛏 Sleeping
8	Colors Central Ladadika	A2
9	Rent Rooms Thessaloniki	D2

✕ Eating
10	Chatzis	B2
11	I Nea Follia	C1
12	Kouzina Kioupia	A2
13	Modiano Market	B2
14	Omikron	A2
15	Paparouna	A2

house with 12 uniquely decorated rooms. The modern pop-art decor and vibrant tones give it an uplifting, contemporary feel, and its location in the heart of Ladadika's restaurant quarter couldn't be better.

Rent Rooms Thessaloniki　HOSTEL **€€**
(☑2310 204 080; www.rentrooms-thessaloniki.com; Konstantinou Melenikou 9; dm/s/d/tr/q incl breakfast €25/55/70/90/115; ❅❒) This excellent-value hostel and apartment accommodation has a charming back-garden

ZAGOROHORIA & VIKOS GORGE

Try not to miss the spectacular Zagori region, with its deep gorges, abundant wildlife, dense forests and snowcapped mountains. Some 46 charming villages, famous for their grey-slate architecture, and known collectively as the Zagorohoria, are sprinkled across a large expanse of the Pindos Mountains north of Ioannina. These beautifully restored gems were once only connected by stone paths and arching footbridges, but paved roads now wind between them. Get information on walks from Ioannina's EOS (Greek Alpine Club; ☑ 26510 22138; www.orivatikos.gr; Smyrnis 15; ⊙ hours vary) office.

Monodendri is a popular departure point for treks through dramatic 12km-long, 900m-deep Vikos Gorge, with its sheer limestone walls. Exquisite inns with attached tavernas abound in remote (but popular) twin villages Megalo Papingo and Mikro Papingo. It's best to explore by rental car from Ioannina.

cafe, where you can tuck into a choice of filling breakfasts with views of the Rotunda of Galerius. Some dorms and rooms have mini-kitchens; all have fridges and bathrooms. Security lockers and luggage storage available. The friendly staff is brimming with local info.

✕ Eating & Drinking

Thessaloniki is a great food town. Tavernas dot Plateia Athonos and cafes pack Leoforos Nikis, and the Ladadika quarter is tops for restaurants and bars. Head to **Modiano Market** (Vassiliou Irakliou or Ermo; ⊙ 7am-6pm) for fresh produce. Thessaloniki is known for its sweets: shop around!

★ Kouzina Kioupia   TAVERNA €
(☑ 2310 553 239; www.kouzina-kioupia.gr; Plateia Morihovou 3-5; mains €5-10; ⊙ 1pm-1am Mon-Sat, to 6pm Sun) Bright, friendly and spilling onto the plaza, this welcoming taverna fills with happy local families and tables full of friends. Straightforward taverna dishes are served with flare, and a good time is had by all. Occasional live music.

Omikron   GREEK €
(☑ 2310 532 774; Oplopiou 3; mains €7-10; ⊙ 1pm-late) This neat and tidy local favourite does excellent fresh fish and inventive grills, but most mouth-watering are the daily specials on the chalkboard by the door. Expect masterful use of oysters, market fish and herb-strewn salads.

Chatzis   SWEETS €
(☑ 2310 221 655; http://chatzis.gr; Mitropoleos 24; sweets €1.40-4; ⊙ 8am-late) Glistening syrup-soaked treats have been luring dessert fans into Chatzis since 1908, back when Thes-

saloniki was still an Ottoman city. Try the moist, sugar-rush-inducing *revani* (syrupy semolina cake), chickpea and raisin halva, or *rizogalo* (rice pudding) scented with cinnamon. There are also branches on Sofouli 73 and Venizelou 50.

★ Paparouna   GREEK €€
(☑ 2310 510 852; www.paparouna.com; Pangaiou 4, cnr Doxis; mains €9-14; ⊙ 11am-3am) Ever-popular Paparouna has dishes as vibrant as its interior design. Bright primary-coloured walls and a checkerboard floor set the tone for bold flavours such as thyme-infused cocktails, salads of sea fennel and spice-crumbed seafood.

I Nea Follia   GREEK €€
(☑ 2310 960 383; cnr Aristomenous & Haritos; mains €9-14; ⊙ 1-11pm; ☑) This is the kind of place Anthony Bourdain would like to discover. A bare-bones taverna opened in 1966 on a nondescript north-side alley, in recent years it was commandeered by three young chefs who serve classic Greek fare with a contemporary twist. Expertly sautéed shrimp, fig-strewn salads and juicy grills are all beautifully presented.

ℹ Information

Check www.enjoythessaloniki.com for current events.

Tourism Office (☑ 2310 229 070; www.visit greece.gr; Plateia Aristotelous; ⊙ 10am-5pm) The tourism office on Plateia Aristotelous can assist with hotel bookings, local information, and arranging tours and excursions beyond Thessaloniki.

❶ Getting There & Away

AIR

Makedonia International Airport (SKG; ☑ 2310 985 000; www.thessalonikiairport. com) is 17km southeast of the centre and served by local bus 78 (€2, one hour, half-hourly from 5am to 10pm with a few night buses; www.oasth.gr). Taxis cost €15 to €20 (more from midnight and 5am).

Aegean Airlines and Astra Airlines (p570) fly throughout Greece and many airlines fly internationally.

BOAT

At the time of writing, travellers were being advised to travel to Kavala for ferry connections to the islands. Double-check online through Thesferry (www.thesferry.gr).

BUS

The **main KTEL bus station** (☑ 2310 595 400; www.ktelmacedonia.gr; Giannitson 244), 3km west of the centre, services Athens (€39, six hours, nine daily), Ioannina (€28, 3½ hours, six daily) and other destinations. For Athens *only* you can also get on buses near the train station at **Monastiriou Bus Station** (☑ 2310 500 111; http://ktelthes.gr; Monastiriou 67). Buses to the Halkidiki Peninsula leave from the **Halkidiki bus terminal** (☑ 2310 316 555; www.ktel-chalkidikis. gr; 9km Thessaloniki-Halkidiki road).

KTEL has direct services to Tirana (€30, nine hours, twice weekly) and Sofia (€20 to €23, five hours, four daily). Small bus companies, such as **Simeonidis Tours** (☑ 2310 540 970; www. simeonidistours.gr; 26 Oktovriou 14; ⊙ 9am-9pm Mon-Fri, to 2pm Sat), opposite the courthouse, serve international destinations like Turkey, Romania and Hungary. **Crazy Holidays** (☑ 2310 237 696; www.crazy-holidays.gr; Aristotelous 10, 1st fl) operates daily buses to İstanbul departing at 10am and 10pm.

TRAIN

The **train station** (☑ 2310 599 421; www. trainose.gr; Monastiriou) serves Athens (€55.40, 5¼ hours, seven daily) and other domestic destinations. International trains go to Skopje and Sofia, and beyond.

CYCLADES   ΚΥΚΛΑΔΕΣ

The Cyclades (kih-*klah*-dez) are the Greek islands of postcards. Named after the rough *kyklos* (circle) they form around the island of Delos, they're lapped by the azure Aegean and speckled with white cubist buildings and blue-domed Byzantine churches. Throw in sun-blasted golden beaches, more than a dash of hedonism and history, and it's easy to see why many find the Cyclades irresistible.

Mykonos   Μύκονος

POP 10,134

Mykonos is the great glamour island of the Cyclades and happily flaunts its sizzling style and party-hard reputation. The high-season mix of good-time holidaymakers, cruise-ship crowds (which can reach 15,000 a day), and posturing fashionistas throngs through Mykonos Town, a traditional Cycladic maze. While it retains authentic cubist charms, it remains a mecca for gay travellers and the well bankrolled, and can get super-packed in high season.

◉ Sights

The island's most popular beaches, thronged in summer, are on the southern coast. **Platys Gialos** has wall-to-wall sun lounges, while nudity is not uncommon at **Paradise Beach**, **Super Paradise**, **Elia** and more secluded **Agrari**.

Without your own wheels, catch buses from Hora or caïques from Ornos and Platys Gialos to further beaches. Mykonos Cruises (p544) has an online timetable of its sea-taxi services.

Hora   TOWN
(Mykonos Town) Hora is a captivating labyrinth that's home to chic boutiques and whiter-than-white houses decked with bougainvillea and geraniums, plus a handful of small museums and photogenic churches. **Little Venice**, where the sea laps up to the edge of the restaurants and bars, and Mykonos' famous hilltop **windmills** should be high on the must-see list.

🛏 Sleeping

Book well ahead in high season. Prices plummet outside of July and August, most hotels close in winter.

Mykonos has two **camping** areas, and both on the south coast – Paradise Beach and **Mykonos Camping** (☑ 22890 25915; www. mycamp.gr; Paraga Beach; campsite per adult/child/tent €10/5/10, dm €25, bungalow per person €35; ⊙ May-Sep; @ 🛜 ☒). Minibuses from both meet the ferries and buses go regularly into town.

Mykonos

Tinos; Syros;
Rafina; Piraeus;
Thessaloniki

Ikaria; Samos;
Patmos

5 km
2.5 miles

Cape
Armenistis

Houlakia
Beach

Agios
Stefanos

Agios Stefanos
Beach

Tourlos
Beach

Tourlos

New Port

Malaliamos
Beach

372m

Old Port

Hora
(Mykonos Town)

Vrissi

Ornos

Korfos

Kapari

Kapari
Beach

Agios
Ioannis
Beach

Nea
Mykonos

Cape
Alogomandra

Naxos; Paros; Iraklio;
Ios; Santorini

Excursion Boat

Delos

Cape
Mavros

Mersini
Bay

Mersini
Beach

Fokos
Beach

Panormos Bay

Agios Sostis
Beach

Panormos
Beach

Lake
Marathi

Marathi

Vothonas

Frelia
Beach

Ano Mera

Moni Panagias
Tourlianis

275m

Psarou
Gialos

Platys
Gialos

Psarou
Beach

Platys
Gialos

Paraga
Beach

Super
Paradise
Beach

Paradise
Beach

Elia
Beach

Agrari
Beach

Elia

Merthias
Bay

Profitis Ilias
Anomeritis
(351m)

Lia Beach

Kalafatis Beach

Cape
Kalafatis

Kalo
Livadi
Beach

Cape
Mavrokefalas

Monastichon Beach

Cape
Evros

Cape
Goni

Dragonisi

AEGEAN
SEA

Hotel Lefteris
PENSION €

(☑22890 23128; www.lefterishotel.gr; Apollonas 9; d from €120; ❄🛜) Tucked uphill and away from the crowds, a colourful entranceway leads to pristine, compact rooms and a warm welcome. A young family now runs this eight-room guesthouse (established by the owner's grandfather in the 1970s). All rooms have TV and air-con, and there's a roof terrace with views. Winter prices drop to €35.

Fresh Hotel
BOUTIQUE HOTEL €€

(☑22890 24670; www.hotelfreshmykonos.com; Kalogera 31; s/d incl breakfast €180/190; ⊙mid-May–Oct; ❄🛜) In the heart of town, with a lush and leafy garden and highly regarded on-site restaurant, Fresh is indeed fresh, with compact and stylishly minimalist rooms. Rates fall to €70/80 in the low season.

Carbonaki Hotel
BOUTIQUE HOTEL €€

(☑22890 24124; www.carbonaki.gr; 23 Panahrantou; s/d €140/200; ⊙Apr-Oct; ❄🛜) This family-run boutique hotel is a delightful oasis with bright, comfortable rooms (of various price categories), relaxing public balconies and sunny central courtyards.

★Semeli Hotel
HOTEL €€€

(☑22890 27466; www.semelihotel.gr; off Rohari; d incl breakfast from €355; ❄🛜🏊) Expansive grounds, a glamorous restaurant terrace and swimming pool, and stylish, contemporary rooms combine to make this one of Mykonos' loveliest (and more affordable) top-end hotels.

✖ Eating

High prices don't necessarily reflect high quality in Mykonos Town. Cafes line the waterfront; you'll find good food and coffee drinks at Kadena (☑22890 29290; Hora; mains €10-20; ⊙8am-late; 🛜). Souvlaki shops dot Enoplon Dynameon and Plateia Yialos (Fabrika Sq). Most places stay open late during high season.

To Maereio
GREEK €€

(☑22890 28825; Kalogera 16; mains €15-20; ⊙noon-3pm & 7pm-midnight) A busy, cosy and well-priced place favoured by many locals, with a small but selective menu of Mykonian favourites. It's heavy on meat – try the meatballs, local ham and/or spicy sausage.

★M-Eating
MEDITERRANEAN €€€

(☑22890 78550; www.m-eating.gr; Kalogera 10; mains €17-35; ⊙7pm-1am daily) Attentive service, soft lighting and relaxed luxury are the hallmarks of this creative restaurant specialising in fresh Greek products prepared with flair. Sample anything from sea bass tartar to rib-eye veal with honey truffle. Don't miss the dessert of Mykonian honey pie.

🍸 Drinking & Entertainment

Folks come to Mykonos to party. Each major beach has at least one beach bar which gets going during the day. Night action in town starts around 11pm and warms up by 1am; in the wee hours revellers often relocate from Hora to Cavo Paradiso (☑22890 26124; www.cavoparadiso.gr; Paradise Beach; ⊙11.30pm-7am) on Paradise Beach. From cool sunset cocktails to sweaty trance dancing, wherever you go bring a bankroll – the high life doesn't come cheap.

Hora's Little Venice quarter has a swath of colourful bars and some excellent clubs. Another prime spot is the Tria Pigadia (Three Wells) area on Enoplon Dynameon.

ℹ Information

Mykonos has no tourist office; visit travel agencies instead. There is information online at www.inmykonos.com and www.mykonos.gr. The **Mykonos Accommodation Centre** (MAC; ☑22890 23408; www.mykonos-accommodation.com; 1st fl, Enoplon Dynameon 10) is helpful for all things Mykonos (accommodation, guided tours, island info). The website is loaded.

ℹ Getting There & Around

AIR

Mykonos Airport (☑22890 79000; www.mykonos-airport.com), 3km southeast of the town centre, has flights year-round to Athens and Thessaloniki with Astra Airlines (www.astra-airlines.gr). Summertime connections to European destinations are plentiful.

BOAT

Year-round ferries serve mainland ports Piraeus and Rafina (the latter is usually quicker if you are coming directly from Athens airport), and nearby islands Tinos and Andros. In the high season, Mykonos is well connected with all neighbouring islands, including Paros and Santorini. Hora is loaded with ticket agents.

Mykonos has two ferry quays: the **Old Port**, 400m north of town, where some smaller fast ferries dock, and the **New Port**, 2km north of town, where the bigger fast ferries and all conventional ferries dock. When buying outgoing tickets double-check which quay your ferry leaves from.

DELOS

Southwest of Mykonos, the island of **Delos** (☑ 22890 22259; museum & site adult/child €12/free; ⊗ 8am-8pm Apr-Oct, to 3pm Nov-Mar), a Unesco World Heritage site, is the Cyclades' archaeological jewel. The mythical birthplace of twins Apollo and Artemis, splendid Ancient Delos was a shrine-turned–sacred treasury and commercial centre. It was inhabited from the 3rd millennium BC and reached its apex of power around the 5th century BC.

Overnight stays are forbidden (as is swimming) and boat schedules allow a maximum of four hours at Delos. A simple cafe is located by the museum, but it pays to bring water and food. Wear a hat, sunscreen and walking shoes.

Boats from Mykonos to Delos (€18 return, 30 minutes) go between 9am and 5pm in summer, and return between noon and 8pm. In Hora (Mykonos Town) buy tickets at the old wharf kiosk or at **Delia Travel** (☑ 22890 22322; Akti Kambani), **Sea & Sky** (☑ 22890 22853; www.seasky.gr; Akti Kambani) or **Mykonos Accommodation Centre** (p543). Sometimes in summer boats go from Tinos and Naxos.

Local Boats

Mykonos Cruises (☑ 22890 23995; www.mykonos-cruises.gr; ⊗ 8am-7pm Apr-Oct) offers services to the island's best beaches. See the timetables online. The main departure point is Platys Gialos.

Sea Bus (☑ 6978830355; www.mykonos-seabus.gr; one way €2) connects the New Port with Hora (€2), running hourly from 9am to 10pm.

BUS

Terminal A, the southern bus station (Fabrika Sq), known as Fabrika, serves Ornos and Agios Ioannis Beach, Platys Gialos, Paraga and Super Paradise beaches.

Terminal B, the northern bus station, sometimes called Remezzo, has services to Agios Stefanos via Tourlos, Ano Mera, and Kalo Livadi, Kalafatis and Elia beaches. Buses for Tourlos and Agios Stefanos stop at the Old and New Ports.

Timetables are on the **KTEL Mykonos** (☑ 22890 26797, 22890 23360; www.mykonosbus.com) website.

CAR & TAXI

Car hire starts at €45 per day in high season. Scooters/quads are €20/40. Avis and Sixt are among agencies at the airport.

Naxos   ΝΑΞΟΣ

POP 12,726

The largest of the Cyclades islands, beautiful, raw Naxos could probably survive without tourism. Green and fertile, with vast central mountains, Naxos produces olives, grapes, figs, citrus, corn and potatoes. Explore its fascinating main town, excellent beaches, remote villages and striking interior.

Naxos Town (Hora), on the west coast, is the island's capital and port.

◉ Sights

★ Kastro   AREA

The most alluring part of Hora is the 13th-century residential neighbourhood of Kastro, which Marco Sanudo made the capital of his duchy in 1207. Located behind the waterfront, get lost in its narrow alleyways scrambling up to its spectacular hilltop location.

Several Venetian mansions survive in the centre of Kastro, and you can see the remnants of his castle, the **Tower of Sanoudos**, which was once surrounded by marble balconies.

★ Temple of Apollo   ARCHAEOLOGICAL SITE

(The Portara) FREE From Naxos Town harbour, a causeway leads to the Palatia islet and the striking, unfinished Temple of Apollo, Naxos' most famous landmark (also known as the Portara, or 'Doorway'). Simply two marble columns with a crowning lintel, it makes an arresting sight, and people gather at sunset for splendid views.

Panagia Drosiani   CHURCH

(donations appreciated; ⊗ 10am-7pm May–mid-Oct) Located 2.5km north of Halki, just below Moni, the small, peaceful Panagia Drosiani is among the oldest and most revered churches in Greece. Inside is a series of cavelike chapels. In the darkest chapels, monks and nuns secretly taught Greek language and religion to local children during the Turkish occupation.

Several frescoes still grace the walls and date from the 7th century. Look for the depiction of Mary in the eastern chapter; the clarity and expression is incredible.

Temple of Demeter
TEMPLE

(Dimitra's Temple) About 1.5km south of Sangri is the impressive 6th-century BC Temple of Demeter. The ruins and reconstructions are not large, but they are historically fascinating. There's also a good site museum with some fine reconstructions of temple features. Signs point the way from Sangri.

Beaches

The popular beach of Agios Georgios is just a 10-minute walk south from the main waterfront. Agia Anna Beach, 6km from town, and Plaka Beach are lined with accommodation and packed in summer. Beyond, wonderful sandy beaches continue as far south as Pyrgaki Beach.

Villages

A hire car or scooter will help reveal Naxos' dramatic and rugged landscape. The Tragaea region has tranquil villages, churches atop rocky crags and huge olive groves. Between Melanes and Kinidaros are the island's famous marble quarries. You'll find two ancient abandoned kouros (youth) statues, signposted a short walk from the road. Little Apiranthos settlement perches on the slopes of Mt Zeus (1004m), the highest peak in the Cyclades, and has a few intermittently open museums. The historic village of Halki, one-time centre of Naxian commerce, is well worth a visit.

Lovely waterside Apollonas near Naxos' northern tip has a beach, taverna, and another mysterious 10.5m kouros from the 7th century BC, abandoned and unfinished in an ancient marble quarry.

🛏 Sleeping

Nikos Verikokos Studios
HOTEL €

(☑22850 22025; www.nikos-verikokos.com; Naxos Town; s/d/tr €90/100/120; ⊙year-round; ❄🛜) Friendly Nikos maintains immaculate rooms in the heart of the old town. Some have balconies and sea views, most have little kitchenettes. They offer port pick-up with pre-arrangement.

Hotel Galini
HOTEL €€

(☑22850 22114; www.hotelgalini.com; d incl breakfast from €90; ❄🛜) A nautical theme lends this super-friendly place loads of character. Updated, spacious rooms have small balconies and wrought-iron beds, plus great decor creatively fashioned from seashells and driftwood. The location is first-rate – close to the old town and the beach – and the breakfast is hearty.

KITRON-TASTING IN HALKI

The historic village of Halki is a top spot to try kitron, a liqueur unique to Naxos. While the exact recipe is top secret, visitors can taste it and stock up on supplies at Vallindras Distillery (☑22850 31220; www.facebook.com/media/set/?-set=o.140729449272799; ⊙10am-10pm Jul & Aug, to 6pm May-Jun & Sep-Oct) in Halki's main square. There are free tours of the old distillery's atmospheric rooms, which contain ancient jars and copper stills. Kitron tastings round off the trip.

Xenia Hotel
HOTEL €€

(☑22850 25068; www.hotel-xenia.gr; Plateia Pigadakia; s/d/tr incl breakfast from €85/90/110; ❄🛜) Sleek and minimalist, this hotel (built 2012) is right in the old-town scene, close to everything. Balconies overlook the bustle of the streets but thick glass keeps the noise out when you decide to call it a night.

🍴 Eating & Drinking

Hora's waterfront is lined with eating and drinking establishments. Head into Market St in the Old Town, just down from the ferry quay, to find quality tavernas. South, only a few minutes' walk away, Main Sq is home to other excellent eateries, some of which stay open year-round.

★ Maro
GREEK €

(☑22850 25113; mains €5-15; ⊙lunch & dinner) There's no sea view here, or old-town romance, but the locals don't care. They're too busy tucking into mammoth portions of delicious, good-value local food (including lots of specialities from the village of Apiranthos). The zucchini balls (fritters, really) are tasty, the mousakas (baked layers of eggplant or zucchini, minced meat and potatoes topped with cheese sauce) enormous. It's just south of Plateia Evripeou.

O Apostolis
GREEK €€

(☑22850 26777; www.facebook.com/pages/Taverna-O-Apostolis/314061735335882; Old Market St; mains €8-15; ⊙lunch & dinner) Right at the heart of labyrinthine Bourgos, O Apostolis serves up tasty dishes in its pretty flagstone coutyard. The kleftiko (lamb wrapped in filo pastry), with sautéed vegetables and feta cheese, is delicious.

GREECE NAXOS

L'Osteria
ITALIAN €€

(☑ 22850 24080; www.osterianaxos.com; mains €10-16; ☉ 7pm-midnight) This authentic Italian eatery is tucked away in a small alley uphill from the harbour, beneath the Kastro walls. Grab a table in the cute courtyard and prepare to be impressed: the appetising menu changes daily, but there's also an unchanging list of bruschetta, salads and delectable *antipasti*.

Naxos Cafe
BAR

(☑ 22850 26343; www.facebook.com/naxos-cafe-47365083135; Old Market St; ☉ 8pm-2am) If you want to drink but don't fancy the club scene, here's your answer. This atmospheric, traditional bar is small and candlelit and spills into the cobbled Bourgos street. Drink Naxian wine with the locals.

ℹ Information

There's no official tourist office on Naxos. Travel agencies can deal with most queries. Handy online resources include www.naxos.gr.

ℹ Getting There & Around

AIR

Naxos Airport (JNX; www.naxos.net/airport) serves Athens daily. The airport is 3km south of town; there are no buses – a taxi costs €15, or arrange hotel pick-up.

BOAT

There are myriad high-season daily ferry and hydrofoil connections to most Cycladic islands and Crete, plus Piraeus ferries (€34.50, five hours) and catamarans (€57.50, 3¾ hours). Reduced services in winter.

BUS

Buses leave from the end of the ferry quay in Hora; timetables are posted across the road outside the **bus information office** (☑ 22850 22291; www.naxosdestinations.com; Harbour). You have to buy tickets from the office or from the machine outside (not from the bus driver).

CAR & MOTORCYCLE

Having your own wheels is a good idea for exploring Naxos. Car (€45 to €65) and motorcycle (€25 to €30) rentals line Hora's port and main streets.

Santorini (Thira)
ΣΑΝΤΟΡΙΝΗ (ΘΗΡΑ)

POP 15,550

Stunning Santorini may well have conquered a corner of your imagination before you've even set eyes on it. The startling sight of the submerged caldera almost encircled by sheer lava-layered cliffs – topped by clifftop towns that look like a dusting of icing sugar – will grab your attention and not let it go. If you turn up in high season, though, be prepared for relentless crowds and commercialism – Santorini survives on tourism.

◉ Sights & Activities

★ Museum of Prehistoric Thera
MUSEUM

(☑ 22860 22217; www.santorini.com/museums/prehistoric_museum.htm; Mitropoleos; adult/child €3/free; ☉ 8.30am-3pm Wed-Mon) Opposite the bus station, this well-presented museum houses extraordinary finds excavated from Akrotiri and is all the more impressive when you realise just how old they are. Most remarkable is the glowing gold ibex figurine, dating from the 17th century BC and in amazingly mint condition. Also look for fossilised olive tree leaves from within the caldera from 60,000 BC.

★ Ancient Akrotiri
ARCHAEOLOGICAL SITE

(☑ 22860 81366; http://odysseus.culture.gr/h/3/eh351.jsp?obj_id=2410; adult/child €12/free; ☉ 8am-8pm Apr-Oct, 8am-3pm Nov-Mar) In 1967, excavations began at the site of Akrotiri. What they uncovered was phenomenal: an ancient Minoan city buried deep beneath volcanic ash from the catastrophic eruption of 1613 BC. Today, the site retains a strong sense of place. Housed within a cool, protective structure, wooden walkways allow you to pass through various parts of the city.

★ Art Space
GALLERY

(☑ 22860 32774; www.artspace-santorini.com; Exo Gonia; ☉ 11am-sunset) **FREE** This unmissable, atmospheric gallery is just outside Kamari, in Argyros Canava, one of the oldest wineries on the island. The old wine caverns are hung with superb artworks, while sculptures transform lost corners and niches. The collection features some of Greece's finest modern artists.

Oia
VILLAGE

At the north of the island, the postcard-perfect village of Oia (ee-ah), famed for its sunsets, is less hectic than Fira and a must-visit. Its caldera-facing tavernas are superb spots for a meal. A path from Fira to Oia along the top of the caldera takes three to four hours to walk; otherwise take a taxi or bus. Beat the crowds in the early morning or late evening.

Santorini (Thira)

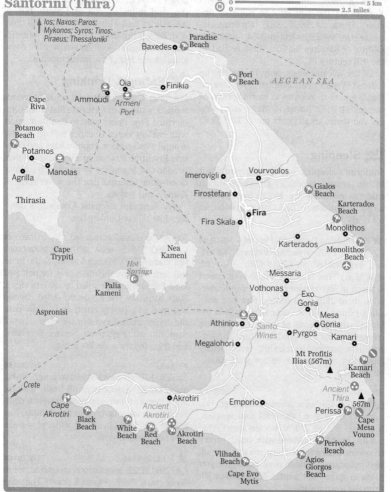

N ↑ Ios; Naxos; Paros;
Mykonos; Syros; Tinos;
Piraeus; Thessaloniki

Paradise Beach
Baxedes
Pori Beach
AEGEAN SEA
Oia
Finikia
Ammoudi
Armeni Port
Cape Riva
Potamos Beach
Potamos
Agrilla
Manolas
Thirasia
Imerovigli
Vourvoulos
Gialos Beach
Firostefani
Karterados Beach
Fira
Monolithos
Fira Skala
Karterados
Monolithos Beach
Cape Trypiti
Nea Kameni
Messaria
Hot Springs
Vothonas
Exo Gonia
Palia Kameni
Mesa Gonia
Aspronisi
Athinios
Santo Wines
Pyrgos
Kamari
Megalohori
Mt Profitis Ilias (567m)
Kamari Beach
Crete
Ancient Thira 567m
Cape Akrotiri
Akrotiri
Emporio
Perissa
Black Beach
Ancient Akrotiri
Cape Mesa Vouno
White Beach
Red Beach
Akrotiri Beach
Perivolos Beach
Vlihada Beach
Agios Giorgos Beach
Cape Evo Mytis

0 — 5 km
0 — 2.5 miles

GREECE SANTORINI (THIRA)

Fira
VILLAGE

Santorini's vibrant main town with its snaking narrow streets full of shops and restaurants perches on top of the caldera. The stunning caldera views from Fira and its neighbouring hamlet Firostefani are matched only by tiny Oia.

SantoWines
WINERY

(☎ 22860 22596; www.santowines.gr; tours & tastings from €12.50; ☺ 9am-9pm) The best place to start your wine adventure. The island's co-operative of grape-growers, it's a large tourist-focused complex on the caldera edge near the port. It has short tours of the production process and lots of tasting options. There are also superb views, a wine bar with food, and a shop full of choice vintages as well as gourmet local products.

◉ Around the Island

Santorini's known for its multihued beaches. The black-sand beaches of **Perissa**, **Perivolos**, **Agios Giorgos** and **Kamari** sizzle – beach mats are essential. **Red Beach**, near Ancient Akrotiri, has impressive red cliffs and smooth, hand-sized pebbles submerged under clear water.

On a mountain between Perissa and Kamari are the atmospheric ruins of **Ancient Thira** ([☑]22860 23217; http://odysseus. culture.gr/h/3/eh351.jsp?obj_id=2454; adult/child €4/free; ⊙8am-3pm Tue-Sun), first settled in the 9th century BC.

Of the volcanic islets, only **Thirasia** is inhabited. Visitors can clamber over lava on **Nea Kameni** then swim in warm springs in the sea at **Palia Kameni**. Many excursions get you there; small boats are at Fira Skala port.

🛏 Sleeping

Santorini's sleeping options are exorbitant in high season, especially anywhere with a caldera view. Many hotels offer free port and airport transfers. Check www.airbnb.com for deals.

★**Karterados Caveland Hostel**   HOSTEL €€
([☑]22860 22122; www.cave-land.com; Karterados; incl breakfast dm €25, d €90; ⊙Mar-Oct; [P][❄][🔊][≋]) This fabulous, chilled-out hostel is based in an old winery complex in Karterados about 2km from central Fira (see website for directions). Accommodation is in the big old wine caves, all of them with creative, colourful decor and good facilities. The surrounding garden is relaxing, with weekly barbecues held, and there are yoga classes on offer too.

Villa Soula   HOTEL €€
([☑]22860 23473; www.santorini-villasoula.gr; Fira; r from €100; [❄][🔊][≋]) Cheerful and spotless, this hotel is a great deal. Rooms aren't large but are freshly renovated with small, breezy balconies. Colourful public areas and a small, well-maintained undercover pool give you room to spread out a little. It's a short walk from the town centre.

★**Zorzis Hotel**   BOUTIQUE HOTEL €€
([☑]22860 81104; www.santorinizorzis.com; Perissa; d incl breakfast from €90; [❄][🔊][≋]) Behind a huge bloom of geraniums on Perissa's main street, Hirohiko and Spiros (a Japanese-Greek couple) run an immaculate 10-room hotel. It's a pastel-coloured sea of calm (no kids), with delightful garden, pool and mountain backdrop.

★**Mill Houses**   BOUTIQUE HOTEL €€€
([☑]22860 27117; www.millhouses.gr; Firostefani; d incl breakfast from €350; [❄][🔊][≋]) Built right into the side of the caldera at Firostefani,

down a long flight of steps, these superb studios and suites are chic and plush. Lots of white linen and whitewashed walls fill them with light. King-sized beds, Bulgari toiletries and private patios looking out over the Aegean are just a few of the lavish touches.

🍴 Eating & Drinking

Overpriced, indifferent food geared towards tourists is still an unfortunate feature of summertime Fira. Prices tend to double at spots with caldera views. Cheaper eateries cluster around Fira's square. Popular bars and clubs line Erythrou Stavrou in Fira. Many diners head to Oia, legendary for its superb sunsets. Good-value tavernas line the waterfronts at Kamari and Perissa.

Try Santorini Brewing Company's offerings like Yellow Donkey beer.

Assyrtico Wine Restaurant   GREEK €€
([☑]22860 22463; www.assyrtico-restaurant.com; Fira; mains €15-30; ⊙lunch & dinner) Settle in on this terrace above the main drag for polished local flavours accompanied by caldera views. Start with, say, the *saganaki* (fried cheese) wrapped in a pastry crust, and follow with the deconstructed gyros or the *mousakas* of Santorini white eggplant. Service is relaxed and friendly; the wine list is big.

Krinaki   TAVERNA €€
([☑]22860 71993; www.krinaki-santorini.gr; Finikia; mains €12-22; ⊙noon-late) All-fresh, all-local ingredients go into top-notch taverna dishes at this homey taverna in tiny Finikia, just east of Oia. Local beer and wine, plus a sea (but not caldera) view.

★**Metaxi Mas**   TAVERNA €€
([☑]22860 31323; www.santorini-metaximas.gr; Exo Gonia; mains €9-19; ⊙lunch & dinner) The *raki* flows at this convivial taverna, a favourite among locals and authenticity-seeking travellers. In the central village of Exo Gonia (between Pyrgos and Kamari), park by the large church and walk down some steps to reach it. Prebooking is a good idea. Enjoy sweeping views and a delicious menu of local and Cretan specialities.

Koukoumavlos   GREEK €€€
([☑]22860 23807; www.koukoumavlos.com; mains €28-34; ⊙dinner Apr–mid-Oct) This terrace is filled with gleeful diners partaking of fresh, modern, Aegean cuisine (including a worthwhile degustation at €65). Creativity reigns

and the menu is poetic, elevating dishes to new heights: 'slow-cooked shoulder of lamb with potato mousseline flavored with jasmine, fig and Greek coffee sauce'. Look for the pink building and wooden doorway. Book ahead.

ⓘ Information

Try www.santorini.net for more information.

Dakoutros Travel (☑ 22860 22958; www. dakoutrostravel.gr; Fira; ☺ 8.30am-10pm) on the main street, just before Plateia Theotokopoulou. Ferry and air tickets sold; assitance with excursions, accommodation and transfers.

ⓘ Getting There & Around

AIR

Santorini Airport (☑ 22860 28400; www. santoriniairport.com) has flights year-round to/from Athens (from €64, 45 minutes). Seasonal European connections are plentiful, including easyJet from London, Rome and Milan.

There are frequent bus connections between Fira's bus station and the airport between 7am and 9pm (€1.60, 20 minutes). Most accommodation providers will arrange (paid) transfers.

BOAT

Thira's main port, Athinios, stands on a cramped shelf of land 10km south of Fira. Buses (and taxis) meet all ferries and then cart passengers up the towering cliffs. Accommodation providers can usually arrange transfers (to Fira per person is around €10).

Multiple boats leave daily for Piraeus (€36 to €59, 5 hours), Naxos (€19.50 to €42, 1½ to two hours) and Mykonos (€60, two to three hours). Less frequent sailing service Rethymno, Rhodes and Kos.

BUS

KTEL Santorini Buses (☑ 22860 25404; http://ktel-santorini.gr) has a good website with schedules and prices. Tickets are purchased on the bus.

In summer, buses leave Fira twice-hourly for Oia, with more services pre-sunset (€1.60). There are also numerous daily departures for Akrotiri (€1.80), Kamari (€1.60), Perissa and Perivolos Beach (€2.20), and a few to Monolithos (€1.60).

Buses leave Fira, Perissa and Kamari for the port of Athinios (€2.20, 30 minutes) a half-dozen times per day. Buses for Fira meet all ferries, even late at night.

CAR & MOTORCYCLE

A car (from €50 per day) or scooter is good for getting out of town. Outlets abound.

CRETE ΚΡΗΤΗ

POP 623,000

With its dramatic landscape, myriad mountain villages, unique cultural identity and some of the best food in Greece, Crete is a delight to explore. As Greece's largest, most southerly island, its size, distance and independent history give it the feel of a different country.

The island is split by a spectacular chain of mountains running east to west. Major towns are on the more hospitable northern coast, while most of the southern coast is too precipitous to support large settlements. The rugged mountainous interior, dotted with caves and sliced by dramatic gorges, offers rigorous hiking and climbing. Small villages like Magarites, a potters' village near Mt Idi, offer a glimpse into traditional life.

Iraklio ΗΡΑΚΛΕΙΟ

POP 140,730

Iraklio (ee-*rah*-klee-oh; often spelt Heraklion), Crete's capital and economic hub, is a bustling modern city and the fifth-largest in Greece. It has a lively city centre, an excellent archaeological museum and is close to Knossos, Crete's major visitor attraction. Other towns are more picturesque, but in a pinch, you can stay over in Iraklio.

Iraklio's harbours face north with the landmark **Koules Venetian Fortress**. Plateia Venizelou, known for its **Lion (Morosini) Fountain**, is the heart of the city, 400m south of the old harbour up 25 Avgoustou.

⊙ Sights & Activities

★ Heraklion

Archaeological Museum MUSEUM

(☑ 2810 279000; http://odysseus.culture.gr; Xanthoudidou 2; adult/child €10/free; ☺ 8am-8pm Apr-Oct, 11am-5pm Mon, 8am-3pm Tue-Sun Nov-Mar) Reopened in 2014 after a long renovation, the Archaeological Museum of Heraklion is Crete's outstanding jewel. The two floors of the restored 1930s Bauhaus building make a gleaming showcase for the exhibits that span 5500 years, from neolithic to Roman times, and an extensive Minoan collection. The rooms are colour coded and artefacts, displayed both chronologically and thematically, are beautifully presented with descriptions in English. A visit here enhances any understanding of Crete's rich history. Don't skip it.

GREECE IRAKLIO

Crete

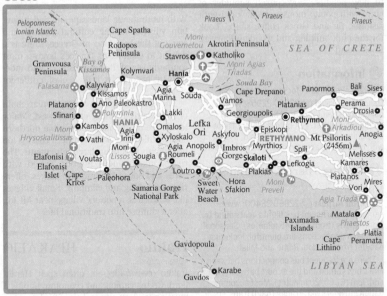

Cretan Adventures OUTDOORS

(☑2810 332772; www.cretanadventures.gr; 3rd fl, Evans 10) 🖉 This well-regarded local company run by friendly and knowledgeable English-speaking Fondas organises hiking tours, mountain biking and extreme outdoor excursions. It also coordinates fabulous self-guided tours with detailed hiking instructions, plus accommodation with breakfast and luggage transfer (from €740 for one week). Fondas' office is up on the 3rd floor and easy to miss.

🛏 Sleeping

Staying in nearby Arhanes offers a chance to see Cretan wine country. Try **Arhontiko** (☑2810 752985; www.arhontikoarhanes.gr; Arhanes; apt €75-95; ❋🛜) with its beautifully kitted-out apartments.

Kronos Hotel HOTEL €

(☑2810 282240; www.kronoshotel.gr; Sofokli Venizelou 2; s €47, d €60-67; ❋@🛜) Good, if noisy, position near the waterfront, the no-frills but pleasant rooms have double-glazed windows to block out noise, as well as a balcony, phone, a tiny TV and a fridge. Some doubles have sea views. An 'only-OK' breakfast costs €7.

Capsis Astoria HOTEL €€

(☑2810 343080; www.capsishotel.gr; Plateia Eleftherias 11; r incl breakfast €100-140; P❋@🛜☀) The hulking exterior doesn't impress, but past the front door the Capsis is a class act, all the way to the rooftop pool from where you enjoy a delicious panorama of Iraklio. Rooms sport soothing neutral tones and dashing historic black-and-white photographs. Thirty of the 131 rooms are 'skylight' rooms, meaning windows but no vistas. Fabulous breakfast buffet.

🍴 Eating & Drinking

Eateries, bars and cafes surround Plateia Venizelou (Lion Fountain) and the El Greco Park area. The old harbour offers seafood options.

Fyllo...Sofies CAFE €

(☑2810 284774; www.fillosofies.gr; Plateia Venizelou 33; snacks €3-7; ⏱6am-late; 🛜) With tables sprawling out towards the Morosini Fountain, this is a great place to sample a breakfast *bougatsa* (creamy semolina pudding wrapped in a pastry envelope and sprinkled with cinnamon and sugar). The less-sweet version is made with *myzithra* (sheep's-milk cheese).

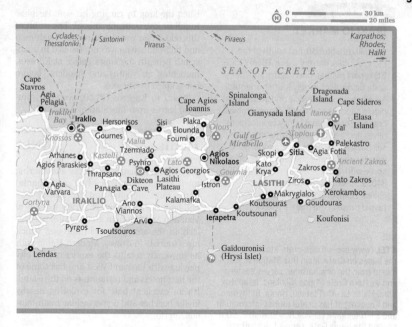

★ **Peskesi** CRETAN €€

(☑ 2810 288887; www.peskesicrete.gr; mains €8-16; ⊙10am-late) One of Iraklio's recent additions to the city's upmarket dining scene, and housed in a smartly converted cottage, this lovely eatery comes with a large dollop of snob value. It's best described as 'postmodern ancient Greek' (say what? we hear you ask). Think smoked pork (*apaki*) hanging off a butcher's hook with smoking herbs beneath and *kandavlos* (an ancient souvlaki).

Ippokambos SEAFOOD €€

(Sofokli Venizelou 3; mains €6-15; ⊙ noon-late Mon-Sat; 🛜) Locals give this smart *ouzerie* (place that serves ouzo and light snacks) an enthusiastic thumbs up and we are only too happy to follow suit. Fish is the thing here – it's freshly caught, simply but expertly prepared and sold at fair prices. In summer, park yourself on the covered waterfront terrace. Look for the seahorse (*ippokambos*) sign.

Parasties GREEK €€

(☑ 2810 225009; www.parasties.gr; Historic Museum Sq, Sofokli Venizelou 19; mains €7-24; ⊙noon-midnight) Parasties' owner Haris is Iraklio's answer to a city's restaurateur who is genuine about serving great-quality local produce and top Cretan wines. And his passion shows in his small but gourmet menu. Beef liver and grilled mushrooms are our top choices, while a great selection of zingy salads and superb meats will keep you munching more than you planned.

ℹ Information

Visit www.heraklion.gr for city information.

ℹ Getting There & Around

AIR

Flights from Iraklio's **Nikos Kazantzakis International Airport** (HER; ☑ general 2810 397800, info 2810 397136; www.heraklion-airport.info) serve Athens, Thessaloniki and Rhodes plus destinations all over Europe. The airport is 5km east of town. In summer, bus 1 travels between the airport and city centre (€1.10) every 15 minutes from 6.15am to midnight. A taxi into town costs around €12 to €15.

BOAT

Daily ferries from Iraklio's **ferry port** (☑ 2810 244956) service Piraeus (€36 to €43, 6½ to 9½ hours), and catamarans head to Santorini and other Cycladic islands. Ferries sail east to Rhodes (€27, 14 hours) via Agios Nikolaos, Sitia, Kasos, Karpathos and Halki. Services are reduced in winter. See www.openseas.gr.

IRAKLIO MARKET

An Iraklio institution, just south of the Lion Fountain, narrow **Odos 1866** (1866 St) is part market, part bazaar and, despite being increasingly tourist-oriented, it's a fun place to browse and stock up on picnic supplies from fruit and vegetables, creamy cheeses and honey to succulent olives and fresh breads. Other stalls sell pungent herbs, leather goods, hats, jewellery and some souvenirs. Cap off a spree with lunch at **Giakoumis** (☑28102 84039; Theodosaki 5-8; mains €6-13; ⊙7am-11pm) or another nearby taverna (avoid those in the market itself).

BUS

KTEL (www.bus-service-crete-ktel.com) runs the buses on Crete. Main Bus Station A, just inland from the new harbour, serves eastern and western Crete (Agios Nikolaos, Ierapetra, Sitia, Malia, Lasithi Plateau, Hania, Rethymno and Knossos). It has useful tourist information and a left-luggage service.Bus Station B, 50m beyond the Hania Gate, serves the southern route (Phaestos, Matala and Anogia).

Knossos   ΚΝΩΣΣΟΣ

Crete's most famous historical attraction is the **Palace of Knossos** (☑28102 31940; http://odysseus.culture.gr; adult/concession/child €15/8/free, incl Heraklion Archaeological Museum €16; ⊙8am-8pm Apr-Oct, to 5pm Nov-Mar), 5km south of Iraklio, and the grand capital of Minoan Crete. Excavation on Knossos (k-nos-*os*) started in 1878 with Cretan archaeologist Minos Kalokerinos, and continued from 1900 to 1930 with British archaeologist Sir Arthur Evans. Today, it's hard to make sense, in the extensive restorations, of what is Evans' interpretation and what actually existed in Minoan times. But the setting is gorgeous and the ruins and recreations impressive, incorporating an immense palace, courtyards, private apartments, baths, lively frescoes and more. Going to the Heraklion Archaeological Museum (p549) in Iraklio (most treasures are there) and taking a guided tour (€10) add needed context.

Knossos was the setting for the myth of the Minotaur. According to legend, King Minos of Knossos was given a magnificent white bull to sacrifice to the god Poseidon, but decided to keep it. This enraged Poseidon, who punished the king by causing his wife Pasiphae to fall in love with the animal. The result of this odd union was the Minotaur – half-man and half-bull – who was imprisoned in a labyrinth beneath the king's palace at Knossos, munching on youths and maidens, before being killed by Theseus.

Bus 2 to Knossos (€1.50, every 20 minutes) leaves from Bus Station A in Iraklio.

Hania   XANIA
POP 54,000

Crete's most romantic, evocative and alluring town, Hania (hahn-*yah*; often spelt Chania) is the former capital and the island's second-largest city. There is a rich mosaic of Venetian and Ottoman architecture, particularly in the area of the old harbour, which lures tourists in droves. Modern Hania with its university retains the exoticism of a city playing with East and West and has some of the best hotels and restaurants on the island. It's an excellent base for exploring nearby idyllic beaches and a spectacular mountainous interior.

◉ Sights

★**Venetian Harbour**   HISTORIC SITE
A stroll around the old harbour is a must for any visitor to Hania. Pastel-coloured historic homes and businesses line the harbour, zigzagging back into narrow lanes lined with shops. The entire area is ensconced in impressive **Venetian fortifications**, and it's worth the 1.5km walk around the sea wall to the **Venetian lighthouse**. On the eastern side of the inner harbour the prominent **Mosque of Kioutsouk Hasan** (Mosque of Janissaries) houses regular exhibitions.

★**Archaeological Museum**   MUSEUM
(☑28210 90334; Halidon 30; adult/child €4/free; ⊙8am-8pm Mon-Fri, to 3pm Sat & Sun) The setting alone in the beautifully restored 16th-century Venetian Church of San Francisco is reason to visit this fine collection of artefacts from neolithic to Roman times. The museum's late-Minoan sarcophagi catch the eye as much as a large glass case with an entire herd of clay bulls (used to worship Poseidon). Other standouts include three Roman floor mosaics, Hellenistic gold jewellery, clay tablets with Linear A and Linear B script, and a marble sculpture of Roman emperor Hadrian.

PHAESTOS

Sixty-three kilometres southwest of Iraklio is Crete's second-most important Minoan palatial site, **Phaestos** (☑28920 42315; http://odysseus.culture.gr; adult/concession/child €8/4/free; ☺8am-8pm Apr-Oct, 8.30am-3pm Nov-Mar). More unreconstructed and moody than Knossos, Phaestos (fes-*tos*) is also worth a visit for its stunning views of the surrounding Mesara plain and Mt Psiloritis (2456m; also known as Mt Ida). The smaller site of **Agia Triada** (☑27230 22448; adult/child €3/free; ☺9.30am-4.30pm summer, 8.30am-3pm winter) is 3km west.

★**Byzantine &
Post-Byzantine Collection**   MUSEUM
(☑28210 96046; Theotokopoulou 82; €2; ☺8am-3pm Tue-Sun) The Byzantine museum is in the impressively restored Venetian Church of San Salvatore. It has a small but fascinating collection of artefacts, icons, jewellery and coins spanning the period from AD 62 to 1913, including a fine segment of a mosaic floor for an early-Christian basilica and a prized icon of St George slaying the dragon. The building has a mixed bag of interesting architectural features from its various occupiers. A joint ticket with the Archaeological Museum costs adult/child €3/free.

★**Maritime Museum of Crete**   MUSEUM
(☑28210 91875; www.mar-mus-crete.gr; Akti Koundourioti; adult/child €4/free; ☺9am-5pm Mon-Sat, 10am-6pm Sun) Part of the hulking Venetian-built Firkas Fortress at the western port entrance, this museum celebrates Crete's nautical tradition with model ships, naval instruments, paintings, photographs, maps and memorabilia. One room is dedicated to historical sea battles while upstairs there's thorough documentation on the WWII-era Battle of Crete. The gate to the fortress itself is open from 8am to 2pm.

🛏 Sleeping

Hania's Old Harbour is loaded with great hotels which can book up, even on winter weekends; reserve ahead.

Pension Theresa   PENSION €
(☑28210 92798; www.pensiontheresa.gr; Angelou 8; r €50-60; ❋ 🤶) Part of the Venetian fortifications, this creaky old house with a steep (and narrow!) spiral staircase and antique furniture delivers snug rooms with character aplenty. The location is excellent and views are stunning from the rooftop terrace with communal kitchen stocked with basic breakfast items. They have another annexe as well.

★**Casa Leone**   BOUTIQUE HOTEL €€€
(☑28210 76762; www.casa-leone.com; Parodos Theotokopoulou 18; d/ste incl breakfast from €135/190; ❋🤶) This Venetian residence has been converted into a classy and romantic family-run boutique hotel. The rooms are spacious and well appointed, with balconies overlooking the harbour. There are honeymoon suites, with classic drape-canopy beds and sumptuous curtains. Discounts for prebooking or cash payments.

🍴 Eating & Drinking

Look beyond the waterfront tourist-traps for some of the best eats on the island. The Splantzia neighbourhood is popular with discerning locals. Nightclubs dot the port and atmospheric **Fagotto Jazz Bar** (☑28210 71877; Angelou 16; ☺12-5pm & 9pm-12am) has occasional live music.

★**Bougatsa tou Iordanis**   CRETAN €
(☑28210 88855; Apokoronou 24; bougatsa €3; ☺6am-2.30pm Mon-Sat, to 1.30pm Sun) You haven't lived until you've eaten the *bougatsa* at this little storefront dedicated to the flaky, sweet-cheesy treat. It's cooked fresh in enormous slabs and carved up in front of your eyes. Pair it with a coffee and you're set for the morning. There's nothing else on the menu!

★**Taverna Tamam**   MEDITERRANEAN €€
(☑28210 96080; Zambeliou 49; mains €7-14; ☺noon-midnight; 🤶) This excellent, convivial taverna in a converted Turkish bathhouse fills with chatting locals at tables spilling out onto the street. Dishes incorporate Middle Eastern spices, and include tasty soups and a superb selection of vegetarian specialities. Cretan delicacies include tender goat with *staka* (a rich goat's milk sauce).

★**To Maridaki**   CRETAN €€
(☑28210 08880; Daskalogianni 33; dishes €7-12; ☺noon-midnight Mon-Sat) This modern seafood *mezedhopoleio* (restaurant specialising in mezedhes) is not to be missed. In a cheerful, bright dining room, happy visitors and locals alike tuck into impeccable local seafood and Cretan specialities. Ingredients

RETHYMNO & MONI ARKADIOU

Rethymno (*reth*-im-no), on the coast between Iraklio and Hania, is one of the island's architectural treasures, due to its stunning fortress and mix of Venetian and Turkish houses in the old quarter. It's worth a stop to explore the area around the old Venetian harbour, and shop in its interesting arts and crafts boutiques.

Moni Arkadiou (Arkadi Monastery; ☑ 28310 22415, 28310 83136; www.arkadimonastery. gr; €3; ⊙ 9am-8pm Jun-Aug, shorter hours Sep-May), in the hills some 23km southeast of Rethymno, has deep significance for Cretans. A potent symbol of human resistance, it was the site of a tragic and momentous stand-off between the Turks and the Cretans in 1866, and considered a spark plug in the struggle towards freedom from Turkish occupation. Arkadiou's most impressive structure, its **Venetian church** (1587), has a striking Renaissance facade marked by eight slender Corinthian columns and topped by an ornate triple-belled tower. Its high mountain valley is beautiful, especially around sunset.

are fresh, the fried calamari is to die for, the house white wine is crisp and delicious, and the complimentary panna cotta to finish the meal is sublime. What's not to love?

★**Thalassino Ageri**　　　SEAFOOD €€€
(☑ 28210 51136; www.thalasino-ageri.gr; Vivilaki 35; fish per kg €55; ⊙ from 7.30pm Apr–mid-Oct) This solitary fish taverna in a tiny port 2km east of the centre among the ruins of Hania's old tanneries is one of Crete's top eateries. Take in the sunset from the superb setting and peruse the changing menu, dictated by the day's catch. Most dishes, like the fisherman's salad, hum with creativity, or transcendent simplicity like melt-in-your-mouth calamari.

ⓘ Information

For information visit www.chania.gr.

ⓘ Getting There & Away

AIR

Hania Airport (☑ 28210 83800; www.chania airport.com) serves Athens, Thessaloniki and seasonally cities around Europe. The airport is 14km east of town. KTEL (www.bus-service-crete-ktel.com) buses link the airport with central Hania up to 27 times daily (€2.30, 30 minutes). Taxis cost €20 (plus €2 per bag).

BOAT

The port is at Souda, 7km southeast of Hania. Once-nightly **Anek** (www.anek.gr) ferries serve Piraeus (€35, nine hours). Frequent buses (€1.50) and taxis (€9) connect the town and Souda. Hania buses meet each boat, as do buses to Rethymno.

BUS

Frequent buses from the **main bus station** (☑ info 28210 93052, tickets 28210 93306; www.bus-service-crete-ktel.com; Kydonias

73-77; ☎) run along Crete's northern coast to Iraklio (€13.80, 2¾ hours, half-hourly) and Rethymno (€6.20, one hour, half-hourly); buses run less frequently to Paleohora, Omalos and Hora Sfakion. Buses for beaches west of Hania leave from the eastern side of Plateia 1866.

Samaria Gorge
ΦΑΡΑΓΓΙ ΤΗΣ ΣΑΜΑΡΙΑΣ

Samaria Gorge (☑ 28210 45570, 28210 67179; www.samaria.gr; adult/child €5/free; ⊙ 7am-sunset May-late Oct) is one of Europe's most spectacular gorges and a superb (very popular) hike. Walkers should take rugged footwear, food, drinks and sun protection for this strenuous five- to six-hour trek. You can do the walk as part of an excursion tour, or independently by taking the Omalos bus from the main bus station in Hania (€6.90, one hour) to the head of the gorge at Xyloskalo (1230m). It's a 16.7km walk (all downhill) to **Agia Roumeli** on the coast, from where you take a boat to Hora Sfakion (€10, 1¼ hours) and then a bus back to Hania (€7.60, 1½ hours). You are not allowed to spend the night in the gorge, so you need to complete the walk in a day, or beat the crowds and stay over in one of the nearby villages. Other gorges, like **Imbros** (€2; ⊙ year-round), also make for fine walking, and are less crowded.

DODECANESE
ΔΩΔΕΚΑΝΗΣΑ

Strung out along the coast of western Turkey, the 12 main islands of the Dodecanese (*dodeca* means 12) have suffered a turbulent past of invasions and occupations that have endowed them with a fascinating diversity.

Conquered successively by the Romans, the Arabs, the Knights of St John, the Turks, the Italians, then liberated from the Germans by British and Greek commandos in 1944, the Dodecanese became part of Greece in 1947. These days, tourists rule.

Rhodes ΡΟΔΟΣ

POP 115,000

Rhodes (Rodos in Greek) is the largest island in the Dodecanese. According to mythology, the sun god Helios chose Rhodes as his bride and bestowed light, warmth and vegetation upon her. The blessing seems to have paid off, for Rhodes produces more flowers and sunny days than most Greek islands. Throw in an east coast of virtually uninterrupted sandy beaches and it's easy to understand why sun-starved northern Europeans flock here in droves. The old town is magnificent.

Rhodes Town

POP 86,000

Rhodes' capital is Rhodes Town, on the northern tip of the island. Its magnificent Old Town, the largest inhabited medieval town in Europe, is enclosed within massive walls and is a delight to explore. Nowhere else in the Dodecanese can boast so many layers of architectural history, with ruins and relics of the classical, medieval, Ottoman and Italian eras entangled in a mind-boggling maze of twisting alleys.

To the north is New Town, the commercial centre. The town beach, which looks out at Turkey, runs around the peninsula at the northern end of New Town. The main port, Commercial Harbour, is east of the Old Town, and is where the big interisland ferries dock. Northwest of here is Mandraki Harbour, lined with excursion boats and smaller ferries, hydrofoils and catamarans. It was the

LINDOS

The **Acropolis of Lindos** (☎ 22413 65200; adult/concession/child €12/6/free; ⊙8am-8pm Tue-Fri, to 3pm Sat-Mon Apr-Oct, 8.30am-3pm Tue-Sun Nov-Mar), 47km south from Rhodes Town, is an ancient city spectacularly perched atop a 116m-high rocky outcrop. Below is the town of Lindos, a tangle of pedestrian streets with elaborately decorated 17th-century captain houses. Nearby is the gorgeous though tiny beach of Agios Pavlos.

supposed site of the **Colossus of Rhodes**, a 32m-high bronze statue of Apollo built over 12 years (294–282 BC). The statue stood for a mere 65 years before being toppled by an earthquake.

◉ Sights

A wander around Rhodes' Unesco World Heritage–listed Old Town is a must. It is reputedly the world's finest surviving example of medieval fortification, with 12m-thick walls. A mesh of Byzantine, Turkish and Latin architecture, the Old Town is divided into the Kollakio (the Knights' Quarter, where the Knights of St John lived during medieval times), the Hora and the Jewish Quarter. The Knights' Quarter contains most of the medieval historical sights while the Hora, often referred to as the Turkish Quarter, is primarily Rhodes Town's commercial sector with shops and restaurants, thronged by tourists.

The Knights of St John lived in the **Knights' Quarter** in the northern end of the Old Town. The cobbled **Avenue of the Knights** (Ippoton) is lined with magnificent medieval buildings, the most imposing of which is the **Palace of the Grand Master** (☎ 22410 23359, 22413 65270; €6; ⊙8am-8pm

GREECE RHODES

THE KNIGHTS OF ST JOHN

Island-hopping in the Dodecanese you'll quickly realise that the Knights of St John left behind a passel of castles. Originally formed as the Knights Hospitaller in Jerusalem in 1080 to provide care for poor and sick pilgrims, the knights relocated to Rhodes (via Cyprus) after the loss of Jerusalem in the First Crusade. They ousted the ruling Genoese in 1309, built a stack of castles in the Dodecanese to protect their new home, then set about irking the neighbours by committing acts of piracy against Ottoman shipping. Sultan Süleyman the Magnificent, not a man you'd want to irk, took offence and set about dislodging the knights from their strongholds. Rhodes finally capitulated in 1523 and the remaining knights relocated to Malta. They set up there as the Sovereign Military Hospitaller of Jerusalem, of Rhodes, and of Malta.

SOUTHWEST COAST VILLAGES

Crete's southern coastline at its western end is dotted with remote, attractive little villages that are brilliant spots to take it easy for a few days.

From Paleohora heading east are Sougia, Agia Roumeli, Loutro and Hora Sfakion. No road links the coastal resorts, but a once-daily boat from Paleohora to Sougia (€9, 50 minutes), Agia Roumeli (€15, 1½ hours), Loutro (€16, 2½ hours) and Hora Sfakion (€17, three hours) connects the villages in summer. See www.sfakia-crete.com/sfakia-crete/ferries.html. In summer three buses daily connect Hania and Hora Sfakion (€7.60, one hour and 40 minutes), two daily to Sougia (€7.10, one hour and 50 minutes). If you're a keen hiker, it's also possible to walk right along this southern coast.

Paleohora This village is isolated on a peninsula with a sandy beach to the west and a pebbly beach to the east. On summer evenings the main street is closed to traffic and the tavernas move onto the road. If you're after a relaxing few days, Paleohora is a great spot to chill out. Stay at Joanna's (☎28230 41801; www.joanna-place.com; studio €50-60; ⊗ Apr-Nov; P ✳ 🛜) spacious, spotless studios.

Sougia At the mouth of the Agia Irini gorge, Sougia (soo-yah) is a laid-back and refreshingly undeveloped spot with a wide curve of sand-and-pebble beach. The 14.5km (six hours) walk from Paleohora is popular, as is the Agia Irini gorge walk which ends (or starts!) in Sougia. It's possible to get here by ferry, by car or on foot. Stay at Santa Irene Apartments (☎28230 51342; www.santa-irene.gr; apt €60-80; ⊗ late Mar-early Nov; P ✳ 🛜), a smart beachside complex with its own cafe.

Agia Roumeli At the mouth of the Samaria Gorge (p554), Agia Roumeli bristles with gorge-walkers from mid-afternoon until the ferry comes to take them away. Once they are gone, this pleasant little town goes into quiet mode until the first walkers turn up in the early afternoon the following day. Right on the waterfront, Paralia Taverna & Rooms (☎28250 91408; www.taverna-paralia.com; d €35-40; ✳ 🛜) offers excellent views, tasty Cretan cuisine, cold beer and simple, clean rooms.

Loutro This tiny village is a particularly picturesque spot, curled around the only natural harbour on the southern coast of Crete. With no vehicle access, the only way in is by boat or on foot. Hotel Porto Loutro (☎28250 91433, 28250 91001; www.hotelportoloutro.com; s/d/tr incl breakfast €55/65/75; ⊗ Apr-Oct; ✳ @ 🛜) has tasteful rooms with balconies overlooking the harbour. The village beach, excellent walks, rental kayaks, and boat transfers to excellent Sweetwater Beach fill peaceful days.

Hora Sfakion Renowned in Cretan history for its rebellious streak, Hora Sfakion is an amiable town. WWII history buffs know this as the place where thousands of Allied troops were evacuated by sea after the Battle of Crete. Hora Sfakion's seafront tavernas serve fresh seafood and unique *Sfakianes pites* which look like crêpes filled with sweet or savoury local cheese. Hotel Stavris (☎28250 91220; www.hotel-stavris-sfakia-crete.com; s/d from €28/33; ✳ 🛜) has simple rooms and breakfast outside in its courtyard.

May-Oct, 8am-4pm Tue-Sun Nov-Apr), which was restored, but never used, as a holiday home for Mussolini. From the palace, explore the D'Amboise Gate, the most atmospheric of the fortification gates which takes you across the moat.

The beautiful 15th-century Knights' Hospital, closer to the seafront, now houses the excellent Archaeological Museum (☎22413 65200; Plateia Mousiou; adult/child €8/free; ⊗ 8am-8pm Tue-Fri, 8am-3pm Sat & Sun, 9am-3pm Mon Apr-Oct, 9am-4pm Tue-Sat Nov-Mar). The splendid building was restored by the Italians and has

an impressive collection that includes the ethereal marble statue *Aphrodite of Rhodes*.

The pink-domed Mosque of Süleyman (Sokratous), at the top of Sokratous, was built in 1522 to commemorate the Ottoman victory against the knights, then rebuilt in 1808.

🛏 Sleeping

★ **Hotel Anastasia** PENSION €€
(☎22410 28007; www.anastasia-hotel.com; 28 Oktovriou 46; s/d/tr €55/65//85; ✳ @ 🛜) The New Town's friendliest and most peaceful accommodation option, this handsome

white-painted villa is set well back from the road and offers charming ochre-coloured ensuite rooms with wooden shutters, tiled floors and traditional furnishings. Some have private balconies and there's an inviting breakfast bar in the lush garden.

★ **Marco Polo Mansion** BOUTIQUE HOTEL €€
(☑ 22410 25562; www.marcopolomansion.gr; Agiou Fanouriou 40; d incl breakfast €80-260; ☺ Apr-Oct; ❄ ☎) In the 15th century, this irresistible garden-set mansion, tucked away on an ancient alleyway, was home to a high Ottoman official. Now it's a gloriously romantic B&B hotel, its cool, high-ceilinged rooms decorated with exquisite taste and old-world flair. Amazing buffet breakfasts are spread out in the flower-filled courtyard, which is open to all every evening as a fabulous restaurant.

★ **Spirit of the Knights** BOUTIQUE HOTEL €€€
(☑ 22410 39765; www.rhodesluxuryhotel.com; Alexandridou 14; s/d incl breakfast €160-200/200-375; ☺ ❄ ☎) Six sumptuous suites in a splendidly transformed old home, nestled close to the Old Town walls. Each has its own historical theme, evoked through lavish linens, hangings and furniture and details such as stained glass, while all share a library inside and a whirlpool spa outside. Linger over breakfast in the tranquil gardens.

✗ Eating & Drinking

Old Rhodes is rife with tourist traps; look in the backstreets. Head further north into New Town for better-value restaurants and bars.

★ **Koykos** GREEK €
(☑ 22410 73022; http://koukosrodos.com; Mandilana 20-26; mains €3-10; ☺ daily early-late; ❄ ☎) This inviting complex, off a pedestrian shopping street, consists of several antique-filled rooms – a couple hold vintage jukeboxes – along with two bougainvillea-draped courtyards and a floral roof terrace. Best known for fabulous homemade pies, it also serves all the classic mezedhes, plus meat and fish dishes, or you can drop in for a coffee or sandwich.

★ **Nireas** SEAFOOD €€
(☑ 22410 21703; Sofokleous 45-47; mains €8-16; ☺ lunch & dinner; ❄) Nireas' status as Rhodes' favourite seafood restaurant owes much to the sheer enthusiasm and verve of genial owner Theo, from Symi – that and the beautifully prepared food, served beneath a vine-shaded canopy outside, or in the candlelit, lemon-walled interior. Be sure to sample the Symi shrimp, salted mackerel and, if you're in the mood, the 'Viagra' salad of small shellfish.

★ **Marco Polo Cafe** MEDITERRANEAN €€
(☑ 22410 25562; www.marcopolomansion.gr; Agiou Fanouriou 40-42; mains €12-25; ☺ 7-11pm) ✔ Magical, irresistibly romantic restaurant in a delightful garden courtyard. The passion and flair of the cuisine is astounding, while the service epitomises *filoxenia* (hospitality). Menus change nightly, with specials such as calamari and prawn balls in a couscous crust, tuna in sesame marinated with orange, or lamb souvlaki on a bed of risotto, plus inventive desserts such as semifreddo of tahini.

Petaladika GREEK €€
(☑ 22410 27319; Menakleous 8; mains €8-15; ☺ noon-late) Petaladika might look like just another tourist trap, tucked into a corner off the main drag, but it has quickly established itself as the finest newcomer on the Old Town dining scene. Locals swoon over highlights such as deep-fried baby squid, zucchini balls and freshly grilled fish.

ⓘ Information

EOT (Greek Tourist Information Office; ☑ 22410 44335; www.ando.gr/eot; cnr Makariou & Papagou; ☺ 8am-2.45pm Mon-Fri) National tourism information, including brochures, maps and transport details.

Rhodes Tourism Office – New Town (☑ 22410 35495; www.rhodes.gr; Plateia Rimini; ☺ 7.30am-3pm Mon-Fri) Conveniently poised between Mandraki Harbour and the Old Town.

Rhodes Tourism Office – Old Town (☑ 22410 35945; www.rhodes.gr; cnr Platonos & Ippoton; ☺ 7am-3pm Mon-Fri) In an ancient building at the foot of the Street of the Knights, this helpful office supplies excellent street maps, leaflets and brochures.

ⓘ Getting There & Around

AIR

Many flights daily connect Rhodes' **Diagoras Airport** (RHO; ☑ 22410 88700; www.rhodes-airport.org) and Athens, plus less-regular flights to Karpathos, Kastellorizo, Thessaloniki, Iraklio, Crete, Santorini and Samos. International flights, budget airlines and charter flights swarm in summer. The airport is on the west coast, 16km southwest of Rhodes Town; 25 minutes and €2.40 by bus, €22 by taxi.

ⓘ BOATS TO TURKEY

Turkey is so close that it looks like you could swim there from many of the Dodecanese and Northeastern Aegean islands. Here are the boat options:

Bodrum from Kos

Çeşme (near İzmir) from Chios

Dikili (near Ayvalık) from Lesvos

Kuşadasi (near Ephesus) from Samos

Marmaris from Rhodes

BOAT

Rhodes is the main port of the Dodecanese and there is a complex array of departures. Most of the daily boats to Piraeus (€44, 18 hours) sail via the Dodecanese, but some go via Karpathos, Crete and the Cyclades. In summer, catamaran services run up and down the Dodecanese daily from Rhodes to Symi or Halki, Kos, Kalymnos, Nisyros, Tilos, Patmos and Leros. Check www.openseas.gr, **Dodekanisos Seaways** (☑ 22410 70590; www.12ne.gr; Afstralias 3, Rhodes Town) and **Blue Star Ferries** (☑ 21089 19800; www.bluestarferries.com). Excursion boats at the harbour also go to Symi.

To Turkey

Catamarans connect Rhodes and Marmaris in Turkey (one-way/return including port taxes €50/75, 50 minutes). Check www.marmarisinfo.com.

BUS

Rhodes Town has two bus stations a block apart next to the New Market. The **Eastern Bus Terminal** (☑ 22410 27706; www.ktelrodou.gr) has frequent services to the airport (€2.40), Kalithea Thermi (€2.20), Ancient Kamiros (€5) and Monolithos (€6). The **Western Bus Terminal** (☑ 22410 26300) services Faliraki (€2.20), Tsambika Beach (€3.50), Stegna Beach (€4) and Lindos (€5).

Kos ΚΩΣ

POP 33,300

Bustling Kos, only 5km from the Turkish peninsula of Bodrum, is popular with history buffs as the birthplace of Hippocrates (460–377 BC), the father of medicine. The island also attracts an entirely different crowd – hordes of sun-worshipping beach lovers from northern Europe who pack the long, sandy stretches in summer.

◉ Sights & Activities

Busy Kos Town has lots of **bicycle paths** and renting a bike along the pretty waterfront is great for seeing the sights. Near the Castle of the Knights is **Hippocrates Plane Tree** (Plateia Platanou, Kos Town) FREE, under which the man himself is said to have taught his pupils. The modern town is built on the vast remains of the ancient Greek one – explore the ruins!

★ **Asklepieion** ARCHAEOLOGICAL SITE
(☑ 22420 28763; adult/child €7/free; ☉ 8am-7pm Tue-Sun Apr-Oct, 8am-3pm Tue-Sun Nov-Mar) The island's most important ancient site stands on a pine-covered hill 3km southwest of Kos Town, commanding lovely views across town towards Turkey. A religious sanctuary devoted to Asclepius, the god of healing, it was also a healing centre and a school of medicine. It was founded in the 3rd century BC, according to legend by Hippocrates himself. He was already dead by then, though, and the training here simply followed his teachings.

Castle of the Knights CASTLE
(☑ 22420 27927; €4; ☉ 8am-8pm Apr-Oct, 8am-3pm Tue-Sun Nov-Mar) Kos' magnificent 15th-century castle was constructed not on a hilltop, but right beside the entrance to the harbour. Access it by the bridge from Plateia Platanou, crossing what was once a seawater-filled moat but is now a road. Visitors can stroll atop the intact outer walls, surveying all activity in the port and keeping a watchful eye on Turkey across the strait. The precinct within, however, is now largely overgrown, with cats stalking through a wilderness of wildflowers.

⌂ Sleeping

★ **Hotel Afendoulis** HOTEL €
(☑ 22420 25321; www.afendoulishotel.com; Evripilou 1; s/d €30/50; ☉ Mar-Nov; ❄ @ ☎) Peaceful Afendoulis has unfailingly friendly staff and sparkling rooms with white walls, small balconies and spotless bathrooms. Downstairs, the open breakfast room and flowery terrace have wrought-iron tables and chairs for enjoying the feast of homemade jams and marmalades. There may be more modern, plusher hotels in Kos, but none with the special soul of this fine, family-run establishment.

Hotel Sonia   HOTEL €€
(☑22420 28798; www.hotelsonia.gr; Irodotou 9; s/d/tr €45/60/75; ❄🛜) A block from the waterfront on a peaceful backstreet, this pension offers a dozen sparkling rooms with parquet floors, fridges, smart bathrooms and an extra bed if required. Room 4 has the best sea view. Breakfast is served on a relaxing communal verandah, there's a decent book exchange and it plans to open up the garden to visitors.

✖ Eating & Drinking

Restaurants line the central waterfront of the old harbour in Kos Town, but backstreets harbour better value. Nightclubs dot Diakon and Nafkliirou, just north of the *agora* (market).

★ Pote Tin Kyriaki   TAVERNA €
(☑22420 27872, 6930352099; Pisandrou 9; ⊙7pm-2am) Named for Melina Mercouri's Oscar-winning 1960 song, 'Never on Sunday' is not the sort of place you expect to find in modern Kos – and it takes a lot of finding. This traditional *ouzerie* (place that serves ouzo and light snacks) serves delicious specialities such as stuffed zucchini flowers, dolmadhes (vine leaves stuffed with rice and sometimes meat) with lemongrass, and steamed mussels. It plans to open for breakfast and lunch too – just never on Sunday.

Elia   GREEK €€
(☑22420 22133; Appelou Ifestou 27; mains €8-15; ⊙12.30pm-late; ❄🛜🖊🍴) 🌿 Friendly restaurant with seating in the garden and venerable interior as well as on the lively pedestrian street. The menu draws on traditional dishes from all over Greece, with standouts including the chunky rustic sausage, bream baked with oregano and rosemary, and drunken pork (cooked in wine). Simple starters such as fava and fried onions are equally tasty.

Petrino Meze Restaurant   MEZEDHES €€
(☑22420 27251; www.petrino-kos.gr; Plateia Theologou 1; mains €9-28; ⊙lunch & dinner; ❄🛜) Peaceful and balmy, this graceful restaurant has a leafy garden shaded by bougainvillea, overlooking Kos Town's western group of archaeological ruins. Highlights on its upscale menu include hearty meat concoctions such as beef stuffed with blue cheese and pork with plums, but it also serves lighter dishes such as steamed swordfish or pasta, as well as mixed mezedhes platters.

ℹ Information

Visit www.kos.gr, www.kosinfo.gr or www.travel-to-kos.com for information.

Fanos Travel & Shipping (☑22420 20035; 11 Akti Koundourioti) Tickets for the hydrofoil service to Bodrum and other ferries, plus yachting services.

Kentrikon Travel (☑22420 28914; Akti Kountouriotou 7) The offical agents for Blue Star Ferries also sells all other ferry and air tickets.

ℹ Getting There & Around

AIR

From **Ippokratis Airport** (KGS; ☑22420 56000; www.kosairportguide.com), there are up to four daily flights to Athens (from €50, 55 minutes) as well as three weekly to Rhodes (€61, 30 minutes), and once weekly in summer to Heraklion in Crete (€69, 50 minutes). The airport is 24km southwest of Kos Town; buses cost €3.20, taxis €30.

BICYCLE

Hire bikes at the harbour to get around town.

BOAT

Kos has services to Piraeus and all islands in the Dodecanese, the Cyclades, Samos and Thessaloniki. Catamarans are run by Dodekanisos Seaways at the interisland ferry quay. Local passenger and car ferries run to Pothia on Kalymnos from Mastihari. For tickets, visit Fanos Travel & Shipping on the harbour.

To Turkey

Catamarans connect Kos Town with both Bodrum (two daily) and Turgutreis in Turkey (one daily). Both journeys take 20 minutes. Tickets cost €18 each way, with same-day returns €24 and longer-stay returns €32. For schedules and bookings, visit www.rhodes.marmarisinf.

BUS

The main **bus station** (☑22420 22292; Kleopatras 7, Kos Town), well back from the waterfront in Kos Town, is the base for services to all parts of the island, including the airport and south-coast beaches, with **KTEL** (☑22420 22292; www.ktel-kos.gr).

> **ℹ ISLAND SHORTCUTS**
>
> If long ferry rides eat into your holiday too much, check Aegean Airlines (p569), Olympic Air (p570), Astra Airlines (p570) and Sky Express (p570) for flights. But beware baggage limits: Sky Express in particular only allows teeny bags.

NORTHEASTERN AEGEAN ISLANDS

ΤΑ ΝΗΣΙΑ ΤΟΥ ΒΟΡΕΙΟ ΑΝΑΤΟΛΙΚΟ ΑΙΓΑΙΟΥ

One of Greece's best-kept secrets, these far-flung islands are strewn across the northeastern corner of the Aegean, closer to Turkey than mainland Greece. They harbour unspoilt scenery, welcoming locals, fascinating independent cultures, and remain relatively calm even when other Greek islands are sagging with tourists at the height of summer.

Samos   ΣΑΜΟΣ

POP 32,820

A lush mountainous island only 3km from Turkey, Samos has a glorious history as the legendary birthplace of Hera, wife and sister of god-of-all-gods Zeus. Samos was an important centre of Hellenic culture, and the mathematician Pythagoras and storyteller Aesop are among its sons. The island has beaches that bake in summer, and a hinterland that is superb for hiking. Spring brings with it pink flamingos, wildflowers, and orchids that the island grows for export, while summer brings throngs of package tourists.

Vathy (Samos Town)   Βαθύ Σάμος

POP 2025

Busy Vathy is an attractive working port town. Most of the action is along Themistokleous Sofouli, the main street that runs along the waterfront. The main square, Plateia Pythagorou, in the middle of the waterfront, is recognisable by its four palm trees and statue of a lion.

The first-rate Archaeological Museum (22730 27469; adult/child €4/free, free 1st Sun Nov-Mar; 8am-3pm Tue-Sun) is one of the best in the islands and the Museum of Samos Wines (22730 87551; www.samoswine.gr; €2; 8am-8pm Mon-Sat) FREE offers tours and taste-testing with one of the island's best vinters. Cleomenis Hotel (22730 23232; Kallistratous 33; d incl breakfast from €50) offers great, simple rooms close to the beach northeast of town. Elegant Ino Village Hotel (22730 23241; www.inovillagehotel.com; Kalami; d incl breakfast €67-150; P✳🛜❄) in the hills north of the ferry quay has Elea Restaurant with views over town and the harbour.

ITSA Travel (22730 23605; www.itsatravel samos.gr; Themistokleous Sofouli 5; 8am-8pm), opposite the quay, is helpful with travel inquiries, excursions, accommodation and luggage storage.

Pythagorio   Πυθαγόρειο

POP 1330

Little Pythagorio, 11km south of Vathy, is where you'll disembark if you've come by boat from Patmos. It is a small, enticing town with a yacht-lined harbour and a busy, holiday atmosphere, overwhelming to some.

The 1034m-long Evpalinos Tunnel (22730 61400; adult/child €4/free; 8am-3pm Tue-Sun), built in the 6th century BC, was dug by political prisoners and used as an aqueduct to bring water from Mt Ampelos (1140m).

Ireon (adult/child €4/free; 8.30am-3pm Tue-Sun), the legendary birthplace of the goddess Hera, is 8km west of Pythagorio. The temple at this World Heritage site was enormous – four times the size of the Parthenon – though only one column remains.

The impeccable Pension Despina (6938120399, 22730 61677; www.samosrooms. gr/despina/more.html; A Nikolaou; r/studio €35/40; ✳🛜) is a relaxing spot with a garden while Polyxeni Hotel (22730 61590; www.polyxeni hotel.com; s/d/tr incl breakfast from €40/55/70; ✳🛜) is in the heart of the waterfront action. Tavernas and bars line the waterfront.

The cordial Tourist Office (22730 61389; Lykourgou Logotheti; 8am-9.30pm, reduced hours in winter) is two blocks from the waterfront on the main street. The bus stop is two blocks further inland on the same street.

Around Samos

Samos is an island of forests, mountains, wildlife and over 30 villages, harbouring excellent, cheap tavernas. The captivating villages of Vourliotes and Manolates, on the slopes of imposing Mt Ampelos, northwest of Vathy, are excellent walking territory and have many marked pathways.

Karlovasi, on the northwest coast, is another ferry port and interesting in its own right. Spend the night at Studios Angela (22730 62198; www.studiosangela. com; Manolates; d €30-40; ✳), with studios built into a hillside overlooking the sea. The beaches south of Karlovasi, like Potami Beach, are tops. Other choice beaches include **Tsamadou** on the north coast, **Votsalakia** in the southwest and **Psili Ammos** to the east of Pythagorio. The latter is sandy and stares straight out at Turkey, barely a couple of kilometres away. Beautiful **Bollos Beach** near Skoureika village is even more off the beaten path.

Hire a car and explore!

ⓘ Getting There & Around

AIR

Daily flights connect Athens with Samos Airport (SMI), 4km west of Pythagorio. Several weekly flights serve Iraklio, Rhodes, Chios and Thessaloniki. Charters serve Chios from Amsterdam, Oslo and Vienna.

Buses (€2) run three to four times daily and taxis to Vathy/Pythagorio cost €25/6.

BOAT

Samos is home to three ports – Vathy (aka Samos), Pythagorio and Karlovasi. The new ferry terminal in Vathy, for ferries to domestic destinations only, is at the harbour's southeast end, 1.7km from the old ferry terminal, which is only for boats to Turkey. A taxi between the terminals is €5.

A maritime hub, Samos offers daily ferries to Piraeus (€32, 12 hours), plus ferries heading north to Chios and west to the Cyclades. In summer, high-speed services head south to Patmos and Kos.

ITSA Travel (p560), directly opposite Vathy's old ferry terminal, provides detailed information and sells tickets. In Pythagorio, check ferry and hydrofoil schedules with the tourist office (p560), the **port police** (☎22730 61225) or **By Ship Travel** (☎22730 80768; www.byshiptravel.gr).

To Turkey

There are daily ferries to Kuşadası (for Ephesus) in Turkey (€35/45 one-way/return, plus €10 port taxes). Day excursions are also available from April to October. Check with **ITSA Travel** (p560) for up-to-date details.

BUS

You can get to most of the island's villages and beaches by bus.

CAR & MOTORCYCLE

Opposite the port entrance in Vathy, **Manos Moto-Auto Rental** (☎6974392157, 22730 23309; www.manos-rentals.gr; Grammou & Kounturioti) runs an efficient service. Another good option is **Pegasus Rent-a-Car** (☎22730 24470, 6978536440; www.samos-car-rental.com; Themistoklis Sofouli 5, Vathy), with good rates on car, 4WD and motorcycle hire.

Lesvos (Mytilini)
ΛΕΣΒΟΣ (ΜΥΤΙΛΗΝΗ)
POP 95,330

Lesvos, or Mytilini as it is often called, tends to do things in a big way. The third-largest of the Greek islands after Crete and Evia, Lesvos produces half the world's ouzo and is home to over 11 million olive trees. Mountainous yet fertile, the island has world-class local cuisine, and presents excellent hiking and birdwatching opportunities, but remains refreshingly untouched in terms of tourism.

Mytilini   Μυτιλήνη
POP 29,650

The capital and main port, Mytilini, is a lively student town with great eating and drinking options, plus eclectic churches and grand 19th-century mansions and museums. It is built between two harbours (north and south) with an imposing fortress on the promontory to the east. All ferries dock at the southern harbour, and most of the town's action is around this waterfront.

◉ Sights

Teriade Museum   MUSEUM
(☎22510 23372; http://museumteriade.gr; Varia; adult €2; ☺9am-2pm & 5-8pm Apr-Oct, 9am-5pm Nov-Mar) Varia, 4km south of Mytilini, is the

---

SAPPHO, LESBIANS & LESVOS

Sappho, one of Greece's great ancient poets, was born on Lesvos during the 7th century BC. Most of her work was devoted to love and desire, and the objects of her affection were often female. Because of this, Sappho's name and birthplace have come to be associated with female homosexuality.

These days, Lesvos is visited by many lesbians paying homage to Sappho. The whole island is very gay-friendly, in particular the southwestern beach resort of **Skala Eresou**, which is built over ancient Eresos, where Sappho was born. The village is well set up to cater to lesbian needs and has a 'Women Together' festival held annually in September. See www.womensfestival.eu and www.sapphotravel.com for details.

unlikely home of the Teriade Museum with its astonishing collection of paintings by artists such as Picasso, Chagall, Miro, Le Corbusier and Matisse. The museum honours the Lesvos-born artist and critic Stratis Eleftheriadis, who brought the work of primitive painter and Lesvos native Theophilos to international attention.

Archaeological Museum
MUSEUM

(22510 40223; 8 Noemvriou; adult/child €3/2; ⊘8am-5pm Jun-Oct, 8.30am-5pm Tue-Sun Nov-May) This handsome and refurbished museum, about 500m above the eastern quay (and the now-closed Old Archaeological Museum), portrays island life from the 2nd century BC to the 3rd century AD, including striking floor mosaics with a walking 'trail' across the protective glass surface.

Fortress
FORTRESS

(Kastro; adult/child €2/free; ⊘8am-3pm Tue-Sun) Mytilini's imposing early Byzantine fortress was renovated in the 14th century by Genoese overlord Francisco Gatelouzo, and then the Turks enlarged it again. Flanked by pine trees, it's popular for a stroll, with great views included.

🛌 Sleeping

★ Alkaios Rooms
PENSION €

(6981314154, 22510 47737; www.alkaiosrooms.gr; Alkaiou 16; s/d/tr incl breakfast €35/45/55; 🅿🌐) This collection of 30 spotless and well-kept rooms nestled discreetly in two renovated traditional buildings is Mytilini's most attractive budget option. It's a two-minute walk up from the west side of the waterfront (and Kitchen 19 cafe). The reception is in a restored mansion, where breakfast is served in a flowery courtyard.

Theofilos Paradise Boutique Hotel
BOUTIQUE HOTEL €€

(22510 43300; www.theofilosparadise.gr; Skra 7; d/ste/f incl breakfast from €120/150/170; 🅿🌐@🌐🌐) This smartly restored, 100-year-old mansion is elegant, cheerful and good value, with modern amenities along with a traditional *hammam*. The 22 swanky rooms (plus two luxe suites) are spread among three adjacent buildings surrounding an inviting courtyard.

Hotel Lesvion
HOTEL €€

(22510 28177; www.lesvion.gr; Kountouriotou 27a, harbour; s/d/tr from €45/60/70; 🌐) The modern and well-positioned Lesvion, smack on the harbour, has friendly service and attractive and spacious rooms, some with excellent port-view balconies. A breakfast bar overlooks the harbour.

🍴 Eating & Drinking

Hit the streets in the bend in the harbour (Plateia Sapphou), around Ladadika, for zippy bars, cafes and creative eats.

★ Taverna Efkaliptos
SEAFOOD €

(22510 32727; old harbour, Panagiouda; mains €6-12; ⊘lunch & dinner) You might be sitting closer to the fishing boats than the kitchen at this first-class fish taverna in Panagiouda, just 4km north of Mytilini but with a distinctly remote feel. Excellent mezedhes and well-priced fresh fish, great service, and white wine from nearby Limnos.

★ To Steki tou Yianni
TAVERNA €

(22510 28244; Agiou Therapodos; mains €5-15; ⊘noon-3pm & 8pm-late) Head up behind the giant Agios Therapon church to this wonderful, welcoming taverna where Yianni dishes out whatever's freshest. All the produce is local, the cheeses delectable, and the fish or meat top quality. Go with the flow...this is a local hang-out, with folks arriving after 9pm. Sip a local ouzo and see what Yianni brings you.

Cafe P
CAFE €

(22510 55594; Samou 2; mains €2-7; ⊘11am-3am) This hip back-alley bistro draws a mostly university crowd for its unusual and well-priced small plates, small menu, eclectic music mix and all-round chill atmosphere. Oven-cooked pork with leeks or baked feta in a fig balsamic, plus a draught beer is €6. About 50m in from Sappho Sq. Look for the single Greek letter, 'Π'.

ℹ Information

See www.lesvos.net and www.greeknet.com for information.

Molyvos (Mithymna)
Μόλυβος (Μήθυμνα)
POP 1500

The gracious, historic town of Mithymna (known by locals as Molyvos), 62km north of Mytilini Town, winds beautifully from the picturesque **old harbour**, up through cobbled streets canopied by flowering vines to the impressive **Byzantine-Genoese Castle** (22530 71803; €2; ⊘8.30am-3pm) on the hilltop, from which you get tremendous views out to Turkey and around the lush valleys.

Ravishing to the eye, Molyvos is well worth a wander, or is a peaceful place to stay.

Eftalou hot springs (☑22530 71245; old/ new bathhouse €4/5; ☺old bathhouse 6-8am & 6-9pm, new bathhouse 9am-5pm), 4km from town on the beach, is a superb bathhouse complex with steaming, pebbled pools. The scenery on the northern coast is extraordinary, as are its tiny villages.

Airy, friendly **Nassos Guest House** (☑6942046279; www.nassosguesthouse.com; d/tr without bathroom from €25/35; ☎) offers shared facilities and a communal kitchen, in an old Turkish house with rapturous views. **Lela's Studios** (☑22530 71285, 6942928224; www.eftalouolivegrove.com/lelas_studios.htm; studio from €40; ❄☎) is set in a courtyard of roses and geraniums with sunset sea views.

From the bus stop, walk towards town 100m to the helpful **municipal tourist office** (☑22530 71347; ☺10am-3pm Mon-Sat May-Jun & Sep, 10am-3pm & 4-9pm Mon-Sat, 10am-3pm Sun Jul-Aug).

Buses to Mithymna (€7.50) take 1½ hours from Mytilini; a rental car is a better option with so much to explore.

Around the Island

Hire a car and tour the incredible countryside. Southern Lesvos is dominated by **Mt Olympus** (968m), and grove-covered valleys. Visit wonderful mountain village **Agiasos**, with its artisan workshops making everything from handcrafted furniture to pottery. **Plomari** in the far south is the land of ouzo distilleries; tour fascinating **Varvagianni Ouzo Museum** (☑22520 32741; www.barbayanni-ouzo.com; Plomari; ☺9am-4pm Mon-Fri Apr-Oct, 10am-2pm Mon-Fri Nov-Mar, by appointment Sat & Sun) FREE.

Western Lesvos is known for its **petrified forest** (☑22510 47033; www.petrifiedforest.gr; €2; ☺park 8am-4pm Tue-Sun Jul-Sep, museum 9.30am-5.30pm Jul-Sep, 9am-5pm Tue-Sun Oct-Jun), with petrified wood at least 500,000 years old, and for the gay-friendly town of **Skala Eresou**, the birthplace of Sappho. You can stay over in peaceful **Sigri**, with its broad beaches, to the southwest.

ⓘ Getting There & Around

Written up on flight schedules as Mytilene, Lesvos' **Odysseas Airport** (MJT; ☑22510 61212, 22510 38700) has daily connections with Athens and Thessaloniki. **Sky Express** (☑28102 23500; www.skyexpress.gr) flies to Limnos,

Chios, Samos and Rhodes (but beware their strict baggage policy). The airport is 8km south of Mytilini town; taxis cost €10, bus €1.60.

BOAT

In summer, daily fast boats leave Mytilini Town for Piraeus (€42, 11 to 13 hours) via Chios. Other ferries serve Chios, Ikaria, Limnos, Thessaloniki and Samos. Check www.openseas.gr.

BUS

The long-distance bus station in Mytilini Town is beside Agia Irinis Park, near the domed church. The local bus station is opposite Plateia Sapphou, the main square.

CAR

It's worth renting a car in Lesvos to explore the vast island. There are several outlets at the airport and many in town.

SPORADES   ΣΠΟΡΑΔΕΣ

Scattered to the southeast of the Pelion Peninsula, to which they were joined in prehistoric times, the 11 islands that make up the Sporades group have similarly mountainous terrain and dense vegetation, and are surrounded by scintillatingly clear seas.

The main ports for the Sporades are Volos and Agios Konstantinos on the mainland.

Skiathos   ΣΚΙΑΘΟΣ

POP 6110

Lush and green, Skiathos has a beach resort feel about it. Charter flights bring loads of package tourists, but the island still oozes enjoyment and is downright mellow in winter. Skiathos Town, with its quaint **old harbour**, and some excellent beaches are on the hospitable south coast.

◉ Sights & Activities

Moni Evangelistrias (☑24270 22012; museum €2; ☺10am-dusk), the most famous of the island's monasteries, was a hilltop refuge for freedom fighters during the War of Independence, and the Greek flag was first raised here, in 1807.

Skiathos has superb beaches, particularly on the south coast. **Koukounaries** is popular with families, and has a wonderful protected **marshland** for water fowl. A stroll over the headland, **Big Banana Beach** is stunning, but if you want an all-over tan, head a tad further to **Little Banana Beach**, where bathing suits are a rarity. Beautiful **Lalaria** on the north coast is accessible only by boat.

At the Old Port in Skiathos Town, **boat excursions** go to nearby beaches (€10), around Skiathos Island (€25) and on full-day trips to Skopelos, Alonnisos and the Alonnisos Marine Park (€35).

🛏 Sleeping

★**Gisela's House-in-Town**   PENSION €

(📋 24270 21370, 6945686542; gisbaunach@ hotmail.com; r from €45; ❋ 🛜) Cosy and quiet on a backstreet off Papadiamanti, this well-managed budget gem has just two rooms, with two twin beds in each, overhead fans, mosquito screens, tables, tea kettles and a flowery verandah.

Hotel Bourtzi   BOUTIQUE HOTEL €€

(📋 24270 21304; www.hotelbourtzi.gr; Moraitou 8, cnr Papadiamanti; d incl breakfast from €90; 🅿 ❋ 🛜 🏊) On upper Papadiamanti, the swank Bourtzi features austere-modern rooms, attentive staff, and an inviting garden and pool.

🍴 Eating & Drinking

Seafood joints line Skiathos' Old Harbour, cafes and bars wrap around the whole waterfront.

★**Taverna-Ouzerie Kabourelia**   TAVERNA €

(📋 24270 21112; Old Harbour; mains €4-12; ⊙noon-midnight; 🛜) Poke your nose into the open kitchen to glimpse the day's catch at this popular year-round eatery at the old port. Perfect fish grills and house wine are served at moderate prices. Grilled octopus and *taramasalata* (a thick purée of fish roe, potato, oil and lemon juice) are just two of several standout mezedhes.

★**La Cucina di Maria**   RISTORANTE €€

(📋 24270 24168; Plateia Trion Ierarhon; €8-15; ⊙dinner) Excellent thin-crust pizza twirled in the air is just the beginning at this popular spot above the old port. Fresh pasta, fine meat and fish grills in a colourful setting under the mulberry tree.

ℹ Information

See skiathosinfo.com for information.

ℹ Getting There & Around

AIR

Skiathos Airport (JSI; 📋 24270 29100) is 2km northeast of Skiathos Town, and has two summertime daily flights to Athens (€88) and charter flights from northern Europe. Taxis cost €6 to €15 depending on where you're headed.

BOAT

Frequent daily hydrofoils serve mainland ports Volos (€37, 1½ hours) and Agios Konstantinos (€37, 1½ hours), as do cheaper ferries. Hydrofoils/ferries serve Skopelos (€17/10, 20/55 minutes) and Alonnisos (€17/11, 1½/two hours). See **Hellenic Seaways** (📋 24270 22209; www. skiathosoe.com; cnr Papadiamantis, waterfront).

Water taxis around Skiathos depart from the Old Harbour.

BUS

Crowded buses ply the south-coast road between Skiathos Town and Koukounaries (€2) every 30 minutes between 7.30am and 11pm year-round, stopping at all the beaches along the way. The bus stop is at the eastern end of the harbour.

IONIAN ISLANDS
ΤΑ ΕΠΤΑΝΗΣΑ

The idyllic cypress- and fir-covered Ionian Islands stretch down the western coast of Greece from Corfu in the north to Kythira, off the southern tip of the Peloponnese. Mountainous, with dramatic cliff-backed beaches, soft light and turquoise water, they're more Italian in feel, offering a contrasting experience to other Greek islands.

Corfu   ΚΕΡΚΥΡΑ

POP 102,071

Many consider Corfu, or Kerkyra (*ker*-kih-rah) in Greek, to be Greece's most beautiful island – the unfortunate consequence of which is that it's overbuilt and often overrun with crowds. Look beyond them to find its core splendour.

Corfu Town   Κέρκυρα

POP 35,000

Built on a promontory and wedged between two fortresses, Corfu's **Old Town** is a tangle of narrow walking streets through gorgeous Venetian buildings. Explore the winding alleys and surprising plazas in the early morning or late afternoon to avoid the hordes of day trippers seeking souvenirs.

⊙ Sights

★**Palaio Frourio**   FORTRESS

(Old Fortress; 📋 26610 48310; adult/concession €4/2; ⊙8am-8pm Apr-Oct, 8.30am-3pm Nov-Mar) Constructed by the Venetians in the 15th century on the remains of a Byzantine castle (and further altered by the British), this spectacular landmark offers respite from the crowds and superb views of the region. Climb to the summit of the inner outcrop, which is crowned by a lighthouse, for a 360-degree panorama. The gatehouse contains a Byzantine museum.

★ Palace of St Michael & St George
PALACE

Originally the residence of a succession of British high commissioners, this palace now houses the world-class Museum of Asian Art (☑ 26610 30443; www.matk.gr; adult/child €6/free, 3-day with Antivouniotissa Museum & Old Fortress €14; ⊙ 9am-4pm Tue-Sun), founded in 1929. Expertly curated with extensive, informative English-language placards, the collection's approximately 10,000 artefacts, collected from all over Asia, include priceless prehistoric bronzes, ceramics, jade figurines, coins and works of art in onyx, ivory and enamel. Additionally, the palace's throne room and rotunda are impressively adorned in period furnishings and art.

★ Church of Agios Spyridon
CHURCH

(Agios Spyridonos; ⊙ 7am-8pm) FREE The sacred relic of Corfu's beloved patron saint, St Spyridon, lies in an elaborate silver casket in the 16th-century basilica.

Mon Repos Estate
PARK

(Kanoni Peninsula; ⊙ 8am-7pm May-Oct, to 5pm Nov-Apr) FREE On the Kanoni Peninsula on the southern outskirts of town, an extensive, wooded parkland estate surrounds an elegant neoclassical villa. It houses the Museum of Palaeopolis (☑ 26610 41369; adult/concession €4/2; ⊙ 8am-3pm), with entertaining archaeological displays and exhibits on the history of Corfu Town. Paths lead through lush grounds to the ruins of two Doric temples; the first is truly a ruin, but the southerly Temple of Artemis is serenely impressive.

Antivouniotissa Museum
MUSEUM

(☑ 26610 38313; www.antivouniotissamuseum. gr; off Arseniou; adult/child €2/free; ⊙ 8.30am-3pm Tue-Sun) The exquisite, timber-roofed, 15th-century Church of Our Lady of Antivouniotissa holds an outstanding collection of Byzantine and post-Byzantine icons and artefacts dating from the 13th to the 17th centuries.

🛏 Sleeping

Accommodation prices fluctuate wildly depending on season; book ahead.

★ Bella Venezia
BOUTIQUE HOTEL €€

(☑ 26610 46500; www.bellaveneziahotel.com; N Zambeli 4; s/d incl breakfast from €115/130; ⊙ ❋ ☎) From the instant you enter this neoclassical former girls' school – with its elegant lobby decked in candelabras, velvet chairs and grand piano – the place will charm you with its pure old-world charm. The Venezia has plush, high-ceilinged rooms with fine city views (some with balcony). Conscientious staff welcome you, and the gazebo breakfast room in the garden is delightful.

★ Siorra Vittoria
BOUTIQUE HOTEL €€

(☑ 26610 36300; www.siorravittoria.com; Stefanou Padova 36; s/d incl breakfast from €118/160; P ❋ ☎) Expect luxury and style at this quiet 19th-century mansion where painstakingly restored traditional architecture meets modern amenities; marble bathrooms, crisp linens and genteel service make for a relaxed stay. Breakfast in the peaceful garden beneath an ancient magnolia tree. The Vittoria suite encompasses the atelier and has views to the sea.

Hermes Hotel
HOTEL €€

(☑ 26610 39268; www.hermes-hotel.gr; Markora 12; s/d/tr from €55/65/75; ❋ ☎) Peaceful Hermes has cool, lime-hued rooms in a central location (though mercifully the windows are double-glazed), with old-fashioned bathrooms, laminate floors and a classy breakfast area. Rooms have TVs, fridges and CD players. Find it up a stairway, overlooking the market.

🍴 Eating & Drinking

Corfu has excellent restaurants. Cafes and bars line the arcaded Liston. Try Corfu Beer.

★ Il Vesuvio
GREEK €

(☑ 26610 21284; Guilford; mains from €10; ⊙ noon-late) The Neapolitan owner of this classy Italian restaurant, which has premises on both sides of the street, won the 'Best Italian Restaurant in Greece' award for his moreish homemade gnocchi, tortellini and ravioli. Eat on the street or inside but don't neglect a taste of their silky-smooth panna cotta – so fresh it will make your taste buds sing.

GREECE CORFU

WORTH A TRIP

IONIAN PLEASURES

Paxi (Πάξοι) Paxi lives up to its reputation as one of the Ionians' most idyllic and picturesque islands. At only 10km by 4km it's the smallest of the main holiday islands and makes a fine escape from Corfu's quicker-paced pleasures.

Kefallonia (Κεφαλλονιά) Tranquil cypress- and fir-covered Kefallonia, the largest Ionian island, is breathtakingly beautiful with rugged mountain ranges, rich vineyards, soaring coastal cliffs and golden beaches. Not yet overrun with package tourism, it remains low-key outside resort areas and is a perfect spot for kayaking.

Ithaki (Ιθάκη) Odysseus' long-lost home in Homer's *Odyssey*, Ithaki (ancient Ithaca) remains a verdant, pristine island blessed with cypress-covered hills and beautiful turquoise coves. It's a walkers' paradise, best reached from Kefallonia.

Lefkada (Λευκάδα) Lefkada has some of the best beaches in Greece, if not the world, and an easygoing way of life.

★ **To Tavernaki tis Marinas** TAVERNA €
(☑ 69816 56001; 4th Parados, Agias Sofias 1; mains €6-16; ◷ noon-midnight) Restored stone walls, hardwood floors and cheerful staff lift the ambience of this taverna. Check daily specials or choose anything from *mousakas* (baked layers of eggplant or zucchini, minced meat and potatoes topped with cheese sauce) or grilled sardines to steak. Accompany it all with a dram of ouzo or *tsipouro* (a spirit similar to ouzo).

Rouvas TAVERNA €
(☑ 26610 31182; S Desilla 13; mains €9; ◷ 9am-5pm) As authentically Greek as it gets, this earthy gourmand's delight is a Corfiot institution. Look out for dishes like beef stew in tomato sauce and roast salmon with potatoes, as well as plenty of veggie dishes. Even celebrity chef Rick Stein was impressed.

★ **La Cucina** ITALIAN €€
(☑ 26610 45029; Guilford 17; mains €13-25; ◷ 7-11pm; ❀ 🛜) A long-established favourite, well-run La Cucina shines for its creative cuisine, with hand-rolled pasta dishes at the fore. The original Guilford location has cosy, warm tones and murals, while the **Moustoxidou** (☑ 26610 45799; cnr Guilford & Moustoxidou; €10-15; ◷ 7-11pm) annexe (with identical menu) is chic in glass and grey.

ℹ Information

Municipal Tourist Kiosk (Palaio Frourio; ◷ 9am-4pm Mon-Sat Jun-Sep) Offers helpful information for things to do around Corfu, accommodation and transport timetables.
Pachis Travel (☑ 26610 28298; www.pachistravel.com; Guilford 7; ◷ 9am-2.30pm & 5.30-9pm, closed Sun) This helpful travel agency can assist with ferry and plane tickets, and hotels. They also organise charter boats and excursions to Paxi.

Around the Island

To explore the island fully your own transport is best. Much of the coast just north of Corfu Town is overwhelmed with beach resorts, the south is quieter, and the west has a beautiful, if popular, coastline. The **Corfu Trail** (www.thecorfutrail.com) traverses the island north to south.

North of Corfu Town, in **Kassiopi**, picturesque **Manessis Apartments** (☑ 6973918416, 26630 81474; www.manessiskassiopi.com; Kassiopi; 4-person apt €80-110; ❀ 🛜) offers water-view apartments.

South of Corfu Town, **Achillion Palace** (☑ 26610 56210; www.achillion-corfu.gr; Gastouri; €7, audio guide €3; ◷ 8am-8pm Apr-Oct, 8.45am-4pm Nov-Mar) pulls 'em in for over-the-top royal bling. Don't miss a dinner at one of the island's best tavernas, **Klimataria** (☑ 26610 71201; www.klimataria-restaurant.gr; Benitses; mains €8-15; ◷ 7pm-midnight Feb-Nov), in nearby **Benitses**.

To gain an aerial view of the gorgeous cypress-backed bays around **Paleokastritsa**, the west coast's main resort, go to the quiet village of **Lakones**. For beautiful rooms just 20m from the pretty beach, check in to **Hotel Zefiros** (☑ 26630 41244; www.hotel-zefiros.gr; Paleokastritsa; d/tr/q from €90/130/145; ❀ 🛜). Further south, good beaches surround tiny **Agios Gordios**, which has famous **Pink Palace** (☑ 26610 53103; www.thepinkpalace.com; Agios Gordios Beach; incl breakfast & dinner dm/d/tr/q from €21/42/63/84, 2-night minimum stay; ❀ @) backpackers and party central.

ℹ️ Getting There & Around

AIR

Ioannis Kapodistrias Airport (CFU; ☑ 26610 89600; www.corfu-airport.com) is 2km south-west of Corfu Town. There are direct flights to Athens daily and regularly to Thessaloniki, throughout the Ionians and (from June to September) to Iraklio, Crete. Charter planes and budget airlines fly internationally in summer. Bus 15 serves the airport (€1.50), taxis cost €10.

BOAT

Neo Limani port lies west of the Neo Frourio (New Fortress). Ferries go to Igoumenitsa (€10, 1¼ hours, hourly). In summer daily ferries and hydrofoils go to Paxi, and ferries to Italy (Bari, Brindisi and Venice) also stop in Patra (€35, six hours); some stop in Kefallonia and Zakynthos. Check www.openseas.gr.

BUS

Blue buses (€1.10 to €1.50) for villages near Corfu Town depart from the **local bus station** (☑ 26610 31595, 26610 39859; www.asti koktelkerkyras.gr; Plateia San Rocco) in Corfu Old Town. Services to other destinations (around Corfu €1.60 to €4.40) and daily buses to Athens (€45, 8½ hours) and Thessaloniki (€35, eight hours) leave from Corfu's **long-distance bus station** (☑ 26610 28900; www.greenbuses.gr; Ioannou Theotoki, Corfu Town).

SURVIVAL GUIDE

ℹ️ Directory A–Z

ACCOMMODATION
Accommodation Types

Hotels Range from basic business lodging to high-end boutique extravaganzas.

Pensions and guesthouses Often include breakfast and are usually owner-operated.

Domatia Rooms for rent; owners greet ferries and buses shouting 'room!'.

Youth hostels In most major towns and on some islands.

Campgrounds Generally open April to October; standard facilities include hot showers, kitchens, restaurants and minimarkets, often a swimming pool. Check out **Panhellenic Camping Association** (☑ 21036 21560; www. greececamping.gr). Wild camping is forbidden.

Mountain refuges Listed in *Greece Mountain Refuges & Ski Centres*, available free from EOT and EOS (Ellinikos Orivatikos Syndesmos; Greek Alpine Club) offices.

Prices

Accommodation is nearly always negotiable (and deeply reduced) outside peak season, especially for longer stays.

CUSTOMS REGULATIONS

It is strictly forbidden to export antiquities (anything over 100 years old) without an export permit.

INTERNET ACCESS

Wi-fi is common at most sleeping and eating venues, ports, airports and some city squares.

INTERNET RESOURCES

EOT (Greek National Tourist Organisation; www.gnto.gr) Concise tourist information.

Greek Travel Pages (www.gtp.gr) Access to ferry schedules and accommodation.

Lonely Planet (www.lonelyplanet.com/greece) Destination information, hotel bookings and traveller forum.

Ministry of Culture (www.culture.gr) For cultural events and sights.

MONEY

➡ ATMs are everywhere except small villages.

➡ Cash is king, especially in the countryside; credit cards are not always accepted in small villages.

➡ Service charge is included on the bill in restaurants, but it is the custom to 'round up the bill'; same for taxis.

OPENING HOURS

Hours decrease significantly in the shoulder and low seasons, when many places shut completely.

Banks 8.30am–2.30pm Monday to Thursday, 8am–2pm Friday

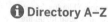
GREECE CORFU

ESSENTIAL FOOD & DRINK

Nutritious and flavourful, the food is one of the great pleasures of travelling in Greece. The country's rich culinary heritage draws from a fusion of mountain village food, island cuisine, flavours introduced by Greeks from Asia Minor, and influences from various invaders and historical trading partners. The essence of classic Greek cuisine lies in fresh, seasonal home-grown produce and generally simple, unfussy cooking that brings out the rich flavours of the Mediterranean.

Savoury appetisers Known as mezedhes (literally, 'tastes'; meze for short), standards include *tzatziki* (yoghurt, cucumber and garlic), *melitzanosalata* (aubergine dip), *taramasalata* (fish-roe dip), dolmadhes (stuffed vine leaves; dolmas for short), *fasolia* (beans) and *oktapodi* (octopus).

Cheap eats *Gyros* is pork or chicken shaved from a revolving stack of sizzling meat and wrapped in pitta bread with tomato, onion, fried potatoes and lashings of *tzatziki*. Souvlaki is skewered meat, usually pork.

Taverna staples You'll find *mousakas* (layers of aubergine and mince, topped with béchamel sauce and baked) on every menu, alongside *moschari* (oven-baked veal and potatoes), *keftedes* (meatballs), *stifado* (meat stew), *pastitsio* (baked dish of macaroni with minced meat and béchamel sauce) and *yemista* (either tomatoes or green peppers stuffed with minced meat and rice).

Sweets Greeks are serious about their sweets, with *zaharoplasteia* (sweet shops) in even the smallest villages. Try variations on baklava (thin layers of pastry filled with honey and nuts). Or go simple: delicious Greek yoghurt drizzled with honey.

Top Tipples Legendary aniseed-flavoured ouzo, sipped slowly, turns a cloudy white when ice or water is added. *Raki*, the Cretan firewater, is produced from grape skins. Greek coffee, a legacy of Ottoman rule, is a favourite pastime.

Bars 8pm–late
Cafes 10am–midnight
Clubs 10pm–4am
Post Offices 7.30am–2pm Monday to Friday (rural); 7.30am–8pm Monday to Friday, 7.30am–2pm Saturday (urban)
Restaurants 11am–noon and 7pm–1am
Shops 8am–3pm Monday, Wednesday and Saturday; 8am–2.30pm and 5–8pm Tuesday, Thursday and Friday

POST

Tahydromia (post offices; www.elta.gr) are easily identified by their yellow sign. To send post abroad, use the yellow post boxes labelled *exoteriko* (for overseas).

PUBLIC HOLIDAYS

Epiphany 6 January
First Sunday in Lent February
Greek Independence Day 25 March
Good Friday March/April
Orthodox Easter Sunday 8 April 2018, 28 April 2019
May Day (Protomagia) 1 May
Whit Monday (Agiou Pnevmatos) 50 days after Easter Sunday
Feast of the Assumption 15 August
Ohi Day 28 October
Christmas Day 25 December
St Stephen's Day 26 December

TELEPHONE

➡ Organismos Tilepikoinonion Ellados, known as OTE (o-teh), public phones abound; phonecards are sold at OTE shops and newspaper kiosks; pressing the 'i' button brings up instructions in English.

➡ Local SIM cards can be used in European and Australian phones. Most other phones can be set to roaming. US/Canadian phones need to have a dual- or tri-band system.

➡ For directory inquiries within Greece, call ☎131; for international inquiries ☎161. Area codes are part of the 10-digit number within Greece.

TIME

Greece is in the Eastern European time zone: two hours ahead of GMT/UTC and three hours ahead on daylight-saving time (last Sunday in March through to last Sunday in October).

ⓘ Getting There & Away

Regular ferry connections shuttle between Greece and the Italian ports of Ancona, Bari, Brindisi and Venice. Similarly, ferries operate between the Greek islands of Rhodes, Kos, Samos, Chios and Lesvos and the Aegean coast of Turkey.

Overland, it's possible to reach Albania, Bulgaria, the Former Yugoslav Republic of Macedonia (FYROM), Romania and Turkey from Greece. If you've got your own wheels, you can drive through border crossings with these four countries. There are train and bus connections with Greece's neighbours, but check ahead, as these have been affected by the financial crisis.

See www.seat61.com for more information on ferry travel.

AIR

Most visitors arrive by air, mostly into Athens. There are 17 international airports in Greece; most handle only summer charter flights to the islands.

There's a growing number of direct scheduled services into Greece by European budget airlines – **Aegean Airlines** (www.aegeanair.com) and its subsidiary, **Olympic Air** (www.olympicair.com), also fly internationally.

LAND
Border Crossings

You can drive or ride through the following border crossings.

Albania Kakavia (60km northwest of Ioannina); Sagiada (28km north of Igoumenitsa); Mertziani (17km west of Konitsa); Krystallopigi (14km west of Kotas)

Bulgaria Promahonas (109km northeast of Thessaloniki); Ormenio (41km from Serres); Exohi (a 448m-tunnel border crossing 50km north of Drama)

Former Yugoslav Republic of Macedonia (FYROM) Evzoni (68km north of Thessaloniki); Niki (16km north of Florina); Doïrani (31km north of Kilkis)

Turkey Kipi (43km east of Alexandroupolis); Kastanies (139km northeast of Alexandroupolis)

Bus

Private companies and KTEL Macedonia run buses from Thessaloniki to İstanbul, Skopje and Sofia.

Albania is served by **Albatrans** (☑ +355 42 259 204; www.albatrans.com.al) and **Euro Interlines** (☑ 21052 34594; www.komatastours.gr).

Bus and tour companies run buses between Greece and Sofia, Bulgaria; Budapest, Hungary; Prague, Czech Republic; and Turkey. See **Simeonidis Tours** (p541), **Dimidis Tours** (☑ 21069 27240; www.dimidistours.gr; 68 Kifissias Av, Athens; ⊙ 9am-8pm Mon-Fri, 9.30am-2.30pm Sat) and **Tourist Service** (www.tourist-service.com).

Train

The Greek railways organisation **OSE** (Organismos Sidirodromon Ellados; ☑ 14511; www.trainose.gr) runs daily trains from Thessaloniki to Sofia and to Belgrade (via Skopje), with a weekly onward train to and from Budapest.

SEA

Check ferry routes and schedules at www.greekferries.gr and www.openseas.gr.

If you are travelling on a rail pass, check to see if ferry travel between Italy and Greece is included. Some ferries are free, others give a discount. On some routes you will need to make reservations.

Albania

For Saranda, **Petrakis Lines** (☑ 26610 38690; www.ionian-cruises.com) has daily hydrofoils to Corfu (25 minutes).

Italy

Routes vary, check online.

Ancona Patra (20 hours, three daily, summer)

Bari Patra (15 hours, daily) via Corfu (10 hours) and Keffalonia (14 hours); also to Igoumenitsa (11½ hours, daily)

Brindisi Patra (15 hours, April to early October) via Igoumenitsa (11 hours)

Venice Patra (30 hours, up to 12 weekly, summer) via Corfu (25 hours)

Turkey

Boat services operate between Turkey's Aegean coast and the Greek islands.

⊙ Getting Around

Greece has a comprehensive transport system and is easy to get around.

AIR

It's sometimes cheaper to fly than take the ferry, especially if you book ahead online. Domestic airlines include the following.

Aegean Airlines (A3; ☑ 801 112 0000; www.aegeanair.com)

COUNTRY FACTS

Area 131,944 sq km

Capital Athens

Country Code ☑ 30

Currency Euro (€)

Emergency ☑ 112

Language Greek

Money Cash is king, ATMs are common except in small villages, and credit cards only sporadically accepted.

Population 10.9 million

Visas Generally not required for stays up to 90 days. Member of Schengen Convention.

Astra Airlines (A2; ☑ 2310 489 392, 800 700 7466; www.astra-airlines.gr) Thessaloniki-based airline.

Olympic Air (☑ 801 801 0101; www.olympicair.com) Partly merged with Aegean.

Sky Express (☑ 28102 23800; www.skyexpress.gr) Cretan airline with flights around Greece. Beware harsh baggage restrictions.

Hellenic Seaplanes (☑ 801 505 5050, 210 647 0180; www.hellenic-seaplanes.com) Charters with planned routes to the islands.

BICYCLE

→ Greece has very hilly terrain and the summer heat can be stifling. In addition, most drivers totally disregard road rules. Bicycles are carried for free on ferries.

→ See www.cyclegreece.gr for bicycle tour ideas.

→ Rental bicycles are available at most tourist centres, but are generally for pedalling around town rather than for serious riding. Prices range from €5 to €12 per day.

BOAT

From state-of-the-art 'superferries' that run on the major routes, to ageing open ferries that operate local services to outlying islands, Greece has an extensive network of ferries – the only means of reaching many of the islands. Schedules are often subject to delays due to poor weather and industrial action, and prices fluctuate regularly. In summer, ferries run regular services between all but the most out-of-the-way destinations; however, services seriously slow down in winter (and in some cases stop completely).

Be flexible. Boats seldom arrive early, but often arrive late. And some don't come at all. You may have the option of 'deck class', which is the cheapest ticket, or 'cabin class' with air-con assigned seats. On larger ferries there are lounges and restaurants for everyone serving fast food or snacks.

Tickets can be bought at the dock, but in high season, boats are often full – plan ahead. Check www.openseas.gr or www.gtp.gr for schedules, costs and links to individual boat company websites.

The Greek Ships app for smartphones tracks ferries in real time.

BUS

Long-distance buses are operated by **KTEL** (www.ktel.org). Fares are fixed by the government and service routes can be found on the company's website or regional websites (listed in our coverage). Buses are comfortable, generally run on time, are reasonably priced and offer frequent services on major routes. Buy tickets at least an hour in advance. Buses don't have toilets or refreshments, but stop for a break every couple of hours.

CAR & MOTORCYCLE

→ A great way to explore areas in Greece that are off the beaten track, but be careful on highways – Greece has the highest road-fatality rate in Europe. The road network is decent, but freeway tolls are fairly hefty.

→ Almost all islands are served by car ferries, but they are expensive; costs vary by the size of the vehicle.

→ The Greek automobile club, **ELPA** (www.elpa.gr), generally offers reciprocal services to members of other national motoring associations. If your vehicle breaks down, dial 104.

→ EU-registered vehicles are allowed free entry into Greece for six months without road taxes being due; a green card (international third-party insurance) is all that's required.

Hire Cars

→ Available throughout Greece, you'll get better rates with local rental-car companies than with the big multinational outfits. Check insurance waivers closely, and how they assist in a breakdown.

→ High-season weekly rates start at about €280 for the smallest models, dropping to €200 in winter – add tax and extras. Major companies request a credit-card deposit.

→ Minimum driving age in Greece is 18, but most firms require a driver of 21 or over.

Hire Mopeds & Motorcycles

→ Available for hire everywhere. Regulations stipulate that you need a valid motorcycle licence for the size of motorcycle you wish to rent – from 50cc upwards.

→ Mopeds and 50cc motorcycles start from €15 per day or from €30 per day for a 250cc motorcycle. Outside high season, rates drop considerably.

Main Ferry Routes

Road Rules

➺ Drive on the right.

➺ Overtake on the left (not all Greeks do this!).

➺ Compulsory to wear seatbelts in the front seats, and in the back if they are fitted.

➺ Drink-driving laws are strict; a blood alcohol content of 0.05% incurs a fine of around €150 and over 0.08% is a criminal offence.

PUBLIC TRANSPORT

All major towns have a local bus system. Athens is the only city with a metro system.

TAXI

➺ Taxis are widely available and reasonably priced. Yellow city cabs are metered; rates double between midnight and 5am. Grey rural taxis do not have meters; settle on a price before you get in.

➺ Athens taxi drivers are gifted in their ability to make a little bit extra with every fare. If you have a complaint, note the cab number and contact the Tourist Police. Rural taxi drivers are better.

TRAIN

➺ Check the **Greek Railways Organisation** (www.trainose.gr) website for the current schedules. Greece has only two main lines: Athens north to Thessaloniki and Alexandroupolis, and Athens to the Peloponnese.

➺ There are a number of branch lines, eg Pyrgos–Olympia line and the spectacular Diakofto–Kalavryta mountain railway.

➺ Inter-Rail and Eurail passes are valid; you still need to make a reservation.

➺ In summer make reservations at least two days in advance.

Hungary

Best Places to Eat

➜ Borkonyha (p580)

➜ Macok Bistro & Wine Bar (p591)

➜ Zeller Bistro (p580)

➜ Barack & Szilva (p580)

➜ Nem Kacsa (p586)

Best Places to Stay

➜ Four Seasons Gresham Palace Hotel (p579)

➜ Hotel Senator Ház (p591)

➜ Shantee House (p577)

➜ Bohem Art Hotel (p579)

➜ Tiszavirág Hotel (p589)

Why Go?

Stunning architecture, vital folk art, thermal spas and Europe's most exciting capital after dark: Hungary is just the place to kick off a European adventure. Lying virtually in the centre of the continent, this land of Franz Liszt and Béla Bartók, paprika-lashed dishes, superb wines and the romantic Danube River continues to enchant visitors. The allure of Budapest, once an imperial city, is immediate at first sight, and it also boasts the region's hottest nightlife.

Pécs, the warm heart of the south, and Eger, wine capital of the north, also have much to offer travellers, as does the Great Plain, where cowboys ride and cattle roam. And how about lazing in an open-air thermal spa while snow patches glisten around you? That's at Hévíz at the western edge of Lake Balaton, continental Europe's largest lake and Hungary's 'inland sea', which offers innumerable opportunities for rest and recreation.

When to Go
Budapest

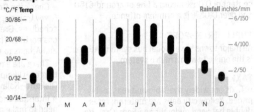

°C/°F Temp — Rainfall inches/mm

30/86 — — 6/150
20/68 — — 4/100
10/50 — — 2/50
0/32 — — 0
-10/14 —

J F M A M J J A S O N D

May Spring is in full swing, meaning reliable weather, cool temperatures and flowers.

Jul–Aug Sunny but often hot; decamp to the hills or Lake Balaton (book ahead).

Sep–Oct Blue skies, mild temperatures and grape-harvest festivals – a rewarding time to visit.

Hungary Highlights

1 Budapest (p573)
Losing yourself in Europe's best nightlife – the 'ruin pubs', wine bars and nightclubs of Hungary's capital.

2 Eger (p590)
Understanding the sobering history of Turkish attacks, and sampling the region's famed Bull's Blood wine.

3 Pécs (p588) Absorbing the Mediterranean-like

climate and historic architecture, including the iconic Mosque Church.

4 Lake Balaton (p585)
Taking a pleasure cruise across Central Europe's largest body of fresh water.

5 Hévíz (p587) Easing your aching muscles year-round in the warm waters of this thermal lake.

6 Hortobágy National Park (p590) Watching Hungarian cowboys' spectacular shows in this romantic region of the Great Plain.

7 Szentendre (p583)
Mill about with artists, freethinkers and day trippers at this too-cute-for-words town.

BUDAPEST

♪ 1 / POP 1.7 MILLION

The beauty of Hungary's capital is both natural and man-made. Straddling a gentle curve in the Danube, the city is flanked by the Buda Hills on the west bank and the beginnings of the Great Plain to the east. Ar-

chitecturally, the city is a treasure trove of baroque, neoclassical, Eclectic and art nouveau buildings. The city is also blessed with an abundance of hot springs, and in recent years Budapest has taken on the role of the region's party town.

Budapest is paradise for explorers; keep your senses primed and you'll discover something wonderful at every turn.

◉ Sights & Activities

⊙ Buda

Castle Hill (Várhegy) is Budapest's biggest tourist draw and a first port of call for any visit to the city. Here, you'll find most of Budapest's remaining medieval buildings, the Royal Palace and sweeping views of Pest across the river.

You can walk to Castle Hill up the **Király lépcső**, the 'Royal Steps' that lead northwest off Clark Ádám tér, or else take the **Sikló** (Map p576; www.bkv.hu; I Szent György tér; one-way/return adult 1200/1800Ft, 3-14yr 700/1100Ft; ⊙7.30am-10pm, closed 1st & 3rd Mon of month; ⊒16, 16A, ⊒19, 41), a funicular railway built in 1870 that ascends from Clark Ádám tér to Szent György tér near the Royal Palace.

★**Fishermen's Bastion**   MONUMENT
(Halászbástya; Map p576; I Szentháromság tér; adult/concession 800/400Ft; ⊙9am-8pm Mar–mid-Oct; ⊒16, 16A, 116) The bastion, a neo-Gothic masquerade that looks medieval and offers some of the best views in Budapest, was built as a viewing platform in 1905 by Frigyes Schulek, the architect behind Matthias Church. Its name was taken from the medieval guild of fishermen responsible for defending this stretch of the castle wall. The seven gleaming white turrets represent the Magyar tribes that entered the Carpathian Basin in the late 9th century.

★**Matthias Church**   CHURCH
(Mátyás templom; Map p576; ⊉1-355 5657; www.matyas-templom.hu; I Szentháromság tér 2; adult/concession 1500/1000Ft; ⊙9am-5pm Mon-Sat, 1-5pm Sun; ⊒16, 16A, 116) Parts of Matthias Church date back 500 years, notably the carvings above the southern entrance. But basically Matthias Church (so named because King Matthias Corvinus married Beatrix here in 1474) is a neo-Gothic confection designed by the architect Frigyes Schulek in 1896.

★**Citadella**   FORT
(Citadel; Map p576; ⊒27) The Citadella is a fortress that never saw a battle. Built by the Habsburgs after the 1848–49 War of Independence to defend the city from further insurrection, the structure was obsolete by the time it was ready in 1851 due to the change in political climate. Today the fortress contains some big guns peeping through the loopholes, but the interior has now been closed to the public while its future is decided.

★**Memento Park**   HISTORIC SITE
(⊉1-424 7500; www.mementopark.hu; XXII Balatoni út & Szabadkai utca; adult/student 1500/1000Ft; ⊙10am-dusk; ⊒101, 150) Home to more than 40 statues, busts and plaques of Lenin, Marx, Béla Kun and others whose likenesses have ended up on trash heaps elsewhere, Memento Park, 10km southwest of the city centre, is truly a mind-blowing place to visit. Ogle the socialist realism and try to imagine that some of these relics were erected as recently as the late 1980s.

ITINERARIES

One Week

Spend at least three days in **Budapest**, checking out the sights, museums, cafes and 'ruin pubs'. On your fourth day take a day trip to a Danube Bend town such as **Szentendre** or **Esztergom**. Day five can be spent getting a morning train to **Pécs** to see Turkish remains, museums and galleries. If you've still got the travel bug, on day six head for **Eger,** a baroque town set in red-wine country. On your last day recuperate back in one of Budapest's wonderful thermal baths.

Two Weeks

After a week in Budapest and the Danube Bend towns, spend two days exploring the towns and grassy beaches around **Lake Balaton**. **Tihany** is a rambling hillside village set on a protected peninsula, **Keszthely** is an old town with a great palace in addition to beaches, and **Hévíz** has a thermal lake. On day 10, head to the **Great Plain** – **Szeged** is a splendid university town on the Tisza River, and **Kecskemét** a centre of art nouveau. Finish your trip in **Tokaj**, home of Hungary's famous sweet wine.

★**Gellért Baths** BATHHOUSE
(Gellért gyógyfürdő; ☎1-466 6166; www.gellert
bath.hu; XI Kelenhegyi út 4, Danubius Hotel Gellért;
with locker/cabin Mon-Fri 5100/5500Ft, Sat & Sun
5300/5700Ft; ◉6am-8pm; ☐7, 86, Ⓜ M4 Szent
Gellért tér, ☐18, 19, 47, 49) Soaking in the art
nouveau Gellért Baths, open to both men
and women in mixed sections (so bring a
swimsuit), has been likened to taking a bath
in a cathedral. The eight thermal pools (one
outdoors) range in temperature from 19°C to
38°C, and the water is said to be good for pain
in the joints, arthritis and blood circulation.

◉ **Margaret Island**

The island's gardens and shaded walkways
are lovely places to stroll or cycle, plus there
is a dense concentration of swimming pools
and spas. The largest and best series of outdoor pools in the capital is **Palatinus Strand**
(☑1-340 4505; www.palatinusstrand.hu; XIII Margit-
sziget; adult/child Mon-Fri 2800/2100Ft, Sat & Sun
3200/2300Ft; ◉9am-7pm May-Sep; ☐26), with
upward of a dozen pools (two with thermal
water), wave machines, water slides and
kids' pools.

◉ **Pest**

★**Parliament** HISTORIC BUILDING
(Országház; Map p578; ☑1-441 4904; www.
hungarianparliament.com; V Kossuth Lajos tér 1-3;
adult/student EU citizen 2200/1200Ft, non-EU
citizen 5400/2800Ft; ◉8am-6pm Mon-Fri, to 4pm
Sat, to 2pm Sun; Ⓜ M2 Kossuth Lajos tér, ☐2)
The Eclectic-style Parliament, designed by
Imre Steindl and completed in 1902, has 691
sumptuously decorated rooms, but you'll
only get to see several of these and other features on a guided tour of the North Wing: the
Golden Staircase; the **Domed Hall**, where
the **Crown of St Stephen**, the nation's most
important national icon, is on display; the
Grand Staircase and its wonderful landing;
Loge Hall; and **Congress Hall**, where the
House of Lords of the one-time bicameral
assembly sat until 1944.

★**Heroes' Square** SQUARE
(Hősök tere; ☐105, Ⓜ M1 Hősök tere) Heroes' Sq
is the largest and most symbolic square in
Budapest, and contains the Millenary Monument *(Ezeréves emlékmű)*, a 36m-high pillar
topped by a golden Archangel Gabriel. Legend has it that he offered Stephen the crown
of Hungary in a dream. At the column's base

are Prince Árpád and other chieftains. The
colonnades behind the pillar feature various illustrious leaders of Hungary. It was
designed in 1896 to mark the 1000th anniversary of the Magyar conquest of the Carpathian Basin.

★**Basilica of St Stephen** CATHEDRAL
(Szent István Bazilika; Map p578; ☑06 30 703
6599, 1-311 0839; www.basilica.hu; V Szent István
tér; requested donation 200Ft; ◉9am-7pm Mon-
Sat, 7.45am-7pm Sun; Ⓜ M3 Arany János utca) Budapest's neoclassical cathedral was built over
half a century and completed in 1905. Much
of the interruption during construction had
to do with a fiasco in 1868 when the dome
collapsed during a storm, and the structure
had to be demolished and then rebuilt from
the ground up. The basilica is rather dark
and gloomy inside, but take a trip to the top
of the **dome** for incredible views.

★**House of Terror** MUSEUM
(Terror Háza; Map p578; ☑1-374 2600; www.
terrorhaza.hu; VI Andrássy út 60; adult/concession
2000/1000Ft, audioguide 1500Ft; ◉10am-6pm
Tue-Sun; Ⓜ M1 Oktogon) The headquarters of
the dreaded secret police is now the startling
House of Terror, focusing on the crimes and
atrocities of Hungary's fascist and Stalinist
regimes in a permanent exhibition called
Double Occupation. But the years after
WWII leading up to the 1956 Uprising get
the lion's share of the exhibition space (almost three-dozen spaces on three levels).
The reconstructed prison cells in the basement and the **Perpetrators' Gallery**, featuring photographs of the turncoats, spies and
torturers, are chilling.

★**Hungarian National
Museum** MUSEUM
(Magyar Nemzeti Múzeum; Map p578; ☑1-338
2122; www.hnm.hu; VIII Múzeum körút 14-16; adult/
concession 1600/800Ft; ◉10am-6pm Tue-Sun;
☐47, 49, Ⓜ M3/4 Kálvin tér) The Hungarian
National Museum houses the nation's most
important collection of historical relics in
an impressive neoclassical building, purpose
built in 1847. Exhibits trace the history of the
Carpathian Basin from earliest times to the
end of the Avar period, and the ongoing story
of the Magyar people from the conquest of
the basin to the end of communism. Don't
miss King Stephen's crimson silk coronation
mantle and the Broadwood piano, used by
both Beethoven and Liszt.

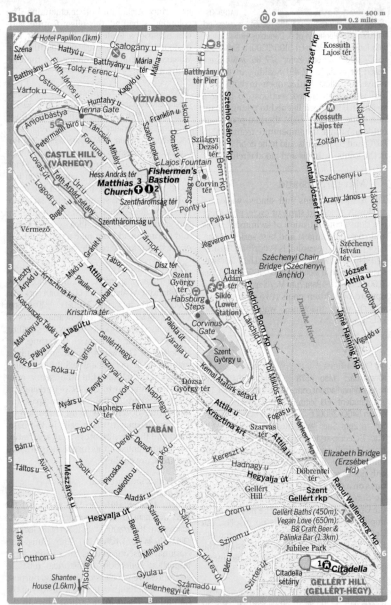

★**Great Synagogue**   SYNAGOGUE
(Nagy Zsinagóga; Map p578; ☎1-462 0477; www.
dohany-zsinagoga.hu; VII Dohány utca 2; adult/
concession incl museum 3000/2000Ft; ⊙10am-
6pm Sun-Thu, to 4pm Fri Mar-Oct, 10am-4pm Sun-
Thu, to 2pm Fri Nov-Feb; ⓂM2 Astoria, ☒47, 49)

Budapest's stunning Great Synagogue is the
largest Jewish house of worship in the world
outside New York City. Built in 1859, the
synagogue has both Romantic and Moorish
architectural elements. Inside, the **Hungarian Jewish Museum & Archives** (Magyar

Buda

◉ **Top Sights**
1 Citadella D6
2 Fishermen's Bastion.............................. B2
3 Matthias Church B2

◉ **Activities, Courses & Tours**
4 Sikló C3

◉ **Sleeping**
5 Baltazár.. A2

◉ **Eating**
6 Csalogány 26... B1
7 Rudas Restaurant & Bar D6

◉ **Drinking & Nightlife**
8 Kávé Műhely C1

Zsidó Múzeum és Levéltár; Map p578; ☑1-343 6756; www.milev.hu; incl in synagogue entry adult/concession 3000/2000Ft) contains objects relating to both religious and everyday life. On the synagogue's north side, the **Holocaust Tree of Life Memorial** (Map p578; Raoul Wallenberg Memorial Park, opp VII Wesselényi utca 6) presides over the mass graves of those murdered by the Nazis.

★**Kerepesi Cemetery**   CEMETERY
(Kerepesi temető; ☑06 30 331 8822; www.nem zetisirkert.hu; VIII Fiumei út 16; ⊙7am-8pm May-Jul, to 7pm Apr & Aug, to 6pm Sep, to 5pm Mar & Oct, 7.30am-5pm Nov-Feb; ⓂM2/4 Keleti train station, 🚌24) FREE Budapest's equivalent of London's Highgate or Père Lachaise in Paris, this 56-hectare necropolis was established in 1847 and holds some 3000 gravestones and mausoleums, including those of statesmen and national heroes Lajos Kossuth, Ferenc Deák and Lajos Batthyány. Maps indicating the location of noteworthy graves are available free at the entrance. Plot 21 contains the graves of many who died in the 1956 Uprising.

★**Széchenyi Baths**   BATHHOUSE
(Széchenyi Gyógyfürdő; ☑1-363 3210; www. szechenyibath.hu; XIV Állatkerti körút 9-11; tickets incl locker/cabin Mon-Fri 4700/5200Ft, Sat & Sun 4900/5400Ft; ⊙6am-10pm; ⓂM1 Széchenyi fürdő) These thermal baths are particularly popular with visitors and have helpful, English-speaking attendants. Its mix of indoor and outdoor pools includes 12 thermal pools (water temperatures up to 40°C), a swimming pool and an activity pool with whirlpool. The baths are open year-round, and it's quite a sight to watch men and women playing chess on floating boards when it's snowing.

★★ **Festivals & Events**

★**Sziget Festival**   MUSIC
(http://szigetfestival.com; ⊙mid-Aug) One of the biggest and most popular music festivals in Europe, held in mid-August on Budapest's Hajógyár (Óbuda) Island, with some 500,000 revellers (in 2016) and a plethora of Hungarian and international bands.

★**Budapest International Wine Festival**   WINE
(www.aborfesztival.hu; ⊙mid-Sep) Hungary's foremost winemakers introduce their wines at this ultrapopular event in the Castle District. The tipples are accompanied by a cornucopia of edibles along the Gastro Walkway.

★**CAFE Budapest**   PERFORMING ARTS
(Contemporary Art Festival; www.budapestbylocals. com/event/budapest-autumn-festival; ⊙Oct) Contemporary art takes on many forms during this two-week-long festival: poetry slams, contemporary fashion design, modern theatre, a jazz marathon and the 'Night of the Contemporary Galleries', to name a few. Design Week, the Art Market Budapest and the Mini Festival of Contemporary Music in Várkert Bazaar are all part of the celebrations.

◉ **Sleeping**

Buda

★**Shantee House**   HOSTEL €
(☑1-385 8946; www.backpackbudapest.hu; XI Takács Menyhért utca 33; beds in yurt €10-13, dm small/large from €12/16, d €38-52; 🅿@🛜; 🚌7, 7A, 🚌19, 49) Budapest's first hostel (originally known as the Back-Pack Guesthouse), the Shantee has added two floors to its colourfully painted suburban 'villa' in south Buda. It's all good and the fun (and sleeping bodies in high season) spills out into a lovely landscaped garden, with hammocks, a yurt and a gazebo. Two of the five doubles are en suite.

★**Hotel Papillon**   HOTEL €€
(☑1-212 4750; www.hotelpapillon.hu; II Rózsahegy utca 3/b; s/d/tr €44/54/69, apt €39-99; 🅿❄🛜🏊; 🚌4, 6) This cosy hotel in Rózsadomb (Rose Hill) has a delightful back garden with a small swimming pool, and some of the 20 rooms have balconies.

Central Pest

HUNGARY BUDAPEST

N 0 ——— 400 m
0 ——— 0.2 miles

Palatinus Strand (2.1km)

Szent István krt

Nyugati Train Station

TERÉZVÁROS

Heroes' Square (950m);
City Park (1km);
Budapest Info (1.1km);
Sparty (1.8km);
Széchenyi Baths (1.8km)

Parliament
5

Kossuth Lajos tér

House of Terror
3

Vörösmarty u

Hunyadi tér

Zeller Bistro (250m)

LIPÓTVÁROS

Szabadság tér

Oktogon
Jókai tér

ERZSÉBETVÁROS

21

Opera
20

Basilica of St Stephen
1

Szent István tér

14

18

Széchenyi Chain Bridge (Széchenyi lánchíd)
9

13

19

15

12

Klauzál tér

16

11

Eötvös tér

József nádor tér

Erzsébet tér

Memento Park Bus

Deák Ferenc tér

10

Jane Haining rkp

Danube River

17

Deák Ferenc u

Vörösmarty tér

Vigadó tér

Károly krt

6

7 2
Great Synagogue

Keleti (1.2km); Kerepesi Cemetery (1.2km); Piety Museum (1.6km)

Rákóczi út

Vigadó tér Pier

Astoria

Kossuth Lajos u

Múzeum krt

JÓZSEFVÁROS

Petőfi tér

Ferenciek tere

Szabadsajtó út

Elizabeth Bridge (Erzsébet híd)

Egyetem tér

Hungarian National Museum
4

Mahart PassNave

8

International Ferry Pier

Kálvin tér

Szent Gellért rkp

Raoul Wallenberg rkp

Liberty Bridge (Szabadság híd)

22

Fővám tér

Liszt

Central Pest

There are also four apartments available in the same building, one boasting a lovely roof terrace, as well as more apartments (studio to three-bedroom) next door. The staff are on the ball and helpful.

★**Baltazár**   BOUTIQUE HOTEL €€€
(Map p576; ☑1-300 7051; http://baltazarbudapest. com/; I Országház utca 31; r/ste from €135/214; ✳🛜; 🚌16, 16A, 116) This family-run boutique hotel at the northern end of the Castle District has 11 individually decorated rooms decked out with vintage furniture and striking wallpaper. Nods to more recent times include street art on the walls and a rain shower in the bathrooms. One of the rooms has a lovely little balcony with views to the castle. Excellent value.

Pest

★**Hive Hostel**   HOSTEL €€
(Map p578; ☑06 30 826 6197; www.thehive. hu; VII Dob utca 19; dm €15-25, d €60-100; @🛜; Ⓜ M1/2/3 Deák Ferenc tér) This enormous and very central place with more than 50 rooms of all sizes and shapes over several levels is for the slightly better-heeled budget traveller. There's a big common area and kitchen and a wonderful rooftop bar that looks down on a courtyard with two large chestnut trees and a popular ruin garden. A wonderful place, with equally great staff.

★**Bohem Art Hotel**   BOUTIQUE HOTEL €€
(Map p578; ☑1-327 9020; www.bohemarthotel. hu; V Molnár utca 35; r/ste incl breakfast from

€95/118; P✳🛜; Ⓜ M4 Fővám tér, M3/4 Kálvin tér, 🚊47, 48, 49) Though the rooms at this delightful small hotel are a little on the compact side, each one is decorated in its own individual style (the suites are done by local artists – we particularly like Room 302), with giant prints, bold touches of colour amid monochrome decor and ultramodern furnishings present throughout. Indulgent buffet breakfast.

★**Four Seasons Gresham Palace Hotel**   HOTEL €€€
(Map p578; ☑1-268 6000; www.fourseasons. com/budapest; V Széchenyi István tér 5-6; r/ste from €295/815; P✳@🛜♨; 🚊16, 105, 🚊2) This one-of-a-kind 179-room hotel was created out of the long-derelict art nouveau Gresham Palace (1907) and a lot of blood, sweat and tears. No expense was spared to piece back together the palace's Zsolnay tiles, mosaics and celebrated wrought-iron Peacock Gates leading north, west and south from the enormous lobby – the hotel is truly worthy of its name.

✖ Eating

Buda

Vegan Love   VEGAN €
(www.veganlove.hu; Bartók Béla út 9; mains 1490-1590Ft; �) 11am-8pm Mon-Sat, noon-8pm Sun; ☑; Ⓜ M4 Móricz Zsigmond körtér, 🚊18, 19, 47, 49) Vegan fast (sorry, street) food doesn't get much better than at this hole-in-the-wall eatery on up-and-coming Bartók Béla út. Try the likes

of sweet potato or curry lentil burgers, or the vegan chilli tofu hotdog. Small/large servings from the salad bar cost 590/1120Ft.

★ Rudas Restaurant & Bar INTERNATIONAL €€

(Map p576; ☑ 06 20 921 4877; www.rudasrestaurant. hu; Döbrentei tér 9, Rudas Baths; mains 2450-4350Ft; ⏱ 11am-10pm; ☐ 7, 86, ☐ 18, 19) We love, love, love this place with its turquoise interior and stunning views of the Danube and bridges. It sits above the Rudas Baths Wellness Centre (ask about inclusive packages) so it's just the ticket after a relaxing massage or treatment. The smallish outside terrace is a delight in summer (though it can be noisy).

★ Csalogány 26 INTERNATIONAL €€

(Map p576; ☑ 1-201 7892; www.csalogany26.hu; I Csalogány utca 26; mains 3800-5300Ft; ⏱ noon-3pm & 7-10pm Tue-Sat; ☐ 11, 111) Definitely one of the better restaurants in town, this intimate place with spartan decor turns its creativity to its superb food. Try the suckling *mangalica* (a kind of pork) with savoy cabbage (4900Ft) or other meat-heavy dishes that make the most of local ingredients. A three-course set lunch is a budget-pleasing 2900Ft.

✗ Pest

The **Nagycsarnok** (Great Market Hall; Map p578; ☑ 1-366 3300; www.piaconline.hu; IX Vámház körút 1-3; ⏱ 6am-5pm Mon, to 6pm Tue-Fri, to 3pm Sat; Ⓜ M4 Fővám tér) is a vast historic market built of steel and glass. Head here for fruit, vegetables, deli items, fish and meat.

Kisharang HUNGARIAN €

(Map p578; ☑ 1-269 3861; www.kisharang.hu; V Október 6 utca 17; mains 1000-2350Ft; ⏱ 11.30am-10pm; ☐ 15, 115) Centrally located 'Little Bell' is an *étkezde* (canteen serving simple Hungarian dishes) that's top of the list with students and staff of the nearby Central European University. The daily specials are something to look forward to and the retro decor is fun. *Főzelék* (370Ft to 490Ft), the traditional Hungarian way of preparing vegetables and sometimes served with meat, is always a good bet.

★ Borkonyha HUNGARIAN €€

(Wine Kitchen; Map p578; ☑ 1-266 0835; www. borkonyha.hu; V Sas utca 3; mains 3150-7950Ft; ⏱ noon-4pm & 6pm-midnight Mon-Sat; ☐ 15, 115, Ⓜ M1 Bajcsy-Zsilinszky út) Chef Ákos Sárközi's approach to Hungarian cuisine at this

Michelin-starred restaurant is contemporary, and the menu changes every week or two. Go for the signature foie gras appetiser wrapped in strudel pastry and a glass of sweet Tokaj wine. If *mangalica* (a special type of Hungarian pork) is on the menu, try it with a glass of dry *furmint*.

★ Barack & Szilva HUNGARIAN €€

(Map p578; ☑ 1-798 8285; www.barackesszilva. hu; VII Klauzál utca 13; mains 3200-5500Ft; ⏱ 6pm-midnight Mon-Sat; Ⓜ M2 Blaha Lujza tér) This is the kind of perfectly formed restaurant that every neighbourhood wishes it could boast. Run by a husband-and-wife team, the 'Peach & Pear' serves high-quality and exceptionally well-prepared Hungarian provincial food in a bistro setting. Try the duck pâté with dried plums and the red-wine beef *pörkölt* (goulash). Lovely terrace in summer too.

★ Zeller Bistro HUNGARIAN €€

(☑ 06 30 651 0880, 1-321 7879; VII Izabella utca 38; mains 2900-5400Ft; ⏱ noon-3pm & 6-11pm Tue-Sat; Ⓜ M1 Vörösmarty utca, ☐ 4, 6) You'll receive a very warm welcome at this lovely candlelit cellar where the attentive staff serve food sourced largely from the owner's family and friends in the Lake Balaton area. The Hungarian home cooking includes some first-rate dishes such as grey beef, duck leg, oxtail and lamb's knuckle. Superb desserts too. Popular with both locals and expats; reservations are essential.

Drinking

🌐 Buda

★ Kávé Műhely COFFEE

(Map p576; ☑ 06 30 852 8517; www.facebook. com/kavemuhely; II Fő utca 49; ⏱ 7.30am-6.30pm Mon-Fri, 9am-5pm Sat & Sun; Ⓜ M2 Batthyány tér, ☐ 19, 41) This tiny coffee shop is one of the best in the city. These guys roast their own beans, and their cakes and sandwiches are fantastic. Too hot for coffee? They've got craft beers and homemade lemonades, too. The attached gallery stages vibrant contemporary art exhibitions.

B8 Craft Beer & Pálinka Bar CRAFT BEER

(B8 Kézműves Sör és Pálinkabár; ☑ 1-791 3462; www. facebook.com/b8pub; Bercsényi utca 8; ⏱ 4-11pm Mon, noon-11pm Tue-Fri, 5-11pm Sat; Ⓜ M4 Móricz Zsigmond körtér, ☐ 18, 19, 47, 49) Our favourite new watering hole in Buda, this pint-sized place (though there are three floors) has

---

LOCAL KNOWLEDGE

BUDAPEST'S RUIN PUBS

Ruin pubs (romkocsmák) began to appear in the city from the early 2000s, when entrepreneurial free thinkers took over abandoned buildings and turned them into pop-up bars. At first a very word-of-mouth scene, the ruin bars' popularity grew exponentially and many have transformed from ramshackle, temporary sites full of flea-market furniture to more slick, year-round fixtures. Start with **Anker't** (Map p578; www.facebook.com/ankertbar; VI Paulay Ede utca 33; ⊙2pm-2am Mon-Wed & Sun, to 4am Thu-Sat; 🛜; Ⓜ M1 Opera), an achingly cool, grown-up courtyard pub surrounded by seriously ruined buildings, and **Füge Udvar** (Fig Court; Map p578; ☑1-782 6990; VII Klauzál utca 19; ⊙4pm-4am; Ⓜ M2 Blaha Lujza tér, 🚃4, 6), an enormous ruin pub with a large covered courtyard (both are on the Pest side).

---

more than two-dozen craft beers available from Hungary's 52 (at last count) breweries. Look for the names Legenda, Monyo and Etyeki and try the last's Belga Búza (Belgian Wheat). Harder stuff? Some 10 types of *pálinka* (fruit brandy), from Japanese plum to Gypsy cherry.

🍷 Pest

⭐ Instant   CLUB
(Map p578; ☑06 30 830 8747, 1-311 0704; www.instant.co.hu; VII Akácfa utca 51; ⊙4pm-6am; Ⓜ M1 Opera) We still love this 'ruin bar' on one of Pest's most vibrant nightlife strips and so do all our friends. It has 26 rooms, seven bars, seven stages and two gardens with underground DJs and dance parties. It's always heaving.

⭐ DiVino Borbár   WINE BAR
(Map p578; ☑06 70 935 3980; www.divinoborbar.hu; V Szent István tér 3; ⊙4pm-midnight Sun-Wed, to 2am Thu-Sat; Ⓜ M1 Bajcsy-Zsilinszky út) Central and always heaving, DiVino is Budapest's most popular wine bar, as the crowds spilling out onto the square in front of the Basilica of St Stephen in the warm weather will attest. Choose from more than 140 wines produced by 36 winemakers under the age of 35, but be careful: those 0.15dL (15mL) glasses (650Ft to 3500Ft) go down quickly.

⭐ Gerbeaud   CAFE
(Map p578; ☑1-429 9001; www.gerbeaud.hu; V Vörösmarty tér 7-8; ⊙noon-10pm; Ⓜ M1 Vörösmarty tér) Founded on the northern side of Pest's busiest square in 1858, Gerbeaud has been the most fashionable meeting place for the city's elite since 1870. Along with exquisitely prepared cakes and pastries, it serves continental/full breakfasts and a smattering of nicely presented Hungarian dishes with international touches. A visit is mandatory.

Tütü Bar   GAY
(Map p578; ☑06 70 353 4074; http://tutubudapest.hu; V Hercegprímás utca 18; ⊙10pm-5am Thu-Sat; Ⓜ M3 Arany János utca) Budapest's newest gay club is a basement bar that serves up a lot more than just drinks and attitude. From pole-dancers and acrobats to drag and fashion shows, they are out to entertain you. A barrel of laughs.

☆ Entertainment

Handy websites for booking theatre and concert tickets are www.kulturinfo.hu and www.jegymester.hu.

Performing Arts

⭐ Liszt Music Academy   CLASSICAL MUSIC
(Liszt Zeneakadémia; Map p578; ☑1-462 4600, box office 1-321 0690; www.zeneakademia.hu; VI Liszt Ferenc tér 8; ⊙box office 10am-6pm; Ⓜ M1 Oktogon, 🚃4, 6) Performances at Budapest's most important concert hall are usually booked up at least a week in advance, but more expensive (though still affordable) last-minute tickets can sometimes be available. It's always worth checking.

⭐ Hungarian State Opera House   OPERA
(Magyar Állami Operaház; Map p578; ☑1-814 7100, box office 1-353 0170; www.opera.hu; VI Andrássy út 22; ⊙box office 10am-8pm; Ⓜ M1 Opera) The gorgeous neo-Renaissance opera house is worth a visit as much to admire the incredibly rich decoration inside as to view a performance and hear the perfect acoustics.

🛍 Shopping

⭐ Ecseri Piac   MARKET
(Ecseri Market; www.piaconline.hu; XIX Nagykőrösi út 156; ⊙8am-4pm Mon-Fri, 5am-3pm Sat, 8am-1pm Sun; 🚌54, 84E, 89E 94E) One of the biggest flea markets in Central Europe, Ecseri sells everything from antique jewellery and Soviet army watches to Fred Astaire–style top hats.

Take bus 54 from Pest's Boráros tér, or for a quicker journey, express bus 84E, 89E or 94E from the Határ út stop on the M3 metro line in Pest and get off at the Fiume utca stop.

ℹ️ Information

There are ATMs everywhere, including in the train and bus stations and at the airport. Avoid moneychangers (especially those on V Váci utca) in favour of banks if possible. Arrive about an hour before closing time to ensure the bureau de change desk is still open.

Budapest Info (☎1-438 8080; www.budapest info.hu; Olof Palme sétány 5, City Ice Rink; ⊗9am-7pm; Ⓜ M1 Hősök tere) Helpful tourist office branch with bicycles for rent.

Déli Gyógyszertár (☎1-355 4691; www. deligyogyszertar.hu; XII Alkotás utca 1/b; ⊗24hr; Ⓜ M2 Déli pályaudvar) All-night pharmacy.

FirstMed Centers (☎1-224 9090; www. firstmedcenters.com; I Hattyú utca 14, 5th fl; ⊗8am-8pm Mon-Fri, to 2pm Sat, urgent care 24hr; Ⓜ M2 Széll Kálmán tér)

SOS Dent (☎1-269 6010, 06 30 383 3333; www.sosdent.hu; VI Király utca 14; ⊗8am-8pm Mon-Sat; Ⓜ M1/2/3 Deák Ferenc tér) Dental consultations from 5000Ft.

Vist@netcafe (☎06 70 585 3924; http:// vistanetcafe.com; XIII Váci út 6; per hour 250Ft; ⊗24hr; Ⓜ M3 Nyugati pályaudvar) One of the very few internet cafes open round the clock.

ℹ️ Getting There & Away

AIR

Budapest's **Ferenc Liszt International Airport** (BUD; ☎1-296 7000; www.bud.hu) has two modern terminals side by side 24km southeast of the city centre.

BOAT

Mahart PassNave (Map p578; ☎1-484 4013; www.mahartpassnave.hu; V Belgrád rakpart; ⊗9am-4pm Mon-Fri; Ⓡ2) runs a hydrofoil service on the Danube River between Budapest and Vienna (5½ to 6½ hours) from late April to late September. Hydrofoils arrive at and depart from the **International Ferry Pier** (Nemzetközi hajóállomás; Map p578; ☎1-484 4013; www. mahartpassnave.hu; V Belgrád rakpart; ⊗9am-4pm Mon-Fri; Ⓡ2), which is between Elizabeth and Liberty Bridges on the Pest side.

BUS

All international buses and domestic ones to/ from western Hungary arrive at and depart from **Népliget bus station** (☎1-219 8030; IX Üllői út 131; Ⓜ M3 Népliget) in Pest. The international ticket office is upstairs. **Eurolines** (www. eurolines.hu) is represented here, as is its Hun-garian associate, **Volánbusz** (☎1-382 0888; www.volanbusz.hu). There are left-luggage lockers on the ground floor. Népliget is on the blue metro M3 (station: Népliget).

Stadion bus station (☎1-219 8086; XIV Hungária körút 48-52; Ⓜ M2 Stadionok, Ⓡ1) generally serves cities and towns in eastern Hungary. The ticket office and left-luggage lock-ers are on the ground floor. Stadion is on the red metro M2 (station: 2 Stadionok).

Árpád Híd bus station (☎1-412 2597; XIII Árbóc utca 1; Ⓜ M3 Árpád Híd), on the Pest side of Árpád Bridge, is the place to catch buses for the Danube Bend and parts of the Northern Uplands.

CAR & MOTORCYCLE

Border formalities with Austria, Slovenia and Slovakia are virtually nonexistent. However, one may only enter or leave Hungary via designated border crossing points during opening hours when travelling to/from Croatia, Romania, Ukraine and Serbia, especially since, in the wake of the Syrian refugee crisis, a controversial bor-der wall now stretches along Hungary's border with Serbia and Croatia. For the latest on border formalities, check www.police.hu.

All major international rental firms, including **Avis** (☎1-318 4240; www.avis.hu; V Arany János utca 26-28; ⊗7am-6pm Mon-Fri, 8am-2pm Sat & Sun; Ⓜ M3 Arany János utca) and **Europcar** (☎1-505 4400; www.europcar.hu; V Erzsébet tér 7-8; ⊗8am-6pm Mon & Fri, to 4.30pm Tue-Thu, to noon Sat; Ⓜ M1/2/3 Deák Ferenc tér), have offices in the city and at the airport.

TRAIN

MÁV (Magyar Államvasutak, Hungarian State Railways; ☎1-349 4949; www.mavcsoport. hu) runs the country's extensive rail network. Contact the **MÁV-Start passenger service centre** (☎1-512 7921; www.mav-start.hu; V József Attila utca 16; ⊗9am-6pm Mon-Fri; Ⓜ M1/M2/M3 Deák Ferenc tér) for information on domestic train departures and arrivals. Its website has a useful timetable in English for planning routes.

Buy tickets at one of Budapest's three main train stations or the passenger service centre. **Keleti train station** (Keleti pályaudvar; VIII Kerepesi út 2-6; Ⓜ M2/M4 Keleti pályaudvar) handles most international trains as well as domestic ones from the north and northeast.

For some international destinations (eg Ro-mania), as well as domestic ones to/from the Danube Bend and Great Plain, head for **Nyugati train station** (Western Train Station; VI Nyugati tér). For trains bound for Lake Balaton and the south, eg Osijek in Croatia and Sarajevo in Bos-nia, go to **Déli train station** (Déli pályaudvar; I Krisztina körút 37; Ⓜ M2 Déli pályaudvar). All three stations are on metro lines.

ℹ Getting Around

TO/FROM THE AIRPORT

To get into the city centre from Ferenc Liszt International Airport, minibuses, buses and trains run from 4am to midnight (350Ft to 3200Ft); taxis cost from 6500Ft.

MiniBUD (☑1-550 0000; www.minibud.hu; one way from 1900Ft) shuttles passengers from the airport directly to their accommodation. Tickets are available at a clearly marked desk in the arrivals hall, though you may have to wait while the van fills up.

PUBLIC TRANSPORT

Public transport operates from 4.15am to between 9am and 11.30pm. After hours some 41 night buses run along main roads. Tram 6 on the Big Ring Rd runs round the clock.

A single ticket for all forms of transport is 350Ft (60 minutes of uninterrupted travel on the same metro, bus, trolleybus or tram line without transferring/changing); a book of 10 tickets is 3000Ft. A 'transfer ticket' allowing unlimited stations with one change within one hour costs 530Ft.

The three-day travel card (4150Ft) or the seven-day pass (4950Ft) make things easier, allowing unlimited travel inside the city limits. The fine for riding without a ticket is 8000Ft on the spot, or 16,000Ft if you pay within 30 days at the **BKK office** (☑1-325 5255; www.bkk.hu; VII Akácfa utca 22; ☉7am-8pm Mon-Fri, 8am-2pm Sat; Ⓜ M2 Blaha Lujza tér).

TAXI

Taxis in Budapest are fully regulated, with uniform flag-fall (450Ft) and per-kilometre charges (280Ft). Never get into a taxi that does not have a yellow licence plate and dashboard identification badge (required by law), plus the logo of a reputable firm on the outside and a table of fares clearly visible on the right-side back door. Reliable companies include **Budapest Taxi** (☑1-777 7777; www.budapesttaxi.hu), **City Taxi** (☑1-211 1111; www.citytaxi.hu), **Fő Taxi** (☑1-222 2222; www.fotaxi.hu) and **Taxi 4** (☑1-444 4444; www.taxi4.hu). Note that rates are higher at night and early morning.

THE DANUBE BEND

The Danube Bend is where hills on both banks force the river to turn sharply and flow southward. It is the most beautiful stretch of the Danube, where several historical towns vie for visitors' attention. Szentendre has its roots in Serbian culture and became an important centre for art early in the 20th century. Round the bend is tiny Visegrád, Hungary's 'Camelot' in the 15th century.

Esztergom is a sleepy town with the nation's biggest cathedral.

ℹ Getting There & Away

BUS & TRAIN

Regular buses serve towns on the west bank of the Danube. Trains reach Szentendre and, on a separate line, Esztergom. For Visegrád, you can take one of the regular trains from Budapest to the opposite bank of the river and then take a ferry across (timings linked to train arrivals).

BOAT

Regular **Mahart PassNave** (☑1-484 4013; www.mahartpassnave.hu; ☉8am-4pm Mon-Fri) boats run to and from Budapest over the summer months. From May to September, a boat departs Budapest's Vigadó tér at 10am Tuesday to Sunday bound for Szentendre (one way/return 2000/3000Ft, 1½ hours), returning at 5pm; the service runs on Saturday only in April. In July and August, the boat continues to Visegrád (one way/return 2500/3750Ft).

Between May and late August there's a daily ferry from Vigadó tér in Budapest at 9am, calling in at Visegrád (noon, 2500/3750Ft) before carrying on to Esztergom (2pm, 3000/4500Ft).

Hydrofoils travel from Budapest to Visegrád (one way/return 4000/6000Ft, one hour) and Esztergom (one way/return 5000/7500Ft, 1½ hours) on Friday, Saturday and Sunday from early May to September; boats leave at 9.30am and return at 5pm from Esztergom and 5.30pm from Visegrád.

Szentendre

☑ 26 / POP 25,542

Pretty little Szentendre (*sen*-ten-dreh), 19km north of Budapest, is an art colony turned tourist centre. The charming old centre around **Fő tér** (Main Square) has plentiful cafes and galleries, as well as beautiful baroque Serbian Orthodox churches. Meanwhile the **Art Mill** (Művészet Malom; ☑26-301 701; www.muzeumicentrum.hu; Bogdányi utca 32; adult/6-26yr 2000/1200Ft; ☉10am-6pm) exhibits cutting-edge art installations across three floors. The **Tourinform** (☑26-317 965; www.szentendreprogram.hu; Dumtsa Jenő utca 22; ☉9am-6pm) office hands out maps.

The most convenient way to get to Szentendre is to take the HÉV suburban train from Buda's Batthyány tér (630Ft, 40 minutes, every 10 to 20 minutes). There are efficient ferry services to Szentendre from Budapest between late March and late October.

Visegrád

☑ 26 / POP 1842

History and spectacular views pull visitors to soporific, leafy Visegrád (*vish*-eh-grahd).

The mighty 13th-century **Citadel** (Fellegvár; ☑ 26-598 080; www.parkerdo.hu; Várhegy; adult/concession 1800/900Ft; ☉ 9am-5pm mid-Mar–Apr & Oct, to 6pm May-Sep, to 3pm Nov–mid-Mar) looms over Visegrád atop a 350m hill; the views are well worth the climb. The partly reconstructed **Royal Palace** (Királyi Palota; ☑ 26-597 010; www.visegrad.hu; Fő utca 29; adult/concession 1100/550Ft; ☉ 9am-5pm Tue-Sun Mar-Oct, 10am-4pm Tue-Sun Nov-Feb) stands at the foot of the hills, closer to the centre of town. Seek information from **Visegrád Info** (☑ 26-597 000; www.palotahaz.hu; Dunaparti út 1; ☉ 10am-6pm Apr-Oct, to 4pm Tue-Sun Nov-Mar).

Buses are very frequent (745Ft, 1¼ hours) to/from Budapest's Újpest-Városkapu train station, Szentendre (465Ft, 45 minutes, every 45 minutes) and Esztergom (560Ft, 45 minutes, hourly). Regular ferry services travel to Visegrád from Budapest between late April and late September.

Esztergom

☑ 33 / POP 27.990

Esztergom's massive basilica sits high above the town and Danube River. But Esztergom's attraction goes deeper than the domed structure: the country's first king, St Stephen, was born here in 975. It was a royal seat from the late 10th to the mid-13th centuries, as well as the seat of Roman Catholicism in Hungary for more than a thousand years.

Hungary's largest church is **Esztergom Basilica** (Esztergomi Bazilika; ☑ 33-402 354; www.bazilika-esztergom.hu; Szent István tér 1; basilica free, crypt 200Ft, dome adult/concession 700/500Ft, treasury adult/concession 900/450Ft; ☉ 8am-6pm, crypt & treasury 9am-5pm, dome 9am-6pm). At the southern end of the hill is the extensive **Castle Museum** (Vármúzeum; ☑ 33-415 986; www.mnmvarmuzeuma.hu; Szent István tér 1; tours adult 1500-2000Ft, tours concession 750-1000Ft, joint ticket with Balassa Bálint Museum 3400/1700Ft; ☉ 10am-6pm Tue-Sun), housed in the former Royal Palace built during Esztergom's golden age. Below Castle Hill in the former Bishop's Palace, the **Christian Museum** (Keresztény Múzeum; ☑ 33-413 880; www.christianmuseum.hu; Mindszenty hercegprímás tere 2; adult/concession 900/450Ft; ☉ 10am-5pm Wed-Sun Mar-Nov; ☎) contains the finest collection of medieval religious art in Hungary.

Frequent buses run to/from Budapest (930Ft, 1¼ hours), Visegrád (560Ft, 45 minutes) and Szentendre (930Ft, 1¼ hours). Trains depart from Budapest's Nyugati train station (1120Ft, 1¼ hours) at least hourly. Ferries travel regularly from Budapest to Esztergom between May and September.

WESTERN HUNGARY

A visit to this region is a boon for anyone wishing to see remnants of Hungary's Roman legacy, medieval heritage and baroque splendour. Because it largely managed to avoid the Ottoman destruction of the 16th and 17th centuries, towns like Sopron retain their medieval cores; exploring their cobbled streets and hidden courtyards is a magical experience.

Sopron

☑ 99 / POP 61.887

Sopron (*showp*-ron) is the most beautiful town in western Hungary. Its medieval Inner Town (*Belváros*) is intact and its cobbled streets are a pleasure to wander. It's also surrounded by flourishing vineyards and famous for its wine.

◉ Sights

★ Storno House   MUSEUM
(Storno Ház és Gyűjtemény; ☑ 99-311 327; www.muzeum.sopron.hu; Fő tér 8; adult/concession Storno Collection 1000/500Ft, Boundless Story 700/350Ft; ☉ 10am-6pm Tue-Sun) Storno House, built in 1417, has an illustrious history: King Matthias stayed here in 1482–83, and Franz Liszt played a number of concerts here in the mid-19th century. Later it was taken over by the Swiss-Italian family of Ferenc Storno, chimney sweep turned art restorer, whose recarving of Romanesque and Gothic monuments throughout Transdanubia divides opinions to this day. Don't miss the **Storno Collection**, the family's treasure trove. The **Boundless Story** exhibition of local history is also worth a peek.

⌂ Sleeping

★ Braun Rooms Deluxe   GUESTHOUSE €€
(☑ 06 70 300 6460; http://braun-rooms-deluxe-sopron.bedspro.com; Deák tér 15; s/d €30/38; ⊜ ❋ ☎) Halfway between the Old Town and the train station, this great place consists of just three spotless, super-comfortable

doubles, with sunken bathtubs, climate control, coffee makers and murals on the walls. And if you want your teeth done, you're in an ideal location – right above a dental surgery.

★ Pauline-Carmelite Monastery of Sopronbanfalva   MONASTERY €€€

(Sopronbánfalvi Pálos-Karmelita; ☑99-505 895; www.banfalvakolostor.hu; Kolostorhegy utca 1; s/d/ste €84/128/164; �) Having worn many hats over the centuries – home for coal miners, Carmelite nunnery, mental hospital, museum – this 15th-century monastery has now been sensitively restored as a beautiful hotel/retreat. The vaulted singles and light-filled doubles look out on to the forest. Upstairs there's an art gallery and a tranquil common space, the library. The **refectory** (Kolostorhegy utca 2; mains 2750-6850Ft; tasting menus 7200Ft; ☯noon-3pm & 6-9pm; ☑) serves the best meals in Sopron.

✗ Eating & Drinking

★ Erhardt   INTERNATIONAL €€

(☑99-506 711; www.erhardts.hu; Balfi út 10; mains 2990-4590Ft; ☯11.30am-10pm Sun-Thu, to 11pm Fri & Sat; ☑) An excellent restaurant where a pleasant garden terrace, a wooden-beamed ceiling and paintings of rural scenes complement imaginative dishes such as paprika catfish with oyster mushrooms and crispy duck leg with cabbage noodles. There's an extensive selection of Sopron wines to choose from (also available for purchase at its wine cellar).

★ Cezár Pince   WINE BAR

(☑99-311 337; www.cezarpince.hu; Hátsókapu utca 2; ☯noon-midnight Mon-Sat, 4-11pm Sun; �) Atmospheric bar in a 17th-century cellar, where you can imbibe a wide selection of local wines while sharing large platters of cured meats, local cheeses, pâtés and salami.

ⓘ Information

OTP Bank (Várkerület 96/a) Handy ATM.

Tourinform (☑99-517 560; http://turizmus. sopron.hu; Liszt Ferenc utca 1, Ferenc Liszt Conference & Cultural Centre; ☯9am-5pm Mon-Fri, to 1pm Sat year-round, 9am-1pm Sun Mar-Sep only) Some information on Sopron and surrounds, including local vintners.

ⓘ Getting There & Away

BUS

There are direct buses to Keszthely (2520Ft, three hours, four daily) and to Balatonfüred (3130Ft, four hours, daily).

TRAIN

Direct services from the **train station** (Állomás utca), a 10-minute walk from the heart of Sopron, run to Budapest's Keleti train station (4735Ft, 2½ hours, six daily) and Vienna's Haufbahnhof and Miedling (5000Ft, 1½ hours, up to 12 daily).

LAKE BALATON

Extending roughly 80km, at first glance Lake Balaton seems to simply be a happy, sunny expanse of fresh water in which to play. But step beyond the beaches of Europe's biggest and shallowest body of water and you'll encounter vine-filled forested hills, a national park and a wild peninsula jutting out 4km, nearly cutting the lake in half.

Balatonfüred

☑87 / POP 13,082

Balatonfüred (*bal*-ah-ton fuhr-ed) is the oldest and most fashionable resort on the lake. In its glory days in the 19th century the wealthy and famous built large villas along its tree-lined streets, hoping to take advantage of the health benefits of the town's thermal waters. The town now sports the most stylish marina on the lake.

✗ Activities

The lake is ideal for water sports, such as windsurfing, kayaking and stand-up paddleboarding. Hire your gear from **Surf Pro Center** (☑06 30 936 6969; www.surfpro.hu; Széchenyi utca 10; ☯9am-6pm Apr-Oct); windsurfing lessons also available. The 210km Balaton cycle path runs through Balatonfüred, and you can rent bicycles from **Eco Bike** (☑06 20 924 4995, 06 70 264 2299; www. greenspark.hu; Széchenyi utca 8; per half-/1/2 days from 1900/2755/5655Ft; ☯9am-8pm) at the western end of the promenade.

Kisfaludy Strand (www.balatonfuredistran dok.hu; Aranyhíd sétány; adult/child 600/400Ft; ☯8.30am-7pm mid-Jun–mid-Aug, 8am-6pm mid-May–mid-Jun & mid-Aug–mid-Sep) is the best of the three public beaches.

🛏 Sleeping

Aqua Haz   PENSION €€

(☑87-342 813; www.aquahaz.hu; Garay utca 2; s/d/tr 9350/11,000/15,500Ft; ᴘ奈) Family-run, mustard-yellow, three-storey house, conveniently located between the lake and the train/bus station. The operators go out of their way

HISTORIC TIHANY

While in Balatonfüred, don't miss the chance to visit Tihany (population 1383), a peninsula jutting 5km into the lake and the place with the greatest historical significance on Lake Balaton. Tihany is home to the celebrated Benedictine Abbey Church (Bencés Apátság Templom; ☑ 87-538 200; http://tihany.osb.hu; András tér 1; adult/concession incl museum 1000/700Ft; ☺ 9am-6pm Apr-Sep, 10am-5pm Oct, 10am-4pm Nov-Mar), filled with fantastic altars, pulpits and screens carved in the mid-18th century by an Austrian lay brother; all are baroque-rococo masterpieces. The church attracts a lot of tourists, but the peninsula itself has an isolated, almost wild feel. Hiking is one of Tihany's main attractions; a good map outlining the trails is available from the Tourinform (☑ 87-448 804; www.tihany.hu; Kossuth Lajos utca 20; ☺ 9am-7pm Mon-Fri, 10am-6pm Sat & Sun mid-Jun–mid-Sep, 10am-4pm Mon-Fri mid-Sep–mid-Jun) office just down from the church. Buses bound for Tihany depart from Balatonfüred's bus/train station (310Ft, 30 minutes, 15 daily).

to make you feel right at home, most rooms feature bright balconies, and free bikes are available for tooling around town. Excellent breakfast.

★ **Club Hotel Füred** RESORT €€€
(☑ 87-341 511, 06 70 458 1242; www.clubhotelfured.hu; Anna sétany 1-3; r/ste from 22,100/60,000Ft; ✳ ☎ ⛱) This stunner of a resort hotel, right on the lake, about 1.5km from the town centre, has 43 rooms and suites in several buildings spread over 2.5 hectares of parkland and lush gardens. There's an excellent spa centre with sauna, steam room and pool, but the real delight is the private beach at the end of the garden. Stellar service.

✗ Eating & Drinking

★ **Nem Kacsa** HUNGARIAN €€
(☑ 06 70 364 7800; www.facebook.com/nemkacsa etterem; Zákonyi Ferenc utca; mains from 3300Ft; ☺ noon-11pm Wed-Sun) The gourmet stylings of chef Lajos Takács stand out against the town's largely mediocre offerings. The kitchen delivers beautifully crafted dishes featuring freshly grown produce from the farm it shares with the chef of Bistro Sparhelt (☑ 06 70 639 9944; http://bistrosparhelt.hu; Szent István tér 7; mains 2790-6390Ft; ☺ noon-10pm Wed-Sun; ☑). Duck stands out, but it's hard to go wrong with other meats or the homemade Italian pasta. Marina views and local wines seal the deal.

Kredenc Borbisztró WINE BAR
(☑ 06 20 518 9960; www.kredencborbisztro.hu; Blaha Lujza utca 7; ☺ noon-10pm Mon-Fri, 10am-midnight Sat & Sun) This family-run combination wine bar and bistro is a peaceful retreat near the lakefront. The menu is stacked with

oodles of local wines and the owner is often on hand to thoughtfully recommend the best tipple according to your tastes. The wine bar sells bottles of everything served, plus an extensive selection of regional wines. Weekend DJ sets.

ℹ Information

Tourinform (☑ 87-580 480; www.balatonfured.info.hu; Blaha Lujza utca 5; ☺ 9am-7pm Mon-Sat, 10am-4pm Sun) is the main tourist office. Useful websites include www.balatonfured.hu and www.welovebalaton.hu.

ℹ Getting There & Away

BOAT

From April to June and September to late October, at least four daily **Balaton Shipping Co** (Balatoni Hajózási Rt; ☑ 84-310 050; www.balatonihajozas.hu; Krúdy sétány 2, Siófok) ferries link Balatonfüred with Siófok and Tihany (adult/concession 1300/650Ft). Up to seven daily ferries serve these ports from July to August.

BUS

Buses reach Tihany (310Ft, 30 minutes, 15 daily) and Keszthely (1300Ft, one to 1½ hours, three daily). Buses and trains to Budapest (both 2520Ft, three hours) are much of a muchness but bus departures are more frequent (up to eight daily).

Keszthely

☑ 83 / POP 19,910

At the very western end of Lake Balaton sits Keszthely (*kest*-hey), the lake's main town and a place of grand townhouses and a gentle ambience.

⊙ Sights & Activities

★ Festetics Palace   PALACE
(Festetics Kastély; ☎ 83-312 194; www.helikon kastely.hu; Kastély utca 1; Palace & Coach Museum adult/6-26yr 2500/1250Ft; ⊙ 9am-6pm) The glimmering white, 100-room Festetics Palace was begun in 1745; the two wings were extended out from the original building 150 years later. Some 18 splendid rooms in the baroque south wing are now part of the Helikon Palace Museum, as is the palace's greatest treasure, the Helikon Library, with its 100,000 volumes and splendid carved furniture.

Helikon Beach   BEACH
(Helikon Strand; adult/concession 500/350Ft; ⊙ 8am-7pm May–mid-Sep) Reedy Helikon Beach, north of City Beach, is good for swimming and sunbathing. It has a unique view of both the north and south shores of the lake.

⌂ Sleeping

★ Ilona Kis Kastély Panzió   PENSION €€
(☎ 83-312 514; Móra Ferenc utca 22; s/d/apt 9400/12,130/16,980Ft; ✳ 🛜) Its pointy turrets covered in creepers, this delightful pension resembles a miniature castle. The rooms might be on the compact side, but some have balconies, while the apartments are positively spacious. A generous, varied breakfast is included. What sets this place apart is the attitude of its owners, who can't do enough to make their guests feel welcome.

✕ Eating

Lakoma Étterem   HUNGARIAN €€
(☎ 83-313 129; Balaton utca 9; mains 1990-3200Ft; ⊙ 11am-10pm; ✐) With a good vegetarian and fish selection (trout with almonds, grilled perch-pike), meaty stews and roasts, plus a back garden that transforms itself into a convivial dining area in the summer months, it's hard to go wrong with Lakoma.

★ Paletta Keszthely   BISTRO €€
(☎ 06 70 431 7413; www.facebook.com/Paletta Keszthely; Libás Strand; mains 1700-3300Ft; ⊙ 9am-11pm May–mid-Oct) On a summer terrace by the marina, this appealing spot mixes international fare such as bouillabaisse and its signature Basalt Burger. The dishes on the succinct menu are well-executed and the staff are friendly and prompt.

WORTH A TRIP

HOT SPRINGS OF HÉVÍZ

Hévíz (population 4721), just 8km northwest of Keszthely, is the most famous of Hungary's spa towns because of the Gyógy-tó (Hévíz Thermal Lake; ☎ 83-342 830; www.spaheviz.hu; Dr Schulhof Vilmos sétány 1; 3hr/4hr/whole day 2600/3000/4500Ft; ⊙ 8am-7pm Jun-Aug, 9am-6pm May & Sep, 9am-5.30pm Apr & Oct, 9am-5pm Mar & Nov-Feb) – Europe's largest 'thermal lake'. A dip into this water lily–filled lake is essential for anyone visiting the Lake Balaton region.

Fed by 80 million litres of thermal water daily, Thermal Lake is an astonishing sight. The temperature averages 33°C and never drops below 22°C in winter, allowing bathing even when there's ice on the fir trees of the surrounding Park Wood.

Buses link Hévíz with Keszthely (250Ft, 15 minutes) every half-hour.

ⓘ Information

Tourinform (☎ 83-314 144; www.keszthely.hu; Kossuth Lajos utca 30; ⊙ 9am-7pm mid-Jun–Aug, to 5pm Mon-Fri, to noon Sat Sep–mid-Jun) An excellent source of information on Keszthely and the west Balaton area. Brochures in English are available, and English spoken. Bicycles for rent, too.

www.welovebalaton.hu A handy listings website.

ⓘ Getting There & Away

BUS
Buses link Keszthely with Hévíz (250Ft, 15 minutes, half-hourly), Budapest (3410Ft, 2½ to four hours, up to nine daily) and Pécs (2830Ft, 3½ hours, up to four daily).

TRAIN
Keszthely has train links to Budapest (3705Ft, three hours, seven daily). To reach towns along Lake Balaton's northern shore, such as Balatonfüred (1490Ft, 1½ hours, 10 daily) by train, you have to change at Tapolca.

SOUTHERN HUNGARY

Southern Hungary is a place to savour life at a slower pace. It's only marginally touched by tourism and touring through the countryside is like travelling back in time.

Pécs

📞72 / POP 145,347

Blessed with a mild climate, an illustrious past and a number of fine museums and monuments, Pécs (pronounced *paich*) is one of the most pleasant and interesting cities to visit in Hungary. Many travellers put it second only to Budapest on their Hungary 'must-see' list.

◉ Sights

★ Zsolnay Cultural Quarter
NOTABLE BUILDING

(📞72-500 350; www.zskn.hu; adult/concession 4500/2500Ft; ⊙9am-6pm Apr-Oct, to 5pm Nov-Mar) The biggest project to evolve out of the 2010 Capital of Culture has been the Zsolnay Cultural Quarter, built on the grounds of the original Zsolnay Family Factory. Divided into four quarters (craftsman, family and children's, creative and university), it's a lovely place to stroll around. Highlights include the street of artisans' shops and the functioning Zsolnay Factory (Zsolnay utca 37, Zsolnay Cultural Quarter; adult/concession 1200/700Ft; ⊙10am-6pm Tue-Sun Apr-Oct, to 5pm Nov-Mar), which now takes up just a section of the grounds.

★ Mosque Church
MOSQUE

(Mecset templom; 📞72-321 976; Hunyadi út 4; adult/concession 1000/500Ft; ⊙9am-5pm Mon-Sat, 1-5pm Sun) The largest building from the time of the Turkish occupation, the former Pasha Gazi Kassim Mosque (now the Inner Town Parish Church) dominates the main square in Pécs. Turks built the square mosque in the mid-16th century with the stones of the ruined Gothic Church of St Bertalan. The Catholics moved back in the early 18th century. The Islamic elements include windows with distinctive Turkish ogee arches, a *mihrab* (prayer niche), faded verses from the Koran and lovely geometric frescos.

🛏 Sleeping

Nap Hostel
HOSTEL €

(📞72-950 684; www.naphostel.com; Király utca 23-25; dm €10-15, d €44; @ 🛜) This friendly hostel has three dorm rooms, with between six and eight beds each, and a double with washbasin on the 1st floor of a former bank (1885). One of the six-bed dorm rooms has a corner balcony, and there's a little garden at the rear. There's a large communal kitchen and great

on-site bar (📞72-585 705; www.facebook.com/nappali.bar; ⊙10am-2am). Enter through the bar's main entrance.

★ Szinbád Panzió
PENSION €€

(📞72-221 110; www.szinbadpanzio.hu; Klimó György utca 9; s/d from €37/48; 🅿🛜) A cosy, standard pension with excellent service and well-maintained, snug, wood-panelled rooms with cable TV, just outside the walls of Old Town. The warm welcome from the staff is much appreciated.

🍴 Eating & Drinking

Cellárium
HUNGARIAN €€

(📞72-314 453; http://cellariumetterem.hu; Hunyadi János út 2; mains 2850-4370Ft; ⊙11am-10pm Mon-Sat) This subterranean eatery with vaulted stone ceilings offers good value for money and imaginative dishes (juniper-braised venison, tarragon lamb with feta...). Weekends bring a variety of live music – often a small folk band or just a guy playing guitar.

★ Csinos Presszó
RUIN PUB

(📞06 30 357 0004; www.facebook.com/csinos presszo; Váradi Antal utca 8; ⊙10am-midnight Mon-Thu, noon-2am Fri & Sat, noon-midnight Sun) Between the alfresco garden with mismatched furniture painted in bright pastels and the Christmas lights strung from the trees it's easy to see why Csinos packs in relaxed patrons. A small snack menu accompanies an inventive drinks menu (a number of the cordials are house-made) and in the afternoon it's also a prime spot to grab a coffee and press pause.

❶ Information

Tourinform (📞06 30 681 7195; www.irany pecs.hu; Széchenyi tér; ⊙8am-8pm Mon-Fri, 9am-8pm Sat, 10am-6pm Sun Apr-Oct, 8am-8pm Mon-Fri, 10am-6pm Sat & Sun Nov-Mar) Knowledgable staff; copious information on Pécs and surrounds.

❶ Getting There & Away

BUS

Daily buses connect Pécs with Budapest (3690Ft, 4½ hours, five daily), Szeged (3690Ft, 3½ hours, two daily) and Kecskemét (3410Ft, 4¼ hours, daily).

TRAIN

Up to nine direct trains daily connect Pécs with Budapest's Keleti station (4485Ft, 237km, three hours). Most destinations in Southern Transdanubia are best reached by bus.

GREAT PLAIN

Like the Outback for Australians or the Wild West for Americans, the Nagyalföld (Great Plain) – also known as the *puszta* – holds a romantic appeal for Hungarians. Many of these notions come as much from the collective imagination, paintings and poetry as they do from history, but there's no arguing the spellbinding potential of big-sky country. The Great Plain is home to cities of graceful architecture and history such as Szeged and Kecskemét.

Szeged

✏ 62 / POP 162,600

Szeged (*seh*-ged) is a bustling border town with a handful of historic sights that line the embankment along the Tisza River and a clutch of sumptuous art nouveau town palaces. Importantly, it's also a big university town, which means lots of culture, lots of partying and an active festival scene that lasts throughout the year.

✥ Festivals & Events

Annual events include the 10-day **Szeged Wine Festival** (Szegedi Borfesztivál; www.szegediborfesztival.hu; ☉May), the pretty (and fragrant) three-day **Rose Festival** (Rózsafesztivál; www.rozsaunnep.hu; ☉Jun), and the tasty, but less fragrant **International Tisza Fish Festival** (Nemzetközi Tiszai Halfesztivál; www.halfesztival.hu; ☉Sep).

★ **Szeged Open-Air Festival**   MUSIC
(Szegedi Szabadtéri Játékok; ✏62-541 205; www.szegediszabadteri.hu; ☉Jul & Aug) The Szeged Open-Air Festival held in Dom tér in July and August is the largest festival in Hungary outside Budapest. The outdoor theatre in front of the Votive Church seats some 6000 people. Main events include an opera, an operetta, a play, folk dancing, classical music, ballet and a rock opera.

◉ Sights & Activities

Reök Palace   ARCHITECTURE
(Reök Palota; ✏62-541 205; www.reok.hu; Tisza Lajos körút 56; ☉10am-6pm Tue-Sun) The Reök Palace is a mind-blowing green-and-lilac art nouveau structure, built in 1907, that looks like a decoration at the bottom of an aquarium. It's been polished up to regain its original lustre in recent years and now hosts regular photography and visual-arts exhibitions.

Anna Baths   SPA
(✏62-553 330; www.szegedsport.hu/intezmenyek/anna-furdo; Tisza Lajos körút 24; adult/child 1650/1350Ft; ☉6am-8pm) The lovely cream-coloured Anna Baths were built in 1896 to imitate the tilework and soaring dome of a Turkish bath. Rich architectural detail surrounds all the modern saunas and bubbly pools you'd expect.

🛏 Sleeping

Familia Vendégház   GUESTHOUSE €€
(Family Guesthouse; ✏62-441 122; www.familia panzio.hu; Szentháromság utca 71; s/d/tr 7500/11,000/14,000Ft; ✳🖩) Families and international travellers often book up this family-run guesthouse with contemporary, if nondescript, furnishings in a great old building close to the train station. The two-dozen rooms have high ceilings, lots of wood and brick walls, and loads of light from tall windows.

★ **Tiszavirág Hotel**   BOUTIQUE HOTEL €€€
(✏62-554 888; http://tiszaviragszeged.hu; Hajnóczy utca 1/b; s/d/ste €80/90/140; ✳🖩🖥) Wow. Our favourite new boutique hotel in Szeged is a jaw-dropper. Set in a historic townhouse built by a wealthy goldsmith in 1859, it counts 12 rooms, many with original features and all with fabulous modern artwork. There's a new wing too, separated from the old one by a splendid glass-enclosed inner courtyard perfect for lounging.

🍴 Eating & Drinking

★ **Malata**   BURGERS €€
(www.facebook.com/malatakezmuves; Somogyi utca 13; mains 1190-3000Ft; ☉2-11pm Mon-Thu, 2pm-1am Fri, noon-1am Sat, noon-11pm Sun) This great new hipster hang-out is part ruin garden, part pub/cafe and counts upwards of two dozen craft beers on tap and by the bottle. The food is mostly gourmet burgers (1450Ft to 1850Ft) though not exclusively so; order and pay at the bar. In winter and rain, sit in the colourful cafe with upended umbrellas dangling from the ceiling.

ℹ Information

Tourinform (✏62-488 690; www.szeged tourism.hu; Dugonics tér 2; ☉9am-5pm Mon-Fri year-round, plus 9am-1pm Sat Apr-Oct) This exceptionally helpful office is tucked away in a courtyard near the university. There is a seasonal **Tourinform kiosk** (Széchenyi tér; ☉8am-8pm Jun-Sep) in Széchenyi tér.

DEBRECEN: CULTURE & COWBOY COUNTRY

Debrecen is Hungary's second-largest city, and its array of museums and thermal baths will keep you busy for a day or two. Start with the colourful **Calvinist College** (Református Kollégium; ☑ 52-614 370; www.reformatuskollegium.ttre.hu; Kálvin tér 16; adult/concession 900/500Ft; ◷ 10am-4pm Mon-Fri, 10am-1pm Sat), before splashing around the slides and waterfalls within **Aquaticum Debrecen Spa** (☑ 52-514 111; www.aquaticum.hu; Nagyerdei Park 1; adult/concession 3000/2450Ft; ◷ 9am-7pm); you can sleep here, too.

Next take a trip to **Hortobágy National Park**, 40km west, once celebrated for its sturdy *csikósok* (cowboys), inns and Gypsy bands. You can see a staged recreation at **Máta Stud Farm** (Mátai Ménes; ☑ 52-589 369, 06 70 492 7655; www.hortobagy.eu/hu/matai-menes; Hortobágy-Máta; adult/child 2600/1400Ft; ◷ 10am, noon & 2pm mid-Mar–Oct, plus 4pm Apr–mid-Oct).

Buses reach Debrecen from Eger (2520Ft, 2½ hours, eight daily) and Szeged (3950Ft, 4½ hours, three daily), while trains go direct from Budapest (3950Ft, 3½ hours, hourly). Six buses stop daily at Hortobágy village on runs between Debrecen (745Ft, 40 minutes) and Eger (1680Ft, 1¾ hours).

🛈 Getting There & Away

BUS

Buses run to Pécs (3410Ft, 3½ hours, seven daily) and Debrecen (3950Ft, five hours, three daily). You can also get to the Serbian city of Novi Sad (2510Ft, 3½ hours) up to four times a day by bus.

TRAIN

Szeged is on the main rail line to Budapest's Nyugati train station (3705Ft, 2½ hours, hourly); many trains also stop halfway along in Kecskemét (1680Ft, one hour).

NORTHEASTERN HUNGARY

This is the home of Hungary's two most famous wines – honey-sweet Tokaj and Eger's famed Bull's Blood – and a region of microclimates conducive to wine production. The chain of wooded hills in the northeast constitutes the foothills of the Carpathian Mountains, which stretch along the Hungarian border with Slovakia.

Eger

☑ 36 / POP 54,500

Filled with baroque buildings, Eger (*egg-air*) is a jewellery box of a town. Explore the bloody history of Turkish occupation and defeat at the hilltop castle, listen to an organ performance at the colossal basilica, or relax in a renovated Turkish bath. Then traipse from cellar to cellar in the Valley of Beautiful Women, tasting celebrated Eger Bull's Blood (Egri Bikavér) from the cask.

◉ Sights & Activities

★ Eger Castle   FORTRESS

(Egri Vár; ☑ 36-312 744; www.egrivar.hu; Vár köz 1; castle grounds adult/child 800/400Ft, incl museum 1600/800Ft; ◷ exhibits 10am-5pm Tue-Sun May-Oct, 10am-4pm Tue-Sun Nov-Apr, castle grounds 8am-8pm May-Aug, to 7pm Apr & Sep, to 6pm Mar & Oct, to 5pm Nov-Feb) Climb up cobbled Vár köz from Tinódi Sebestyén tér to reach the castle, erected in the 13th century after the Mongol invasion. Models, drawings and artefacts like armour and Turkish uniforms in the **Castle History Exhibition**, on the 1st floor of the former Bishop's Palace (1470), painlessly explain the castle's story. On the eastern side of the complex are foundations of the 12th-century **St John's Cathedral**. Enter the **castle casemates** (Kazamata) hewn from solid rock via the nearby **Dark Gate**.

★ Lyceum Library   LIBRARY

(Liceumi Könyvtar; ☑ 36-520 400 ext 2214; Eszterházy tér 1, Lyceum; adult/child 1000/500Ft; ◷ 9.30am-1.30pm Tue-Sun Mar & Apr, 9.30am-3.30pm Tue-Sun May-Sep, by appointment Oct-Feb) This awesome 60,000-volume all-wood library on the 1st floor of the Lyceum's south wing contains hundreds of priceless manuscripts, medical codices and incunabula. The trompe l'oeil ceiling fresco painted by Bohemian artist Johann Lukas Kracker in 1778 depicts the Counter-Reformation's Council of Trent (1545–63), with a lightning bolt setting heretical manuscripts ablaze. It was Eger's

– and its archbishop's – response to the Enlightenment and the Reformation.

★ **Valley of the Beautiful Women**   WINE
(Szépasszony-völgy Hétvége) More than two dozen cellars are carved into rock at the evocatively named Valley of the Beautiful Women, where wine tasting is popular. Try ruby-red Bull's Blood or any of the whites: *leányka*, *olaszrizling* and *hárslevelű* from nearby Debrő. The choice of wine cellars can be a bit daunting so walk around and have a look yourself. The valley is a little over 1km southwest across Rte 25 and off Király utca.

🛏 Sleeping

Agria Retur Vendégház   GUESTHOUSE €
(☑ 36-416 650; www.returvendeghaz.hu; Knézich Károly utca 18; s/d/tr 4200/7600/10,600Ft; @ 🛜) You couldn't receive a warmer welcome than the one you'll get at this guesthouse near the minaret. Walking up three flights of stairs, you enter a cheery communal kitchen/eating area central to four mansard rooms. Out the back is a huge garden with tables and a barbecue at your disposal.

★ **Hotel Senator Ház**   BOUTIQUE HOTEL €€€
(Senator House Hotel; ☑ 36-320 466; www.senatorhaz.hu; Dobó István tér 11; s/d €47/64; ❄ @ 🛜) Eleven warm and cosy rooms with traditional white furnishings fill the upper floors of this delightful 18th-century inn on Eger's main square. The ground floor is shared between a quality restaurant and a reception area stuffed with antiques and curios.

✕ Eating & Drinking

★ **Macok Bistro & Wine Bar**   HUNGARIAN €€€
(Macok Bisztró és Borbár; ☑ 36-516 180; www.imolaudvarhaz.hu/en/the-macok-bisztro-wine-bar.html; Tinódi Sebestyén tér 4; mains 2190-4900Ft; ⊙ noon-10pm Sun-Thu, to 11pm Fri & Sat) This stylish eatery at the foot of the castle, with its inventive menu and excellent wine cellar, has been named among the top dozen restaurants in Hungary.

Bíboros   CLUB
(☑ 06 70 199 2733; www.facebook.com/biboroseger; Bajcsy-Zsilinszky utca 6; ⊙ 11am-3am Mon-Fri, 1pm-3am Sat, 3pm-midnight Sun) A subdued ruin bar by day, the 'Cardinal' transforms into a raucous dance club late in the evening; the cops at the door most weekend nights are a dead giveaway. Enjoy.

ℹ Information

Tourinform (☑ 36-517 715; www.eger.hu; Bajcsy-Zsilinszky utca 9; ⊙ 8am-6pm Mon-Fri, 9am-1pm Sat & Sun Jul & Aug, 8am-5pm Mon-Fri, 9am-1pm Sat May, Jun, Sep & Oct, 8am-5pm Mon-Fri Nov-Apr) Helpful office that promotes both the town and areas surrounding Eger.

ℹ Getting There & Away

BUS
From Eger, buses serve Debrecen (2520Ft, 2¾ hours, six daily), Kecskemét (3130Ft, four hours, two daily) and Szeged (3950Ft, 5½ hours, two daily).

TRAIN
Up to seven direct trains a day head to Budapest's Keleti train station (2905Ft, two hours).

SURVIVAL GUIDE

ℹ Directory A–Z

DISCOUNT CARDS
The **Hungary Card** (www.hungarycard.hu) offers free entry to many museums; 50% off on a number of return train fares and some bus and boat travel; up to 20% off selected accommodation; and 25% off the price of the **Budapest Card** (www.budapestinfo.hu). It's available at Tourinform offices.

INTERNET RESOURCES
Budapest Tourism (www.budapestinfo.hu)
Hungary Museums (www.museum.hu)
Hungarian National Tourist Office (www.gotohungary.com)

COUNTRY FACTS
Area 93,030 sq km
Capital Budapest
Country Code 36
Currency Forint (Ft)
Emergency Ambulance ☑ 104, emergency assistance ☑ 112, fire ☑ 105, police ☑ 107
Language Hungarian
Money ATMs widely available
Population 9.82 million
Visas None for EU, USA, Canada, Australia and New Zealand

EATING PRICE RANGES

The following price ranges refer to a main course in the provinces and the cost of a two-course meal with drink in Budapest.

Budapest

€ less than 3500Ft

€€ 3500Ft–7500Ft

€€€ more than 7500Ft

Provinces

€ less than 2000Ft

€€ 2000Ft–3500Ft

€€€ more than 3500Ft

MONEY

The unit of currency is the Hungarian forint (Ft). Coins come in denominations of five, 10, 20, 50, 100 and 200Ft, and notes are denominated in 500, 1000, 2000, 5000, 10,000 and 20,000Ft. ATMs are everywhere, even in small villages. Tip waiters, hairdressers and bar staff approximately 10% of the total, and round up taxi fares.

TELEPHONE

Hungary's country code is 36. To make an outgoing international call, dial ☑00 first. For an intercity landline call within Hungary and whenever ringing a mobile telephone, dial ☑06, followed by the area code and phone number. All localities in Hungary have a two-digit city code, except for Budapest, where the code is ☑1.

Hungary has extensive mobile phone network coverage. Local SIM cards can be used in European, Australian and some North American phones. Other phones must be set to roaming, which can be pricey (check with your service provider). The three main mobile phone providers are Telenor, T-Mobile and Vodafone. You can purchase a rechargeable or prepaid SIM card from any of the three providers.

TOURIST INFORMATION

The **Hungarian National Tourist Office** (HNTO; http://gotohungary.com) has a chain of some 130 **Tourinform** (☑ from abroad 36 1 438 80 80; www.tourinform.hu; ⊘8am-8pm Mon-Fri) information offices across the country.

VISAS

Citizens of all European countries and of Australia, Canada, Israel, Japan, New Zealand and the USA do not require visas for visits of up to 90 days. Check current visa requirements on the website of the **Ministry of Foreign Affairs** (http://konzuliszolgalat.kormany.hu/).

❶ Getting There & Away

There are direct train connections from Budapest to major cities in all of Hungary's neighbours. International buses head in all directions and in the warmer months you can take a ferry along the Danube to reach Vienna in Austria.

AIR

Ferenc Liszt International Airport (p582) has flights to/from Schengen countries at Terminal 2A, while Terminal 2B serves non-Schengen countries. Between April and November, **Hévíz-Balaton Airport** (SOB; ☑ 83-200 304; www.hevizairport.com; Repülőtér 1, Sármellék) receives flights from German destinations and Moscow.

LAND
Bus

Most international buses arrive at the Népliget bus station (p582) in Budapest and most services are run by **Eurolines** (www.eurolines.com) in conjunction with its Hungarian affiliate, Volánbusz (p582). Useful international routes include buses from Budapest to Vienna in Austria, Bratislava in Slovakia, Subotica in Serbia, Rijeka, Dubrovnik and Split in Croatia, Prague in the Czech Republic, Kraków in Poland and Sofia in Bulgaria.

Car & Motorcycle

Drivers and motorbike riders will need the vehicle's registration papers, liability insurance and an international driver's permit in addition to their domestic licence.

Travel on Hungarian motorways requires pre-purchase of a highway pass *(matrica)* available from petrol stations and post offices (see www.autopalya.hu for more details).

Train

MÁV (p582) links up with international rail networks in all directions, and its schedule is available online. Most larger train stations in

SLEEPING PRICE RANGES

The following price ranges refer to a double room with bathroom in high season:

Budapest

€ less than 15,000Ft

€€ 15,000Ft–33,500Ft

€€€ more than 33,500Ft

Provinces

€ less than 9000Ft

€€ 9000Ft–16,500Ft

€€€ more than 16,500Ft

ESSENTIAL FOOD & DRINK

Traditional Hungarian food is heavy and rich. Meat, sour cream and fat abound and the omnipresent seasoning is paprika. Things are lightening up though, with increasingly available vegetarian, 'New Hungarian' and world cuisines.

Gulyás (goulash) Hungary's signature dish, though here it's more like a soup than a stew and made with beef, onions and tomatoes.

Halászlé Highly recommended fish soup made from poached freshwater fish, tomatoes, green peppers and paprika.

Lángos Street food; fried dough topped with cheese and/or *tejföl* (sour cream).

Palacsinta Thin crêpes eaten as a main course or filled with jam, sweet cheese or chocolate sauce for dessert.

Pálinka A strong brandy distilled from all kinds of fruit but especially plums and apricots.

Paprika The omnipresent seasoning in Hungarian cooking, which comes in two varieties: strong (*erős*) and sweet (*édes*).

Pörkölt Paprika-infused stew; closer to what we would call goulash.

Wine Two Hungarian wines are known internationally: the sweet dessert wine Tokaji Aszú and Egri Bikavér (Eger Bull's Blood), a full-bodied red.

Hungary have left-luggage rooms open from at least 9am to 5pm.

Seat reservations are required for international destinations, and are included in the price of the ticket. Some direct train connections from Budapest include Austria, Slovakia, Romania, Ukraine, Croatia, Serbia, Germany, Slovenia, Czech Republic, Poland, Switzerland, Italy and Bulgaria.

RIVER

Mahart PassNave (p582) runs daily hydrofoil services on the Danube River between Budapest and Vienna (5½ to 6½ hours) from mid-May to late September. Adult one-way/return fares for Vienna are €99/125. For the return journey, consult **Mahart PassNave Wien** (⌐01 72 92 162, 01 72 92 161; Handelskai 265, Reichsbrücke pier, Vienna) in Vienna.

ⓘ Getting Around

Hungary does not have any scheduled domestic flights.

BOAT

In summer there are regular passenger ferries on the Danube from Budapest to Szentendre, Visegrád and Esztergom as well as on Lake Balaton.

BUS

Domestic buses, run by the Volánbusz (p582), an association of coach operators, cover an extensive nationwide network.

CAR & MOTORCYCLE

There is a 100% ban on alcohol when you are driving, and this rule is strictly enforced. Headlights must be on at all times outside built-up areas. Motorcyclists must illuminate headlights

too, but at all times and everywhere. Helmets are compulsory. Most cities and towns require that you pay for street parking (usually 9am to 6pm workdays) by buying temporary parking passes from machines or a warden.

LOCAL TRANSPORT

Public transport is efficient and extensive in Hungary, with bus and, in many towns, trolleybus services. Budapest, Szeged and Debrecen also have trams, and there's an extensive metro and a suburban commuter railway in Budapest. Purchase tickets at newsstands before travelling and validate them once aboard. Inspectors frequently check tickets.

TRAIN

MÁV (p582) operates reliable train services. Schedules are available online and computer information kiosks are popping up at train stations around the country.

IC trains are express trains and are the most comfortable and modern. *Gyorsvonat* and *sebesvonat* ('fast trains', indicated on the timetable by boldface type, a thicker route line and/or an 'S') take longer and use older cars; *személyvonat* (passenger trains) stop at every village along the way. Seat reservations *(helyjegy)* cost extra and are required on IC and some fast trains; these are indicated on the timetable by an 'R' in a box or a circle (a plain 'R' means seat reservations are available but not required).

In all stations a yellow board indicates departures *(indul)* and a white board is for arrivals *(érkezik)*. Express and fast trains are indicated in red, local trains in black.

Both **InterRail** (www.interrail.eu) and **Eurail** (www.eurail.com) passes cover Hungary.

Iceland

Best Places to Eat

➡ Dill (p602)

➡ Messinn (p601)

➡ Matur og Drykkur (p601)

➡ Hótel Húsafell (p609)

➡ Bjargarsteinn Mathús (p609)

Best Places to Stay

➡ Apotek (p601)

➡ Hótel Rangá (p607)

➡ Skjaldarvík (p610)

➡ Hótel Egilsen (p609)

➡ Grand Guesthouse Garðakot (p609)

Why Go?

The energy is palpable on this magical island, where astonishing natural phenomena inspire the welcoming, creative locals and draw an increasing number of visitors in search of its untrammelled splendour. A vast volcanic laboratory, here the earth itself is restless and alive. Admire thundering waterfalls, glittering glaciers carving their way to black-sand beaches, explosive geysers, rumbling volcanoes and contorted lava fields.

In summer, permanent daylight energises the already zippy inhabitants of Iceland's lively capital, Reykjavík, with its wonderful cafe and bar scene. Fashion, design and music are woven into the city's fabric, and the museums are tops. In winter, with luck, you may see the Northern Lights shimmering across the sky. Year-round, though, adventure tours abound, getting you up close and personal with sights and sounds that will stay with you for life.

When to Go
Reykjavík

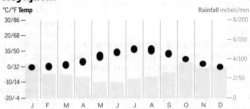

May–Jun Prime birdwatching season happily coincides with the two driest months and fewer crowds.

Aug It's full throttle in Reykjavík, the country teems with visitors and it's almost always light.

Nov–Apr The best months for Northern Lights and bare minimalism.

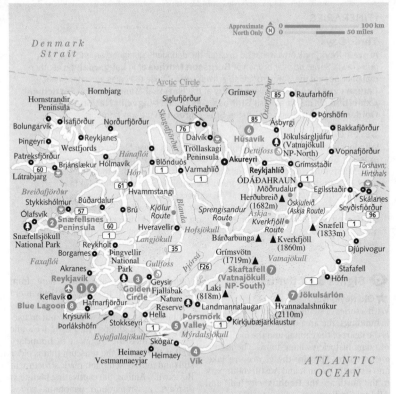

Iceland Highlights

1 **Reykjavík** (p595)
Partying till dawn on the weekend pub crawl *djammið*, then hitting excellent museums, shops and cafes.

2 **Snæfellsnes Peninsula** (p609) Riding horses, climbing glaciers, trekking lava fields, or soaking in hot-pots.

3 **Golden Circle** (p604)
Joining the droves exploring

the scintillating Gullfoss waterfall, exploding geysers, and the nation's birthplace, rift valley Þingvellir.

4 **Vík** (p607) Exploring black-sand beaches and off-shore rock formations.

5 **Þórsmörk** (p607)
Taking a wilderness hike in this dramatic valley.

6 **Húsavík** (p610) Going

whale watching in Húsavík or Reykjavík.

7 **Skaftafell** (p608)
Exhausting your camera's memory card at Skaftafell in Vatnajökull National Park and nearby Jökulsárlón glacial lagoon.

8 **Blue Lagoon** (p605)
Swimming through steam clouds at this world-famous milky-blue geothermal pool.

REYKJAVÍK

POP 209,500

The world's most northerly capital combines colourful buildings, wild nightlife and a capricious soul to brilliant effect. You'll find Viking history, captivating museums, cool music, and off-beat cafes and bars. And it's a superb base for touring Iceland's natural wonders.

Reykjavík's heart lies between Tjörnin (the Pond) and the harbour, and along Laugavegur, with nearly everything for visitors within walking distance.

ITINERARIES

Three Days

Arrive in **Reykjavík** on a weekend to catch the decadent all-night *djammið* (partying pub crawl). Sober up over brunch at **Bergsson Mathús** or in **Laugardalur**'s geothermal pool, admire the views from **Hallgrímskirkja**, cruise the cafes and shops near **Laugavegur**, then absorb Viking history at the **National Museum** or the **Settlement Exhibition**. On day three, visit **Gullfoss**, **Geysir** and **Þingvellir National Park** on a **Golden Circle tour**, and soak in the **Blue Lagoon** on the way home.

Seven Days

With four more days you'll have plenty of time to head to west Iceland for **Borgarnes'** excellent **Settlement Centre**. Next visit **Snæfellsnes Peninsula** with its ravishing **Snæfellsjökull National Park**, or head inland to **Langjökull** with its **ice cave**, and nearby **Viðgelmir lava tube**. Explore further afield in South Iceland: **Hekla** volcano, **Skógar** with its waterfalls and hikes, **Vík** with gorgeous ocean-front landscapes, or take a super-Jeep or amphibious bus to **Þórsmörk**. **Vatnajökull National Park**, **Skaftafell** and **Jökulsárlón glacier lagoon** are worth a trip for amazing scenery and outdoor adventures. Or hop a flight to **Akureyri** and check out the North, or **Ísafjörður** and explore the Westfjords.

⊙ Sights & Activities

★ Old Reykjavík
AREA

With a series of sights and interesting historic buildings, the area dubbed Old Reykjavík is the heart of the capital, and the focal point of many historic walking tours. The area is anchored by **Tjörnin**, the city-centre lake, and sitting between it and Austurvöllur park to the north are the **Raðhús** (city hall) and **Alþingi** (Parliament).

★ National Museum
MUSEUM

(Þjóðminjasafn Íslands; ☑ 530 2200; www.national museum.is; Suðurgata 41; adult/child kr1500/ free; ☉ 10am-5pm May–mid-Sep, closed Mon mid-Sep–Apr; ☐ 1, 3, 6, 12, 14) This superb museum displays artefacts from settlement to the modern age. Exhibits give an excellent overview of Iceland's history and culture, and the audioguide (kr300) adds loads of detail. The strongest section describes the Settlement Era – including how the chieftains ruled and the introduction of Christianity – and features swords, drinking horns, silver hoards and a powerful little **bronze figure of Thor**. The priceless 13th-century **Valþjófsstaðir church door** is carved with the story of a knight, his faithful lion and a passel of dragons.

★ Settlement Exhibition
MUSEUM

(Landnámssýningin; ☑ 411 6370; www.reykjavik museum.is; Aðalstræti 16; adult/child kr1500/free; ☉ 9am-6pm) This fascinating archaeological ruin/museum is based around a 10th-century Viking longhouse unearthed here from 2001 to 2002, and the other settlement-era finds from central Reykjavík. It imaginatively combines technological wizardry and archaeology to give a glimpse into early Icelandic life. Don't miss the fragment of **boundary wall** at the back of the museum that is older still (and the oldest human-made structure in Reykjavík). Among the captivating high-tech displays, a wraparound panorama shows how things would have looked at the time of the longhouse.

★ Hallgrímskirkja
CHURCH

(☑ 510 1000; www.hallgrimskirkja.is; Skólavörðustígur; tower adult/child kr900/100; ☉ 9am-9pm Jun-Sep, to 5pm Oct-May) Reykjavík's immense white-concrete church (1945–86), star of a thousand postcards, dominates the skyline, and is visible from up to 20km away. Get an unmissable view of the city by taking an elevator trip up the 74.5m-high **tower**. In contrast to the high drama outside, the Lutheran church's interior is quite plain. The most eye-catching feature is the vast 5275-pipe **organ** installed in 1992. The church's size and radical design caused controversy, and its architect, Guðjón Samúelsson (1887–1950), never saw its completion.

★ Reykjavík Art Museum
GALLERY

(Listasafn Reykjavíkur; www.artmuseum.is; adult/child kr1500/free; ☎) The excellent Reykjavík Art Museum is split over three well-done sites: the large, modern downtown

Hafnarhús (☏411 6400; Tryggvagata 17; adult/child kr1500/free; ⊙10am-5pm Fri-Wed, to 10pm Thu) focusing on contemporary art; **Kjarvalsstaðir** (☏411 6420; Flókagata 24, Miklatún Park; adult/child kr1300/free; ⊙10am-5pm; 🛜), in a park just east of Snorrabraut, and displaying rotating exhibits of modern art; and **Ásmundarsafn** (Ásmundur Sveinsson Museum; ☏411 6430; www.artmuseum.is; Sigtún; adult/child kr1500/free; ⊙10am-5pm May-Sep, 1-5pm Oct-Apr; 🛜; 🚌2, 5, 15, 17), a peaceful haven near Laugardalur for viewing sculptures by Ásmundur Sveinsson.

One ticket is good at all three sites, and if you buy after 3pm you get a 50% discount should you want a ticket the next day.

★**Old Harbour**   AREA
(Geirsgata; 🚌1, 3, 6, 11, 12, 13, 14) Largely a service harbour until recently, the Old Harbour has blossomed into a hot spot for tourists, with several museums, volcano and Northern Lights films, and excellent restaurants. Whale-watching and puffin-viewing trips depart from the pier. Photo ops abound with views of fishing boats, Harpa concert hall and snowcapped mountains beyond. On the western edge of the harbour, the Grandi area, named after the fish factory there, has burgeoned with eateries and shops as well.

★**Culture House**   GALLERY
(Þjóðmenningarhúsið; ☏530 2210; www.culture house.is; Hverfisgata 15; adult/child kr1200/free; ⊙10am-5pm May–mid-Sep, closed Mon mid-Sep–Apr; 🛜) This fantastic collaboration between the National Museum, National Gallery and four other organisations creates a superbly curated exhibition covering the artistic and cultural heritage of Iceland from settlement to today. Priceless artefacts are arranged by theme, and highlights include 14th-century manuscripts, contemporary art and items including the skeleton of a great auk (now extinct). The renovated 1908 building is beautiful, with great views of the harbour, and a cafe on the ground floor. Check the website for free guided tours.

★**National Gallery of Iceland**   MUSEUM
(Listasafn Íslands; ☏515 9600; www.listasafn.is; Fríkirkjuvegur 7; adult/child kr1500/free; ⊙10am-5pm mid-May–mid-Sep, 11am-5pm Tue-Sun mid-Sep–mid-May; 🛜) This pretty stack of marble atriums and spacious galleries overlooking Tjörnin offers ever-changing exhibits drawn from the 10,000-piece collection. The museum can only exhibit a small sample at any time; shows range from 19th- and 20th-century paintings by Iceland's favourite sons and daughters (including Jóhannes Kjarval and Nína Sæmundsson) to sculptures by Sigurjón Ólafsson and others. The museum ticket also covers entry to the **Ásgrímur Jónsson Collection** (☏515 9625; www.listasafn.is; Bergstaðastræti 74; adult/child kr1000/free; ⊙2-5pm Tue, Thu & Sun mid-May–mid-Sep, 2-5pm Sun mid-Sep–Nov & Feb–mid-May) and **Sigurjón Ólafsson Museum** (Listasafn Sigurjóns Ólafssonar; ☏553 2906; www.lso.is; Laugarnestanga 70; adult/child kr1000/free; ⊙2-5pm Tue-Sun Jun-Aug, 2-5pm Sat & Sun Sep-Nov & Feb-May; 🚌12, 16).

Volcano House   MUSEUM
(☏555 1900; www.volcanohouse.is; Tryggvagata 11; adult/child kr1990/free; ⊙9am-10pm; 🛜) This modern theatre with a hands-on lava exhibit in the foyer screens a 55-minute pair of films (hourly) about the Vestmannaeyjar volcanoes and Eyjafjallajökull. They show in German once daily in summer.

Saga Museum   MUSEUM
(☏511 1517; www.sagamuseum.is; Grandagarður 2; adult/child kr2100/800; ⊙10am-6pm; 🛜; 🚌14) The endearingly bloodthirsty Saga Museum is where Icelandic history is brought to life by eerie silicon models and a multi-language soundtrack with thudding axes and hair-raising screams. Don't be surprised if you see some of the characters wandering around town, as moulds were taken from Reykjavík residents (the owner's daughters are the Irish princess and the little slave gnawing a fish!).

★**Laugardalur**   AREA, PARK
(🚌2, 5, 14, 15, 17) Laugardalur encompasses a verdant stretch of land 4km east of the city centre. It was once the main source of Reykjavík's hot-water supply: it translates as 'Hot-Springs Valley', and in the park's centre you'll find relics from the old wash house. The park is a favourite with locals for its huge **swimming complex** (☏411 5100; Sundlaugavegur 30a, Laugardalur; adult/child kr900/140, suit/towel rental kr850/570; ⊙6.30am-10pm Mon-Fri, 8am-10pm Sat & Sun; 🏊), fed by the geothermal spring, alongside a spa, **cafe** (Flóran; ☏553 8872; www.floran.is; Botanic Gardens; cakes kr950, mains kr1400-3000; ⊙10am-10pm May-Sep; 🅿), skating rink, botanical gardens, sporting and concert arenas, and a kids' zoo/entertainment park.

Central Reykjavík

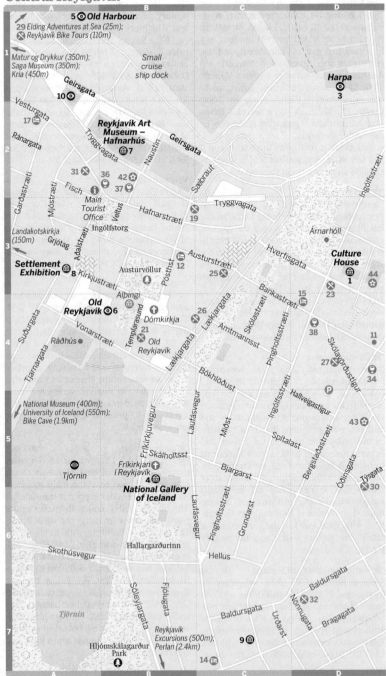

5 ◎ Old Harbour

29 Elding Adventures at Sea (25m);
⊗ Reykjavík Bike Tours (110m)

Matur og Drykkur (350m);
Saga Museum (350m);
Kria (450m)

Small cruise ship dock

Harpa
3 ◎

Geirsgata

10 ◎

Vesturgata

17 🏛

Ránargata

Reykjavík Art Museum – Hafnarhús
🏛 **7**

Geirsgata

Tryggvagata

Naustin

Sæbraut

Garðastræti

Mjóstræti

Fisch

31 ⊗ 36   42 ★
     37 ⊟

ℹ Main Tourist Office

Tryggvagata

19 ⊗

Landakotskirkja (150m)

Grjótag

Aðalstræti

Veltus

Hafnarstræti

Ingólfstorg

Árnarhóll ●

Hverfisgata

Culture House
🏛 **1**

44 ★

Settlement Exhibition 🏛 **8**

Kirkjustræti

Austurvöllur

Pósthst

Austurstræti

12 🏛

25 ⊗

Bankastræti

15 🏛

23 ⊗

Old Reykjavík ◎ **6**

Alþingi

Dómkirkja

Templarasund

21

Old Reykjavík

26 🏛

Lækjargata

Skólastræti

Amtmannsst

Þingholtsstræti

38 ℗

27 ℗

11 ●

34 🏨

Suðurgata

Vonarstræti

Ráðhús ●

Tjarnargata

Lækjargata

Bókhlöðust

Miðst

Spítalast

Ingólfsstræti

Hallveigastígur

Bergstaðastræti

Skólavörðustígur

43 ★

National Museum (400m);
University of Iceland (550m);
Bike Cave (1.9km)

Fríkirkjuvegur

Skálholtsst

Laufásvegur

Bjargarst

Óðinsgata

Týsgata

30 ⊗

Tjörnin ◎

Fríkirkjan í Reykjavík ✝
4 🏛
National Gallery of Iceland

Þingholtsstræti

Grundarst

Skothúsvegur

Hallargarðurinn

Hellus

Baldursgata

Tjörnin

Sóleyjargata

Fjólugata

Laufásvegur

Nönnugata

Urðarst

Bragagata

Baldursgata

32 ⊗

Hljómskálagarður Park
♪

Reykjavík Excursions (500m);
Perlan (2.4km)

9 🏛

14 ⊟

Central Reykjavík

⊙ Top Sights
1 Culture House	D3
2 Hallgrímskirkja	F7
3 Harpa	D1
4 National Gallery of Iceland	B5
5 Old Harbour	A1
6 Old Reykjavík	B4
7 Reykjavík Art Museum – Hafnarhús	B2
8 Settlement Exhibition	A3

⊙ Sights
9 Ásgrímur Jónsson Collection	C7
10 Volcano House	A1

⊕ Activities, Courses & Tours
11 Arctic Adventures	D4

⊜ Sleeping
12 Apotek	B3
13 Forsæla Apartmenthouse	F5
14 Galtafell Guesthouse	C7
15 Loft Hostel	D4
16 REY Apartments	E5
17 Reykjavík Downtown Hostel	A2
18 Reykjavík Residence	F4

⊗ Eating
Apotek	(see 12)
19 Bæjarins Beztu	B3
20 Bakarí Sandholt	F5
21 Bergsson Mathús	B4
22 Brauð & Co	F6
23 Dill	D3
24 Gló	E4
25 Grillmarkaðurinn	C3
26 Messinn	C4
27 Ostabúðin	D4
28 Public House	E5
29 Sægreifinn	A1
30 Snaps	D6
31 Stofan Kaffihús	A2
32 Þrír Frakkar	D7

⊝ Drinking & Nightlife
33 Boston	F5
34 Kaffibarinn	D4
Kaldi	(see 24)
35 Kiki	E4
36 Micro Bar	B2
37 Paloma	B2
38 Prikið	D4
39 Reykjavík Roasters	F6

⊛ Entertainment
40 Bíó Paradís	F4
41 Café Rosenberg	E4
42 Húrra	B2
43 Mengi	D5
44 National Theatre	D3

⊜ Shopping
Fjallakofinn	(see 11)

✦✦ Festivals & Events

Reykjavíkers turn out in force for a day and night of art, music, dance and fireworks in mid-August on **Culture Night** (www.menningarnott.is). In November, the fab **Iceland Airwaves** international music festival (www.icelandairwaves.is) is one of the world's premier showcases for new music (Icelandic and otherwise). The **Secret Solstice** music festival (www.secretsolstice.is) lights up in June.

☞ Tours

Walking, bike and bus tours are the main way to take in the city. Whale-watching, puffin-spotting and sea-angling trips allow a jaunt offshore.

As lovely as the capital's sights are, though, Reykjavík is also the main hub for tours to amazing landscapes and activities around Iceland. Those without wheels, time or the desire to travel the countryside independently can use Reykjavík as a cosmopolitan base for all forms of tours from super-Jeeps and buses to horse riding, snowmobiling and heli or airplane tours. If you have time, though, head out on your own.

Elding Adventures at Sea   WILDLIFE

(☑ 519 5000; www.whalewatching.is; Ægisgarður 5; adult/child kr9900/4950; ☺ harbour kiosk 8am-9pm; 🚌 14) 🖋 The city's most established and ecofriendly whale-watching outfit, with an included whale exhibition and refreshments sold on board. Elding also offers angling (adult/child kr13,800/6900) and puffin-watching (adult/child from kr6500/3250) trips and combo tours, and runs the ferry to Viðey. Offers pick-up.

Reykjavík Excursions   BUS

(Kynnisferðir; ☑ 580 5400; www.re.is; BSÍ Bus Terminal, Vatnsmýrarvegur 10) The largest and most popular bus-tour operator (with large groups) has an enormous booklet full of summer and winter programs (tours from kr9000 to kr47,900). Extras include horse riding, snowmobiling and themed tours tying in with festivals. Also offers 'Iceland on Your Own' bus tickets and passports for transport, and operates the Flybus to the Keflavík International Airport.

Arctic Adventures   ADVENTURE

(☑ 562 7000; www.adventures.is; Laugavegur 11; ☺ 8am-10pm) With young and enthusiastic staff, this company specialises in action-filled tours: kayaking (kr20,000), rafting (from kr14,000), horse riding, quad-biking, glacier walking (kr11,000) and so on. It has a booking office with gear shop **Fjallakofinn** (☑ 510 9505; www.fjallakofinn.is; Laugavegur 11; ☺ 9am-7pm Mon-Fri, 10am-5pm Sat, noon-6pm Sun) in central Reykjavík.

Icelandic Mountain Guides   ADVENTURE

(Iceland Rovers; ☑ 587 9999; www.mountainguides.is; Stórhöfði 33) This full-action outfit specialises in mountaineering, trekking, ice climbing (from kr23,900) and the like. It also markets itself as 'Iceland Rovers' for its super-Jeep tours (Essential Iceland tour kr42,900).

★ Creative Iceland   ART

(☑ 615 3500; www.creativeiceland.is) Get involved with graphic design, cooking, arts, crafts, music...you name it. This service hooks you up with local creative people offering workshops in their art or craft.

🛏 Sleeping

Accommodation prices are for June to September; out of season, rates drop.

★ Loft Hostel   HOSTEL €

(☑ 553 8140; www.lofthostel.is; Bankastræti 7; dm kr7600-8700, d/q kr27,800/37,600; @ 🛜) Perched high above the action on bustling Bankastræti, this modern hostel attracts a decidedly young crowd, including locals who come for its trendy bar and cafe terrace. This sociable spot comes with prim dorms, linen included and en suite bathrooms in each. HI members discount kr700/2800 for a dorm/double.

★ Reykjavík Downtown Hostel   HOSTEL €

(☑ 553 8120; www.hostel.is; Vesturgata 17; dm 4-/10-bed kr9100/6450, d with/without bathroom kr27,800/23,800; @ 🛜) Squeaky clean and well run, this effortlessly charming hostel gets such good reviews that it regularly lures large groups and the nonbackpacker set. Enjoy friendly service, guest kitchen and excellent rooms. Discount kr700 for HI members.

KEX Hostel   HOSTEL €

(☑ 561 6060; www.kexhostel.is; Skúlagata 28; dm 4-/16-bed kr7900/4900, d with/without bathroom kr39,700/25,500; @ 🛜) An unofficial headquarters of backpackerdom and popular local gathering place, KEX is a mega-hostel with heaps of style (think retro Vaudeville meets rodeo) and sociability. Overall it's not as prim as the other hostels – and bathrooms are shared by many – but KEX is a favourite for its lively restaurant-bar with water views and interior courtyard.

★ **Forsæla**

Apartmenthouse GUESTHOUSE, APARTMENT €€
(☑551 6046; www.apartmenthouse.is; Grettisgata 33b; d/tr without bathroom incl breakfast kr22,700/30,800, apt/house from kr38,200/74,000; 🛜) This lovely option in Reykjavík's centre stars a 100-year-old wood-and-tin house for four to eight people, which comes with all the old beams and tasteful mod cons you could want. Three apartments have small, cosy bedrooms and sitting rooms, kitchens and washing machines. Plus there's B&B lodging with shared bathrooms. Minimum three-night stay in apartments and the house.

★ **REY Apartments** APARTMENT €€
(☑771 4600; www.rey.is; Grettisgata 2a; apt kr23,000-49,800; 🛜) For those leaning towards private digs rather than hotel stays, REY is a very handy choice with a huge cache of modern apartments scattered across several Escher-like stairwells. They're well maintained and stylishly decorated.

★ **Grettisborg Apartments** APARTMENT €€
(☑666 0655; www.grettisborg.is; Grettisgata 51; apt kr21,200-51,500; 🛜) Like sleeping in a magazine for Scandinavian home design, these thoroughly modern studios and apartments sport fine furnishings and sleek built-ins. The largest sleeps six or seven.

★ **Galtafell Guesthouse** GUESTHOUSE €€
(☑551 4344; www.galtafell.com; Laufásvegur 46; d with/without bathroom from kr25,300/22,100, apt from kr26,000; 🛜) In a quiet lakeside neighbourhood within easy walking distance of the city centre, the four one-bedroom apartments in this converted historic mansion contain fully equipped kitchens and cosy seating areas. Three doubles share a guest kitchen. The garden and entry spaces feel suitably lovely.

★ **Reykjavík Residence** APARTMENT €€€
(☑561 1200; www.rrhotel.is; Hverfisgata 45; apt from kr33,300-70,200; @🛜) Plush city-centre living feels just right in these two converted historic mansions. Linens are crisp, service attentive and the light a glowing gold. They come in loads of configurations from suites and studios with kitchenettes to two- and three-bedroom apartments.

★ **Apotek** BOUTIQUE HOTEL €€€
(☑512 9000; www.keahotels.is; Austurstræti 16; d incl breakfast from kr44,100; 🛜) This new hotel in a well-renovated 1917 Guðjón Samúelsson building, a former pharmacy, smack in the centre of Old Reykjavík offers slick contemporary rooms in muted tones and a popular ground-floor tapas-style **restaurant-bar** (☑551 0011; www.apotekrestaurant.is; mains kr3000-8000; ⊙11.30am-1am) as well.

🍴 Eating

★ **Sægreifinn** SEAFOOD €
(Seabaron; ☑553 1500; www.saegreifinn.is; Geirsgata 8; mains kr1350-1900; ⊙11.30am-11pm mid-May–Aug, to 10pm Sep–mid-May) Sidle into this green harbourside shack for the most famous lobster soup (kr1350) in the capital, or to choose from a fridge full of fresh fish skewers to be grilled on the spot. Though the original sea baron sold the restaurant some years ago, the place retains a homey, laid-back feel.

★ **Stofan Kaffihús** CAFE €
(☑546 1842; www.facebook.com/stofan.cafe; Vesturgata 3; dishes kr1500-1600; ⊙9am-11pm Mon-Wed, to midnight Thu-Sat, 10am-10pm Sun; 🛜) This laid-back cafe in an historic brick building has a warm feel with its worn wooden floors, plump couches and spacious main room. Settle in for coffee, cake or soup, and watch the world go by.

Bæjarins Beztu HOT DOGS €
(www.bbp.is; Tryggvagata; hot dogs kr420; ⊙10am-2am Sun-Thu, to 4.30am Fri & Sat; 🚶) Icelanders swear the city's best hot dogs are at this truck near the harbour (patronised by Bill Clinton and late-night bar-hoppers). Use the vital sentence *Eina með öllu* (One with everything) to get the quintessential favourite with sweet mustard, ketchup and crunchy onions.

★ **Messinn** SEAFOOD €€
(☑546 0095; www.messinn.com; Lækjargata 6b; lunch mains kr1900-2100, dinner mains kr2500-3800; ⊙11.30am-3pm & 5-10pm; 🛜) Make a beeline to Messinn for the best seafood that Reykjavík has to offer. The speciality is amazing pan-fries where your pick of fish is served up in a sizzling cast-iron skillet accompanied by buttery potatoes and salad. The mood is upbeat and comfortable.

★ **Matur og Drykkur** ICELANDIC €€
(☑571 8877; www.maturogdrykkur.is; Grandagarður 2; lunch mains kr1900-3200, dinner menus kr3000-5000; ⊙11.30am-3pm Mon-Sat, 6-10.30pm Tue-Sat; 🚌14) One of Reykjavík's top high-concept restaurants, Matur Og Drykkur means 'Food and Drink', and you surely will be plied with the best of both. It's the brainchild of

brilliant chef Gísli Matthías Auðunsson, who also owns excellent **Slippurinn** (☑481 1515; www.slippurinn.com; Strandvegur 76; lunch kr 2200-3000, dinner kr3500-4000; ⊘noon-2.30pm & 5-10pm early May–mid-Sep; ⃝) in the Vestmannaeyjar, so expect inventive versions of traditional Icelandic fare. Book ahead in high season and for dinner.

★**Gló**   ORGANIC, VEGETARIAN €€
(☑553 1111; www.glo.is; Laugavegur 20b; mains kr1200-2000; ⊘11am-10pm Mon-Fri, 11.30am-10pm Sat & Sun; ⃝🖉) Join the cool cats in this upstairs, airy restaurant serving fresh, large daily specials loaded with Asian-influenced herbs and spices. Though not exclusively vegetarian, it's a wonderland of raw and organic foods with your choice from a broad bar of elaborate salads, from root veggies to Greek. It also has branches in **Laugardalur** (☑553 1111; Engjateigur 19; mains kr1200-2000; ⊘11am-9pm Mon-Fri; ⃝🖉) 🍴 and **Kópavogur** (Hæðasmári 6; mains kr1200-2000; ⊘11am-9pm Mon-Fri, 11.30am-9pm Sat & Sun; ⃝🖉) 🍴.

Bergsson Mathús   CAFE €€
(☑571 1822; www.bergsson.is; Templarasund 3; mains kr2000-2400; ⊘7am-9pm Mon-Fri, to 5pm Sat & Sun; 🖉) This popular, no-nonsense cafe features homemade breads, fresh produce and filling lunch specials. Stop by on weekends when locals flip through magazines, gossip and devour scrumptious brunch plates. After 4pm there is two-for-one takeaway.

★**Ostabúðin**   DELI €€
(Cheese Shop; ☑562 2772; www.facebook.com/Ostabudin/; Skólavörðustígur 8; mains kr3600-5000; ⊘restaurant 11.30am-9pm Mon-Fri, noon-9pm Sat & Sun, deli 10am-6pm Mon-Thu, to 7pm Fri, 11am-4pm Sat) Head to this gourmet cheese shop and deli, with a large dining room for the friendly owner's cheese and meat platters (from kr1900 to kr4000), or the catch of the day, accompanied by homemade bread. You can pick up other local goods, like terrines and duck confit, on the way out.

★**Snaps**   FRENCH €€
(☑511 6677; www2.snaps.is; Þórsgata 1; dinner mains kr3800-5000; ⊘7-10am daily, 11.30am-11pm Sun-Thu, to midnight Fri & Sat) Reserve ahead for this French bistro that's a mega-hit with locals. Snaps' secret is simple: serve scrumptious seafood and classic bistro mains – think steak or *moules frites* – at surprisingly decent prices. Lunch specials (11.30am to 2pm; kr1990) and brunches (11.30am to 4pm Saturday and Sunday; kr1300 to kr4000) are a big draw, too.

Public House   FUSION, TAPAS €€
(☑555 7333; www.publichouse.is; Laugavegur 24; small plates kr1300-2000; ⊘11.30am-1am) Excellent Asian-style tapas and great local draught beers and cocktails are only part of the draw to this new central gastropub. It's also just a fun place to hang out, with its bustling dining room and tables spilling out onto Laugavegur. A place to see and be seen.

★**Dill**   ICELANDIC €€€
(☑552 1522; www.dillrestaurant.is; Hverfisgata 12; 5-course meal from kr11,900; ⊘6-10pm Wed-Sat) Top 'New Nordic' cuisine is the major drawcard at this elegant yet simple bistro. The focus is very much on the food – locally sourced produce served as a parade of courses. The owners are friends with Copenhagen's famous Noma clan, and take Icelandic cuisine to similarly heady heights. Popular with locals and visitors alike, a reservation is a must.

★**Þrír Frakkar**   ICELANDIC, SEAFOOD €€€
(☑552 3939; www.3frakkar.com; Baldursgata 14; mains kr4000-6000; ⊘11.30am-2.30pm & 6-10pm Mon-Fri, 6-11pm Sat & Sun) Owner-chef Úlfar Eysteinsson has built up a consistently excellent reputation at this snug little restaurant – apparently a favourite of Jamie Oliver's. Specialities range throughout the aquatic world from salt cod and halibut to *plokkfiskur* (fish stew) with black bread. Non-fish items run towards guillemot, horse, lamb and whale.

★**Grillmarkaðurinn**   FUSION €€€
(Grill Market; ☑571 7777; www.grillmarkadurinn.is; Lækargata 2a; mains kr4600-7000; ⊘11.30am-2pm Mon-Fri, 6-10.30pm Sun-Thu, to 11.30pm Fri & Sat) Tippety-top dining is the order of the day here, from the moment you enter the glass atrium with the golden-globe lights to your first snazzy cocktail, and on through the meal. Service is impeccable, and locals and visitors alike rave about the food: locally sourced Icelandic ingredients prepared with culinary imagination by master chefs.

🍷 Drinking & Nightlife

Reykjavík is renowned for its weekend *djammið*, when folks buy booze from Vínbúðin (state alcohol shop), have a preparty at home, then hit the town at midnight. Many of the cool-cat cafes around town morph into bars at night. The 'Appy Hour' smartphone app lists local happy hours. Minimum drinking age is 20.

★**Kaffibarinn** BAR

(www.kaffibarinn.is; Bergstaðastræti 1; ☺3pm-1am Sun-Thu, to 4.30am Fri & Sat; 🛜) This old house with the London Underground symbol over the door contains one of Reykjavík's coolest bars; it even had a starring role in the cult movie *101 Reykjavík* (2000). At weekends you'll feel like you need a famous face or a battering ram to get in. At other times it's a place for artistic types to chill with their Macs.

★**Kaldi** BAR

(www.kaldibar.is; Laugavegur 20b; ☺noon-1am Sun-Thu, to 3am Fri & Sat) Effortlessly cool with mismatched seats and teal banquettes, plus a popular smoking courtyard, Kaldi is awesome for its full range of Kaldi microbrews, not available elsewhere. Happy hour (4pm to 7pm) gets you one for kr700. Anyone can play the in-house piano.

★**Micro Bar** BAR

(www.facebook.com/MicroBarIceland; Vesturgata 2; ☺2pm-12.30am Sun-Thu, to 2am Fri & Sat) Boutique brews is the name of the game at this low-key spot in the heart of the action. Bottles of beer represent a slew of brands and countries, but more importantly you'll discover 10 local draughts on tap from the island's top microbreweries: one of the best selections in Reykjavík. Happy hour (5pm to 7pm) offers kr850 beers.

★**Kaffi Vínyl** CAFE

(☑537 1332; www.facebook.com/vinilrvk; Hverfisgata 76; ☺9am-11pm Mon-Fri, 10am-11pm Sat, noon-11pm Sun; 🛜) This new entry on the Reykjavík coffee, restaurant and music scene is popular for its chill vibe, great music, and delicious vegan and vegetarian food.

Boston BAR

(www.facebook.com/boston.reykjavik; Laugavegur 28b; ☺4pm-1am Sun-Thu, to 3am Fri & Sat) Boston is cool, arty and found up through a doorway on Laugavegur that leads to its laid-back lounge and interior deck with sofas; DJs spin from time to time.

★**Paloma** CLUB

(www.facebook.com/BarPaloma; Naustin 1-3; ☺8pm-1am Thu & Sun, to 4.30am Fri & Sat; 🛜) One of Reykjavík's best late-night dance clubs, with DJs upstairs laying down reggae, electronica and pop, and a dark deep house dance scene in the basement. Find it in the same building as the Dubliner.

Kiki GAY

(www.kiki.is; Laugavegur 22; ☺9pm-1am Thu, to 4.30am Fri & Sat) Ostensibly a queer bar, Kiki is also *the* place to get your dance on (with pop and electronica the mainstays), since much of Reykjavík's nightlife centres around the booze, not the groove.

Prikið PUB

(☑551 2866; www.prikid.is; Bankastræti 12; ☺8am-1am Mon-Thu, to 4.30am Fri, 11am-4.30am Sat, 11am-midnight Sun) Being one of Reykjavík's oldest joints, Prikið feels somewhere between diner and saloon: great if you're up for greasy eats (mains kr2000 to kr3500) and socialising. Things get hip-hop dance-y in the wee hours, and if you survive the night, it's popular for its next-day 'hangover killer' breakfast (kr2590).

★**Reykjavík Roasters** CAFE

(www.reykjavikroasters.is; Kárastígur 1; ☺8am-6pm Mon-Fri, 9am-5pm Sat & Sun) These folks take their coffee seriously. This tiny hipster joint is easily spotted on warm days with its smattering of wooden tables on a small square. Swig a perfect latte with a flaky croissant. It now has a **branch** (Brautarholt 2; ☺8am-6pm Mon-Fri, 9am-5pm Sat & Sun; 🛜) in the Hlemmur area.

☆ Entertainment

The vibrant Reykjavík live-music scene is ever-changing. There are often performances at late-night bars and cafes, and venues such as **Húrra** (Tryggvagata 22; ☺5pm-1am Sun-Thu, to 4.30am Fri & Sat; 🛜), **Mengi** (☑588 3644; www.mengi.net; Óðinsgata 2; ☺noon-6pm Tue-Sat & for performances) and **Café Rosenberg** (☑551 2442; Klapparstígur 25-27; ☺3pm-1am Mon-Thu, 4pm-3am Fri & Sat). Local theatres and **Harpa concert hall** (☑box office 528 5050; www.harpa.is; Austurbakki 2; ☺8am-midnight, box office 10am-6pm; 🛜) bring in all of the performing arts. Reykjavík's **National Theatre** (Þjóðleikhúsið; ☑551 1200; www.leikhusid.is; Hverfisgata 19; ☺closed Jul) stages plays, musicals and operas. Cool, central cinema **Bíó Paradís** (www.bioparadis.is; Hverfisgata 54; adult kr1600; 🛜) screens films with English subtitles.

To see what's on, consult Grapevine (www.grapevine.is; which also has an app called 'Appening'), Visit Reykjavík (www.visitreykjavik.is), What's On in Reykjavík (www.whatson.is/magazine), Musik.is (www.musik.is) or city music shops.

🛍 Shopping

Reykjavík's vibrant design culture makes for great shopping: from sleek, fish-skin purses and knitted *lopapeysur* (traditional Icelandic woollen sweaters) to unique music or lip-smacking Icelandic schnapps *brennivín*. Laugavegur is the most dense shopping street. Fashion concentrates near the Frakkastígur and Vitastígur end of Laugavegur. Skólavörðustígur is strong for arts and jewellery. Bankastræti and Austurstræti have many tourist shops.

ℹ Information

DISCOUNT CARDS

Reykjavík City Card (www.citycard.is; 24/48/72hr kr3500/4700/5500) offers admission to Reykjavík's municipal swimming/thermal pools and to most of the main galleries and museums, plus discounts on some tours, shops and entertainment. Also gives free travel on the city's Strætó buses and on the ferry to Viðey. Get cards at the Main Tourist Office, some travel agencies, 10-11 supermarkets, HI hostels and some hotels.

EMERGENCY

Ambulance, fire brigade, police & search and rescue ☑112

MEDICAL SERVICES

Health Centre (☑585 2600; Vesturgata 7; ⊘ call to arrange appointment) Book in advance.

Landspítali University Hospital (☑543 1000, doctor on duty 1770; www.landspitali.is; Fossvogur) Casualty department open 24/7.

TOURIST INFORMATION

The widely distributed English-language newspaper/website Grapevine (www.grapevine.is) is an irreverent introduction to Reykjavík.

Main Tourist Office (Upplýsingamiðstöð Ferðamanna; ☑590 1550; www.visitreykjavik.is; Aðalstræti 2; ⊘8am-8pm) Friendly staff and mountains of free brochures, plus maps. Reykjavík City Cards and Strætó city bus tickets. Books accommodation, tours and activities.

ℹ Getting Around

BICYCLE

At the Old Harbour, rent bikes at **Reykjavík Bike Tours** (Reykjavík Segway Tours; ☑bike 694 8956, segway 897 2790; www.icelandbike.com; Ægisgarður 7; bike rental per 4hr from kr3500, tours from kr6500; ⊘9am-5pm Jun-Aug, reduced hours Sep-May; ☑14) and get service at **Kría** (www.kriacycles.com; Grandagarður 5; ⊘10am-6pm Mon-Fri, 11am-1pm Sat) bicycle

---

ICELANDIC POP

Iceland produces a disproportionate number of world-class musicians. Björk (and the Sugarcubes) and Sigur Rós are Iceland's most famous musical exports. Sigur Rós' concert movie *Heima* (2007) is a must-see. New sounds surface all the time, ranging from indie-folk Of Monsters and Men, quirky troubadour Ásgeir Trausti and indie band Seabear (which produced hit acts Sin Fang and Sóley), to electronica (FM Belfast, GusGus and múm). Visit www.icelandmusic.is for more info.

---

shop, or do your own repairs at **Bike Cave** (☑770 3113; www.bikecave.is; Einarsnes 36; ⊘9am-11pm; ☑12) cafe.

BUS

Strætó (☑540 2700; www.bus.is, www.straeto.is) operates good buses around Reykjavík and its suburbs, as well aslong-distance buses (operating from the Mjódd terminal). It has online schedules and a smartphone app. Free maps such as *Welcome to Reykjavík City Map* include bus-route maps. The fare is kr420, with no change given.

Buses run from 7am until 11pm or midnight daily (from 11am on Sunday). Services depart at 20-minute or 30-minute intervals. Limited night-bus service runs until 2am on Friday and Saturday. Buses only stop at designated bus stops, marked with a yellow letter 'S'.

TAXI

Taxis prices are high. Flagfall starts at around kr680. Taxis wait outside bus stations, airports and bars (on weekend nights).

AROUND REYKJAVÍK

The Golden Circle

The Golden Circle takes in three popular attractions all within 100km of the capital: Þingvellir, Geysir and Gullfoss. It is an artificial tourist circuit (there is no valley; natural topography marks its extent) that is loved (and marketed) by thousands, and easy to see on one day-long circular drive or tour.

Þingvellir National Park (www.thingvellir.is) is inside an immense rift valley, caused by the separating North American and Eurasian tectonic plates. It's Iceland's most important historical location and a Unesco World Heritage site: early Icelanders established the world's first democratic parliament, the Alþing, here in AD 930.

Geysir FREE, after which all spouting hot springs are named, only erupts rarely. Luckily, alongside it is the ever-reliable **Strokkur**, which spouts up to 30m approximately every five minutes. Ten kilometres east, **Gullfoss** (Golden Falls; www.gullfoss.is) FREE is a spectacular rainbow-tinged double waterfall, which drops 32m before thundering away down a vast canyon.

Laugarvatn makes a good base for overnights and has the swanky lakeside **Fontana** (📞486 1400; www.fontana.is; Hverabraut 1; adult/child kr3800/2000; ☺10am-11pm early Jun-late Aug, 11am-10pm late Aug-early Jun) geothermal spa.

🛏 Sleeping & Eating

Laugarvatn HI Hostel HOSTEL €
(📞486 1215; www.laugarvatnhostel.is; dm/s/d without bathroom kr4100/7000/10,900, s/d kr13,400/16,650; 🅿@🛜) This large hostel, spread over several buildings along the village's main street, is professional and comfortable. There's a newly renovated two-storey building with plenty of kitchen space (great lake views while washing up or from the dining room). Some buildings are much smaller and houselike. There's a kr700 discount for HI members.

Þingvellir Campsites CAMPGROUND €
(www.thingvellir.is; sites per adult/child/tent kr1300/free/100; ☺Jun-Sep) Overseen by the park information centre, the best two areas are at Leirar, near the cafe: Syðri-Leirar is the biggest and Nyrðri-Leirar has laundry facilities. Fagrabrekka and Hvannabrekka are for campers only (no cars). Vatnskot is down by the lake and has toilets and cold water (no electricity).

★**Efstidalur II** GUESTHOUSE €€
(📞486 1186; www.efstidalur.is; Efstidalur 2, Bláskógabyggð; d/tr incl breakfast from kr26,200/29,700; 🅿🛜) Located 12km northeast of Laugarvatn on a working dairy farm, Efstidalur offers wonderfully welcoming digs, tasty meals and amazing ice cream. Adorable semidetached cottages have brilliant views of hulking Hekla, and the **restaurant** (📞486 1186; Efstidalur 2; mains kr2250-5500; ☺7.30am-9.30am & 11.30am-9pm; 🛜) serves beef from the farm and trout from the lake. The ice-cream bar scoops farm ice cream (kr400 per scoop) and has windows looking into the dairy barn.

★**Héraðsskólinn** HOSTEL, GUESTHOUSE €€
(📞537 8060; www.heradsskolinn.is; dm/s/d/q without bathroom from kr5400/14,000/15,300/30,100, d with bathroom kr25,400; 🅿🛜) This sparkling hostel and guesthouse fills an enormous renovated historical landmark school, built in 1928 by Guðjón Samúelsson. The beautiful lakeside building with peaked roofs offers both private rooms with shared bathrooms (some sleep up to six) and dorms, plus a spacious library/living room and a cafe (open 7.30am to 10pm).

Lake Thingvellir Cottages COTTAGE €€
(📞892 7110; www.lakethingvellir.is; Heiðarás; cottages kr18,500, plus per person per night kr2400; 🅿🛜) Four modern pine cottages with views to the lake sit near the national-park entrance along Rte 36.

Ion Luxury Adventure Hotel BOUTIQUE HOTEL €€€
(📞482 3415; www.ioniceland.is; Nesjavellir vid Þingvallavatn; d kr50,100; 🅿@🛜♨) 🌿 A leader in a new breed of deluxe countryside hotels, Ion is all about hip, modern rooms and sustainable practices. Its geothermal pool, organic spa, **restaurant** (Nesjavellir vid Þingvallavatn; mains lunch kr2500-6000, dinner kr5000-7000; ☺11.30am-10pm) with slow-food local ingredients and bar with floor-to-ceiling plate-glass windows are all sumptuous. Rooms are a tad smallish, but kitted out impeccably.

★**Lindin** ICELANDIC €€
(📞486 1262; www.laugarvatn.is; Lindarbraut 2; restaurant mains kr3800-6300, bistro mains kr2200-5600; ☺noon-10pm May-Sep, reduced hours Oct-Apr; 🛜) Owned by Baldur, an affable, celebrated chef, Lindin is the best restaurant for miles. In a sweet little silver house, the restaurant faces the lake and is purely gourmet, with high-concept Icelandic fare featuring local or wild-caught ingredients. The casual, modern bistro serves a more informal menu, from soups to an amazing reindeer burger. Book ahead for dinner in high season.

Blue Lagoon

Arguably Iceland's most famous attraction is the **Blue Lagoon** (Bláa Lónið; 📞420 8800; www.bluelagoon.com; adult/child Jun-Aug from €50/free, Sep-May from €40/free; ☺8am-midnight Jun–mid-Aug, reduced hours mid-Aug–May), a milky-blue geothermal pool set in a massive black lava field, 50km southwest of

Reykjavík on the Reykjanes Peninsula. The futuristic Svartsengi geothermal plant provides an other-worldly backdrop, as well as the spa's water – 70% sea water, 30% fresh water, at a perfect 38°C. Daub yourself in silica mud and loll in the hot-pots with an ice-blue cocktail. The mineral-rich waters dry hair to straw – use plenty of the provided hair conditioner.

You must book in advance, and to beat enormous crowds, go early or very late in the day. Reykjavík Excursions (p613) buses serve the BSÍ bus terminal (or hotels and the airport on request).

SOUTH ICELAND

As you work your way east from Reykjavík, Rte 1 (the Ring Rd) emerges into austere volcanic foothills punctuated by surreal steam vents and hot springs, around **Hveragerði**, then swoops through a flat, wide coastal plain, full of verdant horse farms and greenhouses, before the landscape suddenly begins to grow wonderfully jagged, after **Hella** and **Hvolsvöllur**. Hvolsvöllur's **LAVA – Iceland Volcano & Earthquake Center** (www.lavacentre.is; Austurvegur 14, Hvolsvöllur; adult/child kr2600/free, cinema only kr1200/free; ⊙ exhibition 10am-7pm, LAVA house 9am-10pm) showcases the volcanic terrain with multimedia exhibits, and the museum **Sögusetrið** (Saga Centre; ☑ 487 8781; www.njala.is; Hlíðarvegur 14, Hvolsvöllur; adult/child kr900/free; ⊙ 9am-6pm mid-May–mid-Sep, 10am-5pm Sat & Sun mid-Sep–mid-May) is devoted to the dramatic events of *Njál's Saga*. Mountains thrust upwards on the inland side of the Ring Road, some of them volcanoes wreathed by mist (**Eyjafjallajökull**, site of the 2010 eruption), and the first of the awesome

---

ICELANDIC SETTLEMENT & SAGAS

Rumour, myth and fantastic tales of fierce storms and barbaric dog-headed people kept most explorers away from the great northern ocean, *oceanus innavigabilis*. Irish monks who regularly sailed to the Faroe Islands looking for seclusion were probably the first to stumble upon Iceland. It's thought that they settled around the year 700 but fled when Norsemen began to arrive in the early 9th century.

The Age of Settlement

The Age of Settlement is traditionally defined as between 870 and 930, when political strife on the Scandinavian mainland caused many to flee. Most North Atlantic Norse settlers were ordinary citizens: farmers and merchants who settled across Western Europe, marrying Britons, Westmen (Irish) and Scots.

Among Iceland's first Norse visitors was Norwegian Flóki Vilgerðarson, who uprooted his farm and headed for Snæland (archaic Viking name for Iceland) around 860. He navigated with ravens, which, after some trial and error, led him to his destination and provided his nickname, Hrafna-Flóki (Raven-Flóki). Hrafna-Flóki sailed to Vatnsfjörður on the west coast but became disenchanted with the conditions. On seeing the icebergs in the fjord he dubbed the country Ísland (Iceland) and returned to Norway. He did eventually settle in Iceland's Skagafjörður district.

According to the 12th-century *Íslendingabók* (a historical narrative of the Settlement Era), Ingólfur Arnarson fled Norway with his blood brother Hjörleifur, landing at Ingólfshöfði (southeast Iceland) in 871. He was then led to Reykjavík by a pagan ritual: he tossed his high-seat pillars (a symbol of authority) into the sea as they approached land. Wherever the gods brought the pillars ashore would be the settlers' new home. Ingólfur named Reykjavík (Smoky Bay) after the steam from its thermal springs. Hjörleifur settled near the present town of Vík, but was murdered by his slaves shortly thereafter.

Descendants of the first settlers established the world's first democratic parliament, the Alþing, in 930 at Þingvellir (Parliament Plains).

The Saga Age

The late 12th century kicked off the Saga Age, when the epic tales of the earlier 9th-to-10th-century settlement were recorded by historians and writers. These sweeping prose epics or sagas detail the family struggles, romance, vendettas and colourful characters of the Settlement Era. They are the backbone of medieval Icelandic literature and a rich source for historical understanding. Try *Egil's Saga*, the colourful adventures of a poet-warrior and grandson of a shape-shifter.

glaciers appears, as enormous rivers like the Þjórsá cut their way to the black-sand beaches rimming the Atlantic.

Throughout, roads pierce deep inland, to realms of lush waterfall-doused valleys like Þjórsádalur and Fljótshlíð, and awe-inspiring volcanoes such as Hekla. Two of the most renowned inland spots are Landmannalaugar, where vibrantly coloured rhyolite peaks meet bubbling hot springs; and Þórsmörk, a gorgeous, forested valley tucked away from the brutal northern elements under a series of ice caps. They are linked by the rightly famous 55km Laugavegurinn hike, Iceland's most popular trek (for more information, check Ferðafélag Íslands' website, www.fi.is). Since these areas lie inland on roads impassable by standard vehicles, most visitors access them on tours or amphibious buses from the southern Ring Rd. Þórsmörk, one of Iceland's most popular hiking destinations, can be done as a day trip.

Skógar is the leaping-off point for Þórsmörk and boasts Skógar Folk Museum (Skógasafn; ☑ 487 8845; www.skogasafn.is; adult/child kr2000/free; ☉ 9am-6pm Jun-Aug, 10am-5pm Sep-May), plus nearby waterfalls Seljalandsfoss & Gljúfurárbui and Skógafoss. One of the easiest glacial tongues to reach is Sólheimajökull, just east of Skógar, but only climb onto the glacier accompanied by a local guide – conditions are often, and invisibly, shifting. Vík is surrounded by glaciers, vertiginous cliffs and black beaches such as Reynisfjara with the off-shore rock formation Dyrhólaey. South of the Ring Rd, the tiny fishing villages of Stokkseyri and Eyrarbakki are refreshingly local-feeling.

Churning seas lead to the Vestmannaeyjar archipelago offshore (sometimes called the Westman Islands), with its zippy puffins and small town Heimaey tucked between lava flows, explained at the excellent volcano museum Eldheimar (Pompeii of the North; ☑ 488 2700; www.eldheimar.is; Gerðisbraut 10; adult/child kr2300/1200; ☉ 10.30am-6pm May-mid-Oct, 1-5pm Wed-Sun mid-Oct–Apr; ☎).

Public transport (and traffic) is solid along the Ring Rd. Midgard Adventure (☑ 770 2030; www.midgardadventure.is; Dufþaksbraut 14) and Southcoast Adventure (☑ 867 3535; www.southadventure.is) run excellent hiking, adventure and super-Jeep tours in the region.

The popular southwest area (www.south.is) is developing quickly and infrastructure keeps improving, with family farms offering lovely guesthouses. Nevertheless, it gets very busy in high seasons (eg summer, Christmas), so advanced accommodation booking is essential.

🛏 Sleeping & Eating

For inland camping near Landmannalaugar and Þórsmörk, check Ferðafélag Íslands (Icelandic Touring Association; www.fi.is), which maintains the Laugavegurinn trail and huts. Þórsmörk also has private hostel-guesthouse-campground Húsadalur (☑ 552 8300; www.volcanohuts.com; Húsadalur; sites per person kr2000, dm/s/d & cottages without bathroom kr7500/16,000/25,000; ☎) and Hostelling International campground Slyppugil (☑ 575 6700; www.hostel.is; sites per person kr1200; ☉ mid-Jun–mid-Aug). Book many months ahead.

Hella & Around

★ River Hotel
HOTEL €€

(☑ 487 5004; www.riverhotel.is; Þykkvabæjarvegur (Rte 25); d/f kr22,000/30,000; ☑☎) Relax and watch the river glide by through giant plate-glass windows in the lounge areas of this immaculate new hotel on the banks of the Ytri-Rangá river. Contemporary rooms and a separate cottage are super-comfortable and there's an on-site restaurant for dinner. It's ideal for Northern Lights watching as well, and the owners are avid anglers.

★ Hótel Rangá
HOTEL €€€

(☑ 487 5700; www.hotelranga.is; Suðurlandsvegur; d/ste incl breakfast from kr42,000/65,400; ◎☎) Just south of the Ring Rd 8km east of Hella, Hótel Rangá looks like a log cabin but caters to Iceland's high-end travellers. Service is top-notch, and the wood-panelled rooms and luxurious common areas are cosy. The restaurant (lunch mains kr2600 to kr3900, dinner mains kr4800 to kr7200) has broad windows looking across open pastures. To splash out, go for a 'World Pavilion' suite.

★ Frost & Fire Hotel
BOUTIQUE HOTEL €€€

(Frost og Funi; ☑ 483 4959; www.frostandfire.is; Hverhamar, Hveragerði; d/tr incl breakfast kr31,000/42,700; ☑◎☲) This lovely little hotel sits along a bubbling stream and beneath fizzing geothermal spouts. The comfortable rooms with subtle Scandi-sleek details and original artworks stretch along the river ravine. The heat-pressured sauna and simmering hot-pots are fed by the hotel's private borehole.

WORTH A TRIP

SKAFTAFELL & VATNAJÖKULL NATIONAL PARK

Skaftafell, the jewel in the crown of Vatnajökull National Park (www. vjp.is; www.visitvatnajokull.is), encompasses a breathtaking collection of peaks and glaciers. It's the country's favourite wilderness: 300,000 visitors per year come to marvel at thundering waterfalls, twisted birch woods, the tangled web of rivers threading across the *sandar* (sand deltas) and brilliant blue-white Vatnajökull with its myriad ice tongues.

Icelandic Mountain Guides (IMG; ☑ Reykjavík 587 9999, Skaftafell 894 2959; www.mountainguides.is; ⊙ 8.30am-6pm May-Sep, reduced hours Oct-Apr) and Glacier Guides (☑ Reykjavík 562 7000, Skaftafell 659 7000; www.glacierguides. is; ⊙ 8.30am-6pm Apr-Oct, reduced hours Nov-Mar) lead glacier walks and adventure tours.

Kaffi Krús INTERNATIONAL €€
(☑ 482 1266; www.kaffikrus.is; Austurvegur 7, Selfoss; mains kr2000-3600; ⊙ 10am-10pm Jun-Aug, reduced hours Sep-May) The 'Coffee Mug' is a popular cafe in a charming old house along the main road in the village of Selfoss. There's great outdoor space and a large selection of Icelandic and international dishes, from nachos to excellent pizza and burgers.

🛏 Skógar & Around

Skálakot GUESTHOUSE, FARMSTAY €
(☑ 487 8953; www.skalakot.com; dm kr5500, d/f without bathroom kr13,000/19,500, farmstay with full board kr18,500; ℗ 🕸) The fresh-faced Skálakot horse farm offers dorms, guesthouse rooms and sleeping bag accommodation (kr3800), plus full farmstay experiences. It's 15km west of Skógar on Rte 246.

★ Skógar Campsite CAMPGROUND €
(sites per adult/child kr1200/800; ⊙ May-Sep) Basic grassy lot with a great location, right by Skógafoss; the sound of falling water makes a soothing lullaby. There's a no-frills toilet block (shower kr300); pay at the hostel nearby.

★ Hamragarðar CAMPGROUND €
(☑ 867 3535; sites per adult/child kr1300/free; ⊙ May-Sep) Camp right next to the hidden waterfall at Gljúfurárbui at the start of Rte

249. There's a small cafe (9am to 11pm June to August) that sells cake and coffee, plus a laundry (kr500), showers (kr300), a shared kitchen and an info area for Southcoast Adventure (p607).

★ Skógar Guesthouse GUESTHOUSE €€
(☑ 894 5464; www.skogarguesthouse.is; d/tr without bathroom incl breakfast kr21,000/30,000; 🕸) This charming white farmhouse is tucked back inside the trees, beyond the Hótel Edda, almost to the cliff face. A friendly family offers quaint, impeccably maintained rooms with crisp linens and cosy quilts, a large immaculate kitchen and bathrooms, and a hot tub on a wood deck beneath the maples. It feels well out of the tourist fray despite being in central Skógar.

★ Stóra-Mörk III GUESTHOUSE, COTTAGE €€
(☑ 487 8903; www.storamork.com; d with/without bathroom incl breakfast kr17,000/12,000; 🕸) About 5km along Rte 249 beyond the cluster of traffic at Seljalandsfoss falls, a dirt track leads to historic Stóra-Mörk III farmhouse (mentioned, of course, in *Njál's Saga*), which offers large, homey rooms. The main house has some rooms with private bathrooms, a large kitchen and a dining room with excellent mountain-to-sea views. Sleeping-bag accommodation with/without bathroom costs kr4500/3800.

Country Hotel Anna HOTEL €€
(☑ 487 8950; www.hotelanna.is; Rte 246, Moldnúpur; s/d incl breakfast kr19,900/28,900; 🕸) 🍃 This inn's namesake, Anna, wrote books about her worldwide voyages – and her descendants' country hotel upholds her passion for travel, with seven sweetly old-fashioned rooms furnished with antiques and embroidered bedspreads. The hotel and its little restaurant (open 6.30pm to 9pm; mains kr4200 to kr5200) sit at the foot of Eyjafjallajökull volcano on Rte 246.

🛏 Vík & Around

★ Garðar GUESTHOUSE €
(☑ 487 1260; www.reynisfjara-guesthouses.com; Reynisfjara; cottages kr12,000-18,000) Garðar, at the end of Rte 215, to the west of Vík, is a magical, view-blessed place. Friendly farmer Ragnar rents out self-contained beachside huts: one stone cottage sleeps four, other timber cottages sleep two to four. Linen costs kr1500 per person.

⭐ **Grand Guesthouse Garðakot**   B&B €€
(☑487 1441; www.ggg.is; Garðakot farm; d kr26,000;
📶) Set on a pastoral sheep farm, this small,
tidy house holds four beautiful rooms, two
with private bathrooms and two that share.
Heated hardwood floors downstairs, sweeping views of volcanoes and sea upstairs, and
friendly proprietors, pretty decor, serenity
and flat-screen TVs for all. It's 14km west of
Vík, south of the Ring Rd on Rte 218.

⭐ **Guesthouse Carina**   B&B €€
(☑699 0961; www.guesthousecarina.is; Mýrar-
braut 13; s/d/q without bathroom incl breakfast from
kr16,900/21,900/31,500; 🅿📶) Friendly Carina
and her husband Ingvar run one of the best
lodging options in Vík. Neat-as-a-pin, spacious rooms with good light and clean shared
bathrooms fill a large converted house near
the centre of town.

⭐ **Icelandair Hótel Vík**   HOTEL €€€
(☑487 1480, booking 444 4000; www.iceland
airhotels.com; Klettsvegur 1-5; d/tr/f from
kr24,500/29,000/50,000; 🅿📶) This sleek
black-window-fronted hotel is improbably
tucked just behind the Hótel Edda, on the
eastern edge of town, near the campground.
The hotels share a lobby (and have the same
friendly owners), but that's where the resemblance ends. The Icelandair hotel has suitably
swanky rooms, some with views to the rear
cliffs or the sea. The light, natural decor is inspired by the local environment.

⭐ **Suður-Vík**   ICELANDIC, ASIAN €€
(☑487 1515; www.facebook.com/Sudurvik; Suður-
víkurvegur 1, Vík; mains kr2100-5000; ⏱noon-
10pm) The friendly ambience, hardwood
floors, interesting artwork and smiling staff
help elevate this restaurant beyond the competition. Food is Icelandic hearty, and ranges
from heaping steak sandwiches with bacon
and Béarnaise sauce to Asian (think Thai satay with rice). In a warmly lit silver building
atop town. Book ahead in summer.

WEST ICELAND

Geographically close to Reykjavík yet far, far
away in sentiment, West Iceland (known as
Vesturland; www.west.is) is a splendid microcosm of what Iceland has to offer. The
long arm of **Snæfellsnes Peninsula** is a
favourite for its glacier, Snæfellsjökull. The
area around **Snæfellsjökull National Park**
(☑436 6860; www.snaefellsjokull.is) is tops for

birding, whale watching, lava field hikes and
horse riding.

Inland beyond **Reykholt** you'll encounter
lava tubes such as **Viðgelmir** (☑783 3600;
www.thecave.is; tour per adult/child from kr6500/
free) and remote highland glaciers, including enormous **Langjökull** with its **Into the
Glacier** (Langjökull Ice Cave; ☑578 2550; www.in-
totheglacier.is) ice cave. **Hótel Húsafell** (☑435
1551; www.hotelhusafell.com; d incl breakfast from
kr39,500; 🅿📶) with its top-notch rooms and
gourmet restaurant offer high-end digs and
camping, too.

Icelanders honour West Iceland for its
local sagas: two of the best known, *Laxdæ-
la Saga* and *Egil's Saga,* took place along
the region's brooding waters, marked today by haunting cairns and an exceptional
Settlement Centre (Landnámssetur Íslands;
☑437 1600; www.settlementcentre.is; Brákarbraut
13-15; adult/child 1 exhibition kr1900/free, 2 exhibitions kr2500/free; ⏱10am-9pm; 📶) in lively
Borgarnes, which also has good lodging,
such as **Bjarg** (☑437 1925; bjarg@simnet.is;
Bjarg farm; d with/without bathroom incl breakfast
kr20,400/18,300; 📶) and **Egils's Guesthouse
& Apartments** (www.egilsguesthouse.is; Brákarbraut 11; d with/without bathroom incl breakfast
kr20,000/17,000, studios from kr20,400; 🅿📶),
and fine eats.

West Iceland offers everything from windswept beaches to historic villages and awe-
inspiring terrain in one neat, little package.
Stykkishólmur makes a great base, with its
fine hotels and guesthouses such as **Hótel
Egilsen** (☑554 7700; www.egilsen.is; Aðalgata
2; s/d kr24,000/30,000; @📶), excellent eateries like **Plássið** (☑436 1600; www.plassid.is;
Frúarstígur 1; mains kr2500-5000; ⏱11.30am-10pm
May-Sep; 🍴♿), interesting museums such as
Norska Húsið (Norwegian House; ☑433 8114;
www.norskahusid.is; Hafnargata 5; adult/child kr800/
free; ⏱11am-6pm Jun-Aug, 2-5pm Tue-Thu Sep-May;
📶) and boats around Breiðafjörður operated by **Seatours** (Sæferðir; ☑433 2254; www.
seatours.is; Smiðjustígur 3; ⏱8am-8pm mid-May–
mid-Sep, 9am-5pm mid-Sep–mid-May). Find the
region's top cuisine at **Bjargarsteinn Mathús**
(☑438 6770; www.facebook.com/Bjargarsteinnres-
taurant; Sólvellir 15; mains kr2900-4000; ⏱2-10pm
Jun-Aug, 5-8pm Sep-May, closed mid-Dec–mid-Jan;
📶) in nearby Grundarfjörður.

NORTH ICELAND

Iceland's mammoth and magnificent north
is a wonderland of moonlike lava fields,

WILD WESTFJORDS

Some of Iceland's least touristed but wildest scenery lies in the far northwest of the country, in the craggy rainbow-prone Westfjords (www.westfjords.is). Ísafjörður is the largest city and base, with tiny fjord-side hamlets dotting the rest of the far-flung fjord fingers. Highlights include the remote **Hornstrandir Nature Reserve** (☑591 2000; www. ust.is/hornstrandir), thundering **Dynjandi waterfall** and the gorgeous **Rauðasandur** pink-sand beach with its nearby **Látrabjarg bird cliffs**.

belching mudpots, epic waterfalls, snow-capped peaks and whale-filled bays. The region's top sights are variations on one theme: a grumbling, volcanically active earth.

Húsavík is Iceland's premier whale-watching destination, with up to 11 species coming to feed in summer. Go out whale and puffin spotting with **North Sailing** (☑464 7272; www.northsailing.is; Garðarsbraut; 3hr tour adult/child kr10,500/4200), **Gentle Giants** (☑464 1500; www.gentlegiants.is; Garðarsbraut; 3hr tour adult/child kr10,300/4200) or **Salka** (☑464 3999; www.salkawhalewatching.is; Garðarsbraut 6; 3hr tour adult/child kr9950/4200; ☺May-Sep). **Siglufjörður** on the **Tröllaskagi Peninsula** offers vast vistas and rugged mountainscapes.

Visit otherworldy lake **Mývatn** for its lava castles and hidden fissures. Thunderously roaring **Dettifoss** is one of Iceland's grandest waterfalls. Nearby **Goðafoss** (Waterfall of the Gods) rips straight through the Bárðardalur lava field along Rte 1. Although smaller and less powerful than some of Iceland's other chutes, it's definitely one of the most beautiful.

On the east side of the lake, the giant jagged lava field at **Dimmuborgir** (literally 'Dark Castles') is one of the most fascinating flows in the country. Dominating the lava fields on the eastern edge of Mývatn is the classic tephra ring **Hverfjall** (also called Hverfell). This near-symmetrical crater appeared 2700 years ago in a cataclysmic eruption. The dramatic lava cave at **Lofthellir** is a stunning destination, with magnificent natural ice sculptures (ice trolls?) dominating the interior.

The magical, ochre-toned world of **Hverir** (also called Hverarönd) is a lunar-like landscape of mud cauldrons, steaming vents, radiant mineral deposits and piping fumaroles.

For birdwatching background, swing by **Sigurgeir's Bird Museum** (Fuglasafn Sigurgeirs; ☑464 4477; www.fuglasafn.is; adult/child kr1200/600; ☺9am-6pm Jun-Aug, reduced hours Sep-May), housed in a beautiful lakeside building that fuses modern design with a traditional turf house.

Akureyri

Little Akureyri, with its surprising moments of big-city living is the best base in the north. From here you can explore by car or bus, and tour the region's highlights.

Tours

Saga Travel (☑558 8888; www.sagatravel.is; Kaupvangsstræti 4; ☺booking office 7.30am-6pm Jun-Aug, reduced hours rest of year) offers diverse year-round excursions and activities throughout the north.

Sleeping & Eating

Akureyri

Stay at **Sæluhús** (☑412 0800; www.saeluhus. is; Sunnutröð; studio/house kr25,700/49,000; ☎) with its well-equipped modern studios and houses, or **Skjaldarvík** (☑552 5200; www. skjaldarvik.is; s/d without bathroom incl breakfast kr18,900/23,900; @☎), a slice of guesthouse nirvana, in a farm setting 6km north of town. There's an unexpected touch of the Mediterranean at outstanding **Halllandsnes** (☑895 6029; www.halllandsnes.is; Rte 1; apt from kr28,000; ☎), 6km east of Akureyri along Rte 1.

Akureyri Backpackers (☑571 9050; www. akureyribackpackers.com; Hafnarstræti 98; dm kr5800-6300, d without bathroom kr20,300; ☎) offers great budget digs, and **Icelandair Hotel Akureyri** (☑518 1000; www.icelandairhotels.com; Þingvallastræti 23; d from kr28,100; @☎) hits the top-end mark.

Around Akureyri

On Tröllaskagi Peninsula, Dalvík's excellent **HI Hostel** (☑865 8391, 699 6616; www.dalvik hostel.com; Hafnarbraut 4; dm/d without bathroom kr4900/12,700; ☎) and wonderful cafe **Gísli,**

Eiríkur, Helgi (Kaffihús Bakkabræðra; Grundargata 1; soup & salad buffet kr1990; ⊙10am-10pm) make the sleepy village a good option. The wow factor delights at **Apartment Hótel Hjalteyri** (☑897 7070, 462 2770; www.hotelhjalteyri.is; Hjalteyri; d kr39,000, 2-bedroom apt kr49,000, incl breakfast; ☎), a renovated schoolhouse en route to Hjalteyri's harbour. In Siglufjörður, stay over at charming **Herring Guesthouse** (☑868 4200; www.theherringhouse.com; Hávegur 5; s/d without bathroom kr13,500/17,900, 4-person apt kr44,800; ☎) or **Siglunes Guesthouse** (☑467 1222; www.hotelsiglunes.is; Lækjargata 10; d with/without bathroom from kr19,400/15,900; ☎).

Near Mývatn, **Vogafjós** (☑464 3800; www.vogafjos.net; mains kr2500-5400; ⊙10am-11pm Jun-Aug, shorter hours Sep-May; ☎🅿🏠) in Reykjahlíð serves up top local vittles and offers a nearby guesthouse.

SURVIVAL GUIDE

ℹ Directory A–Z

ACCOMMODATION

For visits between June and August travellers should book accommodation well in advance (no need to prebook campsites). All hostels and some guesthouses and hotels offer cheaper rates if guests use their own sleeping bags. There are many different room styles – we list but a few. Generally, accommodation prices are very high compared to mainland European lodging.

Accommodation Types

Camping is allowed anywhere in Iceland, apart from on private land. However, in national parks and reserves you must stay in marked campsites, and most towns have designated camping areas – generally open mid-May to mid-September. The Camping Card (www.campingcard.is) can be a good deal for longer stays. Private walking clubs and **Ferðafélag Íslands** (Iceland Touring Association; ☑568 2533; www.fi.is; Mörkin 6) maintain *skálar* (mountain huts; singular *skáli*) on many popular hiking tracks – in summer, reservations are essential.

Hostelling International Iceland (www.hostel.is) administers 35 of Iceland's superb youth hostels; Akureyri and Reykjavík have private ones, too.

Gistiheimilið (guesthouses) range from private homes to purpose-built farmstays, and often have shared bathrooms. Many only open mid-May to mid-September. Check Icelandic Farm Holidays (www.farmholidays.is) for great countryside accommodations.

Hotels range from motels to boutique luxury hotels, with more being built constantly.

Summer-only Edda Hótels (www.hoteledda.is), based in schools, often offers dorms.

ACTIVITIES

➤ Hiking and mountaineering is stunning all over the country, especially in national parks and nature reserves. July, August and September are the best months for walking. For details check Ferðafélag Íslands (www.fi.is).

➤ A vast menu of adventure tours combine ice climbing, snowmobiling, caving etc with super-Jeeps or bus tours. Most pick up from Reykjavík – see Tours (p600).

➤ Stables offer everything from 90-minute horse rides to multiday tours, and can combine riding with other activities, such as visiting the Golden Circle or Blue Lagoon. Some offer guesthouse accommodation.

➤ Hvítá river, located along the Golden Circle, is a top spot for white-water rafting and speedboating near Reykjavík. Trips run from Reykholt, but offer Reykjavík pick-ups. Contact **Arctic Rafting** (☑571 2200; www.arcticrafting.com; ⊙mid-May–mid-Sep).

➤ Scuba-diving tours with **Dive.is** (☑578 6200; www.dive.is; 2 dives at Þingvellir kr45,000) and **Scuba Iceland** (☑892 1923; www.scuba.is; Silfra dive tour with 2 dives kr39,900) go to Þingvellir's rift waters, which have astonishing 100m visibility.

➤ Every town has a geothermal public pool, and natural hot-pots abound.

➤ Whale watching is best from mid-May to September. Boats depart from Reykjavík, although northern Húsavík is renowned for whale watching.

➤ Northern Lights tours feature in winter, and flight tours cover the whole country.

CUSTOMS REGULATIONS

For regulations, see www.customs.is.

INTERNET ACCESS

Wi-fi is common at most sleeping and eating venues. Find computers for public internet access at libraries and tourist offices.

INTERNET RESOURCES

Icelandic Tourist Board (www.visiticeland.com) With links to regional websites.

Reykjavík Tourist Office (www.visitreykjavik.is)

ℹ️ SMARTPHONE APPS

There's an incredible range of smartphone apps. Useful ones include 112 Iceland app for safe travel, Veður (weather), and apps for bus companies such as Strætó and Reykjavík Excursions. The Reykjavík Appy Hour app gets special mention for listing happy hours and their prices!

MONEY

Credit cards are ubiquitous, but many transactions (such as purchasing petrol) require a PIN – get one before leaving home. ATMs take MasterCard, Visa, Cirrus, Maestro and Electron cards. VAT and service are included in marked prices. Tipping is not required. Spend over kr6000 in a single shop and claim a tax refund (see www.globalblue.com).

POST

Icelandic postal service (www.postur.is) is reliable. Postcards/letters to Europe cost kr180/310; to places outside Europe kr240/490.

TELEPHONE

Iceland's international access code is 📞 00, country code is 📞 354; no area codes. For international directory assistance and reverse-charge (collect) calls, dial 📞 1811. Mobile coverage is widespread. Visitors with GSM 900/1800 phones can make roaming calls. You can purchase a local SIM card (at grocery stores and petrol stations) if you're staying awhile and have an unlocked mobile.

TIME

Iceland's time zone is the same as GMT/UTC (London), but there is no daylight saving time.

ℹ️ Getting There & Away

AIR

Iceland is connected by year-round flights (including budget carriers) from Keflavík International Airport (KEF; www.kefairport.is), 48km southwest of Reykjavík, to a multitude of European destinations, as well as to the United States and Canada. Icelandair (www.icelandair.com) offers stopovers between the continents, and flights to Akureyri in the north.

Internal flights and those to Greenland and the Faroe Islands use the small Reykjavík Domestic Airport (REK; Reykjavíkurflugvöllur; www.reykjavikairport.is) in central Reykjavík.

SEA

Smyril Line (www.smyrilline.com) operates a weekly car ferry, the *Norröna*, from Hirsthals (Denmark) through Tórshavn (Faroe Islands) to Seyðisfjörður in East Iceland. Schedules vary; check online.

ℹ️ Getting Around

TO/FROM THE AIRPORT

Flybus (📞 580 5400; www.re.is; 📶), **Airport Express** (📞 540 1313; www.airportexpress.is; 📶) and public busline **Strætó** (p604) have buses connecting the airport with Reykjavík or the Blue Lagoon. Flybus and Airport Express offer pick-up/drop-off at many city accommodations (to bus station/hotel from kr2100/2700); Strætó is slightly cheaper (kr1680, to bus station only). Airport Express has a new connection between the airport and Akureyri.

ESSENTIAL FOOD & DRINK

Traditional Icelandic dishes These reflect a historical need to eat every scrap and make it last through winter. *Harðfiskur* (dried strips of haddock with butter), *plokkfiskur* (a hearty fish-and-potato gratin) and delicious, yoghurt-like *skyr* are tasty treats. Brave souls might try *svið* (singed sheep's head), *súrsaðir hrútspungar* (pickled ram's testicles) and *hárkarl* (fermented shark meat).

Succulent specialities Icelandic lamb is among the tastiest on the planet – sheep roam the mountains all summer, grazing on sweet grass and wild thyme. Also, superfresh fish dishes grace most menus. Reindeer meat from the eastern highlands is a high-end treat.

Whale-meat controversy Many restaurants serve whale meat, but 75% of Icelanders never buy whale meat. Tourists are responsible for consuming a significant proportion of these protected species. Similarly, puffins (also found on many menus) and the Greenland shark used in *hárkarl* are facing pressure. While we do not exclude restaurants that serve these meats from our listings, you can opt not to order it, or find whale-free spots at www.icewhale.is/whale-friendly-restaurants.

Favourite drinks The traditional alcoholic brew *brennivín* is schnapps made from potatoes and caraway seeds. It's fondly known as 'black death'. Craft beers are popular: look for brews by Kaldi, Borg Brugghús and Einstök. Coffee is a national institution.

Car-hire chains are at the airport – prebooking is highly recommended. Taxis are rarely used (since they cost about kr15,000 to Reykjavík).

AIR

Iceland has a network of domestic flights, which locals use almost like buses. In winter a flight can be the only way to get between destinations, but winter weather plays havoc with schedules. Note that almost all domestic flights depart from the small domestic airport in Reykjavík (not Keflavík International Airport). Check Air Iceland (Flugfélag Íslands; www.airiceland.is) and Eagle Air (www.eagleair.is).

BICYCLE

Cycling is a fantastic (and increasingly popular) way to see the country's landscapes, but be prepared for harsh conditions. Most buses accept bikes. Reykjavík Bike Tours (www.icelandbike.com) rents touring bikes; others rent bikes for local jaunts. Icelandic Mountain Bike Club (http://fjallahjolaklubburinn.is) links to the annually updated *Cycling Iceland* map.

BOAT

Several year-round ferries operate major routes:
➡ Landeyjahöfn–Vestmannaeyjar (www.herjolfur.is)
➡ Stykkishólmur–Brjánslækur (www.seatours.is)
➡ Dalvík–Hrísey/Grímsey (www.saefari.is)
➡ Arskógssandur–Hrísey (www.hrisey.net)

From June to August, Bolungarvík and Ísafjörður have regular boat services to Hornstrandir (Westfjords).

BUS

➡ Iceland has an extensive network of long-distance bus routes, operated by multiple companies. Many offer bus passes. The free *Public Transport in Iceland* map has an overview of routes – look for it in tourist offices and bus terminals, especially in Reykjavík.

➡ From roughly mid-May to mid-September regularly scheduled buses serve the Ring Rd, popular hiking areas of the southwest and larger Icelandic towns. The rest of the year, services range from daily to nonexistent.

➡ In summer, 4WD buses ply a few F roads (highland roads), including the Kjölur and Sprengisandur routes (inaccessible to 2WD cars).

➡ Many buses can be used as day tours (the bus spends a few hours at the final destination before returning, and may stop at various tourist destinations en route).

➡ Bus companies operate from different pick-up points. In Reykjavík, there are several bus terminals; in small towns buses usually stop at the main petrol station, but it pays to double-check.

Main bus companies:

Strætó (☑ 540 2700; www.bus.is, www.straeto.is)

Reykjavík Excursions (☑ 580 5400; www.re.is)

Sterna (☑ 551 1166; www.icelandbybus.is)

Trex (☑ 587 6000; www.trex.is)

SBA-Norðurleið (☑ 550 0700; www.sba.is)

CAR & CAMPERVAN

Renting a vehicle is expensive but extremely helpful, and gives unparalleled freedom to discover the country. Booking ahead is usually cheapest. The Ring Rd is almost entirely paved, but many backcountry areas are served by dirt tracks. Note that most rental cars are not allowed on highland (F) roads. To hire a car you must be at least 20 years old (23 to 25 years for a 4WD) and hold a valid licence. Campervans offer even more independence – Camper Iceland (www.campericeland.is) is just one of several outfits.

HITCHING

Hitching is never entirely safe and we don't recommend it. Travellers who hitch should understand that they are taking a small but potentially serious risk. In summer hitching is possible, but you may wait a long time in rural areas.

Ireland

Best Traditional Pubs

➡ Kyteler's Inn (p626)

➡ O'Connor's (p631)

➡ Crown Liquor Saloon

➡ Peadar O'Donnell's (p644)

➡ Crane Bar (p635)

Best Places to Eat

➡ Fade Street Social (p622)

➡ Market Lane (p629)

➡ Barking Dog (p639)

➡ Oscar's (p635)

Why Go?

Few countries have an image so plagued by cliché. From shamrocks and *shillelaghs* (Irish fighting sticks) to lepre-chauns and lovable rogues, there's a plethora of platitudes to wade through before you reach the real Ireland. But it's well worth looking beyond the tourist tat, for the Emerald Isle is one of Europe's gems, a scenic extravaganza of lakes, moun-tains, sea and sky. From picture-postcard County Kerry to the rugged coastline of Northern Ireland (part of the UK, distinct from the Republic of Ireland), there are countless opportuni-ties to get outdoors and explore, whether cycling the Cause-way Coast or hiking the hills of Killarney and Connemara.

There are cultural pleasures too in the land of Joyce and Yeats, U2 and the Undertones. Dublin, Cork and Belfast all have world-class art galleries and museums, while you can enjoy foot-stomping traditional music in the bars of Galway and Killarney. So push aside the shamrocks and experience the real Ireland.

When to Go
Dublin

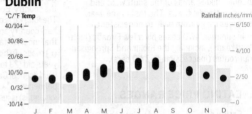

Late Mar Spring flowers every-where, landscape is greening, St Patrick's Day fes-tivities beckon.

Jun Best chance of dry weather, long summer eve-nings, Bloomsday in Dublin.

Sep–Oct Sum-mer crowds thin, autumn colours reign, surf's up on the west coast.

Map labels

ATLANTIC OCEAN

0 — 80 km
0 — 40 miles

Giant's Causeway ③
Carrick-a-Rede Island
Bushmills
Ballycastle
Troon
Lough Foyle
Coleraine
Cairnyan
Derry/Londonderry
Letterkenny
Glens of Antrim
A26
A6
Larne
North Channel
NORTHERN IRELAND
Newtownabbey
Douglas; Liverpool
Glencolumbcille
Slieve League ▲
N15
Donegal
Lower Lough Erne
Omagh
Lough Neagh
⑦ **Belfast**
Bundoran
Ballycastle
N59
Sligo
N26
Enniskillen
Newry
Mourne Mountains
Irish Sea
Lough Feeagh
Dundalk
Westport
N17
Longford
M1
Drogheda
Liverpool; Douglas
Connemara
Lough Corrib
Mullingar
Clifden
Galway ② Burren Village
Athlone
M6
M4
Dublin ①
Holyhead
The Curragh
N7
Dun Laoghaire ⑤
Aran Islands ⑧
The Burren
N18
Doolin
Cliffs of Moher
Portlaoise
Naas
Glendalough
Gleneely
Lugnaquilla Mountain ▲
M11
Wicklow Head
Ennis
Carlow
Donegal Point
M7
Limerick
Kilkenny
N9
Mouth of the Shannon
M8
Rock of Cashel
St George's Channel
N69
Dingle Peninsula
Tralee
N20
Clonmel
Wexford
Fishguard (Wales)
Gap of Dunloe ⑥
IRELAND
Waterford
Rosslare
Dingle
Carrantuohil
Killarney
Blarney
Cork
Caherciveen
N71
N22
④ Skellig Michael
Cobh
Ballinskelligs
Beara Peninsula
Kinsale
ATLANTIC OCEAN
Mizen Head Peninsula
Clear Island
Baltimore
Roscoff (France)
Cherbourg & Roscoff (France)

Ireland Highlights

① **Dublin** (p616)
Meandering through the museums, pubs and literary haunts of the Irish capital.

② **Galway** (p633) Hanging out in bohemian Galway, with its hip cafes and music venues.

③ **Giant's Causeway** (p642) Hiking along the Causeway Coast and clambering across the Giant's Causeway.

④ **Skellig Michael** (p631) Taking a boat trip to the 6th-century monastery.

⑤ **Irish Pubs** (p622) Sipping a pint while tapping your toes to a live music session in one of Dublin's traditional Irish pubs.

⑥ **Gap of Dunloe** (p630) Cycling through spectacular lake and mountain scenery.

⑦ **Titanic Belfast** (p638) Discovering the industrial history of the city that built the famous ocean liner.

⑧ **Aran Islands** (p643) Wandering the wild shores of the remote and craggy islands.

DUBLIN

POP 1,273,069

Sultry rather than sexy, Dublin exudes personality as only those who've managed to turn careworn into carefree can. The halcyon days of the Celtic Tiger (the Irish economic boom of the late 1990s), when cash cascaded like a free-flowing waterfall, have long since disappeared, and the city has once again been forced to grind out a living. But Dubliners still know how to enjoy life. They do so through music, art and literature – things which Dubs often take for granted but, once reminded, generate immense pride.

There are world-class museums, superb restaurants and the best range of entertainment available anywhere in Ireland – and that's not including the pub, the ubiquitous centre of the city's social life and an absolute must for any visitor. And should you wish to get away from it all, the city has a handful of seaside towns at its edges that make for wonderful day trips.

◉ Sights

Dublin's finest Georgian architecture, including its famed doorways, is found around **St Stephen's Green** (⊙dawn-dusk; 🚇all city centre, 🚌St Stephen's Green) and **Merrion Square** (⊙dawn-dusk; 🚇all city centre) just south of Trinity College; both are prime picnic spots when the sun shines.

The grand dame of Dublin thoroughfares is the imperially wide O'Connell St, a street that has played a central role in key episodes of Dublin's – and the nation's – history. None more so than the 1916 Easter Rising, when

---

BOOK OF KELLS

The world-famous *Book of Kells*, dating from around AD 800 and thus one of the oldest books in the world, was probably produced by monks at St Colmcille's Monastery on the remote island of Iona, Scotland. It contains the four gospels of the New Testament, written in Latin, as well as prefaces, summaries and other text. If it were merely words, the *Book of Kells* would simply be a very old book – it's the extensive and amazingly complex illustrations (the illuminations) that make it so wonderful. The superbly decorated opening initials are only part of the story, for the book has smaller illustrations between the lines.

---

the proclamation announcing Ireland's independence was read out to a slightly bemused crowd from the steps of the **General Post Office** (📞01-705 7000; www.anpost.ie; Lower O'Connell St; ⊙8am-8pm Mon-Sat; 🚇all city centre, 🚌Abbey).

★**Trinity College**　　HISTORIC BUILDING
(📞01-896 1000; www.tcd.ie; College Green; ⊙8am-10pm; 🚇all city centre) **FREE** Ireland's most prestigious university is a bucolic retreat in the heart of the city that puts one in mind of the great universities like Oxford, Cambridge or Harvard. Just ambling about its cobbled squares it's easy to imagine it in those far-off days when all good gentlemen (for they were only men) came equipped with a passion for philosophy and a love of empire. The student body is a lot more diverse these days, even if the look remains the same.

★**Long Room**　　NOTABLE BUILDING
(www.tcd.ie/visitors/book-of-kells; East Pavilion, Library Colonnades, Trinity College; adult/student/child €13/10/free; ⊙8.30am-5pm Mon-Sat, 9.30am-5pm Sun May-Sep, 9.30am-5pm Mon-Sat, noon-4.30pm Sun Oct-Apr; 🚇all city centre) Trinity's greatest treasures are kept in the **Old Library's** (www.tcd.ie; Library Sq; adult/student/family €11/9.50/22, fast-track adult/student/family €14/12/28; ⊙8.30am-5pm Mon-Sat, 9.30am-5pm Sun May-Sep, 9.30am-5pm Mon-Sat, noon-4.30pm Sun Oct-Apr; 🚇all city centre) stunning 65m Long Room, which houses about 200,000 of the library's oldest volumes. Included is the **Book of Kells**, a breathtaking, illuminated manuscript of the four Gospels of the New Testament, created around AD 800 by monks on the Scottish island of Iona. Other displays include a rare copy of the **Proclamation of the Irish Republic**, which was read out by Pádraig Pearse at the beginning of the 1916 Easter Rising.

Also here is the so-called harp of **Brian Ború**, which was definitely not in use when the army of this early Irish hero defeated the Danes at the Battle of Clontarf in 1014. It does, however, date from around 1400, making it one of the oldest harps in Ireland. Your entry ticket also includes admission to temporary exhibitions on display in the East Pavilion.

The Long Room gets very busy during the summer months, so it's recommended to go online and buy a fast-track ticket (adult/student/family €13/11/26), which gives timed admission to the exhibition and allows visitors to skip the queue. You'll still get only a

ITINERARIES

One Week
Spend a couple of days in **Dublin** ambling through the excellent national museums, and gorging yourself on Guinness and good company in Temple Bar. Get medieval in **Kilkenny** before heading on to **Cork** and discovering why they call it 'The Real Capital'. Head west for a day or two exploring the scenic **Ring of Kerry** and enchanting **Killarney**.

Two Weeks
Follow the one-week itinerary, then make your way north from Killarney to bohemian **Galway**. Using Galway as your base, explore the alluring **Aran Islands** and the hills of **Connemara**. Finally, head north to see the **Giant's Causeway** and experience the optimistic vibe in fast-changing **Belfast**.

fleeting moment with the *Book of Kells*, as the constant flow of viewers is hurried past.

⭐**National Museum of Ireland – Archaeology**   MUSEUM
(www.museum.ie; Kildare St; ⏰10am-5pm Tue-Sat, 2-5pm Sun; 🚌all city centre) FREE Ireland's most important cultural institution was established in 1877 as the primary repository of the nation's archaeological treasures. These include the most famous of Ireland's crafted artefacts, the **Ardagh Chalice** and the **Tara Brooch**, dating from the 12th and 8th centuries respectively. They are part of the **Treasury**, itself part of Europe's finest collection of Bronze and Iron Age gold artefacts, and the most complete assemblage of medieval Celtic metalwork in the world.

⭐**Guinness Storehouse**   BREWERY, MUSEUM
(www.guinness-storehouse.com; St James's Gate, South Market St; adult/student/child €18/16/6.50, connoisseur experience €48; ⏰9.30am-5pm Sep-Jun, to 6pm Jul & Aug; 🎧; 🚌21A, 51B, 78, 78A, 123 from Fleet St, 🚃James's) The most popular visit in town is this multimedia homage to Guinness, one of Ireland's most enduring symbols. A converted grain storehouse is the only part of the 26-hectare brewery that is open to the public, but it's a suitable cathedral in which to worship the black gold. Across its seven floors you'll discover everything about Guinness before getting to taste it in the top-floor **Gravity Bar**, with its panoramic views. Pre-booking your tickets online will save you money.

⭐**Chester Beatty Library**   MUSEUM
(📞01-407 0750; www.cbl.ie; Dublin Castle; ⏰10am-5pm Mon-Fri, 11am-5pm Sat, 1-5pm Sun year-round, closed Mon Nov-Feb, free tours 1pm Wed, 2pm Sat & 3pm Sun; 🚌all city centre) FREE This world-famous library, in the grounds of **Dublin Castle** (📞01-677 7129; www.dublincastle.ie; Dame St; guided tours adult/child €10/4; self-guided tour adult/child €7/3; ⏰9.45am-5.45pm, last admission 5.15pm; 🚌all city centre), houses the collection of mining engineer Sir Alfred Chester Beatty (1875–1968), bequeathed to the Irish State on his death. And we're immensely grateful for Chester's patronage: spread over two floors, the breathtaking collection includes more than 20,000 manuscripts, rare books, miniature paintings, clay tablets, costumes and other objects of artistic, historical and aesthetic importance.

⭐**Kilmainham Gaol**   MUSEUM
(📞01-453 2037; http://kilmainhamgaolmuseum.ie; Inchicore Rd; adult/child €8/4; ⏰9.30am-6.45pm Jul-Aug, to 5.30pm rest of year; 🚌69, 79 from Aston Quay, 13, 40 from O'Connell St) If you have *any* desire to understand Irish history – especially the juicy bits about resistance to British rule – then a visit to this former prison is an absolute must. This threatening grey building, built between 1792 and 1795, played a role in virtually every act of Ireland's painful path to independence, and even today, despite closing in 1924, it still has the power to chill.

⭐**National Gallery**   MUSEUM
(www.nationalgallery.ie; West Merrion Sq; ⏰9.15am-5.30pm Mon-Wed, Fri & Sat, to 8.30pm Thu, 11am-5.30pm Sun; 🚌4,7, 8, 46A from city centre) FREE A magnificent Caravaggio and a breathtaking collection of works by Jack B Yeats – William Butler's younger brother – are the main reasons to visit the National Gallery, but not the only ones. Its excellent collection is strong in Irish art, and there are also high-quality collections of every major European school of painting.

⭐**St Patrick's Cathedral**   CATHEDRAL
(www.stpatrickscathedral.ie; St Patrick's Close; adult/student/child €6.50/5.50/free; ⏰9.30am-5pm Mon-Fri, 9am-6pm Sat, 9-10.30am & 12.30-

Dublin

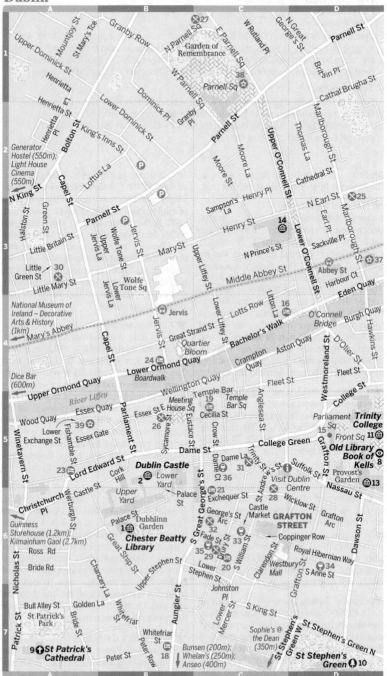

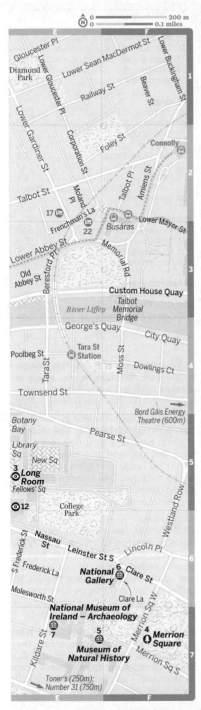

2.30pm Sun; 🚌 50, 50A, 56A from Aston Quay, 54, 54A from Burgh Quay) Ireland's largest church is St Patrick's Cathedral, built between 1191 and 1270 on the site of an earlier church that had stood here since the 5th century. It was here that St Patrick himself reputedly baptised the local Celtic chieftains, making this bit of ground some fairly sacred turf: the well in question is in the adjacent **St Patrick's Park**, which was once a slum but is now a lovely spot to sit and take a load off.

🛏 Sleeping

Hotel rooms in Dublin aren't as expensive as they were during the Celtic Tiger years, but demand is high and booking is highly recommended, especially if you want to stay in the city centre or within walking distance of it.

North of the Liffey

⭐**Isaacs Hostel** HOSTEL €
(📞01-855 6215; www.isaacs.ie; 2-5 Frenchman's Lane; dm/tw from €16/70; @🛜; 🚊 Connolly) The north side's best hostel – hell, for atmosphere alone it's the best in town – is in a 200-year-old wine vault just around the corner from the main bus station. With summer barbecues, live music in the lounge, internet access and colourful dorms, this terrific place generates consistently good reviews from backpackers and other travellers.

⭐**Generator Hostel** HOSTEL €
(📞01-901 0222; www.generatorhostels.com; Smithfield Sq; dm/tw from €16/70; @🛜; 🚊Smithfield) This European chain brings its own brand of funky, fun design to Dublin's hostel scene, with bright colours, comfortable dorms (including women-only) and a lively social scene. It even has a screening room for movies. Good location right on Smithfield Sq, next to the Old Jameson Distillery.

Abbey Court Hostel HOSTEL €
(📞01-878 0700; www.abbey-court.com; 29 Bachelor's Walk; dm/d from €16/80; 🛜; 🚊 all city centre) Spread over two buildings, this large, well-run hostel has 33 clean dorm beds with good storage. Its excellent facilities include a dining hall, a conservatory and a barbecue area. Doubles with bathrooms are in the newer building where a light breakfast is provided in the adjacent cafe. Not surprisingly, this is a popular spot; reservations are advised.

Anchor House B&B €€
(📞01-878 6913; www.anchorhousedublin.com; 49 Lower Gardiner St; r from €125; 🅿🛜; 🚊all city

Dublin

centre, ⎚ Connolly) While most B&Bs round these parts offer pretty much the same stuff – TV, half-decent shower, tea- and coffee-making facilities and wi-fi – the Anchor does all of that with a certain (frayed) elegance, and also has a friendliness the others can't easily match.

Morrison Hotel HOTEL €€€
(⏲ 01-887 2400; www.morrisonhotel.ie; Lower Ormond Quay; r from €260; P @ ⏳; ⎚ all city centre, ⎚ Jervis) Space-age funky design is the template at this hip hotel, recently taken over by the Hilton Doubletree group. King-size beds (with Serta mattresses), 40in LCD TVs, free wi-fi and Crabtree & Evelyn toiletries are just some of the hotel's offerings. Easily the northside's most luxurious address.

🏨 South of the Liffey

Avalon House HOSTEL €
(⏲ 01-475 0001; www.avalon-house.ie; 55 Aungier St; dm/s/d from €10/34/54; @ ⏳; ⎚ 15, 16, 16A, 16C, 19, 19A, 19C, 65, 65B, 83 & 122) One of the city's most popular hostels, welcoming Avalon House has pine floors, high ceilings and large, open fireplaces that create the ambience for a good spot of meet-the-backpack-

er lounging. Some of the cleverly designed rooms have mezzanine levels, which are great for families. Book well in advance.

Barnacles HOSTEL €
(⏲ 01-671 6277; www.barnacles.ie; 19 Lower Temple Lane; dm/d from €20/130; P ⏳; ⎚ all city centre) If you're here for a good time, not a long time, then this bustling Temple Bar hostel is the ideal spot to meet fellow revellers, and tap up the helpful and knowledgeable staff for the best places to cause mischief. Rooms are quieter at the back.

Kinlay House HOSTEL €
(⏲ 01-679 6644; www.kinlaydublin.ie; 2-12 Lord Edward St; dm/d from €20/90; ⏳; ⎚ all city centre) This former boarding house for boys has massive, mixed dormitories (for up to 24), and smaller rooms, including doubles. It's in Temple Bar, so it's occasionally raucous. Staff are friendly, and there are cooking facilities and a cafe. Breakfast is included.

Brooks Hotel HOTEL €€€
(⏲ 01-670 4000; www.brookshotel.ie; 59-62 Drury St; r from €200; P ✿ @ ⏳; ⎚ all cross-city, ⎚ St Stephen's Green) About 120m west of Grafton St, this small, plush place has an emphasis on familial, friendly service. The decor is

nouveau classic with high-veneer-panelled walls, decorative bookcases and old-fashioned sofas, while bedrooms are extremely comfortable and come fitted out in subtly coloured furnishings. The clincher though, is the king- and superking-size beds in all rooms, complete with...a pillow menu.

Central Hotel HOTEL €€
(☑01-679 7302; www.centralhoteldublin.com; 1-5 Exchequer St; r from €110; @ 🛜; ☐all city centre, 🚇St Stephen's Green) The rooms are a modern – if miniaturised – version of Edwardian luxury. Heavy velvet curtains and custom-made Irish furnishings (including beds with draped backboards) fit a little too snugly into the space afforded them, but they do lend a touch of class. Note that street-facing rooms can get a little noisy. Location-wise, the name says it all.

★**Number 31** GUESTHOUSE €€€
(☑01-676 5011; www.number31.ie; 31 Leeson Close; s/d €220/260; P 🛜; ☐all city centre) The city's most distinctive property is the former home of modernist architect Sam Stephenson, who successfully fused '60s style with 18th-century grace. Its 21 bedrooms are split between the retro coach house, with its coolly modern rooms, and the more elegant Georgian house, where rooms are individually furnished with tasteful French antiques and big comfortable beds. Breakfast included. Gourmet breakfasts with kippers, homemade breads and granola are served in the conservatory.

✖ Eating

The most concentrated restaurant area is Temple Bar but, apart from a handful of good places, the bulk of eateries offer bland, unimaginative fodder and cheap set menus for tourists. Better food and service can usually be found on either side of Grafton St, while the top-end restaurants are clustered around Merrion Sq and Fitzwilliam Sq. Fastfood chains dominate the northside, though some fine cafes and eateries are finally appearing there too.

✖ North of the Liffey

★**Oxmantown** CAFE €
(www.oxmantown.com; 16 Mary's Abbey, City Markets; sandwiches €5.50; ⊗7.30am-4pm Mon-Fri; 🚇Four Courts, Jervis) Delicious breakfasts and excellent sandwiches make this relatively new cafe one of the standout places

for daytime eating on the north side of the Liffey. Locally baked bread, coffee supplied by Cloud Nine (Dublin's only micro-roastery) and meats sourced from Irish farms are the ingredients, but it's the way it's all put together that makes it so worthwhile.

★**101 Talbot** MODERN IRISH €€
(www.101talbot.ie; 100-102 Talbot St; mains €18-24; ⊗noon-3pm & 5-11pm Tue-Sat; 🚇all city centre) This Dublin classic has expertly resisted every trendy wave and has been a stalwart of good Irish cooking since opening more than two decades ago. Its speciality is traditional meat-and-two-veg dinners, but with vague Mediterranean and even Middle Eastern influences: roast Wicklow venison with sweet potato, lentil and bacon cassoulet and a sensational Morccocan-style lamb tagine. Superb.

★**Chapter One** MODERN IRISH €€€
(☑01-873 2266; www.chapteronerestaurant.com; 18 N Parnell Sq; 2-course lunch €32.50, 4-course dinner €75; ⊗12.30-2pm Tue-Fri, 7.30-10.30pm Tue-Sat; 🚇3, 10, 11, 13, 16, 19, 22 from city centre) Flawless haute cuisine and a relaxed, welcoming atmosphere make this Michelin-starred restaurant in the basement of the Dublin Writers Museum our choice for best dinner experience in town. The food is French-inspired contemporary Irish, the menus change regularly and the service is top-notch. The three-course pretheatre menu (€37.50) is great if you're going to the **Gate** (www.gatetheatre.ie; 1 Cavendish Row) around the corner.

FREE THRILLS

Dublin is not a cheap city, but there are plenty of attractions that won't bust your budget.

Trinity College (p616) Wander the grounds at Dublin's oldest and most beautiful university.

National Museum of Archaeology (p617) Discover the world's finest collection of prehistoric gold artefacts.

Chester Beatty Library (p617) Explore the library with its collection of oriental and religious art.

National Gallery (p617) Gaze at Irish and European paintings.

St Stephen's Green (p616) Laze at the city's most picturesque public park.

ℹ DUBLIN PASS

If you're planning some heavy-duty sightseeing, you'll save a packet by investing in the **Dublin Pass** (www.dublinpass.com; adult/child 1 day €49/29, 3 day €79/49). It provides free entry to more than 30 attractions, including the Guinness Storehouse and Kilmainham Gaol, and you can also skip queues by presenting your card. It also includes free transfer to and from the airport on the Aircoach. Available from any Dublin Tourism office.

⋇ South of the Liffey

Cornucopia VEGETARIAN €
(www.cornucopia.ie; 19-20 Wicklow St; salads €5.50-10.95, mains €12.50-€13.95; ⊗8.30am-9pm Mon, 8.30am-10pm Tue-Sat, noon-9pm Sun; ⊿; ☐all city centre) Dublin's best-known vegetarian restaurant is this terrific eatery that serves wholesome salads, sandwiches and a selection of hot main courses from a daily changing menu. It's so popular it's recently expanded onto the 2nd floor.

Bunsen BURGERS €
(www.bunsen.ie; 22 Essex St E; burgers €7-10; ⊗noon-9.30pm Mon-Wed, noon-10.30pm Thu-Sat, 1-9.30pm Sun; ☐all city centre) The tagline says Straight Up Burgers, but Bunsen serves only the tastiest, most succulent lumps of prime beef cooked to perfection and served between two halves of a homemade bap. Want fries? You've a choice between skinny, chunky or sweet potato. Order the double at your peril. There are two other branches: on **Wexford Street** (36 Wexford St; ⊗noon-9.30pm Mon-Wed, noon-10.30pm Thu-Sat, 1-9.30pm Sun; ☐all city centre) and South Anne St.

Simon's Place CAFE €
(George's St Arcade, S Great George's St; sandwiches €5-6; ⊗8.30am-5pm Mon-Sat; ⊿; ☐all city centre) Simon's soup-and-sandwich joint is a city stalwart, impervious to the fluctuating fortunes of the world mostly because its doorstep sandwiches and wholesome vegetarian soups are delicious and affordable. As trustworthy cafes go, this is the real deal.

★ Fade Street Social MODERN IRISH €€
(⊿01-604 0066; www.fadestreetsocial.com; 4-6 Fade St; mains €18-32, tapas €5-12; ⊗12.30-10.30pm Mon-Fri, 5-10.30pm Sat & Sun; ☎; ☐all city centre) ⊘ Two eateries in one, courtesy of renowned chef Dylan McGrath: at the front, the buzzy tapas bar, which serves up gourmet bites from a beautiful open kitchen. At the back, the more muted restaurant specialises in Irish cuts of meat – from veal to rabbit – served with home grown, organic vegetables. There's a bar upstairs too. Reservations suggested.

Sophie's @ the Dean ITALIAN €€
(www.sophies.ie; 33 Harcourt St; mains €14-29; ⊗7am-midnight; ☐10, 11, 13, 14 or 15A, ⊟Harcourt) There's perhaps no better setting in all of Dublin – a top-floor glasshouse restaurant with superb views of the city – to enjoy this quirky take on Italian cuisine, where delicious pizzas come with non-traditional toppings (pulled pork with BBQ sauce?) and the 8oz fillet steak is done to perfection. A good spot for breakfast too.

Pichet FRENCH €€
(⊿01-677 1060; www.pichetrestaurant.ie; 15 Trinity St; mains €19-27; ⊗noon-3pm & 5-10pm Mon-Sat, 11am-4pm & 5-9pm Sun; ☐all city centre) Head chef Stephen Gibson (formerly of L'Ecrivain) delivers his version of modern French cuisine to this elongated dining room replete with blue leather chairs and lots of windows to stare out of. The result is pretty good indeed, the food excellent – we expected nothing less – and the service impeccable. Sit in the back for atmosphere.

🍷 Drinking & Nightlife

Temple Bar, Dublin's 'party district', is almost always packed with raucous stag (bachelor) and hen (bachelorette) parties, scantily clad girls and loud guys from Ohio wearing Guinness T-shirts. If you're looking to get smashed and hook up with someone from another country, there's no better place in Ireland. If that's not your style, there's plenty to enjoy beyond Temple Bar. In fact, most of the best old-fashioned pubs are outside the district.

★ Toner's PUB
(⊿01-676 3090; www.tonerspub.ie; 139 Lower Baggot St; ⊗10.30am-11.30pm Mon-Thu, to 12.30am Fri & Sat, 11.30am-11pm Sun; ☐7, 46 from city centre) Toner's, with its stone floors and antique snugs, has changed little over the years and is the closest thing you'll get to a country pub in the heart of the city. Next door, Toner's Yard is a comfortable outside space. The shelves and drawers are reminders that it once doubled as a grocery shop.

The writer Oliver St John Gogarty once brought WB Yeats here, after the upper-class poet – who lived just around the corner – decided he wanted to visit a pub. After a silent sherry in the noisy bar, Yeats turned to his friend and said, 'I have seen the pub, now please take me home.' We always suspected he was a little too precious for normal people, and he would probably be horrified by the good-natured business crowd making the racket these days too. His loss.

★ Grogan's Castle Lounge   PUB
(www.groganspub.ie; 15 S William St; ◷10.30am-11.30pm Mon-Thu, to 12.30am Fri & Sat, 12.30-11pm Sun; ⌨all city centre) This place, known simply as Grogan's (after the original owner), is a city-centre institution. It has long been a favourite haunt of Dublin's writers and painters, as well as others from the alternative bohemian set, who enjoy a fine Guinness while they wait for that inevitable moment when they're discovered.

★ No Name Bar   BAR
(3 Fade St; ◷12.30-11.30pm Sun-Wed, to 1am Thu, to 2.30am Fri & Sat; ⌨all city centre) A low-key entrance just next to the trendy French restaurant L'Gueuleton leads upstairs to one of the nicest bar spaces in town, consisting of three huge rooms in a restored Victorian townhouse plus a sizeable heated patio area for smokers. There's no sign or a name – folks just refer to it as the No Name Bar.

★ Anseo   BAR
(18 Lower Camden St; ◷10.30am-11.30pm Mon-Thu, to 12.30am Fri & Sat, 11am-11pm Sun; ⌨14, 15, 65 or 83) Unpretentious, unaffected and incredibly popular, this cosy alternative bar – which is pronounced 'an-*shuh*', the Irish for 'here' – is a favourite with those who live by the credo that to try too hard is far worse than not trying at all. The pub's soundtrack is an eclectic mix; you're as likely to hear Peggy Lee as Lee 'Scratch' Perry.

★ Kehoe's   PUB
(9 S Anne St; ◷10.30am-11.30pm Mon-Thu, to 12.30am Fri & Sat, noon-11pm Sun; ⌨all city centre) This is one of the most atmospheric pubs in the city centre and a favourite with all kinds of Dubliners. It has a beautiful Victorian bar, a wonderful snug, and plenty of other little nooks and crannies. Upstairs, drinks are served in what was once the publican's living room – and looks it!

Stag's Head   PUB
(www.louisfitzgerald.com/stagshead; 1 Dame Ct; ◷10.30am-1am Mon-Sat, to midnight Sun; ⌨all city centre) The Stag's Head was built in 1770, remodelled in 1895 and thankfully not changed a bit since then. It's a superb pub: so picturesque that it often appears in films, and also featured in a postage-stamp series on Irish bars. A bloody great pub, no doubt.

☆ Entertainment

For events, reviews and club listings, pick up a copy of the fortnightly music review *Hot Press* (www.hotpress.com), or for free cultural events, check out the weekly e-zine *Dublin Event Guide* (www.dublineventguide.com). Friday's *Irish Times* has a pull-out section called 'The Ticket' that has reviews and listings of all things arty.

Smock Alley Theatre   THEATRE
(☏01-677 0014; www.smockalley.com; 6-7 Exchange St) One of the city's most diverse theatres is hidden in this beautifully restored 17th-century building. It boasts a diverse program events (expect anything from opera to murder mystery nights, puppet shows and Shakespeare) and many events also come with a dinner option. The theatre was built in 1622 and was the only Theatre Royal to ever be built outside London. It's been reinvented as a warehouse and a Catholic church and was lovingly restored in 2012 to become a creative hub once again.

Whelan's   LIVE MUSIC
(☏01-478 0766; www.whelanslive.com; 25 Wexford St; ⌨16, 122 from city centre) Perhaps the city's most beloved live-music venue is this midsized room attached to a traditional bar. This is the singer-songwriter's spiritual home: when they're done pouring out the contents of their hearts on stage, you can find them filling up in the bar along with their fans.

Light House Cinema   CINEMA
(☏01-872 8006; www.lighthousecinema.ie; Smithfield Plaza; ⌨all city centre, ⊕Smithfield) The most impressive cinema in town is this snazzy four-screener in a stylish building just off Smithfield Plaza. The menu is strictly art house, and the cafe-bar on the ground floor is perfect for discussing the merits of German Expressionism.

Bord Gáis Energy Theatre   THEATRE
(☏01-677 7999; www.grandcanaltheatre.ie; Grand Canal Sq; ⊕Grand Canal Dock) Forget the uninviting sponsored name: Daniel Libeskind's masterful design is a three-tiered, 2100-capacity auditorium where you're as likely to be entertained by the Bolshoi or a touring state opera as you are to see *Disney on Ice* or

Barbra Streisand. It's a magnificent venue – designed for classical, paid for by the classics.

Abbey Theatre THEATRE
(☑ 01-878 7222; www.abbeytheatre.ie; Lower Abbey St; ⊟ all city centre, ⊟ Abbey) Ireland's national theatre was founded by WB Yeats in 1904 and was a central player in the development of a consciously native cultural identity. Its relevance has waned dramatically in recent decades but it still provides a mix of Irish classics (Synge, O'Casey etc), established international names (Shepard, Mamet) and contemporary talent (O'Rowe, Carr et al).

ⓘ Information

All Dublin tourist offices provide walk-in services only – no phone enquiries. For tourist information by phone call ☑ 1850 230 330 from within the Republic.

Grafton Medical Centre (☑ 01-671 2122; www.graftonmedical.ie; 34 Grafton St; ⊙ 8.30am-6pm Mon-Fri, 11am-2pm Sat; ⊟ all city centre) One-stop shop with male and female doctors and physiotherapists.

Hickey's Pharmacy (☑ 01-679 0467; 21 Grafton St; ⊙ 8.30am-8pm Mon-Wed & Fri, to 8.30pm Thu, 9am-7.30pm Sat, 10.30am-6pm Sun)

St James's Hospital (☑ 01-410 3000; www.st-james.ie; James's St; ⊟ James's) Dublin's main 24-hour accident and emergency department.

Visit Dublin Centre (www.visitdublin.com; 25 Suffolk St; ⊙ 9am-5.30pm Mon-Sat, 10.30am-3pm Sun; ⊟ all city centre) The main tourist information centre, with free maps, guides and itinerary planning, plus booking services for accommodation, attractions and events.

ⓘ Getting There & Away

AIR

Dublin Airport (p646), about 13km north of the city centre, is Ireland's major international gateway, with direct flights from Europe, North America and Asia. Budget airlines such as Ryanair and Flybe land here.

BOAT

There are direct ferries from Holyhead (Wales) to Dublin Port, 3km northeast of the city centre, and to Dun Laoghaire, 13km southeast. Boats also sail direct to Dublin Port from Liverpool and from Douglas, on the Isle of Man.

BUS

Dublin's main bus station Busáras (☑ 01-836 6111; www.buseireann.ie; Store St; ⊟ Connolly) (pronounced buh-saw-ras) is just north of the Liffey. **Aircoach** (www.aircoach.ie) operates a service from O'Connell St in the Dublin city centre, via Dublin Airport to Belfast.

Belfast €18.50, 2½ hours, hourly
Cork €16.50, 3¾ hours, six daily
Galway €15.50, 3¾ hours, hourly
Kilkenny €9.50, 1¾ hours, six daily
Rosslare Europort €19, 3½ hours, five daily
The private company Citylink (www.citylink.ie) has nonstop services from Dublin Airport (picking up in the city centre at Bachelor's Walk, near O'Connell Bridge) to Galway (€13, 2½ hours, hourly).

TRAIN

Connolly station is north of the Liffey, with trains to Belfast, Sligo and Rosslare. **Heuston station** is south of the Liffey and west of the city centre, with trains for Cork, Galway, Killarney, Limerick, and most other points to the south and west. Visit www.irishrail.ie for timetables and fares.

Belfast €38, 2¼ hours, eight daily
Cork €66, 2¾ hours, hourly
Galway €37, 2¾ hours, nine daily
Killarney €70, 3¼ hours, seven daily

ⓘ Getting Around

TO/FROM THE AIRPORT

Aircoach (www.aircoach.ie) Buses every 10 to 15 minutes between 6am and midnight, hourly from midnight until 6am (one way/return €7/12).

Airlink Express (☑ 01-873 4222; www.dublinbus.ie; one-way/return €10/6) Bus 747 runs every 10 to 20 minutes from 5.45am to 11.30pm between the airport, central bus station (Busáras) and the Dublin Bus office on Upper O'Connell St.

Taxi There is a taxi rank directly outside the arrivals concourse. It should take about 45 minutes to get into the city centre by taxi and cost about €25, including a supplementary charge of €3 (not applied when going to the airport).

BICYCLE

Rental rates begin at around €13/70 per day/week; you'll need a €50 to €200 cash deposit and photo ID.

Neill's Wheels (www.rentabikedublin.com; per day €15) Various outlets, including Avalon House and Isaacs Hostel.

Dublinbikes (www.dublinbikes.ie) A pay-as-you-go service similar to London's: cyclists purchase a Smart Card (€5 for three days, €20 for one year, plus a €150 credit-card deposit) either online or at any of more than 40 stations throughout the city centre, and bike use is then free for the first 30 minutes, increasing gradually thereafter (eg €3.50 for up to three hours).

PUBLIC TRANSPORT
Bus

Dublin Bus (www.dublinbus.ie) Local buses cost from €0.75 to €3.30 for a single journey. You must pay the exact fare when boarding;

drivers don't give change. The Freedom Pass (€33) allows three days' unlimited travel on all Dublin buses including Airlink and Dublin Bus hop-on/hop-off tour buses.

Train

Dublin Area Rapid Transport (DART; ☑ 01-836 6222; www.irishrail.ie) Provides quick rail access as far north as Howth and south to Bray; Pearse and Tara St stations are handy for central Dublin. Single fares cost €2.20 to €5.95; a one-day pass costs €11.70.

Tram

Luas (www.luas.ie) Runs on two (unconnected) lines; the green line runs from the eastern side of St Stephen's Green southeast to Sandyford, and the red line runs from Tallaght to Connolly station, with stops at Heuston station, the National Museum and Busáras. Single fares range from €2 to €3.30 depending on how many zones you travel through; a one-day pass is €7.

Taxi

Taxis in Dublin are expensive; flag fall costs €4, plus €1.25 per kilometre. For taxi service, call **National Radio Cabs** (☑01-677 2222; www.nrc.ie).

THE SOUTHEAST

Kilkenny

POP 24,400

Kilkenny (Cill Chainnigh) is the Ireland of many visitors' imaginations. Its majestic riverside castle, tangle of 17th-century passageways, rows of colourful, old-fashioned shopfronts and centuries-old pubs with traditional live music all have a timeless appeal, as does its splendid medieval cathedral. But Kilkenny is also famed for its contemporary restaurants and rich cultural life.

⊙ Sights

★**Kilkenny Castle** CASTLE
(☑ 056-770 4100; www.kilkennycastle.ie; The Parade; adult/child €8/4; ⊙9.30am-5.30pm Apr-Sep, to 5pm Mar, to 4.30pm Oct-Feb) Rising above the River Nore, Kilkenny Castle is one of Ireland's most visited heritage sites. Stronghold of the powerful Butler family, it has a history dating back to the 12th century, though much of its present look dates from Victorian times.

During the winter months (November to January) visits are by 40-minute guided tours only, which shift to self-guided February to October. Highlights include the Long

Gallery with its painted roof and carved marble fireplace. There's an excellent tea room in the former castle kitchens, all white marble and gleaming copper.

★**St Canice's Cathedral** CATHEDRAL
(☑056-776 4971; www.stcanicescathedral.ie; St Canice's Pl; cathedral €4, round tower €3, combined €6; ⊙9am-6pm Mon-Sat, 1-6pm Sun Jun-Aug, shorter hours Sep-May) Ireland's second-largest medieval cathedral (after St Patrick's in Dublin) has a long and fascinating history. The first monastery was built here in the 6th century by St Canice, Kilkenny's patron saint. The present structure dates from the 13th to 16th centuries, with extensive 19th-century reconstruction, its interior housing ancient grave slabs and the tombs of Kilkenny Castle's Butler dynasty. Outside stands a 30m-high round tower, one of only two in Ireland that you can climb.

National Craft Gallery GALLERY
(☑056-779 6147; www.nationalcraftgallery.ie; Castle Yard; ⊙10am-5.30pm Tue-Sun; ▲) FREE Contemporary Irish crafts are showcased at these imaginative galleries, set in former stables across the road from Kilkenny Castle, next to the shops of the **Kilkenny Design Centre** (☑056-772 2118; www.kilkennydesign.com; ⊙10am-7pm). Ceramics dominate, but exhibits often feature furniture, jewellery and weaving from the members of the Crafts Council of Ireland. Family days are held the third Saturday of every month, with a tour of the gallery and free hands-on workshops for children. For additional workshops and events, check the website.

✦ Festivals & Events

Kilkenny is rightly known as the festival capital of Ireland, with several world-class events throughout the year.

Kilkenny Arts Festival ART
(☑056-776 3663; www.kilkennyarts.ie; ⊙Aug; ▲) In August the city comes alive with theatre, cinema, music, literature, visual arts, children's events and street spectacles for 10 action-packed days.

Kilkenny Rhythm & Roots MUSIC
(☑056-776 3669; www.kilkennyroots.com; ⊙Apr/May) More than 30 pubs and other venues participate in hosting this major music festival in late April/early May, with an emphasis on country and 'old-time' American roots music.

🛏 Sleeping

Kilkenny Tourist Hostel   HOSTEL €
(📞 056-776 3541; www.kilkennyhostel.ie; 35 Parliament St; dm/tw from €17/42; @ 🛜) Inside an ivy-covered 1770s Georgian town house, this fairly standard, 60-bed IHH hostel has a sitting room warmed by an open fireplace, and a timber- and leadlight-panelled dining room adjoining the self-catering kitchen. Excellent location.

⭐ Rosquil House   GUESTHOUSE €€
(📞 056-772 1419; www.rosquilhouse.com; Castlecomer Rd; r from €95, 2-person apt from €80; 🅿 🛜) Rooms at this immaculately maintained guesthouse are decorated with darkwood furniture and pretty paisley fabrics, while the guest lounge is similarly tasteful with sink-into sofas, brass-framed mirrors and leafy plants. The breakfast is above average with home-made granola and fluffy omelettes. There's also a well equipped and comfortable self-catering apartment (minimum three-day stay).

Celtic House   B&B €€
(📞 056-776 2249; www.celtic-house-bandb.com; 18 Michael St; r €60-80; 🅿 @ 🛜) Artist and author Angela Byrne extends one of Ireland's warmest welcomes at this spick-and-span B&B. Some of the bright rooms have sky-lit bathrooms, others have views of the castle, and Angela's landscapes adorn many of the walls. Book ahead.

🍴 Eating

Gourmet Store   SANDWICHES €
(📞 056-777 1727; 56 High St; sandwich & coffee €5; ⏲ 8am-6pm Mon-Sat) In this crowded little deli, takeaway sandwiches are assembled from choice imported meats and cheeses (plus a few top-notch locals).

⭐ Foodworks   BISTRO, CAFE €€
(📞 056-777 7696; www.foodworks.ie; 7 Parliament St; lunch mains €14, 3-course dinner €30; ⏲ noon-4.30pm Sun-Wed, noon-9.30pm Thu-Sat; 🛜 ♿) 🍃 The owners of this cool and casual bistro keep their own pigs and grow their own salad leaves, so it would be churlish not to try their pork belly stuffed with black pudding, or confit pig's trotter – and you'll be glad you did. Delicious food, excellent coffee and friendly service make this a justifiably popular venue; best to book a table.

🍷 Drinking & Nightlife

⭐ Kyteler's Inn   PUB
(📞 056-772 1064; www.kytelersinn.com; 27 St Kieran's St; ⏲ 11am-midnight Sun-Thu, to 2am Fri & Sat) Dame Alice Kyteler's old house was built back in 1224 and has seen its share of history: she was charged with witchcraft in 1323. Today the rambling bar includes the original building, complete with vaulted ceiling and arches. There is a beer garden, a courtyard and a large upstairs room for the live bands (nightly March to October), ranging from trad to blues.

☆ Entertainment

Watergate Theatre   THEATRE
(📞 box office 056-776 1674; www.watergatetheatre. com; Parliament St) Kilkenny's top theatre venue hosts drama, comedy and musical performances. If you're wondering why intermission lasts 18 minutes, it's so patrons can nip into **John Cleere's pub** (📞 056-776 2573; www.cleeres.com; 22 Parliament St; ⏲ 11.30am-11.30pm Mon-Thu, to 12.30am Fri & Sat, 1-11pm Sun) for a pint.

ℹ Information

Kilkenny Tourist Office (📞 056-775 1500; www.visitkilkenny.ie; Rose Inn St; ⏲ 9am-6pm Mon-Sat, 10.30am-4pm Sun) Stocks guides and walking maps. Located in Shee Alms House, dating from 1582 and built in local stone by benefactor Sir Richard Shee to help the poor.

ℹ Getting There & Away

BUS

Buses depart from the train station. Services include Cork (€19, three hours, two daily) and Dublin (€9.50, 1¾ hours, six daily).

TRAIN

Kilkenny train station (Dublin Rd) is east of the town centre along John St, next to the MacDonagh Junction shopping mall. Services include Dublin Heuston (€26, 1¾ hours, eight daily) and Galway (€63, 3½ hours, two daily, change at Kildare).

THE SOUTHWEST

Cork

POP 119,230

Ireland's second city is first in every important respect, at least according to the locals, who cheerfully refer to it as the 'real capital of Ireland'. The compact city centre is surrounded by interesting waterways and is chock full of great restaurants fed by arguably the best foodie scene in the country.

◉ Sights

★ **English Market**   MARKET
(www.englishmarket.ie; main entrance Princes St; ⊙8am-6pm Mon-Sat) It could just as easily be called the Victorian Market for its ornate vaulted ceilings and columns, but the English Market is a true gem, no matter what you name it. Scores of vendors sell some of the region's very best local produce, meats, cheeses and takeaway food. On a sunny day, take your lunch to nearby Bishop Lucey Park, a popular al fresco eating spot.

Cork City Gaol   MUSEUM
(✆021-430 5022; www.corkcitygaol.com; Convent Ave; adult/child €8/5; ⊙9.30am-5pm Apr-Sep, 10am-4pm Oct-Mar) This imposing former prison is well worth a visit, if only to get a sense of how awful life was for prisoners a century ago. An audio tour guides you around the restored cells, which feature models of suffering prisoners and sadistic-looking guards. Take a bus to UCC – from there walk north along Mardyke Walk, cross the river and follow the signs uphill (10 minutes).

Crawford Municipal Art Gallery   GALLERY
(✆021-480 5042; www.crawfordartgallery.ie; Emmet Pl; ⊙10am-5pm Mon-Wed, Fri & Sat, to 8pm Thu) FREE Cork's public gallery houses a small but excellent permanent collection covering the 17th century through to the modern day. Highlights include works by Sir John Lavery, Jack B Yeats and Nathaniel Hone, and a room devoted to Irish women artists from 1886 to 1978 – don't miss the pieces by Mainie Jellet and Evie Hone.

🛏 Sleeping

Oscar's Hostel   HOSTEL €
(✆021-241 8380; www.oscarshostel.com; 111 Lower Glanmire Rd; dm €18-22, tw €50-55; 🛜) Small (32-bed) but stylish, this relatively new hostel is set on a busy street just 200m east of the train station and 15-minutes' walk from the city centre. Facilities are good, with a well-equipped modern kitchen, comfy common rooms and bike storage, though the bedrooms are basic.

Brú Bar & Hostel   HOSTEL €
(✆021-455 9667; www.bruhostel.com; 57 MacCurtain St; dm/tw incl breakfast from €17/50; @🛜)

WORTH A TRIP

ROCK OF CASHEL

The **Rock of Cashel** (www.heritageire land.ie; adult/child €8/4; ⊙9am-7pm early Jun–mid-Sep, to 5.30pm mid-Mar–early Jun & mid-Sep–mid-Oct, to 4.30pm mid-Oct–mid-Mar) is one of Ireland's most spectacular archaeological sites. A prominent green hill, banded with limestone outcrops, it rises from a grassy plain on the outskirts of Cashel town and bristles with ancient fortifications. For more than 1000 years it was a symbol of power, and the seat of kings and churchmen who ruled over the region. Sturdy walls circle an enclosure that contains a complete round tower, a roofless abbey and the finest 12th-century Romanesque chapel in Ireland.

Cashel Lodge & Camping Park (✆062-61003; www.cashel-lodge.com; Dundrum Rd; campsite per person €10, s/d from €55/85; P🛜) is a good place to stay, with terrific views of the Rock. Bus Éireann services run every two hours between Cashel and Cork (€15.70, 1¾ hours).

This buzzing hostel has its own internet cafe, with free access for guests, and a fantastic bar, popular with backpackers and locals alike. The dorms (each with a bathroom) have four to six beds and are both clean and stylish – ask for one on the upper floors to avoid bar noise. Breakfast is free.

★ **Garnish House**   B&B €€
(✆021-427 5111; www.garnish.ie; 18 Western Rd; s/d/tr/f from €92/103/119/134; P🛜) Attention is lavished upon guests at this award-winning B&B where the legendary breakfast menu (30 choices) ranges from fresh fish to French toast. Typical of the touches here is freshly cooked porridge, served with creamed honey and your choice of whiskey or Baileys; enjoy it out on the garden terrace. The 14 rooms are very comfortable; reception is open 24 hours.

★ **River Lee Hotel**   HOTEL €€€
(✆021-425 2700; www.doylecollection.com; Western Rd; r from €195; P🛜♨) This modern riverside hotel brings a touch of luxury to the city centre. It has gorgeous public areas with huge sofas, a designer fireplace, a stunning five-storey glass-walled atrium, and superb

Cork

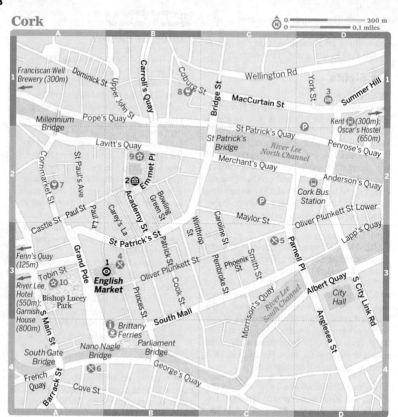

service. There are well-equipped bedrooms (nice and quiet at the back, but request a corner room for extra space) and possibly the best breakfast buffet in Ireland.

🍴 Eating

★ **Farmgate Cafe**   CAFE, BISTRO €
(☎ 021-427 8134; www.farmgate.ie; Princes St, English Market; mains €8-14; ☺ 8.30am-5pm Mon-Sat) 🍃 An unmissable experience at the heart of the English Market, the Farmgate is perched on a balcony overlooking the food stalls below, the source of all that fresh local produce on your plate – everything from crab and oysters to the lamb for an Irish stew. Up the stairs and turn left for table service, right for counter service.

Quay Co-op   VEGETARIAN €
(☎ 021-431 7026; www.quaycoop.com; 24 Sullivan's Quay; mains €5-11; ☺ 10am-9pm; 🍴 👶) 🍃 Flying the flag for alternative Cork, this cafete-

ria offers a range of self-service vegetarian dishes, all organic, including big breakfasts and rib-sticking soups and casseroles. It also caters for gluten-, dairy- and wheat-free needs, and is amazingly child-friendly.

★ **Market Lane**   IRISH, INTERNATIONAL €€
(☑ 021-427 4710; www.marketlane.ie; 5 Oliver Plunkett St; mains €11-27; ☺ noon-9.30pm Mon-Thu, noon-10.30pm Fri & Sat, 1-9.30pm Sun; 🕱 💺) 🍴 It's always hopping at this bright corner bistro. The menu is broad and hearty, changing to reflect what's fresh at the English Market: perhaps gamekeepers pie with celeriac bake, or mushroom and lentil pie with stout gravy? No reservations for fewer than six diners; sip a drink at the bar till a table is free. Lots of wines by the glass.

Fenn's Quay   MODERN IRISH €€
(☑ 021-427 9527; www.fennsquay.net; 5 Fenn's Quay; mains €12-24; ☺ 8.15-11.30am & noon-3pm Mon-Fri, 5-8pm Thu, 5-10pm Fri, 8.30am-3pm & 5-10pm Sat; 💺) 🍴 From breakfast (Rosscarbery black pudding with smoked Gubbeen cheese on home-baked toast) to lunch (spiced beef and pickle sandwiches or fresh fish platters) to dinner (collar of bacon with cabbage and walnuts), this hidden gem of a restaurant serves up the best of local produce, much of it from the English Market – 'Cork on a fork', as their tagline says.

🍷 **Drinking & Nightlife**

In Cork pubs, drink Guinness at your peril, even though Heineken now owns both of the local stout legends, Murphy's and Beamish (and closed down the latter's brewery). Cork's microbrewery, the Franciscan Well Brewery, makes quality beers, including Friar Weisse, popular in summer.

★ **Sin É**   PUB
(www.corkheritagepubs.com; 8 Coburg St; ☺ 12.30-11.30pm Mon-Thu, to 12.30am Fri & Sat, to 11pm Sun) You could easily while away an entire day at this great old place, which is every thing a craic-filled pub should be – long on atmosphere and short on pretension (Sin É means 'that's it!'). There's music most nights (regular sessions Tuesday at 9.30pm, Friday and Sunday at 6.30pm), much of it traditional, but with the odd surprise.

Franciscan Well Brewery   PUB
(www.franciscanwellbrewery.com; 14 North Mall; ☺ 1-11.30pm Mon-Thu, to 12.30am Fri & Sat, to 11pm Sun; 🕱) The copper vats gleaming behind the bar give the game away: the Franciscan

Well brews its own beer. The best place to enjoy it is in the enormous beer garden at the back. The pub holds regular beer festivals together with other small independent Irish breweries.

Rising Sons   MICROBREWERY
(☑ 021-241 1126; www.risingsonsbrewery.com; Cornmarket St; ☺ noon-late) This huge, warehouse-like, red-brick building houses Cork's newest microbrewery. The industrial decor of exposed brick, riveted iron and gleaming copper brewing vessels recalls American West Coast brewpubs. It turns out 50 kegs a week, some of them full of its lip-smacking trademark stout, Mi Daza, and has a food menu that extends as far as pizza, and no further.

⭐ **Entertainment**

Cork's cultural life is generally of a high calibre. To see what's happening grab *WhazOn?* (www.whazon.com), a free monthly booklet available from the tourist office, newsagencies, shops, hostels and B&Bs.

Cork Opera House   OPERA
(☑ 021-427 0022; www.corkoperahouse.ie; Emmet Pl; ☺ box office 10am-5.30pm Mon-Sat, to 7pm preshow, also 6-7pm Sun preshow) Given a modern makeover in the 1990s, this leading venue has been entertaining the city for more than 150 years with everything from opera and ballet to stand-up comedy and puppet shows. Around the back, the **Half Moon Theatre** presents contemporary theatre, dance, art and occasional club nights.

Triskel Arts Centre   ARTS CENTRE
(☑ 021-472 2022; www.triskelart.com; Tobin St; ☺ box office 10am-5pm Mon-Sat; 🕱) A fantastic cultural centre housed partly in a renovated church building – expect a varied program of live music, installation art, photography and theatre at this intimate venue. There's also a cinema (from 6.30pm) and a great cafe.

ℹ **Information**

Cork City Tourist Office (☑ 021-425 5100; www.discoverireland.ie/corkcity; Grand Pde; ☺ 9am-5pm Mon-Sat year-round, plus 10am-5pm Sun Jul & Aug) Souvenir shop and information desk. Sells Ordnance Survey maps.

ℹ **Getting There & Around**

BIKE

Cycle Scene (☑ 021-430 1183; www.cyclescene.ie; 396 Blarney St; per day/week from

€15/80) has bikes for hire from €15/80 per day/week.

BOAT

Brittany Ferries ([☎] 021-427 7801; www.brittanyferries.ie; 42 Grand Pde) sails to Roscoff (France) weekly from the end of March to October. The ferry terminal is at Ringaskiddy, about 15 minutes by car southeast of the city centre along the N28.

BUS

Aircoach ([☎] 01-844 7118; www.aircoach.ie) provides a direct service to Dublin city (€16) and Dublin Airport (€20) from St Patrick's Quay (three hours, hourly). **Cork bus station** (cnr Merchant's Quay & Parnell Pl) is east of the city centre. Services include Dublin (€16.50, 3¾ hours, six daily), Kilkenny (€15.70, three hours, five daily) and Killarney (€21, 1½ hours, hourly).

TRAIN

Cork's **Kent train station** ([☎] 021-450 6766) is across the river. Destinations include Dublin (€67, 2¼ hours, eight daily), Galway (€58, four to six hours, seven daily, two or three changes needed) and Killarney (€28, 1½ to two hours, nine daily).

Around Cork

Blarney Castle
CASTLE

([☎] 021-438 5252; www.blarneycastle.ie; adult/child €15/6; ⊙ 9am-7pm Mon-Sat, to 6pm Sun Jun-Aug, shorter hours Sep-May; [P]) If you need proof of the power of a good yarn, then join the queue to get into this 15th-century castle, one of Ireland's most popular tourist attractions. They're here, of course, to plant their lips on the **Blarney Stone**, which supposedly gives you the gift of the gab – a cliché that has entered every lexicon and tour route. Blarney is 8km northwest of Cork and buses run every half hour from Cork bus station (€7.80 return, 30 minutes).

Killarney

POP 14,220

Killarney is a well-oiled tourism machine set in a sublime landscape of lakes, forests and 1000m peaks. Its manufactured tweeness is renowned, the streets filled with tour-bus visitors shopping for soft-toy shamrocks and countless placards pointing to trad-music sessions. However, it has many charms beyond its proximity to lakes, waterfalls and woodland spreading beneath a skyline of 1000m-plus peaks. In a town that's been practising the tourism game for more than

250 years, competition keeps standards high, and visitors on all budgets can expect to find superb restaurants, great pubs and good accommodation.

◎ Sights & Activities

Most of Killarney's attractions are just outside the town. The mountain backdrop is part of **Killarney National Park** (www.killarneynationalpark.ie) **FREE**, which takes in beautiful Lough Leane, Muckross Lake and Upper Lake. Besides Ross Castle and Muckross House, the park also has much to explore by foot, bike or boat.

In summer the **Gap of Dunloe**, a gloriously scenic mountain pass squeezed between Purple Mountain and Carrauntouhill (at 1040m, Ireland's highest peak), is a tourist bottleneck. Rather than join the crowds taking pony-and-trap rides, **O'Connors Tours** ([☎] 064-663 0200; www.gapofdunloetours.com; 7 High St; ⊙ Mar-Oct) can arrange a bike and boat circuit (€15; highly recommended) or bus and boat tour (€30) taking in the Gap.

🛏 Sleeping

Súgán Hostel
HOSTEL €

([☎] 087 718 8237; www.suganhostelkillarney.com; Lewis Rd; dm/tw from €15/40; [🛜]) Behind its publike front, 250-year-old Súgán is an amiably eccentric hostel with an open fire in the cosy common room, low, crazy-cornered ceilings and hardwood floors. Check in at the next-door pub, a handy spot for a pint of Guinness once you're settled in.

★ Fleming's White Bridge Caravan & Camping Park
CAMPGROUND €

([☎] 064-663 1590; http://killarneycamping.com; White Bridge, Ballycasheen Rd; sites per vehicle plus 2 adults €26, hiker €10; ⊙ mid-Mar−Oct; [🛜]) A lovely, sheltered, family-run campsite about 2km southeast of the town centre off the N22, Fleming's has a games room, bike hire, campers' kitchen, laundry and free trout fishing on the river that runs alongside. Your man Hillary at reception can arrange bus, bike and boat tours, if he doesn't talk the legs off you first!

★ Crystal Springs
B&B €€

([☎] 064-663 3272; www.crystalspringsbandb.com; Ballycasheen Cross, Woodlawn Rd; s/d €75/115; [P][🛜]) The timber deck of this wonderfully relaxing B&B overhangs the River Flesk, where trout anglers can fish for free. Rooms are richly furnished with patterned wallpapers and walnut timber; private bathrooms (most with spa baths) are huge. The glass-enclosed breakfast room also overlooks the rushing river. It's about a 15-minute stroll into town.

Eating

Jam CAFE €
(☑064-663 7716; www.jam.ie; Old Market Lane; mains €4-11; ☺8am-5.30pm Mon-Sat, 9am-5pm Sun; 🖘) Duck down the alley to this local hideout for a changing menu of deli sandwiches, coffee and cake, and hot lunch dishes like shepherd's pie. It's all made with locally sourced produce and there are a few tables out front.

Smoke House STEAK, SEAFOOD €€
(☑064-663 9336; https://thesmokehouse.ie; 8 High St; mains €13-31; ☺5-10pm Mon-Fri, noon-10pm Sat & Sun) One of Killarney's busiest restaurants, this always-crowded bistro was the first establishment in Ireland to cook with a Josper (superhot Spanish charcoal oven). Stylish starters include old-school prawn cocktail, while the Kerry surf'n'turf platter – a half-lobster and fillet steak – is decadence on a plate. Weekend brunch, served from noon till 3pm, includes eggs Florentine and Benedict.

Mareena's Simply Food IRISH €€
(☑066-663 7787; www.mareenassimplyfood.com; East Avenue Rd; mains €19-29; ☺6-9pm Tue-Sun mid-Feb–Dec) The clue is in the name – Mareena's serves the finest of locally sourced produce, from scallops and sea bass to neck of lamb and pork fillet, cooked plainly and simply to let the quality of the food speak for itself. The decor matches the cuisine – unfussy and understated.

🍷 Drinking

★O'Connor's PUB
(http://oconnorstraditionalpub.com; 7 High St; ☺10.30am-11pm Mon-Thu, to 12.30am Fri & Sat, 12.30-11pm Sun) This tiny traditional pub with leaded-glass doors is one of Killarney's most popular haunts. Live music plays every night; good bar food is served daily in summer. In warmer weather, the crowds spill out onto the adjacent lane.

Courtney's PUB
(www.courtneysbar.com; 24 Plunkett St; ☺2-11.30pm Sun-Thu, to 12.30am Fri & Sat Jun-Sep, from 5pm Oct-May) Inconspicuous on the outside, inside this timeless pub bursts at the seams with Irish music sessions many

SKELLIG MICHAEL

Portmagee (an 80km drive west of Killarney) is the jumping-off point for an unforgettable experience: the Skellig Islands, two tiny rocks 12km off the coast. The vertiginous climb up uninhabited **Skellig Michael** inspires an awe that monks could have clung to life in the meagre beehive-shaped stone huts that cluster on the tiny patch of level land on top. From spring to late summer, weather permitting, boat trips run from Portmagee to Skellig Michael; the standard rate is around €60 per person, departing 10am and returning 3pm. Advance booking is essential; there are a dozen boat operators, including **Sea Quest** (☑087 236 2344; www.skelligs-rock.com; Skellig tour €75; ☺Skellig tour 9am mid-May–Sep).

nights year-round. This is where locals come to see their old mates perform and to kick off a night on the town.

ℹ Information

Tourist Office (☑064-663 1633; http://killarney.ie; Beech Rd; ☺9am-5pm Mon-Sat; 🖘) Can handle most queries, especially good with transport intricacies.

ℹ Getting There & Around

BUS
Operating from the bus station on Park Rd, Bus Éireann has regular services to Cork (€21, ½ hours, hourly), Galway via Tralee and Limerick (€28, 3¾ hours, four daily) and Rosslare Harbour (€29, six hours, three daily).

TAXI
Taxis can be found at the taxi rank on College St. A cab from the edge of town (eg Flesk campsite) into the town centre costs around €9 to €10.

TRAIN
Travelling by train to Cork (€28, 1½ to two hours, nine daily) or Dublin (€70, 3¼ hours, seven daily) sometimes involves changing at Mallow.

Ring of Kerry

The Ring of Kerry, a 179km circuit around the dramatic coastal scenery of the Iveragh Peninsula (pronounced eev-raa), is one of Ireland's premier tourist attractions. Most travellers tackle the Ring by bus on guided day trips from Killarney, but you could spend days wandering here.

The Ring is dotted with picturesque villages (Sneem and Portmagee are worth a stop), prehistoric sites (ask for a guide at Killarney tourist office) and spectacular viewpoints, notably at Beenarourke just west of Caherdaniel, and Ladies' View (between Kenmare and Killarney). The Ring of Skellig, at the end of the peninsula, has fine views of the Skellig Rocks and is not as busy as the main route. You can forgo driving completely by walking part of the 200km Kerry Way (www.kerryway.com), which winds through the Macgillycuddy's Reeks mountains past Carrauntuohill (1040m), Ireland's highest mountain.

◉ Sights

Kerry Bog Village Museum
MUSEUM

(www.kerrybogvillage.ie; Ballincleave, Glenbeigh; adult/child €6.50/4.50; ☉9am-6pm) This museum re-creates a 19th-century bog village, typical of the small communities that carved out a precarious living in the harsh environment of Ireland's ubiquitous peat bogs. You'll see the thatched homes of the turf-cutter, blacksmith, thatcher and labourer, as well as a dairy, and meet Kerry bog ponies (a native breed) and Irish wolfhounds. It's on the N70 between Killorglin and Glenbeigh; buy a ticket at the neighbouring Red Fox Inn if no one's at the gate.

Old Barracks Heritage Centre
MUSEUM

(☑066-401 0430; www.oldbarrackscahersiveen.com; Bridge St; adult/child €4/2; ☉10am-5.30pm Mon-Sat, 11am-5.30pm Sun) Established in response to the Fenian Rising of 1867, the Royal Irish Constabulary barracks at Caherciveen were built in an eccentric Bavarian-schloss style, complete with pointy turret and stepped gables. Burnt down in 1922 by anti-Treaty forces, the imposing building has been restored and now houses fascinating exhibitions on the Fenian Rising and the life and works of local hero Daniel O'Connell.

Derrynane National Historic Park
HISTORIC SITE

(☑066-947 5113; www.heritageireland.ie; Derrynane; adult/child €5/3; ☉10.30am-5.15pm mid-Mar–Sep, 10am-5pm Wed-Sun Nov–mid-Dec; ☞) Derrynane House was the home of Maurice 'Hunting Cap' O'Connell, a notorious local smuggler who grew rich on trade with France and Spain. He was the uncle of Daniel O'Connell, the 19th-century campaigner for Catholic emancipation, who grew up here in his uncle's care and inherited the property in 1825, when it became his private retreat. The house is furnished with O'Connell memorabilia, including the impressive triumphal chariot in which he lapped Dublin after his release from prison in 1844.

🛏 Sleeping & Eating

There are plenty of hostels and B&Bs along the Ring. It's wise to book ahead, though, as some places are closed out of season and others fill up quickly.

★ Mannix Point Camping & Caravan Park
CAMPGROUND €

(☑066-947 2806; www.campinginkerry.com; Mannix Point, Cahersiveen; hiker €8.50, vehicle plus 2 adults €26; ☉mid-Mar–mid-Oct; ☞) ✿ Mortimer Moriarty's award-winning waterfront campsite is one of Ireland's finest, with an inviting kitchen, campers' sitting room with peat fire (no TV but regular music sessions), a barbecue area and even a birdwatching platform. And the sunsets are stunning.

★ Smuggler's Inn
MODERN IRISH €€

(☑066-947 4330; www.the-smugglers-inn.com; Cliff Rd; d €95-150; ☉Apr-Oct; ☞) The Smuggler's Inn is a diamond find (it's hard to spot if you're coming from the north; head towards the golf course). Rooms are fresh and understated – try for room 15, with a glassed-in balcony overlooking Ballinskelligs Bay. Breakfasts, including a catch of the day, are cooked to order.

The inn also has a gourmet restaurant where owner/chef Henry Hunt's creations not only span seafood (including sensational chowder) but locally farmed poultry and meat, and elegant desserts.

Moorings
INN €€

(☑066-947 7108; www.moorings.ie; s/d/tr from €70/110/140; ☞) The Moorings is a friendly local hotel, bar and restaurant, with 16 rooms split between modern sea-view choices and simpler options, most refreshingly white. The nautical-themed restaurant (☑066-947 7108; www.moorings.ie; mains €22-26; ☉6-10pm Tue-Sun Mar-Oct; ☝) specialises in excellent seafood, while the Bridge Bar (☑066-947 7108; www.moorings.ie; ☉11am-11.30pm Mon-Sat, noon-11pm Sun) serves superb fish and chips.

QCs Seafood Restaurant & Bar SEAFOOD €€
(☑ 066-947 2244; http://qcbar.com; 3 Main St;
mains €16-26.50, bar food €9-15; ☺ kitchen 12.30-
2.30pm & 6-9.30pm Mon-Sat, 5-9pm Sun, bar
12.30pm-midnight Mon-Sat, 5pm-midnight Sun;
☎) QCs is a modern take on a classic pub
and as such is open pub hours for pints and
craic. But when the kitchen's open, some of
the finest food on the Ring pours forth (especially locally sourced seafood). Hours may
vary – it's best to call ahead and book a table. Upstairs are six boutique B&B bedrooms
(doubles from €109).

ⓘ Getting Around

Bus Éireann runs a once-daily Ring of Kerry bus
service (No 280) from late June to late August.
Buses leave Killarney at 11.30am and stop at
Killorglin, Glenbeigh, Cahersiveen (€16.60, 1½
hours), Waterville, Caherdaniel and Kenmare
(€22, 4½ hours), arriving back at Killarney at
4.45pm.

Travel agencies and hostels in Killarney offer
daily coach tours of the Ring for about €25 year-
round, lasting from 10.30am to 5pm.

THE WEST COAST

Galway

POP 75,600

Arty and bohemian, Galway (Gaillimh) is
legendary around the world for its entertainment scene. Students make up a quarter of the city's population and brightly
painted pubs heave with live music on any
given night. Here, street life is more important than sightseeing – cafes spill out onto
cobblestone streets filled with a frenzy of
fiddles, banjos, guitars and *bodhráns* (hand-
held goatskin drums), while jugglers, painters, puppeteers and magicians in outlandish
masks enchant passers-by.

⦿ Sights

★**Galway City Museum** MUSEUM
(www.galwaycitymuseum.ie; Spanish Parade House,
Merchant's Rd; ☺ 10am-5pm Tue-Sat year-round,
noon-5pm Sun Easter-Sep) **FREE** This modern
museum has exhibits on the city's history
from 1800 to 1950, including an iconic Galway Hooker fishing boat, a collection of *cur-
rachs* (boats made from animal hides) and
sections covering Galway and the Great War
and the city's cinematic connections.

WORTH A TRIP

CLIFFS OF MOHER

Star of a million tourist brochures, the
Cliffs of Moher in County Clare are one
of the most popular sights in Ireland.
But like many an ageing star, you have
to look beyond the famous facade to
appreciate its inherent attributes. In
summer the site is overrun with day
trippers, but there are good rewards if
you're willing to walk along the clifftops
for 10 minutes to escape the crowds.

The landscaped **Cliffs of Moher
Visitor Centre** (☑ 065-708 6141; www.
cliffsofmoher.ie; adult/child including parking €6/free, O'Brien's Tower €2/1; ☺ 9am-
9pm Jul & Aug, 9am-7.30pm Mon-Fri, to 8pm
Sat & Sun June & Sep, shorter hours rest of
year; ☎) has exhibitions about the cliffs
and their natural history. A number of
bus tours leave Galway every morning
for the Cliffs of Moher, including Burren
Wild Tours.

Also check out rotating displays of works
by local artists. The ground floor cafe, with
its Spanish Arch views, is a perfect rest stop.

★**Spanish Arch** HISTORIC SITE
The Spanish Arch is thought to be an extension of Galway's medieval city walls, designed to protect ships moored at the nearby
quay while they unloaded goods from Spain,
although it was partially destroyed by the
tsunami that followed the 1755 Lisbon earthquake. Today it reverberates to the beat of
bongo drums, and the lawns and riverside
form a gathering place for locals and visitors
on sunny days, as kayakers negotiate the tidal rapids of the River Corrib.

✯ Festivals

Galway International Arts Festival ART
(www.giaf.ie; ☺ mid-late Jul) A two-week extravaganza of theatre, music, art and comedy in
mid-July.

**Galway International Oyster
& Seafood Festival** FOOD, DRINK
(www.galwayoysterfest.com; ☺ late Sep) Going
strong for over 60 years, the world's oldest
oyster festival draws thousands of visitors in
late September.

IRELAND GALWAY

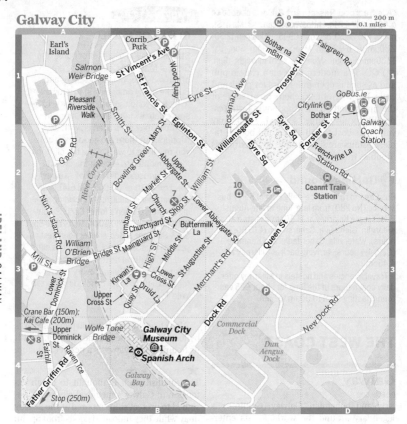

Galway City

🛏 Sleeping

★ Kinlay House
HOSTEL €

(📞091-565 244; www.kinlaygalway.ie; Merchant's Rd, Eyre Sq; dm/d €25/70; @ 🛜) Easygoing staff, a full range of facilities and a cream-in-the-doughnut location just off Eyre Sq make this a top choice, with four- to eight-bed dorms and doubles. Spanning two huge, brightly lit floors, amenities include a self-catering kitchen and a cosy TV lounge, with a pool table. Some rooms have bay views and newer beds have electric sockets and USB points.

Snoozles Tourist Hostel
HOSTEL €

(📞091-530 064; http://snoozleshostelgalway. ie; Forster St; dm/d/q from €17.50/90/117; @ 🛜) Dorms and private rooms all have bathrooms at this hostel west of Eyre Sq and not far from the train and bus stations. Continental breakfast is free and facilities include a barbecue terrace, pool table, lounge with PS2 and kitchen.

★**Stop**   B&B €€
(☑091-586736; www.thestopbandb.com; 38 Father Griffin Rd; s/d/tw/tr/f from €70/100/100/140/180; 🛜) Done up with funky artwork, fun colours and bare floorboards, this tremendous house pulls out all the stops. The owners keep things fresh as a daisy and neat as a pin with 11 shipshape but never dull rooms. Space – at a premium – is wisely used, so no wardrobes (just hangers), small work desk, no TV, but comfy beds. Brekkie is another forte.

★**Heron's Rest**   B&B €€
(☑091-539 574; www.theheronsrest.com; 16a Longwalk; d €140-160; 🛜) Ideally located in a lovely row of houses on the banks of the Corrib, the thoughtful hosts here give you deck chairs so you can sit outside and enjoy the scene. Other touches include holiday-friendly breakfast times (8am to 11am), decanters of port (enough for a glass or two) and more. Double-glazed rooms, all with water views, are small and cute.

✗ **Eating & Drinking**

★**McCambridge's**   CAFE, DELI €
(www.mccambridges.com; 38/39 Shop St; dishes €5-14; ⊘cafe 8.30am-5.30pm Mon-Wed, 8.30am-9pm Thu-Sat, 9.30am-6pm Sun, deli 8am-7pm Mon-Wed, 8am-9pm Thu-Sat, 9.30am-6pm Sun) The long-running food hall here has some superb prepared salads, hot foods and other more exotic treats. Create the perfect picnic or enjoy your pickings at the tables out front. All high ceilings, blond-wood and busy staff, the upstairs cafe is lovely with an ever-changing menu of modern Irish fare plus gourmet sandwiches, salads, silky soups and tip top coffee.

★**Kai Cafe**   CAFE €€
(☑091-526 003; http://kaicaferestaurant.com; 20 Sea Rd; mains lunch €11-12.50, dinner €18.50-26.50; ⊘cafe 9.30am-3pm Mon-Fri, 10.30am-3pm Sat, restaurant 6.30-10.30pm Tue-Sat; 🛜) This fantastic cafe on happening Sea Rd is a delight, whether for a coffee, portions of West Coast Crab or Roscommon hogget and glasses of Galway Hooker Sixty Knots IPA in a relaxed, casual, wholesome and rustic dining environment. Great at any time of the day, but reserve for din-dins.

★**Oscar's**   SEAFOOD €€
(☑091-582 180; www.oscarsseafoodbistro.com; Upper Dominick St; mains €15.50-25.50; ⊘6-9.30pm Mon-Sat) Galway's best seafood restaurant is just west of the tourist bustle. The long and ever-changing menu has a huge range of local specialities, from shellfish to white fish (which make some superb fish and chips), with some bold flavours. There's a two-course dinner menu from Monday to Thursday (€18.50) before 7pm.

★**Tigh Neachtain**   PUB
(www.tighneachtain.com; 17 Upper Cross St; ⊘11.30am-midnight Mon-Thu, 11.30am-1am Fri, 10.30am-1am Sat, 12.30-11.30pm Sun) Painted a bright cornflower blue, this 19th-century pub, known simply as Neáchtain's (*nock-tans*) or Naughtons, has a wraparound string of tables outside, many shaded by a large tree. It's a place where a polyglot mix of locals plop down and let the world pass them by – or stop and join them for a pint. Good lunches.

★**Crane Bar**   PUB
(www.thecranebar.com; 2 Sea Rd; ⊘10.30am-11.30pm Mon-Fri, 10.30am-12.30am Sat, 12.30pm-11pm Sun) This atmospheric old pub west of the Corrib is the best spot in Galway to catch an informal *céilidh* (traditional music and dancing) most nights. Talented bands play its rowdy, goodnatured upstairs bar; downstairs at times it seems straight out of *The Far Side*.

ℹ **Information**

Galway Tourist Office (☑091-537 700; www.discoverireland.ie; Forster St; ⊘9am-5pm Mon-Sat) Large, efficient regional information centre that can help arrange local accommodation and tours.

ℹ **Getting There & Around**

BIKE

On Yer Bike (☑091-563 393; http://onyourbikecycles.com; 42 Prospect Hill; bike rental per day from €20; ⊘9am-7pm Mon-Sat, noon-6pm Sun) Bike hire for €15/90 per day/week.

BUS

Bus Éireann Services depart from outside the train station. **Citylink** (www.citylink.ie; ticket office 17 Forster St; ⊘9am-6pm; 🛜) and **GoBus** (www.gobus.ie; Galway Coach Station; 🛜) use the **coach station** (New Coach Station; Fairgreen Rd) a block northeast. Citylink has buses to Clifden (€15, 1½ hours, five daily) and

Dublin (€15, 2½ hours, hourly). Bus Éireann runs buses to Killarney via Limerick (€28, 4½ hours, four daily).

TRAIN

Trains run to and from Dublin (€38, 2¾ hours, nine daily). You can connect with other trains at Athlone.

Aran Islands

The windswept Aran Islands are one of western Ireland's major attractions. As well as their rugged beauty – they are an extension of The Burren's limestone plateau – the Irish-speaking islands have some of the country's oldest Christian and pre-Christian ruins.

There are three main islands in the group, all inhabited year-round. Most visitors head for the long and narrow (14.5km by a maximum 4km) Inishmór (or Inishmore). The land slopes up from the relatively sheltered northern shores and plummets on the southern side into the raging Atlantic. Inishmaan and Inisheer are much smaller and receive far fewer visitors.

The tourist office (☎ 099-61263; www. aranislands.ie; Kilronan; ☺ 10am-5pm) operates year-round at Kilronan, the arrival point and major village of Inishmór. You can leave your luggage here and change money. Around the corner is a Spar supermarket with an ATM (many places do not accept credit cards).

Inishmór

Three spectacular forts stand guard over Inishmór, each believed to be around 2000 years old. Chief among them is Dún Aengus (Dún Aonghasa; www.heritageireland.ie; site adult/child €5/3, visitor centre €2/1; ☺ 9.30am-6pm Apr-Oct, to 4pm Nov-Mar), which has three massive drystone walls that run right up to sheer drops to the ocean below. It is protected by remarkable *chevaux de frise*, fearsome and densely packed defensive stone spikes. A small visitor centre has displays that put everything in context. A slightly strenuous 900m walkway wanders uphill to the fort itself.

Kilronan Hostel (☎ 099-61255; http:// kilronanhostel.com; Kilronan; dm from €30; ☺ late Feb-late Oct; @ 🛜), perched above Tí Joe Mac's pub, is a friendly hostel just a two-minute walk from the ferry. Kilmurvey House (☎ 099-61218; www.aranislands.ie/ kilmurvey-house/; Kilmurvey; s/d from €60/95; ☺ Apr–mid-Oct; 🛜) offers B&B in a grand 18th-century stone mansion on the path leading to Dún Aengus.

ⓘ Getting There & Away

AIR

Aer Arann Islands (☎ 091-593 034; http:// aerarannislands.ie; one-way/return €25/49) Offers return flights to each of the islands three to six times a day for adult/child €49/27; the flights take about 10 minutes, and groups of four or more can get group rates (€44 each adult). A connecting minibus from the Victoria Hotel in Galway costs €3 one-way.

BOAT

Aran Island Ferries (☎ 091-568 903; www. aranislandferries.com; one-way/return €13/25) Crossings can take up to one hour, subject to cancellation in high seas. Boats leave from Rossaveal, 40km west of Galway City on the

---

WORTH A TRIP

CONNEMARA

With its shimmering black lakes, pale mountains, lonely valleys and more than the occasional rainbow, Connemara in the northwestern corner of County Galway is one of the most gorgeous corners of Ireland. It's prime hillwalking country with plenty of wild terrain, none more so than the Twelve Bens, a ridge of rugged mountains that form part of Connemara National Park (www.connemaranationalpark.ie; off N59; ☺ 24hr) FREE .

Connemara's 'capital', Clifden (An Clochán), is an appealing Victorian-era country town with an oval of streets offering evocative strolls. Right in the centre of town is cheery Clifden Town Hostel (☎ 087 7769 345; http://clifdenbayhostel; 1 Market St; dm €17-23; ☺ reception 9am-5pm), while the gorgeous Dolphin Beach B&B (☎ 095-21204; www.dolphinbeachhouse.com; Lower Sky Rd; s/d from €90/130, dinner €40; 🅿🛜) 🍴 is 5km west of town.

From Galway, Lally Tours (☎ 091-562 905; http://lallytours.com; tours adult/child from €25/15) run day-long coach tours of Connemara.

OTHER IRISH PLACES WORTH A VISIT

Some other places in Ireland you might like to consider for day trips or longer visits:

Dingle (65km west of Killarney) The charms of this special spot have long drawn runaways from across the world, making this port town a surprisingly cosmopolitan and creative place. There are loads of cafes, bookshops and art-and-craft galleries, and a friendly dolphin called Fungie who has lived in the bay for 25 years.

Glendalough (50km south of Dublin) Nestled between two lakes, haunting Glendalough (Gleann dá Loch, meaning 'Valley of the Two Lakes') is one of the most significant monastic sites in Ireland and one of the loveliest spots in the country.

Kinsale (28km south of Cork) This picturesque yachting harbour is one of the many gems that dot the coastline of County Cork, and has been labelled the gourmet capital of Ireland; it certainly contains more than its fair share of international-standard restaurants.

Slieve League (120km southwest of Derry/Londonderry) The awe-inspiring cliffs at Slieve League, rising 300m above the Atlantic Ocean, are one of Ireland's top sights. Experienced hikers can spend a day walking along the top of the cliffs via the slightly terrifying One Man's Path to Malinbeg, near Glencolumbcille.

Sligo (140km north of Galway) William Butler Yeats (1865–1939) was born in Dublin and educated in London, but his poetry is infused with the landscapes, history and folklore of his mother's native Sligo (Sligeach). He returned many times and there are plentiful reminders of his presence in this sweet, sleepy town.

R336. Buses from Queen St in Galway (return adult/child €7/4) connect with most sailings; ask when you book.

Ferries to the Arans (primarily Inisheer) also operate from Doolin.

NORTHERN IRELAND

♪ 028

Dragged down for decades by the violence and uncertainty of the Troubles, Northern Ireland today is a nation rejuvenated. The 1998 Good Friday Agreement laid the groundwork for peace and raised hopes for the future, and since then this UK province has seen a huge influx of investment and redevelopment. Belfast has become a happening place with a famously wild nightlife, and the stunning Causeway Coast gets more and more visitors each year.

There are plenty of reminders of the Troubles – notably the 'peace lines' that divide Belfast – and the passions that have torn Northern Ireland apart over the decades still run deep. But despite occasional setbacks there is an atmosphere of determined optimism.

When you cross from the Republic into Northern Ireland you notice a couple of changes: the accent is different, the road signs are in miles, and the prices are in pounds sterling. But there's no border checkpoint, no guards, not even a sign to mark the crossing point – the two countries are in a customs union, so there's no passport control and no customs declarations. However, the UK's 2016 decision to leave the EU has introduced a note of uncertainty, and no one is quite sure what its long-term effect on the Ireland/Northern Ireland border will be.

Belfast

POP 280,900

Once lumped with Beirut, Baghdad and Bosnia as one of the four 'B's for travellers to avoid, Belfast has pulled off a remarkable transformation from bombs-and-bullets pariah to hip-hotels-and-hedonism party town. The old shipyards on the Lagan continue to give way to the luxury apartments of the Titanic Quarter, whose centrepiece is the stunning, star-shaped Titanic Belfast centre, the city's number-one tourist draw. New venues keep popping up – historic Crumlin Road Gaol and *SS Nomadic* have opened to the public, and WWI warship HMS *Caroline* is set to become a floating museum. They all add to a list of attractions that includes beautifully restored Victorian architecture, a glittering waterfront lined with modern art, a fantastic foodie scene and music-filled pubs.

The city centre is compact, and the imposing City Hall in Donegall Sq is the central landmark. The principal shopping district is north of the square. North again, around Donegall St and St Anne's Cathedral, is the bohemian Cathedral Quarter.

South of the square, the so-called Golden Mile stretches for 1km along Great Victoria St, Shaftesbury Sq and Botanic Ave to Queen's University and the leafy suburbs of South Belfast; this area has dozens of restaurants and bars, and most of the city's budget and midrange accommodation.

○ Sights

★ **Titanic Belfast**   MUSEUM
(www.titanicbelfast.com; Queen's Rd; adult/child £18/8; ⊙ 9am-7pm Jun-Aug, to 6pm Apr, May & Sep, 10am-5pm Oct-Mar; ⊡ Abercorn Basin) The head of the slipway where the *Titanic* was built is now occupied by the gleaming, angular edifice of Titanic Belfast, an unmissable multimedia extravaganza that charts the history of Belfast and the creation of the world's most famous ocean liner. Cleverly designed exhibits enlivened by historic images, animated projections and soundtracks chart Belfast's rise to turn-of-the-20th-century industrial superpower, followed by a high-tech ride through a noisy, smells-and-all re-creation of the city's shipyards.

★ **SS Nomadic**   HISTORIC SITE
(www.nomadicbelfast.com; Hamilton Dock, Queen's Rd; adult/child £7/5; ⊙ 9am-7pm Jun-Aug, to 6pm Apr, May & Sep, 10am-5pm Oct-Mar) Built in Belfast in 1911, the SS *Nomadic* is the last remaining vessel of the White Star Line. The little steamship ferried 1st- and 2nd-class passengers between Cherbourg Harbour and the ocean liners that were too big to dock at the French port. On 10 April 1912 it delivered 172 passengers to the ill-fated *Titanic*. First-come, first-served guided tours run every 30 minutes from 10am until an hour before closing. Alternatively, you're free to roam at will (don't miss the 1st-class toilets!).

★ **Ulster Museum**   MUSEUM
(www.nmni.com; Botanic Gardens; ⊙ 10am-5pm Tue-Sun; ♿; ⊡ Botanic) **FREE** You could spend hours browsing this state-of-the-art museum, but if you're pressed for time don't miss the **Armada Room**, with artefacts retrieved from the 1588 wreck of the Spanish galleon *Girona;* the **Egyptian Room**, with Princess Takabuti, a 2500-year-old Egyptian mummy unwrapped in Belfast in 1835; and the **Early Peoples Gallery**, with the bronze Bann Disc, a superb example of Celtic design from the Iron Age.

Free tours (10 people maximum; first-come, first served) run at 2.30pm Tuesday to Friday and 1.30pm Sunday.

★ **Crown Liquor Saloon**   HISTORIC BUILDING
(www.nationaltrust.org.uk/the-crown-bar; 46 Great Victoria St; ⊙ 11.30am-11pm Mon-Sat, 12.30-10pm Sun; ⊡ Europa Bus Centre) **FREE** There are not too many historical monuments that you can enjoy while savouring a pint of beer, but the National Trust's Crown Liquor Saloon is one of them. Belfast's most famous bar was refurbished by Patrick Flanagan in the late 19th century and displays Victorian decorative flamboyance at its best (he was looking to pull in a posh clientele from the newfangled train station and Grand Opera House across the street).

West Belfast   HISTORIC SITE
(⊡ Falls Rd) Though scarred by three decades of civil unrest, the former battleground of West Belfast is one of the most compelling places to visit in Northern Ireland. Falls Rd and Shankill Rd are adorned with famous **murals** expressing local political and religious passions, and divided by the infamous **Peace Line** (⊡ Falls Rd) barrier separating Catholic and Protestant districts. Take a taxi tour of the district, or pick up a map from the tourist office and explore on foot.

✦ Festivals & Events

Féile An Phobail   CULTURAL
(West Belfast Festival; www.feilebelfast.com; ⊙ early Aug) Said to be the largest community festival in Ireland, the Féile takes place in West Belfast over 10 days. Events include an opening carnival parade, street parties, theatre performances, concerts and historical tours of the City and Milltown cemeteries.

ⓘ BELFAST VISITOR PASS

The Belfast Visitor Pass (one/two/three days £6.50/11/14.50) allows unlimited travel on bus and train services in Belfast and around, and discounts on admission to **Titanic Belfast** and other attractions. You can buy it at airports, main train and bus stations, the Metro kiosk on Donegall Sq and the **Visit Belfast Welcome Centre** (p641).

BELFAST CITY TOURS

Many operators, including **Harpers** (www.harpertaxitours.com; from £30) and **Paddy Campbell's** (☑07990 955227; www.belfastblackcabtours.co.uk; tour per 1-3 people £30), offer guided taxi tours of West Belfast, with an even-handed account of the Troubles. They run daily for around £10 per person based on a group of three to six, or £30 total for one or two, and pick-up can be arranged.

There are a number of walking tours available, including the three-hour **Belfast Pub Crawl** (☑07731 977774; www.belfastcrawl.com; per person £10; ⊙8.30pm Fri & Sat; ▣Queen's Sq), taking in four of the city's historic pubs, and the three-hour **Titanic Tour** (☑028-9065 9971; www.titanictours-belfast.co.uk; ½ day tour £25 per person), visiting various *Titanic* sites.

Belfast International
Arts Festival   PERFORMING ARTS
(www.belfastinternationalartsfestival.com; ⊙mid-late Oct) The UK's second-largest arts festival stretches over two weeks and features theatre, music, dance and talks.

🛏 Sleeping

Many B&Bs are concentrated in the pleasant university district of South Belfast, which is well stocked with restaurants and pubs.

★**Vagabonds**   HOSTEL €
(☑028-9023 3017; www.vagabondsbelfast.com; 9 University Rd; dm £15-17, d & tw £50; @🤶; ▣Shaftesbury Sq) Comfy bunks, lockable luggage baskets, private shower cubicles and a relaxed atmosphere are what you get at one of Belfast's best hostels, run by a couple of experienced travellers. It's conveniently located close to both Queen's and the city centre.

Tara Lodge   GUESTHOUSE €€
(☑028-9059 0900; www.taralodge.com; 36 Cromwell Rd; s/d from £75/85; P@🤶; ▣Upper Crescent Queens University) In a great location on a quiet side street just a few paces from the buzz of Botanic Ave, this B&B feels more like a boutique hotel with its clean-cut, minimalist decor, friendly and efficient staff, and 24 bright and cheerful rooms. Delicious breakfasts include porridge with Bushmills whiskey.

Old Rectory   B&B €€
(☑028-9066 7882; www.anoldrectory.co.uk; 148 Malone Rd; s/d/f from £52/80/132; P@🤶; ▣Myrtlefield Pk) A lovely Victorian villa with lots of original stained glass, this former rectory has five spacious bedrooms, a comfortable drawing room with leather sofa and fancy breakfasts (home-baked bread, homemade Irish-whiskey marmalade, scrambled eggs with smoked salmon, veggie fry-ups, freshly squeezed OJ). A credit card is required to secure your booking but payment is in cash only.

The inconspicuous driveway is on the left, just past Deramore Park S.

🍴 Eating

There are lots of inexpensive eating places along Botanic Ave in South Belfast, and many pubs offer good-value meals.

Maggie May's   CAFE €
(☑028-9032 2662; www.maggiemaysbelfastcafe.co.uk; 50 Botanic Ave; mains £4.50-7.50; ⊙8am-11pm Mon-Sat, 9am-11pm Sun; 🥢👶; ▣Botanic) This is a classic little cafe with cosy wooden booths, murals of old Belfast and a host of hungover students wolfing down huge Ulster fry-ups. The all-day breakfast menu includes French toast and maple syrup, while lunch can be soup and a sandwich or beef lasagne. BYO.

There's a newer branch in **Stranmillis** (☑028-9066 8515; www.maggiemaysbelfastcafe.co.uk; 2 Malone Rd; mains £4.50-7.50; ⊙8am-11pm Mon-Sat, 9am-11pm Sun; ▣Methodist College).

★**Barking Dog**   BISTRO €€
(☑028-9066 1885; www.barkingdogbelfast.com; 33-35 Malone Rd; mains £16-30 tapas 5 dishes £15.50; ⊙noon-2.30pm & 5-10pm Mon-Thu, to 11pm Fri & Sat, noon-4pm & 5-9pm Sun; 🥢👶; ▣Eglantine Ave) Chunky hardwood, bare brick, candlelight and quirky design create the atmosphere of a stylishly restored farmhouse. The menu completes the feeling of cosiness and comfort with simple but sensational dishes such as their signature burger of meltingly tender beef shin with caramelised onion and horseradish cream, and sweet-potato ravioli with carrot and parmesan crisps. It has superb service, too.

Belfast

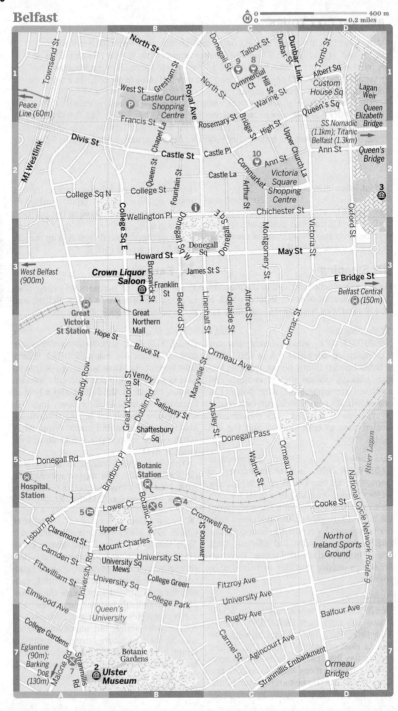

0 _____ 400 m
0 _____ 0.2 miles

Townsend St

North St

West St

Castle Court Shopping Centre

Gresham St

Royal Ave

North St

Donegall St

Talbot St

Dunbar St

Dunbar Link

Tomb St

Albert Sq

Custom House Sq

Lagan Weir

Queen Elizabeth Bridge

Peace Line (60m)

Francis St

Chapel La

Commercial Ct

Waring St

Queen's Sq

SS Nomadic (1.1km); Titanic Belfast (1.3km)

Queen's Bridge

M1 Westlink

Divis St

Castle St

Castle Pl

Rosemary St

Bridge St

High St

Upper Church La

Ann St

Queen's St

Fountain St

Castle La

Cornmarket

Arthur St

Victoria Square Shopping Centre

Oxford St

3

College Sq N

College St

Wellington Pl

Donegall Sq E

Chichester St

Victoria St

College Sq E

Donegall Sq W

Donegall Sq

Montgomery St

May St

West Belfast (900m)

Howard St

James St S

E Bridge St

Crown Liquor Saloon

Brunswick St

Franklin St

Bedford St

Linenhall St

Adelaide St

Alfred St

Cromac St

Belfast Central (150m)

1

Great Victoria St Station

Great Northern Mall

Hope St

Bruce St

Ormeau Ave

Sandy Row

Ventry St

Dublin Rd

Salisbury St

Maryville St

Apsley St

Ormeau Rd

River Lagan

Shaftesbury Sq

Donegall Pass

Walnut St

National Cycle Network Route 9

Donegall Rd

Bradbury Pl

Great Victoria St

Botanic Station

Cooke St

Hospital Station

Lower Cr

Botanic Ave

6

4

Cromwell Rd

North of Ireland Sports Ground

5

Lisburn Rd

Claremont St

Upper Cr

Mount Charles

Lawrence St

Camden St

University Rd

University St

Fitzwilliam St

University Sq Mews

University Sq

College Green

Fitzroy Ave

University Ave

Rugby Ave

Balfour Ave

Elmwood Ave

College Park

Carmel St

Agincourt Ave

College Gardens

Queen's University

Stranmillis Embankment

Ormeau Bridge

Eglantine (90m); Barking Dog (130m)

Malone Rd

Stranmillis Rd

7

Botanic Gardens

2 Ulster Museum

9

8

10

5

7

Belfast

★**Holohan's at the Barge**   MODERN IRISH €€
(☑028-9023 5973; www.holohansatthebarge.
co.uk; Belfast Barge, Lanyon Quay; mains lunch
£5-9, dinner £15-22; ☺5-11pm Tue-Sat, 1-7pm Sun;
🚇Oxford St) Aboard the **Belfast Barge** (www.
facebook.com/TheBelfastBarge; Lanyon Quay;
☺10am-4pm Tue-Sat; 🚇Oxford St) FREE, Holohan's is a sensational find for inspired twists
on seafood (seared scallops with burnt cauliflower purée; roast hake with crayfish and
dulse butter), as well as land-based dishes
such as salt-aged beef with heirloom vegetables, desserts such as plum and ginger
cake with vanilla ice cream, and by-the-glass
wines from around the world.

🍷 Drinking & Nightlife

Belfast's pub scene is lively and friendly, with
the older traditional pubs complemented by
a rising tide of stylish designer bars.

★**Duke of York**   PUB
(☑028-9024 1062; www.dukeofyorkbelfast.com;
11 Commercial Ct; ☺11.30am-midnight Mon, to
1am Tue-Sat, 1-9pm Sun; 🚇Queen's Sq) Down
an inconspicuous alley in the heart of the
city's former newspaper district, the snug,
traditional Duke was a hang-out for print
workers and journalists. Sinn Féin leader
Gerry Adams worked behind the bar here
during his student days in 1971. The entire
alley takes on a street-party atmosphere in
warm weather.

★**Eglantine**   PUB
(www.eglantinebar.com; 32 Malone Rd;
☺11.30am-midnight Sun-Tue, to 1am Wed-Sat; 🛜;
🚇Eglantine Ave) The 'Eg' is a local institution,
and widely reckoned to be the best of Belfast's many student pubs. It serves good beer
and good food, and hosts numerous events:
Monday is quiz night, Tuesday is open-mic
night; other nights see DJs spin and bands
perform. Bonus: Pac-Man machine.

★**Love & Death Inc**   COCKTAIL BAR
(www.loveanddeathinc.com; 10a Ann St; ☺4pm-
1am Mon-Thu, noon-3am Fri-Sat, 2pm-midnight
Sun) More like a cool inner-city house party,
speakeasy-style Love & Death Inc is secreted
up a flight of stairs above a pizza joint. Its
living-room-style bar has outrageous decor,
feisty Latin American–influenced food, feist-
ier cocktails and a wild nightclub in the attic
on weekends.

ℹ Information

Visit Belfast Welcome Centre (☑028-9024
6609; http://visit-belfast.com; 9 Donegall Sq
N; ☺9am-7pm Mon-Sat, 11am-4pm Sun Jun-
Sep, 9am-5.30pm Mon-Sat, 11am-4pm Sun
Oct-May; 🛜; 🚇Donegall Sq) Provides information about the whole of Northern Ireland and
books accommodation. Services include left
luggage (not overnight), currency exchange and
free wi-fi.

ℹ Getting There & Away

AIR

Belfast International Airport (p646) is 30km
northwest of the city, and has flights from the
UK, Europe and the USA. George Best Belfast
City Airport (p646) is 6km northeast of
the city centre, with flights from the UK and
Europe.

BOAT

Stena Line ferries to Belfast from Cairnryan and
Liverpool dock at Victoria Terminal, 5km north of
the city centre; exit the M2 motorway at junction
1. Ferries from the Isle of Man arrive at Albert
Quay, 2km north of the centre.

Other car ferries to and from Scotland dock at
Larne, 37km north of Belfast.

BUS

Europa Bus Centre, Belfast's main bus station,
is behind the Europa Hotel and next door to
Great Victoria St train station; it's reached via
the Great Northern Mall beside the hotel. It's the
main terminus for buses to Derry, Dublin and
destinations in the west and south of Northern
Ireland.

Ballycastle £12, 2¼ hours, four daily on week-days, two on Saturday, change at Ballymena

Derry £12, 1¾ hours, half-hourly

Dublin £15, 2½ hours, hourly

Aircoach (www.aircoach.ie) operates a service from Glengall St, near Europa Bus Centre, to Dublin city centre and Dublin Airport.

TRAIN

Belfast has two main train stations: Great Victoria St, next to the Europa Bus Centre, and Belfast Central, east of the city centre. If you arrive by train at Central Station, your rail ticket entitles you to a free bus ride into the city centre. A local train also connects with Great Victoria St.

Derry £12, 2¼ hours, seven or eight daily

Dublin £30, 2¼ hours, eight daily Monday to Saturday, five on Sunday

Larne Harbour £7.20, one hour, hourly

❶ Getting Around

BIKE

Belfast Bike Tours (☑ 07812 114235; www.bel-fastbiketours.com; per person £15; ☉ 10.30am & 2pm Mon, Wed, Fri & Sat Apr-Aug, Sat only Sep-Mar; ☒ Queen's University) hires out bikes for £15 per day. Credit-card deposit and photo ID are required.

BUS

A short trip on a city bus costs £1.50 to £2.30; a one-day ticket costs £3.90. Most local bus services depart from Donegall Sq, near the City Hall, where there's a ticket kiosk; otherwise, buy a ticket from the driver.

The Causeway Coast

Ireland isn't short of scenic coastlines, but the **Causeway Coast** between Portstewart and Ballycastle – climaxing in the spectacular rock formations of the Giant's Causeway – and the **Antrim Coast** between Ballycastle and Belfast, are as magnificent as they come.

From April to September the **Ulsterbus** (☑ 028-9066 6630; www.translink.co.uk) Antrim Coaster (bus 252) links Larne with Coleraine (£12, four hours, two daily) via the Glens of

GAME OF THRONES TOURS

If you're driving around Northern Ireland, there are *Game of Thrones* filming locations aplenty – visit www.discover-northernireland.com/gameofthrones. Alternatively, day-long bus tours depart from Belfast.

Antrim, Ballycastle, the Giant's Causeway, Bushmills, Portrush and Portstewart.

From Easter to September the Causeway Rambler (bus 402) links Coleraine and Carrick-a-Rede (£6.50, 40 minutes, seven daily) via Bushmills Distillery, the Giant's Causeway, White Park Bay and Ballintoy. The ticket allows unlimited travel in both directions for one day.

There are several hostels along the coast, including **Sheep Island View Hostel** (☑ 028-2076 9391; www.sheepislandview.com; 42a Main St; dm/s/tw £18/25/45; ⓟⓐ🐾), **Ballycastle Backpackers** (☑ 028-2076 3612; www.ballycastlebackpackers.net; 4 North St; dm/tw from £17.50/35, cottage £80; ⓟⓐ🐾) and **Bushmills Youth Hostel** (☑ 028-2073 1222; www.hini.org.uk; 49 Main St; dm £16-20, tr £53; ☉ closed 11.30am-2.30pm Jul & Aug, 11.30am-5pm Mar-Jun, Sep & Oct; ⓐ🐾).

⦿ Sights

★ **Giant's Causeway**   LANDMARK
(www.nationaltrust.org.uk; ☉ dawn-dusk) **FREE**
This spectacular rock formation – Northern Ireland's only Unesco World Heritage site – is one of Ireland's most impressive and atmospheric landscape features, a vast expanse of regular, closely packed, hexagonal stone columns looking for all the world like the handiwork of giants. The phenomenon is explained in the **Giant's Causeway Visitor Experience** (☑ 028-2073 1855; www.nationaltrust.org.uk; 60 Causeway Rd; adult/child £10.50/5.25; ☉ 9am-7pm Jul-Aug, to 6pm Mar-Jun & Sep-Oct, to 5pm Nov-Feb; 🐾) 🍃, a spectacular new ecofriendly building half-hidden in a hillside above the sea.

Visiting the Giant's Causeway itself is free of charge but you pay to use the car park and the visitor centre. (The admission fee is reduced by £2 if you arrive by bus, bike or on foot.)

From the centre it's an easy 10- to 15-minute walk downhill to the Causeway itself, but a more interesting approach is to follow the clifftop path northeast for 2km to the Chimney Tops headland, then descend the Shepherd's Steps to the Causeway. For the less mobile, a minibus shuttles from the visitors centre to the Causeway (£2 return).

★ **Carrick-a-Rede Rope Bridge**   BRIDGE
(☑ 028-2076 9839; www.nationaltrust.org.uk/carrick-a-rede; 119 Whitepark Rd, Ballintoy; adult/child £7/3.50; ☉ 9.30am-6pm Apr-Oct, to 3.30pm Nov-Mar) This 20m-long, 1m-wide bridge of wire

rope spans the chasm between the sea cliffs and the little island of Carrick-a-Rede, swaying 30m above the rock-strewn water. Crossing the bridge is perfectly safe, but frightening if you don't have a head for heights, especially if it's breezy (in high winds the bridge is closed). From the island, views take in Rathlin Island and Fair Head to the east.

There's a small National Trust information centre and cafe at the car park.

Derry/Londonderry

POP 84,340

Northern Ireland's second city comes as a pleasant surprise to many visitors. Derry was never the prettiest of places, and it certainly lagged behind Belfast in terms of investment and redevelopment, but in preparation for its year in the limelight as UK City of Culture 2013, the city centre was given a handsome makeover. The new **Peace Bridge**, Ebrington Sq, and the redevelopment of the waterfront and Guildhall area make the most of the city's riverside setting. And Derry's determined air of can-do optimism has made it the powerhouse of the North's cultural revival.

There's a lot of history to absorb here, from the Siege of Derry to the Battle of the Bogside – a stroll around the 17th-century city walls is a must, as is a tour of the Bogside murals. The city's lively pubs are home to a burgeoning live-music scene. But perhaps the biggest attraction is the people themselves: warm, witty and welcoming.

Derry or Londonderry? The name you use for Northern Ireland's second-largest city can be a political statement, but today most people just call it Derry, whatever their politics. The 'London' prefix was added in 1613 in recognition of the Corporation of London's role in the 'plantation' of Ulster with Protestant settlers.

In 1968 resentment at the long-running Protestant domination of the city council boiled over into a series of (Catholic-dominated) civil-rights marches. In August 1969 fighting between police and local youths in the poor Catholic Bogside district prompted the UK government to send British troops into Derry. In January 1972 'Bloody Sunday' resulted in the deaths of 13 unarmed Catholic civil-rights marchers in Derry at the hands of the British army, an event that marked the beginning of the Troubles in earnest.

◉ Sights

★ **Derry's City Walls**   WALLS

(⊙dawn-dusk) **FREE** The best way to get a feel for Derry's layout and history is to walk the 1.5km circumference of the city's walls. Completed in 1619, Derry's city walls are 8m high and 9m thick and are the only city walls in Ireland to survive almost intact. The four original gates (Shipquay, Ferryquay, Bishop's and Butcher's) were rebuilt in the 18th and 19th centuries, when three new gates (New, Magazine and Castle) were added.

★ **Tower Museum**   MUSEUM

(www.derrystrabane.com/towermuseum; Union Hall Pl; adult/child £4/2; ⊙10am-5.30pm, last admission 4pm) Head straight to the 5th floor of this award-winning museum inside a replica 16th-century tower house for a view from the top. Then work your way down through the excellent **Armada Shipwreck** exhibition, and the **Story of Derry**, where well-thought-out exhibits and audiovisuals lead you through the city's history from the founding of the monastery of St Colmcille (Columba) in the 6th century to the Battle of the Bogside in the late 1960s. Allow at least two hours.

People's Gallery Murals   PUBLIC ART

(Rossville St) The 12 murals that decorate the gable ends of houses along Rossville St, near Free Derry Corner, are popularly referred to as the People's Gallery. They are the work of Tom Kelly, Will Kelly and Kevin Hasson, known as 'the Bogside Artists'. The three men have spent most of their lives in the Bogside, and lived through the worst of the Troubles. The murals can be clearly seen from the northern part of the City Walls.

⌂ Sleeping

★ **Merchant's House**   B&B €€

(☑028-7126 9691; www.thesaddlershouse.com; 16 Queen St; s/d/tr/f from £40/65/90/100; @ �) This historic, Georgian-style town house is a gem of a B&B. It has an elegant lounge and dining room with marble fireplaces and antique furniture, TV, coffee-making facilities, homemade marmalade at breakfast and bathrobes in the bedrooms (some rooms have shared bathroom). Call at **Saddler's House** (☑028-7126 9691; www.thesaddlershouse.com; 36 Great James St; s/d from £55/60; ⌂) first to pick up a key.

ESSENTIAL FOOD & DRINK

Ireland's recently acquired reputation as a gourmet destination is thoroughly deserved, with a host of chefs and producers leading a foodie revolution that has made it easy to eat well on all budgets.

Champ Northern Irish dish of mashed potatoes with spring onions (scallions).

Colcannon Potatoes mashed with milk, cabbage and fried onion.

Farl Triangular flatbread in Northern Ireland and Donegal.

Irish stew Lamb stew with potatoes, onions and thyme.

Irish whiskey Around 100 different types are produced by only four distilleries: Jameson, Bushmills, Cooley and recently reopened Kilbeggan.

Soda bread Wonderful bread – white or brown, sweet or savoury – made from very soft Irish flour and buttermilk.

Stout Dark, almost black beer made with roasted barley; famous brands are Guinness in Dublin, and Murphy's and Beamish & Crawford in Cork.

Abbey B&B
B&B €€

(☑ 028-7127 9000; www.abbeyaccommodation. com; 4 Abbey St; s/d/tr from £50/70/90; ☏) There's a warm welcome waiting at this family-run B&B just a short walk from the walled city, on the edge of the Bogside. The six rooms are stylishly decorated.

Eating & Drinking

★ Pyke 'n' Pommes
STREET FOOD €

(www.facebook.com/PykeNPommes; behind Foyle Marina, off Baronet St; mains £4-16; ☺ noon-4pm Sun-Thu, to 5pm Fri & Sat; ☑ ⊞) ✆ Derry's single-best eatery is this quayside shipping container. Chef Kevin Pyke's amazing, mostly organic burgers span his signature Notorious Pig (pulled pork, crispy slaw, beetroot and crème fraiche), Cheeky Monkey (monkfish, warm potato and smoked-apple purée) and Veganderry (chickpeas, lemon and coriander) to his Legenderry Burger (wagyu beef, pickled onions and honey-mustard mayo). Seasonal specials might include mackerel or oysters.

★ Peadar O'Donnell's
PUB

(www.peadars.com; 59-63 Waterloo St; ☺ 11.30am-1.30am Mon-Sat, 12.30pm-12.30am Sun) Done up as a typical Irish pub/grocery – with shelves of household items, shopkeepers scales on the counter and a museum's-worth of old bric-a-brac – Peadar's has traditional music sessions every night and often on weekend afternoons as well. Its adjacent **Gweedore Bar** (www.peadars.com; 59-61 Waterloo St; ☺ 11.30am-1.30am Mon-Sat, noon-12.30am Sun)

hosts live rock bands every night, and a Saturday night disco upstairs.

ℹ Information

Visit Derry (☑ 028-7126 7284; www.visitderry. com; 44 Foyle St; ☺ 9am-5.30pm Mon-Fri, 10am-5pm Sat & Sun; ☏) Sells books and maps, has a bureau de change and can book accommodation.

ℹ Getting There & Away

BUS

The **bus station** (☑ 028-7126 2261; Foyle St) is just northeast of the walled city.

Belfast £12, 1¾ hours, half-hourly Monday to Friday, hourly Saturday and Sunday

Dublin £20, four hours, every two hours daily

TRAIN

Derry's train station (always referred to as Londonderry in Northern Ireland timetables) is on the eastern side of the River Foyle; a free Rail Link bus connects with the bus station.

Belfast £12, 2½ hours, nine daily Monday to Saturday, six on Sunday

SURVIVAL GUIDE

ℹ Directory A–Z

ACCOMMODATION

Hostels in Ireland can be booked solid in the summer.

From June to September a dorm bed at most hostels costs €15 to €25 (£13 to £20), except for the more expensive hostels in Dublin, Belfast and a few other places.

Typical B&Bs cost around €35 to €45 (£25 to £40) per person a night (sharing a double room), though more luxurious B&Bs can cost upwards of €55 (£45) per person. Most B&Bs are small, so in summer they quickly fill up.

Commercial camping grounds typically charge €12 to €25 (£10 to £20) for a tent or campervan and two people. Unless otherwise indicated, prices quoted for 'campsites' are for a tent, car and two people.

The following are useful resources:

An Óige (www.anoige.ie) Hostelling International (HI)–associated national organisation with 26 hostels scattered around the Republic.

Family Homes of Ireland (www.familyhomes.ie) Lists family-run guesthouses and self-catering properties.

HINI (www.hini.org.uk) HI-associated organisation with six hostels in Northern Ireland.

Independent Holiday Hostels of Ireland (IHH; www.hostels-ireland.com) 80 tourist-board approved hostels throughout Ireland.

Independent Hostel Owners of Ireland (IHO; www.independenthostelsireland.com) Independent hostelling association.

ACTIVITIES

Ireland is great for outdoor activities, and tourist offices have a wide selection of information covering birdwatching, surfing (great along the west coast), scuba diving, cycling, fishing, horse riding, sailing, canoeing and many other activities.

Walking is particularly popular, although you must come prepared for wet weather. There are now well over 20 waymarked trails throughout Ireland, one of the more popular being the 214km Kerry Way.

SLEEPING PRICE RANGES

The following price ranges have been used in our reviews of places to stay. Prices are all based on a double room with private bathroom in high season.

Republic

€ less than €80

€€ €80-180

€€€ more than €180

Northern Ireland

€ less than €50

€€ €50-120

€€€ more than €120

COUNTRY FACTS

Area 84,421 sq km

Capitals Dublin (Republic of Ireland), Belfast (Northern Ireland)

Country Code Republic of Ireland ☑ 353, Northern Ireland ☑ 44

Currency euro (€) in Republic of Ireland; pound sterling (£) in Northern Ireland

Emergency ☑ 112

Languages English, Irish Gaelic

Money ATMs widespread; credit cards widely accepted

Population Republic of Ireland 4.76 million; Northern Ireland 1.87 million

Visas Schengen rules do not apply

INTERNET RESOURCES

Entertainment Ireland (www.entertainment.ie) Countrywide listings for every kind of entertainment.

Failte Ireland (www.discoverireland.ie) Official tourist board website – practical info and a huge accommodation database.

Lonely Planet (www.lonelyplanet.com/ireland) Destination information, hotel bookings, traveller forums and more.

Northern Ireland Tourist Board (www.nitb.com) Official tourist site.

MONEY

The Republic of Ireland uses the euro (€), while Northern Ireland uses the British pound sterling (£). Banks offer the best exchange rates; exchange bureaux, open longer, have worse rates and higher commissions. Post offices generally have exchange facilities and are open on Saturday morning.

In Northern Ireland several banks issue their own Northern Irish pound notes, which are equivalent to sterling but not readily accepted in mainland Britain. Many hotels, restaurants and shops in Northern Ireland accept euros.

Tipping

Fancy hotels and restaurants usually add a 10% or 15% service charge onto bills. Simpler places usually don't add a service charge; if you decide to tip, just round up the bill (or add 10% at most). Taxi drivers do not have to be tipped, but if you do, 10% is more than generous.

EATING PRICE RANGES

The following price indicators are used to indicate the cost of a main course at dinner:

Republic

€ less than €12

€€ €12-25

€€€ more than €25

Northern Ireland

€ less than €12

€€ €12-20

€€€ more than €20

OPENING HOURS

Banks 10am–4pm Monday to Friday (to 5pm Thursday)

Pubs 10.30am–11.30pm Monday to Thursday, 10.30am–12.30am Friday and Saturday, noon–11pm Sunday (30 minutes 'drinking up' time allowed); closed Christmas Day and Good Friday

Restaurants noon–10.30pm; many close one day of the week

Shops 9.30am–6pm Monday to Saturday (until 8pm Thursday in cities), noon–6pm Sunday

PUBLIC HOLIDAYS

The main public holidays in the Republic of Ireland and Northern Ireland are:

New Year's Day 1 January

St Patrick's Day 17 March

Easter (Good Friday to Easter Monday inclusive) March/April

May Holiday First Monday in May

Christmas Day 25 December

St Stephen's Day (Boxing Day) 26 December

Northern Ireland

Spring Bank Holiday Last Monday in May

Orangemen's Day 12 July (following Monday if 12th is on the weekend)

August Bank Holiday Last Monday in August

Republic of Ireland

June Holiday First Monday in June

August Holiday First Monday in August

October Holiday Last Monday in October

TELEPHONE

The mobile- (cell-) phone network in Ireland runs on the GSM 900/1800 system compatible with the rest of Europe and Australia, but not the USA. Mobile numbers in the Republic begin with ☑ 085, ☑ 086 or ☑ 087 (☑ 07 in Northern Ireland). A local pay-as-you-go SIM for your mobile will cost from around €10, but may work out free after the standard phone-credit refund (make sure your phone is compatible with the local provider).

To call Northern Ireland from the Republic, do not use ☑ 0044 as for the rest of the UK. Instead, dial ☑ 048 and then the local number. To dial the Republic from Northern Ireland, however, use the full international code ☑ 00 353, then the local number.

VISAS

If you're a European Economic Area (EEA) national, you don't need a visa to visit (or work in) either the Republic or Northern Ireland. Citizens of Australia, Canada, New Zealand, South Africa and the US can visit the Republic for up to three months, and Northern Ireland for up to six months.

There are currently no border controls or passport checks bcorketween the Republic of Ireland and Northern Ireland.

ⓘ Getting There & Away

AIR

There are nonstop flights from Britain, Continental Europe and North America to Dublin, Shannon and Belfast International, and nonstop connections from Britain and Europe to Cork. International departure tax is normally included in the price of your ticket.

International airports in Ireland:

Belfast International Airport (Aldergrove; ☑ 028-9448 4848; www.belfastairport.com; Airport Rd) Located 30km northwest of the city; flights serve the UK and Europe, and in the USA, Las Vegas, Orlando and New York.

Dublin Airport (☑ 01-814 1111; www.dublinairport.com) Dublin Airport, 13km north of the centre, is Ireland's major international gateway airport. It has two terminals: most international flights (including most US flights) use the newer Terminal 2; Ryanair and select others use Terminal 1. Both terminals have the usual selection of pubs, restaurants, shops, ATMs and car-hire desks.

There is no train service to/from the airport, but there are bus and taxi options.

George Best Belfast City Airport (BHD; ☑ 028-9093 9093; www.belfastcityairport.com; Airport Rd) Located 6km northeast of Belfast's city centre; flights serve the UK and Europe.

Shannon Airport (SNN; ☑ 061-712 000; www.shannonairport.ie; ☜) Has many facilities, including a free observation area for those stuck waiting. Almost everything, including ATMs, currency exchange and car rental, is on one level.

SEA

The main ferry routes between Ireland and the UK and mainland Europe:

- Belfast to Liverpool (England; eight hours)
- Belfast to Cairnryan (Scotland; 1¾ hours)
- Cork to Roscoff (France; 14 hours; April to October only)
- Dublin to Liverpool (England; fast/slow four/8½ hours)
- Dublin & Dun Laoghaire to Holyhead (Wales; fast/slow two hours/3½ hours)
- Larne to Cairnryan (Scotland; two hours)
- Larne to Troon (Scotland; two hours; March to October only)
- Larne to Fleetwood (England; six hours)
- Rosslare to Cherbourg/Roscoff (France; 18/20½ hours)
- Rosslare to Fishguard & Pembroke (Wales; 3½ hours)

Competition from budget airlines has forced ferry operators to discount heavily and offer flexible fares.

A useful website is www.ferrybooker.com, which covers all sea-ferry routes and operators to Ireland.

Main operators include the following:

Brittany Ferries (www.brittanyferries.com) Cork to Roscoff; April to October.

Irish Ferries (www.irishferries.com) It has Dublin to Holyhead ferries (up to four per day year-round); and France to Rosslare (three times per week).

P&O Ferries (www.poferries.com) Daily sailings year-round from Dublin to Liverpool, and Larne to Cairnryan. Larne to Troon runs March to October only.

Stena Line (www.stenaline.com) Daily sailings from Holyhead to Dublin Port, from Belfast to Liverpool and Cairnryan, and from Rosslare to Fishguard.

Discounts & Passes

Eurail Pass Holders get a 50% discount on Irish Ferries crossings to France.

InterRail Pass Holders get a 50% discount on Irish Ferries and Stena Line services.

Britrail Pass Has an option to add on Ireland for an extra fee, including ferry transit.

ⓘ Getting Around

Travelling around Ireland looks simple, as the distances are short and there's a dense network of roads and railways. But in Ireland, getting from A to B seldom uses a straight line, and public transport can be expensive (particularly trains), infrequent or both. For these reasons having your own transport – either car or bicycle – can be a major advantage.

BICYCLE

Ireland's compact size and scenic landscapes make it a good cycling destination. However, dodgy weather, many very narrow roads and some very fast drivers are major concerns. Special tracks such as the 42km Great Western Greenway in County Mayo are a delight. A good tip for cyclists in the west is that the prevailing winds make it easier to cycle from south to north.

Buses will carry bikes, but only if there's room. For trains, bear in mind:

- Bikes are carried free on Intercity and off-peak commuter trains.
- Book in advance (www.irishrail.ie), as there's only room for two bikes per service.

BUS

The Republic of Ireland's national bus line, **Bus Éireann** (📞 1850 836 6111; www.buseireann.ie), operates services all over the Republic and into Northern Ireland. Bus fares are cheaper than train fares. Return trips are usually only slightly more expensive than one-way fares, and special deals (eg same-day returns) are often available. Most intercity buses in Northern Ireland are operated by **Ulsterbus** (📞 028-9066 6630; www.translink.co.uk).

CAR & MOTORCYCLE

The majority of hire companies won't rent you a car if you're under 23 years of age and haven't had a valid driving licence for at least a year. Some companies will not hire to those aged 74 or over. Your own local licence is usually sufficient to hire a car for up to three months.

TRAIN

The Republic of Ireland's railway system, **Iarnród Éireann** (Iarnród Éireann; 📞 1850 366 222; www.irishrail.ie), has routes radiating out from Dublin, but there is no direct north–south route along the west coast. Tickets can be twice as expensive as the bus, but travel times may be dramatically reduced. Special fares are often available, and a midweek return ticket sometimes costs just a bit more than the single fare; the flip side is that fares may be significantly higher on Friday and Sunday. **Rail Users Ireland** (www.railusers.ie) can be more informative than the official website.

Northern Ireland Railways (NIR; 📞 028-9066 6630; www.translink.co.uk/Services/NI-Railways/; Belfast Central Station) has four lines from Belfast, one of which links up with the Republic's rail system.

Italy

Best Places to Eat

→ Pizzeria Gino Sorbillo (p710)

→ All'Osteria Bottega (p691)

→ Trattoria Mario (p698)

→ Marina Grande (p717)

→ Antiche Carampane (p687)

Best Museums & Galleries

→ Vatican Museums (p656)

→ Galleria degli Uffizi (p693)

→ Museo Archeologico Nazionale (p707)

→ Museo del Novecento (p673)

→ Museo e Galleria Borghese (p660)

Why Go?

A favourite destination since the days of the 18th-century Grand Tour, Italy may appear to hold few surprises. Its iconic monuments and masterpieces are known the world over, while cities like Rome, Florence and Venice need no introduction.

Yet Italy is far more than the sum of its sights. Its fiercely proud regions maintain customs and culinary traditions dating back centuries, resulting in passionate festivals and delectable food at every turn. And then there are those timeless landscapes, from Tuscany's gentle hillsides to icy Alpine peaks, vertiginous coastlines and spitting southern volcanoes.

Drama is never far away in Italy and its theatrical streets and piazzas provide endless people-watching, ideally over a leisurely lunch or cool evening drink. This is, after all, the land of *dolce far niente* (sweet idleness) where simply hanging out is a pleasure and time seems to matter just that little bit less.

When to Go

Rome

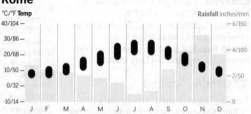

Apr–May Perfect spring weather; ideal for exploring vibrant cities and blooming countryside.

Jun–Jul Summer means beach weather and a packed festival calendar.

Sep–Oct Enjoy mild temperatures, autumn cuisine and the *vendemia* (grape harvest).

Italy Highlights

1 **Rome** (p650) Seeing awe-inspiring art and monuments.

2 **Venice** (p680) Cruising past Gothic palaces, churches and crumbling piazzas.

3 **Florence** (p692) Exploring this exquisite Renaissance time capsule.

4 **Naples** (p707) Working up an appetite for the world's best pizza.

5 **Turin** (p672) Visiting Turin's regal palaces and magnificent museums.

6 **Siena** (p702) Admiring glorious Gothic architecture and Renaissance art.

7 **Amalfi Coast** (p715) Basking in inspiring sea views.

8 **Verona** (p679) Enjoying an open-air opera in one of Italy's most romantic cities.

9 **Bologna** (p690) Feasting on foodie delights and medieval architecture in hedonistic Bologna.

10 **Syracuse** (p721) Revelling in drama at an ancient Greek theatre.

ROME

POP 2.86 MILLION

Ever since its glory days as an ancient super-power, Rome has been astonishing visitors. Its historic cityscape, piled high with haunting ruins and iconic monuments, is achingly beautiful, and its museums and basilicas showcase some of Europe's most celebrated masterpieces. But no list of sights and must-sees can capture the sheer elation of experiencing Rome's operatic streets and baroque piazzas, of turning a corner and stumbling across a world-famous fountain or a colourful neighbourhood market. Its streetside cafes are made for idling and elegant Renaissance *palazzi* (mansions) provide the perfect backdrop for romantic alfresco dining.

◉ Sights

◎ Ancient Rome

★ **Colosseum** RUINS

(Colosseo; Map p652; ☑06 3996 7700; www.coopculture.it; Piazza del Colosseo; adult/reduced incl Roman Forum & Palatino €12/7.50; ⊙8.30am-1hr before sunset; Ⓜ Colosseo) Rome's great gladiatorial arena is the most thrilling of the city's ancient sights. Inaugurated in AD 80, the 50,000-seat Colosseum, also known as the Flavian Amphitheatre, was clad in travertine and covered by a huge canvas awning held aloft by 240 masts. Inside, tiered seating encircled the arena, itself built over

---

ITINERARIES

One Week

A one-week whistle-stop tour of Italy is enough to take in the country's three most famous cities. After a couple of days exploring the unique canalscape of **Venice**, head south to **Florence**, Italy's great Renaissance city. Two days will whet your appetite for the artistic and architectural treasures that await in **Rome**.

Two Weeks

After the first week, continue south for some sea and southern passion. Spend a day admiring art in **Naples**, a day investigating the ruins at **Pompeii**, and a day or two admiring the **Amalfi Coast**. Then backtrack to Naples for a ferry to **Palermo** and the gastronomic delights of Sicily.

---

an underground complex (the hypogeum) where animals were caged and stage sets prepared. Games involved gladiators fighting wild animals or each other.

★ **Palatino** ARCHAEOLOGICAL SITE

(Palatine Hill; Map p652; ☑06 3996 7700; www.coopculture.it; Via di San Gregorio 30, Piazza di Santa Maria Nova; adult/reduced incl Colosseum & Roman Forum €12/7.50; ⊙8.30am-1hr before sunset; Ⓜ Colosseo) Sandwiched between the Roman Forum and the Circo Massimo, the Palatino is an atmospheric area of towering pine trees, majestic ruins and memorable views. It was here that Romulus supposedly founded the city in 753 BC and Rome's emperors lived in unabashed luxury. Look out for the **stadio** (stadium), the ruins of the **Domus Flavia** (imperial palace), and grandstand views over the Roman Forum from the **Orti Farnesiani**.

★ **Roman Forum** ARCHAEOLOGICAL SITE

(Foro Romano; Map p652; ☑06 3996 7700; www.coopculture.it; Largo della Salara Vecchia, Piazza di Santa Maria Nova; adult/reduced incl Colosseum & Palatino €12/7.50; ⊙8.30am-1hr before sunset; ⓠ Via dei Fori Imperiali) An impressive – if rather confusing – sprawl of ruins, the Roman Forum was ancient Rome's showpiece centre, a grandiose district of temples, basilicas and vibrant public spaces. The site, which was originally an Etruscan burial ground, was first developed in the 7th century BC, growing over time to become the social, political and commercial hub of the Roman Empire. Landmark sights include the **Arco di Settimio Severo** (Arch of Septimius Severus), the **Curia** and the **Casa delle Vestali** (House of the Vestal Virgins).

★ **Capitoline Museums** MUSEUM

(Musei Capitolini; Map p652; ☑06 06 08; www.museicapitolini.org; Piazza del Campidoglio 1; adult/reduced €11.50/9.50; ⊙9.30am-7.30pm, last admission 6.30pm; ⓠ Piazza Venezia) Dating to 1471, the Capitoline Museums are the world's oldest public museums. Their collection of classical sculpture is one of Italy's finest, including crowd-pleasers such as the iconic *Lupa capitolina* (Capitoline Wolf), a sculpture of Romulus and Remus under a wolf, and the *Galata morente* (Dying Gaul), a moving depiction of a dying Gaul warrior. There's also a formidable picture gallery with masterpieces by the likes of Titian, Tintoretto, Rubens and Caravaggio.

Ticket prices increase when there's a temporary exhibition on.

ⓘ COLOSSEUM TICKETS

Long waits are the norm at the Colosseum. You'll have to queue for security checks and then to buy a ticket. To save time, get your ticket at the Palatino entrance (about 250m away at Via di San Gregorio 30) or book online at www.coopculture.it (incurs a €2 booking fee).

Vittoriano MONUMENT
(Victor Emmanuel Monument; Map p652; Piazza Venezia; ☉9.30am-5.30pm summer, to 4.30pm winter; 🚇Piazza Venezia) FREE Love it or loathe it, as many Romans do, you can't ignore the Vittoriano (aka the Altare della Patria; Altar of the Fatherland), the massive mountain of white marble that towers over Piazza Venezia. Begun in 1885 to honour Italy's first king, Victor Emmanuel II – who's immortalised in its vast equestrian statue – it incorporates the **Museo Centrale del Risorgimento** (📞06 679 35 98; www.risorgimento.it; adult/reduced €5/2.50; ☉9.30am-6.30pm), a small museum documenting Italian unification, and the **Tomb of the Unknown Soldier**.

For Rome's best 360-degree views, take the **Roma dal Cielo** (adult/reduced €7/3.50; ☉9.30am-7.30pm, last admission 7pm) lift to the top.

Bocca della Verità MONUMENT
(Mouth of Truth; Map p658; Piazza Bocca della Verità 18; ☉9.30am-5.50pm; 🚇Piazza Bocca della Verità) A bearded face carved into a giant marble disc, the *Bocca della Verità* is one of Rome's most popular curiosities. Legend has it that if you put your hand in the mouth and tell a lie, the Bocca will slam shut and bite your hand off.

The mouth, which was originally part of a fountain, or possibly an ancient manhole cover, now lives in the portico of the **Chiesa di Santa Maria in Cosmedin**, a handsome medieval church.

⊙ Centro Storico

★**Pantheon** CHURCH
(Map p658; www.pantheonroma.com; Piazza della Rotonda; ☉8.30am-7.15pm Mon-Sat, 9am-5.45pm Sun; 🚇Largo di Torre Argentina) FREE A striking 2000-year-old temple, now a church, the Pantheon is the best preserved of Rome's ancient monuments and one of the most influential buildings in the Western world. Built by Hadrian over Marcus Agrippa's earlier 27 BC temple, it has stood since around AD 125, and although its greying, pockmarked exterior looks its age, it's still a unique and exhilarating experience to pass through its vast bronze doors and gaze up at the largest unreinforced concrete dome ever built.

★**Piazza Navona** PIAZZA
(Map p658; 🚇Corso del Rinascimento) With its showy fountains, baroque *palazzi* and colourful cast of street artists, hawkers and tourists, Piazza Navona is central Rome's elegant showcase square. Built over the 1st-century **Stadio di Domiziano** (Domitian's Stadium; 📞06 4568 6100; www.stadiodomiziano.com; Via di Tor Sanguigna 3; adult/reduced €8/6; ☉10am-7pm Sun-Fri, to 8pm Sat), it was paved over in the 15th century and for almost 300 years hosted the city's main market. Its grand centrepiece is Bernini's **Fontana dei Quattro Fiumi** (Fountain of the Four Rivers), a flamboyant fountain featuring an Egyptian obelisk and muscular personifications of the rivers Nile, Ganges, Danube and Plate.

Campo de' Fiori PIAZZA
(Map p658; 🚇Corso Vittorio Emanuele II) Noisy, colourful 'Il Campo' is a major focus of Roman life: by day it hosts one of Rome's best-known markets, while at night it morphs into a raucous open-air pub as drinkers spill out from its many bars and eateries. For centuries the square was the site of public executions, and it was here that philosopher Giordano Bruno was burned for heresy in 1600. The spot is marked by a sinister statue of the hooded monk, which was created by Ettore Ferrari in 1889.

★**Galleria Doria Pamphilj** GALLERY
(Map p658; 📞06 679 73 23; www.doriapamphilj.it; Via del Corso 305; adult/reduced €12/8; ☉9am-7pm, last admission 6pm; 🚇Via del Corso) Hidden behind the grimy grey exterior of Palazzo Doria Pamphilj, this wonderful gallery boasts one of Rome's richest private art collections, with works by Raphael, Tintoretto, Titian, Caravaggio, Bernini and Velázquez, as well as several Flemish masters. Masterpieces abound, but the undisputed star is Velázquez' portrait of an implacable Pope Innocent X, who grumbled that the depiction was 'too real'. For a comparison, check out Gian Lorenzo Bernini's sculptural interpretation of the same subject.

ITALY ROME

Ancient Rome

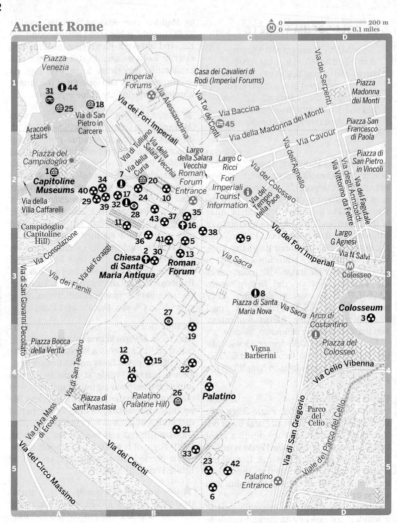

★ **Trevi Fountain**   FOUNTAIN
(Fontana di Trevi; Map p662; Piazza di Trevi; Ⓜ Barberini) The Fontana di Trevi, scene of Anita Ekberg's dip in *La dolce vita*, is a flamboyant baroque ensemble of mythical figures and wild horses taking up the entire side of the 17th-century Palazzo Poli. After a Fendi-sponsored restoration finished in 2015, the fountain gleams brighter than it has for years. The tradition is to toss a coin into the water, thus ensuring that you'll return to Rome – on average about €3000 is thrown in every day.

★ **Palazzo Barberini**   GALLERY
(Galleria Nazionale d'Arte Antica; Map p662; ☏ 06 481 45 91; www.barberinicorsini.org; Via delle Quattro Fontane 13; adult/reduced €5/2.50, incl Palazzo Corsini €10/5; ⊗ 8.30am-7pm Tue-Sun; Ⓜ Barberini) Commissioned to celebrate the Barberini family's rise to papal power, Palazzo Barberini is a sumptuous baroque palace that impresses even before you clap eyes on the breathtaking art. Many high-profile architects worked on it, including rivals Bernini and Borromini; the former contributed a large squared staircase, the latter a helicoidal

Ancient Rome

one. Amid the masterpieces, don't miss Pietro da Cortona's *Il triChiesa della Trinità dei Montionfo della divina provvidenza* (Triumph of Divine Providence; 1632–39), the most spectacular of the *palazzo*'s ceiling frescoes in the 1st-floor main salon.

★ **Piazza di Spagna &**
the Spanish Steps   PIAZZA
(Map p662; Ⓜ Spagna) A magnet for visitors since the 18th century, the Spanish Steps (Scalinata della Trinità dei Monti) provide a perfect people-watching perch. The 135 steps, gleaming after a recent clean-up, rise from Piazza di Spagna to the landmark Chiesa della Trinità dei Monti.

Piazza di Spagna was named after the Spanish Embassy to the Holy See, although the staircase, designed by the Italian Francesco de Sanctis, was built in 1725 with money bequeathed by a French diplomat.

★ **Piazza del Popolo**   PIAZZA
(Map p654; Ⓜ Flaminio) This dazzling piazza was laid out in 1538 to provide a grandiose entrance to what was then Rome's main northern gateway. It has since been remodelled several times, most recently by Giuseppe Valadier in 1823. Guarding its southern approach are Carlo Rainaldi's twin 17th-century churches, Chiesa

di Santa Maria dei Miracoli (Via del Corso 528; ◔ 6.45am-12.30pm & 4.30-7.30pm Mon-Sat, 8am-1.15pm & 4.30-7.45 Sun) and Chiesa di Santa Maria in Montesanto (Chiesa degli Artisti; www.chiesadegliartisti.it; Via del Babuino 198; ◔ 5.30-8pm Mon-Fri, 11am-1.30pm Sun). In the centre, the 36m-high obelisk was brought by Augustus from ancient Egypt; it originally stood in Circo Massimo.

◉ Vatican City, Borgo & Prati

★ **St Peter's Basilica**   BASILICA
(Basilica di San Pietro; Map p654; ☎ 06 6988 5518; www.vatican.va; St Peter's Square; ◔ 7am-7pm summer, to 6.30pm winter; ▣ Piazza del Risorgimento, Ⓜ Ottaviano-San Pietro) FREE In this city of outstanding churches, none can hold a candle to St Peter's (Basilica di San Pietro), Italy's largest, richest and most spectacular basilica. Built atop an earlier 4th-century church, it was consecrated in 1626 after 120 years' construction. Its lavish interior contains many spectacular works of art, including three of Italy's most celebrated masterpieces: Michelangelo's *Pietà,* his soaring dome, and Bernini's 29m-high baldachin over the papal altar.

Expect queues and note that strict dress codes are enforced, so no shorts, miniskirts or bare shoulders.

Greater Rome

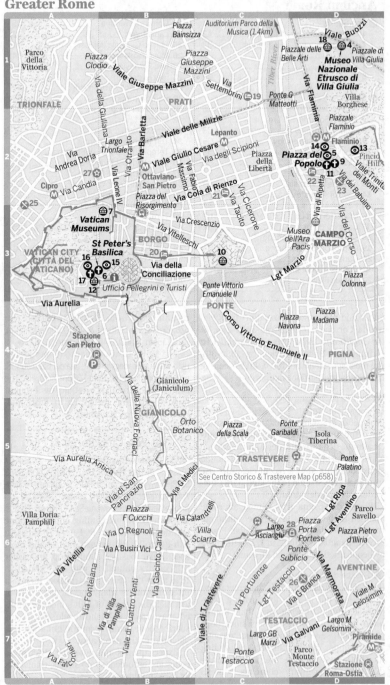

Piazza Bainsizza

Auditorium Parco della Musica (1.4km)

Piazza Clodio

Viale Giuseppe Mazzini

Piazza Giuseppe Mazzini

Via Settembrini

Piazzale delle Belle Arti

18

4 Piazzale di Villa Giulia

Museo Nazionale Etrusco di Villa Giulia

Parco della Vittoria

Via della Giuliana

TRIONFALE

Via Andrea Doria

Largo Trionfale

27

Cipro

Via Candia

25

Via Leone IV

Via Otranto

Via Barletta

PRATI

Viale delle Milizie

Lepanto

Viale Giulio Cesare

Via degli Scipioni

Via Fabio Massimo

Ottaviano-San Pietro

Piazza del Risorgimento

7

Vatican Museums

St Peter's Basilica

VATICAN CITY (CITTÀ DEL VATICANO)

16

17

15

6

12

Ufficio Pellegrini e Turisti

Via Cola di Rienzo

21

Via Tacito

Via Cicerone

Via Crescenzio

Via Vitelleschi

BORGO

20

Via della Conciliazione

10

Via Aurelia

Stazione San Pietro

P

Via delle Nuova Fornaci

Gianicolo (Janiculum)

GIANICOLO

Orto Botanico

Ponte G Matteotti

Tiber River

Via Flaminia

Villa Borghese

Piazzale Flaminio

14 Flaminio

Piazza del Popolo

5 Pincio Hill

13

9

11

22

23

Via di Ripetta

Via del Babuino

Viale Trinità dei Monti

Museo dell'Ara Pacis

CAMPO MARZIO

Via del Corso

Lgt Marzio

Ponte Vittorio Emanuele II

PONTE

Corso Vittorio Emanuele II

Piazza Navona

Piazza Madama

Piazza Colonna

PIGNA

Piazza della Scala

Ponte Garibaldi

Isola Tiberina

TRASTEVERE

See Centro Storico & Trastevere Map (p658)

Ponte Palatino

Lgt Ripa

Lgt Aventino

Parco Savello

Piazza Pietro d'Illiria

Via Aurelia Antica

Via di San Pancrazio

Piazza F Cucchi

Via O Regnoli

Via A Busiri Vici

Via Giacinto Carini

Via G Medici

Villa Doria Pamphilj

Via Vitellia

Via Fonteiana

Via di Villa Pamphilj

Viale di Quattro Venti

Via Falc...

Viale di Trastevere

Via Calandrelli

Villa Sciarra

Largo Ascianghi

28

Piazza Porta Portese

Ponte Sublicio

Via Portuense

Lgt Testaccio

26

Via G Branca

TESTACCIO

Largo GB Marzi

Ponte Testaccio

Via Galvani

Parco Monte Testaccio

Largo M Gelsomini

AVENTINE

Via Marmorata

Viale M Gelosimini

Piramide

Piramide

Stazione Roma-Ostia

Piazza della Libertà

Piazza del Popolo

19

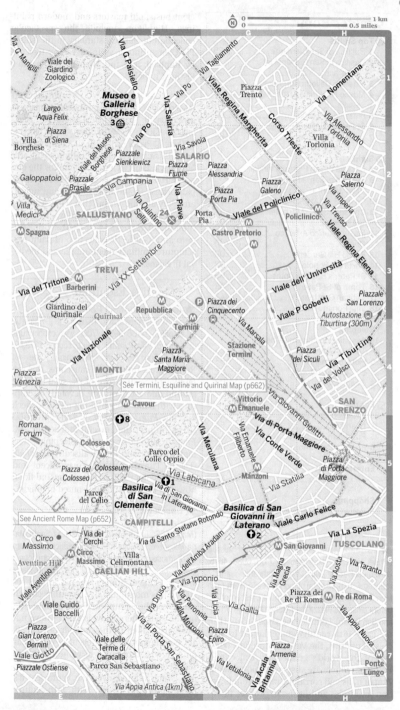

ITALY ROME

0 ─────────── 1 km
0 ─────────── 0.5 miles

Greater Rome

★ Vatican Museums   MUSEUM

(Musei Vaticani; Map p654; ☑06 6988 4676; www.museivaticani.va; Viale Vaticano; adult/reduced €16/8, last Sun of month free; ☉9am-6pm Mon-Sat, 9am-2pm last Sun of month, last entry 2hr before close; 🚇Piazza del Risorgimento, Ⓜ Ottaviano-San Pietro) Founded by Pope Julius II in the early 16th century and enlarged by successive pontiffs, the Vatican Museums boast one of the world's greatest art collections. Exhibits, which are displayed along about 7km of halls and corridors, range from Egyptian mummies and Etruscan bronzes to an-

cient busts, old masters and modern paintings. Highlights include the spectacular collection of classical statuary in the Museo Pio-Clementino, a suite of rooms frescoed by Raphael, and the Michelangelo-painted Sistine Chapel.

Castel Sant'Angelo   MUSEUM, CASTLE

(Map p654; ☑06 681 91 11; www.castelsantangelo. beniculturali.it; Lungotevere Castello 50; adult/reduced €10/5; ☉9am-7.30pm, ticket office to 6.30pm; 🚇Piazza Pia) With its chunky round keep, this castle is an instantly recognisable landmark. Built as a mausoleum for the emperor Hadrian, it was converted into a papal fortress in the 6th century and named after an angelic vision that Pope Gregory the Great had in 590. Nowadays, it houses the **Museo Nazionale di Castel Sant'Angelo** and its eclectic collection of paintings, sculpture, military memorabilia and medieval firearms.

◎ Monti & Esquilino

★ Museo Nazionale Romano: Palazzo Massimo alle Terme   MUSEUM

(Map p662; ☑06 3996 7700; www.coopculture. it; Largo di Villa Peretti 1; adult/reduced €7/3.50; ☉9am-7.45pm Tue-Sun; Ⓜ Termini) One of Rome's great unheralded museums, this is a fabulous treasure trove of classical art. The ground and 1st floors are devoted to sculpture with some breathtaking pieces – check out the *Pugile* (Boxer), a 2nd-century-BC Greek bronze; the graceful 2nd-century-BC *Ermafrodite dormiente* (Sleeping Hermaphrodite); and the idealised *Il discobolo* (Discus Thrower). It's the magnificent and vibrantly coloured frescoes on the 2nd floor, however, that are the undisputed highlight.

★ Basilica di Santa Maria Maggiore   BASILICA

(Map p662; ☑06 6988 6800; Piazza Santa Maria Maggiore; basilica free, adult/reduced museum €3/2, museum & loggia €5/4; ☉7am-7pm, loggia guided tours 9.30am-5.45pm; 🚇Piazza Santa Maria Maggiore) One of Rome's four patriarchal basilicas, this monumental 5th-century church stands on the summit of the Esquiline Hill, on the spot where snow is said to have miraculously fallen in the summer of AD 358. To commemorate the event, every year on 5 August thousands of white petals are released from the basilica's coffered ceiling. Much altered over the centuries, it's an architectural hybrid with 14th-century

---

ℹ SKIP THE LINE AT THE VATICAN MUSEUMS

➡ Book tickets online at http://biglietteriamusei.vatican.va/musei/tickets/do (€4 booking fee).

➡ Time your visit: Tuesdays and Thursdays are quietest; Wednesday mornings are good as everyone is at the pope's weekly audience; afternoon is better than the morning; avoid Mondays when many other museums are shut.

Romanesque belfry, 18th-century baroque facade, largely baroque interior and a series of glorious 5th-century mosaics.

Basilica di San Pietro in Vincoli BASILICA
(Map p654; Piazza di San Pietro in Vincoli 4a; ⏰ 8am-12.30pm & 3-7pm summer, to 6pm winter; Ⓜ Cavour) Pilgrims and art lovers flock to this 5th-century basilica for two reasons: to marvel at Michelangelo's colossal *Moses* (1505) sculpture and to see the chains that supposedly bound St Peter when he was imprisoned in the Carcere Mamertino (near the Roman Forum). Access to the church is via a flight of steps through a low arch that leads up from Via Cavour.

◎ Trastevere

Trastevere is one of central Rome's most vivacious neighbourhoods, a tightly packed warren of ochre *palazzi,* ivy-clad facades and photogenic lanes. Originally working class, it's now a trendy hang-out full of bars and restaurants.

★ Basilica di Santa Maria in Trastevere BASILICA
(Map p658; ☎ 06 581 4802; Piazza Santa Maria in Trastevere; ⏰ 7.30am-9pm Sep-Jul, 8am-noon & 4-9pm Aug; ☒ Viale di Trastevere, ☒ Viale di Trastevere) Nestled in a quiet corner of Trastevere's focal square, this is said to be the oldest church dedicated to the Virgin Mary in Rome. In its original form, it dates to the early 3rd century, but a major 12th-century makeover saw the addition of a Romanesque bell tower and glittering facade. The portico came later, added by Carlo Fontana in 1702. Inside, the 12th-century mosaics are the headline feature.

◎ San Giovanni & Testaccio

★ Basilica di San Giovanni in Laterano BASILICA
(Map p654; Piazza di San Giovanni in Laterano 4; basilica/cloister free/€5 with audio guide; ⏰ 7am-6.30pm, cloister 9am-6pm; Ⓜ San Giovanni) For a thousand years this monumental cathedral was the most important church in Christendom. Commissioned by Constantine and consecrated in AD 324, it was the first Christian basilica built in the city and, until the late 14th century, was the pope's main place of worship. It's still Rome's official cathedral and the pope's seat as the bishop of Rome.

The basilica has been revamped several times, most notably by Borromini in the 17th century, and by Alessandro Galilei, who added the immense white facade in 1735.

VATICAN MUSEUMS ITINERARY

Follow this three-hour itinerary for the museums' greatest hits:

At the top of the escalator after the entrance, head out to the **Cortile della Pigna**, a courtyard named after the Augustan-era bronze pine cone in the monumental niche. Cross the courtyard into the long corridor that is the **Museo Chiaramonti** and head left up to the **Museo Pio-Clementino**, home of the Vatican's finest classical statuary. Follow through the **Cortile Ottagono** (Octagonal Courtyard) onto the **Sala Croce Greca** (Greek Cross Room) from where stairs lead up to the 1st floor. Continue through the **Galleria delle Carte Geografiche** (Map Gallery) to the **Sala di Costantino**, the first of the four **Stanze di Raffaello** (Raphael Rooms) – the others are the **Stanza d' Eliodoro**, the **Stanza della Segnatura**, home to Raphael's superlative *La scuola di Atene* (The School of Athens), and the **Stanza dell'Incendio di Borgo**. Anywhere else these frescoed chambers would be the star attraction, but here they're the warm-up act for the museums' grand finale, the **Sistine Chapel**. Originally built in 1484 for Pope Sixtus IV, this towering chapel boasts two of the world's most famous works of art: Michelangelo's ceiling frescoes (1508–12) and his *Giudizio universale* (Last Judgment; 1535–41).

Centro Storico & Trastevere

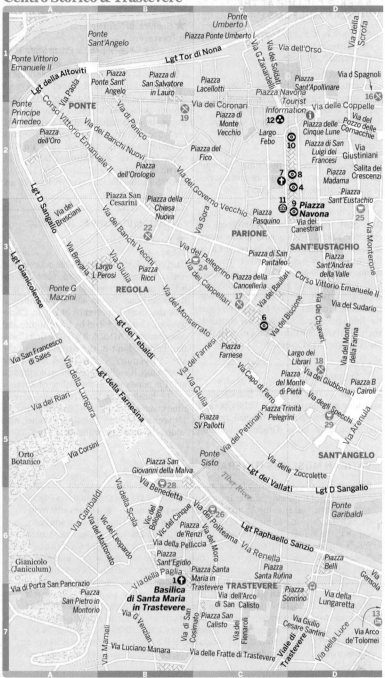

ITALY ROME

N ⌂
0 —————————— 200 m
0 —————————— 0.1 miles

ITALY ROME

★ **Basilica di San Clemente**   BASILICA

(Map p654; www.basilicasanclemente.com; Piazza San Clemente; excavations adult/reduced €10/5; ☉9am-12.30pm & 3-6pm Mon-Sat, 12.15-6pm Sun; ☐Via Labicana) Nowhere better illustrates the various stages of Rome's turbulent past than this fascinating multi-layered church. The ground-level 12th-century basilica sits atop a 4th-century church, which, in turn, stands over a 2nd-century pagan temple and a 1st-century Roman house. Beneath everything are foundations dating from the Roman Republic.

◎ **Villa Borghese**

Accessible from Piazzale Flaminio, Pincio Hill and the top of Via Vittorio Veneto, Villa Borghese is Rome's best-known park.

ℹ ROME FOR FREE

Some of Rome's most famous sights are free:

➡ Trevi Fountain

➡ Spanish Steps

➡ Pantheon

➡ St Peter's Basilica and all of Rome's churches

➡ Vatican Museums on the last Sunday of the month

➡ All state museums and monuments on the first Sunday of the month

★ **Museo e Galleria Borghese**　　　MUSEUM
(Map p654; ☑ 06 3 28 10; www.galleriaborghese. it; Piazzale del Museo Borghese 5; adult/reduced €15/8.50; ☉ 9am-7pm Tue-Sun; ☐ Via Pinciana) If you only have the time (or inclination) for one art gallery in Rome, make it this one. Housing what's often referred to as the 'queen of all private art collections', it boasts paintings by Caravaggio, Raphael and Titian, as well as some sensational sculptures by Bernini. Highlights abound, but look out for Bernini's *Ratto di Proserpina* (Rape of Proserpina) and Canova's *Venere vincitrice* (Venus Victrix).

To limit numbers, visitors are admitted at two-hourly intervals, so you'll need to pre-book your ticket and get an entry time.

★ **Museo Nazionale Etrusco di Villa Giulia**　　　MUSEUM
(Map p654; ☑ 06 322 65 71; www.villagiulia. beniculturali.it; Piazzale di Villa Giulia; adult/reduced €8/4; ☉ 8.30am-7.30pm Tue-Sun; ☐ Via delle Belle Arti) Pope Julius III's 16th-century villa provides the charming setting for Italy's finest collection of Etruscan and pre-Roman treasures. Exhibits, many of which came from tombs in the surrounding Lazio region, range from bronze figurines and black *bucchero* tableware to temple decorations, terracotta vases and a dazzling display of sophisticated jewellery.

Must-sees include a polychrome terracotta statue of Apollo from a temple in Veio and the 6th-century-BC *Sarcofago degli sposi* (Sarcophagus of the Betrothed), found in 1881 in Cerveteri.

🛏 Sleeping

🛏 Ancient Rome

★ **Residenza Maritti**　　　GUESTHOUSE €€
(Map p652; ☑ 06 678 82 33; www.residenza maritti.com; Via Tor de' Conti 17; s/d/tr €120/170/190; ❄ 🛜; Ⓜ Cavour) Boasting stunning views over the nearby forums and Vittoriano, this hidden gem has rooms spread over several floors. Some are bright and modern, others are more cosy in feel with antiques, original tiled floors and family furniture. There's a fully equipped kitchen and a self-service breakfast is provided.

🛏 Centro Storico

Okapi Rooms　　　HOTEL €
(Map p654; ☑ 06 3260 9815; www.okapirooms. it; Via della Penna 57; s/d/tr/q €80/110/140/170; ❄ 🛜; Ⓜ Flaminio) The Okapi is a smart, value-for-money choice near Piazza del Popolo. Rooms, spread over six floors of a narrow townhouse, are simple and airy with cream walls, terracotta floors and the occasional stone frieze. Some are smaller than others and several have little terraces. An optional breakfast (€4.50) is served in a nearby bar; buy a voucher at reception.

Hotel Pensione Barrett　　　PENSION €€
(Map p658; ☑ 06 686 8481; www.pensionebarrett. com; Largo di Torre Argentina 47; s/d/tr €115/135/165; ❄ 🛜; ☐ Largo di Torre Argentina) This exuberant *pensione* is quite unique. Boasting a convenient central location, its decor is wonderfully over the top with statues, busts and vibrant stucco set against a forest of leafy potted plants. Rooms are cosy and come with thoughtful extras like foot spas, coffee machines and fully stocked fridges.

🛏 Vatican City, Borgo & Prati

Le Stanze di Orazio　　　B&B €€
(Map p654; ☑ 06 3265 2474; www.lestanzedi orazio.com; Via Orazio 3; d €110-135; ❄ 🛜; ☐ Via Cola di Rienzo, Ⓜ Lepanto) This friendly boutique B&B makes for an attractive home away from home in the heart of the elegant Prati district, a single metro stop from the Vatican. It has five bright, playfully decorated rooms – think shimmering rainbow wallpaper, lilac accents and designer bathrooms – and a small breakfast area.

Hotel Bramante
HISTORIC HOTEL €€€

(Map p654; ☑ 06 6880 6426; www.hotelbramante.
com; Vicolo delle Palline 24-25; s €140-180, d €200-
240, tr €230-270, q €260-290; ❋ ❧; ☐ Via Tran-
spontina) Nestled under the Vatican walls, the
Bramante exudes country-house charm with
its cosy internal courtyard and classically
attired rooms complete with wood-beamed
ceilings and antique furniture. It's housed
in the 16th-century building where architect
Domenico Fontana once lived.

Monti & Esquilino

★ Beehive
HOSTEL €

(Map p662; ☑ 06 4470 4553; www.the-beehive.
com; Via Marghera 8; dm €35-40, d with shared
€80, s/d/tr €70/100/120; ❧ reception 7am-11pm;
❋ ❧; Ⓜ Termini) ✎ More boutique chic than
backpacker dive, the Beehive is a small and
stylish hostel with glorious summer garden.
Dynamic American owners Linda and Steve
exude energy and organise cooking classes,
storytelling evenings, weekly hostel dinners
around a shared table, pop-up dinners with
chefs, and so on. Pick from a spotless eight-
bed dorm (mixed), a four-bed female dorm,
or private rooms with ceiling fan and hon-
ey-based soap.

Blue Hostel
GUESTHOUSE €

(Map p662; ☑ 340 925 85 03; www.bluehostel.it;
Via Carlo Alberto 13, 3rd fl; d/tr/q €150/160/190;
❋ ❧; Ⓜ Vittorio Emanuele) A hostel in name
only, this small guesthouse has small, hotel-standard rooms with en suite bathroom
and tasteful low-key decor – think beamed
ceilings, wooden floors, French windows,
framed B&W photos. There's also an apartment with kitchen that sleeps up to four. No
lift and no breakfast.

Trastevere

★ Arco del Lauro
GUESTHOUSE €€

(Map p658; ☑ 06 9784 0350; www.arcodellauro.
it; Via Arco de' Tolomei 27; d €95-135, q €135-175;
❋ @ ❧; ☐ Viale di Trastevere, ☐ Viale di Trastevere) Perfectly placed on a peaceful cobbled
lane in the 'quiet side' of Trastevere, this
ground-floor guesthouse sports six gleaming
white rooms with parquet floors, a modern
low-key look and well-equipped bathrooms.
Guests share a kettle, fridge, complimentary
fruit bowl and cakes, and breakfast is served
in a nearby cafe. Daniele and Lorenzo who
run the place could not be friendlier or more
helpful.

✗ Eating

The most atmospheric neighbourhoods to
dine in are the *centro storico* (historic centre) and Trastevere. There are also excellent
choices in boho Monti and Testaccio. Watch
out for overpriced tourist traps around Termini and the Vatican.

✗ Centro Storico

★ Supplizio
FAST FOOD €

(Map p658; ☑ 06 8987 1920; www.facebook.com/
supplizioroma; Via dei Banchi Vecchi 143; suppli €3-7;
❧ noon-8pm Mon-Thu, noon-3.30pm & 6.30-10.30pm
Fri & Sat; ☐ Corso Vittorio Emanuele II) Rome's favourite snack, the *supplì* (a fried croquette
filled with rice, tomato sauce and mozzarella), gets a gourmet makeover at this elegant
street-food joint. Sit back on the vintage leather sofa and dig into a crispy classic or push the
boat out and try something different, maybe
a little fish number stuffed with fresh anchovies, cheese, bread and raisins.

Forno Roscioli
PIZZA, BAKERY €

(Map p658; ☑ 06 686 4045; www.anticoforno
roscioli.it; Via dei Chiavari 34; pizza slices from €2,
snacks €2; ❧ 6am-8pm Mon-Sat, 9am-7pm Sun;
☐ Via Arenula) This is one of Rome's top bakeries, much loved by lunching locals who
crowd here for luscious sliced pizza, prize
pastries and hunger-sating *supplì*. The *pizza margherita* is superb, if messy to eat, and
there's also a counter serving hot pastas and
vegetable side dishes.

Forno di Campo de' Fiori
PIZZA, BAKERY €

(Map p658; www.fornocampodefiori.com; Campo de' Fiori 22; pizza slices around €3; ❧ 7.30am-
2.30pm & 4.45-8pm Mon-Sat, closed Sat dinner Jul

ⓘ **ROMA PASS**
....

A cumulative sightseeing and transport
card, available online or from tourist
information points and participating
museums, the **Roma Pass** (www.roma
pass.it) comes in two forms:

72 hours (€38.50) Provides free admission to two museums or sites, as well as
reduced entry to extra sites, unlimited
city transport, and discounted entry to
other exhibitions and events.

48 hours (€28) Gives free admission to
one museum or site, and then as per the
72-hour pass.

ITALY ROME

Termini, Esquiline and Quirinal

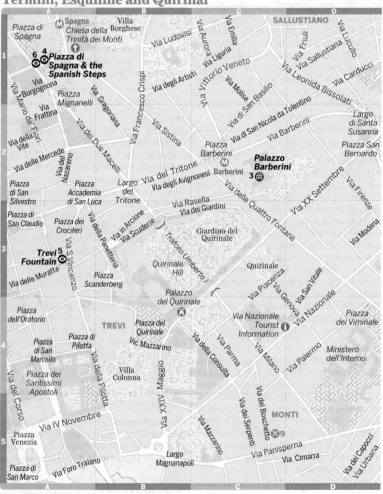

Termini, Esquiline and Quirinal

ITALY ROME

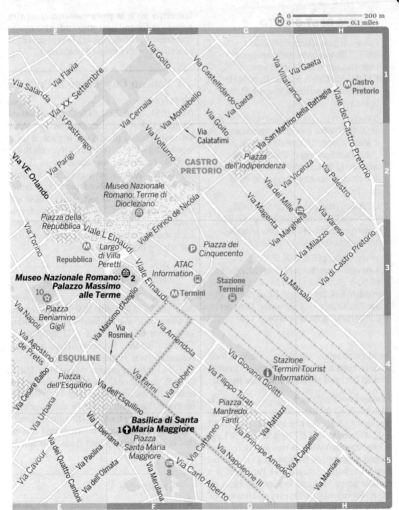

& Aug; 🚊 Corso Vittorio Emanuele II) This buzzing bakery on Campo de' Fiori, divided into two adjacent shops, does a roaring trade in *panini* and delicious fresh-from-the-oven *pizza al taglio* (pizza by the slice). Aficionados swear by the *pizza bianca* ('white' pizza with olive oil, rosemary and salt), but the *panini* and *pizza rossa* ('red' pizza with olive oil, tomato and oregano) taste plenty good too.

★ **La Ciambella** ITALIAN €€

(Map p658; ☎ 06 683 2930; www.la-ciambella. it; Via dell'Arco della Ciambella 20; meals €35-45; ⊙ bar 7.30am-midnight, wine bar & restaurant noon-11pm Tue-Sun; 🚊 Largo di Torre Argentina) Central but largely undiscovered by the tourist hordes, this friendly wine-bar-cum-restaurant beats much of the neighbourhood competition. Its spacious, light-filled interior is set over the ruins of the Terme di Agrippa, visible through transparent floor panels, and

ROME'S BEST GELATO

Fatamorgana (Map p654; ☑ 06 3265 2238; www.gelateriafatamorgana. com; Via Laurina 10; 2/3/4/5 scoops €2.50/3.50/4.50/5; ⊗ noon-11pm; Ⓜ Flaminio) Superb artisanal flavours at multiple central locations.

Gelateria del Teatro (Map p658; ☑ 06 4547 4880; www.gelateriadelteatro. it; Via dei Coronari 65; gelato €2.50-5; ⊗ 10.30am-8pm winter, 10am-10.30pm summer; ☐ Via Zanardelli) Seasonal fruit and spicy chocolate flavours, all made on site.

I Caruso (Map p654; ☑ 06 4201 6420; Via Collina 13-15; cones & tubs from €2.50; ⊗ noon-midnight; Ⓜ Repubblica) A small but perfect selection of creamy flavours.

Venchi (Map p658; ☑ 06 6992 5423; www.venchi.com; Via degli Orfani 87; gelato €2.50-5; ⊗ 10.30am-11pm Sun-Thu, to midnight Fri & Sat summer, 10am-10pm Sun-Thu, to 11pm Fri & Sat winter; ☐ Via del Corso) Nirvana for chocoholics.

its kitchen sends out some excellent food, from tartares and chickpea pancakes to slow-cooked beef and traditional Roman pastas.

Armando al Pantheon ROMAN €€ (Map p658; ☑ 06 6880 3034; www.armandoalpantheon.it; Salita dei Crescenzi 31; meals €40; ⊗ 12.30-3pm Mon-Sat & 7-11pm Mon-Fri; ☐ Largo di Torre Argentina) With its cosy wooden interior and unwavering dedication to old-school Roman cuisine, Armando al Pantheon is a regular go-to for local foodies. It's been on the go for more than 50 years and has served its fair share of celebs, but it hasn't let fame go to its head and remains as popular as ever. Reservations essential.

★ Casa Coppelle RISTORANTE €€€ (Map p658; ☑ 06 6889 1707; www.casacoppelle. it; Piazza delle Coppelle 49; meals €65, tasting menu €85; ⊗ noon-3.30pm & 6.30-11.30pm; ☐ Corso del Rinascimento) Boasting an enviable setting near the Pantheon and a plush, theatrical look – think velvet drapes, black lacquer tables and bookshelves – Casa Coppelle sets a romantic stage for high-end Roman-French cuisine. Gallic trademarks like snails and onion soup feature alongside updated Roman

favourites such as pasta *amatriciana* (with tomato sauce and pancetta) and *cacio e pepe* (pecorino and black pepper), here re-invented as a risotto with prawns. Book ahead.

✗ Vatican City, Borgo & Prati

★ Pizzarium PIZZA € (Map p654; ☑ 06 3974 5416; Via della Meloria 43; pizza slices €5; ⊗ 11am-10pm; Ⓜ Cipro-Musei Vaticani) When a pizza joint is packed on a wet winter's lunch, you know it's something special. Pizzarium, the takeaway of Gabriele Bonci, Rome's acclaimed pizza king, serves Rome's best sliced pizza, bar none. Scissor-cut squares of soft, springy base are topped with original combinations of seasonal ingredients and served on paper trays for immediate consumption. Also worth trying are the freshly fried *supplì*.

✗ Monti & Esquilino

★ L'Asino d'Oro ITALIAN €€ (Map p662; ☑ 06 4891 3832; www.facebook. com/asinodoro; Via del Boschetto 73; weekday lunch menu €16, meals €45; ⊗ 12.30-2.30pm & 7.30-11pm Tue-Sat; Ⓜ Cavour) This fabulous restaurant was transplanted from Orvieto, and its Umbrian origins resonate in Lucio Sforza's exceptional cooking. Unfussy yet innovative dishes feature bags of flavourful contrasts, like lamb meatballs with pear and blue cheese. Save room for the equally amazing desserts. Intimate, informal and classy, this is one of Rome's best deals – its lunch menu is a steal.

✗ Trastevere

★ La Gensola SICILIAN €€ (Map p658; ☑ 06 581 63 12; Piazza della Gensola 15; meals €45; ⊗ 12.30-3pm & 7.30-11.30pm, closed Sun summer; ☐ Viale di Trastevere, ☐ Viale di Trastevere) Enjoy delicious traditional cuisine with an emphasis on seafood at this upmarket trattoria, which can feel a tad overpriced. Begin the feast with a half-dozen oysters or wafer-thin slices of raw tuna, amberjack or seabass carpaccio, followed perhaps by a heap of *spaghellini* with fingernail-sized clams or seared anchovies with chicory. Meat lovers, tuck into Roman classics like *coda alla vaccinara* (oxtail stew) or *trippa* (tripe).

San Giovanni & Testaccio

Pizzeria Da Remo   PIZZA €
(Map p654; ☑ 06 574 62 70; Piazza Santa Maria Liberatrice 44; meals €15; ⊗ 7pm-1am Mon-Sat; 🚇 Via Marmorata) For an authentic Roman experience, join the noisy crowds here, one of the city's best-known and most popular pizzerias. It's a spartan-looking place, but the fried starters and thin-crust Roman pizzas are the business, and there's a cheerful, boisterous vibe. Expect to queue after 8.30pm.

🍷 Drinking & Nightlife

Much of the drinking action is in the *centro storico*: Campo de' Fiori is popular with students, while the area around Piazza Navona hosts a more upmarket scene. Over the river, Trastevere is another favoured spot with dozens of bars and pubs.

Rome's clubbing scene is centred on Testaccio and the Ostiense area, although you'll also find places in Trastevere and the *centro storico*. Admission to clubs is often free, but drinks are expensive.

★ Il Tiaso   BAR
(☑ 06 4547 4625; www.iltiaso.com; Via Ascoli Piceno 25; ⊗ 6pm-2am; 🚻; 🚇 Circonvallazione Casilina) Think living room with zebra-print chairs, walls of indie art, Lou Reed biographies wedged between wine bottles, and 30-something owner Gabriele playing his latest New York Dolls album to neo-beatnik chicks, corduroy-clad professors and the odd neighbourhood dog. Expect well-priced wine, an intimate chilled vibe, regular live music and lovely pavement terrace.

★ Barnum Cafe   CAFE
(Map p658; ☑ 06 6476 0483; www.barnumcafe. com; Via del Pellegrino 87; ⊗ 9am-10pm Mon, to 2am Tue-Sat; 🚻; 🚇 Corso Vittorio Emanuele II) A laid-back *Friends*-style cafe, evergreen Barnum is the sort of place you could quickly get used to. With its shabby-chic vintage furniture and white bare-brick walls, it's a relaxed spot for a breakfast cappuccino, a light lunch or a late afternoon drink. Come evening, a coolly dressed-down crowd sips seriously good cocktails.

Caffè Sant'Eustachio   COFFEE
(Map p658; www.santeustachioilcaffe.it; Piazza Sant'Eustachio 82; ⊗ 8.30am-1am Sun-Thu, to 1.30am Fri, to 2am Sat; 🚇 Corso del Rinascimento) This small, unassuming cafe, generally three deep at the bar, is reckoned by many to serve the best coffee in town. To make it, the bartenders sneakily beat the first drops of an espresso with several teaspoons of sugar to create a frothy paste to which they add the rest of the coffee. It's superbly smooth and guaranteed to put some zing into your sightseeing.

Open Baladin   BAR
(Map p658; ☑ 06 683 8989; www.openbaladin roma.it; Via degli Specchi 6; ⊗ noon-2am; 🚻; 🚇 Via Arenula) For some years, this cool, modern pub near Campo de' Fiori has been a leading light in Rome's craft beer scene, and it's still a top place for a pint with more than 40 beers on tap and up to 100 bottled brews, many from Italian artisanal microbreweries. There's also a decent food menu with *panini,* gourmet burgers and daily specials.

La Casa del Caffè Tazza d'Oro   COFFEE
(Map p658; ☑ 06 678 9792; www.tazzadorocoffee shop.com; Via degli Orfani 84-86; ⊗ 7am-8pm Mon-Sat, 10.30am-7.30pm Sun; 🚇 Via del Corso) A busy, stand-up affair with burnished 1940s fittings, this is one of Rome's best coffee houses. Its espresso hits the mark nicely and there's a range of delicious coffee concoctions, including a cooling *granita di caffè,* a crushed-ice coffee drink served with whipped cream. There's also a small shop and, outside, a coffee *bancomat* for those out-of-hours caffeine emergencies.

Ma Che Siete Venuti a Fà   PUB
(Map p658; ☑ 06 6456 2046; www.football-pub. com; Via Benedetta 25; ⊗ 11am-2am; 🚇 Piazza Trilussa) Named after a football chant, which translates politely as 'What did you come here for?', this pint-sized Trastevere pub is a beer-buff's paradise, packing in around 15 international craft beers on tap and even more by the bottle. Expect some rowdy drinking.

Freni e Frizioni   BAR
(Map p658; ☑ 06 4549 7499; www.freniefrizioni. com; Via del Politeama 4-6; ⊗ 7pm-2am; 🚇 Piazza Trilussa) This perennially cool Trastevere bar is housed in an old mechanic's workshop – hence its name ('brakes and clutches') and tatty facade. It draws a young *spritz*-loving crowd that swells onto the small piazza outside to sip superbly mixed cocktails (€10) and seasonal punches, and fill up on its lavish early-evening *aperitivo* buffet (7pm to 10pm). Table reservations are essential on Friday and Saturday evenings.

ITALY ROME

☆ Entertainment

Rome has a thriving cultural scene, with a year-round calendar of concerts, performances and festivals. Upcoming events are also listed on www.turismoroma.it and www.inromenow.com.

Auditorium Parco della Musica
CONCERT VENUE

(☏06 8024 1281; www.auditorium.com; Viale Pietro de Coubertin; 🚌Viale Tiziano) The Auditorium is the capital's premier concert venue. Its three concert halls offer superb acoustics, and together with a 3000-seat open-air arena, stage everything from classical music concerts to jazz gigs, public lectures and film screenings. The Auditorium is also home to Rome's world-class **Orchestra dell'Accademia Nazionale di Santa Cecilia** (www. santacecilia.it).

Alexanderplatz
JAZZ

(Map p654; ☏06 8377 5604; www.facebook. com/alexander.platz.37; Via Ostia 9; ⊙8.30pm-1.30am; Ⓜ️Ottaviano-San Pietro) Intimate, underground, and hard to find – look for the discreet black door – Rome's most celebrated jazz club draws top Italian and international performers and a respectful cosmopolitan crowd. Book a table for the best stage views or to dine here, although note that it's the music that's the star act not the food.

Teatro dell'Opera di Roma
OPERA, BALLET

(Map p662; ☏06 48 16 01; www.operaroma.it; Piazza Beniamino Gigli 1; ⊙box office 10am-6pm Mon-Sat, 9am-1.30pm Sun; Ⓜ️Repubblica) Rome's premier opera house boasts a plush gilt interior, a Fascist 1920s exterior and an impressive history: it premiered Puccini's *Tosca*, and Maria Callas once sang here. Opera and ballet performances are staged between September and June.

🛍 Shopping

Rome boasts the usual cast of flagship chain stores and glitzy designer outlets, but what makes shopping here fun is its legion of small, independent shops: family-run delis, small-label fashion boutiques, artisans' studios and neighbourhood markets.

Porta Portese Market
MARKET

(Map p654; Piazza Porta Portese; ⊙6am-2pm Sun; 🚌Viale di Trastevere, 🚋Viale di Trastevere) To see another side of Rome, head to this mammoth flea market. With thousands of stalls selling everything from rare books and fell-off-a-lorry bikes to Peruvian shawls and MP3 players, it's crazily busy and a lot of fun. Keep your valuables safe and wear your haggling hat.

ⓘ Information

DANGERS & ANNOYANCES

Rome is not a dangerous city, but petty theft can be a problem. Watch out for pickpockets around the big tourist sites, at Stazione Termini and on crowded public transport – the 64 Vatican bus is notorious.

INTERNET ACCESS

Free wi-fi is widely available in hostels, B&Bs and hotels; some also provide laptops or computers. Many bars and cafes also offer wi-fi .

MEDICAL SERVICES

Farmacrimi Stazione Termini (☏06 474 54 21; Via Marsala 29; ⊙7am-10pm; Ⓜ️Termini) Pharmacy located in Stazione Termini, next to Platform 1.

Policlinico Umberto I (☏06 4 99 71; www. policlinicoumberto1.it; Viale del Policlinico 155; Ⓜ️Policlinico, Castro Pretorio) Rome's largest hospital is located near Stazione Termini.

WORTH A TRIP

VIA APPIA ANTICA

Completed in 190 BC, the Appian Way connected Rome with Brindisi on Italy's Adriatic coast. It's now a picturesque area of ancient ruins, grassy fields and towering pine trees. But it has a dark history – this is where Spartacus and 6000 of his slave rebels were crucified in 71 BC, and where the ancients buried their dead. Well-to-do Romans built elaborate mausoleums while the early Christians went underground, creating a 300km network of subterranean burial chambers – the catacombs.

Highlights include the **Catacombe di San Sebastiano** (☏06 785 03 50; www.catacombe.org; Via Appia Antica 136; adult/reduced €8/5; ⊙10am-5pm Mon-Sat Jan-Nov; 🚌Via Appia Antica) and the nearby **Catacombe di San Callisto** (☏06 513 01 51; www.catacombe.roma. it; Via Appia Antica 110-126; adult/reduced €8/5; ⊙9am-noon & 2-5pm Thu-Tue Mar-Jan; 🚌Via Appia Antica).

To get to the Via, take bus 660 from Colli Albani metro station (line A) or bus 118 from Circo Massimo (line B).

DAY TRIPS FROM ROME

Ostia Antica

An easy train ride from Rome, Ostia Antica is one of Italy's most under-appreciated archaeological sites. The ruins of ancient Rome's main seaport, the **Scavi Archeologici di Ostia Antica** (☑ 06 5635 0215; www.ostiaantica.beniculturali.it; Viale dei Romagnoli 717; adult/reduced €8/4, exhibitions €3; ⊗ 8.30am-6.15pm Tue-Sun summer, shorter hours winter), are spread out and you'll need a few hours to do them justice.

To get to Ostia take the Ostia Lido train (25 minutes, half-hourly) from Stazione Porta San Paolo next to Piramide metro station. The journey is covered by standard public-transport tickets.

Tivoli

Tivoli, 30km east of Rome, is home to two Unesco–listed sites. Five kilometres from Tivoli proper, the ruins of the emperor Hadrian's sprawling **Villa Adriana** (☑ 0774 38 27 33; www.villaadriana.beniculturali.it; adult/reduced €8/4; ⊗ 9am-1hr before sunset) are quite magnificent. Up in Tivoli's hilltop centre, the Renaissance **Villa d'Este** (☑ 0774 33 29 20; www.villadestetivoli.info; Piazza Trento; adult/reduced €8/4; ⊗ 8.30am-1hr before sunset Tue-Sun) is famous for its elaborate gardens and fountains.

Tivoli is accessible by Cotral bus (€1.30, one hour, every 15 to 20 minutes) from Ponte Mammolo metro station. To get to Villa Adriana from Tivoli town centre, take CAT bus 4 or 4X (€1.30, 10 minutes, half-hourly) from Largo Garibaldi.

TOURIST INFORMATION

For phone enquiries, there's a **tourist information line** (☑ 06 06 08; www.060608.it; ⊗ 9am-9pm).

For information about the Vatican, contact the **Centro Servizi Pellegrini e Turisti** (Map p654; ☑ 06 6988 1662; St Peter's Square; ⊗ 8.30am-6.30pm Mon-Sat; Ⓜ Piazza del Risorgimento, Ⓜ Ottaviano-San Pietro).

There are **tourist information points** (☑ 06 06 08; www.turismoroma.it) at **Fiumicino** (International Arrivals, Terminal 3; ⊗ 8am-8.45pm) and **Ciampino** (Arrivals Hall; ⊗ 8.30am-6pm) airports, and at locations across town. These include the following:

Stazione Termini Tourist Information (Map p662; Via Giovanni Giolitti 34; ⊗ 9am-5pm; Ⓜ Termini) Located inside the station next to the Mercato Centrale, not far from the car-rental and left-luggage desk. Pick up city maps and reserve city tours at this efficient tourist office.

Via Nazionale Tourist Information (Map p662; Via Nazionale 184; ⊗ 9.30am-7pm; Ⓠ Via Nazionale) Tourist information kiosk in front of Palazzo delle Esposizioni. Handy for city maps and sells the Roma Pass.

Fori Imperiali Tourist Information (Map p652; Via dei Fori Imperiali; ⊗ 9.30am-7pm; Ⓠ Via dei Fori Imperiali) Has a panel illustrating the Roman and Imperial Forums – photograph it and you've got a useful guide.

Minghetti Tourist Information (Map p658; Via Marco Minghetti; ⊗ 9.30am-7pm; Ⓠ Via del Corso) A tourist information kiosk between Via del Corso and the Trevi Fountain.

Piazza Navona Tourist Information (Map p658; Piazza delle Cinque Lune; ⊗ 9.30am-7pm; Ⓠ Corso del Rinascimento) Actually located just off of Piazza Navona, on Piazza delle Cinque Lune.

USEFUL WEBSITES

060608 (www.060608.it) Rome's official tourist website.

Auditorium (www.auditorium.com) Check concert listings.

Coopculture (www.coopculture.it) Information and ticket booking for Rome's monuments.

Lonely Planet (www.lonelyplanet.com/rome) Destination low-down, hotel bookings and traveller forum.

Vatican Museums (www.vatican.va) Book tickets and avoid the queues.

ⓘ Getting There & Away

AIR

Rome's main international airport, **Leonardo da Vinci** (☑ 06 6 59 51; www.adr.it/fiumicino), better known as Fiumicino, is on the coast 30km west of the city.

The much smaller **Ciampino Airport** (☑ 06 6 59 51; www.adr.it/ciampino), 15km southeast of the city centre, is the hub for European low-cost carrier Ryanair.

BOAT

The nearest port to Rome is Civitavecchia, about 80km north. Ferries sail here from Spain and Tunisia, as well as Sicily and Sardinia. Book tickets at travel agents or online at www.traghettiweb.it. You can also buy directly at the port. Half-hourly trains connect Civitavecchia and Roma Termini (€5 to €15.50, 40 minutes to 1¼ hours).

BUS

Long-distance national and international buses use the **Autostazione Tiburtina** (Tibus; Largo Guido Mazzoni; M Tiburtina). Get tickets at the bus station or at travel agencies.

CAR & MOTORCYCLE

Rome is circled by the Grande Raccordo Anulare (GRA), to which all autostrade (motorways) connect, including the main A1 north–south artery, and the A12, which runs to Civitavecchia and Fiumicino airport.

Car hire is available at the airport and Stazione Termini.

TRAIN

Rome's main station is **Stazione Termini** (www.romatermini.com; Piazza dei Cinquecento; M Termini). It has regular connections to other European countries, all major Italian cities and many smaller towns. **Left luggage** (Stazione Termini; 1st 5hr €6, 6-12hr per hour €0.90, 13hr & over per hour €0.40; ⊙6am-11pm; M Termini) is in the wing on the Via Giolitti side of the station, near the tourist office.

Rome's other principal train stations are Stazione Tiburtina and Stazione Roma-Ostiense.

ℹ Getting Around

TO/FROM THE AIRPORTS
Fiumicino

The easiest way to get to/from Fiumicino is by train, but there are also bus services. The set taxi fare to the city centre is €48 (valid for up to four people with luggage).

Leonardo Express Train (one way €14) Runs to/from Stazione Termini. Departures from Fiumicino airport every 30 minutes between 6.23am and 11.23pm; from Termini between 5.35am and 10.35pm. Journey time is 30 minutes.

FL1 Train (one way €8) Connects to Trastevere, Ostiense and Tiburtina stations, but not Termini. Departures from Fiumicino airport every 15 minutes (half-hourly on Sundays and public holidays) between 5.57am and 10.42pm; from Tiburtina every 15 minutes between 5.01am and 7.31pm, then half-hourly to 10.01pm.

Ciampino

The best option from Ciampino is to take one of the regular bus services into the city centre. The set taxi fare to the city centre is €30.

SIT Bus – Ciampino (☑ 06 591 68 26; www.sitbusshuttle.com; from/to airport €5/6, return €9) Regular departures from the airport to Via Marsala outside Stazione Termini between 7.45am and 11.15pm; from Termini between 4.30am and 9.30pm. Get tickets on the bus. Journey time is 45 minutes.

Schiaffini Rome Airport Bus – Ciampino (☑ 06 713 05 31; www.romeairportbus.com; Via Giolitti; one-way/return €4.90/7.90) Regular departures to/from Via Giolitti outside Stazione Termini. From the airport, services are between 4am and 10.50pm; from Via Giolitti, buses run from 4.50am to midnight. Buy tickets onboard, online, at the airport, or at the bus stop. Journey time is approximately 40 minutes.

PUBLIC TRANSPORT

Rome's public transport system includes buses, trams, metro and a suburban train network.

Tickets are valid on all forms of public transport, except for routes to Fiumicino airport. They come in various forms:

BIT (€1.50) Valid for 100 minutes and one metro ride.

Roma 24h (€7) Valid for 24 hours.

Roma 48h (€12.50) Valid for 48 hours.

Roma 72h (€18) Valid for 72 hours.

Buy tickets at *tabacchi* (tobacconist shops), newsstands or from vending machines.

Bus

➺ Rome's buses and trams are run by **ATAC** (☑ 06 5 70 03; www.atac.roma.it).

➺ The main bus station is in front of Stazione Termini on Piazza dei Cinquecento, where there's an **information booth** (Map p662; ⊙8am-8pm).

➺ Other important hubs are at Largo di Torre Argentina and Piazza Venezia.

➺ Buses generally run from about 5.30am until midnight, with limited services throughout the night.

Metro

➺ Rome has two main metro lines, A (orange) and B (blue), which cross at Termini.

➺ Trains run between 5.30am and 11.30pm (to 1.30am on Fridays and Saturdays).

TAXI

➺ Official licensed taxis are white with an ID number and *Roma Capitale* on the sides.

➺ Always go with the metered fare, never an arranged price (the set fares to and from the airports are exceptions).

➺ There are taxi ranks at the airports, Stazione Termini, Piazza della Repubblica, Piazza Barberini, Piazza di Spagna, the Pantheon, the Colosseum, Largo di Torre Argentina, Piazza Belli, Piazza Pio XII and Piazza del Risorgimento.

NORTHERN ITALY

Italy's well-heeled north is a fascinating area of historical wealth and natural diversity. Bordered by the northern Alps and boasting some of the country's most spectacular coastline, it also encompasses Italy's largest lowland area, the fertile Po valley plain. Glacial lakes in the far north offer stunning scenery, while cities like Venice, Milan and Turin harbour artistic treasures and lively cultural scenes.

Genoa

POP 586,700

Genoa (Genova) is an absorbing city of aristocratic *palazzi,* dark, malodorous alleyways, Gothic architecture and industrial sprawl. Formerly a powerful maritime republic known as La Superba (Christopher Columbus was born here in 1451), it's still an important transport hub, with ferry links to destinations across the Med and train links to the Cinque Terre.

◎ Sights

★ Palazzo Reale   PALACE

(📋 010 271 02 36; www.palazzorealegenova.beniculturali.it; Via Balbi 10; adult/reduced €4/2; ⊘ 9am-7pm Tue-Sat, 1.30-7pm Sun) If you only get the chance to visit one of the Palazzi dei Rolli (a group of palaces belonging to the city's most eminent families), make it this one. A former residence of the Savoy dynasty, it has terraced gardens, exquisite furnishings, a fine collection of 17th-century art and a gilded Hall of Mirrors that is worth the entry fee alone.

Musei di Strada Nuova   MUSEUM

(📋 010 557 21 93; www.museidigenova.it; Via Garibaldi 9; combined ticket adult/reduced €9/7; ⊘ 9am-7pm Tue-Fri, 10am-7.30pm Sat & Sun summer, to 6.30pm winter) Skirting the northern edge of what was once the city limits, pedestrianised Via Garibaldi (formerly called the Strada Nuova) was planned by Galeazzo Alessi in the 16th century. It quickly became the city's most sought-after quarter, lined with the palaces of Genoa's wealthiest citizens. Three of these *palazzi* – Rosso, Bianco and Doria-Tursi – today comprise the Musei di Strada Nuova. Between them, they hold the city's finest collection of old masters.

Cattedrale di San Lorenzo   CATHEDRAL

(Piazza San Lorenzo; ⊘ 8am-noon & 3-7pm) Genoa's zebra-striped Gothic-Romanesque cathedral owes its continued existence to the poor quality of a British WWII bomb that failed to ignite here in 1941; it still sits on the right side of the nave like an innocuous museum piece.

The cathedral, fronted by three arched portals, twisting columns and crouching lions, was first consecrated in 1118. The two bell towers and cupola were added later in the 16th century.

🛏 Sleeping & Eating

★ Palazzo Cambiaso   APARTMENT €

(📋 010 856 61 88; www.palazzocambiaso.it; Via al Ponte Calvi 6; d €80-120, apt €120-240; 🛜) A real attention to design is evident in these rooms and apartments, set on the upper floor of a stately *palazzo.* The larger ones (sleeps up to six) come with full marble kitchens, long dining tables and laundries, but even the cheapest double is spacious, soothing and has the signature Frette linen.

★ Hotel Cairoli   HOTEL €

(📋 010 246 14 54; www.hotelcairoligenova.com; Via Cairoli 14/4; d €65-105, tr €85-125, q €90-150; ✳️@🛜) For five-star service at three-star prices, book at this artful hideaway. Rooms, on the 3rd floor of a towering *palazzo,* are themed on modern artists and feature works inspired by the likes of Mondrian, Dorazio and Alexander Calder. Add in a library, chill-out area, internet point, small gym and terrace, and you have the ideal bolt-hole.

Trattoria Rosmarino   TRATTORIA €€

(📋 010 251 04 75; www.trattoriarosmarino.it; Salita del Fondaco 30; meals €30-35; ⊘ 12.30-2.30pm & 7.30-10.30pm Mon-Sat) Rosmarino cooks up the standard local specialities, yes, but the straight-forwardly priced menu has an elegance and vibrancy that sets it apart. With two nightly sittings, there's always a nice buzz (though there's also enough nooks and crannies that a romantic night for two isn't out of the question). Call ahead for an evening table.

Trattoria della Raibetta   TRATTORIA €€

(📋 010 246 88 77; www.trattoriadellaraibetta.it; Vico Caprettari 10-12; meals €30-35; ⊘ noon-2.30pm & 7.30-11pm Tue-Sun) Totally *typica* Genoese food can be found in the family-run joints hidden in the warren of streets near the cathedral. This, a snug trattoria with a low brick-vaulted ceiling, serves regional classics such as *trofiette al pesto* or octopus salad alongside excellent fresh fish.

ℹ Information

Tourist Office (☑ 010 557 29 03; www.
visitgenoa.it; Via Garibaldi 12r; ⊗ 9am-6.20pm)
Helpful office in the historic centre.

ℹ Getting There & Around

AIR

Genoa's **Cristoforo Colombo Airport** (☑ 010
6 01 51; www.airport.genova.it) is 6km west of
the city.

To get to/from it, the **Volabus** (☑ 848 000
030; www.amt.genova.it; one-way €6) shuttle
connects with Stazione Brignole and Stazione
Principe. Buy tickets on board.

BOAT

Ferries sail to Spain, Sicily, Sardinia, Corsica,
Morocco and Tunisia from the international
passenger terminals, west of the city centre.
Grandi Navi Veloci (GNV; ☑ 010 209 45 91;
www.gnv.it) Ferries to Sardinia (Porto Torres;
from €38) and Sicily (Palermo; from €68). Also
to Barcelona (Spain) and Tunis (Tunisia).
Moby Lines (☑ 199 303040; www.mobylines.
it) Ferries year-round to the Sardinian ports of
Olbia (from €41) and Porto Torres (from €41).

BUS

Buses to international cities depart from Piazza
della Vittoria, as does a daily bus to/from Milan's
Malpensa airport (€25, three hours) and other
interregional services. Tickets are sold at **Geo
travels** (☑ 010 58 71 81; Piazza della Vittoria 57;
⊗ 9am-12.30pm & 3-7pm Mon-Fri, 9am-noon Sat).

TRAIN

Genoa's Stazione Principe and Stazione Brignole
are linked by train to the following destinations:

TO	FARE (€)	DURATION (HR)	FREQUENCY
Milan	13-27	1½	22 daily
Pisa	21-26	2-2½	16 daily
Rome	51-63	4½-5½	9 daily
Turin	12-21	2	19 daily

Cinque Terre

Liguria's eastern Riviera boasts some of Italy's most dramatic coastline, the highlight
of which is the Unesco-listed **Parco Nazionale delle Cinque Terre** (Cinque Terre National Park) just west of La Spezia. Running
for 18km, this awesome stretch of plunging
cliffs and vine-covered hills is named after
its five tiny villages: Riomaggiore, Manarola,
Corniglia, Vernazza and Monterosso.

In October 2011 flash floods along the
Ligurian coast wreaked havoc in Vernazza
and Monterosso, burying historic streets under metres of mud and killing half-a-dozen
people. The villages recovered swiftly, but
some of the walking trails remain closed to
visitors.

🏃 Activities

The Cinque Terre offers excellent hiking
with a 120km network of paths. The best
known is the 12km **Sentiero Azzurro** (Blue
Trail), a one-time mule trail that links all
five villages. To walk it (or any of the national park's trails) you'll need a **Cinque
Terre Card** (one/two days €7.50/14.50), or
a **Cinque Terre Treno Card** (one/two days
€16/29), which also provides unlimited train
travel between La Spezia and the five villages. Both cards are available at park offices.

At the time of writing, two legs of the
Sentiero Azzurro were closed – Riomaggiore
to Manarola (the so-called Via dell'Amore)
and Manarola to Corniglia – and will possibly remain so until 2018. Check www.
parconazionale5terre.it for the current
situation.

If water sports are more your thing, you
can hire snorkelling gear and kayaks at the
Diving Center 5 Terre (☑ 0187 92 00 11; www.
5terrediving.it; Via San Giacomo) in Riomaggiore.

ℹ Information

Parco Nazionale (www.parconazionale5terre.
it; ⊗ 8am-8pm summer, 8.30am-12.30pm &
1-5pm winter) Offices in the train stations of all
five villages and La Spezia station; has comprehensive information about hiking trail closures.

ℹ Getting There & Away

BOAT

Golfo Paradiso SNC (☑ 0185 77 20 91; www.
golfoparadiso.it) In summer, Golfo Paradiso
runs boats to the Cinque Terre from Genoa (one
way/return €20/35).
**Consorzio Marittimo Turistico Cinque Terre
Golfo dei Poeti** (www.navigazionegolfodeipo-
eti.it) From late March to October, La Spezia–
based Consorzio Marittimo Turistico Cinque
Terre Golfo dei Poeti runs daily shuttle boats
between all of the Cinque Terre villages (except
Corniglia), costing €9 one way, including all
stops, or €20 for an all-day ticket.

TRAIN

From Genoa Brignole, direct trains run to Rio-maggiore (€6.80, 1½ to two hours, at least 10 daily), stopping at each of the villages.

From La Spezia, one to three trains an hour run up the coast between 4.30am and 11.10pm. If you're using this route and want to stop at all the villages, get the Cinque Terre Treno Card.

Monterosso

The largest and most developed of the villages, Monterosso boasts the coast's only sandy beach, as well as a wealth of eating and accommodation options.

🛏 Sleeping & Eating

⭐**Hotel Pasquale** HOTEL €€
(📞0187 81 74 77; www.hotelpasquale.it; Via Fegina 4; s €85-170, d €135-255, tr €170-340; ☻Mar-Nov; ❋⛶) Offering soothing views and 15 unusually stylish, modern guest rooms, this friendly seafront hotel is built into Monterosso's medieval sea walls. To find it, exit the train station and go left through the tunnel towards the *centro storico*.

Trattoria da Oscar TRATTORIA €€
(Via Vittorio Emanuele 67; meals €35; ☻noon-2pm & 7-10pm) Behind Piazza Matteoti, in the heart of the old town, this vaulted dining room is run by a young, friendly team. The town's famed anchovies dominate the menu; whether you go for the standard fried-with-lemon, with a white wine sauce or deep-fried, they are all good. No credit cards.

Vernazza

Perhaps the most attractive of the five villages, Vernazza overlooks a small, picturesque harbour.

From near the harbour, a steep, narrow staircase leads up to **Castello Doria** (€1.50; ☻10am-7pm summer, to 6pm winter), the oldest surviving fortification in the Cinque Terre. Dating to around 1000, it's now largely ruined except for the circular tower in the centre of the esplanade, but the castle is well worth a visit for the superb views it commands.

To overnight in Vernazza, try **La Mala** (📞334 287 57 18; www.lamala.it; Via San Giovanni Battista 29; d €140-220; ❋⛶), a contemporary boutique hotel in the cliffside heights of the village.

Corniglia

Corniglia, the only village with no direct sea access, sits atop a 100m-high rocky promontory surrounded by vineyards. To reach the village proper from the railway station you must first tackle the **Lardarina**, a 377-step brick stairway, or jump on a shuttle bus (one way €2.50).

Once up in the village, you can enjoy dazzling 180-degree sea views from the **Belvedere di Santa Maria**, a heart-stopping lookout point at the end of Via Fieschi.

Manarola

One of the busiest of the villages, Manarola tumbles down to the sea in a helter-skelter of pastel-coloured buildings, cafes, trattorias and restaurants.

🛏 Sleeping & Eating

Hotel Marina Piccola BOUTIQUE HOTEL €€
(📞0187 92 07 70; www.hotelmarinapiccola.com; s/d/tr €125/145/190, ste €160-245; ❋⛶) This choice Manarola hotel has 12 big, comfortable, contemporary rooms, with a few looking over the sea. The lovely lobby and lounge area, which sports a surprisingly on-trend interior, is a welcome respite from the busy day-time streets. A real find at this price, although there is a minimum two-day stay in summer.

Da Aristide SEAFOOD €
(📞0187 92 00 00; Via Discovolo 290; meals €25-30; ☻9am-11pm Fri-Wed) Up the hill, not far from the train station, Aristide has tables in an old village house and in a bright, modern terrace on the square. Order a few of the heaped plates of stuffed anchovies or lemon-doused grilled octopus to share or keep one of the fish ravioli or homemade pappardelle with mussels and eggplant for yourself.

Riomaggiore

The Cinque Terre's largest and easternmost village, Riomaggiore acts as the unofficial HQ.

For a taste of classic seafood and local wine, search out **Dau Cila** (📞0187 76 00 32; www.ristorantedaucila.com; Via San Giacomo 65; meals €40; ☻noon-midnight, closed Jan & Feb), a smart restaurant-cum-wine bar perched overlooking the twee harbour.

Turin

POP 890,500

With its regal *palazzi,* baroque piazzas, cafes and world-class museums, Turin (Torino) is a dynamic, cultured city. For centuries, it was the seat of the royal Savoy family, and between 1861 and 1864, it was Italy's first post-unification capital. More recently, it hosted the 2006 Winter Olympics and was European Capital of Design in 2008.

⊙ Sights

★ Museo Egizio   MUSEUM

(Egyptian Museum; ☑011 561 77 76; www.museo egizio.it; Via Accademia delle Scienze 6; adult/reduced €15/11; ⊙9am-6.30pm Tue-Sun, 9am-2pm Mon) Opened in 1824 and housed in the austere Palazzo dell'Accademia delle Scienze, this Turin institution houses the most important collection of Egyptian treasure outside Cairo. Among its many highlights are a statue of Ramses II (one of the world's most important pieces of Egyptian art), the world's largest papyrus collection and over 500 funerary and domestic items found in 1906 in the tomb of royal architect Kha and his wife Merit (from 1400 BC).

Mole Antonelliana   LANDMARK

(www.gtt.to.it/cms/turismo/ascensore-mole; Via Montebello 20; lift adult/reduced €7/5, incl Museo €14/11; ⊙lift 10am-8pm Sun, Mon & Wed-Fri, to 11pm Sat) The symbol of Turin, this 167m tower with its distinctive aluminium spire appears on the Italian two-cent coin. It was originally intended as a synagogue when construction began in 1862, but was never used as a place of worship, and nowadays houses the Museo Nazionale del Cinema (☑011 813 85 60; www.museocinema.it; adult/reduced €10/8, incl lift €14/11; ⊙9am-8pm Sun, Mon & Wed-Fri, to 11pm Sat). For dazzling 360-degree views, take the Panoramic Lift up to the 85m-high outdoor viewing deck.

Cattedrale di San
Giovanni Battista   CATHEDRAL

(www.duomoditorino.it; Via XX Settembre 87; ⊙9am-12.30pm & 3-7pm) Turin's cathedral was built between 1491 and 1498 on the site of three 14th-century basilicas and, before that, a Roman theatre. Plain interior aside, as home to the famous Shroud of Turin (alleged to be the burial cloth in which Jesus' body was wrapped), this is a highly trafficked church. A copy of the cloth is on permanent display to the left of the cathedral altar.

Piazza Castello   PIAZZA

Turin's central square is lined with museums, theatres and cafes. The city's Savoy heart, although laid out from the mid-1300s, was mostly constructed from the 16th to 18th centuries. Dominating it is the part-medieval, part-baroque Palazzo Madama, the original seat of the Italian parliament. To the north is the exquisite facade of the Palazzo Reale, the royal palace built for Carlo Emanuele II in the mid-1600s.

🛏 Sleeping & Eating

★ Via Stampatori   B&B €

(☑339 258 13 30; www.viastampatori.com; Via Stampatori 4; s/d €90/110; 🕾) This utterly lovely B&B occupies the top floor of a frescoed Renaissance building. Six bright, stylish and uniquely furnished rooms overlook either a sunny terrace or a leafy inner courtyard. The owner's personal collection of 20th-century design is used throughout the rooms and several serene common areas. It's central but blissfully quiet.

★ DuParc
Contemporary Suites   DESIGN HOTEL €€

(☑011 012 00 00; www.duparcsuites.com; Corso Massimo D'Azeglio 21; r/ste from €120/140; 🅿❋🕾) A business-friendly location doesn't mean this isn't a great choice for all travellers. Staff are young and friendly, and the building's stark modern lines are softened with a fantastic contemporary art collection, bold colour and tactile furnishings. Best of all, even the cheapest rooms here are sumptuously large, with king beds, ample cupboard space, huge bathrooms and floor-to-ceiling windows.

È Cucina   MODERN ITALIAN €

(☑011 562 90 38; www.cesaremarretti.com; Via Bertola 27a; meals €10-30; ⊙12.30-3pm & 8-11pm) Northern Italians are fond of a 'concept' and Bolognese chef Cesare Marretti's concept here is *sorpesa* (surprise). Beyond the choice of meat, fish or vegetables and the number of courses you want, it's up to the kitchen. What *is* certain is the innovative cooking and excellent produce that will arrive. Local's tip: don't be tempted to over order.

★ Banco vini e alimenti   PIEDMONT €€

(☑011 764 02 39; www.bancoviniealimenti.it; Via dei Mercanti 13f; meals €25-30; ⊙6.30pm-12.30am Mon, 12.30pm-12.30am Tue-Sat) A hybrid restaurant-bar-deli, this smartly designed but low-key place does clever small-dish dining for lunch and dinner. While it might vibe casual wine bar, with young staff in T-shirts and boyfriend jeans, don't underestimate the food: this is serious Piedmontese cooking. Open all day, you can grab a single-origin pour-over here in the morning, or a herbal house *spritz* late afternoon.

Drinking & Nightlife

Aperitivi and more substantial *apericenas* are a Turin institution. If you're on a tight budget, you can fill up on a generous buffet of bar snacks for the cost of a drink.

Nightlife concentrates in the riverside area around Piazza Vittoria Veneto, the Quadrilatero Romano district and increasingly the southern neighbourhoods of San Salvarino and Vanchiglia.

ⓘ Information

Piazza Castello Tourist Office (☏ 011 53 51 81; www.turismotorino.org; Piazza Castello; ☉9am-6pm) Central and multilingual.

ⓘ Getting There & Around

From **Turin Airport** (☏ 011 567 63 61; www. aeroportoditorino.it; Strada Aeroporto 12), 16km northwest of the city centre in Caselle, airlines fly to Italian and European destinations.

Sadem (☏ 800 801 600; www.sadem.it) runs an airport shuttle (€6.50 or €7.50 on board, 50 minutes, half-hourly) to/from Porta Nuova train station.

Trains connect with Milan (€12 to €35, one to two hours, 30 daily), Florence (€55 to €116, three hours, 10 daily), Genoa (€12 to €21, two hours, up to 19 daily) and Rome (€60 to €124, 4¼ hours, up to 16 daily).

Milan

POP 1.34 MILLION

Few Italian cities polarise opinion like Milan, Italy's financial and fashion capital. Some people love the cosmopolitan, can-do atmosphere, the vibrant cultural scene and sophisticated shopping; others grumble that it's dirty, ugly and expensive. Certainly, it lacks the picture-postcard beauty of many Italian towns, but in among the urban hustle are some truly great sights – Leonardo da Vinci's *Last Supper,* the immense Duomo and La Scala opera house.

WORTH A TRIP

MUSEO NAZIONALE DELL'AUTOMOBILE

As the historic birthplace of one of the world's leading car manufacturers – the 'T' in Fiat stands for Torino – Turin is the obvious place for a car museum. And the dashing **Museo Nazionale dell'Automobile** (☏ 011 67 76 66; www.museoauto.it; Corso Unità d'Italia 40; adult/reduced €12/8; ☉10am-7pm Wed, Thu & Sun, to 9pm Fri & Sat, to 2pm Mon, 2-7pm Tue; Ⓜ Lingotto), located roughly 5km south of the city centre, doesn't disappoint with its precious collection of over 200 automobiles – everything from an 1892 Peugeot to a 1980 Ferrari 308 (in red, of course).

◉ Sights

★**Duomo** CATHEDRAL
(☏ 02 7202 3375; www.duomomilano.it; Piazza del Duomo; adult/reduced duomo €2/3, roof terraces via stairs €9/4.50, lift €13/7, archaeological area €7/3; ☉duomo 8am-7pm, roof terraces 9am-7pm; Ⓜ Duomo) A vision in pink Candoglia marble, Milan's extravagant Gothic cathedral, 600 years in the making, aptly reflects the city's creativity and ambition. Its pearly white facade, adorned with 135 spires and 3400 statues, rises like the filigree of a fairy-tale tiara, wowing the crowds with its extravagant detail. The interior is no less impressive, punctuated by the largest stained-glass windows in Christendom, while in the crypt saintly Carlo Borromeo is interred in a rock-crystal casket.

★**Museo del Novecento** GALLERY
(☏ 02 8844 4061; www.museodelnovecento. org; Via Marconi 1; adult/reduced €10/8; ☉2.30-7.30pm Mon, 9.30am-7.30pm Tue, Wed, Fri & Sun, to 10.30pm Thu & Sat; 📷; Ⓜ Duomo) Overlooking Piazza del Duomo, with fabulous views of the cathedral, is Mussolini's Arengario, from where he would harangue huge crowds in his heyday. Now it houses Milan's museum of 20th-century art. Built around a futuristic spiral ramp (an ode to the Guggenheim), the lower floors are cramped, but the heady collection, which includes the likes of Umberto Boccioni, Campigli, de Chirico and Marinetti, more than distracts.

ITALY MILAN

Central Milan

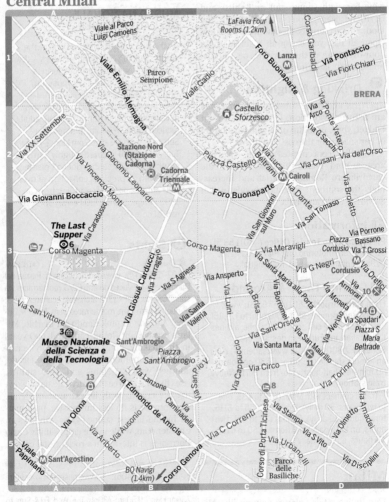

★ **Pinacoteca di Brera** GALLERY

(☎02 722 631; www.pinacotecabrera.org; Via Brera 28; adult/reduced €10/7; ◷8.30am-7.15pm Tue-Wed & Fri-Sun, to 10.15pm Thu; Ⓜ Lanza, Montenapoleone) Located upstairs from the centuries-old Accademia di Belle Arti (still one of Italy's most prestigious art schools), this gallery houses Milan's impressive collection of Old Masters, much of it 'lifted' from Venice by Napoleon. Rubens, Goya and Van Dyck all have a place in the collection, but you're here for the Italians: Titian, Tintoretto, Veronese, and the Bellini brothers. Much of the work has tremendous emotional clout, most notably Mantegna's brutal *Lamentation over the Dead Christ*.

★ **The Last Supper** ARTWORK

(Il Cenacolo; ☎02 9280 0360; www.cenacolovinciano.net; Piazza Santa Maria delle Grazie 2; adult/reduced €10/5, plus booking fee €2; ◷8.15am-6.45pm Tue-Sun; Ⓜ Cadorna) Milan's most famous mural, Leonardo da Vinci's *The Last Supper* is hidden away on a wall of the refectory adjoining the **Basilica di Santa Maria delle Grazie** (☎02 467 6111; www.legraziemilano.it; ◷7am-noon & 3.30-7.30pm Mon-Sat, 7.30am-12.30pm & 4-9pm Sun). Depicting Christ and

at Milan's science museum, the largest of its kind in Italy. It is a fitting tribute in a city where arch-inventor Leonardo da Vinci did much of his finest work. The 16th-century monastery where it is housed features a collection of more than 10,000 items, including models based on da Vinci's sketches, and outdoor hangars housing steam trains, planes and Italy's first submarine, *Enrico Toti*. More recently, the museum added a helicopter flight simulator, in which you can swoop over Milan in a real AW109 cockpit.

🛏 Sleeping

his disciples at the dramatic moment when Christ reveals he's aware of his betrayal, it's a masterful psychological study and one of the world's most iconic images. To see it you must book in advance or sign up for a guided city tour.

★**Museo Nazionale della Scienza e della Tecnologia**　　MUSEUM
(☑02 48 55 51; www.museoscienza.org; Via San Vittore 21; adult/child €10/7.50, submarine tours €8, flight simulator €10; ⊙9.30am-5pm Tue-Fri, to 6.30pm Sat & Sun; 🕿👪; Ⓜ Sant'Ambrogio) Kids and would-be inventors will go goggle-eyed

★**Ostello Bello**　　HOSTEL €
(☑02 3658 2720; www.ostellobello.com; Via Medici 4; dm/d/tr €45/129/149; ❄🕿; 🚌2, 3, 14) A breath of fresh air in Milan's stiffly-suited centre, this is the best hostel in town. Entrance is through its lively bar-cafe, open to nonguests, where you're welcomed with a smile and a complimentary drink. Beds are in mixed dorms or spotless private rooms, and there's a kitchen, a small terrace, and a basement lounge equipped with guitars, board games and table football.

★ **LaFavia Four Rooms**   B&B €€

(☑ 347 7842212; www.lafavia4rooms.com; Via Carlo Farini 4; s €90-105, d €100-125; ❄ 🔊; Ⓜ Garibaldi) Marco and Fabio's four-room B&B in the former Rabarbaro Zucca factory is a multicultural treat with rooms inspired by their travels through India, Mexico and Europe. Graphic wallpapers by Manuela Canova in zippy greens and oranges are complemented by lush window views onto plant-filled verandas. Best of all is the rooftop garden, where an organic breakfast is served in summer.

Antica Locanda Leonardo   HOTEL €€

(☑ 02 4801 4197; www.anticalocandaleonardo.com; Corso Magenta 78; s €95-105, d €158; ❄ @ 🔊; Ⓜ Conciliazione) An old-school, homely B&B in a 19th-century residence near Leonardo's *The Last Supper*. Rooms are small and decorated in an old-fashioned style with faux period furniture, parquet floors and heavy drapes. Managed by the same family for more than 40 years, it's a convenient, affordable place in a great location, although it's starting to need a little TLC.

✖ Eating & Drinking

Local specialities include *risotto alla milanese* (saffron-infused risotto cooked in bone marrow stock) and *cotoletta alla milanese* (breaded veal cutlet).

Luini   FAST FOOD €

(☑ 02 8646 1917; www.luini.it; Via Santa Radegonda 16; panzerotti €2.70; ⊙ 10am-3pm Mon, to 8pm Tue-Sat; 🍴; Ⓜ Duomo) This historic joint is the go-to place for *panzerotti,* delicious pizza-dough parcels stuffed with a combination of mozzarella, spinach, tomato, ham or spicy salami, and then fried or baked in a wood-fired oven.

★ **Un Posto a Milano**   MODERN ITALIAN €€

(☑ 02 545 77 85; www.unpostoamilano.it; Via Cuccagna 2; meals €15-35; ⊙ 12.30-3pm & 7.30-11pm; ☑ 🍴; Ⓜ Porta Romana) A few years ago this country *cascina* (farmhouse) was a derelict ruin until a collection of cooperatives and cultural associations returned it to multifunctional use as restaurant, bar, social hub and hostel. Delicious salads, homemade foccacia, soups and snacks are served throughout the day at the bar, while the restaurant serves simple home cooking using locally sourced ingredients.

Trattoria Milanese   MILANESE €€

(☑ 02 8645 1991; Via Santa Marta 11; meals €35-45; ⊙ noon-2.45pm & 7-10.45pm Mon-Sat; 🚌 2, 14) Like an old friend you haven't seen in years, this trattoria welcomes you with generous goblets of wine, hearty servings of traditional Milanese fare and convivial banter over the vegetable buffet. Regulars slide into their seats, barely needing to order as waiters bring them their usual: meatballs wrapped in cabbage, minestrone or the sinfully good *risotto al salto* (refried risotto).

BQ Navigli   BAR

(Birra Artigianale di Qualità; ☑ 02 8940 3212; www.bqmilano.it; Alzaia Naviglio Grande 44; ⊙ 6pm-3am Wed-Fri, noon-3am Sat & Sun; Ⓜ Porta Genova) This Navigli canalside bar has a fine selection of craft beers, ranging from light lagers to robust hop-heavy bitters. Soak it all up with *panini* and *piadine* (stuffed pitta breads).

☆ Entertainment

Teatro alla Scala   OPERA

(La Scala; ☑ 02 72 00 3744; www.teatroallascala.org; Piazza della Scala; tickets €30-300; Ⓜ Duomo) The opera season at La Scala, one of the most famous opera stages in the world, runs from early December through July. You can also see theatre, ballet and concerts here year-round (except August). Buy tickets online or by phone up to two months before the performance, or from the central box office. On performance days, tickets for the gallery are available from the box office at Via Filodrammatici 2 (one ticket per customer). Queue early.

San Siro Stadium   FOOTBALL

(Stadio Giuseppe Meazza; ☑ 02 4879 8201; www.sansiro.net; Piazzale Angelo Moratti; tickets from €20; 🍴; Ⓜ San Siro Stadio) San Siro Stadium wasn't designed to hold the entire population of Milan, but on a Sunday afternoon amid 80,000 football-mad citizens it can certainly feel like it. The city's two clubs, AC Milan and FC Internazionale Milano (aka Inter), play on alternate weeks from September to May.

🔒 Shopping

Beyond the hallowed streets of the Quadrilatero d'Oro, designer outlets and chains can be found along Corso Buenos Aires and Corso Vercelli; younger, hipper labels live along Via Brera and Corso Magenta; while Corso di Porta Ticinese and Navigli are home of the Milan street scene and subculture shops.

Peck FOOD & DRINKS

(☎ 02 802 31 61; www.peck.it; Via Spadari 9; ⊙ 3-8pm Mon, 9am-8pm Tue-Sat, 10am-5pm Sun; ☎; Ⓜ Duomo) Milan's historic deli is a bastion of the city's culinary heritage with three floors below ground dedicated to turning out the fabulously colourful display of foods that cram every counter. It showcases a mind-boggling selection of cheeses, chocolates, pralines, pastries, freshly made gelato, seafood, meat, caviar, pâté, fruit and vegetables, olive oils and balsamic vinegars.

ⓘ Information

Farmacia Essere Benessere (☎ 02 669 07 35; 2nd fl, Stazione Centrale; ⊙ 7am-10pm Mon-Thu, to 10.45pm Fri & Sat, 8am-10.45pm Sun; Ⓜ Centrale FS) A well-stocked pharmacy with highly qualified staff and long opening hours located in the Central Station shopping arcade.

Milan Tourist Office (☎ 02 8845 5555; www.turismo.milano.it; Galleria Vittorio Emanuele II 11-12; ⊙ 9am-7pm Mon-Fri, to 6pm Sat, 10am-6pm Sun; Ⓜ Duomo) Centrally located in the Galleria with helpful English-speaking staff and tons of maps and brochures.

ⓘ Getting There & Away

AIR

Aeroporto Linate (LIN; ☎ 02 23 23 23; www.milanolinate-airport.com) Located 7km east of Milan city centre; domestic and European flights only.

Aeroporto Malpensa (MXP; ☎ 02 23 23 23; www.milanomalpensa-airport.com; Ⓡ Malpensa Express) About 50km northwest of Milan city; northern Italy's main international airport.

Orio al Serio (☎ 035 32 63 23; www.sacbo.it) Low-cost carriers link Bergamo airport with a wide range of European cities. It has direct transport links to Milan.

TRAIN

Fast trains depart Stazione Centrale for Venice (€44, 2½ hours), Bologna (€34 to €84, one to two hours), Florence (€35 to €74, 1¾ hours), Rome (€89, three hours) and other Italian and European cities.

Most regional trains also stop at Stazione Nord in Piazzale Cadorna.

ⓘ Getting Around

TO/FROM THE AIRPORT
Linate

Airport Bus Express (☎ 02 3391 0794; www.airportbusexpress.it; one way/return €5/9; Ⓜ Centrale) The Autostrada express airport bus departs from Milan's Stazione Centrale for

QUADRILATERO D'ORO

A stroll around the world's most famous shopping district, **Quadrilatero d'Oro** (Golden Quad; Ⓜ Monte Napoleone), is a must. This quaintly cobbled quadrangle of streets – bounded by Via Monte Napoleone, Via Sant'Andrea, Via della Spiga and Via Alessandro Manzoni – has always been synonymous with elegance and money (Via Monte Napoleone was where Napoleon's government managed loans). Even if you don't have the slightest urge to buy, the window displays and people-watching are priceless.

Linate airport every half-hour between 5.30am and 10pm. Buses from the airport to Milan run on the same schedule. Buses from Milan depart from Piazza Luigi di Savoia on the east side of the station. Tickets are sold on board.

Malpensa

Malpensa Shuttle (☎ 02 5858 3185; www.malpensashuttle.it; one way/return €10/16; Ⓜ Centrale) This Malpensa airport shuttle runs at least half-hourly between 5.15am and 10.45pm from Stazione Centrale, and hourly throughout the rest of the night. The journey time is 50 minutes and buses depart from Piazza IV Novembre on the west side of the station. Terminal 2 stops need to be requested.

Malpensa Express (☎ 02 7249 4949; www.malpensaexpress.it; one way €13) Half-hourly trains run from Malpensa airport Terminal 1 to Cadorna Stazione Nord (40 minutes) and Stazione Centrale (60 minutes). Services to Cadorna run between 5.26am and 12.26am; to Stazione Centrale from 5.43am to 10.43pm. The train also serves Terminal 2.

Orio al Serio

Orio al Serio Bus Express (☎ 02 3008 9300; www.airportbusexpress.it; one way/return €5/9; Ⓜ Centrale) This Autostrade service departs Piazza Luigi di Savoia at Stazione Centrale approximately every half-hour between 2.45am and 11.15pm, and from Orio al Serio airport between 7.45am and 11.15am. The journey takes one hour.

PUBLIC TRANSPORT

Milan's metro, buses and trams are run by **ATM** (Azienda Trasporti Milano; ☎ 02 4860 7607; www.atm.it). Tickets (€1.50) are valid for one underground ride and up to 90 minutes' travel on city buses and trams. A day ticket costs €4.50.

The Lakes

Ringed by snowcapped mountains, gracious towns and landscaped gardens, the Italian lake district is an enchanting corner of the country.

Lago Maggiore

Snaking across the Swiss border, Lago Maggiore, the westernmost of the three main lakes, retains the belle époque air of its 19th-century heyday when it was a popular retreat for artists and writers.

Its headline sights are the Borromean islands, accessible from Stresa on the lake's western bank. Isola Bella is dominated by the 17th-century Palazzo Borromeo (☎0323 3 05 56; www.isoleborromee.it; adult/child €16/8.50, incl Palazzo Madre €21/10; ☉9am-5.30pm mid-Mar–mid-Oct), a grand baroque palace with a wonderful art collection and beautiful tiered gardens. Over the water, Palazzo Madre (☎0323 3 05 56; www.isoleborromee.it; adult/child €13/6.50, incl Palazzo Borromeo €21/10; ☉9am-5.30pm mid-Mar–mid-Oct) lords it over Isola Madre.

In Stresa's pedestrianised centre, Piemontese (☎0323 3 02 35; www.ristorante piemontese.com; Via Mazzini 25; meals €40-55; ☉noon-3pm & 7-11pm Tue-Sun) is a refined restaurant serving excellent regional cooking. Nearby, the Hotel Saini Meublè (☎0323 93 45 19; www.hotelsaini.it; Via Garibaldi 10; d €95-125, tr €130-160; ☎) has warm, spacious rooms.

For further information, contact Stresa's tourist office (☎0323 3 13 08; www.stresa turismo.it; Piazza Marconi 16; ☉10am-12.30pm & 3-6.30pm summer, closed Sat pm & Sun winter).

ⓘ Getting There & Around

The easiest way to get to Stresa is by train from Milan (€8.60 to €17, one hour, up to 20 daily).

Between April and September, Saf (☎0323 55 21 72; www.safduemila.com) operates an Alibus shuttle to/from Malpensa airport (€12, one hour, six daily).

Navigazione Lago Maggiore (☎800 551801; www.navigazionelaghi.it) operates ferries across the lake. From Stresa, a return ticket to Isola Bella costs €6.80, to Isola Madre €10.

Lago di Como

Lago di Como, overshadowed by steep wooded hills and snowcapped peaks, is the most spectacular and least visited of the lakes. At its southwestern tip, Como is a prosperous town with an imposing Duomo (Cattedrale di Como; ☎031 331 22 75; Piazza del Duomo; ☉10.30am-5pm Mon-Sat, 1-4.30pm Sun) and a charming medieval core.

For lunch head to the characterful Osteria del Gallo (☎031 27 25 91; www.osteriadel gallo-como.it; Via Vitani 16; meals €26-32; ☉12.30-3pm Mon, to 10pm Tue-Sat).

Also in the medieval centre, the modish Avenue Hotel (☎031 27 21 86; www.avenueho tel.it; Piazzolo Terragni 6; d €190-280, ste €280-310; P❉☎) offers slick four-star accommodation.

You can get more information at the tourist office (☎342 0076403; www.visitcomo.eu; Como San Giovanni, Piazzale San Gottardo; ☉9am-5pm summer, 10am-4pm Wed-Mon winter) at San Giovanni train station.

ⓘ Getting There & Around

Regional trains run to Como San Giovanni from Milan's Stazione Centrale and Porta Garibaldi (€4.80, one hour, half-hourly).

Navigazione Lago di Como (☎800 551801; www.navigazionelaghi.it) operates year-round ferries from the jetty near Piazza Cavour.

Lago di Garda

The largest and most developed of the lakes, Lago di Garda straddles the border between Lombardy and the Veneto.

A good base is Sirmione, a picturesque village on its southern shores. Here you can investigate the Grotte di Catullo (☎030 91 61 57; www.grottedicatullo.beniculturali.it; Piazzale Orti Manara 4; adult/reduced €6/3; ☉8.30am-7.30pm Tue-Sat & 9.30am-6.30pm Sun summer, 8.30am-5pm Tue-Sat & 8.30am-2pm Sun winter), a ruined Roman villa, and enjoy views over the lake's placid blue waters.

There are an inordinate number of eateries crammed into Sirmione's historic centre. One of the best is La Fiasca (☎030 990 61 11; www.trattorialafiasca.it; Via Santa Maria Maggiore 11; meals €30-35; ☉noon-2.30pm & 7-10.30pm Thu-Tue), an authentic trattoria serving flavoursome lake fish.

Sirmione can be visited on a day trip from Verona, but if you want to overnight, Grifone (☎030 91 60 14; www.gardalakegrifonehotel.eu; Via Gaetano Bocchio 4; s €50-80, d €70-110) boasts a superb lakeside location and relaxing views.

Get information from the tourist office (☎030 91 61 14; iat.sirmione@provincia.brescia. it; Viale Marconi 8; ☉10am-12.30pm & 3-6.30pm daily summer, 10am-12.30pm & 3-6pm Mon-Fri, 9.30am-12.30pm Sat winter) outside the medieval walls.

ⓘ Getting There & Around

Regular buses run to Sirmione from Verona (€3.50, one hour, hourly).

Navigazione Lago di Garda (☑ 030 914 9511; www.navigazionelaghi.it) operates the lake's ferries.

Verona

POP 258,800

Wander Verona's atmospheric streets and you'll understand why Shakespeare set *Romeo and Juliet* here – this is one of Italy's most beautiful and romantic cities. Known as *piccola Roma* (little Rome) for its importance in ancient times, its heyday came in the 13th and 14th centuries when it was ruled by the Della Scala (aka Scaligeri) family, who built *palazzi* and bridges, sponsored Giotto, Dante and Petrarch, oppressed their subjects, and feuded with everyone else.

◎ Sights

Roman Arena   RUINS
(☑ 045 800 32 04; Piazza Brà; adult/reduced €10/7.50; ⊙ 8.30am-7.30pm Tue-Sun, from 1.30pm Mon) Built of pink-tinged marble in the 1st century AD, Verona's Roman amphitheatre survived a 12th-century earthquake to become the city's legendary open-air opera house, with seating for 30,000 people. You can visit the arena year-round, though it's at its best during the summer opera festival. In winter months, concerts are held at the **Teatro Filarmonico** (☑ 045 800 28 80; www.arena.it; Via dei Mutilati 4; opera €23-60, concerts €25-50). From January to May and October to December, admission is €1 on the first Sunday of the month.

Casa di Giulietta   NOTABLE BUILDING
(Juliet's House; ☑ 045 803 43 03; Via Cappello 23; adult/reduced €6/4.50, free with VeronaCard; ⊙ 1.30-7.30pm Mon, 8.30am-7.30pm Tue-Sun) Never mind that Romeo and Juliet were completely fictional characters, and that there's hardly room for two on the narrow stone balcony: romantics flock to this 14th-century house to add their lovelorn pleas to the sea of sticky notes lining the courtyard gateway. In truth, Juliet's House is altogether underwhelming, so consider a free glance from the courtyard and search for your Romeo elsewhere.

★Basilica di Sant'Anastasia   BASILICA
(www.chieseverona.it; Piazza di Sant'Anastasia; €2.50; ⊙ 9am-6pm Mon-Sat, 1-6pm Sun Mar-Oct, 10am-1pm & 1.30-5pm Mon-Sat, 1-5pm Sun Nov-Feb) Dating from the 13th to 15th centuries and featuring an elegantly decorated vaulted ceiling, the Gothic Sant'Anastasia is Verona's largest church and a showcase for local art. The multitude of frescoes is overwhelming, but don't overlook Pisanello's story-book-quality fresco *St George and the Princess* above the entrance to the **Pellegrini Chapel**, or the 1495 holy water font featuring a hunchback carved by Paolo Veronese's father, Gabriele Caliari.

🛏 Sleeping & Eating

★Corte delle Pigne   B&B €€
(☑ 333 7584141; www.cortedellepigne.it; Via Pigna 6a; s €60-110, d €90-150, tr €110-170, q €130-190; 🅿❄🛜) In the heart of the historic centre, this three-room B&B is set around a quiet internal courtyard. It offers tasteful rooms and plenty of personal touches: sweet jars, luxury toiletries and even a Jacuzzi for one lucky couple.

Hotel Aurora   HOTEL €€
(☑ 045 59 47 17; www.hotelaurora.biz; Piazzetta XIV Novembre 2; d €110-280, tr €130-300; ❄🛜) Overlooking Piazza delle Erbe, friendly Aurora offers smart rooms, some with piazza views and all with classic wooden furniture and fresh, modern bathrooms. The open-air terrace makes for a perfect spot to enjoy breakfast or a lazy sundowner.

★Locanda 4 Cuochi   MODERN ITALIAN €€
(☑ 045 803 03 11; www.locanda4cuochi.it; Via Alberto Mario 12; meals €40, 3-course set menu €25; ⊙ 12.30-2.30pm & 7.30-10.30pm, closed lunch Mon-Wed; 🛜) With its open kitchen, urbane vibe and hotshot chefs, you're right to expect great things from the Locanda. Culinary acrobatics play second fiddle to prime produce cooked with skill and subtle twists. Whether it's perfectly crisp suckling pig lacquered with liquorice, or an epilogue of *gianduia* ganache with sesame crumble and banana, expect to swoon.

La Taverna di Via Stella   VENETO €€
(☑ 045 800 80 08; www.tavernadiviastella.com; Via Stella 5c; meals €30-35; ⊙ 12.15-2.30pm & 7.15-11pm, closed Wed & Mon evening) Brush past the haunches of prosciutto dangling over the deli bar and make your way into the dining room, decorated Tiepolo-style with rustic murals of chivalric knights and maidens. This is the place you'll want to sample traditional Veronese dishes such as *pastissada*

(horse stew), *bigoli* with duck *ragù* and DOP Lessinia cheeses from Monte Veronese. Cash only for bills under €30.

☆ Entertainment

Performances during the summer opera festival are held at the Roman Arena (☎045 800 51 51; www.arena.it; box office Via Dietro Anfiteatro 6b; opera tickets €22-200; ☉box office 9am-noon Mon-Sat & 3.15-5.45pm Mon-Fri, longer hours during opera festival).

ℹ Information

Tourist Office (☎045 806 86 80; www.tourism.verona.it; Via degli Alpini 9; ☉10am-7pm Mon-Sat, to 3pm Sun) Just off Piazza Brà. Knowledgeable and helpful.

ℹ Getting There & Around

Verona-Villafranca airport (☎045 809 56 66; www.aeroportoverona.it) is 12km outside town and accessible by ATV Aerobus to/from the train station (€6, 15 minutes, every 20 minutes 5.35am to 11.10pm).

From the station, buses 11, 12 and 13 (90, 96, 97 and 98 evenings and Sundays) run to Piazza Brà.

Trains connect with Milan (€12 to €64, one hour 20 minutes to two hours, up to three hourly), Venice (€9 to €26, 50 minutes to 2¼ hours, twice hourly) and Bologna (€10 to €24, 50 minutes to 1½ hours, 20 daily).

Venice

POP 263,300

Venice (Venezia) is a hauntingly beautiful city. At every turn you're assailed by unforgettable images – tiny bridges arching over limpid canals; chintzy gondolas sliding past working barges; towers and distant domes silhouetted against the watery horizon. Its celebrated sights are legion, and its labyrinthine alleyways exude a unique, almost eerie atmosphere, redolent of cloaked passions and dark secrets. Many of the city's treasures date to its time as a powerful medieval republic known as La Serenissima.

◉ Sights

◔ San Marco

★ Basilica di San Marco   CATHEDRAL
(St Mark's Basilica; Map p682; ☎041 270 83 11; www.basilicasanmarco.it; Piazza San Marco; ☉9.45am-5pm Mon-Sat, 2-5pm Sun summer, to 4pm Sun winter; ▣San Marco) **FREE** With its Byzan-

---

ℹ NAVIGATING VENICE

Venice is not an easy place to navigate and even with a smartphone and satellite mapping you're bound to get lost. The main area of interest lies between Santa Lucia train station (signposted as the *ferrovia*) and Piazza San Marco (St Mark's Sq). The path between the two – Venice's main drag – is a good 40- to 50-minute walk. It also helps to know that the city is divided into six *sestieri* (districts): Cannaregio, Castello, San Marco, Dorsoduro, San Polo and Santa Croce.

---

tine domes and 8500 sq metres of luminous mosaics, Venice's basilica is an unforgettable sight. It dates to the 9th century when, according to legend, two merchants smuggled the corpse of St Mark out of Egypt in a barrel of pork fat. When the original burnt down in 932 Venice rebuilt the basilica in its own cosmopolitan image, with Byzantine domes, a Greek cross layout and walls clad in marbles from Syria, Egypt and Palestine.

Campanile   TOWER
(Bell Tower; Map p682; www.basilicasanmarco.it; Piazza San Marco; adult/reduced €8/4; ☉8.30am-9.30pm summer, 9.30am-5.30pm winter, last entry 45min prior; ▣San Marco) The basilica's 99m-tall bell tower has been rebuilt twice since its initial construction in AD 888. Galileo Galilei tested his telescope here in 1609, but modern-day visitors head to the top for 360-degree lagoon views and close encounters with the Marangona, the booming bronze bell that originally signalled the start and end of the working day for the craftsmen (*marangoni*) at the Arsenale shipyards. Today it rings twice a day, at noon and midnight.

★Palazzo Ducale   MUSEUM
(Ducal Palace; Map p682; ☎041 271 59 11; www.palazzoducale.visitmuve.it; Piazzetta San Marco 1; adult/reduced incl Museo Correr €19/12, or with Museum Pass; ☉8.30am-7pm Apr-Oct, to 5.30pm Nov-Mar; ▣San Zaccaria) This grand Gothic palace was the Doge's official residence from the 9th century, and seat of the Venetian Republic's government (and prisons) for nearly seven centuries. The Doge's Apartments are on the 1st floor, but it's the lavishly decorated 2nd-floor chambers that are the real highlight. These culminate in the echoing Sala del Maggior Consiglio (Grand Council Hall), home to the Doge's

Greater Venice

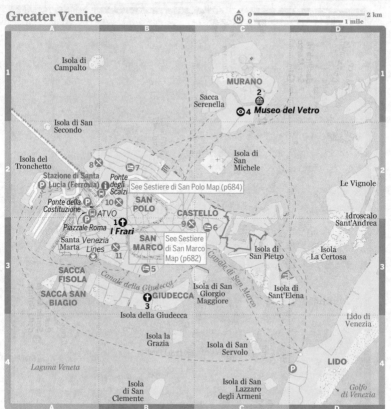

throne and a 22m-by-7m *Paradise* painting by Tintoretto's son Domenico.

Ponte dei Sospiri BRIDGE

(Bridge of Sighs; Map p682; 🚊 San Zaccaria) One of Venice's most photographed sights, the Bridge of Sighs connects Palazzo Ducale to the 16th-century Prigione Nove (New Prisons). It's named after the sighs that condemned prisoners – including Giacomo Casanova – emitted as they were led down to the cells.

◎ Dorsoduro

★ Gallerie dell'Accademia GALLERY

(Map p682; ☏ 041 520 03 45; www.gallerie accademia.org; Campo della Carità 1050, Dorsoduro; adult/reduced €12/6, 1st Sun of month free; ◷ 8.15am-2pm Mon, to 7.15pm Tue-Sun; 🚊 Accademia) Venice's historic gallery traces the development of Venetian art from the 14th to 18th centuries, with works by Bellini, Titian,

Tintoretto, Veronese and Canaletto among others. The former Santa Maria della Carità

Sestiere di San Marco

Ponte Capello

Basilica di San Marco
7 🏛 ✝1

C di Canonica
C Larga San Marco
Piazzetta dei Leoni

Ponte della Paglia

8 ◉

4 🏛

Palazzo Ducale

🏛6

Piazzetta San Marco

Marzaria dell'Orologio

Procuratie Vecchie

Procuratie Nuove

Rio dei Ferali

San Marco Giardinetti

San Marco
ℹ Tourist Office

Bacino di San Marco

C di Fabbri
C dei Fabbri
Frezzeria
Rio Orseolo

Giardini Ex-Reali

San Marco Vallaresso

Canale della Giudecca

C Larga Delle Colonne
Ramo Zorzi
Corte Zorzi
Campo S Gallo
Rio Terà delle Colonne

Fond del Fonteghetto

11

C dei Fuseri

C Fiubera

C de le Locande

C de la Mandola

Frezzaria
C Venier
C d'la Chiesa
Fenice

C d Selvadego
C Frezzaria

Bocca di Piazza

C d'la Frezzeria
Ramo 1ª Cte Contarina

C Vallaresso

C dei 13 Martiri

C Barozzi
Corte Barozzi

Campo di San Moisè

C Bognolo
C del Carro

Fond Dogana alla Salute

Basilica di Santa Maria della Salute
2 ✝

Rio di S Luca
Rio dei Barcaroli
Rio della Veste

Campo S Fantin
Piscina Frezzaria
Cllo della Fenice
C della Fenice

C Squero
C del Traghetto

C Larga XXII Marzo
C della Veste
C del Pestrin

Campo della Salute

Salute

Fond della Salute

SAN MARCO

☆12

Fond Fenice

Campo di Santa Maria del Giglio

C delle Ostreghe

Campo Traghetto

Rio Terà de la Mandola
C degli Avvocati
C de Cristo

Rio di S Angelo
C Caotorta

Santa Maria del Giglio
Grand Canal

C de Lanza

C d Bastion
Rio della Fornace

Campo S Anzolo
C Va In

Campiello
C della Chiesa
C Spezier
Campo S Maurizio

Fond Corner Zaguri
Rio Santa Maria Zobenigo

C Gritti

CS Cristoforo

Rio della Fornace

Fond Ospedaleto

Campo Santo Stefano

C del Dose Da Ponte

10 ℹ

Peggy Guggenheim Collection 🏛5

C del Pestrin
Campiello Nuovo
C de le Botteghe
C del Piovan

Rio dell'Orso

Campo di S Vidal

DORSODURO

Campo San Vio

C d Chiesa

Fond di Ca' Bragadin

Piscina Forner

C Mocenigo Ca' Vecchia
Ramo Grassi
C del Zotti
C de Carrozze
Sotop Squero
Calle le Carrozze
C San Samuele
S Samuele

Campo S Samuele

Ponte dell'Accademia

Accademia

Campo della Carità
3 🏛

Galleria dell'Accademia

C Vitturi
C Giustinian

Rio Terà Antonio Foscarini

Sestiere di San Marco

◎ Top Sights

convent complex housing the collection maintained its serene composure for centuries until Napoleon installed his haul of Venetian art trophies here in 1807. Since then there's been nonstop visual drama inside its walls.

★**Peggy Guggenheim Collection** MUSEUM
(Map p682; ☑041 240 54 11; www.guggenheim-venice.it; Palazzo Venier dei Leoni 704, Dorsoduro; adult/reduced €15/9; ◎10am-6pm Wed-Mon; ▣Accademia) After losing her father on the *Titanic,* heiress Peggy Guggenheim became one of the great collectors of the 20th century. Her palatial canalside home, Palazzo Venier dei Leoni, showcases her stockpile of surrealist, futurist and abstract expressionist art with works by up to 200 artists, including her ex-husband Max Ernst, Jackson Pollock (among her many rumoured lovers), Picasso and Salvador Dalí.

★**Basilica di Santa Maria
della Salute** BASILICA
(La Salute; Map p682; www.basilicasalutevenezia.it; Campo della Salute 1b, Dorsoduro; basilica free, sacristy adult/reduced €4/2; ◎basilica 9.30am-noon & 3-5.30pm, sacristy 10am-noon & 3-5pm Mon-Sat, 3-5pm Sun; ▣Salute) Guarding the entrance to the Grand Canal, this 17th-century domed church was commissioned by Venice's plague survivors as thanks for their salvation. Baldassare Longhena's uplifting design is an engineering feat that defies simple logic; in fact the church is said to have

mystical curative properties. Titian eluded the plague until age 94, leaving 12 key paintings in the basilica's art-slung sacristy.

◎ San Polo & Santa Croce

★**I Frari** CHURCH
(Basilica di Santa Maria Gloriosa dei Frari; Map p681; ☑041 272 86 18; www.basilicadeifrari.it; Campo dei Frari 3072, San Polo; adult/reduced €3/1.50; ◎9am-6pm Mon-Sat, 1-6pm Sun; ▣San Tomà) A soaring Italian-brick Gothic church, I Frari's assets include marquetry choir stalls, Canova's pyramid mausoleum, Bellini's achingly sweet *Madonna with Child* triptych in the sacristy and Longhena's creepy Doge Pesaro funereal monument. Upstaging them all, however, is the small altarpiece. This is Titian's lauded 1518 *Assunta* (Assumption), in which a radiant red-cloaked Madonna reaches heavenward, steps onto a cloud and escapes this mortal coil. Titian himself – lost to the plague in 1576 at the age 94 – is buried here near his celebrated masterpiece.

◎ Giudecca

Chiesa del Santissimo Redentore CHURCH
(Church of the Most Holy Redeemer; Map p681; www.chorusvenezia.org; Campo del SS Redentore 194, Giudecca; adult/reduced €3/1.50, with Chorus Pass free; ◎10.30am-4.30pm Mon-Sat; ▣Redentore) Built to celebrate the city's deliverance from the Black Death, Palladio's Il Redentore was completed under Antonio da Ponte (of Rialto bridge fame) in 1592. Inside there are works by Tintoretto, Veronese and Vivarini, but the most striking is Paolo Piazza's 1619 *Gratitude of Venice for Liberation from the Plague.*

◎ The Islands

Murano ISLAND
(Map p681; ▣Faro) Murano has been the home of Venetian glass-making since the 13th century. Today, artisans ply their trade at workshops along **Fondamenta dei Vetrai**.

To learn about local manufacturing traditions and enjoy a collection of historic glassware, visit the **Museo del Vetro** (Glass Museum; Map p681; ☑041 527 47 18; www.museovetro.visitmuve.it; Fondamenta Giustinian 8, Murano; adult/reduced €10/7.50, free with Museum Pass; ◎10am-5pm; ▣Museo) near the Museo *vaporetto* stop.

ITALY VENICE

Sestiere di San Polo

Strada Nova

RIALTO-MERCATO

RIALTO

SAN POLO

SANTA CROCE

CASTELLO

SAN MARCO

Ponte di Rialto

Grand Canal

200 m
0.1 miles

Sestiere di San Polo

🛏 Sleeping

✴ Eating

⊝ Drinking & Nightlife

Burano   ISLAND

(🚲 Burano) Burano, with its cheery pastel-coloured houses, is renowned for its handmade lace, which once graced the décolletage and ruffs of European aristocracy. These days, however, much of the lace sold in local shops is imported.

Torcello   ISLAND

(🚲 Torcello) Torcello, the republic's original island settlement, was largely abandoned due to malaria and now counts no more than 10 permanent residents. Its mosaic-clad Byzantine cathedral, the **Basilica di Santa Maria Assunta** (🎫 041 73 01 19; Piazza Torcello; adult/reduced €5/4, incl museum €8/6, incl museum, audio guide & campanile €12/10; ⊙10am-5pm), is Venice's oldest.

🏃 Activities

Official gondola rates are €80 for 30 minutes (it's €100 for 35 minutes from 7pm to 8am) for up to six people. Additional time is charged in 20-minute increments (day/night €40/50).

🎊 Festivals & Events

Carnevale   CARNIVAL

(www.carnevale.venezia.it; ⊙Feb) Masquerade madness stretches over two weeks in February before Lent. A Grand Canal flotilla marks the outbreak of festivities which feature masked balls, processions, public parties in every *campo* (square), and all manner of dressing up.

Venice Biennale   ART

(www.labiennale.org; Giardini della Biennale; ⊙mid-May–Nov; 🚲Giardini Biennale) Europe's premier arts showcase since 1907 is something of a

misnomer: the Venice Biennale is actually held every year, but the spotlight alternates between art (odd-numbered years) and architecture (even-numbered years).

Festa del Redentore   RELIGIOUS

(Feast of the Redeemer; http://events.veneziaunica. it; ⊙Jul) Walk on water across the Giudecca Canal to Il Redentore via a wobbly pontoon bridge on the third Saturday and Sunday in July, then watch the fireworks from the Zattere.

Venice International Film Festival   FILM

(Mostra Internazionale d'Arte Cinematografica; www.labiennale.org/en/cinema; Lido; ⊙Aug-Sep) The only thing hotter than a Lido beach in August is the film festival's star-studded red carpet, usually rolled out from the last weekend in August through the first week of September.

Regata Storica   CULTURAL

(www.regatastoricavenezia.it; ⊙Sep) Sixteenth-century costumes, eight-oared gondolas and ceremonial barques feature in this historical procession (usually held in early September) along the Grand Canal, which re-enacts the arrival of the Queen of Cyprus and precedes gondola races.

🛏 Sleeping

🛏 San Marco

★ Hotel Flora   HOTEL €€

(Map p682; 🎫 041 520 58 44; www.hotelflora.it; Calle dei Bergamaschi 2283a; s/d from €134/151; ❄🅿; 🚲Giglio) Down a lane from glitzy Calle Larga XXII Marzo, this ivy-covered retreat quietly outclasses brash designer neighbours with its delightful tearoom and breakfasts around the garden fountain. Guest rooms feature antique mirrors, fluffy duvets atop hand-carved beds, and tiled en-suite bathrooms with apothecary-style amenities. Damask-clad superior rooms overlook the garden. Strollers and kids' teatime are complimentary; babysitting available.

★ Novecento   BOUTIQUE HOTEL €€€

(Map p682; 🎫 041 241 37 65; www.novecento. biz; Calle del Dose 2683/84; r from €200; ❄🅿; 🚲Giglio) Sporting a boho-chic look, the Novecento is a real charmer. Its nine individually designed rooms ooze style with Turkish kilim pillows, Fortuny draperies and 19th-century carved bedsteads. You can mingle with creative fellow travellers around the

ITALY VENICE

ℹ️ VENICE DISCOUNT PASSES

Civic Museum Pass (www.visitmuve.it; adult/reduced €24/18) Valid for single entry to 11 civic museums, or just the four museums around Piazza San Marco (€19/12). Buy online or at participating museums.

Chorus Pass (www.chorusvenezia.org; adult/reduced €12/8) Covers admission to 16 churches. Buy at participating sites.

VeneziaUnica (www.veneziaunica.it) A universal pass covering museum admission, transport, wi-fi and more. There's no standard pass; instead you tailor it to your needs and pay according to the services you include on it. See the website for details.

honesty bar, while outside, its garden is a lovely spot to linger over breakfast.

Dorsoduro

⭐ **B&B Corte Vecchia** B&B €€
(Map p681; ☑ 335 7449238; www.cortevecchia. net; Rio Terà San Vio 462, Dorsoduro; s €60-80, d €100-130; ❄️ 🛜; 🚤 Accademia) Corte Vecchia is a stylish steal, run by young architects Antonella and Mauro and a stone's throw from Peggy Guggenheim, Accademia and Punta della Dogana. Choose from a snug single with en suite, or two good-sized doubles: one with en suite, the other with an external private bathroom. All are simple yet understatedly cool, with contemporary and vintage objects, and a tranquil, shared lounge.

San Polo & Santa Croce

Ca' Angeli BOUTIQUE HOTEL €€
(Map p684; ☑ 041 523 24 80; www.caangeli.it; Calle del Traghetto de la Madoneta 1434, San Polo; d €165-240; ❄️ 🛜; 🚤 San Silvestro) Murano glass chandeliers, a Louis XIV love-seat and namesake 16th-century angels set a refined tone at this restored, canalside *palazzo*. Guest rooms are a picture with beamed ceilings, antique carpets and big bathrooms, while the dining room looks out onto the Grand Canal. Breakfast includes organic products where possible.

Pensione Guerrato PENSION €€
(Map p684; ☑ 041 528 59 27; http://hotelguerrato. com; Calle Drio la Scimia 240a, San Polo; d/tr/q €145/165/185, apt €160-280; ❄️ 🛜; 🚤 Rialto-Mercato) In a 1227 tower that was once a hostel for knights headed to the Third Crusade, the smart guestrooms here haven't lost their sense of history – some have frescoes or glimpses of the Grand Canal. Sparkling modern bathrooms, a prime Rialto Market location and helpful owners add to the package. No lift.

Cannaregio

Hotel Bernardi HOTEL €€
(Map p684; ☑ 041 522 72 57; www.hotelbernardi. com; SS Apostoli Calle de l'Oca 4366; s/d from €80/110, without bathroom from €32/65; ❄️ 🛜; 🚤 Ca' d'Oro) Hospitable owners, a convenient location just off the main thoroughfare, and keen prices mean that the Bernardi is always heavily booked. Some of the best rooms – think timber-beamed ceilings, Murano chandeliers and gilt furniture – are in the annexe round the corner.

Giardino dei Melograni HOTEL €€
(Map p681; ☑ 041 822 61 31; www.pardesrimonim. net; Campo del Ghetto Nuovo 2874; s €80-150, d €100-200; ❄️ 🛜; 🚤 Guglie) Run by Venice's Jewish community, to which all proceeds go, the 'Garden of Pomegranates' is a sparkling kosher residence. It's located on the charming Campo Ghetto Nuovo just a short walk from the train station, and offers 14 bright modern rooms.

Castello

⭐ **B&B San Marco** B&B €
(Map p681; ☑ 041 522 75 89; www.realvenice.it; Fondamenta San Giorgio dei Schiavoni 3385I; r with/without bathroom €135/105; ❄️; 🚤 San Zaccaria) One of the few genuine B&Bs in Venice. Alice and Marco welcome you warmly to their home overlooking Carpaccio's frescoed Scuola di San Giorgio Schiavoni. The 3rd-floor apartment (no lift), with its parquet floors and large windows, is furnished with family antiques and offers photogenic views over the terracotta rooftops and canals. Marco and Alice live upstairs, so they're always on hand with great recommendations.

🍴 Eating

Dorsoduro

⭐ **Ristorante La Bitta** RISTORANTE €€
(Map p681; ☑ 041 523 05 31; Calle Lunga San Barnaba 2753a, Dorsoduro; meals €35-40; ⏱ 6.30-11pm

Mon-Sat; ⊜Ca' Rezzonico) Recalling a cosy, woody bistro, La Bitta keeps punters purring with hearty rustic fare made using the freshest ingredients – no fish, just meat and seasonal veggies. Scan the daily menu for mouthwatering options like tagliatelle with artichoke thistle and Gorgonzola, or juicy pork *salsiccette* (small sausages) served with *verze* (local cabbage) and warming polenta. Reservations essential. Cash only.

San Polo & Santa Croce

★**Antiche Carampane**   VENETIAN €€€
(Map p684; ☑041 524 01 65; www.antiche carampane.com; Rio Terà delle Carampane 1911, San Polo; meals €50; ⊙12.45-2.30pm & 7.30-10.30pm Tue-Sat; ⊜San Stae) Hidden in the once-shady lanes behind Ponte delle Tette, this culinary indulgence is a trick to find. Once you do, say goodbye to soggy lasagne and hello to a market-driven menu of silky *crudi* (raw fish/seafood), surprisingly light *fritto misto* (fried seafood) and *caramote* prawn salad with seasonal vegetables. Never short of a smart, convivial crowd; it's a good idea to book ahead.

★**Osteria Trefanti**   VENETIAN €€
(Map p681; ☑041 520 17 89; www.osteriatrefanti.it; Fondamenta Garzotti 888, Santa Croce; meals €40; ⊙noon-2.30pm & 7-10.30pm Tue-Sun; 🐾; ⊜Riva de Biasio) 🍃 La Serenissima's spice trade lives on at simple, elegant Trefanti, where a dish of marinated prawns, hazelnuts, berries and caramel might get an intriguing kick from garam masala. Furnished with old pews and recycled copper lamps, it's the

domain of the competent Sam Metcalfe and Umberto Slongo, whose passion for quality extends to a small, beautifully curated selection of local and organic wines.

Osteria La Zucca   MODERN ITALIAN €€
(Map p684; ☑041 524 15 70; www.lazucca.it; Calle del Tentor 1762, Santa Croce; meals €35-40; ⊙12.30-2.30pm & 7-10.30pm Mon-Sat; 🐾; ⊜San Stae) With its menu of seasonal vegetarian creations and classic meat dishes, this cosy, woody restaurant consistently hits the mark. Herbs and spices are used to great effect in dishes such as cinnamon-tinged pumpkin flan and chicken curry with yoghurt, lentils and rice. The small interior can get toasty, so reserve canalside seats in summer.

Cannaregio

★**Dalla Marisa**   VENETIAN €€
(Map p681; ☑041 72 02 11; Fondamenta di San Giobbe 692b; set menu lunch €15, dinner €35-40; ⊙noon-2.15pm daily, 8-11pm Wed-Sat; ⊜Crea) At this Cannaregio institution, you'll be seated where there's room and get no menu – you'll have whatever Marisa's cooking. And you'll like it. Lunches are a bargain at €15 for a first, main, side, wine, water and coffee – pace yourself through prawn risotto to finish with steak and grilled zucchini.

Trattoria da Bepi Già "54"   VENETIAN €€
(Map p684; ☑041 528 50 31; www.dabepi.it; Campo SS Apostoli 4550; meals €24-37; ⊙noon-3pm & 7-10pm Fri-Wed; ⊜Ca' d'Oro) Da Bepi is a traditional trattoria in the very best sense. The interior is a warm, wood-panelled cocoon, and the service is efficient and friendly: host

ITALY VENICE

LOCAL KNOWLEDGE

CICHETI

Venice's answer to tapas, *cicheti* are served at lunch and from around 6pm to 8pm with sensational Veneto wines by the glass. They range from basic bar snacks (spicy meatballs, fresh tomato and basil bruschetta) to highly inventive small plates: think white Bassano asparagus and shrimp wrapped in pancetta at **All'Arco** (Map p684; ☑041 520 56 66; Calle dell'Ochialer 436, San Polo; cicheti from €2; ⊙8am-2.30pm Mon, Tue & Sat, to 7pm Wed-Fri summer, 8am-2.30pm Mon-Sat winter; ⊜Rialto-Mercato); Gorgonzola paired with *peperoncino* (chilli) jam at **Dai Zemei** (Map p684; ☑041 520 85 96; www.ostariadaizemei. it; Ruga Vecchia San Giovanni 1045, San Polo; cicheti from €1.50; ⊙8.30am-8.30pm Mon-Sat, 9am-7pm Sun; ⊜San Silvestro); or bite-sized rolls crammed with tuna, chicory and horse-radish at **Al Mercà** (Map p684; ☑346 8340660; Campo Cesare Battisti 213, San Polo; ⊙10am-2.30pm & 6-8pm Mon-Thu, to 9.30pm Fri & Sat; ⊜Rialto-Mercato).

Prices start at €1 for meatballs and range from €3 to €6 for gourmet fantasias, typically devoured standing up or perched atop stools at the bar.

Loris has been welcoming loyal locals and curious culinary travellers for years. Take their advice on the classic Venetian menu and order *spaghetti col nero di seppia* (with cuttlefish ink), grilled turbot and a tiramisu that doesn't disappoint.

Castello

★ Osteria Ruga di Jaffa
OSTERIA €€

(Map p681; ☎ 041 241 10 62; www.osteriarugadi jaffa.it; Ruga Giuffa 4864; meals €29-41; ⏰ 7am-11pm; ⛴ San Zaccaria) Hiding in plain sight on the busy Ruga Giuffa is this excellent *osteria* (casual tavern) with artsy Murano wall lamps. You should be able to spot it by the *gondolieri* packing out the tables at lunchtime; they come to feast on the select menu of housemade pastas and succulent roast pork soaked in its own savoury juices.

Drinking & Nightlife

★ Al Prosecco
WINE BAR

(Map p684; ☎ 041 524 02 22; www.alprosecco. com; Campo San Giacomo dell'Orio 1503, Santa Croce; ⏰ 10am-8pm Mon-Fri, to 5pm Sat Nov-Mar, to 10.30pm Apr-Oct; ⛴ San Stae) ❂ The urge to toast sunsets in Venice's loveliest *campo* is only natural – and so is the wine at Al Prosecco. This forward-thinking bar specialises in *vini naturi* (natural-process wines) – organic, biodynamic, wild-yeast fermented – from enlightened Italian winemakers like Cinque Campi and Azienda Agricola Barichel. So order a glass of unfiltered 'cloudy' *prosecco* and toast to the good things in life.

★ Timon
WINE BAR

(☎ 041 524 60 66; Fondamenta dei Ormesini 2754; ⏰ 6pm-1am; ⛴ San Marcuola) Find a spot on the boat moored out front along the canal and watch the motley parade of drinkers and dreamers arrive for seafood *crostini* (open-face sandwiches) and quality organic and DOC wines by the *ombra* (half-glass of wine) or carafe. Folk singers play sets canalside when the weather obliges; when it's cold, regulars scoot over to make room for newcomers at indoor tables.

Harry's Bar
BAR

(Map p682; ☎ 041 528 57 77; www.harrysbarven-ezia.com; Calle Vallaresso 1323; ⏰ 10.30am-11pm; ⛴ San Marco) Aspiring auteurs hold court at bistro tables well scuffed by Ernest Hemingway, Charlie Chaplin, Truman Capote and Orson Welles, enjoying the signature bellini

(Giuseppe Cipriani's original 1948 recipe: white peach juice and *prosecco*) with a side of reflected glory. Upstairs is one of Italy's most unaccountably expensive restaurants – stick to the bar to save the financing for your breakthrough film.

☆ Entertainment

To find out what's on during your visit, check listings in free mags distributed citywide and online at Venezia da Vivere (www.venezia davivere.com) and 2Venice (www.2venice.it).

★ La Fenice
OPERA

(Map p682; ☎ 041 78 66 72; www.teatrolafenice. it; Campo San Fantin 1977; restricted view from €30; ⛴ Giglio) La Fenice, one of Italy's top opera houses, hosts a rich program of opera, ballet and classical music. With advance booking you can tour the theatre, but the best way to see it is with the *loggionisti* – opera buffs in the cheap top-tier seats. Get tickets at the theatre, online or through Vela Venezia Unica ticket offices.

ⓘ Information

Marco Polo Airport Tourist Office (☎ 041 24 24; www.veneziaunica.it; Arrivals Hall, Marco Polo Airport; ⏰ 8.30am-7pm) Tourist information at the airport.

Ospedale SS Giovanni e Paolo (☎ 041 529 41 11; www.ulss12.ve.it; Campo Zanipolo 6777, Castello; ⛴ Ospedale) Venice's main hospital; for emergency care and dental treatment.

San Marco Tourist Office (Map p682; ☎ 041 24 24; www.veneziaunica.it; Piazza San Marco 71f; ⏰ 9am-7pm; ⛴ San Marco) Near the entrance to the Museo Correr.

Stazione Santa Lucia Tourist Office (Map p681; ☎ 041 24 24; www.veneziaunica.it; ⏰ 7am-9pm; ⛴ Ferrovia)

ⓘ Getting There & Away

AIR

Most flights arrive at and depart from **Marco Polo Airport** (☎ flight information 041 260 92 60; www.veniceairport.it; Via Galileo Gallilei 30/1, Tessera), 12km outside Venice.

Ryanair flies to/from **Treviso Airport** (☎ 0422 31 51 11; www.trevisoairport.it; Via Noalese 63), about 30km away.

BOAT

Anek (☎ 041 528 65 22; www.anekitalia.com; Via Dell 'Elettronica, Fusina) runs regular ferries between Venice and Greece, and **Venezia Lines** (Map p681; ☎ 041 847 09 03; www.

venezialines.com) runs high-speed boats to/from Croatia in summer.

BUS

ACTV (Azienda del Consorzio Trasporti Veneziano; ☑ 041 272 21 11; www.actv.it) buses service surrounding areas. Get tickets and information at the **bus station** (Piazzale Roma).

TRAIN

Regular trains serve Venice's Stazione di Santa Lucia from Padua (€4 to €17, 25 minutes) and Verona (€9 to €26, 50 minutes to 2¼ hours) as well as Bologna, Milan, Rome and Florence.

ⓘ Getting Around

TO/FROM THE AIRPORT
Marco Polo Airport

Alilaguna (☑ 041 240 17 01; www.alilaguna.it; airport transfer one-way €15) operates three boat lines that link the airport with various parts of Venice at a cost of €8 to Murano and €15 to all other landing stages. It takes approximately 1¼ hours to reach Piazza San Marco. Lines:

Blue Stops at Lido, San Marco, Cruise Terminal and points in-between.

Red Stops include Murano, Lido, San Marco and Giudecca.

Orange To Santa Maria del Giglio via Rialto and the Grand Canal.

An **ATVO** (☑ 0421 59 46 71; www.atvo.it; Piazzale Roma 497g, Santa Croce; ⊙ 6.40am-7.45pm) shuttle bus goes to/from Piazzale Roma (one way/return €8/11, 15 minutes, half-hourly), as does ACTV bus 5 (one way/return €8/15, 25 minutes, every 15 minutes).

Treviso Airport

ATVO buses run to/from Piazzale Roma (one way/return €12/22, 70 minutes, 13 daily).

BOAT

The city's main mode of public transport is the *vaporetto* (water bus).

Tickets, available from booths at major landing stations and on Piazzale Roma, cost €7.50 for a single trip. Passes are available for 24/48/72 hours at €20/30/40.

Useful routes:

1 Piazzale Roma to the train station and down the Grand Canal to San Marco and the Lido.

2 San Marco to/from the train station and Piazzale Roma, via the Grand canal and Rialto.

4.1 Joins Murano to Fondamente Nove, then circles the perimeter of Venice in both directions.

Trieste
POP 204,400

Italy's last city before Slovenia, Trieste merits a quick stopover. There are few must-see sights, but its imposing seafront *palazzi* lend it an impressive grandeur and the historic centre buzzes with bars and cafes. Hanging over everything is a palpable Mittel-European air, a hangover of its time as an important Austro-Hungarian port.

⊙ Sights & Activities

Piazza dell'Unità d'Italia   PIAZZA
This vast public space – Italy's largest sea-facing piazza – is an elegant triumph of Austro-Hungarian town planning and contemporary civil pride. Flanked by the city's grandest *palazzi,* including Palazzo del Municipio, Trieste's 19th-century city hall, it's a good place for a drink or a chat, or simply for a quiet moment staring out at ships on the horizon.

★Castello di Miramare   CASTLE
(☑ 040 22 41 43; www.castello-miramare.it; Viale Miramare; adult/reduced €8/5; ⊙ 9am-7pm) Sitting on a rocky outcrop 7km from town, Castello di Miramare is Trieste's elegiac bookend, the fanciful neo-Gothic home of the hapless Archduke Maximilian of Austria. Maximilian originally came to Trieste in the 1850s as the commander-in-chief of Austria's imperial navy, an ambitious young aristocrat known for his liberal ideas. But in 1867 he was shot by a republican firing squad in Mexico, after briefly, and rather foolishly, taking up the obsolete crown.

🛏 Sleeping & Eating

L'Albero Nascosto   BOUTIQUE HOTEL €€
(☑ 040 30 01 88; www.alberonascosto.it; Via Felice Venezian 18; s €80-95, d €105-170; ❀ ☎) A delightful little hotel in the middle of the old town, Nascosto is a model of discreet style. Rooms are spacious and tastefully decked out with parquet floors, original artworks, books and a vintage piece or two; most also have a small kitchen corner. Breakfasts are simple but thoughtful, with local cheeses, top-quality preserves and Illy coffee.

Buffet da Siora Rosa   BUFFET €
(☑ 040 30 14 60; Piazza Hortis 3; meals €25; ⊙ 8am-10pm Tue-Sat) Opened before WWII, the family-run Siora Rosa is one Trieste's

traditional buffets (bar-restaurants). Sit outside or in the wonderfully retro interior and tuck into boiled pork, sauerkraut and other Germanic and Hungarian offerings, or opt for something fishy like *baccalà* (salted cod) with polenta.

ℹ Information

Tourist Office (📞 040 347 83 12; www.turismofvg.it; Via dell'Orologio 1; ⊗9am-6pm)

ℹ Getting There & Around

Trains run to Trieste from Venice (€13 to €19, two to three hours, at least hourly).

From the train station, bus 30 heads down to Piazza dell'Unità d'Italia and the seafront.

National and international buses operate from the **bus station** (📞 040 42 50 20; www.autostazionetrieste.it; Via Fabio Severo 24). These include services to Croatia (Pula, Zagreb, Dubrovnik), Slovenia (Ljubljana) and further afield.

Bologna

POP 386,700

Bologna is one of Italy's great unsung destinations. Its medieval centre is an eye-catching ensemble of red-brick *palazzi,* Renaissance towers and 40km of arcaded porticoes, and there are enough sights to excite without exhausting. A university town since 1088 (Europe's oldest), it's also a prime foodie destination, home to the eponymous bolognese sauce *(ragù)* as well as *tortellini,* lasagne and *mortadella* (Bologna sausage).

⊙ Sights

★**Basilica di San Petronio**   CHURCH
(www.basilicadisanpetronio.org; Piazza Galvani 5; photo pass €2; ⊗7.45am-6.30pm) FREE Bologna's hulking Gothic basilica is the world's 15th-largest church, measuring 132m by 66m by 47m. Work began on it in 1390, but it was never finished and still today its main facade remains incomplete. Inside, look out for the huge sundial that stretches 67.7m down the eastern aisle. Designed in 1656 by Gian Cassini and Domenico Guglielmi, this was instrumental in discovering the anomalies of the Julian calendar and led to the creation of the leap year.

Le Due Torri   TOWER
(The Two Towers; Piazza di Porta Ravegnana) Standing sentinel over Piazza di Porta Ravegnana, Bologna's two leaning towers are the city's main symbol. The taller of the two, the 97.2m-high **Torre degli Asinelli** (€3; ⊗9am-7pm summer, to 5pm winter) is open to the public, although it's not advisable for vertigo-sufferers or owners of arthritic knees (there are 498 steps up a semi-exposed wooden staircase).

★**Basilica di Santo Stefano**   CHURCH
(http://abbaziasstefano.wixsite.com/abbaziasste fano; Via Santo Stefano 24; ⊗8am-7pm) FREE Bologna's most unique religious site is this atmospheric labyrinth of interlocking ecclesiastical structures, whose architecture spans centuries of Bolognese history and incorporates Romanesque, Lombard and even ancient Roman elements. Originally there were seven churches – hence the basilica's nickname Sette Chiese – but only four remain intact today: Chiesa del Crocefisso, Chiesa della Trinità, Santo Sepolcro and Santi Vitale e Agricola.

🛏 Sleeping & Eating

Albergo delle Drapperie   HOTEL €
(📞051 22 39 55; www.albergodrapperie.com; Via delle Drapperie 5; s €58-70, d €85-120, ste €115-150; ❋ �🎧) Offering one of the best quality-to-price ratios in central Bologna, this hotel in the atmospheric Quadrilatero neighbourhood is snugly ensconced in the upper floors of a large building. Buzz in at ground level and climb the stairs to discover 19 attractive rooms with marble floors, wood-beamed ceilings, the occasional brick arch and colourful ceiling frescoes.

★**Bologna nel Cuore**   B&B €€
(📞051 26 94 42; www.bolognanelcuore.it; Via Cesare Battisti 29; s €75-100, d €95-140, apt €125-130; 🅿 ❋ 🎧) This centrally located, immaculate and well-loved B&B features a pair of bright, high-ceilinged rooms with pretty tiled bathrooms and endless mod cons, plus two comfortable, spacious apartments with kitchen and laundry facilities. Owner and art historian Maria generously shares her knowledge of Bologna and serves breakfasts featuring jams made with fruit picked near her childhood home in the Dolomites.

★**Osteria dell'Orsa**   ITALIAN €
(📞051 23 15 76; www.osteriadellorsa.com; Via Mentana 1; meals €10-20; ⊗noon-1am) If you were to make a list of the great wonders of Italy, hidden amid Venice's canals and Rome's Colosseum would be cheap, pretension-free

osterie (casual taverns) like Osteria dell'Orsa, where the food is serially sublime and the prices are giveaway cheap. So what if the waiter's wearing an AC Milan shirt and the wine is served in a water glass?

★ **All'Osteria Bottega** OSTERIA €€
(☑ 051 58 51 11; Via Santa Caterina 51; meals €35-45; ⊙ 12.30-2.30pm & 8-1am Tue-Sat) At this *osteria* truly worthy of the name, owners Daniele and Valeria lavish attention on every table between trips to the kitchen for plates of *culatello di Zibello* ham, tortellini in capon broth, pork shank in red wine reduction and other Slow Food delights. Desserts are homemade by Valeria, from the *ciambella* (Romagnola ring-shaped cake) to fresh fruit sorbets.

❶ Information

Bologna Welcome (Tourist Office; ☑ 051 658 31 11; www.bolognawelcome.it; Piazza Maggiore 1e; ⊙ 9am-7pm Mon-Sat, 10am-5pm Sun) Also has an office at the airport.

❶ Getting There & Around

AIR

European and domestic flights serve **Guglielmo Marconi Airport** (☑ 051 647 96 15; www.bologna-airport.it; Via Triumvirato 84), 8km northwest of the city.

From the airport, an **Aerobus shuttle** (€6, 25 minutes, every 11 to 30 minutes) connects with the train station.

BUS

Bologna has an efficient bus system, run by **TPER** (☑ 051 29 02 90; www.tper.it).

Lines 25 and 30 are among those that connect the train station with the city centre.

TRAIN

Bologna is a major rail hub. From the station on Piazza delle Medaglie d'Oro, there are regular high-speed trains to Milan (€34 to €84, one to two hours), Venice (€32, 1½ hours), Florence (€32, 40 minutes) and Rome (€84, two to 2½ hours).

Ravenna

POP 159,100

A rewarding and worthwhile day trip from Bologna, Ravenna is famous for its Early Christian mosaics. These Unesco-listed treasures have been impressing visitors since the 13th century, when Dante described them in his *Divine Comedy* (much of which was written here).

◎ Sights

Ravenna's mosaics are spread over five sites in the centre: the Basilica di San Vitale, the Mausoleo di Galla Placidia, the Basilica di Sant'Appollinare Nuovo, the Museo Arcivescovile and the Battistero Neoniano. These are covered by a single ticket, available at any of the sites. The website www.ravennamosaici.it gives further information.

On the northern edge of the *centro storico,* the sombre exterior of the 6th-century **Basilica di San Vitale** (www.ravennamosaici.it; Via San Vitale; 5-site combo ticket €9.50; ⊙ 9am-7pm Mar-Oct, 10am-5pm Nov-Feb) hides a dazzling interior with mosaics depicting Old Testament scenes. In the same complex, the small **Mausoleo di Galla Placidia** (www.ravennamosaici.it; Via San Vitale; 5-site combo ticket €9.50 plus summer-only surcharge €2; ⊙ 9am-7pm Mar-Oct, 10am-5pm Nov-Feb) contains the city's oldest mosaics.

Adjoining Ravenna's unremarkable cathedral, the **Museo Arcivescovile** (www.ravennamosaici.it; Piazza Arcivescovado; 5-site combo ticket €9.50; ⊙ 9am-7pm Mar-Oct, 10am-5pm Nov-Feb) boasts an exquisite 6th-century ivory throne, while next door in the **Battistero Neoniano** (www.ravennamosaici.it; Piazza del Duomo; 5-site combo ticket €9.50; ⊙ 9am-7pm Mar-Oct, 10am-5pm Nov-Feb), the baptism of Christ is represented in the domed roof mosaic.

To the east, the **Basilica di Sant'Apollinare Nuovo** (www.ravennamosaici.it; Via di Roma 52; 5-site combo ticket €9.50; ⊙ 9am-7pm Apr-Sep, 9.30am-5.30pm Mar & Oct, 10am-5pm Nov-Feb) boasts, among other things, a superb mosaic depicting a procession of martyrs headed towards Christ and his apostles.

Five kilometres southeast of the city, the **Basilica di Sant'Apollinare in Classe** (Via Romea Sud 224; adult/reduced €5/2.50; ⊙ 8.30am-7.30pm Mon-Sat, 1-7.30pm Sun) is a must-see. Take bus 4 from the train station.

✖ Eating

La Gardela TRATTORIA €€
(☑ 0544 21 71 47; www.ristorantelagardela.com; Via Ponte Marino 3; meals €25-30; ⊙ noon-2.30pm & 7-10.30pm Fri-Wed) Economical prices, formidable home cooking and an attractive front terrace that's good for people-watching mean this bustling trattoria can be crowded, but in a pleasant, gregarious way. Professional waiters

glide by with plates of Italian classics: think risottos, pasta with *ragù*, and good grilled meats and fish. Fixed-price menus including water and coffee (but not wine) start at €15.

ℹ Information

Informazione e Accoglienza Turistica (IAT) - Centro (Tourist Information; ☏ 0544 3 54 04; www.turismo.ravenna.it; Piazza San Francesco 7; ☺ 8.30am-7pm, shorter hours in winter) Helpful office with maps and printed material; can help with booking accommodation.

ℹ Getting There & Around

Regional trains run to/from Bologna (€7.35,1½ hours, hourly) and destinations on the east coast.

TUSCANY & UMBRIA

Tuscany and its lesser-known neighbour, Umbria, are two of Italy's most beautiful regions. Tuscany's fabled landscape of rolling vine-covered hills dotted with cypress trees and stone villas has long been considered the embodiment of rural chic, while its historic cities and hilltop towns are home to a significant portfolio of the world's medieval and Renaissance art.

To the south, the predominantly rural region of Umbria, dubbed the 'green heart of Italy', harbours some of the country's best-preserved historic *borghi* (villages) and many important artistic, religious and architectural treasures.

Florence

POP 382,800

Visitors have been rhapsodising about Florence (Firenze) for centuries, and still today it looms large on Europe's 'must-sees' list. Tourists flock here to feast on world-class art and explore its historic streets, laden with grand palaces, jewel-box churches, trattorias, wine bars and elegant boutiques. Cradle of the Renaissance and home of Machiavelli, Michelangelo and the Medici, it's a magnetic, romantic and brilliantly absorbing place.

The city's golden age came under the Medici family between the 14th and 17th centuries. Later, it served as capital of the newly unified Italy from 1865 to 1870.

◎ Sights

◉ Piazza del Duomo

★ Duomo   CATHEDRAL
(Cattedrale di Santa Maria del Fiore; ☏ 055 230 28 85; www.ilgrandemuseodelduomo.it; Piazza del Duomo; ☺ 10am-5pm Mon-Wed & Fri, to 4.30pm Thu, to 4.45pm Sat, 1.30-4.45pm Sun) FREE Florence's Duomo is the city's most iconic landmark. Capped by Filippo Brunelleschi's red-tiled cupola, it's a staggering construction whose breathtaking pink, white and green marble facade and graceful *campanile* (bell tower) dominate the medieval cityscape. Sienese architect Arnolfo di Cambio began work on it in 1296, but construction took almost 150 years and it wasn't consecrated until 1436. In the echoing interior, look out for frescoes by Vasari and Zuccari and up to 44 stained-glass windows.

★ Cupola del Brunelleschi   LANDMARK
(Brunelleschi's Dome; ☏ 055 230 28 85; www.ilgrandemuseodelduomo.it; Piazza del Duomo; adult/reduced incl cupola, baptistry, campanile, crypt & museum €15/3; ☺ 8.30am-7pm Mon-Fri, to 5pm Sat, 1-4pm Sun) A Renaissance masterpiece, the Duomo's cupola – 91m high and 45.5m wide – was built between 1420 and 1436. Filippo Brunelleschi, taking inspiration from the Pantheon in Rome, designed a distinctive octagonal form of inner and outer concentric domes that rests on the drum of the cathedral rather than the roof itself. Over four million bricks were used, laid in consecutive rings according to a vertical herringbone pattern. Advance reservations, online or at the cathedral's Piazza di San Giovanni ticket office, are obligatory.

★ Campanile   TOWER
(Bell Tower; ☏ 055 230 28 85; www.ilgrandemuseodelduomo.it; Piazza del Duomo; adult/reduced incl campanile, baptistry, cupola, crypt & museum €15/3; ☺ 8.15am-8pm) The 414-step climb up the cathedral's 85m-tall *campanile,* begun by Giotto in 1334, rewards with staggering city views. The first tier of bas-reliefs around the base of its elaborate Gothic facade are copies of those carved by Pisano depicting the Creation of Man and *attività umane* (arts and industries). Those on the second tier depict the planets, cardinal virtues, the arts and the seven sacraments. The sculpted Prophets and Sibyls in the upper-storey niches are copies of works by Donatello and others.

ITALIAN ART & ARCHITECTURE

Italy is littered with architectural and artistic reminders of its convoluted history. **Etruscan** tombs and **Greek** temples tell of glories long past, **Roman** amphitheatres testify to ancient blood lust and architectural brilliance, and **Byzantine** mosaics reveal influences sweeping in from the East.

The **Renaissance** left an indelible mark, giving rise to some of Italy's greatest masterpieces: Filippo Brunelleschi's dome atop Florence's Duomo, Botticelli's *The Birth of Venus*, and Michelangelo's Sistine Chapel frescoes. Contemporaries Leonardo da Vinci and Raphael further brightened the scene.

Caravaggio revolutionised the late 16th-century art world with his controversial and highly influential painting style. He worked in Rome and the south, where **baroque** art and architecture flourished in the 17th century.

In the late 18th and early 19th centuries **neoclassicism** saw a return to sober classical lines. Its main Italian exponent was sculptor Antonio Canova.

In sharp contrast to backward-looking neoclassicism, early 20th-century **futurism** sought new ways to express the dynamism of the machine age, while Italian **rationalism** saw the development of a linear, muscular style of architecture.

Continuing in this modernist tradition are Italy's two contemporary **starchitects**: Renzo Piano, the visionary behind Rome's Auditorium, and Rome-born Massimiliano Fuksas.

Battistero di San Giovanni LANDMARK
(Baptistry; ☑ 055 230 28 85; www.ilgrandemuseo delduomo.it; Piazza di San Giovanni; adult/reduced incl baptistry, campanile, cupola, crypt & museum €15/3; ⊘8.15am-10.15am & 11.15am-7.30pm Mon-Fri, 8.15am-6.30pm Sat, 8.15am-1.30pm Sun) This 11th-century baptistry is a Romanesque, octagonal-striped structure of white-and-green marble with three sets of doors conceived as panels illustrating the story of humanity and the Redemption. Most celebrated are Lorenzo Ghiberti's gilded bronze doors at the eastern entrance, the Porta del Paradiso (Gate of Paradise). What you see today are copies – the originals are in the Grande Museo del Duomo. Buy tickets online or at the ticket office at Piazza di San Giovanni 7, opposite the main baptistry entrance.

⊙ Piazza della Signoria & Around

Piazza della Signoria PIAZZA
(Piazza della Signoria) Florentines flock to this piazza, the hub of local life since the 13th century, to meet friends and chat over early evening *aperitivi* at historic cafes. Presiding over everything is Palazzo Vecchio, Florence's city hall, and the 14th-century **Loggia dei Lanzi** FREE, an open-air gallery showcasing Renaissance sculptures, including Giambologna's *Rape of the Sabine Women* (c 1583), Benvenuto Cellini's bronze *Perseus*

(1554) and Agnolo Gaddi's *Seven Virtues* (1384–89).

★**Palazzo Vecchio** MUSEUM
(☑ 055 276 85 58, 055 27 68 22; www.musefirenze. it; Piazza della Signoria; adult/reduced museum €10/8, tower €10/8, museum & tower €14/12, archaeological tour €4, combination ticket €18/16; ⊘museum 9am-11pm Fri-Wed, to 2pm Thu Apr-Sep, 9am-7pm Fri-Wed, to 2pm Thu Oct-Mar, tower 9am-9pm Fri-Wed, to 2pm Thu Apr-Sep, 10am-5pm Fri-Wed, to 2pm Thu Oct-Mar; ☎) This fortress palace, with its crenellations and 94m-high tower, was designed by Arnolfo di Cambio between 1298 and 1314 for the *signoria* (city government). It remains the seat of the city's power, home to the mayor's office and the municipal council. From the top of the **Torre d'Arnolfo** (tower), you can revel in unforgettable rooftop views. Inside, Michelangelo's *Genio della Vittoria* (Genius of Victory) sculpture graces the Salone dei Cinquecento, a magnificent painted hall created for the city's 15th-century ruling Consiglio dei Cinquecento (Council of 500).

★**Galleria degli Uffizi** GALLERY
(Uffizi Gallery; ☑ 055 29 48 83; www.uffizi.beniculturali.it; Piazzale degli Uffizi 6; adult/reduced €8/4, incl temporary exhibition €12.50/6.25; ⊘8.15am-6.50pm Tue-Sun) Home to the world's greatest collection of Italian Renaissance art, Florence's premier gallery occupies the vast U-shaped Palazzo degli Uffizi, built between

Florence

ITALY FLORENCE

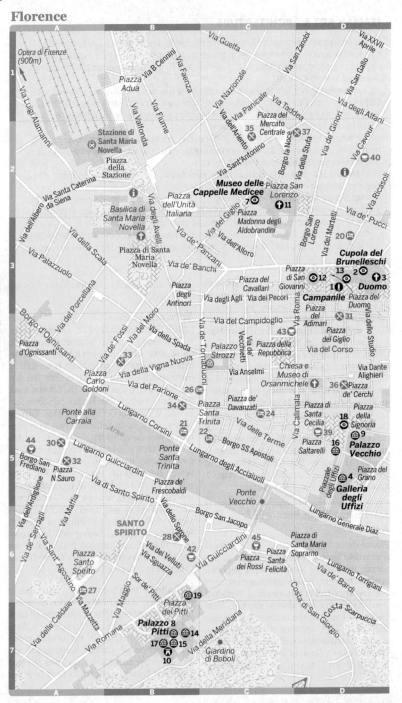

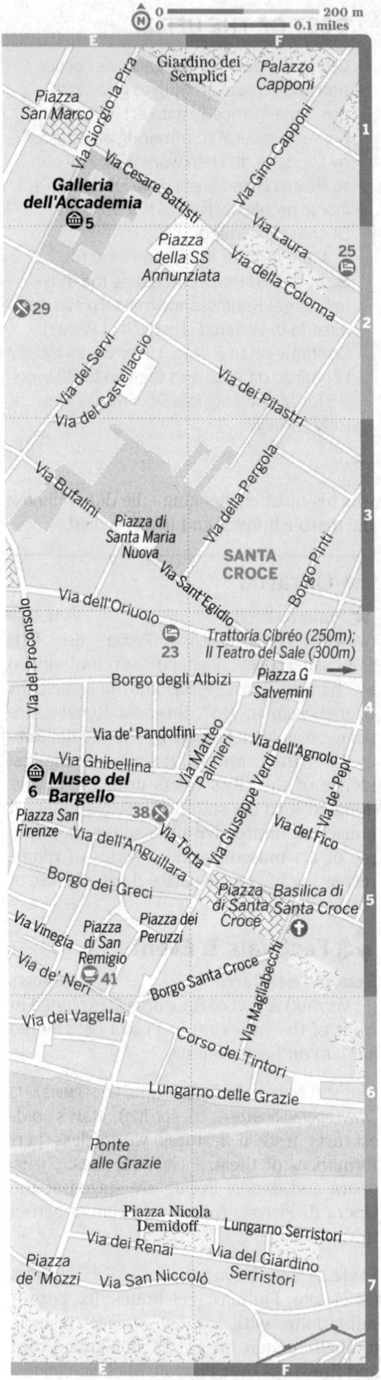

Florence

Top Sights

1 Campanile....D3
2 Cupola del Brunelleschi....D3
3 Duomo....D3
4 Galleria degli Uffizi....D5
5 Galleria dell'Accademia....E1
6 Museo del Bargello....E4
7 Museo delle Cappelle Medicee....C2
8 Palazzo Pitti....B7
9 Palazzo Vecchio....D5

Sights

10 Appartamenti Reali....B7
11 Basilica di San Lorenzo....C2
12 Battistero di San Giovanni....D3
13 Cripta Santa Reparata....D3
14 Galleria d'Arte Moderna....B7
15 Galleria Palatina....B7
16 Loggia dei Lanzi....D5
17 Museo della Moda e del Costume....B7
18 Piazza della Signoria....D5
19 Tesoro del Granduchi....B6

Sleeping

20 Academy Hostel....D3
21 Antica Torre di Via de' Tornabuoni 1....B5
22 Hotel Cestelli....C5
23 Hotel Dalí....E4
24 Hotel Davanzati....C5
25 Hotel Morandi alla Crocetta....F2
26 Hotel Scoti....B4
27 Palazzo Guadagni Hotel....A6

Eating

28 5 e Cinque....B6
29 Carabé....E2
30 Gelateria La Carraia....A5
31 Grom....D4
32 Il Santo Bevitore....A5
33 L'Osteria di Giovanni....B4
34 Mariano....B4
35 Mercato Centrale....C2
36 Osteria Il Buongustai....D4
37 Trattoria Mario....D2
38 Vivoli....E5

Drinking & Nightlife

39 Caffè Rivoire....D5
40 Ditta Al Cinema....D2
41 Ditta Artigianale....E5
42 Ditta Artigianale....B6
43 Gilli....C4
44 La Cité....A5
45 Le Volpi e l'Uva....C6

1560 and 1580 to house government offices. The collection, bequeathed to the city by the Medici family in 1743 on condition that it never leave Florence, contains some of Italy's best-known paintings, including Piero della Francesco's profile portaits of the Duke and Duchess of Urbino and rooms full of masterpieces by Sandro Botticelli.

★ **Museo del Bargello** MUSEUM
(www.bargellomusei.beniculturali.it; Via del Proconsolo 4; adult/reduced €8/4; ⊙8.15am-1.50pm, closed 2nd & 4th Sun & 1st, 3rd & 5th Mon of month) It was behind the stark walls of Palazzo del Bargello, Florence's earliest public building redecorated in neo-Gothic style in 1845, that the *podestà* meted out justice from the 13th century until 1502. Today the building safeguards Italy's most comprehensive collection of Tuscan Renaissance sculpture with some of Michelangelo's best early works and several Donatellos. Michelangelo was just 21 when a cardinal commissioned him to create the drunken grape-adorned *Bacchus* (1496–97), on show at the Bargello.

⊙ San Lorenzo

★ **Museo delle Cappelle Medicee** MAUSOLEUM
(Medici Chapels; www.firenzemusei.it; Piazza Madonna degli Aldobrandini 6; adult/reduced €8/4; ⊙8.15am-1.50pm, closed 1st, 3rd & 5th Mon, 2nd & 4th Sun of month) Nowhere is Medici conceit expressed so explicitly as in the Medici Chapels. Adorned with granite, marble, semi-precious stones and some of Michelangelo's most beautiful sculptures, it is the burial place of 49 dynasty members. Francesco I lies in the dark, imposing **Cappella dei Principi** (Princes' Chapel) alongside Ferdinando I and II and Cosimo I, II and III. Lorenzo il Magnifico is buried in the graceful **Sagrestia Nuova** (New Sacristy), which was Michelangelo's first architectural work.

⊙ San Marco

★ **Galleria dell'Accademia** GALLERY
(www.firenzemusei.it; Via Ricasoli 60; adult/reduced €8/4, incl temporary exhibition €12.50/6.25; ⊙8.15am-6.50pm Tue-Sun) A queue marks the door to this gallery, built to house one of the Renaissance's most iconic masterpieces, Michelangelo's *David*. But the world's most famous statue is worth the wait. The subtle detail of the real thing – the veins in his sinewy arms, the leg muscles, the change in expression as you move around the statue – *is* impressive. Carved from a single block of marble, Michelangelo's most famous work

BEST OF THE UFFIZI

Cut to the quick of the gallery's collection and start by getting to grips with pre-Renaissance Tuscan art in **Room 2**, home to several shimmering alterpieces by Giotto et al. Then work your way on to **Room 8** and Piero della Francesca's iconic profile portrait of the Duke and Duchess of Urbino.

More familiar images await in the **Sala di Botticelli**, including the master's great Renaissance masterpiece, *La nascita di Venere* (The Birth of Venus). Continue on to **Room 15** for works by Leonardo da Vinci and then on to **Room 35** for Michelangelo's *Doni tondi* (The Holy Family).

was his most challenging – he didn't choose the marble himself and it was veined.

⊙ Oltrarno

★ **Palazzo Pitti** MUSEUM
(www.uffizi.beniculturali.it; Piazza dei Pitti; ⊙8.15am-6.50pm Tue-Sun) Commissioned by banker Luca Pitta and designed by Brunelleschi in 1457, this vast Renaissance palace was later bought by the Medici family. Over the centuries, it served as the residence of the city's rulers until the Savoys donated it to the state in 1919. Nowadays it houses an impressive silver museum, a couple of art museums and a series of rooms recreating life in the palace during House of Savoy times.

🎭 Festivals & Events

Scoppio del Carro FIREWORKS
(⊙Mar/Apr) A cart of fireworks is exploded in front of the cathedral in Piazza del Duomo at 11am on Easter Sunday.

Maggio Musicale Fiorentino PERFORMING ARTS
(www.operadifirenze.it; ⊙Apr-Jun) Italy's oldest arts festival features world-class performances of theatre, classical music, jazz, opera and dance. Events are staged at the Opera di Firenze (p699) and venues across town.

Festa di San Giovanni RELIGIOUS
(⊙24 Jun) Florence celebrates its patron saint, John, with a *calcio storico* (historic football) match on Piazza di Santa Croce and fireworks over Piazzale Michelangelo.

🛏 Sleeping

⭐ Hotel Dalí
HOTEL €

(📞 055 234 07 06; www.hoteldali.com; Via dell'Oriuolo 17; d €90, s/d without bathroom €40/70, apt from €95; 🅿 🛜) A warm welcome from hosts Marco and Samanta awaits at this lovely small hotel. A stone's throw from the *duomo*, it has 10 sunny rooms, some overlooking a leafy inner courtyard, decorated in a low-key modern way and equipped with kettles, coffee and tea. No breakfast, but – miraculous for downtown Florence – free parking in the rear courtyard.

⭐ Academy Hostel
HOSTEL €

(📞 055 239 86 65; www.academyhostel.eu; Via Ricasoli 9; dm €32-45, d €80-100; ❄ @ 🛜) This classy 13-room hostel – definitely not a party hostel – sits on the 1st floor of Baron Ricasoli's 17th-century *palazzo*. The inviting lobby, with books to browse and computers to surf, was once a theatre and is a comfy spot to chill on the sofa over TV or a DVD. Dorms sport four, five or six beds, high moulded ceilings and brightly coloured lockers.

Hotel Cestelli
HOTEL €

(📞 055 21 42 13; www.hotelcestelli.com; Borgo SS Apostoli 25; d €100, s/d without bathroom €60/80; ☺ closed 2 weeks Jan & 10 days Aug; 🛜) Housed in a 12th-century *palazzo* a stiletto strut from fashionable Via de' Tornabuoni, this intimate eight-room hotel is a gem. Rooms reveal an understated style, tastefully combining polished antiques with spangly chandeliers, vintage art and silk screens. Owners Alessio and Asumi are a mine of local information and are happy to share their knowledge. No breakfast. Ask about low-season discounts for longer stays.

⭐ Hotel Scoti
PENSION €€

(📞 055 29 21 28; www.hotelscoti.com; Via de' Tornabuoni 7; d/tr/q €130/160/185; ☺ reception 8am-11.30pm; 🛜) Wedged between designer boutiques on Florence's smartest shopping strip, this hidden *pensione* is a fabulous mix of old-fashioned charm and value for money. Its 16 traditionally styled rooms are spread across the 2nd floor of a 16th-century *palazzo;* some have lovely rooftop views. Guests can borrow hairdryers, bottle openers, plug adaptors etc and the frescoed lounge (1780) is stunning. No breakfast.

⭐ Hotel Davanzati
HOTEL €€

(📞 055 28 66 66; www.hoteldavanzati.it; Via Porta Rossa 5; s/d/tr €143/215/281; ❄ @ 🛜) Twenty-two steps lead up to this family-run hotel. A labyrinth of enchanting rooms, frescoes and modern comforts, it has bags of charisma – and that includes Florentine brothers Tommaso and Riccardo, and father Fabrizio, who run the show (Grandpa Marcello surveys proceedings). Rooms come with a mini iPad, meaning free wi-fi around town, direct messaging with the hotel and a handy digital city guide.

⭐ Palazzo Guadagni Hotel
HOTEL €€

(📞 055 265 83 76; www.palazzoguadagni.com; Piazza Santo Spirito 9; d €150-220, tr/q €265/310; ❄ 🛜) This romantic hotel overlooking Florence's liveliest summertime square is legendary – Zeffirelli shot scenes from *Tea with Mussolini* here. Housed in an artfully revamped Renaissance palace, it has 15 spacious if old-fashioned rooms and an impossibly romantic loggia terrace with wicker chairs and predictably dreamy views.

Hotel Morandi alla Crocetta
BOUTIQUE HOTEL €€

(📞 055 234 47 48; www.hotelmorandi.it; Via Laura 50; s €70-120, d €100-170, tr €130-210, q €150-250; 🅿 ❄ 🛜) This medieval convent-turned-hotel away from the madding crowd in San Marco is a stunner. Rooms are refined and traditional in look – think antique furnishings, wood beams and oil paintings – with a quiet, old-world ambience. Pick of the bunch is frescoed room No 29, the former chapel. Garage parking €25 per night.

⭐ Antica Torre di Via de' Tornabuoni 1
BOUTIQUE HOTEL €€€

(📞 055 265 81 61; www.tornabuoni1.com; Via de' Tornabuoni 1; d €350; ❄ 🛜) Footsteps from the Arno, inside the beautiful 14th-century Palazzo Gianfigliazzi on Florence's smartest shopping strip, is this stylish hotel. Rooms

---

ℹ CUT THE QUEUES

➡ Book tickets for the Uffizi and Galleria dell'Accademia, as well as several other museums through **Firenze Musei** (Florence Museums; www.firenzemusei.it). Note that this entails a booking fee of €4 per museum.

➡ Alternatively, the **Firenze Card** (€72, valid for 72 hours) allows you to bypass both advance booking and queues. Check details at www.firenzecard.it.

and various suites are spacious and contemporary, but what completely steals the show is the stunning rooftop breakfast terrace – among the best in the city. Sip cappuccino and swoon over Florence graciously laid out at your feet.

✕ Eating

★ Mercato Centrale FOOD HALL €

(☑ 055 239 97 98; www.mercatocentrale.it; Piazza del Mercato Centrale 4; dishes €7-15; ☺ 10am-midnight; 🛜) Meander the maze of stalls rammed with fresh produce at Florence's oldest and largest food market, on the ground floor of a fantastic iron-and-glass structure designed by architect Giuseppe Mengoni in 1874. Head to the 1st floor's buzzing, thoroughly contemporary food hall with dedicated bookshop, cookery school and artisan stalls cooking steaks, burgers, tripe *panini*, vegetarian dishes, pizza, gelato, pastries and pasta.

★ Trattoria Mario TUSCAN €

(☑ 055 21 85 50; www.trattoria-mario.com; Via Rosina 2; meals €25; ☺ noon-3.30pm Mon-Sat, closed 3 weeks Aug) Arrive by noon to ensure a stool around a shared table at this noisy, busy, brilliant trattoria – a legend that retains its soul (and allure with locals) despite being in every guidebook. Charming Fabio, whose grandfather opened the place in 1953, is front of house while big brother Romeo and nephew Francesco cook with speed in the kitchen. No advance reservations, no credit cards.

★ Osteria Il Buongustai OSTERIA €

(☑ 055 29 13 04; Via dei Cerchi 15r; meals €15-20; ☺ 8am-4pm Mon-Fri, to 11pm Sat) Run with breathtaking speed and grace by Laura and Lucia, this place is unmissable. Lunchtimes heave with locals who work nearby and savvy students who flock here to fill up on tasty Tuscan home cooking at a snip of other restaurant prices. The place is brilliantly no frills – expect to share a table and pay in cash; no credit cards.

★ Mariano SANDWICHES €

(☑ 055 21 40 67; Via del Parione 19r; panini €3.50; ☺ 8am-3pm & 5-7.30pm Mon-Fri, 8am-3pm Sat) Our favourite for its simplicity, around since 1973. From sunrise to sunset, this brick-vaulted, 13th-century cellar gently buzzes with Florentines propped at the counter sipping coffee or wine or eating salads and *panini*. Come here for a coffee-and-pastry breakfast,

light lunch, *aperitivo* with cheese or salami tasting platter (€12), or *panino* to eat on the move.

★ 5 e Cinque VEGETARIAN €

(☑ 055 274 15 83; Piazza della Passera 1; meals €25; ☺ noon-3pm & 7.30-10pm Tue-Sun; 🛜 ☑) The hard work and passion of a photography and antique dealer is behind this highly creative, intimate eating space adored by many a savvy local. Cuisine is vegetarian with its roots in Genova's kitchen – '5 e Cinque' (meaning '5 and 5') is a chickpea sandwich from Livorno and the restaurant's *cecina* (traditional Ligurian flat bread made from chickpea flour) is legendary.

★ Il Santo Bevitore TUSCAN €€

(☑ 055 21 12 64; www.ilsantobevitore.com; Via di Santo Spirito 64-66r; meals €40; ☺ 12.30-2.30pm & 7.30-11.30pm, closed Sun lunch & Aug) Reserve or arrive right on 7.30pm to snag the last table at this ever-popular address, an ode to stylish dining where gastronomes eat by candlelight in a vaulted, whitewashed, bottle-lined interior. The menu is a creative reinvention of seasonal classics: risotto with monkfish, red turnip and fennel; *ribollita* with kale; chicken liver terrine with brioche and a Vin Santo reduction.

★ Il Teatro del Sale TUSCAN €€

(☑ 055 200 14 92; www.teatrodelsale.com; Via dei Macci 111r; lunch/dinner/weekend brunch €15/35/20; ☺ 11am-3pm & 7.30-11pm Tue-Sat, 11am-3pm Sun, closed Aug) Florentine chef Fabio Picchi is one of Florence's living treasures who steals the Sant' Ambrogio show with this eccentric, good-value members-only club (everyone welcome, membership €7) inside an old theatre. He cooks up weekend brunch, lunch and dinner, culminating at 9.30pm in a live performance of drama, music or comedy arranged by his wife, artistic director and comic actress Maria Cassi.

Trattoria Cibrèo TUSCAN €€

(www.cibreo.com; Via dei Macci 122r; meals €40; ☺ 12.50-2.30pm & 6.50-11pm Tue-Sat, closed Aug) Dine here chez Fabio Picchi and you'll instantly understand why a queue gathers outside before it opens. Once inside, revel in top-notch Tuscan cuisine: perhaps *pappa al pomodoro* (a thick soupy mash of tomato, bread and basil) followed by *polpettine di pollo e ricotta* (chicken and ricotta meatballs). No reservations, no credit cards, no pasta and arrive early to snag a table.

★ **L'Osteria di Giovanni** TUSCAN €€

(☑055 28 48 97; www.osteriadigiovanni.it; Via del Moro 22; meals €45; ☺7-10pm Mon-Fri, noon-3pm & 7-10pm Sat & Sun) Cuisine at this smart eatery is timelessly Tuscan. Imagine truffles, tender steaks and delicious pasta such as *pici al sugo di salsicccia e cavolo nero* (thick spaghetti with a sauce of sausage and black cabbage). Throw in a complimentary glass of *prosecco* as aperitif and sweet Vin Santo wine with a plate of almond-studded *cantuccini* to end your meal, and you'll be hooked.

🍷 Drinking & Nightlife

★ **Le Volpi e l'Uva** WINE BAR

(☑055 239 81 32; www.levolpieluva.com; Piazza dei Rossi 1; ☺11am-9pm Mon-Sat) This unassuming wine bar hidden away by Chiesa di Santa Felicità remains as appealing as the day it opened over a decade ago. Its food and wine pairings are first class – taste and buy boutique wines by small producers from all over Italy, matched perfectly with cheeses, cold meats and the best *crostini* in town. Wine-tasting classes too.

★ **Ditta Artigianale** CAFE, BAR

(☑055 274 15 41; www.dittaartigianale.it; Via de' Neri 32r; ☺8am-10pm Sun-Thu, 8am-midnight Fri, 9.30am-midnight Sat; 📶) With industrial decor and welcoming laid-back vibe, this ingenious coffee roastery and gin bar is a perfect place to hang any time of day. The creation of three-times Italian barista champion Francesco Sanapo, it's famed for its first-class coffee and outstanding gin cocktails. If you're yearning a flat white, cold brew tonic or cappuccino made with almond, soy or coconut milk, come here.

Caffè Rivoire CAFE

(☑055 21 44 12; www.rivoire.it; Piazza della Signoria 4; ☺7am-midnight Tue-Sun summer, to 9pm winter) This golden oldie with an unbeatable people-watching terrace has produced some of the city's most exquisite chocolate since 1872. Black-jacketed barmen with ties set the formal tone. Save several euros by joining the local Florentine crowd standing at the bar rather than sitting down at a table.

Gilli CAFE

(☑055 21 38 96; www.gilli.it; Piazza della Repubblica 39r; ☺7.30am-1.30am) The most famous of the historic cafes on the city's old Roman forum, Gilli has been serving utterly delec-

FLORENCE'S BEST GELATO

Vivoli (☑055 29 23 34; www.vivoli.it; Via dell'Isola delle Stinche 7; tubs €2-10; ☺7.30am-midnight Tue-Sat, 9am-midnight Sun, to 9pm winter) Select from the huge choice on offer and scoff it in the pretty piazza opposite.

Grom (☑055 21 61 58; www.grom.it; Via del Campanile 2; cones €2.60-4.60, tubs €2.60-5.50; ☺10am-10.30pm Sun-Thu, to 11.30pm Fri & Sat) Delectable flavours and organic seasonal ingredients.

Gelateria La Carraia (☑055 28 06 95; Piazza Nazario Sauro 25r; cones/tubs €1.50-6; ☺10.30am-midnight summer, 11am-10pm winter) Fantastic gelateria next to Ponte Carraia.

Carabé (☑055 28 94 76; www.parco carabe.it; Via Ricasoli 60r; cones €2.50-4; ☺10am-midnight, closed mid-Dec–mid-Jan) Fill up on Sicilian ice cream as you wait to see *David*.

table cakes, chocolates, fruit tartlets and *millefoglie* (sheets of puff pastry filled with rich vanilla or chocolate Chantilly cream) to die for since 1733 (it moved to this square in 1910 and sports a beautifully preserved art nouveau interior).

☆ Entertainment

La Cité BAR

(☑055 21 03 87; www.lacitelibreria.info; Borgo San Frediano 20r; ☺2pm-2am Mon-Sat, 3pm-2am Sun; 📶) A hip cafe-bookshop with an eclectic choice of vintage seating, La Cité makes a wonderful, intimate venue for book readings, after-work drinks and fantastic live music – jazz, swing, world music. Check its Facebook page for the week's events.

Opera di Firenze OPERA

(☑055 277 93 09; www.operadifirenze.it; Piazzale Vittorio Gui, Viale Fratelli Rosselli 15; ☺box office 10am-6pm Tue-Fri, to 1pm Sat) Florence's strikingly modern opera house with glittering contemporary geometric facade sits on the green edge of city park Parco delle Cascine. Its three thoughtfully designed and multifunctional concert halls seat an audience of 5000 and play host to the springtime Maggio Musicale Fiorentino.

ℹ Information

24-Hour Pharmacy (☑ 055 21 67 61; Stazione di Santa Maria Novella; ⊙ 24hr) Nonstop pharmacy inside Florence's central train station; at least one member of staff usually speaks English.

Dr Stephen Kerr: Medical Service (☑ 335-836 16 82, 055 28 80 55; www.dr-kerr.com; Piazza Mercato Nuovo 1; ⊙ 3-5pm Mon-Fri, or by appointment 9am-3pm Mon-Fri) Resident British doctor.

Tourist Office (☑ 055 29 08 32; www.firenze-turismo.it; Via Cavour 1r; ⊙ 9am-1pm Mon-Fri) Tourist office not far from the historic centre.

Tourist Office (☑ 055 21 22 45; www.firen-zeturismo.it; Piazza della Stazione 4; ⊙ 9am-6.30pm Mon-Sat, to 1.30pm Sun) Tourist office just across the street from Florence's central train station.

ℹ Getting There & Away

AIR

The main airport serving Tuscany is **Pisa International Airport** (p701).

The smaller **Florence Airport** (Aeroporto Amerigo Vespucci; ☑ 055 3 06 15, 055 306 18 30; www.aeroporto.firenze.it; Via del Termine 11) is 5km north of town.

BUS

The main bus station is just west of Piazza della Stazione.

Buses leave for Siena (€7.80, 1¼ hours, at least hourly) and San Gimignano via Poggibonsi (€6.80, 1¼ to two hours, hourly).

TRAIN

Florence's **Stazione di Santa Maria Novella** (Piazza della Stazione) is on the main Rome–Milan line. There are regular direct services to/from Pisa (€8, one hour), Rome (€65, 1½ to 3½ hours), Venice (€40 to €49, two hours) and Milan (€35 to €74, 1¾ hours).

ℹ Getting Around

TO/FROM THE AIRPORT

Volainbus (☑ 800 373760; www.fsbusitalia.it) The Volainbus shuttle runs between the bus station and Florence airport. Going to the airport, departures are roughly half-hourly between 6am and 8.30pm and then hourly until 11.30pm; from the airport between 5.30am and 8.30pm then hourly until 11.45pm. Journey time is 30 minutes and a single/return ticket costs €6/10.

PUBLIC TRANSPORT

City buses are operated by ATAF. Get tickets (€1.20 or €2 if bought on board) at the ticket office at Santa Maria Novella train station, at tobacconists and at news-stands. They are valid for 90 minutes on any bus.

Pisa

POP 89,160

A handsome university city, Pisa is best known as the home of an architectural project gone terribly wrong. However, the Leaning Tower is just one of a number of noteworthy sights in its compact medieval centre.

Pisa's golden age came in the 12th and 13th centuries when it was a maritime power to rival Genoa and Venice.

⊙ Sights

★ Leaning Tower   TOWER

(Torre Pendente; ☑ 050 83 50 11; www.opapisa.it; Piazza dei Miracoli; €18; ⊙ 8am-8pm Apr-Sep, 9am-7pm Oct, to 6pm Mar, 10am-5pm Nov-Feb) One of Italy's signature sights, the Torre Pendente truly lives up to its name, leaning a startling 3.9 degrees off the vertical. The 56m-high tower, officially the Duomo's *campanile* (bell tower), took almost 200 years to build, but was already listing when it was unveiled in 1372. Over time, the tilt, caused by a layer of weak subsoil, steadily worsened until it was finally halted by a major stabilisation project in the 1990s.

★ Duomo   CATHEDRAL

(☑ 050 83 50 11; www.opapisa.it; Piazza dei Miracoli; ⊙ 10am-8pm Apr-Sep, to 7pm Oct, to 6pm Nov-Mar) **FREE** Pisa's magnificent Romanesque Duomo was begun in 1064 and consecrated in 1118. Its striking tiered exterior, with cladding of green-and-cream marble bands, gives on to a vast columned interior capped by a gold wooden ceiling. The elliptical dome, the first of its kind in Europe at the time, was added in 1380.

Note that while admission is free, you'll need an entrance coupon from the ticket office or a ticket from one of the other Piazza dei Miracoli sights.

★ Battistero   CHRISTIAN SITE

(Baptistry; ☑ 050 83 50 11; www.opapisa.it; Piazza dei Miracoli; €5, combination ticket with Camposanto or Museo delle Sinopie €7, Camposanto & Museo

€8; ⊙8am-8pm Apr-Sep, 9am-7pm Oct, to 6pm Mar, 10am-5pm Nov-Feb) Pisa's unusual round baptistry has one dome piled on top of another, each roofed half in lead, half in tiles, and topped by a gilt bronze John the Baptist (1395). Construction began in 1152, but it was remodelled and continued by Nicola and Giovanni Pisano more than a century later and finally completed in the 14th century. Inside, the hexagonal marble pulpit (1260) by Nicola Pisano is the highlight.

🛏 Sleeping & Eating

★Hotel Pisa Tower
HOTEL €€

(📞050 520 00 19; www.hotelpisatower.com; Via Andrea Pisano 23; d €115-125, tr €140-145, q €150-160; 🅿❄🛜) Superb value for money, a superlative location, and spacious, high-ceilinged rooms – this polished three-star is one of Pisa's best deals. Chandeliers, marble floors and old framed prints adorn the classically attired interiors, while out back, a pristine lawn adds a soothing dash of green.

Hotel Bologna
HOTEL €€

(📞050 50 21 20; www.hotelbologna.pisa.it; Via Giuseppe Mazzini 57; s €98-228; 🅿❄🛜) Placed well away from the Piazza dei Miracoli mayhem, this elegant four-star mansion hotel is an oasis of peace and tranquillity. Its big, bright rooms have wooden floors and colour-coordinated furnishings – some are frescoed. Kudos for the small terrace and cypress-shaded garden out back – delightful for lazy summertime breakfasts. Reception organises bike/scooter hire; courtyard parking for motorists costs €10 per night.

★L'Ostellino
SANDWICHES €

(Piazza Cavallotti 1; panini €3.50-7; ⊙noon-4.30pm Mon-Fri, to 6pm Sat & Sun) For a buster-size gourmet *panino* (sandwich) wrapped in crunchy waxed paper, this minuscule deli and *panineria* (sandwich shop) delivers. Take your pick from dozens of different combos written by hand on the blackboard (*lardo di colonnata* with figs or cave-aged pecorino with honey and walnuts are sweet favourites), await construction, then hit the green lawns of Piazza dei Miracoli to picnic with the crowds.

Osteria La Toscana
OSTERIA €€

(📞050 96 90 52; Via San Frediano 10; meals €30; ⊙noon-3pm & 7-11pm Thu-Tue) This relaxed spot is one of several excellent eateries on

Via San Frediano, a lively street off Piazza dei Cavalieri. Subdued lighting, bare brown walls and background jazz set the stage for ample pastas and delectable grilled meats served with a smile and quiet efficiency.

ⓘ Information

Tourist Office (📞050 55 01 00; www.turismo. pisa.it/en; Piazza dei Miracoli 7; ⊙9.30am-5.30pm) Provides city information and various services including bike hire and left luggage.

ⓘ Getting There & Around

Pisa International Airport (Galileo Galilei Airport; 📞050 84 93 00; www.pisa-airport.com) is linked to the city centre by the PisaMover bus (€1.30, eight minutes, every 10 minutes).

Terravision buses link the airport with Florence (one way/return €5/10, 70 minutes, 18 daily).

Frequent trains run to Lucca (€3.50, 30 minutes), Florence (€8.40, one hour) and La Spezia (€7.50 to €15, one to 1½ hours) for the Cinque Terre.

Lucca

POP 89,000

Lucca is a love-at-first-sight type of place. Hidden behind monumental Renaissance walls, its historic centre is chock-full of handsome churches, alluring piazzas and excellent restaurants. Founded by the Etruscans, it became a city state in the 12th century and stayed that way for 600 years. Most of its streets and monuments date from this period.

◎ Sights

City Wall
HISTORIC SITE

Lucca's monumental *mura* (wall) was built around the old city in the 16th and 17th centuries and remains in almost perfect condition. It superceded two previous walls, the first built from travertine stone blocks as early as the 2nd century BC. Twelve metres high and 4.2km long, today's ramparts are crowned with a tree-lined footpath looking down on the *centro storico* and out towards the Apuane Alps. This path is a favourite location for the locals' daily *passeggiata* (traditional evening stroll).

★ Cattedrale di San Martino
CATHEDRAL

(☑0583 49 05 30; www.museocattedralelucca.it; Piazza San Martino; adult/reduced €3/2, incl Museo della Cattedrale & Chiesa e Battistero dei SS Giovanni & Reparata €9/5; ⊙9.30am-6pm Mon-Fri, to 6.45pm Sat, noon-6pm Sun summer, 9.30am-5pm Mon-Fri, to 6.45pm Sat, noon-6pm Sun winter) Lucca's predominantly Romanesque cathedral dates to the 11th century. Its stunning facade was constructed in the prevailing Lucca-Pisan style and designed to accommodate the preexisting *campanile* (bell tower). The reliefs over the left doorway of the portico are believed to be by Nicola Pisano, while inside, treasures include the **Volto Santo** (literally, Holy Countenance) crucifix sculpture and a wonderful 15th-century tomb in the **sacristy**. The cathedral interior was rebuilt in the 14th and 15th centuries with a Gothic flourish.

🛏 Sleeping & Eating

★ Piccolo Hotel Puccini
HOTEL €

(☑0583 5 54 21; www.hotelpuccini.com; Via di Poggio 9; s/d/t €75/95/120; ❋ 🛜) In a brilliant central location, this welcoming three-star hotel hides behind a discreet brick exterior. Its small guest rooms are attractive with wooden floors, vintage ceiling fans and colourful, contemporary design touches. Breakfast, optional at €3.50, is served at candlelit tables behind the small reception area. Rates are around 30% lower in winter.

★ Da Felice
PIZZA €

(☑0583 49 49 86; www.pizzeriadafelice.it; Via Buia 12; focaccias €1-3, pizza slices €1.30; ⊙11am-8.30pm Mon, 10am-8.30pm Tue-Sat) This buzzing spot behind Piazza San Michele is where the locals come for wood-fired pizza, *cecina*

(salted chickpea pizza) and *castagnacci* (chestnut cakes). Eat in or take away, *castagnaccio* comes wrapped in crisp white paper, and, my, it's good married with a chilled bottle of Moretti beer.

★ Ristorante Giglio
TUSCAN €€

(☑0583 49 40 58; www.ristorantegiglio.com; Piazza del Giglio 2; meals €40; ⊙noon-2.30pm & 7.30-10pm Thu-Mon, 7.30-10pm Wed) Don't let the tacky plastic-covered pavement terrace deter. Splendidly at home in the frescoed 18th-century Palazzo Arnolfini, Giglio is stunning. Dine at white-tableclothed tables, sip a complimentary *prosecco,* watch the fire crackle in the marble fireplace and savour traditional Tuscan with a modern twist: think fresh artichoke salad served in an edible parmesan-cheese wafer 'bowl', or risotto simmered in Chianti.

ℹ Information

Tourist Office (☑0583 58 31 50; www.turismo.lucca.it; Piazzale Verdi; ⊙9am-7pm Apr-Sep, to 5pm Mar-Oct) Free hotel reservations, left-luggage service (two bags €1.50/4.50/7 per hour/half-day/day) and guided city tours in English departing at 2pm daily in summer and on Saturdays and Sundays in winter. The two-hour tour costs €10.

ℹ Getting There & Around

Regional trains run to/from Florence (€7.50, 1½ hours, every 30 to 90 minutes) and Pisa (€3.50, 30 minutes, half-hourly).

Siena

POP 53,900

Siena is one of Italy's most enchanting medieval towns. Its walled centre is a beautifully preserved warren of dark lanes punctuated with Gothic *palazzi,* and at its heart, Piazza del Campo (Il Campo), the sloping square that is the venue for the city's famous annual horse race, Il Palio.

In the Middle Ages, the city was a political and artistic force to be reckoned with, a worthy rival for its larger neighbour Florence.

◎ Sights

★ Piazza del Campo
SQUARE

This sloping piazza, popularly known as Il Campo, has been Siena's civic and social centre since being staked out by the ruling Consiglio dei Nove in the mid-12th century. It was built on the site of a Roman marketplace, and its pie-piece paving design is divided into nine sectors to represent the number of members of that ruling council.

Palazzo Pubblico   HISTORIC BUILDING
(Palazzo Comunale; Piazza del Campo) The restrained, 14th-century Palazzo Comunale serves as the grand centrepiece of the square in which it sits – notice how its concave facade mirrors the opposing convex curve. From the *palazzo* soars a graceful bell tower, the **Torre del Mangia** (☑ 0577 29 23 43; www.enjoysiena.it; admission €10; ☺ 10am-6.15pm summer, to 3.15pm winter), 102m high and with 500-odd steps. The views from the top are magnificent.

★ **Museo Civico**   MUSEUM
(Civic Museum; ☑ 0577 29 22 32; Palazzo Pubblico, Piazza del Campo 1; adult/reduced €9/8; ☺ 10am-6.15pm summer, to 5.15pm winter) Siena's most famous museum occupies rooms richly frescoed by artists of the Sienese school. Commissioned by the governing body of the city, rather than by the church, many – unusually – depict secular subjects. The highlight is Simone Martini's celebrated *Maestà* (Virgin Mary in Majesty; 1315) in the **Sala del Mappamondo** (Hall of the World Map). It features the Madonna beneath a canopy surrounded by saints and angels, and is Martini's first known work.

★ **Duomo**   CATHEDRAL
(Cattedrale di Santa Maria Assunta; ☑ 0577 28 63 00; www.operaduomo.siena.it; Piazza Duomo; summer/winter €4/free, when floor displayed €7;

☺ 10.30am-7pm Mon-Sat, 1.30-6pm Sun summer, to 5.30pm winter) Siena's cathedral is one of Italy's most awe-inspiring churches. Construction started in 1215 and over the centuries many of Italy's top artists have contributed: Giovanni Pisano designed the intricate white, green and red marble facade; Nicola Pisano carved the elaborate pulpit; Pinturicchio painted some of the frescoes; Michelangelo, Donatello and Gian Lorenzo Bernini all produced sculptures. Buy tickets from the **duomo ticket office** (☑ 0577 28 63 00; ☺ 10am-6.30pm summer, to 5pm winter).

★ **Museale Santa Maria della Scala**   MUSEUM
(☑ 0577 53 45 71, 0577 53 45 11; www.santamariadellascala.com; Piazza Duomo 1; adult/reduced €9/7; ☺ 10am-5pm Mon, Wed & Thu, to 8pm Fri, to 7pm Sat & Sun, extended hours in summer) This former hospital, parts of which date from the 13th century, was built as a hospice for pilgrims travelling the Via Francigena pilgrimage trail. Its highlight is the upstairs Pellegrinaio (Pilgrim's Hall), with vivid 15th-century frescoes by Lorenzo Vecchietta, Priamo della Quercia and Domenico di Bartolo lauding the good works of the hospital and its patrons.

★★ **Festivals & Events**

Palio   PAGEANT, HORSE RACE
(☺ 2 Jul & 16 Aug) Dating from the Middle Ages, this spectacular annual event includes a series of colourful pageants and a wild

ITALY SIENA

WORTH A TRIP

SAN GIMIGNANO

This tiny hilltop town deep in the Tuscan countryside is a mecca for day trippers from Florence and Siena. Its nickname is the 'Medieval Manhattan' courtesy of the 14 11th-century towers that soar above its pristine *centro storico* (historic centre).

The **tourist office** (☑ 0577 94 00 08; www.sangimignano.com; ☺ 10am-1pm & 3-7pm summer, 10am-1pm & 2-6pm winter) is on Piazza del Duomo. Next door, **Palazzo Comunale** (☑ 0577 99 03 12; www.sangimignanomusei.it; combined Civic Museums ticket adult/reduced €9/7; ☺ 10am-7.30pm summer, 11am-5.30pm winter) houses San Gimignano's art gallery, the **Pinacoteca**, and tallest tower, the **Torre Grossa**.

Overlooking Piazza del Duomo, the **Collegiata** (Duomo or Basilica di Santa Maria Assunta; ☑ 0577 94 01 52; www.duomosangimignano.it; adult/reduced €4/2; ☺ 10am-7pm Mon-Sat, 12.30-7pm Sun summer, 10am-4.30pm Mon-Sat, 12.30-4.30pm Sun winter), San Gimignano's Romanesque cathedral, boasts a series of superb 14th-century frescoes.

For a traditional Tuscan lunch, head to **Locanda Sant'Agostino** (☑ 0577 94 31 41; Piazza Sant'Agostino 15; meals €35, pizzas €8-10; ☺ noon-3pm & 7-10pm Thu-Tue).

Regular buses link San Gimignano with Florence (€6.80, 1¼ to two hours, hourly) via Poggibonsi. There are also services to/from Siena (€6, 1¼ hours, 10 daily Monday to Saturday).

ORVIETO

Strategically located on the main train line between Rome and Florence, this spectacularly sited hilltop town has one major drawcard: its extraordinary Gothic **Duomo** (☑ 0763 34 24 77; www.opsm.it; Piazza Duomo 26; €3; ☉ 9.30am-7pm summer, shorter hours winter), built over 300 years from 1290. The facade is stunning, and the beautiful interior contains Luca Signorelli's awe-inspiring *Giudizio universale* (The Last Judgment) fresco cycle.

For information, the **tourist office** (☑ 0763 34 17 72; www.inorvieto.it; Piazza Duomo 24; ☉ 8.15am-1.50pm & 4-7pm Mon-Fri, 10am-1pm & 3-6pm Sat & Sun) is opposite the cathedral. For a filling meal, search out the **Trattoria del Moro Aronne** (☑ 0763 34 27 63; www. trattoriadelmoro.info; Via San Leonardo 7; meals €25-30; ☉ noon-3pm & 7-10pm Wed-Mon).

Direct trains run to/from Florence (€16, 2¼ hours, hourly) and Rome (€8 to €17.50, 1¼ hours, hourly).

If you arrive by train, you'll need to take the **funicular** (tickets €1.30; ☉ every 10min 7.20am-8.30pm Mon-Sat, every 15min 8am-8.30pm Sun) up to the town centre.

horse race in Piazza del Campo. Ten of Siena's 17 *contrade* (town districts) compete for the coveted *palio* (silk banner). Each *contrada* has its own traditions, symbol and colours, plus its own church and *palio* museum.

🍴 Sleeping & Eating

⭐ Hotel Alma Domus
HOTEL €

(☑ 0577 4 41 77; www.hotelalmadomus.it; Via Camporegio 37; s €55, d €90-140; ✸ @ 🛜) Your chance to sleep in a convent: Alma Domus is owned by the church and is still home to several Dominican nuns. The economy rooms, although supremely comfortable, are styled very simply. But the superior ones are positively sumptuous, with pristine bathrooms, pared-down furniture and bursts of magenta and lime. Many have mini-balconies with uninterrupted Duomo views. Families are welcome.

⭐ Pensione
Palazzo Ravizza
BOUTIQUE HOTEL €€

(☑ 0577 28 04 62; www.palazzoravizza.it; Pian dei Mantellini 34; s €145-230, d €160-295, ste €250-315; 🅿 ✸ 🛜) Heritage features and luxurious flourishes combine at this Renaissance-era *palazzo* to create an irresistible hotel. Frescoed ceilings, stone staircases and gilt mirrors meet elegant furnishings, wooden shutters and (from some bedrooms) captivating views. The greenery-framed rear garden is utterly delightful; settle down in a wicker chair here, gaze out towards the hills and you may never want to leave.

⭐ Morbidi
DELI €

(☑ 0577 28 02 68; www.morbidi.com; Via Banchi di Sopra 75; lunch/aperitivo buffet €12/from €7;

☉ 8am-8pm Mon-Thu, to 10pm Fri & Sat) Possibly the classiest cheap feed in Siena: set in the stylish basement of Morbidi's deli, the lunch buffet on offer here is excellent. For a mere €12, you can join the well-dressed locals sampling antipasti, salads, risottos, pastas and a dessert of the day. Bottled water is supplied; wine and coffee cost extra. Buy your ticket upstairs before heading down.

⭐ Enoteca I Terzi
TUSCAN €€

(☑ 0577 4 43 29; www.enotecaiterzi.it; Via dei Termini 7; meals €35; ☉ 11am-3pm & 6.30pm-1am Mon-Sat, shorter hours in winter) A favourite for many locals who head to this historic *enoteca* (wine bar) to linger over lunches, *aperitivi* and casual dinners featuring top-notch Tuscan *salumi* (cured meats), delicate handmade pasta and wonderful wines.

Osteria Nonna Gina
TUSCAN €€

(☑ 0577 28 72 47; www.osterianonnagina.it; Pian dei Mantellini 2; meals €30; ☉ 12.30-2.30pm & 7.30-10.30pm Tue-Sun) The atmosphere is pure Siena neighbourhood *osteria*: gingham tablecloths, postcards tacked to the rafters and pictures of Palio jockeys on the walls. The menu speaks of fine local traditions too: piles of local meat form the *antipasto Toscano* and the house red is a very decent Chianti, while the ingredients of the 'secret sauce' covering the plump, cheese-filled gnocchi will never be revealed.

ℹ Information

Tourist Office (☑ 0577 28 05 51; www. enjoysiena.it; Santa Maria della Scala, Piazza Duomo 1; ☉ 9am-6pm summer, to 5pm winter) Provides free Siena city maps, reserves accommodation, organises car and scooter hire, and sells train tickets (commission applies). Also takes bookings for a range of day tours.

ⓘ Getting There & Away

Siena Mobilità (☏ 800 922984; www.siena mobilita.it), part of the **Tiemme** (☏ 0577 20 41 11; www.tiemmespa.it) network, links Siena with Florence (€7.80, 1¼ hours, at least hourly) and San Gimignano (€6, 1¼ hours, 10 daily Monday to Saturday), either direct or via Poggibonsi.

Sena (☏ 0861 199 19 00; www.sena.it) operates services to/from Rome Tiburtina (€20, three hours, up to 13 daily), Milan (€32, 4½ hours, three daily), Perugia (€18, 1¾ hours, one daily) and Venice (€27, 5¾ hours, two daily).

Ticket offices are in the basement under the bus station on Piazza Gramsci.

Perugia

POP 166,100

With its hilltop medieval centre and international student population, Perugia is Umbria's largest and most cosmopolitan city. In July, music fans inundate the city for the prestigious **Umbria Jazz festival** (www.umbriajazz. com), and in the third week of October the **Eurochocolate** (www.eurochocolate.com) festival lures chocoholics from across the globe.

Perugia has a dramatic and bloody past. In the Middle Ages, art and culture thrived – both Perugino and Raphael, his student, worked here – as powerful local dynasties fought for control of the city.

⊙ Sights

Cattedrale di San Lorenzo   CATHEDRAL
(Piazza IV Novembre; ☺ 7.30am-12.30pm & 3.30-6.45pm Mon-Sat, 8am-12.45pm & 4-7.30pm Sun) Overlooking Piazza IV Novembre is Perugia's stark medieval cathedral. A church has stood here since the 900s, but the version you see today was begun in 1345 from designs created by Fra Bevignate. Building continued until 1587, although the main facade was never completed. Inside you'll find dramatic late Gothic architecture, an altarpiece by Signorelli and sculptures by Duccio. The steps in front of the facade are where seemingly all of Perugia congregates; they overlook the piazza's centrepiece, the delicate pink-and-white marble **Fontana Maggiore** (Great Fountain).

★ **Palazzo dei Priori**   PALACE
(Corso Vannucci 19) Flanking Corso Vannucci, this Gothic palace, constructed between the 13th and 14th centuries, is architecturally striking with its tripartite windows, ornamental portal and fortress-like crenellations. It was formerly the headquarters of the local magistracy, but now houses the city's main art gallery, the Galleria Nazionale dell'Umbria. Also of note is the **Nobile Collegio del Cambio** (Exchange Hall; www.collegiodelcambio. it; €4.50, incl Nobile Collegio della Mercanzia €5.50; ☺ 9am-12.30pm & 2.30-5.30pm Mon-Sat, 9am-1pm Sun), Perugia's medieval money exchange, with its Perugino frescoes.

Galleria Nazionale dell'Umbria   GALLERY
(www.gallerianazionaleumbria.it; Palazzo dei Priori, Corso Vannucci 19; adult/reduced €8/4; ☺ 8.30am-7.30pm Tue-Sun, noon-7.30pm Mon Apr-Oct) Umbria's foremost art gallery is housed in Palazzo dei Priori on the city's main strip. Its collection, one of central Italy's richest, numbers almost 3000 works, ranging from Byzantine-inspired 13th-century paintings to Gothic works by Gentile da Fabriano and Renaissance masterpieces by hometown heroes Pinturicchio and Perugino.

🛏 Sleeping & Eating

★ **B&B San Fiorenzo**   B&B €
(☏ 393 3869987; www.sanfiorenzo.com; Via Alessi 45; d/qd €70/120; 🖳) Buried in Perugia's medieval maze of a centre is this charming 15th-century *palazzo*, where Luigi and Monica make you welcome in one of three unique rooms. A Florentine architect has carefully incorporated mod cons and marble bathrooms into spacious quarters with brick vaulting, lime-washed walls and antique furnishings, including an apartment with an 11th-century shower and a 13th-century tower room.

Hotel Signa   HOTEL €
(☏ 075 572 41 80; www.hotelsigna.it; Via del Grillo 9; s €34-59, d €49-99, tr €69-104, q €69-135; ❄🖳) Slip down an alley off Corso Cavour to reach Signa, one of Perugia's best budget picks. The petite rooms are simple, bright and well kept; many have balconies with cracking views of the city and countryside. Rooms at the cheaper end of the scale have shared bathrooms. Breakfast costs an extra €7. The owner, Mario, hands out maps and tips freely.

Pizzeria Mediterranea   PIZZA €

(Piazza Piccinino 11/12; pizzas €4-12; ⏱12.30-2.30pm & 7.30-11.30pm; 🍴) A classic pizzeria with a wood-fired oven and bustling atmosphere, this popular spot does the best pizzas in town. Served bubbling hot, they come with light, Neapolitan-style bases and flavoursome toppings. Expect queues at the weekend.

★ **La Taverna**   ITALIAN €€

(☑075 572 41 28; www.ristorantelataverna.com; Via delle Streghe 8; meals €30-40; ⏱12.30-3pm & 7.30-11pm; 🔊) Way up there on the Perugia dining wish list, La Taverna consistently wins the praise of local foodies. Chef Claudio cooks market-fresh produce with flair and precision, while waiters treat you like one of the *famiglia*.

ℹ Information

Informazione e Accoglienza Turistica (IAT)
(Tourist Information; ☑075 573 64 58; http://turismo.comune.perugia.it; Piazza Matteotti 18; ⏱9am-6pm) Housed in the 14th-century Loggia dei Lanari, Perugia's main tourist office has stacks of info on the city, maps (€0.50) and up-to-date bus and train timetables.

ℹ Getting There & Around

BUS

Perugia's bus station is on Piazza dei Partigiani, from where *scale mobili* (escalators) connect with Piazza Italia in the historic centre.
Sulga (☑800 099661; www.sulga.it) Buses run to/from Rome (€17, 2½ hours, up to five daily) and Fiumicino Airport (€22, 3¾ hours, four Monday to Saturday, two Sunday).
Umbria Mobilità (☑075 963 76 37; www.fsbusitalia.it) Operates buses to regional destinations, including Assisi (€4.20, 45 minutes, up to eight daily).

TRAIN

Direct trains connect with Florence (€14.55, 1½ to two hours, 10 daily).

To get to the centre from the train station, take the *minimetrò* (€1.50) to the Pincetto stop just below Piazza Matteotti. Alternatively, take the bus to Piazza Italia (€1.50, €2 on bus) .

Assisi

POP 28,300

The birthplace of St Francis (1182–1226), the medieval town of Assisi is a major destination for millions of pilgrims. The main sight is the Basilica di San Francesco, one of Italy's most visited churches, but the hilltop historic centre is also well worth a look.

◉ Sights

★ **Basilica di San Francesco**   BASILICA
(www.sanfrancescoassisi.org; Piazza di San Francesco; ⏱upper church 8.30am-6.50pm, lower church & tomb 6am-6.50pm) **FREE** Visible for miles around, the Basilica di San Francesco is the crowning glory of Assisi's Unesco World Heritage ensemble. It's divided into an upper church, the **Basilica Superiore**, with a celebrated cycle of Giotto frescoes, and beneath, the lower, older **Basilica Inferiore**, where you'll find frescoes by Cimabue, Pietro Lorenzetti and Simone Martini. Also here, in the **Cripta di San Francesco**, is St Francis' elaborate and monumental tomb.

Basilica di Santa Chiara   BASILICA
(www.assisisantachiara.it; Piazza Santa Chiara; ⏱6.30am-noon & 2-7pm summer, to 6pm winter) Built in a 13th-century Romanesque style, with steep ramparts and a striking pink-and-white facade, this church is dedicated to St Clare, a spiritual contemporary of St Francis and founder of the Sorelle Povere di Santa Chiara (Order of the Poor Ladies), now known as the Poor Clares. She is buried in the church's crypt, alongside the **Crocifisso di San Damiano**, a Byzantine cross before which St Francis was praying when he heard from God in 1205.

🛏 Sleeping & Eating

Hotel Alexander   HOTEL €
(☑075 81 61 90; www.hotelalexanderassisi.it; Piazza Chiesa Nuova 6; s €50-75, d €75-108; ❈🔊) On a small cobbled piazza by the Chiesa Nuova, Hotel Alexander offers nine spacious rooms and a communal terrace with wonderful rooftop views. The modern decor – pale wooden floors and earthy brown tones – contrasts well with the wood-beamed ceilings and carefully preserved antiquity all around.

★ **Osteria Eat Out**   UMBRIAN €€
(☑075 81 31 63; www.eatoutosteriagourmet.it; Via Eremo delle Carceri 1a; meals €40-50; ⏱7.30-10.30pm Mon-Fri, 7.30-10.30pm & 12.30-2.30pm Sat & Sun; 🔊) With such astounding views and minimalist-chic interiors, you might expect the glass-fronted restaurant of the Nun Assisi hotel to prefer style over substance. Not so. Polished service and an exciting wine list are well matched with seasonal Umbrian cuisine flavoured with home-grown herbs. Dishes like *umbricelli* pasta with fresh truffle and fillet of Chianina beef are big on flavour and easy on the eye.

ℹ Information

Informazione e Accoglienza Turistica (IAT)
(Tourist Office; ☎ 075 813 86 80; www.visit-assisi.it; Piazza del Comune 22; ⊗9am-6pm Mon-Fri, to 7pm Sat, to 6pm Sun, shorter hours winter) Stop by here for maps, leaflets and info on accommodation.

ℹ Getting There & Away

It is better to travel to Assisi by bus rather than train.

Buses arrive at and depart from Piazza Matte-otti in the *centro storico*.

Umbria Mobilità (☎075 963 76 37; www.fs-busitalia.it) Buses run to/from Perugia (€4.20, 45 minutes, up to eight daily).

SOUTHERN ITALY

A sun-bleached land of spectacular coastlines and rugged landscapes, southern Italy is a robust contrast to the more genteel north. Its stunning scenery, baroque towns and classical ruins exist alongside ugly urban sprawl and scruffy coastal development, sometimes in the space of just a few kilometres.

Yet for all its flaws, *il mezzogiorno* (the midday sun, as southern Italy is known) is an essential part of every Italian itinerary, offering charm, culinary good times and architectural treasures.

Naples

POP 974,000

A love-it-or-loathe-it sprawl of regal palaces, bombastic churches and chaotic streets, Naples (Napoli) is totally exhilarating. Founded by Greek colonists, it became a thriving Roman city and was later the Bourbon capital of the Kingdom of the Two Sicilies. In the 18th century it was one of Europe's great cities, something you'll readily believe as you marvel at its art-crammed museums and great baroque buildings.

⊙ Sights

★ Museo Archeologico Nazionale   MUSEUM
(☎848 80 02 88, from mobile 06 399 67050; www.museoarcheologiconapoli.it; Piazza Museo Nazionale 19; adult/reduced €12/6; ⊗9am-7.30pm Wed-Mon; Ⓜ Museo, Piazza Cavour) Naples' National Archaeological Museum serves up one of the world's finest collections of Graeco-Roman artefacts. Originally a cavalry barracks and

ℹ THE ARTECARD

The **Campania Artecard** (www.campaniartecard.it) offers discounted museum admission and transport. It comes in various forms, of which the most useful are:

Napoli (€21, valid for three days) Gives free entry to three sights in Naples, then discounts on others, as well as free city transport.

Tutta la regione (€32/34, valid for three/seven days) Provides free entry to two/five sights (three-/seven-day card) across the region and discounts on others. Free public transport is covered by the three-day card, but not by the seven-day version.

Cards can be purchased online, at the dedicated artecard booth inside the tourist office at Stazione Centrale (p711), or at participating sites and museums.

later seat of the city's university, the museum was established by the Bourbon king Charles VII in the late 18th century to house the antiquities he inherited from his mother, Elisabetta Farnese, as well as treasures looted from Pompeii and Herculaneum. Star exhibits include the celebrated *Toro Farnese* (Farnese Bull) sculpture and a series of awe-inspiring mosaics from Pompeii's Casa del Fauno.

★ Cappella Sansevero   CHAPEL
(☎081 551 84 70; www.museosansevero.it; Via Francesco de Sanctis 19; adult/reduced €7/5; ⊗9.30am-6.30pm Wed-Mon; Ⓜ Dante) It's in this Masonic-inspired baroque chapel that you'll find Giuseppe Sanmartino's incredible sculpture, *Cristo velato* (Veiled Christ), its marble veil so realistic that it's tempting to try to lift it and view Christ underneath. It's one of several artistic wonders that include Francesco Queirolo's sculpture *Disinganno* (Disillusion), Antonio Corradini's *Pudicizia* (Modesty) and riotously colourful frescoes by Francesco Maria Russo, the latter untouched since their creation in 1749.

★ Duomo   CATHEDRAL
(☎081 44 90 97; Via Duomo 149; cathedral/baptistry free/€2; ⊗cathedral 8.30am-1.30pm & 2.30-7.30pm Mon-Sat, 8am-1pm & 4.30-7.30pm Sun, baptistry 8.30am-12.30pm & 4-6.30pm Mon-Sat, 8.30am-1pm

Central Naples

N 0 ———————— 400 m
0 ———————— 0.2 miles

Palazzo Reale
di Capodimonte
(1.9km)

**Museo
Archeologico
Nazionale**
2

Museo

Via Foria

Via Maria Longo

Cerasiello B&B (350m);
Casa D'Anna (500m)

Via Santissimi Apostoli

Via S Guiseppe
dei Nudi

Piazza
Museo
Nazionale

Piazza
Cavour

Via d'Anticaglia

Via Santa Maria di Costantinopoli

Via dei Tribunali

Via Tommasi

Via Broggia

Largo
Regina
Coeli

Via Pisanelli

Vico Gigianti

Via Duomo

3

Via Francesco
Saverio Correra

Via della Sapienza

Via Atri

Via San Paolo

Piazza San
Gaetano

Vico Zuroli

Via della Zite

Via Enrico Pessina

Via Bellini

Piazza
Luigi
Miraglia

12

Vico Giuseppe Maffei

Via Vicaria
Vecchia

Via G Brombeis

Vico S Domenico Soriano

5

Via del Sole

Via dei Tribunali

9

Via Nilo

Piazza
Museo
Filangieri

Via Port'Alba

Piazza
Bellini

**Cappella
Sansevero**
1

Via San Biagio dei Librai

Vico S Severino

Via d'Alagno

11

Dante

Piazza Dante

Palazzo dei
Di Sangrio

Piazzetta
del Nilo

Via Montesanto

Via Tarsia

Via San Sebastiano

Via Benedetto Croce

Via B Capasso

Piazza Nicola
Amore

Duomo

3

Via Pellegrini

Funicolare di
Montesanto (170m);
Certosa e Museo
di San Martino (1.5km)

Piazza del
Gesù Nuovo

7

Via Santa Chiara

Via Merzocannone

Via G Paladino

Alibus (Stazione
Central Stop) (850m);
Terminal Metropark (1.1km);
Stazione Centrale (1.2km);
Circumvesuviana (1.2km)

Via Pasquale
Scura

Complesso
Monumentale di
Santa Chiara

Largo
Giusso

Piazzetta
Orefici

Via T
Caravita

Largo
Banchi
Nuovi

Eccelenze
Campane
(1.9km)

Via S Anna dei Lombardi

Via Formale

Via S Liborio

Via Pignasecca

Piazza
Carità

Via Donnalbina

Via Sedile di Porto

Via Nuova Marina

4

Via G Simonelli

Via Monteoliveto

Corso Umberto I

Vico P Galluppi

Via C Battisti

Piazza
Matteotti

Via D Cerriglio

Piazza
Bovio

Università

Via Concezione
a Montecalvario

Via A Diaz

Via D Fiorentini

Via Graziella

Via Bracco

Tirrenia

Toledo

Via A Depretis

Via Alside De Gasperi

5

Via Potracrarese
a Montecalvario

Via S Tommaso d'Aquino

Via F Gioia

Via S Nicola
alla Dogana

Calata Porta
di Massa

Varco
Immacolatella

Via Speranzella

Via S Giacomo

Via Medina

Via S Bartolomeo

Via Cristoforo Colombo

Via Toledo

Piazza del
Municipio

Via G
Melisurgo

4

Bacino del
Piliero

Via P E Imbriani

6

Piazza
Francese

Municipio

Molo
Angioino

8

Via G Verdi

Via Santa Brigida

Via Vittorio
Emanuele III

SNAV

Vico d'Aflitto

Funicolare
Centrale

Castel
Nuovo

Alibus For
Airport

Porto Immacolatella

Piazza
Trieste e
Trento

13

Via San Carlo

Parco
Castello

Alilauro

Caremar

Via Chiaia

10

Muu Muuzzarella
Lounge (600m);
B&B Cappella
Vecchia (700m)

Molo
Beverello

Via A F Acton

7

Piazza del
Plebiscito

Central Naples

Sun; 🚇 E1, E2 to Via Duomo) Whether you go for Giovanni Lanfranco's fresco in the **Cappella di San Gennaro** (Chapel of St Janarius), the 4th-century mosaics in the baptistry, or the thrice-annual miracle of San Gennaro, do not miss Naples' cathedral. Kick-started by Charles I of Anjou in 1272 and consecrated in 1315, it was largely destroyed in a 1456 earthquake, with copious nips and tucks over the subsequent centuries.

★ **Certosa e Museo di San Martino** MONASTERY, MUSEUM
(🕿 081 229 45 03; www.polomusealenapoli.beniculturali.it; Largo San Martino 5; adult/reduced €6/3; ⊙8.30am-7.30pm Thu-Tue; 🚇 Vanvitelli, 🚠 Montesanto to Morghen) The high point (quite literally) of the Neapolitan baroque, this charterhouse turned museum was founded as a Carthusian monastery in the 14th century. Centred on one of the most beautiful cloisters in Italy, it has been decorated, adorned and altered over the centuries by some of Italy's finest talent, most importantly Giovanni Antonio Dosio in the 16th century and baroque master Cosimo Fanzago a century later. Nowadays, it's a superb repository of Neapolitan artistry.

★ **Palazzo Reale di Capodimonte** MUSEUM
(🕿 081 749 91 30; www.museocapodimonte. beniculturali.it; Via Miano 2; adult/reduced €8/4; ⊙8.30am-7.30pm Thu-Tue; 🚇 R4, 178 to Via Capo-

dimonte) Originally designed as a hunting lodge for Charles VII of Bourbon, this monumental palace was begun in 1738 and took more than a century to complete. It's now home to the **Museo Nazionale di Capodimonte**, southern Italy's largest and richest art gallery. Its vast collection – much of which Charles inherited from his mother, Elisabetta Farnese – was moved here in 1759 and ranges from exquisite 12th-century altarpieces to works by Botticelli, Caravaggio, Titian and Andy Warhol.

✸ Festivals & Events

Festa di San Gennaro RELIGIOUS
The faithful flock to the Duomo to witness the miraculous liquefaction of San Gennaro's blood on the Saturday before the first Sunday in May. Repeat performances take place on 19 September and 16 December.

🛏 Sleeping

B&B Cappella Vecchia B&B €
(🕿 081 240 51 17; www.cappellavecchia11.it; Vico Santa Maria a Cappella Vecchia 11; s €50-80, d €75-110, tr €90-140; ❄ @ 🛜; 🚇 C24 to Piazza dei Martiri) Run by a super-helpful young couple, this B&B is a first-rate choice in the smart, fashionable Chiaia district. Rooms are simple and upbeat, with funky bathrooms, vibrant colours and Neapolitan themes. There's a spacious communal area for breakfast, and free internet available 24/7. Check the website for special offers.

Cerasiello B&B B&B €
(🕿 081 033 09 77, 338 926 44 53; www.cerasiello. it; Via Supportico Lopez 20; s €40-85, d €60-100, tr €75-110, q €90-125; ❄ 🛜; 🚇 Piazza Cavour, Museo) This gorgeous B&B consists of four rooms with private bathroom, an enchanting communal terrace and an ethno-chic look melding Neapolitan art with North African furnishings. The stylish kitchen offers a fabulous view of the Certosa di San Martino, a view shared by all rooms (or their bathroom) except Fuoco (Fire), which looks out at a beautiful church cupola.

Hostel of the Sun HOSTEL €
(🕿 081 420 63 93; www.hostelnapoli.com; Via G Melisurgo 15; dm €18-25, s €30-35, d €60-80; ❄ @ 🛜; 🚇 Municipio) HOTS is an ultrafriendly hostel near the hydrofoil and ferry terminals. Located on the 7th floor (have €0.05 for the lift), it's a bright, sociable place with multicoloured dorms, a casual in-house bar (with cheap evening cocktails) and – a few

floors down – a series of hotel-standard private rooms, many with en-suite bathrooms.

★**Hotel Piazza Bellini** BOUTIQUE HOTEL €€
(☑081 45 17 32; www.hotelpiazzabellini.com; Via Santa Maria di Costantinopoli 101; d €58-148; ✳@⑨; ⓂDante) Only steps from buzzing Piazza Bellini, this sharp, contemporary hotel occupies a 16th-century *palazzo*, its mint white spaces spiked with original maiolica tiles and the work of emerging artists. Rooms offer pared-back cool, with designer fittings, chic bathrooms and mirror frames drawn straight onto the wall. Rooms on the 5th and 6th floors feature panoramic terraces.

★**Casa D'Anna** GUESTHOUSE €€
(☑081 44 66 11; www.casadanna.it; Via dei Cristallini 138; s €80-114, d €113-163; ✳⑨; ⓂPiazza Cavour, Museo) Everyone from artists to Parisian fashionistas adore this elegant guesthouse, lavished with antiques, books and original artwork. Its four guestrooms blend classic and contemporary design features of the highest quality, while the lush communal terrace is perfect for an alfresco tête-à-tête. Breakfast includes homemade baked treats and jams. There's a two-night minimum stay...though we doubt you'll be hurrying to leave.

★**La Ciliegina
Lifestyle Hotel** BOUTIQUE HOTEL €€
(☑081 1971 8800; www.cilieginahotel.it; Via PE Imbriani 30; d €115-300, junior ste €144-400; ✳@⑨; ⓂMunicipio) An easy walk from the hydrofoil terminal, this chic, contemporary slumber spot is a hit with fashion-conscious urbanites. Spacious white rooms are splashed with blue and red accents, each with top-of-the-range Hästens beds, flat-screen TVs and marble-clad bathrooms with a water-jet Jacuzzi shower (one junior suite has a Jacuzzi tub).

✖ Eating

★**Pizzeria Gino Sorbillo** PIZZA €
(☑081 44 66 43; www.sorbillo.it; Via dei Tribunali 32; pizzas from €3; ⊙noon-3.30pm & 7pm-11.30pm Mon-Thu, to midnight Fri & Sat; ⑨; ⓂDante) Day in, day out, this cult-status pizzeria is besieged by hungry hordes. While debate may rage over whether Gino Sorbillo's pizzas are the best in town, there's no doubt that his giant, wood-fired discs – made using organic flour and tomatoes – will have you licking

fingertips and whiskers. Head in super early or prepare to queue.

★**Pintauro** PASTRIES €
(☑081 41 73 39; Via Toledo 275; sfogliatelle €2; ⊙9am-8pm, closed mid-Jul–early Sep; ☐R2 to Via San Carlo, ⓂMunicipio) Of Neapolitan *dolci* (sweets), the cream of the crop is the *sfogliatella,* a shell of flaky pastry stuffed with creamy, scented ricotta. This local institution has been selling *sfogliatelle* since the early 1800s, when its founder supposedly brought them to Naples from their culinary birthplace on the Amalfi Coast.

★**Muu Muuzzarella Lounge** NEAPOLITAN €
(☑081 40 53 70; www.muumuuzzarellalounge. it; Vico II Alabardieri 7; dishes €7-16; ⊙12.30pm-midnight Tue-Sun; ⑨; ☐C24 to Riviera di Chiaia) Pimped with milking-bucket lights and cow-hide patterned cushions, playful, contemporary Muu is all about super-fresh Campanian mozzarella, from cheese and charcuterie platters to creative dishes like buffalo bocconcini with creamy pesto and crunchy apple. Leave room for the chef's secret recipe white-chocolate cheesecake, best paired with a glass of Guappa (buffalo-milk liqueur).

★**La Taverna di Santa Chiara** NEAPOLITAN €€
(☑081 048 49 08; Via Santa Chiara 6; meals €25; ⊙1-2.30pm & 8-10.30pm, lunch to 3pm Fri-Sun, closed Tue lunch & Sun dinner; ⑨; ⓂDante) Gragnano pasta, Agerola pork, Benevento *latte nobile:* this intimate, two-level eatery is healthily obsessed with small, local producers and Slow Food ingredients. The result is a beautiful, seasonal journey across Campania. For an inspiring overview, order the *misto di salumi e formaggi* (an antipasto of cheese and cured meats), then tuck into lesser-known classics like *zuppa di soffritto* (spicy meat stew) with a glass of smooth house *vino.*

★**Eccellenze Campane** NEAPOLITAN €€
(☑081 20 36 57; www.eccellenzecampane.it; Via Benedetto Brin 49; pizza from €6, meals around €30; ⊙complex 7am-11pm Sun-Fri, to 12.30am Sat, restaurants 12.30-3.30pm & 7.30-11pm Sun-Fri, to 12.30am Sat; ⑨; ☐192, 460, 472, 475) This is Naples' answer to Turin-based food emporium Eataly, an impressive, contemporary showcase for top-notch Campanian comestibles. The sprawling space is divided into various dining and shopping sections, offering everything from beautifully charred pizzas

and light *fritture* (fried snacks) to finer-dining seafood, coveted Sal Da Riso pastries, craft beers and no shortage of take-home pantry treats. A must for gastronomes. Website in Italian.

 Ristorantino dell'Avvocato NEAPOLITAN €€
([☑] 081 032 00 47; www.ilristorantinodellavvocato.it; Via Santa Lucia 115-117; meals €40-45; ⊙ noon-3pm daily, also 7-11pm Tue-Sat; [☎]; [🚌] 128 to Via Santa Lucia) This elegant yet welcoming restaurant has quickly won the respect of Neapolitan gastronomes. Apple of their eye is affable lawyer turned head chef Raffaele Cardillo, whose passion for Campania's culinary heritage merges with a knack for subtle, refreshing twists – think gnocchi with fresh mussels, clams, crumbed pistachio, lemon, ginger and garlic.

🍷 Drinking & Nightlife

Caffè Mexico CAFE
(Piazza Dante 86; ⊙ 5.30am-8.30pm Mon-Sat; [Ⓜ] Dante) Naples' best (and best-loved) coffee bar – even the local cops stop by for a quick pick-me-up – is a retro-tastic combo of old-school baristas, an orange espresso machine and velvety, full-flavoured *caffè*. The espresso is served *zuccherato* (sweetened), so request it *amaro* if you fancy a bitter hit.

Caffè Gambrinus CAFE
([☑] 081 41 75 82; www.grancaffegambrinus.com; Via Chiaia 1-2; ⊙ 7am-1am Sun-Thu, to 2am Fri & Sat; [🚌] R2 to Via San Carlo, [Ⓜ] Municipio) Grand, chandeliered Gambrinus is Naples' oldest and most venerable cafe. Oscar Wilde knocked back a few here and Mussolini had some of the rooms shut to keep out left-wing intellectuals. The prices may be steep, but the *aperitivo* nibbles are decent and sipping a *spritz* or a luscious *cioccolata calda* (hot chocolate) in its belle époque rooms is something worth savouring.

Spazio Nea CAFE
([☑] 081 45 13 58; www.spazionea.it; Via Constantinopoli 53; ⊙ 9am-2am, to 3am Fri & Sat; [☎]; [Ⓜ] Dante) Aptly skirting bohemian Piazza Bellini, this whitewashed gallery features its own cafe-bar speckled with books, flowers, cultured crowds and alfresco seating at the bottom of a baroque staircase. Eye up exhibitions of contemporary Italian and foreign art, then kick back with a *caffè* or a Cynar *spritz*. Check Nea's Facebook page for upcoming readings, live-music gigs or DJ sets.

☆ Entertainment

Teatro San Carlo OPERA, BALLET
([☑] 081 797 23 31; www.teatrosancarlo.it; Via San Carlo 98; ⊙ box office 10am-5.30pm Mon-Sat, to 2pm Sun; [🚌] R2 to Via San Carlo) One of Italy's top opera houses, the San Carlo stages opera, ballet and concerts. Bank on up to €40 for a place in the sixth tier, €75 to €110 for a seat in the stalls or – if you're under 30 and can prove it – €15 to €30 for a place in a side box. Ballet tickets range from €55 to €95, with €20 to €30 tickets for those under 30.

❶ Information

Travellers should be careful about walking alone late at night near Stazione Centrale and Piazza Dante. Petty theft is also widespread so watch out for pickpockets (especially on the city's public transport) and scooter thieves.

Loreto Mare Hospital (Ospedale S. Maria di Loreto Nuovo; [☑] 081 254 21 11; www.aslnapoli1centro.it/818; Via A Vespucci 26; [🚌] 154) Central city hospital with an emergency department.

Police Station (Questura; [☑] 081 794 11 11; Via Medina 75; [Ⓜ] Università) To check if your car's been removed, call the municipal police on [☑] 081 787 06 37.

Tourist Information Office ([☑] 081 26 87 79; Stazione Centrale; ⊙ 9am-8pm; [Ⓜ] Garibaldi) Tourist office inside Stazione Centrale (Central Station).

Tourist Information Office ([☑] 081 551 27 01; www.inaples.it; Piazza del Gesù Nuovo 7; ⊙ 9am-5pm Mon-Sat, to 1pm Sun; [Ⓜ] Dante) Tourist office in the *centro storico*.

Tourist Information Office ([☑] 081 40 23 94; www.inaples.it; Via San Carlo 9; ⊙ 9am-5pm Mon-Sat, to 1pm Sun; [🚌] R2 to Via San Carlo, [Ⓜ] Municipio) Tourist office at Galleria Umberto I, directly opposite Teatro San Carlo.

❶ Getting There & Away

AIR
Naples International Airport (Capodichino) ([☑] 081 789 62 59; www.aeroportodinapoli.it) Capodichino airport, 7km northeast of the city centre, is southern Italy's main airport. It's served by a number of major airlines and low-cost carriers, including EasyJet, which operates flights to Naples from London, Paris, Berlin and several other European cities.

BOAT
Fast ferries and hydrofoils for Capri, Ischia, Procida and Sorrento depart from **Molo Beverello** in front of Castel Nuovo; hydrofoils also sail from Mergellina, 5km west.

Ferries for Sicily and Sardinia sail from **Molo Angioino** (right beside Molo Beverello) and neighbouring **Calata Porta di Massa**.

As a rough guide, bank on about €20 for the 50-minute jet crossing to Capri, and €12.50 for the 35-minute sail to Sorrento.

Tickets for shorter journeys can be bought at the ticket booths on Molo Beverello, Calata Porta di Massa or at Mergellina. For longer journeys try the offices of the ferry companies or a travel agent.

Hydrofoil and ferry companies include the following:

Alilauro (☑ 081 497 22 38; www.alilauro.it)

Caremar (☑ 081 1896 6690; www.caremar.it)

NLG (NLG; ☑ 081 552 07 63; www.navlib.it)

SNAV (☑ 081 428 55 55; www.snav.it)

Tirrenia (☑ 892 123; www.tirrenia.it)

BUS

Most national and international buses now leave from **Terminal Bus MetroPark** (☑ 800 65 00 06; Corso Arnaldo Lucci; Ⓜ Garibaldi), located on the southern side of Stazione Centrale. The bus station is home to **Biglietteria Vecchione** (☑ 331 88969217, 081 563 03 20; www.big lietteriavecchione.it; ⊙ 6.30am-9.30pm Mon-Fri, to 7.30pm Sat & Sun), a ticket agency selling national and international bus tickets.

TRAIN

Most trains arrive at or depart from **Stazione Centrale** (Piazza Garibaldi).

There are about 40 daily trains to Rome (€11 to €44, 1¼ to 2½ hours), many of which continue northwards.

From Piazza Garibaldi station (adjacent to Stazione Centrale), **Circumvesuviana** (☑ 800 21 13 88; www.eavsrl.it) operates half-hourly trains to Sorrento (€4.50, 65 minutes) via Ercolano (€2.50, 20 minutes) and Pompeii (€3.20, 40 minutes).

❶ Getting Around

TO/FROM THE AIRPORT

Airport shuttle **Alibus** (☑ 800 63 95 25; www. anm.it) connects the airport to **Piazza Garibaldi** (Corso Novara) (Stazione Centrale) and **Molo Beverello** (€4, 45 minutes, every 20 minutes).

PUBLIC TRANSPORT

You can travel around Naples by bus, metro and funicular.

Tickets come in various forms, most usefully:

TIC Standard (Ticket Integrato Campania) Valid for 90 minutes, €1.50

TIC Daily €4.50

Note that these tickets are only valid for Naples city; they don't cover travel on the Circumve-suviana trains to Herculaneum, Pompeii and Sorrento.

Capri

POP 14,100

The most visited of the islands in the Bay of Naples, Capri deserves more than a quick day trip. Beyond the glamorous veneer of chichi cafes and designer boutiques is an island of rugged seascapes, desolate Roman ruins and a surprisingly unspoiled rural in-land.

Ferries dock at Marina Grande, from where it's a short funicular ride up to Capri, the main town. A further bus ride takes you up to Anacapri.

⊙ Sights

Grotta Azzurra   CAVE

(Blue Grotto; €14; ⊙ 9am-5pm) Capri's single most famous attraction is the Grotta Azzurra, a stunning sea cave illuminated by an other-worldly blue light. The easiest way to visit is to take a **tour** (☑ 081 837 56 46; www.motoscafisticapri.com; Private Pier 0, Marina Grande; €15) from Marina Grande; tickets include the return boat trip but the rowing boat into the cave and admission are paid separately. Allow a good hour.

Giardini di Augusto   GARDENS

(Gardens of Augustus; €1; ⊙ 9am-7.30pm) Escape the crowds by seeking out these colourful gardens near the Certosa di San Giacomo. Founded by Emperor Augustus, they rise in a series of flowered terraces to a lookout point offering breathtaking views over to the **Isole Faraglioni**, a group of three limestone stacks that rise out of the sea.

★ Villa Jovis   RUINS

(Jupiter's Villa; Via A Maiuri; €4; ⊙ 10am-7pm Tue-Sun summer, shorter hours rest of year, closed Jan–mid-Mar) A 45-minute walk east of Ca-pri along Via Tiberio, Villa Jovis was the largest and most sumptuous of the island's 12 Roman villas and Tiberius' main Capri residence. A vast pleasure complex, now re-duced to ruins, it famously pandered to the emperor's debauched tastes, and included imperial quarters and extensive bathing are-as set in dense gardens and woodland.

POMPEII & HERCULANEUM

On 24 August AD 79, Mt Vesuvius erupted, submerging the thriving port of Pompeii in lapilli (burning fragments of pumice stone) and Herculaneum in mud. Both places were quite literally buried alive, leaving thousands of people dead. The Unesco-listed ruins of both provide remarkable models of working Roman cities, complete with streets, temples, houses, baths, forums, taverns, shops, and even a brothel.

Pompeii

A stark reminder of the malign forces that lie deep inside Vesuvius, the ruins of ancient **Pompeii** (☑081 857 53 47; www.pompeiisites.org; entrances at Porta Marina, Piazza Esedra & Piazza Anfiteatro; adult/reduced €13/7.50, incl Herculaneum €22/12; ◷9am-7.30pm Apr-Oct, to 5.30pm Nov-Mar) make for one of Europe's most compelling archaeological sites. The remains first came to light in 1594, when the architect Domenico Fontana stumbled across them while digging a canal, but systematic exploration didn't begin until 1748. Since then 44 of Pompeii's original 66 hectares have been excavated.

There's a huge amount to see at the site. Start with the **Terme Suburbane**, a public bathhouse decorated with erotic frescoes just outside **Porta Marina**, the most impressive of the city's original seven gates. Once inside the walls, continue down **Via Marina** to the grassy **foro** (forum). This was the ancient city's main piazza and is today flanked by limestone columns and what's left of the **basilica**, the 2nd-century-BC seat of the city's law courts and exchange. Opposite the basilica, the **Tempio di Apollo** is the oldest and most important of Pompeii's religious buildings, while at the forum's northern end the **Granai del Foro** (Forum Granary) stores hundreds of amphorae and a number of body casts. These were made in the 19th century by pouring plaster into the hollows left by disintegrated bodies. A short walk away, the **Lupanare** (Brothel) pulls in the crowds with its collection of red-light frescoes. To the south, the 2nd-century-BC **Teatro Grande** is a 5000-seat theatre carved into the lava mass on which Pompeii was originally built.

Other highlights include the **Anfiteatro**, the oldest known Roman amphitheatre in existence; the **Casa del Fauno**, Pompeii's largest private house, where many of the mosaics now in Naples' Museo Archeologico Nazionale originated; and the **Villa dei Misteri**, home to the Dionysiac frieze, the most important fresco still on site.

To get to Pompeii, take the Circumvesuviana train to Pompeii Scavi-Villa dei Misteri (€3.20, 40 minutes from Naples; €2.80, 30 minutes from Sorrento) near the main Porta Marina entrance.

Herculaneum

Smaller and less daunting than Pompeii, **Herculaneum** (☑081 857 53 47; www.pompeii sites.org; Corso Resina 187, Ercolano; adult/reduced €11/5.50, incl Pompeii €22/12; ◷8.30am-7.30pm Apr-Oct, to 5pm Nov-Mar; ⊞Circumvesuviana to Ercolano-Scavi) can reasonably be visited in a morning or afternoon.

A modest fishing port and resort for wealthy Romans, Herculaneum, like Pompeii, was destroyed by the Vesuvius eruption. But because it was much closer to the volcano, it drowned in a 16m-deep sea of mud and debris rather than in the lapilli and ash that rained down on Pompeii. This essentially fossilised the town, ensuring that even delicate items like furniture and clothing were well preserved. Excavations began after the town was rediscoverd in 1709 and continue to this day.

There are a number of fascinating houses to explore. Notable among them are the **Casa d'Argo**, a noble residence centred on a porticoed, palm-treed garden; the aristocratic **Casa di Nettuno e Anfitrite**, named after the extraordinary mosaic of Neptune in the nymphaeum (fountain and bath); and the **Casa dei Cervi** with its marble deer, murals, and beautiful still-life paintings.

Marking the sites' southernmost tip, the 1st-century-AD **Terme Suburbane** is a wonderfully preserved baths complex with deep pools, stucco friezes and bas-reliefs looking down on marble seats and floors.

To reach Herculaneum, take the Circumvesuviana train to Ercolano (€2.50, 20 minutes from Naples; €3.40, 45 minutes from Sorrento), from where it's a 500m walk from the station – follow signs downhill to the *scavi* (ruins).

★ **Seggiovia del Monte Solaro**　CABLE CAR
(☑ 081 837 14 38; www.capriseggiovia.it; single/
return €8/11; ⊘ 9.30am-5pm summer, to 3.30pm
winter) A fast and painless way to reach Capri's highest peak, Anacapri's Seggiovia del
Monte Solaro chairlift whisks you to the top
of the mountain in a tranquil, beautiful ride
of just 12 minutes. The views from the top
are outstanding – on a clear day, you can see
the entire Bay of Naples, the Amalfi Coast
and the islands of Ischia and Procida.

🛏 Sleeping & Eating

★ **Hotel La Tosca**　PENSION €€
(☑ 081 837 09 89; www.latoscahotel.com; Via
Dalmazio Birago 5; s €50-105, d €75-165; ✳ 🛜)
Away from the glitz of the town centre, this
charming one-star place is hidden down a
quiet back lane overlooking the Certosa
di San Giacomo. Rooms are airy and comfortable, with pine furniture, light tiles,
striped fabrics and large bathrooms. Several
also have private terraces or garden vistas.
Breakfast is served on the terrace, with a
view of the sea.

★ **Hotel Villa Eva**　HOTEL €€
(☑ 081 837 15 49; www.villaeva.com; Via La Fab-
brica 8; d €120-200, tr €150-220, apt per person
€60-90; ⊘ Apr-Oct; ✳ @ 🛜 🏊) Nestled amid
fruit and olive trees in the countryside near
Anacapri, Villa Eva is an idyllic retreat, complete with swimming pool, lush gardens and
sunny rooms and apartments. Whitewashed
domes, terracotta floors, stained-glass windows and vintage fireplaces add character,
while the location ensures peace and quiet.

★ **È Divino**　ITALIAN €€
(☑ 081 837 83 64; www.edivinocapri.com/divino;
Vico Sella Orta 10a; meals €30-35; ⊘ 8pm-1am
daily Jun-Aug, 12.30-2.30pm & 7.30pm-midnight
Tue-Sun rest of year; 🛜) Look hard for the sign:
this Slow Food restaurant is a well-kept secret. Step inside and you find yourself in
what resembles a traditional sitting room;
the only hints that this is a restaurant are
the tantalising aromas and the distant tinkle
of glasses. The menu changes daily, according to whatever is fresh from the garden or
market.

La Rondinella　ITALIAN €€
(☑ 081 837 12 23; www.ristorantelarondinella.com;
Via Guiseppe Orlandi 295; meals €30; ⊘ noon-
2.30pm & 7-11.30pm Fri-Mon) La Rondinella
has a relaxed, rural feel and remains one

of Anacapri's better restaurants; apparently
Graham Greene had a favourite corner table
here. The menu features a number of Italian
classics such as *saltimbocca alla romana*
(veal slices with ham and sage).

🛈 Information

Tourist Office (☑ 081 837 06 34; www.
capritourism.com; Banchina del Porto, Marina
Grande; ⊘ 8.45am-1.30pm & 3.30-6pm Mon-
Sat, 9am-1pm Sun summer, 8.30am-2.30pm
Mon-Sat winter) Can provide a map of the
island (€1) with town plans of Capri and Anacapri. For hotel listings and other useful information, ask for a free copy of *Capri è*.

🛈 Getting There & Around

There are year-round boats to Capri from Naples
and Sorrento. Timetables and fare details are
available online at www.capritourism.com.
From Naples Regular services depart from
Molo Beverello. Tickets cost €20.50 for jetfoils,
€12.80 for ferries.
From Sorrento Jetfoils cost €18.30, slower
ferries €14.80.

　On the island, buses run from Capri Town
to/from Marina Grande, Anacapri and Marina
Piccola. Single tickets cost €1.80 on all routes,
including the funicular.

Sorrento

POP 16,700

Despite being a popular package-holiday
destination, Sorrento manages to retain a
laid-back southern Italian charm. There
are very few sights to speak of, but there
are wonderful views of Mt Vesuvius, and its
small *centro storico* is an atmospheric place
to explore. Sorrento's relative proximity to
the Amalfi Coast, Pompeii and Capri also
make it a good base for exploring the area.

⊙ Sights & Activities

Museo Correale　MUSEUM
(☑ 081 878 18 46; www.museocorreale.it; Via Correale 50; €8; ⊘ 9.30am-6.30pm Tue-Sat, to 1.30pm
Sun) East of the city centre, this museum
is well worth a visit whether you're a clock
collector, an archaeological egghead or into
embroidery. In addition to the rich assortment of 17th- to 19th-century Neapolitan
art and crafts, there are Japanese, Chinese
and European ceramics, clocks, furniture
and, on the ground floor, Greek and Roman
artefacts.

Chiesa di San Francesco CHURCH

(Via San Francesco; ⊙8am-1pm & 2-8pm) Located next to the Villa Comunale Park, this is one of Sorrento's most beautiful churches. Surrounded by bougainvillea and birdsong, the evocative cloisters have an Arabic portico and interlaced arches supported by octagonal pillars. The church is most famous, however, for its summer program of concerts featuring world-class performers from the classical school. If this strikes a chord, check out the schedule at the tourist office. There are also regular art exhibitions.

🛏 Sleeping & Eating

★Ulisse HOTEL €

(☑081 877 47 53; www.ulissedeluxe.com; Via del Mare 22; dm €20-35, d €60-150; P❋☎☰) Although it calls itself a hostel, the Ulisse is about as far from a backpackers' pad as a hiking boot from a stiletto. Most rooms are plush, spacious affairs with swish if rather bland fabrics, gleaming floors and large en-suite bathrooms. There are two single-sex dorms, and quads for sharers. Breakfast is included in some rates but costs €10 with others.

Casa Astarita B&B €€

(☑081 877 49 06; www.casastarita.com; Corso Italia 67; d €70-140, tr €95-165; ❋☎) Housed in an 18th-century *palazzo* on Sorrento's main strip, this charming B&B has a colourful, eclectic look with original vaulted ceilings, brightly painted doors and maiolica-tiled floors. Its six simple but well-equipped rooms surround a central parlour, where breakfast is served on a large rustic table.

★Da Emilia TRATTORIA €

(☑081 807 27 20; Via Marina Grande 62; meals €21-30; ⊙noon-3pm & 6-10.30pm Mar-Nov; ⊞) Founded in 1947 and still run by the same family, this is a homely yet atmospheric joint overlooking the fishing boats in Marina Grande. There's a large informal dining room, complete with youthful photos of former patron Sophia Loren, a scruffily romantic terrace and a menu of straightforward, no-fail dishes like mussels with lemon, and spaghetti with clams.

Raki GELATO €

(www.rakisorrento.com; Via San Cesareo 48; cones & tubs from €2.50; ⊙11am-late) There are numerous gelaterie in Sorrento, but this place is a hit with its homemade preservative-free ice cream in a number of exciting flavours. Try ricotta, walnut and honey, or vanilla and ginger, which packs a surprisingly spicy punch.

OTHER SOUTHERN SPOTS WORTH A VISIT

Lecce Known as the Florence of the South; a lively university town famous for its ornate baroque architecture.

Matera A prehistoric town set on two rocky ravines, known as *sassi,* studded with primitive cave dwellings.

Aeolian Islands An archipelago of seven tiny islands off Sicily's northeastern coast. Lipari is the largest and the main hub, while Stromboli is the most dramatic, with its permanently spitting volcano.

ℹ Information

Main Tourist Office (☑081 807 40 33; www.sorrentotourism.com; Via Luigi de Maio 35; ⊙9am-6pm Mon-Fri winter, daily summer) In the Circolo dei Forestieri (Foreigners' Club). Ask for the useful publication *Surrentum.*

ℹ Getting There & Away

Circumvesuviana (☑800 21 13 88; www.eavsrl.it) trains run half-hourly between Sorrento and Naples (€4.50, 65 minutes) via Pompeii (€2.80, 30 minutes) and Ercolano (€3.40, 45 minutes from Sorrento).

Regular **SITA** (☑344 103 10 70; www.sitasudtrasporti.it) buses leave from the Circumvesuviana station for the Amalfi Coast, stopping at Positano (€2.20, 50 minutes) and Amalfi (€3.40, 1¾ hours).

From Marina Piccola, regular jetfoils (€18.30) and ferries (€14.80) sail to Capri (25 minutes, up to 16 daily).There are also summer sailings to Naples (€12.30, 35 minutes), Positano (€16, 40 minutes) and Amalfi (€17, 70 minutes).

Amalfi Coast

Stretching 50km along the southern side of the Sorrentine Peninsula, the Unesco-protected Amalfi Coast (Costiera Amalfitana) is a postcard-perfect vision of shimmering blue water fringed by vertiginous cliffs on which whitewashed villages and terraced lemon groves cling.

ℹ Getting There & Away

BOAT

Boat services generally run between April and October.

Alicost (☑ 089 87 14 83; www.alicost.it) Operates daily boats from Salerno (Molo Manfredi) to Amalfi (€8), Positano (€12) and Capri (€22.50).

Travelmar (☑ 089 87 29 50; www.travelmar.it) Has daily sailings from Salerno (Piazza Concordia) to Amalfi (€8) and Positano (€12).

BUS

SITA (☑ 344 103 10 70; www.sitasudtrasporti. it) buses run from Sorrento to Positano (€2.20, 50 minutes) and Amalfi (€3.40, 1¾ hours), and from Salerno to Amalfi (€2.80, 1¼ hours).

Positano

POP 3950

Approaching Positano by boat, you're greeted by an unforgettable view of colourful, steeply stacked houses clinging to near-vertical green slopes. In town, the main activities are hanging out on the small beach, drinking and dining on flower-laden terraces, and browsing the expensive boutiques.

The **tourist office** (☑ 089 87 50 67; www.aziendaturismopositano.it; Via Regina Giovanna 13; ☺ 8.30am-8pm Mon-Sat, to 2pm Sun May-Sep, reduced hrs rest of year) can provide information on walking in the densely wooded Lattari Mountains.

🛏 Sleeping & Eating

★ Villa Nettuno   HOTEL €

(☑ 089 87 54 01; www.villanettunopositano.it; Viale Pasitea 208; d €80-140; ☺ year-round; ❄ 🛜) Hidden behind a barrage of perfumed foliage, Villa Nettuno oozes charm. Go for one of the original rooms in the 300-year-old part of the building with heavy rustic decor and a communal terrace. Rooms in the renovated part of the villa lack the same character.

★ La Fenice   B&B €€

(☑ 089 87 55 13; www.lafenicepositano.com; Via Guglielmo Marconi 8; d €170; ☺ Easter-Oct; ❄ 🛜 ➰) With hand-painted Vietri tiles, white walls and high ceilings, the rooms here are simple but stylish; most have their own balcony or terrace. The views are stunning, but it feels very smartly homely and not super posh. As with everywhere in Positano, you'll need to be good at stomping up and down steps to stay here.

C'era Una Volta   TRATTORIA, PIZZA €

(☑ 089 81 19 30; Via Marconi 127; meals €20-30; ☺ noon-3pm & 6.30-11pm) Up in the high part of town, this authentic trattoria is a good bet for honest, down-to-earth Italian grub. Alongside regional staples like *gnocchi alla sorrentina* (gnocchi served in a tomato and basil sauce), there's a decent selection of pizzas (to eat in or takeaway) and a full menu of pastas and fail-safe mains.

★ Next2   RISTORANTE €€

(☑ 089 812 35 16; www.next2.it; Viale Pasitea 242; meals €50; ☺ 6.30-11.30pm) Understated elegance meets creative cuisine at this contemporary set-up. Local and organic ingredients are put to impressive use in beautifully presented dishes such as ravioli stuffed with aubergine and prawns or sea bass with tomatoes and lemon-scented peas. Desserts are wickedly delicious, and the alfresco sea-facing terrace is summer perfection.

Amalfi

POP 5150

Amalfi, the main hub on the coast, makes a convenient base for exploring the surrounding coastline. It's a pretty place with a tangle of narrow alleyways, stacked whitewashed houses and sun-drenched piazzas, but it can get very busy in summer as day-trippers pour in to peruse its loud souvenir shops and busy eateries.

The **tourist office** (☑ 089 87 11 07; www.amalfitouristoffice.it; Corso delle Repubbliche Marinare 27; ☺ 8.30am-1pm & 2-6pm Mon-Sat Apr-Oct, 8.30am-1pm Mon-Sat Nov-Mar) can provide information about sights, activities and transport.

⊙ Sights

★ Cattedrale di Sant'Andrea   CATHEDRAL

(☑ 089 87 10 59; Piazza del Duomo; ☺ 7.30am-7.30pm) A melange of architectural styles, Amalfi's cathedral, one of the few relics of the town's past as an 11th-century maritime superpower, makes a striking impression at the top of its sweeping flight of stairs. Between 10am and 5pm entrance is through the adjacent **Chiostro del Paradiso** (☑ 089 87 13 24; adult/reduced €3/1; ☺ 9am-7.45pm Jul-Aug, reduced hrs rest of year), a 13th-century cloister.

Grotta dello Smeraldo   CAVE

(€5; ☺ 9am-4pm) Four kilometres west of Amalfi, this grotto is named after the eerie emerald colour that emanates from the water. Stalactites hang down from the 24m-high ceiling, while stalagmites grow up to 10m tall. Buses regularly pass the car park above the cave entrance (from where you take a lift or stairs down to the rowing boats). Alternatively, Coop Sant'Andrea (☑ 089 87 31 90; www.coopsantandrea.com; Lungomare dei Cavalieri 1) runs boats from Amalfi (€10 return, plus cave admission). Allow 1½ hours for the return trip.

🛏 Sleeping & Eating

★**Residenza del Duca**   HOTEL €€
(☑ 089 873 63 65; www.residencedelduca.it; Via Duca Mastalo II 3; r €70-175; ⊗Mar-Oct; ✸ 🛜) This family-run hotel has just six rooms, all of them light, sunny, and prettily furnished with antiques, maiolica tiles and the odd chintzy cherub. The Jacuzzi showers are excellent. Call ahead if you are carrying heavy bags, as it's a seriously puff-you-out-climb up some steps to reach here and a luggage service is included in the price.

Hotel Lidomare   HOTEL €€
(☑ 089 87 13 32; www.lidomare.it; Largo Duchi Piccolomini 9; s €65/145; ✸ 🛜) Family run, this old-fashioned hotel has real character. The large, luminous rooms have an air of gentility, with their appealingly haphazard decor, vintage tiles and fine antiques. Some have Jacuzzi bath-tubs, others have sea views and a balcony, some have both. Rather unusually, breakfast is laid out on top of a grand piano.

Trattoria Il Mulino   TRATTORIA, PIZZA €€
(☑ 089 87 22 23; Via delle Cartiere 36; pizzas €6-11, meals €30; ⊗11.30am-4pm & 6.30pm-midnight Tue-Sun) A TV-in-the-corner, kids-running-between-the-tables sort of place, this is about as authentic an eatery as you'll find in Amalfi. There are few surprises on the menu, just hearty, honest pastas, grilled meats and fish. For a taste of local seafood, try the *scialatielli alla pescatore* (ribbon pasta with prawns, mussels, tomato and parsley).

★**Marina Grande**   SEAFOOD €€€
(☑ 089 87 11 29; www.ristorantemarinagrande. com; Viale Della Regioni 4; tasting menu lunch/dinner €28/60, meals €50; ⊗noon-3pm & 6.30-11pm Wed-Mon Mar-Oct) 🍃 Run by the third generation of the same family, this beachfront restaurant serves fish so fresh it's almost flapping. It prides itself on its use of locally sourced organic produce, which, in Amalfi,

WORTH A TRIP

RAVELLO

Elegant Ravello sits high in the clouds overlooking the coast. From Amalfi, it's a nerve-tingling half-hour bus ride (€1.60, up to three an hour), but once you've made it up, you can unwind in the ravishing gardens of Villa Rufolo (☑ 089 85 76 21; www.villarufolo.it; Piazza Duomo; adult/reduced €7/5; ⊗9am-9pm May-Sep, reduced hrs rest of year, tower museum 11am-4pm) and bask in awe-inspiring views at Villa Cimbrone (☑ 089 85 74 59; www.hotelvillacimbrone.com/gardens; Via Santa Chiara 26; adult/reduced €7/4; ⊗9am-sunset).

means high-quality seafood. Reservations recommended.

Sicily

Everything about the Mediterranean's largest island is extreme, from the beauty of its rugged landscape to its hybrid cuisine and flamboyant architecture. Over the centuries Sicily has seen off a catalogue of foreign invaders, from the Phoenicians and ancient Greeks to the Spanish Bourbons and WWII Allies. All have contributed to the island's complex and fascinating cultural landscape.

ℹ Getting There & Away

AIR

Flights from mainland Italian cities and European destinations serve Sicily's two main airports: Palermo's **Falcone-Borsellino** (☑ 800 541880, 091 702 02 73; www.gesap.it) and Catania's **Fontanarossa** (☑ 095 723 91 11; www.aero porto.catania.it).

BOAT

Regular car and passenger ferries cross to Sicily (Messina) from Villa San Giovanni in Calabria.

Ferries also sail from Genoa, Livorno, Civitavecchia, Naples, Salerno and Cagliari, as well as Malta and Tunisia.

Main operators:

Caronte & Tourist (☑ 090 36 46 01, 800 627414; www.carontetourist.it) To Messina from Salerno.

Grandi Navi Veloci (☑ 010 209 45 91; www. gnv.it) To Palermo from Civitavecchia, Genoa, Naples and Tunis.

Grimaldi (✆ 081 49 64 44; www.grimaldi-ferries.com) To Palermo from Livorno, Salerno and Tunis.

Tirrenia (✆ 892123; www.tirrenia.it) To Palermo from Naples and Cagliari.

BUS

SAIS Trasporti (✆ 091 617 11 41; www.saistrasporti.it) operates long-distance buses between Sicily and Italian mainland destinations including Rome and Naples.

TRAIN

Trenitalia (✆ 06 6847 5475, 892021; www.trenitalia.com) operates direct trains to Sicily from both Rome and Naples, along with direct night trains from Milan, Rome and Naples.

Palermo

POP 678,500

Still bearing the bruises of its WWII battering, Palermo is a compelling and chaotic city. It takes a little work, but once you've acclimatised to the congested and noisy streets you'll be rewarded with some of southern Italy's most imposing architecture, impressive art galleries, vibrant street markets and an array of tempting restaurants and cafes.

☉ Sights

★**Palazzo dei Normanni**   PALACE
(Palazzo Reale; ✆ 091 626 28 33; www.federico-secondo.org; Piazza Indipendenza 1; adult/reduced Fri-Mon €8.50/6.50, Tue-Thu €7/5, plus possible exhibition supplement; ☺ 8.15am-5.40pm Mon-Sat, to 1pm Sun) Home to Sicily's regional parliament, this venerable palace dates to the 9th century. However, it owes its current look (and name) to a major Norman makeover, during which spectacular mosaics were added to its royal apartments and magnificent chapel, the Cappella Palatina. Visits to the apartments, which are off-limits from Tuesday to Thursday, take in the mosaic-lined

Sala dei Venti, and Sala di Ruggero II, King Roger's 12th-century bedroom.

★**Cappella Palatina**   CHAPEL
(Palatine Chapel; www.federicosecondo.org; Piazza Indipendenza; adult/reduced Fri-Mon €8.50/6.50, Tue-Thu €7/5, plus possible exhibition supplement; ☺ 8.15am-5.40pm Mon-Sat, 8.15-9.45am & 11.15am-1pm Sun) Designed by Roger II in 1130, this extraordinary chapel is Palermo's top tourist attraction. Located on the mid-level of Palazzo dei Normanni's three-tiered loggia, its glittering gold mosaics are complemented by inlaid marble floors and a wooden *muqarnas* ceiling, the latter a masterpiece of Arabic-style honeycomb carving reflecting Norman Sicily's cultural complexity.

Note that queues are likely, and that you'll be refused entry if you're wearing shorts, a short skirt or a low-cut top.

★**Mercato di Ballarò**   MARKET
(☺ 7.30am-8pm Mon-Sat, to 1pm Sun) Snaking for several city blocks southeast of Palazzo dei Normanni is Palermo's busiest street market, which throbs with activity well into the early evening. It's a fascinating mix of noises, smells and street life, and the cheapest place for everything from Chinese padded bras to fresh produce, fish, meat, olives and cheese – smile nicely for *un assaggio* (a taste).

★**Cattedrale di Palermo**   CATHEDRAL
(✆ 091 33 43 73; www.cattedrale.palermo.it; Corso Vittorio Emanuele; cathedral free, tombs €1.50, treasury & crypt €2, roof €5, all-inclusive ticket adult/reduced €7/3; ☺ cathedral 7am-7pm Mon-Sat, 8am-1pm & 4-7pm Sun, royal tombs, treasury & roof 9am-5pm summer, 9am-1.30pm winter) A feast of geometric patterns, ziggurat crenellations, maiolica cupolas and blind arches, Palermo's cathedral has suffered aesthetically from multiple reworkings over the

---

BARI

Most travellers visit Puglia's regional capital to catch a ferry. And while there's not a lot to detain you, it's worth taking an hour or so to explore Bari Vecchia (Old Bari). Here, among the labyrinthine lanes, you'll find the Basilica di San Nicola (www.basilicasannicola.it; Piazza San Nicola; ☺ 7am-8.30pm Mon-Sat, to 10pm Sun), the impressive home to the relics of St Nicholas (aka Santa Claus).

For lunch, Terranima (✆ 080 521 97 25; www.terranima.com; Via Putignani 213/215; meals €25-30; ☺ noon-3pm & 7-11pm) serves delicious Puglian food.

Regular trains run to Bari from Rome (€20 to €79, four to 6½ hours, six daily).

Ferries sail to Greece, Croatia, Montenegro and Albania from the port, accessible by bus 20/ from the train station.

centuries, but remains a prime example of Sicily's unique Arab-Norman architectural style. The interior, while impressive in scale, is essentially a marble shell whose most interesting features are the royal Norman tombs (to the left as you enter), the treasury (home to Constance of Aragon's gem-encrusted 13th-century crown) and the panoramic views from the roof.

La Martorana
CHURCH

(Chiesa di Santa Maria dell'Ammiraglio; Piazza Bellini 3; adult/reduced €2/1; ◉9am-1pm & 3.30-5.30pm Mon-Sat, 9-10.30am Sun) On the southern side of Piazza Bellini, this luminously beautiful 12th-century church was endowed by King Roger's Syrian emir, George of Antioch, and was originally planned as a mosque. Delicate Fatimid pillars support a domed cupola depicting Christ enthroned amid his archangels. The interior is best appreciated in the morning, when sunlight illuminates magnificent Byzantine mosaics.

★Teatro Massimo
THEATRE

(◨tour reservations 091 605 32 67; www.teatromassimo.it; Piazza Giuseppe Verdi; guided tours adult/reduced €8/5; ◉9.30am-6pm) Taking over 20 years to complete, Palermo's neoclassical opera house is the largest in Italy and the second-largest in Europe. The closing scene of *The Godfather: Part III,* with its visually arresting juxtaposition of high culture, crime, drama and death, was filmed here and the building's richly decorated interiors are nothing short of spectacular. Guided 30-minute tours are offered throughout the day in English, Italian, French, Spanish and German.

⟃ Sleeping

★Stanze al Genio Residenze
B&B €

(◨340 097 15 61; www.stanzealgeniobnb.it; Via Garibaldi 11; s/d €74/90; ❇❄) Speckled with Sicilian antiques, this B&B offers four gorgeous bedrooms, three with 19th-century ceiling frescoes. All four are spacious and thoughtfully appointed, with Murano lamps, old wooden wardrobes, the odd balcony railing turned bedhead, and top-quality, orthopaedic beds. That the property features beautiful maiolica tiles is no coincidence; the B&B is affiliated with the wonderful Museo delle Maioliche (Stanze al Genio; adult/reduced €7/5; ◉by appointment) downstairs.

B&B Panormus
B&B €

(◨091 617 58 26; www.bbpanormus.com; Via Roma 72; s €45-75, d €50-85, tr €75-120; ❇❄) Popular for its keen prices, charming host and convenient location between the train station and the Quattro Canti, this B&B offers five high-ceilinged rooms decorated in elegant Liberty style, each with double-glazed windows, flat-screen TV and a private bathroom down the passageway.

★BB22 Palace
B&B €€

(◨091 32 62 14; www.bb22.it; cnr Via Roma & Via Bandiera; d €120-180, whole apt €700-950) Occupying a flouncy *palazzo* in the heart of the city, BB22 Palace offers four chic, contemporary rooms, each with its own style. Top billing goes to the Stromboli room, complete with spa bath and a bedroom skylight offering a glimpse of its 15th-century neighbour. Peppered with artworks, coffee-table tomes and an honour bar, the communal lounge makes for an airy, chi-chi retreat.

✕ Eating & Drinking

Touring Café
CAFE €

(◨091 32 27 26; Via Roma 252; arancino €1.70; ◉6.15am-11pm Mon-Fri, to midnight Sat & Sun) Don't let the gleaming Liberty-style mirrored bar and array of picture-perfect pastries distract you. You come here for the *arancine,* great fist-sized rice balls stuffed with *ragù,* spinach or butter, and fried to a perfect golden orange.

★Trattoria al Vecchio Club Rosanero
SICILIAN €

(◨091 251 12 34; Vicolo Caldomai 18; meals €15; ◉1-3.30pm Mon-Sat & 8-11pm Thu-Sat; ❄) A veritable shrine to the city's football team (*rosa nero* refers to the team's colours, pink and black), cavernous Vecchio Club scores goals with its bargain-priced, flavour-packed grub. Fish and seafood are the real fortes here; if it's on the menu, order the *caponata e pesce spada* (caponata with swordfish), a sweet-and-sour victory. Head in early to avoid a wait.

Osteria Ballarò
SICILIAN €€

(◨091 32 64 88; www.osteriaballaro.it; Via Calascibetta 25; meals €30-45; ◉noon-3.15pm & 7-11.15pm) A slinky, buzzing restaurant-cum-wine bar, Osteria Ballarò marries an atmospheric setting with sterling, Slow Food island cooking. Bare stone columns, exposed brick walls and vaulted ceilings set an evocative scene for arresting *crudite di pesce* (local sashimi) and seafood *primi,* elegant local wines and memorable Sicilian *dolci* (sweets). Reservations recommended. Slow Food recommended.

★ **Enoteca Buonivini**   WINE BAR
(📞 091 784 70 54; Via Dante 8; ☺ 9.30am-1.30pm & 4pm-midnight Mon-Thu, to 1am Fri & Sat) Serious oenophiles flock to this bustling, urbane *enoteca* (wine bar), complete with bar seating, courtyard and a generous selection of wines by the glass. There's no shortage of interesting local drops, not to mention artisan cheese and charcuterie boards, beautiful pasta dishes and grilled meats. When you're done, scan the shelves for harder-to-find craft spirits (Australian gin, anyone?) and Sicilian gourmet pantry essentials.

ℹ Information

Hospital (Ospedale Civico; 📞 091 666 11 11; www.arnascivico.it; Piazza Nicola Leotta; ☺ 24hr) Emergency facilities.

Police (Questura; 📞 091 21 01 11; Piazza della Vittoria 8) Main police station.

Municipal Tourist Office (📞 091 740 80 21; http://turismo.comune.palermo.it; Piazza Bellini; ☺ 8am-8pm Mon-Thu, to 6.30pm Fri, 9am-7pm Sat, 9.30am-6.30pm Sun) The main branch of Palermo's city-run information booths. Other locations include Teatro Politeama, Via Cavour, the Port of Palermo and Mondello, though these are only intermittently staffed, with unpredictable hours.

ℹ Getting There & Away

AIR

Falcone-Borsellino Airport (📞 800 541880, 091 702 02 73; www.gesap.it) is at Punta Raisi, 35km northwest of Palermo on the A29 motorway. There are regular flights between Palermo and most mainland Italian cities.

BOAT

Numerous ferry companies operate from Palermo's port, just east of the New City. These include the following:

Grandi Navi Veloci (📞 010 209 45 91, 091 6072 6162; www.gnv.it; Calata Marinai d'Italia)

Grimaldi Lines (📞 091 611 36 91, 081 49 64 44; www.grimaldi-lines.com; Via del Mare)

Tirrenia (📞 892123; www.tirrenia.it; Calata Marinai d'Italia)

BUS

The main **bus terminal** is on Piazzetta Cairoli, to the side of the train station. Other intercity buses depart from **Via Paolo Balsamo**, two blocks due east of the train station.

Main bus companies:

Cuffaro (📞 091 616 15 10; www.cuffaro.info; Via Paolo Balsamo 13) Services to Agrigento (€9, two hours, three to eight daily).

Interbus (📞 091 616 79 19; www.interbus.it; Piazzetta Cairoli Bus Terminal) To/from Syracuse (€13.50, 3½ hours, two to three daily).

SAIS Autolinee (📞 800 211020, 091 616 60 28; www.saisautolinee.it; Piazzetta Cairoli Bus Station) To/from Catania (€12.50, 2¾ hours, nine to 12 daily) and Messina (€15, 2¾ hours, three to six daily).

TRAIN

Regular services leave from **Palermo Centrale train station** (Piazza Giulio Cesare; ☺ 6am-9pm) to Messina (from €12.80, three to 3¾ hours, eight to 14 daily), Catania (from €13.50, 2¾ to 5½ hours, five to 10 daily) and Agrigento (€9, two hours, six to 10 daily). There are also Intercity trains to Reggio di Calabria, Naples and Rome.

ℹ Getting Around

TO/FROM THE AIRPORT

Prestia e Comandè (📞 091 58 63 51; www.prestiaecomande.it; one way/return €6.30/11) Runs an efficient half-hourly bus service between 5am and 12.30pm that transfers passengers from the airport to the centre of Palermo, dropping people off outside the Teatro Politeama Garibaldi and Palermo Centrale train station. To find the bus, follow the signs past the downstairs taxi rank and around the corner to the right.

BUS

Walking is the best way to get around Palermo's centre, but if you want to take a bus, most stop outside or near the train station. Tickets cost €1.40 (€1.80 on board) and are valid for 90 minutes.

Taormina

POP 11,085

Spectacularly perched on a clifftop terrace overlooking the Ionian Sea and Mt Etna, this sophisticated town has attracted socialites, artists and writers ever since Greek times. Its pristine medieval core, proximity to beaches, grandstand coastal views and chic social scene make it a hugely popular summer holiday destination.

⊙ Sights & Activities

★ **Teatro Greco**   RUINS
(📞 0942 2 32 20; Via Teatro Greco; adult/reduced €10/5; ☺ 9am-1hr before sunset) Taormina's premier sight is this perfect horseshoe-shaped theatre, suspended between sea and sky,

with Mt Etna looming on the southern horizon. Built in the 3rd century BC, it's the most dramatically situated Greek theatre in the world and the second largest in Sicily (after Syracuse). In summer, it's used to stage international arts and film festivals. In peak season, the site is best explored early in the morning to avoid the crowds.

Corso Umberto I   STREET

Taormina's chief delight is wandering this pedestrian-friendly, boutique-lined thoroughfare. Start at the tourist office in **Palazzo Corvaja** (Piazza Santa Caterina), which dates back to the 10th century, before heading southwest for spectacular panoramic views from **Piazza IX Aprile**. Facing the square is the early-18th-century **Chiesa San Giuseppe** (☉usually 8.30am-8pm). Continue west through **Torre dell'Orologio**, the 12th-century clock tower, into **Piazza del Duomo**, home to an ornate baroque fountain (1635) that sports Taormina's symbol, a two-legged centaur with the bust of an angel.

Villa Comunale   PARK

(Parco Duchi di Cesarò; Via Bagnoli Croce; ☉9am-midnight summer, 9am-sunset winter) To escape the crowds, wander down to these stunningly sited public gardens. Created by Englishwoman Florence Trevelyan in the late 19th century, they're a lush paradise of tropical plants and delicate flowers, punctuated by whimsical follies. You'll also find a children's play area.

🛏 Sleeping & Eating

Le 4 Fontane   B&B €

(☑333 679 38 76; www.le4fontane.com; Corso Umberto I 231; s €40-70, d €60-110; ❄🌐) An excellent budget B&B on the top floor of an old *palazzo*, Le 4 Fontane is run by a friendly couple and has three spacious, well-equipped rooms, two of which have views of Piazza del Duomo.

Isoco Guest House   GUESTHOUSE €€

(☑0942 2 36 79; www.isoco.it; Via Salita Branco 2; r €130-220; ☉Mar-Nov; 🅿❄@🌐) Each room at this welcoming, LGBT-friendly guesthouse is dedicated to an artist, from Botticelli to Keith Haring. While the older rooms are highly eclectic, the newer suites are chic and subdued, each with a modern kitchenette. Breakfast is served around a large table, while a pair of terraces offer stunning sea views and a hot tub. Multinight or prepaid stays earn the best rates.

⭐ **Osteria Nero D'Avola**   SICILIAN €€

(☑0942 62 88 74; Piazza San Domenico 2b; meals €40; ☉12.30-3pm & 7-11pm Tue-Sun Sep-Jun, 7pm-midnight Jul & Aug) Not only does affable owner Turi Siligato fish, hunt and forage for his smart *osteria*, he'll probably greet you at your table, share anecdotes about the day's bounty and play a few tunes on the piano. Here, seasonality, local producers and passion underscore arresting dishes like the signature *cannolo di limone Interdonato* (thinly sliced Interdonato lemon with roe, tuna, tomato and chives).

ℹ Information

Tourist Office (☑0942 2 32 43; Palazzo Corvaja, Piazza Santa Caterina; ☉8.30am-2.15pm & 3.30-6.45pm Mon-Fri year-round, also 8.30am-2.15pm & 3.30-6.45pm Sat & Sun summer) Has plenty of practical information, including transport timetables and a free map.

ℹ Getting There & Away

Bus is the easiest way to reach Taormina. The bus station is on Via Luigi Pirandello, 400m east of Porta Messina, the northeastern entrance to the old town. **Interbus** (www.interbus.it; Via Luigi Pirandello) services leave daily for Messina (€4.30, 55 minutes to 1¾ hours, up to six daily), Catania (€5.10, 1¼ hours, up to 16 daily) and Catania airport (€8.20, 1½ hours, up to 12 daily).

Syracuse

POP 122,500

A tumultuous past has left Syracuse (Siracusa) a beautiful baroque centre and some of Sicily's finest ancient ruins. Founded in 734 BC by Corinthian settlers, it became the dominant Greek city state on the Mediterranean and was known as the most beautiful city in the ancient world. A devastating earthquake in 1693 destroyed most of the city's buildings, paving the way for a citywide baroque makeover.

◉ Sights

⭐ **Piazza del Duomo**   PIAZZA

Syracuse's showpiece square is a masterpiece of baroque town planning. A long, rectangular piazza flanked by flamboyant *palazzi*, it sits on what was once Syracuse's ancient acropolis (fortified citadel). Little remains of the original Greek building but if you look along the side of the Duomo, you'll see a number of thick Doric columns incorporated into the cathedral's structure.

★ **Parco Archeologico della Neapolis** ARCHAEOLOGICAL SITE
(☑ 0931 6 62 06; Viale Paradiso 14; adult/reduced €10/5, incl Museo Archeologico €13.50/7; ☺ 9am-1hr before sunset Mon-Sat, 9am-1pm Sun) For the classicist, Syracuse's real attraction is this archaeological park, home to the pearly white 5th-century-BC **Teatro Greco**. Hewn out of the rocky hillside, this 16,000-capacity amphitheatre staged the last tragedies of Aeschylus (including *The Persians*), first performed here in his presence. In late spring it's brought to life with an annual season of classical theatre.

★ **Museo Archeologico Paolo Orsi** MUSEUM
(☑ 0931 48 95 11; www.regione.sicilia.it/beniculturali/museopaoloorsi; Viale Teocrito 66; adult/reduced €8/4, incl Parco Archeologico €13.50/7; ☺ 9am-6pm Tue-Sat, to 1pm Sun) About 500m east of the archaeological park, this modern museum contains one of Sicily's largest and most interesting archaeological collections. Allow plenty of time to investigate the four sectors charting the area's prehistory, as well as Syracuse's development from foundation to the late Roman period.

🛏 Sleeping & Eating

B&B dei Viaggiatori, Viandanti e Sognatori B&B €
(☑ 0931 2 47 81; www.bedandbreakfastsicily.it; Via Roma 156; s €35-50, d €55-70, tr €75-85, q €100; ✳ ☎) Decorated with verve and boasting a prime Ortygia location, this relaxed B&B exudes an easy, boho vibe. It's a homely place, graced with books, antique furniture and imaginatively decorated rooms. The sunny roof terrace – complete with sweeping sea views – is a fine place for breakfast, whose offerings include biological bread and homemade marmalades.

★ **Hotel Gutkowski** HOTEL €€
(☑ 0931 46 58 61; www.guthotel.it; Lungomare Vittorini 26; d €90-140, tr €140; ✳ @ ☎) Book well in advance for one of the sea-view rooms at this stylish, eclectic hotel on the Ortygia waterfront, at the edge of the Giudecca neighbourhood. Divided between two buildings, its rooms are simple yet chic, with pretty tiled floors, walls in teals, greys, blues and browns, and a sharply curated mix of vintage and industrial details.

Sicily PIZZA €
(☑ 392 9659949; www.sicilypizzeria.it; Via Cavour 67; pizzas €4.50-12; ☺ 7pm-midnight Tue-Sun) Experimenting with pizzas is something you do at your peril in culinary-conservative Sicily. But that's what they do, and do well, at this funky retro-chic pizzeria. So if you're game for wood-fired pizzas topped with more-ish combos like sausage, cheese, Swiss chard, pine nuts, sun-dried tomatoes and raisins, this is the place for you.

★ **Bistrot Bella Vita** ITALIAN €€
(☑ 348 1939792; Via Gargallo 60; sweets €1.50, meals €25; ☺ cafe 8am-1am summer, to 11pm winter, restaurant noon-3pm & 6.30-11pm, closed Mon) Owned by affable Lombard expat Norma and her Sicilian pastry-chef husband Salvo, this casually elegant cafe-restaurant is one of Ortygia's latest stars. Stop by for good coffee (soy milk available) and made-from-scratch *cornetti, biscotti* and pastries (try the sour orange-and-almond tart). Or book a table in the intimate back dining room, where local, organic produce drives beautifully textured, technically impressive dishes.

WORTH A TRIP

PADUA

Were it just for Padua's medieval centre and lively university atmosphere, the city would be a rewarding day trip from Venice. But what makes a visit so special is the **Cappella degli Scrovegni** (Scrovegni Chapel; ☑ 049 201 00 20; www.cappelladegliscrovegni.it; Piazza Eremitani 8; adult/reduced €13/8, night ticket €8/6; ☺ 9am-7pm), home to a remarkable cycle of Giotto frescoes. Considered one of the defining masterpieces of early Renaissance art, this extraordinary work consists of 38 colourful panels, painted between 1303 and 1305, depicting episodes from the life of Christ and the Virgin Mary. Note that visits to the chapel must be booked in advance.

To fuel your wanderings, lunch on hearty local fare at the **Osteria dei Fabbri** (☑ 049 65 03 36; Via dei Fabbri 13; meals €30; ☺ noon-3pm & 7-11pm, closed Sun dinner).

Trains leave for Padua (Padova) from Venice (€4 to €17, 25 minutes) every 20 minutes or so.

MT ETNA

The dark silhouette of Mt Etna (3329m) broods ominously over Sicily's east coast, more or less halfway between Taormina and Catania. One of Europe's highest and most volatile volcanoes, it erupts frequently, most recently in May 2016.

To get to Etna by public transport, take the AST bus from Catania (at 8.15am daily). This departs from in front of the train station (returning at 4.30pm; €6.60 return) and drops you at the Rifugio Sapienza (1923m), where you can pick up the **Funivia dell'Etna** (☑ 095 91 41 41; www.funiviaetna.com; return €30, incl bus & guide €63; ☺9am-4.15pm Apr-Nov, to 3.45pm Dec-Mar) to 2500m. From there buses courier you up to the crater zone (2920m). If you want to walk, allow up to four hours for the round trip.

Gruppo Guide Alpine Etna Sud (☑ 389 3496086, 095 791 47 55; www.etnaguide.eu) is one of many outfits offering guided tours. Bank on around €85 for a full-day excursion.

Further Etna information is available from Catania's **tourist office** (☑ 095 742 55 73; www.comune.catania.it; Via Vittorio Emanuele 172; ☺8am-7.15pm Mon-Sat, 8.30am-1.30pm Sun).

ⓘ Information

Tourist Office (☑ 0931 46 29 46; http://turismo.provsr.it; Via Roma 31; ☺9am-12.30pm Mon-Fri) City maps and brochures.

ⓘ Getting There & Around

Buses are a better bet than trains, serving a **terminal** (Corso Umberto I) close to the **train station** (Via Francesco Crispi).

Interbus (☑ 0931 6 67 10; www.interbus. it) runs services to/from Catania (€6.20, 1½ hours, 18 Monday to Friday, nine Saturday, seven Sunday) and its airport, and Palermo (€13.50, 3¼ to 3½ hours, two to three daily).

Up to 11 trains depart daily for Catania (from €7, one to 1½ hours) and Messina (from €10, 2½ to 3½ hours).

Sd'a Trasporti (www.siracusadamare.it; ticket/day pass/week pass €1/3/10) runs three lines of electric buses, the most useful of which is the red No 2 line, which links Ortygia with the train station and archaeological zone. Tickets, available on board, cost €1.

Agrigento

POP 59,600

Seen from a distance, Agrigento doesn't bode well, with rows of unsightly apartment blocks crowded onto the hillside. But behind the veneer, the city boasts a small but attractive medieval core and, down in the valley, one of Italy's greatest ancient sites, the Valley of the Temples (Valle dei Templi).

Founded around 581 BC by Greek settlers, the city was an important trading centre under the Romans and Byzantines.

For maps and information, ask at the **tourist office** (☑ 800 236837, 800 315555; www.livingagrigento.it; Piazzale Aldo Moro 1;

☺8am-1pm & 2-7pm Mon-Fri, to 1pm Sat) in the Provincia building.

⊙ Sights

★ **Valley of the Temples** ARCHAEOLOGICAL SITE (Valle dei Templi; www.parcovalledeitempli.it; adult/reduced €10/5, incl Museo Archeologico €13.50/7; ☺8.30am-7pm year-round, plus 7.30-10pm Mon-Fri, 7.30-11pm Sat & Sun mid-Jul–mid-Sep) Sicily's most enthralling archaeological site encompasses the ruined ancient city of Akragas, highlighted by the stunningly well-preserved **Tempio della Concordia** (Temple of Concordia), one of several ridge-top temples that once served as beacons for homecoming sailors. The 13-sq-km park, 3km south of Agrigento, is split into eastern and western zones. Ticket offices with car parks are at the park's southwestern corner (the main Porta V entrance) and at the northeastern corner near the Temple of Hera (Eastern Entrance).

🛏 Sleeping & Eating

★ **PortAtenea** B&B €
(☑ 349 093 74 92; www.portatenea.com; Via Atenea, cnr Via C Battisti; s €39-50, d €59-75, tr €79-95; ⧉ 🕏) This five-room B&B wins plaudits for its panoramic roof terrace overlooking the Valley of the Temples, and its super-convenient location at the entrance to the old town, five minutes' walk from the train and bus stations. Best of all is the generous advice about Agrigento offered by hosts Sandra and Filippo (witness Filippo's amazing Google Earth tour of nearby beaches!).

★ **Aguglia Persa** SEAFOOD €€
(☑ 0922 40 13 37; Via Francesco Crispi 34; meals €25-40; ☺noon-3.30pm & 7-11pm Wed-Mon) Set

ESSENTIAL FOOD & DRINK

Italian cuisine is highly regional in nature and wherever you go you'll find local specialities. That said, some staples are ubiquitous:

Pizza There are two varieties: Roman, with a thin crispy base; and Neapolitan, with a higher, more doughy base. The best are always prepared in a *forno a legna* (wood-fired oven).

Pasta Comes in hundreds of shapes and sizes and is served with everything from thick meat-based sauces to fresh seafood.

Gelato Classic flavours include *fragola* (strawberry), *pistacchio* (pistachio), *nocciola* (hazelnut) and *stracciatella* (milk with chocolate shavings).

Wine Ranges from big-name reds such as Piedmont's *Barolo* and Tuscany's *Brunello di Montalcino* to sweet Sicilian *Malvasia* and sparkling *prosecco* from the Veneto.

Caffè Italians take their coffee seriously, drinking cappuccino only in the morning, and espressos whenever, ideally standing at a bar.

Eat Like an Italian

A full Italian meal consists of an *antipasto*, a *primo* (first course; pasta or rice dish), *secondo* (main course; usually meat or fish) with an *insalata* (salad) or *contorno* (vegetable side dish), *dolce* (dessert) and coffee. Most Italians only eat a meal this large at Sunday lunch or on a special occasion, and when eating out it's fine to mix and match and order, say, a *primo* followed by an *insalata* or *contorno*.

Italians are late diners, often not eating until after 9pm.

Where to Eat & Drink

Trattorias are traditional, often family-run places serving local food and wine; *ristoranti* (restaurants) are more formal, with greater choice and smarter service; pizzerias, which usually open evenings only, often serve a full menu alongside pizzas.

At lunchtime bars and cafes sell *panini* (bread rolls), and many serve an evening *aperitivo* (aperitif) buffet. At an *enoteca* (wine bar) you can drink wine by the glass and snack on cheese and cured meats. Some also serve hot dishes. For a slice of pizza search out a *pizza al taglio* joint.

in a mansion with leafy courtyard just below the train station, this place is a welcome addition to Agrigento's fine-dining scene. Opened in 2015 by the owners of Porto Empedocle's renowned Salmoriglio restaurant, it specialises in fresh-caught seafood in dishes such as citrus-scented risotto with shrimp and wild mint, or marinated salmon with sage cream and fresh fruit.

ⓘ Getting There & Away

The bus is the easiest way to get to Agrigento. The **intercity bus station** and ticket booth are on Piazza Rosselli, from where you can catch local bus 1, 2 or 3 to the Valley of the Temples (€1.20).

Cuffaro (📞 091 616 15 10; www.cuffaro.info) runs buses to/from Palermo (€9, two hours, three to eight daily) and **SAIS Trasporti** (📞 0922 2 60 59; www.saistrasporti.it) services go to Catania (€13.40, three hours, hourly).

SURVIVAL GUIDE

ⓘ Directory A–Z

ACCOMMODATION

➡ The bulk of Italy's accommodation is made up of *alberghi* (hotels) and *pensioni* (small, often family run hotels). Other options are hostels, campgrounds, B&Bs, *agriturismi* (farm-stays), mountain *rifugi* (Alpine refuges), monasteries and villa/apartment rentals.

➡ High-season rates apply at Easter, in summer (mid-June to August), and over the Christmas to New Year period.

➡ Many places in coastal resorts close between November and March.

B&Bs

➡ Often great value, can range from rooms in family houses to self-catering studio
➡ apartments.

➡ Prices typically range from about €60 to €140 for a double room.

» Check www.bbitalia.it and www.bed-and-breakfast.it.

Camping

» Most Italian campgrounds are major complexes with on-site supermarkets, restaurants and sports facilities.

» In summer expect to pay up to €20 per person, and a further €25 for a tent pitch.

» Useful resources include www.campeggi.com, www.camping.it and www.italcamping.it.

Convents & Monasteries

Basic accommodation is often available in convents and monasteries. See www.monasterystays.com, a specialist online booking service.

Farm-Stays

» An *agriturismo* (farm-stay) is a good option for a country stay, although you'll usually need a car to get there.

» Accommodation varies from spartan billets on working farms to palatial suites at luxury retreats.

» For lists check out www.agriturist.it or www.agriturismo.com.

Hostels

» Official HI-affiliated *ostelli per la gioventù* (youth hostels) are run by the **Italian Youth Hostel Association** (AIG; Map p654; ☎06 487 11 52; www.aighostels.it; Via Nicotera 1, entrance Via Settembrini 4, Rome; ☺8am-5.30pm Mon-Fri; ☐Viale delle Milizie). A valid HI card is required for these; you can get a card in your home country or directly at hostels.

» There are also many excellent private hostels offering dorms and private rooms.

» Dorm rates are typically between €15 and €40, with breakfast usually included.

Hotels & Pensioni

» A *pensione* is a small, often family-run, hotel. In cities, they are often in converted apartments.

» Hotels and *pensioni* are rated from one to five stars. As a rule, a three-star room will come with an en-suite bathroom, air-con, hairdryer, minibar, safe and wi-fi.

» Many city-centre hotels offer discounts in August to lure clients from the crowded coast.

ACTIVITIES

Cycling Tourist offices can provide details on trails and guided rides. The best time is spring. Favourite areas include Tuscany, the flatlands of Emilia-Romagna, and the peaks around Lago Maggiore and Lago del Garda.

Hiking Thousands of kilometres of *sentieri* (marked trails) criss-cross the country. The hiking season is from June to September. The Italian Parks organisation (www.parks.it) lists walking trails in Italy's national parks.

COUNTRY FACTS

Area 301,230 sq km

Capital Rome

Currency Euro (€)

Emergency ☑112

Language Italian

Money ATMs widespread; credit cards widely accepted

Population 61 million

Telephone Country code ☑39, international access code ☑00

Visas Schengen rules apply

Skiing Italy's ski season runs from December through to March. Prices are generally high, particularly in the top Alpine resorts – the Apennines are cheaper. A popular option is to buy a *settimana bianca* (literally 'white week') package deal, covering accommodation, food and ski passes.

FOOD

» On the bill expect to be charged for *pane e coperto* (bread and cover charge). This is standard and is added even if you don't ask for or eat the bread.

» Service (*servizio*) is generally included in restaurants – if it's not, a euro or two is fine in pizzerias, 10% in restaurants.

» Restaurants are nonsmoking.

GAY & LESBIAN TRAVELLERS

» Homosexuality is legal in Italy. It's well tolerated in major cities, but overt displays of affection could attract a negative response.

» Italy's main gay and lesbian organisation is **Arcigay** (☑051 095 72 00; www.arcigay.it; Via Don Minzoni 18, Cassero LGBT Center).

 HOTEL TAX

Most Italian hotels apply a room occupancy tax *(tassa di soggiorno)*, which is charged on top of your regular hotel bill. The exact amount, which varies from city to city, depends on your type of accommodation, but as a rough guide reckon on €1 to €3 per person per night in a one-star hotel, €3 to €3.50 in a B&B, €3 to €4 in a three-star hotel etc.

Prices quoted in accommodation reviews do not include the tax.

SLEEPING PRICE RANGES

The following price ranges refer to a double room with private bathroom (breakfast included) in high season.

€ under €110
(under €120 in Rome & Venice)

€€ €110–€200
(€120–€250 in Rome, €120–€220 in Venice)

€€€ over €200
(over €250 in Rome, over €220 in Venice)

INTERNET ACCESS

➤ Most hotels, hostels, B&Bs and *pensioni* offer free wi-fi, as do many bars and cafes.

➤ Public wi-fi is available in many large cities, but you'll generally need an Italian mobile number to register for it.

MONEY

ATMs Known as *bancomat,* are widely available and most will accept cards tied into the Visa, MasterCard, Cirrus and Maestro systems.

Credit cards Good for payment in most hotels, restaurants, shops, supermarkets and toll-booths. Major cards such as Visa, MasterCard, Eurocard, Cirrus and Eurocheques are widely accepted. Amex is also recognised, though less common.

Tipping If *servizio* is not included, leave 10% in restaurants, a euro or two in pizzerias. It's not necessary in bars or cafes, but many people leave small change if drinking at the bar.

OPENING HOURS

Opening hours vary throughout the year. We've provided high-season opening hours; hours will generally decrease in the shoulder and low seasons. 'Summer' times generally refer to the period from April to September or October, while 'winter' times generally run from October or November to March.

Banks 8.30am–1.30pm and 2.45–3.45pm or 4.30pm Monday to Friday

Restaurants noon–2.30pm and 7.30–11pm or midnight

Cafes 7.30am–8pm

Bars and clubs 10pm–4am or 5am

Shops 9am–1pm and 4–8pm Monday to Saturday, some also open Sunday

PUBLIC HOLIDAYS

Most Italians take their annual holiday in August, with the busiest period occurring around 15 August, known locally as Ferragosto. As a result, many businesses and shops close for at least part of that month. Settimana Santa (Easter Holy Week) is another busy holiday period for Italians.

National public holidays:

Capodanno (New Year's Day) 1 January

Epifania (Epiphany) 6 January

Pasquetta (Easter Monday) March/April

Giorno della Liberazione (Liberation Day) 25 April

Festa del Lavoro (Labour Day) 1 May

Festa della Repubblica (Republic Day) 2 June

Ferragosto (Feast of the Assumption) 15 August

Festa di Ognisanti (All Saints' Day) 1 November

Festa dell'Immacolata Concezione (Feast of the Immaculate Conception) 8 December

Natale (Christmas Day) 25 December

Festa di Santo Stefano (Boxing Day) 26 December

SAFE TRAVEL

Italy is generally a safe country, but petty theft is prevalent. Be on your guard against pickpockets in popular tourist centres such as Rome, Florence, Venice and Naples.

TELEPHONE

➤ Area codes must be dialled even when calling locally.

➤ To call Italy from abroad, dial ☏ 0039 and then the area code, including the first zero.

➤ To call abroad from Italy, dial ☏ 00, then the relevant country code followed by the telephone number.

➤ Italian mobile phone numbers are nine or 10 digits long and start with a three-digit prefix starting with a 3.

Mobile Phones

➤ Local SIM cards can be used in European, Australian and some unlocked US phones. Other phones must be set to roaming.

➤ You can get SIMs from **TIM** (Telecom Italia Mobile; ☏187; www.tim.it), **Wind** (☏155; www.

EATING PRICE RANGES

The following price ranges refer to a meal of two courses (antipasto/*primo* and *secondo*), a glass of house wine, and *coperto* (cover charge) for one person.

€ under €25

€€ €25–€45

€€€ over €45

wind.it) and **Vodafone** (☎190; www.vodafone.it) outlets. You'll need a passport or ID when you buy one.

⇒ Schengen visa rules apply for entry to Italy.

⇒ Unless staying in a hotel/B&B/hostel etc, all foreign visitors are supposed to register with the local police within eight days of arrival.

⇒ A *permesso di soggiorno* (permit to stay) is required by all non-EU nationals who stay in Italy longer than three months. Check details on www.poliziadistato.it.

⇒ EU citizens do not require a *permesso di soggiorno*.

ⓘ Getting There & Away

Italy is well served by international airlines and European low-cost carriers, and there are plenty of bus, train and ferry routes into the country.

Flights, tours and rail tickets can be booked online at lonelyplanet.com/bookings.

AIR

There are direct intercontinental flights to/from Rome and Milan. European flights also serve regional airports.

Italy's national carrier is **Alitalia** (☎89 20 10; www.alitalia.com).

Italy's principal airports:

Leonardo da Vinci (☎06 6 59 51; www.adr.it/fiumicino) Italy's main airport, in Rome; also known as Fiumicino.

Rome Ciampino (☎06 6 59 51; www.adr.it/ciampino) Rome's second airport.

Milan Malpensa(☎02 23 23 23; www.milanomalpensa-airport.com) Northern Italy's principal hub.

Venice Marco Polo (☎flight information 041 260 92 60; www.veniceairport.it) Venice's main airport.

Pisa International (Galileo Galilei Airport; ☎050 84 93 00; www.pisa-airport.com) Gateway for Florence and Tuscany.

Naples Capodichino (☎081 789 62 59; www.aeroportodinapoli.it) Southern Italy's main airport.

Catania Fontanarossa (☎095 723 91 11; www.aeroporto.catania.it) Sicily's largest airport.

LAND
Bus

Eurolines (☎0861 199 19 00; www.eurolines.it) operates buses from European destinations to many Italian cities.

Train

Milan and Venice are Italy's main international rail hubs. International trains also run to/from Rome, Genoa, Turin, Verona, Bologna and Florence.

Main routes:

Milan To/from Paris, Geneva, Zürich and Vienna.

Rome To/from Munich and Vienna.

Venice To/from Paris, Munich and Vienna.

Voyages-sncf (☎0844 848 58 48; http://uk.voyages-sncf.com) can provide fare information

MAIN INTERNATIONAL FERRY ROUTES

FROM	TO	COMPANY	HIGH SEASON FARE (€)	DURATION (HR)
Ancona	Igoumenitsa, Greece	Minoan, Superfast, Anek	64-109	16½-22
Ancona	Patra, Greece	Minoan, Superfast, Anek	64-109	22-29
Ancona	Split, Croatia	Jadrolinija, SNAV	42-58	10¾
Bari	Igoumenitsa, Greece	Superfast	67-96	8-12
Bari	Patra, Greece	Superfast	67-96	16
Bari	Dubrovnik, Croatia	Jadrolinija	48-58	10-12
Bari	Bar, Montenegro	Montenegro	50-55	9
Brindisi	Igoumenitsa, Greece	Grimaldi	55-101	8
Brindisi	Patra, Greece	Grimaldi	55-101	14
Genoa	Barcelona, Spain	GNV	42-87	19½
Genoa	Tunis, Tunisia	GNV	83-142	23½
Venice	Igoumenitsa, Greece	Superfast, Anek	69-99	14½-21

USEFUL WEBSITES

Lonely Planet (www.lonelyplanet.com/italy) Destination information, hotel bookings, traveller forum and more.

Trenitalia (www.trenitalia.com) Italian railways website.

Enit Italia (www.italia.it) Official Italian-government tourism website.

on journeys from the UK to Italy, most of which require a change at Paris. Another excellent resource is www.seat61.com.

Eurail and Inter-Rail passes are valid in Italy.

SEA

➡ Ferries serve Italian ports from across the Mediterranean. Timetables are seasonal, so always check ahead.

➡ For routes, companies and online booking try www.traghettiweb.it.

➡ Holders of Eurail and Inter-Rail passes should check with the ferry company if they are entitled to a discount or free passage.

➡ Major ferry companies:

Anek Lines (☑ 071 207 22 75; www.anekitalia.com)

GNV (☑ 010 209 45 91; www.gnv.it)

Grimaldi Lines (☑ 0831 54 81 16; www.grimaldi-lines.com; Costa Morena Terminal)

Jadrolinija (☑ Ancona 071 207 24 97, Bari 080 521 76 43; www.jadrolinija.hr)

Minoan Lines (☑ 071 20 17 08; www.minoan.it)

Montenegro Lines (☑ Bar 382 3030 3469; www.montenegrolines.net)

SNAV (☑ 081 428 55 55; www.snav.it)

Superfast (☑ Ancona 071 20 20 33, Bari 080 528 28 09; www.superfast.com)

❶ ADMISSION PRICES

Admission to state-run museums, galleries, monuments and sites is free to under-18s. People aged between 18 and 25 are entitled to a discount. To get it, you'll need proof of your age, ideally a passport or ID card.

Admission is free to everyone on the first Sunday of each month.

❶ Getting Around

BICYCLE

➡ Bikes can be taken on regional and certain international trains carrying the bike logo, but you'll need to pay a supplement (€3.50 on regional trains, €12 on international trains).

➡ Bikes can be carried free if dismantled and stored in a bike bag.

➡ Bikes generally incur a small supplement on ferries, typically €10 to €15.

BOAT

Craft *Navi* (large ferries) service Sicily and Sardinia, while *traghetti* (smaller ferries) and *aliscafi* (hydrofoils) service the smaller islands. Most ferries carry vehicles; hydrofoils do not.

Routes Main embarkation points for Sicily and Sardinia are Genoa, Livorno, Civitavecchia and Naples. Ferries for Sicily also leave from Villa San Giovanni and Reggio Calabria. Main arrival points in Sardinia are Cagliari, Arbatax, Olbia and Porto Torres; in Sicily they're Palermo, Catania, Trapani and Messina.

Timetables and tickets Direct Ferries (www.directferries.co.uk) allows you to search routes, compare prices and book tickets for ferry routes in Italy.

BUS

➡ Italy boasts an extensive and largely reliable bus network.

➡ Buses are not necessarily cheaper than trains, but in mountainous areas they are often the only choice.

➡ In larger cities, companies have ticket offices or operate through agencies, but in villages and small towns tickets are sold in bars or on the bus.

➡ Reservations are only necessary for high-season long-haul trips.

CAR & MOTORCYCLE

➡ Italy's roads are generally good, and there's an extensive network of toll autostrade (motorways).

➡ All EU driving licences are recognised in Italy. Holders of non-EU licences should get an International Driving Permit (IDP) through their national automobile association.

➡ Traffic restrictions apply in most city centres.

➡ To hire a car you'll require a driving licence (plus IDP if necessary) and credit card. Age restrictions vary, but generally you'll need to be 21 or over.

ITALY GETTING AROUND

→ If driving your own car, carry your vehicle registration certificate, driving licence and proof of third-party liability insurance cover.

→ For further details, see the website of Italy's motoring organisation **Automobile Club d'Italia** (ACI; ☑ 803116, from a foreign mobile 800 116 800; www.aci.it).

→ ACI provides 24-hour roadside assistance: call ☑ 803 116 from a landline or Italian mobile, ☑ 800 116 800 from a foreign mobile.

TRAIN

Italy has an extensive rail network. Most services are run by **Trenitalia** (☑ 892021; www.trenitalia.com) but **Italo** (☑ 89 20 20; www.italotreno.it) also operates high-speed trains.

There are several types of train:

Regionale/interregionale Slow local services.

InterCity (IC) Faster services between major cities.

Alta Velocità (AV) State-of-the-art, high-velocity trains: Frecciarossa, Frecciargento, Frecciabianca and Italo trains.

Tickets

→ InterCity and Alta Velocità trains require prior reservation.

→ If your ticket doesn't include a reservation with an assigned seat, you must validate it before boarding by inserting it into one of the machines dotted around stations.

Kosovo

Includes ➜

Best Places to Eat

➜ Tiffany (p734)

➜ Renaissance (p734)

➜ Soma Book Station (p734)

➜ Art Design (p737)

Best Places to Stay

➜ Swiss Diamond Hotel (p733)

➜ Dukagjini Hotel (p736)

➜ Driza's House (p737)

➜ Han Hostel (p733)

Why Go?

Europe's newest country, Kosovo is a fascinating land at the heart of the Balkans rewarding visitors with welcoming smiles, charming mountain towns, incredible hiking opportunities and 13th-century domed Serbian monasteries – and that's just for starters. It's perfectly safe to travel here now, but despite this, Kosovo remains one of the last truly off-the-beaten-path destinations in Europe.

Kosovo declared independence from Serbia in 2008, and while it has been diplomatically recognised by 112 countries, there are still many nations that do not accept Kosovan independence, including Serbia. The country has been the recipient of massive aid from the international community, particularly the EU and NATO, which effectively run the entity politically and keep peace between the ethnic Albanian majority and the minority Serbs. Barbs of its past are impossible to miss, however: roads are dotted with memorials to those killed in 1999, while NATO forces still guard Serbian monasteries.

When to Go
Pristina

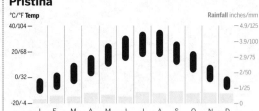

Dec–Mar
Hit the powder on the still largely virgin ski slopes of Brezovica.

May–Sep
Pleasant weather for hiking in the Rugova Mountains.

Aug
The excellent DokuFest in Prizren is Kosovo's best arts event.

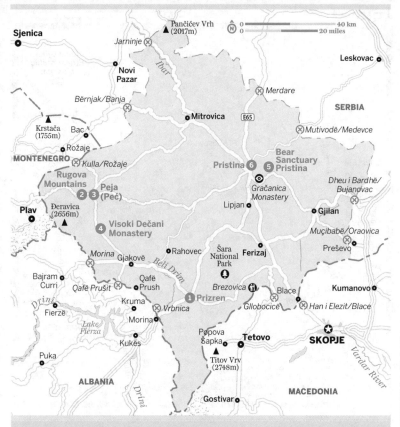

Kosovo Highlights

1 Prizren's old town
(p737) Discovering the picturesque, mosque-studded streets of Prizren's charming old quarter and getting a breathtaking view from the fortress.

2 Rugova Mountains
(p736) Trekking around the stunning landscapes of Kosovo's most impressive mountains, which rise to the west of Peja.

3 Peja's Cheese Market
(p736) Breathing deep at Peja's Saturday Cheese Market inside the town's colourful bazaar.

4 Visoki Dečani Monastery (p736) Taking in gorgeous frescoes and then buying monk-made wine and cheese at this serene 14th-century Serbian monastery.

5 Bear Sanctuary Pristina (p735) Visiting the rescued bears living in excellent conditions at this wonderful lakeside sanctuary that's just a short trip from the capital.

6 Pristina (p731)
Exploring Europe's youngest country through its plucky and idiosyncratic capital city, and enjoying its excellent dining and nightlife.

PRISTINA

038 / POP 211,000

Pristina (pronounced 'prish-*tee*-na') is a city changing fast and one that feels full of optimism and potential, even if its traffic-clogged streets and mismatched architectural styles

don't make it an obviously attractive place. Far more a provincial town than great city, Pristina makes for an unlikely national capital, and yet feels more cosmopolitan than the capitals of many larger Balkan nations due to the number of foreigners working here: the UN

Pristina

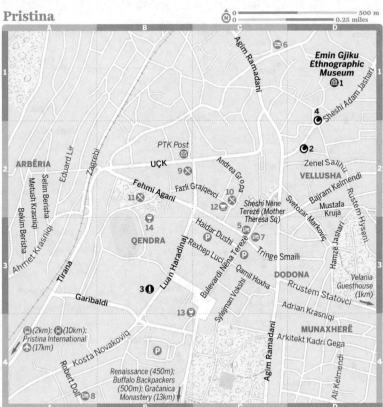

Pristina

⊚ **Top Sights**

and EU both have large presences and the city feels rich and more sophisticated as a result.

⊙ Sights

★ **Emin Gjiku Ethnographic Museum**　　　HISTORIC BUILDING
(Rr Iliaz Agushi; ⊘10am-5pm Tue-Sat, to 3pm Sun) **FREE** This wonderful annex of the Muse-um of Kosovo is located in two beautifully preserved Ottoman houses enclosed in a large walled garden. The English-speaking staff will give you a fascinating tour of both properties and point out the various unique pieces of clothing, weaponry, jewellery and household items on display in each. There's no better introduction to Kosovar culture.

Jashar Pasha Mosque
MOSQUE

(Rr Ylfete Humolli; ☉ dawn-dusk) This mosque, which was fully renovated as a gift from the Turkish government, reopened in 2015 and has vibrant interiors that exemplify Turkish baroque style.

Sultan Mehmet Fatih Mosque
MOSQUE

(Xhamia e Mbretit; Rr Ilir Konushevci; ☉ dawn-dusk) The 'imperial mosque' (Xhamia e Mbretit), as locals call it, was built on the orders of Mehmed the Conqueror around 1461, and although it was converted to a Catholic church during the Austro-Hungarian era, it was renovated again after WWII and is now the city's most important mosque. It has some beautiful interiors, as well as striking painted ceilings over the main entrance.

Newborn Monument
MONUMENT

These iconic block letters in downtown Pristina look a bit scrappy and worn these days, but they captured the imagination of the fledgling nation when they were unveiled on 17 February 2008, the day Kosovo declared its independence from Serbia and began its painful (and still incomplete) journey to full international recognition.

🏃 Activities

Be In Kosovo
TOURS

(☏ 049 621 768; www.beinkosovo.com) This ambitious and fast-growing company offers tours and services throughout Kosovo, and its Kosovar guides know the country well – including the Serbian monasteries and the Serb minorities of North Mitrovica. The company also has offices in neighbouring countries and can easily organise multinational itineraries.

Traveks
ADVENTURE

(☏ 044 484 444; www.traveks.com) This operator offers a variety of tours including horse riding around the village of Brod in southern Kosovo, and 'Taste of Kosovo' cultural tours which include raki and wine tasting.

🛏 Sleeping

★ Han Hostel
HOSTEL €

(☏ 044 396 852, 044 760 792; www.hostelhan.com; Rr Fehmi Agani 2/4; dm €12-14, s/d €20/30; @ ☎) Pristina's best hostel is on the 4th floor of a residential building right in the heart of town. Cobbled together from two apartments that have been joined and converted, this great space has a large communal kitchen, balconies and smart rooms with clean

ITINERARIES

Two to Three Days

Spend a day in cool little **Pristina** and get to know Kosovo's chaotic but somehow charming capital. The next day, visit **Visoki Dečani Monastery** and then head on to **Prizren**, to see the old town's Ottoman sights and enjoy the view from the castle.

One Week

After a couple of days in the capital, and a visit to **Gračanica Monastery** and the **Bear Sanctuary Pristina**, loop to lovely **Prizren** for a night before continuing to **Peja** (Peć) for monasteries and markets. Then end with a few days of hiking in the beautiful **Rugova Mountains**.

bathrooms. It's well set up for backpackers and run by an extremely friendly local crew.

White Tree Hostel
HOSTEL €

(☏ 049 166 777; www.whitetreehostel.com; Rr Mujo Ulqinaku 15; dm €9-12, d €30; ❄ ☎) This hostel is run by a group of well-travelled locals who took a derelict house into their care, painted the tree in the courtyard white and gradually began to attract travellers with a cool backpacker vibe. It feels more like an Albanian beach resort than a downtown Pristina bolthole.

Buffalo Backpackers
HOSTEL €

(☏ 377 643 261; www.buffalobackpackers.com; Rr Musine Kokalari 25; dm/camping incl breakfast €12/6; ☎) This charming dorm-only hostel has some of the cheapest and most chilled-out accommodation in the country, as well as friendly staff and a pleasant location in a house south of Pristina's busy city centre.

Hotel Begolli
HOTEL €€

(☏ 038 244 277; www.hotelbegolli.com; Rr Maliq Pashë Gjinolli 8; s/d incl breakfast €40/50, apt from €50; ❄ @ ☎) While it may have gone overboard with its '90s-style furniture, Begolli is a pleasant, rather sprawling place to stay. The apartment has a Jacuzzi and a kitchen and is good value, while the normal rooms are on the small side but comfy. Staff are friendly, and a good breakfast is served in the ground-floor bar.

★ Swiss Diamond Hotel
LUXURY HOTEL €€€

(☏ 038 220 000; www.swissdiamondhotelprishtina.com; Sheshi Nënë Tereza; s/d incl breakfast from

KOSOVO PRISTINA

€145/165; 🄿🕭❄@📶🌊) This international-standard five-star hotel is the choice of those who can afford it. Opened in 2012 in the heart of the city, this place is all marble floors, obsequious staff and liveried attendants. The rooms are lavish and the suites are immense, all decorated with expensive furnishings and many enjoying great city views.

✘ Eating

★ Soma Book Station MEDITERRANEAN €€
(4/A Fazli Grajqevci; mains €5-11; ⊘8am-midnight Mon-Sat; 📶) Despite existing for just a couple of years, Soma is already a local institution, and nearly all visitors to Pristina end up here at some point. The shady garden hums with activity at lunchtime, while the interior has a club-like atmosphere. Food combines various tastes of the Mediterranean, including tuna salad, beef carpaccio, grilled fish, steaks and burgers.

★ Tiffany BALKAN €€
(📱038 244 040; off Rr Fehmi Agani; meals €12; ⊘9am-10.30pm Mon-Sat, from 6pm Sun; 📶) The organic menu here (delivered by efficient, if somewhat terse, English-speaking staff) is simply dazzling: sit on the sun-dappled terrace and enjoy the day's grilled special, beautifully cooked seasonal vegetables drenched in olive oil, and freshly baked bread. Understandably much prized by the foreign community, this brilliant place is unsigned and somewhat hidden behind a well-tended bush on Fehmi Agani.

ESSENTIAL FOOD & DRINK

'Traditional' food is generally Albanian – most prominently, stewed and grilled meat and fish. Kos (goat's-cheese yoghurt) is eaten alone or with almost anything. Turkish kebabs and *gjuveç* (baked meat and vegetables) are common.

Byrek Pastry with cheese or meat.

Gjuveç Baked meat and vegetables.

Fli Flaky pastry pie served with honey.

Kos Goat's-milk yoghurt.

Pershut Dried meat.

Qofta Flat or cylindrical minced-meat rissoles.

Tavë Meat baked with cheese and egg.

Vranac Red wine from the Rahovec region of Kosovo.

★ Renaissance BALKAN €€
(Renesansa; 📱044 118 796; Rr Musine Kokollari; set meals €15; ⊘6pm-midnight) This atmospheric place might just be Pristina's best-kept secret, if only for the fact that it seems to move premises with alarming speed. At its newest location, wooden doors open to a traditional dining room where tables are brimming with local wine and delicious meze and meaty main courses prepared by the family's matriarch. Vegetarians can be catered for but should call ahead. The restaurant can be rather tricky to find, as it's unsigned: taxi drivers usually know it.

Home Bar & Restaurant INTERNATIONAL €€
(Rr Luan Haradinaj; mains €5-12; ⊘7am-11pm Mon-Sat, 11am-11pm Sun; 📶✏) Having been here since the dark days of 2001, this is the closest Pristina has to an expat institution. It lives up to its name, too: it's exceptionally cosy and friendly and is peppered with curios and antiques. The menu, which has some Lebanese influence, includes comfort foods such as spring rolls, hummus, curries, wraps, burgers and fajitas.

🍷 Drinking

★ Dit' e Nat' CAFE
(www.ditenat.com/en; Rr Fazli Grajqevci 5; ⊘8am-midnight Mon-Sat, noon-midnight Sun; 📶) 'Day and night', a bookshop-cafe-bar-performance space, is a home away from home for bookish expats and locals alike. There's a great selection of books in English, strong espresso, excellent cocktails, friendly English-speaking staff and occasional live music in the evenings, including jazz. Recently the establishment has started serving vegetarian food to boot.

Sabaja Craft Brewery BREWERY
(Stadioni i Prishtinës; ⊘9am-11pm; 📶) This American-Kosovar venture is Pristina's first microbrewery; its several wonderful brews include an IPA and a Session pale ale. There are also various seasonal products available. To complement that, there's a relaxed vibe and a good international menu (mains €2 to €5) available.

Rooftop 13 CLUB
(📱045 628 628; www.rooftop13.com; 13th fl, Grand Hotel, Blvd Nënë Tereza; ⊘11pm-5am Wed, Fri & Sat) Despite its rather unlikely location on top of the gargantuan and grotesque state-run Grand Hotel, Rooftop 13 pulls off the impressive feat of being a smart and stylish club. Revelers come to drink cocktails until the early hours while enjoying incredible views of

GRAČANICA MONASTERY & BEAR SANCTUARY PRISTINA

Explore beyond Pristina by heading southeast to two of the country's best sights. Dusty fingers of sunlight pierce the darkness of Gračanica Monastery (☉6am-5pm) FREE, completed in 1321 by Serbian King Milutin. It's an oasis in a town that is the cultural centre of Serbs in central Kosovo. Take a Gjilan-bound bus (€0.50, 15 minutes, every 30 minutes); the monastery's on your left. Do dress respectably (that means no shorts or sleeveless tops for anyone, and head scarves for women) and you'll be very welcome to look around this historical complex and to view the gorgeous icons in the main church.

Further along the road to Gjilan is the excellent Bear Sanctuary Pristina (☑045 826 072; www.vier-pfoten.eu; Mramor; adult/student €1.50/0.50c; ☉9am-6pm Apr-Oct, 10am-4pm Nov-Mar), in the village of Mramor. Here you can visit a number of brown bears that were rescued from cruel captivity by the charity Four Paws. All the bears here were once kept in tiny cages as mascots for restaurants, but when the keeping of bears was outlawed in Kosovo in 2010, Four Paws stepped in to care for these wonderful animals. Sadly some of them still suffer from trauma and don't socialise well, but their excellent conditions are heartening indeed. Ask to be let off any Gjilan-bound bus by the Delfina gas station at the entrance to Mramor, then follow the road back past the lakeside, and then follow the track around to the right.

the city. Dress to impress – locals do and you'll feel out of place if you don't make an effort.

ⓘ Information

American Hospital (☑038 221 661; www. ks.spitaliamerikan.com; Rr Shkupi) The best hospital in Kosovo offers American-standard healthcare, although not always the language skills to match. It's just outside the city in the Serbian-majority town of Gračanica.

Barnatore Pharmacy (Blvd Nënë Tereza; ☉8am-10pm)

PTK Post (Rr UÇK; ☉8am-8pm Mon-Sat) Post and special delivery services.

ⓘ Getting There & Around

AIR

There is currently no public transport from **Pristina International Airport** (☑038 501 502 1214; www.airportpristina.com), so you'll have to get a taxi into the city. Taxis charge €25 for the 20-minute, 18km trip to the city centre.

BUS

The **bus station** (Stacioni i Autobusëve; ☑038 550 011; Rr Lidja e Pejes) is 2km southwest of the centre off Blvd Bil Klinton. Taxis to the centre should cost €2.

International buses from Pristina include Belgrade (€21, seven hours, 11pm) and Novi Pazar (€5.50, three hours, 10am) in Serbia; Tirana, Albania (€10.50, five hours, every one to two hours), Skopje, Macedonia (€5.50, two hours, hourly from 5.30am to 5pm); Podgorica (€15.50, seven hours, 7pm) and Ulcinj (€15.50, seven hours, 8am & 9pm) in Montenegro .

Domestically there are buses to all corners of the country, including Prizren (€4, 75 minutes, every 20 minutes) and Peja (€4, 1½ hours, every 20 minutes).

TRAIN

Trains run from Pristina to Peja (€3, at 8.01am and 4.41pm, two hours) and, internationally, to Skopje in Macedonia (€4, 7.22am, three hours).

AROUND PRISTINA

Kosovo is a small country, which can be crossed by car in any direction in around an hour. Not far in distance, but worlds away from the chaotic capital, the smaller towns of Peja and Prizren both offer a different pace and a new perspective on Kosovar life.

Peja (Peć)

☑ 039 / POP 97,000

Peja (known as Peć in Serbian) is Kosovo's third-largest city and one flanked by sites vital to Orthodox Serbians. With a Turkish-style bazaar at its heart and the dramatic but increasingly accessible Rugova Mountains all around it, it's a diverse and progressive place that's fast becoming Kosovo's tourism hub.

◉ Sights

Patriarchate of Peć   MONASTERY
(Pećka Patrijaršija; ☑044 150 755; ☉9am-6pm) This church and nunnery complex on the outskirts of Peja are a slice of Serbian Orthodoxy that has existed here since the late 13th

DON'T MISS

VISOKI DEČANI MONASTERY

This imposing whitewashed **monastery** (☏ 049 776 254; www.decani.org; ⊙ 11am-1pm & 4-5.30pm), 15km south of Peja, is one of Kosovo's absolute highlights. Located in an incredibly beautiful spot beneath the mountains and surrounded by a forest of pine and chestnut trees, the monastery has been here since 1327 and is today heavily guarded by Nato's Kosovo Force (KFOR). Despite occasional attacks from locals who'd like to see the Serbs leave – most recently a grenade attack in 2007 – the 25 Serbian monks living here in total isolation from the local community have stayed.

Buses go to the town of Dečani from Peja (€1, 30 minutes, every 15 minutes) on their way to Gjakovë. It's a pleasant 1km walk to the monastery from the bus stop. From the roundabout in the middle of town, take the second exit if you're coming from Peja. You'll need to surrender your passport while visiting.

century. You're welcome to enter to visit the church, which is divided into four separate chapels containing superb frescoes. The entire complex dates from between the 1230s and the 1330s. Since 2013, the buildings have been guarded by Kosovo's police force, and you will need your passport to enter.

Cheese Market
MARKET

(⊙ 8am-4pm Sat) The town's bustling daily bazaar makes you feel like you've just arrived in İstanbul, and it's a great place to see local farmers and artisans hawking their wares. The highlight is when farmers gather in a busy courtyard at the centre of the market area each Saturday with wooden barrels of goat's cheese. You can actually just follow your nose and you'll find it.

🏃 Activities

Peja has established itself as the country's tourism hub and there's an impressive number of activities on offer in the nearby Rugova Mountains, including rock climbing, mountain biking, skiing, hiking and white-water rafting.

★ Rugova Experience
ADVENTURE

(☏ 044 137 734, 044 350 511; www.rugovaexperience.org; Rr Mbretëreshë Teuta) 🖉 This excellent, locally run company is championing the Rugova region for hikers and cultural tourists. It organises homestays in mountain villages, runs very good trekking tours, enjoys great local access and works with English-speaking guides. Its helpful office has maps and plenty of information about Peja's local trekking opportunities.

Balkan Natural Adventure
ADVENTURE

(☏ 049 661 105; www.bnadventure.com) Balkan Natural Adventure is the best local resource to book your via ferrata, zipline, caving, rock climbing or snowshoeing adventure in the Rugova region. It also leads the Peaks of the Balkans hiking tours.

Rugova Hiking
HIKING

(☏ 049 126 443; www.rugovahiking.com; Rr Filip Shiroka 16) This highly regarded local firm offers hiking, biking and skiing tours of the Rugova Mountains to groups of up to 20 people. There's a number of tried and tested itineraries on offer, but tailor-made tours are also possible. One popular tour is a 43km downhill biking tour (€39 per person, 4-5 hours) run with Belgian cycling tour operator Cyclistes Sans Frontières.

🛏 Sleeping

Hostel Saraç
HOSTEL €

(☏ 049 247 391; hostelsarac@gmail.com; Vëllezërit Bakir e Adem Gjuka 22; dm €10; 🛜) Opened in 2015, this new hostel inside a family home has a spacious garden and a common area scattered with traditional Albanian musical instruments. The accommodation is in one big dorm upstairs, which is partially divided into two areas that all share a small kitchen and bathroom. Private rooms are planned. It's central, English-speaking and ideal for groups.

★ Dukagjini Hotel
HOTEL €€

(☏ 038 771 177; www.hoteldukagjini.com; Sheshi i Dëshmorëve 2; s/d incl breakfast €50/70; ❄🛜💨) The regal Dukagjini boasts international standards, which you probably didn't expect in a small city in Kosovo. Rooms can be rather small but are grandly appointed and have supremely comfortable beds; many on the 1st floor have huge terraces overlooking the central square. There's a pool and gym and a huge restaurant with views of the river.

✖ Eating

★ Art Design
BALKAN €

(☑049 585 885; Rr Enver Hadri 53; mains €2.50-6; ☺8am-midnight) Despite sounding flash and modern, Art Design is actually an old house brimming with character and full of local arts and crafts. Choose between dining outside over a little stream or in one of the two rather chintzy dining rooms. Traditional dishes here include *sarma* (meat and rice rolled in grape leaves) and *speca dollma* (peppers filled with meat and rice).

Kulla e Zenel Beut
BALKAN €€

(Rr William Walker; mains €3-7; ☺8am-midnight; 🐾) This charming option in the centre of town has a pleasant terrace and a cosy dining room. The dishes to go for here are the *tava* (various traditional specialties served in clay pots), though fresh fish, baked mussels, grills and even a breakfast menu are on offer, too. There's only one English menu, so you may have to wait your turn.

ℹ Information

Tourist Information Centre (☑039 423 949; www.pejatourism.org; Rr Mbretëreshë Teuta; ☺8am-noon & 1-4pm Mon-Fri) This little office in the centre of town is run by friendly English-speaking staff. They can offer you lots of advice, maps and other information about exploring Peja and the surrounding region, and help organise trips into the Rugova Mountains.

ℹ Getting There & Away

BUS

The town's bus station is on Rr Adem Jashari, a short walk from the town centre. Frequent buses run to Pristina (€4, 1½ hours, every 20 minutes), Prizren (€4, 80 minutes, hourly), Gjakova (€2.50, 50 minutes, hourly) and Dečani (€1, 20 minutes, hourly). International buses link Peja with Ulclinj (€16, 10 hours, 10am and 8.30pm) and Podgorica in Montenegro (€15, seven hours, 10am).

TRAIN

Trains depart Peja for Pristina (€3, two hours, twice daily) from the town's small train station. To find the station, walk away from the Dukagjini Hotel down Rr Emrush Miftari for 1.4km.

Prizren

☑029 / POP 185,000

Picturesque Prizren is Kosovo's second city and it shines with post-independence enthusiasm that's infectious. If you're passing through between Albania and Pristina, the charming mosque- and church-filled old town is well worth setting aside a few hours to wander about in. It's also worth making a special journey here if you're a documentary fan: Prizren's annual DokuFest is Kosovo's leading arts event and attracts documentary makers and fans from all over the world every August.

◉ Sights

Prizren Fortress
CASTLE

(Kalaja; ☺dawn-dusk) **FREE** It's well worth making the steep 15-minute hike up from Prizren's old town (follow the road past the Orthodox church on the hillside; it's well signed and pretty obvious) for the superb views over the city and on into the distance. The first fortress here was built by the Byzantines and was expanded by successive Serbian kings in the 12th to 14th centuries before becoming a seat of power for the Ottoman rulers of Kosovo until their expulsion in 1912.

Sinan Pasha Mosque
MOSQUE

(Xhamia e Sinan Pashës; Vatra Shqiptare; ☺dawn-dusk) Dating from 1615, the Sinan Pasha Mosque is the most important in Prizren, and it sits right at the heart of the old town, overlooking the river and the town's Ottoman Bridge. Its impressive dome, minaret and colonnaded facade form a fabulous sight from the street, though it's also well worth going inside (outside of prayer times) to see the striking interior.

Church of Our Lady of Ljeviš
CHURCH

(Bogorodica Ljeviška; Rr Xhemil Fluku; admission €3) Prizren's most important site is the Orthodox Church of Our Lady of Ljeviš, a 14th-century Serbian church that was used as a mosque by the local population until 1911. The church was badly damaged in 2004 by the town's Albanian population and placed on Unesco's World Heritage in Danger list in 2006. Restoration work on its magnificent frescoes has recently begun.

🛏 Sleeping

★ Driza's House
HOSTEL €

(☑049 618 181; www.drizas-house.com; Remzi Ademaj 7; dm €9-15, tw/tr €25/40; ❋🐾) New in 2016, this former family home in a courtyard just off the river embankment is an atmospheric option full of local charm. Made up of two dorms with custom-made bunk beds (which include curtains, reading lights, personal electricity plugs and lockable storage cupboards), the place feels very communal – but worlds away from your average hostel.

Prizren City Hostel
HOSTEL €

(☑ 049 466 313; www.prizrencityhostel.com; Rr Iljaz Kuka 66; dm incl breakfast €11, d incl breakfast with/without bathroom €33/28; ❂ ❄ 🛜) Over four floors and a short wander from the heart of the old town, Prizren's original hostel is a great place to stay, with a friendly, international vibe and a chilled-out roof terrace bar complete with hammocks, awesome city views and regular BBQs. There are good bathrooms, tours can be arranged and the friendly owner decidedly encourages drinking.

Classic Hotel
HOTEL €€

(☑ 029 223 333; www.classic-hotel-prizren.com; Shuaip Spahiu; s/d €49/69; P ❄ 🛜) This plush and atmospheric spot in the heart of the old town is an ideal place to stay if you'd like some comfort and a bit of pampering. The spacious rooms have safes, flat-screen TVs, minibars and marble bathrooms. Gold flourishes abound, and service is gracious and attentive.

✖ Eating

Ego
INTERNATIONAL €

(Sheshi i Shadërvanit; mains €2.50-7; ❂ 8am-11pm Mon-Fri, 11am-11pm Sat & Sun; 🛜) Right on Prizren's pretty main cobblestone square, this place stands out from the many cafes and restaurants here with its sophisticated international menu, abundant vegetarian options, smart decor and charming staff. Have lunch on the terrace, drinks inside or a more formal dinner in the upstairs dining room.

Ambient
BALKAN €€

(Rr Vatrat Shqiptare; mains €3-9; ❂ 8am-midnight; 🛜) With views over the old town and by far the most charming location in Prizren – beside a waterfall cascading down the cliffside by the river – this is a place to come for a romantic dinner or sundowner. The menu includes a Pasha burger, steaks, seafood and a catch of the day cooked to your specification.

🍺 Drinking

Te Kinezi
PUB

(Sheshi i Shadërvanit; ❂ noon-midnight Sun-Thu, until 2am Fri & Sat) This little place is riotously popular and rightly so: it has excellent brews on tap from Pristina's Sabaja Craft Brewery (p734). There's a full range of other drinks, too, and an in-the-know crowd that's more bohemian and interesting than most you'll meet in town.

Corner Bar
BAR

(Sheshi i Shadërvanit; ❂ noon-11pm) In the thick of the bars that surround the old town's main square, this raucous and popular place stands out for its young, cool crowd and eclectic local DJs. There's a big cocktail list, and the owner will often join in the fun himself while the crowds spill out onto the street during the summer.

❶ Getting There & Away

Prizren is well connected by bus to Pristina (€4, two hours, every 20 minutes), Peja (€4, two hours, six daily), Skopje in Macedonia (€6, three hours, two daily) and Tirana in Albania (€12, three hours, seven daily). The bus station is on the right bank of the river, a short walk from the old town: follow the right-hand side of the river embankment away from the castle until you come to the traffic circle, then turn left onto Rr De Rada. The bus station will be on your left after around 200m.

SURVIVAL GUIDE

❶ Directory A–Z

ACCOMMODATION

Accommodation is booming in Kosovo, with most large towns now offering a good range of options.

INTERNET RESOURCES

UN Mission in Kosovo Online (http://unmik.unmissions.org) A good overview of the UN's work in Kosovo and the latest security situation.

Balkan Insight (www.balkaninsight.com) Quality news and analysis about the Balkans, with a good section on Kosovo.

Kosovo Guide (www.kosovoguide.com) An excellent Kosovo travel wiki.

Balkanology (www.balkanology.com) A popular website about the Balkans with strong Kosovo coverage.

Lonely Planet (www.lonelyplanet.com/kosovo) Destination information, hotel bookings, traveller forum and more.

MONEY

Kosovo's currency is the euro, despite not being part of the eurozone or the EU. It's best to arrive with small denominations, and euro coins are particularly useful. ATMs are common and established businesses accept credit cards.

OPENING HOURS

Opening hours vary, but these are the usual hours of business.

Banks 8am–5pm Monday to Friday, until 2pm Saturday

KOSOVO DIRECTORY A–Z

Bars 8am–11pm

Shops 8am–6pm Monday to Friday, until 3pm Saturday

Restaurants 8am–midnight

POST

PTK post and telecommunications offices operate in Kosovo's main towns.

PUBLIC HOLIDAYS

New Year's Day 1 January

Independence Day 17 February

Kosovo Constitution Day 9 April

Labour Day 1 May

Europe Day 9 May

Note that traditional Islamic and Orthodox Christian holidays are also observed, including Ramadan.

TELEPHONE

Kosovo's country code is ☑ 381.

VISAS

Kosovo is visa-free for EU, Australian, Canadian, Japanese, New Zealand, South African and US passport holders. All passports are stamped on arrival for a 90-day stay.

🛈 Getting There & Away

AIR

Pristina International Airport (p735) is 18km from the centre of Pristina. Airlines flying to Kosovo include Air Pristina, Adria, Austrian Airlines, easyJet, Norwegian, Pegasus and Turkish Airlines.

LAND

Kosovo has good bus connections between Albania, Montenegro and Macedonia, with regular services from Pristina, Peja and Prizren to Tirana (Albania), Skopje (Macedonia) and Podgorica (Montenegro). There's also a train line from Pristina to Macedonia's capital, Skopje. You can take international bus trips to and from all neighbouring capital cities; note that buses to and from Belgrade in Serbia travel via Montenegro.

Border Crossings

Albania There are three border crossings between Kosovo and Albania. To get to Albania's Koman Ferry, use the Qafa Morina border crossing west of Gjakova. A short distance further south is the Qafë Prush crossing, though the road continuing into Albania is bad here. The busiest border is at Vërmicë, where a modern motorway connects to Tirana.

Macedonia There are crossings to Blace from Pristina and Gllobocicë from Prizren.

Montenegro The main crossing is the Kulla/Rožaje crossing on the road between Rožaje and Peja.

> ## COUNTRY FACTS
>
> **Area** 10,887 sq km
>
> **Capital** Pristina
>
> **Country Telephone Code** 381
>
> **Currency** Euro (€)
>
> **Emergency** Ambulance 94, fire 93, police 92
>
> **Language** Albanian, Serbian
>
> **Money** ATMs in larger towns; banks open Monday to Friday
>
> **Population** 1.88 million
>
> **Visas** Kosovo is visa-free for most nationalities. All passports are stamped on arrival for a 90-day stay.

Serbia There are six border crossings between Kosovo and Serbia. Be aware that Kosovo's independence is not recognised by Serbia, so if you plan to continue to Serbia but entered Kosovo via Albania, Macedonia or Montenegro, officials at the Serbian border will deem that you entered Serbia illegally and you will not be let in. You'll need to exit Kosovo to a third country and then enter Serbia from there. If you entered Kosovo from Serbia, there's no problem returning to Serbia.

🛈 Getting Around

BUS

Buses stop at distinct blue signs, but can be flagged down anywhere. Bus journeys are generally cheap, but the going can be slow on Kosovo's single-lane roads.

CAR

Drivers should carry their licences with them whenever on the road, as police checks are not uncommon. Road conditions in Kosovo are generally good, though watch out for potholes on some poorly maintained stretches.

European Green Card vehicle insurance is not valid in the country, so you'll need to purchase vehicle insurance at the border when you enter with a car; this is a hassle-free and inexpensive procedure.

It's perfectly easy to hire cars here and travel with them to neighbouring countries (with the exception of Serbia). Note that Serbian-plated cars have been attacked in Kosovo, and rental companies do not let cars hired in Kosovo travel to Serbia and vice versa.

TRAIN

The train system is something of a novelty, but services connect Pristina to Peja and to Skopje in Macedonia. Locals generally take buses.

Latvia

Best Places to Eat

➜ Vincents (p747)

➜ Fazenda Bazārs (p747)

➜ 36.Line (p750)

➜ 3 Pavaru (p747)

➜ Skroderkrogs (p753)

Best Places to Stay

➜ Ekes Konvents (p746)

➜ Hotel Bergs (p747)

➜ Neiburgs (p746)

➜ Hotel Cēsis (p751)

➜ 2 Baloži (p752)

Why Go?

A tapestry of sea, lakes and woods, Latvia is best described as a vast unspoilt parkland with just one real city – its cosmopolitan capital, Rīga. The country might be small, but the amount of personal space it provides is enormous. You can always secure a chunk of pristine nature all for yourself, be it for trekking, cycling or dreaming away on a white-sand beach amid pine-covered dunes. Having been invaded by every regional power, Latvia has more cultural layers and a less homogenous population than its neighbours. People here fancy themselves to be the least pragmatic and the most artistic of the Baltic lot. They prove the point with myriad festivals and a merry, devil-may-care attitude – well, a subdued Nordic version of it.

When to Go
Rīga

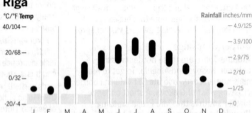

Jun–Aug Summer starts with an all-night solstice romp, then it's off to the beach.

Sep Refusing to let summer go, Rīgans sip lattes under heat lamps at al fresco cafes.

Dec Celebrate the festive season in the birthplace of the Christmas tree.

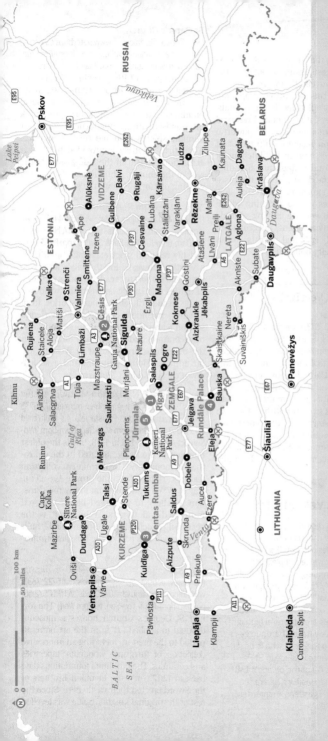

Latvia Highlights

1 Rīga (p742)
Clicking your camera at the nightmarish menagerie of devilish gargoyles, mythical beasts, praying goddesses and twisting vines that inhabits the city's surplus of art nouveau architecture.

2 Cēsis (p751)
Launching lighting raids into Gauja National Park from the castle fortress.

3 Ventas Rumba (p752) Joining swarms of fish trying to jump over the waterfall, the widest (and possibly the shortest) in Europe.

4 Rundāle Palace (p742) Sneaking away from the capital and indulging in aristocratic decadence.

5 Jūrmala (p749) Hobnobbing with Russian jetsetters in the heart of the swanky spa scene.

RĪGA

POP 643,000

The Gothic spires that dominate Rīga's cityscape might suggest austerity, but it is the flamboyant art nouveau that forms the flesh and the spirit of this vibrant cosmopolitan city, the largest of all three Baltic capitals. Like all northerners, it is quiet and reserved on the outside, but there is some powerful chemistry going on inside its hip bars and modern art centres, and in the kitchens of its cool experimental restaurants. Standing next to a gulf named after itself, Rīga is a short drive from jet-setting sea resort, Jūrmala, which comes with a stunning white-sand beach. But if you are craving solitude and a pristine environment, gorgeous sea dunes and blueberry-filled forests, begin right outside the city boundaries.

◉ Sights

◉ Old Rīga (Vecrīga)

★ Rīga Cathedral   CHURCH
(Rīgas Doms; ☑ 6722 7573; www.doms.lv; Doma laukums 1; admission €3; ☺ 10am-5pm Oct-Jun, 9am-6pm Sat-Tue, 9am-5pm Wed-Fri Jul-Sep) Founded in 1211 as the seat of the Rīga diocese, this enormous (once Catholic, now Evangelical Lutheran) cathedral is the largest medieval church in the Baltic. The architecture is an amalgam of styles from the 13th to the 18th centuries: the eastern end, the oldest portion, has Romanesque features; the tower is 18th-century baroque; and much of the rest dates from a 15th-century Gothic rebuilding.

WORTH A TRIP

THE BALTIC VERSAILLES

Built as a grand residence for the Duke of Courland, the magnificent **Rundāle Palace** (Rundāles pils; ☑ 6396 2274; www.rundale.net; whole complex/house longroute/short route/garden/short route & garden €9/6/4/4/7.50; ☺ 10am-5pm Nov-Apr, 10am-6pm May-Oct) is a monument-to 18th-century aristocratic ostentation, and rural Latvia's architectural highlight. It was designed by Italian baroque genius Bartolomeo Rastrelli, who is best known for the Winter Palace in St Petersburg. About 40 of the palace's 138 rooms are open to visitors, as are the wonderful formal gardens, inspired by those at Versailles.

St Peter's Church   CHURCH
(Sv Pētera baznīca; www.peterbaznica.riga.lv; Skārņu iela 19; adult/child €9/3; ☺ 10am-6pm Tue-Sat, noon-6pm Sun, to 7pm May-Aug) Forming the centrepiece of Rīga's skyline, this Gothic church is thought to be around 800 years old, making it one of the oldest medieval buildings in the Baltic. Its soaring red-brick interior is relatively unadorned, except for heraldic shields mounted on the columns. A colourful contrast is provided by the art exhibitions staged in the side aisles. At the rear of the church, a lift whisks visitors to a viewing platform 72m up the steeple.

★ Art Museum Rīga Bourse   MUSEUM
(Mākslas muzejs Rīgas Birža; ☑ 6732 4461; www.lnmm.lv; Doma laukums 6; adult/child €6/3; ☺ 10am-6pm Tue-Thu, Sat & Sun, to 8pm Fri) Rīga's lavishly restored stock exchange building is a worthy showcase for the city's art treasures. The elaborate facade features a coterie of deities that dance between the windows, while inside, gilt chandeliers sparkle from ornately moulded ceilings. The Oriental section features beautiful Chinese and Japanese ceramics and an Egyptian mummy, but the main halls are devoted to Western art, including a Monet painting and a scaled-down cast of Rodin's *The Kiss*.

Rīga History & Navigation Museum MUSEUM
(Rīgas vēstures un kuģniecības muzejs; ☑ 6735 6676; www.rigamuz.lv; Palasta iela 4; adult/child €4.27/0.71; ☺ 10am-5pm May-Sep, 11am-5pm Wed-Sun Oct-Apr) Founded in 1773, this is the oldest museum in the Baltic, situated in the old cathedral monastery. The permanent collection features artefacts from the Bronze Age all the way to WWII, ranging from lovely pre-Christian jewellery to preserved hands removed from Medieval forgers. A highlight is the beautiful neoclassical Column Hall, built when Latvia was part of the Russian empire.

Museum of Decorative
Arts & Design   MUSEUM
(Dekoratīvi lietišķās mākslas muzejs; ☑ 6722 7833; www.lnmm.lv; Skārņu iela 10/20; adult/child €5/2.50; ☺ 11am-5pm Tue & Thu-Sun, till 7pm Wed) The former St George's Church houses a museum devoted to applied art from the art nouveau period to the present, including an impressive collection of furniture, woodcuts, tapestries and ceramics. The building's foundations date back to 1207 when the Livonian Brothers of the Sword erected their castle here. Since the rest of the original knights' castle was levelled

by rioting citizens at the end of the same century, it is the only building that remains intact since the birth of Rīga.

★**Blackheads House** HISTORIC BUILDING
(Melngalvju nams; ☑6704 3678; www.melngalvjunams.lv; Rātslaukums 7) Built in 1344 as a veritable fraternity house for the Blackheads guild of unmarried German merchants, the original house was decimated in 1941 and flattened by the Soviets seven years later. Somehow the original blueprints survived and an exact replica of this fantastically ornate structure was completed in 2001 for Rīga's 800th birthday.

★**Arsenāls Exhibition Hall** GALLERY
(Izstāžu zāle Arsenāls; ☑6732 4461; www.lnmm.lv; Torņa iela 1; adult/child €3.50/2; ☺11am-6pm Tue, Wed & Fri, to 8pm Thu, noon-5pm Sat & Sun) Behind a row of spooky granite heads depicting Latvia's most prominent artists, the imperial arsenal, constructed in 1832 to store weapons for the Russian tzar's army, is now a prime spot for international and local art exhibitions, which makes it worth a visit whenever you are in Rīga. Also check out the massive wooden stairs at the back of the building – their simple yet funky geometry predates modern architecture.

◉ **Central Rīga (Centrs)**

Freedom Monument MONUMENT
(Brīvības bulvāris) Affectionately known as 'Milda', Rīga's Freedom Monument towers above the city between Old and Central Rīga. Paid for by public donations, the monument was designed by Kārlis Zāle and erected in 1935 where a statue of Russian ruler Peter the Great once stood.

Latvian National Museum of Art GALLERY
(Latvijas Nacionālā mākslas muzeja; ☑6732 4461; www.lnmm.lv; K Valdemāra iela 10a; adult/child €6/3; ☺10am-6pm Tue-Thu, to 8pm Fri, to 5pm Sat & Sun) Latvia's main gallery, sitting within the Esplanāde's leafy grounds, is an impressive building built in a baroque-classical style in 1905. Well-displayed paintings form a who's who of Latvian art from the 18th to late 20th centuries. Temporary exhibitions supplement the permanent collection.

★**Alberta iela** ARCHITECTURE
It's like a huge painting, which you can spend hours staring at, as your eye detects more and more intriguing details. But in fact this must-see Rīga sight is a rather functional street with residential houses, restaurants

ITINERARIES

Three Days
Fill your first two days with a feast of Rīga's architectural eye candy, then take a day trip to opulent **Rundāle Palace**.

One Week
Spend day four lazing on the beach and coveting the gracious wooden houses of **Jūrmala**. The following morning head west to **Kuldīga** before continuing on to **Ventspils**. Spend your last days exploring **Sigulda** and **Cēsis** within the leafy confines of **Gauja National Park**.

and shops. Art nouveau, otherwise known as Jugendstil, is the style, and the master responsible for most of these is Mikhail Eisenstein (father of filmmaker Sergei Eisenstein). Named after the founder of Rīga, Bishop Albert von Buxthoeven, the street was the architect's gift to Rīga on its 700th anniversary.

Nativity of Christ Cathedral CHURCH
(Kristus Piedzimšanas katedrāle; ☑6721 1207; www.pravoslavie.lv; Brīvības bulvāris 23; ☺7am-7pm) With gilded cupolas peeking through the trees, this Byzantine-styled Orthodox cathedral (1883) adds a dazzling dash of Russian bling to the skyline. During the Soviet period the church was converted into a planetarium but it's since been restored to its former use. Mind the dress code – definitely no shorts; women are asked to cover their heads.

◉ **Moscow Suburb (Maskavas forštate)**

This old part of Rīga takes its name from the main road to Moscow which runs through it. During the Nazi occupation it was the site of the Rīga Ghetto. In October 1941 the city's entire Jewish population (around 30,000 people) was crammed into the blocks east of Lāčplēša iela and enclosed by barbed wire. Later that year most of them were marched 10km to the Rumbula Forest where they were shot and buried in mass graves.

★**Rīga Central Market** MARKET
(Rīgas Centrāltirgus; ☑6722 9985; www.rct.lv; Nēģu iela 7; ☺7am-6pm) Haggle for your huckleberries at this vast market, housed in a series of WWI Zeppelin hangars and spilling outdoors as well. It's an essential Rīga experience, providing bountiful opportunities both

Rīga

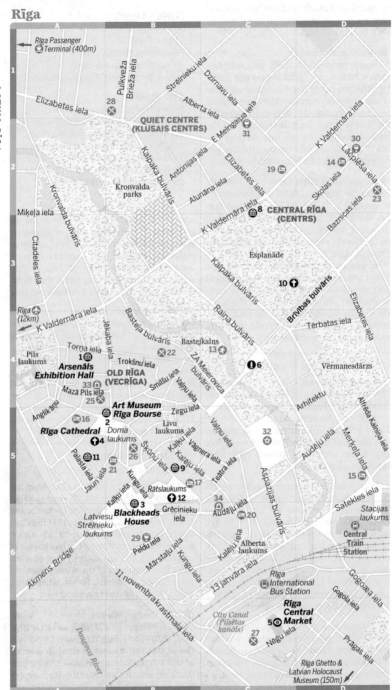

Scale: 0 — 400 m / 0 — 0.2 miles

Piens (550m)

Brīvības iela

Miera iela

Matīsa iela

Bruņinieku iela

Stabu iela

Ģertrūdes iela

Brīvības iela

Akas iela

Tērbatas iela

Martas

Blaumaņa iela

Dzirnavu iela

K Barona iela

Ģertrūdes iela

Lāčplēša iela

Baltā Pirts (1.5km)

A Čaka iela

Elizabetes iela

Mārijas iela

Blaumaņa iela

E Birznieka Upīša iela

Satekles iela

Turgeņeva iela

Timoteja iela

MOSCOW SUBURB (MASKAVAS FORŠTATE)

Rīga

◎ Top Sights

1	Arsenāls Exhibition Hall	A4
2	Art Museum Rīga Bourse	B5
3	Blackheads House	B6
4	Rīga Cathedral	A5
5	Rīga Central Market	C7

◎ Sights

6	Freedom Monument	C4
7	Latvian Academy of Science	E7
8	Latvian National Museum of Art	C2
9	Museum of Decorative Arts & Design	B5
10	Nativity of Christ Cathedral	C3
11	Rīga History & Navigation Museum	A5
12	St Peter's Church	B5

✪ Activities, Courses & Tours

13	Rīga By Canal	C4

⬚ Sleeping

14	Art Hotel Laine	D2
15	Cinnamon Sally	D5
16	Dome Hotel	A5
17	Ekes Konvents	B5
18	Hotel Bergs	E4
19	Hotel Valdemārs	C2
20	Naughty Squirrel	C6
21	Neiburgs	B5

✗ Eating

22	3 Pavaru	B4
23	Fazenda Bazārs	D2
24	Kasha Gourmet	E2
25	Ķiploku Krogs	A4
	Le Dome Fish Restaurant	(see 16)
26	LIDO Alus Sēta	B5
27	Siļķītes un Dillītes	C7
28	Vincents	B1

⊙ Drinking & Nightlife

29	Folksklub Ala Pagrabs	B6
30	Kaņepes Kultūras Centrs	D2
31	Left Door Bar	C2

✪ Entertainment

32	Latvian National Opera	C5

⬛ Shopping

33	Hobbywool	A4
34	Latvijas Balzāms	C6

for people-watching and to stock up for a picnic lunch. Although the number of traders is dwindling, the dairy and fish departments, each occupying a separate hangar, present a colourful picture of abundance that activates ancient foraging instincts in the visitors.

Rīga Ghetto &
Latvian Holocaust Museum MUSEUM
(☑ 6799 1784; www.rgm.lv; Maskavas iela 14A; adult/child €5/3; ⊘10am-6pm Sun-Fri) FREE The centrepiece of this rather modest museum is a wooden house with a reconstructed flat, like those where Jews had to move into when in 1941 the Nazis established a ghetto in this area of Rīga. Models of synagogues that used to stand in all major Latvian towns are exhibited in the ground floor of the house. Outside, there is a photographic exhibition detailing the Holocaust in Latvia.

🖝 Tours

E.A.T. Rīga WALKING, CYCLING
(☑ 22469888; www.eatriga.lv; tours from €15) Foodies may be initially disappointed to discover that the name stands for 'Experience Alternative Tours' and the focus is on off-the-beaten-track themed walking tours (Old Rīga, Art Nouveau, Alternative Rīga, Retro Rīga). But don't fret – Rīga Food Tasting is an option. It also offers a cycling tour of Jūrmala.

Rīga By Canal BOATING
(☑ 2591 1523; www.rigabycanal.lv; adult/child €18/9; ⊘10am-8pm May–mid-Oct) Enjoy a different perspective of the city aboard the century-old *Darling,* a charming wooden canal cruiser that belonged to the family of ABBA producer Stig Anderson and saw the entire band on board. There are three other boats in the fleet that paddle along the same loop around the city canal and Daugava River.

🛏 Sleeping

🛏 Old Rīga (Vecrīga)

★Naughty Squirrel HOSTEL €
(☑ 6722 0073; www.thenaughtysquirrel.com; Kalēju iela 50; dm €10-12, f €48-58; ✳@⊚) Slashes of bright paint and cartoon graffiti brighten up the city's capital of backpackerdom, which buzzes with travellers rattling the foosball table and chilling out in the TV room. Sign up for regular pub crawls, day trips to the countryside and summer BBQs.

★Cinnamon Sally HOSTEL €
(☑ 22042280; www.cinnamonsally.com; Merķeļa iela 1; dm €10-14; @⊚) Convenient for the train/bus stations, Cinnamon Sally comes with perfectly clean rooms, very helpful staff and a common area cluttered with sociable characters. It might feel odd to be asked to take off your shoes at the reception, but it's

all part of its relentless effort to create a homey atmosphere.

★Ekes Konvents HOTEL €€
(☑ 6735 8393; www.ekekonvents.lv; Skārņu iela 22; r €60; ⊚) Not to be confused with Konventa Sēta next door, the 600-year-old Ekes Konvents oozes wobbly medieval charm from every crooked nook and cranny. Curl up with a book in the adorable stone alcoves on the landing of each storey. Breakfast is served down the block.

★Dome Hotel HOTEL €€€
(☑ 6750 9010; www.domehotel.lv; Miesnieku iela 4; r €149-380; ⊚) It's hard to imagine that this centuries-old structure was once part of a row of butcheries. Today a gorgeous wooden staircase leads guests up to a charming assortment of uniquely decorated rooms that sport eaved ceilings, wooden panelling, upholstered furniture and picture windows with city views.

★Neiburgs HOTEL €€€
(☑ 6711 5522; www.neiburgs.com; Jaun iela 25/27; r €194-244; ✳⊚) Occupying one of Old Rīga's finest art nouveau buildings, Neiburgs blends preserved details with contemporary touches to achieve its signature boutique-chic style. Try for a room on one of the higher floors – you'll be treated to a view of a colourful clutter of gabled roofs and twisting medieval spires.

🛏 Central Rīga (Centrs)

★Art Hotel Laine HOTEL €€
(☑ 6728 8816; www.laine.lv; Skolas iela 11; s €55, d €65-77, superior d €126; P⊚) Embedded into an apartment block, with an antiquated lift taking guests to the reception on the 3rd floor, this place brings you closer to having your own home in Rīga than most hotels can or indeed wish to do. Dark green walls and armchair velvet, art on the walls, yesteryear bathtubs and furniture only complement the overall homey feeling.

Hotel Valdemārs HOTEL €€
(☑ 6733 4462; www.nordicchoicehotels.com; K Valdemāra iela 23; s/d €130/146; ✳⊚) Hidden within an art nouveau block, this Clarion Collection hotel is an excellent choice for those happy to trade fancy decor for reasonable rates. Most surprisingly, the hotel lays on breakfast, afternoon snacks and a simple dinner buffet for all guests. Prices drop significantly outside July.

Hotel Bergs   HOTEL €€€
(☑6777 0900; www.hotelbergs.lv; Elizabetes iela
83/85; ste from €187; P✳🐾🛜) A refurbished
19th-century building embellished with a
Scandi-sleek extension, Hotel Bergs embod-
ies the term 'luxury'. The spacious suites
are lavished with high-quality monochro-
matic furnishings and some have kitchens.
There's even a 'pillow menu', allowing guests
to choose from an array of different bed pillows based on material and texture.

✕ Eating

✕ Old Rīga (Vecrīga)

LIDO Alus Sēta   LATVIAN €
(☑6722 2431; www.lido.lv; Tirgoņu iela 6; mains
around €5; ⊙11am-10pm; 🛜) The pick of the
LIDO litter (Rīga's ubiquitous smorgasbord
chain), Alus Sēta feels like an old Latvian
brew house. It's popular with locals as well
as tourists – everyone flocks here for cheap
but tasty traditional fare and homemade
beer. Seating spills onto the cobbled street
during the warmer months.

Ķiploku Krogs   EUROPEAN €€
(Garlic Pub; ☑6721 1451; www.kiplokukrogs.lv;
Jēkaba iela 3/5; mains €7-14; ⊙noon-11pm) Vam-
pires beware – *everything* at this joint contains garlic, even the ice cream. The menu is
pretty hit-and-miss, but no matter what, it's
best to avoid the garlic pesto spread – it'll
taint your breath for days (trust us). Enter
from Mazā Pils.

★3 Pavaru   MODERN EUROPEAN €€€
(☑20370537; www.3pavari.lv; Torņa iela 4; mains
€17-28; ⊙noon-11pm) The stellar trio of chefs
who run the show have a jazzy approach to
cooking, with improvisation at the heart of
the compact and ever-changing menu. The
emphasis is on experiment (baked cod with
ox-tail stew, anyone?) and artful visual presentation that could have made Joan Miró
gasp in admiration.

Le Dome Fish Restaurant   SEAFOOD €€€
(☑6755 9884; www.zivjurestorans.lv; Miesnieku iela
4; mains €18-30; ⊙7am-11pm Mon-Fri, 8am-11pm
Sat & Sun; 🛜) The Dome Hotel's restaurant
quickly reminds diners that Rīga sits near a
body of water that's full of delicious fish. Service is impeccable and dishes (including some
meat and vegetarian options) are expertly
prepared, reflecting the eclectic assortment of
recipes in the modern Latvian lexicon.

ART NOUVEAU IN RĪGA

If you ask any Rīgan where to find the city's
world-famous art nouveau architecture, you
will always get the same answer: 'Look up!'

Rīga has the greatest number of art
nouveau buildings of any city in Europe.
More than 750 buildings boast this flamboyant style of decor which is also known
as Jugendstil, meaning 'youth style'. It
was named after Munich-based magazine, *Die Jugend*, which popularised it
around the turn of the 20th century.

Rīga's art nouveau district (known
more formally as the 'Quiet Centre') is
anchored around **Alberta iela** (p743)
– check out 2a, 4 and 13 in particular –
but you'll find fine examples throughout
the city. Don't miss the renovated facades of **Strēlnieku 4a** and **Elizabetes 10b** and **33**.

✕ Central Rīga (Centrs)

★Fazenda Bazārs   MODERN EUROPEAN €€
(☑6724 0809; www.fazenda.lv; Baznīcas iela 14;
mains €7-12; ⊙9am-10pm Mon-Fri, 10am-10pm
Sat, 11am-10pm Sun) Although right in the centre, this place feels like you've gone a long
way and suddenly found a warm tavern in
the middle of nowhere. Complete with a
tiled stove, this wooden house oozes mega-
tonnes of charm and the food on offer feels
as homey as it gets, despite its globalist fusion nature.

★Kasha Gourmet   MODERN EUROPEAN €€
(☑20201444; www.kasha-gourmet.com; Stabu iela
14; mains €8-17; ⊙10am-10pm Mon-Thu, 10am-11pm
Fri & Sat, 10am-8pm Sun) It might be that it does
succeed in making the food feel tastier by
turning the plate into a piece of modern art,
or perhaps it's the post-modernist mixture of
ingredients, but this is one of the most unusual and undervalued restaurants in Rīga.
We are particularly fond of its set breakfasts
beautifully laid out on wooden slabs.

★Vincents   EUROPEAN €€€
(☑6733 2830; www.restorans.lv; Elizabetes iela 19;
mains €28-37; ⊙6-10pm Tue-Sat) 🌿 Rīga's ritz-
iest restaurant has served royalty and rock
stars (Emperor Akihito, Prince Charles, El-
ton John) amid its eye-catching van Gogh–
inspired decor. The head chef, Martins Rit-
ins, is a stalwart of the Slow Food movement

AN ENCHANTING FOREST

If you don't have time to visit the Latvian countryside, a stop at the **Latvian Ethnographic Open-Air Museum** (Latvijas etnogrāfiskais brīvdabas muzejs; ☑ 6799 4106; www.brivdabasmuzejs.lv; Brīvības gatve 440; adult/child €4/1.40; ⊙ 10am-5pm, to 8pm May-Oct) is a must. Sitting along the shores of Lake Jugla just northeast of the city limits, this stretch of forest contains more than 100 wooden buildings (churches, windmills, farmhouses etc) from each of Latvia's four cultural regions. Take bus 1 from the corner of Merķeļa iela and Tērbatas iela to the 'Brīvdabas muzejs' stop.

and crafts his ever-changing menu mainly from produce sourced directly from small-scale Latvian farmers.

Moscow Suburb (Maskavas forštate)

Siļķītes un Dillītes　　　　　SEAFOOD €€
(www.facebook.com/SilkitesUnDillites; Centrāltirgus iela 3; mains €7-10; ⊙ 9am-5pm) Having explored fish stalls at the Rīga Central Market, one might ask: Where do I get it cooked? Well, Herring & Dill, as the name of this grungy kitchen-cum-bar translates, is right here and it'll do the cooking for you. Pick your fish and some minutes later it will be fried and served with veggies and chips. It's located in the passage between the fish and vegetable departments of the market.

Drinking & Nightlife

★**Folksklub Ala Pagrabs**　　　　BEER HALL
(☑ 27796914; www.folkklubs.lv; Peldu iela 19; ⊙ noon-midnight Sun, to 1am Mon & Tue, to 3am Wed, to 4am Thu & Fri, 2pm-4am Sat) A huge cavern filled with the bubbling magma of relentless beer-infused joy, folk-punk music, dancing and Latvian nationalism, this is an essential Rīga drinking venue, no matter what highbrowed locals say about it. The bar strives to reflect the full geography and diversity of Latvian beer production, but there is also plenty of local cider, fruit wine and *šmakouka* moonshine.

Left Door Bar　　　　　　　COCKTAIL BAR
(☑ 26300368; www.theleftdoorbar.lv; Antonijas iela 12; ⊙ noon-midnight Mon-Thu, noon-1am Fri,

6pm-1am Sat, 6pm-midnight Sun) Rīga's grand lodge of cocktails masters masquerades as an assuming bar in the art nouveau district. Never satisfied with past achievements, the award-winning prodigies in charge are constantly experimenting with the aim to impress globetrotting connoisseurs, not your average Joe. Each cocktail comes in individually shaped glasses.

★**Kaņepes Kultūras Centrs**　　　　　BAR
(☑ 29404405; www.kanepes.lv; Skolas iela 15; ⊙ 1pm-2am or later) The crumbling building of a former musical school, which half of Rīgans over 40 seem to have attended, is now a bar with a large outdoor area filled with an artsy studenty crowd. Wild dancing regularly erupts in the large room, where the parents of the patrons once suffered through their violin drills.

Piens　　　　　　　　　　　BAR, CLUB
(Milk; www.klubspiens.lv; Aristida Briāna iela 9; noon-midnight Sun-Tue, to 4pm Wed-Sat) Located up in the Miera iela area, this bar-club hybrid occupies a large chunk of industrial land. There's an appealing mix of eclectic decor, old sofas and sunny terraces.

☆ Entertainment

Latvian National Opera　　　OPERA, BALLET
(Latvijas Nacionālajā operā; ☑ 6707 3777; www.opera.lv; Aspazijas bulvāris 3) With a hefty international reputation as one of the finest opera companies in all of Europe, the national opera is the pride of Latvia. It's also home to the Rīga Ballet; locally born lad Mikhail Baryshnikov got his start here.

Arena Rīga　　　　　　　　　LIVE MUSIC
(☑ 6738 8200; www.arenariga.com; Skantes iela 21) This is the main venue for the most popular spectator sports, ice hockey and basketball. The 10,000-seat venue hosts dance revues and pop concerts when it is not being used for sporting events.

🔒 Shopping

Hobbywool　　　　　　　　ARTS & CRAFTS
(☑ 27072707; www.hobbywool.com; Mazā Pils iela 6; ⊙ 10am-6pm Mon-Sat, 11am-3pm Sun) It feels like walking into a Mark Rothko painting – the little shop is filled from top to bottom with brightly coloured knitted shawls, mittens, socks and jackets.

Latvijas Balzāms　　　　　　　DRINKS
(☑ 6708 1213; www.lb.lv; Audēju iela 8; ⊙ 9am-10pm) One of myriad branches of a popular

chain of liquor stores selling the trademark Latvian Black Balzām.

ⓘ Getting There & Away

Rīga is connected by air, bus, train and ferry to various international destinations.

BUS

Buses depart from **Rīga International Bus Station** (Rīgas starptautiskā autoosta; ☑ 9000 0009; www.autoosta.lv; Prāgas iela 1), located behind the railway embankment just beyond the southeastern edge of Old Rīga. Destinations include Sigulda (€2.15, one hour, every 45 minutes), Cēsis (€4.15, two hours, hourly), Kuldīga (€6.40, 2½ to 3½ hours, 11 daily) and Ventspils (€7.55, three hours, hourly).

TRAIN

Rīga's **central train station** (Centrālā stacija; ☑ 6723 2135; www.pv.lv; Stacijas laukums 2) is housed in a conspicuous glass-encased shopping centre near the Central Market. Destinations include Jūrmala (€1.40, 30 minutes, half-hourly), Sigulda (€2.35, 1¼ hours, 10 daily) and Cēsis (€3.50, 1¾ hours, five daily).

ⓘ Getting Around

TO/FROM THE AIRPORT

Rīga International Airport (Starptautiskā Lidosta Rīga; ☑1817; www.riga-airport.com; Mārupe District; ☐ 22) is in Skulte, 20km west of the city centre.

The cheapest way to get to central Rīga is bus 22 (€2, 25 minutes), which runs every 10 to 30 minutes and stops at several points around town. Taxis cost €12 to €15 and take about 15 minutes.

BICYCLE

Zip around town with **Sixt Bicycle Rental** (Sixt velo noma; ☑ 6767 6780; www.sixtbicycle.lv; per 30min/day €0.90/9). A handful of stands are conveniently positioned around Rīga and Jūrmala; simply choose your bike, call the rental service and receive the code to unlock your wheels.

PUBLIC TRANSPORT

The centre of Rīga is too compact for most visitors even to consider public transport, but trams, buses or trolleybuses may come in handy if you are venturing further out. For routes and schedules, consult www.rigassatiksme.lv. Tickets cost €1.15 (€0.30 for ISIC-holding students). Unlimited tickets are available for 24 hours (€5), three days (€10) and five days (€15). Tickets are available from Narvessen newspaper kiosks as well as vending machines on board new trams and in the underground pass by the train station.

TAXI

Taxis charge €0.60 to €0.80 per kilometre. Insist on having the meter on before you set off. Meters usually start running at around €1.50. It shouldn't cost more than €5 for a short journey (like crossing the Daugava for dinner in Ķīpsala). There are taxi ranks outside the bus and train stations, at the airport and in front of a few major hotels in Central Rīga, such as Radisson Blu Hotel Latvija.

AROUND RĪGA

If you're on a tight schedule, it's easy to get a taste of the Latvian countryside on day trips from Rīga. Within 75km of the capital are national parks, the country's grandest palace and long stretches of flaxen beach.

Jūrmala

POP 56,600

The Baltic's version of the French Riviera, Jūrmala is a long string of townships with grand wooden beach houses belonging to Russian oil tycoons and their supermodel trophy wives. Even during the height of communism, Jūrmala was a place to see and be seen. On summer weekends, jet-setters and day-tripping Rīgans flock to the resort town for some serious fun in the sun.

If you don't have a car or bicycle, you're best to head straight to the townships of Majori and Dzintari, the heart of the action. A 1km-long pedestrian street, Jomas iela, connects the two and is considered to be Jūrmala's main drag.

The highway connecting Rīga to Jūrmala was known as '10 Minutes in America' during Soviet times, because locally produced films set in the USA were always filmed on this busy asphalt strip. Motorists driving the 15km into Jūrmala must pay a €2 toll per day, even if they are just passing through. Keep an eye out for the multilane self-service toll stations sitting at both ends of the resort town.

◉ Sights

Jūrmala City Museum   MUSEUM
(☑ 6776 1915; www.facebook.com/JurmalasPilsetasMuzejsJurmalaCityMuseum; Tirgoņu iela 29; ◉10am-6pm Wed-Sun) FREE After a pricey renovation, this museum now features a beautiful permanent exhibit detailing Jūrmala's colourful history as *the* go-to resort town in the former USSR.

EAT LIKE A LATVIAN

Black Balzām The jet-black, 45%-proof concoction is a secret recipe of more than a dozen fairy-tale ingredients including oak bark, wormwood and linden blossoms. A shot a day keeps the doctor away, so say most of Latvia's pensioners. Try mixing it with a glass of cola to take the edge off.

Mushrooms A national obsession; mushroom-picking takes the country by storm during the first showers of autumn.

Alus For such a tiny nation there's definitely no shortage of *alus* (beer) – each major town has its own brew. You can't go wrong with Užavas (Ventspils' contribution).

Smoked fish Dozens of fish shacks dot the Kurzeme coast – look for the veritable smoke signals rising above the tree line. Grab 'em to go; they make the perfect afternoon snack.

Kvass Single-handedly responsible for the decline of Coca Cola at the turn of the 21st century, Kvass is a beloved beverage made from fermented rye bread. It's surprisingly popular with kids!

Rye Bread Apart from being tasty and arguably healthier than their wheat peers, these large brown loafs have aesthetic value too, matching nicely the dark wood of Latvia's Nordic interiors.

🛏 Sleeping & Eating

⭐**Hotel MaMa**   BOUTIQUE HOTEL **€€€**
(☑ 6776 1271; www.hotelmama.lv; Tirgoņu iela 22; r €175-360; 🖥) The bedroom doors have thick, mattress-like padding on the interior (psycho-chic?) and the suites themselves are a veritable blizzard of white drapery. A mix of silver paint and pixie dust accents the ultramodern furnishings and amenities. If heaven had a bordello, it would look something like this.

⭐**36.Line**   LATVIAN **€€€**
(☑ 22010696; www.36line.com; Līnija 36; mains €14-33; ⊙ 11am-11pm; ☑) Popular local chef Lauris Alekseyevs delivers modern twists on traditional Latvian dishes at this wonderful restaurant, occupying a slice of sand at the eastern end of Jūrmala. Enjoy the beach, then switch to casual attire for lunch or glam up for dinner. In the evening it's not uncommon to find DJs spinning beats.

ℹ Getting There & Away

Two to three trains per hour link central Rīga to the sandy shores of Jūrmala. Most visitors disembark at Majori station (€1.50, 30 minutes).

The river boat *New Way* departs from Rīga Riflemen Sq and docks in Majori near the train station. The journey takes one hour, and only runs on weekends.

Sigulda

POP 16,700

With a name that sounds like a mythical ogress, it's fitting that the gateway to Gauja National Park is an enchanted little spot. Locals proudly call their pine-peppered town the 'Switzerland of Latvia', but if you're expecting a mountainous snowcapped realm, you'll be rather disappointed. Instead, Sigulda is a magical mix of scenic walking and cycling trails, extreme sports and 800-year-old castles steeped in colourful legends.

👁 Sights

⭐**Turaida Museum Reserve**   CASTLE
(Turaidas muzejrezervāts; ☑ 67971402; www.turaida-muzejs.lv; Turaidas iela 10; adult/child €5/1.15, in winter €3/0.70; ⊙ 9am-8pm May-Sep, 9am-7pm Oct, 10am-5pm Nov-Mar, 10am-7pm Apr) Turaida means 'God's Garden' in ancient Livonian, and this green knoll capped with a fairy-tale castle is certainly a heavenly place. The redbrick castle with its tall cylindrical tower was built in 1214 on the site of a Liv stronghold. A museum inside the castle's 15th-century granary offers an interesting account of the Livonian state from 1319 to 1561, and additional exhibitions can be viewed in the 42m-high Donjon Tower, and the castle's western and southern towers.

🏃 Activities

Bobsled Track   ADVENTURE SPORTS
(Bob trase; ☑ 6797 3813; www.bobtrase.lv; Šveices iela 13; ⊙ noon-5pm Sat & Sun) Sigulda's 1200m bobsled track was built for the Soviet team. In winter you can fly down the 16-bend track at 80km/h in a five-person Vučko **soft bob** (per adult/child €10/7, from November to March). Summer speed fiends can ride

a wheeled **summer bob** (per adult/child €10/7, from May to September).

Aerodium   ADVENTURE SPORTS
(☑ 28384400; www.aerodium.lv; 2min/4min €45/65) The one-of-a-kind aerodium is a giant wind tunnel that propels participants up into the sky as though they were flying. Instructors can get about 15m high, while first-timers usually rock out at about 3m. To find the site, look for the sign along the A2 highway, 4km west of Sigulda.

Cable Car Bungee Jump   ADVENTURE SPORTS
(☑ 28383333; www.bungee.lv; Poruka iela 14; bungee jump from €40; ⊙ 6.30pm, 8pm & 9.30pm Wed-Sun Apr-Oct) Take your daredevil shenanigans to the next level with a 43m bungee jump from the bright-orange cable car that glides over the Gauja River. For an added thrill, jump naked.

Tarzāns Adventure Park   ADVENTURE SPORTS
(Piedzīvojumu Parks Tarzāns; ☑ 27001187; www.tarzans.lv; Peldu iela 1; adult/child combo €35/25, toboggan €3.50/1.50, ropes course €17/10; ⊙ 10am-8pm May-Oct) Head here to swish down a toboggan track or monkey around on the 'Tarzan' ropes course. There's also a chairlift, tube-sliding, reverse bungee, giant swing, jungle climb and archery.

🛏 Sleeping & Eating

Līvkalni   B&B €€
(☑ 22825739; livkalnisigulda@gmail.com; Pēteralas iela 2; s/d from €45/55; 🅿 ❄ 🛜) No place is more romantically rustic than this idyllic retreat next to a pond on the forest's edge. The rooms are pine-fresh and sit among a campus of adorable thatch-roof manors.

★ Mr Biskvīts   CAFE, BAKERY €
(☑ 6797 6611; www.mr.biskvits.lv; Ausekļa iela 9; mains €4-8; ⊙ 8am-9pm Mon-Fri, 9am-9pm Sat, 9am-7pm Sun) Naughty Mr Biskvīts' candy-striped lair is filled with delicious cakes and pastries, but it's also a good spot for a cooked breakfast, a lunchtime soup or sandwich, and an evening pasta or stir-fry. The coffee's great too.

❶ Getting There & Around

Trains run to/from Rīga (€2.35, one or 1¼ hours) and Cēsis (€2, 40 minutes, five daily).

There are also buses to Rīga (€2.15, one hour, every 30 minutes between 8am and 10.30pm) and Cēsis (€1.85, 1½ hours, daily).

Cēsis

With its stunning medieval castle, cobbled streets, green hills and landscaped garden, Cēsis is simply the cutest little town in the whole of Latvia. There is a lot of history there, too. The place started eight centuries ago as a Livonian Order's stronghold in the land of unruly pagans and saw horrific battles right under (or inside) the castle walls. Although it's an easy day trip from Rīga, Cēsis is definitely worth a longer stay, especially since there is the whole of Gauja National Park around it to explore.

◉ Sights

★ Cēsis Castle   CASTLE
(Cēsu pils; ☑ 6412 1815; www.cesupils.lv; both castles adult/student €5/2.50, tours from €35; ⊙ 10am-6pm daily May-Sep, 10am-5pm Tue-Sat, 10am-4pm Sun Oct-Apr) It is actually two castles in one. The first is the sorrowful dark-stone towers of the old Wenden castle. Founded by Livonian knights in 1214, it was sacked by Russian tsar Ivan the Terrible in 1577, but only after its 300 defenders blew themselves up with gunpowder. The other is the more cheerful castle-like 18th-century manor house once inhabited by the dynasty of German counts von Sievers. It houses a museum that features original fin de siècle interiors.

🛏 Sleeping & Eating

Hotel Cēsis   HOTEL €€
(☑ 6412 0122; www.facebook.com/hotelcesis; Vienības laukums 1; s/d €45/60; @ 🛜) The exterior is vaguely neoclassical while the inside features rows of standard upmarket rooms. The in-house restaurant serves top-notch Latvian and European cuisine in a formal setting or outdoors in the pristine garden.

★ Izsalkušais Jānis   MODERN EUROPEAN €€
(☑ 29262001; www.izsalkusaisjanis.lv; Valmieras iela 1; mains €9-16; ⊙ noon-11pm) The town's old fire depot has changed profession and now helps to extinguish hunger and thirst with a compact but powerful menu that takes Cēsis to a metropolitan level of culinary sophistication. Hot trout salad is our personal fave. It also bakes its own delicious bread.

❶ Getting There & Away

Four to five trains a day travel to/from Rīga (€3.50, 1¾ hours) and Sigulda (€2, 45 minutes).

There are also buses to Rīga (€4.15, two hours, hourly) and Sigulda (€1.85, 1½ hours, daily).

WESTERN LATVIA

Latvia's westernmost province, Kurzeme (Courland), offers the simple delights of beautiful beaches and a scattering of historic towns. It's hard to imagine that this low-key region once had imperial aspirations but during the 17th century, while still a semi-independent vassal of the Polish-Lithuanian Commonwealth, the Duchy of Courland had a go at colonising Tobago and the Gambia. The Great Northern War put paid to that, after which the Duchy was subsumed into the Russian Empire.

Kuldīga

Lovely old Kuldīga would be a hit even if it didn't have its own Niagara of sorts, with salmon flying over its chute for good measure. Home to what Latvians brand 'the widest waterfall in Europe', Kuldīga is also the place where your immersion into the epoch of chivalry won't be spoiled by day-tripping camera-clickers – the place is simply too far from Rīga.

In its heyday, Kuldīga (or Goldingen, as its German founders called it) served as the capital of the Duchy of Courland (1596–1616), but it was badly damaged during the Great Northern War and never quite able to regain its former lustre. Today, this blast from the past is a favourite spot to shoot Latvian period-piece films.

◎ Sights

Ventas Rumba
(Kuldīga Waterfall) WATERFALL
In a country that is acutely short of verticals but rich on horizontals, landscape features appear to be blatantly two-dimensional – even waterfalls. Spanning 240m, Ventas Rumba is branded Europe's widest, but as it is hardly taller than a basketball player, it risks being dismissed by vile competitors as a mere rapid, if it decides to attend an international waterfall congress. That said, it does look like a cute toy Niagara, when observed from the Kuldīga castle hill.

⊨ Sleeping & Eating

★2 Baloži GUESTHOUSE €€
(☑29152888; www.facebook.com/2balozi; Pasta iela 5; r from €50) Perched above the Alekšupīte stream, this old wooden house has newly refurbished rooms designed in the laconic Scandinavian style with lots of aged wood that creates a pleasant nostalgic ambience. Goldingen Room restaurant across the square serves as the reception.

★Pagrabiņš INTERNATIONAL €€
(☑6632 0034; www.pagrabins.lv; Baznīcas iela 5; mains €5-15; ⊙11am-11pm Mon-Thu, to 3am Fri & Sat, noon-11pm Sun; ☑) Pagrabiņš inhabits a cellar that was once used as the town's prison. Today a combination of Latvian and Asian dishes are served under low-slung alcoves lined with honey-coloured bricks. In warmer weather, enjoy your snacks on the small verandah, which sits atop the trickling Alekšupīte stream out the back.

❶ Getting There & Away

Buses run to/from Rīga (€6.40, three hours, 11 daily) and Ventspils (€6, 1¼ hours, six daily).

Ventspils

Fabulous amounts of oil and shipping money have given Ventspils an economic edge over Latvia's other small cities, and although locals coddle their Užavas beer and claim that there's not much to do, tourists will find a weekend's worth of fun in the form of brilliant beaches, well-maintained parks and interactive museums.

◎ Sights

Open-Air Museum of the Coast MUSEUM
(Ventspils jūras zvejniecības brīvdabas muzejs; ☑6322 4467; www.muzejs.ventspils.lv; Riņķu iela 2; adult/child €1.40/0.60; ⊙10am-6pm Tue-Sun May-Oct, by appointment winter) For centuries, life in Kurzeme revolved around seafaring and fishing. Occupying vast parkland territory, the museum features a collection of fishing crafts, anchors and traditional log houses, brought from coastal villages north and south of Ventspils. A bonus attraction is a narrow-gauge railway, built by the occupying Germans in 1916.

⊨ Sleeping & Eating

Kupfernams B&B €€
(☑27677107; www.hotelkupfernams.lv; Kārļa iela 5; s/d €44/65; ☎) Our favourite spot to spend the night, this charming wooden house at the centre of the Old Town has a set of cheery upstairs rooms with slanted ceilings, opening onto a communal lounge. Below, there's a cafe and a hair salon.

Skroderkrogs LATVIAN €€
(☑ 6362 7634; Skroderu iela 6; mains €6-13; ☉ 11am-10pm) If you're after big serves of Latvian comfort food in a pleasant local setting (candles and flowers on tables fashioned from old sewing machines), this is the place to come.

ⓘ Getting There & Away

Ventspils is served by buses to/from Rīga (€7.50, 2¾ to four hours, hourly) and Kuldīga (€3, 1¼ hours, five daily).

SURVIVAL GUIDE

ⓘ Directory A–Z

FESTIVALS & EVENTS
Check out Kultura (www.culture.lv) for a yearly listing of festivals and events across the country. At midsummer, the cities empty out as locals head to the countryside for traditional celebrations.

GAY & LESBIAN TRAVELLERS
Homosexuality was decriminalised in 1992 and an equal age of consent applies (16 years). However, negative attitudes towards gays and lesbians are the norm and violent attacks occasionally occur. Rīga has a few gay venues and in 2015 it became the first former-Soviet city to host Europride.

INTERNET RESOURCES
Latvia Travel www.latvia.travel
Latvian Institute www.li.lv
Latvian Yellow Pages www.1188.lv

TELEPHONE
There are no area codes in Latvia. All telephone numbers have eight digits; landlines start with 6 and mobile numbers with 2.

ⓘ Getting There & Away

AIR
Fifteen European airlines fly into Rīga, including the national carrier airBaltic.

LAND
In 2007 Latvia acceded to the Schengen Agreement, which removed all border control between Estonia and Lithuania. Carry your travel documents with you at all times, as random border checks do occur.

Bus
Ecolines Routes include Rīga–Parnu–Tallinn (€17, four to 4¾ hours, seven daily), Rīga–Tartu (€7, four hours, two daily), Rīga–Vilnius (€17, four hours, seven daily), Rīga–Vilnius–Minsk (€24, eight hours, daily) and Rīga–Moscow (€60, 14 hours, daily).

Kautra/Eurolines (www.eurolines.lt) Operates buses on the Rīga–Vilnius–Warsaw–Berlin–Cologne route (€116, 29 hours).

Lux Express & Simple Express Routes include Rīga–Pärnu–Tallinn (from €13, 4½ hours, 11 daily), Rīga–Tartu–St Petersburg (from €23, 12 hours, four daily), Rīga–Vilnius (from €11, four hours, 10 daily) and Rīga–Kaliningrad (€20, eight hours, daily).

Train
International trains head from Rīga to Moscow (16 hours), St Petersburg (15 hours) and Minsk (12 hours) daily. There are no direct trains to Estonia; you'll need to change at Valka.

ⓘ Getting Around

BUS
⇒ Buses are generally more frequent than trains and serve more of the country.
⇒ Updated timetables are available at www.1188.lv and www.autoosta.lv.

CAR & MOTORCYCLE
⇒ Driving is on the right-hand side.
⇒ Headlights must be on at all times.
⇒ Local car-hire companies usually allow you to drive in all three Baltic countries but not beyond.

TRAIN
⇒ There are train services from Rīga to Jūrmala, Sigulda and Cēsis.
⇒ Timetables are online at www.1188.lv and www.ldz.lv.

COUNTRY FACTS
Area 64,589 sq km
Capital Rīga
Country Telephone Code ☑ 371
Currency euro (€)
Emergency ☑ 112
Language Latvian
Money ATMs easy to find.
Population 2 million
Visas Not required for citizens of the EU, Australia, Canada, New Zealand and the USA, among others, for stays of up to 90 days. For further information, visit www.mfa.gov.lv.

Lithuania

Includes ➔

Best Places to Eat

➔ Balzac (p759)

➔ Senoji Kibininė (p761)

➔ Lokys (p759)

➔ Sweet Root (p759)

Best Places to Stay

➔ Bernardinu B&B (p757)

➔ Miško Namas (p765)

➔ Litinterp Guesthouse (p764)

➔ Domus Maria (p758)

Why Go?

Little Lithuania has so much to offer. Those with a passion for baroque architecture, ancient castles and archaeological treasures will find plenty in the capital and beyond. There are sculpture parks and interactive museums for the historically curious; modern art spaces for the more contemporary-minded; and all-night clubbing for those requiring something less cerebral.

Away from the cities, the pristine beaches and giant sand dunes on the west coast are a must-see. The Hill of Crosses is an unexpected delight. Elsewhere, the country's woods and lakes come alive in summer with cyclists, berry pickers and campers.

When to Go
Vilnius

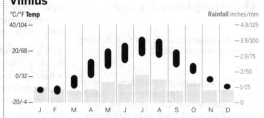

Apr Some of the world's best jazz performers are at the Kaunas International Jazz Festival.

Jun & Jul The loveliest time to explore the forests and sand dunes of the Curonian Spit.

Sep Vilnius Capital Days, a celebration of the capital with street theatre, music and fashion.

Lithuania Highlights

1 Vilnius (p755) Exploring Lithuania's beautiful baroque capital with its cobbled streets, church spires, bars and bistros.

2 Curonian Spit (p765) Breathing pure air amid fragrant pine forests and high sand dunes.

3 Hill of Crosses (p763) Hearing the wind whistle between thousands of crosses at this eerie pilgrimage site, near Šiauliai.

4 Trakai (p761) Wandering this historic city, home of the Karaite people and a stunning island castle.

5 Grūtas Park (p761) Experiencing a taste of Lithuania's communist past.

6 Ninth Fort (p762) Taking in the poignant WWII history of Kaunas' memorial.

VILNIUS

♪ 5 / POP 546,700

Lithuania's capital, Vilnius, doesn't get the attention it deserves. The city's surprising Old Town is a dazzling assemblage of bright baroque houses, inviting alleyways and colourful churches built around quiet courtyards. But this is no museum piece. The city's cosmopolitan heritage, enriched by Polish, Jewish and Russian influences, lends a sophisticated vibe, and thousands of students keep the energy level high.

⊙ Sights

◉ Cathedral Square & Gediminis Hill

Cathedral Square (Katedros aikštė), dominated by Vilnius Cathedral (p756) and its

57m-tall belfry, marks the centre of Vilnius and is home to the city's most important sights.

Gediminas Castle & Museum MUSEUM

(Gedimino Pilis ir Muziejus; ☑ 5-261 7453; www.lnm.lt; Gediminas Hill, Arsenalo gatvė 5; adult/child €2/1; ☺ 10am-7pm daily Apr-Sep, 10am-5pm Tue-Sun Oct-Mar) With its prime hilltop location above the junction of the Neris and Vilnia rivers, Gediminas Castle is the last of a series of settlements and fortified buildings occupying this site since Neolithic times. This brick version, built by Grand Duke Vytautas in the early 15th century, offers commanding 360-degree views of Vilnius, and an exhibition tracing the history of the castle across the centuries, complete with scale models.

★ Palace of the Grand Dukes of Lithuania MUSEUM

(Valdovų Rumai; ☑ 5-212 7476; www.valdovurumai.lt; Katedros aikštė 4; adult/student €3/1.50, guided tour €22; ☺ museum 10am-6pm Tue, Wed, Fri & Sat, to 8pm Thu, to 4pm Sun) On a site that has been settled since at least the 4th century AD stands the latest in a procession of fortified palaces, repeatedly remodelled, extended, destroyed, and rebuilt over the centuries. What visitors now see is a painstaking restoration of its final grand manifestation, the baroque palace built for the Grand Dukes in the 17th century. While the gleamingly white complex is evidently new, it contains fascinating historical remains, and is a potent symbol of revitalised, independent Lithuania.

ITINERARIES

Three Days

Devote two days to exploring the baroque heart of **Vilnius**, then day trip to **Trakai** for its island castle and the homesteads of the Karaite people, stopping off at **Paneriai** on the way.

One Week

Spend four nights in **Vilnius**, with day trips to both **Trakai** and the **Kernavė Cultural Reserve**. Travel cross-country to the **Hill of Crosses**, near Šiauliai, then explore some serious nature on the **Curonian Spit** for two or three days. Head back east via **Klaipėda** and **Kaunas**.

National Museum of Lithuania MUSEUM

(Lietuvos Nacionalinis Muziejus; ☑ 5-262 7774; www.lnm.lt; Arsenalo gatvė 1; adult/child €2/1; ☺ 10am-6pm Tue-Sun) FREE Building on the collections complied by the Museum of Antiquities since 1855, this splendid museum shows artefacts from Lithuanian life from Neolithic times to the 20th century. It has special collections devoted to the country's different folk traditions, to numismatics (including some of the very first Lithuanian coins) and to burial goods. A statue of Mindaugas, Lithuania's sole king, stands guard over the entrance.

Vilnius Cathedral CATHEDRAL

(Vilniaus Arkikatedra; ☑ 5-261 0731; www.katedra.lt; Katedros aikštė 1; crypts adult/child €4.50/2.50; ☺ 7am-7pm, crypts 10am-4pm Mon-Sat) Known in full as the Cathedral of St Stanislav and St Vladislav, this national symbol occupies a spot originally used for the worship of Perkūnas, the Lithuanian thunder god. Seventeenth-century St Casimir's Chapel, with its a baroque cupola, coloured marble and frescoes of the saint's life, is the showpiece, while the crypts (10am to 4pm Monday to Saturday, adult/child €4.50/2.50) are the final resting place of many prominent Lithuanians, including Vytautas the Great (1350–1430). The website has details of Mass.

◉ Old Town

★ Vilnius University HISTORIC BUILDING

(Vilniaus Universitetas; ☑ 5-268 7298; www.muziejus.vu.lt; Universiteto gatvė 3; architectural ensemble adult/child €1.50/0.50; ☺ 9am-6pm Mon-Sat Mar-Oct, 9.30am-5.30pm Mon-Sat Nov-Feb) Founded in 1579 during the Counter-Reformation, Vilnius University was run by Jesuits for two centuries and became one of the greatest centres of Polish learning. It produced many notable scholars but was closed by the Russians in 1832 and didn't reopen until 1919. Today it has 23,000 students and Lithuania's oldest library, shelving five million books (including one of two originals of *The Catechism* by Martynas Mažvydas, the first book ever published in Lithuanian).

Gates of Dawn HISTORIC BUILDING

(Aušros Vartai; ☑ 5-212 3513; www.ausrosvartai.lt; Aušros Vartų gatvė 12; ☺ 6am-7pm) FREE The southern border of Old Town is marked by the last-standing of five portals that were once built into the city walls. A suitably grand way to enter one of the best-preserved

JEWISH VILNIUS

Over the centuries Vilnius developed into one of Europe's leading centres of Jewish life and scholarship until the community was brutally wiped out by the occupying Nazis and their Lithuanian sympathisers during WWII. The former Jewish quarter lay in the streets west of Didžioji gatvė, including present-day Žydų gatvė (Jews St) and Gaono gatvė, named after Vilnius' most famous Jewish resident, Gaon Elijahu ben Shlomo Zalman (1720–97).

The **Tolerance Centre** (☑5-262 9666; www.jmuseum.lt; Naugarduko gatvė 10/2; adult/concession €3/1.50; ☉10am-6pm Mon-Thu, to 4pm Fri & Sun), a beautifully restored former Jewish theatre, houses thought-provoking displays on the history and culture of Jews in Lithuania before the Shoah (Holocaust) and occasional art exhibitions. The **Holocaust Museum** (Holokausto Muziejus; ☑5-262 0730; www.jmuseum.lt; Pamėnkalnio gatvė 12; adult/child €3/1.50; ☉9am-5pm Mon-Thu, 9am-4pm Fri, 10am-4pm Sun), in the so-called Green House, is an unvarnished account detailing the suffering of the Lithuanian Jews in an unedited display of horrific images and letters by local Holocaust survivors.

Vilnius' only remaining synagogue, the **Choral Synagogue** (Choralinė Sinagoga; ☑5-261 2523; Pylimo gatvė 39; donations welcome; ☉10am-2pm Mon-Fri) **FREE**, was built in a Moorish style in 1903 and survived only because the Nazis used it as a medical store.

---

sections of the Old Town, it's also the site of the Gate of Dawn Chapel of Mary the Mother of Mercy and the 'Vilnius Madonna', a 17th-century painting of Our Lady said to work miracles.

St Anne's Church   CHURCH

(Šv Onos Bažnyčia; ☑8-698 17731; www.onosbaznycia.lt; Maironio gatvė 8-1; ☉10.30am-6.30pm Tue-Sat, 8am-5pm May-Sep, 4.30-6.30pm Tue-Fri, 10.30am-6.30pm Sat, 8am-5pm Sun Oct-Apr) This gorgeous, late-15th-century Gothic church is a tiny confection of red brick, glass and arches, dwarfed by the Bernadine Church outside which it stands. Marrying 33 different kinds of brick into a whole that many regard as the most beautiful in Vilnius, it's reputed that Napoleon was so charmed by St Anne's that he wanted to relocate it to Paris.

⊙ New Town & Outside the City Centre

★Museum of Genocide Victims   MUSEUM

(Genocido Aukų Muziejus; ☑5-249 8156; www.genocid.lt/muziejus; Aukų gatvė 2a; adult/discount €4/1; ☉10am-6pm Wed-Sat, to 5pm Sun) This former headquarters of the KGB (and before them the Gestapo, Polish occupiers and Tsarist judiciary) houses a museum dedicated to thousands of Lithuanians who were murdered, imprisoned or deported by the Soviet Union from WWII until the 1960s. Memorial plaques honouring those who perished tile the outside of the building. Inside, floors cover the harsh realities of Soviet occupa-

tion, including gripping personal accounts of Lithuanian deportees to Siberia.

★Antakalnis Cemetery   CEMETERY

(off Karių kapų gatvė; ☉9am-dusk) One of Eastern Europe's most beautiful graveyards lies in this leafy suburb, a short stroll east of the centre. Those killed by Soviet special forces on 13 January 1991 are buried here; a sculpture of the Madonna cradling her son memorialises them. Another memorial honours Napoleonic soldiers who died of starvation and injuries in Vilnius while retreating from the Russian army. The remains of 2000 of them were only found in 2002.

🛏 Sleeping

Jimmy Jumps House   HOSTEL €

(☑5-231 3847; www.jimmyjumpshouse.com; Savičiaus gatvė 12-1; dm €11-13, r from €30; ❂@🛜) This clean, well-run, centrally located hostel is justifiably popular among backpackers. The pine-wood bunks are modest in four- to 12-bed rooms, but extras like free walking tours, themed pub crawls and a free breakfast add up to money well spent. Offers discounts if booked directly via email. No credit cards.

★Bernardinu B&B   GUESTHOUSE €€

(☑5-261 5134; www.bernardinuhouse.com; Bernardinų gatvė 5; r without bathroom €45-50, r with bathroom €50-70; P❊🛜) This charming family-owned guesthouse is on one of the most picturesque lanes in the Old Town. The 18th-century townhouse has been sensitively renovated, preserving elements like

Central Vilnius

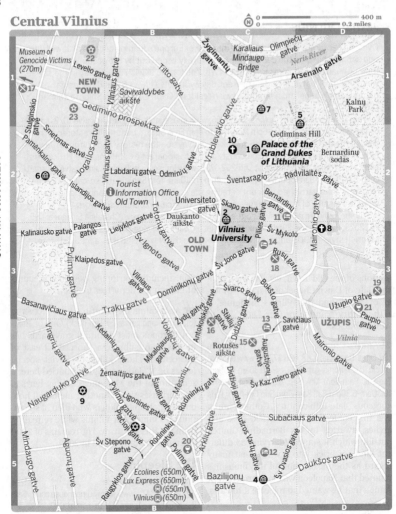

old timber flooring and ceilings, and with stripped patches of brick allowing you to see through the patina of the years. Breakfast (€4) is brought to your door on a tray.

Domus Maria   GUESTHOUSE **€€**
(☎5-264 4880; www.domusmaria.lt; Aušros Vartų gatvė 12; s/d €62/85; P⊜@🖥) The guesthouse of the Vilnius archdiocese is housed in a former monastery dating to the 17th century and oozes charm. Accommodation is in the monks' chambers, but they've been given a thorough, stylish makeover. Two rooms, 207 and 307, have views of the Gates of Dawn and are usually booked far in advance. Breakfast is served in the vaulted refectory.

★ Narutis   HISTORIC HOTEL **€€€**
(☎5-212 2894; www.narutis.com; Pilies gatvė 24; r €109-139; P❋@🖥) Housed in a red-brick townhouse built in 1581, this classy pad has been a hotel since the 16th century. Breakfast and dinner are served in a vaulted Gothic cellar, there's wi-fi access throughout, and free apples at reception add a tasty touch. Booking over the internet can yield substantial savings.

Central Vilnius

✗ Eating

★Senamiesčio Krautuvė LITHUANIAN €
(☑5-231 2836; www.senamiesciokrautuve.lt; Literatų gatvė 5; ☉10am-8pm Mon-Sat, 11am-5pm Sun) Look no further than this wonderful, quiet hobbit-hole for the very best Lithuanian comestibles, many unique to the country. Cured meats, fresh sausages, cheeses, fresh fruit and vegetables, honey and preserves, breads and pastries: all are arranged in irresistible profusion around the walls of this snug trove on Literatų gatvė.

Radharanė VEGETARIAN €
(☑5-212 3186; www.radharane.lt; Gediminio prospektas 32; mains €4; ☉11am-9pm Mon-Fri, 11.30am-9pm Sat & Sun; ☑) In a town where light, tasty vegetarian fare isn't thick on the ground, Radharanė's Indian-with-a-Lithuanian-twist fare is a godsend. Try the kofta, paneer with eggplant, channa dahl: all served with rice and salad, it's all good.

★Balzac FRENCH €€
(☑8-614 89223; www.balzac.lt; Savičiaus gatvė 7; mains €12-15; ☉11.30am-11pm Mon-Thu, to midnight Fri & Sat, to 9pm Sun) This classic French bistro serves what may be the best French food in Vilnius. Alongside bistro staples, such as *tournedos de boeuf* and duck confit, you'll find a great selection of seafood, some flown fresh from France. While there's a summer terrace, the dining area is small, so book to avoid disappointment.

★Lokys LITHUANIAN €€€
(☑5-262 9046; www.lokys.lt; Stiklių gatvė 8; mains €10-19; ☉noon-midnight) Track down the big wooden bear to find this Vilnius institution, making merry in the vaulted 16th-century cellars of a former merchant's house since 1972. As a 'hunters' restaurant', it does a strong line in game, including roast venison and boar, game sausages, quail with pear and cowberry, and even beaver stewed with mushrooms. Folk musicians play in summer.

Sweet Root LITHUANIAN €€€
(☑8-685 60767; www.sweetroot.lt; Užupio gatvė 22; 7-course degustation €65; ☉6-11pm Tue-Sat) Sweet Root is proof that the (ironically international) trend towards 'locavorism' has reached high-end dining in Vilnius. In a smart if formulaic modern dining room (complete with open kitchen and tattooed chefs) you can enjoy modern dishes using Lithuanian ingredients, such as dock leaves, catmint, snails, beetroot leaves and freshwater fish.

☕ Drinking & Nightlife

Bukowski BAR
(☑8-640 58855; www.facebook.com/bukowski-pub; Visų Šventų gatvė 7; ☉11am-midnight Sun-Wed, to 5am Thu-Sat) The eponymous Barfly is the spiritual patron of this charismatic boho bar in a less-trodden pocket of the Old Town. It has a back terrace for finer weather, great beers on tap, a full program of poetry, music and other events, and a welcoming, unpretentious atmosphere. One of Vilnius' best.

Špunka BAR
(☑8-652 32361; www.spunka.lt; Užupio gatvė 9; ☉3-10pm Tue-Sun, from 5pm Mon) This tiny, charismatic bar does a great line in craft

ales from Lithuania and further afield. If you need sustenance to keep the drink and chat flowing, local cheese and charcuterie are on hand.

☆ Entertainment

Lithuanian National Opera & Ballet Theatre OPERA
(Lietuvos Nacionalinis Operos ir Baleto Teatras; ☑ 5-262 0727; www.opera.lt; Vienuolio gatvė 1; ⊙ box office 10am-7pm Mon-Fri, to 6.30pm Sat, to 3pm Sun) This stunning (or gaudy, depending on your taste) Soviet-era building, with its huge, cascading chandeliers and grandiose dimensions, is home to Lithuania's national ballet and opera companies. You can see world-class performers for as little as €4 (or as much as €200...).

Small Theatre of Vilnius THEATRE
(Vilniaus Mažasis Teatras; ☑ 5-249 9869; www.vmt.lt; Gedimino prospektas 22) Founded just before Lithuania achieved legal Independence from the Soviet Union, in March 1990, the Small Theatre has occupied its present premises since 2005. The brainchild of artistic director Rimas Tuminas, it stages productions of classic works (Chekov, Beckett) alongside plays by Lithuanian writers and Tuminas' own repertoire.

ℹ Information

Tourist Information Office Old Town (☑ 5-262 9660; www.vilnius-tourism.lt; Vilniaus gatvė 22; ⊙ 9am-6pm) The head office of Vilnius' tourist information service is great for brochures, advice and accommodation bookings.

University Emergency Hospital (☑ 5-236 5000; www.santa.lt; Santariškių gatvė 2; ⊙ 24hr) This teaching hospital takes serious and emergency cases.

ℹ Getting There & Away

BUS

The **bus station** (Autobusų Stotis; ☑ information 1661; www.autobusustotis.lt; Sodų gatvė 22) handles both domestic and international

coach services and is situated about 1km south of Old Town, across the street from the train station. The main international bus operators include **Ecolines** (☑ 5-213 3300; www.ecolines.net; Geležinkelio gatvė 15; ⊙ 8am-9.30pm Mon-Fri, 9am-9.30pm Sat & Sun), **Lux Express** (☑ 5-233 6666; www.luxexpress.eu; Sodų 20b-1; ⊙ 8am-7pm Mon-Fri, 9am-7pm Sat & Sun) or one of the affiliated carriers under **Eurolines** (☑ 5-2335 2774; www.eurolines.lt; Sodų gatvė 22; ⊙ 6.30am-9.30pm).

TRAIN

From the **train station** (Geležinkelio Stotis; ☑ information 233 0088; www.litrail.lt; Geležinkelio gatvė 16), Vilnius is linked by rail to various international destinations, including Warsaw, Minsk and Moscow, though most trains run through Belarus and require a transit visa.

ℹ Getting Around

TO/FROM THE AIRPORT

Bus 1 runs between **Vilnius International Airport** (p766), 5km south of the city centre, and the train station. A shuttle train service runs from the train station 17 times daily between 5.44am and 9.07pm (around €0.75). A taxi from the airport to the city centre should cost around €15.

BICYCLE

Vilnius is becoming increasingly bike-friendly, although bike lanes are rarer outside the Old Town and along the banks of the Neris. Orange Cyclocity stations dot the city, the Tourist Office has free cycling maps, and BaltiCCycle (www.balticcycle.lt) is good for ideas and information.

PUBLIC TRANSPORT

The city is efficiently served by buses and trolleybuses from 5.30am or 6am to midnight; Sunday services are less frequent. Single-trip tickets cost: €1 from the driver; €0.64 if you have a Vilniečio Kortelė (an electronic ticket sold at kiosks); or nothing if you have a Vilnius City Card with public transport included (sold in tourist information centres).

TAXI

Taxi rates in Vilnius can vary, and are generally cheaper if ordered in advance by telephone than if hailed directly off the street or picked up at a taxi stand. Ask the hotel reception desk or restaurant to call one for you.

ℹ VILNIUS CITY CARD

If you're planning to do epic amounts of sightseeing within a short period of time, the Vilnius City Card provides free or discounted entry to many attractions, as well as free transport.

PANERIAI

During WWII the Nazis – aided by Lithuanian accomplices – murdered 100,000 people, around 70,000 of them Jews, at this site in the forest, 8km southwest of Vilnius.

GRŪTAS PARK – THE GRAVEYARD OF COMMUNISM

Both entertaining and educational, **Grūtas Park** (Grūto Parkas; ☑ 6824 2320; www.grutoparkas.lt; Grūtas; adult/child €6/3 Oct-Apr, €7.50/4 May-Sep; ⊗ 9am-10pm summer, to 5pm rest of year; 🖷), 125km south of Vilnius, near the spa town of Druskininkai, has been an enormous hit since it opened in 2001. The sprawling grounds, built to resemble a Siberian concentration camp, feature the entire Marxist pantheon and dozens of other statuesque examples of Soviet realism, as well as assorted communist paraphernalia, exhibits on Soviet history (with a focus on the oppression of Lithuania) and loudspeakers bellowing Soviet anthems.

From the entrance a path leads to the small **Paneriai Museum** (☑ tours 6999 0384; www.jmuseum.lt; Agrastų gatvė 15; ⊗ 9am-5pm Tue-Sun May-Sep, by appointment Oct-Apr) **FREE**, with a graphic display of photographs and personal belongings of those who died here, and the grassed-over pits where the Nazis burnt the exhumed bodies of their victims.

TRAKAI

☑ 528 / POP 5400

With its picturesque red-brick castle, Karaite culture, quaint wooden houses and pretty lakeside location, Trakai is a highly recommended day trip, within easy reach of the capital.

The Karaite people are named after the term *kara,* which means 'to study the scriptures' in both Hebrew and Arabic. The sect originated in Baghdad and practices strict adherence to the Torah (rejecting the rabbinic Talmud). In around 1400 the grand duke of Lithuania, Vytautas, brought about 380 Karaite families to Trakai from Crimea to serve as bodyguards. Only a dozen families remain in Trakai today and their numbers are dwindling rapidly.

Trakai's trophy piece is the fairy-tale **Trakai Castle** (Trakų Pilis; www.trakaimuziejus.lt; adult/senior/student & child €6/4/3; ⊗ 10am-7pm May-Sep, 10am-6pm Tue-Sun Mar, Apr & Oct, 9am-5pm Tue-Sun Nov-Feb; 🖷), occupying a small island in Lake Galvė. A footbridge links the island castle to the shore. The red-brick Gothic castle, painstakingly restored from original blueprints, dates from the late 14th century. Inside the castle, the Trakai History Museum tells the story of the structure. There's a bewildering variety of objects on show – hoards of coins, weaponry and porcelain, as well as interactive displays.

You can sample *kibinai* (meat-stuffed Karaite pastries similar to empanadas or Cornish pasties) either at **Senoji Kibininė**

(☑ 528-55 865; www.kibinas.lt; Karaimų gatvė 65; mains €4-8; ⊗ 10am-10pm) or at **Kybynlar** (☑ 8-698 06320; www.kybynlar.lt; Karaimų gatvė 29; mains €7-12; ⊗ noon-9pm Mon, 11am-9pm Tue-Thu, 11am-10pm Fri & Sat, 11am-9pm Sun).

KAUNAS

☑ 37 / POP 353,000

Lithuania's second city has a compact Old Town, an entertaining array of museums and plenty of vibrant, youthful energy provided by its large student population. A good time to visit is in late April, during the Kaunas Jazz Festival (www.kaunasjazz.lt), when homegrown and international artists perform in venues across the city.

⊙ Sights

◎ Old Town

The heart of Kaunas' lovely Old Town is **Rotušės Aikštė**, home of the city's former **Town Hall** (Kauno rotušė; ☑ 37-203 572; www.kaunas.lt; Rotušės aikštė 15), now known as the 'Palace of Weddings', and surrounded by 15th- and 16th-century German merchants' houses.

St Francis Xavier Church & Monastery   CHURCH
(☑ 37-432 098; www.jesuit.lt; Rotušės aikštė 7-9; tower €1.50; ⊗ 4-6pm Mon-Fri, 7am-1pm & 4-6pm Sun) The southern side of Rotušės aikštė is dominated by the twin-towered St Francis Xavier Church, college and Jesuit monastery complex, built between 1666 and 1720. Take a peek inside and then climb the tower for the best aerial views of Kaunas.

Maironis Lithuanian Literary Museum   MUSEUM
(Maironio Lietuvos Literatūros Muziejus; ☑ 37-206 842; www.maironiomuziejus.lt; Rotušės aikštė 13;

adult/child €1.45/0.58; ⊙ 9am-6pm Tue-Sat) This 18th-century mansion was, between 1910 and 1932, the home of Jonas Mačiulis (Maironis), the Kaunas poet-priest who stirred Lithuania's national ambitions in the late 19th and early 20th centuries. It's now a museum dedicated to his life and works, and Lithuanian literature more broadly.

⊙ New Town

Laisvės alėja, a 1.7km-long pedestrian street lined with bars, shops and restaurants, runs east from Old Town to New Town, ending at the white, neo-Byzantine **St Michael the Archangel Church** (Šv Archangelo Mykolo Rektoratas; ☑ 37-226 676; www.kaunoarkivyskupija.lt; Nepriklausomybės aikštė 14; ⊙ 9am-6pm).

★MK Čiurlionis National Museum of Art   GALLERY
(MK Čiurlionio Valstybinis Dailės Muziejus; ☑ 37-229 475; www.ciurlionis.lt; Putvinskio gatvė 55; adult/child €4/2; ⊙ 11am-5pm Tue, Wed & Fri-Sun, to 7pm Thu) In this, Kaunas' leading gallery, you'll find extensive collections of the romantic paintings of Mikalojus Konstantinas Čiurlionis (1875–1911), one of Lithuania's greatest artists and composers, as well as Lithuanian folk art and 16th- to 20th-century European applied art.

Museum of the Ninth Fort   MUSEUM
(IX Forto Muziejus; ☑ 37-377 750; www.9fortomuziejus.lt; Žemaičių plentas 73; adult/child €3/1.50; ⊙ 10am-6pm Wed-Mon Apr-Oct, 10am-4pm Wed-Sun Nov-Mar) A poignant memorial to the tens of thousands of people, mainly Jews, who were murdered by the Nazis, the excellent Museum of the Ninth Fort, 7km north of Kaunas, comprises an old WWI-era fort and the bunker-like church of the damned. Displays cover deportations of Lithuanians by the Soviets and graphic photo exhibitions track the demise of Kaunas' Jewish community. Various guided tours of different aspects of the fort are offered.

Kaunas Picture Gallery   GALLERY
(Kauno Paveikslų Galerija; ☑ 37-221 779; www.ciurlionis.lt; Donelaičio gatvė 16; adult/student €2/1; ⊙ 11am-5pm Tue, Wed & Fri-Sun, to 7pm Thu) This underrated gem, another branch of the many-tentacled MK Čiurlionis National Museum of Art, exhibits works by late-20th-century Lithuanian artists, with a room devoted to Jurgis Mačiūnas, the father of the Fluxus avant-garde movement.

🛏 Sleeping

Kauno Arkivyskupijos Svečių Namai   GUESTHOUSE €
(☑ 37-322 597; www.kaunas.lcn.lt/sveciunamai; Rotušės aikštė 21; s/d/tr without bathroom €15/25/32, d with bathroom €35-48; ⓟ ✳ @) 🍃 This Catholic archdiocesan guesthouse couldn't have a better location, snuggled between venerable churches and overlooking the Old Town square. Rooms are spartan but spacious, and breakfast is not included. Book well in advance, since it fills up fast.

Daugirdas   BOUTIQUE HOTEL €€
(☑ 37-301 561; www.daugirdas.lt; T Daugirdo gatvė 4; s/d/tr €60/72/90; ✳ 🛜) This stylish boutique hotel, wedged between central Old Town and the Nemunas, is one of the most charismatic in Kaunas. The standard doubles are perfectly acceptable, with good-quality beds and bathrooms (with heated floors), but for something a little out of the ordinary, try the timber ceiling, enormous bed and Jacuzzi of the Gothic Suite.

Radharanė   GUESTHOUSE €€
(☑ 37-320 800; www.radharane.lt; M Daukšos gatvė 28; d €48-60; ⓟ @ 🛜) Atmospheric guesthouse with an excellent Old Town location. The rooms have been recently renovated and the vegetarian restaurant below is well worth investigating.

🍴 Eating

Motiejaus Kepyklėlė   BAKERY €
(☑ 8-616 15599; Vilniaus gatvė 7; ⊙ 8am-7pm Mon-Sat, 9am-6pm Sun) Perhaps the best bakery in Kaunas, Motiejaus has settled into grand new red-brick digs in the heart of Vilniaus gatvė. Alongside Lithuanian cookies and pastries you'll find excellent international dainties, such as canelles, cupcakes, macaroons and croissants. The coffee can also be counted on.

★Moksha   INDIAN, THAI €€
(☑ 8-676 71649; www.facebook.com/cafemoksha; Vasario 16-osios gatvė 6; mains €5-8; ⊙ 11am-10pm Mon-Sat; 🍴) This tiny place with whitewashed brick walls and fresh flowers everywhere lures you in with exotic smells. You can expect such daily specials as lamb kofta curry or crispy duck with persimmon salad, and there are even vegan options such as lentil soup. On top of that, the service is super-friendly; a rarity in these parts.

THE HILL OF CROSSES

One of Lithuania's most awe-inspiring sights is the legendary **Hill of Crosses** (Kryžių kalnas; ☑41-370 860; Jurgaičiai). The sound of the thousands of crosses – which appear to grow on the hillock – tinkling in the breeze is wonderfully eerie.

Planted here since at least the 19th century and probably much older, the crosses were bulldozed by the Soviets, but each night people crept past soldiers and barbed wire to plant more, risking their lives or freedom to express their national and spiritual fervour.

Some of the crosses are devotional, others are memorials (many for people deported to Siberia) and some are finely carved folk-art masterpieces.

Senieji Rūsiai EUROPEAN €€
(Old Cellars; ☑37-202 806; www.seniejirusiai.lt; Vilniaus gatvė 34; mains €9-16; ⊙11am-midnight Mon-Thu, 11am-1am Fri, noon-1am Sat, noon-11pm Sun; 🐱) Named for its 17th-century subterranean vaults, lined with candlelit frescoes, 'Old Cellars' is one of the most atmospheric places in Kaunas to eat substantial pan-European dishes. Alongside frogs' legs, trout and other local delicacies, you can shell out extra for fillet with *foie gras,* or steak flame grilled at your table.

🍷 Drinking & Nightlife

Kultūra Kavinė CAFE
(☑8-676 25546; www.facebook.com/kauno.kultura; Donelaičio gatvė 14-16; ⊙noon-10pm Sun-Thu, noon-2am Fri & Sat; 🐱) It calls itself a cafe, but this alternative meeting spot covers the bases from pub to cocktail bar to cosy spot to grab a cup of coffee. The clientele is skewed towards students and thinkers, and the space is a bit of fresh air for anyone looking to escape trendier, commercial bars. Excellent bar food, salads and wings, too.

Skliautas BAR
(☑37-6864 2700; www.skliautas.com; Rotušės aikštė 26; ⊙11am-midnight Mon-Thu, to 2am Fri & Sat, to 11pm Sun) Great for cheap Lithuanian food and a boisterous atmosphere, Skliautas bursts with energy most times of the day and night, and in summer its crowd basically takes over the adjoining alley. Also good for coffee and cake.

❶ Information

Tourist Office (☑37-323 436; www.visit. kaunas.lt; Laisvės alėja 36; ⊙9am-7pm Mon-Fri, 10am-3pm Sat & Sun Apr-Oct, 9am-6pm Mon-Thu, 9am-5pm Fri Nov-Mar) Books accommodation, sells maps and guides, and arranges bicycle rental and guided tours of the Old Town.

❶ Getting There & Away

Kaunas' bus and train stations are located not far from each other, about 2km south of the city centre. From the bus station, frequent services leave for Klaipėda (€14, three hours) and Vilnius (€6, 1¾ hours). From the train station there are plenty of trains each day to Vilnius (€5-6, 1¼ to 1¾ hours).

KLAIPĖDA

☑46 / POP 161,300

Klaipėda, Lithuania's main seaport, is known mainly as the gateway to the Curonian Spit, though it has a fascinating history as the East Prussian city of Memel long before it was incorporated into modern Lithuania in the 1920s. It was founded in 1252 by the Teutonic Order, who built the city's first castle, and has served as a key trading port through the centuries to modern times. It was retaken by Nazi Germany in WWII and housed a German submarine base. Though it was heavily bombed in the war, it retains a unique Prussian feel, particularly in the quiet backstreets of the historic **Old Town**.

◉ Sights

Klaipėda Castle Museum MUSEUM
(Klaipėda Pilies Muziejus; ☑46-410 527; www. mlimuziejus.lt; Pilies gatvė 4; adult/child €1.74/0.87; ⊙10am-6pm Tue-Sat) This small museum is based inside the remains of Klaipėda's old moat-protected castle, which dates back to the 13th century. It tells the castle's story through the ages until the 19th century, when most of the structure was pulled down. You'll find fascinating photos from WWII and the immediate postwar years, when the city was rebuilt by Soviet planners.

History Museum of Lithuania Minor   MUSEUM

(Mažosios Lietuvos Istorijos Muziejus; ☑46-410 524; www.mlimuziejus.lt; Didžioji Vandens gatvė 6; adult/child €1.45/0.72; ⊙10am-6pm Tue-Sat) This small museum traces the origins of 'Lithuania Minor' (Kleinlitauen) – as this coastal region was known during several centuries as part of East Prussia. It exhibits Prussian maps, coins, artefacts of the Teutonic order, traditional weaving machines and traditional folk art.

🛏 Sleeping

Litinterp Guesthouse   GUESTHOUSE €

(☑46-410 644; www.litinterp.com; Puodžių gatvė 17; s without/with bathroom €23/28, d without/with bathroom €40/46; 🅿🛜) A commercial building since the 18th century, this guesthouse retains timber stairs, brick arches and other lovely old touches. Its 19 rooms are spotless, with light pine furnishings. The breakfast (€3) is spartan, but with overall value this good we're not complaining.

★Hotel Euterpė   HOTEL €€

(☑46-474 703; www.euterpe.lt; Daržų gatvė 9; s/d €73/93; 🅿😊@🛜) Our bet for the best small hotel in Klaipėda is this upscale number, tucked among former German merchant houses in the Old Town. Expect a warm welcome at reception and snug rooms in earthy colours and a neat, minimalist look. The downstairs restaurant is excellent and there's a small terrace to enjoy your morning coffee.

🍴 Eating & Drinking

Friedricho Pasazas   INTERNATIONAL €€

(☑46-301 070; www.pasazas.lt; Tiltų gatvė 26a; mains €5-10; ⊙11am-1am Mon-Sat, noon-midnight Sun; 🛜) Lining this snug carriageway on the southern side of the Old Town you'll find Friedricho Pasazas – not just one restaurant, but a whole complex of them. Friedricho Restoranas, the main show, is top of the pile, with creative Mediterranean dishes and wine to match. Following closely behind, there's a pizzeria, a steakhouse and a Lithuanian tavern.

★Momo Grill   STEAK €€€

(☑8-693 12355; www.momogrill.lt; Liepų gatvė 20; mains €10-18; ⊙11am-10pm Tue-Fri, noon-10pm Sat; 😊🛜) This tiny, modern, minimalist steakhouse is foodie heaven and the hardest table to book in town. The small menu consists of just three cuts of beef plus grilled fish and leg of duck, and allows the chef to focus on what he does best. The austere interior of white tiles is soothing and the wine list is excellent.

Žvejų Baras   BAR

(☑8-686 60405; www.zvejubaras.lt; Kurpių gatvė 8; ⊙5pm-midnight Sun-Wed, to 2am Thu, to 4am Fri & Sat) The beautiful, lead-lit, timbered interior of this portside pub (the name means 'Fisherman's Bar') is one of Klaipėda's nicest places to catch live music, or chat over a few interesting beers.

ℹ Information

Tourist Office (☑46-412 186; www.klaipedainfo.lt; Turgaus gatvė 7; ⊙9am-7pm Mon-Fri, 10am-4pm Sat & Sun Apr-Oct, 9am-6pm

---

ESSENTIAL FOOD & DRINK

Beer and mead Šytutys, Utenos and Kalnapilis are top beers; midus (mead) is a honey-tinged nobleman's drink.

Beer snacks No drinking session is complete without a plate of smoked pigs' ears and *kepta duona* (deep-fried garlicky bread sticks).

Beetroot delight Cold, creamy *šaltibarščiai* (beetroot soup) is a summer speciality, served with a side of fried potatoes.

Potato creations Try the cepelinai (potato-dough 'zeppelin' stuffed with meat, mushrooms or cheese), bulviniai blynai (potato pancakes) or žemaičių blynai (heart-shaped mashed potato stuffed with meat and fried), or the vedarai (baked pig intestines stuffed with mashed potato).

Smoked fish The Curonian Spit is famous for its smoked fish, particularly the superb rukytas unguris (smoked eel).

Unusual meat Sample the game, such as beaver stew or bear sausages.

Mon-Fri Nov-Mar) Exceptionally efficient tourist office selling maps and locally published guidebooks, and arranging accommodation, tours and more. Operates reduced hours outside high season, closing on Sundays.

🛈 Getting There & Away

The train and bus stations are situated near each in the modern part of town, about 2km north of Old Town. Three daily trains run to Vilnius (€18, four hours). There's also regular bus services to Vilnius (€18, four to 5½ hours) and Kaunas (€14, 2¾ to four hours).

CURONIAN SPIT

🗓 469 / POP 3100

This magical sliver of land, covered by pine forest, hosts some of Europe's most precious sand dunes and a menagerie of elk, deer and avian wildlife. Recognised by Unesco as a World Heritage Site, the fragile spit is divided evenly between Lithuania and Russia's Kaliningrad region, with Lithuania's half protected as **Curonian Spit National Park** (🗓 46-402 256; www.nerija.lt; Smiltynės gatvė 11, Smiltynė; ⊙ 9am-5pm Sun-Thu, to 6pm Fri & Sat).

Smiltynė, where the ferries from Klaipėda dock, draws weekend crowds with the delightful aquarium and the **Ethnographic Sea Fishermen's Farmstead** (Smiltynės gatvė; ⊙ dusk-dawn) FREE. Further south, the village of Juodkrantė is awaft with the tempting smells of smoked fish (*žuvis*), while picture-perfect Nida is home to the unmissable 52m-high **Parnidis Dune** (Parnidžio kopos), with its panoramic views of the 'Lithuanian Sahara' – coastline, forest and sand extending towards Kaliningrad. Stay in one of the town's handsomely painted fisherman's houses and eat the famous Curonian smoked fish at **Tik Pas Jona** (🗓 8-620 82084; www.facebook.com/RukytosZuvysTikPasJona; Naglių gatvė 6-1; mains €3; ⊙ 10am-10pm Apr-Nov, Sat & Sun only Dec-Mar).

A flat cycling trail runs all the way from Nida to Smiltynė, passing the massive colony of grey herons and cormorants near Juodkrantė, and you stand a good chance of seeing wild boar and other wildlife along the path. Bicycles are easy to hire (around €9/12 per 12/24 hours) in Nida.

The tourist office in Klaipėda can help arrange transport and accommodation; **Miško Namas** (🗓 469-52 290; www.miskonamas.com; Pamario gatvė 11; d €75-85, 2-/4-person apt €95/100; 🅿 @ 🛜 🛝) and **Vila Banga** (🗓 8-686 08073; www.nidosbanga.lt; Pamario gatvė 2; d/apt €98/135; 🛜) are both fine choices.

WITCHES' HILL

Juodkrantė's biggest attraction is the macabre **Witches' Hill** (Raganų Kalnas; 🛝) – wooded sculpture trails lined with devils, witches and other grotesque wooden carvings from Lithuanian folklore.

🛈 Getting There & Away

To get to the Spit, board a ferry at the **Old Ferry Port** (Senoji perkėla; 🗓 46-311 117; www.keltas.lt; Danės gatvė 1; per passenger/bicycle €0.80/free) just west of Klaipėda's Old Town (€0.90, 10 minutes, half-hourly). Vehicles must use the **New Ferry Port** (Naujoji perkėla; 🗓 46-311 117; www.keltas.lt; Nemuno gatvė 8; per passenger/car €0.80/11.05, bicycle free), 2.5km south of the passenger terminal (per car €12, at least hourly).

SURVIVAL GUIDE

🛈 Directory A–Z

ACCOMMODATION

➡ Book ahead in the high season for Vilnius and the Curonian Spit. High-season prices are around 30% higher than low-season prices. Prices are higher in Vilnius.

➡ Vilnius has numerous youth hostels. Budget accommodation is easy to find outside the capital.

RESOURCES

Lithuania Travel (www.lithuania.travel) The State Department of Tourism's visitor portal

Vilnius Tourism (www.vilnius-tourism.lt/en/) Handy, always-up-to-date site covering most of what the capital has to offer

Lithuania Railways (www.litrail.lt/en) Train schedules, fares and information.

Autobusubilietai (www.autobusubilietai.lt) Bus fares, schedules and information.

SLEEPING PRICE RANGES

The following price ranges refer to the cost of a double room with private bathroom

€ less than €50

€€ €50–100

€€€ more than €100

COUNTRY FACTS

Area 65,303 sq km

Capital Vilnius

Country Code ☑ 370

Currency euro (€)

Emergency ☑ 112

Language Lithuanian

Money ATMs everywhere

Population 2.9 million

Visas Not required for citizens of the EU, Australia, Canada, Israel, Japan, New Zealand, Switzerland or the US for stays of 90 days

MONEY

Lithuania adopted the euro (€) on 1 January 2015.

➡ Exchange money with your credit or debit card at ATMs located around the country or at major banks.

➡ Credit cards are widely accepted for purchases.

➡ Some banks still cash travellers cheques, though this is increasingly uncommon.

➡ Tip 10% in restaurants to reward good service.

OPENING HOURS

Banks 8am to 3pm Monday to Friday

Bars 11am to midnight Sunday to Thursday, 11am to 2am Friday and Saturday

Clubs 10pm to 5am Thursday to Saturday

Post offices 8am to 8pm Monday to Friday, 10am to 9pm Saturday, 10am to 5pm Sunday

Restaurants noon to 11pm; later on weekends

Shops 9am or 10am to 7pm Monday to Saturday; some open on Sunday

TELEPHONE

➡ Dial 8 and wait for the tone before calling both landlines (followed by the city code and phone number) and mobile phones (followed by the eight-digit number).

➡ To make an international call dial 00 before the country code.

➡ Mobile companies **Bitė** (www.bite.lt), **Omnitel** (www.omnitel.lt) and **Tele 2** (www.tele2.lt) sell prepaid SIM cards; Tele2 offers free roaming with its prepaid cards – making it the best choice for those also travelling in Estonia, Latvia and Poland – and has the cheapest rates.

➡ Payphones – increasingly rare given the widespread use of mobiles – only accept phonecards, sold at newspaper kiosks.

ℹ Getting There & Away

Lithuania has frequent air, bus, train and ferry links to neighbouring countries, though be sure to route your travel to avoid Belarus or the Russian province of Kaliningrad if you don't have the right transit visas. Latvia and Poland are both members of the EU's Schengen zone and there are no passport controls at these borders. Vilnius is the country's hub for air travel, with an increasing number of direct services to many European cities. Sweden and Germany can be reached by ferry from Klaipėda, Lithuania's international seaport.

Flights, tours and rail tickets can be booked online at www.lonelyplanet.com/bookings.

AIR

Most international traffic to Lithuania goes through **Vilnius International Airport** (Tarptautinis Vilniaus Oro Uostas; ☑ 6124 4442; www.vno.lt; Rodūnios kelias 10a; ☎; ☐ 1, 2), which has connections to a good cross-section of Europe's cities..

➡ Major carriers that service Vilnius include airBaltic, Austrian Airlines, Lufthansa, LOT and Scandinavian Airlines.

➡ Budget carriers include Ryanair and Wizz Air.

BOAT

From Klaipėda's **International Ferry Port** (☑ 46-395 051; www.dfdsseaways.lt; Perkėlos gatvė 10), **DFDS Seaways** (☑ 46-395 000; www.dfdsseaways.com; Šaulių gatvė 19) runs passenger ferries to/from Kiel (from €80, six weekly, 22 hours) in Germany and Karlshamn, Sweden (from €75, 14 hours, daily).

BUS

The main international bus companies operating in Lithuania are **Lux Express** (https://luxexpress.eu) and **Ecolines** (https://ecolines.net).

CAR & MOTORCYCLE

➡ There are no passport or customs controls if entering from Poland or Latvia.

➡ A valid entry or transit visa is required to enter or drive through Belarus and the Russian province of Kaliningrad.

TRAIN

➡ Many international train routes, including to Warsaw and Moscow, pass through Belarus and require a transit visa.

➡ Consult the timetable at **Lithuanian Railways** (www.litrail.lt/en) for further information.

ⓘ Getting Around

BICYCLE
→ Lithuania is mostly flat and easily explored by bike.

→ Large cities and areas popular with visitors have bike-rental and repair shops.

→ Information about bike touring in Lithuania can be found on **BaltiCCycle** (www.balticcycle.lt)

BUS
→ The bus network is extensive, efficient and relatively inexpensive.

→ See www.autobusubilietai.lt for national bus timetables.

CAR & MOTORCYCLE
→ Drivers must be at least 18 years old and have a valid driving licence (with photo) in their country of residence.

→ The speed limit is 50km/h in cities, 70km/h to 90km/h on two-lane highways, and 110km/h to 130km/h on motorways.

→ The blood-alcohol limit is 0.04% (or 0.2% for drivers of less than two years' experience).

→ International and local car-rental agencies are well represented at Vilnius International

---

EATING PRICE RANGES

The following Lithuanian budgets are based on a typical main meal offered.

€ less than €7

€€ €7–14

€€€ more than €14

Airport. Expect to pay around €150 per week for a basic compact manual.

LOCAL TRANSPORT
→ Lithuanian cities generally have good public transport, based on buses, trolleybuses and minibuses.

→ A ride usually costs around €1.

TRAIN
→ The country's efficient train network, **Lithuanian Rail** (see www.litrail.lt, with timetables in English) links Vilnius to Kaunas, Klaipėda and Trakai, though for some journeys, including Kaunas to Klaipėda, buses are faster.

Macedonia

Best Places to Eat

➡ Letna Bavča Kaneo (p780)

➡ Hotel Tutto (p777)

➡ Vila Raskrsnica (p784)

➡ Kebapčilnica Destan (p773)

Best Places to Stay

➡ Vila Raskrsnica (p784)

➡ Villa Dihovo (p784)

➡ Sunny Lake Hostel (p779)

➡ Villa Jovan (p779)

➡ Urban Hostel & Apartments (p772)

Why Go?

Part Balkan, part Mediterranean and rich in Greek, Roman and Ottoman history, Macedonia (Македонија) has a fascinating past and complex national psyche. Glittering Lake Ohrid and the historic waterside town of Ohrid itself have etched out a place for Macedonia on the tourist map, but this small nation is far more than just one great lake.

Skopje may be the Balkans' most bonkers and unfailingly entertaining capital city, thanks to a government-led building spree of monuments, museums and fountains. What has emerged is an intriguing jigsaw where ancient history and buzzing modernity collide.

The rest of Macedonia is a stomping ground for adventurers. Mountains are omnipresent and walking trails blissfully quiet. The national parks of Mavrovo, Galičica and Pelister are also cultivating some excellent cultural and food tourism initiatives; these gorgeous regions are criminally underexplored. If you want to get off the beaten track in Europe, this is it.

When to Go
Skopje

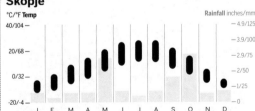

Jun–Aug Enjoy Ohrid's Summer Festival and dive into its 300m-deep lake.

Sep–Oct Partake in Skopje's jazz festival or the Tikveš region's Kavadarci Wine Carnival.

Dec–Feb Ski Mavrovo, snuggle up in chalet-style lodges and experience Ohrid out of season.

Macedonia Highlights

1 **Ohrid Old Town**
(p777) Exploring the distinctive historic quarter, right to the end of the boardwalk and pebble beach, and up to the clifftop Church of Sveti Jovan.

2 **Skopje** (p769) Diving into the historic Čaršija (Old Turkish Bazaar) of Macedonia's capital, then marvelling at its super-sized new riverside monuments.

3 **Pelister National Park**
(p783) Eating your fill at food-focused village tourism initiatives in this underrated national park, and walking it off the next day.

4 **Golem Grad** (p782)
Chasing ghosts, pelicans and tortoises around this eerie Lake Prespa island, fecund with overgrown ruins.

5 **Popova Kula** (p781)
Sipping and slurping your way through Macedonia's premier wine region, Tikveš, using this could-be-in-Italy winery hotel as your base.

6 **Sveti Jovan Bigorski Monastery** (p776) Taking tea with monks at this majestic complex, teetering in the hills of Mavrovo National Park.

SKOPJE СКОПЈЕ

⚲ 02 / POPULATION 2.02 MILLION

In the past few years, the central riverside area of Skopje has hammered out the look of a set design for an ancient civilisation. Towering warrior statues gaze down on you and gleaming Italianate power buildings make visitors feel very small indeed. Marble-clad museums have mushroomed alongside hypnotic new mega-fountains, and the Macedonian capital has become a thoroughly entertaining Balkan metropolis – a bit surreal and at times garish, maybe, but never dull.

Yet peel back the veneer and Skopje has a genuine historic core that warrants just as much attention as its new wonders. Ottoman- and Byzantine-era sights are focused around the city's delightful Čaršija (old Turkish bazaar), bordered by the 15th-century Kameni Most (Stone Bridge) and Tvrdina Kale Fortress – Skopje's guardian since the 5th century.

⊙ Sights

⊚ Ploštad Makedonija & the South Bank

Ploštad Makedonija   SQUARE
(Macedonia Sq) This gigantic square is the centrepiece to Skopje's audacious nation-building-through-architecture project and has massive statues dedicated to national heroes in it, as well as an incongruous Triumphal Arch in the southeast corner. The towering, central Warrior on a Horse is bedecked by fountains that are illuminated at night. Home to a number of cafes and hotels, it's a popular stomping ground for locals as well as tourists, particularly when the sun goes down.

Memorial House of Mother Teresa MUSEUM
(🖉02 3290 674; ul Makedonija 9; ⊙9am-8pm Mon-Fri, to 2pm Sat-Sun) FREE This extraordinary retro-futuristic memorial is the most unique church you'll see in Macedonia. Inside the building there's a small 1st-floor museum displaying memorabilia relating to the famed Catholic nun of Calcutta, born in Skopje in 1910. On the 2nd floor there is a mind-boggling chapel, with glass walls wrought in filigree (a revered traditional craft of Skopje). Silhouettes of doves are worked into the filigree to symbolise peace, as a homage to Mother Teresa.

⊚ North Bank & Čaršija

★**Čaršija**   AREA
(Old Turkish Bazaar) Čaršija is the hillside Turkish old town of Skopje and evokes the city's Ottoman past with its winding lanes filled with teahouses, mosques, craftsmen's stores, and even good nightlife. It also boasts Skopje's best historic structures and a handful of museums, and is the first place any visitor should head. Čaršija runs from the Stone Bridge to the Bit Pazar, a big vegetable and household goods market. Expect to get pleasantly lost in its maze of narrow streets.

★**Archaeological Museum of Macedonia** MUSEUM
(www.amm.org.mk; Bul Goce Delčev; adult/student & child 300/150MKD; ⊙10am-6pm Tue-Sun) All gleaming and shiny new, this supersized pile of Italianate-styled marble has been a giant receptacle for Skopje's recent splurge on government-led monuments to boost national pride. Inside, there are three floors displaying the cream of Macedonian archaeological excavations beneath the dazzle of hundreds of tiny lights. Highlights include Byzantine treasures; sophisticated 3D reconstructions of early Macedonian faces from skulls; a pint-sized replica of an early Christian basilica showing the life phases of mosaic conservation; and a Phoenician royal necropolis.

Sveti Spas Church   CHURCH
(Church of the Holy Saviour; Makarije Frčkoski 8; adult/student 120/50MKD; ⊙9am-5pm Tue-Fri, to 3pm Sat & Sun) Partially submerged 2m underground (the Ottomans banned churches from being taller than mosques), this church dates from the 14th century and is the most historically important in Skopje. Its sunken design means it doesn't look like a church, so you might not notice it at first: it's opposite the Old Town Brewery – look for the pretty bell tower that watches over it, built into its outer courtyard wall. Inside the church an elaborate carved iconostasis shines out of the dark.

★**Tvrdina Kale Fortress**   FORTRESS
(Samoilova; ⊙7am-7pm) FREE Dominating the skyline of Skopje, this *Game of Thrones*–worthy 6th-century AD Byzantine (and later, Ottoman) fortress is an easy walk up from the Čaršija and its ramparts offer great views over the city and river. Inside the ruins, two mini museums were being built at the time of writing to house various archaeological finds from neolithic to Ottoman times. This will be a welcome addition to the site, as there are no information boards at the fortress at present.

National Gallery of Macedonia   GALLERY
(Daut Paša Amam; www.nationalgallery.mk; Kruševska 1a; admission adult/student & child 50/20MKD; ⊙10am-8pm Tue-Sun Apr-Sep, to 6pm Oct-Mar) The Daut Paša Amam (1473) were once the largest Turkish baths outside of İstanbul and they make a magical setting for the permanent collection of Skopje's national art gallery, just by the entrance to the

Skopje

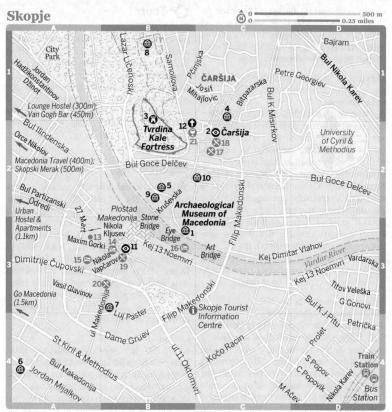

MACEDONIA SKOPJE

Čaršija (Old Turkish Bazaar). The seven restored rooms house mainly modern art and sculpture from Macedonia, brought to life by the sun piercing through the small star-shaped holes in the domed ceilings.

Museum of the Macedonian Struggle for Statehood & Independence
MUSEUM

(Iljo Vojvodo; adult/child 300/120MKD; ⊘10am-6pm, closed 1st Mon of month) Part history museum, part national propaganda machine, this is a formidable memorial to Macedonia's historic occupation, land struggles and revolutionary heroes. The museum is dark, literally (the walls are black and lighting is low) and figuratively (gruesome giant oil paintings depict scenes of battle and betrayal, and physical reconstructions include a bloodied child's cradle and a dead revolutionary hung from the rafters). It's not suitable for children. The guides are interesting and knowledgeable (despite offering a rather one-sided perspective on events).

Holocaust Memorial Center for the Jews of Macedonia
MUSEUM

(Iljo Vojvoda; ⊘9am-7pm Tue-Fri, to 3pm Sat & Sun) FREE The mirrored-glass entrance is bizarrely unwelcoming, but once inside this is a moving museum with fascinating displays that commemorate the all-but-lost Sephardic Jewish culture of Macedonia through a range of photos, English-language wall texts, maps and video. The exhibition documents the Jewish community's history in the Balkans, ending in WWII when some 98% of Macedonian Jews perished in the Holocaust. In the central atrium, 7144 beads hang to represent the individuals who died.

Museum of Contemporary Art
MUSEUM

(NIMoCA; ☑02 3117 734; www.msuskopje.org.mk; Samoilova 17; admission 300MKD, free 1st Fri of month; ⊘10am-5pm Tue-Sat, 9am-1pm Sun) This museum was formed in the aftermath of Skopje's devastating 1963 earthquake, with artists and collections around the world donating works to form a collection that now includes works by Picasso, Léger, Hockney, Meret Oppenheim and Bridget Riley. It's housed in an impressive contemporary building with floor-to-ceiling windows, perched atop a hill with wonderful city views. Unfortunately, its collection isn't always on display – you may come here and find its exhibitions extraordinary or mundane, depending on what's been put on display.

Tours

Skopje Walks
WALKING

(www.skopjewalks.com; ul Makedonija; donations welcome; ⊘10am daily) FREE These excellent free tours run for 2½ hours and cover every important corner of Skopje's inner city. Highly recommended for an insight into the city, its history and its residents from local guides who are passionate about showing Skopje off. Tours meet outside the Memorial House of Mother Teresa (p770) – look out for the blue ID badge.

🛏 Sleeping

★Urban Hostel & Apartments
HOSTEL €

(☑078 432 384, 02 6142 785; www.urbanhostel.com.mk; Adolf Ciborovski 22; dm €10-13, s/d €24/35, apt €35-70; 🕸🛜) In a converted residential house with a sociable front garden for summer lounging, Urban is an excellent budget option on the outskirts of the leafy Debar Maalo neighbourhood, a 15-minute walk west of central Skopje. Decor is eclectic, with a fireplace for cosy winter nights and even a piano. The hostel's modern apartments are great value.

Lounge Hostel
HOSTEL €

(☑076 547 165; www.loungehostel.mk; Naum Naumovski Borče 80, 1st fl; dm €9-12, s/d €17/25; 🕸🛜) A lovely large common area, orthopaedic mattresses and bright, breezy balconies attached to every room (privates and dorms) are some of the highlights of this sociable retro-styled hostel with a view over the City Park. Staff are a little less clued-up here than at some other hostels, but will bend over backwards to help make guests' lives easier.

Bed & Breakfast London
BOUTIQUE HOTEL €€

(☑02 3116 146; www.londonbnb.mk; Maksim Gorki 1; s/d/ste €50/60/90; 🕸🛜) The theme at this hotel is a little random, but all is forgiven when you see the front-row Ploštad view it has – rooms at the front are in gawping distance of the Alexander the Great fountain, though the hotel is set back slightly from the main square and windows are thick enough that sound from the cafe-bar below doesn't disturb too much.

Senigallia
HOTEL €€

(☑02 3224 044; www.senigallia.mk; Kej 13 Noemvri 5S; s/d €65/75 ste €90-110; 🕸🛜) You see that splendid ship docked opposite the grand Archaeological Museum? It's not a pirate ship; it's a rather swish hotel that just so happens to blend in perfectly with the government's weird and wonderful building drive along the Vardar river. The hotel's interior is all wood panelling, rooms have mini fridges and there's a terrace bar on the top deck.

★ **Hotel Solun** HOTEL €€€
(☑ 02 3232 512, 071 238 599; www.hotelsolun.com; Nikola Vapčarov 10; s/d from €83/103; ❄ @ 🛜 🏊) The 55-room Solun sits in a different stratosphere to most of Macedonia's faded 'high-end' hotels (though you wouldn't know it from the dated hotel signage around the Ploštad). It's a stylish and design-conscious property that wouldn't feel out of place in any European capital, accessed through an alley just off the main square.

✗ Eating

★ **Kebapčilnica Destan** KEBAB €
(ul 104 6; set meal 180MKD; ⊘ 7am-11pm) Skopje's best beef kebabs, accompanied by seasoned grilled bread, peppers and a little raw onion, are served at this classic Čaršija place. There's no menu, everyone gets the same thing, but the terrace is usually full – that's how good it is. Ten stubby kebabs constitute a serious meat feast (180MKD); or you can ask for a half portion (120MKD).

Rock Kafana Rustikana GRILL €
(☑ 02 72 561 450; off Dimitrije Čupovski; 140-300MKD; ⊘ 8am-midnight Mon-Sat; 🛜 🍴) Just a block from the Ploštad but rocking a decidedly more local vibe, this humble bar-restaurant prides itself on good music, friendly service and simple dishes of grilled meats, sandwiches and inventive bar snacks such as zucchini with sour cream and garlic. Its setting amid an unkempt, mildly post-apocalyptic green space behind the Rekord Hostel only adds to its kooky charm.

Restaurant Pelister INTERNATIONAL €€
(Ploštad Makedonija; mains 260-400MKD; ⊘ 7am-1am daily Jun-Sep, 7am-1am Fri-Sat, to midnight Sun-Thu Oct-May; 🛜 🍴) This cafe-restaurant is a real local fixture with a prime spot on Skopje's Ploštad and the feel of a Mitteleuropa grand cafe, attracting a diverse crowd. It's a good spot for coffee and people-watching, and it also serves a vast array of decent pastas.

★ **Pivnica An** MACEDONIAN €€€
(Beerhouse An; ☑ 02 3212 111; www.pivnicaan.mk; Kapan An; mains 250-750MKD; ⊘ 10am-midnight; 🛜 🍴) Skopje's Čaršija is still home to a couple of *ans* – ancient Ottoman inns, similar to desert *caravanserai* – and the Kapan An houses this upmarket restaurant, serving some of the city's best Macedonian fare. Try butter-soft *sarma* (stuffed vine leaves) or roasted pork ribs and observe history echoing through the sumptuous central courtyard, where Pivnica's partially covered patio offers a tranquil bolt-hole. It's tricky to find: it's through an archway off the busy little square in the heart of the Čaršija where the kebab restaurants are concentrated.

Skopski Merak MACEDONIAN €€€
(☑ 02 3212 215; Debarca 51; mains 200-1000MKD; ⊘ 8am-1am; 🛜 🍴) This hugely popular place packs locals in with its pretty timber-framed terrace, live music most evenings and huge menu of *skara* (grilled meats) and other Macedonian specialities. Its chef's choice platters of smoked meats, local cheeses and grilled veg are particularly impressive, but not on the menu: ask for *daska* (around 500MKD for two people). It's worth booking for dinner.

MACEDONIA SKOPJE

ITINERARIES

One Week

Plan to spend at least a couple of days in the capital **Skopje** (p769) marvelling at the statues and visiting its **Čaršija** (p770). Leave time for a day trip to **Canyon Matka** (p775), then head southwest to historic **Ohrid** (p777) for some R&R by the lake.

Complete the week with a couple of nights at a village guesthouse on the edge of **Pelister National Park** (p783), and a visit to **Golem Grad** (p782) island.

Two Weeks

Between Skopje and Ohrid, add in a trip through **Mavrovo National Park** (p776), stay in a village and visit the impressive **Sveti Jovan Bigorski Monastery** (p776). From Pelister National Park take a trip to the cultured city of Bitola, with its ancient **Heraclea Lyncestis** (p784) ruins. Before heading back to Skopje, spend a night at Macedonia's fabulous winery hotel, **Popova Kula** (p781).

🍷 Drinking & Nightlife

The steep Čaršija street called Teodosij Gologanov is the centre of Skopje's nightlife.

★ Old Town Brewery
CRAFT BEER

(Gradište 1; ⊙10am-1am; 🛜) The siren call of tasty craft beer sings to locals and tourists alike at Skopje's only microbrewery, which is justifiably popular for its Weiss beer, IPA, Golden Ale and dark beer – all brewed on-site and accompanied by a dependable menu of international pub grub. Its sunny terrace, sandwiched between the fortress walls and the Sveti Spas Church, crowns its appeal.

Van Gogh Bar
BAR

(📞02 3121 876; Mikhail Cokov 4; ⊙8am-1am) Whisky nights, cocktail nights, live-music nights...there's something going on every day of the week at Van Gogh, a poky bar with a lively local crew that spills onto the street. The bar is a haunt of local bikers, but all sorts of characters drink here and it's always good fun. It's close to the City Park, in Debar Maalo.

ℹ️ Information

INTERNET ACCESS

Free wi-fi is widespread in cafes, restaurants and hotels, though it's often unadvertised – don't feel cheeky asking staff for password details. Some hotels have desktop computers for guest use.

MEDICAL SERVICES

City Hospital (📞02 3235 000; 11 Oktomvri 53; ⊙24hr)

Neuromedica Private Clinic (📞02 3133 313; www.neuromedica.com.mk; Partizanski Odredi 42; ⊙24hr)

TOURIST INFORMATION

Skopje's tourist offices are neglected, not always open and not very useful. The staff in your hotel are likely to be far better sources of information.

Skopje Tourist Office (Filip Makedonski; ⊙8.30am-4.30pm)

TRAVEL AGENCIES

Go Macedonia (📞02 3064 647; www.gomacedonia.com; ul Ankarska 29a)

Macedonia Experience (📞075 243 944; www.macedoniaexperience.com; ul Nikola Kljusev 3, Skopje)

Macedonia Travel (📞02 3112 408; www.macedoniatravel.com; Orce Nikolov 109/1, 3rd fl)

ℹ️ Getting There & Away

AIR

Skopje Alexander the Great Airport (📞02 3148 333; www.airports.com.mk; 1043, Petrovec) is located 21km east of the city centre. Skopje has direct air services to many cities throughout Europe, Turkey and the Gulf.

BUS

Skopje's **bus station** (📞02 2466 313; www.sas.com.mk in Macedonian; bul Nikola Karev), with ATM, exchange office and English-language information office, adjoins the train station. Bus schedules are only available online in Macedonian (your hotel/hostel staff should be more than happy to translate for you, though). Buy tickets on the day or in advance from the window counters inside the station.

Domestic Buses

Bitola (480MKD, three hours, 11 daily)
Kavadarci (270MKD, two hours, 10 daily)
Mavrovo (350MKD, two hours, two Monday to Saturday)
Ohrid (500MKD, three hours, 14 daily)

International Buses

Belgrade (1400MKD, six to eight hours, 10 daily)
İstanbul (1900MKD, 12 hours, five daily)
Ljubljana (3800MKD, 14 hours, one daily)
Pristina (330MKD, two hours, 14 daily)
Sarajevo (3170MKD, 14 hours, 8pm Wednesday and Sunday)
Sofia (1040MKD, 5½ hours, five daily)
Thessaloniki (1300MKD, four hours, 6am and 5pm Monday, Wednesday and Friday)
Zagreb (3200MKD, 12 hours, 5pm daily)

CAR

For car hire try **Balkan Rent-A-Car** (📞02 6091 112, 070 206 157; balkanrentacar@yahoo.com; Vladimir Polezinovski 30; 1-5 days from €27 per day).

TRAIN

The **train station** (Železnička Stanica; bul Jane Sandanski) serves local and international destinations.

Domestic Trains

The 5.10pm daily service to Bitola is an express train, taking two hours 40 minutes. All trains to Bitola stop at Prilep first.

Bitola (320MKD, 3½ hours, four daily)
Negotino (200MKD, 1¾ hours, two daily)
Prilep (250MKD, three hours, four daily)

International Trains

Disagreements with the Greek government have led to periodically suspended train routes with Greece. At the time of writing, the Skopje–Thessaloniki ticket being sold by the train station involved a train to Gevgelija and then a bus across the border to Thessaloniki (760MKD, five hours, 4.45am daily).

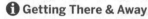

A train serves Belgrade (1430MKD, 10 hours, 10.19pm daily), and another heads for Pristina (three hours, 4.10pm daily) in Kosovo; for Pristina, the train station will only sell you a ticket to the border (100MKD) and at the border you need to buy another ticket for your onward travel to the capital, costing €2.50.

ⓘ Getting Around

TO/FROM THE AIRPORT

Airport shuttle bus **Vardar Express** (📞 02 3118 263; www.vardarexpress.com) runs between the airport and the city; check the website for its timetable. Taxis to the airport cost 800MKD to 1000MKD. From the airport to the city centre, taxis cost 1200MKD.

BUS

Skopje's public city buses cost 35MKD and follow numbered routes. You can buy and validate tickets on board. Buses congregate under the bus/train station.

TAXI

Skopje's taxis aren't bad value, with the first kilometre costing just 40MKD, and 25MKD for subsequent kilometres. Drivers rarely speak English, but they do use their meters (if they don't, just ask or point). Central destinations cost 60MKD to 150MKD.

Around Skopje

Monasteries, mountains plunging into a spectacular canyon and an impressive new ethno village surround Skopje's urban core, and make worthwhile day trips.

⊙ Sights

Macedonian Village   MUSEUM, HOTEL
(📞 02 3077 600; www.macedonianvillage.mk; Gorno Nerezi village) **FREE** Across the road from ancient **Sveti Pantelejmon Monastery** (Gorno Nerezi village; admission 120MKD; ⊙10am-5pm Tue-Sun), it is something of a surprise to come face to face with this elaborate, no-money-spared reconstruction of a Macedonian village. The village – also a quirky heritage hotel with restaurants and a bar – consists of 12 houses typical of each region of Macedonia, showcasing traditional styles of architecture. Tours of the village are free and finish at a small ethnographic museum. A taxi from Skopje city centre takes about 20 minutes and should cost around 350MKD.

Mt Vodno   MOUNTAIN
(gondola round-trip 100MKD) Framing Skopje to the south, Vodno's towering mass – pin-

pointed by the 66m Millennium Cross – is an enduring symbol of the city. A popular (shaded) hiking trail cuts a swathe up its wooded slopes and there's also a gondola that climbs the mountainside from halfway up, where a couple of restaurants cater to day-trippers. To get here, take the 'Millennium Cross' special bus (35MKD, 12 daily) from the bus station to the gondola. A taxi to the gondola costs about 200MKD.

ⓘ Getting There & Away

At the time of writing, there were plans to run a bus line up to the Sveti Pantelejmon Monastery and ethno village, but it wasn't yet in operation.

Canyon Matka (Матка)

Ah, Matka. Early Christians, ascetics and anti-Ottoman revolutionaries picked a sublime spot when they retreated into the hills here from Ottoman advances: the setting is no less than reverential.

Churches, chapels and monasteries have long been guarded by these forested mountains, though most have now been left to rack and ruin.

These days, locals and tourists alike come to take the breadth of the canyon and dip a toe in the tempting clear waters of the dammed lake. Brace yourself: the temperature hovers at around 14°C year-round.

Canyon Matka is a popular day trip from Skopje and crowded at weekends; if you want peace and quiet, come very.

⊙ Sights

There are also several atmospheric churches (mostly ruins) scaling the canyon cliffs but getting to them is tricky. **Sveti Spas**, close to the village of Gorna Matka, has a modern bell tower and crumbling, ancient chapel (often locked), with the ruins of **Sveta Trojca** adjoining the site; **Sveta Nedela** is the highest and most spectacularly located atop a rocky outcrop, but the scramble up there is scary indeed.

Church of Sveti Andrej   CHURCH
(Lake Matka; ⊙9/10am-4pm) **FREE** The most easily accessible of Canyon Matka's 14th-century churches and also one of the finest, the petite Church of St Andrew (1389) is practically attached to the Canyon Matka Hotel and backed by the towering massif of the canyon walls. Inside, well-preserved painted frescoes depict apostles, holy warriors and archangels. Opening hours can be a bit erratic.

Sveta Bogorodica Monastery MONASTERY
(Lake Matka; ☺8am-8pm) FREE Bogorodica is an extremely sweet spot. Framed by mountains and blessed with some interesting architectural features, the monastery is still home to nuns and an air of peace prevails (cover shoulders and knees when visiting). The wooden-balustraded living quarters date to the 18th century and the frescoed chapel to the 14th century, though a church has stood on this spot since the 6th century. Bogorodica is clearly signposted from the road that leads to the Canyon Matka car parks.

Cave Vrelo CAVE
(Matka boat kiosk; 400MKD; ☺9am-7pm) A team of scuba divers from Italy and Belgium have explored Matka's underwater caverns to a depth of 212m and still not found the bottom, making these caves among the deepest in Europe. Cave Vrelo is open to the public and the chug down the canyon by boat to reach it is a popular excursion – offering visitors a chance to get out on the water as well as enter the inky depths of the bat-inhabited cave. Boats depart from Canyon Matka Hotel.

🏃 Activities

While it's theoretically possible to do some hiking at Lake Matka, most of the trails are not maintained and it's not recommended you attempt any serious walking without a guide (book in Skopje) or reliable GPS.

The area's easiest amble is a 5km walkway that clings precariously to one side of the steep canyon walls, though tragically its appeal is dampened by the volume of cigarette butts carelessly littering the path.

You can rent kayaks (single/double kayak per 30 mins 150/250MKD; ☺9am-7pm) at the boat kiosk for a gentle paddle.

🛏 Sleeping & Eating

Canyon Matka Hotel LODGE €€
(☎02 2052 655; www.canyonmatka.mk; Lake Matka; d €40-50) Its premium lakefront setting by the canyon walls makes this hotel a fine place for a night's rest, but it's a bit more rough around the edges than might be expected and ultimately feels like an adjunct to the excellent restaurant below. Rooms on the 2nd floor have characterful wooden beams but are slightly smaller than those on the 1st floor.

ⓘ Getting There & Away

From Skopje, catch bus 60 from bul Partizanski Odredi or from the bus/train station (return 70MKD, 40 minutes, nine daily). From the bus and taxi (450MKD) drop-off point at Matka, it's a scenic 10- to 15-minute walk to the main lake area. There are also two free car parks here.

WESTERN MACEDONIA

Mavrovo National Park
Маврово Национален Парк

The gorges, pine forests, karst fields and waterfalls of Mavrovo National Park offer a breath of fresh, rarefied air for visitors travelling between Skopje and Ohrid. Locally the park is best known for its ski resort (the country's biggest) near Mavrovo town, but by international standards the skiing is fairly average. In summertime, this area is glorious.

Driving in the park is extremely scenic, but a word of caution: car GPS doesn't work well here and signposting is poor.

◉ Sights & Activities

★**Sveti Jovan Bigorski Monastery** MONASTERY
(☺services 5.30am, 4pm, 6pm) FREE This revered 1020 Byzantine monastery is located, fittingly, up in the gods along a track of switchbacks off the Debar road, close to Janče village. Legend attests an icon of Sveti Jovan Bigorski (St John the Baptist) miraculously appeared here; since then the monastery has been rebuilt often – the icon occasionally reappearing too. The complex went into demise during Communist rule but has been painstakingly reconstructed and today is as impressive as ever, with some excellent views over Mavrovo's mountains. Hang about and the monks might approach for a chat and offer a tea or coffee. The monastery also offers comfy hostel accommodation (☑Father Serges 070 304 316, Father Silvan 078 383 771; www.bigorski.org; Mavrovo National Park; dm €15-20; ❄ ☎); call a day ahead to book.

Janče VILLAGE
The small village of Janče is one of the few places in Mavrovo (beside the ski resort) where it's possible to get decent accommodation (p777). It's a picturesque spot that scales the hillside, with awesome views and some fascinating examples of decaying rural architecture.

Note that although Janče and Galičnik are very close to each other as the crow flies (6km), there is no road between the two and to visit both involves a drive of about 1½ hours looping through the national park. A picturesque walking trail connects the two villages but some parts can be tricky to follow; if at all possible, take a GPS with you if you plan to do this walk.

Galičnik
VILLAGE

Up a winding, tree-lined road ending in a rocky moonscape 17km southwest of Mavrovo, almost depopulated Galičnik features traditional houses along the mountainside. It's also famed for its traditional cheese making. The village is placid except for during the Galičnik Wedding Festival in mid-July.

Horse Club Bistra Galičnik
HORSE RIDING

(☑077 648 679; www.horseriding.com.mk) Offers daily rides (as well as multiday excursions) through Mavrovo's mountain valleys, departing from the village of Galičnik and dropping by traditional villages. The shortest treks offered are two, three or four hours and involve a stop for cheese tasting.

🛏 Sleeping & Eating

Hotel Tutto
HOTEL €€

(☑042 470 999; www.tutto.com.mk; Janče; s/d/t €30/50/60; P❋🛜🐾) A foodie hotel with a broad brushstroke of a dining terrace wrapped around it, fronting a ramshackle village of crumbling 19th-century stone houses high in the hills of Mavrovo: welcome to one of Macedonia's most enterprising community projects. Service is a bit hit and miss, but the 1st-floor rooms are exceedingly comfy: ask for one at the front to appreciate the view from your balcony. Tutto's owner also rents a handful of nice apartments (one- to two-bed, €40 to €50; email for details) in two restored houses in the village and has grand ambitions to help support the community by turning the entire village into an eco-project.

❶ Getting There & Away

Without your own wheels, it's difficult to reach the various places of interest in the national park independently, or do any hiking.

Two buses a day run from Skopje to Mavrovo town Monday to Saturday (350MKD, 9.30am and 2.45pm).

For Sveti Jovan Bigorski Monastery, buses transiting Debar for Ohrid or Struga will be able to drop you off. The monastery is very close to the village of Janče, so you would no doubt be able to make it to the village if you can get as far as the monastery (even if it means walking between the two – it's about 5km).

Ohrid
Охрид
POP 55,749

Sublime Ohrid is Macedonia's most seductive destination, with an atmospheric old quarter cascading down a graceful hill, crammed full of beautiful churches and topped by the bones of a medieval castle. Its cobbled streets are flanked by traditional restaurants and lakeside cafes, but it's not a complete tourist circus just yet and still has a lived-in feel.

Best of all is that you can be skipping through historic monuments one minute and lying on a deck chair with your toes in the water the next – its location right on the edge of serene Lake Ohrid is hard to beat. A holiday atmosphere prevails all summer; Ohrid's busiest time is from mid-July to mid-August, during the popular summer festival (☑046 262 304; www.ohridsummer.com.mk; Kej Maršal Tito; ⊙box office 9am-10pm Jul & Aug).

◉ Sights

★Church of Sveti Jovan at Kaneo
CHURCH

(Kaneo; 100MKD; ⊙9am-6pm) This stunning 13th-century church is set on a cliff over the lake, about a 15-minute walk west of Ohrid's port area, and is possibly Macedonia's most photographed structure. Peer down into the azure waters and you'll see why medieval monks found spiritual inspiration here. The small church has original frescoes behind the altar. Little bobbing boats cluster beneath the church around the cliff base, waiting to whisk passengers back to the harbour (300MKD) if you don't fancy the walk.

★Ohrid Boardwalk & City Beach
BEACH

Skimming the surface of the water along Ohrid's shore, snaking towards Kaneo fishing village and the town's most famous church, this over-water boardwalk propels people towards a gorgeous outcrop of rocky beaches and a handful of small restaurants and bars. On a hot day, the area is thronged by bathers, drinkers and diners. The cool waters are translucent and inviting, the cliff-backed setting is sublime and strolling this stretch of coast up to the Church of Sveti Jovan is an Ohrid must.

Plaošnik
CHURCH

(adult/student & child 100/30MKD; ⊙8am-7pm) Saluting the lake from Ohrid's hilltop, Plaošnik is home to the multidomed medieval Church of Sveti Kliment i Pantelejmon, the foundations of a 5th-century basilica and a garden of intricate Early Christian

Ohrid

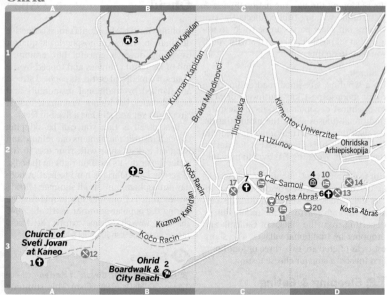

flora-and-fauna mosaics. The central church was restored in 2002; though it lacks the ancient wall frescoes of many other Macedonian churches, it is unusual in having glass floor segments revealing the original foundations and framed relics from the medieval church, which dated to the 9th century. At the time of writing, Plaošnik's once-woody environs were a building site, paving the way for the construction of a ginormous School of Theology that will also house a museum and gallery of icons.

Sveta Bogorodica Bolnička & Sveti Nikola Bolnički   CHURCH

(off Car Samoil; admission to each church 50MKD; ⊘9am-1pm) *Bolnica* means 'hospital' in Macedonian; during plagues visitors faced 40-day quarantines inside the confines of these petite churches that are thought to date to the 14th century. Sandwiched between Car Samoil and Kosta Abras in the Old Town, the churches have somewhat irregular opening hours, but are worth a look if you're passing and they are accessible. Both churches are small and low-lying, but have intricate interiors heaving under elaborate icons.

Sveta Sofija Cathedral   CHURCH

(Car Samoil; adult/student & child 100/30MKD; ⊘9am-7pm) Ohrid's grandest church, 11th-century Sveta Sofija is supported by columns and decorated with elaborate, if very faded, Byzantine frescoes, though they are well preserved and very vivid in the apse, still. Its superb acoustics mean it's often used for concerts. To one side of the church there's a peaceful, manicured garden providing a small oasis of green in the heart of the Old Town.

National Museum   MUSEUM

(Robev Family House Museum; Car Samoil 62; adult/student & child 100/50MKD; ⊘9am-3pm Tue-Sun) Ohrid's National Museum is housed over three floors of this remarkably well-preserved Old Town house, which dates to 1863 and was once owned by the Robev family of merchants. The creaking timbered building has just been renovated; on the top two floors displays include Roman archaeological finds, a 5th-century golden mask from Ohrid and local wood carving, while the ground floor is reserved for art exhibitions. Across the road the Urania Residence, a further part of the museum, has an ethnographic display.

Car Samoil's Fortress   CASTLE

(Kuzman Kapidan; 30MKD; ⊘9am-7pm) The massive, turreted walls of Ohrid's 10th-century castle indicate the power of the medieval Bulgarian state. The ramparts offer fantastic views over the town and lake, but there's lit-

N 0 — 200 m
0 — 0.1 miles

City Hostel (300m);
Green Market (350m);
(1.3km)

Galeb Ticket Office

Harbour

MACEDONIA OHRID

tle else to come here for – the site itself is in a bit of a woeful state.

🏃 Activities

Free Pass Ohrid   TOURS
(☑ 070 488 231; www.freepassohrid.mk; Kosta Abraš 74) This alternative tourism company organises stacks of cultural and adventure tours from its base in Ohrid, including winery tours to Tikveš, hiking in Galičica National Park and paragliding over Lake Ohrid.

🛏 Sleeping

★ **Sunny Lake Hostel**   HOSTEL €
(☑ 075 629 571; www.sunnylakehostel.mk; 11 Oktombri 15; dm €10-12, d €25 Jul–mid-Sep, dm €8-9, d €22 mid-Sep–Jun; ❄ 🛜) This excellent hostel is a bustling hub for backpackers stopping off in Ohrid. Space is a little cramped, but nobody cares because they have such a good time here. The common areas are a highlight: a snug upstairs terrace with lake views and a garden down below for beer drinking. Facilities include laundry, free breakfast, a kitchen, lockers and bike hire (€5 per day).

★ **Villa Jovan**   HISTORIC HOTEL €
(☑ 076 236 606; vila.jovan@gmail.com; Car Samoli 44; s/d/ste €25/35/49; ❄ 🛜) There are nine rooms within this 1856 mansion in the heart

of Ohrid's Old Town, and they're charmingly rustic with old-world furnishings and wooden beams. The rooms are a little on the small side but they're bright and have more character than anything else in town. Two of the rooms have quirky sunken baths and tiny sun-trap terraces.

City Hostel   HOSTEL €
(☑ 078 208 407; jedidooel@yahoo.com; bul Makedonski Prosvetiteli 22; dm/d €10/€30 incl breakfast; ❄ ❄ 🛜) In a modern block a 10-minute walk north of Ohrid's harbour, everything at this family-run hostel feels fresh and new. The quirky interior takes inspiration from Ohrid's timbered Old Town houses – even down to the lanterns. The common area is a little dark and there's no communal outside chilling space, but the rooms are bright and all have balconies and ensuite bathrooms.

Villa Lucija   GUESTHOUSE €
(☑ 046 265 608, 077 714 815; www.vilalucija.com.mk; Kosta Abraš 29; s/d/tr/apt €25/35/40/55; ❄ 🛜) Lucija is in the thick of the Old Town with

possibly the most enviable location: right on the lake front with a patio and decking by the water's edge, complete with lounge chairs. A homely feel pervades, with a communal kitchen and lovingly decorated, breezy rooms with lake-view balconies. Rooms cost €5 less per night from mid-September to mid-June.

★ **Jovanovic Guest House** GUESTHOUSE **€€**
(📞 070 589 218; jovanovic.guesthouse@hotmail.com; Boro Sain 5; apt €40-65; ❋ 🛜 🛗) This property has two studio apartments, both of which sleep four, set in the heart of the Old Town. Each is well equipped and comes with a shady balcony. The apartment on the 1st floor is slightly bigger, but the top-floor apartment's balcony is more private and has one of the best views in town, right over the lake and Sveta Sofija Cathedral.

✗ Eating

The best place for self-caterers to stock up is the **fruit and vegetable market** (off Goce Delčev; ⊙ 7am-9pm Mon-Sat, to 2pm Sun, closes 2 hrs earlier Mon-Sat in winter), just north of the Činar tree, and the **supermarkets** (bul Makedonski Prosvetiteli) at the foot of Makedonski Prosvetiteli, by the harbour.

Via Sacra PIZZA **€**
(📞 075 440 211; www.viasacra.mk; Ilindenska 36; mains 160-350MKD; ⊙ 9am-1am; 🛜 🛗) Pleasantly fusing the best of Italian and Macedonian fare, Via Sacra offers up crisp and tasty pizzas as well as a good selection of Macedonian national cooking and wines. Service is excellent and its location is a big draw too: facing the lovely Sveta Sofija Cathedral on

---

LAKE CONSERVATION: OHRID SOS

Lake Ohrid's growing popularity as a stop-off on the tourist circuit has come at a price. Thanks in part to an increase in cheap international flights to Ohrid, plans have been drawn up to create a marina, artificial Mediterranean-style beaches and new apartments by draining an important marshland that acts as a natural filter to the lake. A local initiative called Ohrid SOS was set up in 2015 to help challenge the proposals, and the struggle to find a balance between commercial desires and conservation imperatives continues.

---

a cobbled Old Town street. Breakfast is also served, a rarity in Ohrid.

★ **Letna Bavča Kaneo** SEAFOOD **€€**
(📞 046 250 975; Kočo Racin 43; mains 220-370MKD; ⊙ 9am-midnight; 🛜) There are three terrace restaurants dipping their toes in the water at Kaneo and this one is marginally considered the best. A fry-up of *plasnica* (a diminutive fish commonly eaten fried in the Balkans; 190MKD), plus salad, feeds two cheaply, or try other Lake Ohrid specialities such as eel, carp or local lake fish *belvica* – the location doesn't come much better than this.

Restoran Cun MACEDONIAN **€€**
(📞 046 255 603; Kosta Abraš 4; mains 180-480MKD; 🛗) There's a vaguely nautical air about this whitewashed restaurant with large lakefront windows and a breezy elevated terrace, housed in a traditional-style Ohrid Old Town building. Of all the restaurants on this prime strip, Cun is the classiest. Across the road there's a strip of streetside tables close enough to dive into the harbour; a great spot for breakfast.

Restaurant Antiko MACEDONIAN **€€**
(Car Samoil 30; mains 200-800MKD; ⊙ 11am-11pm; 🛗) In an old Ohrid mansion in the middle of the Old Town, the famous Antiko has great traditional ambience and is a good place to try classic Macedonian dishes such as *tavče gravče* (beans cooked in spices and peppers), and top-quality Macedonian wines.

🍷 Drinking & Nightlife

Ohrid's main nightclub is **Havana Club** (www.cubalibreohrid.com; Partizanska 2; ⊙ 1am-5am) **FREE**, just outside the Old Town.

★ **Jazz Inn** BAR
(Kosta Abraš 74; ⊙ 9pm-1am) This unassuming little jazz-themed bar sways to a different rhythm than the strip of bars down on Ohrid's lakefront, with an alternative vibe, a different soundtrack and grungier clientele. Tucked down a cobbled backstreet away from the touristy hubbub, the low-lit interior has a speakeasy feel, though revellers can be found spilling out onto the road by midnight on weekends and throughout summer.

Liquid CAFE
(Kosta Abraš 17; ⊙ 10am-1am; 🛜 🛗) Ohrid's most stylish lakefront bar is a relaxed chillout place by day, serving coffee and drinks (no food). At night it morphs into the town's most lively bar with a beautiful crowd and

TASTING TIKVEŠ WINES

On the cusp of eastern Macedonia, Tikveš is the country's most lauded and well-developed wine region. Although many vineyards are theoretically open for tastings, beware that in practice it's difficult to tour them independently. Signposting is extremely poor and virtually none of the wineries accept walk-ins. If you want to visit, you'll need to plan appointments to taste and tour by calling ahead (and arrange a taxi, at a cost of about €25 per car for five or so hours, to escort you around).

If you want to visit this area, your best bet is to book a night at the region's excellent winery hotel and restaurant, **Popova Kula** (☑ 043 367 400; www.popovakula.com.mk; bul Na Vinoto 1, Demir Kapija; s €35–€45, d €45-60) in Demir Kapija. Tours of the property are held four times a day for guests and non-guests, rooms have wonderful vineyard views and its restaurant offers food and wine pairing menus.

If you don't have time to stay over, it's also possible to take a tour of the region from Ohrid (a long day) with **Free Pass Ohrid** (p779).

---

pumping music. Its patio jutting into the lake has the best views and ambience on this strip. During the day this place is kid-friendly, too.

ℹ Information

Ohrid no longer has an official tourist office (despite the fact that many city maps suggest it does); www.visitohrid.org is the municipal website.

Once you leave Ohrid town, ATMs are surprisingly hard to find elsewhere around the lake. There's a reliable one in the foyer of Hotel Bellevue, just south of Ohrid town.

ℹ Getting There & Around

AIR

Ohrid's **St Paul the Apostle Airport** (☑ 046 252 820; www.airports.com.mk) is 10km north of the town.

There is no public transport to and from the airport. Taxis cost 500MKD one way (it's a set fare) and are easy to pick up without pre-booking.

BUS

Ohrid's **bus station** (cnr 7 Noemvri & Klanoec) is 1.5km northeast of the town centre. Tickets can either be bought at the station itself or from the **Galeb** (www.galeb.mk; Partizanska; ⊙ 9am-5pm) bus company ticket office just outside Ohrid Old Town. A taxi to Ohrid's bus station from the port area on the edge of the Old Town is a set fare of 150MKD. Destinations include the following:

Skopje via Kičevo (490MKD, three hours, seven daily)

Skopje via Bitola (550MKD, five hours, two daily)

Bitola (190MKD, 1½ hours, six daily)

Kavadarci/Tikveš (420MKD, 3¼ hours, one daily)

Belgrade, Serbia Three buses a day but only one direct, departing at midday (1790MKD, nine hours)

Tirana, Albania (1000MKD, four hours, one daily)

Kotor, Montenegro (1530MKD, 8½ hours, one daily)

It's also possible to cross into Albania by taking the bus or a taxi to Sveti Naum, from where you can cross the border and take a taxi (€5, 6km) to Pogradeci.

Around Ohrid

The rippling, rock-crested massif of Galičica lies to the east of Ohrid, separating Lakes Ohrid and Prespa. To the south, a long, wooded coast conceals pebble beaches, churches and a **camp site** (per tent €10; ⊙ 24hr reception) at Gradište. Much of the area surrounding Lake Ohrid is protected within the 228-sq-km **Galičica National Park**, stretching down to Sveti Naum.

At 300m deep, 34km long and three million years old, Lake Ohrid is among Europe's deepest and oldest. The Macedonian portion is inscribed on the Unesco World Heritage list and is considered the most biodiverse lake of its size in the world.

◉ Sights

★ **Sveti Naum Monastery**   MONASTERY
(Lake Ohrid; 100MKD, parking 50MKD; ⊙ 7am-8pm Jun-Aug, closes at sunset rest of year) Sveti Naum, 29km south of Ohrid, is an imposing sight on a bluff near the Albanian border and a popular day trip from Ohrid. Naum was a contemporary of St Kliment, and their monastery an educational centre. The iconostasis inside the church date to 1711 and the frescoes to the 19th century, and it's well worth paying the fee to enter. Sandy beaches hem the mon-

astery in on two sides and are some of the best places to swim around Lake Ohrid.

Surrounding the core of the complex is a tranquil garden looped by fountains, with roses and peacocks (mind the peacocks – they're cranky!). Boat trips to the **Springs of St Naum** (per boat 600MKD) are also worthwhile, and there's a good-value **hotel** (☑046 283 080; www.hotel-stnaum.com.mk; s/d/ste from €30/40/50; ☏).

If you come by car, you have to pay for parking at the entrance to the monastery.

★ Golem Grad   ISLAND

(Lake Prespa) Adrift on Lake Prespa, Golem Grad was once the summer playground of Car Samoil but is now home to wild tortoises, cormorants and pelicans, and perhaps a few ghosts. A settlement endured here from the 4th century BC to the 6th century AD and during medieval times there was a monastery complex. The ruins, birdlife and otherworldly beauty make it well worth exploration. Trips can be organised through Vila Raskrsnica (p784) in the village of Brajčino or Dzani Dimovski (☑070 678 123), who owns the cafe at Dupeni Beach.

An hour or so on the island and return boat transfers from Dupeni Beach costs €65 for up to three to four people.

Museum on Water – Bay of the Bones   MUSEUM

(☑078 909 806; adult/student & child 100/30MKD; ☺9am-7pm Jul-Aug, to 4pm rest of year, closed Mon Oct-Apr) In prehistoric times Lake Ohrid was home to a settlement of pile dwellers who lived literally on top of the water, on a platform supported by up to 10,000 wooden piles anchored to the lake bed. The remains of the settlement were discovered at this spot and between 1997 and 2005 they were gradually excavated by an underwater team – the Museum on Water is an elaborate reconstruction of the settlement as archaeologists think it would have looked between 1200 and 600 BC.

Vevčani   VILLAGE

(Lake Ohrid) Keeping one sleepy eye on Lake Ohrid from its mountain perch, Vevčani dates to the 9th century and is a quiet rural settlement beloved by locals for its traditional restaurants and **natural springs** (Vevchani, Lake Ohrid; adult/child 20/10MKD; ☺9am-5pm). The old brick streets flaunt a distinctive 19th-century rural architecture and the village is watched over by the Church of St Nicholas. Vevčani lies 14km north of Struga, at the northerly edge of the lake. Buses from Struga run hourly (50MKD); a taxi should cost around 400MKD.

🛏 Sleeping

Robinson Sunset House   HOSTEL €

(☑075 727 252; www.ohridhotel.org; Lagadin, Lake Ohrid; dm/d/apt €12/30/45; ❀☏⊞) Sweeping lake views, free surfboards (for paddling) and a sprawling garden with lots of relaxing nooks and crannies make this ramshackle hostel a winner if you don't fancy the bustle of Ohrid itself. It sits on a hill above the village of Lagadin, a short bus ride south of Ohrid town. Rooms are spacious and charming, if a little rough around the edges.

✖ Eating & Drinking

Kutmičevica   MACEDONIAN €€

(☑046 798 399; kutmicevica@yahoo.com; Vevčani; mains 250-900MKD; ☺10am-11pm; 🖬) This restaurant, which reverberates with the chatter of locals, is a great find: the views from its dining room are immense, right out over the lake, and it spills onto a terrace on sunny days. The traditional wood-beamed setting

---

ESSENTIAL FOOD & DRINK

Ajvar Sweet red-pepper dip; accompanies meats and cheeses.

Lukanci Homemade chorizo-like pork sausages, laced with paprika.

Pita A pie made of a coil of flaky pastry stuffed with local cheese and spinach or leek.

Rakija Grape-based fruit brandy.

Šopska salata Tomatoes, onions and cucumbers topped with grated sirenje (white cheese).

Tavče gravče Baked beans cooked with spices, onions and herbs and served in earthenware.

Vranec and **Temjanika** Macedonia's favourite red/white wine varietals.

matches the menu, where you'll see some Macedonian specialities you won't see on the menus in Ohrid, and some inventive takes on classic foods.

If you want to stay in Vevčani, this place also offers a few rooms.

Restaurant Ostrovo MACEDONIAN €€
(Острово; Sveti Naum Monastery; mains 120-850MKD; ⊗8am-9pm) Of all the restaurants at Sveti Naum, this one has the prettiest setting by the water. Cross the little bridge and there's a seemingly endless garden for dining as well as a unique feature: moored pontoons that you can eat on. Staff speak very little English but are friendly and helpful. Fish features heavily on the menu and breakfast here is good.

Orevche Beach Bar BAR
(Orevche, Lake Ohrid; ⊗10am-8pm; 🛜) A twisted cliffside path sloping steeply downwards into the unknown makes Orevche feel like a secret hideaway, and really it is because hardly anybody knows it's here. The Lake Ohrid water is clear and it would be easy to lose a few hours lounging on the rustic beach bar's day beds and swimming, particularly at sunset. It's not quite Ibiza, but it's lovely.

As well as alcohol, coffee and a short lunch menu is served, or there are toasted sandwiches outside of lunch hours.

❶ Getting Around

Frequent buses ply the Ohrid–Sveti Naum route (€1) in summer, stopping off at various points along the lake road, including the village of Lagadin and the Bay of Bones.

From Ohrid town harbour, boats run to Sveti Naum (€10 return) every day at 10am, returning at 4pm, and it's 1.5 hours each way; taxis take half an hour and cost €16 one way or €32 return, and for that price the driver will stop at the Bay of Bones as well.

CENTRAL MACEDONIA

Pelister National Park
Пелистер

Macedonia's oldest national park, created in 1948, Pelister covers 125 sq km of the country's third-highest mountain range. Eight peaks top 2000m, crowned by Mt Pelister (2601m). Two glacial lakes, known as 'Pelister's Eyes', sit at the top.

Pelister has excellent village guesthouses in its foothills and the historic town of Bitola is just 30 minutes away by car. With its fresh alpine air and good day hikes, the park is an underrated Macedonian stopover.

⦿ Sights & Activities

Dihovo VILLAGE
Propping up the base of Pelister, just 5km from Bitola, the 830m-high mountainside hamlet of Dihovo is a charming spot, surrounded by thick pine forests and rushing mountain streams. The village's proximity to the main access road into Pelister National Park makes it a popular base for walkers, and locals have shown impressive initiative in developing their traditional community into a pioneering village tourism destination.

Brajčino VILLAGE
Cradled by the foothills on the western edge of Pelister, little Brajčino's lungs are fit to bursting with fresh mountain air, making it a thoroughly idyllic place to pitch up. Rushing water resounds around the village, cherry trees blossom in summer and migrating swallows stop by; traditional rural architecture adds further charm. There are five churches and a monastery hidden in the leafy environs circling this well-kept village and a two- to -three-hour, well-marked trail takes in all of them.

Mt Pelister & Lakes WALKING
Pelister's signature hike is the full-day ascent to the national park's highest peak (2601m) and nearby mountain lakes – Big Lake and Small Lake – that puncture the mountain top like a pair of deep blue eyes, hence their nickname, 'Pelister's Eyes'. There are numerous starting points for the hike but none are reliably marked so it's advisable to take a guide.

Guides can be arranged for about €50 through Villa Dihovo (p784) or Vila Raskrsnica (p784) and most speak English. If your budget won't stretch to a guide at the very least take a detailed map, which can be purchased from the national park information centre for 120MKD.

First World War Trail WALKING
During WWI the Macedonian Front was stationed in and around Bitola and tasked with fighting off Bulgarian and German forces. Villages in the shadow of Pelister were dragged into the turmoil and suffered greatly. This gentle trail starting at the national park's headquarters meanders uphill through Pelister's cool alpine forests, and

MACEDONIA PELISTER NATIONAL PARK

BITOLA & HERACLEA LYNCESTIS

Buttressing Pelister National Park, elevated Bitola (Битола; 660m) has a sophistication inherited from its Ottoman days as the 'City of Consuls'. Macedonians wax lyrical about its elegant 18th- and 19th-century buildings, nationally important ruins and cafe culture.

The main promenade and heart of the city is pedestrianised Širok Sokak. Bitola's quaint, workaday Čaršija (Old Turkish Bazaar) is worth a look, particularly for its interesting food market in the eastern corner. Bitola's headline attraction is the **Heraclea Lyncestis** (adult/child 100MKD/20MKD; ⊙ daylight-8pm) ruins, 1km south of the city centre. It is among Macedonia's best archaeological sites – though the neglected state of the on-site museum might make you think otherwise.

The bus and train stations are adjacent on Nikola Tesla, 1km south of the centre and within walking distance of Heraclea Lyncestis. Buses serve Skopje (450MKD, 3¼ hours, hourly) and Ohrid (210MKD, 1¾ hours, four daily). There are five trains a day to Skopje (314MKD to 365MKD, 3¼ hours).

is accompanied by engaging information boards (in English) exploring this chapter in Macedonian history. The trail is easy enough to follow without a map or GPS.

🛏 Sleeping & Eating

★ **Vila Raskrsnica**　　　　BOUTIQUE HOTEL €
(☑ 047 482 322; vila.raskrsnica@gmail.com; Brajčino; d €40; P❋🗗🛈) It's worth detouring from the tourist trail between Skopje and Ohrid just to stay at this utterly lovely village hotel, which offers five rooms in a chalet-style house and lip-smacking country food. Rooms are relatively luxurious, with exposed stone walls and wooden floors, but it's the expansive mountain-backed garden, its rustic picnic tables and peeping view of Lake Prespa that make Raskrsnica so special.

★ **Villa Dihovo**　　　　　GUESTHOUSE €€
(☑ 070 544 744, 047 293 040; www.villadihovo.com; Dihovo; 🛈) A remarkable guesthouse, Villa Dihovo comprises three traditionally decorated rooms in a historic house that's home to former professional footballer Petar Cvetkovski and family. There's a big, private flowering lawn and cosy living room with open fire place for winter. The only fixed prices are for the homemade wine, beer and *rakija* (fruit brandy); all else, room price included, is your choice.

Petar himself is a mine of information, deeply involved in the Slow Food movement, and can arrange everything from food tastings to hikes to Pelister's lakes, to mountain-bike rides to an evening of wine tasting in his cellar. Ask about cooking classes (€20 per person).

ℹ Information

Pelister National Park Information Centre
(☑ 047 237 010; www.park-pelister.com; ⊙9am-3pm Tue-Sun) The information centre at Pelister National Park sells a detailed map of the park and its trails (120MKD) and has information on various routes and their starting points. There's also an exhibition of the park's flora and fauna inside, though unfortunately it's not free (20MKD). The centre is accessible from the Dihovo road shortly after you enter the park.

ℹ Getting There & Away

There is one main road into Pelister, which enters from the eastern side coming from Bitola and skirts very close to the village of Dihovo. If you enter the park in your own car, you'll be stopped at a checkpoint and charged 50MKD.

Public transport does not service the park. If you're staying in one of the surrounding villages, your host will be able to organise transfers. A taxi from Bitola or Dihovo costs 360MKD one way.

SURVIVAL GUIDE

ℹ Directory A–Z

MONEY

Most tourist businesses, including lower to mid-range hotels, accept cash only. ATMs are wide-

---

SLEEPING PRICE RANGES

The following price indicators are for a high-season double room:

€ less than 3000MKD/€50

€€ 3000MKD/€50 – 5000MKD/€80

€€€ more than 5000MKD/€80

spread in major towns, but surprisingly hard to find around Lake Ohrid except in Ohrid town itself.

ℹ Getting There & Away

Skopje and Ohrid are well connected to other Balkan tourist hubs, as well as some international destinations further afield.

AIR

The long-awaited arrival of budget airlines has improved Skopje's modest number of air connections, and it's now connected pretty well to major European cities. International flights to Ohrid have also increased in the past few years, particularly coming from the UK (with Wizz Air).

LAND
Bus

International routes from Macedonia generally arrive and depart from Skopje or Ohrid. Pristina, Tirana, Sofia, Belgrade and Thessaloniki are the most common connections.

From Skopje it's also possible to get to Ljubljana, İstanbul and Zagreb; some Ohrid buses travel to various destinations in Montenegro.

Train

Macedonian Railway runs antiquated trains. They are often the cheapest mode of transport, however the network is limited and trains are less frequent than buses.

Trains connect Skopje to Pristina, Belgrade and Thessaloniki (though the last is currently via a train-and-bus combo because of the fraught relationship with Greece).

ℹ Getting Around

BUS

Skopje serves most domestic destinations. Larger buses are new and air-conditioned; *kombi* (minibuses) are usually not. During summer, pre-book for Ohrid. Sunday is often the busiest day for inter-city bus travel among locals, so if you plan to travel that day book ahead if you can.

CAR & MOTORCYCLE

There are occasional police checkpoints; make sure you have the correct documentation. Call 196 for roadside assistance.

Motorway toll points are common in the north of Macedonia on roads leading from and to Skopje.

The toll is usually 40MKD to 60MKD and cheaper if you pay in denars (you can also pay in euros). The toll can be paid in cash or by credit card.

Driver's Licence

Your national driver's licence is fine, though an International Driving Permit is best.

Hire

Economy cars (small) average €25 a day, including basic insurance, but you can negotiate down to €20 to €21 a day if you're renting for one to two weeks. Bring your passport, driver's licence and credit card; some agencies will even drop the car off at your hotel door (ask!).

Note that it's virtually impossible to hire a car with automatic transmission in Macedonia: manual-only here.

Road Rules

➡ Drive on the right.

➡ Speed limits are 120km/h on motorways, 80km/h for open road and 50km/h to 60km/h in towns. Speeding fines start from 1500MKD.

➡ Seatbelt and headlight use is compulsory (yes – headlights even during the day).

➡ Cars must carry replacement bulbs, two warning triangles and a first-aid kit (usually supplied by the hire company – if you're driving your own car, this kit is available to buy at big petrol stations).

➡ From 15 November to 15 March snow tyres must be used, otherwise you can be fined, and chains should be on-board too.

➡ Police also fine for drink driving (blood alcohol limit 0.05%). Fines are payable immediately.

TRAIN

Domestic trains are reliable but slow. From Skopje, one train line runs to Negotino and another to Bitola via Veles and Prilep. A smaller line runs Skopje–Kičevo. Ohrid does not have a train station.

Moldova

Best Places to Eat

➡ Grill House (p790)

➡ Gok-Oguz (p789)

➡ Kumanyok (p796)

➡ Vatra Neamului (p791)

➡ Pani Pit (p791)

Best Places to Stay

➡ Art Rustic Hotel (p789)

➡ City Park Hotel (p789)

➡ Eco-Resort Butuceni (p793)

➡ Hotel Russia (p796)

➡ Hotel Codru (p789)

Why Go?

The world is finally waking up to the charms of this little nation wedged between Romania and Ukraine. Famously dubbed the world's least happy place in a bestselling book almost a decade ago, Moldova is increasingly known more for its unspoiled countryside and superb wine tours.

As one of Europe's least visited countries, Moldova retains a certain off-the-beaten-track charm. But even that's changing as budget flights from London and other European cities make the lively capital, Chişinău, a popular weekend break. Meanwhile, those looking to plant the flag in a land few others have visited still have their Shangri-La in the form of the breakaway republic of Transdniestr, where the Soviet Union still reigns supreme.

As for Moldova's 'unhappy' reputation? Well it's shed that, too, thank you very much. According to the most recent UN survey on the subject, Moldova is now the world's 55th *happiest* country.

When to Go
Chişinău

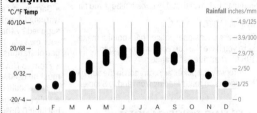

Jun Parks and restaurant terraces fill with students, and the weather is warm.

Jul High season hits its peak with hiking, wine tours and camping in full operation.

Oct The wine festival takes place during the first weekend of October in Chişinău.

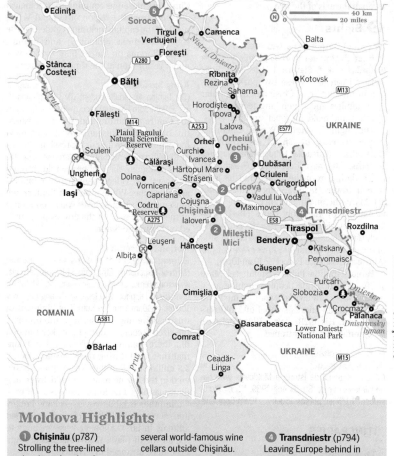

Moldova Highlights

❶ **Chişinău** (p787) Strolling the tree-lined streets and parks of Moldova's friendly capital.

❷ **Wineries** (p793) Designating a driver for tours of Cricova, one of several world-famous wine cellars outside Chişinău.

❸ **Orheiul Vechi** (p788) Exploring this historic cave monastery, burrowed by 13th-century monks.

❹ **Transdniestr** (p794) Leaving Europe behind in this surreal, living homage to the Soviet Union.

❺ **Soroca** (p794) Ogling gypsy-king mansions in Moldova's Roma capital, and visiting its medieval fortress.

CHIŞINĂU

📞 22 / POP 750,000

The capital Chişinău is by far Moldova's largest and liveliest city and its main transport hub. While the city's origins date back six centuries to 1420, much of Chişinău was levelled in WWII and a tragic earthquake that struck in 1940. The city was rebuilt in Soviet style from the 1950s onwards, and is dominated by utilitarian (and frankly not very attractive) buildings.

That said, Chişinău does have a few architectural gems remaining, and is surprisingly green and peaceful. It's a pleasant city to wander about and discover as you go – with frequent cafe breaks and all-you-can-carry wine-shopping sprees.

Most visitors confine their stay to the centre, defined by two large, diagonally opposed parks. The best museums, hotels, restaurants and cafes are no more than a leisurely 10- or 15-minute walk away. The impressive main artery, B-dul Ștefan cel Mare, cuts right through the axis of the two parks.

Sights

Parcul Catedralei & Grădina Publică Ștefan cel Mare și Sfînt   PARK

(Cathedral Park & Ștefan cel Mare Park; B-dul Ștefan cel Mare; ⊞) These two parks, smack dab in the middle of Chișinău, are popular with families and canoodling teenagers on benches, and make for great strolling.

The highlight of the Parcul Catedralei is the **Nativity of Christ Metropolitan Cathedral** (Catedrala Mitropolitană Nașterea Domnului; http://en.mitropolia.md; ⊙9am-8pm), **FREE**, dating from the 1830s, and its lovely bell tower (1836). Along B-dul Ștefan cel Mare the main entrance to the park is marked by the Holy Gates (1841), also known as Chișinău's own **Arc de Triomphe** (Holy Gates) **FREE**. On the northwestern side of the park is a colourful **Flower Market** (Str Mitropolit G Bănulescu-Bodoni; ⊙10am-10pm).

Parcul Grădina Publică Ștefan cel Mare și Sfînt is a first-rate people-watching area. Ștefan was Moldavia's greatest medieval prince and ubiquitous symbol of Moldova's brave past. His 1928 **statue** (B-dul Ștefan cel Mare) lords over the entrance.

National Archaeology & History Museum   MUSEUM

(Muzeul Național de Istorie a Moldovei; www.nationalmuseum.md; Str 31 Aug 1989, 121a; adult/student 10/5 lei, photos 15 lei; ⊙10am-6pm Sat-Thu, to 5pm Nov-Mar; ⊛) The grandaddy of Chișinău's museums contains archaeological artefacts from the region of Orheiul Vechi, north of the capital, including Golden Horde coins; Soviet-era weaponry; and a huge WWII diorama on the 1st floor (which was under restoration at the time of research).

Army Museum   MUSEUM

(Str Tighina 47; adult/student 10/3 lei, photos 10 lei; ⊙9am-5pm Tue-Sun) Occupying one end of the Centre of Culture and Military History, this once-musty museum now hosts a moving exhibit on Soviet-era repression. Stories of Red Terror, forced famines, mass deportations and gulag slave labor are told through photographs, videos, newspaper clippings and dioramas. While little is in English, the museum nevertheless gives you a good sense of the horrific scale of the crimes perpetrated by Lenin and Stalin.

National Museum of Ethnography & Natural History   MUSEUM

(Muzeul Național de Etnografie și Istorie Naturală; www.muzeu.md; Str M Kogălniceanu 82; adult/student 15/10 lei, photos 10 lei, English-language tour 100 lei; ⊙10am-6pm Tue-Sun) The highlight of this massive and wonderful exhibition is a life-sized reconstruction of the skeleton of a dinothere – an 8-tonne elephant-like mammal that lived during the Pliocene epoch – 5.3 million to 1.8 million years ago – discovered in the Rezine region in 1966. Sweeping dioramas depict national customs and dress, while other exhibits cover geology, botany and zoology (including bizarre deformed animals in jars). Allow at least an hour to see all the displays. English-language tours need to be arranged in advance.

Pushkin Museum   MUSEUM

(☎022 924 138; Str Anton Pann 19; adult/student 10/5 lei, per photo 10 lei, excursion 100 lei; ⊙10am-4pm Tue-Sun) This is where Russia's national poet Alexander Pushkin (1799–1837) spent three years exiled between 1820 and 1823. You can view his tiny cottage, filled with original furnishings and personal items, including a portrait of his beloved Byron on his writing desk. There's also a three-room literary museum in the building facing the cottage, which documents Pushkin's dramatic life.

Tours

Chișinău has several highly competent travel agencies that specialise in day or multi-day trips out of the capital. All do the

---

ITINERARIES

Three Days

Use the capital **Chișinău** as your base for a long-weekend getaway. Make day trips out to the stunning cave monastery at **Orheiul Vechi** (Butuceni) and, if you don't mind a bit of driving, the intriguing Roma capital **Soroca**. On day three take a day trip to one of the big-name **vineyards** around Chișinău for a tour and tasting.

One Week

Spend a night or two in surreal **Transdniestr**, a bastion of Russian-ness on the fringes of Europe-leaning Moldova. Take an overnight trip to **Soroca** to see the impressive fortress on the lazy Dniestr River. Lastly, reserve two or three days to explore Moldova's great outdoors.

standard wine and monastery tours in addition to more specialised offerings. **Tatra-Bis** (📱 022 844 304; www.tatrabis.md; Str Alexandru Bernardazzi 59; ⊙ 9am-7pm Mon-Fri) and **Amadeus Travel** (Lufthansa City Center; 📱 022 221 644; www.amadeus.md; Str Puşkin 24; ⊙ 9am-7pm Mon-Fri) are two of the better ones. **Valery Bradu** (📱 079 462 986, 022 227 850; valbradu@ yahoo.com) is a recommended English-speaking driver for excursions outside Chişinău.

🛏 Sleeping

Rates on business hotels tend to go down at the weekends, so be sure to inquire. Renting an apartment is always an option - check out **Adresa** (📱 022 544 392; www.adresa.md; B-dul Negruzzi 1; 1-bedroom apt €35-70), **Marisha.net** (📱 022 488 258, 069 155 753; www.marisha.net; apt 500-600 lei) or **Natalia Raiscaia** (📱 079 578 217; www.domasha.net; per person €8-15). The latter offers homestays.

Tapok Hostel　　　　　　HOSTEL €
(📱 068 408 626; www.tapokhostel.com; Str Armenească 27a; dm €8-10, d €20; P ⊜ 🛜) This friendly, modern youth hostel offers accommodation in four-, six- and eight-bed dorms in a quiet location near the centre and handy to the city's best bars and restaurants. The kitchen is tiny but the tall dark-wood bunks with individual plugs and lights are a bonus.

⭐**Art Rustic Hotel**　　　　HOTEL €€
(📱 022 232 593; www.art-rustic.md; Str Alexandru Hajdeu 79/1; s/d incl breakfast from €35/45; P ⊜ ❄ 🛜) This small boutique hotel, a 10- to 15-minute walk from the centre, offers excellent value. The 13 rooms are individually and imaginatively furnished (some feature antiques). Rooms come in two classes: 'standart' and cheaper 'econom', with the former being much bigger, and the latter boasting balconies. And a dalmatian greets you at the entrance. Note there's no lift.

⭐**City Park Hotel**　　　　HOTEL €€
(📱 022 249 249; www.citipark.md; Str E Doga 2; s/d incl breakfast €70/80; P ⊜ 🛜) This fashionable hotel on the main walking street in town is very popular, so book ahead if you want to enjoy its bold, bright rooms, crisp English-speaking service and excellent breakfast in its street-side beer restaurant. Phone or walk-in bookings net a substantial discount, just make sure you ask for it.

Hotel Codru　　　　　　HOTEL €€
(📱 022 208 104; www.codru.md; Str 31 August 1989, 127; s/d incl breakfast from €70/79; P ⊜

WORTH A TRIP

GAGAUZIA

The autonomous region of Gagauzia (Gagauz Yeri) lies 100km due south of Chişinău but is a world apart from the cosmopolitan capital. This Turkic-influenced Christian ethnic minority forfeited full independence for autonomy in the early '90s, thus making it subordinate to Moldova constitutionally and for defence. But politically the Gagauz generally look toward Russia for patronage.

Comrat, the capital, is little more than an intriguing cultural and provincial oddity, but makes an easy day trip from Chişinău, with hourly *marshrutky* departures from the South Bus Station (45 lei, two hours). The Chişinău-based owner of Tiraspol Hostel (p796) runs excellent tours to Gagauzia that cover both Comrat and smaller villages, with plenty of Gagauzian food and wine consumed along the way.

❄ @ 🛜) Go through the cavernous lobby and ascend the tiny lift to find no-nonsense, business-standard rooms that become downright plush when you reach 'luxury' classification. The location, across the street from the park and near the main entertainment and dining strip, is just about perfect.

🍴 Eating

Chişinău has a surprising number of good restaurants. Most are clustered in the centre in the shady neighbourhood along Str Bucureşti and Str 31 August 1989. Pedestrianised Str E Doga is another cafe and restaurant row.

⭐**Gok-Oguz**　　　　GAGAUZIAN €
(📱 022 468 852; Str Calea Orheiului 19a; mains 75-125 lei; ⊙ 10am-11pm) It's well worth the short taxi ride north of the centre to Chişinău's only Gagauzian restaurant. Gagauzian food has Turkic, Romanian and Russian influences, and the offerings here include *carne de miel po Gheorhievski* (baked mutton with rice and vegetables), lamb *cavurma* (a spicy stew) and *ghiozlemea* (gözleme – or Turkic pastries) with ewes' milk cheese.

⭐**Coffee Molka**　　　　CAFE €
(Str Alexandru cel Bun; ⊙ 8am-10pm; 🛜) The charismatic owner's love of coffee is on dis-

Central Chişinău

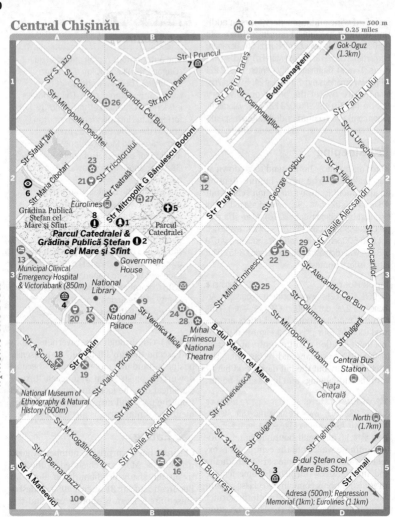

play everywhere at Coffee Molka, from Turkish coffee faithfully prepared according to an ancient style, to shelves of antique coffee grinders that make up part of the on-site coffee 'museum' and library. Vintage furniture and groovy lighting only add to the ambience. Light bites available.

Propaganda Cafe INTERNATIONAL €
(✆060 096 666; Str Alexei Şciusev 70; mains 85-150 lei; ⏱11am-1am; ⊕🛜🚼) This highly recommended, popular student-oriented cafe serves very good mains built around chicken, pork and beef, as well as inventive salads and des-

serts – all at very reasonable prices. The playfully antique interior, done up like a 19th-century dollhouse, is worth the trip alone.

★**Grill House** INTERNATIONAL €€
(✆022-224 509; Str Armeneasca 24/2; mains 100-250 lei; ⏱11am-midnight; ⊕🛜) It may not look like much from the street, but inside this sleek place you'll find the best steaks in town served up by attentive staff from the glassed-in, fire-oven kitchen. Creative pasta dishes complement the array of hearty meat, seafood and fish, and there's a great wine list to boot. Go down the atmospheric alley off the street.

Central Chişinău

Vatra Neamului MOLDOVAN €€
(☑ 022 226 839; www.vatraneamului.md; Str Puşkin 20b; mains 115-230 lei; ⊙ 11am-11pm; ☻☎) This superb place boasts charming old-world decor, unfailingly genial staff and – by night – a duet strumming traditional Moldovan instruments. A long menu of imaginatively dressed-up meats – think stewed pork with *mămăligă* (boiled corn meal), baked rabbit and salmon in pastry, not to mention *varenyky* (Ukrainian dumplings) and *plăcintă* (stuffed pastries) – may prompt repeat visits.

Pani Pit MOLDOVAN €€
(☑ 022 240 127; Str 31 August 1989, 115; mains 100-300 lei; ⊙ 11am-11pm; ☎) In the heart of Chişinău's main drinking and dining area is this charming courtyard restaurant with cushioned cast-iron chairs, vines and a small waterfall. It features peasant-uniformed staff serving Moldovan dishes with a modern twist, such as pork and apples in teriyaki sauce, beef tartare and trout fried in almonds.

🍷 Drinking & Nightlife

Teatru Spălătorie CLUB
(Str Mihai Eminescu 72; ⊙ 9pm-late Thu-Sat) This chic, grey-slate basement joint is the nightclub of choice for the young creative set, who gather to listen to great DJs and occasional live music. Usually closes for most of the summer.

Mojito BAR
(Str Tricolorului; ⊙ 24hr) Love it or hate it, you have to acknowledge there's a reason for its unbridled popularity. That patio was put there by the gods, broad and beckoning with warm blankets when it gets chilly, and the cocktails are almost grotesquely large. Tack on an absurdly good location flanking the opera house? No wonder it draws the cool crowd.

Military Pub CLUB
(Str 31 August 1989, 68; 100 lei; ⊙ 10pm-6am Fri & Sat) This is the most happening spot in town, conveniently located in the middle of the bar-packed alley off Str 31 Aug 1989. It gets packed early and stays that way until the wee hours, drawing all kinds.

☆ Entertainment

Opera & Ballet Theatre OPERA
(www.nationalopera.md; B-dul Ştefan cel Mare 152; ⊙ box office 10am-6pm) Home to the esteemed national opera and ballet company, which puts on productions from September to June.

Organ Hall CLASSICAL MUSIC
(Sala cu Orgă; www.organhall.md; B-dul Ştefan cel Mare 81; ⊙ box office 11am-6pm, performances 6pm) Classical concerts and organ recitals

are held in the neoclassical Organ Hall, one of Chişinău's fin de siècle architectural gems.

Shopping

The main tourist sites have souvenir shops attached, or head to **Kishinösky Arbat** (B-dul Ştefan cel Mare 81; ☺9am-6.30pm), a row of souvenir vendors next to the Organ Hall. **Carpe Diem** (www.wineshop.md; Str Columna 136, 3a; ☺11am-11pm) is the best wine shop in town, with highly knowledgeable, English-speaking owners.

ⓘ Information

Moldinconbank (B-dul Ştefan cel Mare 123; ☺6am-6pm Mon-Sat, 9am-2pm Sun) All banking services, including Western Union and Moneygram.

Municipal Clinical Emergency Hospital (☑903; cnr Str 31 August 1989 & Str Toma Ciorba; ☺24hr) Has emergency services, although finding English-speaking staff could be a challenge.

ⓘ Getting There & Away

AIR

Moldova's only international airport is the modern **Chişinău International Airport** (KIV; ☑022 525 111; www.airport.md; Str Aeroportului 80/3), 13km southeast of the city centre, with regular flights to many major European capitals. There are no domestic flights.

Marshrutka No 165 departs every 20 minutes until 9pm between the airport and the **B-dul Ştefan cel Mare bus stop** (cnr B-dul Ştefan cel Mare & Str Ismail) in the centre (3 lei, 35 minutes). Taxis from the airport cost a fixed 100 lei.

BUS

Buses heading south to Bucharest and east to Transdniestr and Odesa (via Tiraspol) use the

Central Bus Station (Gara Centrala; ☑022 271 476; www.autogara.md; Str Mitropolit Varlaam). The **North Bus Station** (Autogara Nord; ☑022 411 338) serves Soroca and points north, and has international departures to Kyiv, Moscow and Odesa via Palanca (these avoid Transdniestr). The **South Bus Station** (Autogara Sud; ☑022 713 983; Şoseaua Hînceşti 143) serves Comrat and most southern destinations, and also serves Iaşi, Romania.

With offices at the **train station** (☑022 549 813; www.eurolines.md; Aleea Garii 1; ☺9am-6pm Mon-Fri) and in the **centre** (☑022 222 827; www.eurolines.md; Str Teatrului 4/1), Eurolines has nicer buses to major cities around Europe.

TRAIN

International trains depart from the beautiful, recently renovated **train station** (Gara Feroviară Chişinău; Aleea Gării).

From Chişinău trains serve Bucharest (from 720 lei, 14 hours, 4.45pm daily); Odesa (200 lei, five hours, 7.45am Saturday & Sunday) via Tiraspol; Moscow (from 1710 lei, 29 to 32 hours, two to three daily) via Kyiv; and St Petersburg (2100 lei, 37 hours, odd days) via Vinnytsia, Ukraine, and Zhlobin, Belarus.

ⓘ Getting Around

Buses (2 lei), trolleybuses (2 lei) and *marshrutky* (3 lei) run from 6am until about midnight. Trolleybuses 4, 5, 8 and 28 connect the train station with the centre via main drag B-dul Ştefan cel Mare. From the centre, bus 11 serves the South Bus Station while buses 24 and 38 go to the North Bus Station.

Taxis ordered by phone are dirt cheap – only 25 lei or so for trips around the centre. Call 14 222, 14 009, 14 022 or 14 700.

BUSES FROM CHIŞINĂU

DESTINATION	PRICE (LEI)	DURATION (HR)	DEPARTURES
Bucharest	260-340	8-9	hourly
Comrat (marshrutky)	45	2	hourly
Iaşi	140	4	hourly
Kyiv	300	12	several daily
Moscow	600	28hr	several daily
Odesa	150	5	hourly
Soroca (marshrutky)	75	2½	every 30min
Tiraspol (via Bendery; marshrutky)	37	1¾	every 20min

TOURING MOLDOVA'S WINE COUNTRY

Moldova was the Rhone Valley of the Soviet Union, and two of the largest wineries in the world are within 20km of Chişinău. More intimate wine-tasting experiences are also possible, though you'll have to travel a bit further to reach these. Moldova's **wine festival** (⊘ Oct) kicks off the first weekend in October in downtown Chişinău and elsewhere. A run-down of the top wineries:

Cricova (☑ 069 077 734; www.cricova.md; Str Ungureanu 1, Cricova; ⊘ 10am-5pm Mon-Fri) This underground wine kingdom 15km north of Chişinău is one of Europe's biggest. Some 60km of the 120km-long underground limestone tunnels – dating from the 15th century – are lined wall-to-wall with bottles. Reserve well in advance as these tours are often booked out. The basic tour with tasting costs 310 lei; it's 410 lei with snacks, and 695 lei (minimum four persons) with lunch.

Mileştii Mici (www.milestii-mici.md; Str Vasile Alecsandri 137; ⊘ 9am-7pm Mon-Fri, to 5pm Sat, to 3pm Sun) The impressive wine cellars at Mileştii Mici, 20km south of Chişinău, stretch for some 200km, holding about 1.5 million bottles – which makes this the world's largest wine collection, according to the *Guinness Book of World Records*. You must email or call ahead to book a tour, and you'll need to arrive in a private car to navigate the vast underground cave network.

Château Vartely (☑ 022 829 891; Str Eliberării 170b, Orhei (New Orhei)) This up-and-coming winery, established in 2008, offers not just very good whites and reds, but excellent food and cosy accommodation (rooms from €82) in one of 12 pretty wooden bungalows, just 50km north of Chişinău.

Château Purcari (☑ 024 230 411; www.purcari.md; Purcari) Nestled in the extreme southeast corner of Moldova, about 115km from Chişinău and 95km west of Odesa, Purcari's wines are arguably Moldova's finest. Tours here can last from one to several days, with luxurious lakeside accommodation (single/double rooms from €46/56), excellent food and an array of activities to squeeze in between tastings.

AROUND CHIŞINĂU

Even the furthest reaches of Moldova are a reasonable day trip from Chişinău, though an overnight somewhere is a good idea to experience the tranquil rural atmosphere. Moldova Holiday (www.moldovaholiday. travel) lists rural guesthouses in Trebujeni, Mileştii Mici and elsewhere.

Orheiul Vechi

The archaeological and ecclesiastical complex at Orheiul Vechi (Old Orhei), about 50km north of Chişinău, is the country's most important historical site and a place of stark natural beauty. Occupying a remote cliff high above the Răut River, the complex is known for its **Cave Monastery** (Mănăstire în Peşteră; Orheiul Vechi; voluntary donation; ⊘ 8am-6pm) **FREE**, but also includes baths, fortifications and ruins dating back as much as 2000 years.

The complex is in the village of Butuceni, where a small bridge over the Răut takes you to the trailhead for a 15-minute hike up to the Cave Monastery, dug by Orthodox monks in the 13th century. Dress appropriately at the monastery: long skirts or pants for women, long shorts or trousers for men, and no tank tops.

Excursions in English (150 lei) are possible via the **Orheiul Vechi Exhibition Centre** (☑ 079 292 125, 068 440 761; Butuceni; museum adult/student 10/5 lei; ⊘ 9am-5pm Tue-Sun), located just before the bridge. The exhibition centre also has a museum and some basic rooms, but you are better off staying in Butuceni proper at **Eco-Resort Butuceni** (☑ 079 617 870, 023 556 906; www.pensiuneabutuceni.md; Butuceni; d with/without meals 1200/1000 lei; ☎ ⊛), a rambling complex with fantastic cottage-style rooms and a swimming pool.

From Chişinău, *marshrutky* to Butuceni depart from Str Mitropolit Varlaam directly opposite the Central Bus Station entrance (27 lei, 1¼ hours, five or six daily). Placards will say 'Butuceni', 'Trebujeni' or 'Orheiul Vechi'. The last trip back is at 4.15pm (6.20pm in the summer). A taxi round-trip shouldn't cost more than €35.

SOROCA

✔230 / POP 37,000

The northern city of Soroca occupies a prominent position on the Dniestr River and is Moldova's unofficial 'Roma capital'. The incredibly gaudy, fantastical mansions of the Roma 'kings' that line the streets up on the hill above the centre are a sight to behold.

◉ Sights

Soroca Fortress FORTRESS
(Cetatea Soroca; ✔069 323 734; Str Petru Rareş 1; adult/student 5/3 lei, photos 3 lei, tours in English 100 lei; ⊙9am-1pm & 2-6pm Wed-Sun) This gloriously solid behemoth on the Dniestr dates from 1499 when Moldavian Prince Ştefan cel Mare built a wooden fortress here. It was rebuilt in stone less than 50 years later and given its circular shape, with five bastions. Today those bastions contain medieval-themed exhibits, with a few English placards posted about that shed light on the history of the fortress.

Candle of Gratitude MONUMENT
You can get fantastic views of the Dniestr and the perfectly partitioned fields of Ukraine beyond from this curious obelisk, which was erected in 2004 to honour the 'anonymous heroes' responsible for preserving Moldova's culture over the years. It's accessible by a 660-step (not an exact count) stairway on the town's southern outskirts.

🛏 Sleeping & Eating

Hotel Central HOTEL €
(✔0230 23 456; www.soroca-hotel.com; Str M Kogâlniceanu 20; s/d from €20/30; ☺🌐📶) The best lodging in town is this small, partly renovated hotel opposite the mothballed Dacia Theatre in the centre of town. The ground level rooms are mediocre, but the situation improves dramatically upstairs, where amenities such as spruced-up bathrooms, balconies and luggage racks await.

Andy's Pizza PIZZA €
(Parcu Central; mains 60-100 lei; ⊙9am-11pm) The local branch of this national chain is a burst of fresh air on the bleak Soroca dining scene. Besides the eponymous pizza, you'll find burgers, salmon and a range of Russian and Moldovan favourites on the menu. You can't miss it in the very centre of town opposite the central park.

❶ Getting There & Away

There are *marshrutky* to Chişinău's North Bus Station every 45 minutes or so until 6pm (75 lei, 2½ hours).

TRANSDNIESTR

POP 505,000

The self-declared republic of Transdniestr (sometimes called Transnistria), a narrow strip of land on the eastern bank of the Dniestr River, is one of the strangest places in Eastern Europe. Unrecognised by anybody else, it's a ministate with its own currency, police force, army and borders.

From the Moldovan perspective, Transdniestr is still officially part of its sovereign territory that was illegally grabbed in the early 1990s with Russian support. Officials in Transdniestr see it differently and proud-

---

❶ CROSSING INTO TRANSDNIESTR

Entering Transdniestr is fairly straightforward and formalities take about five minutes. You'll be given a 'migration card' that allows for a stay of up to 24 hours. You're required to keep this paper with your passport and surrender it when leaving (so don't lose it!).

It's easy to extend your stay beyond the 24-hour time frame. The better hotels and hostels do this automatically, or you or your host can handle it at the OVIR (✔053 379 038; ul Kotovskogo 2a; ⊙9am-5pm Mon-Tue & Thu-Fri) immigration office in Tiraspol.

If you are entering Transdniestr from Ukraine and continuing on to Moldova proper, you will not obtain a Moldovan entry stamp upon exiting Transdniestr. Register instead at one of the following within three days of arriving in Moldova proper:

➡ **Center for State Information Resources 'Registru'** (Str Puşkin 42, Chişinău)

➡ **Bureau for Migration and Asylum** (B-dul Ştefan cel Mare 124, Chişinău)

➡ Any local passport office outside of Chişinău.

Be prepared to present valid proof of arrival in the form of a bus or train ticket. You may be fined or worse when leaving Moldova if you fail to comply.

ly point to the territory having won its 'independence' in a bloody civil war in 1992. A bitter truce has ensued ever since.

Tiraspol

☑ 533 / POP 136,000

The 'capital' of Transdniestr is also, officially at least, the second-largest city in Moldova. But don't expect it to be anything like the chaotic Moldovan capital: here time seems to have stood still since the end of the Soviet Union. Tiraspol (from the Greek, meaning 'town on the Nistru') will be one of the strangest places you'll ever visit.

If you get here, be sure to add neighbouring Bendery to your itinerary. Site of a wonderful old fortress on the Dniestr River, this pleasantly provincial town is an easy 20-minute drive from Tiraspol.

◎ Sights & Activities

Do have a stroll along the river, where a pedestrian bridge behind the War Memorial leads to a public beach, and party boats depart on one-hour river cruises (per person 25 roubles) in the summer. The main drag, ul 25 Oktober, has some foreboding Soviet buildings, including the Presidential Palace (⊘ closed to the public) and the House of Soviets, both fronted by Lenin statues.

Bendery Fortress   FORTRESS
(Tighina Fortress; ☑ 055 248 032, 077 908 728; www.bendery-fortress.com; ul Kosmodemyanskoi 10; admission 50 roubles, tours in English 75 roubles; ⊘ 9am-6pm Tue-Sun) This impressive Ottoman fortress on the outskirts of Bendery was built in the 16th century, and saw keen fighting between Turkish and Russian forces before falling to Tsarist Russia permanently in the early 19th century. Today it's Transdniestr's top tourist attraction. You can walk along the ramparts taking in the fine views of the Dniestr River, have a picnic on the grounds, and visit several museums onsite that document the fort's long and rich history.

Noul Neamţ Monastery   MONASTERY
(Kitskany Monastery; Kitskany Village) A stunning 70m bell tower marks this serene monastery (1861) 7km south of Tiraspol. You can climb the bell tower for a birds'-eye view of the monastery's four churches and a sweeping panorama of the countryside. You'll need to ask around for the key to be let up. To get here, cross the Dniestr via the classic Sovi-

OFF THE BEATEN TRACK

INTO THE WILD

Moldova has several playgrounds for lovers of the great outdoors, but to experience it you'll want to find a capable guide with the right equipment. The travel agents in Chişinău providing guided tours (p788) all offer some variety of outdoor fun. Another option is to base yourself at Costel Hostel (☑ 069 072 674; www.costelhostel.com; Rosu Village, Cahul; s/d from €10/20; ☎), just north of Cahul; owner Constantin knows the lower Prut River basin inside and out.

But to really get into the wild, you're best off contacting English-speaking Leonid at Explore Moldova (☑ 069 258 006; leonidros@gmail.com) in Chişinău. Leonid has fleets of kayaks and mountain bikes, and you can combine both with hiking or rock-climbing on a multi-day excursion. Highlights include a three-day kayaking and camping expedition on the Dniestr River in the northern Soroca District; birdwatching with professional ornithologists in the Prutul de Jos (lower Prut) Natural Scientific Reserve; and biking or cross-country skiing along the Troyanov Val – a defence wall in the extreme south that dates back to Roman times.

et-era car ferry (car/passenger 10/1.50 roubles) near the Hotel Aist in Tiraspol, then pick up a *marshrutka* on the other side (4 roubles, 15 minutes, frequent).

Tiraspol National
History Museum   MUSEUM
(ul 25 Oktober 46; 39 roubles; ⊘ 8.30am-5pm Mon-Fri, 9.30am-6.30pm Sat & Sun) No period of Transdniestran history is ignored at this relatively interesting museum, starting with photos of late-19th-century Tiraspol, moving to the Soviet period and the Great Patriotic War, to the war of 1992.

Kvint Factory   FACTORY
(☑ 053 392 025; www.kvint.biz; ul Lenina 38; ⊘ store 8am-9pm) Since 1897, Kvint has been making some of Moldova's finest brandies. Book private tasting tours in English a day in advance (US$32 to US$100 per person, depending on what you're tasting), or join one-hour standard tours of the factory (in Russian), which take place Monday to Friday at 3pm (180 roubles per person).

MOLDOVA TIRASPOL

ESSENTIAL FOOD & DRINK

Brânză Moldova's most common cheese is a slightly salty-sour sheep's milk product that often comes grated. Put it on *mămăligă*.

Fresh produce Moldova is essentially one big, very rewarding farmers market.

Mămăligă Cornmeal mush with a consistency between porridge and bread that accompanies many dishes.

Muşchi de vacă/porc/miel A cutlet of beef/pork/lamb.

Piept de pui The ubiquitous chicken breast.

Sarma Cabbage-wrapped minced meat or pilau rice packages, similar to Turkish dolma or Russian *goluptsy*.

🛌 Sleeping

Both hostels in town arrange interesting tours of the city and beyond.

Go Tiraspol Hostel   HOSTEL €
(📞 068 188 352, 077 758 005; www.gotiraspol. wordpress.com; ul Lenina 28; dm €13) Tiraspol's newest hostel has nine beds a few floors up in a large apartment building between the train station and the centre. You'll need to call ahead to access the entrance, which is around the back.

Tiraspol Hostel   HOSTEL €
(📞 068 571 472; www.moldovahostels.com; ul Krasnodonskaya 46/22; dm €15; ☻ 🛜) This welcoming hostel occupies a homey apartment in a quiet residential area a bit outside the centre. Prices include a tour. There are just a few dorm beds and a small but well-appointed kitchen. It's hard to find, so call for a pick-up.

Hotel Russia   HOTEL €€
(📞 053 338 000; www.hotelrussia.biz; ul Sverdlova 69; r from €50; 🅿 ☻ ❄ 🛜) This large and smartly furnished hotel is definitely the mainstay for business people and anyone wanting comfort. It has a super-central location near the House of Soviets. Rooms come with flat-screen TVs, smart bathrooms and comfortable beds. Breakfast costs €10.

🍴 Eating & Drinking

★ Kumanyok   UKRAINIAN €
(📞 053 372 034; ul Sverdlova 37; mains 50-100 roubles; ⊙ 9am-11pm; 🛜) This smart, super-friendly, traditional Ukrainian place is set in a kitsch faux-countryside home, where diners are attended to by a fleet of peasant-dressed waitresses. The menu is hearty Ukrainian fare; think *varenyky, bliny, golubtsi* (stuffed cabbage rolls), fish, mutton and, above all, excellent, authentic borscht.

Cafe Larionov   INTERNATIONAL €
(ul K Liebknechta 397; mains 25-70 roubles; ⊙ 8am-11pm Mon-Fri, noon-midnight Sat & Sun; 🛜) Named for Tiraspol's own avant-garde modernist painter Mikhail Larionov (1881–1964), this cafe has a menu featuring local cuisines drawing from the cultural influences (Russian, Jewish, Moldovan) common in Larionov's time, with an emphasis on soups, stews and grilled meats.

Vintage   CLUB
(www.clubvintage.ru; ul Klary Tsetkin 14/2; free weekdays, from 100 roubles weekends; ⊙ 7pm-6am) The hottest club in Tiraspol, often pulling top DJs from Moscow and elsewhere. Serious fun.

ℹ Information

You can exchange dollars, euros, Russian roubles or Moldovan lei for Transdniestran roubles at exchange kiosks and banks. Credit cards are not accepted in the republic. The Bank of the Republic of Transdniestr (www.cbpmr.net) posts daily exchange rates.

ℹ Getting There & Around

The bus station and train station share a parking lot about 1.5km north of the centre. Trolleybus 1 takes you into the centre via ul Lenina and ul 25 Oktober (2.50 roubles).

From the bus station, *marshrutky* go to Odesa in Ukraine (60 roubles, 2½ hours to three hours, at least five daily) and Chişinău (40 roubles, 1¾ hours, every 20 minutes).

To get from Tiraspol to Bendery, hop on trolleybus 19 (3 roubles, 25 minutes) or various *marshrutky* (3.50 roubles, 20 minutes) heading west along ul 25 Oktober.

EATING PRICE RANGES

The following price indicators are based on the average cost of a main course.

€ less than 110 lei

€€ 110–220 lei

€€€ more than 220 lei

COUNTRY FACTS

Area 33,851 sq km

Capital Chişinău

Country Code ☑373

Currency Moldovan leu (plural lei)

Emergency Ambulance ☑903, fire ☑901, police ☑902

Language Moldovan

Money ATMs abundant in Chişinău; less common in smaller cities and towns.

Population 3.5 million (including Transdniestr)

Visas None for EU, USA, Canada, Japan, Australia and New Zealand citizens, but required for South Africa and many other countries.

SURVIVAL GUIDE

❶ Directory A–Z

BUSINESS HOURS

Banks 9am to 3pm Monday to Friday

Businesses 8am to 7pm Monday to Friday, to 4pm Saturday

Shops 9am or 10am to 6pm or 7pm Monday to Saturday

MONEY

Moldova's currency, the leu (plural lei), has been stable for several years. Use ATMs to withdraw lei, or exchange dollars, euros or pounds for lei at banks or higher-end hotels.

The only legal tender in Transdniestr is the wonderfully quirky Transdniestran rouble, not recognised anywhere outside Transdniestr.

PUBLIC HOLIDAYS

New Year's Day 1 January

Orthodox Christmas 7 January

International Women's Day 8 March

Orthodox Easter April/May

Victory (1945) Day 9 May

Independence Day 27 August

National Language Day 31 August

VISAS

The maximum stay for visa-free countries is 90 days within a six-month period. For South Africans (and some others), visa on arrival is available at Chişinău International Airport and at the following land border crossings with Romania:

SLEEPING PRICE RANGES

The following price ranges denote one night's accommodation in a double room with bathroom.

€ less than €25

€€ €25–80

€€€ more than €80

Sculeni/Sculeni; Leuşeni/Albiţa; Oancea/Cahul. South Africans and others who require visas also require letter of invitation, obtainable from a travel agent, hotel or individual. Visas on arrival are not available if arriving by train.

❶ Getting There & Away

AIR

Moldova's only **international airport** (p792) is in Chişinău.

LAND
Bus

Chişinău is well linked by bus (p792) to Romania, Russia and Ukraine. For bus journeys between Chişinău and Odesa, we advise taking the route going through the southeast Palanca border crossing, circumnavigating Transdniestr.

Car & Motorcyle

On arriving at the border, drivers need to show valid vehicle registration, insurance (Green Card), driving licence (US and EU licences OK) and passport. Motorists must purchase a highway sticker (vignette) to drive on Moldovan roads. Buy these at the border crossing. Rates per 7/15/30 days are €2/4/7.

Train

Only a handful of international trains serve Moldova, all of them terminating in Chişinău.

❶ Getting Around

Moldova has a comprehensive network of buses running to most towns and villages. *Marshrutky*, or fixed-route minivans (also known by their Romanian name, maxitaxis), follow the same routes as the buses and are quicker.

Car hire makes sense as Moldova's roads are in great shape these days and you can reach just about any part of the country on a day trip out of Chişinău. Car hire is readily available at Chişinău International Airport (p792).

Montenegro

Best Places to Eat

➡ Grill Bistro Parma (p801)
➡ Restoran Galerija (p804)
➡ Konoba Školji (p805)
➡ Byblos (p805)
➡ Jadran kod Krsta (p801)

Best Places to Stay

➡ Hotel Hippocampus (p804)
➡ Avala Resort & Villas (p801)
➡ Etno Selo Šljeme (p808)
➡ Hotel Poseidon (p801)
➡ Old Town Hostel (p804)

Why Go?

If all the world's a stage, then Montenegro struts upon it, continuously playing out the most dramatic act. There's not an iota of the insipid to be found here; from its backdrop of majestic mountains and captivating coastline to its passionate populace and lively, living history, this is a country with charisma.

Most visitors make a beeline to Montenegro's spectacular seaside, where mountains jut sharply from crystal-clear waters, ancient walled towns cling to the rocks and cosmopolitan jetsetters mingle with traditional fisherfolk. But there's more to Montenegro than sun and sand; its native name – Crna Gora (Црна Гора) – means 'Black Mountain', and it's in the rugged highlands that the country's profound and adventurous soul reveals itself.

Smaller than the state of Connecticut and roughly two-thirds the size of Wales, miniscule Montenegro proves once and for all that good things do indeed come in small packages.

When to Go

Podgorica

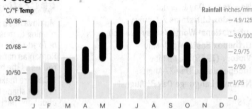

Jun Enjoy balmy weather without the peak season prices and crowds.

Sep Warm water but fewer bods to share it with; shoulder season prices.

Oct The leaves turn golden, making a rich backdrop for walks in the national parks.

Montenegro Highlights

① Kotor (p802) Randomly roaming the atmospheric streets until you're at least a little lost.

② Lovćen National Park (p805) Driving the vertiginous route from Kotor to the Njegoš Mausoleum.

③ Perast (p804) Admiring the baroque palaces and churches.

④ Ostrog Monastery (p806) Seeking out the spiritual at this impressive cliff-clinging monastery.

⑤ Tara Canyon (p807) Floating through paradise,

rafting between the plunging walls of this canyon.

⑥ Cetinje (p806) Diving into Montenegro's history, art and culture in the old royal capital.

⑦ Budva (p800) Watching the beautiful people over the rim of a coffee cup in the cobbled Old Town lanes.

COASTAL MONTENEGRO

It's not even 300km from tip to toe, but Montenegro's coastline crams in some of Europe's most stunning seaside scenery. The commanding cliffs and dazzling waters of the Bay of Kotor (Boka Kotorska) are brain-blowingly beautiful; the Adriatic Coast's beautiful beaches and charismatic Old Towns are equally enrapturing.

Budva Будва

033 / POP 13,400

Budva is the poster child of Montenegrin tourism. Easily the country's most-visited destination, it attracts hordes of holidaymakers intent on exploring its atmospheric Stari Grad (Old Town), sunning themselves on the bonny beaches of the Budva Riviera and partying until dawn; with scores of buzzy bars and clanging clubs, it's not nicknamed 'the Montenegrin Miami' for nothing.

Sights

Budva's best feature and star attraction is the Stari Grad (Old Town) – a mini-Dubrovnik with marbled streets and Venetian walls rising from the clear waters below. Much of it was ruined by two earthquakes in 1979 but it has since been completely rebuilt and now houses more shops, bars and restaurants than residences.

Citadela FORTRESS

(admission €2.50; 9am-midnight May-Oct, to 5pm Nov-Apr) At the Stari Grad's seaward end, the old citadel offers striking views, a small museum and a library full of rare tomes and maps. It's thought to be built on the site of the Greek acropolis, but the present incarnation dates to the 19th century Austrian occupation. Its large terrace serves as the main stage of the annual Theatre City festival.

Town Walls FORTRESS

(admission €1.50) A walkway about a metre wide leads around the landward walls of the Stari Grad, offering views across the rooftops and down on some beautiful hidden gardens. Admission only seems to be charged in the height of summer; at other times it's either free or locked. The entrance is near the Citadela.

Ričardova Glava BEACH

(Richard's Head) Immediately south of the Old Town, this little beach has the ancient walls as an impressive backdrop. Wander around the headland and you'll come to a **statue** of a naked dancer, one of Budva's most-photographed landmarks. Carry on and you'll find the quiet, double-bayed **Mogren Beach**. There's a spot near here where the fearless or foolhardy leap from the cliffs into the waters below.

Jaz Beach BEACH

The blue waters and broad sands here look spectacular when viewed from high up on the Tivat road. While it's not built up like Budva and Bečići, the beach is still lined with loungers, sun umbrellas and beach bars; head down the Budva end of the beach for a little more seclusion. If peace and privacy is what you're after, steer clear in mid-July, when Jaz is overrun by more than 100,000 merrymakers boogeying it up at the **Sea Dance Festival** (www.seadancefestival.me).

Sleeping

★**Montenegro Freedom Hostel** HOSTEL €

(067-523 496; montenegrofreedom@gmail.com; Cara Dušana 21; dm/tw/d €18/50/66;) In a quieter section of the Old Town, this beloved, sociable hostel has tidy little rooms scattered between three buildings. The terraces and small courtyard are popular spots for impromptu guitar-led singalongs.

Montenegro Hostel HOSTEL €

(069-039 751; www.montenegrohostel.com; Vuka Karadžića 12; dm €17.50, r per person from €20;) With a right-in-the-thick-of-it Old Town location (pack earplugs), this colourful little hostel provides the perfect base for hitting the bars and beaches. Each floor has its own kitchen and bathroom, and there's a communal space at the top for fraternisation.

ITINERARIES

Five Days

Basing yourself in **Kotor**, spend an afternoon in Perast and a whole day in Budva. Allow another day to explore **Lovćen National Park** and **Cetinje**.

One Week

For your final two days, head north to **Durmitor National Park**, making sure to stop at **Ostrog Monastery** on the way. Spend your time hiking, rafting (in season) and canyoning.

Sailor House
GUESTHOUSE €€

(www.sailor-house-guest-house-budva.bedspro.com; Vuka Karadžića 25; r from €50; ❄ 🛜) Come for the budget prices and great Old Town location, stay for the warm hospitality. The five cosy rooms are kept immaculate, and there's a shared kitchen for socialising. Bike rentals available. Online bookings only.

⭐ Hotel Poseidon
HOTEL €€€

(📞 033-463 134; www.poseidon-jaz.com; Jaz Beach; d/apt per person €59/47; 🅿 ❄ 🛜) This glorious seaside hotel has been sitting by the sands of Jaz Beach since 1967, and while the clean, spacious rooms don't show their age, its excellent service certainly echoes decades of experience. The views from every room – many of which have kitchens – are picture-perfect, and the hotel has its own small slice of private beach with sunbeds and umbrellas free for guests' use.

⭐ Avala Resort & Villas
RESORT €€€

(www.avalaresort.com; Mediteranska 2; d/villa/ste from €225/316/360; 🅿 ❄ 🛜 🏊) Stunning, breathtaking, luxurious: and that's just the views from the sea-facing rooms. This modern resort is a decadent delight, with a prime location right on Ričardova Glava, and an array of simple yet elegant rooms and sumptuous suites to choose from. The eye-smartingly blue outdoor pool makes direct eye contact with the Old Town and Sveti Nikola; you'd better waterproof your camera, as this is prime selfie scenery.

🍴 Eating

⭐ Grill Bistro Parma
MONTENEGRIN €€

(📞 069-028 076; Mainski Put 70; mains €3-10; ⏲ 24hr) A good grill *(roštilj)* is easy to find in meat-loving Montenegro, but if you're looking for one that's great, get your carnivorous self to Parma post-haste. Everything from *ćevapi* to chicken is barbecued to perfection here; their *punjena pljeskavica* (stuffed spicy hamburger) will inspire daydreams and drooling for months after your meal. Portions are massive. The restaurant is friendly and often packed; they also do deliveries.

⭐ Mercur
MONTENEGRIN €€

(Katunska Trpeza; 📞 067-570 483; Budva bus station; mains €3-12) Bus stations and top nosh are usually mutually exclusive territories, but this marvellous restaurant is the exception to the rule. For starters, it sits in a gorgeous green oasis populated by peacocks, deer and goats; there's also a playground. The menu is

Montenegrin to the core, with superb grilled and baked *(ispod sač)* meats, spicy soups and local seafood. The prices are ridiculously low.

Jadran kod Krsta
MONTENEGRIN, SEAFOOD €€

(📞 069-030 180; www.restaurantjadran.com; Šetalište bb; mains €6-20; ⏲ 7am-1am; 🛜) With candlelit tables directly over the water, this extremely popular, long-standing restaurant offers all the usual seafood suspects along with classic Montenegrin dishes from the interior. It may seem incongruous, but there's a rip-roaring bar – the Beer & Bike Club – out the back.

Konoba Portun
MONTENEGRIN, SEAFOOD €€

(📞 068-412 536; Mitrov Ljubiše 5; mains €7-20; ⏲ noon-midnight) Hidden within the Old Town's tiny lanes, this atmospheric eatery has only three outdoor tables and a handful inside; it feels like you're eating in a long-lost relative's home. The traditional dishes are beautifully presented. Don't miss out on their house speciality, *hobotnica ispod sača* (octopus cooked under a metal lid with hot coals on top).

Taste of Asia
ASIAN €€

(📞 033-455 249; Popa Jola Zeca bb; mains €7-15; ⏲ 11am-11pm) Spicy food is virtually non-existent in Montenegro, which makes this attractive little eatery such a welcome surprise. The menu ambles through Southeast Asia, with dishes from Indonesia, Malaysia, Singapore and Vietnam, but lingers longest in Thailand and China.

🍷 Drinking & Nightlife

Greco
BAR

(Njegoševa bb; ⏲ 9am-2am) On summer nights, the little square that Greco shares with its neighbour/rival Cafe Jef is packed from wall to wall with revellers. It's easily the busiest spot in the Old Town.

Top Hill
CLUB

(www.tophill.me; Topliški Put; events €10-25; ⏲ 11pm-5am Jul & Aug) The top cat of Montenegro's summer party scene attracts up to 5000 revellers to its open-air club atop Topliš Hill, offering them top-notch sound and lighting, sea views, big-name touring DJs and performances by local pop stars.

ℹ️ Information

Tourist Office (📞 033-452 750; www.budva.travel; Njegoševa 28; ⏲ 9am-9pm Mon-Sat, 5-9pm Sun Jun-Aug, 8am-8pm Mon-Sat Sep-May) Small but helpful office in the Old Town.

ℹ Getting There & Away

The **bus station** (☎ 033-456 000; Popa Jola Zeca bb) has frequent services to Kotor (€3.75, 40 minutes) and Cetinje (€3.75, 40 minutes), and a daily bus to Žabljak (€16, five hours).

Kotor   Котор

☎ 032 / POP 5340

Wedged between brooding mountains and a moody corner of the bay, the achingly atmospheric Kotor is perfectly at one with its setting. Hemmed in by staunch walls snaking improbably up the surrounding slopes,

the town is a Middle Ages maze of museums, churches, cafe-strewn squares and Venetian palaces and pillories. Come nightfall, Kotor's spectacularly lit-up walls glow as serenely as a halo; behind the bulwarks, the streets buzz with bars, live music – from soul to serenades – and castle-top clubbing.

◉ Sights & Activities

The best thing to do in Kotor is to let yourself get lost and found again in the maze of winding streets. You'll soon know every nook and cranny, but there are plenty of old churches to pop into, palaces to ogle and

Kotor

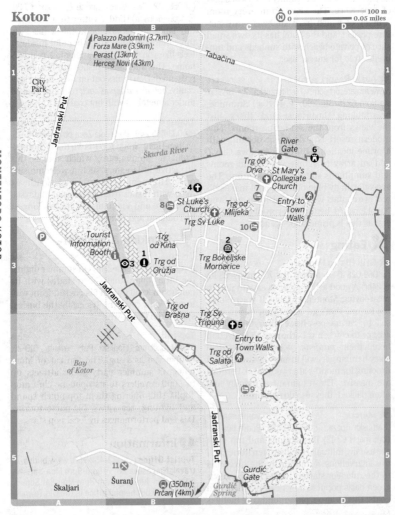

many coffees and/or vinos to be drunk in the shady squares.

Sea Gate
GATE

(Vrata od Mora) The main entrance to the town was constructed in 1555 when it was under Venetian rule (1420–1797). Look out for the winged lion of St Mark, Venice's symbol, which is displayed prominently on the walls here and in several other spots around the town. Above the gate, the date of the city's liberation from the Nazis is remembered with a communist star and a quote from Tito. An enormous (and inexplicable) bench outside the entrance makes for amusing happy snaps.

As you pass through the gate, look for the 15th-century stone relief of the Madonna and Child flanked by St Tryphon and St Bernard. Stepping through onto Trg od Oružja (Weapons Sq), you'll see a strange stone pyramid in front of the **clock tower** (1602); it was once used as a pillory to shame wayward citizens.

Town Walls
FORTRESS

(admission €3; ⊘24hr, fees apply 8am-8pm May-Sep) Kotor's fortifications started to head up St John's Hill in the 9th century and by the 14th century a protective loop was completed, which was added right up until the 19th century. The energetic can make a 1200m ascent up the fortifications via 1350 steps to a height of 260m above sea level; the views from up here are glorious. There are entry points near the North Gate and behind Trg od Salate; avoid the heat of the day and bring lots of water.

St Tryphon's Cathedral
CHURCH

(Katedrala Sv Tripuna; Trg Sv Tripuna; admission €2.50; ⊘8am-7pm) Kotor's most impressive

building, this Catholic cathedral was consecrated in the 12th century but reconstructed after several earthquakes. When the entire frontage was destroyed in 1667, the baroque bell towers were added; the left one remains unfinished. The cathedral's gently hued interior is a masterpiece of Romanesque architecture with slender Corinthian columns alternating with pillars of pink stone, thrusting upwards to support a series of vaulted roofs. Its gilded silver bas-relief altar screen is considered Kotor's most valuable treasure.

St Nicholas' Church
CHURCH

(Crkva Sv Nikole; Trg Sv Luke) Breathe in the smell of incense and beeswax in this relatively unadorned Orthodox church (1909). The silence, the iconostasis with its silver bas-relief panels, the dark wood against bare grey walls, the filtered light through the dome and the simple stained glass conspire to create a mystical atmosphere.

Maritime Museum of Montenegro
MUSEUM

(Pomorski muzej Crne Gore; www.museummaritimum.com; Trg Bokeljske Mornarice; adult/child €4/1; ⊘8am-6.30pm Mon-Sat, 9am-1pm Sun Apr-Oct, 9am-5pm Mon-Sat, to noon Sun Nov-Mar) Kotor's proud history as a naval power is celebrated in three storeys of displays housed in a wonderful early 18th-century palace. An audio guide helps explain the collection of photographs, paintings, uniforms, exquisitely decorated weapons and models of ships.

Kotor Open Tour
BUS

(tickets €20; ⊘9am-5pm, departing every 30min) On sunny days during summer, these open-top, hop-on-hop-off sightseeing buses ply the busy road between Kotor, Perast and Risan, showing off the hot spots (apart from the pedestrian-free Stari Grad, of course) and providing histories and explanations via multi-language audio guides. The ticket price includes admission to the museums in Perast and Risan.

You can't pre-book a ticket; just look out for the women wearing red T-shirts near the Sea Gate, or ask at the tourism information booth.

🛏 Sleeping & Eating

Although the Stari Grad is a charming place to stay, you'd better pack earplugs. In summer, the bars blast music onto the streets until 1am every night, rubbish collectors clank around at 6am and the chattering starts at the cafes by 8am. Some of the best options are just out of Kotor in quieter Dobrota.

MONTENEGRO KOTOR

★**Old Town Hostel** HOSTEL €
(☑032-325 317; www.hostel-kotor.me; near Trg od Salata; dm €18-22, d with/without bathroom €50/30, apt €55; ❋ ☎) If the ghosts of the Bisanti family had any concerns when their 13th-century palazzo was converted into a hostel, they must be overjoyed now. Sympathetic renovations have brought the place to life, and the ancient stone walls now echo with the cheerful chatter of happy travellers, mixing and mingling beneath the Bisanti coat of arms.

★**Palazzo Drusko** GUESTHOUSE €€
(☑032-325 257; www.palazzodrusko.me; near Trg od Mlijeka; s/d from €50/88; ❋ ☎) Loaded with character and filled with antiques, this venerable 600-year-old palazzo is a memorable place to stay, right in the heart of the Old Town. Thoughtful extras include a guest kitchen, 3D TVs and old-fashioned radios rigged to play Montenegrin music.

Hotel Marija HOTEL €€
(☑032-325 062; www.hotelmarija.me; Stari Grad; r €65-130; ❋) This charming little hotel occupies a beautiful palazzo in the centre of the Old Town. Although the decor of the rooms is a little old-fashioned, it's very comfortable, clean and has a romantic feel, despite its dated furnishings. One room has a balcony. The location is unbeatable, but be warned: the walls aren't soundproofed.

★**Hotel Hippocampus** BOUTIQUE HOTEL €€€
(☑068-889 862; www.hotelhippocampus.com; near Trg od Mlijeka; d €140-260; ❋ ☎) The hippocampus is the part of the brain responsible for memories, and you'll have plenty of those after a stay at this gorgeous boutique hotel. The owner is an architect, and it shows: every inch of the place is elegant, interesting and evocative. They haven't placed style over substance, though: the beds are comfortable, the rooms are spacious and the staff attentive.

Restoran Galerija MONTENEGRIN, SEAFOOD €€
(☑068-825 956; www.restorangalerija.com; Šuranj bb; mains €7-20; ☺11am-11.30pm) This bustling place on the waterfront excels in both meat and seafood, as well as fast and attentive service (along the coast, you'll often find these things are mutually exclusive). Try the prawns or mixed seafood in *buzara* sauce, a deceptively simple – yet spectacularly sublime – blend of olive oil, wine, garlic and mild spices.

❶ Information

Tourist Information Booth (☑032-325 950; www.tokotor.me; outside Vrata od Mora; ☺8am-8pm Apr-Nov, 8am-5pm Dec-Mar) Stocks free maps and brochures, and can help with contacts for private accommodation.

❶ Getting There & Away

The **bus station** (☑032-325 809; ☺ticket sales 6am-8pm) is to the south of town, just off the road leading to the Tivat tunnel. Buses head to Budva (€4, 55 minutes) at least hourly and to Žabljak (€17, 4 hours) twice daily.

A taxi to Tivat airport should cost between €7 to €10.

Perast   Пераст
☑032 / POP 350

Looking like a chunk of Venice that has floated down the Adriatic and anchored itself onto the bay, Perast hums with melancholy memories of the days when it was rich and powerful. Despite having only one main street, this tiny town boasts 16 churches and 17 formerly grand palazzos. Perast's most famous landmarks aren't on land at all: two peculiarly picturesque islands with equally peculiar histories.

◉ Sights

Gospa od Škrpjela ISLAND
(Our-Lady-of-the-Rock Island) This iconic island was artificially created (on 22 July 1452, to be precise) around a rock where an image of the Madonna was found; every year on that same day, the locals row over with stones to continue the task. The magnificent church was erected in 1630 and has sumptuous Venetian paintings, hundreds of silver votive tablets and a small museum (admission €1). The most unusual – and famous – exhibit is an embroidered icon of the Madonna and Child partly made with the hair of its maker.

Boats (€5 return) run between Perast and the island during summer.

Sveti Djordje ISLAND
(St George's Island) Sveti Djordje, rising from a natural reef, is the smaller of Perast's two islands. It houses a Benedictine monastery shaded by cypresses, and a large cemetery, earning it the local nickname 'Island of the Dead'. Legend has it that the island is cursed...but it looks pretty heavenly to us.

Perast Museum
MUSEUM

(Muzej grada Perasta; adult/child €2/1; ⊙9am-7pm) The Bujović Palace, dating from 1694, has been lovingly preserved and converted into a museum showcasing the town's proud seafaring history. It's worth visiting for the building alone and for the wondrous photo opportunities afforded by its balcony.

🛏 Sleeping & Eating

Bogišić Rooms & Apartments APARTMENT €
(☑067-440 062; www.bogisicroomsapartment. com; Obala Marka Martinovića bb; s €25, d without bathroom €42, apt €70; P❋🛜) This welcoming place offers great value for money. The rooms aren't massive, but they're comfortable, cute and right on the waterfront. The hosts have Montenegrin hospitality down pat; you'll want for naught here. The single room and two-bedroom apartment have kitchenettes.

★ **Palace Jelena** BOUTIQUE HOTEL €€€
(☑032-373 549; www.palacejelena-perast.com; Obala Marka Martinovića bb; d €80-140; ❋🛜) This quaint, family-run hotel isn't suffering from delusions of grandeur; its four atmospheric rooms and lovely restaurant are actually located within a palace (the Lučić-Kolović-Matikola Palace to be precise). It's so close to the shore that you can hear waves lapping from your room. All rooms have gorgeous sea and island views; the most expensive has a balcony.

★ **Konoba Školji** SEAFOOD, MONTENEGRIN €€
(☑069-419 745; Obala Marka Martinovića bb; mains €7-17; ⊙11am-11pm) This cute, traditional waterfront restaurant is all about the thrill of the grill; fresh seafood and falling-off-the-bone meats are barbecued to perfection in full view of salivating diners. Thankfully, they're not shy with the portion sizes; the delightful/maddening smell of the cooking and the sea air will have you ravenous by the time your meal arrives.

ⓘ Getting There & Away

Paid parking is available on either approach to town; car access into the town centre is restricted.

There's no bus station but buses to and from Kotor (€1.50, 25 minutes) stop at least every 30 minutes on the main road at the top of town

CENTRAL MONTENEGRO

The heart of Montenegro – physically, spiritually and politically – is easily accessed as a

---

WORTH A TRIP

TIVAT

With bobbing super yachts, a posh promenade and rows of elegant edifices, visitors to Tivat could be forgiven for wondering if they're in Monaco or Montenegro. The erstwhile village's impossibly glamorous **Porto Montenegro** (www.portomontenegro.com) complex houses boutiques, bars, an excellent naval museum (Zbirka Pomorskog Nasljeđa; Porto Montenegro; adult/child €2/1; ⊙9am-4pm Mon-Fri, 1-5pm Sat) and a marina. It's also home to some of the country's most eclectic eateries, including the luxurious **Byblos** (☑063-222 023; www.byblos.me; Porto Montenegro; mains €8-27; ⊙7am-1am) Lebanese restaurant. Tivat, renowned as one of the sunniest spots in Boka Kotorska, is an easy day trip from Kotor (11km away).

---

day trip from the coast, but it's well deserving of a longer exploration. This really is the full monty, with soaring peaks, hidden monasteries, steep river canyons and historic towns

Lovćen National Park
Ловћен

Directly behind Kotor is Mt Lovćen (1749m), the black mountain that gave Crna Gora (Montenegro) its name; *crna/negro* means 'black', and *gora/monte* means 'mountain' in Montenegrin and Italian respectively. This locale occupies a special place in the hearts of all Montenegrins. For most of its history it represented the entire nation – a rocky island of Slavic resistance in an Ottoman sea. The old capital of Cetinje nestles in its foothills.

The national park's 6220 hectares are criss-crossed with well-marked hiking paths.

⊙ Sights

★ **Njegoš Mausoleum** MONUMENT
(Njegošev Mauzolej; admission €3; ⊙8am-6pm) Lovćen's star attraction, this magnificent mausoleum (built 1970–1974) sits at the top of its second-highest peak, Jezerski Vrh (1657m). Take the 461 steps up to the entry where two granite giantesses guard the tomb of Montenegro's greatest hero. Inside under a golden mosaic canopy, a 28-ton Petar II Petrović Njegoš rests in the wings of an eagle, carved from a single block of black granite.

OSTROG MONASTERY

Clinging improbably – miraculously? – to a cliff face 900m above the Zeta valley, the gleaming white Ostrog Monastery (1665) is a strangely affecting place that attracts up to one million visitors each year.

A guesthouse near the Lower Monastery offers tidy single-sex dorm rooms (€5); in summer, sleeping mats are provided for free to pilgrims in front of the Upper Monastery. There's no public transport but numerous tour buses head here from the coast.

Njeguši   VILLAGE

On the northern edge of the park, this endearing collection of stone houses is famous for being the home village of the Petrović dynasty, Montenegro's most important rulers, and for making the country's best *pršut* (smoke-dried ham) and *sir* (cheese). Roadside stalls sell both, along with honey, *rakija* (fruit brandy), hand-woven mats and souvenirs. In the nearby village of Erakovic, Petar II Petrović Njegoš' birth house has been turned into a small museum (admission €2).

ℹ Information

National Park Visitor Centre (www.nparkovi. me; Ivanova Korita; ⊙ 9am-5pm) The centre has loads of information on the national park, and it also rents bikes (per hour €2) and offers accommodation in four-bed bungalows (€40).

ℹ Getting There & Away

If you're driving, the park (entry €2) can be approached from either Kotor (20km) or Cetinje (7km). Tour buses are the only buses that head into the park.

Cetinje   Цетиње

📞 041 / POP 16,700

Rising from a green vale surrounded by rough grey mountains, Cetinje is an odd mix of erstwhile capital (it was the seat of Montenegro until 1946) and overgrown village, where single-storey cottages and stately mansions share the same street.

◉ Sights

Cetinje's collection of four museums and two galleries is known collectively as the National Museum of Montenegro. A joint ticket (adult/child €10/5) will get you into all of them or you can buy individual tickets.

Biljarda   PALACE

(Njegoš Museum, Njegošev muzej; www.mnmuseum. org; Dvorski Trg; adult/child €3/1.50; ⊙ 9am-5pm) This castle-like palace was the residence of Montenegro's favourite son, prince-bishop and poet Petar II Petrović Njegoš. It was built and financed by the Russians in 1838 and housed the nation's first billiard table (hence the name). The bottom floor is devoted to military costumes, photos of soldiers with outlandish moustaches and exquisitely decorated weapons. Upstairs are Njegoš' personal effects, including his bishop's cross and garments, documents, fabulous furniture and, of course, the famous billiard table.

History Museum   MUSEUM

(Istorijski muzej; 📞 041-230 310; www.mnmuseum. org; Novice Cerovića 7; adult/child €3/1.50; ⊙ 9am-5pm) Housed in the imposing former parliament building (1910), this fascinating museum follows a timeline from the Stone Age to 1955. There are few English signs but the enthusiastic staff will give you an overview. Bullet holes are a theme of some of the most interesting relics: there are three in the back of the tunic that Prince Danilo was wearing when assassinated; Prince Nikola's standard from the battle of Vučji Do has 396; while, in the communist section, there's a big gaping one in the skull of a fallen comrade.

Montenegrin Art Gallery   GALLERY

(Crnogorska galerija umjetnosti; www.mnmuseum. org; Novice Cerovića 7; adult/child €4/2; ⊙ 9am-5pm) All of Montenegro's great artists are represented here, with the most famous (Milunović, Lubarda, Đurić etc) having their own separate spaces. There's a small collection of icons, the most important being the precious 9th-century Our Lady of Philermos, traditionally believed to be painted by St Luke himself. It's spectacularly presented in its own blue-lit 'chapel', but the Madonna's darkened face is only just visible behind its spectacular golden casing mounted with diamonds, rubies and sapphires.

Cetinje Monastery   MONASTERY

(Cetinjski Manastir; ⊙ 8am-6pm) It's a case of four times lucky for the Cetinje Monastery, having been repeatedly destroyed during Ottoman attacks and rebuilt. This sturdy incarnation dates from 1786, with its only exterior ornamentation being the capitals of columns recycled from the original building, founded in 1484. The chapel to the right of the courtyard holds the monastery's proudest possessions: a shard of the True Cross (the pièce de résistance of many of Europe's churches) and the mummified right hand of St John the Baptist.

🛏 Sleeping & Eating

⭐**La Vecchia Casa**   B&B **€**
(☑067-629 660; www.lavecchiacasa.com; Vojvode Batrica 6; s/d/apt €17/28/40; P ❄ 🛜) With its gorgeous garden, traditional hospitality and pervading sense of tranquility, this remarkably renovated period house wouldn't be out of place in a quaint mountain village. Instead, it's right in the centre of Cetinje, offering a rural-feeling retreat with all of the historical capital's attractions, shops and restaurants a short stroll away. Clean, simple rooms retain a sense of the home's history; good-sized apartments have kitchens.

⭐**Kole**   MONTENEGRIN, EUROPEAN **€€**
(☑041-231 620; www.restaurantkole.me; Bul Crnogorskih Junaka 12; mains €4-15; ⊙7am-midnight) They serve omelettes and pasta at this snazzy modern eatery, but it's the local specialities that truly shine. Try the memorable Njeguški *ražanj,* smoky spit-roasted meat stuffed with *pršut* and cheese.

ℹ Information

Tourist Information (☑041-230 250; www. cetinje.travel; Novice Cerovića bb, Njegošev Park; ⊙8am-6pm Mar-Oct, to 4pm Nov-Feb) Helpful tourist information, though be aware that they often charge for brochures that elsewhere might be free. The website could use an update, but it's a good place to start your pre-Cetinje research.

ℹ Getting There & Away

Buses stop at the run-down Trg Goloatočkih Žrtava, two blocks from the main street. There are regular services to Budva (€4, 40 minutes) and Kotor (€5, 1½ hours).

Durmitor National Park
Дурмитор

The impossibly rugged and dramatic Durmitor National Park (entry €3) is one of Montenegro's – and Mother Nature's – showpieces. Carved out by glaciers and underground streams, the Durmitor range has 48 limestone peaks soaring to over 2000m; the highest, **Bobotov Kuk**, hits 2523m. Scattered in between are 18 glacial lakes known as *gorske oči* (mountain eyes); the largest, **Black Lake** (Crno jezero), is a 3km walk from **Žabljak**, the park's principal gateway. Slicing through the mountains at the northern edge of the national park, the **Tara River** forms one of the world's deepest canyons (1300m; the Grand Canyon plummets a mere 200m deeper).

From December to March, Durmitor is a major ski resort, while in summer it's popular for hiking, rafting and other active pursuits.

🏃 Activities

Durmitor is rough, rugged and ripe for adventure, with tons of outdoor activities on offer, from canyoning to high-altitude hiking; the visitors centre can help with thrill-seeking quests. Rafting along the Tara is the country's

MONTENEGRO DURMITOR NATIONAL PARK

WORTH A TRIP

MORE TO EXPLORE

Herceg Novi A bustling waterfront promenade runs below a small fortified centre, with cafes and churches set on sunny squares.

Sveti Stefan Gazing down on this impossibly picturesque walled island village (now an exclusive luxury resort) provides one of the biggest 'wow' moments on the entire Adriatic coast.

Ulcinj Minarets and a hulking walled town dominate the skyline, providing a dramatic background for the holidaymakers on the beaches.

Podgorica The nation's modern capital has a buzzy cafe scene, lots of green space and some excellent galleries.

Lake Skadar National Park The Balkans' largest lake is dotted with island monasteries and provides an important sanctuary for migrating birds.

Prokletije National Park The 'Accursed Mountains' offer heavenly hiking in a forgotten corner of Europe.

ESSENTIAL FOOD & DRINK

Loosen your belt; you're in for a treat. By default, most Montenegrin food is local, fresh and organic, and hence very seasonal. The food on the coast is virtually indistinguishable from Dalmatian cuisine: lots of grilled seafood, garlic, olive oil and Italian dishes. Inland it's much more meaty and Serbian-influenced. The village of Njeguši in the Montenegrin heartland is famous for its *pršut* (prosciutto, air-dried ham) and *sir* (cheese). Anything with Njeguški in its name is going to be a true Montenegrin dish and stuffed with these goodies. Eating in Montenegro can be a trial for vegetarians and almost impossible for vegans. Pasta, pizza and salad are the best fallback options.

Here are some local favourites:

Riblja čorba Fish soup, a staple of the coast.

Crni rižoto Black risotto, coloured and flavoured with squid ink.

Lignje na žaru Grilled squid, sometimes stuffed *(punjene)* with cheese and smoke-dried ham.

Jagnjetina ispod sača Lamb cooked (often with potatoes) under a metal lid covered with hot coals.

Rakija Domestic brandy, made from nearly anything. The local favourite is grape-based *loza*.

Vranac & Krstač The most famous indigenous red and white wine varietals (respectively).

premier outdoor attraction (May to October). Most of the day tours from the coast traverse only the last 18km of the river – this is outside the national park and hence avoids hefty fees. This section also has the most rapids – but don't expect much in the way of white water.

Summit Travel Agency ADVENTURE
(☑ 069-016 502; www.summit.co.me; Njegoševa 12, Žabljak; half-/1-/2-day rafting trip €45/110/200) As well as rafting trips, this long-standing agency can arrange 4WD tours, mountain-bike hire and canyoning expeditions. It also has accommodation in the form of cabins (€70) and a guesthouse (from €15) in Žabljak.

🛏 Sleeping

★ Eko-Oaza

Suza Evrope CABINS, CAMPGROUND €
(☑ 069-444 590; ekooazatara@gmail.com; Dobrilovina; campsites per tent/person/campervan €5/1/10, cabins €50; ☉ Apr-Oct) Consisting of four comfortable wooden cottages (each

EATING PRICE RANGES

The following price categories refer to a standard main meal. Tipping isn't expected, though it's common to round up to the nearest euro.

€ up to €5

€€ €5 to €8

€€€ over €9

sleeping five people) and a fine stretch of lawn above the river, this magical, family-run 'eco oasis' offers a genuine experience of Montenegrin hospitality. Home-cooked meals are provided on request, and rafting trips and 4WD safaris can be arranged.

★ Hikers Den HOSTEL €
(☑ 067-854 433; www.hostelzabljak.com; Božidara Žugića bb, Žabljak; dm €13-15, s/d €22/35; 🔊) Split between three neighbouring houses, this laid-back and sociable place is by far the best hostel in the north. If you're keen on a rafting or canyoning trip, the charming English-speaking hosts will happily make the arrangements.

★ Etno Selo Šljeme CABIN €€
(☑ 063-229 294; www.etnoselosljeme.com; Smrčevo brdo bb, Žabljak; cabin €90; 🅿🔊) With majestic mountain views and lashings of local cuisine on offer, a stay here is a wonderful way to soak up the scenic splendour of Durmitor. The five two-bedroom cabins are more swish than some of the other 'etno' offerings in the area; there's also a playground and bikes for hire. It's close to the ski centres and Žabljak town, but isolated enough to get a feel for the northern wilderness.

❶ Information

National Park Visitors Centre (☑ 052-360 228; www.nparkovi.me; ☉ 7am-5pm Mon-Fri, 10am-5pm Sat & Sun Jan & Jun–mid-Sep, 7am-3pm Mon-Fri mid-Sep–Dec & Feb-May) On the road to the Black Lake, this centre has a wonderful micromuseum focusing on the park's flora and fauna. Maps, books and permits are sold here; they can also organise local guides (from €60).

 Getting There & Away

The bus station is at the southern edge of Žabljak, on the Šavnik road. Destinations include Kotor (€17, four hours, two daily) and Budva (€16, five hours, daily).

SURVIVAL GUIDE

Directory A–Z

ACCOMMODATION

Private accommodation and hotels form the bulk of the sleeping options, although there are some hostels in the more touristed areas. Campgrounds operate in summer and some of the mountainous areas have cabin accommodation in 'eco villages' or mountain huts. In the peak summer season, some places require minimum stays (three days to a week). Many establishments on the coast close during winter. An additional tourist tax (usually less than €1 per night) is added to the rate for all accommodation types.

INTERNET RESOURCES

Montenegrin National Tourist Organisation (www.montenegro.travel)
National Parks of Montenegro (www.nparkovi.me)
Visit Montenegro (www.visit-montenegro.com)

Getting There & Away

AIR

Montenegro has two international airports – Tivat (TIV; ☑ 032-670 930; www.montenegroairports.com) and Podgorica (TGD; ☑ 020-444 244; www.montenegroairports.com) – although many visitors use Croatia's Dubrovnik Airport, which is very near the border.

Montenegro Airlines (www.montenegroairlines.com) is the national carrier.

SLEEPING PRICE RANGES

The following price indicators refer to a double room in the shoulder season (June and September). Expect to pay more in the absolute peak months (July and August).

€ less than €45

€€ €45 to €100

€€€ more than €100

COUNTRY FACTS

Area 13,812 sq km

Capital Podgorica

Country Code ☑ 382

Currency euro (€)

Emergency Ambulance ☑124, fire ☑123, police ☑122

Language Montenegrin

Money ATMs in larger towns.

Population 676,870

Visas None for citizens of EU, Canada, USA, Australia, New Zealand and many other countries.

LAND
Bus

There's a well-developed bus network linking Montenegro with major cities in the neighbouring countries, including Dubrovnik, Sarajevo, Belgrade, Pristina and Shkodra.

Car & Motorcycle

Vehicles need a locally valid insurance policy (such as European Green Card vehicle insurance); otherwise, insurance must be bought at the border.

Train

At least two trains head between Bar and Belgrade daily (€21, 11 hours); see www.zcg-prevoz.me for details.

SEA

Montenegro Lines (www.montenegrolines.com) operates car ferries between Bar to Bari, Italy, at least twice weekly from May to September.

Getting Around

BUS

The bus network is extensive and reliable. Buses are usually comfortable and air-conditioned, and are rarely full.

CAR & MOTORCYCLE

Cars drive on the right-hand side and headlights must be kept on at all times. Drivers are recommended to carry an International Driving Permit (IDP) as well as their home country's driving licence. Traffic police are everywhere, so stick to speed limits. Sadly requests for bribes do happen (especially around the Durmitor area), so don't give the police any excuse to pull you over.

Allow more time than you'd expect for the distances involved, as the terrain will slow you down.

The major international car-hire companies have a presence in various centres.

The Netherlands

Best Places to Eat

➡ Ron Gastrobar (p817)
➡ Bisschopsmolen (p832)
➡ Restaurant Allard (p823)
➡ Tante Nel (p827)
➡ Brick (p821)

Best Places to Stay

➡ Hoxton Amsterdam (p817)
➡ King Kong Hostel (p827)
➡ Mary K Hotel (p831)
➡ Pincoffs (p827)
➡ Collector (p817)

Why Go?

Old and new intertwine in the Netherlands. The legacies of great Dutch artists Rembrandt, Vermeer and Van Gogh, beautiful 17th-century canals, windmills, tulips and quaint brown cafes lit by flickering candles coexist with ground-breaking contemporary architecture, cutting-edge fashion, homewares, design and food scenes, phenomenal nightlife and a progressive mindset.

Much of the Netherlands is famously below sea level and the pancake-flat landscape offers idyllic cycling. Locals live on bicycles and you can too. Rental outlets are ubiquitous throughout the country, which is crisscrossed with dedicated cycling paths.

Allow plenty of time to revel in the magical, multifaceted capital Amsterdam, to venture further afield to charming canal-laced towns such as Leiden and Delft. Check out Dutch cities such as exquisite Maastricht, with its city walls, ancient churches and grand squares, and the pulsing port city of Rotterdam, currently undergoing an urban renaissance.

When to Go
Amsterdam

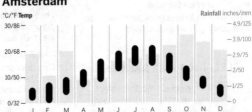

Mar–May
Colour explodes as billions of bulbs bloom.

Jul Mild summer temps and long daylight hours keep you outside cycling and drinking.

Dec–Feb
When the canals freeze, the Dutch passion for ice skating is on display nationwide.

AMSTERDAM

📞020 / POP 813,000

World Heritage–listed canals lined by gabled houses, candlelit cafes, whirring bicycles, lush parks, monumental museums, colourful markets, diverse dining, quirky shopping and legendary nightlife make the free-spirited Dutch capital one of Europe's great cities.

Amsterdam has been a liberal place since the Netherlands' Golden Age, when it was at the forefront of European art and trade. Centuries later, in the 1960s, it again led the pack – this time in the principles of tolerance, with broad-minded views on drugs and same-sex relationships taking centre stage.

Explore its many worlds-within-worlds, where nothing ever seems the same twice.

⊙ Sights

Amsterdam is compact and you can roam the city on foot but there's also an excellent public transport network.

◉ City Centre

Crowned by the Royal Palace (p811), the square that puts the 'Dam' in Amsterdam anchors the city's oldest quarter, which is also home to its infamous Red Light District.

★**Royal Palace**　PALACE
(Koninklijk Paleis; 📞020-620 40 60; www.paleis amsterdam.nl; Dam; adult/child €10/free; ◎10am-5pm; 🚊4/9/16/24 Dam) Opened as a town hall in 1655, this building became a palace in the 19th century. The interiors gleam, especially the marble work – at its best in a floor inlaid with maps of the world in the great *burgerzaal* (citizens' hall), which occupies the heart of the building. Pick up a free audio tour at the desk after you enter; it will ex-

plain everything you see in vivid detail. King Willem-Alexander uses the palace only for ceremonies; check the website for periodic closures.

★**Begijnhof**　SQUARE
(📞020-622 19 18; www.nicolaas-parochie.nl; off Gedempte Begijnensloot; ◎9am-5pm; 🚊1/2/5 Spui) 𝐅𝐑𝐄𝐄 This enclosed former convent dates from the early 14th century. It's a surreal oasis of peace, with tiny houses and postage-stamp gardens around a well-kept courtyard. The beguines were a Catholic order of unmarried or widowed women who cared for the elderly and lived a religious life without taking monastic vows. The last true beguine died in 1971.

◉ Canal Ring

Amsterdam's Canal Ring was built during the 17th-century after the seafaring port grew beyond its medieval walls, and authorities devised a ground-breaking expansion plan.

Wandering here amid architectural treasures and their reflections on the narrow waters of the Prinsengracht, Keizersgracht and Herengracht can cause days to vanish.

★**Anne Frank Huis**　MUSEUM
(📞020-556 71 05; www.annefrank.org; Prinsengracht 267; adult/child €9/4.50; ◎9am-10pm Apr-Oct, 9am-7pm Sun-Fri, to 9pm Sat Nov-Mar; 🚊13/14/17 Westermarkt) The Anne Frank Huis draws almost one million visitors annually (prepurchase tickets online to minimise the queues). With its reconstruction of Anne's melancholy bedroom and her actual diary – sitting alone in its glass case, filled with sunnily optimistic writing tempered by quiet despair – it's a powerful experience.

ITINERARIES

One Week
Spend three days canal exploring, museum hopping and cafe crawling in **Amsterdam**. Work your way through the ancient towns of the **Randstad** and the contemporary vibe of **Rotterdam**, and save a day for the grandeur of **Maastricht**.

Two Weeks
Allow four days for Amsterdam's many delights, plus a day trip to the old towns of the north, and a day or two exploring some of the region's smaller towns. Then add a day each at beautiful **Delft**, regal **Den Haag** (The Hague), student-filled **Utrecht** and buzzing **Rotterdam**. Finish off with two days in historic **Maastricht**.

Netherlands Highlights

① Amsterdam (p811) Cruising the canals while soaking up one of Europe's most enchanting old cities.

② Markthal Rotterdam (p829) Marvelling at the architecture, a highlight of the Netherlands' hip-and-happening 'second city'.

③ Fort Sint Pieter (p832) Exploring the centuries-old

tunnels below the resplendent city of Maastricht.

④ Vermeer Centrum Delft (p824) Learning about Vermeer's life and work in his evocative hometown.

⑤ Den Haag (p822) Discovering the beautiful tree-lined boulevards, classy museums and the palatial Binnenhof buildings.

⑥ Keukenhof Gardens (p822) Delving into the cache of museum in Leiden and dazzling tulip displays at its nearby gardens.

⑦ Zaanse Schans (p821) Watching windmills twirl and mee the millers at the delightful open-air museum.

⑧ Cycling (p825) Following canals or touring the tulip fields of the Randstad on the world's best network of cycling routes.

Museumplein

Amsterdam's big three museums fan out around the grassy expanse of Museumplein, in the Old South neighbourhood.

⭐ **Van Gogh Museum** MUSEUM
(☑ 020-570 52 00; www.vangoghmuseum.com; Museumplein 6; adult/child €17/free, audioguide €5; ☺ 9am-7pm Sun-Thu, to 9pm Sat mid-Jul-Aug, to 6pm Sat-Thu Sep–mid-Jul, to 5pm Jan-Mar, to 10pm Fri; ☎; ☐ 2/3/5/12 Van Baerlestraat) Framed by a gleaming new glass entrance hall, the world's largest Van Gogh collection offers a superb line-up of masterworks. Trace the artist's life from his tentative start through his giddy-coloured sunflower phase, and on to the black cloud that descended over him and his work. There are also paintings by contemporaries Gauguin, Toulouse-Lautrec, Monet and Bernard.

Queues can be huge; prebooked e-tickets and discount cards expedite the process with fast-track entry.

⭐ **Rijksmuseum** MUSEUM
(National Museum; ☑ 020-674 70 00; www.rijksmuseum.nl; Museumstraat 1; adult/child €17.50/free; ☺ 9am-5pm; ☎; ☐ 2/5 Rijksmuseum) The Rijksmuseum is the Netherlands' premier art trove, splashing Rembrandts, Vermeers and 7500 other masterpieces over 1.5km of galleries. To avoid the biggest crowds, come after 3pm. Or prebook tickets online, which provides fast-track entry.

The Golden Age works are the highlight. Feast your eyes on still lifes, gentlemen in ruffled collars and landscapes bathed in pale yellow light. Rembrandt's *The Night Watch* (1642) takes pride of place.

⭐ **Stedelijk Museum** MUSEUM
(☑ 020-573 29 11; www.stedelijk.nl; Museumplein 10; adult/child €18/free, audio guide €5; ☺ 10am-6pm Sat-Thu, to 10pm Fri; ☎; ☐ 2/3/5/12 Van Baerlestraat) Built in 1895 to a neo-Renaissance design by AM Weissman, the Stedelijk Museum is the permanent home of the National Museum of Modern Art. Amassed by postwar curator Willem Sandberg, the modern classics here are among the world's most admired. The permanent collection includes all the blue chips of 19th- and 20th-century painting – Monet, Picasso and Chagall among them – as well as sculptures by Rodin, abstracts by Mondrian and Kandinsky, and much, much more.

JORDAAN

A densely populated *volksbuurt* (district for the common people) until the mid-20th century, the intimate Jordaan is now one of Amsterdam's most desirable addresses. The neighbourhood is a pastiche of modest 17th- and 18th-century merchants' houses and humble workers' homes squashed in a grid of tiny lanes peppered with bite-sized cafes and shops. There's a handful of small-scale museums (houseboat museum, tulip museum) but the real pleasure here is simply losing yourself in its charming canal-side backstreets.

⭐ **Vondelpark** PARK
(www.hetvondelpark.net; ☐ 2/5 Hobbemastraat) The lush urban idyll of the Vondelpark is one of Amsterdam's most magical places – sprawling, English-style gardens with ponds, lawns, footbridges and winding footpaths. On a sunny day, an open-air party atmosphere ensues when tourists, lovers, cyclists, in-line skaters, pram-pushing parents, cartwheeling children, football-kicking teenagers, spliff-sharing friends and champagne-swilling picnickers all come out to play.

De Pijp

Immediately south of the Canal Ring, villagey De Pijp is Amsterdam's most spontaneous and creative quarter. Bohemian cafes, restaurants and bars spill out around its festive street market.

⭐ **Albert Cuypmarkt** MARKET
(www.albertcuyp-markt.amsterdam; Albert Cuypstraat, btwn Ferdinand Bolstraat & Van Woustraat; ☺ 9.30am-5pm Mon-Sat; ☐ 16/24 Albert Cuypstraat) The best place to marvel at De Pijp's colourful scene is the Albert Cuypmarkt, Amsterdam's largest and busiest market. Vendors loudly tout their odd gadgets and their arrays of fruit, vegetables, herbs and spices. They sell clothes and other general goods too, often cheaper than anywhere else. Snack vendors tempt passers-by with herring sandwiches, egg rolls, doughnuts and caramel-syrup-filled *stroopwafels* (waffles). If you have room after all that, the surrounding area teems with cosy cafes and eateries.

Central Amsterdam

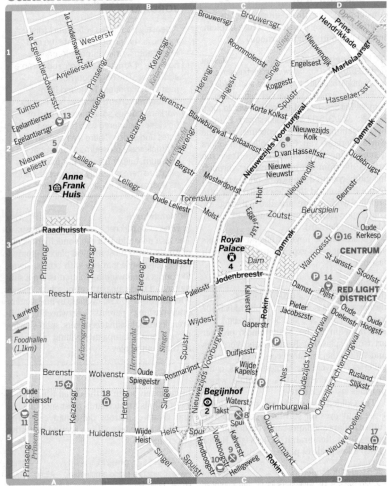

★ **Heineken Experience** BREWERY
(☎ 020-523 92 22; www.heineken.com; Stadhouderskade 78; adult/child €18/14.50; ⊙ 10.30am-9pm daily Jul & Aug, to 7.30pm Mon-Thu, to 9pm Fri-Sun Sep-Jun; ☐ 16/24 Stadhouderskade) On the site of the company's old brewery, the crowning glory of this self-guided 'Experience' (samples aside) is a multimedia exhibit where you 'become' a beer by getting shaken up, sprayed with water and subjected to heat. True beer connoisseurs will shudder, but it's a lot of fun. Admission includes a 15-minute shuttle boat ride to the Heineken Brand Store near Rembrandtplein. Prebooking tickets online saves you €2 on the entry fee and allows you to skip the ticket queues.

◉ Nieuwmarkt & Plantage

The streets around the Rembrandt House are prime wandering territory, offering a vibrant mix of old Amsterdam, canals and quirky shops and cafes.

★ **Museum het Rembrandthuis** MUSEUM
(Rembrandt House Museum; ☎ 020-520 04 00; www.rembrandthuis.nl; Jodenbreestraat 4; adult/

Central Amsterdam

👉 Tours

Amsterdam's **canal boats** are a relaxing way to tour the town. Avoid steamed-up glass windows by choosing boats with open seating areas.

Those Dam Boat Guys   BOATING
(☏06 1885 5219; www.thosedamboatguys.com; per person €25; ⊙1pm, 3pm & 5pm; 🚊13/14/17 Westermarkt) Here's your least-touristy canal-cruise option. The guys offer cheeky small tours (no more than 11 people) on electric boats. Feel free to bring food, beer, smoking material and whatever else you want for the 90-minute jaunt. Departure is from Cafe Wester (Nieuwe Leliestraat 2).

Yellow Bike   CYCLING
(☏020-620 69 40; www.yellowbike.nl; Nieuwezijds Kolk 29; city/countryside tours from €22.50/32.50; 🚊1/2/5/13/17 Nieuwezijds Kolk) The original. Choose from city tours or the longer countryside tour through the pretty Waterland district to the north.

---

child €13/4; ⊙10am-6pm; 🚊9/14 Waterlooplein) You almost expect to find the master himself at the Museum het Rembrandthuis, where Rembrandt van Rijn ran the Netherlands' largest painting studio, only to lose the lot when profligacy set in, enemies swooped and bankruptcy came a-knocking. The museum has scores of etchings and sketches. Ask for the free audio guide at the entrance. You can buy advance tickets online, though it's not as vital here as at some of the other big museums.

Southern Canal Ring

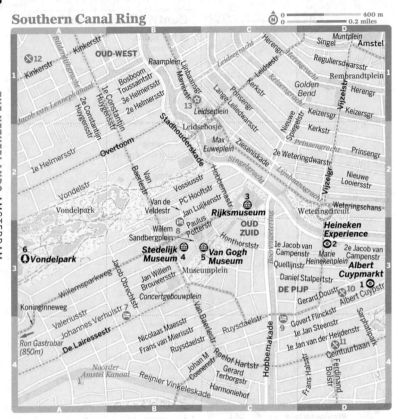

🛏 Sleeping

Book ahead for summer and weekends year-round. Many cheaper places cater specifically to party animals with general mayhem around the clock. Others exude refined old-world charm. Wi-fi is near universal but lifts/elevators are not.

Generator Amsterdam   HOSTEL €
(☏ 020-708 56 00; www.generatorhostels.com; Mauritskade 57; dm/d/q €54/144/360; 🚇 9/14 9/10/14 Alexanderplein) Generator continues its push into the upscale hostel market: set in a century-old university building right by Oosterpark, this design-savvy property has 566 beds spread over 168 twin and quad rooms, all with en-suite bathrooms. Guests can socialise in the cafe with terrace overlooking the park, in a bar carved from the old lecture hall or in a basement speakeasy.

★ **Collector** B&B €€

(📞 020-673 67 79; www.the-collector.nl; De Lairess-estraat 46; s/d from €90/125; @ 🛜; 🚋 5/16/24 Museumplein) This spotless B&B near the Concertgebouw is furnished with muse-um-style displays of clocks, wooden clogs and ice skates – things the owner, Karel, col-lects. Each of the three rooms has balcony access and a TV. Karel stocks the kitchen for guests to prepare breakfast at their leisure (the eggs come from his hens in the garden).

★ **Hotel Fita** HOTEL €€

(📞 020-679 09 76; www.fita.nl; Jan Luijkenstraat 37; s/d from €116/136; 🛜; 🚋 2/3/5/12 Van Bae-rlestraat) Family-owned Fita, on a quiet street off the Museumplein and PC Hooftstraat, has 15 handsome rooms with nicely appoint-ed bathrooms; a bountiful free breakfast of eggs, pancakes, cheeses and breads; and a lift/elevator. The dynamic young owner keeps the property in mint condition (new furniture, new artwork, fresh paint), and ser-vice could not be more attentive.

★ **Hoxton Amsterdam** DESIGN HOTEL €€€

(📞 020-888 55 55; www.thehoxton.com; Heren-gracht 255; s/d from €159/199; ✳ 🛜; 🚋 13/14/17 Westermarkt) Part of a European-based chain known for high style at affordable prices, the Hoxton opened in 2015 to great hipster fan-fare. The 111 rooms splash through five canal houses and come in sizes from 'shoebox' to 'roomy'. The breakfast snack, speedy wi-fi, free international calls and low-priced can-teen items are nice touches.

★ **Sir Albert Hotel** DESIGN HOTEL €€€

(📞 020-305 30 20; www.sirhotels.com/albert; Albert Cuypstraat 2-6; d from €209; ✳ @ 🛜; 🚋 16 Ruys-daelstraat) A 19th-century former diamond factory houses this glitzy design hotel. Its 90 creative rooms and suites have soaring ceil-ings and large windows, with custom-made linens and Illy espresso machines; iPads are available for guest use in the Persian-rug-floored study. Energetic staff are genuine and professional in equal measure.

✖ **Eating**

Amsterdam abounds with eateries. Superb streets for hunting include Utrechtsestraat, near Rembrandtplein; Amstelveenseweg, along the Vondelpark's western edge; and any of the little streets throughout the west-ern canals.

★ **Gartine** CAFE €

(📞 020-320 41 32; www.gartine.nl; Taksteeg 7; mains €7.25-11.50, high tea €17.50-24.75; ⊘ 10am-5pm Wed-Sun; 🍴; 🚋 4/9/14/16/24 Spui/Rokin) Gartine is magical, from its covert location in an alley off busy Kalverstraat to its mis-matched antique tableware and its sublime breakfast pastries, sandwiches and salads (made from produce grown in its garden plot). The sweet-and-savoury high tea is a scrumptious bonus.

★ **Foodhallen** FOOD HALL €

(www.foodhallen.nl; Hannie Dankbaar Passage 3, De Hallen; dishes €5-15; ⊘ 11am-11.30pm Sun-Thu, to 1am Fri-Sat; 🚋 17 Ten Katestraat) Inside De Hallen, this glorious international food hall has 21 stands surrounding an airy open-plan eating area. Some are offshoots of popular Amsterdam eateries, such as the Butcher (📞 020-470 78 75; http://the-butcher.com; Albert Cuypstraat 129; burgers €7.50-11.50; ⊘ 11am-midnight; 🚋 16/24 Albert Cuypstraat); also look out for Viet View Vietnamese street food, Ja-bugo Iberico Bar ham, Pink Flamingo pizza, Bulls & Dogs hot dogs, Rough Kitchen ribs and De Ballenbar *bitterballen* (croquettes).

★ **Vleminckx** FAST FOOD €

(http://vleminckxdesausmeester.nl; Voetboogstraat 33; fries €2.30-4.50, sauces €0.70; ⊘ noon-7pm Sun & Mon, 11am-7pm Tue, Wed, Fri & Sat, 11am-8pm Thu; 🚋 1/2/5 Koningsplein) Vleminckx has been frying up *frites* (French fries) since 1887, and doing it at this hole-in-the-wall takeaway shack near the Spui for more than 50 years. The standard is smothered in mayonnaise, though you can also ask for ketchup, peanut sauce or a variety of spicy toppings.

★ **Ron Gastrobar** DUTCH €€

(📞 020-496 19 43; www.rongastrobar.nl; Sophia-laan 55; dishes €15, desserts €9; ⊘ noon-2.30pm & 5.30-10.30pm; 🛜; 🚋 2 Amstelveenseweg) Ron Blaauw ran his two-Michelin-star restau-rant in these stunning designer premises before trading the stars in to transform the space into an egalitarian 'gastrobar', serving around 25 one-flat-price tapas-style dishes such as steak tartare with crispy veal brains, mushroom ravioli with sweet-potato foam, barbecue-smoked bone marrow, Dutch as-paragus with lobster-and-champagne sauce, and wagyu burgers – with no minimum order restrictions.

Dèsa INDONESIAN €€

(📋 020-671 09 79; www.restaurantdesa.com; Ceintuurbaan 103; mains €12.50-22, rijsttafel €18.50-35; ⊙5-10.30pm; 🍴; 🚋3 Ferdinand Bolstraat) Named for the Indonesian word for 'village' (apt for this city, but especially this 'hood), Dèsa is wildly popular for its rijsttafel ('rice table') banquets. À la carte options include *serundeng* (spiced fried coconut), *ayam besengek* (chicken cooked in saffron and coconut milk), *sambal goreng telor* (stewed eggs in spicy Balinese sauce) and *pisang goreng* (fried banana) for dessert.

🍸 Drinking & Nightlife

In addition to the Medieval Centre and Red Light District, party hotspots include Rembrandtplein and Leidseplein, both awash with bars, clubs, *coffeeshops* (cafe authorised to sell cannabis) and pubs.

To truly experience the unique Dutch quality of *gezellig* (conviviality/cosiness), head to a history-steeped *bruin café* (brown cafe, ie pub, traditional drinking establishments named for the nicotine-stained walls). Many serve food.

★Brouwerij 't IJ BREWERY

(www.brouwerijhetij.nl; Funenkade 7; ⊙brewery 2-8pm, English tour 3.30pm Fri-Sun; 🚋10 Hoogte Kadijk) 🍴 Beneath the creaking sails of the 1725-built De Gooyer windmill, Amsterdam's leading organic microbrewery produces delicious (and often very potent) standard, seasonal and limited-edition brews. Pop in for a beer in the tiled tasting room, lined by an amazing bottle collection, or on the plane tree-shaded terrace. A beer is included in the 30-minute brewery tour (€5).

★'t Smalle BROWN CAFE

(www.t-smalle.nl; Egelantiersgracht 12; ⊙10am-12.30am Sun-Thu, to 2am Fri & Sat; 🚋13/14/17 Westermarkt) Dating back to 1786 as a *jenever* (Dutch gin) distillery and tasting house,

and restored during the 1970s with antique porcelain beer pumps and lead-framed windows, locals' favourite 't Smalle is one of Amsterdam's charming *bruin cafés*. Dock your boat right by the pretty stone terrace, which is wonderfully convivial by day and impossibly romantic at night.

★Wynand Fockink DISTILLERY

(www.wynand-fockink.nl; Pijlsteeg 31; ⊙3-9pm; 🚋4/9/16/24 Dam) This small tasting house (dating from 1679) serves scores of *jenever* (Dutch gin) and liqueurs in an arcade behind Grand Hotel Krasnapolsky. Although there are no seats or stools, it's an intimate place to knock back a shot glass or two of gin. Guides give an English-language tour of the distillery and tastings (six samples) on weekends at 3pm, 4.30pm, 6pm and 7.30pm (€17.50, reservations not required).

★SkyLounge COCKTAIL BAR

(www.skyloungeamsterdam.com; Oosterdoksstraat 4; ⊙11am-1am Sun-Tue, to 2am Wed & Thu, to 3am Fri & Sat; 🚋1/2/4/5/9/14/16/24 Centraal Station) An unrivalled 360-degree panorama of Amsterdam extends from the glass-walled

---

RED LIGHT DISTRICT

Just southeast of Centraal Station, on and around the parallel neon-lit canals Oudezijds Voorburgwal and Oudezijds Achterburgwal, the warren of medieval alleyways making up Amsterdam's Red Light District (locally known as De Wallen), is a carnival of vice, seething with skimpily clad prostitutes in brothel windows, raucous bars, haze-filled 'coffeeshops', strip shows, sex shows, mind-boggling museums and shops selling everything from cartoonish condoms to S&M gear and herbal highs.

The area is generally safe, but keep your wits about you and don't photograph or film prostitutes in the windows – out of respect, and to avoid having your camera flung in a canal by their enforcers. Seriously.

SkyLounge on the 11th floor of the Double-Tree Amsterdam Centraal Station hotel – and just gets better when you head out to its vast, sofa-strewn SkyTerrace, with an outdoor bar. Deliberate over more than 500 different cocktails; DJs regularly hit the decks.

Coffeeshops

In the Netherlands, 'coffeeshops' are where one buys marijuana.

Dampkring COFFEE

(www.dampkring-coffeeshop-amsterdam.nl; Handboogstraat 29; ☺10am-1am; 🔊; 🚋1/2/5 Koningsplein) With an interior that resembles a larger-than-life lava lamp, Dampkring is a consistent Cannabis Cup winner, and known for having the most comprehensive menu in town (including details about smell, taste and effect). Its name references the ring of the earth's atmosphere where smaller items combust.

La Tertulia COFFEE

(☏020-623 85 03; www.coffeeshoptertulia.com; Prinsengracht 312; ☺11am-7pm Tue-Sat; 🚋7/10/17 Elandsgracht) A backpackers' favourite, this mother-and-daughter-run *coffeeshop* has a greenhouse feel. You can sit outside by the Van Gogh–inspired murals, play some board games or contemplate the Jurassic-sized crystals by the counter. Bonus: Tertulia actually has good coffee, made with beans from a Dutch speciality roaster.

☆ Entertainment

Find out what's on at I Amsterdam (www.iamsterdam.com).

For tickets, including last-minute discounts, head to **Uitburo** (www.lastminuteticketshop.nl; ☺online ticket sales from 10am on day of performance; 🚋1/2/5/7/10 Leidseplein).

Melkweg LIVE MUSIC

(www.melkweg.nl; Lijnbaansgracht 234a; ☺6pm-1am; 🚋1/2/5/7/10 Leidseplein) In a former dairy, the nonprofit 'Milky Way' is a dazzling galaxy of diverse music. One night it's electronica, the next reggae or punk, and next heavy metal. Roots, rock and mellow singer-songwriters all get stage time too. Check out the website for cutting-edge cinema, theatre and multimedia offerings.

Felix Meritis THEATRE

(☏626 23 21; www.felix.meritis.nl; Keizersgracht 324; ☺box office 9am-7pm; 🔊; 🚋1/2/5 Spui) Amsterdam's centre for arts, culture and science puts on innovative modern theatre,

music and dance, as well as talks on politics, diversity, art, technology and literature. Its adjoining cafe is exceptional for coffee or cocktails by the huge windows or outside overlooking the canal.

🛍 Shopping

The ultimate pleasure of shopping in Amsterdam is discovering some tiny shop selling something you'd find nowhere else. In the Western Canal Ring, the 'nine little streets' making up the **Negen Straatjes** (Nine Streets; www.de9straatjes.nl; 🚋1/2/5 Spui) are dotted with them.

Markets of just about every description are scattered across the city, including Amsterdam's largest and busiest, De Pijp's Albert Cuypmarkt (p813).

★ Droog DESIGN, HOMEWARES

(www.droog.com; Staalstraat 7; ☺9am-7pm; 🚋4/9/14/16/24 Muntplein) Droog means 'dry' in Dutch, and this slick local design house's products are strong on dry wit. You'll find all kinds of smart items you never knew you needed, such as super-powerful suction cups. Also here is a gallery space, whimsical blue-and-white cafe, and fairy tale–inspired courtyard garden that Alice in Wonderland would love, as well as a top-floor apartment (double €278).

★ Waterlooplein Flea Market MARKET

(www.waterlooplein.amsterdam; Waterlooplein; ☺9.30am-6pm Mon-Sat; 🚋9/14 Waterlooplein) Covering the square once known as Vlooienburg (Flea Town), the Waterlooplein Flea Market draws bargain hunters seeking everything from antique knick-knacks to designer knock-offs. The street market started in 1880 when Jewish traders living in the neighbourhood began selling their wares here.

Food vendors waft falafel sandwiches, *frites* and other quick bites around the market's periphery.

> **ⓘ I AMSTERDAM CARD**
>
> The **I Amsterdam Card** (www.
> iamsterdam.com; per 24/48/72hr
> €55/65/75) provides admission to
> more than 30 museums, a canal cruise
> and discounts at shops, entertainment
> venues and restaurants. Also includes
> a GVB transit pass. Available at VVV I
> Amsterdam Visitor Centres and some
> hotels.

★**Condomerie Het Gulden Vlies**   ADULT
(https://condomerie.com; Warmoesstraat 141;
⊙11am-9pm Mon & Wed-Sat, 11am-6pm Tue,
1-6pm Sun; ⊠4/9/14/16/24 Dam) Perfectly
positioned for the Red Light District, this
boutique sells condoms in every imaginable
size, colour, flavour and design (horned
devils, marijuana leaves, Delftware tiles...),
along with lubricants and saucy gifts.

ⓘ Information

I Amsterdam Visitor Centre (☑020-702 60
00; www.iamsterdam.com; Stationsplein 10;
⊙9am-5pm Mon-Sat; ⊠4/9/16/24 Centraal
Station) Outside Centraal Station. Sells maps,
attraction tickets, and transit passes.

ⓘ Getting There & Away

AIR

Most major airlines serve Schiphol (p834),
18km southwest of the city centre.

BUS

Buses arrive at Amsterdam Duivendrecht train
station, 7.5km southeast of the centre, which
has an easy metro link to Centraal Station (about
a 20-minute trip).

 Eurolines' ticket office (www.euro-
lines.nl; Rokin 38a; ⊙9am-5pm Mon-Sat;
⊠4/9/14/16/24 Dam) is near the Dam.

TRAIN

Amsterdam's main train station is fabled **Centraal Station**, with extensive services to the rest
of the country and major European cities.

 For domestic destinations, visit the Dutch
national train service, **NS** (www.ns.nl). **NS International** (www.nsinternational.nl) operates
many international services.

ⓘ Getting Around

TO/FROM THE AIRPORT

Taxi To Amsterdam from Schiphol airport takes
20 to 30 minutes and costs about €47.

Trains To Centraal Station depart every 10
minutes or so from 6am to 12.30am; the trip
takes 17 minutes and costs €5.20.

BICYCLE

Amsterdam is cycling nirvana. The city has more
bicycles (881,000) than residents (813,000).
About 80,000 bicycles are stolen each year, so
always lock up.

BOAT

Canal Bus (☑020-217 05 00; www.canal.nl;
day pass adult/child €24/12; ⊙10am-6pm; 🚲;
⊠1/2/5 Leidseplein) Offers a handy hop-on,
hop-off service. Its 20 docks around the city are
located near the big museums and landmarks.

PUBLIC TRANSPORT

Public transport in Amsterdam uses the
OV-chipkaart. Rides cost €2.90 when bought on
board. Unlimited-ride passes are available for
one to seven days (€7.50 to €33) and are valid
on trams, most buses and the metro.

TAXI

Amsterdam taxis are expensive, even over short
journeys. Try **Taxicentrale Amsterdam** (TCA;
☑020-777 77 77; www.tcataxi.nl).

THE RANDSTAD

One of the most densely populated places on
the planet, the Randstad stretches from Amsterdam to Rotterdam and is crammed with
classic Dutch towns and cities such as Den
Haag, Utrecht, Leiden and Delft. A cycling
network links the towns amid tulip fields.

Haarlem

☑023 / POP 157,900

Just 15 minutes by train from Amsterdam,
Haarlem's canals and cobblestone streets
filled with gabled buildings, grand churches,
terrific museums, cosy bars, fine cafes and
antique shops draw scores of day trippers.

◉ Sights

Haarlem's centre radiates out from the **Grote
Markt**. The **Town Hall** (Grote Markt 2) is worth
a look, as is the cathedral, **Grote Kerk van St
Bavo** (www.bavo.nl; Oude Groenmarkt 22; adult/
child €2.50/free; ⊙10am-5pm Mon-Sat, noon-5pm
Sun Jul & Aug, 10am-5pm Mon-Sat Sep-Jun).

★**Frans Hals Museum**   MUSEUM
(www.franshalsmuseum.nl; Groot Heiligland 62;
adult/child €15.50/free; ⊙11am-5pm Tue-Sat, from
noon Sun; 🚲) A short stroll south of Grote
Markt, the Frans Hals Museum is a must

ZAANSE SCHANS

The working, inhabited village Zaanse Schans functions as an open-air **windmill gallery** (www.dezaanseschans.nl; site free, per windmill adult/child €4/2; ⊘ windmills 10am-5pm Apr-Nov, hours vary Dec-Mar) on the Zaan river. Popular with tourists, its mills are completely authentic and operated with enthusiasm and love. You can explore the windmills at will, seeing the vast moving parts first-hand.

The impressive **Zaans Museum** (⌧ 075-616 28 62; www.zaansmuseum.nl; Schansend 7; adult/child €10/6; ⊘ 10am-5pm; ☎) shows how wind and water were harnessed.

Trains (€3.10, 17 minutes, four per hour) run from Amsterdam Centraal Station (direction Alkmaar) to Koog Zaandijk, from where it's a well-signposted 1.5km walk.

for anyone interested in the Dutch Masters. Located in the poorhouse where Hals spent his final years, the collection focuses on the 17th-century Haarlem School; its pride and joy are eight group portraits of the Civic Guard that reveal Hals' exceptional attention to mood and psychological tone. Look out for works by other greats such as Pieter Bruegel the Younger and Jacob van Ruisdael.

✖ Eating & Drinking

Cafes and restaurants abound along Zijl-straat, Spaarne and especially Lange Veer-straat, as well as around the Grote Markt. The Saturday morning market here is one of the Netherlands' best; there's a smaller market on Monday.

★ Brick   MODERN EUROPEAN €€

(⌧ 023-551 18 70; www.restaurantbrick.nl; Breestraat 24-26; mains lunch €6-10.50, dinner €15.50-21; ⊘ 6-9.30pm Mon-Thu, noon-4pm & 6-10pm Fri-Sun) You can watch Brick's chefs creating inspired dishes such as duck and hazelnut ravioli with black truffle and foie-gras sauce, not only from the street-level dining room but also the 1st-floor space, which has a glass floor directly above the open kitchen. There are pavement tables out front but in summer the best seats are on the roof terrace.

★ Jopenkerk   BREWERY

(www.jopenkerk.nl; Gedempte Voldersgracht 2; ⊘ brewery & cafe 10am-1am, restaurant 5.30pm-late Tue-Sat) Haarlem's most atmospheric place to drink is this independent brewery inside a stained-glass-windowed 1910 church. Enjoy brews such as citrusy Hopen, fruity Lente Bier or chocolatey Koyt along with classic Dutch bar snacks (*bitterballen,* cheeses) beneath the gleaming copper vats. Or head to the mezzanine for dishes made from locally sourced, seasonal ingredients and Jopenkerk's beers, with pairings available.

ℹ Getting There & Away

Trains serve Haarlem's stunning art-nouveau station, a 10-minute walk north of the centre. Destinations include:
Amsterdam (€4.20, 15 minutes, four to eight per hour)
Den Haag (€8.30, 40 minutes, four to six per hour)
Rotterdam (€12.20, one hour, four to six per hour).

Leiden

⌧ 071 / POP 122,500

Vibrant Leiden is renowned for being Rembrandt's birthplace, the home of the Netherlands' oldest university (and 23,000 students) and the place America's pilgrims raised money to lease the *Mayflower* that took them to the New World in 1620. Beautiful 17th-century buildings line its canals.

◉ Sights

The best way to experience Leiden is by strolling the historic centre, especially along the Rapenburg canal.

★ Hortus Botanicus Leiden   GARDENS

(www.hortusleiden.nl; Rapenburg 73; adult/child €7.50/3; ⊘ 10am-6pm daily Apr-Oct, 10am-4pm Tue-Sun Nov-Mar) The lush Hortus Botanicus is one of Europe's oldest botanical gardens (1590; the oldest was created in Padua, Italy, in 1545), and is home to the Netherlands' oldest descendants of the Dutch tulips. It's a wonderful place to relax, with explosions of tropical colour and a fascinating (and steamy) greenhouse.

★ Rijksmuseum van Oudheden   MUSEUM

(National Museum of Antiquities; www.rmo.nl; Rapenburg 28; adult/child €12.50/4; ⊘ 11am-5pm Tue-Sun plus Mon during school holidays; ☎) This museum has a world-class collection of Greek, Roman

DON'T MISS

KEUKENHOF GARDENS

One of the Netherlands' top attractions is near Lisse, between Haarlem and Leiden. Keukenhof (www.keukenhof. nl; Stationsweg 166; adult/child €16/8, parking €6; ⊘ 8am-7.30pm mid-Mar–mid-May, last entry 6pm; 🐛) is the world's largest bulb-flower garden, attracting nearly 800,000 visitors during a season almost as short-lived as the blooms on the millions of multicoloured tulips, daffodils and hyacinths.

Special buses link Keukenhof with Amsterdam's Schiphol airport and Leiden's Centraal Station in season; combination tickets covering entry and transport are available (adult/child €24/12.50). Pre-purchase tickets online to help avoid huge queues.

and Egyptian artefacts, the pride of which is the extraordinary **Temple of Taffeh**, a gift from former Egyptian president Anwar Sadat to the Netherlands for helping to save ancient Egyptian monuments from floods.

Pieterskerk   CHURCH
(www.pieterskerk.com; Pieterskerkhof 1; admission €3; ⊘ 11am-6pm) Crowned by its huge steeple, Pieterskerk is often under restoration – a good thing as it has been prone to collapse since it was built in the 14th century.

Museum De Lakenhal   MUSEUM
(www.lakenhal.nl; Oude Singel 28-32) Leiden's foremost museum, the Lakenhal, displaying works by native son Rembrandt among others, has closed its doors between 2016 and 2019 while it undergoes a major renovation and expansion. Check online or with the tourist office for updates.

🛏 Sleeping & Eating

The city-centre canals and narrow old streets teem with choices. Saturday's market sprawls along Nieuwe Rijn.

Huys van Leyden   BOUTIQUE HOTEL €€
(☑ 071-260 07 00; www.huysvanleyden.nl; Oude Singel 212; d from €109; 🐛) Steeped in history, this 1611 canal house has luxurious rooms and amenities including a sauna, roof terrace, and Nespresso machines in each of the five Golden-Age-meets-21st-century rooms richly decorated with shimmering fabrics and canopied beds. Its sister property,

De Barones van Leyden (www.debarones vanleyden.nl; Oude Herengracht 22; d from €109; 🐛), is, incredibly, even more opulent.

David's Burger   BURGERS €€
(www.davidsburger.nl; Steenstraat 57; burgers €12.50-15.50; ⊘ 4-11pm Tue-Sun) 🍴 Cowhide covers the timber booths, and horseshoes and farm equipment hang on the walls at David's, serving Leiden's best, all-organic burgers such as the gaucho (beef with grilled pepper, courgette and chimichurri), spicy veggie (bean and chipotle-pepper patty with guacamole and cheese), lams (lamb with red-onion relish) and classic (beef with lettuce, tomato and pickles), plus corn on the cob.

⭐ **In den Doofpot**   MODERN EUROPEAN €€€
(☑ 071-512 24 34; www.indendoofpot.nl; Turfmarkt 9; mains €22-35, 3-/4-course lunch menu €39/45, 4-/5-/6-/8-course dinner menu €55/65/70/80; ⊘ noon-3pm & 5-10pm Mon-Fri, 5-10pm Sat) Given the sky-high calibre of chef Patrick Brugman's cooking, In den Doofpot's prices are a veritable steal. Pork belly with smoked eel, grilled lobster with truffle butter and micro-herb salad, organic Dutch beef fillet with Madeira sauce, potatoes and caramelised orange and other intense flavour combinations are all executed with artistic vision. Wines cost €8 per course.

🛈 Information

Tourist Office (☑ 071-516 60 00; www.visit leiden.nl; Stationsweg 26; ⊘ 7am-7pm Mon-Fri, 10am-4pm Sat, 11am-3pm Sun) Across from the train station.

🛈 Getting There & Away

Buses leave from directly in front of Centraal Station.

Train destinations include:

Amsterdam (€9, 35 minutes, six per hour)
Den Haag (€3.50, 15 minutes, six per hour)
Schiphol Airport (€5.80, 15 minutes, six per hour)

Den Haag

☑ 070 / POP 518,600

Flanked by wide, leafy boulevards, Den Haag (The Hague) – officially known as 's-Gravenhage (Count's Hedge) – is the Dutch seat of government (although Amsterdam is the capital). Embassies and various international courts of justice give the city a worldly air.

Conversely, its seaside suburb of Scheveningen (pronounced as s'CHay-fuh-ninger) has a loud and lively kitsch, and a long stretch of beach. It sprawls about 5km northwest.

◉ Sights

★ Mauritshuis   MUSEUM
(www.mauritshuis.nl; Plein 29; adult/child €14/free, combined ticket with Galerij Prins Willem V €17.50/2.50; ☺1-6pm Mon, 10am-6pm Tue, Wed & Fri-Sun, 10am-8pm Thu) For a comprehensive introduction to Dutch and Flemish Art, visit the Mauritshuis, a jewel-box of a museum in an old palace and brand-new wing. Almost every work is a masterpiece, among them Vermeer's *Girl with a Pearl Earring*, Rembrandt's wistful self-portrait from the year of his death, 1669, and *The Anatomy Lesson of Dr Nicolaes Tulp*. A five-minute walk southwest, the recently restored **Galerij Prins Willem V** (Buitenhof 35; adult/child €5/2.50, combined ticket with Mauritshuis €17.50/2.50; ☺noon-5pm Tue-Sun) contains 150 old masters (Steen, Rubens, Potter, et al).

★ Binnenhof   PALACE
The Binnenhof's central courtyard (once used for executions) is surrounded by parliamentary buildings. The splendid 17th-century North Wing is still home to the Upper Chamber of the **Dutch Parliament**. The Lower Chamber formerly met in the ballroom, in the 19th-century wing; it now meets in a modern building on the south side. A highlight of the complex is the restored 13th-century **Ridderzaal** (Knights' Hall).

To see the buildings you need to join a tour through visitor organisation **ProDemos** (☎070-757 02 00; www.prodemos.nl; Hofweg 1; 45min Ridderzaal tour €5, 90min Ridderzaal & House of Representative tour €8.50, 75min Ridderzaal & Senate tour €8.50, 90min Ridderzaal, House of Rep-

resentative & Senate tour €10; ☺office 10am-5pm Mon-Sat, tours by reservation).

Afterwards, stroll around the **Hofvijver**, where the reflections of the Binnenhof and the Mauritshuis have inspired countless snapshots.

★ Escher in Het Paleis Museum   MUSEUM
(www.escherinhetpaleis.nl; Lange Voorhout 74; adult/child €9.50/6.50; ☺11am-5pm Tue-Sun) The Lange Voorhout Palace was once Queen Emma's winter residence. Now it's home to the work of Dutch graphic artist MC Escher. The permanent exhibition features notes, letters, drafts, photos and fully mature works covering Escher's entire career, from his early realism to the later phantasmagoria. There are some imaginative displays, including a virtual reality reconstruction of Escher's impossible buildings.

🛏 Sleeping & Eating

Expats on expense accounts support a diverse and thriving cafe culture. The cobbled streets and canals off Denneweg are an excellent place to start wandering.

Hotel Sebel   HOTEL €€
(☎070-345 92 00; www.hotelsebel.nl; Prins Hendrikplein 20; s/d/tr from €89/99/139; 🛜) This 33-room hotel spreads out across three proud art-nouveau corner buildings. The cheapest rooms are minuscule but others have balconies, and studios have kitchenettes. Everything has been tastefully updated, including the minimalist lobby.

Bloem   CAFE €
(www.bloemdenhaag.nl; Korte Houtstraat 6; dishes €3.50-9, high tea per person €20; ☺11am-4pm Tue, to 6pm Wed-Sun) Across the Plein from the Binnenhof, this cute little cafe has white tables, chairs and flowers out front. Housemade tarts are superb; it also has great sandwiches and smoothies. Stop by for afternoon high tea.

★ Restaurant Allard   BISTRO €€
(☎070-744 79 00; www.restaurantallard.nl; Jagerstraat 6; mains €19-29, 2-/3-/4-course menus €35/42/49; ☺5-11pm Tue-Sat) Tucked down a charming alleyway with outdoor tables, Allard is a diamond find for flavour-packed creations such as tuna tartare with sun-dried tomato crème, lamb fillet with honey and fig jus, truffle risotto with wild mushrooms, and grilled sea bass with spinach and potato gratin in a cosy, cellar-like space with exposed brick walls, low-lit chandeliers and black-and-white chessboard-tiled floors.

HOLLAND OR THE NETHERLANDS?

'Holland' is a popular synonym for the Netherlands, yet it only refers to the combined provinces of Noord (North) and Zuid (South) Holland. Amsterdam is Noord-Holland's largest city; Haarlem is the provincial capital. Rotterdam is Zuid-Holland's largest city; Den Haag is its provincial capital. The rest of the country is not Holland, even if locals themselves often make the mistake.

🛍 Shopping

Grote Markstraat is fittingly the street for large stores. Enticing boutiques line Hoogstraat, Noordeinde, Heulstraat and especially Prinsestraat.

Museumshop Den Haag   GIFTS & SOUVENIRS
(www.museumshopdenhaag.com; Lange Voorhout 58b; ⊙noon-5pm Sun & Mon, 11am-5pm Tue-Sat) The Netherlands' first-ever independent museum shop is a one-stop-shop for books, prints, postcards, gifts and accessories of artworks and exhibitions from some of the country's most prestigious museums including Amsterdam's Rijksmuseum and Van Gogh Museum, as well as the Mauritshuis, and Escher in Het Paleis Museum.

ℹ Information

Tourist Office (VVV; ☑070-361 88 60; www.denhaag.com; Spui 68; ⊙noon-8pm Mon, 10am-8pm Tue-Fri, 10am-5pm Sat & Sun; 🛜) On the ground floor of the public library in the landmark New Town Hall.

ℹ Getting There & Around

A day pass for local trams costs €6.50.

Most trains use Den Haag Centraal Station (CS), but some through trains only stop at Den Haag Hollands Spoor (HS) station just south of the centre.

Services include:

Amsterdam (€11.50, one hour, up to six per hour)

Rotterdam (€4.80, 25 minutes, up to six per hour) Also accessible by metro.

Schiphol airport (€8.30, 30 minutes, up to six per hour)

Delft

☑015 / POP 101,600

Compact and charming, Delft is synonymous with its blue-and-white-painted porcelain. It's *very* popular with day-trip visitors strolling its narrow canals, gazing at the remarkable old buildings and meditating on the career of Golden Age painter Johannes Vermeer, who was born here and lived here, so getting an early start helps beat the crowds.

◉ Sights

The town hall and the Waag on the Markt are right out of the 17th century.

★**Vermeer Centrum Delft**   MUSEUM
(www.vermeerdelft.nl; Voldersgracht 21; adult/child €9/5; ⊙10am-5pm) As the place where Johannes Vermeer was born, lived and worked, Delft is 'Vermeer Central' to many art-history and old-masters enthusiasts. Along with viewing life-sized images of Vermeer's oeuvre, you can tour a replica of Vermeer's studio, which reveals the way the artist approached the use of light and colour in his craft. A 'Vermeer's World' exhibit offers insight into his environment and upbringing, while temporary exhibits show how his work continues to inspire other artists.

★**Oude Kerk**   CHURCH
(Old Church; www.oudeennieuwekerkdelft.nl; Heilige Geestkerkhof 25; adult/child incl Nieuwe Kerk €4/2.50, Nieuwe Kerk tower additional €4/2.50, combination ticket €7/4.50; ⊙9am-6pm Mon-Sat Apr-Oct, 11am-4pm Mon-Fri, 10am-5pm Sat Nov-Jan, 10am-5pm Mon-Sat Feb & Mar) The Gothic Oude Kerk, founded in 1246, is a surreal sight: its 75m-high tower leans nearly 2m from the vertical due to subsidence caused by its canal location, hence its nickname Scheve Jan ('Leaning Jan'). One of the tombs inside the church is Vermeer's.

★**Nieuwe Kerk**   CHURCH
(New Church; www.oudeennieuwekerkdelft.nl; Markt 80; adult/child incl Oude Kerk €4/2.50, Nieuwe Kerk tower additional €4/2.50, combination ticket €7/4.50; ⊙9am-6pm Mon-Sat Apr-Oct, 11am-4pm Mon-Fri, 10am-5pm Sat Nov-Jan, 10am-5pm Mon-Sat Feb & Mar) Construction on Delft's Nieuwe Kerk began in 1381; it was finally completed in 1655. Amazing views extend from the 108.75m-high tower: after climbing its 376 narrow, spiralling steps you can see as far as Rotterdam and Den Haag on a clear day. It's the resting place of William of Orange (William the Silent), in a mausoleum designed by Hendrick de Keyser.

De Candelaer   FACTORY
(☑015-213 1848; www.candelaer.nl; Kerkstraat 13; ⊙9.30am-5.30pm Mon-Fri, to 5pm Sat May-Sep, 10am-4pm Mon-Sat Oct-Apr) FREE The most central and modest Delftware outfit is de Candelaer, just off the Markt. It has five artists, a few of whom work most days. When it's quiet they'll give you a detailed tour of the manufacturing process.

THE NETHERLANDS BY BIKE

The Netherlands has more than 32,000km of dedicated bike paths *(fietspaden)*, which makes it one of the most bike-friendly places on the planet. You can crisscross the country on the motorways of cycling: the LF routes. Standing for *landelijke fietsroutes* (long-distance routes), but virtually always simply called LF, they cover approximately 4500km. All are well marked by distinctive green-and-white signs.

The best overall maps are the widely available Falk/VVV *Fietskaart met Knooppunt-ennetwerk* (cycling network) maps, an easy-to-use series of 22, with keys in English, that blanket the country in 1:50,000 scale, and cost €9. Every bike lane, path and other route is shown, along with distances.

Comprehensive cycling website Nederland Fietsland (www.nederlandfietsland.nl) has route planners and downloadable GPS tracks, and lists every bike-rental outlet in the country.

Bike Rentals

Bicycle hire is available all over the Netherlands at hotels, independent rental outlets and train stations. Prices average around €12 per 24 hours. You'll need to show ID and leave a deposit (usually €25 to €100).

On Trains

You may bring your bicycle onto any train outside peak hours (6.30am to 9am and 4.30pm to 6pm Monday to Friday) as long as there is room. Bicycles require a day pass *(dagkaart fiets;* €6.10).

THE NETHERLANDS DELFT

🛏 Sleeping & Eating

Hotel de Plataan   BOUTIQUE HOTEL €€
(☑ 015-212 60 46; www.hoteldeplataan.nl; Doelenplein 10; s/d from €110/120, themed d from €155; 🅿 🛜) On a pretty canal-side square in the old town, this family-run gem has small but elegant standard rooms and wonderfully opulent theme rooms, including the 'Garden of Eden'; the Eastern-style 'Amber', with a Turkish massage shower; or the desert-island 'Tamarinde'. Modesty alert: many en suites are only partially screened from the room. Rates include breakfast and secure parking.

Stads-Koffyhuis   CAFE €
(www.stads-koffyhuis.nl; Oude Delft 133; mains €8-15, sandwiches €6.50-9, pancakes €6.25-12.75; ⊙9am-8pm Mon-Fri, 9am-6pm Sat, 11am-6pm Sun Jun-Sep, shorter hours Oct-May) The most coveted seats at this delightful cafe are on the terrace, aboard a barge moored out front. Tuck into award-winning bread rolls, with fillings such as aged artisan Gouda with apple sauce, mustard, fresh figs and walnuts, or house-speciality pancakes, while admiring possibly the best view of the Oude Kerk, just ahead at the end of the canal.

⭐**Brasserie 't Crabbetje**   SEAFOOD €€
(☑ 015-213 88 50; www.crabbetjedelft.nl; Verwersdijk 14; mains €18.50-34.50, 3-/4-course tasting menus €35.50/42.50; ⊙5.30-10pm Wed-Sun; 🛜)

Seafood is given the gourmet treatment at this cool, sophisticated restaurant. From scallops with leek and lobster reduction to skate wing with hazelnut crumb and beurre noisette (warm butter sauce), salmon carpaccio with smoked-eel croquette, and grilled lobster with tomato and truffle oil. Lavish seafood platters cost €41.50. Desserts are exquisite, too.

Spijshuis de Dis   DUTCH €€
(☑ 015-213 17 82; www.spijshuisdedis.com; Beestenmarkt 36; soups €6-7.50, mains €17-24.50; ⊙5-10pm Tue-Sat) Fresh fish and amazing soups served in bread bowls take centre stage at this romantic foodie haven, but meat eaters and vegetarians are well catered for too. Creative starters include smoked, marinated mackerel on sliced apple with horseradish. Don't skip the Dutch pudding served in a wooden shoe.

🍺 Drinking & Nightlife

Locus Publicus   BROWN CAFE
(www.locuspublicus.nl; Brabantse Turfmarkt 67; ⊙11am-1am Mon-Thu, 11am-2am Fri & Sat, noon-1am Sun) Cosy little Locus Publicus is filled with cheery locals quaffing their way through the 200-strong beer list including 13 on tap. There's great people-watching from the front terrace.

ℹ️ Information

Tourist Office (VVV; ☎ 015-215 40 51; www.delft.nl; Kerkstraat 3; ⊙10am-4pm Sun & Mon, 10am-5pm Tue-Sat Apr-Sep, noon-4pm Mon, 10am-4pm Tue-Sat, 11am-3pm Sun Oct-Mar) Sells excellent walking-tour brochures.

ℹ️ Getting There & Away

Delft's gleaming new train station opened in 2015. Services include:

Amsterdam (€13, one hour, four per hour)
Den Haag (€2.50, 15 minutes, six per hour)
Rotterdam (€3.30, 15 minutes, eight per hour)

Rotterdam

☎ 010 / POP 626,900

Futuristic architecture, a proliferation of art, and a surge of drinking, dining and nightlife venues make Rotterdam one of Europe's most exhilarating cities right now. The Netherlands' second-largest metropolis has a diverse, multiethnic community, an absorbing maritime tradition centred on Europe's busiest port and a wealth of top-class museums.

Rotterdam is a veritable open-air gallery of modern, postmodern and contemporary construction. It's a remarkable feat for a city largely razed to the ground by WWII bombers. Rebuilding has continued unabated ever since with ingenuity and vision.

Split by the vast Nieuwe Maas shipping channel, Rotterdam is crossed by a series of tunnels and bridges. On the north side of the water, the city centre is easily strolled.

◉ Sights & Activities

Not only is Rotterdam an architectural gallery, its streets are also filled with art. Well over 60 sculptures are scattered all over town. For a full list and an interactive map of their locations, visit Sculpture International Rotterdam (www.sculptureinternationalrotterdam.nl).

⭐**Museum Boijmans van Beuningen**　MUSEUM
(www.boijmans.nl; Museumpark 18-20; adult/child €15/7.50; ⊙11am-5pm Tue-Sun) Among Europe's finest museums, the Museum Boijmans van Beuningen has a permanent collection spanning all eras of Dutch and European art, including superb old masters. Among the highlights are *The Marriage Feast at Cana* by Hieronymus Bosch, the *Three Maries at the Open Sepulchre* by Van Eyck, the minutely detailed *Tower of Babel* by Pieter Brueghel

the Elder, and *Portrait of Titus* and *Man in a Red Cap* by Rembrandt.

Overblaak Development　NOTABLE BUILDING
(Overblaak) Designed by Piet Blom and built from 1978 to 1984, this mind-bending development facing the Markthal Rotterdam is marked by its pencil-shaped tower, **De Kolk**, and 'forest' of 45-degree-tilted, cube-shaped apartments on hexagonal pylons. One apartment, the **Kijk-Kubus Museum-House** (www.kubuswoning.nl; Overblaak 70; adult/child €2.50/1.50; ⊙11am-5pm), is open to the public; the **Stayokay Rotterdam** (☎010-436 57 63; www.stayokay.com; Overblaak 85-87; dm/d/tr from €21.50/59/93; 🛜) youth hostel occupies the supersized cube at the southern end.

Euromast　VIEWPOINT
(www.euromast.nl; Parkhaven 20; adult/child €9.75/6.25; ⊙9.30am-10pm Apr-Sep, 10am-10pm Oct-Mar) A 1960-built landmark, the 185m Euromast offers unparalleled 360-degree views of Rotterdam from its 100m-high observation deck, reached by elevator in 30 seconds.

Extra diversions include a brasserie serving lunch, high tea, high wine, dinner and Sunday brunch, as well as summertime abseiling (€55). Accommodation in the tower's two suites start from €385 each, including breakfast.

Erasmusbrug　BRIDGE
A symbol of the city, this graceful bridge dubbed 'the Swan' was designed by architect Ben van Berkel in 1996 and spans 802m across the Maas river.

Maritiem Museum Rotterdam　MUSEUM
(Maritime Museum; www.maritiemmuseum.nl; Leuvehaven 1; adult/child €11.50/7.50; ⊙10am-5pm Tue-Sat, 11am-5pm Sun, plus Mon during school holidays) This comprehensive, kid-friendly museum looks at the Netherlands' rich maritime traditions through an array of models that any youngster would love to take into the tub. There are great explanatory displays such as Mainport Live, giving a 'real time' view of the port's action in miniature, and a raft of fun temporary exhibitions.

⭐**Urban Guides**　WALKING
(☎010-433 22 31; www.urbanguides.nl; Schiekade 205, Hofplein; ⊙office 10am-6pm Mon-Sat, noon-5pm Sun Apr-Oct, 10am-6pm Mon-Fri Nov-Mar) Based in the Schieblock, this hip young outfit of passionate Rotterdammers runs a fantastic selection of tours, from 2½ hour 'By Cycle' tours (per person €25) to architectural

DON'T MISS

DELFSHAVEN

Just 3km southwest of Rotterdam's centre, Delfshaven, once the official seaport for the city of Delft, survived the war and retains a village-like atmosphere. Take trams 4 or 8, or the metro to the Delfshaven station.

Oude Kerk (☑010-477 41 56; www.oudeofpelgrimvaderskerk.nl; Aelbrechtskolk 22; ⊘noon-4pm Sat & every 2nd Fri) The Pilgrims prayed for the last time at Delfshaven's 1417-founded Oude Kerk (aka Pilgrim Fathers Church) before leaving the Netherlands for America aboard the *Speedwell* on 22 July 1620. They could barely keep the leaky boat afloat and, in England, eventually transferred to the *Mayflower* – the rest is history. Models of their vaguely seaworthy boats are inside. It closes for events such as weddings and concerts.

Stadsbrouwerij De Pelgrim (www.pelgrimbier.nl; Aelbrechtskolk 12; ⊘noon-midnight Wed-Sat, to 10pm Sun) The heady scent of hops greets you at this vintage brewery abutting the Oude Kerk, with bubbling copper vats by the entrance. Here you can take a voyage through its wonderful seasonal and standard beers such as Rotterdams Stoombier and Mayflower Tripel in the bar, canal-side terrace or courtyard. A tasting flight of five beers costs €5. Ask and they'll usually let you peek at the tanks. There's a restaurant too.

Windmill (www.molendelfshaven.nl; Voorhaven 210) A reconstructed 18th-century windmill overlooks the water at Delfshaven. It still mills grain; the interior is closed to the public.

cycling tours (including an option led by architecture students), walking tours, building tours such as the **Van Nelle Fabriek** (Van Nelle Factory; www.vannellefabriek.com; Van Nelleweg 1), boat tours, exhibition tours and more. It also rents bikes (per day €10).

🛏 Sleeping

⭐**King Kong Hostel**   HOSTEL €
(☑010-818 87 78; www.kingkonghostel.com; Witte de Withstraat 74; dm/d/q from €17.50/70/101; @🛜) Outdoor benches made from salvaged timbers and garden hoses by Sander Bokkinga sit outside King Kong, a design haven on Rotterdam's coolest street. Artist-designed rooms and dorms are filled with vintage and industrial furniture; fab features include hammocks, lockers equipped with device-charging points, a gourmet self-catering kitchen, roof garden and barbecue area, and Netflix.

⭐**Pincoffs**   BOUTIQUE HOTEL €€
(☑010-297 45 00; www.hotelpincoffs.nl; Stieltjesstraat 34; d/ste from €133/195; 🅿❄🛜) A former customs house dating from 1879 encases this exquisite sanctum that blends recycled and vintage art and furniture with 21st-century style. Romantic rooms come with luxuries such as Egyptian cotton robes and towels. A wood-burning fireplace blazes in the bar, and there's a water-taxi stop outside the front door.

Hotel New York   HISTORIC HOTEL €€€
(☑010-439 05 55; www.hotelnewyork.nl; Koninginnenhoofd 1; d €105-287.50; @🛜) An art-nouveau showpiece, the Holland-America passenger-ship line's former HQ has sweeping vistas, superb dining options including an oyster bar, a barber shop and a water taxi ferrying guests across the Nieuwe Maas to the city centre. Rooms retain original, painstakingly restored fittings and decor; styles range from standard to timber-panelled suites in the old boardrooms with fireplaces.

🍴 Eating

Rotterdam's foodie scene is booming. Look out for new openings all over the city and especially in hotspots like **Station Hofplein** (www.stationhofplein.nl). The stunning Markthal Rotterdam (p829) has sit-down and takeaway eating options galore.

⭐**Tante Nel**   FAST FOOD €
(www.tante-nel.com; Pannekoekstraat 53a; dishes €2.25-13.50; ⊘noon-10pm Tue-Sat, to 9pm Sun) New-generation Tante Nel is as tiny as a traditional *frites* (fries) stand but decked out with a stunning Dutch-design painted brick interior and marquee-style canopied terrace for savouring its organic, hand-cut fries (topped by nine different sauces), along with house-speciality milkshakes, beer, wine and 13 different gins.

Rotterdam

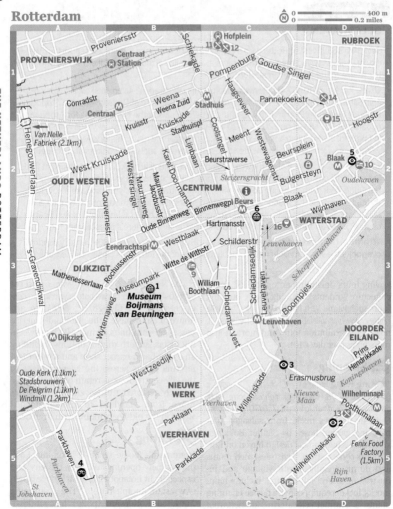

⭐ **Fenix Food Factory**   MARKET €

(www.fenixfoodfactory.nl; Veerlaan 19d; ⊙10am-11pm Tue-Sat, noon-11pm Sun, individual stall hours vary) 🍴 Almost everything in this vast former warehouse is made locally and sold by separate vendors making their mark on the food scene. They include Booij Kaasmakers (cheese), Cider Cider (cider), Jordy's Bakery (bread and baked goods), Stielman Koffiebranders (coffee roasters), Kaapse Brouwers (craft beer) and Rechtstreex (locally grown fruit and veggies).

HMB   INTERNATIONAL €€

(☑010-760 06 20; www.hmb-restaurant.nl; Holland Amerika Kade 104; mains €20-22, 3-course lunch menu €37.50 Tue-Fri, 4-/5-/6-course dinner menu €57/67/77; ⊙noon-3pm & 5.30-10pm Tue-Fri, 5.30-10pm Sat, closed late Dec-early Jan) On the ground floor of the glitzy 'vertical city' **De Rotterdam** (www.derotterdam.nl), with dazzling views of the Erasmusbrug, chic HMB serves artistically presented contemporary cuisine (veal meatballs with truffled potatoes; foie gras with eel and apple) at impressively reasonable prices. Afterwards, head to the terrace of the building's 7th-floor cocktail bar.

★ **FG Food Labs**   GASTRONOMY €€€
(☎010-425 05 20; www.fgfoodlabs.nl; Katshoek 41; 3-course lunch menu Mon-Fri €42.50, snacks €6.50-27.50, 4-/5-/6-/7-/8-/9-course menus €32/40/48/56/64/72; ⏰noon-2pm & 6-10pm, closed early–mid-Jan) François Geurds' one-Michelin-star molecular gastronomy lab sits under timber and silvery pressed-tin ceilings within Station Hofplein. Dine on his evolving cuisine or even take a culinary electric-bike tour (€95) around Rotterdam starting from the lab and finishing with a three-course lunch at his flagship two-Michelin-star premises, **FG** (www.fgrestaurant.nl; Katshoek 37b).

🍷 Drinking & Nightlife

★ **Bokaal**   BAR
(www.bokaalrotterdam.nl; Nieuwmarkt 11; ⏰11am-1am Sun-Thu, to 2am Fri & Sat) In a *bokaal* (trophy) location at the heart of the enclave around pedestrian Nieuwmarkt and Pannekoekstraat locally dubbed 'Soho Rotterdam', Bokaal's spectacularly designed bar has butcher-shop tiling, raw concrete floors, and an oak bar and huge all-day-sun terrace. Beer (craft and Trappist) is its speciality, with nine on tap, and more than 80 in bottles, along with charcuterie and cheese.

Vessel 11   PUB
(www.vessel11.nl; Wijnhaven 101; ⏰noon-10pm Tue-Thu, noon-2am Fri, 11am-2am Sat, 11am-10pm Sun) This fire-engine-red, 1951-built lighthouse vessel (with a working gas light and fog horn) is now a Brit-influenced pub which brews its own ale, hosts live gigs (mainly rock) and barbecues, and serves full English breakfasts and Sunday roasts. It also rents Rotterdam-designed HotTug hot-tub boats (per two hours for two/eight people €139/259) to pilot around the harbour while you soak.

🛍 Shopping

Brand-name shops line the bustling, open-air, semi-subterranean Beurstraverse, nicknamed *de Koopgoot* ('buying trench'). More alternative options congregate on and around Meent, as well as Nieuwmarkt, Pannekoekstraat, OudeBinnenweg and Nieuwe Binnenweg.

★ **Markthal Rotterdam**   FOOD & DRINKS
(www.markthalrotterdam.nl; Nieuwstraat; ⏰10am-8pm Mon-Thu & Sat, to 9pm Fri, noon-6pm Sun) The Netherlands' inaugural indoor food market hit international headlines when it opened in 2014 due to its extraordinary inverted-U-shaped design, with glass-walled apartments arcing over the food hall's 40m-high fruit- and vegetable-muralled ceiling. There's a tantalising array of produce, prepared food and drinks; shops continue downstairs.

ℹ Information

Tourist Office (☎010-790 01 85; www.rotterdam.info; Coolsingel 114; ⏰9am-5.30pm; 📶) Main tourist office.

ℹ Getting There & Away

Completed in 2014, Rotterdam's Centraal Station is an architectural stunner. There are direct services to Brussels and Paris; from late 2017, Eurostar trains linking Amsterdam with London will stop here.

Major services:

Amsterdam regular (€15.10, 70 minutes, eight per hour)

Amsterdam high speed (€17.50, 40 minutes, four per hour)

Schiphol airport (€12.20–14.60, 20–50 minutes, eight per hour)

Utrecht (€10.30, 40 minutes, four per hour)

ℹ Getting Around

Rotterdam's trams, buses and metro are operated by **RET** (www.ret.nl). Most converge in front of Centraal Station, where there's an **information booth** (www.ret.nl; Stationsplein 20, Centraal Station; ☉7am-10pm Mon-Fri, 9.30am-5.30pm Sat & Sun) that also sells tickets. Day passes are available for varying durations (one/two/three days €7.50/12.50/16.50). A single-ride ticket purchased from a bus driver or tram conductor costs €3.

Utrecht

♪ 030 / POP 338,500

One of the Netherlands' oldest cities, Utrecht retains a beautiful old-world city centre, ringed by unique 13th-century canal wharves below street level. Canal-side streets brim with shops, restaurants and cafes. Its spirited student community of 40,000 is the country's largest.

While the canals form Utrecht's restful core, elsewhere the city is busy reinventing itself, and part of the excitement is witnessing this ongoing transformation. Roads such as Catharijnebaan are being turned back into the canals they once were and the spectacular new train station adds a vital complement to the old town.

◉ Sights

Focus your wanderings on the **Domplein** and south along the tree-lined **Oudegracht**.

★**Domtoren** HISTORIC BUILDING
(Cathedral Tower; www.domtoren.nl; Domplein 9; tower tour adult/child €9/5; ☉11am-5pm Tue-Sat, noon-4pm Sun) A remnant of Utrecht's original 14th-century **cathedral** (Cathedral; www.domkerk.nl; Achter de Dom 1; donation requested; ☉10am-4pm Mon-Fri, to 3.30pm Sat, 12.30-4pm Sun Jul-Sep, 11am-4pm Mon-Fri, to 3.30pm Sat, 12.30-4pm Sun Oct-Jun), this tower is 112m high, with 50 bells. It's worth the 465-step climb to the top for unbeatable city views; on a clear day you can see Amsterdam. Visit is by guided tour only, departing on the hour.

WORTH A TRIP

OTHER DUTCH DESTINATIONS WORTH A VISIT

Other Netherlands highlights worth considering for day trips or longer visits:

Alkmaar Although touristy, its cheese ceremony (Fridays from first Friday of April to the first Friday of September) dates from the 17th century.

Hoge Veluwe National Park Beautiful landscape of forests, dunes and marshes, with a bonus of a Van Gogh-rich art museum on site.

Kinderdijk & Dordrecht A good day trip by fast ferry from Rotterdam is to visit Kinderdijk's Unesco-listed windmills then Dordrecht's medieval canals.

Gouda The perfect little Dutch town.

Texel Largest of the Frisian Islands, with endless walks along dune-backed beaches and excellent local seafood.

Tickets can be purchased online or at the Tourist Office across the square.

★**Centraal Museum** MUSEUM
(♪030-236 23 62; www.centraalmuseum.nl; Agnietenstraat 1; adult/child €11/5, incl admission to Rietveld Schröderhuis plus €3 surcharge; ☉11am-5pm Tue-Sun; ☎) Applied arts are at the heart of a wide-ranging collection that also features paintings by artists of the Utrecht School and a bit of De Stijl to boot. Here too is the world's most extensive Gerrit Rietveld collection, a dream for all minimalists. There's even a Viking longboat that was dug out of the local mud, plus a sumptuous 17th-century doll's house.

★**Museum Catharijneconvent** MUSEUM
(♪030-231 38 35; www.catharijneconvent.nl; Lange Nieuwestraat 38; adult/child €12.50/7; ☉10am-5pm Tue-Fri, 11am-5pm Sat & Sun) Museum Catharijneconvent is the pick of Utrecht's museums, with the finest collection of medieval religious art in the Netherlands – virtually the history of Christianity, in fact – housed in a Gothic former convent and an 18th-century canalside house. Marvel at the many beautiful illuminated manuscripts, look for the odd Rembrandt and hope for one of the often salacious special exhibitions.

Miffy Museum
MUSEUM

(Nijntje Museum; ☑030-236 23 62; www.nijntje museum.nl; Agnietenstraat 2; adult/child €3.50/ 8.50; ☺10am-5pm Tue-Sun) One of Utrecht's favourite sons, author and illustrator Dick Bruna is the creator of the beloved cartoon rabbit Miffy (Nijntje as she's known in Dutch) and she naturally takes pride of place at the artist's former studio, across the street from the Centraal Museum. The museum was renovated in 2015 to make it more toddler-friendly (ages two to six).

🛏 Sleeping

Strowis Hostel
HOSTEL €

(☑030-238 02 80; www.strowis.nl; Boothstraat 8; dm from €20, s/d with bathroom €70/75, s/d/ tr without bathroom €60/65/87.50; @☎) This 17th-century building is near the town centre and has been lovingly restored and converted into a hostel (with four- to 14-bed rooms). There's a fine rear garden that is a focus of activity. It's loose and lively and around the corner from its slacker sister, the ACU (p831).

★ Mary K Hotel
HOTEL €€

(☑030-230 48 88; www.marykhotel.com; Oude-gracht 25; d from €125; ☎) 🍃 A bevy of Utrecht artists decorated the rooms at this ideally situated canal house. Rooms come in three basic sizes (cosy, medium and large), but no two are alike. All make use of the original 18th-century features and you may find a timber beam running through your bathroom or a stuffed animal snoozing in the rafters.

🍴 Eating & Drinking

Gys
CAFE €

(☑030-259 17 88; www.gysutrecht.nl; Voorstraat 77; dishes €5-10; ☺10am-9.30pm; ☎🍴) 🍃 Everything's organic at this bright bistro, from the burgers (tofu or lamb) and sandwiches (smoked mackerel with beet mousse, tempeh with sweet potato, avocado and watercress) to the salads and eggplant schnitzel.

★ Lokaal Negen
FRENCH €€€

(☑030-231 13 18; www.lokaalnegen.nl; Trans 7; 3-/4-/5-course menus €35/39.50/45; ☺5-10pm) Around the corner from the Domtoren, this long-standing option offers intimate dining in the living room of a sturdy old house with an interior garden. Instead of ordering, let yourself be pleasantly surprised by the multi-course set meals, each with an assortment of original starters.

ACU
BAR

(www.acu.nl; Voorstraat 71; ☺6-11pm Tue & Wed, 6pm-3am Thu, 8pm-4am Fri, 6pm-4am Sat, 2-11pm Sun) An anarcho-slacker reference point in Utrecht, ACU combines bar, music venue, lecture hall and more. Argue about whether Trotsky was too conservative while downing organic vegan food by the inimitable Kitchen Punx (6pm to 9pm Tuesday to Saturday).

ℹ️ Information

Tourist Office (VVV; ☑030-236 00 04; www. visit-utrecht.com; Domplein 9; ☺11.45am-5pm Mon, 10am-5pm Tue-Sat, noon-5pm Sun, to 6pm mid-Jul–Aug) Sells Domtoren tickets. Another tourist info point is in the corridor between the train station and Hoog Catharijne shopping centre.

ℹ️ Getting There & Away

Utrecht's train station is a major connection point, including for Germany. Key services include the following:

Amsterdam (€7.50, 30 minutes, four per hour)

Cologne (€29-44, two hours, six direct services per day)

Maastricht (€23.60, two hours, two per hour)

Rotterdam (€10.30, 40 minutes, four per hour)

THE SOUTH

Actual hills rise on the Netherlands' southern edge, where Belgium and Germany are within range of a tossed wooden shoe. The star here is Maastricht.

Maastricht

☑043 / POP 123,000

In the far-flung south, the grand old city of Maastricht is well worth the journey from Amsterdam and the pearls of the Randstad, and you can easily continue to Belgium and Germany.

Among Maastricht's 1650 listed historic buildings, look for Spanish and Roman ruins, French and Belgian architectural twists, splendid food and the cosmopolitan flair that made Maastricht the location for the signing of the namesake treaty, which created the modern EU in 1992.

It's at its most exuberant during carnaval (February/March), from the Friday before Shrove Tuesday until late Wednesday.

⊙ Sights

Maastricht's delights are scattered along both banks of the Maas and reward walkers.

Ringed by grand cafes, museums and churches, the large **Vrijthof** square is a focal point. Intimate **Onze Lieve Vrouweplein** is a cafe-filled square named after its church, which still attracts pilgrims. The arched stone footbridge **Sint Servaasbrug** dates from the 13th-century and links Maastricht's centre with the Wyck district.

★ **Sint Servaasbasiliek**   CHURCH
(www.sintservaas.nl; Keizer Karelplein 3; basilica free, treasury adult/child €4.50/free; ⊙10am-6pm Jul & Aug, to 5pm Sep-Nov & Apr-Jun, 10am-5pm Mon-Sat, 12.30-5pm Sun Dec-Mar) Built around the shrine of St Servatius, the first bishop of Maastricht, the basilica presents an architectural pastiche dating from 1000. Its beautiful curved brick apse and towers dominate the Vrijthof. The **Treasury** is filled with medieval gold artwork. Be sure to duck around the back to the serene cloister garden.

★ **Bonnefantenmuseum**   MUSEUM
(☑043-329 01 90; www.bonnefanten.nl; Ave Cèramique 250; adult/child €12/free; ⊙11am-5pm Tue-Sun) Maastricht's star museum, in the Ceramique district east of the Maas, is easily recognisable by its rocket-shaped tower. Designed by the Italian Aldo Rossi, the distinctive E-shaped structure displays early European painting and sculpture on the 1st floor and contemporary works by Limburg artists on the next, linked by a dramatic sweep of stairs. The dome of the tower is reserved for large-scale installations.

Fort Sint Pieter   FORTRESS
(☑043-325 21 21; www.maastrichtunderground.nl; Luikerweg 71; fort tour adult/child €6.40/5, combination tour €9.95/6.95; ⊙English tours 12.30pm) Looming atop a marlstone hill with commanding views of the Maas, the five-sided Fort Sint Pieter formed the city's southern defence and is linked to a network of underground tunnels. It's been fully restored to its original 1701 appearance. Visit is by guided tour only, which can be combined with a tunnel tour. Purchase tickets at the visitor centre below the fort. It's a 2km walk south of Maastricht, or take bus 7 and get off at 'Mergelweg'.

🛏 Sleeping

Botel Maastricht   HOTEL €
(☑043-321 90 23; www.botelmaastricht.nl; Maasboulevard 95; dm €35, s/d with bathroom €63/70, without bathroom €57/64) Realise your dream of staying on a houseboat in one of the 34 compact cabins on this ship moored on the Maas' west bank. Most feature tiny but well-equipped bathrooms. Enjoy breakfast or a sunset drink on deck and admire the barges rolling down the river. Rates drop mid-week.

Kaboom Hotel   HOTEL €€
(☑043-321 11 11; www.kaboomhotel.nl; Stationsplein 1; s/d from €63/126; 🕸) This just-unwrapped hotel bills itself as 'a touch rebellious', and its minimal decor strikes an irreverent tone without sacrificing such comforts as flat-screen TVs and hair dryers. It's right across the street from the station.

✗ Eating & Drinking

Excellent restaurants are even more common than old fortifications in Maastricht.

★ **Bisschopsmolen**   BAKERY €
(www.bisschopsmolen.nl; Stenebrug 3; vlaai €2.40, baguette sandwiches €6; ⊙9am-6pm Tue-Sat, 10am-5pm Sun) A working 7th-century water wheel powers a vintage flour mill that supplies its adjoining bakery. Spelt loaves and *vlaai* (seasonal fruit pies) come direct from the ovens out back. You can dine on-site at the cafe, and, if it's not busy, self-tour the mill and see how flour's been made for aeons.

Café Sjiek   DUTCH €€
(www.cafesjiek.nl; St Pieterstraat 13; mains lunch €12.50-19.50, dinner €14.50-26; ⊙kitchen 5-11pm Mon-Thu, noon-11pm Fri-Sun, bar to 2am; 🕸) Traditional local fare at this cosy spot ranges from *zuurvlees* (sour stew made with horsemeat) with apple sauce to hearty venison, fresh fish and Rommedoe cheese with pear syrup and rye bread. It doesn't take reservations and is always busy, but you can eat at the bar.

★ **Take One**   BROWN CAFE
(www.takeonebiercafe.nl; Rechtstraat 28; ⊙4pm-2am Thu-Mon) This narrow, eccentric 1930s tavern has well over 100 beers from the most obscure parts of the Benelux. It's run by a husband-and-wife team who help you select the beer most appropriate to your taste. The Bink Blonde is sweet, tangy and very good.

❶ Information

Tourist Office (VVV; ☎ 043-325 21 21; www.
vvvmaastricht.nl; Kleine Straat 1; ⊙10am-6pm
Mon-Sat, 11am-5pm Sun May-Oct, 10am-6pm
Mon-Fri, 10am-5pm Sat, 11am-5pm Sun Nov-
Apr) In the 15th-century Dinghuis; cycling tours
offered.

❶ Getting There & Away

There is an hourly international train service to
Liège (30 minutes), from where fast trains depart for Brussels, Paris and Cologne.

Domestic services include:

Amsterdam (€25.50, 2½ hours, two per hour)
Utrecht (€23.60, two hours, two per hour)

SURVIVAL GUIDE

❶ Directory A–Z

ACCOMMODATION

Always book accommodation ahead, especially
during high season. The tourist offices operate
booking services.

Many Dutch hotels have steep, perilous stairs
but no lifts/elevators, although most top-end
and some midrange hotels are exceptions.

Stayokay (www.stayokay.com) is the Dutch
hostelling association. A youth-hostel card costs
€17.50; nonmembers pay an extra €2.50 per
night and after six nights you become a member.
The usual HI discounts apply.

DISCOUNT CARDS

Museumkaart (Museum Card; www.museum
kaart.nl; adult/child €60/32.50, plus for 1st
registration €5) Free and discounted entry to
some 400 museums all over the country for
one year. Purchase at participating museum
ticket counters or from ticket shops.

INTERNET RESOURCES

Lonely Planet (www.lonelyplanet.com/
the-netherlands)

Netherlands Tourism Board (www.holland.
com)

Windmill Database (www.molendatabase.org)

LEGAL MATTERS

Drugs are actually illegal in the Netherlands.
Possession of soft drugs up to 5g is tolerated
but larger amounts can get you jailed. Hard
drugs are treated as a serious crime.

Smoking is banned in all public places. In a
uniquely Dutch solution, you can still smoke
tobacco-free pot in *coffeeshops*.

SLEEPING PRICE RANGES

The following price ranges refer to a
double room with bathroom in high season. Unless otherwise stated, breakfast
is not included in the price.

€ less than €100
€€ €100–180
€€€ more than €180

MONEY

ATMs

ATMs proliferate outside banks, inside supermarkets and at train stations.

Credit Cards

Most hotels, restaurants and large stores accept
major international cards. Some establishments, however, don't accept non-European
credit cards – check first.

OPENING HOURS

Banks 9am–4pm Monday to Friday, some
Saturday morning.

Cafes and Bars Open noon (exact hours vary);
most close 1am Sunday to Thursday, 3am
Friday and Saturday.

Museums Some closed Monday.

Restaurants Lunch 11am–2.30pm, dinner
6–10pm.

Shops 10am or noon to 6pm Tuesday to Friday,
10am to 5pm Saturday and Sunday, noon or
1pm to 5pm or 6pm Monday (if at all).

PUBLIC HOLIDAYS

Nieuwjaarsdag New Year's Day
Goede Vrijdag Good Friday
Eerste Paasdag Easter Sunday
Tweede Paasdag Easter Monday
Koningsdag (King's Day)27 April
Bevrijdingsdag (Liberation Day) 5 May
Hemelvaartsdag Ascension Day
Eerste Pinksterdag Whit Sunday (Pentecost)
Tweede Pinksterdag Whit Monday
Eerste Kerstdag (Christmas Day) 25 December
Tweede Kerstdag (Boxing Day) 26 December

SAFE TRAVEL

The Netherlands is a safe country, but be sensible all the same and *always* lock your bike.
Never buy drugs on the street: it's illegal. And
don't light up joints just anywhere – stick to
coffeeshops.

ESSENTIAL FOOD & DRINK

Vlaamse frites Iconic French fries smothered in mayonnaise or myriad other sauces.

Cheese The Dutch consume almost 19kg of cheese per person per year, nearly two-thirds of which is Gouda. The tastiest hard, rich *oud* (old) varieties have strong, complex flavours.

Seafood Street stalls sell seafood snacks including raw, slightly salted *haring* (herring) cut into bite-sized pieces and served with onion and pickles.

Indonesian The most famous meal is arijsttafel (rice table): an array of spicy savoury dishes such as braised beef, pork satay and ribs served with rice.

Kroketten Croquettes are crumbed, deep-fried dough balls with various fillings, such as meat-filled *bitterballen*.

Beer Big names like Heineken are ubiquitous; small brewers like De Drie Ringen and Gulpener are the best.

Jenever Dutch gin is made from juniper berries and drunk chilled from a tulip-shaped shot glass. *Jonge* (young) *jenever* is smooth; strongly flavoured *oude* (old) *jenever* can be an acquired taste.

TELEPHONE

Country code 📞 31
International access code 📞 00

ⓘ Getting There & Away

AIR

Huge **Schiphol International Airport** (AMS; www.schiphol.nl) is the Netherlands' main international airport. **Rotterdam The Hague Airport** (RTM; www.rotterdamthehagueairport. nl) and budget airline hub **Eindhoven Airport** (EIN; www.eindhovenairport.nl; Luchthavenweg 25) are small.

LAND

Bus

European bus network **Eurolines** (www. eurolines.com) serves 11 destinations across the Netherlands including the major cities.

Car & Motorcycle

Drivers need vehicle registration papers, third-party insurance and their domestic licence. The national auto club, **ANWB** (www.anwb.nl), has offices across the country and will provide info if you can show an auto-club card from your home country (eg AAA in the US or AA in the UK).

Train

International train connections are good. All Eurail and Inter-Rail passes are valid on the Dutch national train service, **NS** (Nederlandse Spoorwegen; www.ns.nl).

Many international services are operated by **NS International** (www.nsinternational.nl). In addition, **Thalys** (www.thalys.com) fast trains serve Brussels (where you can connect to the Eurostar) and Paris. From December 2017, direct Eurostar services will link Amsterdam, Schiphol airport and Rotterdam with London.

The high-speed line from Amsterdam (via Schiphol and Rotterdam) speeds travel times to Antwerp (1¼ hours), Brussels (two hours) and Paris (3¼ hours). German ICE high-speed trains run six direct services per day between Amsterdam and Cologne (2½ hours) via Utrecht. Many continue on to Frankfurt (four hours) via Frankfurt airport.

In peak periods, it's wise to reserve seats in advance. Buy tickets online at **SNCB Europe** (www.b-europe.com).

SEA

Several companies operate car/passenger ferries between the Netherlands and the UK:

Stena Line (www.stenaline.co.uk) Sails between Harwich and Hoek van Holland, 31km northwest of Rotterdam, linked to central Rotterdam by train (30 minutes).

P&O Ferries (www.poferries.com) Operates an overnight ferry every evening (11¾ hours) between Hull and Europoort, 39km west of central Rotterdam. Book bus tickets (40 minutes) to/ from Rotterdam when you reserve your berth.

DFDS Seaways (www.dfdsseaways.co.uk) Sails between Newcastle and IJmuiden, 30km northwest of Amsterdam, linked to Amsterdam by bus; the 15-hour sailings depart every day.

EATING PRICE RANGES

The following price ranges refer to a main course:

€ less than €12

€€ €12–25

€€€ more than €25

ⓘ Getting Around

BOAT

Ferries connect the mainland with the five Frisian Islands, including Texel. Other ferries span the Westerschelde in the south of Zeeland, providing a link between the southwestern expanse of the country and Belgium. These are popular with people using the Zeebrugge ferry terminal and run frequently year-round.

CAR & MOTORCYCLE

Hire

You must be at least 23 years of age to hire a car in the Netherlands.

Outside Amsterdam, car-hire companies can be in inconvenient locations if you're arriving by train.

Road Rules

Traffic travels on the right and the minimum driving age is 18 for vehicles and 16 for motorcycles. Seat belts are required and children under 12 must ride in the back if there's room. Trams always have the right of way and, if turning right, bikes have priority.

Speed limits are generally 50km/h in built-up areas, 80km/h in the country, 100km/h on major through-roads, and 130km/h on freeways (variations are clearly indicated). Hidden speeding cameras are everywhere and they will find you through your rental car company.

LOCAL TRANSPORT

National public transport info is available in English at **9292** (www.9292.nl), which has an excellent smartphone app.

Local transport tickets are smart cards called the OV-chipkaart (www.ov-chipkaart.nl).
➡ Either purchase a reusable OV-chipkaart in advance at a local transport-information office, or purchase a disposable one when you board a bus or tram.

ⓘ TIPS FOR BUYING TRAIN TICKETS

➡ Tickets can be bought at NS service counters or at ticketing machines. The ticket windows are easiest to use, though there is often a queue.

➡ Pay with cash, debit or credit card. Visa and Mastercard are accepted, though there is a €0.50 surcharge to use them, and they must have embedded chips (even then, international cards sometimes do not work).

➡ There is a €1 surcharge for buying a single-use disposable ticket.

➡ If you want to use a ticketing machine and pay cash, know that they accept coins only (no paper bills).

➡ There are basically two types of domestic train: Intercity (faster, with fewer stops) and Sprinter (slower, stops at each station).

➡ When you enter *and* exit a bus, tram or metro, hold the card against a reader at the doors or station gates. The system then calculates your fare and deducts it from the card.

➡ Fares for the reusable cards are much lower than the disposable ones (though you do have to pay an initial €7.50 fee; the card is valid for five years).

➡ You can also buy OV-chipkaarts for unlimited use for one or more days, and this often is the most convenient option. Local transport operators sell these.

➡ Stored-value OV-chipkaarts can be used on trains throughout the Netherlands.

TRAIN

The train network is run by NS (Nederlandse Spoorwegen; www.ns.nl). First-class sections are barely different from 2nd-class areas, but they are less crowded. Trains are fast and frequent and serve most places of interest. Distances are short. The high-speed line between Amsterdam, Schiphol and Rotterdam requires a small supplement (around €3). Most train stations have lockers operated by credit cards (average cost €6).

Norway

Best Places to Stay

➡ The Thief (p840)
➡ Hotel Park (p845)
➡ Westerås Gard (p850)
➡ Svinøya Rorbuer (p853)
➡ Tromsø Bed & Books (p855)

Best Places to Eat

➡ Markveien Mat & Vinhus (p841)
➡ Pingvinen (p847)
➡ Torget Fish Market (p845)
➡ Baklandet Skydsstasjon (p852)
➡ Renaa Matbaren (p848)

Why Go?

Norway is a once-in-a-lifetime destination and the essence of its appeal is remarkably simple: this is one of the most beautiful countries on earth. Impossibly steep-sided fjords cut deep gashes into the interior; grand and glorious glaciers snake down from Europe's largest ice fields; and the appeal of the Arctic is primeval. The counterpoint to so much natural beauty is found in the country's vibrant cultural life. Norwegian cities are cosmopolitan and brimful of architecture that showcases the famous Scandinavian flair for design. Yes, Norway is one of the most expensive countries on the planet, but it'll pay you back with never-to-be-forgotten experiences many times over.

When to Go

Oslo

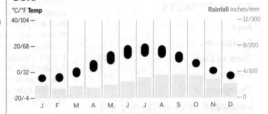

| **Mar** There's still plenty of snow on the ground, but enough daylight to enjoy winter sports. | **Jun–Aug** Scandinavian summers are short, and beyond the Arctic Circle, the sun never sets. | **Sep** The stunning colours of autumn make this prime hiking time. |

OSLO

POP 647,676

Oslo is home to world-class museums and galleries to rival anywhere else on the European art trail and is fringed with forests, hills and lakes. Add to this mix a thriving cafe and bar culture, and top-notch restaurants and the result is a thoroughly intoxicating place in which to forget about the fjords for a while.

◉ Sights

★ Oslo Opera House   ARCHITECTURE

(Den Norske Opera & Ballett; ☑ 21 42 21 21; www. operaen.no; Kirsten Flagstads plass 1; foyer free; ⊙ foyer 10am-9pm Mon-Fri, 11am-9pm Sat, noon-9pm Sun) Hoping to transform the city into a world-class cultural centre, the city leaders have embarked on a massive waterfront redevelopment project (which is scheduled to last until 2020), the centrepiece of which is the magnificent Opera House – a creation that is fast becoming one of the iconic modern buildings of Scandinavia.

★ Astrup Fearnley Museet   GALLERY

(Astrup Fearnley Museum; ☑ 22 93 60 60; www. afmuseet.no; Strandpromenaden 2; adult/student/child Nkr120/80/free, guided tours Nkr50; ⊙ noon-5pm Tue, Wed & Fri, to 7pm Thu, 11am-5pm Sat & Sun) Recently re-opened in a stunning architectural creation at the centre of Oslo's waterfront, this museum, which contains all manner of zany contemporary art, is Oslo's latest flagship project and the artistic highlight of the city.

Akershus Festning   FORTRESS

(Akershus Fortress; ⊙ 6am-9pm) FREE Strategically located on the eastern side of the harbour, dominating the Oslo harbourfront, are the medieval castle (Akershus Castle; ☑ 22 41 25 21; www.nasjonalefestningsverk.no; Kongens gate; adult/child Nkr70/30, with Oslo Pass free; ⊙ 10am-4pm Mon-Sat, noon-4pm Sun May-Aug, noon-5pm Sat & Sun Sep-Apr) and fortress, arguably Oslo's architectural highlights. The complex as a whole is known as Akershus Festning. Inside the expansive complex are a couple of museums and interesting buildings.

Nasjonalgalleriet   GALLERY

(National Gallery; ☑ 21 98 20 00; www.nasjonalmuseet.no; Universitetsgata 13; adult/child Nkr100/free, Thu free; ⊙ 10am-6pm Tue, Wed & Fri, to 7pm Thu, 11am-5pm Sat & Sun) One of Oslo's major highlights, the National Gallery houses the nation's largest collection of art. Some of Edvard Munch's best-known creations are on display here, including his most renowned work, *The Scream*. There's an impressive collection of other European art, with works by Gauguin, Picasso and El Greco, plus impressionists such as Manet, Degas, Renoir, Matisse, Cézanne and Monet. Norwegian artists have a strong showing, too, including key figures such as JC Dahl and Christian Krohg.

Munchmuseet   GALLERY

(Munch Museum; ☑ 23 49 35 00; www.munchmuseet.no; Tøyengata 53; adult/child Nkr100/free; ⊙ 10am-4pm, to 5pm mid-Jun–late Sep; ☐ 20, Ⓜ Tøyen) Fans of Edvard Munch (1863–1944) won't want to miss the Munch Museum, which houses the largest collection of his work in the world: 1100 paintings and 4500 watercolours, many of which were gifted to the city by Munch himself (although the best-known pieces, including *The Scream*, are actually in the National Gallery).

Royal Palace & Slottsparken   PALACE, PARK

(Det Kongelige Slott; ☑ 81 53 31 33; www.royalcourt.no; Slottsparken; park free, palace tours adult/child Nkr95/85; ⊙ guided tours in English noon, 2pm & 2.20pm Mon-Thu & Sat, 2pm, 2.20pm & 4pm Fri & Sun late Jun–mid-Aug) FREE Rising up above the western end of central Oslo is the sloping parkland of Slottsparken. Filled with stately royal trees and a duck pond or three, it's a lovely place for a quiet walk. The Norwegian royal family liked the park so much they moved in – the Royal Palace sits grandly at the top.

ITINERARIES

One Week

Begin in **Oslo** and soak up the Scandinavian sophistication of the city's museums, waterfront and culinary scene. Join the Norway in a Nutshell tour, travelling by train across the stunning roof of Norway, down to **Sognefjorden** then on to **Bergen** via **Gudvangen**, **Stalheim** and **Voss**. Three days in Bergen will give you a taste of this beguiling city, then jump back on the train back to Oslo.

Two Weeks

With an extra week, allow for two days in **Stavanger** (including the day excursion to **Pulpit Rock** above Lysefjord), a couple more days in **Trondheim**, then three days exploring the length and breadth of the **Lofoten Islands** before flying back to **Oslo**.

Norway Highlights

1 **Oslo** (p837)
Enjoying the capital's cosmopolitan charms and the stunning Opera House.

2 **Geiranger** (p850) Exploring Norway's No 1 fjord on the ferry from Hellesylt.

3 **Bergen** (p844) Lingering amid enchanted Bryggen buildings along the waterfront.

4 **Oslo to Bergen railway** (p844) Hopping aboard the train for Norway's most spectacular rail trip.

5 **Pulpit Rock** (p849) Hiking high above Lysefjord to Norway's most breathtaking lookout.

Svalbard (550km)
(see inset)

200 km
100 miles

N

RUSSIA

Vardø
Vadsø
Kirkenes
Båtsfjord
Kjøllefjord
Knivskjelodden (71°11'08"N)
Repvåg
Nordkapp
Honningsvåg
Hammerfest
Lakselv
Hasvik
Alta
Karasjok
Kautokeino

FINLAND

Oulu

E63
E75
E8
E10
E4
E6
45

NORWEGIAN SEA

Ringvassøy
Tromsø **7**
Skibotn
Finnsnes
Harstad
Narvik
Kiruna
Andenes
Vesterålen
Lofoten Islands **8**
Svolvær
Henningsvær
Værøy
Å
Vestvågøy
Bodø
Fauske
Ørnes
Vedøya
Saltfjellet-Svartisen National Park **6**
Mo i Rana
Sandnessjøen
Mosjøen
Brønnøysund
Grong
Namsos
E6
E12
R17

Jan Mayen (1200km)

Svalbard inset

Kvitøya
Storøya
Nordaustlandet
Kong Karls Land
Svenskøya
Barentsøya
Edgeøya
Prins Karls Forlandet
Svalbard
Longyearbyen
Spitsbergen
Storfjorden
Magdalenefjord
Erik Eriksenstretet
Olgastretet

300 km
200 miles

Norway mainland

TOURS

For maximum sights in minimal time, it's hard to beat the popular **Norway in a Nutshell** (Fjord Tours; ☑81 56 82 22; www.norwaynutshell.com); book at tourist offices or train stations. From Oslo, the typical route includes train across Hardangervidda to Myrdal, descent along the dramatic Flåmbanen, cruise along Nærøyfjorden to Gudvangen, bus to Voss, connecting train to Bergen for a short visit, then an overnight return rail trip to Oslo (including a sleeper compartment); the return tour costs Nkr2890.

Vikingskipshuset   MUSEUM
(Viking Ship Museum; ☑ 22 13 52 80; www.khm.uio.no; Huk Aveny 35; adult/child Nkr80/free; ⊙9am-6pm May-Sep, 10am-4pm Oct-Apr) Some 1100 years ago, Vikings dragged up two longships, *Oseberg* and *Gokstad*, from the shoreline and used them as the centrepiece for grand ceremonial burials, probably for an important chieftain or noble. Along with the ships, they buried many items for the afterlife: food, drink, jewellery, furniture, carriages, weapons, and even a few dogs and servants for companionship. Discovered in Oslofjord in the late 19th century, they're beautifully preserved and offer an evocative insight into the vanished world of the Vikings.

🛏 Sleeping

★Saga Poshtel Oslo   HOSTEL €
(☑23 10 08 00; www.sagahoteloslocentral.no; Kongens gate 7; dm Nkr395-485, d Nkr895-1025; ☎) There's a growing trend for this kind of crossover hostel-hotel, which allows budget travellers a dash of designer luxury. And it works brilliantly – it's smartly designed and very central, and there's a big social lounge with decent wi-fi. Rooms are basic but spotless; there are lots of doubles, plus four- and six-bunk-bed dorms, all with en suites.

Citybox Oslo   HOTEL €
(☑ 21 42 04 80; www.citybox.no/oslo; Prinsens gate 6; r Nkr699-1199; ☎) This functional city chain comes to Oslo with its trademark brand of no-frills, bare-bones rooms at bargain prices (well, at least for Norway). But don't expect prison-block chic – it's surprisingly smart, with plain all-white rooms, Scandi-style furniture, free wi-fi and an on-site cafe, as well as a great downtown location. Plush: no; practical: very.

★Ellingsens Pensjonat   PENSION €€
(☑22 60 03 59; www.ellingsenspensjonat.no; Holtegata 25; s/d from Nkr700/990, without bathroom Nkr550/800, apt s/d Nkr700/1200; ☎) Located in a quiet, pleasant neighbourhood, this homey B&B offers one of the best deals in the capital. The building dates from 1890 and many of the original features (high ceilings, rose designs) remain. Rooms are bright, airy and beautifully decorated, with fridges and kettles, and there's a small garden to lounge about in on sunny days.

Cochs Pensjonat   PENSION €€
(☑23 33 24 00; www.cochspensjonat.no; Parkveien 25; s/d with kitchenette from Nkr650/850, without bathroom Nkr530/720; ☎) Opened as a guesthouse for bachelors in the 1920s, this olde-worlde yellow-brick hotel offers sparsely furnished rooms, some with kitchenettes. It's ideally located behind the Royal Palace, although it's on a busy intersection, so expect some noise. The rear rooms overlooking the Slottsparken are especially spacious, but cost a little more; cheaper rooms share corridor bathrooms.

★The Thief   BOUTIQUE HOTEL €€€
(☑24 00 40 00; www.thethief.com; Landgangen 1; d from Nkr3390; ☎⊠) Despite its distinctly peculiar name, the Thief is the place to splash your cash on Oslo accommodation. It's in the redeveloped waterfront overlooking the Astrup Fearnley Museum, and it's packed with playful touches, from moving images in the elevators to gold knitting clocks that don't tell the time. As you'd expect, rooms are sleek, chic and seriously expensive.

🍴 Eating

Kasbah   MIDDLE EASTERN €
(☑21 94 90 99; www.thekasbah.no; Kingos gate 1b; mains Nkr85-189, meze platter Nkr145; ⊙11am-1am Mon-Fri) A popular neighbourhood hang-out with a Middle Eastern flavour, specialising in filling falafels, filled pittas and meze platters. It's as relaxing as a pair of Moroccan slippers, with sofas to lounge around on, reggae on the stereo and thrift-store decor to match.

Nighthawk Diner   BURGERS €€
(☑96 62 73 27; www.nighthawkdiner.com; Seilduksgata 15; mains Nkr139-198; ⊙7am-11pm or midnight Mon-Thu, to 1am Fri, 10am-1am Sat, 10am-11pm Sun) 🍴 Every hipster district needs its burger joint, and in Grünerløkka it's the Nighthawk – a thoroughly convincing impression of an all-American diner, right down to the booth seats, jukebox, ketchup

caddies and art deco–style mirrored bar. There's even a mural of Edward Hopper's *Nighthawks* on one wall. Burgers, shakes and dogs are excellent, and use locally sourced beef and homemade sauces.

Asylet
NORWEGIAN €€

(✍ 22 17 09 39; www.asylet.no; Grønland 28; mains Nkr124-169; ☉ 11am-11.30pm Mon-Tue, to 12.30am Wed-Fri, noon-12.30am Sat, to 10.30pm Sun) In the multicultural area around Grønland, this classic hostelry (dating from 1730) comes as a real surprise. Head through the arch into the cobbled courtyard, surrounded by wooden galleries, then head inside to the low-ceilinged, half-timbered pub, complete with flagstones, beams and a decidedly wonky-looking fireplace. The food is filling and traditional – it's particularly known for its *smørbrød* (open-faced sandwiches).

Albert Bistro
FRENCH €€

(✍ 21 02 36 30; www.albertbistro.no; Stranden 3, Aker Brygge; mains Nkr185-285; ☉ 7.30am-11pm Mon-Fri, 9am-11pm Sat & Sun) Located in Oslo's flashy new waterfront area, this French-inspired bistro specialises in Gallic cuisine, from croque monsieur for breakfast right through to bistro classics such as *carré d'agneau* (lamb cutlet) and *entrecôte* (steak). It's light and bright, and not absurdly pricey.

★ Markveien Mat & Vinhus
NORWEGIAN €€€

(✍ 22 37 22 97; www.markveien.no; Torvbakkgt 12; mains Nkr258-296, 3 courses Nkr435; ☉ 4pm-1am Mon-Sat) For cosy Norwegian dining, this lovely spot on the southern edge of Grünerløkka is hard to better. Settle in at one of the candlelit tables and tuck into hearty, traditional dishes such as lamb shank with root vegetables, green-crab soup or monkfish with roasted squash.

Dr Kneipp's Vinbar
NORWEGIAN €€€

(✍ 22 37 22 97; www.markveien.no; Torvbakkgt 12; mains Nkr199-259; ☉ 4pm-1am Mon-Sat) Slightly more relaxed than its sister restaurant, Markveien Mat & Vinhus (p841), Dr Kneipp's is the place for sipping wines by the glass (there are around 400 wines to choose from) accompanied by light, snacky dishes. The cheesecake is legendary.

🍷 Drinking & Entertainment

The best neighbourhood bar scene is along Thorvald Meyers gate and the surrounding streets in Grünerløkka. The Youngstorget area has some of the most popular places close to the city centre, while the Grønland neighbourhood has a more alternative feel.

★ Fuglen
COCKTAIL BAR

(www.fuglen.com; Universitetsgaten 2; ☉ 7.30am-10pm Mon & Tue, to 1am Wed & Thu, to 3am Fri, 11am-3am Sat, to 10pm Sun) Despite its slightly odd location on a busy thoroughfare, this cool cafe-bar is well worth a visit. It's like a cross between a mid-century antiques shop and a cocktail lounge – and if you're sold on the decor, you can just take it home with you, since everything's for sale.

★ Blå
JAZZ

(www.blaaoslo.no; Brenneriveien 9c; Nkr100-270) Blå features on a global list of 100 great jazz clubs compiled by US jazz magazine *Down Beat;* as one editor put it, 'To get in this list means that it's quite the club'. Sometimes it offers other musical styles (like salsa); occasionally DJs get the crowds moving instead of live musicians.

★ Tim Wendelboe
CAFE

(✍ 40 00 40 62; www.timwendelboe.no; Grüners gate 1; ☉ 8.30am-6pm Mon-Fri, 11am-5pm Sat & Sun) World-renowned barista Tim W has opened his own eponymous Oslo coffee shop, and it really is a must-visit for aficionados of the holy bean. All the coffees are self-sourced and hand-roasted (the roaster takes up half the floor space), and as you'd expect, the latte art is world-class.

Grünerløkka Brygghus
PUB

(www.brygghus.no; Thorvald Meyers gate 30; beers from Nkr450; ☉ 3pm-1am Mon-Tue, to 2pm Wed-Thu, to 3am Fri, noon-3am Sat, to midnight Sun) Like all northern Europeans, the Norwegians like nothing more than a good beer, and this ale-house and microbrewery caters to its clientele with a range of home brews from Pilsners to weissbiers.

Supreme Roastworks
COFFEE

(✍ 22 71 42 02; www.srw.no; Thorvald Meyers gate 18A; coffee Nkr250-450; ☉ 7am-5pm) Run by award-winning barista Odd-Steinar Tøllefsenis, named the World Brewers Cup Champion in Sweden in 2015, this ubertrendy coffee-bar and microroastery is the place in Grünerløkka to get your flat white or cold-brewed, single origin drip-filter. Choose from the superb espresso-based drinks or your choice of hand-filters (J60 or Chemex), and watch the beans being roasted while you drink.

Bar Boca
BAR

(Thorvald Meyers gate 30; ☉ 11am-1am Mon-Thu, to 3am Fri & Sat, noon-1am Sun) This trendy, tiny Grünerløkka hang-out has the '80s vibe down pat, from the colourful cocktails

Oslo

500 m
0.25 miles

Marcus Thranes gate
Finnmarkgata
Helgesens gate
Sannergata
Toftes gate
Sofienberggata
Sars gate
Botanisk Hage
Jens Bjelkes gate
Rathkes gate
Trondheimsveien
Monrads gate
Tøyen T-bane Station
5
Akebergvn.
Tøyengata
Lakkegata
Motzfeldts gate
Grønland
Grønland T-bane Station
14
Tøyenbekken
Nylandsveien
Galleri Oslo
Bus Terminal
Storgata
Vaterlands bru
Brugata
Oslo S Information Desk
Biskop Gunnerus gate
Oslo Sentralstasjon
Oslo Visitor Centre

17
18
20
21
Thorvald Meyers gate
GRÜNELØKKA
Olaf Ryes plass
22
Gruneriagen Park
Nordre gate
Korsgata
Markveien
Torvbakkgt.
Søndre gate
Hausmanns gate
Øvre Elvebakke
Møllergata
Torggata
(Hammersborggata)
Torggata
Jernbanetorget S (Oslo S)
Use-It

15
Sannergata
Maridalsveien
Akersbakken
Tåsenveien
Waldemar Thranes gate
Møllerveien
Brenneriveien
Akersveien
Damstredet
23
16

Ullevalsveien
St Hanshaugen
Ullevalsveien
Vår Frelsers Gravlund
Stensberggata
Nordahl Bruns gate
Pilestredet
19
6
Kristian IV's gate
Karl Johans gate
Stortinget T-bane Station
Prinsens gate
Tollbugata
Nedre Vollgate
Tordenskiolds gate

Theresesgate
Louises gate
Pilestredet
Suhms gate
Parkveien
Holbergs plass
Holbergs gate
St Olavs gate
Wergelandsveien
Slottsparken
Nationaltheatret T-bane Station
Haakon VII's gate
Rådhusgata
Rådhus
Cort Adelers gate

Majorstuen T-bane Station
Vibes gate
Bogstadveien
Josefines gate
Oscars gate
Hegdehaugsveien
9
Camilla Colletts vei
Uranienborgveien
Inkognitogata
Riddervoldsgata
Colbjørnsens gate
Henrik Ibsens gate
Hansteens gate
Huitfeldts gate
Ruseløkkveien

Kirkeveien
Middelthuns gate
Gyldenløves gate
Holtegata
Niels Juels gate
Skovveien
Frognerveien
Bygdøy allé
Drammensveien
Munkedamsveien

10
7

A   B   C   D

1   2   3   4

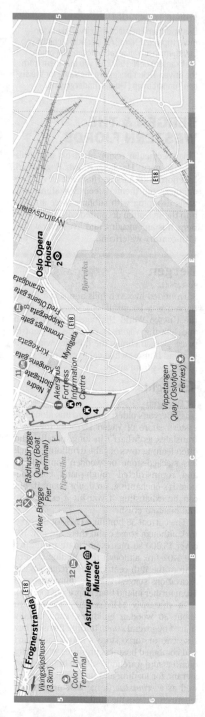

through to the kitsch lounge-bar vibe. It gets very busy at weekends.

ℹ Information

Oslo Visitor Centre (☎ 81 53 05 55; www.visitoslo.com; ⊙ 9am-6pm) Now located at the train station, Oslo's excellent main tourist office is tucked away in a corner of the Østbahnhallen station hall. It can help you with accommodation, activities, cruises and cross-country trips, and also sells transport tickets and the Oslo Pass. Pick up one of their free city guides.

ℹ Getting There & Away

AIR

Oslo Gardermoen International Airport (www.osl.no), the city's main airport, is 50km north of the city. It's linked to the city by high-speed trains, as well as buses and taxis. It's used by international carriers, including Norwegian, SAS and British Airways.

ℹ OSLO PASS

Oslo Pass, sold at the tourist office, is one popular way of cutting transport and ticket costs around the city. The majority of the city's museums are free with the pass, as is public transport within the city limits (barring late-night buses). Other perks include restaurant and tour discounts.

Note that many budget flights, including those run by SAS Braathens, Widerøe and Ryanair operate from **Torp International Airport**, some 123km southwest of Oslo, or **Rygge Airport**, around 60km southeast of the centre. Check carefully which airport your flight is going to!

BUS

Long-distance buses arrive and depart from the **Galleri Oslo Bus Terminal** (☑ 23 00 24 00; Schweigaards gate 8). The train and bus stations are linked via a convenient overhead walkway for easy connections.

Nor-Way Bussekspress (☑ 81 54 44 44; www. nor-way.no) provides timetables and booking. International services also depart from the bus terminal. Destinations include:

Bergen (Nkr 695, 11 hours, three daily)

Stavanger (Nkr5810, seven hours, usually one daily) Via Kristiansand.

Trondheim (Nkr560, nine hours, two per week)

TRAIN

All trains arrive and depart from **Oslo S** in the city centre. It has **reservation desks** (Jernbanetorget 1; ⊙ 6.30am-11pm) and an **information desk** (☑ 81 50 08 88; Jernbanetorget 1) that provides details on routes and timetables throughout Norway.

Bergen (Nkr865, 6½ to 7½ hours, four daily)

Røros (Nkr787, five hours, every two hours)

Stavanger (Nkr968, seven hours 40 minutes, six daily)

Trondheim (Nkr937, 6½ to 7½ hours, six daily)

ℹ Getting Around

TO/FROM AIRPORT

FlyToget (www.flytoget.no; adult/child Nkr180/90) Trains connect Gardermoen airport with Oslo's central station in just 19 minutes. Most standard **NSB** (www.nsb.no) trains also stop at Gardermoen (Nkr90, from 26 minutes, hourly but fewer on Saturday).

Flybussen (www.flybussen.no), runs from the airport to the bus terminal at Galleri Oslo, as well as a few other stops in the city every 20 minutes from 4am to around 10pm. The trip costs adult/child Nkr160/80 and takes about 40 minutes.

PUBLIC TRANSPORT

Bus and tram lines lace the city. Tickets for most trips cost Nkr32/16 per adult/child if you buy them in advance (at 7-Eleven, Narvesen, Trafikanten) or Nkr50/25 if you buy them from the driver. Ticket prices are the same for the six-line Tunnelbanen (T-bane) underground.

BERGEN & THE WESTERN FJORDS

This spectacular region has truly indescribable scenery. Hardangerfjord, Sognefjord, Lysefjord and Geirangerfjord are all variants on the same theme: steep crystalline rock walls dropping with sublime force straight into the sea, often decorated with waterfalls. Bergen is an engaging and lively city with a 15th-century waterfront.

Bergen

POP 275,112

Surrounded by seven hills and seven fjords, Bergen is a beautiful, charming city. With the Unesco World Heritage–listed Bryggen and buzzing Vågen Harbour as its centrepiece, Bergen climbs the hillsides with timber-clad houses, while cable cars offer stunning views from above.

⊙ Sights

★ **Bryggen**   HISTORIC SITE

FREE Bergen's oldest quarter runs along the eastern shore of Vågen Harbour (*bryggen* translates as 'wharf') in long, parallel and often leaning rows of gabled buildings. Each has stacked-stone or wooden foundations and reconstructed rough-plank construction. It's enchanting, no doubt about it, but can be exhausting if you hit a cruise-ship and bus-tour crush.

The current 58 buildings (25% of the original, although some claim there are now 61) cover 13,000 sq metres and date from after the 1702 fire, although the building pattern is from the 12th century. The archaeological excavations suggest that the quay was once 140m further inland than its present location.

In the early 14th century, there were about 30 wooden buildings, each usually shared by several *stuer* (trading firms). They rose two or three storeys above the wharf and combined business premises with living quarters and warehouses. Each building had a crane for loading and unloading ships, as well as a *schøtstue* (large assembly room) where employees met and ate.

The wooden alleyways of Bryggen have become a haven for artists and craftspeople, and there are shops and boutiques at every turn. The atmosphere of an intimate waterfront community remains intact, and losing yourself here is one of Bergen's pleasures.

★ **KODE** GALLERY

(☑53 00 97 04; www.kodebergen.no; Rasmus Meyers allé; adult/child Nkr100/free; ☉10am-5pm daily mid-May–Aug, 11am-4pm Sep–mid-May) Bergen's art museums are collected under the umbrella institution KODE and form one of the largest art-and-design collections in Scandinavia. Four separate, and architecturally unique, buildings line up along the Lille Lungegård lake, each with its own focus. Key highlights include a large selection of the strange, fantastical works of Nikolai Astrup, as well as a selection of pieces by Picasso, Munch and JC Dahl. One ticket includes admission to all the galleries for two days.

★ **Edvard Grieg Museum** MUSEUM

(Troldhaugen; ☑55 92 29 92; http://griegmuseum.no; Troldhaugvegen 65, Paradis-Bergen; adult/child Nkr100/free; ☉9am-6pm May-Sep, 10am-4pm Oct-Apr) Composer Edvard Grieg and his wife Nina Hagerup spent summers at this charming Swiss-style wooden villa from 1885 until Grieg's death in 1907. Surrounded by fragrant, tumbling gardens and occupying a semi-rural setting – on a peninsula by coastal Nordåsvatnet lake, south of Bergen – it's a truly lovely place to visit. Apart from Grieg's original home, there is a modern exhibition centre, a 200-seat concert hall and perhaps the most compelling feature of them all, a tiny, lake-side **Composer's Hut**.

Fløibanen Funicular CABLE CAR

(☑55 33 68 00; www.floibanen.no; Vetrlidsalmenning 21; adult/child return Nkr85/43; ☉7.30am-11pm Mon-Fri, 8am-11pm Sat & Sun) For an unbeatable view of the city, ride the 26-degree Fløibanen funicular to the top of Mt Fløyen (320m), with departures every 15 minutes. From the top, well-marked hiking tracks lead into the forest; the possibilities are mapped out on the free *Walking Map of Mount Fløyen,* available from the Bergen tourist office (p847).

🛏 **Sleeping**

Citybox HOSTEL, HOTEL **€**

(☑55 31 25 00; www.citybox.no; Nygårdsgaten 31; s/d from Nkr550/799, without bathroom from Nkr450/599; ☎) Norway's first hostel-hotel mini-chain began in Bergen, and it's still doing brisk business. It's located in an impressive turreted building, and its spacious, colourful rooms make maximum use of high ceilings and architectural features (family rooms even have small kitchenettes). The hostel is being extended and renovated in early 2017, but should be open again by May – check the website.

★ **Hotel Park** HISTORIC HOTEL **€€**

(☑55 54 44 00; www.hotelpark.no; Harald Hårfagresgate 35; s/d Nkr1190/1390; ☎) Two 19th-century houses combined comprise this family-run beauty, still managed by the daughters of the long-time owner. Packed with curios and antiques, it's a lovely, welcoming place to stay – all 33 rooms are slightly different, with quirky layouts and surprising design touches; corner rooms have the best views over Bergen's rooftops and Mt Fløyen.

Hotel No.13 BOUTIQUE HOTEL **€€€**

(☑55 36 13 00; www.nordicchoicehotels.no/nordic-resort/hotel-no13/; Torgalmenningen 13; d/ste Nkr2000/3500; ✳☎) You couldn't ask for a better location than at this smart, pale-grey building, on a pedestrianised thoroughfare just a short walk from the waterfront. Now owned by the Nordic Choice chain, it's a smart offering, with a bold decor choice combining black floors with puce furnishings and splashes of art. The suite's a real beauty, with a curving glass skylight.

✖ **Eating**

Torget Fish Market SEAFOOD **€**

(Torget; lunches Nkr99-169; ☉7am-7pm Jun-Aug, 7am-4pm Mon-Sat Sep-May) For most of its history, Bergen has survived on the fruits of the sea, so there's no better place for lunch than the town's lively fish market. Here you'll find everything from salmon to calamari, fish and chips, prawn baguettes and seafood salads. If you can afford it, the sides of smoked salmon are some of the best in Norway.

FJORD TOURS FROM BERGEN

There are dozens of tours of the fjords from Bergen; the tourist office (p847) has a full list and you can buy tickets there or online. Most offer discounts if you have a Bergen Card. For a good overview, pick up the *Round Trips – Fjord Tours & Excursions* brochure from the tourist office, which includes tours offered by a range of private companies.

Bergen

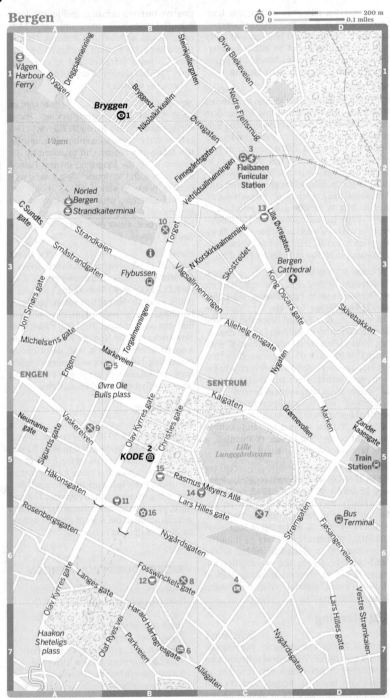

0 ————— 200 m
0 ————— 0.1 miles

Vågen Harbour Ferry

Bryggen 1

Steinkjellergaten

Øvre Blekeveien

Nedre Fjellsmug

Dreggsallmenning

Bryggestr.

Nikolaikirkeallm

Øvregaten

Finnegårdsgaten

Vetrlidsallmenningen

Fløibanen Funicular Station 3

Norled Bergen

Strandkaiterminal

C. Sundts gate

Strandkaien

Småstrandgaten

10 Torget

Flybussen

Vågsallmenningen

N Korskirkeallmenning

Skostredet

Lille Øvregaten 13

Bergen Cathedral

Kong Oscars gate

Skivebakken

Jon Smørs gate

Michelsens gate

Torgallmenningen

Markeveien

Engen

5

Allehelgensgate

Nygaten

Marken

ENGEN

Øvre Ole Bulls plass

SENTRUM

Kaigaten

Grønnevollen

Zander Kaaesgate

Neumanns gate

Vaskerelven

Sigurds gate

Olav Kyrres gate

Christies gate

9

Lille Lungegårdsvann

Train Station

KODE 2

15

Rasmus Meyers Allé

14

7

Håkonsgaten

11

16

Lars Hilles gate

Rosenbergsgaten

Nygårdsgaten

Strømgaten

Bus Terminal

Fløsangerveien

Olav Kyrres gate

Langes gate

Fosswinckels gate

12

8

4

Vestre Strømkaien

Lars Hilles gate

Haakon Sheteligs plass

Olaf Ryes vei

Harald Hårfagresgate

Parkveien

6

Allégaten

Nygårdsgaten

Bergen

Pingvinen NORWEGIAN €€
(📞55 60 46 46; www.pingvinen.no; Vaskerelven 14; daily specials Nkr119, mains Nkr159-269; ⊙noon-3am) Devoted to Norwegian home cooking, and with a delightfully informal ambience, Pingvinen is the old favourite of *everyone* in Bergen. They come for meals their mothers and grandparents used to cook, and although the menu changes regularly, there'll be at least one of the following: fish-cake sandwiches, reindeer, fish pie, whale, salmon, lamb shank and *raspeballer* (sometimes called *komle*) – west-coast potato dumplings.

Marg & Bein BISTRO €€€
(📞55 32 34 32; www.marg-bein.no; Fosswinckels gate 18; mains Nkr255-279; ⊙5-9.30pm Tue-Thu, 5-10pm Fri & Sat, 5-9.30pm Sun) Light, bright and enormously inviting, this attractive bistro in the student area around Fosswinckels gate is a super place for supper. The menu is modern, playing with traditional meat, veg and fish but giving them a modern spin – celeriac purées, beetroot reductions and homemade chutneys abound. Wooden tables, big windows and Scandi furniture complete the swish package.

🍷 Drinking & Nightlife

⭐ **Landmark** BAR, CAFE
(📞94 01 50 50; Bergen Kunsthalle, Rasmus Meyers allé 5; ⊙cafe 11am-5pm Tue-Sun, bar 7pm-1am Tue-Thu, to 3.30am Fri & Sat) This large, airy room is a beautiful example of 1930s Norwegian design and is named for architect Ole Landmark. It multitasks: day-time cafe, lecture and screening hall; live-performance space, bar and venue for Bergen's best club nights. It's a favourite with the city's large creative scene. The cafe serves yummy lunches, with a choice of open-faced sandwiches and a weekly melt (Nkr99 to Nkr129).

Apollon BAR
(📞55 31 59 43; www.apollon.no; Nygårdsgaten 2a; ⊙10am-midnight Mon-Sat, noon-midnight Sun) Sink a beer while you browse for vintage vinyl at this too-cool-for-school record store and late-night hang-out, in business since the early 80s. Racks of records take up one side of the shop, with the other side occupied by a well-stocked bar serving local beers. The shop sometimes hosts in-store performances.

Blom CAFE
(John Lunds plass 1; ⊙8.30am-5pm Mon-Fri, 11am-5pm Sat & Sun; 🛜) This cafe is known for its excellent coffee (this is where off-duty baristas come for a pour-over) and attracts a fashionable, young crowd. It's a simple, warm place, with sweet service, lots of room to pull out your laptop, big sandwiches and more-ish homemade muesli slices, brownies and fruit crumbles.

Garage LIVE MUSIC
(www.garage.no; Christies gate 14; ⊙3pm-3am Mon-Sat, 5pm-3am Sun) Garage has taken on an almost mythical quality for music lovers across Norway. They do have the odd jazz and acoustic act, but this is a rock and metal venue at heart, with well-known Norwegian and international acts drawn to the cavernous basement. Stop by for their Sunday jam sessions in summer.

ℹ Information

Bergen Tourist Information Centre (📞55 55 20 00; www.visitbergen.com; Strandkaien 3; ⊙8.30am-10pm Jun-Aug, 9am-8pm May & Sep, 9am-4pm Mon-Sat Oct-Apr) You can't miss Bergen's tourist office – it's in a hulking edifice on the waterfront. The staff are superb, helping organise fjord tours, public transport, hiking routes and who knows what else. They publish the free *Bergen Guide*, and sell admission, excursion and public-transport tickets. It gets very, very busy: arrive early or be prepared to queue.

NORWAY BERGEN

❶ Getting There & Away

BOAT

International ferries to/from Bergen dock at **Skoltegrunnskaien** (Skoltegrunnskaien), northwest of the Rosenkrantz tower, while the *Hurtigruten* coastal ferry leaves from the Hurtigruteterminalen, southwest of the centre. A number of operators offer express boat services, leaving from the Strandkaiterminalen.

Norled (📞 51 86 87 00; www.norled.no; Kong Christian Frederiks plass 3) offers at least one daily ferry service to Sognefjord. It departs from Bergen and terminates at Flåm (adult/child Nkr795/398, 5½ hours), stopping at towns including Vik, Balestrand and Sogndal.

BUS

Flybussen (www.flybussen.no; one-way/return adult Nkr90/160, child Nkr50/80) Runs up to four times hourly between the airport, the Radisson Blu Royal Hotel, the main bus terminal and opposite the tourist office on Vågsallmenningen.

Bergen's bus terminal is located on Vestre Strømkaien.

Ålesund (two daily, Nkr 721, 10 hours)

Oslo (four daily, Nkr695, 11 hours)

Stavanger (six daily, Nkr600,5½ hours)

Stryn (three daily, Nkr571, 6½ hours)

TRAIN

The spectacular train journey between Bergen and Oslo (Nkr349 to Nkr849, 6½ to eight hours, five daily) runs through the heart of Norway. Other destinations include Voss (Nkr199, one hour, hourly) and Myrdal (Nkr300, 2¼ hours, up to nine daily) for connections to the Flåmsbana railway.

Stavanger

POP 124,936

Said by some to be the largest wooden city in Europe, Stavanger's old quarter climbs up the slopes around a pretty harbour. Stavanger is also one of Norway's liveliest urban centres and an excellent base to explore stunning Lysefjord.

◉ Sights

★ Gamle Stavanger   AREA

Gamle (Old) Stavanger, above the western shore of the harbour, is a delight. The Old Town's cobblestone walkways pass between rows of late 18th-century whitewashed wooden houses, all immaculately kept and adorned with cheerful, well-tended flower boxes. It well rewards an hour or two of ambling.

★ Norsk Oljemuseum   MUSEUM

(Oil Museum; www.norskolje.museum.no; Kjeringholmen; adult/child Nkr120/60; ⊙10am-7pm daily Jun-Aug, 10am-4pm Mon-Sat, to 6pm Sun Sep-May) Admittedly, the prospect of an 'oil museum' doesn't sound like the most promising prospect for an afternoon out. But this state-of-the-art place is well worth visiting – both for its striking, steel-clad architecture, and its high-tech displays exploring the history of North Sea oil exploration. Highlights include the world's largest drill bit, simulated rigs, documentary films, archive testimony and a vast hall of oil-platform models. There are also exhibitions on natural history, energy use and climate change.

🛏 Sleeping

Comfort Hotel Square   HOTEL €

(📞 51 56 80 00; www.nordicchoicehotels.no; Løkkeveien 41; d from Nkr699 at weekends, Nkr1247 mid-week; ❄ 🛜) It's part of a massive chain, yes, but this place in Gamle Stavanger offers more individuality than most. Outside, a wavy, wooden facade and a super roof terrace; inside, colourful rooms, exposed concrete and giant wall murals. Rates drop at weekends (often half-price compared to mid-week), and include breakfast. You can sleep in on Sundays and check out by 6pm, should you wish.

★ Darby's Inn   B&B €€

(📞 47 62 52 48; www.darbysbb.com; Oscars gate 18; r Nkr1180-1280; 🅿 ❄ 🛜) The two front rooms at this understated, opulent B&B might be Stavanger's nicest, even without a sea view. Traditional interiors in this historic house combine dark wood with antique furniture, paintings, Persian rugs and a baby grand in the lounge and dining room. The large guest rooms are simpler but still have luxury linen, plump cushions and suitably heavy curtains.

🍴 Eating

★ Renaa Matbaren   INTERNATIONAL €€

(📞 51 55 11 11; www.restaurantrenaa.no; Breitorget 6, enter from Bakkegata; small dishes Nrk59-135, mains Nkr165-395; ⊙11am-1am Mon-Sat, 1pm-midnight Sun) Run by top chef Sven Erik Renaa, this smart bistro offers a taste of his food at (reasonably) affordable prices. The menu is classic – mussels in beer, rib-eye with rosemary fries, squid with fennel and shallots, all with a Nordic twist. The glass and wood feels uber-Scandi, and the art collection is stellar (yes, that's an Antony Gormley statue).

LYSEFJORD & PULPIT ROCK

This 42km-long fjord is many visitors' favourite, and there's no doubt that it has a captivating beauty. The area's most popular outing is the two-hour hike to the top of incredible 604m-high Preikestolen (Pulpit Rock), 25km east of Stavanger. The usual involves catching a boat from Stavanger to Tau, and a bus to the hike's starting point at Preikestolhytta Vandrerhjem. It's best done between April and September.

For general information on the region, check out www.lysefjordeninfo.no and www.visitlysefjorden.no.

The cheapest option is to book a ticket through **Norled** (www.norled.no), or through **Tide** (www.tide.no), which uses the regular ferry from Stavanger's Fiskespiren Quay to Tau. The trip costs adult/child Nkr300/150, including the bus fare between Tau and Preikestolhytta, and the return ferry fares between Stavanger and Tau. Tickets can be bought online, at the tourist office or at Fiskespiren Quay. **Rødne Fjord Cruises** (☑51 89 52 70; www.rodne.no; Skagenkaien 35-37, Stavanger) runs its own cruise-and-hike excursions (adult Nkr780/500).

If you've got your own vehicle, you can take the car ferry (adult/child/car Nkr52/26/155, 40 minutes, roughly every 40 minutes, fewer ferries at weekends) from Stavanger's Fiskespiren Quay to Tau. From the pier in Tau, a well-signed road (Rv13) leads 19km to Preikestolhytta Vandrerhjem (take the signed turn-off after 13km).

Døgnvill BURGERS €€
(☑51 89 10 00; www.dognvillburger.no; Skagen 13; burgers Nkr139-179; ⊙11am-11pm Mon-Wed, 11am-midnight Thu-Sat, noon-11pm Sun; 🅿) 🍴
The hot spot for Stavanger's hipsters (and everyone else, in fact), this slinky burger joint does everything right – from its artisan buns through to its locally sourced meats, cheeses and salads. Go for a classic, spice things up with BBQ sauce or chipotle, add blue cheese or taleggio, or go veggie with baked beetroot or smoked aubergine and portobello mushroom. Mmm.

ℹ Information

Tourist Office (☑51 85 92 00; www.regionstavanger.com; Strandkaien 61; ⊙9am-8pm Jun-Aug, 9am-4pm Mon-Fri, 9am-2pm Sat Sep-May) Local information and advice on Lysefjord and Preikestolen.

ℹ Getting There & Away

BUS
Most services to Oslo change at Kristiansand.
Bergen (Nkr600, 5½ hours,hourly)
Haugesund (Nkr290,two hours ,hourly)
Kristiansand (Nkr410, 4½ hours, four daily)
Oslo (Nkr900, 9½ hours,three daily)

TRAIN
Most train services to Oslo change at Kristiansand.
Egersund (Nkr172, 1¼ hours, hourly)
Kristiansand (Nkr498,three hours, five daily)
Oslo (Nkr968,eight hours,up to five daily)

Sognefjorden

The world's second-longest (203km) and Norway's deepest (1308m) fjord, Sognefjorden cuts a deep slash across the map of western Norway. In places, sheer walls rise more than 1000m above the water, while elsewhere a gentler shoreline supports farms, orchards and villages. The broad, main waterway is impressive but cruise into its narrower arms, such as the deep and lovely Nærøyfjord to Gudvangen, for idyllic views of abrupt cliff faces and cascading waterfalls.

Flåm
POP 450

Scenically set at the head of Aurlandsfjorden, Flåm is a tiny village that's a jumping-off spot for travellers exploring the area. It all gets a little overrun with people when a cruise ship's in port, and sees an amazing 500,000 visitors every summer.

◉ Sights

★**Flåmsbana Railway** RAIL
(www.visitflam.com/en/flamsbana; adult/child one-way Nkr340/170, return Nkr440/170) A 20km-long engineering wonder hauls itself up 864m of altitude gain through 20 tunnels. At a gradient of 1:18, it's the world's steepest railway that runs without cable or rack wheels. It takes a full 45 minutes to climb to Myrdal on the bleak, treeless Hardangervidda Plateau, past thundering waterfalls

SOGNEFJORDEN BY BOAT

From Flåm, boats head out to towns around Sognefjorden. The most scenic trip from Flåm is the passenger ferry up Nærøyfjord to Gudvangen (one way/ return Nkr315/420). At Gudvangen, a connecting bus takes you on to Voss, where you can pick up the train for Bergen or Oslo. The tourist office sells all ferry tickets, plus the Flåm–Voss ferry-bus combination.

From May to September, **Norled** (p848) also runs a direct ferry to Bergen (Nkr795, 5½ hours).

(there's a photo stop at awesome Kjosfossen). The railway runs year-round, with up to 10 departures daily in summer, dropping to four in winter.

🛌 Sleeping

★Flåm Camping & Hostel
HOSTEL, CAMPGROUND **€**

(☑94032681; www.flaam-camping.no; Nedre Brekkevegen 12; 1-/2-person tent Nkr120/205, en suite dm/s/tw/q Nkr335/550/920/1315, with shared bathroom dm/s/tw/q Nkr260/450/720/995; ☺Mar-Nov; 🛜) It's part of the HI network, but this wood-clad hostel and campsite is still family-run and has a good dose of Norwegian charm. There's a comprehensive choice of rooms, from bunk-bed dorms to singles, twins, triples and quads, all with a cosy feel, colourful fabrics, stripped wood floors and views over green countryside. It's handy for the railway, too.

🍷 Drinking

Ægir Bryggeri
BREWERY

(☑57 63 20 50; www.flamsbrygga.no/aegir-bryggeripub/; Flåmsbrygga; ☺noon-10pm May–mid-Sep, 6-10pm mid-Sep–Apr) Looking for all the world like a stave church, Ægir Brewery, all appealing woodwork and flagstones, offers six different kinds of draught beer, all brewed on the spot. It also does a tasty, creative take on Norwegian comfort food as well as burgers and pizzas (Nkr160 to Nkr210).

ℹ Information

Tourist Office (☑57 63 33 13; www.visitflam. com; Stasjonsvegen; ☺8.30am-8pm Jun-Aug, 8.30am-4pm May & Sep) Inside the Flåm train station.

Geirangerfjorden

Scattered cliffside farms, most long abandoned, still cling to the towering, near-sheer walls of twisting, 20km-long emerald-green Geirangerfjord, a Unesco World Heritage site. Waterfalls – the Seven Sisters, the Suitor, the Bridal Veil and more – sluice and tumble. The one-hour scenic ferry trip along its length between Geiranger and Hellesylt is as much mini-cruise as means of transport – take it even if you've no particular reason to get to the other end.

Sights & Activities

★Geiranger Fjordservice
BOATING

(☑70 26 30 07; www.geirangerfjord.no; Homlong; tours adult/child Nkr110/45) This operation offers one and 1½-hour sightseeing **boat tours** (1½-hour adult/child Nkr 250/165, sailing four times daily April to mid-Oct). Its kiosk is within the Geiranger tourist office. From mid-June to August, it also operates a smaller, 15-seater RIB boat (Nkr695/395) that scuds deeper and faster into the fjord. They also offer kayaking tours (from adult/child Nkr470/420) from their base at Homlong, 2km from Geiranger. If you don't have a car, you can arrange a minibus or bike rental to get there, otherwise it's a 30-minute walk.

Flydalsjuvet
VIEWPOINT

Somewhere you've seen that classic photo, beloved of brochures, of the overhanging rock Flydalsjuvet, usually with a figure gazing down at a cruise ship in Geirangerfjord. The car park, signposted Flydalsjuvet, about 5km uphill from Geiranger on the Stryn road, offers a great view of the fjord and the green river valley, but doesn't provide the postcard view down to the last detail.

🛌 Sleeping & Eating

★Westerås Gard
CABIN **€€**

(☑93 26 44 97; www.geiranger.no/westeras; 2-bed cabins Nkr950, apt Nkr1150; ☺May-Sep) This beautiful old working farm, 4km along the Rv63 towards Grotli, sits at the end of a narrow road dizzingly high above the bustle. Stay in one of the two farmhouse apartments, or there's five pine-clad cabins. The barn, dating to 1603, is home to a restaurant, where Arnfinn and Iris serve dishes made with their own produce.

Brasserie Posten
BRASSERIE **€€**

(☑70 26 13 06; www.brasserieposten.no; lunch Nkr99-135, dinner Nkr165-249; ☺noon-11pm

Apr-Sep, shorter hours rest of year) 🍴 A simple menu of salads, burgers, steaks, fish and pizza is elevated above the norm by a passionate local chef who sources his Heelsylt, organic dairy from Røros and makes the most of fresh herbs and vegetables. The modern Scando interior is bright and atmospheric, but the fjord-side terrace wins.

ℹ Information

Tourist Office (☎70 26 30 99; www.geiranger. no; ⊙9am-6pm mid-May–mid-Sep) Located right beside Geiranger's pier.

ℹ Getting There & Away

The car ferry between Geiranger and Hellysylt is a stunner. There are four to eight sailings a day between May and early October; the trip takes about 90 minutes. Standard fares are adult/child Nkr250/125 one-way, or Nkr 340/170 return. With a car, the fare is Nkr755 for one passenger, or Nkr990 with up to five people.

NORTHERN NORWAY

With vibrant cities and some wondrous natural terrain, you'll be mighty pleased with yourself for undertaking an exploration of this huge territory that spans the Arctic Circle. An alternative to land travel is the *Hurtigruten* coastal ferry, which pulls into every sizeable port, passing some of the best coastal scenery in Scandinavia.

Trondheim

POP 184,960

With its colourful warehouses, waterways and wooded hills, Trondheim is without doubt one of Norway's most photogenic towns, and served as Norway's capital from 1030 to 1217. These days, Norway's third largest city is a pleasure to explore, with wide boulevards and a partly pedestrianised heart, as well as some great cafes, restaurants and museums to visit – plus Europe's northernmost Gothic cathedral.

⊙ Sights

★**Nidaros Domkirke**   CATHEDRAL
(www.nidarosdomen.no; Kongsgårdsgata; adult/child/family Nkr90/40/220, tower Nkr40, combination ticket with Archbishop's Palace & crown jewels Nkr180/90/440; ⊙9am-6pm Mon-Fri, to 2pm Sat, to 5pm Sun mid-Jun–mid-Aug, shorter hours rest of year) Nidaros Cathedral is Scandinavia's largest medieval building, and the northernmost

Gothic structure in Europe. Outside, the ornately embellished, altar-like west wall has top-to-bottom statues of biblical characters and Norwegian bishops and kings, sculpted in the early 20th century. Several are copies of medieval originals, nowadays housed in the museum. Note the glowing, vibrant colours of the modern stained-glass in the rose window at the west end, a striking contrast to the interior gloom.

Sverresborg Trøndelag Folkemuseum   MUSEUM, ARCHITECTURE
(☎73 89 01 00; www.sverresborg.no; Sverresborg Allé 13; adult/5-15yr/child incl guided tour Nkr150/110/free mid-Jun–Aug, Nkr110/90/free Sep–mid-Jun; ⊙10am-5pm daily Jun-Aug, 10am-3pm Tue-Fri, noon-4pm Sat & Sun Sep-May; 🅿18, 🚌8) Three kilometres west of the centre, this folk museum is one of the best of its kind in Norway. The indoor exhibition, Livsbilder (Images of Life), displays artefacts in use over the last 150 years – from clothing to school supplies to bicycles. The rest of the museum is open-air, comprising over 60 period buildings, adjoining the ruins of King Sverre's castle and giving fine views of the city.

🏃 Activities

Trondheim Kajakk   KAYAKING
(☎48 33 83 18; www.trondheimkajakk.no; 2hr tour incl rental Nkr400; 🚌3, 🚌4, 🚌9, 🚌46) A fine way to get an alternative perspective on Trondheim, these kayak tours paddle from where the Nidelven River meets the fjord and then right through the old town. Prices vary with the number of people. Most trips depart from the Tempe football field, on Bostadvegen, about 4km south of the train station. Ask the bus driver to let you off at Valøyvegen. From here it's a two minute walk to the football field.

🛏 Sleeping

Pensjonat Jarlen   GUESTHOUSE €
(☎73 51 32 18; www.jarlen.no; Kongens gate 40; s/d Nkr540/690; 🛜) Price, convenience and value for money are a winning combination here. After a recent overhaul, the rooms at this central spot have a contemporary look and are outstanding value, although some bathrooms could do with a spruce-up. Some rooms have polished floorboards, others carpet, and most have a hot plate and fridge thrown in.

P-Hotel   HOTEL €€
(☎73 80 23 50; www.p-hotels.no; Nordre gate 24; s/d from Nkr595/795; @🛜) This efficient hotel

NORWAY TRONDHEIM

is a short walk from the train station and the main shopping street. It's part of the Norwegian P-Hotels chain, so it's short on imagination – but rooms are comfortable and simply appointed. Upper floors are preferable to avoid noise from the restaurant underneath. Breakfast-in-a-bag (a bottle of juice and a sandwich) is delivered to your door.

Scandic Bakklandet   HOTEL €€€

(✆72 90 20 00; Nedre Bakklandet 60; r from Nkr1249, ste from Nkr1749; P ☎) At the northern end of Bakklandet, this upmarket choice has plenty in its favour: a great waterside location overlooking the river, an excellent Norwegian restaurant and a very decent bar. The rooms aren't terribly exciting – expect generic furniture and neutral colour schemes, partnered with occasionally adventurous wallpaper. River-view rooms are the best here.

🍴 Eating

Fairytale Cupcakes   NORWEGIAN, INTERNATIONAL €

(✆40 05 61 08; www.fairytalecupcakes.no; Thomas Angells gate 10b; 1 or 2 smørbrød Nkr119/179, cupcakes Nkr45-55; ⊙10am-6pm Mon-Sat) While the cupcakes are a major draw here – light, impeccably frosted and frankly irresistible – it's the fantastic lunchtime *smørbrød* (open sandwiches) that really sell this cafe, with tempting options like smoked trout with poached egg and hollandaise, or chicken with chipotle aioli. It's a lovely space too, dressed in slinky greys and pinks, with oversized lightbulbs dangling overhead.

Bror   DINER €

(✆45 83 15 26; www.brorbar.no; Olav Tryggvasons gate 29; burgers Nkr98-119, tacos Nkr139-149; ⊙11am-12.30am Mon-Thu, 11am-2.30 Fri & Sat, noon-2.30am Sun) There are two choices at this trendy brewpub – burgers or tacos – but the variety of flavours is impressive, taking in everything from chicken with mango chutney and smoked-paprika mayo,

to smoked-cod tacos with radish, lemon and cayenne-spiced nuts. You get a digi-beeper that tells you when your order's ready to be collected from the hatch.

⭐**Baklandet Skydsstasjon**   NORWEGIAN €€

(✆73 92 10 44; www.skydsstation.no; Øvre Bakklandet 33; mains Nkr158-275; ⊙11am-1am Mon-Fri, noon-1am Sat & Sun) If you're still searching for that quintessentially Norwegian meal out, then you won't get much more traditional than this. Originally an 18th-century coaching inn, it's now everyone's favourite homely hang-out in Trondheim, with rambling rooms rammed with old furniture and clad in flock wallpaper. The menu is stuffed with comforting classics like fish soup, reindeer soup, baked salmon and liver paste.

⭐**Folk & Fe**   NORWEGIAN €€€

(✆97 51 81 80; www.folkogfe-bistro.no; Øvre Bakklandet 66; 3-/5-course menu Nkr525/815; ⊙noon-4pm & 5-10pm Tue-Sun) Rustic-chic is the modus operandi at the Folk and Fairy. Lauded by the *White Guide* (Scandinavia's equivalent of the *Michelin Guide*), it's vintage New Nordic, with a taste for minimalist presentation and seasonal dishes maxing out on local ingredients. The menu changes constantly, but expect smoked fish, reindeer carpaccio, farm cheeses and foraged berries, served on wooden platters.

❶ Information

Tourist Office (✆73 80 76 60; www.visittrondheim.no; Nordre gate 11; ⊙9am-6pm daily mid-Jun–mid-Aug, 9am-6pm Mon-Sat rest of year) In the heart of the city, with stacks of information and an accommodation booking service. It's on the 1st floor.

❶ Getting There & Away

BOAT

Trondheim is a major stop on the *Hurtigruten* coastal ferry route.

BUS

The **intercity bus terminal** (Fosenkaia) (Rutebilstasjon) adjoins Trondheim Sentralstasjon (train station, also known as Trondheim S).

Nor-Way Bussekspress (p844) services run to/from destinations including:

Bergen (Nkr876, 14½ hours) One overnight bus.

Oslo (Nkr560, 8¾ hours) One daily bus.

TRAIN

There are two to four trains daily to/from Oslo (Nkr937, 6½ hours). Two trains head north to Bodø (Nkr1088, 9¾ hours).

Lofoten Islands

You'll never forget approaching Lofoten by ferry. The islands spread their tall, craggy physique against the sky like some spiky sea dragon, and you wonder how humans eked a living in such inhospitable surroundings.

The four main islands are all linked by bridges or tunnels, with buses running the entire length of the Lofoten road (E10) from Fiskebøl in the north to Å at the road's end in the southwest. The official website (www.lofoten.info) is rich in information on the whole archipelago.

Sights & Activities

The islands' principal settlement is Svolvær, and is a good spot to base your explorations, with steep mountains rising sharply in the background and a busy harbour. Also worth seeking out is the fishing village of Henningsvær, and tiny Å, on the western tip of Lofoten, lined with red-painted *rorbuer* (fishermen's huts) jutting out into the sea.

★ Lofotr Viking Museum   MUSEUM
(☑76 15 40 00; www.lofotr.no; adult/child incl guided tour mid-Jun–mid-Aug Nkr200/150, rest of year Nkr140/100; ⊙10am-7pm Jun–mid-Aug, shorter hours rest of year) In 1981 at Borg, near the centre of Vestvågøy, a farmer's plough hit the ruins of the 83m-long dwelling of a powerful Viking chieftain, the largest building of its era ever discovered in Scandinavia. The resulting Lofotr Viking Museum, 14km north of Leknes, offers a glimpse of life in Viking times. You can walk 1.5km of trails over open hilltops from the replica of the chieftain's longhouse (the main building, shaped like an upside-down boat) to the Viking-ship replica on the water.

★ Svolværgeita   HIKING, CLIMBING
You'll see it on postcards all over Lofoten – some daring soul leaping between two fingers of rock high above Svolvær. To hike up to a point just behind the two pinnacles (355m), walk northeast along the E10 towards Narvik, pass the marina, and then turn left on Nyveien, and right on Blatind veg. The steep climb begins just behind the children's playground. The climb takes around 30 minutes, or onehour if you continue up to the summit of Floya. To actually climb Svolværgeita and take the leap, you'll need to go with a climbing guide – ask the tourist office for recommendations or try Northern Alpine Guides (☑94 24 91 10; www.alpineguides.no; Havnegata 3).

Sleeping & Eating

★ Svinøya Rorbuer   CABIN €€€
(☑76 06 99 30; www.svinoya.no; Gunnar Bergs vei 2; cabins & ste Nkr1600-3500) Across a bridge on the islet of Svinøya, site of Svolvær's first settlement, are several cabins, some historic, most contemporary, all cosy and comfortable. Reception is a veritable museum, a restored and restocked *krambua* (general store), constructed in 1828, which was Svolvær's first shop. They have properties all over the area and some of the best *rorbuer* in Lofoten.

★ Henningsvær Bryggehotel   HOTEL €€€
(☑76 07 47 19; www.henningsvaer.no; Hjellskjæret; d from Nkr1395-1795; 🐾) In a beautiful wood-clad building by the harbour, this heritage hotel is hands down the best place to stay in Henningsvær. The rooms are decked out in cool greys and creams; most have watery views, and some have fun loft-space beds for the kids. Its restaurant, the Bluefish, is excellent – the menu prides itself on serving fish species 'you've probably never heard of'.

★ Fiskekrogen   SEAFOOD €€€
(☑76 07 46 52; www.fiskekrogen.no; Dreyersgate 29; mains Nkr195-345, lunch dishes Nkr145-275; ⊙1-4pm & 6-11pm Sun, 6-11pm Mon-Sat Jun-Aug, shorter hours rest of year) At the end of a slipway overlooking the harbour, this dockside restaurant – a favourite of the Norwegian royal family – is Henningsvær's other culinary claim to fame. Try, in particular, the outstanding fish soup (Nkr195), but there's everything else on the menu from fish and chips, to fried cod tongues. They also serve smoked whale.

ℹ Information

Tourist Office (☑76 07 05 75; www.lofoten.info; Torget; ⊙9am-9pm Mon-Fri, 9am-7pm Sat & Sun mid-Jun–mid-Aug, shorter hours rest of year) The largest tourist office in the islands provides a wealth of information on the entire archipelago, and organises accommodation bookings.

ℹ Getting There & Away

AIR

Lofoten's main airports are in Svolvær and Leknes. **Norwegian** (www.norwegian.no) and **SAS** (www.flysas.com) offer a good range of flights from major Norwegian airports, nearly all connecting through the small town of Bodø, from where **Widerøe** (www.wideroe.no) offers connecting flights to the islands.

From April 2017, Widerøe is also operating direct flights at least twice a week from Oslo to Svolvær and Leknes.

BOAT

The cheapest way to get to Lofoten is usually via ferry, although it can be a notoriously rough crossing, especially outside summer. There are various routes, the most useful of which are from:

Bodø Foot-passenger express ferry to Svolvær (Nkr443, three to 3½ hours), and a car ferry to Moskenes (one car and passenger Nkr705 to Nkr1001, passenger-only Nkr196, 3 to 3½ hours) via Røst and Værøy.

Skutvik Car ferry to Svolvær (car/passenger Nkr355/103, 1¾ hours).

The Lofoten Islands are also a regular stop on the *Hurtigruten* ferry route.

Tromsø

POP 72.681

Sitting 400km north of the Arctic Circle at 69°N, the small town of Tromsø bills itself as Norway's gateway to the Arctic, and there's definitely more than a hint of polar atmosphere around town. These days it's best known as one of the best places in northern Norway to spot the northern lights. It's also a notoriously lively city, with a large university, a lively cultural calendar and an animated nightlife.

⊙ Sights

★ **Polar Museum**   MUSEUM
(Polarmuseet; ☑77 62 33 60; www.polarmuseum.no; Søndre Tollbodgata 11; adult/child Nkr60/30; ⊙9am-6pm mid-Jun–mid-Aug, 11am-5pm rest of year) Fittingly for a town that was the launchpad for many pioneering expeditions to the Pole, this fascinating museum is a rollicking romp through life in the Arctic, taking in everything from the history of trapping to the groundbreaking expeditions of Nansen and Amundsen. There are some fascinating artefacts and black-and-white archive photos; the stuffed remains of various formerly-fuzzy, once-blubbery polar creatures are rather less fun. It's in a harbourside building that served as Tromsø's customs house from 1833 to 1970.

★ **Polaria**   MUSEUM, AQUARIUM
(☑77 75 01 11; www.polaria.no; Hjalmar Johansens gate 12; adult/child Nkr125/60; ⊙10am-7pm mid-May–Aug, to 5pm Sep–mid-May) This Arctic-themed attraction provides a multimedia introduction to northern Norway and Svalbard. Kick things off by watching the two films *In the Land of the Northern Lights* and *Spitsbergen – Arctic Wilderness*, then follow the Arctic walkway past exhibits on shrinking sea ice, the aurora borealis, aquariums of cold-water fish and – the big draw

– some yapping, playful bearded seals (feeding time is at noon year-round, plus either 3pm in summer or 3.30pm in winter).

★ **Fjellheisen**   CABLE CAR
(☑77 63 87 37; www.fjellheisen.no; Solliveien 12; adult/child Nkr170/60; ⊙10am-1am late May–mid-Aug, shorter hours rest of year; ☑26) For a fine view of the city and the midnight sun, take the cable car to the top of Mt Storsteinen (421m). There's a restaurant at the top, from where a network of hiking routes radiates. You can buy a combined bus and cable-car ticket (adult/child Nkr145/65).

Arctic Cathedral   CHURCH
(Ishavskatedralen; ☑47 68 06 68; Hans Nilsens veg 41; adult/child Nkr40/free, organ recitals Nkr70-150; ⊙9am-7pm Mon-Sat, 1-7pm Sun Jun–mid-Aug, 3-6pm mid-Aug–mid-May, opens at 2pm Feb; ☑20, ☑24) The 11 triangles of the Arctic Cathedral (1965), aka Tromsdalen Church, suggest glacial crevasses and auroral curtains. The glowing stained-glass window that occupies the east end depicts Christ descending to earth. The west end is filled by a futuristic organ and icicle-like lamps of Czech crystal. Unfortunately, its position beside one of Tromsø's main thoroughfares somewhat spoils the serenity outside. It's on the southern side of the Bruvegen bridge, about 1km from town.

🏃 Activities

Active Tromsø   ADVENTURE
(☑48 13 71 33; www.activetromso.no) An excellent company offering the full range of summer and winter activities, with dog-sledding expeditions a particular speciality – including overnight husky trips with the chance to spot the aurora en route.

Arctic Guide Service   SCENIC DRIVE
(☑92 20 79 01; www.arcticguideservice.com; Bankgata 1; adult/student/child Nkr 950/800/475) This guide company runs a nightly aurora-hunting trip at 6.15pm between mid-September and March. Minibus trips last six hours and visit several locations around Tromsø, using the latest weather forecasts to maximise your chances of seeing the show. Obviously there's no guarantees, but if there's solar activity and clear skies, there's a chance. The office is underneath the Radisson Blu Hotel.

🛏 Sleeping

Smart Hotel Tromsø   HOTEL **€**
(☑41 53 65 00; www.smarthotel.no; Vestregata 12; d from Nkr695; ☎) The northernmost outpost of this budget mini-chain offers some

of the best rates in town, and it's a fine base – as long as you don't mind the boxy rooms, basic facilities and institutional decor (battleship-grey is the colour of choice, combined with graffiti-style slogans like 'You Are Smart'). It's popular, so book ahead. The buffet breakfast costs Nkr110.

★ **Tromsø Bed & Books**   GUESTHOUSE €€

(☑77 02 98 00; www.bedandbooks.no; Strandvegen 45; s Nkr850, d Nkr950; 🛜) Run by a pair of seasoned globetrotters, this lovely guesthouse has two 'homes' – a Fisherman's and a Writer's – all stuffed with books, retro furniture, old maps and curios, and all thoughtfully designed for budget travellers. The rooms can feel cramped when full, and noisy, but that's part of the budget trade-off. No breakfast, but both houses have shared kitchens.

✗ Eating

★ **Riso**   CAFE €

(☑416 64 516; www.risoe-mk.no; 32 Strandgata; mains Nkr95-149; ⊙7.30am-5pm Mon-Fri, 9am-5pm Sat) You'll find this popular new coffee- and lunch-bar packed throughout most of the day: young trendies come in for their hand-brewed Chemex coffee, while local workers pop in for the daily specials, open-faced sandwiches and delicious cakes. It's small, and the tables are packed in tight, so you might have to queue.

Driv   CAFE €€

(☑77 60 07 76; www.driv.no; Sondre Tollbodgata 3; mains Nkr165-185; ⊙noon-1.30am Mon-Thu, to 3am Fri & Sat, kitchen shuts 9pm) This student-run converted warehouse serves meaty burgers (try its renowned Driv burger) and great salads. It organises musical and cultural events and has a disco every Saturday. In winter you can steep yourself in good company within its open-air hot tub.

★ **Emma's Under**   NORWEGIAN €€

(☑77 63 77 30; www.emmasdrommekjokken. no; Kirkegata; mains Nkr155-365; ⊙11am-10pm Mon-Fri, noon-10pm Sat) Homely and down-to-earth Norwegian cuisine is the dish of the day here. You'll find hearty dishes like fish gratin, king crab and baked clipfish on the lunch menu, served in a cosy space designed to echo a traditional kitchen à la grand-ma. Upstairs is the more formal Emma's Drømekjøkken (mains Nkr175-355, 3-course menu Nkr390; ⊙6pm-midnight Mon-Sat), which shares its menu with Emma's Under after 5.30pm.

🍷 Drinking & Nightlife

Tromsø enjoys a thriving nightlife, with many arguing that it's the best scene in Norway. On Friday and Saturday, most nightspots stay open to 3.30am.

Ølhallen Pub   PUB

(☑77 62 45 80; www.olhallen.no; Storgata 4; ⊙10am-7.30pm Mon-Wed, to 12.30am Thu-Sat) Reputedly the oldest pub in town, and once the hang out for salty fishermen and Arctic sailors, this is now the brewpub for the excellent Mack Brewery. There are 67 ales to try, including around eight on tap – so it might take you a while (and a few livers) to work your way through them all.

Blå Rock Café   BAR

(☑77 61 00 20; Strandgata 14/16; ⊙11.30am-2am) The loudest, most raving place in town has theme evenings, almost 50 brands of beer, occasional live bands and weekend DJs. The music is rock, naturally. Every Monday hour is a happy hour.

ℹ Information

Tourist Office (☑77 61 00 00; www.visittromso.no; Kirkegata 2; ⊙9am-7pm Mon-Fri, 9am-6pm Sat, 10am-6pm Sun Jan-Mar & mid-May–Aug, shorter hours rest of year; 🛜) Tromsø's busy, efficient tourist office is in a detached building beside the harbour, and provides booking services and local info. Wi-fi is free.

ℹ Getting There & Away

AIR

Tromsø Airport (☑77 64 84 00; www.avinor. no/flyplass/tromso) is the main airport for the far north.

Norwegian (www.norwegian.no) Flies to/from most major cities in Norway, plus UK destinations including London Gatwick, Edinburgh and Dublin.

Wideroe (www.wideroe.no) Several flights a day to Svolvær and Leknes in the Lofoten Islands (from around NKr1638 one-way). All flights are via Bodø.

BOAT

Tromsø is a major stop on the *Hurtigruten* coastal ferry route.

BUS

The main **bus terminal** (Samuel Arnesens gate) (sometimes called Prostneset) is on Kaigata, beside the **Hurtigruten quay** (Samuel Arnesens gate). There are up to three daily express buses to/from Narvik (Nkr385, 4¼ hours) and one to/from Bodø (Nkr500, 6½ hours).

SURVIVAL GUIDE

ℹ️ Directory A–Z

ACCOMMODATION

Norway offers a wide range of accommodation, from camping, hostels and pensions to international-standard hotels. You'll pay a lot more for what you get compared with other countries, but standards are high. Most places have wi-fi access. Norway has more than 1000 campsites, mostly open only from mid-May to late August. For a comprehensive list, pick up a copy of the free *Camping* (available at some tourist offices, campsites and from **Norsk Camping** (www. camping.no)..

ACTIVITIES

On the water Every waterside town has a place where you can rent a canoe, kayak or rowing boat. Rafting is common around Sjoa in central Norway. Options range from short, Class II doddles to Class III and IV adventures, and rollicking Class V punishment.

Hiking Norway has some of Europe's best hiking, best done from June to September. Wilderness huts line the northern trails.

Skiing The ski season runs from late November to early May and slightly longer in the north.

Dog-sledding Expeditions can range from two-hour tasters to multiday trips with overnight stays in remote forest huts.

GAY & LESBIAN TRAVELLERS

Norwegians are generally tolerant of alternative lifestyles. Homosexuality has been legal in Norway since 1973. That said, public displays of affection are not common, except perhaps in some areas of Oslo. Oslo has the liveliest gay scene, and it's

SLEEPING PRICE RANGES

The following price ranges relate to a double room with private bathroom in high season and, unless stated otherwise, include breakfast:

€ less than Nkr750

€€ Nkr750 to Nkr1400

€€€ more than Nkr1400

worth stopping by **Use-It** (📞24 14 98 20; www. use-it.no; Møllergata 3; ⊙11am-5pm Mon-Fri, noon-5pm Sat), where you can pick up its *Streetwise* booklet, which has a 'Gay Guide' section.

INTERNET ACCESS

➡ Public libraries usually have at least one free internet terminal; may need to be reserved ahead.

➡ Tourist offices often have an internet terminal that you can use (usually 15 minutes).

➡ Wi-fi is widely available at most hotels, cafes and tourist offices, as well as some restaurants; it's generally (but not always) free.

MONEY

➡ ATMs can be found even in small villages.

➡ Credit cards are widely accepted; Norwegians are dedicated users of plastic even to buy a beer or cup of coffee.

➡ Travellers cheques and cash can be exchanged at banks; in the big cities, independent exchange facilities usually offer better rates.

➡ Service is generally considered to be included in bills, so there's no need to tip at all unless you want to reward exceptional service.

ESSENTIAL FOOD & DRINK

Norwegian food is delicious, but as always in Norway, you'll have to pay dearly to sample it.

Cheeses Norwegian cheeses have come to international attention as a result of the mild but tasty Jarlsberg. Try also the disconcertingly brown Gudbrandsdalsost made from the whey of goat's and/or cow's milk and with a slightly sweet flavour.

Coffee If Norway has a national drink, it's coffee. Most Norwegians drink it black and strong, but foreigners requiring milk and/or sugar are normally indulged.

Elk Known elsewhere in the world as moose, elk (elg) comes in a variety of forms, including as a steak or burger.

Meatballs Traditional Norwegian meatballs served with mushy peas, mashed potatoes and wild-berry jam is a local, home-cooked favourite.

Reindeer Roast reindeer (*reinsdyrstek*) is something every non-vegetarian visitor to Norway should try at least once: best eaten rare to medium-rare.

Salmon The national fish comes two ways: grilled (*laks*) or smoked (*røykelaks*). It's made by marinating salmon in sugar, salt, brandy and dill, and usually served in a creamy sauce.

Wild berries The most popular edible wild berries include strawberries, blackcurrants, red currants, raspberries, blueberries (huckleberries) and the lovely amber-coloured *moltebær* (cloudberries).

OPENING HOURS

These standard hours are for high season (mid-June to mid-September) and tend to decrease outside that time.

Banks 8.15am-3pm Monday to Wednesday and Friday, 8.15am-5pm Thursday.

Central post offices 8am-8pm Monday to Friday, 9am-6pm Saturday; otherwise 9am-5pm Monday to Friday, 10am-2pm Saturday.

Restaurants noon-3pm and 6-11pm.

Shops 10am-5pm Monday to Wednesday and Friday, 10am-7pm Thursday, 10am-2pm Saturday.

Supermarkets 9am-9pm Monday to Friday, 9am-6pm Saturday.

TELEPHONE

➡ You can buy a prepaid SIM card easily. You should pick up a card for as little as Nkr200, including some call credit. Top the credit up at the same outlets, online or at ATMs.

➡ You can buy cut-rate phone cards that lower the cost of making international calls.

Getting There & Away

Norway is well linked to other European countries by air. There are regular bus and rail services from neighbouring Sweden and Finland (from where there are connections further afield to Europe), with less regular (and more complicated) services to/from Russia. Regular car and passenger ferries also connect southern Norwegian ports with Denmark, Sweden and Germany.

AIR

Norwegian (www.norwegian.com) Low-cost airline with domestic and international network.

SAS (www.sas.no) The largest international network of Norway's carriers.

Widerøe (www.wideroe.no) Predominantly operates between smaller towns and cities, provides flights to the Lofoten Islands and the far north.

SEA

Ferry connections are possible between Norway and Denmark, Germany, Iceland, the Faroe Islands and Sweden.

Getting Around

Norway has an extremely efficient public transport system and its trains, buses and ferries

COUNTRY FACTS

Area 386,224 sq km

Capital Oslo

Country Code 47

Currency Krone

Emergency 112

Language Norwegian

Population 5.15 million

Time One hour ahead of UTC/GMT (two hours ahead late March to late October)

Visas Schengen visa rules apply

are often timed to link with each other, although services vary with the season. Rail lines reach as far north as Bodø (you can also reach Narvik by rail from Sweden); further north you're limited to buses and ferries. A fine alternative to land travel is the *Hurtigruten* coastal ferry, which calls in at every sizable port between Bergen and Kirkenes.

AIR

Norway has an extensive domestic air network and the major Norwegian domestic routes are quite competitive, meaning that it is possible to travel for little more than the equivalent train fare.

BOAT

Norway's excellent system of ferries connects otherwise inaccessible, isolated communities with an extensive network of car ferries criss-crossing the fjords; express boats link the country's offshore islands to the mainland. Most ferries accommodate motor vehicles.

BUS

Buses on Norway's extensive long-distance bus network are comfortable and efficient.

CAR & MOTORCYCLE

Main highways, such as the E16 from Oslo to Bergen and the entire E6 from Oslo to Kirkenes, are open year-round; smaller, often more scenic mountain roads generally only open from June to September, snow conditions permitting.

Both fuel and car rental is expensive; all the major international car-rental companies have offices throughout Norway.

Older roads and mountain routes are likely to be narrow, with multiple hairpin bends and very steep gradients. Watch for wandering reindeer in the far north.

TRAIN

Norwegian State Railways (Norges Statsbaner, NSB; press 9 for English 81 50 08 88; www.nsb.no) operates a limited system of lines connecting Oslo with Stavanger, Bergen, Åndalsnes, Trondheim, Fauske and Bodø.

EATING PRICE RANGES

The following prices refer to a standard main course.

€ less than Nkr130

€€ Nkr130 to Nkr200

€€€ more than Nkr200

Poland

Best Places to Eat

➡ Warszawa Wschodnia (p864)

➡ Glonojad (p869)

➡ Kardamon (p872)

➡ Drukarnia (p879)

➡ Tawerna Mestwin (p882)

Best Places to Stay

➡ Hotel Rialto (p863)

➡ Mundo Hostel (p868)

➡ Hotel Piast (p876)

➡ Hotel Stare Miasto (p878)

➡ Hotel Petite Fleur (p884)

Why Go?

If they were handing out prizes for 'most eventful history', Poland would score a gold medal. The nation has spent centuries at the pointy end of history, grappling with war and invasion. Nothing, however, has succeeded in suppressing Poles' strong sense of nationhood and cultural identity. As a result, bustling centres like Warsaw and Kraków exude a sophisticated energy that's a heady mix of old and new.

Away from the cities, Poland is surprisingly diverse, from its northern beaches to a long chain of mountains on its southern border. In between, towns and cities are dotted with ruined castles, picturesque market squares and historic churches.

Although prices have steadily risen in the postcommunist era, Poland is still good value. As the Poles continue to reconcile their distinctive national identity with their location at the heart of Europe, it's a fascinating time to pay a visit.

When to Go
Warsaw

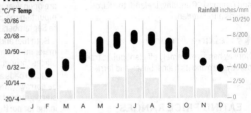

May–Jun Stately Kraków returns to life after a long winter.

Jul–Aug A brief but hot summer is good for swimming in the Baltic Sea or hiking in the mountains.

Sep–Oct Warm and sunny enough for an active city break to Warsaw.

Poland Highlights

1 Kraków (p865)
Experiencing the beauty and history of the Old Town.

2 Wrocław (p875)
Enjoying the city's student-fuelled party vibe.

3 Auschwitz-Birkenau
(p871) Remembering the victims of the Nazi German genocide.

4 European Solidarity Centre (p882) Reliving Poland's inspirational anticommunist struggle in Gdańsk.

5 Zakopane (p873)
Skiing or hiking the Tatra mountains from this alpine resort.

6 Museum of the History of Polish Jews (p861)
Being dazzled by the museum in Warsaw.

WARSAW

POP 1.74 MILLION

Once you've travelled around Poland, you realise this: Warsaw is different. Rather than being centred on an old market square, the capital is spread across a broad area with diverse architecture: restored Gothic, communist concrete, modern glass and steel.

This jumble is a sign of the city's tumultuous past. Warsaw has suffered the worst history could throw at it, including virtual destruction at the end of World War II – and survived. As a result, it's a fascinating collection of neighbourhoods, landmarks and fine museums charting its culture and history.

It's not all about the past, however, as Warsaw's restaurant and entertainment scene is the best in Poland. This gritty city knows how to have fun.

⊙ Sights

⊙ Old Town

Warsaw's Old Town looks old but dates from the post-WWII era. It was rebuilt from the ground up after being reduced to rubble during the conflict. The reconstruction, which took place between 1949 and 1963, aimed at restoring the appearance of the city from the 17th and 18th centuries. Its centre is the rebuilt **Old Town Square** (Rynek Starego Miasta).

★**Royal Castle**   CASTLE
(Zamek Królewski; ☑ 22 3555 338; www.zamek-krolewski.pl; Plac Zamkowy 4; adult/concession 30/20zł; ⊙10am-6pm Mon-Sat, 11am-6pm Sun) This massive brick edifice, a copy of the original blown up by the Germans in WWII, began life as a wooden stronghold of the dukes of Mazovia in the 14th century. Its heyday came in the mid-17th century, when it became one of Europe's most splendid royal residences. It then served the Russian tsars and, in 1918, after Poland regained independence, became the residence of the president. Today it is filled with period furniture and works of art.

Highlights of the castle tour include the Great Apartment and its magnificent Great Assembly Hall, which has been restored to its 18th-century decor of dazzling gilded stucco and golden columns. The enormous ceiling painting, *The Disentanglement of Chaos,* is a postwar re-creation of a work by Marcello Bacciarelli showing King Stanisław bringing order to the world. The king's face also appears in a marble medallion above the main door, flanked by the allegorical figures of Peace and Justice.

The neighbouring National Hall was conceived by the king as a national pantheon; the six huge canvases (surviving originals) depict pivotal scenes from Polish history. A door leads off the hall into the smaller Marble Room, decorated in 16th-century style with coloured marble and trompe l'oeil paintwork. The room houses 22 portraits of Polish kings, from Bolesław Chrobry to a large gilt-framed image of Stanisław August Poniatowski himself.

Further on from the National Hall is the lavishly decorated Throne Room. Connected by a short corridor is the King's Apartment, the highlight of which is the Canaletto Room at the far end. An impressive array of 23 paintings by Bernardo Bellotto (1721–80), better known in Poland as Canaletto, captures Warsaw's mid-18th-century heyday in great detail. The works were of immense help in reconstructing the city's historic facades.

Barbican   FORTRESS
(Barbakan; ul Nowomiejska) Heading north out of the Old Town along ul Nowomiejska you'll soon see the redbrick Barbican, a semicircular defensive tower topped with a decorative Renaissance parapet. It was partially dismantled in the 19th century, but reconstructed after WWII, and is now a popular spot for buskers and art sellers.

⊙ Royal Way

This 4km historic route connects the Old Town with the modern city centre, running south from about Plac Zamkowy along elegant ul Krakowskie Przedmieście and ul Nowy Świat all the way to busy Al Jerozolimskie.

Church of the Holy Cross   CHURCH
(Kościół św Krzyża; ☑ 22 826 8910; ul Krakowskie Przedmieście 3; ⊙10am-4pm) FREE Of Warsaw's many impressive churches, this is the one most visitors want to visit. Not so much to admire the fine Baroque altarpieces that miraculously survived the Warsaw

---

ITINERARIES

One Week

Spend a day exploring **Warsaw**, with a stroll around the Old Town and a stop at the Museum of the History of Polish Jews. Next day, head to historic **Kraków** for three days, visiting the beautiful Old Town, Wawel Castle and former Jewish district of Kazimierz. Take a day trip to **Auschwitz-Birkenau**, the former Nazi German extermination camp. Afterward, head to **Zakopane** for a day in the mountains.

Two Weeks

Follow the above itinerary, then travel to **Wrocław** for two days, taking in its graceful town square. Head north to Gothic **Toruń** for a day, then onward to **Gdańsk** for two days, exploring the museums and bars of the main town and visiting the magnificent castle at **Malbork**.

Rising reprisals, but to glimpse a small urn by the second pillar on the left side of the nave. This urn, adorned with an epitaph to Frédéric Chopin, contains what remains of the composer's heart. It was brought here from Paris after the great man's death.

★**Chopin Museum**   MUSEUM
(✆22 441 6251; www.chopin.museum; ul Okólnik 1; adult/concession 22/13zł, Sun free; ⊙11am-8pm Tue-Sun) High-tech, multimedia museum within the Baroque Ostrogski Palace, showcasing the work of the country's most famous composer. You're encouraged to take your time through four floors of displays, including stopping by the listening booths in the basement where you can browse Chopin's oeuvre to your heart's content. Limited visitation is allowed each hour; your best bet is to book your visit in advance by phone or email.

⊙ **City Centre & Beyond**

★**Palace of Culture
& Science**   HISTORIC BUILDING
(Pałac Kultury i Nauki; www.pkin.pl; Plac Defilad 1; observation terrace adult/concession 20/15zł; ⊙9am-8.30pm) Love it or hate it, every visitor to Warsaw should visit the iconic, socialist realist PKiN (as its full Polish name is abbreviated). This 'gift of friendship' from the Soviet Union was built in the early 1950s, and at 231m high remains the tallest building in Poland. It's home to a huge congress hall, theatres, a multiscreen cinema and museums. Take the high-speed lift to the 30th-floor (115m) observation terrace to take it all in.

The building has never sat well with the locals, who have branded it with one uncomplimentary moniker after another; the 'Elephant in Lacy Underwear', a reference both to the building's size and the fussy sculptures that frill the parapets, is a particular favourite. However, though there are occasional calls for it to be demolished, the Palace is gradually becoming accepted (even embraced) as a city icon.

★**Warsaw Rising Museum**   MUSEUM
(Muzeum Powstania Warszawskiego; www.1944. pl; ul Grzybowska 79; adult/concession 20/16zł, Sun free; ⊙8am-6pm Mon, Wed & Fri, to 8pm Thu, 10am-6pm Sat & Sun; Ⓜ Rondo Daszyńskiego, 🚌9, 22 or 24 along al Jerozolimskie) One of Warsaw's best, this museum traces the history of the city's heroic but doomed uprising against the German occupation in 1944 via three levels of interactive displays, photographs,

film archives and personal accounts. The volume of material is overwhelming, but the museum does an excellent job of instilling in visitors a sense of the desperation residents felt in deciding to oppose the occupation by force, and of illustrating the dark consequences, including the Germans' destruction of the city in the aftermath.

The ground floor begins with the division of Poland between Nazi Germany and the Soviet Union in 1939 and moves through the major events of WWII. A lift then takes you to the 2nd floor and the start of the uprising in 1944. The largest exhibit, a Liberator bomber similar to the planes that were used to drop supplies for insurgents, fills much of the 1st floor.

★**Łazienki Park**   GARDENS
(Park Łazienkowski; www.lazienki-krolewskie.pl; ul Agrykola 1; ⊙dawn-dusk) Pronounced wah-zhen-kee, this park is a beautiful place of manicured greens and wild patches. Its popularity extends to families, peacocks and fans of classical music, who come for the alfresco Chopin concerts on Sunday afternoons at noon and 4pm from mid-May through September. Once a hunting ground attached to Ujazdów Castle, Łazienki was acquired by King Stanisław August Poniatowski in 1764 and transformed into a splendid park complete with palace, amphitheatre, and various follies and other buildings.

⊙ **Former Jewish District**

The suburbs northwest of the Palace of Culture & Science were once predominantly inhabited by Warsaw's Jewish community.

★**Museum of the
History of Polish Jews**   MUSEUM
(Polin; ✆22 471 0301; www.polin.pl; ul Anielewicza 6; adult/concession 25/15zł, incl temporary exhibits 30/20zł; ⊙10am-6pm Mon, Wed-Fri & Sun, to 8pm Sat; 🚌4, 15, 18 or 35 along ul Marszałkowska) This exceptional museum's permanent exhibition opened in late 2014. Impressive multimedia exhibits document 1000 years of Jewish history in Poland, from accounts of the earliest Jewish traders in the region through waves of mass migration, progress and pogroms, all the way to WWII and the destruction of Europe's largest Jewish community. It's worth booking online first, and you can hire an audioguide (10zł) to get the most out of the many rooms of displays, interactive maps, photos and videos.

Central Warsaw

0 ____ 500 m
0 ____ 0.25 miles

Museum of the History of Polish Jews (500m); Hotel Maria (1.4km)

Świętojerska

Polyester (250m)

2 Old Town Square

Długa

Miodowa

Warsaw Tourist Office

Świętojańska

Jezuicka

Bugaj

8

Podwale

4 **Royal Castle**

Vistula

Generała Andersa

Długa

Al Solidarności

Senatorska

Kozia

Bednarska

Furmańska

Dobra

M Ratusz-Arsenał

Senatorska

Wierzbowa

Trębacka

Moliera

Krakowskie Przedmieście

Browarna

Elektoralna

12

Saxon Gardens

Plac Piłsudskiego

Plac Małachowskiego

Traugutta

Oboźna

Seweryńów

Dynasy

6

Marszałkowska

Królewska

Kredytowa

Plac Dąbrowskiego

13

Czackiego

Warsaw Rising Museum (1.4km)

Grzybowska

Jasna

15

Nowy Świat - Uniwersytet **M**

Chopin Museum

1

Plac Próźna Grzybowski

Zielna

Jasna

9

Świętokrzyska

Mazowiecka

Świętokrzyska

Tamka

Ordynacka

Okólnik

Kopernika

Twarda

Świętokrzyska **M**

Moniuszki

14

Sienkiewicza

Warecka

Plac Powstańców Warszawy

Nowy Świat

11

Foksal

Szpitalna

Górskiego

Plac Defilad

Złota

Zgoda

Chmielna

7

Smolna

Palace of Culture & Science

Sienna

Emilii Plater

3

M Warsaw Tourist Office

Bracka

10

Centrum **M**

Widok

Al Jerozolimskie

Złota

Warszawa Śródmieście Train Station

Nowogrodzka

P

Książęca

Plac Trzech Krzyży

Warszawa Centralna Train Station

Al Jerozolimskie

Żurawia

Wspólna

Hoża

Warszawa Zachodnia Terminal (2.2km)

Emilii Plater

Wspólna

Poznańska

Marszałkowska

Krucza

Hoża

Wilcza

Mokotowska

Al Ujazdowskie

Wiejska

Niepodległości

Hoża

Hotel Riałto (100m)

Charlotte Chleb i Wino (500m)

Łazienki Park (1km)

POLAND **WARSAW**

Central Warsaw

◉ Praga

★ Neon Museum · MUSEUM

(Muzeum Neonów; ☑ 665 711635; www.neon-muzeum.org; ul Mińska 25; adult/concession 10/8zł; ⊙ 12-5pm Wed-Sun; 🚊 22 from al Jerozolimskie) Situated within the cool Soho Factory complex of old industrial buildings housing designers and artists, this museum is devoted to the preservation of the iconic neon signs of the communist era. The collection is arrayed within a historic factory, with many large pieces fully lit. Other exhibits are dotted around the complex and are illuminated after dark. It's well worth the trek across the river. Alight the tram at the Bliska stop.

🛏 Sleeping

Apartments Apart (☑ 22 351 2250; www.apartmentsapart.com; ul Nowy Świat 29/3; apt from 200zł; 🛜) offers short-term apartment rentals in the Old Town and city centre.

★ Oki Doki Hostel · HOSTEL €

(☑ 22 828 0122; www.okidoki.pl; Plac Dąbrowskiego 3; dm 29-90zł, s/d from 100/128zł; 🛜) Arguably Warsaw's most popular hostel, and certainly one of the best. Each of its bright, large rooms is individually named and dec-

orated. Accommodation is in three- to eight-bed dorms, with a special three-bed dorm for women only. The owners are well travelled and know the needs of backpackers, providing a kitchen and a laundry service. Breakfast available (15zł).

★ Castle Inn · HOTEL €€

(☑ 22 425 0100; www.castleinn.pl; ul Świętojańska 2; s/d from 280/300zł; 🅿️❄🛜) Nicely decorated 'art hotel', housed in a 17th-century town house. All rooms overlook either Castle Sq or St John's Cathedral, and come in a range of playful styles. Our favourite would be No 121, 'Viktor', named for a reclusive street artist, complete with tasteful graffiti and a gorgeous castle view. Breakfast costs an extra 35zł.

Hotel Maria · HOTEL €€

(☑ 22 838 4062; www.hotelmaria.pl; al Jana Pawła II 71; s/d 323/384zł; 🅿️❄🛜) Rambling old house masquerading as a hotel set on three floors (no lifts, just steep wooden stairs), with friendly staff, a delightful restaurant and breakfast nook, and spacious rooms. The location is outside the centre, but convenient to the Jewish sights and just a few tram stops away from the Old Town.

Rooms at the back are slightly quieter than those at the front, along busy al Jana Pawła II. Weekend bookings slice about 100zł off the price.

★ Hotel Rialto · HOTEL €€

(☑ 22 584 8700; www.rialto.pl; ul Wilcza 73; s/d from 279/319zł; 🅿️❄🛜) This converted town house is a monument to early 20th-century design. Each room is individually decorated in Art Nouveau or Art Deco style, with antique and reproduction furniture, period fittings, and tiled or marbled baths. There are plenty of modern touches where it counts, such as power showers, and a sauna and steam room. Cheaper rates click into place at weekends.

🍴 Eating

★ Charlotte Chleb i Wino · FRENCH €

(www.bistrocharlotte.pl; al Wyzwolenia 18; mains 8-18zł; ⊙ 7am-midnight Mon-Thu, to 1am Fri, 9am-1am Sat, 9am-10pm Sun; 🛜) Dazzling French bakery and bistro facing Plac Zbawiciela. It dishes up tantalising croissants and pastries at the break of dawn, then transitions to big salads and crusty sandwiches through the lunch and dinner hours, and finally to wine on the terrace in the evening. Great value for money.

POLAND WARSAW

★ **Mango** VEGAN €
([☎]535 533 629; www.mangovegan.pl; ul Bracka 20; mains 13-25zł; [⊙]11am-10pm Sun-Thu, to 10.30pm Fri & Sat; [奈][✐]) Mango is a stylish all-vegan eatery with a simple contemporary interior and pleasant outdoor seating. Excellent menu items range from veggie burgers to mango sticky rice. The 'Mango Plate' (Talerz Mango) of hummus, mango, falafel, eggplant, olives, sweet peppers and harissa paste served with pita bread is top value at 22zł.

Socjal MEDITERRANEAN €€
([☎]787 181 051; ul Foksal 18; mains 18-39zł; [⊙]noon-midnight) Hypercool restaurant and bar with pared-back interiors and an open kitchen. The menu is Mediterranean-influenced, with *piadine* (stuffed Italian flatbreads), pasta, and pizzas of a more adventurous stripe (asparagus pizza, anyone?). The outdoor deck is a great people-watching space.

★ **Warszawa Wschodnia** EUROPEAN €€€
([☎]22 870 2918; www.sohofactory.pl; ul Mińska 25; mains 25-80zł; [⊙]24hr; [奈]) Fabulous restaurant within a huge industrial building in the Soho Factory complex, taking its name from a neon sign salvaged from the nearby train station of the same name. Serves a modern interpretation of Polish cuisine, with French influences. Mains are priced between 60zł and 80zł, so you can't beat the 25zł three-course set lunch menu served noon to 4pm Monday to Friday.

🍷 **Drinking & Nightlife**

Good places for pub crawls include along ul Mazowiecka in the centre, in Praga across the Vistula River, and the Powiśle district near the university.

Capitol CLUB
([☎]608 089 504; ul Marszałkowska 115; [⊙]10pm-late Fri & Sat) If scarcity excites you, squeeze through the doors of this oh-so-cool club on the two nights of the week it's open – Friday and Saturday. Low lighting gleams off pillars, retro decor and the shining faces of Warsaw's beautiful people as they gyrate within the dance-floor throng.

Polyester BAR
(ul Freta 49/51; [⊙]noon-midnight; [奈]) Smooth establishment with fashionably retro furnishings and a laid-back vibe – arguably the hippest cocktail bar in the vicinity of the Old Town. Serves excellent cocktails, as well as a range of coffee drinks and light food. Also hosts regular jazz and other live music.

Enklawa CLUB
([☎]22 827 3151; www.enklawa.com; ul Mazowiecka 12; [⊙]10pm-4am Tue-Sat) Blue and purple light illuminates this space with comfy plush seating, mirrored ceilings, two bars and plenty of room to dance. Check out the extensive drinks menu, hit the dance floor or observe the action from a stool on the upper balcony. Wednesday night is 'old school' night, with music from the '70s to the '90s.

☆ **Entertainment**

Filharmonia Narodowa CLASSICAL MUSIC
(National Philharmonic; [☎]22 551 7127; www.filharmonia.pl; ul Jasna 5; [⊙]box office 10am-2pm & 3-7pm Mon-Sat) Home of the world-famous National Philharmonic Orchestra and Choir of Poland, founded in 1901, this venue has a concert hall (enter from ul Sienkiewicza 10) and a chamber-music hall (enter from ul Moniuszki 5), both of which stage regular concerts. The box office entrance is on ul Sienkiewicza.

Tygmont LIVE MUSIC
([☎]22 828 3409; www.tygmont.com.pl; ul Mazowiecka 6/8; [⊙]9pm-late) Hosting both local and international acts, the live music here (occasionally including jazz) is both varied and plentiful. Concerts start around 10pm; it fills up early, so either reserve a table or turn up at opening time. Dinner is also available.

🛈 **Information**

Warsaw Tourist Information (www.warsawtour.pl) operates three helpful branches at various points around town: **Old Town** (www.warsawtour.pl; Rynek Starego Miasta 19/21; [⊙]9am-8pm May-Sep, to 6pm Oct-Apr; [奈]), the **Palace of Culture & Science** (www.warsawtour.pl; Plac Defilad 1, enter from ul Emilii Plater; [⊙]8am-8pm May-Sep, to 6pm Oct-Apr; [奈]) and **Warsaw-Frédéric Chopin Airport** (www.warsawtour.pl; Terminal A, Warsaw Frédéric Chopin Airport, ul Żwirki i Wigury 1; [⊙]9am-7pm). They offer free city maps as well as advice on what to see and where to stay.

🛈 **Getting There & Away**

AIR
Warsaw's main international airport, **Warsaw-Frédéric Chopin Airport** (Lotnisko Chopina Warszawa; [☎]22 650 4220; www.lotnisko-chopina.pl; ul Żwirki i Wigury 1), 10km from the city centre, handles most flights in and out of the city. The terminal has ATMs, restaurants and a branch of the Warsaw Tourist Information office.

Some budget flights, including Ryanair services, use outlying **Warsaw Modlin** ([☎]801 80

1880; www.modlinairport.pl; ul Generała Wiktora Thommée 1a), 35km north of the city.

BUS

Warsaw's main bus station is **Warszawa Zachodnia** (☑708 208 888; www.dworzeconline.pl; al Jerozolimskie 144; ⊘ information & tickets 6am-9pm), southwest of the centre and adjoining Warszawa Zachodnia train station. This sprawling terminal handles most (but not all) international and domestic routes.

Trains are usually more convenient than buses to Poland's major cities, with the exception of the comfortable coach services run by private company Polski Bus. These usually depart from the small **Wilanowska bus station** (Dworzec Autobusowy Wilanowska; ul Puławska 145) near the Wilanowska metro station. Check the bus company's website (www.polskibus.com) for further information and give yourself plenty of time to find the bus station. Fares vary by date and demand, so buy your tickets online.

TRAIN

Warsaw has several train stations and is connected directly to a number of international destinations. The station most travellers use is **Warszawa Centralna** (Warsaw Central; www.pkp.pl; al Jerozolimskie 54; ⊘24hr), but it's not always where trains start or finish so be sure to board promptly.

Regular international train services run to Berlin (from €60, six hours, five daily), Prague (€50, eight hours, three daily), Bratislava (€90, eight hours, daily), Kyiv (from €90, 11 hours, daily), Minsk (from €80, 10 hours, daily) and Moscow (€130, 19 hours).

ℹ Getting Around

TO/FROM THE AIRPORT

Regular train services run between the airporT's **Warszawa Lotnisko Chopina** (ul Żwirki i Wigury) station and Warszawa Centralna (4.40zł, 20 minutes). Some trains also link the airport to **Warszawa Śródmieście station** (al Jerozolimskie), next to the Palace of Culture.

Bus 175 (4.40zł) terminates at Plac Piłsudskiego, about a 500m walk from the Old Town. A taxi fare between the airport and city centre is around 50zł.

From Warsaw Modlin, the easiest way to the centre is aboard the regular **Modlin bus** (☑22 290 5090; www.modlinbus.com) (33zł). A taxi will cost from 160zł to 200zł.

PUBLIC TRANSPORT

Warsaw has a reliable system of trams, buses and metro cars. Trams running east–west across busy Al Jerozolimskie are particularly handy.

Buy tickets from machines (have coins or small bills handy) or from news kiosks near

stops. A standard ticket (4.40zł) is valid for one ride by bus, tram or metro. Day passes are available for 15zł. Be sure to validate the ticket on boarding.

MAŁOPOLSKA

Małopolska (literally 'Lesser Poland') covers southeastern Poland from the former royal capital of Kraków to the eastern Lublin Uplands. The name does not refer to size or relative importance, but rather that Lesser Poland was mentioned in atlases more recently than Wielkopolska ('Greater Poland'). It's a colourful region filled with remnants of traditional life and historic cities.

Kraków

POP 761,000

Many Polish cities are centred on an attractive Old Town, but none compare to Kraków (pronounced krak-oof) for effortless beauty. As it was the royal capital of Poland until 1596 and miraculously escaped destruction in WWII, Kraków is packed with appealing historic buildings and streetscapes. One of the most important sights is Wawel Castle, from where the ancient Polish kingdom was once ruled.

South of the castle lies the former Jewish quarter of Kazimierz. Its silent synagogues are a reminder of the tragedy of WWII. These days, the quarter has been injected with new life and is home to some of the city's best bars and clubs.

◉ Sights

◎ Wawel Hill

South of Old Town, this prominent hilltop is crowned with the former Royal Castle and Cathedral – both enduring symbols of Poland.

★ **Wawel Royal Castle**   CASTLE
(Zamek Królewski na Wawelu; ☑Wawel Visitor Centre 12 422 5155; www.wawel.krakow.pl; Wawel Hill; grounds admission free, attractions priced separately; ⊘grounds 6am-dusk; 🚊6, 8, 10, 13, 18)
As the political and cultural heart of Poland through the 16th century, Wawel Castle is a potent symbol of national identity. It's now a museum containing five separate sections: Crown Treasury & Armoury; State Rooms; Royal Private Apartments; Lost Wawel; and the Exhibition of Oriental Art. Each

Kraków – Old Town & Wawel

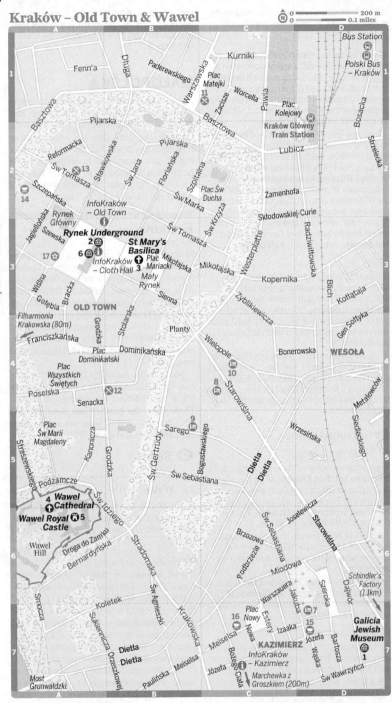

Kraków – Old Town & Wawel

requires a separate ticket. Of the five, the State Rooms and Royal Private Apartments are most impressive. There's also a special display here of the city's most valuable painting, Leonardo da Vinci's *The Lady with an Ermine*.

The Renaissance palace you see today dates from the 16th century. An original, smaller residence was built in the early 11th century by King Bolesław I Chrobry. Kazimierz III Wielki (Casimir III the Great) turned it into a formidable Gothic castle, but when it burned down in 1499, Zygmunt I Stary (Sigismund I the Old; 1506–48) commissioned a new residence. Within 30 years, the current Italian-inspired palace was in place. Despite further extensions and alterations, the three-storey structure, complete with a courtyard arcaded on three sides, has been preserved to this day.

Repeatedly sacked and vandalised by the Swedish and Prussian armies, the castle was occupied in the 19th century by the Austrians, who intended to make Wawel a barracks, while moving the royal tombs elsewhere. They never got that far, but they did turn the royal kitchen and coach house into a military hospital and raze two churches. They also built a new ring of massive brick walls, largely ruining the original Gothic fortifications.

After Kraków was incorporated into re-established Poland after WWI, restoration work began and continued until the outbreak of WWII. The work was resumed after the war and has been able to recover a good deal of the castle's earlier external form and interior decoration.

★ **Wawel Cathedral** CHURCH
(☑ 12 429 9515; www.katedra-wawelska.pl; Wawel 3, Wawel Hill; cathedral free, combined entry for crypts, bell tower & museum adult/concession 12/7zł; ☺9am-5pm Mon-Sat, from 12.30pm Sun; 🚌6, 8, 10, 13, 18) The Royal Cathedral has witnessed many coronations, funerals and burials of Poland's monarchs and strongmen over the centuries. This is the third church on this site, consecrated in 1364. The original was founded in the 11th century by King Bolesław I Chrobry and replaced with a Romanesque construction around 1140. When that burned down in 1305, only the Crypt of St Leonard survived. Highlights include the Holy Cross Chapel, Sigismund Chapel, Sigismund Bell, and the Crypt of St Leonard and Royal Crypts.

⊙ Old Town

This vast Rynek Główny (main square) is the focus of the Old Town, and is Europe's largest medieval town square (200m by 200m).

Cloth Hall HISTORIC BUILDING
(Sukiennice; www.mnk.pl; Rynek Główny 1/3; 🚌1, 6, 8, 13, 18) **FREE** Dominating the middle of Rynek Główny, this building was once the centre of Kraków's medieval clothing trade. Created in the early 14th century when a roof was put over two rows of stalls, it was extended into a 108m-long Gothic structure, then rebuilt in Renaissance style after a 1555 fire; the arcades were a late 19th-century addition. The ground floor is now a busy trading centre for crafts and souvenirs; the upper floor houses the recently renovated **Gallery of 19th-Century Polish Painting** (☑ 12 433 5400; www.mnk.pl; Rynek Główny 1; adult/concession 14/8zł, Sun free; ☺10am-6pm Tue-Sun; 🚌1, 6, 8, 13, 18).

The gallery's collection features works by Józef Chełmoński, Jacek Malczewski, Aleksander Gierymski and the leader of monumental historic painting, Jan Matejko.

POLAND KRAKÓW

★ **Rynek Underground** MUSEUM
(☑ 12 426 5060; www.podziemiarynku.com; Rynek Główny 1; adult/concession 19/16zł; ⊙ 10am-8pm Mon, to 4pm Tue, to 10pm Wed-Sun; 🚊 1, 6, 8, 13, 18) This fascinating attraction beneath the market square consists of an underground route through medieval market stalls and other long-forgotten chambers. The 'Middle Ages meets 21st century' experience is enhanced by holograms and audiovisual wizardry. Buy tickets at an office on the western side of the Cloth Hall (Sukiennice 21), where an electronic board shows tour times and tickets available. The entrance to the tunnels is on the northeastern end of the Cloth Hall.

★ **St Mary's Basilica** CHURCH
(Basilica of the Assumption of Our Lady; ☑ 12 422 0737; www.mariacki.com; Plac Mariacki 5, Rynek Główny; adult/concession church 10/5zł, tower 15/10zł; ⊙ 11.30am-6pm Mon-Sat, 2-6pm Sun; 🚊 1, 6, 8, 13, 18) Overlooking Rynek Główny, this striking brick church, best known simply as St Mary's, is dominated by two towers of different heights. The first church here was built in the 1220s and following its destruction during a Tatar raid, construction of the basilica began. Tour the exquisite interior, with its remarkable carved wooden altarpiece, and in summer climb the tower for excellent views. Don't miss the hourly *hejnał* (bugle call) from the taller tower.

⊙ **Kazimierz & Podgórze**

Founded by King Kazimierz III Wielki in 1335, Kazimierz was originally an independent town and then became a Jewish district. During WWII, the Germans relocated Jews south across the Vistula River to a walled ghetto in Podgórze. They were exterminated in the nearby Płaszów Concentration Camp, as portrayed in the Steven Spielberg film *Schindler's List*. In addition to the attractions below, many synagogues are still standing and can be visited individually.

★ **Schindler's Factory** MUSEUM
(Fabryka Schindlera; ☑ 12 257 0096; www.mhk.pl; ul Lipowa 4; adult/concession 21/16zł, free Mon; ⊙ 10am-4pm Mon, 9am-8pm Tue-Sun; 🚊 3, 9, 19, 24, 50) This impressive interactive museum covers the German occupation of Kraków in WWII. It's housed in the former enamel factory of Oskar Schindler, the Nazi Germany industrialist who famously saved the lives of members of his Jewish labour force during the Holocaust. Well-organised, innovative

exhibits tell the moving story of the city from 1939 to 1945.

From the main post office in the Old Town, catch any tram down ul Starowiślna and alight at the first stop over the river at Plac Bohaterów Getta. From here, follow the signs east along ul Kącik, under the railway line to the museum.

★ **Galicia Jewish Museum** MUSEUM
(☑ 12 421 6842; www.galiciajewishmuseum.org; ul Dajwór 18; adult/concession 16/11zł; ⊙ 10am-6pm; 🚲; 🚊 3, 9, 19, 24, 50) This museum both commemorates Jewish victims of the Holocaust and celebrates the Jewish culture and history of the former Austro-Hungarian region of Galicia. It features an impressive photographic exhibition depicting modern-day remnants of southeastern Poland's once-thriving Jewish community, called *Traces of Memory*, along with video testimony of survivors and regular temporary exhibits. The museum also leads guided tours of the Jewish sites of Kazimierz. Call or email for details.

🛌 Sleeping

Kraków is unquestionably Poland's major tourist destination, with prices to match. **Hamilton Suites** (☑ 12 346 4670; www.krakow-apartments.biz; apt 300-600zł; 🚲) is one of several companies offering good-value, short-term apartment rentals.

★ **Mundo Hostel** HOSTEL €
(☑ 12 422 6113; www.mundohostel.eu; ul Sarego 10; dm 60-65zł, d 170-190zł; @ 🚲; 🚊 6, 8, 10, 13, 18) Attractive, well-maintained hostel in a quiet courtyard location neatly placed between the Old Town and Kazimierz. Each room is decorated for a different country; for example, the Tibet room is decked out with colourful prayer flags. Barbecues take place in summer. There's a bright, fully equipped kitchen for do-it-yourself meals.

★ **Wielopole** HOTEL €€
(☑ 12 422 1475; www.wielopole.pl; ul Wielopole 3; s/d 260/360zł; 🌸 🚲; 🚊 3, 10, 19, 24, 52) Wielopole's selection of bright, modern rooms – all of them with spotless bathrooms – is housed in a renovated block with a great courtyard on the eastern edge of the Old Town, within easy walk of Kazimierz. The breakfast spread here is impressive.

Hotel Eden HOTEL €€
(☑ 12 430 6565; www.hoteleden.pl; ul Ciemna 15; s/d 240/320zł; 🚲; 🚊 3, 9, 19, 24, 50) Located

WORTH A TRIP

A UNESCO-PROTECTED SALT MINE

Some 14km southeast of Kraków, **Wieliczka** (🖉12 278 7302; www.kopalnia.pl; ul Daniłow-icza 10; adult/concession 84/64zł; ⊙7.30am-7.30pm Apr-Oct, 8am-5pm Nov-Mar) – pronounced vyeh-leech-kah – is famous for its deep salt mine. It's an eerie world of pits and chambers, and everything within its depths has been carved by hand from salt blocks. A section of the mine, some 22 chambers, is open to the public and it's a fascinating trip.

You visit three upper levels of the mine, from 64m to 135m below ground. Some have been made into chapels, with altarpieces and figures, others are adorned with statues and monuments – and there are even underground lakes.

Guided tours take about two hours. Wear comfortable shoes and dress warmly as the temperature in the mine is 14°C. In summer, English-language tours depart every half-hour. During the rest of the year, tours are less frequent.

Minibuses to Wieliczka (3zł) depart Kraków frequently from ul Pawia near the Galeria Krakowska shopping mall next to Kraków Główny train station.

within three meticulously restored 15th-century townhouses, the Eden has comfortable rooms and comes complete with a sauna and the only *mikvah* (traditional Jewish bath) in Kraków. Kosher meals are available on request.

★**Hotel Pugetów**   BOUTIQUE HOTEL €€€
(🖉12 432 4950; www.donimirski.com; ul Starowiśl-na 15a; s/d 330/460zł; 🅿❉🛜; 🚌1, 3, 19, 24, 52) This charming boutique hotel stands proudly next to the 19th-century neo-Renaissance palace of the same name. It offers just seven rooms with distinctive names (Conrad, Bonaparte) and identities. Think embroidered bathrobes, black-marble baths and a fabulous breakfast room in the basement.

✗ Eating

★**Glonojad**   VEGETARIAN €
(🖉12 346 1677; www.glonojad.com; Plac Matejki 2; mains 16-20zł; ⊙8am-10pm; 🛜✗; 🚌2, 4, 14, 19, 20, 24) Attractive and much-lauded, this vegetarian restaurant has a great view onto Plac Matejki, just north of the Barbican. The diverse menu has a variety of tasty dishes including samosas, curries, potato pancakes, burritos, gnocchi and soups. There's also an all-day breakfast menu, so there's no need to jump out of that hotel bed too early.

★**Marchewka z Groszkiem**   POLISH €€
(🖉12 430 0795; www.marchewkazgroszkiem.pl; ul Mostowa 2; mains 11-29.50zł; ⊙9am-10pm; 🛜; 🚌6, 8, 10, 13) Traditional Polish cooking, with hints of influence from neighbouring countries like Ukraine (beer), Hungary (wine) and Lithuania. Excellent potato pancakes and a delicious boiled beef with horseradish sauce highlight the menu. There are a few sidewalk

tables to admire the parade of people down one of Kazimierz' up-and-coming streets.

Trufla   ITALIAN €€
(🖉12 422 1641; ul Św Tomasza 2; mains 25-43zł; ⊙9am-11pm Mon-Fri, 10am-11pm Sat & Sun; 🛜; 🚌2, 4, 14, 18, 20, 24) Affordable yet quality Italian food, including steaks, seafood, pasta and risotto – but no pizza. The decor is uncluttered: think hardwood floors and simple, wooden tables. Yet the overall ambience is relaxing. In summer, there's a pretty garden out back (to access the garden, walk through a corridor to the left of the main entrance).

★**Miód Malina**   POLISH €€€
(🖉12 430 0411; www.miodmalina.pl; ul Grodzka 40; mains 24-69zł; ⊙noon-11pm; 🛜; 🚌1, 6, 8, 13, 18) The charmingly named 'Honey Raspberry' serves Polish dishes in colourful surrounds. Grab a window seat and order the wild mushrooms in cream, and any of the duck or veal dishes. There's a variety of beef steaks on the menu as well. The grilled sheep's cheese appetiser, served with cranberry jelly, is a regional speciality. Reservations essential.

🍷 Drinking & Nightlife

There are hundreds of pubs and bars in Kraków's Old Town, many housed in ancient vaulted cellars. Kazimierz also has a lively bar scene, centred on Plac Nowy.

★**Café Bunkier**   CAFE
(🖉12 431 0585; http://en.bunkiercafe.pl; Plac Szczepański 3a; ⊙9am-late; 🛜; 🚌2, 4, 14, 18, 20, 24) The 'Bunker' is a wonderful cafe with a positively enormous glassed-in terrace tacked onto the Bunkier Sztuki (Art Bunker), a cutting-edge gallery northwest of the Rynek. The garden space is heated in winter

and seems to always have a buzz. Excellent coffee, non-filtered beers and homemade lemonades, as well as light bites like burgers and salads. Enter from the Planty.

★ **Cheder** CAFE
(✉ 515 732 226; www.cheder.pl; ul Józefa 36; ☺ 10am-10pm; 🚌 3, 9, 19, 24, 50) Unlike most of the other Jewish-themed places in Kazimierz, this one aims to entertain *and* educate. Named after a traditional Hebrew school, the cafe offers access to a decent library in Polish and English, regular readings and films, as well as real Israeli coffee, brewed in a traditional Turkish copper pot with cinnamon and cardamom, and snacks like homemade hummus.

Mleczarnia CAFE
(✉ 12 421 8532; www.mle.pl; ul Meiselsa 20; ☺ 10am-late; 🚌 6, 8, 10, 13) Wins the prize for best courtyard cafe – located across the street. Shady trees and blooming roses make this place tops for a sunny-day drink. If it's rainy, never fear, for the cafe is warm and cosy, with crowded bookshelves and portrait-covered walls. Interesting beverages available here include mead and cocoa with cherry vodka. Self-service.

☆ Entertainment

★ **Harris Piano Jazz Bar** JAZZ
(✉ 12 421 5741; www.harris.krakow.pl; Rynek Główny 28; ☺ 3pm-late Mon-Fri, from 1pm Sat & Sun; 🚌 1, 6, 8, 13, 18) This lively jazz haunt is housed in an atmospheric, intimate cellar space right on the Rynek Główny. Harris hosts jazz and blues bands most nights of the week from around 9.30pm, but try to arrive an hour earlier to get a seat (or book in advance by phone). Wednesday nights see weekly (free) jam sessions.

Filharmonia Krakowska CLASSICAL MUSIC
(Filharmonia im. Karola Szymanowskiego w Krakowie; ✉ reservations 12 619 8722, tickets 12 619 8733; www.filharmonia.krakow.pl; ul Zwierzyniecka 1; ☺ box office 10am-2pm & 3-7pm Tue-Fri; 🚌 1, 2, 6) Home to one of Poland's best orchestras. Tickets start at 25zł.

ℹ Information

The official tourist information office, **Info-Kraków** (www.infokrakow.pl), maintains branches around town, including at the **Cloth Hall** (✉ 12 354 2716; www.infokrakow.pl; Cloth Hall, Rynek Główny 1/3; ☺ 9am-7pm May-Sep, to 5pm Oct-Apr; 🚌 1, 6, 8, 13, 18), **Kazimierz** (✉ 12 354 2728; www.infokrakow.pl; ul Józefa 7; ☺ 9am-5pm; 🚌 6, 8, 10, 13), the **Old Town**

(✉ 12 354 2725; www.infokrakow.pl; ul Św Jana 2; ☺ 9am-7pm; 🚌 1, 6, 8, 13, 18) and the **Airport** (✉ 12 285 5341; www.infokrakow.pl; John Paul II International Airport, Balice; ☺ 9am-7pm).

ℹ Getting There & Away

AIR

Kraków's **John Paul II International Airport** (KRK; ✉ information 12 295 5800; www.krakowairport.pl; Kapitana Mieczysława Medweckiego 1, Balice; 🚕) is located in the town of Balice, about 15km west of the centre. A regular train service (8zł, 17 minutes), departing once or twice an hour between 4am and 11.30pm, runs to Kraków Główny station. Taxis to the centre cost about 80zł.

The main Polish carrier LOT (p887) flies to Warsaw and other large cities. Budget operators connect Kraków to cities in Europe.

BUS

Kraków's modern **bus station** (✉ 703 403 340; www.mda.malopolska.pl; ul Bosacka 18; ☺ information 7am-8pm Mon-Fri, 9am-5pm Sat & Sun; 🚌 2, 3, 4, 10, 14, 19, 24, 52) is conveniently located next to the main train station, Kraków Główny, on the fringe of the Old Town.

Bus travel is the best way to reach Zakopane (16zł, two hours, hourly). Modern **Polski Bus** (✉ emergencies 703 502 504; www.polskibus.com) coaches depart from here to Warsaw (five hours, several daily) and Wrocław (three hours, several daily); check fares and book tickets online.

TRAIN

Newly remodelled and gleaming **Kraków Główny** (Dworzec Główny; ✉ information 703 202 025; www.pkp.pl; Plac Dworcowy; 🚌 2, 3, 4, 10, 14, 19, 24, 52) train station, on the northeastern outskirts of the Old Town, handles all international trains and most domestic rail services.

Useful domestic destinations include Gdańsk (80zł, eight hours, three daily), Lublin (62zł, four hours, two daily), Poznań (80zł, eight hours, three daily), Toruń (73zł, seven hours, three daily), Warsaw (60zł to 130zł, three hours, at least hourly) and Wrocław (50zł, 5½ hours, hourly).

Popular international connections include Bratislava (7½ hours, one daily), Berlin (10 hours, one daily), Budapest (10½ hours, one daily), Lviv (7½ to 9½ hours, two daily) and Prague (10 hours, one daily).

Lublin

POP 342,000

Poland's eastern metropolis admittedly lacks the grandeur of Gdańsk or Kraków, but does have an attractive Old Town, with beautiful churches and tiny alleyways. It's a natural jumping-off point for exploring southeast-

AUSCHWITZ-BIRKENAU

Many visitors pair a trip to Kraków with a visit to the **Auschwitz-Birkenau Museum & Memorial** (Auschwitz-Birkenau Miejsce Pamięci i Muzeum; 🗐 guides 33 844 8100; www. auschwitz.org; ul Więźniów Oświęcimia 20; tours 45zł; ⊗7.30am-7pm Jun-Aug, to 6pm Apr-May & Sep, to 5pm Mar & Oct, 8am-4pm Feb, to 3pm Jan & Nov, to 2pm Dec) FREE – or as it's known officially the 'Auschwitz-Birkenau: German Nazi Concentration & Extermination Camp' – in the town of Oświęcim. More than a million Jews as well large numbers of ethnic Poles and Roma were systematically murdered here by occupying Germans during WWII.

Both the main camp at Auschwitz (Auschwitz I) and a larger outlying camp at Birkenau (Auschwitz II), about 2km away, are open to the public and admission is free (though if arriving between 10am and 3pm from May to October, a guided tour is compulsory). A visit is essential to understanding the Holocaust, though the scope and nature of the crimes are horrifying and may not be suitable for children under 14.

The tour begins at the main camp, Auschwitz I, which began life as a Polish military barracks but was co-opted by the Nazi Germans in 1940 as an extermination camp. Here is the infamous gate, displaying the grimly cynical message: 'Arbeit Macht Frei' (Through Work Freedom). Some 13 of 30 surviving prison blocks house museum exhibitions.

From here, the tour moves to Birkenau (Auschwitz II), where most of the killings took place. Massive and purpose-built to be efficient, the camp had more than 300 prison barracks. Here you'll find the remnants of gas chambers and crematoria.

Auschwitz-Birkenau is a workable day trip from Kraków. Most convenient are the approximately hourly buses to Oświęcim (12zł, 1½ hours), departing from the bus station in Kraków. There are also numerous minibuses to Oświęcim (10zł, 1½ hours) from the minibus stands off ul Pawia, next to Galeria Krakowska.

ern Poland. Thousands of students make for a lively restaurant, bar and club scene.

Lublin plays an important role in Polish and Jewish history. It was here in 1569 that the Lublin Union was signed, uniting Poland and Lithuania to form one of the largest and most powerful entities in Europe in its day. For those interested in Jewish heritage, for centuries Lublin served as a centre of European Jewish culture. The Holocaust ended this vibrant community, and one of the most notorious Nazi German extermination camps, Majdanek, lies at Lublin's doorstep.

⊙ Sights

Lublin Castle MUSEUM
(🗐81 532 5001; www.zamek-lublin.pl; ul Zamkowa 9; adult/concession museum 6.50/4.50zł, chapel 6.50/4.50zł; ⊗10am-6pm Tue-Sun Jun-Aug, 9am-5pm Sep-May) Lublin's royal castle dates from the 12th and 13th centuries, though it's been rebuilt many times over the years. It was here in 1569 that the union with Lithuania was signed. The castle is home to both the **Lublin Museum** and the surviving **Gothic Chapel of the Holy Trinity**, which dates from the 14th century. Each requires a separate entry ticket. The museum's permanent collection features mainly art, folk art and weaponry. The 14th-century chapel is con-

sidered a masterpiece of the Middle Ages, with Russian-Byzantine-inspired frescos. Painted in 1418, only to be later plastered over, they were rediscovered in 1897 and painstakingly restored over a 100-year period. These are possibly the finest examples of medieval wall paintings in the country.

During WWII the occupying German army used the castle as a prison, holding as many as 40,000 inmates. The darkest day of the war here came in July 1944, just ahead of the prison's liberation by the Soviet Red Army, when the Germans executed 300 prisoners on the spot.

Kraków Gate MUSEUM
(Brama Krakowska; 🗐81 532 6001; www.muzeum lubelskie.pl; Plac Łokietka 3; adult/concession 5.50/4.50zł; ⊗10am-6pm Tue-Sun Jun-Aug, to 5pm Sep-May) The only significant surviving remnant of the fortified walls that once surrounded the Old Town is the 14th-century Gothic-style Kraków Gate. It was conceived during the reign of Kazimierz III Wielki following the Mongol attack in 1341. It received its octagonal Renaissance superstructure in the 16th century, and its Baroque crown in 1782. These days it's home to the **Historical Museum of Lublin** and its small collection of documents and photographs of the town's history.

Cathedral of St John the Baptist CHURCH

(www.archidiecezjalubelska.pl; Plac Katedralny; ⏱dawn-sunset, treasury 10am-2pm & 3-5pm Tue-Sun) **FREE** This former Jesuit church dates from the 16th century and is the largest in Lublin. There are many impressive details to behold, including the Baroque trompe l'oeil frescos (the work of Moravian artist Józef Majer) and the 17th-century altar made from a black Lebanese pear tree. The acoustic vestry (so called for its ability to project whispers) and the **treasury** (*skarbiec*), behind the chapel, also merit attention.

The painting of the *Black Madonna* is said to have shed tears in 1945, making it a source of much reverence for local devotees.

Majdanek HISTORIC SITE

(Państwowe Muzeum na Majdanku; ☑81 710 2833; www.majdanek.eu; Droga Męczenników Majdanka 67; admission free; ⏱9am-6pm Apr-Oct, to 4pm Nov-Mar, museum closed Mon) **FREE** Four kilometres southeast of the centre of Lublin is the Nazi German Majdanek extermination camp, where tens of thousands of people, mainly Jews, were murdered during WWII. The Germans went to no effort to conceal Majdanek, as they did at other extermination camps. A 5km walk starts at the visitors centre, passes the foreboding Monument of Fight & Martyrdom, goes through parts of the barracks and finishes at the mausoleum. The camp is accessible by public transport: from the Krakowska Gate, take bus 23.

☞ Tours

Underground Route WALKING

(☑tour bookings 81 534 6570; Rynek 1; adult/concession 10/8zł; ⏱10am-4pm Tue-Fri, noon-5pm Sat & Sun) This 280m trail winds its way through connected cellars beneath the Old Town, with historical exhibitions along the way. Entry is from the neoclassical Old Town Hall in the centre of the pleasant Market Sq (Rynek) at approximately two-hourly intervals; check with the tourist office for exact times.

🛏 Sleeping

Hostel Lublin HOSTEL €

(☑792 888 632; www.hostellublin.pl; ul Lubartowska 60; dm/r 40/95zł; ☎) The city's first modern hostel is situated within a former apartment building and contains neat, tidy dorms, a basic kitchenette and a cosy lounge. Take trolleybus 156 or 160 north from the Old Town; after you cross busy al Tysiąclecia, exit at the second stop.

Vanilla Hotel HOTEL €€

(☑81 536 6720; www.vanilla-hotel.pl; ul Krakowskie Przedmieście 12; s 265-330zł, d 315-395zł; P@☎) The name must be tongue-in-cheek. This beautiful boutique, just off the main pedestrian thoroughfare, is anything but vanilla. The rooms are filled with inspired, even bold, styling: vibrant colours, big headboards behind the beds, and stylish, retro lamps and furniture. There's lots of attention to detail here, which continues into the chic restaurant and coffee bar. Lower prices on weekends.

Hotel Waksman HOTEL €€

(☑81 532 5454; www.waksman.pl; ul Grodzka 19; s/d 210/230zł, apt from 290zł; P@☎) Hotel Waksman deserves a blue ribbon for many reasons, not least of which is the atmospheric Old Town location. Each standard room (named 'yellow', 'blue', 'green' or 'red' for its decor) has individual character. The two apartments on top are special; they offer ample space for lounging or working, and views over the Old Town and castle.

🍴 Eating

★Kardamon INTERNATIONAL €€

(☑81 448 0257; www.kardamon.eu; ul Krakowskie Przedmieście 41; mains 24-69zł; ⏱noon-11pm Mon-Sat, to 10pm Sun; ☎) By many accounts, Lublin's best restaurant is this lush, cellar affair on the main street. The menu is a mix of international staples such as grilled pork tenderloin, along with Polish favourites such as duck served in cranberry sauce, and some rarer regional specialities. The 'gooseneck', a regional dish served with liver stuffing and buckwheat, is a particular favourite.

Mandragora JEWISH €€

(☑81 536 2020; www.mandragora.lublin.pl; Rynek 9; mains 20-49zł; ⏱noon-10pm Sun-Thu, to midnight Fri & Sat; ☎) There's good kitsch and there's bad kitsch, and at Mandragora, it's all good. Sure they're going for the *Fiddler on the Roof* effect with the lace tablecloths, knick-knacks and photos of old Lublin, but in the romantic Rynek locale, it works wonderfully. The food is a hearty mix of Polish and Jewish, featuring mains such as goose and duck.

🍷 Drinking & Nightlife

Szklarnia CAFE

(Centrum Kultury w Lublinie; ☑81 466 6140; www.ck.lublin.pl; ul Peowiaków 12; ⏱10am-11pm Mon-Fri, noon-midnight Sat & Sun; ☎) It's not easy

ZAMOŚĆ: POLAND'S RENAISSANCE HEART

While most Polish cities' attractions centre on their medieval heart, Zamość (zah-moshch) is pure 16th-century Renaissance. It was founded in 1580 by nobleman Jan Zamoyski and designed by an Italian architect. The splendid architecture of Zamość's Old Town escaped serious destruction in WWII and was added to Unesco's World Heritage List in 1992.

The **Rynek Wielki** (Great Market Square; Rynek Wielki) is the heart of Zamość's attractive Old Town. This impressive Italianate Renaissance square (exactly 100m by 100m) is dominated by a lofty, pink town hall and surrounded by colourful, arcaded burghers' houses. The **Museum of Zamość** (Muzeum Zamojskie; ☑ 84 638 6494; www.muzeum-zamojskie.pl; ul Ormiańska 30; adult/concession 10/6zł; ⊙ 9am-5pm Tue-Sun) is based in two of the loveliest buildings on the square and houses interesting exhibits, including paintings, folk costumes and a scale model of the 16th-century town.

The city's **synagogue** (☑ 84 639 0054; www.zamosc.fodz.pl; ul Pereca 14; admission 7zł; ⊙ 10am-6pm Tue-Sun Mar-Oct, 9am-2pm Nov-Feb) was recently reopened to the public after a long renovation. It was built around 1620 and served as the Jewish community's main house of worship until WWII, when it was shuttered by the Germans. The highlight of the exhibition is a gripping computer presentation on the history of the town's Jewish community, including its roots in Sephardic Judaism.

The helpful **tourist office** (☑ 84 639 2292; www.travel.zamosc.pl; Rynek Wielki 13; ⊙ 8am-6pm Mon-Fri, 10am-5pm Sat & Sun May-Sep, 8am-5pm Mon-Fri, 9am-3pm Sat & Sun Oct-Apr) in the town hall has maps, brochures and souvenirs. Zamość makes for an easy day trip from Lublin. Buses and minibuses make the 80km trip (15zł) in around 90 minutes.

finding good coffee in Lublin. This sleek cafe in the recently refurbished Lublin Cultural Centre has great coffee as well as a daily selection of cakes. There's live entertainment some nights, and a nice terrace at the back in warm weather.

Czarna Owca PUB
(☑ 81 532 4130; ul Narutowicza 9; ⊙ noon-midnight Sun-Tue, to 3am Wed-Sat) The 'Black Sheep' is a legendary Lublin watering hole, going strong until the wee morning hours from Wednesday to Saturday. In addition to beers and shots of vodka chasers, it has decent pub food, pizzas and toasts to munch on.

ⓘ Information

Tourist Information Centre (LOITiK; ☑ 81 532 4412; www.lublin.eu; ul Jezuicka 1/3; ⊙ 9am-7pm Mon-Fri, 10am-7pm Sat & Sun May-Oct, 9am-5pm Mon-Fri, 10am-5pm Sat & Sun Nov-Apr) Extremely helpful English-speaking staff. There are souvenirs for sale and lots of brochures, including handy maps of the most popular walking tours in Lublin. There's also a computer on hand for short-term web-surfing.

ⓘ Getting There & Away

BUS

PKS buses run from the **bus station** (☑ 703 402 900; lublin.pks.busportal.pl; ul Hutnicza 1,

cross al Tysiąclecia), opposite the castle. From here, Polski Bus (www.polskibus.com) heads to Warsaw (25zł, three hours, five daily). Private minibuses run to various destinations, including Zamość (15zł, 1½ hours, hourly), from a minibus station north of the bus terminal.

TRAIN

The **train station** (Dworzec Kolejowy Lublin Główny; ☑ info 703 202 025; www.pkp.pl; Plac Dworcowy 1) is 1.8km south of the Old Town. Useful direct train connections included to Kraków (62zł, four hours, two daily) and Warsaw (37zł, 2¾ hours, five daily).

CARPATHIAN MOUNTAINS

The Carpathians (Karpaty) stretch from the southern border with Slovakia into Ukraine, and their wooded hills and snowy mountains are a magnet for hikers, skiers and cyclists. The most popular destination here is the resort of Zakopane.

Zakopane

POP 27,000

Zakopane, 100km south of Kraków, is Poland's main alpine resort, situated at the foot of the Tatra Mountains. It's a popular jumping-off spot for **trekking and mountain hikes**, as well as **skiing**. The busy high street, ul Krupówki, is a jumble of souvenir shops, bars and restaurants, but away from the centre, the pace slows down. This was an artists' colony in the early 20th century, and the graceful timbered villas from those days – built in what's known as the 'Zakopane style' – are still scattered around town.

◎ Sights & Activities

Museum of Zakopane Style   MUSEUM
(Willa Koliba; ☑18 201 3602; www.muzeumtatrzanskie.pl; ul Kościeliska 18; adult/concession 7/5.50zł; ⊙10am-6pm Tue-Sat, 9am-3pm Sun Jul & Aug, 9am-5pm Wed-Sat, 9am-3pm Sun Sep-Jun) Housed in the Willa Koliba, this was the first of several grand wooden villas designed by the noted Polish painter and architect Stanisław Witkiewicz in his 'Zakopane Style' (similar to the Arts and Crafts movement that swept the US and Britain at the turn of the 20th century). The interior has been restored to its original state, complete with highlander furnishings and textiles, all designed for the villa.

Old Church & Cemetery   CHURCH
(Stary Kościół, Pęksowy Brzyzek National Cemetery; ul Kościeliska; ⊙dawn-dusk) **FREE** This small wooden church and adjoining atmospheric cemetery date from the mid-19th century. The Old Church has charming carved wooden decorations and pews, and the Stations of the Cross painted on glass on the windows. Just behind, the old cemetery is certainly one of the country's most beautiful, with a number of amazing wood-carved headstones, some resembling giant chess pieces. The noted Polish painter and creator of the Zakopane Style, Stanisław Witkiewicz, is buried here beneath a modest wooden grave marker.

Morskie Oko   LAKE
(☑18 202 3300; www.tpn.pl; park 5zł) The most popular outing near Zakopane is to this emerald-green mountain lake, about 20km southeast of the centre. Buses regularly depart from ul Kościuszki, across from the main bus station, for Polana Palenica (45 minutes), from where a 9km-long road continues uphill to the lake. Cars, bikes and buses are not allowed, so you'll have to walk (about two hours each way). Travel agencies organise day trips.

Kasprowy Wierch Cable Car   CABLE CAR
(☑18 201 5356; www.pkl.pl; Kuźnice; adult/concession return 63/48zł; ⊙7.30am-4pm Jan-Mar, 7.30am-6pm Apr-Jun & Sep-Oct, 7am-9pm Jul & Aug, 9am-4pm Nov-Dec) The cable-car trip from Kuźnice (2km south of Zakopane) to the Mt Kasprowy Wierch summit (1985m) is a classic tourist experience. At the end of the ascent (20 minutes, climbing 936m), you can get off and stand with one foot in Poland and the other in Slovakia. The view from the top is spectacular (clouds permitting). The cable car normally closes for two weeks in May, and won't operate if the snow or wind conditions are dangerous.

🛌 Sleeping

Travel agencies in Zakopane can usually arrange private rooms. Expect a double to cost about 80zł in the high season in the town centre, and about 60zł for somewhere further out.

Target Hostel   HOSTEL €
(☑730 955 730, 18 207 4596; www.targethostel.pl; ul Sienkiewicza 3b; dm 29-55zł; @ 🛜) This private, well-run hostel is within easy walking distance of the bus station, which is convenient if you're arriving from Kraków. Accommodation is in four- to 10-bed dorms, with the smaller rooms priced slightly higher. Dorms are classic light wood, with wooden floors. There's a common room and collective kitchen, as well as niceties such as free wi-fi and computers to check email.

Czarny Potok   HOTEL €€
(☑18 202 2760; www.czarnypotok.pl; ul Tetmajera 20; s/d from 270/320zł; P 🛜 🏊) The 'Black Stream', set upon a pretty brook amid lovely gardens, is a 44-room pension-like hostelry along a quiet street just south of the pedestrian mall. It has a great fitness centre with two saunas.

Hotel Sabała   HOTEL €€€
(☑18 201 5092; www.sabala.zakopane.pl; ul Krupówki 11; s/d from 300/400zł; ❄ 🛜 🏊) Built in 1894 but thoroughly up to date, this striking timber hotel has a superb location overlooking the picturesque pedestrian thoroughfare. The hotel offers 51 cosy, attic-style rooms, and there's a sauna, solarium and swimming pool. The restaurant here serves both local specialities and international favourites.

🍴 Eating

Pstrąg Górski   SEAFOOD €€
(☑512 351 746; www.pstrag-zakopane.pl; ul Krupówki 6a; mains 20-40zł; ⊙10am-10pm; ❄ 🛜) This fish restaurant, done up in timber-rich traditional style and overlooking a narrow stream, serves some of the freshest trout, salmon and sea fish in town. Trout is priced

POLAND ZAKOPANE

at 5zł and up per 100g (whole fish), bringing the price of a standard fish dinner to around 30zł, not including sides.

Karczma Zapiecek POLISH €€
(✆18 201 5699; www.karczmazapiecek.pl; ul Krupówki 43; mains 17-29zł; ☺10am-11pm) One of the better choices among a group of similar highlander-style restaurants along ul Krupówki, with great food, an old stove and a terrace. Traditional dishes on offer include *hałuski* (noodles) with *bryndza* (sheep's cheese) and baked trout.

ⓘ Information

Tatra National Park Headquarters (Tatrzański Park Narodowy; ✆18 200 0308; www.tpn.pl; ul Chałubińskiego 42; ☺office 9am-4pm Mon-Fri) The information office of the Tatra National Park is located in a small building near the Rondo Kuźnickie on the southern outskirts of the city. It's a good place for maps, guides and local weather and hiking information.

Tourist Information Centre (✆18 201 2211; www.zakopane.pl; ul Kościuszki 17; ☺9am-5pm Mar-Aug, 9am-5pm Mon-Fri Sep-Feb) Small but helpful municipal tourist office just south of the bus station on the walk toward the centre. It has free city maps and sells more-detailed hiking maps.

ⓘ Getting There & Away

Though Zakopane has a small train station, the majority of visitors arrive by bus from Kraków. Coaches make the journey (16zł, 1¾ hours) every 30 to 60 minutes during the day. The leading bus company is **Szwagropol** (✆12 271 3550; www.szwagropol.pl). Buy tickets bound for Kraków at Zakopane **bus station** (PKS; ✆666 396 090; www.zdazakopane.pl; ul Kościuszki 23).

SILESIA

Silesia (Śląsk in Polish; pronounced *shlonsk*), in the far southwest of the country, is a traditional industrial and mining region with a fascinating mix of landscapes.

Wrocław

POP 635,000

Everyone loves Wrocław (vrots-wahf) and it's easy to see why. The city's gracious Old Town is a mix of Gothic and Baroque styles, and its large student population ensures a healthy number of restaurants, bars and nightclubs. Wrocław has been traded back and forth between various domains over the centuries, but began life around 1000 AD.

History buffs may know the city better as Breslau, the name it had as part of Germany until the end of WWII. When the city went over to Polish hands after the war, Wrocław was a shell of its former self. Sensitive restoration has returned the historic centre to its former beauty.

⊙ Sights

The hub of city life is the city's magnificent market square, the **Rynek**.

⊙ Old Town

⭐**Old Town Hall** HISTORIC BUILDING
(Stary Ratusz; Rynek) This grand edifice took almost two centuries (1327–1504) to complete, and work on the 66m-high tower and decoration continued for another century.

The eastern facade reflects three distinct stages of the town hall's development. The segment to the right, with its austere early Gothic features, is the oldest, while the delicate carving in the section to the left shows elements of the early Renaissance style. The central 16th-century section is topped by an ornamented triangular roof adorned with pinnacles.

Wrocław Dwarves PUBLIC ART
(Wrocławskie Krasnale; www.krasnale.pl) See if you can spot the diminutive statue of a resting dwarf at ground level, just to the west of the **Hansel and Gretel houses** (Jaś i Małgosia; ul Odrzańska 39/40) off Wrocław's main square. A few metres away you'll spot firemen dwarves, rushing to put out a blaze. These figures are part of a collection of over 300 scattered through the city. Though whimsical, they're also a reference to the symbol of the Orange Alternative, a communist-era dissident group that used ridicule as a weapon. They're sometimes identified in English as gnomes, as the Polish folkloric character they're based on (the leprechaun-like *krasnoludek*) resembles a cross between a dwarf and a gnome. Buy a 'dwarf map' (6zł) from the tourist office and go dwarf-spotting.

⊙ Outside the Old Town

⭐**Panorama of Racławice** MUSEUM
(Panorama Racławicka; www.panoramaraclawicka.pl; ul Purkyniego 11; adult/concession 30/23zł; ☺9am-5pm mid-Apr–Sep, to 4pm Tue-Sun Oct–mid-Apr) Wrocław's pride and joy is this giant painting of the battle for Polish independence fought at Racławice on 4 April 1794,

POLAND WROCŁAW

between the Polish army led by Tadeusz Kościuszko and Russian troops under General Alexander Tormasov. The Poles won but it was all for naught: months later the nationwide insurrection was crushed by the tsarist army. The canvas measures 15m by 114m, and is wrapped around the internal walls of a rotunda.

Visits are by guided tour, departing every half-hour. You move around the balcony, inspecting each scene in turn, while an audioguide provides recorded commentary. The small rotunda behind the ticket office features a model of the battlefield and the uniforms of forces engaged in the battle.

The painting came into being when, a century after the battle, a group of patriots in Lviv (then the Polish city of Lwów) commissioned the panorama. The two main artists, Jan Styka and Wojciech Kossak, were helped by seven other painters who did the background scenes and details. They completed the monumental canvas in just over nine months, using 750kg of paint.

After WWII the painting was sent to Wrocław, but since it depicted a defeat of the Russians (Poland's then official friend and liberator), the communist authorities were reluctant to put it on display. The pavilion built for the panorama in 1967 sat empty until 1985, when the canvas was shown for the first time in more than four decades.

National Museum   MUSEUM

(Muzeum Narodowe; ☑ 71 372 5150; www.mnwr. art.pl; Plac Powstańców Warszawy 5; adult/concession 15/10zł; ⊙ 10am-5pm Tue-Sun, to 6pm Sat) A treasure trove of fine art, 200m east of the Panorama of Racławice. Medieval stone sculpture is displayed on the ground floor; exhibits include the Romanesque tympanum from the portal of the Church of St Mary Magdalene, depicting the Assumption of the Virgin Mary, and 14th-century sarcophagi from the Church of SS Vincent and James. There are also collections of Silesian paintings, ceramics, silverware and furnishings from the 16th to 19th centuries.

Cathedral of St John the Baptist   CHURCH

(Archikatedra Św Jana Chrzciciela; www.katedra.archidiecezja.wroc.pl; Plac Katedralny 18; tower adult/concession 5/4zł; ⊙ tower 10am-5.30pm Mon-Sat, from 2pm Sun) The centrepiece of Cathedral Island, this three-aisled Gothic basilica was built between 1244 and 1590. Seriously damaged during WWII, it was reconstructed in its previous Gothic form, complete with dragon guttering. The high altar boasts a gold and silver triptych from 1522 attributed to the school of Veit Stoss, and the western portico is a medieval gem. For once you don't need strong legs to climb the 91m-high tower, as there is a lift.

🛏 Sleeping

⭐ Hotel Piast   HOTEL €

(☑ 71 343 0033; www.piastwroclaw.pl; ul Piłsudskiego 98; s/d from 130/180zł; 🛜) Known as the Kronprinz (Crown Prince) in German times, this former hostel has recently been upgraded to a neat and tidy two-star hotel. Its fully renovated rooms are clean and light, great value for the price and very handy for the train station. There's a restaurant on the premises, and breakfast costs an additional 20zł.

Hostel Mleczarnia   HOSTEL €

(☑ 71 787 7570; www.mleczarniahostel.pl; ul Włodkowica 5; dm from 35zł, r 220zł; 🛜) On a quiet road not far from the Rynek, this hostel has bags of charm, having been decorated in a deliberately old-fashioned style within a former residential building. There's a women-only dorm available, along with a kitchen and free laundry facilities. Downstairs is the excellent Mleczarnia cafe-bar.

Hotel Patio   HOTEL €€

(☑ 71 3750 400; www.hotelpatio.pl; ul Kiełbaśnicza 24; s/d from 300/340zł; 🅿 ❄ 🛜) The Patio offers pleasant lodgings a short hop from the main square, within two buildings linked by a covered, sunlit courtyard. Rooms are clean and light, sometimes small but with reasonably high ceilings, and there's a spectacular breakfast spread.

Hotel Monopol   HOTEL €€€

(☑ 71 772 3777; www.monopolwroclaw.hotel.com. pl; ul Modrzejewskiej 2; s/d 600/650zł; ❄ 🛜 🌊) In its heyday the elegant Monopol hosted such luminaries as Pablo Picasso and Marlene Dietrich (along with unsavoury characters such as Adolf Hitler). It's opposite the opera house, 350m south of the Rynek off ul Świdnicka. It boasts restaurants, bars, a cafe, a spa and boutiques, so you won't be short of pampering – though you might soon be short of cash.

🍴 Eating

Bar Wegetariański Vega   VEGETARIAN €

(☑ 71 344 3934; www.barvega.wroclaw.pl; Rynek 1/2; mains 5.50-10.50zł; ⊙ 8am-7pm Mon-Thu, 8am-9pm Fri, 9am-9pm Sat, 9am-7pm Sun; 🍴) Cheap, meat-free cafeteria on two floors in the centre of the Rynek, offering vegetarian and vegan dishes in a light green space.

There's a good choice of soups and crêpes. Set menu options run from 10zł to 22zł.

Bernard CZECH, INTERNATIONAL €€
(📞71 344 1054; www.bernard.wroclaw.pl; Rynek 35; mains 32-75zł; ⊙10.30am-11pm; 🛜) This lively split-level bar-restaurant is inspired by the Czech beer of the same name, and the menu features some Czech dishes such as rabbit and pork knee. There's upmarket comfort food including burgers, steak and fish dishes, as well as plenty of beer. The stylish interior is conducive to a quiet evening or group outing. Breakfast is served from 10.30am to noon.

Restauracja Jadka POLISH €€€
(📞71 343 6461; www.jadka.pl; ul Rzeźnicza 24/25; mains 56-86zł; ⊙1-11pm) Well-regarded fine-dining option presenting impeccable modern versions of Polish classics such as wild boar in cranberry sauce and pork knuckle, and with silver-service table settings (candles, crystal, linen) in delightful Gothic surrounds. Bookings are recommended, especially at weekends.

Drinking & Nightlife

★ Vinyl Cafe BAR
(📞508 260 288; ul Kotlarska 35/36; ⊙10am-late; 🛜) Hitting the retro button hard, this cool cafe-bar is a jumble of mismatched furniture, old framed photos and stacks of vinyl records. It's a great place to grab a drink, both day and night.

Mleczarnia BAR
(📞71 787 7576; www.mle.pl; ul Włodkowica 5; ⊙8am-4am; 🛜) Hidden away in an area that was once the city's main Jewish neighbourhood, this atmospheric place is stuffed with chipped old wooden tables bearing lace doilies and candlesticks. It turns out good coffee and light meals, including breakfast. At night the cellar opens, adding another moody dimension. There's a beautiful back garden in summer.

Bezsenność CLUB
(www.bezsennoscklub.com; ul Ruska 51; ⊙7pm-late) With its alternative/rock/dance line-up and distressed decor, 'Insomnia' attracts a high-end clientele and is one of the most popular clubs in town. It's located in the Pasaż Niepolda, home to a group of bars, clubs and restaurants, just off ul Ruska.

☆ Entertainment

Filharmonia CLASSICAL MUSIC
(Philharmonic Hall; 📞tickets 71 715 9700; www.nfm.wroclaw.pl; ul Piłsudskiego 19) Hear classical music at this venue, located 800m southwest of the Rynek.

ℹ Information

Intermax (📞71 794 0573; www.imx.pl; ul Psie Budy 10/11; per hr 4zł; ⊙9am-11pm Mon-Sat, from 10am Sun) Internet access. Enter from ul Kazimierza Wielkiego.

Tourist Office (📞71 344 3111; www.wroclaw-info.pl; Rynek 14; ⊙9am-7pm) Provides advice and assistance to visitors to Wrocław.

ℹ Getting There & Away

BUS

The **bus station** (Dworzec Centralny PKS; 📞703 400 444; ul Sucha 1/11) is south of the train station. For most destinations the train is a better choice, though handy Polski Bus services run from here to Warsaw (five hours, hourly) and Prague (five hours, four daily). Book these via www.polskibus.com.

TRAIN

Wrocław Main Train Station (📞32 428 8888; www.pkp.pl; ul Piłsudskiego 105) was opened in 1857 as a lavish architectural confection. It's easily Poland's most attractive railway station and worth visiting even if you're not travelling by train. Sample destinations include Warsaw (150zł, 3¾ hours, seven daily), Kraków (40zł, 3½ hours, eight daily) and Poznań (34zł, 2¾ hours, hourly).

WIELKOPOLSKA

Wielkopolska (Greater Poland) is the region where Poland came to life in the Middle Ages. As a result of this ancient eminence, its cities and towns are full of historic and cultural attractions. The battles of WWII later caused widespread destruction in the area, though Poznań has resumed its prominent economic role.

Poznań

POP 546,000

Stroll into Poznań's central market square on any evening and you'll receive an instant introduction to the characteristic energy of Wielkopolska's capital. The city's Old Town district is buzzing at any time of the day, and positively jumping by night.

The city is strongly associated with the formation of the Polish kingdom in the 10th century. From the late 18th century to 1945, Poznań was the German-ruled city of Posen. Much of Poznań, including the main square

(Stary Rynek), was destroyed in fighting in WWII and painstakingly rebuilt in the decades after. These days, Poznań is a vibrant university city. There's a beautiful Old Town, with a number of interesting museums and a range of lively bars, clubs and restaurants.

◎ Sights

◎ Old Town

Town Hall   HISTORIC BUILDING
(Ratusz; Stary Rynek 1) Poznań's Renaissance town hall, topped with a 61m-high tower, instantly attracts attention. Its graceful form replaced a 13th-century Gothic structure, which burned down in the early 16th century. Every day at noon two metal goats appear through a pair of small doors above the clock and butt their horns together 12 times, in deference to an old legend. These days, the town hall is home to the city's Historical Museum. The building was designed by Italian architect Giovanni Battista Quadro and built from 1550 to 1560; only the tower is a later addition, built in the 1780s after its predecessor collapsed. The crowned eagle on top of the spire, with an impressive wingspan of 2m, adds some Polish symbolism.

Concerning the legend of the goats: apparently two goats intended for a celebratory banquet escaped and ended up clashing horns above the about-to-be-unveiled clock, much to the amusement of the assembled dignitaries. The clockmaker was duly ordered to add the errant animals' images to his piece.

★**Historical Museum of Poznań**   MUSEUM
(Muzeum Historii Miasta Poznania; ☑ 61 8568 000; www.mnp.art.pl; Stary Rynek 1; adult/concession 7/5zł, Sat free; ◎ 11am-5pm Tue-Thu, noon-9pm Fri, 11am-6pm Sat & Sun) Inside the town hall, this museum displays an interesting and well-presented exhibition on the town's history, and the building's original interiors are worth the entry price on their own. The Gothic vaulted cellars are the only remains of the first town hall. They were initially used for trade but later became a jail.

◎ Ostrów Tumski

The island of Ostrów Tumski, east of the main square and across the Warta River, is the place where Poznań was founded, and with it the Polish state.

★**Poznań Cathedral**   CHURCH
(Katedra Poznańska; ☑ 61 8529 642; www.katedra. archpoznan.pl; ul Ostrów Tumski 17; crypt adult/ concession 3.50/2.50zł; ◎ 9am-6pm) Ostrów Tumski is dominated by this monumental double-towered cathedral. Basically Gothic with additions from later periods, most notably the Baroque tops of the towers, the cathedral was damaged in 1945 and took 11 years to rebuild. The aisles and the ambulatory are ringed by a dozen chapels containing numerous tombstones. The most famous is the Golden Chapel behind the high altar, which houses the remains of the first two Polish rulers: Mieszko I and Bolesław Chrobry.

The rulers' original burial site was the crypt, accessible from the back of the left-hand aisle. Apart from the fragments of what are thought to have been their tombs, you can see the relics of the first pre-Romanesque cathedral dating from 968 and of the subsequent Romanesque building from the second half of the 11th century, along with dozens of coins tossed in by more recent Polish visitors.

★**Porta Posnania**
Interactive Heritage Centre   MUSEUM
(Brama Poznania ICHOT; www.bramapoznania.pl; ul Gdańska 2; adult/concession 15/9zł, audioguide 5/3zł; ◎ 9am-6pm Tue-Fri, 10am-7pm Sat & Sun; 🖱) Cutting-edge multimedia museum that opened in 2014, telling the tale of Tumski island's eventful history and the birth of the Polish nation via interactive displays and other technological gadgetry. It's located opposite the island's eastern shore and is linked to the cathedral area by footbridge. The exhibitions are multilingual, but opt for an audioguide to help put everything together. To reach the museum from the city centre, take tram 8 eastward to the Rondo Śródka stop.

🛏 Sleeping

Frolic Goats Hostel   HOSTEL €
(☑ 61 852 4411; www.frolicgoatshostel.com; ul Wrocławska 16/6; dm 30-50zł, d 210zł; 🖱) Named after the feisty goats who fight above the town hall clock, this popular hostel is aimed squarely at the international backpacker. The pleasant lounge complements tidy, reasonably uncrowded dorms, there's a washing machine and bike hire is available for 50zł per day. Enter from ul Jaskółcza.

★**Hotel Stare Miasto**   HOTEL €€
(☑ 61 663 6242; www.hotelstaremiasto.pl; ul Rybaki 36; s 229zł, d 269-329zł; 🅿🌸🖱) Stylish value-for-money hotel with a tastefully chandeliered foyer and spacious breakfast room. Rooms can be small but are clean and bright with lovely starched white sheets.

Some upper rooms have skylights in place of windows.

Blow Up Hall 5050   HOTEL €€

(☑61 657 9980; www.blowuphall5050.com; ul Kościuszki 42; r from 450zł; ᴾ❋🕾) Wild art hotel housed within the solid ex-brewery walls of the Stary Browar shopping mall, 750m south of the Rynek. Each room has an individual hyper-modern design with colour schemes from dazzling white to gleaming black, with shiny angular furniture and fittings. The restaurant and bar are equally impressive.

✗ Eating

Apetyt   CAFETERIA €

(ul Szkolna 4; mains 4-13zł; ⊙9am-8pm Mon-Sat, 11am-10pm Sun; 🖋) This late-closing *bar mleczny* (milk bar) enjoys a good central location. The Polish cafeteria food is exactly what you'd expect – cheap serves of unfussy, filling food such as *pierogi* (dumplings) and *zupy* (soups), with *naleśniki* (crêpe) choices galore. Includes several good vegetarian items.

★Drukarnia   INTERNATIONAL €€

(☑61 850 1420; www.poznan-drukarnia.pl; ul Podgórna 6; mains 15-79zł; ⊙7am-10pm Mon-Wed, to midnight Thu, to 1am Fri, 11am-1am Sat, 11am-10pm Sun) Some Polish restaurants are finally opening for breakfast, and this sleek eatery with exposed beams above concrete floors is a top early-bird's choice. Choices include a full English breakfast with sausage, bacon, eggs and beans, and a more adventurous pasta with smoked mackerel. Later on there's a menu featuring steaks and burgers, as well as a long wine list.

Ludwiku do Rondla   JEWISH, POLISH €€

(ul Woźna 2/3; mains 28-40zł; ⊙1-10pm) Small, cosy place east of the main square, specialising in Jewish and Polish cooking – particularly where the two intertwine. Menu items are helpfully marked if an item is Polish or Jewish in origin, and include such items as herring in oil (Polish/Jewish) and stuffed meat roulade with buckwheat (Polish). The lunchtime set menu is top value at around 25zł.

🍷 Drinking & Nightlife

★Stragan   CAFE

(☑789 233 965; ul Ratajczaka 31; ⊙8am-10pm Mon-Fri, 11am-10pm Sat, 11am-8pm Sun; 🕾) Cool, contemporary cafe in which even the most bearded hipster would feel at home. Coffee ranges from Chemex brews to flat whites, complemented by excellent cakes and light meals. Also serves breakfast.

Chmielnik   BAR

(☑790 333 946; ul Żydowska 27; ⊙noon-late) Ideal place to sample the output of the booming Polish craft-beer scene, with over 150 beers in stock. Lounge and sip in the pleasant wood-lined interior or in the ambient beer garden out the back.

Van Diesel Music Club   CLUB

(☑515 065 459; www.vandiesel.pl; Stary Rynek 88; ⊙9pm-5am Fri & Sat) Happening venue on the main square, with DJs varying their offerings between pop, house, R&B, soul and dance. Given the variety, you're sure to find a night that will get you on the dance floor.

☆ Entertainment

Centrum Kultury Zamek   CONCERT VENUE

(Castle Cultural Centre; ☑61 646 5260; www.zamek.poznan.pl; ul Św Marcin 80/82; 🕾) Within the grand neo-Romanesque **Kaiserhaus**, built from 1904 to 1910 for German emperor Wilhelm II, this active cultural hub hosts cinema, art and music events.

ℹ Information

City Information Centre (☑61 852 6156; www.poznan.travel; Stary Rynek 59/60; ⊙10am-8pm Mon-Sat, 10am-6pm Sun May-Sep, 10am-5pm Oct-Apr) Located conveniently on the main square.

ℹ Getting There & Away

BUS

The **bus station** (Dworzec PKS; ☑703 30 3330; www.pks.poznan.pl; ul Dworcowa 1) is located next to the train station and is part of the Poznań City Centre transport and shopping complex. It's 1.5km southwest of the Old Town and can be reached on foot in 15 minutes, or by tram to stop 'Most Dworcowy'.

Polski Bus (www.polskibus.com) runs services to Warsaw (four to 5½ hours, seven daily) and Wrocław (3½ hours, three daily). Buy tickets online.

TRAIN

Busy **Poznań Main Train Station** (ul Dworcowa 1) is 1.5km southwest of the Old Town and can be reached on foot in 15 minutes, or by tram to stop 'Most Dworcowy'.

Useful domestic train connections include to Gdańsk (60zł, 3¾ hours, eight daily), Kraków (67zł, six hours, hourly), Toruń (26zł, 2½ hours, nine daily), Wrocław (34zł, 2½ hours, hourly) and Warsaw (95zł, three hours, hourly). Poznań is a natural jumping-off spot for Berlin (168zł, 2¾ hours, five daily).

POMERANIA

Pomerania (Pomorze in Polish) is an attractive region with diverse drawcards, from beautiful beaches to architecturally pleasing cities. The historic port city of Gdańsk is situated at the region's eastern extreme, while the attractive Gothic city of Toruń lies inland.

Gdańsk

POP 460,000

The Hanseatic port of Gdańsk grew wealthy during the Middle Ages, linking inland cities with seaports around Europe. That wealth is on display in the form of a bustling riverbank, mammoth red-brick churches and lively central streets.

Gdańsk has played an outsized role in history. The creation of the 'Free City of Danzig', at the conclusion of World War I, served as a pretext for Hitler to invade Poland at the start of WWII. The Germans fired the first shots of the war here on 1 September 1939 at the Polish garrison at Westerplatte.

In August 1980, the city became the centre of Poland's anticommunist movement with the establishment of the Solidarity trade union, led by its charismatic leader (and future Polish president), Lech Wałęsa.

⊙ Sights

Gdańsk's major sights are situated in the **Main Town** (Główne Miasto). Much of what you see, including the dazzling palaces that line the central promenade, **Long St** (ul Długa), was rebuilt from rubble after the bombardment of WWII.

⊙ Main Town

Historical Museum of Gdańsk　　MUSEUM
(Town Hall; www.mhmg.pl; Długa 46/47; adult/concession 12/6zł, tower 5zł; ⊙9am-1pm Tue, 10am-4pm Wed, Fri & Sat, to 6pm Thu, from 11am Sun) This museum is located in the historic **town hall**

Gdańsk

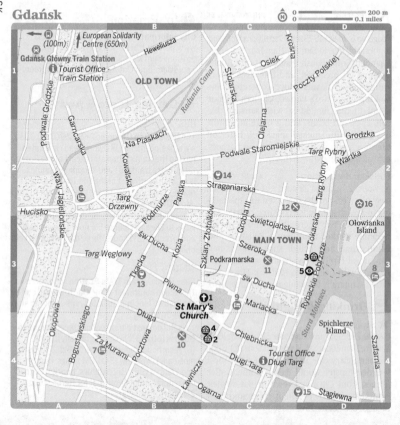

(Długi Targ), which claims Gdańsk's highest tower at 81.5m. The showpiece is the Red Room (Sala Czerwona), done up in Dutch Mannerist style from the end of the 16th century. The 2nd floor houses exhibitions related to Gdańsk's history, including mock-ups of old Gdańsk interiors. From here you can access the tower for great views across the city.

The Red Room's interior is not an imitation but the real deal; it was dismantled in 1942 and hidden outside the city until the end of the bombing. The richly carved fireplace (1593) and the marvellous portal (1596) all attract the eye, but the centre of attention is the ornamented ceiling – 25 paintings dominated by an oval centrepiece entitled *The Glorification of the Unity of Gdańsk with Poland*. Other striking rooms include the Winter Hall with its portraits of Gdańsk's mayors up to the 17th century and the Great Council Chamber with its huge oils of Polish kings.

★St Mary's Church   CHURCH
(www.bazylikamariacka.gdansk.pl; ul Podkramarska 5; adult/concession 4/2zł, tower 6/3zł; ☉8.30am-6.30pm Mon-Sat, 11am-noon & 1-5pm Sun May-Sep, slightly shorter hours Oct-Apr) Dominating the heart of the Main Town, St Mary's is often cited as the largest brick church in the world. Some 105m long and 66m wide at the transept, its massive squat tower climbs 78m high into the Gdańsk cityscape. Begun in 1343, St Mary's didn't reach its present proportions until 1502. Don't miss the 15th-century astronomical clock, placed in the northern transept, and the church tower (405 steps above the city).

On first sight, the church looks almost empty, but walk around its 30-odd chapels to discover how many outstanding works of art have been accumulated. In the floor alone, there are about 300 tombstones. In the chapel at the back of the left (northern) aisle is a replica of Memling's *The Last Judgment* – the original is in the National Museum's Department of Early Art. The extraordinary Baroque organ manages enough puff to fill the space with its tones.

The church's elephantine size is arresting and you feel even more antlike when you enter the building. Illuminated with natural light passing through 37 large windows (the biggest is 127 sq metres), the three-naved interior, topped by an intricate Gothic vault, is bright and spacious. It was originally covered with frescos, the sparse remains of which are visible in the far right corner.

The high altar boasts a Gothic polyptych from the 1510s, with the Coronation of the Virgin depicted in its central panel. Large as it is, it's a miniature in this vast space. The same applies to the 4m crucifix high up on the rood beam.

National Maritime Museum   MUSEUM
(Narodowe Muzeum Morskie w Gdańsku; ☑ Maritime Cultural Centre 58 329 8700, information 58 301 8611; www.nmm.pl; ul Ołowianka 9-13; all sites adult/concession 18/10zł; ☉10am-6pm daily) This is a sprawling exhibition of maritime history and Gdańsk's role through the centuries as a Baltic seaport. Headquarters is the multi-million-euro Maritime Cultural Centre, with a permanent interactive exhibition 'People-Ships-Ports'. Other exhibitions include the MS *Sołdek*, the first vessel to be built at the Gdańsk shipyard in the postwar years, and the Żuraw (Crane; www.nmm.pl; ul Szeroka 67/68; adult/concession 8/5zł; ☉10am-6pm daily Jul & Aug, closed Mon and shorter hours Sep-Jun), a 15th-century loading crane that was the biggest in its day. The granaries across the river house more displays, which are highly recommended.

POLAND GDAŃSK

Outside the Centre

★European Solidarity Centre   MUSEUM
(Europejskie Centrum Solidarności; ☑58 772 4112; www.ecs.gda.pl; Plac Solidarności 1; adult/concession 17/13zł; ☉10am-8pm Jun-Sep, to 6pm Oct-May) Housed in a mind-bogglingly ugly, oh-so 21st-century hulk of architecture, the exhibition in this unmarked centre (finding the entrance will be your first task) has quickly become one of Gdańsk's unmissables since it opened in 2014. Audioguide clamped to ears, the seven halls examine Poland's postwar fight for freedom, from the strikes of the 1970s to the round-table negotiations of the late 1980s and beyond. The displays are a blend of state-of-the-art multimedia experiences and real artefacts. Allow at least two hours.

🛏 Sleeping

3 City Hostel   HOSTEL €
(☑58 354 5454; www.3city-hostel.pl; Targ Drzewny 12/14; dm from 49zł, r 170zł; @☎) Big, modern, colourful hostel near the train station, with high ceilings, pleasant common areas, a kitchen, and a lounge with a view. Breakfast is included, plus there are computers on-hand for internet use. Reception runs round the clock.

Dom Harcerza   HOSTEL €
(☑58 301 3621; www.domharcerza.pl; ul Za Murami 2/10; dm/s/d from 25/60/100zł; ☎) Though occupying a former cinema, the 75-bed 'Scouts' House' has a decidedly un-Hollywood feel. There's dirt-cheap student-oriented dorm accommodation and rooms for one to three people with and without bathrooms. The simple, snug rooms are nothing fancy, but they're clean and tidy. The location near ul Długa is a winner.

Kamienica Gotyk   HOTEL €€
(☑58 301 8567; www.gotykhouse.eu; ul Mariacka 1; s/d 280/310zł; P☎) Wonderfully located at the St Mary's Church end of ul Mariacka, Gdańsk's oldest house is filled by this neat, clean, Gothic-themed guesthouse. The seven rooms have Gothic touches such as broken-arched doorways and hefty drapery, though most are thoroughly modern creations and bathrooms are definitely of the third millennium. Breakfast is served in your room.

★Hotel Podewils   HOTEL €€€
(☑58 300 9560; www.podewils.pl; ul Szafarnia 2; s/d 530/620zł; P☎) The view from the Podewils across the river to the Main Town can't be beaten, though the owners probably wish they could take its cheery Baroque facade and move it away from the incongruously soulless riverside development that's sprouted next door. Guestrooms are a confection of elegantly curved timber furniture, classic prints and distinctive wallpaper.

🍴 Eating

Bar Mleczny Neptun   CAFETERIA €
(☑058 301 4988; www.barneptun.pl; ul Długa 33/34; mains 4-9zł; ☉7.30am-7pm Mon-Fri, 10am-6pm Sat & Sun, 1hr later Jul & Aug; ☎▣) It's surprising just where some of Poland's communist-era milk bars have survived and this one, right on the tourist drag, is no exception. However, the Neptun is a cut above your run-of-the-mill *bar mleczny*, with potted plants, decorative tiling and free wi-fi. Popular with foreigners on a budget, it even has an English menu of Polish favourites such as *naleśniki* (crêpes) and *gołąbki* (cabbage rolls).

★Tawerna Mestwin   POLISH €€
(☑58 301 7882; ul Straganiarska 20/23; mains 20-40zł; ☉11am-10pm Tue-Sun, to 6pm Mon; ☎) The speciality here is Kashubian regional cooking from the northwest of Poland, and dishes like potato dumplings and stuffed cabbage rolls have a pronounced homemade quality. There's usually a fish soup and fried fish as well. The interior is done out like a traditional cottage and the exposed beams and dark-green walls create a cosy atmosphere.

Restauracja Pod Łososiem   POLISH €€€
(☑58 301 7652; www.podlososiem.com.pl; ul Szeroka 52/54; mains 40-110zł; ☉noon-11pm; ▣) Founded in 1598 and famous for salmon, this is one of Gdańsk's most highly regarded restaurants. Red leather seats, brass chandeliers and a gathering of gas lamps fill out the rather sober interior, illuminated by the speciality drink – Goldwasser. This gooey, sweet liqueur with flakes of gold was produced in its cellars from the 16th century until WWII.

🍷 Drinking & Nightlife

★Józef K   BAR
(☑058 550 4935; ul Piwna 1/2; ☉10am-last customer; ☎) Is it a bar or a junk shop? You decide as you relax with a cocktail or a glass of excellent Polish perry (pear cider) on one of the battered sofas, illuminated by an old theatre spotlight. Downstairs is an open

area where the party kicks off at weekends; upstairs is more intimate with lots of soft seating and well-stocked bookcases.

Lamus BAR
(Lawendowa 8, enter from Straganiarska; ⊗noon-1am Mon-Fri, to 3am Sat, to midnight Sun) This fun retro-drink halt has a random scattering of 1970s furniture, big-print wallpaper from the same period, and a menu of Polish craft beers, cider and coffee. There's also a spillover bar for the Saturday-night crowd.

Miasto Aniołów CLUB
(📞58 768 5831; www.miastoaniolow.com.pl; ul Chmielna 26) The City of Angels covers all the bases – late-night revellers can hit the spacious dance floor, crash in the chill-out area or hang around the atmospheric deck overlooking the Motława River. Nightly DJs play disco and other dance-oriented sounds.

☆ Entertainment

Baltic Philharmonic Hall CLASSICAL MUSIC
(📞58 320 6262; www.filharmonia.gda.pl; ul Ołowianka 1) The usual home of chamber music concerts also organises many of the major music festivals throughout the year.

ℹ️ Information

Tourist Office Train station (📞58 721 3277; www.gdansk4u.pl; ul Podwale Grodzkie 8; ⊗9am-7pm May-Sep, to 5pm Oct-Apr); Main Town (📞58 301 4355; www.gdansk4u.pl; Długi Targ 28/29; ⊗9am-7pm May-Sep, to 5pm Oct-Apr); Airport (📞58 348 13 68; www.gdansk4u.pl; ul Słowackiego 210, Gdańsk Lech Wałęsa Airport; ⊗24hr) Relatively efficient but occasionally visitor-weary info points. The train station branch is hidden in the underpass leading to the city centre.

ℹ️ Getting There & Away

BUS

The **bus station** (PKS Gdańsk; 📞801 055 900; www.pks.gdansk.pl; ul 3 Maja 12) is behind the main train station. PKS buses head to Warsaw (50zł, 5¼ hours, hourly), as do services of Polski Bus (4½ to 5½ hours, seven daily). Book tickets for the latter at www.polskibus.com.

TRAIN

The city's train station, **Gdańsk Główny** (Gdańsk Główny; www.pkp.pl; ul Podwale Grodzkie 1), is located on the western outskirts of the Old Town. Most long-distance trains actually start or finish at Gdynia, so make sure you get on/off quickly here.

Useful direct train connections include to Toruń (40zł, three hours, nine daily), Poznań

WORTH A TRIP

MALBORK

Magnificent **Malbork Castle** (📞tickets 55 647 0978; www.zamek.malbork.pl; ul Starościńska 1; adult/concession 39.50/29.50zł; ⊗9am-7pm May-Sep, 10am-3pm Oct-Apr) makes a great day trip from Gdańsk. It's the largest Gothic castle in Europe and was once headquarters for the medieval Teutonic Knights. Its sinister form looms over the relatively small town and Nogat River. Trains run regularly from Gdańsk Główny station (14zł, 45 minutes, twice hourly). Once you get to Malbork station, turn right, cross the highway and follow ul Kościuszki to the castle. Compulsory tours come with an audio tour in English. There are places to eat at the castle and in the town.

(60zł, 3½ hours, eight daily) and Warsaw (60zł to 119zł½, three to six hours, hourly).

Toruń
POP 205,000

Toruń escaped major damage in WWII and is famous for its well-preserved Gothic architecture, along with the quality of its famous gingerbread. The city is also renowned as the birthplace of Nicolaus Copernicus, who revolutionised the field of astronomy in 1543 by asserting the Earth travelled around the Sun. He's a figure you will not be able to escape – you can even buy gingerbread men in his likeness.

◎ Sights

The usual starting point on Toruń's Gothic trail is the **Old Town Market Square** (Rynek Staromiejski), lined with finely restored houses. At the southeast corner, look for the picturesque **Statue of Copernicus**.

Old Town Hall MUSEUM
(Ratusz Staromiejski; www.muzeum.torun.pl; Rynek Staromiejski 1; adult/concession museum 12/8zł, tower 12/8zł, combined ticket 19/14zł; ⊗museum 10am-6pm Tue-Sun, tower 10am-8pm May-Sep, shorter hours Oct-Apr) The Old Town Hall dates from the 14th century and hasn't changed much since, though some Renaissance additions lent an ornamental touch to the sober Gothic structure. Today, it houses the main branch of the Toruń Regional Museum

POLAND TORUŃ

GREAT MASURIAN LAKES

The northeastern corner of Poland features a beautiful postglacial landscape dominated by thousands of lakes. About 200km of canals connect these bodies of water, making the area a prime destination for canoeists, as well as those who love to hike, fish and mountain bike.

The towns of Giżycko and Mikołajki make good bases. Both the Giżycko tourist office (☑87 428 5265; www.gizycko.turystyka.pl; ul Wyzwolenia 2; ☺8am-5pm Mon-Fri, 10am-2pm Sat & Sun Mar-May & Sep-Oct, 9am-6pm Mon-Fri, 10am-4pm Sat & Sun Jun-Aug, shorter hours Nov-Feb) and the Mikołajki tourist office (☑87 421 6850; www.mikolajki.pl; Plac Wolności 7; ☺10am-6pm Jun-Aug, 10am-6pm Mon-Sat May & Sep) supply useful maps for sailing and hiking, provide excursion boat schedules, and assist in finding accommodation.

Nature aside, there are some interesting fragments of history in this region. A grim reminder of the past is the Wolf's Lair (Wilczy Szaniec; ☑89 752 4429; www.wolfsschanze. pl; adult/concession 15/10zł; ☺8am-dusk). Located at Gierłoż, 8km east of Kętrzyn, this ruined complex was Hitler's wartime headquarters for his invasion of the Soviet Union. In 1944, a group of high-ranking German officers tried to assassinate Hitler here. These dramatic events were reprised in the 2008 Tom Cruise movie *Valkyrie*.

boasting displays of Gothic art (painting and stained glass), a display of local 17th- and 18th-century crafts and a gallery of Polish paintings from 1800 to the present, including a couple of Witkacys and Matejkos. Climb the tower for a fine panoramic view of Toruń's Gothic townscape.

Cathedral of SS John the Baptist & John the Evangelist
CHURCH

(www.katedra.diecezja.torun.pl; ul Żeglarska 16; ☺9am-5.30pm Mon-Sat, 2-5.30pm Sun) Toruń's mammoth Gothic cathedral was begun around 1260 but only completed at the end of the 15th century. Its massive tower houses Poland's second-largest historic bell, the Tuba Dei (God's Trumpet). On the southern side of the tower, facing the Vistula, is a large 15th-century clock; its original face and single hand are still in working order. Check out the dent above the VIII – it's from a cannonball that struck the clock during the Swedish siege of 1703.

Toruń Gingerbread Museum
MUSEUM

(Muzeum Toruńskiego Piernika; www.muzeum. torun.pl; ul Strumykowa 4; adult/concession 12/8zł; ☺10am-6pm Tue-Sun May-Sep, to 4pm Oct-Apr) Not to be confused with the commercial Gingerbread Museum (Muzeum Piernika; ☑56 663 6617; www.muzeumpiernika.pl; ul Rabiańska 9; adult/child15/10zł; ☺10am-6pm, tours every hour, on the hour) across town, this branch of the Toruń Regional Museum is housed in a former gingerbread factory and looks at the 600-year-long history of the city's favourite sweet.

🛏 Sleeping

Toruń Główny Hostel
HOSTEL €

(☑606 564 600; www.hosteltg.com; Toruń Główny train station; dm/d 39/70zł; 🖳) This 56-bed hostel is housed in the old post office building right on the platform at Toruń's recently renovated main train station. The six- and eight-bed dorms are spacious with suitcase-size lockers and reading lamps; free breakfast is taken in the basement kitchen. There are attractive wall frescos of Toruń's old town and, surprisingly, no train noise to keep you awake at night.

★ Hotel Petite Fleur
HOTEL €€

(☑56 621 5100; www.petitefleur.pl; ul Piekary 25; s/d from 180/210zł; 🖳) One of the better midrange options in Toruń has understated rooms containing slickly polished timber furnishings and elegant prints, though the singles can be a touch small. The French brick-cellar restaurant is one of Toruń's better hotel dining options and the buffet breakfast is one of the best in the north.

Hotel Karczma Spichrz
HOTEL €€

(☑56 657 1140; www.spichrz.pl; ul Mostowa 1; s/d 250/310zł; ✴🖳) Wonderfully situated within a historic waterfront granary, this hotel's 19 rooms are laden with personality, featuring massive exposed beams above characterful timber furniture and contemporary bathrooms. The location by the river is within walking distance of the sights but away from the crowds. Good restaurant next door.

Eating

Karrotka
VEGETARIAN €

(Łazienna 9; mains 5-12zł; ⊘noon-7pm Mon-Sat, to 5pm Sun; 🖉) Enjoy tasty vegetarian dishes under a large wall mural of painted carrots crossed in meat-free defiance at this small vegetarian milk bar.

Oberża
POLISH €

(🖉606 664 756; www.gotujemy.pl; ul Rabiańska 9; mains 8-17zł; ⊘11am-10pm Mon-Thu, to 11pm Fri & Sat, to 9pm Sun; 🐦) This large self-service canteen stacks 'em high and sells 'em cheap for a hungry crowd of locals and tourists. Find your very own thatched mini cottage or intimate hideout lost amid stained-glass windows, cartwheels, bridles and other rural knick-knacks of yesteryear to enjoy 11 types of *pierogi* (dumplings), soups, salads and classic Polish mains from a menu tuned to low-cost belly-packing.

★ Szeroka 9
INTERNATIONAL €€€

(🖉56 622 8424; www.szeroka9.pl; ul Szeroka 9; mains 32-49zł; ⊘noon-11pm Mon-Fri, from 10am Sat & Sun; 🖻) Arguably Toruń's top restaurant, it offers a changing menu of seasonal gourmet-style fare with everything from rabbit in apple and cream sauce to house tagliatelle. The dessert to plump for is local gingerbread in plum sauce. The decor is contemporary urban and the staff is friendly and knowledgeable about what's on the plate. Reservations are recommended for dinner.

🍷 Drinking & Nightlife

Cafe Molus
CAFE

(🖉56 621 1107; www.cafemolus.pl; Rynek Staromiejski 36; ⊘8am-last customer) This stylish cafe fulfils the desires of the sweet-toothed and caffeine-cravers under broken Gothic arches, painted ceilings and some of the chunkiest beamery you've ever seen. The highlight here is the secluded Renaissance-style courtyard out back where you can leave the city behind as you take cake.

Jan Olbracht
BREWERY

(www.browar-olbracht.pl; ul Szczytna 15; ⊘10am-11pm Sun-Thu, to midnight Fri & Sat) Take a seat in an egg-shaped indoor booth or at the street-side mini beer garden to sip some of this microbrewery's unusual beers. These include pils, wheat beer, a special ale and, this being Toruń, gingerbread beer, all brewed in the huge copper vats at the front of the huge building.

☆ Entertainment

Dwór Artusa
CLASSICAL MUSIC

(🖉56 655 4929; www.artus.torun.pl; Rynek Staromiejski 6) The Artus Court, one of the most impressive mansions on the main square, is now a major cultural centre and has an auditorium hosting musical events, including concerts and recitals.

❶ Information

Tourist Office (🖉56 621 0930; www.torun.pl; Rynek Staromiejski 25; ⊘9am-6pm Mon-Fri, to 4pm Sat & Sun; 🐦) Free wi-fi access, heaps of info and professional staff who know their city.

❶ Getting There & Away

BUS

The **bus station** (Dworzec Autobusowy Arriva; www.rozklady.com.pl; ul Dąbrowskiego 8-24) is a 10-minute walk north of the Old Town. From here, Polski Bus connects to Warsaw (3½ hours, four daily) and Gdańsk (two hours, five daily); fares vary, so book online at www.polskibus. com. For other places, it's usually better to take the train.

TRAIN

Toruń's **main train station** (Toruń Główny; www. pkp.pl; Kujawska 1; 🚋22, 27) is located on the opposite side of the Vistula River and linked to the Old Town by bus 22 or 27 (or a 2km walk). Useful direct train connections include those to Gdańsk (45zł, three hours, nine daily), Kraków (65zł, seven hours, three daily), Poznań (26zł, 2½ hours, nine daily) and Warsaw (45zł, 2¾ hours, eight daily).

ESSENTIAL FOOD & DRINK

Barszcz Famous beetroot soup comes in two varieties: red (made from beetroot) and white (with wheat flour and sausage).

Bigos Thick stew with sauerkraut and meat.

Pierogi Flour dumplings, usually stuffed with cheese, mushrooms or meat.

Szarlotka Apple cake with cream; a Polish classic.

Wódka Vodka: try it plain, or ask for *myśliwska* (flavoured with juniper berries).

Żurek Hearty, sour rye soup includes sausage and hard-boiled egg.

SURVIVAL GUIDE

ℹ️ Directory A–Z

ACCOMMODATION

➡ Polish accommodation runs the gamut from youth hostels, bungalows and mountain cabins to modest hotels and pensions all the way to up-market boutiques and business-oriented chains.

➡ Youth hostels are divided into 'older-style', where accommodation is offered in basic dorms, and modern hostels, geared toward international backpackers. A dorm bed can cost anything from 40zł to 60zł per person per night.

➡ A handy campsite resource is the website of the **Polish Federation of Camping and Caravanning** (www.pfcc.eu).

➡ Hotel prices vary substantially depending on the day of the week or season. In cities, expect higher rates during the week and weekend discounts. In heavily touristed areas, rates may rise over the weekend.

➡ In big cities like Warsaw, Kraków and Gdańsk, private apartments with washing machines are available for short-term rentals. These can offer an affordable alternative to hotels, and compensate for the lack of laundromats in Poland.

GAY & LESBIAN TRAVELLERS

➡ Homosexual activity is legal in Poland and overt discrimination is banned, though public attitudes are generally not supportive.

➡ Warsaw and Kraków are the best places to find gay-friendly bars and clubs.

➡ A decent source of online information: www.gayguide.net.

INTERNET ACCESS

➡ Nearly all hotels and hostels offer internet, usually wi-fi.

COUNTRY FACTS

Area 312,679 sq km

Capital Warsaw

Country Code ☑ 48

Currency Złoty (zł)

Emergency Ambulance ☑ 999, fire ☑ 998, police ☑ 997; from mobile phones ☑ 112

Language Polish

Money ATMs all over; banks open Monday to Friday

Population 38.5 million

Visas Not required for citizens of the EU, US, Canada, New Zealand and Australia.

SLEEPING PRICE RANGES

Accommodation listings are grouped by price then ordered by preference. Prices listed are for an average double room in high season, with private bathroom and including breakfast.

€ less than 150zł

€€ 150–400zł

€€€ more than 400zł

➡ Many cafes, restaurants and bars offer free wi-fi for customers.

➡ Internet cafes are not as abundant as they were, but normally charge around 6zł per hour.

MONEY

➡ Poland's currency is the złoty (*zwo-ti*), abbreviated as zł (international currency code PLN). It's divided into 100 groszy (gr).

➡ *Bankomats* (ATMs) accept most international credit cards and are easily found. Private *kantors* (foreign-exchange offices) are also everywhere.

➡ Tipping isn't common in Poland, but feel free to leave 10% extra for waitstaff or taxi drivers if you've had good service.

OPENING HOURS

Banks 9am–4pm Monday to Friday, 9am–1pm Saturday (varies)

Offices 9am–5pm Monday to Friday, 9am–1pm Saturday (varies)

Post Offices 8am–7pm Monday to Friday, 8am–1pm Saturday (cities)

Restaurants 11am–10pm daily

Shops 8am–6pm Monday to Friday, 10am–2pm Saturday

PUBLIC HOLIDAYS

New Year's Day 1 January

Epiphany 6 January

Easter Sunday March or April

Easter Monday March or April

State Holiday 1 May

Constitution Day 3 May

Pentecost Sunday Seventh Sunday after Easter

Corpus Christi Ninth Thursday after Easter

Assumption Day 15 August

All Saints' Day 1 November

Independence Day 11 November

Christmas 25 and 26 December

TELEPHONE

All Poland phone numbers have nine digits. Landlines are written ☑ 12 345 6789, while mobile phone numbers are written ☑ 123 456 789. To call abroad from Poland, dial the international access code (00), then the country code, then the area code (minus any initial zero) and the number. To dial Poland from abroad, dial your country's international access code, then ☑ 48 (Poland's country code) then the nine-digit local number.

VISAS

EU citizens do not need visas and can stay indefinitely. Citizens of the USA, Canada, Australia, New Zealand, Israel, Japan and many other countries can stay in Poland for up to 90 days without a visa. Other nationalities should check with their local Polish embassy or at the Polish Ministry of Foreign Affairs website (www.msz.gov.pl).

❶ Getting There & Away

AIR

➡ Warsaw-Frédéric Chopin Airport (p864) is the nation's main international gateway, while other important airports include Kraków, Gdańsk, Poznań and Wrocław.

➡ The national carrier **LOT** (☑ 22 577 7755; www.lot.com) flies to major European cities and select destinations further afield.

➡ A vast array of budget carriers, including **Ryanair** (www.ryanair.com) and **Wizz Air** (www.wizzair.com), fly into Poland from airports across Europe, including regional airports in Britain and Ireland.

LAND
Border Crossings

➡ As Poland is a member of the EU's Schengen Zone, there are no passport or customs controls if arriving from Germany, the Czech Republic, Slovakia or Lithuania.

➡ Expect border delays if arriving from Ukraine, Belarus or Russia's Kaliningrad province.

Bus

➡ International buses head in all directions, including eastward to the Baltic States. From Zakopane, it's easy to hop to Slovakia via bus or minibus.

➡ Several companies operate long-haul coach service. Two reliable operators include **Eurolines Polska** (☑ 146 571 777; www.eurolines.pl) and Polski Bus (www.polskibus.com).

Car & Motorcycle

➡ The minimum legal driving age is 18.

➡ The maximum blood-alcohol limit is 0.02%.

➡ All drivers are required to carry their home driving licence, along with identity card, vehicle registration and liability insurance.

Train

There are direct rail services from Warsaw to several surrounding capitals, including Berlin, Prague, Minsk and Moscow. Kraków also has useful international rail connections.

EATING PRICE RANGES

The following price ranges refer to the cost of an average main-course item.

€ less than 20zł

€€ 20–40zł

€€€ more than 40zł

SEA

Ferry services operated by **Polferries** (☑ 801 003 171; www.polferries.pl), **Stena Line** (☑ 58 660 9200; www.stenaline.pl) and **Unity Line** (☑ 91 359 5600; www.unityline.pl) connect Poland's Baltic coast ports of Gdańsk, Gydnia and Świnoujscie to destinations in Scandinavia.

❶ Getting Around

AIR

LOT flies between Warsaw, Gdańsk, Kraków, Poznań, Wrocław and Lublin.

BUS

➡ Most buses are operated by the state bus company, PKS. It operates both ordinary buses (marked in black on timetables) and fast buses (marked in red).

➡ Buy tickets at bus terminals or directly from the driver.

➡ Private company Polski Bus offers modern, comfortable long-haul coach service to select large Polish cities and beyond; buy tickets from its website (www.polskibus.com).

CAR

Major international car-rental companies are represented in larger cities and airports.

TRAIN

Polish State Railways (PKP; ☑ information 703 202 020; www.pkp.pl) operates trains to nearly every tourist destination; its online timetable is helpful, providing routes, fares and intermediate stations in English.

➡ EIC (Express InterCity) and EC (EuroCity) trains link large cities and offer the best and fastest connections. Reservations are obligatory.

➡ TLK (Tanie Linie Kolejowe) trains tend to be as fast as EC, but are cheaper. Trains are often crowded and no reservations are taken for 2nd class on some trains.

➡ IR (InterRegio) and R (Regio) are cheap and slow local trains.

➡ Buy tickets at ticket machines, station ticket windows or at special PKP passenger-service centres, located in major stations. Also buy online at the Polish State Railways (PKP) website.

Portugal

Best Places to Eat

➡ Ti-Natércia (p897)

➡ Mercado da Ribeira (p897)

➡ A Eira do Mel (p906)

➡ Cafe Santa Cruz (p911)

➡ Flor dos Congregados (p917)

Best Places to Stay

➡ Lisbon Destination Hostel (p894)

➡ Casa do Príncipe (p896)

➡ Moon Hill Hostel (p900)

➡ Canto de Luz (p916)

➡ 6 Only (p916)

Why Go?

With medieval castles, frozen-in-time villages, captivating cities and golden-sand bays, the Portuguese experience can mean many things. History, terrific food and wine, lyrical scenery and all-night partying are just the beginning.

Portugal's cinematically beautiful capital, Lisbon, and its soulful northern rival, Porto, are two of Europe's most charismatic cities. Both are a joy to stroll, with river views, rattling trams and tangled lanes hiding boutiques, new-wave bars and a seductive mix of restaurants, fado (traditional Portuguese melancholic song) clubs and open-air cafes.

Beyond the cities, Portugal's landscape unfolds in all its beauty. Stay in converted hilltop fortresses fronting age-old vineyards, hike amid granite peaks or explore medieval villages in the little-visited hinterland. More than 800km of coast shelters some of Europe's best beaches: gaze out over dramatic end-of-the-world cliffs, surf Atlantic breaks off dune-covered beaches or laze on sandy islands fronting the ocean.

When to Go
Lisbon

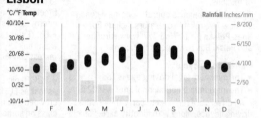

Apr & May Sunny days and wildflowers set the stage for hiking and outdoor activities.

Jun–Aug Lovely and lively, with a packed festival calendar and steamy beach days.

Late Sep & Oct Crisp mornings and sunny days; prices dip, crowds disperse.

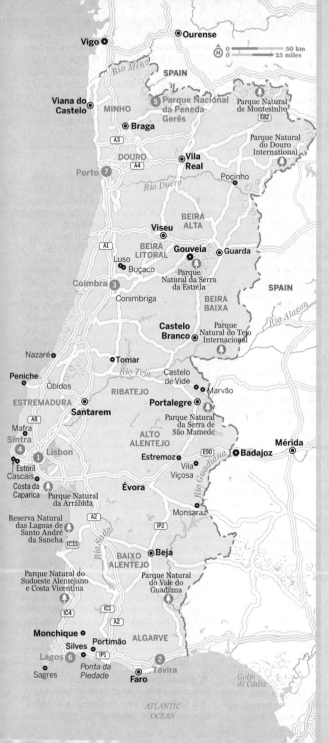

Portugal Highlights

1 **Alfama** (p902) Following the sound of fado spilling from the lamplit lanes of this enchanting old-world neighbourhood in the heart of Lisbon.

2 **Tavira** (p903) Taking in the laid-back charms, before hitting some of the Algarve's prettiest beaches.

3 **Coimbra** (p910) Catching live music in a backstreet bar in this festive university town with a stunning medieval centre.

4 **Sintra** (p900) Exploring the wooded hills, studded with fairy tale–like palaces, villas and gardens.

5 **Parque Nacional da Peneda-Gerês** (p920) Conquering the park's ruggedly scenic trails.

6 **Lagos** (p904) Enjoying heady beach days in this surf-loving town with a vibrant drinking and dining scene.

7 **Porto** (p913) Exploring the Unesco World Heritage–listed city centre, sampling velvety ports at riverside wine lodges.

LISBON

POP 547,733

Spread across steep hillsides that overlook the Rio Tejo, Lisbon has captivated visitors for centuries. Windswept vistas at breathtaking heights reveal the city in all its beauty: Roman and Moorish ruins, white-domed cathedrals and grand plazas lined with sun-drenched cafes. The real delight of discovery, though, is delving into the narrow cobblestone lanes.

As bright-yellow trams clatter through curvy tree-lined streets, Lisboetas (residents of Lisbon) stroll through lamplit old quarters, much as they've done for centuries. Village-life gossip is exchanged over fresh bread and wine at tiny patio restaurants as fado singers perform in the background. In other parts of town, Lisbon reveals her youthful alter ego at stylish dining rooms and lounges, late-night street parties, riverside nightspots, and boutiques selling all things classic and cutting-edge.

⊙ Sights

⊙ Baixa & Alfama

Alfama is Lisbon's Moorish time capsule: a medina-like district of tangled alleys, hidden palm-shaded squares and narrow terracotta-roofed houses that tumble down to the glittering Tejo.

★ Castelo de São Jorge   CASTLE

(www.castelodesaojorge.pt; adult/student/child €8.50/5/free; ⊙9am-9pm Mar-Oct, to 6pm Nov-Feb) Towering dramatically above Lisbon, the mid-11th-century hilltop fortifications of Castelo de São Jorge sneak into almost every snapshot. Roam its snaking ramparts and pine-shaded courtyards for superlative views over the city's red rooftops to the river. Three guided tours daily (Portuguese, English and Spanish) at 1pm and 5pm are included in the admission price.

Sé de Lisboa   CATHEDRAL

(Largo de Sé; ⊙9am-7pm Tue-Sat, to 5pm Mon & Sun) FREE One of Lisbon's icons is the fortress-like Sé de Lisboa, built in 1150 on the site of a mosque soon after Christians recaptured the city from the Moors.

It was sensitively restored in the 1930s. Despite the masses outside, the rib-vaulted interior, lit by a rose window, is calm. Stroll around the cathedral to spy leering gargoyles peeking above the orange trees.

Museu do Fado   MUSEUM

(www.museudofado.pt; Largo do Chafariz de Dentro; adult/child €5/3; ⊙10am-6pm Tue-Sun) Fado (traditional Portuguese melancholic song) was born in the Alfama. Immerse yourself in its bittersweet symphonies at Museu do Fado. This engaging museum traces fado's history from its working-class roots to international stardom.

⊙ Belém

This quarter, 6km west of Rossio, whisks you back to Portugal's Age of Discoveries with its iconic sights. Besides heritage architecture, Belém bakes some of the country's best *pastéis de nata* (custard tarts).

To reach Belém, hop aboard tram 15 from Praça da Figueira or Praça do Comércio.

★ Mosteiro dos Jerónimos   MONASTERY

(www.mosteirojeronimos.pt; Praça do Império; adult/child €10/5, 1st Sun of month free; ⊙10am-6.30pm Tue-Sun, to 5.30pm Oct-May) Belém's undisputed heart-stealer is this Unesco-listed monastery. The *mosteiro* is the stuff of pure fantasy: a fusion of Diogo de Boitaca's creative vision and the spice and pepper dosh of Manuel I, who commissioned it to trumpet Vasco da Gama's discovery of a sea route to India in 1498.

Torre de Belém   TOWER

(www.torrebelem.pt; adult/child €6/3, 1st Sun of month free; ⊙10am-6.30pm Tue-Sun, to 5.30pm Oct-Apr) Jutting out onto the Rio Tejo, this Unesco World Heritage–listed fortress epitomises the Age of Discoveries. You'll need to breathe in to climb the narrow spiral staircase to the tower, which affords sublime views over Belém and the river.

Museu Colecção Berardo   MUSEUM

(www.museuberardo.pt; Praça do Império; ⊙10am-7pm) FREE Culture fiends get their contemporary-art fix for free at Museu Colecção Berardo, the star of the Centro Cultural de Belém. The ultrawhite, minimalist gallery displays millionaire José Berardo's eye-popping collection of abstract, surrealist and pop art, including Hockney, Lichtenstein, Warhol and Pollock originals.

⊙ Saldanha

★ Museu Calouste Gulbenkian   MUSEUM

(www.museu.gulbenkian.pt; Av de Berna 45; adult/child €5/free, Sun free; ⊙10am-6pm Wed-Mon) Famous for its outstanding quality and breadth, the world-class Museu Calouste Gulbenkian showcases an epic collection of Western and Eastern art – from Egyptian treasures to Old Master and Impressionist paintings.

Centro de Arte Moderna   MUSEUM
(Modern Art Centre; CAM; www.cam.gulbenkian.pt; Rua Dr Nicaulau de Bettencourt; adult/child €5/ free, free Sun; ⊙10am-6pm Wed-Mon) Situated in a sculpture-dotted garden, the Centro de Arte Moderna reveals a stellar collection of 20th-century Portuguese and international art.

◉ Santa Apolónia & Lapa

The museums listed here are west and east of the city centre, but are well worth visiting.

Museu Nacional do Azulejo   MUSEUM
(www.museudoazulejo.pt; Rua Madre de Deus 4; adult/child €5/2.50, free 1st Sun of the month; ⊙10am-6pm Tue-Sun) Housed in a sublime 16th-century convent, Lisbon's Museu Nacional do Azulejo covers the entire *azulejo* (hand-painted tile) spectrum. Star exhibits feature a 36m-long panel depicting pre-earthquake Lisbon, a Manueline cloister with web-like vaulting and exquisite blue-and-white *azulejos*, and a gold-smothered baroque chapel.

★Museu Nacional de Arte Antiga   MUSEUM
(Ancient Art Museum; www.museudearteantiga.pt; Rua das Janelas Verdes; adult/child €6/3, 1st Sun of month free; ⊙10am-6pm Tue-Sun) Set in a lemon-fronted, 17th-century palace, the Museu Nacional de Arte Antiga is Lapa's biggest draw. It presents a star-studded collection of European and Asian paintings and decorative arts.

LX Factory   ARTS CENTRE
(www.lxfactory.com; Rua Rodrigues de Faria 103) Lisbon's hub of cutting-edge creativity hosts a dynamic menu of events from live concerts and film screenings to fashion shows and art exhibitions. There's a rustically cool cafe as well as a restaurant, bookshop and design-minded shops. Weekend nights see parties with a dance- and art-loving crowd.

◉ Parque das Nações

The former Expo '98 site, this revitalised 2km-long waterfront area in the northeast equals a family fun day out, packed

HEAVENLY VIEWS

Lisbon's *miradouros* (lookouts) lift spirits with their heavenly views. Some have outdoor cafes for lingering.

Largo das Portas do Sol (Largo das Portas do Sol) Moorish gateway with stunning views over Alfama's rooftops.

Miradouro da Graça (Largo da Graça) Pine-fringed square that's perfect for sundowners.

Miradouro da Senhora do Monte (Rua da Senhora do Monte) The highest lookout, with memorable castle views.

Miradouro de São Pedro de Alcântara (Rua São Pedro de Alcântara; viewpoint 24hr, kiosk 10am-midnight Mon-Wed, to 2am Thu-Sun) Drinks and sweeping views on the edge of Bairro Alto.

Miradouro de Santa Catarina (Rua de Santa Catarina; ⊙24hr) FREE Youthful spot with guitar-playing rebels, artful graffiti and far-reaching views.

with public art, gardens and kid-friendly attractions.

Take the metro to **Oriente station** (Oriente Station; Av Dom João II) – a stunner designed by star Spanish architect Santiago Calatrava.

Oceanário   AQUARIUM
(www.oceanario.pt; Doca dos Olivais; adult/child €14/9, incl temporary exhibition €17/11; ⊙10am-8pm, to 7pm winter) The closest you'll get to scuba diving without a wetsuit, Lisbon's Oceanário is mind-blowing. No amount of hyperbole, where 8000 marine creatures splash in 7 million litres of seawater, does it justice. Huge wrap-around tanks make you feel as if you are underwater, as you eyeball zebra sharks, honeycombed rays, gliding mantas and schools of neon fish.

Pavilhão do Conhecimento   MUSEUM
(Pavilion of Knowledge; www.pavconhecimento.pt; Living Science Centre; adult/child €9/5; ⊙10am-6pm Tue-Fri, 11am-7pm Sat & Sun) Kids won't grumble about science at the interactive Pavilhão do Conhecimento, where they can experience the gravity on the moon (or lack thereof, rather) and get dizzy on a high-wire bicycle. Budding physicists have fun whipping up tornadoes and blowing massive soap bubbles, while tots run riot in the adult-free unfinished house.

Central Lisbon

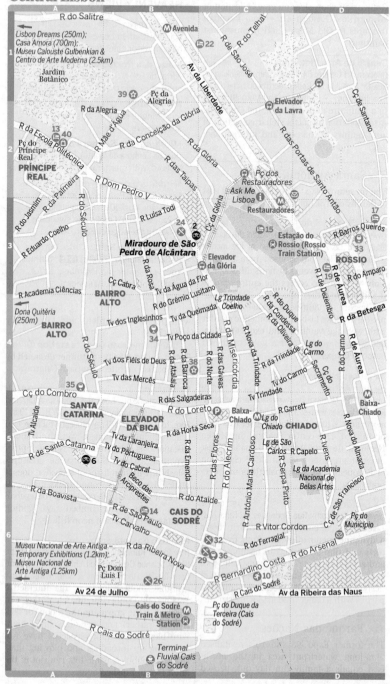

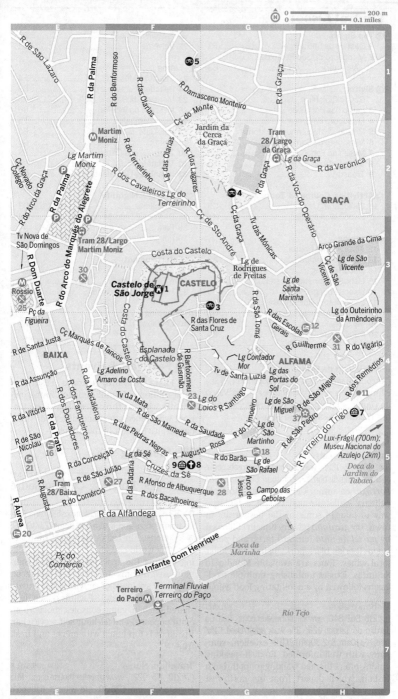

0   200 m
0   0.1 miles

R de São Lázaro

R da Palma

R do Benformoso

R das Olarias

R Damasceno Monteiro

R da Graça

Martim Moniz

R do Terreirinho

Jardim da Cerca da Graça

Tram 28/Largo da Graça

Lg da Graça

R da Verónica

Cç Novado Colégio

R do Arco da Graça

R da Palma

Lg Martim Moniz

R do Marquês do Alegrete

R dos Cavaleiros Lg do Terreirinho

Cç de Sto André

R dos Lagares

Cç da Graça

R da Graça

R da Voz do Operário

GRAÇA

Tv Nova de São Domingos

R Dom Duarte

Tram 28/Largo Martim Moniz

Costa do Castelo

Lg de Rodrigues de Freitas

Arco Grande da Cima

Cç de São Vicente

Lg de São Vicente

Rossio

Pç da Figueira

CASTELO

Castelo de São Jorge

R de São Tomé

Lg de Santa Marinha

Lg do Outeirinho da Amêndoeira

R de Santa Justa

Cç Marquês de Tancos

R das Flores de Santa Cruz

R das Escolas Gerais

R Guilherme

R do Vigário

BAIXA

Costa do Castelo

Esplanada do Castelo

R Bartolomeu de Gusmão

Lg Contador Mor

ALFAMA

R da Assunção

Lg Adelino Amaro da Costa

Tv de Santa Luzia

Lg das Portas do Sol

R da Vitória

R dos Fanqueiros

Tv da Mata

R de São Mamede

R da Saudade

Lg de São Miguel

R de São Miguel

R dos Remédios

R de São Nicolau

R da Madalena

R das Pedras Negras

Lg do Loios

R Santiago

R do Limoeiro

Lg de São Pedro

R Terreiro do Trigo

Lux-Frágil (700m);
Museu Nacional do Azulejo (2km)

R da Prata

R da Conceição

R Augusto Rosa

Lg de São Martinho

Doca do Jardim do Tabaco

R de São Julião

Lg da Sé

Cruzes da Sé

R do Barão

Lg de São Rafael

Tram 28/Baixa

R da Padaria

R Afonso de Albuquerque

Arco de Jesus

R do Comércio

R dos Bacalhoeiros

Campo das Cebolas

R Áurea

R da Alfândega

Pç do Comércio

Doca da Marinha

Av Infante Dom Henrique

Terreiro do Paço

Terminal Fluvial Terreiro do Paço

Rio Tejo

Central Lisbon

Ponte Vasco da Gama   BRIDGE
(Vasco da Gama Bridge; www.lusoponte.pt) Vanishing into a watery distance, Ponte Vasco da Gama is Europe's longest bridge, stretching 17.2km across the Rio Tejo.

☞ Tours

Culinary Backstreets   FOOD & DRINK
(☑963 472 188; www.culinarybackstreets.com/culinary-walks/lisbon; 3/6hr tour €85/118) *Eat Portugal* co-author Célia Pedroso leads epic culinary walks through Lisbon, a fantastic way to take in some of the best treats in town. Try *ginjinha* (cherry liqueur) followed by *pastel de nata* (custard tarts) and *porco preto* (Iberian black pork), paired with killer local wines. Tours are available Monday to Saturday. Expect tantalising multiple food-gasms followed by a debilitating food coma.

Lisbon Walker   WALKING
(☑218 861 840; www.lisbonwalker.com; Rua do Jardim do Tabaco 126; 3hr walk adult/child €15/free; ⊙10am & 2.30pm) This excellent company, with well-informed, English-speaking guides, offers themed walking tours through Lisbon, which depart from the northwest corner of Praça do Comércio.

✹ Festivals & Events

The **Festa de Santo António** (Festival of Saint Anthony), from 12 June to 13 June, culminates with the three-week **Festas de Lisboa**, with processions and dozens of street parties; it's liveliest in the Alfama.

🛏 Sleeping

🛏 Baixa, Rossio & Cais do Sodré

Lisbon Destination Hostel   HOSTEL €
(☑213 466 457; www.destinationhostels.com; Rossio train station, 2nd fl; dm/s/d from €23/40/80; @🕾) Housed in Lisbon's loveliest train station, this world-class hostel has a glass ceiling lighting the spacious plant-filled common area. Rooms are crisp and well-kept, and there are loads of activities (bar crawls, beach day trips, etc). Facilities include a shared kitchen, game consoles, movie room (with popcorn) and 24-hour self-service bar. Breakfast is top-notch with crêpes and fresh fruit.

Travellers House   HOSTEL €
(☑210 115 922; www.travellershouse.com; Rua Augusta 89; dm €28-30, s/d without bathroom

€40/70, d €80-90; ❄ @ 🛜) Travellers enthuse about this super-friendly hostel set in a converted 250-year-old house on Rua Augusta. As well as cosy dorms and a wealth of comfortable private rooms (some more minimalist than others), there's a retro lounge with beanbags, an internet corner and a communal kitchen. Newly installed CCTV and heaters keep everyone safe and warm.

Lisbon Lounge Hostel HOSTEL €
(📋 213 462 061; www.lisbonloungehostel.com; Rua de São Nicolau 41; dm/d with shared bath from €22/64, d €84; ❄ @ 🛜) Lisbon Lounge Hostel has artfully designed dorms, and a slick lounge complete with faux moose head, plastic-bottle chandeliers and an old salon hood dryer. Three-course dinners, bike hire, walking tours and DJ nights are all part and parcel of these nicely chilled Baixa digs.

★**Lisbon Story Guesthouse** GUESTHOUSE €€
(📋 218 879 392; www.lisbonstoryguesthouse.com; Largo de São Domingos 18; d €80-100, without bathroom €50-70, apt €120; @ 🛜) 🍃 Overlooking Largo de São Domingos, Lisbon Story is a small, extremely welcoming guesthouse with nicely maintained, light-drenched rooms, all of which sport Portuguese themes (the Tejo, tram 28, fado etc) and working antique radios, record players and the like. The shoe-free lounge, with throw pillows and low tables, is a great place to chill.

My Story Rossio BOUTIQUE HOTEL €€
(📋 213 400 380; www.mystoryhotels.com; Praça Dom Pedro IV 59; s/d from €127/137; ❄ 🛜) This 2015 newcomer gets a gold star for its central location right on Rossio Sq. Carpeted hallways depicting Google Maps views of Lisbon lead to rooms (and bathrooms) that tend to be cramped (you'll be happier in a roomier superior), but travellers enjoy hitech mod cons such as TV/mirror hybrids, quirky themes (Fado, Amor, Lisboa) and value for money.

Pousada de Lisboa BOUTIQUE HOTEL €€€
(📋 210 407 650; www.pestana.com/en/hotel/pousada-lisboa; Praça do Comércio 31; r from €210; ❄ @ 🛜 ♒) Location, location, location! Portugal's Pestana chain hit triple 7s with this 2015 newcomer's privileged position on Praça do Comércio. A €70-million renovation turned the former Ministry of Internal Affairs into a cosy *pousada* (upmarket inn) with museum-like qualities. Sculptures throughout represent epic moments in Portuguese history and, yes, you can sit on those 13th-century *liteiras* (litters).

🛏 Alfama

Alfama Patio Hostel HOSTEL €
(📋 218 883 127; www.alfama.destinationhostels.com; Rua das Escolas Gerais 3; dm €18-24, s/d without bathroom from €30/45, d €60; @ 🛜) In Alfama's heart, this beautifully run hostel offers custom-made, Cappadocia-inspired particle-board dorms with privacy curtains and lockable drawers. From the upper-floor rooms, you can practically file your fingernails across the top of the tram as it rattles past. A bevy of activities (fado, street art and surfing tours) and barbecues on the garden-like patio mean it's notably social.

★**Memmo Alfama** BOUTIQUE HOTEL €€€
(📋 210 495 660; www.memmoalfama.com; Travessa Merceeiras 27; r €170-350; ❄ 🛜 ♒) Slip down a narrow alley to reach these gorgeous boutique Alfama sleeps, a stunning conversion of a shoe-polish factory and former bakery. The rooms are an ode to whitewashed minimalism and staff are as sleek as the decor with their uniform-issued Chuck Taylor All-Stars and hipster aura. The view down to the Tejo from the roof terrace is phenomenal.

🛏 Chiado, Bairro Alto & Príncipe Real

Lisbon Calling HOSTEL €
(📋 213 432 381; www.lisboncalling.net; Rua de São Paulo 126, 3rd fl; dm/d with shared bathroom €16/55, d €75; @ 🛜) This fashionable, unsigned backpacker favourite near Santa Catarina features original frescoes, *azulejos* and hardwood floors – all lovingly restored

PORTUGAL LISBON (vertical side tab)

CYCLING THE TEJO

A **cycling/jogging path** courses along the Tejo for 7km, between Cais do Sodré and Belém. Complete with artful touches – including the poetry of Pessoa printed along parts of it – the path takes in ageing warehouses, weathered docks, and open-air restaurants and nightspots.

A handy place to rent bikes is a short stroll from Cais do Sodré: **Bike Iberia** (📋 969 630 369; www.bikeiberia.com; Largo Corpo Santo 5; bike hire per hr/day from €5/14; ⊙ 9.30am-7pm).

by friendly Portuguese owners. The bright, spacious dorms and a brick-vaulted kitchen are easy on the eyes, but the private rooms – specifically room 1812 – will floor you: boutique-hotel-level dens of style and comfort that thunderously out-punch their price point.

⭐**Casa do Príncipe**   B&B €€

(☑ 218 264 183; www.casadoprincipe.com; Praça do Príncipe Real 23; r €99-150; ❄ 🖥) Perfectly located, exquisitely restored and priced to shock, this new nine-room B&B is housed inside what once was the same 19th-century neo-Moorish palace as **Embaixada** (www.embaixadalx.pt; Praça do Príncipe Real 26; ⊙ noon-8pm, restaurants to 2am) next door. Original frescoes, *azulejos* and ornate moulded ceilings adorn the hardwood halls and spacious rooms, which are themed after the life of King Dom Pedro V. Indeed, you'll sleep like a king here yourself.

🏠 **Avenida de Liberdade, Rato & Marquês de Pombal**

⭐**Casa Amora**   GUESTHOUSE €€

(☑ 919 300 317; www.casaamora.com; Rua João Penha 13; d €90-180, apt €120-220; ❄ 🖥) ✒ Casa Amora has 11 beautifully designed guestrooms and studio apartments, with eye-catching art and iPod docks. There's a lovely garden patio where the first-rate breakfast is served. It's located in the peaceful neighbourhood of Amoreiras, a few steps from one of Lisbon's prettiest squares.

Lisbon Dreams   GUESTHOUSE €€

(☑ 213 872 393; www.lisbondreamsguesthouse.com; Rua Rodrigo da Fonseca 29; s/d without bathroom €50/60, d €90; ❄ @ 🖥) On a quiet street lined with jacaranda trees, Lisbon Dreams offers excellent value for its bright, modern rooms with high ceilings and excellent mattresses. The green apples are a nice touch, and there are attractive common areas to unwind in. All bathrooms are shared except one, but are spotlessly clean.

Valverde   BOUTIQUE HOTEL €€€

(☑ 210 940 300; www.valverdehotel.com; Av da Liberdade 164; d €200-325, ste €305-600; 🅿 ❄ @ 🖥 ☐) Exquisite Valverde feels like a boutique town house (which of course it once was). Its facade is not showy, but once inside, an urban oasis of discerning design and personalised service is subtlety unveiled.

The 25 rooms, reached by black-dominated, hushed hallways, are awash in cultured European art and unique mid-century modern pieces, and elicit style, form and function.

🍴 **Eating**

In addition to creative newcomers, you'll find inexpensive, traditional dining rooms home to classic Portuguese fare.

🍴 **Baixa, Rossio & Cais do Sodré**

⭐**Mercado da Baixa**   MARKET €

(www.adbaixapombalina.pt; Praça da Figueira; ⊙ 10am-10pm Fri-Sun) This tented market/glorious food court on Praça da Figueira has been slinging cheese, wine, smoked sausages and other gourmet goodies since 1855. It takes place on the last weekend of each month and it is fantastic fun to stroll the stalls eating and drinking yourself into a gluttonous mess.

Povo   PORTUGUESE €

(www.povolisboa.com; Rua Nova do Carvalho 32; small plates €7-11; ⊙ 6pm-2am Mon-Wed & Sun, to 4am Thu-Sat) On bar-lined Rua Nova do Carvalho, Povo serves tasty Portuguese comfort food in the form of *petiscos* (tapas/snacks). There's also outdoor seating, plus live performances a few times per week from in-house *fadista* Marta de Sousa (Thursdays are best; from 9.30pm).

Nova Pombalina   PORTUGUESE €

(www.facebook.com/anovapombalina; Rua do Comércio 2; sandwiches €2.20-4; ⊙ 7am-7.30pm, closed Sun) The reason this bustling traditional restaurant is always packed around midday is its delicious *leitão* (suckling pig) sandwich, served on freshly baked bread in 60 seconds or less by the lightning-fast crew behind the counter.

Vicente by Carnalentejana   PORTUGUESE €€

(☑ 218 237 126; www.restaurantecarnalentejana.com; Rua das Flores 6; mains €9-14; ⊙ noon-11pm; 🖥) This sexy newcomer dishes up succulent beef and pork dishes made with ultra-premium Carnalentejana DOP-certified meat from the Alentejo along with wines, cheeses, olive oils and other treats produced by the same artisan farmers. A former coal shop turned carnivore's den of decadence, the original low-slung stone walls, exposed air ducts and filament light bulbs are notably atmospheric.

✕ Alfama

⭐ Ti-Natércia
PORTUGUESE €

(📞 218 862 133; Rua Escola Gerais 54; mains €5-12; ⏰ 7pm-midnight Mon-Fri, noon-3pm & 7pm-midnight Sat) A decade in and a legend in the making, 'Aunt' Natércia and her downright delicious Portuguese home cooking is a tough ticket: there are but a mere six tables and they fill up fast. She'll talk your ear off (and doesn't mince words!) while you devour her excellent take on the classics. Reservations essential (and cash only).

Pois Café
CAFE €

(www.poiscafe.com; Rua de São João da Praça 93; mains €7-10; ⏰ noon-11pm Mon, 10am-11pm Tue-Sun; 📶) Boasting a laid-back vibe under dominant stone arches, atmospheric Pois Café has creative salads, sandwiches and fresh juices, plus a handful of heartier daily specials (salmon quiche, sirloin steak). Its sofas invite lazy afternoons spent reading novels and sipping coffee, but you'll fight for space with the laptop brigade.

Chapitô à Mesa
PORTUGUESE €€

(📞 218 875 077; www.facebook.com/chapitoamesa; Rua Costa do Castelo 7; mains €18-21; ⏰ noon-11pm Mon-Fri, 7.30-11pm Sat-Sun; 📶) Up a spiral iron staircase from this circus school's casual cafe, the decidedly creative menu of Chef Bertílio Gomes is served alongside views worth writing home about. His modern takes include classic dishes (bacalhau à Brás, stewed veal cheeks, suckling pig), plus daring ones (rooster testicles – goes swimmingly with a drop of Quinta da SilveiraReserva).

Tasca Zé dos Cornos
PORTUGUESE €€

(📞 218 869 641; www.facebook.com/ZeCornos; Beco Surradores 5; mains €10-15; ⏰ 8am-11pm Mon-Sat) This family-owned tavern welcomes regulars and first-timers with the same undivided attention. Lunchtime is particularly busy but the service is whirlwind quick and effective. Space is tight so sharing tables is the norm. The menu is typical Portuguese cuisine with emphasis on pork and bacalhau (dried salt cod) grilled on the spot, served in very generous portions.

✕ Chiado, Bairro Alto & Príncipe Real

⭐ Mercado da Ribeira
MARKET €

(www.timeoutmarket.com; Av 24 de Julho; ⏰ 10am-midnight Sun-Wed, to 2am Thu-Sat; 📶) Doing trade in fresh fruit and veg, fish and flowers since 1892, this oriental-dome-topped market hall is the word on everyone's lips since *Time Out* transformed half of it into a gourmet food court in 2014. Now it's like Lisbon in microcosm, with everything from Garrafeira Nacional wines to Conserveira de Lisboa fish, Arcádia chocolate and Santini gelato.

Dona Quitéria
PORTUGUESE €

(📞 213 951 521; Travessa de São José 1; small plates €5-12; ⏰ 7pm-midnight Tue-Sun) Locals do their best to keep this quaint corner *petiscaria* (small plates restaurant), a former grocery store from 1870, all to themselves – no such luck. Pleasant palate surprises such as tuna *pica-pau* instead of steak, or a pumpkin-laced cream-cheese mousse for dessert, put tasty creative spins on tradition. It's warm, welcoming and oh so tiny – so reserve ahead.

Decadente
PORTUGUESE €€

(📞 213 461 381; www.thedecadente.pt; Rua de São Pedro de Alcântara 81; mains €9-16; ⏰ noon-11pm Sun-Wed, to midnight Thu-Sat; 📶) This beautifully designed restaurant inside a boutique hotel overlooking the stunning São Pedro de Alcântara lookout, with touches of industrial chic, geometric artwork and an enticing back patio, serves inventive dishes showcasing high-end Portuguese ingredients at excellent prices. The changing three-course lunch menu (€10) is first-rate. Start with creative cocktails in the front bar.

✕ Belém

Antiga Confeitaria de Belém
PASTRIES €

(📞 213 637 423; www.pasteisdebelem.pt; Rua de Belém 84-92; pastries from €1.05; ⏰ 8am-11pm Oct-Jun, to midnight Jul-Sep) Since 1837 this patisserie has been transporting locals to sugar-coated nirvana with heavenly *pastéis de belém*. The crisp pastry nests are filled with custard cream, baked at 200°C for that perfect golden crust, then lightly dusted with cinnamon. Admire *azulejos* in the vaulted rooms or devour a still-warm tart at the counter and try to guess the secret ingredient.

🍷 Drinking & Nightlife

All-night street parties in Bairro Alto, sunset drinks from high-up terraces and sumptuous art deco cafes scattered about Chiado –

Lisbon has many enticing options for imbibers.

Lux-Frágil CLUB

(www.luxfragil.com; Av Infante Dom Henrique, Armazém A - Cais de Pedra, Santo Apolónia; ⊘11pm-6am Thu-Sat) Lisbon's ice-cool, must-see club, Lux hosts big-name DJs spinning electro and house. It's run by ex-Frágil maestro Marcel Reis and part-owned by John Malkovich. Grab a spot on the terrace to see the sun rise over the Tejo; or chill like a king on the throne-like giant interior chairs.

★Park BAR

(www.facebook.com/00park; Calçada do Combro 58; cocktails €6.50-8; ⊘1pm-2am Tue-Sat, 1-8pm Sun; 🎵) If only all multistorey car parks were like this... Take the elevator to the 5th floor, and head up and around to the top, which has been transformed into one of Lisbon's hippest rooftop bars, with sweeping views reaching right down to the Tejo and over the bell towers of Santa Catarina Church.

★Pensão Amor BAR

(www.pensaoamor.pt; Rua do Alecrim 19; cocktails €5.50-13; ⊘noon-3am Mon-Wed, to 4am Thu-Sat, to 3am Sun) Set inside a former brothel, this cheeky bar pays homage to its passion-filled past with colourful wall murals, a library of erotic-tinged works, and a small stage where you can sometimes catch burlesque shows. The Museu Erótico de Lisboa (MEL) was on the way at time of research.

★A Ginjinha BAR

(Largo de Saõ Domingos 8; ⊘9am-10pm) Hipsters, old men in flat caps, office workers and tourists all meet at this microscopic *ginjinha* (cherry liqueur) bar for that moment of cherry-licking, pip-spitting pleasure (€1.40 a shot).

★BA Wine Bar do Bairro Alto WINE BAR

(✆213 461 182; bawinebar@gmail.com; Rua da Rosa 107; wines from €3, tapas from €12; ⊘6-11pm Tue-Sun; 🎵) Reserve ahead unless you want to get shut out of Bairro Alto's best wine bar, where the genuinely welcoming staff will offer you three fantastic choices to taste based on your wine proclivities. The cheeses (from small artisanal producers) and charcuterie (melt-in-your-mouth black-pork *presuntos*) are not to be missed, either. You could spend the night here.

☆ Entertainment

For the latest goings-on, pick up the weekly *Time Out Lisboa* (www.timeout.pt) from bookstores, or the free monthly *Follow me Lisboa* from the tourist office.

Live Music

Hot Clube de Portugal JAZZ

(✆213 460 305; www.hcp.pt; Praça da Alegria 48; ⊘10pm-2am Tue-Sat) As hot as its name suggests, this small, poster-plastered cellar (and newly added garden) has staged top-drawer jazz acts since the 1940s. It's considered one of Europe's best.

A Baîuca FADO

(✆218 867 284; Rua de São Miguel 20; ⊘8pm-midnight Thu-Mon) On a good night, walking into A Baîuca is like gate-crashing a family party. It's a special place with *fado vadio*, where locals take a turn and spectators hiss if anyone dares to chat during the singing. There's a €25 minimum spend, which is as tough to swallow as the food, though the fado is spectacular. Reserve ahead.

A Tasco do Chico FADO

(✆961 339 696; www.facebook.com/atasca.dochico; Rua Diário de Notícias 39; ⊘noon-2am, to 3am Fri-Sat) This crowded dive (reserve ahead), full of soccer banners and spilling over with people of all ilk, is a fado free-for-all. It's not uncommon for taxi drivers to roll up, hum a few bars, and hop right back into their cabs, speeding off into the night. Portugal's most famous fado singer, Mariza, brought us here in 2005. It's still legit.

Sport

Lisbon's football teams are Benfica, Belenenses and Sporting. Euro 2004 led to the upgrading of the 65,000-seat **Estádio da Luz** (Estádio do Sport Lisboa e Benfica; ✆707 200 100; www.slbenfica.pt; Av General Norton de Matos) and the construction of the 54,000-seat **Estádio Nacional** (✆214 197 212; http://jamor.idesporto.pt; Av Pierre de Coubertin, Cruz Quebrada). State-of-the-art stadium **Estádio José de Alvalade** (www.sporting.pt; Rua Prof Fernando da Fonseca) seats 54,000 and is just north of the university. Take the metro to Campo Grande.

❶ Information

EMERGENCY

Police Station (✆213 403 410; www.psp.pt; Rua da Atalaia 138) Police station in the heart of Bairro Alto, though non-Portuguese-speaking tourists are better off visiting the tourist police (Esquadra de Turismo; 📞213 421 623; www.psp.pt; Palácio Foz, Praça dos Restauradores; ⏲24hr) in non-emergency situations.

MEDICAL SERVICES

British Hospital (📞800 271 271; www.british-hospital.pt; Rua Tomás da Fonseca) English-speaking staff and English-speaking doctors.

Farmácia Estácio (Praça Dom Pedro IV 62; ⏲8.30am-8pm Mon-Fri, 10am-7pm Sat-Sun) A central pharmacy.

POST

Main Post Office (CTT; www.ctt.pt; Praça dos Restauradores 58; ⏲8am-10pm Mon-Fri, 9am-6pm Sat)

Post Office (CTT; www.ctt.pt; Praça do Município 6; ⏲8.30am-6.30pm) Central post office.

TOURIST INFORMATION

Ask Me Lisboa (📞213 463 314; www.askmelisboa.com; Praça dos Restauradores, Palácio Foz; ⏲9am-8pm) The largest and most helpful tourist office. Can book accommodation or reserve rental cars. There's also an office (📞218 450 660; www.askmelisboa.com; Aeroporto de Lisboa, Arrivals Hall; ⏲7.30am-9.30am Tue-Sat) in the arrivals hall at the airport.

ℹ Getting There & Away

AIR

Around 6km north of the centre, **Aeroporto de Lisboa** (Lisbon Airport; 📞218 413 700; www.ana.pt; Alameda das Comunidades Portuguesas) operates direct flights to many European cities.

BUS

Lisbon's long-distance bus terminal is **Sete Rios** (Praça General Humberto Delgado, Rua das Laranjeiras), conveniently linked to both Jardim Zoológico metro station and Sete Rios train station. The big carriers, **Rede Expressos** (📞707 223 344; www.rede-expressos.pt) and **Eva** (📞707 223 344; www.eva-bus.com), run frequent services to almost every major town.

The other major terminal is **Gare do Oriente** (at Oriente metro and train station), concentrating on services to the north and to Spain. The biggest companies operating from here are **Renex** (📞218 956 836; www.renex.pt; Gare do Oriente) and the Spanish operator **Avanza** (📞912 722 832; www.avanzabus.com).

TRAIN

Santa Apolónia station is the terminus for northern and central Portugal. You can catch trains from Santa Apolónia to **Gare do Oriente train station**, which has departures to the Algarve and international destinations. **Cais do Sodré station** is for Belém, Cascais and Estoril. **Rossio station** is the terminal for trains to Sintra via Queluz.

For fares and schedules, visit www.cp.pt.

ℹ Getting Around

TO/FROM THE AIRPORT

The **AeroBus** (www.aerobus.pt; 1-way adult/child €3.50/2) runs every 20 minutes from 7am to 11pm, taking 30 to 45 minutes between the airport and Cais do Sodré.

A metro station on the red line gives convenient access to downtown. Change at Alameda (green line) to reach Rossio and Baixa. A **taxi** into town is about €15.

PUBLIC TRANSPORT

A 24-hour **Bilhete Carris/Metro** (€6.15) gives unlimited travel on all buses, trams, metros and funiculars. Pick it up from Carris kiosks and metro stations.

Bus, Tram & Funicular

Buses and trams run from 6am to 1am, with a few all-night services. Pick up a transport map from tourist offices or Carris kiosks. A single ticket costs more if you buy it on board (€2.85/1.80/3.60 for tram/bus/funicular), and much less (€1.40 per ride) if you buy a refillable **Viva Viagem** card (€0.50), available at Carris offices and in metro stations.

There are three funiculars: Elevador da Bica, Elevador da Glória and Elevador do Lavra.

Don't leave the city without riding tram 28 from Largo Martim Moniz through the narrow streets of the Alfama; tram 12 goes from Praça da Figueira out to Belém.

Ferry

Car, bicycle and passenger ferries leave frequently from the Cais do Sodré ferry terminal to Cacilhas (€1.20, 10 minutes). From Terreiro do Paço terminal, catamarans zip across to Montijo (€2.75, every 30 minutes) and Seixal (€2.35, every 30 minutes).

Metro

The **metro** (www.metro.transporteslisboa.pt; single/day ticket €1.40/6; ⏲6.30am-1am) is useful for hops across town and to the Parque das Nações. Buy tickets from metro ticket machines, which have English-language menus.

AROUND LISBON

Sintra

POP 26,000

Lord Byron called this hilltop town a 'glorious Eden' and, although best appreciated at dusk when the coach tours have left, it *is* a magnificent place. Less than an hour west of Lisbon, Sintra was the traditional summer retreat of Portugal's kings. Today, it's a fairytale setting of stunning palaces and manors surrounded by rolling green countryside.

◎ Sights & Activities

Although the whole town resembles a historical theme park, there are several compulsory eye-catching sights.

★ Quinta da Regaleira
NOTABLE BUILDING, GARDENS

(www.regaleira.pt; Rua Barbosa du Bocage; adult/child €6/3; ☉10am-8pm high season, shorter hours in low season) This magical villa and gardens is a neo-Manueline extravaganza, dreamed up by Italian opera-set designer Luigi Manini, under the orders of Brazilian coffee tycoon António Carvalho Monteiro, aka 'Monteiro dos Milhões' ('Moneybags Monteiro'). The villa is surprisingly cosy inside, despite its ferociously carved fireplaces, frescoes and Venetian-glass mosaics. Keep an eye out for mythological and Knights Templar symbols.

★ Palácio Nacional de Sintra
PALACE

(www.parquesdesintra.pt; Largo Rainha Dona Amélia; adult/child €10/8.50; ☉9.30am-7pm, shorter hours in low season) The star of Sintra-Vila is this palace, with its iconic twin conical chimneys and lavish interior. The whimsical interior is a mix of Moorish and Manueline styles, with arabesque courtyards, barley-twist columns and 15th- and 16th-century geometric *azulejos* that figure among Portugal's oldest.

★ Castelo dos Mouros
CASTLE

(www.parquesdesintra.pt; adult/child €8/6.50; ☉10am-6pm) Soaring 412m above sea level, this mist-enshrouded ruined castle looms high above the surrounding forest. When the clouds peel away, the vistas over Sintra's palace-dotted hill and dale, across to the glittering Atlantic are – like the climb – breathtaking.

The 10th-century Moorish castle's dizzying ramparts stretch across the mountain ridges and past moss-clad boulders the size of small buses.

★ Palácio Nacional da Pena
PALACE

(www.parquesdesintra.pt; combined ticket with Parque Nacional da Pena adult/child €14/12.50; ☉10am-6pm) Rising from a thickly wooded peak and often enshrouded in swirling mist, Palácio Nacional da Pena is a wacky confection of onion domes, Moorish keyhole gates, writhing stone snakes and crenellated towers in pinks and lemons. It is considered the greatest expression of 19th-century romanticism in Portugal.

⬛ Sleeping & Eating

★ Moon Hill Hostel
HOSTEL €

(☎219 243 755; www.moonhillhostel.com; Rua Guilherme Gomes Fernandes 19; dm €19, d with/without bathroom €89/59; ✳@🖥) This design-forward, minimalist newcomer easily outshines the Sintra competition. Whether you book a boutique-hotel-level private room, with colourful reclaimed-wood headboards and wall-covering photos of enchanting Sintra forest scenes (go for 10 or 14 for Pena National Palace views, 12 or 13 for Moorish castle views), or a four-bed mixed dorm (lockers), you are sleeping in high style.

★ Sintra 1012
B&B €€

(☎918 632 997; www.sintra1012.com; Rua Gil Vicente 10; d €60-120; ✳@🖥) You'll probably need to go to war to book one of the four spacious and smart rooms in this highly recommended guesthouse run by a young Portuguese-American couple. Behind original medieval walls, it's a modern minimalist retreat which, in Roman times, was Sintra's first theatre. Today, it's all comfort and class right down to the basement studio, an astonishing deal (€60).

INcomum
PORTUGUESE €€

(☎219 243 719; www.incomumbyluissantos.pt; Rua Dr Alfredo Costa 22; mains €14.50-15.50; ☉noon-midnight; 🖥) Chef Luis Santos is shaking up the scene in Sintra with his modern upgrades to Portuguese cuisine, served amid the muted greys and greens of his synchronic dining room. INcomum quickly established itself as the anti-traditional choice among serious foodies, first by dangling an unbeatable €9.50, three-course lunch carrot, then by letting the food seal the deal.

ℹ Information

Ask Me Sintra (Turismo; ☑219 231 157; www.
askmelisboa.com/sintra; Praça da República
23; ⊙9.30am-6pm) Near the centre of Sintra-Vila, Turismo de Lisboa's helpful multilingual office has expert insight on Sintra and the
surrounding areas, as well as the interactive
'Myths & Legends' presentation (€4.50).
However, keep in mind this is a member-driven
organisation, which only promotes those who
pay. There's also a small train station (☑211
932 545; www.askmelisboa.com/sintra; Sintra train station; ⊙10am-noon & 2.30-6pm)
branch, often overrun by arriving visitors.

ℹ Getting There & Away

Train services (€2.20, 40 minutes, every 15
minutes) run between Sintra and Lisbon's Rossio
station.

ℹ Getting Around

A handy bus for accessing the castle is the hop-
on, hop-off **Scotturb bus 434** (☑219 230 381;
www.scotturb.com; Av Dr Miguel Bombarda 59;
⊙9am-6pm) (€5), which runs from the train
station via Sintra-Vila to Castelo dos Mouros
(10 minutes), Palácio da Pena (15 minutes), and
back.

A taxi to Pena or Monserrate costs around €8
one way.

Cascais

POP 35,000

Cascais is a handsome seaside resort with
elegant buildings, an atmospheric Old Town
and a happy abundance of restaurants and
bars.

◎ Sights & Activities

Cascais' three sandy bays – **Praia da Con-
ceição**, **Praia da Rainha** and **Praia da
Ribeira** – are great for a sunbake or a tingly
Atlantic dip, but attract crowds in summer.

The sea roars into the coast at **Boca do
Inferno** (Hell's Mouth), 2km west of Cascais. Spectacular **Cabo da Roca**, Europe's
westernmost point, is 16km from Cascais
and Sintra, and is served by buses from both
towns.

Casa das Histórias Paula Rego　MUSEUM
(www.casadashistoriaspaularego.com; Av da
República 300; adult/child €3/free; ⊙10am-6pm
Tue-Sun, to 7pm summer) ⌀ The Casa das
Histórias Paula Rego showcases the disturb-
ing, highly evocative paintings of Portugal's

finest living artist. Biannually changing exhibits span Rego's career, from early work
with collage in the 1950s to the twisted fairy
tale–like tableaux of the 1980s, and up to the
disturbing realism of more recent years.

**Museu Condes de
Castro Guimarães**　MUSEUM
(www.cm-cascais.pt/equipamento/museu-condes
-de-castro-guimaraes; Parque Marechal Camona;
adult/child €3/free; ⊙10am-5pm Tue-Sun) This
whimsical early-19th-century mansion, complete with castle turrets and Arabic cloister,
sits in the grounds of the **Parque Marechal
Carmona** (www.cm-cascais.pt/equipamento/par
que-marechal-carmona; A⊙8.30am-6pm, to 8pm
summer).

🛏 Sleeping & Eating

Perfect Spot Lisbon　HOSTEL €
(☑924 058 643; www.perfectspot-lisbon.com;
Av de Sintra 354; 3-/4-/7-day packages from
€155/205/365; ℙ☎) New parents Jon and
Rita run this lovely hostel – perfect for families in addition to surfers and climbers – in
a large home just a smidgen outside the
tourist zone. Spacious rooms and dorms are
themed with unique art, but the real coup is
the closed-in garden, a supreme hang space
with day beds and a BBQ lounge.

Villa Cascais　BOUTIQUE HOTEL €€€
(☑214 863 410; www.thealbatrozcollection.com;
Rua Fernandes Tomás 1; d from €145; ❋@☎) If
you like your hotels with a jolting dose of
personality, the newly made-over, so-very-
blue Villa Cascais (blue walls, blue couches
and blue ceilings!) should sit quite well.
Striking brass staircases lead to 11 beautiful
and spacious rooms in three colours (two
of which are not blue), each with discerning lounge furniture. Trendy, bright and
beautiful!

★**Café Galeria House
of Wonders**　CAFE €€
(www.facebook.com/houseofwonders; Largo da
Misericórdia 53; buffet 1/2 people €14.95/24.50,
light meals €2.50-9.75; ⊙10am-midnight; ☎✍)
⌀ This fantastically whimsical, Dutch-
owned cafe is tucked away in the old quarter. Its astonishingly good Middle Eastern/
Mediterranean vegetarian meze buffet
downstairs includes a hot-dish add-on for
€9.95 (aubergine moussaka, zucchini lasagne etc) amid a warm, welcoming ambience
and artwork-filled interior. Don't miss it!

PORTUGAL CASCAIS

ℹ Information

Ask Me Cascais (Turismo; ☑ 912 034 214; www.visitcascais.com; Largo Cidade Vitória; ⊙ 9am-8pm summer, to 6pm winter) The official Cascais tourist information booth has a handy map and events guide (*What's in Cascais*), and is helpful to an extent.

ℹ Getting There & Around

Trains run frequently to Cascais via Estoril (€2.15, 40 minutes) from Cais do Sodré station in Lisbon.

THE ALGARVE

It's easy to see the allure of the Algarve: breathtaking cliffs, golden sands, scalloped bays and long sandy islands. Although overdevelopment has blighted parts of the coast, head inland and you'll land solidly in lovely Portuguese countryside once again. Algarve highlights include the riverside town of Tavira, party-loving Lagos and windswept Sagres. Faro is the regional capital.

Faro

POP 50,000

Faro is an attractive town with a palm-clad waterfront, well-maintained plazas and a small pedestrianised centre sprinkled with outdoor cafes. There are no beaches in Faro itself, though it's an easy jaunt by ferry to picturesque beaches nearby. A boat trip through the Parque Natural da Ria Formosa is another highlight.

◎ Sights & Activities

★ **Parque Natural da Ria Formosa**   NATURE RESERVE
(www.icnf.pt) This sizeable system of lagoons and islands stretches for 60km along the Algarve coastline from west of Faro to Cacela Velha. It encloses a vast area of *sapal* (marsh), *salinas* (salt pans), creeks and dune islands. The marshes are an important area for migrating and nesting birds. You can see a huge variety of wading birds here, along with ducks, shorebirds, gulls and terns. This is the favoured nesting place of the little tern and the rare purple gallinule.

★ **Formosamar**   BOATING
(☑ 918 720 002; www.formosamar.com; Clube Naval, Faro Marina) ✐ This recommended outfit genuinely embraces and promotes environmentally responsible tourism. Among the excellent tours it provides are two-hour birdwatching trips around the Parque Natural da Ria Formosa (€25), dolphin watching (€45), cycling (€37), and a two-hour small-boat trip that penetrates some of the narrower lagoon channels (€25). All trips have a minimum number of participants (usually two or three).

🛏 Sleeping

★ **Casa d'Alagoa**   HOSTEL €
(☑ 289 813 252; www.farohostel.com; Praça Alexandre Herculano 27; dm not incl breakfast €22-30, d €80; 🛜) Housed in a renovated mansion on a pretty square, this commendable budget option has all the elements of today's sophisticated hostel: it's funky, laid-back and cool (and clean!). There's a range of spacious dorms, a great lounge and an upstairs terrace, plus a communal kitchen...but hey, why do you need it when dinner is on offer? Bike rental also available.

Hotel Eva   HOTEL €€
(☑ 800 8585 1234; www.hotel-eva-faro.h-rez.com; Avenida da República 1; d €88-105; P ❄ 🛜 ⊠) Upmarket Eva has 134 spacious, pleasant rooms, with rates varying according to whether the view from the window is of sea, marina or city. There's a rooftop swimming pool for more marina gazing, and various meal plans are available for a fairly reasonable cost.

🍴 Eating

★ **Faz Gostos**   PORTUGUESE, FRENCH €€
(☑ 289 878 422; www.fazgostos.com; Rua do Castelo 13; mains €13-19.50; ⊙ noon-3pm & 7-11pm Mon-Fri, 7-11pm Sat; 🛜) Elegantly housed in the old town, this restaurant offers high-class French-influenced Portuguese cuisine in a spacious, comfortably handsome dining area. There's plenty of game, fish and meat on offer with rich and seductive sauces, and a few set menus are available.

Gengibre e Canela   VEGETARIAN €
(Travessa da Mota 10; buffet €7.50; ⊙ noon-3pm Mon-Sat, groups only evenings; 🛜 🍴) Give the taste buds a break from meat and fish dishes and veg out (literally) at this Zen-like restaurant. The buffet changes daily; there may be vegetable lasagne, vegetarian *feijoada* (bean casserole) and tofu dishes, but there's only the occasional curry. Wine and desserts are extra.

ℹ Information

Turismo (www.visitalgarve.pt; Rua da Misericórdia 8; ⊘9am-1pm & 2-6pm) Busy but efficient office with friendly staff.

ℹ Getting There & Away

Faro airport has both domestic and international flights.

From the **bus station**, just west of the centre, there are at least hourly express coaches to Lisbon (€20, five hours), plus several slower services, and frequent buses to other coastal towns.

The **train station** is a few minutes' walk west of the bus station. Five trains run daily to Lisbon's Sete Rios station (€21.20 to €22.20, 3¾ hours) and there are hourly services to all points along the Algarve coast.

ℹ Getting Around

Próximo (☑289 899 700; www.proximo.pt) city buses 14 and 16 run to the bus station (€2.22, 20 minutes, half-hourly June to August, slightly less frequently in low season). From here it's an easy stroll to the centre.

A taxi into town costs around €13.

Tavira

POP 15,100

Set on either side of the meandering Rio Gilão, Tavira is arguably the Algarve's most charming town, with a hilltop castle, an old Roman bridge and a smattering of Gothic churches. The pretty sands of Ilha da Tavira are a short boat ride away.

☉ Sights & Activities

Núcleo Islâmico   MUSEUM

(Praça da República 5; adult/child €2/1, with Palácio da Galeria €3/1.50; ⊘10am-12.30pm & 3-6pm mid-Jun–mid-Sep, 10am-4.30pm Tue-Sat mid-Sep–mid-Jun) Built around the globulous remains of an Islamic-era structure, this small 21st-century museum exhibits impressive Islamic pieces discovered in various excavations around the old town. There's a six-minute introductory video downstairs; one of the most important finds on display upstairs is the Tavira vase, an elaborate ceramic work with figures and animals around the rim. Multilingual handouts are available at reception.

The top floor of the museum is dedicated to temporary exhibitions with a local theme.

Igreja da Misericórdia   CHURCH

(Largo da Misericórdia; ⊘9.30am-1pm & 2-6pm Mon-Sat) Built in the 1540s, this church is the Algarve's most important Renaissance monument, with a magnificent carved, arched doorway. Inside, the restrained Renaissance arches contrast with the cherub-heavy baroque altar; tiled panels depict the works of mercy. Behind is a museum with a rather effeminate St John, salvers, chalices, and a hall with an interesting 18th-century apple-wood ceiling and elegant furniture.

🛏 Sleeping & Eating

⭐**Pousada de Juventude Tavira**   HOSTEL €

(☑281 326 731; www.pousadasjuventude.pt; Rua Dr Miguel Bombarda 36; dm €17, d €38-47; ⊘Jan-Nov; 🛜) Forget the stereotypical youth hostel: this hip, modern spot is a comfortable haven for the budget traveller. It features a lovely living room decked out in a Moorish theme, spacious four-bed dorms, a fabulous kitchen and a laundry. Its ingenious design even allows for attractive hotel-style doubles. What's more, it's bang in the centre of town.

⭐**Casa Beleza do Sul**   APARTMENT €€

(☑960 060 906; www.casabelezadosul.com; Rua Dr Parreira 43; apt €90-120; 🛜) A gorgeous historical house in central Tavira is showcased to full advantage in this beautiful conversion. The result is a cute studio and three marvellous suites of rooms, all different, with original tiled floors and modern bathrooms. All have a kitchenette and there are numerous thoughtful touches that put this well above the ordinary. Minimum stays apply.

O Tonel   PORTUGUESE €€

(☑963 427 612; Rua Dr Augo Silva Carvalho; mains €9.50-14; ⊘noon-3pm & 7-11pm Wed-Mon) Gourmet-style food for a decent price is the mantra at this brand-new restaurant where traditional dishes such as codfish *cataplana* (stew) and grilled meat and seafood dominate the menu. Dishes are served with hipster-esque imagination, though some may not appreciate their food served on slates and in jars.

ℹ Information

Turismo (☑281 322 511; www.visitalgarve.pt; Praça da República 5; ⊘9am-6pm daily Jul & Aug, 9am-6pm Mon-Wed, 9am-1pm & 2-6pm Thu-Sat Sep-Jun) Provides local and some regional information and has accommodation listings.

ⓘ Getting There & Away

Some 15 trains run daily between Faro and Tavira (€3.15, 35 minutes).

Lagos

POP 22,000

In summer, the pretty fishing port of Lagos has a party vibe; its picturesque cobbled streets and pretty nearby beaches, including Meia Praia to the east and Praia da Luz to the west, are packed with revellers and sun-seekers.

🏃 Activities

Blue Ocean DIVING

(📞964 665 667; www.blue-ocean-divers.de) For those who want to go diving or snorkelling. Offers a half-day discovery experience (€30), a full-day dive (€90) and a Divemaster PADI scuba course (€590). It also offers kayak safaris (half-/full day €30/45, children under 12 half price).

Dizzy Dolphins BOATING

(📞938 305 000; www.dizzydolphin.com) Run by a former BBC wildlife-documentary producer, this small outfit offers excellent 90-minute summer dolphin-spotting trips on a rigid inflatable.

🛏 Sleeping

Old Town Hostel HOSTEL €

(📞282 087 221; Rua da Barroca 70; dm €23; @🛜) If you're in town to party, this highly rated hostel is the place to sleep it all off during the day. Located in atmospheric Rua da Barroca, it has a kitchen, terrace and small common room, but the dorms are a little cramped and often full. The friendly staff is more than willing to show you the best bars.

★ Hotel Mar Azul GUESTHOUSE €€

(📞282 770 230; www.hotelmarazul.eu; Rua 25 de Abril 13; s €50-60, d €60-85; ❄@🛜) This little gem is one of Lagos' best-value spots. It's a central, well-run and delightfully welcoming place, with tidy, modern, compact rooms, some even boasting sea views. The simple breakfast is a mean €5 extra.

★ Inn Seventies GUESTHOUSE €€

(📞967 177 590; www.innseventies.com; Rua Marquês de Pombal; d €90-129; P❄🛜🏊) Though the entrance and stairwell don't give a great first impression, the rooms here are sexy suites with a vaguely 70s theme. They come well equipped with big TV, fridge and Nespresso machine, and there's a nice rooftop deck with views and plunge pool. The central location is fabulous and prices include the town's best buffet breakfast.

🍴 Eating

Café Gombá CAFE €

(📞282 762 188; Rua Cândido dos Reis 56; ⊙8am-7pm Mon-Sat year round, Sun mid-Jun–mid-Sep) Although around since 1964, this traditional cafe-bakery with 21st-century decor looks more like it opened in 2014. Elderly locals hang out here for the best cakes, coffees and sandwiches in town, and it's correspondingly cheap.

★ A Forja PORTUGUESE €€

(📞282 768 588; Rua dos Ferreiros 17; mains €8-17.50; ⊙noon-3pm & 6.30-10pm Sun-Fri) Like an Italian trattoria, this buzzing *adega tipica* (wine bar) pulls in the crowds – locals, tourists and expats – for its hearty, top-quality traditional food served in a bustling environment at great prices. Plates of the day are always reliable, as are the simply prepared fish dishes.

ⓘ Information

Turismo (📞282 763 031; www.visitalgarve.pt; Praça Gil Eanes; ⊙9am-7pm Jul & Aug, to 6pm Easter-Jun & Sep, to 5pm Oct-Easter) The very helpful staff offer excellent maps and leaflets.

ⓘ Getting There & Away

Bus services depart frequently for other Algarve towns including Faro (€5.90, two hours 10 minutes, six daily), and around 10 times daily to Lisbon (€20, four hours). Lagos is the western terminus of the trans-Algarve line with hourly services to all coastal points east.

Silves

POP 11,000

The one-time capital of Moorish Algarve, Silves is a pretty town of jumbled orange rooftops scattered above the banks of the Rio Arade. It boasts one of the best-preserved castles in the Algarve, attractive redstone walls and winding, sleepy backstreets on a hillside.

⊙ Sights

★ Castelo
CASTLE

(☑282 440 837; adult/concession/under 10yr €2.80/1.40/free, joint ticket with Museu Municipal de Arqueologia €3.90; ⊙9am-8pm Jun-Aug, to 6.30pm Mar-May & Sep-Nov, to 5pm Dec-Feb) This russet-coloured, Lego-like castle – originally occupied in the Visigothic period – has great views over the town and surrounding countryside. What you see today dates mostly from the Moorish era, though the castle was heavily restored in the 20th century. Walking the parapets and admiring the vistas is the main attraction, but you can also gaze down on the excavated ruins of the Almohad-era palace. The whitewashed 12th-century water cisterns, 5m deep, now host temporary exhibitions.

Museu Municipal de Arqueologia
MUSEUM

(☑282 444 838; Rua das Portas de Loulé; adult/under 10yr €2.10/free, joint ticket with Castelo €3.90; ⊙10am-6pm) Built tight against the defensive walls, this archaeological museum has a mix of interesting finds from the town and around. The modern building was constructed around an 18m-deep Moorish well with a spiral staircase heading into the depths that you can follow for a short stretch. Otherwise this is another Algarve museum that starts at the very prehistoric beginning but soon moves on to focus on the Almohad period of the 12th and 13th centuries.

🛏 Sleeping & Eating

Duas Quintas
INN €€

(☑282 449 311; www.duasquintas.com; Santo Estevão; d/studios €105/130; 🅿🛜🏊) Set among orange groves and rolling hills, this utterly charming converted farmhouse has six pleasant rooms, a living space, terraces and a pool. Some of the furniture is antique and there are big discounts for staying a week or more. It's 6km northeast of Silves along the N124.

Pastelaria Rosa
CAFE, DESSERTS €

(Largo do Município; pastries €1.50-3; ⊙7.30am-10pm Mon-Sat; 🛜) On the ground floor of the town-hall building, this quaint, tile-lined place is Silves' oldest cafe and the best place to try Algarvian sweets. The table service is excellent and the extra you pay for the coffee and cakes here is worth it for the location and atmosphere. It's next to the tourist office.

★ Restaurante O Barradas
PORTUGUESE €€€

(☑282 443 308; www.obarradas.com; Palmeirinha; mains €8.50-25; ⊙6-10pm Thu-Tue; 🚸) 🌿 The star choice for foodies is this delightful converted farmhouse run by Luís and his German wife, Andrea. They take pride in careful sourcing, and use organic fish, meat and fruit in season. Luís is a winemaker, so you can be assured of some fine wines. Follow the road to Lagoa and then to Palmeirinha; it's 3km from Silves.

ⓘ Information

Centro de Interpretaçao do Património Islâmico (☑282 440 800; Largo do Município; ⊙9am-1pm & 2-5pm Mon-Fri)

Turismo (☑282 098 927; www.visitalgarve.pt; Parque das Merendas; ⊙9am-1pm & 2-6pm Tue-Sat)

ⓘ Getting There & Away

Silves **train station** is 2km from town; trains from Lagos (€2.90, 35 minutes) stop nine times daily (from Faro, change at Tunes), to be met by local buses.

Sagres

POP 1900

The small, elongated village of Sagres has an end-of-the-world feel with its sea-carved cliffs and empty, wind-whipped fortress high above the ocean. This coast is ideal for surfing; hire windsurfing gear at sand-dune-fringed Praia do Martinhal.

Visit Europe's southwesternmost point, the **Cabo de São Vicente** (Cape St Vincent), 6km to the west. A solitary lighthouse stands on this barren cape.

⊙ Sights & Activities

Fortaleza de Sagres
FORT

(☑282 620 140; adult/child €3/1.50; ⊙9.30am-6.30pm Apr, 9am-8pm May, Jun & Sep, 9am-8.30pm Jul & Aug, 9am-5pm Oct-Mar) Blank, hulking and forbidding, Sagres' fortress offers breathtaking views over the sheer cliffs, and all along the coast to Cabo de São Vicente. According to legend, this is where Prince Henry the Navigator established his navigation school and primed the early Portuguese explorers. It's quite a large site, so allow at least an hour to see everything.

Cabo de São Vicente
LANDMARK

(⊙lighthouse complex 10am-6pm Tue-Sun Apr-Sep, to 5pm Oct-Mar) Five kilometres from Sagres,

Europe's southwesternmost point is a barren headland, the last piece of home that Portuguese sailors once saw as they launched into the unknown. It's a spectacular spot: at sunset you can almost hear the hissing as the sun hits the sea. A red lighthouse houses the small but excellent Museu dos Faróis (adult/child €1.50/1; ⊗10am-6pm Tue-Sun Apr-Sep, to 5pm Oct-Mar), showcasing Sagres' role in Portugal's maritime history.

★ Walkin'Sagres   WALKING
(☑925 545 515; www.walkinsagres.com) ✐ Multilingual Ana Carla offers recommended guided walks in the Sagres area, explaining the history and other details of the surrounds. The walks head through pine forests to the cape's cliffs, and vary from shorter 7.7km options (€25, three hours) to a longer 15km walk (€40, 4½ hours). There's also a weekend walk for parents with young children (€15, children free).

🍽 Sleeping & Eating

Mareta View
Boutique B&B   BOUTIQUE HOTEL €€
(☑282 620 000; www.maretaview.com; Beco D Henrique; s/d from €88.50/112.50; ❋@🤶) The Mareta View brings sleek – and classy – attitude to Sagres. White- and aquamarine-hued decor gives it a futuristic feel (the funky mood lighting in the rooms rivals the Cabo de São Vicente lighthouse beacon). It offers wonderful sea views, excellent breakfasts and a convenient location on the old plaza.

★ A Eira do Mel   PORTUGUESE €€€
(☑282 639 016; Estrada do Castelejo, Vila do Bispo; mains €16-22; ⊗noon-2.30pm & 7.30-10pm Tue-Sat) It's worth driving 10km north of Sagres to Vila do Bispo to enjoy José Pinheiro's creations at this much-lauded slow-food restaurant. The meat leans towards the Algarvian; the seafood has a more contemporary touch. Think rabbit in red-wine sauce (€16), octopus *cataplana* (seafood stew) with sweet potatoes (€35 for two people), curried Atlantic wild shrimps (€22) and *javali* (wild boar; €17). Mouth-watering.

ℹ Information

Turismo (☑282 624 873; www.cm-viladobispo. pt; Rua Comandante Matoso; ⊗9am-1pm & 2-6pm Tue-Sat, extended hours summer) Situated on a patch of green lawn, 100m east of Praça da República. Buses stop nearby.

ℹ Getting There & Away

The bus stop (Rua Comandante Matoso) is by the *turismo*. You can buy tickets on the bus.

Buses come from Lagos via Salema (€3.85, one hour, six daily). On weekends there are fewer services. It's only 10 minutes to Cabo de São Vicente (twice daily on weekdays only; €2).

CENTRAL PORTUGAL

The vast centre of Portugal is a rugged swathe of rolling hillsides, whitewashed villages, and olive groves and cork trees. Richly historic, it is scattered with prehistoric remains and medieval castles. It's also home to one of Portugal's most architecturally rich towns, Évora, as well as several spectacular walled villages. There are fine local wines and, for the more energetic, plenty of outdoor exploring in the dramatic Beiras region.

Évora

POP 49,000

Évora is an enchanting place to delve into the past. Inside the 14th-century walls, Évora's narrow, winding lanes lead to a striking medieval cathedral, a Roman temple and a picturesque town square. These old-fashioned good-looks are the backdrop to a lively student town surrounded by wineries and dramatic countryside.

◉ Sights & Activities

Templo Romano   RUINS
(Temple of Diana; Largo do Conde de Vila Flor) Once part of the Roman Forum, the remains of this temple, dating from the 2nd or early 3rd century, are a heady slice of drama right in town. It's among the best-preserved Roman monuments in Portugal, and probably on the Iberian Peninsula. Though it's commonly referred to as the Temple of Diana, there's no consensus about the deity to which it was dedicated, and some archaeologists believe it may have been dedicated to Julius Caesar.

Igreja de São Francisco   CHURCH
(Praça 1 de Maio) Évora's best-known church is a tall and huge Manueline-Gothic structure, completed around 1510 and dedicated to St Francis. Legend has it that the Portuguese playwright Gil Vicente is buried here.

Sé
CATHEDRAL

(Largo do Marquês de Marialva; €1.50, with cloister & towers €3.50, with museum €4.50; ⊙9am-5pm) Guarded by a pair of rose granite towers, Évora's fortress-like medieval cathedral has fabulous cloisters and a museum jam-packed with ecclesiastical treasures. It was begun around 1186, during the reign of Sancho I, Afonso Henriques' son; there was probably a mosque here before. It was completed about 60 years later. The flags of Vasco da Gama's ships were blessed here in 1497.

🛏 Sleeping

Hostel Namaste
HOSTEL €

(☑266 743 014; www.hostelnamasteevora.pt; Largo Doutor Manuel Alves Branco 12; dm/s/d €17/30/45; 🛜) Maria and Carla Sofia are the kind souls who run these welcoming digs in the historic Moorish quarter. Rooms are bright, spotlessly clean and decorated with splashes of art and colour, and there's a lounge, library, kitchen and bike hire. Breakfast costs €4.

⭐Albergaria do Calvario
BOUTIQUE HOTEL €€€

(☑266 745 930; www.albergariadocalvario.com; Travessa dos Lagares 3; r €116-133; 🅿❄🛜) Unpretentiously elegant, discreetly attentive and comfortable, this beautifully designed guesthouse has an ambience that travellers adore. The staff leave no service stone unturned and breakfasts are among the region's best, with locally sourced organic produce, homemade cakes and egg dishes.

✗ Eating & Drinking

Botequim da Mouraria
PORTUGUESE €€

(☑266 746 775; Rua da Mouraria 16A; mains €14-17; ⊙12.30-3pm & 7-10pm Mon-Fri, noon-3pm Sat) Poke around the old Moorish quarter to find some of Évora's finest food and wine – gastronomes believe this is Évora's culinary shrine. Owner Domingos will expertly guide you through the menu, which also features an excellent variety of wines from the Alentejo. There are no reservations and just nine stools at a counter. It is extremely popular, and lines are long. To have any chance of getting a seat, arrive before it opens.

Vinho e Noz
PORTUGUESE €€

(☑266 747 310; Ramalho Orgião 12; mains €11-13; ⊙noon-10pm Mon-Sat) This unpretentious place is run by a delightful family and offers professional service, a large wine list and good-quality cuisine. It's been going for over 30 years and is one of the best-value places in town.

Art Cafe
CAFE

(Rua Serpa Pinto 6; ⊙11am-midnight Tue-Sat, to 9pm Sun & Mon) Set in the cloisters of the old Palácio Barrocal, this bohemian cafe and drinking spot has outdoor tables, hipster wait staff and ambient electronic grooves. The outdoor tables are a fine spot to unwind with a sangria after a day exploring. Tasty veg-friendly snacks too (gazpacho, *tostas*, lasagne).

ℹ Information

Turismo (☑266 777 071; www.cm-evora.pt; Praça do Giraldo 73; ⊙9am-7pm Apr-Oct, to 6pm Nov-Mar) This helpful, central tourist office offers a great town map.

ℹ Getting There & Away

Regular trains go direct to Lisbon (€12.20, 1½ hours, four daily) and indirectly, via Pinhal Novo, to Faro (€25.30, four to five hours, two daily) and Lagos (€26.30, 4½ to five hours, three daily). The train station is 600m south of the Jardim Público.

Peniche
POP 14,700

Popular for its nearby surfing beaches and also as a jumping-off point for Berlenga Grande, part of the beautiful Ilhas Berlengas nature reserve, the coastal city of Peniche remains a working port, giving it a slightly grittier and more 'lived-in' feel than its beach-resort neighbours. It has a walled historic centre and lovely beaches east of town.

From the bus station, it's a 10-minute walk west to the historic centre.

◉ Sights

Baleal
BEACH

About 5km to the northeast of Peniche is this scenic island-village, connected to the mainland village of Casais do Baleal by a narrow causeway (note: it's accessed through a car park). The fantastic sweep of sandy beach here offers some fine surfing. Surf schools dot the sands, as do several bar-restaurants.

Berlenga Grande
ISLAND

Sitting about 10km offshore from Peniche, and part of the Berlenga archipelago, Berlenga Grande is a spectacular, rocky and remote island, with twisting, shocked-rock formations and gaping caverns.

Fortaleza
FORT

(☑ 262 780 116; ⊘ 9am-12.30pm & 2-5.30pm Tue-Fri, from 10am Sat & Sun) **FREE** Dominating the south of the peninsula, Peniche's imposing 16th-century fortress was used in the 20th century as one of dictator Salazar's infamous jails for political prisoners.

🏃 Activities

Surfing

Surf camps offer week-long instruction as well as two-hour classes, plus board and wetsuit hire. Well-established names include **Baleal Surfcamp** (☑ 262 769 277; www.baleal surfcamp.com; Rua Amigos do Baleal 2; 1-/3-/5-day course €60/95/145) and **Peniche Surfcamp** (☑ 962 336 295; www.penichesurfcamp.com; Avenida do Mar 162, Casais do Baleal; ⊘ 1/2/10 surf classes €35/60/250).

Diving

There are good diving opportunities around Peniche, and especially around Berlenga. Expect to pay about €65 to €75 for two dives (less around Peniche) with **Acuasuboeste** (☑ 918 393 444; www.acuasuboeste.com; Porto de Pesca; diving intro course €80, two dives €65) or **Haliotis** (☑ 262 781 160; www.haliotis.pt; Casal da Ponte S/N, Atouguia da Baleia; single-/double-dive trip €35/75).

🛏 Sleeping & Eating

Peniche Hostel
HOSTEL €

(☑ 969 008 689; www.penichehostel.com; Rua Arquitecto Paulino Montês 6; dm €18-20, d €50; @ 🛜) This older-style little hostel run by friendly staff, only steps from the tourist office and a five-minute walk from the bus station, has colourfully decorated rooms with a hippie element. Front rooms have windows while some smaller, more claustrophobic rooms do not.

★ Casa das Marés
B&B €€

(☑ Casa 1 262 769 200, Casa 2 262 769 255, Casa 3 262 769 371; www.casadasmares1.com; Praia do Baleal; d €80-89; 🛜) At the picturesque, wind-swept tip of Baleal stands one of the area's most unique accommodation options. Three sisters inherited this imposing house from their parents and divided it into three parts – each of which now serves as its own little B&B. Breezy, inviting rooms all have great close-up sea views, and the sound of the breaking waves below is magical.

★ Nau dos Corvos
MODERN PORTUGUESE €€€

(☑ 262 783 168; www.naudoscorvos.com; Marginal Norte, Cabo Carvoeiro; mains €19.50-37; ⊘ noon-3pm & 7-10.30pm) It's just you and the sea out here at Cabo Carvoeiro, 2.5km from the town centre at the tip of the peninsula. But as you gaze out at the Atlantic from the windy platform, it's nice to know that under your feet is an excellent, upmarket seafood restaurant (and Peniche's best). It boasts some of the best sunset views in Portugal.

ℹ Getting There & Away

Peniche's **bus station** (☑ 968 903 861; Rua Dr Ernesto Moreira) is served by **Rodotejo** (www.rodotejo.pt) and **Rede Expressos** (www.rede-expressos.pt). Destinations include Coimbra (€14.70, 2¾ hours, hourly), Leiria (€12.80, two hours, three to four daily), Lisbon (€9, 1½ hours, every one to two hours) and Óbidos (€3.20, 40 minutes, six to eight daily).

Óbidos

POP 3100

Surrounded by a classic crenellated wall, Óbidos' gorgeous historic centre is a labyrinth of cobblestoned streets and flower-bedecked, whitewashed houses livened up with dashes of vivid yellow and blue paint. It's a delightful place to pass an afternoon, but there are plenty of reasons to stay overnight, as there's excellent accommodation including a hilltop castle now converted into one of Portugal's most luxurious *pousadas* (upmarket hotels).

◉ Sights

Castelo, Walls & Aqueduct
HISTORIC SITE

FREE You can walk around the unprotected **muro** (wall) for uplifting views over the town and surrounding countryside. The walls date from Moorish times (later restored), but the **castelo** (castle) itself is one of Dom Dinis' 13th-century creations. It's a stern edifice, with lots of towers, battlements and big gates. Converted into a palace in the 16th century (some Manueline touches add levity), it's now a deluxe **pousada** (☑ 262 955 080; www.pousadas.pt; d/ste from €220/350; ❀ 🛜).

The impressive 3km-long **aqueduct**, southeast of the main gate, dates from the 16th century.

Igreja de Santa Maria CHURCH

(Praça de Santa Maria; ⊙ 9.30am-12.30pm & 2.30-7pm summer, to 5pm winter) The town's elegant main church, near the northern end of Rua Direita, stands out for its interior, with a wonderful painted ceiling and walls done up in beautiful blue-and-white 17th-century *azulejos* (hand-painted tiles). Paintings by the renowned 17th-century painter Josefa de Óbidos are to the right of the altar. There's a fine 16th-century Renaissance tomb on the left, probably carved by French sculptor Nicolas Chanterène.

🛏 Sleeping & Eating

★Casa d'Óbidos HOTEL €€

(☑ 262 950 924; www.casadobidos.com; Quinta de São José; s/d €75/90, 2-/4-/6-person apt without breakfast €90/140/175; 🅿 🛜 ⊠) In a white-washed, 19th-century villa below town, this delightful option features spacious, breezy rooms with good new bathrooms and period furnishings, plus a tennis court, swimming pool and lovely grounds with sweeping views of Óbidos' bristling walls and towers. Breakfast is served at a common dining table. Trails lead through orchards up to town.

★Ja!mon Ja!mon PORTUGUESE €

(☑ 916 208 162; mains €5; ⊙ 10am-late Tue-Sun) Just outside Porta da Vila, before the tourist office, don't miss this cute little eatery. Six tables are crammed into a quaint room, a former *padeiria* (bakery), and fresh bread is baked in the wood-fired oven (along with other dishes). Each day brings a small selection of daily specials. We suggest just sitting back and letting the experience happen.

ℹ Information

Turismo (☑ 262 959 231; www.obidos.pt; ⊙ 9.30am-7.30pm summer, to 6pm winter) Outside Porta da Vila, near the bus stop, with helpful multilingual staff offering town brochures and maps in five languages.

ℹ Getting There & Away

There are direct buses Monday to Friday from Lisbon (€8.15, 65 minutes).

Nazaré

POP 10,500

Nazaré has a bustling coastal setting with narrow cobbled lanes running down to a wide, cliff-backed beach. The town centre is jammed with seafood restaurants and bars; expect huge crowds in July and August.

◉ Sights & Activities

The **beaches** here are superb, although swimmers should be aware of dangerous currents. Climb or take the funicular to the clifftop **Sítio**, with its cluster of fishermen's cottages and great view.

🛏 Sleeping & Eating

Many townspeople rent out rooms; doubles start at €35. Ask around near the seafront at Avenida da República.

ℹ Information

Turismo (☑ 262 561 194; www.cm-nazare.pt; Avenida Vieira Giumarães, Edifício do Mercado Municipal; ⊙ 9.30am-1pm & 2.30-6pm Oct-Mar, 9.30am-12.30pm & 2.30-6.30pm Apr-Jun, 9am-9pm Jul & Aug) In the front offices of the food market. Helpful, multilingual staff.

ℹ Getting There & Away

Nazaré has numerous bus connections to Lisbon (€11, 1¾ hours).

Tomar

POP 16,000

Tomar is one of central Portugal's most appealing small towns. With its pedestrian-friendly historic centre, its pretty riverside park frequented by swans, herons and families of ducks, and its charming natural setting adjacent to the lush Mata Nacional dos Sete Montes (Seven Hills National Forest), it wins lots of points for aesthetics.

◉ Sights

★Convento de Cristo MONASTERY

(www.conventocristo.pt; Rua Castelo dos Templários; adult/under 12yr €6/free, with Alcobaça & Batalha €15; ⊙ 9am-6.30pm Jun-Sep, 9am-5.30pm Oct-May) Wrapped in splendour and mystery, the Knights Templar held enormous power in Portugal from the 12th to 16th centuries, and largely bankrolled the Age of Discoveries. Their headquarters sit on wooded slopes above the town and are enclosed within 12th-century walls. The Convento de Cristo is a stony expression of magnificence, founded in 1160 by Gualdim Pais, Grand Master of the Templars. It has chapels, cloisters and choirs in diverging styles, added over

PORTUGAL NAZARÉ

the centuries by successive kings and Grand Masters.

🍴 Sleeping & Eating

⭐**Hostel 2300 Thomar** HOSTEL €
(☑249 324 256; www.hostel2300thomar.com; Rua Serpa Pinto 43; dm €18-20, d €40; 🛜) One of Portugal's funkiest hostels, this cleverly renovated mansion right in the heart of town celebrates Portugal, with each room brightly decorated in the country's theme: from the Lisbon tram to sardines. Airy dorms (and doubles), lockers, modern bathrooms and a cool and fun living space are enough to convert those after luxe experiences into a backpacker instead.

⭐**Hotel dos Templários** HOTEL €€
(☑249 310 100; www.hoteldostemplarios.pt; Largo Cândido dos Reis 1; s/d from €79/99, superior s/d from €99/132; 🅿❄🛜🏊) At the river's edge, just outside the historic centre, this spacious, efficient hotel offers excellent facilities including gym, sauna, and indoor and outdoor pools (the last adjacent to a small but stylish hotel bar). The rooms are large and very comfortable; most have balconies, some of which overlook the river. Service is five-star and the breakfast spread is great.

Restaurante Tabuleiro PORTUGUESE €€
(Rua Serpa Pinto 140; mains €8-12; ☺noon-3pm & 7-10pm Mon-Sat; 🍴) Located just off Tomar's main square, this family-friendly local hangout features warm, attentive service, good traditional food and ridiculous (read: more-than-ample) portions. A great spot to experience local fare. The cod pie is a standout.

ℹ Information

Turismo (☑249 329 823; www.cm-tomar.pt; Avenida Dr Cândido Madureira; ☺9.30am-12.30pm & 2-6pm) Offers a good town map, an accommodation list and information about a historical trail.

ℹ Getting There & Away

Frequent trains run to Lisbon (€9.65 to €10.85, 1¾ to two hours).

Coimbra

POP POP 101,455

Coimbra is a dynamic, fashionable, yet comfortably lived-in city, with a student life centred on the magnificent 13th-century university. Aesthetically eclectic, there are elegant shopping streets, ancient stone walls and backstreet alleys with hidden *tascas* (taverns) and fado bars. Coimbra was the birth and burial place of Portugal's first king, and was the country's most important city when the Moors captured Lisbon. It's also home to a slightly different kind of *fado* music.

◉ Sights

⭐**Universidade de Coimbra** UNIVERSITY
(☑239 242 744; www.uc.pt/en/informacaopara/visit/paco; adult/student €9/7, tower €1; ☺9am-7.30pm mid-Mar–Oct, 9.30am-1pm & 2-5.30pm Nov–mid-Mar) The city's high point, the university nucleus, consists of a series of remarkable 16th- to 18th-century buildings, all set within and around the vast Páteo das Escolas ('patio' or courtyard). These include the **Paço das Escolas (Royal Palace)**, **clock tower**, **Prisão Acadêmica (prison)**, **Capela de São Miguel (chapel)** and **Biblioteca Joanina** (João V Library; ☑239 859 818). Visitors to the library are admitted in small groups every 20 minutes. Buy your ticket at the university's visitor centre near the Porta Férrea. With the exception of the library, you can enter and explore on your own, or head off with a knowledgable university tour guide on one of three different tours (€12.50/15/20). These take place daily at 11am and 3pm.

⭐**Museu Nacional de Machado de Castro** MUSEUM
(☑239 853 070; www.museumachadocastro.pt; Largo Dr José Rodrigues; adult/child €6/free, cryptoportico only €3, with audio guide €7.50; ☺2-6pm Tue, 10am-7pm Wed-Sun Apr-Sep, 2-6pm Tue, 10am-6pm Wed-Sun Oct-Mar) This great museum is a highlight of central Portugal. It's built over the Roman forum, the remains of which can be seen and cover several levels. Part of the visit takes you down to the vaulted, spooky and immensely atmospheric galleries of the cryptoportico that allowed the forum to be level on such a hilly site. The artistic collection is wide-ranging and superb. The route starts with sculpture, from the architectural (column capitals) through Gothic religious sculpture and so on.

⭐**Sé Velha** CATHEDRAL
(Old Cathedral; ☑239 825 273; www.sevelha-coimbra.org; Largo da Sé Velha, Rua do Norte 4; €2.50; ☺10am-6pm Mon-Sat, 1-6pm Sun) Coimbra's stunning 12th-century cathedral is one of Portugal's finest examples of Romanesque architecture. The main portal and facade are

exceptionally striking. Its crenellated exterior and narrow, slit-like lower windows serve as reminders of the nation's embattled early days, when the Moors were still a threat. These buildings were designed to be useful as fortresses in times of trouble.

🛏 Sleeping

★**Serenata Hostel**   HOSTEL €

(☏239 853 130; www.serenatahostel.com; Largo da Sé Velha 21; dm/d without bathroom €15/38, d/ste/f with bathroom €49/55/79; 🛜) In the pretty heart of the (noisy-at-night) old town, this noble building with an intriguingly varied history has been converted to a fabulous hostel, chock-full of modern comforts and facilities while maintaining a period feel in keeping with this historic zone. Great lounge areas, a cute, secluded sun terrace, spacious dorms and a modern kitchen complete a very happy picture.

★**Casa Pombal**   GUESTHOUSE €€

(☏239 835 175; www.casapombal.com; Rua das Flores 18; s with/without bathroom €55/40, d with/without bathroom €65/54; @🛜) In a lovely old-town location, this winning, Dutch-run guesthouse squeezes tons of charm into a small space. You can forgive the odd blip for the delicious breakfast (served in a gorgeous blue-tiled room) and the friendly staff who provide multilingual advice. Nine cosy wood-floored rooms (five with shared bathroom) are individually decorated in historical style; a couple boast magnificent views.

★**Quinta das Lágrimas**   HOTEL €€€

(☏239 802 380; www.quintadaslagrimas.pt; Rua António Augusto Gonçalves; r €160-260; 🅿❄🛜🏊) This splendid historical palace is now one of Portugal's most enchanting upper-crust hotels. Choose between richly furnished rooms in the old palace, or Scandinavian-style minimalism in the modern annexe – complete with Jacuzzi. A few rooms look out on to the garden where Dona Inês de Castro reputedly met her tragic end. Discounts are sometimes available online, even in high season, and it's cheaper midweek.

🍴 Eating & Drinking

★**Tapas Nas Costas**   TAPAS €€

(☏239 157 425; www.tapasnascostas.pt; Rua Quebra Costas 19; tapas €3.50-6.60; ⊙noon-midnight Tue-Sat) *The* 'hotspot' about town at the time of research, this sophisticated tapas joint delivers delicious tapas. Decor is stylish, as

ROMAN RUINS
. . . .
Conimbriga (ruins & museum adult/child €4.50/free; ⊙10am-7pm), 16km south of Coimbra, is the site of the well-preserved ruins of a Roman town, including mosaic floors, elaborate baths and trickling fountains. It's a fascinating place to explore, with a **museum** that describes the once-flourishing and later abandoned town. Frequent buses run to Condeixa, 2km from the site; there are also two direct buses from Coimbra.

are the gourmet-style goodies, such as *ovo com alheira de caça e grelos* (sausage with turnip greens and egg; €5.60). What are 'small-to-medium' sized servings for Portuguese are possibly 'normal' for anyone else, so share plates are a satisfying experience.

Restaurante Zé Neto   PORTUGUESE €€

(☏239 826 786; Rua das Azeiteiras 8; mains €9-14; ⊙9am-3pm & 7pm-midnight Mon-Sat) This marvellous family-run place specialises in homemade Portuguese standards, including *cabrito* (kid; half portions €6). Things have been modernised by the elderly owner's daughter, who is the chef (until recently her father used to tap out the menu on a vintage typewriter), but thankfully, it hasn't lost its flair for producing great meats.

★**Café Santa Cruz**   CAFE

(☏239 833 617; www.cafesantacruz.com; Praça 8 de Maio; ⊙7.30am-midnight Mon-Sat) One of Portugal's most atmospheric cafes, where the elderly statesmen meet for their daily cuppas. Santa Cruz is set in a dramatically beautiful high-vaulted former chapel, with stained-glass windows and graceful stone arches. The terrace grants lovely views of Praça 8 de Maio. Don't miss the *crúzios,* award-winning, egg- and almond-based conventual cakes for which the cafe is famous.

★**Galeria Santa Clara**   BAR

(☏239 441 657; www.galeriasantaclara.com; Rua António Augusto Gonçalves 67; ⊙1pm-2am Mon-Fri, to 3am Sat & Sun) Arty tearoom by day and chilled-out bar by night, this terrific place across the Mondego has good art on the walls, a series of sunny rooms and a fine terrace. It's got a great indoor-outdoor vibe and can feel like a party in a private house when things get going.

PORTUGAL COIMBRA

☆ Entertainment

Coimbra-style fado is more cerebral than the Lisbon variety, and its adherents are staunchly protective.

★ Fado ao Centro   FADO

(☑ 910 679 838; www.fadoaocentro.com; Rua Quebra Costas 7; show incl drink €10) At the bottom of the old town, this friendly fado centre is a good place to introduce yourself to the genre. There's a performance every evening at 6pm. Shows include plenty of explanation, in Portuguese and English, about the history of Coimbra fado and the meaning of each song. It's tourist-oriented, but the performers enjoy it and do it well.

ⓘ Information

Turismo Largo da Portagem (☑ 239 488 120; www.turismodecoimbra.pt; Largo da Portagem; ⊙ 9am-6pm Mon-Fri, 9am-1pm & 2-6pm Sat & Sun mid-Sep–mid-Jun, 9am-8pm Mon-Fri, 9am-6pm Sat & Sun mid-Jun–mid-Sep) By the bridge, in the centre of things.

ⓘ Getting There & Away

BUS

From the rather grim **bus station** (Av Fernão de Magalhães), a 15-minute walk northwest of the centre, **Rede Expressos** (☑ 239 855 270; www.rede-expressos.pt) runs at least a dozen buses daily to Lisbon (€14.50, 2½ hours) and to Porto (€12, 1½ hours), with almost as many to Braga (€14, 2¾ hours) and to Faro (€27, six to nine hours).

TRAIN

Long-distance trains stop only at **Coimbra B** station, north of the city. Cross the platform for quick, free connections to more-central **Coimbra A** (called just 'Coimbra' on timetables).

Coimbra is linked by regular Alfa Pendular (AP) and *intercidade* (IC) trains to Lisbon (AP/IC €22.80/19.20, 1¾/two hours) and Porto (€16.70/13.20, one/1¼ hours); IC trains also stop at intermediate destinations north and south. Trains run roughly hourly to Figueira da Foz (€2.65, one hour) and Aveiro (€5.25, one hour).

Luso & the Buçaco Forest

This sylvan region harbours a lush forest of century-old trees surrounded by countryside that's dappled with heather, wildflowers and leafy ferns. There's even a fairy-tale **palace** (☑ 231 937 970; www.themahotels.pt; Mata Nacional do Buçaco; mains €11.50-15; ⊙ 8-10.30am, 1-3pm & 8-10pm; ☑) here, a 1907 neo-Manueline extravagance, where deep-pocketed visitors can dine or stay overnight. The palace lies amid the Mata Nacional do Buçaco, a forest criss-crossed with trails, dotted with crumbling chapels and graced with ponds, fountains and exotic trees. Buçaco was chosen as a retreat by 16th-century monks, and it surrounds the lovely spa town of Luso. From the centre, it's a 2km walk through forest up to the palace.

The **Maloclinic Spa** (www.maloclinictermasluso.com; Rua Álvaro Castelões; ⊙ 8am-1pm & 2-7pm daily high season, 9am-1pm & 2-6pm Mon-Sat low season) offers a range of soothing treatments.

🛏 Sleeping & Eating

Alegre Hotel   BOUTIQUE HOTEL €

(☑ 231 930 256; www.alegrehotels.com; Rua Emídio Navarro 2, Luso; s/d €45/55; P 🎵 ☎) This grand, atmospheric, pinkish-coloured 19th-century town house has large doubles with plush drapes, decorative plaster ceilings and polished period furniture. Its appeal is enhanced by an elegant entryway, formal parlour and pretty vine-draped garden with pool.

Palace Hotel do Buçaco   HOTEL €€€

(☑ 231 937 970; www.themahotels.pt; Mata Nacional do Buçaco; s €148-199, d €169-225; P) This sumptuous royal palace was originally a hunting lodge (completed in 1907). It sits in the middle of the forest and offers a delightfully ostentatious place to stay. Common areas are stunning – particularly the tilework above the grand staircase – though some rooms feel a little musty and threadbare. Don't expect flatscreen TVs or period furniture, but do expect stunning marble bathrooms.

ⓘ Information

Turismo (☑ 231 939 133; Rua Emídio Navarro 136, Luso; ⊙ 9.30am-1pm & 2.30-5.30pm) Has accommodation information, internet access, and town and forest maps, and is helpful.

ⓘ Getting There & Away

Buses to/from Coimbra (around €4, 40 minutes) run four times daily each weekday and twice daily on Saturdays. Trains to/from Coimbra B station (€2.60, 25 minutes) run several times daily; it's a 15-minute walk to town from the station.

THE NORTH

Beneath the edge of Spanish Galicia, northern Portugal is a land of lush river valleys, sparkling coastline, granite peaks and virgin forests. This region is also gluttony for wine lovers: it's the home of the sprightly *vinho verde* wine (a young, slightly sparkling white or red wine) and ancient vineyards along the dramatic Rio Douro. Gateway to the north is Porto, a beguiling riverside city blending both medieval and modern attractions. Smaller towns and villages also offer cultural allure, from majestic Braga, the country's religious heart, to the seaside beauty Viana do Castelo.

Porto

POP 237,600

From across the Rio Douro at sunset, romantic Porto looks like a pop-up town – a colourful tumbledown dream with medieval relics, soaring bell towers, extravagant baroque churches and stately beaux-arts buildings piled on top of one another, illuminated by streaming shafts of sun. If you squint you might be able to make out the open windows, the narrow lanes and the staircases zigzagging to nowhere.

A lively walkable city with chatter in the air and a tangible sense of history, Porto's old-world riverfront district is a Unesco World Heritage site. Across the water twinkle the neon signs of Vila Nova de Gaia, the headquarters of the major port manufacturers.

☉ Sights & Activities

Perfect for a languid stroll, the **Ribeira** district – Porto's riverfront nucleus – is a remarkable window into the city's history. Along the riverside promenade, *barcos rabelos* (the traditional boats used to ferry port wine down the Douro) bob beneath the shadow of the photogenic Ponte de Dom Luís I.

A few kilometres west of the city centre, the seaside suburb of **Foz do Douro** is a prime destination on hot summer weekends. It has a long beach promenade and a smattering of oceanfront bars and restaurants.

★**Palácio da Bolsa**   HISTORIC BUILDING
(Stock Exchange; www.palaciodabolsa.com; Rua Ferreira Borges; tours adult/child €8/4.50; ☉9am-

6.30pm Apr-Oct, 9am-12.30pm & 2-5.30pm Nov-Mar) This splendid neoclassical monument (built from 1842 to 1910) honours Porto's past and present money merchants. Just past the entrance is the glass-domed **Pátio das Nações** (Hall of Nations), where the exchange once operated. But this pales in comparison with rooms deeper inside; to visit these, join one of the half-hour guided tours, which set off every 30 minutes.

★**Sé**   CATHEDRAL
(Terreiro da Sé; cloisters adult/student €3/2; ☉9am-12.30pm & 2.30-7pm Apr-Oct, to 6pm Nov-Mar) From Praça da Sé rises a tangle of medieval alleys and stairways that eventually reach the hulking, hilltop fortress of the cathedral. Founded in the 12th century, it was largely rebuilt a century later and then extensively altered during the 18th century. However, you can still make out the church's Romanesque origins in the barrel-vaulted nave. Inside, a rose window and a 14th-century Gothic cloister also remain from its early days.

★**Igreja de São Francisco**   CHURCH
(Praça Infante Dom Henrique; adult/child €4/2; ☉9am-8pm Jul-Sep, to 7pm Mar-Jun & Oct, to 6pm Nov-Feb) Sitting on Praça Infante Dom Henrique, Igreja de São Francisco looks from the outside to be an austerely Gothic church, but inside it hides one of Portugal's most dazzling displays of baroque finery. Hardly a centimetre escapes unsmothered, as otherworldly cherubs and sober monks are drowned by nearly 100kg of gold leaf. If you see only one church in Porto, make it this one.

★**Jardim do Palácio de Cristal**   GARDENS
(Rua Dom Manuel II; ☉8am-9pm Apr-Sep, to 7pm Oct-Mar) Sitting atop a bluff, this gorgeous botanical garden is one of Porto's best-loved escapes, with lawns interwoven with sun-dappled paths and dotted with fountains, sculptures, giant magnolias, camellias, and cypress and olive trees. It's actually a mosaic of small gardens that open up little by little as you wander – as do the stunning views of the city and Rio Douro.

★**Serralves**   MUSEUM
(www.serralves.pt; Rua Dom João de Castro 210; adult/child museums & park €10/free, park only €5/free, 10am-1pm 1st Sun of the month free; ☉10am-7pm Tue-Fri, to 8pm Sat & Sun May-Sep, reduced hours Oct-Mar) This fabulous cultural

Porto

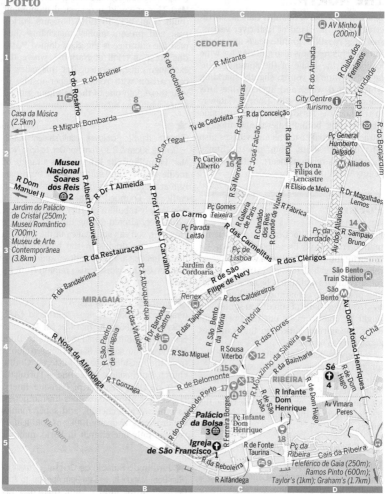

institution combines a museum, a mansion and extensive gardens. Cutting-edge exhibitions, along with a fine permanent collection featuring works from the late 1960s to the present, are showcased in the **Museu de Arte Contemporânea**, an arrestingly minimalist, whitewashed space designed by the eminent Porto-based architect Álvaro Siza Vieira. The delightful pink **Casa de Serralves** is a prime example of art deco, bearing the imprint of French architect Charles Siclis. One ticket gets you into both museums.

⭐**Museu Nacional**
Soares dos Reis   MUSEUM
(www.museusoaresdosreis.pt; Rua Dom Manuel II 44; adult/child €5/free,1st Sun of the month free; ⊙10am-6pm Tue-Sun) Porto's best art museum presents a stellar collection ranging from Neolithic carvings to Portugal's take on modernism, all housed in the formidable Palácio das Carrancas.

Teleférico de Gaia   CABLE CAR
(www.gaiacablecar.com; one-way/return €5/8; ⊙10am-8pm May-Sep, to 6pm Oct-Mar) Don't miss a ride on the Teleférico de Gaia, an

PORTUGAL PORTO

aerial gondola that provides fine views over the Douro and Porto on its short, five-minute jaunt. It runs between the southern end of the Ponte Dom Luís I and the riverside.

★ **Taste Porto Food Tours** TOURS
(⌨ 967 258 750; www.tasteportofoodtours.com; food tour adult/child €59/39; ⊙ food tours 10am, 10.30am & 4pm Tue-Sat) Loosen a belt notch for these superb half-day food tours, where you'll sample everything from Porto's best slow-roast-pork sandwich to éclairs, fine wines, cheese and coffee. Friendly, knowledgeable André and his team lead these indulgent 3½-hour walking tours, which take in viewpoints, historic back lanes and the Mercado do Bolhão en route to restaurants, grocery stores and cafes.

★ **Other Side** TOURS
(⌨ 916 500 170; www.theotherside.pt; Rua Souto 67; ⊙9am-8pm) Well-informed, congenial guides reveal their city on half-day walking tours of hidden Porto (€19), *petisco* (tapas) trails (€25), and e-bike tours of Porto and Foz (€29). They can also venture further afield with full-day trips to the Douro's vineyards (€85) and to Guimarães and Braga (€69).

🎊 Festivals & Events

Festa de São João RELIGIOUS
(St John's Festival) Porto's biggest party. For one night in June, on the 24th, the city erupts into music, competitions and riotous parties; this is also when merrymakers pound each other on the head with squeaky plastic mallets (you've been warned).

Serralves Em Festa
CULTURAL

(www.serralvesemfesta.com; ⊙ Jun) This huge (free) celebration runs for 40 hours nonstop over one weekend in early June. Parque de Serralves hosts the main events, with concerts, avant-garde theatre and kiddie activities. Other open-air events happen all over town.

🛏 Sleeping

★ Gallery Hostel
HOSTEL €

(📞 224 964 313; www.gallery-hostel.com; Rua Miguel Bombarda 222; dm/d/tr/ste from €22/64/80/90; ❋ 🛜) A true travellers' hub, this hostel-gallery has clean and cosy dorms and doubles, a sunny, glass-enclosed back patio, a grassy terrace, a cinema room, a shared kitchen and a bar-music room. Throw in its free walking tours, homemade dinners on request, port-wine tastings and concerts, and you'll see why it's booked up so often – reserve ahead.

★ Canto de Luz
B&B €€

(📞 225 492 142; www.cantodeluz.com; Rua do Almada 539; r €70-95; 🛜) *Ah oui,* this French-run guesthouse, just a five-minute walk from Trindade metro, is a delight. Rooms are light, spacious and make the leap between classic and contemporary, with vintage furnishings used to clever effect. Your kindly hosts André and Brigitte prepare delicious breakfasts, with fresh-squeezed juice, pastries and homemade preserves. There's also a pretty garden terrace.

★ 6 Only
GUESTHOUSE €€

(📞 222 013 971, 926 885 187; www.6only.pt; Rua Duque de Loulé 97; r €60-80, ste €75-100; 🛜) This beautifully restored guesthouse has just six rooms – so get in early. All flaunt simple but stylish details that effortlessly blend traditional elements (such as high stucco ceilings and polished-wood floors) with understated contemporary design. There's a lounge, a Zen-like courtyard and friendly staff. Fresh pastries and juice and eggs to order feature at breakfast.

★ Maison Nos B&B
B&B €€

(📞 222 011 683, 927 537 457; www.maisonnos.com; Rua Dr Barbosa de Castro 36; d €70-90; 🛜) Stéphane and Baris go the extra mile to make you feel at home at their sweet, understatedly stylish B&B, nuzzled in among 14th-century walls in the Vitória district. The parquet-floored rooms are light and uniquely furnished – some with petite balconies, others with free-standing tubs. Fresh juice, homemade cake and strong coffee at breakfast kick-start the day perfectly.

★ Guest House Douro
BOUTIQUE HOTEL €€€

(📞 222 015 135; www.guesthousedouro.com; Rua da Fonte Taurina 99-101; r from €140; ❋ @ 🛜) In a restored relic overlooking the Douro, these eight rooms have been blessed with gorgeous wooden floors, plush queen beds and marble baths; the best have dazzling river views. But it is the welcome that makes this place stand out from the crowd – your charming hosts Carmen and João bend over backwards to please.

ESSENTIAL FOOD & DRINK

Cod for all seasons The Portuguese have dozens of ways to prepare bacalhau (dried salt cod). Try bacalhau a brás (grated cod fried with potatoes and eggs), bacalhau espiritual (cod soufflé) or bacalhau com natas (baked cod with cream and grated cheese).

Drink Port and red wines from the Douro valley, alvarinho and vinho verde (crisp, semi-sparkling wine) from the Minho and great, little-known reds from the Alentejo and the Beiras (particularly the Dão region).

Field & fowl Porco preto (sweet 'black' pork), leitão (roast suckling pig), alheira (bread and meat sausage – formerly Kosher), cabrito assado (roast kid) and arroz de pato (duck risotto).

Pastries The pastel de nata (custard tart) is legendary, especially in Belém. Other delicacies: travesseiros (almond and egg pastries) and queijadas (mini-cheese pastries).

Seafood Char-grilled lulas (squid), polvo (octopus) or sardinhas (sardines). Other treats: cataplana (seafood and sausage cooked in a copper pot), caldeirada (hearty fish stew) and açorda de mariscos (bread stew with shrimp).

✖️ Eating

Taberna do Largo PORTUGUESE €
(📋 222 082 154; Largo de São Domingos 69; petiscos €2-14; ⊘5pm-midnight Tue-Thu, to 1am Fri, noon-1am Sat, noon-midnight Sun; 📶) Lit by wine-bottle lights, this sweet grocery store, deli and tavern is run with passion by Joana and Sofia. Tour Portugal with your taste buds with their superb array of hand-picked wines, which go brilliantly with tasting platters of smoked tuna, Alentejo *salpicão* sausage, Azores São Jorge cheese, Beira *morcela* (blood sausage), *tremoços* (lupin beans) and more.

⭐Flor dos Congregados PORTUGUESE €€
(📋 222 002 822; www.flordoscongregados.pt; Travessa dos Congregados 11; mains €8-16; ⊘7-10pm Mon, 10am-10pm Tue-Sat) Tucked away down a narrow alley, this softly lit, family-run restaurant brims with stone-walled, wood-beamed, art-slung nooks. The frequently changing blackboard menu goes with the seasons.

⭐Cantina 32 PORTUGUESE €€
(📋 222 039 069; www.cantina32.com; Rua das Flores 32; petiscos €5-15; ⊘12.30-2.30pm & 7.30-11pm; 📶) Industrial-chic meets boho at this delightfully laid-back haunt, with its walls of polished concrete, mismatched crockery, verdant plants, and vintage knick-knacks ranging from a bicycle to an old typewriter. The menu is just as informal – *petiscos* such as *pica-pau* steak (bite-sized pieces of steak in a garlic and white-wine sauce), quail-egg croquettes, and cheesecake served in a flower pot reveal a pinch of creativity.

⭐DOP GASTRONOMY €€€
(📋 222 014 313; www.ruipaula.com; Largo de São Domingos 18; menus €20-56; ⊘7-11pm Mon, 12.30-3pm & 7-11pm Tue-Sat; 📶) Housed in the Palácio das Artes, DOP is one of Porto's most stylish addresses, with its high ceilings and slick, monochrome interior. Much-feted chef Rui Paula puts a creative, seasonal twist on outstanding ingredients, with dish after delicate, flavour-packed dish skipping from octopus carpaccio to cod with lobster rice. The three-course lunch is terrific value at €20.

🍷 Drinking & Nightlife

The bar-lined Rua Galeira de Paris and nearby streets are packed with revellers most nights. Down by the water, the open-air bar scene on Praça da Ribeira is great for drinks with a view.

TASTING PORT WINE

Sitting just across the Rio Douro from Porto, **Vila Nova de Gaia** is woven into the city's fabric by stunning bridges and a shared history of port-wine making. Since the mid-18th century, port-wine bottlers and exporters have maintained their lodges here.

Today, some 30 of these lodges clamber up the riverbank and most open their doors to the public for cellar tours and tastings. Among the best are **Taylor's** (📋 223 772 956, 223 742 800; www.taylor.pt; Rua do Choupelo 250; tours incl tasting €12; ⊘10am-6pm), **Graham's** (📋 223 776 484; www.grahams-port.com; Rua do Agro 141; tours incl tasting €10-100; ⊘9.30am-6pm) and **Ramos Pinto** (📋 936 809 283; www.ramospinto.pt; Av Ramos Pinto 400; tours incl tasting €6; ⊘10am-6pm May-Oct, reduced hours Nov-Apr).

⭐Prova WINE BAR
(www.prova.com.pt; Rua Ferreira Borges 86; ⊘4pm-2am Wed-Mon; 📶) Diogo, the passionate owner, explains the finer nuances of Portuguese wine at this chic, stone-walled bar, where relaxed jazz plays. Stop by for a two-glass tasting (€5), or sample wines by the glass – including beefy Douros, full-bodied Dãos and crisp Alentejo whites. These marry well with sharing plates of local hams and cheeses (€14). Diogo's port tonics are legendary.

⭐Aduela BAR
(Rua das Oliveiras 36; ⊘3pm-2am Mon, 1pm-2am Tue-Sat, 2pm-midnight Sun) Retro and hip but not self-consciously so, chilled Aduela bathes in the nostalgic orange glow of its glass lights, which illuminate the green walls and mishmash of vintage furnishings. Once a sewing machine warehouse, today it's where friends gather to converse over wine and appetising *petiscos* (€3 to €8).

Vinologia WINE BAR
(www.vinologia.pt; Rua de São João 28-30; ⊘11am-midnight) This cosy wine bar is an excellent place to sample the fine quaffs of Porto, with over 200 different ports on offer. If you fall in love with a certain wine, you can usually buy a whole bottle (or even send a case home).

☆ Entertainment

★ Casa da Música CONCERT VENUE
(House of Music; ☑ 220 120 220; www.casadamusica.com; Avenida da Boavista 604; ☺ box office 9.30am-7pm Mon-Sat, to 6pm Sun) Grand and minimalist, sophisticated yet populist, Porto's cultural behemoth boasts a shoebox-style concert hall at its heart, meticulously engineered to accommodate everything from jazz duets to Beethoven's Ninth.

FC Porto FOOTBALL
(www.fcporto.pt) The Estádio do Dragão is home to Primeira Liga heroes FC Porto. It's northeast of the centre, just off the VCI ring road (metro stop Estádio do Dragão).

❶ Information

City Centre Turismo (☑ 223 393 472; www.visitporto.travel; Rua Clube dos Fenianos 25; ☺ 9am-8pm May-Oct, to 7pm Nov-Apr) The main city *turismo* has a detailed city map, a transport map and the *Agenda do Porto* cultural calendar, among other printed materials.

Post Office (Praça General Humberto Delgado 320; ☺ 8am-9pm Mon-Fri, 9am-6pm Sat) Across from the main tourist office.

Santo António Hospital (☑ 222 077 500; www.chporto.pt; Largo Prof Abel Salazar) Has English-speaking staff.

❶ Getting There & Away

AIR

Porto's **airport** (OPO; ☑ 229 432 400; www.ana.pt) is connected by daily flights from Lisbon and London, and has direct links from other European cities, particularly with EasyJet and Ryanair.

BUS

Porto has many private bus companies leaving from different terminals; the main tourist office can help. In general, for Lisbon and the Algarve, the choice is **Renex** (www.renex.pt; Rua Campo Mártires de Pátria 37) or **Rede Expressos** (☑ 222 006 954; www.rede-expressos.pt; Rua Alexandre Herculano 366).

Three companies operate from or near Praceto Régulo Magauanha, off Rua Dr Alfredo Magalhães: **Transdev-Norte** (www.transdev.pt; Garagem Atlântico, Rua de Alexandre Herculano 366) goes to Braga (€6); **AV Minho** (www.avminho.pt) to Viana do Castelo (€8).

TRAIN

Porto is a northern Portugal rail hub. Most international trains, and all intercity links, start at Campanhã, 2km east of the centre.

At São Bento, you can book tickets to any other destination.

❶ Getting Around

TO/FROM THE AIRPORT

The metro's 'violet' E line provides handy service to the airport. A one-way ride to the centre costs €1.85 and takes about 45 minutes. A daytime **taxi** costs €20 to €25 to/from the centre.

PUBLIC TRANSPORT

Save money on transport by purchasing a refillable **Andante Card** (€0.60), valid for transport on buses, metro, funicular and tram. You can buy them from STCP kiosks or newsagents. A 24-hour ticket for the entire public transport network, excluding trams, costs €7.

Bus

Central hubs of Porto's extensive bus system include Jardim da Cordoaria, Praça da Liberdade and São Bento station. Tickets purchased on the

---

WORTH A TRIP

THROUGH THE GRAPEVINES OF THE DOURO

Portugal's best-known river flows through the country's rural heartland. In the upper reaches, port-wine grapes are grown on steep terraced hills, punctuated by remote stone villages and, in spring, splashes of dazzling white almond blossom.

The Rio Douro is navigable right across Portugal. Highly recommended is the train journey from Porto to Pinhão (€11, 2½ hours, five daily), the last 70km clinging to the river's edge; trains continue to Pocinho (from Porto €13.30, 3¼ hours). **Porto Tours** (☑ 222 000 045; www.portotours.com; ☺ 10am-7pm), situated next to Porto's cathedral, can arrange tours, including idyllic Douro cruises.

Cyclists and drivers can choose river-hugging roads along either bank, and can visit wineries along the way (check out www.dourovalley.eu for an extensive list of wineries open to visitors). You can also stay overnight in scenic wine lodges among the vineyards.

bus are one way €1.20/€1.85 with/without the Andante Card.

Funicular

The panoramic **Funicular dos Guindais** (one-way €2.50; ☺8am-10pm May-Oct, to 8pm Nov-Apr) shuttles up and down a steep incline from Avenida Gustavo Eiffel to Rua Augusto Rosa.

Metro

Porto's **metro** (http://en.metrodoporto.pt) currently comprises six metropolitan lines that all converge at the Trinidade stop. Tickets cost €1.20 with an Andante Card. There are also various 24-hour passes (from €4.15) available.

Tram

Porto has three antique trams that trundle around town. The most useful line, 1E, travels along the Douro towards the Foz district. A single tram ticket costs €2.50, a day pass €8.

Viana do Castelo

POP 15,600

The jewel of the Costa Verde (Green Coast), Viana do Castelo has both an appealing medieval centre and lovely beaches just outside the city. In addition to its natural beauty, Viana do Castelo whips up some excellent seafood and hosts some magnificent traditional festivals, including the spectacular Festa de Nossa Senhora da Agonia in August.

◉ Sights

The stately heart of town is Praça da República, with its delicate fountain and grandiose buildings, including the 16th-century Misericórdia, a former almshouse.

Monte de Santa Luzia   HILL

There are two good reasons to visit Viana's 228m eucalyptus-clad hill. One is the wondrous view down the coast and up the Lima valley. The other is the fabulously over-the-top, 20th-century, neo-Byzantine Templo do Sagrado Coração de Jesus (Temple of the Sacred Heart of Jesus; ☺9am-6pm). You can get a little closer to heaven on its graffiti-covered roof, via a lift, followed by an elbow-scraping stairway – take the museum entrance on the ground floor.

Praia do Cabedelo   BEACH

(☺ferry 9am-6pm) This is one of the Minho's best beaches: a 1km-long arch of blond, powdery sand that folds into grassy dunes backed by a grove of wind-blown pines. It's across the river from town, best reached on

a five-minute ferry trip (one way/return adult €1.40/2.80, half-price/free under-12/under-six; ☺to Praia do Cabedelo 9am-6pm) from the pier south of Largo 5 de Outubro.

🛏 Sleeping & Eating

★Ó Meu Amor   GUESTHOUSE €

(☑258 406 513; www.omeuamor.com; Rua do Poço 19; s/d without bathroom €25/45; @🖥) Top choice in town right in the historic centre, this hideaway in a rambling town house full of nooks and crannies has nine adorable rooms with shared bathrooms. Guests can use the kitchen and cosy living room. Each room has a theme – such as the India and Africa rooms in the attic – and some have tiny balconies with rooftop and mountain views.

★Margarida da Praça   GUESTHOUSE €€

(☑258 809 630; www.margaridadapraca.com; Largo 5 de Outubro 58; s €60-75, d €78-88; @🖥) Fantastically whimsical, this boutique inn offers thematic rooms in striking pinks, sea greens and whites, accented by stylish floral wallpaper, candelabra lanterns and lush duvets. The equally stylish lobby glows with candlelight in the evening.

O Pescador   SEAFOOD €€

(☑258 826 039; Largo de São Domingos 35; mains €9.50-15.50; ☺noon-3pm & 7-10pm Tue-Sat, noon-3pm Sun) A simple, friendly, family-run restaurant admired by locals for its good seafood, and tasty lunch specials (from €6.50).

ℹ Getting There & Away

Five to 10 trains go daily to Porto (€5 to €6.65, two hours), as well as express buses (€6.50, two hours).

Braga

POP 136,885

Portugal's third-largest city boasts a fine array of churches, their splendid baroque facades looming above the old plazas and narrow lanes of the historic centre. Lively cafes, trim little boutiques, and some good restaurants add to the appeal.

◉ Sights

Sé   CATHEDRAL

(www.se-braga.pt; Rua Dom Paio Mendes; ☺9am-7pm high season, 9am-6.30pm low season) Braga's extraordinary cathedral, the oldest in Portugal, was begun when the archdiocese was restored in 1070 and completed in the following century. It's a rambling complex made up of differing styles, and architecture buffs could spend half a day happily distinguishing the Romanesque bones from Manueline musculature and baroque frippery.

Museu dos Biscainhos MUSEUM
(Rua dos Biscainhos; adult/student €2/1, first Sun of the month free; ⊙9.30am-12.45pm & 2-5.30pm Tue-Sun) An 18th-century aristocrat's palace is home to the enthusiastic municipal museum, with a nice collection of Roman relics and 17th- to 19th-century pottery and furnishings. The palace itself is the reason to come, with its polychrome, chestnut-panelled ceilings and 18th-century *azulejos* depicting hunting scenes. The ground floor is paved with deeply ribbed flagstones on which carriages would have once rattled through to the stables.

🛌 Sleeping

★ Collector's Hostel HOSTEL €
(☑253 048 124; www.collectorshostel.com; Rua Francisco Sanches 42; dm €19-22, s/d €26/39) A lovely hostel, lovingly run by two well-travelled women who met in Paris (one of whom was born in the hostel's living room), restored the family house and all the furniture inside, and turned the three floors into a cosy hideaway where guests feel like they're in their grandparents' home, with a twist.

Tea 4 Nine GUESTHOUSE €€
(☑914 004 606; www.tea4nine.pt; Praça Conde Agrolongo 49; s/d €80/105) A swish new guesthouse with four stunning suites featuring clean-lined contemporary decor, pine floors and a full range of top-of-the-line amenities. Two face the square, two are out back, and three more sit in another building facing the square. Note that there's no elevator. The sweet downstairs bistro with a garden does great lunch menus and a Sunday brunch (€7.50).

🍴 Eating

Anjo Verde VEGETARIAN €
(Largo da Praça Velha 21; mains €7.50-8.60; ⊙noon-3pm & 7.30-10.30pm Mon-Sat; ☑) Braga's vegetarian offering serves generous, elegantly presented plates in a lovely, airy dining room. Vegetarian lasagne, risotto and vegetable tarts are among the choices. Mains can be bland, but the spiced chocolate tart is a superstar.

Casa de Pasto das Carvalheiras FUSION €€
(☑253 046 244; Rua Dom Afonso Henriques 8; mains €4.50-14; ⊙noon-3pm & 7pm-midnight) This funky eatery with lots of colourful details and a long bar serves up flavourful fusion food served as *pratinhos* (small plates). The menus change weekly and feature dishes like salmon ceviche, *alheira* (a light garlicky sausage of poultry or game) rolls with turnip sprouts and black octopus polenta. Weekday lunch menus are a great deal (€8 or €12, depending on the number of dishes you order).

ℹ Information

Turismo (☑253 262 550; www.cm-braga.pt; Avenida da Liberdade 1; ⊙9am-7pm Mon-Fri, 9am-12.30pm & 2-5.30pm Sat & Sun Jun-Sep, shorter hours in low season) Braga's helpful tourist office is in an art-deco-style building facing the fountain.

ℹ Getting There & Away

Trains run to/from Lisbon (€31, four hours, two to four daily), Coimbra (€19.80, 2¼ hours, five to seven daily) and Porto (€3.10, about one hour). Eight buses a day go to Viana do Castelo (€4.45, 1½ hours).

Parque Nacional da Peneda-Gerês

Spread across four impressive granite massifs, this vast park encompasses boulder-strewn peaks, precipitous valleys, gorse-clad moorlands and forests of oak and pine. It also shelters more than 100 granite villages that, in many ways, have changed little since Portugal's founding in the 12th century. For nature lovers, the stunning scenery here is unmatched in Portugal for camping, hiking and other outdoor adventures. The park's main centre is at **Vila do Gerês**, a sleepy, hot-springs village.

🏃 Activities

Hiking
There are trails and footpaths through the park, some between villages with accommodation. Leaflets detailing these are available from the park offices.

Day hikes around Vila do Gerês are popular. An adventurous option is the **old Roman road** from Mata do Albergaria (10km up-valley from Vila do Gerês), past the **Vilarinho das Furnas** reservoir to Campo do Gerês. More distant destinations include Ermida and Cabril, both with simple accommodation.

Cycling & Horse Riding

Mountain bikes can be hired in Campo do Gerês (15km northeast of Vila do Gerês) from Equi Campo (⌫253 161 405; www.equicampo.com; ⊙9am-7pm Jun-Aug, 9am-7pm weekends Sep-May). Guides here also lead horse-riding trips, hikes and combination hiking/climbing/abseiling excursions.

Water Sports

Rio Caldo, 8km south of Vila do Gerês, is the base for water sports on the Caniçada Reservoir. English-run AML (⌫253 391 779; www.aguamontanha.com; Lugar de Paredes) rents kayaks, pedal boats, rowing boats and small motorboats. It also organises kayaking trips along the Albufeira de Salamonde.

🛏 Sleeping & Eating

Vila do Gerês has plenty of *pensões* (guesthouses), but you may find vacancies are limited; many are block-booked by spa patients in summer.

Pousada do Gerês-Caniçada/São Bento POUSADA €€€
(⌫210 407 650; www.pousadas.pt; Caniçada; s/d €180/190; P❄🕸🏊) This lovely place has a spectacular setting. High above the Albufeira, it offers a splendid retreat at eagle's-nest heights. The rooms have wood-beamed ceilings and comfy furnishings; some have verandahs with magnificent views. There's a pool, gardens, a tennis court, and an excellent restaurant serving local delicacies (trout, roasted goat). To get here head south 3km from Rio Caldo along the N304, following signs to Caniçada.

ℹ Information

The head park office is **Adere-PG** (⌫258 452 250; www.adere-pg.pt; Rua Dom Manuel I; ⊙9am-12.30pm & 2.30-6pm Mon-Fri) in Ponte de Barca. Obtain park information and reserve cottages and other park accommodation here.

ℹ Getting There & Away

Because of the lack of transport within the park, it's good to have your own wheels. You can rent cars in **Braga** (⌫253 203 910; Rua Gabriel Pereira de Castro 28; ⊙9am-7pm Mon-Fri, 9am-12.30pm Sat).

SURVIVAL GUIDE

ℹ Directory A–Z

PORTUGAL DIRECTORY A–Z

ACCOMMODATION

Portugal offers outstanding value by and large. Budget places provide some of Western Europe's cheapest digs, while you'll find atmospheric accommodation in converted castles, mansions and farmhouses.

Seasons

High season Mid-June to mid-September.
Mid-season May to mid-June and mid-September to October.
Low season November to April.

Ecotourism & Farmstays

Turismo de Habitação is a private network of historic, heritage or rustic properties, ranging from 17th-century manors to quaint farmhouses or self-catering cottages. Doubles run from €60 to €120.

Pousadas

These are government-run former castles, monasteries or palaces, often in spectacular locations. For details, contact tourist offices or Pousadas de Portugal.

Guesthouses

The most common types are the *residencial* and the *pensão*: usually simple, family-owned operations. Some have cheaper rooms with shared bathrooms. Double rooms with private bathroom typically run €40 to €60.

Hostels

Portugal has a growing number of cool backpacker digs, particularly in Lisbon. Nationwide, Portugal has over 30 pousadas da juventude within the Hostelling International (HI) system. The average price for a dorm room is about €20.

Camping

For detailed listings of campsites nationwide, pick up the Roteiro Campista, updated annually and sold at bookshops. Some of the swishest

---

SLEEPING PRICE RANGES

The following price ranges refer to a double room with bathroom in high season. Unless otherwise stated. breakfast is included in the price.

€ less than €60
€€ €60–€120
€€€ more than €120

places are run by **Orbitur** (☑ 226 061 360; www.orbitur.pt).

MONEY

ATMs are widely available, except in the smallest villages. Credit cards accepted in midrange and high-end establishments.

OPENING HOURS

Opening hours vary throughout the year. We provide high-season opening hours; hours will generally decrease in the shoulder and low seasons.

Banks 8.30am–3pm Monday to Friday

Bars 7pm–2am

Cafes 9am–7pm

Clubs 11pm–4am Thursday to Saturday

Restaurants noon–3pm and 7–10pm

Shopping malls 10am–10pm

Shops 9.30am–noon and 2–7pm Monday to Friday, 10am–1pm Saturday

PUBLIC HOLIDAYS

Banks, offices, department stores and some shops close on the public holidays listed here. On New Year's Day, Easter Sunday, Labour Day and Christmas Day, even *turismos* close.

New Year's Day 1 January

Carnaval Tuesday February/March – the day before Ash Wednesday

Good Friday March/April

Liberty Day 25 April

Labour Day 1 May

Corpus Christi May/June – ninth Thursday after Easter

Portugal Day 10 June – also known as Camões and Communities Day

Feast of the Assumption 15 August

Republic Day 5 October

All Saints' Day 1 November

Independence Day 1 December

Feast of the Immaculate Conception 8 December

Christmas Day 25 December

TELEPHONE

Portugal's country code is ☑ 351. There are no regional area codes. Mobile phone numbers

---

within Portugal have nine digits and begin with ☑ 9.

For general information, dial ☑ 118, and for reverse-charge (collect) calls dial ☑ 120.

ℹ Getting There & Away

AIR

Most international flights arrive in Lisbon, though Porto and Faro also receive some. For more information, including live arrival and departure schedules, see www.ana.pt.

LAND

Bus

The major long-distance carriers that serve European destinations are Busabout (www.busabout.com) and Eurolines (www.eurolines.com); though these carriers serve Portugal, it is not currently included in the multicity travel passes of either company.

For some European routes, Eurolines is affiliated with the big Portuguese operators **Internorte** (☑ 707 200 512; www.internorte.pt) and **Eva Transportes** (☑ 289 899 760; www.eva-bus.com).

Train

The most popular train link from Spain is on the Sud Express, operated by Renfe, which has a nightly sleeper service between Madrid and Lisbon.

Two other Spain–Portugal crossings are at Valença do Minho and at Caia (Caya in Spain), near Elvas.

ℹ Getting Around

AIR

TAP Portugal has daily Lisbon–Porto and Lisbon–Faro flights (taking less than one hour) year round.

BUS

A host of small bus operators, most amalgamated into regional companies, run a dense network of services across the country. Among the largest companies are **Rede Expressos** (☑ 707 223 344; www.rede-expressos.pt), **Rodonorte** (☑ 259 340 710; www.rodonorte.pt) and the Algarve line **Eva** (p922).

Most bus-station ticket desks will give you a computer printout of fares, and services and schedules are usually posted at major stations.

Classes

Bus services are of four general types:

Alta Qualidade A fast deluxe category offered by some companies.

Carreiras Marked 'CR'; slow, stopping at every crossroad.

Expressos Comfortable, fast buses between major cities.

Rápidas Quick regional buses.

CAR & MOTORCYCLE
Automobile Associations

Automóvel Clube de Portugal (ACP; ☑ 213 180 100, 24hr emergency assistance 808 222 222; www.acp.pt) has a reciprocal arrangement with better-known foreign automobile clubs, including AA and RAC. It provides medical, legal and breakdown assistance. The 24-hour emergency help number is %707 509 510.

Hire

To hire a car in Portugal you must be at least 25 years old and have held your home licence for over a year. To hire a scooter of up to 50cc you must be over 18 years old and have a valid driving licence.

Road Rules

The various speed limits for cars and motorcycles are 50km/h within cities and public centres, 90km/h on normal roads and 120km/h on motorways.

The legal blood-alcohol limit is 0.5g/L, and there are fines of up to €2500 for drink-driving. It's also illegal in Portugal to drive while talking on a mobile phone.

TRAIN

Caminhos de Ferro Portugueses is the statewide train network and is generally efficient.

There are four main types of long-distance service. Note that international services are marked 'IN' on timetables.

Alfa Pendular Deluxe, marginally faster and much pricier service.

Interregional (IR) Reasonably fast trains.

Intercidade (IC) or Rápido Express trains.

Regional (marked R on timetables) Slow trains that stop everywhere.

Romania

Best Places to Eat

➜ Lacrimi şi Sfinţi (p929)

➜ Bistro de l'Arte (p932)

➜ Crama Sibiul Vechi (p936)

➜ Roata (p939)

➜ Caruso (p942)

Best Places to Stay

➜ Little Bucharest Old Town Hostel (p928)

➜ Rembrandt Hotel (p929)

➜ Casa Georgius Krauss (p935)

➜ Youthink Hostel (p938)

Why Go?

Beautiful and beguiling, Romania's rural landscape remains relatively untouched by the country's urban evolution. It's a land of aesthetically stirring hand-ploughed fields, sheep-instigated traffic jams and lots of homemade plum brandy.

Most visitors focus their attention on Transylvania, with its legacy of fortified Saxon towns like Braşov and Sighişoara, plus tons of eye-catching natural beauty. Similar in character but even more remote, the region of Maramureş offers authentic folkways and villages marked by memorable wooden churches. Across the Carpathians, the Unesco-listed painted monasteries dot southern Bucovina. The Danube Delta has more than 300 species of birds, including many rare varieties, and is an ideal spot for birdwatching.

Energetic cities like Timişoara, Sibiu, Cluj-Napoca and, especially, Bucharest offer culture – both high- and low-brow – and showcase Romania as a rapidly evolving European country.

When to Go
Bucharest

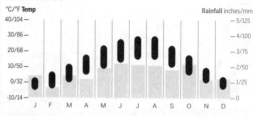

May Trees in full blossom; bird-watching in the Danube Delta at its best.

Jun Mountain hiking starts in mid-June; castles and museums are open and in high gear.

Sep The summer heat is gone, but sunny days are perfect for exploring big cities.

Romania Highlights

1 Braşov (p931) Basing yourself here to ascend castles and mountains (and castles on top of mountains).

2 Southern Bucovina (p940) Following the Unesco World Heritage line of painted monasteries.

3 Sibiu (p935) Soaking in this beautifully restored Saxon town.

4 Sighişoara (p934) Exploring this medieval citadel and birthplace of Dracula.

5 Danube Delta (p938) Rowing through the tributaries and the riot of nature.

6 Bucharest (p925) Enjoying the museums and cacophonous nightlife of the capital.

BUCHAREST

📞 021 / POP 1,900,000

Romania's capital gets a bad rap, but in fact it's dynamic, energetic and fun. It's where still-unreconstructed communism meets unbridled capitalism; where the soporific forces of the EU meet the passions of the Balkans. Many travellers give the city just a night or two before heading off to Transylvania, but that's not enough. Budget at least a few days to take in the good museums, stroll the parks and hang out at trendy cafes.

👁 Sights

👁 South of the Centre

⭐ **Palace of Parliament** HISTORIC BUILDING
(Palatul Parlamentului, Casa Poporului; 📞 tour bookings 0733-558 102; http://cic.cdep.ro; B-dul Națiunile Unite; adult/student complete tours 55/28 lei,

Central Bucharest

◉Ⓝ 0 _____ 200 m
0 _____ 0.1 miles

A **B** **C** **D**

Midland Youth Hostel (350m)

Shift Pub (250m)

Icoanei Garden

Grigore Antipa Natural History Museum (1.2km); Museum of 🏛16 the Romanian Peasant & Gift Shop (1.5km); Atlassib (1.6km); Seneca Anticafe (2.1km)

Str Mendeleev

🏛13

B-dul Gen Magheru

Str Nicolae Golescu

Str Georges Clemenceau

Str Episcopiei

12 18

Str Pictor Verona

Str Pictor Verona

1

Str George Enescu

Str Pitar Moş

Str Dionisie Lupu

Str Luterană

Calea Victoriei

Romanian Atheneaum 🏛1

Str Franklin

Vila Arte (500m)

Str Ştirbei Vodă

Piaţa George Enescu

Str C A Rosetti

B-dul Nicolae Bălcescu

Str C A Rosetti

10 ✕

Str Ion Câmpineanu

🏛2

Piaţa Revoluţiei

Str D I Dobrescu

Str Nicolae Filipescu

Str Tudor Arghezi

!
4

Str Boteanu

🔒17

Piaţa Walter Mărăcineanu

Str Ion Câmpineanu

Str Ion Brezoianu

✉ Str Matei Millo

Str E Quinet

Universitate Ⓜ

University (Piaţa Universităţii) ℹ

Cişmigiu Garden

Str Constantin Mille

15 ✪

Str Academiei

B-dul Regina Elisabeta

Bucharest National Opera House (1.2km)

Str Domniţa Anastasia

Str Eforie

Romanian National Library

Str Ion Ghica

Str Colţei

Str Lipscani

Str Lipscani

14 🏛

Str M Vodă

Bucharest Financial Plaza

Str Doamnei

Spl Independenţei

Str Ilfov

Calea Victoriei

✕8
Str Stavropoleos

5

Str Lipscani

🏛7

Str Blănari

🏛6

Str Hanul cu Tei

Str Gabroveni

B-dul I C Brătianu

Str Poştei

HISTORIC QUARTER

🏛11

9 ✕

Str Covaci

Palace of Parliament (400m)

B-dul Naţiunile Unite

Piaţa Naţiunile Unite

Str Franceză

Str Smârdan

Str Şelari

3 🕆

Great Synagogue (800m)

Dâmboviţa River

Central Bucharest

standard tours 35/18 lei, photography 30 lei; ⊙ 9am-5pm Mar-Oct, to 4pm Nov-Feb; Ⓜ Izvor) The Palace of Parliament is the world's second-largest administrative building (after the Pentagon) and former dictator Nicolae Ceauşescu's most infamous creation. Started in 1984 (and still unfinished), the building has more than 3000 rooms and covers 330,000 sq metres. Entry is by guided tour only (book in advance). Entry to the palace is from B-dul Naţiunile Unite on the building's northern side (to find it, face the front of the palace from B-dul Unirii and walk around the building to the right). Bring your passport.

Great Synagogue SYNAGOGUE
(☑ 0734-708 970; Str Adamache 11; ⊙ 9am-3pm Mon-Thu, to 1pm Fri & Sun; Ⓜ Piaţa Unirii) FREE This important synagogue dates from the mid-19th century and was established by migrating Polish Jews; entry is free, but a donation (10 lei) is expected. It's hard to find, hidden on three sides by public housing blocks, but worth the effort to see the

meticulously restored interior and to take in the main exhibition on Jewish life and the Holocaust in Romania.

◉ Historic Centre & Piaţa Revoluţiei

Bucharest's Historic Centre *(Centrul Istoric)*, sometimes referred to as the Old Town, lies south of Piaţa Revoluţiei. It was the seat of power in the 15th century but today is filled with clubs and bars.

Piaţa Revoluţiei saw the heaviest fighting in the overthrow of communism in 1989. Those days are commemorated by the **Rebirth Memorial** (Memorialul Renaşterii; Calea Victoriei, Piaţa Revoluţiei; ⊙ 24hr; Ⓜ Universitate) in the centre of the square.

Old Princely Court Church CHURCH
(Biserica Curtea Veche; Str Franceză; ⊙ 7am-8pm; Ⓜ Piaţa Unirii) FREE The Old Princely Court Church, built from 1546 to 1559 during the reign of Mircea Ciobanul (Mircea the Shepherd), is considered to be Bucharest's oldest church. The faded 16th-century frescoes next to the altar are originals. The carved stone portal was added in 1715.

Stavropoleos Church CHURCH
(☑ 021-313 4747; www.stavropoleos.ro; Str Stavropoleos 4; ⊙ 7am-8pm; Ⓜ Piaţa Unirii) FREE The tiny and lovely Stavropoleos Church, which dates from 1724, perches a bit oddly a block over from some of Bucharest's craziest Old Town carousing. It's one church, though, that will make a lasting impression, with its courtyard filled with tombstones, ornate wooden interior and carved wooden doors.

★ **Romanian Athenaeum** HISTORIC BUILDING
(Ateneul Român; ☑ box office 021-315 6875; www.fge.org.ro; Str Benjamin Franklin 1-3; tickets 20-65 lei; ⊙ box office noon-7pm Tue-Fri, 4-7pm Sat, 10-11am Sun; Ⓜ Universitate, Piaţa Romană) The exquisite Romanian Athenaeum is the majestic heart of Romania's classical music tradition. Scenes from Romanian history are featured on the interior fresco inside the Big Hall on the 1st floor; the dome is 41m high. A huge appeal dubbed 'Give a Penny for the Athenaeum' saved it from disaster after funds dried up in the late 19th century. Today it's home to the George Enescu Philharmonic Orchestra and normally only open during concerts, but you can often take a peek inside.

ITINERARIES

One Week

Spend a day ambling around the capital, then take a train to Braşov – Transylvania's main event – for castles, activities and beer at streetside cafes. Spend a day in Sighişoara's medieval citadel, then catch a train back to Bucharest or on to Budapest.

Two Weeks

Arrive in Bucharest by plane or Timişoara by train, then head into Transylvania, devoting a day or two each to Braşov, Sighişoara and Sibiu. Tour southern Bucovina's painted monasteries, then continue on to Bucharest.

National Art Museum   MUSEUM

(Muzeul Naţional de Artă; ☑ information 021-313 3030; www.mnar.arts.ro; Calea Victoriei 49-53; 15 lei; ☉ 11am-7pm Wed-Sun; Ⓜ Universitate) Housed in the 19th-century Royal Palace, this massive, multipart museum – all signed in English – houses two permanent galleries: one for National Art and the other for European Masters. The national gallery is particularly strong on ancient and medieval art, while the European gallery includes some 12,000 pieces and is laid out by nationality.

◉ North of the Centre

Luxurious villas and parks line grand Şos Kiseleff, which begins at Piaţa Victoriei. The major landmark is the Triumphal Arch (Arcul de Triumf; Piaţa Arcul de Triumf; ☉ closed to the public; Ⓜ Aviatorilor) FREE, which stands halfway up Şos Kiseleff.

★ Former Ceauşescu Residence   HISTORIC BUILDING

(Primăverii Palace; ☑ 021-318 0989; www.palatulprimaverii.ro; B-dul Primăverii 50; guided tours in English adult/child 45/30 lei; ☉ 10am-6pm Wed-Sun; Ⓜ Aviatorilor) This restored villa is the former main residence of Nicolae and Elena Ceauşescu, who lived here for around two decades up until the end of 1989. Everything has been returned to its former lustre, including the couple's bedroom and the private apartments of the three Ceauşescu children. Highlights include a cinema in the basement, Elena's opulent private chamber, and the

back garden and swimming pool. Reserve a tour in advance by phone or on the website.

★ Grigore Antipa Natural History Museum   MUSEUM

(Muzeul de Istorie Naturală Grigore Antipa; ☑ 021-312 8826; www.antipa.ro; Şos Kiseleff 1; adult/student 20/5 lei; ☉ 10am-8pm Wed-Sun; 🚼; Ⓜ Piaţa Victoriei) One of the few attractions in Bucharest aimed squarely at kids, this natural history museum has been thoroughly renovated and features modern bells and whistles such as video displays, games and interactive exhibits. Much of it has English signage.

Museum of the Romanian Peasant   MUSEUM

(Muzeul Ţăranului Român; ☑ 021-317 9661; www.muzeultaranuluiroman.ro; Şos Kiseleff 3; adult/child 8/2 lei; ☉ 10am-6pm Tue-Sun; Ⓜ Piaţa Victoriei) The collection of peasant bric-a-brac, costumes, icons and partially restored houses makes this one of the most popular museums in the city. There's not much English signage, but insightful little cards in English posted in each room give a flavour of what's on offer. An 18th-century church stands in the back lot, as does a great gift shop (www.muzeultaranuluiroman.ro; Şos Kiseleff 3; ☉ 10am-6pm Tue-Sun; Ⓜ Piaţa Victoriei) and restaurant.

🛏 Sleeping

Hotels in Bucharest are typically aimed at businesspeople, and prices are higher here than the rest of the country. Cert Accommodation (☑ 0720-772 772; www.cert-accommodation.ro; apt 250-500 lei) offers good-value private apartment stays starting at around 200 lei per night.

★ Little Bucharest Old Town Hostel   HOSTEL €

(☑ 0786-329 136; www.littlebucharest.ro; Str Smârdan 15; dm 50-60 lei, r 250 lei; ❀@🛜; Ⓜ Piaţa Unirii) Bucharest's most central hostel, in the middle of the lively Historic Centre, is super clean well-run. Accommodation is over two floors, with dorms ranging from six to 12 beds. Private doubles are also available. The staff is travel friendly and youth oriented, and can advise on sightseeing and fun. Book over the website or by email.

Midland Youth Hostel   HOSTEL €

(☑ 021-314 5323; www.themidlandhostel.com; Str Biserica Amzei 22; dm 40-60 lei; ❀❄@🛜; Ⓜ Piaţa Romană) A happening hostel, with an excellent central location not far from popular Piaţa Amzei. Accommodation is in four-, eight- or 12-bed dorms. There's a common kitchen too.

★ Rembrandt Hotel   HOTEL €€

(☎021-313 9315; www.rembrandt.ro; Str Smârdan 11; s/d tourist 180/230 lei, standard 260/300 lei, business 350/380 lei; ❄❖@☎; Ⓜ Universitate) It's hard to say enough good things about this place. Stylish beyond its three-star rating, this 16-room, Dutch-run hotel faces the landmark National Bank in the Historic Centre. Rooms come in three categories – tourist, standard and business – with the chief difference being size. Book well in advance.

Vila Arte   BOUTIQUE HOTEL €€€

(☎021-210 1035; www.vilaarte.ro; Str Vasile Lascăr 78; s/d 260/320 lei; ❄❖@☎; Ⓜ Piaţa Romană, ⛟5, 21) A renovated villa transformed into an excellent-value boutique hotel stuffed with original art that pushes the envelope on design and colour at this price point. The services are top drawer and the helpful reception makes every guest feel special. The 'Ottoman' room is done in an updated Turkish style, with deep-red spreads and fabrics, and oriental carpets.

✗ Eating

★ Caru' cu Bere   ROMANIAN €€

(☎021-313 7560; www.carucubere.ro; Str Stavropoleos 3-5; mains 20-45 lei; ⊙8am-midnight Sun-Thu, to 2am Fri & Sat; ☎; Ⓜ Piaţa Unirii) Despite a decidedly touristy-leaning atmosphere, with peasant-girl hostesses and sporadic traditional song-and-dance numbers, Bucharest's oldest beer house continues to draw in a strong local crowd. The colourful belle-époque interior and stained-glass windows dazzle, as does the classic Romanian food. Dinner reservations are essential.

Shift Pub   INTERNATIONAL €€

(☎021-211 2272; www.shiftpub.ro; Str General Eremia Grigorescu 17; mains 25-40 lei; ⊙noon-2am; Ⓜ Piaţa Romană) Great choice for salads and burgers as well as numerous beef and pork dishes, often sporting novel Asian, Middle Eastern or Mexican taste touches. Try to arrive slightly before meal times to grab a coveted table in the tree-covered garden.

Lente Praporgescu   INTERNATIONAL €€

(☎021-310 7424; www.lente.ro; Str Gen Praporgescu 31; mains 25-40 lei; ⊙11.30am-1am; ☎; Ⓜ Piaţa Romană) The main branch of three 'Lente' restaurants scattered around the city centre. The recipe for all three is broadly the same: inventive soups and salads, an eclectic design of mismatched chairs and old books, and a relaxed, vaguely alternative vibe. A ter-

rific choice for lunch or a casual dinner. The garden terrace offers respite on a hot day.

★ Lacrimi şi Sfinţi   ROMANIAN €€€

(☎0725-558 286; www.lacrimisisfinti.com; Str Şepcari 16; mains 30-50 lei; ⊙12.30pm-2am Tue-Sun, 6pm-2am Mon; ☎; Ⓜ Piaţa Unirii) A true destination restaurant in the Historic Centre, Lacrimi şi Sfinţi takes modern trends such as farm-to-table freshness and organic sourcing and marries them to old-school Romanian recipes. The philosophy extends to the simple, peasant-inspired interior, where the woodwork and decorative elements come from old farmhouses. The result is authentic and food that is satisfying. Book in advance.

♟ Drinking & Nightlife

★ Grădina Verona   CAFE

(☎0732-003 060; www.facebook.com/GradinaVerona; Str Pictor Verona 13-15; ⊙9am-midnight May-Sep; ☎; Ⓜ Piaţa Romană) A garden oasis hidden behind the Cărtureşti bookshop, serving standard-issue but excellent espresso drinks and some of the wackiest iced-tea infusions ever concocted in Romania, such as peony flower, mango and lime (it's not bad).

M60   CAFE

(☎031-410 0010; www.facebook.com/m60cafeamzei/; Str Mendeleev 2; ⊙10am-1am; ☎; Ⓜ Piaţa Romană) M60 is a category-buster, transforming through the day from one of the city's pre-eminent morning coffee houses to a handy lunch spot (healthy salads and vegetarian options) and then morphing into a meet-up and drinks bar in the evening. It's been a hit since opening day, as city residents warmed to its clean, minimalist Scandinavian design and living-room feel.

Origo   CAFE

(☎0757-086 689; https://origocoffee.ro; Str Lipscani 9; ⊙7.30am-8pm Mon, to midnight Tue-Fri, 9am-midnight Sat & Sun; ☎; Ⓜ Piaţa Unirii) Arguably the best coffee in town and *the* best place to hang out in the morning, grab a table and check your email. Lots of special coffee roasts and an unlimited number of ways to imbibe. There are a dozen pavement tables for relaxing on a sunny day.

Fire Club   BAR

(☎0732-166 604; www.fire.ro; Str Gabroveni 12; ⊙10am-4am Sun-Thu, to 6am Fri & Sat; ☎; Ⓜ Piaţa Unirii) A crowded student-oriented bar and rock club that's much less flash and more relaxed than some of the other venues around the Historic Centre.

☆ Entertainment

Control
LIVE MUSIC

(☑ 0733-927 861; www.control-club.ro; Str Constantin Mille 4; ☺ noon-4am; 🛜; Ⓜ Universitate) This is a favourite among club-goers who like alternative, turbo-folk, indie and garage sounds. Hosts both live acts and DJs, depending on the night.

Green Hours 22
LIVE MUSIC

(☑ bar reservations 0751-772 275; www.greenhours. ro; Calea Victoriei 120; ☺ 9am-4am; Ⓜ Piaţa Romană) This old-school basement jazz club runs a lively programme of jazz and experimental theatre most nights through the week, and hosts an international jazz fest in May/June. There's also a popular bar, bistro and garden terrace. Check the website for the schedule during your trip and book in advance by email.

Bucharest National Opera House
OPERA

(Opera Naţională Bucureşti; ☑ box office 021-310 2661; www.operanb.ro; B-dul Mihail Kogălniceanu 70-72; tickets 10-70 lei; ☺ box office 9am-1pm & 3-7pm; Ⓜ Eroilor) The city's premier venue for classical opera and ballet. Buy tickets online or at the venue box office.

🛍 Shopping

★ Anthony Frost
BOOKS

(☑ 021-311 5136; www.anthonyfrost.ro; Calea Victoriei 45; ☺ 10am-8pm Mon-Fri, to 7pm Sat, to 2pm Sun; Ⓜ Universitate) Serious readers will want to make time for arguably the best small English-language bookshop in Eastern Europe. Located in a small passage next to the Creţulescu Church, this shop has a carefully chosen selection of highbrow contemporary fiction and nonfiction.

Cărtureşti Verona
BOOKS

(☑ 0728 828 916; www.carturesti.ro; Str Pictor Verona 13-15, cnr B-dul Nicolae Bălcescu; ☺ 10am-10pm; Ⓜ Piaţa Romană) This bookshop, music store, tearoom and funky backyard garden is a must-visit. Amazing collection of design, art and architecture books, as well as carefully selected CDs and DVDs, including many classic Romanian films with English subtitles. Also sells Lonely Planet guidebooks.

ℹ Information

You'll find hundreds of bank branches and ATMs in the centre. Banks usually have currency exchange offices, but bring your passport as you'll have to show it to change money.

Bucharest Tourist Information Center (☑ 021-305 5500, ext 1003; http://seebucharest.ro; Piaţa Universităţii; ☺ 10am-5pm Mon-Fri, to 2pm Sat & Sun; Ⓜ Universitate) Not much information, though the English-speaking staff can field basic questions.

Central Post Office (☑ 021-315 9030; www. posta-romana.ro; Str Matei Millo 10; ☺ 7.30am-8pm Mon-Fri; Ⓜ Universitate)

Emergency Clinic Hospital (☑ 021-599 2300; www.scub.ro; Calea Floreasca 8; ☺ 24hr; Ⓜ Ştefan cel Mare) Arguably the city's, and country's, best emergency hospital.

Seneca Anticafe (☑ 0720-331 100; www. senecanticafe.ro; Str Arhitect Ion Mincu 1; per hr 8 lei; ☺ 9am-10pm; 🛜; 🚌 24, 42, 45) Coffee and internet access.

ℹ Getting There & Away

AIR

All international and domestic flights use **Henri Coandă International Airport** (OTP, Otopeni; ☑ arrivals 021-204 1220, departures 021-204 1210; www.bucharestairports.ro; Şos Bucureşti-Ploieşti; 🚌 783), often referred to by its previous name, Otopeni. Henri Coandă is 17km north of Bucharest on the road to Braşov. The airport is a modern facility, with restaurants, newsagents, currency exchange offices and ATMs.

It's also the hub for national carrier **Tarom** (☑ call centre 021-204 6464, office 021-316 0220; www.tarom.ro; Spl Independenţei 17, City Centre; ☺ 9am-5pm Mon-Fri; Ⓜ Piaţa Unirii). Tarom has a comprehensive network of internal flights to major Romanian cities as well as to capitals and big cities around Europe and the Middle East.

BUS

It's possible to get just about anywhere in the country by bus from Bucharest, but figuring out where your bus or maxitaxi departs from can be tricky. Bucharest has several bus stations and they don't seem to follow any discernible logic. The best bet is to consult the websites www. autogari.ro and www.cdy.ro.

Sample domestic destinations and fares from Bucharest include Braşov (from 35 lei, three hours, hourly), Cluj-Napoca (90 lei, nine hours, six daily), Sibiu (55 lei, 4½ hours, 10 daily) and Tulcea/Danube Delta (45 lei, five hours, 10 daily).

CAR & MOTORCYCLE

Driving in Bucharest is lunacy and you won't want to do it for more than a few minutes before you stow the car and use the metro. If you're travelling around by car and want to visit Bucharest for the day, park at a metro station on the outskirts and take the metro in.

Gara de Nord (✆ phone reservations 021-9522; www.cfrcalatori.ro; Piaţa Gara de Nord 1; Ⓜ Gara de Nord) is the main station for most national and all international trains. The station is accessible by metro from the centre.

Buy tickets at station ticket windows. A seat reservation is compulsory if you are travelling with an InterRail or Eurail pass.

Check the latest train schedules on either www.cfr.ro or the reliable German site www.bahn.de. Sample fares from Bucharest on fast IC trains include Braşov (50 lei, 2½ hours, several daily), Cluj-Napoca (92 lei, 7½ hours, four daily), Sibiu (85 lei, six hours, two daily), Timişoara (101 lei, nine hours, three daily) and Suceava (90 lei, seven hours, three daily).

❶ Getting Around

TO/FROM THE AIRPORT
Bus

Express bus 783 leaves every 30 minutes from the airport arrivals hall to various points in the centre, including Piaţa Victoriei and Piaţa Unirii. A single journey on the express bus costs 7 lei.

Taxi

Order a taxi by touchscreen at the arrivals terminal. Simply choose a company and rate (all are about the same), and you'll get a ticket and number. Pay the driver. A reputable taxi to the centre should cost no more than 50 lei.

PUBLIC TRANSPORT

Bucharest's public transport system of metro, buses, trams and trolleybuses is operated by the transport authority **RATB** (Regia Autonomă de Transport Bucureşti; ✆ 021-9391; www.ratb.ro). The system runs daily from about 4.30am to approximately 11.30pm.

The ticketing situation differs for street transport (buses, trams and trolleybuses) and for the metro system. To use buses, trams or trolleybuses, you must first purchase an **Activ** card (3.70 lei) from any RATB street kiosk, which you then load with credit that is discharged as you enter the transport vehicles. Trips cost 1.30 lei each.

Metro stations are identified by a large letter 'M'. To use the metro, buy a magnetic-strip ticket available at ticketing machines or cashiers inside station entrances (have small bills handy). Tickets valid for two journeys cost 5 lei. A 10-trip ticket costs 20 lei.

TRANSYLVANIA

After a century of being name-checked in literature and cinema, the word 'Transylvania' enjoys worldwide recognition. The mere mention conjures a vivid landscape of mountains, castles, spooky moonlight and at least one well-known count with a wicked overbite. Unexplained puncture wounds notwithstanding, Transylvania is all those things and more. A melange of architecture and chic sidewalk cafes punctuate the towns of Braşov, Sighişoara and Sibiu, while the vibrant student town Cluj-Napoca has some vigorous nightlife.

Braşov

POP 275,000

Gothic spires, medieval gateways, Soviet blocks and a huge Hollywood-style sign: Braşov's skyline is instantly compelling. A number of medieval watchtowers still glower over the town. Between them sparkle baroque buildings and churches, while easy-going cafes line main square Piaţa Sfatului. Visible from here is forested Mt Tâmpa, sporting 'Braşov' in huge white letters.

◉ Sights

In addition to the sights below, explore the Old Town Fortifications that line the centre on the eastern and western flanks. Many have been restored.

Black Church   CHURCH
(Biserica Neagră; ✆ 0268-511 824; www.honterusgemeinde.ro; Curtea Johannes Honterus 2; adult/student/child 9/6/3 lei; ⊙10am-7pm Tue-Sat & noon-7pm Sun Apr-Oct, 10am-3pm Tue-Sat & noon-3pm Sun Nov-Mar) Romania's largest Gothic church rises triumphantly over Braşov's old town. Built between 1385 and 1477, this German Lutheran church was named for its charred appearance after the town's Great Fire in 1689. Restoration of the church took a century. Today it towers 65m high at its bell tower's tallest point. Organ recitals are held in the church three times a week during July and August, usually at 6pm Tuesday, Thursday and Saturday.

St Nicholas' Cathedral   CHURCH
(Biserica Sfântul Nicolae; Piaţa Unirii 1; ⊙7am-7pm) With forested hills rising behind its prickly Gothic spires, St Nicholas' Cathedral is one of Braşov's most spectacular views. First built in wood in 1392, it was replaced by a Gothic stone church in 1495 and later embellished in Byzantine style. It was once enclosed by military walls; today the site has a small cemetery. Inside are murals of Romania's last king and queen, covered by

plaster to protect them from communist leaders and uncovered in 2004.

Mt Tâmpa
MOUNTAIN

(Muntele Tâmpa) Rising 940m high and visible around Braşov, Mt Tâmpa is adorned with its very own Hollywood-style sign. Hard as it is to imagine, it was the site of a mass-impaling of 40 noblemen by Vlad Ţepeş. Banish such ghoulish images from your head as you take the cable car (Telecabina; ☑0268-478 657; Aleea Tiberiu Brediceanu; adult one way/return 10/16 lei, child one way/return 6/9 lei; ☺9.30am-5pm Tue-Sun, noon-6pm Mon), or hike (about an hour), to reach a small viewing platform offering stunning views over the city. There's a slightly drab cafe at the top.

Activities

★ Transylvanian Wolf
TOURS

(☑0744-319 708; www.transylvanian.ro; ☺year-round) This family-run nature-tour company, with award-winning Romanian guide Dan Marin at its helm, leads walks on the trail of animals such as wolves, bears and lynx (€40 per person, minimum two people). Adventurous rambles in pure nature are guaranteed, though sightings aren't. Alternatively, sightings are very likely on excursions to a bear hide (€55 per person for two hours; price includes transfers).

Sleeping

Rolling Stone Hostel
HOSTEL €

(☑0268-513 965; www.rollingstone.ro; Str Piatra Mare 2A; dm/r €10/30; P@🛜) Powered by enthusiastic staff, Rolling Stone has clean dorm rooms that sleep between six and 10. Most rooms have high ceilings and convenient touches like lockers and reading lamps for each bed. Private doubles are comfy, or you can sleep in the wood-beamed attic for a stowaway vibe. Maps and excellent local advice are supplied the moment you step through the door.

★ Bella Muzica
HOTEL €€

(☑0268-477 956; www.bellamuzica.ro; Piaţa Sfatului 19; s/d/apt from 220/270/540 lei; ❄🛜) A regal feel permeates Bella Muzica, housed within a 400-year-old building, thanks to its tastefully restored wooden beams, exposed brick, high ceilings and occasional antiques. The main square location of this refined hotel is hard to top.

Casa Reims
B&B €€

(☑0368-467 325; www.casareims.ro; Str Castelului 85; s/d from €48/56; P❄🛜) Pastels and acid tones mingle beautifully with bare brick and wooden beams at this boutique B&B. Personalised service from the friendly owners adds to the VIP feel, and most rooms have views of Mt Tâmpa.

Eating

Sergiana
ROMANIAN €€

(☑0268-419 775; www.sergianagrup.ro; Str Mureşenilor 28; mains 25-40 lei; ☺11am-11pm) Steaming soups in hollowed-out loaves of bread, paprika-laced meat stews, and the most generous ratio of cheese and sour cream we've ever seen in a polenta side dish – do not wear your tight jeans for a feast at Sergiana. The subterranean dining hall, lined with brick and wood, is lively and casual – fuelled by ample German beer and loud conversation.

★ Bistro de l'Arte
BISTRO €€

(☑0720-535 566; www.bistrodelarte.ro; Piaţa Enescu 11; mains 15-35 lei; ☺9am-midnight Mon-Sat, noon-midnight Sun; 🛜🍴) Tucked down a charming side street, this bohemian joint can be spotted by the bike racks shaped like penny-farthings. There's an almost Parisian feel in Bistro de l'Arte's arty decor and champagne breakfasts (59 lei), though its menu picks the best from France, Italy and beyond: bruschetta, fondue, German-style cream cake, and a suitably hip cocktail list.

Drinking

Croitoria de Cafea
COFFEE

(☑0770-263 333; Str Iuliu Maniu 17; ☺8am-7pm Mon-Fri, 9.30am-6pm Sat, to 4pm Sun) The best coffee in town can be sipped at this hole-in-the-wall cafe, which has a few wooden stools for you to perch amid bulging bags of beans.

Festival 39
BAR

(☑0743-339 909; www.festival39.com; Str Republicii 62; ☺7am-midnight) Jazz flows from this vintage-feel watering hole and restaurant, an art-deco dream of stained-glass, high ceilings, wrought-iron finery, candelabra and leather banquettes. As good for clanking together beer glasses as for cradling a hot chocolate over your travel journal.

Information

You'll find numerous ATMs and banks on and around Str Republicii and B-dul Eroilor.

Central Post Office (Str Nicolae Iorga 1; ☺8am-7pm Mon-Fri, 9am-1pm Sat) Opposite the Heroes' Cemetery.

ROMANIA BRAŞOV

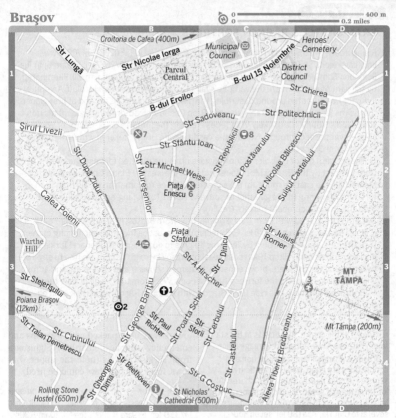

Braşov

⊙ **Sights**
1 Black Church	B3
2 Old Town Fortifications	B3

⊕ **Activities, Courses & Tours**
3 Mt Tâmpa Cable Car	D3

⊖ **Sleeping**
4 Bella Muzica	B3
5 Casa Reims	D1

⊗ **Eating**
6 Bistro de l'Arte	B2
7 Sergiana	B2

⊕ **Drinking & Nightlife**
8 Festival 39	C2

County Hospital (Spitalul Judetean; ☏ 0268-135 080; www.hospbv.ro; Calea Bucureşti 25-27; ⊗ 24hr) Hospital with emergency clinic, northeast of the centre.

Tourist Information Centre (www.brasovtourism.eu; Str Prundului 1; ⊗ 9am-5pm Mon-Fri) Cordial staff offer maps and local advice. Check www.brasovtravelguide.ro for general info.

🛈 Getting There & Around

BUS

Maxitaxis are the best way to reach places near Braşov, including Bran and Râşnov. The most accessible station is **Bus Station 1** (Autogara 1; ☏ 0268-427 267; www.autogari.ro; B-dul Gării 1), next to the train station.

From 6am to 7.30pm, maxitaxis leave every half-hour for Bucharest (from 35 lei, 2½ to 3½ hours). About 12 daily buses or maxitaxis leave for Sibiu (30 lei, 2½ hours). Three go daily to Sighişoara (30 lei). Less frequent buses reach Cluj-Napoca (65 lei, five to 5½ hours, three daily).

TRAIN

The **train station** (Gara Braşov; ☏ 0268-410 233; www.cfrcalatori.ro; B-dul Gării 5) is 2km

BRAN CASTLE & RÂSNOV FORTRESS

Rising above the town on a rocky promontory, Bran Castle (☎0268-237 700; www.bran-castle.com; Str General Traian Moşoiu 24; adult/student/child 35/20/7 lei; ☉9am-6pm Tue-Sun, noon-6pm Mon Apr-Sep, same hours to 4pm Oct-Mar) holds visitors in thrall. Illuminated by the light of a pale moon, the vampire's lair glares down from its rocky bluff. An entire industry has sprouted around describing the pile as 'Dracula's Castle', and at first glance the claims look legit. Regrettably, though, Bran Castle's blood-drinking credentials don't withstand scrutiny. It's unlikely Vlad Ţepeş – either 'the Impaler' or 'protector of Wallachia' – ever passed through. Nor did the castle inspire Bram Stoker in writing his iconic Gothic novel *Dracula*.

These seem minor quibbles when you gaze up at the turreted fortress, guarded from the east by the Bucegi Mountains and from the west by Piatra Craiului massif. Meanwhile, the castle's museum pays greater homage to Romanian royals than immortal counts. Ignoring this, a gauntlet of souvenir sellers hawk fang-adorned mugs and Vlad-the-Impaler compact mirrors (really).

Commonly paired with Bran Castle on day trips from Braşov, nearby Râşnov Fortress (Cetatea Râşnov; adult/child 12/6 lei; ☉9am-6pm) might just be the more enchanting of the two. The medieval citadel, built by Teutonic Knights to guard against Tatar and Turkish invasion, roosts on a hilltop 19km southwest of Braşov by road. Visitors are free to stroll between sturdy watchtowers, browse medieval-themed souvenir and craft stalls, and admire views of rolling hills from the fortress' highest point. Walk from the village or take the lift.

Bran is a 45-minute bus ride from Braşov, with a stop in Râşnov, and makes an easy day trip.

---

northeast of the centre. Buy tickets at the station. There are ATMs and a left-luggage office.

Braşov is an important train junction and connections are good. Daily domestic train service includes hourly trains to Bucharest (49 lei, three hours), seven daily to Sighişoara (40 lei, 2½ hours), six to Sibiu (45 lei, four hours) and several to Cluj-Napoca (80 lei, seven hours).

Sighişoara

POP 28,100

So resplendent are Sighişoara's pastel-coloured buildings, stony lanes and medieval towers, you'll rub your eyes in disbelief. Fortified walls encircle Sighişoara's lustrous merchant houses, now harbouring cafes, hotels and craft shops. Lurking behind the gingerbread roofs and turrets of the Unesco-protected old town is the history of Vlad Ţepeş, the country's most notorious ruler; he was allegedly born in a house here that is visitable to this day.

◉ Sights

Citadel
FORTRESS

Sighişoara's delightful medieval buildings are enclosed within its citadel, a Unesco-listed complex of protective walls and watchtowers. Walking in the citadel is today a tranquil, fairytale-like experience, but these

towers were once packed with weapons and emergency supplies, guarding Sighişoara from Turkish attacks (note the upper windows, from which arrows could be fired).

Clock Tower
MUSEUM

(Turnul cu Ceas; Piaţa Muzeului 1; adult/child 14/3.50 lei; ☉9am-6.30pm Tue-Fri, 10am-5.30pm Sat & Sun) The multicoloured tiled roof of Sighişoara's Clock Tower glitters like the scales of a dragon. The tower was built in the 14th century and expanded 200 years later. It remains the prettiest sight in town, offering a magnificent panorama from the top. The views are as good a reason to visit as the museum inside, a patchy collection of Roman vessels, scythes and tombstones, and a scale model of the fortified town (English-language explanation is variable).

Casa Vlad Dracul
HISTORIC BUILDING

(www.casavladdracul.ro; Str Cositorarilor 5; 5 lei; ☉10am-10pm) Vlad Ţepeş (aka Dracula) was reputedly born in this house in 1431 and lived here until the age of four. It's now a decent restaurant, but for a small admission fee the staff will show you Vlad's old room (and give you a little scare). Bubble-burster: the building is indeed centuries old, but has been completely rebuilt since Vlad's days.

🛏 Sleeping

Burg Hostel   HOSTEL **€**
(📞 0265-778 489; www.burghostel.ro; Str Bastionului 4-6; dm 45 lei, s/d 90/110 lei, without bathroom 85/100 lei; 🖥🏊) A great budget choice without compromising on charm, Burg Hostel has spacious dorms (with handy touches like plug sockets close to beds). Common areas have chandeliers made from old cartwheels, ceramic lamps, vaulted ceilings and other rustic touches. Staff are friendly and there's a relaxing courtyard cafe. Breakfast isn't included, but you can buy meals from the cafe.

Pensiunea Legenda   GUESTHOUSE **€€**
(📞 0748-694 368; www.legenda.ro; Str Bastionului 8; r €26-39; 🖥) The owners of this historic guesthouse whisper that Vlad Țepeș once wooed a beautiful young woman within these walls, a myth that will either charm or chill you. All five rooms at this well-run guesthouse have snug beds and occasional vampiric twists like black chandeliers and dungeon-like doors. Breakfast not included.

★Casa Georgius Krauss BOUTIQUE HOTEL **€€€**
(📞 0365-730 840; www.casakrauss.com; Str Bastionului 11; r 243-450 lei; 🅿🍴🖥) This dazzling boutique hotel is hived out of an old burgher's house at the northern end of the citadel. The restoration left period details like wood-beamed ceilings, while adding tasteful modern bathrooms and plush-linened beds. The Krauss Room, number 2, has original paintings including a medieval coat of arms, plus a four-poster bed.

🍴 Eating

Central Park   INTERNATIONAL **€€**
(📞 0365-730 006; www.hotelcentralpark.ro; Central Park Hotel, Piața Hermann Oberth 25; mains 25-40 lei; ⊘ 11am-11pm; 🖥) Even if you're not staying at the Central Park **hotel** (📞 0365-730 006; www.hotelcentralpark.ro; Piața Hermann Oberth 25; s/d/ste €77/90/110; 🅿🍴@🖥), plan a meal here. Sighișoara is short on good restaurants and this is one of the best. The food is a mix of Romanian and international dishes, and the carefully selected wine list offers the best domestic labels. Dress up for the lavish dining room or relax on the terrace.

Casa Vlad Dracul   ROMANIAN **€€**
(📞 0265-771 596; www.casavladdracul.ro; Str Cositorarilor 5; mains 24-35 lei; ⊘ 11am-11pm; 🍴) The link between Dracula and tomato soups, or medallions with potato and chicken roulade, we'll never quite understand. But the house where Vlad was born could have been dealt a worse blow than this atmospheric, wood-panelled restaurant. The menu of Romanian, Saxon and grilled specials is dotted with Dracula references. With a little embellishing from you, your kids will love it.

🔒 Shopping

★Arts & Crafts   ARTS & CRAFTS
(www.thespoonman.ro; Str Cositorarilor 5; ⊘ 10am-6pm) Inside Casa Vlad Dracul, this wondrous handicraft shop is the brainchild of self-styled 'Spoonman' Mark Tudose, who employs traditional woodcarving methods to fashion Transylvanian spoons (each with a local legend behind it), as well as painted-glass icons, clay statues, painted eggs and much more. It's a beautiful place to browse, and your best bet for finding a culturally meaningful souvenir.

ℹ Information

There are numerous ATMs and banks lining Sighișoara's main street, Str 1 Decembrie 1918.
Tourist Information Centre (📞 0788-115 511; Piața Muzeului 6; ⊘ 9am-5pm) Cordial, multilingual information service adjoining the Clock Tower, with maps and transport information.

ℹ Getting There & Away

BUS

Next to the train station on Str Libertății, the **bus station** (Autogara Sighișoara; 📞 0265-771 260; www.autogari.ro; Str Libertății 53) sends buses around the country, including to Brașov (18 to 25 lei, 2½ hours, three daily) and Sibiu (20 lei, 2½ hours, four daily).

TRAIN

Sighișoara is on a main international line and direct trains connect the town's **train station** (📞 0265-771 130; www.cfrcalatori.ro; Str Libertății 51) with Brașov (18 to 40 lei, 2½ to 3½ hours, six daily), Bucharest (67 lei, five to 5½ hours, three daily; more via Brașov), Cluj-Napoca (30 to 60 lei, 4½ to six hours, four daily; more via Teius) and Sibiu (13 lei, 2½ to three hours, two daily; more via Mediaș).

Sibiu

POP 154,890

Sibiu is awash in aristocratic elegance. Noble Saxon history emanates from every art-nouveau façade and gold-embossed church, all parked elegantly around graceful squares. Renowned composers Strauss, Brahms and Liszt all played here during the 19th century, and Sibiu has stayed at the forefront of Romania's cultural scene. Houses with distinctive eyelid-shaped windows (imagine a benign *Amityville Horror* House) watch a cast of artists and buskers bustling below them. Cafes and bars inhabit brick-walled cellars and luminously decorated attics.

◉ Sights

★St Mary's Evangelical Church   CHURCH
(Catedrala Evanghelică Sfânta Maria; Piața Huet; adult/child 5/2 lei, with tower 8/3 lei; ☉9am-8pm Mon-Sat, 11.30am-8pm Sun) Sibiu's Gothic centrepiece rises more than 73m over the old town. Inside, marvel at ghoulish stone skeletons, 17th-century tombs and the largest organ in Romania, all framed by a magnificent arched ceiling. Built in stages from the mid-1300s to 1520, the church was planted atop the site of an older 12th-century sanctuary. The four turrets on its tower once signified the right of the town to sentence criminals to death.

Brukenthal Palace   GALLERY
(European Art Gallery; ☎0269-217 691; www.brukenthalmuseum.ro/europeana; Piața Mare 5; adult/student 20/5 lei; ☉10am-6pm Tue-Sun summer, closed Tue winter) Brukenthal Palace is worth visiting as much for its resplendent period furnishings as for the European art within. Duck beneath the Music Room's chandeliers to admire colourful friezes and 18th-century musical instruments, before sidling among chambers exhibiting 17th-century portraits amid satin chaise longues and cases packed with antique jewellery. Sumptuously curated.

History Museum   MUSEUM
(Casa Altemberger; www.brukenthalmuseum.ro/istorie; Str Mitropoliei 2; adult/child 20/5 lei; ☉10am-6pm Tue-Sun Apr-Oct, 10am-6pm Wed-Sun Nov-Mar) This impressive museum begins with re-enactments of cave dwellers squatting in the gloom and dioramas of Dacian life. Out of these shadowy corridors, the museum opens out to illuminating exhibitions about Saxon guilds and local handicrafts (most impressive is the 19th-century glassware from Porumbacu de Sus). There's plenty of homage to Saxon efficiency: you could expect a fine for improperly crafting a copper cake tin.

ASTRA National Museum Complex   MUSEUM
(Muzeul Civilizației Populare Tradiționale ASTRA; ☎0269-202 447; www.muzeulastra.ro; Str Pădurea Dumbrava 16-20; adult/child 17/3.50 lei; ☉8am-8pm May-Sep, 9am-5pm Oct-Apr) Five kilometres from central Sibiu, this is Europe's largest open-air ethnographic museum, where churches, mills and traditional homes number among 400 folk architecture monuments on-site. In summer, ASTRA hosts numerous fairs, dance workshops and musical performances, so it's worthwhile checking the website for events. There's also a nice gift shop and restaurant with creekside bench seats. Get there via bus 13 from Sibiu's train station.

🛏 Sleeping

Welt Kultur   HOSTEL €
(☎0269-700 704; www.weltkultur.ro; Str Nicolea Bălcescu 13; dm 45-53 lei, d from 137 lei; ❋@🛜) Almost too chic to be dubbed a hostel, Welt has elegant wrought-iron bunks in its spotless four-, six- and eight-bed dorms (one is women-only). Meanwhile doubles are plain but easily as comfortable as Sibiu's pricier midranges. The best rooms face the street: they have more light and better views. There are lockers and a friendly chill-out room.

The Council   BOUTIQUE HOTEL €€
(☎0369-452 524; www.thecouncil.ro; Piața Mică 31; s/d/apt from €50/55/109; ❋🛜) Tapping into Sibiu's medieval lifeblood, this opulent hotel occupies a 14th-century hall in the heart of the old town. Individually designed rooms are equipped with desks, security safes and plenty of contemporary polish, but there are aristocratic touches like crimson throws, bare wooden rafters and Turkish-style rugs.

Am Ring   HOTEL €€
(☎0269-206 499; www.amringhotel.ro; Piața Mare 14; s/d/ste 250/290/390 lei; ❋🛜) Centrally located and decorated in a smorgasbord of styles, this is Sibiu's most lavish place to sleep. From the vaulted brick dining room to bedrooms styled with original wooden beams, throne-like chairs and baroque touches like gold candelabra, Am Ring exudes old-world elegance.

🍴 Eating

★Crama Sibiul Vechi   ROMANIAN €€
(☎0269-210 461; www.sibiulvechi.ro; Str Papiu-Ilarian 3; mains 25-30 lei; ☉11am-10pm) Hidden in an old wine cellar, this is the most evocative restaurant in Sibiu. Explore Romanian fare such as cheese croquettes, minced meatballs

and peasant's stew with polenta. Show up early, or reserve ahead; it's very popular.

★ **Kulinarium** ROMANIAN, EUROPEAN €€
(☑0721-506 070; www.kulinarium.ro; Piața Mică 12; mains 25-35 lei; ⊙noon-midnight) Fresh, well-presented Italy- and France-leaning cuisine, using seasonal ingredients, graces plates at Kulinarium. The restaurant has an intimate, casual feel, with roughly painted stone walls and dangling modern lampshades. Choose from smoky Austrian sausages, spinach soup with quail eggs, ra-re-beef salad, trout with polenta or well-exe-cuted pasta dishes.

Weinkeller ROMANIAN €€
(☑0269-210 319; www.weinkeller.ro; Str Turnului 2; mains 20-30 lei; ⊙noon-midnight) Mixing traditional Romanian mains such as stuffed cabbage leaves with Austro-Hungarian-influenced fare like *Tafelspitz* (boiled beef) and goulash, this romantic wine cellar and restaurant is the best date spot in Sibiu.

🍷 Drinking & Nightlife

Music Pub BAR
(☑0369-448 326; www.musicpubsibiu.ro; Piața Mică 23; ⊙8am-3am Mon-Fri, from 10am Sat & Sun) Skip down the graffitied corridor and rub your eyes in astonishment as a cellar bar and airy verandah opens up. One of the merriest spots in town, Music Pub sparkles with straw lamps and little candles, while '90s dance and rock plays on. There's table service, it's friendly, and there's occasional live music: a sure-fire winning night out.

Cafe Wien CAFE
(☑0269-223 223; www.cafewien.ro; Piața Huet 4; ⊙10am-2am Mon, 9am-2am Tue-Sun; 🛜) There's no more genteel Viennese tradition than *Kaffee und Kuchen* (coffee and cake), and Cafe Wien has just the right blend of re-finement and relaxation to accompany your strudel or Sachertorte (chocolate cake).

☆ Entertainment

State Philharmonic CLASSICAL MUSIC
(www.filarmonicasibiu.ro; Str Cetății 3-5; tickets 16-30 lei; ⊙box office noon-4pm Mon-Fri) Founded in 1949, this has played a key role in main-taining Sibiu's prestige as a main cultural centre of Transylvania. It's the key venue for performances at the annual opera festival (www.filarmonicasibiu.ro; ⊙mid-Sep).

ℹ Information

ATMs are located all over the centre.
Hospital (☑0269-215 050; www.scjs.ro; Str Izvorului) Has an accident and emergency department.
Tourist Information Centre (☑0269-208 913; www.turism.sibiu.ro; Piața Mare 2; ⊙9am-8pm Mon-Fri, to 6pm Sat & Sun May-Sep, 9am-5pm Mon-Fri, to 1pm Sat & Sun Oct-Apr) Based at the town hall, staff can offer free maps and plenty of local transport advice.

ℹ Getting There & Around

BUS
The main **bus station** (Autogara Sibiu; ☑0269-217 757; www.autogari.ro; Piața 1 Decembrie 1918) is opposite the train station. Bus and max-itaxi services include Brașov (28 lei, 2½ hours, 12 daily), Bucharest (55 lei, 4½ hours, 10 daily), Cluj-Napoca (35 lei, 3½ hours, several daily) and Timișoara (65 lei, six hours, seven daily).

TRAIN
There are nine daily direct trains to Brașov (40 lei, three hours), four trains to Bucharest (61 lei, six hours) and two to Timișoara (61 lei, six hours). To get to/from Cluj-Napoca (56 lei, five hours, several daily), you'll usually change at Copșa Mică or Mediaș.

The **train station** (Gara Sibiu; ☑0269-211 139; www.cfrcalatori.ro; Piața 1 Decembrie 1918, 6) is 2km east of the centre, about 20 minutes on foot.

Cluj-Napoca
POP 324,500

Bohemian cafes, music festivals and vigor-ous nightlife are the soul of Cluj-Napoca, Romania's second-largest city. With increas-ing flight links to European cities, Cluj is welcoming more and more travellers, who usually shoot off to the Apuseni Mountains, Maramureș or more popular towns in south-ern Transylvania. But once arrived, first-time visitors inevitably lament their failure to allow enough time in Cluj.

👁 Sights

St Michael's Church CHURCH
(Biserica Sfantul Mihail; ☑0264-592 089; Piața Un-irii; ⊙8am-6pm) The showpiece of Piața Unirii is 14th- and 15th-century St Michael's, the second-biggest Gothic church in Romania (after Brașov's Black Church). Its neo-Gothic clock tower (1859), 80m high, with original Gothic features – such as the 1444 front por-tal – can still be admired. Inside, soaring rib vaults lift the gaze towards fading frescoes.

DANUBE DELTA

After passing through several countries and absorbing countless lesser waterways, the Danube River empties into the Black Sea in eastern Romania, just south of the Ukrainian border.

The Danube Delta (Delta Dunării), included on Unesco's World Heritage list, is one of Romania's leading attractions. At the port of **Tulcea** (pronounced tool-cha), the river splits into three separate channels: the Chilia, Sulina and Sfântu Gheorghe arms, creating a constantly evolving 4187 sq km wetland of marshes, floating reed islets and sandbars. The region provides sanctuary for 300 species of bird and 160 species of fish. Reed marshes cover 1563 sq km, constituting one of the largest single expanses of reed beds in the world.

The delta is a haven for wildlife lovers, birdwatchers, fishers and anyone wanting to get away from it all. There are beautiful, secluded beaches at both **Sulina** and **Sfântu Gheorghe**, and the fish and seafood, particularly the fish soup, are the best in Romania.

Tulcea is the largest city in the delta and the main entry point for accessing the region. It's got good bus and minibus connections to the rest of the country, and is home to the main passenger ferries.

There is no rail service in the delta and few paved roads, meaning the primary mode of transport is ferry boat. Regularly scheduled ferries, both traditional 'slow' ferries and faster (and more expensive) hydrofoils, leave from Tulcea's main port on select days throughout the week and access major points in the delta.

The helpful staff at the **Tourism Information Centre** (☑0240-519 130; www.cnipt tulcea.ro; Str Gării 26; h8am-4pm Mon-Fri) in Tulcea

Pharmacy History Collection MUSEUM
(Piața Unirii 28; adult/child 6/3 lei; ◷10am-4pm Mon-Wed & Fri, noon-6pm Thu) Cluj-Napoca's oldest pharmacy building holds an intriguing collection of medical miscellany. 'Crab eyes' skulls, and powdered mummy are just a few of the cures on display in these antique-filled rooms. The prettiest is the Officina, a polished room with dark filigree swirling around its walls. You'll also learn that the 18th-century recipe for a love potion sounds suspiciously like mulled wine...

It's just past the northeast corner of the square, towards Str Regele Ferdinand I.

Fabrica de Pensule ARTS CENTRE
(Paintbrush Factory; ☑0727-169 569; www.fabricadepensule.ro; Str Henri Barbusse 59-61; ◷tours 4-8pm Mon-Sat) FREE More of a living, breathing creative space than a gallery, Fabrica de Pensule teems with just-made artwork by local and foreign creators who use this former paintbrush factory as a studio. Visits are by free guided tour, and depending on when you visit you'll spy anything from haunting urban photography to surreal Icelandic ceramics. You'll either adore visiting this artistic community in a post-industrial setting,

or be bemused by the work-in-progress art within boxy gallery spaces.

Parcul Etnografic Romulus Vuia MUSEUM, PARK
(www.muzeul-etnografic.ro; Aleea Muzeului Etnografic; adult/child 6/3 lei; ◷10am to 6pm summer, 9am to 4pm winter) Traditional architecture from around Romania has been faithfully reassembled at this open-air museum, 5km northwest of central Cluj. Most impressive is the Cizer Church; get the attention of a caretaker to allow you inside to view frescoes covering its wooden interior.

🛏 Sleeping

★**Youthink Hostel** HOSTEL €
(☑0745-202 911; www.youthinkhostel.com; Str Republicii 74; dm/d €15/35; [P][🕸]) 🐾 A labour-of-love restoration project has transformed a 1920 building, abandoned for a decade, into something between a hostel and an ecotourism retreat. Original wood beams, fireplace and hardwood floors retain the building's early-20th-century splendour, while the seven- and eight-bed dorms are clean and modern. Aptly for such a cheery and eco-conscious hostel, you'll be greeted by friendly dogs and a cat.

★ **Lol & Lola** BOUTIQUE HOTEL €€
(📞0264-450 498; www.loletlolahotel.ro; Str Neagră 9; s/d €67/79; 🅿 ❄ 🛜) This enjoyably zany hotel has a rainbow of individually styled rooms to choose from, with themes ranging from Hollywood, ballet, and a rock 'n' roll room with vinyl and guitars. It's ultra-modern with friendly service.

Hotel Confort HOTEL €€
(📞0264-598 410; www.hotelconfort.ro; Calea Turzii 48; s/d/ste 200/220/255 lei; 🅿 ❄ 🛜) Huge rooms with wooden floors and fuzzy rugs are accented with flower arrangements and arty prints at this chic hotel. Four rooms have balconies, and most have big windows and billowy drapes. It's a car-friendly location, a 15-minute walk outside central Cluj. Parking is free but limited; ask ahead. Breakfast is an extra 12 lei.

 Eating

★ **Roata** ROMANIAN €€
(📞0264-592 022; www.restaurant-roata.ro; Str Alexandru Ciurea 6; mains 20-28 lei; ☺noon-11pm; 🚲) Transylvanian cuisine just like Granny made it, in an untouristed part of Cluj. Settle in beneath the vine-covered trellis in the outdoor area, and agonise between roasted pork ribs and pike with capers. Or go all out with a 'Transylvanian platter' for two (52 lei), with homemade sausages, meatballs, sheep's cheese, aubergine stew and spare elastic for when your pants snap (we wish).

Camino INTERNATIONAL €€
(📞0749-200 117; Piaţa Muzeului 4; mains 20-30 lei; ☺9am-midnight; 🛜) This boho restaurant has a raffish charm, its peeling interior decked in candelabra and threadbare rugs, and outdoor seating spilling into monumental Piaţa Muzeului. Italian, Spanish and Indian dishes grace the menu. Ideal for solo book-reading over a pressed lemonade or alfresco tapas for two.

Bricks – (M)eating Point Restaurant STEAK €€€
(📞0364-730 615; www.bricksrestaurant.ro; Str Horea 2; mains 33-58 lei; ☺11am-11pm; 🛜) Jazz flows right along with the cocktails at this chic steakhouse overhanging the river. Italian pasta dishes, burgers and barbecued meats dominate the menu, alongside a couple of vegetarian options and plump desserts like cottage-cheese pancakes. Lunch specials (15 lei) offer the best value.

🍷 **Drinking & Nightlife**

Insomnia BAR, BEER GARDEN
(www.insomniacafe.ro; Str Universităţii 2; ☺9am-1am Mon-Fri, 11am-1am Sat & Sun) Squeezed into a narrow courtyard, a jaunty beer garden adjoins this zanily decorated bohemian cafe. Insomnia is one of a slew of bars catering to Cluj's arty crowd (which seems to be half the city) within the student quarter.

Joben Bistro CAFE
(www.jobenbistro.ro; Str Avram Iancu 29; ☺8am-2am Mon-Thu, noon-2am Fri-Sun; 🛜) This steampunk cafe will lubricate the gears of any traveller with a penchant for Victoriana. Aside from the fantasy decor, with skull designs, taxidermied deer heads and copper pipes on bare brick walls, it's a laid-back place to nurse a lavender-infused lemonade or perhaps the potent 'Drunky Hot Chocolate'.

Roots CAFE
(B-dul Eroilor 4; ☺7.30am-11.30pm Mon-Fri, 9am-11.30pm Sat, to 5pm Sun) Competition for Cluj's best brew is stiff, but Roots' silky coffee is the front runner. Staff are as friendly as the flat whites are smooth.

Irish & Music Pub BAR
(📞0729-947 133; www.irishmusicpub.ro; Str Horea 5; ☺10am-4am Mon-Sat, 6pm-4am Sun) Before you flee from the hackneyed 'Irish pub abroad' theme, know that this subterranean place has plenty of atmosphere resounding from its cavernous brick walls, plus a menu of steak sandwiches and veggie-friendly bar snacks to line your stomach.

☆ **Entertainment**

National Theatre THEATRE
(Teatrul Naţional Lucian Blaga; www.teatrulnationalcluj.ro; Piaţa Ştefan cel Mare 2-4; tickets from 20 lei) From Molière and Shakespeare through to modern drama, the Romanian-language performances at the National Theatre are the slickest productions in town. Buy tickets at the nearby **box office** (📞tickets 0264-595 363; Piaţa Ştefan cel Mare 14; ☺11am-2pm & 3-5pm Tue-Sun & 1 hour before performances).

Flying Circus CONCERT VENUE, CLUB
(www.flyingcircus.ro; Str Iuliu Maniu 2; entry before/after 1am 7/10 lei; ☺5pm-dawn) Arrive around midnight to see this student-oriented club begin to swing. Punters come for the music rather than to pose, so check the theme before you rock up: events vary from doom

WORTH A TRIP

PAINTED MONASTERIES OF SOUTHERN BUCOVINA

The painted monasteries of southern Bucovina are among the greatest artistic monuments of Eastern Europe. In 1993 they were collectively designated a Unesco World Heritage site.

Erected in the 15th and 16th centuries, when Moldavia was threatened by Turkish invaders, the monasteries were surrounded by strong defensive walls. Biblical stories were portrayed on the church walls in colourful pictures so that illiterate worshippers could better understand them.

The most impressive collection of monasteries is located west of Suceava. It includes the Arbore, Humor, Voroneţ and Moldoviţa monasteries.

Arbore Monastery (Manastirea Arbore; ☑0740-154 213; www.manastireaarbore.ro; Hwy DN2K 732, Arbore; adult/student 5/2 lei, photography 10 lei; ☺8am-7pm May-Sep, to 4pm Oct-Apr) (1503), the smallest of the main monasteries, receives a fraction of the visitors the others receive. The smaller scale allows you to study the paintings up close, to appreciate the skills and techniques.

Humor Monastery (Mănăstirea Humorului; Gura Humorului; adult/student 5/2 lei, photography 10 lei; ☺8am-7pm May-Sep, to 4pm Oct-Apr) (1530), near the town of Gura Humorului, boasts arguably the most impressive interior frescoes.

Voroneţ Monastery (Mănăstirea Voroneţ; ☑0230-235 323; Str Voroneţ 166, Voroneţ; adult/child 5/2 lei, photography 10 lei; ☺8am-7pm May-Sep, to 4pm Oct-Apr), also not far from Gura Humorului, is the only one to have a specific colour associated with it. 'Voroneţ Blue', a vibrant cerulean colour created from lapis lazuli, is prominent in its frescoes. The monastery was built in just three months and three weeks by Ştefan cel Mare following a 1488 victory over the Turks.

Moldoviţa Monastery (Mânăstirea Moldoviţa; Vatra Moldoviţei; adult/student 5/2 lei, photography 10 lei; ☺8am-7pm May-Sep, to 4pm Oct-Apr) (1532), 35km northwest of the Voroneţ Monastery, occupies a fortified quadrangular enclosure with tower, gates and flowery lawns. The central painted church has been partly restored, and features impressive frescoes from 1537.

The main gateway to the monasteries is **Suceava**, reachable by direct train from both Bucharest (91 lei, seven hours, six daily) and Cluj-Napoca (73 lei, seven hours, four daily).

metal to euphoric drum and bass. There's usually a free shot with the entry fee.

❶ Information

There are many banks and ATMs scattered around the centre.

Tourist Information Office (☑0264-452 244; www.visitcluj.ro; B-dul Eroilor 6; ☺8.30am-8pm Mon-Fri, 10am-6pm Sat & Sun) Super-friendly office with free maps, thoughtful trekking advice, and tons of info on transport links, accommodation, events and more.

❶ Getting There & Around

BUS

Domestic and international bus services depart mostly from **Bus Station 2** (Autogara 2, Autogara Beta; ☑0264-455 249; www.autogara-beta-cluj.ro; Str Giordano Bruno 1-3). The bus station is 350m northwest of the train station (take the overpass). Popular destinations include Braşov (65 lei, five hours, four daily),

Bucharest (90 lei, nine hours, six daily) and Sibiu (35 lei, four hours, almost hourly).

TRAIN

Cluj has decent train connections. Sample destinations include five daily trains to Bucharest (87 lei, 10 hours), six to Braşov (75 lei, seven hours) and four to Sighişoara (52 lei, four hours). Change at Teiuş or Mediaş for Sibiu (46 lei, four hours).

The **train station** (www.cfrcalatori.ro; Str Căii Ferate) is 1km north of the centre. Buy tickets at the station or in town at the **Agenţia de Voiaj CFR** (☑0264-432 001; Piaţa Mihai Viteazu 20; ☺8.30am-8pm Mon-Fri).

BANAT

Western Romania, with its geographic and cultural ties to neighbouring Hungary and Serbia and its historical links to the Austro-Hungarian Empire, enjoys an ethnic diversity that much of the rest of the country lacks. Timişoara, the regional hub, has a nationwide reputation as a beautiful and lively metropolis, and for a series of 'firsts'. It was the world's first city to adopt electric street lights (in 1884) and, more importantly, the first city to rise up against dictator Nicolae Ceauşescu in 1989.

Timişoara

POP 319,280

Romania's third-largest city (after Bucharest and Cluj-Napoca) is also one of the country's most attractive urban areas, built around a series of beautifully restored public squares and lavish parks and gardens. The city's charms have been recognised by the EU, which named Timişoara as the European Capital of Culture for 2021. Locally, Timişoara is known as 'Primul Oraş Liber' (The First Free City), for it was here that anti-Ceauşescu protests first exceeded the Securitate's capacity for violent suppression in 1989, eventually sending Ceauşescu and his wife to their deaths.

◎ Sights

◎ Piaţa Unirii & Around

Piaţa Unirii is Timişoara's most picturesque square, featuring the imposing sight of the Catholic and Serbian **churches** facing each other.

★**Museum of the 1989 Revolution**   MUSEUM
(📞0256-294 936; www.memorialulrevolutiei.ro; Strada Popa Şapcă 3-5; entry by donation; ⊗8am-4pm Mon-Fri, 10am-2pm Sat) This is an ideal venue to brush up on the December 1989 anticommunist revolution that began here in Timişoara. Displays include documentation, posters and photography from those fateful days, capped by a graphic 20-minute video (not suitable for young children) with English subtitles. Enter from Str Oituz 2.

Synagogue in the Fortress   SYNAGOGUE
(Sinagoga din Cetate; Str Mărăşeşti 6) Built in 1865 by Viennese architect Ignatz Schuhmann, the synagogue acts as an important keynote in Jewish history – Jews in the Austro-Hungarian Empire were emancipated in 1864, when permission was given to build the synagogue. It was closed at the time of research for a massive renovation, but the fine exterior is worth taking in.

Timişoara Art Museum   MUSEUM
(Muzeul de Artă Timişoara; 📞0256-491 592; www. muzeuldeartatm.ro; Piaţa Unirii 1; adult 10 lei, child free; ⊗10am-6pm Tue-Sun) This museum displays a representative sample of paintings and visual arts over the centuries as well as regular, high-quality temporary exhibitions. It's housed in the baroque **Old Prefecture Palace** (built 1754), which is worth a look inside for the graceful interiors alone.

◎ Piaţa Victoriei & Around

Piaţa Victoriei is a beautifully green pedestrian mall, dotted with fountains and lined on both sides by shops and cafes.

Orthodox Metropolitan Cathedral   CATHEDRAL
(Catedrala Ortodoxă Mitropolitană; www.mitropolia-banatului.ro; B-dul Regele Ferdinand I; ⊗6am-8pm) The Orthodox cathedral was built between 1936 and 1946. It's unique for its Byzantine-influenced architecture, which recalls the style of the Bucovina monasteries; the floor tiles recall traditional Banat carpets. At 83m, the dome is the highest in Romania.

Reformed Church   CHURCH
(Biserica Reformată; Str Timotei Cipariu 1) The 1989 revolution began at the Reformed Church, where Father László Tőkés spoke out against Ceauşescu. You can sometimes peek in at the church, and it is usually open during times of worship.

🛏 Sleeping

★**Hostel Costel**   HOSTEL €
(📞0356-262 487; www.hostel-costel.ro; Str Petru Sfetca 1; dm 50-60 lei, d 135 lei; @🔊) This charming 1920s art-nouveau villa is the city's best-run hostel. The vibe is relaxed and congenial. There are three dorm rooms with six to 10 beds and one private double, plus ample chill rooms, a kitchen and a big garden with hammocks for relaxing.

★**Pensiunea Casa Leone**   PENSION €€
(📞0723-329 612, 0256-292 621; www.casaleone. ro; B-dul Eroilor de la Tisa 67; s/d/tr 140/160/225 lei; 🅿❄✳🔊) This lovely, very welcoming 10-room *pensiune* offers exceptional service and individually decorated rooms. The surrounding garden is a cool and leafy oasis in summer. To find it, take tram 8 from the train station, alight at Deliblata station and walk one block northeast to B-dul Eroilor. Or phone ahead to arrange transport.

★ **Vila La Residenza** HOTEL €€€
(☎0256-401 080; www.laresidenza.ro; Str Independenţei 14; s/d/ste €80/92/108; [P][❄][@][🛜][🏊])
This converted villa recalls an English manor, with a cosy reading room and library off the lobby and an enormous, well-tended garden in the back with swimming pool. Its 15 rooms are comfort-driven in a similar understated way. A first choice for visiting celebrities and *the* place to stay if price is no object.

✖ Eating

★ **Casa Bunicii** ROMANIAN €€
(☎0356-100 870; www.casa-bunicii.ro; Str Virgil Onitiu 3; mains 20-50 lei; ☺noon-midnight; [♿])
The names translate to 'Granny's House' and indeed this casual, family-friendly restaurant specialises in home cooking and regional specialities from the Banat, with an emphasis on dishes based on *spätzle* (egg noodles). The duck soup with dumplings (10 lei) and grilled chicken breast served in sour cherry sauce (20 lei) both come recommended. Folksy surrounds.

★ **Caruso** INTERNATIONAL €€€
(☎0256-224 771; www.restaurantcaruso.ro; Str Enrico Caruso 2; mains 56-115 lei; ☺noon-midnight)
Probably Timişoara's finest restaurant, Caruso serves superb international and New Romanian cuisine that puts a 21st-century spin on old favourites. Foie gras with cocoa? Breast of pigeon with pear mouse? Or try veal sweetbreads with bacon mash and morel sauce. Seating on two levels and minimalist decor with lots of photos of the celebrated Italian tenor.

🍷 Drinking & Nightlife

Scârţ loc lejer CAFE
(☎0751-892 340; www.facebook.com/scartloclejer; Str Laszlo Szekely 1; ☺9am-11pm Mon-Fri, 11am-11pm Sat, 2-11pm Sun; [🛜]) An old villa that's been retro-fitted into a funky coffee house called something like the 'Creaky Door', with old prints on the walls and chill tunes on the turntable. There are several cosy rooms in which to read and relax, but our favourite is the garden out back, with shady nooks and even hammocks to stretch out on.

Aethernativ CAFE
(☎0724-012 364; www.facebook.com/Aethernativ; Str Mărăşeşti 14; ☺10am-1am Mon-Fri, noon-1am Sat, 5pm-1am Sun) This trendy art club, cafe and bar occupies a courtyard of an old building two blocks west of Piaţa Unirii and has eclectic furnishings and an alternative, student vibe. There are no signs to let you know you're here; simply find the address and push open the door. Always a fun crowd on hand.

☆ Entertainment

La Căpiţe LIVE MUSIC
(☎0720-400 333; www.lacapite.ro; B-dul Pârvan Vasile; ☺10am-1am Mon-Sat, 10am-noon Sun; [🛜])
Shaggy riverside beer garden and alternative hang-out strategically located across the street from the university, ensuring lively crowds on warm summer evenings. Most nights have live music or DJs. The name translates as 'haystack', and bales of hay strewn everywhere make for comfy places to sit and chill.

National Theatre & Opera House THEATRE, OPERA
(Teatrul Naţional şi Opera Română; ☎opera 0256-201 286, theatre 0256-499 908; www.tntimisoara.com; Str Mărăşeşti 2) The National Theatre and Opera House features both dramatic works and classical opera, and is highly regarded. Buy tickets (from around 40 lei) at the **box office** (☎0256-201 117; www.ort.ro; Str Mărăşeşti 2; ☺11am-7pm Tue-Sun) or via email, but note that most of the dramatic works will be in Romanian.

ℹ Information

County Emergency Hospital (Spitalul Clinic Judeţean de Urgenţă Timişoara; ☎0356-433 111; www.hosptm.ro; B-dul Iosif Bulbuca 10) Modern hospital, located 2km south of the centre, with 24-hour emergency service.

Tourist Information Centre (Info Centru Turistic; ☎0256-437 973; www.timisoara-info.ro; Str Alba Iulia 2; ☺9am-7pm Mon-Fri, 10am-4pm Sat May-Sep, 9am-6pm Mon-Fri, 10am-3pm Sat Oct-Apr) This great tourist office can assist with accommodation and trains, and provide maps and regional information on the Banat.

ℹ Getting There & Away

BUS

Timişoara lacks a centralised bus station. Buses and minibuses are privately operated and depart from several points around the city. Consult the website www.autogari.ro for departure points. Sample fares include Arad (15 lei), Cluj-Napoca (75 lei) and Sibiu (65 lei).

International buses leave from the **East Bus Station** (Gara de Est; www.autogari.ro). The main international operators include **Atlassib** (☎0256-226 486, local office 0757-112 370; www.atlassib.ro; Calea Stan Vidrighin 12) and

Eurolines (0256-288 132, 0372-766 478; www.eurolines.ro; Str M Kogălniceanu 20). Belgrade-based **Gea Tours** (0316-300 257; www. geatours.rs) offers daily minibus service between Timişoara and Belgrade (one way/return €15/30); book over the website.

TRAIN

Trains depart from the **Northern Train Station** (Gara Timişoara-Nord; 0256-200 457; www. cfrcalatori.ro; Str Gării 2), though it's actually 'west' of the centre. Daily express trains include services to Bucharest (112 lei, nine hours, two daily), Cluj-Napoca (80 lei, six hours, two daily), Arad (18 lei, one hour, four daily) and Oradea (49 lei, three hours, three daily).

SURVIVAL GUIDE

ⓘ Directory A–Z

ACCOMMODATION

Romania has a wide choice of accommodation to suit most budgets. Book summer lodging along the Black Sea coast well in advance. Elsewhere, it's usually not necessary to reserve ahead.

Budget properties include hostels, camping grounds and cheaper guesthouses. Midrange accommodation includes three-star hotels and pensions. Top-end means fancy hotels, corporate chains and boutiques.

GAY & LESBIAN TRAVELLERS

Public attitudes towards homosexuality remain generally negative. In spite of this, Romania has made significant legal progress in decriminalising homosexual acts and adopting antidiscrimination laws.

➡ Bucharest remains the most tolerant city, though here too open displays of affection between same-sex couples are rare.

➡ The Bucharest-based **Accept Association** (www.acceptromania.ro) promotes rights of gays and lesbians at the national level. Each year in June the group helps to organise the six-day festival **Bucharest Pride** (www.bucharestpride.ro; ☉ Jun), with films, parties, conferences and a parade.

SLEEPING PRICE RANGES

The following price ranges refer to a double room with a bathroom, including breakfast (Bucharest prices tend to be higher).

€ less than 150 lei

€€ 150–300 lei

€€€ more than 300 lei

COUNTRY FACTS

Area 237,500 sq km

Capital Bucharest

Country code 40

Currency Romanian leu

Emergency 112

Language Romanian

Money ATMs abundant

Population 19.9 million

Visas Not required for citizens of the EU, USA, Canada, Australia, New Zealand

---

INTERNET RESOURCES

Bucharest Life (www.bucharestlife.net)

Romania National Tourism Office (www.romaniatourism.com)

Bus Timetable (www.autogari.ro)

Train Timetable (www.cfrcalatori.ro)

MONEY

The currency is the leu (plural: lei). One leu is divided into 100 bani. Banknotes come in denominations of one, five, 10, 50, 100, 200 and 500 lei. Coins come in 50 and 10 bani.

➡ Romania is a member of the European Union, but the euro does not circulate.

➡ ATMs are nearly everywhere and give 24-hour withdrawals in lei on most international bank cards. ATMs require a four-digit PIN.

➡ The best place to exchange money is a bank. You can also change money at a private exchange booth (*casa de schimb*), but be wary of commission charges.

➡ International credit and debit cards are widely accepted in cities. In rural areas, bring cash.

TELEPHONE

➡ All Romanian numbers have 10 digits, consisting of a 0, plus a city code and number. Mobile phone numbers have a three-digit prefix starting with 7.

➡ Romanian mobiles use the GSM 900/1800 network, the standard throughout Europe as well as in Australia and New Zealand, but not compatible with mobile phones in North America or Japan.

➡ To reduce expensive roaming fees, buy a prepaid local SIM card from one of three main carriers: **Vodafone** (www.vodafone.ro), **Telekom Romania** (www.telekom.ro) and **Orange** (www.orange.ro).

ROMANIA DIRECTORY A–Z

ESSENTIAL FOOD & DRINK

Romanian food borrows heavily from its neighbours, including Turkey, Hungary and the Balkans, and is centred on pork and other meats. Farm-fresh, organically raised fruits and vegetables are in abundance, lending flavour and colour to a long list of soups and salads. Condiments typically include sour cream, garlic sauce and grated sheep's cheese.

Ciorbă Sour soup that's a mainstay of the Romanian diet.

Covrigi Oven-baked pretzels served warm from windows around town.

Mămăligă Cornmeal mush, sometimes topped with sour cream or cheese.

Sarmale Spiced meat wrapped in cabbage or grape leaves.

Țuică Fiery plum brandy sold in water bottles at roadside rest stops.

➡ Public phones require a magnetic-stripe phonecard bought at post offices and newspaper kiosks. Phonecard rates start at about 10 lei.

VISAS

Citizens of EU countries do not need visas to visit Romania and can stay indefinitely. Citizens of the USA, Canada, Australia, New Zealand, Israel, Japan and some other countries can stay for up to 90 days without a visa. Other nationalities check with the Romanian **Ministry of Foreign Affairs** (www.mae.ro) before departure.

ℹ Getting There & Away

AIR

Romania has good air connections to Europe and the Middle East. At the time of research there were no direct flights to Romania from North America or Southeast Asia.

Airports

The majority of international flights to Romania arrive at Bucharest's **Henri Coandă International Airport**. Other international airports:

Cluj Avram Iancu International Airport (CLJ; ☎0264-307 500, 0264-416 702; www.airport-cluj.ro; Str Traian Vuia 149)

Sibiu International Airport (SBZ; ☎0269-253 135; www.sibiuairport.ro; Șoseaua Alba Iulia 73)

Timișoara Traian Vuia International Airport (TSR; ☎0256-386 089; http://aerotim.ro/en; Str Aeroport 2, Ghiroda)

EATING PRICE RANGES

The following price ranges refer to an average main course.

€ less than 20 lei

€€ 20–40 lei

€€€ more than 40 lei

LAND

Romania shares a border with five countries: Bulgaria, Hungary, Moldova, Serbia and Ukraine. Most crossings follow international highways or national roads. Romania has two bridge and three car-ferry crossings with Bulgaria over the Danube River. Highway border posts are normally open 24 hours, though some smaller crossings may only be open from 8am to 8pm.

Romania is not a member of the EU's common customs and border area, the Schengen area, so even if you're entering from an EU member state (Bulgaria or Hungary), you'll still have to show a passport or valid EU identity card.

Bus

Long-haul bus services remain a popular way of travelling from Romania to Western Europe as well as to parts of southeastern Europe and Turkey. Bus travel is comparable in price to train travel, but can be faster and require fewer connections.

Bus services to and from Western Europe are dominated by two companies: **Eurolines** (www.eurolines.ro) and **Atlassib** (☎021-222 8971, call centre 080-10 100 100; www.atlassib.ro; Str Gheorghe Duca 4, Bucharest; Ⓜ Gara de Nord). Both maintain vast networks from cities throughout Europe to destinations all around Romania. Check the companies' websites for the latest schedules, prices and departure points.

For sample prices, a one-way ticket from Vienna to Bucharest costs roughly €70. From Paris, the trip is about €100.

Car & Motorcycle

Romania has decent road and car-ferry connections to neighbouring countries, and entering the country by car or motorcycle will present no unexpected difficulties.

At border crossings, drivers should be prepared to show the vehicle's registration, proof of insurance (a 'green' card) and a valid driver's license.

All foreigners, including EU nationals, are required to show a valid passport (or EU identity card).

Train

Romania is integrated into the European rail grid, and there are decent connections to Western Europe and neighbouring countries. Nearly all of these arrive at and depart from Bucharest's main station, **Gara de Nord**.

Budapest is the main rail gateway in and out of Romania from Western Europe. There are two daily direct trains between Budapest and Bucharest, with regular onward direct connections from Budapest to Prague, Munich and Vienna.

Getting Around

AIR

Given the distances and poor state of the roads, flying between cities is a feasible option if time is a primary concern.

➡ The Romanian national carrier **Tarom** (www.tarom.ro) operates a comprehensive network of domestic routes and has a network of ticket offices around the country. The airline flies regularly between Bucharest and Cluj-Napoca, Iaşi, Oradea, Suceava and Timişoara.

➡ The budget carrier **Blue Air** (www.blueair-web.com) has a network of domestic destinations that overlaps with Tarom, but includes Sibiu and Constanţa.

BUS

A mix of buses and maxitaxis form the backbone of the national transport system. If you understand how the system works, you can move around easily and cheaply, but finding updated information without local help can be tough. The website www.autogari.ro is a helpful online timetable.

CAR & MOTORCYCLE

Roads are generally crowded and in poor condition. The country has only a few stretches of motorway (autostrada), meaning most of your travel will be along two-lane national highways (DN, drum naţional) or secondary roads (DJ, drum judeţean). These pass through every village en route and are choked with cars and trucks, and even occasionally horse carts and tractors pulling hay racks. When calculating arrival times, figure on covering about 50km per hour.

Western-style petrol stations are plentiful, but be sure to fill up before heading on long trips through the mountains or in remote areas. A litre of unleaded 95 octane costs about 5 lei.

Road Rules

Motorists are required to buy and display a sticker, called a **rovinieta** (www.roviniete.ro), purchased on the border, at petrol stations or online. A vignette valid for one week costs 15 lei.

Other traffic rules:

Speed limits 50km/h in town; 90km/h on national roads; 130km/h on expressways

Minimum driving age 18

Blood-alcohol limit 0.00%

Seat belts compulsory

Headlights on day and night

LOCAL TRANSPORT

Romanian cities have good public-transport systems comprised of buses, trams, trolleybuses and, in some cases, maxitaxis. Bucharest is the only city with an underground metro. The method for accessing the systems is broadly similar. Purchase bus or tram tickets at newsagents or street kiosks marked bilete or casă de bilete before boarding, and validate the ticket once onboard. For maxitaxis, you usually buy a ticket directly from the driver. Tickets generally cost from 1 to 3 lei per ride.

Taxis

Taxis are cheap, reliable and a useful supplement to the public-transport systems. Drivers are required by law to post their rates on car doors or windscreens. The going rate varies from city to city but ranges from 1.39 to 1.79 lei per kilometre. Any driver posting a higher fare is likely looking to rip off unsuspecting passengers.

TRAIN

Trains are slow but reliable for getting around Romania. The extensive network covers much of the country, including most of the main tourist sights and key destinations. The national rail system is run by **Căile Ferate Române** (CFR; www.cfrcalatori.ro); the website has a handy online timetable (mersul trenurilor). Buy tickets at train-station windows, specialised **Agenţia de Voiaj CFR** ticket offices, private travel agencies or online at www.cfrcalatori.ro.

Russia

Best Places to Eat

➡ Lavka-Lavka (p954)

➡ Delicatessen (p954)

➡ Duo Gastrobar (p963)

➡ Clean Plates Society (p964)

Best Places to Stay

➡ Hotel Metropol (p954)

➡ Blues Hotel (p953)

➡ Soul Kitchen Hostel (p963)

➡ Rachmaninov Antique Hotel (p963)

Why Go?

Could there be a more iconic image of Eastern Europe than the awe-inspiring architectural ensemble of Moscow's Red Square? The brash, exciting and oil-rich capital of Russia (Россия) is a must on any trip to the region.

St Petersburg, on the Baltic coast, is another stunner. The former imperial capital is still Russia's most beautiful and alluring city, with its grand Italianate mansions, wending canals and enormous Neva River. Also make time for Suzdal to get a glimpse of old Russia with its golden cupolas and fortress-like monasteries. Emulating the tourist-friendly nature of its Baltic neighbours is little Kaliningrad, wedged between Poland and Lithuania on the Baltic Sea. It's a fascinating destination, combining all the best elements of its enormous mother.

Visa red tape deters many travellers from visiting – don't let it keep you from experiencing the incredible things to see and do in the European part of the world's largest country.

When to Go
Moscow

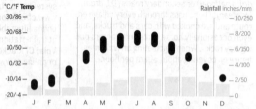

May Big military parades and a public holiday mark the end of WWII.

Jun–Jul Party during St Petersburg's White Nights, and bask on the beaches of Kaliningrad.

Dec–Jan Snow makes Moscow and St Petersburg look magical, while hotel rates drop.

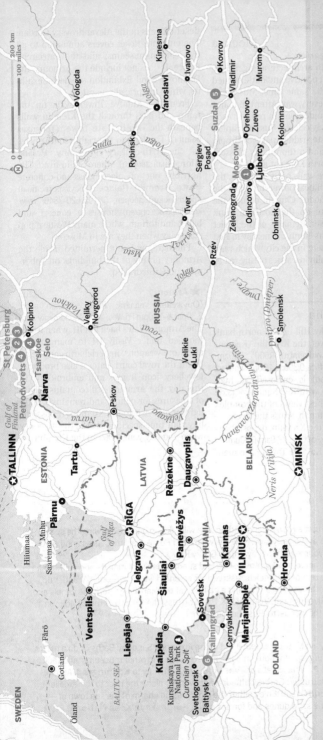

Russia

① **Moscow** (p948)
Being awe-inspired by the massive scale and riches of Russia's brash, energetic capital.

② **St Petersburg** (p959) Taking a walking, bike or boat tour of a glorious Italianate slice of Old Europe incongruously placed in Russia.

③ **State Hermitage Museum** (p963) Ogling the seemingly endless collection of masterpieces in St Petersburg's unrivalled museum.

④ **Petrodvorets** and **Tsarskoe Selo** (p965) Taking a day trip out of St Petersburg to see the imperial country estates in these spectacular sights.

⑤ **Suzdal** (p958) Crisscrossing this beautiful town by bicycle or on foot, listening to the music of church bells and nightingales.

⑥ **Kaliningrad** (p966) Exploring this historic city, once part of the Prussian empire, and home to the pristine beaches of the Kurshskaya Kosa National Park.

Moscow   Москва

✓ 495 & 499 / POP 12.2 MILLION

Huge and prone to architectural gigantism, full of energy, both positive and dark, refined and tasteless at the same time, Moscow is overwhelming in every way. After the major spruce-up it has undergone in recent years, the mind-bogglingly eclectic Russian capital may look like hipster-ridden parts of Brooklyn at one point and a thoroughly glossed-over version of North Korea at another.

The sturdy stone walls of the Kremlin, the apex of Russian political power and once the centre of the Orthodox Church, occupy the city's founding site on the northern bank of the Moscow River. Remains of the Soviet state, such as Lenin's Tomb, are nearby in Red Square and elsewhere in the city, which radiates from the Kremlin in a series of ring roads.

⊙ Sights

⊙ The Kremlin

Covering Borovitsky Hill on the north bank of the Moscow River, the **Kremlin** (Кремль; ✓ 495-695 4146; www.kreml.ru; R500; ⊙10am-5pm Fri-Wed, ticket office 9.30am-4.30pm Fri-Wed; Ⓜ Aleksandrovsky Sad) is enclosed by high walls 2.25km long, with Red Square outside the east wall. The best views of the complex are from Sofiyskaya nab across the river.

Before entering the Kremlin, deposit bags at the **left-luggage office** (⊙9am-6.30pm Fri-Wed), beneath the Kutafya Tower. The main ticket office is in the Alexandrovsky Garden. The entrance ticket covers admission to all five church-museums, and the Patriarch's Palace. It does not include the Armoury, the Diamond Fund Exhibition or special exhibits, which are priced separately.

From the Kutafya Tower, walk up the ramp and pass through the Kremlin walls beneath the **Trinity Gate Tower** (Троицкая башня). The lane to the right (south) passes the 17th-century **Poteshny Palace** (Потешный дворец), where Stalin lived. The horribly out of place glass-and-concrete **State Kremlin Palace** (Государственный кремлёвский дворец; ✓ 495 620 7846; www.kremlinpalace.org/en) houses a concert and ballet auditorium, where many Western pop stars play when they are in Moscow.

Photography is not permitted inside the Armoury or any of the buildings on Sobornaya pl (Cathedral Sq).

★ **Armoury**   MUSEUM
(Оружейная палата; R700; ⊙10am, noon, 2.30pm & 4.30pm Fri-Wed; Ⓜ Aleksandrovsky Sad) The Armoury dates back to 1511, when it was founded under Vasily III to manufacture and store weapons, imperial arms and regalia for the royal court. Later it also produced jewellery, icon frames and embroidery. To this day, the Armoury still contains plenty of treasures for ogling, and remains a highlight of any visit to the Kremlin. If possible, buy your time-specific ticket to the Armoury when you buy your ticket to the Kremlin.

ITINERARIES

One Week

In **Moscow**, touring the Kremlin and Red Square will take up one day, viewing the spectacular collections at the Tretyakov, New Tretyakov and Pushkin art museums another. On day three stretch your legs in the revamped Gorky Park.

Take the night train to **Veliky Novgorod** and spend a day exploring its ancient kremlin and churches. The rest of the week is reserved for splendid **St Petersburg**. Wander up Nevsky pr, see Dvortsovaya pl, and spend a half-day at the Hermitage. Tour the canals and the mighty Neva River by boat. Visit Peter & Paul Fortress, the Church of the Saviour on Spilled Blood and the wonderful Russian Museum.

Two Weeks

With two extra days in Moscow, sweat it out in the luxurious Sanduny Baths or do a metro tour. In St Petersburg, spend more time in the Hermitage and other museums, and tack on an excursion to **Petrodvorets** or **Tsarskoe Selo**. Then fly to **Kaliningrad**. Admire the capital's reconstructed Gothic Cathedral and wander along the river to the excellent Museum of the World Ocean. Enjoy either the old Prussian charm of the spa town of **Svetlogorsk** or the sand dunes and forests of the **Kurshskaya Kosa National Park**.

★**Red Square**   HISTORIC SITE

(Красная площадь; Krasnaya pl; Ⓜ Ploshchad Revolyutsii) Immediately outside the Kremlin's northeastern wall is the celebrated Red Square, the 400m by 150m area of cobblestones that is at the very heart of Moscow. Commanding the square from the southern end is **St Basil's Cathedral** (Покровский собор, Храм Василия Блаженного; www.saintbasil.ru; adult/student R350/100; ⊙ticket office 11am-4.30pm; Ⓜ Ploshchad Revolyutsii) This panorama never fails to send the heart aflutter, especially at night.

★**Lenin's Mausoleum**   MEMORIAL

(Мавзолей Ленина; www.lenin.ru; ⊙10am-1pm Tue-Thu & Sat; Ⓜ Ploshchad Revolyutsii) FREE Although Vladimir Ilych requested that he be buried beside his mum in St Petersburg, he still lies in state at the foot of the Kremlin wall, receiving visitors who come to pay their respects. Line up at the western corner of the square (near the entrance to Alexander Garden) to see the embalmed leader, who has been here since 1924. Note that photography is not allowed and stern guards ensure that all visitors remain respectful and silent.

State History Museum   MUSEUM

(Государственный исторический музей; www.shm.ru; Krasnaya pl 1; adult/student R350/100, audioguide R300; ⊙ticket office 10am-5pm Wed & Fri-Mon, 11am-8pm Thu; Ⓜ Okhotny Ryad) At the northern end of Red Square, the State History Museum has an enormous collection covering the whole Russian empire from the time of the Stone Age. The building, dating from the late 19th century, is itself an attraction – each room is in the style of a different period or region, some with highly decorated walls echoing old Russian churches.

◉ South of the Moscow River

★**State Tretyakov Gallery Main Branch**   GALLERY

(Главный отдел Государственной Третьяковской галереи; www.tretyakovgallery.ru; Lavrushinsky per 10; R400; ⊙10am-6pm Tue, Wed & Sun, to 9pm Thu, Fri & Sat, last tickets 1hr before closing; Ⓜ Tretyakovskaya) The exotic boyar castle on a little lane in Zamoskvorechie contains the main branch of the State Tretyakov Gallery, housing the world's best collection of Russian icons and an outstanding collection of other pre-revolutionary Russian art. Show up early to beat the queues.

THE BANYA

Taking a traditional Russian *banya* is a must. These wet saunas are a social hub and a fantastic experience for any visitor to Russia. Leave your inhibitions at home and be prepared for a beating with birch twigs (far more pleasant than it sounds). Ask at your accommodation for the nearest public *banya*. In Moscow, try the luxurious **Sanduny Baths** (☑495-782 1808; www.sanduny.ru; Neglinnaya ul 14; R1600-2500; ⊙8am-10pm Wed-Mon, Second Male Top Class 10am-midnight Tue-Fri, 8am-10pm Sat & Sun; Ⓜ Kuznetsky Most) and in St Petersburg the traditional **Mytninskiye Bani** (Мытнинские бани; www.mybanya.spb.ru; ul Mytninskaya 17-19; per hr R200-300; ⊙8am-10pm Fri-Tue; Ⓜ Ploshchad Vosstaniya).

★**Gorky Park**   PARK

(Парк Горького; ⊙24hr; 🛜🚻; Ⓜ Oktyabrskaya) FREE Moscow's main escape from the city within the city is not your conventional expanse of nature preserved deep inside an urban jungle. It is not a fun fair either, though it used to be one. Its official name says it all – Maxim Gorky's Central Park of Culture & Leisure. That's exactly what it provides: culture and leisure in all shapes and forms. Designed by avant-garde architect Konstantin Melnikov as a piece of communist utopia in the 1920s, these days it showcases the enlightened transformation Moscow has undergone in the recent past.

New Tretyakov Gallery   GALLERY

(Новая Третьяковская галерея; www.tretyakovgallery.ru; ul Krymsky val 10; R400; ⊙10am-6pm Tue, Wed & Sun, to 9pm Thu-Sat, last tickets 1hr before closing; Ⓜ Park Kultury) The premier venue for 20th-century Russian art is this branch of the State Tretyakov Gallery, better known as the New Tretyakov. This place has much more than the typical socialist realist images of muscle-bound men wielding scythes and busty women milking cows (although there's that, too). The exhibits showcase avant-garde artists such as Malevich, Kandinsky, Chagall, Goncharova and Popova.

Art Muzeon & Krymskaya Naberezhnaya   PUBLIC ART

(ul Krymsky val 10; Ⓜ Park Kultury) FREE Now fully revamped and merged with the wonderfully reconstructed Krymskaya

RUSSIA MOSCOW

Central Moscow

0.5 miles
1 km

G
Izmaylovsky Market (7.7km)
Rusakovskaya ul
Yaroslavsky Vokzal
Leningradsky Vokzal
Komsomolskaya pl
Komsomolskaya
Kazansky Vokzal
Novoryazanskaya ul
Elokhovsky Hotel (750m)
Park im Baumana
Novaya Basmannaya ul
Ryazansky per
Kalanchevskaya ul
Kalanchevskaya
Orlikov per
Sadovaya-Spasskaya ul
Staraya Basmannaya ul
ul Zemlyanoy Val (Garden Ring)
Kursky Vokzal
Kurskaya
Bolshoy Kazenny per
Lyapin per
Chkalovskaya
Vorontsovo Pole (Garden Ring)
Yauzsky bul
Winzavod 10
ArtPlay 2
Bolshoy Polyaroslavsky per

F
Bolshoy Balkansky per
Bolshoy Spasskaya ul
Dokuchaev per
Grokholsky per
1-y Koptelsky per
pr Akademika Sakharova
ul Mashi Poryvaevoy
ul Myasnitskaya
Pl Krasnye Vorota
Krasnye Vorota
(Garden Ring)
ul Sadovaya-Chernogryazskaya
ul Chaplygina
ul Pokrovka
P Pokrovka
Bolshoy Kharitonevsky per
Chistye Prudy
43
Chistoprudny bul
48
Pokrovsky bul
KITAY-GOROD
Kolpachny per
Podkolokolny per
ul Solyanka

E
pr Mira
ul Durova
ul Gilyarovskogo
ul Shchepkina
Sukharevskaya ul
Sukharevskaya
Sukharevskaya pl
Sretenka
ul Sretenka
Sretensky Bulvar
Turgenevskaya
Turgenevskaya pl
Bolshoy Kiselny per
Kuznetsky Most
ul Bolshaya Lubyanka
ul Malaya Lubyanka
Lubyanka
Armyansky per
Myasnitskaya ul
Lubyanskaya pl
31
Novaya pl
Ploshchad Revolyutsii
Kitay-Gorod
Lubyansky proezd
Staraya pl
Slavyanskaya pl
ul Varvarka
ul Ilyinka
Kitay-Gorod

D
Delegatskaya ul
pl Shchepkina
Samotechnaya
Troitskaya ul
Sadovaya-Sukharevskaya ul
Sadovaya-Samotechnaya ul
Tsvetnoy bul
Tsvetnoy Bulvar
37
32
Trubnaya ul
Trubnaya
Trubnaya pl
Posledny per
Pushkarev per
Pechatnikov per
Rozhdestvensky bul
Zvonarsky per
ul Neglinnaya
Pushechnaya ul
Teatralny proezd
34
Teatralnaya pl
49
Okhotny Ryad
Teatralnaya
Manezhnaya pl
38
See Kremlin
Left-Luggage Office
Saviour Gate Tower
Aleksandrovsky Sad
Biblioteka imeni Lenina

C
Olimpiysky pl
Samotechnaya ul
Delegatskaya ul
Bolshoy Karetny per
ul Karetny Ryad
Hermitage Gardens
41
Uspensky per
Petrovsky bul
42
40
ul Petrovka
ul Petrovka
Petrovka
Kuznetsky most
Bolshaya Dmitrovka
Okhotny Ryad
Teatralnaya pl
Gazetny per
Tverskaya ul
Bolshaya Nikitskaya ul
Bolshoy Kislovsky per
Mokhovaya ul
Biblioteka imeni Lenina
Borovitskaya

B
Dolgorukovskaya ul
MAYAKOVSKAYA
Sadovaya-Triumfalnaya ul
Oruzheyny per
Tverskaya ul
Chekhovskaya
Chekhovskaya
Strastnoy bul
Pushkinskaya
Pushkinskaya ul
Tverskaya
Tverskaya ul
Malaya Dmitrovka
ul Malaya Dmitrovka
Tverskaya
46
50
47
Bryusov per
Voznesensky per
Gazetny per
Tverskaya ul
33
36
39
Bolshaya Bronnaya ul
Bolshoy Gnezdnikovsky per
Nezhdanovoy per
Bolshoy Kozikhinsky per
Malaya Bronnaya ul
European Medical Centre
ul Spiridonovka
Granatny per
Malaya Nikitskaya ul
Bolshaya Nikitskaya ul
pl Nikitskie Vorota
Maly Kislovsky per
Nikitsky bul
Arbatskaya
Arbatskaya

A
Belorusskaya
Belorusskaya
Belorussky vokzal
Vasilevskaya ul
ul Fadeeva
1-ya Tverskaya-Yamskaya ul
1-ya Brestskaya ul
1-ya Tverskaya-Yamskaya ul
ul Yuliusa Fuchika
Tishinskaya pl
Mayakovskaya
Triumfalnaya pl
Bolshaya Sadovaya ul
Sadovaya-Kudrinskaya ul
ul Krasina
Patriarch's Pond
Sixteen Tons (900m)
Bolshaya Gruzinskaya ul
Zoologicheskaya ul
Barrikadnaya
Barrikadnaya
Kudrinskaya pl
Bolshaya Nikitskaya ul
Povarskaya ul
ul Novy Arbat
Skaternyy per
Khlebnyy per
Trubnikovsky per
Novinsky bul
Spasopeskovskaya pl
Radisson River Cruises (950m)

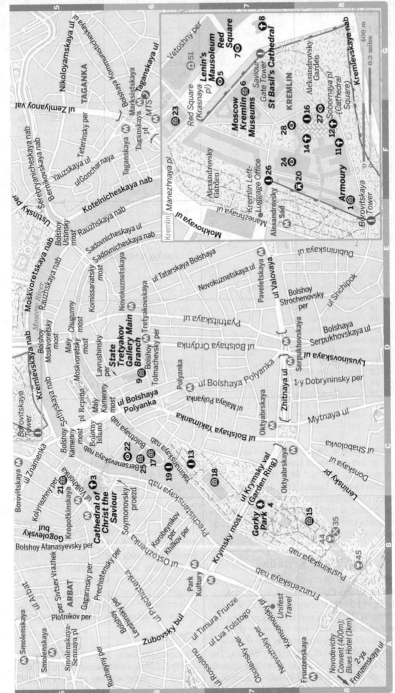

RUSSIA MOSCOW

Central Moscow

Naberezhnaya embankment is this motley collection of (mostly kitschy) sculpture and monuments to Soviet idols (Stalin, Sverdlov, a selection of Lenins and Brezhnevs) that were ripped from their pedestals in the post-1991 wave of anti-Soviet feeling. All of these stand in lovely gardens with boardwalks and many inviting benches.

◎ West of the Kremlin

★**Cathedral of Christ the Saviour** CHURCH
(Храм Христа Спасителя; www.xxc.ru; ul Volkhonka 15; ⊙1-5pm Mon, 10am-5pm Tue-Sun; ⑩Kropotkinskaya) **FREE** This gargantuan cathedral was completed in 1997 – just in time to celebrate Moscow's 850th birthday. It is amazingly opulent, garishly grandiose and truly historic. The cathedral's sheer size and splendour guarantee its role as a love-it-or-hate-it landmark. Considering Stalin's plan for this site (a Pal-

ace of Soviets topped with a 100m statue of Lenin), Muscovites should at least be grateful they can admire the shiny domes of a church instead of the shiny dome of Ilyich's head.

**Pushkin Fine Arts
Museum Main Building**   MUSEUM
(Главное здание; ul Volkhonka 12; adult/student R300/150; ⑩Kropotkinskaya) Moscow's premier foreign-art museum displays a broad range of European works. The main building is the original location of the museum, which opened in 1912 as the museum of Moscow University. The highlights of the museum are the Dutch masterpieces from the 17th century.

◎ Tours

Moscow Free Tour   WALKING
(☑495-222 3466; www.moscowfreetour.com; Nikolskaya ul 4/5; guided walk free, paid tours from €35) Every day these enthusiastic ladies offer an

informative, inspired two-hour guided walk around Red Square and Kitay Gorod – and it's completely free. It's so good, that (they think) you'll sign up for one of their excellent paid tours, covering the Kremlin, the Arbat and the Metro, or more thematic tours, such as communist Moscow or mystical Moscow.

Radisson River Cruises BOATING
(www.radisson-cruise.ru; 2½hr cruise R750; Ⓜ Kievskaya) The Radisson operates big river boats that cart 140 people up and down the Moscow River from the dock in front of the hotel and from the dock in Gorky Park. In summer, there are five or six daily departures from each location (check the website for times). Boats are enclosed (and equipped with ice cutters), so the cruises run year-round, albeit less frequently in winter.

🛏 Sleeping

Godzillas Hostel HOSTEL €
(☑ 495-699 4223; www.godzillashostel.com; Bolshoy Karetny per 6; dm from R750; s/d R2500/2800; ❄ @ 🛜; Ⓜ Tsvetnoy Bulvar) Tried and true, Godzillas is Moscow's best-known hostel, with dozens of beds spread out over four floors. The rooms come in various sizes, but they are all spacious and light-filled and painted in different colours. To cater to the

many guests, there are bathroom facilities on each floor, three kitchens and a big living room with satellite TV.

Comrade Hostel HOSTEL €
(☑ 499-709 8760; www.comradehostel.com; ul Maroseyka 11; dm/s/d R650/2200/2700; ⊖ @ 🛜; Ⓜ Kitay-Gorod) It's hard to find this tiny place – go into the courtyard and look for entrance No 3, where you might spot a computer-printed sign in the 3rd-floor window. Inside is a great welcoming atmosphere, although the place is usually packed. Ten to 12 beds are squeezed into the dorm rooms, plus there are mattresses on the floor if need be.

★ **Blues Hotel** BOUTIQUE HOTEL €€
(☑ 495-961 1161; www.blues-hotel.ru; ul Dovatora 8; r from R4600; ⊖ ❄ 🛜; Ⓜ Sportivnaya) The location is not exactly central, but is not a disadvantage. It is steps from the red-line metro (five stops to Red Square) and a few blocks from Novodevichy, with several worthwhile restaurants in the vicinity. Considering that, this friendly, affordable boutique hotel is a gem, offering stylish, spotless rooms with king-size beds and flat-screen TVs.

Elokhovsky Hotel HOTEL €€
(Отель Елоховский; ☑ 495-632 2300; www.elo-hotel.ru; ul Spartakovskaya 24; s/d R4500/5300;

SOBORNAYA PLOSHCHAD

On the northern side of Sobornaya pl, with five golden helmet domes and four semicircular gables facing the square, is the **Assumption Cathedral** (Успенский собор), built between 1475 and 1479. As the focal church of prerevolutionary Russia, it's the burial place of most heads of the Russian Orthodox Church from the 1320s to 1700. The iconostasis dates from 1652, but its lowest level contains some older icons, including the Virgin of Vladimir (Vladimirskaya Bogomater), an early-15th-century Rublyov-school copy of Russia's most revered image, the Vladimir Icon of the Mother of God (Ikona Vladimirskoy Bogomateri).

The delicate little single-domed church beside the west door of the Assumption Cathedral is the **Church of the Deposition of the Robe** (Церковь Ризоположения), built between 1484 and 1486 by masons from Pskov.

With its two golden domes rising above the eastern side of Sobornaya pl, the 16th-century **Ivan the Great Bell Tower** (Колокольня Ивана Великого; R250) is the Kremlin's tallest structure. Beside the bell tower stands the **Tsar Bell** (Царь-колокол), a 202-tonne monster that cracked before it ever rang. North of the bell tower is the mammoth **Tsar Cannon** (Царь-пушка), cast in 1586 but never shot.

The 1508 **Archangel Cathedral** (Архангельский собор), at the square's southeastern corner, was for centuries the coronation, wedding and burial church of tsars. The tombs of all of Russia's rulers from the 1320s to the 1690s are here bar one (Boris Godunov, who was buried at Sergiev Posad).

Finally, the **Annunciation Cathedral** (Благовещенский собор), at the southwest corner of Sobornaya pl and dating from 1489, contains the celebrated icons of master painter Theophanes the Greek. He probably painted the six icons at the right-hand end of the diesis row, the biggest of the six tiers of the iconostasis. Archangel Michael (the third icon from the left on the diesis row) and the adjacent St Peter are ascribed to Russian master Andrei Rublyov.

✳ 🛜; Ⓜ Baumanskaya) Admittedly not very central and occupying the top floor of a shopping arcade, this hotel is nevertheless about the best value for money you can find in Moscow. Room themes are based on the world's major cities, and are painted in soothing, homey colours. The coffee machine in the lobby is available 24 hours. Baumanskaya metro and Yelokhovsky Cathedral are a stone's throw away.

★**Hotel de Paris** BOUTIQUE HOTEL €€
(☑ 495-777 0052; www.hotel-deparis.ru; Bolshaya Bronnaya ul 23, bldg 3; s/d from R6400/6800; ℙ➌✳🛜; Ⓜ Pushkinskaya) Steps from the madness of Tverskaya, this is a delightfully stylish hotel tucked into a quiet courtyard off the Boulevard Ring. Situated on the lower floors, the rooms do not get much natural light, but they feature king-size beds, jacuzzi tubs and elegant design. Service is consistently friendly. Prices drop by 40% on weekends, offering terrific value.

★**Hotel Metropol** HISTORIC HOTEL €€€
(☑ 499-501 7800; www.metropol-moscow.ru; Teatralny proezd 1/4; r from R15,500; ➌✳@✉; Ⓜ Teatralnaya) Nothing short of an art nouveau masterpiece, the 1907 Metropol brings an artistic, historic touch to every nook and cranny, from the spectacular exterior to the grand lobby to the individually decorated (but small) rooms. The breakfast buffet (R2000) is ridiculously priced, but it's served under the restaurant's gorgeous stained-glass ceiling.

✖ Eating

Danilovsky Market MARKET €€
(www.danrinok.ru; Mytnaya ul 74; mains R400-600; ⏱8am-8pm; Ⓜ Tulskaya) A showcase of the ongoing gentrification of Moscow, this giant So-viet-era farmers market is now largely about deli food cooked and served in a myriad of little eateries, including such gems as a Dagestani dumpling shop and a Vietnamese pho soup kitchen. The market itself looks very orderly, if a tiny bit artificial, with uniformed vendors and thoughtfully designed premises.

★**Delicatessen** INTERNATIONAL €€
(Деликатесы; www.newdeli.ru; Savodvaya-Karetnaya ul 20; mains R500-800; ⏱noon-midnight Tue-Sun; 🛜📱; Ⓜ Tsvetnoy Bulvar) The affable (and chatty) owners of this place travel the world and experiment with the menu a lot, turning burgers, pizzas and pasta into artfully constructed objects of modern culinary art. The other source of joy is a cabinet filled with bottles of ripening fruity liquors, which may destroy your budget if consumed uncontrollably (a pointless warning, we know).

★**Khachapuri** GEORGIAN €€
(☑ 8-985-764 3118; www.hacha.ru; Bolshoy Gnezdnikovsky per 10; mains R400-600; ➌🛜📱; Ⓜ Pushkinskaya) Unassuming, affordable and appetising, this urban cafe exemplifies what people love about Georgian culture: the warm hospitality and the freshly baked *khachapuri* (cheese bread). Aside from seven types of delicious *khachapuri,* there's also an array of soups, shashlyki (kebabs), *khinkali* (dumplings) and other Georgian favourites.

Gran Cafe Dr Zhivago RUSSIAN €€
(☑ 499-922 0100; www.drzhivago.ru; ul Mokhovaya 15/1; mains R540-1200; ⏱24hr; Ⓜ Okhotny Ryad) An excellent breakfast choice before visiting the Kremlin, this round-the-clock place mixes Soviet nostalgia with a great deal of mischievous irony in both design and food. The chef has upgraded the menu of a standard pioneer camp's canteen to near haute cuisine level, with masterfully cooked porridge, pancakes, *vareniki* (dumplings) and cottage-cheese pies.

★**Lavka-Lavka** INTERNATIONAL €€
(Лавка-Лавка; ☑ 8-903-115 5033; www.restoran.lavkalavka.com; ul Petrovka 21 str 2; mains R500-950; ⏱noon-midnight Tue-Thu & Sun, to 1am Fri & Sat; ♿; Ⓜ Teatralnaya) ✿ Welcome to the Russian Portlandia – all the food here is organic and hails from little farms where you may rest assured all the lambs and chickens lived a very happy life before being served to you on a plate. Irony aside, this is a great place to sample local food cooked in a funky improvisational style.

METRO TOUR

For just R40 you can spend the day touring Moscow's magnificent metro stations. Many of the stations are marble-faced, frescoed, gilded works of art. Among our favourites are **Komsomolskaya**, a huge stuccoed hall, its ceiling covered with mosaics depicting military heroes; **Novokuznetskaya**, featuring military bas-reliefs done in sober khaki, and colourful ceiling mosaics depicting pictures of the happy life; and **Mayakovskaya**, Grand Prize winner at the 1939 World's Fair in New York.

★ **Café Pushkin** RUSSIAN €€€
(Кафе Пушкинъ; ☎495-739 0033; www.ca-fe-pushkin.ru; Tverskoy bul 26a; business lunch from R620, mains R800-1800; ⊗24hr; ⊜🛜📶; Ⓜ Pushkinskaya) The tsarina of *haute-russe* dining, with an exquisite blend of Russian and French cuisines – service and food are done to perfection. The lovely 19th-century building has a different atmosphere on each floor, including a richly decorated library and a pleasant rooftop cafe.

RUSSIA MOSCOW

🍷 **Drinking**

★ **32.05** CAFE
(☎905-703 3205; www.veranda3205.ru; ul Karetny Ryad 3; ⊗11am-3am; Ⓜ Pushkinskaya) The biggest drinking/eating establishment in Hermitage Gardens, this verandah positioned at the back of the main building looks a bit like a greenhouse. In summer, tables (and patrons) spill out into the park, making it one of the city's best places for outdoor drinking. With its long bar and joyful atmosphere, the place also heaves in winter.

Cafe Mart CAFE
(Кафе Март; www.cafemart.ru; ul Petrovka 25; meals R800-1200; ⊗11am-midnight Sun-Wed, 11am-6am Thu-Sat, jazz concert 9pm Thu; 🚸; Ⓜ Chekhovskaya) It looks like another cellar bar, but if you walk all the way through the underground maze you'll find yourself in the huge overground 'orangerie' hall with mosaic-covered walls, warm lighting and possibly a jazz concert. When the weather is fine, Mart spills into the sculpture-filled courtyard of the adjacent Moscow Museum of Contemporary Art.

★ **Noor / Electro** BAR
(☎8-903-136 7686; www.noorbar.com; ul Tverskaya 23/12; ⊗8pm-3am Mon-Wed, to 6am Thu-Sun; Ⓜ Pushkinskaya) There is little to say about this misleadingly unassuming bar, apart from the fact that everything in it is close to perfection. It has it all – prime location, convivial atmosphere, eclectic DJ music, friendly bartenders and superb drinks. Though declared 'the best' by various magazines on several occasions, it doesn't feel like they care.

Time-Out Bar COCKTAIL BAR
(www.timeoutbar.ru; 12th fl, Bolshaya Sadovaya ul 5; ⊗noon-2am Sun-Thu, noon-6am Fri & Sat; Ⓜ Mayakovskaya) On the upper floors of the throwback Pekin Hotel, this trendy bar is nothing but 'now'. That includes the bartenders sporting plaid and their delicious concoctions, especially created for different times of the day. The

decor is pretty impressive – particularly the spectacular city skyline. Perfect place for sundowners (or sun-ups, if you last that long).

Ukuleleshnaya BAR
(Укулелешная; ☎495-642 5726; www.uku-uku.ru; ul Pokrovka 17 str 1; ⊗noon-midnight Sun-Thu, to 4am Fri & Sat; Ⓜ Chistye Prudy) In its new location, this is now more of a bar than a musical instrument shop, although ukuleles still adorn the walls, prompting an occasional jam session. Craft beer prevails on the drinks list, but Ukuleleshnaya also serves experimental cocktails of its own invention. Live concerts happen regularly and resident Pomeranian Spitz Berseny (cute dog) presides over the resulting madness.

Coffee Bean CAFE
(www.coffeebean.ru; ul Pokrovka 21; ⊗8am-11pm; Ⓜ Chistye Prudy) Winds of change brought US national Jerry Ruditser to Moscow in the early 1990s on a mission to create the nation's first coffee chain, in which he succeeded long before Starbucks found Russia on the map. Some argue it's still the best coffee served in the capital. That might be disputed, but on the friendliness front Coffee Bean is unbeatable.

☆ **Entertainment**

To find out what's on, see the entertainment section in Thursday's *Moscow Times*. Most theatres, including the Bolshoi, are closed between late June and early September.

★ **Bolshoi Theatre** BALLET, OPERA
(Большой театр; ☎495-455 5555; www.bolshoi.ru; Teatralnaya pl 1; tickets R100-12,000; ⊗closed Jul & Aug; Ⓜ Teatralnaya) An evening at the Bolshoi

DON'T MISS

MOSCOW'S WHITE-HOT ART SCENE

Revamped old industrial buildings and other spaces in Moscow are where you'll find gems of Russia's super-creative contemporary art scene. Apart from the following recommended spots, also see www.artguide.ru.

Garage Museum of Contemporary Art (☑ 495-645 0520; www.garagemca.org; ul Krymsky val 9/32; adult/student R400/200; 11am-10pm; Ⓜ Oktyabrskaya) Having moved into a permanent Gorky Park location, a Soviet-era building renovated by the visionary Dutch architect Rem Koolhaas, Garage hosts exciting exhibitions by top artists.

Vinzavod (Винзавод; www.winzavod.ru; 4 Syromyatnichesky per 1; Ⓜ Chkalovskaya) **FREE** A former wine factory has morphed into this postindustrial complex of prestigious galleries, shops, a cinema and trendy cafe. Nearby, another converted industrial space, the **Artplay** (☑ 495-620 0882; www.artplay.ru; Nizhny Syromyatnichesky per 10; ⊙ noon-8pm Tue-Sun; Ⓜ Chkalovskaya) **FREE** ,is home to firms specialising in urban planning and architectural design, as well as furniture showrooms and antique stores.

Proekt_Fabrika (www.proektfabrika.ru; 18 Perevedenovsky per; ⊙ 10am-8pm Tue-Sun; Ⓜ Baumanskaya) **FREE** A still-functioning paper factory is the location for this nonprofit set of gallery and performance spaces enlivened by arty graffiti and creative-industry offices.

Red October (Завод Красный Октябрь; Bersenevskaya nab; Ⓜ Kropotkinskaya) **FREE** The red-brick buildings of this former chocolate factory now host the **Lumiere Brothers Photography Centre** (www.lumiere.ru; Bolotnaya nab 3, bldg 1; R200-430; ⊙ noon-9pm Tue-Fri, to 10pm Sat & Sun) plus other galleries, cool bars and restaurants. In an adjacent building the **Strelka Institute for Media, Architecture and Design** (www.strelkainstitute.ru; bldg 5a, Bersenevskaya nab 14/5; Ⓜ Novokuznetskaya) is worth checking out for its events, bookshop and bar. Also, look out for **GES-2**, a new large contemporary art space that was due to open in an old power station in 2017.

is still one of Moscow's most romantic and entertaining options for a night on the town. The glittering six-tier auditorium has an electric atmosphere, evoking over 240 years of premier music and dance. Both the ballet and opera companies perform a range of Russian and foreign works here. After the collapse of the Soviet Union, the Bolshoi was marred by politics, scandal and frequent turnover. Yet the show must go on – and it will.

Tchaikovsky Concert Hall   CLASSICAL MUSIC
(Концертный зал имени Чайковского; ☑ 495-232 0400; www.meloman.ru; Triumfalnaya pl 4/31; tickets R300-3000; ⊙ closed Jul & Aug; Ⓜ Mayakovskaya) Home to the famous Moscow State Philharmonic (Moskovskaya Filharmonia), the capital's oldest symphony orchestra, Tchaikovsky Concert Hall was established in 1921. It's a huge auditorium, with seating for 1600 people. This is where you can expect to hear the Russian classics such as Stravinsky, Rachmaninov and Shostakovich, as well as other European favourites. Look out for special children's concerts.

Sixteen Tons   LIVE MUSIC
(Шестнадцать тонн; ☑ 495-253 1550; www.16tons.ru; ul Presnensky val 6; cover R600-1200;

⊙ 11am-6am; ☎; Ⓜ Ulitsa 1905 Goda) Downstairs, the brassy English pub-restaurant has an excellent house-brewed bitter. Upstairs, the club gets some of the best Russian bands that play in Moscow and an occasional first-rate or semi-obscure Western visitor. Show times are subject to change so check the website for details.

🔒 Shopping

Ul Arbat has always been a tourist attraction and is littered with souvenir shops and stalls.

GUM   MALL
(ГУМ; www.gum.ru; Krasnaya pl 3; ⊙ 10am-10pm; Ⓜ Ploshchad Revolyutsii) The elaborate 240m facade on the northeastern side of Red Square, GUM is a bright, bustling shopping mall with hundreds of fancy stores and restaurants. With a skylight roof and three-level arcades, the spectacular interior was a revolutionary design when it was built in the 1890s, replacing the Upper Trading Rows that previously occupied this site.

Izmaylovsky Market   MARKET
(www.kremlin-izmailovo.com; Izmaylovskoye shosse 73; ⊙ 10am-8pm; Ⓜ Partizanskaya) Never mind the kitschy faux 'tsar's palace' it surrounds,

Izmaylovsky flea market is the ultimate place to shop for *matryoshki* (nesting dolls), military uniforms, icons, Soviet badges and some real antiques. Huge and diverse, it is almost a theme park, including shops, cafes and a couple of not terribly exciting museums.

Serious antiquarians occupy the 2nd floor of the wooden trade row surrounding the palace, but for really good stuff you need to come here at an ungodly hour on Saturday morning and compete with pros from Moscow galleries. Keep in mind that Russia bans the export of any item older than 100 years.

ⓘ Information

Wireless access is ubiquitous and almost always free.

36.6 A chain of 24-hour pharmacies with many branches all around the city.

European Medical Centre (☑ 495-933 6655; www.emcmos.ru; Spiridonevsky per 5; ☺ 24hr; Ⓜ Mayakovskaya) Offers 24-hour emergency service, consultations and a full range of medical specialists.

Main Post Office (Myasnitskaya ul 26; ☺ 24hr; Ⓜ Chistye Prudy)

Moscow Times Best locally published English-language newspaper, widely distributed free of charge.

Unifest Travel (☑ 495-234 6555; www.unifest. ru; Komsomolsky pr 16/2 str 3-4; ☺ 9am-7pm Mon-Fri, visa department 10am-6pm Mon-Fri) On-the-ball travel company offers rail and air tickets, visa support and more.

ⓘ Getting Around

TO/FROM THE AIRPORT

All three Moscow airports (Domodedovo, Sheremetyevo or Vnukovo) are accessible by the convenient **Aeroexpress Train** (☑ 8-800 700 3377; www.aeroexpress.ru; R420; ☺ 6am-midnight) from the city centre; reduced rates are available for online purchase.

Alternatively, order an official airport taxi from the dispatcher's desk in the terminal (R2000 to R2200 to the city centre). If you can order a taxi by phone or with a mobile phone app (you'll need a Russian SIM card and some knowledge of the language) it will be about 50% cheaper. Consider asking fellow Russian travellers on your plane – someone should be able to help if you ask nicely.

PUBLIC TRANSPORT

The **Moscow Metro** (www.mosmetro.ru) is by far the easiest, quickest and cheapest way of getting around the city. Stations are marked outside by 'M' signs. Magnetic tickets (R55) are sold at ticket booths. Save time by buying unlimited travel tickets (one day R210, three days R400, seven days R800) or multiple-ride tickets (five rides for R160, 20 rides for R720).

The ticket is a contactless smart card, which you must tap on the reader before going through the turnstile.

Buses, trolleybuses and trams are useful along a few radial or cross-town routes that the metro misses, and are necessary for reaching sights away from the city centre. Same tickets as in the metro apply and you can buy them from the driver. Boarding is only through the first door, where you need to apply the magnetic card at a turnstile.

TAXI

Taxi cabs are affordable, but not that easy for casual visitors to Moscow to use as you can't really flag down an official metered taxi in the street. These days, most people use mobile phone apps (such as Uber, Gett and Yandex Taxi) to order a cab.

You can also order an official taxi by phone or book it online, or ask a Russian-speaker to do this for you. **Taxi Tsel** (☑ 495-204 2244; www. taxicel.ru) is a reliable company, but operators don't speak English.

Golden Ring
Золотое Кольцо

The Golden Ring is textbook Russia: onion-shaped domes, kremlins and gingerbread cottages with cherry orchards. It is a string of the country's oldest towns that formed the core of eastern Kyivan Rus. Too engrossed in fratricide, they failed to register the rise of Moscow, which elbowed them out of active politics. Largely untouched by Soviet industrialisation, places like Suzdal now attract flocks of Russian tourists in search of the lost idyll. The complete circular route, described in the Lonely Planet guide to Russia, requires about a week to be completed. But several gems can be seen on one- or two-day trips from Moscow.

Vladimir
Владимир

Vladimir may look like another Soviet Gotham City, until you pass the medieval Golden Gate and stop by the cluster of exquisite churches and cathedrals, some of the oldest in Russia. Hiding behind them is an abrupt bluff with spectacular views of the Oka Valley. Prince Andrei Bogolyubsky chose Vladimir as his capital in 1157 after a stint in the Holy Land where he befriended European crusader kings, such as Friedrich Barbarossa. They sent him their best architects, who designed the town's landmarks, fusing Western and Kyivan traditions. The main jewel, Assumption Cathedral (Успенский собор; ☑ 4922-325 201; www.vladmuseum.ru; pl Sobornaya; R100; ☉ services 7am-8pm, visitors 1pm-4.45pm Tue-Sun), features frescoes by Russia's most prominent icon painter, Andrei Rublyov. Vladimir flourished for less than a century under Andrei's successor, Vsevolod III, until a series of devastating Tatar-Mongol raids led to its decline and dependence on Moscow. The last, a 1408 siege, is vividly if gruesomely reenacted in Andrei Tarkovsky's film *Andrei Rublyov*. Vsevolod's legacy is the exquisite Cathedral of St Dmitry (Дмитриевский собор; www.vladmuseum.ru; Bolshaya Moskovskaya ul 60; R80; ☉ 10am-5pm Wed-Mon Apr-Oct, to 4pm Nov-Mar), its exterior covered in an amazing profusion of images carved in limestone.

Most people don't overnight in Vladimir, preferring the charming Suzdal 35km away. But if you need to, head to Voznesenskaya Sloboda (Вознесенская слобода; ☑ 4922-325 494; www.vsloboda.ru; ul Voznesenskaya 14b; d R4800; P ✿ ⛄) , a mansion dramatically set on the high bank of the Oka and featuring a decent restaurant. For lunch or dinner, check out Piteyny Dom Kuptsa Andreyeva (☑ 4922-232 6545; www.andreevbeer.com/dom; Bolshaya Moskovskaya ul 16; mains R350-600; ☉ 11am-midnight; ⛄ ⛄) that serves traditional Russian fare, like *shchi* cabbage soup and *bliny* pancakes, as well as home-brewed beer.

❶ Getting There & Away

Vladimir is on the main Trans-Siberian line between Moscow and Nizhny Novgorod and the parallel highway. There are four train services a day from Moscow, with modern Strizh and slightly less comfortable Lastochka trains (R900 to R1100, 1¾ hours). Buses for Suzdal (R87, one hour, half-hourly) depart from the bus station, located across the square from the train station.

Suzdal   Суздаль

The Golden Ring comes with a diamond and that's Suzdal. If you have only one place to visit near Moscow, come here – even though everyone else will do the same. In 1864, local merchants failed to coerce the government into building the Trans-Siberian Railway through their town. Instead it went through Vladimir, 35km away. As a result, Suzdal was bypassed not only by trains, but by the 20th century altogether. This is why the place remains largely the same as ages ago – its cute

wooden cottages mingling with golden cupolas that reflect in the river, which meanders through gentle hills and meadows.

A grandfather of its Moscow namesake, Suzdal's Kremlin (Кремль; joint ticket excluding Nativity cathedral adult/child R250/100; ☉ 10am-6pm Wed-Mon) was the seat of Prince Yury Dolgoruky, who founded both Suzdal and the Russian capital, a rather unimportant outpost in his times. An even more grandiose sight is the Saviour Monastery of St Euthymius (Спасо-Евфимиев мужской монастырь; ☑ 49231-20 746; adult/student R400/200; ☉ 10am-6pm Tue-Sun), which harks back to the times of Ivan the Terrible.

Suzdal has plenty of accommodation, from quaint two- or three-room guesthouses to vast holiday resorts. One of the latter, Pushkarskaya Sloboda (Пушкарская слобода; ☑ 49231-23 303; www.pushkarka.ru; ul Lenina 45; hotel d from R3750, village d from R5400; ✿ ⛄ ⛄), is arguably the most reliable and centrally located option for a short stay. Equally reliable, the unpretentious Kharchevnya (Харчевня; ☑ 49231-20 722; ul Lenina 73; R200-400), serves traditional Russian staples.

❶ Getting There & Away

The bus station is 2km east of the centre on Vasilievskaya ul. Some long-distance buses pass the central square on the way. A train/bus combination via Vladimir is by far the best way of getting from Moscow. Buses run every 45 minutes to/from Vladimir (R87, one hour) and there is a daily bus to Moscow (R500, five hours).

Sergiev Posad   Сергиев Посад

Blue and golden cupolas offset by snow-white walls – this colour scheme lies at the heart of the Russian perception of divinity and Sergiev Posad's Trinity Monastery of St Sergiy (Troitse-Sergieva Lavra; ☑ 496-544 5356; www.stsl.ru; ☉ 5am-9pm) FREE is a textbook example. It doesn't get any holier than here in Russia, for the place was founded in 1340 by the country's most revered saint, St Sergius of Radonezh. Since the 14th century, pilgrims have been journeying to this place to pay homage to him.

Although the Bolsheviks closed the monastery, it was reopened following WWII as a museum, residence of the patriarch and a working monastery. The patriarch and the church's administrative centre moved to the Danilovsky Monastery in Moscow in 1988, but Sergiev Posad remains one of the most important spiritual sites in Russia.

Sergiev Posad is an easy day trip from Moscow and that's how most people visit it.

ℹ️ Getting There & Away

Considering horrendous traffic jams on the approaches to Moscow, train is a much better way of getting to Sergiev Posad from the capital. The fastest option is the express commuter train that departs from Moscow's Yaroslavsky vokzal (R210, one hour, six daily). Bus 388 to Sergiev Posad from Moscow's VDNKh metro station departs hourly from 7am to 10pm (R206).

St Petersburg
Санкт Петербург

🎵 812 / POP 4.9 MILLION

Affectionately known as Piter to locals, St Petersburg is a visual delight. The Neva River and surrounding canals reflect unbroken facades of handsome 18th- and 19th-century buildings that house a spellbinding collection of cultural storehouses, culminating in the incomparable Hermitage. Home to many of Russia's greatest creative talents (Pushkin, Dostoevsky, Tchaikovsky), Piter still inspires a contemporary generation of Russians, making it a liberal, hedonistic and exciting place to visit.

The city covers many islands, some real, some created through the construction of canals. The central street is Nevsky pr, which extends some 4km from the Alexander Nevsky Monastery to the Hermitage.

◉ Sights

Dvortsovaya Ploshchad HISTORIC SITE
(Palace Sq) The monumental **Dvortsovaya pl** is one of the most impressive and historic spaces in the city. Stand well back to admire the palace and the central 47.5m **Alexander Column**, named after Alexander I and commemorating the 1812 victory over Napoleon. It has stood here, held in place by gravity alone, since 1834. It was in this square that tsarist troops fired on peaceful protestors in 1905 (on a day now known as Bloody Sunday), sparking the revolution of that year. At least once a year, in summer, the square is used for free outdoor concerts; the Rolling Stones and Roger Waters have played here.

★ Russian Museum MUSEUM
(Русский музей; 🎵 812-595 4248; www.rusmuseum.ru; Inzhenernaya ul 4; adult/student R450/200, 4-palace ticket adult/student R600/300; ◉10am-6pm Mon, Wed & Fri-Sun, 1-9pm Thu; Ⓜ Nevsky

Prospekt) The handsome Mikhailovsky Palace is home to the country's biggest collection of Russian art. After the Hermitage you may feel you have had your fill of art, but try your utmost to make some time for this gem of a museum. There's also a lovely garden behind the palace.

★ Church of the Saviour on the Spilled Blood CHURCH
(Церковь Спаса на Крови; www.cathedral.ru; Konyushennaya pl; adult/student R250/150; ◉10.30am-6pm Thu-Tue; Ⓜ Nevsky Prospekt) This five-domed dazzler is St Petersburg's most elaborate church with a classic Russian Orthodox exterior, and an interior decorated with some 7000 sq metres of mosaics. Officially called the Church of the Resurrection of Christ, its far more striking colloquial name references the assassination attempt on Tsar Alexander II here in 1881.

★ St Isaac's Cathedral MUSEUM
(Isaakievsky Sobor; www.cathedral.ru; Isaakievskaya pl; cathedral adult/student R250/150, colonnade R150; ◉cathedral 10.30am-6pm Thu-Tue, colonnade 10.30am-10.30pm May-Oct, to 6pm Nov-Apr, 3rd Wed of month closed; Ⓜ Admiralteyskaya) The golden dome of St Isaac's Cathedral dominates the St Petersburg skyline. Its obscenely lavish interior is open as a museum, although services are held in the cathedral on major religious holidays. Most people bypass the museum to climb the 262 steps to the *kolonnada* (colonnade) around the drum of the dome, providing superb city views.

★ Peter & Paul Fortress FORTRESS
(Петропавловская крепость; www.spbmuseum.ru; grounds free, Peter & Paul Cathedral adult/child R450/250, combined ticket for 5 exhibitions R600/350; ◉grounds 8.30am-8pm, exhibitions 11am-6pm Mon & Thu-Sun, 10am-5pm Tue; Ⓜ Gorkovskaya) Housing a cathedral where the Romanovs are buried, a former prison and various exhibitions, this large defensive fortress on Zayachy Island is the kernel from which St Petersburg grew into the city it is today. History buffs will love it and everyone will swoon at the panoramic views from atop the fortress walls, at the foot of which lies a sandy riverside beach, a prime spot for sunbathing.

★ Kunstkamera MUSEUM
(Кунсткамера; www.kunstkamera.ru; Tamozhenny per; adult/child R250/50; ◉11am-6pm Tue-Sun; Ⓜ Admiralteyskaya) Also known as the Museum of Ethnology and Anthropology, the

Central St Petersburg

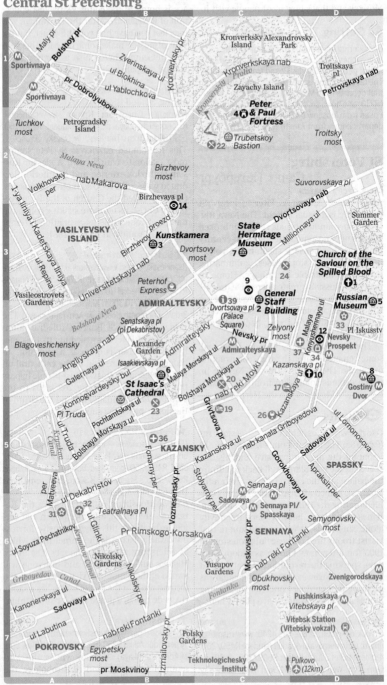

Maly pr

Bolshoy pr

Ⓜ Sportivnaya

Zverinskaya ul

ul Blokhina

pr Dobrolyubova

Ⓜ Sportivnaya

ul Yablochkova

Tuchkov most

Petrogradsky Island

Malaya Neva

nab Makarova

VASILYEVSKY ISLAND

1-ya liniya
1-ya liniya

ul Repina

Volkhovsky per

Kadetskaya liniya

Vasileostrovets Gardens

Universitetskaya nab

Bolshaya Neva

Blagoveshchensky most

Angliyskaya nab

Galernaya ul

Kronverksky pr

Kronverksky Alexandrovsky Island Park

Kronverksky Proliv

Kronverkskaya nab

Zayachy Island

Peter **4** ⊕ & Paul Fortress

⊗ 22 ⊞ Trubetskoy Bastion

Birzhevoy most

Birzhevaya pl
◉ 14

Birzhevoy proezd

Kunstkamera
🏛 **3**

Dvortsovy most

Peterhof Express ⊗

ADMIRALTEYSKY

Senatskaya pl
(pl Dekabristov)

Alexander Garden

Isaakievskaya pl

🏛 **6**

St Isaac's Cathedral

⊗ 23

Pochtamtskaya ul

Konnogvardeysky bul

Pl Truda

ul Truda

per Matveeva

ul Dekabristov

🌟 **32**

31 🌟

Teatralnaya Pl

ul Glinki

Nikolsky Gardens

Griboyedov Canal

Kanonerskaya ul

POKROVSKY

ul Labutina

nab reki Fontanki

Egypetsky most

pr Moskvinoy

Troitskaya pl

Petrovskaya nab

Troitsky most

Suvorovskaya pl

Dvortsovaya ul

Millionnaya ul

Summer Garden

State Hermitage Museum
🏛 **7**

Dvortsovy most

Church of the Saviour on the Spilled Blood
❶ **1**

Russian Museum 🏛 **5**

⊗ 24

◉ 9

General Staff Building
ℹ **39**
2

Dvortsovaya pl (Palace Square)

33

Pl Iskusstv

Zelyony most

Nevsky pr

Ⓜ **Admiralteyskaya**

Malaya Konyushennaya ul

◉ **12**

Nevsky Prospekt

37 ⊗

34

Admiralteysky pr

Malaya Morskaya ul

Bolshaya Morskaya ul

Kazanskaya pl

❶ **10**

Ⓜ **8**
🏛

Gostiny Dvor

nab reki Moyki

⊞ 20

🏛 19

Grivtsova per

17 ⊞

26 ⊗

nab kanala Griboyedova

ul Lomonosova

Kazanskaya ul

⊕ **36**

KAZANSKY

Fonarny per

Voznesensky pr

Stolyarny per

Sadovaya ul

Gorokhovaya ul

SPASSKY

Apraksin per

Sennaya pl

Ⓜ Sadovaya

Ⓜ **Sennaya Pl/ Spasskaya**

Semyonovsky most

SENNAYA

Moskovsky pr

Yusupov Gardens

nab reki Fontanki

Obukhovsky most

Zvenigorodskaya Ⓜ

Pushkinskaya Ⓜ
Vitebskaya pl

Vitebsk Station (Vitebsky vokzal) 🚃

Polsky Gardens

Fontanka

Izmailovsky pr

Tekhnologichesky Institut Ⓜ

↓ Pulkovo
✈ (12km)

Kryukov Canal

Pr Rimskogo-Korsakova

ul Soyuza Pechatnikov

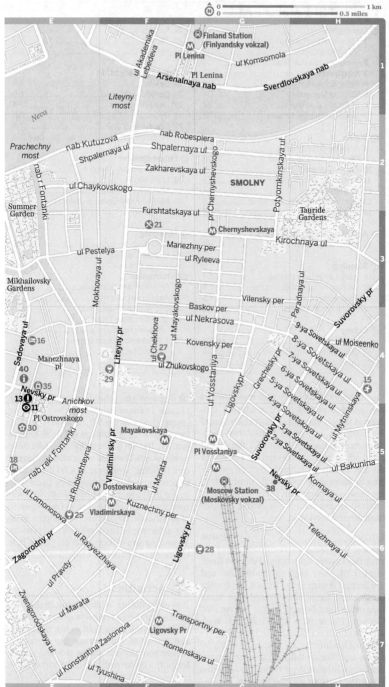

Central St Petersburg

Kunstkamera is the city's first museum and was founded in 1714 by Peter himself. It is famous largely for its ghoulish collection of monstrosities, preserved 'freaks', two-headed mutant foetuses, deformed animals and odd body parts, all collected by Peter with the aim of educating the notoriously superstitious Russian people. While most rush to see these sad specimens, there are also very interesting exhibitions on native peoples from around the world.

Strelka
LANDMARK

Among the oldest parts of Vasilyevsky Island, this eastern tip is where Peter the Great wanted his new city's administrative and intellectual centre to be. In fact, the Strelka became the focus of St Petersburg's maritime trade, symbolised by the colonnaded Customs House (now the Pushkin House). The two Rostral Columns, archetypal St Petersburg landmarks, are studded with ships' prows and four seated sculptures representing four of Russia's great rivers: the Neva, the Volga, the Dnieper and the Volkhov.

★ **General Staff Building** MUSEUM

(Здание Главного штаба; www.hermitagemuseum.org; Dvortsovaya pl 6-8; R300; incl main State Hermitage & other buildings; R600; ☉10.30am-6pm Tue, Thu, Sat & Sun, to 9pm Wed & Fri; Ⓜ Admiralteyskaya) The east wing of this magnificent building, wrapping around the south of Dvortsovaya pl and designed by Carlo Rossi in the 1820s, marries restored interiors with contemporary architecture to create a series of galleries displaying the Hermitage's amazing collection of Impressionist and post-Impressionist works. Contemporary art is here, too, often in temporary exhibitions by major artists.

🏃 Activities

Especially during White Nights, cycling is a brilliant and economical way to get around St Petersburg's spread-out sights, restaurants and bars. Off main drags like Nevsky pr (where you can ride on the sidewalk), St Petersburg's backstreets are quiet and sublime.

🛏 Sleeping

High season is May to September, with some hotels increasing their rates even further in June and July. You can get great deals in the low season, when hotel prices drop 30% on average.

⭐ **Soul Kitchen Hostel**　　　HOSTEL €

(📞8-965-816 3470; www.soulkitchenhostel.com; nab reki Moyki 62/2, apt 9, Sennaya; dm/d from R985/2700; 🔄@🛜; Ⓜ Admiralteyskaya) Soul Kitchen blends boho hipness and boutique-hotel comfort, scoring perfect 10s in many key categories: private rooms (chic), dorm beds (double-wide with privacy-protecting curtains), common areas (vast), kitchen (vast *and* beautiful) and bathrooms (downright inviting). There is also bike hire, table football, free Macs to use, free international phone calls and stunning Moyka River views from a communal balcony.

⭐ **Baby Lemonade Hostel**　　　HOSTEL €

(📞812-570 7943; Inzhenernaya ul 7; dm/d with shared bathroom from R500/1700, d from R2200; @🛜; Ⓜ Gostiny Dvor) The owner of Baby Lemonade is crazy about the 1960s and it shows in the pop-art, psychedelic design of this friendly, fun hostel with two pleasant, large dorms and a great kitchen and living room. However, it's worth splashing out for the boutique-hotel-worthy private rooms that are in a separate flat with great rooftop views.

⭐ **Rachmaninov Antique Hotel**　　　BOUTIQUE HOTEL €€

(📞812-327 7466; www.hotelrachmaninov.com; Kazanskaya ul 5; s/d from R3100/4200; @🛜; Ⓜ Nevsky Prospekt) The long-established Rachmaninov still feels like a secret place for those in the know. Perfectly located and run by friendly staff, it's pleasantly old world with hardwood floors and attractive Russian furnishings, particularly in the breakfast salon, which has a grand piano.

⭐ **Rossi Hotel**　　　BOUTIQUE HOTEL €€€

(📞812-635 6333; www.rossihotels.com; nab reki Fontanki 55; d/ste from R6700/15,500; ❄@🛜; Ⓜ Gostiny Dvor) Occupying a beautifully restored building on one of St Petersburg's prettiest squares, the Rossi's 53 rooms are all designed differently, but their brightness and moulded ceilings are uniform. Antique beds, super-sleek bathrooms, exposed brick walls and lots of cool designer touches create a great blend of old and new.

🍴 Eating

⭐ **Duo Gastrobar**　　　FUSION €

(📞812-994 5443; www.duobar.ru; ul Kirochnaya 8A; mains R350-500; ⏱1pm-midnight; 🔄; Ⓜ Chernyshevskaya) This light-bathed place, done out

---

DON'T MISS

STATE HERMITAGE MUSEUM

Mainly set in the magnificent Winter Palace and adjoining buildings, the **Hermitage** (Государственный Эрмитаж; www.hermitagemuseum.org; Dvortsovaya pl 2; joint ticket R600; ⏱10.30am-6pm Tue, Thu, Sat & Sun, to 9pm Wed & Fri; Ⓜ Admiralteyskaya) fully lives up to its sterling reputation. You can be absorbed by its treasures for days and still come out wanting more.

The enormous collection (over three million items, only a fraction of which are on display in around 360 rooms) almost amounts to a comprehensive history of Western European art. Viewing it demands a little planning, so choose the areas you'd like to concentrate on before you arrive.The museum consists of five connected buildings. From west to east they are:

Winter Palace Designed by Bartolomeo Rastrelli, its opulent state rooms, Great Church, Pavilion Hall and Treasure Rooms shouldn't be missed.

Small Hermitage and Old Hermitage Both were built for Catherine the Great, partly to house the art collection started by Peter the Great, which she significantly expanded. Here you'll find works by Rembrandt, Da Vinci and Caravaggio.

New Hermitage Built for Nicholas II, to hold the still-growing art collection. The Old and New Hermitages are sometimes grouped together and labelled the Large Hermitage.

State Hermitage Theatre Built in the 1780s by the Giacomo Quarenghi. Concerts and ballets are still performed here.

RUSSIA'S MOST FAMOUS STREET

Walking **Nevsky Prospekt** is an essential St Petersburg experience. Highlights along it incude the **Kazan Cathedral** (Казанский собор; http://kazansky-spb.ru; Kazanskaya pl 2; ⊘8.30am-7.30pm; Ⓜ Nevsky Prospekt) FREE, with its curved arms reaching out towards the avenue.

Opposite is the **Singer Building** (Nevsky pr 28; Ⓜ Nevsky Prospekt), a Style Moderne (art deco) beauty restored to all its splendour when it was the headquarters of the sewing-machine company; inside is the bookshop **Dom Knigi** (www.spbdk.ru; Nevsky pr 28; ⊘9am-1am; ☎; Ⓜ Nevsky Prospekt) and **Café Singer** (Nevsky pr 28; ⊘9am-11pm; ☎; Ⓜ Nevsky Prospekt), serving good food and drinks with a great view over the street.

Further along are the covered arcades of Rastrelli's historic **Bolshoy Gostiny Dvor** (Большой Гостиный Двор; http://bgd.ru; Nevsky pr 35; ⊘10am-10pm; Ⓜ Gostiny Dvor) department store, while on the corner of Sadovaya ul is the Style Moderne classic **Kupetz Eliseevs** (http://kupetzeliseevs.ru; Nevsky pr 56; ⊘10am-10pm; ☎; Ⓜ Gostiny Dvor) reincarnated as a luxury grocery and cafe.

An enormous **statue of Catherine the Great** stands at the centre of **Ploshchad Ostrovskogo** (Площадь Островского; Ⓜ Gostiny Dvor), commonly referred to as the Catherine Gardens; at the southern end of the gardens is **Alexandrinsky Theatre** (☑ 812-710 4103; www.alexandrinsky.ru; pl Ostrovskogo 2; Ⓜ Gostiny Dvor), where Chekhov's *The Seagull* premiered (to tepid reviews) in 1896.

in wood and gorgeous glass lampshades, has really helped put this otherwise quiet area on the culinary map. Its short fusion menu excels, featuring such unlikely delights as passionfruit and gorgonzola mousse and salmon with quinoa and mascarpone. There are also more conventional choices such as risottos, pastas and salads.

★**Clean Plates Society**   INTERNATIONAL €
(Общество чистых тарелок; www.cleanplates-cafe.com; Gorokhovaya ul 13; mains R350-500; ⊘11am-1am; ☎ ▣; Ⓜ Admiralteyskaya) Burgers, curry, borsch and burritos all get a look-in on this stylish and relaxed restaurant's menu. The horseshoe bar and the inventive cocktail and drinks list are its prime attractions. The name derives from a short story by Vladimir Bonch-Bruyevich about Lenin's visit to a kindergarten.

★**Yat**   RUSSIAN €€
(Ять; ☑ 812-957 0023; www.eatinyat.com; nab reki Moyki 16; mains R370-750; ⊘11am-11pm; ☎ �ⓙ; Ⓜ Admiralteyskaya) Perfectly placed for eating near the Hermitage, this country-cottage-style restaurant has a very appealing menu of traditional dishes, presented with aplomb. The *shchi* (cabbage-based soup) is excellent, and there is also a tempting range of flavoured vodkas. There's a fab kids area with pet rabbits for them to feed.

★**Teplo**   MODERN EUROPEAN €€
(☑ 812-570 1974; www.v-teple.ru; Bolshaya Morskaya ul 45; mains R280-840; ⊘9am-midnight; ☺ ☻ ☑ ▣; Ⓜ Admiralteyskaya) This much-feted, eclectic and original restaurant has got it all just right. The venue itself is a lot of fun to nose around, with multiple small rooms, nooks and crannies. Service is friendly and fast (when it's not too busy) and the peppy, inventive Italian-leaning menu has something for everyone. Reservations are usually required, so call ahead.

Koryushka   RUSSIAN, GEORGIAN €€
(Корюшка; ☑ 812-640 1616; www.ginza.ru/spb/restaurant/korushka; Petropavlovskaya krepost 3, Zayachy Island; mains R550-1300; ⊘noon-midnight; ☎ ▣ ⓙ; Ⓜ Gorkovskaya) Lightly battered and fried smelt *(koryushka)* is a St Petersburg speciality every April, but you can eat the small fish year-round at this relaxed, sophisticated restaurant beside the Peter and Paul Fortress. There are plenty of other very appealing Georgian dishes on the menu to supplement the stunning views across the Neva.

🍷 Drinking

★**Borodabar**   COCKTAIL BAR
(☑ 8-911-923 8940; Kazanskaya ul 11; ⊘5pm-2am Sun-Thu, to 4am Fri & Sat; ☎; Ⓜ Nevsky Prospekt) Boroda means beard in Russian, and sure enough you'll see plenty of facial hair and

tattoos in this hipster cocktail hang-out. Never mind, as the mixologists really know their stuff – we can particularly recommend their smoked old fashioned, which is infused with tobacco smoke, and their colourful (and potent) range of shots.

Bekitser　　　　　　　　　　　　BAR

(Бекицер; ☑ 812-926 4342; www.facebook.com/bktzr; ul Rubinshteyna 41; ⊙ noon-6am; Ⓜ Dostoyevskaya) Always crowded and spilling out into the street, this Israel-themed bar cum falafel shop has instantly become the flagship of St Peterburg's main bar row – ul Rubinshteyna. Not kosher, and open on Saturdays, the place lures hip and joyful people with its trademark Shabad Sholom cocktail, Israeli Shiraz and the best falafel wraps this side of the Baltic Sea.

Dead Poets Bar　　　　　COCKTAIL BAR

(☑ 812-449 4656; www.deadpoetsbar.com; ul Zhukovskogo 12; ⊙ 2pm-2am Sun-Thu, to 8am Fri & Sat; 🛜; Ⓜ Mayakovskaya) This very cool place has a sophisticated drinks menu and an almost unbelievable range of spirits stacked along the long bar and served up by a committed staff of mixologists. It's more of a quiet place, with low lighting, a jazz soundtrack and plenty of space to sit down.

★**Union Bar & Grill**　　　　　　　BAR

(www.facebook.com/barunion; Liteyny pr 55; ⊙ 6pm-6am; 🛜; Ⓜ Mayakovskaya) The Union is a glamorous and fun place, characterised by one enormous long wooden bar, low lighting and a New York feel. It's all rather adult, with a serious cocktail list and designer beers on tap. It's crazy at the weekends, but quiet during the week, and always draws a cool twenty- and thirty-something crowd.

Warszawa　　　　　　　　　　　BAR

(ul Kazanskaya 11; ⊙ 10am-2am Sun-Thu, to 4am Fri & Sat; Ⓜ Nevsky Prospekt) Russian urbanites have always harboured a special admiration for the quaint provincialism of Eastern Europe, hence this smallish bar with old-fashioned wallpaper, vintage furniture and portraits of 20th-century Polish film stars. Polish beer is on tap and cocktails are based on liquors you may have never heard of. Good for deep, vodka-infused philosophical conversations.

Dyuni　　　　　　　　　　　　　BAR

(Дюны; www.facebook.com/dunes.on.ligovsky; Ligovsky pr 50; ⊙ 4pm-midnight Sun-Thu, to 6am Fri & Sat; 🛜; Ⓜ Ploshchad Vosstaniya) What looks like a small suburban house sits rather incongruously here amid repurposed warehouses in this vast courtyard. There's a cosy indoor bar and a sand-covered outside area with table

RUSSIA ST PETERSBURG

WORTH A TRIP

PETERHOF & TSARSKOE SELO

Several palace estates around St Petersburg, country retreats for the tsars, are now among the most spectacular sights in Russia.

Peterhof (Петергоф; also known as Petrodvorets), 29km west of the city and built for Peter the Great, is best visited for its **Grand Cascade** (⊙ 11am-5pm Mon-Fri, to 6pm Sat & Sun May-early Oct) and Water Avenue, a symphony of over 140 fountains and canals located in the **Lower Park** (Нижний парк; www.peterhofmuseum.ru; adult/student May-Oct R700/350, Nov-Apr free; ⊙ 9am-7pm). There are several additional palaces, villas and parks here, each of which charges its own hefty admission price.

Tsarskoe Selo (Царское Село), 25km south of the city in the town of Pushkin, is home to the baroque **Catherine Palace** (Екатерининский дворец; www.tzar.ru; Sadovaya ul 7; adult/student R1000/290, audioguide R150; ⊙ 10am-4.45pm Wed-Sun), expertly restored following its near destruction in WWII. From May to September individual visits to Catherine's Palace are limited to noon to 2pm and 4pm to 5pm, other times being reserved for tour groups.

Buses and *marshrutky* (fixed-route minibuses) to Petrodvorets (R55, 30 minutes) run frequently from outside metro stations Avtovo and Leninsky Prospekt. From May to September, the **Peterhof Express** (www.peterhof-express.com; single/return adult R750/1300, student R500/900; ⊙ 10am-6pm) hydrofoil leaves from jetties behind the Hermitage and the Admiralty.

The easiest way to get to Tsarskoe Selo is by *marshrutka* (R35) from Moskovskaya metro station.

KALININGRAD REGION

Sandwiched by Poland and Lithuania, the Kaliningrad Region is a Russian exclave that's intimately attached to the Motherland yet also a world apart. In this 'Little Russia' – only 15,100 sq km with a population of 941,873 – you'll also find beautiful countryside, charming old Prussian seaside resorts and splendid beaches. Citizens of Japan and many European countries can visit Kaliningrad on a 72-hour visa.

The capital, **Kaliningrad** (Калининград; formerly Königsberg), was once a Middle European architectural gem equal to Prague or Kraków. Precious little of this built heritage remains but there are attractive residential suburbs and remnants of the city's old fortifications that evoke the Prussian past. The most impressive building is the Gothic **Kaliningrad Cathedral** (Кафедральный собор Кёнигсберга; ☑ 4012-631 705; www.sobor-kaliningrad.ru; Kant Island; adult/student R200/100, photos R50, concerts from R150; ⊙ 10am-6pm Mon-Thu, to 7pm Fri-Sun), founded in 1333 and restored after almost being destroyed during WWII. West of the cathedral along the river also make time for the fascinating **Museum of the World Ocean** (Музей Мирового Океана; www.world-ocean.ru; nab Petra Velikogo 1; adult/student R300/150, individual vessels adult/student R150/100; ⊙ 10am-6pm Wed-Mon).

The best places to stay are the budget **Oh, my Kant** (☑ 4012-390 278; www.ohmykant.ru; ul Yablonevaya Alleya 34; dm from R300, d from R1200; ☜) , with local born German philosopher Immannuel Kant in the name, and the midrange **Skipper Hotel** (Гостиница Шкиперская; ☑ 4012-307 237; www.skipperhotel.ru; ul Oktyabrskaya 4a; r from R4300; ❈☜) in the attractive, slightly kitsch Fish Village riverside development. There are plenty of good places to eat and drink including **Fish Club** (Рыбный клуб; ul Oktyabrskaya 4a; mains R500-1500; ⊙ noon-midnight), **Zarya** (Заря; ☑ 4012-300 388; pr Mira 43; mains R200-540; ⊙ 10am-3am; ☜) and the hip apartment-cum-cafe **Kvartira** (Apartment; ☑ 4012-216 736; www.vk.com/kvartira_koloskova13; ul Serzhanta Koloskova 13; ☜).

It's easy to access the region's other key sights on day trips from Kaliningrad, but if you did want to spend time away from the city, base yourself in the seaside resort of **Svetlogorsk** (Светлого́рск), which is only a few hours' drive down the Baltic coast from the pine forests and Sahara-style dunes of the **Kurshskaya Kosa National Park** (Национальный парк Куршская коса; www.park-kosa.ru; admission per person/car R40/300), a Unesco World Heritage site.

---

football and ping pong, which keeps the cool kids happy all night in the summer months. To find it, simply continue in a straight line from the courtyard entrance.

☆ Entertainment

From July to mid-September the big theatres like the Mariinsky and the Mikhailovsky close but plenty of performances are still staged. Check the *St Petersburg Times* for comprehensive listings.

Mariinsky Theatre   BALLET, OPERA

(Мариинский театр; ☑ 812-326 4141; www.mariinsky.ru; Teatralnaya pl 1; tickets R1000-6000; Ⓜ Sadovaya) St Petersburg's most spectacular venue for ballet and opera, the Mariinsky Theatre is an attraction in its own right. Tickets can be bought online or in person, but they should be bought in advance during the summer months. The magnificent interior is the epitome of imperial grandeur, and any evening here will be an impressive experience.

Mariinsky II   THEATRE

(Мариинский II; ☑ 812-326 4141; www.mariinsky.ru; ul Dekabristov 34; tickets R300-6000; ⊙ ticket office 11am-7pm; Ⓜ Sadovaya) Finally opening its doors in 2013 after more than a decade of construction, legal wrangles, scandal and rumour, the Mariinsky II is a showpiece for St Petersburg's most famous ballet and opera company. It is one of the most technically advanced music venues in the world, with superb sightlines and acoustics from all of its 2000 seats.

Mikhailovsky Opera & Ballet Theatre   BALLET, OPERA

(☑ 812-595 4305; www.mikhailovsky.ru; pl Iskusstv 1; tickets R300-4000; Ⓜ Nevsky Prospekt) While not quite as grand as the Mariinsky, this illustrious stage still delivers the Russian ballet or operatic experience, complete with multi-tiered theatre, frescoed ceiling and elaborate concerts. Pl Iskusstv (Arts Sq) is a lovely setting for this respected venue, which is home to the State Academic Opera & Ballet Company.

❶ Information

Free wi-fi access is common across the city.

American Medical Clinic (☎812-740 2090; www.amclinic.ru; nab reki Moyki 78; ⊗24hr; Ⓜ Admiralteyskaya) One of the city's largest private clinics.

Apteka Petrofarm (Nevsky pr 22; ⊗24hr) An excellent, all-night pharmacy.

Main Post Office (Pochtamtskaya ul 9; ⊗24hr; Ⓜ Admiralteyskaya) Worth visiting for its elegant Style Moderne interior.

Ost-West Kontaktservice (☎812-327 3416; www.ostwest.com; Nevsky pr 100; ⊗10am-6pm Mon-Fri; Ⓜ Ploshchad Vosstaniya) Can find you an apartment to rent and organise tours and tickets.

St Petersburg Times (www.sptimes.ru) Published every Tuesday and Friday, when it has an indispensable listings and arts review section.

Tourist Information Bureau (☎812-310 2822; http://eng.ispb.info; Sadovaya ul 14/52; ⊗10am-7pm Mon-Fri, noon-6pm Sat; Ⓜ Gostiny Dvor) There are also branches outside the **Hermitage** (Dvortsovaya pl; ⊗10am-7pm; Ⓜ Admiralteyskaya) and **Pulkovo airport** (⊗9am-8pm Mon-Fri).

❶ Getting Around

TO/FROM THE AIRPORT

From St Petersburg's superb new airport, an official taxi to the centre should cost between R900 and R1400, or you can take bus 39 (35 minutes) or 39A (20 minutes) to Moskovskaya metro station for R30, then take the metro from Moskovskaya (Line 2) all over the city for R35.

PUBLIC TRANSPORT

The metro is usually the quickest way around the city. *Zhetony* (tokens) and credit-loaded cards can be bought from booths in the stations (R45). Multiride cards are also available (R355 for 10 trips, R680 for 20 trips).

Buses, trolleybuses and *marshrutky* (fixed-route minibuses fare R34) often get you closer to the sights and are especially handy to cover long distances along main avenues like Nevsky pr.

TAXI

Taxi apps, such as Uber, Gett and Yandex Taxi, are all the rage in St Petersburg and they've brought down the prices while improving the service a great deal. You need a Russian SIM card to use them. Otherwise, the best way to get a taxi is to order it by phone. **Taxi Million** (☎812-600 0000; www.6-000-000.ru) has English-speaking operators.

SURVIVAL GUIDE

❶ Directory A–Z

ACCOMMODATION

The devaluation of the rouble in 2014 has suddenly made hotels in Russia considerably more affordable, with prices similar to those in Central Europe. The hotel scene has improved a great deal over recent years in terms of quality and diversity of choice – from youth hostels and B&Bs to Western chains and boutique hotels.

There has been a boom in budget-friendly hostels in both Moscow and St Petersburg, and if you're on a budget you'll want to consider these – even if you typically don't 'do' hostels, most offer a few private rooms.

Apartment Rental

Booking an apartment is a good way to save money on accommodation, especially for small groups. They typically cost around R4300 to R8600 per night. The following agencies can make bookings in Moscow and/or St Petersburg.

Enjoy Moscow (www.enjoymoscow.com; per night from US$155; ☎)

HOFA (www.hofa.ru; apt from per night €44; ☎)

Moscow Suites (www.moscowsuites.ru; studio per night from US$199; ☎)

Ost-West Kontaktservice (p967)

BUSINESS HOURS

Restaurants and bars often stay open later than their stated hours if the establishment is full. In fact, many simply say that they work *do poslednnogo klienta* (until the last customer leaves).

Note that most museums close their ticket offices one hour (in some cases 30 minutes) before the official closing time.

Banks 9am–6pm Monday to Friday, some open 9am–5pm Saturday

Bars noon–midnight, to 5am Friday and Saturday

Restaurants noon–midnight

Shops 10am–8pm

SLEEPING PRICE RANGES

The following price ranges are for high season and include private bathroom unless otherwise stated. Prices exclude breakfast unless otherwise stated.

€ less than R1500 (less than R3000 in Moscow & St Petersburg)

€€ R1500–R4000 (R3000–R8000 in Moscow & St Petersburg)

€€€ more than R4000 (more than R8000 in Moscow & St Petersburg)

INTERNET RESOURCES

Afisha (www.afisha.ru) Extensive restaurant, bar, museum and event listings for all major cities; in Russian only.

Lonely Planet (www.lonelyplanet.com/russia) Destination information, hotel bookings, traveller forum and more.

Moscow Expat Site (www.expat.ru) Mine expat knowledge of Russia.

Way to Russia (www.waytorussia.net) Comprehensive online travel guide.

MONEY

The Russian currency is the rouble, written as 'рубль' and abbreviated as 'руб' or 'р'. Roubles are divided into 100 almost worthless *kopeyki* (kopecks). Coins come in amounts of R1, R2, R5 and R10 roubles, with banknotes in values of R10, R50, R100, R200, R500, R1000, R2000 and R5000.

ATMs that accept all major credit and debit cards are everywhere, and most restaurants, shops and hotels in major cities gladly accept plastic. Visa and MasterCard are the most widespread card types, while American Express can be problematic in some hotels and shops. You can exchange dollars and euros (and some other currencies) at most banks; when they're closed, try the exchange counters at top-end hotels. You may need your passport. Note that crumpled or old banknotes are often refused.

POST

The Russian post service is **Pochta Rossia** (www.russianpost.ru). The main offices are open from 8am to 8pm or 9pm Monday to Friday, with shorter hours on Saturday and Sunday. To send a postcard or letter up to 20g anywhere in the world by air costs R37.

COUNTRY FACTS

Area 17,098,242 sq km

Capital Moscow

Country Code 7

Currency Rouble (R)

Emergency Stationary/mobile phone –ambulance 03/103, fire 01/101, police 02/102

Language Russian

Money Plenty of ATMs, most accepting foreign cards

Population 143.8 million

Visas Required by all – apply at least a month in advance of your trip

PUBLIC HOLIDAYS

Many businesses are closed from 1 to 7 January. Russia's main public holidays:

New Year's Day 1 January
Russian Orthodox Christmas Day 7 January
Defender of the Fatherland Day 23 February
International Women's Day 8 March
International Labour Day/Spring Festival 1 May
Victory Day 9 May
Russian Independence Day 12 June
Unity Day 4 November

SAFE TRAVEL

Travellers have nothing to fear from Russia's 'mafia' – the increasingly respectable gangster classes are not interested in such small fry. However, petty theft and pickpockets are prevalent in both Moscow and St Petersburg, so be vigilant with your belongings.

Some police officers can be bothersome, especially to dark-skinned or foreign-looking people. Other members of the police force target tourists, though reports of tourists being hassled about their documents and registration have declined. Still, you should always carry a photocopy of your passport, visa and registration stamp. If you are stopped for any reason – legitimate or illegitimate – you will surely be hassled if you don't have these.

Sadly, racism is a problem in Russia, though the number of hate attacks against people of Central Asian, Mideastern and African appearance has declined considerably in recent years. Exercise extra caution, but don't succumb to paranoia, if you are dark-skinned. Try not to venture into dodgy outlying areas of large cities on your own. Avoid domestic football (soccer) games unless accompanied by Russian friends. Security standards at major international fixtures are high, so don't be worried about attending the World Cup in 2018.

TELEPHONE

The international code for Russia is 7. The international access code from landline phones in Russia is 8, followed by 10 after the second tone, followed by the country code.

The four main mobile phone companies, all with prepaid and 4G internet options, are **Beeline**, **Megafon** (www.megafon.ru), **Tele 2** (www.tele2.ru) and **MTS** (www.mts.ru). Company offices are everywhere. It costs almost nothing to purchase a SIM card, but bring your passport.

Internal roaming that still existed in Russia at the time of writing was due to be abolished by the end of 2017. But you may still have to pay more for calling from one Russian region to another, if this long overdue decision is for some reason postponed.

VISAS

Everyone needs a visa to visit Russia. For most travellers a tourist visa (single- or double-entry, valid for a maximum of 30 days) will be sufficient. If you plan to stay longer than a month, you can apply for a business visa or – if you are a US citizen – a three-year multi-entry visa.

Applying for a visa is undeniably a headache, but the process is actually quite straightforward. There are three stages: invitation, application and registration.

Invitation

To obtain a visa, everyone needs an invitation also known as 'visa support'. Hotels and hostels will usually issue anyone staying with them an invitation voucher free or for a small fee (typically around €20 to €30). If you are not staying in a hotel or hostel, you will need to buy an invitation – this can be done through most travel agents or via specialist visa agencies, also for around €20.

Application

Invitation voucher in hand, you can then apply for a visa. Wherever in the world you are applying you can start by entering details in the online form of the Consular Department of the Russian Ministry of Foreign Affairs (https://visa.kdmid.ru/PetitionChoice.aspx).

Take care in answering the questions accurately on this form, including listing all the countries you have visited in the last 10 years and the dates of visits – stamps in your passport will be checked against this information and if there are anomalies you will likely have to restart the process. Keep a note of the unique identity number provided for your submitted form – if you have to make changes later, you will need this to access it without having to fill in the form from scratch again.

Russian embassies in the UK and US have contracted separate agencies to process the submission of visa applications; these companies use online interfaces that direct the relevant information into the standard visa application form. In the UK, the agency is **VFS. Global** (http://ru.vfsglobal.co.uk) with offices in London and Edinburgh; in the US it's **Invisa Logistic Services** (http://ils-usa.com) with offices in Washington, DC, New York, San Francisco, Houston and Seattle.

Consular offices apply different fees and slightly different application rules country by country. Avoid potential hassles by checking well in advance what these rules might be. Among the things that you will need:

➡ a printout of the invitation/visa support document

➡ a passport-sized photograph for the application form

➡ if you're self-employed, bank statements for the previous three months showing you have sufficient funds to cover your time in Russia

➡ details of your travel insurance.

The charge for the visa will depend on the type of visa applied for and how quickly you need it.

We highly recommend applying for your visa in your home country rather than on the road.

Registration

Every visitor to Russia must have their visa registered *within seven days of arrival*, excluding weekends and public holidays. Registration is handled by your accommodating party. If staying in a homestay or rental apartment, you'll either need to make arrangements with the landlord or a friend to register you through the post office. See http://waytorussia.net/RussianVisa/Registration.html for how this can be done.

Once registered, you'll receive a registration slip. Keep this safe – that's the document that any police who stop you will ask to see. You do not need to register more than once unless you stay in additional cities for more than seven days, in which case you'll need additional registration slips.

72-Hour Visa-Free Travel

To qualify for this visa for St Petersburg, you need to enter and exit the city on a cruise or ferry such as that offered by **St Peter Line** (☑ 812-386 1147; www.stpeterline.com). For Kaliningrad, make arrangements in advance with locally based tour agencies.

Immigration Form

Immigration forms are produced electronically by passport control at airports. Take good care of your half of the completed form as you'll need it for registration and could face problems while travelling in Russia – and certainly will on leaving – if you can't produce it.

ℹ Getting There & Away

AIR

International flights land and take off from Moscow's three airports – **Domodedovo** (Домодедово; ☑ 495-933 6666; www.domodedovo.ru), **Sheremetyevo** (Шереметьево; ☑ 495-578 6565; www.svo.aero) and **Vnukovo**

ESSENTIAL FOOD & DRINK

Russia's rich black soil provides an abundance of grains and vegetables used in a wonderful range of breads, salads, appetisers and soups. Its waterways yield a unique range of fish and, as with any cold-climate country, there's a great love of fat-loaded dishes – Russia is no place to go on a diet!

Soups For example, the lemony, meat *solyanka* or the hearty fish *ukha*.

Bliny (pancakes) Served with *ikra* (caviar) or *tvorog* (cottage cheese).

Salads A wide variety usually slathered in mayonnaise, including the chopped potato Olivier.

Pelmeni (dumplings) Stuffed with meat and eaten with sour cream and vinegar.

Central Asian dishes Try *plov* (Uzbek pilaf), *shashlyk* (kebab) or *lagman* (noodles).

Vodka The quintessential Russian tipple.

Kvas A refreshing, beer-like drink, or the red berry juice mix *mors*.

(Внуково; ☑ 495-937 5555; www.vnukovo. ru) – and St Petersburg's **Pulkovo** (LED; ☑ 812-337 3822; www.pulkovoairport.ru) airport. International flights to Kaliningrad's **Khrabrovo** (☑ 4012-610 620; www.kgd.aero) airport are rarer.

LAND

Russia has excellent train and bus connections with the rest of Europe. However, many routes connecting St Petersburg and Moscow with points west – including Kaliningrad – go through Belarus, for which you'll need a transit visa. Buses are the best way to get from St Petersburg to Tallinn. St Petersburg to Helsinki can be done by bus or train.

Adjoining 13 countries, the Russian Federation has a huge number of border crossings. From Eastern Europe you are most likely to enter from Finland near Vyborg; from Estonia at Narva; from Latvia at Rēzekne; from Belarus at Krasnoye or Ezjaryshcha; and from Ukraine at Chernihiv. You can enter Kaliningrad from Lithuania and Poland at any of seven border posts, but visa-free arrangements are limited to the two checkpoints on the Polish border.

SEA

Between early April and late September, international passenger ferries connect Stockholm and Tallinn with St Petersburg's **Morskoy Vokzal** (Морской вокзал; pl Morskoy Slavy 1).

❶ Getting Around

Getting around Russia is a breeze thanks to a splendid train network and a packed schedule of flights between all major and many minor towns and cities. In the summer months many rivers and lakes are navigable and have cruises and ferry operations. For hops between towns, there are buses, most often *marshrutky* (fixed-route minibuses).

AIR

Safety paranoia associated with Russian airlines is largely a thing of the past. The prime concern these days is the petty nastiness of budget carriers and problems associated with it – delays, cancellations and torturously insufficient legroom.

Major Russian airlines, including Aeroflot (www.aeroflot.com), Rossiya (www.rossiya-airlines.com), S7 Airlines (www.s7.ru), Ural Airlines (www.uralairlines.com), UTAir (www.utair.ru) and the new budget airline Pobeda (wwww.pobeda.aero), have online booking, with the usual discounts for advance purchases. Otherwise, it's no problem buying a ticket at ubiquitous *aviakassa* (ticket offices), which may be able to tell you about flights that you can't easily find out about online overseas. Online agencies specialising in Russian air tickets with English interfaces include **Anywayanyday** (☑ 8-800 775 7753; www. anywayanyday.com), www.onetwotrip.ru and www.tickets.ru. Skyscanner.ru is a great aggregator that compares prices on different sites.

Whenever you book airline tickets in Russia you'll need to show your passport and visa. Tickets can also be purchased at the airport right up to the departure of the flight and sometimes even if the city centre office says that the plane is full. Return fares are usually double the one-way fares.

Most internal flights in Moscow use either Domodedovo or Vnukovo airports; if you're connecting to Moscow's Sheremetyevo international airport, allow a few hours to cross town (at least three hours if you need to go by taxi, rather than train and metro). Small town airports offer facilities similar to the average bus shelter.

BUS

Long-distance buses tend to complement rather than compete with the rail network. They generally serve areas with no railway or routes on which trains are slow, infrequent or overloaded.

Most cities have an intercity bus station (автовокзал; *avtovokzal*). Tickets are sold at the station or on the bus. Fares are normally listed on the timetable and posted on a wall.

Marshrutky (a Russian diminutive form of *marshrutnoye taksi*, meaning a fixed-route taxi) are minibuses that are sometimes quicker than larger buses and rarely cost much more.

CAR & MOTORCYCLE

Bearing in mind erratic road quality, lack of adequate signposting and fine-seeking highway police officers, driving in Russia can be a challenge. But if you've a sense of humour, patience and a decent vehicle, it's an adventurous way to go. That said, both road quality and driving culture have improved a great deal in the last decade, so driving has become much more pleasant than previously.

You can bring your own vehicle into Russia, but expect delays, bureaucracy and the attention of the roundly hated GIBDD (traffic police), who take particular delight in stopping foreign cars for document checks.

To enter Russia with a vehicle you will need a valid International Driving Permit as well as the insurance and ownership documents for your car.

As you don't really need a car to get around big cities, hiring a car comes into its own for making trips out of town where public transport may not be so good. All the major agencies have offices in Moscow and St Petersburg.

Driving is on the right-hand side, and at an intersection traffic coming from the right generally (but not always) has the right of way. The maximum legal blood-alcohol content is 0.03%, a rule that is strictly enforced.

TAXI

Normal yellow taxis, which one could hail in the street and which used meters, disappeared after the fall of communism. The taxi situation was a pain until a few years ago, when Uber and its competitors, such as Gett and Yandex Taxi, made cabs much more affordable and easy to use.

Elsewhere, taxis are ordered by phone, which is usually advertised on branded cabs, so you can find one by simply standing still and watching the traffic for five minutes. But English-speaking operators are rare.

It's less common these days, but it's still possible to flag down a taxi, or just a random driver whose owner needs some extra cash, in the street. Check with locals to determine the average taxi fare in that city at the time of your visit; taxi prices around the country vary widely.

TRAIN

Russia's extensive train network is efficiently run by **Russian Railways** (РЖД; ☑ 8-800 775 0000; www.rzd.ru). High-speed trains connect Moscow with St Petersburg in the west and Nizny Novgorod (via Vladimir) in the east. Slower sleeper trains service other long-distance lines around the country.

There are a number of options on where to buy, including online from RZD. Bookings open 45 days before the date of departure. You'd be wise to buy well in advance over the busy summer months and holiday periods such as New Year and early May, when securing berths at short notice on certain trains can be difficult.

For long-distance trains, unless otherwise specified we quote 2nd-class sleeper *(kupe)* fares. Expect 1st-class (SV) fares to be double this, and 3rd class *(platskartny)* to be about 40% less. Children under five travel free if they share a berth with an adult; otherwise, children under 10 pay a reduced fare for their own berth.

You'll need your passport (or a photocopy) to buy tickets. You can buy tickets for others if you bring their passports or photocopies. Queues can be very long and move with interminable slowness. At train ticket offices ('*Zh/D kassa*', short for '*zheleznodorozhnaya kassa*'), which are all over most cities, you can pay a surcharge of around R200 and avoid the queues. Alternatively, most travel agencies will organise the reservation and delivery of train tickets for a substantial mark-up.

Prigorodny (suburban) or short-distance trains – also known as *elektrichky* – do not require advance booking: you can buy your ticket at the *prigorodny poezd kassa* (suburban train ticket offices) at train stations.

Serbia

Best Places to Eat

➡ Lorenzo & Kakalamba (p978)

➡ Radost Fina Kuhinjica (p978)

➡ Fish i Zeleniš (p984)

➡ Čarda Aqua Doria (p984)

Best Places to Stay

➡ Yugodom (p977)

➡ Narrator (p984)

➡ Varad Inn (p984)

➡ Hostelche (p975)

Why Go?

Warm, welcoming and a hell of a lot of fun – everything you never heard about Serbia (Србија) is true. Exuding a feisty mix of élan and *inat* (Serbian trait of rebellious defiance), this country doesn't do 'mild': Belgrade is one of the world's wildest party destinations, Novi Sad hosts the rocking EXIT festival, and even its hospitality is emphatic – expect to be greeted with *rakija* (fruit brandy) and a hearty three-kiss hello.

While political correctness is as commonplace as a non-smoking bar, Serbia is nevertheless a cultural crucible: the art nouveau town of Subotica revels in its proximity to Hungary, bohemian Niš echoes to the clip-clop of Roma horse carts, and minaret-studded Novi Pazar nudges some of the most sacred sites in Serbian Orthodoxy. For something truly wild, head to the stunningly scenic Tara, Djerdap and Fruška Gora National Parks.

Forget what you think you know: come and say *zdravo* (hello)...or better yet, *živeli* (cheers)!

When to Go
Belgrade

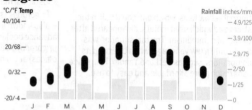

Apr Watch winter melt away with a scenic ride on the nostalgic Šargan 8 railway.

Jul & Aug Rock out at Novi Sad's EXIT, go wild at Guča and get jazzy at Nišville.

Dec–Mar Head to Tara National Park and Zlatibor for alpine adventure.

Serbia Highlights

① **Kalemegdan Citadel**
(p974) Soaking up Belgrade's
bloody, bawdy history at this
formidable fortress.

② **EXIT Festival** (p984)
Joining thousands of
party people for beats and
bacchanalia in Novi Sad.

③ **Tara National Park**
(p981) Hiking, biking or

paddling around this slice of
Serbia. Watch out for bears!

④ **Mokra Gora** (p985)
Escaping reality in the
village of Drvengrad and on a
whimsical Šargan 8 train ride.

⑤ **Guča Festival** (p972)
Steeling your eardrums (and
liver) at this frenetic music
festival.

⑥ **Fruška Gora National Park**
(p983) Rambling the ranges
of this gentle region studded
with ancient monasteries and
ancestral vineyards.

⑦ **Niš** (p985) Getting a
Balkan-flavoured taste of old
Rome at the birthplace of
Constantine the Great.

BELGRADE БЕОГРАД

☑ 011 / POP 1.6 MILLION

Outspoken, adventurous, proud and audacious: Belgrade is by no means a 'pretty' capital, but its gritty exuberance makes it one of the most happening cities in Europe. While it hurtles towards a brighter future, its chaotic past unfolds before your eyes: socialist blocks are squeezed between art nouveau masterpieces, and remnants of the Habsburg legacy contrast with Ottoman relics.

It's here where the Sava River meets the Danube, contemplative parkland nudges hectic urban sprawl, and old-world culture gives way to new-world nightlife.

Grandiose coffee houses and smoky dives all find their rightful place along Knez Mihailova, a lively pedestrian boulevard flanked by historical buildings all the way to the ancient Kalemegdan Citadel, crown of the city. The old riverside Savamala quarter has gone from ruin to resurrection, and is the city's creative headquarters. Deeper in Belgrade's bowels are museums guarding the cultural, religious and military heritage of the country.

'Belgrade' literally translates as 'White City', but Serbia's colourful capital is red hot.

⊙ Sights & Activities

★ **Kalemegdan Citadel** FORTRESS
(Kalemegdanska tvrđava; www.beogradskatvrdjava. co.rs) FREE Some 115 battles have been fought over imposing, impressive Kalemegdan; the citadel was destroyed more than 40 times throughout the centuries. Fortifications began in Celtic times, and the Romans extended

---

ITINERARIES

One Week

Revel in three days of cultural and culinary exploration in Belgrade, allowing for at least one night of hitting the capital's legendary nightspots. Carry on to Novi Sad for trips to the vineyards and monasteries of Fruška Gora National Park and Sremski Karlovci.

Two Weeks

Follow the above itinerary, then head north for the art nouveau architecture of Subotica, before either slicing southwest to Tara National Park en route to traditional Serbian villages, or southeast via Djerdap National Park to lively Niš.

---

it onto the flood plains during the settlement of 'Singidunum', Belgrade's Roman name. Much of what stands today is the product of 18th-century Austro-Hungarian and Turkish reconstructions. The fort's bloody history, discernible despite today's plethora of jolly cafes and funfairs, only makes Kalemegdan all the more fascinating. Kalemegdan is littered with museums, monuments and absorbing architecture. Must-sees include the **Military Museum** (www.muzej.mod.gov.rs; adult/child 150/70DIN; ⊙10am-5pm Tue-Sun), **Gunpowder Magazine** (200DIN; ⊙11am-7pm), **Nebojša Tower** (200DIN; ⊙11am-7pm Wed-Sun) and the creepy, mysterious **Roman Well** (120DIN; ⊙11am-7pm).

★ **Museum of Yugoslav History** MUSEUM
(www.mij.rs; Botićeva 6; incl Maršal Tito's Grave 400DIN; ⊙10am-8pm Tue-Sun May-Oct, to 6pm Nov-Apr) This must-visit museum houses an invaluable collection of more than 200,000 artefacts representing the fascinating, tumultuous history of Yugoslavia. Photographs, artworks, historical documents, films, weapons, priceless treasure; it's all here. It can be a lot to take in; English-speaking guides are available if booked in advance via email, or you can join a free tour on weekends (11am and noon).

Tito's Mausoleum is also on the museum grounds; admission is included in the ticket price.

Take trolleybus 40 or 41 at the south end of Parliament on Kneza Miloša. It's the second stop after turning into Bul Mira: ask the driver to let you out at Kuća Cveća.

Zepter Museum GALLERY
(☑ 011 328 3339; www.zeptermuseum.rs/; Knez Mihailova 42; 200DIN; ⊙10am-8pm Tue, Wed, Fri & Sun, noon-10pm Thu & Sat) This impressive collection of works by contemporary Serbian artists became Serbia's first private museum in 2010, but remains somewhat hidden even though it's housed in a magnificent 1920s building in the heart of pedestrianised Knez Mihailova. The interior's eclectic design is a perfect backdrop to the broad range of styles on display. The permanent collection is a great introduction to the main trends in Serbian art from the second half of the 20th century. The museum also hosts temporary exhibitions and other events.

★ **Nikola Tesla Museum** MUSEUM
(www.nikolateslamuseum.org; Krunska 51; admission incl guided tour in English 500DIN; ⊙10am-6pm Tue-Sun) Meet the man on the 100DIN note at

BELGRADE'S HISTORIC 'HOODS

Skadarska or 'Skadarlija' is Belgrade's Montmartre. This cobblestoned strip east of Trg Republike was the bohemian heartland at the turn of the 20th century; local artistes and dapper types still gather in its legion of cute restaurants and cafes.

Savamala, cool-Belgrade's destination du jour, stretches along the Sava down ul Karadjordjeva. Constructed in the 1830s for Belgrade's smart set, the neighbourhood now houses cultural centres, ramshackle, photogenic architecture, nightspots and a buzzing vibe.

Dorćol, an Ottoman-era multicultural marketplace, is now dotted with mega-hip sidewalk cafes, boutiques and cocktail bars.

Zemun, 6km northwest of central Belgrade, was the most southerly point of the Austro-Hungarian Empire when the Turks ruled Belgrade. These days it's known for its fish restaurants and quaint, non-urban ambience.

one of Belgrade's best museums, where you can release your inner nerd with some wondrously sci-fi-ish interactive elements. Tesla's ashes are kept here in a glowing, golden orb: debate has been raging for years between the museum (and its secular supporters) and the church as to whether the remains should be moved to Sveti Sava Temple.

Royal Compound
PALACE

(☑ 011 2635 622; www.royalfamily.org; Bul Kneza Aleksandra Karađorđevića, Dedinje; 450DIN; ⊘ 11am & 2pm Sat & Sun Apr-Oct) The Royal and White Palaces (1929 and 1937, respectively) were residences of King Peter II and used by the communist regime after WWII; today, they're home to the descendants of the Karađorđević dynasty. The white-marble Royal Palace's most impressive rooms include the fresco-covered Entrance Hall and the baroque Blue Drawing Room. The classicist White Palace houses a notable art collection and a vast basement (with a wine cellar, billiards room and cinema) featuring scenes from Serbian national mythology. Bookings essential.

Sveti Sava Temple
CHURCH

(www.hramsvetogsave.com; Svetog Save; ⊘ 7am-7pm) **FREE** Sveti Sava is the Balkans' biggest (and the world's second-biggest) Orthodox church, a fact made entirely obvious when looking at the city skyline from a distance or standing under its dome. The church is built on the site where the Turks apparently burnt relics of St Sava. Work on the interior (frequently interrupted by wars) continues today.

Ada Ciganlija
BEACH

(www.adaciganlija.rs) In summertime, join the hordes of sea-starved locals (up to 250,000 a day) for sun and fun at this artificial island on the Sava. Cool down with a swim, kayak

or windsurf after a leap from the 55m bungee tower. Take bus 52 or 53 from Zeleni Venac.

National Museum
MUSEUM

(Narodni Muzej; www.narodnimuzej.rs; Trg Republike 1a; adult/child 200/100DIN; ⊘ 10am-5pm Tue-Wed & Fri, noon-8pm Thu & Sat, 10am-2pm Sun) Trg Republike (Republic Sq), a meeting point and outdoor exhibition space, is home to the National Museum. Lack of funding for renovations has kept it mostly shuttered for more than 10 years, though some exhibitions are occasionally open to the public. Some of its collections are available for viewing in other museums around town, including the **Historical Museum of Serbia** (Istorijski Muzej Srbije; www.imus.org.rs; Trg Nikole Pašića 11; 200DIN; ⊘ noon-8pm Tue-Sun) and the **Gallery of the Natural History Museum** (www.nhmbeo. rs; Kalemegdan Citadel; adult/child 100/80DIN; ⊘ 10am-9pm Tue-Sun summer, to 5pm winter).

Yugotour
DRIVING

(☑ 066 900 8386; http://yugotour.com/; per person €45; ⊘ from 11am daily) Yugotour is a mini road trip through the history of Yugoslavia and the life of its president Tito. Belgrade's communist years are brought to life in the icon of Yugo-nostalgia: a Yugo car! Tours are led by young locals happy to share their own perceptions of Yugoslavia; they take in the communist-era architecture of New Belgrade, the Museum of Yugoslav History and Tito's mausoleum, among other locations.

🛏 Sleeping

★ Hostelche
HOSTEL €

(☑ 011 263 7793; www.hostelchehostel.com; Kralja Petra 8; dm from €10, private r from €25; ﹡🔊) A bend-over-backwards staff, homey atmosphere, free walking tours and a super

Central Belgrade

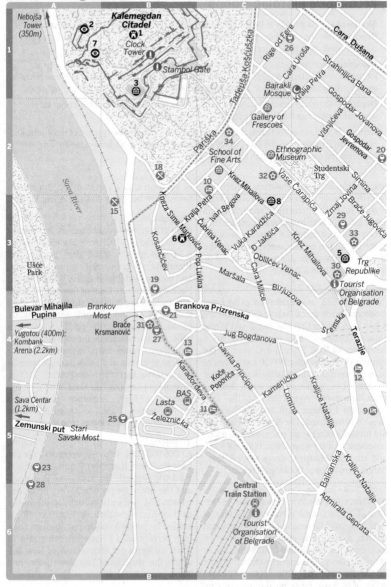

Neboйša Tower (350m)

Kalemegdan Citadel

Clock Tower

Stambol Gate

Rige od Fere

Cara Dušana

Cara Uroša

Strahinjića Bana

Bajrakli Mosque

Kralja Petra

Gospodar Jovanova

Gallery of Frescoes

Višnjićeva

Gospodar Jevremova

Ethnographic Museum

Studentski Trg

Simina

School of Fine Arts

Knez Mihailova

Vase Čarapića

Zmaj Jovina

Braće Jugovića

Pariška

Kneza Sime Markovića

Kralja Petra

Ivan Begova

Čubrina Venac

Vuka Karadžića

Đ Jakšića

Knez Mihailova

Trg Republike

Kosančićev

Pop Lukina

Oblićev Venac

Cara Mince

Birjuzova

Tourist Organisation of Belgrade

Ušće Park

Sava River

Bulevar Mihajila Pupina

Brankov Most

Brankova Prizrenska

Sremska

Terazije

Yugotou (400m); Kombank Arena (2.2km)

Braće Krsmanović

Jug Bogdanova

Karađorđeva

Gavrila Principa

Koče Popovića

Kamenička

Lomina

Kraljice Natalije

Sava Centar (1.2km)

BAS

Lasta

Železnička

Balkanska

Kraljice Natalije

Zemunski put

Stari Savski Most

Central Train Station

Tourist Organisation of Belgrade

Admirala Geprata

---

location make this award-winner popular for all the right reasons. There is also a branch in **Smederevo** (☏064 984 3861; www.hostelchehostel.com/SD; Beogradski put 88, Smederevo; dm/r from €6/20).

★ Hostel Bongo
HOSTEL €

(☏011 268 5515; www.hostelbongo.com; ul Terazije 36; dm/d from €20/34; ❄ ☎) Guests at the modern, brightly painted Bongo can take their pick: plunge into the tonne of attractions, bars and restaurants nearby, or hide from it all in

brilliant B&B is all early 1900s charm out the front, nouveau-Savamala graffiti-murals out the back. As hip as you'd expect from its location in Belgrade's coolest quarter, the digs here are furnished with a mix of period furniture and the work of up-and-coming Belgrade designers. It's close to the city's main sights, and there are tonnes of happening bars and restaurants within staggering distance.

Hotel Bristol   HISTORIC HOTEL €€

(☑ 011 262 2128; www.vudedinje.mod.gov.rs; Karađorđeva 50, Savamala; s 2947-3467DIN, d/tr 4624/6561DIN, day rate d 1728DIN; 🛜) If slick service and shiny spaces are your bag, don't even think about dropping yours here. But if you revel in retro ramshackelry, this Savamala icon is for you. The delightfully unrenovated hotel hosts an eclectic crowd here for the cheap (drab) rooms, in-the-thick-of-it location and a surprisingly good restaurant. The bar is a great spot for drinks with eccentric locals. Built in 1912 and run by an army agency, the Bristol was once a haven for the rich and famous, including the Rockefeller and British royal families. Day rates (10am to 6pm) available.

★**Yugodom**   GUESTHOUSE €€€

(☑ 065 984 6366; www.yugodom.com; Strahinjica Bana 80; r €80; ✳) This remarkable, evocative guesthouse offers more than a comfortable and stylish place to sleep; it's also a vessel for time travel. Billed as a 'stayover museum', Yugodom (*dom* means 'house' in Serbian) is decked out with gorgeous art and furnishings from the Tito era (though you'll find all the mod cons and self-catering facilities you need disguised among the retro trappings).

The location is as impeccable as the surrounds; smack in the middle of Dorćol and across the road from Bajloni farmers market.

★**Hotel Moskva**   HISTORIC HOTEL €€€

(Hotel Moscow; ☑ 011 364 2069; www.hotelmoskva. rs; Terazije 20; s/d/ste from €129/139/210; ✳🛜) Art nouveau icon and proud symbol of the best of Belgrade, the Moskva has been wowing guests – including Albert Einstein, Indira Gandhi and Alfred Hitchcock – since 1906. Laden with ye olde glamour, this is the place to write your memoirs at a big old desk.

✖ Eating

★**To Je To**   BALKAN €

(bul Despota Stefana 21; mains 220-800DIN; ☺ 8am-midnight) 'To je to' means 'that's it', and in this case, they're talking about meat.

the hostel's sweet garden terrace. Fantastic staff with oodles of hostelling experience.

★**Savamala Bed & Breakfast**   B&B €€

(☑ 011 406 0264; www.savamalahotel.rs; Kraljevića Marka 6, Savamala; s/d from €38/50; ✳🛜) This

Central Belgrade

Piles of the stuff, grilled in all its juicy glory, make up the menu here in the forms of Sarajevo-style *ćevapi* (spicy skinless sausages), turkey kebab, sweetbreads and more. It serves homemade *sarma* (stuffed cabbage rolls) on the weekends. Cheap, scrumptious and highly recommended by locals.

★**Radost Fina Kuhinjica**   VEGETARIAN €€
(☑060 603 0023; www.facebook.com/Radost-FinaKuhinjica; Pariska 3; mains 420-1240DIN; ⊙2pm-midnight Tue-Sat, 1-9pm Sun; ☑) Barbecue-obsessed Serbia isn't the easiest place for vegetarians, but thanks to this cheery eatery, you'll never have to settle for eating garnish and chips again. Its ever-changing menu features curries, veg burgers, innovative pastas and meat substitutes galore, some of which are vegan. The healthy cupcakes are a delight.

Dva Jelena   SERBIAN €€
(Two Deer; ☑011 723 4885; www.dvajelena.rs; Skadarska 32; mains 620-1650DIN; ⊙11am-1am) A local icon, Dva Jelena has been dishing up hearty fare for over 180 years. Rustic, homespun and with the obligatory violin serenades, it ticks all the Skadarlija boxes.

★**Little Bay**   EUROPEAN €€
(www.littlebay.rs; Dositejeva 9a; mains 595-1390DIN; ⊙11am-1am) Little wonder locals and visitors have long been singing the praises of this gem: it's one of the most interesting dining experiences in Belgrade. Tuck yourself into a private opera box and let any of the meaty treats melt in your mouth as a live opera singer does wonderful things to your ears. It does a traditional English roast lunch (795DIN) on Sundays.

★**Lorenzo & Kakalamba**   INTERNATIONAL €€€
(☑011 329 5351; www.lk.rs; Cvijićeva 110; mains 900-1950DIN; ⊙noon-midnight) Covered from floor to ceiling in a riot of out-there artworks and marvellous miscellany, and staffed (and frequented) by peculiar characters, to step inside here is to fall down the rabbit-hole to Wonderland. The food is as much of a masterpiece as the interior, with an extensive menu split between Italian (the handmade pastas are to die for) and southern Serbian cuisines; the starters alone are worth a trip.

★**Ambar**   BALKAN €€€
(☑011 328 6637; www.ambarrestaurant.com; Beton Hala; mains 510-3300DIN; ⊙10am-2am) Traditional Balkan cuisine has been given a contemporary spin at this chic spot; even the *pljeskavica* (hamburger) gets the five-star treatment. Service is helpful and attentive; put your meal choices in the hands of the staff and you won't be disappointed. Ambar is one of many upmarket restaurants in Beton Hala, a once-derelict concrete warehouse overlooking the Sava.

🍷 **Drinking & Nightlife**

Bars

⭐ **Blaznavac**   BAR
(www.facebook.com/blaznavac; Kneginje Ljubice 18, Dorćol; ⊙9am-1am) Part cafe, part bar, part wonderfully wacko gallery, this pocket-sized place is one of the city's best spots for pre-drink drinks. Plastered in murals and quirky collectables, it's used as an exhibition space for young Belgrade artists; it also hosts live music and spoken-word events. Blaznavac's appeal isn't limited to night-time jams and cocktails; it also makes a mean coffee, and is a great spot for a snack.

⭐ **Kafana Pavle Korčagin**   TAVERNA
(📞011 240 1980; www.kafanapavlekorcagin.rs; Ćirila i Metodija 2a; ⊙7.30am-1am Mon-Fri, 10am-1am Sat, 11am-11.30pm Sun) Raise a glass to Tito at this frantic, festive *kafana* (tavern). Lined with communist memorabilia and packed to the rafters with revellers and grinning accordionists, this table-thumping throwback fills up nightly; reserve a table via the website.

Dvorištance   BAR
(www.facebook.com/klub.dvoristance; Cetinjska 15; ⊙9am-midnight Sun-Thu, to 1am Fri & Sat) Whimsical little Dvorištance is a rainbow-bright cafe by day, absolute ripper of a bar/performance space by night. It regularly hosts live gigs and alternative/indie DJ parties.

Rakia Bar   BAR
(www.rakiabar.com; Dobračina 5, Dorćol; ⊙9am-midnight Sun-Thu, to 1am Fri & Sat) An ideal spot for *rakija* rookies to get their first taste of the spirit of Serbia. English-speaking staff will gently guide you through the extensive drinks menu, but beware: this stuff is strong.

Miners Pub   PUB
(www.miners-pub.com; Rige od Fere 16, Dorćol; ⊙2pm-midnight Sun-Thu, to 1am Fri-Sun) With a huge assortment of craft beers, cool art on the walls, rock'n'roll on the stereo and a pinball machine, this little place is a gem of a hang-out. Happy hour daily (2pm to 7pm).

Nightclubs

Belgrade has a reputation as one of the world's top party cities, with a wild club scene limited only by imagination and hours in the day. Many clubs move to river barges in summertime.

⭐ **Kenozoik**   CLUB
(www.facebook.com/kenozoik.beograd; Cetinjska 15; ⊙8pm-2am winter) Housed within an abandoned brewery, Kenozoik is Cetinjska 15's cool-culture HQ, with live music, diverse DJ sets, movie screenings and art exhibitions drawing a more alternative crowd than the flashier Belgrade beats. You've got to be 23 and up to enter.

Kenozoik is a winter club; come summer, it moves the party to the **Favela** (www.facebook.com/favela.beograd; Ušće bb; ⊙6pm-late summer) river barge.

Drugstore   CLUB
(www.facebook.com/drugstore.beograd; Bul Despota Stefana 115; ⊙11pm-late Fri & Sat) This cavernous space – formerly a slaughterhouse – can hold up to 1000 people, and its wild popularity means that it often does. Playing techno, underground house and genre-defying tunes to an avant-garde crowd, Drugstore's industrial-arty vibe is an intriguing blend of Belgrade and Berlin.

ESSENTIAL FOOD & DRINK

Serbia is famous for grilled meats; regional cuisines range from spicy Hungarian goulash in Vojvodina to Turkish kebabs in Novi Pazar. Vegetarians should try asking for *posna hrana* ('meatless food'); this is also suitable for vegans.

Kajmak Along the lines of a salty clotted cream, this dairy delight is lashed on to everything from bread to burgers.

Ćevapčići The ubiquitous skinless sausage and *pljeskavica* (spicy hamburger) make it very easy to be a carnivore in Serbia.

Burek Flaky meat, cheese or vegetable pie eaten with yoghurt.

Karađorđeva šnicla Similar to chicken Kiev, but with veal or pork and lashings of *kajmak* and tartar.

Rakija Distilled spirit most commonly made from plums. Treat with caution: this ain't your grandpa's brandy.

Plastic
CLUB

(www.klubplastic.rs; cnr Dalmatinska & Takovska; ◉10pm-6am Wed-Sat Oct-May) A perennial favourite among electro-heads and booty shakers, this slick venue is frequented by top local and international DJs. The more intimate Mint Club is within Plastic.

River Barges

Belgrade is famous for its Sava and Danube river-barge clubs, known collectively as *splavovi*. Most are open only in summer.

The Sava boasts a 1.5km strip of *splavovi* on its west bank: these are the true wild-and-crazy party boats. Walk over Brankov Most or catch tram 7, 9 or 11 from the city.

Adjacent to Hotel Jugoslavija in Novi Belgrade, the 1km strip of Danube barges are a bit more sophisticated; many are restaurants that get their dancing shoes on later in the evening. Take bus 704 or 706 from Zeleni Venac and get out by Hotel Jugoslavija.

★ Povetarac
RIVER BARGE

(Brodarska bb, Sava River; ◉11pm-late) This rusting cargo ship attracts a fun indie crowd for its eclectic playlist, cheap drinks and exceedingly welcoming atmosphere. Open year-round (8pm to late winter).

★ Blek Panters
RIVER BARGE

(Crni Panteri; Ada Ciganlija bb; ◉8pm-late Wed-Mon) If wild, reeling Balkan music floats your boat, make your way to this legendary *splav*

for an unforgettable night of dancing and drinking. Run by the Roma band that gives the club its name, this is one of Belgrade's most famous nightspots. The party gets into full swing about midnight. Open year-round.

Freestyler
RIVER BARGE

(www.freestyler.rs; Brodarska bb, Sava River; ◉midnight-6am) Freestyler has been a symbol of *splav* saturnalia for years, not least for its infamous foam parties.

☆ Entertainment

For concert and theatre tickets, go to Bilet Servis (☑0900 110 011; www.eventim.rs; Trg Republike 5; ◉10am-8pm Mon-Fri, noon-8pm Sat). Large venues for visiting acts include Sava Centar (☑011 220 6060; www.savacentar.net; Milentija Popovića 9; ◉box office 10am-8pm Mon-Fri, to 3pm Sat) and Kombank Arena (☑011 220 2222; www.kombankarena.rs; Bul Arsenija Čarnojevića 58; ◉box office 10am-8pm Mon-Fri, to 3pm Sat).

Mikser House
CULTURAL CENTRE

(www.house.mikser.rs; Žorža Klemansoa, IMK Building; ◉noon-midnight) Innovative, outré and hip as hell, Mikser House is Belgrade's creative hub. Located in an industrial-chic complex in Dorćol, it has a shop, artistic workspaces, a cafe and galleries showcasing the talents of local designers; come nighttime, it morphs into a bar, restaurant and music venue hosting live acts and DJs from Serbia and around the world.

THE SAVAMALA SCENE

The once-derelict, now-dapper Savamala creative district is Belgrade's hip HQ, with bars, clubs and cultural centres that morph into achingly cool music/dance venues come sundown. Dress codes and attitudes are far more relaxed here than in other parts of the city; music-wise, indie, electro, rock and '90s disco are the go. Don't let the bedraggled buildings fool you; there's magic going down inside. Some happening haunts:

KC Grad (www.gradbeograd.eu; Braće Krsmanović 4, Savamala; ◉noon-midnight Mon-Thu, to 2am Fri & Sat, 2pm-midnight Sun) This wonderful warehouse space promotes local creativity with workshops, exhibitions, a restaurant and nightly avant-garde music events.

Brankow (www.facebook.com/brankow; Crnogorska 12, Savamala; ◉11.30pm-5am winter) This uber-urbane winter club inside one of the pillars of Brankov Most (bridge) attracts a trendy crowd for its miscellany of music and sophisticated surrounds. In summer, the party moves to Lasta (www.facebook.com/LastaGradskiSplav; Hercegovačka bb, Savamalski kej; ◉11pm-5am Thu-Sat, 6pm-3am Sun) – Belgrade's first city-side *splav* (river-barge nightclubs).

Bašta (www.jazzbasta.com; Karadjordjeva 43, Savamala; ◉5pm-1am Mon-Thu, noon-2am Fri-Sun) Hidden in an old building with a whimsical courtyard, creative cocktails and frequent live jazz, Bašta is so very Savamala.

Mladost i Ludost (www.mladost-ludost.com; Karadjordjeva 44, Savamala; ◉9pm-6am) These two bars are within the same building; punters hepped up on old-school DJ tunes criss-cross between them at their leisure.

GO WILD: TARA & DJERDAP NATIONAL PARKS

Serbia's cities offer fun, festivals and possibly the nattiest nightlife in Europe. But if you need a breather from bacchanalia, two spectacular national parks offer fresh-air fun in droves.

The sprawling **Djerdap National Park** (636 sq km) is home to one of Serbia's 'seven wonders', the awe-inspiring **Iron Gates gorge** (*Djerdapska klisura*). Its formidable cliffs – some of which soar over 500m – dip and dive for 100km along the Danube to form a natural border with Romania. Though the Iron Gates presented a rugged barrier to trade and travel – hence the name – the hulking **Golubac Fortress** (Tvrđava Golubački Grad), ancient settlement of **Lepenski Vir** (www.lepenski-vir.org; adult/child 400/250DIN; ⊗9am-8pm) and **Tabula Traiana** (a water-level plaque commemorating an AD 103 Roman bridge across the Danube) are testimony to old-time tenacity.

With 220 sq km of forested slopes, dramatic ravines, jewel-like waterways and rewarding views, **Tara National Park** is scenic Serbia at its best. Pressed up against – and affording gorgeous glimpses into – Bosnia and Herzegovina, this western wonderland attracts both adventurers eager for escapism and exploration. The park's main attraction is the vertigo-inducing **Drina River canyon**, the third-largest of its kind in the world. The gloriously green river of the same name slices through its cliffs, offering prime panoramas and ripper rafting; Tara's two artificial lakes – **Perućac** and **Zaovine** – are ideal for calm-water kayaking.

National Theatre
THEATRE

(⌨011 262 0946; www.narodnopozoriste.rs; Trg Republike; ⊗box office 11am-3pm & 5pm-performance time) This glorious 1869 building hosts operas, dramas and ballets during autumn, winter and spring.

Bitef Art Cafe
LIVE MUSIC

(www.bitefartcafe.rs; Mitropolita Petra 8; ⊗9am-4am) There's something for everyone at this delightful hotchpotch of a cafe-club. Funk, soul and jazz get a good airing, as do rock, world music and classical. In summer, Bitef moves its stage to Kalemegdan Fortress.

Cultural Centre of Belgrade
ARTS CENTRE

(Kulturni Centar Beograda, KCB; www.kcb.org.rs; Trg Republike 5) The KCB hosts a miscellany of alternative events, including art-house film screenings, exhibitions, experimental music concerts and various hip happenings.

Madlenianum
Opera & Theatre
OPERA, THEATRE

(⌨box office 011 316 2797; www.operatheatremadlenianum.com; Glavna 32, Zemun) The first private opera house in southeastern Europe hosts regular musicals, plays, ballets and – of course – operas. Be sure to book ahead, as this intimate venue (maximum capacity 524) often sells out.

Kolarac University Concert Hall
LIVE MUSIC

(⌨011 2630 550; www.kolarac.rs; Studentski Trg 5; ⊗box office 10am-2.30pm & 3-8.30pm Mon-Fri,

10am-2pm Sat, plus 6-8pm for weekend concerts) The hall is home to the Belgrade Philharmonica; other classical music performances are also held here. A gallery, bookshop and cinema are also on-site.

Yugoslav Cinematheque
CINEMA

(⌨011 3286 723; www.kinoteka.org.rs; Uzun Mirkova 1; ⊗hours vary) The Yugoslav Cinematheque's impressive and recently renovated building across from the Ethnographic Museum screens everything from the classics of world cinema to art-house productions and cult Yugoslav-era movies. There are also regular screenings in its other building in Kosovska street. Check the website for the current program.

ℹ Information

TOURIST INFORMATION

Tourist Organisation of Belgrade (www.tob. rs) has locations at **Trg Republike 5** (⌨011 263 5622; Trg Republike 5; ⊗9am-9pm Mon-Sat, 10am-3pm Sun), the **train station** (⌨011 361 2732; Train Station; ⊗7am-8pm Mon-Fri, 7am-2.30pm Sat & Sun) and **Nikola Tesla Airport**. You will find helpful folk with a raft of brochures, city maps and all the info you could need.

WEBSITES

Belgrade Cat (www.belgradecat.com)
Belgrade My Way (www.belgrademyway.com)
Lonely Planet (www.lonelyplanet.com/serbia/belgrade)

ℹ Getting There & Away

BUS

Belgrade has two adjacent bus stations, near the eastern banks of the Sava River: **BAS** (Central Bus Station; ☏ 011 263 6299; www.bas.rs; Železnička 4) and **Lasta** (☏ 011 334 8555, freecall 0800 334 334; www.lasta.rs; Železnička 2). Buses run from both to international and Serbian destinations. Sample daily routes include Belgrade to Sarajevo (2585DIN, eight hours, three daily), Ljubljana (4300DIN, 7½ hours, two daily), Priština (3075DIN, seven hours, six daily) and Vienna (4430DIN, nine hours, two daily); frequent domestic services include Subotica (800DIN, three hours), Novi Sad (570DIN, one hour), Niš (1240DIN, three hours) and Novi Pazar (1470DIN, three hours).

CAR & MOTORCYCLE

There are many rental car offices at Nikola Tesla Airport, including **Budget** (☏ 011 228 6361; www.budget.rs; ⊙ 6am-11pm), **Avis** (☏ 011 209 7062; www.avis.com; ⊙ 7am-11pm Mon-Fri, 8am-10pm Sat & Sun) and **Avaco** (☏ 011 243 3797; www.avaco.rs; ⊙ 9am-9am). See www.beg.aero/en for a full list of agencies.

TRAIN

The **central train station** (Savski Trg 2) has an information office on Platform 1, tourist information office, **exchange bureau** (⊙ 6am-10pm) and **sales counter** (Savski Trg 2; ⊙ 24hr).

Frequent trains go to Novi Sad (288DIN, 1½ hours, hourly), Subotica (560DIN, three hours, at least five daily) and Niš (784DIN, four hours, at least five daily). International destinations include Bar (2954DIN, 11½ hours, two daily), Budapest (1846DIN, eight hours, four daily) and Zagreb (2338DIN, seven hours, two daily). See www.serbianrailways.com for updated timetables and fares.

ℹ Getting Around

TO/FROM THE AIRPORT

Nikola Tesla Airport (☏ 011 209 4444; www.beg.aero) is 18km from Belgrade. Local bus 72 (89DIN to 150DIN, half-hourly, 4.50am to midnight from airport, 4am to 11.40pm from town) connects the airport with Zeleni Venac; the cheapest tickets must be purchased from news stands. A minibus also runs between the airport and the central Slavija Sq (300DIN, 5am to 3.50am from the airport, 4.20am to 3.20am from the square).

Don't get swallowed up by the airport taxi shark pit. Head to the taxi information desk (near baggage claim area); they'll give you a taxi receipt with the name of your destination and the fare price. A taxi from the airport to Knez Mihailova should be around 1800DIN.

CAR & MOTORCYCLE

Parking in Belgrade is regulated by three parking zones – red (one hour, 56DIN), yellow (two hours, 48DIN per hour) and green (three hours, 41DIN per hour). Tickets must be bought from kiosks or via SMS (in Serbian).

PUBLIC TRANSPORT

Trams and trolleybuses ply limited routes but buses chug all over town. Rechargeable BusPlus cards can be bought and topped up (89DIN per ticket) at kiosks across the city; they're 150DIN if you buy from the driver.

Tram 2 connects Kalemegdan Citadel with Trg Slavija, bus stations and the central train station.

Zemun is a 45-minute walk from central Belgrade (across Brankov Most, along Nikole Tesle and the Kej Oslobođenja waterside walkway). Alternatively, take bus 15 or 84 from Zeleni Venac market, or bus 83 or 78 from the main train station.

TAXI

Move away from obvious taxi traps and flag down a distinctly labelled cruising cab, or get a local to call you one. Flagfall is 170DIN; reputable cabs should charge about 70DIN per kilometre. Make absolutely sure the meter is turned on.

VOJVODINA ВОЈВОДИНА

Home to more than 25 ethnic groups, six languages and the best of Hungarian and Serbian traditions, Vojvodina's pancake plains mask a diversity unheard of in the rest of the country. Affable capital Novi Sad hosts the eclectic EXIT festival – the largest in southeast Europe – while the hilly region of Fruška Gora keeps the noise down in hushed monasteries and ancestral vineyards. Charming Subotica, 10km from Hungary, is an oasis of art nouveau delights. Compact and well linked by good roads, the region's tranquil nature, mellow villages and unhurried vibe make Vojvodina an ideal slow-travel destination.

Novi Sad Нови Сад

☏ 021 / POP 250,440

As convivial as a *rakija* toast – and at times just as carousing – Novi Sad is a chipper town with all the spoils and none of the stress of the big smoke. Locals sprawl in pretty parks and outdoor cafes, and laneway bars on pedestrian thoroughfare, Zmaj Jovina, which stretches from the town square (Trg Slobode) to Dunavska street, pack out nightly.

SREM DISTRICT

Nicknamed 'the jewel of Serbia', **Fruška Gora** is an 80km stretch of rolling hills where cloistered life has endured since monasteries were built between the 15th and 18th centuries to safeguard Serbian culture and religion from the Turks. Of the 35 original monasteries, 16 remain, and they're open to visitors. Fruška Gora is also famous for its small but select wineries; grapes were first planted here in AD 3 by the Roman Emperor Probus.

The park is an easy 11km drive (20 to 30 minutes) from Novi Sad. If you're relying on public transport, catch a bus in Novi Sad bound for Irig (175DIN, 40 minutes) and ask to be let out at the **Novo Hopovo Monastery** (Irig; ⊙9am-5pm). From here, walk or catch local buses to other points such as Vrdnik and Iriški Venac.

At the edge of Fruška Gora on the banks of the Danube is the photogenic village of **Sremski Karlovci**. It's lined with stunning structures like the **St Nicholas Orthodox cathedral** (1758–62), the working **Karlovci Orthodox Theological Seminary** (1794) – the second of its kind in the world – and the magnificent **Four Lions fountain**; the round yellow **Chapel of Peace** at the southern end of town is where the Turks and Austrians signed the 1699 Peace Treaty. Sremski Karlovci is also at the heart of a famed wine region and hosts a **grape harvesting festival** in late September. Visit the **Museum of Beekeeping & Wine Cellar** (☑021 881 071; www.muzejzivanovic.com; Mitropolita Stratimirovića 86) to try famous *bermet* wine, or drop in at any of the family-owned cellars around town. Take frequent buses 60, 61 or 62 from Novi Sad (145DIN, 30 minutes) and visit the tourist organisation just off the main square.

Sremska Mitrovica, in the western corner of Srem, was once Sirmium, one of the Roman Empire's four capitals and, at its peak, one of the largest cities in the world. You can visit what remains of old Rome at the **Sirmium Imperial Palace Complex** (☑022 621 568; www.carskapalata.rs; Pivarska 2, Sremska Mitrovica; adult/child 150/100DIN; ⊙9am-5pm), a 50km drive from Sremski Karlovci.

Novi Sad is 2019's European Youth Capital, and in 2021 it will become the first non-EU city to spend a year with the prestigious title of European Capital of Culture.

⊙ Sights

⭐**Petrovaradin Citadel**　　　FORTRESS
(Tvrdjava) Towering over the river on a 40m-high volcanic slab, this mighty citadel is aptly nicknamed 'Gibraltar on the Danube'. Constructed with slave labour between 1692 and 1780, its dungeons have held notable prisoners including Karađorđe (leader of the first uprising against the Turks and founder of a royal dynasty) and Tito. Have a good gawk at the iconic clock tower: the size of the minute and hour hands are reversed so far-flung fisherfolk can tell the time.

Within the citadel walls, a **museum** (Muzej Grada Novog Sada; ☑021 6433 145; www.museumns.rs; 150DIN; ⊙9am-5pm Tue-Sun) offers insight into the site's history. The museum can also arrange tours (in English; 500DIN per person) of Petrovaradin's 16km of creepy, but cool, unlit underground tunnels known locally as *katakombe*. While their official use was for military purposes, rumours abound of mysterious treasure troves, tunnel-dwelling reptiles and still-roaming ghosts.

Petrovaradin hosts Novi Sad's wildly popular EXIT Festival each July.

⭐**Gallery of Matica Srpska**　　MUSEUM
(www.galerijamaticesrpske.rs; Trg Galerija 1; 100DIN; ⊙10am-6pm Tue-Thu & Sat, noon-8pm Fri) First established in Pest (part of modern Budapest) in 1826 and moved to Novi Sad in 1864, this is one of Serbia's most important and long-standing cultural institutions. It's not a mere gallery, but rather a national treasure, with three floors covering priceless Serbian artworks from the 18th, 19th and 20th centuries in styles ranging from Byzantine to the baroque, with countless icons, portraits, landscapes and early graphic art (and more) in between.

Museum of Vojvodina　　　MUSEUM
(Muzej Vojvodine; www.muzejvojvodine.org.rs; Dunavska 35-7; 200DIN, free Sun; ⊙9am-7pm Tue-Fri, 10am-6pm Sat & Sun) This museum houses historical, archaeological and ethnological exhibits. Building 35 covers Vojvodinian history from Palaeolithic times to the late 19th century. Building 37 takes the story to 1945 with a harrowing emphasis on WWI and WWII.

Štrand   BEACH

(50DIN) One of Europe's best by-the-Danube beaches, this 700m-long stretch morphs into a city of its own come summertime, with bars, stalls and all manner of recreational diversions attracting thousands of sun- and fun-seekers from across the globe. It's also the ultimate Novi Sad party venue, hosting everything from local punk gigs to EXIT raves.

It's also great for kids (watch them by the water: the currents here are strong), with playgrounds, trampolines and dozens of ice-cream and fast-food stalls.

✦✦ Festivals & Events

The Petrovaradin Citadel is stormed by thousands of revellers each July during the epic **EXIT Festival** (www.exitfest.org; ⊘ Jul). The first festival in 2000 lasted 100 days and galvanised a generation of young Serbs against the Milošević regime. The festival has been attended by the likes of Chemical Brothers, Gogol Bordello and Patti Smith...and an annual tally of about 200,000 merrymakers.

🛏 Sleeping

★ Varad Inn   HOSTEL €

(⌨ 021 431 400; www.varadinn.com; Štrosmajerova 16, Petrovaradin; dm €10-13, r €30; ✳ 🛜) Sitting in the shadow of Petrovaradin Fortress, this excellent budget option is housed in a gorgeous yellow baroque-style building constructed in 1714. Completely renovated but making beautiful use of salvaged historical bits and bobs, the Varad Inn (get it?) has beautiful feel-at-home rooms (all with their own bathrooms, lockers and towels), a lovely garden cafe and communal kitchen.

★ Narrator   APARTMENT €€

(⌨ 060 6767 886; www.en.narator.rs; Dunavska 17; apt from €30; ✳ 🛜) The super-central designer digs at Narrator do indeed tell a story; eight of them, in fact, one for every themed, individually decorated apartment. With names like 'The Chambermaid from Eden', 'The Bookworm' and 'Captain Honeymoon', each room's tale unfolds via a series of exquisite, original naive-style portraits scattered across the walls. All apartments are self-contained.

★ Hotel Veliki   HOTEL €€

(⌨ 021 4723 840; www.hotelvelikinovisad.com; Nikole Pašića 24; s/d €34/50, apt from €69; P✳🛜) Sitting atop an absolutely stupendous Vojvodinian restaurant of the same name, the Veliki ('Big') lives up to its name: some of the rooms are truly huge. Staff are delightful, and the location, around the corner from Zmaj Jovina, is top-notch. Bonus: free breakfast downstairs!

🍴 Eating

★ Fish i Zeleniš   MEDITERRANEAN €€

(Fish and Greens; ⌨ 021 452 000; www.fishizelenis. com; Skerlićeva 2; mains 690-1740DIN; ⊘ noon-midnight; 🍴) This bright, snug little nook serves up the finest vegetarian/pescatarian meals in northern Serbia (don't fret, meat lovers – there's plenty here for you, too). Organic, locally sourced ingredients? Ambient? Ineffably delicious? Tick, tick, tick. A three-minute walk from Zmaj Jovina.

Alla Lanterna   ITALIAN €€

(www.allalanterna.rs; Dunavska 27; pizzas from 600DIN, mains 500-1400DIN; ⊘ 8am-midnight) Come for the toothsome pastas, pizzas and Italian-influenced mains, stay for the jaw-dropping decor; thousands of polished pebbles and tiles have been meticulously arranged into psychedelic swirling patterns that run from the vaulted ceiling to the polished floorboards.

★ Čarda Aqua Doria   SEAFOOD €€€

(⌨ 021 6430 949; www.carda.rs; Petrovaradin Fortress; mains 560-1700DIN; ⊘ 8am-midnight) All

---

MADNESS, MADE IN SERBIA

On the surface, the **Dragačevo Trumpet Assembly** (an annual gathering of brass musicians) sounds harmless; nerdily endearing even. But band camp this ain't: it *is*, however, the most boisterous music festival in all of Europe, if not the world.

Known simply as 'Guča', after the western Serbian village that has hosted it each August since 1961, the four-day debauch is hedonism at its most rambunctious: tens of thousands of beer-and-brass-addled visitors dance wild *kola* (fast-paced circle dances) through the streets, gorging on spit-meat and slapping dinar on the sweaty foreheads of the (mostly Roma) *trubači* performers. See www.guca.rs for information on accommodation and transport.

ZLATIBOR

Zlatibor is a romantic region of gentle mountains, traditions and hospitality. It's also a popular skiing destination. Quirky adventures await in the village of Mokra Gora. There's the mini-village of Drvengrad (Küstendorf; www.mecavnik.info; Mećavnik hill, Mokra Gora; adult/child 250/100DIN; ⊙7am-7pm), built by Serbian director Emir Kusturica for his film *Life is a Miracle*, offering surreal fun and prime panoramas. And there's the joy of a 2½-hour journey on the Šargan 8 railway (☑Mon-Fri 031 510 288, Sat-Sun 031 800 003; www.serbianrailways.com; Mokra Gora; adult/child 600/300DIN; ⊙daily Apr-Oct, by appointment Nov-Mar) tourist train and its disorienting twists, turns and tunnels (all 22 of them).

Reach these sights via bus from Užice or through Zlatibor Tours (☑031 845 957; zlatibortours@gmail.com; Tržni centar, bus station; ⊙8am-10pm).

aboard for romance, river views and rich fish dishes! Bobbing in the shadow of Petrovaradin Fortress, this beautiful barge restaurant is popular with locals looking to splurge on exquisitely prepared *čorba* (fish stew), smoked fish and other Danube delights. Impeccable service, top-notch *rakija* (fruit brandy), sublime views and live *tamburaši* (musicians playing mandolin-like instruments) make meals here utterly memorable.

🍷 Drinking & Nightlife

Laze Telečkog (pedestrian side street running off Zmaj Jovina) is lined with bars to suit every whim. The ramshackle Chinese Quarter (Kineska Četvrt; Bul Despota Stefana) houses Novi Sad's alternative-scene clubs and secret saloons.

★Martha's Pub   BAR
(Laze Telečkog 3; ⊙8am-3am) One of the best in a street of top bars, Martha's is a small, smoky and stupendously sociable den famous for its divine *medovača* (honey brandy). Crowbar yourself inside, or get there early to nab a table outside to watch the party people of Laze Telečkog romp by.

The Quarter   CLUB
(www.facebook.com/ClubQuarter; Bul Despota Stefana 5, Chinese Quarter; ⊙hours vary) Hosting regular exhibitions, live music gigs and all manner of avant-garde performances, the Quarter is also a top spot for a drink and hanging out with the offbeat locals that the Chinese Quarter attracts. Pop next door to Fabrika, the neighbourhood's arty-crew HQ.

Culture Exchange   CAFE
(www.facebook.com/cultureexchangeserbia; Jovana Subotića 21; ⊙9am-11pm; 🛜) Run by well-travelled volunteers, Culture Exchange offers coffees, cakes and pretty much everything else you can imagine: free bike repairs, Serbian

language classes, live music gigs, film screenings and art exhibitions. It's also a top spot for pre-big-night-out drinks. There's nowhere quite like it in town (or indeed, Serbia!).

ℹ️ Information

Novi Sad Greeters (☑021 530 231; www. novisadgreeters.rs)
Tourist Information Centre (www.novisad. travel/en; Jevrejska 10; ⊙9am-5pm Mon-Fri, 10am-3pm Sat)

ℹ️ Getting There & Away

The bus station (Bul Jaše Tomića; ⊙information counter 6am-11pm) has regular departures to Belgrade (570DIN, one hour, every 10 minutes) and Subotica (600DIN, 1½ hours), plus services to Užice (1230DIN, five hours) and Zlatibor (1330DIN, six hours).

From the station, four stops on bus 4 will take you to the town centre: nip down the underpass and you'll see Trg Slobode on emerging.

Frequent trains leave the train station (Bul Jaše Tomića 4), next door to the bus station, for Belgrade (288DIN, 1½ hours) and Subotica (384DIN, 1½ hours). At least four trains go daily to Budapest (1479DIN, 6½ hours).

SOUTH SERBIA

Niš   Ниш
☑018 / POP 183,000

Serbia's third-largest metropolis is a lively city of curious contrasts, where Roma in horse-drawn carriages trot alongside new cars, and posh cocktails are sipped in antiquated alleyways. Niš was settled in pre-Roman times and flourished during the time of local-boy-made-good Emperor Constantine (AD 280–337).

⊙ Sights

Niš Fortress
FORTRESS

(Niška tvrđava; Jadranska; ⊘24hr) Though its current incarnation was built by the Turks in the 18th century, there have been forts on this site since ancient Roman times. Today, it's a sprawling recreational area with restaurants, cafes, market stalls and ample space for moseying. It hosts the **Nišville International Jazz Festival** (www.nisville.com; ⊘Aug) each August and **Nišomnia** (www.facebook.com/festivalnisomnia; ⊘Sep), featuring rock and electro acts, in September. The city's main pedestrian boulevard, Obrenovićeva, stretches before the citadel.

Ćele Kula
MONUMENT

(Tower of Skulls; Bul Zoran Đinđić; 150DIN; ⊘9am-7pm Tue-Fri, to 5pm Sat & Sun) With Serbian defeat imminent at the 1809 Battle of Čegar, the Duke of Resava kamikazed towards the Turkish defences, firing at their gunpowder stores, killing himself, 4000 of his men and 10,000 Turks. The Turks triumphed regardless, and to deter future acts of rebellion, they beheaded, scalped and embedded the skulls of the dead Serbs in this tower. Only 58 of the initial 952 skulls remain. Contrary to Turkish intention, the tower serves as proud testament to Serbian resistance.

Get there on any bus marked 'Niška Banja' from the stop opposite the abandoned Ambassador Hotel: ask to be let out at Ćele Kula.

Medijana
RUINS

(Bul Cara Konstantina; 150DIN; ⊘10am-6pm Tue-Fri, to 3pm Sat & Sun) FREE Medijana is what remains of Constantine the Great's luxurious 4th-century Roman palace. The recently unveiled 1000 sq metres of gorgeous mosaics are the highlight here; they were hidden from public view until protective renovations were completed in 2016. Digging has revealed a palace, a forum, a church and an expansive grain-storage area. There's not much in the way of signage, but knowledgeable staff are on hand to talk visitors through the complex. Medijana is a short walk from Ćele Kula.

Red Cross Concentration Camp
MUSEUM

(Crveni Krst; Bul 12 Februar; 150DIN; ⊘9am-4pm Tue-Fri, 10am-3pm Sat & Sun) One of the best-preserved Nazi camps in Europe, the deceptively named Red Cross held about 30,000 Serbs, Roma, Jews and Partisans during the German occupation of Serbia (1941–45). Harrowing displays tell their stories, and those of the prisoners who attempted to flee in the biggest-ever breakout from a concentration camp. The English-speaking staff are happy to provide translations and explain the exhibits in depth. The camp is a short walk north of the Niš bus station.

🛏 Sleeping

Aurora Hostel
HOSTEL €

(☑018 214 642; www.aurorahostel.rs; Dr Petra Vučinića 16; dm/r from 790/1190DIN; ❋🐾) Set within a 19th-century former Turkish consulate, Aurora offers charm and comfort by the ladle-load. Though the building has been renovated, its wood-heavy interiors and hospitable host are redolent of a more gentle era. Rooms are spic, and there's a good communal kitchen and a lovely garden area.

⭐ ArtLoft Hotel
BOUTIQUE HOTEL €€

(☑018 305 800; www.artloft.rs; Oblačića Rada 8; s/d/ste from €42/55/66; ❋🐾) Central and chic, this designer hotel takes its name literally, with original murals and paintings by local artists dominating every room. The modern feel extends to the professional staff, who take service to the next level by offering friendly assistance, advice and little touches including complimentary fruit and drinks. It's a short stroll from here to Trg Republike and Kopitareva.

🍴 Eating & Drinking

The cobblestoned Kopitareva (Tinkers' Alley) is full of eating and drinking options.

⭐ Hamam
BALKAN €€

(Niš Fortress; mains 520-2400DIN; ⊘8am-midnight) This former Turkish bathhouse once provided respite for weary travellers from Istanbul; today, it welcomes visitors from all over with lashings of Ottoman-influenced treats. The menu is chock-a-block with spicy meats, hearty stews and perennial Balkan classics; its location by the fortress gate makes it a good spot for just a drink and a spot of people-watching as well.

EATING PRICE RANGES

The following price categories are based on the cost of a main course:

€ less than 600DIN

€€ 600DIN–1000DIN

€€€ more than 1000DIN

Saloon Tvrdjava
BAR

(Niš Fortress; ⏲10am-late) As dark and dingy as any self-respecting rock-and-roll bar should be, this fortress bar packs out regularly, especially on nights when there's live music. Escape the crowds (and cigarette smoke) by making a beeline for the beer garden.

❶ Information

Tourist Organisation of Niš (☏018 250 222; www.visitnis.com; Tvrđava; ⏲7.30am-7pm Mon-Fri, 9am-1pm Sat) Helpful info within the citadel gates. There's another branch at Vožda Karađorđa 7 in the city centre.

❶ Getting There & Away

Behind Niš Fortress, the **bus station** (Bul 12 Februar) has frequent services to Belgrade (1240DIN, three hours) and Brus (720DIN, 1½ hours) for Kopaonik, and three daily to Novi Pazar (1200DIN, four hours).

From the **train station** (Dimitrija Tucovića), there are seven trains to Belgrade (784DIN, 4½ hours) and two to Sofia (730DIN, five hours).

Niš Constantine The Great Airport (www. nis-airport.com) is 4km from downtown Niš, serving destinations including Germany, Italy, Slovakia and the Netherlands. Get here on bus 34.

SURVIVAL GUIDE

❶ Directory A–Z

MONEY

Serbia retains the dinar (DIN); though accommodation prices are often quoted in euro, you must pay in dinar.

VISAS

Tourist visas for stays of less than 90 days aren't required by citizens of EU countries, most other European countries, Australia, New Zealand, Canada and the USA. Officially, all visitors must register with the police. Hotels and hostels will do this for you but if you're camping or staying in a private home, you are expected to register within 24 hours of arrival. Unofficially? This is rarely enforced, but being unable to produce

---

SLEEPING PRICE RANGES

The following price categories are based on the cost of a high-season double room:

€ less than 3000DIN

€€ 3000DIN–7000DIN

€€€ more than 7000DIN

COUNTRY FACTS

Area 77,474 sq km

Capital Belgrade

Country Code (☏381

Currency Dinar (DIN)

Emergency Ambulance (☏194, fire (☏193, police (☏192

Language Serbian

Money ATMs in all main and midsized towns

Population 7.13 million

Visas None for citizens of the EU, UK, Australia, New Zealand, Canada and the USA

---

registration documents upon leaving Serbia could result in a fine.

❶ Getting There & Away

AIR

Belgrade's **Nikola Tesla Beograd Airport** (p982) handles most international flights. Serbia's national carrier is Air Serbia (www. airserbia.com).

LAND

Because Serbia does not acknowledge crossing points into Kosovo as international border crossings, it may not be possible to enter Serbia from Kosovo unless you first entered Kosovo from Serbia. Driving Serbian-plated cars into Kosovo isn't advised, and is often not permitted by rental agencies or insurers.

Drivers need International Driving Permits. If you're in your own car, you'll need your vehicle registration, ownership documents and locally valid insurance (such as European Green Card vehicle insurance). Otherwise, border insurance costs about €150 for a car, €95 for a motorbike; www.registracija-vozila.rs has updated price lists.

Bus services to both Western Europe and Turkey are well developed.

International rail connections leaving Serbia originate in Belgrade. For more information, visit **Serbian Railways** (www.serbianrailways.com).

❶ Getting Around

Bus services are extensive, though outside major hubs connections can be sporadic. Reservations are only worthwhile for international buses and during festivals.

Serbian Railways serves Novi Sad, Subotica, Užice and Niš from Belgrade.

Bicycle paths are improving in larger cities.

Slovakia

Best Places to Eat

➡ Vino & Tapas (p997)

➡ Modrá Hviezda (p994)

➡ Republika Východu (p1004)

➡ Med Malina (p1004)

Best Places to Stay

➡ Hotel Marrol's (p993)

➡ Hotel Bankov (p1004)

➡ Penzión Sabato (p997)

➡ Grand Hotel Kempinski (p999)

Why Go?

Right in the heart of Europe, Slovakia is a land of castles and mountains, occasionally interrupted by concrete sprawl. More than two decades after Czechoslovakia's break-up, Slovakia has emerged as a self-assured, independent nation. Capital city Bratislava draws the most visitors, thanks to its excellent nightlife, resplendent old town and sheer ease of access from around Europe. Beyond Bratislava are countless gingerbread-style villages, a clear sign that modern Slovakia still reveres its folk traditions.

Slovakia shines brightest for lovers of the outdoors. The High Tatras are heavenly for walking or winter sports, and national parks like Slovenský Raj sparkle with waterfalls. Castles worthy of a Disney princess perch on hills, and quaint churches speckle the less-discovered east around friendly second city Košice. Within a long weekend in this small country, you can hike or ski epic mountains, blink in astonishment at socialist-era oddities and clink glasses in cellar restaurants.

When to Go
Bratislava

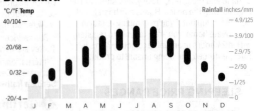

Jun & Jul Cultural festivals amp up, and all hiking trails are open.

Sep & Oct Fewer crowds but clement walking weather, plus festivals galore.

Late Dec–Feb Christmas markets twinkle in Bratislava, skiers flock to Poprad and High Tatras.

BRATISLAVA

🎵 02 / POP 5.45 MILLION

Bratislava doesn't provoke admiring swoons; it intrigues. In the midst of Slovakia's capital, a flying saucer hovers above forest-fringed riverbanks. Its castle presides over a pastel-hued old town, but a concrete jungle looms behind. Despite the march of modernism, Bratislava is green. It banks the Danube River, by the Austrian border, and its hilly parks are threaded with hiking and biking trails. The Male Karpaty (Small Carpathians) roll north, with vineyards in their lowlands.

No wonder Bratislava feels like a frenetic mix of wild and urban, classic and contemporary: it became capital of newly independent Slovakia only in 1993. Bratislava preserved spires and squares from its 18th-century heyday, but now socialist-era monuments (and an eyebrow-raising cast of statues) have joined the party. Speaking of which, Bratislava's nightlife is crowd-pleasing whether you prefer beer halls, rooftop cocktails or stag-party mayhem. In a city this exciting, who needs postcard pretty?

History

First inhabited by Slavs during the 6th century, the earliest mention of Bratislava and its castle was in AD 907. By the 12th century Bratislava (then called Poszony in Hungarian or Pressburg in German) was a large city in greater Hungary. King Matthias Corvinus founded a university here, Academia Istropolitana. Many of the imposing baroque palaces you see date to the reign of Austro-Hungarian empress Maria Theresa (1740–80), when the city flourished. From the 16th-century Turkish occupation of Budapest to the mid-1800s, the Hungarian parliament met locally and monarchs were crowned in St Martin's Cathedral.

'Bratislava' was officially born as the second city of a Czechoslovakian state after WWI and became capital of the new nation of Slovakia in 1993.

⊙ Sights

★ Bratislava Castle CASTLE
(www.snm.sk; grounds free, museum adult/student €7/4; ⊙grounds 9am-9pm, museum 10am-6pm Tue-Sun) Square, a brilliant shade of white and flanked by four stocky towers, bold Bratislava Castle looks as though it has been transplanted straight from a children's picturebook. The fortification's history dates to the 9th century, though today's incarnation is a 1960s rebuild in Renaissance style; the castle had lain in ruins after a fire in 1811. Exhibitions feature a picture gallery, model reconstruction of the castle and Middle Ages history.

Hlavné Námestie SQUARE
The nucleus for Bratislava's history, annual festivals and cheerful cafe culture is Hlavné nám (Main Sq). Roland Fountain (Hlavné nám), at the square's heart, is thought to have been built in 1572 as a public water supply. Flanking the northeast side of the square is the 14th-century Old Town Hall (www.muzeum.bratislava.sk; Primaciálne nám 3; adult/child €6/3; ⊙10am-5pm Tue-Fri, 11am-6pm Sat & Sun), home to the Municipal Museum.

★ St Martin's Cathedral CHURCH
(Dóm sv Martina; http://dom.fara.sk; cnr Kapitulská & Staromestská; ⊙9-11.30am & 1-6pm Mon-Sat, 1.30-4pm Sun May-Sep, until 4pm Mon-Sat Oct-Apr) The crown at the top of St Martin's Cathedral is 300kg of real gold. By comparison, its interior is rather modest, though 19 royal coronations have been held within its 14th-century walls.

SLOVAKIA BRATISLAVA

ITINERARIES

Three Days
Spend three days in Bratislava. It's enough to enjoy the main sights – Bratislava Castle, Hlavné nam, Soviet oddities – and take excursions to Devín Castle and Danubiana Meulensteen Art Museum.

One Week
After three days in Bratislava and its surrounds, venture east to Starý Smokovec for two glorious days of hiking. Press on to dramatic Spiš Castle, then spend a final day or two in culture-packed Košice.

Slovakia Highlights

1 Bratislava (p989)
Strolling from hilltop castles to sci-fi monuments en route to your next cafe or beer stop.

2 High Tatras (p998)
Thundering down ski slopes,

or hiking between huts, in this extraordinary mountainscape.

3 Slovenský Raj National Park (p1002) Clinging to ladders and being splashed by

waterfalls along treks through this dramatic reserve.

4 Spiš Castle (p1002)
Strutting along the ramparts of a 13th-century castle.

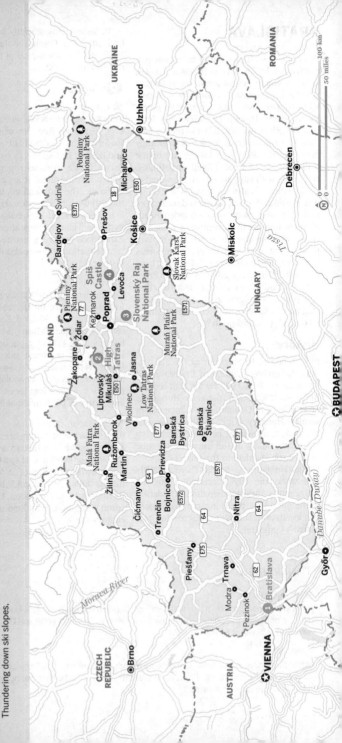

Museum of Jewish Culture MUSEUM
(www.snm.sk; Židovská 17; adult/child €7/2; ☉11am-5pm Sun-Fri) This enriching museum unveils the lives of Bratislava's once-thriving Jewish community through photographs and objects from daily life, with a focus on the impressive Jewish architecture lost both during and after WWII. Most moving are the oil paintings of death marches, created by Jewish survivors of the war, and timelines of the community's destruction by the Nazis.

Blue Church CHURCH
(Kostol Svätej Alžbety; Bezručova 2) The early-20th-century Church of St Elizabeth, known as the Blue Church, unites 50 shades of blue into an art nouveau delight. From the outside you can admire its powder-blue clock tower, glinting sapphire-tinged ceramic roof and columns that look rolled in icing. During the erratic and infrequent opening hours, you can see baby-blue pews and gold decoration.

🏃 Activities

Bratislava Bike Point CYCLING
(☑0944 103 432; www.bratislavabikepoint.com; bike rental per hr/day €6/15; ☉10am-6pm mid-Apr–Sep) Hire a bike from this summer rental outfit beneath the UFO (Most SNP). You can also book an Iron Curtain–themed three-hour bike tour (from €29).

🧭 Tours

★Authentic Slovakia CULTURAL
(☑0908 308 234; www.authenticslovakia.com; per person per 2/4hr tour from €22/32) Always with ribald humour and an eye for the dark side, Authentic Slovakia leads you into Bratislava's seamy history and wacky architecture (usually aboard a retro Škoda car). Want to see 'Bratislava's Beverly Hills', Brutalist cityscapes or drink your way around Devín Castle? You're in safe hands.

🎉 Festivals & Events

Fjúžn CULTURAL
(Festival of Minorities; www.fjuzn.sk; ☉Apr) Concerts, debates and food festivals form the varied program of this annual celebration of Slovak minorities and their cultures.

Bratislava Music Festival MUSIC
(www.bhsfestival.sk; ☉Oct/Nov) One of Slovakia's most important music festivals; international classical music performances take place from October or November.

Christmas Markets CHRISTMAS MARKET
(☉Nov-Dec) From late November, Hlavné and Hviezdoslavovo nám fill with food and drink, crafts for sale and festive performances. Towards the end you can buy a tree or live carp for Christmas dinner (locals keep them in the bath, but we don't recommend it).

🛏 Sleeping

Getting a short-term rental flat in the old town is a great way to stay central without paying hotel prices, plus you can self-cater. Managed by a friendly, family team, **Apartments Bratislava** (☑0918 397 924; www.apartmentsbratislava.com; apt €55-69; ☎) has 12 modern properties in the old-town centre and near the Blue Church.

Hostel Possonium HOSTEL €
(☑02-2072 0007; www.possonium.sk; Šancová 20; dm €9-20, d €40-70; ☎) A friendly traveller bolthole just five minutes' walk from the train station, Possonium has an underground and outdoor bar, as well as well-tended dorm rooms and essentials like a shared kitchen and washing machine. Modern, smooth-running and worth booking in advance. Rates vary by season.

Penzión Portus GUESTHOUSE €
(☑0911 978 026; www.portus.sk; Paulínyho 10; d/tr/q incl breakfast from €40/60/80; ☎) Resisting the encroaching embassies and modern buildings, rose-pink Portus somehow retains its old-timey vibe. Simple rooms roost above a restaurant, in a hard-to-beat location less than 100m south of Hviezdoslavovo nám.

Central Bratislava

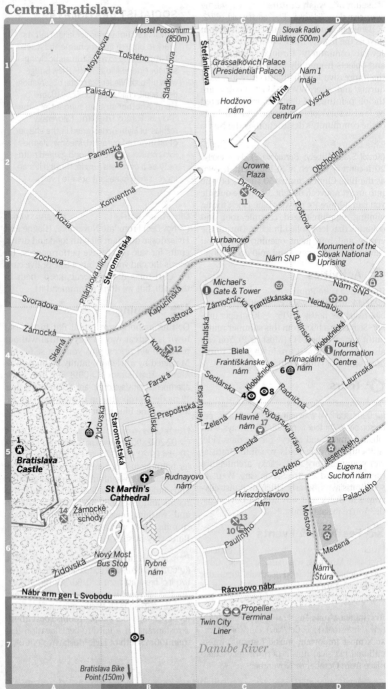

Hostel Possonium
(850m)

Slovak Radio
Building (500m)

Štefánikova

Moyzesova
Tolstého
Palisády

Sládkovičova

Grassalkovich Palace
(Presidential Palace)

Nám 1
mája

Vysoká

Hodžovo
nám

Mýtna

Tatra
centrum

Panenská
16

Crowne
Plaza

Obchodná

Konventná

Drevená
11

Kozia

Hurbanovo
nám

Nám SNP

Monument of the
Slovak National
Uprising

Zochova

Poštová

23

Svoradova

Michael's
Gate & Tower

Nám SNP

20

Zámocká

Kapucínska

Zámočnícka

Františkánska

Nedbalova

Skalná

Baštová

Michalská

Biela

Uršulínska

Klobučnícka

Tourist
Information
Centre

12
Klariská

Františkánske
nám

Primaciálne
6   nám

Laurinská

Farská

Sedlárska

Klobučnícka

4   8

Radničná

Kapitulská

Prepoštská

Ventúrska

Zelená

Hlavné
nám
17

Rybárska brána

1
Bratislava
Castle

7
Židovská

Staromestská

Úzka

Panská

Gorkého

21
Jesenského

Eugena
Suchoň nám

Palackého

St Martin's
Cathedral

2

Rudnayovo
nám

Hviezdoslavovo
nám

Mostová

14   Žámocké
schody

13
10

Paulínyho

22
Medená

Židovská

Nový Most
Bus Stop

Rybné
nám

Nám L
Štúra

Nábr arm gen L Svobodu

Rázusovo nábr

Propeller
Terminal

Twin City
Liner

5

Danube River

Bratislava Bike
Point (150m)

Central Bratislava

Hotel Arcus GUESTHOUSE €€
(☏02-5557 2522; www.hotelarcus.sk; Moskovská 5; s €54-66, d €80-100, tr €109-127, all incl breakfast; P☎) There is a relaxing ambience at this place, tucked away on a residential street. Room sizes vary, but all have a good amount of space, and there's a garden out the back to relax in. Most rooms are doubles but one family room can sleep up to four.

★Hotel Marrol's BOUTIQUE HOTEL €€€
(☏02-5778 4600; www.hotelmarrols.sk; Tobrucká 4; d incl breakfast from €138; P☎☒) Even travellers with aristocratic tastes will raise an approving eyebrow at the art deco furnishings, elegant Jasmine spa (treatments by arrangement) and exemplary service at Marrol's. Rooms are plush, in soft shades of ivory and gold, or you can linger by the fireplace in the lobby bar.

SLOVAKIA BRATISLAVA

✗ Eating

Hviezdoslavovo nám and Laurinská are well-touristed, but have plenty of choice. Set-lunch menus usually offer the best value.

★ **Modrá Hviezda**　　　　　　　SLOVAK €
(📞 0948 703 070; www.modrahviezda.sk; ul Beblavého 14; mains €9-20; ⊙ 11am-11pm) The 'Blue Star' specialises in rich, regally executed Slovak dishes: rabbit in red wine, baked trout, and mangalica pork (from woolly pigs) on a silky purée of chestnuts. Seasonal ingredients inform the changing menu, and the brick-lined cellar space, twinkling with candlelight, feels equal parts romantic and rustic. A must-eat.

Funki Punki　　　　　　　　CRÊPES €
(www.funkipunki.sk; Klariská 12; mains €5; ⊙ 10am-10pm Mon-Fri, noon-10pm Sun; 🚲🐕) Dig in to sweet or savoury crêpes at this bohemian spot with schoolroom seating and pretty murals. Pancakes are stuffed with classic Slovak flavours like bacon and *bryndza* cheese, plenty of veggie options, and tempting sweet chestnut and kiwi, and you can choose the type of batter (including gluten-free buckwheat). Wash it down with a homemade lemonade and drift off to the ethereal soundtrack.

Štúr　　　　　　　　　　　　　CAFE €
(www.sturcafe.sk; Štúrova 8; snacks €4-7; ⊙ 8.30am-10pm Mon-Fri, 9am-10pm Sat, 9am-9pm Sun; 📶🚲🐕) Wonderful coffee, gateaus from coconut sponge to caramel cheesecake, and soups served in a comforting, bookish *kaviareň* (cafe or coffee shop). It's named for L'udovít Štúr, pioneer of the Slovak literary language.

Bratislavský Meštiansky Pivovar　　　　　　　　　SLOVAK €€
(📞 0944 512 265; www.mestianskypivovar.sk; Drevená 8; mains €7-22; ⊙ 11am-midnight Mon-Thu & Sat, to 1am Fri, 11am-11pm Sun; 📶🐕) Continuing Bratislava's 600-year-old brewing tradition, Meštiansky Pivovar offers local and German beers to accompany its menu of Central European stomach liners (sometimes infusing it into the dishes). Within the elegantly vaulted beer hall, choose from trout with bacon, beer and onion goulash, strudels, and moreish snacks from cheese plates to crackling pork.

Lemon Tree　　　THAI, MODERN EUROPEAN €€€
(📞 0948 109 400; www.lemontree.sk; Hviezdoslavovo nám 7; mains €10-20; ⊙ 11am-midnight Mon-Fri, from noon Sat & Sun; 🚲🐕) If panang curry duck followed by poppyseed cake sounds like a match made in heaven, head to this top-end Thai and European restaurant. Thai dishes like green papaya salad and pad thai are beautifully executed, while European flavours like pheasant soup and poached rabbit are just as much of a tastebud adventure.

🍷 Drinking & Nightlife

From mid-April to October, sidewalk cafe tables sprout all over the pedestrian old town. Hviezdoslavovo nám has good options. Admission prices for Bratislava's clubs are usually low (free to €5).

Slovak Pub　　　　　　　　　　PUB
(www.slovakpub.sk; Obchodná 62; ⊙ 10am-midnight Tue-Thu & Sat, to 2am Fri, noon-11pm Sun, 10am-11pm Mon; 📶) Touristy but difficult to resist, Slovak Pub serves every national dish you can think of (mains €3.50 to €11) in a big, wood-walled tavern. Before you get beer goggles, you might even learn something about Slovak culture from wall decorations like knightly regalia, antlers and embroidered folk costumes.

Cork　　　　　　　　　　　　WINE BAR
(www.cork.sk; Panská 4; ⊙ 5pm-midnight Sun-Thu, to 2am Fri & Sat) Lost your taste for beer after too many hoppy nights in Bratislava? This intimate wood-lined wine cellar, with bottles displayed floor to ceiling, offers pan-European wines as a sophisticated alternative.

Nu Spirit Bar　　　　　　　　　BAR
(www.nuspirit.sk; Medená 16; ⊙ 5pm-3am Mon-Sat, to 1am Sun) Deservedly popular cellar bar with regular live music as underground as its location: jazz, reggae, electronica, soul.

Apollon Club　　　　　GAY & LESBIAN
(www.gdisco.sk; Panenská 24; ⊙ 8pm-3am Tue & Thu, to 5am Wed, Fri & Sat) Slovakia's oldest gay club, friendly Apollon has themed nights from disco to karaoke and 'beach parties'.

☆ Entertainment

Check **Kam do Mesta** (www.kamdomesta.sk/bratislavsky-kraj) for the latest.

Slovak National Theatre　　　THEATRE
(Slovenské Národné Divadlo; SND; 📞 02-2047 2299; www.snd.sk; Hviezdoslavovo nám) The national theatre company stages quality operas (Slavic and international), ballets and dramas in two venues: the gilt decoration of the landmark **Historic SND** (📞 box office 02-2049 4290; www.snd.sk; Hviezdoslavovo nám, booking office cnr

SLOVAKIA BRATISLAVA

Jesenského & Komenského; tickets €4-20; ⊘ box office 8am-7pm Mon-Fri, 9am-noon & 2-7pm Sat & Sun, plus 1hr before performances) is a show in itself; the modern New SND (☑02-2047 2111; www. snd.sk; Pribinova 17) has a cafe and guaranteed English-speaking reservation line.

Slovak Philharmonic THEATRE
(www.filharmonia.sk; Eugena Suchoň nám; tickets €5-20; ⊘ 9am-2pm Mon, 1-6pm Tue-Fri & before performances) Neo-baroque Reduta Palace houses the Slovak Philharmonic. Tickets can be reserved online.

Dunaj PERFORMING ARTS
(www.kcdunaj.sk; Nedbalova 3; ⊘ noon-1am Mon-Wed, to 3am Thu, to 4am Fri, 4pm-4am Sat, 4pm-midnight Sun; 🛜) Cultural centre hosting some of Slovakia's most interesting drama and music performances, as well as comedy, club nights, visual arts and the odd literary evening. Something is on almost nightly, plus there is a terrace bar with panoramic old-town views.

🛍 Shopping

Find craft and jewellery stores around Hlavné nám, as well as souvenir booths (fancy a brassiere-themed 'Bra-tislava' T-shirt?). Artisan galleries and antique shops inhabit alleyways off old-town streets.

ÚľuV ARTS & CRAFTS
(Centre for Folk Art Production; www.uluv.sk; Námestie SNP 12; ⊘ 10.30am-6pm Mon-Fri, to 2pm Sat) Shops in Bratislava's old town overflow with mass-produced souvenirs, so ÚľuV's handcrafted folk art is a breath of fresh air. This branch of Slovakia's handicraft cooperative is a delightful place to rummage for pottery jugs, framed pieces of lace, and sheep-shaped money banks, painted by hand.

At the time of research, ÚľuV's **main branch** (www.uluv.sk; Obchodná 64; ⊘ 10.30am-6pm Mon-Fri, to 2pm Sat) in Bratislava was being renovated but was expected to reopen in the near future.

ℹ Information

Most cafes have wi-fi access; Hlavné nám and Hviezdoslavovo nám are free wi-fi zones. Bratislava's old town has banks and ATMs, especially along Poštova. The train and bus stations, and airport, have ATMs/exchange booths.

Main Police Station (☑ 0961 01 1111, emergency 112, emergency 158; Hrobákova 44) Main police station for foreigners, in Petržalka, about 3.5km south of Most SNP.

Main Post Office (Nám SNP 34-35; ⊘ 7am-8pm Mon-Fri, to 6pm Sat) In a beautiful building.

Poliklinika Ruzinov (☑ 02-4827 9111; www. ruzinovskapoliklinika.sk; Ružinovská 10) Hospital with emergency services and 24-hour pharmacy, 3km east of the old town.

Tatra Banka (Dunajská 4; ⊘ 8am-6pm Mon-Fri) English-speaking staff.

Tourist Information Centre (☑ 02-5441 9410; http://visit.bratislava.sk; Klobučnícka 2; ⊘ 9am-7pm Apr-Oct, to 6pm Nov-Mar) Helpful and multilingual official tourist office. Brochures galore, including a small Bratislava guide and maps.

ℹ Getting There & Away

Bratislava is the main hub for trains, buses and the few planes that head in and out of the country.

AIR
Keep in mind that Vienna's much busier international airport is only 60km west.

Bratislava Airport (BTS; ☑ 02-3303 3353; www.bts.aero; Ivanská cesta) A 15km drive northeast of central Bratislava. Direct flights to Dubai, Germany, Greece, Ireland, Italy, Russia, Spain, UK cities and more.

BOAT
From April to October, plying the Danube is a cruisey way to get between Bratislava and Vienna.

Twin City Liner (☑ 0903 610 716; www.twincity liner.com; Propeller Terminal, Rázusovo nábr) Up to four boats daily to Vienna (one way €20 to €35, 1½ hours). You can also book through the office of **Flora Tours** (☑ 02-5443 5803; www. floratour.sk; Kúpelná 6; ⊘ 9am-5pm Mon-Fri).

BUS
Direct destinations include cities throughout Slovakia and Europe, but the train is usually comparably priced and more convenient. The **Bratislava bus station** (Mlynské nivy; 🚌 Autobusová stanica, AS) is 1km east of the old town; locals call it 'Mlynské Nivy' (the street name). For schedules, see cp.atlas.sk.

Eurolines (☑ Bratislava office 02-5556 2195; www.eurolines.sk; Bratislava bus station, Mlynské Nívy) Contact for most international buses with services to Budapest (€12, three to 3¾ hours, two daily) and Vienna (€5, 1¼ hours, four daily). Less-frequent long-distance services operate to Paris (€75, 18¾ hours) and Venice (€55, 10 hours).

Slovak Lines (☑ 02-5542 2734; www.slovak lines.sk; Bratislava bus station, Mlynské Nivy; ⊘ ticket sales 6.30am-6.30pm) Services throughout the country as well as daily buses to Vienna (€5, 1¼ hours, half-hourly), Budapest (€12, three to 3¾ hours, five daily), Prague

WORTH A TRIP

THE VILLAGE TIME FORGOT

The tiny mountain hamlet of **Vlkolínec** (www.vlkolinec.sk; adult/child €2/1; ⊘9am-6pm Mon-Fri, to 7pm Sat & Sun) has an otherworldly atmosphere, somewhere between medieval Europe and a Hobbit village. Vlkolínec, 80km west of Poprad, earned its Unesco listing thanks to 45 traditional buildings. Cottages are painted shades from peach to powder blue, there's an 18th-century timber bell tower, neoclassical Catholic chapel, and dozens of woodcarved sculptures representing village life and folklore.

Vlkolínec opens its doors to visitors but it remains a functioning village (population 19), so don't wander into gardens or photograph through windows.

(€14, 4¼ hours, eight daily) and even occasional services to Clermont-Ferrand in France (€92, 25½ hours).

TRAIN

Rail is the main way to get around Slovakia and to neighbouring countries. Intercity (IC) and Eurocity (EC) trains are quickest. *Ryclík* (R; 'fast' trains) take slightly longer, but run more frequently and cost less. For schedules see cp.atlas.sk.

Domestic trains run to Poprad (€15, 4½ hours, 12 daily, some with changes) and Košice (€19, 5½ hours, eight daily, more with changes).

International trains run to Vienna (return €17.50; includes Vienna city transport, one hour, hourly), Prague (from €15, 4¼ hours, six daily) and Budapest (from €15, 2¾ hours, six daily).

Main Train Station (Hlavná Stanica; www.slovakrail.sk; Franza Liszta nám)

🛈 Getting Around

TO/FROM THE AIRPORT

➡ City bus 61 links Bratislava Airport with the main train station (20 minutes).

➡ Standing taxis (over)charge to town, some as much as an eye-watering €25; ask the price before you get in.

➡ Buses (€5 to €7.50, one hour, 14 daily) connect Vienna International Airport to Bratislava Airport (also stopping at Most SNP); find timetables on www.flixbus.com.

CAR

Numerous international car-hire companies such as Hertz and Sixt have offices at Bratislava Airport.

Abrix (📞0905 405 405; www.abrix.sk; Pestovateľská 1; ⊘8am-6pm Mon-Fri) Rates around €18 to €25 per day for short hires and as low as €16 for 20 days or more.

PUBLIC TRANSPORT

Bratislava has an extensive tram, bus and trolleybus network; though the old town is small, so you won't often need it. **Dopravný Podnik Bratislava** (DPB; www.dpb.sk) is the public transport company; you'll find a route map online. Check www.imhd.zoznam.sk for city-wide schedules.

Tickets cost €0.70/0.90/1.20 for 15/30/60 minutes. Buy at machines next to stops and news stands, and always validate on board (or risk a legally enforceable €50 to €70 fine). Passes start at €3.50/8 for 24/72 hours.

Bus 93 Main train station to Hodžovo nám then Petržalka train station.

Trolleybus 207 Hodžovo nám to Bratislava Castle.

Trolleybus 210 Bratislava bus station to main train station.

TAXI

Standing cabs compulsively overcharge foreigners; an around-town trip should never cost above €10. To save money ask someone to help you order a taxi (not all operators speak English). Uber operates in Bratislava.

AA Euro Taxi (📞0903 807 022, in Slovakia 02-16 022; www.aataxieuro.sk; minimum fare €3.89, per km €1.45)

Around Bratislava

If you don't manage at least a half-day trip out of the city, you're doing Bratislava wrong. **Devín Castle** (www.muzeum.bratislava.sk; adult/child €4/2; ⊘10am-6pm Tue-Fri, to 7pm Sat & Sun May-Sep, to 5pm Tue-Sun Apr-Oct), 9km west, has stood since the 9th century. The castle's name originates from the Slavic *deva* (girl), and its Maiden Watchtower has acquired various legends of tragic young ladies across its long history. Wave at Austria, just across the river from the castle. Bus 29 links Devín with Bratislava's Nový Most bus stop, under Most SNP.

Some 15km south of Bratislava is **Danubiana Meulensteen Art Museum** (www.danubiana.sk; Via Danubia, Čunovo; adult/child €10/5; ⊘11am-7pm Tue-Sun May-Sep, 10am-6pm Tue-Sun Oct-Apr), innovatively designed on a spit of land jutting into the Danube. Boat trips run from the city centre on weekends from May to October (return tickets are adult/child €12/8, including the gallery ticket; see www.lod.sk for details). Otherwise take bus 90 (€1.20) from Nový Most bus stop to Čunovo and walk from the terminus (2.5km).

TATRAS MOUNTAINS

Poprad

☑ 052 / POP 55,000 / ELEV 672M

Gateway to the High Tatras, Poprad is the place to mug up on hiking or skiing information before you head into the wilds. Mountain trails, forests and gorges lie in its surrounds: by road, hike hub Starý Smokovec is 14km north, tranquil lake spot Štrbské Pleso 26km west and Hrabušice (for Slovenský Raj National Park) 15km south.

◉ Sights & Activities

Spišská Sobota   AREA

Renaissance-style merchant houses dating as far back as the 15th century line Spišská Sobota town square, 2km north of Poprad's modern centre, Sv Egídia nám. A 13th-century church and baroque column are planted in the centre, and placards around the square detail each building's links to Hungarian kings and nobles. A worthy ramble.

Adventoura   ADVENTURE SPORTS

(☑ 0903 641 549; www.adventoura.eu) Dog sledding, walking and adventure holidays, ski packages...this energetic outfit can arrange the works. Day rates for private trips around the Tatras and its surroundings begin at around €30 per person. Book at least four weeks ahead of your trip, particularly in the busy summer and winter seasons.

Aqua City   SPA

(☑ 052-785 1111; www.aquacity.sk; Športová 1397; day pass adult/child €22/19, 3hr pass adult/child €19/16; ⊗ 8am-9pm; 🅟) 🏊 Poprad's thermal water park not only has saunas, pools and Mayan-themed outdoor water slides (summer only), it's something of an eco pioneer in Central Europe. Its heat and electricity derive from geothermal and solar sources; knowing this will give you an additional glow as you soak in 30°C to 35°C pools. Book ahead for Thai massage and other treatments.

🛏 Sleeping & Eating

★ Penzión Sabato   B&B €€

(☑ 052-776 9580; www.sabato.sk; Sobotské nám 6; r incl breakfast €60-90; 🅟🛜) Within this peach-coloured mansion, dating to 1730, find eight romantic rooms with billowy drapes, wood-beamed ceilings and handsome Renaissance-era furniture. Each one is different (they're priced by size) and five have fireplaces.

FOLK CULTURE FRENZY

Soak up the best Slovak folk culture at **Východná Folk Festival** (www.festival vychodna.sk/en; Východná; ⊗ late Jun/ early Jul), an extravaganza of music, dance, craft workshops and mountain cuisine. The annual event is one of the largest of its kind in Slovakia, assembling as many as 1400 performers. Expect oversized musical instruments, choirs, wood-chopping, loom demonstrations and more accordions than you've ever seen assembled in one place. Východná is 32km west of Poprad.

★ Vino & Tapas   INTERNATIONAL €€€

(☑ 0918 969 101; Sobotské nám 38; mains €13-15; ⊗ 5-11pm Tue-Sat) Truffled eggs, delicate ravioli, flower-strewn desserts...Vino & Tapas offers an exceptional dining experience in an atmospheric, brick-walled restaurant. Opt for a set menu with amuse-bouche (€39) to savour the best stuff. Phone ahead as it's rightly popular.

ℹ Information

City Information Centre (☑ 052-16 186; www.visitpoprad.sk; Svätého Egídia nám 86; ⊗ 8am-8pm Mon-Fri, 9am-1pm Sat year-round, plus 2-5pm Sun Jun-Sep) Helpful, multilingual visitors centre; also sells stamps.

ℹ Getting There & Away

AIR

Poprad-Tatry International Airport (☑ 052-776 3875; www.airport-poprad.sk; Na Letisko 100), 4km west of town, has links to London, Moscow, Riga, Kyiv and Antalya. There is no public transport to the airport from Poprad town. **Taxis** (☑ 052-772 3623) cost about €4.

BUS

Buses serve Levoča (€1.70, 45 minutes, almost hourly), Bardejov (€4.50, 2½ hours, seven daily, more via Prešov) and Zakopane in Poland (€5.50, two hours, two to four daily mid-June to mid-October).

CAR

Rates from €22 per day are offered by well-established **Car Rental Poprad** (☑ 0903 639 179; http://carrental-poprad.com; Nálepkova 11, Batizovce; ⊗ 8am-6pm Mon-Fri, to 2pm Sat, other times by arrangement).

TRAIN

Poprad is accessible by direct train from Bratislava (€15, 4¾ hours, seven daily) and Košice (€5.30, 1¼ to two hours, at least hourly). Buses also reach Poprad from Košice (€6.90, 2½ hours, five daily), with more services via Prešov.

HIGH TATRAS

 052

The High Tatras (Vysoké Tatry), the tallest range in the Carpathian Mountains, tower over most of Eastern Europe. Some 25 peaks measure above 2500m, but the massif is only 25km wide and 78km long, with pristine snowfields, ultramarine mountain lakes, thundering waterfalls, undulating pine forests and shimmering alpine meadows.

The highest trails are closed because of snow from November to mid-June. June and July can be especially rainy; July and August are the warmest (and most crowded) months.

◉ Sights & Activities

The High Tatras hiking routes are colour-coded, and distances for hikes in Slovak national parks are officially given in hours rather than kilometres. Pick up one of numerous maps and hiking guides from bookshops and information offices.

Many hiking routes criss-cross, or form part of, the 65km-long Tatranská Magistrála. This mighty trail starts at the base of the Western (Západné) Tatras, but mostly runs beneath the peaks (between 1300m and 1800m) of the High Tatras, with mountain hut stop-offs and cable-car/ski-lift access.

◎ Smokovec Resort Towns

If you're looking for an easy access point to half-day hikes, head to Hrebienok (1280m), which is connected by funicular railway to Starý Smokovec. East and west from here, the red Tatranská Magistrála Trail transects the southern slopes of the High Tatras for 65km start to finish. Bilíkova Chata (p999), a log-cabin lodge and restaurant, is a short walk from the funicular railway terminus. Heading west, you can hike along the base of Slavkovsky štít to lakeside Sliezsky dom hotel (red, two hours), then down a small connector trail to the yellow-marked trail back to Starý Smokovec (four hours total). An easy and well-signposted northbound walk-

ing trail (green) leads from Bilíkova Chata to Studený potok waterfalls (Vodopády Studeného Potoka), taking about 30 minutes; 30 additional minutes brings you up to Zamkovského chata hut.

This is also a good base for more adventurous trekkers: mountain climbers scale to the top of Slavkovský štít (2452m) via the blue trail from Starý Smokovec (eight to nine hours return). To ascend the peaks without marked hiking trails (Gerlachovský štít included), you must hire a guide. Contact the Mountain Guide Society (p998): rates for these experienced mountain guides vary according to the length and difficulty of a hike (or ice climb), starting at €175.

◎ Tatranská Lomnica & Around

While in the Tatras, you shouldn't miss the precipitous Lomnický štít Ascent (www.vt.sk; return adult/child €46/30; ☺8.30am-5.30pm Jul & Aug, to 3.30pm Sep-Jun) (bought as a single ticket). Gondolas rise from Lomnica to Štart, where you can change cable cars up to the skiing zone and lake of Skalnaté pleso. Another cable car climbs an additional 855m to Lomnický štít, a perilous 2634m at its summit. There is a high price tag for these majestic views, though this doesn't deter visitors (arrive early, as tickets sell out on sunny days). Timed tickets allow 50 minutes at the summit, enough to take photos, walk the observation platforms, and grab a drink or snack before returning.

Alternatively, at Skalnaté pleso you can change to a quadlift (one way adult/child €19/14, 9am to 4pm) towards Lomnické sedlo, a 2190m saddle below the peak of Lomnický štít.

Štrbské Pleso & Around

Condo and hotel development continue unabated in the village but the namesake clear-blue glacial lake *(pleso)* remains beautiful. Hire row boats (per 40min/1hr €15/25; ☺10am-6pm May-Sep) outside Grand Hotel Kempinski and bob across Slovakia's most postcard-perfect waters.

Sleeping

Wild camping isn't permitted, but there is a camping ground near Tatranská Lomnica. For the quintessential Slovak mountain experience, you can't beat hiking from one *chata* (mountain hut; anything from a shack to a chalet) to the next, high up among the peaks. Food (optional meal service or restaurant) is always available. Beds fill up, so book ahead.

Smokovec Resort Towns

The main road running through Nový Smokovec to Horný Smokovec is lined with places to stay, ranging from no-frills pensions to spa hotels. Starý Smokovec is most convenient (and popular); it's quieter in the towns on either side. Book far in advance for July and August, and for ski season.

Bilíkova Chata HUT€
(☏0949 579 777; www.bilikovachata.sk; Hrebienok 14; r from €46, without bathroom €28, apt from €80; �) A 300m walk from Hrebienok funicular station, this log cabin is basic but its lofty location compensates (1225m), planting you in the heart of hiking trails. There's a restaurant (open 7am to 8pm) serving filling Slovak fare, and there are big low-season discounts.

Villa Siesta SPA HOTEL €€
(☏052-478 0931; www.villasiesta.com; Nový Smokovec 88; s/d/ste €54/81/103; P奎) This contemporary mountain villa is a romantic choice, with 18 airy rooms and a spa featuring a silky hot tub and sauna. The restaurant serves light, seasonally driven Slovak cuisine.

Grand Hotel Starý Smokovec HOTEL €€
(☏044-290 1339; www.grandhotel.sk; Starý Smokovec 38; d incl breakfast from €77; P奎逻) Starý Smokovec's *grande dame* is this 1904 man-

sion with a mountain backdrop. Staff are eager to please, and the rooms retain art deco stylings (the chic deluxe rooms, from €97, are worth a splurge). The pool and wellness area is leafy and warm-hued, and treatments start from a reasonable €15.

Tatranská Lomnica & Around

Look for private rooms *(privat* or *zimmer frei)*, from €15 per person, on the back streets south and east of the train station.

Zamkovského Chata HUT €
(☏0905 554 471, 052-442 2636; www.zamka. sk; per person €19; ☺year-round) Atmospheric wood chalet at 1475m above sea level, with 23 bunk beds and a restaurant with steaming soups and traditional dumplings. A great hike stop midway between Skalnaté Pleso and Hrebienok (it's an hour's hike from the latter). Breakfast is €5 and half board is a reasonable €13.

Grandhotel Praha HOTEL €€
(☏044-290 1338; www.ghpraha.sk; Tatranská Lomnica; d/ste incl breakfast from €81/131; P奎逻) Stepping into this 1905 art nouveau hotel, the indignities of ski-lift queues and mud-spattered hikes melt away. The marble staircase and sparkling chandeliers set the tone. The ample rooms are similarly lavish, with gilt-edged mirrors and burnished wallpaper, and the spa is fragrant with mountain herbs, oils and healing salt lamps.

Štrbské Pleso & Around

★**Grand Hotel Kempinski** HOTEL €€€
(☏052-326 2222; www.kempinski.com/hightatras; Kupelna 6, Štrbské Pleso; d €180-210, ste from €320; P奎@奎逻) Everything you'd expect from this sumptuous hotel chain, with the bonus of dreamy lake views, the Kempinski is Štrbské Pleso's best address. Elegantly furnished rooms have balconies that lean towards lake and spruce forest. Every luxury is here, from a heated indoor pool with chandeliers and mountain views, to the dining room where waiters whisk quinoa risotto and grilled tiger prawns to the tables.

Eating

The resort towns are close enough that it's easy to sleep in one and eat in another. There's at least one grocery store per town.

ℹ️ MULTIRESORT SKI PASSES

Ski areas in Štrbské Pleso, Starý Smokovec and Tatranská Lomnica have joined forces to offer multi-resort lift passes (adult one-/six-day €35/167, child one-/six-day €25/116). They're cheaper outside the late-December to mid-March rush, though snow conditions will be more of a gamble. Small savings are available if you buy online (www.gopass.sk).

🍴 Smokovec Resort Towns

Reštaurácia Svišť SLOVAK €€
(📞 0918 195 811; www.kupelens.sk; Nový Smokovec 30; ⊗ 11am-10pm) Stuffed pancakes, stuffed chicken breasts, stuffed diners. The food in this log-lined haunt will have you full to bursting; fortunately, its traditional decor is worth lingering in while you recover.

Pizzeria La Montanara ITALIAN €€
(Starý Smokovec 22; mains €5-12; ⊗ 11am-10pm) Pizza, lasagne, tiramisu: the holy trinity of carb-loading satisfies many a hiker at this simple Italian joint. It's above a grocery store at the east end of town.

🍴 Štrbské Pleso & Around

⭐ **Koliba Patria** SLOVAK €€
(http://hotelpatria.sk; eastern lakeshore, Štrbské Pleso; mains €8-18; ⊗ 11.30am-10.30pm) On a pretty lakeshore perch with an outdoor terrace, wood-lined Koliba Patria exceeds expectations with refined (though comforting) takes on Slovak shepherd cuisine. Chilled strawberry soup, chicken salads and hulking portions of smoky pork allow for anything from light refreshment to a pre-hike feast.

🍷 Drinking & Nightlife

Humno Tatry BAR
(www.humnotatry.sk; Tatranská Lomnica; ⊗ 11am-11pm Thu, noon-4am Fri & Sat, noon-11pm Sun, closed Mon-Wed) Roll straight from the cable-car station base into this club, diner and cocktail bar, where the sound of clunking ski boots is as loud as the soundtrack within. It's an enormous, wood-beamed temple to après-ski that gets wild at weekends.

U Vlka CAFE
(www.kaviarenacajovnauvlka.sk; Cesta Slobody 4d, Starý Smokovec; ⊗ 9am-9pm) Near Sport 2000 and La Montanara, 'The Wolf' is a ramshackle, hippie-chic hang-out with coffee, snacks and a huge range of teas. Film and cultural events take place in summer; keep an eye on the posters outside.

ℹ️ Information

All three main resort towns have ATMs on the main street.

EMERGENCY

Mountain Rescue Service (📞 052-442 2820, emergency 18 300; www.hzs.sk; Starý Smokovec 23) The website has mountain weather forecasts, while avalanche warnings can be checked on www.laviny.sk.

TOURIST INFORMATION

High Tatras Tourist Trade Association (www.tatryinfo.sk) Lists chalets and other hiking accommodation options, and gives an overview of the region.

T-Ski Travel (📞 052-442 3201; www.slovakiatravel.sk; Starý Smokovec 46; ⊗ 9am-4pm Mon-Thu, to 5pm Fri-Sun) Books lodgings, arranges ski and snowboard instruction, runs mountain-biking programs, and rents wintersports gear.

Tatras Information Office (Tatranská informačná kancelária; 📞 052-442 3440; www.tatry.sk; Starý Smokovec 23; ⊗ 8am-6pm Jan-Mar, to 4pm Apr-Dec) Starý Smokovec information office, with helpful English-speaking staff and vast quantities of brochures.

Tatry.sk (www.tatry.sk) Official website of Tatra towns, with thorough information on accommodation, outdoor activities and transport.

ℹ️ Getting There & Around

To reach the Tatras by public transport, switch in Poprad. From the main train station there, a narrow-gauge electric train runs up to Starý Smokovec, then makes numerous stops in the resort towns along the main road; buses go to smaller, downhill villages as well. Either way, to get between Štrbské Pleso and Tatranská Lomnica, change in Starý Smokovec. Check schedules at cp.atlas.sk.

BUS

The main bus routes from Poprad include to Starý Smokovec (€0.90, 20 minutes, hourly), Tatranská Lomnica (€1.30, 30 minutes, hourly), Štrbské Pleso (€1.70, one hour, four daily) and Ždiar (€2, one hour, seven daily, or change in Kežmarok).

TRAIN

Electric trains (TEŽ) run more or less hourly. Buy individual TEŽ tickets at stations and block tickets at tourist offices. Validate all on board. Bringing bikes on board costs €1.50, large luggage costs €1, but skis and snowboards incur no charge.

Regular trains run from Poprad up to Starý Smokovec (€1.50, 25 minutes). From here reach Tatranská Lomnica (€1,15 minutes) and Štrbské Pleso (€1.50, 40 minutes).

EAST SLOVAKIA

Welcome to Slovakia's untrammelled east. Freethinking Košice, Slovakia's second-largest city, is the prime reason to visit, with waterfall-kissed Slovenský Raj National Park close behind. Combine these with architectural gems like Levoča and Bardejov, and you have one unforgettable road trip.

Levoča

📞 053 / POP 14,800

Levoča's Unesco-listed centre packs centuries of history between its high medieval walls. A Gothic church and fine town hall compete for attention in the main square, Majstra Pavla nám, which is hemmed by burgher mansions with gabled roofs. Presiding over it all is the celestial apparition of the Church of Mariánska Hora, on a hilltop 2km north of town. Take a day trip from Poprad, or stop en route to Spiš Castle, and see what all the fuss is about.

◎ Sights

Majstra Pavla Nám SQUARE
Gothic and Renaissance eye candy abound on Levoča's main square, including the **Historic Town Hall** (📞053-451 2449; Majstra Pavla nám 2; adult/child €4/2; ⊙9am-5pm) and private **Thurzov House**, at No 7, with a characteristically frenetic Spiš Renaissance roofline and turn-of-the-20th-century window decorations.

Church of Mariánska Hora CHURCH
(📞053-451 2347; http://rkc.levoca.sk; Bazilika Panny Márie; ⊙hours vary, services 2.30pm Sun summer; 🅿) Glowing beatifically from a hill 2km north of Levoča, the Church of Mariánska Hora is Slovakia's most famous Catholic pilgrimage site. For hundreds of years on the first Sunday in July, worshippers from around the country have filed towards this church. You can drive up to the church, or it's

a 30-minute hike from town. Just as heavenly as the church itself are the views of Levoča, nestled in the meadowlands beneath.

🛏 Sleeping & Eating

Hotel U Leva HOTEL €
(📞053-450 2311; www.uleva.sk; Majstra Pavla nám 25; s/d/ste incl breakfast €33/43/89; 🅿🐾) Cutting a dapper silhouette in the main square, Levoča's best hotel is spread across two pyramid-roofed buildings. Rooms are painted in warming sunset shades, with rustic accents in the form of wooden beams. Each room is unique, and most suites have a kitchenette. Book ahead for disability-accessible hotel rooms.

U Leva's fine restaurant (mains €6 to €12) muddles Mediterranean flavours among time-honoured Slovak recipes (like chicken stuffed with cheese and pesto, and broccoli soup with almonds).

❶ Information

Everything you're likely to need, banks and post office included, is on the main square.

Tourist Information Office (📞053-451 3763; http://eng.levoca.sk; Majstra Pavla nám 58; ⊙9am-noon & 12.30-5pm)

❶ Getting There & Away

Levoča is on the main E50 motorway between Poprad (25km) and Košice (90km).

BUS

The **bus station** (Železničný riadok 31) is 1km by foot from the main square. Direct services reach Košice (€5, two hours, four daily), Poprad (€2, 45 minutes, every one to two hours), Spišská Nová Ves (€0.90 to €2, up to one hour, half-hourly) and Spišské Podhradie (€1, 30 minutes, one to two per hour).

Spišské Podhradie

📞053 / POP 4000

Spišské Podhradie snoozes contentedly between two Unesco World Heritage sites. Rising above the village is Spiš Castle, the former stomping ground of medieval watchmen and Renaissance nobles. This spellbinding ruin is perched on a rocky ridge, surrounded by verdant meadows, and is likely Slovakia's most-photographed sight. While the castle is unquestionably the main draw, it's worth lingering to see 'Slovakia's Vatican', a Gothic ecclesiastical settlement west of the village.

◉ Sights

★ Spiš Castle   CASTLE
(Spišský hrad; adult/student/child €6/4/3; ☺ 9am-6pm May-Sep, to 4pm Apr & Oct, 10am-4pm Nov, closed Dec-Mar) Crowning a travertine hill above Spišské Podhradie village, this vast castle is one of Slovakia's most impressive medieval fortifications. Spiš Castle spreads over 4 hectares, making it one of the largest in Central Europe. Its bulwarks and thick defensive walls date to the 12th century (at the latest), and once housed Hungarian royals and nobles. Highlights are views from the 22m-high tower, and a museum of medieval history within the former palace.

Spiš Chapter   CATHEDRAL
(Spišská kapitula; Levočská cesta) On the west side of Spišské Podhradie is still-active Spiš Chapter, a 13th-century Catholic complex fondly referred to as 'Slovakia's Vatican'. Encircled by a 16th-century wall, its pièce de résistance is St Martin's Cathedral (1273), towering above a huddle of Gothic houses. If you're travelling by bus from Levoča, get off 1km before Spišské Podhradie, at Kapitula.

⌂ Sleeping & Eating

This is best experienced as a day trip from the High Tatras or Košice.

Penzión Podzámok   GUESTHOUSE €
(☎053-454 1755; www.penzionpodzamok.sk; Podzámková 28; s/d from €18/27; [P][🛜][🐾]) Simple but snug rooms within a homely (though slightly worn) guesthouse. Ceramics and wall-mounted antlers give a farmhouse feel to the attached restaurant, and the view of Spiš Castle from the yard is spectacular. The pool is open in summer. Breakfast is €4.

Spišsky Salaš   SLOVAK €
(☎053-454 1202; http://spisskysalas.sk; Levočská cesta 11; mains from €4; ☺10am-9pm; [📷][🍴]) An almost mandatory refuelling stop before or after Spiš Castle, this folksy dining room (complete with cow bells) hurries plates of *pirohy* (dumplings), lamb stew and barbecued meat to its wooden tables. There is ample outdoor dining space, overlooking a big play area for kids. Informal, with occasionally chaotic service, but satisfying nonetheless.

Spišsky Salaš is 1km northwest of Spiš Chapter, on a hill overlooking the E50 Hwy towards Levoča.

❶ Getting There & Away

Spišské Podhradie is 15km east of Levoča and 78km northwest of Košice.

BUS
Buses connect with Levoča (€1, 20 to 30 minutes, regular), Poprad (€2.35, one hour, one to two hourly) and Košice (€4.30, 1½ hours, four daily, more via Prešov or Levoča).

TRAIN
Spišské Podhradie is connected by bus to Spišské Vlachy (€0.90, 15 minutes, 10 daily), which has direct rail links west to Spišská Nová Ves (for Slovenský Raj) and east to Košice.

Slovenský Raj & Around
🗹 053

You don't simply visit Slovenský Raj National Park. It's more accurate to say that you clamber, scramble and get thoroughly drenched in this dynamic landscape of caves, canyons and waterfalls. Hikers in 'Slovak Paradise' climb ladders over gushing cascades, trek to ruined monasteries and shiver within an ice cave – and that's just on day one.

The park is hugged by the Low Tatras and the Slovak Ore Mountains, with deep gorges sliced by the Hornád River. The nearest major town is Spišská Nová Ves, 23km southeast of Poprad. Closer to the action are the park's three major trailhead villages, each with food and accommodation options: most popular is Podlesok, outside Hrabušice (a 16km drive southeast of Poprad); pretty and low-key Čingov is 5km west of Spišská Nová Ves; and lakeside Dedinky fringes the park's southern edge.

◉ Sights & Activities

Before hiking, pick up VKÚ's 1:25,000 Slovenský Raj hiking map (No 4) or 1:50,000 regional map (No 124). Cycling trails crisscross the park, and swimmers can take a dip in Dedinky. During winter, ski at small resorts like Gugel, which has 5km of pistes and 35km of cross-country trails.

★ Slovenský Raj National Park   PARK
(www.slovenskyraj.sk; Jul & Aug €1.50, Sep-Jun free) In Slovenský Raj, rocky plateaus, hills and primeval forests are interlaced with thrashing streams and waterfalls. This is some of the most thrilling hiking terrain in Slovakia, and not for the timid: treks usually involve

scaling metal ladders or balancing on footbridges over cascades. Aside from the exhilaration of being lashed with crystal water, the rewards are breathtakingly green views. Trails are challenging but well-marked, and multilingual staff at the information centres offer excellent advice.

Dobšinská Ice Cave CAVE
(Dobšinská ľadová jaskyňa; www.ssj.sk; adult/child €8/4; ⊙9am-4pm Tue-Sun by hourly tour late May-Sep, closed Oct–mid-May) More than 110,000 cubic metres of ice are packed into the gleaming walls of this Unesco-listed ice cave, near the southern edge of Slovenský Raj National Park. Frosty stalagmites and chambers where tendrils of ice sparkle from the ceiling create an otherworldly atmosphere. The departure point is a half-hour walk from the car park, so arrive in good time ahead of guided tours (on the hour).

🛏 Sleeping & Eating

Camping grounds and budget guesthouses are good value in these parts, and most are fabulous for families. Many lodgings have restaurants, and there are several eateries and a small grocery store in Podlesok. Spišská Nová Ves has several large supermarkets.

Autocamping Podlesok CAMPGROUND €
(✉053-429 9165; www.podlesok.sk; per adult/child/tent €4/2.50/3, hut from €50; P🐕🐾) The office at this well-located camping ground provides substantial trail info. Pitch a tent or choose from fairly up-to-date two to 12-bed huts and cottages with bathrooms. Book huts well in advance.

★ **Relax Farma Mariánka** GUESTHOUSE €
(✉0905 714 583; www.relaxfarmamarianka.sk; Betlanovce 83; d/tr from €28/38; P🐕🐾🍴) 🍴 The hospitable owners of this big, well-kept eight-room pension can advise you about outdoor activities. Relax in the hot tub, meet the pigs or enjoy Janka's scrumptious organic cooking (breakfast €4). Family-friendly perks include games rooms, a communal kitchen and a sauna (for exhausted parents). From Hrabušice, it's just past the Podlesok turn-off where the road kinks sharp right.

Reštaurácia Rumanka SLOVAK €
(✉0907 289 262; www.podlesok.com; Podlesok; mains €5-8) Enormously popular Rumanka serves enough varieties of *halušky* (dumplings) to satisfy ravenous hikers, as well as

crispy fried *pirohy* (stuffed with mushrooms or meat), pork chops, and sheep's cheese in handy takeaway portions (from €0.95).

❶ Information

Outside Spišská Nová Ves, guesthouses and camping grounds are an excellent source of information. The park info centre is only open in July and August. Get cash before you arrive in the park; there is an ATM and exchange at Spišská Nová Ves train station.

Mountain Rescue Service (✉053-429 7902, emergency 183 00; http://his.hzs.sk) For emergencies in the park.

National Park Information Centre (www.npslovenskyraj.sk; Hlavná, Hrabušice; ⊙7.30am-3pm Mon-Fri, 9.30am-4.30pm Sat & Sun Jul & Aug, closed Sep-Jun) Friendly staff can advise on activities and hiking trails.

❶ Getting There & Around

During low season especially, you may consider hiring a car in Košice; connections to the park can be a chore. You'll have to transfer at least once, usually in Spišská Nová Ves.

BUS

Buses are most frequent in July and August, and services thin out on weekends. Carefully check schedules at cp.atlas.sk.

Buses run from Slovenský Raj's transport hub of Spišska Nová Ves to Poprad (€1.70, 45 minutes, at least hourly Monday to Friday and every one to two hours Saturday and Sunday), sometimes with a change in Spišský Štvrtok. Other buses run from Spisška Nová Ves to Levoča (€0.90 to €2, 30 minutes, hourly) and Čingov (€0.60, 15 minutes, four daily), and there are bus connections to Hrabušice (for Podlesok; €1.10, 30 minutes, six daily) and Dedinky (€2.60, 80 minutes, four daily or change in Poprad).

TRAIN

Trains run from Spisška Nová Ves to Poprad (€1.55, 20 minutes, at least hourly) and Košice (€4, one hour, every one to two hours).

Košice

✉055 / POP 242,000
Equal parts pretty and gritty, Košice lures you with its dazzling historic core but holds your interest with free-spirited nightlife. The pride of Eastern Slovakia's largest city is Hlavná, the central square with the country's largest concentration of historic monuments. Since its tenure as European Capital of Culture 2013, Košice has grown increasingly

SLOVAKIA KOŠICE

confident. The cultural scene continues to bloom in unconventional ways: offbeat bars, Soviet city tours and vegan dining share the limelight with well-established draws like the showstopping Gothic cathedral, philharmonic orchestra and, yes, ice hockey.

⊙ Sights & Activities

★ Cathedral of St Elizabeth CHURCH
(Dóm Sv Alžbety; Hlavné nám; tower adult/child €1.50/1; ⊙1-4pm Mon, 9.30am-4.30pm Tue-Sat) This 14th-century cathedral dominates the main square, resplendent with elaborate tracery, prickly turrets and colourful roof tiles. One of Europe's easternmost Gothic cathedrals, 60m-long St Elizabeth is the largest in the country. Ascend the narrow, circular stone steps up the church's 59m-tall tower for city views.

Hlavné Nám SQUARE
Much of Košice's finery is assembled along Hlavná, a long plaza lined with floral gardens, and flanked with cafes on either side. Stroll past the central musical fountain to hear its hourly chimes, across from the 1899 State Theatre (Štátne divadlo Košice; ☑055-245 2269; Hlavné nám 58). Look for the turn-of-the-20th-century, art nouveau Hotel Slávia at No 63. The 1779 Shire Hall (Župný Dom; Hlavné nám 27), crowned with a coat of arms, is today home to the East Slovak Gallery (☑055-681 7511; www.vsg.sk; Hlavná 27; adult/child full admission €5/3, special exhibitions €2/1; ⊙10am-6pm Tue-Sun).

Hrnčiarska HISTORIC SITE
(Ulička Remesiel; Hrnčiarska) FREE Arts and crafts workshops line quaint Hrnčiarska, such as herbalists, potters and purveyors of precious stones, whose methods haven't changed in 200 years. Some buildings along this cobbled lane have traditional crafts demonstrations, others house arty coffee shops.

★ Authentic Košice CULTURAL
(☑0908 808 848, 0905 848 750; http://authentic kosice.com; per person 2hr tour €23-35, 4hr tour €32-49) Let locals lead you to Košice's less discovered corners. These witty and intriguing tours take in Soviet landmarks, concrete housing estates, factories, breweries and sites of intrigue, usually in a retro Czechoslovak car like a Škoda. Nostalgic snacks are included. Prices depend on group size.

🛏 Sleeping

Košice Hostel HOSTEL €
(☑055-633 5192, 0907 933 462; www.kosice hostel.sk; Jesenského 20; dm €11-13, s/d €22/28; 🅿@🛜) This well-run hostel has clean, airy dorm rooms, a couch-filled common room, shared kitchen and backpacker essentials, like lockers and 24-hour reception.

★ Hotel Bankov HISTORIC HOTEL €€
(☑ext 4 055-632 4522; www.hotelbankov.sk; Dolný Bankov 2; s/d incl breakfast from €59/74; 🅿✳🛜🏊) Effortlessly uniting 19th-century elegance with modern luxuries, Slovakia's oldest hotel (1869) lies 4km northwest of central Košice in a verdant location. Rooms ooze old-world charm (beams, period furniture), and there's an excellent restaurant serving upmarket European fare (pork with figs, oyster mushroom risotto). The wellness centre has an elemental feel, thanks to saunas and treatment chambers lined in stone and wood.

🍴 Eating

★ Republika Východu INTERNATIONAL, CAFE €
(www.republikavychodu.sk; Hlavná 31; mains €5-8; ⊙8am-11pm Mon-Thu, to midnight Fri & Sat, to 10pm Sun; 🛜☑♿) Proudly proclaiming independence from Western Slovakia and indeed anywhere else, Republika Východu (Republic of the East) tempts you with coffees, cakes, health-boosting quinoa salads, avocado on toast and zesty smoothies. The cafe is lined with bookshelves, there's a children's game area, and friendly service welcomes regulars and tourists alike.

Med Malina POLISH, SLOVAK €€
(☑055-622 0397; www.medmalina.sk; Hlavná 81; mains €6-14; ⊙11am-11pm Mon-Sat, to 10pm Sun; ☑) Dumplings with sheep's cheese, duck with potato pancakes, and *bigos* (cabbage and mushroom stew, flavoured with sausage meat): a medley of Polish and Slovak specialities are served with cheer in a simple but homely setting. Worth reserving on weekends.

Karczma Mlyn SLOVAK €€
(☑055-622 0547; www.karczmamlyn.sk; Hlavná 86; mains €7-10; ⊙11am-11pm Mon-Thu, to midnight Fri & Sat, 11.30am-10pm Sun; 🛜) Like dining inside the prettiest of barns, sheepskin rugs and cartwheels surround you, while you settle in on a tree-trunk stool for Goral (mountain) cuisine: plates of buckwheat dumplings with curd cheese, pork steaks and raw cakes. Traditional live music on Friday nights.

Drinking & Entertainment

Nightlife options range from sidewalk cafes and boho wine bars along the main square to beer halls and nightclubs. Browse entertainment listings on www.kamdomesta.sk/kosice.

Retro Cult Club CLUB
(http://retro.cultclub.sk; Kováčska 49; ⊙9pm-2am Mon-Sat, sometimes to 4am) Dance and drink under neon lights and sparkling disco balls at this cocktail bar and club, whose events roam from local DJs to student nights.

Jazz Club CLUB
(www.jazzclub-ke.sk; Kováčska 39; ⊙bar 11.30am-midnight Mon-Fri, 6pm-midnight Sat & Sun, club 9am-4am Tue & Wed-Sat) Part cafe-bar, part nightclub, Jazz Club has something to suit most revellers. It's an appealing mix of medieval-style arches, steampunk brass and wood decor and bright lights. A youthful crowd totters along to student nights and dance parties, or you can stick to the charismatic bar and terrace.

State Philharmonic Košice CLASSICAL MUSIC
(Štátna filharmónia Košice, House of the Arts; ☑ ticket office 055-622 0763; www.sfk.sk; Moyzesova 66; ⊙2-4pm Mon, to 5pm Tue-Thu, plus 1hr before concerts) Jazz, choral and orchestral music fill this concert hall on evenings around the year. Check the events calendar online, or time your Košice trip for the **Spring Music Festival** (www.filharmonia.sk; ⊙mid-Apr) to enjoy a wealth of musical performances.

ℹ Information

Most hotels, cafes and restaurants have free wi-fi. Lots of banks with ATMs are scattered around Hlavné nám.
City Information Centre (☑055-625 8888; www.visitkosice.eu; Hlavná 59; ⊙10am-6pm Mon-Fri, to 3pm Sat & Sun) Offers excellent local advice, and can arrange accommodation, themed city tours (including Jewish history) and more.
Ľudová Banka (Mlynská 29)
Nemocnica Košice-Šaca (☑055-723 4111; www.nemocnicasaca.sk; Lúčna 9, Košice-Šaca) Private healthcare, 12km southwest of central Košice.
Police Station (☑158; Pribinova 6)

ℹ Getting There & Away

Check bus and train schedules at www.cp.atlas.sk.

Košice International Airport (KSC; www.airportkosice.sk; Košice-Barca) is 7km southwest of the city centre by road; bus 23 connects them hourly.

BUS

Buses reach Levoča (€5, two hours, 12 to 14 daily), with many routes requiring a change in Prešov. For Poprad, you'll usually need to switch buses in Prešov or Zvolen. Book ahead for Ukraine-bound buses through **Eurobus** (☑055-680 7306; www.eurobus.sk; Staničné nám 9); services reach Uzhhorod (€7, three hours, twice daily). Getting to Poland is easier from Poprad.

CAR

Several international car-hire companies such as Avis and Eurocar have representatives at the airport.
Buchbinder (☑055-683 2397, 0911 582 200; www.buchbinder.sk; Košice International Airport; ⊙8am-4.30pm Mon-Fri)

TRAIN

Trains from Košice run to Bratislava (€19, five to seven hours, every 1½ hours), Poprad in the High Tatras (€5, 1¼ to two hours, hourly) and Spišská Nová Ves for Slovenský Raj (€3 to €4, one hour, hourly). There are also trains over the border to Miskolc, Hungary (€7, 1½ hours, one to two daily) continuing to Budapest (€15, 3½ hours).

ℹ Getting Around

The old town is small and walkable. Transport tickets (30-/60-minute ticket €0.60/0.70) cover most buses and trams; buy them at news stands and machines and validate as soon as you board. Bus 23 runs between the airport and train station; buy tickets on board for €1.

SURVIVAL GUIDE

ℹ Directory A–Z

Advance booking is advisable in July and August, and in mountain areas during ski season (mid-December through to mid-March). Bratislava has the country's best choice of accommodation, including excellent hostels, though centrally located hotel bargains are hard to find; check out **Bratislava Hotels** (www.bratislavahotels.com). Outside the capital, you'll find plenty of reasonable *penzióny* (guesthouses). Breakfast is usually available (often included) at all lodgings and wi-fi is near ubiquitous. Many lodgings offer nonsmoking rooms. Parking is only a problem in Bratislava.

COUNTRY FACTS

Area 49,035 sq km

Capital Bratislava

Country Code ☎ 00421

Currency Euro (€)

Emergency ☎ 112 (general), ☎ 150 (fire), ☎ 155 (ambulance), ☎ 158 (police)

Language Slovak

Money ATMs widely available in cities

Population 5.45 million

Visas Not required for most visitors staying less than 90 days

INTERNET ACCESS

Wi-fi is widely available at lodgings and cafes across the country; so much so that internet cafes are becoming scarce. For the laptopless, some hotels (especially four-stars) have computers guests can use.

MONEY

➡ In January 2009 Slovakia's legal tender became the euro. Previously, it was the Slovak crown, or Slovenská koruna (Sk).

➡ Slovaks don't tip consistently, but rounding off the bill or leaving an extra 10% is becoming increasingly common (and is often expected of foreign tourists).

POST

For outgoing mail, bank on five working days to reach other parts of Europe and seven for the US/Australia. Post offices are found across Slovakia, including the main post office (p995) in Bratislava.

TELEPHONE

Landline numbers can have either seven or eight digits. Mobile phone numbers (10 digits) are often used for businesses; they start with 09. When dialling from abroad, you need to drop the zero from both city area codes and mobile phone numbers. Purchase local and international phonecards at newsagents. Dial ☎ 00 to call out of Slovakia.

Mobile Phones

Slovakia has very good network coverage and you only need to bring a passport to buy a local SIM card. Major providers include Orange, T-Mobile and O2.

TOURIST INFORMATION

Association of Information Centres of Slovakia (AICES; ☎ 044-551 4541; www.aices.sk) Runs an extensive network of city information centres.

Slovak Tourist Board (http://slovakia.travel/en) The country's overarching tourist resource is online.

VISAS

For a full list of visa requirements, see www.mzv.sk (under 'Consular Info').

➡ No visa is required for EU citizens.

➡ Visitors from Australia, New Zealand, Canada, Japan and the US do not need a visa for up to 90 days.

➡ Visas are required for South African nationals, among others. For the full list see www.slovak-republic.org/visa-embassies.

❶ Getting There & Away

Bratislava and Košice are the country's main entry and exit points by air, road and rail. Poprad is in distant third place. Entering Slovakia from the EU is a breeze. Lengthy customs checks make arriving from Ukraine more tedious.

Bratislava has the most international flights, and well-connected Vienna International Airport is just 60km away. By train from Bratislava, Budapest (2¾ hours) and Prague (4¼ hours) are easily reachable, as is Vienna (one hour). Buses connect to Uzhhorod in Ukraine (three hours) from Košice.

AIR

Bratislava Airport (p995), 9km northeast of the city centre, has direct flights to Dubai, Ireland, Italy, Germany, Greece, Russia, Spain, UK cities and more. Dedicated buses run between Bratislava and **Vienna International Airport** (VIE; ☎ 01-700 722 233; www.viennaairport.com; ☎) in Austria, the nearest big international air hub. A few international routes reach Košice and Poprad.

Airports

Bratislava Airport (p995)

Košice International Airport (p1005)

Poprad-Tatry International Airport (p997)

Airlines

Austrian Airlines (www.austrian.com) Connects Košice with Vienna.

Czech Airlines (www.csa.cz) Flies between Košice, Bratislava and Prague.

LOT (www.lot.com) Flies between Warsaw and Košice.

SLEEPING PRICE RANGES

The following price ranges refer to a double room with bathroom.

€ less than €60

€€ €60–€130

€€€ more than €130

Ryanair (www.ryanair.com) Connects Bratislava with numerous destinations across the UK and Italy, coastal Spain, Dublin, Paris and Brussels.

Wizz Air (http://wizzair.com) Connects Košice to a few UK airports, and Poprad to London Luton.

LAND

Border posts between Slovakia and fellow EU Schengen member states – Czech Republic, Hungary, Poland and Austria – are almost nonexistent. Checks at the Ukrainian border are much more stringent, as you will be entering the EU. By bus or car, expect at least one to two hours' wait.

Bus

Local buses connect Poprad with Poland during the summer season. Eurolines (p995) and Košice-based Eurobus (p1005) handle international routes across Europe from Bratislava and heading east to Ukraine from Košice.

Car & Motorcycle

Private vehicle requirements for driving in Slovakia are vehicle registration papers, proof of third-party liability insurance and a nationality sticker. Vehicles must carry a first-aid kit, reflective jacket and warning triangle, and a toll sticker for highways.

Train

See www.cp.atlas.sk for domestic and international train schedules. Direct trains connect Bratislava to Austria, the Czech Republic, Poland, Hungary and Russia; from Košice, trains connect to the Czech Republic, Poland, Ukraine and Russia.

RIVER

Danube riverboats offer an alternative way to get between Bratislava and Vienna.

❶ Getting Around

AIR

Czech Airlines (www.csa.cz) offers the only domestic air service, between Bratislava and Košice.

BICYCLE

Roads can be narrow and potholed, and in towns cobblestones and tram tracks can prove dangerous for bike riders. Bike rental outfits aren't very common. Charges apply for bringing bikes aboard trains.

EATING PRICE RANGES

The following price ranges refer to a main course.

€ less than €7

€€ €7–€12

€€€ more than €12

ESSENTIAL FOOD & DRINK

Sheep's cheese Sample *bryndza* (tangy, soft and spreadable) and *oštiepok* (salty and chewy), or sip *žinčina*, a traditional sheep's-whey drink (like sour milk).

Soups Slurp *vývar* (chicken/beef broth served with *slížiky*, thin pasta strips, or liver dumplings) or *kapustnica* (thick sauerkraut and meat soup, often with ham or mushrooms).

Dumplings Varieties include *halušky* (mini-dumplings in cabbage or *bryndza* sauce topped with bacon) or *pirohy* (pocket-shaped dumplings stuffed with *bryndza* or smoked meat).

Fruity firewater Liquor made from berries and pitted fruits, such as *borovička* (from juniper) and *slivovica* (from plums).

BUS

Read timetables carefully; different schedules apply for weekends and holidays. Find up-to-date schedules online at cp.atlas.sk.

CAR & MOTORCYCLE

➡ Driving with a blood alcohol level above zero is an offence. If fined for a traffic offence, ask for a receipt.

➡ Toll stickers are required on *all* green-signed motorways. Buy at petrol stations or border crossings (per 10 days/month €10/14). Rental cars usually have them.

➡ City streetside parking restrictions are eagerly enforced. In some places you can pay by SMS (Slovak SIM cards only).

➡ Headlights stay on permanently and drivers must respect pedestrian priority at crossings.

➡ Winter tyres or snow chains are compulsory in some snowy destinations.

➡ Car hire is easily available in Bratislava, Košice and Poprad.

LOCAL TRANSPORT

Towns all have efficient bus systems; most villages have surprisingly good services. Bratislava and Košice have trams and trolleybuses; the High Tatras also has an efficient electric railway.

➡ Public transport generally operates from 5am to 10.30pm (4.30am to 11pm in Bratislava).

➡ City transport tickets are good for all local buses, trams and trolleybuses. Buy at news stands and validate on board or risk serious fines.

Slovenia

Best Places to Eat

➡ Druga Violina (p1011)

➡ Prince of Orange (p1011)

➡ Cantina Klet (p1022)

➡ Restaurant Proteus (p1020)

➡ Štrud'l (p1018)

Best Places to Stay

➡ Hostel Vrba (p1011)

➡ Adora Hotel (p1011)

➡ Rustic House 13 (p1018)

➡ Old Parish House (p1016)

➡ Hostel Soča Rocks (p1019)

Why Go?

It's a pint-sized place, with a surface area of just over 20,000 sq km, and two million people. But 'good things come in small packages', and never was that old chestnut more appropriate than in describing Slovenia. The country has everything – from beaches, snowcapped mountains, hills awash in grape vines and wide plains blanketed in sunflowers to Gothic churches, baroque palaces and art-nouveau buildings. Its incredible mixture of climates brings warm Mediterranean breezes up to the foothills of the Alps, where it can snow in summer.

The capital, Ljubljana, is a culturally rich city that values liveability and sustainability over unfettered growth. This sensitivity towards the environment also extends to rural and lesser-developed parts of the country.

When to Go
Ljubljana

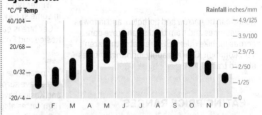

Apr–Jun A great time to be in the lowlands and the flower-carpeted valleys of the Julian Alps.

Sep This is the month made for everything – still warm enough to swim and tailor-made for hiking.

Dec–Mar Everyone (and their grandma) dons their skis in this winter-sport-mad country.

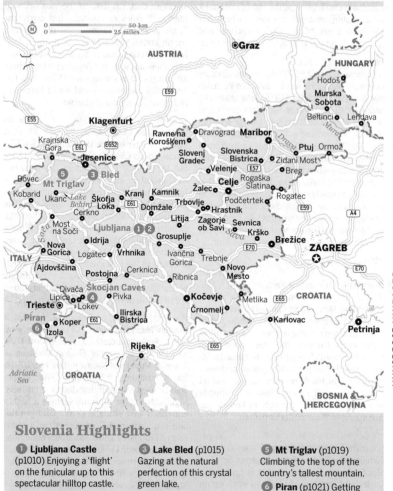

Slovenia Highlights

1 Ljubljana Castle
(p1010) Enjoying a 'flight' on the funicular up to this spectacular hilltop castle.

2 National & University Library (p1010)
Considering the genius of architect Jože Plečnik at Ljubljana's historic library.

3 Lake Bled (p1015)
Gazing at the natural perfection of this crystal green lake.

4 Škocjan Caves (p1020)
Gawking in awe at the 100m-high walls of this incredible cave system.

5 Mt Triglav (p1019)
Climbing to the top of the country's tallest mountain.

6 Piran (p1021) Getting lost wandering the narrow Venetian alleyways of this seaside town.

LJUBLJANA

01 / POP 278,800

Slovenia's capital and largest city also happens to be one of Europe's most liveable capitals. Car traffic is restricted in the centre, leaving the leafy banks of the emerald-green Ljubljanica River, which flows through the city's heart, free for pedestrians and cyclists. In summer, cafes set up terrace seating along the river, lending the feel of a perpet-

ual street party. Slovenia's master of early-Modern, minimalist design, Jože Plečnik, graced Ljubljana with beautiful bridges and buildings. The museums, hotels and restaurants are among the best in the country.

⊙ Sights

The easiest way to see Ljubljana is on foot. The oldest part of town, with the most important historical buildings and sights (including

Ljubljana Castle), lies on the right (east) bank of the Ljubljanica River. Center, which has the lion's share of the city's museums and galleries, is on the left (west) side of the river.

★ Ljubljana Castle   CASTLE

(Ljubljanski Grad; ☑ 01-306 42 93; www.ljubljanskigrad.si; Grajska Planota 1; adult/child incl funicular & castle attractions €10/7, castle attractions only €7.50/5.20; ☺ castle 9am-11pm Jun-Sep, to 9pm Apr, May & Oct, 10am-8pm Jan-Mar & Nov, to 10pm Dec) Crowning a 375m-high hill east of the Old Town, the castle is an architectural mishmash, but most of it dates to the early 16th century when it was largely rebuilt after a devastating earthquake. It's free to ramble around the castle grounds, but you'll have to pay to enter the Watchtower, the Chapel of St George, to see the worthwhile Exhibition on Slovenian History, visit the new Puppet Theatre and take the Time Machine tour.

★ National & University Library   ARCHITECTURE

(Narodna in Univerzitetna Knjižnica (NUK); ☑ 01-200 11 10; www.nuk.uni-lj.si; Turjaška ulica 1; ☺ 8am-8pm Mon-Fri, 9am-2pm Sat) This library is Jože Plečnik's masterpiece, completed in 1941. To appreciate this great man's philosophy, enter through the main door (note the horse-head doorknobs) on Turjaška ulica – you'll find yourself in near darkness, entombed in black marble. As you ascend the steps, you'll emerge into a colonnade suffused with light – the light of knowledge, according to the architect's plans.

★ Central Market   MARKET

(Centralna Tržnica; Vodnikov trg; ☺ open-air market 6am-6pm Mon-Fri, 6am-4pm Sat summer, 6am-4pm Mon-Sat winter) Central Market is Ljubljana's larder and worth a trip both to stock up on provisions or just have a good snoop (and sniff) around. Go first to the vast open-air market (Tržnica na Prostem) just across the Triple Bridge to the southeast of Prešernov trg on Vodnikov trg. Here you'll find a daily farmers market (except Sunday). In the next neighbouring square – Pogačarjev trg – there are always stalls selling everything from foraged wild mushrooms and forest berries to honey and homemade cheeses.

City Museum of Ljubljana   MUSEUM

(Mestni Muzej Ljubljana; ☑ 01-241 25 00; www.mgml.si; Gosposka ulica 15; adult/child €4/2.50, special exhibits €6/4; ☺ 10am-6pm Tue, Wed & Fri-Sun, to 9pm Thu) The excellent city museum established in 1935 focuses on Ljubljana's history, culture and politics via imaginative multimedia and interactive displays. The reconstructed street that once linked the eastern gates of the Roman colony of Emona (today's Ljubljana) to the Ljubljanica River and the collection of well-preserved classical artefacts in the basement treasury are worth a visit in themselves. So too are the models of buildings that the celebrated architect Jože Plečnik never got around to erecting.

National Museum of Slovenia   MUSEUM

(Narodni Muzej Slovenije; ☑ 01-241 44 00; www.nms.si; Prešernova cesta 20; adult/student €6/4, with National Museum of Slovenia Metelkova or Slovenian Museum of Natural History €8.50/6, 1st Sun of month free; ☺ 10am-6pm Fri-Wed, to 8pm Thu) Housed in a building dating from 1888, highlights at this museum include a highly embossed Vače situla, a Celtic pail from the late 6th century BC unearthed in a town east of Ljubljana, and a Stone Age bone flute discovered near Cerkno in western Slovenia in 1995. There are also examples of Roman glass and jewellery found in 6th-century Slavic graves as well as a huge glass-enclosed Roman lapidarium outside to the north.

SLOVENIA ITINERARIES

Three Days

Spend a couple of days in Ljubljana, then head north to unwind in romantic Bled or Bohinj beside idyllic mountain lakes. Alternatively, head south to visit the caves at Škocjan or Postojna.

One Week

A full week will allow you to see the country's top highlights. After two days in the capital, head for Bled and Bohinj. Depending on the season, take a bus or drive over the hair-raising Vršič Pass into the valley of the vivid-blue Soča River and take part in some adventure sports in Bovec. Continue south to the caves at Škocjan and Postojna and then to the sparkling Venetian port of Piran on the Adriatic.

🛏 Sleeping

Accommodation prices in Ljubljana are the highest in the country. Ljubljana Tourist Information Centre (TIC) (www.visitljubljana. com) maintains a list of hotels and sleeping options, including private rooms (single/double/triple from €30/50/75). A few are in the centre, but most require a bus trip.

★ Hostel Vrba   HOSTEL €
(☑ 064 133 555; www.hostelvrba.si; Gradaška ulica 10; dm €13-22, d €40; @ 🛜) Probably our favourite new budget accommodation in Ljubljana, this nine-room hostel on the Gradiščica Canal is just opposite the bars and restaurants of delightful Trnovo. There are three doubles, dorms with four to eight beds, hardwood floors and always a warm welcome. Free bikes, too, in summer.

★ Hostel Tresor   HOSTEL €€
(☑ 01-200 90 60; www.hostel-tresor.si; Čopova ulica 38; dm €15-24, s/d €40/70; 🏵 @ 🛜) This new 28-room hostel in the heart of Center is housed in a Secessionist-style former bank, and the money theme continues right into rooms named after currencies and financial aphorisms on the walls. Dorms have between four and 12 beds but are spacious. The communal areas (we love the atrium) are stunning; breakfast is in the vaults.

★ Adora Hotel   HOTEL €€
(☑ 082 057 240; www.adorahotel.si; Rožna ulica 7; s €85-125, d €170-250, apt €85-155; P 🏵 @ 🛜) This small hotel below Gornji trg is a welcome addition to accommodation in the Old Town. The 10 rooms are small but fully equipped, with lovely hardwood floors and tasteful furnishings. The lovely breakfast room looks out onto a small garden, bikes are free for guests' use and the staff are overwhelmingly friendly and helpful.

★ Vander Urbani Resort   BOUTIQUE HOTEL €€€
(☑ 01-200 90 00; www.vanderhotel.com; Krojaška ulica 6; r €120-207; 🏵 @ 🛜 🏊) This stunning new boutique hotel in the heart of Ljubljana's Old Town was formed from four 17th-century buildings. But history stops there, for this hostelry – with 16 rooms over three floors – is as modern as tomorrow. Designed by the trendsetting Sadar Vuga architectural firm, the rooms are not huge but each is unique and makes use of natural materials.

★ Antiq Palace Hotel & Spa   BOUTIQUE HOTEL €€€
(☑ 083 896 700, 040 638 163; www.antiqpalace. com; Gosposka ulica 10; s/d €180/210; 🏵 @ 🛜) The city's most luxurious sleeping option, the Antiq Palace occupies a 16th-century townhouse, about a block from the river. Accommodation is in 21 individually designed rooms and suites, some stretching to 250 sq metres in size and with jacuzzi. Many retain their original features (hardwood floors, floor-to-ceiling windows) and are furnished in an eclectic manner with quirky rococo touches.

🍴 Eating

Ljubljana has Slovenia's best selection of restaurants; even the more expensive restaurants usually offer an excellent-value three-course *dnevno kosilo* (set lunch) for under €10.

★ Prince of Orange   ITALIAN €
(☑ 083 802 447; Komenskega ulica 30; dishes €4.50-9; ⊙ 7.30am-9.30pm Mon-Fri) This true find – a bright and airy cafe just above Trubarjeva cesta – serves outstanding shop-made soups and bruschetta. Ask for some of the farmer's goat cheese and about the link between the cafe and England's King William III (the pub sign on the wall is a clue).

★ Druga Violina   SLOVENIAN €
(☑ 082 052 506; Stari trg 21; mains €4.50-10; ⊙ 8am-midnight) Just opposite the Academy of Music, the 'Second Fiddle' is an extremely pleasant and affordable place for a meal in the Old Town. There are lots of very Slovenian dishes like *ajdova kaša z jurčki* (buckwheat groats with ceps) and *obara* (a thick stew of chicken and vegetables) on the menu. It's a social enterprise designed to help those with disabilities.

★ Taverna Tatjana   SEAFOOD €€
(☑ 01-421 00 87; www.taverna-tatjana.si; Gornji trg 38; mains €9-25; ⊙ 5pm-midnight Mon-Sat) This charming little tavern bordering Old Town specialises in fish and seafood (though there's beef and foal on the menu too). Housed in several vaulted rooms of an atmospheric old townhouse with wooden ceiling beams, the fish is fresher than a spring shower. Go for something you wouldn't normally find elsewhere like *brodet* (Croatian fish stew with polenta) or cuttlefish black risotto.

SLOVENIA LJUBLJANA

Ljubljana

SLOVENIA LJUBLJANA

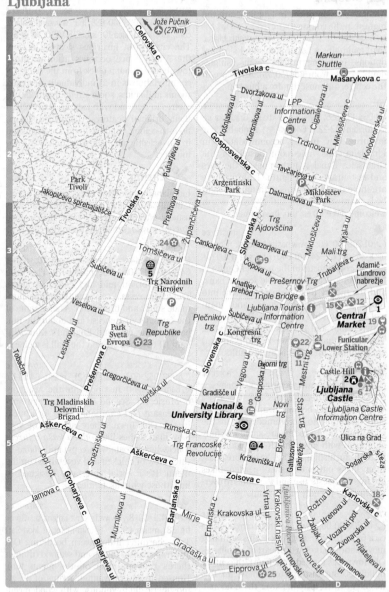

★**Strelec**
(Archer; ☑031 687 648; www.kaval-group.si/
strelec.asp; Grajska Planota 1; mains €12-28;
⊙noon-10pm Mon-Sat) This is haute cuisine
from on high – Ljubljana Castle's Archer's
Tower, no less – with a menu that traces the
city's history chosen by ethnologist Janez
Bogataj and prepared by Igor Jagodic, recognised as one of the top chefs in Slovenia.
Tasting menus are priced from €32 to €77
for between three and nine courses.

Ljubljana

SLOVENIA LJUBLJANA

🍷 Drinking & Nightlife

Ljubljana offers a dizzying array of drinking options, whether your tipple is beer, wine and spirits, or tea and coffee.

★ Pritličje   CAFE
(Ground Floor; ☑ 040 204 693; www.pritlicje.si; Mestni trg 2; ⊘ 9am-1am Sun-Wed, to 3am Thu-Sat) Ultra-inclusive cultural centre 'Ground Floor' offers something for everyone: cafe, bar, live music, cultural centre and comic-book shop, and is one of the very few LGBT-friendly places in town. Events are scheduled almost nightly and the location next to the Town Hall, with good views across Mestni trg, couldn't be more perfect.

★ Slovenska Hiša   COCKTAIL BAR
(Slovenian House; ☑ 083 899 811; www.slovenska-hisa.si; Cankarjevo nabrežje 13; ⊘ 8am-1am Sun-

Self-Catering

Covered Market   MARKET €
(Pokrita Tržnica; Dolničarjeva ulica; ⊘ 7am-4pm Mon-Fri, 7am-2pm Sat) The covered part of central market sells meats and cheeses.

Thu, to 3am Fri & Sat) Our favourite new boozer along the river is so cute it's almost twee. Sourcing only Slovenian products makes the cocktails that much more inventive (gin – yes, tonic – no), meat and cheese plates (€4 to €7) are worthy blotter, and should you want cigarettes, you must buy from a Kompas 'Duty-Free Shop', as they're not made in Slovenia.

★ **Klub Daktari**   BAR
(☑ 059 055 538; www.daktari.si; Krekov trg 7; ☺ 8am-1am Mon-Sat, 9am-midnight Sun) This rabbit warren of a watering hole at the foot of the funicular to Ljubljana Castle is so chilled there's practically frost on the windows. The decor is retro-distressed, with shelves full of old books and a player piano in the corner. More of a cultural centre than club, Daktari hosts live music sets and an eclectic mix of other cultural events.

☆ Entertainment

Buy tickets for shows and events at the venue's box office, online through Eventim (☑ 430 24 05; http://www.eventim.si/en/), or at the Ljubljana Tourist Information Centre. Expect to pay €10 to €20 for tickets to live acts.

★ **Sax Pub**   JAZZ
(☑ 040 168 804; www.saxhostelljubljana.com/sax-pub.html; Eipprova ulica 7; ☺ 8am-1am Mon-Fri, 9am-1am Sat & Sun) More than a quarter-century in Trnovo and decorated with colourful murals and graffiti outside, the tiny and convivial Sax has live jazz as well as blues,

METELKOVA MESTO

For a scruffy alternative to trendy clubs, head for Metelkova Mesto (Metelkova Town; www.metelkovamesto.org; Masarykova cesta 24), an ex-army garrison taken over by squatters in the 1990s and converted into a free-living commune. In this two-courtyard block, a dozen idiosyncratic venues hide behind brightly tagged doorways, coming to life generally after midnight daily in summer and on Friday and Saturday the rest of the year. While it's certainly not for the genteel and the quality of the acts and performances varies with the night, there's usually a little of something for everyone.

folk and hip-hop at 8pm on Thursday year-round. Canned stuff rules at other times.

Opera Ballet Ljubljana   OPERA
(☑ 01-241 59 00, box office 01-241 59 59; www.opera.si; Župančičeva ulica 1; ☺ box office 10am-1pm & 2-6pm Mon-Fri, 10am-1pm Sat, 1hr before performance) Home to the Slovenian National Opera and Ballet companies, this historic neo-Renaissance theatre has been restored to its former glory in recent years. Enter from Cankarjeva cesta.

Cankarjev Dom   CLASSICAL MUSIC
(☑ 01-241 71 00, box office 01-241 72 99; www.cd-cc.si; Prešernova cesta 10; ☺ box office 11am-1pm & 3-8pm Mon-Fri, 11am-1pm Sat, 1hr before performance) Ljubljana's premier cultural and conference centre has two large auditoriums (the Gallus Hall is said to have perfect acoustics) and a dozen smaller performance spaces offering a remarkable smorgasbord of performance arts.

ⓘ Information

There are ATMs at every turn, including several outside the main Ljubljana Tourist Information Centre office. At the train station you'll find a **bureau de change** (☑ 01-432 10 14; ☺ 8am-8pm) changing cash for no commission, but not travellers cheques.

Ljubljana Tourist Information Centre (TIC; ☑ 01-306 12 15; www.visitljubljana.com; Adamič-Lundrovo nabrežje 2; ☺ 8am-9pm Jun-Sep, to 7pm Oct-May) Knowledgeable and enthusiastic staff dispense information, maps and useful literature and help with accommodation. Maintains an excellent website.

Slovenian Tourist Information Centre (STIC; ☑ 01-306 45 76; www.slovenia.info; Krekov trg 10; ☺ 8am-9pm Jun-Sep, 8am-7pm Mon-Fri, 9am-5pm Sat & Sun Oct-May) Good source of information for the rest of Slovenia, with internet and bicycle rental also available.

ⓘ Getting There & Away

BUS

Buses to destinations both within Slovenia and abroad leave from the **bus station** (Avtobusna Postaja Ljubljana; ☑ 01-234 46 00; www.ap-ljubljana.si; Trg Osvobodilne Fronte 4; ☺ 5am-10.30pm Mon-Fri, to 10pm Sat, 5.30am-10.30pm Sun) in front of the train station. Next to the ticket windows are multilingual information phones and a touch-screen computer. Frequent buses serve Bohinj (€8.70, two hours, 91km, hourly) via Bled (€6.30, 1¼ hours, 57km), Piran (€12, 2½ hours, 140km, up to seven daily) and Postojna (€6, one hour, 53km, half-hourly).

TRAIN

Domestic and international trains arrive at and depart from central Ljubljana's **train station** (Železniška Postaja; ☑ 01-291 33 32; www.slo-zeleznice.si; Trg Osvobodilne Fronte 6; ⊙ 5am-10pm), where you'll find a separate information centre on the way to the platforms. Buy domestic tickets from windows No 1 to 8 and international ones from either window No 9 or the information centre. Useful domestic destinations include Bled (€6.60, one hour, half-hourly) and Divača (€5.80, one hour, several daily).

❶ Getting Around

TO/FROM THE AIRPORT

The cheapest way to Ljubljana's **Jože Pučnik Airport** (Aerodrom Ljubljana; ☑ 04-206 19 81; www.lju-airport.si/eng; Zgornji Brnik 130a, Brnik) is by public bus (€4.10, 45 minutes, 27km) from stop No 28 at the bus station. These run at 5.20am and hourly from 6.10am to 8.10pm Monday to Friday; at the weekend there's a bus at 6.10am and then one every two hours from 9.10am to 7.10pm. Buy tickets from the driver.

Two airport-shuttle services that get consistently good reviews are **GoOpti** (☑ 01-320 45 30; www.goopti.com) and **Markun Shuttle** (☑ 051 321 414, 041 041 792 865; www.prevozi-markun.com), which will transfer you from Brnik to central Ljubljana for €9 in half an hour. Book by phone or online.

A taxi from the airport to Ljubljana will cost €35 to €45.

BICYCLE

Ljubljana is a pleasure for cyclists, and there are bike lanes and special traffic lights.

Ljubljana Bike (☑ 01-306 45 76; www.visitljubljana.si; Krekov trg 10; per 2hr/day €2/8; ⊙ 8am-7pm Mon-Fri, 9am-5pm Sat & Sun Apr, May & Oct, 8am-9pm Jun-Sep) rents two-wheelers in two-hour or full-day increments from April through October from the **Slovenia Tourist Information Centre**. For short rides, you can hire bicycles as needed from 32 **Bicike(lj)** (☑ 080 23 34; www.bicikelj.si; subscription weekly/yearly €1/3 plus hourly rate; ⊙ 24hr) stations with 300 bikes located around the city. To rent a bike requires pre-registration and subscription over the company website plus a valid credit or debit card.

PUBLIC TRANSPORT

Ljubljana's city buses, many running on methane, operate every five to 15 minutes from 5am (6am on Sunday) to around 10.30pm. There are also a half-dozen night buses. A flat fare of €1.20 (good for 90 minutes of unlimited travel, including transfers) is paid with a stored-value magnetic **Urbana** (☑ 01-474 08 00; www.jhl.si/en/single-city-card-urbana) card, which can be purchased at news stands, tourist offices and the **LPP Information Centre** (☑ 01-430 51 74; www.lpp.si/en; Slovenska cesta 56; ⊙ 7am-7pm Mon-Fri) for €2; credit can then be added (€1 to €50). **Kavalir** (☑ 031 666 331, 031 666 332; ⊙ 8am-8pm) is an LPP-run transport service that will pick you up and drop you off anywhere in the pedestrianised Old Town free of charge. All you have to do is call (and wait – there are only three golf cart-like vehicles available April to October and just one the rest of the year).

JULIAN ALPS

The Julian Alps – named in honour of Caesar himself – form Slovenia's dramatic northwest frontier with Italy. Triglav National Park, established in 1924, includes almost all of the Alps lying within Slovenia, including triple-peaked Mt Triglav, at 2864m Slovenia's highest mountain. Along with an abundance of fauna and flora, the area offers a wide range of adventure sports.

Bled

☑ 04 / POP 5120

Yes, it's every bit as lovely in real life. With its emerald-green lake, picture-postcard church on an islet, a medieval castle clinging to a rocky cliff and some of the highest peaks of the Julian Alps and the Karavanke as backdrops, Bled is Slovenia's most popular resort, drawing everyone from honeymooners lured by the over-the-top romantic setting to backpackers, who come for the hiking, biking, water sports and canyoning possibilities.

◉ Sights

★ Lake Bled   LAKE

(Blejsko jezero) Bled's greatest attraction is its exquisite blue-green lake, measuring just 2km by 1.4km. The lake is lovely to behold from almost any vantage point, and makes a beautiful backdrop for the 6km walk along the shore. Mild thermal springs warm the water to a swimmable 26°C (79°F) from June through August. The lake is naturally the focus of the entire town: you can rent boats, go diving or simply snap countless photos.

★ Bled Island   ISLAND

(Blejski Otok; www.blejskiotok.si) Tiny, tear-shaped Bled Island beckons from the shore. There's the Church of the Assumption and a small museum, but the real thrill is the ride out by *pletna* (gondola). The *pletna* will set you down on the south side at the monumental South Staircase (Južno Stopnišče), built in 1655. The staircase comprises 99 steps – a local tradition is for the husband to carry his new bride up them.

★ Bled Castle CASTLE
(Blejski Grad; ☑ 04-572 97 82; www.blejski-grad.si; Grajska cesta 25; adult/child €10/5; ☺ 8am-9pm mid-Jun–mid-Sep, to 8pm Apr–mid-Jun & mid-Sep–Oct, to 6pm Nov-Mar) Perched atop a steep cliff more than 100m above the lake, Bled Castle is how most people imagine a medieval fortress to be, with towers, ramparts, moats and a terrace offering magnificent views. The castle houses a museum collection that traces the lake's history from earliest times to the development of Bled as a resort in the 19th century.

★ Vintgar Gorge PARK
(Soteska Vintgar; ☑ 031 344 053; www.vintgar. si; adult/child €5/2.50; ☺ 8am-7pm late Apr-Oct) One of the easiest and most satisfying half-day trips from Bled is to Vintgar Gorge, some 4km to the northwest of Bled village. The highlight is a 1600m wooden walkway through the gorge, built in 1893 and continually rebuilt since. It criss-crosses the swirling Radovna River four times over rapids, waterfalls and pools before reaching 16m-high Šum Waterfall.

★ Activities

Several local outfits organise a wide range of outdoor activities in and around Bled, including trekking, mountaineering, rock climbing, ski touring, cross-country skiing, mountain biking, rafting, kayaking, canyoning, caving, horse riding and paragliding.

★ 3glav Adventures ADVENTURE SPORTS
(☑ 041 683 184; www.3glav.com; Ljubljanska cesta 1; ☺ 9am-noon & 4-7pm mid-Apr–Sep) The number-one adventure-sport specialists in Bled for warm-weather activities. 3glav Adventures' most popular trip is the Emerald River Adventure (from €80), an 11-hour hiking and swimming foray into Triglav National Park and along the Soča River that covers a huge sightseeing loop of the region (from Bled over the Vršič Pass and down the Soča Valley, with optional rafting trip).

⭐ Sleeping & Eating

Bled has a wide range of accommodation – from Slovenia's original hostel to a five-star hotel in a villa that was once Tito's summer retreat. Private rooms and apartments are offered by dozens of homes in the area. Both Kompas and the TIC have lists, with prices for singles ranging from €16 to €33 and doubles €24 to €50.

★ Jazz Hostel & Apartments HOSTEL, GUESTHOUSE €
(☑ 040 634 555; www.jazzbled.com; Prešernova cesta 68; dm €35, d without/with bathroom €50/60, apt d/q €80/85; P@⑨) If you don't mind being a little way (a short walk) from the action, this is a first-class budget choice. Guests rave about Jazz, mainly thanks to Jani, the superbly friendly owner who runs a sparkling, well-kitted-out complex. There are dorms (bunk-free, and with underbed storage) and colourful en suite rooms, plus family-sized apartments with full kitchen.

★ Old Parish House GUESTHOUSE €€
(☑ 045 741 203; www.blejskiotok.si/hotel; Riklijeva cesta 22; s/d from €45/98; P⑨) In a privileged position, the Old Parish House (Stari Farovž) belonging to the Parish Church of St Martin has been newly transformed into a simple, welcoming guesthouse, with timber beams, hardwood floors and neutral, minimalist style. Pros include car parking, lake views and waking to church bells.

★ Garden Village Bled RESORT €€€
(☑ 083 899 220; www.gardenvillagebled.com; Cesta Gorenjskega odreda 16; pier tent €110, treehouse €290, glamping tent €340; ☺ Apr-Oct; P@⑨▣) Garden Village embraces and executes the eco-resort concept with aplomb, taking glamping to a whole new level and delivering lashings of wow factor. Accommodation ranges from small two-person tents on piers over a trout-filled stream (shared bathroom), to family-sized treehouses and large safari-style tents. Plus there are beautiful grounds, a natural swimming pool and an organic restaurant. Superb.

★ Finefood – Penzion Berc SLOVENIAN €€€
(☑ 04-574 18 38; www.penzion-berc.si; Želeška cesta 15; mains €16-30; ☺ 5-11pm late Apr-late Oct) In a magical garden setting, Penzion Berc sets up a summertime restaurant, with local produce served fresh from its open kitchen. Try sea bass with asparagus soufflé, homemade pasta with fresh black truffle, deer entrecôte or Black Angus steak. Finefood's reputation for high-class flavour and atmosphere is growing: book ahead.

ESSENTIAL FOOD & DRINK

Little Slovenia boasts an incredibly diverse cuisine, with as many as two dozen different regional styles of cooking. Here are some highlights:

Brinjevec A strong brandy made from fermented juniper berries.

Gibanica Layer cake stuffed with nuts, cheese and apple.

Jota Hearty bean-and-cabbage soup.

Postrv Trout, particularly from the Soča River, is a real treat.

Potica A nut roll eaten at teatime or as a dessert.

Prekmurska gibanica A rich concoction of pastry filled with poppy seeds, walnuts, apples and cheese and topped with cream.

Pršut Air-dried, thinly sliced ham from the Karst region.

Štruklji Scrumptious dumplings made with curd cheese and served either savoury as a main course or sweet as a dessert.

Wine Distinctively Slovenian tipples include peppery red Teran from the Karst region and Malvazija, a straw-colour white from the coast.

Žganci The Slovenian stodge of choice – groats made from barley or corn but usually *ajda* (buckwheat).

Žlikrofi Ravioli-like parcels filled with cheese, bacon and chives.

★ **Castle Restaurant** SLOVENIAN €€€
(☑04-620 34 44; www.jezersek.si/en/bled-castle-restaurant; Grajska cesta 61; mains €15-30; ☉11am-10pm) It's hard to fault the superb location of the castle's restaurant, with a terrace and views straight from a postcard. What a relief the food is as good as it is: black risotto with octopus, lake trout fillet, veal fillet with tarragon dumplings. Book in advance to score a table with a view – note: with a reservation, you don't pay to enter the castle.

ℹ Information

Tourist Information Centre (☑04-574 11 22; www.bled.si; Cesta Svobode 10; ☉8am-9pm Mon-Sat, 9am-5pm Sun Jul & Aug, reduced hours Sep-Jun) Occupies a small office behind the Casino at Cesta Svobode 10; sells maps and souvenirs, rents bikes and has internet access. It's open year-round: until at least 6pm Monday to Friday, to 3pm Sunday.

ℹ Getting There & Around

BUS

Bled is well connected by bus; the **bus station** (Cesta Svobode 4) is a hub of activity at the lake's northeast. Popular services include Lake Bohinj (€3.60, 37 minutes, 29km, up to 12 daily) and Ljubljana (€6.30, 80 to 90 minutes, 57km, up to 15 daily).

TRAIN

Bled has two train stations, though neither is close to the centre. Mainline trains to/from Ljubljana (€5.08 to €6.88, 40 minutes to one hour, 51km, up to 20 daily) and Austria use Lesce-Bled station, 4km to the east of town. Trains to/from Bohinjska Bistrica (€1.85, 20 minutes, 18km, seven daily), from where you can catch a bus to Lake Bohinj, use the smaller Bled Jezero station, 2km west of central Bled.

Bohinj

☑04 / POP 5300

Many visitors to Slovenia say they've never seen a more beautiful lake than Bled...that is, until they've seen Lake Bohinj, just 26km to the southwest. We'll refrain from weighing in on the Bled versus Bohinj debate other than to say we see their point. Admittedly, Bohinj lacks Bled's glamour, but it's less crowded and in many ways more authentic. People come primarily to chill out or to swim in the crystal-clear, blue-green water, with leisurely cycling and walking trails to occupy them.

◉ Sights & Activities

Mt Triglav is visible from Bohinj and there are activities galore – from kayaking and mountain biking to trekking up Triglav via one of the southern approaches.

★ **Church of St John the Baptist** CHURCH
(Cerkev Sv Janeza Krstnika; Ribčev Laz; ☉ 10am-4pm Jul & Aug, group bookings only May & Sep) This postcard-worthy church, at the head of the lake and right by the stone bridge, is what every medieval church should be: small, surrounded by natural beauty, and full of exquisite frescoes. The nave is Romanesque, but the Gothic presbytery dates from about 1440. Many walls and ceilings are covered with 15th- and 16th-century frescoes.

★ **Savica Waterfall** WATERFALL
(Slap Savica; Ukanc; adult/child €3/1.50; ☉ 8am-8pm Jul & Aug, 9am-7pm Apr-Jun, 9am-5pm Sep-Nov) The magnificent Savica Waterfall, which cuts deep into a gorge 78m below, is 4km from Ukanc and can be reached by a walking path from there in 1½ to two hours. By car, you can continue past Ukanc via a sealed road to a car park beside the Savica restaurant, from where it's a 20-minute walk up more than 500 steps and over rapids and streams to the falls. Wear decent shoes for the slippery path.

Alpinsport ADVENTURE SPORTS
(☑ 04-572 34 86, 041 596 079; www.alpinsport.si; Ribčev Laz 53; ☉ 9am-noon & 3-7pm) Rents equipment: canoes, kayaks, SUPs and bikes in summer, skis and snowboards in winter. It also operates guided rafting and canyoning trips. Its base is opposite Hotel Jezero in Ribčev Laz.

🛏 Sleeping & Eating

The TICs can arrange accommodation: private rooms (€14 to €20 per person), plus apartments and holiday houses. Apartments for two/six in summer start at €48/116. The website www.bohinj.si has more details.

★ **Camp Zlatorog** CAMPGROUND €
(☑ 059 923 648; www.camp-bohinj.si; Ukanc 5; per person €10-15; ☉ May-Sep; ℗ 🐾) This tree-filled campground can accommodate up to 750 guests and sits photogenically on the lake's southwestern corner, 5km from Ribčev Laz. Prices vary according to site location, with the most expensive (and desirable) sites right on the lake. Facilities are very good – including restaurant, laundry and water-sport rentals, and the tourist boat docks here. Tents can be hired.

★ **Rustic House 13** PENSION €€
(Hiša 13; ☑ 031 466 707; www.studor13.si; Studor 13; d/q €70/110; ℗ 🐾) Cosy and rustic down to the last detail (from the wooden balcony to the garden area), Rustic House gives you a delightful taste of village life. It's owned by

an Australian-Slovenian couple and houses two super suites that each sleep up to four. There's a shared kitchen and lounge – admire Andy's photos of the surrounds (he also offers photography tours).

★ **Vila Park** BOUTIQUE HOTEL €€€
(☑ 04-572 3300; www.vila-park.si; Ukanc 129; d €100-120; ℗ 🐾) Vila Park creates a great first impression, with sunloungers set in expansive riverside grounds, and balconies overflowing with flowers. The interior is equally impressive, with eight elegant rooms plus a handsome lounge and dining area. Note: it's a kid-free zone.

★ **Štrud'l** SLOVENIAN €
(☑ 041 541 877; www.strudl.si; Triglavska cesta 23; mains €6-12; ☉ 8am-9pm Sun-Thu, to 10pm Fri & Sat) This modern take on traditional farmhouse cooking is a must for foodies keen to sample local specialities. Overlook the incongruous location in the centre of Bohinjska Bistrica, and enjoy dishes like *ričet s klobaso* (barley porridge with sausage and beans).

Gostišče Erlah SLOVENIAN €€
(☑ 04-572 33 09; www.erlah.com; Ukanc 67; mains €8-18; ☉ 11am-9pm Sun-Fri, to 10pm Sat) Local trout is king at this relaxed eatery, and it comes perfectly prepared: smoked, grilled or *en brochette* (skewered). There's a rustic, timber-lined terrace, and families will be happy with the kids' playground right next door. Rooms are also available.

ℹ Information

Tourist Information Centre Ribčev Laz (TIC; ☑ 04-574 60 10; www.bohinj-info.com; Ribčev Laz 48; ☉ 8am-8pm Mon-Sat, 8am-6pm Sun Jul & Aug, 9am-5pm Mon-Sat, 9am-3pm Sun Nov & Dec, 8am-6pm Mon-Sat, 9am-3pm Sun Jan-Jun & Sep & Oct)

TNP Center Bohinj (☑ 04-578 0245; www.tnp.si; Stara Fužina 37-38; ☉ 10am-6pm late Apr-Jun & Sep–mid-Oct, 9am-7pm Jul-Aug, 10am-3pm mid-Oct–late Apr, closed 1 Nov) A brand-new national park info centre about 1km north of the Church of St John the Baptist, full of exhibits, maps and books. There's a summer program of free events that includes talks, walks and stargazing. You can also arrange a trekking guide here, or a guide for an ascent of Mt Triglav.

ℹ Getting There & Away

BUS
Buses run regularly from Ljubljana (€8.30, two hours, 86km, hourly). Around 12 buses daily go from Bled (€3.60, 40 minutes) to Bohinj Jezero (via Bohinjska Bistrica) and return.

TRAIN

A half-dozen daily trains make the run to Bohinjska Bistrica from Ljubljana (€7.17, two hours, 74km), though this route requires a change in Jesenice. There are also frequent trains between Bled's small Bled Jezero station (€1.85, 20 minutes, 18km, seven daily) and Bohinjska Bistrica.

SOČA VALLEY

The Soča Valley region (Posočje) stretches from Triglav National Park to Nova Gorica, including the outdoor activity centres of Bovec and Kobarid. Threading through it is the magically aquamarine Soča River. Most people come here for the rafting, hiking and skiing though there are plenty of historical sights and locations, particularly relating to WWI, when millions of troops fought on the mountainous battlefront here.

Bovec

☑ 05 / POP 1593

Soča Valley's de facto capital, Bovec offers plenty for adventure-sports enthusiasts. With the Julian Alps above, the Soča River below and Triglav National Park all around, you could spend a week here rafting, hiking, kayaking, mountain biking and, in winter, skiing, without ever doing the same thing twice.

🏃 Activities

You'll find everything you need on the compact village square, Trg Golobarskih Žrtev, including a half-dozen adrenaline-raising adventure-sports companies. Among the best are Aktivni Planet (☑ 040 639 433; http://aktivniplanet.si; Trg Golobarskih Žrtev 19)

THE GREAT OUTDOORS

Slovenes have a strong attachment to nature, and most lead active, outdoor lives from an early age. As a result, the choice of activities and range of facilities on offer are endless. From skiing and climbing to canyoning and cycling, Slovenia has it all and it's always affordable. The major centres are Bovec, Lake Bled and Lake Bohinj. The Slovenian Tourist Board publishes specialist brochures on skiing, hiking, cycling, golfing and horse riding as well as top spas and heath resorts.

---

and Soča Rafting (☑ 05-389 62 00, 041 724 472; www.socarafting.si; Trg Golobarskih Žrtev 14).

Rafting, kayaking and canoeing on the beautiful Soča River are major draws. The season lasts from April to October. Rafting trips on the Soča over a distance of around 8km (1½ hours) cost €35 to €40; longer trips may be possible when water levels are high. Prices include guiding, transport to/from the river, a neoprene suit, boots, life jacket, helmet and paddle. Wear a swimsuit; bring a towel.

A canyoning trip, in which you descend through gorges and jump over falls near the Soča attached to a rope, costs around €45.

🛏 Sleeping & Eating

The TIC has dozens of private rooms and apartments (from €20) on its lists.

⭐ **Hostel Soča Rocks**　　　　HOSTEL €

(☑ 041 317 777; http://hostelsocarocks.com; Mala Vas 120; dm €13-15, d €34-40; P @ 🖛) This welcome new arrival sleeps 68 and is a new breed of hostel: colourful, spotlessly clean and social, with a bar that never seems to quit. Dorms sleep maximum six; there are also a few doubles (all bathrooms shared). Cheap meals are served (including summertime barbecue dinners), and a full activity menu is offered: the hostel is affiliated with Aktivni Planet.

⭐ **Dobra Vila**　　　　BOUTIQUE HOTEL €€€

(☑ 05-389 64 00; www.dobra-vila-bovec.si; Mala Vas 112; d €120-165; P ✳ @ 🖛) This stunning 10-room boutique hotel is housed in an erstwhile telephone-exchange building dating from 1932. Peppered with art deco flourishes, interesting artefacts and objets d'art, it has its own library and wine cellar, and a fabulous restaurant with a winter garden and outdoor terrace.

Martinov Hram　　　　SLOVENIAN €€

(☑ 05-388 62 14; www.martinov-hram.si; mains €8-18; ⏱ 10am-10pm Tue-Fri, to midnight Sat & Sun) This traditional restaurant gets mixed reviews, but on a good day you'll enjoy well-prepared local specialities including venison, Soča trout and mushroom dishes. The best place to enjoy them is from the street-front terrace, under the grapevines.

ℹ Information

Tourist Information Centre (TIC; ☑ 05-384 19 19; www.bovec.si; Trg Golobarskih Žrtev 22; ⏱ 8am-8pm Jul & Aug, 9am-7pm Jun & Sep, 9am-6pm May, shorter hours Oct-Apr) The TIC is open year-round. Winter hours will depend on the reopening of the local ski centre – expect long hours when the ski season is in full swing.

ℹ️ Getting There & Away

There are a couple of daily buses to Ljubljana (€13.60, 3¾ hours, 151km) via Kobarid and Idrija. From late June to August a service to Kranjska Gora (€6.70, 1¾ hours, 46km) via the Vršič Pass departs several times a day, continuing on to Ljubljana.

KARST & COAST

Slovenia's short coast (47km) is an area for both recreation and history; the town of Piran, famed for its Venetian Gothic architecture and picturesque narrow streets, is among the main drawcards here. En route from Ljubljana or the Soča Valley, you'll cross the Karst, a huge limestone plateau and a land of olives, ruby-red Teran wine, *pršut* (air-dried ham), old stone churches and deep subterranean caves, including those at Postojna and Škocjan.

Postojna & Škocjan Caves

☎ 05 / POP 9366

As much of a draw as the mountains and the sea in Slovenia are two world-class but very different cave systems in the Karst area.

◉ Sights

⭐ **Postojna Cave** CAVE
(Postojnska Jama; ☎ 05-700 01 00; www.postojnska-jama.eu; Jamska cesta 30; adult/child €23.90/14.30, with Predjama Castle €31.90/19.10; ⊘ tours hourly 9am-5pm or 6pm Jul & Aug, 9am-5pm May, Jun & Sep, 10am, noon or 3pm Nov-Mar, 10am-noon & 2-4pm Apr & Oct) The jaw-dropping Postojna Cave system, a series of caverns, halls and passages some 24km long and two million years old, was hollowed out by the Pivka River, which enters a subterranean tunnel near the cave's entrance.

Visitors get to see 5km of the cave on 1½-hour tours; 3.2km of this is covered by a cool electric train. Postojna Cave has a temperature of 8°C to 10°C with a humidity of 95%, so a warm jacket and decent shoes are advised.

⭐ **Škocjan Caves** CAVE
(Škocjanske Jame; ☎ 05-708 21 00; www.park-skocjanske-jame.si; Škocjan 2; cave tour adult/child €16/7.50; ⊘ tours hourly 10am-5pm Jun-Sep, 10am, 1pm & 3.30pm Apr, May & Oct, 10am & 1pm Mon-Sat,

10am, 1pm & 3pm Sun Nov-Mar) Touring the huge, spectacular subterranean chambers of the 6km-long Škocjan Caves is a must. This remarkable cave system was carved out by the Reka River, which enters a gorge below the village of Škocjan and eventually flows into the Dead Lake, a sump at the end of the cave where it disappears. It surfaces again as the Timavo River at Duino in Italy, 34km northwest, before emptying into the Gulf of Trieste. Dress warmly and wear good walking shoes.

🛏️ Sleeping & Eating

⭐ **Youth Hostel Proteus Postojna** HOSTEL €
(☎ 05-850 10 20; www.proteus.sgls.si; Tržaška cesta 36; dm/d/s €15/17/23; [P] [@] [🛜]) Don't be fooled by the institutional exterior – inside, this place is a riot of colour. It's surrounded by parkland and is a fun, chilled-out space, with three-bed rooms (shared bathrooms), kitchen and laundry access, and bike rental. The year-round hostel shares the building with student accommodation, so facilities are good. It's about 500m southwest of Titov trg.

⭐ **Lipizzaner Lodge** GUESTHOUSE €€
(☎ 040 378 037; www.lipizzanerlodge.com; Landol 17; s/d/q from €55/80/100; [P] [🛜]) In a relaxing rural setting 9km northwest of Postojna Cave, a Welsh-Finnish couple have established this very hospitable, affordable guesthouse. They offer seven well-equipped rooms (including family-sized, and a self-catering apartment); great-value evening meals on request (€14); and brilliant local knowledge (check out their comprehensive website for an idea). Forest walks (including to Predjama in 40 minutes) plus bike rental.

⭐ **Restaurant Proteus** SLOVENIAN €€
(☎ 081 610 300; Titov trg 1; mains €12-20; ⊘ 8am-10pm) The fanciest place in town: inside is modern and white, with booths fringed by curtains, while the terrace overlooking the main square is a fine vantage point. Accomplished cooking showcases fine regional produce – house specialities include venison goulash and steak with Teran (red wine) sauce. It's hard to go past the four-course Chef's Slovenian Menu (€35) for value and local flavour.

Information

Tourist Information Centre Postojna (TIC; ☎ 064 179 972; tic.postojna.info@gmail.com; Tržaška cesta; ⊘ 9am-9pm Jul & Aug, to 6pm Jun & Sep, shorter hours Oct, Nov, Apr & May, closed Jan-Mar) A smart new pavilion

PREDJAMA CASTLE

Nine kilometres from Postojna is **Predjama Castle** (☑05-700 01 00; www.postojnska-jama.eu; Predjama 1; adult/child €11.90/7.10, with Postojna Cave €23.90/19.10; ☺9am-7pm Jul & Aug, to 6pm May, Jun & Sep, 10am-5pm Apr & Oct, 10am-4pm Nov-Mar), one of the world's most dramatic castles. It teaches a clear lesson: if you want to build an impregnable fortification, put it in the gaping mouth of a cavern halfway up a 123m cliff. Its four storeys were built piecemeal over the years from 1202, but most of what you see today is from the 16th century. It looks simply unconquerable.

An audioguide (available in 15 languages) details the site's highlights and history. The castle holds great features for kids of any age – holes in the ceiling of the entrance tower for pouring boiling oil on intruders, a very dank dungeon, a 16th-century chest full of treasure (unearthed in the cellar in 1991), and an eyrie-like hiding place at the top called Erazem's Nook, named for Erazem (Erasmus) Lueger, a 15th-century robber-baron who, like Robin Hood, stole from the rich to give to the poor.

The cave below the castle is part of the 14km Predjama cave system. It's open to visitors from May to September (closed in winter so as not to disturb its colony of bats). Tours need to be booked at least three days in advance; caving tours range in price from €24 to €80.

---

has been built in the town's west, on the road into town (by the supermarket Mercator). It's ideal for motorists, not so good for those on public transport, so there is a small info area inside the library at Trg Padlih Borcev 5, not far southwest of Titov trg.

ⓘ Getting There & Away

Buses from Ljubljana en route to Piran stop in Postojna (€6, one hour, 54km, hourly) and Divača (€7.90, 1½ hours, 82km, seven daily). Postojna is on the main train line linking Ljubljana (€5.80, one hour, 67km) with Sežana and Trieste via Divača. In July and August there is a free shuttle bus from the train station to Postojna Cave.

Piran

☑05 / POP 3975

Picturesque Piran (Pirano in Italian), sitting pretty at the tip of a narrow peninsula, is everyone's favourite town on the Slovenian coast. Its Old Town – one of the best-preserved historical towns anywhere on the Adriatic – is a gem of Venetian Gothic architecture, but it can be a mob scene at the height of summer. In quieter times, it's hard not to fall instantly in love with the atmospheric winding alleyways, the sunsets and the seafood restaurants.

☉ Sights

★**Cathedral of St George**　　CATHEDRAL
(Župnijska Cerkev Sv Jurija; www.zupnija-piran.si; Adamičeva ulica 2) A cobbled street leads from behind the Venetian House to Piran's hilltop cathedral, baptistery and bell tower. The cathedral was built in baroque style in the early 17th century, on the site of an earlier church from 1344.

The cathedral's doors are usually open and a metal grille allows you to see some of the richly ornate and newly restored interior, but full access is via the **Parish Museum of St George** (☑05-673 34 40; Adamičeva ulica 2; adult/child €1.50/0.75; ☺10am-4pm Wed-Mon), which includes the church's treasury and catacombs.

★**Bell Tower**　　TOWER
(Zvonik; Adamičeva ulica; €1; ☺10am-8pm summer) The Cathedral of St George's freestanding, 46.5m bell tower, built in 1609, was clearly modelled on the campanile of San Marco in Venice and provides a fabulous backdrop to many a town photo. Its 147 rickety stairs can be climbed for superb views of the town and harbour. Next to it, the octagonal 17th-century **baptistery** (*krstilnica*) contains altars and paintings. It is now sometimes used as an exhibition space. To the east is a 200m-long stretch of the 15th-century **town wall**.

★**Sergej Mašera**
Maritime Museum　　MUSEUM
(☑05-671 00 40; www.pomorskimuzej.si; Cankarjevo nabrežje 3; adult/child €3.50/2.10; ☺9am-noon & 5-9pm Tue-Sun Jul & Aug, 9am-5pm Tue-Sun Sep-Jun) Located in the 19th-century **Gabrielli Palace** on the waterfront, this museum's focus is the sea, with plenty of salty-dog stories relating to Slovenian seafaring. In the archaeological section, the 2000-year-old Roman amphorae beneath the glass floor are impressive. The antique model ships

upstairs are very fine; other rooms are filled with old figureheads and weapons, including some lethal-looking blunderbusses. The folk paintings are offerings placed by sailors on the altar of the pilgrimage church at Strunjan for protection against shipwreck.

🛏 Sleeping & Eating

Prices are higher in Piran than elsewhere on the coast, and it's not a good idea to arrive without a booking in summer. If you need to find a private room, start at the Maona Tourist Agency or Turist Biro (☎ 05-673 25 09; www.turistbiro-ag.si; Tomažičeva ulica 3; ⊗ 9am-1pm & 4-7pm Mon-Sat, 10am-1pm Sun).

★ PachaMama   GUESTHOUSE, APARTMENT €€
(☎ 059 183 495; www.pachamama.si; Trubarjeva 8; per person €30-35; ❋ 🛜) Built by travellers for travellers, this excellent new guesthouse ('PachaMama Pleasant Stay') sits just off Tartinijev trg and offers 12 simple, fresh rooms, decorated with timber and lots of travel photography. Cool private bathrooms and a 'secret garden' add appeal. There are also a handful of studios and family-sized apartments under the PachaMama umbrella, dotted around town and of an equally high standard.

★ Max Piran   B&B €€
(☎ 041 692 928, 05-673 34 36; www.maxpiran.com; Ulica IX Korpusa 26; d €65-70; ❋ 🛜) Piran's most romantic accommodation has just six handsome, compact rooms, each bearing a woman's name rather than a number, in a delightful, coral-coloured, 18th-century

townhouse. It's just down from the Cathedral of St George, and excellent value.

★ Cantina Klet   SEAFOOD €
(Trg 1 Maja 10; mains €5-9; ⊗ 10am-11pm) This small wine bar sits pretty under a grapevine canopy on Trg 1 Maja. You order drinks from the bar (cheap local wine from the barrel or well-priced beers), but we especially love the self-service window (labelled 'Fritolin pri Cantini') where you order from a small blackboard menu of fishy dishes, like fish fillet with polenta, fried calamari or fish tortilla.

ℹ Information

Tourist Information Centre (TIC; ☎ 05-673 44 40; www.portoroz.si; Tartinijev trg 2; ⊗ 9am-10pm Jul & Aug, to 7pm May, to 5pm Sep-Apr & Jun) In the impressive Municipal Hall.

ℹ Getting There & Away

BUS

At least three buses a day make the run to/from Ljubljana (€12, three hours, 140km via Divača and Postojna). One bus a day heads to Trieste (€5.90, 1½ hours, 43km) in Italy. One bus a day heads south for Croatian Istria from late June to September, stopping at the coastal towns of Umag, Poreč and Rovinj (€9, 2¾ hours).

SURVIVAL GUIDE

ℹ Directory A–Z

MONEY
The official currency is the euro. Exchanging cash is simple at banks, major post offices, travel agencies and a *menjalnica* (bureau de change), although many don't accept travellers cheques. Major credit and debit cards are accepted almost everywhere, and ATMs are ubiquitous.

TELEPHONE
Slovenia uses GSM 900, which is compatible with the rest of Europe and Australia but not with the North American GSM 1900 or the Japanese system.

TOURIST INFORMATION
The **Slovenian Tourist Board** (Slovenska Turistična Organizacija, STO; ☎ 01-589 85 50; www.slovenia.info; Dimičeva 13), based in Ljubljana, is the umbrella organisation for tourist promotion in Slovenia, and produces a number of excellent brochures, pamphlets and booklets in English. In addition, the organisation oversees dozens of tourist information centres (TICs) across the country.

COUNTRY FACTS

Area 20,273 sq km

Capital Ljubljana

Country code ☎ 386

Currency Euro (€)

Emergency Ambulance ☎ 112, fire ☎ 112, police ☎ 113

Language Slovene

Money ATMs are everywhere; banks open Monday to Friday and (rarely) Saturday morning

Population 2.06 million

Visas Not required for citizens of the EU, Australia, USA, Canada or New Zealand

---

ⓘ Getting There & Away

AIR

Slovenia's main international airport is Jože Pučnik Airport, located 27km north of Ljubljana. In the arrivals hall there's a **Slovenia Tourist Information Centre desk** (STIC; www.visitl-jubljana.si; Jože Pučnik Airport; ☺8am-7pm Mon-Fri, 9am-5pm Sat & Sun Oct-May, 8am-9pm Jun-Sep), travel agencies and an ATM.

Adria Airways (☑04-259 45 82, 01-369 10 10; www.adria-airways.com), the Slovenian flag-car-rier, serves more than 20 European destinations on regularly scheduled flights. Budget carriers include **EasyJet** (☑04-206 16 77; www.easyjet. com) and **Wizz Air** (☑ in UK 44-330 977 0444; www.wizzair.com).

LAND
Bus

International bus destinations from Ljubljana include Serbia, Germany, Croatia, Bosnia & Hercegovina, Macedonia, Italy and Scandinavia. You can also catch buses to Italy and Croatia from coastal towns, including Piran.

Train

It is possible to travel to Italy, Austria, Germany, Croatia and Hungary by train; Ljubljana is the main hub, although you can hop on international trains in certain other cities. International train travel can be expensive. It is sometimes cheaper to travel as far as you can on domestic routes before crossing borders.

Sea

Piran sends catamarans to Trieste daily and to Venice at least twice a week in season.

ⓘ Getting Around

BICYCLE

Cycling is a popular way of getting around. Bikes can be transported for €3.50 in the baggage compartments of some IC and regional trains. Larger buses can also carry bikes as luggage. Most towns and cities have dedicated bicycle lanes and traffic lights.

EATING PRICE RANGES

The following price ranges refer to a two-course, sit-down meal, including a drink, for one person. Many restaurants also offer an excellent-value set menu of two or even three courses at lunch.

€ less than €15

€€ €16–€30

€€€ more than €31

SLEEPING PRICE RANGES

The following price ranges refer to a double room with en suite toilet and bath or shower, and include tax and breakfast.

€ less than €50

€€ €51–€100

€€€ more than €100

BUS

You can buy your ticket at the *avtobusna postaja* (bus station) or simply pay the driver as you board. In Ljubljana you should book your seat (€1.50/3.70 domestic/international) a day in advance if you're travelling on Friday, or to destinations in the mountains or on the coast on a public holiday. A range of bus companies serve the country, but prices are uniform: €3.10/5.60/9.20/16.80 for 25/50/100/200km of travel.

CAR & MOTORCYCLE

Roads in Slovenia are generally good. Tolls are no longer paid separately on the motor-ways. Instead, cars must display a *vinjeta* (road-toll sticker) on the windscreen. It costs €15/30/110 for a week/month/year for cars and €7.50/30/55 for motorbikes and is available at petrol stations, post offices and certain news stands and tourist information centres. Failure to display a sticker risks a fine of up to €300.

Renting a car in Slovenia allows access to cheaper out-of-centre hotels and farm or village homestays. Rentals from international firms such as Avis, Budget, Europcar and Hertz vary in price; expect to pay from €38/200 per day/week, including unlimited mileage, taxes and required insurance. Some smaller agencies have more competitive rates; booking on the internet is always cheaper.

Dial ☑1987 for roadside assistance.

TRAIN

Much of the country is accessible by rail, run by the national operator, **Slovenian Railways** (Slovenske Železnice, SŽ; ☑ 01-291 33 32; www. slo-zeleznice.si). The website has an easy-to-use timetable.

Figure on travelling at about 65km/h except on the fastest InterCity Slovenia (ICS) express trains that run at an average speed of 90km/h.

Purchase your ticket at the *železniška postaja* (train station) itself; buying it from the conduc-tor on the train costs an additional €3.60. An invalid ticket or fare dodging earns a €40 fine.

Spain

Best Places to Eat

➜ Casa Delfín (p1054)

➜ La Cuchara de San Telmo (p1063)

➜ Cinc Sentits (p1055)

➜ El Poblet (p1070)

➜ Adolfo (p1044)

Best Places to Stay

➜ Un Patio en Santa Cruz (p1079)

➜ Balcón de Córdoba (p1082)

➜ Barceló Raval (p1053)

➜ Hotel Costa Vella (p1067)

➜ Hospedería La Gran Casa Mudéjar (p1042)

Why Go?

Passionate, sophisticated and devoted to living the good life, Spain is at once a stereotype come to life and a country more diverse than you ever imagined.

Spanish landscapes stir the soul, from the jagged Pyrenees and wildly beautiful cliffs of the Atlantic northwest to charming Mediterranean coves, while astonishing architecture spans the ages at seemingly every turn. Spain's cities march to a beguiling beat with cutting-edge architecture and unrivalled nightlife, even as time-capsule villages serve as beautiful signposts to Old Spain. And then there's one of Europe's most celebrated (and varied) gastronomic scenes.

But, above all, Spain lives very much in the present. Perhaps you'll sense it along a crowded after-midnight street when all the world has come out to play. Or maybe that moment will come when a flamenco performer touches something deep in your soul. Whenever it happens, you'll find yourself nodding in recognition: *this* is Spain.

When to Go
Madrid

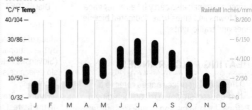

Mar–Apr Spring wildflowers, Semana Santa processions and mild southern temps.

May, Jun & Sep Balmy weather but without the crowds of high summer.

Jul–Aug Spaniards hit the coast in the summer heat, but quiet corners still abound.

MADRID

POP 3.3 MILLION

No city on earth is more alive than Madrid, a beguiling place whose sheer energy carries a simple message: this city really knows how to live. Explore the old streets of the centre, relax in the plazas, soak up the culture in Madrid's excellent art museums, and spend at least one night in the city's legendary nightlife scene.

◉ Sights

★ Museo del Prado — MUSEUM

(Map p1030; www.museodelprado.es; Paseo del Prado; adult/child €15/free, 6-8pm Mon-Sat & 5-7pm Sun free, audio guides €3.50, admission plus official guidebook €24; ⏲10am-8pm Mon-Sat, 10am-7pm Sun; 🚇; Ⓜ Banco de España) Welcome to one of the world's premier art galleries. The more than 7000 paintings held in the Museo del Prado's collection (although only around 1500 are currently on display) are like a window onto the historical vagaries of the Spanish soul, at once grand and imperious in the royal paintings of Velázquez, darkly tumultuous in *Las pinturas negras* (The Black Paintings) of Goya, and outward looking with sophisticated works of art from all across Europe.

★ Centro de Arte Reina Sofía — MUSEUM

(Map p1034; ☎91 774 10 00; www.museoreinasofia. es; Calle de Santa Isabel 52; adult/concession €8/free, 1.30-7pm Sun, 7-9pm Mon & Wed-Sat free; ⏲10am-9pm Mon & Wed-Sat, 10am-7pm Sun; Ⓜ Atocha) Home to Picasso's *Guernica,* arguably Spain's most famous artwork, the Centro de Arte Reina Sofía is Madrid's premier collection of contemporary art. In addition to plenty of paintings by Picasso, other major drawcards are works by Salvador Dalí (1904–89) and Joan Miró (1893–1983). The collection principally spans the 20th century up to the 1980s. The occasional non-Spaniard artist makes an appearance (including Francis Bacon's *Lying Figure;* 1966), but most of the collection is strictly peninsular.

★ Plaza Mayor — SQUARE

(Map p1034; Ⓜ Sol) Madrid's grand central square, a rare but expansive opening in the tightly packed streets of central Madrid, is one of the prettiest open spaces in Spain, a winning combination of imposing architecture, picaresque historical tales and vibrant street life coursing across its cobblestones. At once beautiful in its own right and a reference point for so many Madrid days, it also hosts the city's main tourist office, a Christmas market in December and arches leading to laneways leading out into the labyrinth.

★ Museo Thyssen-Bornemisza — MUSEUM

(Map p1034; ☎902 760511; www.museothyssen. org; Paseo del Prado 8; adult/child €12/free, Mon free; ⏲10am-7pm Tue-Sun, noon-4pm Mon; Ⓜ Banco de España) The Thyssen is one of the most extraordinary private collections of predominantly European art in the world. Where the Prado or Reina Sofía enable you to study the body of work of a particular artist in depth, the Thyssen is the place to immerse yourself in a breathtaking breadth of artistic styles. Most of the big names are here, sometimes with just a single painting, but the Thyssen's gift to Madrid and the art-loving public is to have them all under one roof.

SPAIN MADRID

ITINERARIES

One Week

Marvel at the art nouveau–influenced Modernista architecture and seaside style of Barcelona before taking the train to San Sebastián. Head on to Bilbao for the Guggenheim Museum and end the trip living it up inthelegendary night-life scene of Madrid.

One Month

Fly into Seville and embark on a route exploring this and Andalucía's other magical cities, Granada and Córdoba. Take the train to Madrid, from where you can check out Toledo, Salamanca and Segovia. Make east for the coast and Valencia. Head up to the Basque Country to see the epoch-making Guggenheim Museum in Bilbao and feast on some of the world's best food in San Sebastián, then head east via the medieval villages of Aragón and the dramatic Pyrenees to Catalonia, spending time in Tarragona before reaching Barcelona. Take a plane or boat for some R and R on the beautiful Balearic Islands before catching a flight home.

Spain Highlights

1 Alhambra
(p1083) Exploring the exquisite Islamic palace complex in Granada.

2 La Sagrada Família (p1049)
Visiting Gaudí's singular work in progress in Barcelona, a cathedral that truly defies imagination.

3 Mezquita
(p1081) Wandering amid the horseshoe arches of Córdoba's great medieval mosque, close to perfection wrought in stone.

4 San Sebastián
(p1062) Eating your way through a food-lover's paradise with an idyllic setting.

5 Santiago de Compostela (p1066)
Joining the pilgrims in Galicia's magnificent cathedral city.

6 Seville (p1076)
Soaking up the scent of orange blossom, being carried away by the passion of flamenco and surrendering to the party atmosphere in this sunny southern city.

7 Menorca
(p1073) Discovering the impossibly beautiful beaches and coves of this less-developed Mediterranean island.

8 Madrid (p1025)
Spending your days in some of Europe's best art galleries and nights amid its best nightlife.

BAY OF BISCAY

Avilés
Gijón
Santander

A Coruña
Ferrol
Oviedo
Torrelavega

Santiago de Compostela **5**
Lugo
GALICIA
ASTURIAS
Reinosa

AP9
A6
AP66

Pontevedra
Ourense
León

Vigo
Valença do Minho
Benavente
Palencia
A62

Zamora
Valladolid

Porto
Salamanca
Segovia

Ávila
A6

Coimbra
PORTUGAL
Plasencia
Talavera de la Reina
8
Madrid

A5
Toledo
CASTILLA-LA MANCHA

Cáceres
Trujillo
Ciudad Real

EXTREMADURA

LISBON
Badajoz
Mérida
Almadén

Zafra
Puertollano

Barrancos
N432
N420

Aracena
A66
Córdoba **3**
Jaén

Seville **6**
A4
ANDALUCÍA

Huelva
Jerez de la Frontera
Arcos de la Frontera
Ronda

Faro
Cádiz
Marbella
Málaga

AP7
Costa del Sol

Algeciras
Gibraltar (UK)

Tarifa
Sea of Gibraltar
Ceuta (Spain)

Tangier

ATLANTIC OCEAN

MOROCCO

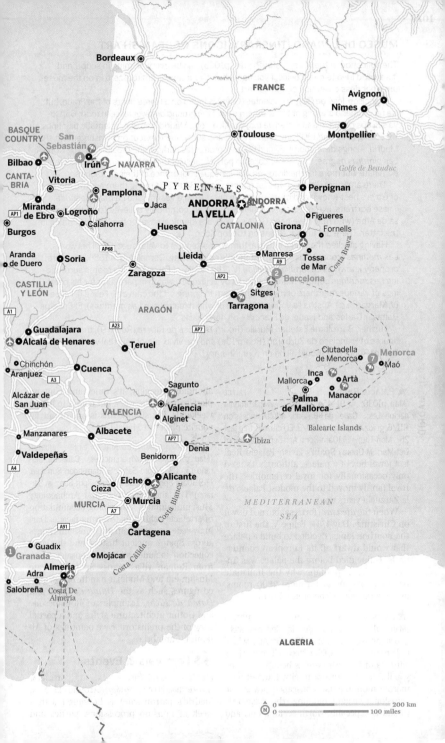

MUSEO DEL PRADO ITINERARY: ICONS OF SPANISH ART

The collection of the Museo del Prado (p1025) can be overwhelming in scope, and it's a good idea to come twice if you can – but if your time is limited, zero in on the museum's peerless collection of Spanish art.

Francisco José de Goya y Lucientes (Goya) is found on all three floors of the Prado, but we recommend starting at the southern end of the ground or lower level. In room 65, Goya's *El dos de mayo* and *El tres de mayo* rank among Madrid's most emblematic paintings; they bring to life the 1808 anti-French revolt and subsequent execution of insurgents in Madrid. Alongside, in rooms 67 and 68, are some of his darkest and most disturbing works, *Las pinturas negras*; they are so called in part because of the dark browns and black that dominate, but more for the distorted animalesque appearance of their characters.

There are more Goyas in rooms 34 to 37. Among them are two more of Goya's best-known and most intriguing oils: *La maja vestida* and *La maja desnuda*. These portraits, in room 36, of an unknown woman, commonly believed to be the Duquesa de Alba (who may have been Goya's lover), are identical save for the lack of clothing in the latter. There are further Goyas on the top floor.

Having studied the works of Goya, turn your attention to Velázquez. Of all his works, *Las meninas* (room 12) is what most people come to see. Completed in 1656, it is more properly known as *La família de Felipe IV* (The Family of Felipe IV). The rooms surrounding *Las meninas* contain more fine works by Velázquez: watch in particular for his paintings of various members of royalty who seem to spring off the canvas – Felipe II, Felipe IV, Margarita de Austria (a younger version of whom features in *Las meninas*), El Príncipe Baltasar Carlos and Isabel de Francia – on horseback.

Further, Bartolomé Esteban Murillo (Room 17), José de Ribera (Room 9), the stark figures of Francisco de Zurbarán (Room 10a) and the vivid, almost surreal works of El Greco (Room 8b) should all be on your itinerary.

★ **Palacio Real**   PALACE
(Map p1030; ✆91 454 88 00; www.patrimonio nacional.es; Calle de Bailén; adult/concession €11/6, guide/audio guide €4/3, EU citizens free last 2hr Mon-Thu; ◷10am-8pm Apr-Sep, 10am-6pm Oct-Mar; Ⓜ Ópera) Spain's lavish Palacio Real is a jewel box of a palace, although it's used only occasionally for royal ceremonies; the royal family moved to the modest Palacio de la Zarzuela years ago.

When the *alcázar* (fortress) burned down on Christmas Day 1734, Felipe V, the first of the Bourbon kings, decided to build a palace that would dwarf all its European counterparts. Felipe died before the palace was finished, which is perhaps why the Italianate baroque colossus has a mere 2800 rooms, just one-quarter of the original plan.

★ **Parque del Buen Retiro**   GARDENS
(Map p1030; Plaza de la Independencia; ◷6am-midnight May-Sep, to 10pm Oct-Apr; Ⓜ Retiro, Príncipe de Vergara, Ibiza, Atocha) The glorious gardens of El Retiro are as beautiful as any you'll find in a European city. Littered with marble monuments, landscaped lawns, the occasional elegant building (the Palacio de Cristal is especially worth seeking out) and abundant greenery, it's quiet and contemplative during the week but comes to life on weekends. Put simply, this is one of our favourite places in Madrid.

Museo Arqueológico Nacional   MUSEUM
(Map p1030; http://man.mcu.es; Calle de Serrano 13; €3, 2-8pm Sat & 9.30am-noon Sun free; ◷9.30am-8pm Tue-Sat, 9.30am-3pm Sun; Ⓜ Serrano) The showpiece National Archaeology Museum contains a sweeping accumulation of artefacts behind its towering facade. Daringly redesigned within, the museum ranges across Spain's ancient history and the large collection includes stunning mosaics taken from Roman villas across Spain, intricate Muslim-era and Mudéjar handiwork, sculpted figures such as the *Dama de Ibiza* and *Dama de Elche,* examples of Romanesque and Gothic architectural styles and a partial copy of the prehistoric cave paintings of Altamira (Cantabria).

✦ Festivals & Events

Fiesta de San Isidro   CULTURAL
(www.esmadrid.com; ◷May) Around 15 May, Madrid's patron saint is honoured with a week of nonstop processions, parties and

bullfights. Free concerts are held throughout the city, and this week marks the start of the city's bullfighting season.

🛏 Sleeping

Plaza Mayor & Royal Madrid

⭐ **Central Palace Madrid**   HOTEL €€
(Map p1034; ✆ 91 548 20 18; www.centralpalace-madrid.com; Plaza de Oriente 2; d with/without view €119/99; ❄ 🛜; Ⓜ Ópera) Now here's something special. The views alone would be reason enough to come and definitely worth paying extra for – rooms with balconies look out over the Palacio Real and Plaza de Oriente. But the rooms themselves are lovely and light-filled, with tasteful, subtle faux-antique furnishings, comfortable beds, light wood floors and plenty of space.

La Latina

⭐ **Posada del León de Oro** BOUTIQUE HOTEL €€
(Map p1034; ✆ 91 119 14 94; www.posadadelleondeoro.com; Calle de la Cava Baja 12; r from €130; ❄ 🛜; Ⓜ La Latina) This rehabilitated inn has muted colour schemes and generally large rooms. There's a *corrala* in its core, and thoroughly modern rooms (some on the small side) along one of Madrid's best-loved streets. The downstairs bar is terrific.

Sol, Santa Ana & Huertas

⭐ **Lapepa Chic B&B**   B&B €
(Map p1034; ✆ 648 474742; www.lapepa-bnb.com; 7th fl, Plaza de las Cortes 4; s/d from €63/69; ❄ 🛜; Ⓜ Banco de España) A short step off the Paseo del Prado and on a floor with an art nouveau interior, this fine little B&B has lovely rooms with a contemporary, clean-lined look so different from the dour *hostal* furnishings you'll find elsewhere – modern art or even a bedhead lined with flamenco shoes gives this place personality in bucketloads.

⭐ **Hotel Alicia**   BOUTIQUE HOTEL €€
(Map p1034; ✆ 91 389 60 95; www.room-mateho-teles.com; Calle del Prado 2; d €135-175, ste from €200; ❄ 🛜; Ⓜ Sol, Sevilla, Antón Martín) One of the landmark properties of the designer Room Mate chain of hotels, Hotel Alicia overlooks Plaza de Santa Ana with beautiful, spacious rooms. The style (the work of designer Pascua Ortega) is a touch more

muted than in other Room Mate hotels, but the supermodern look remains intact, the downstairs bar is oh-so-cool, and the service is young and switched on.

⭐ **Praktik Metropol**   BOUTIQUE HOTEL €€
(Map p1034; ✆ 91 521 29 35; www.hotelpraktik metropol.com; Calle de la Montera 47; s/d from €100/110; ❄ 🛜; Ⓜ Gran Vía) You'd be hard-pressed to find better value anywhere in Europe than here in this recently overhauled hotel. The rooms have a fresh, contemporary look with white wood furnishings, and some (especially the corner rooms) have brilliant views down to Gran Vía and out over the city.

Malasaña & Chueca

⭐ **Hostal Main Street Madrid**   HOSTAL €
(Map p1034; ✆ 91 548 18 78; www.mainstreet-madrid.com; 5th fl, Gran Vía 50; r from €68; ❄ 🛜; Ⓜ Callao, Santo Domingo) Excellent service is what travellers rave about here, but the rooms – modern and cool in soothing greys – are also some of the best *hostal* rooms you'll find anywhere in central Madrid. It's an excellent package and not surprisingly it's often full, so book well in advance.

⭐ **Only You Hotel**   BOUTIQUE HOTEL €€
(Map p1034; ✆ 91 005 22 22; www.onlyyouhotels.com; Calle de Barquillo 21; d €180-260; ❄ @ 🛜; Ⓜ Chueca) This stunning boutique hotel makes perfect use of a 19th-century Chueca mansion. The look is classy and contemporary and is the latest project by respected interior designer Lázaro Rosa-Violán. Nice touches include all-day à la carte breakfasts and a portable router that you can carry out into the city to stay connected.

⭐ **Hotel Orfila**   HOTEL €€€
(Map p1030; ✆ 91 702 77 70; www.hotelorfila.com; Calle de Orfila 6; r from €230; 🅿 ❄ 🛜; Ⓜ Alonso Martínez) One of Madrid's best hotels, Hotel Orfila has all the luxuries of any five-star hotel – supremely comfortable rooms, for a start – but it's the personal service that elevates it into the upper echelon; regular guests get bathrobes embroidered with their own initials. An old-world elegance dominates the decor, and the quiet location and sheltered garden make it the perfect retreat at day's end.

Madrid

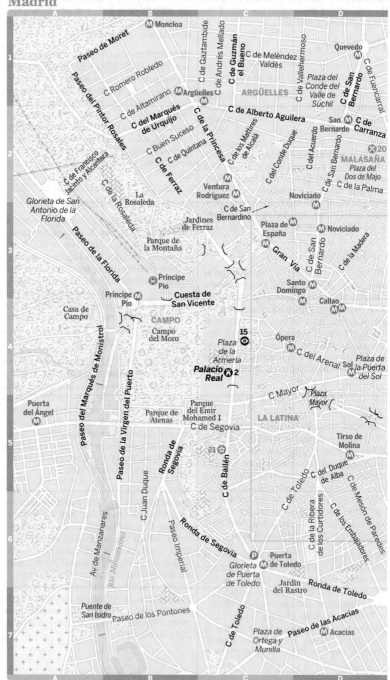

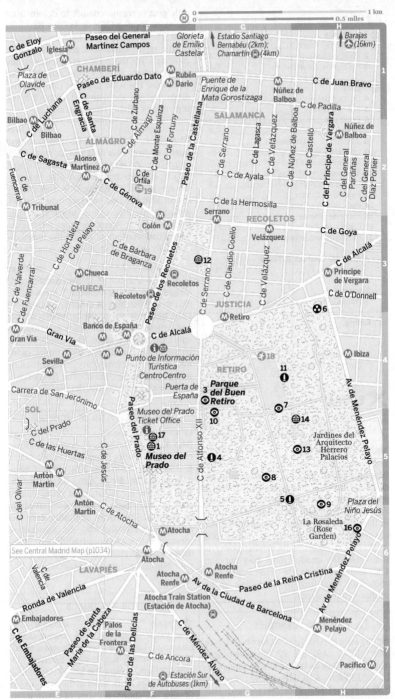

✖ Eating

Plaza Mayor & Royal Madrid

★ Restaurante Sobrino de Botín
CASTILIAN €€€

(Map p1034; ☎ 91 366 42 17; www.botin.es; Calle de los Cuchilleros 17; mains €19-27; ⊙1-4pm & 8pm-midnight; Ⓜ La Latina, Sol) It's not every day that you can eat in the oldest restaurant in the world (the *Guinness Book of Records* has recognised it as the oldest – established in 1725). The secret of its staying power is fine *cochinillo asado* (roast suckling pig; €25) and *cordero asado* (roast lamb; €25) cooked in wood-fired ovens. Eating in the vaulted cellar is a treat.

La Latina & Lavapiés

★ Taberna Matritum
MODERN SPANISH €€

(Map p1034; ☎ 91 365 82 37; www.taberna matritum.es; Calle de la Cava Alta 17; mains €13-17; ⊙1.30-4pm & 8.30pm-midnight Wed-Sun, 8.30pm-midnight Mon & Tue; Ⓜ La Latina) This little gem is reason enough to detour from the more popular Calle de la Cava Baja next door. The seasonal menu here encompasses terrific tapas, salads and generally creative cooking – try the *cocido* croquettes or the winter *calçots* (large spring onions) from Catalonia. The wine list runs into the hundreds and it's sophisticated without being pretentious. Highly recommended.

El Estragón
VEGETARIAN €€

(Map p1034; ☎ 91 365 89 82; www.elestragon-vegetariano.com; Plaza de la Paja 10; mains €8-15; ⊙1pm-1am; ⏧; Ⓜ La Latina) A delightful spot for crêpes, vegie burgers and other vegetarian specialities, El Estragón is undoubtedly one of Madrid's best vegetarian restaurants, although attentive vegans won't appreciate the use of butter. Apart from that, we're yet to hear a bad word about it, and the *menú del día* (daily set menu; from €12) is a bargain.

La Buga del Lobo
SPANISH €€

(Map p1034; ☎ 91 528 88 38; www.facebook.com/labugadellobo; Calle de Argumosa 11; mains €12-21; ⊙11am-2am Wed-Mon; Ⓜ Lavapiés) La Buga del Lobo has been one of the 'in' places in cool and gritty Lavapiés for years now and it's still hard to get a table. The atmosphere is bohemian and inclusive, with funky, swirling murals, contemporary art exhibitions and jazz or lounge music. The food's traditional with a few creative detours.

✖ Sol, Santa Ana & Huertas

La Finca de Susana
SPANISH €

(Map p1034; ☎ 91 429 76 78; www.grupandilana.com; Calle del Príncipe 10; mains €8-14; ⊙1-3.45pm & 8.30-11.30pm Sun-Wed, 1-3.45pm & 8.15pm-midnight Thu-Sat; ⏧; Ⓜ Sevilla) It's difficult to find a better combination of price, quality cooking and classy atmosphere anywhere in Huertas. The softly lit dining area has a sophisticated vibe and the sometimes-innovative, sometimes-traditional food draws a hip young crowd. The duck confit with plums, turnips and couscous is a fine choice. No reservations.

✖ Malasaña & Chueca

★ Bazaar
MODERN SPANISH €

(Map p1034; ☎ 91 523 39 05; www.restaurant bazaar.com; Calle de la Libertad 21; mains €6.50-10; ⊙1.15-4pm & 8.30-11.30pm Sun-Wed, 1.15-4pm & 8.15pm-midnight Thu-Sat; ⏧; Ⓜ Chueca) Bazaar's popularity among the well-heeled Chueca set shows no sign of abating. Its

SPAIN MADRID

pristine white interior design, with theatre-style lighting and wall-length windows, may draw a crowd that looks like it's stepped out of the pages of *¡Hola!* magazine, but the food is extremely well priced and innovative, and the atmosphere is casual.

⭐ Yakitoro by Chicote   JAPANESE, SPANISH €€
(Map p1034; ☑91 737 14 41; www.yakitoro.com; Calle de la Reina 41; tapas €3-8; ⊘1pm-midnight; Ⓜ Banco de España) Based around the idea of a Japanese tavern, driven by a spirit of innovation and a desire to combine the best in Spanish and Japanese flavours, Yakitoro is a hit. Apart from salads, it's all built around brochettes cooked over a wood fire, with wonderful combinations of vegetable, seafood and meat.

🍷 Drinking & Nightlife

The essence of Madrid lives in its streets and plazas, and bar-hopping is a pastime enjoyed by young and old alike. If you're after the more traditional, with tiled walls and flamenco tunes, head to Huertas. For gay-friendly drinking holes, Chueca is the place. Malasaña caters to a grungy, funky crowd, while La Latina has friendly bars that guarantee atmosphere most nights of the week. In summer, the terrace bars that pop up all over the city are unbeatable.

The bulk of Madrid bars open to 2am Sunday to Thursday, and to 3am or 3.30am Friday and Saturday. As the bars wind down, the nightclubs *(discotecas)* that have brought such renown to Madrid start to open. Don't expect them to get going until after 1am at the earliest. Standard entry fee is €12, which usually includes the first drink, although megaclubs and swankier places charge a few euros more.

⭐ Delic   BAR
(Map p1034; ☑91 364 54 50; www.delic.es; Costanilla de San Andrés 14; ⊘11am-2am Sun & Tue-Thu, 11am-2.30am Fri & Sat; Ⓜ La Latina) We could go on for hours about this long-standing cafe-bar, but we'll reduce it to its most basic elements: nursing an exceptionally good mojito (€8) or three on a warm summer's evening at Delic's outdoor tables on one of Madrid's prettiest plazas is one of life's great pleasures. Bliss.

⭐ La Venencia   BAR
(Map p1034; ☑91 429 73 13; Calle de Echegaray 7; ⊘12.30-3.30pm & 7.30pm-1.30am; Ⓜ Sol, Sevilla) La Venencia is a *barrio* classic, with *manzanilla* (chamomile-coloured sherry) from Sanlúcar and sherry from Jeréz poured straight from the dusty wooden barrels, accompanied by a small selection of tapas with an Andalucian bent. Otherwise, there's no music, no flashy decorations; it's all about you, your *fino* (sherry) and your friends. As one reviewer put it, it's 'a classic among classics'.

SPAIN MADRID

MADRID'S BEST PLAZAS

A royal palace that once had aspirations to be the Spanish Versailles. Sophisticated cafes watched over by apartments that cost the equivalent of a royal salary. The **Teatro Real** (Map p1034; ☑902 24 48 48; www.teatro-real.com; Plaza de Oriente; Ⓜ Ópera), Madrid's opera house and one of Spain's temples to high culture. Some of the finest sunset views in Madrid... Welcome to **Plaza de Oriente** (Map p1030; Plaza de Oriente; Ⓜ Ópera), a living, breathing monument to imperial Madrid.

On the other hand, the intimate **Plaza de la Villa** (Map p1034; Plaza de la Villa; Ⓜ Ópera) is one of Madrid's prettiest. Enclosed on three sides by wonderfully preserved examples of 17th-century *barroco madrileño* (Madrid-style baroque architecture – a pleasing amalgam of brick, exposed stone and wrought iron), it was the permanent seat of Madrid's city government from the Middle Ages until recent years, when Madrid's city council relocated to the grand Palacio de Cibeles on **Plaza de la Cibeles** (Map p1034; Ⓜ Banco de España).

Plaza de Santa Ana (Map p1034; Plaza de Santa Ana; Ⓜ Sevilla, Sol, Antón Martín) is a delightful confluence of elegant architecture and irresistible energy. It presides over the upper reaches of the Barrio de las Letras and this literary personality makes its presence felt with the statues of the 17th-century writer Calderón de la Barca and Federico García Lorca, and in the **Teatro Español** (Map p1034; ☑91 360 14 84; www.teatroespanol.es; Calle del Príncipe 25; Ⓜ Sevilla, Sol, Antón Martín), formerly the Teatro del Príncipe, at the plaza's eastern end. Apart from anything else, the plaza is the starting point for many a long Huertas night.

Central Madrid

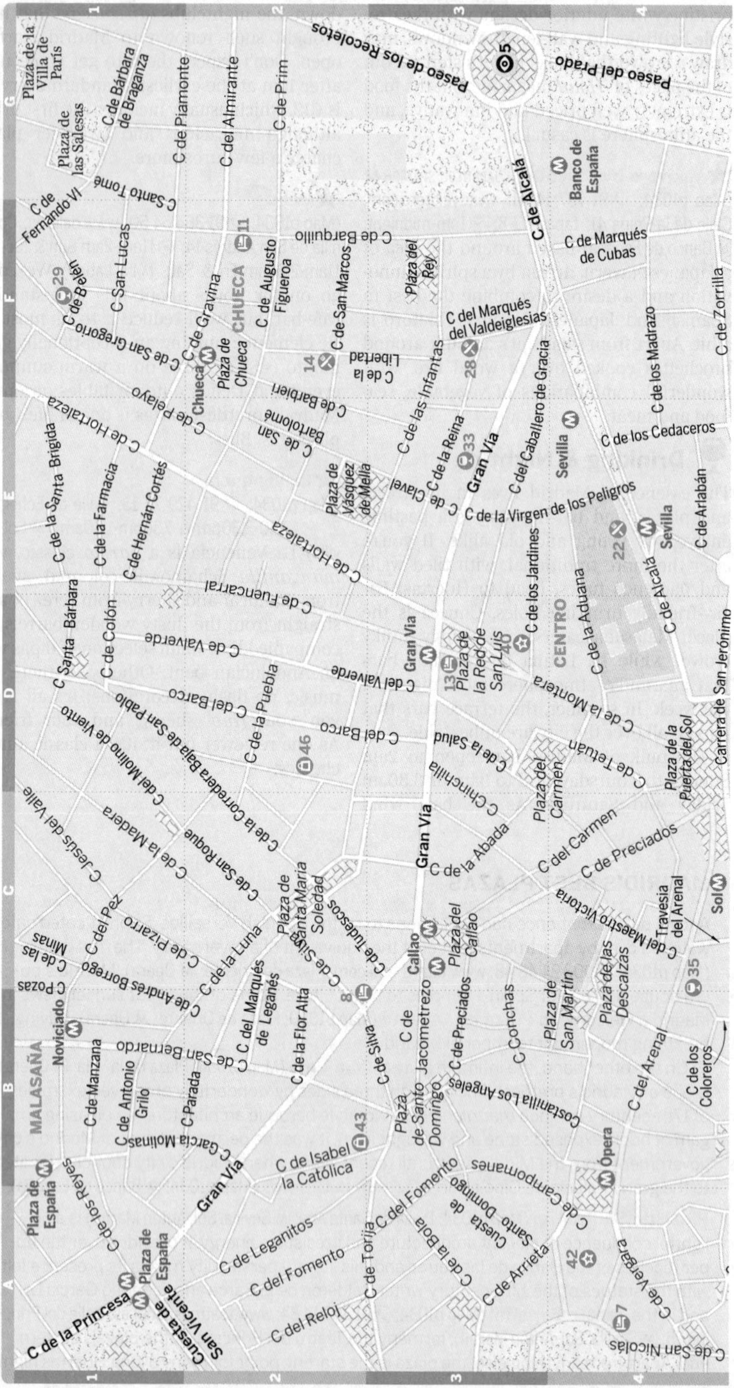

SPAIN MADRID

Map locations and labels:

Plaza de la Villa de París
Plaza de las Salesas
C de Bárbara de Braganza
C de Piamonte
C del Almirante
C de Prim
Paseo de los Recoletos
Paseo del Prado

C de Fernando VI
C de Santo Tomé
C de San Lucas
C de San Gregorio
C de Belén
C de Augusto Figueroa
C de Gravina
CHUECA
C de Bárbaro
C de San Marcos
Plaza del Rey
Banco de España
C de Alcalá
C de Marqués de Cubas
C de los Madrazo
C de Zorrilla

C de la Santa Brígida
C de la Farmacia
C de Hernán Cortés
C de Hortaleza
C de Pelayo
Chueca
C de San Bartolomé
C de Barbieri
C de la Libertad
C del Marqués del Valdeiglesias
Plaza de Vázquez de Mella
C de Chueca
C de las Infantas
C de la Reina
Gran Vía
C del Clavel
C de la Virgen de los Peligros
C del Caballero de Gracia
Sevilla
C de los Cedaceros
C de los Jardines
C de la Aduana
C de Alcalá
C de Ariabán
Sevilla

C Santa Bárbara
C de Colón
C de Valverde
C de Fuencarral
C del Valverde
Gran Vía
Plaza de la Red de San Luis
CENTRO
C de la Montera

C del Barco
C de la Puebla
C del Barco
C de la Salud
Chinchilla
Plaza del Carmen
C de Tetuán
Plaza de la Puerta del Sol

C Jesús del Valle
C del Molino de Viento
C de San Pablo
C de la Corredera Baja de San Pablo
C de la Madera
C de San Roque
C de la Luna
Plaza de Santa María Soledad
C de Tudescos
C de la Abada
C del Carmen
C de Preciados
Plaza del Carmen
Carrera de San Jerónimo

C de las Minas
C de Andrés Borrego
C del Pez
C de Pizarro
C del Marqués de Leganés
C de la Flor Alta
C de San Bernardo
Callao
Plaza del Callao
C de Silva
C de Jacometrezo
C de Conchas
Plaza de San Martín
Plaza de las Descalzas
Sol
Travesía del Arenal
C del Maestro Victoria

Novicado
C Pozas
MALASAÑA
C de Manzana
C de Antonio Grilo
C Parada
García Molinas
C de la Flor Alta
Plaza de Santo Domingo
Costanilla Los Ángeles
C del Arenal
C de los Coloreros

Plaza de España
C de los Reyes
Plaza de España
Cuesta de San Vicente
C de la Princesa
C de Isabel la Católica
Gran Vía
C de Leganitos
C de Torija
C del Fomento
C de la Bola
Cuesta de Santo Domingo
C del Fomento
C de Campomanes
Ópera
C de Vergara

C del Reloj
C del Relol
C de Arrieta
C de San Nicolás

29
11
14
28
5
33
22
13
46
8
43
42
7
35

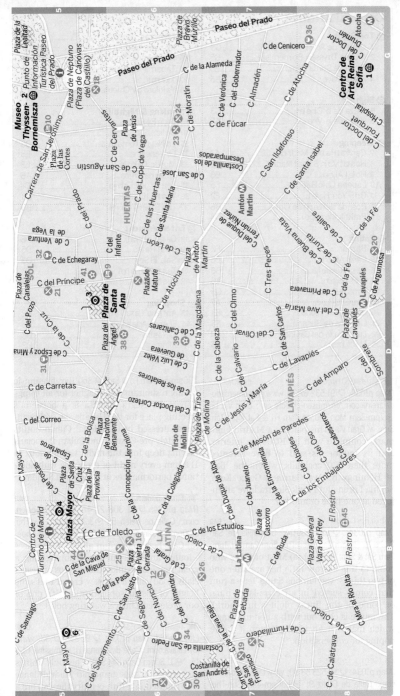

SPAIN MADRID

Paseo del Prado

Plaza de la Lealtad

Museo Thyssen-Bornemisza 10

2 Punto de Información Turística Paseo del Prado

Plaza de Neptuno (Plaza de Cánovas del Castillo) 18

Paseo del Prado

Plaza de Bravo Murillo

C de Cenicero 36

Centro de Arte Reina Sofía 1

M Atocha

C del Doctor Drumen

Carrera de San Jerónimo

Plaza de las Cortes

C de Cervantes

Plaza de Jesús

C de la Alameda

C de Moratín 24

C de Verónica

C del Gobernador

C de Almadén

C de Atocha

C del Doctor Fourquet

C Hospital

C de San Agustín

C de Lope de Vega

C de Jesús

C de Fúcar

Costanilla de los Desamparados

C de San Ildefonso

C de Santa Isabel

HUERTAS

C del Prado

C de las Huertas

C de Santa María

C de San José

M Antón Martín

C de la Fe

C de Ventura de la Vega 32

C del Infante

C del Duque de Fernán Núñez

C de Zurita

C de Salitre

Plaza de las Cortes

C de Echegaray

C de León

Plaza de Antón Martín

C de Buena Vista

C de la Fe 20

SOL

C del Príncipe 41

9

Plaza de Santa Ana 3

Plaza de Matute

C de Atocha

C de Tres Peces

C de Primavera

M Lavapiés 45

C de Argumosa

Plaza de Canalejas 21

Plaza del Ángel 38

39

C de Cañizares

C del Olmo

C del Ave María

LAVAPIÉS

C del Pozo

31 C de Espoz y Mina

C de la Cruz

C de Luis Vélez de Guevara

C de la Magdalena

C del Olivar

C de San Carlos

Plaza de Lavapiés

C del Amparo

C de Carretas

C de los Relatores

C del Doctor Cortezo

C de la Cabeza

C del Calvario

C de Jesús y María

C de Lavapiés

C de Sombrerete

C del Correo

Plaza de Jacinto Benavente

Plaza de Tirso de Molina

C de Mesón de Paredes

C de Abades

C del Oso

C de Cabestreros

C de la Bolsa

Tirso de Molina M

C de Juanelo

C de la Encomienda

C de los Embajadores

C Mayor

C de Pozas

C de Esparteros

Plaza de la Concepción Jerónima

C de la Colegiata

C del Duque de Alba

Plaza de Cascorro

El Rastro

Plaza de Santa Cruz

Plaza de la Provincia

4

Plaza Mayor

C de Toledo

C de los Estudios

C de Ruda

El Rastro

Centro de Turismo de Madrid

C de la Cava de San Miguel

Plaza de Puerta Cerrada 16

25

C del Grafal

26

LA LATINA M La Latina

Plaza General Vara del Rey

37

C de la Pasa

12

C de Toledo

Plaza de la Cebada

C de San Justo

C del Nuncio

C del Almendro

Plaza de Cascorro

C de Segovia

6

C del Sacramento

Costanilla de San Pedro

34

Costanilla de la Cava Baja

19 27

C de Humilladero

C Mra l Río Alta

C de Toledo

C de Santiago

C Mayor

Carrera de San Francisco

Costanilla de San Andrés

17 30

C de Calatrava

Central Madrid

★ **Museo Chicote** COCKTAIL BAR
(Map p1034; ☑ 91 532 67 37; www.grupomercado-delareina.com/en/museo-chicote-en/; Gran Vía 12; ⊗7pm-3am Mon-Thu, to 4am Fri & Sat, 4pm-1am Sun; ⓜGran Vía) This place is a Madrid landmark, complete with its 1930s-era interior, and its founder is said to have invented more than 100 cocktails, which the likes of Hemingway, Ava Gardner, Grace Kelly, Sophia Loren and Frank Sinatra have all enjoyed at one time or another.

Taberna Chica BAR
(Map p1034; ☑ 683 269114; Costanilla de San Pedro 7; ⊗8pm-2am Mon-Thu, 5pm-2am Fri, 1pm-2am Sat & Sun; ⓜLa Latina) Most of those who come to this narrow little bar are after one of two things: the famous Santa Teresa rum that comes served in an extra-large mug, or some of the finest mojitos in Madrid. The music is chill-out with a nod to lounge, which makes it an ideal pit stop if you're hoping for conversation.

La Negra Tomasa BAR
(Map p1034; ☑ 91 523 58 30; www.lanegratomasa. com; Calle de Cádiz 9; ⊗1.30pm-4am Sun-Thu, 1.30pm-5.30am Fri & Sat; ⓜSol) Bar, live-music venue, restaurant and magnet for all things Cuban, La Negra Tomasa is a boisterous meeting place for the Havana set, with waitresses dressed in traditional Cuban outfits (definitely pre-Castro) and Cuban musicians playing deep into the night. Groups start at 11.30pm every night of the week, with additional performances at 3.30pm on Sundays.

★ **Café Belén** BAR
(Map p1034; ☑ 91 308 27 47; www.elcafebelen. com; Calle de Belén 5; ⊗3.30pm-3am Tue-Thu, 3.30pm-3.30am Fri & Sat, 7-10pm Sun; ☎; ⓜChueca) Café Belén is cool in all the right places – lounge and chill-out music, dim lighting, a great range of drinks (the mojitos are especially good) and a low-key crowd that's the height of casual sophistication. It's one of our preferred Chueca watering holes.

★ **Teatro Joy Eslava** CLUB
(Joy Madrid; Map p1034; ☑ 91 366 37 33; www. joy-eslava.com; Calle del Arenal 11; admission €12-15; ⊗11.30pm-6am; ⓜSol) The only things guaranteed at this grand old Madrid dance club (housed in a 19th-century theatre) are a

crowd and the fact that it'll be open (it claims to have operated every single day since 1981). The music and the crowd are a mixed bag, but queues are long and invariably include locals and tourists, and even the occasional *famoso* (celebrity).

Teatro Kapital CLUB
(Map p1034; ☏ 91 420 29 06; www.grupo-kapital. com; Calle de Atocha 125; admission from €17; ☉ midnight-6am Thu-Sat; Ⓜ Atocha) One of the most famous megaclubs in Madrid, this seven-storey venue has something for everyone: from cocktail bars and dance music to karaoke, salsa, hip hop and chilled spaces; there's even a 'Kissing Room'.

☆ Entertainment

★ Casa Patas FLAMENCO
(Map p1034; ☏ 91 369 04 96; www.casapatas. com; Calle de Cañizares 10; admission incl drink €38; ☉ shows 10.30pm Mon-Thu, 8pm & 10.30pm Fri & Sat; Ⓜ Antón Martín, Tirso de Molina) One of the top flamenco stages in Madrid, this *tablao* (choreographed flamenco show) always offers flawless quality that serves as a good introduction to the art. It's not the friendliest place in town, especially if you're only here for the show, and you're likely to be crammed in a little, but no one complains about the standard of the performances.

★ Café Central JAZZ
(Map p1034; ☏ 91 369 41 43; www.cafecentral-madrid.com; Plaza del Ángel 10; admission €12-18; ☉ 12.30pm-2.30am Mon-Thu, to 3.30am Fri, 11.30am-3.30am Sat, performances 9pm; Ⓜ Antón Martín, Sol) In 2011 the respected jazz magazine *Down Beat* included this art deco bar on its list of the world's best jazz clubs – the only place in Spain to earn the prestigious accolade (said by some to be the jazz equivalent of earning a Michelin star). With well over 1000 gigs under its belt, it rarely misses a beat.

★ Corral de la Morería FLAMENCO
(Map p1030; ☏ 91 365 84 46; www.corraldela moreria.com; Calle de la Morería 17; admission incl drink from €49; ☉ 7pm-12.15am, shows 8.30pm & 10.20pm; Ⓜ Ópera) This is one of the most prestigious flamenco stages in Madrid, with 50 years' experience as a leading venue and top performers most nights. The stage area has a rustic feel, and tables are pushed up close. Set menus from €47.

★ Sala El Sol LIVE MUSIC
(Map p1034; ☏ 91 532 64 90; www.elsolmad.com; Calle de los Jardines 3; admission incl drink €10, concert tickets €8-25; ☉ midnight-5.30am Tue-Sat Jul-Sep; Ⓜ Gran Vía) Madrid institutions don't come any more beloved than Sala El Sol. It opened in 1979, just in time for *la movida madrileña* (the Madrid scene), and quickly established itself as a leading stage for all the icons of the era, such as Nacha Pop and Alaska y los Pegamoides.

★ Estadio Santiago Bernabéu STADIUM
(☏ tickets 902 324324, tours 91 398 43 00/70; www.realmadrid.com; Av de Concha Espina 1; tours adult/child €24/18; ☉ tours 10am-7pm Mon-Sat, 10.30am-6.30pm Sun, except match days; Ⓜ Santiago Bernabéu) Football fans and budding Madridistas (Real Madrid supporters) will want to make a pilgrimage to the Estadio Santiago Bernabéu, a temple to all that's extravagant and successful in football. The self-guided tours take you into the stands, dressing rooms, trophy exhibit and out through the players' tunnel onto the pitch. Better still, attend a game alongside 80,000 delirious fans. For bigger games, tickets are hard to get. For less important matches, tickets can be purchased online, by phone or in person from the ticket office at gate 42 on Av de Concha Espina; for the last option, turn up early in the week before a scheduled game (eg a Monday morning for a Sunday game).

🔒 Shopping

Salamanca is the home of Spanish fashion. For offbeat boutiques, poke around La Latina and Lavapiés. Malasaña is the place for retro fashions, while nearby Chueca deals in more upmarket styles. For the best souvenirs, explore the Sol, Santa Ana and Huertas area.

★ El Rastro MARKET
(Map p1034; Calle de la Ribera de los Curtidores; ☉ 8am-3pm Sun; Ⓜ La Latina) A Sunday morning at El Rastro is a Madrid institution. You could easily spend an entire morning inching your way down the hill and the maze of streets that host El Rastro flea market each week. Cheap clothes, luggage, old flamenco records, even older photos of Madrid, faux designer purses, grungy T-shirts, household goods and electronics are the main fare. For every 10 pieces of junk, there's a real gem (a lost masterpiece, an Underwood typewriter) waiting to be found.

SPAIN MADRID

★ Antigua Casa Talavera   CERAMICS
(Map p1034; ☎91 547 34 17; www.antiguacasa
talavera.com; Calle de Isabel la Católica 2; ☺10am-
1.30pm & 5-8pm Mon-Fri, 10am-1.30pm Sat; Ⓜ Santo Domingo) The extraordinary tiled facade of
this wonderful old shop conceals an Aladdin's cave of ceramics from all over Spain.
This is not the mass-produced stuff aimed at
a tourist market, but comes from the small
family potters of Andalucía and Toledo, ranging from the decorative (tiles) to the useful
(plates, jugs and other kitchen items). The
old couple who run the place are delightful.

Kling   FASHION & ACCESSORIES
(Map p1034; ☎91 522 51 45; www.kling.es; Calle de la
Ballesta 6; ☺11am-9pm Mon-Sat; Ⓜ Gran Vía) Like
a classy version of Zara but with just a hint
of attitude, Kling is housed in a reconceived
former sex club (prostitutes still scout for clients outside) and is one of Madrid's best-kept
secrets. It's ideal for fashion-conscious women
who can't afford Salamanca's prices.

★ El Arco Artesanía   ARTS & CRAFTS
(Map p1034; ☎913 65 26 80; www.artesaniaelarco.
com; Plaza Mayor 9; ☺11am-9pm Sun-Thu, to 11pm
Fri & Sat; Ⓜ Sol, La Latina) This original shop
in the southwestern corner of Plaza Mayor
sells an outstanding array of homemade designer souvenirs, from stone, ceramic and
glass work to jewellery and home fittings.
The papier mâché figures are gorgeous, but
there's so much else here to turn your head.

ⓘ Information

SAFE TRAVEL
Madrid is a generally safe city, although you
should, as in most European cities, be wary of
pickpockets on transport and around major
tourist sights. You're most likely to fall foul of
pickpockets in the most heavily touristed parts
of town, notably the Plaza Mayor and surrounding streets, the Puerta del Sol, El Rastro and
around the Museo del Prado. Be wary of jostling
on crowded buses and the metro and, as a general rule, dark, empty streets are to be avoided;
luckily, Madrid's most lively nocturnal areas are
generally busy with crowds having a good time.

To report thefts or other crime-related matters, your best bet is the **Servicio de Atención
al Turista Extranjero** (Foreign Tourist Assistance Service; ☎91 548 80 08, 91 548 85 37;
www.esmadrid.com/informacion-turistica/sate;
Calle de Leganitos 19; ☺9am-midnight; Ⓜ Plaza
de España, Santo Domingo), where specially
trained police officers work alongside representatives from the Tourism Ministry.

TOURIST INFORMATION
Centro de Turismo de Madrid (Map p1034;
☎010, 91 578 78 10; www.esmadrid.com; Plaza
Mayor 27; ☺9.30am-8.30pm; Ⓜ Sol) The Madrid government's Centro de Turismo is terrific.
Housed in the Real Casa de la Panadería on
the north side of the Plaza Mayor, it allows free
access to its outstanding website and city database, and offers free downloads of the metro
map to your mobile; staff are helpful.

ⓘ Getting There & Away

AIR
Adolfo Suárez Madrid-Barajas Airport
(☎902 404704; www.aena.es; Ⓜ Aeropuerto
T1, T2 & T3, Aeropuerto T4) The airport lies
15km northeast of the city and is Europe's
sixth-busiest hub, with almost 50 million passengers passing through here every year. It has
four terminals. Terminal 4 (T4) deals mainly
with flights of Iberia and its partners (eg British
Airways, American Airlines and Vueling), while
the remainder leave from the conjoined T1, T2
and (rarely) T3.

BUS
Estación Sur de Autobuses (☎91 468 42
00; Calle de Méndez Álvaro 83; Ⓜ Méndez
Álvaro) Just south of the M30 ring road, this is
the city's principal bus station. It serves most
destinations to the south and many in other
parts of the country. Most bus companies have
a ticket office here, even if their buses depart
from elsewhere.

TRAIN
All trains are run by **Renfe** (☎902 320320;
www.renfe.es/cercanias/madrid). High-speed
AVE (Tren de Alta Velocidad Española) services
connect Madrid with Alicante, Barcelona, Córdoba, Huesca, León, Málaga, Segovia, Seville,
Tarragona, Toledo, Valencia, Valladolid, Zaragoza and some towns en route.

Estación de Chamartín (☎902 432343;
Ⓜ Chamartín) North of the city centre, Estación de Chamartín has numerous long-distance
rail services, especially those to/from northern
Spain. This is also where long-haul international
trains arrive from Paris and Lisbon.

Puerta de Atocha (www.renfe.es; Av de la
Ciudad de Barcelona; Ⓜ Atocha Renfe) Madrid's
main train station is at the southern end of the
city centre. The bulk of trains for Spanish destinations depart from Atocha, especially those
going south. For bookings, contact Renfe.

ⓘ Getting Around

TO/FROM THE AIRPORT
Bus
The 24-hour Exprés Aeropuerto (Airport Express; bus 203; www.emtmadrid.es; €5, 40

minutes) runs between Puerta de Atocha train station and the airport. From 11.30pm until 6am, departures are from the Plaza de Cibeles, not the train station. Departures take place every 13 to 20 minutes from the station or at night-time every 35 minutes from Plaza de Cibeles.

Metro

The easiest way into town from the airport is line 8 of the metro (entrances in T2 and T4) to the Nuevos Ministerios transport interchange, which connects with lines 10 and 6. It operates from 6.05am to 1.30am. A one-way ticket to/from the airport costs €4.50. The journey to Nuevos Ministerios takes around 15 minutes, around 25 minutes from T4.

Taxi

There is a fixed rate of €30 for taxis from the airport to the city centre.

PUBLIC TRANSPORT

Madrid's modern metro (www.metromadrid.es) is a fast, efficient and safe way to navigate Madrid, and generally easier than getting to grips with bus routes. There are 11 colour-coded lines in central Madrid and colour maps showing the metro system are available from any metro station or online. The metro operates from 6.05am to 1.30am. Single-journey metro or bus tickets cost €1.50; Metrobús tickets valid for 10 rides on the metro or buses are €12.20.

TAXI

You can pick up a taxi at ranks throughout town or simply flag one down. From 7am to 9pm Monday to Friday, flag fall is €2.40 and you pay €1.05 per kilometre. The rest of the time flag fall is €2.90 and the per-kilometre charge is €1.20. Several supplementary charges, usually posted inside the taxi, apply; these include €3 from taxi ranks at train and bus stations.

CASTILLA Y LEÓN

Salamanca

POP 148,000

Whether floodlit by night or bathed in late afternoon sunlight, there's something magical about Salamanca. This is a city of rare architectural splendour, awash with golden sandstone overlaid with Latin inscriptions in ochre, and with an extraordinary virtuosity of plateresque and Renaissance styles. The monumental highlights are many, with the exceptional Plaza Mayor (illuminated to stunning effect at night) an unforgettable highlight. But this is also Castilla's liveliest city, home to a massive Spanish and inter-national student population who throng the streets at night and provide the city with youth and vitality.

⊙ Sights

★ Plaza Mayor   SQUARE

Built between 1729 and 1755, Salamanca's exceptional grand square is widely considered to be Spain's most beautiful central plaza. The square is particularly memorable at night when illuminated (until midnight) to magical effect. Designed by Alberto Churriguera, it's a remarkably harmonious and controlled baroque display. The medallions placed around the square bear the busts of famous figures.

★ Universidad Civil   HISTORIC BUILDING

(☑ 923 29 44 00, ext 1150; www.salamanca.es; Calle de los Libreros; adult/concession €10/5, audio guide €2; ⊙ 10am-6.30pm Mon-Sat, to 1.30pm Sun) Founded initially as the Estudio General in 1218, the university reached the peak of its renown in the 15th and 16th centuries. The visual feast of the entrance facade is a tapestry in sandstone, bursting with images of mythical heroes, religious scenes and coats of arms. It's dominated by busts of Fernando and Isabel. Behind the facade, the highlight of an otherwise-modest collection of rooms lies upstairs: the extraordinary university library, the oldest one in Europe.

★ Catedral Nueva   CATHEDRAL

(☑ 923 21 74 76; www.catedralsalamanca.org; Plaza de Anaya; adult/child incl audio guide & admission to Catedral Vieja €4.75/3; ⊙ 10am-8pm Apr-Sep, 10am-5.15pm Oct-Mar) The tower of this late-Gothic cathedral lords over the city centre, its compelling churrigueresque (an ornate style of baroque architecture) dome visible from almost every angle. The interior is similarly impressive, with elaborate choir stalls, main chapel and retrochoir, much of it courtesy of the prolific José Churriguera. The ceilings are also exceptional, along with the Renaissance doorways – particularly the Puerta del Nacimiento on the western face, which stands out as one of several miracles worked in the city's native sandstone.

★ Catedral Vieja   CATHEDRAL

(☑ 923 28 10 45; www.catedralsalamanca.org; Plaza de Anaya; adult/child incl audio guide & admission to Catedral Nueva €4.75/3; ⊙ 10am-8pm Apr-Sep, 10am-5.15pm Oct-Mar) The Catedral Nueva's largely Romanesque predecessor, the Catedral Vieja is adorned with an exquisite

15th-century altarpiece, one of the finest outside Italy. Its 53 panels depict scenes from the lives of Christ and Mary and are topped by a haunting representation of the Final Judgement. The cloister was largely ruined in an earthquake in 1755, but the Capilla de Anaya houses an extravagant alabaster sepulchre and one of Europe's oldest organs, a Mudéjar work of art from the 16th century.

Sleeping

Hostal Concejo
HOSTAL €

(☑ 923 21 47 37; www.hconcejo.com; Plaza de la Libertad 1; s €25-45, d €35-60; P ✱ 🛜) A cut above the average *hostal*, the stylish Concejo has polished-wood floors, tasteful furnishings, light-filled rooms and a superb central location. Try to snag one of the corner rooms, such as room 104, which has a traditional, glassed-in balcony, complete with a table, chairs and people-watching views.

★ Microtel Placentinos
BOUTIQUE HOTEL €€

(☑ 923 28 15 31; www.microtelplacentinos.com; Calle de Placentinos 9; s/d incl breakfast Sun-Thu €57/73, Fri & Sat €88/100; ✱ 🛜) One of Salamanca's most charming boutique hotels, Microtel Placentinos is tucked away on a quiet street and has rooms with exposed stone walls and wooden beams. The service is faultless, and the overall atmosphere one of intimacy and discretion. All rooms have a hydromassage shower or tub and there's an outside whirlpool spa (open summer only).

★ Salamanca Suite Studios
APARTMENT €€

(☑ 923 27 24 65; www.salamancasuitestudios.com; Plaza de la Libertad 4; r €59-110; ✱ 🛜) This excellent place has smart and contemporary modern suites and apartments with kitchens; some have Nespresso coffee machines, and all have bucketloads of style with their white-and-turquoise colour schemes. The

---

FIND THE FROG

The facade of the University of Salamanca is an ornate mass of sculptures and carvings, and hidden among this 16th-century plateresque creation is a tiny stone frog. Legend says that those who find the frog will have good luck in studies, life and love. If you don't want any help, look away now... It's sitting on a skull on the pillar that runs up the right-hand side of the facade.

---

location is lovely and central and the service is discreet but attentive.

🍴 Eating & Drinking

★ La Cocina de Toño
TAPAS €€

(☑ 923 26 39 77; www.lacocinadetoño.es; Calle Gran Via 20; tapas from €1.60, menú €17, mains €18-23; ⊙ noon-4.30pm & 8-11.30pm Tue-Sat, noon-4.30pm Sun; 🛜) This place owes its loyal following to its creative *pinchos* (tapas-like snacks) and half-servings of dishes such as escalope of foie gras with roast apple and passionfruit gelatin. The restaurant serves more traditional fare as befits the decor, but the bar is one of Salamanca's gastronomic stars. Slightly removed from the old city, it draws a predominantly Spanish crowd.

Mesón Las Conchas
CASTILIAN €€

(☑ 923 21 21 67; Rúa Mayor 16; mains €10-21; ⊙ bar 8am-midnight, restaurant 1-4pm & 8pm-midnight; 📶) Enjoy a choice of outdoor tables, an atmospheric bar or the upstairs, wood-beamed dining area. The bar caters mainly to locals who know their *embutidos* (cured meats). For sit-down meals, there's a good mix of roasts, *platos combinados* and *raciones* (full-size tapas). The restaurant serves a highly rated oven-baked turbot.

Doctor Cocktail
COCKTAIL BAR

(☑ 923 26 31 51; Calle del Doctor Piñuela 5; ⊙ 4pm-late) Excellent cocktails, friendly bar staff and a cool crowd make for a fine mix just north of the Plaza Mayor. Apart from the creative list of cocktails, it has 32 different kinds of gin to choose from and above-average tonic to go with it.

ℹ Information

Municipal & Regional Tourist Office (☑ 923 21 83 42; www.salamanca.es; Plaza Mayor 32; ⊙ 9am-2pm & 4.30-8pm Mon-Fri, 10am-8pm Sat, 10am-2pm Sun Easter–mid-Oct, 9am-2pm & 4-6.30pm Mon-Fri, 10am-6.30pm Sat, 10am-2pm Sun mid-Oct–Easter) The municipal tourist office shares an office with the regional office, on Plaza Mayor. An audio guide to city sights can be accessed on your smartphone from www.audioguiasalamanca.es.

ℹ Getting There & Away

The bus and train stations are 10 and 15 minutes' walk, respectively, from Plaza Mayor.

BUS

There are buses to Madrid (regular/express €17/23, 2½ to 3½ hours, once or twice hourly) and Ávila (€9.25, 1½ hours, four daily).

BURGOS & LEÓN – A TALE OF TWO CATHEDRALS

Burgos and León are cathedral towns par excellence, and both are well connected by train and bus to Madrid.

Burgos

Catedral (☎ 947 20 47 12; www.catedraldeburgos.es; Plaza del Rey Fernando; adult/under 14yr incl audio guide €7/1.50, 4.30-6pm Tue free; ⏱ 9.30am-7.30pm) This Unesco World Heritage–listed cathedral, once a former modest Romanesque church, is a masterpiece. Work began on a grander scale in 1221; remarkably, within 40 years most of the French Gothic structure had been completed. You can enter from Plaza de Santa María for free for access to the Capilla del Santísimo Cristo, with its much-revered 13th-century crucifix, and the Capilla de Santa Tecla, with its extraordinary ceiling. However, we recommend that you visit the cathedral in its entirety.

Hotel Norte y Londres (☎ 947 26 41 25; www.hotelnorteylondres.com; Plaza de Alonso Martínez 10; s €32-55, d €36-70; P @ ⏱) Set in a former 16th-century palace and decorated with understated period charm, this fine, family-run hotel promises spacious rooms with antique furnishings and polished wooden floors. All rooms have pretty balconies; those on the 4th floor are more modern. The bathrooms are exceptionally large and the service friendly and efficient.

Cervecería Morito (☎ 947 26 75 55; Calle de Diego Porcelos 1; tapas/raciones from €3.50/5.00; ⏱ 12.30-3.30pm & 7-11.30pm) Cervecería Morito is the undisputed king of Burgos tapas bars and as such it's always crowded. A typical order is *alpargata* (lashings of cured ham with bread, tomato and olive oil) or the *revueltos Capricho de Burgos* (scrambled eggs served with potatoes, blood sausage, red peppers, baby eels and mushrooms) – the latter is a meal in itself.

León

Catedral (☎ 987 87 57 70; www.catedraldeleon.org; Plaza de Regia; adult/concession/under 12yr €6/5/free; ⏱ 9.30am-1.30pm & 4-8pm Mon-Fri, 9.30am-noon & 2-6pm Sat, 9.30-11am & 2-8pm Sun Jun-Sep, 9.30am-1.30pm & 4-7pm Mon-Sat, 9.30am-2pm Sun Oct-May) León's 13th-century cathedral, with its soaring towers, flying buttresses and breathtaking interior, is the city's spiritual heart. Whether spotlit by night or bathed in glorious northern sunshine, the cathedral, arguably Spain's premier Gothic masterpiece, exudes a glorious, almost luminous quality. The show-stopping facade has a radiant rose window, three richly sculpted doorways and two muscular towers. The main entrance is lorded over by a scene of the Last Supper, while an extraordinary gallery of *vidrieras* (stained-glass windows) awaits you inside.

Panteón Real (www.turismoleon.org; Plaza de San Isidoro; €5, 4-6.30pm Thu €1; ⏱ 10am-1.30pm & 4-6.30pm Mon-Sat, 10am-2pm Sun) Attached to the Real Basílica de San Isidoro (☎ 987 87 61 61; Plaza de San Isidro; ⏱ 7.30am-11pm), the stunning Panteón Real houses royal sarcophagi, which rest with quiet dignity beneath a canopy of some of the finest Romanesque frescos in Spain. Colourful motifs of biblical scenes drench the vaults and arches of this extraordinary hall, held aloft by marble columns with intricately carved capitals. The pantheon also houses a small museum where you can admire the shrine of San Isidoro, a mummified finger(!) of the saint and other treasures.

La Posada Regia (☎ 987 21 31 73; www.regialeon.com; Calle de Regidores 9-11; incl breakfast s €54-70, d €59-130; ❄ ⏱) This place has the feel of a *casa rural* (village or farmstead accommodation) despite being in the city centre. The secret is a 14th-century building, magnificently restored (with wooden beams, exposed brick and understated antique furniture), with individually styled rooms and supremely comfortable beds and bathrooms. As with anywhere in the Barrio Húmedo, weekend nights can be noisy.

TRAIN

Trains run to Madrid's Chamartín station (€12 to €24, two to three hours, 10 trains daily), Ávila (€12, 1¼ hours, seven trains) and Segovia (€9.50 to €32, 1¼ hours, two to four trains).

Segovia

POP 52,700

Unesco World Heritage–listed Segovia has a stunning monument to Roman grandeur and a castle said to have inspired Walt Disney, and is otherwise a city of warm terracotta and sandstone hues set amid the rolling hills of Castilla.

Sights

★ Acueducto LANDMARK

(www.turismodesegovia.com) Segovia's most recognisable symbol is El Acueducto (Roman Aqueduct), an 894m-long engineering wonder that looks like an enormous comb plunged into Segovia. First raised here by the Romans in the 1st century AD, the aqueduct was built with not a drop of mortar to hold the more than 20,000 uneven granite blocks together. It's made up of 163 arches and, at its highest point in Plaza del Azoguejo, rises 28m high.

★ Alcázar CASTLE

(☑921 46 07 59; www.alcazardesegovia.com; Plaza de la Reina Victoria Eugenia; adult/concession/child under 6yr €5.50/5/free, tower €2.50; ◉10am-6.30pm Oct-Mar, to 7.30pm Apr-Sep; ◉) Rapunzel towers, turrets topped with slate witches' hats and a deep moat at its base make the Alcázar a prototype fairy-tale castle – so much so that its design inspired Walt Disney's vision of Sleeping Beauty's castle. Fortified since Roman days, the site takes its name from the Arabic *al-qasr* (fortress). It was rebuilt in the 13th and 14th centuries, but the whole lot burned down in 1862. What you see today is an evocative, over-the-top reconstruction of the original.

★ Catedral CATHEDRAL

(☑921 46 22 05; www.turismodesegovia.com; Plaza Mayor; adult/concession €3/2, Sun morning free, tower tour €5; ◉9.30am-6.30pm Apr-Oct, 9.30am-5.30pm Mon-Sat, 1.15-5.30pm Sun Nov-Mar, tower tours 10.30pm & 12.30pm year-round plus 4.30pm Apr-Oct, 4pm Nov-Mar) Started in 1525 on the site of a former chapel, Segovia's cathedral is a powerful expression of Gothic architecture that took almost 200 years to complete.

The austere three-nave interior is anchored by an imposing choir stall and enlivened by 20-odd chapels, including the Capilla del Cristo del Consuelo, with its magnificent Romanesque doorway, and the Capilla de la Piedad, containing an important altarpiece by Juan de Juni. Join an hour-long guided tour to climb the tower for fabulous views.

Plaza Mayor SQUARE

The shady Plaza Mayor is the nerve centre of old Segovia, lined by an eclectic assortment of buildings, arcades and cafes and with an open pavilion in its centre. It's also the site of the cathedral and the regional tourist office.

Sleeping

Häb Urban Hostel HOSTAL €

(☑921 46 10 26; www.habhostel.com; Calle de Cervantes 16; r €48-75; ❄@🛜) This bright and welcoming *hostal* – think doubles with private bathrooms rather than dorms with bunk beds, despite the name – is modern and has a fine location just where the pedestrian street begins the climb up into the old town. Some rooms are on the small side, but the look is light and contemporary.

★ Hospedería La Gran Casa Mudéjar HISTORIC HOTEL €€

(☑921 46 62 50; www.lacasamudejar.com; Calle de Isabel la Católica 8; r €45-95; ❄@🛜) Spread over two buildings, this place has been magnificently renovated, blending genuine 15th-century Mudéjar carved wooden ceilings in some rooms with modern amenities. In the newer wing, top-floor rooms have fine mountain views out over the rooftops of Segovia's old Jewish quarter. Adding to the appeal is a small spa. The restaurant comes highly recommended.

Eating

★ Restaurante El Fogón Sefardí JEWISH €€

(☑921 46 62 50; www.lacasamudejar.com; Calle de Isabel la Católica 8; tapas from €2.50, mains €14-25, set menus €18.50-24.50; ◉1.30-4.30pm & 5.30-11.30pm) Located within the Hospedería La Gran Casa Mudéjar, this is one of the most original places in town. Sephardic Jewish cuisine is served either on the intimate patio or in the splendid dining hall with original 15th-century Mudéjar flourishes. The theme in the bar is equally diverse. Stop here for a taste of the award-winning tapas. Reservations recommended.

ÁVILA

Ávila's old city, 1½ hours from Madrid by train or bus, and about halfway between Segovia and Salamanca, is one of Spain's best-preserved medieval bastions, surrounded by imposing walls with eight monumental gates, 88 watchtowers and more than 2500 turrets. Ávila is also famed as the home town of the 16th-century mystic and religious reformer, Santa Teresa de Ávila.

Murallas (www.murralladeavila.com; adult/child under 12yr €5/free; ⊙10am-8pm Apr-Oct, to 6pm Nov-Mar; 🚻) Ávila's splendid 12th-century walls stretch for 2.5km atop the remains of earlier Roman and Muslim battlements and rank among the world's best-preserved medieval defensive perimeters. Two sections of the walls can be climbed – a 300m stretch that can be accessed from just inside the **Puerta del Alcázar**, and a longer (1300m) stretch from **Puerta de los Leales** that runs the length of the old city's northern perimeter. The admission price includes a multilingual audio guide.

Catedral del Salvador (📱920 21 16 41; Plaza de la Catedral; admission incl audio guide €5; ⊙10am-7pm Mon-Fri, 10am-8pm Sat, noon-6.30pm Sun) Ávila's 12th-century cathedral is both a house of worship and an ingenious fortress: its stout granite apse forms the central bulwark in the historic city walls. The sombre, Gothic-style facade conceals a magnificent interior with an exquisite early 16th-century **altar frieze** showing the life of Jesus, plus Renaissance-era carved choir stalls and a **museum** with an El Greco painting and a splendid silver monstrance by Juan de Arfe. (Push the buttons to illuminate the altar and the choir stalls.)

Hotel El Rastro (📱920 35 22 25; www.elrastroavila.com; Calle Cepedas; s/d €35/55; ❄🅿🛜) This atmospheric hotel occupies a former 16th-century palace with original stone, exposed brickwork and a natural, earth-toned colour scheme exuding a calm, understated elegance. Each room has a different form, but most have high ceilings and plenty of space. Note that the owners also run a marginally cheaper *hostal* (budget hotel) of the same name around the corner.

⭐**Casa Duque** SPANISH €€€
(📱921 46 24 87; www.restauranteduque.es; Calle de Cervantes 12; mains €19.50-24, set menus €35-40; ⊙12.30-4.30pm & 8.30-11.30pm) Segovia's famed speciality *cochinillo asado* (roast suckling pig) has been served at this atmospheric *mesón* (tavern) since the 1890s. For the uninitiated, try the *menú de degustación* (€40), which includes *cochinillo*. Downstairs is the informal *cueva* (cave), where you can get tapas and full-bodied *cazuelas* (stews). Reservations recommended.

❶ Information

Centro de Recepción de Visitantes (📱921 46 67 20; www.turismodesegovia.com; Plaza del Azoguejo 1; ⊙10am-8pm Mon-Sat, to 7pm Sun Apr-Sep, 10am-6.30pm Mon-Sat, to 5pm Sun Oct-Mar) Segovia's main tourist office runs at least two guided tours of the city's monumental core daily (€11 to €14 per person), usually departing at 10.30am and 4.30pm (although check as this schedule can change). Reserve ahead.

Regional Tourist Office (📱921 46 60 70; www.segoviaturismo.es; Plaza Mayor 10; ⊙9.30am-2pm & 5-8pm Mon-Sat, 9.30am-5pm Sun Jul–mid-Sep, 9.30am-2pm & 4-7pm Mon-Sat, 9.30am-5pm Sun mid-Sep–Jun)

❶ Getting There & Away

BUS

The bus station is just off Paseo de Ezequiel González. Buses run half-hourly to Segovia from Madrid's Intercambiador de Moncloa bus stop (€7.90, 1½ hours). Buses depart to Ávila (€6.20, one hour, eight daily) and Salamanca (€14, three hours, four daily), among other destinations.

TRAIN

Up to five normal trains run daily from Madrid to Segovia (€8.25, two hours), leaving you at the main train station 2.5km from the aqueduct. The faster option is the 25 daily high-speed Avant (€13, 27 minutes) and Alvia (€24, 28 minutes) trains which deposit you at Segovia-Guiomar station, 5km from the aqueduct.

CASTILLA-LA MANCHA

Toledo

POP 85,600

Though one of Spain's smallest regional capitals, Toledo looms large in the nation's history and consciousness as a bulwark of the Spanish church and symbol of a flourishing multicultural medieval society where, tradition has it, Muslim, Christian and Jewish communities coexisted peacefully. The old town today is a treasure chest of churches, museums, synagogues and mosques set in a labyrinth of narrow streets, plazas and inner patios in a lofty setting high above the Río Tajo. Toledo's other forte is art, in particular the haunting canvases of El Greco, the impossible-to-classify painter with whom the city is synonymous. Crowded by day, Toledo changes dramatically after dark when the streets take on a moody, other-worldly air.

◉ Sights

★**Catedral**   CATHEDRAL
(www.catedralprimada.es; Plaza del Ayuntamiento; adult/child €12.50/free; ⊙10am-6pm Mon-Sat, 2-6pm Sun) Toledo's illustrious main church ranks among the top 10 cathedrals in Spain. An impressive example of medieval Gothic architecture, its humongous interior is full of the classic characteristics of the style, rose windows, flying buttresses, ribbed vaults and pointed arches among them. Equally visit-worthy is the art. The cathedral's sacristy is a veritable art gallery of old masters, with works by Velázquez, Goya and – of course – El Greco.

★**Alcázar**   FORTRESS
(Museo del Ejército; www.toledo-turismo.com; Calle Alféreces Provisionales; adult/child €5/free, Sun free; ⊙10am-5pm Thu-Tue) At the highest point in the city looms the forbidding Alcázar. Rebuilt under Franco, it has been reopened as a vast military museum. The usual displays of uniforms and medals are here, but the best part is the exhaustive historical section, with an in-depth overview of the nation's history in Spanish and English.

★**Sinagoga del Tránsito**   SYNAGOGUE, MUSEUM
(✆925 22 36 65; http://museosefardi.mcu.es; Calle Samuel Leví; adult/child €3/1.50, after 2pm Sat & all day Sun free; ⊙9.30am-7.30pm Tue-Sat Mar-Oct, 9.30am-6pm Tue-Sat Nov-Feb, 10am-3pm Sun year-round) This magnificent synagogue was built in 1355 by special permission from Pedro I. The synagogue now houses the Museo Sefardí. The vast main prayer hall has been expertly restored and the Mudéjar decoration and intricately carved pine ceiling are striking. Exhibits provide an insight into the history of Jewish culture in Spain, and include archaeological finds, a memorial garden, costumes and ceremonial artefacts.

🍴 Sleeping & Eating

La Posada de Manolo   BOUTIQUE HOTEL €
(✆925 28 22 50; www.laposadademanolo.com; Calle de Sixto Ramón Parro 8; s/d from €55/77; ❇☎) This memorable hotel has themed each floor with furnishings and decor reflecting one of the three cultures of Toledo: Christian, Islamic and Jewish. There are stunning views of the old town and cathedral from the terrace.

★**Hacienda del Cardenal**   HISTORIC HOTEL €€
(✆925 22 49 00; www.haciendadelcardenal.com; Paseo de Recaredo 24; r incl breakfast €95-135; ❇☎) This wonderful 18th-century mansion has soft ochre-coloured walls, arches and columns. Some rooms are grand, others are spartan, and all come with dark furniture, plush fabrics and parquet floors. Several overlook the glorious terraced gardens.

La Abadía   CASTILIAN, TAPAS €€
(www.abadiatoledo.com; Plaza de San Nicolás 3; raciones €7-15; ⊙bar 8am-midnight, restaurant 1-4pm & 8.30pm-midnight) In a former 16th-century palace, this atmospheric bar and restaurant has arches, niches and coloured bottles lined up as decoration, spread throughout a warren of brick-and-stone-clad rooms. The menu includes lightweight dishes and tapas, but the 'Menú de Montes de Toledo' (€20) is a fabulous collection of tastes from the nearby mountains.

★**Adolfo**   MODERN EUROPEAN €€€
(✆925 22 73 21; www.adolforestaurante.com; Callejón Hombre de Palo 7; mains €25-28; ⊙1-4pm & 8pm-midnight Mon-Sat, 1-4pm Sun) Toledo doffs its hat to fine dining at this temple of good food and market freshness. Run by notable La Mancha–born chef Adolfo Muñoz, the restaurant has been around for over 25 years, and in that time has morphed into one of Spain's best gourmet establishments. The king of Spain – no less – has sung the praises of Adolfo's partridge.

❶ Information

Main Tourist Office (☑ 925 25 40 30; www.toledo-turismo.com; Plaza Consistorio 1; ⊘10am-6pm) Within sight of the cathedral. There's another branch (⊘9.30am-3pm) at the train station.

❶ Getting There & Away

For most major destinations, you'll need to backtrack to Madrid.

BUS

Buses run from Madrid's Plaza Elíptica to Toledo's **bus station** (☑ 925 21 58 50; www.alsa.es; Avenida de Castilla La Mancha), and back, roughly every half-hour (€5.40, 45 minutes to 1½ hours), some going direct, some via villages.

TRAIN

High-speed trains run about hourly from Madrid's Puerta de Atocha station (one way/return €13/21, 33 minutes) to Toledo's pretty **train station** (☑ 902 24 02 02; www.renfe.es; Paseo de la Rosa).

CATALONIA

Barcelona

POP 1.6 MILLION

Barcelona is one of Europe's coolest cities. Despite two millennia of history, it's a forward-thinking place, always at the cutting edge of art, design and cuisine. Whether you explore its medieval palaces and plazas, admire the Modernista masterpieces of Antoni Gaudí and others, shop for designer fashions along its bustling boulevards, sample its exciting nightlife or just soak up the sun on the beaches, you'll find it hard not to fall in love with this vibrant city.

As much as Barcelona is a visual feast, it will also lead you into culinary temptation. Anything from traditional Catalan cooking to the latest in avant-garde new Spanish cuisine will have your appetite in overdrive.

◉ Sights & Activities

◉ La Rambla & El Raval

Spain's most famous boulevard, La Rambla is pure sensory overload. Stretching from Plaça de Catalunya to the waterfront, it's always a hive of activity, with buskers, hawkers, human statues and con artists (watch out!) mingling amid the sunlit cafes, flower stalls, historic buildings, markets, shops and a ceaseless parade of saunterers from all corners of the globe.

★Mercat de la Boqueria   MARKET
(Map p1050; ☑ 93 412 13 15; www.boqueria.info; La Rambla 91; ⊘8am-8.30pm Mon-Sat; Ⓜ Liceu) Mercat de la Boqueria is possibly La Rambla's most interesting building, not so much for its Modernista-influenced design (it was actually built over a long period, from 1840 to 1914, on the site of the former St Joseph Monastery), but for the action of the food market within.

Gran Teatre del Liceu   ARCHITECTURE
(Map p1050; ☑ 93 485 99 00; www.liceubarcelona.cat; La Rambla 51-59; tours 45/30min €9/6; ⊘45min tours hourly from 2-6pm Mon-Fri, from 9.30am Sat, 30min tours 1.30pm; Ⓜ Liceu) If you can't catch a night at the opera, you can still have a look around one of Europe's greatest opera houses, known to locals as the Liceu. Smaller than Milan's La Scala but bigger than Venice's La Fenice, it can seat up to 2300 people in its grand horseshoe auditorium.

◉ Barri Gòtic

You could easily spend several days or even a week exploring the medieval streets of the Barri Gòtic, Barcelona's oldest quarter. In addition to major sights, its tangle of narrow lanes and tranquil plazas conceals some of the city's most atmospheric shops, restaurants, cafes and bars.

★La Catedral   CATHEDRAL
(Map p1050; ☑ 93 342 82 62; www.catedralbcn.org; Plaça de la Seu; free, 'donation entrance' €7, choir €3, roof €3; ⊘8am-12.45pm & 5.15-7.30pm Mon-Fri, 8am-8pm Sat & Sun, entry by donation 1-5.30pm Mon,1-5pm Sat, 2-5pm Sun; Ⓜ Jaume I) Barcelona's central place of worship presents a magnificent image. The richly decorated main facade, laced with gargoyles and the stone intricacies you would expect of northern European Gothic, sets it quite apart from other churches in Barcelona. The facade was actually added in 1870, although the rest of the building was built between 1298 and 1460. The other facades are sparse in decoration, and the octagonal, flat-roofed towers are a clear reminder that, even here, Catalan Gothic architectural principles prevailed.

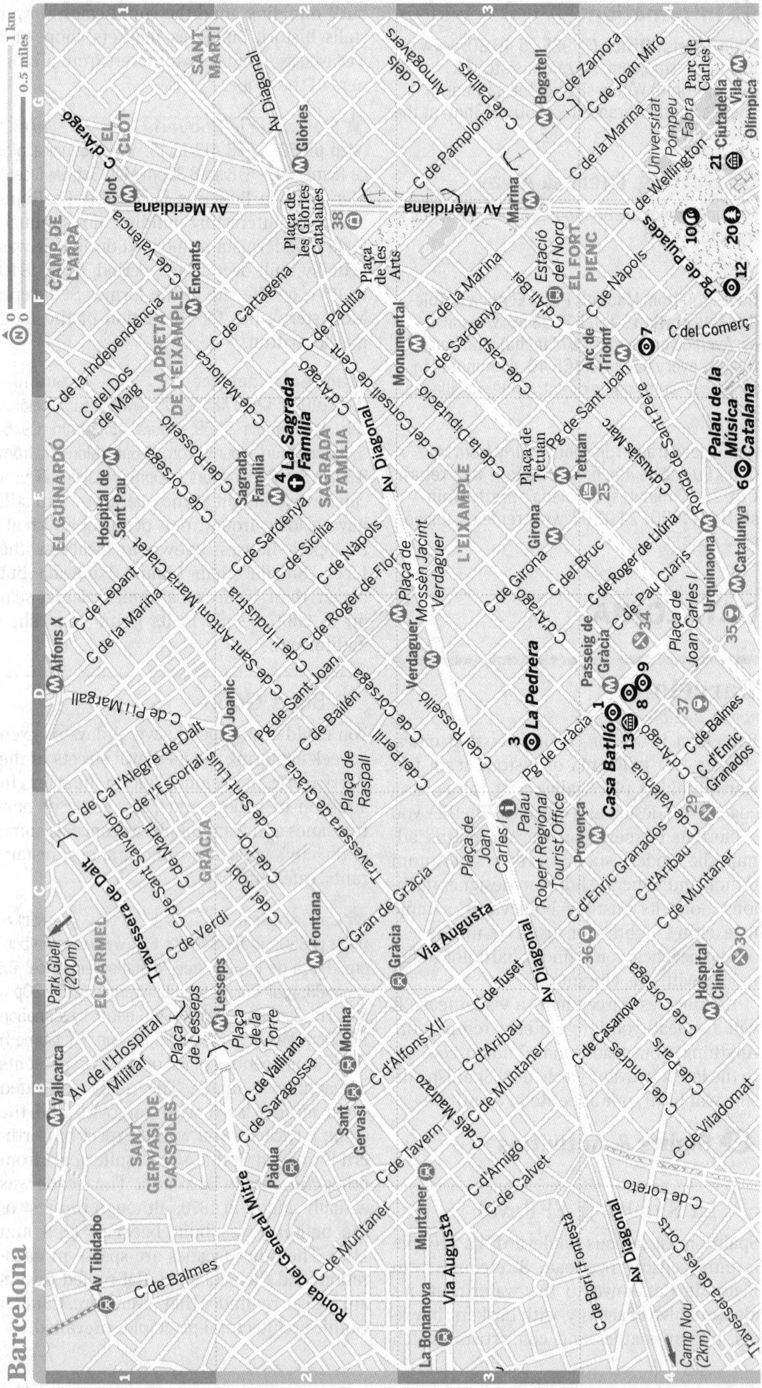

Barcelona
0.5 miles
1 km
Av Tibidabo
C de Balmes
Ronda del General Mitre
C de Muntaner
La Bonanova
Via Augusta
Muntaner
C de Tavern
C dels Madrazo
C d'Amigó
C de Calvet
C de Bori i Fontestà
Av Diagonal
Travessera de les Corts
Camp Nou (2km)
C de Loreto
C de Viladomat
C de Londres
C de París
C de Casanova
C de Corsega
Hospital Clínic
C de Muntaner
C d'Aribau
C de Tuset
C d'Alfons XII
Sant Gervasi
Pàdua
SANT GERVASI DE CASSOLES
C de Saragossa
C de Vallirana
Molina
Plaça de la Torre
Plaça de Lesseps
Lesseps
Av de l'Hospital Militar
Vallcarca
Park Güell (200m)
EL CARMEL
Travessera de Dalt
C de Verdi
Fontana
C Gran de Gràcia
Gràcia
Via Augusta
C de Sant Salvador
C de Martí
GRÀCIA
C de Ca l'Alegre de Dalt
C de l'Escorial
C de Sant Lluís
C del Robí
C de l'Or
Travessera de Gràcia
Plaça de Raspall
C del Perill
Plaça de Joan Carles I
Palau Robert Regional Tourist Office
Provença
C d'Enric Granados
C d'Aribau
C de Muntaner
36
30
29
C de Valencia
C de Balmes
C d'Enric Granados
Casa Batlló
13
1
8
9
37
C d'Aragó
Pg de Gràcia
3
La Pedrera
C del Rosselló
C de Corsega
C de Bailèn
Pg de Sant Joan
Joanic
C de Pi i Margall
Alfons X
C de la Marina
C de Lepant
C de Sant Antoni Maria Claret
C de l'Indústria
C de Roger de Flor
Verdaguer
Plaça de Mossèn Jacint Verdaguer
Passeig de Gràcia
34
35
Plaça de Joan Carles I
C de Pau Claris
C de Roger de Llúria
C del Bruc
C d'Aragó
C de Girona
Girona
Urquinaona
Catalunya
L'EIXAMPLE
Tetuan
25
Plaça de Tetuan
Pg de Sant Joan
Ronda de Sant Pere
C d'Ausiàs Marc
6
Palau de la Música Catalana
C de Nàpols
C de Sicília
C de Sardenya
SAGRADA FAMÍLIA
Sagrada Família
4
La Sagrada Família
Av Diagonal
C del Consell de Cent
C de la Diputació
C de Casp
C de Sardenya
Monumental
C de Padilla
C de Mallorca
C del Rosselló
C de Corsega
Hospital de Sant Pau
EL GUINARDÓ
C del Dos de Maig
LA DRETA DE L'EIXAMPLE
C de la Independència
C de Cartagena
Encants
CAMP DE L'ARPA
C de València
Clot
EL CLOT
C d'Aragó
Av Meridiana
Plaça de les Glòries Catalanes
38
Glòries
Av Diagonal
SANT MARTÍ
C dels Almogàvers
C de Pallars
C de Pamplona
Plaça de les Arts
C de la Marina
Estació del Nord
C d'Alí Bei
EL FORT PIENC
C de Nàpols
Arc de Triomf
7
C del Comerç
Marina
Av Meridiana
Bogatell
C de Zamora
C de Joan Miró
C de la Marina
C de Wellington
Universitat Pompeu Fabra
Parc de Carles I
Ciutadella Vila Olímpica
21
10
20
12
Pg de Pujades

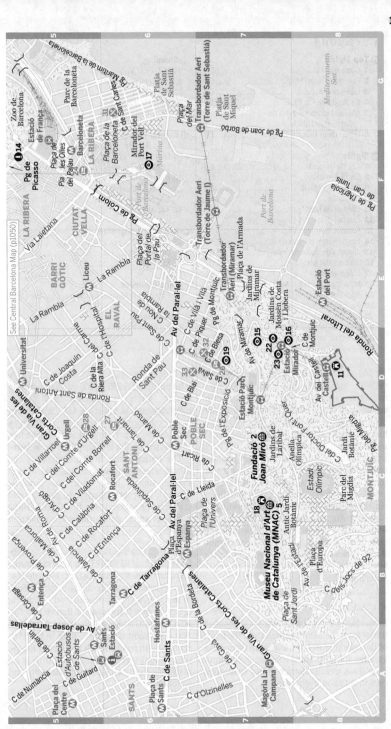

SPAIN BARCELONA

Barcelona

⊙ Top Sights
1 Casa Batlló	D4
2 Fundació Joan Miró	C7
3 La Pedrera	D3
4 La Sagrada Família	E2
5 Museu Nacional d'Art de Catalunya (MNAC)	C7
6 Palau de la Música Catalana	E4

⊙ Sights
7 Arc de Triomf	F4
8 Casa Amatller	D4
9 Casa Lleó Morera	D4
10 Cascada	F4
11 Castell de Montjuïc	D8
12 Castell dels Tres Dragons	F4
13 Fundació Antoni Tàpies	D4
14 Homenatge a Picasso	F5
15 Jardins de Joan Brossa	D7
16 Jardins del Mirador	D7
17 L'Aquàrium	F6
18 Mirador del Palau Nacional	C7
19 MUHBA Refugi 307	D7
20 Parc de la Ciutadella	F4
21 Parlament de Catalunya	G4
22 Plaça de la Sardana	D7
23 Telefèric de Montjuïc	D7

⊙ Sleeping
24 H10 Port Vell	F5
25 Hostal Center Inn	E4
26 Hotel Brummell	D7
27 Hotel Market	D6
28 Pars Tailor's Hostel	C5

⊗ Eating
29 Cinc Sentits	C4
30 Disfrutar	C4
31 La Cova Fumada	G6
32 Palo Cortao	D7
33 Quimet i Quimet	D6
Speakeasy	(see 36)
34 Tapas 24	D4

⊙ Drinking & Nightlife
35 City Hall	D4
36 Dry Martini	C4
37 Monvínic	D4

⊛ Entertainment
Palau de la Música Catalana	(see 6)

⊙ Shopping
38 Els Encants Vells	F2

★**Museu d'Història de Barcelona** MUSEUM
(MUHBA; Map p1050; ☑93 256 21 00; www.museuhistoria.bcn.cat; Plaça del Rei; adult/concession/child €7/5/free, 3-8pm Sun & 1st Sun of month free; ☉10am-7pm Tue-Sat, to 2pm Mon, to 8pm Sun; ☎; Ⓜ Jaume I) One of Barcelona's most fascinating museums takes you back through the centuries to the very foundations of Roman Barcino. You'll stroll over ruins of the old streets, sewers, laundries and wine- and fish-making factories that flourished here following the town's founding by Emperor Augustus around 10 BC. Equally impressive is the building itself, which was once part of the Palau Reial Major (Grand Royal Palace) on Plaça del Rei, among the key locations of medieval princely power in Barcelona.

⊙ La Ribera

In medieval days, La Ribera was a stone's throw from the Mediterranean and the heart of Barcelona's foreign trade, with homes belonging to numerous wealthy merchants. Now it's a trendy district full of boutiques, restaurants and lively bars.

★**Museu Picasso** MUSEUM
(Map p1050; ☑93 256 30 00; www.museupicasso.bcn.cat; Carrer de Montcada 15-23; adult/concession/child all collections €14/7.50/free, permanent collection €11/7/free, temporary exhibitions €4.50/3/free, 3-7pm Sun & 1st Sun of month free; ☉9am-7pm Tue-Sun, to 9.30pm Thu; ☎; Ⓜ Jaume I) The setting alone, in five contiguous medieval stone mansions, makes the Museu Picasso unique (and worth the probable queues). The pretty courtyards, galleries and staircases preserved in the first three of these buildings are as delightful as the collection inside.

★**Basílica de Santa Maria del Mar** CHURCH
(Map p1050; ☑93 310 23 90; www.santamaria-delmarbarcelona.org; Plaça de Santa Maria del Mar; €8; ☉guided tours 1.15pm, 2pm, 3pm, 5.15pm; Ⓜ Jaume I) At the southwest end of Passeig del Born stands the apse of Barcelona's finest Catalan Gothic church, Santa Maria del Mar (Our Lady of the Sea). Built in the 14th century with record-breaking alacrity for the time (it took just 54 years), the church is remarkable for its architectural harmony and simplicity.

★Palau de la Música Catalana ARCHITECTURE
(Map p1046; ☎93 295 72 00; www.palaumusica.
cat; Carrer de Palau de la Música 4-6; adult/
concession/child €18/11/free; ⊙guided tours
10am-3.30pm, to 6pm Easter, Jul & Aug; ⓂUr-
quinaona) This concert hall is a high point
of Barcelona's Modernista architecture, a
symphony in tile, brick, sculpted stone and
stained glass. Built by Domènech i Montaner
between 1905 and 1908 for the Orfeo Català
musical society, it was conceived as a temple
for the Catalan Renaixença (Renaissance).

Parc de la Ciutadella PARK
(Map p1046; Passeig de Picasso; ⊙8am-9pm
May-Sep, to 7pm Oct-Apr; ⚑; ⓂArc de Triomf)
Come for a stroll, a picnic, a boat ride on
the lake or to inspect Catalonia's regional
parliament, but don't miss a visit to this, the
most central green lung in the city. Parc de la
Ciutadella is perfect for winding down.

◉ L'Eixample

Modernisme, the Catalan version of art nouveau, transformed Barcelona's cityscape in
the early 20th century. Most Modernista
works, including Antoni Gaudí's unfinished
masterpiece, La Sagrada Família, were built
in the elegant, if traffic-filled, L'Eixample

(pronounced 'lay-sham-pluh'), a grid-plan
district that was developed from the 1870s on.

★La Sagrada Família CHURCH
(Map p1046; ☎93 208 04 14; www.sagradafamilia.
cat; Carrer de Mallorca 401; adult/concession/
under 11yr €15/13/free; ⊙9am-8pm Apr-Sep, to
6pm Oct-Mar; ⓂSagrada Família) If you have
time for only one sightseeing outing, this
should be it. La Sagrada Família inspires
awe by its sheer verticality, and in the manner of the medieval cathedrals it emulates,
it's still under construction after more than
130 years. When completed, the highest tower will be more than half as high again as
those that stand today.

★La Pedrera ARCHITECTURE
(Casa Milà; Map p1046; ☎902 202138; www.
lapedrera.com; Passeig de Gràcia 92; adult/
concession/under 13yr/under 7yr €22/16.50/11/
free; ⊙9am-6.30pm & 7pm-9pm Mon-Sun; ⓂDi-
agonal) This undulating beast is another
madcap Gaudí masterpiece, built in 1905–10
as a combined apartment and office block.
Formally called Casa Milà, after the busi-
nessman who commissioned it, it is better
known as La Pedrera (the Quarry) because of
its uneven grey stone facade, which ripples
around the corner of Carrer de Provença.

LA SAGRADA FAMÍLIA HIGHLIGHTS

Roof The roof of La Sagrada Família is held up by a forest of extraordinary angled pillars. As the pillars soar towards the ceiling, they sprout a web of supporting branches, creating the effect of a forest canopy.

Nativity Facade The artistic pinnacle of the building. You can climb high up inside some of the four towers by a combination of lifts and narrow spiral staircases – a vertiginous experience.

Passion Facade The southwest Passion Facade, on the theme of Christ's last days and death, was built between 1954 and 1978 based on surviving drawings by Gaudí, with four towers and a large, sculpture-bedecked portal by Josep Subirachs.

Glory Facade The Glory Facade is under construction and will, like the others, be crowned by four towers – the total of 12 representing the Twelve Apostles.

Museu Gaudí The Museu Gaudí, below ground level, includes interesting material on Gaudí's life and other works, as well as models and photos of La Sagrada Família.

Exploring La Sagrada Família Booking tickets online avoids what can be very lengthy queues (La Sagrada Família gets around 2.8 million visitors a year). Although the church is essentially a building site, the completed sections and museum may be explored at leisure. Fifty-minute guided tours (€9) are offered. Alternatively, pick up an audio tour (€7), for which you need ID. Enter from Carrer de Sardenya or Carrer de la Marina. Once inside, €14 (which includes the audio tour) will get you into lifts that rise up inside towers in the Nativity and Passion facades.

Central Barcelona

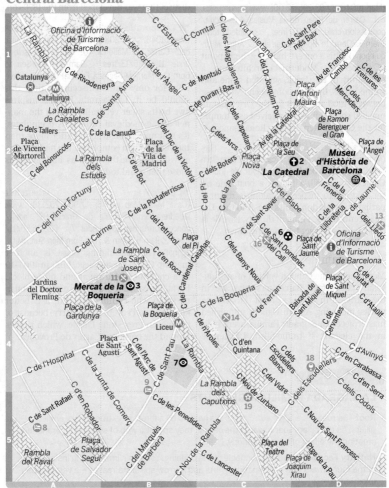

★ **Casa Batlló** ARCHITECTURE
(Map p1046; ☎93 216 03 06; www.casabatllo.es; Passeig de Gràcia 43; adult/concession/under 7yr €23.50/20.50/free; ☺9am-9pm, last admission 8pm; Ⓜ Passeig de Gràcia) One of the strangest residential buildings in Europe, this is Gaudí at his hallucinatory best. The facade, sprinkled with bits of blue, mauve and green tiles and studded with wave-shaped window frames and balconies, rises to an uneven blue-tiled roof with a solitary tower.

Fundació Antoni Tàpies GALLERY
(Map p1046; ☎93 487 03 15; www.fundaciotapies. org; Carrer d'Aragó 255; adult/concession €7/5.60; ☺10am-7pm Tue-Sun; Ⓜ Passeig de Gràcia) The Fundació Antoni Tàpies is both a pioneering Modernista building (completed in 1885) and the major collection of leading 20th-century Catalan artist Antoni Tàpies. A man known for his esoteric work, Tàpies died in February 2012, aged 88; he left behind a powerful range of paintings and a foundation intended to promote contemporary artists.

SPAIN BARCELONA

◎ Montjuïc

Southwest of the city centre, the hillside overlooking the port has some of the city's finest art collections, and also serves as a Central Park of sorts, a great place for a jog or stroll. The closest metro stops are Espanya, Poble Sec and Paral·lel. From Paral·lel a funicular railway runs up to Estació Parc Montjuïc, from where a cable car, the Telefèric de Montjuïc (Map p1046; www.telefericdemontjuic.cat; Av de Miramar 30; adult/child one way €8/6.20; ☺10am-9pm Jun-Sep, to 7pm Oct-May; 🚌55, 150), climbs to the Castell de Montjuïc. Bus 150 does a circle trip from Plaça d'Espanya to Castell de Montjuïc.

★ **Museu Nacional
d'Art de Catalunya (MNAC)**   MUSEUM
(Map p1046; ☏93 622 03 76; www.museunacional.cat; Mirador del Palau Nacional; adult/student/child €12/8.40/free, after 3pm Sat & 1st Sun of

★**Park Güell**   PARK
(☏93 409 18 31; www.parkguell.cat; Carrer d'Olot 7; adult/child €8/6; ☺8am-9.30pm May-Aug, to 8pm Sep-Apr; 🚌24, Ⓜ Lesseps, Vallcarca) North of Gràcia and about 4km from Plaça de Catalunya, Park Güell is where Gaudí turned his hand to landscape gardening. It's a strange, enchanting place where his passion for natural forms really took flight – to the point where the artificial almost seems more natural than the natural.

month free; ⊘10am-8pm Tue-Sat, to 3pm Sun May-Sep, to 6pm Tue-Sat Oct-Apr; ⊛; Ⓜ Espanya) From across the city, the bombastic neobaroque silhouette of the **Palau Nacional** (Map p1046) can be seen on the slopes of Montjuïc. Built for the 1929 World Exhibition and restored in 2005, it houses a vast collection of mostly Catalan art spanning the early Middle Ages to the early 20th century. The high point is the collection of extraordinary Romanesque frescos.

★ **Fundació Joan Miró**   MUSEUM
(Map p1046; ☑93 443 94 70; www.fmirobcn.org; Parc de Montjuïc; adult/child €12/free; ⊘10am-8pm Tue-Wed & Fri, to 9pm Thu, to 3pm Sun Apr-Oct, shorter hours rest of the year; ⊛; ⊒55, 150, ⊠Paral·lel) Joan Miró, the city's best-known 20th-century artistic progeny, bequeathed this art foundation to his hometown in 1971. Its light-filled buildings, designed by close friend and architect Josep Lluís Sert (who also built Miró's Mallorca studios), are crammed with seminal works, from Miró's earliest timid sketches to paintings from his last years.

Castell de Montjuïc   FORTRESS
(Map p1046; ☑93 256 44 45; www.bcn.cat/castelldemontjuic; Carretera de Montjuïc 66; adult/child €5/free, after 3pm Sun free; ⊘10am-8pm Apr-Oct, to 6pm Nov-Mar; ⊠150, Telefèric de Montjuïc, Castell de Montjuïc) This forbidding *castell* (castle or fort) dominates the southeastern heights of Montjuïc and enjoys commanding views over the Mediterranean. It dates, in its present form, from the late 17th and 18th centuries. For most of its dark history, it has been used to watch over the city and as a political prison and killing ground.

⊙ **La Barceloneta & the Waterfront**

Barcelona's formerly industrial waterfront has been transformed in recent decades, with sparkling beaches, seaside bars and restaurants, elegant sculptures, yacht-filled marinas and long esplanades popular with walkers, runners and cyclists. Port Vell, at the foot of La Rambla, is where many visitors first lay eyes on Barcelona's slice of the Mediterranean. The pedestrian bridge of Rambla de Mar leads out to the Maremàgnum mall and one of Europe's biggest aquariums, **L'Aquàrium** (Map p1046; ☑93 221 74 74; www.aquariumbcn.com; Moll d'Espanya; adult/child

€20/15, dive €300; ⊘9.30am-11pm Jul & Aug, to 9pm Sep-Jun; Ⓜ Drassanes), next door.

East of there, where the old fishing quarter of La Barceloneta abuts the sea, you'll find open-air restaurants offering views out over the promenade and the artificial beaches beyond.

⭐ Festivals & Events

Festes de Santa Eulàlia   CULTURAL
(http://lameva.barcelona.cat/santaeulalia; ⊘Feb) Around 12 February this big winter fest celebrates Barcelona's first patron saint with a week of cultural events, including parades of *gegants* (giants), open-air art installations, theatre, *correfocs* (fire runs) and *castells* (human castles).

Festes de la Mercè   CULTURAL
(www.bcn.cat/merce; ⊘Sep) The city's biggest party involves four days of concerts, dancing, *castellers* (human-castle builders), a fireworks display synchronised with the Montjuïc fountains, dances of giants on the Saturday, and *correfocs* – a parade of firework-spitting dragons and devils – from all over Catalonia, on the Sunday. Held around 24 September.

🛏 Sleeping

Accommodation in Barcelona is more expensive than anywhere else in Spain except Madrid. La Rambla, the Barri Gòtic and El Raval can be noisy but are close to the action with a big selection of boxy hotels, glorious boutique options, hostels and fleapits. You'll find a few attractive boutique-style guesthouses and hostels in Poble Sec and up-and-coming Sant Antoni. L'Eixample has the greatest range of hotels in most classes, including some classic hotels and a long list of decent midrange places, though some are a bit far from the old city.

🛏 **El Raval**

Hotel Peninsular   HOTEL €
(Map p1050; ☑93 302 31 38; www.hotelpeninsular. net; Carrer de Sant Pau 34; s/d €50/70; ❋⊛; Ⓜ Liceu) An oasis on the edge of the slightly dicey Barri Xino, this former convent (which was connected by tunnel to the Església de Sant Agustí) has a plant-draped atrium extending its height and most of its length. The 60 rooms are simple, with tiled floors and whitewash, but mostly spacious and well kept. There are some great bargains to be had during quiet periods.

★ **Barceló Raval**   DESIGN HOTEL €€

(Map p1050; ☑ 93 320 14 90; www.barceloraval. com; Rambla del Raval 17-21; r from €125; ❀ ☎; Ⓜ Liceu) Part of the city's plans to pull El Raval district up by the bootstraps, this oval-shaped designer hotel tower makes a 21st-century splash. The rooftop terrace offers fabulous views and the B-Lounge bar-restaurant is the toast of the town for meals and cocktails. Rooms have slick aesthetics (white with lime green or ruby-red splashes of colour), Nespresso machines and iPod docks.

Barri Gòtic

Serras Hotel   BOUTIQUE HOTEL €€€

(Map p1050; ☑ 93 169 18 68; www.hoteltheserras-barcelona.com; Passeig de Colom 9; r from €302; ❀ ☎ ⚄; Ⓜ Barceloneta) A fresh and funky five-star that has every comfort – including a rooftop bar with a small dipping pool and a terrific view over the port – but never feels stuffy. Rooms at the front are brighter and have a better view (from the bathtub, in some cases) but rooms at the side are spared the traffic noise.

Poble Sec & Sant Antoni

Pars Tailor's Hostel   HOSTEL €

(Map p1046; ☑ 93 250 56 84; www.tailors-hostel. com; Carrer de Sepúlveda 146; dm €18-20; ❀ ☎; Ⓜ Urgell, Sant Antoni) Decorated like a mid-20th-century tailor's shop, this popular hostel has uncommon style, with old sewing machines, lovingly framed brassieres and vintage fixtures adorning the common areas. Aside from admiring the aesthetics, there's much afoot at Tailor's: you can shoot a round on the old billiards table, mingle with other guests in the comfy lounge, or join one of the many activities on offer.

★ **Hotel Brummell**   BOUTIQUE HOTEL €€

(Map p1046; ☑ 93 125 86 22; www.hotelbrummell. com; Carrer Nou de la Rambla 174; d from €150; ❀ ☎ ⚄; Ⓜ Paral·lel) This stylish addition to Barcelona has been turning heads since its 2015 opening. It's a thoughtfully designed hotel with a creative soul and great atmosphere. The 20 rooms are bright with a cheerful, minimalist design, and the best of the bunch have sizeable terraces with views and even outdoor soaking tubs. The smallest (the Brummell Classic rooms) feel a little tight.

Hotel Market   BOUTIQUE HOTEL €€

(Map p1046; ☑ 93 325 12 05; www.andilanahotels. com; Carrer del Comte Borrell 68; r from €80; ❀ @ ☎; Ⓜ Sant Antoni) Attractively located in a renovated building along a narrow lane just north of the grand old Sant Antoni market, this place has an air of simple chic, with wide plank floors, oversized armoires, bold art prints and nicely designed bathrooms (stone basins, rain showers). Some rooms have tiny (two-seat) balconies.

L'Eixample

Hostal Center Inn   HOTEL €€

(Map p1046; ☑ 93 265 25 60; www.centerinnbarce-lona.com; Gran Via de les Corts Catalanes 688; s/d €75/85; ❀ ☎ ☎; Ⓜ Tetuan) Simple rooms have quirky touches – wrought-iron bedsteads, Moroccan mosaic tables on the ample balconies, stripey Tim Burton wallpaper in one room, an antique escritoire in another. The bathrooms carry a vaguely Andalucian flavour. Get a back room if you can, as the Gran Via is noisy.

La Barceloneta & the Waterfront

H10 Port Vell   BOUTIQUE HOTEL €€

(Map p1046; ☑ 93 310 30 65; www.h10hotels.com; Pas de Sota Muralla 9; d from €188; ❀ @ ☎ ⚄; Ⓜ Barceloneta) The location is excellent at this 58-room hotel within a short stroll of El Born and Barceloneta. Sleek, modern rooms have a trim, minimalist design with black and white bathrooms, and the best rooms (not all) have fine views over the marina. The rooftop terrace is the best feature, with sun loungers, a tiny plunge pool and cocktails by evening.

✖ Eating

Barcelona is foodie heaven, fuelled by a combination of world-class chefs, imaginative recipes and magnificent ingredients fresh from farms and the sea. Catalan culinary masterminds like Ferran Adrià and Carles Abellan have reinvented haute cuisine, while classic old-world Catalan seafood and meat recipes continue to earn accolades in dining rooms and tapas bars across the city.

✖ El Raval

★ **Bar Pinotxo**   TAPAS €€

(Map p1050; www.pinotxobar.com; Mercat de la Boqueria; mains €8-17; ☉ 7am-4pm Mon-Sat; Ⓜ Liceu) Bar Pinotxo is arguably La Boqueria's, and even Barcelona's, best tapas bar. It sits among the half-dozen or so informal eateries within the market, and the popular owner, Juanito, might serve up chickpeas with pine nuts and raisins, a soft mix of potato and spinach sprinkled with salt, soft baby squid with cannellini beans, or a quivering cube of caramel-sweet pork belly.

★ Barri Gòtic

★ La Vinateria del Call   SPANISH €€
(Map p1050; ☑ 93 302 60 92; www.lavinateriadel call.com; Carrer de Sant Domènec del Call 9; raciones €7-12; ⊙ 7.30pm-1am; Ⓜ Jaume I) In a magical setting in the former Jewish quarter, this tiny jewel box of a restaurant serves up tasty Iberian dishes including Galician octopus, cider-cooked chorizo and the Catalan *escalivada* (roasted peppers, aubergine and onions) with anchovies. Portions are small and made for sharing, and there's a good and affordable selection of wines.

★ Cafè de l'Acadèmia   CATALAN €€
(Map p1050; ☑ 93 319 82 53; Carrer dels Lledó 1; mains €15-20; ⊙ 1-3.30pm & 8-11.30pm Mon-Fri; 🔊; Ⓜ Jaume I) Expect a mix of traditional Catalan dishes with the occasional creative twist. At lunchtime, local Ajuntament (town hall) office workers pounce on the *menú del día* (daily set menu; €15.70). In the evening it is rather more romantic, as low lighting emphasises the intimacy of the beamed ceiling and stone walls. On warm days you can also dine on the pretty square at the front.

Can Culleretes   CATALAN €€
(Map p1050; ☑ 93 317 30 22; www.culleretes.com; Carrer Quintana 5; mains €10-18; ⊙ 1.30-4pm & 9-11pm Tue-Sat, 1.30-4pm Sun; Ⓜ Liceu) Founded in 1786, Barcelona's oldest restaurant is still going strong, with tourists and locals flocking here to enjoy its rambling interior, old-fashioned tile-filled decor and enormous helpings of traditional Catalan food, including fresh seafood and sticky stews.

★ Poble Sec & Sant Antoni

★ Palo Cortao   TAPAS €€
(Map p1046; ☑ 93 188 90 67; www.palocortao. es; Carrer de Nou de la Rambla 146; mains €10-15; ⊙ 8pm-1am Tue-Sun, 1-5pm Sat & Sun; Ⓜ Paral·lel) Palo Cortao has a solid reputation for its beautifully executed seafood and meat dishes, served at fair prices. Highlights include octopus with white bean hummus, skirt

steak with foie Armagnac, and tuna tataki tempura. You can order half sizes of all plates – which will allow you to try more dishes.

★ Quimet i Quimet   TAPAS €€
(Map p1046; ☑ 93 442 31 42; Carrer del Poeta Cabanyes 25; tapas €4-10, montaditos around €3; ⊙ noon-4pm & 7-10.30pm Mon-Fri, noon-4pm Sat; Ⓜ Paral·lel) Quimet i Quimet is a family-run business that has been passed down from generation to generation. There's barely space to swing a *calamar* in this bottle-lined, standing-room-only place, but it is a treat for the palate, with *montaditos* (tapas on a slice of bread) made to order.

★ La Ribera

Bormuth   TAPAS €
(Map p1050; ☑ 93 310 21 86; Carrer del Rec 31; tapas €4-10; ⊙ 12.30pm-1.30am Sun-Thu, to 2.30am Fri & Sat; 🔊; Ⓜ Jaume I) Located on the pedestrian Carrer del Rec, Bormuth has tapped into the vogue for old-school tapas with modern-day service and decor, and serves all the old favourites – *patatas bravas, ensaladilla* (Russian salad) and tortilla – along with some less predictable and superbly prepared numbers (try the chargrilled red pepper with black pudding).

★ Casa Delfín   CATALAN €€
(Map p1050; ☑ 93 319 50 88; www.tallerdetapas. com; Passeig del Born 36; mains €10-15; ⊙ 8am-midnight Sun-Thu, to 1am Fri & Sat; 🔊; Ⓜ Barceloneta) One of Barcelona's culinary delights, Casa Delfín is everything you dream of when you think of Catalan (and Mediterranean) cooking. Start with the tangy and sweet *calçots* (a cross between a leek and an onion; February and March only) or salt-strewn *padron* peppers, moving on to grilled sardines speckled with parsley, then tackle the meaty monkfish roasted in white wine and garlic.

★ L'Eixample

★ Tapas 24   TAPAS €
(Map p1046; ☑ 93 488 09 77; www.carlesabellan. com; Carrer de la Diputació 269; tapas €4-9.50; ⊙ 9am-midnight; 🔊; Ⓜ Passeig de Gràcia) Carles Abellan, master of the now-defunct Comerç 24 in La Ribera, runs this basement tapas haven known for its gourmet versions of old faves. Specials include the *bikini* (toasted ham and cheese sandwich – here the ham is cured and the truffle makes all the difference)

and a thick black *arròs negre de sípia* (squid-ink black rice).

★ **Cinc Sentits**   INTERNATIONAL €€€
(Map p1046; ✆ 93 323 94 90; www.cincsentits.com; Carrer d'Aribau 58; tasting menus €100-120; ◷ 1.30-3pm & 8.30-10pm Tue-Sat; Ⓜ Passeig de Gràcia) Enter the realm of the 'Five Senses' to indulge in a jaw-dropping tasting menu consisting of a series of small, experimental dishes (there is no à la carte, although dishes can be tweaked to suit diners' requests). There is a lunch *menú* for €55.

★ **Disfrutar**   MODERN EUROPEAN €€€
(Map p1046; ✆ 93 348 68 96; www.en.disfrutarbarcelona.com; Carrer de Villarroel 163; tasting menus €110-180; ◷ 1-2.30pm & 8-9.30pm Tue-Sat; Ⓜ Hospital Clínic) In its first few months of life, Disfrutar rose stratospherically to become the city's finest restaurant – book now while it's still possible to get a table. Run by alumni of Ferran Adrià's game-changing El Bulli restaurant, it operates along similar lines.

La Barceloneta & the Waterfront

★ **La Cova Fumada**   TAPAS €
(Map p1046; ✆ 93 221 40 61; Carrer del Baluard 56; tapas €4-8; ◷ 9am-3.20pm Mon-Wed, 9am-3.20pm & 6-8.15pm Thu & Fri, 9am-1pm Sat; Ⓜ Barceloneta) There's no sign and the setting is decidedly downmarket, but this tiny, buzzing family-run tapas spot always packs in a crowd. The secret? Mouthwatering *pulpo* (octopus), *calamar, sardines* and 15 or so other small plates cooked to perfection in the small open kitchen. The *bombas* (potato croquettes served with *alioli*) and grilled *carxofes* (artichokes) are good, but everything is amazingly fresh.

🍷 Drinking & Nightlife

Barcelona is a night-lover's town, with an enticing spread of candlelit wine bars, old-school taverns, stylish lounges and kaleidoscopic nightclubs. Clubs mostly open from midnight until 6am, Thursday to Saturday. Entry can cost from nothing to over €20 (one drink usually included).

The best streets and plazas for bar-hopping include Plaça Reial and Carrer dels Escudellers in the Barri Gòtic, Carrer de Joaquín Costa in bohemian El Raval, Carrer Nou de la Rambla and Carrer del Parlament in hipster/bohemian Poble Sec and Sant An-

toni, Passeig del Born in stylish La Ribera, and Carrer d'Aribau in L'Eixample.

Barcelona's vibrant gay and lesbian scene is concentrated in the 'Gaixample', an area in L'Eixample around Carrer del Consell de Cent, five or six blocks southwest of Passeig de Gràcia.

Barri Gòtic

Marula Café   BAR
(Map p1050; ✆ 93 318 76 90; www.marulacafe.com; Carrer dels Escudellers 49; ◷ 11pm-6am Wed-Sun; Ⓜ Liceu) A fantastic find in the heart of the Barri Gòtic, Marula will transport you to the 1970s and the best in funk and soul. James Brown fans will think they've died and gone to heaven. It's not, however, a monothematic place and DJs slip in other tunes, from breakbeat to house. Samba and other Brazilian dance sounds also penetrate here.

La Ribera

El Born Bar   BAR
(Map p1050; ✆ 93 319 53 33; www.elbornbar.neositios.com; Passeig del Born 26; ◷ 10am-2am Mon-Thu, to 3am Fri & Sat, noon-2.30am Sun; 📶; Ⓜ Jaume I) El Born Bar effortlessly attracts everyone from cool thirty-somethings from all over town to locals who pass judgement on Passeig del Born's passing parade. Its staying power depends on a good selection of beers, spirits, and *empanadas* and other snacks.

L'Eixample

★ **Dry Martini**   BAR
(Map p1046; ✆ 93 217 50 80; www.drymartiniorg.com; Carrer d'Aribau 162-166; ◷ 1pm-2.30am Mon-Thu, 6pm-3am Fri & Sat, 7pm-2.30am Sun; Ⓜ Diagonal) Waiters with a discreetly knowing smile will attend to your cocktail needs and make uncannily good suggestions, but the house drink, taken at the bar or in one of the plush green leather banquettes, is a safe bet. The gin and tonic comes in an enormous mug-sized glass – one will take you most of the night.

★ **Monvínic**   WINE BAR
(Map p1046; ✆ 93 272 61 87; www.monvinic.com; Carrer de la Diputació 249; ◷ 1-11pm Tue-Fri, 7-11pm Mon & Sat; Ⓜ Passeig de Gràcia) Apparently considered unmissable by El Bulli's sommelier, Monvínic is an ode, a rhapsody even, to wine loving. The interactive wine list sits on the bar for you to browse, on a digital tablet similar to an iPad, and boasts more than 3000 varieties.

SPAIN BARCELONA

DON'T MISS

SEEING AN FC BARCELONA MATCH

Football in Barcelona has the aura of religion and for much of the city's population, support of FC Barcelona is an article of faith. FC Barcelona is traditionally associated with the Catalans and even Catalan nationalism.

Tickets to FC Barcelona matches are available at Camp Nou (☑902 189900; www.fcbarcelona.com; Carrer d'Arístides Maillol; Ⓜ Palau Reial), online (through FC Barcelona's official website), and through various city locations. Tourist offices sell them (the branch at Plaça de Catalunya is a centrally located option) as do FC Botiga stores. Tickets can cost anything from €39 to upwards of €250, depending on the seat and match. On match day the ticket windows (at gates 9 and 15) are open from 9.15am until kick-off.

Fans who can't get to a game will still enjoy the self-guided stadium tour Camp Nou Experience (☑902 189900; www.fcbarcelona.com; Gate 9, Avinguda de Joan XXIII; adult/child €25/20; ☺9.30am-7.30pm daily Apr-Sep, 10am-6.30pm Mon-Sat, to 2.30pm Sun Oct-Mar; Ⓜ Palau Reial).

City Hall CLUB
(Map p1046; ☑932380722; www.cityhallbarcelona.com; Rambla de Catalunya 2-4; cover €10-15, incl 1 drink; ☺midnight-5am Wed & Thu, midnight-6am Fri & Sat, 11pm-5am Sun; Ⓜ Catalunya) A long corridor leads to the dance floor of this venerable and popular club, located in a former theatre. House and other electric sounds dominate, with occasional funk nights. Check the website for details.

☆ Entertainment

★ Palau de la Música Catalana CLASSICAL MUSIC
(Map p1046; ☑93 295 72 00; www.palaumusica.cat; Carrer de Palau de la Música 4-6; tickets from €15; ☺box office 9.30am-9pm Mon-Sat, 10am-3pm Sun; Ⓜ Urquinaona) A feast for the eyes, this Modernista confection is also the city's most traditional venue for classical and choral music, although it has a wide-ranging program, including flamenco, pop and – particularly – jazz. Just being here for a performance is an experience. In the foyer, its tiled pillars all a-glitter, sip a pre-concert tipple.

Jamboree LIVE MUSIC
(Map p1050; ☑93 319 17 89; www.masimas.com/jamboree; Plaça Reial 17; tickets €10-20; ☺8pm-6am; Ⓜ Liceu) For over half a century, Jamboree has been bringing joy to the jivers of Barcelona, with high-calibre acts featuring jazz trios, blues, Afrobeats, Latin sounds and big-band sounds. Two concerts are held most nights (at 8pm and 10pm), after which Jamboree morphs into a DJ-spinning club at midnight. WTF jam sessions are held Mondays (entrance a mere €5).

🔒 Shopping

Most mainstream fashion stores are along a shopping 'axis' that runs from Plaça de Catalunya along Passeig de Gràcia, then left (west) along Avinguda Diagonal.

In La Ribera, El Born and Carrer del Rec are the places for cool designer boutiques that sell high-end fashion. There are plenty of shops scattered throughout the Barri Gòtic (stroll Carrer d'Avinyò). El Raval is a haven for vintage fashion (especially Carrer de la Riera Baixa) and all kinds of original and arty independent shops.

Coquette FASHION & ACCESSORIES
(Map p1050; ☑93 310 35 35; www.coquettebcn.com; Carrer de Bonaire 5; ☺11am-3pm & 5-9pm Mon-Fri, 11.30am-9pm Sat; Ⓜ Barceloneta) Elegant women's store with designers from around the globe, but particularly Spain.

Custo Barcelona FASHION & ACCESSORIES
(Map p1050; ☑93 268 78 93; www.custo.com; Plaça de les Olles 7; ☺10am-9pm Mon-Sat, noon-8pm Sun; Ⓜ Barceloneta) The psychedelic decor and casual atmosphere lend this avant-garde Barcelona fashion store a youthful edge. Custo presents daring new women's and men's collections each year on the New York catwalks. The dazzling colours and cut of everything from dinner jackets to hot pants are for the uninhibited. It has three other stores around town.

Els Encants Vells MARKET
(Fira de Bellcaire; Map p1046; ☑93 246 30 30; www.encantsbcn.com; Plaça de les Glòries Catalanes; ☺9am-8pm Mon, Wed, Fri & Sat; Ⓜ Glòries) In a gleaming open-sided complex near Plaça de les Glòries Catalanes, the 'Old Charms' flea market is the biggest of its kind in Barcelona. Over 500 vendors ply their wares beneath massive mirror-like panels. It's all here, from antique furniture through to secondhand clothes. A lot of it is junk, but occasionally you'll stumble across a *ganga* (bargain).

❶ Information

Purse snatching and pickpocketing are major problems, especially around Plaça de Catalunya, La Rambla and Plaça Reial. Report thefts to the **Guàrdia Urbana** (Local Police; ☑ 092/93 256 24 30; www.bcn.cat/guardiaurbana; La Rambla 43; ⏰24hr; Ⓜ Liceu) on La Rambla. You're unlikely to recover your goods but you will need to make this formal *denuncia* (police report) for insurance purposes. Avoid walking around El Raval and the southern end of La Rambla late at night.

Oficina d'Informació de Turisme de Barcelona (Map p1050; ☑ 93 285 38 34; www.barcelona-turisme.com; Plaça de Catalunya 17; ⏰9.30am-9.30pm; Ⓜ Catalunya) The main Barcelona tourist information office sells walking tours, bus tours, discount cards, transport passes and tickets to shows, and can help book accommodation. It's underground at the Plaça de Catalunya.

Palau Robert Regional Tourist Office (Map p1046; ☑ 93 238 80 91; www.palaurobert. gencat.cat; Passeig de Gràcia 107; ⏰10am-8pm Mon-Sat, to 2.30pm Sun; Ⓜ Diagonal) A host of material on Catalonia, audiovisual resources, a bookshop and a branch of Turisme Juvenil de Catalunya (for youth travel).

❶ Getting There & Away

AIR

El Prat Airport (☑ 902 404704; www.aena.es) Barcelona's El Prat airport lies 17km southwest of Plaça de Catalunya at El Prat de Llobregat. The airport has two main terminal buildings: the new T1 terminal and the older T2, itself divided into three terminal areas (A, B and C).

BOAT

Barcelona has ferry connections to the Balearic Islands and Italy. Boats depart from the port just south of the old city.

Trasmediterranea (☑ 902 454645; www. trasmediterranea.es; Ⓜ Drassanes) Passenger and vehicular ferries operated by Trasmediterranea to/from the Balearic Islands dock around the Moll de Barcelona wharf in Port Vell. Information and tickets are available at the terminal buildings along Moll de Sant Bertran and on Moll de Barcelona or from travel agents.

BUS

Long-distance buses leave from Estació del Nord. A plethora of companies service different parts of Spain; many come under the umbrella of **Alsa** (☑ 902 422242; www.alsa.es). For other companies, ask at the bus station. There are frequent services to Madrid, Valencia and Zaragoza (20 or more a day) and several daily departures to distant destinations such as Burgos, Santiago de Compostela and Seville.

Eurolines (www.eurolines.com), in conjunction with local carriers all over Europe, is the main international carrier. Its website provides links to national operators; it runs services across Europe and to Morocco from **Estació del Nord** (Map p1046; ☑ 902 26 06 06; www.barcelona-nord.cat; Carrer d'Ali Bei 80; Ⓜ Arc de Triomf), and from **Estació d'Autobusos de Sants** (Map p1046; ☑ 93 339 73 29; www.adif.es; Carrer de Viriat; Ⓜ Estació Sants), next to Estació Sants Barcelona.

TRAIN

The main station is **Estació Sants** (www.adif.es; Plaça dels Països Catalans; Ⓜ Estació Sants), 2.5km west of La Rambla. About 30 daily high-speed trains to Madrid via Zaragoza take as little as 2½ hours; prices vary from €50 to over €200 (book well ahead for lowest fares). Other daily trains run to Valencia (€12 to €45, three to 4½ hours, up to 19 daily), Pamplona, San Sebastián, Bilbao, Santiago de Compostela, Seville and Málaga. Direct overnight trains from Paris, Geneva, Milan and Zürich also arrive at Estació Sants.

❶ Getting Around

TO/FROM THE AIRPORT

The frequent Aerobús (www.aerobusbcn.com) runs every five or 10 minutes between both airport terminals and Plaça de Catalunya (€5.50, 35 minutes), from 5.30am to 1am. The L9 Sud line of the Barcelona metro also serves both terminals (€4.50) but you need a couple of changes to reach central areas. Taxis cost around €30.

WORTH A TRIP

ANDORRA

This mini-country wedged between France and Spain offers by far the best ski slopes and resort facilities in all the Pyrenees. Once the snows melt, there's an abundance of great walking, ranging from easy strolls to demanding day hikes in the principality's higher, more remote reaches. Strike out above the tight valleys and you can walk for hours, almost alone.

The only way to reach Andorra is by road from Spain or France. If driving, fill up in Andorra; fuel is substantially cheaper there. There are buses to/from Barcelona's Estació del Nord, Estació Sants and airport, Lleida, La Seu d'Urgell and Toulouse (France). All bus services arrive at and leave from Andorra la Vella.

WORTH A TRIP

GIRONA

A tight huddle of ancient arcaded houses, grand churches, climbing cobbled streets and medieval baths, all enclosed by defensive walls and a lazy river, constitutes a powerful reason for visiting northern Catalonia's largest city, Girona (Castilian: Gerona). From Girona station there are at least 15 trains per day to Figueres (€4.10 to €5.45, 30 to 40 minutes) and 30 to Barcelona (from €9.30, 40 minutes to 1¼ hours).

Catedral (www.catedraldegirona.org; Plaça de la Catedral; adult/student incl Basílica de Sant Feliu €7/5, Sun free; ⊙10am-6.30pm Apr-Oct, 10am-5.30pm Sep-Mar) Towering over a flight of 86 steps rising from Plaça de la Catedral, this edifice is far more ancient than its billowing baroque facade suggests. Built over an old Roman forum, parts of the cathedral's foundations date from the 5th century. Today, Gothic styling – built over the Romanesque church during the 14th century – dominates, though a fine, double-columned Romanesque **cloister** dates from the 12th century. It's a surprisingly formidable sight to explore, but an audio guide is included in the price.

Museu d'Història dels Jueus de Girona (www.girona.cat/call; Carrer de la Força 8; adult/child €4/free; ⊙10am-6pm Mon-Sat, to 2pm Sun Sep-Jun, to 8pm Jul & Aug) Until 1492 Girona was home to Catalonia's second most important medieval Jewish community (after Barcelona), and one of the finest Jewish quarters in the country. The Call was centred on the narrow Carrer de la Força for 600 years, until relentless persecution forced the Jews out of Spain. This excellent museum shows genuine pride in Girona's Jewish heritage without shying away from the less salubrious aspects, such as persecution by the Inquisition and forced conversions.

Bells Oficis (☎972 22 81 70; www.bellsoficis.com; Carrer dels Germans Busquets 2; r incl breakfast €42-93; ❀☎) A lovingly restored, 19th-century flat just by the Rambla in the heart of Girona makes a stylish and ultra-welcoming place to stop. It's the former home of Catalan artist Jaume Busquets i Mollera, and retains period details in each of the five individually styled rooms. Some rooms share bathrooms, while those with en suite have no bathroom door. The largest room has ample room for four people.

Nu (☎972 22 52 30; www.nurestaurant.cat; Carrer d'Abeuradors 4; mains €16-18; ⊙1.15-3.45pm & 8.15-10.45pm Tue-Sat, 1.15-3.45pm Mon; ☎) Sleek and confident, this handsome contemporary old-town spot has innovative, top-notch plates prepared in view by the friendly team. Flavour combinations keep things interesting: sample tuna tataki with red fruit glaze, tandoori pork cheeks with mango, and orange flower crème brûlée. Great value for this quality.

PUBLIC TRANSPORT

Barcelona's metro system spreads its tentacles around the city in such a way that most places of interest are within a 10-minute walk of a station. Buses and suburban trains are needed only for a few destinations. A single metro, bus or suburban train ride costs €2.15, but a T-10 ticket, valid for 10 rides, costs €10.30.

TAXI

Taxis charge €2.10 to €2.30 flagfall plus meter charges of €1.10 to €1.40 per kilometre (the higher rates are for nights and weekends). You can flag a taxi down in the street or call one:

Fonotaxi (☎93 300 11 00; www.fonotaxi.net)

Radio Taxi 033 (☎93 303 30 33; www.radio-taxi033.com)

The call-out charge is between €3.40 and €4.50.

Tarragona

POP 132,200

In this effervescent port city, Roman history collides with beaches, nightlife and a food scene that perfumes the air with freshly grilled seafood. The biggest lure is the wealth of remains from one of Spain's most important Roman cities, including mosaic-packed museums and a seaside amphitheatre. A roll-call of excellent places to eat gives you good reason to linger in the knot of lanes in the medieval centre, flanked by a broad cathedral with Gothic flourishes.

☉ Sights

★**Catedral de Tarragona**   CATHEDRAL
(www.catedraldetarragona.com; Plaça de la Seu; adult/child €5/3; ⊙10am-7pm Mon-Sat mid-Mar–

Oct, 10am-5pm Mon-Fri, 10am-7pm Sat Nov–mid-Mar) Sitting grandly atop town, Tarragona's cathedral has both Romanesque and Gothic features, as typified by the main facade. The cloister has Gothic vaulting and Romanesque carved capitals, one of which shows rats conducting a cat's funeral...until the cat comes back to life! It's a lesson about passions seemingly lying dormant until they reveal themselves. Chambers off the cloister incorporate the Museu Diocesà, with its large collection extending from Roman hairpins to some lovely 12th- to 14th-century polychrome woodcarvings of a breastfeeding Virgin.

Passeig Arqueològic Muralles   WALLS
(www.tarragonaturisme.cat; adult/child €3.30/free; ☉ sites 9am-9pm Tue-Sat, 10am-3pm Sun Easter-Sep, 10am-7pm Tue-Sat, 10am-3pm Sun Oct-Easter) A peaceful walk takes you around part of the perimeter of the old town between two lines of city walls. The inner ones are mainly Roman and date back to the 3rd century BC, while the outer ones were put up by the British in 1709 during the War of the Spanish Succession. The earliest stretches are a mighty 4m thick. Prepare to be awed by the vast gateways built by the Iberians and clamber up onto the battlements from the doorway to the right of the entrance for all-encompassing views of the city.

★ Museu Nacional Arqueològic de Tarragona   MUSEUM
(www.mnat.cat; Plaça del Rei 5; adult/child €4.50/free; ☉ 9.30am-6pm Tue-Sat, to 8.30pm Jun-Sep, 10am-2pm Sun) This excellent museum does justice to the cultural and material wealth of Roman Tarraco. The mosaic collection traces the changing trends – from simple black-and-white designs to complex full-colour creations; a highlight is the large, almost complete *Mosaic de Peixos de la Pineda*, showing fish and sea creatures. Explanation in the museum is in Catalan and Spanish, but there is a multilingual audio guide included in the price.

Amfiteatre Romà   RUINS
(www.tarragonaturisme.cat; Parc de l'Anfiteatre; adult/child €3.30/free; ☉ 9am-9pm Tue-Sat, 10am-3pm Sun Easter-Sep, 10am-7pm Tue-Sat, 10am-3pm Sun Oct-Easter) Near the beach is this well-preserved amphitheatre, where gladiators hacked away at each other, or wild animals. In its arena are the remains of 6th- and 12th-century churches built to commemorate the martyrdom of the Christian bishop Fructuosus and two deacons, believed to have been burnt alive here in AD 259. Much of the amphitheatre was picked to bits, with the stone used to build the port, so what you see now is a partial reconstruction.

🛏 Sleeping & Eating

Look for tapas bars and inexpensive cafes on the Plaça de la Font. The quintessential Tarragona seafood experience can be had in Serrallo, the town's fishing port, where a dozen bars and restaurants sell the day's catch.

Tarragona Hostel   HOSTEL €
(☏ 877 05 58 96; www.tarragonahostel.com; Carrer de la Unió; dm/d €12/30; ☏) All the backpacker essentials are well executed at this dead-centre hostel with chirpy staff. Choose from eight-bed dorms or a double room, and avail yourself of free wi-fi, a comfy common room, shared kitchen and laundry facilities (€4).

Hotel Plaça de la Font   HOTEL €€
(☏ 977 24 61 34; www.hotelpdelafont.com; Plaça de la Font 26; s/d €60/75; ✳☏) Comfortable modern rooms, decorated in individual styles with photos of Tarragona monuments, fill this cheerful hotel on popular Plaça de la Font. Rooms at the front are pretty well soundproofed from the sociable murmur below and have tiny balconies for people-watching. Breakfast is an extra €6.

Barquet   SEAFOOD €€
(☏ 977 24 00 23; www.restaurantbarquet.com; Carrer del Gasometre 16; mains €12-20; ☉ 1-3.30pm & 9-10.30pm Tue-Sat, 1-3.30pm Mon) This popular neighbourhood restaurant is a short downhill stroll from the centre. It's deservedly famous for its excellent rice dishes bursting with maritime flavour, and also has great *raciones* (large plates) of seafood. Don't be fooled by the nautical warehouse interior, fish dishes and jewel-like desserts are executed with finesse.

AQ   MEDITERRANEAN, FUSION €€
(☏ 977 21 59 54; www.aq-restaurant.com; Carrer de les Coques 7; mains €11-22; ☉ 1.30-3.30pm & 8.30-11pm Tue-Sat) The crisp interior design of this stone-walled restaurant promises fine dining, and AQ amply delivers. Its impeccably crafted fusion dishes – taking inspiration from Catalan, Italian and Asian cuisines – are playfully executed. Treat your taste buds to Iberico pork burgers, squid carbonara or chop suey lobster. The three-course lunch *menú* (€19.80) is excellent value.

SPAIN TARRAGONA

DALÍ'S CATALONIA

The only name that could come into your head when you set eyes on the red castle-like building in central Figueres, topped with giant eggs and stylised Oscar-like statues and studded with plaster-covered croissants, is Salvador Dalí. With its entrance watched over by medieval suits of armour balancing baguettes on their heads, the Teatre-Museu Dalí (www.salvador-dali.org; Plaça de Gala i Salvador Dalí 5; adult/child under 9yr incl Museu de l'Empordà €14/free; ⊙9am-8pm Tue-Sun Jul-Sep, 10.30am-6pm Tue-Sun Oct-Jun, closed Mon) is an entirely appropriate final resting place for the master of surrealism. 'Theatre-museum' is an apt label for this trip through the incredibly fertile imagination of one of the great showmen of the 20th century. It's full of surprises, tricks and illusions, and contains a substantial portion of Dalí's life's work.

Port Lligat, a 1.25km walk from Cadaqués, is a tiny settlement around a lovely cove, with fishing boats pulled up on its beach. The Casa Museu Dalí (☎972 25 10 15; www.salvador-dali.org; adult/under 8yr €11/free; ⊙10.30am-6pm Tue-Sun, closed mid-Jan–mid-Feb) started life as a fisherman's hut, but was steadily enlarged by Dalí and his wife Gala during their residence here from 1930 to 1982 (apart from a dozen or so years abroad around the Spanish Civil War). It provides a fascinating insight into the lives of the (excuse the pun) surreal couple. We probably don't need to tell you that it's the house with a lot of little white chimneypots and two egg-shaped towers, overlooking the western end of the beach. You must book ahead.

ⓘ Information

Tourist Office (☎977 25 07 95; www.tarragonaturisme.es; Carrer Major 39; ⊙10am-2pm & 3-5pm Mon-Fri, 10am-7pm Sat, 10am-2pm Sun) Good place for booking guided tours of the city. Opens extended hours in high season.

ⓘ Getting There & Away

BUS

The **bus station** (www.alsa.es; Plaça Imperial Tarraco) is 1.5km northwest of the old town along Rambla Nova. Destinations include Barcelona (€8.80, 1½ hours, up to 16 daily) and Valencia (€19 to €22, three to 4½ hours, six daily).

TRAIN

Tarragona station is a 10-minute walk from the old town while fast AVE trains stop at Camp de Tarragona station, 10km north. Departures from Tarragona station include trains to Barcelona (€7 to €21, one to 1½ hours, about half-hourly) and Valencia (€14 to €38, 2½ hours, 17 daily).

ARAGÓN, BASQUE COUNTRY & NAVARRA

Zaragoza

POP 679,600

Zaragoza (Saragossa), on the banks of the mighty Río Ebro, is a vibrant, elegant and fascinating city. Its residents, who form over half of Aragón's population, enjoy a lifestyle that revolves around some superb tapas bars, great shopping and a vigorous nightlife. But Zaragoza is much more than just a good-time city: its host of historical sights spans all the great civilisations that have left their mark on the Spanish soul. This is also a good place to get acquainted with the artistic genius of Francisco de Goya, who was born a short horse-ride away in 1746.

◉ Sights

★Basílica de Nuestra Señora del Pilar CHURCH (www.basilicadelpilar.es; Plaza del Pilar; ⊙6.45am-8.30pm Mon-Sat, to 9.30pm Sun) FREE Brace yourself for this great baroque cavern of Catholicism. The faithful believe that it was here on 2 January AD 40 that Santiago saw the Virgin Mary descend atop a marble *pilar* (pillar). A chapel was built around the remaining pillar, followed by a series of ever-more-grandiose churches, culminating in the enormous basilica. A lift (admission €3; ⊙10am-2pm & 4-8pm Apr-Oct, to 6pm Nov-Mar) whisks you most of the way up the north tower from where you climb to a superb viewpoint over the domes and city.

★Aljafería PALACE (☎976 28 96 83; www.turismodezaragoza.es; Calle de los Diputados; €5, Sun free; ⊙10am-2pm & 4-6.30pm Mon-Sat, 10am-2pm Sun) The Aljafería is Spain's finest Islamic-era edifice outside Andalucía. Built as a pleasure palace for

Zaragoza's Islamic rulers in the 11th century, it underwent its first alterations in 1118 when the city passed into Christian hands. In the 1490s, the Catholic Monarchs, Fernando and Isabel, tacked on their own palace, whereafter the Aljafería fell into decay. Twentieth-century restorations brought the building back to life, and in 1987 Aragón's regional parliament was established here. Tours take place throughout the day (multilingual in July and August).

La Seo   CATHEDRAL
(Catedral de San Salvador; ☑ 976 29 12 31; www.turismodezaragoza.es; Plaza de la Seo; adult/child €4/free; ⊙ 10am-2pm & 4-6.30pm Tue-Fri, 10am-12.30pm & 4-6.30pm Sat, 10am-noon & 4-6.30pm Sun) Dominating the eastern end of Plaza del Pilar, La Seo was built between the 12th and 17th centuries and displays a fabulous spread of architectural styles from Roman-esque to baroque. The cathedral stands on the site of Islamic Zaragoza's main mosque (which in turn stood upon the temple of the Roman forum). The admission price includes entry to La Seo's Museo de Tapices (☑ 976 29 12 38), a collection of 14th- to 17th-century Flemish and French tapestries considered the best of its kind in the world.

Museo del Foro de Caesaraugusta   MUSEUM
(☑ 976 72 12 21; www.turismodezaragoza.es; Plaza de la Seo 2; adult/child €4/free; ⊙ 10am-2pm & 5-9pm Tue-Sat, 10am-2.30pm Sun) The trapezoi-dal building on Plaza de la Seo is the entrance to an excellent reconstruction of part of Ro-man Caesaraugusta's forum, now well below ground level. The remains of porticoes, shops, a great *cloaca* (sewer) system, and a limited collection of artefacts from the 1st century AD are on display. An multilingual 15-minute audiovisual show breathes life into it all.

★ Museo Goya –
Colección Ibercaja   MUSEUM
(☑ 976 39 73 28; www.museogoya.ibercaja.es; Calle de Espoz y Mina 23; with/without audio guide €6/4; ⊙ 10am-2pm & 4-8pm Mon-Sat, 10am-2pm Sun) Outside of Madrid's Museo del Prado, this excellent museum contains what is arguably the best exposé of the work of one of Spain's most revered artists. The place is exceeding-ly well laid-out with each of its three floors carrying a different theme.

★ Museo del Teatro
de Caesaraugusta   MUSEUM
(☑ 976 72 60 75; www.turismodezaragoza.es; Calle de San Jorge 12; adult/child €4/free; ⊙ 10am-2pm & 5-9pm Tue-Sat, 10am-2.30pm Sun) The finest

in the quartet of Zaragoza's Roman muse-ums was discovered during the excavation of a building site in 1972. The crumbling but precious theatre once seated 6000 spec-tators, and great efforts have been made to help visitors reconstruct the edifice's former splendour, including evening projections of a virtual performance (May to October) and an entertaining audiovisual production. The theatre is visible from the surrounding streets and an on-site cafe. The all-round aes-thetics are fabulous.

🛏 Sleeping

Hotel Río Arga   HOTEL €
(☑ 976 39 90 65; www.hotelrioarga.es; Calle Con-tamina 20; s/d €40/45; ⓟ❈ 🛜) Río Arga offers comfortable, spacious rooms with easy-on-the-eye decor and large bathrooms with tubs. The private parking is a real boon given this central city location. Breakfast costs €3.75.

★ Hotel Sauce   BOUTIQUE HOTEL €€
(☑ 976 20 50 50; www.hotelsauce.com; Calle de Espoz y Mina 33; s from €45, d €51-66; ❈ 🛜) This chic, small hotel with a great central loca-tion has a hip feel thanks largely to its white wicker, painted furniture, stripy fabrics and tasteful watercolours on the walls. The su-perior rooms are well worth the few euros extra. There's a thoroughly pleasant 24-hour coffee shop/cafe on the ground floor with a cake display case that's rarely left empty.

Catalonia El Pilar   HOTEL €€
(☑ 976 20 58 58; www.hoteles-catalonia.com; Calle de la Manifestación 16; r from €78; ❈@🛜) Ten out of ten for the facade, a magnificent Mod-ernista construction that has been artfully renovated to house this eminently comfort-able contemporary hotel. Inside, rooms are spacious and decorated in restful muted earth tones with elegant marble-clad bath-rooms. Some of the beds are king-size.

🍴 Eating & Drinking

Head to the tangle of lanes in El Tubo, north of Plaza de España, for one of Spain's richest gatherings of tapas bars.

Calle del Temple, southwest of Plaza del Pilar, is the spiritual home of Zaragoza's roar-ing nightlife. This is where the city's students head out to party, with more bars lined up cheek to jowl than anywhere else in Aragón.

★ Restaurante Méli Mélo   TAPAS €
(☑ 976 29 46 95; www.restaurantemelimelozaragoza. com; Calle Mayor 45; tapas €2.50-6; ⊙ 1-4pm &

8pm-midnight Mon-Sat, 1-4pm Sun) Typically, *pintxos* are Basque-style tapas presented on small slices of bread, but in Méli Mélo they are stacked up so high they look like mini-skyscrapers topped with creative arrangements of cured hams, breaded cod, octopus and aubergine. Come here at 8pm before the rush and you'll see a veritable Manhattan of *pintxos* lined up on the bar all ready for tasting.

Los Xarmientos ARAGONESE **€€**
(✐ 976 29 90 48; www.facebook.com/xarmientos; Calle de Espoz y Mina 25; mains €12-19; ⊙ 1.30-4.30pm & 8-11.30pm Wed-Sat, 1-4pm Tue & Sun) Aragonese meat dishes are a speciality at this artfully designed restaurant. It styles itself as a *parrilla*, meaning the dishes are cooked on a barbecue-style grill. It's a fine place to sample the local *ternasco* (lamb), Aragon's most emblematic dish, served here with a jacket potato on the side.

ℹ Information

Municipal Tourist Office (✐ 976 20 12 00; www.zaragozaturismo.es; Plaza del Pilar; ⊙ 9am-9pm mid-Jun–mid-Oct, 10am-8pm mid-Oct–mid-Jun; 🛜) Has branch offices around town, including the train station.

Oficina de Turismo de Aragón (✐ 976 28 21 81; www.turismodearagon.com; Plaza de España 1; ⊙ 9am-2pm & 5-8pm Mon-Fri, from 10am Sat & Sun; 🛜) Has plenty of brochures on the region.

ℹ Getting There & Away

BUS

Dozens of bus lines fan out across Spain from the bus station attached to the Estación Intermodal Delicias train station, 3km northwest of the centre. **ALSA** (✐ 902 42 22 42; www.alsa.es) runs to/from Madrid (€17 to €23, 3¾ hours, 17 daily buses) and Barcelona (€16 to €22, 3¾ hours, 15 buses). **Alosa** (✐ 902 490690; http://alosa.avanzabus.com) runs half-hourly buses to/from Huesca (€7.80, 1¼ hours) and seven daily buses to Jaca (€16, 2½ hours).

TRAIN

Zaragoza's futuristic **Estación Intermodal Delicias** (✐ 902 404 704; www.renfe.com; Calle Rioja 33; ⊙ 5.30am-midnight) is connected by almost hourly high-speed AVE services to Madrid (€21 to €65, 1½ hours) and Barcelona (€18 to €100, 1¾ hours). Other destinations include Huesca (from €7, one hour, seven trains daily), Jaca (€15, 3¼ hours, two trains) and Teruel (€20, 2½ hours, four trains).

Around Aragón

Aragón is a beautiful and fascinating region to explore if you have a few days to do so. In the south, little visited Teruel is home to some stunning Mudéjar architecture. Nearby, Albarracín is one of Spain's prettiest villages.

In the north, the Parque Nacional de Ordesa y Monte Perdido is the most spectacular stretch of the Spanish Pyrenees, with dramatic mountain scenery and superb hiking; the pretty village of Torla is the main gateway (though it gets overrun with visitors in July and August). En route to the mountains are several towns and villages with enchanting medieval quarters or fascinating medieval monuments, such as Aínsa, Jaca and Huesca.

In Aragón's northwest, Sos del Rey Católico is another gorgeous stone village draped along a ridge.

San Sebastián

POP 186,100

With Michelin stars apparently falling from the heavens onto its restaurants, not to mention a *pintxo* (tapas) culture almost unmatched anywhere else in Spain, stylish San Sebastián (Donostia in Basque) frequently tops lists of the world's best places to eat. Charming and well-mannered by day, cool and happening by night, the city has an idyllic location on the shell-shaped Bahía de la Concha, with crystalline waters, a flawless beach and green hills on all sides.

◎ Sights & Activities

★ **Playa de la Concha** BEACH
(Paseo de la Concha) Fulfilling almost every idea of how a perfect city beach should be formed, Playa de la Concha (and its westerly extension, Playa de Ondarreta), is easily among the best city beaches in Europe. Throughout the long summer months a fiesta atmosphere prevails, with thousands of tanned and toned bodies spread across the sands. The swimming is almost always safe.

Monte Igueldo VIEWPOINT
(www.monteigueldo.es; ⊙ 10am-10pm Jun-Sep, shorter hours rest of year) The views from the summit of Monte Igueldo, just west of town, will make you feel like a circling hawk staring down over the vast panorama of the Bahía de la Concha and the surrounding

coastline and mountains. The best way to get there is via the old-world **funicular railway** (Plaza del Funicular; return adult/child €3.15/2.35; ⊙10am-9pm Jun-Aug, shorter hours rest of year) to the **Parque de Atracciones** (📞943 21 35 25; Paseo de Igeldo; adult/child €3.15/2.35; ⊙11am-2pm & 4-8.30pm Mon-Fri, to 9pm Sat & Sun Jul-Sep, shorter hours rest of year), a slightly tacky theme park at the top of the hill.

San Telmo Museoa   MUSEUM
(📞943 48 15 80; www.santelmomuseoa.com; Plaza Zuloaga 1; adult/student/child €6/3/free; ⊙10am-8pm Tue-Sun) Although it's one of the newest museums in the Basque Country, the San Telmo Museoa has actually been around since the 1920s. It was closed for many years, but after major renovation work it reopened in 2011. The displays range from historical artefacts to the squiggly lines of modern art, with all pieces reflecting Basque culture and society.

🛏 Sleeping

Pensión Altair   PENSIÓN €
(📞943 29 31 33; www.pension-altair.com; Calle Padre Larroca 3; s/d €55/75; ❇@🛜) This *pensión* is in a beautifully restored town house, with unusual church-worthy arched windows and modern, minimalist rooms that are a world away from the fusty decor of the old-town *pensiones*. Interior rooms lack the grandiose windows but are much larger.

Pensión Amaiur   BOUTIQUE HOTEL €€
(📞943 42 96 54; www.pensionamaiur.com; Calle de 31 de Agosto 44; d with/without bathroom €60/75; @🛜) A top-notch guesthouse in a prime old-town location, Amaiur has bright floral wallpapers and bathrooms tiled in Andalucían blue and white. The best rooms are those that overlook the main street, where you can sit on a little balcony and be completely enveloped in blushing red flowers. Some rooms share bathrooms.

**Hotel de Londres
y de Inglaterra**   HISTORIC HOTEL €€
(📞943 44 07 70; www.hlondres.com; Calle de Zubieta 2; d from €124; P❇🛜) Sitting pretty on the beachfront, Hotel de Londres y de Inglaterra (Hotel of London and England) is as proper as it sounds. Queen Isabel II set the tone for this hotel well over a century ago, and things have stayed pretty regal ever since. The place exudes elegance; some rooms have stunning views over Playa de la Concha.

🍴 Eating & Drinking

As if 16 Michelin stars weren't enough, San Sebastián is overflowing with bars weighed down under mountains of *pintxos* (Basque tapas, typically towering creations pinned in place on pieces of bread by large toothpicks) that almost every Spaniard will tell you (sometimes grudgingly) are the best in country.

Do what the locals do – crawl the city centre's bars. *Pintxo* etiquette is simple. Ask for a plate and point out what *pintxos* you want. Keep the toothpicks and go back for as many as you'd like. Accompany with *txakoli*, a cloudy white wine poured like cider to create a little fizz. When you're ready to pay, hand over the plate with all the toothpicks and tell bar staff how many drinks you've had. It's an honour system that has stood the test of time. Expect to pay €2.50 to €3.50 per *pintxo*.

⭐La Fábrica   BASQUE €€
(📞943 98 05 81; www.restaurantelafabrica.es; Calle del Puerto 17; mains €15-20, menús from €28; ⊙12.30-4pm & 7.30-11.30pm Mon-Fri, 1-4pm & 8-11pm Sat-Sun) The red-brick interior walls and white tablecloths lend an air of class to this restaurant, whose modern takes on Basque classics have been making waves with San Sebastián locals over the last couple of years. At just €25, the multi-dish tasting *menú* is about the best-value deal in the city. Advance reservations are essential.

⭐La Cuchara de San Telmo   BASQUE €€
(📞043 44 16 55; www.lacucharadesantelmo.com; Calle de 31 de Agosto 28; pintxos from €2.50; ⊙7.30-11pm Tue, noon-3.30pm & 7.30-11pm Wed-Sun) This unfussy, hard-to-find bar offers miniature *nueva cocina vasca* (Basque nouvelle cuisine) from a supremely creative kitchen. Unlike many San Sebastián bars, this one doesn't have any *pintxos* (Basque

---

SAN SEBASTIÁN SPLURGE

With three shining Michelin stars, acclaimed chef Juan Mari Arzak takes some beating when it comes to *nueva cocina vasca* (Basque nouvelle cuisine) and his restaurant is considered one of the best places to eat in the world. **Arzak** (📞943 27 84 65; www.arzak.info; Avenida Alcalde Jose Elosegui 273; meals around €195; ⊙Tue-Sat, closed Nov & late Jun) is now assisted by his daughter Elena and they never cease to innovate. Reservations, well in advance, are obligatory.

tapas) laid out on the bar top; instead you must order from the blackboard menu behind the counter.

Astelena BASQUE €€
(☑943 42 58 67; www.restauranteastelena.com; Calle de Iñigo 1; pintxos from €2.50; ⊙1-4.30pm & 8-11pm Tue & Thu-Sat, 1-4.30pm Wed) The *pintxos* (Basque tapas) draped across the counter in this bar, tucked into the corner of Plaza de la Constitución, stand out. Many of them are a fusion of Basque and Asian inspirations, but the best of all are the foie-gras-based treats. The great positioning means that prices are slightly elevated.

Restaurante Kokotxa MODERN SPANISH €€€
(☑943 42 19 04; www.restaurantekokotxa.com; Calle del Campanario 11; mains €25-35, menús from €60; ⊙1.30-3.30pm & 8.45-11pm Tue-Sat) This Michelin-star restaurant is hidden away down an overlooked alley in the old town, but the food rewards those who search. Most people opt for the *menú de mercado* (€60) and enjoy the flavours of the traders from the busy city market. It's closed for parts of February, June and October.

❶ Information

Oficina de Turismo (☑943 48 11 66; www.sansebastianturismo.com; Alameda del Boulevard 8; ⊙9am-8pm Mon-Sat, 10am-7pm Sun Jul-Sep, shorter hours rest of year) Friendly office with comprehensive information on the city and the Basque Country in general.

❶ Getting There & Away

BUS
Services leave for Bilbao (from €6.50, 1½ hours, frequent), Bilbao Airport (€17, 1¼ hours, hourly), Biarritz (France; €5 to €7, one hour, six daily), Madrid (€36, six hours, nine daily) and Pamplona (€8, one to two hours, 12 daily).

TRAIN
Euskotren (www.euskotren.eus) runs local trains half-hourly from Amara station, about 1km south of San Sebastián centre, to Hendaye (Hendaya; €2.45, 40 minutes), just across the border in France, from where there are frequent trains to Paris and other French destinations. San Sebastián's Renfe station, opposite the bus station on the east side of the Río Urumea, has six departures daily to Madrid (from €16, 5½ to eight hours) and two to Barcelona (from €19, six hours).

Bilbao
POP 346,600

The commercial hub of the Basque Country, Bilbao (Bilbo in Basque) is best known for the magnificent Guggenheim Museum. An architectural masterpiece by Frank Gehry, the museum was the catalyst of a turnaround that saw Bilbao transformed from an industrial port city into a vibrant cultural centre (without losing its down-to-earth soul). After visiting this must-see temple to modern art, spend time exploring Bilbao's Casco Viejo (Old Quarter), a grid of elegant streets dotted with shops, cafes, *pintxo* bars and several small but worthy museums.

❍ Sights

★ **Museo Guggenheim Bilbao** GALLERY
(☑944 35 90 16; www.guggenheim-bilbao.es; Avenida Abandoibarra 2; adult/student/child from €13/7.50/free, depends on exhibits; ⊙10am-8pm, closed Mon Sep-Jun) Shimmering titanium Museo Guggenheim Bilbao is one of modern architecture's most iconic buildings. It has almost single-handedly lifted Bilbao out of its post-industrial depression and into the 21st century – and with sensation. It boosted the city's already inspired regeneration, stimulated further development and placed Bilbao firmly in the international art and tourism spotlight. Inside, the often excellent temporary exhibitions are usually the chief attraction – but it's the building itself that is the star of the show.

★ **Museo de Bellas Artes** GALLERY
(☑944 39 60 60; www.museobilbao.com; Plaza del Museo 2; adult/student/child €9/7/free, Wed free; ⊙10am-8pm Wed-Mon) The Museo de Bellas Artes houses a compelling collection that includes everything from Gothic sculptures to 20th-century pop art. There are three main subcollections: classical art, with works by Murillo, Zurbarán, El Greco, Goya and van Dyck; contemporary art, featuring works by Paul Gauguin, Francis Bacon and Anthony Caro; and Basque art, with works of the great sculptors Jorge Oteiza and Eduardo Chillida, and strong paintings by the likes of Ignacio Zuloaga and Juan de Echevarría.

Casco Viejo OLD TOWN
The compact Casco Viejo, Bilbao's atmospheric old quarter, is full of charming streets, boisterous bars and plenty of quirky and independent shops. At the heart of the Casco are

Bilbao's original seven streets, Las Siete Calles, which date from the 1400s. The 14th-century Gothic **Catedral de Santiago** (www.bilbaoturismo.net; Plaza de Santiago; ⊗10am-1pm & 5-7.30pm Tue-Sat, 10am-1pm Sun & holidays) has a splendid Renaissance portico and pretty little cloister.

Euskal Museoa   MUSEUM
(Museo Vasco; ☑944 15 54 23; www.euskal-museoa.org/es/hasiera; Plaza Miguel Unamuno 4; adult/child €3/free, Thu free; ⊗10am-7pm Mon & Wed-Fri, 10am-1.30pm & 4-7pm Sat, 10am-2pm Sun) This is probably the most complete museum of Basque culture and history in all of Spain. The story begins in prehistory; from this murky period the displays bound rapidly up to the modern age, in the process explaining just how long the Basques have called this corner of the world home. Explanatory matter is in Spanish and Basque only, however.

🛏 Sleeping & Eating

The Bilbao tourism authority has a useful **reservations department** (☑902 87 72 98; www.bilbaoreservas.com; ⊗10am-9pm) for accommodation.

Pintxos (Basque tapas) are as good in Bilbao as they are in San Sebastián, and slightly cheaper (from around €2.50). Plaza Nueva, on the edge of the Casco Viejo, offers especially rich pickings, as do Calle de Perro and Calle Jardines.

Casual Bilbao Gurea   PENSION €
(☑944 16 32 99; www.casualhoteles.com; Calle de Bidebarrieta 14; s/d from €45/55; ☎) The family-run Gurea has arty, modern rooms with wooden floors and large bathrooms (most of which have bathtubs) and exceptionally

friendly staff. Add it all up and you get what is easily one of the best deals in the old town.

Hostal Begoña   GUESTHOUSE €
(☑944 23 01 34; www.hostalbegona.com; Calle de la Amistad 2; s/d from €50/65; P @ ☎) Friendly Begoña has guestrooms with modern artwork, wrought-iron beds and colourful tiled bathrooms. The cosy common areas have plenty of books and information about local culture and attractions. It's a great place to meet other travellers, too.

Miró Hotel   DESIGN HOTEL €€
(☑946 61 18 80; www.mirohotelbilbao.com; Alameda Mazarredo 77; d from €137; ❋ @ ☎) This hip hotel, facing the Museo Guggenheim Bilbao, is the passion project of fashion designer Antonio Miró. It's filled with modern photography and art, quirky books, and minimalist decor – a perfect fit with arty Bilbao.

★La Viña del Ensanche   PINTXOS €
(☑944 15 56 15; www.lavinadelensanche.com; Calle de la Diputación 10; pintxos from €1.35, menú €30; ⊗8.30am-11.30pm Mon-Fri, noon-1am Sat) Hundreds of bottles of wine line the walls of this outstanding octogenarian *pintxos* (Basque tapas) bar. This could very well be the best place to eat *pintxos* in the entire city. If you can't decide what to sample, opt for the €30 tasting menu.

★Agape Restaurante   BASQUE €€
(☑944 16 05 06; www.restauranteagape.com; Calle de Hernani 13; menú del día €12.90, menús €21-36; ⊗1-4pm Sun-Wed, 1-4pm & 8.30-11.30pm Thu-Sat; ☎) With a solid reputation among locals for good-value meals that don't sacrifice quality, this is a great place for a slice of real Bilbao

---

PAMPLONA & SANFERMINES

Immortalised by Ernest Hemingway in *The Sun Also Rises*, the pre-Pyrenean city of Pamplona (Iruña in Basque) is home of the wild Sanfermines festival, but is also an extremely walkable city that's managed to mix the charm of old plazas and buildings with modern shops and a lively nightlife.

The Sanfermines festival is held from 6 to 14 July, when Pamplona is overrun with thrill-seekers, curious onlookers and, yes, bulls. The Encierro (Running of the Bulls) begins at 8am daily, when bulls are let loose from the Coralillos Santo Domingo. The 825m run through the streets to the bullring lasts just three minutes.

Since records began in 1924, 16 people have died during Pamplona's bullrun. Many of those who run are full of bravado (and/or drink) and have little idea of what they're doing. For dedicated *encierro* news, check out www.sanfermin.com.

Animal rights groups oppose bullrunning as a cruel tradition, and the participating bulls will almost certainly all be killed in the afternoon bullfight. PETA (www.peta.org.uk) organises eye-catching protests in Pamplona at every Sanfermines.

culinary life. It's away from the standard tourist circuit, but worth the short walk.

ℹ Information

Main Tourist Office (☑ 944 79 57 60; www.bilbaoturismo.net; Plaza Circular 1; ⊙ 9am-9pm; 🛜)

ℹ Getting There & Away

BUS

Bilbao's main bus station, **Termibus** (☑ 944 39 50 77; www.termibus.es; Gurtubay 1, San Mamés), is west of the centre. Services operate to San Sebastián (from €6.50, 1½ hours, frequent), Madrid (from €31, four to five hours, 15 buses daily), Barcelona (€47, eight hours, four daily), Pamplona (€15, 2½ hours, seven buses), Santander (from €6.60, 1½ hours, frequent) and Santiago de Compostela (from €20, nine hours, four buses).

TRAIN

Two Renfe trains run daily to Madrid (€15 to €50, 5¼ hours) and Barcelona (€20 to €85, seven hours) from the Abando station. Slow **FEVE** (www.renfe.com/viajeros/feve) trains from Concordia station next door head west to Santander (€8.90, three hours, three daily), where you can connect for places further west in Cantabria, Asturias and Galicia.

CANTABRIA, ASTURIAS & GALICIA

With a landscape reminiscent of parts of the British Isles, 'Green Spain' offers great walks and scenery in mountainous national and regional parks, seafood feasts in sophisticated towns or quaint fishing villages, and a spectacular coastline strung with oodles of beautiful beaches washed by the chilly waters of the north Atlantic.

Santillana del Mar

Thirty kilometres west of the Cantabrian capital, Santander, Santillana del Mar is a bijou medieval village and the obvious overnight base for visiting nearby Altamira. Buses run three or more times a day from Santander to Santillana del Mar.

Spain's finest prehistoric art, in the **Cueva de Altamira**, 2.5km southwest of Santillana, was discovered in 1879. It took more than 20 years, after further discoveries of cave art in France, before scientists accepted that these wonderful paintings of bison, horses

and other animals really were the handiwork of primitive people many thousands of years ago. A replica cave here in the **Museo de Altamira** (☑ 942 81 88 15; http://museode altamira.mcu.es; Avenida Marcelino Sanz de Sautuola; adult/child €3/free, Sun & from 2.30pm Sat free; ⊙ 9.30am-8pm Tue-Sat May-Oct, to 6pm Tue-Sat Nov-Apr, to 3pm Sun & holidays year-round; Ⓟ 🚻) now enables everyone to appreciate the inspired, 13,000 to 35,000-year-old paintings – advance bookings advisable.

Santiago de Compostela

POP 80,000

The supposed burial place of St James (Santiago), this unique cathedral city and goal of pilgrims for nearly 1200 years is a bewitching place. The hundreds of thousands who walk here every year along the Camino de Santiago are often struck mute with wonder on entering the city's medieval centre. Fortunately, they usually regain their verbal capacities over a celebratory nocturnal foray into the city's lively bar scene.

◎ Sights & Activities

⭐**Catedral de Santiago de Compostela**   CATHEDRAL

(www.catedraldesantiago.es; Praza do Obradoiro; ⊙ 7am-8.30pm) The grand heart of Santiago, the cathedral soars above the city centre in a splendid jumble of spires and sculpture. Built piecemeal over several centuries, its beauty is a mix of the original Romanesque structure (constructed between 1075 and 1211) and later Gothic and baroque flourishes. The tomb of Santiago beneath the main altar is a magnet for all who come to the cathedral. The artistic high point is the Pórtico de la Gloria inside the west entrance, featuring 200 masterly Romanesque sculptures.

⭐**Cathedral Rooftop Tour**   TOURS

(☑ 902   557812;   www.catedraldesantiago.es; adult/senior, pilgrim, unemployed & student/child €12/10/free, combined ticket with Museo da Catedral €15/12/free; ⊙ tours hourly 10am-1pm & 4-6pm or 7pm; 🚻) For unforgettable bird's-eye views of the cathedral interior from its upper storeys, and of the city from the cathedral roof, take the rooftop tour, which starts in the visitor reception centre beneath the Obradoiro facade. The tours are popular, so book beforehand, or book online. One of the afternoon tours is usually given in English; the rest are in Spanish.

⭐ **Praza do Obradoiro**   PLAZA

The grand square in front of the cathedral's west facade earned its name (Workshop Sq) from the stonemasons' workshops set up here while the cathedral was being built. It's free of both traffic and cafes, and has a unique, magical atmosphere.

⭐ **Museo da Catedral**   MUSEUM

(Colección Permanente; www.catedraldesantiago.es; Praza do Obradoiro; adult/senior, pilgrim, unemployed & student/child €6/4/free; ⊙9am-8pm Apr-Oct, 10am-8pm Nov-Mar) The Museo da Catedral spreads over four floors and includes the cathedral's large, 16th-century, Gothic/plateresque cloister. You'll see a sizeable section of Maestro Mateo's original carved stone choir (destroyed in 1604 but recently pieced back together), an impressive collection of religious art (including the *botafumeiros,* in the 2nd-floor library), the lavishly decorated 18th-century *sala capitular* (chapter house), a room of tapestries woven from designs by Goya, and, off the cloister, the Panteón de Reyes, with tombs of kings of medieval León.

⭐ **Museo das Peregrinacións e de Santiago**   MUSEUM

(http://museoperegrinacions.xunta.gal; Praza das Praterías; adult/pilgrim & student/senior & child €2.40/1.20/free, Sat afternoon & Sun free; ⊙9.30am-8.30pm Tue-Fri, 11am-7pm Sat, 10.15am-2.45pm Sun) Installed in a newly converted premises on Praza das Praterías, the brightly displayed Museum of Pilgrimages & Santiago gives fascinating insights into the phenomenon of Santiago (man and city) down the centuries. Much of the explanatory material is in English as well as Spanish and Galician. There are also great close-up views of some of the cathedral's towers from the 3rd-floor windows.

🛏 **Sleeping**

The Last Stamp   HOSTEL €

(El Último Sello; ☑981 563 525; www.thelaststamp.es; Rúa Preguntoiro 10; dm €18-20; ⊙closed late Dec-late Feb; ⊖@🗫) A purpose-designed hostel, the Last Stamp occupies a 300-year-old, five-storey house (with lift) in the heart of the old town. The cleverly designed dorms feature semi-private modules with ultra-solid bunks, good mattresses and individual reading lights. Some rooms enjoy cathedral views. Bathrooms and kitchen are good and big – and Camino-themed murals add a bit of fun.

WORTH A TRIP

PICOS DE EUROPA

These jagged mountains straddling corners of Asturias, Cantabria and Castilla y León amount to some of the finest walking country in Spain. They comprise three limestone massifs (the highest peak rises to 2648m). The 671-sq-km **Parque Nacional de los Picos de Europa** covers all three massifs and is Spain's second-biggest national park.

There are numerous places to stay and eat all around the mountains, with Cangas de Onís (Asturias) and Potes (Cantabria) the main centres for accommodation and information. Getting here and around by public transport can be slow going but the Picos are accessible by bus from Oviedo and Santander (the former is easier).

The official websites, www.mapama.gob.es and www.parquenacionalpicoseuropa.es, are mostly in Spanish, but www.picosdeeuropa.com and www.liebanaypicosdeeuropa.com are useful for the Asturias and Cantabria sides respectively.

⭐ **Hotel Costa Vella**   BOUTIQUE HOTEL €€

(☑981 569 530; www.costavella.com; Rúa da Porta da Pena 17; s/d €59/81; ⊖❋🗫) Tranquil, thoughtfully designed rooms (some with typically Galician *galerías* – glassed-in balconies), a friendly welcome, super-helpful management and staff, and a lovely garden cafe (breakfast €6; ⊙8am-11pm; 🗫) make this family-run hotel in an old stone house a wonderful option – and the €6 breakfast is substantial.

⭐ **Parador Hostal dos Reis Católicos**   HISTORIC HOTEL €€€

(☑981 582 200; www.parador.es; Praza do Obradoiro 1; r incl breakfast €166-294, ste from €347; P⊖❋@🗫) Opened in 1509 as a pilgrims' hostel, and with a claim to be the world's oldest hotel, this palatial *parador* occupies a wonderful building that is one of Santiago's major monuments in its own right, just steps from the cathedral. Even standard rooms are regal, with canopied beds, wooden floors, original art and generously sized bathrooms with bathtubs and big glass showers.

If you're not staying, stop in for a look round and coffee and cakes at the elegant cafe, or dine at one of the two restaurants.

✕ Eating

★ Abastos 2.0
GALICIAN €€

(📞654 015937; www.abastosdouspuntocero.es; Rúa das Ameas 3; dishes €3-12, menú €21; ⊙noon-3.30pm & 8-11pm Mon-Sat) This highly original and incredibly popular marketside eatery offers new dishes concocted daily from the market's offerings. Go for small individual items, or plates to share, or a six-item *menú* that adds up to a meal for €21. The seafood is generally fantastic, but whatever you order you're likely to love the great tastes and delicate presentation – if you can get a seat!

★ O Curro da Parra
GALICIAN €€

(www.ocurrodaparra.com; Rúa do Curro da Parra 7; mains €10-18, tapas & starters €6-13; ⊙1.30-3.30pm & 8.30-11.30pm Tue-Sun) With a neat little stone-walled dining room upstairs and a narrow tapas and wine bar below, always-busy Curro da Parra serves a broad range of tasty, thoughtfully created, market-fresh fare. You might go for crunchy prawn-and-soft-cheese rolls with passion-fruit sauce, or the free-range chicken skewers with mayonnaise-style *grebiche* sauce – or just ask about the fish and seafood of the day.

La Bodeguilla de San Roque
SPANISH €€

(📞981 564 379; www.bodeguilladesanroque.com; Rúa de San Roque 13; raciones & mains €5-16; ⊙9am-11.30am Mon-Fri, from 10.30am Sat & Sun) A busy two-storey restaurant-cum-wine-bar just northeast of the old town, the Bodeguilla serves an eclectic range of excellent dishes ranging from salads to casseroles of shrimp, mushroom and seaweed, Galician beef sirloin in port, or plates of cheeses, sausages or ham.

ℹ Information

Turismo de Santiago (📞981 555 129; www.santiagoturismo.com; Rúa do Vilar 63; ⊙9am-9pm Apr-Oct, 9am-7pm Mon-Fri, 9am-2pm & 4-7pm Sat & Sun Nov-Mar) The efficient main municipal tourist office.

ℹ Getting There & Around

Santiago has direct flights to/from some 20 European and Spanish cities, many of them operated by budget airlines EasyJet, Ryanair and Vueling.

BUS

The **bus station** (📞981 542 416; www.alsa.es; Praza de Camilo Díaz Baliño; 📶) is 1.5km northeast of the city centre. There are services to León (€30, six hours, one daily), Madrid (€46, eight to 10 hours, four daily), Porto (Portugal; €33, 3¼ hours, one daily), Santander (€50, nine to 10 hours, two daily) and many places around Galicia.

TRAIN

From the **train station** (www.renfe.es; Rúa do Hórreo), plentiful trains run up and down the Galician coast as far as A Coruña and Vigo. High-speed AVE service to/from Madrid is due to start during 2018; in the meantime there are three daily trains (from €17, 5¼ hours).

Around Galicia

Galicia's dramatic coastline is one of Spain's best-kept secrets, with wild and precipitous cliffs, long inlets running far inland, splendid beaches and isolated fishing villages. The lively port city of A Coruña has a lovely city beach and fabulous seafood (a recurring Galician theme). It's also a gateway to the stirring landscapes of the Costa da Morte and Rías Altas; the latter's highlight among many is probably Cabo Ortegal. Inland Galicia is also worth exploring, especially the old town of Lugo, surrounded by what many consider the world's best preserved Roman walls.

VALENCIA

POP 786.200

Spain's third-largest city is a magnificent place, content for Madrid and Barcelona to grab the headlines while it gets on with being a wonderfully liveable city with thriving cultural, eating and nightlife scenes. The star attraction is the strikingly futuristic buildings of the Ciudad de las Artes y las Ciencias, designed by local-boy-made-good Santiago Calatrava. Valencia also has a fistful of fabulous Modernista architecture, great museums and a large, characterful old quarter. Surrounded by fertile fruit-and-veg farmland, the city is famous as the home of rice dishes like paella, but its buzzy dining scene offers plenty more besides.

◉ Sights & Activities

★ Ciudad de las Artes y las Ciencias
NOTABLE BUILDING

(City of Arts & Sciences; 📞902 100031; www.cac.es; ♿) The aesthetically stunning City of Arts & Sciences occupies a massive 35-hectare swath of the old Turia riverbed. It's mostly the work of world-famous, locally born architect Santiago Calatrava. He's a controversial figure for many Valencians, who complain about the expense, and various design flaws that have necessitated major repairs here. Nevertheless, if your taxes weren't involved, it's awe-inspiring stuff, and pleasingly family-oriented.

Oceanogràfic AQUARIUM
(☑902 100031; www.oceanografic.org; Camino de las Moreras; adult/child €29.10/22, audio guide €3.70, combined ticket with Hemisfèric & Museo de las Ciencias €37.40/28.40; ☉10am-5pm Sun-Fri, 10am-7pm Sat, 10am-midnight Jul & Aug; 🚼) Spain's most famous aquarium is the southernmost building of the City of Arts & Sciences. It's an impressive display; the complex is divided into a series of climate zones, reached overground or underground from the central hub building. The sharks, complete with tunnel, are an obvious favourite, while a series of beautiful tanks present species from temperate, Mediterranean, Red Sea and tropical waters. Less happily, the aquarium also keeps captive dolphins and belugas: research suggests that this is detrimental to their welfare.

★**Catedral** CATHEDRAL
(☑963 91 81 27; www.catedraldevalencia.es; Plaza de la Virgen; adult/child incl audio guide €7/5.50; ☉10am-6.30pm Mon-Sat, 2-5.30pm Sun, to 5.30pm Nov-Mar, closed Sun Nov-Feb; 🕾) Valencia's cathedral was built over the mosque after the 1238 reconquest. Its low, wide, brick-vaulted triple nave is mostly Gothic, with neoclassical side chapels. Highlights are rich Italianate frescos above the altarpiece, a pair of Goyas in the Capilla de San Francisco de Borja, and...ta-dah...in the flamboyant Gothic Capilla del Santo Cáliz, what's claimed to be the Holy Grail from which Christ sipped during the Last Supper. It's a Roman-era agate cup, later modified, so at least the date is right.

★**La Lonja** HISTORIC BUILDING
(☑962 08 41 53; www.valencia.es; Calle de la Lonja; adult/child €2/1, Sun free; ☉9.30am-7pm Mon-Sat, 9.30am-3pm Sun) This splendid building, a Unesco World Heritage site, was originally Valencia's silk and commodity exchange, built in the late 15th century when Valencia was booming. It's one of Spain's finest examples of a civil Gothic building. Two main structures flank a citrus-studded courtyard: the magnificent Sala de Contratación, a cathedral of commerce with soaring twisted

pillars, and the Consulado del Mar, where a maritime tribunal sat. The top floor boasts a stunning coffered ceiling brought here from another building.

★**Mercado Central** MARKET
(☑963 82 91 00; www.mercadocentralvalencia.es; Plaza del Mercado; ☉7.30am-3pm Mon-Sat) Valencia's vast Modernista covered market, constructed in 1928, is a swirl of smells, movement and colour. Spectacular seafood counters display cephalopods galore and numerous fish species, while the fruit and vegetables, many produced locally in Valencia's *huerta* (area of market gardens), are of special quality. A tapas bar lets you sip a wine and enjoy the atmosphere.

★**Museo de Bellas Artes** GALLERY
(San Pío V; ☑963 87 03 00; www.museobellasartesvalencia.gva.es; Calle de San Pío V 9; ☉10am-8pm Tue-Sun) FREE Bright and spacious, this gallery ranks among Spain's best. Highlights include a collection of magnificent late-medieval altarpieces, and works by several Spanish masters, including some great Goya portraits, a haunting Velázquez selfie, an El Greco *John the Baptist*, Murillos, Riberas and works by the Ribaltas, father and son. Downstairs, an excellent series of rooms focuses on the great, versatile Valencian painter Joaquín Sorolla (1863–1923), who, at his best, seemed to capture the spirit of an age through sensitive portraiture.

Beaches
Valencia's town beaches are 3km east of the centre. Playa de las Arenas runs north into Playa de la Malvarrosa and Playa de la Patacona, forming a wide strip of sand some 4km long. It's bordered by the Paseo Marítimo promenade and a string of restaurants and cafes. One block back, lively bars and discos thump out the beat in summer.

🛏 Sleeping

★**Russafa Youth Hostel** HOSTEL €
(☑963 28 94 60; www.russafayouthhostel.com; Calle Padre Perera 5; dm/d €18/40; @🕾) You'll feel instantly at home in this super-welcoming, cute hostel set over various floors of a venerable building in the heart of vibrant Russafa. It's all beds, rather than bunks, and with a maximum of three to a room, there's no crowding. Sweet rooms and spotless bathrooms make for a mighty easy stay.

SPAIN AROUND GALICIA

★ **Hostal Antigua Morellana**   HOSTAL €€
(☑ 963 91 57 73; www.hostalam.com; Calle En Bou
2; s/d €50/60; ❉ 🛜) This friendly, family-run,
18-room spot occupies a renovated 18th-
century *posada* (where wealthier merchants
bringing their produce to the nearby food
market would spend the night), and has
cosy, good-sized rooms, most with balconies.
It's kept extremely shipshape by the rightly
house-proud owners and there are loads of
great features including memory-foam mattresses and hairdryers. Higher floors have
more natural light. Good value.

★ **Caro Hotel**   HOTEL €€€
(☑ 963 05 90 00; www.carohotel.com; Calle
Almirante 14; r €156-330; 🅿 ❉ 🛜) Housed in
a sumptuous 19th-century mansion, this
hotel sits atop two millennia of Valencian
history, with restoration revealing a hefty
hunk of the Arab wall, Roman column bases
and Gothic arches. Each room is furnished
in soothing dark shades, and has a great
king-sized bed and varnished cement floors.
Bathrooms are tops. For special occasions,
reserve the 1st-floor grand suite, once the
ballroom.

✕ Eating

The number of restaurants has to be seen to
be believed! In the centre there are numerous
traditional options, as well as trendy tapas
choices. The main eating zones are the Barrio
del Carmen, L'Eixample and, above all, the vibrant tapas-packed streets of Russafa.

★ **Navarro**   VALENCIAN €€
(☑ 963 52 96 23; www.restaurantenavarro.com;
Calle del Arzobispo Mayoral 5; rices €11-18, set menu
€22; ☺ 1.30-4pm daily, 8.30-11pm Sat; 🛜) A byword in the city for decades for its quality
rice dishes, Navarro is run by the grandkids
of the original founders and it offers plenty
of choice, outdoor seating and a set menu,
including one of the rices as a main.

★ **Refugio**   FUSION €€
(☑ 690 61 70 18; www.refugiorestaurante.com;
Calle Alta 42; mains €14-22, set menu €12-15; ☺ 2-
4pm & 9pm-midnight; 🛜) Named for the civ-
il-war hideout opposite and simply decorated in whitewashed brick, Refugio preserves
some of the Carmen *barrio's* former revolutionary spirit. Excellent Med-fusion cuisine
is presented in lunchtime menus of surprising quality: there are some stellar plates on
show, though the vegie options aren't always

quite as flavoursome. Evening dining is high
quality and innovative.

★ **Delicat**   TAPAS €€
(☑ 963 92 33 57; Calle Conde Almodóvar 4; lunch
menú €14.50, mains €10-15; ☺ 1.45-3.30pm &
8.45pm-12.30am Tue-Sat, 1.45-3.45pm Sun; 🛜) At
this particularly friendly, intimate option,
Catina, up front, and her partner, Paco, on
full view in the kitchen, offer an unbeata-
ble-value, five-course menu of samplers for
lunch and a range of truly innovative tapas plates, designed for sharing, anytime.
There's a range of influences at play; the
decor isn't lavish but the food is memorable.

★ **El Poblet**   GASTRONOMY €€€
(☑ 961 11 11 06; www.elpobletrestaurante.com;
Calle de Correos 8; menus €58-118; ☺ 1.30-3.30pm
Tue, 1.30-3.30pm & 8.30-10.30pm Wed-Sat & Mon;
🛜) Run by noted chef Luis Vallis Rozalén,
this upstairs restaurant offers elegance and
fine gastronomic dining at prices that are
very competitive for this quality. Modern
French and Spanish influences combine to
create sumptuous degustation menus. Some
of the imaginative presentation has to be
seen to be believed, and staff are genuinely
welcoming and helpful.

🍷 Drinking & Nightlife

Russafa has the best bar scene, with a huge
range of everything from family-friendly cultural cafes to quirky bars, and also a couple
of big clubs. The Barrio del Carmen is also
famous nightlife territory. In summer the
port area and Malvarrosa beach leap to life.

Radio City   CLUB
(☑ 963 91 41 51; www.radiocityvalencia.es; Calle de
Santa Teresa 19; ☺ 10.30pm-3.30am, from 8.30pm
Thu & Fri) Almost as much mini cultural centre as club, Radio City, which gets packed
from around 1am, pulls in the punters
with activities such as language exchange,
and DJs or live music every night. There's
everything from flamenco (Tuesday) to reggae and funk, and the crowd is eclectic and
engaged.

L'Umbracle Terraza/Mya   BAR, CLUB
(www.umbracleterraza.com; Avenida del Professor
López Piñero 5; admission €10; ☺ midnight-7.30am
Thu-Sat) At the southern end of the Umbracle walkway within the Ciudad de las Artes
y las Ciencias, this is a cool, sophisticated
spot to spend a hot summer night. Catch
the evening breeze under the stars on the

terrace (from 6pm Thursday to Sunday May to October), then drop below to Mya, a top-of-the-line club with an awesome sound system. Admission covers both venues.

La Fustería BAR
(⏲ 633 100428; www.lafusteriaruzafa.com; Calle de Cádiz 28; ⏰ 7-11.30pm Mon-Thu, 7pm-2.30am Fri & Sat; 🐾) This former carpentry workshop is now a likeable jumbled bar and restaurant with mismatched furniture and exposed brick walls. It's a great venue for an after-dinner drink, with an amiable mix of folk, and regular events – flamenco when we were last there – out the back.

ℹ Information

Tourist Kiosk (☎ 963 52 49 08; www.turis valencia.es; Plaza del Ayuntamiento; ⏰ 9am-7pm Mon-Sat, 10am-2pm Sun)
Regional Tourist Office (☎ 963 98 64 22; www.comunitatvalenciana.com; Calle de la Paz 48; ⏰ 10am-6pm Mon-Fri, 10am-2pm Sat & Sun) A fount of information about the Valencia region.

ℹ Getting There & Away

AIR
Valencia's **airport** (VLC; ☎ 902 40 47 04; www.aena.es) is 10km west of the city centre along the A3, towards Madrid. Budget flights serve major European destinations including London, Paris and Berlin.

BOAT
Trasmediterranea (☎ 902 45 46 45; www.trasmediterranea.es) operates car and passenger ferries to Ibiza, Mallorca and Menorca. **Baleària** (☎ 902 16 01 80, from overseas 966 42 87 00; www.balearia.com) goes to Mallorca and Ibiza.

BUS
Valencia's **bus station** (☎ 963 46 62 66; Avenida Menéndez Pidal) is beside the riverbed. Bus 8 connects it to Plaza del Ayuntamiento.
Avanza (www.avanzabus.com) Operates 10 daily buses to/from Madrid (€27 to €36, 4¼ hours).
ALSA (www.alsa.es) Has nine daily buses to/from Barcelona (€26 to €36, four to 5¼ hours) and services to Andalucian cities including Granada, Málaga and Seville.

TRAIN
Thirteen daily high-speed AVE trains to Madrid (€22 to €72, 1¾ hours), eight fast Euromed trains to Barcelona (€16 to €45, 3¼ hours), and one AVE to Seville (€37 to €56, four hours), go from Valencia Joaquín Sorolla station, 800m south of the old town. A few slower but not necessarily cheaper trains to the same and other destina-

WORTH A TRIP

LAS FALLAS

In mid-March, Valencia hosts one of Europe's wildest street parties: **Las Fallas de San José** (www.fallas.com; ⏰ Mar). From 15 to 19 March the city is engulfed by an anarchic swirl of fireworks, music, festive bonfires and all-night partying. On the final night, hundreds of giant effigies (fallas), many of them representing political and social personages, are torched.

If you're not in Valencia then, see the ninots (figurines placed at the base of the fallas) that have been saved from the flames by popular vote (one per year) at the **Museo Fallero** (☎ 963 52 54 78; www.valencia.es; Plaza Monteolivete 4; adult/child €2/free, Sun free; ⏰ 9.30am-7pm Mon-Sat, 9.30am-3pm Sun).

tions go from Estación del Norte, 500m away. The two stations are linked by free shuttle bus.

ℹ Getting Around

Valencia has an integrated bus, tram and metro network. Rides are €1.50; one-/two-/three-day travel cards cost €4/6.70/9.70. Metro lines 3 and 5 connect the airport, central Valencia and the port. The tram is a pleasant way to get to the beach and port. Pick it up at Pont de Fusta or where it intersects with the metro at Benimaclet.

BALEARIC ISLANDS

The Balearic Islands (Illes Balears in Catalan) adorn the glittering Mediterranean waters off Spain's eastern coastline. Beach tourism destinations par excellence, each of the islands has a quite distinct identity and they have managed to retain much of their individual character and beauty. All boast beaches second to none in the Med, but each offers reasons for exploring inland too.

Check out websites like www.illesbalears.es and www.platgesdebalears.com.

ℹ Getting There & Away

AIR
In summer, charter and regular flights converge on Palma de Mallorca and Ibiza from all over Europe.

BOAT
The major ferry companies are **Trasmediterranea** (p1057) and **Baleària** (☎ 902 16 01 80;

www.balearia.com). Compare prices and look for deals at Direct Ferries (www.directferries.com).

The main ferry routes to the mainland, most operating only from Easter to late October, include the following:

Ibiza (Ibiza City) To/from Barcelona and Valencia (Trasmediterranea, Balearia) and Denia (Balearia)

Ibiza (Sant Antoni) To/from Denia and Valencia (Balearia)

Mallorca (Palma de Mallorca) To/from Barcelona and Valencia (Trasmediterranea, Balearia) and Denia (Balearia)

Mallorca (Port d'Alcúdia) To/from Barcelona (Balearia)

Menorca (Maó) To/from Barcelona (Trasmediterranea, Balearia) and Valencia (Trasmediterranea)

The main interisland ferry routes include the following:

Ibiza (Ibiza City) To/from Palma de Mallorca (Trasmediterranea, Balearia)

Mallorca (Palma de Mallorca) To/from Ibiza City (Trasmediterranea, Balearia) and Maó (Trasmediterrnea)

Mallorca (Port d'Alcúdia) To/from Ciutadella (Trasmediterranea, Balearia)

Menorca (Ciutadella) To/from Port d'Alcúdia (Trasmediterranea, Balearia)

Menorca (Maó) To/from Palma de Mallorca (Trasmediterranea)

Mallorca

The sunny, warm hues of the medieval heart of Palma de Mallorca, the archipelago's capital, make a great introduction to the islands. Getting beyond the beach developments and out to some of the more secluded bays, and into the mountains and pretty inland towns, is the key to enjoying the island if you have time to venture beyond Palma. The northwest coast, dominated by the limestone Serra de Tramuntana mountain range, is a beautiful region of olive groves, pine forests and ochre villages, with a spectacularly rugged coastline. Most of Mallorca's best beaches are on the north and east coasts, and although many have been swallowed up by tourist developments, you can still find the occasional deserted cove.

Palma de Mallorca

Palma de Mallorca is a graceful and historic Mediterranean city with some world-class attractions and equally impressive culinary, art and nightlife scenes.

 Sights

⭐ **Catedral de Mallorca** CATHEDRAL
(La Seu; www.catedraldemallorca.org; Carrer del Palau Reial 9; adult/child €7/free; ⊙10am-6.15pm Mon-Fri Jun-Sep, to 5.15pm Apr, May & Oct, to 3.15pm Nov-Mar, 10am-2.15pm Sat year-round) Palma's vast cathedral ('La Seu' in Catalan) is the city's major architectural landmark. Aside from its sheer scale and undoubted beauty, its stunning interior features, designed by Antoni Gaudí and renowned contemporary artist Miquel Barceló, make this unlike any cathedral elsewhere in the world. The awesome structure is predominantly Gothic, apart from the main facade, which is startling, quite beautiful and completely mongrel.

⭐ **Palau de l'Almudaina** PALACE
(www.patrimonionacional.es; Carrer del Palau Reial; adult/child €7/4, audio guide/guided tour €3/4; ⊙10am-8pm Apr-Sep, to 6pm Oct-Mar) Originally an Islamic fort, this mighty construction opposite the cathedral was converted into a residence for the Mallorcan monarchs at the end of the 13th century. The King of Spain resides here still, at least symbolically. The royal family are rarely in residence, except for the occasional ceremony, as they prefer to spend summer in the Palau Marivent (in Cala Major). At other times you can wander through a series of cavernous stone-walled rooms that have been lavishly decorated.

⭐ **Palau March** MUSEUM
(☎971 71 11 22; www.fundacionbmarch.es; Carrer del Palau Reial 18; adult/child €4.50/free; ⊙10am-6.30pm Mon-Fri Apr-Oct, to 2pm Nov-Mar, to 2pm Sat year-round) This house, palatial by any definition, was one of several residences of the phenomenally wealthy March family. Sculptures by 20th-century greats including Henry Moore, Auguste Rodin, Barbara Hepworth and Eduardo Chillida grace the outdoor terrace. Within lie many more artistic treasures from such luminaries of Spanish art as Salvador Dalí and Barcelona's Josep Maria Sert and Xavier Corberó. Not to be missed are the meticulously crafted figures of an 18th-century Neapolitan *belén* (nativity scene).

⭐ **Es Baluard** GALLERY
(Museu d'Art Modern i Contemporani; ☎971 90 82 00; www.esbaluard.org; Plaça de Porta de Santa Catalina 10; adult/temporary exhibitions/child €6/4/free; ⊙10am-8pm Tue-Sat, to 3pm Sun; 🖗) Built with flair and innovation into the shell of the Renaissance-era seaward walls, this contemporary art gallery is one of the finest

SPAIN MALLORCA

MENORCA

Renowned for its pristine beaches and archaeological sites, tranquil Menorca was declared a Biosphere Reserve by Unesco in 1993. Maó absorbs most of the tourist traffic. North of Maó, a drive across a lunar landscape leads to the lighthouse at Cap de Faváritx. South of the cape stretch some fine remote sandy bays and beaches reachable only on foot, including Cala Presili and Platja d'en Tortuga.

Ciutadella, with its smaller harbour and historic buildings, has a more Spanish feel to it and is the more attractive of the island's two main towns. A narrow country road leads south of Ciutadella (follow the 'Platges' sign from the *ronda*, or ring road) and then forks twice to reach some of the island's loveliest beaches: (from west to east) Arenal de Son Saura, Cala es Talaier, Cala en Turqueta and Cala Macarella. As with most beaches, you'll need your own transport.

In the centre of the island, the 357m-high Monte Toro has great views; on a clear day you can see Mallorca. On the northern coast, the picturesque town of Fornells is on a large bay popular with windsurfers.

The ports in both Maó and Ciutadella are lined with bars and restaurants.

on the island. Its temporary exhibitions are worth viewing, but the permanent collection – works by Miró, Barceló and Picasso – give the gallery its cachet. Entry on Fridays is by donation, and anyone turning up on a bike, on any day, is charged just €2.

★ **Museu Fundación Juan March**   GALLERY
(☑ 91 435 42 40; www.march.es; Carrer de Sant Miquel 11; ⏰ 10am-6.30pm Mon-Fri, 10.30am-2pm Sat) FREE The 17th-century Can Gallard del Canya, a 17th-century mansion overlaid with minor Modernist touches, now houses a small but significant collection of painting and sculpture. The permanent exhibits – some 80 pieces held by the Fundación Juan March – constitute a veritable who's who of modern Spanish art, including Miró, Picasso, fellow cubist Juan Gris, Dalí, and the sculptors Eduardo Chillida and Julio González.

🛏 Sleeping

★ **Misión de San Miguel**   BOUTIQUE HOTEL €€
(☑ 971 21 48 48; www.urhotels.com; Carrer de Can Maçanet 1A; d/ste €140/175; 🅿 ❄ @ 🛜) This boutique hotel, with its 32 stylish designer rooms gathered discreetly around a quiet inner courtyard, is a real bargain. Good-quality mattresses and rain shower heads are typical of a place where the little things are always done well, although some rooms open onto public areas and can be a tad noisy. Service is friendly and professional.

★ **Hotel Tres**   BOUTIQUE HOTEL €€€
(☑ 971 71 73 33; www.hoteltres.com; Carrer dels Apuntadors 3; s/d/ste €187/258/300; ❄ @ 🛜 ⬛) Hotel Tres swings joyously between

16th-century town palace and fresh-faced Scandinavian design. Centred on a courtyard with a single palm, the rooms are cool and minimalist, with cowhide benches, anatomy-inspired prints, and nice details like rollaway desks and Durance aromatherapy cosmetics. Head up to the roof terrace at sunset for a steam and dip as the cathedral begins to twinkle.

🍴 Eating

★ **Can Cera Gastro-Bar**   MEDITERRANEAN €€
(☑ 971 71 50 12; www.cancerahotel.com; Carrer del Convent de Sant Francesc 8; tapas €9-22; ⏰ 12.30-11pm) This restaurant spills onto a lovely inner patio at the Can Cera hotel, housed in a *palau* (palace) that dates originally to the 13th century. Dine by lantern light on tapas-sized dishes such as *frito mallorquín* (seafood fried with potato and herbs), Cantabrian anchovies, and pork ribs with honey and mustard. The vertical garden attracts plenty of attention from passers-by.

★ **Toque**   INTERNATIONAL €€
(☑ 971 28 70 68; www.restaurante-toque.com; Carrer Federico García Lorca 6; mains €17-19, 3-course lunch menú €14.50; ⏰ 1-4pm & 7-11pm Tue-Sat; 🍴) A father-and-son team run this individual little place with real pride and warmth. The food is Belgian-meets-Med (perhaps cauliflower cream with *butifarrón* sausage, raisins and pine nuts, or pork cheeks with peach) and has generated a loyal following among *palmeros*. Wines are well chosen and modestly priced, and the €14.50 lunch *menú* is a dead-set bargain.

★ **Marc Fosh**   MODERN EUROPEAN €€€
(☑ 971 72 01 14; www.marcfosh.com; Carrer de la Missió 7A; menús lunch €28-40, dinner €68-89; ☺ 1-4.30pm & 7.30pm-midnight) The flagship of Michelin-starred Fosh's burgeoning flotilla of Palma restaurants, this stylish gastronomic destination introduces novel twists to time-honoured Mediterranean dishes and ingredients, all within the converted refectory of a 17th-century convent. The weekly lunch *menú*, three/five courses for €28/40, is a very reasonable way to enjoy dishes such as foie gras and duck terrine, or truffled pasta with burrata.

ⓘ Information

Consell de Mallorca Tourist Office (☑ 971 17 39 90; www.infomallorca.net; Plaça de la Reina 2; ☺ 8.30am-8pm Mon-Fri, to 3pm Sat; 📶)

Around Palma de Mallorca

Mallorca's northwestern coast is a world away from the high-rise tourism on the other side of the island. Dominated by the dramatic, razorback Serra de Tramuntana, it's a beautiful region of olive groves, pine forests and small villages with shuttered stone buildings. There are a couple of highlights for drivers: the hair-raising road down to the small port of **Sa Calobra**, and the amazing trip along the peninsula at the island's northern tip, **Cap Formentor**.

Sóller is a good place to base yourself for hiking and the nearby village of **Fornalutx** is one of the prettiest on Mallorca.

From Sóller, it's a 10km walk to the beautiful hilltop village of **Deià**, where Robert Graves, poet and author of *I Claudius*, lived for most of his life. From the village, you can scramble down to the small shingle beach of **Cala de Deià**. The pretty streets of **Valldemossa**, further southwest down the coast, are crowned by a fine monastery.

Further east, **Pollença** and **Artà** are attractive inland towns. Nice beaches include those at **Cala Sant Vicenç**, **Platja des Coll Baix** hidden on Cap des Pinar, **Cala Agulla** and others near Cala Ratjada, **Cala Mondragó** and **Cala Llombards**.

Buses and/or trains cover much of the island, but hiring a car (in any town or resort) is best for exploring the remoter beaches, hill towns and mountains.

Ibiza

Ibiza (Eivissa in Catalan) is an island of extremes. Its formidable party reputation is completely justified, with some of the world's greatest clubs attracting hedonists from the world over. The interior and northeast of the island, however, are another world. Peaceful country drives, hilly green territory, a sprinkling of mostly laid-back beaches and coves, and some wonderful inland accommodation and eateries are light years from the throbbing all-night dance parties that dominate the west.

Ibiza City

◉ Sights

Ibiza City's port and nightlife area **Sa Penya** is crammed with funky and trashy clothing boutiques and arty-crafty market stalls. From here, you can wander up into **D'Alt Vila**, the atmospheric old walled town.

★ **Ramparts**   HISTORIC SITE
Encircling D'Alt Vila, Ibiza's colossal protective walls reach over 25m in height and include seven bastions. Evocatively floodlit at night, these fortifications were constructed to safeguard Ibiza's residents against the threat of pirate attack. You can walk the entire perimeter of these impressive Renaissance-era ramparts, designed to withstand heavy artillery. Along the way, enjoy great views over the Port Area and south to Formentera.

Catedral   CATHEDRAL
(Plaça de la Catedral; ☺ 9.30am-1.30pm & 4-8pm) FREE Ibiza's cathedral, which sits close to the highest ground in D'Alt Vila, elegantly combines several styles: the original 14th-century structure is Catalan Gothic, the sacristy was added in 1592, and a major baroque renovation took place in the 18th century. Inside, the **Museu Diocesà** (€1.50; ☺ 9.30am-1.30pm Tue-Sun, closed Dec-Feb) contains some impressive religious art.

🛏 Sleeping

Many of Ibiza City's hotels and *hostales* are closed in winter and heavily booked between April and October. Make sure you book ahead.

SPAIN IBIZA

Hostal Parque
HOSTAL **€€**

(☑ 971 30 13 58; www.hostalparque.com; Plaça des Parc 4; s €61-83, d €83-143, tr €132; ✳ 🖨) Overlooking palm-dotted Plaça des Parc, this *hostal's* rooms have been spruced up with boutique touches such as wood floors, contemporary art and ultramodern bathrooms. There's a price hike for *ático* (penthouse) rooms, but their roof terraces with D'Alt Vila views are something else. Street-facing rooms might be a tad noisy for light sleepers.

 Urban Spaces
DESIGN HOTEL **€€€**

(☑ 871 51 71 74; Carrer de la Vía Púnica 32; ste €200-270; ✳ 🖨) Ira Francis-Smith is the brains behind this design hotel with an alternative edge. Some of the world's most prolific street artists (N4T4, INKIE, JEROM, et al) have pooled their creativity in the roomy, mural-splashed suites, with clever backlighting, proper workstations and balconies with terrific views. Extras such as yoga on the roof terrace and clubber-friendly breakfasts until 1pm are sure-fire people-pleasers.

✖ Eating

⭐ **S'Escalinata**
MEDITERRANEAN, CAFE **€**

(☑ 971 30 61 93; www.sescalinata.es; Carrer Portal Nou 10; snacks/meals from €5/9; ☺ 10.30am-3.30am Apr-Oct; 🖨) Enjoying an incredibly picturesque location inside D'Alt Vila, this casual cafe-restaurant's low tables and cushioned seating (on the steps of a steep stone staircase) create a relaxed vibe. Healthy breakfasts, tapas, *bocadillos* (filled rolls) and a satisfying dinner menu are offered. It's open late into the night, doubling as a bar with good house sangria and cocktails.

S'Ametller
IBIZAN **€€€**

(☑ 971 31 17 80; www.restaurantsametller.com; Carrer de Pere Francès 12; menús €24-38; ☺ 8pm-11pm Mon-Sat Jun-Sep, 1-4pm Mon-Sat, 8pm-11pm Wed-Sat Oct-May) The 'Almond Tree' specialises in local, market-fresh cooking. The daily *menú* is inventive and superb value. For dessert, choose the house *flaó*, a mint-flavoured variant of cheesecake and a Balearic Islands speciality. S'Ametller also offers cookery courses – including one that imparts the secrets of that *flaó*.

🍷 Drinking & Nightlife

Sa Penya is the nightlife centre. Dozens of bars keep the port area jumping. Alternatively, various bars at Platja d'en Bossa combine sounds, sand, sea and sangria.

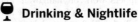

CLUBBING IN IBIZA

Ibiza's clubs are the stuff of legend. From late May to the end of September, the west of the island is one big, nonstop dance party from sunset to sunrise and back again. Space, Amnesia and Pacha were Nos 1, 3 and 4 in *DJ Mag*'s top 100 clubs for 2016.

The major clubs operate nightly from around midnight to 6am from mid-May or June to early October. Theme nights, fancy-dress parties and foam parties are regular features.

Entertainment Ibiza-style doesn't come cheaply. Admission can cost anything from €15 to €75 (mixed drinks and cocktails then go for around €10 to €15).

Pacha (www.pachaibiza.com; Avinguda 8 d'Agost; admission from €20, drinks from €10; ☺ 11pm-6am daily May-Sep, 11pm-6am Sat Oct-Apr) Going strong since 1973, Pacha is Ibiza's original and most classy nightclub. Built around the shell of a farmhouse, it boasts an amazing main dance floor, the Funky Room (for soul and disco sounds), a huge VIP section and myriad other places to groove or chill, including a fab open-air terrace and a Global Room for hip hop and R & B.

Amnesia (www.amnesia.es; Carretera Ibiza a Sant Antoni Km 5; €35-70; ☺ midnight-6am end May-Oct) Amnesia is arguably Ibiza's most influential club, its decks welcoming such DJ royalty as Sven Väth, Paul Van Dyk, Paul Oakenfold and Avicii. There's a warehouse-like main room and a terrace topped by a graceful atrium. Big nights include techno-fest Cocoon; Cream; foam-filled Espuma, which always draws a big local crowd; and La Troya, the biggest gay night on the island.

Ushuaïa (www.ushuaiabeachhotel.com; Platja d'en Bossa 10; €40-75; ☺ 3pm or 5pm-midnight; 🖨) Queen of daytime clubbing, ice-cool Ushuaïa is an open-air megaclub. The party starts early with superstar DJs such as David Guetta, Luciano and Sven Väth, and poolside lounging by a lagoon with Bali beds. Check out the Sky Lounge for sparkling sea views, or stay the night in the minimalist-cool hotel (there are even swim-up rooms!).

Much cheaper than a taxi, the Discobus (www.discobus.es; per person €3; ☺ midnight-6am Jun-Sep) does an all-night whirl of the major clubs, bars and hotels in Ibiza City, Platja d'en Bossa, Sant Rafel, Es Canar, Santa Eulària and Sant Antoni.

★ Bar 1805   BAR
(☑ 651 625972; www.bar1805ibiza.com; Carrer Santa Lucía 7; ☺ 8pm-3.30am May-Oct; ☎) Tucked away on a Sa Penya backstreet, this terrific boho bar has the best cocktails in town. There's lots of absinthe action on the list – try a Green Beast (served in a punch bowl) or the house margarita (with mescal instead of tequila), which packs a mean Mexican punch. There's a great outdoor terrace for quaffing.

Bora Bora Beach Club   BAR
(www.boraboraibiza.net; Carrer d'es Fumarell 1, Platja d'en Bossa; ☺ noon-6am May-Sep) This is *the* place – a long beachside bar where sun and fun worshippers work off hangovers and prepare new ones. Entry's free and the ambience is chilled, with low-key club sounds wafting over the sand.

Around Ibiza City

Ibiza has numerous unspoiled and relatively undeveloped beaches. On the east coast, north of Santa Eulària d'es Riu, are the small and serene Cala Llenya and Cala Mastella. A bit further north, Cala Boix is the only black-sand beach on the island, and a few kilometres further is the lovely, clothing-optional Aigües Blanques.

On the north coast near Portinatx, Cala d'en Serra is one of Ibiza's most beautiful cove beaches, and near Sant Miquel de Balansat is the spectacular Benirrás beach.

In the southwest, Cala d'Hort is a long arc of sand in a spectacular setting overlooking the 380m-high limestone islet Es Vedrá.

The best thing about rowdy Sant Antoni, the island's second-biggest town, north of Ibiza City, is heading to the small rock-and-sand strip on the north shore to join hundreds of others for sunset drinks at a string of chilled bars, among them the island's most famous bar, Café del Mar (www.cafedelmar music.com; Carrer Vara de Rey 27; ☺ 4pm-midnight May–mid-Oct).

Check out rural accommodation at www. ibizaruralvillas.com. For more standard accommodation, start at www.ibizahotels-guide.com.

Local buses (www.ibizabus.com) run to most destinations between May and October.

ANDALUCÍA

So many of the most powerful images of Spain emanate from Andalucía that it can be difficult not to feel a sense of déjà vu. It's almost as if you've already been there in your dreams: the flashing fire of a flamenco dancer, the scent of orange blossom, a festive summer fair, magical nights in the shadow of the Alhambra. In the bright light of day, the picture is no less magical.

Seville
POP 703,000

It takes a stony heart not to be captivated by stylish but ancient, proud yet fun-loving Seville – home to two of Spain's most colourful festivals, fascinating and distinctive *barrios* (neighbourhoods) such as the flower-decked Santa Cruz, great historic monuments, and a population that lives life to the fullest. Being out among the celebratory, happy crowds in the tapas bars and streets on a warm spring night in Seville is an unforgettable experience. But try to avoid July and August, when it's so hot that most locals flee to the coast!

◉ Sights

★ Alcázar   FORTRESS
(☑ tours 954 50 23 24; www.alcazarsevilla.org; adult/child €9.50/free; ☺ 9.30am-7pm Apr-Sep, to 5pm Oct-Mar) If heaven really *does* exist, then let's hope it looks a little bit like the inside of Seville's Alcázar. Built primarily in the 14th century during the so-called 'dark ages' in Europe, the fortress' intricate architecture is anything but dark. Indeed, compared to our modern-day shopping malls, the Alcázar marks one of history's architectural high points. Unesco agreed, making it a World Heritage site in 1987.

Catedral & Giralda   CATHEDRAL
(www.catedraldesevilla.es; adult/child €9/free; ☺ 11am-3.30pm Mon, 11am-5pm Tue-Sat, 2.30-6pm Sun) Seville's immense cathedral, one of the largest Christian churches in the world, is awe-inspiring in its scale and sheer majesty. It stands on the site of the great 12th-century Almohad mosque, with the mosque's minaret (the Giralda) still towering beside it.

Museo de Bellas Artes   GALLERY
(Fine Arts Museum; ☑ 955 54 29 31; www.museode-bellasartesdesevilla.es; Plaza del Museo 9; EU citizens/other free/€1.50; ☺ 10am-8.30pm Tue-Sat, to 5pm Sun) Housed in the beautiful former

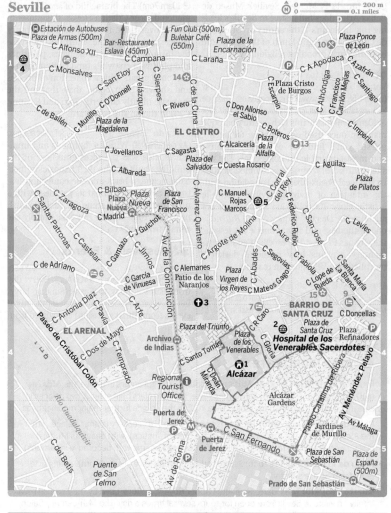

Seville

◉ Top Sights
1 Alcázar	C4
2 Hospital de los Venerables Sacerdotes	C4

◉ Sights
3 Catedral & Giralda	C3
4 Museo de Bellas Artes	A1
5 Museo del Baile Flamenco	C2

🛏 Sleeping
6 Hotel Adriano	A3
7 Hotel Casa 1800	C4
8 Oasis Backpackers' Hostel	A1

9 Un Patio en Santa Cruz	D3

✖ Eating
10 El Rinconcillo	D1
11 La Brunilda	A3
12 Restaurante Oriza	D5

🍷 Drinking & Nightlife
13 El Garlochi	D2

✪ Entertainment
14 Casa de la Memoria	B1
15 La Casa del Flamenco	D3

Convento de la Merced, Seville's Museo de Bellas Artes does full justice to Seville's leading role in Spain's 17th-century artistic Siglo de Oro (Golden Age). Much of the work here is of the dark, brooding religious type.

★ **Hospital de los**
Venerables Sacerdotes GALLERY
(☑954 56 26 96; www.focus.abengoa.es; Plaza de los Venerables 8; adult/child incl audio guide €8/3.75; ⊘10am-4pm) Inside this 17th-century baroque mansion once used as a hospice for ageing priests, you'll find one of Seville's greatest and most admirable art collections. The on-site Centro Velázquez was founded in 2007 by the local Focus-Abengoa Foundation with the intention of reviving Seville's erstwhile artistic glory. Its collection of masterpieces anchored by Diego Veláquez' *Santa Rufina* is one of the best and most concise art lessons the city has to offer. The excellent audio commentary explains how medieval darkness morphed into Velázquezian realism.

Museo del Baile Flamenco MUSEUM
(☑954 34 03 11; www.museoflamenco.com; Calle Manuel Rojas Marcos 3; adult/concession €10/8; ⊘10am-7pm) The brainchild of *sevillana* flamenco dancer Cristina Hoyos, this museum spread over three floors of an 18th-century palace makes a noble effort to showcase the mysterious art with sketches, paintings and photos of erstwhile (and contemporary) flamenco greats, plus a collection of dresses and shawls. Even better than that are the fantastic nightly concerts (7pm and 8.45pm; €20) in the on-site courtyard.

Plaza de España HISTORIC BUILDING
(Av de Portugal) With its fountains and mini-canals, this was the most grandiose of the buildings built for the 1929 Exposición Iberoamericana, a brick-and-tile confection featuring Seville tilework at its gaudiest, with a map and historical scene for each Spanish province. You can hire row boats to ply the canals from only €5.

🎊 Festivals & Events

Semana Santa HOLY WEEK
(www.semana-santa.org; ⊘Mar/Apr) Every day from Palm Sunday to Easter Sunday, large, life-sized *pasos* (sculptural representations of events from Christ's Passion) are carried from

---

DON'T MISS

ALCÁZAR HIGHLIGHTS

Founded in AD 913 as a fort for Muslim Córdoba's local governors in Seville, the Alcázar (p1076) has been revamped many times since. Muslim rulers built at least two palaces inside it and after the Christians took Seville in 1248 they made further major modifications.

Patio del León (Lion Patio) The garrison yard of an 11th-century Islamic palace within the Alcázar. Off here is the Sala de la Justicia (Hall of Justice), with beautiful Mudéjar plasterwork and an *artesonado* (ceiling of interlaced beams with decorative insertions).

Patio de la Montería The rooms surrounding this patio are filled with interesting artefacts from Seville's history.

Cuarto Real Alto The Cuarto Real Alto (Upper Royal Quarters; used by the Spanish royal family on visits to Seville) are open for tours several times a day. The 14th-century Salón de Audiencias is still the monarch's reception room.

Palacio de Don Pedro Built by the Castilian king Pedro I ('the Cruel') in the 1360s, this is the single most stunning building in Seville. At its heart is the wonderful Patio de las Doncellas (Patio of the Maidens), surrounded by beautiful arches, plasterwork and tiling. The Alcoba Real (Royal Quarters), on the patio's northern side, has stunningly beautiful ceilings. The little Patio de las Muñecas (Patio of the Dolls), the heart of the palace's private quarters, features delicate Granada-style decoration. The Salón de Embajadores (Hall of Ambassadors), at the western end of the Patio de las Doncellas, was the throne room. Its fabulous wooden dome of multiple star patterns, symbolising the universe, was added in 1427.

Salones de Carlos V Reached via a staircase at the southeastern corner of the Patio de las Doncellas, these are the much-remodelled rooms of Alfonso X's 13th-century Gothic palace.

Gardens From the Salones de Carlos V you can go out and wander in the Alcázar's large and sleepy gardens, some with pools and fountains.

Seville's churches through the streets to the cathedral, accompanied by processions that may take more than an hour to pass. The processions are organised by more than 50 different *hermandades* or *cofradías* (brotherhoods, some of which include women).

Feria de Abril SPRING FAIR
(www.turismosevilla.org; ☺ Apr) The April fair, held in the second half of the month (sometimes edging into May), is the jolly counterpart to the sombre Semana Santa. The biggest and most colourful of all Andalucía's ferias (fairs) is less invasive (and also less inclusive) than the Easter celebration. It takes place on El Real de la Feria, in the Los Remedios area west of the Río Guadalquivir.

🛏 Sleeping

Oasis Backpackers' Hostel HOSTEL €
(☏ 955 26 26 96; www.oasissevilla.com; Calle Almirante Ulloa 1; dm/d incl breakfast from €13/44; ✻ @ 🛜 ☲) It's not often you get to backpack in a palace. A veritable oasis in the busy city-centre district, this place is a friendly welcoming hostel set in a palatial 19th-century mansion with some private room options, a cafe-bar and a rooftop deck with a small pool.

★ Hotel Adriano HOTEL €€
(☏ 954 29 38 00; www.adrianohotel.com; Calle Adriano 12; s/d €65/75; P ✻ 🛜) A solid Arenal option with great staff, rooms with attractive *sevillano* features and one of the best coffee shops in Seville out front.

Un Patio en Santa Cruz HOTEL €€
(☏ 954 53 94 13; www.patiosantacruz.com; Calle Doncellas 15; s €65-85, d €65-120; ✻ 🛜) Feeling more like an art gallery than a hotel, this place has starched white walls coated in loud works of art, strange sculptures and preserved plants. The rooms are immensely comfortable, staff are friendly, and there's a cool rooftop terrace with mosaic Moroccan tables. It's easily one of the hippest and best-value hotels in town.

★ Hotel Casa 1800 LUXURY HOTEL €€€
(☏ 954 56 18 00; www.hotelcasa1800sevilla.com; Calle Rodrigo Caro 6; r from €195; ✻ @ 🛜) Reigning as number one in Seville's 'favourite hotel' charts is this positively regal Santa Cruz pile where the word *casa* (house) is taken seriously. This really is your home away from home (albeit a posh one), with charming staff catering for your every need. Historic highlights include a complimentary after-

noon-tea buffet, plus a quartet of penthouse garden suites with Giralda views.

🍴 Eating

★ Bar-Restaurante

Eslava FUSION, ANDALUCIAN €€
(☏ 954 90 65 68; www.espacioeslava.com; Calle Eslava 3; medias raciones €9-13; ☺ 1.30-4pm & 9-11.30pm Tue-Sat, 12.30-4pm Sun) A legend in its own dinnertime, Eslava shirks the traditional tilework and bullfighting posters of tapas-bar lore and delivers where it matters: fine food backed up with equally fine service.

★ La Brunilda TAPAS €€
(☏ 954 22 04 81; www.labrunildatapas.com; Calle Galera 5; tapas €4-7.50; ☺ 1-4pm & 8.30-11.30pm Tue-Sat, 1-4pm Sun) Seville's crown as Andalucía's tapas capital is regularly attacked by well-armed rivals from the provinces, meaning it constantly has to reinvent itself and offer up fresh competition. Enter La Brunilda, a newish font of fusion tapas sandwiched into an inconspicuous backstreet in the Arenal quarter where everything – including the food, staff and clientele – is pretty.

El Rinconcillo TAPAS €€
(☏ 954 22 31 83; www.elrinconcillo.es; Calle Gerona 40; tapas/raciones €3/12; ☺ 1pm-1.30am) Some say the Rinconcillo is resting on its laurels. Maybe so; but, with more than 345 years of history, there is a lot to rest on. Seville's oldest bar first opened in 1670, when the Inquisition was raging and tapas were still just tops you screwed on bottles.

Restaurante Oriza CONTEMPORARY SPANISH €€€
(☏ 954 22 72 54; www.restauranteoriza.com; Calle San Fernando 41; mains €22-32; ☺ noon-11.30pm Mon-Sat, noon-5pm Sun) Say Basque and you've got a byword for fine dining these days, so it's not surprising that Basque-run Oriza is regarded as one of the city's standout restaurants. Situated close to the Prado de San Sebastián bus station, this could be your first (and best) culinary treat in Seville. There's an equally posh tapas spot on the ground floor.

🍷 Drinking & Nightlife

Drinking and partying really get going around midnight on Friday and Saturday (daily when it's hot). Classic drinking areas include Plaza de la Alfalfa (cocktail and dive bars), the Barrio de Santa Cruz and the Alameda de Hércules. The latter is the hub for young *sevillanos* and the city's gay nightlife. In summer, dozens of open-air

SPAIN SEVILLE

late-night bars (*terrazas de verano*) spring up along both banks of the river.

El Garlochi   BAR

(Calle Boteros 4; ⊙ 9pm-3am) Dedicated entirely to the iconography, smells and sounds of Semana Santa, the ultracamp El Garlochi is a true marvel. Taste the rather revolting sounding cocktail Sangre de Cristo (Blood of Christ) or the Agua de Sevilla, both heavily laced with vodka, whisky and grenadine, and pray they open more bars like this.

Bulebar Café   BAR

(☑ 954 90 19 54; www.facebook.com/Bulebar Cafe; Alameda de Hércules 83; ⊙ 9am-2am) This place gets pretty *caliente* (hot) at night but is pleasantly chilled in the early evening, with friendly staff. Don't write off its spirit-reviving alfresco breakfasts that pitch early birds with up-all-nighters. It's in the uber-cool Alameda de Hércules.

☆ Entertainment

Seville is arguably Spain's flamenco capital and there are many opportunities to experience live performances.

★ Casa de la Memoria   FLAMENCO

(☑ 954 56 06 70; www.casadelamemoria.es; Calle Cuna 6; admission €18; ⊙ shows 7.30pm & 9pm) Neither a *tablao* (choreographed flamenco show) nor a private *peña* (club, usually of flamenco aficionados), this cultural centre offers what are, without doubt, the most intimate and authentic nightly flamenco shows in Seville. It's accommodated in the old stables of the Palacio de la Condesa de Lebrija.

It's perennially popular and space is limited to 100, so reserve tickets a day or so in advance by calling or visiting the venue.

La Casa del Flamenco   FLAMENCO

(☑ 954 50 05 95; www.lacasadelflamencose villa.com; Calle Ximénez de Enciso, 28; adult/child €18/10; ⊙ shows 8.30pm) This beautiful patio in an old Sephardic Jewish mansion in Santa Cruz is home to La Casa del Flamenco and the performances on a stage hemmed in by seating on three sides are mesmerising.

Fun Club   LIVE MUSIC

(☑ 958 25 02 49; www.funclubsevilla.com; Alameda de Hércules 86; admission €5; ⊙ midnight-late Thu-Sun, from 9.30pm live-band nights) Positively ancient by live music club standards, the emblematic Fun Club has been entertaining the nocturnal Alameda de Hércules crowd since

the late 1980s. Its speciality is live bands. This is ground zero for Seville's alternative music scene.

❶ Information

Regional Tourist Office (☑ 954 22 14 04; www.turismosevilla.org; Avenida de la Constitución 21; ⊙ 9am-7pm Mon-Fri, 10am-2pm & 3-7pm Sat, 10am-2pm Sun, closed holidays) The Constitución office is well informed but often very busy. There is also a branch at the airport (☑ 954 44 91 28; Aeropuerto San Pablo; ⊙ 9am-8.30pm Mon-Fri, 10am-6pm Sat, 10am-2pm Sun, closed holidays).

❶ Getting There & Away

AIR

Seville's **airport** (SVQ; ☑ 954 44 90 00; www. aena.es; A4, Km 532) has a fair range of international and domestic flights.

BUS

Buses to Córdoba (€12, two hours, seven daily), Granada (€23 to €29, three hours, nine daily), Málaga (€19 to €24, 2½ to four hours, six daily), Madrid (€22, 6½ hours, eight daily) and Lisbon (€45 to €50, 7½ hours, two daily) go from the **Estación de Autobuses Plaza de Armas** (☑ 902 45 05 50; www.autobusesplazadear mas.es; Avenida del Cristo de la Expiración).

TRAIN

Estación Santa Justa (☑ 902 43 23 43; www. renfe.es; Avenida Kansas City) is 1.5km north-east of the centre. Up to 20 AVE and other high-speed trains whiz daily to/from Madrid (€29 to €125, 2½ to 2¾ hours). Other destinations include Córdoba (€12 to €30, 45 minutes to 1¼ hours, more than 30 trains daily), Granada (€30, 3½ hours, four daily), Málaga (€24 to €44, two to 2¾ hours, 11 daily) and Barcelona (€19 to €117, 5½ to 11½ hours, five daily).

Córdoba

POP 326,600

A little over a millennium ago Córdoba was the capital of Islamic Spain and Western Europe's biggest, most cultured city, where Muslims, Jews and Christians coexisted peaceably. Its past glories place it among Andalucía's top draws today. The centrepiece is the mesmerising, multiarched Mezquita. Surrounding it is an intricate web of winding streets, geranium-sprouting flower boxes and cool intimate patios that are at their most beguiling in late spring.

⊙ Sights

★ Mezquita MOSQUE, CATHEDRAL
(Mosque; ☑ 957 47 05 12; www.catedraldecordoba.
es; Calle Cardenal Herrero; adult/child €10/5, 8.30-
9.30am Mon-Sat Mar-Oct free; ⊗ 8.30-9.30am
& 10am-7pm Mon-Sat, 8.30-11.30am & 3-7pm
Sun Mar-Oct, 10am-6pm Mon-Sat, 8.30-11.30am
& 3-6pm Sat & Sun Nov-Feb) It's impossible to
overemphasise the beauty of Córdoba's great
mosque, with its remarkably serene (despite
tourist crowds) and spacious interior. One
of the world's greatest works of Islamic architecture, the Mezquita hints, with all its
lustrous decoration, at a refined age when
Muslims, Jews and Christians lived side by
side and enriched their city with a heady in-
teraction of diverse, vibrant cultures.

★ Alcázar de los Reyes Cristianos FORTRESS
(Fortress of the Christian Monarchs; ☑ 957 42 01
51; www.alcazardelosreyescristianos.cordoba.es;
Campo Santo de Los Mártires; admission 8.30am-
2.30pm €4.50, other times incl water, light & sound
show adult/child €7/free; ⊗ 8.30am-8.45pm Tue-
Fri, to 4.30pm Sat, to 2.30pm Sun Sep-Jun, to 3pm
Tue-Sun Jul-Aug; ⊕) Built under Castilian
rule in the 13th and 14th centuries on the
remains of a Moorish predecessor, this fort-
cum-palace hosted both Fernando and Isabel, who made their first acquaintance with
Columbus in 1486. One hall displays
some remarkable Roman mosaics, dug up
from the Plaza de la Corredera in the 1950s.
The Alcázar's terraced gardens – full of fish
ponds, fountains, orange trees and flowers –
are a delight to stroll around.

★ Museo Arqueológico MUSEUM
(☑ 957 35 55 17; www.museosdeandalucia.es; Plaza
de Jerónimo Páez 7; EU citizen/other free/€1.50;
⊗ 9am-8pm Tue-Sat, to 3pm Sun mid-Sep–mid-
Jun, 9am-3.30pm Tue-Sun mid-Jun–mid-Sep) The
excellent Archaeological Museum traces
Córdoba's many changes in size, appearance
and lifestyle from pre-Roman to early Re-
conquista times, with some fine sculpture,
an impressive coin collection, and interesting exhibits on domestic life and religion. In
the basement you can walk through the excavated remains of the city's Roman theatre.

★ Centro Flamenco Fosforito MUSEUM
(Posada del Potro; ☑ 957 47 68 29; www.centro
flamencofosforito.cordoba.es; Plaza del Potro;
⊗ 8.30am-7.30pm Tue-Fri, 8.30am-2.30pm Sat &
Sun) **FREE** Possibly the best flamenco museum in Andalucía, the Fosforito centre has
exhibits, film and information panels in

MEZQUITA HIGHLIGHTS

Emir Abd ar-Rahman I founded the
Mezquita in AD 785. Three later extensions nearly quintupled its original
size and brought it to the form you see
today – except for one major alteration:
a 16th-century cathedral plonked right
in the middle.

Torre del Alminar You can climb inside
the 54m-tall bell tower (originally the
Mezquita's minaret) for fine panoramas.

Patio de los Naranjos This lovely courtyard, with its orange and palm trees and
fountains, was the site of ritual ablutions
before prayer in the mosque.

Prayer Hall Divided into 19 'naves' by
lines of two-tier arches striped in red
brick and white stone. Their simplicity
and number give a sense of endlessness
to the Mezquita.

Mihrab & Maksura The arches of the
maksura (the area where the caliphs
and their retinues would have prayed)
are the mosque's most intricate and
sophisticated, forming a forest of interwoven horseshoe shapes. The portal of
the mihrab itself is a sublime crescent
arch in glittering gold mosaic.

The Cathedral 16th-century construction in the Mezquita's heart.

English and Spanish telling you the history
of the guitar and all the flamenco greats.
Touch-screen videos demonstrate the important techniques of flamenco song, guitar,
dance and percussion – you can test your
skill at beating out the *compás* (rhythm) of
different *palos* (song forms). Regular live
flamenco performances are held here, too.

★ Madinat al-Zahara ARCHAEOLOGICAL SITE
(Medina Azahara; ☑ 957 10 49 33; www.museosde
andalucia.es; Carretera Palma del Río Km 5.5; EU
citizen/other free/€1.50; ⊗ 9am-7.30pm Tue-Sat
Apr–mid-Jun, to 3.30pm mid-Jun–mid-Sep, to 6pm
mid-Sep–Mar, 9am-3pm Sun year-round; ⓟ) Eight
kilometres west of Córdoba stands what's
left of Madinat al-Zahra, the sumptuous pal-
ace-city built by Caliph Abd ar-Rahman III
in the 10th century. The complex spills down
a hillside with the caliph's palace (the area
you visit today) on the highest levels overlooking what were gardens and open fields.
The residential areas (still unexcavated) were

SPAIN CÓRDOBA

JEWISH CÓRDOBA

Jews were among the most dynamic and prominent citizens of Islamic Córdoba. The medieval *judería* (Jewish quarter), extending northwest from the Mezquita almost to Avenida del Gran Capitán, is today a maze of narrow streets and whitewashed buildings with flowery window boxes. The **Sinagoga** (☑957 74 90 15; www.turismodecordoba.org; Calle de los Judíos 20; EU citizen/other free/€0.30; ☺9am-3.30pm Tue-Sun mid-Jun–mid-Sep, to 8pm Tue-Sat mid-Sep–mid-Jun), built in 1315, is one of the few surviivng testaments to the Jewish presence in Andalucía. Across the street is the **Casa de Sefarad** (☑957 42 14 04; www.casadesefarad.es; cnr Calles de los Judíos & Averroes; €4; ☺10am-6pm Mon-Sat, 11am-6pm Sun), an interesting museum on the Sephardic (Iberian Peninsula Jewish) tradition.

set away to each side. A fascinating modern museum has been installed below the site.

🛏 Sleeping

Option Be Hostel
HOSTEL €

(☑661 420733; www.bedandbe.com; Calle Leiva Aguilar 1; dm €15-25, d €20-40; ✳🛜) Contemporary-design hostel in the old city, with mostly private bathrooms and a delightful communal terrace, kitchen and lounge area, run by the Bed and Be team.

Casa de los Azulejos
HOTEL €€

(☑957 47 00 00; www.casadelosazulejos.com; Calle Fernando Colón 5; incl breakfast s €78, d €89-134; ✳@🛜🏊) Mexican and Andalucian styles converge in this stylish nine-room hotel, where the patio is all banana trees, ferns and potted palms bathed in sunlight. Colonial-style rooms feature tall antique doors, big beds, walls in lilac and sky blue, and floors adorned with the beautiful old *azulejos* (tiles) that give the place its name.

★Balcón de Córdoba
BOUTIQUE HOTEL €€€

(☑957 49 84 78; www.balcondecordoba.com; Calle Encarnación 8; r incl breakfast €165-260; ✳🛜) Offering top-end boutique luxury, the 10-room Balcón is a riveting place with a charming *cordobés* patio, slick rooms, antique doorways, and ancient stone relics dotted around as if it were a wing of the nearby archaeological museum. Service doesn't miss a beat and the rooms have tasteful, soothing, contemporary decor with a little art but no clutter.

🍴 Eating

★Garum 2.1
ANDALUCIAN €€

(☑957 48 76 73; Calle de San Fernando 122; tapas €3-7, raciones €7-17; ☺noon-midnight, to 2am Fri & Sat) Garum serves up traditional meaty, fishy and vegie ingredients in all sorts of creative, tasty new concoctions. We recommend the *presa ibérica con herencia del maestro*

(Iberian pork with potatoes, fried eggs and ham). Service is helpful and friendly.

★La Boca
FUSION €€

(☑957 47 61 40; www.facebook.com/restaurante. laboca; Calle de San Fernando 39; mains €10-18; ☺noon-midnight Wed-Mon, to 5pm Tue) Trendy for a reason, this cutting-edge eatery whips up exciting global variations from traditional ingredients, then presents them in eye-catching ways: Iberian pork cheeks with red curry and basmati? Battered cod chunks with almonds and garlic? It's very well done, though portions are not for giant appetites. Reservations advisable at weekends.

★Bodegas Campos
ANDALUCIAN €€

(☑957 49 75 00; www.bodegascampos.com; Calle de Lineros 32; mains & raciones €12-25; ☺1.30-4.30pm daily, 8-11.30pm Mon-Sat) This atmospheric warren of rooms and patios is popular with smartly dressed *cordobeses*. The restaurant and more informal *taberna* (tavern) serve up delicious dishes, putting a slight creative twist on traditional Andalucian fare – the likes of cod-and-cuttlefish ravioli or pork sirloin in grape sauce. Campos also produces its own house Montilla.

ℹ Information

Centro de Visitantes (Visitors Centre; ☑902 201774, 957 35 51 79; www.turismodecordoba. org; Plaza del Triunfo; ☺9am-2.30pm & 5pm-7.30pm Mon-Fri, 9.30am-3pm Sat & Sun) The main tourist-information centre, with an exhibit on Córdoba's history, and some Roman and Visigothic remains downstairs.

ℹ Getting There & Away

BUS

The **bus station** (☑957 40 40 40; www. estacionautobusescordoba.es; Avenida Vía Augusta) is 2km northwest of the Mezquita, behind the train station. Destinations include Seville

(€12, two hours, seven buses daily), Granada (€15 to €17, 2¾ hours, eight daily) and Málaga (€12 to €15, 2½ to three hours, four daily).

TRAIN

Córdoba's **train station** (📞 902 24 05 05; www. renfe.com; Glorieta de las Tres Culturas) is on the high-speed AVE line between Madrid and Seville/Málaga. Rail destinations include Seville (€12 to €30, 45 minutes to 1¼ hours, more than 30 trains daily), Madrid (€25 to €105, 1¾ hours, 29 daily), Málaga (€17 to €41, one hour, 17 daily) and Barcelona (€18 to €120, five to 10 hours, six or more daily). Trips to Granada (€18 to €36, two to 2¾ hours, four or more daily) include changing to a train or bus at Antequera.

Granada

ELEV 690M / POP 258,000

Granada's eight centuries as a Muslim city are symbolised in its keynote emblem, the remarkable Alhambra, one of the most graceful achievements of Islamic architecture. Granada is chock-full of history, the arts and life, with tapas bars filled to bursting and flamenco dives resounding to the heart-wrenching tones of the south. Today, Islam is more present here than for many centuries in the shops, tearooms and mosque of a growing North African community around the maze of the Albayzín.

⊙ Sights

★**Alhambra**   PALACE
(📞 902 441221; www.granadatur.com/la-alhambra; adult/under 12yr €14/free, Generalife only €7; ⊙ 8.30am-8pm mid-Mar–mid-Oct, to 6pm mid-Oct–mid-Mar, night visits 10-11.30pm Tue-Sat mid-Mar–mid-Oct, 8-9.30pm Fri & Sat mid-Oct–mid-Mar) The Alhambra is Granada's – and Europe's – love letter to Moorish culture, a place where fountains trickle, leaves rustle, and ancient spirits seem to mysteriously linger. Part palace, part fort, part World Heritage site, part lesson in medieval architecture, the Alhambra has long enchanted a never-ending line of expectant visitors. As a historic monument, it is unlikely it will ever be surpassed – at least not in the lifetime of anyone reading this.

★**Capilla Real**   HISTORIC BUILDING
(📞 958 22 78 48; www.capillarealgranada.com; Calle Oficios; €4; ⊙ 10.15am-1.30pm & 3.30-6.30pm Mon-Sat, 11am-1.30pm & 2.30-5.30pm Sun) Here they lie, Spain's notorious Catholic Monarchs, entombed in a chapel adjoining Granada's cathedral; far more peaceful in death than their tumultuous lives would have suggested. Isabel and Fernando commissioned the elaborate Isabelline-Gothic-style mausoleum that was to house them, but it was not completed until 1521, hence their temporary interment in the Alhambra's Convento de San Francisco.

⊙ Albayzín

On the hill facing the Alhambra across the Darro valley, the Albayzín is an open-air museum in which you can lose yourself for most of a day. The cobbled streets are lined with gorgeous *cármenes* (large mansions with walled gardens). It survived as the Muslim quarter for several decades after the Christian conquest in 1492.

Calle Calderería Nueva   STREET
Linking the upper and lower parts of the Albayzín, Calle Calderería Nueva is a narrow

SPAIN GRANADA

DON'T MISS

ALHAMBRA HIGHLIGHTS

It was Granada's Nasrid emirs of the 13th and 14th centuries who turned a relatively modest fortress-palace into the fairytale **Alhambra** we see today.

Palacios Nazaríes The central palace complex is the pinnacle of the Alhambra's design, a harmonious synthesis of space, light, shade, water and greenery that sought to conjure the gardens of paradise for the rulers who dwelt here.

Patio de los Leones (Courtyard of the Lions) Glorious, recently restored patio in the Palacios Nazaríes with a famous fountain and exceptional rooms around the perimeter.

Palacio de Carlos V Renaissance-era circle-in-square ground plan. Inside, the Museo de la Alhambra displays Alhambra artefacts.

Generalife These gardens are a soothing arrangement of pathways, patios, pools, fountains, trees, topiary and, in season, flowers of every imaginable hue.

Alcazaba The Alhambra's main fortifications.

Granada

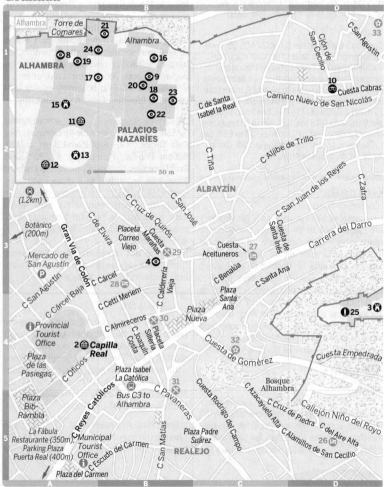

street famous for its *teterías* (teahouses), but also a good place to shop for slippers, hookahs, jewellery and North African pottery from an eclectic cache of shops redolent of a Moroccan souk.

Mirador San Nicolás VIEWPOINT
(Callejón de San Cecilio) Callejón de San Cecilio leads to the Mirador San Nicolás, a lookout with unbeatable views of the Alhambra and Sierra Nevada. Come back here for sunset (you can't miss the trail then!). At any time of day take care: skilful, well-organised wallet-lifters and bag-snatchers operate here.

Don't be put off – it is still a terrific atmosphere, with buskers and local students intermingling with camera-toting tourists.

Colegiata del Salvador CHURCH
(958 27 86 44; www.granadatur.com; Plaza del Salvador; €0.75; 10am-1pm & 4.30-6.30pm) Plaza del Salvador, near the top of the Albayzín, is dominated by the Colegiata del Salvador, a 16th-century church on the site of the Albayzín's former main mosque, the patio of which still survives at the church's western end.

SPAIN GRANADA

🛏 Sleeping

Hotel Posada del Toro　　　　　HOTEL €

(☑ 958 22 73 33; www.posadadeltoro.com; Calle de Elvira 25; d incl breakfast from €50; ❄ 🛜) A lovely small hotel with rooms set around a tranquil central patio. Walls are coloured like Italian gelato in pistachio, peach and cream flavours. The rooms are similarly tasteful with parquet floors, Alhambra-style stucco, rustic-style furniture and small but perfectly equipped bathrooms with double sinks and hydromassage showers. A bargain – especially considering its central location.

★**Carmen de la Alcubilla del Caracol**　　　　HISTORIC HOTEL €€

(☑ 958 21 55 51; www.alcubilladelcaracol.com; Calle del Aire Alta 12; s/d €110/130; ⊙ mid-Jul-31-Aug; ❄ @ 🛜) This much-sought-after small hotel inhabits a traditional *carmen* on the slopes of the Alhambra. It feels more like a B&B than a hotel thanks to the attentiveness of its Granada-loving host, Manuel. The seven rooms are furnished luxuriously, but not ostentatiously.

ℹ ALHAMBRA TICKETS

Up to 6600 tickets to the Alhambra are available for each day. About one-third of these are sold at the entrance on the day, but they sell out early and if you're here between March and October you need to start queuing by 7am to be reasonably sure of getting one. Fortunately, it's also possible to buy tickets up to three months ahead, online or by phone, from Alhambra Advance Booking (☑ 902 88 80 01, for international calls +34 958 92 60 31; www.alhambra-tickets.es), for €1.40 extra per ticket.

For internet or phone bookings you need a Visa card, MasterCard Maestro card or Eurocard. Tickets can be collected from ATMs of La Caixa bank throughout Andalucía, or from ticket machines or ticket windows at the Alhambra entrance. You'll need your booking reference number and your payment card (or ID document if collecting at Alhambra ticket windows).

The Palacios Nazaríes are open for night visits, good for atmosphere rather than detail.

It's a pleasant (if uphill) walk of just over 1km from Plaza Nueva to the Alhambra's main entrance. Alternatively, buses C3 and C4 (€1.20) run every few minutes from Plaza Isabel La Católica. By car, follow 'Alhambra' signs from the highway to the car park, just uphill from the ticket office.

Hotel Casa del Capitel Nazarí HISTORIC HOTEL €€
(☑ 958 21 52 60; www.hotelcasacapitel.com; Cuesta Aceituneros 6; s/d €68/85; ※ @ 🖙) Another slice of Albayzín magic in a 1503 Renaissance palace that's as much architectural history lesson as midrange hotel. Rooms have Moroccan inflections and the courtyard hosts art exhibits. It's just off Plaza Nueva.

🍴 Eating

Granada is a bastion of that fantastic practice of free tapas with every drink, and some have an international flavour. The labyrinthine Albayzín holds a wealth of eateries tucked away in the narrow streets. Calle Calderería Nueva is a fascinating muddle of *teterías* (tearooms) and Arabic-influenced takeaways.

Bodegas Castañeda TAPAS €
(☑ 958 21 54 64; Calle Almireceros; tapas €2-3, raciones €6-9; ⊙ 11.30am-4.30pm & 7.30pm-1.30am) A relic much loved by locals and tourists alike, the buzzing Castañeda is the Granada tapas bar to trump all others. Don't expect any fancy new stuff here, but do expect lightning-fast service, booze from big casks mounted on the walls, and eating as a contact sport.

⭐ Carmela Restaurante TAPAS €€
(☑ 958 22 57 94; www.restaurantecarmela.com; Calle Colcha 13; tapas €5-10; ⊙ 8am-midnight) Long a bastion of traditional tapas, Granada has taken a leaf out of Seville's book and come up with something a little more out-of-the-box at this streamlined restaurant, guarded by the statue of Jewish philosopher Yehuba ibn Tibon at the jaws of the Realejo quarter. The best of Carmela's creative offerings is the made-to-order tortilla and cured-ham croquettes.

Arrayanes MOROCCAN €€
(☑ 958 22 84 01; www.rest-arrayanes.com; Cuesta Marañas 4; mains €15; ⊙ 1.30-4.30pm & 7.30-11.30pm Sun-Fri, 1.30-4.30pm Sat; ☑) The best Moroccan food in a city that is well known for its Moorish throwbacks. Recline on lavish patterned seating, try the rich, fruity tagine casseroles and make your decision. Note that Arrayanes does not serve alcohol.

⭐ La Fábula Restaurante MODERN EUROPEAN €€€
(☑ 958 25 01 50; www.restaurantelafabula.com; Calle de San Antón 28; mains €24-28, degustation menu €75-90; ⊙ 1.30-4.30pm & 8.30-11pm Tue-Sat) In Fábula it's hard to avoid the pun – the place is pretty fabulous. Hidden in the highly refined confines of the Hotel Villa Oniria, the setting matches the food, which is presented like art and tastes equally good. Standouts are the venison with chestnuts and quince, or the baby eels with basil in venere rice.

🍷 Drinking & Entertainment

The best street for drinking is the rather scruffy Calle de Elvira, but other chilled bars line the Río Darro at the base of the Albayzín and Calle Navas in Realejo.

Botánico BAR
(☑ 958 27 15 98; www.botanicocafe.es; Calle Málaga 3; ⊙ 10am-1am Mon-Fri, noon-1am Sat & Sun) A haven for cool dudes with designer beards, students finishing off their Lorca dissertations, and anyone else with arty inclinations, Botánico is a casual snack restaurant by day,

a cafe at *merienda* time (5pm to 7pm), and a bar and club come dusk, with DJs or live music emphasising jazz and blues.

The bright colour scheme screams 'orange', while the name comes from the peaceful botanical garden across the road.

Peña La Platería FLAMENCO
(☑958 21 06 50; www.laplateria.org.es; Placeta de Toqueros 7) Buried in the Albayzín warren, Peña La Platería claims to be the oldest flamenco aficionados' club in Spain, founded in 1949. Unlike other more private clubs, it regularly opens its doors to nonmembers for performances on Thursday nights (and sometimes Saturdays) at 10.15pm. Tapas and drinks are available. Reservations recommended.

Jardines de Zoraya FLAMENCO
(☑958 20 60 66; www.jardinesdezoraya.com; Calle Panaderos 32; tickets with drink/dinner €20/43; ⊙shows 8pm & 10.30pm) A little larger than some of Andalucía's new flamenco cultural centres, and hosted in a restaurant that serves food and drink, the Jardines de Zoraya appears, on first impression, to be a touristy *tablao* (choreographed flamenco show). But reasonable entry prices, topnotch performers and a highly atmospheric patio make the Abayzín venue a worthwhile stop for any aficionado.

Casa del Arte Flamenco FLAMENCO
(☑958 56 57 67; www.casadelarteflamenco.com; Cuesta de Gomérez 11; tickets €18; ⊙shows 7.30pm & 9pm) A small newish flamenco venue that is neither *tablao* (choreographed flamenco show) nor *peña* (private club), but something in between. The performers are invariably top-notch, while the atmosphere depends largely on the tourist-local make-up of the audience.

ⓘ Information

Municipal Tourist Office (☑958 24 82 80; www.granadatur.com; Plaza del Carmen; ⊙9.30am-7pm Mon-Sat, 9.30am-2pm Sun) New digs in the Town Hall.

Provincial Tourist Office (☑958 24 71 28; www.granadatur.com; Cárcel Baja 3; ⊙9am-8pm Mon-Fri, 10am-7pm Sat, 10am-3pm Sun) Information on all of Granada province.

ⓘ Getting There & Away

BUS

Granada's **bus station** (☑902 42 22 42; www.alsa.es; Carretera de Jaén; ⊙6.30am-1.30am) is 3km northwest of the city centre. Destinations

include Córdoba (€15 to €17, 2¾ hours, eight buses daily), Seville (€23 to €29, three hours, seven daily), Málaga (€11 to €14, 1¾ hours, 15 daily) and Madrid (€19 to €45, five hours, 13 daily).

TRAIN

The **train station** (☑958 24 02 02; Avenida de Andaluces) is 1.5km west of the centre. Services run to Seville (€30, 3¼ hours, four daily), Almería (€20, 2½ hours, four daily), Madrid (€27 to €77, four hours, five daily) and Barcelona (€35 to €117, eight hours, two daily). Due to line construction work west of Granada, all these except Almería include a bus transfer as far as Antequera until at least 2018.

Málaga

POP 568,500

Málaga is a world apart from the adjoining, overdeveloped Costa del Sol: an exuberant, historic port city that has rapidly emerged as a city of culture, its so-called 'mile of art' being compared to Madrid, and its dynamism and fine dining to Barcelona.

The tastefully restored historic centre is a delight, with a Gothic cathedral surrounded by narrow pedestrian streets flanked by traditional and modern bars, and shops that range from idiosyncratic and family owned to urban-chic and contemporary. The city's terrific bars and nightlife, the last word in Málaga *joie de vivre*, stay open very late.

◉ Sights

★**Museo Picasso Málaga** MUSEUM
(☑902 443377; www.museopicassomalaga.org; Calle San Agustín 8; €7, incl temporary exhibition €10; ⊙10am-8pm Jul-Aug, to 7pm Mar-Jun & Sep-Oct, to 6pm Nov-Feb; ☎) The Museo Picasso has an enviable collection of 204 works, 155 donated and 49 loaned to the museum by Christine Ruiz-Picasso (wife of Paul, Picasso's eldest son) and Bernard Ruiz-Picasso (his grandson), and includes some wonderful paintings of the family, including the heartfelt *Paulo con gorro blanco* (Paulo with a White Cap), a portrait of Picasso's eldest son painted in the 1920s.

Don't miss the Phoenician, Roman, Islamic and Renaissance archaeological remains in the museum's basement, discovered during construction works.

★**Catedral de Málaga** CATHEDRAL
(☑952 21 59 17; www.malagaturismo.com; Calle Molina Lario; cathedral & museum €5, tower €6; ⊙10am-6pm Mon-Sat) Málaga's cathedral was

SPAIN MÁLAGA

ANDALUCÍA'S QUIETEST BEACHES

The coast east of Almería in eastern Andalucía is perhaps the last section of Spain's Mediterranean coast where you can (sometimes) have a beach to yourself. This is Spain's sunniest region – even in March it can be warm enough to strip off and take in the rays. The best thing about it is the wonderful coastline and semidesert scenery of the Cabo de Gata promontory. All along the 50km coast from El Cabo de Gata village to Agua Amarga, some of the most beautiful beaches on the Mediterranean, from long sandy strands to tiny rock-girt coves, alternate with precipitous cliffs and scattered villages. The main base is laid-back San José, with excellent beaches nearby, such as Playa de los Genoveses, Playa de Mónsul and the four isolated little beaches of the Calas de Barronal. The former gold-mining village of Rodalquilar, a few kilometres inland, is a bit of a boho-chic hideaway.

started in the 16th century on the site of the former mosque. Of the mosque, only the Patio de los Naranjos survives, a small courtyard of fragrant orange trees.

Inside, the fabulous domed ceiling soars 40m into the air, while the vast colonnaded nave houses an enormous cedar-wood choir. Aisles give access to 15 chapels with gorgeous 18th-century retables and religious art. Climb the tower (200 steps) to enjoy stunning panoramic views of the city skyline and coast.

★ Alcazaba   CASTLE
(☑ 630 932987; www.malagaturismo.com; Calle Alcazabilla; €2.20, incl Castillo de Gibralfaro €3.40; ⊙ 9.30am-8pm Tue-Sun) No time to visit Granada's Alhambra? Then Málaga's Alcazaba can provide a taster. The entrance is next to the Roman amphitheatre, from where a meandering path climbs amid lush greenery: crimson bougainvillea, lofty palms, fragrant jasmine bushes and rows of orange trees. Extensively restored, this palace-fortress dates from the 11th-century Moorish period; the caliphal horseshoe arches, courtyards and bubbling fountains are evocative of this influential period in Málaga's history.

★ Centre Pompidou Málaga   MUSEUM
(☑ 951 92 62 00; www.centrepompidou.es; Pasaje Doctor Carrillo Casaux, Muelle Uno; €7, incl temporary exhibition €9; ⊙ 9.30am-8pm Wed-Mon; 🐾) Opened in 2015 in the port, this offshoot of the Paris Pompidou Centre is housed in a low-slung modern building crowned by a playful multicoloured cube. The permanent exhibition includes the extraordinary *Ghost,* by Kader Attia, depicting rows of Muslim women bowed in prayer and created from domestic aluminium foil, plus works by such modern masters as Frida Kahlo, Francis Bacon and Antoni Tàpies. There are also audiovisual installations, talking 'heads' and temporary exhibitions.

Castillo de Gibralfaro   CASTLE
(☑ 952 22 72 30; www.malagaturismo.com; Camino Gibralfaro; €2.20, incl Alcazaba €3.40; ⊙ 9am-9pm Apr-Sep) One remnant of Málaga's Islamic past is the craggy ramparts of the Castillo de Gibralfaro, spectacularly located high on the hill overlooking the city. Built by Abd ar-Rahman I, the 8th-century Cordoban emir, and later rebuilt in the 14th century when Málaga was the main port for the emirate of Granada, the castle originally acted as a lighthouse and military barracks.

Nothing much is original in the castle's interior, but the airy walkway around the ramparts affords the best views over Málaga.

Museo Automovilístico Málaga   MUSEUM
(☑ 951 13 70 01; www.museoautomovilmalaga. com; Avenida Sor Teresa Prat 15; adult/child €7.50/ free; ⊙ 10am-7pm Tue-Sun; 🐾) Petrol heads and fashionistas will love this museum, housed in a former tobacco factory, which combines the history of the automobile with 20th-century fashion from style gurus such as Chanel, Yves Saint Laurent and Dior. Around 85 cars have been immaculately restored, including a Bugatti, a Bentley and a fabulous flower-power-painted Rolls. From Málaga Centre Alameda Principal, take bus 3, 15 or 16 and get off at Avenida La Paloma (€1.35, 10 minutes).

🛏 Sleeping

★ Dulces Dreams   HOSTEL €
(☑ 951 35 78 69; www.dulcesdreamshostel.com; Plaza de los Mártires 6; r incl breakfast €45-60; ❄🐾) Run by an enthusiastic young team, the rooms at Dulces (sweet) Dreams are appropriately named after desserts; 'Cupcake'

is a good choice with its terrace overlooking the imposing red-brick church across the way. This is an older building so there's no lift and the rooms vary in size, but they are bright and whimsically decorated using recycled materials as far as possible.

El Riad Andaluz   GUESTHOUSE €
(☑952 21 36 40; www.elriadandaluz.com; Calle Hinestrosa 24; s/d/tr €45/55/75; ✲@🛜) This French-run guesthouse, in the historic part of town, has eight rooms set around the kind of atmospheric patio that's known as a *riad* in Morocco. The decoration is Moroccan but each room is different, including colourful tiled bathrooms. Breakfast is available.

✗ Eating & Drinking

Málaga has a staggering number of tapas bars and restaurants, particularly around the historic centre (over 400 at last count). One of the city's biggest pleasures is a slow crawl round its numerous tapas bars and old bodegas (cellars). The best bar-hop areas are from Plaza de la Merced in the northeast to Calle Carretería in the northwest, plus Plaza Mitjana and Plaza de Uncibay.

**★El Mesón
de Cervantes**   TAPAS, ARGENTINIAN €€
(☑952 21 62 74; www.elmesondecervantes.com; Calle Álamos 11; mains €13-16; ⊘7pm-midnight Wed-Mon) Cervantes started as a humble tapas bar run by expat Argentinian Gabriel Spatz (the original bar is still operating around the corner), but has expanded into plush spacious digs with an open kitchen, fantastic family-style service and incredible meat dishes.

★Óleo   FUSION €€
(☑952 21 90 62; www.oleorestaurante.es; Edificio CAC, Calle Alemania; mains €12-16; ⊘10am-midnight Mon-Sat; 🛜) Located at the city's contemporary art museum with white-on-white minimalist decor, Óleo provides diners with the unusual choice of Mediterranean or Asian food with some subtle combinations such as duck breast with a side of seaweed with hoisin, as well as more purist Asian and gourmet palate-ticklers such as candied, roasted piglet.

Los Patios de Beatas   WINE BAR
(☑952 21 03 50; www.lospatiosdebeatas.com; Calle Beatas 43; ⊘1-5pm & 8pm-midnight Mon-Sat, 1-6pm Sun; 🛜) Two 18th-century mansions have metamorphosed into this sumptuous

space where you can sample fine wines from a selection reputed to be the most extensive in town. Stained-glass windows and beautiful resin tables inset with mosaics and shells add to the overall art-infused atmosphere. Innovative tapas and *raciones* (full-plate servings) are also served.

☆ Entertainment

Kelipe   FLAMENCO
(☑692 829885; www.kelipe.net; Muro de Puerta Nueva 10; €24-35; ⊘9.30pm show Thu-Sat) Málaga's substantial flamenco heritage has its nexus to the northwest of Plaza de la Merced. This flamenco centre puts on authentic performances Thursday to Saturday at 9.30pm; €24 entry includes two drinks – reserve ahead.

ℹ Information

Municipal Tourist Office (☑951 92 60 20; www.malagaturismo.com; Plaza de la Marina; ⊘9am-8pm Mar-Sep, to 6pm Oct-Feb) Offers a range of city maps and booklets. It also operates information kiosks at the Alcazaba entrance (Calle Alcazabilla), at the main train station (Explanada de la Estación), on Plaza de la Merced and on the eastern beaches (El Palo and La Malagueta).

JAMÓN – A PRIMER

Unlike Italian prosciutto, Spanish *jamón* is a bold, deep red and well marbled with buttery fat. Like wines and olive oil, Spanish *jamón* is subject to a strict series of classifications. *Jamón serrano* refers to *jamón* from white-coated pigs introduced to Spain in the 1950s. Originally it was salted and semidried by the cold, dry winds of the Spanish sierras (mountain ranges), hence the name; most now goes through a similar process of curing and drying in a climate-controlled shed for around a year. *Jamón serrano* accounts for approximately 90% of cured ham in Spain.

Jamón ibérico – more expensive and generally regarded as the elite of Spanish hams – comes from a black-coated pig indigenous to the Iberian Peninsula and a descendant of the wild boar. If the pig gains at least 50% of its body weight during the acorn-eating season, it can be classified as *jamón ibérico de bellota*, the most sought-after designation for *jamón*.

ANDALUCÍA BEYOND THE CITIES

The Andalucian countryside, with its white villages, rugged mountains, winding country roads and appealing small towns, is every bit as magical as the region's famed cities – and packs in huge variety.

On the south flank of the Sierra Nevada (mainland Spain's highest mountain range), the jumble of valleys known as **Las Alpujarras** juxtaposes arid mountainsides and deep ravines with oasis-like, Berber-style villages set amid orchards and woodlands. There's great walking, a unique ambience derived from the area's Moorish past, and plenty of good accommodation in and around scenic villages like **Capileira**, **Ferreirola**, **Trevélez** and **Cádiar**, one to two hours' drive south from Granada.

Further afield, 200km northeast from Granada, the **Parque Natural Sierras de Cazorla, Segura y Las Villas** is 2099 sq km of craggy mountains, remote hilltop castles and deep green river valleys with some of the most abundant and visible wildlife in Spain – including three types of deer, ibex, wild boar, mouflon (a wild sheep), griffon vultures and golden eagles. The picturesque medieval town of **Cazorla** is a great base, and en route you shouldn't miss the gorgeous towns of **Úbeda** and **Baeza**, World Heritage–listed for their outstanding Renaissance architecture.

If you're starting from Seville, it's about an hour's drive west to the vast wetlands of the **Parque Nacional de Doñana**, Western Europe's biggest roadless region, where flocks of flamingos tinge the sky pink, huge herds of deer and boar roam the woodlands, and the iberian lynx fights for survival. Four-hour minibus safaris into the park go from **El Rocío**, **Sanlúcar de Barrameda** and **El Acebuche** visitors centre.

Along back roads between Seville and Málaga, hung from the skies between the spectacular clifftop towns of **Arcos de la Frontera** and **Ronda**, the gorgeously green limestone gorges and crags of the **Sierra de Grazalema** are crisscrossed by beautiful, marked trails between charming white villages such as **Grazalema**, **Benaoján** and **Zahara de la Sierra**.

All these areas have plenty of good accommodation including many charming country guesthouses or small hotels. They can be reached by bus with a bit of effort: a car is the ideal way to get to and around them.

❶ Getting There & Around

AIR

Málaga's **airport** (AGP; ☑ 952 04 88 38; www.aena.es), 9km southwest of the city centre, is the main international gateway to Andalucía, served by top global carriers as well as budget airlines. Buses (€3, 15 minutes) and trains (€1.80, 12 minutes) run every 20 or 30 minutes between airport and city centre.

BUS

Málaga's **bus station** (☑ 952 35 00 61; www.estabus.emtsam.es; Paseo de los Tilos) is 1km southwest of the city centre. Destinations include Seville (€19 to €24, 2¾ hours, six buses daily), Granada (€11 to €14, 1½ to two hours, 18 buses), Córdoba (€12, 2¼ to four hours, five buses) and Ronda (€11, two to three hours, 13 buses).

TRAIN

The main station, **Málaga María Zambrano Train Station** (☑ 902 43 23 43; www.renfe.es; Explanada de la Estación; ⏰ 5am-12.45am), is around the corner from the bus station. The superfast AVE service runs to Madrid (€32 to €134, 2¾ hours, 13 daily). Trains also go to Córdoba (€17 to €41, one hour, 19 daily) and Seville (€24 to €44, two to 2¾ hours, 11 daily).

EXTREMADURA

Cáceres

POP 95,600

Few visitors make it to the region of Extremadura, bordering Portugal, but those who do are rewarded with some true gems of old Spain, especially Roman Mérida and the 16th-century towns of Trujillo and Cáceres. The Ciudad Monumental, Cáceres' old centre, is truly extraordinary. Narrow cobbled streets twist and climb among ancient stone walls lined with palaces and mansions, while the skyline is decorated with turrets, spires, gargoyles and enormous storks' nests. Protected by defensive walls, it has survived almost intact from its 16th-century heyday.

◉ Sights

★ Palacio de los
Golfines de Abajo   HISTORIC BUILDING

(☑ 927 21 80 51; www.palaciogolfinesdeabajo. com; Plaza de los Golfines; tours adult/senior/child €2.50/1.50/free; ⊘ tours hourly 10am-1pm & 5-7pm Tue-Sat, 10am-1pm Sun May-Sep, 4.30-6.30pm Tue-Sat Oct-Apr) The sumptuous home of Cáceres' prominent Golfín family has been beautifully restored. Built piecemeal between the 14th and 20th centuries, it's crammed with historical treasures: original 17th-century tapestries and armoury murals, a 19th-century bust of Alfonso XII, a signed 1485 troops request from the Reyes Católicos (Catholic Monarchs) to their Golfín stewards. But it's the detailed, theatrical tours (Spanish, English, French or Portuguese), through four richly decorated lounges, an extravagant chapel and a fascinating documents room, that make it a standout.

★ Museo de Cáceres   MUSEUM

(☑ 927 01 08 77; www.museodecaceres.gobex.es; Plaza de las Veletas; EU citizens/other free/€1.20; ⊘ 9am-3.30pm & 5-8.30pm Tue-Sat, 10.15am-2.30pm Sun mid-Apr–Sep, 9am-7pm Tue-Sat, 10am-3.30pm Sun Oct–mid-Apr) The excellent Museo de Cáceres, spread across 12 buildings in a 16th-century mansion built over an evocative 12th-century *aljibe* (cistern), is the only surviving element of Cáceres' Moorish castle. The impressive archaeological section includes an elegant stone boar dated to the 4th to 2nd centuries BC, while the equally appealing fine-arts display (behind the main museum; open only in the mornings) showcases works by such greats as Picasso, Miró, Tàpies and El Greco.

⌇ Sleeping & Eating

★ Hotel Casa
Don Fernando   BOUTIQUE HOTEL €€

(☑ 927 21 42 79, 927 62 71 76; www.casadonfernando. com; Plaza Mayor 30; s €55-75, d €63-85; 🅿 ❋ 🛜) Cáceres' smartest midrange choice sits on Plaza Mayor right opposite the Arco de la Estrella. Boutique-style rooms, spread over four floors, are tastefully modern, with gleaming bathrooms through glass doors. Pricier 'superiors' enjoy the best plaza views (though weekend nights can be noisy), and attic-style top-floor rooms are good for families. Service hits that perfect professional-yet-friendly note.

★ La Cacharrería   TAPAS €€

(☑ 927 03 07 23; lacacharreria@live.com; Calle de Orellana 1; tapas €4.50, raciones €10-14.50; ⊘ restaurant 12.30-4pm & 8.30-midnight Thu-Mon, cafe 4pm-1.30am Thu-Sat, 4-11pm Sun; 🖉) Local flavours and ingredients combine in exquisite, international-inspired concoctions at this packed-out, minimalist-design tapas bar tucked into an old-town house. *Solomillo* (tenderloin) in Torta del Casar cheese arrives in martini glasses. Delicious guacamole, hummus, falafel and 'salsiki' are a godsend for vegetarians. No advance reservations: get here by 1.45pm or 8.30pm.

❶ Information

Oficina de Turismo Regional (☑ 927 25 55 97; www.turismocaceres.org; Palacio Carvajal, Calle Amargura 1; ⊘ 8am-8.45pm Mon-Fri, 10am-1.45pm & 5-7.45pm Sat, 10am-1.45pm Sun) Covers Cáceres city and province; very helpful.

❶ Getting There & Away

BUS

The **bus station** (☑ 927 23 25 50; www. estacionautobuses.es; Calle Túnez 1; ⊘ 6.30am-10.30pm) has services to Madrid (€25, four hours, seven daily), Seville (€20, 3¾ hours, six daily), Salamanca (€16, three hours, seven daily) and Trujillo (€3.66, 40 minutes, six daily).

TRAIN

Trains run to Madrid (€28 to €33, four hours, five daily), Mérida (€6.10, one hour, six daily) and Seville (€27, 4¾ hours, 6.50am).

SURVIVAL GUIDE

❶ Directory A–Z

ACCOMMODATION

Budget options range from backpacker hostels to family-style *pensiones* and slightly better-heeled *hostales*. At the upper end of this category you'll find rooms with air-conditioning and private bathrooms. Midrange *hostales* and hotels are more comfortable and most offer standard hotel services. Business hotels, trendy boutique hotels and luxury hotels are usually in the top-end category.

Camping

Spain has around 1000 officially graded *campings* (camping grounds) and they vary greatly in service, location, cleanliness and style. They're officially rated as 1st class (1ªC), 2nd class (2ªC)

SPAIN CÁCERES

SLEEPING PRICE RANGES

The following price brackets refer to a double room with private bathroom:

€ less than €65

€€ €65–€140

€€€ more than €140

The price ranges for Madrid and Barcelona are inevitably higher:

€ less than €75

€€ €75–€200

€€€ more than €200

or 3rd class (3ªC). Camping grounds usually charge per person, per tent and per vehicle – typically €5 to €10 for each. Many camping grounds close from around October to Easter.

Campings Online (www.campingsonline.com/espana) Booking service.

Guía Camping (www.guiacampingfecc.com) Online version of the annual *Guía Camping* (€14), which is available in bookshops around the country.

Hotels, Hostales & Pensiones

Most accommodation options fall into the categories of hotels (one to five stars; full amenities, everything from classic luxury to designer to boutique to family-run), *hostales* (high-end guesthouses with private bathroom; one to three stars) or *pensiones* (guesthouses, usually with shared bathroom; one to three stars). The **paradores** (☑ in Spain 902 54 79 79; www.parador.es) are a state-funded chain of luxury hotels often in historical monuments (castles, monasteries...) and/or stunning locations.

Hostels

Spain has a good supply of international backpacker hostels, often with private rooms as well as dorms, in addition to the 250 or so hostels of the **Red Española de Albergues Juveniles** (www.reaj.com), Spain's Hostelling International (HI) organisation. The latter can be heavily booked with school groups and may have curfews.

Typical dorm rates are between €15 and €25. A good resource is Hostel World (www.hostelworld.com).

Seasons & Reservations

Most of the year is high season in Barcelona and Madrid. July and August can be dead in the cities, but are high season along the coasts. Spring, early summer and autumn are high season in some inland areas. Reserving a room is always recommended in high season.

ACTIVITIES

Hiking

➺ Top walking areas include the Pyrenees, Picos de Europa, Las Alpujarras (Andalucía) and the Galician coast.

➺ Best season is June to September in most areas, but April to June and September–October in most of Andalucía.

➺ Region-specific walking guides are published by Cicerone Press (www.cicerone.co.uk).

➺ GR (*Gran Recorrido;* long distance) trails are indicated with red-and-white markers; PR (*Pequeño Recorrido;* short distance) trails have yellow-and-white markers.

➺ Good hiking maps are published by Prames (www.prames.com), Editorial Alpina (www.editorialalpina.com) and the Institut Cartogràfic de Catalunya (www.icgc.cat).

➺ The Camino de Santiago pilgrim route to Santiago de Compostela has many variations starting from all over Spain (and other countries). Most popular is the Camino Francés, running 783km from Roncesvalles, on Spain's border with France. Good websites: Caminolinks (www.santiago-compostela.net/caminos), Mundicamino (www.mundicamino.com), Camino de Santiago (www.caminodesantiago.me).

Skiing

Skiing is cheaper but less varied than in much of the rest of Europe. The season runs from December to mid-April. The best resorts are in the Pyrenees, especially in northwest Catalonia and in Aragón. The Sierra Nevada in Andalucía offers the most southerly skiing in Western Europe.

Surfing, Windsurfing & Kitesurfing

The Basque Country has good surf spots, including San Sebastián, Zarautz and the legendary left at Mundaka. Tarifa in Andalucía, with its long beaches and ceaseless wind, is generally considered to be the kitesurfing and windsurfing capital of Europe.

GAY & LESBIAN TRAVELLERS

Homosexuality is legal in Spain. Same-sex marriages were legalised in 2005. Madrid, Barcelona, Sitges, Torremolinos and Ibiza have particularly active and lively gay scenes. Gay Iberia (www.gayiberia.com) has gay guides to the main destinations.

INTERNET ACCESS

➺ Wi-fi is available at most hotels and in some cafes, restaurants and airports; generally (but not always) free.

INTERNET RESOURCES

Fiestas.net (www.fiestas.net) Festivals around the country.

Lonely Planet (www.lonelyplanet.com/spain) Destination information, hotel bookings, traveller forums and more.

Renfe (Red Nacional de los Ferrocarriles Españoles; www.renfe.com) Spain's rail network.

Turespaña (www.spain.info) Spanish tourist office's site.

Oh Hello, Spain (www.ohhellospain.blogspot.co.uk) English-language blog, aimed at youngish travellers.

MONEY

➡ Many credit and debit cards can be used for withdrawing money from *cajeros automáticos* (ATMs) and for making purchases. The most widely accepted cards are Visa and Master-Card.

➡ Most banks will exchange major foreign currencies and offer the best rates. Ask about commissions and take your passport.

➡ Exchange offices, indicated by the word *cambio* (exchange), offer longer opening hours than banks, but worse exchange rates and higher commissions.

➡ Value-added tax (VAT) is known as IVA *(impuesto sobre el valor añadido)*. Non-EU residents are entitled to a refund of the 21% IVA on purchases costing more than €90.16 from any shop if they are taking them out of the EU within three months.

➡ Menu prices include a service charge. Most people leave some small change. Taxi drivers don't have to be tipped but a little rounding up won't go amiss.

OPENING HOURS

Banks 8.30am to 2pm Monday to Friday; some also open 4pm to 7pm Thursday and 9am to 1pm Saturday

Central post offices 8.30am to 9.30pm Monday to Friday, 8.30am to 2pm Saturday

Nightclubs midnight or 1am to 5am or 6am

Restaurants lunch 1pm to 4pm, dinner 8.30pm to midnight or later

Shops 10am to 2pm and 4.30pm to 7.30pm or 5pm to 8pm Monday to Saturday; big supermarkets and department stores generally open from 9am or 10am to 9pm or 10pm Monday to Saturday

PUBLIC HOLIDAYS

The two main periods when Spaniards go on holiday are Semana Santa (the week leading up to Easter Sunday) and July or August. At these times accommodation can be scarce and transport heavily booked.

Everywhere in Spain has 14 official holidays a year, some observed nationwide, others just locally. The following are commonly observed nationwide:

Año Nuevo (New Year's Day) 1 January

Epifanía (Epiphany) or **Día de los Reyes Magos** (Three Kings' Day) **6 January**

Jueves Santo (Holy Thursday) March/April (not observed in Catalonia)

Viernes Santo (Good Friday) March/April

Fiesta del Trabajo (Labour Day) 1 May

La Asunción (Feast of the Assumption) 15 August

Fiesta Nacional de España (National Day) 12 October

Todos los Santos (All Saints' Day) 1 November

Día de la Constitución (Constitution Day) 6 December

La Inmaculada Concepción (Feast of the Immaculate Conception) 8 December

Navidad (Christmas) 25 December

The following are observed in many regions and localities:

Lunes de Pascua (Easter Monday) March/April

Día de San José (St Joseph's Day) 19 March

Día de San Juan Bautista (Feast of St John the Baptist) 24 June

Día de Santiago Apóstol (Feast of St James the Apostle) 25 July

SAFE TRAVEL

Most visitors to Spain never feel remotely threatened, but you should be aware of the possibility of petty theft (which may of course not seem so petty if your passport, cash, credit card and phone go missing). Stay alert and you can avoid most thievery techniques. Barcelona, Madrid and Seville are the worst offenders, as are popular beaches in summer (never leave belongings unattended).

TELEPHONE

The once widespread, but now fast disappearing, blue payphones accept coins, *tarjetas telefónicas* (phonecards) issued by the national phone company Telefónica and, in some

SPAIN DIRECTORY A–Z

COUNTRY FACTS

Area 505,370 sq km

Capital Madrid

Country Code 📞 34

Currency Euro (€)

Emergency 📞 112

Languages Spanish (Castilian), Catalan, Basque, Galician (Gallego)

Money ATMs everywhere

Population 48 million

Visas Schengen rules apply

ESSENTIAL FOOD & DRINK

Paella This signature rice dish comes in infinite varieties, although Valencia is its true home.

Cured meats Wafer-thin slices of *chorizo*, *lomo*, *salchichón* and *jamón serrano* appear on most Spanish tables.

Tapas These bite-sized morsels range from uncomplicated Spanish staples to pure gastronomic innovation.

Olive oil Spain is the world's largest producer of olive oil.

Wine Spain has the largest area of wine cultivation in the world. La Rioja and Ribera del Duero are the best-known wine-growing regions.

Seafood Plentiful everywhere and best in Galicia at Spain's northwest corner.

cases, various credit cards. Calling from your smartphone, tablet or computer using an internet-based service such as Skype or FaceTime is generally the cheapest and easiest option.

Mobile Phones

Local SIM cards are widely available and can be used in unblocked European and Australian mobile phones but are not compatible with many North American or Japanese systems. The Spanish mobile-phone companies (Telefónica's MoviStar, Orange and Vodafone) offer *prepagado* (prepaid) accounts for mobiles. The SIM card costs from €10, to which you add some prepaid phone time.

Phone Codes

Spain has no area codes. All numbers are nine digits and you just dial that nine-digit number.

Numbers starting with ☎900 are national toll-free numbers, while those starting with ☎901 to ☎905 come with varying costs; most can only be dialled from within Spain.

TOURIST INFORMATION

Most towns and large villages of any interest have a helpful *oficina de turismo* (tourist office) where you can get maps and brochures.

Turespaña (www.spain.info) is the country's national tourism body.

VISAS

Spain is one of 26 member countries of the Schengen Convention and Schengen visa rules apply.

Citizens or residents of EU & Schengen countries No visa required.

Citizens or residents of Australia, Canada, Israel, Japan, NZ and the USA No visa required for tourist visits of up to 90 days.

Other countries Check with a Spanish embassy or consulate.

To work or study in Spain A special visa may be required – contact a Spanish embassy or consulate before travel.

ⓘ Getting There & Away

Flights, cars and tours can be booked online at lonelyplanet.com/bookings.

ENTERING THE COUNTRY

Immigration and customs checks usually involve a minimum of fuss, although there are exceptions. Your vehicle could be searched on arrival from Morocco; they're looking for controlled substances. Expect long delays at these borders, especially in summer.

The tiny principality of Andorra is not in the EU, so border controls (and rigorous customs checks for contraband) remain in place.

AIR

Flights from all over Europe (including numerous budget airlines), plus direct flights from North and South America, Africa, the Middle East and Asia, serve main Spanish airports. All of Spain's airports share the user-friendly website and flight information telephone number of **Aena** (☎91 321 10 00, 902 404 704; www.aena.es), the national airports authority. Each airport's page on the website has details on practical information (such as parking and public transport) and a list of (and links to) airlines using that airport.

Madrid's Aeropuerto de Barajas is Europe's sixth-busiest airport. Other major airports include Barcelona's Aeroport del Prat and the airports of Palma de Mallorca, Málaga, Alicante, Ibiza, Valencia, Seville, Bilbao, Menorca and Santiago de Compostela.

LAND

Spain shares land borders with France, Portugal and Andorra.

Bus

Aside from the main cross-border routes, numerous smaller services criss-cross Spain's borders with France and Portugal. Regular buses connect Andorra with Barcelona (including winter ski buses and direct services to the airport) and other destinations in Spain (including Madrid) and France.

Eurolines (www.eurolines.com) is the main operator of international bus services to Spain from most of Western Europe and Morocco. Services from France include Nice to Madrid, and Paris to Barcelona.

Avanza (www.avanzabus.com) runs three buses daily each way between Lisbon and Madrid (€41, 8½ hours).

Train

France to Barcelona A high-speed service runs from Paris' Gare de Lyon (from €59, 6½ hours, two daily) via Nimes, Montpellier, Perpignan, Figueres and Girona. High-speed services also run from Toulouse (from €35, 3¼ hours), Lyon (from €44, five hours) and Marseille (from €39, five hours).

France to Madrid You can take a high-speed train to Barcelona and change there to a Spanish high-speed AVE (total fare from €144, 9¾ hours). Or take a high-speed train from Paris-Montparnasse to Hendaye, walk across the border to Irún and board a Spanish train there (total fare from €68, 15 hours). High-speed service runs from Marseille to Madrid (from €59, 7¾ hours).

Lisbon to Madrid (seat/sleeper from €24/34, 10 hours, 9.30pm) via Salamanca and Ávila.

Lisbon to Irún (seat/sleeper from €28/38, 13 hours, 9.30pm)

Porto to Vigo (€15, 2½ hours, two daily)

SEA

Trasmediterranea (www.trasmediterranea.es) Many Mediterranean ferry services are run by the Spanish company Trasmediterranea.

Brittany Ferries (www.brittany-ferries.co.uk) Services between Spain and the UK.

Grandi Navi Veloci (www1.gnv.it) High-speed luxury ferries between Barcelona and Genoa.

Grimaldi Lines (www.grimaldi-lines.com) Barcelona to Civitavecchia (near Rome), Savona (near Genoa) and Porto Torres (northwest Sardinia).

ℹ Getting Around

Students and seniors are eligible for discounts of 30% to 50% on most types of transport within Spain.

AIR

Air Europa (www.aireuropa.com) Madrid to Ibiza, Palma de Mallorca, Málaga, Bilbao, Barcelona and Vigo as well as other routes between Spanish cities.

Iberia (www.iberia.com) Spain's national airline has an extensive domestic network.

Ryanair (www.ryanair.com) Extensive Spanish network including to Santiago de Compostela and Ibiza from Barcelona, Madrid, Málaga and Seville, and to Barcelona from Seville and Málaga.

Volotea (www.volotea.com) Budget airline with domestic routes taking in Alicante, Bilbao, Ibiza, Málaga, Maó, Oviedo, Palma de Mallorca, Santander, Valencia and Zaragoza (but not Madrid or Barcelona).

Vueling (www.vueling.com) Spanish low-cost company with loads of domestic flights, especially from Barcelona.

BOAT

Regular ferries connect the Spanish mainland with the Balearic Islands.

BUS

Spain's bus network is operated by countless independent companies and reaches into the most remote towns and villages. Many towns and cities have one main bus station where most buses arrive and depart.

It is not necessary, and often not possible, to make advance reservations for local bus journeys. It is, however, a good idea to turn up at least 30 minutes before the bus leaves to guarantee a seat. For longer trips, you can and should buy your ticket in advance.

ALSA Countrywide bus network.

CONNECTIONS

Spanish airports are among Europe's best connected, while the typical overland route leads many travellers from France over or round the Pyrenees into Spain. Numerous roads and the Madrid–Lisbon rail line connect Spain with Portugal.

The most obvious sea journeys lead across the Strait of Gibraltar to Morocco. The most common routes connect Algeciras or Tarifa with Tangier, from where there's plenty of transport deeper into Morocco. Car ferries also connect Barcelona with Italian ports, and the northern ports of Santander and Bilbao with the UK.

There are two main rail lines to Spain from Paris: a high-speed route to Barcelona (with direct trains taking 6½ hours), and another to Madrid and the north via the Basque Country, requiring a change of trains at the border.

Avanza Buses from Madrid to Extremadura, western Castilla y León and Valencia.

Socibus Services between Madrid and western Andalucía including Seville.

CAR & MOTORCYCLE

Spain's roads vary enormously but are generally good. Fastest are the *autopistas;* on some, you have to pay hefty tolls.

Every vehicle should display a nationality plate of its country of registration and you must always carry proof of ownership of a private vehicle. Third-party motor insurance is required throughout Europe. A warning triangle and a reflective jacket (to be used in case of breakdown) are compulsory.

Driving Licences

All EU member states' driving licences are recognised. Other foreign licences should be accompanied by an International Driving Permit (although in practice local licences are usually accepted). These are available from automobile clubs in your country and valid for 12 months.

Hire

To rent a car in Spain you have to have a licence, be aged 21 or over and have a credit or debit card. Rates vary widely: the best deals tend to be in major tourist areas, including airports. Prices are especially competitive in the Balearic Islands.

Road Rules

➡ The blood-alcohol limit is 0.05%.

➡ The legal driving age for cars is 18. The legal driving age for motorcycles and scooters is

---

FERRIES TO SPAIN

A useful website for comparing routes and finding links to the relevant ferry companies is www.ferrylines.com.

From Algeria

ROUTE	DURATION	FREQUENCY
Ghazaouet to Almería	9hr	2-3 weekly

From Italy

ROUTE	DURATION	FREQUENCY
Genoa to Barcelona	18hr	1-2 weekly
Civitavecchia (near Rome) to Barcelona	20hr	6 weekly
Porto Torres (Sardinia) to Barcelona	12hr	5 weekly
Savona (near Genoa) to Barcelona	20hr	2 weekly

From Morocco

ROUTE	DURATION	FREQUENCY
Tangier to Algeciras	1-2hr	15 or more daily
Tangier to Barcelona	27-33hr	2-3 weekly
Tangier to Tarifa	35–60min	13 or more daily
Nador to Almería	6hr	2-3 daily

From the UK

ROUTE	DURATION	FREQUENCY
Plymouth to Santander	21hr	weekly Apr-Oct
Portsmouth to Santander	24hr	1-2 weekly
Portsmouth to Bilbao	24hr	2-3 weekly

16 (80cc and over) or 14 (50cc and under). A licence is required.

⇒ Motorcyclists must use headlights at all times and wear a helmet if riding a bike of 125cc or more.

⇒ Drive on the right.

⇒ In built-up areas, the speed limit is 50km/h (and in some cases, such as inner-city Barcelona, 30km/h), which increases to 100km/h on major roads and up to 120km/h on *autovías* and *autopistas* (toll-free and tolled dual-lane highways, respectively). Cars towing caravans are restricted to a maximum speed of 80km/h.

TRAIN

The national railway company is **Renfe** (☏ 902 243 402; www.renfe.com). Trains are mostly modern and comfortable, and late arrivals are the exception. The high-speed network is in constant expansion.

Passes are valid for all long-distance Renfe trains; Inter-Rail users pay supplements on Talgo, InterCity and AVE trains. All pass-holders making reservations pay a small fee.

Among Spain's numerous types of train:

Altaria, Alvia and Avant Long- and medium-distance intermediate-speed services.

AVE (Tren de Alta Velocidad Española) High-speed trains that link Madrid with Alicante, Barcelona, Córdoba, Cuenca, Huesca, León, Lleida, Málaga, Segovia, Seville, Tarragona, Valencia, Valladolid and Zaragoza. There are also Barcelona–Seville, Barcelona–Málaga and Valencia–Seville services. In coming years Madrid–Granada, Madrid–Cádiz and Madrid–Bilbao should come on line.

Cercanías For short hops and services to outlying suburbs and satellite towns of Madrid, Barcelona and 12 other cities.

Euromed Similar to AVE trains, they connect Barcelona with Valencia and Alicante.

Regionales Trains operating within one region, usually stopping at all stations.

Talgo Slower long-distance trains.

Trenhotel Overnight trains with sleeper berths, operating to Galicia from Madrid and Barcelona.

Classes & Costs

⇒ Fares vary enormously depending on the service (faster trains cost considerably more) and, for many long-distance trains, on the time and day of travel and how far ahead you book (the earlier the better).

⇒ Long-distance trains have 2nd and 1st classes, known as *turista* and *preferente*, respectively. The latter is 20% to 40% more expensive.

⇒ Children aged between four and 14 years are entitled to a 40% discount; those aged under four travel for free (but on long- and medium-distance trains only if they share a seat with a fare-paying passenger). Buying a return ticket gives a 20% discount on most long- and medium-distance trains. Students and people up to 25 years of age with a Euro<26 or GO 25 card are entitled to 20% off most ticket prices.

Reservations

Reservations are recommended for long-distance trips, and you can make them in train stations, **Renfe** offices and travel agencies, as well as online. In a growing number of stations, you can pick up prebooked tickets from machines scattered about the station concourse.

SPAIN GETTING AROUND

Sweden

Best Places to Eat

➜ Woodstockholm (p1105)

➜ Camp Ripan Restaurang (p1119)

➜ Mrs Saigon (p1110)

➜ Thörnströms Kök (p1114)

Best Places to Stay

➜ Rival Hotel (p1104)

➜ Mäster Johan Hotel (p1109)

➜ Icehotel (p1118)

➜ STF Göteborg City (p1112)

Why Go?

As progressive and civilised as it may be, Sweden is a wild place. Its scenery ranges from barren moonscapes and impenetrable forests in the far north to sunny beaches and lush farmland further south. Its short summers and long winters mean that people cling to every last speck of summer sunshine, while in winter locals rely on candlelight and *glögg* (mulled wine) to warm their spirits. But lovers of the outdoors will thrive here in any season: winter sees skiing and dog-sledding, while the warmer months invite long hikes, swimming and sunbathing, canoeing, cycling, you name it – if it's fun and can be done outdoors, you'll find it here. For less rugged types, there's always restaurant- and nightclub-hopping and museum-perusing in cosmopolitan Stockholm, lively Göteborg and beyond.

When to Go
Stockholm

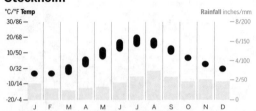

Mar There's still plenty of snow, but enough daylight to enjoy winter sports.

Jun–Aug Swedish summers are short but intense, and the White Nights beyond the Arctic Circle are magical.

Sep The stunning colours of the autumn season make this prime hiking time up north.

STOCKHOLM

📋 08 / POP 910,000

Beautiful capital cities are no rarity in Europe, but Stockholm is near the top of the list for sheer loveliness. The saffron-and-cinnamon buildings that cover its 14 islands rise starkly out of the surrounding ice-blue water, honeyed in sunlight and frostily elegant in cold weather. The city's charms are irresistible. From its movie-set Old Town (Gamla Stan) to its ever-modern fashion sense and impeccable taste in food and design, the city acts like an immersion school in aesthetics.

◎ Sights

Once you get over the armies of tourists wielding ice-cream cones and shopping bags, you'll discover that Gamla Stan, the oldest part of Stockholm, is also its most beautiful. The city emerged on this tiny island in the 13th century.

★Kungliga Slottet   PALACE

(Royal Palace; 📋 08-402 61 30; www.theroyalpalace. se; Slottsbacken; adult/child Skr160/80; guided tour in English Skr20; ⏰ 8.30am-5pm Jul & Aug, 10am-5pm May-Jun & Sep, shorter hours rest of year; 🚌 2 Slottsbacken, Ⓜ Gamla Stan) Kungliga Slottet was built on the ruins of Tre Kronor castle, which burned down in 1697. The north wing survived and was incorporated into the new building. Designed by court architect Nicodemus Tessin the Younger, it took 57 years to complete. Highlights include the decadent Karl XI Gallery, inspired by Versailles' Hall of Mirrors, and Queen Kristina's silver throne in the Hall of State.

★Vasamuseet   MUSEUM

(www.vasamuseet.se; Galärvarvsvägen 14; adult/child Skr130/free; ⏰ 8.30am-6pm Jun-Aug, 10am-5pm Sep-May; 🅿 🚻; 🚌 67) A good-humoured glorification of some dodgy calculations, Vasamuseet is the custom-built home of the massive warship *Vasa*; 69m long and 48.8m tall, it was the pride of the Swedish crown when it set off on its maiden voyage on 10 August 1628. Within minutes, the top-heavy vessel tipped and sank to the bottom of Saltsjön, along with many of the people on board.

Tour guides explain the extraordinary and controversial 300-year story of its death and resurrection, which saw the ship painstakingly raised in 1961 and reassembled like a giant 14,000-piece jigsaw. Almost all of what you see today is original.

On the entrance level is a model of the ship at scale 1:10 and a cinema screening a 25-minute film (in English at 9.30am and 1.30pm daily in summer) covering topics not included in the exhibitions. There are four other levels of exhibits covering artefacts salvaged from the *Vasa*, life on board, naval warfare, and 17th-century sailing and navigation, plus sculptures and temporary exhibitions. The bottom-floor exhibition is particularly fascinating, using modern forensic science to recreate the faces and life stories of several of the ill-fated passengers.

Guided tours are in English every 30 minutes in summer, less frequently the rest of the year.

★Historiska Museet   MUSEUM

(📋 08-51 95 56 20; www.historiska.se; Narvavägen 13-17; ⏰ 11am-6pm Jun-Sep, to 8pm Wed Sep, shorter hours rest of year; Ⓜ Karlaplan | Östermalmstorg, 🚌 Djurgårdsbron-sillalle) FREE The national historical collection awaits at this enthralling museum. From Iron Age skates and a Viking boat to medieval textiles and Renaissance triptychs, it spans over 10,000 years of Swedish culture and history. There's an exhibit about the medieval Battle of Gotland (1361), an excellent multimedia display on the Vikings, a room of breathtaking altarpieces from the Middle Ages, a vast textile collection and a section on prehistoric culture.

An undisputed highlight is the subterranean Gold Room, a dimly lit chamber gleaming with Viking plunder and other treasures, including the jewel-encrusted Reliquary of St Elisabeth (who died at 24 and was canonised in 1235). The most astonishing artefact, however, is the 5th-century seven-ringed gold collar discovered in Västergötland in the 19th century. Weighing 823g, it is decorated with 458 symbolic figures.

Moderna Museet   MUSEUM

(📋 08-52 02 35 00; www.modernamuseet.se; Exercisplan 4; ⏰ 10am-8pm Tue & Fri, to 6pm Wed-Thu, to 5pm Sat & Sun; 🅿 🛜; 🚌 65, ⛴ Djurgårdsfärjan) FREE Moderna Museet is Stockholm's modern-art maverick, its permanent collection ranging from paintings and sculptures to photography, video art and installations. Highlights include works by Pablo Picasso, Salvador Dalí, Andy Warhol, Damien Hirst and Robert Rauschenberg. There are important pieces by Francis Bacon, Marcel Duchamp and Matisse, as well as their Scandinavian contemporaries, plus work by lesser known contemporary artists.

Sweden
Highlights

① Icehotel
(p1118) Hiking wild reindeer-filled landscapes, exploring Sami culture and sleeping in the world-famous Icehotel in Jukkasjärvi.

② Stockholm
(p1099) Touring urban waterways, exploring top-notch museums and wandering the labyrinthine Old Town in the capital city.

③ Malmö (p1109) Heading south to this beautiful city for edgy museums, good food and a dynamic, multicultural vibe.

Nobelmuseet MUSEUM

(☑08-54 43 18 00; www.nobelmuseet.se; Stortorget; adult/child Skr100/free; ☉9am-8pm Jun-Aug, shorter hours rest of year; ☐53, Ⓜ Gamla Stan) Nobelmuseet presents the history of the Nobel Prizes and their recipients, with a focus on the intellectual and cultural aspects of invention. It's a slick space with fascinating displays, including short films on the theme of creativity, interviews with laureates like Ernest Hemingway and Martin Luther King, and cafe chairs signed by the visiting prize recipients (flip them over to see!).

Skansen MUSEUM

(www.skansen.se; Djurgårdsvägen; adult/child Skr180/60; ☉10am-4pm, extended hours in summer; Ⓟ 🚻; ☐69, 🛳 Djurgårdsfärjan) The world's first open-air museum, Skansen was founded in 1891 by Artur Hazelius to provide an insight into how Swedes once lived. You could easily spend a day here and not see it all. Around 150 traditional houses and other exhibits dot the hilltop – it's meant to be 'Sweden in miniature', complete with villages, nature, commerce and industry. Note that prices and opening hours vary seasonally; check the website before you go.

🏃 Activities

Sjöcaféet CYCLING

(☑08-660 57 57; www.sjocafeet.se; Djurgårdsvägen 2; bicycles per hr/day Skr80/275, canoes Skr150/400, kayaks Skr125/400; ☉9am-9pm Apr-Sep; 🚻; ☐7) Rent bicycles from the small wooden hut below this huge restaurant, cafe and cocktail bar-cum-tourist-info centre beside Djurgårdsbron; it also offers canoes and kayaks for hire.

🛌 Sleeping

Expect high-quality accommodation in Stockholm, although it can be expensive. Major hotel chains are invariably cheaper booked online and in advance. A number of services, including **Guestroom B&B** (☑070- 206 71 69; www.gastrummet.com/eng/; Magnus Ladulåsgatan 9; ☉9am-7pm Mon-Fri, to 1pm Sat) and **c/o Stockholm** (www.costockholm.com) can arrange apartment or B&B accommodation from around Skr400 per person per night.

Stockholm's Svenska Turistföreningen (STF) hostels are affiliated with Hostelling International (HI); a membership card yields a Skr50 discount. Many have options for single, double or family rooms.

★ Vandrarhem af Chapman & Skeppsholmen HOSTEL €

(☑08-463 22 66; www.stfchapman.com; Flaggmansvägen 8; dm/r from Skr375/840; ☉@🛜; ☐65 Skeppsholmen) The *af Chapman* is a storied vessel that has done plenty of travelling of its own. It's anchored in a superb location, swaying gently off Skeppsholmen. Bunks are in dorms below deck. Apart from showers and toilets, all facilities are on dry land in the Skeppsholmen hostel, including a good kitchen, a laid-back common room and a TV lounge.

Hotel Tegnérlunden HOTEL €€

(☑08-54 54 55 50; www.hoteltegnerlunden.se; Tegnérlunden 8, Norrmalm; s/d Skr865/1025; Ⓟ ❄🛜; ☐69, Ⓜ T-Centralen) This chic small hotel enjoys a choice location, overlooking the leafy Tegnérlunden park and near the vibrant Drottningatan pedestrian shopping street. Rooms are tight on space but are an excellent example of efficient Swedish design with swivel bedside lamps, decent work desks, comfy armchairs, full-length mirrors and slick black-and-white decor. The 6th-floor breakfast room offers sweeping panoramic views.

Hotel Hellsten HOTEL €€

(☑08-661 86 00; www.hellsten.se; Luntmakargatan 68, Vasatan; s/d from Skr1090/1400; Ⓟ ❄@🛜; Ⓜ Rådmansgatan) Hip Hellsten is owned by anthropologist Per Hellsten, whose touch is evident in the rooms and common areas, which are furnished and decorated with objects from his travels and life, including Congan tribal masks and his grandmother's chandelier. Rooms are comfortable and individually styled, but do vary considerably in size. Themes range from rustic Swedish to Indian exotica, with some rooms even featuring original tile stoves.

Hotel Anno 1647 HISTORIC HOTEL €€

(☑08-442 16 80; www.anno1647.se; Mariagränd 3; s/d economy from Skr925/970, standard from Skr1500/1700; Ⓟ☉@🛜; Ⓜ Slussen) Just off buzzing Götgatan, with many rooms overlooking the colourful roofs of Gamla Stan, this historical hotel in two beautiful buildings has labyrinthine hallways, gorgeous wooden floors and spiral staircases, plus affable staff. The economy rooms are swing-a-cat size, while the most expensive have antique rococo wallpaper, all modern amenities and the occasional chandelier.

Stockholm

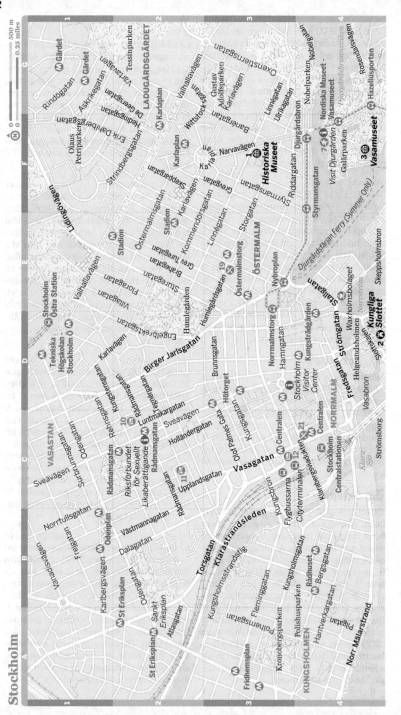

500 m
0.25 miles

Stockholm

Nordic 'C' Hotel
HOTEL €€

(☑ 08-50 56 30 00; www.nordicchotel.com; Vasaplan 4; s/d from Skr795/850; ❂❄@❂; Ⓜ T-Centralen) A fantastic deal if you time it right and book ahead, this sister hotel to the slightly more upmarket Nordic Light has smallish but sleek rooms, great service and a cool lobby lounge area. The cheapest rooms are windowless and tiny but efficiently designed and totally comfortable. One of the two hotel bars is the famous Icebar (p1106).

The breakfast buffet is enormous. The Arlanda Express (p1107) is just steps from the lobby, and you can buy tickets at the front desk.

★ Rival Hotel
HOTEL €€€

(☑ 08-54 57 89 00; www.rival.se; Mariatorget 3; s/d from Skr2695/2895; ❂❄@❂; Ⓜ Mariatorget) Owned by ABBA's Benny Andersson and overlooking leafy Mariatorget, this ravishing design hotel is a chic retro gem, complete with vintage 1940s movie theatre and art deco cocktail bar. The super-comfy rooms feature posters from great Swedish films and a teddy bear to make you feel at home. All rooms have luxurious, well-equipped bathrooms.

✗ Eating

Stockholm is a city of foodies. The city has more than half a dozen Michelin-starred restaurants. Its epicurean highlights don't come cheap, but you can find great value in the abundant cafes, coffee shops and vegetarian buffets.

Hälsocafet
VEGAN €

(☑ 08-42 05 65 44; www.halsocafet.se; Hornsgatan 61; meals Skr55-105; ⊙9am-7pm Mon-Fri, 10am-7pm Sat & Sun; Ⓜ Mariatorget) ✐ Taking an imaginative twist on modern classics, Hälsocafet delivers exciting, healthy, ethical food, with a focus on ecological and vegan-friendly products. Salads, cakes, coffee and smoothies are all served up by friendly staff in a warm and relaxed atmosphere. Perfect for lunch, a coffee or simply to indulge your sweet tooth while keeping a clean conscience.

Chokladkoppen
CAFE €

(www.chokladkoppen.se; Stortorget 18; cakes Skr40-80; ⊙9am-11pm Jun-Aug, shorter hours rest of year; ❂; Ⓜ Gamla Stan) Arguably Stockholm's best-loved cafe, hole-in-the-wall Chokladkoppen sits slap bang on Gamla Stan's enchanting main square. It's an atmospheric spot with a sprawling terrace and pocket-sized interior with low beamed ceilings, custard-coloured walls and edgy artwork. The menu includes savoury treats like broccoli-and-blue-cheese pie and scrumptious cakes.

★ Hermitage
VEGETARIAN €€

(www.hermitage.gastrogate.com; Stora Nygatan 11; buffet lunch/dinner Skr120/130; ⊙11am-8pm Mon-Fri, noon-8pm Sat & Sun, to 9pm Jun-Aug; ☑; Ⓜ Gamla Stan) Herbivores love Hermitage for its simple, tasty, vegetarian buffet, easily one of the best bargains in Gamla Stan. Salad, homemade bread, tea and coffee are included in the price. Pro tip: don't miss the drawers of hot food hiding under the main buffet tabletop. Vegan fare also available.

Under Kastanjen
SWEDISH €€

(🖉08-21 50 04; www.underkastanjen.se; Kindstugatan 1, Gamla Stan; mains Skr200-280; ⊙8am-10pm Mon-Fri, from 9am Sat, 9am-7pm Sun; 🛜; Ⓜ Gamla Stan) This has to be just about the most picturesque corner of Gamla Stan, with tables set on a cobbled square under a beautiful chestnut tree surrounded by storybook-style houses in shades of ochre and yellow. Enjoy classic Swedish dishes like homemade meatballs with mashed potato; the downstairs wine bar has a veritable Spanish bodega feel with its whitewashed brick arches and moody lighting.

Lisa Elmqvist
SEAFOOD €€

(🖉08-55 34 04 10; www.lisaelmqvist.se; Östermalmstorg, Östermalms Saluhall; mains from Skr180; ⊙11am-11pm Mon-Sat; Ⓜ Östermalmstorg) Seafood fans, look no further. This Stockholm legend is never short of a satisfied lunchtime crowd. Located inside the temporary Östermalms Saluhall (the historic market across the road is under restoration until the summer of 2018), it has a menu that changes daily, so let the waiters order for you; classics include shrimp sandwiches (Skr180) and a gravadlax plate (Skr195). It also has an excellent selection of wine.

Blå Dörren
SWEDISH €€

(🖉08-743 07 43; www.bla-dorren.se; Södermalmstorg 6; mains Skr150-250; ⊙10.30am-11pm Mon, to midnight Tue-Thu, to 1am Fri, 1pm-1am Sat, 1-11pm Sun; Ⓜ Slussen) A stone's throw from Gamla Stan and facing Stockholm City Museum, Blå Dörren (The Blue Door) honours its historic surroundings with a variety of traditional Swedish dishes. You can't go wrong with the pan-fried herring or elk meatballs, both accompanied with fresh lingonberries.

The Market
SWEDISH €€

(🖉07-21 80 23 03; www.scandichotels.com; Klarabergsgatan 41, Norrmalm; mains Skr165-275; ⊙6.30am-9.30pm Mon-Fri, 7am-midnight Sat & Sun; Ⓜ T-Centralen) Handy for the station, this restaurant is particularly good for a buffet lunch with a superb spread of salads and hot dishes (including vegetarian options) plus dessert, salad and mineral water all for just Skr140. The atmosphere is rustic chic with wooden shelves, racks of wine and arty lamps; squeeze in at the bar, at a cosy table for two or at the communal tables.

Meatballs
SWEDISH €€

(🖉08-466 60 99; www.meatballs.se; Nytorgsgatan 30, Södermalm; mains Skr125-250; ⊙11am-10pm Mon-Thu, to midnight Fri & Sat; 🛜; Ⓜ Medborgarplatsen) The name says it all. This restaurant serves serious meatballs, including moose, deer, wild boar and lamb. Served with creamed potatoes and pickled vegetables, washed down with a pint of Sleepy Bulldog craft beer, it's a traditional Swedish dining experience, accentuated by the rustic decor and delightful waiting staff. You can even buy a Meatballs logo T-shirt here to impress the folks back home.

★ Woodstockholm
SWEDISH €€€

(🖉08-36 93 99; www.woodstockholm.com; Mosebacke Torg 9, Södermalm; mains from Skr200; ⊙11.30am-2pm Mon, 11.30-2pm & 5-11pm Tue-Sat; 🛜; Ⓜ Slussen) This restaurant combines a wine bar, hip dining spot, and designer furniture store showcasing chairs and tables by local designers. The menu changes weekly and is themed, somewhat wackily: think Salvador Dalí or Aphrodisiac; the latter including scallops with oyster mushrooms and sweetbreads with yellow beets and horseradish cream. This is fast becoming one of the city's classic foodie destinations. Reservations essential.

🍸 Drinking & Entertainment

Stockholm is a stylish place to drink, whether you're after cocktails or coffee. The coolest and most casual drinking holes are on Södermalm, the bohemian island in the southern part of town. For a moneyed, glamorous scene, head to Östermalm's late-night clubs. Even the hotel bars draw an ultrachic cocktail crowd.

Note that many places charge a mandatory Skr30 to Skr50 coat-check fee.

Himlen
COCKTAIL BAR

(🖉08-660 60 68; www.restauranghimlen.se; Götgatan 78, Södermalm; cocktails from Skr140; ⊙11.30am-midnight Mon, to 1am Tue & Thu, to 3am Fri & Sat; 🛜; Ⓜ Medborgarplatsen) Cruise up by elevator to the dizzy heights of the 27th floor to this elegant cocktail bar in what is easily the tallest building in Södermalm. After you have finished ogling the view, go for the splurge and indulge in a fabulous cocktail, accompanied by oysters (Skr175 for six) or a plate of *pata negra* Iberian ham (Skr225).

STOCKHOLM ARCHIPELAGO

Buffering the city from the open Baltic Sea, the archipelago is a wonderland of thousands of rocky isles and little red cottages. And it's more accessible than many visitors imagine, with regular ferry services and tours.

Waxholmsbolaget (☑08-686 24 65; www.waxholmsbolaget.se; Strömkajen; single trip Skr75-130, 5-/30-day pass Skr420/Skr750; ☺8am-6pm; Ⓜ Kungsträdgården), the main provider for island traffic, offers standard commuter routes and tours, as does **Strömma Kanalbolaget** (☑08-12 00 40 00; www.stromma.se; Svensksundsvägen 17; Skr220-400; 🖱).

Vaxholm is the gateway to the archipelago (just 35km northeast of Stockholm; take bus 670 from the Tekniska Högskolan tunnelbana station). On a sunny spring day, its crooked streets and storybook houses are irresistible. It has a thriving restaurant scene and popular Christmas market.

To the south, **Utö** has sandy beaches, fairy-tale forests, abundant bird life and an excellent **bakery** (Gruvbrggan; breakfast Skr80-120, lunch Skr150, sandwiches Skr45-75; ☺8am-5pm; 🚢 Waxhombolaget). Tiny Gruvbryggan is the main ferry stop. Ask at the guest harbour about cycle hire. Don't miss Sweden's oldest **iron mine** (Utö Gruvbryggan, Haninge; ☺24hr).

Equally charming is **Arholma** in the northern section. Once a popular resort, it has a moneyed yet agricultural feel, with green pastures, walking trails, rocky bathing spots and the delightful **Bull-August Vandrarhem** (☑0176-560 18; www.bullaugust.se; Arholma Södra Byväg 8; s/d from Skr345/650; 🅿🖱).

Kvarnen
BAR
(☑08-643 03 80; www.kvarnen.com; Tjärhovsgatan 4; ☺11am-1am Mon & Tue, to 3am Wed-Fri, noon-3am Sat, noon-1am Sun; Ⓜ Medborgarplatsen) An old-school Hammarby football fan hang-out, Kvarnen is one of the best bars in Söder. The gorgeous beer hall dates from 1907 and seeps tradition; if you're not the clubbing type, get here early for a nice pint and a meal (mains from Skr210). As the night progresses, the nightclub vibe takes over. Queues are fairly constant but justifiable.

Icebar
BAR
(☑08-50 56 35 20; www.icebarstockholm.se; Vasaplan 4, Nordic 'C' Hotel; entry & 1 drink Skr205; ☺3.45pm-midnight Sun-Thu, to 1am Fri & Sat) It's touristy. Downright gimmicky! And you're utterly intrigued, admit it: a bar built entirely out of ice, where you drink from glasses carved of ice on tables made of ice. The admission price gets you warm booties, mittens, a parka and one drink. Refill drinks cost Skr95; entry is cheaper if you book online.

❶ Information

Stockholm Visitors Center (☑08-508 28 508; www.visitstockholm.com; Kulturhuset, Sergels Torg 3; ☺9am-7pm Mon-Fri, to 4pm Sat, 10am-4pm Sun May-Sep, shorter hours rest of year; Ⓜ T-Centralen) The main visitors centre occupies a space inside Kulturhuset on Sergels Torg.

Visit Djurgården (☑08-667 77 01; www.visit djurgarden.se; Djurgårdsvägen 2; ☺9am-dusk) With tourist information specific to Djurgården, this office at the edge of the Djurgården bridge is attached to **Sjöcaféet** (p1101), so you can grab a bite or a beverage as you plot your day.

❶ Getting There & Away

AIR

Stockholm Arlanda (☑10-109 10 00; www.swedavia.se/arlanda) Stockholm's main airport, 45km north of the city centre, is reached from central Stockholm by bus and express train. Terminals two and five are for international flights; three and four are domestic; there is no terminal one.

BUS

Cityterminalen (www.cityterminalen.com; ☺7am-6pm) Most long-distance buses arrive and depart from Cityterminalen, which is connected to Centralstationen. The **main counter** (7am to 6pm) sells tickets for several bus companies, including Flybussarna (airport coaches), Swebus Express, Svenska Buss, Eurolines and Y-Buss.

TRAIN

Stockholm is the hub for national and international train services run by SJ (Sveriges Järnväg). Ticket offices are inside **Centralstationen** (Centralplan; Ⓜ T-Centralen).

ⓘ Getting Around

TO/FROM THE AIRPORT

The **Arlanda Express** (www.arlandaexpress.com; Centralstation; one-way Skr280) train from Centralstationen (Skr280, 20 minutes, every 15 minutes) links the city centre with Arlanda.

A cheaper option is the **Flygbussarna** (www.flygbussarna.se; Cityterminalen) bus service between Arlanda and Cityterminalen (Skr99, 40 minutes, every 10 to 15 minutes).

PUBLIC TRANSPORT

Storstockholms Lokaltrafik (SL; ☑ 08-600 10 00; www.sl.se; Centralstationen; single trip Skr36-72, unlimited 24hr/72hr/7-day pass Skr115/230/300, students & seniors half-price) SL runs all tunnelbana (metro) trains, local trains and buses within Stockholm county. You can buy tickets and passes at SL counters, ticket machines at tunnelbana stations, and Pressbyrå and 7-Eleven stores, as well as with the smartphone app SL-biljetter. Tickets cannot be bought on buses. Fines are steep (Skr1200) for travelling without a valid ticket. Refillable SL travel cards (Skr20) can be loaded with single-trip or unlimited-travel credit.

UPPSALA

☑ 018 / POP 186,000

The historical and spiritual heart of the country, Uppsala has the upbeat party vibe of a university town to balance the weight of its castle, cathedral and university. Peaceful by day and lively by night, it makes an easy day trip from Stockholm, though it's worth lingering overnight to wander the deserted streets and soak up the atmosphere.

⊙ Sights

★**Gamla Uppsala**   ARCHAEOLOGICAL SITE
(www.arkeologigamlauppsala.se; ⊙24hr; **P**; 🚌2) **FREE** One of Sweden's largest and most important burial sites, Gamla Uppsala (4km north of Uppsala) contains 300 mounds from the 6th to 12th centuries. The earliest are also the three most impressive. Legend has it they contain the pre-Viking kings Aun, Egil and Adils, who appear in *Beowulf* and Icelandic historian Snorre Sturlason's *Ynglingsaga*. More recent evidence suggests the occupant of Östhögen (East Mound) was a woman, probably a female regent in her 20s or 30s.

According to Olof Rudbeck's 1679 book *Atlantica*, Gamla Uppsala was the seat of Western culture. Rudbeck (1630–1702), a scientist, writer and all-around colourful character, amassed copious evidence proving that Old Uppsala was, in fact, the mythical lost city of Atlantis. In retrospect this seems unlikely, but the area is a fascinating attraction nevertheless. You can learn more in the adjoining Gamla Uppsala Museum (www.raa.se; adult/child Skr80/free; ⊙10am-4pm Apr-late Jun & mid-Aug–Sep, 11am-5pm late Jun–mid-Aug, noon-4pm Mon, Wed, Sat & Sun Oct-Mar; **P**), or wander on your own; there are informative plaques throughout the site.

Speculation has surrounded the burial site from the beginning. Early press reports include that of medieval chronicler Adam of Bremen – who never actually visited – describing a vast golden temple in Gamla Uppsala in the 10th century. Allegedly, animal and human sacrifices were strung up in a sacred grove outside.

When Christianity arrived around 1090, Thor, Odin and the other Viking gods began to fade. From 1164, the archbishop of Uppsala had his seat in a cathedral on the site of the present church.

If you feel like a stroll or a bicycle ride, Eriksleden is a 6km 'pilgrims path' between the cathedral in Uppsala and the church in Gamla Uppsala. Its namesake, Erik the Holy, was king of Sweden from around 1150 until the Danes beheaded him 10 years later. The story is that his head rolled down the hill, and where it stopped a spring came up. The main trail also provides access to a ridged wilderness area called Tunåsen, with a panoramic viewpoint (follow signs along Eriksleden just south of Gamla Uppsala to '*utsiktsleden*').

Buses for Gamla Uppsala leave from the bus stop on Vaksalagatan.

Domkyrka   CHURCH
(Cathedral; www.uppsaladomkyrka.se; Domkyrkoplan; ⊙8am-6pm, tours in English 11am & 2pm Mon-Sat, 4pm Sun Jul & Aug) **FREE** The Gothic Domkyrka dominates the city and is Scandinavia's largest church, with towers soaring some 119m. The interior is imposing, with the French Gothic ambulatory flanked by small chapels. Tombs here include those of St Erik, Gustav Vasa and the scientist Carl von Linné. Tours are available in English.

Uppsala Slott   CASTLE
(www.uppsalaslott.se; admission by guided tour only, adult/child Skr90/15; ⊙tours in English 1pm & 3pm Tue-Sun late Jun-Sep) Uppsala Slott was built by Gustav Vasa in the 1550s. It contains the state hall where kings were enthroned

and Queen Kristina abdicated. It was also the scene of a brutal murder in 1567, when King Erik XIV and his guards killed Nils Sture and his two sons, Erik and Svante, after accusing them of high treason. The castle burned down in 1702 but was rebuilt and took on its present form in 1757.

🛏 Sleeping

Hotel & Vandrarhem Central Station
HOSTEL €

(☑ 018-444 20 10; www.hotellcentralstation.se; Bangårdsgatan 13; dm/s/d Skr250/550/650; @ 🛜) The location of this hotel-cum-hostel is excellent, across from the train and bus station and close to the tourist office. The hostel rooms and dorms are tiny but spotless; the lack of windows may be a consideration for some, although there is adequate ventilation. The shared bathrooms are spacious and clean.

Sunnersta Herrgård
HOSTEL €€

(☑ 018-32 42 20; www.sunnerstaherrgard.se; Sunnerstavägen 24; dm Skr270, s/d from Skr760/880; ⊙ Jan–mid-Dec; P @ 🛜 🛁; 🚌 20) In a historic manor house about 6km south of the city centre, this hostel has a park-like setting at the water's edge and a good restaurant on-site. You can rent bikes (per day/week Skr50/200) or borrow a boat, and there's free wi-fi. Hotel-standard rooms include breakfast and share a bathroom with one other room; hostel guests can add breakfast for Skr95.

Best Western Hotel Svava
HOTEL €€

(☑ 018-13 00 30; www.bestwestern.se; Bangårdsgatan 24; s/d Skr1350/1450; P 🏿 🛜) Named after one of Odin's Valkyrie maidens, Hotel Svava, right opposite the train station, is a very comfortable top-end business-style hotel with recently renovated, carpeted rooms and great summer and weekend discounts.

🍴 Eating

Ofvandahls
CAFE €

(Sysslomansgatan 3-5; cakes Skr35, snacks Skr55-75; ⊙ 8am-6pm Mon-Fri, 9am-5pm Sat, 11am-5pm Sun) Something of an Uppsala institution, this classy but sweet *konditori* (bakery-cafe) dates back to the 19th century and is a cut above your average coffee-and-bun shop. It's been endorsed by no less a personage than the king, and radiates old-world charm with antique furniture and fittings. Try the star turn – homemade blueberry cake.

Storken
SWEDISH €

(Stora Torget 3; snacks from Skr75; ⊙ 9.30am-10pm; 🛜 🛁) The frontage is deceptive here; it's tucked into the corner of Stora Torget, but climb the stairs and you are transported to a series of eclectically furnished rooms with sink-into sofas, grandfather clocks, antique radios and typewriters, groaning bookshelves and an overall ambience of old-style comfort. The menu is brief but well prepared and includes sandwiches, soups, moussaka, pizza and salads.

Hambergs Fisk
SEAFOOD €€

(www.hambergs.se; Fyristorg 8; mains Skr125-295; ⊙ 11.30am-10pm Tue-Sat) Let the aromas of dill and seafood tempt you into this excellent fish restaurant, in a tiny storefront facing the river. Self-caterers should check out the fresh fish counter at the back of the dining room.

Frenchi
FRENCH €€€

(☑ 018-15 01 55; www.frenchi.se; Stora Torget 10; mains Skr200-385; ⊙ 10am-10pm Mon-Sat, to 6pm Sun; 🛜) Situated in the city's former law courts, this sophisticated restaurant is a delight. Although the cuisine is essentially French (fried frogs' legs anyone?), there are some nods towards Asian cuisine with dishes such as miso chicken and spring rolls with tuna, coriander and a killer hit of wasabi. Kickstart your meal with a cocktail at the classy downstairs bar with its chic black-and-white decor.

ℹ Information

Tourist Office (☑ 018-727 48 00; www.destinationuppsala.se; Kungsgatan 59; ⊙ 10am-6pm Mon-Fri, to 3pm Sat, plus 11am-3pm Sun Jul & Aug) Located directly in front of the train station, the tourist office has helpful advice, maps and brochures for the whole county.

ℹ Getting There & Away

Swebus Express runs regular direct services to Stockholm (from Skr79, one hour, six daily), which is also connected by frequent SJ trains (Skr89 to Skr124, 35 to 55 minutes one way).

SOUTHERN SWEDEN

Artists adore southern Sweden. Down here, the light is softer, the foliage brighter and the shoreline more dazzling. Sweden's southernmost county, Skåne (Scania), was Danish property until 1658 and still flaunts its differences.

Malmö

⚡ 040 / POP 324,000

Sweden's third-largest city has a progressive, contemporary feel. Home to beautiful parks, edgy contemporary museums and some seriously good cuisine, this dynamic city has also felt more directly connected to cool Copenhagen and the rest of Europe since the opening of the Öresund bridge in 2000.

◉ Sights

★**Malmö Museer**   MUSEUM
(www.malmo.se/museer; Malmöhusvägen; adult/child Skr40/free, audio guides Skr20; ⊙10am-5pm; 🖼) Various museums with diverse themes, including handicrafts, military material, art and transport, are located in and around Malmöhus Slott and make up the so-called Malmö Museer. There are gift shops and cafes inside all the museums, and plenty to keep the tots interested, including an aquarium. Don't miss the stunning nocturnal hall, wriggling with everything from bats to electric eels, plus local swimmers like cod and pike.

The Malmö Konstmuseum boasts a fabulous collection of Swedish furniture and handicrafts, as well as Scandinavia's largest collection of 20th-century Nordic art, while the Stadsmuseum (City Museum) combines exhibitions on the region's cultural history with more international themes. The Knight's Hall contains various late-medieval and Renaissance exhibits, such as the regalia of the order of St Knut. The northwest cannon tower is an atmospheric mix of cannons and shiny armour.

A short distance to the west of Malmöhus Slott, the technology and maritime museum Teknikens och Sjöfartens Hus is home to aircraft, vehicles, a horse-drawn tram, steam engines, and the amazing 'U3' walk-in submarine, outside the main building. The submarine was launched in Karlskrona in 1943 and decommissioned in 1967. Upstairs, a superb hands-on experiment room will keep kids (of all ages) suitably engrossed.

The old Kommendanthuset (Commandant's House) arsenal, opposite the castle, hosts regular photography exhibitions.

★**Moderna Museet Malmö**   MUSEUM
(www.modernamuseet.se/malmo; Gasverksgatan 22; ⊙11am-6pm Tue-Sun; 🕾) 🆓 Architects Tham & Videgård chose to make the most of the distinct 1901 Rooseum, once a power-

LUND

The centrepiece of the appealing university town of Lund, just 15 minutes from Malmö by train, is the splendid Romanesque Domkyrkan (www.lundsdomkyrka.se; Kyrkogatan; ⊙8am-6pm Mon-Fri, 9.30am-5pm Sat, 9.30am-6pm Sun), with some fantastic gargoyles over the side entrances, a giant turned to stone in the eerie crypt and an astronomical clock that sends the wooden figures whirring into action (at noon and 3pm Monday to Saturday, 1pm and 3pm on Sunday).

The town's most engaging museum, Kulturen (www.kulturen.com; Tegnerplatsen; adult/child Skr120/free, Skr90 in winter; ⊙10am-5pm May-Aug, noon-4pm Tue-Sun Sep-Apr; 🕾🖼), is a huge open-air space where you can wander among birch-bark hovels, perfectly preserved cottages, churches, farms and grand 17th-century houses.

generating turbine hall, by adding a contemporary annexe, complete with a bright, perforated orange-red facade. Venue aside, the museum's galleries are well worth visiting, with the permanent exhibition including works by Matisse, Dalí and Picasso.

🛏 Sleeping

STF Vandrarhem Malmö City   HOSTEL €
(⚡040-611 62 20; www.svenskaturistforeningen.se; Rönngatan 1; dm/d from Skr270/680; @ 🕾) Don't be put off by the exterior; this is a sparkling hostel right in the city centre with a bright and airy communal kitchen and an outdoor patio. Staff are enthusiastic and helpful.

Best Western Hotel Royal   HOTEL €€
(⚡040-664 25 00; www.bestwestern.se; Nora Vallgatan 94; s/d Skr850/950; 🅿@🕾) This small hotel has rooms spread over a historic 16th-century building and its modern counterpart. Either choice is a sound one, with excellent facilities, although the modern rooms are more spacious. Rooms have parquet floors and earthy toned decor. Comfortable chairs and sofas add to the appeal.

★**Mäster Johan Hotel**   HOTEL €€€
(⚡040-664 64 00; www.masterjohan.se; Mäster Johansgatan 13; r/ste from Skr1490/1990; 🅿@🕾) Just off Lilla Torg is one of Malmö's finest slumber spots, with spacious, elegantly

understated rooms featuring beautiful oak floors and fabrics in snowy white and cobalt blue. Bathrooms flaunt Paloma Picasso–designed tiles, there's a sauna and gym, and the faultless breakfast buffet is served in a glass-roofed courtyard.

✖ Eating

There's a good **produce market** (⊘8am-5pm Mon-Sat) on Möllevångstorget.

★Mrs Saigon   VIETNAMESE €€

(☑040-788 35; www.mrs-saigon.se; Engelbrektsgatan 17; mains Skr90-130; ⊘11.30am-3pm & 5.30-11pm Tue-Sat, noon-3pm Mon; 🔊) If you come here for lunch be sure to choose the superb signature rice noodle soup spiced with coriander, onion, basil and lime and served with chicken, beef or tofu; it will not disappoint. Other Vietnamese specialities include crispy shrimp rolls, homemade fish balls and stir-fried chicken flavoured with curry, lime leaves, lemongrass and chilli; the cuisine is authentically Southeast Asian.

Atmosfär   SWEDISH €€

(☑040-12 50 77; www.atmosfar.com; Fersensväg 4; mains Skr130-185; ⊘11.30am-11pm Mon-Fri, to 2am Sat; 🔊) This classy neighbourhood restaurant changes its menu regularly depending on what's in season, but you can depend on flavourful, innovative combinations like salads topped with young nasturtium leaves and pike with a fennel, leek and lobster sauce. The cocktails (Skr105) are similarly irresistible. Elderflower fizz, anyone?

Mrs Brown   SWEDISH €€€

(☑040-97 22 50; www.mrsbrown.nu; Storgatan 26; mains from Skr220; ⊘noon-3.30pm & 5-10.30pm Mon-Fri, 6-10.30pm Sat; 🖋) 🍽 Demure little Mrs Brown is the kind of neighbourhood place you dream will open up near you. The open kitchen churns out modern Scandinavian home cooking using local and organic ingredients like Greenland prawns in chilli sauce. Service is attentive but not overbearing and the dining room is decorated in a minimalist fashion that is both comforting and modish.

❶ Information

Malmö Airport Visitor Centre (www.malmoairport.se; Sturup airport; ⊘8am-6pm, varies slightly according to flight arrival times) Helpful tourist office at the airport. You can also purchase Flygbuss tickets here.

THE BRIDGE

The **Öresund Bridge** (www.oresundsbron.com; motorcycle/car/minibus Skr235/440/880) is the planet's longest cable-tied road and rail bridge, measuring 7.8km from Lernacken (on the Swedish side, near Malmö) to the artificial island of Peberholm (Pepper Island), south of Saltholm (Salt Island).

Local commuters pay via an electronic transmitter, while tolls for everyone else are payable by credit card, debit card or in euros, Danish or Swedish currency at the Lernacken tollbooths.

Tourist Information (☑040-34 12 00; www.malmotown.com; Skånegårdsvägen 5; ⊘9am-5pm Mon-Fri, 10am-2.30pm Sat & Sun) On the E20, 800m from the Öresund bridge tollgate.

Tourist Office (☑040-34 12 00; www.malmotown.com; Skeppsbron 2; ⊘9am-7pm Mon-Fri, 10am-4pm Sat & Sun, shorter hours in winter) Across from the Centralstationen, with an excellent range of flyers and information about the city.

Tourism in Skåne (www.skane.com) Regional website with lots of information, tips, maps and booking service.

❶ Getting There & Away

BUS

Swebus Express (☑0771-21 82 18; www.swebus.se) runs two to four times daily to Stockholm (from Skr549, 8½ hours) and up to 10 times daily to Göteborg (from Skr199, three to four hours); five continue to Oslo (from Skr319, eight hours).

TRAIN

Pågatågen (local trains) operated by **Skånetrafiken** (www.skanetrafiken.se; Centralstationen; ⊘6.30am-8pm Mon-Fri, 7am-6pm Sat, 10am-6pm Sun) run regularly to Helsingborg (Skr103, one hour), Lund (Skr48, 15 minutes) and other towns in Skåne.

The Malmö to Copenhagen central station train leaves every 20 minutes (Skr110, 35 minutes).

The high-speed SJ2000 (from Skr270, 2½ hours) and regional (from Skr351, 3¼ hours) trains run several times daily to/from Göteborg. The SJ2000 (from Skr539, 4½ hours, hourly) and Intercity (from Skr479, five hours, frequently) trains run between Stockholm and Malmö.

GÖTEBORG

📞 031 / POP 550,000

Often caught in Stockholm's shadow, gregarious Göteborg (yur-te-*borry*; Gothenburg in English) packs a mighty good punch of its own. Stockholm may represent the 'big time', but many of the best and brightest ideas originate in this grassroots town.

◉ Sights

The Haga district (www.hagashopping.se; 🚋 25 Hagakyrkan, 🚋 2 Handelshögskolan), south of the canal, is Göteborg's oldest suburb, dating back to 1648. In the 1980s and '90s, the area was thoroughly renovated and is now a cute, cobblestone maze of precious cafes and boutique shops.

★ Konstmuseum   GALLERY
(www.konstmuseum.goteborg.se; Götaplatsen; adult/child Skr40/free; ⊙ 11am-6pm Tue & Thu, to 8pm Wed, 11am-5pm Fri-Sun; 🚻; 🚋 4 Berzeliigatan) Göteborg's premier art collection, Konstmuseum hosts works by the French Impressionists, Rubens, Van Gogh, Rembrandt and Picasso; Scandinavian masters such as Bruno Liljefors, Edvard Munch, Anders Zorn and Carl Larsson have pride of place in the Fürstenburg Galleries.

Other highlights include a superb sculpture hall, the Hasselblad Center with its annual *New Nordic Photography* exhibition, and temporary displays of next-gen Nordic art.

The unveiling of the bronze Poseidon fountain out front scandalised the city's strait-laced citizens, who insisted on drastic penile-reduction surgery.

★ Universeum   MUSEUM
(www.universeum.se; Södra Vägen 50; adult/3-16yr Skr245/185; ⊙ 10am-6pm, to 8pm Jul & Aug; 🅿 🚻; 🚋 2 Korsvägen) In what is arguably the best museum for kids in Sweden, you find yourself in the midst of a humid rainforest, complete with trickling water, tropical birds and butterflies flitting through the greenery and tiny marmosets. On a level above, roaring dinosaurs maul each other, while next door, denizens of the deep float through the shark tunnel and venomous beauties lie coiled in the serpent tanks. In the 'technology inspired by nature' section, stick your children to the Velcro wall.

★ Röda Sten Konsthall   GALLERY
(www.rodastenkonsthall.se; Röda Sten 1; adult/under 26yr Skr40/free; ⊙ noon-5pm Tue & Thu-Sun, to 7pm Wed; 🚋 3 Vagnhallen Majorna) Occupying a defunct power station beside the giant Älvsborgsbron, Röda Sten's four floors are home to such temporary exhibitions as edgy Swedish photography and cross-dressing rap videos by Danish-Filipino artist Lillibeth Cuenca Rasmussen that challenge sexuality stereotypes in Afghan society. The indie-style cafe hosts weekly live music and club nights, and offbeat one-offs like punk bike races, boxing matches and stand-up comedy. To get there, walk towards the Klippan precinct, continue under Älvsborgsbron and look for the brown-brick building.

Liseberg   AMUSEMENT PARK
(www.liseberg.se; Södra Vägen; 1-day pass adult/child under 110cm Skr645/free; ⊙ 11am-11pm Jun–mid-Aug; 🅿 🚻; 🚋 2 Korsvägen) The attractions of Liseberg, Scandinavia's largest amusement park, are many and varied. Adrenalin blasts include the venerable wooden roller coaster Balder; its 'explosive' colleague Kanonen, where you're blasted from 0km/h to 75km/h in under two seconds; AtmosFear, Europe's tallest (116m) free-fall tower; and the park's biggest new attraction, Loke, a fast-paced spinning 'wheel' that soars 42m into the air. Softer options include carousels, fairy-tale castles, an outdoor dance floor, adventure playgrounds, and shows and concerts.

Entry to the park grounds is reasonable (Skr95), which is ideal for those who just want to enjoy the charming landscaped grounds studded with impressive sculptures, but note that you pay for individual rides using coupons. Each ride costs between one and four coupons (Skr20 each) per go, so costs can mount up and you may be better off getting a day pass. Opening hours are varied – check the website.

When it comes to refuelling in between rides, Lisberg is also the first theme park in the world to offer a very high-quality, delicious, exclusively vegetarian/vegan buffet lunch (Skr159) at the Green Room.

Mölndals Museum   MUSEUM
(📞 031-431 34; www.museum.molndal.se; Kvarnbygatan 12; ⊙ noon-6pm Tue-Sun; 🅿 🚻; 🚋 752, 756, 🚋 Mölndal) FREE Located in an old police station, the Mölndals Museum is like a

Göteborg

vast warehouse, with a 10,000-strong booty of local nostalgia spanning a 17th-century clog to kitchen kitsch and a recreated 1930s worker's cottage. With a focus on memories and feelings, it's an evocative place where you can plunge into racks of vintage clothes, pull out hidden treasures and learn the individual items' secrets on the digital catalogue.

From Göteborg, catch a Kungsbacka-bound train to Mölndal station, then bus 752 or 756.

🛏 Sleeping

★**STF Göteborg City**   HOSTEL **€**
(☎031-756 98 00; www.svenskaturistforeningen. se; Drottninggatan 63-65; s/d from Skr655/1000; @🛜; 🚌1 Brunnsparken) This large supercentral hostel is all industrial chic in the cafe/dining area and lounge and elegant comfort on each of its individually themed floors. All rooms are private, with en suite bathroom, plush carpeting and comfortable bed-bunks, and – rarity of rarities! – your bed linen and towels are provided for you. Breakfast costs an additional Skr85.

Hotel Flora   BOUTIQUE HOTEL **€€**
(☎031-13 86 16; www.hotelflora.se; Grönsakstorget 2; r from Skr910; @🛜; 🚌1 Grönsakstorget) Fabulous Flora's slick, individually themed rooms flaunt black, white and spot-colour interiors, designer chairs, flat-screen TVs and sparkling bathrooms, though lack of storage facilities may dismay those with extensive sartorial needs. The top-floor rooms have air-con, several rooms offer river views, and rooms overlooking the chic split-level courtyard are for night owls rather than early birds.

★**Dorsia Hotel**   BOUTIQUE HOTEL **€€€**
(☎031-790 10 00; www.dorsia.se; Trädgårdsgatan 6; s/d/ste from Skr1950/2550/5850; P❄@🛜; 🚌3 Kungsportsplatsen) If Heaven had a bordello, it would resemble this lavish, flamboyant establishment that combines old-world

decadence with cutting-edge design. Rooms delight with their heavy velvet curtains, a purple-and-crimson colour scheme and opulent beds; thick carpet in the corridors muffles your footsteps; and the fine art adorning the walls comes from the owner's personal collection.

✗ Eating

Göteborg's chefs are at the cutting edge of Sweden's Slow Food movement and there are no fewer than seven Michelin-starred restaurants. Happily, there are also more casual options for trying old-fashioned *husmanskost* (home cooking). Cool cafes, cheap ethnic gems and foodie favourites abound in the Vasastan, Haga and Linné districts. For self-caterers, there's a supermarket in the Nordstan shopping complex.

Saluhall Briggen   MARKET €
(www.saluhallbriggen.se; Nordhemsgatan 28; ⊗9am-6pm Mon-Fri, to 3pm Sat; 🚋1 Prinsgatan) This covered market will have you drooling over its bounty of fresh bread, cheeses, quiches, seafood and ethnic treats. It's particularly handy for the hostel district.

Smaka   SWEDISH €€
(📞031-13 22 47; www.smaka.se; Vasaplatsen 3; mains Skr175-265; ⊗5pm-late; 🔊; 🚋1 Vasaplatsen) For top-notch Swedish *husmanskost*, like the speciality meatballs with mashed potato and lingonberries, it's hard to do better than this smart yet down-to-earth restaurant-bar. Mod-Swedish options might include hake with suckling pig cheek or salmon tartar with pickled pear.

Magazzino   ITALIAN €€
(www.magazzino.se; Magasinsgatan 3; mains Skr170-190; ⊗5pm-11pm; 🔊; 🚋1 Domkyrkan) Expect to wait for a table at this perennially popular Italian restaurant on this pedestrian stretch of restaurants and bars. With Italians in the kitchen you can expect authentic cuisine, plus some gourmet additional ingredients like pasta with pecorino cheese infused with truffle oil. The interior is lined with giant-sized photos of Italian film stills with moody lighting and a boisterous bustling atmosphere.

Orange n Blk   INTERNATIONAL €€
(www.orangenblk.com; Västra Hamngatan 24; mains
Skr110-235; ⏲7am-7pm; 🛜; 🚊3 Kungsportsplatsen) The menu here is short and sassy, with
a focus on globally themed wraps like the
Tangier, Tijuana or Beirut with associated
emphasis on that country's spices and ingredients. There's also fresh fruit juices and
smoothies and delicious fresh salads. Seating
takes the form of sofas surrounded by palms
and tropical greenery.

★**Thörnströms Kök**   SCANDINAVIAN €€€
(📞031-16 20 66; www.thornstromskok.com; 3 Te-
knologgatan; mains Skr675/895/1175; ⏲6pm-1am Mon-Sat;
🛜; 🚊7 Kapellplatsen) Specialising in modern
Scandinavian cuisine, chef Håkan shows you
how he earned that Michelin star through
creative use of local, seasonal ingredients
and flawless presentation. Feast on the likes
of rabbit with pistachios, pickled carrots
and seaweed; don't miss the remarkable
milk-chocolate pudding with goat's-cheese
ice cream. A la carte dishes are available if a
multi-course menu overwhelms you.

🍷 Drinking & Nightlife

★**Champagne Baren**   WINE BAR
(www.forssenoberg.com; Kyrkogatan; ⏲5-11pm
Tue-Thu, 4pm-midnight Fri, noon-midnight Sat; 🛜;
🚊1 Domkyrkan) What's not to like? This champagne bar has an idyllic setting on an inner
courtyard with uneven cobbles, picturesque
buildings and plenty of greenery. Along with
glasses of bubbly, there are platters of cheese,
oysters and cold cuts. Very popular with the
boho-chic set; you can expect some cool background beats, as well as occasional live jazz.

ℹ️ Information

Cityguide Gothenburg (www.goteborg.com/
apps) Info on the city's attractions, events and
more, available as an Android and iPhone app.
City map available offline.

Tourist Office (www.goteborg.com; Nils
Eriksongatan; ⏲10am-8pm Mon-Fri, to 6pm
Sat, noon-5pm Sun) Branch office inside the
Nordstan shopping complex.

Tourist Office (📞031-368 42 00; www.
goteborg.com; Kungsportsplatsen 2;
⏲9.30am-8pm late Jun–mid-Aug, shorter
hours rest of year) Central and busy; has a
good selection of free brochures and maps.

RFSL Göteborg (📞031-13 83 00; www.rfsl.se/
goteborg; Stora Badhugatan 6) Comprehensive
information on the city's gay scene, events and
more.

GOTLANDSLEDEN CYCLE PATH

Renting a bicycle and following the well-
marked Gotlandsleden cycle path is one
of the best ways to spend time on Gotland. It loops all around the island, mostly
winding through quiet fields and forests.
Hire bikes and get maps harbourside in
Visby. There's an excellent hostel network along the route, with good facilities
in Bunge, Lummelunda, Lärbro and Fårö.

ℹ️ Getting There & Away

AIR

The **Göteborg Landvetter Airport** (www.
swedavia.se/landvetter) is located 25km east of
the city. It has daily flights to/from Stockholm
Arlanda and Stockholm Bromma airports, as
well as weekday services to Umeå.

BOAT

Göteborg is a major entry point for ferries, with
several car/passenger services to Denmark and
Germany.

For a special view of the region, jump on a boat
for an unforgettable journey along the Göta
Canal. Starting in Göteborg, you'll pass through
Sweden's oldest lock at Lilla Edet, opened in
1607. From there the trip crosses the great lakes
Vänern and Vättern through the rolling country
of Östergötland and on to Stockholm.

BUS

Swebus Express (📞0771-21 82 18; www.
swebusexpress.com) operates from the bus
terminal (adjacent to the train station).
Services include the following:
Malmö (Skr199, 3½ to four hours, seven to
nine daily)
Oslo (Skr289, 3½ hours, five to 10 daily)
Stockholm (Skr369, 6½ to seven hours, four
to five daily)

TRAIN

From Centralstationen trains run to:
Copenhagen (Skr450, 3¾ hours, hourly)
Malmö (Skr195, 2½ to 3¼ hours, hourly)
Östersund (Skr820, 12 hours, daily)
Stockholm (Skr419, three to five hours, one to
two hourly)

ℹ️ Getting Around

Västtrafik runs the city's public transport
system of buses, trams and ferries. The most
convenient way to travel around Göteborg is by
tram. Colour-coded lines, numbered one to 13,

converge near Brunnsparken (a block from Centralstationen). Holders of the Göteborg City Card travel free, including on late-night transport. Otherwise a city transport ticket costs Skr28/22 per adult/child (Skr48 on late-night transport).

GOTLAND

Gorgeous Gotland, adrift in the Baltic, has much to brag about: a Unesco-lauded medieval capital, truffle-sprinkled woods, A-list dining hot spots, talented artisans and more hours of sunshine than anywhere else in Sweden. It's also one of the country's richest historical regions, with around 100 medieval churches and countless prehistoric sites.

ℹ Getting There & Away

Year-round car ferries between Visby and both Nynäshamn and Oskarshamn are operated by **Destination Gotland** (📞0771-22 33 00; www.destinationgotland.se; Korsgatan 2, Visby). There are departures from Nynäshamn one to six times daily (about three hours). From Oskarshamn, there are one or two daily departures in either direction (three to four hours). **Gotlandsbåten** (www.gotlandsbaten.se; Färjeleden 2, Visby) runs daily foot-passenger ferries (June to August) from Västervik to Visby (from Skr275, about three hours).

ℹ Getting Around

In Visby, hire bikes from Skr100 per 24 hours at **Gotlands Cykeluthyrning** (📞0498-21 41 33; www.gotlandscykeluthyrning.com; Skeppsbron 2; per day Skr120; ☺9am-6pm Jun-Aug, shorter hours rest of year), at the harbour. **Kollektiv Trafiken** (📞0498-21 41 12; www.gotland.se/kollektivtrafiken; Kung Magnus Väg 1) runs buses via most villages to all corners of the island (tickets up to Skr80).

Visby

📞0498 / POP 24,000

The port town of Visby is medieval eye candy and enough to warrant a trip to Gotland all by itself. Inside its thick city walls await twisting cobbled streets, fairy-tale wooden cottages and evocative ruins. And with more restaurants per capita than any other Swedish city, it's a food-lovers' paradise.

⊙ Sights

★**Gotlands Museum**   MUSEUM
(www.gotlandsmuseum.se; Strandgatan 14; incl Konstmuseet adult/child Skr120/free; ☺11am-4pm Tue-Sun; 🚼) Gotlands Museum is one of the

mightiest regional museums in Sweden. While highlights include amazing 8th-century pre-Viking picture stones, human skeletons from chambered tombs and medieval wooden sculptures, the star turn is the legendary Spillings treasure horde. At 70kg it's the world's largest booty of preserved silver treasure.

🛏 Sleeping

Visby has a solid choice of sleeping options, ranging from budget digs to the truly luxurious. Book in advance, particularly during the summer months and **Medeltidsveckan** (Medieval Week; www.medeltidsveckan.se; ☺Aug), when Stockholm's city dwellers descend in droves. The tourist office can help out with accommodation if you're stuck, plus there are a couple of campsites near town if you are prepared to hammer down some pegs.

Fängelse Vandrarhem   HOSTEL €
(📞0498-20 60 50; www.visbyfangelse.se; Skeppsbron 1; dm/s/d Skr300/450/750; 🛜) This hostel offers beds year-round in the small converted cells of an old prison. It's in a handy location, between the ferry dock and the harbour restaurants, and there's an inviting terrace bar in summer. Reception is open from 9am to 2pm, so call ahead if you are arriving outside these times.

Hotel Stenugnen   HOTEL €€
(📞0498-21 02 11; www.stenugnen.nu; Korsgatan 6; s/d Skr1000/1350, annexe r Skr1000; 🅿🛜🚼) At this inviting small hotel, bright, white-washed rooms are designed to make you feel as if you're sleeping on a yacht, and the location is practically on top of the medieval wall. Plenty of rainy-day distractions are provided for kids and the homemade bread is just delicious. Cheaper doubles come with shared bathrooms in the annexe.

★**Clarion Hotel Wisby**   HISTORIC HOTEL €€€
(📞0498-25 75 00; www.clarionwisby.com; Strandgatan 6; s/d from Skr1880/2180; 🅿@🛜❄) Top of the heap in Visby is the luxurious, landmark Wisby. Medieval vaulted ceilings and sparkling candelabras contrast with eye-catching contemporary furnishings. The gorgeous pool (complete with medieval pillar) occupies a converted merchant warehouse. Don't miss the 11th-century chapel, just inside the entrance. The hotel's **Kitchen & Table** restaurant receives rave reviews from readers.

SWEDEN ÖSTERSUND

✕ Eating

Visby has plenty of eating options – more per capita than any other town in Sweden. The majority are located around the main square, Wallérs plats; explore the backstreets and you'll find tucked-away cafes where you can sit in a flower-filled garden. Be sure to try the traditional *saffranspankaka* (a saffron-based pancake topped with berries and cream).

Bolaget   FRENCH €€
(www.bolaget.fr; Stora Torget 16; mains Skr180-230; ☉ 1pm-11pm Mon-Fri, from 1pm Sat; ☎) Take a defunct Systembolaget shop, chip the 'System' off the signage, and reinvent the space as a buzzing, French bistro-inspired hot spot (fried frogs' legs, anyone?). Staff members are amiable and the summertime square-side bar seating is perfect for a cool break.

Amarillo   INTERNATIONAL €€
(www.amarillovisby.se; Schweitzergränd 5; mains Skr110-135; ☉ 5pm-11pm Tue-Thu, to midnight Fri & Sat; ☎) This is a relaxed, unpretentious place with distressed wood panelling, stylish art work and a menu of small tapas-style dishes with Pacific, Swedish and Mexican influences. Expect tasty bites like shrimp tacos, pork buns and scallops, with sides including dill and Parmesan fries and cheesy cornbread. There is an excellent range of craft and imported beers, including several available on tap.

Jessens Saluhall & Bar   SWEDISH €€
(www.saluhallochbar.se; Hästgatan 19; mains Skr125-145; ☉ 11am-6pm Mon-Thu, to 8pm Fri, to 4pm Sat) Although the seating area here is very plain diner-style, the fact that this venue doubles as a deli and sells fresh seafood and meat means that the ingredients are top quality. Daily specials are chalked up on a board and generally include the perennially popular fish soup. Meat is sourced locally, with lamb and beef dishes generally taking centre stage.

ⓘ Information

Tourist Office (☎ 0498-20 17 00; www.gotland.info; Donners Plats 1; ☉ 8am-7pm daily in summer, 9am-5pm Mon-Fri, 10am-4pm Sat rest of year) The tourist office is conveniently located at Donners Plats and can help with accommodation and advise on what is going on during your stay. It also organises free tours during the summer months.

NORRLAND

Norrland, the northern half of Sweden, is a paradise for nature lovers who enjoy hiking, skiing and other outdoor activities; in winter the landscape is transformed by snowmobiles, dog-sleds and the eerie natural phenomenon known as the aurora borealis (northern lights). The north is home to the Sami people and their reindeer.

Östersund

✓ 063 / POP 61,280

This pleasant town by Storsjön lake, in whose chilly waters is said to lurk Sweden's answer to the Loch Ness monster, is an excellent activity base and gateway town for further explorations of Norrland.

◉ Sights

★ Jamtli   MUSEUM
(www.jamtli.com; Museiplan; adult/child Skr70/free, entry late Aug-late Jun free; ☉ 11am-5pm daily late Jun-late Aug, Tue-Sun rest of year; ℗ ♿; 🚌 2) Jamtli, 1km north of the centre, consists of two parts. One is an open-air museum comprising painstakingly reconstructed wooden buildings, complete with enthusiastic guides wearing 19th-century period costume.

The second is the indoor museum, home to the **Överhogdal Tapestries**, the oldest of their kind in Europe – Christian Viking relics from AD 1100 that feature animals, people, ships and dwellings. Another fascinating display is devoted to Storsjöodjuret (reputed lake monster), including taped interviews with those who've seen the beast, monster-catching gear and a pickled monster embryo.

🛌 Sleeping

★ Hotel Emma   HOTEL €€
(☎ 063-51 78 40; www.hotelemma.com; Prästgatan 31; s/d Skr950/1095; ℗ ☎) The individually styled rooms at super-central Emma nestle in crooked hallways on two floors, with homey touches like squishy armchairs and imposing ceramic stoves; some rooms have French doors facing the courtyard. The breakfast spread is a delight. Reception hours are limited, so call ahead if arriving late or early.

Hotel Jämteborg   HOTEL €€
(☎ 063-51 01 01; www.jamteborg.se; Storgatan 54; hostel d/tr Skr600/850, B&B s/d/tr Skr600/700/900, hotel s/d from Skr1075/1300;

LAPONIA WORLD HERITAGE AREA

The vast **Laponia World Heritage Area** (www.laponia.nu) stretches for 9400 sq km, comprising the mountains, forests and marshlands of Padjelanta, Sarek, Stora Sjöfallet and Muddus National Parks. Unusually for a World Heritage Area, it's recognised for both its cultural and its natural wealth.

Established in 1996, Laponia encompasses ancient reindeer-grazing grounds of both the Mountain and the Forest Sami, whose seven settlements and herds of around 50,000 reindeer are located here. The Sami still lead relatively traditional lives, following the reindeer during their seasonal migrations.

P ⊛) Just imagine: you're travelling with friends but you're all on different budgets. Hotel Jämteborg comes to the rescue, with its catch-all combo of hostel beds, B&B rooms and hotel rooms in several adjacent buildings. The cheerful hotel rooms come in cream-and-crimson, defying Sweden's 'earth tones only' rule. The hostel is only open from June to September.

✖ Eating

Östersund is one of just five Unesco-designated cities of gastronomy in the world. The harsh climate means that produce rarely found elsewhere thrives here and most of it is farmed organically. Wild moose and reindeer can also be found on menus, as well as trout and other fresh water fish; the region is famed for its great fishing.

Wedemarks   CAFE €
(www.wedemarks.se; Prästgatan 27; snacks Skr60-80; ⊙8am-6pm Mon-Fri, 10am-4pm Sat, noon-4pm Sun; ⊛) This glorious cafe has been sweet-toothing its customers since 1924; this the place to try a slice of such typical Swedish delights as the traditional Princess layer cake with its topping of bright green marzipan.

ℹ Information

Tourist Office (☑ 063-701 17 00; www.visit ostersund.se; Rådhusgatan 44; ⊙9am-5pm Mon-Fri, 10am-3pm Sat & Sun) Opposite the town hall.

ℹ Getting There & Away

Daily bus 45 runs north at 7.15am from Östersund to Gällivare (Skr532, 11¼ hours) via Arvidsjaur (Skr460, seven hours) and Jokkmokk (Skr574, 9½ hours) and south to Mora (Skr284, 5¼ hours, two daily).

SJ connections include two trains daily to Stockholm (Skr701, five hours) via Uppsala and up to six daily trains west to Åre (Skr146, 1¼ hours). In summer the **Inlandsbanan** (☑ 0771-53 53 53; www.inlandsbanan.se; Storsjöstråket 19, Östersund) train runs once daily north and south.

Umeå

☑ 090 / POP 119,613

With the vibrant feel of a college town (it has around 30,000 students), Umeå is a welcome outpost of urbanity in the barren north. Since the title of Culture Capital of Europe was bestowed on it in 2014, it's really been strutting its stuff, showcasing northern and Sami culture.

◎ Sights

★**Västerbottens Museum**   MUSEUM
(www.vbm.se; Helena Elizabeths väg, Gammliavägen; ⊙10am-5pm Tue-Fri, to 9pm Wed, 11am-5pm Sat & Sun; P ♿; ☐2, 7) FREE The star of the Gammlia museum complex, the engrossing Västerbottens Museum traces the history of the province from prehistoric times to today. Exhibitions include an enormous skis-through-the-ages collection starring the world's oldest ski (5400 years old), and an exploration of Sami rock art and shaman symbols. The exhibits are complemented by audiovisual presentations and there are excellent temporary exhibitions as well as regular workshops and activities for children. There is also a superb cafe specialising in organic fare.

⊨ Sleeping

STF Vandrarhem Umeå   HOSTEL €
(☑090-771650; www.umeavandrarhem.com; Västra Esplanaden 10; dm/s/d from Skr230/475/600; @⊛) This busy hostel has rooms of varying quality: try to nab a space in one of the newer rooms with beds, as opposed to the rather basic dorms with bunks. It's in a great location, in a residential neighbourhood at the edge of the town centre, and the facilities (kitchen, laundry) are very handy for self-caterers. Reception hours are limited.

ICEHOTEL

The winter wonderland that is the **Icehotel** (☑ 0980-668 00; www.icehotel.com; Marnadsvägen 63; s/d/ste from Skr2400/3300/5400, cabins from Skr2000; ☉ Dec-Apr; P ☎; ☒ 501 Kiruna) in Jukkasjärvi, 18km east of Kiruna, is an international phenomenon.

The enormous hotel is built using 30,000 tonnes of snow and 4000 tonnes of ice, with international artists and designers contributing innovative ice sculptures every year.

In the ice rooms, the beds are made of compact snow and covered with reindeer skins and serious sleeping bags, guaranteed to keep you warm despite the -5°C temperature inside the rooms. Come morning, guests are revived with a hot drink and a sauna.

The attached Ice Church is popular for weddings, and the much-copied Absolut Icebar serves drinks in ice glasses.

In summer you can visit the smaller replica inside a chilled warehouse.

★ **Stora Hotellet Umeå**   BOUTIQUE HOTEL €€
(☑ 090-77 88 70; www.storahotelletumea.se; Storgatan 46; s/d/ste from Skr1000/1150/6000; P ☎) We love the muted colours and the plush, old-style furnishings that give you the impression that you're adrift aboard a luxurious ship. Of the six categories of rooms, even the modest 'Superstition' presents you with luxurious queen-size bunks that real sailors could only dream of, while 'Passion' offers grander surroundings, velvet couches and his 'n' hers showers.

✖ Eating

Pinchos   INTERNATIONAL €
(www.pinchos.se; Kungsgatan 48; pinchos Skr35-45; ☉ 4-10pm Sun-Mon, to 11pm Tue-Thu, to 1am Fri, to midnight Sat; ☎) Circus-style decor and Spanish tapas combined with the novel idea of placing orders via an inhouse app (easy to load and use) equals a fun and different experience. Pinchos also offers a chance for friends to taste a relatively inexpensive large variety of different dishes, ranging from mushroom risotto and sweet-potato fries to Asian-style dumplings and a spicy south-of-the-border chilli.

Två Fiskare   SEAFOOD €€
(www.tvafiskare.se; Storgatan 44; mains Skr95-135; ☉ 10am-6pm Mon-Fri, to 4pm Sat) These folk take their fish very seriously indeed. Not only do they sell it fresh, they also prepare a handful of exquisite seafood and fish dishes daily for those in the know. Crabcakes, fish soup, smoked salmon...the dishes will depend on what is flapping fresh that day. Undecided? Then opt for the classic fish and chips, served in newspaper, the traditional way.

★ **Koksbaren Umea**   SWEDISH €€€
(www.koksbaren.com; Raadhusesplanaden 17; mains Skr275-350; ☉ 11am-10pm Mon, to 11pm Tue-Thu, 11am-midnight Sat, noon-midnight Sun; ☎) Expect stunning culinary combinations at this sophisticated restaurant near the train station. From lemon sole and truffle risotto to beetroot burgers with all the trimmings – and virtually everything is made here, including the ketchup and the 'smoked' mayonnaise. The speciality is dry cured steaks with a choice of rib eye, sirloin or filet mignon. The bright yet classy dining area adds to the agreeable eating experience.

Reservations recommended.

❶ Information

Tourist Office (☑ 090-16 16 16; www.visit umea.se; Rådhusesplanaden 6a; ☉ 9am-7pm Mon-Fri, 10am-4pm Sat, noon-4pm Sun) Centrally located with helpful staff who can advise on places to stay and what's going on.

❶ Getting There & Away

Umeå Airport (☑ 01-109 50 00; www.swedavia.com/umea; Flygplatsvägen) is 5km south of the city centre. SAS and Norwegian fly daily to Stockholm's Arlanda and Bromma, Malmö Aviation to Göteborg and Stockholm, and Direktflyg to Östersund and Luleå.

Airport buses run to the city centre (Skr45, 20 minutes).

Kiruna & Around

☑ 0980 / POP 23,000

Thousands of visitors flock to the workaday mining town of Kiruna every year to see the Icehotel in nearby Jukkasjärvi – northern Sweden's biggest attraction – and to take part in all manner of outdoor adventures: dog-sledding, snowmobiling and aurora borealis tours in winter, and biking, hiking and canoeing in summer.

☞ Tours

Active Lapland SNOW SPORTS
(☑ 076-104 55 08; www.activelapland.com; Solbacksvägen 22; tours from Skr1250; ☺ Nov-Mar) This experienced operator offers 2½-hour dogsled rides (Skr1250), rides under the northern lights (highly recommended), and airport pick-ups by dog sleigh (Skr5400). They'll even let you drive your own dogsled (Skr3200).

Kiruna Guidetur OUTDOORS
(☑ 0980-811 10; www.kirunaguidetur.com; Vänortsgatan 8) These popular all-rounders organise anything from overnighting in a self-made igloo, snowmobile safaris and cross-country skiing outings in winter to overnight mountain-bike tours, rafting and quad-biking in summer. Book via the website.

🛏 Sleeping

STF Vandrarhem & Hotell City HOSTEL €
(☑ 0980-17 000; www.spiskiruna.se; Bergmästaregatan 7; dm/d from Skr265/465, hotel s/d Skr995/1095; P 🛜) This catch-all hotel-and-hostel combo has a gleaming red-and-white colour scheme in its modern hotel rooms and cosy dorms. Sauna and breakfast cost extra for hostel guests, but there is a communal guest kitchen and an even handier supermarket just a few minutes stroll away.

Hotel Arctic Eden BOUTIQUE HOTEL €€
(☑ 0980-611 86; www.hotelarcticeden.se; Föraregatan 18; s/d Skr950/1250; P 🛜🏊) At Kiruna's fanciest lodgings the rooms are a chic blend of Sami decor and modern technology, there's a plush spa and indoor pool, and the friendly staff can book all manner of outdoor adventures. A fine breakfast spread is served in the morning and the on-site Arctic Thai & Grill is flooded with spice-seeking customers on a daily basis.

✗ Eating

There is plenty of cuisine choice here, but if you can, try to taste some Sami-inspired dishes, like smoked and salted reindeer meat and grouse with local berries, which you can find in several local restaurants.

★ **Camp Ripan Restaurang** SWEDISH €€
(☑ 0980-630 00; www.ripan.se; Campingvägen 5; lunch buffet weekday/weekend Skr100/125, dinner mains Skr245-355; ☺ 11am-2pm & 6-9.30pm Mon-Fri, noon-2pm & 6-9.30pm Sat & Sun; 🛜) The unusually veggie-heavy lunch buffet is good value, but the real draw is the Sami-inspired à la carte menu featuring local, seasonal produce. Dishes change regularly, but you can expect treats like a creamy crayfish soup with shiitake mushrooms and carpaccio of smoked reindeer with Parmesan cheese and mushroom mayonnaise. The restaurant is located at the local campground.

ℹ Information

Tourist Office (☑ 0980-188 80; www.kiruna lapland.se; Lars Janssonsgatan 17; ☺ 8.30am-9pm Mon-Fri, to 6pm Sat & Sun) Inside the Folkets Hus visitor centre; has internet access and can book various tours.

ℹ Getting There & Away

AIR
Kiruna airport (☑ 010-109 46 00; www. swedavia.com/kiruna), 7km east of the town, has direct flights to Stockholm.

BUS
Daily bus 91 runs to Narvik (Norway; Skr320, 2¾ hours) via Abisko (Skr215, 1¼ hours). Bus 501 goes to Jukkasjärvi (Skr48, 30 minutes, two to six daily).

TRAIN
There is a daily overnight train to Stockholm (from Skr696, 17½ hours).

CONNECTIONS

Getting to the rest of Scandinavia and further into Europe from Sweden is easy. From Stockholm there are train and bus connections to London or Berlin as well as to Denmark, Finland and Norway. Ferries are another option, with frequent connections between many Swedish ports and the rest of Europe. Airports in Stockholm and Göteborg connect Sweden with the rest of the world.

SURVIVAL GUIDE

 Directory A–Z

ACCOMMODATION

At hostels, HI members save a substantial amount at affiliated places – called **STF** (☑ 070-695 21 16; www.svenskaturistforeningen.se) in Sweden. You'll save extra by bringing your own sleep sheet.

Accommodation in Sweden is generally of a high standard.

CHILDREN

Sweden makes it easy to travel with children, with many kid-friendly attractions and outdoor activities. Museum admission is often free for those aged under 20. Hotels will put extra beds in rooms, restaurants have family-friendly features and there are substantial transport discounts for kids.

GAY & LESBIAN TRAVELLERS

Sweden is famously liberal; since 2009 its gender-neutral marriage law has given same-sex married couples the same rights and obligations as heterosexual married couples. The national organisation for gay and lesbian rights is **Riksförbundet för Sexuellt Likaberättigande** (RFSL; ☑ 08-501 62 900; www.rfsl.se; Sveavägen 59; ☺10am-5pm Mon-Fri).

For entertainment listings, club nights and other local information, visit www.qx.se.

INTERNET ACCESS

Most hotels and hostels have wi-fi. Free wi-fi at coffee shops is common; ask for the code when you order. Many tourist offices offer a computer terminal for visitor use (sometimes for a fee).

INTERNET RESOURCES

Visit Sweden (www.visitsweden.com) Official tourism website.

Swedish Institute (www.si.se/English) Scholarly info on Swedish culture.

The Local (www.thelocal.se) News from Sweden in English.

Lonely Planet (www.lonelyplanet.com/sweden) For planning and inspiration.

MONEY

Credit and debit cards can be used almost everywhere, and ATMs are plentiful. Visa and MasterCard are standard; American Express and Discover are less widely accepted.

The default system uses cards with microchips; if your card has no chip or pin, ask the clerk to swipe it.

TELEPHONE

Public telephones are increasingly rare, although you may find them at transport hubs, including train and bus stations. They accept phonecards or credit cards.

Telia phonecards (*telefonkort*) cost Skr50 and Skr120 (for 50 and 120 units, respectively) and can be bought from Telia phone shops and newsagents.

Local SIM cards for mobile phones are available (around Skr100); you then load them with at least Skr110 in credit. Top-ups are available at petrol stations and Pressbyrån shops.

ESSENTIAL FOOD & DRINK

Scandinavian cuisine, once viewed as meatballs, herring and little else, is now at the forefront of modern gastronomy. New Nordic cuisine showcases local produce, blending traditional techniques and contemporary experimentation.

Swedish menu essentials:

Coffee To fit in, eight or nine cups a day is about right; luckily, the region's cafes are a delight.

Reindeer & Game Expect to see reindeer and other delicious game, especially up north in Sami cooking.

Alcohol Beer is everywhere, and improving; but try a shot of *brännvin* (aquavit) with your pickled herring, too.

Fish Salmon is ubiquitous and delicious, and smoked, cured, pickled or fried herring is fundamental. Tasty lake fish include Arctic char and pike-perch.

TIME

Sweden is one hour ahead of UTC/GMT (two hours from late March to late October).

VISAS

Schengen visa rules apply.

🛈 Getting There & Away

AIR

Sweden's main airport is Stockholm Arlanda. Entry is straightforward; most visitors simply need to fill out and hand over a brief customs form and show their passport at immigration.

LAND

Numerous trains connect Copenhagen in Denmark to Sweden via the **Öresund bridge** (p1110).

SEA

Baltic and Atlantic ferries connect Sweden with eastern and northern European nations: Germany, Poland, Estonia, Latvia, Lithuania, Finland, Russia and the UK. Book ahead if travelling with a vehicle. Many ferry lines offer 50% discounts for holders of rail passes. The website www.directferries.com is useful for routes and discounted tickets.

🛈 Getting Around

BICYCLE

Bikes can be carried on many trains (though not Stockholm's tunnelbana) and most buses and ferries, but it's wise to reserve space in advance. Sweden is one of the world's most cycle-friendly destinations, with numerous places to hire bikes, cycle lanes in every city, and excellent long-distance trail networks.

BUS

Swebus Express (☎ 0771-21 82 18; www.swebus.se) has a large network of express buses serving the southern half of the country.

Svenska Buss (☎ 0771-67 67 67; www.svenskabuss.se) and **Nettbuss** (☎ 0771-15 15 15; www.nettbuss.se) connect many southern towns and cities with Stockholm.

COUNTRY FACTS

Area 450,295 sq km

Capital Stockholm

Country Code ☎ 46

Emergency ☎ 112

Currency Krona (Skr)

Language Swedish, Finnish, Sami dialects, English

Money ATMs very common; plastic taken everywhere

Population 9.59 million

Several smaller operators, including **Ybuss** (☎ 060-17 19 60; www.ybuss.se), have services to Östersund and Umeå.

CAR & MOTORCYCLE

If you're bringing your own car, you'll need vehicle registration documents, unlimited third-party liability insurance and a valid driving licence. A right-hand-drive vehicle brought from the UK or Ireland should have deflectors fitted to the headlights to avoid dazzling oncoming traffic. You must carry a reflective warning breakdown triangle.

Hire

To hire a car you have to be at least 20 (sometimes 25) years of age, with a recognised driving licence and a credit card. Avis, Hertz and Europcar have desks at Stockholm Arlanda airport and offices in most major cities. The lowest car-hire rates are generally from larger petrol stations (like Statoil and OKQ8).

TRAIN

Sweden has an extensive and reliable railway network, and trains are almost always faster than buses.

Train Passes

The Sweden Rail Pass, Eurodomino tickets and international passes, such as InterRail and Eurail, are accepted on SJ services and most regional trains.

The **Eurail Scandinavia Pass** (www.eurail.com) entitles you to unlimited rail travel in Denmark, Finland, Norway and Sweden; it is valid in 2nd class only and is available for four, five, six, eight or 10 days of travel within a two-month period (prices start at youth/adult US$295/395). The X2000 trains require all rail-pass holders to pay a supplement of Skr70. The pass provides free travel on Scandlines' Helsingør to Helsingborg route and discounts on other ship routes.

EATING PRICE RANGES

The following price categories for eating listings refer to the average price of a main dish, not including drinks.

€ less than Skr100

€€ Skr100–Skr200

€€€ more than Skr200

Switzerland

Best Places to Eat

➡ Chez Vrony (p1132)

➡ Volkshaus Basel (p1142)

➡ Restaurant 1903 (p1137)

➡ Buvette des Bains (p1125)

➡ Alpenrose (p1140)

Best Places to Stay

➡ Esther's Guest House (p1138)

➡ Gletschergarten (p1137)

➡ Guesthouse Castagnola (p1145)

➡ Il Fuorn (p1144)

➡ Backpackers Villa Sonnenhof (p1135)

Why Go?

What giddy romance Zermatt, St Moritz and other glitterati-encrusted names evoke. This is Sonderfall Schweiz ('special-case Switzerland'), a privileged neutral country set apart from others, proudly idiosyncratic, insular and unique. It's blessed with gargantuan cultural diversity: its four official languages alone speak volumes.

The Swiss don't do half measures: Zürich, their most gregarious urban centre, has cutting-edge art, legendary nightlife and one of the world's highest living standards. The national passion for sharing the great outdoors provides access (by public transport, no less!) to some of the world's most inspiring panoramic experiences.

So don't depend just on your postcard images of Bern's and Lucerne's chocolate-box architecture, the majestic Matterhorn or those pristine lakes – Switzerland is a place so outrageously beautiful it simply must be seen to be believed.

When to Go
Bern

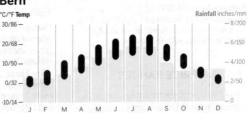

Dec–early Apr Carve through powder and eat fondue at an Alpine resort.

Jun–Sep Hike in the shadow of the mesmerising Matterhorn and be wowed by its perfection.

Aug Celebrate Swiss National Day on 1 August and witness Swiss national pride in full force.

Switzerland Highlights

1 Zürich (p1138) Discovering this zesty city via a daytime stroll along the city's sublime lake followed by a rollicking night out.

2 Zermatt (p1130) Marvelling at the iconic Matterhorn and wandering around this car-free Alpine village.

3 Bern (p1132) and **Lucerne** (p1133) Enjoying

the charm of these famous beauties: think medieval Old Town appeal, folkloric fountains and art.

4 Jungfraujoch (p1137) Being wowed by the Eiger's monstrous north face on a ride to the 'top of Europe', 3471m Jungfraujoch.

5 Geneva (p1123) Boarding a boat in this sophisticated city for a

serene Lake Geneva cruise to medieval **Lausanne** (p1128).

6 Bernina Express (p1131) Riding one of Switzerland's legendary scenic trains, such as the Bernina Express.

7 Lugano (p1144) Going Italian at Lugano, with its lovely, temperate lake setting.

GENEVA

POP 198,072

The whole world seems to be in Geneva, Switzerland's second city. The UN, the International Red Cross, the World Health Organization – 200-odd governmental and nongovernmental international organisations fill the city's plush hotels with big-name guests, who feast on an extraordinary choice of cuisine and help prop up the overload of banks, jewellers and chocolate shops for which Geneva is known.

⊙ Sights & Activities

The city centre is so compact it's easy to see many of the main sights on foot. Begin your explorations on the southern side of Lake Geneva and visit the **Jardin Anglais** (Quai du Général-Guisan) to see the **Horloge Fleurie** (Flower Clock). Crafted from 6500 flowers,

the clock has ticked since 1955 and sports the world's longest second hand (2.5m).

★**Jet d'Eau**   FOUNTAIN

(Quai Gustave-Ador) When landing by plane, this lakeside fountain is the first dramatic glimpse you get of Geneva. The 140m-tall structure shoots up water with incredible force – 200km/h, 1360 horsepower – to create the sky-high plume, kissed by a rainbow on sunny days. At any one time, 7 tonnes of water is in the air, much of which sprays spectators on the pier beneath. Two or three times a year it is illuminated pink, blue or another colour to mark a humanitarian occasion.

★**Cathédrale St-Pierre**   CATHEDRAL

(www.cathedrale-geneve.ch; Cour St-Pierre; towers adult/child Sfr5/2; ⊙9.30am-6.30pm Mon-Sat, noon-6.30pm Sun Jun-Sep, 10am-5.30pm Mon-Sat, noon-5.30pm Sun Oct-May) Begun in the 11th century, Geneva's cathedral is predominantly Gothic with an 18th-century neoclassical facade. Between 1536 and 1564 Protestant John Calvin preached here; see his seat in the north aisle. Inside the cathedral, 96 steps spiral up to the **northern tower and attic** – offering a fascinating glimpse at the cathedral's architectural construction. From here, another 60 steps climb into the **southern tower**, revealing close-up views of the bells and panoramic city vistas up top.

★**CERN** RESEARCH CENTRE
(☑ 022 767 84 84; www.cern.ch; Meyrin; ⊘ guided tours in English 11am & 1pm Mon-Sat) **FREE** Founded in 1954, the European Organisation for Nuclear Research, 8km west of Geneva, is a laboratory for research into particle physics. It accelerates protons down a 27km circular tube (the Large Hadron Collider, the world's biggest machine) and the resulting collisions create new matter. Two exhibitions shed light on its work and two-hour guided tours in English delve deeper; reserve online up to 15 days ahead and bring photo ID. From the train station take tram 18 (Sfr3, 20 minutes).

Musée International de la Croix-Rouge et du Croissant-Rouge MUSEUM
(International Red Cross & Red Crescent Museum; ☑ 022 748 95 11; www.redcrossmuseum.ch; Av de la Paix 17; adult/child Sfr15/7; ⊘ 10am-6pm Tue-Sun Apr-Oct, to 5pm Nov-Mar) Compelling multimedia exhibits at Geneva's fascinating International Red Cross and Red Crescent Museum trawl through atrocities perpetuated by humanity. The litany of war and nastiness, documented in films, photos, sculptures and soundtracks, is set against the noble aims of the organisation created

by Geneva businessmen and philanthropists Henri Dunant and Henri Dufour in 1864. Excellent temporary exhibitions command an additional entrance fee.

Take bus 8 from Gare de Cornavin to the Appia stop.

★**Patek Philippe Museum** MUSEUM
(☑ 022 807 09 10; www.patekmuseum.com; Rue des Vieux-Grenadiers 7; adult/child Sfr10/free; ⊘ 2-6pm Tue-Fri, 10am-6pm Sat) This elegant museum by one of Switzerland's leading luxury watchmakers displays exquisite timepieces and enamels from the 16th century to the present.

🛏 Sleeping

When checking in, ask for your free Public Transport Card, covering unlimited bus travel for the duration of your hotel stay.

★**Hôtel Bel'Esperance** HOTEL €€
(☑ 022 818 37 37; www.hotel-bel-esperance.ch; Rue de la Vallée 1; s/d/tr/q from Sfr150/170/210/250; ⊘ reception 7am-10pm; @ 🛜) This two-star hotel is extraordinary value. Rooms are quiet and cared for, those on the 1st floor share a kitchen, and there are fridges for guests to store picnic supplies – or sausages – in! Ride the lift to the 5th floor to flop on its wonderful flower-filled rooftop terrace, complete with barbecue.

Hôtel N'vY HOTEL €€
(☑ 022 544 66 66; www.hotelnvygeneva.com; Rue de Richemont 18; r weekend/weekday from Sfr175/260; ❄ @ 🛜) Contemporary flair abounds at this modish four-star northeast of the train station, from the purple-lit bar downstairs to in-room amenities like international power outlets, Bluetooth connec-

---

ITINERARIES

One Week

Starting in vibrant **Zürich**, shop famous Bahnhofstrasse, then eat, drink and be merry. Next, head to the **Jungfrau region** to explore some kick-ass Alpine scenery, whether it be by hiking or skiing. Take a pit stop in beautiful **Lucerne** before finishing up in Switzerland's delightful capital, **Bern**.

Two Weeks

As above, then head west for a French flavour in **Geneva** or lakeside **Lausanne**. Stop in **Gruyères** to dip into a cheesy fondue and overdose on meringues drowned in thick double cream. Zip to **Zermatt** or across to **St Moritz** to frolic in snow or green meadows, then loop east to taste the Italian side of Switzerland at lakeside **Lugano**.

GENEVA'S TOP PICNIC SPOTS

With mountains of fine views to pick from, Geneva is prime picnicking terrain for those reluctant to pay too much to eat. Shop for supplies at downtown *boulangeries* (bakeries) and delis, or at the takeaway food hall in the **Globus** (www.globus.ch/fr/store/116/globus-geneve; Rue du Rhône 48; ⊙ 9am-7pm Mon-Wed, to 9pm Thu, to 7.30pm Fri, to 6pm Sat; food hall 7.30am-10pm Mon-Fri, 8.30am-10pm Sat) department store, and head for one of these classic picnic spots:

➡ In the contemplative shade of Henry Moore's voluptuous sculpture *Reclining Figure: Arch Leg* (1973) in the park opposite the Musée d'Art et d'Histoire.

➡ Behind the cathedral on **Terrasse Agrippa d'Abigné**, a tree-shaded park with benches, sandpit and see-saw for kids, and a fine rooftop and cathedral view.

➡ On a bench on **Quai du Mont-Blanc** with Mont Blanc view (sunny days only).

➡ On the world's longest bench (126m long) on chestnut-tree-lined Promenade de la Treille in the **Parc des Bastions**.

tivity and chromotherapy lighting. Among the five room categories, all but the standards come with big-screen TV, espresso machine and parquet wood floor. Upper-floor executive rooms have views of Lake Geneva and the Alps.

Hôtel Beau-Rivage   HISTORIC HOTEL €€€
(☑ 022 716 66 66; www.beau-rivage.ch; Quai du Mont-Blanc 13; d weekend/weekday from Sfr550/670; P❄@🖱) Run by the Mayer family for five generations, this grand hotel with its evocative setting at the meeting of the Rhône and Lake Geneva is a 19th-century jewel dripping in opulence.

Eating

Eateries crowd Place du Bourg-de-Four, Geneva's oldest square, in the lovely Old Town. Otherwise, head down the hill towards the river and Place du Molard, packed with tables and chairs for much of the year. In Pâquis, there's a tasty line-up of more affordable restaurants on Place de la Navigation.

★**Buvette des Bains**   CAFETERIA €
(☑ 022 738 16 16; www.bains-des-paquis.ch; Quai du Mont-Blanc 30, Bains des Pâquis; mains Sfr14-23; ⊙ 7am-10.30pm) Meet Genevans at this earthy beach bar – rough and hip around the edges – at the Bains des Pâquis lakeside pool and sauna complex. Grab breakfast, a salad or the *plat du jour* (dish of the day), or dip into a *fondue au crémant* (Champagne fondue).

Cottage Café   MEDITERRANEAN €
(☑ 022 731 60 16; www.cottagecafe.ch; Rue Adhémar-Fabri 7; tapas & mezze Sfr9-16; ⊙ 7.30am-midnight Mon-Fri, 9am-midnight Sat) Hovering near the waterfront, this quaint cottage hides in a park guarded by two stone lions and a mausoleum (Geneva's Brunswick Monument, no less). On clear days, views of Mont Blanc from its garden are swoonworthy, and lunching or lounging inside is akin to hanging out in your grandma's book-lined living room.

★**Le Relais d'Entrecôte**   STEAK €€
(☑ 022 310 60 04; www.relaisentrecote.fr; Rue Pierre Fatio 6; steak, salad & chips Sfr42; ⊙ noon-2.30pm & 7-11pm) Key vocabulary at this timeless classic where everyone eats the same dish is *à point* (medium), *bien cuit* (well done) and *saignant* (rare). It doesn't even bother with menus, just sit down, say how you like your steak cooked and wait for it to arrive – two handsome servings pre-empted by a green salad and accompanied by perfectly crisp, skinny fries.

★**Brasserie des Halles de l'Île**   EUROPEAN €€
(☑ 022 311 08 88; www.brasseriedeshallesdelile.ch; Pl de l'Île 1; weekday lunch specials Sfr18.90, dinner mains Sfr20-35; ⊙ 10.30am-midnight Sun & Mon, to 1am Tue & Wed, to 2am Thu-Sat) At home in Geneva's old market hall on an island, this industrial-style venue cooks up a buzzing cocktail of after-work aperitifs with music, after-dark DJs and seasonal fare of fresh veggies and regional products – look for

Geneva

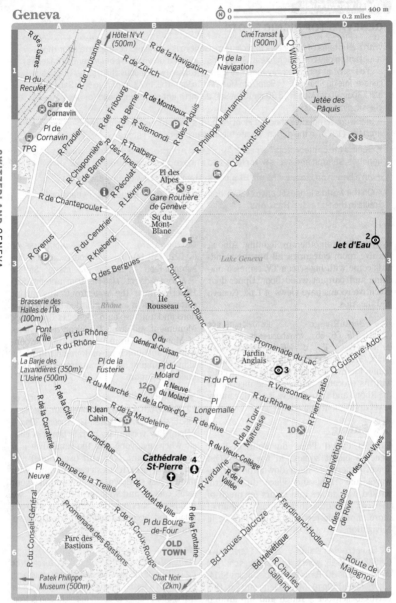

0 ——— **400 m**
0 ——— **0.2 miles**

R des Gares
Pl du Reculet
R de Lausanne
Hôtel N'vY (500m)
R de Zürich
R de la Navigation
Pl de la Navigation
CinéTransat (900m)
Q Wilson
Jetée des Pâquis
Gare de Cornavin
R de Fribourg
R de Monthoux
R de Berne
R des Pâquis
R Philippe Plantamour
Pl de Cornavin
TPG
R Pradier
R Sismondi
Q du Mont-Blanc
⊗8
R Chaponnière
R des Alpes
R de Berne
R Thalberg
R Pécolat
Pl des Alpes
6
⊗9
R de Chantepoulet
R Lévrier
Gare Routière de Genève
R du Cendrier
R Kléberg
Sq du Mont-Blanc
R Grenus
Q des Bergues
●5
Jet d'Eau 2 ◎
Pont du Mont-Blanc
Lake Geneva
Brasserie des Halles de l'Île (100m)
Rhône
Île Rousseau
Pont d'Île
Pl du Rhône
R du Rhône
Q du Général-Guisan
Promenade du Lac
Q Gustave-Ador
La Barje des Lavandières (350m); L'Usine (500m)
R de la Cité
Pl de la Fusterie
Pl du Molard
R Neuve du Molard
Pl du Port
Jardin Anglais
◎3
R Versonnex
R du Rhône
R de la Corraterie
R du Marché
12
R de la Croix-d'Or
Pl Longemalle
R de Rive
R de la Tour-Maîtresse
R Pierre-Fatio
R Jean Calvin
R de la Madeleine
11
R du Vieux-Collège
10⊗
Grand-Rue
Pl Neuve
Rampe de la Treille
Cathédrale St-Pierre 4 ⊕
1
R Verdaine
7
R de la Vallée
Bd Helvétique
Pl des Eaux-Vives
R du Conseil-Général
Promenade des Bastions
R de l'Hôtel-de-Ville
R de la Fontaine
Pl du Bourg-de-Four
OLD TOWN
Bd Jaques-Dalcroze
R Ferdinand-Hodler
R des Glacis de Rive
Parc des Bastions
Bd Helvétique
Route de Malagnou
Patek Philippe Museum (500m)
Chat Noir (2km)
Bd Helvétique
R Charles Galland

the Appellation d'Origine Contrôllée (AOC) products flagged on the menu. Arrive early to snag the best seat in the house – a superb terrace hanging over the water.

Drinking & Entertainment

Pâquis, the district in-between the train station and lake, is particularly well endowed with bars. For a dose of Bohemia, head to Carouge on tram 12. This shady quarter of

Geneva

17th-century houses and narrow streets has galleries, funky shops and hip nightlife.

In warm weather, waterfront bars pop up along the banks of the Rhône and Lake Geneva. In July and August, catch free movies under the stars at **CinéTransat** (www.cinetransat.ch; ⊘ lounge chair rental from 7pm, films start at sunset).

★**Chat Noir**   BAR
(✆ 022 307 10 40; www.chatnoir.ch; Rue Vauthier 13; ⊘ 6pm-4am Tue-Thu, to 5am Fri & Sat) One of the busiest night spots in Carouge, the Black Cat is packed most nights thanks to its all-rounder vibe: arrive after work for an aperitif with a selection of tapas to nibble on, and stay until dawn for dancing, live music and DJ sets.

La Barje des Lavandières   BAR
(www.labarje.ch; Promenade des Lavandières; ⊘ 11am-midnight Mon-Fri, noon-midnight Sat, noon-11pm Sun May-Sep) This summertime address is not a barge at all, but rather a vintage caravan with tin roof and candy-striped facade, parked on the grassy banks of the Rhône near the Bâtiment des Forces Motrices. The beer and music are plentiful, outside concerts and art performances pull huge crowds, and proceeds go towards helping young people in difficulty.

L'Usine   PERFORMING ARTS
(www.usine.ch; Pl des Volontaires 4) At the gritty heart of Geneva's alternative culture scene, this nonprofit collection of 18 arts-related initiatives is housed beside the Rhône in a former gold-processing factory. On any given night, expect to see cutting-edge theatre at **TU** (www.theatredelusine.ch), live music at **Le Zoo** (www.lezoo.ch) or up-and-coming VJ artists at **Kalvingrad** (www.kalvingrad.com).

Alhambra   LIVE MUSIC
(✆ 078 966 07 97; www.alhambra-geneve.ch; Rue de la Rôtisserie 10) Reopened in 2015 after extensive renovations, this gorgeous historic theatre with its cut-glass chandeliers, embossed silver ceilings and scarlet chairs makes a classy venue for live concerts ranging from Brazilian 'electrotropical' to African drumming, disco to salsa, and Afro-Caribbean to R&B.

🛍 Shopping

Designer shopping is wedged between Rue du Rhône and Rue de Rive; the latter has lots of chain stores. Grand-Rue in the Old Town and Carouge boast artsy boutiques.

ⓘ Information

Tourist Office (✆ 022 909 70 00; www.geneve.com; Rue du Mont-Blanc 18; ⊘ 10am-6pm Mon, 9am-6pm Tue-Sat, 10am-4pm Sun) Helpful, well-stocked office just downhill from the train station.

ⓘ Getting There & Away

AIR

Geneva Airport (p1147), 4km northwest of the town centre, is served by a wide variety of Swiss and international airlines.

BOAT

CGN (Compagnie Générale de Navigation; ✆ 0900 929 929; www.cgn.ch; Quai du Mont-Blanc) runs steamers from Jardin Anglais and Pâquis to other Lake Geneva villages. Many only sail May to September, including those to/from Lausanne (Sfr66, 3½ hours). Eurail and Swiss passes are valid on CGN boats.

BUS

Buses to neighbouring France depart from **Gare Routière de Genève** (✆ 0900 320 230, 022 732 02 30; www.coach-station.com; Pl Dorcière).

TRAIN

More-or-less-hourly trains run from Geneva's central station, **Gare de Cornavin** (Pl de Cornavin), to Swiss cities including Lausanne

(Sfr23, 35 to 50 minutes), Bern (Sfr51, 1¾ hours) and Zürich (Sfr89, 2¾ hours).

International daily rail connections from Geneva include Paris by TGV (3¼ hours) and Milan (four hours).

ⓘ Getting Around

TO/FROM THE AIRPORT

Getting from the airport is easy with regular trains into Gare de Cornavin (Sfr3, seven minutes). Slower bus 10 (Sfr3, 30 minutes) does the same 4km trip. Grab a free public transport ticket from the machine inside the airport's luggage hall. A metered taxi costs Sfr35 to Sfr50.

BICYCLE

Pick up a bike at **Genèveroule** (☑ 022 740 13 43; www.geneveroule.ch; Pl de Montbrillant 17; 4hr free, then per hour Sfr2; ⊙ 8am-9pm May-Oct, to 6pm Nov-Apr) just outside the train station.

PUBLIC TRANSPORT

Buses, trams, trains and boats operated by **TPG** (www.tpg.ch; Rue de Montbrillant; ⊙ 7am-7pm Mon-Fri, 9am-6pm Sat) serve the city, and ticket dispensers are found at all stops. A one-hour ticket costs Sfr3; a day pass offering unlimited rides costs Sfr10 (Sfr8 if purchased after 9am).

LAKE GENEVA REGION

Lausanne

POP 135,629

In a fabulous location overlooking Lake Geneva, Lausanne is an enchanting beauty with several distinct personalities: the former fishing village of Ouchy, with its lakeside bustle; the Vieille Ville (Old Town), with charming cobblestone streets and covered staircases; and Flon, a warehouse district of bars and boutiques.

⦿ Sights & Activities

★ Musée Olympique   MUSEUM

(Olympic Museum; ☑ 021 621 65 11; www.olympic.org/museum; Quai d'Ouchy 1; adult/child Sfr18/10; ⊙ 9am-6pm daily May–mid-Oct, 10am-6pm Tue-Sun mid-Oct–Apr) Musée Olympique is easily Lausanne's most lavish museum and an essential stop for sports buffs (and kids). Thoroughly revamped in 2014, the state-of-the-art installations recount the Olympic story from its inception to the present day through video, interactive displays, memorabilia and temporary themed exhibitions. Other attractions include tiered landscaped gardens, site-specific sculptural works and a fabulous cafe with champion lake views from its terrace.

★ Cathédrale de Notre Dame   CATHEDRAL

(Pl de la Cathédrale; ⊙ 9am-7pm Apr-Sep, to 5.30pm Oct-Mar) Lausanne's Gothic cathedral, Switzerland's finest, stands proudly at the heart of the Old Town. Raised in the 12th and 13th centuries on the site of earlier, humbler churches, it lacks the lightness of French Gothic buildings but is remarkable nonetheless. Pope Gregory X, in the presence of Rudolph of Habsburg (the Holy Roman Emperor) and an impressive following of European cardinals and bishops, consecrated the church in 1275.

Place de la Palud   SQUARE

In the heart of the Old Town, this 9th-century medieval market square – pretty as a picture – was originally bogland. For five centuries it has been home to the city government, now housed in the 17th-century Hôtel de Ville (town hall). A fountain pierces one end of the square, presided over by a brightly painted column topped by the allegorical figure of Justice, clutching scales and dressed in blue.

🛏 Sleeping

Hotel guests get a Lausanne Transport Card providing unlimited use of public transport for the duration of their stay.

Lhotel   BOUTIQUE HOTEL €

(☑ 021 331 39 39; www.lhotel.ch; Pl de l'Europe 6; r from Sfr130; ▣❋☎) This smart small hotel is ideally placed for the city's lively Flon district nightlife. Rooms are simple and startlingly white, and come with iPads; breakfast costs Sfr14. There's a fab rooftop terrace and your stay gives you access to the spa at the five-star Lausanne Palace & Spa nearby for Sfr55.

★ Hôtel Beau-Rivage
Palace   HISTORIC HOTEL €€€

(☑ 021 613 33 33; www.brp.ch; Pl du Port 17-19; r from Sfr510; ▣@☎❋) Easily the most stunningly located hotel in town, this luxury lakeside address is sumptuous. A beautifully maintained early 19th-century mansion set in immaculate grounds, it tempts with magnificent lake and Alp views, a grand spa, and a number of bars and upmarket restaurants (including a superb gastronomic temple headed by Anne-Sophie Pic, the only French female chef with three Michelin stars).

MONTREUX

This tidy lakeside town boasts Switzerland's most extraordinary castle.

Originally constructed on the shores of Lake Geneva in the 11th century, **Château de Chillon** (☑ 021 966 89 10; www.chillon.ch; Av de Chillon 21; adult/child Sfr12.50/6; ☺ 9am-7pm Apr-Sep, 9.30am-6pm Mar & Oct, 10am-5pm Nov-Feb, last entry 1hr before close) was brought to the world's attention by Lord Byron and the world has been filing past ever since. Spend at least a couple of hours exploring its numerous courtyards, towers, dungeons and halls filled with arms, period furniture and artwork.

The castle is a lovely 45-minute lakefront walk from Montreux. Alternatively, take bus 201 (10 minutes) or a CGN steamer (15 minutes).

Crowds throng to the legendary (and not all-jazz) **Montreux Jazz Festival** (www. montreuxjazz.com; ☺ Jul) for a fortnight in early July. Free concerts take place every day, but big-name gigs cost Sfr75 to Sfr250. Lovers of Freddie Mercury should hightail it to the **Queen Studio Experience** (www.mercuryphoenixtrust.com/studioexperience; Rue du Théâtre 9, Casino Barrière de Montreux; ☺ 10.30am-10pm) FREE and also to the **Freddie Mercury statue** on Place du Marché.

There are frequent trains to Lausanne (Sfr13, 20 to 35 minutes) and other lakeside points. Make the scenic journey to Interlaken via the **GoldenPass Line** (www.goldenpass. ch; 2nd class one way Sfr54, three hours, daily; rail passes valid).

✖ Eating & Drinking

★ Holy Cow   BURGERS €

(www.holycow.ch; Rue Cheneau-de-Bourg 17; burger with chips & drink Sfr16-25; ☺ 11am-11pm; 🚭) A Lausanne success story, with branches in Geneva, Zürich and France, burgers (beef, chicken or veggie) feature local ingredients, creative toppings and witty names. Grab a beer, sit at a shared wooden table, and wait for your burger and fab fries to arrive in a straw basket. A second outlet can be found at Rue des Terreaux 10.

Café Romand   SWISS €

(☑ 021 312 63 75; www.cafe-romand.ch; Pl St François 2; mains Sfr18-41; ☺ 9am-midnight Mon-Sat) Tucked away in an unpromising-looking arcade, this Lausanne legend dating to 1951 is a welcome blast from the past. Locals pour into the broad, somewhat sombre dining area filled with timber tables to revel in fondue, *cervelle au beurre noir* (brains in black butter), tripe, *pied de porc* (pork trotters) and other feisty traditional dishes.

★ Great Escape   PUB

(☑ 021 312 31 94; www.the-great.ch; Rue Madeleine 18; ☺ 11.30am-late Mon-Fri, from 10am Sat, from noon Sun) Everyone knows the Great Escape, a busy student pub with pub grub (great burgers) and an enviable terrace with a view over Place de la Riponne. From the aforementioned square, walk up staircase Escaliers de l'Université and turn right.

ℹ Information

Tourist Office (☑ 021 613 73 73; www. lausanne-tourisme.ch; Pl de la Gare 9; ☺ 9am-7pm) Conveniently located in Lausanne's train station. Other branches are at Lausanne's **cathedral** (Pl de la Cathédrale; ☺ 9.30am-6.30pm Mon-Sat, 1-5.30pm Sun Jun-Aug, shorter hours Sep-May) and lakeside in **Ouchy** (☑ 021 613 73 21; Pl de la Navigation 6; ☺ 9am-7pm Apr-Sep, to 6pm Oct-Mar).

ℹ Getting There & Away

BOAT

The **CGN** (Compagnie Générale de Navigation; www.cgn.ch) steamer service runs from early April to mid-September to/from Geneva (Sfr45, 3½ hours) via Nyon. Other services lace the lake, including to Montreux (Sfr27, 1½ hours, up to six daily).

TRAIN

There are frequent trains to/from Geneva (Sfr23, 35 to 50 minutes) and Bern (Sfr34, 70 minutes).

ℹ Getting Around

Lausanne spans several steep hillsides, so prepare for some good walks.

Buses and trolley buses service most destinations; the vital m2 Métro line (single trip/day pass Sfr2.30/9.30) connects the lake (Ouchy) with the train station (Gare), cathedral area and Flon.

A DAY AT CHARLIE CHAPLIN'S MANSION

Opened in 2016, the engaging **Chaplin's World** (www.chaplinsworld.com; Route de Fenil 2, Corsier-sur-Vevey; adult/child Sfr23/17; ⊙10am-6pm) museum celebrates the life and work of iconic London-born film star Charlie Chaplin. Split between the neoclassical Manoir de Ban – the Corsier-sur-Vevey mansion where Chaplin spent his last quarter century – and a purpose-built interactive studio, the exhibits include multimedia displays, excerpts from Chaplin's films, recreations of film sets, family photos and other evocative memorabilia, right down to Chaplin's trademark hat and cane. A tour of the mansion's splendid gardens rounds out the visit.

From Lausanne, catch a train to Vevey (15 minutes), then bus 212 to the museum (11 minutes, total cost Sfr11.20).

Gruyères

POP 2153

Cheese and featherweight meringues drowned in thick cream are what this dreamy village is all about. Named after the emblematic *gru* (crane) brandished by the medieval Counts of Gruyères, it is a riot of 15th- to 17th-century houses tumbling down a hillock. Its heart is cobbled, a castle is its crowning glory and hard AOC Gruyère (the village is Gruyères, but the 's' is dropped for the cheese) has been made for centuries in its surrounding Alpine pastures. Fondueserving cafes line the main square.

◉ Sights

Château de Gruyères CASTLE
(✆026 921 21 02; www.chateau-gruyeres.ch; Rue du Château 8; adult/child Sfr12/4; ⊙9am-6pm Apr-Oct, 10am-5pm Nov-Mar) This bewitching turreted castle, home to 19 different Counts of Gruyères, who controlled the Sarine Valley from the 11th to 16th centuries, was rebuilt after a fire in 1493. Inside you can view period furniture, tapestries and modern 'fantasy art', plus watch a 20-minute multimedia film about Gruyères' history. Don't miss the short footpath that weaves its way around the castle. Combined tickets covering the château and other area attractions are available.

La Maison du Gruyère FARM
(✆026 921 84 00; www.lamaisondugruyere.ch; Place de la Gare 3; adult/child Sfr7/6; ⊙9am-6.30pm Jun-Sep, to 6pm Oct-May) The secret behind Gruyère cheese is revealed in Pringy, directly opposite Gruyères train station (1.5km below town). Cheesemaking takes place three to four times daily between 9am and 11am and 12.30pm to 2.30pm. A combined ticket for both the dairy and Château de Gruyères costs Sfr16 (no child combo).

❶ Getting There & Away

Gruyères is served by hourly trains from Montreux (Sfr20.40, 1¼ hours, via Montbovon). The village is a 10-minute walk uphill from the station (or take the free shuttle bus).

VALAIS

This is Matterhorn country, an intoxicating land that seduces the toughest of critics with its endless panoramic vistas and breathtaking views. Switzerland's 10 highest mountains rise to the sky here, while snow fiends ski and board in one of Europe's top resorts, Zermatt.

Zermatt

POP 5759

Since the mid-19th century, Zermatt has starred among Switzerland's glitziest resorts. Today. it attracts intrepid mountaineers and hikers, skiers who cruise at a snail's pace, spellbound by the scenery, and styleconscious darlings flashing designer togs in the lounge bars. But all are smitten with the **Matterhorn** (4478m), the Alps' most famous peak and an unfathomable monolith synonymous with Switzerland that you simply can't quite stop looking at.

◉ Sights & Activities

Zermatt is skiing heaven, with mostly long, scenic red runs, plus a smattering of blues for ski virgins and knuckle-whitening blacks for experts. The main skiing areas in winter are Rothorn, Stockhorn and Klein Matterhorn – 350km of ski runs in all, with a link from Klein Matterhorn to the Italian resort of Cervinia and a freestyle park with half-pipe for snowboarders. Summer skiing (20km of runs) and boarding (gravity park at Plateau Rosa on the Theodul glacier) is Europe's most extensive. One-/two-day summer ski passes are Sfr84/125.

Zermatt is also excellent for **hiking**, with 400km of summer trails through some of the most incredible scenery in the Alps – the tourist office has trail maps. For Matterhorn close-ups, nothing beats the highly dramatic **Matterhorn Glacier Trail** (two hours, 6.5km) from Trockener Steg to Schwarzsee; 23 information panels en route tell you everything you could possibly need to know about glaciers and glacial life.

★**Gornergratbahn** RAILWAY
(www.gornergrat.ch; Bahnhofplatz 7; adult/child round trip Sfr94/47; ⊙7am-7.15pm) Europe's highest cogwheel railway has climbed through picture-postcard scenery to **Gornergrat** (3089m) – a 30-minute journey – since 1898. On the way up, sit on the right-hand side of the little red train to gawp at the Matterhorn. Tickets allow you to get on and off en route; there are restaurants at Riffelalp (2211m) and Riffelberg (2582m). In summer an extra train runs once a week at sunrise and sunset – the most spectacular trips of all.

★**Matterhorn Glacier Paradise** CABLE CAR
(www.matterhornparadise.ch; adult/child return Sfr100/50; ⊙8.30am-4.20pm) Views from Zermatt's cable cars are all remarkable, but the Matterhorn Glacier Paradise is the icing on the cake. Ride Europe's highest-altitude cable car to 3883m and gawp at 14 glaciers and 38 mountain peaks over 4000m from the **Panoramic Platform** (only open in good weather). Don't miss the **Glacier Palace**, an ice palace complete with glittering ice sculptures and an ice slide to swoosh down bum first. End with some exhilarating **snow tubing** outside in the snowy surrounds.

🍴 Sleeping & Eating

Most places close May to mid- (or late) June and again from October to mid-November.

★**Hotel Bahnhof** HOTEL **€**
(☑027 967 24 06; www.hotelbahnhof.com; Bahnhofstrasse; dm Sfr35-50, s/d from Sfr80/120; ⊙closed May–mid-Jun & mid-Oct–Nov; 🖧) Opposite the train station, these five-star budget digs have comfy beds, spotless bathrooms and family-perfect rooms for four. Dorms (Sfr5 liner obligatory) are cosy and there's a stylish lounge with armchairs to flop in and books to read. No breakfast, but feel free to prepare your own in the snazzy, open-plan kitchen.

SWITZERLAND'S SCENIC TRAINS

Swiss trains, buses and boats are more than a means of getting from A to B. Stunning views invariably make the journey itself the destination. Switzerland boasts the following routes among its classic sightseeing journeys.

You're able to choose just one leg of the trip. Also, scheduled services often ply the same routes for standard fares; these are cheaper than the named trains, which often have cars with extra-large windows and require reservations.

Glacier Express (www.glacierexpress.ch) Hop aboard this red train with floor-to-ceiling windows for the famous eight-hour journey between St Moritz and Zermatt. Scenic highlights include the climb through Alpine meadows to Oberalp Pass (2033m) – the journey's high point between Disentis/Mustér and Andermatt – and the crossing of the iconic 65m-high Landwasser Viaduct between St Moritz and Chur.

Bernina Express (www.rhb.ch) This unforgettable four-hour train ride cuts 145km through the Engadine's glaciated realms, linking Chur, St Moritz and Tirano, Italy. Between May and October, continue 2½ hours by bus from Tirano to Lugano along Italy's Lake Como and Ticino's palm-fringed Lake Lugano.

Jungfrau Region (www.jungfrau.ch) You can spend days ogling stunning Alpine scenery from the trains, cable cars and more here.

GoldenPass Line (www.goldenpass.ch) Travels between Lucerne and Montreux. The journey is in three legs, and you must change trains twice. Regular trains, without panoramic windows, work the whole route hourly.

Centovalli Express (www.centovalli.ch) An underappreciated gem of a line (two hours) that snakes along fantastic river gorges in Switzerland and Italy, from Locarno to Domodossola. Trains run through the day and it is easy to connect to Brig and beyond from Domodossola in Italy.

★ Snowboat Bar & Yacht Club
INTERNATIONAL €

(☏ 027 967 43 33; www.zermattsnowboat.com; Vispastrasse 20; mains Sfr22-39; ⊘ noon-midnight) This hybrid eating-drinking riverside address, with marigold-yellow deckchairs sprawled across its rooftop sun terrace, is a blessing. When fondue tires, head here for barbecue-sizzled burgers (not just beef, but crab and veggie burgers too), super-power creative salads (the Omega 3 buster is a favourite) and great cocktails. The vibe? 100% friendly, fun and funky.

★ Chez Vrony
SWISS €€

(☏ 027 967 25 52; www.chezvrony.ch; Findeln; breakfast Sfr15-28, mains Sfr25-45; ⊘ 9.15am-5pm Dec-Apr & mid-Jun–mid-Oct) Ride the Sunnegga Express funicular (one-way/round trip Sfr 16/24) to 2288m, then ski down blue piste 6 or summer-hike 15 minutes to Zermatt's tastiest slope-side address in the Findeln hamlet. Keep snug in a blanket or lounge on a sheepskin-cushioned chaise longue and revel in the effortless romance of this century-old farmhouse with potted edelweiss, first-class Matterhorn views and exceptional organic cuisine.

❶ Getting There & Around

CAR

Zermatt is car-free. Motorists have to park in **Täsch** (☏ 027 967 12 14; www.matterhorn terminal.ch; per 24hr Sfr15.50) and ride the Zermatt Shuttle train (adult/child Sfr8.40/4.20, 12 minutes, every 20 minutes from 6am to 9.40pm) the last 5km to Zermatt.

TRAIN

Trains depart regularly from Brig – a major rail hub (Sfr38, 1½ hours), stopping at Visp en route. Zermatt is also the starting point of the popular Glacier Express to Graubünden.

BERN

POP 131,554

One of the planet's most underrated capitals, Bern is a fabulous find. With the genteel old soul of a Renaissance man and the heart of a high-flying 21st-century gal, the riverside city is both medieval and modern. The 15th-century Old Town is gorgeous enough to sweep you off your feet and make you forget the century (it's definitely worthy of its 1983 Unesco World Heritage Site status).

◉ Sights

Bern's flag-bedecked medieval centre is an attraction in its own right, with 6km of covered arcades and cellar shops and bars descending from the streets. After a devastating fire in 1405, the wooden city was rebuilt in today's sandstone. The city's 11 decorative fountains (1545) depict historical and folkloric characters. Most are along Marktgasse as it becomes Kramgasse and Gerechtigkeitsgasse, but the most famous lies in Kornhausplatz: the Kindlifresserbrunnen (Ogre Fountain) of a giant snacking...on children.

★ Zytglogge
TOWER

(Marktgasse) Bern's most famous Old Town sight, this ornate clock tower once formed part of the city's western gate (1191–1256). Crowds congregate to watch its revolving figures twirl at four minutes before the hour, after which the chimes begin. Tours enter the tower to see the clock mechanism from May to October; contact the tourist office for details. The clock tower supposedly helped Albert Einstein hone his special theory of relativity, developed while working as a patent clerk in Bern.

Münster
CATHEDRAL

(www.bernermuenster.ch; Münsterplatz 1; tower adult/child Sfr5/2; ⊘ 10am-5pm Mon-Sat, 11.30am-5pm Sun Apr–mid-Oct, noon-4pm Mon-Fri, 10am-5pm Sat, 11.30am-4pm Sun mid-Oct–Mar) Bern's 15th-century Gothic cathedral boasts Switzerland's loftiest spire (100m); climb the 344-step spiral staircase for vertiginous views. Coming down, stop by the Upper Bells (1356), rung at 11am, noon and 3pm daily, and the three 10-tonne Lower Bells (Switzerland's largest). Don't miss the main portal's Last Judgement, which portrays Bern's mayor going to heaven, while his Zürich counterpart is shown into hell. Afterwards, wander through the adjacent Münsterplattform, a bijou clifftop park with a sunny pavilion cafe.

★ Zentrum Paul Klee
MUSEUM

(☏ 031 359 01 01; www.zpk.org; Monument im Fruchtland 3; adult/child Sfr20/7; ⊘ 10am-5pm Tue-Sun) Bern's answer to the Guggenheim, Renzo Piano's architecturally bold 150m-long wave-like edifice houses an exhibition space that showcases rotating works from Paul Klee's prodigious and often playful career. Interactive computer displays and audioguides help interpret the Swiss-born artist's work. Next door, the fun-packed **Kindermuseum Creaviva** (☑031 359 01 61; www.creaviva-zpk.org; ⊘10am-5pm Tue-Sun; 🖼) `FREE` lets kids experiment with hands-on art exhibits or create original artwork with the atelier's materials during the weekend **Five Franc Studio** (www.creaviva-zpk.org/5-franc-studio; Sfr5; ⊘10am-4.30pm Sat & Sun; 🖼).

Bus 12 runs from Bubenbergplatz direct to the museum.

🛏 Sleeping

Hotel Landhaus
HOTEL €

(☑031 348 03 05; www.landhausbern.ch; Altenbergstrasse 4; dm Sfr38, s Sfr115-130, d Sfr160-180, s/d without bathroom from Sfr85/120; 🅿🖼@🛜) Fronted by the river and Old Town spires, this well-run boho hotel offers a mix of stylish six-bed dorms, family rooms and doubles. Its buzzing ground-floor cafe and terrace attracts a cheery crowd. Breakfast (included with private rooms) costs Sfr10 extra for dorm-dwellers.

Hotel Schweizerhof
LUXURY HOTEL €€€

(☑031 326 80 80; www.schweizerhof-bern.ch; Bahnhofplatz 11; s Sfr359-640, d Sfr449-790; 🅿🖼@🛜) This classy five-star offers lavish accommodation with excellent amenities and service. A hop, skip and a jump from the train station, it's geared for both business and pleasure.

🍴 Eating & Drinking

Look for interesting cafes and bistros scattered amid the arcades on Old Town streets including Zeughausgasse, Rathausgasse, Marktgasse and Kramgasse.

Altes Tramdepot
SWISS €€

(☑031 368 14 15; www.altestramdepot.ch; Grosser Muristalden 6, Am Bärengraben; mains Sfr18-44; ⊘11am-12.30am Mon-Fri, from 10am Sat & Sun) At this cavernous microbrewery, Swiss specialities compete against wok-cooked stir-fries for your affection, and the microbrews go down a treat: sample three different varieties for Sfr10.90, four for Sfr14.60, or five for Sfr18.20.

Café des Pyrénées
BAR

(☑031 311 30 63; Kornhausplatz 17; ⊘9am-11.30pm Mon-Wed, to 12.30am Thu-Sat, noon-9pm Sun) This bohemian corner joint, under new ownership as of 2016, remains a beloved Bern institution for its traditional Parisian cafe-bar vibe. Its central location near the tram tracks makes for good people-watching.

ℹ Information

Tourist Office (☑031 328 12 12; www.bern.com; Bahnhoftplatz 10a; ⊘9am-7pm Mon-Sat, to 6pm Sun) Street-level floor of the train station. City tours, free hotel bookings, internet access. There's also a branch near the bear park (Grosser Muristalden 6, Bärengraben; ⊘9am-6pm Jun-Sep, 10am-4pm Mar-May & Oct, 11am-4pm Nov-Feb).

ℹ Getting There & Around

Frequent trains connect to most Swiss cities, including Geneva (Sfr51, 1¾ hours), Basel (Sfr41, 55 minutes) and Zürich (Sfr51, 55 minutes to 1½ hours).

Buses and trams are operated by **BernMobil** (www.bernmobil.ch); many depart from stops near Bahnhofplatz.

CENTRAL SWITZERLAND & BERNESE OBERLAND

These two regions should come with a health warning – caution: may cause breathlessness as the sun rises and sets over Lake Lucerne, trembling before the north face of Eiger and uncontrollable bouts of euphoria at the foot of Jungfrau.

Lucerne

POP 81,295

Recipe for a gorgeous Swiss city: take a cobalt lake ringed by mountains of myth, add a medieval Old Town and sprinkle with covered bridges, sunny plazas, candy-coloured houses and waterfront promenades. Bright, beautiful Lucerne has been Little Miss Popular since the likes of Goethe, Queen Victoria and Wagner savoured her views in the 19th century.

◉ Sights

Your first port of call should be the medieval Old Town, with its ancient rampart walls and towers. Wander the cobblestone lanes and squares, pondering 15th-century buildings with painted facades and the two much-photographed covered bridges over the Reuss.

★Kapellbrücke
BRIDGE

(Chapel Bridge) You haven't really been to Lucerne until you have strolled the creaky 14th-century Kapellbrücke, spanning the Reuss River in the Old Town. The octagonal water tower is original, but its gabled roof is

WORTH A TRIP

MOUNTAIN DAY TRIPS FROM LUCERNE

Among the several (heavily marketed) day trips from Lucerne, consider the one to 2132m-high **Mt Pilatus** (www. pilatus.com). From May to October, you can reach the peak on a classic 'golden round-trip'. Board the lake steamer from Lucerne to Alpnachstad, then rise with the world's steepest cog railway to Mt Pilatus. From the summit, cable cars bring you down to Kriens via Fräkmüntegg and Krienseregg, where bus 1 takes you back to Lucerne. The return trip costs Sfr106 (less with valid Swiss, Eurail or InterRail passes).

a modern reconstruction, rebuilt after a disastrous fire in 1993. As you cross the bridge, note Heinrich Wägmann's 17th-century triangular roof panels, showing important events from Swiss history and mythology. The icon is at its most photogenic when bathed in soft golden light at dusk.

★**Museum Sammlung Rosengart** MUSEUM
(☎041 220 16 60; www.rosengart.ch; Pilatusstrasse 10; adult/child Sfr18/10; ☉10am-6pm) Lucerne's blockbuster cultural attraction is the Sammlung Rosengart, occupying a graceful neoclassical pile in the heart of town. It showcases the outstanding stash of Angela Rosengart, a Swiss art dealer and close friend of Picasso. Alongside works by the great Spanish master are paintings and sketches by Klee, Cézanne, Renoir, Chagall, Kandinsky, Miró, Matisse, Modigliani and Monet, among others. Complementing this collection are some 200 photographs by David Douglas Duncan documenting the last 17 years of Picasso's life.

★**Lion Monument** MONUMENT
(Löwendenkmal; Denkmalstrasse) By far the most touching of the 19th-century sights that lured so many British to Lucerne is the Lion Monument. Lukas Ahorn carved this 10m-long sculpture of a dying lion into the rock face in 1820 to commemorate Swiss soldiers who died defending King Louis XVI during the French Revolution. Mark Twain once called it the 'saddest and most moving

piece of rock in the world'. For *Narnia* fans, it often evokes Aslan at the stone table.

Verkehrshaus MUSEUM
(Swiss Museum of Transport; ☎0900 333 456; www.verkehrshaus.ch; Lidostrasse 5; adult/child Sfr30/15; ☉10am-6pm Apr-Oct, to 5pm Nov-Mar; ✪) A great kid-pleaser, the fascinating interactive Verkehrshaus is deservedly Switzerland's most popular museum. Alongside rockets, steam locomotives, aeroplanes, vintage cars and dugout canoes are hands-on activities such as pedalo boats, flight simulators, broadcasting studios and a walkable 1:20,000-scale map of Switzerland.

The museum also shelters a **planetarium** (adult/child Sfr15/9), Switzerland's largest **3D cinema** (www.filmtheater.ch; adult/child Sfr18/14), and the **Swiss Chocolate Adventure** (adult/child Sfr15/9), a 20-minute ride that whirls visitors through multimedia exhibits on the origins, history, production and distribution of chocolate, from Ghana to Switzerland and beyond.

Spreuerbrücke BRIDGE
(Spreuer Bridge; btwn Kasernenplatz & Mühlenplatz) Downriver from Kapellbrücke, this 1408 structure is darker and smaller but entirely original. Lore has it that this was the only bridge where Lucerne's medieval villagers were allowed to throw *Spreu* (chaff) into the river. Here, the roof panels consist of artist Caspar Meglinger's movie-storyboard-style sequence of paintings, *The Dance of Death,* showing how the plague affected all levels of society.

🛏 Sleeping

Backpackers Lucerne HOSTEL €
(☎041 360 04 20; www.backpackerslucerne.ch; Alpenquai 42; dm/tr Sfr33/111, tw Sfr78-84; ☉reception 7.30-10am & 4-11pm; @☎) Just opposite the lake, a 15-minute walk southeast of the station, this is a soulful place to crash, with art-slung walls, bubbly staff and immaculate dorms with balconies. There's no breakfast, but guests have access to a well-equipped kitchen.

Hotel Waldstätterhof HOTEL €€
(☎041 227 12 71; www.hotel-waldstaetterhof.ch; Zentralstrasse 4; s Sfr190, d Sfr270-300, ste Sfr340-380; ℗☎) Opposite the train station, this hotel with faux-Gothic exterior offers smart, modern rooms with hardwood-style floors and high ceilings, plus excellent service.

The Hotel
HOTEL €€€

(☑ 041 226 86 86; www.the-hotel.ch; Sempacherstrasse 14; r Sfr255-395, ste Sfr555-595; ✳ @ 🛜) This shamelessly hip hotel, bearing the imprint of architect Jean Nouvel, is all streamlined chic, with refined suites featuring stills from movie classics on the ceilings. Downstairs, the hotel boasts one of Lucerne's trendiest restaurants, and the gorgeous green park across the street is a cool place to idle.

✖ Eating & Drinking

★ Grottino 1313
ITALIAN €€

(☑ 041 610 13 13; www.grottino1313.ch; Industriestrasse 7; lunch menus Sfr20-38, dinner menu Sfr64; ⊘ 11am-2pm & 6-11.30pm Mon-Fri, 6-11.30pm Sat & Sun) Offering a welcome escape from Lucerne's tourist throngs, this relaxed yet stylish eatery serves ever-changing 'surprise' menus featuring starters like chestnut soup with figs, creative pasta dishes, meats cooked over an open fire and scrumptious desserts. The gravel-strewn, herb-fringed front patio is lovely on a summer afternoon, while the candlelit interior exudes sheer cosiness on a chilly evening.

★ Wirtshaus Galliker
SWISS €€

(☑ 041 240 10 02; Schützenstrasse 1; mains Sfr21-51; ⊘ 11.30am-2pm & 6-8.30pm Tue-Sat) Passionately run by the Galliker family for over four generations, this old-style, wood-panelled tavern attracts a lively bunch of regulars. Motherly waitresses dish up Lucerne soul food (rösti, *chögalipaschtetli* and the like) that is batten-the-hatches filling.

Rathaus Bräuerei
BREWERY

(☑ 041 410 52 57; Unter den Egg 2; ⊘ 11.30am-midnight Mon-Sat, to 11pm Sun) Sip home-brewed beer under the vaulted arches of this buzzy tavern near Kapellbrücke, or nab a pavement table and watch the river flow.

ℹ Information

Lake Lucerne Region Visitors Card (Vierwaldstättersee Gästekarte; www.luzern.com/en/festivals-events/visitors-card) Stamped by your hotel, this free card entitles visitors to discounts on various museums, sporting facilities, cable cars and lake cruises in Lucerne and the surrounding area.

Tourist Office (☑ 041 227 17 17; www.luzern.com; Zentralstrasse 5; ⊘ 8.30am-7pm Mon-Fri, 9am-7pm Sat, 9am-5pm Sun May-Oct, shorter hours Nov-Apr) Reached from Zentralstrasse or platform 3 of the Hauptbahnhof. Offers city walking tours (Sfr18). Call for hotel reservations.

ℹ Getting There & Around

Frequent trains serve Interlaken Ost (Sfr33, 1¾ hours), Bern (Sfr36 to Sfr40, one hour), Lugano (Sfr61, two hours) and Zürich (Sfr26, 45 minutes to one hour).

SGV (www.lakelucerne.ch) operates extensive boat services on Lake Lucerne (including some paddle steamers). Rail passes are good for free or discounted travel.

Interlaken

POP 5692

Once Interlaken made the Victorians swoon with its dreamy mountain vistas, viewed from the chandelier-lit confines of its grand hotels. Today, it makes daredevils scream with its adrenalin-loaded adventures. Straddling the glittering Lakes Thun and Brienz (thus the name), and dazzled by the pearly whites of Eiger, Mönch and Jungfrau, Interlaken boasts exceptional scenery.

◉ Sights & Activities

Switzerland is the world's second-biggest adventure-sports centre and Interlaken is its busiest hub. Sample prices are Sfr120 for rafting or canyoning, Sfr140 for hydrospeeding, Sfr130 to Sfr180 for bungee or canyon jumping, Sfr170 for tandem paragliding, Sfr180 for ice climbing, Sfr220 for hang-gliding and Sfr430 for skydiving. A half-day mountain-bike tour will set you back around Sfr25.

Harder Kulm
MOUNTAIN

(www.jungfrau.ch/harderkulm; adult/child Sfr16/8) For far-reaching views to the 4000m giants, take the eight-minute **funicular ride** (adult/child return Sfr32/16) to 1322m Harder Kulm. Many hiking paths begin here, and the vertigo-free can enjoy the panorama from the **Zweiseensteg** (Two Lake Bridge) jutting out above the valley. The wildlife park near the valley station is home to Alpine critters, including marmots and ibex.

🛏 Sleeping

★ Backpackers Villa Sonnenhof
HOSTEL €

(☑ 033 826 71 71; www.villa.ch; Alpenstrasse 16; dm Sfr39.50-47, d Sfr110-148; 🅿 🛜) Repeatedly voted one of Europe's best hostels, Sonnenhof is a slick, ecofriendly combination of ultramodern chalet and elegant art-nouveau villa. Dorms are immaculate, and some have balconies with Jungfrau views. There's also a relaxed lounge, a well-equipped kitchen, a kids' playroom and a vast backyard for mountain gazing. Special family rates are available.

★ **Victoria-Jungfrau**
Grand Hotel & Spa   LUXURY HOTEL €€€
(☏ 033 828 28 28; www.victoria-jungfrau.ch; Höheweg 41; d Sfr479-749, junior ste from Sfr539, ste from Sfr950; P @ 🎙 🏊) The reverent hush and impeccable service here (as well as the prices) evoke an era when only royalty and the seriously wealthy travelled. A perfect melding of well-preserved art-nouveau features and modern luxury make this Interlaken's answer to Raffles – with plum views of Jungfrau, three first-class restaurants and a gorgeous spa to boot.

✗ Eating & Drinking

Höheweg, east of Interlaken Ost train station, is lined with ethnic eateries with reasonable prices.

Sandwich Bar   SANDWICHES €
(www.sandwichbar.ch; Rosenstrasse 5; sandwiches Sfr6-9.50; ⏰ 7.30am-7pm Mon-Fri, 8am-5pm Sat) Choose your bread and get creative with fillings like air-dried ham with sun-dried tomatoes and brie with walnuts. Or try the soups, salads, toasties and locally made ice cream.

❶ Information

Tourist Office (☏ 033 826 53 00; www.inter-lakentourism.ch; Marktgasse 1; ⏰ 8am-7pm Mon-Fri, to 5pm Sat, 10am-4pm Sun Jul & Aug, shorter hours Sep-Jun) Relocated next to the post office in 2017, Interlaken's well-stocked, well-staffed tourist office also provides hotel booking services.

❶ Getting There & Away

There are two train stations. Interlaken West is slightly closer to the centre and is a stop for trains to Bern (Sfr29, 50 minutes). Interlaken Ost (East) is the rail hub for all lines, including the scenic ones up into the Jungfrau region and the lovely GoldenPass Line to Lucerne (Sfr33, 1¾ hours).

Jungfrau Region

If the Bernese Oberland is Switzerland's Alpine heart, the Jungfrau region is where yours will skip a beat. Presided over by glacier-encrusted monoliths Eiger, Mönch and Jungfrau (Ogre, Monk and Virgin), the scenery stirs the soul and strains the neck muscles. It's a magnet for skiers and snowboarders with its 214km of pistes, 44 lifts and much more; a one-day ski pass for either

Grindelwald-Wengen or Mürren-Schilthorn costs adult/child Sfr63/32.

Come summer, hundreds of kilometres of walking trails allow you to capture the landscape from many angles, but it never looks less than astonishing.

❶ Getting There & Around

Hourly trains (www.jungfrau.ch) depart for the Jungfrau region from Interlaken Ost station. Sit in the front half of the train for Lauterbrunnen (Sfr7.60) or the back half for Grindelwald (Sfr11.40).

From Grindelwald, trains ascend to Kleine Scheidegg (Sfr31), where you can transfer for Jungfraujoch. From Lauterbrunnen, trains ascend to Wengen (Sfr6.80) and continue to Kleine Scheidegg (Sfr24) for Jungfraujoch.

You can reach Mürren two ways from Lauterbrunnen: with a bus and cable car via Stechelberg (Sfr16.40) or with a cable car and train via Grütschalp (Sfr11.40). Do a circle trip for the full experience. Gimmelwald is reached by cable car from Stechelberg and Mürren.

Many cable cars close for servicing in April and November.

Grindelwald

POP 3740

Grindelwald's charms were discovered by skiers and hikers in the late 19th century, making it one of Switzerland's oldest resorts and the Jungfrau's largest. It has lost none of its appeal over the decades, with archetypal Alpine chalets and verdant pastures set against the chiselled features of the Eiger north face.

🏃 Activities

The **Grindelwald-First** skiing area has a mix of cruisy red and challenging black runs stretching from Oberjoch at 2486m to the village at 1050m, plus 15.5km of well-groomed cross-country ski trails. In the summer it caters to hikers with 90km of trails at about 1200m, 48km of which are open year-round.

★ **Kleine Scheidegg Walk**   HIKING
One of the region's most stunning day hikes is this 15km trek from Grindelwald Grund to Wengen via Kleine Scheidegg, which heads up through wildflower-freckled meadows to skirt below the Eiger's north face and reach Kleine Scheidegg, granting arresting views of the 'Big Three'. Allow around 5½ to six

JUNGFRAU REGION HIKING 101

There are hundreds of hikes along the hundreds of kilometres of trails in the Jungfrau region; all include some of the world's most stunning scenery. Every skill and fortitude level is accommodated and options abound. Here are two to get you started:

Grütschalp to Mürren Ride the cable car up from Lauterbrunnen and follow the trail along the railway tracks. The walk to Mürren takes about an hour and is mostly level. There are unbeatable views, Alpine woods and babbling glacier-fed streams.

Männlichen to Kleine Scheidegg Reach the Männlichen lift station by cable car from Wengen or Grindelwald. Now follow the well-marked, spectacular path down to Kleine Scheidegg. It takes about 90 minutes and you have nothing but Alps in front of you.

hours. The best map is the SAW 1:50,000 *Interlaken* (Sfr22.50).

Grindelwald Sports ADVENTURE SPORTS
(☎033 854 12 80; www.grindelwaldsports.ch; Dorfstrasse 103; ⏲8.30am-7pm) Opposite the tourist office, this outfit arranges mountain climbing, ski and snowboard instruction, canyon jumping and glacier bungee jumping at the Gletscherschlucht. It also houses a cosy cafe and sells walking guides.

Sleeping

Mountain Hostel HOSTEL €
(☎033 854 38 38; www.mountainhostel.ch; Grundstrasse 58; dm Sfr35-39, d Sfr98, q Sfr156; P 📶) In a bright blue building halfway between Grindelwald Grund train station and the Männlichen cable-car station, this is an ideal base for sports junkies, with well-kept dorms and a helpful crew. There's a beer garden, ski storage, TV lounge and mountain and e-bike rental.

★ **Gletschergarten** HISTORIC HOTEL €€
(☎033 853 17 21; www.hotel-gletschergarten.ch; Obere Gletscherstrasse 1; s Sfr130-170, d Sfr230-320; P 📶) The sweet Breitenstein family make you feel at home in their rustic timber chalet, brimming with heirlooms from landscape paintings to snapshots of Elsbeth's grandfather who had 12 children (those were the days…). Decked out in pine and flowery fabrics, the rooms have balconies facing Unterer Gletscher at the front and Wetterhorn (best for sunset) at the back.

Wengen

POP 1300

Photogenically poised on a mountain ledge, Wengen has celestial views of the glacier-capped giant peaks' silent majesty as well as the shimmering waterfalls spilling into the Lauterbrunnen Valley below.

The village is car-free and can only be reached by train. It's a fabulous hub for **hiking** for much of the year as well as **skiing** in winter.

From Wengen's train station, loop back under the tracks and head three minutes downhill to **Hotel Bären** (☎033 855 14 19; www.baeren-wengen.ch; s Sfr190-280, d Sfr220-310, f Sfr340-470, all incl half-board; 📶), a snug log chalet with bright, cosy rooms; the affable Brunner family serves a hearty breakfast and delicious seasonal cuisine in the attached restaurant. For superb regional fare in an even dreamier setting, check out the leafy mountain-facing terrace or the pine-clad, candlelit dining room at **Restaurant 1903** (☎033 855 34 22; www.hotel-schoenegg.ch; mains Sfr35-58; ⏲6.30-10pm, closed May & mid-Oct–mid-Dec), a 250m walk uphill from the station.

Jungfraujoch

Jungfraujoch (3471m) is a once-in-a-lifetime trip and there's good reason why two million people a year visit Europe's highest train station. Clear good weather is essential; check www.jungfrau.ch for current conditions, and don't forget warm clothing, sunglasses and sunscreen.

From Interlaken Ost, the journey time is two to 2½ hours each way (Sfr210.80 return, discounts with rail passes). The last train back sets off at 6.43pm in summer and 4.43pm in winter. From May to October there's a cheaper Good Morning Ticket costing Sfr145 if you take one of the first two trains from Interlaken Ost (6.35am or 7.05am) and leave the summit by 1pm.

Gimmelwald

POP 130

Decades ago some anonymous backpacker scribbled these words in the guestbook at the Mountain Hostel: 'If heaven isn't what it's cracked up to be, send me back to Gimmelwald'. Enough said. When the sun is out in Gimmelwald, this pipsqueak of a village will simply take your breath away. Sit outside and listen to the distant roar of avalanches on the sheer mountain faces arrayed before you.

The charming, spotless **Esther's Guest House** (☑ 033 855 54 88; www.esthersguesthouse. ch; Kirchstatt; s Sfr60-90, d Sfr120-180, apt Sfr240-250; 🖥) is run with love and care. For an extra Sfr16, you'll be served a delicious breakfast of homemade bread, cheese and yoghurt.

Mürren

POP 450

Arrive on a clear evening when the sun hangs low on the horizon, and you'll think you've died and gone to heaven. Car-free Mürren *is* storybook Switzerland.

Sleeping options near the train station include **Eiger Guesthouse** (☑ 033 856 54 60; www.eigerguesthouse.com; s Sfr95-140, d Sfr120-200, q Sfr180-250; 🖥), with its downstairs pub serving tasty food, and **Hotel Eiger** (☑ 033 856 54 54; www.hoteleiger.com; s Sfr183-228, d Sfr275-370, ste Sfr420-1250; 🖥🏊), a huge wooden chalet with swimming pool and picture-windows perfectly framing the Eiger, Mönch and Jungfrau.

Schilthorn

There's a tremendous 360-degree panorama available from the 2970m Schilthorn. On a clear day, you can see over 200 peaks, from Titlis to Mont Blanc and across to the German Black Forest. Note that this was the site of Blofeld's HQ in the under-appreciated 1969 James Bond film *On Her Majesty's Secret Service*. The **Bond World 007** (www. schilthorn.ch; Schilthorn; free with cable-car ticket; ⊙ 8am-6pm) interactive exhibition gives you the chance to pose for photos secret-agent style and relive movie moments in a helicopter and bobsled.

From Interlaken Ost, take a Sfr129.60 excursion to Schilthorn via Lauterbrunnen, Grütschalp and Mürren, returning via Stechelberg to Interlaken. A return from Lauterbrunnen costs Sfr102 via Grütschalp and Mürren, or Sfr111 via the Stechelberg cable car. A return from Mürren is Sfr80. Ask about discounts for early-morning trips. There are discounts with rail passes.

ZÜRICH

POP 396.955

Culturally vibrant, efficiently run and attractively set at the meeting of river and lake, Zürich is regularly recognised as one of the world's most liveable cities. Long known as a savvy, hard-working financial centre, Switzerland's largest and wealthiest metropolis has also emerged in the 21st century as one of central Europe's hippest destinations, with an artsy, post-industrial edge that is epitomised in its exuberant summer Street Parade.

⊙ Sights & Activities

The cobbled streets of the pedestrian Old Town line both sides of the river, while the bank vaults beneath Bahnhofstrasse, the city's most elegant shopping street, are said to be crammed with gold. On Sunday all of Zürich strolls around the lake – on a clear day you'll glimpse the Alps in the distance.

★**Fraumünster**   CATHEDRAL
(www.fraumuenster.ch/en;   Münsterhof;   Sfr5 incl audioguide; ⊙ 10am-6pm Mar-Oct, to 5pm Nov-Feb) The 13th-century cathedral is renowned for its stunning stained-glass windows, designed by the Russian-Jewish master Marc Chagall (1887–1985), who executed the series of five windows in the choir stalls in 1971 and the rose window in the southern transept in 1978. The rose window in the northern transept was created by Augusto Giacometti in 1945. Admission includes a multilingual audioguide.

★**Kunsthaus**   MUSEUM
(☑ 044 253 84 84; www.kunsthaus.ch; Heimplatz 1; adult/child Sfr16/free, Wed free; ⊙ 10am-8pm Wed & Thu, to 6pm Tue & Fri-Sun) Zürich's impressive fine-arts gallery boasts a rich collection of largely European art. It stretches from the Middle Ages through a mix of Old Masters to Alberto Giacometti stick figures, Monet and Van Gogh masterpieces, Rodin sculptures, and other 19th- and 20th-century art. Swiss Rail and Museum Passes don't provide free admission but the ZürichCard does.

Zürich

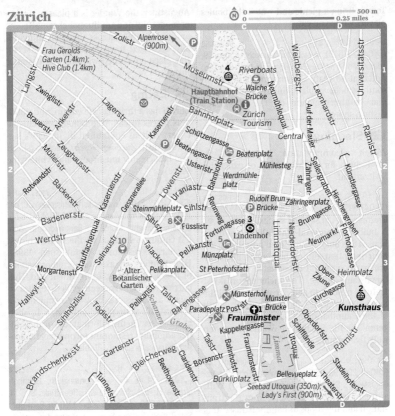

Zürich

◎ Top Sights

◎ Sights

🛏 Sleeping

✕ Eating

☕ Drinking & Nightlife

Schweizerisches Landesmuseum MUSEUM
(Swiss National Museum; ☎ 058 466 65 11; www.
nationalmuseum.ch/e/zuerich; Museumstrasse 2;
adult/child Sfr10/free; ⊙ 10am-5pm Tue, Wed & Fri-
Sun, to 7pm Thu) Inside a purpose-built cross
between a mansion and a castle sprawls this
eclectic and imaginatively presented museum. The permanent collection offers an
extensive tour through Swiss history, with
exhibits ranging from elaborately carved
and painted sleds to household and religious
artefacts to a series of reconstructed historical rooms spanning six centuries. In August
2016 the museum celebrated a major expansion with the opening of its new archaeology
section in a brand-new wing.

Lindenhof SQUARE
Spectacular views across the Limmat to the
Grossmünster from a tree-shaded hilltop
park, smack in the heart of the Aldstadt (Old

Town). Bring a picnic and watch the boules players while you eat.

Seebad Utoquai SWIMMING

(☑ 044 251 61 51; www.bad-utoquai.ch; Utoquai 49; adult/child Sfr8/4; ☺ 7am-8pm mid-May–late Sep) Adjacent to leafy Zürichhorn park, 400m south of Bellvueplatz, this is the most popular bathing pavilion on the Zürichsee's eastern shore.

🛏 Sleeping

Zürich accommodation prices are fittingly high for the main city of expensive Switzerland.

SYHA Hostel HOSTEL €

(☑ 043 399 78 00; www.youthhostel.ch; Mutschellenstrasse 114; dm Sfr43-46, s/d Sfr120/144; @ 🛜) A bulbous, Band-Aid-pink 1960s landmark houses this busy, institutional hostel with 24-hour reception, dining hall, sparkling modern bathrooms and dependable wi-fi in the downstairs lounge. The included breakfast features miso soup and rice alongside all the Swiss standards. It's about 20 minutes south of the Hauptbahnhof. Take tram 7 to Morgental, or the S-Bahn to Wollishofen, then walk five minutes.

★ Townhouse BOUTIQUE HOTEL €€

(☑ 044 200 95 95; www.townhouse.ch; Schützengasse 7; s Sfr195-395, d Sfr225-425; 🛜) With a dream location only steps from the train station and the shops of Bahnhofstrasse, this stylish five-storey hotel offers friendly service and a host of welcoming touches. The 21 rooms come in an assortment of sizes from 15 sq metres to 35 sq metres, with luxurious wallpapers, wall hangings, parquet floors, retro furniture, DVD players and iPod docking stations.

Lady's First HOTEL €€

(☑ 044 380 80 10; www.ladysfirst.ch; Mainaustrasse 24; r Sfr180-338; 🛜) Despite the name, discerning guests of all genders are welcome at this attractive hotel near the opera house and lake – though the attached wellness centre with its rooftop terrace is open to women only. The immaculate, generally spacious rooms abound in aesthetic touches such as traditional parquet flooring and designer furnishings.

Hotel Widder HOTEL €€€

(☑ 044 224 25 26; www.widderhotel.ch; Rennweg 7; s/d from Sfr523/625; P ❀ @ 🛜) A supremely stylish hotel in the equally grand district of Augustiner, the Widder is a pleasing fusion of modernity and traditional charm. Rooms and public areas across the eight individually decorated town houses that make up this place are stuffed with art and designer furniture.

✖ Eating

Zürich has a thriving cafe culture and 2000-plus places to eat. Traditional local cuisine is very rich, as epitomised by the city's signature dish, *Zürcher Geschnetzeltes* (sliced veal in a creamy mushroom and white wine sauce).

★ Haus Hiltl VEGETARIAN €

(☑ 044 227 70 00; www.hiltl.ch; Sihlstrasse 28; per 100g takeaway/cafe/restaurant Sfr3.50/4.50/5.50; ☺ 6am-midnight Mon-Sat, 8am-midnight Sun; ☑) Guinness-certified as the world's oldest vegetarian restaurant (established 1898), Hiltl proffers an astounding smorgasbord of meatless delights, from Indian and Thai curries to Mediterranean grilled veggies to salads and desserts. Browse to your heart's content, fill your plate and weigh it, then choose a seat in the informal cafe or the spiffier adjoining restaurant (economical takeaway service is also available).

★ Café Sprüngli SWEETS €

(☑ 044 224 46 46; www.spruengli.ch; Bahnhofstrasse 21; hot chocolate & coffee drinks Sfr5-14, sweets Sfr8-16; ☺ 7am-6.30pm Mon-Fri, 8am-6pm Sat, 9.30am-5.30pm Sun) Sit down for cakes, chocolate, ice cream and exquisite coffee drinks at this epicentre of sweet Switzerland, in business since 1836. You can have a light lunch too, but whatever you do, don't fail to check out the heavenly chocolate shop around the corner on Paradeplatz.

★ Alpenrose SWISS €€

(☑ 044 431 11 66; www.restaurantalpenrose.ch; Fabrikstrasse 12; lunch menus Sfr21-25, dinner mains Sfr22-38; ☺ 9am-11.30pm Tue-Fri, 5-11.30pm Sat & Sun) With its tall stencilled windows, warm wood panelling and stucco ceiling ornamentation, the Alpenrose exudes cosy old world charm, and the cuisine here lives up to the promise. Hearty Swiss classics such as herb-stuffed trout with homemade *Spätzli* (egg noodles) and buttered carrots are exquisitely prepared and presented, accompanied by a good wine list and a nice selection of desserts.

Zeughauskeller SWISS €€
(☎ 044 220 15 15; www.zeughauskeller.ch; Bahnhofstrasse 28a; mains Sfr19-37; ☉ 11.30am-11pm; 🖉) The menu (in eight languages) at this huge, atmospheric beer hall with ample sidewalk seating offers more than a dozen varieties of sausage, along with numerous other Swiss specialities, including some vegetarian options.

Drinking & Entertainment

Options abound across town, but the bulk of the more animated drinking dens are in Züri-West, especially along Langstrasse in Kreis 4 and Hardstrasse in Kreis 5.

★ **Frau Gerolds Garten** BAR
(www.fraugerold.ch; Geroldstrasse 23/23a; ☉ bar-restaurant 11am-midnight Mon-Sat, noon-10pm Sun Apr-Sep, 6pm-midnight Mon-Sat Oct-Mar, market & shops 11am-7pm Mon-Fri, to 6pm Sat year-round; 🖈) Hmm, where to start? The wine bar? The margarita bar? The gin bar? Whichever poison you choose, this wildly popular focal point of Zürich's summer drinking scene is pure unadulterated fun and one of the best grown-up playgrounds in Europe.

Strewn with shipping containers, overhung with multicoloured fairy lights and sandwiched between cheery flower beds and a screeching railyard, its outdoor seating options range from picnic tables to pillow-strewn terraces to a 2nd-floor sundeck. In winter, the restaurant moves indoors to a funky pavilion and great fondue warms the soul.

★ **Rimini Bar** BAR
(www.rimini.ch; Badweg 10; ☉ 7.15pm-midnight Sun-Thu, 6.45pm-midnight Fri, 2pm-midnight Sat Apr-Oct) Secluded behind a fence along the Sihl River, this bar at the Männerbad public baths is one of Zürich's most inviting open-air drinking spots. Its vast wood deck is adorned with red-orange party lights, picnic tables and throw cushions for lounging, accompanied by the sound of water from the adjacent pools. Open in good weather only.

Hive Club CLUB
(☎ 044 271 12 10; www.hiveclub.ch; Geroldstrasse 5; ☉ 11pm-4am Thu, to 7am Fri, to 9am Sat) Electronic music creates the buzz at this artsy, alternative club adjacent to Frau Gerolds Garten in Kreis 4. Enter through an alley strung with multicoloured umbrellas, giant animal heads, mushrooms and watering cans. Big-

name DJs keep things going into the wee hours three nights a week.

Rote Fabrik LIVE MUSIC
(☎ music 044 485 58 68, theatre 044 485 58 28; www.rotefabrik.ch; Seestrasse 395) With a fabulous lakeside location, this multifaceted performing-arts centre stages rock, jazz and hip-hop concerts, original-language films, theatre and dance performances. There's also a bar and a restaurant. Take bus 161 or 165 from Bürkliplatz.

ℹ Information

Zürich Tourism (☎ 044 215 40 00, hotel reservations 044 215 40 40; www.zuerich.com; train station; ☉ 8am-8.30pm Mon-Sat, 8.30am to 6.30pm Sun May-Oct, 8.30am-7pm Mon-Sat, 9am-6pm Sun Nov-Apr)

ℹ Getting There & Away

AIR
Zürich Airport (ZRH; ☎ 043 816 22 11; www.zurich-airport.com), 9km north of the centre, is Switzerland's main airport.

TRAIN
Direct trains run to Stuttgart (Sfr63, three hours), Munich (Sfr96, 4¼ hours), Innsbruck (Sfr76, 3½ hours) and other international destinations.

There are regular direct departures to most major Swiss towns, such as Lucerne (Sfr26, 45 to 50 minutes), Bern (Sfr51, one to 1¼ hours) and Basel (Sfr34, 55 minutes to 1¼ hours).

ℹ Getting Around

TO/FROM THE AIRPORT
Up to nine trains an hour run in each direction between the airport and the main train station (Sfr6.80, nine to 13 minutes).

BICYCLE
Züri Rollt (☎ 044 415 67 67; www.schweizrollt.ch) allows visitors to borrow or rent bikes from a handful of locations, including Velostation Nord across the road from the north side of the Hauptbahnhof. Bring ID and leave Sfr20 as a deposit. Rental is free if you bring the bike back on the same day and Sfr10 a day if you keep it overnight.

PUBLIC TRANSPORT
The comprehensive, unified bus, tram and S-Bahn public transit system **ZVV** (☎ 0848 988 988; www.zvv.ch) includes boats plying the Limmat River. Short trips under five stops are Sfr2.60; typical trips are Sfr4.30. A 24-hour pass for the city centre is Sfr8.60.

NORTHERN SWITZERLAND

With businesslike Basel at its heart, this region also prides itself on having the country's finest Roman ruins (at Augusta Raurica) and a gaggle of proud castles and pretty medieval villages scattered across the rolling countryside of Aargau Canton.

Basel

POP 169,916

Tucked up against the French and German borders in Switzerland's northwest corner, Basel straddles the majestic Rhine. The town is home to art galleries, 30-odd museums and avant-garde architecture, and it boasts an enchanting Old Town centre.

◎ Sights & Activities

Old Town   AREA

(Altstadt) Begin exploring Basel's delightful medieval Old Town in **Marktplatz**, dominated by the astonishingly vivid red facade of the 16th-century **Rathaus** (Town Hall). From here, climb 400m west along Spalenberg through the former artisans' district to the 600-year-old **Spalentor** city gate, one of only three to survive the walls' demolition in 1866. Along the way, linger in captivating lanes such as Spalenberg, Heuberg and Leonhardsberg, lined by impeccably maintained, centuries-old houses.

★ Fondation Beyeler   MUSEUM

(☑061 645 97 00; www.fondationbeyeler.ch; Baselstrasse 101, Riehen; adult/child Sfr25/6; ⊙10am-6pm Thu-Tue, to 8pm Wed) This astounding private-turned-public collection, assembled by former art dealers Hildy and Ernst Beyeler, is housed in a long, low, light-filled, open-plan building designed by Italian architect Renzo Piano. The varied exhibits juxtapose 19th- and 20th-century works by Picasso and Rothko against sculptures by Miró and Max Ernst and tribal figures from Oceania. Take tram 6 to Riehen from Barfüsserplatz or Marktplatz. Admission is reduced to Sfr20 Wednesday after 5pm and all day Monday.

⌂ Sleeping

Hotels are often full during Basel's trade fairs and conventions; book ahead. Guests receive a pass for free travel on public transport.

★ SYHA Basel St Alban Youth Hostel   HOSTEL €

(☑061 272 05 72; www.youthhostel.ch; St Alban-Kirchrain 10; dm Sfr41-46.50, s/d Sfr120/132; ⊛) Designed by Basel-based architects Buchner & Bründler, this swank modern hostel in a very pleasant neighbourhood is flanked by tree-shaded squares and a rushing creek. It's only a stone's throw from the Rhine, and 15 minutes on foot from the SBB Bahnhof (or take tram 2 to Kunstmuseum and walk five minutes downhill).

★ Hotel Krafft   HOTEL €€

(☑061 690 91 30; www.krafftbasel.ch; Rheingasse 12; s Sfr99-162, d Sfr158-284; ⊛) Design-savvy urbanites will love this renovated historic hotel. Sculptural modern chandeliers dangle in the creaky-floored dining room overlooking the Rhine, and minimalist Japanese-style tea bars adorn each landing of the spiral stairs.

✕ Eating & Drinking

Head to the Marktplatz for a daily market and several stands selling excellent quick bites, such as local sausages and sandwiches.

★ Volkshaus Basel   BRASSERIE, BAR €€

(☑061 690 93 10; www.volkshaus-basel.ch; Rebgasse 12-14; mains Sfr29-54; ⊙restaurant noon-2pm & 6-10pm Mon-Sat, bar 10am-midnight Mon-Wed, to 1am Thu-Sat) This stylish Herzog & de Meuron–designed venue is part resto-bar, part gallery and part performance space. For relaxed dining, head for the atmospheric beer garden, in a cobblestoned courtyard decorated with columns, vine-clad walls and light-draped rows of trees. The menu ranges from brasserie classics (*steak-frites*) to more innovative offerings (house-pickled wild salmon with mustard, dill and beetroot).

❶ Information

Basel Tourismus (☑061 268 68 68; www.basel.com) SBB Bahnhof (Centralbahnstrasse 10; ⊙8-6pm Mon-Fri, 9am-5pm Sat, 9am-3pm Sun); Stadtcasino (Steinenberg 14; ⊙9am-6.30pm Mon-Fri, to 5pm Sat, 10am-3pm Sun) The Stadtcasino branch organises two-hour city walking tours (adult/child Sfr18/9) in English and German (or French upon request) starting at 2.30pm Monday to Saturday May through October, and on Saturdays the rest of the year.

LIECHTENSTEIN

If Liechtenstein (population 37,937) didn't exist, someone would have invented it. A tiny German-speaking mountain principality (160 sq km) governed by an iron-willed monarch in the heart of 21st-century Europe, it certainly has novelty value. Only 25km long by 12km wide (at its broadest point) – just larger than Manhattan – Liechtenstein is mostly visited by people who want a glimpse of the castle and a spurious passport stamp. Stay a little longer and you can escape into its pint-sized Alpine wilderness.

Vaduz

Vaduz is a postage-stamp-size city with a postcard-perfect backdrop. Crouching at the foot of forested mountains, hugging the banks of the Rhine and crowned by a turreted castle, the city has a visually stunning location.

The centre itself is curiously modern and sterile, yet just a few minutes' walk brings you to traces of the quaint village that existed just 50 years ago and quiet vineyards where the Alps seem that bit closer.

Vaduz Castle is closed to the public but is worth the climb for the vistas.

Information

Liechtenstein's international phone prefix is ☑ 423.

The **Liechtenstein Center** (www.tourismus.li) offers brochures, souvenir passport stamps (Sfr3) and the **Philatelie Liechtenstein**, which will interest stamp collectors.

Getting There & Around

The nearest train stations are in the Swiss border towns of Buchs and Sargans. From each of these towns there are frequent buses to Vaduz (Sfr4.80/9.60 from Buchs/Sargans). Buses traverse the country. Single fares (buy tickets on the bus) are Sfr3/4/6/8 for one/two/three/four zones. Swiss Passes are valid on all main routes.

ℹ Getting There & Away

AIR

The **EuroAirport** (MLH or BSL; ☑ +33 3 89 90 31 11; www.euroairport.com), 5km northwest of town in France, is the main airport for Basel. It is a hub for easyJet and there are flights to major European cities.

TRAIN

Basel is a major European rail hub. The main station has TGVs to Paris (three hours) and fast ICEs to major cities in Germany.

Services within Switzerland include frequent trains to Bern (Sfr41, one hour) and Zürich (Sfr34, one hour).

ℹ Getting Around

Bus 50 links the airport and Basel's main train station (Sfr4.40, 20 minutes). Trams 8 and 11 link the station to Marktplatz. Tram and bus tickets cost Sfr2.30 for short trips (maximum four stops), Sfr3.80 for longer trips within Basel and Sfr9.90 for a day pass.

TICINO

Switzerland meets Italy: in Ticino the summer air is rich and hot, and the peacock-proud posers propel their scooters in and out of traffic. Italian weather, Italian style. Not to mention the Italian ice cream, Italian pizza, Italian architecture and Italian language.

Locarno

POP 15,968

Italianate architecture and the northern end of Lago Maggiore, plus more hours of sunshine than anywhere else in Switzerland (2300 hours, to be precise), give this laid-back town a summer resort atmosphere.

Locarno is on the northeastern corner of Lago Maggiore, which mostly lies in Italy's Lombardy region. **Navigazione Lago Maggiore** (www.navigazionelaghi.it) operates boats across the entire lake.

SWISS NATIONAL PARK

The Engadine's pride and joy is the Swiss National Park, easily accessed from Scuol, Zernez and S-chanf. Spanning 172 sq km, Switzerland's only national park is a nature-gone-wild swath of dolomitic peaks, shimmering glaciers, larch woodlands, pastures, waterfalls and high moors strung with topaz-blue lakes. This was the first national park to be established in the Alps, on 1 August 1914, and more than 100 years later it remains true to its original conservation ethos, with the aims to protect, research and inform.

Given that nature has been left to its own devices for a century, the park is a glimpse of the Alps before the dawn of tourism. There are some 80km of well-marked hiking trails, where, with a little luck and a decent pair of binoculars, ibex, chamois, marmots, deer, bearded vultures and golden eagles can be sighted. The Swiss National Park Centre (☑081 851 41 41; www.nationalpark.ch; exhibition adult/child Sfr7/3; ☉8.30am-6pm Jun-Oct, 9am-noon & 2-5pm Nov-May) should be your first port of call for information on activities and accommodation. It sells an excellent 1:50,000 park map (Sfr14, or Sfr20 with guidebook), which covers 21 walks through the park.

You can easily head off on your own, but you might get more out of one of the informative guided hikes (Sfr25) run by the centre from late June to mid-October. These include wildlife-spotting treks to the Val Trupchun and high-alpine hikes to the Offenpass and Lakes of Macun. Most are in German, but many guides speak a little English. Book ahead by phone or at the park office in Zernez.

Entry to the park and its car parks is free. Conservation is paramount here, so stick to footpaths and respect regulations prohibiting camping, littering, lighting fires, cycling, picking flowers and disturbing the animals.

For an overnight stay in the heart of the park, look no further than Il Fuorn (☑081 856 12 26; www.ilfuorn.ch; s/d Sfr120/196, without bathroom Sfr95/150, half-board extra Sfr35; ☉closed Nov, 2nd half Jan & Easter–late Apr), an idyllically sited guesthouse that serves fresh trout and game at its excellent on-site restaurant.

◉ Sights & Activities

Piazza Grande   AREA
Locarno's Italianate Old Town fans out from Piazza Grande, a photogenic ensemble of arcades and Lombard-style houses. A craft and fresh-produce market takes over the square every Thursday.

★Santuario della Madonna del Sasso   CHURCH
(www.madonnadelsasso.org; ☉7.30am-6pm) Overlooking the town, this sanctuary was built after the Virgin Mary supposedly appeared in a vision to a monk, Bartolomeo d'Ivrea, in 1480. There's a highly adorned church and several rather rough, near-life-size statue groups (including one of the Last Supper) in niches on the stairway. The best-known painting in the church is *La Fuga in Egitto* (Flight to Egypt), painted in 1522 by Bramantino.

A funicular (one way/return adult Sfr4.80/7.20, child Sfr2.20/3.60; ☉8am-10pm May, Jun & Sep, to midnight Jul & Aug, to 9pm Apr & Oct, to 7.30pm Nov-Mar) runs every 15 minutes from the town centre past the sanctuary to Orselina, but a more scenic, pilgrim-style approach is the 20-minute walk up the chapel-lined Via Crucis (take Via al Sasso off Via Cappuccini).

❶ Getting There & Away

Locarno is well linked to Ticino and the rest of Switzerland via Bellinzona, or take the scenic **Centovalli Express** (www.centovalli.ch) to Brig via Domodossola in Italy.

Lugano

POP 63,583

Ticino's lush, mountain-rimmed lake isn't its only liquid asset. Lugano is also the country's third-most-important banking centre. Suits aside, it's a vivacious city, with bars and pavement cafes huddling in the spaghetti maze of steep cobblestone streets that untangle at the edge of the lake and along the flowery promenade.

⊙ Sights & Activities

The **Centro Storico** (Old Town) is a 10-minute walk downhill from the train station; take the stairs or the funicular (Sfr1.30).

Wander through the mostly porticoed lanes woven around the busy main square, **Piazza della Riforma** (which is even more lively when the Tuesday- and Friday-morning markets are held).

Cattedrale di San Lorenzo   CATHEDRAL
(St Lawrence Cathedral; Via San Lorenzo; ⊙ 6.30am-6pm) Freshly renovated in 2016, Lugano's early 16th-century cathedral conceals some fine frescoes and ornate baroque statues behind its Renaissance facade. Out front are far-reaching views over the Old Town's jumble of terracotta rooftops to the lake and mountains.

**Società Navigazione del
Lago di Lugano**   BOATING
(☑ 091 971 52 23; www.lakelugano.ch; Riva Vela; ⊙ Apr-Oct) A relaxed way to see the lake's highlights is on one of these cruises, including one-hour bay tours (Sfr27.40) and three-hour morning cruises to Ponte Tresa at the lake's western end (Sfr45.60). Visit the website for timetables.

🛏 Sleeping & Eating

Many hotels close for part of the winter.

Hotel & Hostel Montarina   HOTEL, HOSTEL €
(☑ 091 966 72 72; www.montarina.ch; Via Montarina 1; dm/s/d Sfr29/105/140; P 🛜 ▨) Occupying a pastel-pink villa dating to 1860, this hotel/hostel duo extends a heartfelt welcome. Mosaic floors, high ceilings and wrought-iron balustrades are lingering traces of old-world grandeur. There's a shared kitchen-lounge, toys to amuse the kids, a swimming pool set in palm-dotted gardens and even a tiny vineyard. Breakfast costs an extra Sfr15.

★ **Guesthouse Castagnola**   GUESTHOUSE €€
(☑ 078 632 67 47; www.gh-castagnola.com; Salita degli Olivi 2; apt Sfr125-180; P 🛜) Kristina and Maurizio bend over backwards to please at their B&B, lodged in a beautifully restored 16th-century townhouse. Exposed stone, natural fabrics and earthy colours dominate in three rooms kitted out with Nespresso coffee machines and flat-screen TVs. There's also a family-friendly apartment with washing machine and full kitchen.

Bottegone del Vino   ITALIAN €€
(☑ 091 922 76 89; Via Magatti 3; mains Sfr20-42; ⊙ 11.30am-midnight Mon-Sat) Favoured by Lugano's downtown banking brigade, this place has a season-driven menu, with ever-changing lunch and dinner options scrawled on the blackboard daily. Expect specialities such as ravioli stuffed with fine Tuscan Chianina beef, accompanied by a wide selection of local wines. Knowledgeable waiters fuss around the tables and are only too happy to suggest the perfect Ticino tipple.

❶ Getting There & Away

Lugano is on the main line connecting Milan to Zürich and Lucerne. Services from Lugano include Milan (Sfr27, 1¼ hours), Zürich (Sfr68, 2½ hours) and Lucerne (Sfr61, two hours).

GRAUBÜNDEN

St Moritz

POP 5067

Switzerland's original winter wonderland and the cradle of Alpine tourism, St Moritz (San Murezzan in Romansch) has been luring royals, celebrities and moneyed wannabes since 1864. With its shimmering aquamarine lake, emerald forests and aloof mountains, the town looks a million dollars.

🎿 Activities

With 350km of slopes, ultramodern lifts and spirit-soaring views, **skiing** in St Moritz is second to none, especially for confident intermediates. The general ski pass covers all the slopes.

If cross-country skiing is more your scene, you can glide across sunny plains and through snowy woods on 220km of groomed trails. In summer, the region has excellent hiking trails.

Schweizer Skischule   SKIING
(☑ 081 830 01 01; www.skischool.ch; Via Stredas 14; ⊙ 8am-noon & 2-6pm Mon-Sat, 8-9am & 4-6pm Sun) The first Swiss ski school was founded in St Moritz in 1929. Today, you can arrange skiing or snowboarding lessons for Sfr120/85 per day for adults/children.

🛏 Sleeping & Eating

Jugendherberge St Moritz   HOSTEL €
(📞 081 836 61 11; www.youthhostel.ch/st.moritz; Via Surpunt 60; dm/s/d/q Sfr41/136/161/216; 🛜) On the edge of the forest, this hostel has clean, quiet four-bed dorms and doubles. There's a children's toy room, bike hire and laundrette. Bus 3 offers door-to-door connections with the town centre (five minutes) and train station (10 minutes).

Chesa Spuondas   HOTEL €€
(📞 081 833 65 88; www.chesaspuondas.ch; Via Somplaz 47; s/d/f incl half board Sfr155/280/290; P🛜) This family hotel nestles amid meadows at the foot of forest and mountains, 3km southwest of the town centre. Rooms are in keeping with the Jugendstil villa, with high ceilings, parquet floors and the odd antique. Kids are the centre of attention here, with dedicated meal times, activities, play areas and the children's ski school a 10-minute walk away.

Chesa Veglia   ITALIAN €€€
(📞 081 837 28 00; www.badruttspalace.com; Via Veglia 2; pizza Sfr25-39, mains Sfr45-60; ⊙noon-11.30pm) This slate-roofed, chalk-white chalet restaurant dates from 1658. The softly lit interior is all warm pine and creaking wood floors, while the terrace affords lake and mountain views. Go for pizza or regional specialities such as *Bündner Gerstensuppe* (creamy barley soup) and venison medallions with *Spätzli* (egg noodles).

ℹ Getting There & Away

Regular hourly trains make the scenic run to/from the rail hub of Chur (Sfr42, two hours).

St Moritz is also an end point on the much-hyped **Glacier Express** (www.glacierexpress.ch; one way adult/child Sfr153/76.50), which takes in some spellbinding Alpine scenery on its eight-hour run to Zermatt.

The **Bernina Express** (www.berninaexpress. ch; one way Chur-Tirano Sfr64; ⊙ mid-May–early Dec) provides seasonal links to Lugano from St Moritz, which include the stunning Unesco-recognised train line over the Bernina Pass to Tirano, Italy.

SURVIVAL GUIDE

ℹ Directory A–Z

ACCOMMODATION

Switzerland sports traditional and creative accommodation in every price range. Many budget hotels have cheaper rooms with shared toilet and shower facilities. From there, truly, the sky is the limit. Breakfast buffets can be extensive and tasty but are not always included in room rates. Rates in cities and towns stay constant most of the year. In mountain resorts prices are seasonal (and can fall by 50% or more outside high season).

Low season Mid-September to mid-December, mid-April to mid-June

Mid-season January to mid-February, mid-June to early July, September

High season July to August, Christmas, mid-February to Easter

DISCOUNT CARDS

Swiss Museum Pass (www.museumspass.ch; adult/family Sfr166/288) Regular or long-term visitors to Switzerland may want to buy this pass, which covers entry to 500 museums countrywide.

Visitors' Cards Many resorts and cities have a visitors' card (*Gästekarte*), which provides benefits such as reduced prices for museums, pools, public transit or cable cars, plus free local public transport. Cards are issued by your accommodation.

ESSENTIAL FOOD & DRINK

Fondue Switzerland's best-known dish, in which melted Emmental and Gruyère cheese are combined with white wine in a large pot and eaten with small bread chunks.

Raclette Another popular artery-hardener of melted cheese served with potatoes.

Rösti German Switzerland's national dish of fried shredded potatoes is served with everything.

Veal Highly rated throughout the country; in Zürich, veal is thinly sliced and served in a cream sauce (*Zürcher Geschnetzeltes*).

Bündnerfleisch Dried beef, smoked and thinly sliced.

Chocolate Good at any time of day and available seemingly everywhere.

SLEEPING PRICE RANGES

The following price ranges refer to a double room with a private bathroom, except in hostels or where otherwise specified. Quoted rates are for high season and include breakfast, unless otherwise noted:

€ less than Sfr170

€€ Sfr170–Sfr350

€€€ more than Sfr350

ELECTRICITY

Electrical current in Switzerland is 230V, 50Hz. Swiss sockets are recessed, three-holed, hexagonally shaped and incompatible with many plugs from abroad. They usually, however, take the standard European two-pronged plug.

INTERNET ACCESS

Free wi-fi hot spots can be found at airports, dozens of Swiss train stations and in many hotels and cafes. Public wi-fi (provided by Swisscom) costs Sfr5 per day.

INTERNET RESOURCES

MySwitzerland (www.myswitzerland.com)
Swiss Info (www.swissinfo.ch)

MONEY

➡ Swiss francs are divided into 100 centimes (*Rappen* in German-speaking Switzerland). There are notes for 10, 20, 50, 100, 200 and 1000 francs, and coins for five, 10, 20 and 50 centimes, as well as for one, two and five francs. Euros are accepted by many tourism businesses.

➡ Exchange money at large train stations.

➡ Tipping is not necessary, given that hotels, restaurants, bars and even some taxis are legally required to include a 15% service charge in bills. You can round-up the bill after a meal for good service, as locals do.

OPENING HOURS

We list high-season opening hours for sights and attractions; hours tend to decrease during low season. Most businesses shut completely on Sunday.

Banks 8.30am–4.30pm Monday to Friday
Restaurants noon–2.30pm and 6–9.30pm; most close one or two days per week
Shops 10am–6pm Monday to Friday, to 4pm Saturday
Museums 10am–5pm, many close Monday and open late Thursday

PUBLIC HOLIDAYS

New Year's Day 1 January
Easter Sunday & Monday March/April
Ascension Day 40th day after Easter
Whit Sunday & Monday (Pentecost) 7th week after Easter
National Day 1 August
Christmas Day 25 December
St Stephen's Day 26 December

TELEPHONE

➡ The country code for Switzerland is 🖉41. When calling Switzerland from abroad, drop the initial zero from the number; hence to call Bern, dial 🖉41 31 (preceded by the overseas access code of the country you're dialling from).

➡ The international access code from Switzerland is 🖉00. To call Britain (country code 🖉44), start by dialling 🖉00 44.

➡ Most mobile phones brought from overseas will function in Switzerland. Prepaid local SIM cards are available from network operators Salt (www.salt.ch), Sunrise (www.sunrise.ch) and Swisscom Mobile (www.swisscom.ch/mobile).

VISAS

For up-to-date details on visa requirements, go to www.sem.admin.ch.

Visas are not required for passport holders from the UK, the EU, Ireland, the USA, Canada, Australia, New Zealand, Norway and Iceland.

ⓘ Getting There & Away

AIR

The main international airports:

Geneva Airport (GVA; Aéroport International de Genève; www.gva.ch) Geneva's airport is 4km northwest of the town centre.

Zürich Airport (ZRH; 🖉 043 816 22 11; www.zurich-airport.com) The airport is 9km north of the centre, with flights to most European capitals as well as some in Africa, Asia and North America.

LAND

Bus

Eurolines (www.eurolines.com) has buses with connections across Western Europe.

Train

Switzerland is a hub of train connections to the rest of the Continent. Zürich is the busiest international terminus, with service to all neighbouring countries. Destinations include Münich (4¼ hours), and Vienna (eight hours), from where there are extensive onward connections to cities in Eastern Europe.

COUNTRY FACTS

Area 41,285 sq km

Capital Bern

Country Code ⌁41

Currency Swiss franc (Sfr)

Emergency Ambulance ⌁144, fire ⌁118, police ⌁117

Languages French, German, Italian, Romansch

Money ATMs readily available

Population 8.18 million

Visas Schengen rules apply

→ Numerous TGV trains daily connect Paris to Geneva (3¼ hours), Lausanne (3¾ hours), Basel (three hours) and Zürich (four hours).

→ Nearly all connections from Italy pass through Milan before branching off to Zürich, Lucerne, Bern or Lausanne.

→ Most connections from Germany pass through Zürich or Basel.

→ **Swiss Federal Railways** (www.sbb.ch) accepts internet bookings but does not post tickets outside of Switzerland.

❶ Getting Around

Swiss public transport is an efficient, fully integrated and comprehensive system, which incorporates trains, buses, boats and funiculars.

Marketed as the Swiss Travel System, the network has a useful website (www.swiss travelsystem.ch). Excellent free maps covering the country are available at train stations and tourist offices.

PASSES & DISCOUNTS

Convenient discount passes make the Swiss transport system even more appealing. For extensive travel within Switzerland, the following national travel passes generally offer better savings than Eurail or InterRail passes.

Swiss Travel Pass This entitles the holder to unlimited travel on almost every train, boat and bus service in the country, and on trams and buses in 41 towns, plus free entry to 500-odd museums. Reductions of 25% to 50% apply on funiculars, cable cars and private railways. Different passes are available, valid between three (Sfr216) and 15 (Sfr458) consecutive days.

Swiss Travel Pass Flex This pass allows unlimited travel for a certain number of days within a one-month period – from three (Sfr248) to 15 (Sfr502) days.

Half-Fare Card As the name suggests, you pay only half the fare on trains with this card (Sfr120 for one month), plus you get some discounts on local-network buses, trams and cable cars.

BICYCLE

→ **Rent-a-Bike** (www.rentabike.ch) allows you to rent bikes at 80 train stations in Switzerland. For a Sfr10 surcharge you can collect from one station and return to another.

→ **Suisseroule** (Schweizrollt; www.schweizrollt. ch) lets you borrow a bike for free or cheaply in places like Geneva, Bern and Zürich. Bike stations are usually next to the train station or central square.

→ Local tourist offices often have good cycling information.

BOAT

Ferries and steamers link towns and cities on many lakes, including Geneva, Lucerne, Lugano and Zürich.

BUS

→ Yellow **post buses** (www.postbus.ch) supplement the rail network, linking towns to difficult-to-access mountain regions.

→ Services are regular, and departures (usually next to train stations) are linked to train schedules.

→ Swiss national travel passes are valid.

→ Purchase tickets on board; some scenic routes over the Alps (eg the Lugano–St Moritz run) require reservations.

CAR & MOTORCYCLE

→ Headlights must be on at all times, and dipped (set to low-beam) in tunnels.

→ The speed limit is 50km/h in towns, 80km/h on main roads outside towns, 100km/h on single-lane freeways and 120km/h on dual-lane freeways.

EATING PRICE RANGES

Price indicators refer to the average cost of a main meal.

$ less than Sfr25

$$ Sfr25–Sfr50

$$$ more than Sfr50

ℹ️ TRANSPORT CONNECTIONS

Landlocked between France, Germany, Austria, Liechtenstein and Italy, Switzerland is well linked, especially by train. Formalities are minimal when entering Switzerland by air, rail or road thanks to the Schengen Agreement. Fast, well-maintained roads run from Switzerland through to all bordering countries; the Alps present a natural barrier, meaning main roads generally head through tunnels to enter Switzerland. Switzerland can be reached by steamer from several lakes: from Germany, arrive via Lake Constance and from France via Lake Geneva. You can also cruise down the Rhine to Basel.

➡️ Some minor Alpine passes are closed from November to May – check with the local tourist offices before setting off.

TRAIN

The Swiss rail network combines state-run and private operations. The **Swiss Federal Railway** (www.sbb.ch) is abbreviated to SBB in German, CFF in French and FFS in Italian.

➡️ All major train stations are connected to each other by hourly departures, at least between 6am and midnight.

➡️ Second-class seats are perfectly acceptable, but cars are often close to full. First-class carriages are more comfortable and spacious and have fewer passengers.

➡️ Ticket vending machines accept most major credit cards from around the world.

➡️ The SBB smartphone app is an excellent resource and can be used to store your tickets electronically.

➡️ Check the SBB website for cheap Supersaver tickets on major routes.

➡️ Most stations have 24-hour lockers, usually accessible from 6am to midnight.

➡️ Seat reservations (Sfr5) are advisable for longer journeys, particularly in the high season.

Turkey

Best Places to Eat

➡ Antiochia (p1160)

➡ Ayşa (p1165)

➡ Bi Lokma (p1171)

➡ Ocakbaşı Restoran (p1177)

➡ Vanilla (p1173)

Best Places to Stay

➡ Pera Palace Hotel (p1157)

➡ Hotel Empress Zoe (p1157)

➡ El Vino Hotel (p1168)

➡ Hotel Unique (p1169)

➡ Koza Cave Hotel (p1176)

Why Go?

Turkey walks the tightrope between Europe and Asia with ease. Its cities pack in towering minarets and spice-trading bazaars but also offer buzzing, modern street life. Out in the countryside, this country's reputation as a bridge between continents is laid bare. Its expansive steppes and craggy mountain slopes are scattered with the remnants of once-mighty empires. Lycian ruins peek from the undergrowth across the Mediterranean coast, the Roman era's pomp stretches out before you in Ephesus, while the swirling rock valleys of Cappadocia hide Byzantine monastery complexes whittled out by early Christian ascetics.

Of course, if you just want to sloth on a prime piece of beach, Turkey has you covered. But when you've brushed off the sand, this land where east meets west and the ancient merges seamlessly with the contemporary is a fascinating mosaic of culture, history and visceral natural splendour.

When to Go

İstanbul

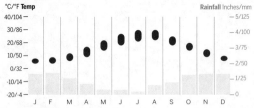

Apr & May İstanbul is a colourful kaleidoscope of tulips and it's prime hiking time on the coast.

Jun–Aug Summer temperatures sizzle and the Mediterranean resorts are in full swing.

Sep & Oct Plenty of crisp clear-sky days but the crowds have dispersed.

İSTANBUL

📞EUROPEAN SIDE 0212 / 📞ASIAN SIDE 0216 / POP 14.6 MILLION

Former capital of both the Byzantine and Ottoman empires, İstanbul manages to doff its cap to its grand past while stridently forging a vibrant, modern path. Stately mosques, opulent palaces and elaborately decorated domed churches cram into the Old City quarter while the hilly streets of Beyoğlu host state-of-the-art museums and art galleries, chic boutiques and funky cafes. Hop on a commuter ferry to cross between Europe and Asia. Haggle your heart out in the Grand Bazaar. Join the gregarious crowds bar-hopping in the alleys off İstiklal Caddesi. This marvellous metropolis is a showcase of Turkey at its most energetic, innovative and cosmopolitan.

The Bosphorus strait, between the Black Sea and the Sea of Marmara, divides Europe from Asia. On its western shore, European İstanbul is further divided by the Golden Horn (Haliç) into the Old City in the southwest and Beyoğlu in the northeast.

👁 Sights

👁 Sultanahmet & Around

The Sultanahmet area is the centre of the Old City, a World Heritage site jam-packed with wonderful historic sights.

★Aya Sofya
MUSEUM

(Hagia Sophia; Map p1158; 📞0212-522 0989, 0212-522 1750; http://ayasofyamuzesi.gov.tr/en; Aya Sofya Meydanı 1; adult/child under 12yr ₺40/free; ⏰9am-7pm Tue-Sun mid-Apr–mid-Oct, to 5pm mid-Oct–mid-Apr, last entry 1hr before closing; 🚊Sultanahmet) There are many important monuments in İstanbul, but this venerable structure – which was commissioned by the great Byzantine emperor Justinian, consecrated as a church in 537, converted to a mosque by Mehmet the Conqueror in 1453 and declared a museum by Atatürk in 1935 – surpasses the rest due to its innovative architectural form, rich history, religious importance and extraordinary beauty.

★Topkapı Palace
PALACE

(Topkapı Sarayı; Map p1158; 📞0212-512 0480; www.topkapisarayi.gov.tr; Babıhümayun Caddesi; palace adult/child under 12yr ₺40/free, Harem adult/child under 6yr ₺25/free; ⏰9am-6.45pm Wed-Mon mid-Apr–Oct, to 4.45pm Nov–mid-Apr, last entry 45min before closing; 🚊Sultanahmet) Topkapı is the subject of more colourful stories than most of the world's museums put together. Libidinous sultans, ambitious courtiers, beautiful concubines and scheming eunuchs lived and worked here between the 15th and 19th centuries when it was the court of the Ottoman Empire. A visit to the palace's opulent pavilions, jewel-filled Treasury and sprawling Harem gives a fascinating glimpse into their lives.

Grand Bazaar
MARKET

(Kapalı Çarşı, Covered Market; Map p1158; www.kapalicarsi.org.tr; ⏰8.30am-7pm Mon-Sat, last entry 6pm; 🚊Beyazıt Kapalıçarşı) The colourful and chaotic Grand Bazaar is the heart of İstanbul's Old City and has been so for centuries. Starting as a small vaulted *bedesten* (warehouse) built by order of Mehmet the Conqueror in 1461, it grew to cover a vast area as lanes between the *bedesten,* neighbouring shops and *hans* (caravanserais) were roofed and the market assumed the sprawling, labyrinthine form that it retains today.

TURKEY İSTANBUL

ITINERARIES

One Week

Spend two days exploring İstanbul then head south to laid-back Selçuk and the grandiose ruins of Ephesus. After a two-night stop, catch a flight from nearby İzmir to the wacky fairy-chimney countryside of Cappadocia.

Two Weeks

Follow the one-week itinerary to Selçuk then scoot to the Aegean coast for a day or two of chichi beach action in Bodrum. Next, trail south along the coast to Fethiye, for boat-trip fun and discovering the ghost village in nearby Kayaköy; or Kaş, to explore Kekova's submerged ruins. Move onto Antalya to crane your neck at Aspendos' theatre and traipse through the old-district streets, before bussing it across the steppe to Cappadocia for cave-hotel quirkiness and hot-air ballooning.

BLACK SEA
(KARADENIZ)

BULGARIA

Burgas

ISTANBUL

Kapıkule
Edirne
Kırklareli

Cide
İnebolu
Sinop

Amasra

GREECE
İpsala
Tekirdağ
Çorlu
İstanbul
Kocaeli
(İzmit)
Adapazarı

Zonguldak
Safranbolu
Kastamonu

Karabük
Tosya
Osmancık

The Bosphorus

Keşan
Darıca
Yalova
İznik
Bolu
Gerede
Kurşunlu
İlgaz
Çankırı
Çorum

Gelibolu
Gemlik

Gallipoli
Peninsula
Lapseki
Bandırma
Bursa

Sungurlu

Troy (Truva)
Çanakkale
Uludağ
(2543m)
Sakarya River
Gordion
ANKARA
Hattuşa

Eskişehir
Kırıkkale
Yozgat

Ayvacık
Edremit
Balıkesir
Polatlı

Assos
Lesvos
Ayvalık
Kütahya

Bergama
Pergamum
Kırşehir
Göreme

Yeni
Foça
Aliağa
Manisa
Uşak
Afyon
Cappadocia
Nevşehir

Chios
Çeşme
İzmir
Sardis
Akşehir
Aksaray
Ürgüp

Selçuk
Odemiş
Çivril
Eğirdir
Gölü
Beyşehir
Gölü
Tuz Gölü
(Salt Lake)
Derinkuyu
Yahyalı

Kuşadası
Aydın
Nazilli
Hierapolis
Niğde

Ikaria
Priene
Ephesus
Afrodisias
Denizli
Isparta
Beyşehir
Suğla
Gölü
Karaman
Ereğli

Didyma
Milas
Yatağan
Burdur
Adana

Güllük
Bodrum
Gökova
(Akyaka)
Muğla
Çavdır
Çavrur
Termessos
Köprülü Kanyon
Akseki
Kırobası
Tarsus
Mersin
(İçel)

Kos
Marmaris
Ortaca
Dalaman
Antalya
Side
Uzuncaburç
Kızkalesi
Silifke
Olukbaşı

Lycian
Way
Fethiye
Ölüdeniz
Çıralı
Kemer
Alanya

Patara
Beach
Kaş
Çıralı
Finike
Olympos
Anamurium
Anamur

Crete

NICOSIA
(LEFKOSIA)

CYPRUS

MEDITERRANEAN SEA
(AKDENİZ)

Sea of
Marmara
The Dardanelles

Turkey Highlights

1 İstanbul (p1151) Ferry-hopping from Europe to Asia with your camera at the ready to capture the city's famous minaret-studded skyline.

2 Cappadocia (p1175)

Bedding down in a cave-hotel to savour modern troglodyte style amid the bizarre lunarscape.

3 Ephesus (p1166) Fulfilling your toga-loaded

daydreams in one of the world's greatest surviving Graeco-Roman cities.

4 Lycian Way (p1170) Exploring the ruins of empires while relishing ridiculously

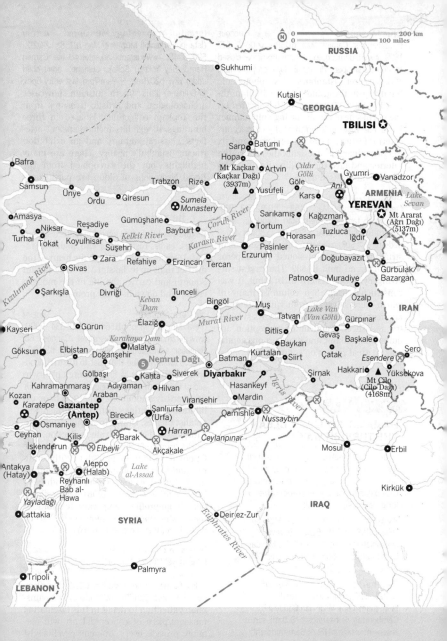

gorgeous coastal views along the long-distance trail.

⑤ Nemrut Dağı (p1177) (Mt Nemrut) Marvelling at one king's egotism, amid

the toppled statues on the summit.

⑥ Kaş (p1170) Paddling over Kekova's sunken city on a kayaking trip out of this fun-activity vortex.

⑦ Antalya (p1172) Strolling the narrow lanes between Ottoman mansions and chunks of Roman wall in the old town quarter.

Blue Mosque   MOSQUE
(Sultanahmet Camii; Map p1158; ☑0545 577
1899; www.bluemosque.co; Hippodrome; ⊘closed
to non-worshippers during 6 daily prayer times;
🖪Sultanahmet) İstanbul's most photogenic
building was the grand project of Sultan Ahmet I (r 1603–17), whose tomb is located on
the north side of the site facing Sultanahmet
Park. The mosque's wonderfully curvaceous
exterior features a cascade of domes and six
slender minarets. Blue İznik tiles adorn the
interior and give the building its unofficial
but commonly used name.

Basilica Cistern   HISTORIC SITE
(Yerebatan Sarnıçı; Map p1158; ☑0212-512 1570;
www.yerebatan.com; Yerebatan Caddesi; ₺20;
⊘9am-6.30pm mid-Apr–Sep, to 5.30pm Nov–
mid-Apr; 🖪Sultanahmet) This subterranean
structure was commissioned by Emperor
Justinian and built in 532. The largest surviving Byzantine cistern in İstanbul, it was
constructed using 336 columns, many of
which were salvaged from ruined temples
and feature fine carved capitals. Its symme-
try and sheer grandeur of conception are
quite breathtaking, and its cavernous depths
make a great retreat on summer days.

DON'T MISS

HAMAMS: SQUEAKY-CLEAN THE TURKISH WAY

İstanbul's hamams may be pricey but
it's not often you get to soap-up amid
such historic finery. Our top three Old
City picks for sudsy relaxation after a
long day of sightseeing:

Ayasofya Hürrem Sultan Hamamı
(Map p1158; ☑0212-517 3535; www.
ayasofyahamami.com; Aya Sofya Meydanı 2;
bath treatments €85-170, massages €40-75;
⊘8am-10pm; 🖪Sultanahmet)

Çemberlitaş Hamamı (Map p1158;
☑0212-522 7974; www.cemberli-
tashamami.com; Vezir Han Caddesi 8,
Çemberlitaş; self-service ₺70, bath, scrub
& soap massage ₺115; ⊘6am-midnight;
🖪Çemberlitaş)

Cağaloğlu Hamamı (Map p1158; ☑0212-
522 2424; www.cagalogluhamami.com.tr; Prof
Kazım İsmail Gürkan Caddesi 24; bath, scrub &
massage packages €40-120, self-service €30;
⊘8am-10pm; 🖪Sultanahmet)

İstanbul Archaeology Museums   MUSEUM
(İstanbul Arkeoloji Müzeleri; Map p1158; ☑0212-
520 7740; www.istanbularkeoloji.gov.tr; Osman
Hamdi Bey Yokuşu Sokak, Gülhane; adult/child
under 12yr ₺20/free; ⊘9am-7pm, last entry 6pm;
🖪Gülhane) This superb museum showcases
archaeological and artistic treasures from
the Topkapı collections. Housed in three
buildings, its exhibits include ancient artefacts, classical statuary and an exhibition
tracing İstanbul's history. There are many
highlights, but the sarcophagi from the
Royal Necropolis of Sidon are particularly
striking.

⊚ Beyoğlu

Beyoğlu is kilometre zero for galleries, boutiques, cafes, restaurants and nightlife. İs-
tiklal Caddesi runs through the heart of the
district right up to Taksim Meydanı (Taksim
Square) and carries the life of the modern
city up and down its lively promenade.

★**Pera Museum**   MUSEUM
(Pera Müzesi; Map p1156; ☑0212-334 9900;
www.peramuseum.org; Meşrutiyet Caddesi 65,
Tepebaşı; adult/student/child under 12yr ₺20/10/
free; ⊘10am-7pm Tue-Thu & Sat, to 10pm Fri, noon-
6pm Sun; Ⓜ Şişhane, 🖪 Tünel) There's plenty to
see at this impressive museum, but its major
drawcard is undoubtedly the 2nd-floor exhibition of paintings featuring Turkish Ori-
entalist themes. Drawn from Suna and İnan
Kıraç's world-class private collection, the
works provide fascinating glimpses into the
Ottoman world from the 17th to 20th centuries and include the most beloved painting
in the Turkish canon – Osman Hamdı Bey's
The Tortoise Trainer (1906). Other floors
host high-profile temporary exhibitions
(past exhibitions have showcased Warhol,
de Chirico, Picasso and Botero).

Museum of Innocence   MUSEUM
(Masumiyet Müzesi; Map p1156; ☑0212-252 9738;
www.masumiyetmuzesi.org; Çukurcuma Caddesi,
Dalgıç Çıkmazı 2; adult/student ₺25/10; ⊘10am-
6pm Tue-Sun, to 9pm Thu; 🖪Tophane) The painstaking attention to detail in this fascinating
museum/piece of conceptual art will certainly provide every amateur psychologist
with a theory or two about its creator, Nobel
Prize–winning novelist Orhan Pamuk. Vit-
rines display a quirky collection of objects
that evoke the minutiae of İstanbullu life in
the mid- to late 20th century, when Pamuk's
novel *The Museum of Innocence* is set.

İstanbul

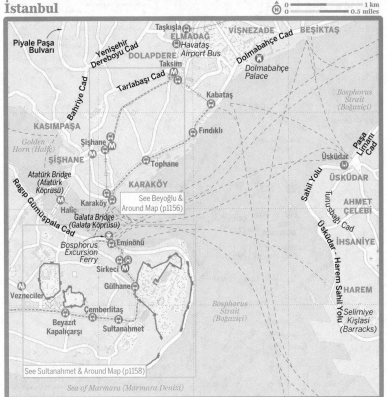

0 _____ **1 km**
0 _____ **0.5 miles**

Piyale Paşa Bulvarı
Yenişehir Dereboyu Cad
ELMADAĞ
Taşkışla
VİŞNEZADE
BEŞİKTAŞ
Havataş Airport Bus
DOLAPDERE
Dolmabahçe Cad
Taksim
Dolmabahçe Palace
Bahriye Cad
Tarlabaşı Cad
Kabataş
Bosphorus Strait (Boğaziçi)
KASIMPAŞA
Golden Horn (Haliç)
Şişhane
Fındıklı
Paşa Limanı Cad
ŞİŞHANE
Tophane
Üsküdar
ÜSKÜDAR
Atatürk Bridge (Atatürk Köprüsü)
KARAKÖY
Tünusbağı Cad
AHMET ÇELEBİ
Ragıp Gümüşpala Cad
Karaköy
See Beyoğlu & Around Map (p1156)
İHSANİYE
Haliç
Galata Bridge (Galata Köprüsü)
Üsküdar - Harem Sahil Yolu
Bosphorus Excursion Ferry
Eminönü
Sirkeci
Veznecilier
Gülhane
Bosphorus Strait (Boğaziçi)
HAREM
Çemberlitaş
Sahil Yolu
Selimiye Kışlası (Barracks)
Beyazıt Kapalıçarşı
Sultanahmet
See Sultanahmet & Around Map (p1158)
Sea of Marmara (Marmara Denizi)

🏃 Activities & Tours

İstanbul Walks (Map p1158; ☎0212-516 6300, 0554 335 6622; www.istanbulwalks.com; 1st fl, Şifa Hamamı Sokak 1; tours adult €35-75, child under 2/7yr free/30% discount; 🚇Sultanahmet) and **Urban Adventures** (☎0532 641 2822; www.urbanadventures.com; tours adult €27-82, child €22-79) offer good guided walking tours. The latter also runs foodie walking tours and gastronomic evenings, while **Cooking Alaturka** (Map p1158; ☎0212-458 5919; www.cookingalaturka.com; Akbıyık Caddesi 72a, Cankurtaran; classes per person incl meal €65; ⏱10.30am & 4.30pm by reservation Mon-Sat; 🚇Sultanahmet) gives convivial 2½-hour cookery classes.

🛏 Sleeping

Sultanahmet & Around

The Sultanahmet area (particularly the quarter of Cankurtaran) has bucketfuls of accommodation across all budgets. It's also only a hop-skip-and-jump from all the Old City sights.

★Marmara Guesthouse   PENSION €

(Map p1158; ☎0212-638 3638; www.marmaraguesthouse.com; Terbıyık Sokak 15, Cankurtaran; d €65-85, tr €80-100, f €95-115; ⊕❄🐱; 🚇Sultanahmet) Few of Sultanahmet's family-run pensions can compete with the Marmara's cleanliness, comfort and thoughtful details. Owner Elif and team go out of their way to welcome guests, offering advice aplenty and serving a delicious breakfast on the vine-covered, sea-facing roof terrace. Rooms have four-poster beds with Turkish hangings, good bathrooms (small in some cases) and double-glazed windows.

Metropolis Hostel   HOSTEL €

(Map p1158; ☎0212-518 1822; www.metropolishostel.com; Terbıyık Sokak 24, Cankurtaran; dm €15-16, d €60-65, s/d/tw/tr without bathroom

Beyoğlu & Around

€44/46/49/68; (P❄✳✉; 🚇Sultanahmet) Located in a quiet street where a good night's sleep is assured, the friendly Metropolis offers four- to six-bed dorms, including a female-only en-suite option with six beds and sweeping Sea of Marmara views. The rooftop terrace has a bar and sea views to equal many pricier hotels, and the busy entertainment program includes summer barbecues and belly dancing.

Beyoğlu & Around

◎ **Top Sights**
  1 Pera Museum A3

◎ **Sights**
  2 İstanbul Araştırmaları
     Enstitüsü...A2
  3 Museum of Innocence.........................C3

🛏 **Sleeping**
  4 Casa di Bava...C3
  5 Pera Palace Hotel A3

🍴 **Eating**
  6 Antiochia..A4
  7 Cuma...C3
  8 Hamdi Restaurant Pera A3
     Pera Café ....(see 1)

🍷 **Drinking & Nightlife**
  9 Mikla A3
  10 Unter...B5

🎭 **Entertainment**
  11 Galata Mevlevi Museum......................A4

★**Hotel Empress Zoe**   BOUTIQUE HOTEL €€
(Map p1158; 🖉0212-518 2504; www.emzoe.
com; Akbıyık Caddesi 10, Cankurtaran; s €60-90, d
€140-160, tr €150, ste €180-300; ❄✳︎🛜; 🚇Sultanahmet) Named after the feisty Byzantine
empress, this is one of İstanbul's most impressive boutique hotels. The four buildings
house 26 diverse rooms. The enticing garden suites overlook a 15th-century hamam
and the gorgeous flower-filled courtyard
where breakfast is served in warm weather.
You can enjoy an early-evening drink there,
or while admiring the sea view from the
terrace.

Hotel Ibrahim Pasha   BOUTIQUE HOTEL €€
(Map p1158; 🖉0212-518 0394; www.ibrahimpasha.com; Terzihane Sokak 7, Sultanahmet; r standard/deluxe €125/175; ❄✳︎@🛜; 🚇Sultanahmet)
Cultural tomes are piled in reception and
throughout the 24 rooms of this exemplary
design hotel, which also has a comfortable
lounge with open fire, and a terrace bar with
knockout views of the nearby Blue Mosque
and Hippodrome. Rooms are gorgeous but
some are small, with more space in the deluxe options and those in the new section.

📖 Beyoğlu & Around

The newer part of central İstanbul's European side is across the Golden Horn from the
Old City's sights, but better for restaurants
and nightlife.

Casa di Bava   BOUTIQUE HOTEL €€
(Map p1156; 🖉0538 377 3877; www.casadibavaistanbul.com; Bostanbaşı Caddesi 28, Çukurcuma; economy ste €140, 1-bedroom apt €180,
2-bedroom penthouse €320; ❄✳︎🛜; 🚇Taksim)
The two-bedroom penthouse apartment at
this recently opened suite hotel is an absolute knockout, and the 11 one-bedroom
apartments in the 1880s building are impressive, too. All are stylishly decorated and
well appointed, with original artworks, fully
equipped kitchenettes and washing machines. The basement suites are smaller and
less expensive; all have daily maid service.
In-room breakfast costs €6 per person.

★**Pera Palace Hotel**   HISTORIC HOTEL €€€
(Map p1156; 🖉0212-377 4000; www.perapalace.
com; Meşrutiyet Caddesi 52, Tepebaşı; r €150-325,
ste €330-550; 🅿❄✳︎@🛜✴︎; 🚇Şişhane) This
famous hotel underwent a €23-million restoration in 2010 and the result is simply
splendiferous. Rooms are luxurious and extremely comfortable, and facilities include
an atmospheric bar and lounge (the latter
often closed for private functions), spa, gym
and restaurant. The most impressive feature
of all is the service, which is both friendly
and efficient. Breakfast costs €25.

✖ Eating

İstanbul is a food-lover's paradise. Head to
Beyoğlu for the cream of the city's dining
scene. Check out www.istanbuleats.com for
bundles of options.

Sefa Restaurant   TURKISH €
(Map p1158; 🖉0212-520 0670; www.sefarestaurant.com.tr; Nuruosmaniye Caddesi 11, Cağaloğlu;
portions ₺8-14, kebaps ₺20; ⊙7am-5pm; 🖉; 🚇Sultanahmet) Describing its cuisine as Ottoman,
this popular place offers *hazır yemek* (ready-
made dishes) and kebaps at reasonable pric-

ⓘ **MUSEUM PASS**

The **Museum Pass İstanbul** (www.
muze.gov.tr/en/museum-card) offers a
possible ₺175 saving on entry to İstanbul's major sights, and allows holders to
skip admission queues.
   You can also buy passes covering
Cappadocia, the Aegean, the Mediterranean and the whole of Turkey.

Sultanahmet & Around

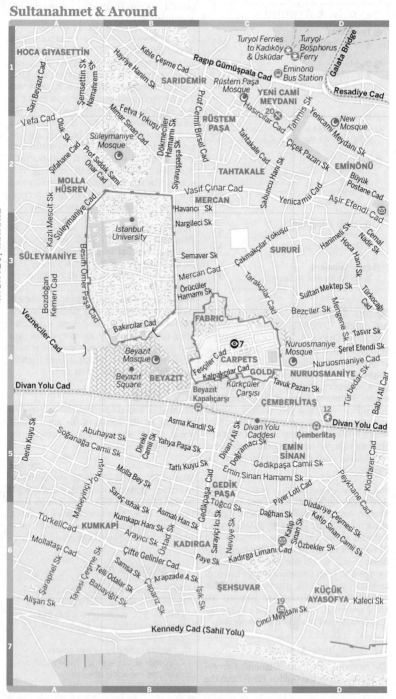

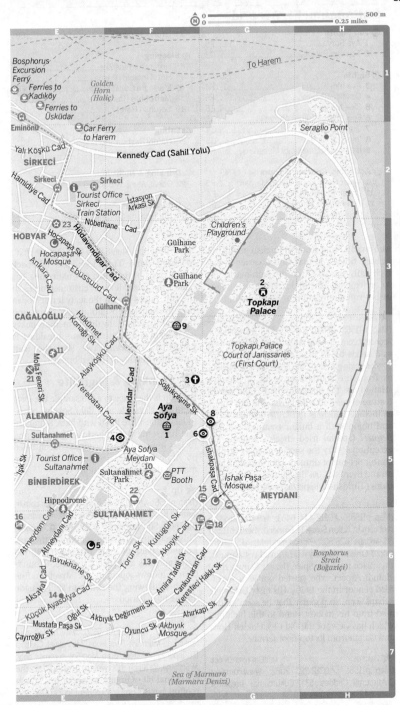

0   500 m
0   0.25 miles

Bosphorus
Excursion
Ferry
Ferries to
Kadıköy
Ferries to
Üsküdar
Eminönü
Car Ferry
to Harem

To Harem

Golden
Horn
(Haliç)

Seraglio Point

Yalı Köşkü Cad

Kennedy Cad (Sahil Yolu)

SİRKECİ

Sirkeci

Hamidiye Cad

Sirkeci
Tourist Office –
Sirkeci
Train Station
Nöbethane Cad

İstasyon
Arkası Sk

HOBYAR
23
Hocapaşa Sk
Hocapaşa
Mosque

Hüdavendigar Cad

Ebussuud Cad

Ankara Cad

Children's
Playground

Gülhane Park

Gülhane
Park

CAĞALOĞLU

Gülhane

Hükümet
Konağı Sk

Alayköşkü Cad

Yerebatan Cad

Alemdar Cad

11

Molla Fenerí Sk

21

ALEMDAR

Sultanahmet

Tourist Office –
Sultanahmet

BINBIRDIREK

Soğukçeşme Sk

3

Aya
Sofya

1

4

Aya Sofya
Meydanı

Sultanahmet
Park

10

22

8

6

PTT
Booth

2
Topkapı
Palace

9

Topkapı Palace
Court of Janissaries
(First Court)

İshakpaşa Cad

İshak Paşa
Mosque

15

MEYDANI

Hippodrome

16

Atmeydanı Cad

Atmeydanı Cad

5

SULTANAHMET

Kutlugün Sk

17 18

Tavukhane Sk

Torun Sk

13

Akbıyık Cad

Amiral Tafdili Sk

Cankurtaran Cad

Keresteci Hakkı Sk

Bosphorus
Strait
(Boğaziçi)

Akçakal Cad

14

Küçük Ayasofya Cad

Oğul Sk

Akbıyık Değirmeni Sk

Mustafa Paşa Sk

Çayıroğlu Sk

Oyuncu Sk Akbıyık
Mosque

Ahırkapı Sk

Sea of Marmara
(Marmara Denizi)

Sultanahmet & Around

es. You can order from an English menu, but at busy times you may find it easier to just pick daily specials from the bain-marie. Try to arrive early-ish for lunch because many dishes run out by 1.30pm. No alcohol.

★**Antiochia** ANATOLIAN €€
(Map p1156; ☑0212-244 0820; www.antiochia-concept.com; General Yazgan Sokak 3, Tünel; mezes & salads ₺13-18, pides ₺21-22, kebaps ₺24-52; ☺noon-midnight Mon-Sat; ☜⊞; 龠Tünel) Dishes from the southeastern city of Antakya (Hatay) are the speciality here. Cold mezes feature olives and wild herbs, and hot choices include delicious *içli köfte* (ground lamb and onion with a bulgur coating) and *özel peyniri* (special fried cheese). Kebaps are exceptional – try the succulent *şiş et* (grilled lamb). Set-menu dinners offer excellent value and there's a 20% discount at lunch, when pides (Turkish-style pizzas) reign supreme.

Hamdi Restaurant KEBAP €€
(Map p1158; ☑0212-444 6463; www.hamdirestorant.com.tr; Kalçın Sokak 11, Eminönü; mezes ₺11.50-26, kebaps ₺28-50; ☺noon-midnight; ⊞; 龠Eminönü) One of the city's best-loved restaurants, this place near the Spice Bazaar is owned by Hamdi Arpacı, who started out as a streetfood vendor in the 1960s. His tasty Urfa-style kebaps were so popular that he soon graduated from his modest stand to this building, which has views of the Old City, Golden Horn and Galata from its top-floor terrace.

★**Cuma** MODERN TURKISH €€€
(Map p1156; ☑0212-293 2062; www.cuma.cc; Çukurcuma Caddesi 53a, Çukurcuma; breakfast plate ₺42, lunch dishes ₺19-34, dinner mains ₺30-36; ☺9am-11pm Mon-Sat, to 8pm Sun; ☜⊿⊞; MTaksim) Banu Tiryakioğulları's laid-back foodie oasis in the heart of Çukurcuma has one of the most devoted customer bases in the city. Tables are on the leafy terrace or in the atmospheric upstairs dining space, and the healthy, seasonally driven menu is heavy on flavour and light on fuss – breakfast is particularly delicious (we love the fruit smoothies and house-baked bread).

🍷 Drinking & Nightlife

Beyoğlu is the place to go to sample the local nightlife. Nevizade and Balo Sokaks, off İstiklal Caddesi, are lined with bars. Sultanahmet has some atmospheric tea gardens and its less impressive bar scene is concentrated on Akbıyık Caddesi, a stone's throw from most of the accommodation.

★**Unter** BAR
(Map p1156; ☑0212-244-5151; www.unter.com.tr; Kara Ali Kaptan Sokak 4, Karaköy; ☺9am-midnight Tue-Thu & Sun, to 2am Fri & Sat; ☜; 龠Tophane) This scenester-free zone epitomises the new Karaköy style: it's glam without trying too hard, and has a vaguely arty vibe. Ground-floor windows open to the street in fine weather, allowing the action to spill outside during busy periods.

★**Mikla** BAR
(Map p1156; ☑0212-293 5656; www.miklarestaurant.com; Marmara Pera Hotel, Meşrutiyet Caddesi 15, Tepebaşı; ☺from 6pm Mon-Sat summer only; MŞişhane, 龠Tünel) It's worth overlooking the occasional bit of uppity service at this stylish rooftop bar to enjoy excellent cocktails and

what could well be the best view in İstanbul. In winter the drinking action moves to the bar in the upmarket restaurant one floor down.

Derviş Aile Çay Bahçesi   TEA GARDEN
(Map p1158; cnr Dalbastı Sokak & Kabasakal Caddesi; ⊙7am-midnight Apr-Oct; 🚇Sultanahmet) Superbly located directly opposite the Blue Mosque, the Derviş beckons patrons with its comfortable cane chairs and shady trees. Efficient service, reasonable prices and peerless people-watching opportunities make it a great place for a leisurely çay (₺3), nargile (water pipe; ₺22), *tost* (toasted sandwich; ₺7) and a game of backgammon.

☆ Entertainment

Hodjapasha Cultural Centre PERFORMING ARTS
(Map p1158; ☎0212-511 4626; www.hodjapasha. com; Hocapaşa Hamamı Sokak 3b, Sirkeci; performances adult ₺70-80, child under 12yr ₺40-50; 🚇Sirkeci) Occupying a beautifully converted 550-year-old hamam, this cultural centre stages a one-hour whirling dervish performance at 7pm on Tuesday, Thursday and Saturday year-round, with additional performances in busy months (daily in April, May, September and October). Note that children under seven are not admitted; and switch off your phone, as readers have reported draconian crowd-control here.

Galata Mevlevi Museum   PERFORMING ARTS
(Galata Mevlevihanesi Müzesi; Map p1156; galatamevlevihanesimuzesi.gov.tr; Galipdede Caddesi 15, Tünel; ₺70; ⊙performances 5pm Sun; 🚇Şişhane, 🚇Tünel) The 15th-century *semahane* (whirling-dervish hall) at this *tekke* (dervish lodge) is the venue for a one-hour *sema* (ceremony) held on Sundays throughout the year. Come early to buy your ticket.

❶ Information

Banks, ATMs and exchange offices are widespread.

American Hospital (Amerikan Hastenesi; ☎0212-311 2000, 0212-444 3777; www. americanhospitalistanbul.com; Güzelbahçe Sokak 20, Nişantaşı; ⊙24hr; 🚇Osmanbey) Private hospital with English-speaking staff and a 24-hour emergency department.

Tourist Office – Sirkeci Train Station
(Map p1158; ☎0212-511 5888, 0555 675 2674; Sirkeci Gar, Ankara Caddesi, Sirkeci; ⊙9.30am-6pm mid-Apr–Sep, 9am-5.30pm Oct–mid-Apr; 🚇Sirkeci) English and German are spoken at this helpful office with maps and brochures available.

❶ Getting There & Away

AIR

İstanbul's **Atatürk International Airport** (IST, Atatürk Havalımanı; ☎+90 444 9828; www. ataturkairport.com) is 23km west of Sultanahmet. A new airport north of the city is set to replace Atatürk in 2018; visit www.igairport. com/en for updates.

Sabiha Gökçen International Airport (SAW, Sabiha Gökçen Havalımanı; ☎0216-588 8888; www.sgairport.com) is 50km east, on the Asian side of the city.

BOAT

Yenikapı is the main dock for **İDO** (İDO; ☎0850 222 4436; www.ido.com.tr) car and passenger ferries across the Sea of Marmara to Yalova, Bursa and Bandırma (from where you can catch a train to İzmir or a bus to Çanakkale).

BUS

Büyük İstanbul Otogarı (Big İstanbul Bus Station; ☎0212-658 0505; www.otogaristanbul. com), 10km northwest of Sultanahmet, is the city's main otogar (bus station) and has buses to towns and cities across the country, as well as to European destinations.

Many bus companies offer a free *servis* (shuttle bus) to/from the otogar. The metro stops here (₺4; Otogar stop) en route between Atatürk International Airport and Aksaray; the latter

DON'T MISS

THE BOSPHORUS EXCURSION BOAT

İstanbul's soul is the Bosphorus. Don't miss seeing the city's iconic skyline and riverside views from the city's real highway aboard the **Bosphorus Excursion Ferry** (Map p1158; www.sehirhatlari. istanbul; Boğaz İskelesi; long tour one way/ return ₺15/25; short tour ₺12; ⊙long tours 10.35am year-round, 1.35pm Apr–Oct & 6.25pm Sat summer, short tours 2.30pm Apr-Oct). Boats depart from Eminönü and stop at various points before turning around at Anadolu Kavağı. Along the way you soak up sights such as the ornate **Dolmabahçe Palace** (Dolmabahçe Sarayı; ☎0212-327 2626; www.millisaraylar. gov.tr; Dolmabahçe Caddesi, Beşiktaş; adult Selâmlık ₺30, Harem ₺20, joint ticket ₺40; ⊙9am-4pm Tue, Wed & Fri-Sun; 🚇Kabataş) and majestically modern Bosphorus Bridge, along with plenty of lavish *yalı* (seafront mansions).

TURKEY HIGHLIGHTS

stop intersects with the tram line to Sultanahmet and Kabataş/Taksim.

TRAIN

Due to ongoing maintenance work, the train network in and out of İstanbul has been severely curtailed. At the time of writing, the daily 10pm Bosfor Ekspresi from İstanbul to Bucharest (₺125) via Sofia (€65) was by bus as far as Sofia.

A new fast train service to Ankara (from ₺70, 3½ hours) currently leaves, inconveniently, from Pendik Station, 25km southeast of Kadıköy on the Asian side of town.

Check **Turkish State Railways** (www.tcdd. gov.tr) and **The Man in Seat Sixty-One** (www. seat61.com/turkey2) for updates.

ⓘ Getting Around

Rechargeable **İstanbulkarts** (travel cards) can be used on public transport citywide. Purchase (₺10) and recharge them at kiosks and machines at metro and tram stops, bus terminals and ferry docks. If you're only using public transport for a few city journeys, *jetons* (single-trip travel tokens, ₺4) can be purchased from machines at tram and metro stops.

BOAT

İstanbul's commuter ferries ply the Bosphorus between the city's European and Asian sides.

Ferries for Üsküdar and Kadıköy on the Asian shore and up the Bosphorus leave from Eminönü dock; they also leave from Kabataş (Adalar İskelesi dock) for the Princes' Islands. Services also depart for Üsküdar and Kadıköy from Karaköy and from Beşiktaş (near Dolmabahçe Palace).

ⓘ GETTING INTO İSTANBUL FROM THE AIRPORTS

Bus Havataş Airport Bus (☑ 444 2656; http://havatas.com) travels between the airports and Cumhuriyet Caddesi, just off Taksim Meydanı. Buses leave Atatürk (₺11, one hour) every 30 minutes between 4am and 1am. Its service between Sabiha Gökçen (₺14, 1½ hours) and Taksim leaves every 30 minutes between 3.30am and 1am – easily the cheapest way to get to the city from Sabiha Gökçen.

Metro From Atatürk to Zeytinburnu, where you can connect with the tram to Sultanahmet (total ₺8, one hour).

Shuttle Most hotels can book airport shuttles to/from both Atatürk (₺25) and Sabiha Gökçen (₺75). Check shuttle schedules at reception.

Taxi From Atatürk/Sabiha Gökçen to Sultanahmet costs around ₺45/155.

BUS

İstanbul's efficient bus system runs between 6am and 11pm. You must have an İstanbulkart to use the buses. The major bus terminals are at Taksim Meydanı and at Beşiktaş, Kabataş, Eminönü, Kadıköy and Üsküdar.

METRO

The most useful metro service is the M1A Line connecting Yenikapı with Atatürk International Airport, stopping at 16 stations including Otogar (for the main bus station) along the way. Services leave every five minutes between 6am and midnight.

TAXI

İstanbul is full of yellow taxis, all of them with meters – insist that drivers use them. It costs around ₺15 to travel between Beyoğlu and Sultanahmet.

TRAM & FUNICULAR

A *tramvay* (tramway) service runs from Zeytinburnu (where it connects with the M1A Metro) to Kabataş (connecting with the funicular to Taksim) via Sultanahmet, Eminönü and Karaköy (connecting with the funicular to Tünel). Trams run every five minutes from 6am to midnight.

An antique tram rattles up and down İstiklal Caddesi between Tünel funicular station and Taksim Meydanı.

The one-stop Tünel funicular between Karaköy and the bottom of İstiklal Caddesi runs between 7am and 10.45pm. Another funicular runs from Kabataş (where it connects with the tram) up to the metro station at Taksim.

AEGEAN COAST

Turkey's Aegean coast can convincingly claim more ancient ruins per square kilometre than any other region in the world. Since time immemorial, conquerors, traders and travellers have beaten a path to the mighty monuments, and few leave disappointed.

Gallipoli (Gelibolu) Peninsula

Antipodeans and many Brits won't need an introduction to Gallipoli; it's the backbone of the 'Anzac legend', in which an Allied campaign in 1915 to knock Turkey out of WWI and open a relief route to Russia turned into one of the war's greatest fiascos. Some 130,000 men died, roughly a third from Allied forces and the rest Turkish.

Today the battlefields are part of the **Gallipoli Historical National Park** (Gelibolu Yarımadası Tarihi Milli Parkı; http://gytmp.milliparklar.gov.tr) and tens of thousands of Turks and foreigners alike come to pay their respects on pilgrimage every year. The Turkish officer responsible for the defence of Gallipoli was Mustafa Kemal (the future Atatürk); his victory is commemorated in Turkey on 18 March. On **Anzac Day** (25 April), a dawn service marks the anniversary of the Allied landings.

The easiest way to see the battlefields is with your own transport or on a tour from Çanakkale or Eceabat; try **Crowded House Tours** (☑ 0286-814 1565; www.crowdedhousegallipoli.com; Zubeyde Hanim Meydani 28, Eceabat).

If you want to sleep on the peninsula, options in Eceabat include hilltop **Hotel Casa Villa** (☑ 0286-814 1320; www.otelcasavilla.com; Çamburnu Sokak 75; r ₺160; ❄ 🛜).

Çanakkale

☑ 0286 / POP 123,000

This sprawling harbour town has a fun and youthful vibe that would be worth visiting for even if it didn't lie across the Dardanelles from the Gallipoli Peninsula and wasn't within easy day-tripping distance to Troy. After you've finished exploring these nearby sights' modern and ancient historical significance, check out this university town's hip and alternative nightlife scene in the bars and cafes cramming the cobbled lanes around the five-storey Ottoman *saat kulesi* (clock tower), or go for a sunset stroll along the *kordon* (waterfront promenade).

🛏 Sleeping & Eating

Anzac House Hostel   HOSTEL ₡
(☑ 0286-213 5969; www.anzachouse.com; Cumhuriyet Meydanı 59; dm/s/d/tw ₺30/50/80/80; ❄ 🛜) Operated by the excellent Hassle Free Tours, Çanakkale's only backpacker hostel has been made-over to re-emerge as the area's best option for budget travellers. Not all of the simple rooms have windows, but they are well kept. Tours around the battlefields, Troy and further afield are all on tap downstairs, and Çanakkale's best bars and cafes are nearby.

Anzac Hotel   HOTEL ₡₡
(☑ 0286-217 7777; www.anzachotel.com; Saat Kulesi Meydanı 8; s €25-30, d €33-40; ❄ 🛜) An extremely professional management team ensures that this renovated and keenly priced hotel opposite the clock tower is well maintained and has high levels of service. Rooms are a good size, include tea- and coffee-making facilities and have double-glazed windows. The convivial bar on the mezzanine shows the movies *Gallipoli* and *Troy* nightly.

★ **Sardalya**   SEAFOOD ₡
(Küçük Hamam Sokak 24b; snacks from ₺6; ☺ 8am-11pm) Named after a type of fish, the no-frills Sardalya is a popular local joint serving everything from superfresh *balık ekmek* (fish sandwiches) to plates of fried mussels or calamari, and deep-fried sardines with salad. Pull up a seat at the counter and chat with the locals between tasty mouthfuls, or ask for takeaway and stroll the short distance to the waterfront.

Cafe du Port   INTERNATIONAL ₡₡
(☑ 0286-217 2908; Yalı Caddesi 12; mains ₺22-28; ☺ 8am-11pm) The restaurant at Hotel Limani is popular for good reason. The glass-fronted building on the *kordon* (waterfront promenade) is stylish and inviting; the chefs are the most versatile in Çanakkale; and the service is brilliant. Specialities include steaks, salads, pastas and whatever else inspires the manager during his regular İstanbul sojourns. If nothing else, settle in for an end-of-day mojito.

❶ Getting There & Away

Regular buses go to İstanbul (₺55, six hours) and İzmir (₺45, 5¾ hours).

To Eceabat and the Gallipoli Peninsula there's an hourly ferry service (₺3/35 per person/car, 25 minutes) from the harbour dock.

Troy (Truva)

Not much remains of the great city of **Troy** (☑ 0286-283 0536; adult/child under 12yr ₺25/free; ☺ 8am-7.30pm Apr-Oct, to 5pm Nov-Mar) and you'll have to use your imagination to envision the fateful day when the Greeks tricked the Trojans with their wooden horse. For history buffs and fans of Homer's *Iliad* though, this is one of the most important stops on the Aegean.

The site is rather confusing for nonexpert eyes – informative audio guides (₺10) are available – but the most conspicuous features, apart from the reconstruction of the **Trojan Horse**, include the **walls** from various periods; the Graeco-Roman Temple of Athena; the Roman Odeon; and the Bouleuterion (Council Chamber), built around Homer's time (c 800 BC). The new state-of-the-art Troy archaeological museum, located nearby in the village of Tevfikiye, is set to open by the end of 2017.

Tour companies in Çanakkale and Eceabat offer half-day Troy tours (€35) and full-day Gallipoli battlefields and Troy excursions (around €75).

From Çanakkale, dolmuşes (minibuses) leave hourly to Troy (₺5, 35 minutes, between 9.30am and 5pm) from a station at the northern end of the bridge over the Sarı River.

Bergama (Pergamum)

📞 0232 / POP 63,825

This workaday market town sits slap-bang below the remarkable ruins of Pergamum, site of ancient Rome's pre-eminent medical centre. During Pergamum's heyday (between Alexander the Great and the Roman domination of Asia Minor), it was one of the Middle East's richest and most powerful small kingdoms.

In town itself are the imposing remains of the Red Hall (Kızıl Avlu; Kınık Caddesi; ₺5; ⊙8am-7pm Apr-Sep, to 5pm Oct-Mar), a 2nd-century temple dedicated to the Egyptian gods Serapis, Isis and Harpocrates. Upon the windswept hilltop, 5km from the Red Hall, and linked by a cable car (Bergama Akropolis Teleferik; 📞0232-631 0805; www.akropolisteleferik.com.tr; Akropol Caddesi; return ₺15; ⊙8am-5pm Apr-Sep, to 7pm Oct-Mar), is the Acropolis (Bergama Akropol; Akropol Caddesi 2; ₺25; ⊙8am-5pm Oct-Mar, to 7pm Apr-Sep), with its spectacular sloping theatre. The Asklepion (Prof Dr Friedhelm Korte Caddesi 1; ₺20; ⊙8am-4.45pm Oct-Mar, to 6.45pm Apr-Sep), 2.5km uphill from town, was Pergamum's famed medical centre. The work Greek physician Galen did here in the 2nd century was the basis for Western medicine well into the 16th century. Back in town, Bergama Archaeology Museum (Bergama Müze Müdürlüğü; 📞0232-483 5117; Cumhuriyet Caddesi 6; ₺5; ⊙8am-5pm Tue-Sun Nov-Mar, to 5pm Apr-Oct) has a small but impressive collection of artefacts.

Odyssey Guesthouse (📞0232-631 3501; www.odysseyguesthouse.com; Abacıhan Sokak 13; dm/s/d/tr ₺25/65/85/120, s/d without bathroom ₺40/70; ⊙closed Jan–mid-Feb; 🅿⊛@🛜) has superb views of the archaeological sites and Aristonicus Boutique Hotel (📞0232-632 4141; www.aristonicus.com; Taksim Caddesi 37;

s/d/ste ₺85/165/215; 🅿⊛🛜) occupies two converted old stone houses.

Regular buses run to İzmir (₺10, two hours) and Çanakkale (₺30 to ₺35, 4½ hours), and there are nightly buses to Ankara (₺85, 8½ hours).

İzmir

📞 0232 / POP 2.89 MILLION

Turkey's third-largest city is a sprawling harbourside hub with a proud history as one of the Mediterranean's cosmopolitan trading metropolises when it was known as Smyrna. Head to the ruins of the Roman agora (Agora Caddesi; ₺10; ⊙8am-4.30pm; Ⓜ Çankaya) to see one of İzmir's few reminders of its grand past, and leave time for İzmir Museum of History & Art's (İzmir Tarih ve Sanat Müzesi; 📞0232-445 6818; near Montrö Meydanı entrance, Kültürpark; ₺5; ⊙8am-4.45pm; 🚌12, 253, Ⓜ Basmane) rich repository of ancient artefacts. Afterwards sniff out a bargain (or five) within Kemeraltı Market (Kemeraltı Çarşısı; ⊙8am-7pm Mon-Sat; Ⓜ Çankaya, Konak), then soak up the city's energetic modern pulse along the kordon (waterfront promenade) and amid the student nightlife haunts of Alsancak district.

🛏 Sleeping & Eating

İzmir's waterfront is dominated by large high-end business hotels, while most midrange and budget options are located in Alsancak or Basmane. In the latter, the accommodating 1296 Sokak is known as 'Oteller Sokak' (Hotel Street).

For bundles of hip cafes and bars, head to the area around Kıbrıs Şehitleri Caddesi in Alsancak.

InHouse Hostel   HOSTEL €
(📞0232-404 0014; www.inhousehostel.com; 1460 Sokak 75, Alsancak; dm ₺36-42, d ₺120, s/d without bathroom ₺75/110; ⊛@🛜; 🚌12, 253, 🚇 Alsancak) Opened in 2015, this hostel offers 56 beds in private rooms and in dorms sleeping between four and 10. Dorms have under-bed lockers, hard bunk beds and clean but limited shared bathrooms. There's 24-hour reception, a kitchen for common use, a small foyer lounge and an entertainment program predominantly consisting of nightly pub crawls. The Alsancak location is excellent.

★ Swissôtel Büyük Efes   HOTEL €€
(📞0232-414 0000; www.swissotel.com/hotels/izmir; Gazi Osmanpaşa Bulvarı 1; s/d €140/150, executive s/d €190/200; 🅿⊛@🛜🏊; Ⓜ Çankaya)

Guests here have been known not to leave the premises at all during their city stay. Frankly, we're not at all surprised. Rooms are comfortable and well appointed, but it's the hotel's gorgeous garden and impressive facilities that are the real attraction. These include indoor and outdoor swimming pools, tennis court, spa, gym and rooftop bar with panoramic bay views.

Ayşa TURKISH €
(☎0232-489 8485; www.bosnakborekcisiaysa.com; Abacıoğlu Han, Anafartalar Caddesi 228, Kemeraltı Market; meze plates ₺8-9, portions from ₺10; ⊙8am-6pm Mon-Sat; 🅥; Ⓜ Konak, Çankaya) Serving Bosnian food that is remarkably similar to Turkish home cooking, this stylish *lokanta* (eatery with ready-made food) in the pretty Abacıoğlu Han offers both indoor and outdoor seating. Choose from the DIY meze display (yum!) and be sure to snaffle a piece of *börek* (filled pastry) if it's on offer. Main dishes are displayed in the bain-marie and include both meat and vegetable choices.

Information

Banks, ATMS and the post office can be found on and around Cumhuriyet Bulvarı, locally called İkinci (Second) Kordon, a block inland from the waterfront.

Getting There & Away

BUS

Bus company ticket offices mostly cluster on Dokuz Eylül Meydanı in Basmane. They usually provide a free *servis* to/from İzmir's mammoth otogar, 6.5km from the centre. Buses head to points across the country including frequent services to Bergama (₺10, two hours), Bodrum (₺30, three hours) and Selçuk (₺10, one hour).

TRAIN

Most intercity trains arrive and depart from Alsancak Garı (train station) including daily services to Ankara (₺44, 14 hours) and Konya (₺45.50, 14 hours). From Basmane Garı there are seven trains daily to Selçuk (₺6, 1½ hours) between 7.45am and 6.25pm.

Selçuk

☎0232 / POP 29,190

This chilled-out provincial town is just the ticket if you want to take a break from your travels for a couple of days. The monumental ruins of Ephesus sit right on its doorstep, storks nest atop a preserved Roman-Byzantine aqueduct that runs right through the middle of town, and the quaint village vibe of the centre is complemented by a scattering of interesting sights hidden down the cobblestone lanes.

Sights

Ephesus Museum MUSEUM
(www.ephesus.us/ephesus/ephesusmuseum.htm; Uğur Mumcu Sevgi Yolu Caddesi; ₺10; ⊙8am-6.30pm Apr-Oct, to 4.30pm Nov-Mar) This fine museum, which reopened in 2014 with nine reorganised galleries after a massive renovation, contains artefacts from Ephesus' **Terraced Houses** (₺20) and the **Temple of Artemis** (Temple of Artemision, Artemis Tapınağı; off Dr Sabrı Yayla Bulvarı; ⊙8am-7pm Apr-Oct, 8.30am-6pm Nov-Mar) FREE, including scales, jewellery and cosmetic boxes as well as coins, funerary goods and ancient statuary. The famous terracotta effigy of phallic god Priapus is in **gallery 2** and most of **gallery 4** is given over to Eros in sculpted form. The two multibreasted marble statues of Artemis in **gallery 8** are very fine works.

Basilica of St John CHURCH
(Aziz Yahya Kilisesi; St Jean Caddesi; incl Ayasuluk Fortress ₺10; ⊙8am-6.30pm Apr-Oct, to 4.30pm Nov-Mar) Despite a century of restoration, the once-great basilica built by Byzantine Emperor Justinian (r 527–65) remains a skeleton of its former self. Nonetheless, it is an atmospheric site with excellent hilltop views, and the best place in the area for a sunset photo. The information panels and scale model highlight the building's original grandeur, as do the marble steps and monumental gate.

Ayasuluk Fortress FORTRESS
(Ayasuluk Kalesi; St Jean Caddesi; incl Basilica of St John ₺10; ⊙8am-6.30pm Apr-Oct, to 4.30pm Nov-Mar) Selçuk's crowning achievement is accessed on the same ticket as the Basilica of St John, the citadel's principal structure. Earlier and extensive excavations here, concluded in 1998 after a quarter of a century, proved that there were castles on Ayasuluk Hill going back beyond the original Ephesian settlement to the Neolithic age. The fortress' partially restored remains, about 350m north of the church, date from Byzantine, Seljuk and Ottoman times and are well worth a visit.

Sleeping & Eating

★**Homeros Pension** PENSION €€
(☎0535 310 7859, 0232-892 3995; www.homerospension.com; 1048 Sokak 3; s/d ₺60/120; ❄@🛜) This long-time favourite offers

DON'T MISS

EPHESUS (EFES)

Ephesus (www.ephesus.us; main site adult/child ₺40/free, Terraced Houses ₺20, parking ₺7.50; ☺8am-7pm Apr-Oct, to 5pm Nov-Mar, last entry 1hr before close) is a dazzlingly complete classical metropolis, once the capital of the Roman province of Asia Minor. A trip here is the closest you'll get to being able to conjure up daily life in the Roman age. There are a wealth of monuments to explore, but don't miss:

Curetes Way Named for the demigods who helped Lena give birth to Artemis and Apollo, the Curetes Way was Ephesus' main thoroughfare, 210m long and lined with statuary, religious and civic buildings, rows of shops selling incense, silk and other goods, along with workshops and even restaurants. Walking this street is the best way to understand Ephesian daily life.

Library of Celsus This magnificent library dating from the early 2nd century AD, the best-known monument in Ephesus, has been extensively restored. Originally built as part of a complex, the library looks bigger than it actually is: the convex facade base heightens the central elements, while the middle columns and capitals are larger than those at the ends. Facade niches hold replica statues of the Four Virtues. From left to right, they are: Sophia (Wisdom), Arete (Goodness), Ennoia (Thought) and Episteme (Knowledge).

Temple of Hadrian One of Ephesus' star attractions and second only to the Library of Celsus, this ornate, Corinthian-style temple honours Trajan's successor and originally had a wooden roof when completed in AD 138. Note its main arch; supported by a central keystone, this architectural marvel remains perfectly balanced, with no need for mortar. The temple's designers also covered it with intricate decorative details and patterns: Tyche, goddess of chance, adorns the first arch, while Medusa wards off evil spirits on the second.

Great Theatre Originally built under Hellenistic King Lysimachus, the Great Theatre was reconstructed by the Romans between AD 41 and 117, and it is thought St Paul preached here. However, they incorporated original design elements, including the ingenious shape of the *cavea* (seating area), part of which was under cover. Seating rows are pitched slightly steeper as they ascend, meaning that upper-row spectators still enjoyed good views and acoustics – useful, considering that the theatre could hold an estimated 25,000 people.

Dolmuşes (minibuses that stop anywhere along their prescribed route) serve the Lower Gate (₺2.5) every half-hour in summer, hourly in winter.

A taxi to/from either gate costs about ₺20. Selçuk is roughly a 3.5km walk from both entrances.

---

10 rooms in two buildings, with colourful hanging textiles and handcrafted furniture made by owner Derviş, a carpenter, antiques collector and ultrawelcoming host. Enjoy dinner and some of the best views in town on the roof terraces. The four rooms in the older building are more romantic but the six in the newer one offer better views.

Boomerang Guesthouse GUESTHOUSE €€
(☑0232-892 4879, 0534 055 4761; www.boomerangguesthouse.com; 1047 Sokak 10; dm/s/d/tr/f from €10/30/40/60/70; ❄@🛜) People keep coming back to this welcoming Turkish/Australian-Chinese operation to spend chilled-out evenings among the trees in the stone courtyard with its excellent bar-restaurant. Some of the 10 rooms have balconies (ie Nos

11 and 14) and No 4 has its own courtyard; all have fridges. Bathroom-sharing budget options are also available (single/double/triple €20/30/45).

Wallabies Aquaduct Restaurant TURKISH €€
(☑0535 669 0037, 0232-892 3204; www.wallabiesaquaductrestaurant.com; Cengiz Topel Caddesi 2; mezes ₺10-14, mains ₺15-35; ☺11am-midnight) This hotel-restaurant spills out onto the square beneath the aqueduct, guaranteeing atmospheric summer dining at almost 36 tables. The traditional Anatolian fare is complemented by more international offerings, including vegie dishes and fish. Try the house speciality, *tavuklu krep sarması* (₺20), a seasoned chicken dish, baked under

a ridge of mashed potatoes and dolloped with béchamel sauce.

ⓘ Getting There & Away

At least two buses head to İstanbul (₺85, 10 hours) daily and there are frequent services to İzmir (₺10, one hour). For Pamukkale and destinations along the Mediterranean coast, you usually have to change buses at Denizli (₺35, three hours).

Eight trains head to İzmir (₺6.50, 1½ hours) daily via the city's Adnan Menderes Airport, and to Denizli (₺16.50, three hours). Note that the train's airport stop is a 20-minute walk from the departures terminal.

Pamukkale

☑ 0258 / POP 2630

Inland from Selçuk is one of Turkey's premier natural wonders. Pamukkale's surreal hillside cascade of gleaming white calcite travertines (₺35; ⊙ 9am-7pm summer), enclosing turquoise pools, has been a tourist attraction since the classical age. On the summit, the ruins of the ancient spa resort of Hierapolis lay testament to this area's enduring appeal.

The attendant farming-turned-tourist village is less impressive, so aim to pass straight through between Selçuk and the Mediterranean, or spend just one night if you'd like to experience the travertines at sunset. Beyaz Kale Pension (☑ 0258-272 2064; www.beyazkalepension.com; Oguzkaan Caddesi 4; s/d/q/f ₺70/90/140/160; ❄ 🛜 ⊛) has 10 spotless rooms on two floors, with some of the best local pension fare served on the relaxing rooftop terrace, and Melrose House (☑ 0258-272 2250; www.melrosehousehotel.com; Vali Vekfi Ertürk Caddesi 8; s €35-55, d €40-55; ❄ 🛜 ⊛) is the closest thing to a boutique hotel in Pamukkale.

Most services to/from Pamukkale involve changing in Denizli. Bus companies should provide a free *servis* from Denizli otogar to Pamukkale's main square. Otherwise, there are frequent dolmuşes (₺4, 40 minutes) between Pamukkale and Denizli otogar.

The convenient Selçuk-Fethiye Bus (☑ 0543-779 4732; www.selcukfethiyebus.com; ₺40; ⊙ departs Fethiye/Pamukkale 9am/4pm Mon, Wed, Fri & Sun) links Fethyie and Pamukkale. Transport leaves Fethiye at 9am, arriving at Pamukkale at 1pm, before returning to Fethiye from Pamukkale at 4pm.

Bodrum

☑ 0252 / POP 37,815

The beating heart of Turkey's holiday-resort peninsula, Bodrum hums with action during the summer months. Its natty whitewashed cottages all sporting blue trims are a postcard-maker's dream while the harbour is a hive for yachties and travellers alike.

⊙ Sights

Bodrum Castle   CASTLE
(Bodrum Kalesi; ☑ 0252-316 2516; www.bodrum-museum.com; İskele Meydanı; ₺30, audio guide ₺15; ⊙ 8.30am-6.30pm Apr-Oct, to 4.30pm Nov-Mar) There are splendid views from the battlements of Bodrum's magnificent castle, built by the Knights Hospitaller in the early 15th century and dedicated to St Peter. Today it houses the Museum of Underwater Archaeology (Sualtı Arkeoloji Müzesi), arguably the most important museum of its type in the world and a veritable lesson in how to bring ancient exhibits to life. Items are creatively displayed and well lit, and information panels, maps, models, drawings, murals, dioramas and videos all help to animate them.

🛏 Sleeping

Kaya Pansiyon   PENSION €
(☑ 0535 737 7060, 0252-316 5745; www.kayapansiyon.com.tr; Eski Hükümet Sokak 10; s/d ₺180/250; ⊙ Apr-Oct; ❄ 🛜) One of Bodrum's better pensions, the very central Kaya has 12 clean, simple rooms plus a studio apartment with hairdryer, safe and TV; six rooms count a balcony as well. There is a roof terrace with a castle view for breakfast, a flowering courtyard with a bar for lounging, and helpful owners Mustafa and Selda can arrange activities.

Su Otel   BOUTIQUE HOTEL €€
(☑ 0252-316 6906; www.bodrumsuhotel.com; Turgutreis Caddesi, Sokak 1201; s/d/ste from €65/95/135; ❄ @ 🛜 ⊛) Epitomising Bodrum's white-and-sky-blue aesthetic from the outside, the relaxing 'Water Hotel' has 25 rooms and suites, most with balconies giving on to a courtyard pool, an Ottoman restaurant open to the skies and a bar. The colour scheme within (think blue and red and yellow) and artwork decorating the premises is just this side of kitsch but it works.

★ **El Vino Hotel** BOUTIQUE HOTEL €€€
(☑ 0252-313 8770; www.elvinobodrum.com; Pamili Sokak; r/ste €185/235; 🅿️ 🎐 🛜 🏊) This beautiful 'urban resort' with 31 rooms is contained in several stone buildings spread over an enormous garden in the backstreets of Bodrum that you'd never know was there. Try for a room with views of both the pool/garden and the sea (eg room 303). The rooftop restaurant is one of the best hotel ones in Bodrum.

✖ Eating & Drinking

The loud bars and clubs of Bar Street (Dr Alim Bey Caddesi and Cumhuriyet Caddesi) get packed during summer nights. More refined nightspots to rub tanned shoulders with the Turkish glitterati include White House (☑ 0536 889 2066; www.facebook.com/WhiteHouseBodrum; Cumhuriyet Caddesi 147; ⊙ 9am-5am) and Helva (☑ 0252-313 2274, 0533 652 7766; www.facebook.com/helvabar; Neyzen Tevfik Caddesi 54; ⊙ 8pm-4am).

★ **Nazik Ana** TURKISH €
(☑ 0252-313 1891; www.nazikanarestaurant.com; Eski Hükümet Sokak 5; mezes ₺7-10, kebaps ₺11-20; ⊙ 8.30am-11pm) This simple back-alley place with folksy, rustic decor offers hot and cold prepared dishes, viewable *lokanta*-style at the front counter, allowing you to sample different Turkish traditional dishes at shared tables. You can also order kebaps and *köfte* (meatballs). It gets busy with workers at lunchtime, offering one of Bodrum's most authentic eating experiences.

Kalamare SEAFOOD €€
(☑ 0252-316 7076, 0544 316 7076; www.facebook.com/kalamare48; Sanat Okulu Sokak 9; mezes ₺10-15, mains ₺18-35; ⊙ noon-1am) Though a bit cramped and inland, this distressed-looking place, with whitewashed tables and pastel-coloured walls, is one of our favourite seafood restaurants in Bodrum. Serving octopus, calamari, sea bass et al (as well as meat dishes for ichthyophobes), Kalamare attracts a cool young crowd, who hold court beneath the extravagant, Gaudí-style chimney.

❶ Information

ATMs and banks congregate on Cevat Şakir Caddesi.

❶ Getting There & Away

Bodrum otogar has numerous services including two buses daily to Antalya (₺60, eight hours);

four to İstanbul (₺90, 12 hours); and hourly buses to İzmir (₺25, 3½ hours).

Daily year-round ferries link Bodrum with Kos in Greece (one way/return from €17/19, 45 minutes). There are also Saturday and Sunday ferries to Rhodes (one way/return from €50/60, two hours) from July to September. For information and tickets, contact the **Bodrum Ferryboat Association** (Bodrum Feribot İşletmeciliği; ☑ 0252-316 0882; www.bodrumferryboat.com; Kale Caddesi 22; ⊙ 8am-7pm May-Sep, to 6pm Oct-Apr).

MEDITERRANEAN COAST

This slice of Turkey – known as the Turquoise Coast – is one of the Mediterranean's most beautiful coastlines. Rugged forest-clad hills, laden with ancient ruins, roll down to a shoreline of sandy coves lapped by clear green-blue waters, all backed by craggy snow-topped mountain peaks. For hikers, sun sloths, yachties and history fiends, this achingly gorgeous region encapsulates Turkey's neverending appeal.

Fethiye

☑ 0252 / POP 82,000

Thanks to the 1958 earthquake, most of the ancient city of Telmessos was destroyed, but the vibrant town of Fethiye – which rose in its place – is now the hub of the western Mediterranean. Its natural harbour, in a broad bay scattered with dinky islands, is one of the finest in the region, and the town's lively vibe makes it an excellent base for forays both on and off the water.

◉ Sights & Activities

Tomb of Amyntas TOMB
(⊙ 8am-7pm) FREE Fethiye's most recognisable sight is the mammoth Tomb of Amyntas, an Ionic temple facade carved into a sheer rock face in 350 BC, in honour of 'Amyntas son of Hermapias'. Located south of the centre, it is best visited at sunset. Other, smaller rock tombs lie about 500m to the east.

Fethiye Museum MUSEUM
(☑ 0252-614 1150; www.lycianturkey.com/fethiye-museum.htm; 505 Sokak; admission ₺5; ⊙ 8am-7pm mid-Apr–mid-Oct, to 5pm mid-Oct–mid-Apr) Focusing on Lycian finds from Telmessos as well as the ancient settlements of Tlos and Kaunos, this museum exhibits pottery, jewellery, small statuary and votive stones (including the important Grave Stelae and the Stelae of Promise). Its most prized sig-

nificant possession, however, is the so-called Trilingual Stele from Letoön, dating from 338 BC, which was used partly to decipher the Lycian language with the help of ancient Greek and Aramaic.

Kayaköy
HISTORIC SITE

(Karmylassos; admission ₺5; ☺ 9am-8pm Apr-Oct, 8am-5pm Nov-Mar) Dolmuşes run to this nearby open-air museum, an evocative Ottoman Greek 'ghost town' that was abandoned after the population exchange of 1923. You can also walk over the hill and through the forest (5km, 1½ hours).

12-Island Tour Excursion Boats
BOATING

(per person incl lunch ₺30-35, on sailboat ₺50; ☺ 10.30am-6.30pm mid-Apr–Oct) Many visitors not joining the longer Blue Voyages opt for the 12-Island Tour, a day-long boat trip around Fethiye Körfezi (Fethiye Bay). The boats usually stop at five or six islands and cruise by the rest, but either way it's a great way to experience the coastline.

🛏 Sleeping & Eating

Most accommodation is up the hill behind the two Karagözler marinas.

Duygu Pension
PENSION €

(☑ 0535 796 6701, 0252-614 3563; www.duygupension.com; Ordu Caddesi 54; s/d/tr ₺60/80/120; P ☺ ❋ @ 🛜 🗙) Cute as a button, this warm and welcoming family-run pension near the Karagözler 2 marina has 10 homely rooms brightened by colourful wall stencils and frilly touches, while the rooftop terrace has

blinding sea views. Birol is your man and a great source of information.

★ Hotel Unique
BOUTIQUE HOTEL €€€

(☑ 0252-612 1145; www.hoteluniqueturkey.com; 30 Sokak 43a; r €130-260; P ☺ ❋ 🛜 🗙) Opened in 2014, this stone building with colourful shutters seems considerably older, offering a contemporary seaside take on Ottoman-village chic. The service and attention to detail are impressive, with wooden beams, floors and hand-carved doors from Black Sea houses in the rooms and pebbles from the beach in the bathroom floors.

Meğri Lokantası
TURKISH €€

(☑ 0252-614 4047; www.megrirestaurant.com; Çarşı Caddesi 26; plates ₺7-14; ☺ 11am-10pm; ☑) Looking for us at lunchtime in Fethiye? We're usually here. Packed with locals who spill onto the streets, this *lokanta* (eatery serving ready-made food) offers excellent and hearty homestyle cooking at very palatable prices. Mix and match your meal by choosing from the huge glass display window of vegetable (₺7) and meat (₺14) dishes. It's pretty much all delicious.

Fish Market
SEAFOOD €€€

(Balık Pazarı, Balık Halı; Hal ve Pazar Yeri; ☺ 11am-10pm) This circle of fishmongers ringed by restaurants is Fethiye's most atmospheric eating experience: buy fresh fish (per kilo ₺10 to ₺35) and calamari (₺45), take it to a restaurant to have them cook it, and watch the fishmongers competing for attention with the waiter-touts, flower sellers and roaming *fasıl* (gypsy music) buskers.

BLUE VOYAGE

Fethiye is the hub of Turkey's cruising scene, and the most popular route is the 'Blue Voyage' *(Mavi Yolculuk)* to Olympos: a four-day, three-night journey on a *gület* (Turkish yacht). Boats usually call in at Ölüdeniz and Butterfly Valley and stop at Kaş, Kalkan and/or Kekova, with the final night at Gökkaya Bay opposite the eastern end of Kekova.

Prices vary by season; in summer they range from around €200 to €300 including food (but water, soft drinks and alcohol are extra). Thoroughly check out your operator before signing up – shoddy companies abound selling Blue Voyage trips with bad food, crews that speak no English and added extras that never materialise. Many people who end up disappointed have bought their trip from an agency in İstanbul; hold off on booking until you get to Fethiye. These owner-operated outfits run a tight ship:

Alaturka (☑ 0252-612 5423; www.alaturkacruises.com; Fevzi Çakmak Caddesi 21A; 3-night cruise per person €220)

Before Lunch Cruises (☑ 0535 636 0076; www.beforelunch.com; 3-night cruise per person €275-350)

Ocean Yachting (☑ 0252-612 4807; www.gofethiye.com; Fevzi Çakmak Caddesi)

DON'T MISS

WALKING THE LYCIAN WAY

Acclaimed as one of the world's top 10 long-distance walks, Turkey's Lycian Way follows way-marked trails down the Mediterranean coast from Fethiye to Antalya. The route leads through pine and cedar forests in the shadow of mountains rising almost 3000m, past villages, stunning coastal views and an embarrassment of ruins at ancient Lycian cities.

Get information on walking all, or some sections, of the Lycian Way at www.cultureroutesinturkey.com.

ⓘ Information

Plentiful banks and ATMs line Atatürk Caddesi, the main street. The **tourist office** (☏0252-614 1527; İskele Meydanı; ⊙8am-noon & 1-5pm) is opposite the marina.

ⓘ Getting There & Away

Fethiye's otogar is 2.5km east of the centre. Buses head to Antalya (₺35, six hours) via Kaş (₺20, two hours) at least hourly.

Local dolmuşes for Ölüdeniz (₺5.50, 25 minutes), Kayaköy (₺4.50, 20 minutes) and surrounding villages leave from the dolmuş stop near the new mosque just off Atatürk Caddesi in the centre.

Catamarans sail daily to Rhodes in Greece (one way/return from €50/60, 1½ hours) from Fethiye pier, opposite the tourist office.

Patara

☏0242 / POP 950

There's always plenty of room to throw down your towel on Turkey's longest uninterrupted beach. Patara has 18km of sandy shore to stretch out on, and when you've finished with sun sandcastles, the remnants of Ancient Patara (admission incl Patara Beach ₺15; ⊙9am-7pm mid-Apr–Oct, 8am-5pm Nov–mid-Apr) sprawl along the beach access road. If those ruins aren't enough, Patara is also within easy day-tripping distance to more ancient Lycian cities, including Letoön (admission ₺8; ⊙9am-7pm mid-Apr–Oct, 8am-5pm Nov–mid-Apr), which has three temples to Apollo, Artemis and Leto, and impressive Xanthos (☏0242-871 6001; admission ₺10; ⊙9am-7pm mid-Apr–Oct, 8am-5pm Nov–mid-Apr, ticket office shuts 30min before closure), with a Roman theatre and Lycian pillar tombs.

All the accommodation is in the postage stamp-sized village of Gelemiş, 1.5km from the beachfront. Akay Pension (☏0242-843 5055, 0532 410 2195; www.pataraakaypension.com; s/d/tr/apt ₺70/100/130/180; 🅿🔅❄🛜🏊) and Flower Pension (☏0530 511 0206, 0242-843 5164; www.pataraflowerpension.com; s/d/tr/studio €30/40/50/50, apt €60-85; 🅿🔅❄@🛜🏊) both have well-maintained rooms and balconies overlooking citrus groves.

Buses on the Fethiye–Kaş route drop you on the highway 3.5km from the village. From here dolmuşes run to the village (₺3) every 30 to 40 minutes between May and October.

Kaş

☏0242 / POP 7558

While other Mediterranean towns bank on their beaches for popularity, Kaş is all about adventure activities. This is Turkey's diving centre and a bundle of kayaking, hiking and boating trips are also easily organised here. It's a mellow kind of place with a squiggle of old town lanes wrapping around the small harbour, which is dominated by the craggy Greek island of Meis (Kastellorizo) just offshore.

⊙ Sights & Activities

Kaş' adventure operators specialise in kayaking and boat trips to the nearby Kekova area with its sunken city ruins, pretty coastal scenery and charming hamlets of Üçağız and Kaleköy. Kaş is also home to Turkey's best diving opportunities and nearly all the adventure operators in town offer dive trips.

Antiphellos Ruins   RUINS

FREE Antiphellos was a small settlement and the port for Phellos, the much larger Lycian town further north in the hills. Its small Hellenistic theatre (Hastane Caddesi) **FREE**, 500m west of the main square, could seat 4000 spectators and is in very good condition. You can also walk to the rock tombs (Likya Caddesi) cut into the sheer cliffs above town, which are illuminated at night. The walk is strenuous so go at a cool time of day.

Dragoman   OUTDOORS

(☏0242-836 3614; www.dragoman-turkey.com; Uzun Çarşı Sokak 15) This dynamic outdoor activities centre has built a reputation for its diving, offering underwater packages from PADI and CMAS courses to snorkelling with a marine biologist. Its outdoor activities include many interesting and unique options, such as 'mermaid' tours, stand-up paddleboarding (SUP), botanical excursions, horse riding and coasteering. It also offers excellent day and multiday sea-kayaking, hiking and mountain-biking routes.

Bougainville Travel   OUTDOORS
(☑0242-836 3737; www.bougainville-turkey.com; İbrahim Serin Caddesi 10, Kaş) This reputable English-Turkish tour operator has much experience in organising any number of activities and tours, including Kekova island boat tours (€30), canyoning (€50), mountain biking (€40), tandem paragliding (€80 for flight lasting 20 to 30 minutes), scuba diving (€23 for one dive including equipment, €30 for a sample dive and €300 for a PADI course) and sea kayaking (€35).

🛏 Sleeping & Eating

Most accommodation is west and northwest of the centre along the waterfront and up the hill around the Yeni Camii (New Mosque).

★ Hideaway Hotel   HOTEL €€
(☑0242-836 1887; www.hotelhideaway.com; Anfitiyatro Sokak 7; s €45, d €55-65, ste €80; [P]🐾❄
@🛜🏊) Run by the unstoppable Ahmet, a fount of local information, this lovely hotel has large, airy rooms (some with sea views) with a fresh white-on-white minimalist feel and gleaming modern bathrooms. There's a pool for cooling off and a chilled-out roof terrace that's the venue for morning yoga and sundowners at the bar with Meis views.

Ateş Pension   PENSION €€
(☑0242-836 1393, 0532 492 0680; www.atespension.com; Anfitiyatro Sokak 3; dm/s/d/tr/f ₺50/130/145/185/210; [P]🐾❄🛜) Offering four-bed dorms and private rooms in two buildings, 'Hot Pension' is a cut above Kaş' other pensions, with snugly duvets and modern bathrooms. Owners Recep and Ayşe are superfriendly hosts and serve Turkish feasts (₺30) and breakfasts of 55 items on the partly covered roof terrace, which is a relaxing lounge with a book exchange and partial sea views.

Bi Lokma   ANATOLIAN €€
(☑0242-836 3942; www.bilokma.com.tr; Hükümet Caddesi 2; mains ₺20-28; ⊙9am-midnight; 🍽) Also known as 'Mama's Kitchen', this place has green tables in a terraced garden high above the harbour. The 'mama' in question

is Sabo, whose daughters have taken the culinary baton, turning out great traditional Turkish soul food, including excellent mezes (go for the ₺25 selection of 10), famous house *mantı* (Turkish ravioli; ₺20) and *börek* (filled pastry; ₺18).

❶ Getting There & Away

The otogar is along Atatürk Bulvarı, 350m north of the centre. Dolmuşes leave half-hourly to Antalya (₺30, 3½ hours) via Olympos (₺15, 2½ hours). Buses to Fethiye (₺20, 2½ hours) leave every two hours.

Ferries to Meis (Kastellorizo; same-day return €25, 20 minutes) leave daily at 10am and return at 4pm. Buy tickets at the **Meis Express** (☑0242-836 1725; www.meisexpress.com; Cumhuriyet Meydanı) office near the harbour.

Olympos & Çıralı

☑0242

The tiny beach hamlets of Olympos and Çıralı are where you head if you're looking for days of beach action. Olympos is an old hippy hang-out with an all-night party reputation in summer and the vine-covered ancient **Olympos ruins** (☑0242-238 5688; www.muze.gov.tr; admission incl Olympos Beach ₺20, parking ₺4; ⊙9am-7pm Apr-Oct, 8am-5pm Nov-Mar) lining the dirt track to the beach.

A couple of kilometres down the beach is more sedate Çıralı, where a clutch of pensions sit back from the sand and life is simplified to a choice between swinging in a hammock or sunning yourself on the beach.

In the evening, trips to the famed **Chimaera** (admission ₺6; ⊙24hr), a cluster of natural flames on the slopes of Mt Olympos, are the major activity. At night the 20-odd flames are visible at sea. Most Olympos accommodation run nightly tours (it's around 7km from Olympos) or you can follow the signs 3.5km up the hill from Çıralı.

🛏 Sleeping & Eating

Olympos's 'tree house' camps, which line the track along the valley down to the ruins, have long been the stuff of travel legend. The 'tree houses' are actually rustic, platformed bungalows, and accommodation prices generally include breakfast and dinner. Most camps also offer bungalows with en suite.

Çıralı has better sleeping and eating options, from rustic pensions to beachfront lodges, and free access to Olympos Beach.

TURKEY ANTALYA

🛏 Olympos

★ Şaban Pension   BUNGALOW €
(☑0242-892 1265; www.sabanpansion.com; Yazırköyü, Olympos; dm ₺45, bungalows s/d/tr ₺100/140/180, tree houses without bathroom s/d ₺75/100; 🅿😊❄🛜) Our personal favourite, this is the place to lounge in a hammock in the orchard or on a wooden platform by the stream enjoying sociable owner Meral's home cooking. Şaban isn't a party spot; it's a tranquil getaway where relaxed conversations strike up around the bonfire at night. Accommodation is in charming cabins and tree houses. Rates include half board.

🛏 Çıralı

Orange Motel   PENSION €€€
(☑0242-825 7328; www.orangemotel.net; Yanartaş Yolu, Çıralı; s/d €50/70, 2-bedroom bungalows €105; 🅿😊❄🛜) In the middle of an orange grove, the Orange feels like a farm despite its central location. Come here in spring and you'll never forget the overwhelming scent and buzz of bees. The garden is hung with hammocks, rooms are veritable wooden suites and there's a house travel agency. Breakfast features homemade orange and lemon marmalades and orange-blossom honey.

🛈 Getting There & Away

Buses and dolmuşes plying the Fethiye–Antalya coast road will stop at the Olympos and Çıralı junctions. From there, dolmuşes (₺6) serve Olympos (10km) half-hourly from 8am to 8pm between May and October; and Çıralı (7km) roughly hourly in summer. Outside these months, ring your guesthouse beforehand to check dolmuş times or organise a pickup.

Antalya
☑0242 / POP 1,027,500

The cultural capital of the Mediterranean, Antalya is a bustling modern city with a wonderfully preserved historic core. The old town of Kaleiçi is an atmospheric maze of Ottoman architecture, Roman ruins and Seljuk hamams, leading to an impressive harbour beneath a soaring cliff topped with cafes and bars– all overlooked by the snow-capped Beydağları (Bey Mountains). Just outside town, a clutch of dazzling ancient ruins sit on craggy slopes in easy reach for day trippers, providing another reason to dally here.

⊙ Sights

★ Antalya Museum   MUSEUM
(☑0242-238 5688; www.antalyamuzesi.gov.tr/en; Konyaaltı Caddesi; admission ₺20; ⊙9am-7pm Apr-Oct, 8am-5pm Nov-Mar, ticket office shuts 30min before closure) Do not miss this comprehensive museum with exhibitions covering everything from the Stone and Bronze Ages to Byzantium. The Hall of Regional Excavations exhibits finds from ancient cities in Lycia (such as Patara and Xanthos) and Phrygia, while the Hall of Gods displays beautiful and evocative statues of 15 Olympian gods, many in excellent condition. Most of the statues were found at Perge, including the sublime Three Graces and the towering Dancing Woman dominating the first room.

Suna & İnan Kıraç Kaleiçi Museum MUSEUM
(☑0242-243 4274; www.kaleicimuzesi.org; Kocatepe Sokak 25; adult/child ₺3/1.50; ⊙9am-noon & 1-5pm Thu-Tue) This small ethnography museum is housed in a lovingly restored Antalya mansion. The 2nd floor contains a series of life-size dioramas depicting some of the most important rituals and customs of Ottoman Antalya. More impressive is the collection of Çanakkale ceramics housed in the former Greek Orthodox church of Aya Yorgi (St George), just behind the main house, which has been fully restored and is worth a look in itself.

Yivli Minare   HISTORIC SITE
(Fluted Minaret; Cumhuriyet Caddesi) This handsome and distinctive 'fluted' minaret, erected by Seljuk Sultan Aladdin Keykubad I in the early 13th century, is Antalya's symbol. The adjacent mosque (1373) is still in use.

🛏 Sleeping

Sabah Pansiyon   PENSION €
(☑0242-247 5345, 0555 365 8376; www.sabahpansiyon.com; Hesapçı Sokak 60; s/d/tr €25/30/45, 2-bedroom self-catering apt €75-100; ❄🛜📶) The Sabah has long been the first port of call for travellers watching their kuruş, thanks to the Sabah brothers who run the show and organise transport and tours aplenty. Rooms vary in size but all are sweet, simple and superclean. The shaded courtyard is prime territory for meeting other travellers, and breakfast takes place across the lane in Yemenli (☑0242-247 5345; Zeytin Sokak 16; mains ₺20, set menu ₺15).

White Garden Pansion PENSION €€
(📷 0242-241 9115; www.whitegardenpansion.com; Hesapçı Geçidi 9; s/d €40/60, self-catering apt €95-140; ⊜ ✳ @ 🛜 ≋) A positively delightful place to stay, combining quirky Ottoman character, modern rooms with an old-world veneer, and excellent service from Metin and team. The building itself is a fine restoration and the courtyard is particularly charming with its large pool. The breakfast also gets top marks.

★**Tuvana Hotel** BOUTIQUE HOTEL €€€
(📷 0242-247 6015; www.tuvanahotel.com; Karanlık Sokak 18; s/d from ₺250/270; P⊜✳@🛜≋) This discreet compound of six Ottoman houses has been stylishly converted into a refined city hotel with 47 rooms and suites. The plush rooms have a historic feel, with varnished floorboards, rugs and wall hangings, plus mod-cons such as DVD players and safes. The swimming pool is a bonus and there are three on-site restaurants: Seraser (📷 0242-247 6015; www.seraserrestaurant.com; Karanlık Sokak 18; mains ₺25-55; ⊙noon-midnight), Il Vicino and Pio.

✕ Eating & Drinking

For cheap eating, walk east to the Dönerciler Çarşısı (Market of Döner Makers; İnönü Caddesi).

ÇaY-Tea's CAFE €
(📷 0542 732 7000; www.cayteas.com; Hıdırlık Sokak 3; mains ₺20; ⊙9am-midnight mid-Apr–mid-Oct, 2-10pm Mon-Fri, 9am-midnight Sat & Sun mid-Oct–mid-Apr) Çay comes with lemons, fake flower garnish and a biscuit in a heart-shaped dish at this eclectic Dutch-Turkish cafe, where vintage furniture spills into the street and a wine cellar houses an inviting country-kitchen-style space. The menu includes sandwiches (₺12), omelettes, pancakes, homemade cakes, high tea and more substantial dishes.

★**Vanilla** INTERNATIONAL €€€
(📷 0242-247 6013; www.vanillaantalya.com; Hesapçı Sokak 33; mains ₺30-50; ⊙11.30am-midnight) This outstanding, ultramodern restaurant, led by British chef Wayne, has a streamlined and unfussy atmosphere with its banquettes, glass surfaces and pleasant outside area dotted with cane-backed chairs. On the menu are Mediterranean-inspired international dishes, including a good pizza selection (₺25).

WORTH A TRIP

ASPENDOS & PERGE

There are several magnificent Graeco-Roman ruins to explore around Antalya. Rent a car, join a group tour or organise a taxi tour from the city. Two of the best, which can easily be visited together, are Aspendos (admission ₺25, parking ₺5; ⊙9am-7pm mid-Apr–mid-Oct, 8am-5pm mid-Oct–mid-Apr), its wonderfully pre-served Roman theatre built by Emperor Marcus Aurelius (AD 161–80) and later used as a caravanserai by the Seljuks; and Perge (admission ₺25; ⊙9am-7pm mid-Apr–mid-Oct, 8am-5pm mid-Oct–mid-Apr), one of the most important towns of ancient Pamphylia, with a Roman Gate, nymphaeum, baths, agora, Hellenistic Gate and colonnaded street.

Castle Café CAFE, BAR
(📷 0242-248 6594; Hıdırlık Sokak 48/1; ⊙8am-11pm) This lively hang-out along the cliff edge is a local favourite, attracting a crowd of young Turks with its affordable drinks (300mL beer ₺11). Service can be slow, but the terrace's jaw-dropping views of the beaches and mountains west of town more than compensate, as do generous bar snacks such as fish and chips and burgers (₺24).

ℹ Information

Atatürk/Cumhuriyet Caddesi is lined with banks and ATMs. The **tourist office** (📷 0242-241 1747; Cumhuriyet Caddesi 55; ⊙8am-6pm) is just west of Cumhuriyet Meydanı.

ℹ Getting There & Away

The otogar is 4km north of the centre. A tram (₺1.80) runs from here to the city centre (İsmet Paşa stop). From the otogar, buses whizz to destinations across the country, including two overnight services to Göreme (₺55, nine hours); several daily to Konya (₺49, five hours); and frequent dolmuşes and buses to Fethiye, via either the inland route (₺30, 3½ hours) or the coastal towns (₺35, six hours).

CENTRAL ANATOLIA

This is the region where the whirling dervishes first swirled, Atatürk began his revolution, Alexander the Great cut the Gordion Knot and Julius Caesar uttered his famous line, '*Veni, vidi, vici*' ('I came, I saw, I conquered').

Turkey's central plains are both alive with mind-boggling history and the place where you'll best capture a sense of modern Anatolian life.

Ankara

☑0312 / POP 4.7 MILLION

İstanbullus may quip that the best view in Ankara is the train home, but the Turkish capital has more substance than its reputation as a staid administrative centre suggests. The capital established by Atatürk boasts two of the country's most important sights, its hilltop *hisar* (citadel) district is full of old-fashioned charm, and the cafe-crammed Kızılay neighbourhood is one of Turkey's hippest urban quarters.

◎ Sights

★**Museum of Anatolian Civilisations**   MUSEUM
(Anadolu Medeniyetleri Müzesi; ☑0312-324 3160; www.anadolumedeniyetlerimuzesi.gov.tr; Gözcü Sokak 2; ₺20; ◎8.30am-6.45pm; MUlus) The superb Museum of Anatolian Civilisations is the perfect introduction to the complex weave of Turkey's ancient past, with beautifully curated exhibits housing artefacts cherry-picked from just about every significant archaeological site in Anatolia.

The central hall houses reliefs and statuary, while the surrounding halls take you on a journey of staggering history from Palaeolithic, Neolithic, Chalcolithic, Bronze Age, Assyrian, Hittite, Phrygian, Urartian and Lydian periods. Downstairs is a collection of Roman artefacts unearthed at excavations in and around Ankara.

★**Anıt Kabir**   MONUMENT
(Atatürk Mausoleum & Museum; www.anitkabir. org; Gençlik Caddesi; audioguide ₺10; ◎9am-5pm; MTandoğan) FREE The monumental mausoleum of Mustafa Kemal Atatürk (1881–1938), the founder of modern Turkey, sits high above the city with its abundance of marble and air of veneration. The tomb itself actually makes up only a small part of this fascinating complex, which consists of museums and a ceremonial courtyard. For many Turks a visit is virtually a pilgrimage, and it's not unusual to see people visibly moved. Allow at least two hours in order to visit the whole site.

⌂ Sleeping

The Ulus area's budget and low-end midrange hotels are convenient for the Museum of Anatolian Civilisations and citadel; Kızılay's midrange hotels are better for restaurants and nightlife.

Deeps Hostel   HOSTEL €
(☑0312-213 6338; www.deepshostelankara. com; Ataç 2 Sokak 46; dm/s/d without breakfast ₺30/55/90; ⊛⊜; MKızılay) At Ankara's best budget choice, friendly owner Şeyda has created a colourful, light-filled hostel with spacious dorms and small private rooms with squeaky-clean, modern shared bathrooms. It's all topped off by masses of advice and information, a fully equipped kitchen and a cute communal area downstairs where you can swap your Turkish travel tales.

★**Angora House Hotel**   HISTORIC HOTEL €€€
(☑0312-309 8380; www.angorahouse.com.tr; Kale Kapısı Sokak 16; s/d/tr €44/60/75; ⊛⊜; MUlus) Be utterly charmed by this restored Ottoman house, which oozes subtle elegance at every turn. The six spacious rooms are infused with loads of old-world atmosphere, featuring dark wood accents, creamy 19th-century design textiles and colourful Turkish carpets, while the walled courtyard garden is the perfect retreat from the citadel streets. Delightfully helpful staff add to the appeal.

✕ Eating & Drinking

It's all about street stalls, hip bistros and cafe culture in Kızılay, where terraces line virtually every inch of space south of Ziya Gökalp Caddesi. Kızılay's tall, thin buildings also pack in up to five floors of nightspots.

Leman Kültür   INTERNATIONAL €
(☑0312-310 8617; www.lmk.com.tr; Bestekar Sokak 80; mains ₺10-25; ◎11am-midnight; ⊜) Named after a cult Turkish comic strip – and decorated accordingly – this is the pre-party pick for a substantial feed and for spotting beautiful young educated things. The food is generally of the meatballs, burgers, pizza and grilled meats variety. Drinks are reasonably priced and the speakers crank everything from indie-electro to Türk pop. The closest metro station is Kızılay.

Zenger Paşa Konağı   TURKISH €€
(☑0312-311 7070; www.zengerpasa.com; Doyran Sokak 13; mains ₺15-25; MUlus) Crammed with Ottoman ephemera, the Zenger Paşa at first

looks like a deserted ethnographic museum, but climb up the rickety stairs and you'll find views of the city that are worth a visit alone. The menu of pide (Turkish-style pizza), meze and grills isn't going to get marks for originality but it's a solid lunch bet within the citadel area.

ⓘ Information

The main road is Atatürk Bulvarı, which connects Ulus with Kızılay and contains plenty of ATMs, banks and the main post office.

ⓘ Getting There & Away

BUS

From Ankara's huge **AŞTİ otogar** (Ankara Şehirlerarası Terminali İşletmesi; Mevlâna Bulvarı), buses depart to all corners of Turkey day and night. Services to İstanbul (₺40 to ₺45, six hours) leave numerous times daily. The AŞTİ is at the western end of Ankara's Ankaray metro line (fare ₺4), by far the easiest way to travel between the otogar and the centre.

TRAIN

Ankara Train Station (Ankara Garı; Talat Paşa Bulvarı) has high-speed trains to Konya (economy/business class ₺30/43, two hours, seven daily); and to Pendik, a suburb 25km east of İstanbul (₺70, 3½ hours). Slow, long-distance trains run overnight to İzmir and eastern Anatolia.

Konya

🎵 0332 / POP 1.2 MILLION

The home of the whirling dervish orders is both a modern economic boom town and a bastion of Seljuk culture. The centre is dotted with imposing historic monuments all topped off by the city's turquoise-domed **Mevlâna Museum** (🎵 0332-351 1215; Asanlı Kışla Caddesi; audioguide ₺10; ⊙10am-6.30pm Mon, 9am-6.30pm Tue-Sun; 🚊Mevlâna) **FREE**; the former dervish lodge is one of Turkey's finest sights and most important centres of pilgrimage.

Try to visit on a Saturday to see a whirling dervish *sema* ceremony at the **Mevlâna Culture Centre** (Whirling Dervish Performance; www.emav.org; Aslanlı Kışla Caddesi; ⊙7pm Sat; 🚊Mevlâna Kültür Merkezi) **FREE**, and don't miss the **Tile Museum** (Karatay Medresesi Çini Müzesi; 🎵0332-351 1914; Alaaddin Meydanı; ₺5; ⊙9am-6.40pm), a former Seljuk theological school (1251) with finely preserved blue-and-white tilework and an outstanding ceramic collection.

For accommodation, **Ulusan Otel** (🎵0532 488 2333, 0332-351 5004; ulusanhotel@hotmail.com; Çarşi PTT Arkasi 4; s/d ₺40/80; ❄🕸) is the pick of the Konya cheapies and **Derviş Otel** (🎵0332-350 0842; www.dervishotel.com; Güngör Sokak 7; r €50-75, f €100; ❄✳🕸) is a 200-year-old house converted into a rather wonderful boutique hotel. You can feast on Turkish classics at **Konak Konya Mutfağı** (🎵0332-352 8547; Piriesat Caddesi 5; mains ₺10-22; ⊙11am-10pm; 🍴), run by well-known food writer Nevin Halıcı, while nearby **Somatçi** (🎵0332-351 6696; www.somatci.com; Mengüc Sokak 36; dishes ₺6.50-25; ⊙9am-11pm; 🍴) rekindles old Seljuk and Ottoman recipes.

Konya otogar is 7km north of the centre and connected by tram. There are frequent buses to all major destinations, including Ankara (₺30, 3½ hours); İstanbul (₺70, 11½ hours); and Nevşehir, Cappadocia (₺30, three hours).

Seven express trains run to/from Ankara daily (economy/business class ₺30/43, two hours).

CAPPADOCIA

Cappadocia's cascading rock formations look like they've been plucked straight out of a fairy tale. Explore these rippling valleys, studded with cone-like rocks (called fairy chimneys), and you'll find the human history here just as fascinating as the geological wonderland. Rock-hewn churches covered in Byzantine frescoes are secreted into cliffs, the villages are honeycombed out of hillsides and vast subterranean complexes, where early Christians once hid, are tunnelled under the ground.

Göreme

🎵 0384 / POP 2200

Surrounded by epic sweeps of moonscape valley, this remarkable honey-coloured village hollowed out of the hills may have long since grown beyond its farming-hamlet roots, but its charm has not diminished. Nearby, **Göreme Open-Air Museum** (Göreme Açık Hava Müzesi; 🎵0384-271 2167; Müze Caddesi; ₺30; ⊙8.30am-6.45pm Apr-Nov, to 4.45pm Dec-Mar) is a rock-cut Byzantine monastic settlement that housed some 20 monks, while if you wander out of town you'll find storybook landscapes and little-visited churches in the likes of Güllüdere (Rose) Valley. With its easy-going allure and stunning setting, it's no wonder Göreme continues to send travellers giddy.

⏱ Tours

Most Göreme tour companies offer two standard full-day tours referred to locally as the **Red Tour** (including visits to Göreme Open-Air Museum, Uçhisar rock castle, Paşabağı and Devrent Valleys, and Avanos) and the **Green Tour** (including a hike in Ihlara Valley and a trip to an underground city).

Heritage Travel   TOURS
(☑ 0384-271 2687; www.turkishheritagetravel.com; Uzundere Caddesi; day tours per person cash/credit card €45/55) This highly recommended local agency offers different day-tour itineraries to most operators in Cappadocia, including an 'Undiscovered Cappadocia' trip which visits Soğanlı, Mustafapaşa, Keslik Monastery and Derinkuyu Underground City. There's a range of more off-beat activities as well, including jeep safaris, cooking classes in King's Valley, and grape harvesting and *pekmez* (syrup made from grape juice) – making day trips during harvest season (September to October).

Yama Tours   TOURS
(☑ 0384-271 2508; www.yamatours.com; Müze Caddesi 2; group day tours ₺110-120) This popular backpacker-friendly travel agency runs daily Cappadocia North (Göreme Open-Air Museum, Paşabağı and Avanos) and South (Ihlara Valley and Derinkuyu Underground City) tours, and can organise a bagful of other Cappadocia adventures and activities for you. It also runs tours to Hacıbektaş and Soğanlı that take in plenty of sights along the way.

DON'T MISS

CAPPADOCIA FROM ABOVE

Göreme is one of the best places in the world to go hot-air ballooning. Flight conditions are especially favourable here and seeing this remarkable landscape from above is a truly magical experience. The following ballooning agencies have good credentials:

Butterfly Balloons (☑ 0384-271 3010; www.butterflyballoons.com; Uzundere Caddesi 29)

Royal Balloon (☑ 0384-271 3300; www.royalballoon.com; Dutlu Sokak 9)

🛏 Sleeping & Eating

Köse Pension   PENSION €
(☑ 0384-271 2294; www.kosepension.com; Ragıp Üner Caddesi; dm ₺20, rooftop hut per person ₺35, d/tr ₺120/135; ☀🗫🛋) It may have no cave character, but traveller favourite Köse is still the pick of Göreme's budget digs. Ably managed by Sabina, this friendly place provides a range of spotless rooms featuring brilliant bathrooms, bright linens and comfortable beds, more basic rooms and a spacious rooftop dorm. The swimming pool is a bonus after a long, hot hike.

Kelebek Hotel   BOUTIQUE HOTEL €€
(☑ 0384-271 2531; www.kelebekhotel.com; Yavuz Sokak 31; fairy chimney s/d €44/55, deluxe €56/70, ste from €68/85; P☀❄🗫🛋) Local guru Ali Yavuz leads a charming team at one of Göreme's original boutique hotels, which has seen a travel industry virtually spring from beneath its stunning terraces. Exuding Anatolian inspiration at every turn, the rooms are spread over a labyrinth of stairs and balconies interconnecting two gorgeous stone houses, each with a fairy chimney protruding skyward.

★ Koza Cave Hotel   BOUTIQUE HOTEL €€€
(☑ 0384-271 2466; www.kozacavehotel.com; Çakmaklı Sokak 49; d €80-90, ste €110-175; ☀❄🗫) 🖉 Bringing a new level of eco-inspired chic to Göreme, Koza Cave is a masterclass in stylish sustainable tourism. Passionate owner Derviş spent decades living in Holland and has incorporated Dutch eco-sensibility into every cave crevice of the 10 stunning rooms. Grey water is reused, and recycled materials and local handcrafted furniture are utilised in abundance to create sophisticated spaces. Highly recommended.

Nostalji Restaurant   ANATOLIAN €€
(☑ 0384-271 2906; Kale Sokak 4; mains ₺12-15, testi kebap ₺35-45; ⊙ 11am-10pm) Bring your appetite and prepare to feast on the soul food that fuelled Cappadocian farmers for centuries. Nostalji has brought the homespun flavours of village dishes into a fine dining environment. It gets major brownie points for complimentary meze and salad with meals, and for the free pickup and drop-off service (reserve in advance); perfect if you're feeling too lazy to walk up the hill.

Seten Restaurant   MODERN TURKISH €€€
(☑ 0384-271 3025; www.setenrestaurant.com; Aydınlı Sokak; mains ₺16-45; ⊙ 11am-11pm; 🖉)

Brimming with an artful Anatolian aesthetic, Seten is a feast for the eye as well as for the stomach. Named after the old millstones used to grind bulgur wheat, this restaurant is an education for newcomers to Turkish cuisine and a treat for well-travelled palates. Attentive service complements classic main dishes and myriad luscious and unusual meze.

ⓘ Getting There & Away

Kayseri Airport (Kayseri Erkilet Havalimanı; ☑ 0352-337 5494; www.kayseri.dhmi.gov.tr; Kayseri Caddesi) and **Nevşehir Airport** (Nevşehir Kapadokya Havalimanı; ☑ 0384-421 4451; www.kapadokya.dhmi.gov.tr; Nevşehir Kapadokya Havaalanı Yolu, Gülşehir) serve central Cappadocia and have several daily flights to/from İstanbul.

Airport shuttle buses to Göreme from either airport must be prebooked. All hotels can do this for you or you can book directly through **Helios Transfer** (☑ 0384 271 2257; www.heliostransfer.com; Adnan Menderes Caddesi 24/A, Göreme; per passenger to/from either airport €10).

BUS

Most long-distance buses from western Turkey terminate in Nevşehir, where a free bus-company *servis* takes you on to Göreme. Make sure your ticket states your final destination, not Nevşehir. Beware of touts at Nevşehir otogar and only use the bus company's official *servis* shuttle.

The major bus companies all have offices in Göreme otogar and service destinations nationwide.

EASTERN TURKEY

Vast, remote and rugged, eastern Anatolia is a place apart. Here you'll find spectacular archaeological sites devoid of other visitors, harshly beautiful steppe countryside, and a fascinating cultural heritage that intermingles Turkish, Kurdish, Arabic and Iranian flavours.

Sadly, fighting between the PKK (Kurdistan Workers Party) and Turkish government forces, along with possible effects of the Syrian conflict in territory near the border, have rendered much of southeastern Anatolia risky for travellers. Check your government's travel advice before considering travelling here.

Nemrut Dağı Milli Parkı

Two thousand years ago, a megalomaniac Commagene king erected his own memorial sanctuary on Nemrut Dağı (Mt Nemrut; 2106m), the centrepiece of today's stunning national park (Nemrut Dağı National Park; www.milliparklar.gov.tr/mp/nemrutdagi; ₺12). The fallen heads of the gigantic decorative statues of gods and kings, toppled by earthquakes, form one of the country's most enduring images.

Most people arrive on a sunrise or sunset tour arranged from Malatya or Kahta, or on a tour from Cappadocia. Note that the Cappadocia tours contain an extremely long drive there and back. In Kahta the pick of the accommodation is the Kommagene Hotel (☑ 0416-725 9726, 0532 200 3856; www.kommagenehotel.com; Mustafa Kemal Caddesi; s/d/tr €20/35/45, camping per car/tent €10/6; P ❄ 🎅), which organises decent Nemrut Dağı tours.

The closest base is the pretty village of Karadut, 12km from the summit. Accommodation here including Karadut Pension (☑ 0533 616 4564, 0416-737 2169; karadutpansiyon@hotmail.com; Karadut; per person without meals ₺30-40, campsite ₺5; P ❄ 🎅) and Nemrut Kervansaray Hotel (☑ 0416-737 2190; osmanaydin.44@hotmail.com; Karadut; s/d half board €44/64; P 🎅 ❄) can arrange pickups from Kahta otogar as well as transport to the summit if you don't have your own car.

Kars

☑ 0474 / POP 79,300

The medieval fortress and stately, pastel-coloured Russian buildings are well worth a look, but most people come to the setting of Orhan Pamuk's novel *Snow* to visit the dramatic ruins of Ani (₺8; ⏱ 8am-7pm Apr-Oct, to 5pm Nov-Mar; P), 45km east of the city.

Formerly a Silk Road entrepôt and capital of the Armenian kingdom, Ani was deserted after a Mongol invasion in 1236. The ghost city, with its lightning-cleaved Church of the Redeemer, now lies amid undulating grass overlooking the Armenian border. The site exudes an eerie ambience that is simply unforgettable.

In Kars, Hotel Katerina Sarayı (☑ 0474-223 0636; www.katerinasarayi.com; Celalbaba Caddesi 52; s/d/tr ₺120/180/220; P 🎅) is all tsarist-style elegance and comfort, occupying a large 1879 Russian stone building, and the classy 40-year-old Ocakbaşı Restoran

TURKEY NEMRUT DAĞI MILLI PARKI

WORTH A TRIP

IHLARA VALLEY

A beautiful canyon full of greenery and scattered with Byzantine rock-cut churches, **Ihlara Valley** (Ihlara Vadısı; admission incl Selime Monastery, Güzelyurt's Monastery Valley & Aksaray Museum ₺20; ⊙8am-6.30pm) is an excellent spot for a ramble. A trail follows the course of the river, which flows between Selime village with its craggy **monastery** (Selime village; admission incl Ihlara Valley, Güzelyurt's Monastery Valley & Aksaray Museum ₺20; ⊙8am-6pm) and Ihlara village.

Most people visit as part of a day tour which takes in the section of the gorge with the most churches. If you want to walk the entire valley – and it's definitely worth the effort – you'll need to stay overnight or have your own transport as having to change buses in both Nevşehir and Aksaray makes it tricky to do as a day trip on public transport.

In Ihlara village, **Akar Pansion** (✆0382-453 7018; www.ihlara-akarmotel.com; Ihlara village; s/d/tr ₺50/90/120; 🛜) has tidy rooms and helpful management while **Star Restaurant** (✆0382-453 7020; Ihlara village; mains ₺15-20; ⊙10am-9pm; 🛜✆) has tasty trout meals with a great riverside setting, as well as a good camping spot.

On weekdays, six dolmuşes travel to/from Aksaray (₺5, 45 minutes) stopping at Selime, Belisırma and Ihlara village. On weekends there are fewer services.

(✆0474-212 0056; www.kaygisizocakbasi.com; Atatürk Caddesi; mains ₺13-22; ⊙8am-11pm; 🛜✆) serves tasty and unusual regional and Turkish dishes.

From the otogar, 4km northeast of central Kars and linked by *servis*, there are daily buses to destinations including Ankara (₺70, 17 hours) and İstanbul (₺100, 22 hours).

The easiest way to get to Ani is to take a taxi minibus (₺150 for one or two people and ₺50 per person for three or more). This includes three hours' waiting time and can be organised through English-speaking driver-guide **Celil Ersözoğlu** (✆0532 226 3966; celilani@hotmail.com).

SURVIVAL GUIDE

ℹ Directory A–Z

ACCOMMODATION

Budget travellers will find backpacker hostels with dorm beds in İstanbul, along the Aegean and Mediterranean coasts, and in Cappadocia. Camping grounds are also found along the coasts and in Cappadocia. There are plentiful hotels of all standards and family-run pensions in tourist areas. Pensions generally represent better value.

Outside tourist areas, solo travellers of both sexes should be cautious about the cheapest hotel options. Suss out the staff and atmosphere in reception; theft and even sexual assaults have occurred in budget establishments (albeit very rarely).

The most interesting midrange and top-end options are Turkey's numerous boutique hotels, often in restored Ottoman mansions (such as

in İstanbul and Antalya), and Cappadocia's cave-hotels.

MONEY

➡ Turkish lira (₺) comes in notes of five, 10, 20, 50, 100 and 200; and coins of one, five, 10, 25 and 50 kuruş and one lira.

➡ Hotels and restaurants in more popular tourist destinations often quote their rates in euro.

➡ ATMs are widespread and dispense Turkish lira, and occasionally euros and US dollars, to Visa, MasterCard, Cirrus and Maestro cardholders.

➡ Credit cards (Visa and MasterCard) are widely accepted by hotels, shops and restaurants, although often not by establishments outside the main tourist areas. You can also

SLEEPING PRICE RANGES

Ranges are based on the cost of a double room in high season (June to August, apart from İstanbul, where high season is April, May, September, October, Christmas and Easter) and include breakfast, en-suite bathroom and taxes unless otherwise stated.

İstanbul & Bodrum Peninsula

€ less than €90

€€ €90 to €200

€€€ more than €200

Rest of Turkey

€ less than ₺90

€€ ₺90 to ₺180

€€€ more than ₺180

get cash advances on these cards. Amex is less commonly accepted.

⇒ US dollars and euros are the easiest currencies to change. You'll get better rates at exchange offices than at banks.

Tipping & Bargaining

⇒ Tipping is customary in restaurants, hotels and for services such as guided tours.

⇒ Round up metered taxi fares to the nearest 50 kuruş.

⇒ Leave waiters around 10% to 15% of the bill.

⇒ Check a *servis ücreti* (service charge) hasn't been automatically added to restaurant bills.

⇒ Hotel prices are sometimes negotiable, especially outside of peak season.

⇒ Bargaining for souvenirs is normal in bazaars.

OPENING HOURS

The working day shortens during the holy month of Ramazan (Ramadan). Friday is a normal working day in Turkey. Opening hours of tourist attractions and tourist information offices may shorten in the low season.

Information 8.30am-noon and 1.30-5pm Monday to Friday

Eating 11am-10pm

Drinking 4pm-late

Nightclubs 11pm-late

Shopping 9am-6pm Monday to Friday (longer hours in tourist areas and big cities – including weekend opening)

Government departments, offices and banks 8.30am-noon and 1.30-5pm Monday to Friday

POST

⇒ Turkish *postanes* (post offices) are indicated by black-on-yellow 'PTT' signs. Postcards sent abroad cost about ₺2.80.

SAFE TRAVEL

Despite the recent terrorist attacks, Turkey is not a dangerous country to visit, but it's always wise to be a little cautious, especially if you're travelling alone. To stay safe, you should watch out in particular for the following:

⇒ A string of terrorist attacks by Islamic State (Isis) and Kurdish insurgents hit Ankara and İstanbul throughout 2016. The likelihood of being caught in such incidents remains statistically low, and the usual targets are government and military installations, but be vigilant and avoid political rallies and large gatherings of people.

⇒ Protests are common in major cities. Keep well away from demonstrations as tear gas and water cannons are often used.

⇒ Do not visit areas in close proximity to the Syrian border, which are the most dangerous parts of Turkey. Here, there is the risk of being caught in the Turkish–Kurdish conflict and of being kidnapped or harmed by terrorists from Syria.

COUNTRY FACTS

Area 783,562 sq km

Capital Ankara

Country Code [%]90

Currency Turkish lira (₺); one Turkish lira is worth 100 kuruş

Emergency Ambulance [%]112, fire [%]110, police [%]155

Language Turkish, Kurdish

Money ATMs widespread; credit and debit cards accepted in cities and tourist areas

Visas Tourist visas (90 days) must be purchased before travel on Turkey's electronic visa website www.evisa.gov.tr

⇒ For the same reasons, large areas of southeastern Anatolia were risky for travellers at the time of writing. Nemrut Dağı National Park was not among the areas considered risky, but check your government's travel advice before visiting the region.

⇒ In İstanbul, single men are sometimes approached and lured to a bar by new 'friends'. The victim is then made to pay an outrageous bill, regardless of what he drank. Drugging is another occasional risk, especially for lone men. It pays to be a tad wary of who you befriend, especially when you're new to the country.

⇒ Although rare, sexual assaults have occurred against travellers of both sexes in hotels in central and eastern Anatolia. If a place seems leery, trust your instincts and go elsewhere.

TELEPHONE

⇒ Payphones require cards that can be bought at telephone centres or, for a small mark-up, at some shops. Some accept credit cards.

⇒ If you set up a roaming facility with your home phone provider, you should be able to connect your mobile to a network.

⇒ Local SIM cards are widely available and cost from ₺65, including ₺35 credit; take your passport to activate. Data bundles cost from ₺20 for 1GB.

⇒ If you buy a local SIM and use it in your home mobile, the network detects and bars foreign phones within 120 days.

VISAS

⇒ Nationals of countries including Denmark, Finland, France, Germany, Israel, Italy, Japan, New Zealand, Sweden and Switzerland don't need a visa to visit Turkey for up to 90 days.

⇒ Nationals of countries including Australia, Austria, Belgium, Canada, Ireland, the Nether-

ESSENTIAL FOOD & DRINK

Turkish food is a celebration of community and life, and is made memorable by the use of seasonal ingredients, ensuring freshness and flavour.

Kebaps and köfte (meatballs) in all their variations are the mainstay of restaurant meals. Look out for regional specialities such as the Adana kebap (spicy *köfte* grilled on a skewer and served with onions, sumac, parsley, barbecued tomatoes and pide bread), many available nationwide.

Meze is where Turkish cuisine really comes into its own. *Acılı ezme* (spicy tomato and onion paste), *fasulye pilaki* (white beans cooked with tomato paste and garlic) and *yaprak sarma* (vine leaves stuffed with rice, herbs and pine nuts) are just a few of the myriad meze dishes on offer.

For quick cheap eats, try *pide* (Turkish pizza), *lahmacun* (Arabic-style pizza), *gözleme* (savoury pancakes) and *börek* (filled pastries).

Popular non-kebap mains include *mantı* (Turkish ravioli), *saç kavurma* (stir-fried cubed meat dishes) and *güveç* (meat and vegetable stews cooked in a terracotta pot).

The national hot drink is **çay**, served black in tulip-shaped glasses. The Turkish liquor of choice is **rakı**, a fiery aniseed drink similar to Greek ouzo; do as the Turks do and cut it by half with water. **Ayran** is a refreshing yoghurt drink made by whipping up yoghurt with water and salt, and is the perfect accompaniment to a kebab.

lands, Norway, Portugal, Spain, the UK and USA need a visa, which should be purchased online at www.evisa.gov.tr before travelling.

➡ Most nationalities, including the above, are given a 90-day multiple-entry visa.

➡ In some cases, the 90-day visa stipulates 'per period 180 days'. This means you can spend three months in Turkey within a six-month period; when you leave after three months, you can't re-enter for three months.

➡ At the time of writing, the e-visa charge was US$20 for most nationalities, with a few exceptions including Australians and Canadians, who paid US$60, and South Africans, who received one month free.

➡ Your passport must be valid for at least six months from the date you enter the country.

WOMEN TRAVELLERS

Travelling in Turkey is straightforward for women, provided you follow some simple guidelines:
➡ Tailor your behaviour and dress to your surroundings. Outside of İstanbul and heavily touristed destinations, you should dress modestly.

EATING PRICE RANGES

Price ranges reflect the cost of a standard main-course dish.

€ less than ₺20

€€ ₺20 to ₺35

€€€ more than ₺35

➡ Cover your hair when visiting mosques or religious buildings.

➡ In more conservative areas (particularly out east) your contact with men should be polite and formal, not chatty and friendly or they are likely to get the wrong idea about your intentions.

➡ Very cheap hotels are not recommended for single women travellers. If a place has a bad vibe, find somewhere else.

🛈 Getting There & Away

AIR

The main international airports are in western Turkey. **Turkish Airlines** (☑ 0850-333 0849; www.turkishairlines.com), the national carrier, has an extensive international network.

Antalya International Airport (Antalya Havalimanı; ☑ 444 7423; www.aytport.com)

Bodrum International Airport (BJV; www.bodrumairport.com)

Dalaman International Airport (☑ 0252-792 5555; www.yda.aero/Dalaman_en/index.php)

İstanbul Atatürk International Airport (p1161)

İstanbul Sabiha Gökçen International Airport (p1161)

İzmir Adnan Menderes Airport (☑ 0232-455 0000; www.adnanmenderesairport.com)

LAND

There are direct bus services to İstanbul from European destinations including Austria, Albania, Bulgaria, Georgia, Germany, Greece, Kosovo, Macedonia and Romania.

The major bus companies that operate these routes are **Metro Turizm** (☑ 0850-222 3455; www.metroturizm.com.tr), **Ulusoy** (p1181) and **Varan** (☑ 0850-811 1999; www.varan.com.tr).

Currently the only train route operating between Europe and İstanbul is the daily Bosfor/Balkan Ekspresi to/from Bucharest (Romania) and Sofia (Bulgaria). See **Turkish State Railways** and **The Man in Seat 61** (www.seat61.com/turkey) for details.

SEA

Departure times and routes change between seasons, with fewer ferries generally running in the winter. **Ferrylines** (www.ferrylines.com) is a good starting point for information. The following is a list of ferry routes from Turkey:

➡ Ayvalık–Lesvos (Midilli), Greece
➡ Bodrum–Kalymnos, Kos, Rhodes and Symi, Greece
➡ Çeşme–Chios, Greece
➡ İstanbul–Illyichevsk (Odessa), Ukraine
➡ Kaş–Meis (Kastellorizo), Greece
➡ Kuşadası–Samos, Patmos and Ikaria, Greece
➡ Marmaris–Rhodes, Greece
➡ Taşucu–Girne, Northern Cyprus
➡ Turgetreis–Kalymnos, Kos and Leros (İleriye), Greece

ℹ Getting Around

AIR

Turkey is a vast country and domestic flights are an affordable way of reducing travel time, with more route choices if flying to/from İstanbul.

There are numerous regional airports, so it's well worth checking what's close to your Turkish destination. In addition to the international airports we've listed above, **Denizli Çardak Airport** (www.cardak.dhmi.gov.tr) is useful for visiting Pamukkale and **Kars Harakani Airport** (http://kars.dhmi.gov.tr/havaalanlari/home.aspx?hv=26) for visiting Ani and northeastern Anatolia.

BUS

Turkey's intercity bus system is as good as any you'll find, with modern, comfortable coaches crossing the country at all hours and for very reasonable prices.

Major companies with extensive networks include **Kamil Koç** (☑ 444 0562; www.kamilkoc.com.tr), **Metro Turizm** and **Ulusoy** (☑ 0850-811 1888; www.ulusoy.com.tr).

A town's otogar is often on the outskirts, but most bus companies provide a *servis* (free shuttle bus) to/from the centre.

Local routes are usually operated by dolmuşes (minibuses), which might run to a timetable or set off when full.

CAR & MOTORCYCLE

Turkey has the world's second-highest petrol prices. Petrol/diesel cost about ₺5 per litre.

An international driving permit (IDP) is not obligatory, but handy if your driving licence is from a country likely to seem obscure to a Turkish police officer.

You must be at least 21 years old to hire a car. Rental charges are similar to those in Europe. Try **Economy Car Rentals** (www.economycarrentals.com).

You must have third-party insurance if you are bringing your own car into the country. Buying it at the border is a straightforward process (one month €80).

Road accidents claim about 10,000 lives each year. To survive on Turkish roads:

➡ Drive defensively and cautiously.
➡ Don't expect fellow motorists to obey traffic signs or use indicators.
➡ Avoid driving at night, when you won't be able to see potholes, animals, vehicles driving without lights or stopped in the middle of the road.

TRAIN

The **Turkish State Railways** (☑ 444 8233; www.tcdd.gov.tr) network covers the country fairly well, with the notable exception of the coastlines. Most train journey times are notoriously long, but the entire system is currently being overhauled. Check out **The Man in Seat Sixty-One** (www.seat61.com/turkey2) for details on Turkish train travel.

High-Speed Routes

➡ Ankara–Konya
➡ İstanbul Pendik–Eskişehir–Ankara
➡ İstanbul Pendik–Eskişehir–Konya

Useful Long-Haul Routes (all departing from Ankara)

➡ Adana via Kayseri
➡ Diyarbakır via Kayseri, Sivas and Malatya
➡ İzmir via Eskişehir
➡ Kars via Kayseri, Sivas and Erzurum

InterRail Global and One Country passes and Balkan Flexipass cover the Turkish railway network, as do the Eurail Global and Select passes. ISIC cardholders get a 20% discount and Train Tour Cards are available at major stations.

Ukraine

Best Places to Eat

➡ Trapezna Idey (p1191)

➡ Arbequina (p1188)

➡ Dim Lehend (p1191)

➡ Baczewski (p1191)

➡ Kanapa (p1188)

Best Places to Stay

➡ Sunflower B&B (p1188)

➡ Villa Stanislavsky (p1190)

➡ Leopolis Hotel (p1190)

➡ Dream House Hostel (p1183)

Why Go?

Shaped like a broken heart, with the Dnipro River dividing it into two, this Slavic hinterland is a vast swath of sage-flavoured steppe filled with sunflowers and wild poppies. Blessed with a near-ideal climate and the richest soil in Europe, it's one huge garden of a country where flowers are blossoming, fruit are ripening and farmers markets sing hymns of abundance.

If only its history were as idyllic. Just over two decades into a very troubled independence, Ukraine (Україна) is dogged by a conflict with neighbouring Russia that has left Crimea and a small chunk of its eastern territory off limits to most travellers. But the country's main attractions, including eclectic and rebellious Kyiv, architecturally rich Lviv and flamboyant Odesa, are well away from the conflict zone. A long stretch of the Black Sea coast invites beach fun, while the Carpathians draw skiers in winter and cyclists in summer.

When to Go
Kyiv

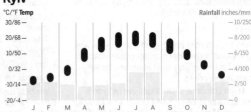

Jan Party on New Year's Eve then repent at an Orthodox Christmas service a week later.

May A great time to visit Kyiv when its countless horse chestnut trees are in blossom.

Aug Sip Ukraine's best coffee in one of Lviv's many outdoor cafes.

Kyiv   Київ

☎ 044 / POP 2.9 MILLION

Sometimes chaotic central Asia, other times quaint central Europe, Kyiv (many agree) is the former USSR's most pleasant metropolis. A pretty spot amid the wooded hills hemming the wide River Dnipro, this eclectic capital has preserved the legacy of its former possessors, from Viking chieftains to post-Soviet dictators. Despite its starring role in the 2014 Maidan Revolution which toppled the last of those rulers, only the very centre around Maidan Nezalezhnosti bears any scars, the rest of the city being untouched by the tumultuous events that have put the geopolitical spotlight firmly on Ukraine.

◎ Sights

★**Kyevo-Pecherska Lavra**   MONASTERY
(Києво-печерська лавра | Caves Monastery; ☎ 044-406 6375; kplavra.kiev.ua; vul Lavrska 9; grounds 20uah, caves & exhibitions adult/child 60/30uah; ☉ 8am-7pm Apr-Oct, 9am-6pm Nov-Mar; Ⓜ Arsenalna) Tourists and Orthodox pilgrims alike flock to the Lavra. Set on 28 hectares of grassy hills above the Dnipro River, the monastery's cluster of gold-domed churches is a feast for the eyes, the hoard of Scythian gold rivals that of the Hermitage in St Petersburg, and the underground labyrinths lined with mummified monks are exotic and intriguing. That's from a tourist's perspective, but for pilgrims this is simply the holiest ground in three East Slavic countries – Ukraine, Russia and Belarus.

Andriyivsky Uzviz   HISTORIC SITE
(Ⓜ Kontraktova pl) According to legend, a man walked up the hill here, erected a cross and prophesied: 'A great city will stand on this spot'. That man was the Apostle Andrew, hence the name of Kyiv's quaintest thoroughfare, a steep cobbled street that winds its way up from Kontraktova pl to vul Volodymyrska, with a vaguely Monparnasse feel. Its highlight is the stunning gold and blue **St Andrew's Church** (Andriyivsky uzviz; ☉ 10am-6pm; Ⓜ Kontraktova pl) `FREE`, a five-domed, cross-shaped baroque masterpiece that celebrates the apostle legend.

★**St Sophia's Cathedral**   CHURCH
(n.sophiakievska.org; pl Sofiyska; grounds/cathedral/bell tower 20/60/30uah; ☉ grounds 9am-7pm, cathedral 10am-6pm Thu-Tue, to 5pm Wed; Ⓜ Maydan Nezalezhnosti) The interior is the most astounding aspect of Kyiv's oldest standing church. Many of the mosaics and frescoes are original, dating back to 1017–31, when the cathedral was built to celebrate Prince Yaroslav's victory in protecting Kyiv from the Pechenegs (tribal raiders). While equally attractive, the building's gold domes and 76m-tall wedding-cake bell tower are 18th-century baroque additions.

★**Maidan Nezalezhnosti**   SQUARE
(майдан Незалежності | Independence Sq; Ⓜ Maydan Nezalezhnosti) Independent Ukraine has a short history, and pretty much all of it was written here. Popularly known as Maidan, the square was the site of pro-independence protests in the 1990s and the Orange Revolution in 2004. But all of that was eclipsed by the Revolution of Dignity in the winter of 2013–14, when the square was transformed into an urban guerrilla camp besieged by government forces. Makeshift memorials to fallen revolutionaries on vul Instytutska serve as a sombre reminder.

🛏 Sleeping

Dream House Hostel   HOSTEL €
(☎ 095 703 2979; www.dream-family.com; Andriyivsky uzviz 2D; dm/d from 170/650uah, d with bathroom from 820uah; ✳ @ 🛜; Ⓜ Kontraktova pl) Ky-

UKRAINE KYIV

ITINERARIES

Two Days

A couple of days are just enough to 'do' Kyiv, starting at its stellar attraction, the Kyevo-Pecherska Lavra (aka the Caves Monastery). Follow this with a hike up artsy Andriyivsky uzviz for a taste of prewar Ukraine, before plunging into the beeswax-perfumed Byzantine interior of Unesco-listed St Sophia's Cathedral.

Five Days

Having seen the sights in Kyiv, hop aboard a slow night train to Lviv, Ukraine's most central European city complete with bean-scented coffee houses, Gothic and baroque churches, and quaintly rattling trams.

Ukraine Highlights

1 Kyevo-Pecherska Lavra (p1183) Inspecting Kyiv's collection of mummified monks by candlelight.

2 Andriyivsky Uzviz (p1183) Making an ascent of Kyiv's most atmospheric street.

3 Lviv (p1189) Doing a spot of cobble-surfing in the historical centre packed with churches, museums and eccentric restaurants.

4 Lychakiv Cemetery (p1189) Exploring Lviv's final resting place of Ukraine's great and good.

Central Kyiv

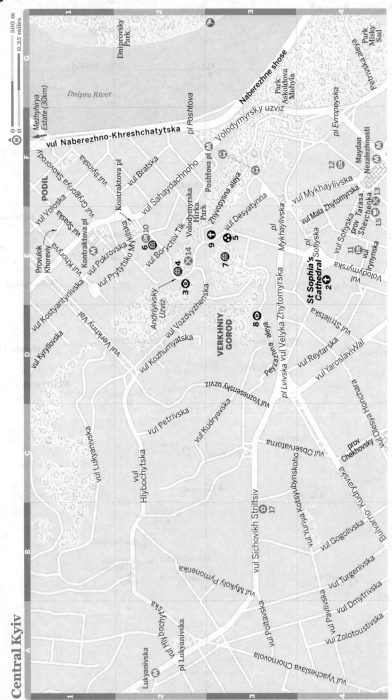

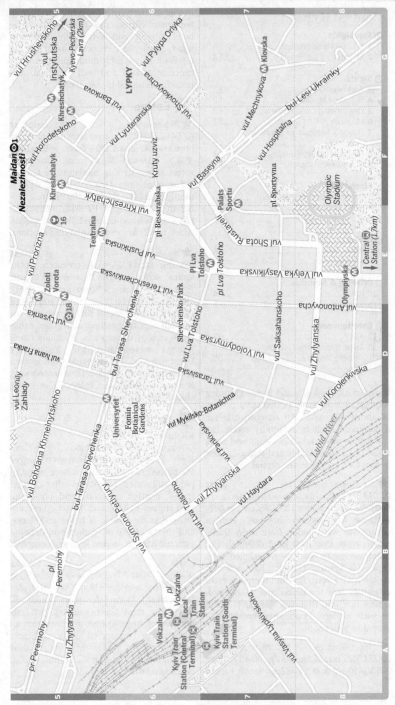

Central Kyiv

iv's most happening hostel is this gleaming 100-bed affair superbly located at the bottom of Andriyivsky uzviz. An attached cafe-bar, a basement kitchen, a laundry room, key cards, bike hire, and daily events and tours make this a comfortable and engaging base from which to explore the capital.

★ **Sunflower B&B Hotel**   B&B €€
(☑044 279 3846; www.sunflowerhotel.kiev.ua; vul Kostyolna 9/41; s/d from 1200/1450uah; ✳@🛜; ⓂMaydan Nezalezhnosti) Just off Maidan square but well hidden from noisy traffic and crowds, this B&B (and definitely not hotel) seems to have been designed by a super-tidy granny. The airy, light-coloured rooms have a retro feel and there are extra amenities like umbrellas and a shoe-polishing machine that you wouldn't expect in such a place. Continental breakfast is served in your room.

★ **Hotel Bontiak**   BOUTIQUE HOTEL €€€
(☑284 0475; bontiak.com; vul Irynynska 5; s/d from 2050/2450uah; ✳@🛜; ⓂZoloti Vorota) Tucked in a quiet courtyard a five-minute walk from both main city squares, this cosy boutique hotel is built into Kyiv's hilly landscape, which is why the reception is located at the top floor. The stylishly minimalist rooms are generously sized and well equipped, and breakfast is served in your room.

✗ Eating

★ **Arbequina**   SPANISH, SEAFOOD €€
(☑044-223 9618; arbequina.com.ua; vul Borysa Hrinchenka 4; mains 120-160uah; ⊙9am-11pm; 🛜🅿; ⓂMaydan Nezalezhnosti) Barcelona meets Odesa in this miniature restaurant a few steps from Maidan square. Food is mostly Spanish – think *paella* and *fideua* – but the chef successfully experiments with Black Sea fish and Eastern European staples, which results in most unusual combinations.

★ **Kanapa**   UKRAINIAN €€
(Канапа; ☑044-425 4548; borisov.com.ua/uk/kanapa; Andriyivsky uzviz 19; mains 80-400uah; ⊙9am-11pm; 🛜🅿; ⓂKontraktova pl) Sneak away from the busy uzviz and you'll find yourself in what seems like a treehouse – a wooden terrace perched above the dense green canopy underneath. A unique place, Kanapa serves gentrified, 21st-century Ukrainian food, largely made from its own farm's produce. Traditional it is not: *borshch* is made of nettlle and chicken Kiev is not chicken but pheasant.

🍷 Drinking

Kupidon   PUB
(Купідон | Cupid; vul Pushkinska 1-3/5; ⊙10am-10pm; 🛜; ⓂKhreshchatyk) Perhaps no longer the hotbed of nationalism it once was, Cupid is still a great Lviv-styled cellar *knaypa* (pub), abutting a secondhand bookshop. Well-crafted coffees and Lvivske beer are enjoyed at the jumble of tables and chairs, and there's plenty of reading and drawing material lying around to keep you occupied.

Kaffa   COFFEE
(Каффа; ☑044-270 6505; www.kaffa.ua; prov Tarasa Shevchenka 3; ⊙10am-10pm; ⓂMaydan Nezalezhnosti) Around for years, Kaffa still serves the most heart-pumping, rich-tasting brew in town. Coffees and teas from all over the world are served in a pot sufficient for two or three punters in a whitewashed African-inspired interior – all ethnic masks, beads and leather.

☆ Entertainment

Atlas CONCERT VENUE
(Атлас; ☑ 067 155 2255; facebook.com/Atlas37/; vul Sichovikh Striltsiv 37-41; Ⓜ Lukyanivska) This industrial-style multistorey venue, complete with roof terrace, caters to all musical tastes from techno to heavy metal with a sprinkling of theatre and poetry readings. The best of the best in Ukrainian and foreign music gravitate here these days.

Taras Shevchenko
National Opera Theatre OPERA
(☑ 044-235 2606; www.opera.com.ua; vul Volodymyrska 50; Ⓜ Zoloti Vorota) Performances at this lavish theatre (opened 1901) are grandiose affairs, but tickets are cheap. True disciples of Ukrainian culture should not miss a performance of *Zaporozhets za Dunaem* (Zaporizhzhyans Beyond the Danube), a sort of operatic, purely Ukrainian version of *Fiddler on the Roof*.

ℹ Information

Almost every cafe and restaurant offers free wi-fi and there are hotspots throughout the city centre.

ℹ Getting There & Away

AIR

Most international flights use Boryspil International Airport, 35km east of the city. Some domestic airlines and Wizzair use **Zhulyany airport** (☑ 044 585 7254; www.airport.kiev.ua), 7km southwest of the centre. There's at least one flight a day to all regional capitals and international flights serve many European cities.

Plane tickets are sold at **Kiy Avia** (www.kiyavia.com; pr Peremohy 2; ◷ 8am-9pm Mon-Fri, 8am-8pm Sat, 9am-6pm Sun; Ⓜ Vokzalna).

BUS

A couple of overnight coaches (eight hours, 250uah) make the Lviv run from the **Central Bus Station** (Tsentralny Avtovokzal; pl Moskovska 3).

TRAIN

Kyiv's **train station** (☑ 044 503 7005; pl Vokzalna 2; Ⓢ Vokzalna) handles domestic services as well as international trains to Moscow, Warsaw, Berlin, Chişinău and Bucharest.

The quickest way to Lviv is on the Intercity+ express (330uah, five hours, one daily), which leaves early evening. Cheaper overnight passenger trains and a few daytime services (165uah to 250uah, eight to 10 hours) are more popular.

Buy tickets at the station or the **advance train ticket office** (bul Tarasa Shevchenka 38/40; ◷ 7am-9pm; Ⓢ Universytet).

WORTH A TRIP

MEZHYHIRYA

Kyiv's newest tourist attraction is Mezhyhirya, the estate that once 'belonged' to ex-president and wannabe Ukrainian dictator, Viktor Yanukovych, famously ousted in the Maidan Revolution of 2014. A wander through the opulent mansion and grounds costing millions of dollars to create gives visitors an idea of just how corrupt the Yanukovych regime had become. Mezhyhirya lies 30km north of Kyiv. Take the metro to the terminus at Heroyiv Dnipra from where buses shuttle visitors to the estate.

ℹ Getting Around

TO/FROM THE AIRPORT

A taxi to the city centre costs around 400uah.

SkyBus (63uah, one hour) departs round the clock from behind the train station's South Terminal every 20 to 40 minutes.

Trolleybus 22 runs to Zhulyany airport from Shulyavska metro station.

PUBLIC TRANSPORT

Kyiv's metro runs between around 6am and midnight. Plastic tokens (*zhetony*; 4uah) are sold at windows and dispensers at stations.

Buy tickets (3uah) for buses, trolleybuses, trams and *marshrutky* (fixed-route minibuses) from the driver or conductor.

Lviv Львів

☑ 032 / POP 729,800

If you've done time in any other Ukrainian region, Lviv will come as a shock. Mysterious and architecturally lovely, this Unesco World Heritage–listed city is the country's least Soviet and exudes the same central European charm as pre-tourism Prague or Kraków once did. Its quaint cobbles, aromatic coffee houses and rattling trams feel a continent away from the war-torn badlands of Ukraine's east. It's also a place where the candle of Ukrainian national identity burns brightest.

◉ Sights

★ **Lychakiv Cemetery** CEMETERY
(Личаківське кладовище; ☑ 032 275 5415; www.lviv-lychakiv.ukrain.travel; vul Pekarska; adult/student 25/15uah; ◷ 9am-6pm Oct-Mar, to 9pm Apr-Sep) Don't leave town until you've seen

this amazing cemetery, only a short ride on tram 7 from the centre. This is the Père Lachaise of Eastern Europe, with the same sort of overgrown grounds and Gothic aura as the famous Parisian necropolis (but containing less-well-known people). Laid out in the late 18th century, it's packed full of western Ukraine's great and good. Pride of place goes to the grave of revered nationalist poet Ivan Franko.

Ploshcha Rynok SQUARE

`FREE` Lviv was declared a Unesco World Heritage site in 1998, and this old market square lies at its heart. The square was progressively rebuilt after a major fire in the early 16th century destroyed the original. The 19th-century **Ratusha** (Town Hall; city-adm.lviv.ua/; pl Rynok 1; ⊙9am-6pm Mon-Thu, to 5pm Fri) stands in the middle of the plaza, with fountains featuring Greek gods at each of its corners. Vista junkies can climb the 65m-high neo-Renaissance **tower** (pl Rynok 1; 10uah; ⊙9am-9pm Apr-Oct, to 6pm Nov-Mar). The ticket booth is on the 4th floor.

Latin Cathedral CATHEDRAL

(pl Katedralna 1; ⊙7.30am-7pm, closed 2-3pm Mon-Fri) With various chunks dating from between 1370 and 1480, this working cathedral is one of Lviv's most impressive churches. The exterior is most definitely Gothic, while the heavily gilded interior, one of the city's highlights, has a more baroque feel, with colourfully wreathed pillars hoisting frescoed vaulting and mysterious side chapels glowing in candlelit half-light. Services are in four languages, including English.

🛏 Sleeping

★ Old City Hostel HOSTEL €

(☑032 294 9644; www.oldcityhostel.lviv.ua; vul Beryndy 3; dm/d from 170/500uah; @ 🖙) Occupying two floors of an elegantly fading tenement just steps from pl Rynok, this expertly run hostel with period features and views of the Shevchenko statue from the wraparound balcony has long since established itself as the city's best. Fluff-free dorms hold four to 16 beds, shower queues are unheard of, sturdy lockers keep your stuff safe and there's a well-equipped kitchen.

★ Villa Stanislavsky BOUTIQUE HOTEL €€

(☑032-275 2505; villastanislavskyi.com.ua/; vul Henerala Tarnavskoho 75; r from 1215uah; P ✳) This hilltop villa stands amid the splendid decay of what used to be a posh fin de siècle residential neighbourhood, 20 minutes on foot from the centre. The dark, polished wood of the stairs and furniture and the placid surroundings provide much-needed respite from the old town's hustle and bustle. A dedicated chess room is the cherry on the sundae.

★ Leopolis Hotel HOTEL €€€

(☑032-295 9500; www.leopolishotel.com; vul Teatralna 16; s/d from 3100/3500uah; ☞✳@🖙) One of the historical centre's finest places to catch some Zs. Every guest room in this 18th-century edifice is different, but all have a well-stocked minibar, elegant furniture and an Italian-marble bathroom with underfloor heating. Wheelchair-friendly facilities, a new spa/fitness area in the cellars and a pretty decent brasserie are extras you won't find anywhere else.

CHORNOBYL

The world's most unlikely tourist attraction, and one of dark tourism's most sinister day's out, a tour of Chornobyl will be the most thought-provoking nine hours you'll spend in Ukraine – few fail to be stirred, scared and/or angered by the apocalyptic site of the world's worst nuclear accident. Chornobyl is located 110km north of Kyiv city centre as the crow flies, around two hours' drive. You can only realistically visit as part of a guided tour from Kyiv and you need to book around 10 days in advance to give the authorities time to run security checks. Different people react in different ways to the tour. Whether it be the sight of reactor No 4, or the plight of the 'liquidators', the nonchalance of the Soviet authorities or the tragedy of the model Soviet town of Pripyat that leaves the biggest impression, you're likely to be in a pensive mood by the end of the tour. Expect to pay $150 to $500 per person, depending on the number of people in your party and which tour company you choose.

ODESA (ОДЕСА)

Ukraine's window on the Black Sea, lively Odesa is a vibrant, Russian-speaking city that attracts surprising numbers of foreign visitors.

With Crimea off limits Odesa these days is packed with Ukrainian holidaymakers. Apart from the **sandy beaches**, the first place many head to is the seafront **Potemkin Steps** (Потьомкінські сходи), star of the most famous scene in the Soviet-era film *Battleship Potemkin*. In the city centre you'll find the **Museum of Western & Eastern Art** (Музей західного та східного мистецтва; www.oweamuseum.odessa.ua; vul Pushkinska 9; adult/child & student 50/30uah; ⊙10.30am-6pm Thu-Tue) occupying a beautifully renovated mid-19th-century palace. Top attraction here is Caravaggio's painting *The Taking of Christ*, famously stolen in 2008 in Ukraine's biggest art heist. Now safely recovered, it's undergoing restoration. Odesa's main commercial street, pedestrian **vul Derybasivska** (Дерибасівська вулиця), is jam-packed with restaurants, bars and, in the summer high season, tourists.

Bus is by far the quickest way to travel from Kyiv (330uah to 430uah, six to seven hours, five daily). For Lviv train is better (260uah, 12 hours, four daily).

✗ Eating

★Baczewski   EASTERN EUROPEAN €€
(Ресторація Бачевських; ☎032-224 4444; kumpelgroup.com; Shevska 8; mains 60-200; ⊙8am-midnight) Here's how you compress your Lviv cultural studies into one evening out. Start with Jewish *forschmak* (herring pâté), eased down by Ukrainian *nalivki* (digestives) and followed by Hungarian fish soup. Proceed to Polish *pierogi* (dumplings) and finish with Viennese *Sachertorte* with Turkish coffee. An essential Lviv experience. Be sure to reserve a table for dinner at this mega-popular place.

★Trapezna Idey   UKRAINIAN €€
(Трапезна идей; ☎032-254 6155; idem.org.ua; mains 50-100uah; ⊙11am-11pm; 🖾) An unmarked door behind the paper-aeroplane monument leads into the bowels of a Bernardine monastery, where this lovely local-intelligentsia fave is hiding, together with a modern art gallery called the Museum of Ideas. People flock here for the hearty *bohrach* (a Ukrainian version of goulash) and *banosh* (Carpathian polenta with salty cottage cheese).

Dim Lehend   UKRAINIAN €€
(Дім легенд; vul Staroyevreyska 48; mains 55-140uah; ⊙11am-2am; 🖾) Dedicated to the city of Lviv, there's nothing dim about the 'House of Legends'. The five floors contain a library stuffed with Lviv-themed volumes, a room showing live webcam footage of Lviv's underground river, rooms dedicated to lions and cobblestones, and another featuring the city

in sounds. The menu is limited to Ukrainian staples. Excellent desserts are a bonus.

🍷 Drinking

Dzyga   CAFE
(Дзиґа; www.dzyga.com.ua; vul Virmenska 35; ⊙10am-midnight; 🛜) This cafe–art gallery in the shadow of the Dominican Cathedral has a relaxed vibe. It's particularly popular with bohemian, alternative types but seems to attract pretty much everyone, really. The summertime outdoor seating is gathered around the city's Monument to the Smile. If it's full, there are other attractive options nearby on postcard-pretty vul Virmenska.

Lvivska Kopalnya Kavy   CAFE
(pl Rynok 10; ⊙8am-midnight Mon-Thu, to 2am Fri-Sun; 🛜) Lviv is Ukraine's undisputed coffee capital, and the 'Lviv Coffee Mine' is where the stratum of arabica is excavated by local colliers from deep beneath pl Rynok. You can tour the mine or just sample the heart-pumping end product at tables as dark as the brews inside, or out in the courtyard beneath old timber balconies.

ℹ️ Information

Tourist Information Centre (☎032-254 6079; www.touristinfo.lviv.ua; pl Rynok 1, Ratusha; ⊙10am-8pm Mon-Fri, to 7pm Sat, to 6pm Sun May-Sep, shorter hours Oct-Apr) Ukraine's best tourist information centre. Branches at the airport (☎067 673 9194; ⊙10am-8pm Mon-Fri, to 7pm Sat, to 6pm Sun May-Sep, shorter hours Oct-Apr) and the train station (☎032-226 2005; Ticket Hall; ⊙10am-8pm Mon-Fri, to 7pm Sat, to 6pm Sun May-Sep, shorter hours Oct-Apr).

ESSENTIAL FOOD & DRINK

'Borshch and bread – that's our food.' With this national saying, Ukrainians admit that theirs is a cuisine of comfort, full of hearty, mild dishes designed for fierce winters rather than one of gastronomic zing. Here are some of the Ukrainian staples you are certain to find on restaurant menus:

Borshch The national soup made with beetroot, pork fat and herbs.

Salo Basically raw pig fat, cut into slices and eaten with bread.

Varenyky Pasta pockets filled with everything from mashed potato to sour cherries.

Kasha Buckwheat swimming in milk and served for breakfast.

Vodka Also known as horilka, it accompanies every celebration and get-together – in copious amounts.

ⓘ Getting There & Away

AIR

Lviv's new **Danylo Halytskyi International Airport** (☎ 032-229 8112; www.lwo.aero; vul Lyubinska 168) stands 7km west of the city centre. UIA operates flights to Borispil airport in Kyiv (1½ hours, two daily). Dniproavia flies to Kyiv's Zhulyany airport as well as to Ivano-Frankivsk, Dnipro, Kharkiv and Odesa. Book through **Kiy Avia** (☎ 032-255 3263; www.kiyavia.com; vul Hnatyuka 24; ⊘ 8am-8pm Mon-Fri, 9am-5pm Sat, 10am-3pm Sun).

Lviv attracts a good number of international flights. There are currently services to/from Vienna, İstanbul, Munich, Warsaw and Madrid.

BUS

Take trolleybus 25 to the **main bus station** (Holovny Avtovokzal; ☎ 032-263 2497; vul Stryska 109) 8km south of the centre.

There are overnight services to Kyiv (275uah, nine hours, five daily).

TRAIN

The quickest way to Kyiv is on the Intercity+ express (360uah, five hours, one daily) departing early morning. There are also cheaper overnight and daytime passenger trains (165uah to 250uah, eight to 10 hours).

Buy tickets from the station or city centre **train ticket office** (Залізничні Квіткові Каси; vul Hnatyuka 20; ⊘ 8am-2pm & 3-8pm Mon-Sat, to 6pm Sun).

ⓘ Getting Around

From the train station, take tram 1, 6 or 9 to the centre. Trolleybus 9 goes to/from the university to the airport. Bus 48 also runs to the airport from pr Shevchenko.

SURVIVAL GUIDE

ⓘ Directory A–Z

ACCOMMODATION

Ukraine has hundreds of hostels with Lviv and Kyiv boasting tens each. There's also a bewildering array of hotel and room types from Soviet-era budget crash pads to 'six-star' over-priced luxury. Everything in between can be hit and miss, and there are no national standards to follow.

Booking ahead isn't normally essential except around New Year. Accommodation is the single biggest expense in Ukraine, but with the virtual collapse of the hryvnya rooms are very affordable.

BUSINESS HOURS

Banks 9am–5pm

Restaurants 11am–11pm

Shops 9am–6pm, to 8pm or 9pm in cities

Sights 9am–5pm or 6pm, closed at least one day a week

CUSTOMS REGULATIONS

You are allowed to bring in up to US$10,000, 1L of spirits, 2L of wine, 5L of beer, 200 cigarettes or 250g of tobacco, and food up to the value of €50.

INTERNET ACCESS

Most hotels offer free wi-fi and free hotspots are much more common than in much of Western Europe. Many restaurants and cafes have wi-fi. Internet cafes are not as common as they once were.

INTERNET RESOURCES

Lonely Planet (www.lonelyplanet.com/ukraine) Info, hotel bookings, traveller forum and more.

Ukraine.com (www.ukraine.com) Gateway site with news and lots of background info.

Ukraine Encyclopaedia (www.encyclopediao-fukraine.com) One of the largest sources of info on Ukraine.

MONEY

US dollars, the euro and Russian roubles are the easiest currencies to exchange. Ukraine remains primarily a cash economy.

➡ Coins: one, five, 10, 25 and 50 kopecks and one hryvnya.

➡ Notes: one, two, five, 10, 20, 50, 100, 200 and 500 hryvnya.

➡ Hryvnya are virtually impossible to buy pre-departure.

➡ ATMs are common.

POST

The national postal service is run by **Ukrposhta** (www.ukrposhta.com).

➡ Sending a postcard or a letter of up to 20g costs 4.30uah to anywhere outside Ukraine.

➡ Mail takes about a week or less to reach Europe, and two to three weeks to the USA or Australia.

PUBLIC HOLIDAYS

Currently the main public holidays in Ukraine are the following:

New Year's Day 1 January
Orthodox Christmas 7 January
International Women's Day 8 March
Orthodox Easter (Paskha) April/May
Labour Day 1–2 May
Victory Day (1945) 9 May
Constitution Day 28 June
Independence Day (1991) 24 August
Defender of Ukraine Day 14 October

SAFE TRAVEL

Despite the recent conflict, Western Ukraine and Kyiv remain safe. Donetsk, Luhansk and Crimea are off limits to foreigners and care should be taken when visiting other Russian-speaking cities in the east and south.

TELEPHONE

All numbers in Ukraine start with 0 and there are no pre-dialling codes.

SLEEPING PRICE RANGES

The following price indicators apply for a high-season double room:

€ less than 400uah

€€ 400uah–800uah

€€€ more than 800uah

COUNTRY FACTS

Area 603,628 sq km

Capital Kyiv

Country Code ☑ 380

Currency Hryvnya (uah)

Emergency ☑ 112

Language Ukrainian, Russian

Money ATMs common; credit cards widely accepted.

Population 44.6 million

Visas Not required for EU, UK, US and Canadian citizens for stays of up to 90 days.

Ukraine's country code is ☑ 0038. To call Kyiv from overseas, dial ☑ 00 38 044 and the subscriber number.

To call internationally from Ukraine, dial ☑ 0, wait for a second tone, then dial 0 again, followed by the country code, city code and number.

European GSM phones work in Ukraine. Local SIM cards work out much cheaper if making several calls.

VISAS

Tourist visas for stays of less than 90 days aren't required by citizens of the EU/EEA, Canada, the USA and Japan. Australians and New Zealanders still need a visa.

ℹ Getting There & Away

The majority of visitors to Ukraine fly – generally to Kyiv. Flights, tours and rail tickets can be booked online through Lonely Planet (www.lonelyplanet.com/bookings).

AIR

Only a couple of low-cost airlines fly to Ukraine.

Most international flights use Kyiv's main airport, **Boryspil International Airport** (☑ 044 393 4371; www.kbp.aero). **Lviv International Airport** (LWO; ☑ 032-229 8112; www.lwo.aero) also has a few international connections.

Ukraine International Airlines (www.flyuia.com) is Ukraine's flag carrier.

LAND

Ukraine is well linked to its neighbours. Kyiv is connected by bus or train to Minsk, Warsaw and Budapest, as well as other Eastern European capitals. Lviv is the biggest city servicing the Polish border – it's possible to take a budget flight to Poland then cross the border to Lviv by bus or train.

UKRAINE GETTING THERE & AWAY

EATING PRICE RANGES

The following price indicators are for a main meal:

€ less than 50uah

€€ 50uah–150uah

€€€ more than 150uah

Bus

Buses are slower, less frequent and less comfortable than trains for long-distance travel.

Car & Motorcycle

To bring your own vehicle into the country, you'll need your original registration papers and a 'Green Card' International Motor Insurance Certificate.

 Getting Around

AIR

Flying is an expensive way of getting around. Overnight train is cheaper and more reliable.

Kiy Avia (www.kiyavia.com) has branches across the country.

BUS

Buses and minibuses serve every city and small town, but are best for short trips (three hours or less). Buses resembling shop-till receipts are sold at bus stations up to departure.

LOCAL TRANSPORT

Trolleybus, tram, bus and metro run in Kyiv. A ticket for one ride by bus, tram or trolley-bus costs 2uah to 5uah. There are no return, transfer, timed or day tickets available. Tickets must be punched on board (or ripped by the conductor).

Metro barriers take plastic tokens (zhetony), sold at counters inside stations.

TRAIN

For long journeys, overnight train is best. **Ukrainian Railways** (www.uz.gov.ua) features timetables and an online booking facility.

All trains have assigned places. Carriage (vahon) and bunk (mesto) numbers are printed on tickets.

Survival Guide

Directory A-Z

Accommodation

Price Ranges

Rates in our reviews are for high season and often drop outside high season by as much as 50%. High season in ski resorts is usually between Christmas and New Year and around the February to March winter holidays. Price categories are broken down differently for individual countries – see each country for full details.

Reservations

During peak holiday periods, particularly Easter, summer and Christmas – and any time of year in popular destinations such as London, Paris and Rome – it's wise to book ahead. Most places can be reserved online. Always try to book directly with the establishment; this means you're paying just for your room, with no surcharge going to a hostel- or hotel-booking website.

B&Bs & Guesthouses

Guesthouses (pension, *Gasthaus, chambre d'hôte* etc) and B&Bs (bed and break-

fasts) offer greater comfort than hostels for a marginally higher price. Most are simple affairs, normally with shared bathrooms.

In some destinations, particularly in Eastern Europe, locals wait in train stations touting rented rooms. Just be sure such accommodation isn't in a far-flung suburb that requires an expensive taxi ride to and from town. Confirm the price before agreeing to rent a room and remember that it's unwise to leave valuables in your room when you go out.

B&Bs in the UK and Ireland often aren't really budget accommodation – even the lowliest tend to have midrange prices and there is a new generation of 'designer' B&Bs which are positively top end.

Camping

Most camping grounds are some distance from city centres; we list easily accessible camping grounds only, or include sites where it's common for travellers to bed down en masse under the stars (for example, on some Greek islands).

National tourist offices provide lists of camping grounds and camping organisations. Also see www. coolcamping.co.uk for details on prime campsites across Europe.

There will usually be a charge per tent or site, per person and per vehicle. In busy areas and in busy seasons, it's sometimes necessary to book.

Camping other than at designated grounds is difficult in Western Europe, because it's hard to find a suitably private spot.

Camping is also illegal without the permission of the local authorities (the police or local council office) or the landowner. Don't be shy about asking; you might be pleasantly surprised.

In some countries, such as Austria, the UK, France and Germany, free camping is illegal on all but private land, and in Greece it's illegal altogether but not enforced. This doesn't prevent hikers from occasionally pitching their tent, and you'll usually get away with it if you have a small tent, are discreet, stay just one or two nights, decamp during the day and don't light a fire or leave rubbish. At worst, you'll be woken by the police and asked to move on.

In Eastern Europe, free camping is more widespread.

BOOK YOUR STAY ONLINE

For more accommodation reviews by Lonely Planet authors, check out http://lonelyplanet.com/hotels/. You'll find independent reviews, as well as recommendations on the best places to stay. Best of all, you can book online.

Homestays & Farmstays

You needn't volunteer on a farm to sleep on it. In Switzerland and Germany, there's the opportunity to sleep in barns or 'hay hotels'. Farmers provide cotton undersheets (to avoid straw pricks) and woolly blankets for extra warmth, but guests need their own sleeping bag and torch. For further details, visit Abenteuer im Stroh (www.schlaf-im-stroh.ch).

Italy has a similar and increasingly popular network of farmstays called *agriturismi*. Participating farms must grow at least one of their own crops. Otherwise, accommodation runs the gamut from small rustic hideaways to grand country estates. See www.agriturismo.it for more details.

Hostels

There's a vast variation in hostel standards across Europe.

HI Hostels (those affiliated to Hostelling International; www.hihostels.com), usually offer the cheapest (secure) roof over your head in Europe and you don't have to be particularly young to use them. That said, if you're over 26 you'll frequently pay a small surcharge (usually about €3) to stay in an official hostel.

Hostel rules vary per facility and country, but some ask that guests vacate the rooms for cleaning purposes or impose a curfew. Most offer a complimentary breakfast, although the quality varies. Hostels are also great places to meet other travellers and pick up all kinds of information on the region you are visiting. They often usurp tourist offices in this respect.

You need to be a YHA or HI member to use HI-affiliated hostels, but nonmembers can stay by paying a few extra euros, which will be set against future membership. After sufficient nights (usually six), you automatically

become a member. To join, ask at any hostel or contact your national hostelling office, which you'll find on the HI website – where you can also make online bookings.

Europe has many private hostelling organisations and hundreds of unaffiliated backpacker hostels. These have fewer rules, more self-catering kitchens and fewer large, noisy school groups. Dorms in many private hostels can be mixed sex. If you aren't happy to share mixed dorms, be sure to ask when you book.

Hotels

Hotels are usually the most expensive accommodation option, though at their lower end there is little to differentiate them from guesthouses or even hostels.

Cheap hotels around bus and train stations can be convenient for late-night or early-morning arrivals and departures, but some are also unofficial brothels or just downright sleazy. Check the room beforehand and make sure you're clear on the price and what it covers.

Discounts for longer stays are usually possible and hotel owners in southern Europe *might* be open to a little bargaining if times are slack. In many countries it's common for business hotels (usually more than two stars) to slash

their rates by up to 40% on Friday and Saturday nights.

University Accommodation

Some university towns rent out their student accommodation during the holiday periods. This is a popular practice in France, the UK and many Eastern European countries. University accommodation will sometimes be in single rooms (although it's more commonly in doubles or triples) and might have cooking facilities. For details ask at individual colleges or universities, at student information offices or local tourist offices.

Customs Regulations

The European Union (EU) has a two-tier customs system: one for goods bought duty-free to import to or export from the EU, and one for goods bought in another EU country where taxes and duties have already been paid.

➡ Entering or leaving the EU, you are allowed to carry duty-free: 200 cigarettes, 50 cigars or 250g of tobacco; 2L of still wine plus 1L of spirits over 22% alcohol or another 4L of wine (sparkling or otherwise); 50g of perfume, 250cc of eau de toilette.

➡ Travelling from one EU country to another, the duty-paid limits are: 800 cigarettes, 200 cigars, 1kg of tobacco, 10L of spirits, 20L of fortified wine, 90L of wine (of which not more than 60L is sparkling) and 110L of beer.

➡ Non-EU countries often have different regulations and many countries forbid the export of antiquities and cultural treasures.

Discount Cards

Camping Cards

The Camping Card International (CCI; www.camping-cardinternational.com) is an ID that can be used instead of a passport when checking into a camping ground. Many camping grounds offer a small discount if you sign in with one and it includes third-party insurance.

Rail Passes

If you plan to visit more than a few countries, or one or two countries in-depth, you might save money with a rail pass.

European citizens or residents qualify for a one-month **InterRail pass** (www.interrail.eu). There are special rates if you're under 26 years old. Children under 12 are free.

Non-European citizens can apply for a **Eurail pass** (www.eurail.com) valid in 28 countries for up to three months.

Student Cards

The International Student Identity Card (www.isic.org), available for students, teachers and under-26s, offers thousands of worldwide discounts on transport, museum entry, youth hostels and even some restaurants. Apply for the cards online or via issuing offices, which include **STA Travel** (www.statravel.com).

For under-26s, there's also the **European Youth Card** (www.euro26.org). Many countries have raised the age limit for this card to under 30.

Electricity

Europe generally runs on 220V, 50Hz AC, but there are exceptions. The UK runs on 230/240V AC, and some old buildings in Italy and Spain have 125V (or even 110V in Spain). The continent is moving towards a 230V standard. If your home country has a vastly different voltage you will need a transformer for delicate and important appliances.

The UK and Ireland use three-pin square plugs. Most of Europe uses the 'europlug' with two round pins. Greece, Italy and Switzerland use a third round pin in a way that the two-pin plug usually – but not always in Italy and Switzerland – fits. Buy an adapter before leaving home; those on sale in Europe generally go the other way, but ones for visitors to Europe are also available – airports are always a good place to buy them.

Type F
230V/50Hz

Type C
220V/50Hz

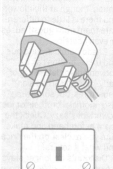

Type G
230V/50Hz

Embassies & Consulates

Generally speaking, your embassy won't be much help in emergencies if the trouble you're in is remotely your own fault. Remember, you're bound by the laws of the country you're in.

In genuine emergencies you might get some assistance, but only if other channels have been exhausted. For example, if you need to get home urgently, a free ticket is exceedingly unlikely – the embassy would expect you to have insurance. If you have all your money and documents stolen, it might assist with getting a new passport, but a loan for onward travel is out of the question.

Gay & Lesbian Travellers

Across Western Europe you'll find very liberal attitudes towards homosexuality. London, Paris, Berlin, Munich, Amsterdam, Madrid and Lisbon have thriving gay communities and pride events. The Greek islands of Mykonos and Lesvos are popular gay beach destinations. Gran Canaria and Ibiza in Spain are big centres for both gay clubbing and beach holidays.

Eastern Europe, and in particular Russia, tends to be far less progressive. Outside the big cities, attitudes become more conservative and discretion is advised, particularly in Turkey and most parts of Eastern Europe.

Health

Before You Go

No jabs are necessary for Europe. However, the World Health Organization (WHO) recommends that all travellers be covered for diphtheria, tetanus, measles, mumps, rubella and polio, regardless of their destination. Since most vaccines don't produce immunity until at least two weeks after they're given, visit a physician at least six weeks before departure.

Health Insurance

It is unwise to travel anywhere in the world without travel insurance. A good policy should include comprehensive health insurance including medical care and emergency evacuation. If you are engaging in hazardous sports, you may need to pay for extra cover.

If you're an EU citizen, the free EHIC (European Health Insurance Card) covers you for most medical care in the 28 EU member states, including maternity care and care for chronic illnesses such as diabetes (though not for emergency repatriation). However, you will normally have to pay for medicine bought from pharmacies, even if prescribed, and perhaps for some tests and procedures. The EHIC does not cover private medical consultations and treatment out of your home country; this includes nearly all dentists, and some of the better clinics and surgeries. In the UK, you can apply for an EHIC online, by telephone, or by filling out a form available at post offices.

Non-EU citizens should find out if there is a reciprocal arrangement for free medical care between their country and the EU country they are visiting.

Availability & Cost of Healthcare

Good health care is readily available in Western Europe and, for minor illnesses, pharmacists can give valuable advice and sell over-the-counter medication. They can also advise if you need specialised help and point you in the right direction. The standard of dental care is usually good.

While the situation in Eastern Europe is improving since the EU accession of many countries, quality medical care is not always readily available outside major cities, but embassies, consulates and five-star hotels can usually recommend doctors or clinics.

Condoms are widely available in Europe, however emergency contraception may not be, so take the necessary precautions.

Insurance

It's foolhardy to travel without insurance to cover theft, loss and medical problems. There are a wide variety of policies, so check the small print.

Some policies specifically exclude 'dangerous activities', which can include scuba diving, motorcycling, winter sports, adventure sports or even hiking.

Check that the policy covers ambulances or an emergency flight home.

Worldwide travel insurance is available online at www.lonelyplanet.com/travel-insurance. You can buy, extend and claim online anytime – even if you're already on the road.

HEALTH RESOURCES

The **World Health Organization** (www.who.int/ith/en) publishes the annually revised, free online book *International Travel and Health*. **MD Travel Health** (www.mdtravelhealth.com) provides up-to-date travel-health recommendations for every country.

It's usually a good idea to consult your government's website before departure, if one is available:

➡ **Australia** (www.smartraveller.gov.au)

➡ **Canada** (www.phac-aspc.gc.ca)

➡ **UK** (www.gov.uk/foreign-travel-advice)

➡ **USA** (www.cdc.gov/travel)

Internet Access

Internet access varies enormously across Europe. In most places, you'll be able to find wireless (wi-fi, also called WLAN in some countries), although whether it's free varies greatly.

Where the wi-fi icon appears, it means that the establishment offers free wi-fi that you can access immediately, or by asking for the access code from staff.

Access is generally straightforward, although a few tips are in order. If you can't find the @ symbol on a keyboard, try AltGr + 2, or AltGr + Q. Watch out for German and some Balkans keyboards, which reverse the Z and the Y positions. Using a French keyboard is an art unto itself.

Where necessary in relevant countries, click on the language prompt in the bottom right-hand corner of the screen or hit Ctrl + Shift to switch between the Cyrillic and Latin alphabets.

Legal Matters

You can generally purchase alcohol (beer and wine) from between 16 and 18 (usually 18 for spirits), but if in doubt, ask. Although you can drive at 17 or 18, you might not be able to hire a car until you're 25.

Drugs are often quite openly available in Europe, but that doesn't mean they're legal. The Netherlands is most famed for its liberal attitudes, with coffeeshops openly selling cannabis even though the drug is *not* technically legal. However, a blind eye is generally turned to the trade as the possession and purchase of small amounts (5g) of 'soft drugs' (ie marijuana and hashish) is allowed and users won't be prosecuted for smoking or carrying this amount. Don't take this relaxed attitude as an invitation to buy harder drugs;

if you get caught, you'll be punished. Since 2008 magic mushrooms have been banned in the Netherlands.

Spain also has pretty liberal laws regarding marijuana although its use is usually reserved for private 'cannabis clubs'.

In Belgium, the possession of up to 3g of cannabis is legal, but selling the drug isn't, so if you get caught at the point of sale, you could be in trouble. Switzerland, Portugal, Ukraine, Malta, Luxembourg, Estonia, Austria and the Czech Republic have also decriminalised possession of marijuana, however, selling remains illegal.

Getting caught with drugs in some parts of Europe can lead to imprisonment. If in any doubt, err on the side of caution, and don't even think about taking drugs across international borders.

Money

ATMs

Across major European towns and cities international ATMs are common, but you should always have a back-up option, as there can be

glitches. In some remote areas, ATMs might be scarce.

Much of Western Europe now uses a chip-and-pin system for added security. You will have problems if you don't have a four-digit PIN number and might have difficulties if your card doesn't have a metallic chip. Check with your bank.

Always cover the keypad when entering your PIN and make sure there are no unusual devices attached to the machine, which can copy your card's details or cause it to stick in the machine. If your card disappears and the screen goes blank before you've even entered your PIN, don't enter it – especially if a 'helpful' bystander tells you to do so. If you can't wbank's emergency number, if you can, before leaving the ATM.

Cash

It's a good idea to bring some local currency in cash, if only to cover yourself until you get to an exchange facility or find an ATM. The equivalent of €150 should usually be enough. Some extra cash in an easily exchanged currency is also a good idea, especially in Eastern Europe.

USEFUL WEBSITES

Blue Flag (www.blueflag.org) Ecolabel for sustainably developed beaches and marinas.

Budget Traveller's Guide to Sleeping in Airports (www.sleepinginairports.net) Funny and useful resource for backpackers flying standby.

Currency Conversions (www.xe.com) Up-to-the-second exchange rates for hundreds of currencies.

Guide for Europe (www.guideforeurope.com) Has a handy hostel review page posted by visitors.

Lonely Planet (www.lonelyplanet.com/thorntree) On Lonely Planet's message board you can usually get your travel questions answered by fellow travellers in a matter of hours.

Money Saving Expert (www.moneysavingexpert.com) Excellent tips on the best UK travel insurance, mobile phones and bank cards to use abroad. The flight-checker facility shows the latest cheap flights available.

The euro, used in 19 EU states as well as four other non-EU states (Andorra, Monaco, San Marino and Vatican City), is made up of 100 cents. Notes come in denominations of €5, €10, €20, €50, €100, €200 and €500, though any notes above €50 are rarely used on a daily basis. Coins come in 1c, 2c, 5c, 10c, 20c, 50c, €1 and €2.

Denmark, the UK and Sweden have held out against adopting the euro for political reasons, while non-EU nations, such as Albania, Belarus, Norway, Russia, Switzerland, Turkey and Ukraine, also have their own currencies.

Credit Cards

Visa and MasterCard/Eurocard are more widely accepted in Europe than Amex and Diners Club; Visa (sometimes called Carte Bleue) is particularly strong in France and Spain.

There are, however, regional differences in the general acceptability of credit cards; in Germany for example, it's rare for restaurants to take credit cards. Cards are not widely accepted off the beaten track.

To reduce the risk of fraud, always keep your card in view when making transactions; for example, in restaurants that do accept cards, pay as you leave, following your card to the till. Keep transaction records and either check your statements when you return home, or check your account online while still on the road.

Letting your credit-card company know roughly where you're going lessens the chance of fraud – or of your bank cutting off the card when it sees (your) unusual spending.

Debit Cards

It's always worthwhile having a Maestro-compatible debit card, which differs from a credit card in deducting money straight from your bank account. Check with your bank or MasterCard (Maestro's parent) for compatibility.

Exchanging Money

Euros, US dollars and UK pounds are the easiest currencies to exchange. You may have trouble exchanging some lesser-known ones at small banks.

Importing or exporting some currencies is restricted or banned, so try to get rid of any local currency before you leave. Get rid of Scottish pounds before leaving the UK; nobody outside Britain will touch them.

Most airports, central train stations, big hotels and many border posts have banking facilities outside regular business hours, at times on a 24-hour basis. Post offices in Europe often perform banking tasks, tend to open longer hours and outnumber banks in remote places. While they always exchange cash, they might baulk at handling travellers cheques not in the local currency.

The best exchange rates are usually at banks. *Bureaux de change* usually – but not always – offer worse rates or charge higher commissions. Hotels and airports are almost always the worst places to change money.

International Transfers

International bank transfers are good for secure one-off movements of large amounts of money, but they might take three to five days and there will be a fee (about £25 in the UK, for example). Be sure to specify the name of the bank, plus the sort code and address of the branch where you'd like to pick up your money.

In an emergency it's quicker but more costly to have money wired via an Amex office (www.americanexpress.com), Western Union (www.westernunion.com) or MoneyGram (www.money-gram.com).

Taxes & Refunds

When non-EU residents spend more than a certain amount (around €75, but amounts vary from country to country) they can usually reclaim any sales tax when leaving the country.

Making a tax-back claim is straightforward. First, make sure the shop offers duty-free sales (often a sign will be displayed reading 'Tax-Free Shopping'). When making your purchase, ask the shop attendant for a tax-refund voucher, filled in with the correct amount and the date. This can be used to claim a refund directly at international airports, or stamped at ferry ports or border crossings and mailed back for a refund.

Tipping & Bargaining

➡ 'Service charges' are increasingly added to bills. In theory this means you're not obliged to tip. In practice that money often doesn't go to the server. Don't pay twice. If the service charge is optional, remove it and pay a tip. If it's not optional, don't tip.

➡ Tipping isn't such a big deal in Europe as it is say in North America. If you tip, 5% to 10% will usually suffice.

Travellers Cheques

It's become more difficult to find places that cash travellers cheques. In parts of Eastern Europe only a few banks handle them, and the process can be quite bureaucratic and costly.

That said, having a few cheques is a good back-up. If they're stolen you can claim a refund, provided you have a separate record of cheque numbers.

Amex and Thomas Cook are reliable brands of travellers cheques, while cheques in US dollars, euros or British pounds are the easiest to cash. When changing them ask about fees and commissions as well as the exchange rate.

Post

From major European centres, airmail typically takes about five days to North America and about a week to Australasian destinations, although mail from such countries as Albania or Russia is much slower.

Courier services such as DHL are best for essential deliveries.

Safe Travel

Travelling in Europe is usually very safe.

Discrimination

In some parts of Europe travellers of African, Arab or Asian descent might encounter unpleasant attitudes that are unrelated to them personally. In rural areas travellers whose skin colour marks them out as foreigners might experience unwanted attention.

Attitudes vary from country to country. People tend to be more accepting in cities than in the country. Race is also less of an issue in Western Europe than in parts of the former Eastern Bloc. For example, there has been a spate of racially motivated attacks in St Petersburg and other parts of Russia in recent years.

Druggings

Although rare, some drugging of travellers does occur in Europe. Travellers are especially vulnerable on trains and buses where a new 'friend' may offer you food or a drink that will knock you out, giving them time to steal your belongings.

Gassings have also been reported on a handful of overnight international trains. The best protection is to lock the door of your compartment (use your own lock if there isn't one) and to lock your bags to luggage racks,

preferably with a sturdy combination cable.

If you can help it, never sleep alone in a train compartment.

Pickpockets & Thieves

Theft is definitely a problem in parts of Europe and you have to be aware of unscrupulous fellow travellers. The key is to be sensible with your possessions.

➡ Don't store valuables in train-station lockers or luggage-storage counters and be careful about people who offer to help you operate a locker. Also be vigilant if someone offers to carry your luggage: they might carry it away altogether.

➡ Don't leave valuables in your car, on train seats or in your room. When going out, don't flaunt cameras, laptops and other expensive electronic goods.

➡ Carry a small day pack, as shoulder bags are an open invitation for snatch-thieves. Consider using small zipper locks on your packs.

➡ Pickpockets are most active in dense crowds, especially in busy train stations and on public transport during peak hours. Be careful in these situations.

➡ Spread valuables, cash and cards around your body or in different bags.

➡ A money belt with your essentials (passport, cash, credit cards, airline tickets) is usually a good idea. However, so you needn't delve into it in public, carry a wallet with a day's worth of cash.

➡ Having your passport stolen is less of a disaster if you've recorded the number and issue date or, even better, photocopied the relevant data pages. You can also scan them and email them to yourself. If you lose your passport, notify the police immediately to get a

statement and contact your nearest consulate.

➡ Carry photocopies of your credit cards, airline tickets and other travel documents.

Scams

Most scams involve distracting you – either by kids running up to you, someone asking for directions or spilling something on you – while another person steals your wallet. Be alert in such situations.

In some countries, especially in Eastern Europe, you may encounter people claiming to be from the tourist police, the special police, the supersecret police, whatever. Unless they're wearing a uniform and have good reason for accosting you, treat their claims with suspicion.

Needless to say, never show your passport or cash to anyone on the street. Simply walk away. If someone flashes a badge, offer to accompany them to the nearest police station.

Unrest & Terrorism

Civil unrest and terrorist bombings are relatively rare in Europe, all things considered, but they do occur. Attacks by Muslim extremists in the UK, France, Germany, Belgium and Russia have occurred in recent years. Keep an eye on the news and avoid areas where any flare-up seems likely.

Telephone

Emergency Numbers

The generic emergency call number for all European countries is 📞112.

Mobile Phones

If your mobile phone is European, it's often perfectly feasible to use it on roaming throughout the continent.

If you're coming from outside Europe, it's usually worth buying a prepaid local SIM in one European country. Even if you're not staying there long, calls across Europe will still be cheaper if they're not routed via your home country and the prepaid card will enable you to keep a limit on your spending. In several countries you need your passport to buy a SIM card.

In order to use other SIM cards in your phone, you'll need to have your handset unlocked by your home provider. Even if your phone is locked, you can use apps such as 'whatsapp' to send free text messages internationally wherever you have wi-fi access, or Skype to make free international calls whenever you're online.

Europe uses the GSM 900 network, which also covers Australia and New Zealand, but is not compatible with the North American GSM 1900 or the totally different system in Japan and South Korea. If you have a GSM phone, check with your service provider about using it in Europe. You'll need international roaming, but this is usually free to enable.

You can call abroad from almost any phone box in Europe. Public telephones accepting phonecards (available from post offices, telephone centres, news stands or retail outlets) are virtually the norm now; coin-operated phones are rare if not impossible to find.

Without a phonecard, you can ring from a telephone booth inside a post office or telephone centre and settle your bill at the counter. Reverse-charge (collect) calls are often possible. From many countries the Country Direct system lets you phone home by billing the long-distance carrier you use at home. These numbers can often be dialled from public phones without even inserting a phonecard.

Time

Nearly all of Europe, with several exceptions (Russia, Belarus, Iceland), observes daylight saving time on synchronised dates in late March (clocks go forward an hour) and late October (clocks go back an hour).

➡ Britain, Ireland and Portugal (GMT)

➡ Central Europe (GMT plus one hour)

➡ Greece, Turkey and Eastern Europe (GMT plus two hours)

➡ Russia (GMT plus three hours)

Toilets

Many public toilets require a small fee either deposited in a box or given to the attendant. Sit-down toilets are the rule in the vast majority of places. Squat toilets can still be found in rural areas, although they are definitely a dying breed.

Public-toilet provision is changeable from city to city. If you can't find one, simply drop into a hotel or restaurant and ask to use theirs.

Tourist Information

Unless otherwise indicated, tourist offices are common and widespread, although their usefulness varies enormously.

Travel with Children

Hidden in the huge labyrinth that is Europe, there are literally tonnes of things that will appeal to kids, youths and teenagers, especially if you're willing to look beyond the obvious (Disneyland Paris, Costa del Sol) and seek out the obscure (cycling in Normandy or horse riding on the west coast of Ireland).

It is hard to generalise about kid-friendliness in Europe. For more details, check the Lonely Planet website and search the specific countries you will be visiting.

My Little Nomads (www. mylittlenomads.com) Has a comprehensive list of family-friendly hotels plus plenty of other advice.

Lonely Planet (www.lonely planet.com/family-travel) The website has regularly updated family travel information, articles and advice. There are also numerous kid's books including *Not For Parents: Europe*.

Practicalities

➡ Europe, in particular Mediterranean Europe, is very kid-orientated. Expect waitstaff to ruffle your kid's hair and bank on seeing young children sitting around at family meals in restaurants until late.

➡ Nappies (diapers) are widely available; baby-changing facilities vary from country to country, but are generally pretty comprehensive.

➡ Baby formula and baby food are widely available in all European countries. However, brands differ. You might want to bring your own stash as back-up.

➡ For cheap rooms, check out Europe's hostels, many of which have at least one family room.

➡ Plan ahead and select a few preplanned big-ticket items aimed specifically at kids before you leave, such as Disneyland Paris or Legoland in Denmark.

➡ Don't write off the less obvious sights. Many of Europe's art galleries and iconic monuments give out kid's activity books that lay out special interactive itineraries for children.

➡ Hit a festival. Many European festivals have a strong family bias and have been entertaining children for centuries from Seville's Feria de Abril to France's Bastille Day.

➡ Most European countries have a pretty relaxed attitude to breastfeeding in public despite the fact that European women are less likely to breastfeed than women elsewhere.

➡ Cots are usually provided free of charge for young children in hotels on request. Reserve when booking.

➡ In the EU, some form of protective car seat must be used by all children under 1.35m (4ft 5 in). Check when booking a vehicle for seat availability.

Travellers with Disabilities

Cobbled medieval streets, 'classic' hotels, congested inner cities and underground subway systems make Europe a tricky destination for people with mobility impairments. However, the train facilities are good and some destinations boast new tram services or lifts to platforms. Download Lonely Planet's free Accessible Travel guide from http://lptravel.to/AccessibleTravel. The following websites can help with specific details.

Accessible Europe (www.accessibleurope.com) Specialist European tours with van transport.

DisabledGo.com (www.disabledgo.com) Detailed access information to thousands of venues across the UK and Ireland.

Mobility International Schweiz (www.mis-ch.ch) Good site (only partly in English) listing 'barrier-free' destinations in Switzerland and abroad, plus wheelchair-accessible hotels in Switzerland.

Mobility International USA (www.miusa.org) Publishes guides and advises travellers with disabilities on mobility issues.

Society for Accessible Travel & Hospitality (SATH; www.sath.org) Reams of information for travellers with disabilities.

Visas

➡ Citizens of the USA, Canada, Australia, New Zealand and the UK need only a valid passport to enter

THE SCHENGEN AREA

Twenty-six European countries are signatories to the Schengen Agreement, which has effectively dismantled internal border controls between them. They are Austria, Belgium, the Czech Republic, Denmark, Estonia, Finland, France, Germany, Greece, Iceland, Italy, Hungary, Latvia, Liechtenstein, Lithuania, Luxembourg, Malta, the Netherlands, Norway, Poland, Portugal, Slovenia, Slovakia, Spain, Sweden and Switzerland.

The UK and Ireland, as well as Russia and much of Eastern Europe, are not part of the Schengen Agreement. Visitors from non-EU countries will have to apply for visas to these countries separately.

Citizens of the US, Australia, New Zealand, Canada and the UK only need a valid passport to enter Schengen countries (as well as the UK and Ireland). However, other nationals, including South Africans, can apply for a single visa – a Schengen visa – when travelling throughout this region.

Non-EU visitors (with or without a Schengen visa) should expect to be questioned, however perfunctorily, when first entering the region. However, later travel within the zone is much like a domestic trip, with no border controls.

If you need a Schengen visa, you must apply at the consulate or embassy of the country that's your main destination, or your point of entry. You may then stay up to a maximum of 90 days in the entire Schengen area within a six-month period. Once your visa has expired, you must leave the zone and may only reenter after three months abroad. Shop around when choosing your point of entry, as visa prices may differ from country to country.

If you're a citizen of the US, Australia, New Zealand or Canada, you may stay visa-free a total of 90 days, during six months, within the entire Schengen region.

If you're planning a longer trip, you need to enquire personally as to whether you need a visa or visas. Your country might have bilateral agreements with individual Schengen countries allowing you to stay there longer than 90 days without a visa. However, you will need to talk directly to the relevant embassies or consulates.

While the UK and Ireland are not part of the Schengen area, their citizens can stay indefinitely in other EU countries, only needing paperwork if they want to work long-term or take up residency.

nearly all countries in Europe, including the entire EU.

→ Belarus and Russia require a prearranged visa before arrival and even an 'invitation' from (or booking with) a tour operator or hotel. It's simpler and safer to obtain these visas before leaving home.

→ Australians and New Zealanders can obtain a visa on arrival in Ukraine from Boryspil International Airport (Kyiv).

→ Transit visas are usually cheaper than tourist or business visas but they allow only a very short stay (one to five days) and can be difficult to extend.

→ All visas have a 'use-by' date and you'll be refused entry afterwards. In some cases it's easier to get visas as you go along, rather than arranging them all beforehand. Carry spare passport photos (you may need from one to four every time you apply for a visa).

→ Visas to neighbouring countries are usually issued immediately by consulates in Eastern Europe, although some may levy a hefty surcharge for 'express service'.

→ Consulates are generally open weekday mornings (if there's both an embassy and a consulate, you want the consulate).

→ Because regulations can change, double-check with the relevant embassy or consulate before travelling.

Volunteering

If you want to spend more time living and working in Europe, a short-term volunteer project might seem a good idea, say, teaching English in Poland or building a school in Turkey. However, most voluntary organisations levy high charges for airfares, food, lodging and recruit-

ment (from about €250 to €800 per week), making such work impractical for most shoestringers. One exception is WWOOF International (www.wwoof.org) which helps link volunteers with organic farms in Germany, Slovenia, the Czech Republic, Denmark, the UK, Austria and Switzerland. A small membership fee is required to join the national chapter but in exchange for your labour you'll receive free lodging and food.

For more information, Lonely Planet publishes *Volunteer: A Traveller's Guide to Making a Difference Around the World*.

Women Travellers

→ Women might attract unwanted attention in Turkey, rural Spain and southern Italy, especially Sicily, where many men view whistling and catcalling as flattery. Conservative dress can help to deter lascivious gazes and wolf whistles; dark sunglasses help avoid unwanted eye contact.

→ Marriage is highly respected in southern Europe, and a wedding ring can help, along with talk about 'my husband'. Hitchhiking alone is not recommended anywhere.

→ Female readers have reported assaults at Turkish hotels with shared bathrooms, so women travelling to Turkey might want to consider a more expensive room with private bathroom.

→ Journeywoman (www.journeywoman.com) maintains an online newsletter about solo female travels all over the world.

Work

EU citizens are allowed to work in any other EU country, but there can still

be tiresome paperwork to complete. Other nationalities require special work permits that can be almost impossible to arrange, especially for temporary work. However, that doesn't prevent enterprising travellers from topping up their funds by working in the hotel or restaurant trades at beach or ski resorts, or teaching a little English – and they don't always have to do this illegally.

The UK, for example, issues special 'Youth Mobility Scheme' visas to citizens from Australia, Canada, New Zealand, Japan, Hong Kong, South Korea and Taiwan aged between 18 and 30, valid for two years of work (see www.gov.uk/tier-5-youth-mobility/overview). Your national student-exchange organisation might be able to arrange temporary work permits to several countries.

If you have a grandparent or parent who was born in an EU country, you may have certain rights of residency or citizenship. Ask that country's embassy about dual citizenship and work permits. With citizenship, also ask about any obligations, such as military service and residency. Beware that your home country may not recognise dual citizenship.

Seasonal Work

→ *Work Your Way Around the World* by Susan Griffith gives practical advice.

→ Typical tourist jobs (picking grapes in France, working at a bar in Greece) often come with board and lodging, and the pay is essentially pocket money, but you'll have a good time partying with other travellers.

→ Busking is fairly common in major European cities, but it's illegal in some parts of Switzerland and Austria. Crackdowns even occur in Belgium and Germany, where it has been tolerated in the past. Some other cities, including London, require permits and security checks. Talk to other buskers first.

EuroJobs (www.eurojobs.com) Links to hundreds of organisations looking to employ both non-Europeans (with the correct work permits) and Europeans.

Natives (www.natives.co.uk) Summer and winter resort jobs, and various tips.

Picking Jobs (www.pickingjobs. com) Includes some tourism jobs.

Season Workers (www.season-workers.com) Best for ski-resort work and summer jobs, although it also has some childcare jobs.

Ski-jobs.co.uk (www.ski-jobs. co.uk) Mainly service jobs such as chalet hosts, bar staff and porters. Some linguistic skills required.

Teaching English

Most schools prefer a bachelor's degree and a TEFL (Teaching English as a Foreign Language) certificate.

It is easier to find TEFL jobs in Eastern Europe than in Western Europe. The British Council (www.britishcouncil.org) can provide advice about training and job searches. Alternatively, try the big schools such as Berlitz (www.berlitz.com) and Wall Street English (www.wallstreetenglish.com).

Transport

GETTING THERE & AWAY

Flights, cars and tours can be booked online at lonely planet.com/bookings.

Entering Europe

Europe is one of the world's major destinations sporting many of its busiest airports with routes fanning out to the far corners of the globe. More adventurous travellers can enter from Asia on some epic long-distance train routes. Numerous ferries jockey across the Mediterranean between Europe and Africa.

Air

To save money, it's best to travel off-season. This means, if possible, avoid mid-June to early September, Easter, Christmas and school holidays. Regardless of your ultimate destination, it's sometimes better to pick a recognised transport 'hub' as your initial port of entry, where high traffic volumes help keep prices down. The busiest, and therefore most obvious, airports are London, Frankfurt, Paris and Rome. Sometimes tickets to Amsterdam, Athens, Barcelona, Berlin, İstanbul, Madrid and Vienna are worth checking out.

Long-haul airfares to Eastern Europe are rarely a bargain; you're usually better flying to a Western European hub and taking an onward budget-airline flight or train. The main hubs in Eastern Europe are Budapest, Moscow, Prague and Warsaw.

Most of the aforementioned gateway cities are also well serviced by low-cost carriers that fly to other parts of Europe.

Main European airports:

➡ **Schiphol Airport, Amsterdam** (www.schiphol.nl)

➡ **Frankfurt Airport, Frankfurt** (www.frankfurt-airport.com)

➡ **Heathrow Airport, London** (www.heathrow.com)

➡ **Barajas Airport, Madrid** (www.aeropuertomadrid-barajas.com)

➡ **Aéroport de Charles de Gaulle, Paris** (www.easycdg.com)

➡ **Leonardo da Vinci Airport, Rome** (www.adr.it)

Land

It's possible to reach Europe by various different train routes from Asia. Most common is the Trans-Siberian Railway, connecting Moscow to Siberia, the Russian Far East, Mongolia and China.

It is also possible to reach Moscow from several Central Asian states and İstanbul from Iran and Jordan. See www.seat61.com for more information about these adventurous routes.

CLIMATE CHANGE & TRAVEL

Every form of transport that relies on carbon-based fuel generates CO_2, the main cause of human-induced climate change. Modern travel is dependent on aeroplanes, which might use less fuel per kilometre per person than most cars but travel much greater distances. The altitude at which aircraft emit gases (including CO_2) and particles also contributes to their climate change impact. Many websites offer 'carbon calculators' that allow people to estimate the carbon emissions generated by their journey and, for those who wish to do so, to offset the impact of the greenhouse gases emitted with contributions to portfolios of climate-friendly initiatives throughout the world. Lonely Planet offsets the carbon footprint of all staff and author travel.

Sea

There are numerous ferry routes between Europe and Africa, including links from Spain to Morocco, Italy and Malta to Tunisia, and France to Morocco and Tunisia. Check out www.traghettiweb. it for comprehensive information on all Mediterranean ferries. Ferries are often filled to capacity in summer, especially to and from Tunisia, so book well in advance if you're taking a vehicle across.

Passenger freighters (typically carrying up to 12 passengers) aren't nearly as competitively priced as airlines. Journeys also take a long time. However, if you have your heart set on a transatlantic journey, **TravLtips Cruise** and **Freighter** (www. travltips.com) has information on freighter cruises.

GETTING AROUND

Air

Airlines

In recent years low-cost carriers have revolutionised European transport. Most budget airlines have a similar pricing system – namely that ticket prices rise with the number of seats sold on each flight, so book as early as possible to get a decent fare.

Some low-cost carriers – Ryanair being the prime example – have made a habit of flying to smaller, less convenient airports on the outskirts of their destination city, or even to the airports of nearby cities, so check the exact location of the departure and arrival airports before you book. Many flights also leave at the crack of dawn or arrive inconveniently late at night.

Departure and other taxes (including booking fees, checked-baggage fees and other surcharges) soon add up and are included in the final price by the end of the

online booking process – usually a lot more than you were hoping to pay – but with careful choosing and advance booking you can get excellent deals.

In the face of competition from low-cost airlines, many national carriers have decided to drop their prices and/ or offer special deals. Some, such as British Airways, have even adopted the low-cost model of online booking, where the customer can opt to buy just a one-way flight, or can piece together their own return journey from two one-way legs.

For a comprehensive overview of which low-cost carriers fly to or from which European cities, check out the excellent www.flycheapo.com.

Air Passes

Various travel agencies and airlines offer air passes including the three main airline alliances: **Oneworld** (www.oneworld.com), **Star Alliance** (www.staralliance. com), and **SkyTeam** (www. skyteam.com). Check with your travel agent for current promotions.

Bicycle

Much of Europe is ideally suited to cycling. Popular cycling areas include the whole of the Netherlands, the Belgian Ardennes, the west of Ireland, the upper reaches of the Danube in southern Germany and anywhere in northern Switzerland, Denmark or the south of France. Exploring the small villages of Turkey and Eastern Europe also provides up-close access to remote areas.

A primary consideration on a cycling trip is to travel light, but you should take a few tools and spare parts, including a puncture-repair kit and an extra inner tube. Panniers are essential to balance your possessions on either side of the bike frame. Wearing a helmet is not com-

pulsory in most countries, but is certainly sensible.

Seasoned cyclists can average 80km a day, but it depends on what you're carrying and your level of fitness.

Cyclists' Touring Club (CTC; www.ctc.org.uk) The national cycling association of the UK runs organised trips to Continental Europe.

European Cyclists' Federation (www.ecf.com) Has details of 'EuroVelo', the European cycle network of 12 pan-European cycle routes, plus tips for other tours.

SwitzerlandMobility (www. veloland.ch/en/cycling-in-switzerland.html) Details of Swiss national routes and more.

Rental & Purchase

It is easy to hire bikes throughout most of Europe. Many Western European train stations have bike-rental counters. It is sometimes possible to return the bike at a different outlet so you don't have to retrace your route. Hostels are another good place to find cheap bike hire.

There are plenty of places to buy bikes in Europe, but you'll need a specialist bicycle shop for a bike capable of withstanding a European trip. Cycling is very popular in the Netherlands and Germany, and those countries are good places to pick up a well-equipped touring bicycle.

European prices are quite high (certainly higher than in North America), however non-European residents should be able to claim back value-added tax (VAT) on the purchase.

A growing number of European cities have bike-sharing schemes where you can casually borrow a bike from a docking station for short hops around the city for a small cost. Most schemes have daily rates, although you usually need a credit card as deposit. Large bike-sharing schemes include Paris' *Vélib* (Europe's biggest), London's *Santander Cycles* and Barcelona's *Bicing*.

Transporting a Bicycle

For major cycling trips, it's best to have a bike you're familiar with, so consider bringing your own rather than buying on arrival. If coming from outside Europe, ask your airline's policy on transporting bikes before buying your ticket.

From the UK to the Continent, Eurostar (the train service through the Channel Tunnel) charges £30 to send a semidismantled bike as registered luggage with you. Book ahead. You can also transport your bicycle with you on Eurotunnel through the Channel Tunnel for around £20. With a bit of tinkering and dismantling (eg removing wheels), you might be able to get your bike into a bag or sack and take it on a train as hand luggage.

Alternatively, the **European Bike Express** (www.bike-express.co.uk) is a UK-based coach service where cyclists can travel with their bicycles to various drop-off and pick-up points in France and northern Spain.

Once on the Continent, local and regional trains usually allow bikes to be transported as luggage, subject to space and a small supplementary fee (€5 to €15). Off-peak hours are best. Some cyclists have reported that Italian and French train attendants have refused bikes on slow trains, so be prepared for regulations to be interpreted differently in different countries.

Fast trains and international trains can rarely accommodate bikes; they might need to be sent as registered luggage and may end up on a different train from the one you take. This is often the case in France and Spain.

Boat

Several different ferry companies compete on the main ferry routes, resulting in a comprehensive but complicated service. The same ferry company can have a host of different prices for the same route, depending on the time of day or year, validity of the ticket and length of your vehicle. Vehicle tickets usually include the driver and often up to five passengers free of charge.

It's worth booking ahead where possible as there may be special reductions on off-peak crossings and advance-purchase tickets. On English Channel routes, apart from one-day or short-term excursion returns, there is little price advantage in buying a return ticket versus two singles.

Rail-pass holders are entitled to discounts or free travel on some lines. Food on ferries is often expensive (and lousy), so it is worth bringing your own. Also be aware that if you take your vehicle on board, you are usually denied access to it during the voyage.

Lake and river ferry services operate in many countries, Austria and Switzerland being just two. Some of these are very scenic.

Bus

International Buses

Often cheaper than trains, sometimes substantially so, long-distance buses also tend to be slower and less comfortable. However in Portugal, Greece and Turkey, buses are often a better option than trains.

Europe's biggest organisation of international buses operates under the name **Eurolines** (www.eurolines.com), comprised of various national companies. A **Eurolines Pass** (www.eurolines.com/en/eurolines-pass) is offered for extensive travel, allowing passengers to visit

---

EUROPE'S BORDER CROSSINGS

Border formalities have been relaxed in most of the EU, but still exist in all their original bureaucratic glory in the more far-flung parts of Eastern Europe.

In line with the Schengen Agreement, there are officially no passport controls at the borders between 26 European states, namely: Austria, Belgium, the Czech Republic, Denmark, Estonia, Finland, France, Germany, Greece, Iceland, Italy, Hungary, Latvia, Liechtenstein, Lithuania, Luxembourg, Malta, the Netherlands, Norway, Poland, Portugal, Slovakia, Slovenia, Spain, Sweden and Switzerland. Sometimes, however, there are spot checks on trains crossing borders, so always have your passport. The UK was a nonsignatory to Schengen and thus maintains border controls over traffic from other EU countries (except Ireland, with which it shares an open border), although there is no customs control. The same goes for Ireland.

Bulgaria, Croatia, Cyprus and Romania are prospective Shengen area members – for up-to-date details see www.schengenvisainfo.com.

Most borders in Eastern Europe will be crossed via train, where border guards board the train and go through compartments checking passengers' papers. It is rare to get hit up for bribes, but occasionally in Belarus or Moldova you may face a difficulty that can only be overcome with a 'fine'. Travelling between Turkey and Bulgaria typically requires a change of trains and is subject to a lengthy border procedure.

a choice of 53 cities across Europe over 15 or 30 days. In the high season (mid-June to mid-September) the pass costs €315/405 for those aged under 26, or €375/490 for those 26 and over. It's cheaper in other periods.

Busabout (www.busabout. com) offers a 'hop-on, hop-off' service around Europe, stopping at major cities. Buses are often oversubscribed, so book each sector to avoid being stranded. It departs every two days from May to the end of October.

National Buses

Domestic buses provide a viable alternative to trains in most countries. Again, they are usually slightly cheaper and somewhat slower. Buses are generally best for short hops, such as getting around cities and reaching remote villages, and they are often the only option in mountainous regions.

Reservations are rarely necessary. On many city buses you usually buy your ticket in advance from a kiosk or machine and validate it on entering the bus.

Car & Motorcycle

Travelling with your own vehicle gives flexibility and is the best way to reach remote places. However, the independence does sometimes isolate you from local life. Also, cars can be a target for theft and are often impractical in city centres, where traffic jams, parking problems and getting thoroughly lost can make it well worth ditching your vehicle and using public transport. Various car-carrying trains can help you avoid long, tiring drives.

Campervan

One popular way to tour Europe is for a group of three or four people to band together and buy or rent a campervan. London is the usual embarkation point. Look at the ads in London's free magazine

TNT (www.tntmagazine.com) if you wish to form or join a group. *TNT* is also a good source for purchasing a van, as is **Loot** (www.loot.com).

Some secondhand dealers offer a 'buy-back' scheme for when you return from the Continent, but check the small print before signing anything and remember that if an offer is too good to be true, it probably is. Buying and reselling privately should be more advantageous if you have time. In the UK, **DUInsure** (www.duinsure.com) offers a campervan policy.

Fuel

➡ Fuel prices can vary enormously (though fuel is always more expensive than in North America or Australia).

➡ Unleaded petrol only is available throughout Europe. Diesel is usually cheaper, though the difference is marginal in Britain, Ireland and Switzerland.

➡ Ireland's Automobile Association maintains a webpage of European fuel prices at www.theaa.ie/aa/motoring-advice/petrol-prices.aspx.

Leasing

Leasing a vehicle involves fewer hassles than purchasing and can work out much cheaper than hiring for longer than 17 days. This program is limited to certain types of new cars, including Renault and Peugeot, but you save money because leasing is exempt from VAT and inclusive insurance plans are cheaper than daily insurance rates.

To lease a vehicle your permanent address must be outside the EU. In the USA, contact **Renault Eurodrive** (www.renault-eurodrive.com) for more information.

Insurance

➡ Third-party motor insurance is compulsory. Most UK policies automatically provide this for EU countries. Get your

insurer to issue a Green Card (which may cost extra), an internationally recognised proof of insurance, and check that it lists every country you intend to visit. You'll need this in the event of an accident outside the country where the vehicle is insured.

➡ Ask your insurer for a European Accident Statement form, which can simplify things if worst comes to worst. Never sign statements that you can't read or understand – insist on a translation and sign that only if it's acceptable.

➡ For non-EU countries, check the requirements with your insurer. Travellers from the UK can obtain additional advice and information from the **Association of British Insurers** (www.abi.org.uk).

➡ Take out a European motoring assistance policy. Non-Europeans might find it cheaper to arrange international coverage with their national motoring organisation before leaving home. Ask your motoring organisation for details about the free services offered by affiliated organisations around Europe.

➡ Residents of the UK should contact the **RAC** (www.rac.co.uk) or the **AA** (www.theaa.co.uk) for more information. Residents of the US, contact **AAA** (www.aaa.com).

Purchase

Buying a car and then selling it at the end of your European travels may work out to be a better deal than renting one, although this isn't guaranteed and you'll need to do your sums carefully.

The purchase of vehicles in some European countries is illegal for non-nationals or non-EU residents. Britain is probably the best place to buy as secondhand prices are good there. Bear in mind that British cars have steering wheels on the right-hand side. If you wish to have left-hand drive and can afford to buy a new car, prices are generally reasonable in Greece, France, Germany, Belgium, Luxembourg and the Netherlands.

Paperwork can be tricky wherever you buy, and many countries have compulsory roadworthiness checks on older vehicles.

Rental

➡ Renting a car is ideal for people who will need cars for 16 days or less. Anything longer, it's better to lease.

➡ Big international rental firms will give you reliable service and good vehicles. National or local firms can often undercut the big companies by up to 40%.

➡ Usually you will have the option of returning the car to a different outlet at the end of the rental period, but there's normally a charge for this and it can be very steep if it's a long way from your point of origin.

➡ Book early for the lowest rates and make sure you compare rates in different cities. Taxes range from 15% to 20% and surcharges apply if rented from an airport.

➡ If you rent a car in the EU you might not be able to take it outside the EU, and if you rent the car outside the EU, you will only be able to drive within the EU for eight days. Ask at the rental agencies for other such regulations.

➡ Make sure you understand what is included in the price (unlimited or paid kilometres, tax, injury insurance, collision damage waiver etc) and what your liabilities are. We recommend taking the collision damage waiver, though you can probably skip the injury insurance if you and your passengers have decent travel insurance.

➡ The minimum rental age is usually 21 years and sometimes 25. You'll need a credit card and to have held your licence for at least a year.

➡ Motorcycle and moped rental is common in some countries, such as Italy, Spain, Greece and southern France.

Road Conditions & Road Rules

➡ Conditions and types of roads vary across Europe. The fastest routes are generally four- or six-lane highways known locally as motorways, autoroutes, autostrade, autobahnen etc. These tend to skirt cities and plough through the countryside in straight lines, often avoiding the most scenic bits.

➡ Some highways incur tolls, which are often quite hefty (especially in Italy, France and Spain), but there will always be an alternative route. Motorways and other primary routes are generally in good condition.

➡ Road surfaces on minor routes are unreliable in some countries (eg Greece, Albania, Romania, Ireland, Russia and Ukraine), although normally they will be more than adequate.

➡ Except in Britain and Ireland, you should drive on the right. Vehicles brought to the Continent from any of these locales should have their headlights adjusted to avoid blinding oncoming traffic (a simple solution on older headlight lenses is to cover up a triangular section of the lens with tape). Priority is often given to traffic approaching from the right in countries that drive on the right-hand side.

➡ Speed limits vary from country to country. You may be surprised at the apparent disregard for traffic regulations in some places (particularly in Italy and Greece), but as a visitor it is always best to be cautious. Many driving infringements are subject to an on-the-spot fine. Always ask for a receipt.

➡ European drink-driving laws are particularly strict. The blood-alcohol concentration (BAC) limit when driving is usually between 0.05% and 0.08%, but in certain areas (such as Gibraltar, Bulgaria and Belarus) it can be zero.

➡ Always carry proof of ownership of your vehicle (Vehicle Registration Document for British-registered cars). An EU driving licence is acceptable for those driving through Europe. If you have any other type of licence, you should obtain an International Driving Permit (IDP) from your motoring organisation. Check what type of licence is required in your destination prior to departure.

➡ Every vehicle that travels across an international border should display a sticker indicating its country of registration. A warning triangle, to be used in the event of breakdown, is compulsory almost everywhere.

➡ Some recommended accessories include a first-aid kit (compulsory in Austria, Slovenia, Croatia, Serbia, Montenegro and Greece), a spare bulb kit (compulsory in Spain), a reflective jacket for every person in the car (compulsory in France, Italy and Spain) and a fire extinguisher (compulsory in Greece and Turkey).

Hitching

Hitching is never entirely safe and we don't recommend it. Travellers who decide to hitch should understand that they are taking a small but potentially serious risk. It will be safer if they travel in pairs and let someone know where they plan to go.

➡ A man and woman travelling together is probably the best combination. A woman hitching on her own is taking a larger than normal risk.

➡ Don't try to hitch from city centres; take public

transport to the suburban exit routes.

➡ Hitching is usually illegal on highways – stand on the slip roads or approach drivers at petrol stations and truck stops.

➡ Look presentable and cheerful, and make a cardboard sign indicating your intended destination in the local language.

➡ Never hitch where drivers can't stop in good time or without causing an obstruction.

➡ It is often possible to arrange a lift in advance: scan student noticeboards in colleges, or check out services such as www.carpooling.co.uk or www.drive2day.de.

Local Transport

European towns and cities have excellent local-transport systems, often encompassing trams as well as buses and metro/subway/underground-rail networks.

Most travellers will find areas of interest in European cities can be easily traversed by foot or bicycle. In Greece and Italy, travellers sometimes rent mopeds and motorcycles for scooting around a city or island.

Taxi

Taxis in Europe are metered and rates are usually high. There might also be supplements for things such as luggage, time of day, location of pick-up and extra passengers.

Good bus, rail and underground-railway networks often render taxis unnecessary, but if you need one in a hurry, they can be found idling near train stations or outside big hotels. Lower fares make taxis more viable in some countries such as Spain, Greece, Portugal and Turkey.

HITCHING FOR CASH

In parts of Eastern Europe including Russia, Ukraine and Turkey, traditional hitchhiking is rarely practised. Instead, anyone with a car can be a taxi and it's quite usual to see locals stick their hands out (palm down) on the street, looking to hitch a lift. The difference with hitching here, however, is that you pay for the privilege. You will need to speak the local language (or at least know the numbers) to discuss your destination and negotiate a price.

Train

Comfortable, frequent and reliable, trains are *the* way to get around Europe.

➡ Many state railways have interactive websites publishing their timetables and fares, including www.bahn.de (Germany) and www.sbb.ch (Switzerland), which both have pages in English. **Eurail** (www.eurail.com) links to 28 European train companies.

➡ The very comprehensive, **Man in Seat 61** (www.seat61.com) is a gem, while the US-based **Budget Europe Travel Service** (www.budgeteuropetravel.com) can also help with tips.

➡ European trains sometimes split en route to service two destinations, so even if you're on the right train, make sure you're also in the correct carriage.

➡ A train journey to almost every station in Europe can be booked via Voyages-sncf.com (http://uk.voyages-sncf.com/en), which also sells InterRail and other passes.

Express Trains

Eurostar (www.eurostar.com) links London's St Pancras International station, via the Channel Tunnel, with Paris' Gare du Nord (2¼ hours, up to 25 a day) and Brussels' international terminal (one hour 50 minutes, up to 12 a day). Some trains also stop at Lille and Calais in France. There are also several trains a week from London to Disneyland Paris; London to Mar-

seilles via Lyon and Avignon; and London to the French ski resorts (the latter only runs December to April).

From December 2017, Eurostar trains will also link Amsterdam Centraal Station with London St Pancras.

The train stations at St Pancras International, Paris and Brussels are much more central than the cities' airports. So, overall, the journey takes as little time as the equivalent flight, with less hassle.

Eurostar in London also sells tickets onward to some Continental destinations. Holders of Eurail and InterRail passes are offered discounts on some Eurostar services; check when booking.

Within Europe, express trains are identified by the symbols 'EC' (EuroCity) or 'IC' (InterCity). The French TGV, Spanish AVE and German ICE trains are even faster, reaching up to 300km/h. Supplementary fares can apply on fast trains (which you often have to pay when travelling on a rail pass), and it is a good idea (sometimes obligatory) to reserve seats at peak times and on certain lines. The same applies for branded express trains, such as the Thalys (between Paris and Brussels, Bruges, Amsterdam and Cologne), and the Freccia trains in Italy.

If you don't have a seat reservation, you can still obtain a seat that doesn't have a reservation ticket attached to it. Check which destination a seat is reserved for – you might be able to sit in it until the person boards the train.

International Rail Passes

If you're covering lots of ground, you should get a rail pass. But do some price comparisons of point-to-point ticket charges and rail passes beforehand to make absolutely sure you'll break even. Also shop around for rail-pass prices as they do vary between outlets. When weighing up options, look into cheap deals that include advance-purchase reductions, one-off promotions or special circular-route tickets, particularly over the internet.

Normal point-to-point tickets are valid for two months, and you can make as many stops as you like en route; make your intentions known when purchasing and inform train conductors how far you're going before they punch your ticket.

Supplementary charges (eg for some express and overnight trains) and seat reservation fees (mandatory on some trains, a good idea on others) are not covered by rail passes. Always ask. Note that European rail passes also give reductions on Eurostar, the Channel Tunnel and on certain ferries.

Pass-holders must always carry their passport with them for identification purposes. The railways' policy is that passes cannot be replaced or refunded if lost or stolen.

NON-EUROPEAN RESIDENTS

Eurail (www.eurail.com) passes can be bought only by residents of non-European countries and should be purchased before arriving in Europe.

The most comprehensive of the various Eurail passes is the 'Global Pass' covering 28 countries. While the pass is valid on some private train lines in the region, if you plan to travel extensively in Switzerland, be warned that the many private rail networks and cable cars, especially in the Jungfrau region around

Interlaken, don't give Eurail discounts. A Swiss Pass or Half-Fare Card might be an alternative or necessary addition.

The pass is valid for a set number of consecutive days or a set number of days within a period of time. Those under 26 years of age can buy a Eurail Youth pass, which only covers travel in 2nd-class compartments. Those aged 26 and over must buy the full-fare Eurail pass, which entitles you to travel 1st class.

Alternatively, there is the Select pass, which allows you to nominate two, three or four bordering countries in which you wish to travel, and then buy a pass allowing five, six, eight or 10 travel days in a two-month period. The five- and six-day passes offer an attractive price break, but for more expensive options, the continuous pass becomes better value.

There are also Eurail National Passes for just one country.

Two to five people travelling together can get a Saver version of all Eurail passes for a 15% discount.

EUROPEAN RESIDENTS

InterRail (www.interrail.eu) offers passes to European residents for unlimited rail travel through 30 European and North African countries (excluding the pass-holder's country of residence). To qualify as a resident, you must have lived in a European country for six months.

While an InterRail pass will get you further than a Eurail pass along the private rail networks of Switzerland's Jungfrau region (near Interlaken), its benefits are limited. A Swiss Pass or Half-Fare Card might be a necessary addition if you plan to travel extensively in that region.

For a small fee, European residents can buy a Railplus Card, entitling the holder to a 25% discount on many (but not all) international train journeys. It is available

from counters in main train stations.

National Rail Passes

National rail operators might also offer their own passes, or at least a discount card, offering substantial reductions on tickets purchased (eg the Bahn Card in Germany or the Half-Fare Card in Switzerland).

Look at individual train-operator sites via http://uk.voyages-sncf.com/en to check. Such discount cards are usually only worth it if you're staying in the country a while and doing a lot of travelling.

Overnight Trains

There are usually two types of sleeping accommodation: dozing off upright in your seat or stretching out in a sleeper. Again, reservations are advisable, as sleeping options are allocated on a first-come, first-served basis. Couchette bunks are comfortable enough, if lacking in privacy. There are four per compartment in 1st class, six in 2nd class.

Sleepers are the most comfortable option, offering beds for one or two passengers in 1st class, or two or three passengers in 2nd class. Charges vary depending upon the journey, but they are significantly more costly than couchettes.

In the former Soviet Union, the most common options are either 2nd-class *kupeyny* compartments – which have four bunks – or the cheaper *platskartny*, which are open-plan compartments with reserved bunks. This 3rd-class equivalent is not great for those who value privacy.

Other options include the very basic bench seats in *obshchiy* (*zahalney* in Ukrainian) class and 1st-class, two-person sleeping carriages (*myagki* in Russian). In Ukrainian, this last option is known as *spalney*, but is usually abbreviated to CB in Cyrillic (pronounced *es-ve*). First class is not

Language

This chapter offers basic vocabulary to help you get around Europe. Read our coloured pronunciation guides as if they were English, and you'll be understood just fine. The stressed syllables are indicated with italics. Note the use of these abbreviations: (m) for masculine, (f) for feminine, (pol) for polite and (inf) for informal.

ALBANIAN

Note that uh is pronounced as the 'a' in 'ago'. Also, ll and rr in Albanian are pronounced stronger than when they are written as single letters. Albanian is also understood in Kosovo.

Hello.	Tungjatjeta.	toon·dya·tye·ta
Goodbye.	Mirupafshim.	mee·roo·paf·sheem
Please.	Ju lutem.	yoo loo·tem
Thank you.	Faleminderit.	fa·le·meen·de·reet
Excuse me.	Më falni.	muh fal·nee
Sorry.	Më vjen keq.	muh vyen kech
Yes./No.	Po./Jo.	po/yo
Help!	Ndihmë!	ndeeh·muh
Cheers!	Gëzuar!	guh·zoo·ar

I don't understand.
Unë nuk kuptoj.   oo·nuh nook koop·toy

Do you speak English?
A flisni anglisht?   a flees·nee ang·leesht

How much is it?
Sa kushton?   sa koosh·ton

Where's ...?
Ku është ...?   koo uhsh·tuh ...

Where are the toilets?
Ku janë banjat?   koo ya·nuh ba·nyat

BULGARIAN

Note that uh is pronounced as the 'a' in 'ago' and zh as the 's' in 'pleasure'.

Hello.	Здравейте.	zdra·vey·te
Goodbye.	Довиждане.	do·veezh·da·ne
Please.	Моля.	mol·ya
Thank you.	Благодаря.	bla·go·dar·ya
Excuse me.	Извинете.	iz·vee·ne·te
Sorry.	Съжалявам.	suh·zhal·ya·vam
Yes./No.	Да./Не.	da/ne
Help!	Помощ!	po·mosht
Cheers!	Наздраве!	na·zdra·ve

I don't understand.
Не разбирам.   ne raz·bee·ram

Do you speak English?
Говорите ли
английски?   go·vo·ree·te lee
ang·lees·kee

How much is it?
Колко струва?   kol·ko stroo·va

Where's ...?
Къде се намира ...?   kuh·de se na·mee·ra ...

Where are the toilets?
Къде има тоалетни?   kuh·de ee·ma to·a·let·nee

CROATIAN & SERBIAN

Croatian and Serbian are very similar and mutually intelligible (and using them you'll also be understood in Bosnia and Hercegovina, Montenegro and parts of Kosovo). In this section the significant differences between Croatian and Serbian are indicated with (C) and (S) respectively. Note that r is rolled and zh is pronounced as the 's' in 'pleasure'.

Hello.	Dobar dan.	daw·ber dan
Goodbye.	Zbogom.	zbo·gom
Please.	Molim.	mo·lim
Thank you.	Hvala.	hva·la
Excuse me.	Oprostite.	o·pro·sti·te
Sorry.	Žao mi je.	zha·o mi ye
Yes./No.	Da./Ne.	da/ne
Help!	Upomoć!	u·po·moch
Cheers!	Živjeli!	zhi·vye·li

I don't understand.
Ja ne razumijem.   ya ne ra·zu·mi·yem

Do you speak English?
Govorite/Govoriš li   go·vo·ri·te/go·vo·rish
engleski? (pol/inf)   li en·gle·ski

How much is it?
Koliko stoji/   ko·li·ko sto·yi/
košta? (C/S)   kosh·ta

Where's ...?
Gdje je ...?   gdye ye ...

Where are the toilets?
Gdje se nalaze   gdye se na·la·ze
zahodi/toaleti? (C/S)   za·ho·di/to·a·le·ti

CZECH

An accent mark over a vowel in written Czech indicates it's pronounced as a long sound. Note that oh is pronounced as the 'o' in 'note', uh as the 'a' in 'ago', and kh as the 'ch' in the Scottish loch. Also, r is rolled in Czech and the apostrophe (') indicates a slight y sound.

Hello.	Ahoj.	uh·hoy
Goodbye.	Na shledanou.	nuh·skhle·duh·noh
Please.	Prosím.	pro·seem
Thank you.	Děkuji.	dye·ku·yi
Excuse me.	Promiňte.	pro·min'·te
Sorry.	Promiňte.	pro·min'·te
Yes./No.	Ano./Ne.	uh·no/ne
Help!	Pomoc!	po·mots
Cheers!	Na zdraví!	nuh zdruh·vee

I don't understand.
Nerozumím.   ne·ro·zu·meem

Do you speak English?
Mluvíte anglicky?   mlu·vee·te uhn·glits·ki

How much is it?
Kolik to stojí?   ko·lik to sto·yee

Where's ...?
Kde je ...?   gde ye ...

Where are the toilets?
Kde jsou toalety?   gde ysoh to·uh·le·ti

DANISH

All vowels in Danish can be long or short. Note that aw is pronounced as in 'saw', and ew as the 'ee' in 'see' with rounded lips.

Hello.	Goddag.	go·da
Goodbye.	Farvel.	faar·vel
Please.	Vær så venlig.	ver saw ven·lee
Thank you.	Tak.	taak
Excuse me.	Undskyld mig.	awn·skewl mai
Sorry.	Undskyld.	awn·skewl
Yes./No.	Ja./Nej.	ya/nai
Help!	Hjælp!	yelp
Cheers!	Skål!	skawl

I don't understand.
Jeg forstår ikke.   yai for·stawr i·ke

Do you speak English?
Taler De/du   ta·la dee/doo
engelsk? (pol/inf)   eng·elsk

How much is it?
Hvor meget koster det?   vor maa·yet kos·ta dey

Where's ...?
Hvor er ...?   vor ir ...

Where's the toilet?
Hvor er toilettet?   vor ir toy·le·tet

DUTCH

It's important to distinguish between the long and short versions of each vowel sound. Note that ew is pronounced as the 'ee' in 'see' with rounded lips, oh as the 'o' in 'note', uh as the 'a' in 'ago', and kh as the 'ch' in the Scottish loch (harsh and throaty).

Hello.	Dag.	dakh
Goodbye.	Dag.	dakh
Please.	Alstublieft.	al·stew·bleeft
Thank you.	Dank u.	dangk ew
Excuse me.	Pardon.	par·don
Sorry.	Sorry.	so·ree
Yes./No.	Ja./Nee.	yaa/ney
Help!	Help!	help
Cheers!	Proost!	prohst

I don't understand.
Ik begrijp het niet.   ik buh·khreyp huht neet

Do you speak English?
Spreekt u Engels?   spreykt ew eng·uhls

How much is it?
Hoeveel kost het?   hoo·veyl kost huht

Where's ...?
Waar is ...?   waar is ...

Where are the toilets?
Waar zijn de toiletten?   waar zeyn duh twa·le·tuhn

ESTONIAN

Double vowels in written Estonian indicate they are pronounced as long sounds. Note that air is pronounced as in 'hair'.

Hello.	Tere.	te·re
Goodbye.	Nägemist.	nair·ge·mist
Please.	Palun.	pa·lun
Thank you.	Tänan.	tair·nan
Excuse me.	Vabandage. (pol)	va·ban·da·ge
	Vabanda. (inf)	va·ban·da
Sorry.	Vabandust.	va·ban·dust
Yes./No.	Jaa./Ei.	yaa/ay
Help!	Appi!	ap·pi
Cheers!	Terviseks!	tair·vi·seks

I don't understand.
Ma ei saa aru.   ma ay saa a·ru

Do you speak English?
Kas te räägite   kas te rair·git·te
inglise keelt?   ing·kli·se keylt

How much is it?
Kui palju see maksab?   ku·i pal·yu sey mak·sab

Where's ...?
Kus on ...?   kus on ...

Where are the toilets?
Kus on WC?   kus on ve·se

FINNISH

In Finnish, double consonants are held longer than their single equivalents. Note that ew is pronounced as the 'ee' in 'see' with rounded lips, and uh as the 'u' in 'run'.

Hello.	Hei.	hay
Goodbye.	Näkemiin.	na·ke·meen
Please.	Ole hyvä.	o·le hew·va
Thank you.	Kiitos.	kee·tos
Excuse me.	Anteeksi.	uhn·tayk·si
Sorry.	Anteeksi.	uhn·tayk·si
Yes./No.	Kyllä./Ei.	kewl·la/ay
Help!	Apua!	uh·pu·uh
Cheers!	Kippis!	kip·pis

I don't understand.
En ymmärrä.   en ewm·mar·ra

Do you speak English?
Puhutko englantia?   pu·hut·ko en·gluhn·ti·uh

How much is it?
Mitä se maksaa?   mi·ta se muhk·saa

Where's ...?
Missä on ...?   mis·sa on ...

Where are the toilets?
Missä on vessa?   mis·sa on ves·suh

FRENCH

The French r sound is throaty. French also has nasal vowels (pronounced as if you're trying to force the sound through the nose), indicated here with o or u followed by an almost inaudible nasal consonant sound m, n or ng. Syllables in French words are, for the most part, equally stressed.

Hello.	Bonjour.	bon·zhoor
Goodbye.	Au revoir.	o·rer·vwa
Please.	S'il vous plaît.	seel voo play
Thank you.	Merci.	mair·see
Excuse me.	Excusez-moi.	ek·skew·zay·mwa
Sorry.	Pardon.	par·don
Yes./No.	Oui./Non.	wee/non
Help!	Au secours!	o skoor
Cheers!	Santé!	son·tay

I don't understand.
Je ne comprends pas.   zher ner kom·pron pa

Do you speak English?
Parlez-vous anglais?   par·lay·voo ong·glay

How much is it?
C'est combien?   say kom·byun

Where's ...?
Où est ...?   oo ay ...

Where are the toilets?
Où sont les toilettes? oo son ley twa·let

GERMAN

Note that aw is pronounced as in 'saw', ew as the 'ee' in 'see' with rounded lips, while kh and r are both throaty sounds in German.

Hello.		
(in general)	Guten Tag.	goo·ten taak
(Austria)	Servus.	zer·vus
(Switzerland)	Grüezi.	grew·e·tsi
Goodbye.	Auf Wiedersehen.	owf vee·der·zey·en
Please.	Bitte.	bi·te
Thank you.	Danke.	dang·ke
Excuse me.	Entschuldigung.	ent·shul·di·gung
Sorry.	Entschuldigung.	ent·shul·di·gung
Yes./No.	Ja./Nein.	yaa/nain
Help!	Hilfe!	hil·fe
Cheers!	Prost!	prawst

I don't understand.
Ich verstehe nicht.   ikh fer·shtey·e nikht

Do you speak English?
Sprechen Sie Englisch?   *shpre*·khen zee *eng*·lish

How much is it?
Wie viel kostet das?   vee feel *kos*·tet das

Where's ...?
Wo ist ...?   vaw ist ...

Where are the toilets?
Wo ist die Toilette?   vo ist dee to·a·*le*·te

GREEK

Note that dh is pronounced as the 'th' in 'that', and that gh and kh are both throaty sounds, similar to the 'ch' in the Scottish *loch*.

Hello.	Γεια σου.	yia su
Goodbye.	Αντίο.	a·*di*·o
Please.	Παρακαλώ.	pa·ra·ka·*lo*
Thank you.	Ευχαριστώ.	ef·kha·ri·*sto*
Excuse me.	Με συγχωρείτε.	me sing·kho·*ri*·te
Sorry.	Συγνώμη.	si·*ghno*·mi
Yes./No.	Ναι./Όχι.	ne/o·hi
Help!	Βοήθεια!	vo·*i*·thia
Cheers!	Στην υγειά μας!	stin i·*yia* mas

I don't understand.
Δεν καταλαβαίνω.   dhen ka·ta·la·*ve*·no

Do you speak English?
Μιλάς Αγγλικά;   mi·*las* ang·gli·*ka*

How much is it?
Πόσο κάνει;   *po*·so *ka*·ni

Where's ...?
Που είναι ...;   pu *i*·ne ...

Where are the toilets?
Που είναι η τουαλέτα;   pu *i*·ne i tu·a·*le*·ta

HUNGARIAN

A symbol over a vowel in written Hungarian indicates it's pronounced as a long sound. Double consonants should be drawn out a little longer than in English. Note that aw is pronounced as in 'law', eu as the 'u' in 'nurse', and ew as 'ee' with rounded lips. Also, r is rolled in Hungarian and the apostrophe (') indicates a slight y sound.

Hello. (to one person)
Szervusz.   *ser*·vus
Hello. (to more than one person)
Szervusztok.   *ser*·vus·tawk

Goodbye.	*Viszlát.*	*vis*·lat
Please.	*Kérem.* (pol)	*key*·rem
	Kérlek. (inf)	*keyr*·lek
Thank you.	*Köszönöm.*	*keu*·seu·neum

Excuse me.   *Elnézést*   *el*·ney·zeysht
             kérek.   *key*·rek

Sorry.	*Sajnálom.*	*shoy*·na·lawm
Yes.	*Igen.*	*i*·gen
No.	*Nem.*	nem
Help!	*Segítség!*	she·geet·sheyg

Cheers! (to one person)
Egészségedre!   e·geys·shey·ged·re

Cheers! (to more than one person)
Egészségetekre!   e·geys·shey·ge·tek·re

I don't understand.
Nem értem.   nem *eyr*·tem

Do you speak English?
Beszél/Beszélsz   be·*seyl*/be·*seyls*
angolul? (pol/inf)   *on*·gaw·lul

How much is it?
Mennyibe kerül?   *men*'·nyi·be ke·rewl

Where's ...?
Hol van a ...?   hawl von o ...

Where are the toilets?
Hol a vécé?   hawl o *vey*·tsey

ITALIAN

The r sound in Italian is rolled and stronger than in English. Most other consonants can have a more emphatic pronunciation too (in which case they're written as double letters).

Hello.	*Buongiorno.*	bwon·*jor*·no
Goodbye.	*Arrivederci.*	a·ree·ve·*der*·chee
Please.	*Per favore.*	per fa·*vo*·re
Thank you.	*Grazie.*	*gra*·tsye
Excuse me.	*Mi scusi.* (pol)	mee *skoo*·zee
	Scusami. (inf)	*skoo*·za·mee
Sorry.	*Mi dispiace.*	mee dees·*pya*·che
Yes.	*Sì.*	see
No.	*No.*	no
Help!	*Aiuto!*	ai·*yoo*·to
Cheers!	*Salute!*	sa·*loo*·te

I don't understand.
Non capisco.   non ka·*pee*·sko

Do you speak English?
Parla inglese?   *par*·la een·*gle*·ze

How much is it?
Quant'è?   kwan·*te*

Where's ... ?
Dov'è ... ?   do·*ve* ...

Where are the toilets?
Dove sono i   *do*·ve so·no ee
gabinetti?   ga·bee·*ne*·tee

LATVIAN

A line over a vowel in written Latvian indicates it's pronounced as a long sound. Note that air is pronounced as in 'hair', ea as in 'ear', wa as in 'water', and dz as the 'ds' in 'adds'.

Hello.	Sveiks.	svayks
Goodbye.	Atā.	a·taa
Please.	Lūdzu.	loo·dzu
Thank you.	Paldies.	pal·deas
Excuse me.	Atvainojiet.	at·vai·nwa·yeat
Sorry.	Piedodiet.	pea·dwa·deat
Yes./No.	Jā./Nē.	yaa/nair
Help!	Palīgā!	pa·lee·gaa
Cheers!	Priekā!	prea·kaa

I don't understand.
Es nesaprotu.   es ne·sa·prwa·tu

Do you speak English?
Vai Jūs runājat   vai yoos ru·naa·yat
angliski?   ang·li·ski

How much is it?
Cik maksā?   tsik mak·saa

Where's ...?
Kur ir ...?   kur ir ...

Where are the toilets?
Kur ir tualetes?   kur ir tu·a·le·tes

LITHUANIAN

Symbols on vowels in written Lithuanian indicate that they're pronounced as long sounds. Note that ow is pronounced as in 'how'.

Hello.	Sveiki.	svay·ki
Goodbye.	Viso gero.	vi·so ge·ro
Please.	Prašau.	pra·show
Thank you.	Ačiū.	aa·choo
Excuse me.	Atleiskite.	at·lays·ki·te
Sorry.	Atsiprašau.	at·si·pra·show
Yes./No.	Taip./Ne.	taip/ne
Help!	Padėkit!	pa·dey·kit
Cheers!	Į sveikatą!	ee svay·kaa·taa

I don't understand.
Aš nesuprantu.   ash ne·su·pran·tu

Do you speak English?
Ar kalbate angliškai?   ar kal·ba·te aang·lish·kai

How much is it?
Kiek kainuoja?   keak kain·wo·ya

Where's ...?
Kur yra ...?   kur ee·ra ...

Where are the toilets?
Kur yra tualetai?   kur ee·ra tu·a·le·tai

MACEDONIAN

Note that r is pronounced as a rolled sound in Macedonian.

Hello.	Здраво.	zdra·vo
Goodbye.	До гледање.	do gle·da·nye
Please.	Молам.	mo·lam
Thank you.	Благодарам.	bla·go·da·ram
Excuse me.	Извинете.	iz·vi·ne·te
Sorry.	Простете.	pros·te·te
Yes./No.	Да./Не.	da/ne
Help!	Помош!	po·mosh
Cheers!	На здравје!	na zdrav·ye

I don't understand.
Јас не разбирам.   yas ne raz·bi·ram

Do you speak English?
Зборувате ли англиски?   zbo·ru·va·te li an·glis·ki

How much is it?
Колку чини тоа?   kol·ku chi·ni to·a

Where's ...?
Каде е ...?   ka·de e ...

Where are the toilets?
Каде се тоалетите?   ka·de se to·a·le·ti·te

NORWEGIAN

In Norwegian, each vowel can be either long or short. Generally, they're long when followed by one consonant and short when followed by two or more consonants. Note that aw is pronounced as in 'law', ew as 'ee' with pursed lips, and ow as in 'how'.

Hello.	God dag.	go·daag
Goodbye.	Ha det.	haa·de
Please.	Vær så snill.	veyr saw snil
Thank you.	Takk.	tak
Excuse me.	Unnskyld.	ewn·shewl
Sorry.	Beklager.	bey·klaa·geyr
Yes./No.	Ja./Nei.	yaa/ney
Help!	Hjelp!	yelp
Cheers!	Skål!	skawl

I don't understand.
Jeg forstår ikke.   yai fawr·stawr i·key

Do you speak English?
Snakker du engelsk?   sna·ker doo eyng·elsk

How much is it?
Hvor mye koster det?   vor mew·e kaws·ter de

Where's ...?
Hvor er ...?   vor ayr ...

Where are the toilets?
Hvor er toalettene?   vor eyr to·aa·le·te·ne

POLISH

Polish vowels are generally pronounced short. Nasal vowels are pronounced as though you're trying to force the air through your nose, and are indicated with n or m following the vowel. Note also that r is rolled in Polish.

Hello.	Cześć.	cheshch
Goodbye.	Do widzenia.	do vee·dze·nya
Please.	Proszę.	pro·she
Thank you.	Dziękuję.	jyen·koo·ye
Excuse me.	Przepraszam.	pshe·pra·sham
Sorry.	Przepraszam.	pshe·pra·sham
Yes./No.	Tak./Nie.	tak/nye
Help!	Na pomoc!	na po·mots
Cheers!	Na zdrowie!	na zdro·vye

I don't understand.
Nie rozumiem.   nye ro·zoo·myem

Do you speak English?
Czy pan/pani mówi   chi pan/pa·nee moo·vee
po angielsku? (m/f)   po an·gyel·skoo

How much is it?
Ile to kosztuje?   ee·le to kosh·too·ye

Where's ...?
Gdzie jest ...?   gjye yest ...

Where are the toilets?
Gdzie są toalety?   gjye som to·a·le·ti

PORTUGUESE

Most vowel sounds in Portuguese have a nasal version (ie pronounced as if you're trying to force the sound through your nose), which is indicated in our pronunciation guides with ng after the vowel.

Hello.	Olá.	o·laa
Goodbye.	Adeus.	a·de·oosh
Please.	Por favor.	poor fa·vor
Thank you.	Obrigado. (m)	o·bree·gaa·doo
	Obrigada. (f)	o·bree·gaa·da
Excuse me.	Faz favor.	faash fa·vor
Sorry.	Desculpe.	desh·kool·pe
Yes./No.	Sim./Não.	seeng/nowng
Help!	Socorro!	soo·ko·rroo
Cheers!	Saúde!	sa·oo·de

I don't understand.
Não entendo.   nowng eng·teng·doo

Do you speak English?
Fala inglês?   faa·la eeng·glesh

How much is it?
Quanto custa?   kwang·too koosh·ta

Where's ...?
Onde é ...?   ong·de e ...

Where are the toilets?
Onde é a casa de   ong·de e a kaa·za de
banho?   ba·nyoo

ROMANIAN

Note that ew is pronounced as the 'ee' in 'see' with rounded lips, uh as the 'a' in 'ago', and zh as the 's' in 'pleasure'. The apostrophe (') indicates a very short, unstressed (almost silent) i. Moldovan is the official name of the variety of Romanian spoken in Moldova.

Hello.	Bună ziua.	boo·nuh zee·wa
Goodbye.	La revedere.	la re·ve·de·re
Please.	Vă rog.	vuh rog
Thank you.	Mulţumesc.	mool·tsoo·mesk
Excuse me.	Scuzaţi-mă.	skoo·za·tsee·muh
Sorry.	Îmi pare rău.	ewm' pa·re ruh·oo
Yes./No.	Da./Nu.	da/noo
Help!	Ajutor!	a·zhoo·tor
Cheers!	Noroc!	no·rok

I don't understand.
Eu nu înţeleg.   ye·oo noo ewn·tse·leg

Do you speak English?
Vorbiţi engleza?   vor·beets' en·gle·za

How much is it?
Cât costă?   kewt kos·tuh

Where's ...?
Unde este ...?   oon·de yes·te ...

Where are the toilets?
Unde este o toaletă?   oon·de yes·te o to·a·le·tuh

RUSSIAN

Note that zh is pronounced as the 's' in 'pleasure'. Also, r is rolled in Russian and the apostrophe (') indicates a slight y sound.

Hello.	Здравствуйте.	zdrast·vuyt·ye
Goodbye.	До свидания.	da svee·dan·ya
Please.	Пожалуйста.	pa·zhal·sta
Thank you.	Спасибо	spa·see·ba
Excuse me./ Sorry.	Извините, пожалуйста.	eez·vee·neet·ye pa·zhal·sta
Yes./No.	Да./Нет.	da/nyet
Help!	Помогите!	pa·ma·gee·tye
Cheers!	Пей до дна!	pyey da dna

I don't understand.
Я не понимаю.   ya nye pa·nee·ma·yu

Do you speak English?
Вы говорите   vi ga·va·reet·ye
по-английски?   pa·an·glee·skee

How much is it?
Сколько стоит? | skol'·ka sto·eet

Where's ...?
Где (здесь) ...? | gdye (zdyes') ...

Where are the toilets?
Где здесь туалет? | gdye zdyes' tu·al·yet

SLOVAK

An accent mark over a vowel in written Slovak indicates it's pronounced as a long sound. Note also that uh is pronounced as the 'a' in 'ago', and kh as the 'ch' in the Scottish *loch*. The apostrophe (') indicates a slight y sound.

Hello.	*Dobrý deň.*	do·bree dyen'
Goodbye.	*Do videnia.*	do vi·dye·ni·yuh
Please.	*Prosím.*	pro·seem
Thank you.	*Ďakujem*	dyuh·ku·yem
Excuse me.	*Prepáčte.*	pre·pach·tye
Sorry.	*Prepáčte.*	pre·pach·tye
Yes./No.	*Áno./Nie.*	a·no/ni·ye
Help!	*Pomoc!*	po·mots
Cheers!	*Nazdravie!*	nuhz·druh·vi·ye

I don't understand.
Nerozumiem. | nye·ro·zu·myem

Do you speak English?
Hovoríte po anglicky? | ho·vo·ree·tye po uhng·lits·ki

How much is it?
Koľko to stojí? | kol'·ko to sto·yee

Where's ...?
Kde je ...? | kdye ye ...

Where are the toilets?
Kde sú tu záchody? | kdye soo tu za·kho·di

SLOVENE

Note that r is pronounced as a rolled sound in Slovene.

Hello.	*Zdravo.*	zdra·vo
Goodbye.	*Na svidenje.*	na svee·den·ye
Please.	*Prosim.*	pro·seem
Thank you.	*Hvala.*	hva·la
Excuse me.	*Dovolite.*	do·vo·lee·te
Sorry.	*Oprostite.*	op·ros·tee·te
Yes./No.	*Da./Ne.*	da/ne
Help!	*Na pomoč!*	na po·moch
Cheers!	*Na zdravje!*	na zdrav·ye

I don't understand.
Ne razumem. | ne ra·zoo·mem

Do you speak English?
Ali govorite | a·lee go·vo·ree·te

angleško? | ang·lesh·ko

How much is it?
Koliko stane? | ko·lee·ko sta·ne

Where's ...?
Kje je ...? | kye ye ...

Where are the toilets?
Kje je stranišče? | kye ye stra·neesh·che

SPANISH

Note that the Spanish r is strong and rolled, th is pronounced 'with a lisp', and v is soft, pronounced almost like a 'b'.

Hello.	*Hola.*	o·la
Goodbye.	*Adiós.*	a·dyos
Please.	*Por favor.*	por fa·vor
Thank you.	*Gracias.*	gra·thyas
Excuse me.	*Perdón.*	per·don
Sorry.	*Lo siento.*	lo syen·to
Yes./No.	*Sí./No.*	see/no
Help!	*¡Socorro!*	so·ko·ro
Cheers!	*¡Salud!*	sa·loo

I don't understand.
Yo no entiendo. | yo no en·tyen·do

Do you speak English?
¿Habla/Hablas inglés? (pol/inf) | a·bla/a·blas een·gles

How much is it?
¿Cuánto cuesta? | kwan·to kwes·ta

Where's ...?
¿Dónde está ...? | don·de es·ta ...

Where are the toilets?
¿Dónde están los servicios? | don·de es·tan los ser·vee·thyos

SWEDISH

Swedish vowels can be short or long – generally the stressed vowels are long, except when followed by double consonants. Note that aw is pronounced as in 'saw', air as in 'hair', eu as the 'u' in 'nurse', ew as the 'ee' in 'see' with rounded lips, and oh as the 'o' in 'note'.

Hello.	*Hej.*	hey
Goodbye.	*Hej då.*	hey daw
Please.	*Tack.*	tak
Thank you.	*Tack.*	tak
Excuse me.	*Ursäkta mig.*	oor·shek·ta mey
Sorry.	*Förlåt.*	feur·lawt
Yes./No.	*Ja./Nej.*	yaa/ney
Help!	*Hjälp!*	yelp

Cheers! *Skål!* skawl

I don't understand.
Jag förstår inte. yaa feur·*shtawr* in·te

Do you speak English?
Talar du engelska? taa·lar doo eng·el·ska

How much is it?
Hur mycket kostar det? hoor mew·ke kos·tar de

Where's ...?
Var finns det ...? var finns de ...

Where are the toilets?
Var är toaletten? var air toh·aa·le·ten

TURKISH

Double vowels are pronounced twice in Turkish. Note also that eu is pronounced as the 'u' in 'nurse', ew as the 'ee' in 'see' with rounded lips, uh as the 'a' in 'ago', r is rolled and v is a little softer than in English.

Hello. *Merhaba.* mer·ha·ba

Goodbye. *Hoşçakal.* hosh·*cha*·kal
(when leaving)

Güle güle. gew·le gew·le
(when staying)

Please. *Lütfen.* lewt·fen

Thank you. *Teşekkür* te·shek·*kewr*
ederim. e·de·reem

Excuse me. *Bakar* ba·*kar*
mısınız. muh·suh·*nuhz*

Sorry. *Özür* eu·*zewr*
dilerim. dee·le·reem

Yes./No. *Evet./Hayır.* e·*vet*/ha·*yuhr*

Help! *İmdat!* eem·dat

Cheers! *Şerefe!* she·re·*fe*

I don't understand.
Anlamıyorum. an·*la*·muh·yo·room

Do you speak English?
İngilizce een·gee·*leez*·je
konuşuyor ko·noo·*shoo*·yor

musunuz? moo·soo·*nooz*

How much is it?
Ne kadar? ne ka·*dar*

Where's ...?
... nerede? ... ne·re·de

Where are the toilets?
Tuvaletler nerede? too·va·let·*ler* ne·re·de

UKRAINIAN

Ukrainian vowels in unstressed syllables are generally pronounced shorter and weaker than they are in stressed syllables. Note that ow is pronounced as in 'how' and zh as the 's' in 'pleasure'. The apostrophe (') indicates a slight y sound.

Hello. Добрий день. do·bry den'

Goodbye. До побачення. do po·*ba*·chen·nya

Please. Прошу. *pro*·shu

Thank you. Дякую. *dya*·ku·yu

Excuse me. Вибачте. vy·bach·te

Sorry. Перепрошую. pe·re·*pro*·shu·yu

Yes./No. Так./Ні. tak/ni

Help! Допоможіть! do·po·mo·*zhit'*

Cheers! Будьмо! bud'·mo

I don't understand.
Я не розумію. ya ne ro·zu·*mi*·yu

Do you speak English?
Ви розмовляєте vy roz·mow·*lya*·ye·te
англійською an·*hliys'*·ko·yu
мовою? *mo*·vo·yu

How much is it?
Скільки це він/вона *skil'*·ki tse vin/vo·*na*
коштує? (m/f) ko·shtu·ye

Where's ...?
Де ...? de ...

Where are the toilets?
Де туалети? de tu·a·le·ti

Behind the Scenes

SEND US YOUR FEEDBACK

We love to hear from travellers – your comments keep us on our toes and help make our books better. Our well-travelled team reads every word on what you loved or loathed about this book. Although we cannot reply individually to your submissions, we always guarantee that your feedback goes straight to the appropriate authors, in time for the next edition. Each person who sends us information is thanked in the next edition – the most useful submissions are rewarded with a selection of digital PDF chapters.

Visit **lonelyplanet.com/contact** to submit your updates and suggestions or to ask for help. Our award-winning website also features inspirational travel stories, news and discussions.

Note: We may edit, reproduce and incorporate your comments in Lonely Planet products such as guidebooks, websites and digital products, so let us know if you don't want your comments reproduced or your name acknowledged. For a copy of our privacy policy visit lonelyplanet.com/privacy.

OUR READERS

Many thanks to the travellers who used the last edition and wrote to us with helpful hints, useful advice and interesting anecdotes: Geoff Clarke, Luke Attard, Marek Zajac, Seokhwan Jeon, Soufiane Laachach

WRITER THANKS

Greg Bloom

Big thanks to pop for tagging along and lending anecdotes, insight and much bar research. To Callie, who couldn't wait until after my deadline to arrive: you were so worth the sleepless nights. To her mama, Windi, T.Y. for keeping it together while I was away. To Callie's sister, Anna, thanks always for keeping me sane. On the road, thanks to Nikolai (Minsk) and Leonid (Chişinău), and to Mike T and Fabian M, respectively, for setting me up with them.

Mark Elliott

Countless kind Bosnians (and Hercegovinians, too) offered more help than I have space to acknowledge. Enormous thanks to the great philosophers at Savat, to Kate Hunt for so much emotion, Wangdi for the space and sustenance, and to Harriet Einsiedel, Izzy and Shashka for the amazing coincidences. Love and endless gratitude beyond words to my unbeatable family.

Anita Isalska

My research in Slovakia was hugely enriched by the people I met on the road. I'm especially thankful for the tips and insights from Slavo Stankovič, Marek Leskovjanský, Erik Ševčík, Jiri Sikora, the incredibly helpful tourist office teams in Bratislava, Žilina and Martin, and pretty much everyone in friendly Košice. Big hugs to Normal Matt for being an invaluable write-up morale-booster.

Catherine Le Nevez

Kiitos paljon/tack så mycket first and foremost to Julian, and to all of the locals, tourism professionals and fellow travellers who provided insights, inspiration and good times. And thanks to Finland itself for the Northern Lights displays in Inari and Rovaniemi. Huge thanks too to Destination Editor Gemma Graham, and all at LP. As ever, *merci encore* to my parents, brother, belle-sœur and neveu.

Tom Masters

Many thanks to Valmir, Emin, Esra, Granit, Shemsi and Lorik in Pristina, to Shpendi, Joard, Mateo, Renato and Rita in Tirana, and to dozens of hostel owners around both countries who supplied such helpful information, especially to Walter in Gjirokastra, Catherine in Valbona, Roza in Shkodra, and the crews at Driza's House in Prizren, Tirana Backpacker's Hostel in Tirana and Hostel Saraç in Peja. Special thanks also to Jimmy in Theth for being a good Samaritan when I had car trouble!

Lorna Parkes

A huge thank you to the friendly people of Macedonia who helped guide me through bad signposting, lost trail markers, GPS black holes and the basics of Cyrillic. Your warmth and good nature is a testament to your country. Equal thanks go to my husband, Rob, without whom I would not have been able to do this job, both mentally and physically, and my beautiful son, Austin, who patiently waited for my return.

Josephine Quintero

Thanks to all the helpful folk at the various tourist information offices, as well as to Sven Jacobsen for his warm welcome and generosity in Copenhagen, and Frederik Serger, a valuable contact in southern Sweden. Thanks too to Destination Editor Gemma Graham and all those involved in the title from the Lonely Planet offices, as well as to my Scandinavian friends in Spain who provided endless advice, contacts and tips.

Leonid Ragozin

Huge thanks to Olexiy Skrypnik, Serhiy Savchuk and Yevhen Stepanenko for helping me to explore Lviv. Another jumbo plane of gratitude goes to Lena Lebedinskaya, Ruslan Popkov and their wonderful friends in Odesa. Finally, thank you, Masha Makeeva, for enduring my long absences.

Tamara Sheward

Every time I go to Serbia, the *hvala* list gets outrageously longer; if I keep this up, I'll be trying to cram 7.13 million names into this tiny space. To whittle down the numbers somewhat, I'll offer my undying gratitude to the Lučić and Eremić families, Srdjan (the lifesaver) and Gordana, the NS Kitchen Collective, the wonderful folks of Šekspirova, and Brana Vladisavljevic at LP. My Dušan and Masha, may 10000 *trubači* bands forever toot in your honour: *poljupci zauvek!*

BEHIND THE SCENES

ACKNOWLEDGEMENTS

Climate map data adapted from Peel MC, Finlayson BL & McMahon TA (2007) 'Updated World Map of the Köppen-Geiger Climate Classification', *Hydrology and Earth System Sciences*, 11, 163344.

Cover photograph: Lavender, Provence, France. Luigi Vaccarella / 4Corners ©

THIS BOOK

This 2nd edition of Lonely Planet's *Europe* guidebook was curated by Alexis Averbuck, James Bainbridge, Mark Baker, Oliver Berry, Greg Bloom, Gregor Clark, Marc Di Duca, Peter Dragicevich, Duncan Garwood, Anita Isalska, Catherine Le Nevez, Anne Mason, Tom Masters, Hugh McNaughtan, Korina Miller, John Noble, Becky Ohlsen, Lorna Parkes, Leonid Ragozin, Tim Richards, Simon Richmond, Andrea Schulte-Peevers, Tamara Sheward, Andy Symington, Anna Tyler, Donna Wheeler, Neil Wilson and Karla Zimmerman.

This guidebook was produced by the following:

Destination Editors Daniel Fahey, Gemma Graham, Lauren Keith, James Smart, Tom Stainer, Anna Tyler, Branislava Vladisavljevic

Product Editors Anne Mason, Jenna Myers

Senior Cartographer Mark Griffiths

Book Designer Mazzy Prinsep

Assisting Editors Janet Austin, Sarah Bailey, Michelle Bennett, Kate Chapman, Katie Connolly, Melanie Dankel, Bruce Evans, Carly Hall, Trent Holden, Kate James, Amy Karafin, Kellie Langdon, Sam Forge, Jodie Martire, Anne Mulvaney, Rosie Nicholson, Lauren O'Connell, Kristin Odijk, Charlotte Orr, Sarah Reid, Gabbi Stefanos, Saralinda Turner, Fionnuala Twomey

Assisting Cartographer Valentina Kremenchutskaya

Cover Researcher Naomi Parker

Thanks to Cheree Broughton, Jennifer Carey, David Carroll, Kate Chapman, Neill Coen, Daniel Corbett, Joel Cotterell, Shona Gray, Jane Grisman, Andi Jones, Ivan Kovanovic, Borbála Molnár-Ellis, Catherine Naghten, Claire Naylor, Karyn Noble, Bridget Nurre Jennions, Martine Power, Rachel Rawling, Kirsten Rawlings, Kathryn Rowan, Ellie Simpson, Tony Wheeler, Dora Whitaker

Index

INDEX M

Map Legend

Sights

- Beach
- Bird Sanctuary
- Buddhist
- Castle/Palace
- Christian
- Confucian
- Hindu
- Islamic
- Jain
- Jewish
- Monument
- Museum/Gallery/Historic Building
- Ruin
- Shinto
- Sikh
- Taoist
- Winery/Vineyard
- Zoo/Wildlife Sanctuary
- Other Sight

Activities, Courses & Tours

- Bodysurfing
- Diving
- Canoeing/Kayaking
- Course/Tour
- Sento Hot Baths/Onsen
- Skiing
- Snorkelling
- Surfing
- Swimming/Pool
- Walking
- Windsurfing
- Other Activity

Sleeping

- Sleeping
- Camping

Eating

- Eating

Drinking & Nightlife

- Drinking & Nightlife
- Cafe

Entertainment

- Entertainment

Shopping

- Shopping

Information

- Bank
- Embassy/Consulate
- Hospital/Medical
- Internet
- Police
- Post Office
- Telephone
- Toilet
- Tourist Information
- Other Information

Geographic

- Beach
- Gate
- Hut/Shelter
- Lighthouse
- Lookout
- Mountain/Volcano
- Oasis
- Park
- Pass
- Picnic Area
- Waterfall

Population

- Capital (National)
- Capital (State/Province)
- City/Large Town
- Town/Village

Transport

- Airport
- Border crossing
- Bus
- Cable car/Funicular
- Cycling
- Ferry
- Metro station
- Monorail
- Parking
- Petrol station
- S-Bahn/Subway station
- Taxi
- T-bane/Tunnelbana station
- Train station/Railway
- Tram
- Tube station
- U-Bahn/Underground station
- Other Transport

Note: Not all symbols displayed above appear on the maps in this book

Routes

- Tollway
- Freeway
- Primary
- Secondary
- Tertiary
- Lane
- Unsealed road
- Road under construction
- Plaza/Mall
- Steps
- Tunnel
- Pedestrian overpass
- Walking Tour
- Walking Tour detour
- Path/Walking Trail

Boundaries

- International
- State/Province
- Disputed
- Regional/Suburb
- Marine Park
- Cliff
- Wall

Hydrography

- River, Creek
- Intermittent River
- Canal
- Water
- Dry/Salt/Intermittent Lake
- Reef

Areas

- Airport/Runway
- Beach/Desert
- Cemetery (Christian)
- Cemetery (Other)
- Glacier
- Mudflat
- Park/Forest
- Sight (Building)
- Sportsground
- Swamp/Mangrove

Karla Zimmerman

The Netherlands Karla lives in Chicago, where she eat doughnuts, yells at the Cubs, and writes stuff for books, magazines, and websites when she's not doing the first two things. She has contributed to 40-plus guidebooks and travel anthologies covering destinations in Europe, Asia, Africa, North America, and the Caribbean – all of which are a long way from the early days, when she wrote about gravel for a construction magazine and got to trek to places like Fredonia, Kansas. To learn more, follow her on Instagram and Twitter (@karlazimmerman).

Contributing Writers & Researchers

Kate Armstrong (Portugal)
Bret Atkinson (Turkey)
Carolyn Bain (Iceland & Slovenia)
Jean-Bernard Carrillet (France)
Kerry Christiani (France)
Fionn Davenport (Britain & Ireland)
Belinda Dixon (Britain)
Mark Elliott (Bosnia & Hercegovina)
Steve Fallon (Hungary, Slovenia, Romania & Turkey)
Damian Harper (Britain & Ireland)
Anna Kaminksi (Hungary)
Jessica Lee (Turkey)
Virginia Maxwell (Turkey)
Anja Mutić (Croatia & Portugal)
Isabella Noble (Britain)
Christopher Pitts (France)
Daniel Robinson (France)
Regis St Louis (Portugal & France)
Ryan Ver Berkmoes (Ireland)
Nicola Williams (France)

Andrea Schulte-Peevers

Germany Born and raised in Germany and educated in London and at UCLA, Andrea has travelled the distance to the moon and back in her visits to some 75 countries. She has earned her living as a professional travel writer for over two decades and authored or contributed to nearly 100 Lonely Planet titles as well as to newspapers, magazines and websites around the world. She also works as a travel consultant, translator and editor. Andrea's destination expertise is especially strong when it comes to Germany, Dubai and the UAE, Crete and the Caribbean Islands. She makes her home in Berlin.

Tamara Sheward

Montenegro & Serbia After years of freelance travel writing, rock'n'roll journalism and insalubrious authordom, Tamara leapt at the chance to join the Lonely Planet ranks in 2009. Since then, she's worked on guides to an incongruous jumble of countries including Montenegro, Australia, Serbia, Russia, the Samoas, Bulgaria and Fiji. She's written a miscellany of travel articles for the BBC, *The Independent*, *Sydney Morning Herald* et al; she's also fronted the camera as a documentary presenter for Lonely Planet TV, Nat Geo and Al-Jazeera. Tamara's based in far northern Australia, but you're more likely to find her roaming elsewhere, tattered notebook in one hand, the world's best-travelled toddler in the other.

Andy Symington

Belgium & Luxembourg, Britain, Estonia, Latvia, Lithuania, Portugal Andy has written or worked on over a hundred books and other updates for Lonely Planet (especially in Europe and Latin America) and other publishing companies, and has published articles on numerous subjects for a variety of newspapers, magazines, and websites. He part-owns and operates a rock bar, has written a novel and is currently working on several fiction and non-fiction writing projects. Andy, from Australia, moved to Northern Spain many years ago. When he's not off with a backpack in some far-flung corner of the world, he can probably be found watching the tragically poor local football side or tasting local wines after a long walk in the nearby mountains.

Donna Wheeler

Austria Donna has written guidebooks for Lonely Planet for ten years, including the Italy, Norway, Belgium, Africa, Tunisia, Algeria, France, Austria and Melbourne titles. She is the author of Paris Precincts, a curated photographic guide to the city's best bars, restaurants and shops and is reporter for Italian contemporary art publisher My Art Guides. Donna's work on contemporary art, architecture and design, food, wine, wilderness areas and cultural history also can be found in a variety of other publications. She became a travel writer after various careers as a commissioning editor, creative director, digital producer and content strategist.

Neil Wilson

Britain, Czech Republic & Ireland Neil was born in Scotland and has lived there most of his life. Based in Perthshire, he has been a full-time writer since 1988, working on more than 80 guidebooks for various publishers, including the Lonely Planet guides to Scotland, England, Ireland and Prague. An outdoors enthusiast since childhood, Neil is an active hill-walker, mountain-biker, sailor, snowboarder, fly-fisher and rock-climber, and has climbed and tramped in four continents, including ascents of Jebel Toubkal in Morocco, Mount Kinabalu in Borneo, the Old Man of Hoy in Scotland's Orkney Islands and the Northwest Face of Half Dome in California's Yosemite Valley.

Lorna Parkes

Macedonia Londoner by birth, Melburnian by palate and ex-Lonely Planet staffer in both cities, Lorna has spent more than 10 years exploring the globe in search of the perfect meal, the friendliest B&B, the best-value travel experience, and the most spectacular lookout point – both for her own pleasure and other people's. She's discovered she writes best on planes, and has contributed to numerous Lonely Planet books and magazines. Wineries and the tropics (not at the same time!) are her go-to happy places. Follow her @Lorna_Explorer.

Josephine Quintero

Denmark, Spain & Sweden Josephine first got her taste of not-so-serious travel when she slung a guitar on her back and travelled in Europe in the early 70s. She eventually reached Greece and caught a ferry to Israel where she embraced kibbutz life and the Mexican-American she was to subsequently wed. Josephine primarily covers Spain and Italy for Lonely Planet.

Leonid Ragozin

Latvia, Russia & Ukraine Leonid studied beach dynamics at the Moscow State University, but for want of decent beaches in Russia, he switched to journalism and spent 12 years voyaging through different parts of the BBC, with a break for a four-year stint as a foreign correspondent for the Russian *Newsweek*. Leonid is currently a freelance journalist focusing largely on the conflict between Russia and Ukraine (both his Lonely Planet destinations), which prompted him to leave Moscow and find a new home in Rīga.

Tim Richards

Poland Tim is a travel writer whose work has appeared in a variety of newspapers, magazines and websites. He also researches and writes guidebooks for Lonely Planet. Tim lived in Egypt for two years, and Poland for a year, while teaching English as a foreign language in the mid-1990s. Nowadays he lives in the city centre of Melbourne, Australia, with his wife, Narrelle Harris.

Simon Richmond

Journalist and photographer Simon Richmond has specialised as a travel writer since the early 1990s and first worked for Lonely Planet in 1999 on their Central Asia guide. He's long since stopped counting the number of guidebooks he's researched and written for the company, but countries covered including Australia, China, India, Iran, Japan, Korea, Malaysia, Mongolia, Myanmar (Burma), Russia, Singapore, South Africa and Turkey. For Lonely Planet's website he's penned features on topics from the world's best swimming pools to the joys of Urban Sketching - follow him on Instagram to see some of his photos and sketches. Simon contributed to the Plan and Survival Guide chapters.

Brendan Sainsbury

Originally from Hampshire, England, Brendan first experienced continental Europe using an inter-rail pass in the late 1980s. He's been back many times since travelling to and through 23 European countries. Since 2005, Brendan has contributed to nearly 50 Lonely Planet guidebooks including multiple editions of Spain and Italy. Brendan contributed to the Plan and Survival Guide chapters.

Catherine Le Nevez

Austria, Britain, Finland, France, Ireland & The Netherlands Catherine's wanderlust kicked in when she roadtripped across Europe from her Parisian base aged four, and she's been hitting the road at every opportunity since, travelling to around 60 countries and completing her Doctorate of Creative Arts in Writing, Masters in Professional Writing, and postgrad qualifications in Editing and Publishing along the way. Over the past dozen-plus years she's written scores of Lonely Planet guides and articles covering Paris, France, Europe and far beyond. Her work has also appeared in numerous online and print publications. Topping Catherine's list of travel tips is to travel without any expectations.

Tom Masters

Albania & Kosovo Dreaming since he could walk of going to the most obscure places on earth, Tom has always had a taste for the unknown. This has led to a writing career that has taken him all over the world, including North Korea, the Arctic, Congo and Siberia. Despite a brief spell living in the English countryside, Tom has always called London, Paris and Berlin home. He currently lives in Berlin and can be found online at www.tommasters.net.

Hugh McNaughtan

Britain, France, Lithuania & Turkey A former English lecturer, Hugh swapped grant applications for visa applications, and turned his love of travel intro a full-time thing. A long-time castle tragic with an abiding love of Britain's Celtic extremities, he jumped at the chance to explore Wales, from the Cambrian Mountains to the tip of Anglesey. He's never happier than when on the road with his two daughters. Except perhaps on the cricket field...

Korina Miller

Greece Korina first ventured to Greece as a backpacking teenager, sleeping on ferry decks and hiking in the mountains. Since then, she's found herself drawn back to soak up the timelessness of the old towns and drink coffee with locals in seaside *kafeneio*. Korina grew up on Vancouver Island and has been exploring the globe independently since she was 16, visiting or living in 36 countries and picking up a degree in Communications and Canadian Studies and an MA in Migration Studies en route. Korina has written nearly 40 titles for Lonely Planet and also works as a children's writing coach.

John Noble

Spain & Turkey John has been travelling since his teens and doing so as a Lonely Planet writer since the 1980s. The number of LP titles he's written or co-written is well into three figures, covering a somewhat random selection of countries scattered across the globe, predominantly ones where Spanish, Russian or English are spoken (usually alongside numerous local languages). He still gets as excited as ever about heading out on the road to unfamiliar experiences, people and destinations, especially remote, off-the-beaten-track ones. Above all, he loves mountains, from the English Lake District to the Himalaya. See his pics on Instagram: @johnnoble11.

Becky Ohlsen

Sweden Becky is a freelance writer, editor and critic based in Portland, Oregon. She writes guidebooks and travel stories about Scandinavia, Portland and elsewhere for Lonely Planet.

Greg Bloom

Belarus & Moldova Greg is a freelance writer, tour operator and travel planner based out of Siem Reap, Cambodia, and Manila, Philippines. Greg began his writing career in the late '90s in Ukraine, working as a journalist and later editor-in-chief of the *Kyiv Post,* an English-language weekly. As a freelance travel writer, he has contributed to some 35 Lonely Planet titles, mostly in Eastern Europe and Asia. In addition to writing, he now organises adventure trips in Cambodia and Palawan (Philippines) through his tour company, Bearcat Travel.

Gregor Clark

France, Switzerland & Liechtenstein Gregor is a US-based writer whose love of foreign languages and curiosity about what's around the next bend have taken him to dozens of countries on five continents. Chronic wanderlust has also led him to visit all 50 states and most Canadian provinces on countless road trips through his native North America. Since 2000, Gregor has regularly contributed to Lonely Planet guides, with a focus on Europe and the Americas.

Marc Di Duca

Britain, Croatia, Germany, Poland, Portugal & Ukraine A travel author for the last decade, Marc has worked for Lonely Planet in Siberia, Slovakia, Bavaria, England, Ukraine, Austria, Poland, Croatia, Portugal, Madeira and on the Trans-Siberian Railway, as well as writing and updating tens of other guides for other publishers. When not on the road, Marc lives between Sandwich, Kent and Mariánské Lázně in the Czech Republic with his wife and two sons.

Peter Dragicevich

Britain, Croatia, Estonia After a successful career in niche newspaper and magazine publishing, both in his native New Zealand and in Australia, Peter finally gave into Kiwi wanderlust, giving up staff jobs to chase his diverse roots around much of Europe. Over the last decade he's written literally dozens of guidebooks for Lonely Planet on an oddly disparate collection of countries, all of which he's come to love. He once again calls Auckland, New Zealand his home – although his current nomadic existence means he's often elsewhere.

Mark Elliott

Bosnia & Hercegovina Mark Elliott had already lived and worked on five continents when, in the pre-Internet dark ages, he started writing travel guides. He has since authored (or co-authored) around 60 books including dozens for Lonely Planet. He also acts as a travel consultant, occasional tour leader, video presenter, speaker, interviewer and blues harmonicist.

Duncan Garwood

Italy From facing fast bowlers in Barbados to sidestepping hungry pigs in Goa, Duncan's travels have thrown up many unique experiences. These days he largely dedicates himself to Italy, his adopted homeland where he's been living since 1997. From his base in the Castelli Romani hills outside Rome, he's clocked up endless kilometres exploring the country's well-known destinations and far-flung reaches, working on guides to Rome, Sardinia, Sicily, Piedmont, and Naples & the Amalfi Coast. Other LP titles include *Italy's Best Trips*, the *Food Lover's Guide to the World*, and *Pocket Bilbao & San Sebastian*. He also writes on Italy for newspapers, websites and magazines.

Anita Isalska

Bulgaria, France, Hungary, Romania & Slovakia Anita is a travel journalist, editor and copywriter whose work for Lonely Planet has taken her from Greek beach towns to Malaysian jungles, and plenty of places in between. After several merry years as an in-house editor and writer – with a few of them in Lonely Planet's London office – Anita now works freelance between the UK, Australia and any Balkan guesthouse with a good wi-fi connection. Anita writes about travel, food and culture for a host of websites and magazines. Read her stuff on www.anitaisalska.com.

OUR STORY

A beat-up old car, a few dollars in the pocket and a sense of adventure. In 1972 that's all Tony and Maureen Wheeler needed for the trip of a lifetime – across Europe and Asia overland to Australia. It took several months, and at the end – broke but inspired – they sat at their kitchen table writing and stapling together their first travel guide, *Across Asia on the Cheap*. Within a week they'd sold 1500 copies. Lonely Planet was born.

Today, Lonely Planet has offices in Franklin, London, Melbourne, Oakland, Dublin, Beijing and Delhi, with more than 600 staff and writers. We share Tony's belief that 'a great guidebook should do three things: inform, educate and amuse'.

OUR WRITERS

Alexis Averbuck

Iceland Alexis has travelled and lived all over the world, from Sri Lanka to Ecuador, Zanzibar and Antarctica. In recent years she's been living on the Greek island of Hydra and exploring her adopted homeland; sampling oysters in Brittany and careening through hill-top villages in Provence; and adventuring along Iceland's surreal lava fields, sparkling fjords and glacier tongues. A travel writer for over two decades, Alexis has lived in Antarctica for a year, crossed the Pacific by sailboat and written books on her journeys through Asia, Europe and the Americas. She's also a painter – visit www.alexisaverbuck.com – and promotes travel and adventure on video and television.

James Bainbridge

Turkey James is a British travel writer and journalist based in Cape Town, South Africa, from where he roams the globe and contributes to publications world-wide. He has been working on Lonely Planet projects for over a decade, updating dozens of guidebooks and TV hosting everywhere from the African bush to the Great Lakes. The managing author of several editions of Lonely Planet's *South Africa, Lesotho & Swaziland*, *Turkey* and *Morocco* guides, his articles on travel, culture and investment appear in the likes of BBC Travel, the UK *Guardian* and *Independent*, *Condé Nast Traveller* and *Lonely Planet Traveller*.

Mark Baker

Czech Republic, Slovenia Mark is a freelance travel writer with a penchant for offbeat stories and forgotten places. He's originally from the United States, but now makes his home in the Czech capital, Prague. He writes mainly on Eastern and Central Europe for Lonely Planet as well as other leading travel publishers, but finds real satisfaction in digging up stories in places that are too remote or quirky for the guides. Prior to becoming an author, he worked as a journalist for *The Economist*, Bloomberg News and Radio Free Europe, among other organisations.Instagram: @markbakerprague Twitter: @markbakerprague

Oliver Berry

France & Norway Oliver is a writer and photographer from Cornwall. He has worked for Lonely Planet for more than a decade, covering destinations from Cornwall to the Cook Islands, and has worked on more than 30 guidebooks. He is also a regular contributor to many newspapers and magazines, including *Lonely Planet Traveller*. His writing has won several awards, including The Guardian Young Travel Writer of the Year and the TNT Magazine People's Choice Award. His latest work is published at www.oliverberry.com.

Published by Lonely Planet Global Limited
CRN 554153
2nd edition – October 2017
ISBN 978 1 78657 146 5
© Lonely Planet 2017   Photographs © as indicated 2017
10 9 8 7 6 5 4 3 2 1
Printed in China